Mercer Commentary on the Bible

In grateful acknowledgment of the

Warren P. and Ava F. Sewell Foundation, Inc.,

whose genuine interest and generous support
in large measure enabled the publication of
the *Mercer Commentary on the Bible*.

Mercer Commentary on the Bible

GENERAL EDITORS
Watson E. Mills
Richard F. Wilson

ASSOCIATE EDITORS
Roger A. Bullard
Walter Harrelson
Edgar V. McKnight

MERCER UNIVERSITY PRESS EDITOR
Edd Rowell

WITH MEMBERS OF THE
National Association
of Baptist Professors of Religion

MERCER UNIVERSITY PRESS ■ MACON, GEORGIA

ISBN 0-86554-406-9 (printed cover, casebound) MUP/H329

Mercer Commentary on the Bible
Copyright ©1995
Mercer University Press, Macon, Georgia 31210-3960 USA
Printed in Hong Kong
First printing, November 1994

The paper used in this publication meets the minimum requirements
of American National Standard for Information Sciences—
Permanence of Paper for Printed Library Materials, ANSI Z39.48–1984.

Mercer University
Mercer University Press
6316 Peake Road
Macon, Georgia 31210-3960 USA
Telephone 912-752-2880 • FAX 912-752-2264

Library of Congress Cataloging-in-Publication Data
Mercer commentary on the Bible / general editors, Watson E. Mills
and Richard F. Wilson; associate editors, Walter Harrelson . . . [et al.].
xxii+1,347pp. 7x10" (17.8x25.4cm.).
ISBN 0-86554-406-9.
1. Bible—commentaries. I. Mills, Watson Early. II. Mercer University Press.
III. National Association of Baptist Professors of Religion.

[CIP data was not available at press time,
and will be included in subsequent printings.]

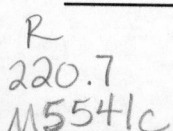

Contents

Apocryphal and Deuterocanonical Books

New Testament

Foreword

The publication of the *Mercer Commentary on the Bible* represents the completion and fulfillment of the most challenging and important project ever undertaken by the Mercer University Press. This volume has been made possible through the generous support of the Warren P. and Ava F. Sewell Foundation, Inc., and by the encouragement, friendship, and support of Lamar Plunkett.

The *Commentary*, by intent and design, is a companion volume to the *Mercer Dictionary of the Bible*. Already in its fourth printing, MDB is serving thousands of Bible students in university and seminary classrooms, in a variety of Christian education settings in churches, and in private study and personal devotion. MDB has been cited as a "truly balanced, thorough, and useful reference work" (*Choice*). It is our hope and expectation that the *Commentary* will serve alongside MDB as a balanced, thorough, and useful guide to and through the Scriptures.

We come to the study of Scripture in a world of increasing religious conflict struggling alongside and within a culture that often dismisses altogether the relevance of religion. Our human situation calls upon us to enter the serious study of Scripture with renewed urgency so that we may understand what the Scriptures actually mean and how their meaning bears upon our living in a world of such dramatic religious pluralism. As we engage the Scriptures, it becomes apparent that we cannot appreciate or claim the depth and insight of Scriptures today unless we are prepared to probe the faith and witness from which our Scriptures sprang. It is from this desire and commitment to study, to understand, and to claim the relevance of Scripture for living that the *Commentary* has been born. The contributions of the sixty-three writers and editors of the *Commentary* come together as a celebration of both the compelling message of Scripture and the inexhaustible wellspring from which the message flows. As one scholar and teacher said of the 247 contributors to the *Dictionary*, the authors and editors of the *Commentary* also are "first-rate scholars who hold in effective relation their faith and their impressive critical learning." It is, we think, this creative tension—between the timeliness and timelessness of Scripture, between seri-

ous faith and sane scholarship—that also distinguishes the *Mercer Commentary on the Bible*. In "wholeheartedly and warmly" recommending MDB, *ADRIS Newsletter* observed that "the work is marked by integrity, balance, scholarship, and, above all, by love of the Bible." The *Mercer Commentary on the Bible* has the same markings.

The pedigree of MDB and MCB reflects the same heritage of faith and scholarship. The editors and contributors of both come from the ranks of the National Association of Baptist Professors of Religion, a fraternity of "teachers of Bible" and/or "teachers of religion." This community of scholars traces its beginnings to 1928 when the founding constitution defined its purpose as "the promotion of fellowship, the investigation of problems, and the formation of ideals in the field of religious education." Recently the NABPR resolved to reaffirm the connection of "our heritage . . . our faith . . . and our responsibility." In the *Mercer Commentary on the Bible*, as in MDB, heritage, faith, and responsibility have again been merged into a new and significant resource for serious Bible study.

At no time in history has it been more important than today that we hear and understand the compelling message of the Scriptures. The Bible's message has become garbled by conflicting and even opposing interpretations, sometimes from sources whose agenda is decidedly unscriptural if not antiscriptural. We earnestly hope that the *Mercer Commentary on the Bible* will take its place alongside MDB as a helpful and trustworthy guide beyond the morass of clamoring, often conflicting pronouncements *about* the Bible to the enduring truths *of* the Bible. Indeed, the publication of this work comes with the earnest hope that teachers and students alike can and will say of the *Mercer Commentary on the Bible* what Walter Brueggemann has said of the *Mercer Dictionary of the Bible*: "In the midst of current controversy about the Bible, this publication stands boldly for sanity, intelligence, and moderation."

R. Kirby Godsey
President, Mercer University

Dedication

Lamar Rich Plunkett

statesman, educator, benefactor, friend

Preface

In 1990 Mercer University Press in association with the National Association of Baptist Professors of Religion published the *Mercer Dictionary of the Bible*. The dictionary received the LMP Literary Award for best reference work published in 1990 (see *Publishers' Weekly*, 28 January 1991) and is now in its fourth printing. The *Mercer Dictionary of the Bible* (MDB) includes approximately 1,500 articles written by members of the NABPR. While firmly grounded in an initial and ongoing commitment to the scholarly community, with the publication of the dictionary Mercer University Press and the National Association of Baptist Professors of Religion undertook a new level of endeavor with regard to the development of scholarly religious literature. The *Mercer Commentary on the Bible* is another tangible result of a continuing commitment by both MUP and the NABPR.

The *Mercer Commentary on the Bible* (MCB) is a companion volume to the MDB. Thus the commentary has been conceived somewhat differently from other one-volume commentaries. A basic assumption was that MCB would not repeat information already contained in MDB since the two will be used in tandem; that is, the goal of creating companion volumes guided the work from the outset. Regular use has been made of specific terms already defined and discussed in MDB. Such references are easily identified since they appear in MCB in small capital letters. For example, when an author refers in the text to JUSTIFICATION, the reader knows that there is an article by that name in MDB. The number of introductory articles also is greatly reduced in comparison to other single-volume commentaries since the excellent work already produced in the MDB has been consciously taken into consideration.

The almost three million words of MDB and MCB spread over more than 2,200 large double-column pages do not claim to convey to the reader all one needs to know about the Bible. Rather, our hope is that the MDB and MCB will together provide accurate, relevant, and interesting information regarding the history, traditions, and interpretation of the literature collected in what we know as Scripture. Since both MDB and MCB are products of a professional community of scholars (the NABPR and MUP), they reflect a broad range of opinions and approaches to the critical issues involved in the study of the Bible. There has been a studied attempt *not* to require contributors to follow any specific school of interpretation. Likewise, every effort has been made to avoid pressing for a particular hermeneutical or theological position.

Neither the MDB nor the MCB are substitutes for the Scripture itself. To encourage study of the Scripture itself, both MDB and MCB reference a variety of tools, including thousands of specific references to the biblical materials, canonical and noncanonical. Further, these volumes do not pretend to supplant the more comprehensive standard Bible dictionaries or the multivolume commentaries that are readily available to the serious student. Rather they seek to fill a real need for single-volume resources that are intended for use by both beginning and advanced Bible students in college, university, and seminary, as well as professional parish ministers and laypersons interested in serious study of the Bible. Our intention is that these two volumes begin and end with a classroom perspective without appearing "bookish." The editors and publishers of and contributors to these works are all either directly involved in teaching beginning and advanced Bible students or serve in support of those who are teaching; they are also involved in the life of the church. The needs of students, whether in formal academic settings or not, have shaped the structure and content of the *Mercer Dictionary of the Bible* and the *Mercer Commentary on the Bible*.

Abbreviations

We generally have followed the abbreviations for biblical books, apocrypha, and other extracanonical books as found in the widely used Society of Biblical Literature list. Bibliographies, where included, are necessarily brief. To save space, we give only the essential bibliographic information: the author's last name and initial(s), date, and the title of the work. Periodical citations include sufficient information to locate the reference, while encyclopedia and dictionary references include only the author, title, and referenced work (if arranged alphabetically; in cases where a reference work arranges articles in some other way, volume and/or page or column numbers are supplied).

Acknowledgments

With Mercer University Press and the National Association of Baptist Professors of Religion, we wish to acknowledge the generous support of Mr. Lamar R. Plunkett and the Warren P. and Ava F. Sewell Foundation, Inc., who have underwritten the publication of this volume. As a loyal Baptist and a distinguished educator himself, it is entirely fitting that this work bears the imprint of Mr. Plunkett's lifelong support of the work of Baptists and of Mercer University. We are honored to dedicate this work to him.

A project as large as this one is finally shaped by the efforts of more people than those listed as editors and contributors. In the final year of production Mrs. Nancy Stubbs, secretary for the Roberts Department of Christianity at Mercer University, has been tireless in her efforts to retype manuscripts as needed, and to enter corrections on computer disks that finally were used by editors and compositors. Her eagerness and cheerfulness has made a daunting task less so.

As the last months and weeks before publication slipped by, a small contingent from MUP joined the efforts to assure that the final volume would be as readable and free from typographical error as possible. Under the leadership of MUP Managing Editor R. Scott Nash, Jackie B. Riley, Nancy E. Hollomon, Vaughn CroweTipton, and Jon Peede logged untold hours of valuable assistance. We are grateful to them for their contributions.

Finally, we wish to acknowledge the continuing support and encouragement of the president of Mercer University, R. Kirby Godsey. His willing support of the Mercer University Press over the years is acknowledged and appreciated. We at Mercer are fortunate to be associated with an institution that respects and encourages the kind of scholarly endeavor reflected in the companion volumes, the *Mercer Dictionary of the Bible* and the *Mercer Commentary on the Bible*.

It is our hope that the *Mercer Commentary on the Bible* will be of real help in the larger world of biblical scholarship, and thus reflect well upon this great university.

Watson E. Mills
Richard F. Wilson
Mercer University
October 1994

Editors

WATSON E. MILLS, general editor, is Professor of New Testament Studies in the Roberts Department of Christianity at Mercer University, Macon, Georgia. He founded the Mercer University Press in 1979 and for twelve years served as its publisher. From 1984 until 1991 he was vice president for research and publication at Mercer University. He is a graduate of the University of Richmond (BA), the University of Louisville (MA), the Southern Baptist Theological Seminary (BD, ThM, ThD), and Baylor University (PhD). He has published widely, having written or edited more than twenty-five books and scores of articles. He is the editor of the *Mercer Dictionary of the Bible* and of the Mellen Intertextual Commentary series. He served for nineteen years as editor of *Perspectives in Religious Studies*, and for five years as the managing editor of *Religious Studies Review* and the *Bulletin of the Council of Societies for the Study of Religion*.

He served on the faculty at Averett College, Danville, Virginia from 1968 until 1979. He has been at Mercer University since 1979.

Mills was the executive officer of the Council of Societies for the Study of Religion (1985–1992) and executive secretary-treasurer of the National Association of Baptist Professors of Religion (1981–1992). He is a member of the Society of New Testament Studies, the Catholic Biblical Association, the Paul Seminar (Westar), and the Society of Biblical Literature.

RICHARD F. WILSON, general editor, is Associate Professor in the Roberts Department of Christianity at Mercer University, where he is also Dean of the Chapel. He is a graduate of Mississippi College (BA), and The Southern Baptist Theological Seminary (MDiv and PhD). He has completed additional studies at the University of Louisville, the University of Kentucky, and the University of Arizona. In the spring of 1994 he was visiting scholar at the International Baptist Theological Seminary in Buenos Aires, Argentina.

Prior to joining the faculty at Mercer in 1988 Wilson taught at Gardner-Webb College, where he also served as assistant academic dean for one year.

Since 1992 Wilson has served the National Association of Baptist Professors of Religion as the executive secretary-treasurer; from 1990 until 1992 he was the assistant executive secretary-treasurer of the NABPR. He is also a member of the American Academy of Religion, and the Society of Biblical Literature.

Wilson was a contributor and assistant editor for the *Mercer Dictionary of the Bible*. He also contributes to journals and other scholarly publications.

ROGER A. BULLARD, associate editor of the apocryphal and deuterocanonical works section, was educated at Union University (BA in English), the University of Kentucky (MA in Classics), Southeastern Baptist Theological Seminary (BD), and Vanderbilt University (PhD in Biblical Studies). From 1965 until 1994 he was on the faculty of Barton College (formerly Atlantic Christian College) in Wilson, North Carolina, where he was Professor of Religion and Philosophy. He has served as visiting professor at Southeastern Seminary and at Brite Divinity School.

He is an associate editor of the *Abingdon Dictionary of Living Religions* (now published as the *Perennial Dictionary of World Religions*). He served on the translation committee preparing the Old Testament and the Deuterocanonicals/Apocrypha of Today's English Version of the Bible and is the author of *The Hypostasis of the Archons: The Coptic Text with English Translation and Commentary* and *Messiah: the Gospel according to Handel's Oratorio*, as well as numerous articles and reviews.

Bullard is a member of the National Association of Baptist Professors of Religion, the Society of Biblical Literature, the American Association of University Professors, and the North Carolina Teachers of Religion. He has served as Corresponding Member of the Institute for Antiquity and Christianity, working on the Coptic Gnostic Project. He has received awards from the Christian Research Foundation, the American Council of Learned Societies, and the National Endowment for the Humanities.

WALTER HARRELSON, associate editor of the Old Testament section, is University Professor at Wake Forest University, and Distinguished Professor emeritus of Hebrew Bible at Vanderbilt University. His undergraduate studies were at Mars Hill College and the University of North Carolina, Chapel Hill, and his graduate studies were at Union Theological Seminary (New York), and the University of Basel. He taught at Andover Newton Theological School, and the Divinity School of the University of Chicago before coming to Vanderbilt in 1960, where he served for most of his academic career.

He is the author of seven books and has published extensively in biblical and theological encyclopedias, dictionaries, and periodicals. His most recent book (with Bruce M. Metzger and Robert C. Dentan) is *The Making of the New Revised Standard Version of the Bible*. A forthcoming book, written with Rabbi Randall M. Falk, deals with Jewish and Christian ethics.

He was vice chair of the committee that produced the New Revised Standard Version of the Bible; he served on two occasions as the rector of the Ecumenical Institute for Theological Research in Jerusalem; he has served as dean of the Divinity Schools of the University of Chicago and of Vanderbilt University; and he is currently assisting Wake Forest University in the creation of its new divinity school.

EDGAR V. MCKNIGHT, associate editor for the New Testament section, is the William R. Kenan, Jr. Professor of Religion at Furman University. He received his undergraduate education in Charleston, graduating from the College of Charleston in 1953. After professional and graduate studies at the Southern Baptist Theological Seminary (MDiv, 1956; PhD, 1960) and a brief appointment as chaplain at Chowan College in Murfreesboro, North Carolina, he joined the faculty of Furman University in 1963. At Furman he has taught in the departments of Classical Languages and Religion, chaired the Department of Classical Languages, served as associate dean of Academic Affairs, and was appointed to the Kenan chair in 1982. Early publications include a *History of Chowan College*; *Opening the Bible*; *A Guide to Understanding the Scriptures*; *What Is Form Criticism?*; and *Introduction to the New Testament*.

During his first sabbatical (1973–1974), McKnight studied philosophical theology with John Macquarrie of Christ Church, Oxford. Early studies and writings in the biblical field were thereby supplemented by work in philosophical and theological hermeneutics. *Meaning in Texts: The Historical Shaping of a Narrative Hermeneutics* resulted from this work. A senior Fulbright professorship at the University of Tübingen in 1981–1982 provided opportunity for further study and writing in the relationship between biblical and literary studies. Two books grew out of this work: *The Bible and the Reader: An Introduction to Literary Criticism* and *Postmodern Use of the Bible*. McKnight is presently at work on a manuscript entitled "Theology and the Revolution in Biblical Studies."

EDD ROWELL is senior editor of Mercer University Press. He earned his AB in religious studies and languages at Howard College (Samford University) and his BD/MDiv at Southeastern Baptist Theological Seminary. From 1958 until 1980 he was pastor of Baptist churches in Alabama and Virginia. He has written numerous curriculum materials for the Sunday School Board and has contributed articles and reviews to a variety of journals. He was author of the two-volume study of Acts in the Bible Book Study Commentary series and of *Apostles—Jesus' Special Helpers* in the BibLearn series for children. He wrote the first unit for and was coeditor of the inaugural issue of Smyth & Helwys's *Formations Commentary* (1992). He was an assistant editor of and contributor to the *Mercer Dictionary of the Bible*. He was until 1993 an assistant editor of *Perspectives in Religious Studies*, and is advisory editor for the International Kierkegaard Commentary and advisory editor for the New Gospel Studies series. Rowell has been an instructor in the University College of Mercer University. He is a member of the Society of Biblical Literature and of the American Academy of Religion, an associate of the National Association of Baptist Professors of Religion, and an associate of the International Institute for the Renewal of Gospel Studies.

Contributors

Samuel E. Balentine
Professor of Old Testament
Baptist Theological Seminary at Richmond
Richmond, Virginia 23227

Jon L. Berquist
Assistant Professor of Old Testament
Phillips Graduate Seminary
Tulsa, Oklahoma 74104

Gerald L. Borchert
T. Rupert and Lucille Coleman Professor
    of New Testament Interpretation
The Southern Baptist Theological Seminary
Louisville, Kentucky 40280

Margaret Dee Bratcher
Associate Professor
Roberts Department of Christianity
Mercer University
Macon, Georgia 31207

Linda McKinnish Bridges
Associate Professor of New Testament and Greek
Baptist Theological Seminary at Richmond
Richmond, Virginia 23227

Edwin K. Broadhead
Whitley College
University of Melbourne
Pikeville Victoria 3052 Australia

J. Bradley Chance
Professor of Religion
Department of Religion
William Jewell College
Liberty, Missouri 64062

Charles H. Cosgrove
Associate Professor of New Testament
Northern Baptist Theological Seminary
Lombard, Illinois 60148

Kenneth M. Craig, Jr.
E. Lee Oliver Fagan Chair of Bible and Religion
Department of Religion and Philosophy
Chowan College
Murfreesboro, North Carolina 27855

Jerome F. D. Creach
Assistant Professor of Religion
Department of Religion and Philosophy
Barton College
Wilson, North Carolina 27893

James L. Crenshaw
Robert L. Flowers Professor of Old Testament
Duke Divinity School
Durham, North Carolina 27706

R. Alan Culpepper
Professor
Department of Religion
Baylor University
Waco, Texas 76798

Bruce T. Dahlberg
Professor of Religion and Biblical Literature
Smith College
Northhampton, Massachusetts 01063

Sharyn E. Dowd
Professor of New Testament
Lexington Theological Seminary
Lexington, Kentucky 40508

Joel F. Drinkard, Jr.
Professor of Old Testament
The Southern Baptist Theological Seminary
Louisville, Kentucky 40280

Paul D. Duke
Senior Pastor
Kirkwood Baptist Church
St. Louis, Missouri 63122

Robert C. Dunston
Professor and Chair
Department of Religion and Philosophy
Cumberland College
Williamsburg, Kentucky 40769

John I Durham
Pastor
Greenwich Baptist Church
Greenwich, Connecticut 06830

W. Hulitt Gloer
Professor of New Testament
Midwestern Baptist Theological Seminary
Kansas City, Missouri 64118

Carol Stuart Grizzard
Associate Professor of Religion
Pikeville College
Pikeville, Kentucky 41501

Thomas O. Hall, Jr.
Professor Emeritus
Department of Philosophy and Religious Studies
Virgina Commonwealth University
Richmond, Virginia 23284

Walter Harrelson
Distinguished Professor Emeritus of Hebrew Bible
Vanderbilt University
Nashville, Tennessee 37240, and
University Professor
Wake Forest University
Winston-Salem, North Carolina 27109

John H. Hayes
Professor of Old Testament
Emory University
Atlanta, Georgia 30322

E. Glenn Hinson
Professor of Spirituality, Worship, and Church History
Baptist Theological Seminary at Richmond
Richmond, Virginia 23227

Stephenson Humphries-Brooks
Associate Professor
Department of Religious Studies
Hamilton College
Clinton, New York 13323

Marie E. Isaacs
Head of the Department of Biblical Studies
Heythrop College
London University, England

John C. H. Laughlin
Professor and Chair
Department of Religion
Averett College
Danville, Virginia 24541

Claude F. Mariottini
Professor of Old Testament
Northern Baptist Theological Seminary
Lombard, Illinois 60148

Molly T. Marshall
Associate Professor of Christian Theology
The Southern Baptist Theological Seminary
Louisville, Kentucky 40280

Calvin Mercer
Associate Professor of Religious Studies
Department of Philosophy
East Carolina University
Greenville, North Carolina 27834

J. Ramsey Michaels
Professor
Department of Religious Studies
Southwest Missouri State University
Springfield, Missouri 65804

Watson E. Mills
Professor
Roberts Department of Christianity
Mercer University
Macon, Georgia 31207

John Joseph Owens
Professor Emeritus,
    Old Testament Interpretation
The Southern Baptist Theological Seminary
Louisville, Kentucky 40280

Mikeal C. Parsons
Assistant Professor
Department of Religion
Baylor University
Waco, Texas 76798

Jack G. Partain
Professor
Department of Religious Studies and Philosophy
Gardner-Webb University
Boiling Springs, North Carolina 28017

David Penchansky
Assistant Professor
Department of Theology
University of Saint Thomas
Saint Paul, Minnesota 55104

Leo G. Perdue
Professor of Hebrew Bible and Dean
Brite Divinity School
Texas Christian University
Forth Worth, Texas 76129

John B. Polhill
James Buchanan Harrison Professor
    of New Testament Interpretation;
Associate Dean of ThM/PhD Programs
The Southern Baptist Theological Seminary
Louisville, Kentucky 40280

Kandy M. Queen-Sutherland
Associate Professor
Religion Department
Stetson University,
DeLand, Florida 32720

Mitchell G. Reddish
Associate Professor and Chair
Religion Department
Stetson University
Deland, Florida 32720

Jeffrey S. Rogers
Dana Assistant Professor
Department of Religion
Furman University
Greenville, South Carolina 29613

Max Gray Rogers
Professor of Old Testament
Southeastern Baptist Theological Seminary
Wake Forest, North Carolina 27587

Edd Rowell
Senior Editor, Mercer University Press
Macon, Georgia 31207

John C. Shelley
Professor
Department of Religion
Furman University
Greenville, South Carolina 29613

David A. Smith
Professor Emeritus
Department of Religion
Furman University
Greenville, South Carolina 29613

Thomas Smothers
Professor of Old Testament
The Southern Baptist Theological Seminary
Louisville, Kentucky 40280

Marion L. Soards
Professor of New Testament Studies
Louisville Presbyterian Theological Seminary
Louisville, Kentucky 40205

Richard A. Spencer
Assistant Professor
Department of Foreign Language and Literature, and
Department of Philosophy and Religion
Appalachian State University
Boone, North Carolina 28608

Frank Stagg
Professor Emeritus, New Testament
The Southern Baptist Theological Seminary
Louisville, Kentucky 40280

Cecil P. Staton, Jr.
Publisher, Mercer University Press, and
President and Publisher
Smyth & Helwys Publishing Inc.
Macon, Georgia 31207

William P. Steeger
W. O. Vaught Professor of Bible and Chair
Division of Religion and Philosophy
Department of Religion
Ouachita Baptist University
Arkadelphia, Arkansas 71923

Charles H. Talbert
Wake Forest Professor of Religion
Wake Forest University
Winston-Salem, North Carolina 27109

Marvin E. Tate
John R. Sampey Professor of Old Testament
The Southern Baptist Theological Seminary
Louisville, Kentucky 40280

Joseph L. Trafton
Professor of Christian Origins
Department of Philosophy and Religion
Western Kentucky University
Bowling Green, Kentucky 42101

John H. Tullock
Professor Emeritus
Department of Religion
Belmont University
Nashville, Tennessee 37212

Dan O. Via
Professor Emeritus of New Testament
The Divinity School
Duke University
Durham, North Carolina 27708

James W. Watts
Assistant Professor
Department of Religion and Philosophy
Hastings College
Hastings, Nebraska 68902

John D. W. Watts
Senior Professor of Old Testament
The Southern Baptist Theological Seminary
Louisville, Kentucky 40280

Mona West
Academic Dean
Samaritan College
Lewisville, Texas 75067

John Keating Wiles
School of Law
University of North Carolina
Chapel Hill, North Carolina 27581

Richard F. Wilson
Associate Professor
Roberts Department of Christianity
Mercer University
Macon, Georgia 31207

Abbreviations

Periodicals/Journals

AASOR	Annual of the American Schools of Oriental Research
ADAJ	Annual of the Dept. of Antiquities of Jordan
AJA	American Journal of Archaeology
AnBib	Analecta biblica
Arch	Archaeology
AS	Asiatische Studien
ASORN	ASOR Newsletter
ATR	Anglican Theological Review
AUSS	Andrews University Seminary Studies
BA	Biblical Archaeologist
BAR	Biblical Archaeology Review
BASOR	Bulletin of the ASOR
BETL	Bibliotheca ephemeridum theologicarum lovaniensium
BHH	Baptist History and Heritage
BI	Biblical Illustrator (formerly SSLI)
Bib	Biblica
BibRev	Bible Review
BJRL	Bulletin of the John Rylands University Library
BJS	British Journal of Sociology
BL	Bible und Leben
BR	Biblical Research
BS	Bibliotheca Sacra
BT	Bible Today
BTB	Biblical Theology Bulletin
BTS	Bible et terre sainte
BYUS	Brigham Young University Studies
CBQ	Catholic Biblical Quarterly
CJ	Concordia Journal
Conc	Concilium
CQR	Church Quarterly Review
CSBSB	Canadian Society of Biblical Studies Bulletin
CTQ	Concordia Theological Quarterly
CTR	Criswell Theological Review
DA	Dissertation Abstracts International
DTT	Dansk teologisk tidsskrift
DR	Downside Review
EB	Estudios biblocos
ETL	Ephemerides théologicae lovannienses
ETR	Études théologiques et religieuses
EvQ	Evangelical Quarterly
ExpTim	Expository Times
GOTR	Greek Orthodox Theological Review
HAR	Hebrew Annual Review
HeyJ	Heythrop Journal
HR	History of Religions
HTR	Harvard Theological Review
HUCA	Hebrew Union College Annual
IEJ	Israel Exploration Journal
Int	Interpretation
IR	Iliff Review
ITQ	Irish Theological Quarterly
JAAR	Journal of the American Academy of Religion
JAOS	Journal of the American Oriental Society
JBL	Journal of Biblical Literature
JCS	Journal of Cuneiform Studies
JCU	Judenten Christentum Urkirche
JEA	Journal of Egyptian Archaeology
JJS	Journal of Jewish Studies
JLR	Journal of Law and Religion
JNES	Journal of Near Eastern Studies
JPH	Journal of Presbyterian History
JQR	Jewish Quarterly Review
JR	Journal of Religion
JRH	Journal of Religious History
JSJ	Journal for the Study of Judaism
JSNT	Journal for the Study of the New Testament
JSOT	Journal for the Study of the Old Testament
JSOTsup	JSOT supplement series
JSS	Journal of Semitic Studies
JSSR	Journal for the Scientific Study of Religion
JTC	Journal for Theology and the Church
JTS	Journal of Theological Studies
Jud	Judaism
KD	Kerygma und Dogma
NKZ	Neue kirchliche Zeitschrift
NovT	Novum Testamentum
NovTsup	NovT supplements
NTS	New Testament Studies
NTT	Nederlands Theologisch Tijdschrift
OTS	Oudtestamentische Studien
PEQ	Palestine Exploration Quarterly
PJ	Perkins (School of Theology) Journal
Proof	Prooftexts
PRS	Perspectives in Religious Studies
PRZ	Patristic and Byzantine Review
PSB	Princeton Seminary Bulletin
PTR	Princeton Theological Review
QDAP	Quarterly of the Dept. of Antiquities of Palestine
RB	Revue biblique
RE	Review and Expositor
RefR	Reformed Review
RevQ	Revue de Qumran
RHR	Revue de l'historie des religions
RL	Religion in Life
RQ	Reformation Quarterly
RSR	Religious Studies Review
Scr	Scripture
SecCen	Second Century
SJT	Scottish Journal of Theology
SLJ	Saint Luke Journal
SMS	Syro-Mesopotamian Studies
SR	Sciences religieuses/Studies in Religion
SSLI	Sunday School Lesson Illustrator (currently BI)

ST	*Studia theologica*	HolmBD	*Holman Bible Dictionary*
SVSQ	*St. Vladimir's Seminary Quarterly* (now SVTQ)	HDB	*Hastings Dictionary of the Bible*
SVTQ	*St. Vladimir's Theological Quart.* (was SVSQ)	HDBsup	*Hastings Dictionary of the Bible* supplement
SWJT	*Southwestern Journal of Theology*	HDBrev	*HDB*, rev. 1-vol. ed.
TJT	*Taiwan Journal of Theology*	IDB	*Interpreter's Dictionary of the Bible*
TLZ	*Theologische Literaturzeitung*	IDBsup	IDB supplementary volume
Trad	*Tradition*	ISBE	*International Standard Bible Enc.*, 3rd rev. ed.
TRu	*Theologische Rundschau*	LionEB	*The Lion Encyclopedia of the Bible*
TS	*Theological Studies*	MDB	*Mercer Dictionary of the Bible*
TT	*Theology Today*	NBD	*New Bible Dictionary*, 2nd ed. rev.
TTE	*The Theological Educator*	NCE	*New Catholic Encyclopedia*
TynBul	*Tyndale Bulletin*	NIBD	*Nelson's Illustrated Bible Dictionary*
UF	*Ugarit-Forschungen*	NIDNTT	*New International Dictionary of NT Theology*
USQR	*Union Seminary Quarterly Review*	OComB	*The Oxford Companion to the Bible*
VC	*Vigiliae christianae*	RGG	*Die Religion in Geschichte und Gegenwart*
VT	*Vetus Testamentum*	TRE	*Theologische Realenzyklopädie*
VTSup	VT supplements	UJEnc	*Universal Jewish Encyclopedia*
WTJ	*Westminster Theological Journal*	WBE	*Wycliff Bible Encyclopedia*
ZAW	*Zeitschrift für die alttestamentliche Wissenschaft*	WDCE	*Westminster Dictionary of Christian Ethics*
ZMR	*Zeitschrift für Missionskunde und Religionswissenschaft*	ZPED	*Zondervan Pictorial Enclopedia of the Bible*
ZNW	*Zeitsch. für die neutestamentliche Wissenschaft*		

Reference Works

Annotated or Study Bibles

CASB	*Cambridge Annotated Study Bible* (NRSV)
CathSB	*The Catholic Study Bible* (NAB)
HCSB	*HarperCollins Study Bible* (NRSV)
HSB	*Harper's Study Bible* rev. ed. (NRSV)
JB	*The Jerusalem Bible* (JB)
NJB	*The New Jerusalem Bible* (NJB)
NIVSB	*The NIV Study Bible*
NOAB	*The New Oxford Annotated Bible* (RSV, NRSV)
OrthSB	*The Orthodox Study Bible* (NKJV)
OSE	*The NEB. Oxford Study Edition* (NEB)
OxSB	*The Oxford Study Bible* (REB)

Dictionaries and Encyclopedias

ADLR	*Abingdon Dictionary of Living Religions*
AEHL	*Archaeological Encyclopedia of the Holy Land*
AncBD	*Anchor Bible Dictionary*
CAH	*Cambridge Ancient History*
ComB	*A Companion to the Bible*, von Allmen
DBA	*Dictionary of Biblical Archaeology*
DBR	*The Dictionary of Bible and Religion*
DCB	*Dictionary of Christian Biography*
DNT	*Dictionary of the New Testament*
EAEHL	*Ency. of Arch. Excavations in the Holy Land*
EB	*Encyclopaedia Biblica*
EBD	*Eerdman's Bible Dictionary*
EBL	*Encyclopedia of Bible Life* (Harper's) 3rd ed.
EncBri	*Encyclopaedia Britannica*
EncJud	*Encyclopedia Judaica*
EncRel	*Encyclopedia of Religion*
EvDTh	*Evangelical Dictionary of Theology*
HBD	*Harper's Bible Dictionary*

Lexicons and Wordbooks

BAGD	Bauer/Arndt/Gingrich/Danker, *A Greek-English Lexicon of the N.T.,* revised edition
BDB	(Gesenius)/Brown/Driver/Briggs, *A Hebrew and English Lexicon of the Old Testament*
GELNT	*Greek-English Lexicon of the New Testament Based on Semantic Domains*
KB	Koehler/Baumgartner, *Lexicon in Veteris Testamenti libros.*
RdA	*Reallexikon der Assyriologie*
TDNT	*Theological Dict. of the NT* (ET of TWNT)
TDOT	*Theological Dict. of the OT* (ET of TWAT)
TWAT	*Theologisches Wörterbuch zum Alten Testament*
TWBB	Richardson, *Theological Wordbook of the Bible*
TWNT	*Theologisches Wörterbuch zum Neuen testament*

Commentaries

AmCNT	An American Commentary on the NT
AncB	Anchor Bible
AugCNT	Augsburg Commentary on the NT
BBC	*Broadman Bible Commentary*
BKAT	Biblischer Kommentar: Altes Testament
BNTC	Black's NT Commentaries (= HNTC [USA])
CBC	Cambridge Bible Commentary
CCHS	*A Catholic Comm. on Holy Scripture*, 1 vol.
DNEB	Die Neue Echter Bibel
EBC	*Eerdman's Bible Commentary* (=NBC)
EGT	The Expositor's Greek Testament
FOTL	Forms of the Old Testament Literature
HBC	*Harper's Bible Commentary*
Herm	Hermeneia
HNTC	Harper's NT Commentaries (= BNTC [UK])
HTKNT	Herders theologischer Kommentar zum N.T.

IB	*Interpreter's Bible*
ICC	International Critical Commentary
Interp	Interpretation. A Bible Commentary
IOVC	*Interpreter's One-Vol. Comm. on the Bible*
ITC	International Theological Commentary
JBC	*Jerome Biblical Commentary* (see NJBC)
JPSTC	JPS Torah Commentary
LBC	*The Layman's Bible Commentary*
MCB	*Mercer Commentary on the Bible*
MNTC	Moffatt New Testament Commentary
NAC	New American Commentary
NBC	*New Bible Commentary*, 3rd ed. (=EBC)
NCB	New Century Bible
NCCHS	*A New Catholic Comm. on H.S.*, new ed. CCHS
NICNT	New International Commentary on the NT
NICOT	New International Commentary on the OT
NIGTC	New International Greek Testament Commentary
NJBC	*New Jerome Biblical Comm.*, 1 vol. (rev. JBC)
NTD	Das Neue Testament Deutsch
OTL	Old Testament Library
SacPag	Sacra Pagina
Str-B	(Strack and) Billerbeck, *Kommentar zum N.T.*
TBC	Torch Bible Commentaries
THKNT	Theologischer Handkommentar zum N.T.
TNTC	Tyndale New Testament Commentaries
TOTC	Tyndale Old Testament Commentaries
WBC	Word Biblical Commentary
WmBC	*The Women's Bible Commentary*
WPelC	Westminster Pelican Commentaries

Essay Collections

AAR/SBLA	*AAR/SBL Abstracts* (SBLASP, AARASP)
BARead	*Biblical Archaeology Reader*
BZAW	Beihefte zur ZAW
BZNW	Beihefte zur ZNW
CHJ	*Cambridge History of Judaism*
CHB	*Cambridge History of the Bible*
SBLASP	*Society of Biblical Literature Abstracts and Seminar Papers* (now AAR/SBLA)

Series

CRINT	*Compendia Rerum Iudaicarum ad Novum Testamentum*
GBS/NT	Guides to Biblical Scholarship, NT series
HDR	Harvard Dissertations in Religion
LEC	Library of Early Christianity
NABPR/SS	NABPR Special Studies series
NHS	Nag Hammadi Studies
OBT	Overtures to Biblical Theology
SBLDS	SBL Dissertation Series
SBLMS	SBL Monograph Series
SBT	Studies in Biblical Theology
SJLA	Studies in Judaism in Late Antiquity

Pseudepigrapha

ApocAb	*Apocalypse of Abraham*
ApocBar	*Apocalypse of Baruch*
ApocMos	*Apocalypse of Moses*
ApocZeph	*Apocalypse of Zephaniah*
AscIsa	*Ascension of Isaiah*
AsMos	*Assumption of Moses*
(BibAnt	*Biblical Antiquities* = PsPhilo)
EpArist	*Epistle of Aristeas*
Hom	*Homilies*, Pseudo-Clement
JosAsen	*Joseph and Asenath*
Jub	*Jubilees*
Life	*Life of Adam and Eve*
LivProph	*Lives of the Prophets*
MartIsa	*Martrydom of Isaiah*
OdeSol	*Odes of Solomon*
PsPhilo	Pseudo-Philo, *Biblical Antiquities*
PssSol	*Psalms of Solomon*
Recog	*Recognitions*, Pseudo-Clement
SibOr	*Sibylline Oracles*
SyrMen	*Syriac Meander*
TMos	*Testament of Moses*
TSol	*Testament of Solomon*
T12Pat	*Testaments of the Twelve Patriarchs*
TAsher	*Testament of Asher*
TBenj	*Testament of Benjamin*
TDan	*Testament of Dan*
TGad	*Testament of Gad*
TIss	*Testament of Issachar*
TJos	*Testament of Joseph*
TJud	*Testament of Judah*
TLevi	*Testament of Levi*
TNaph	*Testament of Naphtali*
TReu	*Testament of Reuben*
TSim	*Testament of Simeon*
TZeb	*Testament of Zebulun*

New Testament Apocrypha

ActPet	*Act of Peter*, Berlin codex 8502
ActsJn	*Acts of John*
ActsPet	*Acts of Peter*
DialSav	*Dialogue of the Savior* (NH)
PistS	*Pistos Sophia*
POxy	*Oxyrhunchus Papyri*
ProtJs	*Protoevangelium of James*
SMark	*The Secret Gospel of Mark*

Dead Sea Scrolls and Related Texts

CD	(Cairo) *Damascus Document* (Zadokite Frag's)
1QapGen	*Genesis Apocryphon*
1QH	*Thanksgiving Hymns*, cave 1
1QM	*War Scroll*
1QpHab	*Pesher on Habakkuk*, cave 1

1QS	Manual of Discipline
1QSa	App. A to 1QS: *Rule of the Congregation*
4QAgesCreat	*The Ages of Creation*
4QFlor	*Florilegium*, cave 4
4QMMT	*Miqsat Ma'aseh Torah*, cave 4
4QPBles	*Patriarchal Blessings*
4QPEzek	*Pseudo-Ezekiel*, cave 4
4QpNah	*Pesher on Nahum*, cave 4
4QPssJosh	*Psalms of Joshua*, cave 4
4QMess	Aramaic "Messianic" text, cave 4
4QShirShabb	*Song of the Sabbath Sacrifice*, cave 4
4QTestim	Testimonia text, cave 4
4QTLevi	*Testament of Levi*, cave 4
11QMelch	*Melchizedek*, cave 11
11QPs[a]	Psalter (first copy), cave 11
11QPs[b]	Psalter (ssecond copy), cave 11
11QPsAp[a]	Apocryphal psalms (first copy), cave 11
11QTem	*Temple Scroll*, cave 11
11QtgJob	*Targum of Job*, cave 11

Nag Hammadi Codices

AcPet12	*Acts of Peter and the Twelve Apostles*
Allog	*Allogenes*
ApJas	*Apocryphon of James*
ApJohn	*Apocryphon of John*
ApocAdam	*Apocalypse of Adam*
1,2 ApocJas	*1,2 Apocalypse of James*
ApocPaul	*Apocalypse of Paul*
ApocPet	*Apocalypse of Peter*
Disc8-9	*Discourse on the Eighth and Ninth*
EpPetPhil	*Epistle of Peter to Philip*
GosEg	*Gospel of the Egyptians*
GosMary	*Gospel of Mary*
GosPhil	*Gospel of Philip*
GosThom	*Gospel of Thomas*
GosTruth	*Gospel of Truth*
HypArch	*Hypostasis of the Archons*
Mars	*Marsanes*
Melch	*Melchizedek*
NHC	Nag Hammadi Codices
Norea	*Thought of Norea*
OnBapA,B,C	*On Baptism A, B, or C*
OnEuchA,B	*On the Eucharist A or B*
OrigWorld	*On the Origin of the World*
ParaphShem	*Paraphrase of Shem*
PrThanks	*Prayer of Thanksgiving*
SentSextus	*Sentences of Sextus*
SophJC	*Sophia of Jesus Christ*
SteleSeth	*Three Steles of Seth*
TeachSilv	*Teachings of Silvanus*
TestTruth	*Testimony of Truth*
ThomCont	*Book of Thomas the Contender*
Thund	*Thunder, Perfect Mind*
TJob	*Testament of Job*
TreatRes	*Treatise on the Resurrection*

TreatSeth	*The Treatise of Seth*
TrimProt	*Trimorphic Protennoia*
TriTrac	*Tripartite Tractate*
ValExp	*A Valentinian Exposition*
Zost	*Zostrianos*

Tractates of the Mishnah and Talmud

BQam	*Baba Qamma*	Middot	*Middot*
Ed	*'Eduyyot*	Ned	*Nedarim*
Erub	*'Erubin*	Šab	*Šabbat*
GenR	*Genesis Rabbah*	Sanh	*Sanhedrin*
Git	*Gittin*	Taan	*Ta'anit*
Meg	*Megilla*	Yad	*Yadayim*

Miscellaneous Texts

ANEATP	*The ANE. An Anthology*, ed. Pritchard
ANEP	*Ancient Near East in Pictures*, ed. Pritchard
ANET	*Ancient Near Eastern Texts*, ed. Pritchard
ANESTP	*Ancient Near East. Supplement*ary, ed. Pritchard
ApocNT	*The Apocryphal New Testament*, ed. James
ApocOT	*The Apocryphal Old Testament*, ed. Sparks
APOT	*Apoc and Pseudepigrapha of the OT*, ed. Charles
InscrGr	*Inscriptiones Graecae*
NTApoc	*The NT Apocrypha*, ed. Hennecke et al.
OTP	*OT Pseudepigrapha*, ed. Charlesworth
RST	*Ras Shamra Texts*

Apostolic Fathers

Barn	*Epistle of Barnabas*
1 Clem	*First Clement*
Did	*Didache*
IgnEph	Ignatius, *Epistle to the Ephesians*
Magn	Ignatius, *Epistle to the Magnesians*
Philad	Ignatius, *Epistle to the Philadelphians*
IgnRom	Ignatius, *Epistle to the Romans*
Smyrn	Ignatiue, *Epistle to the Smyrnaeans*
Vis	*Shepherd of Hermas, Vision(s)*

Other Ancient Authors

AdFam	Cicero, *Ad familares*
AdvHaer	Irenaeus, *Adversus omnes haereses*
AdvMarc	Tertullian, *Adversus Marcionem*
AgPrax	Tertullian, *Against Praxeas*
Anab	Xenophon, *Anabasis*
Ann	Tacitus, *Annals*
Ant	Josephus, *Antiquities of the Jews*
ApChOrd	*Apostolic Church Order*
Apol	Aristides, *Apologia*
Apol	Justin Martyr, *Apologia*
Apol	Tertullian, *Apologeticum*
AppWo	Tertullian, *Apparel of Women*
BJ	Josephus, *Jewish Wars*
CAp	Josephus, *Contra Apionem*
CCel	Origen, *Contra Celsum*

CEph	Jerome, *Commentary on Ephesians*
CEzek	Jerome, *Commentary on Ezekiel*
ChrDoc	Augustine, *On Christian Doctrine*
CIsa	Jerome, *Commentary on Isaiah*
CivDei	Augustine, *City of God*
2 Clem	*Second Clement*
CMatt	Jerome, *Commentary on Matthew*
CMic	Jerome, *Commentary on Micah*
Cohort15	Pseudo-Justin, *Cohortatio 15*
DePat	Tertullian, *De patientia*
DeVir	Jerome, *De viris illustribus*
DivInst	Lactaantius, *Divinae institutiones*
EccHist	Eusebius, *Ecclesiastical History*
Ep	Augustine, *Epistles*
EvGood	Philo, *Every Good Man Is Free*
ExcTheod	*Excerpts from Theodotus*
Frag	Heraclitus, *Fragment*
Geog	Strabo, *Geography*
Haer	Theodoret, *Haereticarum*
Haer	Epiphanius, *Adversus lxxx haereses*
Hist	Tacitus, *Historiae*
Hist	Herodotus, *History*
HLuke	Origen, *Homily on Luke*
HMatt	Chrysostom, *Homily on Matthew*
HJere	Origen, *Homily on Jeremiah*
Hyp	Philo, *Hypothetica*
CJohn	Origen, *Commentary on John*
LAB	Pseudo-Philo, *Liber Antiquitatum Biblicarum*
Lives	Suetonius, *Lives of the Twelve Caesars*
MartPol	*Martyrdom of Polycarp*
Mon2	Pseudo-Justin, *Monarchia 2*
NatHist	Pliny the Elder, *Naturalis historia*
Od	Homer, *Odyssey*
OnAnt	Hippolytus, *On Antichrist*
OnFF	Philo, *On Flight and Finding*
Onom	Eusebius, *Onomasticon*
OnPrin	Origen, *On First Principles*
OpHist	Nicephorus, *Opuscula Historica*
Pan	Epiphanius, *Panarion*
Phaed	Plato, *Phaedrus*
Plot	Porphyry, *Life of Plotinus*
PraepEv	Eusebius, *Praeparatio Evangelica*
PraeschHaer	Tertullian, *De praescriptione haereticorum*
Protrept	Clement of Alexandria, *Protrepticus*
Ref	*Refutatio omnium haeresium*
RomHist	Dio Cassius, *Roman History*
Scorp	Tertullian, *Scorpiace*
SpecLeg	Philo, *De Spelialibus Legibus*
Strom	Clement of Alexandria, *Stromata*
Trypho	Justin, *Dialogue with Trypho*

English Versions

ASV	American Standard Version (USA ed. of ERV)
AT	An American Translation (aka "Goodspeed" and "Chicago Bible")

AV	Authorized Version (UK; =KJV)
Beck	*NT in the Language of Today*
CCD	Confraternity of Christian Doctrine (RCC NT; see NCE; see also NCB = NAB)
CEV	Contemporary Eng. Ver. (NT w/Pss, Prov 1991)
CPV	Cotton Patch Version (Jordan, NT portions)
CTNT	*Centenary Trans. of the NT*
ERV	English Revised Version (rev. KJV; =RV in UK)
GNB	*Good News Bible* (=TEV)
JB	Jerusalem Bible (=annotated; see NJB)
KJV	King James Version (=AV in UK)
Moffatt	*Holy Bible, a New Translation*
NAB	New American Bible (RCC)
NASB	New American Standard Bible (=NASV)
NASV	New American Standard Version (=NASB)
NCB	(New Confraternity Bible) =NAB
NCE	New Catholic Edition
NEB	New English Bible (see REB)
NIV	New International Version
NJT, NJV	New Jewish Translation, NJVersion (=TNK)
NJB	New Jerusalem Bible (rev. JB; =annotated)
NKJB	New King James Bible (=NKJV)
NKJV	New King James Version (=NKJB)
NRSV	New Revised Standard Version (rev. RSV)
ONT	*Original New Testament*
PME	*NT in Modern English*
RV	Revised Version (usu. in UK; =ERV)
REB	Revised English Bible (rev. NEB)
RSV	Revised Standard Version (rev. ASV/ERV)
TEV	Today's English Version (=GNB)
TNK	TaNaKh (new JPS Hebrew Bible; =NJT =NJV)
Williams	*NT in the Language of the People*

Biblical Texts

Old Testament

Gen	Genesis	Cant	Song of Solomon
Exod	Exodus	Isa	Isaiah
Lev	Leviticus	Jer	Jeremiah
Num	Numbers	Lam	Lamentations
Deut	Deuteronomy	Ezek	Ezekiel
Josh	Joshua	Dan	Daniel
Judg	Judges	Hos	Hosea
Ruth	Ruth	Joel	Joel
1,2 Sam	1, 2 Samuel	Amos	Amos
1,2 Kgs	1, 2 Kings	Obad	Obadiah
1,2 Chr	1, 2 Chronicles	Jonah	Jonah
Ezra	Ezra	Mic	Micah
Neh	Nehemiah	Nah	Nahum
Esth	Esther	Hab	Habakkuk
Job	Job	Zeph	Zephaniah
Ps/Pss	Psalms	Hag	Haggai
Prov	Proverbs	Zech	Zechariah
Eccl (or Qoh)	Ecclesiastes (or Qoholet)	Mal	Malachi

Apocryphal and Deuterocanonical Books

Tob	Tobit
Jdt	Judith
Add Esth	Additions to Esther
Wis	Wisdom of Solomon
Sir	Ecclesiasticus, or Wisdom of Jesus Son of Sirach
Bar	Baruch
Ep Jer	Letter of Jeremiah
Pr Azar*	Prayer of Azariah and the Song of the Three Jews
(Song Thr*	Song of the Three Jews)
Sus*	Susanna
Bel*	Bel and the Dragon
1,2 Macc	1, 2 Maccabees
1 Esdr	1 Esdras
Pr Man	Prayer of Manasseh
Ps 151	Psalm 151
3 Macc	3 Maccabees
2 Esdr	2 Esdras
4 Macc	4 Maccabees

*(Pr Azar, Sus, and Bel are often treated as a composite unit: Add Dan = Additions to Daniel.)

New Testament

Matt	Matthew
Mark	Mark
Luke	Luke
John	John
Acts	Acts of the Apostles
Rom	Romans
1,2 Cor	1, 2 Corinthians
Gal	Galatians
Eph	Ephesians
Phil	Philippians
Col	Colossians
1,2 Thes	1, 2 Thessalonians
1,2 Tim	1, 2 Timothy
Titus	Titus
Phlm	Philemon
Heb	Hebrews
Jas	James
1,2 Pet	1, 2 Peter
1,2,3 John	1, 2, 3 John
Jude	Jude
Rev	Revelation

Miscellaneous

ABS	American Bible Society
app.	appendix(es)
ASOR	American Schools of Oriental Research
b.	born
B.C.E.	before the common/Christian era (=B.C.)
ca.	*circa*, approximately
C.E.	of/during the common/Christian era (=A.D.)
chap(s).	chapter(s)
cf.	*confer*, compare
d.	died
ed(s).	edition, editor(s), edited by
e.g.	*exempli gratia*, for example
esp.	especially
fl.	flourished
frag.	fragment
ft.	foot/feet
Gk.	Greek
Heb.	Hebrew
ibid.	*ibidem*, in that place, in the same place
i.e.	*id est*, that is
in.	inch(es)
JPS	Jewish Publication Society
km.	kilometer(s)
lit.	literally
log.	logion
LXX	Septuagint
m.	meter(s)
ms(s).	manuscript(s)
mg.	margin, marginal reading
mi.	mile(s)
MT	Masoretic Text (Heb. OT)
NABPR	National Association of Baptist Professors of Religion
NCC	National Council of the Churches of Christ in the USA (also NCC/USA)
NCCJ	National Council of Christians and Jews
NT	New Testament
OT	Old Testament
oz(s).	ounce(s)
r.	reigned, regnal period (dates for rulers)
par.	parallel(s)
Rab	Rabbinic interpretation
rev.	revised, revision, revised by
SBL	Society of Biblical Literature
UBS	United Bible Societies
v(v).	verse(s)
vs.	versus

The Nature of Scripture

Richard F. Wilson

In his 1983 presidential address before the Society of Biblical Literature, Krister Stendahl probed the topic "The Bible as a Classic and the Bible as Holy Scripture" (1984). The "and" in Stendahl's proposal is significant because he argues against all attempts to separate an understanding of the Old and New Testaments as "classics" of Western culture from the appropriation of those same bodies of literature as "Holy Scripture" for synagogues and churches throughout the last twenty-five centuries. The Bible is a classic of Western culture, Stendahl argues, precisely because it is revered as Scripture in communities of faith across the centuries. The reverence accorded Scripture precedes its status as a classic, or as Stendahl puts it: "it is its recognition that makes a classic a classic, not its inner qualities" (1984, 4). Failure to acknowledge the Bible as Scripture ignores the precise reason it has become a classic of Western culture. The Bible, with all its diversity of setting, genre, and confession, *"becomes important* for those to whom *the scriptures function* as the bearer of revelation" (Stendahl 1984, 5; emphasis added).

While the dominant emphasis of Stendahl's address is a challenge to biblical scholars to remember the confessional and revelatory nature of Scripture, there is nonetheless a serious challenge to *all* who pick up the books of the Old and New Testaments (and, if one is so inclined, the apocryphal and deuterocanonical writings) to remember that they are handling pieces of literature that are infused with the very identity of the communities of faith that undergird the synagogue and the church. The communities—ancient and contemporary—who "recognize" the revelatory function of Scripture both shape it and are shaped by their recognition of it. These books—the Old and New Testaments, and the apocryphal and deuterocanonical books for some—are more than literary survivors in the face of changing history. They are, by virtue of their status as Scripture, the shadows and echoes of communities of faith that stretch as far back as the time of ABRAHAM, MOSES, DAVID, JEREMIAH, EZRA, Judas Maccabeus, JESUS, PAUL, JAMES, and JOHN.

They are, however, more than mere shadows and echoes. The Bible is the lifeblood and breath of the community of faith. Before the Bible became the Bible the stories and exhortations that fill its pages were the common language of memory in the community of faith. Rooted in the claim "A wandering Aramean was my ancestor" (Deut 26:5), and underscored with force in the Johannine confession on the lips of Thomas, "My Lord and my God!" (John 20:28), Scripture has become the mirror in which the community of faith glimpses its rich and diverse heritage, as well as its ultimate hopes. The two, heritage and hope, are different sides of the same coin. Any attempt to separate the history of the communities of faith in synagogue and church from the contemporary expressions of the people of God is a woeful perversion of the unity of God's revelatory presence in history. God is not solely revealed in history through literature; neither is God revealed in history merely in the life of the assembled body of those who seek God's presence. Both the community of faith and the literature of confession are required for a satisfactory foundation for understanding the Bible as Scripture.

In this essay we will explore the nature of Scripture in the context of the persistent reality of a community of faith that draws identity from the confession that the God of Abraham and Sarah shapes and transforms the community in each generation. Telling the stories of Abraham and Sarah, and the stories of all of those models of faithful pilgrims who came after them, is more than recounting the past. Telling the stories also is a way of enlivening the present. In the stories of Abraham and Sarah, and those like them, the community of faith experiences a unique opportunity to look backward and forward at the same time. Looking backward enriches the community's sense of heritage, which in turn stimulates the hope for a destination at the end of the pilgrimage. The writer of Hebrews captures the possibility of a simultaneous backward and forward perspective in the image of the runner in the arena: "Since we are surrounded by so great a cloud of witnesses, . . . let us run with perseverance the race that is set before us" (12:1).

Because the primary intent of this essay takes seriously the integral relationship between the community of faith and its confessional literature, there are three issues that will not receive the sort of detailed treatment some readers may expect. Readers will have to look elsewhere for in-depth discussions of the formation of CANON (Hinson 1990 offers a concise treatment), the structures of canon (there *is* more than one), and those thorny issues that surround the claims of the authority of Scripture (see Angell 1990). That is not to suggest that the history of the canon, the structures of canon, and the confessions of the authority of Scripture are not important. They are important indeed. Giving those issues only passing attention in this essay stems from the conviction that too much time and energy have been devoted to the historical and theological issues *about* the Bible at the expense of genuine explorations into the nature *of* the Bible.

James A. Sanders and Stanley Hauerwas are correct in their challenges to those in the academy and the church who would objectify Scripture as the focus of study rather than recognize the inseparable relationship between the Bible and the practicing community of faith. Sanders observes that "the Bible reaches its true stature in church . . . not in the university or even the pastor's study alone" (1987, xi). In his refreshingly confrontational manner Hauerwas claims that "fundamentalism and biblical criticism are both aberrations of the Christian tradition" because "both camps assume an objectivity of the text in order to the make the Bible available to anyone" (1993, 29, 36). To say that the Bible matures in the church recognizes that the nature of Scripture both draws from and feeds into the community of believers who, in each generation, attempt to see, experience, articulate, and model life lived in the presence of God.

Scripture by its nature is *more than* literature, although it is at least literature. Scripture by its nature is *more than* history, although it is at least history. Perhaps most important of all, Scripture by its nature is *more than* a guidebook for the community of faith when they are gathered for worship or dispersed throughout the larger communities from which they come. Scripture is at least a guide for worship, theology, and ethics, but it is no mere manual or "recipe

book" for the community seeking to live life in the presence of God.

Scripture in a Quilted Community

Most treatments of the formation of canon focus on the crises that prompted communities of faith to identify the core of the traditions that told them who they were, where they came from, and how they should live in relation to God, one another, and their world. The result is that Scripture becomes objectified as the end product of a relatively well-defined historical circumstance. As a corollary, attention and emphasis fall upon a significant person, or group, who exerts a power of influence over both the community and the literature it finally accepts as Scripture. For example, then, the name of Ezra is virtually synonymous with TORAH, and the name of IRENEAUS is inseparable from the collection of a fourfold Gospel.

The major motif of this essay argues against the dominance of such a patchwork of historical crises and charismatic leaders that effect the recognition of certain pieces or collections of literature as Scripture for the community. The patchwork exists, of course, and the historical events and personalities *do* deserve careful consideration. There is another side, however, that should receive primary consideration: the community of faith as it persistently exists through the ages. Conceive of Scripture as a richly crafted quilt, the sort of work grandmothers and aunts of days gone by invested months and years creating. The patchwork side of the quilt is clearly the more interesting with its variety of textures, patterns, and colors. If the quilt is a family project it also bears reminders of the traditions that give the family its identity. Without argument the patchwork side is the more interesting, but the other side—often a plain, but sturdy, seamless stretch of heavy flannel—is what gives the quilt its strength, its durability, and its usefulness.

An exploration into the nature of Scripture requires a primary acknowledgment of the community of faith that provides the constant context that holds together the changing history, diverse styles, and conflicting theologies found throughout the Bible. The authentic community of faith is the constant that gives Scripture its strength, durability, and usefulness precisely because it is the authentic community of faith that continually listens to and hears the words of Scripture as the word of God spoken afresh for each generation.

Textures in the Pentateuch. The first stop on the exploration of canon formation is usually the Water

Gate in Jerusalem during the days of Ezra and Nehemiah (see Neh 8:1-8). The crisis of the EXILE, and then the return to Jerusalem and the struggle to rebuild the city walls and the Temple, had forced the community to ask the foundational questions of identity: Who are we? Where have we come from? and How do we relate to God, to one another, and to our world?

With Ezra's reading of the book of the law, which most readers of the Bible agree was very close to the Pentateuch as read today (Sanders 1972, 51), a closing date for the first division of the Hebrew Bible and Christian Scripture is established near the turn of the fourth century B.C.E. In the drama of the moment, however, it often seems that the great crowds that *heard and recognized* the event as the reading and hearing of the word of God are lost. The emphasis falls first of all upon the literature, and secondarily upon Ezra, frequently cited as the "Father of the Torah" or the "Father of Judaism."

But what of the community that heard and recognized the words as authoritative for their lives? Their hearing and recognizing the words as *more than literature* and the stories of the Pentateuch as *more than history* is certainly the most enduring feature of this scrap of antiquity. An emphasis on the community who hears and recognizes Scripture may, perhaps, correct the imbalance of emphasis that has crept into discussions of Scripture. The literature and history of the Bible is not distinct from the life of the community that reveres it as revelatory; neither can the life of the community that reveres Scripture afford to separate itself from the persistent questions asked through Scripture: Who are we? Where have we come from? and How do we relate to God, to one another, and to our world?

The other stops along the path of exploring the formation of canon look much like the first stop at the Water Gate in Jerusalem during the days of Ezra and Nehemiah. A major crisis catches the attention of the historian because of the way it forces a refocusing of the questions of identity for the community of faith. Through the adaptations of the identifying traditions in a new context, the stability of the community of faith—and its identity that allows it not only to survive but to flourish in the time of crisis—is once again secured. With the passing of the crisis a new division of sacred writings emerges as authoritative for the community.

Textures in the Prophets. The second division of the Hebrew Bible—the Prophets—takes its final shape in the prolonged crises of the growth of Hellenism in the second and third centuries B.C.E. There is widespread agreement that both the Former and Latter Prophets achieved literary stability as much as two centuries before they achieved canonical status. Happily there are no overpowering personalities to undermine the significance of the community of faith during this stage of development. The canonization of the Prophets lacks the sort of clear precipitating factors that make it easy to slight the significance of the community in the process. There is no Exile and no Ezra, as in the case of the Torah. There is no destruction of Jerusalem and no so-called "Council of Jamnia," as in the case of the Writings. Neither are there a MARCION and an Ireneaus, as in the case of the Gospels; nor is there a letter from a powerful bishop of the church, as is the case for the remainder of the NT.

The emergence of the Prophets as Scripture is, therefore, an excellent place to look for the nature of Scripture in the combination of an active community of faith, its heritage and hopes, and the literature that sharpens its identity. Faced with the threat of assimilation into a very appealing Hellenistic world, it appears that the Prophets provided the means by which the community of faith was able to adapt its Torah faith to the present in a way that maintained the integrity of its Torah heritage.

The narratives of the Former Prophets (Joshua–Kings, but not Ruth; the Book of Ruth properly belongs with the Writings), for example, helped the community of faith understand how Torah faith could provide a bulwark against the cultural influences that surrounded them. Taking their cues from the stories of JOSHUA, the judges, ELIJAH and ELISHA, and the like, fourth-, third-, and second-century Jews in the SYNAGOGUE apparently learned how to distance themselves, somewhat, from the Hellenists and their ways.

Both the Former Prophets and the Latter Prophets (Isaiah, Jeremiah, Ezekiel, and the Book of the Twelve) helped forge the Torah faith, with its focus on the role of Moses as the giver of God's law, into a Torah faith with a distinctly monarchical accent with David as the paradigm of God's presence in the midst of the people. The David narratives—the centerpiece of the Former Prophets—do not eclipse the covenants with Abraham and Moses that give the Torah its central identifying story. Rather the David narratives contemporize the community's identity as the people of God, giving a simultaneous glimpse of a rich heritage in the Davidic Kingdom and an exciting hope in the coming KINGDOM OF GOD. The Latter Prophets' point of departure in the David story as the clearest expression of the community's understanding of its relationship to God is a powerful illustration of how the Torah faith of the Exile was adapted in those communities of faith that survived and flourished in the centuries following the return to Jerusalem. Even the prophets of the Northern Kingdom, that is, AMOS and HOSEA, and the postexilic prophets' use of the Davidic ideal as the most appropriate way to understand the relationship between God and the people, whether in political or merely cultural terms, is testimony to the power and authority of the second division of the Hebrew Bible.

Without doubt the Maccabean Revolt (167–164 B.C.E.) drew upon the narratives of conquest found in the Books of Joshua, Judges, and Samuel. There the MACCABEES, and those that followed their leadership, found justification and authority for their resistance to the oppressive demands of the Syrians under the leadership of Antiochus IV. In the crucible of contemporary crisis the community of faith *heard and recognized* the word of God in a productive way. Their understanding of (the oral and) written traditions from their past transformed the meaning of Scripture into a foundational document that answered for them the questions: Who are we? Where have we come from? and How do we relate to God, to one another, and to our world?

Of course an exclusively political hearing and reading of the Torah and Prophets would cause problems for faithful Jews to follow, most notably the Zealots of the first century C.E. Nonetheless, adapting the traditions of the community of faith by recognizing the authority of another collection of literature alongside the Torah would serve to enrich an understanding of identify in the midst of a changing world.

Textures in the Septuagint. Alongside the emergence of the second division of the Hebrew Bible, the Prophets, some mention and discussion of the SEPTUAGINT (LXX) is needed. The LXX is a significant example of how the believing Jewish community attempted to adapt to the influences of Hellenism *without* being thoroughly assimilated. The language of the LXX, Greek, attests to the tensions in the community of faith that called it into existence. On the one hand they recognized that they were living in a world dominated by things Greek, language being the most pervasive example. On the other hand the community of faith continued to strain to *hear and recognize* their identi-

fying traditions, rooted in a Hebrew culture. In the LXX, members of contemporary communities of faith may glimpse reflections of earlier communities actively engaged in hearing, recognizing, and living according to the word of God in their midst.

From the middle of the third century B.C.E. until near the end of the first century C.E. the LXX functioned as Scripture for communities of faith, including those identified with the Jewish synagogues and, later, the early Christians and their churches. As had been the case before, this Scripture was the means through which the community *heard and recognized* the word of God in their midst as they attempted to answer the questions Who are we? Where have we come from? and How do we relate to God, to one another, and to our world?

Texture in the Writings. First-century JUDAISM, the soil from which Christianity sprang, thrived as a far-flung community of faith. Although members of that community participated in a variety of socicocultural settings from Rome, Corinth, Alexandria, throughout Asia Minor, Damascus, Jerusalem, and on to the East, they shared a common tradition that had been woven through the narratives, codes, and poetry of the Torah and the Prophets—and those other pieces of literature that filled out the LXX, many of which were included later in the Writings of the Hebrew Bible, the Christian OT, and the apocryphal and deuterocanonical works. That there was a common core tradition recognized as Scripture in spite of the deep and wide varieties among individual communities underscores the thesis of this essay. Both the community of faith and the literature of confession are required for a satisfactory foundation for understanding the Bible as Scripture.

By the end of the first century, however, the internal divisions of and the external threats to Judaism would result in a major transformation of the community of faith. Of the many faces of first-century Judaism—including those of SADDUCEES, PHARISEES, ESSENES, HERODIANS, ZEALOTS, and followers of "The Way" (see Acts 9:1)—only rabbinic Judaism, the legacy of the Pharisees, and Christianity survived. Remarkably, even with the demise of many expressions of Judaism, and the ultimate separation of the two that remained, the common core tradition recognized as Scripture remained intact. How could that be? Because the community of faith, even in disarray and fractured, continued to *hear and recognize* the word of God as it was used in the community. The community that preserved the traditions stretching back to the days of Abraham and Sarah was once again preserved to a large degree by those same traditions, now recognized as Scripture. The nature of Scripture is woven deep into the fabric of the community of faith. Only when the community uses the Scripture with integrity can it find out who it is *and* come to a genuine understanding of the nature of Scripture.

The common core of tradition found in the Torah and Prophets remained intact, but there were other developments in the community of faith that resulted in a reconsideration of the extent of the authoritative literature for its life. Until a generation ago those "other developments" at the end of the first century of the Common Era were finely focused around the destruction of the Temple in Jerusalem by the Romans in 70 C.E.

The standard explanation for the closing of the third and final division of the Hebrew Bible was the so-called Council of Jamnia. There a group of rabbis allegedly gathered to salvage what was left of their heritage. With the Temple gone all that remained were the Torah and the Prophets and collections of other literature (including the LXX). The outcome of the gathering was the "canonization" of the Writings.

The work of "canonical criticism" during the last twenty years has challenged the neat package of Jamnia in favor of an appreciation of the living community of faith that allows for a more fluid concept of canonization (see esp. Sanders 1987, 77–86). Thus the modern reader of Scripture may acknowledge that at some point during the end of the first and beginning of the second centuries of the Common Era the literature of the Hebrew Bible and the OT of Christian Scripture became a stable body of literature that could rightly be identified as Scripture. What is important to recognize is that no group of rabbis (or bishops) authorized the inclusion of the literature called Scripture. Rather, Scripture emerges in the context of the life of the community of faith as it seeks answers to the primary questions: Who are we? Where have we come from? and How do we relate to God, to one another, and to our world?

James Sanders rightly insists that "adaptability" is the "major characteristic" in the process of canon formation (1987, 22, 83). The traditions around which Scripture takes shape, primarily those of the EXODUS and of the Sinai COVENANT, are stable. Nonetheless, the life of the community of faith is focused and refocused in ever-changing ways. Its central traditions are

interpreted in light of the dramatic changes that the community has faced throughout the centuries. With the emergence of the Prophets and the Writings the community of faith continues to find its identity in terms of the God who called Abraham and Moses, and who made a covenant with the people at SINAI. The Prophets and Writings do not eclipse the Torah faith. Instead they show how the community of faith adapted their Torah faith to a changing world.

The historical contexts that shaped the emergence of the three divisions of the Hebrew Bible span half a century; the literature itself was shaped over two millennia. The traditions of Abraham, Moses, and David that emerged as the central traditions of the community of faith that endured for those two thousand years provide the broad textures of both the Hebrew Bible and the Christian OT (the differences will be explored, in part, in the next section). Pressing the metaphor of the quilt, the primary motif of this essay, the textures of the Torah, Prophets, and Writings are the most obvious ones in the Bible. There are more, less dramatic, textures in the division of Christian Scripture called the NT. To those textures we now turn attention.

Textures in the New Testament. Paul the Apostle was what modern readers of the NT would call a "church planter." The letters he wrote, and those that were written under his influence, are specifically related to particular communities of faith, their particular circumstances, and their particular needs. Those letters are excellent reminders that the nature of Scripture is *always* directed to the needs of the community of faith. In the context of the NT, the particularity of the community of faith, then, is the constant feature of Scripture.

Perhaps contemporaneous with Paul—or at least in the next generation—another collection of letters circulated among the community of faith. These GENERAL LETTERS were not so tied to specific communities and were, therefore, broader treatments of the themes that demanded the attentions of the Christian church as it was being formed. By the end of the century there was also an apocalypse that many in the community looked to for hope and encouragement.

During the generation following Paul's activity as church planter and letter writer another type of literature emerged. The GOSPEL appeared in response to questions and confusion in the community about the Jesus story (see, e.g., Luke 1:1-4; John 20:30-31 and 21:20-25). That the broad community came to accept four distinct versions of the story (see below) is further evidence that the gospel genre was an important texture in the emergence of Scripture.

The NT as modern readers know it took its initial turn toward "canon" with the work of Marcion who, it seems, was the first to make a list of accepted writings for the Christian community. His selection of literature is well known—the Gospel of Luke, edited, and ten letters that bear the name of Paul (the PASTORAL EPISTLES were not included; some say Marcion did not know them), also edited—but what is sometimes lost in his wake is the widespread recognition of Pauline works. Because Marcion only identified the Gospel of Luke as authoritative for the community, most of the attention given to Marcion centers on the way his critics defended a broader collection of Gospels.

One of the most frequently noted critics of Marcion—and the Gnostics with whom he is associated—is Ireneaus, whose name is synonymous with the fourfold Gospel collection in the NT. Ireneaus did develop a rationale for seeing the Gospels of Matthew, Mark, Luke, and John as authoritative for the larger community, but in all likelihood his work was a reflection of the broad acceptance of the community of faith. Ireneaus did not establish the fourfold Gospels; he merely articulated one set of theological reasons behind a prior acceptance of those works (see *AdvHaer* 3.11.8).

The Pauline corpus never seems to have been disputed in the early communities of faith. Marcion included ten works; the MURATORIAN CANON includes them and the Pastoral Epistles. Later, in the *EccHist*, EUSEBIUS hesitated on five of the General Letters, but his hesitation was probably on the basis of the use of that literature in the community of faith. Eusebius was also ambivalent on the inclusion of the Revelation; again the ambivalence was a reflection of the attitudes of the community of faith. The point is that in the context of the early Christian church the community of faith seems to have directed in an obvious manner the acknowledgment of the literature that would, or would not, function as the authority of the community in that generation and for generations to come.

ATHANASIUS, bishop of Alexandria during the last half of the fourth century C.E. is credited with punctuating the canon of the NT. His Festal Letter of 367 included the first known enumeration of the twenty-seven pieces of literature currently included in the NT. Once again, however, it is significant to note that his work was directed to the community of faith as it was spread throughout the ROMAN EMPIRE of the day.

Athanasius did not create the canon. He did, however, reflect the ways the community of faith had been using the literature that modern readers call the NT.

The textures of Scripture underscore its particularity in communities of faith all the way from Ezra to Athanasius. The constant feature over that eight hundred years is a vibrant community of faith seeking to answer the important questions of Who are we? Where have we come from? and How do we relate to God, to one another, and to our world?

The nature of Scripture, then, is imbedded in the nature of the community of faith as it matured, was challenged, and revived. Scripture is the basic structure around which the community of faith finds refuge in changing times. Scripture cannot be divorced from the community and neither should it become an authority *above* the community. Rather Scripture should always be seen as the authority *within* the community of faith for every generation.

Scripture in a Diverse Community

In the foregoing section the textures that are apparent in Scripture were sketched in broad strokes, emphasizing that the textures themselves are clues to the nature of Scripture. Pursuing the motif of the quilt, the textures of Torah, Prophets, and Writings for the Hebrew Bible and Christian OT, and the textures of Epistles, Gospels, and Apocalypse for the Christian NT remind contemporary readers of Scripture that the Bible is inseparable from the history of the communities of faith that *heard and recognized* its words as the word of God in their midst.

Texture is only one part of the nature of Scripture. There are also present well-defined patterns and colors that allow the reader to see the rich diversity of the texts—and the communities—that comprise the Bible. This section of the essay will continue the motif of the quilt with specific attention given to the patterns and colors woven into the fabric of the community of faith and, subsequently, into the pages of Scripture.

Patterns in the Old Testament. For more than a century language derived from the so-called "documentary hypothesis" has had a place in discussions of the Pentateuch. While the initial assessment of literary diversity in the Torah was couched in terms of "documents" and, therefore, left the impression of individual authors or editors, "the process is now seen as communal" and "in terms of traditions which are linked to an ongoing community whose perceptions and understandings are related to their historical experience"

(Brueggemann 1976, 971–72). With a renewed perspective on the community of faith as a thriving organism with varied accents and emphases, the terms YAHWIST, ELOHIST, DEUTERONOMIST, and PRIESTLY WRITERS now point to the rich diversity within the community, rather than to competing voices within the community struggling to be heard. Such an emphasis upon diversity rather than competition makes it easier to understand how these varied patterns of expression can be found in the unified literature called Scripture.

In the same way the textures of Scripture provide glimpses of the community of faith in particular historical and political contexts, so too, the patterns of Scripture allow contemporary readers to observe and participate in the history and life of their forebears. Woven through the pages of the Pentateuch are the testimonies of the community of faith stimulated by five hundred years of continuity and change. The patterns of the Yahwist reflect life under the seemingly endless optimism that stamped the early days of Solomon's reign. That optimism is tempered by the cautions of the Elohist that flowed into Judah on the lips of refugees from the Northern Kingdom following its destruction by Assyria in 722 B.C.E.

The critical theological judgments that became vogue during the days of JOSIAH and his sweeping reforms of the nation punctuate the Pentateuch in the form of the Book of Deuteronomy. The Priestly writers offer a series of introductions and comments on the whole story of Abraham, Sarah, and their descendants from their perspective of hopeful theological reconstructions of faith that were forged in the period of the Exile.

Two features of the diverse patterns of the Pentateuch are particularly remarkable. Each underscores the primary place of the community of faith as the bearer of its own traditions, as opposed to the traditions being imposed upon the community by some force, whether that of a single charismatic leader or a powerful group within the community. First is the fact that these patterns are crafted around the same set of historic circumstances and events. The second is the fact that the patterns exist side by side without any apparent attempt to make the traditions uniform.

The stories of Abraham and Sarah illustrate the first point. Three episodes in the Genesis narratives provide shades of meaning to the idea of Abraham and Sarah as bearers of the covenant promise: the promise of COVENANT (Gen 15); CIRCUMCISION as the sign of the covenant (Gen 17); and the command to Abraham to sacrifice Isaac as the point where the covenant faith of Abraham matures (Gen 22). The first episode bears the accent of the Yahwist; the second episode carries the perspective of the Priestly writers; the final scene conveys the cautions of the Elohist, cautions against confusing popular cultural practices and the word of God (von Rad 1972; cf. Westermann 1986). These three narratives from Genesis each make a confession about Abraham and Sarah as the bearers of the covenant promise that was important to the community of faith.

That these three episodes are found in the Book of Genesis with their distinct features intact is an illustration of the second point. Readers of these stories hear the unmistakable confession that covenants with God are "cut"; yet there is no attempt to regulate an understanding of "cutting the covenant." These stories are *unified* around the figures of Abraham and Sarah in relation to God, but there is no attempt to make the stories *uniform*. The diversity in the story of Abraham and Sarah reflects a diversity in the community of faith that sought in the Abraham story answers to the crucial questions: Who are we? Where have we come from? and How do we relate to God, to one another, and to our world? Those questions can have *unified* responses without having a *uniform* one.

Also significant in this trio of narratives is the point that the traditions they carry look back to the Abraham and Sarah story in order to clarify an identity in the present, and to find a point of departure from which to focus a hope for the future. The accents, or patterns, of three different moments in the life of the same community of faith are preserved. The accent of the Yahwist community from the tenth century does not drown out that of the Priestly writers of the fifth; neither of them eclipses the accent of the Elohist community from the eighth century. Pressing again the motif of this essay, these moments from three different periods in the life of the community of faith are held in place with their vibrant patterns and colors intact precisely by the continuity of the community, and its ability to adapt its understandings of its identity and purpose for each generation. The nature of Scripture is inseparable from the life of the community of faith. What gives the Scripture its strength, durability, and usefulness, then, is the willingness of the community of faith to *hear and recognize* the words of Scripture as the word of God in their midst.

The Pentateuch is the foundation for Scripture and for any understanding of the nature of Scripture. What is apparent in an examination of the Pentateuch is also applicable for the remaining literature that comprises an understanding of Scripture. The literature of the Bible reflects the diversity of the community of faith that *heard and recognized* the word of God in the stories of the patriarchs, the liberators (Moses, Joshua, and the judges), the kings, and the prophets. In each generation the narratives took on particular significance as Scripture when the people found in them identity and hope.

The Former Prophets do not present a uniform narrative of the work of God in the period preceding the establishment of the monarchy. The faithfulness of GIDEON (Judg 6–8), for example, stands in sharp contrast to the faithlessness of JEPHTHAH (Judg 10–12) and SAMSON (Judg 13–16). Likewise the narratives of SAMUEL and SAUL that surround the formation of the monarchy are ambivalent. On the one hand Saul appears as the perfect choice to lead Israel (1 Sam 9:1–10:16); on the other hand Saul is a dubious choice (1 Sam 10:17-27). Similar ambivalence is found throughout the episodes of DAVID and SOLOMON.

The Later Prophets also are unified around the themes of God's challenging presence in the midst of the people in changing times. Thus, for example, JEREMIAH's harsh interpretations of the Babylonian invasion of Jerusalem (Jer 29) finds a balance in the words of ISAIAH welcoming the returning exiles to Jerusalem (Isa 60). Both interpretations are included in Scripture, emphasizing the diversity of Scripture in response to changing circumstance of the community of faith. The Book of the Twelve includes the tirades of OBADIAH against Edom, promising destruction for its response to Judah's fall to Babylon; it also includes God's stinging rebuke to JONAH, and others like him, for taking glee in threats of destruction rather than seeking compassion and tolerance.

As is the case in the Pentateuch, the Prophets present a montage of narrative content, style, genre, and theology. These varying stories, the different manner in which they are told, and the wide range of theological emphases found in them draw attention to the community of faith once again. As it persisted across the ages the community was able to hear and recognize the word of God in its midst in a number of ways. That the richness of confessions within the community remains intact with all their patterns, colors, and accents still vivid is remarkable indeed. The nature of Scripture finds its greatest expression as it is stretched across the community of faith that continues to hear and recognize in Scripture the word of God.

Perhaps the starkest contrast within the OT literature comes when one compares the Writings to the Torah and Prophets. The themes introduced in the Book of Deuteronomy, and that also dominate the books of Joshua through Kings (recall, again, that the Book of Ruth is not included in the Prophets), are directly challenged by the WISDOM LITERATURE, especially the Book of Job and some of the Psalms. The deuteronomist is firm in the conclusion that suffering and defeat are the direct result of sinfulness, yet the writer of the Book of Job is adamant that Job is without sin (1:1, 8, 22 passim). Something happened in the community of faith that caused it to reconsider its conclusions about health and suffering, and success and failure. That "something" was probably the Exile; and so alongside the deuteronomic history there emerged a more reflective, poetic confession of the relationship between God and the community.

The Prophets also include a challenge to the notion that suffering is the result of sin and disobedience. How else are we to understand the Servant Songs that appear in Isa 40–55? But the thoroughgoing reversal of the dominant theology of the deuteronomist is most apparent in the Book of Job, and Psalms such as Pss 37, 49, and 73.

Five pieces of literature within the Writings specifically draw attention to the community of faith as it sought to hear and recognize the word of God it its midst, not only in a particular period of history, but in the recurring cycles observed in worship. These "festival scrolls," or *Megilloth*, are Song of Songs (read at Passover), Ruth (read during Pentecost), Ecclesiastes (read during Tabernacles or "Booths"), Esther (read during Purim), and Lamentations (read to commemorate the destruction of the Temple on the ninth of Ab, and on the Day of Atonement). Their presence in Scripture is a poignant reminder that the use of the literature of faith is inseparable from its status as Scripture. First of all these five scrolls found their way into the regular life of the community at worship; subsequently they were included in the canon.

What is remarkable about the *Megilloth* is its diversity. The Book of Ruth is as broadly tolerant of those outside of JUDAISM as the Book of Esther is intolerant. Likewise the Book of Ecclesiastes is as sanguine in the face of progress as the Book of Lamentations is passionate in the face of defeat. And the eroticism of the Song of Songs seems to have carried the unqualified confession of joy in the presence of the God of history who comes to the people in an unexpected manner. That these scrolls are included in the collection of the Writings is testimony to the rich colors and patterns found in Scripture. These scrolls are unified around the confession that God is at work it the community, but there is no effort to make the confession uniform.

Patterns in the New Testament. Turning to the NT one is struck by the sharp distinctions among the portrayals of the Jesus story, and those among the encouragements for the actual living of the Christian life. Even a casual reader of the Gospels is aware that the first three Gospels (usually identified as the Synoptics because they share a common perspective and chronology) see the Jesus story through a different lens than the writer of the Gospel of John. In the Synoptics Jesus has an intense and vigorous ministry that lasts no longer than eighteen months, and he dies in Jerusalem during his first visit there as an adult. By contrast, Jesus in the Gospel of John has a less intense ministry that allows him to make at least four trips to Jerusalem to celebrate the PASSOVER—thus the popular notion of a three-year ministry.

The diversity of perspective between the Synoptics and the Gospel of John is further evident in such features as the absence of narratives relating the TEMPTATION OF JESUS and the TRANSFIGURATION in the Gospel of John (which are key components in the Synoptics), and the absence of a clearly stated identity of Jesus as the Messiah in the Synoptics (which is the central, explicit confession of the Gospel of John [see John 20:30-31; cf. Mark 8:27-33 and par. where the title "Messiah" is cautiously shunted to the side]). The Gospels are unified around the figure of Jesus, but they do not present a uniformity in the telling of the Jesus story.

The remainder of the NT also reflects the diversity within the first broad community of Christians. While the Pauline materials dominate the collections of letters in the NT (some would even say that PAUL has overshadowed JESUS as the primary influence in the contemporary CHURCH) there are also the distinct patterns and colors that make the Book of James and the Johannine Letters, for example, so noticeable.

The Pauline materials are directed to that segment of early Christianity that came to the faith on a path other than historic Judaism (see, e.g., Gal 2:1-9; 1 Cor 6:9-11; Rom 9–11). Consequently, the content and tone of the Pauline letters establish a foundation for a community of faith less concerned with ritual demands than it was concerned with the liberating experience of being justified by God's grace. Furthermore, the Pauline materials acknowledge the need to mature in one's thinking (see, e.g., 1 Cor 12–14). Thus through the letters that bear the name of Paul readers of Scripture glimpse the communities that heard and recognized Paul's confessions and encouragement as the word of God for them.

The reluctance in James to separate confessions of faith from faithful living is often placed in sharp contrast to the Pauline emphasis on "justification by faith." The conflict between James and Paul is more apparent than real: James is primarily interested in the *practice* of faith among confessing Christians, and Paul is interested in the *efficacy* of faith that leads to one's inclusion in the community of Christians (cf. Jas 2:17-18 and Eph 2:8-10). That both the Pauline material and James exist in the NT highlights the diversity of the community of faith. Clearly the community of faith was unified around the desire to model appropriate responses to the questions: Who are we? Where have we come from? and How do we relate to God, to one another, and to our world? Equally evident is that there was no effort to make the responses to those questions uniform. The acceptance of diversity takes precedence over any demand for uniformity.

Whereas the Pauline materials and the Letter of James probably reflect the same era (the 50s and 60s), the Johannine Letters (as well as the Gospel and the Apocalypse) belie a segment of the community of faith at least a generation later. The passing of time, especially beyond the significant threshold of the Roman destruction of Jerusalem in 70 C.E., establishes a context that is very different from the earlier days of broad tension between Christians from gentile and Jewish backgrounds. The Johannine Letters, as well as the Gospel of John (see esp. chap. 21), offer glimpses of a more narrowly defined community of faith beset with intramural squabbles about leadership and theological foundations (see Kysar 1992a and 1992b).

The Johannine materials underscore the diversity found in the NT less in their relationship to the rest of the literature than in the way they cohere. Within the confines of the Johannine collection, for example, the confessions about Jesus and the encouragement to live faithfully according to the model of Jesus (cf. John 13:31-35; 1 John 2:7-17; 3:11-24; 2 John 4-6) provide points of departure through which a particular community of faith is identified. The pattern established between "new commandment" and "love" is one of the sharpest patterns developed in the NT. The Johannine materials (and community) are clearly unified around such themes as new commandments and love—other themes also contribute to the coherence of the collection. In the broader collection of NT literature, however, there is no effort either to make Johannine perspectives conform to other patterns, or to reshape the Johannine collection in light of other collections. The confession of the Jesus story and encouragement for faithful living provide a unifying center without demanding a uniformity of confession and encouragement, not only for the Johannine materials, but for the whole NT.

Patterns in the Septuagint (and in the apocryphal and deuterocanonical works). Attention to the LXX as a precursor to the various canonical collections in contemporary Christianity (e.g., Eastern, Roman Catholic, and Protestant) is also an instructive glimpse at the diversity of the communities of faith that grew out of Hellenistic Judaism. The textures of the LXX have already been noted in relationship to the process of communities of faith accepting the Prophets and Writings as Scripture. What now captures our attention is the way that the LXX was transformed in the contexts of change within the communities of faith.

The LXX of the third century B.C.E. was a less than critical collection of diverse literature arranged in a manner that combines an interest in chronology and genre. The chronological impetus is reflected in the pattern of inserting the Book of Ruth between the Book of Judges and Kingdoms 1–4 (subsequently identified as 1–2 Samuel and 1–2 Kings), the inclusion of Judith, Tobit, and 1–4 Maccabees after Esther, and the longer versions of Jeremiah (the Additions to Jeremiah and the Letter of Baruch) and Daniel (the Prayer of Azariah, Susanna, and Bel and the Dragon). The attention to genre is seen in the insertion of Psalm 151 and the Prayer of Manasseh between Psalms and Proverbs, and the inclusion of the Wisdom of Solomon, Sirach, and another collection of psalms after the Book of Job.

The LXX included all of the pieces of literature that were subsequently identified as apocryphal or deuterocanonical. It also modelled an arrangement of texts that was ultimately accepted by the Christian community of faith, but rejected by the Jewish community of faith at the end of the first century C.E. (see Harrelson 1995).

More significant than the rearrangement of the texts of the Jewish Bible and the Christian OT (in its most narrow version) is the excision of certain books, such as the Maccabean literature, the additions to Daniel, Jeremiah, and Esther, and the poetic works of the Wisdom of Solomon and Sirach. Some segments of the community of faith apparently ceased to regard certain pieces of literature as Scripture. Even though the LXX functioned as Scripture for both Jewish and Christian communities during the second half of the first century, by the end of the century a retrenchment of the canon had occurred. In the synagogue Scripture was understood to be comprised of Torah, Prophets, and Writings; in the Christian churches Scripture was conceived along the lines of the LXX with or without the various additions of historical and poetic materials.

As James Sanders observes (1987), the canon is adaptable, even to the extent of being pared back. The emergence of the LXX in Hellenistic Judaism, its acceptance as Scripture in the synagogue and churches, and its subsequent downsizing by both Jews (by the end of the first century C.E.) and Christians (from the time of Jerome in the fourth century to that of Luther in the sixteenth [see Charlesworth 1992]) demonstrates, again, the relationship between Scripture and the communities that *heard and recognized* the literature as revelatory—or not!

That some pieces of literature were at one time considered Scripture by the community of faith, and later were assigned to the status of apocryphal and deuterocanonical works throws in sharp relief the boundaries between an authoritative collection of literature and the community (or communities) that regarded the literature "as the bearer of revelation" (Stendahl 1983, 5). The apocryphal and deuterocanonical works reveal the fluidity of the nature of Scripture as it was (and is) used in the broad center of faithful communities. Those communities that value the apocryphal and deuterocanonical works alongside the canons of the Old and New Testaments are part of the durable background that gives the patchwork of Scripture its stability. At the same time, however, those communities prove that there is no firm, impenetrable line to separate the communities and the literature they regard as revelatory.

Although it falls beyond the scope of this essay, it is important to note that vast collections of noncanonical literature have been used as supplements to Scripture by a variety of faithful communities through the centuries. The OT pseudepigrapha, the NT Apocrypha, the APOSTOLIC FATHERS, the DEAD SEA SCROLLS (which also contain canonical works), and the library discovered at NAG HAMMADI are the major examples of such supplemental literature. Interested readers would find exploration of the above-mentioned collections intriguing and instructive.

Scripture as Active Memory

The foregoing development of the nature of Scripture conceived through the metaphor of the quilt rests upon the conviction that the community of faith, as it has persisted through the centuries in synagogue and church, is both the preserver of the Word of God and the product of the Word of God. As the community has *heard and recognized* God's presence through Scripture, Scripture has emerged as the canon for the broader community of faith that spans time, geography, and cultures.

Leander Keck accurately draws attention to the relationship between Scripture and canon: "The Bible's standing in the church depends upon the church's experience of it as Scripture. When the Bible ceases to function as Scripture, as special, it ceases to be the canon and becomes instead a resource book on a shelf of great religious classics" (1983, 9). As noted above, all attempts to objectify Scripture—attempts to make the Bible a book on the shelf—undermine its mature nature. Critics who explore the historical, cultural, structural, and literary aspects of the Bible without also identifying the way Scripture functions in communities of faith through the centuries, fall short of understanding the true nature of Scripture. Likewise those who use the Bible as a tool to be used to corral the community, or as a weapon to wield against the opponents of the community, fail to experience the nature of Scripture. They fail to appreciate Scripture as the product of a persistent and diverse community of faith as reflected in synagogue and church over the last twenty-five centuries.

Attempting to objectify Scripture either as an esoteric focus of scholarship or as the devotional focus of the self-consciously religious finally ends with Scripture being read and used nostalgically. A nostalgic approach to Scripture is reductionistic at best and obscurantist at worst. The problem with nostalgia is twofold. First, what is wistfully recalled probably never actually existed. The Davidic Kingdom was not all peace and prosperity; the primitive church was not a paradigm of progress and harmony. Second, nostalgic forays are attempts to retreat rather than they are efforts to move forward.

The mature nature of Scripture is found in the way it stirs active memory in the life of the community of faith. In contrast to a nostalgic use of Scripture, the Bible as active memory confronts the multifaceted reality of the present even as it provides a lens through which the community of faith may glimpse the future. Nostalgia is that insidious inclination to be seduced by something dead and gone. The nostalgic impulse sucks the life breath out of the present and tries to blow it into the atrophied lungs of yesterday's corpse.

Memory, on the other hand, is the recognition that there is a continuity in what was alive and meaningful in the past and is still vibrant in the present. To preserve a memory is to broaden and deepen the very values that made life worth living in the past and to tap the same values for the present and future (cf. Buechner 1973, 58).

Scripture as active memory links the historic communities who *heard and recognized* the word of God in their midst with the contemporary community of faith in synagogues and churches who continues to *hear and recognize* the word of God in their midst. Scripture as active memory is at least literature and history, but it is more than that. Scripture as active memory is at least a guide for the community of faith, but it is more than that, too. The mature stature of Scripture emerges in the life of the community that acknowledges it as revelatory without thoroughly objectifying and externalizing it.

For Further Study

In the *Mercer Dictionary of the Bible*: APOCRYPHA, MODERN; APOCRYPHAL LITERATURE; APOSTOLIC FATHERS; BIBLE; BIBLE, AUTHORITY OF; CANON; DEAD SEA SCROLLS; NAG HAMMADI; REVELATION; TEXTS, MANUSCRIPTS, AND VERSIONS. In other sources: See the works cited, below, and P. Achtemeier, *The Inspiration of Scripture*; J. Barr, *Holy Scripture: Canon, Authority, Criticism*; J. Sanders, "The Strangeness of the Bible." *USQR* 42/1-2 (1988): 33-77; D. Tracy, *The Analogical Imagination*; J. Trafton, "The Importance of Noncanonical Literature," MCB.

Works Cited

Angell, J. William. 1990. "Bible, Authority of." MDB.

Brueggemann, Walter. 1976. "Yahwist." *IDBSup*.

Buechner, Frederick. 1973. *Wishful Thinking: A Theological ABC*.

Charlesworth, James H. 1992. "Old Testament Apocrypha," s.v. "Apocrypha." AncBD.

Harrelson, Walter. 1995. "The Hebrew Bible." MCB.

Hauerwas, Stanley. 1993. *Unleashing the Scripture*.

Hinson, E. Glenn. 1990. "Canon." MDB.

Keck, Leander E. 1983. "Scripture and Canon." *Quarterly Review* (Winter): 8–20.

Kysar, Robert. 1992a. "John, Epistles of." AncBD; 1992b. "John, Gospel of." AncBD.

Rad, Gerhard von. 1972. *Genesis*, rev. ed. OTL.

Sanders, James A. 1987. *From Sacred Story to Sacred Text*; 1974. *Torah and Canon*.

Stendahl, Krister. 1984. "The Bible as a Classic and the Bible as Holy Scripture." *JBL* 103/1:3-10.

Westermann, Claus. 1986. *Genesis 12–36: A Commentary*.

The Hebrew Bible

Walter Harrelson

The term "Hebrew Bible" is currently the most commonly used designation for the Christian Old Testament and the Jewish Bible. In the Jewish community the Hebrew Bible is also called by the acronym *Tanakh*, created by using the opening letter of the Hebrew names of the three parts of Jewish Scripture: *T* for the divine Law or Teaching (*Torah*), *N* for the Prophets (*Nevi'im*), and *K* for the Writings (*Ketuvim*). Many Christians today look for terms more suitable than "Old Testament" to refer to the Scriptures of the Jews, since "Old" has often been understood to mean "old and outmoded." Terms other than "Hebrew Bible" that are suitable are "First Testament" (which then allows Christians to refer to the New Testament as the "Second Testament") and "Jewish Bible."

The problem is complicated further by the fact that the Christian community preserved as a part of its OT a number of works not found in the Bible of the Jews. These works, routinely called Apocrypha by Protestants (Roman Catholics regard most of them as "deuterocanonical" and Eastern churches include one to three more such books as [deutero]canonical), generally have had somewhat less standing than the books in the Jewish Bible, chiefly because they were *not* claimed as canonical by the Jewish community. Most Christian Bibles today, however, include these apocryphal writings, together with some (e.g., 3 and 4 Maccabees and Psalm 151) that were not included in Roman Catholic and Protestant Bibles. While the Apocrypha and other ancient Jewish literature are widely used in Jewish scholarship, they are not a part of sacred Scripture in the same way the oral Torah, found in the Talmud (see RABBINIC LITERATURE), is understood as authoritative. Some Christian communities continue to leave the apocryphal writings out of their CANON of sacred Scripture.

The *order* of the Jewish Bible and Christian OT is also distinct. Both communities agree that the first five books are Genesis, Exodus, Leviticus, Numbers, and Deuteronomy, the books that comprise the Jewish TORAH. The Jewish designation for the next block of books is, as we saw above, the "Prophets," which include two groups of books—the "former" or "earlier" prophets Joshua, Judges, 1–2 Samuel, and 1–2 Kings—and the "latter" or "later" prophets Isaiah, Jeremiah, Ezekiel, and the Book of the Twelve (Amos, Hosea, Micah, etc.). The final block of writings in the Jewish Bible is the (sacred) Writings: Job, Psalms, Proverbs; the small festal scrolls Ruth, Song of Solomon, Ecclesiastes, Lamentations, and Esther; and the late writings Daniel, Ezra and Nehemiah (treated as one book in ancient times), and 1–2 Chronicles.

In the Christian Bible, the collection is organized differently, an arrangement that began already in the Jewish community in Egypt. This Jewish translation of the Hebrew Scriptures into Greek (which began in the third century B.C.E.) is found today in the Christian Greek OT called the SEPTUAGINT. Its arrangement has continued to be used in virtually all Christian Bibles. The arrangement clearly shows the desire of the translators to organize the material by subject matter, with little attention being given to the chronological development of the literature. The Book of Ruth is placed after the Book of Judges because the story of RUTH and NAOMI is set in the period when the judges ruled. The Books of 1–2 Chronicles are placed directly after the Books of 1–2 Kings because they cover much of the same ground covered in 1–2 Kings. Ezra, Nehemiah, and Esther are placed at the end of the historical collection that includes Joshua, Judges, Ruth, 1–2 Samuel, 1–2 Kings, and 1–2 Chronicles because Ezra, Nehemiah, and Esther continue the story of Israel's history in EXILE and tell of the return from exile to Judah. The festal scrolls are placed with the other poetic and wisdom materials, and Daniel is included as one of Israel's great prophets because Daniel, too, receives oracles from God for the people of Israel.

This difference in arrangement has had consequences to this day. Since the early Christian community understood itself as having inherited God's promise made to Abraham and his descendants, it only made sense for their "Old Testament" to end with the promise of Elijah's return to usher in a definitive epoch in Israel's history (Mal 4:5-6). And since the Jewish community had only recently (66–70 C.E.) witnessed the destruction of Jerusalem and its temple with the loss of thousands of lives and the scattering of the Jewish people, it only made sense for Jewish scholars in the following decades to place at the end of their collection the Book of 2 Chronicles, which spoke of the edict of the Persian king CYRUS that allowed Jews in Babylonian exile to return to their homeland. Christians found that their "Old Testament" led directly into the world of the NT, while Jews could note that their Scripture ended with continuing confidence that God had not abandoned the people of the covenant. Just as God had brought their ancestors back from Babylonian captivity to reclaim the LAND, so God could be counted upon to bring deliverance to the faithful once more. The order of Scripture carries a message of its own.

The Torah

The term "Torah" means "guidance" or "teaching" as well as "Law." The fundamental teaching found in the first five books of the Torah is clear: God is the creator of all that exists, and God guides the course of human life through divine promises and demands. Human life itself is sheer gift of divine love, for God could and did manage even when there were no human beings to serve their appointed ends. But human life is purposive and good, and in the garden God enjoys the companionship of the first human pair, is grieved to see disobedience and wickedness break out, and takes steps, even through severe punishment, to direct the human community toward God's purposed ends.

This theme finds expression throughout all the parts of the Torah (see the commentary on each of the five books). The development can be followed as a divine promise on the way to realization but never fully realized. God's promise to ABRAHAM and to ISAAC and JACOB is concrete and practical: descendants, land, prosperity. The demand is that the people of the Covenant *be* a blessing to others even as they are blessed. The people of the COVENANT develop institutions, forms of worship, laws to regulate conduct, and procedures for rallying the tribes to defend the people against enemies. All of these are duly recorded in the complex literary traditions that comprise the Torah.

The whole is dominated by a few personalities, many of whom are portrayed in sagas that offer little by way of personal biography. Others, like MOSES and AARON and MIRIAM and JOSHUA, stand out in their individuality, their gifts and their failings evident. The society portrayed in the Torah is ostensibly in the control of the male population, but women keep breaking out of the encrusted patriarchy to claim dominant positions of leadership over and again. And God exercises restraint, unwilling to give up the choice of a people of God even though it often seems that the people are bent on flaunting the divine will and neglecting or perverting the divine promise.

As the Torah comes to an end, Moses is still in the land of Moab, where he is permitted to see the land of promise from afar. God buries Moses outside that promised land, hiding the location of his burial place from all (Deut 34:6). Even so, the Torah does not end tragically; Joshua has already been commissioned and prepared to take over. Although Moses—unlike Abraham and SARAH, Isaac and REBEKAH, and Jacob and LEAH and RACHEL—is buried outside the land that God is giving to the people of the covenant, still the story is not a tragedy. This extraordinary ending for the most sacred part of the Hebrew Bible, the Torah, makes clear that God's fulfilling of the Promise comes over time, comes through the agency of a *people*, and is not thwarted finally by human failings—even though it is clearly furthered by human fidelity and obedience. God remains sovereign over the divine promise.

We can see, therefore, that while the Torah was the product of centuries of experience, containing narratives, poems, lists, genealogies, priestly instructions, legal collections, and some circumstantial accounts of historical events, it is much more than the history of the beginnings of earth, of human life, and of the people Israel. The Torah offers an affirmation of faith: that everything that has being owes its being to the action and purposes of the one God; that the people of God are charged to live in covenant with the one God, seeing to it—under God's guidance—that divine blessing spreads over all the earth, reaching all of earth's peoples. Torah can be called the "gospel" of the Hebrew Bible.

The Former Prophets

It is generally recognized today that the Books of Joshua, Judges, 1–2 Samuel, and 1–2 Kings were brought together and recast to form a great historical account, the theme of which is the fate and fortunes of God's word of guidance, demand, and judgment. Much of the material is very ancient, handed down orally for some centuries, while other parts existed in written form and were brought together to form large literary unities long before the historical collection was made in the seventh century B.C.E.

The Book of Joshua has lists of tribal boundaries interwoven with lists of the major towns and cities of the various tribes. It also has vivid accounts of some battles against Canaanite cities and peoples, along with other generalizations about the course of battle. The book claims a total CONQUEST OF CANAAN, but then quickly notes that not all of the large Canaanite cities could, in fact, be captured. The actual course of Israel's settlement in Canaan may have involved some battles led by incoming Israelite tribes, but much of the land was claimed by peasants living in Canaan and oppressed by the city-state system of the time who got together, made common cause, and secured their freedom, joining forces with the Moses group later on.

The story that Joshua tells is a grim and bloody one. The tellers of the story were confident that God ordered the destruction of the population of Canaan and Israel's replacement of Canaan on the land. It is good to learn, from the Book of Joshua itself, that the settlement also involved peaceful treaty making, intermarriage, and a long and slow weaving together of the peoples and cultures and languages and religions of the population of Canaan.

In Joshua's farewell address (chap. 24) the point is made. Some among the Israelites continued to worship the traditional deities of Israel's ancestors in Mesopotamia, while others were worshipers of BAAL and Ashera and Anath, deities of Canaan. And still others worshiped God under the personal name YHWH, called the LORD. From this amalgam of religious customs, ideas, and traditions there developed our present account of the conquest of Canaan.

The Book of Judges personalizes the struggles for land and blessing and a secure place within Canaan. Again, the historian stylized the events, offering an account of how disobedience to the divine Word brought about historical disaster. Suffering under oppression by one or other of Israel's enemies, the people would cry out to God for help. God would raise up a deliverer, male or female, from one tribe or another, and with God's direction of affairs, the "judge" would prove victorious and the land would have rest once more. Here too we can see how God's promise is threatened, whether by Israel's failings or by the avarice of others, how human beings must do their part in preserving the promise, and how God stood ready to intervene when called upon by the people of the covenant.

Some of the stories in Joshua and Judges (and elsewhere in the Bible) tell of wholesale slaughter done in the name of God. Such a religious teaching is not central to the religious understandings of the Hebrew Scriptures and is generally rejected by readers of the Bible today. The God of Jewish and Christian faith neither requires nor commends such acts of violence. The same must be said about the violence done to women (e.g., in the case of the concubine of the Levite from the tribe of Ephraim [Judg 19–21]).

The Books of Samuel and Kings introduce us to historical personalities who are more clearly etched than those of the earlier traditions. The difference probably lies with the coming of the Israelite kingship, which brought many baneful developments to Israel (distinctions of class and loss of personal freedom; a widening gap between the poor and the wealthy; new notions of deity that threatened the idea that God's special concern was with the lowly and the oppressed, etc.), but which also brought a richer and more sophisticated understanding of Israel's social and economic and religious world. In the Books of Samuel, for example, the struggle between SAMUEL and SAUL is told in such a way as to enable readers to see the strengths and weaknesses of both; neither is a hero, and neither is a villain. The same obtains in the portrayal of the struggles between Saul and DAVID. Was Saul a person promoted beyond his actual abilities, pathologically driven to maintain a position as king that he should simply have yielded to the better qualified David? Or was Saul a faithful worshiper of YHWH, determined not to adopt a form of royal life and leadership that would be religiously inappropriate, but taken advantage of by a much cleverer and more ruthless David, skilled in *using* the religious traditions to his own ends?

The remarkable fact is that the traditions justify our saying yes to both portrayals! Here we find profound discernment of the struggles and posturings and acts of heroism and of cruelty that take us into the political world of any time. Here, good and evil appear intertwined in all of Israel's leaders. And here too, the literary genius enables us to see our own world, and frequently our own selves, in these figures who also, in their distinctive ways, struggle with the promise of God for blessing and security and a purposeful destiny. A great leader, beloved by almost everyone, loses his sense of purpose when there are no more enemies to conquer. The remarkable political and economic and religious community that he has helped to form begins to disintegrate before his and our eyes. He would only need to rally in order to put an end to rebellion and corruption within his own family, but, alas, he has lost the will to do so. The greatness is still present, for God is with him; but the will to serve God is gone, and all else is thereby threatened.

The story continues in the Books of Kings, where occasional extended narratives (stories of ELIJAH, ELISHA, and MICAIAH SON OF IMLAH [1 Kgs 22] in particular) are woven into a rather subtle story-outline. The outline is about what happened to this kingship set up by David with such promise and with so much achieved. The narrator clearly sees things from a Judean vantage point, judging events in North Israel harshly, for the most part. But the historian is too honest to whitewash Judean events. Only two kings stand out as genuinely faithful to God (which is the author's chief criterion): HEZEKIAH and JOSIAH. The story ends with the last of Judah's kings in regular succession, JEHOIACHIN, who had been exiled to Babylonia along with much of the surviving population of Jerusalem, being released from prison and united with his family, apparently completely at the mercy of the foreign king. But the historian knows, as JEREMIAH also knew, that the promise of God has not run its course: "There is hope for your future, says the LORD" (Jer 31:17).

The Latter Prophets

Much of the treasure of Israelite literature and thought appears in the four prophetic collections called the Latter Prophets. The Book of Isaiah contains material composed over two and one half centuries, in all probability, all of it bearing Isaiah's name in the manuscripts. Isaiah's own words are found largely in the first thirty-two chapters, although these too have been supplemented by his disciples. But all of the sixty-six chapters claim the ISAIAH heritage and build upon it. If we think, then, of an Isaiah *tradition*, we can with confidence treat Isa 40–55 (a great literary masterpiece from the time shortly before the return of Jews from Babylonian exile, which began in the last half of the sixth century B.C.E.) as an exilic reclaiming of Isaiah's message and heritage. Similarly Isa 33 and 35 and Isa 56–66 are a rich reclaiming of Isaiah's message and heritage by disciples of Isaiah living in Judah (who associated themselves with the Isaiah tradition long after the prophet's death) in the period after the return from exile.

Isaiah of Jerusalem (last third of the eighth century B.C.E.) took with great seriousness both the demands of the covenant and its promises. In chapter after chapter, the Book of Isaiah affirms the divine glory and transcendence, calls on the community of Israel and its leaders to entrust their lives to God's care, even as they amend their ways and begin to practice the faith that they profess, and offers a variety of magnificent word pictures of what it will be like when God does bring the divine purposes and promises to their consummation. Much of the message of the prophet Isaiah and his followers has been captured in the liturgy and hymnody of synagogue and church. Whether the PROPHET is denouncing ISRAEL (Isa 1:2-20) or Israel's enemy ASSYRIA (Isa 10:5-19) or is offering promise to Israel and to the world (Isa 2:2-4; 9:1-7; 11:1-9), his words and images have gained a place in the consciousness of Jews and Christians that transcends the generations.

Jeremiah, too, has such a place in the religious consciousness of succeeding generations. This immensely long book (the longest in the Hebrew Scriptures) also was augmented by later disciples of the prophet, but there is much from the prophet himself and there is much *about* the prophet that can be taken to be historically reliable. Jeremiah's special contribution to Israelite religion is his lyrical account of the love with which God loved and still loves the people Israel. Even as the prophet denounces Israel and its leaders for acts of faithlessness, the prophet's own love for and identification with the people are unmistakable. He affirms with confidence that the exile to Babylon is not the end of God's dealings with Israel. Who can know, humanly speaking, how valuable for Israel's survival this faith of Jeremiah actually was? We have testimony that Jeremiah encouraged the first exiles from Jerusalem (598/7) to build houses, plant vineyards, settle in, and pray for the welfare of the land in which they were living as captives. Jeremiah was convinced that a faithful life could be lived in exile, but he also was fully convinced that God intended that the people of the Covenant return to the land promised to Israel's ancestors.

The prophet EZEKIEL apparently spent his entire career as a prophet among the Babylonian exiles, but his message was addressed to the entire community of Israel, those who were still in Jerusalem and Judah after he had been taken into EXILE, along with many other Israelite leaders, in 598/7 B.C.E., and those who were in exile with him. As the number of exiles swelled following Jerusalem's destruction in 587/6 B.C.E., Ezekiel's message included them as well, and it is remarkable to see how sharply his message changed after the fall of Jerusalem—from threats of divine punishment for sin to promises of restoration and a fresh start.

The message of Ezekiel is couched in rich and often strange symbolism. The prophet also uses strong and often violent language, denouncing the people as no prophet before him had done, while also making grand promises that seem to sweep aside any need for human repentance or amendment of life. The reasons for such sweeping language are not hard to identify. Ezekiel's own personality must surely have been a contributing factor, but in addition, Israel's desperate plight was largely responsible. Ezekiel had to convince those still living in Judah and Jerusalem that their having been spared in 598/7 was no indication that they were favored by God or that they could delay amendment of life.

Especially offensive to the priest Ezekiel were the non-Israelite religious rites being practiced in Jerusalem—in the name of the one God, YHWH. But he had to convince those in exile with him that God had not finished with Israel: the covenant with Israel and with David still held, although Ezekiel, like Isaiah and the other prophets, did much to transform the notion of kingship that was characteristic of ancient Near Eastern views. While God had not abandoned the promise made to David, new conquerors and potentates were not in God's plan and purpose, according to the prophets. A new kind of Davidic ruler was to come to Israel, one whose rule was characterized by justice for all and peace among the nations.

Ezekiel's speech and actions were forceful, graphic, and must often have been found to be offensive. He spoke of Jerusalem's beginnings as a result of a union of two different peoples (chap. 16). The result of the union was the birth of the child Jerusalem, abandoned beside the road, uncared for, left to die. It was God who came to do the duties of a midwife for Jerusalem (Jerusalem clearly includes the whole people Israel), to care for her, and eventually to return and claim Jerusalem as bride. The people's APOSTASY is the more shocking precisely because of these past demonstrations of the divine love.

But the future includes Israel's building up, reconstitution as a people, with God's Spirit breathed in to give life to all (Ezek 37). It includes the reconstitution of the very inner disposition and will of the people, as God removes the stony heart and inserts a heart of flesh (Ezek 36). And above all, it includes the transformation of the entire land, the resettlement of all the tribes, most of them in new locations, with the temple restored and its activities closely regulated, and with blessing and fertility extending throughout the entire land of the Promise (Ezek 40–48).

Many of the treasures of prophetic literature and thought are found in the collection called the Book of the Twelve (Prophets). Chief among these are the Books of Amos (the earliest of the twelve prophets), Hosea, Micah, Habakkuk, and Jonah. As the commentaries below will make clear, each has its distinct emphasis and setting within the life and faith of Israel.

AMOS is known for the rigor of his denunciation of the social and economic evils of Israel in his day and for the power and vitality of his language and imagery. While his message is addressed to North Israel in large part, his words are clearly intended for the whole people of God. As God's messenger, he pronounces divine judgment upon a faithless people, not for religious sins but for socioeconomic and political ones.

HOSEA too follows in that line, as does the prophet MICAH, but for Hosea the great crime is infidelity to God's searching and unrelenting love. God demands faithfulness of the people of the covenant, but God will go to the greatest of lengths to bring an errant people to faithfulness. Especially painful to the prophet was the corruption of the priests, the prophets, and other religious institutions.

HABAKKUK too has a distinctive word of faith to utter. In the period when Judah was about to be destroyed by the Babylonians for their faithlessness to the covenant, the prophet pressed God to show how Israel's destruction can be fair. Is Israel *really* more evil than Assyria or Babylonia? Can God not find some way of bringing divine judgment on faithless Israel that is not itself an act of injustice? The prophet summons hearers to place their utter trust in God, anticipating new things in the near future.

And the Book of Jonah offers a critique of prophetic religion when that religion gets too rigorous and self-righteous, when prophets are bent upon seeing God's judgment fall upon the sinners of earth who deserve punishment. The whole narrative is designed to help hearers and readers feel the oppressive weight of a religious faith that demands that God stick to the divine demands, punishing sinners when they sin. The author's Jonah is a prophet who is never happier than when God brings deserved judgment upon sinners and sticks to the judgment. The problem presented by the Book of Jonah is that God keeps insisting upon finding ways to show mercy, compromising therefore the clean and rigorous judgment that means death to sinners and life to the righteous. The author knows well enough that *all* stand condemned, if God should insist upon exact retribution for human misdeeds (Ps 130).

The Writings

As we follow the order of the Hebrew Bible, we come next to the sacred Writings, all those books that do not belong with the Torah or the Prophets. This collection developed last, with the latest of the books (in their present form) perhaps taking that shape in the early second century B.C.E. (the Book of Daniel, e.g.). Here, we have the poetic and wisdom texts of the Septuagint (Psalms, Proverbs, Job, Song of Solomon, Ecclesiastes) plus the books placed in earlier collections of the Septuagint (Ruth, which follows Judges in the Septuagint, and the additions to the "Prophets": 1–2 Chronicles, Ezra, Nehemiah, and Esther, plus Lamentations and Daniel).

The Psalms contain actual prayers and praises of the people, given here with all their beauty, power, passion, and frequent expressions of hatred for enemies, disappointment in God, indications of self-satisfaction, and all the rest. Clearly, no one has sought to "edit" the collection to make it express only positive sentiments expressive of the love of God and neighbor that was Israel's mandate from the Torah.

Similarly, in the wisdom traditions, exalted pictures of Lady Wisdom and her part in the divine creation (Prov 8; see Sir 1 and 24, and Wisdom of Solomon) appear alongside practical guidance that often seems flat and banal. The wisdom collections appealed to common sense, held in general to the view that God's created universe operated on the basis of a divine *order* that could be depended upon. The wisdom collections offer perspectives and insights for all peoples, not just for the people of the covenant, and it was recognized by the wisdom teachers that this was so.

Two wisdom collections stand out because they seem not to fit the normal features of ancient Near Eastern wisdom. The first of these is the Book of Job, a powerful declaration of the truth, observable by all, that the claims made for a God of justice and fairness seem not to fit the actual experiences of human beings. The author of this seventh-sixth century B.C.E. classic seems to be affirming that God may indeed be just in governing the universe, but that the divine justice is by no means evident in public affairs. Righteous persons and groups suffer while lawless and cruel persons and groups often escape judgment for their misdeeds. But deeper than this observation is the question raised whether religion is not, after all, a bargain with God that the faithful strike, only to withdraw from the bargain if God does not deliver just what the worshipers believe is their due. Is there such a thing as devotion to God that is not based upon received or anticipated gain? Or is religion just another of the world's deals: one does certain things for God with the anticipation that God will return the favor. (The early theologians spoke of this by means of the Latin term *do ut des*: "I act in order that you [God] may act").

The resolution found in the Book of Job is itself mysterious. Does the deity accept Job's repentance once Job has experienced an actual vision of the deity (Job 42:1-6)? Or is the point of the author that there is the true and gracious and just God *behind* the notions of God that human beings create, a deity who lives and suffers with the faithful in their struggles but does not always miraculously intervene to spare them pain and the experiences of injustice and meaninglessness? It may be that the author of the Book of Job is pressing hearers and readers to trust their actual experience of God, an experience that is itself blessedness and peace and the promise of justice, even in the midst of personal and social injustices and evils.

The other book that stands out is the Book of Ecclesiastes, called in Hebrew *Qoheleth* ("the Preacher" or "the Assembler"—"the Teacher" in NRSV). This small book has much material that is like that found in the Book of Proverbs and in other wisdom collections, but throughout Ecclesiastes there is voiced the relentless insistence that human activities and strivings and accomplishments are but "vanity . . . a chasing after wind" (an image used at least nine times in the book). But here too at one point the author seems to show that God is engaging this vain world, along with human beings, bringing out of the struggles of life those features and meanings that are enduring. Ecclesiastes sees vanity all around, but the invitation to dig more deeply, to search for meaning (see 3:15), continues to be pressed upon hearers and readers. It is a powerful, prophetic book, shattering religious complacency.

The Types of Literature

The variety of OT literature is described in the commentary on the particular books. Here we need only point to the major features of that variety.

Among the oldest pieces are ancient victory hymns such as the Song of Miriam (Exod 15:21) and the larger Song of Moses (Exod 15:1-18) that precedes it. The Song of Deborah is probably of about the same age (Judg 5), and some of the poetic "blessings" of the tribes (Gen 49 and Deut 33) are also quite ancient. Akin to these are shorter blessings and long or short cursings, such as the blessings of Isaac on his sons (Gen 27:27-29 and 27:39-40), the taunt-song of LAMECH (Gen 4:23-24) that is almost a curse, and the self-curse of the tribes found near the end of the Book of Deuteronomy (Deut 27:15-26).

But by far the best known of the poetic pieces of the Hebrew Bible are the prayers and praises of the community (esp. the Book of Psalms), the wisdom collections, most of which are in the form of proverbs (see, e.g., the Book of Proverbs and the deuterocanonical Book of Sirach), and the prophetic utterances, many of which are poetic, covering a large variety of forms. The prophets made use of literary forms employed in legal proceedings, others used in the community's worship, some taken from the world of diplomacy and royal ceremonies, and many that came from daily life and work. In addition, they created new forms and often modified and transformed existing forms of speaking and writing.

Highly original speakers and writers in ancient Israel created distinct masterpieces, such as the poetry of the Book of Job, especially Job 3–27, 29–31, and 38:1–42:6, and the rich and often lyric poetry of Isa 40–55. Also original and distinctive are many of the classic narratives of the Hebrew Bible, among which the narratives of Genesis such as chaps. 16, 18, 22, and 24 stand out, as do some of the stories of the heroes and villains of the books of Judges, 1–2 Samuel, and 1–2 Kings. To these one must add the powerful stories of Ruth and Jonah, the love lyrics of the Song of Solomon (Song of Songs), and the iconoclastic wisdom collection known as Ecclesiastes.

But in addition there are those collections of laws, directions for the observation of religious rites, lists of the tribes and families of Israel, and accounts of the history of Israel and of Judah that make up the contents of much of the Hebrew Bible. There are also texts that portray the piety and faith of persons facing persecution (Esther and Daniel 1–6), and there are visionary portrayals of the fulfillment of God's purposes for the creation. In the prophetic collections these visions of the end of the age are still firmly rooted in history; they sketch out, with a variety of images, God's bringing to its intended purpose the life of Israel and of the nations of the world, on a transformed earth, and sometimes following severe judgment upon Israel for its faithlessness to the divine covenant.

Another kind of literature also describes the consummation of God's purposes—APOCALYPTIC LITERATURE. The second half of the Book of Daniel describes wars among the nations of earth that virtually wipe out all hostility to the divine will and purpose and prepare the way for God's blessing to fall upon the faithful people of God who will have been spared in the conflicts. Similar visions appear in Ezek 38–39 and Isa 24–27. This type of literature, widely represented in Jewish texts outside the canon of the Hebrew Bible but preserved in the canons of various Christian churches (texts such as the books of *Enoch*, parts of *4 Ezra*, and the *Testament of Moses*), is also found in NT literature (Mark 13 and par. and the Book of Revelation).

These two types of visions of the consummation of the divine purpose are both of great strength and value. The prophetic pictures of the end of the age offer the greater challenge to the community to public action, so that the structures of public life can be made to conform, here and now, more closely with the political and social structure that God purposes. Prophetic eschatology, that is to say, is a direct summons to social action on the part of the faithful community. Apocalyptic eschatology, too, is a summons to action, but this type of VISION of the triumph of God's purpose seems to arise in situations in which the social and political structures seem impervious to reformation and renewal. The community, even so, is not to lose heart, for what may be impossible to mortals is by no means impossible to God.

Actually, apocalyptic eschatology, as we know from our own day, can flourish in any kind of political community. The Christian community has continued to give a larger place to apocalyptic visions than the Jewish community has. Even the horrors of the Holocaust in Europe under Nazism did not issue in the adoption of an apocalyptic religious outlook among Jews. It is wise to acknowledge that the appeal of apocalyptic visions lies not only in external social and political circumstances; apocalyptic appeals to a distinct kind and quality of religious life, a reality that can appear and reappear quite apart from prosperity or adversity.

Literary and Theological Qualities of the Old Testament

The OT is a *literary* collection and should be treated as such. From the opening, sonorous lines of the creation story of Gen 1 to the circumstantial account of Israel's exile and promised return from exile in 2 Chronicles, we are dealing with a body of materials of varied literary forms and with varied tendencies and aims. It would be unwise to overlook this variety in our reading, just as it would be unwise to overlook this variety in a commentary on the entire Hebrew Bible. The first creation story (Gen 1) is intended to *teach* us, to make things clear, to avoid error and mis-understanding in interpretation. The second creation story (Gen 2) also teaches, but it does so by its captivating *story*, its delight in developing character, its show of the play of human emotions, its picture of how human beings, precisely when they are attempting to be creative and claim their place in God's world, ever so easily overstep the bounds and make grave difficulty for themselves. The story of the first human sin, similarly, tells us not only about the first sin; it tells us about the nature of sin as such. Human beings are *prompted* to fall into sin by realities and forces outside themselves (Gen 3, the snake stands for such forces). But they are also tempted *from within* to disobey the divine will. Human sin is a human act, but it also gets prompted by the very character of life in community, life on an earth for which humans are appointed to take responsibility.

Theological and literary strength and subtlety characterize the great narratives of the books of Genesis, Judges, and 1–2 Samuel as well. The story of Abraham's readiness to offer his son Isaac on one of the mountains in the land of Moriah (Gen 22) displays utter faithfulness, love, and trust—in God by Abraham, in his father by Isaac. The repeated clause "and they went, the two of them, together . . . " (Gen 22:6, 8) is at once heartbreaking and sublime.

And the complex and rich narratives of David reveal the grandeur and the baseness both of David himself and of those surrounding him.

But the literary qualities are equally important and impressive in wisdom texts (Job, Prov 8 and 31, Sir 39, 44–50, Bar 3–5), in prophecy (Isa 1, 35, 40–55, Jonah), in classic narratives of the later period such as Ruth, Esther, Tobit, Susanna, and Judith, and above all in the Psalms. In the treatment of particular books within this commentary, the attention of readers is called to some elements of this literary artistry and theological subtlety. But nothing takes the place of the reading of the Bible itself.

The Hebrew Bible and the New Testament

Christians through the centuries have resisted the temptation to lay aside the Hebrew Scriptures and claim the NT alone as their Bible. The story of the Hebrew Bible is Israel's story; it is also the story of the CHURCH. The Christian community has used various interpretive schemes to make this truth clear, some of which have contributed to Christian misunderstanding of Judaism and Christian mistreatment of the Jewish people. When the church has seen itself as the "new" Israel, the successor people to the people of the first covenant, it has been tempted to claim (against PAUL in Rom 9–11) that God has rejected Israel and passed the divine mission on to the church alone.

The NT writers, especially the authors of the Gospel of Matthew and the Letter to the Hebrews, underscore the continuities between JUDAISM and Christianity even as they assert the primacy of the new covenant over the old covenant. The author of Matthew stresses the continuing validity of the Torah, and the author of Hebrews shows how Jesus the HIGH PRIEST of a better covenant has brought to consummation the divine purposes for Israel and for the nations of earth.

The Book of Revelation draws heavily from Psalms and from prophetic texts to portray the consummation of God's work, which for this author centers in Jerusalem, the Zion of the last days spoken of so frequently by Israel's prophets. The representatives of the twelve tribes of Israel enter the heavenly Jerusalem through twelve gates that stand open continually, and so do the elect of God from all the nations and families of earth. In that city there is light eternal, for night is banished forever.

Conclusion

Theologically, the Hebrew Bible contributes richly to Christian understanding. It is *the* Bible of the earliest Christians, and its strong emphasis upon God's demand for public justice was surely presupposed by Jesus and by the earliest Christians. The OT teaching that God demands justice for all, care for the oppressed, the needy, and the stranger, and diligent care for the whole of the creation is a central part of Christian faith and morals. While the NT concentrates upon the new dimensions of the divine work in Jesus as the Christ, its message is inseparably linked, for Christians, to the literature, the history, and the thought of the people of Israel.

Christian Scripture is different from Jewish Scripture both in scope and understanding. But Christian Scripture has always included—to the great good of the Christian community—that part of Scripture called by Christians "The Old Testament."

For Further Study

In the *Mercer Dictionary of the Bible:* APOCALYPTIC LITERATURE; BIBLE IN WESTERN LITERATURE; CANON; LITERATURE, BIBLE AS; OLD TESTAMENT; ORAL TRADITION; POETRY; RABBININC LITERATURE; SEPTUAGINT; SOCIOLOGY OF THE OT; THEOLOGY OF THE OT; TORAH; WISDOM LITERATURE. In other sources: B. Anderson, *Understanding the Old Testament*, 4th ed; J. Blenkinsopp, *A History of Prophecy in Israel*; J. Crenshaw, *Old Testament Wisdom*; D. N. Freedman, ed.-in-chief, *Anchor Bible Dictionary*; N. K. Gottwald, *The Hebrew Bible: A Socio-Literary Introduction*. W. Harrelson, "Introduction to the Old Testament," in B. Anderson, ed., *The Books of the Bible*, vol. 1; A. J. Heschel, *The Prophets*; H. Ringgren, *Israelite Religion*; R. de Vaux, *Ancient Israel: Its Life and Institutions*.

A History of Interpretation

John H. Hayes

Inner-Biblical Interpretation

The earliest interpretation of biblical materials occurs within the Bible itself. This is especially the case if one considers the OT and NT together. Earlier texts are often reused, reinterpreted, reapplied, and reunderstood in later texts (often, of course, there is some difficulty in knowing which is earlier and which later). This reuse may be either overt, generally with some clear indication that earlier material is being used, or covert when allusion is made through borrowed image or verbal parallels.

In some cases the interpretation of a text will appear as a gloss, that is, as an explanatory note that has been added to aid the reader (it is, of course, difficult to know if the explanatory note was a secondary gloss or whether it belonged to the original stratum of a text). For example, Judg 1:10 speaks of Hebron and adds the statement "the name of Hebron was formerly Kiriath-arba." Numerous such glosses appear in the OT, where the intent is to elucidate and explain.

Interpretation sometimes involves a direct quotation of an earlier text. Daniel 9:1-2, 24-27 refers to the prophecy of Jeremiah concerning the seventy years of exile (see Jer 25:11-12; 29:10). The author of Daniel quotes Jeremiah as a respected text but offers an interpretation that assumes that the original prediction by Jeremiah contained a hidden meaning. The seventy years are then understood as referring to seventy *times* seven years. Here the reinterpretation of the earlier text is made so as to extend its frame of reference down to the time of the author of Daniel.

The numerous parallels between the laws in Deut 12–26 and other legal texts probably indicate that the author of Deuteronomy was reusing earlier legal collections. Many of the laws in this section have parallels in Exod 21–23. For example, the law on the Hebrew slave in Exod 21:11 is given a broader and a more humane application in Deut 15:12-18. Here the purpose would be a reapplication of an earlier law for later, changed conditions.

Most scholars assume that 1-2 Chronicles, where these overlap with the history in Samuel-Kings, is a retelling, a rewriting, of this earlier material (it may be that 1-2 Chronicles and Samuel-Kings both draw on a common source). The Chronicles material has different emphases (more priestly and religiously oriented) than the parallel texts in Samuel-Kings. This reuse of material would thus be intended to bring the presentation into line with a different portrayal of the history of Israel.

In the superscriptions to thirteen psalms (3, 7, 18, 34, 51, 52, 54, 56, 57, 59, 60, 63, 142), there are references to events in the life of David. All but one of the these (Ps 7) allude to events described in 1-2 Samuel. If these were added later as interpretive glosses then they serve two functions. On the one hand, the psalm material has been given a historical context against which it can be read and to which its sentiments can be related. On the other hand, a person reading the narratives about David could utilize the psalms to understand how David felt and reacted in the episodes.

Nehemiah 8:1-8 indicates that the law needed interpretation after a public reading. It is entirely possible that some of these early interpretations have found their way into the biblical texts themselves.

The prophets occasionally allude to stories and events also described in the Pentateuch. For example, Hos 9:10 seems to refer to Baal-peor about which there is a narrative in Num 25:1-18. Hosea 12:3-6 parallels Gen 25:26; 32:22-30; 28:11-17; and 35:5-8. Is Hosea alluding to and interpreting the Genesis accounts? Or do both draw upon common stories? Or has the pentateuchal material been composed to fill out the allusions in the prophetic references? We cannot be certain which is the case but clearly there are interplays between the texts and some element of intertextuality must be taken into consideration.

In the NT, the use of, quotation of, and allusion to OT texts and events becomes commonplace. There are hundreds of such quotations and allusions. The writers of the NT clearly wanted Jesus and the Christian movement to be seen in light of the OT. The early church understood the OT as divine word and Jesus and the new community as predicted in its contents.

Often a NT text will clearly indicate that some event or occurrence is a fulfillment of an OT passage. The clearest case is the Gospel of Matthew, which notes in eleven passages that something "fulfills what had been spoken."

At other times, OT texts are quoted to buttress an argument or a position. For example, Paul may conclude a point by quoting a biblical text (e.g., Rom 3:4) or even a collage of texts (see Rom 3:10-18).

In Stephen's speech in Acts, there is a retelling of much of the biblical story but obviously reinterpreted to present the history of Israel as one of constant rebellion. This is what might be called a Christian homily that applies the text to a contemporary audience.

Frequently the NT writers have Jesus dialoguing with Jewish leaders over the interpretation of some particular law (e.g., Mark 10:1-12, 17-31). In these episodes, Jesus is shown offering a rereading of the material. It is clear the early church wished to present Jesus as an interpreter of scripture whose interpretations agreed with the church's reading. In Luke 24:44-49, the resurrected Christ refers to "everything written about [him] in the law of Moses, the prophets, and the psalms." He is said to have "opened [their] minds to understand the scriptures."

Christians not only saw in the OT foreshadowings and predictions of Christ and the church but also the actual activity of the preexistent Christ. In 1 Cor 10:1-4, Paul not only describes OT events using the Christian symbol of baptism but he also identifies the "rock" in the wilderness from which the Israelites drank as Christ.

It was possible for Christians to deny the straightforward reference of an OT text in order to relate the text to new realities. According to Paul the reference to not muzzling an ox (Deut 25:4) does not really have to do with oxen but with whether Christians should receive payment for their services (1 Cor 9:3-10).

OT "prophecies" could be interpreted by Christians not only with reference to the first coming of Christ but also to the parousia or second coming. The son of man saying in Dan 7:13-14 was frequently used this way in the teachings attributed to Jesus.

Paul introduced terminology into his discussion of the OT that was greatly to influence later Christian interpretation. In places, he speaks of OT events as types or allegories (1 Cor 10:6, 11; Gal 4:21-26). Early events are viewed as types paralleling present realities and the account of these "were written down to instruct us" (1 Cor 10:11). In Gal 4:21-26, Hagar and Sarah are taken as allegories of the Jewish and Christian covenants or the present and heavenly Jerusalems. The obvious referent of the OT text is seen to contain a deeper, hidden reference.

Paul also spoke of the letter that kills and the Spirit that makes alive (2 Cor 3:6; cf. Rom 7:6). Although Paul here does not necessarily have reference to a twofold sense in a text, he nonetheless used terminology that could be so interpreted.

Early Jewish and Christian Interpretation

As noted above, Jewish and Christian interpretation of the Bible is already reflected in the Bible itself. Here we are concerned with a later phase in the process. The Jewish ordering of the Hebrew Bible—Torah, Prophets, Writings—already reflects an interpretive principle, namely, the TORAH takes precedence over all other biblical materials (the Christian shaping of the OT with the prophets at the end emphasized that the center of interpretation had shifted). The 613 commandments collected by the later rabbis are all drawn from the Torah and no prophet was said to be able to add to the Mosaic law. However, there grew up around the written law an oral law that was considered binding and was declared to have been given to Moses on Sinai. This presence of a dual law demonstrates that in Judaism the Torah was understood as both a closed entity and an expanding entity. What was authoritative was both the text *and* its traditional understanding. Judaism was thus a religion based on textual exegesis *and* interpretation. The interpreters, the scribes, raised their interpretations to the level of scripture.

Jewish rabbis recognized that interpretation of a text was necessary when it contained textual problems, was not clear, appeared to contradict other texts or traditional understanding, or needed clarification or supplementation to adapt it to changing conditions.

Examples of Jewish interpretation may be seen in the Aramaic translations of scripture (the targums) as well as in the Greek translation (especially of the Pentateuch but also in the Prophets), in the Mishnah where scripture is appealed to for substantiating a view or position, in the rewritten form of biblical materials, and in various types of commentaries (see RABBINIC LITERATURE). Since early Judaism, especially before 70 C.E., was not a homogeneous phenomenon, not all interpretation is identical.

The Qumran community was part of an eschatologically oriented Jewish sect which could read the scriptures much like the early Christians, namely, as a collection of oracles concerned with the founder and the present and future life of the community. The Temple Scroll from cave 11 represents a rewriting of the Pentateuch to incorporate the views of the sectarians. Among the Qumran scrolls are *pesharim* in which biblical texts are given an interpretation (i.e., its *pesher*) in terms of the community's beliefs (see PESHARIM, QUMRAN). Such *pesharim* could take the form of a running commentary on a book or commentary on a collection of texts. In the *pesharim* the biblical text is assumed to contain cryptic allusions to the future that concerned the sect. The Qumran community could also interpret scripture to formulate *halaka*, rules and regulations for observing the law.

Rabbinical Judaism whose schools produced the midrashim was less eschatologically oriented. In the midrashim, represented by such works as the *Mekhilta* of Rabbi Ishmael on Exodus, the *Sifra* on Leviticus, the *Sifre* on Numbers and Deuteronomy, and the *Pesiqta* of Rab Kahana on biblical readings for festivals and special days, one sees true commentary work that argues a case, offers divergent opinions, and sometimes leaves an issue or interpretation open. These commentaries contain both legal type material (*halaka*) and homiletical/narrative material (*aggada*). The former was intended to establish and aid in keeping the legal requirements while the latter was inspirational and edifying.

The Targums originated, as perhaps did the earliest Greek translations of the Torah, as translations into the vernacular so non-Hebrew speakers could comprehend the text. The Targums are often quite expansive and explanatory rather than literal translations.

As a rule, the material in the commentaries gives a straightforward interpretation of the text, especially in the legal portions although passages are often brought together on the basis of particular terms, general allusions, and incidental matters which might call another text to mind. The texts occasionally resort to typological and allegorical reading. This was especially the case with the Song of Songs where the two lovers were understood as God and Israel. The rabbis concluded that "the law speaks according to human language" (Babylonian Talmud *Berakoth* 31b) and that "no verse could ever lose its plain (*peshat*) sense" (Babylonian Talmud *Shabbath* 63a).

Various rules (*middot*) were formulated that were to be used in interpreting Torah. Seven such rules were attributed to Rabbi Hillel and thirteen to Rabbi Ishmael. These overlap somewhat and appear to be deductions drawn from how the rabbis already worked.

Of a totally different class were such Jewish exegetes as PHILO of Alexandria (ca. 20 B.C.E.–42 C.E.). Living in a thoroughly Hellenistic culture, Philo sought to harmonize Greek philosophy (Platonic and Stoic morality and natural philosophy) with the Bible. The scriptures were read as if they pointed to higher things; persons and events became symbols of other realities.

Early Christian interpretation, already reflected in the NT, drew upon both Jewish and Hellenistic exegetical techniques. The Greeks possessed a long tradition of reading Homer both grammatically and allegorically. Early Christian interpreters picked up on Paul's terminology and read the OT looking for types and allegories about Christ and the church. The apostolic writings, like the letter of Barnabas and 1 Clement, used typological exegesis as did JUSTIN MARTYR (ca. 100–ca. 165) and Melito of Sardis (late second century). In his *Dialogue with Trypho the Jew*, Justin sought to demonstrate the truth of Christianity on the basis of proof from prophecy.

In the course of the second century, what were considered variant forms of Christianity developed. One such was represented by MARCION (d. ca. 160) who put together a canon consisting of the Gospel of Luke and ten Pauline letters. Both the gospel and the letters were edited by Marcion to remove what he considered to be interpolations (a common practice among Hellenistic scholars). For Marcion these interpolations represented judaistic material. Since Marcion stressed the difference between the NT God of love and the alien deity of the OT, he rejected the Hebrew scriptures and anything Jewish. Marcion's position represented a dualism and the rejection of the OT as scripture, neither of which was acceptable to mainline Christians.

A second variant form of Christianity was represented by GNOSTICISM. Gnosticism read even the Christian texts, especially the Gospel of John, in the light of a doctrine of sin and salvation that the church found unacceptable.

In response to such threats, church leaders argued that scriptural interpretation is a prerogative of the church, and must be in agreement with accepted, traditional teaching (the rule of faith) and under the supervision of episcopal authority (see esp. IRENAEUS's *Against Heresies*).

The first major Christian treatise on biblical interpretation in found in book 4 of *On First Principles* by Origen (ca. 185–ca. 254). Origen advocated a multilevel reading of the scriptures although at times he vigorously defended the literal reading where others resorted to allegory. Drawing upon texts such as the Greek of Prov 22:20-21 and a tripartite anthropology, Origen argued that scripture has a body, soul, and spirit, a literal and a twofold spiritual sense. Some texts he argued contain no literal sense because their statements are absurd. Difficulties in the text have been placed there to challenge the interpreter. The spiritual meaning is intended to be appropriated by the Christians as they grow toward the heavenly world and as an aid in that growth.

Exegetes influenced by Origen (such as Gregory of Nyssa [ca. 335–395] and Didymus the Blind [d. 398]) laid great weight on the spiritual and allegorical reading of the text. In contrast to this Alexandrian school, exegetes in the region of Antioch were advocates of a more literal reading of the Bible, probably being influenced by Jewish exegesis, Aristotelian philosophy, and conservative Hellenistic grammarians. The most significant members of this school were Diodore of Tarsus (d. ca. 394) and Theodore of Mopsuestia (ca. 350–428). They argued that allegorical interpretation was without controls and emptied history of meaning. The Antiochians argued for what they called *theoria* which appears to have been spiritual truths that did not abrogate history. Theodore tried to prove that what Paul meant by allegory was *theoria*. Perhaps *allegoria* was oriented to spiritual knowledge while *theoria* was more morally based. The Antiochians greatly limited the number of messianic texts in the OT.

The two most influential early Christian interpreters were Jerome (347–420) and Augustine (354–430). Both stood somewhat midway between the Alexandrians and the Antiochians. Both produced many commentaries. (The fourth and early fifth centuries were the golden age of Christian commentaries. Only Cassiodurus [485–580] and Gregory the Great [540–604] produced notable commentaries in the sixth century.) Jerome mastered Hebrew with the help of Jewish instructors and went back to the Hebrew to produce his translation of the OT. Augustine's *On Christian Doctrine* contains his fullest statements on biblical interpretation. He argued that the arts and other aids must be applied in the study of scripture and that one should know the original languages (though he didn't). For Augustine the primary purpose of scripture was to teach love and if the literal sense of a text was not edifying, then it must be taken nonliterally. Augustine's works, even his "literal commentary" on Genesis is filled with allegory.

The early Christian exegetes bequeated to the Middle Ages the view that the scriptures were a multilayered embodiment of all truth. Christian exegetes advanced various expressions to delineate the multifold levels of meaning in, and means for the understanding of scripture, sometimes threefold, sometimes fourfold. Jerome spoke of *historia*, *tropologica*, and *intelligentia spiritualis* (*Epistolae* 120.12); Gregory the Great, of *historia*, *significatio typica*, and *moralitas* (*Moralium libri Epistula missoria* 3); and Augustine, of *historia*, *allegoria*, *analogia*, and *aetiologia* (*De Genesi ad litteram* 1.1.1; and *De utilitate credendi* 3.5-9). Augustine's terminology—etiology and analogy—was never especially utilized either by himself or others (see Aquinas, *Summa Theologiae* Ia.1,10). Nevertheless, Augustine, along with Gregory, greatly influenced the medieval exegetes' search for more than one "higher" meaning in scripture. At the beginning of his unfinished literal commentary on Genesis, he wrote:

Four ways of expounding the Law are handed down by certain men who treat the Scriptures. Their names can be set forth in Greek, while they are defined and explained in Latin: in accord with history, allegory, analogy, and etiology. It is a matter of history when deeds done—whether by men or by God—are reported. It is a matter of allegory when things spoken in figures are understood. It is a matter of analogy, when the conformity of the Old and New Testaments is shown. It is a matter of etiology when the causes of what is said or done are reported. (*De Genesi ad litteram liber imperfectus*, 2.5)

The terminology and scheme of multiple meanings in scripture that were to become almost standard in medieval times was formulated by John Cassian (ca. 360–435):

[T]he practical side of knowledge is hived off among many professions and disciplines. The contemplative side is divided into two parts, namely, historical interpretation and spiritual interpretation.

Hence, Solomon, having listed the multiform grace present in the Church, goes on to say, "All those of her household are clothed twice over' (Prov. 31:21). Now there are three kinds of spiritual lore, namely, tropology, allegory, and anagoge. . . .

History embraces the knowledge of things which are past and which are perceptible. . . . What follows is allegorical, because the things which actually happened are said to have prefigured another mystery. . . . Anagoge climbs up from spiritual mysteries to the higher and more august secrets of heaven. . . . Tropology is moral teaching designed for the amendment of life and for instruction in asceticism. . . . And if we wish it, these four modes of interpretation flow into a unity so that the one Jerusalem can be understood in four different ways, in the historical sense as the city of the Jews, in allegory as the church of Christ, in anagoge as the heavenly city of God . . . , in the tropological sense as the human soul. . . . " (*Conferences*, 14.8)

In the later Middle Ages, this fourfold interpretation (the *Quadriga*) was expressed in a widely used rhyme first attested in the *Rotulus pugillaris*, an aid to preaching by the Dominican Augustine of Dacia (d. 1285).

> *Littera gesta docet; quid credas allegoria;*
> *moralitas quid agas; quid speres anagogia.*

> The letter teachs what happened;
>   allegory what to believe;
> morality how to behave;
>   anagogy what to hope for.

The Medieval Period

New impluses in Christian biblical studies were characteristic of the late eighth and most of the ninth centuries, the Carolingian period, and again beginning in the twelfth century. Jewish work on the scriptures during the early Middle Ages witnessed not only the completion of the work of the Masoretes but also extensive philological and commentary study of the Bible precipitated partially by the rise of the Karaites ("Scripturalists") in the eighth century and partially by the influence of Arabic grammarians and theologians/philosophers.

The Bible was of course the central text in the medieval monasteries where its reading and exposition (*lectio divina*) nurtured and structured the life of the monks and centered around homiletical and meditative interests. The monastic focus was on the text as sacred page (*sacra pagina*) with its passive role toward the text through which God addressed the reader and hearer, shaping and forming the recipient in the search for divine wisdom and the beatific vision.

The most significant figure in Christian scholarship between late antiquity and the Carolingian era was the Venerable Bede (ca. 673–735). A native of Northumbria, Bede spent his life at the twin monasteries of Wearmouth and Jarrow where their founder Benedict Biscop (ca. 628–689) and his successor Coelfrid (d. 716) had accumulated an impressive library including Old Latin, Vulgate, and Latin-Greek texts as well as patristic and classical sources, and had produced manuscript copies of the Bible (e.g., *Codex Amiatinus*).

Bede wrote across a broad spectrum of subjects including commentaries on several OT and NT books (Gen 1–20; Samuel, Kings, Ezekiel, Ezra-Nehemiah, Song of Songs, Tobit, Luke, Acts, Revelation). His separate works on the tabernacle and the temple of Solomon texts represent the first time these materials were subjected to detailed commentary. Bede allegorized this material as prefiguring the church as the house of God. Bede apparently knew some Greek and utilized the *Laudian Acts*, a Latin-Greek bilingual text (see Gibson 1993, 22–23), in writing his retractions on his Acts commentary. His *De schematibus et tropis* was written to facilitate biblical studies and to offer help in reconciling difficulties in content. He described his primary work as follows:

> I have made it my business, for my own benefit and that of my brothers, to make brief extracts from the books of the venerable Fathers on Holy Scripture, or to add notes of my own to clarify their sense and interpretation.
>
> (*Ecclesiastical History* 5.24)

Although at points Bede displays exegetical originality and offers clarification of the fathers, he was heavily dependent upon patristic sources, drawing especially upon Ambrose, Augustine, Jerome, and Gregory the Great, whom he was the first to declare the four great doctors of the Latin church (in the prologue to his *In Lucae evangelium expositio*). His use of quotations of the fathers in running commentary anticipated the accumulation of patristic materials in the Carolingian period and subsequently.

The widespread reforms—political, religious, and educational—carried out by Pepin III (d. 768), Charlemagne (d. 814), and their successors greatly impacted biblical study. For the first time in church history, political and religious authorities cooperatively pushed for reform and improvement in the total educational enterprise. The Carolingian program, announced in the *Admonitio generalis* and *Epistola de litteris* called for the instruction of students in reading, chant, *computus*, and grammar with special attention to be given to the study and copying of the scriptures. Charlemagne recruited scholars widely to advise and supervise court and cathedral education life: the Italian Paul the Deacon (ca. 720–ca. 800), the Visigoth from Islamic Spain Theodulf of Orleans (ca. 750–821), and the Anglo-Saxon Alcuin (ca. 735–804).

Charlemagne's grandson Charles the Bald (d. 877) patronized the Irish philosopher John Scotus Erigena (ca. 810–ca. 877) who was made head of the palace school at Laon. An exceptional scholar of the Carolingian world, Erigena was noted for his knowledge of Greek and his translation of works by Maximus the Confessor, Gregory of Nyssa, and Pseudo-Dionysius. His direct approach to scripture, inquisitive mentality, and resort to the Greek text can be seen in his homily on the prologue and his commentary on the Gospel of John, his only exegetical works.

Several factors in the Carolingian renaissance are worthy of note. First, the production of texts of the Bible reached a new level. In addition to requisitioning books from elsewhere, especially Rome, Charlemagne expressed his desire for a grammatically and orthographically correct text of the Bible, just as his father Pepin had sponsored the production of a correct lectionary. St. Martin's monastery at Tours under Alcuin and his successors produced numerous biblical "pandects" and "gospelbooks," perhaps partially dependent upon the earlier work of Maurdramnus, abbot of Corbie (772–781). The pandects were massive folio lectern Bibles apparently based on a common text, although Alcuin and his disciples did not seek to produce a revision of the Latin text. Equally impressive are the texts produced under the direction of Theodulf with their smaller size and minuscular handwriting, obviously intended for scholarly use. Although Theodulfian manuscripts occasionally contain marginal variants, some in the psalms apparently based on the Hebrew, their texts are basically eclectic and all known copies show textual differences.

Second, aids to biblical study were also provided. Theodulf and Alcuin provided prefaces to the books of the Bible. Rabanus Maurus (780–856), in chapter 10 of book 2 of his handbook for clergy training (*De institutione clericorum libri tres*, ca. 819), provided a section outlining a program for biblical studies. Theodulfian Bibles included certain aids for biblical study: Isidore of Seville's *Chronica minora* containing an outline of world history to the seventh century C.E.; the second book of Eucherius of Lyon's *Instructiones* which offers explanations of various biblical names, places, and other facts and matters; Pseudo-Melito's *Clavis* which provided allegorical explanations and interpretations of biblical terminology; and Pseudo-Augustine's *Liber de divinis scripturis* which offered moral understanding of various biblical texts. These provided the interpreter with historical, allegorical, and tropological insights.

Third, Carolingian exegetes produced an exceptional number of biblical commentaries—the twenty or so volumes in J.-P. Migne's *Patrologia Latina* are far from exhaustive. Among the commentators were Alcuin, Rabanus Maurus, Paschasius Radbertus (ca. 790–865), Walafrid Strabo (ca. 808–849), Haimo (d. ca. 855), Heiric (ca. 841–ca. 885), Remigius of Auxerre (ca. 841–908), and John Scotus. For the first time in Christian history, there now existed full-fledged running commentaries on all the books of the Bible. No small role in this was played by Rabanus Maurus who produced commentaries on all the OT books except Baruch and on most of the NT. Two special factors should be noted about these commentaries. First, the Carolingian exegetes worked with an extraordinary veneration for the church fathers and treated their opinions about the meaning of biblical texts with what approached a dogmatic orthodoxy. Compilation, clarification, summation, and harmonization of patristic sources are thus typical of the commentaries. Which fathers are quoted often depended upon the availability of sources. Second, many of the commentaries were written at the requests and to meet the desires of particular patrons. Thus they display significant diversity in the handling of materials.

Two developments that were to culminate in the twelfth and thirteenth centuries have their roots in the Carolingian period. First, the glossing of biblical texts, a technique probably first used on classical secular texts, makes its appearance. Marginal notes, explanatory of the text and intentionally planned and executed by the scribe producing the biblical text, appear in manuscripts, especially of the psalter. Interlinear notations also appear in some manuscripts from the period but these were added by subsequent readers or later editors. The glossing of the Bible would reach its apex in the great *Glossa ordinaria* of the twelfth century. Second, although the use of questions and responses addressed to or arising out of the text was already present in the patristic period, this becomes more noticeable and begins to point to what would flourish in later scholastic exegesis.

Jewish biblical scholarship in the medieval period was both extensive and impressive. By the ninth century, the masoretes had completed their work of producing a pointed (voweled) text based on traditional pronunciation and interpretation. The masoretic text included not only vowel points but also accent markings and notes written in the margins, at the top and bottom of pages and at the end of books. These notes (the *masorah*) call attention to variant textual readings (the *kethiv* and *qere*), to the number of times an unusual word form occurs, and so on, as well as the number of words and letters in a book to aid in the correct copying of manuscripts. Three major schools of masoretes existed; the Tiberian and its system of vocalization and *masorah* became dominant.

The Muslim conquest of the Middle East in the seventh and eighth centuries brought many Jews into contact with an alien Semitic faith. Arabic-speaking Jews became conversant not only with the Islamic faith but also with Islamic science and philosophy where the thought of Aristotle was still known and influential. Jewish and Muslim dialogue over the Hebrew scriptures occurred and Hebrew studies were influenced by the work of Arabic grammarians.

In the mid-eighth century, a new Jewish sect arose, the Karaites ("scripturalists"), founded by Anan ben David. The Karaites argued that the Bible should be read and interpreted without reliance on, or even with the rejection of, the classical rabbinic interpretations. This "back to the Bible" movement argued for *sola scriptura* and sought to interpret scripture, without preconceived notions, though correlation of the Bible's contents.

Jewish response to these new impulses as well as a renewed interest in biblical studies in general found embodiment in the work of a number of outstanding scholars. Among the more philosophically oriented were Saadiah Gaon (882–942), Judah Halevi (ca. 1075–ca. 1140), and Moses Maimonides (1135–1204). Maimonides sought to reconcile biblical faith and human reason in a modified Aristotelianism. His *Guide for the Perplexed* (1190), which contains much biblical interpretation, was translated into Latin early in the thirteenth century and greatly influenced later Christian thought especially that of Albertus Magnus (ca. 1200–1280) and Thomas Aquinas (ca. 1225–1274).

Jewish biblical scholarship was especially cultivated in two regions, Spain-Provence and northern France (see Sarna 1971). The most famous French exegete was Rashi (Rabbi Solomon ben Isaac, 1040–1105) who drew upon rabbinic tradition but sought to expound the literal (*peshat*) meaning of the text. His commentaries remind one, at least in form, of the glossing of the Bible carried out by contemporary Christians.

Another important Jewish exegete was the Spanish Abraham Ibn Ezra (1089–1164) who travelled and wrote widely. In the introduction to his work *Sefer Ha-Yashar* (*The Book of the Upright*), a commentary on the Pentateuch, Ibn Ezra described five different types of Jewish biblical interpretation. These are widely assumed to reflect the various approaches to scripture taken by Jews in medieval times, but described of course from Ibn Ezra's distinctive perspective (see Jacobs 1973, from whom the translation is derived).

> The first method is lengthy and diffuse, remote from the souls of the men of our generation. If we use the illustration of a circle and place the truth at its center point, then this method can only be compared to the periphery of the circle, which goes round and round only to return to the place where it began. . . . Rabbi Saadiah, Gaon of the Exile, trod this path. . . . The same applies to Rabbi Samuel ben Hofni [d. 1034].

According to Ibn Ezra, these commentators interspersed their discussion of the text with long, extraneous treatises and digressions on all sorts of subjects only tangentially related to the text.

> The second method is that chosen by the distorters, albeit they are Jews. They imagine that they have reached the very point of the circle but in reality they have not the faintest idea where it is to be found. This is the way of the Sadducees [the Karaites] such as Anan [and others] . . . and the way of whoever does not believe in the words of the bearers of religious traditions. . . . Each of these men interprets the Bible as he sees fit and this applies even to the commandments and the laws. . . . How can anyone rely on their opinions . . . because you will not find a single precept explained fully in the Torah itself.

Here he argues against those who believe that scripture can interpret scripture adequately without recourse to traditional views.

> The third view is a way of darkness and obscurity. It lies entirely beyond the circle. This is the method of those who invent mysterious interpretations for all the passages in Scripture. It is their belief that the Torah and the precepts are riddles. . . . The words of the Torah are never less than straightforward. In one thing only are these people right. That is that every precept of the Torah, whether great or small, must be measured in the balance of the heart into which God has implanted some of His wisdom. Therefore if there appears something in the Torah which seems to contradict reason or to refute the evidence of our senses then here one should seek for the solution in a figurative interpretation. For reason is the foundation of everything. . . . the figurative meaning is evident on the surface.

Here Ibn Ezra is condemning those who read the text allegorically. Perhaps he would have included in this group the later qabbalists (cabalists).

> The fourth method is near to the point. A whole group of commentators have followed it. This is the method pursued by the sages . . . who are not overmuch concerned with a balanced view but rely on the homiletical method.

Ibn Ezra describes those who engage in rabbinic exegesis of a midrashic-homiletical nature especially adaptable to preaching.

> My commentary is based on the fifth method. . . . First I shall investigate with all the power at my command the grammatical form of each word and then I shall explain its meaning to the best of my ability. . . . Also a correct interpretation does not involve any textual emendation. The Targum of the Torah in Aramaic is accurate. The authority of this work explains every difficulty. Even though he is addicted to the Midrashim we recognize that even more was he devoted to the true sense of the Hebrew language. . . . The plain meaning of a verse is not affected by its Midrashic interpretation for there are seventy faces to the Torah. . . . the bearers of the tradition, all of whom were righteous men, . . . with all the strength we have we must rely on the accuracy of what they say.

Ibn Ezra represents an approach that stresses the plain/literal sense which is to be modified only where such a reading would directly clash with the received tradition. For him, scripture is not a homogeneous whole consistent throughout. Thus one must use reason as well as the wisdom of the past sages, that is, grammatical focus, the cumulative tradition, and an intellectual independence of judgment must be combined.

Beginning in the twelfth century, new developments and emphases became characteristic of Christian biblical interpretation: an increased concern for the accuracy and authenticity of the text, an awakened interest in the original languages of the biblical text, a greater focus on the literal or historical reading of texts with a concomitant concern with the human authors, new developments in the manufacture of biblical texts, the production of new tools for study and employment of the biblical text, the introduction of scholastic methodology into the commentary tradition, as well as the development of new theological emphases.

Some of the reasons behind these new developments in Christian biblical study were similar to those that influenced forms of medieval Jewish interpretation. Renewed contact with ancient Greek philosophy, especially that of Aristotle, growth in the strength and number of monastic and cathedral schools and eventually the founding of universities, a greater utilization of the liberal arts (the *trivium*—grammar, rhetoric, and logic; and the *quadrivium*—arithmethic, geometry, astronomy, and music) in biblical study, the presence of heretics (e.g., the Cathari and the Waldenses), and other factors made their contribution.

Throughout the early Middle Ages, the Latin text produced by Jerome had been subject to various corruptions. Harmonizations with the Old Latin and changes and additions to bring the text into line with patristic readings had produced a very fluid and eclectic text. The Psalter, for example, circulated in various forms—the Old Roman and variations thereof, the Gallican, and Jerome's final revision (the *Hebraica veritas*) which was the least popular of all. Alcuin's and Theodulf's textual work was not an attempt to produce a critically corrected text but it did aid somewhat in creating a stabler text. John Scotus had compared the Latin text of John with Greek exemplars and some evidence exists for similar work on the psalter.

A new stage of textual comparison and revision is evident beginning in the early twelfth century. Odo (ca. 879–942) while abbot at St. Martin's prepared a quadruple psalter with the transliterated Greek paralleling the three Latin versions. The most thorough attempt to correct the Latin text was associated with the Cistercians and especially the work of Stephen Harding (d. 1134) early in the twelfth century and of Nicholas Manjacoria of Rome about mid-century. Both operated on the assumption that the fuller text is not necessarily the more original. Harding deleted material not found in the Hebrew. Subsequently in the thirteenth century various *correctoria* were circulated by the Dominicans and Franciscans.

Very few scholars in the Middle Ages were competent in Hebrew and Greek. Beginning in the twelfth century, interest in if not a thorough knowledge of Hebrew became rather widespread, more so than for Greek. Abelard (1079–1142) recommended to the nuns of the convent of the Paraclete that they study Hebrew, Greek, and Latin. The presence of Hebrew-speaking Jewish communities in many of the large medieval cities allowed Christians the opportunity for contact, conversation, and even instruction with Jews over the interpretation of the Hebrew scriptures. The existence of Hebrew-Latin psalters with commentary and the exegetical work on the psalms by Herbert of Bosham (fl. ca. 1160–1186) illustrate that some progress was made in this area. Robert Grossteste (ca. 1175–1253) mastered Greek sufficently to translate numerous works into Latin including the *Testaments of the Twelve Patriarchs* and utilized the Greek texts of both testaments in his commentaries. The Council of Vienne (1311–1312) decreed, primarily to facilitate missionary activity and through the influence of Raymond Lull (ca. 1233–ca. 1315), that the study of Oriental languages—Arabic, Hebrew, and Aramaic—be established at the universities in Paris, Oxford, Salamanca, Bologna, and at the Roman court. Although the idea was supported by Popes Clement V (1305–1314) and John XXII (1316–1334), the goal of trilingual education was not realized until the sixteenth century.

A greater concern with the literal meaning of texts and the placing of texts within an original historical frame of reference become more noticeable in the literature of the twelfth and thirteenth centuries. A number of factors perhaps contributed to this development. The use of the *Quadriga* had of course always recognized the existence of the historical or literal sense or level in scripture and had certainly not ignored this completely. Paradoxically, at the same time that some scholars focused on the literal sense the allegorical reading was disseminated more widely than ever in lay circles through the preaching of the Domin-

ican and Franciscan mendicants, the appearance and widespread usage of preaching manuals (*Artes praedicandi*), and various forms of the *Bible moralisée* (probably of Parisian origin, early thirteenth century) and the so-called *Biblia pauperum* (probably of South German origin, mid-thirteenth century, one of the earliest books printed, ca. 1460).

A certain weariness with some allegorical readings becomes evident. Although no exact system of allegorical correspondences between OT events and characters and Christian figures and beliefs ever became standard, such allegorical reading as the widespread association of David with Christ, Bathsheba with the church, and Uriah with the devil was hard to justify for some interpreters. Alain of Lille (1120–1202) referred to the Bible as a "nose of wax," that is, something that could be shaped and used to fit one's conceptions and beliefs through allegory (this image appears frequently in the late sixteenth and seventeenth centuries).

Two clearly evident factors contributed to the focus on the literal. One was the increased contact between Jews and Christians. Acquaintance with Jews and Jewish interpretation with its concern for the *peshat* (plain or literate) level of reading and a subdued messianic emphasis forced Christians to recognize a more straightforward and less spiritual form of interpretation of the Hebrew scriptures than was traditional. The second factor was the introduction of Aristotelian thought into the mainstream of Christian scholarship in the late twelfth and thirteenth centuries. Aristotle's works on logic and dialetic with their emphasis on the univocality of language resisted the appeal to secondary levels of meaning in statements and argumentation. Further, the Aristotelian theory of causality with its concern for the analysis of efficient, material, formal, and final causes was highly significant. The adoption of this theory of causality led to a new form of prologue (*accesus*) in biblical commentaries and also to a sharper focus on the human author (the efficient cause) and the writer's method of treatment and organization of the material (the material cause; see Minnis 1988, 28–159; Minnis-Scott 1991, 197–276).

Hugh (ca. 1096–1141) and others associated with the abbey of St. Victor in Paris laid stress on the importance of history and the literal. Hugh's *Didascalicon* (late 1120s), a textbook on the arts and learning disciplines, in books 4–6, lays out a program of biblical study discussing such matters as the order in which biblical books should be read, how to read, the canon, and so forth, and throughout stresses the importance of the historical/literal level of meaning as an indispensable foundation for interpretation. His pupil Andrew (d. 1175), more familiar with Jewish scholarship than Hugh, laid greater stress on the historical meaning, saw Jewish exegesis as reflective of the literal sense, and generally refused to offer a Christological/ecclesiological reading of OT texts. For example, he understood Isa 7:14 as referring to the prophet's wife (as did Rashi).

Others than the Victorines focused on the literal reading. Peter Lombard (ca. 1100–1160) exegeted the Pauline epistles in a literal fashion, often introducing historical considerations about Paul and his times into the discussion so as to relativize some of Paul's positions (see Colish 1994; in his psalms exegesis, Lombard was more traditional). William of Auvergne (ca. 1180–1249) wrote on OT law and sought to understood the prescriptions in terms of their original function.

By the time of Aquinas (ca. 1225–1274), the nature and role of the literal sense of scripture had become a significant issue of controversy. In answering Andrew, Richard of St. Victor (d. 1173) had argued in *De Emmanuele* that the literal meaning of Isa 7:14 is its reference to the Virgin Mary. In the opening sections of his *Summa theologiae* (Ia.1,9–10), Aquinas restates some of Augustine's positions: that words can signify things (the literal emphasis) and that these things can then signify other things (the spiritual emphasis) and that theological arguments and conclusions should be based on the literal.

> [A]ll meanings are based on one, namely, the literal sense. . . . nothing necessary for faith is contained under the spiritual sense that is not also conveyed through the literal sense elsewhere.

Aquinas argued that the literal sense is what the author intended but he also held that God is the ultimate author of scripture which allowed for an open-endedness in interpretation so long as conclusions remained within the realm of traditional faith. Aquinas continued to find both literal and figurative meanings in OT texts, especially those concerning ceremonial laws:

> The ceremonies of the Old Law had two causes: one, literal, in that they were directed to the worship of God; the other, figurative, as directed to the prefiguring of Christ. . . . All the sacrifices of the Old Law were offered to prefigure this [Christ's] unique and principal sacrifice, the perfect prefigured by the imperfect. . . . And since the reason for the figure is to be drawn from what it figures, the

reasons for the figurative sacrifices of the Old Law are to be drawn from the true sacrifice of Christ. (*Summa theologiae* Ia2ae.102,3)

Since Christian interpreters were not content to read the OT without reference to its prefiguration, allegorization, and prophecy of the New, exegetes began to speak of a double literal meaning or a double intentionality of the author. In his psalms commentary based on Jerome's *Hebraica veritas* (written ca. 1317–1320) Nicholas Trevet spoke of the literal sense as the author's primary intention and the spiritual/mystical as a secondary intention. William of Nottingham (active at Oxford ca. 1312–1336) wrote of a double literal sense, the proper literal sense derived from the initial signification and a figurative literal sense derived from the metaphorical or secondary signification.

Nicholas of Lyra (ca. 1270–1349), knowledgeable in Hebrew and Jewish and Christian exegesis, and the most literalistic and ultimately the most influential of medieval exegetes, hypothesized a *duplex sensus litteralis* for some texts, namely a reference to OT times and to NT realities. Nicholas produced a *Postilla litteralis* (with two prologues on hermenuetics, ca. 1322–1331) on the entire Bible (the first commentary to be printed, in 1471–1472, five volumes, and running into more than one hundred different editions and printings by 1600). Although Nicholas stressed the historical/literal sense and made critical observations throughout his work, he placed many interpretations into the literal category which had previously been understood as spiritual readings and also still held the view that much of the OT was literally Christological or ecclesiological in its signification. (Nicholas also wrote a spiritual commentary on scripture, the *Postilla moralis*, 1339.) The controversy over the nature and role of the literal sense of scripture was to continue on into the reformation period and later (see Froehlich 1977).

Several new developments in Bible production occurred in the medieval period (see Gibson 1993 and Gameson 1994). Generally, single biblical manuscripts contained only a portion of the text, most frequently divided according to the nine-volume pattern recommended by Cassiodorus (*Institutiones divinarum et saecularium Litterarum* I.11.3): Genesis-Ruth, six books of the Kings (1-2 Samuel, 1-2 Kings, 1-2 Chronicles), prophets, Psalms, wisdom literature, lives of great men and women (Job, Tobit, Esther, Judith, 1-2 Maccabees, Ezra-Nehemiah), four gospels, Pauline and Catholic epistles, and Acts and Revelation.

Few Latin pandects (*complete* Bibles, like the *Codex Amiatinus* from the eighth century) have survived from or were produced during the early Middle Ages. Following the productions of Alcuin and Theodulf, intended for lectern use, large display bibles were produced, especially in the late eleventh and early twelfth centuries, generally in two volumes and lavishly illustrated.

With the founding of the universities and the development of scholarly work on the scriptures, new efforts were made to produce a scholarly reference Bible. The result, to which many scholars and schools contributed, especially that at Laon, was the *Glossa ordinaria* (in nine or ten volumes) with carefully produced marginal and interlinear glosses derived primarily from the Latin fathers (see Gibson-Froehlich 1992). The *Glossa* reached its classic form in the second quarter of the twelfth century and remained rather stable thereafter. A product of the monastic scriptorium, the *Glossa* was intended for institutional libraries to be consulted and cribbed by the scholar. Manuscripts of the *Glossa* were produced for more than a century and the work was widely used until the shift to the use of Greek and Hebrew rendered it rather obsolete (no manuscript form in which all the volumes match in script and decoration is extant; the work was first printed in 1480–1481 and about a dozen different editions were produced by 1617). Various other glossed portions of the Bible were produced, the so-called *Magna glossatura* by Peter Lombard on the Psalms and the Pauline epistles being preferred over the *Glossa ordinaria*.

In the early thirteenth century, the production of biblical texts moved out of the monastic scriptorium and into secular workshops. The demands associated with higher education and university life created a sizeable market. In Paris and northern France, the so-called "Paris Bible" received wide circulation. Although varying somewhat in text and illumination, these one-volume Bibles utilized a thin parchment page and a small script. Placing all the books in a single volume necessitated a standard order and grouping for the biblical books. The Paris edition made the personal ownership of the Bible available to a wide audience—wealthy bourgeoisie, university teachers, and members of religious orders. A small or pocket-size, one-volume edition of the Bible, less than seven inches high, often containing a summary of the Christian faith expressed in selected biblical texts in an appendix, also appeared in the thirteenth century.

These were probably used by mendicant preachers and others defending and proclaiming the faith to heretics and outsiders.

New tools, in facts-reference works, for biblical study and use, were introduced in the late twelfth and thirteenth centuries. These were intended as guides for locating information rather than works for continuous reading. Several forms of biblical *distinctiones* were produced. This was a form of dictionary that listed various theological terms and subdivisions within the thought asssociated with the term. The term was provided with various supporting and illustrative biblical texts. These were of great aid to the preacher in preparing sermons.

A verbal concordance to the Bible, arranged alphabetically, was produced under the direction of Hugh of St. Cher (ca. 1195–1263) by the Dominicans at St. Jacques in Paris. This concordance used the chapter divisions current in Paris at the time, generally attributed to Stephen Langton (d. 1228). The enumeration of the chapters used Arabic numbers, adopted in Europe in the twelfth century. Since the enumeration of verses was not yet in use, chapters were divided into lettered sections (a-g). The concordance gave only the biblical references for words; later English Dominicans revised the work providing a sentence of context where terms occurred, thus giving the user the verbal contexts. The latter work was overly bulky, and late in the century a version with shorter contexts and with short chapters divided into only four units (a–d) was produced. At any rate, an indispensable tool for biblical study, the concordance, had come into being.

(Division of the NT into the verse divisions used today dates from 1551, when the printer-scholar Robert Estienne (Stephanus) published a Greek-Latin edition of the NT. The masoretic text of the Hebrew Bible was already divided into verses but not numbered. Estienne's 1555 Latin edition of the Bible, including the Apocrypha, utilized verse enumeration throughout. Rabbi Isaac Nathan (ca. 1440) had earlier produced a Hebrew concordance that used numbered verses for the masoretic text.)

A further tool that should be noted is the *Historia scholastica* of Peter Comestor (d. ca. 1179). This was a presentation of history from creation to the end of the Book of Acts that drew upon both biblical and patristic-classical sources. The work was one of the most widely used texts in medieval times. Comestor's work in a French translation was interlaced with the text of a French Bible to produce the *Bible historiale complétée* early in the fourteenth century. This work was also widely used and circulated.

The twelfth and thirteenth centuries saw the triumph of the scholastic approach to biblical studies and theology. The heavy utilization of logic and dialectic in theology by Abelard (1079–1142) and others led to a treatment of the scripture as *sacra doctrina*. Biblical expositors utilized the *quaestio* to address the text, which was then interrogated along the lines of the questions asked. Rather than merely interacting with the text, the scholastic method tended to subject the text to a series of inquisitions. This method of examining the text remained in use for years, reaching its apex in the enormous exegetical output of the Spanish Alfonso Tostado (ca. 1400–1455). (The approach is even found in modified form in Protestant exegetical works of the seventeenth century.)

Although most medieval theologians viewed their work as exposition of biblical faith, some like John Wyclif (ca. 1330–1384) and John Huss (ca. 1372–1415), wished to reform the church and the orders and did so by stressing biblical faith and life as the ideal. In his *De veritate Sacrae Scripturae*, *De ecclesia*, *De protestate Papae* (1377–1378), and *De apostasis* (ca. 1382), Wyclif maintained that the scriptures were the eternal exemplar of the Christian faith and should be used as the sole criterion of faith. He also concluded that the papacy and monastic orders were either ill-founded or without any foundation in scripture. Both Wyclif (and his followers, the Lollards) and Huss were persecuted by the church. Wyclif's followers rendered the Latin Bible into English. Wyclif's writings had great influence on Huss.

Renaissance and Reformation

New developments in the attitude toward and in the study of ancient texts, including the Bible, arose in the fifteenth century. These new developments, with many links to earlier attitudes, were part of what has been called the Renaissance or early humanism. Although this movement was complex and involved many areas of life, the focus here is on some literary dimensions, namely, the concern for and interpretation of ancient texts. Three general characteristics should be noted.

First, throughout the century, concerted efforts were made to recover texts from antiquity. This search for manuscripts was concerned not only to recover texts of works unavailable (and even unknown) at the time but also to recover source texts older than those from which contemporary editions were made.

Second, there was a desire to study ancient texts, including both the Bible and the church fathers, in their original form and language. This desire, even stated as a requirement, had been stressed by many important figures in the Middle Ages such as Roger Bacon (ca. 1220–1292) who made harsh criticisms of the contemporary Latin editions of the Bible and their deviations from the originals. The issue was now taken far more seriously and viewed not just as an idealized goal but as a potential that could be realized. Instruction in Greek was offered at Florence before the beginning of the fifteenth century and an increasing number of Christian scholars were learning Hebrew from Jews or Jewish converts (this of course became more difficult with the expulsion of Jews from most European countries).

Third, there was a new interest in encountering classical writings, including bibical and patristic texts, directly rather than reading than through a filter of glosses and comments. Such study of texts involved, on the practical level, a bypassing of tradition and traditional interpretations. Interpretation of a text had to start from the original and not from a translation. The characteristic slogan of the Renaissance, *Ad fontes*, "to the sources," expressed the view that later translations and commentaries were streams that flowed from the springs (sources) but that the purest waters were at the sources.

It was widely assumed at the time that the days when ancient texts were produced were better and more simplistic than the present. This produced a nostalgia about the past and the desire to "reproduce" classical times and the primitive church in the present as well as a critical attitude toward contemporary conditions and thought.

The growing interest in texts and their interpretation coincided with the development of the printing press utilizing movable type. In 1454(?), Johannes Gutenberg (ca. 1390–1468) printed a Latin Bible inaugurating the age of printed books. The printing press proved to be a major change agent in society and a great catalyst in biblical study (see Eisenstein 1979). The impact of the printing press was enormous.

First, it provided for a more rapid production of texts than previous manuscript workshops, in a standardized form, and at less cost. Second, availability of books and a reduced price meant that texts were distributed more widely. A teacher's influence, in the form of published lectures, could suddenly become widely known. Estimates suggest that Luther's writings sold more than 300,000 copies between 1517 and 1520. Third, private ownership of a book, especially of the Bible, allowed one to read the text and interact directly and subjectively with its content. Prior to the printing press, it is difficult to imagine Christianity as a religion of the book. Individualistic and subjective reading of the text embodied the possibility of practically everyone becoming their own interpreter. Fourth, printers and publishing houses were not only to encourage writing and even the creation of controversy so as to increase sales but also to function as clearing houses and educational institutions supporting research and writing and aiding in the collection and editing of texts. They became centers and gathering places for scholars. Printers themselves were often scholars and belonged to what came to be called the Republic of Letters (see below).

Two examples from the middle of the fifteenth century illustrate the nature and impact of textual work in biblical study. Giannozzo Manetti (1396–1459), eventually in the service of the king of Naples, put together a library of Jewish manuscripts, which later formed a part of the Vatican collection. Included were Hebrew manuscripts of the OT and works and commentaries by Rashi, Ibn Ezra, David Kimchi, and Gersonides. Manetti knew both Hebrew and Greek and prepared a new translation of the Psalter and the NT (neither ever published). He placed his Latin translation of the Psalter in parallel columns to the Gallican and *Hebraica veritas* of Jerome. His goal was to produce an accurate translation of the Bible, over against the widely used Latin Vulgate. Although his work was not published, Manetti illustrates the type of activity beginning to be undertaken.

Italian philologist Lorenzo Valla (1407–1457) compared several Greek manuscripts with the contemporary Latin translation and offered numerous instances where the Latin text did not adequately reflect the Greek. Valla's *Collatio Novi Testamenti* (1442/1443) was later, in his 1453/1457 rewrite, to be highly influential upon NT studies and especially upon Erasmus, who discovered a copy of Valla's manuscript in 1504 and edited and published it in 1505 as *Adnotationes in Novum Testamentum*. Not only was Valla a textual critic of the Latin Bible, but also a critic of ecclesiastical documents; his work, utilizing textual-historical criticism, on the so-called *Donation* of Constantine proved this document to be inauthentic. Valla criticized theologians who based their arguments on a Latin translation of the NT. If the Vulgate translation was faulty so might be theological conclusions based upon it.

In the last half of the fifteenth century, numerous publications made available biblical texts in Hebrew and Greek, but initially almost exclusively of the OT. The Hebrew psalter (with David Kimchi's commentary) was published in 1477, the Pentateuch (with the Targum Onkelos [see RABBINIC LITERATURE] and Rashi's commentary) in 1482, the prophets in 1485–1486, and the writings in 1486–1487. The complete Hebrew Bible appeared in 1488. In September 1481, Johannes Crastonus published the psalms in Greek with his Latin translation in parallel columns (the first biblical polyglot—actually a diglot—to be printed). In the preface Crastonus concluded that the text of Jerome's translation could no longer be established since the Vulgate text had become so contaminated.

Various forms of polyglots appeared early in the sixteenth century. Jacques Lefèvre (ca. 1455–1536) published *Quincuplex Psalterium* (1509), giving the psalms in five versions, and Agostino Giustiniani (1470–1536) published *Psalterium octaplum* (1516) which incorporated Hebrew, Greek, Arabic, and Aramaic versions of the psalms. (According to Giustiniani, Columbus's discovery of the New World fulfilled the prophecy of Ps 19:4.)

Pride of place as a scholarly tool was the *Complutensian Polyglot*, conceived in 1502 by Cardinal Ximenes de Cisneros (1436–1517) who had founded the trilingual university at Alcalà (Complutum) in Spain. Printed in 1514–1517, although not released until the early 1520s, the six volumes of this work contain the first printed edition of the Greek NT (completed 10 January 1514 but not published until 22 March 1520). For the Pentateuch, the Latin text is printed in a center column with the Greek (with interlinear translation) and the Hebrew versions on either side (see Gibson 1993, 84–85; in the preface Ximenes wrote: "Like Christ between two thieves"). Hebrew words in the text are coded to the Latin text and word roots are provided in the margin. The Aramaic targum with Latin translation is given at the bottom of the page (see Gibson 1993, 84–85). In addition to the text, the volumes offered various guides, word lists, and so forth, including the first Greek-Latin glossary of the NT. The value of the polyglot was not the aids it offered, mostly extracts and summaries of medieval material, but the parallel texts that allowed for comparative reading.

The humanist Desiderius Erasmus (ca. 1469–1536) was the first to publish an edition of the Greek NT

(*Novum instrumentum omne*, March 1516), but it was rushed to market and was not based on a very broad manuscript base.

Tools for learning the languages and using the Hebrew and Greek texts of the Bible were produced. Lascaris's Greek grammar appeared in 1495, to be followed by those of Theodore of Gaza (translated by Erasmus) in 1516, Melanchthon in 1518, Budé in 1520. The first significant Hebrew grammar published in Latin was Conrad Pellican's *De modo legendi et intelligendi Hebraeum* (1503 or 1504). This limited grammar was followed by Johannes Reuchlin's *De rudimentis Hebraicis* (1506), basically a translation and rewrite of David Kimchi's medieval grammar. The bulk of Reuchlin's work (pp. 32–451) consisted of a Hebrew-Latin dictionary. Reuchlin was recognized as one of the greatest humanistic scholars of his day and is remembered especially for his fight against elements in the church that sought the destruction of Jewish works, especially the Talmud.

The production of educational and scholarly tools for study of the Hebrew and Greek Bible texts was paralleled by efforts to produce reliable texts for the writings of the church fathers, which led to the recognition that many works had been falsely attributed.

Scholars such as Erasmus, Reuchlin, and Lefèvre, working with the new humanistic tools, produced new approaches to exegesis that were less dependent upon traditional views and were simultaneously the produce of direct engagement with the text in its original languages. Erasmus was highly critical of the scholastic method and of many traditions and practices of the church. These movements, it should be noted, had their origin and early development within Catholicism itself before the beginning of the Protestant Reformation.

The Protestant Reformation was engendered in the midst of this exciting and exhilarating period of academic and educational developments. The catalysts for the Reformation were indeed numerous: the need of the church for reform in both theology and practice; nostalgia for the idealized early days of Christendom; rising nationalism and regional consciousness; the inclinations and strengths of particular individuals; the recovery of Augustine's theology; and so forth. Certainly the new methods of Renaissance scholarship and the new approaches to the scriptures played a significant role. Luther welcomed the new "sacred philology." Most of the early reformers utilized and followed, to a lesser or greater degree, the same philological and linguistic tools and methods as their humanistic colleagues who remained within Roman Catholicism.

Certain positions were shared by practically all Protestants. (1) The church had drastically gone wrong at some point in its earlier history and departed from the original purity of the church reflected in the NT. They differed as to when this deviation from the true path had occurred. The magisterial reformation (Lutheranism and Calvinism) placed it after the early major church confessions. Others, like the Socinians and the more radical groups, placed the decay prior to the major church confessions, even at the close of NT history. Protestants were unanimously agreed that the Bible was the primary instrument for reforming the church and for returning it to its original purity.

(2) Theology and the church's institutional life should be based on the principle of *sola scriptura*. All theological doctrines and church and Christian practices should be rooted in and sanctioned by scripture, with scripture serving as its own interpreter, that is, interpretation of difficult texts should be done in light of other, clearer texts.

(3) The authoritative form of the Bible should be the Hebrew and Greek, with translations in the vernacular to be based on the original languages. (Many vernacular translations in various languages existed prior to the Reformation without church disapproval and often with church sanction, but these were made from the Latin.)

(4) People should have the right to read and interpret the Bible on their own. The individual's prerogative to interpret scripture was often played off against the authority of the pope and church councils.

(5) Most protestant reformers denied the multilevel reading of scripture and emphasized the literal sense, but the latter they generally understood as having a more Christological and ecclesiological dimension than would later be the case. The perspectives on the OT found in the writings of the NT were generally considered indicative of a literal reading. Many reformers, even Luther himself, continued to use allegorical and tropological readings and interpretations in making the connection between texts, especially those of the OT, and contemporary life and situations. This was also true of post-Reformation exegetes, who often spoke of the "spiritual" dimension of a text. The use of analogy between the text and the contemporary situation tended to become more common with the passage of time.

(6) The individual reader of the scriptures should personally encounter and engage the scriptures in an

existential manner, being directed by the Holy Spirit who had inspired the biblical writings in their original encodement. To some extent, this parallels the older monastic attitude toward the Bible as *sacra pagina*.

(7) The central doctrine of the Christian faith and the central thrust of the biblical materials were understood as "justification by faith" through the gracious act of God in Jesus Christ. Thus Luther distinguished among biblical writings, depending upon how much emphasis a certain work placed on Christology and justification by faith. For Luther, there was clearly "a canon within the canon" with Romans, Galatians, and the Gospel of John being the most favored NT books.

The sixteenth century witnessed an enormous output of biblical commentaries of diverse sorts (see Williams 1988). Martin Luther (1483–1546) and John Calvin (1509–64) were the most productive in this area. Luther, trained in medieval theology, wrote commentaries that expounded and narrated the faith, often with a great deal of anti-Catholicism incorporated. Calvin, educated in the humanistic disciplines, gave greater attention to the straightforward sense of the text and wrote commentaries with a distinctive modern cast (Calvin's first published work was a commentary on Seneca's *De Clementia* [1532] which he hoped would gain him a reputation over against Erasmus).

The humanist Erasmus worked with a somewhat reduced version of Christianity: he was interested in the *philosophia Christi* and in the Bible as *sacra littera*. His paraphrases of biblical texts sought to make the NT available in an easily digestible form (in spite of his emphasis on educating the common person, Erasmus wrote in Latin, hardly the language of everyday discourse).

Catholics such as Cardinal Cajetan (Thomas de Vio, 1469–1534), one of Luther's inquisitors in 1518, wrote numerous commentaries stressing the literal sense of scripture and seeking to show that the NT supported Catholic positions.

Protestants translated the scriptures into numerous vernacular languages, basing their translations on the Hebrew and Greek. Latin translations from the original languages were also popular among Protestant scholars and remained in use until well into the eighteenth century. After the Reformation was underway and especially after the Council of Trent, Catholics took a dim view of vernacular translations with their accompanying potential for private interpretation. An official edition of the Vulgate was issued under the authority of Pope Sixtus V in 1590 and reissued with more than

3,000 corrections as the Clementine edition by Pope Clement VIII in 1592.

Controversy over the nature, role, and interpretation of the Bible was a common staple of the sixteenth century. There was not only a Protestant-Catholic debate but also internal struggles within Protestantism. Luther, followed by the other reformers, accepted as the canonical OT only those writings found in the Hebrew Bible (but not in its order). Luther's decision was based partially on the fact that some doctrines (e.g., prayers and offerings for the dead) were taught in some of the deleted books with which he did not agree. To justify the shorter canon, the reformers appealed to the authority of Jerome (and some medieval writers) who had spoken of OT books not in the Hebrew canon as "Apocrypha."

The first defense and explanation of the Protestant canon was written by Andreas Bodenstein (Carlstadt): *De canonicis scripturis libellus* (August 1520; followed by a slimmer volume, *Welche Bucher biblisch seint*, November 1520). Carlstadt placed the books of the Bible into three categories, placing Hebrews, James, 2 Peter, 2-3 John, Jude, and Revelation (the *antilegomena* of Eusebius of Caesarea) into the third category and the last chapter of Mark and the Letter to the Laodiceans in the Apocrypha (he also argued on literary grounds that Moses could not have written the entire Pentateuch, a view already hinted at by Ibn Ezra). This subordination of certain previously contested NT writings was shared by many Lutheran reformers. Niels Hemmingsen (1513–1600) wrote in 1555:

All these books of the New Testament are in the canon except Second Peter, Second and Third John, the Epistles of James and Jude along with the Apocalypse. Some also place the Epistle to the Hebrews outside the canon. (Steinmetz 1990, 188)

Books could thus be in the Bible without being canonical. The issue of the disputed books as well as Luther's attitude toward James ("a right strawy epistle") probably explains why no early Lutheran confession contains a separate section on the scripture with an enumeration of the biblical books. The fourth session of the Council of Trent (8 April 1546) set the Catholic OT canon once and for all by enumerating the books (including Tobit, Judith, Wisdom of Solomon, Ecclesiasticus, Baruch, and 1-2 Maccabees) and placing under anathema those who did not accept this list. Later, the Jewish convert to Christianity Sixtus Senensis coined the phrase "deuterocanonical" (secondarily canonical) with reference to these works (*Bibliotheca sancta*, 1566); this term has been widely used, especially in recent years.

Catholics and Protestants differed over who had the right to interpret scripture with the latter initially arguing for every person (at least those trained in the original languages). Catholics argued, prophetically, that such a broad endowment of the right to interpret would produce a plethora of interpretations and create divisiveness in the church. Again the Council of Trent declared authoritatively:

> In matters of faith and morals pertaining to the edification of the Christian doctrine, no one, relying on his own judgment and distorting the Sacred Scriptures according to his own conceptions, shall dare to interpret them contrary to that sense which Holy Mother Church, to whom it belongs to judge their true sense and meaning, has held and does hold, or even contrary to the unanimous agreement of the Fathers, even though such interpretations should never at any time be published.

To enforce its decree, the council declared that all publications "dealing with sacred matters" must be approved by the church (the basis for the later *Index librorum prohibitorum*).

The debate over "Holy Writ versus Holy Church" which had already troubled theological waters in the fourteenth and fifteenth centuries sharply divided Catholics and Protestants. Protestants argued for the priority of scripture and Catholics for the priority of the church and its tradition. Catholics argued that before any NT book was written, the church already was and that before the NT was written the faith was carried through the traditions and the oral proclamation. After lengthy debate, the Council of Trent denied the principle of *sola scriptura* but refused to declare that revelation comes partly through scripture and partly through tradition, opting instead for

> Truths and rules are contained in the written books and in the unwritten traditions which, received by the Apostles from the mouth of Christ Himself or from the Apostles themselves, the Holy Spirit dictating, have come down to us, transmitted as it were from hand to hand.

Catholics thus acknowledged that what is authoritative is the text and the faith which has grown up around the text, a view similar to that of Judaism and a position operative in practice for most "book religions."

It is interesting to note that Protestants soon created their own "tradition" by which the scriptures were to be read, namely, confessions of faith and theological treatises. In the preface to his *Institutes* (first edition, 1536), Calvin declared he had written the work so the reader of the Bible would know what to look for as one read. Most early English translations of the Bible were issued with extensive marginal notes, prologues, and summaries to guide the reader. Those in Tyndale's translation of the NT and Pentateuch (1520s) and in the complete Geneva Bible (1560) were strongly theological and highly influential. At the direction of King James, the authorized version of 1611 contained only marginal notes related to text and translation.

Protestants argued that the Bible was sufficiently clear to be understood by the normal reader (presumably in a vernacular translation) at least on all matters necessary for salvation. Many Catholics argued against this view and declared that the difficulties in understanding the scriptures should drive one to fideism and acceptance of the faith on the basis of the church's authority.

Protestants argued for the authority of the Hebrew and Greek forms of the scriptures but Catholics defended the Vulgate. The Council of Trent declared that

> the old Latin Vulgate edition, which has been approved for use in the Church for so many centuries, is to be taken as authentic in public lectures, disputations, and expositions, and that no one should dare or presume to reject it under any circumstances whatsoever.

Disputes within Protestantism over biblical interpretation occured early on in the movement. The mainline European reform movements could not agree on the nature of the Eucharist and whether the words of Jesus "this is my body" were to be interpreted literally or not (Catholics used this debate to show that Protestants did not read and believe the Bible literally). Socinians and others argued that the NT did not teach either a doctrine of the vicarious death of Jesus or a doctrine of the Trinity. For holding the latter position, Michael Servetus (1511–1553) was burned at the stake under Calvin's supervision on 27 October 1553. Sebastian Castellio (1515–1563) was forced out of Geneva, primarily over his humanist views and his conclusion that the Song of Songs was merely love poetry and should not be a part of the OT canon. In the annotations to his translation of the Bible into Ciceronian Latin (*Biblia Sacra Latina*, 1551) and his *De Haereticis* (1554) Castellio argued for unrestricted religious toleration and complete freedom of interpretation.

Already in the sixteenth century, there seem to have been people who did not share the general religious view that the Bible was the Word of God. Calvin and others allude to persons, whose voices have not been passed along, that denied the truthfulness of biblical content and challenged the religious opinion about the Bible. This disparagement of the Bible may explain the appearance of several harmonies of the gospels produced during the century, the first by Andreas Osiander (1498–1552). Others were published by Jansen, Codmann, Chemnitz, and Mercator. Most of these harmonies acknowledged an apologetic quality to their work—to defend the gospel accounts from those who repudiated their trustworthiness because of their contradictions and differences.

In 1646, Bishop John Wilkins (1614–1672), later to serve as secretary for the Royal Society, in his *Ecclesiastes, or a Discourse concerning the Gift of Preaching*, offered an extensive bibliography on the Bible. At the beginning he noted that the preacher should own two or three harmonizers, that is, works that showed how to overcome difficulties and problems in the text. At least at this time, it was assumed that the Bible properly understood could stand up against its despisers. It was not long thereafter that the Bible and its worldview would be put on the defensive.

Seventeenth and Eighteenth Centuries

In many respects, the seventeenth century represents the watershed in the interpretation of the Bible. In addition to the continued internecine warfare over biblical interpretation among Christians, new developments in science, philosophy, world exploration, and other areas presented challenges to the worldview derived from the Bible (travel books took second place to theology in popularity). In addition, study of the Bible itself presented scholars with the necessity to deal with the fact that the scriptures were not the unified document that had once been believed. On the one hand, some Protestant scholars took a rigid stance toward new assessments and expositions of the Bible and sought to defend the scriptures against Catholics and non-Christians through a highly developed form of scholasticism, a path that proved eventually to be a dead end (see Muller 1993 for a sympathetic treatment). On the other hand, more humanistic work on the scriptures, by both Catholics and Protestants, in the

tradition of Valla, Reuchlin, and Erasmus, made significant contributions to the field.

In the foreground of much research and publication throughout the seventeenth century was what was called the Republic of Letters (*Respublica litterarum*). This was an unorganized but self-conscious stratum of scholars that transcended national and confessional boundaries, interested in scholarship and new developments and discoveries. Theologians, jurists, scientists, philosophers, philologists, and persons interested in experimental science and world exploration made up its number. A network of correspondence in Latin kept the members informed of each other's work and in touch with one another.

The roots of this association may go back to humanist groups of the fifteenth century and the scholar-printers of the sixteenth and seventeenth centuries whose printing shops served as international houses, message centers, meeting places, and sanctuaries. Mutual cooperation and distribution of work as well as scholarly aid were characteristic of the group.

Throughout the century, two general conditions are noteworthy. First, there was a gradual erosion of the biblical worldview as the all-encompassing key for understanding human life and history. Accumulation of new knowledge expanded the biblical worldview to the breaking point. Second, after years of warfare and strife fought over the intricacies of theology and biblical interpretation, many sought to focus on the essentials of religion, on those doctrines on which all or most could agree, in hopes of creating more peaceful conditions. That is, a minimum of doctrine rather than a maximalist view gradually came to be stressed. Lord Herbert of Cherbury (1583–1648) in his *De Veritate* (1624) and subsequent writings argued that there are five essential inborn notions common to all religions: (1) there is a God, (2) who ought to be worshipped, (3) virtue and morality are the chief elements in service to the divine, (4) but since humans fail, repentance for sin is a duty, and (5) there is a future life of rewards and punishments. Near the end of the century, John Locke (1632–1704) concluded that, in the last analysis, Christianity could be reduced to one central tenet: belief in Jesus as the messiah.

Early in the century, the Galileo affair reflected the coming tensions that would occur between science and a worldview based on the Bible (see Blackwell 1991). In 1543, Nicolas Copernicus (1473–1543) had published his *De revolutionibus orbium coelestium* in which he advocated a heliocentric view of the universe. The full impact of his work was modified by Andreas Osiander (1498–1565) who attached a preface stating that Copernicus's views were proposed as a hypothesis, not as a statement of how things really were.

Utilizing the work of John Kepler (1571–1630) and his own astronomical observations, Galileo Galilei (1564–1642) proposed a heliocentric view of the universe as scientific fact. As part of his defense against the church which claimed his views were contrary to biblical teachings, Galileo wrote his famous *Letter to Madame Christina . . . Concerning the Use of Biblical Quotations in Matters of Science* (1615). Galileo argued that the primary purpose of the sacred writings was the service of God and the salvation of souls, not scientific facts and theories that are based on experimentation, observation, and reason: "The intention of the Holy Ghost is to teach us how one goes to heaven, not how heaven goes." Galileo proposed that some biblical statements should be taken allegorically or figuratively when they conflicted with scientific truths and that God was accommodating to human knowledge at the time in statements which imply a geocentric universe.

Galileo appealed to various church fathers and contemporary masters but especially to Augustine's *De Genesi ad literam* where Augustine had argued that one should not believe things inadvisedly perchance they later be proven to be untrue and that if something was disproved by most certain truth, then it was not holy scripture that ever affirmed it, but human ignorance that imagined it. In spite of his defense, Galileo was condemned. The church at the time interpreted scripture very literally (Josh 10:12-14—"the sun stood still and the moon stopped"—was the main text in the affair). Protestants did not have the same difficulties with the new astronomy.

Issues of world history and problems of chronology also moved outside the perimeters of the biblical worldview in the first half of the sixteenth century. Both Luther and Melanchthon as well as others had written on biblical chronology. Knowledge of other cultures and nonbiblical chronological schemes, however, began to create problems for understanding world history within biblical frames of reference. In 1632, J. d'Auzoles tabulated that there were 122 different interpretations of world chronology with seventy-nine different dates for creation ranging from 3083 to 6984 B.C.E. (*La sainte chronologie*). (Bishop James Ussher's [1581–1656] system with creation in 4004 B.C.E. was published in 1650–1654 in his *Annales*

Veteris et Novi Testamenti). Simultaneous with the debates over chronology, the discovery of new worlds and people unmentioned in the Bible cast doubt on the accuracy of biblical contents. The issue of astronomy might be minor since the Bible never discusses the topic directly, but history and chronology were different matters. Biblical interpretation had to respond to outside impulses.

The Frenchman Isaac de la Peyrére (ca. 1596–1676) sought to meet the growing dilemma and offered an explanation of the origin of peoples and nations not mentioned in the Bible in his *Men before Adam. . . . By which are prov'd that the first men were created before Adam* (1655) which had circulated in manuscript form in the 1640s. Peyrére's theses were that Adam was not the first human but the tribal ancestor of Israel, Noah's flood was a local affair, and the Pentateuch was a hodgepodge of materials not written by Moses in its entirety. The work became widely known, appeared in an English translation in 1656, and introduced the polygenetic anthropology of pre-Adamic humans into Western thought (see Popkin 1987).

The Englishman Thomas Hobbes (1588–1679) published his *Leviathan* in 1651, offering an analysis of the Bible, how it should be used in politics, and suggestions about its study, especially in the third part (books 32–43). Hobbes concluded that it should be the prerogative of the sovereign power to set the contents of the canon for the realm and to serve as its ultimate interpreter. Hobbes argued that the authorship and antiquity of the biblical writings cannot be determined by tradition. The issue must be guided by the evidence drawn from the books themselves, "and this light, though it show us not the writer of every book, yet it is not unuseful to give us knowledge of the time, wherein they were written." On this basis, he concluded that anachronistic statements indicate that Moses did not produce the Pentateuch but probably only what the Bible says he wrote, namely, Deut 12–26, a book later discovered by Hilkiah the priest which was the basis for Josiah's reform (2 Kgs 22–23). Hobbes thus argued that good biblical study should bypass traditional views and reach decisions on the basis of internal evidence. Neither Galileo, nor Peyrère, nor Hobbes were biblical scholars per se, yet their concerns were issues interpreters soon had to face.

One issue that was of great concern and discussion in the Republic of Letters in the seventeenth century was the origin and date of the Hebrew vowel points. The debate had surfaced earlier, in 1538, when the

Jewish scholar Elias Levita (ca. 1468–1549) published his *Massoreth ha-Massoreth* which was translated into Latin the following year by the great Christian semiticist Sebastian Münster (1489–1522). Levita's work denied the widely assumed theory of the antiquity of the pointing and argued that the vowel points dated from post-Talmud times (after 600 C.E.). The issue first agitated Jewish scholars. Levita was answered by Azariah de Rossi (ca. 1514–1577) in 1574. At the turn of the century, the issue came to occupy Christians.

The reason the matter was of concern to the church had to do with the inspiration of the biblical text and the question of which OT text had the greatest claim to antiquity and authenticity. If the vowels were added as late as Levita claimed, then it was assumed they represented a late human addition to the text. Also if they were this late, then the Catholic Vulgate was translated from an older and thus more authentic text than the Masoretic text. Matters were further complicated when Pietro della Valle brought to Europe in 1616 a copy of the Samaritan Pentateuch, written in ancient Hebrew characters but without vowel points and differing from the Masoretic text at about 6,000 points.

Catholics seized on the argument that the Septuagint text and Jerome's Vulgate were really older than the Masoretic text and that the Protestant OT (the Hebrew text) was a later and likely a corrupt text. The debate raged for years (see Laplanche 1986). The antiquity of the vowel points was argued by many Protestants especially Johann Buxtorf (1564–1629) and his son (1599–1664). The lateness of the pointing was defended especially by Louis Cappell (1585–1658), an Arminian Protestant. Cappell, in his *Arcanum punctationis revelatum* (published anonymously in Holland by Thomas Erpenius in 1624) and *Critica sacra* (1650) established his case conclusively. *Critica sacra* was published through the efforts of the Catholic scholar Jean Morinus (1591–1659). For the first time since the Reformation, real scholarly cooperation in biblical study crossed Christian confessional boundaries. A new movement was underway: biblical criticism.

(The use of the term "criticism" with reference to the study, evaluation, and correction of texts came into widespread usage in the late sixteenth century, primarily in regard to nonbiblical classical texts. In his *History of the Royal Society*, 1667, Thomas Sprat could already write that "we have had enough of criticism"— but he had an axe to grind.)

In spite of Cappell's work conservative Swiss Protestants included belief in the antiquity and inspiration of the vowel points in the *Formula Consensus* (1675) and ruled (in 1678) that no one could be licensed to preach without publicly declaring a belief in the integrity of the Hebrew text and the divinity of the vowel points.

Two trajectories characterize mid-seventeenth biblical interpretation. On one hand, from the point of scholarship, it was one of the most productive periods in history. The Paris Polyglot, adding the Samaritan Pentateuch and an Arabic version, was produced during 1629–1645, in ten mammoth volumes (the Antwerp Polyglot [1569–1572, eight volumes] had added the Syriac NT). The London Polyglot, the finest ever produced, appeared in six volumes in 1655–1657 (there is a commonwealth and a royalist edition varying only in the preface and the time of binding). This included the Hebrew, Greek, Vulgate, Syriac, Ethiopic, Arabic, and Persian versions with Latin translations as well as the Samaritan Pentateuch, various Targums, and readings from Codex Alexandrinus (acquired by the British in 1627) along with various aids. Companion volumes to the London Polyglot included Castell's Heptaglot lexicon (two volumes, 1669) and the *Critici sacri* (nine volumes, 1660) which provided a commentary and annotations on the entire Bible (Apocrypha included) drawn from scores of sixteenth- and seventeenth-century commentators and several dozen dissertations on diverse topics, texts, and problems. Matthew Poole produced his *Synopsis criticorum* in 1669–1674 (five volumes) a recasting and supplementation of the *Critici sacri* which brought the number of commentators excerpted to about 150. In addition, the famous annotated Bible, generally associated with the Assembly of Divines, appeared in 1651.

Four of the most famous British interpreters published during this period were Edward Pococke (1604–1691) who published major commentaries on three of the minor prophets and was the first scholar to utilize Arabic extensively as an interpretive aid; John Lightfoot (1602–1675) who published numerous works on the Bible, being the first person to draw extensively on rabbinic literature to elucidate the NT (in his *Horae Hebraicae et Talmudicae*, six volumes, 1658–1678, and still in print); Henry Ainsworth (1560–1622) whose translation and commentary on the Pentateuch, Psalms, and Song of Songs appeared in 1639; and Henry Hammond (1605–1660) who published *A Paraphrase and Annotations upon all the Books of the New Testament* (1653), a widely used and respected volume and the first to raise Gnosticism as an important issue in understanding the NT. Bishop James Ussher's (1581–1656) study of the letters of Polycarp and Ignatius appeared in 1644 and his *Annales Veteris et Novi Testamenti* in 1650–1654. The work of the Dutch scholar Hugo Grotius (1583–1645), *Annotationes* to the entire Bible (six volumes, 1641–1650), employed all the humanistic tools and offered a historical reading of the Bible drawing upon innumerable ancient sources while still respecting scriptural authority. Probably no period in history has witnessed such scholarly achievements in the field. Biblical criticism had come of age.

On the other hand, the period of the English revolution and the Commonwealth (1640–1660), when press censorship was lifted, witnessed the use of the Bible to support practically every conceivable political and social form of life and behavior (see Hill 1993). Radical Millenarianism was rampant (Joseph Mede's *Clavis Apocalyptica* appeared in 1627). Quakerism and the appeal to the "inner light"—even over against the Bible—emerged. Oliver Cromwell (1599–1658) read his career in light of Psalm 110. John Milton (1608–1674) sought to reason away the NT prohibition against divorce (*The Doctrine and Discipline of Divorce*, 1643), and worked on his heterodox *De doctrina Christiana* (published posthumously) which contains more than 8,000 biblical references and declares in regard to biblical interpretation:

> No one else can usefully interpret for him, unless that person's interpretation coincides with the one he makes for himself and his own conscience. . . . Every man is his own arbitrator. . . . All things are eventually to be referred to the Spirit and the unwritten word. (*Complete Prose Works of Milton*, 6:583–90)

The doctrine of "the priesthood of the believer" had been stretched to its limit and applied to biblical interpretation. Biblical authority came out of the period somewhat shattered.

Two seventeenth-century figures, the excommunicated Dutch Jewish philosopher Baruch Spinoza (1632–1677) and the French Catholic Oratorian Richard Simon (1638–1712), have generally been considered precursors of the modern phase of biblical study. Spinoza wrote in the wake of the Cartesian revolution in philosophy and placed reason and philosophy above religion and faith as the arbiter of truth. In his *Tractatus theologico-politicus* (1670), he considered the Bible to be a humanly produced book which must be studied like any other book and its truths

assessed by reason. Spinoza explained biblical miracles as extraordinary events whose causes were unknown to the observers. Spinoza outlined a program of biblical studies: (1) knowledge of the original languages (he also wrote a Hebrew grammar and pointed to the Hebraic quality of NT Greek); (2) analysis of each book; (3) the Bible must be interpreted by the Bible (which for Spinoza allowed one to critique speculative conclusions about the Bible and its authority); (4) knowledge of the environment and intention of the author ("who was the speaker, what was the occasion, and to whom were the words addressed"); and (5) investigation of all that has happened to every book in the Bible (i.e., its transmission, corruption, copyist's errors, etc.).

For Spinoza, the Bible contains truths that could have been discovered through reason; it has a very persuasive character and is often imaginative literature; and the laws of the Torah were intended for a specific time for people in their childhood. He considered much of the OT to have been edited late, in the time of Ezra and afterward. Although Spinoza's book was almost universally condemned, banned, and placed on the Index of Forbidden Books, the work and his philosophy were highly influential.

Oratorian Richard Simon published an enormous amount of literature as well as a new translation of the NT: critical histories of the OT and the NT and the versions, and biblical commentators. His most influential work was *Histoire critique du Vieux Testament* (already printed in 1678 but most copies were destroyed by the censor; second edition, 1685). One of Simon's goals in this work was to prove to Protestants that the Hebrew OT (and all versions and translations) and its text were too unreliable and uncertain to be the basis of the faith, thus affirming the long-held Catholic view. Simon was caustic in his assessment of other commentators, even the patristic fathers (which got him into trouble with his church and order). Simon not only denied that Moses was the author of the Pentateuch but also proposed a theory regarding its origin along with the historical books: public scribes recorded events and happenings and their records served as the basis of the biblical books. Practically all of Simon's works were translated into English shortly after being published.

By the end of the seventeenth century, the historical-critical method (the quest for the *sensus historicus*) was reasonably well developed (though not necessarily widely accepted) resting on the following presumptions. (1) The Bible is a book of antiquity separated from the present both chronologically and conceptually. (2) The Bible should be studied and read like any other book, that is, in a straightforward fashion. Individual books or groupings of books must be read on their own, not filtered through the Bible as a whole or church/synagogue tradition (John Locke wrote "an essay for the understanding of St. Paul's Epistles, by consulting St. Paul himself"). (3) A biblical text is the product of a human author(s) living in a particular time and place. (4) The form and content of a text reflect and are intelligible only in light of the author's conceptions, intentions, and beliefs, which are conditioned by the time and context of the original writer's and readers' environment and thought world. (5) The authenticity and validity of the Bible or a biblical text depend, in no small measure, on how they and their content measure up to the canons of human thought and reason. (6) The causes and nature of events in the Bible must be understood in terms of historical analogy, what was possible then is possible now and vice versa (the latter perspective was more hinted at than declared).

The eighteenth century witnessed the Bible and biblical worldview under attack and, before the century was over, even ridiculed, as had not been the case since the days of Celsus, Porphyry, and Emperor Julian the Apostate (Muslim attacks on the Bible in the Middle Ages had been pointed but superficial). The broad movement behind this attitude toward the Bible (and "revealed" religion in general) was what has been broadly called Deism. The Deists sought greater liberty in civil life, increased freedom to publish without censorship, and the right, as Spinoza had already said, to "think what one likes, and say what one thinks." Deists denied the particularistic favoritism implied in all religions based on "special" revelation and argued for belief in a deity that treated all humans alike. The movement drew upon (1) the thought of Lord Herbert, Hobbes, and Spinoza; (2) the classics, especially the Greek skeptics with their critiques of religion; (3) Latitudinarian thinkers and theologians like Isaac Newton (1642–1727), John Locke (1632–1704), Samuel Clarke (1675–1729), and Archbishop John Tillotson (1630–1694) who sought to reconcile faith and reason and the new science, a movement that found embodiment in the famous Boyle Lectures; (4) certain elements in Calvin and Calvinism (Deism has been described as Calvinism without the anxiety, tears, and determinism); (5) the philosophy of Francis Bacon's (1561–1626)

empiricism with its desire to undertake "a total reconstruction of the sciences, arts, and all human knowledge, raised upon proper foundations"; and (6) the methods of Protestant anti-Catholic polemic (which had challenged such topics as the mystery of transubstantiation and continuing miracles in the church) which were then applied to the Protestant faith and primitive church, and to the biblical literature. Deism expounded a religion of nature ("Adamic religion") which was assumed to have been based on reason, was morally oriented and monotheistic, and had been perverted by the priestly hierarchy with innumerable superstitions to keep the common lot in ignorance, bondage, and servitude to the advantage of the priestly caste (see Byrne 1989). With the end of English government press censorship in 1696, the publication of deistic works became more widespread.

Before his suicide, Charles Blount (1654–1693) published something of a Deist Manifesto outlining the seven essential articles of natural religion. In 1696, John Toland (1670–1722) published *Christianity not Mysterious* in which he denied that either God or revelation were beyond human comprehension. By 1698, English Deism had become so widespread that Charles Leslie (1650–1722) wrote *A Short and Easy Method with the Deists, wherein the Certainty of the Christian Religion is demonstrated by Infallible Proof from Four Rules, which are Incompatible to any Imposture that ever yet has been, or that can possibly be.* Leslie outlined a method for the evidential-factual investigation of biblical events seeking to show how their historicity could be affirmed by appealing to certain characteristics of the events, their public nature, and their attestation in publicly available documents deriving from the time of the events. Something like Leslie's arguments has been a staple of much British biblical scholarship ever since.

The three issues related to biblical studies most attacked by the Deists were the fulfillment of prophecy, biblical miracles, and the Protestant understanding of the early church. The following are some of the representative works. Anthony Collins (1676–1729) published *A Discourse on the Grounds and Reasons of the Christian Faith* (1724) and *A Scheme of Literal Prophecy Considered* (1725) in which he argued that OT prophecies could be seen as fulfilled in Jesus and the early church only if understood allegorically, a common method of exegesis in the Judaism of Jesus' day. Thus there was no miraculous fulfillment of predictions to support the authenticity and uniqueness of the Bible and Christian faith but only an exegetical method.

The issue of OT prophecies and their fulfillment had been one of the basic elements in Christian apologetics and a hotly debated issue at the turn of the century. William Whiston (1667–1752) who succeded Newton as Lucasian professor of mathmatics at Cambridge had written *Accomplishment of Scripture Prophecies* (1708) arguing that prophecies had but one fulfillment but ended up arguing that the OT prophetical texts had been corrupted by the Jews thus explaining the differences between OT predictions and NT fulfillments. Thomas Woolston (1669–1731) wrote a series of discourses and defenses of these (in the 1620s) challenging the historicity of the gospel miracles (see Burns 1981). Woolston and other deistic writers discussed the gospels as theological statements, not factual reports.

Eventually the resurrection of Christ, the central NT miracle, became the center of debate. Thomas Sherlock (1678–1761) defended its historicity (*Tryal of the Witnesses of the Resurrection of Jesus*, 1729) and Peter Annet (1693–1769) offered the challenge (*The Resurrection of Jesus Considered*, 1743; *The Resurrection Reconsidered: The Resurrection Defenders Stript of All Defence*, 1745). Annet pointed to the difficulties in reconciling the gospel accounts of the resurrection to the fact that even witnesses may be deceived, and claimed that in any case "a historical fact [even a miracle] is not part of true and pure religion, which is founded only on truth and purity. That it [true religion] does not consist in the belief of any history."

The Deists, especially Toland (*Nazarenus, or Jewish, Gentile, and Mahometan Christianity*, 1718) and Thomas Morgan (d. 1743; *The Moral Philosopher*, three volumes, 1737–1740), offered a reconstruction of early church history. In the beginning, there was Jesus and his followers with a simple message ("purest morals," "reasonable worship," and "just conceptions of Heaven and Heavenly Things"). This movement was perverted by the introduction into the church of elements of Jewish ceremonial and Gentile mystery. Morgan formulated the issue in terms of a Pauline proclamation of Jesus as universal savior in conflict with a group represented by Peter and others which was strongly influenced by exclusivistic Jewish elements. Although Jewish Christianity prevailed for a time, Gentile and Jewish Christians eventually combined in the time of Christian persecution to produce what became Catholic Christianity, with the more strongly Pauline elements going over to Gnosticism.

The NT writings cover up this movement and contain corruptions and additions to bring them into line with developing thought.

If the reformers may be said to have concluded that medieval theologians and scholasticism had misunderstood biblical religion, the Socinians and radicals that all later theologians had misunderstood the Bible, and the Latitudianarians that the early creeds had misunderstood the NT, then the deistic movement may be said to have advocated the view that the NT writers had misunderstood Jesus. The way was now open for not only a detailed examination of the biblical writings in terms of the history of the early church and Christian thought but also for the study of the historical Jesus and the relationship of these writings to him.

The writings of the Deists themselves were representative of what might be called "coffee house" theology—disorganized, evocative, personalized, argumentative. (Coffee was first introduced into Europe in the year that Luther "nailed" his theses to the Wittenberg church door. The first coffee house opened in England at Oxford in 1650. Such houses became centers of dialogue and diatribe.) None of the English Deists held academic positions. Most were free floaters. Only Conyers Middleton (1683–1750) had university connections—he was librarian at Cambridge.

Deism was far more influential on the continent than in England. Most of their works were translated into French and German. Throughout most of the century European theology and biblical studies drew their stimulus from England. A massive nineteen-volume biblical commentary was produced by the Germans (1749–1770) consisting solely of translations from English in order to bring German scholarship abreast of work in England (initially edited by D. R. Teller). No deistic work was included, because no English Deist wrote commentaries or any systematic treatise on the Bible.

A movement that developed contemporaneously with Deism was Pietism, part of a transdenominational phenomenon represented in Judaism by Hasidism, in Catholicism by the Jansenists, and in Protestantism by the Moravian Brethen and Methodism. Within the German church the movement had its beginning in the publication of *Pia Desideria* (1675) by Philipp Jakob Spener (1635–1705) who sought revival of the church through biblical piety. Biblical study was fostered in frequent devotional meetings. The university of Halle and A. H. Francke (1663–1727) became rallying points for the movement which stressed the *sensus spiritualis* and the subjective, experiential reading of the text illumined by the Holy Spirit. Pietism produced a number of significant contributors to biblical studies, since its focus on the interpreter freed one to engage in even critical work on the text.

J. A. Bengel (1687–1752) published an edition of the Greek NT (1734) noting variant readings among texts of the NT in a critical apparatus (the first such critical apparatus was in Estienne's Greek NT, 1550). Bengel's commentary on the NT, *Gnomon Novi Testamenti* (1742) proved to be a classic. Textual criticism in which variant readings among Greek manuscripts were noted tended to relativize any doctrine of an inspired text as well as the widely held view that God would not allow his word to be corrupted in its transmission. John Mill (1645–1707) had published a Greek NT in 1707 with about 30,000 variant readings drawn from about one hundred manuscripts. J. J. Wettstein (1693–1754) published a still-valuable Greek NT (two volumes, 1751–1752) with a critical apparatus using *sigla* for the various texts and detailed exegetical notes (neither Mill nor Wettstein were pietists but NT textual criticism owed much to Pietism).

Two works published in 1753, one by a Frenchman and the other by an Englishman, marked new departures in biblical studies. Jean Astruc (1684–1766), physician at the court of Louis XV and professor of medicine at the royal college in Paris, published *Conjectures sur les Mémoires originaux dont il paroit que Moyse s'est servi pour composer le Livre de la Genèse*. Astruc, at least in his stated intent, set out to explain how Moses composed the book of Genesis and how it came to be in the corrupted form we possess, so as to silence biblical detrators. He divided the material in Genesis into a number (primarily four) of sources that Moses used in putting together the book. Moses used sources since he was no eyewitness to the events before his day. Astruc divided the sources primarily on the basis of the names used for God (Yahweh and Elohim). Source criticism of the Pentateuch was thus introduced into biblical studies.

Between 1741 and 1750, Robert Lowth (1710–1787), Oxford professor of poetry, delivered a series of lectures on Hebrew poetry that was published in 1753 as *De sacra poesi Hebraeorum* (English translation in 1787). Lowth argued that much of the OT was poetry (Psalms and Prophets especially) and must be understood aesthetically. His emphasis fell on literary appreciation of the Hebrew poetic genius which he identi-

fied with the work of the Holy Spirit. Lowth's work exerted enormous influence, especially in Germany.

Beginning in the second half of the eighteenth century, German scholarship came increasingly to dominate biblical studies. The emphasis on natural theology, reason, and the downplaying of revelation that undergirded English Deism had found expression in Germany in the work of Christian Wolff (1679–1754) who sought to synchronize reason and revelation. Historical criticism erupted in Germany in radical but scholarly form, being heavily dependent on ideas derived from English Deists.

After writing a dissertation defending the orthodox interpretation of prophecy and its fulfillment (1731), H. S. Reimarus (1694–1768) fell under the sway of rationalistic natural theology. At his death, Reimarus left behind a major work, partially published anonymously in 1774–1778 by G. E. Lessing (1729–1881). Reimarus reached radical conclusions about such events as the Exodus from Egypt as described in the Bible but his most controversial positions concerned the nature of Jesus' ministry and the resurrection. According to Reimarus, Jesus taught a natural, rational, and practical religion but saw himself as the messiah of a coming political realm, which of course never came into being. Following this failure, the disciples stole the body of Jesus, proclaimed his resurrection, and then edited his teachings to have Jesus proclaim his death and resurrection and his coming kingdom as a heavenly, spiritual realm. This alteration in the message of Jesus and the fabrication of the resurrection allowed the disciples to preserve their vocations as travelling clerics (again the perversion of the truth by the established hierarchy). Reimarus stressed that what was preached about Jesus was not identical with what Jesus preached and he felt that the differences among the gospels, particularly with regard to the resurrection, meant that they must all be false (therefore falsified).

At the same time that radical criticism was beginning to be openly published, the Bible was subjected to radical ridicule by extreme Deists such as Voltaire (1694–1778) and Thomas Paine (1737–1809). For both, the Bible, through not necessarily the real teachings of Jesus, was a collection of superstititions, incongruities, primitive mentality, and priestcraft.

In this context, one must understand the flowering of historical criticism in the late eighteenth century as not only the continuation of the mainstream of philological, textual, and historical criticism which had begun in the Renaissance but also as a major apologetic activity aimed at offering more reasonable discussion of the Bible and explanations of its problems than that of its despisers. The so-called historical-critical method, generally traced to the eighteenth century, is frequently presented as an attempt to undercut the Bible's authority, to bring it into line with modern thought, and to free biblical study from dogmatic dominance. In some respects, just the opposite is probably a more accurate description. The practitioners of the method were primarily Protestant scholars; they were not anti-biblical although their work was frequently anti-Catholic and anti-Jewish (see Moore 1921) and often at variance with traditional Christianity.

The second half of the eighteenth century witnessed the production of the first systematic introductions to the Bible, generally to the two testaments separately. These works discussed such matters as the development of the canon, origin and character of the individual books, and the history of the text. Such works took into account and subjected to judgment traditional views and opinions on these matters. J. D. Michaelis's (1717–1791) introduction to the NT appeared in 1750 (fourth edition, two volumes, 1788; English translation, four volumes, 1793–1801, with supplementation by Herbert Marsh [1757–1839]). The Englishman Nathaniel Lardner (1684–1768) in his *The Credibility of the Gospel History* (seventeen volumes, 1727–1757) had collected patristic evidence in defending traditional dates, circumstances, and authorship as well as on problem texts, providing scholarship with an invaluable resource. The first major OT introduction was published by J. G. Eichhorn (1752–1827; three volumes, 1780–1783, with subsequent editions). Eichhorn also published introductions to the Apocrypha (1795) and the NT (two volumes, 1804–1812). In these manuals, practically all the major issues of biblical interpretation were raised. Later work would restate the questions and/or provide different solutions to the problems or view the problems slightly differently. Radical solutions were already part of the discussion before the end of the century. Reimarus's work provides one illustration. Another is Edward Evanson (1731–1805), an English Unitarian, who, in *The Dissonance of the Four Generally Received Evangelists* (1792) and other works, argued that the only genuine first-century NT writings were Luke-Acts (minus interpolations), 1-2 Corinthians, Galatians, Philippians, 1-2 Thessalonians, 1-2 Timothy, Titus, Philemon, and the Apocalypse (minus the letters to the seven churches). All the rest were spurious second-century documents. An edition of the NT was published in 1807 containing only what Evanson had declared authentic.

The Nineteenth Century

As in previous centuries, a wide variety of biblical interpretations were practiced during this period. The older form of Protestant orthodoxy was continued (and lived on into the twentieth century as the so-called "Princeton School"). Pietistic and devotional use persisted as did mystical reading. Most movements cut across the boundaries of Jewish, Catholic, and Protestant categories. In general, orthodox, pietistic, and mystical reading of the Bible continued patterns and practices already long in existence. Here only new developments in biblical criticism can be noted.

Biblical criticism was to a large extent the domain of German Protestantism during the century (see Rogerson 1988). Following the French Revolution (1789), England was very resistant to European currents. Only a few isolated British scholars were open to German scholarship until well past the half century mark. The Catholic Alexander Geddes (1737–1802) and Hebert Marsh were two of the exceptions.

The program outlined by Charles Leslie in the fight against the Deists was used by British scholars against the new developments in German thought. The works of William Paley (1743–1805), *Horae Paulinae* (1790) and *View of the Evidences of Christianity* (1794), typify this view. In the United States, a circle associated with Theodore Parker (1810–1860) and the New England Unitarians accepted and publicized German scholarship for a short time but the group itself made no lasting contribution to biblical interpretation. In Judaism the development of the "Science of Judaism" (*Wissenschaft des Judentums*) beginning in the 1820s gradually moved some Jewish research into the mainstream of biblical interpretation.

In OT studies, the pivotal issue was the source analysis of the Pentateuch, already inaugurated by Astruc and developed by Eichhorn. (Theories that the Pentateuch was composed of numerous unrelated fragments or that it was composed of one major document with extensive supplementation were advocated but not widely followed.) Once the idea of source analysis became an operating principle, then the sources had to be delineated on the basis of some criteria, the sources had to be related to each other, and in some fashion associated with the history of Israel.

The pivotal figure in early eighteenth-century OT studies was W. M. L. de Wette (1780–1849). In his 1805 dissertation on Deuteronomy, he isolated Deuteronomy from the rest of the Pentateuch, argued that it was the latest stratum, and hinted at its association with Josiah's reform (2 Kgs 22–23). In two contributions on introduction to the OT (1806–1807), he sought to demonstrate that 1-2 Chronicles are much later than Samuel-Kings (whose narrative they retell so as to show that the full Mosaic law was operative from the time of David and Solomon) and that they were unreliable as documents for reconstructing the history of Israel. (A comparable move in NT studies was the treatment of the Gospel of John with its self-assertion of Christology by Jesus as an unhistorical source.)

The pentateuchal material was gradually divided into four sources, later called Priestly (P), Elohistic (E), Yahwistic (J), and Deuteronomic (D). After the differentiation of sources, the major question was their literary and chronological relationship. The idea that the priestly material (P) was the latest stratum was discussed in lectures by Edward Reuss (1804–1891) in 1833–1834, suggested in books written by Wilhelm Vatke (1806–1882) and J. F. L. George (1811–1873) in 1835, and then argued by K. H. Graf (1815–1869), Abraham Kuenen (1828–1891), and others in the 1860s. Involved in the problem of the relationship of the sources were the questions of the nature of early Israelite life and religion and the relationship of the prophets to OT law.

In 1878, Julius Wellhausen (1844–1918) published his *Prolegomena to the History of Israel* and laid out in convincing style the evidence supporting the following conclusions.

(1) the three pentateuchal law codes (in J(E), D, and P) are to be related to the history of Israel as reconstructed from the OT historical and prophetical books (minus 1-2 Chronicles); (2) this history suggests that the J(E) law code belongs to the middle monarchic (preclassical prophetic) period, D to the time of Josiah's reform, and P to the exilic period; (3) early Israel was a society that lived without written law, in freedom and only according to custom; (4) the major prophets preceded the ceremonical law and introduced the elements of morality and divine universalism into Israelite life; and (5) the law with its stifling quality is characteristic of postexilic times and Judaism in general (Wellhausen's Lutheranism, anti-Judaism, and romanticism are all reflected in the tone of his writings if not in his use of evidence).

Source and historical criticism were also applied to other books in the Hebrew Bible. The Book of Isaiah was divided into two halves following chap 39, and assigned to the eighth and sixth centuries BCE respectively. The Book of Daniel was dated to the time of the Maccabean revolt (ca. 165–164 B.C.E.) and so on.

The early practitioners of the historical-critical approach to the OT in Britain and the United States lost their posts or suffered church sanction, W. Robertson Smith (1846–94) in Britain and Charles Augustus Briggs (1841–1913) in America. By the end of the century, the English-speaking world had made something of a truce with the historical-critical method even if not with all its conclusions. The appointment of the moderate critic S. R. Driver (1846–1914) at Oxford and his reverent attitude toward the Bible helped the movement gain general acceptance.

Comparative texts from other cultures, first Egyptian and then Mesopotamian, led to the recognition of how much cultural and literary sharing there was between Israel and its neighbors. Babylonian creation and flood stories and law codes showed striking parallels to the Bible, so much so that "pan-Babylonianism," a movement tracing much in the Bible to Babylonian influence arose and climaxed in the *Bibel-Babel* (Bible-Babylon) controversy. Archaeological activity in Palestine exposed the artifacts of Israelite culture, and relating the "evidence of the spade" to biblical events became and remains a major field of inquiry.

The nineteenth-century preoccupation with history and the reading of the scriptures in terms of the original author-reader context led to a temporary demise in the writing of OT theologies, their place being taken by histories of Israelite and Hebrew religion.

In NT studies, the nineteenth century was especially preoccupied with the authentiticy and dating of NT writings, the relationship among the gospels, and the quest for the historical Jesus. The dominant figure for much of the century was F. C. Baur (1792–1860), the founder of the Tübingen School.

Baur inherited the view—from J. S. Semler (1725–1791) who in turn was influenced by Thomas Morgan—that the early church was a scene of conflict between Jewish and Gentile sentiments or the Pauline and Petrine parties (first advocated by Baur in an article in 1831). Party strife eventually resulted in a synthesis that became Catholic Christianity. Baur's pro-Pauline and anti-Catholic sympathies were combined with a Hegelian dialectic. In 1835, a vintage year in biblical scholarship, Baur published his work challenging the Pauline authorship of the pastoral epistles (not a view previously unheard of since Eichhorn ·had finally come to this position). Eventually Baur challenged all the letters attributed to Paul except Galatians, 1-2 Corinthians, and Romans. Acts was viewed by the Tübingen school as late, an attempt to downplay the conflict between Peter and Paul. The gospel of John was considered inauthentic (so already K. G. Bretschneider [1776–1848] in 1820) and placed in the middle of the second century as a synthesizing work. Matthew and Revelation were placed early as representative of Jewish, exclusivistic Christianity.

The relationship of the four gospels to each other was related both to the issue of the date and authenticity of the books as well as the quest for the historical Jesus. Generally church tradition had assumed the gospels were written in the order in which we have them, with Mark being an epitome of Matthew (a view probably falsely attributed to Augustine by Martin Chemnitz [1522–1586]). In 1782, J. B. Koppe (1750–1791) challenged the view of Matthew's priority and that Mark was a summary based on Matthew. Since J. J. Griesbach (1745–1812) had published his Greek NT text of the first three gospels in parallel columns (1774) there had been no doubt that some sort of relationships existed between these three (the synoptic) gospels. Various theories had been proposed and continued to be supported: all three synoptic gospels depended on oral tradition; a primitive (written or oral), probably Aramaic, gospel lay behind all three; various fragments of tradition were utilized independently; and the three depended upon each other in some way (e.g., Mark copied Matthew). Marcan priority as the solution to the synoptic problem was proposed by G. G. Wilke (1786–1854) in 1838 and eventually defended by H. J. Holtzmann (1832–1910) in 1863 along with idea that Matthew and Luke shared a common sayings source (traditionally designated "Q"). It was widely argued that the Gospel of Mark provided access to the Jesus of history.

The nineteenth-century quest for the historical Jesus reached its crisis point in the *Leben Jesu* (two volumes, 1835) of D. F. Strauss (1804–1874). Strauss ignored the Gospel of John and argued that the synoptic gospel portraits of Jesus are based on myths that express the sentiments of his early followers and their rereading of OT texts. Jesus is taken as a person who is the symbolic reflection of the unity between divinity and humanity. Very little can be known about the actual person of Jesus of Nazareth. The answers to and critiques of Strauss were numerous.

In spite of Strauss's work, the output of "lives of Jesus" was enormous (see Schweitzer 1910 and Pals 1985). Conservative, liberal, and pietistic "biographies" were written. Some opted to focus only on the "Christ of faith," that is, Jesus as presented in the gospels.

Near the end of the century, the Catholic Modernist Movement, saw several scholars, including Marie Joseph Lagrange (1855–1938) and Alfred F. Loisy (1857–1940), adopting the historical-critical approach to the scriptures. Pope Leo XIII had given encouragement to the study of the Bible in the encyclical *Providentissimus Deus* (18 November 1893). The movement was suppressed in 1907 by Pope Pius X, but a new day was dawning for Catholic biblical scholarship.

The Twentieth Century

Stimuli for much biblical study in this century have their roots in the last two decades of the nineteenth century. (1) First, the widespread liberalism that viewed the kingdom of God in terms of morality and community (e.g., Albert Ritschl [1822–1889]) and the preaching of Jesus as emphasizing certain central general ideas (the father of God, brotherhood of humanity, and infinite value of the individual; e.g., Adolf Harnack [1851–1930]) was already breaking down. (2) The apocalyptic orientation of the early church and also of the historical Jesus was beginning to be stressed. The last half of the nineteenth century witnessed the recovery of nonbiblical apocalyptic literature. In 1892, Johannes Weiss (1863–1914) wrote *Jesus' Proclamation of the Kingdom of God* (English translation, 1971) arguing that Jesus' preaching was consistently eschatological, a proclamation of the imminent appearance of the transcendent kingdom of God. (3) The rise of the history-of-religions school (*Religionsgeschichtliche Schule*) in the 1880s led to a focus on religion as a historical phenomenon understandable only in light of its origin and roots. Comparative religious phenomena and literature, not modern doctrinal concepts, it was argued, must be utilized to understand Christianity without appeal to special revelation. (4) New emphasis on the role of the community in the creation and shaping of literature and the role of literature in social contexts was replacing focus on individuality so characteristic of much of nineteenth-century thought. (5) Study of literature in terms of genre analysis rather than in terms of authorship was current in the general study of literature and was beginning to make headway into biblical study.

In 1906, Albert Schweitzer (1875–1965) published his *Quest of the Historical Jesus* (English translation, 1910) in which he presented a thoroughly eschatological Jesus while critiquing all earlier efforts at reconstruction. According to Schweitzer, only the spirit of the historical Jesus can challenge modern man; the historical Jesus cannot be made to fit into modern times.

> The study of the Life of Jesus has had a curious history. It set out in quest of the historical Jesus, believing that when it had found Him it could bring Him straight into our time as a Teacher and Saviour. It loosed the bands by which He had been riveted for centuries to the stony rocks of ecclesiastical doctrine, and rejoiced to see life and movement coming into the figure once more, and the historical Jesus advancing, as it seemed, to meet it. But He does not stay; He passes by our time and returns to His own. What surprised and dismayed the theology of the last forty years was that, despite all forced and arbitrary interpretations, it could not keep Him in our time, but had to let Him go. He returned to His own time, not owing to the application of any historical ingenuity, but by the same inevitable necessity by which the liberated pendulum returns to its original position. (Schweitzer 1910, 399)

Schweitzer felt he had written the obituary for the quest, but time has shown that he succeeded only in writing another life of Jesus. Nonetheless Schweitzer's "Jesus" was indicative of new impulses in biblical study.

Two methodologies dominated biblical scholarship in the first half of the century: form criticism and the history of tradition. Both disciplines share an emphasis on the importance of tradition and the community in the formation, structuring, and production of biblical writings (although not done consciously, this move represented an acceptance of the older Catholic position that before the Bible there was the believing community and tradition). A name associated with both methods is Hermann Gunkel (1862–1932). Gunkel was concerned with both genre (form) analysis and how material develops from its earliest oral phase to final canonical form. Gunkel argued that the biblical material can be classified into genres according to its mood and thought, stylistic features and linguistic structure, and its *Sitz im Leben* (the life situations in which the

material originated and was used). He believed the earliest genres could be isolated—short story, psalm (various types), law, wise saying, etiology, and so on—and that a history of tradition or literature, how the genres developed, could be written. Gunkel was also very much interested in early cultures and comparative literature and thought.

Form criticism became a significant factor in NT studies through the work of Martin Dibelius (1883–1947), K. L. Schmidt (1891–1956), and Rudolf Bultmann (1884–1976). The analysis of the material of the NT into various genres raised questions about the role of the church in shaping and creating tradition, about what could be traced back to Jesus, and about the structure of the gospels and whether this had any relationship to the actual course of events in the life of Jesus or was a theological construct.

In OT studies, the history of tradition became a special concern of a circle associated with Albrecht Alt (1883–1956). Martin Noth (1902–1968) and Gerhard von Rad (1901–1971) investigated how Israel's traditions originated and developed. Noth was concerned with the impact of the approach for understanding the history of Israel and von Rad for writing a theology of the OT in terms of the use and reinterpretation of traditions.

The most controversial development in NT study was Bultmann's program of demythologization. Bultmann argued that the biblical thought world and much of its content presuppose a mythological worldview that is in sharp contrast to contemporary thought. Bultmann argued that this mythological worldview should be transposed into an existentialist key so the texts can address the contemporary human understanding. For Bultmann, only the fact of the human existence of Jesus was necessary as a historical datum. For him, the life and preaching of Jesus was part of the Jewish background to Christianity since Jesus was, as Wellhausen had earlier noted, a Jew not a Christian.

In the wake of Bultmann's work, a new quest of the historical Jesus was pursued. The focus of this endeavor was to understand the movement from what Jesus preached and taught to what was preached and taught about Jesus. (A so-called third quest for the historical Jesus has begun in the 1990s.)

Nonbiblical texts and archaeological data have played a greater role in biblical studies in the twentieth century than ever before in history. New textual discoveries such as the Ugaritic texts, the Qumran (Dead Sea) Scrolls, and the Nag Hammadi texts have supplied scholars with new material. In addition, Hellenistic papyri, Eygptian and Mesopotamian texts, as well as Syro-Palestinian inscriptions can now be utilized in understanding the Bible. Palestine has become one of the most excavated areas in the world and people like W. F. Albright (1891–1971) and his students and Israeli scholars especially have worked to integrate this material.

Comparative study of ancient Near Eastern materials has led to seeing common patterns or at least analogous beliefs and practices that Israel and the early church shared with other cultures. The Myth and Ritual School in England and the Uppsala School in Scandinavia have highlighted these parallels. Gnosticism and its relationship to NT writings and early church life raises a similar set of issues.

Since the 1930s, Protestants and Catholics have concerned themselves with biblical theology, with formulating an approach that would allow a systematic presentation of the theology of the individual testaments and the Bible as a whole. Various methods and schemes have been employed. In spite of the failure of biblical theologians to arrive at a commonly shared approach and description, the effort has contributed to a better understanding of the biblical materials.

A distinctive feature of twentieth-century biblical interpretation has been its ecumenical dimension. The first half of the century saw the *Wissenschaft des Judentums* mature. Pope Pius XII's encyclical *Divino*

Afflante Spiritu (30 September 1943) gave greater freedom to Catholic scholars, a movement extended at the Second Vatican Council (1962–1965). Catholics, Protestants, and Jews now study the Bible, often cooperatively, utilizing similar methods and often arriving at similar conclusions.

A second new feature of bibical study is the diversity of methods employed. In the last four decades of the century, a great variety of interests and approaches have characterized biblical study. The old historical-critical paradigm that stressed the original historical sense of the text as the center of interpretation has last its dominance. New developments in literary analysis, sociocultural concerns, linguistics, and philosophy have made their impact on biblical interpretation. Thus one can approach the text with a wide variety of methods and questions realizing that interpretation is a multilevel and complex phenomenon. No one single approach is assumed to exhaust the text. In addition to the old fields of textual, source, form, and historical criticisms, new criticisms are now part of the scene—redaction, structural, reader response, rhetorical, canonical—each concerned with different emphases and goals. Simultaneously, the Bible is read with sensitivity toward and advocacy of the concerns of various social groups; thus we may now include liberation, third-world, feminist, and black hermeneutics among the many modern "schools" of biblical interpretation.

For Further Study

In the *Mercer Dictionary of the Bible*: BIBLE AND WESTERN LITERATURE; HERMENEUTICS; INTERPRETATION, HISTORY OF; LITERATRURE, BIBLE AS; PATRISTIC LITERATURE. In other sources: (See also works cited, below.)

<u>General.</u> P. R. Ackroyd et al., eds., *Cambridge History of the Bible*, 3 vols.; L. Diestel, *Geschichte des Alten Testamentes in der Christlichen Kirche*; *Enchiridion biblicum. Documenta ecclesiastica Sacram Scripturam spectantia*, 4th ed.; F. W. Farrar, *History of Interpretation*; R. M. Grant and D. Tracy, *A Short History of the Interpretation of the Bible*; F. E. Greenspahn, ed., *Scripture in the Jewish and Christian Traditions: Authority, Interpretation, Relevance*; C. Kannengiesser, ed., *Bible de tous les temps*. 8 vols.; D. E. Nineham, ed., *The Church's Use of the Bible: Past and Present*; D. Norton, *A History of the Bible as Literature*. 2 vols.

<u>Inner-Biblical Interpretation.</u> G. L. Archer and G. C. Chirichigno, *O.T. Quotations in the N.T.: A Complete Survey*; D. A. Carson and H. G. M. Williams,

eds., *It is Written: Scripture Citing Scripture*; D. Daube, *The N.T. and Rabbinic Judaism*; C. H. Dodd, *According to the Scriptures: The Sub-Structure of N.T. Theology*; E. E. Ellis, *The O.T. in Early Christianity*; M. Fishbane, *Biblical Interpretation in Ancient Israel*; L. Goppelt, *Typos: The Typological Interpretation of the O.T. in the New*; A. T. Hanson, *Living Utterances of God: The N.T. Exegesis of the Old*; D. H. Juel, *Messianic Exegesis: Christological Interpretation of the O.T. in Early Christianity*; B. Lindars, *N.T. Apologetic: The Doctrinal Significance of the O.T. Quotations*; J. Weingreen, *From Bible to Mishna: The Continuity of Tradition*.

<u>Early Jewish and Christian Interpretation.</u> J. Barton, *Oracles of God: Perceptions of Ancient Prophecy in Israel after the Exile*; J. Braverman, *Jerome's Commentary on Daniel: A Study of Comparative Jewish and Christian Interpretation of the Hebrew Bible*; G. J. Brooke, *Exegesis at Qumran: 4Q Florilegium in Its Jewish Context*; J. C. Endres, *Biblical Interpretation in the Book of Jubilees*; R. M. Grant, *Heresy and Criticism: The Search for Authenticity in Early Christian*

Literature; G. M. Hahneman, *The Muratorian Fragment and the Development of the Canon*; R. P. C. Hanson, *Allegory and Event: A Study of The Sources and Significance of Origen's Interpretation of Scripture*; M. P. Horgan, *Pesharim: Qumran Interpretations of Biblical Books*; J. L. Kugel and A. G. Rowan, *Early Biblical Interpretation*; B. de Margerie, *Introduction a l'histoire de l'exégèse*. 3 vols.; M. J. Mulder, ed., *Mikra: Text, Translation, Reading and Interpretation of the Hebrew Bible in Ancient Judaism and Early Christianity*; J. Neusner, *What is Midrash?*; D. Patte, *Early Jewish Hermeneutic in Palestine*; H. G. Reventlow, *Epochen der Bibelauslegung*, vol. 1, *Vom Alten Testament bis Origenes*; M. Simonetti, *Biblical Interpretation in the Early Church: An Historical Introduction to Patristic Exegesis*; H. L. Strack and G. Stemberger, *Introduction to the Talmud and Midrash*; T. H. Tobin, *The Creation of Man: Philo and the History of Interpretation*; J., W. Trigg, *Biblical Interpretation*; G. Vermes, *Scripture and Tradition in Judaism*; D. Winston, ed., *Philo of Alexandria*.

Medieval Period. A. Berlin, *Biblical Poetry through Medieval Jewish Eyes*; W. Chomsky, *David Kimhi's Hebrew Grammar (Mikhlol)*; I. Contreni, "Carolingian Biblical Studies," *Carolingian Essays*, ed. U.-R. Blumenthal; N. van Deusen, ed., *The Place of the Psalms in the Intellectual Culture of the Middle Ages*; R. K. Emmerson and B. McGinn, eds., *The Apocalypse in the Middle Ages*; G. R. Evans, *The Language and Logic of the Bible: The Earlier Middle Ages*; H. Feld, *Die Anfänge der modernen biblischen Hermeneutik in der spätmittelalterlichen Theologie*; B. Fischer, *Lateinische Bibelhandschriften im frühen Mittelalter*; K. Froehlich, "'Always to Keep the Literal Sense in Holy Scripture Means to Kill One's Soul': The State of Biblical Hermeneutics at the Beginning of the Fifteenth Century," in *Literary Uses of Typology from the Late Middle Ages to the Present*, ed. E. Miner; A. Funkenstein, *Theology and the Scientific Imagination from the Middle Ages to the Seventeenth Century*; H. Hailperin, *Rashi and The Christian Scholars*; B. Holtz, B., ed., *Back to The Sources: Reading The Classic Jewish Texts*; F. Kropatschek, *Das Schriftprinzip der lutherischen Kirche I: Die Vorgeschichte: Das Erbe des Mittelalters*; W. Lourdaux and D. Verhelst, eds., *The Bible and Medieval Culture*; de Lubac, H., *Exégèse Médiévale: Les quatre sens de l'écriture*. 4 vols; R. E. McNalley, *The Bible in The Early Middle Ages*; A. J. Minnis, *Medieval Theory of Authorship: Scholastic Literary Attitudes in the Later Middle Ages*. 2nd ed.; A. J. Minnis and A. B. Scott, *Medieval Literary Theory and Criticism ca. 1100-ca. 1375: The Commentary Tradition*, rev. ed.; J. S. Preus, *From Shadow to Promise: O.T. Interpretation from Augustine to the Young Luther*; H. Rost, *Die Bibel im Mittelalter*; H. Schüssler, *Der Primät der Heiligen Schrift als theologisches und kanonistisches Problem im Spätmittalter*; U. Simon, *Four Approaches to the Book of Psalms: From*

Saadiah Gaon to Abraham Ibn Ezra; B. Smalley, *Medieval Exegesis of Wisdom Literature: Essays by Beryl Smalley*, ed. R. E. Murphy; *Studies in Medieval Thought and Learning: From Abelard to Wyclif*; *The Study of the Bible in the Middle Ages*, 3rd ed.; and *The Gospels in the Schools ca. 1100-ca. 1280*; P. C. Spicq, *Esquisse d'une historie de l'exégèse latine du moyen age*; K. Walsh and D. Wood, eds., *The Bible in The Medieval World: Essays in Memory of Beryl Smalley*.

Renaissance-Reformation. D. C. Allen, *The Legend of Noah: Renaissance Rationalism in Art, Sciences and Letters*; J. H. Bentley, *Humanists and Holy Writ: N.T. Scholarship in the Renaissance*; G. R. Evans, *The Language and Logic of the Bible: The Road to Reformation*; O. Fatio and P. Fraenkel, eds., *Histoire de l'exégèse au XVI° siècle*; J. Friedman, *The Most Ancient Testimony: Sixteenth-Century Christian-Hebraica in the Age of Renaissance Nostalgia*; E. A. Gosselin, *The King's Progress to Jerusalem: Some Interpretations of David during The Reformation and Their Patristic and Medieval Background*; K. Hagen, *Luther's Approach to Scripture as Seen in His "Commentaries" on Galatians 1519-1538*; A. McGrath, *The Intellectual Origins of the European Reformation*; J. Pelikan, *Luther the Expositor: Introduction to the Reformer's Exegetical Writings*; W. Schwarz, *Principles and Problems of Biblical Translation: Some Reformation Controversies and Their Background*; D. C. Steinmetz, ed., *The Bible in the Sixteenth Century*; G. H. Tavard, *Holy Writ or Holy Church: The Crisis of the Protestant Reformation*.

Seventeenth and Eighteenth Centuries. W. Baird, *A History of N.T. Research*, vol. 1, *From Deism to Tübingen*; A. Barnes, *Jean Leclerc (1657-1736) et la république des lettres*; S. G. Burnett, *The Christian Hebraism of Johann Buxtorf (1564-1629)*; H. Chadwick, *Lessing's Theological Writings: Selections in Translation with an Introductory Essay*; M.-H. Cotoni, *Exégèse du Nouveau Testament dans la philosophie francaise du dix-huiteme siecle*; J. Drury, *Critics of the Bible 1724-1873*; H. W. Frei, *The Eclipse of Biblical Narrative: A Study in Eighteenth and Nineteenth Century Hermeneutics*; D. Freiday, *The Bible: Its Criticism, Interpretation and Use in 16th and 17th Century England*; R. C. Fuller, *Alexander Geddes 1737-1802: Pioneer of Biblical Criticism*; G. L. Jones, *The Discovery of Hebrew in Tudor England: A Third Language*; E. G. Kraeling, *The O.T. Since the Reformation*; H.-J. Kraus, *Die Biblische Theologie. Ihr Geschichte und Problematik*; H.-J. Kraus, *Geschichte der historisch-kritischen Erforschung des Alten Testaments*, 3rd ed.; W. G. Kümmel, *The N.T.: The History of the Investigation of Its Problems*; R. H. Popkin, *The History of Skepticism from Erasmus to Spinoza*; R. H. Popkin and J. E. Force, *Essays on the Context, Nature, and Influence of Isaac Newton's Theology*; R. Preus, *The Inspiration of Scripture: A Study of the Seventeenth Century Lutheran Dogmaticians*; G. Reedy, *The*

Bible and Reason: Anglicans and Scripture in Late Seventeenth-Century England; H. G. Reventlow, The Authority of the Bible and the Rise of The Modern World; H. G. Reventlow, et al. (eds.), Historische Kritik und biblischer Kanon in der deutschen Aufklärung; D. Ritschl, "Johann Salomo Semler: The Rise of the Historical-Critical Method in Eighteenth-Century Theology on the Continent," Introduction to Modernity: A Symposium on Eighteenth-Century Thought, ed. Robert Mollenauer; K. Scholder, The Birth of Modern Critical Theory: Origins and Problems of Biblical Criticism in the Seventeenth Century; E. S. Shaffer, "Kubla Khan" and the Fall of Jerusalem: The Mythological School in Biblical Criticism and Secular Literature 1770-1880; L. Stephen, History of English Thought in the Eighteenth Century, 2 vols.; B. Willey, The Seventeenth Century Background: Studies in the Thought of the Age in Relation to Poetry and Religion.

Nineteenth Century. C. Brown, Jesus in European Protestant Thought 1778-1860; J. W. Brown, The Rise of Biblical Criticism in America, 1800-1870; J. E. Carpenter, The Bible in the Nineteenth Century; T. K. Cheyne, Founders of O.T. Criticism; R. E. Clements, "The Study of the O.T.," in Nineteenth Century Religious Thought in the West, ed. N. Smart et al., 3 vols.; H. Detering, Paulusbriefe ohne Paulus? Die Paulusbriefe in der holländisehen Radikalkritik; S. J. De Vries, Bible and Theology in the Netherlands: Dutch O.T. Criticism under Modernist and Conservative Auspices, 1850 to World War I, 2nd ed.; G. B. Glover, Evangelical Nonconformists and Higher Criticism in the Nineteenth Century; E. Krentz, The Historical-Critical Method; M. C. Massey, Christ Unmasked: The Meaning of The Life of Jesus in German Politics; J. C. O'Neill, "The Study of the N.T.," in Nineteenth Century Religious Thought, ed. N. Smart et al. 3 vols.; J. C. O'Neill, The Bible's Authority: A Portrait Gallery of Thinkers from Lessing to Bultmann; R. A. Riesen, Criticism and Faith in Late Victorian Scotland: A. B. Davidson, William Robertson Smith, and George Adam Smith; J. W. Rogerson, O.T. Criticism in the Nineteenth Century: England and Germany; J. W. Rogerson, W. M. L. de Wette, Founder of Modern Biblical Criticism: An Intellectual Biography; R. J. Thompson, Moses and the Law in a Century of Criticism since Graf.

Twentieth Century. J. Barton, Reading the O.T.: Method in Biblical Study; H. Boers, What is N.T. Theology?; R. E. Clements, A Century of O.T. Study, rev. ed.; E. J. Epp and G. W. MacRae, eds., The N.T. and Its Modern Interpreters; H. F. Hahn, The O.T. in Modern Research, 2nd ed.; J. H. Hayes, Introduction to Old Testament Study; D. A. Knight and G. M. Tucker, eds., The O.T. and Its Modern Interpreters; I. H. Marshall, ed., N.T. Interpretation; R. Morgan (with J. Barton), Biblical Interpretation; S. Neill and T.

Wright, The Interpretation of the N.T. 1861-1986; O. C. Ollenburger, et al., eds., The Flowering of O.T. Theology; J. K. Riches, A Century of N.T. Study; H. G. Reventlow, Problems of Old Testament Theology in the Twentieth Century; H. G. Reventlow, Problems of Biblical Theology in the Twentieth Century; R. Smend, Deutsche Alttestamentler in Drei Jahrhunderten.

Works Cited

Blackwell, R. 1991. Galileo, Bellarmine, and the Bible.

Burns, R. M. 1981. The Great Debate on Miracles: From Joseph Glanville to David Hume.

Byrne, P. 1989. Natural Religion and the Nature of Religion: The Legacy of Deism.

Colish, M. L. 1994. Peter Lombard. Two volumes.

Eisenstein, E. L. 1979. The Printing Press as an Agent of Change.

Froehlich, K., ed. 1984. Biblical Interpretation in the Early Church.

Gameson, R. G., ed. 1994. The Early Medieval Bible: Its Production, Decoration, and Use.

Gibson, M. T. 1993. The Bible in the Latin West.

Gibson, M. T., and K. Froehlich, eds. 1992. Biblia Latina cum Glossa Ordinaria: Facsimile Reprint of the Editio Princeps by Adolf Rusch of Strassburg, ca. 1480. Four volumes.

Hill, C. 1993. The English Bible and the Seventeenth Century Revolution.

Jacobs, L. 1973. Jewish Biblical Exegesis.

Jordan, M. D. and K. Emery, eds. 1992. Ad Litteram: Authoritative Texts and Their Medieval Readers.

Laplanche, F. J. M. 1986. L'Ecriture, le sacré et l'histoire. Erudits et politiques protestants devant la Bible en France au XVIIᵉ siecle.

Moore, G. F. 1921. "Christian Writers on Judaism," HTR 14:197-254.

Muller, R. A. 1993. Post-Reformation Reformed Dogmatics. Vol. 2. Holy Scripture: The Cognitive Foundation of Theology.

Pals, D. 1982. The Victorian "Lives" of Jesus.

Popkin, R. H. 1987. Isaac La Peyrère (1596-1676): His Life, Work, and Influence.

Rogerson, J., C. Rowland, and B. Lindars. 1988. The Study and Use of the Bible.

Sarna, N. M. 1971. "Hebrew and Bible Studies in Medieval Spain," in The Sephardi Heritage, ed. R. D. Barnett.

Schweitzer, A. 1910. The Quest of the Historical Jesus.

van Rooden, P. T. 1989. Theology, Biblical Scholarship, and Rabbinical Studies in the Seventeenth Century: Constantijn L'Empereur (1591-1648) Professor of Hebrew and Theology at Leiden.

Williams, A. 1948. The Common Expositor: An Account of the Commentaries on Genesis 1527-1633.

Biblical Theology

Molly T. Marshall

Biblical theology is that discipline that articulates the message of Scripture, the ways of God with creation and humanity, in its own historical setting. Unlike systematic, philosophical, or dogmatic theology, biblical theology does not utilize categories drawn from the church's historic faith, systems of philosophy, or conciliar formulations or creeds. Rather, biblical theology seeks to understand the message of the BIBLE, which itself arises from varied voices in a wide range of historical contexts.

This form of theology necessarily includes exegetical, hermeneutical, and systematic (in terms of an orderly exposition of the biblical materials) dimensions; however, in its contemporary dress biblical theology often utilizes auxiliary disciplines such as literary criticism and sociology.

The question of the theological unity and diversity of the teachings of Scripture has made biblical theology a much debated enterprise, and establishing the central theme or forging agreement about key integrating motifs has been difficult. Thus, theologies of the whole Bible are rare; indeed, as Reventlow (1986) has observed, a " 'biblical theology' has yet to be written." Usually a scholar has attempted to treat the Hebrew Scriptures or the New Testament, or perhaps some body of literature within these testamental frameworks.

The contemporary status of biblical theology is fraught with conflicting perspectives concerning a terminal or healthy prognosis for the discipline. Representative of the former perspective are scholars such as Childs (1970), Barr (1976), Strecker (1991), and Reventlow (1986) who argue the discipline is in crisis (or at least is methodologically muddled) and needs a radical recasting. A more promising diagnosis is offered by Smart (1979), Mauser (1991), Trible (1978), and Reumann (1991), who see many creative possibilities on the horizon. The last few decades have witnessed the fragmentation of a once coherent if diverse movement that emerged during the 1940s and figured prominently in the period following the Second World War. The wide consensus concerning the tasks and methods of biblical theology that claimed scholars earlier in this century is no longer valid.

In this article, this development is charted by a brief history of the roots of biblical theology, a survey of the chief characteristics of the Biblical Theology Movement, an analysis of its decline due to tensions and methodological problems, and perspectives on the possibility of recovering or reorienting biblical theology in the present. Because many essays and monographs have been devoted to analyzing this movement (see the bibliography), this treatment will focus more on new approaches and trends in biblical theology.

The Historical Roots of Biblical Theology

The roots of biblical theology can be traced to the Reformation, or, perhaps, to the forerunner of the Reformation, John Wyclif (some scholars have even pointed as far back as the writings of IRENAEUS or Origen). For Wyclif the whole Bible was to be understood as the sole criterion of doctrine, a radical departure from the Medieval Schoolmen. Clearly, biblical teaching was not equal to ecclesiastical dogma in early Christianity and the Middle Ages.

The Reformers' renewed attention to biblical exegesis evoked understandings that conflicted with the magisterial tradition of the CHURCH, leading to one of the Reformation's overarching watchwords, *Sola Scriptura*. Yet neither the Reformers nor their followers produced a biblical theology. Instead, the subordination of the Bible to dogmatic theology (collections of texts under doctrinal headings) continued, now in the form of Protestant Orthodoxy. The Pietist Philipp Spener (1635–1705) in his *Pia Desideria* (*Pious Desires*, 1675) challenged this dogmatic control, urging a simple openness to the Bible that would allow it to function as the basis and norm for all theology.

The Enlightenment fostered powerful intellectual forces that called forth a major reorientation in biblical

and theological study. As a new historical consciousness took form, eighteenth-century theologians began
to call for a critical study of the Bible for its own
sake, not as simply a ready compendium of proof texts
for the dogmatic teaching of the church. In his inaugural address at the University of Altdorf in 1787, Johann Philipp Gabler (1753–1826) distinguished between *biblical* and *dogmatic* theology. Biblical theology, according to Gabler's rationalist program, is

> of historical origin, conveying what the holy writers
> felt about divine things; on the other hand, there is
> dogmatic theology of didactic origin, teaching what
> each theologian . . . philosophizes rationally about
> divine things.

Gabler is not suggesting that pure biblical theology can
serve all needs for doctrinal teaching, but Scripture
must not be interpreted through the dogmatic lens. His
line of demarcation between historical and theological
study of the Bible has been difficult to secure, as subsequent writings have demonstrated.

Gabler wanted the Bible to serve as the foundation
of all theology. He argued that the Bible did not contain theology in the sense of a rigorous second-order
reflection; rather, it offers religion that he understood
to be the ordinary conceptions, beliefs, and teachings
of persons responding to the divine revelation in their
specific historical settings. He envisioned biblical theology as a purely historical discipline that should
correct the errors of dogmatic theology. This clear delineation between biblical and dogmatic theology set
forth by Gabler did not result in cooperation within
these areas of study—the goal he desired—but rather
in an ever-widening chasm between them until the
emergence of the Biblical Theology Movement.

William Wrede (1859–1906) followed the impulse
of Gabler's distinction to its logical conclusion. Wrede
argued in 1897 in his little book *Concerning the Task
and Method of the So-called New Testament Theology*
that biblical theology as it pertains to the NT should not
be bound to the dogmatic category of "canon." Further, the NT ought not be interpreted as a doctrinal system. This contention led to the development of the history-of-religions school that examined a variety of religious traditions without giving a privileged status to
the religion of the NT. Historians of religion such as
Wernle, Bousset, and Weiss, to mention only a few,
interpreted the history of faith in Christ in the broad
framework of the religious environment surrounding
Christianity. Sources for this study included in addition

to the NT writings extrabiblical materials from the early
centuries. Rudolf Bultmann's magisterial *Theology of
the New Testament* (1949, 1953; ET 1951, 1955) demonstrates the full flowering and perhaps final example
of this approach.

As might be expected, reactions against the history-
of-religions approach were voiced by scholars concerned for the theological meaning of the Bible for the
church. About the turn of the century Adolf von
Schlatter (1852–1938), an able representative of this
conservative reaction, resisted the separation between
historical and dogmatic work, contending that while a
person of faith may approach these tasks as methodologically distinct, he or she cannot (and should not)
bracket out the presuppositions that such faith contains. It is a chief responsibility of the Christian scholar to work out of a theological method that is not imposed by the culture.

Schlatter did not presume that the Scriptures provided theology in the strict sense of the term, but in
his judgments more could be found than the simple
ethical religion purported by the *Religionsgeschichtliche Schule*. The interpreter could not escape theological questions. In what way, for example, is the truth
conveyed by the Scriptures in an earlier historical
setting relevant for the Christian today? In many ways
Schlatter anticipated some aspects of neoorthodoxy and
the contemporary understanding in Gospel studies of
the inseparable intertwining of the historical and theological materials, yet his own biblical theology remains
in the fetters of dogmatics.

The Biblical Theology Movement

Robert C. Dentan (1963) suggests three factors that
contributed to a move beyond the history-of-religions
and liberal approaches of the late nineteenth and early
twentieth centuries: (1) a loss of faith in evolutionary
naturalism; (2) a reaction against the purely historical
method that claimed complete objectivity and presumed the adequacy of the "bare facts" to convey
historical truth; and (3) the recovery of the idea of
revelation.

Identifying biblical theology as the "biblical companion" to dialectical theology, James Barr (1976) sees
in these concomitant movements a strong reaction to
the biblical interpretation of liberal theology that was
ostensibly controlled by the History of Religions
School. In neoorthodox theology and biblical theology
the convergence of theological concern with renewed
biblical study is evident.

The Distinctiveness of Biblical Thought

Biblical theology has characteristically been opposed to any philosophical system as the interpretative framework in which Scripture must be understood. Along with avoiding categories that Scripture itself does not provide, biblical theology has resisted the systematic impulses of dogmatic theology that follows the Lombardian order in *Sententiarum libri IV* (*Four Books of Sentences*, ca. 1148–1151), a theological method foreign to the Bible.

Biblical theology places considerable emphasis upon the distinctive Hebraic thought patterns and view of history found in the Bible. It considers Greek thought an alien and corrupting influence on the semitic structure found in Scripture. On the one hand, considering the NT apart from its sociocultural and religious setting in contradistinction to the history-of-religions approach heightened the distinctiveness of Christian faith; but on the other hand, it diminished the contribution that an understanding of context often makes to informed hermeneutics and theological construction.

The Unity of the Bible

Biblical theology assumes the unity of the Bible although individual scholars have construed this unity in disparate ways. An abiding problem has been the relationship between the testaments—a problem that has contributed to the almost insuperable task of writing a theology of the whole Bible. Christian scholars have at times sacrificed the original meaning and integrity of the Hebrew Scriptures in their historical situation in their haste to appropriate them for the church's teaching under the lordship of Christ, or they have regarded the OT as inferior revelation that has little consequence for theology and doctrine.

The relationship between the OT and the NT has been configured by biblical theologians in the following representative approaches (see the useful surveys by Barr [1976], Reventlow [1986], and Hasel [1984]).

Salvation-History. The model of an ongoing salvation history is an attempt to embrace both testaments under the theme of the continuity of God's redemptive activity. Under this rubric the tradition-history method of OT scholar Gerhard von Rad (1962, 1965) saw the historical traditions of the faith of Israel in an ineluctable process of reinterpretation in new contexts. The traditions of the OT logically lead into the NT, for the view of history in the biblical writings is open to a future.

Starting from a NT perspective, Oscar Cullmann (*Chrsit and Time*, 1945; ET 1949, ³1962) offered a different approach. He argued that the center of God's saving acts was the Christ-event that is itself in continuity with the salvation-history of the OT where God acted through key events.

Typology. The typological approach was revivified by the Biblical Theology Movement through the efforts of scholars such as von Rad and Leonard Goppelt. Long thought to have been made obsolete by historical-critical studies, biblical theologians returned to a method prized by exegetes of the early church. Patterns or types are said to occur in the OT that prefigure some truth connected with Christianity.

Goppelt insisted that the typological approach of the OT in the NT (as the key method of interpretation and theological understanding) showed "the New Testament's consciousness of its own place in redemptive history." Roman Catholic theology has shared this interest in the typological method. Jean Daniélou (1960) argued for typology as a means of a spiritual reading of Scripture. He extended his exegetical work to both testaments since typology may be seen within the OT itself as well as in the NT's method of interpreting Scripture.

Sensus Plenior. Catholic scholarship has debated a third method of relating the OT and the NT during the decades following the Second World War. The *Sensus Plenior* or "fuller meaning" approach suggests that because Scripture is inspired by God there is a deeper meaning in the texts than any human author can know. This meaning can only be discerned in light of further revelation. Thus the whole Bible exists in an organic relationship and is best understood when related to the Christ event. This concept sought to interface traditional interpretations with renewed biblical study, for example, Isa 7:14 was discerned by Matthew (1:23) to be referring to the virgin birth.

Promise and Fulfillment. A fourth means of postulating the unity of Scripture is found in the scheme of promise and fulfillment. This could take the form of examining the "messianic promises" of the OT that find their fulfillment in the life of Jesus Christ. Biblical theologians using this method are not of one mind about whether the OT only points beyond itself to future actualization of prophecy or if there is a provisional level of fulfillment within the OT itself. Further, in what way can the biblical interpreter claim final fulfillment in the activity of Jesus, the expectation of the kingdom of God, and eschatological hope?

The Superiority of the Old Testament. A rather novel approach has been offered by A. A. van Ruler (1971), a Reformed theologian, who argued for the superiority of the OT. The integrating motif of the Bible is the theocratic Rule of God demonstrated in concrete earthly circumstances, which he maintains is evident in the OT. The NT's "spiritualization" of the Rule not only diminishes the robust character of the Reign of God, but cannot stand alone. Without Israel's understanding of their identity as the people of God, the land, the posterity, and supremely the Sovereign Rule of God, as found in the OT, the story of Jesus has no grounding. Indeed, van Ruler warns against doing violence to the OT by trying to find Jesus Christ within its pages; rather, one should read it to, for example, legitimate his messiahship, not to conscript it as a Christian text.

Word Studies

Bible dictionaries and word studies have been characteristic of biblical theology, and at times word studies have been *equated* with biblical theology. The Kittel-Friedrich ten-volume NT dictionary (1933–1976; ET 1964–1976), which features rich studies of Hebrew and Greek words, is the abiding fruit of this movement. Although the conception of language upon which this work was based (and its adherence to a salvation-history orientation) has been severely criticized, the word studies continue to shape the prospects for biblical theology.

Popular approaches included studying all the Hebrew names for God or the titles ascribed to Jesus as a means of discerning the theological content of texts. This atomistic method of interpretation neglected the narrative character of the biblical material and the interthematic connections within Scripture.

Revelation in History

Articulating a fully orbed understanding of revelation has been of chief interest to the Biblical Theology Movement. The emphasis on history as the locus for revelation has allowed biblical theologians to steer between a fundamentalist notion of the Bible as the deposit of doctrine and the liberal notion that Scripture merely reflects the progressive religious consciousness of a particular group of people. Selectively appropriating biblical material to reinforce the notion of the Hebrew view of history, scholars accentuated revelation through history. This perspective presupposes a special stream of saving history within the larger flow of world history, and the mighty acts of God were accessible only to those participating in the salvation history of Israel and the church.

Yet the construct of two realms of history seems to imply that while God is especially at work in "holy history" the rest of history (as well as nature) is marked by its exclusion from the redemptive activity of God. Further, the inaccessibility of this revelation to canons of historical criticism as put forward by the influential Ernst Troeltsch has rendered dubious the coherence of the idea of revelation in history, as the sustained work of Wolfhart Pannenberg manifests.

The Decline of Biblical Theology

Many reasons are cited for the dissipation of the Biblical Theology Movement (at least in its particularly American form), some of which have already been noted. Brevard Childs (1970) suggests that unresolved methodological problems led to the cracking of the walls and the erosion of the foundation of the movement. Central to Childs's critique of biblical theology is its "problem with the Bible."

There has been a prevailing uncertainty and awkwardness about how to use the Bible because of the lack of interface between historical criticism and theological interpretation. Consequently, locating biblical theology courses in the seminary curricula proved problematic. For example, in what way should these courses relate to biblical studies and to systematic theology?

The continuing separation of the study of the OT from the NT further retarded biblical theology. Beyond formal theological education, biblical theology did not serve congregational life effectively either. Childs argues that no "new genre of preaching" emerged and the claims for the "mighty acts of God" in history seemed overdrawn for the conventional life of the church. The relevance of the Bible for the life of modern Christianity was contestable—the nadir of what the Biblical Theology Movement has promised.

Fissures in the foundational affirmations of biblical theology concerning the significance of words studies, the concept of history, the Hebrew-Greek dichotomy, the distinctiveness of the Bible over against its environment, and the unity of the Bible, led to destructive divisions and decline. John Reumann (1991) observes a similar demise of the popularity of Barthian theology, for which biblical theology had a close affinity. Their common repudiation of philosophy and hostility to historical context could not withstand new developments in theological studies, and they were left behind.

Barr (1976) has maintained that biblical theology lacked a scientific method that could sustain its enterprise. Word studies and linguistic analysis came closest to such a method, but much of the work of biblical theologians was done in reaction to the guiding assumptions and critical tools of earlier liberal scholarship. Setting their work over against these academic forebears, they failed to justify their own approach adequately. Concepts such as the "Word of God," God's "mighty acts," or even "history" were left only vaguely defined or a common understanding was merely assumed.

Contemporary Perspectives on Biblical Theology

The period from about 1970 forward has seen a resurgence in biblical studies among Roman Catholics, following the direction set by Vatican II. Two contemporary Roman Catholic scholars, Karl Rahner and Edward Schillebeeckx demonstrate their conviction that dogmatic theology cannot avoid engaging in biblical theology. The theological content of the biblical writings must be joined with the larger Christian tradition, yet remain the *norma non normata* for theology and the Church. The Church's traditional emphases on canon and authority were easily compatible with renewed attention to the canonical shape and form of Scripture, and lectionary reform ensued.

Other significant methodological contributions to biblical theology have come in the form of new interest in the sociocultural context of the biblical writings (something of a return to the history-of-religions approach) as well as the social location of those who are reading the texts. This latter aspect, "reader-oriented" criticism, has been particularly accentuated by liberation and feminist theologians.

The current epoch is characterized by a paradigm shift from the *historical* era to the *literary* era in biblical studies. New methods drawn from literary criticism have fulminated a variety of new directions in biblical theology. Narrative criticism, rhetorical approaches, and structuralism are calling attention in a fresh way to the nature of the biblical story.

In 1973 Walter Brueggemann and John R. Donahue initiated a new monograph series entitled Overtures to Biblical Theology. In the series foreword they wrote: "The certainties of the older biblical theology *in service* of dogmatics, as well as of the more recent biblical theology movement *in lieu* of dogmatics, are no longer present" (Brueggemann 1977, xi). Hence, there is great variation in the blueprints for constructing the bridge between the biblical texts and a coherent theological program (which is a strength); though some remain under construction, these bridges are proving that they can bear the weight of biblical theology.

In the remainder of this article, a brief overview of selected new methods will be offered. Distinctive approaches, each has significant implications for the promise of biblical theology for the future.

Feminist Hermeneutics

A "feminist biblical theology" has been emerging over the past two decades among Jewish and Christian scholars. Although there are pluriform critical strategies being employed among those who refuse to see the Bible as irredeemably misogynistic, the following methodological assumptions shape this new approach.

First, feminist biblical theology is conceived of as "advocacy" scholarship; feminist scholars believe descriptive treatments do little to further the liberation of women, a group regularly marginated in the Bible and society. Critics of this approach charge these scholars with subjective bias, coming to the biblical texts with a particular agenda; their response is that there is no neutral scholarship and biblical studies heretofore have been shaped by androcentric biases and concerns of mostly male students of Scripture. Feminist scholars are quite intentional about their purpose of studying the Bible in order to find liberating insights concerning God's intention for women. They cannot leave their own experience of "otherness" in a society where men have been the primary interpreters of reality behind as they pursue their exegetical and theological work.

Second, a critical feminist hermeneutics allows the reader to hear again the biblical stories of mostly silent women within patriarchal cultures. Through historical reconstruction of Christian origins (Elisabeth Schüssler Fiorenza 1983), discerning a "prophetic-liberating tradition" within Scripture (Rosemary Radford Ruether 1983), or careful linguistic and literary work (Phyllis Trible 1978; Mary Ann Tolbert 1983), the Bible is allowed to sing its song of God's care for the oppressed. This "reclamation project" is necessary for many for whom Scripture has become "unholy" (Trible's term). Numerous recent monographs and articles have focused on individual women of the Bible as well as their social and political circumstances.

Third, feminist approaches to biblical theology involve both a "hermeneutics of suspicion" and a "herme neutics of consent." The former prompts the interpreter to bring new questions to the biblical material, for example, why was Abraham's son Isaac spared while Jephthah's daughter—whose name we do not know—was not? What does this say about the status of women among the people of God and God's seeming legitimation of such oppression? The latter coordinate, a "hermeneutics of consent," privileges the biblical material as the horizon of the Christian community's faith and experience, and seeks to discern its dimensions of authority in the life of the church, and particularly in the lives of contemporary women.

Feminist approaches are rapidly changing the terrain traversed by biblical theologians. Burgeoning literature by feminist scholars reflecting creative interpretation and theological construction is making the pursuit of biblical theology both livelier and more complex. As a specialization within the larger field of liberation theology, feminist biblical theology gives voice to the urgent message of God's justice for the oppressed and forsaken found in the Bible.

The Jewishness of Jesus

Some recent scholars have suggested that a third "quest" for the historical Jesus is underway presently, the quest for the "Jewish Jesus." Yet this quest does not depend upon earlier historical methods that sought to unearth "bare facts" untainted by confessional or theological material. The map for this quest is charted by a new alliance with social sciences that offers a new perspectival window on the social setting and patterns of first-century JUDAISM. A new confidence about the possibility of learning a great deal about the life of Jesus accompanies these new methods.

The current interest in the Jewishness of Jesus is framed by the larger discussion of the relationship of Judaism to Christianity. Thus both Jewish (Pinchas Lapide 1983; David Flusser 1991; Geza Vermes 1973) and Christian (Marcus J. Borg 1987; Robert Funk 1975; E. P. Sanders 1985) scholars are contributing new insights to biblical studies that presage significant theological interpretation of a textual world they share.

How direct was Jesus about claiming messiahship? What was Jesus relationship to his people and to the official structures of Judaism? What was the purpose of Jesus' ministry within Judaism? How does the death of Jesus relate to his messianic status? Questions such as these are receiving new scrutiny and correcting certain biases with which biblical theologians in the Christian tradition have worked. Too often Christian

exegetes have been preoccupied with who Jesus was for Christianity rather than the prior question of Jesus' relationship to Judaism. A perjorative attitude toward and ignorance of Judaism has eviscerated much Christian scholarship of balanced perception. Indeed, the remarkable revival of interest in Jesus by Jewish as well as Christian scholars gives new depth to theological understanding of the Scriptures as a whole.

Theology in Canonical Context

A key response to the conundrum of the Biblical Theology Movement was a renewed interest in the meaning of canon for theology. Several methodological avenues vector out from this method: interest in biblical narrative, the literary character of the Bible, the canonical shaping of texts in their final form, intertextual reading, and the role of the canon in the church. The canon as the only appropriate context for doing biblical theology is due to its authoritative status because of the church's theological decision, according to Childs (1993), a foremost pioneer in this method.

Comprehensive in its treatment of Scripture, this strategy employs the whole Bible: both parts of the canon comprise the church's book. Hence, no "center" or "canon within the canon" can function as the hermeneutical key. Theology of the OT is treated as a Christian discipline because the Hebrew Scriptures are permanently joined to the NT by the church; likewise, the NT cannot be understood if severed from its place in the canon.

Important to this approach is an intertextual reading of the biblical materials. Worship, with its use of the lectionary, and doctrine, with its construal of texts drawn from the whole Bible, reflect the close relationship that biblical theology must forge with dogmatic theology.

Narrative theology owes its primary orientation to the emphasis on the final form of the text as proposed by this method. Rather than conducting an archaeological dig to discern the history behind the text, narrative theology reclaims an emphasis of the Reformers, that is, the perspicuity or the self-evident sense of Scripture for the community of faith. The literary-narrative shift promises to garner continuing attention.

Actualizing Interpretation

A final approach seeks to widen the aperture of vision for those pursuing biblical theology that they might address the present-day significance of their historical findings. The primary advocate of this method,

Heikki Räisänen (1990; although many others share his basic concern), seeks to repristinate Gabler's concern that *historical* and *theological* tasks be assigned to two different stages of work, but that both be done by *biblical* theologians. Averring that the unwieldy separation of the historical and theological tasks seen, for example, in Krister Stendahl's article on "Contemporary Biblical Theology" in *IDB* (1962), was doomed to failure, Räisänen contends for an approach that will allow biblical theology to actualize its constructs in a way that benefits universal human intellectual and religious needs. Biblical theology must not be a sequestered academic pursuit with primary attention devoted to the life of the church.

Biblical theology cannot rest with the descriptive task, yet what is its proper relationship to creeds, church tradition, and contemporary developments in Christian thought? Moreover, are there aspects of the theological task in which biblical theology has a normative role for humanity as a whole? These questions are probed by an actualizing interpretation that reflects on the biblical material from an ecumenical and global point of view. Perhaps the continuing vitality of the discipline is in large measure dependent upon such breadth of concern.

Conclusion

Biblical theology has changed graphically since its inception a little more than 200 years ago. Remarkable strides in the critical study of Scripture have sparked new insights into the biblical message; usually the trends have followed the larger cultural and theological trends in the academy and church.

The Biblical Theology Movement that held the field during the middle of this century has ended. Although a few scholars want to revive its major concerns (and a few more long for its unbridled confidence), biblical theology today is marked by vigorous new strategies and a bit more humility about the possibility of a holistic biblical theology.

Some of the same problems lurk as contemporary scholars attempt to relate the historical and theological components of the discipline to the contemporary church's need for dogmatic teaching. The diversity of Scripture wards off simple or forced harmonization, and its rich pluralism points beyond itself to the richness of divine revelation, indeed, to the mystery of God. Nevertheless, biblical theology remains a necessary and foundational partner for constructing a theological vision for the waning of this century and the

beginning of the next. New means of access to these ancient texts are allowing them to speak their messages afresh.

For Further Study

In the *Mercer Dictionary of the Bible*: BIBLE; BIBLICAL THEOLOGY; CANON; FEMINIST HERMENEUTICS; HERMENEUTICS; THEOLOGY OF THE NT; THEOLOGY OF THE OT. In other sources: See the works cited below and H. Boers, *What Is N.T. Theology?*; H. Gese, *Essays on Biblical Theology*; L. Goppelt, *Theology of the N.T.*; W. Harrington, *The Path of Biblical Theology*; J. Lawson, *The Biblical Theology of St. Irenaeus*; R. Morgan, *The Nature of N.T. Theology*; P. Stuhlmacher, *Historical Criticism and Theological Interpretation of Scripture*; M. Tate, "Promising Paths toward Biblical Theology," *RE* 78/2 (1981): 169–85.

Works Cited

Barr, James. 1976. "Biblical Theology." *IDBSup.*

Borg, Marcus J. 1987. *Jesus: A New Vision.*

Brueggemann, Walter. 1977. *The Land: Place as Gift, Promise, and Challenge in Biblical Faith.* OBT.

Childs, Brevard S. 1970. *Biblical Theology in Crisis.* 1993. *Biblical Theology of the Old and New Testaments.*

Cullmann, Oscar. 1945; ET 1949, ³1962.

Daniélou, Jean. 1960. *From Shadows to Reality.*

Denten, Robert C. 1963. *Preface to Old Testament Theology.* Rev. ed.

Flusser, David. 1991. "Jesus, His Ancestry, and the Commandment of Love," in *Jesus' Jewishness*, ed J. H. Charlesworth.

Funk, Robert. 1975. *Jesus as Precursor.*

Hasel, G. F. 1984. "Biblical Theology Movement," *Evangelical Dictionary of Theology.*

Lapide, Pinchas. 1983. *The Resurrection of Jesus: A Jewish Perspective.*

Mauser, Ulrich. 1991. "Historical Criticism: Liberator or Foe of Biblical Theology," in Reumann 1991, 99-113.

Rad, Gerhard von. 1962. *Old Testament Theology.* Vol. 1. 1965. *Old Testament Theology.*Vol. 2.

Räisänen, Heikki. 1990. *Beyond New Testament Theology.*

Reumann, John, ed. 1991. *The Promise and Practice of Biblical Theology.*

Reventlow, Henning Graf. 1986. *Problems of Biblical Theology in the Twentieth Century.*

Ruether, Rosemany Radford. 1983. *Sexism and God-Talk: Toward a Feminist Theology.*

Ruler, Arnold Albert van. 1971. *The Christian Church and the O.T.*

Sanders, E. P. 1985. *Jesus and Judaism.*

Schüssler Fiorenza, Elisabeth. 1983. *In Memory of Her: A Feminist Theological Reconstruction of Christian Origins.*

Smart, James D. 1979. *The Past, Present, and Future of Biblical Theology.*

Strecker, Georg. 1991. "The Law in the Sermon on the Mount, and the Sermon on the Mount as Law," in Reumann 1991, 35–49.

Tolbert, Mary Ann. 1983. "Defining the Problem: The Bible and Feminist Hermeneutics," *Semeia* 28: 113–26.

Trible, Phyllis. 1978. *God and the Rhetoric of Sexuality.* OBT.

Vermes, Geza. 1973. *Jesus the Jew.*

The Importance of Noncanonical Literature

Joseph L. Trafton

Scholars frequently use the expression "noncanonical literature" to refer to specific groupings of Jewish and Christian writings that are not included in the biblical CANON. This article focuses on the five main groupings—the OT Apocrypha, the OT Pseudepigrapha, the Dead Sea Scrolls, the NT Apocrypha, and the Nag Hammadi library—and their importance for understanding the canonical literature.

Classification of Noncanonical Literature

The OT Apocrypha is a relatively fixed collection of Jewish writings found in the OT canons of Roman Catholic and Eastern Orthodox Christianity but not of Protestants. Roman Catholics call the books "Deuterocanonical"—secondarily canonical, or added later to the canon. The Deuterocanonical books are Tobit, Judith, Additions to Esther, Additions to Daniel (including Prayer of Azariah and the Song of the Three Jews, Susanna, and Bel and the Dragon), Wisdom of Solomon, Ecclesiasticus (Sirach), Baruch (or 1 Baruch), Letter of Jeremiah (=Baruch chap. 6), 1 Maccabees, and 2 Maccabees. The Greek Orthodox Church adds 1 Esdras, Psalm 151, Prayer of Manasseh, and 3 Maccabees, with 4 Maccabees in an appendix. The Russian Orthodox Church adds 1 Esdras, 2 Esdras, Psalm 151, and 3 Maccabees. The Roman Catholic canon places Prayer of Manasseh, 1 Esdras, and 2 Esdras in an appendix without implying canonicity.

The OT Pseudepigrapha is a modern collection of documents of primarily Jewish origin based mainly on the OT and frequently attributed (falsely) to OT figures. Most of the books were written between 200 B.C.E. and 200 C.E., although some were later. Many of them have been reworked by Christians, and some probably were composed by Christians. The separation of Jewish and Christian elements in many of these writings is a longstanding problem in Pseudepigrapha studies. The Pseudepigrapha are sometimes classified by literary form into APOCALYPTIC LITERATURE (e.g., *1 Enoch, 2 Enoch, 4 Ezra, 2 Baruch, 3 Baruch, Apocalypse of Abraham, Apocalypse of Zephaniah,* and *Apocalypse of Elijah*), testaments (e.g., *Testaments of the Twelve Patriarchs, Testament of Job, Testament of Abraham, Testament of Moses,* and *Testament of Solomon*), expansions of the OT and legends (e.g., *Letter of Aristeas, Jubilees, Martyrdom of Isaiah, Joseph and Asenath, Life of Adam and Eve, Pseudo-Philo, Lives of the Prophets, 4 Baruch,* and *Jannes and Jambres*), wisdom and philosophical literature (e.g., *Ahiqar* and *4 Maccabees*), and prayers, psalms, and odes (e.g., *Prayer of Manasseh, Psalms of Solomon,* and *Odes of Solomon*), but such a classification is not precise.

The DEAD SEA SCROLLS is a vast collection of more than 800 ancient Jewish manuscripts discovered beginning in 1947 in caves along the DEAD SEA. These scrolls are the remains of a library that belonged to a group of sectarian Jews, probably ESSENES, who lived by the Dead Sea at a site called Qumran from ca. 141 B.C.E. to 68 C.E. In addition to containing the oldest known Hebrew OT manuscripts and portions of previously known apocrypha (apocryphal psalms, Letter of Jeremiah, Tobit, and Sirach) and pseudepigrapha (*Jubilees, 1 Enoch,* and *Testaments of the Twelve Patriarchs*), the scrolls contain other pseudepigrapha (e.g., *Genesis Apocryphon, Book of Giants, Book of Noah, Testament of Amram, Words of Moses, Samuel Apocryphon, Prayer of Nabonidus,* and *Pseudo-Daniel*), sectarian documents, including rules (e.g., *Manual of Discipline, Rule of the Congregation, Damascus Rule, War Rule, Temple Scroll,* and *Miqsat Ma'aseh Torah*), poetical-liturgical texts (e.g., *Thanksgiving Scroll, Angelic Liturgy, Blessings, Words of the Heavenly Lights*), and documents concerned with biblical interpretation (e.g., commentaries or *pesharim* on Isaiah, Habakkuk, Nahum, Hosea, Micah, and Psalm 37; *Florilegium* and *Testimonia*; *Patriarchal Blessings*; and *Melchizedek*), and miscellaneous writings (e.g., *New Jerusalem* and *Copper Scroll*).

The NT Apocrypha is a modern collection of writings composed by Christians between the first and fourth centuries C.E. They are about, or are pseudonymously attributed to, NT figures. These books are generally modeled after the literary forms found in the NT: there are apocryphal gospels (e.g., *Gospel of Peter, Infancy Gospel of Thomas, Protevangelium of James*, and *Gospel of Nicodemus*), apocryphal acts (e.g., *Acts of Peter, Acts of Paul, Acts of John, Acts of Andrew*, and *Acts of Thomas*), apocryphal letters (e.g., *3 Corinthians, Letter to the Laodiceans, Pseudo-Titus*, and *Letter of Barnabas*), and apocryphal revelations (e.g., *Apocalypse of Peter, Apocalypse of Paul* [ANT], and *Apocalypse of Thomas*).

The NAG HAMMADI library consists of thirteen codices discovered in 1945 near Nag Hammadi, Egypt. These codices, which date from the fourth century C.E., are the remains of a library that apparently belonged to a Christian monastery at nearby Chenoboskian. The codices contain fifty-two tractates, forty of which were unknown prior to this discovery. Most of the documents reflect the viewpoints of the syncretistic religious movement known as GNOSTICISM. Some are neither Jewish nor Christian (e.g., *Discourse on the Eighth and Ninth, Three Steles of Seth, Zostrianos*, and *Allogenes*); one, *Apocalypse of Adam*, is Jewish. Most, however, are Christian: there are gospels (e.g., *Gospel of Truth, Gospel of Thomas, Gospel of Philip*, and *Gospel of the Egyptians*), acts (e.g., *Acts of Peter and the Twelve Apostles* and *Letter of Peter to Philip*), letters (e.g., *Treatise on the Resurrection* and *Eugnostos*), and apocalypses (e.g., *Apocalypse of Peter, Apocalypse of Paul* (NH), *First Apocalypse of James*, and *Second Apocalypse of James*), as well as dialogues (e.g., *Sophia of Jesus Christ* and *Dialogue of the Savior*), "secret" books (e.g., *Apocryphon of James* and *Apocryphon of John*), and other miscellaneous writings (e.g., *Hypostasis of the Archons, On the Origin of the World, Exegesis on the Soul*, and *Teaching of Silvanus*).

Contributions of Noncanonical Literature

Generally speaking, Jewish noncanonical literature fills in the gap between the OT and the NT, often called the "intertestamental period." These writings are crucial for understanding JUDAISM of the era. Their primary importance for the study of the Bible is, therefore, as background material for the NT. Christian noncanonical literature is, with a few possible exceptions, later than the NT writings. These documents are very important for discerning certain nuances in the development of Christianity in its early centuries. They can also shed light on the NT, but the question of dating is always problematic, since most were composed later. The contributions of noncanonical literature to the study of the Bible can be grouped under four headings: historical events, religious movements, religious concepts and practices, and literary features.

Historical events

While the works of the first-century Jewish historian JOSEPHUS constitute the most important single source for knowledge of Jewish history between the OT and the NT, information about some historical events can be gleaned from the noncanonical Jewish writings.

The most important historical works in this literature are 1 and 2 MACCABEES. First Maccabees is the main source for reconstructing the history of the Jews in Palestine between 167 and 134 B.C.E., the period of the Maccabean Revolt and its immediate aftermath, and of the beginnings of the Hasmonean dynasty of Jewish kings. Second Maccabees traces the revolt only to 161 B.C.E. but gives a much more extensive account of the events leading up to the Maccabean period (ca. 180–167 B.C.E.). Although not without theological tendencies, these books together are indispensable for understanding this critical period in the history of the Jewish people. Some scholars, for instance, read the Book of Daniel as a response to the Maccabean crisis; if such an approach is valid, then a knowledge of the period is necessary for understanding Daniel. But the events of the Maccabean era are also important for the study of the NT. Although the right of self-determination gained by the Jews during the Maccabean Revolt had given way to Roman rule by the time of Jesus, the Jews' remembrance of their heroic ancestors encouraged at least some of them to work toward throwing off the Roman yoke, as the Maccabees had liberated themselves from the Seleucids 200 years earlier. Such thinking is reflected in the NT (cf. Luke 23:19; Acts 5:36-37) and resulted in the revolt against Rome in 66–70 C.E., with its disastrous consequences for the Jewish people.

Third Maccabees is obviously misnamed since it has nothing to do with the Maccabees. Rather, it narrates two crises faced by the Jews during the reign of Ptolemy IV Philopator of Egypt (221–204 B.C.E.), the first taking place in Jerusalem and the second in Alexandria. Whether these events actually occurred is not known.

The *Letter of Aristeas* purports to tell how the Hebrew Torah was translated into Greek in Alexandria during the reign of the Egyptian king Ptolemy II (285–247 B.C.E.)—by seventy-two Jewish scholars in seventy-two days. Although *Aristeas* is quite tendentious theologically and is probably not to be trusted as a factual account, it is nonetheless true that sometime during the last century or two before the Christian era, some Jews, perhaps in Alexandria, translated the Hebrew Scriptures into Greek. This translation, known as the SEPTUAGINT (LXX) was used by most of the NT writers when quoting the OT.

The *Letter of Aristeas* is a good example of the character of many, if not most, of the noncanonical writings: they are less valuable for *history* than they are for *tradition*. We learn from them not so much what actually happened as what people apparently *believed* to have happened.

Most of the Pseudepigrapha, for example, claims to *add to* the stories about OT figures. A good example is *Enoch*. Enoch is mentioned only briefly in the OT in a genealogy in Gen 5. Yet he is said not to have died because he "walked with God" (v. 24). Because he was seen as such a righteous man, pious Jews began to construct stories about him—stories, they felt, to develop and extend the minimal references to him in the Book of Genesis. The results are three long books, *1, 2,* and *3 Enoch,* not to mention speculations about Enoch in other writings.

Other perceived gaps in the OT narrative are addressed in other writings. What did Adam and Eve do *after* the fall? Read the *Life of Adam and Eve.* What was Abraham like *before* God called him? Try the *Apocalypse of Abraham.* How did Joseph meet his Egyptian wife? *Joseph and Asenath* tells the story. Why was Satan so upset with Job? The answer can be found in *Testament of Job.* The list goes on and on, and so do the traditions about OT figures.

What is the value of these traditions for understanding the Bible? Little, as far as the OT reader is concerned. These books are certainly interesting, but their date is so much later than the events they relate that it is improbable that they add any historical facts to the OT narratives. The writings, however, do provide a sharp contrast to what is actually *present* in the OT

narratives and, hence, how limited our knowledge about certain OT individuals and events really is.

The NT writers, on the other hand, were familiar with at least some of these traditions. The Book of Jude, for example, alludes to an extracanonical account of the death of Moses (v. 9), presumably a lost fragment of *Testament of Moses,* and provides a direct quotation of "Enoch" from *1 Enoch* 1:9 (vv. 14-15). The naming of the two Egyptian magicians who opposed Moses as JANNES AND JAMBRES (cf. the *Damascus Document*) is reflected in 2 Tim 3:8-9. The legend of Isaiah being sawn asunder (*Martyrdom of Isaiah; Lives of the Prophets*) is echoed in Heb 11:37.

In a similar way the noncanonical Christian writings provide numerous extracanonical traditions about Jesus and the disciples. The *Protevangelium of James,* for example, relates the story of Mary's birth, childhood, and eventual marriage to Joseph (a widower with children), culminating in a detailed account of the birth of Jesus (in a cave). The *Infancy Gospel of Thomas* describes Jesus' childhood from age five to age twelve. It presents the child Jesus performing numerous miracles—some of which are rather absurd (e.g., bringing clay sparrows to life). The *Gospel of Nicodemus* (also known as *Acts of Pilate*), provides a detailed account of the trial of Jesus and of Jesus' DESCENT INTO HELL. The *Gospel of Peter,* presents, after an otherwise straightforward account of the crucifixion, a vivid narration of the resurrection of Jesus, complete with a talking cross exiting the tomb.

Books such as *Gospel of Thomas, Gospel of Mary,* and *Dialogue of the Savior* claim to give "secret" teachings of Jesus. The apocryphal acts purport to trace the journeys of the apostles, with Thomas going all the way to India. Throughout these narratives, miracles abound, especially the raising of the dead. In the *Acts of Paul* even a talking lion is baptized. Only John is spared a martyr's death (*Acts of John*): Andrew is crucified (*Acts of Andrew*), Paul is beheaded (*Acts of Paul*), Peter is crucified upside down (*Acts of Peter*).

As in the case of the Pseudepigrapha, the dating of these documents raises serious doubt about their overall historical reliability. Yet their dates (typically second to third centuries C.E.) are not so far removed from the events themselves as to make it impossible that kernels of historical truth may be reflected in these otherwise legendary narratives. For instance, the notion that Jesus was born in a cave is also attested by the early second-century church father JUSTIN MARTYR, and it is certainly possible that Thomas, for example, went to India, or that John died in Ephesus of old age. How many, if any, such kernels remain, especially in the apocryphal acts, is unknown. As with the traditions about OT figures, these stories primarily serve to throw into sharp relief for the NT reader what is actually present in the NT narratives and, in many cases, how restrained the NT accounts actually are.

Some scholars believe the situation is more encouraging for at least some of the apocryphal gospels. The *Gospel of Thomas*, for example, is a collection of 114 sayings purportedly given by Jesus to Thomas. Some of these sayings are found—albeit sometimes in different (some scholars would say "earlier") forms—in the canonical Gospels. For example, *Gospel of Thomas* contains the parable of the sower (Matt 13:1-9) and the parable of the wheat and the tares (Matt 13:24-30), but both are without Jesus' interpretation (cf. Matt 13:18-23, 37-43). Some scholars have used this observation to support a longstanding argument that these interpretations in the canonical Gospels are not authentic, but were composed by the early church. It is also possible that the interpretations are authentic, but the community that produced the *Gospel of Thomas* did not find them to their liking and, hence, excluded them.

Also, *Gospel of Thomas* contains some sayings that sound like some of the sayings found in the canonical Gospels. For example, the kingdom of heaven is compared to a woman carrying a jar of meal; the handle breaks, the meal pours out behind her, and it is not until she reaches her house that she discovers her jar to be empty. Some scholars argue, then, that *Gospel of Thomas* contains authentic sayings of Jesus not found in the NT. If so, it would be potentially a very important document for recovering the teachings of Jesus.

On the other hand, *Gospel of Thomas* in its present form does contain a number of strange sayings that have been attributed to Gnostic or ascetic sources. Furthermore, the earliest extant manuscript of *Gospel of Thomas* dates from ca. 200 C.E. Thus, to project some early version of this document back to the first century C.E. (i.e., early enough to contain independent authentic traditions of Jesus) is highly speculative. Such a speculative approach, however, is precisely what is employed by those scholars who wish to propose that the apocryphal gospels contain independent historical material for studying the life and teaching of Jesus.

The most ambitious proposal of this type is that of J. D. Crossan, who classifies the traditions about Jesus into four chronological strata (Crossan 1991, 427–34). A simplified version of his scheme, focusing on the relative positions of the canonical and noncanonical gospels, follows. The first stratum (30–60 C.E.) contains the first edition of *Gospel of Thomas*, *Egerton Gospel*, two fragmentary papyrus gospels, *Gospel of the Hebrews*, the sayings gospel Q, a collection of miracles now embedded in Mark and John, an apocalyptic source behind Matt 24, and a cross gospel now embedded in *Gospel of Peter*. The second stratum (60–80 C.E.) includes *Gospel of the Egyptians*, *Secret Gospel of Mark*, Mark, another fragmentary papyrus gospel, the second edition of *Gospel of Thomas*, a dialogue collection now embedded in *Dialogue of the Savior*, and a signs gospel now embedded in John. The third stratum (80–120 C.E.) contains Matthew, Luke, and the first edition of John. The fourth stratum (120–150 C.E.) includes the second edition of John, *Apocryphon of James*, *Gospel of the Nazareans*, *Gospel of the Ebionites*, and *Gospel of Peter*. If Crossan's analysis is correct, then a number of apocryphal gospels (although admittedly some are quite fragmentary) are at least as important as, and in some cases even more than, the canonical Gospels for reconstructing the life and teachings of Jesus.

To be sure, Crossan's hypothesis is highly speculative. While other scholars affirm, in varying degrees, the significance of certain apocryphal gospels for shedding light on the historical Jesus, many more would agree with C. H. Talbert's cautious assessment of these writings: "It seems safe to say that, with the possible exception of the Coptic *Gospel of Thomas*, they provide us with no authentic traditions of words or deeds of Jesus, except insofar as they reproduce the canonical tradition" (Talbert 1990, 41).

Religious Movements

Noncanonical literature also provides important information concerning the diversity within both early JUDAISM and the early Church.

Readers familiar with the NT Gospels are well aware that Judaism at this time was characterized by a certain party spirit. The Gospel writers refer frequently to Sadducees and Pharisees, and occasionally to Herodians (e.g., Mark 3:6). Scholars have sometimes sought to identify certain noncanonical Jewish writings with a particular Jewish group. Sirach, for example, a collection (in a form resembling that of the Book of Proverbs) of the teachings of a second-century B.C.E. Jewish scribe named Jesus ben Sira, has sometimes been viewed as a proto-Sadducean book. The *Psalms of Solomon*, a first-century B.C.E. collection of eighteen psalms that clearly reflect the perspective of a particular group of Jews, and Judith, a captivating (though fictitious) story about the heroic exploits of a beautiful widow by the same name, have often been attributed to the Pharisees.

But scholars increasingly have come to recognize that the classic identification of Jewish parties into four groups that is based on Josephus—SADDUCEES, PHARISEES, ESSENES, and ZEALOTS—is probably an over-simplification of a very complex situation. Rather than assign documents to one of these four groups, scholars are more apt to speak more generally: 1 Maccabees, for example, is pro-Hasmonean, while *Psalms of Solomon* is anti-Hasmonean. Other writings. especially the apocalypses, apparently reflect the views of un-named Jewish groups.

The point is that the noncanonical Jewish literature gives ample evidence of a rich diversity within early Judaism; many groups existed and left their mark on the literary remains of this period.

Yet there is one sect of Jews that seems to come into much clearer focus through at least some of this literature: the Essenes. Most scholars believe the DEAD SEA SCROLLS represent the library of an Essene community. Indeed, the discovery of the scrolls has led some scholars to suggest that virtually all of the noncanonical Jewish literature was composed by the Essenes, but this suggestion has little to commend it. Yet the discovery of fragments of *Jubilees*, *1 Enoch*, and *Testaments of the Twelve Patriarchs* among the scrolls, combined with certain parallels between some of their teachings and those of the scrolls, makes it likely that these three documents, at least, are proto-Essenic writings.

Veiled references in the scrolls suggest that the origins of the sect centered around differences with the Temple leadership. The key figure in the early history of the Essenes was the Teacher of Righteousness, an otherwise unnamed individual who gave the sect direction and focus in its early stages. The Essenes believed God had revealed to the Teacher of Righteousness the mysteries concerning the Law. Thus, he alone could properly interpret the Law; other Jews misunderstood it. Led by the Teacher of Righteousness, who was himself a priest, the sect rejected the Temple cult in Jerusalem as it was currently practiced and probably even the ruling priesthood as being illegitimate. Guided by the command in Isa 40:3 to prepare a way for the Lord "in the wilderness" (cf. Matt 3:3), the sect removed itself to the desert area by the Dead Sea to await the final war, from which, with God's help, they as the true Israel would emerge victorious and after which they would restore the sacrificial cult and proper priest-hood to Jerusalem.

The Essenes saw themselves as the "sons of light"; outsiders were the "sons of darkness," from whom they were called to separate. The community was governed by stringent entrance procedures, a detailed code of conduct, and a strict organizational hierarchy under the leadership of the priests. The sectarians had a communal lifestyle, sharing property and work, study-ing the Law, and meeting together for discussion of community matters and for ceremonies. Worship was an important aspect of communal life; the sect under-stood itself as participating in the angelic worship of God. Especially significant was the sacred meal. Cere-monial washings for purification were routine, and em-phasis was placed on the use of the solar calendar, rather than the lunar calendar of official Judaism. Un-able to offer sacrifices in the defiled Jerusalem Tem-ple, the community viewed prayer and obedience as acceptable offerings. Other aspects of personal piety included a deep sense of human frailty and sinfulness and thanksgiving to God for his GRACE and ELECTION.

A number of concepts in the scrolls have striking NT parallels. The centrality of a founding Teacher re-minds one of Jesus. The sacred meal calls to mind the LORD'S SUPPER (cf. 1 Cor 11:17-34). Aspects of the organizational structure (elders, overseer) are reminis-cent of that found in the Pastorals. The dependence on God's grace has been linked by some to justification by faith in Paul. The teaching that God created Two Spirits in which people must walk—the Prince of Light/Angel of Truth/Spirit of Truth and the Angel of Darkness/Spirit of Falsehood (cf. 1 John 4:6)—and that those led by the Two Spirits are characterized by cer-tain attitudes are reminiscent of Gal 5:19-23. Other NT parallels, just to note a few, include the identification of the sect as the Way (cf. Acts 9:2) and as the com-munity of the new covenant (Luke 22:20; 2 Cor 3:6; Heb 8:7-13), the use of Isa 40:3 to justify a movement "in the wilderness" (cf. Mark 1:2), and a number of similarities between *War Rule* and certain parts of Revelation, including the idea of a final war depicted in cosmic terms (cf. Rev 12:7; 16:13-16; 19:11-21), songs celebrating the defeat of the enemy (cf. Rev 18), an interest in the role of trumpets (cf. Rev 8–9) and in precise specifications and precious stones (cf. Rev 21:12-21), and a significant role for the archangel Michael (cf. Rev 12:7).

While the Essenes are not mentioned in the NT (some would see them, however, in the HERODIANS) such parallels have resulted in far-reaching speculation regarding "connections" between the scrolls and Christianity. But most conjectures of any direct link (e.g., that JESUS and/or JOHN THE BAPTIST were at one time a part of the sect) have little support. On the other hand, it is quite possible Jesus knew about the Essenes.

The closest parallel in pre-Christian Judaism, for example, to the command to hate one's enemies (opposed by Jesus in Matt 5:43-44 with a directive to love one's enemies) is found in *Manual of Discipline*, where members of the community are commanded to love the sons of light and to hate the sons of darkness. It is also possible that certain NT writers, in particular John, might have been influenced by Essene beliefs.

Noncanonical Christian literature testifies to the diversity within the early Church. The apocryphal acts, for example, promote a celibate lifestyle, even among husbands and wives. In the *Acts of Thomas*, for example, Jesus appears to a bride and groom on their wedding night and convinces them to refrain from consummating their marriage. In the *Acts of Paul* Paul is banished from Iconium for teaching women not to marry. Although later than the NT, they remind one of the ascetic groups opposed in Col 2:20-23 or in 1 Tim 4:3.

Some of the apocryphal acts also promote a docetic view of Jesus, that is, that he was not really human, but only appeared to be so. In the *Acts of John*, for example, "John" observes that Jesus would change his appearance and that he never left a footprint. Important to the docetic perspective was the affirmation that Jesus, since he was not human, did not really die on the cross. In the *Acts of John*, while Jesus is appearing to be crucified, he appears to John in a cave on the Mount of Olives and reveals to John that he is not in fact experiencing anything that will be said about his crucifixion. John thus descends from the mountain and laughs at the those who "witness" the crucifixion (cf. *SecTreatSeth*). Such a perspective is combatted in 1 John 4:2-3 and 2 John 7, and, perhaps, in John 1:14.

The *Pseudo-Clementine Homilies* and *Recognitions* testify to a rather conservative Jewish-Christian movement, perhaps the Ebionites, in the second and third centuries C.E., somewhat reminding one of the Judaizers in Acts and Galatians. Also Jewish-Christian, though perhaps not all relating to the same movement, are *Gospel of the Hebrews*, *Gospel of the Ebionites*, and *Gospel of the Nazareans*.

But the group about which the noncanonical Christian writings provide the most information is GNOSTICISM. The NAG HAMMADI library, in particular, consists mostly of Gnostic texts. Gnosticism itself was a diverse movement. Indeed, some of the Nag Hammadi tractates have been identified with Valentinian Gnosticism (e.g., *Apocryphon of James*, *Gospel of Truth*, *Tripartite Tractate*, *Gospel of Philip*, and *A Valentinian Exposition*), others with Sethian Gnosticism (e.g., *Apocryphon of John*, *Hypostasis of the Archons*, *Gospel of the Egyptians*, *Apocalypse of Adam*, *Three Steles of Seth*, *Zostrianos*, *Melchizedek* [NH], *Thought of Norea*, *Marsanes*, *Allogenes*, and *Trimorphic Protennoia*), while others cannot at present be connected with any known Gnostic sect (e.g., *Gospel of Thomas* and *Thunder, Perfect Mind*).

Yet the various Gnostic sects shared certain basic beliefs, most importantly a world-rejecting outlook and an emphasis on knowledge (i.e., *gnosis*, the Gk. word from which the term "Gnosticism" derives) as the means to salvation. Gnostics believed that the Creator-god of the material world is an inferior, even evil, spiritual being who has created an inferior, evil world. This Creator-god, in collaboration with his various, and equally evil, spiritual cohorts, conspires to keep humans trapped in ignorance of the higher spiritual realm. The Creator-god's evil designs are ultimately thwarted when beneficent spiritual beings of this higher realm send an emissary (Christ, in Christian forms of Gnosticism) into the lower world to bring the *gnosis* that illuminates and liberates. The Gnostic systems that incorporated these basic beliefs were highly complex, typically going to great lengths to name and to describe the various spiritual entities, both good and evil.

The extent to which the NT writers encountered some form of Gnosticism is difficult to determine. Scholars have proposed that Gnosticism is opposed, for example, in Luke-Acts, the Corinthian letters, Ephesians, Colossians, 2 Peter, and Jude. First and Second Timothy seem particularly open to such an interpretation. The false teaching opposed in these letters is characterized by a concern with "myths" (1 Tim 1:4; 4:7; 2 Tim 4:4), "genealogies" (1 Tim 1:4), "disputes about words" (1 Tim 6:4; 2 Tim 2:14, 23), "speculations" (1 Tim 1:4; 6:4), "knowledge" (1 Tim 6:20), "meaningless talk" (1 Tim 1:6), and "profane chatter" (1 Tim 6:20; 2 Tim 2:16). The false teachers teach false doctrines (1 Tim 1:3; 4:1; 6:3), which include the prohibition of marriage and of certain foods (1 Tim 4:3) and the belief that "the resurrection has already taken place" (2 Tim 2:18). A number of these features—for example, the specific doctrinal teachings (cf. *Treatise on the Resurrection*), the interest in myths and genealogies (cf., e.g., *Apocryphon of John, Hypostasis of the Archons, On the Origin of the World, Thought of Norea, Sophia of Jesus Christ, Tripartite Tractate*, and *A Valentinian Exposition*), and the concern for "knowledge"—suggest that the false teaching might have been an early form of Gnosticism. However, some of the more characteristic aspects of later Gnosticism are lacking, and other explanations have been offered. Since the Gnostic writings date from the second century C.E. and later, a large part of the problem is determining the extent to which Gnosticism was present, if at all, during the first century. Perhaps further analysis of the Nag Hammadi texts will help to clarify these questions.

Religious Concepts and Practices

The OT was written in Hebrew and Aramaic. The fact that the NT was composed in Greek is itself testimony to significant changes that took place in JUDAISM during the centuries after Alexander. As evidenced by the widespread use of the Greek language, there was a certain penetration into Judaism of Greek ideas and practices, a process known as Hellenization. The extent to which Jews adopted Greek ideas and practices differed from place to place and even from Jew to Jew, but it was widespread, nonetheless.

The noncanonical Jewish writings testify, in various ways, to the process of Hellenization. Second Maccabees recounts in some detail Hellenistic inroads into Jewish culture, such as the establishment of a gymnasium for Jewish youth to participate in Greek athletic contests, in Jerusalem prior to the Maccabean Revolt. Fourth Maccabees, an imaginative retelling of a series of Jewish martyrdoms already recorded in 2 Maccabees, employs Stoic ideas in an attempt to demonstrate that inspired reason, guided by the Law, is supreme ruler over the passions. The Wisdom of Solomon, a wisdom book written to strengthen the faith of Jews living in Egypt, affirms such Greek concepts as the preexistence and the immortality of the soul and employs the Greek method of allegorical interpretation. Allegorical interpretation is also used extensively in the *Letter of Aristeas*, where the Jewish dietary laws are understood to refer to universal human virtues and vices. The Jewish composers of the *Sibylline Oracles* adopt both a Greek literary form (epic hexameter) and figure (the prophetess Sibyl) to set forth a series of oracles on the future of the world.

Many more examples of Hellenization in Jewish noncanonical writings could be given, especially in the ethical sections of these documents. But these are sufficient to indicate that the Hellenization of Judaism is something of which the NT reader must be aware. Both Jesus and his disciples encountered and conversed with gentiles. Thus, they must have been able to speak not only Aramaic, the common language of Palestinian Jews at that time, but also Greek. Furthermore, certain early Christians, apparently associated with Jerusalem synagogues populated by Jewish immigrants from Hellenistic regions, were known as "the Hellenists" (Acts 6:1). Paul demonstrated his ability to interact with Greek culture through both his preaching (Acts 17:22-32) and his letters; indeed, the extent to which Paul's theology was influenced primarily by Jewish or by Greek thought has been long debated. Scholars typically view the author of Hebrews as a Jewish Christian trained in Hellenistic rhetoric and learning. The list could continue, but the point is clear: the interaction between Judaism and Hellenism is an important part of the background of the NT.

Another area where noncanonical Jewish literature is important for the study of the NT is that of the religious practices of the Jews. In John 10:22-23 Jesus is in the Temple during the FEAST OF DEDICATION. An examination of the OT reveals no such feast. The reason is that the feast has it roots not in the OT, but in the Maccabean Revolt. As part of his policy of Hellenization of the Jews, the Seleucid king Antiochus IV profaned the Temple by desecrating the altar with sacrifices to Zeus in December 168/7 B.C.E. Three years later, the Maccabees, following their initial victories, reconsecrated the Temple and established the annual Feast of Dedication (also called Hanukkah, which means "dedication"). The story is told in 1 and 2 Maccabees.

In the Gospels and Acts the Jewish practice of almsgiving is assumed (e.g., Matt 6:1-4; Acts 10:2, 4). Although the OT contains numerous exhortations to provide for the poor (e.g., Exod 23:10-11; Lev 19:9-10; Deut 24:29-22), there is perhaps no finer example of a Jew who cared for the poor than Tobit (see also Job in *Testament of Job*), whose inordinate burden to help the needy leads to his own blindness and sets the stage for God's resolution of the plight of two pious families in Tobit. This delightful story, more than any mere exhortation, gives a vivid picture of the high esteem in which almsgiving was held among Jews.

A major aspect of Judaism in any period is OT interpretation. The noncanonical Jewish writings reveal a variety of methods used by Jews to interpret the scriptures during the intertestamental period. The use of allegorical interpretation in the Wisdom of Solomon and the *Letter of Aristeas* has already been mentioned. This method is also found among the DEAD SEA SCROLLS, especially in the *Damascus Rule*. Allegorical interpretation looks beyond the literal meaning of a text to some supposed "symbolic" meaning. In the *Letter of Aristeas*, for example, animals with a cloven or divided hoof symbolize the separation of human actions for good rather than evil. Allegorical interpretation became a favorite method of OT interpretation in the early Church, as exhibited, for example, in the *Letter of Barnabas*, and was occasionally used in the NT (e.g., 1 Cor 10:4).

One of the most striking characteristics of the Dead Sea Scrolls is the distinctive manner of interpreting the OT found in many of the scrolls. Members of the Dead Sea sect (probably Essenes) believed the OT books were full of mysteries that were fulfilled in the history of the community. The meaning of these mysteries was hidden until God revealed them to the founder of the sect, the Teacher of Righteousness, and some of his followers—hence the need for *pesher*, or interpretation. One approach to such interpretation was the production of continuous commentaries, called *pesharim*, on OT books, including Habakkuk, Micah, Psalms, Isaiah, Hosea, Nahum, and Zephaniah. The commentaries are filled with enigmatic historical allusions to figures related to the history of the sect and thus illustrate the sect's method of viewing the OT as fulfilled in itself. Another interpretive strategy of the sect was to collect and interpret OT passages in accordance with a particular theme. The *Testimonia*, for example, seems to be an anthology of messianic texts, the *Florilegium* an amalgam of eschatological texts and interpretations, and *Melchizedek* a collection of OT texts and interpretations centering around the mysterious OT person of the same name (cf. Gen 14:18-20; Heb 5:10; 6:20–7:17).

Similarities between the interpretive strategies found in the Dead Sea Scrolls, especially the *pesharim*, and those found in the NT are obvious. On a number of occasions Matthew, for example, introduces a citation from the OT with an expression to the effect that an event took place "to fulfill what had been spoken through the prophet . . ." (e.g., Matt 1:22-23; 2:15, 17-18, 23). At the opening of his public ministry in Luke, Jesus interprets in a Nazareth synagogue Isa 61:1-2 as being fulfilled in himself (Luke 4:16-21). Similar passages can be found throughout the NT. To be sure, no NT writer wrote a continuous commentary on an OT book, as did the writers of the scrolls, but it is clear that the NT writers employed a strategy similar to that of the Essenes by interpreting much of the OT as having been fulfilled in the events relating to Jesus and the early Church. Some scholars have even proposed that, like the anthologies among the scrolls, collections of key OT texts viewed as relating to Jesus were drawn up by and circulated among the early Christians.

No treatment of OT interpretive strategies in the noncanonical literature would be complete without some mention of the method of interpretation used in certain Gnostic texts (e.g., the *Apocryphon of John*, *Hypostasis of the Archons*, and *On the Origin of the World*). The most startling feature of the approach of these texts to the OT is that they turn the early chapters of Genesis on their head, so to speak. In accordance with the Gnostic view of the universe, they understand the Creator-god as evil, the serpent as good, and the "Fall" of Adam and Eve as a positive step towards overcoming the Creator-god's evil schemes. The relevance of this rather bizarre method of reading the OT for studying the NT is primarily one of contrast: the NT writers understood Genesis quite traditionally (cf. Rom 5).

The noncanonical literature also sheds light on certain Jewish institutions. Throughout the Gospels and Acts there are references to scribes, or teachers of the Law. Paul studied under one such teacher, Gamaliel (Acts 22:3; cf. 5:34). Sirach presents in some detail the teachings of such a scribe, Jesus ben Sira, who devoted himself to the study of Wisdom and the Law, and who shared his learning with his students. The Gospels and Acts also testify to the preeminence of the priesthood, and especially the high priest, in Jewish life. Second Maccabees recounts the growing influence (and politicization) of the high priesthood prior to the Maccabean Revolt. The transferral of the high priesthood to a new family, the Hasmoneans, during the revolt (cf. 1 Maccabees) and the results for Temple worship are harshly criticized in the *Psalms of Solomon*. Similarly, the strong priestly concern running throughout the sectarian Dead Sea Scrolls (cf. especially *Miqsat Ma'aseh Torah*) suggests that the sect probably had its origins in a dispute over the priesthood and Temple worship in the middle of the second century B.C.E. All of this provides insight not only into the NT narratives, but also into certain theological developments in the NT, such as the portrayal of Jesus as the superior high priest in Hebrews or the identification of Christians as priests in 1 Pet 2:9 and Rev 1:6; 5:10; 20:6.

Examples such as the one just given indicate that it is the conceptual world of the NT that is most illuminated by noncanonical literature. The following survey is by no means exhaustive, but is merely suggestive of the kinds of conceptual parallels to the NT that can be found in these writings.

In 2 Cor 12:1-4 Paul speaks of being "caught up to the third heaven," which he identifies as "Paradise." In Rev 4:1-2 John is invited to come up into heaven; he does so "in the Spirit" and spends the time of the rest of the book there. While there are precedents for this in the OT (e.g., Ezek 1; Isa 6), such heavenly travel becomes a major motif in the noncanonical literature. Journeys through the heavens are made, for example, by Enoch (*1, 2,* and *3 Enoch*), Abraham (*Apocalypse of Abraham* and *Testament of Abraham*), Isaac (*Testament of Isaac*), Jacob (*Testament of Jacob*), Levi (*Testament of Levi*), Isaiah (*Ascension of Isaiah*), Baruch (*3 Baruch*), Ezra (*Greek Apocalypse of Ezra* and *Vision of Ezra*), Sedrach (*Apocalypse of Sedrach*), Zephaniah (*Apocalypse of Zephaniah*), Peter (*Apocalypse of Peter*), and Paul (*Apocalypse of Paul* [ANT] and *Apocalypse of Paul* [NH]). But the heavens are also sometimes numbered: there are three (*Apocalypse of Sedrach* and *Apocalypse of Paul* [ANT]), five (*3 Baruch* and *Apocalypse of Zephaniah*), seven (*2 Enoch* [short recension], *Apocalypse of Abraham, Testament of Levi, Ascension of Isaiah*), eight (*Hypostasis of the Archons* and *On the Origin of the World*), or even ten (*2 Enoch* [long recension]; *Apocalypse of Paul* [NH]). As in 2 Corinthians, *Paradise* is in the third heaven (*2 Enoch* and *Life of Adam and Eve*).

John's apocalyptic vision begins with his observance of the worship directed by the "twenty-four elders" and the "four living creatures" towards "the one who sits on the throne" and towards the "Lamb" (Rev 4:8–5:14). In other writings, the seer often experiences the heavenly worship that the angels direct towards God (cf. also from Qumran the *Angelic Liturgy* and the *Blessings* [*1QSb*]). Some scholars have proposed that visions of angelic worship are part of the problem underlying Colossians (cf. Col 2:18).

John also sees a great white throne, where people are judged by what they have done, as recorded in "books," and by the absence of their names from "the book of life" (Rev 20:11-19). Other heavenly travelers record some striking depictions of judgment. In the *Testament of Abraham*, for example, the heavenly judge is Abel, and the one keeping the record of people's deeds is Enoch (recension B; cf. *Jubilees, Ascension of Isaiah, 2 Baruch*, and *4 Ezra*). Individuals are judged in two ways: their righteous deeds are weighed on a balance scale against their sins (cf. *1* and *2 Enoch, Apocalypse of Zephaniah*) and their works are tested by fire (cf. 1 Cor 3:12-15). In the *Apocalypse of Zephaniah* it is two groups of angels who write down the deeds of people: the angels of God record the good deeds and the angels of the accuser the sins, so that the accuser might accuse the dead at the judgment. This latter scenario serves as a striking background for the portrayal of Jesus both in Revelation, where by his blood he casts down the accuser of his followers (12:10-11), and in Colossians, where he nails to the cross the bond that stood against Christians, thereby disarming the principalities and powers (2:13-15). As for *the book of life*, it is mentioned, for example, in *Jubilees, Joseph and Asenath, Apocalypse of Zephaniah*, and *Testament of Jacob*.

Another striking feature of Revelation is its frequent references to angels, including a climactic battle waged by Michael and his angels against the devil and his angels (12:7-9). Angels appear elsewhere in the NT (e.g., Matt 1–2; Luke 1 [Gabriel] and 2) and are mentioned, for example, by Paul and the author of Hebrews. In the noncanonical writings there is a great interest in angels, especially Michael (the *War Scroll, 1* and *2 Enoch, Apocalypse of Abraham, Testament of Abraham, 3* and *4 Baruch, Joseph and Asenath, Apocalypse of Sedrach, Life of Adam and Eve, Sibylline Oracles, Testament of Moses, Ascension of Isaiah, Testament of Jacob*, and *Testament of Solomon*), who in *1 Enoch* is identified, along with Gabriel, Raphael, and Uriel, as one of the four archangels (cf. *Sibylline Oracles*). In Tobit the angel Raphael even (in disguise) accompanies Tobias on his journey.

The NT writers also speak often of Satan, and demons are plentiful in the Gospels. Several noncanonical books seek to explain the origins of the evil angels. In the *Life of Adam and Eve*, for example, the devil explains that he was cast out of heaven for refusing to worship Adam. *First Enoch* opens with a lengthy narrative of how a group of angels, called the Watchers, who desired human women, took them as wives, and produced malevolent giants as offspring (cf. Gen 6:1-4). This story, to which Jude alludes (6), was widely known (cf. *Genesis Apocryphon, 2 Enoch, Jubilees, Apocalypse of Abraham, Pseudo-Philo, Sibylline Oracles, 2 Baruch, Testament of Naphtali, Testament of Reuben*).

A favorite name for the devil in this literature is Beliar/Belial (*Damascus Document, Manual of Discipline, War Scroll, Thanksgiving Hymns, Jubilees, Sibylline Oracles, Lives of the Prophets, Martyrdom of Isaiah, Testament of the Twelve Patriarchs*; cf. 2 Cor 6:15). Speculations about demons and their roles continued after the NT period, as can be seen in the *Testament of Solomon*, a legendary work about Solomon's building of the Temple that describes in considerable detail the astrological signs and characteristic activities of various demons over which Solomon gained mastery through a magic ring.

The NT writers do not always blame sin upon the evil one. Paul, for example, can argue that humans are responsible for their own sins (e.g., Rom 1-2; Eph 2:1-3; Col 1:21), but he can also point the finger at Adam (Rom 5; cf. 1 Cor 15:21-22). Eve even receives the blame in 1 Tim 2:14. *Fourth Ezra* also affirms the effect of Adam's sin upon his descendants by infecting them with an evil heart (cf. *3 Baruch*), while *2 Baruch* explicitly rejects such a notion, affirming the individual's free choice (cf. *Sirach*). Sirach and the *Life of Adam and Eve* stress the role of Eve. The deep sense of personal sin over against God's grace that pervades Paul's thought finds parallels in some of the Dead Sea Scrolls such as *Manual of Discipline* and *Thanksgiving Hymns*. While the importance of repentance is affirmed in many documents (e.g., *Testament of Abraham* and *Joseph and Asenath*), the most beautiful example is the Prayer of Manasseh, a short prayer of confession for individual sin combining trust in the forgiving mercy of God with confidence in the efficacy of heartfelt repentance.

The NT writers emphasize the hope of the resurrection of the body (e.g., 1 Cor 15; 1 Thes 4:13-18), to be followed by eternal life (e.g., Matt 25:46; John 3:15-16; Rom 5:21). The noncanonical books typically share the hope of resurrection (e.g., *2 Maccabees, Life of Adam and Eve, 1 and 2 Enoch, Testament of Abraham, Testament of Benjamin, Testament of Judah, Pseudo-Philo, Sibylline Oracles, Psalms of Solomon, Testament of Job, 4 Ezra, 2 Baruch*, and *Lives of the Prophets*), although some of the more Hellenized

Jewish writings focus on the immortality of the soul (e.g., *4 Maccabees, Wisdom*) and the Gnostic writings understand the resurrection in spiritual terms (e.g., *Treatise on the Resurrection*). Eternal life is affirmed as well (e.g., *2 Enoch, Testament of Abraham, Joseph and Asenath*, and *Pseudo-Philo*). On the other hand, the reality of death is nowhere more graphically portrayed than in the *Testament of Abraham*, a legendary account of Abraham's death in which God sends Michael to prepare Abraham for his death. Abraham refuses to go. Eventually, God sends personified Death, who comes to Abraham in great glory and youthful beauty. Abraham refuses to follow him as well. At Abraham's request, Death reveals himself in all his ugliness and horror. Abraham still resists. Finally, Death tricks Abraham, and Abraham dies. There is no more fitting context in which to read Paul's celebration of death being swallowed up in victory (1 Cor 15:54-55) than *Testament of Abraham*.

In the NT detailed descriptions of heaven are relatively few. The most extensive is Rev 21:1-22:5, which vividly depicts a glorified "new" Jerusalem, complete with the tree of life. In the noncanonical writings there are numerous pictures of the state of the righteous in heaven (e.g., *1 and 2 Enoch, Apocalypse of Zephaniah, Testament of Jacob, Apocalypse of Peter* [ANT], and *Apocalypse of Paul* [ANT]), including portrayals, often in even greater detail than in Revelation, of a glorified Jerusalem and Temple (e.g., *Tobit, Sirach, Sibylline Oracles, 4 Ezra, 2 Baruch*, and *New Jerusalem* [5Q15]; cf. *Temple Scroll*), the latter of which is conspicuously missing in John's picture (Rev 21:22). There is also frequent mention of the tree of life (*4 Maccabees, Life of Adam and Eve, 1 and 2 Enoch, Testament of Levi, Jubilees, Pseudo-Philo, 4 Ezra*, and *Apocalypse of Sedrach*).

The NT writers are even more restrained when in comes to depicting hell, a concept only hinted at in the OT. There are a few pictorial references to fire (e.g., Matt 3:12; 13:42; 18:8; Mark 9:48; Rev 20:10-15), as well as to outer darkness, with weeping and gnashing of teeth (e.g., Matt 8:12). But elsewhere the focus is more generally on the wrath of God (e.g., John 3:36; Rom 5:9) or eternal punishment (Matt 25:46) and/or exclusion from God's presence (2 Thes 1:8-9). Eternal punishment of the wicked is assumed in many of the noncanonical writings (e.g., *Judith, 4 Maccabees*, and *Wisdom*), and fire is a standard part of the picture (e.g., in *1 and 2 Enoch, Testament of Isaiah, Testament of Jacob, Joseph and Asenath, Jannes and*

Jambres, Sibylline Oracles, 2 Baruch, 4 Ezra, Greek Apocalypse of Ezra, and *Vision of Ezra*). But some Jewish and especially Christian writers were more than eager to provide a graphic description of the place where sinners are punished (e.g., *Apocalypse of Zephaniah, Testament of Isaiah, Testament of Jacob, Greek Apocalypse of Ezra, Vision of Ezra, Acts of Thomas, Apocalypse of Peter* [ANT], *Apocalypse of Paul* [ANT], and *Book of Thomas the Contender*). The *Apocalypse of Peter* (ANT) is an excellent example of such a document. In this second century C.E. writing Jesus purportedly gives Peter a lengthy tour of hell, followed by a brief tour of heaven. In hell Peter sees sinners being punished in accordance with their sins: blasphemers, for example, hang by their tongues over a blazing fire, while murderers are cast into a pit full of poisonous snakes. Such pictures of hell had, through later authors such as Dante, a great influence on the development of the Christian concept of hell.

Leading up to the end of the age, the NT writers sometimes predict a series of eschatological woes (e.g., Mark 13; 2 Thes 2; Rev). In 2 Thes 2 these woes include the lawless one, and in Rev 13 the beast, popularly called the Antichrist. Noncanonical writings also predict eschatological plagues (e.g., *Apocalypse of Abraham, Sibylline Oracles, 4 Ezra, 2 Baruch, Testament of Moses, Martyrdom of Isaiah, Apocalypse of Elijah, Greek Apocalypse of Ezra, Epistula Apostolorum*, and *Apocalypse of Thomas*), and several Christian documents speculate on the Antichrist (*Martyrdom of Isaiah, Apocalypse of Elijah*, and *Greek Apocalypse of Ezra*). The *Apocalypse of Elijah*, for example, describes Antichrist as skinny-legged, with a tuft of gray hair at the front of his bald head, eyebrows reaching to his ears, and a leprous spot on the front of his hands. The *Sibylline Oracles* and the *Martyrdom of Isaiah* portray him in terms of the Nero-redivivus myth, which was a rumor widely circulated in the late first century C.E. to the effect that the Roman emperor Nero would return from the dead. Some scholars view this myth as standing behind certain passages in Revelation (e.g., Rev 13, 17).

Central to the NT, of course, is the affirmation that Jesus is the Messiah or Christ. Closely connected with this affirmation is that Jesus is the long-awaited son of David (cf. 2 Sam 7:12-16; Isa 9:2-7; 11:1-16; Jer 33:14-18; Ezek 34:23-24), that is, the king (e.g., Matt 1:1; Acts 2:30-31; Rom 1:3; Rev 1:5). One of the characteristics of Judaism in the intertestamental period is the reemergence of the hope for the Messiah after several centuries of domination by foreign powers. Not all Jews were looking for a Messiah: books such as Tobit, for example, exhibit a staunch hope for a glorified Jerusalem, without any reference to a Messiah. But other writings depict, in varying ways, the Messianic hopes of at least some Jews.

The Dream Visions section of *1 Enoch*, probably written in the late 160s B.C.E. against the backdrop of the Maccabean Revolt, presents the figure of a conquering ram. The expectation is clearly one of military leadership. In *Psalms of Solomon* (first century B.C.E.), the psalmist looks forward to the day when Messiah, the son of David, will come and rid the nation of its enemies and restore Jerusalem to its proper place (cf. *Sibylline Oracles* and *2 Baruch*). Yet the psalmist does not really see the Messiah as a military leader: his trust will be in God, not in horse or rider or bow. Rather, the psalmist, building on Ps 2 (cf. Rev 19:15) and Isa 11 (cf. Rev 22:16), sees him as king, judge, and shepherd. The *Testaments of the Twelve Patriarchs* (first century B.C.E.), especially *Testament of Levi* and *Testament of Judah* affirm a dual Messianic expectation: the kingship from Judah and the priesthood from Levi, with the kingship being subject to the priesthood (cf. *Jubilees*).

The most unusual picture of Messiah is found in *4 Ezra* (end of the first century C.E.). The Messiah, identified as "my [God's] son," will be revealed for a 400-year period of rejoicing (cf. Rev 20:4-6), after which he, along with everyone else, will die. He will also free the remnant of God's people by destroying their enemies through the execution of final judgment according to the standard of the Law.

The Messianic hope found in the Dead Sea Scrolls is extremely complex, testifying perhaps to changing Messianic views over the 200-year history of the sect. Like the *Testaments of the Twelve Patriarchs*, the *Manual of Discipline* (and presumably *Rule of the Congregation* and the *Damascus Document*) anticipates two Messiahs: a priestly Messiah and a royal Messiah, with the priestly Messiah given preeminence. *Patriarchal Blessings* speaks of a single, royal Messiah, who is identified further as the Branch of David. An eschatological Branch of David is also in view in *Florilegium*, where he is associated with the Interpreter of the Law, and in *Pesher on Isaiah*. *Manual of Discipline* speaks further of the coming of the Prophet (cf. *Testimonia*); *Damascus Document* and *Blessings* (i.e, *1QSb*) speak of the appearance of the Prince of the Congregation; and *Testimonia* speaks of the Star of

Jacob and the Scepter of Israel. The precise relationship among these figures is not clear. By contrast, *Melchizedek* views MELCHIZEDEK as the key figure in the final jubilee (cf. Lev 25; Luke 4:16-21) who will restore and make atonement for the sons of light and will execute God's judgment against Belial and his lot (cf. Heb 5:5–7:28).

Given the immense publicity the Dead Sea Scrolls have received and the sensationalistic claims often propounded in connection with them, it is necessary to make a few more observations about them here. First, despite claims to the contrary, there is no evidence that the Dead Sea sect viewed the Teacher of Righteousness as the Messiah, believed him to have met a violent death, or awaited his return at the end of time.

The Teacher of Righteousness and Jesus are indeed similar in certain ways—for example, each founded a movement and each claimed to provide the proper interpretation of the Law (cf. Matt 5–7)—but the differences are equally striking. Second, although there is a fragmentary text that mentions "the Son of God" (*4Q246*), it is not clear whether the text is speaking of a Messianic figure or an evil ruler, such as Antiochus IV. Third, the so-called "pierced Messiah" text (*4Q285*) probably refers not to the slaying of a Messianic figure, but to that of an enemy of the sect.

The most-common self-designation used by Jesus in the Gospels is SON OF MAN (e.g., Matt 9:6). In the "Similitudes of Enoch" section of *1 Enoch* there is extensive development of the concept of the Son of Man as an exalted figure who will come to execute judgment, long recognized for containing striking parallels with the Gospels. The evidence from the Dead Sea Scrolls, however, indicates that this section was not originally part of *1 Enoch*. Whether or not it was written before the coming of Jesus and thus serves as background material for the Son of Man concept in the Gospels, therefore, is uncertain.

John, Paul, and the author of Hebrews affirm the involvement of the preexistent Christ in the creation of the universe (John 1:12; Col 1:15-16; Heb 1:1-2). Such an affirmation is based upon the personification of Wisdom in the OT and the belief that Wisdom was involved in creation (Prov 8; cf. *Wisdom*). Over against those Jews who came to identify Wisdom with the Law (e.g., *1 Baruch* and Sirach), these NT writers instead identified Wisdom with Christ.

The NT writers make much of the importance of Jesus' death in providing atonement for sins. While 2 Maccabees implies that the suffering of martyrs atones for the sins of the nation, 4 Maccabees makes the connection explicit, using the words "ransom" (cf. Mark 10:45) and "atoning sacrifice" or "sacrifice of atonement" ("expiation" in RSV; cf. Rom 3:25).

As already indicated, the portrayal of Jesus as the authoritative interpreter of the Law is similar to that of the Teacher of Righteousness. Indeed, a number of interesting parallels to the teachings of Jesus can be discovered in the intertestamental Jewish writings. For example, the Golden Rule (Matt 7:12) is found in a negative form ("What you hate, do not do to anyone") in the *Letter of Aristeas* and in Tobit. The commands to love God and to love others (Matt 22:37-40) are combined in the *Testament of Issachar* and the *Testament of Daniel*.

The equating of lust with adultery (Matt 5:28) is found in the *Testament of Issachar* and the *Testament of Benjamin*. Tobit, the *Testament of Joseph*, and *2 Enoch* all have passages reminiscent of Jesus' comments in the parable of the sheep and the goats concerning being hungry, naked, in prison, and the like (Matt 25:35-36). The teaching of two ways, a narrow path leading to life and a wide one leading to destruction (Matt 7:13-14), is found in the *Testament of Abraham* (cf. *2 Enoch*). Many more examples could be given.

Such parallels show, on the one hand, the Jewishness of Jesus and his teachings. But they also provide a context in which the distinctiveness of Jesus' teachings becomes clearer. For example, Jesus' positive restatement of the Golden Rule (*In everything do to others as you would have them do to you*—Matt 7:12) marks a very different orientation to living than that of the negative form: the one is active and focuses on what is desirable, the other is passive and focuses on what is undesirable.

A number of other interesting parallels to the NT in noncanonical literature can be noted briefly. Hostility to the Samaritans (cf. John 4:9) is exhibited in Sirach. First Maccabees draws attention to the long absence of prophets among the Jewish people (cf. the coming of JOHN THE BAPTIST). The ability to speak angelic languages (cf. 1 Cor 13:1) is described in a strange passage in the *Testament of Job*. *Joseph and Asenath* on several occasions mentions the bread of life and the cup of immortality (cf. the LORD'S SUPPER). The *Lives of the Prophets* testifies to the veneration of Jewish heroes of old (cf. Matt 23:29). In addition, there are numerous parallels between John and the *Odes of Solomon*, James and Sirach, and Revelation and 2 Esdras.

Literary Features

Noncanonical literature provides background for understanding various literary genres used in the NT. For example, Luke 1–2 and Revelation contain a number of songs in poetic form. Writings such as the *Apocryphal Psalms*, the *Psalms of Solomon, Thanksgiving Scroll, War Rule,* and *Manual of Discipline* provide a context for recovering Jewish poetic techniques and conventions in this period. Also, books such as the *Testaments of the Twelve Patriarchs* and the *Testament of Job,* with their emphasis on the moral teaching contained in the last words of their purported authors, give cause for viewing 2 Timothy and 2 Peter as "testaments." The *Gospel of Thomas,* with its collection of Jesus' sayings apart from a narrative framework, provides an example of what Q, the sayings source widely supposed by scholars to have been used by Matthew and Luke, might have been.

Probably the best example of the value of noncanonical writings for understanding literary genre is Revelation. More important than the ongoing scholarly debate as to whether Revelation is "prophecy" or "apocalyptic" is the recognition that the literary and conceptual world in which Revelation resides is that of the apocalyptic writings (e.g., the *War Scroll, 1* and *2 Enoch, Sibylline Oracles, Apocalypse of Zephaniah, Apocalypse of Abraham, 4 Ezra,* and *2* and *3 Baruch*) and the apocalyptic sections of other writings (e.g., *Testaments of the Twelve Patriarchs* and *Testament of Moses*). These writings are filled with visionary experiences, not to mention symbolic language, not unlike that found in Revelation.

For example, in *4 Ezra* the seer has a vision, described at length, of an eagle, with twelve feathered wings and three heads, rising from the sea "with ten horns and seven heads," that comes to reign over the earth. Though the details differ, the vision bears similarities to John's vision of the beast rising from the sea (Rev 13). The vision is explained to the seer cryptically, as is John's vision in Rev 17. In another vision the seer observes a man against whom an innumerable multitude gathers to make war. The man holds no weapon of war, but rather sends forth from his mouth a stream of fire, a flaming breath, and a storm of sparks, which together incinerate his enemies. This vision bears a striking resemblance to the vision in Rev 19 of the rider on the white horse who comes with the armies of heaven; the kings of the earth and their armies gather together to make was against him,

but he slays them with the only weapon he bears—a sword coming out of his mouth. What is noteworthy about the vision in *4 Ezra* is that the seer is given a *figurative* interpretation of the vision, that is, it is a vivid picture not of a literal war but of final judgment meted out by the Messiah. Such an interpretation is entirely plausible for Rev 19 (v. 11: *in righteousness he judges and makes war*). Nevertheless, the point is that only by immersing oneself in similar literature of the time can one grasp the literary conventions John employed and understand the way he used language.

Another literary feature that characterizes much of the noncanonical literature is pseudonymity: the self-attribution of a writing to someone who was not actually the author. In noncanonical but scripture-related literature, such attribution of course was usually to biblical characters such as Enoch, Abraham, Moses, Ezra, Peter, or Paul. Reasons for pseudonymity were varied—for example, to lend authority to a writing or to attribute ideas to the biblical character who inspired them. At one time or another, some scholars have proposed most of the NT books as being pseudonymous, yet the authenticity of all of the NT books, even those widely viewed as pseudonymous, such as the Pastorals and 2 Peter, continues to be defended by many scholars. The issue of pseudonymity raises a further theological question: does pseudonymity disqualify a book from being useful and/or inspired? Many scholars would answer that it does not. Others would disagree, arguing that while a pseudonymous writing might indeed be useful for understanding the beliefs and perspective of its actual author, pseudonymity is by definition deception and, therefore, eliminates a book from being inspired; thus, they would argue, no canonical writing is, in fact, pseudonymous. In any event, the practice of pseudonymity was widespread during the biblical period and provides the necessary literary and historical, if not theological, context for such a discussion.

To read the noncanonical literature is to enter into the worlds of intertestamental Judaism and postapostolic Christianity. Some of the writings provide a backdrop against which the NT should be read; others throw the OT and NT into relief by showing how ideas and movements developed *after* the canonical books were composed. Some of the writings are difficult; some are informative; and some are simply fun to read. Serious readers of the Bible will want to introduce themselves to the vast, and fascinating, realm of noncanonical literature.

For Further Study

In the *Mercer Dictionary of the Bible*: APOCALYPTIC LITERATURE; APOCRYPHAL ACTS; APOCRYPHAL LITERATURE; CANON; DEAD SEA SCROLLS; GNOSTICISM; NAG HAMMADI; TESTAMENTS, APOCRYPHAL.

In other sources: R. H. Charles, ed., *Apocrypha and Pseudepigrapha of the Old Testament*, 2 vols.; J. H. Charlesworth, ed., *The Old Testament Pseudepigrapha*, 2 vols., and *The Old Testament Pseudepigrapha and the New Testament*; J. Dart, *The Jesus of Heresy and History: The Discovery and Meaning of the Gnostic Nag Hammadi Library*; J. K. Elliott, ed., *The Apocryphal New Testament*; E. Hennecke and W. Schneemelcher, eds., *New Testament Apocrypha*, 2 vols.; B. M. Metzger, *An Introduction to the Apocrypha*; G. W. E. Nickelsburg, *Jewish Literature between the Bible and the Mishnah*; J. M. Robinson, ed., *The Nag Hammadi Library*, rev. ed.; E. Schürer, *The History of the Jewish People in the Age of Jesus Christ*, vol. 3, rev. and ed. G. Vermes, F. Millar, and M. Goodman; H. F. D. Sparks, ed., *The Apocryphal Old Testament*; G. Vermes, *The Dead Sea Scrolls in English*, 3rd ed.

Works Cited

Crossan, J. D. 1991. *The Historical Jesus: The Life of a Mediterranean Jewish Peasant*.

Talbert, C. H. 1990. "Apocryphal Gospels," MDB.

The Bible and the Church

Paul D. Duke

The force of fundamentalism in recent years has set the agenda for much of our conversation concerning the BIBLE. The results have been tragic. Believers who are not biblicists have fallen into defensive positions with regard to the Scriptures. Leaning hard against the onslaughts of a fundamentalism that claims too much for the Bible and at the same time too little, we have insisted much on what the Bible is not. To our great harm, the energy spent on these denials has become energy largely lost to the real work of coming to terms with what the Bible must be for us. Denouncing the worship of the book, we are distracted from sufficient hearing of what the book would say. In Abraham Heschel's words, "we have so much to say *about the Bible* that we are not prepared to hear what the Bible has to say about us" (Heschel 1972, 171).

To be sure, these are idolatrous times, requiring us to declare faithfully what the Bible is *not*. It is not God. It is not a perfect book bearing pure and perfect disclosures of God. It is not without the contingencies of particular cultures and times. It is not without the real limits of human knowledge, speech, and imagination. The Bible is not a monolithic code of belief and behavior, whose every discrete text is uniformly inspired. It is not equivalent to the living Word of God. Recent reports to the contrary, the Trinity has not expanded to name the Bible the Fourth Person of the Godhead, nor has Holy Scripture replaced Holy Spirit as the Third. The Bible performs its servant work and witness well beneath the majesty of God, the lordship of Christ, and the power of Holy Spirit.

To say these things, however, is without any virtue. It is a very small thing indeed, though the times require it, to name what Scripture is not. Beyond these purely preliminary delineations lies the vast and proper labor of attending to Scripture's word, granting it the reverence of our offered minds, immersing ourselves in its story, meditating on its precepts, discerning its patterns, preaching its claims, praying its prayers, receiving its correction, permitting it to give steady and authoritative shape to the individuals and communities of faith that we are becoming.

The Relationship of Community and Scripture

The relationship between the Bible and the faith community is one of absolute and subtle interdependence. Neither exists without the other. The community came first, of course. Both Israel and the CHURCH were given birth well before their distinctive Scriptures developed. These Scriptures were composed by the community, for the community, to bear witness to the community's experience of God, to address specific moments and needs within the community's history. Furthermore, the community chose which of its writings to include in its CANON, and which to exclude. Having chosen, the community ever since has exercised the right to interpret these texts, making choices in the location of meaning and nuance, often assigning relative values to different texts, interpreting some passages in the light of others. In these ways it can be asserted that the Bible very much belongs to the church.

In other ways, however, it must be affirmed that the church belongs to the Bible. Although the Scriptures flowed from the community, the same divine initiative that was the impetus of the community was also the impetus of the Scriptures. The Bible not only bears witness to the community-creating initiatives of God, it continues to call forth, to critique, to correct, to give new existence and shape to communities of faith. As surely as the church made its Scripture, so Scripture makes the church. Samuel Terrien expressed the relationship in this way:

> The church did not really "canonize" her own canon. She officially recognized that the Scripture was canonical because it already constituted for her a test, a standard, a norm, a critique. Both the church and the Bible are different and complimen-

tary manifestations of the Word. The Bible remains the record of the church's origin, the "yardstick" of her fidelity. It is the Bible that judges the church, not the contrary. In the testimony of the Bible, the church finds the cloth of her worship, the substance of her thought, and the nerve of her action.

(Terrien 1962, 81)

The church then lives under biblical authority. The Scriptures, composed, canonized, and interpreted by the community, speak decisively to the community, whose experience again and again affirms that in these words is heard the Word of the Living God.

The church fails its heritage, however, if its submission to Scripture's word is slavish. There is a distinct liberty in the life we live under Scripture's authority. This liberty stems, on the one hand, from the fact that the Bible is so big. With so many different layers, traditions, times, and voices represented in Scripture, there is no question of simple obedience to each chapter and verse. The vast and variegated fabric of Scripture requires us instead to interpret, to locate the crucial within Scripture's witness, and having submitted ourselves to the crucial, to wrestle—in freedom, honesty, and humility—with those texts that are in apparent tension with it. This is our necessary freedom under the authority of so big a Bible.

Our liberty stems, on the other hand, from the fact that as big as the Bible is, God's living Word is bigger. We live in "a new covenant, not of letter but of spirit; for the letter kills, but the Spirit gives life. . . . and where the Spirit of the Lord is, there is freedom" (2 Cor 3:6, 17). God is free to do a new thing, and the Christ who came not to abolish the law but fulfill it, has embodied the freedom of God both to fulfill Scripture's promise and to surpass what Scripture can foresee. As John Barton says,

> The tension between the new faith and the old Scriptures therefore is . . . part of the essence of Christianity from the beginning. Christians are people who have a book, in order to be able to proclaim their freedom from it; yet the character of that freedom is deeply shaped by the book from which they have been freed, and it is the God who gave the book who also gives the freedom.
>
> (Barton 1988, 9–10)

The enormous challenge to the church is to find its submission to Scripture in ways that do not forfeit the real freedom of the Gospel, and to find its freedom under the real authority of Scripture's word.

The Functions of Authority

Perhaps we do well to understand Scripture's *authority* for the community in terms of Scripture's *functions* in the community. How do we experience Scripture authoritatively?

We do so first in the experience of Scripture's function as the church's *memory*. The Bible tells the story that tells us who we are. We are cherished people, created good in God's image to live as partners with God in creation. We are tragic people, self-absorbed and deceived, refusing freedom, forfeiting vocation, enslaved by death. We are fortunate people, recipients of GRACE, God's amazing initiative to set us free, most decisively given in the life, death and resurrection of JESUS, the Word made flesh. We are empowered people, led by the Holy Spirit to live glad and prophetic lives, bearing witness to God's peace. We are expectant people, looking in hope for the final triumph of God's purpose.

This story of creation, fall, redemption, Pentecost, and consummation is the story of who we were, who we are, who we shall be. Hearing the Scriptures restores our memory. We learn our names. We locate ourselves in the story of God, and so recover our purpose. This recovery takes place in hearing the Bible's stories as our own stories. We are ABRAHAM and SARAH, called to forsake security for an impossible promise. We are slaves oppressed by PHARAOH, we are Pharaoh oppressing slaves, we are MOSES seized by God to call Pharaoh to justice and slaves to freedom. We are ZACCHAEUS up a tree. We are Peter shattered by failure and forgiveness. We are Mary Magdalene blinded by tears, stumbling over smiling angels. We are John of Patmos hearing heaven's final laughter.

But the church's memory resides not only in the stories. We remember ourselves also in Scripture's hymns and prayers, in its oracles and pronouncements, and powerfully in its commandments, which give gracious boundaries and definition to our life together. The function of commandment as a guarantor of faithful memory is strikingly illustrated in a text addressed to the kings of Israel. The king "must not acquire many horses for himself" and "he must not acquire many wives for himself, or else his heart will turn away; also silver and gold he must not acquire in great quantity for himself" (Deut 17:16-17). These limits having been given, the text goes on:

> When he has taken the throne of his kingdom, he shall have a copy of this law written for him. . . .

It shall remain with him and he shall read in it all the days of his life, so that he may learn to fear the LORD his God. . . .   (Deut 17:18-19)

The text, knowing kings to be forgetful, requires the king to read daily the commandment that tells him who he is and who he is not. The church lives under the same danger and the same restorative instruction. In Scripture's law, as in its story, the church may find and nourish its memory.

In a related way the Bible functions as the church's fiercest *critic*. The community is always tempted to domesticate its Bible, perverting it into false comfort, reading selectively and conveniently by a dishonest assumption of ownership. The fact is that from the beginning these writings functioned confrontationally against the communities to whom they were given.

I hate, I despise your festivals,
and I take no delight in your solemn assemblies. . . .
But let justice roll down like waters,
    and righteousness like an everflowing stream.
    (Amos 5:21, 24)

Not everyone who says to me, "Lord, Lord," will enter the kingdom of heaven, but only the one who does the will of my Father in heaven.   (Matt 7:21)

It may safely be said that no church can read Scripture honestly and be comfortable with it. Nor has Scripture ever been comfortable with us, for never has the community of faith been fully faithful. As Leander Keck has said,

New Testament Christianity must not be confused with early Christianity; in fact, Christianity according to the New Testament is a fundamental critique of the early Christianity that was actually developing. Precisely the same point must be made for much of the Old Testament. Old Testament faith and religion is not the same as Israelite faith and religion, but a series of critiques of it.
    (Keck 1978, 94–95)

The adversarial relationship of the Bible to the church is a central and nonnegotiable function, for the church is both a community of sinners and the inevitable institutionalizing of the community's sins. We cannot hope to be fully faithful. Being human, we will be idolatrous, often in ways we cannot see. At the very least we can confess it, and in humility grant to the Bible its authority to question us, to accuse us and call us to repentance. Our racism, our militarism, our abuse of the poor, our violence against the earth, all our failures of faith, all our idolatries, especially the ones we commit inside the temple—God rages in Scripture against them all. No reformation of the church has ever come that did not begin with a new hearing of Scripture's sharp correction. The church has little hope for itself unless the church's book remain the church's critic.

A third experience of Scripture's authority lies in the discovery of the Bible as the church's *voice*. The church is in need not only of a saving word to hear, but of a proper word to say. Scripture offers both. Not only bearing God's word to our ears, it places our own truest words on our tongues.

We may not know our own hearts but the Scriptures do. We are mute with fears we cannot name, sorrows we cannot grasp, unarticulated sins, unutterable longings and joys. Uncannily, Scripture names them. The Bible astonishes us by its keen articulation of our hearts, and so liberates us to be truthful, and so teaches us to pray. The Psalms, called by Calvin "the anatomy of all parts of the soul," are the centerpiece of this articulation. Here we learn how to sigh, how to rage, how to ask our darkest questions of God, how to confess, how to sing, how to be silent.

To find the human voice of Scripture is, of course, to discover voices other than our own. We may not have numbered ourselves among the poor, the outcast, the ones who suffer unjustly; but Scripture supplies for them the clearest voice of all and invites the whole church to take up their voice. The Bible speaks for all who are denied a voice in the world. Some of these "little ones" are members of the household of faith, many are not; regardless, Scripture speaks for them. In this respect the Bible is far more than the church's book, "the Bible is everybody's book" (Merton 1970, 28, 39). Its agenda is not the church but the whole of creation (Brueggemann 1978, 143). The church finds its faithfulness in learning from Scripture to speak with and for all creation.

This cannot be done apart from finding also in Scripture our voice for speaking *to* the world. This is commanded: we are witnesses, we are advocates, we have news. In the words of the prophets to the nations, in the words of the apostles to the councils and the crowds, in the words of Jesus to the poor, to the powerful, to the lost, we have our mandate and our pattern for lifting a voice to the world. The Bible is far more than what the church needs to hear. It is what the church needs to say (see Craddock 1985, 26).

A fourth way of describing Scripture's authoritative function is to speak of the Bible as the church's *vision*. Our human confusion is characterized by distorted visions of our neighbors and ourselves, the creation and the Creator. Incorrigible idol-makers, we are hemmed in by false images. We may improve our speech to be "politically correct," we may adjust our outward behaviors to be circumspect and civil, but if our minds are filled with deep and ancient, distorted images, we are in Jesus' words, "like whitewashed tombs" (Matt 23:27).

Here is the taproot of all prejudice, anxiety, and distorted desire: we see neighbor, world, ourselves, and God in false images. "But if your eye is unhealthy, your whole body will be full of darkness" (Matt 6:23).

Scripture's gift is to offer a world of alternative images. The Bible gleams with new pictures of God and humankind. To stand together before these pictures, to gaze on them steadily, to let them recast our speech and our imaginations is to be in time reformed. No transformation of human consciousness occurs apart from replacing old mental pictures with new ones. Immersion into Scripture's world may grant such a transformation, for "the Bible is a lens through which all of life is to be discerned" (Brueggemann 1978, 154).

Through the lens of Scripture we come to see ourselves no longer as owners, competitors, animals, or angels, but as fortunate guests, forgiven transgressors, trusted partners in a sacred vocation. We come to see other persons no longer as the enemy, the problem, or the object, but as neighbors and kin, honored embodiments of the actual Christ. We come to see the future not as fate, but as a new city, a great feast, the triumph of a great love. And though always through a glass darkly, we see more and more of God: true father, mother, lover, friend, servant, host, enthroned in the heavens, hung from a cross, heartbreaking splendor, ineffable light.

With this slow dawning of new vision comes light enough to walk by. Scripture becomes a real source for daily discernment, reliable guidance in the habits and choices that lead to life. The Gospels of Matthew and Luke relate a powerful paradigm for the church as described in the experience of Jesus. In the wilderness tempted by the devil, who sets before him false images and idolatrous choices, Jesus locates his alternative way again and again in quotations from Scripture. By this light he sees his way.

Your word is a lamp to my feet
and a light to my path.   (Ps 119:105)
   . . . in your light we see light.   (Ps 36:9)

We may speak of a final function of Scripture's experienced authority in the church: the Bible as *communion*. We have said unequivocally that the Bible is not God, nor does it merit our worship. It is a book, and the book itself may not rightly be called holy. But the church has had good reason to call these writings Holy Scripture, for in reading and reflecting on Scripture's word, the church has found itself again and again encountered by the Holy One. Not by any abstract doctrine of inspiration, but by the testimony of long experience, the church gives thankful witness that the Bible is a meeting place. Always on its own terms, not ours, never automatically or predictably, still the Bible bears us in time to a presence. When the community of faith brings itself to Scripture in humility and constancy, when this open book is met with open minds and hearts, the Spirit often speaks, and we are on holy ground.

In this respect we have warrant to speak of the sacrament of Scripture as a mediating instrument of the presence of God (see Wainwright 1980, 178–81). Like the sacrament of the table, which likewise brings us to our memory, our critic, our voice, our vision, and our communion, the sacrament of the word may nourish us and transform us. It is an outward and visible sign of an inner, invisible grace. The church reads the Scriptures with reverence ("This is the word of the Lord") and with gratitude ("Thanks be to God"), for the Bible is an instrument of the real presence of God among us.

The Bible in the Church's Worship

Because the Bible serves these authoritative functions in the church, the book is opened, read, and proclaimed whenever the community gathers for worship. Scripture itself provides the forms of our worship, the pattern of our prayers, the substance of our preaching, and much of the very language we employ in the worship of God. Being in particular the church's memory and the church's voice, the Bible is the church's book of worship.

It should go without saying that Christian worship will include times for Scripture, without added commentary, to be publicly read. The liturgical churches follow ancient tradition in the reading of an OT lesson, an Epistle lesson, a Gospel lesson, and a Psalm in each service of worship. Some churches, however, read Scripture hardly at all in their worship, with tragic results. It is common in these churches to attend worship and hear nothing of Scripture itself, apart from a few verses read by a preacher as introduction to the sermon. The Bible itself urges: "Give attention to the public reading of Scripture" (1 Tim 4:13).

The reason for separate, sustained reading of the Bible in worship is that Scripture makes its own witness, "independent of current interpretation and application" (Wainwright 1980, 168). These are the ancient words heard by the ancient communities of faith and by every generation that has followed them. They are the words that have preceded us, waiting all these centuries to speak to our new situation. To read them in the hearing of the congregation, entirely apart from the sermon, is to recognize that Scripture stands apart from its interpretation. It is to grant space for the Bible to function as the critic of the church, the judgment of God on our worship and practice. Such reading also permits the Spirit to make its own witness within the hearts of the hearers, who may understand and apply the word in ways the preacher cannot begin to know.

Because of the weight of Scripture's word, careful attention will be given to the manner of its public reading. The readings should most often be done by laypersons, since the Bible is not the clergy's but the community's book. It should be read clearly, simply and without haste. Dietrich Bonhoeffer suggested that "the situation of the reader of Scripture is probably closest to that in which I read to others a letter from a friend," showing an attentive regard for the friend's word and conveying it as the friend's word, not one's own. In any way to call attention to the self instead of the word "is to commit the worst of sins in presenting the Scriptures" (Bonhoeffer, 1954, 56).

Then comes the word-event called preaching. That the sermon should rise from and be formed by biblical texts is not accepted by all who preach. Fortunately for the church, however, biblical preaching has been widely renewed in recent years. The disciplines of biblical scholarship and homiletics have been engaged in the most fruitful new conversations and mergers. New resources are abundant to assist pastors in the preaching of sermons that are faithful to the forms and intentions of biblical texts.

Because Scripture is the church's memory, its critic, its voice, its vision, and an instrument of its communion with God, the sermon should impart Scripture's word. The people did not come to church to learn what was on the minister's mind, they came

hoping for some glimpse, however brief, of God. They are hungry for a Word. Preachers desiring to be "relevant" may be tempted week by week to shuttle from one psychological or political issue to another, hoping at best to tie in a text at the end. They may manage to be interesting and even helpful, but they will not have preached, nor will they have been relevant. Attending to Scripture reveals what is relevant to God. Biblical preaching will invariably speak to the issues of the day. But only by beginning with Scripture do we discern which questions are God's questions. Only by proceeding from Scripture do the people discern their relevant agenda from the prior word that has preceded them, foreseen them and called them to a purpose.

Which texts shall be preached? Some preachers are fastened to a narrow strip of Scripture. Like MARCION, their canon includes little but PAUL. Or perhaps they have settled into the Synoptics. Or perhaps again, they choose texts from all over the canon, but only those texts that can serve—or be forced to serve—two or three endlessly recapitulated themes. Though it is natural enough for preachers to preach most what they know best, it is crucial that they learn the discipline of preaching from the full range of Scripture's witness—texts and themes from all parts of the canon. Otherwise preaching is not biblical. It is precisely the nature of Scripture to be a vast and variegated witness, bearing in its numerous perspectives and even in its tensions with itself, the many colors of real life, the many names and faces of God.

Preaching from the lectionary can assist in this discipline. The ancient practice of preaching from assigned texts, which over the course of the church year celebrates the many themes of Scripture's whole story, has been newly embraced by a great many congregations and preachers. Among other gifts, the lectionary can add a keen sense of the vital relationship between the Bible and the church, as an ever-growing portion of the church stands before the same texts on the same day. Not all preachers will use the lectionary. A full and faithful proclamation of Scripture's witness can be made without it. Many wonderful texts can only be preached without it. Preachers who do not use the lectionary should only be sure that their preaching includes texts that they themselves would not naturally choose, but that are in some sense imposed upon them.

As a servant of the word, the preacher will give faithful, scrupulous attention to the study of the texts to be preached. This is work, and it is indispensable work. The discipline of study will include coming to terms with the historical setting of the text, the function of its literary form, the meaning of its words, its intended work among those to whom it is addressed. Without any display of this scaffolding of scholarship, the sermon should take its purpose and its shape from these real structures and movements within the text. Biblical preaching does not consist of repeated quotations from the Bible, but of faithfully pursuing the intentions of biblical texts.

It should always be clear that proclamation is not so much the function of the preacher as of the community. The whole church shares in the partnership of preaching, and a congregation can be invited in many ways to enter into the preacher's conversations with a text, to share in the ownership of the sermon. It should certainly be clear that the church's preaching is in complete continuity with what the Bible itself has been from the beginning. The Bible began as preaching. Most of its units are thoroughly oral in form, shaped by preaching and intended to be heard in worshiping communities. Furthermore, the texts not only bear witness to received tradition; they proceed, as preaching does, to interpret and apply the tradition. In its preaching the church continues what Scripture has always been and what it will always invite: a witness to the gracious initiatives of God and a struggle to interpret and apply this news for living in the world, an enfleshment of the word again and again.

The Bible in the Church's Study

It is not enough for the church to hear and proclaim Scripture in its weekly worship. Because it is the community's book, the community seeks regular times and ways to open it together, to question and be questioned by it, to exchange insights, to grapple with its implications for ordinary life.

We are speaking of what is often called the church's ministry of Christian education. Like preaching, this enterprise has often missed its mark, drifting into pedantic, moralistic little Sunday School lessons, closer to indoctrination than to communal conversation and study. But also like preaching, the field of Christian education has experienced a recent renewal in many sectors of the church. The communal study of Scripture is a vital source of the church's life and health. Recent research has found, in fact, that "effective Christian education is the most powerful single influence congregations have on maturity of faith" (Roehlkepartain 1990, 496).

Scripture insists on this enterprise. The great commandment to "love the LORD your God with all your heart, and with all your soul, and with all your might" (Deut 6:5) is instantly followed by a homely call to communal reflection and study:

> Keep these words that I am commanding you today in your heart. Recite them to your children and talk about them. . . .   (Deut 6:6-7)

The purpose is transformation. By keeping Scripture's word in the community's conversation, by inquiring of it, recalling it to each other, pressing it against the ongoing issues of the day and the ordinary circumstances of our lives, we bind it to our heads and hands and write it on our gates. We are altered. Annie Dillard has written of her experience as a child at church camp and Sunday school.

> I had miles of Bible in memory: some perforce, but most by hap, like the words to songs. There was no corner of my brain where you could not find, among the files of clothing labels and heaps of rocks and minerals, among the swarms of protozoans and shelves of novels, whole tapes and snarls and reels of Bible. . . .
>
> Why did they spread this scandalous document before our eyes? If they had read it, I thought, they would have hid it. They did not recognize the lively danger that we would, through repeated exposure catch a dose of its virulent opposition to their world.   (Corn 1990, 28, 35)

Scripture can be privately read and studied, of course; but there is particular and irreplaceable value in communal study. Rising out of communities, the Bible remains a community book. Its implications are best discerned among and between believers and seekers. In communal study we can be delivered from some of our personal predispositions to a text, corrected or confirmed in our understandings and regularly surprised by meanings and applications we could never have guessed. The Spirit interprets Scripture to us through the word and experience of the sister and brother.

> The Bible speaks to us today, as in the past, not by means of a miracle, not by means of audiovisual magic, but by communal effort.
>
>   (Visotzky 1991, 10)

Communal study will therefore maintain an openness to all questions and perspectives. Naturally the community arrives at a certain consensus of meanings that holds idiosyncratic or exotic readings in check. But no question is disallowed. Every perspective is heard and weighed. The church has much to learn from the ancient rabbis, who gloried in multiple readings of texts and rejoiced in the Torah as a gem with at least seventy facets in every word (Visotzky 1991, 228). The Bible gives multiple perspectives on itself. It asks a thousand questions of itself. So the community gathers to hear Scripture afresh by hearing each other's questions, insights, hunches, and stories. In this pooling of light the church finds more of its way.

The Bible in Devotion

The community imparts the word to the individual, but in doing so does not relieve the individual of the necessity of a personal confrontation with the word. In fact, the community relies on each member to attend privately to Scripture. This is so because each member of the community is a priest, personally accountable to the word and personally accountable to exert the word's witness in the community. Each member reads the Bible for the sake of her own soul and for the sake of the church.

For this reason we encourage one another to the daily practice of reading and meditating on Scripture. This need not be considered a legalism. It is a transforming discipline, a sacred duty and privilege. It is not the quest for a certain daily devotional feeling. On many days it yields little feeling at all. It is simply a commitment over time to saturate the mind with Scripture's word, to let it penetrate the heart and have new openings to extend itself in one's thought and behavior.

Among our many aversions to this discipline is that the Bible's words may already be familiar to us. Why devote time to reading words that we know? This is, of course, an illusion. It is precisely our familiarity with Scripture's words that most often keeps us from knowing them. "Let us not be too sure we know the Bible just because we have learned not to be astonished by it" (Merton 1970, 27). There are ways to reopen our minds to amazement, there are new insights and fresh applications to be discovered.

[The Bible] is still at the very beginning of its career, the full meaning of its content having hardly touched the thresholds of our minds; like an ocean at the bottom of which countless pearls lie, waiting to be discovered, its spirit is still to be unfolded. Though its words seem plain and its idiom translu-

cent, unnoticed meanings, undreamed-of intimations break forth constantly. . . . Today it is as if . . . we had not even begun to read it.

(Heschel 1955, 242)

The Bible does not yield its secrets to casual, perfunctory reading. Layers of meaning will also be lost to those who read only with the intellect. The place of critical thinking in the study of Scripture, as we have seen, is crucial. But for Scripture to speak in its fullness, another kind of reading is required. This is meditative reading, reading that takes place in the shape of prayer.

Jewish piety has a long tradition of meditation upon the words of Scripture, as do the Roman Catholic and Orthodox Christian communities. More recently, Dietrich Bonhoeffer did Protestants a great service by calling them, in the tradition of Luther, to the practice of such meditation. He urged not only an ongoing regimen of daily reading from the Bible, but also the choice of a shorter text for use in meditation throughout each week. The text is read again and again. It is surrounded with reflective silence and pondered prayerfully. The thoughts it generates are written down, the prayers it invokes are prayed; the word is kept.

Ponder this word in your heart as Mary did. That is all. That is meditation . . . ponder this word in your heart at length until it is entirely within you and has taken possession of you.

(Bonhoeffer 1986, 32–33)

Whether or not Bonhoeffer's particular method is employed, the regular practice of some form of personal reflection on biblical texts is worthy and is commended by Scripture itself (e.g., Ps 1:2; 119). Much of the Bible is meant to be prayed or to be read on the verge of prayer. Those who permit Scripture's word to bear them into prayer and meditation will have joined in a vital portion of the conversation that Scripture means to have with us.

On this subject a particular word belongs to pastors and others whose profession entails much public use of Scripture. We of all persons are subject to a disinclination to hear Scripture for ourselves. Having labored to hear it and speak it for others, we grow weary and set it aside. Having handled it too often for our professional purposes, we are embarrassed to face it and hear it tell us who we are. As George McDonald said, "Nothing is so deadening to the divine as an habitual dealing with the outsides of holy things" (Doberstein 1986, 248).

We are not only among those who are most at risk, we are also among those whose need to be corrected and formed by Scripture is most urgent. In what profession does ego insinuate itself more insidiously than in ours? And who holds more power to lead the people into making idols than Aaron the priest? Our profession is dangerous, both to ourselves and to the church. Thomas Merton once suggested that the phenomenon of "unconscious revolt against the Bible" on the part of pastors and priests probably accounts for "much that is rigid, callous, inhuman, fanatical in the religious sphere" (Merton 1970, 17–18).

So the pastor, not looking for a sermon, not imagining how a text might be used in the work, will sit before the Scriptures to hear them honestly, correctively, intimately. This appointment may grant many unforeseen gifts to a minister, not the least of which may be a new measure of freedom from the tyrannical grip of the church itself. We who interpret the Bible most often must permit it to interpret us to ourselves and lead us to the offering of our own most secret and saving prayers.

The Bible in the Formation of the Church's Life

We have spoken of Scripture's capacity to give shape to the church. As in the first creation story of Genesis, where the universe is created by a Word, so this same Word—not equivalent to Scripture but borne by it to open hearts—continues to create the church and give it new shape for its vocation in the world.

Clearly the Bible's capacity to give better shape to human lives and institutions is in no way automatic. It is entirely possible in reading the Bible to feel confirmed in one's own preferences and bigotries. Some of the meanest people on earth read the Bible every day and find themselves justified. Most of the cruellest movements in the history of the Western world have taken Scripture as their warrant. Dedicated servants of the Nazi regime, assisting cheerfully in the death camps, could open their Bibles daily and see no contradiction. Baptist deacons in the American South could pose for a photograph by the body of a lynched man, holding Bibles in their hands. Endless is the church's capacity to neglect, pervert, and demonize the Scriptures.

The Bible may be very much like a mirror: self-righteousness looking in will see self-righteousness looking back. In this respect Scripture can be a peculiar instrument of God's wrath upon its readers. In Karl Barth's words,

> The Bible gives to every man and to every era such answers to their questions as they deserve. We shall always find in it as much as we seek and no more. (Barth 1956, 32)

Nothing we can say about the Bible's capacity to transform us can overlook the equal capacities of our own intransigence.

Throughout the church's history, however, where individuals and communities have stood before the Scriptures in humility and openness, an answering power has given a better shape to character, behavior, and life. Scripture's own pattern in speaking of itself says very little of what it *is*, but a great deal about what it *does*. It is not so much a book with a status as with a function. More than repositories of truth, these texts have intensions. "My word . . . will *accomplish* that which I purpose" (Isa 55:11).

There is a kind of organic force ascribed to Scripture, the power of planted seed to stir and grow to a conquering profusion. "Welcome with meekness the implanted word that has the power to save your souls" (Jas 1:21). It is understood as "useful for teaching, for reproof, for correction, and for training in righteousness" (2 Tim 3:16)—*useful*, a "low-key word, strikingly contrasted with what has been made of this text in later times" (Barr 1980, 119), pointing us again to the pragmatic servant-function of Scripture to do real work among us.

We do not learn Scripture for the sake of learning Scripture. The church reads, proclaims, studies, and meditates on Scripture so that these words may do the long and steady work of forming us into communities that embody more of the Christ in the world. Stanley Hauerwas has spoken of the church as a "Story-Formed Community" (Hauerwas 1981, 9–35). Learning Scripture's story, submitting to its pressure and promise, we are formed by it. We are sculpted to the cruciform. Our vocation of character, our ethics and relationships, our evangelical and prophetic mission to the world take their shape as we give ourselves into the hands of Scripture. Witness the definitive shaping force exerted by the biblical story of the exodus upon the African-American churches in the 1960s. Similarly, churches in Latin America, Africa, and Eastern Europe have given striking recent examples of how cruciform communities, shaped by biblical memory and hope, may bear revolutionary witness to their time. Scripture takes hold of the church and shapes it toward Christ that the church may take hold of and give shape to the world.

For the Bible to serve this function we must, above all, take seriously it's strangeness, its tensions with us. Many of its precepts are frankly alien to our sensibilities. Many of its voices and figures—supremely Jesus himself—are baffling to us. Our inclination to soften these tensions, to flatten these bewildering and often offensive voices to a more manageable, falsely coherent system of faith, must at all costs by rejected. Scripture cannot form the church unless the hard words of Scripture are permitted to press against the church. Confronted by difficult words on such subjects as sexuality, marriage and divorce, war and peace, rich and poor, church and state, believers are free under the Holy Spirit to interpret these texts, to struggle with them and argue with them, to note where they may be culturally tinged, to place them ultimately under the higher lordship of Christ. We are not free to dismiss them. The tensions of Scripture within itself and with us must be felt, honored, and permitted to press against the church. By this submission the community and its members are formed for their vocation.

Encountered and amazed by the living God, the ancient church wrote words bearing witness to what it had seen and heard, expressing in many voices and forms the implications of its news. When today's church reads the ancient church's book as our book and as a book of God—granting it diligent study, reverent reflection, and obedient service—the Encounter recurs. Again and again the church is met and amazed.

For Further Study

In the *Mercer Dictionary of the Bible*: BIBLE; BIBLE AND LIBERATION MOVEMENTS; BIBLE AND WESTERN LITERATURE; CANON; CHURCH; CHURCH AND LAW; HERMENEUTICS; INTERPRETATION, HISTORY OF; LITERATURE, BIBLE AS. In other sources: See works cited, below.

Works Cited

Barr, James. 1980. *The Scope and Authority of the Bible.*

Barth, Karl. 1956. *The Word of God and the Word of Man.*

Barton, John. 1988. *People of the Book? The Authority of the Bible in Christianity.*

Bonhoeffer, Dietrich. 1954. *Life Together.* 1986. *Meditating on the Word.*

Brueggemann, Walter. 1978. *The Bible Makes Sense.*

Corn, Alfred, ed. 1990. *Incarnation: Contemporary Writers on the New Testament.*

Craddock, Fred B. 1985. *Preaching.*

Doberstein, John W., ed. 1986. *Minister's Prayer Book.*

Hauerwas, Stanley. 1981. *A Community of Character.*

Heschel, Abraham Joshua. 1955. *God in Search of Man.* 1972. *The Insecurity of Freedom.*

Keck, Leander E. 1978. *The Bible in the Pulpit.*

Merton, Thomas. 1970. *Opening the Bible.*

Roehlkepartain, Eugene C. 1990. "What Makes Faith Mature?" *The Christian Century* (9 May): 496–99.

Terrien, Samuel. 1962. *The Bible and the Church.*

Visotzky, Burton L. *Reading the Book: Making the Bible a Timeless Text.*

Genesis

Bruce T. Dahlberg

Introduction

Falling topically into two main parts of unequal length, the Book of Genesis begins with an account of some of Israel's central beliefs about God's creation of the heavens and the earth and about the earliest history of the human race (1:1–11:32). It then relates in its longer part—beginning with traditions about Abraham and Sarah—the legendary deeds of those patriarchs and matriarchs of Israel who lived in CANAAN until, with Joseph and his generation, they moved to Egypt (12:1–50:26).

Israel's origins, moreover, are presented in Genesis not only as directed toward Israel's destiny in history, but as intimately connected with and auspicious for world history generally (e.g., Gen 12:1-3 passim), while Israel's life, anticipated and symbolized by the primordial SABBATH, is seen to derive from the very order of creation itself (2:2-3).

Genesis tells an epic story, anonymously composed from a great variety of oral and written traditions from the ancient Near East and especially from ancient Israel and earliest JUDAISM.

Genesis in the Old Testament

Jewish and Christian tradition refer to the first five books of the OT, including Genesis, as the Law—a somewhat misleading translation of the Hebrew *tôrâ* (TORAH). Torah is rendered in English better by "teaching," "instruction," or, in some cases, "revelation," although "law" in the narrower sense of ritual or civil regulation describes significant parts of the Torah.

In its written form the Torah is also referred to as the Pentateuch (Gk., "five scrolls") and traditionally, although unhistorically, as the Five Books of Moses.

Because some important threads of the story line begun in Genesis seem not to reach their conclusion until the Book of Joshua (see, e.g., commentary at Gen 12:4-9), many modern biblical interpreters refer to the first six OT books (Genesis–Joshua) together as a broad literary unit called the Hexateuch (Gk., "six scrolls").

Genesis in Early Jewish and Christian Religious Texts

Besides the relatively well-known citations and interpretations of Genesis found in the NT, the Christian patristic writers, the Talmud, and other rabbinical literature, there are other instances of Genesis receiving attention. For example, revisionist expansions and retellings of certain portions of Genesis appear among Jewish and Christian religious writings of the last two centuries B.C.E. and the first two or three centuries C.E. at Qumran, NAG HAMMADI and elsewhere.

Among surviving examples of such texts are the Jewish *Book of Jubilees* (treated as canonical in some OT mss.; see Wintermute 1985; Trafton 1990b) and *The Genesis Apocryphon* (from Qumran; cf. Vermes 1987, 252–59; Trafton 1990a). There are also the Gnostic-Christian *Hypostasis of the Archons* (Layton 1988; Bullard 1990a) and *On the Origin of the World* (Bethge et al. 1988; Bullard 1990b). Of inherent interest in themselves and for the history of Judaism and Christianity, these apocryphal works exhibit the variety and fluidity that obtained in the interpretation of Genesis in the early period of synagogue and church.

Title

The Hebrew title of Genesis is the book's first word, *berêsît*, usually translated as *in the beginning* (Gen 1:1). To name a writing by its opening word or phrase was common in ancient times and is often the practice today with hymns and other poetry.

The English title, Genesis, reproduces the title of the ancient Greek translation of the book. The word has several related meanings, including "origin," "beginning," "generation," and "descendant." The third-century B.C.E. Greek version of the Hebrew Scriptures, the SEPTUAGINT (LXX), chose "Genesis" as the title apparently because in the LXX the word introduces major sections of the book (e.g., 2:4a; 5:1; 10:1; etc.).

Authorship and Date

The ancient but mistaken ascription of the Pentateuch to the authorship of Moses may have been due to a misunderstanding of Deut 31:9 ("Then Moses wrote down this law [*torah*]") as a reference to everything in the five books now called the Torah.

It has long been recognized that Genesis, along with the rest of the Pentateuch, cannot have been written by one author but is, instead, the end result of a process of oral and literary development over at least half a millennium, in which many individuals and groups had a share.

The earliest traditions. Although in its present form Genesis is one continuous narrative, examination of the successive narrative episodes gives clear indication of their having been drawn from quite diverse traditions, many of them originally independent of each other and belonging to diverse literary genres—legends, songs, proverbial sayings, blessings, curses, folk genealogies, ritual laws, etiologies of sacred sites and customs, and other types of shorter or longer literary units. Such units may have been written or originally oral (see Gunkel 1901; Coates 1983; Knight 1990b).

Further, some of the component traditions clearly are drawn from the wider Near Eastern society and culture older than or contemporary with Israel, reworked in Genesis to express Israel's own distinctive beliefs (see, e.g., commentary at Gen 1:1–2:4 and 6:5–8:22).

Narrative compilations prior to Genesis. Before Genesis—and the rest of the Pentateuch—would receive its final form there was an intermediate stage of development in which these diverse and variegated traditions were placed in ordered arrangement in the form of narrative histories. Those predecessor recensions or editions were reworked and incorporated into the final redaction (edition) that is the present Book of Genesis.

Arising from separate geographical regions and time periods, these predecessor documents (or relatively fixed oral cycles of stories) were conflated. Earlier traditions were reworked and expanded by later developments, eventually constituting the present work.

The particular literary and theological features that distinguish each collection or "source" from the others have not been obliterated in the final text. They were editorially harmonized with each other only to a limited extent. As a consequence, although now interwoven, their presence can still be traced as narrative strands or threads distinguishable not only in Genesis but throughout much of the Pentateuch.

The Yahwist source or "J". The earliest such narrative strand begins with the Eden story (Gen 2–3) and as it now proceeds through Genesis it is interwoven with later strands. In Genesis this anonymous source tends to favor the name "Yahweh," which is Israel's particular name for the covenant God (see Humphreys 1990). The name is rendered in most modern English translations as "the LORD." Nineteenth-century German scholars named the source "J" for "Jahveh," the German spelling of "Yahweh." The anonymous final author of this source is thus conventionally referred to now as the YAHWIST. One identifying mark of this strand or source is its typically anthropomorphic representations of the deity, who walks in the garden (Gen 3:8) or dines at table with Abraham (18:1-8).

The J material is supposed by many scholars to be the earliest strand, composed in JUDAH soon after the secession of ISRAEL (i.e., the Northern Kingdom) in the late tenth century B.C.E. (see 1 Kgs 12 and commentary at Gen 13:1-18). The question of date remains open, however. More recently a date as late as the exilic period (sixth-century B.C.E.) has been proposed (Van Seters 1992).

The Elohist source or "E". Interspersed in the text along with J is a second strand of tradition which interpreters have designated as the E or ELOHIST source (derived from Heb. *elohim*, "God," the name this strand favors for the deity). Typically E represents God "calling from heaven" (21:17; 22:11) or speaking through dreams (15:12-16; 20:1-18). The "source" is believed to have been composed in the Northern Kingdom some time after the split with Judah. Where J and E are not clearly distinguishable from each other, as is frequently the case, reference is made simply to JE. It is possible that E is the earlier source of the two, from which J has extracted and reworked certain portions.

The Priestly source or "P". The third and latest major narrative strand is thought to be the end product of the work of a particular community or "school" of tradition. Modern scholarship calls it the "Priestly" source (P) because of its evident interest in the divine origin and validation of particular Jewish religious observances and rituals. Attention to the Sabbath (Gen 2:2-3), dietary laws (9:3-4), and the rite of CIRCUMCISION (17:9-14) are particular examples in Genesis.

Like the E source, P also favors the generic name "God" (Heb. *elohim*) for the deity; both sources apparently hold that the name Yahweh was not known until revealed to Moses; cf. Exod 3:15 (E), and 6:2-3 (P). On the other hand, the J narrator seems to believe God was known as Yahweh from earliest times (Gen 4:26).

The P source appears not only to have been composed after J but, as pointed out in the commentary, certain passages in P seem to be directed at J as a kind of commentary. Although P preserves some very old traditions, it reflects religious rituals and beliefs associated elsewhere in the OT especially with the Jewish late-exilic or early postexilic community in Babylon (late sixth or early fifth centuries B.C.E.), so its final written form is most plausibly dated within that period.

The writers or compilers of P also are thought to have been the final redactors who brought to completion the Book of Genesis, as well as the rest of the Pentateuch. At the latest, this work must have been accomplished by the time EZRA brought the "law of Moses"—believed to be the Pentateuch—from Babylon to Jerusalem (see Ezra 7:1-10; Neh 8:1-12).

The "Documentary Hypothesis." The foregoing treatment is a condensed account of what has been known to several generations of biblical scholars as the "Documentary Hypothesis." Although the work of many scholars contributed to the formulation of the hypothesis, it was most notably set forth by the nineteenth-century German scholar, Julius Wellhausen (Wellhausen 1885; see Gregory 1990 and Gottwald 1985, 150–78, 325–34, 469–82).

While the Documentary Hypothesis has undergone considerable criticism and rethinking over the last century, it remains a watershed in the history of Genesis and Pentateuchal studies, and is still very much a critical point of departure for scholarship in that field. The commentary that follows will indicate sources when appropriate by including a J, E, or P after citations.

A diachronic reading of Genesis. To recognize the process of compilation and editing that led to the present narrative work of Genesis is to realize that it, with the rest of the Pentateuch, has preserved side by side different understandings in tension with each other. The tensions exist between earlier and later generations, and between different regional groups concerning particular matters of public issue in Israel's life and faith.

On these terms Genesis can be read with attention to—and appreciation for—its chronologically different layers of tradition and their respective differing empha-

ses as these developed across many generations. Reading Genesis in light of different eras is what scholars identify as a diachronic (i.e., "through time") approach to the text. It is in many ways comparable to reading the NT in terms of the gospel "according to Matthew" or "according to Luke," and so on. Although in Genesis the demarcation between traditional sources is less neat, it is no less legitimate, and illuminating, to speak of Israel's faith "according to J" or "according to P."

A diachronic reading does not at all require drawing invidious comparisons between earlier and later traditions in either chronological direction—that is, from either a Hegelian notion of historical progress from "lower" to "higher" ideas, or (the reverse notion) a romantic idealization of an earlier period's understanding over one that develops later (cf. Rosenberg and Bloom 1990, 9–55). In this respect the method itself is value neutral. Von Rad suggests that:

> source analysis is not the final conclusion of wisdom; but once we know about the differences in the sources we can no longer have the whole without knowing the exact nature of its parts (1972, 11).

A synchronic reading of Genesis. Genesis as a whole also has been given the form of a single epic story. Even though the separate sources behind the present narrative are still delineable, they have been shaped in certain ways and brought together by a final redactor into a mostly-unified literary and theological work possessed of its own interior logic. Genesis can, therefore, also be read synchronically (i.e., as a total statement and a finished work of art, struck off as it were at one telling by a single anonymous narrator). Robert Alter gives voice to such a reading:

> The very mode of narration conveys a double sense of a total coherent knowledge available to God (and by implication, to His surrogate, the anonymous authoritative narrator) and the necessary incompleteness of human knowledge, for which much about character, motive, and moral status will remain shrouded in ambiguity (1981, 184).

Narrative Structure and Major Themes

Episodic arrangement of the narrative. The divisions adopted here for an outline of Genesis are intentionally broad, and overlap to some extent.

The topical and typological variety and complexity of the many traditions, and the way they have been brought together in the book, make tentative and somewhat arbitrary every scheme for outlining Genesis, whether based on subject matter, story-cycles clustering around a particular character, or virtually any other criterion.

The difficulty arises due largely to the fact that in Genesis the different traditions often stand in stark juxtaposition to each other with only the slightest transitional statement or word (if any) to indicate their logical connection.

The logical literary unit often appears freestanding in relation to what precedes or follows—it is not anticipated by anything said beforehand nor is it alluded to in the narrative afterward. The narratives of CAIN AND ABEL (Gen 4:1-16), the binding of ISAAC (22:1-19), JUDAH and TAMAR (38:1-30) are examples of such episodic arrangement.

Israel's destiny in human history. The Book of Genesis falls into two distinct parts that stand in dramatic tension with each other. The stories of the patriarchs and matriarchs (chaps. 12–50), beginning with Abraham's obedience to the divine command to migrate to Canaan (12:1-3), reverse the pattern of recurrent usurpation and violation, alienation, expulsion and scattering abroad—away from God's presence and from each other—that is humanity's typical behavior and experience as described in chaps. 1–11 (see, e.g., 3:1-24; 4:1-16; 6:1-7; 9:20-27; 11:1-9).

God's ELECTION of the patriarchs, and thus of Israel, to be the object of divine promise in history is at the same time represented as restorative for the whole troubled human race: *I will bless you, and make your name great . . . and in you all the families of the earth shall be blessed* (Gen 12:2-3; cf. 18:18; 22:18; 26:3-5; 28:14). The ancestral history is thus understood to have particular meaning not only to Israel, but through Israel for all humanity.

The genealogical framework. The final redactors of the Genesis sources and their diverse traditions have integrated the whole by superimposing a framework of folk genealogies, tables of nations, king lists and the like (principally Gen 5:1-31; 10:1-32; 11:10-32; 25:12-18; 36:1-43). Each such list marks a transition in subject matter at that point in the narrative, from one generation's adventures and deeds to those of another.

A great number of the personal NAMES in these lists are most likely eponymous (i.e., names of peoples, nations, cities, clans or families personified as individuals [see Redditt 1990]). On the related and problematic matter of the artificial or symbolic chronologies cited within Genesis (5:1-32; 15:13, etc.) see Barrois 1952, 142–45 and Christensen 1990, 147–48.

Life under covenant. The most comprehensive term used in Genesis to express Israel's formal understanding of the divine-human relation is COVENANT. The primeval history (Gen 1–11) represents God as entering into covenant with NOAH and his descendants—that is, with all humankind (9:1-17 [P]).

The ancestral history (chaps. 12–50) twice represents God as entering into covenant with Abraham and his descendants (15:17-21 [E somewhat reworked by J] and 17:1-27 [P]).

The analogy or model for the theological concept of a divine-human covenant is the social institution of covenant-making between human parties, widely attested in the ancient Near East, including examples in Genesis (cf. 25:31-32; 26:26-33; 31:43-54).

Covenants are "a variety of solemn, binding obligations or agreements involving two or more parties in a relationship" (Hayes 1990). A covenant relationship—even more than a pact or treaty—is intentional and existential, based on an explicitly declared promises and on the good faith of the parties to it. It is only secondarily a legal arrangement. Primarily covenant is a moral commitment arising out of an occasion of encounter or resolution of conflict. It is well suited, therefore, to express Israel's belief that its God acts in history and can be encountered there.

Promise and judgment. Together, the stories in Genesis present the history of Israel and the human race as a mixed experience of judgment and grace. There is tension between the divine promises to Israel and their postponed fulfillment. Possession of the land of Canaan, promised to Abraham and his descendants (Gen 13:14-17 passim), is delayed by the sojourn in Egypt and the wilderness experience (15:13-16). The promised posterity that Israel will become a great nation is thrown into doubt by the rivalry between Jacob and Esau (27:41-45; chaps. 32–33) and by the strife between Joseph and his brothers (chaps. 37–50).

Blessing and curse. An analogous structure underlies the primeval history of humankind in chaps. 1–11. The goodness of creation, epitomized by the divine image in humankind (1:27, 31) appears compromised by a perplexing human distrust of God (3:1-7), and acts of pride and self-will (4:1-16 passim). Distrust and pride bring upon human history a curse that overshadows the intended blessing (1:28; 3:14-19; 5:29). The blessing and curse dialectic also runs through the ancestral history (12:3; 27:29).

Reversal of the expected. Paradoxically, however, events in Genesis take on the character of epiphanies in which divine purposes are seen as being accomplished in spite of the intentions and expectations of the human actors. A motif typical of the J source, for example, is the recurrent override or reversal, from one generation to the next, of the right of primogeniture—in antiquity, the traditional right of the first-born son to inherit the father's estate.

Contrary to such expectation, the patriarchal inheritance—essentially, God's promise of the land and a famous posterity—passes from Abraham to the younger son Isaac instead of the first-born Ishmael 17:20-21); from Isaac to Jacob instead of the elder Esau (27:36); from Jacob to Joseph's younger son Ephraim instead of the older brother, Manasseh (48:17-20).

In another way the story of Joseph, which concludes Genesis, testifies explicitly to "reversal of the expected" as the mode of divine action in history: "You meant evil against me, but God meant it for good . . . that many people should be kept alive, as they are today" (50:20 RSV).

The deliverance *from* Egypt, the central theme of the Book of Exodus, is preceded by this concluding tale in Genesis of deliverance *in* Egypt. The Joseph story itself would appear to have been composed intentionally to instil such "hope of reversal" in its initial readers, who in all likelihood were Jews exiled from their land into Babylonia in the sixth century B.C.E.

For Further Study

In the *Mercer Dictionary of the Bible*: ANTHROPOMORPHISM; BABEL, TOWER OF; CREATION; ELOHIST; ETIOLOGY; FLOOD; GENESIS, BOOK OF; HERMENEUTICS; PATRIARCHS; PRIESTLY WRITERS; SOURCES OF THE PENTATEUCH; YAHWIST. In other sources: R. Alter, *The Art of Biblical Narrative*; D. Rosenberg and H. Bloom, *The Book of J*; U. Cassuto, *A Commentary on the Book of Genesis*; G. W. Coats, *Genesis: With an Introduction to Narrative Literature*; E. Fox, "Can Genesis Be Read as a Book?" *Semeia* 46:31–40; H. Gunkel, *The Legends of Genesis*; R. S. Hendel, *The Epic of the Patriarch: The Jacob Cycle and the Narrative Traditions of Canaan and Israel*; D. A. Knight, ed., *Julius Wellhausen and His "Prolegomena to the History of Israel,"* *Semeia* 25; J. S. Kselman, "The Book of Genesis: A Decade of Scholarly Research," *Int* 45:380–92; S. Niditch, *Chaos to Cosmos*; G. von Rad, *Genesis*; N. M. Sarna, *Genesis*; D. Steinmetz, *From Father to Son: Kinship, Conflict, and Continuity in Genesis*; E. A. Speiser, *Genesis*, AncB; J. Van Seters, *Prologue to History: The Yahwist as Historian in Genesis*; J. Wellhausen, *Prolegomena to the History of Ancient Israel*.

Commentary

An Outline

I. The Primeval History, 1:1–11:32
   A. Creation of the World, 1:1–2:4a
   B. The Beginning of Human Life, 2:4b–3:24
   C. From Adam to Noah, 4:1–9:29
   D. From Noah to Abraham, 10:1–11:32
II. The Ancestral History of Israel, 12:1–50:26
   A. Abraham, Sarah, and Hagar, 12:1–23:20
   B. Isaac and Rebekah, 24:1–26:35
   C. Jacob, Rachel, and Leah, 27:1–36:36
   D. Joseph and His Brothers, 37:1–50:26

The Primeval History, 1:1–11:32

Creation of the World, 1:1–2:4a

Genesis 1:1–2:4a belongs chronologically to the latest of the Genesis sources—the sixth-century B.C.E. Priestly source. It functions in some ways as an "editor's foreword" to the rest of Genesis and the Pentateuch and thus to the whole OT. Not as science, but as a narrative theology of creation, these chapters set the tone for all the story and history that is to follow.

Somewhat incongruously chap. 1 now ends before what seems clearly to be the actual end of the creation account at 2:4a. Chapter and verse numbers were not added to the text until some time in the Middle Ages, when perception of the limits of a logical literary unit in a text differed in some cases from what might be perceived today.

Of the several different scenarios proposed in the OT for God's creation of the world, the one with which Genesis opens is the best known. It is instructive, however, to compare it with the others—principally Gen 2:4b-25; Job 38:4-33; Ps 104; Prov 8:22-31 and Isa 48:7. Although alike in their degree of profundity and their agreement that creation brings order out of chaos (see Niditch 1985), these portrayals differ considerably from each another in concept, imagery and descriptive detail.

This wide variation suggests that the biblical writers were not concerned primarily with gaining an objective understanding of how the physical world originally came about or how it unfolded in space and time. That would become a primary objective of investigators working in the natural sciences elsewhere and at a later time.

To take the Genesis account of creation as a substitute for (or an option to) today's scientific reconstructions of nature's origin and evolution is anachronistic and reflects a basic misunderstanding of the biblical creation story's purpose and meaning. The biblical accounts are "not a theory but a credo" (Speiser 1964, 8).

To the extent that the world-picture reflected in Gen 1:1–2:4a is scientific, it is heavily indebted to ancient Near Eastern science and myth, in particular to the Babylonian *Epic of Creation* (see Heidel 1951, 82–140; Speiser 1964, 9–11; cf. Gottwald 1985, 476; Knight 1990a, 175–76).

Compared to the approximately 923 lines of the Babylonian text, however, the thirty-five-verse length of the Genesis account signals major substantive differences between the two. The P redactors have radically reinterpreted or "remythologized" the Babylonian mythic elements, and in Genesis the latter have become "broken" myths (Childs 1960, 30–42).

Creation in the Babylonian text, moreover, is an extravagantly portrayed polytheistic warfare among divine powers in nature. The PRIESTLY WRITERS, on the other hand, with laconic and austere understatement, portray the grandeur and also the simplicity of a created order established by one transcendent God.

1:1-2. In the beginning. The traditional rendition of Gen 1:1 as an independent clause, "In the beginning God created the heavens and the earth" (KJV; RSV; cf. John 1:1), although not to be ruled out absolutely, is problematic by the rules of classical Hebrew syntax and grammar (Speiser 1964, 12–13; Sarna 1989, 5).

The NRSV alternative reading has much in its favor: "When God began to create" (mg.) *the heavens and the earth* (v. 1). Not only is it a grammatically sounder option in terms of the Hebrew, but it rhetorically anticipates—and is thus more consistent with—the concluding statement in 2:2, *God finished the work that he had done*. That is, "God began" and "God finished," in 1:1 and 2:2 respectively, form an INCLUSIO to the overall account of creation.

Why the translation of Gen 1:1 has mattered to Jewish and Christian interpreters is its perceived trou-

blesomeness for a theology of creation. If 1:1 is read in the traditional way—as an independent declarative sentence—then, in Gen 1:2, the earth as *a formless void* and *the deep* covered by darkness would appear to be the initial result—the first stage—of God's work, consistent with a theology of creation *ex nihilo* ("out of nothing").

Alternative translations, on the other hand—including the one opted for above—seem to represent the chaotic earth and the deep of 1:2 as existing before creation and alongside of God—a formless "stuff" out of which God formed the world—implying a dualistic view of eternity. Creation out of an unexplained, pre-existent and uncreated "something" poses a co-eternal "something" alongside of God.

It is unwise, however, to make too much of the philosophical and theological issues that came only later to be associated with translating Gen 1:1-2. It is not clear that the Hebrew writer of 1:1-2 had these particular questions in mind. In these opening lines the writer is using a necessarily mythic mode of expression: "The 'beginning' refers to the period before creation and is a designation, more qualitative than temporal, of the sphere of God" (Brown 1978, 4).

In any case the Hebrew syntax of Gen 1:1-2 and the description of a demythologized CREATION that follows do not preclude that God's creation be understood finally as *ex nihilo*. A monotheistic theology would seem to require such a perspective. The earliest explicit documentation of this understanding known so far occurs in 2 Macc 7:28.

1:2a. Before God spoke. The earth is described as *tohû wa-bohû—formless void*—a devastated wasteland. The same distinctive Hebrew expression is used by Jeremiah, not long before the Babylonian destruction of Jerusalem, to describe the approaching devastation of Judah as the very reversal of creation (Jer 4:23-26).

Jeremiah frames that entire vision in words so clearly reminiscent of Gen 1:1-31 that many have supposed him to be quoting but reversing the latter—foreseeing that the creation described in Genesis will be undone for Judah so that it reverts to wasteland. If, however, the Priestly writers composed the opening chapter of Genesis during or shortly after the EXILE (which would be later than Jeremiah's utterances) the possibility must be considered that the Genesis text is remembering and recasting the words of Jeremiah. The *tohû wa-bohû* that Israel's land and people have at the hands of Babylon actually experienced—not merely imagined or speculated about—will give way to God's work of creation. In the words of a possible contemporary or near contemporary of the Priestly writers, creation is "now, not long ago" (Isa 48:7).

1:2b. Darkness covered the face of the deep. This phrase is further contemplative imaging of the scene prevailing before creation. Hebrew *tehôm* (*the* [watery] *deep*) is a term cognate to Babylonian TIAMAT, the name of the hostile chaos-goddess according to the Babylonian *Epic of Creation*. In Genesis, by contrast, *the deep* is desacralized. With it divine underpinnings removed it is a "broken" myth.

Although the *darkness* will later be called *night* and will be separated from the created *light* (1:4), the *darkness* of v. 2 is more than "the opposite of light" since light has not yet been created. The *darkness*

> is a figure for invisibility. . . . It is out of the darkness of v. 2 that God's voice comes, uttering the first word in v. 3: "Let there be light!" whose climactic nature is due precisely to its surprising implication that the light proceeds from the darkness (Wyatt 1993, 548; cf. Deut 5:23).

1:2c. A wind from God. Alternatively the phrase may be rendered "the spirit of God" (NRSV mg.) or "a mighty wind." The word for "spirit" (*rûah*) can also be translated as "wind" or "breath"; in concept these are not sharply distinguishable in Hebrew usage. Whether "wind" or "spirit," *rûah* can be God's "messenger" (Ps 104:4), and it can be God's agent of creation and itself an aspect of God (Ps 104:30). Here, it sweeps ("hovers" is better; cf. the same verb at Deut 32:11) *over the face of the waters*.

1:3-31. The six days of creation. Among the many striking features of these lines is the repeated use of the same set of formulaic phrases to frame each successive description of a stage or day of creation: *And God said, "Let . . .; And it was so . . .; And God saw that it was good . . .; And there was evening and there was morning . . .* (cf. Gottwald 1985, 475).

The litany-like pattern suggests an originally ritual setting for the narrative, composed to be used in worship, possibly at the new year. Such would be consistent with celebrations throughout most of the ancient Near East, including Babylon, associating the new year with creation by the gods (cf. Heidel 1951, 16–17; Dalley 1989, 231–32; Bjornard 1990).

For the Jewish exilic or early postexilic community in Babylon, however, the narrative would have done double duty—expressing praise of the creator God, and at the same time putting forward a liturgical answer to the polytheistic rituals of their alien rulers. It thus becomes a manifesto of faith challenging the religious and, implicitly, also the political assumptions of the Babylonian host-culture.

The picture of the world in vv. 3-31 is architectonic, stressing the different and distinct identities that differentiate the respective elements of creation making up the whole. Every creature or created entity is given its unique place and function in what is perceived as an elegant order of creation. Reinforcing this perception are the precisely repeated sequences of particular words or phrases describing the work of creation in terms of "separating" one thing from another (vv. 4, 6, 7, 14, 18); "gathering together" (vv. 9, 10); distinguishing *every kind* of creature (vv. 11, 12, 21, 24, 25). Quite special terms—the *image* and *likeness* of God—set human beings apart from all other creatures (vv. 26-27).

The belief is asserted emphatically—seven times—that everything created is *good* in the eyes of the creator (vv. 4, 10b, 12b, 18b, 21b, 25b, 31a). Nature is seen as not opposed to spirit but as the work of spirit (cf. 1:2). In particular, a high view is taken of human nature as having an original goodness (vv. 26-27, 31).

In light of the attention given to sin and evil in the J account of creation to follow (2:4b–3:24), P's emphasis on an original human goodness perhaps can be seen as an intentional commentary on J, prefaced by P to the chronologically earlier source. J's dark psychology of human character is not denied so much as fundamentally qualified by P's affirmative theology of creation and human nature.

1:5b. Evening and morning. As in Jewish observance still, the day is measured from sundown to sundown. *Evening* and *morning* are more than merely "before bedtime" and "before noon" respectively; here they are more broadly the equivalent of "nighttime" and "daytime."

1:6-8. Separating the waters. *Dome* is a more graphic translation than the older "firmament" (e.g., KJV, RSV). God names *the dome Sky* (v. 8a), behind which is the same Hebrew word that is rendered in 1:1 (with the definite article) by *the heavens*. On the dividing of the waters above and below the sky, and the conception of the world presupposed by such imagery, see Heidel 1951, 114–15; Gottwald 1985, 476 (esp. fig. 1); Knight 1990a, 175–76.

1:14-19. Heavenly bodies. The *lights in the dome of the sky* are created *for signs and for seasons and for days and years*—they are time dividers and sources of light. The COSMOLOGY is geocentric and thus prescientific by modern measure, but the Priestly writers have a distinct theological agenda. Tablet V of the Babylonian *Epic of Creation* mentions the stars first ahead of the moon and sun, and gives them considerable descriptive attention, connecting them to gods—attesting to the Babylonian interest in ASTROLOGY (Heidel 1951, 44; 116–17; Dalley 1989, 255). Perhaps because of that connection the Priestly writers barely mention the stars, and put them last in order (v. 16).

There is, on the other hand, a provocative parallelism between what God does and what the celestial luminaries do: both they and God *separate the light from the darkness* (v. 18;cf. 1:4) and *the day from the night* (v. 14; cf. 1:5). God creates light and darkness, however—and day and night—on the first day, while the sources of light *in the dome of the sky* are not made until the fourth day. In the Babylonian parallel, again, the celestial lights are gods, light being their attribute. The Genesis account, however, "puts them in their place" as creatures and views the ultimate source of light as independent of them.

1:26-31. Humankind in the image and likeness of God. *Humankind* translates Hebrew *adam*, literally "a human"; here it is not a personal name. The Hebrew word is for P grammatically but not semantically gender-specific. Its meaning clearly embraces both *female* and *male*; P states this here and even more explicitly later, in Gen 5:2. Translation of the Hebrew term by *humankind* is intended to preserve the inclusive meaning.

In our image, according to our likeness (v. 26) is an example of hendiadys—two words used to express a single notion. For P *image* and *likeness* are not two separate or distinguishable qualities but are seen as interchangeable (cf. v. 27 with 5:1). On the one hand humankind is related to the animal world—created on the same day (1:24-25) or sharing the same blessing of life (1:22, 28)—on the other hand, humans are set above the other creatures (vv. 26-28) and likened to the creator. In the human being nature and spirit intersect.

The assertion of humanity's *dominion* over all other living creatures has been misunderstood by some as human arrogance on the part of the Genesis writers and as having provided in later times a justification for humanity's increasingly destructive behavior toward the earth's ecology. The assertion that *dominion* over the creatures has been delegated to humankind is simply descriptive of humanity's actual and obvious situation in the world. It is scarcely a claim to privilege; rather, it is a sober statement of human responsibility for the world and its life, to be ignored only with peril to the world and humankind alike. Inherent to this perspective is human freedom seen as a responsible instrument for the stewardship of life rather than a license for its exploitation.

The particular placement of *male and female* in apposition with *the image of God* (v. 27) suggests that relationships between the sexes are not only a metaphor but also a particular testing ground for the "godlikeness" at the heart of human existence in the world (cf. Trible 1978, 12–23).

Like all language about God, this language is metaphorical. While it points toward God, it does not warrant the conclusion that God contains male and female elements any more than would metaphors for deity elsewhere in the OT warrant the notion that God is part faunal and floral (e.g., Hos 13:8; 14:8).

What v. 27c does suggest is that humans are relational beings, not merely a race of individuals. The *imago dei* (image of God) applies not to humanity in the abstract but to actual sexual persons, political persons, family persons, artistic persons, craftpersons, good citizens, outlaws, and everyone. Human sin and error do not remove this image but are judged by it.

It cannot be merely coincidental that here (elsewhere in the OT only rarely; cf. Gen 3:22; Isa 6:8) God is represented as speaking in the first person plural: *Let us make . . . in our image, according to our likeness.* The language and imagery is that of a divine council in heaven (Ps 82:1; cf. 1 Kgs 22:19-22; Job 1:6; 2:1; 38:7).

Thus the relational or societal notion of the image of God in human beings is paralleled by another relational metaphor—the deity conceived of in terms of a "celestial society." The Christian metaphor of the Trinity—"one God in three persons"—is not promulgated in Gen 1:26, but neither is it inconsistent with it.

2:1-3. The seventh day. That in v. 2 God is said both to have *finished* work and to have *rested* (or ceased) from work on the seventh day might seem a contradiction. Verse 1, however, represents creation of the heavens and the earth (which in 1:2 was a *formless void*) as completed in six days.

The noun form of the twice-repeated Hebrew verb "rest" is *shabbat*, SABBATH. Although not specifically named, the sabbath is clearly alluded to and represented here as modeled in heaven.

Each of the six days was a time of work; the seventh is marked by cessation from work and is *blessed,* given the power of life, *and hallowed* or declared holy. Holy literally means to separate or to set aside.

The Priestly writers' implication seems to be that in the celestial sabbath—God's cessation or rest from work—God separates himself from work, that is, God declares his transcendence of the created world. God pronounces the world and its creatures *good*, but the created order is not considered divine, as it was thought to be by Israel's neighbors and by many in Israel, as the OT prophets attest.

Analogously, in the sabbath on earth, humans separate themselves from their work. What they have done or made is not to be considered divine. Works of human creation, however good, are not to be worshipped (a prohibition against IDOLATRY). Sabbath observance both celebrates creation and distances the sabbath observer from idol worship.

The Beginning of Human Life, 2:4b–3:24

Introduced at this point in Genesis is a second account of creation unmistakably and significantly different from what has preceded. The name used to speak of the deity suddenly changes. In the P narrative it was "God" (Heb. *elohim*). Here (2:4b–3:24) it is *the LORD God* (*Yahweh elohim*), and scholars accordingly attribute this second account to the J or YAHWIST writer or "source."

How the work of creation is conceived, and the sequence of events in it, are both markedly different from the previous account. Here, for example, a human being is formed before any other creature (2:7); in the P account humans are formed last (1:26-27).

The portrayals of God also are radically different: for P God is a disembodied voice from heaven. In the J, God's voice and actions are described as having a kind of anthropomorphic physicality (e.g., 2:7; 3:8). God engages in dialogue with the human actors (3:9-13) and also seems troubled and taken by surprise at the precocity and godlikeness of the human creature (3:22). In the P account such qualities of humankind were by God's intent and design (1:26-27).

Where P's account of creation showed a contemplative priestly concern and awe for cosmic order (e.g., light and darkness; sea and dry land; sun, moon and stars; the variety of living creatures; human beings overseeing it all, etc.), J focuses on the psychology of the human heart becoming self-aware and estranged both from the creator and other creatures.

Here and elsewhere in the primeval history (chaps. 1–11), a recurrent motif for P is God's blessing of na-ture and humankind (1:28; cf. 5:2; 9:1). For J, it is Yahweh's curse of the ground (3:17; cf. 4:11; 5:29; 8:21).

The mythic mode of this story means that the *man* (v. 7) and the *woman* (v. 22) are understood by the J writer as "Everyman"—every human being. Their experience, from hearing the voice of the serpent (3:1-5) and the voice of God (3:8-22) to their expulsion from the garden (3:23-24), is understood as experience of the universal human situation.

The mystery of what it means to be *a living being* (2:7) is thus thematic to J's story of creation. Beginning with the earth unwatered and lifeless (2:5), the J narrative concludes with particular reference to Eve as *the mother of all living* (3:20); to God's discovery that the human being has become like God (*like one of us*; 3:22; cf. 1:26-27) and to God's consequent (and troubling) measures to keep human beings from *the tree of life* lest they *live forever* (3:22, 24; cf. 6:3). Finally, humanity is thrust out by *the LORD God* from an ideal, timeless *garden of Eden* into life in history, that is, life in real time (3:23-24).

2:4b-7. The first man. Like P, the J writer draws on pottery-making imagery and well-known ideas from ancient Near Eastern culture and shapes them for a particular purpose. The notion of a human being formed by a god or goddess, as by a potter, from moistened dust or clay is attested in the *Epic of Gilgamesh*, a Mesopotamian legend going well back into the second millennium B.C.E. (see Speiser 1969, 74; Dalley 1989, 52).

2:7. Humanity shaped from the ground. There is an obvious pun between the Hebrew words *adam*, *man*, and *adamâ*, *ground*; the terms are appropriately rendered as "earth creature" or "earthling" and "earth" (Trible 1978, 80, 140). The J writer exploits the connection in various ways throughout the story.

The generic *adam* is not properly the personal name "Adam" until it appears without the definite article, as in MT and in the NRSV alternative translation at 3:17. The KJV wrongly uses the personal name first at 2:19 (cf. LXX, 2:16).

The man became a *living being* when God *breathed* (lit. "blew") *into his nostrils the breath of life*.

2:8-11. Eden. The LXX translates *garden* as *parádeisos*, "paradise." *Eden* is a Hebrew term meaning "delight"; thus the garden contains trees that are *pleasant to the sight and good for food, the tree of life also in the midst of the garden* (v. 9). There are precious stones and gold nearby (v. 12).

Elsewhere in the OT, exilic or postexilic prophets cite Eden to draw contrast with the wasteland resulting from the military destruction of nations in their own time (Ezek 28:11-19; 31:8-9; Isa 51:3; Joel 2:3).

A potential threat to the felicity of life in the garden is latent at this point. With typical subtle artfulness the J narrator appends an enumeration of trees, almost as if an afterthought—"[Oh yes,] *and the tree of the knowledge of good and evil*" (v. 9).

J gives Eden a geographical location, however vague, *in the east* (v. 8), but consistent with J's terrestriality. The four rivers that branch out from the *river* that *flows out of Eden*, and the geographical regions in or around which they flow (vv. 10-14) are also consistent with J's world-picture.

Given the inherent fluidity of mythic imagery, it is possible the J writer believes Eden to have included the geographical regions he names. Since the river of v. 10 *flows out of Eden to water the garden*, the lands surrounded by the *four branches* of the river could be thought of as embracing the garden (vv. 11-13).

Havilah (v. 11) is Hebrew for *Haulan*, an ancient tribal group in the region of Yemen. *Cush* (v. 13) is not Ethiopia (as in 2 Kgs 19:9) but is connected with early Babylon (Gen 10:8-10) and is also the eponymous father of Havilah (Gen 10:7). *Assyria* (v. 14) is the region of Mesopotamia north of Babylon. These lands, like Eden, are *in the east* (v. 8), and possibly thought of by the J author as part of Eden. Mythic Eden would be understood then not as a chronologically and anciently sequestered place on earth, but as the primeval paradise that is any earthly place before being drawn into historical time. The distinction between Eden and elsewhere is finally qualitative, not spatial.

2:15-17. Life in the garden. Analogous to P's view of humans as having *dominion* over the creatures (1:26, 28), J represents the first human being as caretaker of the garden, *to till it and keep it* (v. 15). He is *freely* to enjoy the fruit of *every tree of the garden* (v. 16) except one, *the tree of the knowledge of good and evil*, to eat of which God warns will mean having to die (v. 17). Since at this point in the story neither the crime nor the punishment are yet part of the human's experience, the warning is enigmatic. Nonetheless, it suggests a dark side to Eden. Narrative ground is being prepared for the confrontation to ensue later over disobedience of the prohibition (cf. 3:1-19).

2:18-22. Woman. The J narrator writes as if privy to God's innermost thought: It is not good that the man should be alone (v. 18). To find for the man *a helper as his partner* (lit. "a helper corresponding to him"), God resorts to experiment. Animals and birds, like the man, are formed *out of the ground* and brought to the man, who gives them their names (vv. 19-20), but none makes a suitable partner for the man (v. 20b). Then, from *one of [the man's] ribs*, taken after the creature is first put into *a deep sleep* (v. 21; cf. the same expression in Gen 15:12, regarding Abraham), God forms the first woman (v. 21; cf. Rosenberg and Bloom 1990, 178-80).

Animals as initial companions of man before he found the companionship of woman is another example of a motif appropriated from ancient Near Eastern tradition but given a considerably different nuance by the J writer (cf. the character Enkidu in the Epic of Gilgamesh [Dalley 1989, 53–6; Speiser 1969, 74–5]). In the latter story, however, the motif depicts relations with the woman as merely preparing Enkidu for comradeship with the hero Gilgamesh. J, on the other hand, presents companionship between the sexes as good for its own sake.

2:22b-25. Man and woman brought together. J utilizes a proverbial folk etymology for the words *Woman* and *Man* (v. 23). The man's exclamatory *This at last . . .* (v. 23) indicates an Edenic delight with the woman as his opposite, centering on their mutually happy and innocent discovery of their sexuality—as explained in J's appended comments (vv. 24-5); they *were both naked, and were not ashamed* (v. 25). The implication that erotic attraction between the sexes reflects their longing to return to an original unity (vv. 23-24) is a greatly attenuated version of an elaborate and archetypal myth to that effect cited also by Plato (*Symp* 189d–193d; cf. Gunkel 1901, 94).

3:1-24. Godlikeness as the knowledge of good and evil. Whatever is finally to be comprehended by the expression, *knowing good and evil* (v. 5), according to J, it is recognized by both the serpent and God as tantamount to becoming *like God* (v. 5, cf. v. 22). As might be expected, God and the serpent in this particular story hold divergent views of such an outcome. The J writer does not moralize but, rather, presents both views with cool detachment.

In classical Hebrew, to "know good and evil" is a generic idiom for human knowledge in general—both objective and experiential knowledge. Depending on context it can have any one of several related meanings or nuances such as knowledge of right and wrong (Isa 5:20), the distinction between political competence and incompetence (1 Kgs 3:9), the ability to discern human character and motive (2 Sam 14:17), or, in a more general sense, to grow up, mature, or come of age (Isa 7:15).

Here, in view of what is to follow in chaps. 4–11 concerning the emergence of human civilization, culture and a necessary worldly wisdom, the knowledge of good and evil must be read as "the entirety of knowledge" (NOAB v. 5n.) or "the totality of all possible experience," well described (though judged as futility) by a later OT writer coming out of the Wisdom tradition (cf. Eccl 1:12–2:10).

Thus the knowledge of good and evil is here not a particular body of knowledge among others, but a particular way of knowing. It implies control of one's world, and to be complete it requires foreknowledge, or control of the future—for human creaturehood a goal doomed to failure however much it may attract and mesmerize. Moreover, the attempt to possess such an ultimate and independent control, according to the J writer, must by definition be in God's eyes hubris, the inclination to play God (3:22).

Such an understanding lies behind Ezekiel's rhetorical use of the Eden tradition. His "lamentation over the king of Tyre" (Ezek 28:11-19, esp. v. 13) paints an elaborate picture of "Eden, the garden of God" from which the king, like Adam, has been driven because of a self-aggrandizement such as in Genesis is symbolized by eating from the forbidden tree.

3:1-5. The serpent's interpretation. Under the serpent's tutelage, however, the strictures placed on humanity by God's wisdom are weighed by the woman and man against the possibilities held out for them by their vision and imagination. God will denounce the serpent (3:14), but there is no sign of the narrator doing so. J is matter-of-fact and nonjudgmental toward the actors in the Eden story. In matters of the divine-human relation J does not take sides.

The serpent is described in Hebrew as *arum*, translated by NRSV somewhat pejoratively as *crafty*. "Subtle" (KJV, RSV) or "perceptive" (author trans.) are better alternatives in the context. The Hebrew word is clearly a play on the description in 2:25 of the man and woman as both *arom* ("naked"; *erom* in 3:7, 10, 11). The wordplay, and the serpent's possession of human speech (one of two occasions in the OT in which an animal speaks; cf. Numb 22:28-30 and commentary at 3:14-19) associate the serpent with the voice of human imagination and possibility.

As such, the serpent's role in the story is ambiguous. The J writer sees it, to be sure, as leading the hu-

mans into provoking divine judgment (3:11, 22). Perhaps less obviously, what will follow in Gen 4–11 suggests that J sees it also as leading the man and woman from the passive obedience of Eden out into the world of taking life's risks of initiative and responsibility—ingredients basic to a life of faith. It could be said that what God sees as hubris the serpent sees as initiative.

The chronologically later P account of creation will hold that such initiative and responsibility was God's true intent for humankind in the first place and will expand J's problematic expression, *like God*, into the more positive *image and likeness* of God (1:26-28).

Identification of the serpent as the devil or Satan does not appear until the first century B.C.E. (Wis 2:24; cf. Rev 12:9; 20:2). In some second-century C.E. Gnostic or Gnostic-Christian circles the serpent was portrayed in a positive light as "the instructor" of humankind (Layton 1988, 164–65; Bethge et al. 1988, 184–85).

That the serpent's counsel leads to the denial of immortality for humankind (3:4, 22-24) is reminiscent of the snake's role in the *Epic of Gilgamesh* (Tablet XI; cf. Dalley 1989, 119; Speiser 1969, 96)—stealing from Gilgamesh the plant that would give immortality or at least rejuvenation.

3:6-7. The fall. As an event, eating from the forbidden tree would be designated by later Christian interpretation as the "fall from God's grace" of the first humans, and the character of the act as "original sin." Literal interpretations view this episode as a particular act of disobedience at the beginning of temporal history, through which all the descendants of Adam and Eve have genetically inherited the taint of sin and for which all humanity is now held responsible.

More mystical or mythic interpretations see "the Fall" as happening "before" historical time—in effect, before every human action at any time. Thus it amounts to a state or condition of humankind universally (see Niebuhr 1941, 241–64).

In the OT, nowhere is human sin or guilt referred to events narrated in Gen 3:1-6. Related to the more mystical understanding of "original sin," however, is the notion of the "evil inclination" in all humankind (Gen 6:5; 8:21; see Jacobs 1901, 601–602, and commentary at 6:5).

The Hebrew verb translated to know (3:5, 7) is sometimes in classical Hebrew an idiom for sexual intercourse (see Gen 4:1, 25). In the Eden narrative the various connotations of the term are obviously played off each other.

Contrary to some later interpretations, the sin of the man and woman is not represented in Genesis as sexual. This could scarcely be the case given the high view of human sexuality expressed in 2:23-25. That sexual relationships, like all of human life, can become estranged or distorted because of antecedent or attendant human sin and guilt (3:16) is a different matter (cf. Price 1990).

3:8-13. God searches out the man. With irony typical of the J writer, it is precisely in the context of knowledge presumed to be Godlike that J represents God's knowledge as something other than simple foreknowledge or omniscience.

Some ancient rabbinical and Christian patristic interpretations notwithstanding, this and subsequent questions asked by God (vv. 11, 13; cf. 4:9; 18:21) are not rhetorical formalities for the sake of opening a dialogue. The Genesis writers present the human creature as God's experimental "project" by which God can be genuinely surprised either in satisfaction or dismay (cf. 2:18 with v. 20b; 3:22; 6:5-6; 11:5-7; 18:26; 19:21; 22:12).

3:14-19. Judgment. The poetic and proverbial tenor of the three punishment-pronouncements mark them as sayings probably ancient and time-honored well before the J writer adapted them. The writer uses them selectively, but realistically, to describe the hard life in nature and society in contrast to the lost good of Eden.

That the fall of humankind is prelude to the forging of a deeper relationship between humans and God in history—thematic for Genesis as a whole—remains at this point in the story still to be discovered.

The serpent is *cursed . . . among all animals* (v. 14), and expelled from the society of animals and humans known in Eden. A tradition in the second-century B.C.E. *Book of Jubilees* holds that the animals in Eden "used to speak with one another with one speech and one language," and seems to imply that the language was Hebrew (*Jub* 3:28; 12:26; cf. Wintermute 1985, 60, 82).

Concerning what is said to the woman, erotic interaction between humans is not itself condemned. Rather, this human relationship, as every other, is now distorted and corrupted because of the human desire to know *good and evil* (3:5) in such a way as to possess and have control over the other—to play god. Eros, an intended good, has "disintegrated" (Trible 1978, 128; cf. 72–143; see also commentary at 3:20).

3:17-19. The curse of the ground. God's pronouncement on Adam brings the whole Eden narrative

full cycle. *The ground* (Heb. *adama*) from which God made the man (cf. 2:7, *adam*) is now *cursed*—its power of life and fertility is weakened and diminished. Nature and the earth thus also suffer in the fall, human stewardship of them (2:15; cf. 1:26-28) compromised by their being exploited by the steward's pursuit of *the knowledge of good and evil* (cf. Hos 4:1-3). The life of human beings and the life-supporting ground from which they are taken are yoked (v. 19).

Relief from the curse of the ground becomes a leitmotif for the rest of the primeval history (Gen 4:2, 11-12; 5:29; 8:21; 9:20, 25; see commentary at 4:1-16).

3:20. Eve. The explanation of the woman's name is a folk etymology—in Hebrew the name "Eve" resembles the word for "living." Of more interest is the import of this particular etymological folk tradition, which sees the woman as *the mother of all living* that is, of "all living creatures" (cf. the same expression at Gen 8:21c). Whether the J writer takes this to mean only human beings or is recalling traditions of a divine woman is not clear.

According to Gen 2:7 and 2:19, both man and animal are formed from the ground; according to 3:20, Eve is their common mother. It may be that J intends with this alternative tradition of woman's status to correct or mitigate the misogynic implications of 3:16. In the midst of a portrait of Yahweh as creator and judge this citation concerning Eve is remarkable.

It should not be overlooked that in the J narratives in Genesis it is women who more often than not drive the action of the story (3:2, 6; 16:1-15; 19:30-38; 21:6-21; 27:5-17, 42-46; 31:19, 33-35; 38:1-30).

3:21. Life under judgment and grace. Being held divinely accountable for whatever they have done is experienced by the man and woman as punishment for hubris or presumption, but they also experience God's compassion. That God makes garments and clothes them may at first thought seem a merely quaint image and a minimal gesture of grace. The *garments of skins*, however, are symmetrical in the story to the futile fig leaves by which the pair sought to hide their nakedness and vulnerability from themselves and from God (3:7, 10). Clothing concretely provides, and in a more general sense symbolizes, protection against the physical rigors and psychological anxieties of human existence, illustrated but not exhausted by the punishment pronouncements of 3:14-19.

3:22-24. The expulsion from Eden. The couple is driven out of the garden of Eden lest they *take also from the tree of life, and eat, and live forever*. It must be understood that "living forever" does not mean "life after death" but living forever in this world.

The OT does not speak of a life in heaven after death. Even the very late notion of resurrection (Dan 12:2) seems to expect a restoration to life in this world, except that there it is understood to be brought about by God, not achieved by humans.

The J writer thus suggests that to live *forever* (Heb. *olam*, i.e., for all time), would transform a knowledge of good and evil like God's to total knowledge that is God's. The expulsion from Eden is a cautionary tale against the inevitable disillusionment for human beings attracted to any idea of knowledge as the way to forestalling death forever.

A similar observation is made by Qoholeth who may have meditated on the Genesis narrative, if indeed he was not a contributor to it: "[God] has put eternity ['all time'] into man's mind, yet so that he cannot find out what God has done from the beginning to the end" (Eccl 3:11 RSV).

Cherubim and *a sword flaming and turning* (v. 24) cut off the way back into Eden. Cherubim are mythic winged beasts. Carved figures of cherubim guard the inner sanctuary of the temple (1 Kgs 6:23-28); elsewhere Yahweh is represented as enthroned on the cherubim (e.g., 1 Sam 4:4). The picture of cherubim as angelic infants or children is a medieval image, not found in the OT.

The whirling sword is not held by one of the cherubim; it is present in addition to them. The iconography of Eden is paralleled and much elaborated in Ezekiel's "lamentation over the king of Tyre" (Ezek 28:11-19; cf. esp. vv. 14-16), but a sword is not mentioned there.

Possibly the image is related to that of the drawn sword in the hand of the mysterious figure guarding the way into the "holy ground" of Canaan (Josh 5:13-15; cf. Judg 7:20; Jer 47:6).

From Adam to Noah, 4:1–9:29

4:1-22. Cain and Abel. Reference to an established and developed system of sacrifice (vv. 3-4), a generally populated world (vv. 14-15), a wife for Cain (v. 17) and cultural developments apparently uninterrupted to the present (vv. 20-22) indicate that at one time the story of CAIN AND ABEL must have been a freestanding tradition independent of both the preceding Eden narrative, to which it is now attached, as well as the flood tradition that follows in chaps. 6-8.

That the narrative opens with a folk etymology of the name *Cain* but not *Abel* suggests that Abel is mostly a foil to the main actor in the story, who is Cain. (*Abel* renders a Heb. word meaning "vanity," in the sense of being feckless or useless; cf. Eccl 1:2).

The present story seems actually to combine two earlier and quite different traditions—that of Cain the farmer (vv. 2-16) and Cain as metalworker (vv. 17-22).

The folk-explanation—which the narrator attributes to Eve—for the name "Cain" (*"I have produced a man with the help of the LORD"* [v. 1]) relates the name to the Hebrew word for "produced." It need not be taken to imply divine parentage for Cain, as some have suggested. The simplest understanding is that it expresses a common view of childbirth in the OT as well as in many other cultures, that the human parents' biological role is necessary to, but not of itself sufficient for conception in the womb, which ultimately happens only with divine assistance or intervention (cf. e.g., Gen 17:7; 18:10; 30:2; 1 Sam 1:19-20; Ps 139:13).

The original purpose of vv. 1-16 may have been etiological—to account for the traditional rivalry between shepherds and farmers for the land, but in the story as now deployed the J writer's interest lies elsewhere. Considering the outcome of events in Eden (chap. 3), the significant connection for J would seem to be the detail that Cain is *a tiller of the ground* (v. 2) which is now cursed (3:17). This is surely the logic behind Yahweh's otherwise gratuitous rejection of Cain's *offering of the fruit of the ground* (v. 3).

That Cain is warned to restrain his anger and dismay over the situation (v. 7) is another example of the paradox of having to take responsibility for conditions not altogether of one's own making, paralleling the description of human existence in the Eden story. The tenor of Yahweh's inquiries put to Cain after the murder of Abel (vv. 9-15) are reminiscent of the exchange between Yahweh and the first man and woman earlier (3:9-19).

Cain's answer to God's inquiry about Abel—*"I do not know"* (v. 9) is of course a lie, and his question, *"Am I my brother's keeper?"* is rhetorically dissembling and disingenuous, if not insolent. In the context, contrary to some popular interpretations, it is scarcely meant to launch a discussion of ethics.

Cain is *cursed from the ground* (v. 11) because he shed the blood of his brother Abel, and, like his parents, is driven "away from the ground" (v. 14a RSV) and from God's presence. The curse in these several stories early in Genesis is thus portrayed as a universal sickness passing back and forth between the ground and the humans who come from the ground (3:19).

To protect him from any avenger of Abel's death and thus to relieve Cain from having to become *a fugitive and a wanderer on the earth* (v. 14b), God *put a mark on Cain* (v. 15). The nature of the mark is not clear, but in this story it extends the pattern of divine judgment tempered by grace that started with Yahweh's sewing of protective garments for Adam and Eve (see commentary at 3:21).

That Cain *settled in the land of Nod* (v. 16) seems an oxymoron—*Nod* means "wandering"—contradicting the statement that Cain *settled* there. This may be an example of J's proclivity for irony, or it may be another indication that the original tradition had an meaning different from what J gives it. Perhaps J introduces the detail about God's protection of Cain, which appears to obviate Cain's having to become *a fugitive and a wanderer on the earth*. (In place of *Nod*, LXX has "Naid," which has no recognizable meaning.)

Where Cain could obtain a wife (v. 17) in a world empty except for his parents becomes a question only if the story's original independence of the preceding Eden narrative is not recognized. Some ancient Jewish and Christian interpretations thus took recourse to an expansion of the Cain story in which he marries two of his sisters (*Jub* 4:9-12), whose existence seemed allowed for by the reference in Gen 5:4 to Adam's *other sons and daughters*.

In distinction to the popular explanation of the name in v. 1, "Cain" is actually derived linguistically from the Hebrew gentilic term "Kenite," meaning "smith" (i.e., metalworker). Kenites as a people are represented as enemies of Israel in Gen 15:19 and Num 24:21-22; elsewhere they seem to be viewed favorably (Judg 1:16; 4:11; cf. Matthews 1990).

The connection of his name with metallurgy seems in any case consistent with the description of Cain as builder of a city (v. 17), perhaps implicitly a swordsman (vv. 23-24), and progenitor of *Tubal-cain*, who shares his ancestor's name and is a metalsmith (v. 22). J's anachronistic reference to *iron tools* appearing in so ancient a time is one of many details that distinguish this source's archaic knowledge of history from that of modern archaeologists and historians.

The informal genealogy is interrupted here and there to note selected features of emergent civilization (vv. 21-22) in both urban and nomadic culture (vv. 17, 20). Some names in this list of J's plus *Seth* and *Enosh* (vv. 25-26) will be repeated, some only approximated, and others omitted in the Priestly writers' longer list of Adam's descendants through Seth in chap. 5.

4:23-24. The Song of Lamech. The story of Cain ends with an ancient boasting or battle song that recalls his murderous deed (vv. 8-16). From the J writer's ironic perspective, *Lamech* perversely celebrates Cain's violence and mocks Yahweh's words of compassion to Cain by turning them to his own self-glorification (cf. vv. 24, 15a). The song illustrates and dramatizes the worsening condition of human society after Eden and before the Flood.

4:25. Birth of Seth. Seth is the third son of Adam according to this genealogy. Seth's name is chosen by his mother because, as she declares, *"God has appointed for me another child instead of Abel."* In P's variant list of Adam's descendants to follow (5:1-28, 30-32), neither Abel nor Cain are mentioned; there the line of Seth supplants them altogether.

4:26. Enosh and the worship of Yahweh. The meaning of the name *Enosh* is synonymous with *Adam*—"human being"—although it lacks the "earthling" connotations of the latter (see 2:7). Here the name is used in a kind of theological double-entendre: to say that the worship (invocation of the name) of Yahweh (*the LORD*) began with Enosh is also a way of saying that it began with the birth of humankind (see discussion of P's different view in remarks on the Priestly source, under "Authorship and Date," above). For J, Yahweh has always been known.

5:1-32. Adam's descendants through Seth. The rhetorical shape and vocabulary of 5:1 (cf. 1:26-28) and the repetitious form of citation that follows identify the genealogy of chap. 5 as belonging to the P source, with the exception of v. 29, in which the style and subject matter suggests P has drawn from J (see commentary at 3:14-19).

In contrast to J's lineage of Adam (chap. 4), this variant tradition goes through Seth, represented as Adam's firstborn. P either is unfamiliar with the traditions about Cain or—more likely—ignores or suppresses them. The name *Kenan* (5:12-14), except for the final *-an*, is spelled in Hebrew the same as "Cain" and could be a hypocoristic form of the latter, but Kenan is not the firstborn of Adam.

The ancient Near Eastern tradition that human ancestors in earliest times were extraordinarily long-lived was not an invention of the biblical writers. The pre-biblical *Sumerian King List*, a text dating from ca. 2000 B.C.E., lists Mesopotamian kings of legend said to have lived "[before] the Flood swept over the earth," each of whose ages is reckoned in tens of thousands of years (Oppenheim 1969, 265–66).

The names on the two lists are different, although their respective repetitious and formulaic styles are similar. The relevance of the comparison, however, is that the Priestly writers in Gen 5 appear not first of all concerned to make the point that humans once lived to fabulous ages. That tradition would in P's time seem to have been taken more or less for granted. Conceivably, the P writers may even have considered that aspect of the tradition archaic and open to question, while they exploit it for their own purposes.

What is added to the citation of each name in Gen 5 is a notation not present in the Sumerian list, namely, that each long-lived ancestor died (vv. 5, 8, etc.). That these "obituary notices" do not occur in the later continuation of this genealogy through the line of Shem (11:10-32)—a list which otherwise has the same formulaic structure as here—suggests that there is a particular purpose for them here.

The P writers seem concerned to make the point that longevity was not to be confused with immortality. Specifically they may be seeking in this connection to forestall misunderstandings concerning the intimation of immortality for humans implied in the J tradition preserved in Gen 6:1-4.

That such is their main concern at this point is supported by the case of *Enoch* (vv. 21-24)—whom P cites as an exception to the others in Adam's line in that Enoch did not die; rather, he *walked with God; then he was no more, because God took him* (v. 24). The Hebrew language here is precise, and describes not Enoch's death or dying but his bodily translation into the presence of God. The only other such exception in the OT tradition is the prophet Elijah (2 Kgs 2:11). In general the OT lacks any doctrine of resurrection until its very latest writing, from the late post-exilic period (e.g., Dan 12:1-3).

To "walk with God" is idiomatic in biblical Hebrew for living righteously and in keeping faith with God and one's fellow humans (e.g., Mic 6:8; Gen 6:9; Deut 26:17). Thus the lineage given in Gen 5 serves not only a genealogical interest but also theological, in which the P writers correlate righteousness with life (and by implication, sin with death) in a curious but striking way: on the one hand Enoch, remembered as righteous, has the shortest life on earth among those listed but is granted immortality. Having *walked with God*, Enoch lives forever (vv. 23-24). On the other hand, this righteous but relatively short-lived figure is father to *Methuselah* who, of all Adam's descendants,

enjoys the longest life on earth but does not live forever (v. 27).

That the years of Enoch's lifespan number 365 may also be intended by P as significant, since that is the number of days in a solar year. The sun is a widespread symbol for deity in the ancient Near East, including in the OT (Deut 33:2; Judg 5:31; Hab 3:3-4; Mal 4:2 [MT 3:20]).

Possibly P's particular treatment of the Enoch tradition has the purpose of qualifying the theology of J concerning the denial of immortality to humankind (3:22-23). That P has J thus in mind is supported by the use of J's explanation for the name *Noah*, with its hope that Noah will bring relief from the curse of the ground, to conclude P's lineage of Adam (v. 29).

6:1-4. Divine beings cohabit with women. An unusual fragment of mythic tradition now returns the narrative to its theme of humankind overreaching itself—the affront to Yahweh that provoked the expulsion from Eden (3:22-24) and now will provoke a universal flood (6:5–7:24).

That the world's depravity somehow has roots in heaven (referring to the *sons of God*; vv. 1, 4) is but one puzzling aspect of this particular tradition. On the other hand, J seems to represent Yahweh as distancing himself from these *sons of God*.

The identity of the *Nephilim* (v. 4) is unclear; translated in some English versions as "giants" (KJV), the term also can be translated "fallen ones." Possibly the association of this race of semi-divine beings with *the heroes that were of old* (v. 4) is intended to recall the long-lived ancestors cited in Gen. 5, with the particular stress there on their mortal nature.

The final meaning of this somewhat lurid fragment seems in any case to be that the moral situation in human society on earth has become intolerable and must be brought to an end. (On Gen 6:1-4 in relation to its analogues in ancient Near Eastern mythology, cf. Speiser 1964, 45–46.)

6:5–8:21. The flood. As has been known for well over a century, the flood story in Genesis is unmistakably indebted in considerable detail to older versions of the tradition of a worldwide catastrophic flood, copies of which are extant due to archaeological recovery of them in the nineteenth century. The best preserved of these is found in *The Epic of Gilgamesh* (Tablet XI; cf. Speiser 1969, 93–5; Dalley 1989, 109–16). This extrabiblical version explains the legendary disaster as brought about by mere caprice owing to rivalries among the gods, with humans as merely pawns.

By contrast, the biblical version sees the flood from a moral perspective. The narrative in Genesis is bracketed with explicit reference at its beginning and end to the perennial "evil inclination" of the human heart (6:5; 8:21-22) which provoked both the flood and the curse of the ground. God's lifting of the curse is seen as happening in spite of the continued presence of the "evil inclination" and because of the offerings sacrificed to God by Noah (8:20-22; cf. 6:9).

References in 6:5 and 8:21 to a chronic "evil inclination" (*yeser hara*) in the human heart gave rise later to the Jewish rabbinical doctrine of "the evil inclination" (or "evil imagination"), more or less a counterpart to the Christian doctrine of "original sin" (cf. Jacobs 1901, 601–602).

The flood narrative is a composite of the J and P sources which are here for the most part intertwined rather than presented in parallel blocks as with the creation narratives (1:1–2:4a and 2:4b–3:24) or the line of Adam's descendants (4:17-26 and 5:1-32).

According to J, rain falls *for forty days and forty nights* (7:4, 12, 17; 8:6). In P's account, *the waters swelled on the earth for one hundred fifty days* (7:24; 8:3); for P, the flood is not only a matter of heavy rain, but *the fountains of the great deep burst forth and the windows of heavens were opened* (7:11). P thinks of the deluge as a reversal of the dividing of the waters at creation; the world returns to the watery chaos out of which it first came (cf. 1:6-7).

P's version has two of every creature enter the ark (6:19-20); J's has fourteen (seven pairs) of *all clean animals*, two (a pair) of the *animals that are not clean* and *seven pairs of the birds of the air* (7:2-3). For a detailed tabulation of the editorial deployment of the J and P sources in the flood narrative, see Gottwald 1985, 326, 470.

The *ark*, or "chest-like boat" built by Noah is not to be confused with the later ark or chest that Moses made, in which the tablets of the Law were kept (Exod 25:10; Deut 10:5). The word "ark" derives from Latin *arca*, "chest," or "cellroom." In Hebrew, the words for the two objects are different. The Hebrew term for Noah's ark (*teba*) is the same as that for the basket or chest in which the infant Moses' mother kept him hidden and afloat among the reeds of the Nile (Exod 2:3, 5). It is one of a number of motifs shared in common between the Genesis flood narrative and the first fifteen chapters of Exodus.

As the flood waters recede, the ark comes *to rest on the mountains of Ararat* (8:4). Exactly where the ark was believed to have grounded is thus not clear in the story; a region is indicated, not a particular mountain slope (extrabiblical versions of the flood give other geographical locations).

Like the location of Eden (2:8), the location of the grounded ark is finally a place in mythic vision, as is the flood on which it floated that submerged even the highest mountains (7:19). The biblical narrative relegates the universal flood to the realm of myth when God is portrayed as excluding it from the range of what will happen in the world of nature and history (8:21-22; 9:8-17).

The occasional searches for physical remains of Noah's ark undertaken in modern times only demonstrate someone's basic misunderstanding of the mythic character of the ark in sacred symbol and story. Such efforts are not viewed as serious archaeology by most biblical scholars and archaeologists today (cf. Bailey 1989, 28–115, 203–206).

9:1-17. God's covenant with Noah. The distinctive writing style and vocabulary throughout this section are those of the Priestly source (esp. vv. 1-2, 6-7; cf. 1:28-30; 5:1-2).

Life on earth is seen not as merely starting over with the emergence of Noah and his family from the ark, but as entering a qualitatively different history under a COVENANT relationship established by God with the human race and the world of nature (vv. 8-17).

As God undertakes that *never again shall all flesh be cut off by the waters of a flood* (v. 11), so likewise, under this covenant, obligations are laid upon Noah and his descendants, that is, the whole human race, concerning the slaughter of animals and the shedding of human blood (vv. 4-6). Blood is understood as the residence of life.

Therefore living flesh shall not be eaten, which is defined as *flesh with its life, that is, its blood* (v. 4). In Jewish tradition this principle is the basis for the ritual slaughter of animals by draining the blood from the body, so that the meat will be "kosher," "ritually proper," or "correct." Coupled with this injunction is the prohibition against human bloodshed (vv. 5-6).

Since all Noah's descendants fall under this covenant (v. 9), there arose in later Judaism a tradition of the Noachian laws (sometimes, NOACHIC LAWS or "Noahide laws"), obligating not only Israel but all humankind. In its final form the tradition included some but not all of the divine injunctions to humankind in Genesis and added some others. According to the later rabbis, there are seven: prohibitions against idolatry, blasphemy, bloodshed, sexual sins, theft, and eating from a living animal; and the injunction to establish a legal system (Schwarzschild 1972, 1189).

The perpetual sign of this covenant is the *bow in the clouds* appearing after rain (vv. 12-17). The RAIN-BOW is understood as an archer's bow, representing God's weapon put aside or "hung up" in the rain clouds, unneeded since the battle of the flood is permanently over (v. 15).

9:18-29. Drunkenness of Noah and the curse upon Canaan. The language and style now become that of the J writer. Noah becomes the first vintner (v. 20). The description in English of Noah as *a man of the soil* loses a nuance of MT, where "soil" is the same word translated as "ground" (Heb. *adama*) earlier (cf. 3:17; 5:29; 8:21).

Once again the J writer has fitted out his narrative episode with an artful closure; here it has a sardonic cast. Noah, first introduced as one who *out of the ground that the LORD has cursed . . . shall bring us relief from our work and from the toil of our hands* (5:29), is found at the end of the story as a *man of the soil* (lit., "of the ground") bringing relief from work to the descendants of Shem and Japheth by placing upon Canaan the curse of being their slave (vv. 25-27). A further twist is the association of the curse with Noah's nakedness, covered by a blanket instead of fig leaves or a garment of skins (vv. 22-23; cf. 3:7, 21).

At some point in the development of the tradition the curse upon Canaan and the contrasting blessing on Shem (v. 26) would seem to reflect later history, when the descendants of Shem (Israel) subdued the Canaanites—this being read back into the primeval period as a state of affairs destined from the beginning, as told in this tale.

As used now by the J writer, however, the story of Noah's drunkenness and his cursing of Canaan appears to be saying that the "evil inclination" of the human heart remains alive and well after the flood (cf. 8:21), and the human disorder attendant on it will still have to be dealt with.

From Noah to Abraham, 10:1–11:32

10:1-32. Nations descended from Noah. The descendants of Noah's three sons populate the earth, and the three lines are organized here into a "table of nations." It is a mixed list of political states and ethnic or language groups, some named as such directly;

others are "eponyms," that is names of peoples, nations, cities, clans, personified as individuals (cf. Redditt 1990).

The various groupings conform to the understanding of what was seen as already "ancient history" in the time of the J and P writers, whose work is once again intermingled. By the research standards of modern historical study the table is of course precritical and cannot by itself provide a reliable record. As an example of historical understanding in ancient times, however, it is of interest to modern biblical and historical study (cf. Speiser 1964, 71-3).

That *Nimrod . . . a mighty hunter before the LORD* (v. 9) should be the sole individual among the descendants of Noah singled out for extended comment may have something to do with an inference that Nimrod's hunting prowess (presumably with a bow) threatened rebellion against the covenant between God and Noah, the sign of which was God's own hunting bow (cf. Dahlberg 1990).

Consistent with this interpretation is that as legendary founder of the great city-states in Babylonia (*the land of Shinar*) and *Assyria* (vv. 10-12), Nimrod points ahead to the next and last episode in the troubled primeval history, the tower of Babel.

11:1-9. The tower of Babel. The tower is generally understood to mean a ziggurat, or "temple tower"—a pyramid-shaped mound of considerable height with steps ascending to a temple at the summit. The present narrative associates the name *Babel* (v. 9) with the Hebrew word for "confusion." The actual meaning is "gate of God," which the narrator may have known very well—in which case he is simply mocking the name with a derisive etymology.

In contrast to the account in chap. 10 of the orderly spread of populations across the earth, the story of the tower of Babel explains the world's profusion of languages and scattering of peoples (vv. 7-9) as a confusion imposed by Yahweh intentionally, to stem a rising tide of human technological ambition and achievement viewed as an assault upon heaven (vv. 4, 6).

The notion that prior to the building of the tower *the whole earth had one language and the same words* (v. 1) contradicts the picture of linguistic diversity presupposed earlier in the narrative (10:5). The inconsistency, however, only points to the original independence of the present story from the overall narrative in which it is now stands.

Within the primeval history according to the J version, the tower of Babel story provides an ironic conclusion for the "history of religion" up·to this point, which had begun with J's assertion that the name of Yahweh was invoked in worship from the beginning of history (4:2-3, 26). Religion itself is shown to have become infected by troublemaking human pride, represented by its attempt to build the ultimate sacred edifice.

For the Priestly editors of the final work, however, the tower of Babel story provides closure to the overall primeval history in a way not unrelated to but nevertheless different from the purposes of the J writer.

It was suggested earlier that P's account of creation (1:1–2:4a), besides being a celebration of God's creation through worship, provided a liturgical challenge to the religious assumptions of the Babylonian culture under which P's exilic Jewish community lived This story of a world thrown back into chaos because of Babylonian religion and culture, must therefore have seemed for P an ultimately fitting conclusion to the primeval history and a confirmation of the priestly theology that informs it.

11:10-26, 32. Genealogy from Shem to Abraham. The repetitive and formulaic format marks this genealogy as a continuation, through Noah's son Shem, of P's earlier list of long-lived ancestors of the human race (5:1-28, 30-32). Noticeably absent are the explicit reminders of mortality appended to each citation in the earlier list (5:5, 8, 11, etc.), probably because the reminder was not thought to be needed in the new context. In spite of the 120-year limit Yahweh placed on human life according to the J narrative (6:3), the persons in Shem's line according to P continue to enjoy very long lifetimes, although considerably shorter than the antediluvian heroes named in chap. 5.

P's genealogical table concludes at the names of *Terah* and his three sons, *Abram, Nahor, and Haran* (v. 26). For the sake of convenience, and because it does not significantly affect interpretation, the present commentary everywhere (except in direct quotation of the NRSV text) renders the names Abram and Sarai by their respective dialectical variants, Abraham and Sarah, even though the latter forms are not introduced until Gen 17:5.

11:27-31. The sons of Terah. The non-formulaic, more discursive style of this section suggests the J source. Abraham is the chief human protagonist in the first chapters of the ancestral history (Gen 12–23), from which position he is remembered today, although in different ways, by three world religions as historically and spiritually their first ancestor—by Judaism

through Abraham's son Isaac by Sarah (chaps. 17–18); by Christianity through its Jewish heritage (Gal 3:7), and by Islam through Abraham's son Ishmael by Hagar (Gen 17:20; 21:13).

Sarah's ancestry is omitted, which is curious, since that of Nahor's wife is given (v. 29; cf. 20:12). Sarah's barrenness (v. 30) will prove to stand in dramatic tension with God's promise of a great posterity to Abraham (15:5-6).

Haran is an eponym and does double duty in the story as the name both of Abraham's brother and of the city or region in central MESOPOTAMIA to which Terah brings his family (v. 31) and from which Abraham will migrate to Canaan (12:4-5).

Nahor is apparently likewise an eponym, the name of Abraham's brother and also of a city in which the brother lives, near Haran (cf. Gen 24:10). His granddaughter Rebekah later becomes the wife of Abraham's son Isaac (chap. 24).

Lot, Haran's son and Abraham's nephew, presumably comes under Abraham's protection following Haran's death (v. 28) and therefore will go with Abraham to Canaan (12:4) where he will play a supporting role in that unfolding drama.

The city of *Ur* in southern Mesopotamia did not become associated with *the Chaldeans* (a late synonym for "Babylonians") until some time in the first millennium B.C.E., later than the supposed time of Abraham. It was already a metropolis, however, before 2000 B.C.E., well before Abraham. The tradition of Terah and his family in relation to *Ur of the Chaldeans* has seemed to some scholars as therefore an anachronism, or else as a reference to another place with the same name (Sarna 1989, 87). The tradition appears again at Gen 15:7, however, without reference at all to Haran. Anachronistic reference to a region or its population by a name associated with it only much later than the period being referred is not unusual (cf. references to PHILISTINES at 21:32-34 and in chap. 26).

There may be literary and theological reasons for P's insertion from J of the *Ur of the Chaldeans* tradition just at this point—it is consistent with the scattering of peoples as recounted in the tower of Babel story (11:8-9). "It is a common feature of such ancestors to achieve their final destination in stages" (Van Seters 1992, 202–203; cf. Gen 12:6-9; 13:3; Deut 26:3, 5). That Abraham puts Babylonian religion and culture behind him also fits well with P's critical stance toward things Babylonian (see commentary at 1:3-31 and 11:1-9).

The Ancestral History of Israel, 12:1–50:26

The legendary aspects of the Genesis patriarchal-matriarchal traditions leave us without clear synchronisms with historical events or characters known from extrabiblical sources. Chapter 14 may contain such a synchronism, but the particular events it may connect with are not identifiable. This means that proposals for historically dating the ancestral period (as distinguished from dating the Genesis sources which now tell about it—see "Authorship and Date," above) must be considered tentative. For various reasons, chronological details within the ancestral history itself (e.g., 15:13; 35:28) cannot be relied on for this purpose (Andrews 1990, 653–54; Christensen 1990, 148; Barrois 1952, 143–45).

Most scholars, nevertheless, locate the ancestral period somewhere in the Middle Bronze Age (between 2000 and 1500 C.E.) since certain features of the ancestral history strongly support even if they do not absolutely compel such a conclusion. To begin with, passing comments made here and there by the anonymous narrators about the story being told indicate their own awareness that events in the ancestral history belong to an age much earlier than theirs (see e.g., Gen 12:6; 13:7; 32:32; 35:20).

Additionally, a number of customs and social institutions appearing in the narrative have parallels attested in ancient Near Eastern law codes of the early and middle second millenium (see Daube 1969, 1–73). Further, the personal names of the patriarchs and matriarchs and their families in Genesis are all pre-Yahwistic—containing no theophorous element derived from the name Yahweh (in English transliteration, names beginning with *Jo-* or *Jeho-*, or ending with *-iah* or *-jah*).

Finally, a date in early antiquity for the period in question is suggested by the fact that even though the patriarchal traditions have been revised in the light of the later Mosaic tradition, distinctive non-Yahwistic names for God remain embedded in many of the Genesis patriarchal traditions—especially in those connected with particular sacred sites. Examples include *El Elyon* (*God Most High*, 14:18); *El-roi* ("God of Seeing," 16:13 [mg.]); *El Shaddai* (*God Almighty* or "Mountain God," 17:1; 28:3 [mg.]); *El Olam* (*Everlasting God*, 21:33 [mg.]); and *El Bethel* (*God of Bethel*, 31:13). Collectively these ancient names and understandings of the divine seem to be connected

retrospectively in Exod 3:14 to Yahweh, by Yahweh's self-disclosure to Moses as "the God of your ancestors" (cf. Humphreys 1990; Alt 1966, 10–11).

Abraham, Sarah, and Hagar, 12:1–23:20

12:1-4. Abraham's call. Yahweh's summons to Abraham to *go . . . to the land that I will show you* (v. 1), with its attendant promise of becoming *a great nation*, and the promise of blessing to fall upon Abraham and *all the families of the earth* (vv. 2-3) marks a pivotal point for the entire narrative in Genesis. The call to Abraham and his response (v. 4) reverses the pattern of recurrent expulsion, alienation and scattering abroad that characterizes the human experience portrayed in the first eleven chapters. The promise of CANAAN replaces the loss of Eden.

Without idealizing the human actors—indeed, it portrays them at their human worst and best—the ancestral history, culminating in the story of Joseph (chaps. 37–50), sketches a particular historical option to the conditions of human history recounted in the narrative up to this point.

To bless is to bestow life and empowerment; to curse is to invoke or impose misfortune and evil. The blessing and curse formula used here occurs also in Isaac's blessing of Jacob (27:29) and in the prophet BALAAM's oracle concerning Israel (Num 24:9). It echoes a similar pronouncement made to Noah concerning the shedding of human blood (Gen 9:6; cf. 2 Sam 22:26-27).

The genre or form of the pronouncement thus appears to be a proverbial one in the tradition. The use of the CURSE AND BLESSING motif here expresses the seriousness and gravity with which Israel as Abraham's posterity views its vocation. Put in the form of a pronouncement by God, it functions as a confession of faith in God's providence. Like comparable confessional sayings elsewhere in the OT and NT (and in all religions) it runs the risk of being co-opted by ideological self-interest of one type or another, as warrant for privileged status in society or history.

12:5-9. Abraham's entry into Canaan. The boundaries of the land of Canaan are not precisely or consistently defined in the OT. Those given in Gen 15:18 are not geographical but political, designating the claimed boundaries of the empire of David and Solomon (2 Sam 8:3; 1 Kgs 4:21). The Genesis narratives make clear that Canaan was thought of by later generations as having long been occupied by a variety of indigenous and migrant ethnic groups, among whom Abraham, Sarah, and their nephew Lot arrived as strangers, perhaps during the first half of the second millennium B.C.E. (cf. 15:19-20).

Canaan as a geographical region is generally construed as the territory west of the Jordan River to the Mediterranean Coast, bounded on the south by Egypt and on the north by Lebanon, roughly what was referred to in Roman times as PALESTINE.

Abraham's first stop in Canaan is SHECHEM, in the HILL COUNTRY of Samaria below the slopes of Mount Gerizim, about thirty-six miles north of Jerusalem. Shechem was a major Canaanite city and sacred site before Israel's appearance in the land, and it came to play a religious and political role in Israel throughout its history (see, e.g., Judg 9:1-57; 1 Kgs 12:1, 25; John 4:20-24).

In the Hexateuch (Genesis–Joshua) Shechem in Gen 12 marks the beginning of a narrative itinerary that will conclude with Israel's return to Shechem under Joshua for the great covenant ceremony (Josh 24) that concludes Israel's conquest of Canaan.

Lying about twelve miles north of Jerusalem, BETHEL was an ancient city and temple site in what became Israel's Northern Kingdom after its secession from rule by the Davidic house of Judah (cf. Gen 28:17-18; 1 Kgs 12:28). That Abraham *built . . . an altar to the LORD* at these principal holy places (vv. 7, 8; cf. 13:8) implies his laying hold of the promise of the land.

12:10-20. Abraham and Sarah in Egypt. Abraham's brief sojourn in Egypt because of famine in Canaan seems to be a rehearsal for the enlargement of this motif in the eventual movement of Jacob's (Israel's) descents into Egypt because of worldwide famine in the time of Joseph (chaps. 37–50). The Egyptian connection threads through the entire ancestral history in Genesis, requiring the narrator to explain why, unlike his father Abraham and his son Jacob, Isaac does not go down into Egypt in a time of famine (26:2).

The account of Abraham and Sarah in Egypt is dominated by the story of Abraham attempting to pass off Sarah as his sister. The rationale behind this tradition from J and its parallels (20:1-18 [E] and 26:6-11 [J], regarding Isaac) remains enigmatic. It is possible that the narrators themselves passed on a tradition they did not fully understand but used for their own purposes (see Speiser 1964, 91–4).

The J and E writers seem to take the wife-as-sister tradition to illustrate a precariousness in Abraham's and Sarah's situation (or Isaac's and Rebekah's in 26:6-11) from which God delivers them. The detail

that deliverance included Pharaoh's bestowal of wealth on Abraham (v. 16) is the first appearance of a tradition associated with the EXODUS, that Israel plundered ("despoiled," RSV) the Egyptians (Gen 15:14; Exod 3:21-22; 11:2; 12:35-36). This tradition may in fact be the real clue to understanding the "wife as sister" tradition (see commentary at 20:1-18).

13:1-18. The promised land; Abraham and Lot separate. The agreement between Abraham and Lot to separate and to divide the region between them is made presumably at Bethel (v. 3), from whose height much of the Jordan Valley is visible (vv. 13-16). The tradition serves an etiological purpose in explaining the eventual political divisions along the Jordan Rift between Israel on the western side and the nations of Ammon and Moab, whose common ancestor was Lot (19:30-38), on the east.

The story nevertheless betrays a bias in favor of the later Davidic and Solomonic Israelite hegemony over the area in that God's promise of the land to Abraham and his posterity (vv. 14-17) appears to include all of the region presumably divided between Abraham and Lot (vv. 8-12).

That in this context Abraham finally settles *at Hebron* (v. 18), which will one day become King David's capital in the territory of Judah (2 Sam 2:1-4) before he moves it to Jerusalem, reinforces the impression of hegemonic bias. It will be reinforced further by the immediately following account of Abraham's military rescue of Lot from his capture by invaders from the east (14:1-16).

Consistent with the favorable Israelite and Judahite slant, the Ammonites and Moabites seem implicitly derogated in the narrative. Their ancestor Lot is shown for the most part as a foil to Abraham, who is always the central character in the stories concerning them both. Lot is little more than a cipher. Where he shares the narrative stage with Abraham, he never speaks. He comes to life only in the story of the destruction of Sodom (chap. 19), in which his character is portrayed as weak and ineffectual.

14:1-24. Abraham's rescue of Lot. This chapter is unique in the sense that it clearly belongs to none of the literary sources traceable in the book (principally J, E, or P). It, therefore, must be considered an independent source.

For example, it portrays Abraham as military commander and warrior, a role he plays nowhere else in Genesis. Further, its name for the Deity is Canaanite—*God Most High* (Heb. *El Elyon*; vv. 18, 20, 22).

The priest is *King Melchizedek* whose sanctuary is at *Salem* (v. 18), identified by later tradition—whether correctly or not—as Jerusalem (or "Zion"; cf. Ps 76:2 [MT 76:3]), which was a Canaanite (Jebusite) city in the ancestral period.

Such features of the account would seem to imply that chap. 14 is a very old source. Its association with Jerusalem (v. 18) suggests that the tradition was preserved there. The particular event that it originally referred to, however, and the warring kings that are named, are not now identifiable (see Speiser 1964, 105–109).

The present purpose of the tradition in Genesis, however, seems designed further to contrast invidiously the character of Lot, the progenitor of Ammon and Moab—here associated with Sodom and Gomorrah (vv. 11-12)—with Abraham, the progenitor of Israel and Judah. Lot and his neighbors are portrayed as dependent on Abraham for recovery of their wealth (v. 16); on the other hand, Abraham is portrayed as proudly and virtuously refusing to be made wealthy by anything associated with Sodom (vv. 21-24).

The name *Melchizedek* means "righteous (or rightful) king" (Noth 1928, 161–62; cf. Sarna 1989, 380). Perhaps because of the uniqueness of the tradition in which he appears, and because he predates Israel and is the first priest to be mentioned in the OT, early Jewish and Christian tradition cast the mysterious priest-king MELCHIZEDEK in a messianic role (Ps 110:4; Heb 7:1-17). In Genesis, however, Melchizedek's actions and his association with ancient pre-Davidic Jerusalem are no doubt meant as validation for Davidic Jerusalem's claim to Abraham as ancestor.

15:1-21. God's covenant with Abraham (J). The ceremonial and mythic elements in this passage (vv. 9-12, 17, which interweave the J and E sources) give it the impression of great antiquity (Alt 1966, 84–5). In its present position in Genesis it appears to have been intentionally juxtaposed alongside what is now chap. 14, to counterbalance or even correct the military representation of Abraham given there. In chap. 15, not prowess on the battlefield (14:14-16) but Yahweh is Abraham's *shield* (v. 1; cf. Zech 4:6). Here, Abraham's *reward shall be very great*, not as the booty of war (14:16, 24) but as fulfilment of the promises now to be made.

Perhaps the most significant contrast with the Abraham of chap. 14 is drawn by the twice repeated statement that *the word of the LORD came to Abram* (vv. 1, 4). The expression *word of the LORD*, which occurs

only here in Genesis (and only seven times elsewhere in the Pentateuch), is a specific technical term in the OT for divine REVELATION through a PROPHET (e.g., 1 Kgs 17:2; Hos 1:1; Jer 1:2). Its occurrence here anticipates the explicit assertion later in Genesis that Abraham *is a prophet* (20:7 [E]). The designation of Abraham as a prophet is the first reference to that vocation in the Bible.

Metaphorically speaking, the authentic prophet in the classical OT tradition has, by definition, access to the divine council (Jer 23:18, 22). As the messenger of God, the prophet's words and the actions associated with them are considered by the prophet and his or her disciples to be not the prophet's but God's.

Assigning the office of prophet to Abraham at this point in the narrative is the tradition's way of saying that the three promises—a posterity as many in number as the stars (v. 5), the predicted release from Egyptian bondage (vv. 13-14), and the promise of the land (vv. 18-19) are truly promises of God and not—the inventions of Abraham.

It is worth noting also that the *vision* (v. 1) is associated simply with Abraham himself—the person. The VISION is not associated with a particular place as are theophanies elsewhere in the Genesis ancestral history.

The name (if it is a personal name and not a title) *Eliezer of Damascus* (v. 3) is already obscure in the MT and its translation is conjectural. The possible connection with Abraham's pursuit of the coalition of armies to a location *north of Damascus* (14:15) makes the NRSV translation at least plausible. *Eliezer* would then be a servant or aide of some kind, or possibly—at least potentially—an adopted son. This associate of Abraham is not elsewhere mentioned in the OT.

In contrast to the righteousness of a royalty or priesthood—a meaning embedded in the name Melchizedek (14:18, above)—Abraham's righteousness (or "rightful reputation") rests on his trust in Yahweh: *he believed the LORD; and the LORD reckoned it to him as righteousness* (v. 6; cf. Rom 4:3; Gal 3:6).

Jewish rabbinical tradition refers to the central event in this chapter as "the covenant between the pieces" (Sarna 1989, 111–12). The ceremony is quite strange. Verses 7-12, 17-21 appear to be J, while vv. 13-16, appear to be E. The carefully specified and divided animal bodies (vv. 9-11), and the *smoking fire pot* and *flaming torch* that *passed between these pieces* (v. 17) while *a deep sleep* and *a deep and terrifying darkness* descend upon Abraham (v. 12; the Heb. word for the supernatural "deep sleep" is also used regarding

Adam in Gen 2:21) effectively portray a trance-like episode. The *flaming torch* and *smoking fire pot*—literally "oven" (perhaps in this case a smoking censor used by a priest, if this ceremony is actually performed) represent the holy presence of God. Fire and smoke are typical representations of the divine presence (cf. Exod 3:2, 4; 19:18).

The logic of the ceremony seems to be that the flame and smoke symbolize Yahweh's presence and his acknowledgement of Abraham's offering, and that if Abraham or his posterity fail to keep covenant trust (v. 6), they will become like these divided pieces. An analogous ceremony is so interpreted in Jer 34:18. There also may be a more gruesome symbolism in the implicitly covenental context of the dividing of the body of the Levite's concubine (Judg 19:27-30; see Trible 1984, 79–82 for a further link between this brutal story and the Abraham traditions).

In form though not in substance, the Christian symbol of the New Covenant sacrifice—bread broken as the "body broken for you" (1 Cor 11:24 KJV; NRSV mg.)—seems related to the type of covenant ceremony in Gen 15.

The Amorites were a people indigenous to the land of Canaan; Genesis uses "Amorite" (lit. "Westerner") as more or less synonymous with "Canaanite." That their *iniquity . . . is not yet complete* (v. 16; i.e., not fully exposed) reflects one of a number of theological explanations in the Pentateuch for God's promise of the land to Israel. In this case, the view is that it is not because of Israel's righteousness but because of the "wickedness of these nations" (Deut. 9:4-5) that Israel will be blessed with the land. On the boundaries of Canaan (v. 18), see commentary at 12:5-9. On the clans and peoples named in vv. 19-21 as occupying the land before Israel, see Laughlin 1990.

16:1-6. Birth of Ishmael to Hagar. Sarah's barrenness introduces a recurrent motif regarding the ancestral matriarchs (cf. REBEKAH, 25:21; RACHEL, 29:31). Reference to infertility here creates dramatic tension regarding how and whether the promise made to Abraham of a great posterity (15:5-6) will be fulfilled. It underlines the belief expressed often in the OT, not that the divine role displaces the role of human parents in the conception of life in the womb, but it is what finally makes the human role fruitful (Gen 17:7; 18:10; 30:2; 1 Sam 1:19-20; cf. Ps 139:13).

Sarah's recourse to providing her *Egyptian slave-girl . . . Hagar* to Abraham as Sarah's surrogate (v. 2), so that he will have posterity, may reflect social custom and family law attested in the fifteenth-century B.C.E. tablets from NUZI (Speiser 1964, 120–21). It appears that in the story Sarah offers Hagar to Abraham out duty rather than with any joy.

Hagar's pride in her pregnancy (v. 4) prompts jealousy and harsh treatment from Sarah; when Abraham indulges Sarah's inclinations Hagar runs away (v. 6).

Although his form is not described, *the angel of the LORD* (vv. 7, 9, 10, 11) is a figure more terrestrial than celestial in most of the OT—a human or humanlike representation of God's presence. The word translated "angel" literally merans "messenger," which is also the meaning of the Greek *angelos*, from which "angel" is derived.

In contrast to the several patriarchs in Genesis who receive the promise of innumerable offpring (15:5; 26:4; 28:14; 48:19), Hagar, who will become a single parent (21:14) is the only matriarch to receive that promise.

Form and appearance aside, as a messenger represents the message-sender, so in an even more close association, the angel ("messenger") of the LORD (or of God) stands for God's presence. And often where the angel of God has been speaking, suddenly at the next point in the narrative it is God (or Yahweh) who has been speaking (cf. vv. 13 and 16:1; 18:2 with 18:18; Exod 3:2 with 3:4). The distinction between Yahweh and an angel or messenger is fluid—God and angel flow into and out of each other in human perception.

Hagar, accordingly, marvels that she has *really seen God and remained alive after seeing him* (v. 13). The reality is that the otherness, and therefore strangeness, of God is by its very nature a threat to anyone who encounters it whether rashly or by inadvertence (cf. Gen 32:30; Exod 19:18, 21; Judg 6:22-23; 13:22). An analogy is with the danger of being careless with fire: it is a question of fire's nature, not its evil intent.

The name *Ishmael* (vv. 11, 15) means "God (El) hears." His descendants are the peoples listed in 25:12-18 (cf. 17:20), and they are mostly from the Syrian and Transjordanian desert regions, and from the Arabian peninsula. In the Islamic tradition, Abraham is the first ancestor of the Muslims through Ishmael, as in the Jewish tradition he is of Israel through Isaac.

17:1-27. God's covenant with Abraham (P). The interest in rite and ritual as divinely ordained—in this case, circumcision (17:10ff.)—and the distinctive rhetorical style, make this chapter easy to recognize as belonging to the P source. P's style is characterized by a fastidious concern for exact and correct form— achieved in part by near-verbatim repetition of the same words and phrases for a given object or idea each time it is mentioned. P typically shows a statistical bent also (1:1a; 24-25; cf. chap. 5). The style and content of this chapter contrast strongly with J's account of the Abrahamic covenant given in 15:7-21.

Insofar as this section deals, as well, with God's promise that Sarah in her old age will bear a son (vv. 15-22), it forms a doublet with the account of the same subject in 18:1-15, which is recognizeably J.

Parenthetically, it might be supposed the occurrence of the name *the LORD* in v. 1 is anomalous in a passage assigned on other grounds to P, but in fact it supports the assignment. P never supposes Yahweh was not the ancestors' God, only that before Moses the ancestors knew Yahweh by other names. Here, Yahweh himself asserts that he is *El Shaddai*—"God Almighty." It is consistent with a statement elsewhere attributed by P to Yahweh, that he disclosed himself to the ancestors as "God Almighty," but he did not make himself known to them as "the LORD" (Exod 6:3).

Meaning literally "to cut around," CIRCUMCISION is the removal by careful cutting away of the foreskin, or loose fold of skin, that covers the end of the penis. Circumcision was in ancient times (and continues today) a religious rite of initiation of the male into the group or community. It was practiced in the ancient Near East before it was introduced to the Hebrews (by Abraham, according to the present tradition), and is practiced still today by Jews and Muslims, and other peoples in the world. It is also viewed and used by some as a merely sanitary measure, carrying no particular religious connotation.

Like other religious rites favored in Genesis by the P source—sabbath observance (Gen 2:3) and dietary regulations (9:4)—circumcision is a practice that can be observed in any place; it does not require presence in the temple or any other particular place. This may well be relevant to the fact that the P source is concerned for the religious identity of a people in EXILE.

Sarai and *Sarah* (v. 15) are linguistic variants of each other; the name means "princess." *Abraham* may also be simply a linguistic variant of *Abram* (v. 5), which means "exalted father," although here *Abraham* is taken by the writer to mean father *of a multitude*. The P narrator cites these as changes of name associated with a significant change in status—in this case, entering into covenant with God. The change of Jacob's name to "Israel" is analogous (Gen 32:27-28).

J's account of the covenant with Abraham (15:7-21) did not mention a change in name. That all three sources (J, E, P) together use the "old" forms Sarai and Abram until v. 5 (the P source), and then the "new" forms thereafter, is an interesting example of P's redactional shaping of J and E.

That Abraham *laughed* on being told Sarah would bear a son (v. 17) makes a wordplay on the name of *Isaac* (v. 19), which means "he laughs." There is immediately another wordplay on the name Ishmael, when God says *"As for Ishmael, I have heard you"* (v. 20; "Ishmael" means "God hears").

18:1-15. Yahweh's promise of a son to Abraham and Sarah (J). The self-disclosure of Yahweh to Abraham (v. 1) in this tradition is a showcase example of the J writer's sophisticated way of representing God. On the one hand Yahweh is Abraham's guest at dinner (v. 8). The portrayal is on the other hand subtle and nuanced: for all that Yahweh is understood to be present, his appearance is not described. There is a calculated ambiguity of identity between Yahweh and his representative. *The Lord* appears, but Abraham sees *three men* (v. 2). Later it is implied that one of the three is the LORD and the other two men are angels (18:22; 19:1), but nowhere is this made explicit, least of all while Abraham plays host to God in vv. 1-8 (NRSV smoothes over the ambiguity of identity in vv. 9-10; cf. KJV or RSV, which are closer to the MT).

This scene of promise takes place *by the oaks of Mamre* (v. 1). Earlier Abraham built an altar at MAMRE (13:18); later he will purchase a burial plot for Sarah in the same area (23:19).

Excluded from the presence of male guests, Sarah is *listening at the tent entrance* (v. 12). Hearing the declaration that she would bear a child at her age, she laughs (cf. 17:17 and Abraham's laughter). The ensuing byplay of challenge and denial about her having laughed stresses the laughter theme—Isaac's name means "he laughs." The extended wordplay over Sarah's laughter (vv. 12-15; contrast 17:17) conveys the narrator's sober suggestion that Isaac's birth—the birth of the people destined to be Israel—is an improbable, unlikely happening, in the sense of being of miraculous origin, a singular work of God.

18:16-33. Problems in Sodom. Whether or not God should disclose to Abraham the fate of Sodom is decided in Abraham's favor (vv. 17-19) on the grounds that it will serve as a cautionary tale to his children *to keep the way of the LORD . . . so that the LORD may bring about for Abraham what he has promised him*

(v. 19). The divine promise is conditioned on Abraham's and his children's fidelity to *righteousness and justice.*

Yahweh's decision to make Abraham privy to the approaching destruction of Sodom suddenly casts Abraham in a priestly role, and he intercedes earnestly for the city. The concept that righteousness of the few can be redemptive for sins of the many emerges clearly in this portrayal of Yahweh being persuaded to spare Sodom if even ten righteous people are found there.

Although the historical connection cannot now be traced, this episode may be the source (or an early example of) the Jewish tradition that ten persons constitute a *minyan,* the number of adults necessary for public worship to take place in the synagogue.

19:1-14. Depravity of Sodom. The beginning of J's account of events in Sodom, where Lot is hosting two of the men—now referred to as *angels* (v. 1; cf. 16:7-14)—at dinner in his house, counterpoints the adjacent account of their recent enjoyment of Abraham's hospitality at his tent (18:1-8). The contrast between nomadic tent and urban house is probably intentional. Rightly or wrongly, cities tend to be viewed from the rustic perspective as centers of evil.

It seems clear enough that the attempted assault on Lot's guests threatens homosexual violation of them. The full meaning of the episode may be less obvious, however. References to Sodom and Gomorrah elsewhere in the OT use the cities either as a simile for total destruction (e.g., Jer 50:39-40; Deut 29:22-23; Isa 1:9; 13:19), or as a standard of comparison regarding false worship, social injustice, or general lawlessness (Isa 1:10-17; Ezek 16:48-50). None of the references cite homosexuality as defining the wickedness of Sodom (see Lance 1989, 141–43).

Three central features of the episode outside the door of Lot's house can be stated simply. First, the evil portrayed is not homosexuality per se, but an attempt at gang rape. Second, Lot's offer of his daughters to the mob, in place of his guests, seems outrageous from any perspective. It also suggests there is a social pattern working at some level that subordinates women to the perceived interest of men. In this connection, it must be pointed out that Abraham, and later Isaac, are willing to put their wives at risk for the sake of their own welfare (Gen 12:12-13; 20:11; 26:7).

The third noteworthy feature of the assault on Lot's guests is no mere stereotype of lust run amok, but a more troublesome "type scene" (see Alter 1981,

37–62). What is dramatized is the cruel practice—attested from time to time in human society—to subject strangers and newcomers to homosexual humiliation as a way of impressing upon them their subordinate status (see Lance 1989, 143). Thus the particular act threatened in vv. 4-9 is that of a proud and self-righteous citizenry (cf. v. 9).

A comparable and even more barbaric example of such a pattern is preserved in the story of the Levite's concubine (Judg 19:22-26).

That the messengers' urge Lot to warn members of his family of the imminent destruction—a warning that falls on deaf ears (v. 14)—may be to show that not as many as ten righteous people could be found, whose presence might have spared the city (cf. 18:32). The skepticism of Lot's *sons-in-law, who were to marry his daughters* (v. 14a) insures their own doom and, in turn, becomes the rationale for the subsequent incest between Lot and his daughters (vv. 31-32).

19:15-29. Destruction of Sodom and Gomorrah. An "act of God"—in the modern use of that phrase for a natural disaster (earthquake, flood, volcanic action, or the like)—destroyed Sodom and Gomorrah and the other cities of the plain (cf. 13:12; 14:1-12). This does not preclude understanding it as an act of God in the sense of judgment, which is the way it is interpreted in the present tradition, principally for didactic purposes (see Wiles 1990).

In spite of the brevity of her cameo appearance in the story, Lot's wife, who *looked back* and *became a pillar of salt* (v. 26), is more remembered in tradition than Lot himself. That this is "an old tradition to account for bizarre salt formations in the area" (NOAB v. 26n.) may well be true, but artistically and theologically not especially relevant to J's use of it here. The "looking back" and the "salt" suggest tears and a heart of compassion.

It is possible, further, that by bracketing his story of Sodom with the reference to Lot's wife on the one hand, and to Abraham's intercession for Sodom (18:22-33) on the other, the J writer himself conveys discomfort with the tradition in chap. 19 about Sodom's destruction.

19:30-38. Birth of Ammon and Moab. That the account of the birth of sons to Lot's daughters by incest with their father is placed so closely alongside the prediction of the birth of Isaac to Sarah and Abraham invites a comparison of the traditions with each other. It is hard not to see it as intended by the narrator to be an invidious comparison favoring Israel, descended miraculously from Abraham and Sarah, over the nations Ammon and Moab, descended from Lot and his own daughters, who have been pushed to desperate measures for the sake of their father's posterity.

20:1-18. Sarah as Abraham's sister, again. This brief narrative puzzles readers. *Gerar* is identified as the cite of Abraham's encouter of *King Abimelech*, but GERAR is very difficult to locate in the ancient world. Similar problems surround the king; nothing is known beyond what is said about him here, in 21:22-34 and chap. 26. Whether these citations all refer to the same person is not clear because the personal name is fairly common in West Semitic literature.

This particular tradition is clearly a variant (attributed to E) of the like tradition in 12:10-20 (attributed to J). Both are somehow related to another such episode involving Isaac and Rebekah (26:6-11). Each such encounter finds Abraham or Isaac misrepresenting a wife as a sister because the husband believes his life to be in danger.

In all three cases it turns out, however, that the husbands' lives were not in danger, because when it is discovered that the women are their wives, no harm befalls the husbands. On the contrary, they acquire wealth and protection from their hosts (20:14; cf. 12:16; 26:11-14).

The true point of these particular stories seems to be that Abraham and Isaac, by pretending that their lives are in danger, shrewdly use their wives to place persons of power and wealth in the husbands' moral debt (20:6, 9; cf. 12:18-19; 26:10). The stories reflect the shrewd wisdom of the ancestors who are viewed as having been able to dupe the rulers of the land into enriching them. There may well be here an ironic play on the proverbial admonition: "Say to wisdom, you are my sister" (Prov 7:4).

Abraham is identified as *a prophet* (v. 7). This is the first canonical mention of the prophetic office in the OT (see commentary at 15:1-6).

21:1-7. Birth of Isaac. The report of Isaac's birth combines brief notations from each of the three major sources. That Sarah conceived and bore Isaac *at the time of which God had spoken* (v. 2) recalls 18:10 (J). Reference to Isaac's circumcision recalls 17:9-14 (P). Wordplay between the name Isaac and "laughter" occurs for the third time (cf. 17:17; 18:12-15) but with a theocentric reference, in contrast to the derisive laughter in the previous occurrences: *"God has brought laughter for me; everyone who hears will laugh with me"* (v. 6; see commentary at 18:9-15). This appears to be from the E source.

21:8-21. Expulsion of Hagar and Ishmael. The threat to the life of Ishmael in being exposed to the elements (vv. 15-16) parallels the threat to the life of Isaac in being bound on the altar (chap. 22; both traditions bear the characteristics of E). On both occasions, the threat arises when God tells Abraham to do that which will endanger the son—send Hagar and Ishmael away (v. 12), and offer Isaac on the altar (22:2). On both occasions, the threat is resolved at the last moment by the miraculous provision of *a well of water* for Ishmael to drink from (v. 19), and *a ram caught in a thicket by its horns* to be substituted for Isaac on the altar (22:13).

The two traditions exhibit a striking differences between themselves also: the women, Sarah and Hagar, are the primary human actors in the drama of Hagar's and Ishmael's expulsion, and Abraham is merely compliant (v. 14). In the story of the binding of Isaac (chap. 22), however, Abraham is the chief actor, and Sarah, who would seem to have a stake in what will happen to Isaac, is not even mentioned.

Nothing is said of Abraham's emotions or inner thoughts as he prepares to sacrifice Isaac; Hagar, on the other hand, says to no one in particular, *"Do not let me look on the death of the child,"* and sitting a long way off, *she lifted up her voice and wept* (v. 16).

Except for references to his descendants (see commentary at 16:15) and to his helping Isaac with the burial of their father (25:9; see commentary at 25:8-10), no more is told of Ishmael than the brief details here. Living *in the wilderness of Paran* (v. 21) locates the tribe or clan, of which Ishmael is the eponymous ancestor, in a region somewhere between the southern end of the Dead Sea and the northern border of the Wilderness of Sinai. Ishmaelite caravaneers will appear in the story of Joseph, where they buy Joseph from his brothers as a slave to be sold in Egypt (Gen 37:25-28).

21:22-34. Abraham's covenant at Beer-sheba. The name *Beer-sheba* can be translated as both "well of seven" (cf. the thrice-repeated *seven ewe lambs* [vv. 28-30] and "well of the oath" [v. 31]). The like-sounding words in Hebrew both derive from the same verbal root, so that to take an oath concerning something may be said, as it were, to "seven" it—the number is believed a good omen.

The tradition is essentially an etiological tale concerning the founding of BEERSHEBA, a major urban center today on the northern edge of Israel's NEGEB which dates back at least to the Iron II period (i.e., ca. 1000 B.C.E. and later). Based on available archaeological evidence, its association as an urban center in the ancestral period would seem to be traditional but lacking historical support (Sarna 1989, 389).

The name for God as *the Everlasting God* (v. 33) appears only here in the OT. Thought originally to have been the name of one of the ancestral pre-Israelite deities worshipped in Canaan, it is now made an epithet of Yahweh: *the LORD, the Everlasting God* (Alt 1966, 10–11, 34). The *tamarisk tree* that Abraham plants is presumably a memorial to the covenant with Abimelech (v. 32); it may also have been a sacred tree, in the context of Abraham's worship.

Abimelech and *Phicol* appear again in the doublet of this tradition at 26:26-33, where the naming of Beer-sheba is associated with Isaac. It is possible that these are not personal names but titles, for it seems unlikely that both men could be associated with both Abraham and then, considerably later, with Isaac. More likely is it that the two stories are simply doublets of each other in the tradition.

22:1-19. The binding of Isaac. The belief narrated here, that Abraham was commanded by God to offer Isaac as a burnt offering, is traditionally referred to in the Jewish tradition as "the binding of Isaac," or simply as "the *Akedah*." Several important features of the way this tale is told have been mentioned above in the comparison of it with the story of the expulsion of Hagar and Ishmael (see commentary at 21:8-21). Coming mainly from the E source (vv. 1-13, 19, although vv. 14-18 appear to be J), this narrative is a showcase example of the classically laconic, allusive, and introverted style of Hebrew narrative in the OT.

Paradoxically, in the absence of reference to the characters' emotions, the laconic reporting of a word or a gesture (e.g., vv. 1, 3, 7-8) forces the reader-listener to reflect on what must be happening emotionally "behind the scenes." The narrator relies heavily on the involvement of audience imagination (for a study of the impact of the narrative style in this passage see Auerbach 1953, 7–12).

No further identification of the site of the Akedah is given other than *the land of Moriah* (v. 2). Identification is made more of a puzzle by the literal wording in Hebrew: "the land of *the* Moriah." Later biblical tradition associates MORIAH with the temple site in Jerusalem (2 Chr 3:1), as does Islamic tradition. Samaritan tradition holds that the altar for Isaac was on Mount Gerizim, above Shechem.

God tested Abraham (v. 1) makes it explicit that the command to offer up Isaac is from God. The syntax of this Hebrew sentence has "God" in the emphatic position, that is, before the verb. Usually in Hebrew the noun-subject follows the verb.

The story sets forth and explores the enigma that God claims the offering up of the very life he has given. That it is meant to show that sacrifice of the firstborn human is not finally God's wish, is a possible and understandable way of reading it. Yet if God is willing to forgo such an offering, it remains troublesome that Abraham's faith should be measured by his willingness to offer up Isaac if called to do so (vv. 15-18). The story can also be interpreted to mean that God alone can ask for such a sacrifice, in which case the lesson is directed against humanity's readiness to sacrifice its children on some lesser altar such as the nation in war.

Søren Kierkegaard's extended and profound meditation on the import of God's testing of Abraham, and the meaning of Abraham's faith in being prepared to obey, found in *Fear and Trembling*, offers a classic perspective on this difficult story.

That at the end of the story Abraham rejoins his servants and returns with them to Beer-sheba, but nothing is said of Isaac's return, led some Jewish interpreters to the disturbing speculation that this perhaps implies that Isaac was indeed sacrificed by Abraham after all. (On this view, and for a comprehensive history of Jewish and Christian interpretations of the tale, including Christian interpretations of it as pointing to the sacrifice of Jesus Christ, see Spiegel 1967.)

22:20-24. Descendants of Nahor. The inclusion in this genealogy of *Bethuel . . . the father of Rebekah* suggests that the twelve sons of Abraham's brother Nahor are included at this point in anticipation of the story of Isaac and Rebekah that will follow shortly (chap. 24).

23:1-20. Death and burial of Sarah at Hebron. Although it contains dialogue more animated than is elsewhere found in the P source, this story seems on the whole to be in the style of P (careful attention to detail in general, and legal procedural detail in particular).

Kirath-arba is an older name for *Hebron* (v. 2), located about nineteen miles south of Jerusalem. HEBRON would later become the first capital of the Davidic kingdom, before David moved his capital to Jerusalem (2 Sam 2:1-4).

The *Hittites* (v. 3) are literally "children of Heth." These are not the HITTITES of Anatolia (the region of modern Turkey), but "a late and very minor element in the ethnic mix of Iron Age Canaan" (Dever 1990a).

The cave of Machpelah (v. 9) is the burial site not only of Sarah, but, in due course at their deaths, of Abraham, Isaac, and Jacob. Two of the other three matriarchs, Rebekah and Leah will also find rest here (49:29-32; 50:13). Rachel would be buried near Bethlehem (35:19-20) or, according to another tradition, in the territory of Benjamin north of Jerusalem (1 Sam 10:2). (For a concise overview of the importance of MACHPELAH in the tradition, see Sarna 1989, 156–57.)

Isaac and Rebekah. 24:1–26:35

24:1-67. Betrothal of Isaac and Rebekah. This lovely story from the J source speaks for itself and requires little explanation. A wife for Isaac is not to be found not among the Canaanites, viewed as corrupt and idolatrous, but from Abraham's *country* and *kindred* (vv. 3-4). Abraham (and later Isaac; 28:1-2) remains oriented to the Mesopotamian lands of his origin even as he consolidates residence in the land of Canaan.

Consistent with tradition, it will be an arranged marriage—Isaac takes no part in the mission of Abraham's steward, who brings negotiation with Rebekah's family successfully to conclusion. Before the betrothal is finally agreed to by the family, however, Rebekah is asked whether she is willing to go with Abraham's servant. Her response, *"I will,"* (24:58), matches in both its faith and its brevity of expression Abraham's own ready response (*and he went*; 12:4) when called to leave his *country and . . . kindred* to go to Canaan (12:1).

The story thus marks the transition between the generation of Abraham and Sarah and the generation of Isaac and Rebekah. At the story's beginning, Abraham inaugurates the action; at its consummation, with the servant's return, having carried out Abraham's wishes, Isaac and Rebekah are in the foreground, and Abraham is not mentioned (24:62-67). The name *Rebekah* in Hebrew may mean "link" or "connection" between people (Noth 1966, 10).

The phrase describing the servant's oath-taking—he *put his hand under the thigh of Abraham* (v. 9)—is a euphemism meaning that he touched Abraham's genitals. Such a gesture was apparently a traditional sign signifying that the person's life will be served faithfully by the oath-taker's fulfilment of the oath. The sign in this case underscores the importance of finding a wife for Isaac (cf. 47:29).

The home of Rebekah and her father, Bethuel and brother, Laban is *Aram-naharaim* (v. 10). The name means "Aram of the two rivers"; the region would therefore appear to be somewhere in northern Mesopotamia. It is apparently synonymous with Paddan-Aram (25:20).

25:1-18. Abraham's many lines of descendants, at his death. This genealogical list, cited along with notice of Abraham's death and burial (vv. 8-10), recalls the covenant promise to Abraham that his posterity would be as many as *the stars* of heaven (15:5). The citation also intends to confirm, however, that Isaac and his posterity, not other descendants (or their posterity), are the true heirs of Abraham (v. 5).

25:8-10. Abraham's death and burial. On *the cave of Machpelah* (v. 9) see commentary at 23:9. An affecting detail in this citation is the reference to fraternal collaboration between Isaac and Ishmael in the burial of their father.

25:12-18. Descendants of Ishmael. The names found here reflect the earlier material from 16:15 (see commentary there). These verses bring closure to the story of Ishmael (he will be mentioned in passing when Easu arranges to marry one of Ishmael's daughters [28:9]) in a manner that preserves his heritage and dignity. Although he is the "son of right" and not the "son of promise" (Brueggeman 1982, 203) Ishmael is assured a place among the descendants of Abraham.

25:19-28. Birth of Esau and Jacob. Whereas the list of Ishmael's descendants brings closure to his role in Genesis, the mention of Isaac's offspring hearlds the beginning of an important new phase of the partriarchal story. Isaac's sons, Esau and Jacob, are the ancestors, respectively, of Edom and Israel (25:30; 36:1; 32:28); hence the oracle to Rebekah, *"Two nations are in your womb"* (25:23). By the late postexilic period and in NT times Edomites have moved from Transjordan into southern Judah where the region becomes referred to by the Roman (Latin) form of the name Edom—Idumea. Herod the Great, at the end of whose reign Jesus was born, was Idumean.

The tradition that Israel and Edom are brother nations is widely attested and is unlike any relationship claimed with other nations or peoples in the OT (cf. Deut 23:8; Numb 20:14; Obad 10; Mal 1:2). Edom is the only people that shares with Israel the same ancestral parents. It is possible that buried in the tradition is a memory that somewhere in their early history the two peoples shared a common cultic tradition.

A number of references to Yahweh in the OT associate God positively with the region of Edom (or Seir, another name for Edom; cf. Gen 36:9)—see, for example Judg 5:4; Deut 2:5; 33:2; Hab 3:3. It is possible, but not demonstrable, that the name of the Edomite deity *Qos* (or *Qaus*) appears in the priestly name Kushaiah (1 Chr 15:17), which, if so, would imply the existence at some point in history of a community that identified *Qos* with Yahweh.

The folk etymology of Jacob's name plays on the similarity in Hebrew between the word *heel* and the name *Jacob*, which means "he supplants." The oracle predicting Jacob's ascendancy over Esau (v. 23) is already being fulfilled. Similarly, the name *Esau* is related to his redness at birth; that etymology is underscored in the following passage where Esau trades his heritage for some *red stuff* Jacob had prepared (25:30).

25:29-34. Esau sells his birthright. Sibling rivalry is anticipated by parental favoritism: *Isaac loved Esau . . . but Rebekah loved Jacob* (v. 28). The oracular prediction to Rebekah that *the elder shall serve the younger* (v. 23) is complemented by the narrator's moralizing observation that *Esau despised his birthright* (v. 34), the inheritance rights of the eldest son. The implication is that Esau didn't deserve his birthright. This judgment about Esau becomes embedded in later tradition (cf. Heb 12:15-17).

26:1-5. Promise of the land reaffirmed to Isaac. Here and in the rest of chap. 26 Isaac's experiences repeat in a relatively close way those of Abraham earlier. Since it is unlikely that Isaac's career would have been in lockstep with Abraham's, the respective duplications must be variants of each other—one variant featuring Abraham; its doublet featuring Isaac. Which narrative in each of these cases is the earlier cannot be determined with any certainty.

Editorial awareness that variants are being dealt with is suggested by reference to *a famine* besides the one in Abraham's day (v. 1) and by the seemingly gratuitous admonition to Isaac not to *go down to Egypt* (v. 2).

King Abimelech of the Philistines (v. 1) is probably the same figure mentioned in 20:1-18. Reference to the PHILISTINES, who did not enter the region until after the ancestral period, is anachronistic—unless it is taken vaguely to mean merely the people who lived where the Philistines at the time of the recording of the narrative.

My charge, my commandments, my statutes, and my laws (v. 5) is the conclusion of a long quotation attributed to Yahweh (beginning at v. 2). This particular combination of technical terms for divine law in Israel appears only here in Genesis, but with small variation is typical elsewhere in the Pentateuch and the historical books of the OT of the legal language of the D source (for "Deuteronomist"; cf. Deut 7:11; 11:1; 1 Kgs 6:12; see also Gregory 1990). This is the source responsible for the editing of Deuteronomy and the so-called Deuteronomistic History (Joshua–2 Kings).

Genesis 26:5 may be the one place in Genesis rather clearly attributable to the D source—probably by way of editing by P.

26:6-33. A pair of doublets. These passages are doublets of the previous stories about Abraham and Sarah. See commentary at 20:1-18 and 21:22-34.

26:34-35. Esau's Hittite wives. See commentary at 23:3.

Jacob, Rachel, and Leah, 27:1–36:43

27:1-46. Jacob steals Esau's blessing. Besides having induced Esau to surrender his birthright (25:29-34), Jacob—pushed by his mother Rebekah's initiative—now tricks Isaac into bestowing on him the blessing that was rightfully Esau's.

As the story now stands it is more than a little contrived. Jacob's disguise (vv. 15-16) would scarcely appear capable of fooling anyone, even one whose *eyes were dim*, like Isaac's (v. 1). Isaac's credulity, especially in the face of his own suspicions (vv. 20, 22, 24), seems a bit improbable. Contrived or not, the narrative is very entertaining.

The story may originally have carried a merely chauvinistic and perhaps comic thrust, expressing ancient Israel's delight over a story of a rival people or ancestor outwitted by one of their own. It was probably firmly planted in the tradition before its appropriation by the J writer, who uses it now to show how Israel's destiny under God according to the oracle in 25:23 was working itself out in the relationship between the brothers. On the blessing and curse formula in v. 29b, see commentary at 12:3.

The notion that a blessing (or for that matter, a curse), once uttered, cannot be withdrawn or transferred to another (v. 33, 35), reflects a general view held in the OT literature of the gravity and power of the spoken word. Thus when Isaac responds to Esau's pleas for a blessing it is only a dark saying (vv. 39-40), not a blessing like the eloquent invocation of success and prosperity spoken to Jacob (vv. 27-29). Neither is it a curse, however (vv. 39-40). What is said to Esau hints at some future recovery of Esau's (and Edom's) fortunes (v. 40b)—the J writer here perhaps alluding to events in the days of Solomon or later (cf. 1 Kgs 11:14-22, 25; 2 Kgs 8:20-22).

Esau's plan to kill Jacob in revenge for what he has done comes to the attention of Rebekah, who warns Jacob to flee to her own family in Paddan-Aram (vv. 43-44). Rebekah then advises Isaac that she will not have Jacob marry *one of the Hittite women* (v. 46). The purity of the stock of Abraham is once again assured (cf. 26:34-35 and commentary at 23:3).

28:1-22. Jacob's journey to Paddan-aram. This narrative is a conflation of the J and E sources, with an introduction by P (vv. 1-9). P's form of Isaac's blessing is less ebullient than J's (27:27-29) and brings the blessing explicitly into line with the Abrahamic tradition (v. 4). P's citation of Esau's desire to please his father by not marrying *one of the Canaanite women* (vv. 6, 8) is probably motivated more by P's dislike of the Canaanites (or of what they represent for him) than by a desire to treat Esau sympathetically.

Jacob's dream at Bethel (vv. 10-22) is an etiological legend associating the founding of the temple at BETHEL with Jacob. It is a mixture of the sources J (vv. 10-11a, 13-16, 19) and E (11b-12, 17-18, 20-22). Bethel is also one of the places where Abraham built an altar to Yahweh on his inital exploration of the land of promise (see 12:8).

The Hebrew word for *ladder* also means "stairway" or "ramp" (v. 12, NRSV mg.) Rather than a runged ladder, therefore, what Jacob sees in his dream may indeed be steps leading up a steep incline like that leading up the side of a ziggurat or temple tower (see commentary at 11:1-9). Consistent with the foregoing observation, the *angels* in Jacob's dream would not be winged celestial beings (who would not need a ladder or stairway), but quite possibly would be priests in temple service.

The heart of this narrative appears to be the reaffirming to Jacob of promises made to Abraham (vv. 13-16). The renewal establishs Jacob, later named "Israel," as heir to the promises to Abraham and Isaac.

The Hebrew name for God at this point is *elohim*—not *el*, as in the name *Bethel* (v. 19). It would appear that the E writer is concerned not to imply that Jacob worshiped the Canaanite god El. It is the J writer who associates Bethel explicitly with God in Jacob's dream.

29:1-14. Jacob meets Rachel. In contrast to the story of Isaac's betrothal to Rebekah (chap. 24), the story of Jacob's winning of Rachel moves relatively quickly and with passion. Unlike Isaac, who remained offstage while Abraham's servant arranged everything, Jacob represents himself, and would appear to have swept Rachel off her feet (vv. 9-12). The source is J.

29:15-30. Laban rewards Jacob with Leah, then Rachel. Here the source is E—note the introduction of Rachel as if for the first time (v. 16), ignoring her appearance earlier (vv. 9-12).

Laban's deception of his nephew in substituting Leah for Rachel on the wedding night (v. 23) lends a touch of the farcical to the narrative—*when morning came, it was Leah!* (v. 24). The narrative suggests poetic justice for Jacob who had substituted himself for Esau (27:18-29). The entire saga of Jacob's and Laban's relationship (chaps. 29–31) will prove to be a battle of wits, which Jacob ultimately wins.

29:31–30:24. Birth of Jacob's sons and daughter. To these announcements of the birth of Jacob's first eleven sons and his daughter, *Dinah* (30:21), must be added the later report of the birth of *Benjamin* (35:16-18). The several traditions more or less speak for themselves and need not receive special comment.

It is generally recognized that the traditional list of the twelve tribes represented here by their eponymous ancestors is an "official" list, and somewhat artificial, coming from some time during the monarchic period (see Devries 1990, 932–33).

What may be less obvious on the printed page, however, is that the sons (or the tribes of which they are the eponymous ancestors) that are descended from Jacob's wives—Leah and Rachel, and their respective servantmaids Zilpah and Bilhah—can be seen on a map (e.g., MDB Plate 11, or Gottwald 1985, 130) to form rough geographical groupings according to the particular mothers by whom they are related in the genealogical passages under consideration.

The Rachel tribes—Joseph (subdivided between Ephraim and Manasseh) and Benjamin—form together the major territorial region north of Jerusalem. The Leah tribes—Reuben, Simeon, Judah, Issachar, and Zebulon (omitting Levi, who has no territory)—together frame the Rachel tribes to the north and south of the latter, with Judah and Reuben sharing the whole region south of Jerusalem, on either side of the Jordan. The Zilpah tribes—Gad and Asher—are separated from each other and are relegated to the northern and eastern fringe of Israel. The Bilhah tribes—Dan (after the migration northward; cf. Judg 17–18) and Naphtali—lie at the northern extremity of Israel.

The correlations are imperfect or incomplete at some points, but marked enough to suggest that the Genesis writers have sought to order the birth narratives artificially by associating the mothers with particular geographical regions.

Dinah, whose birth is noted in v. 21, is identified with no tribe. Her place in the narrative is apparently to prepare for the story of Dinah and Shechem in chap. 34. She is mentioned after that only in Gen 46:15.

30:25-43. Jacob acquires wealth through magic. Once more an element of farce is injected into the narrative. In a spirited contest between Laban's mendacity and Jacob's skill with magic, Jacob outwits his uncle. Agreeing between them that Jacob's wages shall be only the *speckled and spotted* among the sheep and goats, and *every black lamb* (v. 32), Laban proceeds to remove all such animals from his flock and sends them off with his sons three days' journey away from Jacob.

Using "sympathetic magic" (the peeled rods are presumed somehow to influence genetically the color of the animals when they breed at the watering trough where Jacob has placed the rods) Jacob builds his own flock, which he sequesters from Laban's (vv. 37-44).

The acquisition of wealth ascribed here to Jacob is hyperbolic (v. 43) and seems to exemplify a heightened stage in a programatic movement through the whole of Genesis from the initial blessing of Abraham (12:1-3) to what will become finally the spectacle of Joseph administering the wealth of *all the world* (41:57).

31:1-18. Jacob departs for Canaan. Jacob's explanation to Rachel and Leah (v. 4) of how he came by his wealth constitutes E's version of the preceding account from J. There the outcome depended altogether on Jacob's cleverness; here it is ascribed to the working of God (vv. 9-13). His wives support Jacob's decision (vv. 14-16), and Jacob sets out for Canaan with his family and herds.

31:19-42. Rachel's theft of the household gods. The story of Rachel's theft of Laban's images of the household gods, and her prevention of Laban's discovery of them—by sitting on them and declining to rise, claiming that she is in her menstrual period (v. 35)—is clearly designed to discredit the gods in the eyes of those who worship them.

31:43-55. The covenant at Mizpah. Laban's frustrated capitulation to Jacob's manifest success (v. 43) leads him to propose a covenant between himself and Jacob. Laban's invocation, *"The LORD watch between you and me, when we are absent one from the other"*

(v. 49), is not a kind of benediction commending the parties to divine care while they are apart. Rather, as the context requires (vv. 50, 52) it is a warning not to do any harm to one another's interests while out of each other's sight. It is a covenant between parties who remain suspicious of each other.

32:1[MT 32:2]–33:17. Jacob makes peace with Esau. The cycle of stories now returns to unfinished business. Jacob had been sent away to escape Esau's wrath; now that he is returning, he must confront his brother. While the narrative plot is not complicated, there are certain wordplays apparent in MT that seem to lend a mystical dimension to the story, which are not preserved in translation, as follows:

The Hebrew word translated as *angels* (32:1) is the same word that is translated *messengers* in 32:3, 6 (see commentary at 16:7-14). Thus, Jacob is met by God's messengers, and sends his own messengers to meet Esau.

The Hebrew word translated *camp* (32:2) is the singular form of the same word that is left here untranslated, *Mahanaim*, which in turn is the same word that is translated as *two companies* in 32:7, 10. Thus *God's camp* is paralleled by Jacob's *two companies*. Jacob and his family will later be divided, with his family on one side of the Jabbok (32:23) and he alone on the other, to wrestle with God (32:24, 30).

Peniel (32:30) literally means "face of God [*el*]." As Jacob gives this name to the place, he declares, *"For I have seen God [elohim] face to face, and yet my life is preserved."* When Jacob finally meets his sibling rival, Esau, he declares, *"To see your face is like seeing the face of God"* (33:10). Jacob's struggle with Esau (cf. 25:22) is paralleled by his wrestling with God (vv. 24-26) and in both instances Jacob has prevailed. The mysterious wrestler summarizes the story: *"You have struggled with God and with humans, and have prevailed"* (32:28). At this point, *Jacob* is renamed *Israel* (32:28).

Verses 25 and 31 bracket Jacob's struggle with reference to his limping, because of his hip, struck by the wrestler (32:25). This may be an etiological element from an earlier form of the tradition to account for a limping dance performed at the site sacred to the Canaanite god El. In the present use of the tradition, it implies Jacob is marked by his struggle. The reference to the dietary tradition (32:32) is an etiological footnote, possibly placed there by the narrator to deflect attention from his more serious purpose—in the nature of metaphorical understatement.

Following the intense description of Jacob's struggle the narrative shifts to a scene of reconciliation. Esau appears to have forgiven Jacob, or at least to have been so impressed by the size of his family and his herds (cf. 29:10) that he prudently gives up further thought of revenge. Jacob, however, remains distrustful or fearful of Esau—he clearly wants to avoid having Esau or his men accompany him (33:12-15). Like the peace with Laban (31:43-55), Jacob's peace with Esau is uneasy. Esau was quick to relinquish his birthright (25:29-34) and now seems equally eager to offer forgiveness.

33:18-20. Jacob at Shechem. These verses stand out as a crude seam at the intersection of two rich patches in the Jacob stories. There are two ways to read this brief account of Jacob settling in Shechem. It may be the conclusion to the narrative that began at 32:1. If so, the account of purchasing land and building an altar punctuates Jacob having come full circle since his dispute with Esau (25:27-34; 27:1-45; see Westermann 1985, 527–30). Because the following narrative is set in Shechem some would see these verses as an introduction to a new movement in the Jacob stories (see Brueggemann 1982, 275).

Whether the ending of one narrative or the beginning of another, vv. 18-20 present puzzles of their own. *Shechem* is a son *of Hamor* from whom Jacob buys land (in 34:2 Hamor is further identified as *the Hivite, prince of the region*). Shechem must be understood as the eponymous ancestor of the region; the attentive reader will also know that Jacob is the eponymous ancestor of Israel.

Also curious is the altar that is called *El-Elohe-Israel*. The altar building recalls Abraham's survey of the land in Gen 12–13, suggesting that Jacob now lays claim to the land. If *Israel* is a specific reference to Jacob (cf. 32:28) then the altar is an outpost. If *Israel*, however, is taken as a reference to all the people of God, then the altar "is the beginning of a permanent cult of the God of Israel" (Westermann 1985, 529). Both readings are appropriate.

34:1-31. The rape of Dinah. The narrative is less about Dinah than it is about the total destruction of the city of Shechem by Simeon and Levi. The rape of Dinah leads to what follows and seems to be an etiological explanation for the Shechem's destruction.

By the time of the J writer—the source for this tradition—the tribe of Simeon has become more or less scattered within the territory of Judah, and the tribe of Levi has no territory but has been reduced to the status of servant priests. Consequently this must be a very old tradition that preserves the memory of a time well before the Israelite monarchy, when Simeon and Levi were marauding bands to be reckoned with. This is consistent with their portrayal in Gen 49:5-7, where their cruel violence is recalled and their ultimate decline predicted.

35:1-15. Jacob's return to Bethel. In its present form this section is something of an appendix to the narrative cycle up to this point. The *foreign gods* (vv. 2-4) in Jacob's household recall those brought to Canaan by Rachel (31:19-42). The hiding of them *under the oak that was near Shechem* (v. 4) may be a tendentious thrust against Canaanite cults at Shechem; the events of chap. 34 seem unrelated here. Verse 9-15 contain P's version of God's reiteration to Jacob of the covenant promises made to Abraham (cf. 17:1-8).

35:16-20. Birth of Benjamin; death of Rachel. Rachel's death in childbirth as she bears Benjamin (v. 18) suggests somehow a status apart for Rachel, Jacob's most-loved wife (29:30) and for Benjamin, Jacob's youngest son and the only one to be born in Canaan. Benjamin will be a significant figure in the story of Joseph and his brothers (cf. 43:1–44:34). Rachel is the only one of the matriarchs and patriarchs of Israel not to be buried at Machpelah (see commentary at 23:9).

35:21-22a. Reuben's immorality with Bilhah. Why this brief notice should be placed just here seems a bit arbitrary, except that it does prepare the way for the allusion to this event in Jacob's deathbed "blessing" of Reuben (cf. 49:1-4; cf. Deut 33:6). The tradition may reflect the memory of a sortie in earliest times by the Reubenites against one or both of the small Bilhah tribes.

35:22b-26. The twelve sons of Jacob. This somewhat perfunctorily offered list is apparently from P. The inclusion of Benjamin among *the sons that were born to [Jacob] in Paddan-aram* (v. 26b) ignores or overlooks what appears the much more authoritative tradition concerning Benjamin in 35:16-20.

35:27-29. Death of Isaac. *Esau and Jacob* assist each other at the burial of their father Isaac, as Isaac and Ishmael had done at the burial of Abraham (25:9). By this point in the narrative we have grown comfortable with Jacob's importance over Esau. For that reason the naming of Esau first in the burial narrative is a jolt. Since 25:23 we have expected the brothers to fight. Now they are reconciled in the face of a solemn task.

36:1-43. Descendants of Esau. The genealogy is a combination of several lists, the sources of which are not easily recognized (see Speiser 1964, 280–83). What is remarkable about this genealogy is that the Jacob stories conclude with a thorough acknowledgment of Esau! Even though the narratives from Gen 25–33 make it plain that the son of right (Esau) is not the son of promise (Jacob), this list of Esau's descendants serves as a caution to Israel to avoid an arrogant appropriation of their ELECTION (see Brueggemann 1982, 285–87).

Joseph and His Brothers, 37:1–50:26

The story of Joseph and his brothers is the longest single narrative unit in Genesis. In form it is a *novella*—a short prose tale that typically stresses moral teaching. It is a composite work, combining the sources J and E, with a few brief insertions by P (presumably the final redactor; see Gottwald 1985, 151–53).

Certain distinctive literary and theological features that set the story of Joseph apart from what precedes it call for preliminary commentary that helps frame the story. There are two notable absences in the Joseph stories and four points of correlation with the rest of the book.

(1) The absence of a matriarch. Although in the story Joseph marries the daughter of an Egyptian priest, *Asenath* (41:45), who bears him *two sons* (41:50-52), Asenath does not otherwise play a role in the narrative. Thus, in spite of the prominence of Joseph, the story has no matriarch among its cast of characters—unlike the typical ancestral traditions surround Abraham and Sarah, Isaac and Rebekah, and Jacob, Rachel, and Leah.

(2) Absence of THEOPHANY. A more striking feature is that unlike the patriarchal experience, and in spite of Joseph's many and sincerely pious references to God (e.g., 39:9; 40:8; 50:19), nowhere in the Joseph story is Joseph explicitly addressed by God. Neither does God appear to him directly. Whatever Joseph's inner experience, there is no explicit theophany for Joseph in the story. God does address Jacob (Israel) *in visions of the night* (46:2-4), but this is a true case of the exception proving the rule. God remains in the background in the Joseph narratives. In every episode it is Joseph as a human being who is in the foreground.

The relation of the Joseph story to the primeval history (Gen 1–11) raises the question of the overall unity of Genesis. Granted that the whole work has a composite character, there is the assumption that there is an interior logic to the work in its present redaction. The end, therefore, must somehow answer to the beginning. Affirmations made in the beginning must somehow be confirmed or validated (or exposed as invalid) by the way things turn out at the end. Questions raised or problems posed at the start must be shown as dealt with by what happens at the finish. When this is undertaken with Genesis, evidence for the book's unity emerges at four points.

(1) Joseph and the Eden story. In the oldest of the two creation accounts (2:4b–3:24 [J])—and its exploration of the mystery of human sin and guilt—the dialogue between the serpent and the woman is prominent. The serpent says to the woman, *You will not die; for God knows that when you eat of [the forbidden tree] your eyes will be opened, and you will be like God, knowing good and evil* (3:4-5).

It seems more than coincidence that in the concluding chapter of Genesis, when the brothers appeal to Joseph for forgiveness, he responds as follows: "Do not be afraid! Am I in the place of God? As for you, you meant evil against me, but God meant it for good, to bring it about that many should be kept alive, as they are today" (50:19-20 RSV, a more accurate rendering of the MT than the NRSV).

Here then is a significant correspondence between beginning and ending. The serpent had declared, *You will be like God*; Joseph exclaims, *Am I in the place of God?* The serpent had promised, . . . *knowing good and evil*; Joseph declares, "You meant evil against me but God meant it for good" (RSV). The serpent had said, *You will not die*; Joseph declares, "God meant to bring it about, that many should be kept alive as they are today" (RSV).

The use of these specific words in Joseph's conversation with his brothers, in which he seems to speak to the serpent's argument (3:4-5) point for point, is intended to serve as a dramatic theological reversal of the Eden scene. Thus the Joseph story serves as a resolution of the human situation exposed in Eden.

(2) Joseph as opposite in character to the primeval ancestors. In the early narratives, the human ("Adam") was entrusted with caring for the earth (1:26-28; 2:15) but is described as forfeiting the trust (e.g., 3:17-19; 6:1-4). Humans in the primeval history fail to meet the responsibilities demanded of them. By contrast Joseph, who has become the manager of Egypt's economy and to that degree a savior of the world (41:53-57; 47:13-

26), is seen to be the kind of human being the first ancestors were intended to be but fell short of becoming.

(3) Joseph and the ancestral history. The blessing of the patriarchs, seen in its universal aspect as meant for all the peoples of the earth (*In you all the families of the earth shall be blessed* [12:3b; cf. 18:18; 22:18; 28:14]), is for Abraham, Isaac, and Jacob a promise for the future. In the Joseph story, this promise is being fulfilled—*The LORD blessed the Egyptian's house for Joseph's sake* (39:5; cf. 41:53-57; 50:20b).

(4) Joseph as model for humankind. The question, finally, is not whether Joseph is psychologically or socially a universally appealing or likeable human character, but how he or the tradition about him is used to express what the compilers of the Genesis narratives are trying to say. The Joseph story is integrated in an artful way with the events and theological affirmations of the preceding Genesis material and serves as its artistic and theological culmination.

A work that began with troublesome humankind's infidelity to the Spirit by which it was created—a universal situation (chaps. 1–11) to which God responds with the call to Abraham and his posterity (chaps. 12–36), finds its end in the career of Joseph. Joseph is represented in Genesis as an ideal for Israel and the human race, and it is toward the incarnation of this ideal in Joseph that the whole Genesis narrative moves. Pharaoh himself sums it up, as he exclaims rhetorically: *Can we find anyone else like this—one in whom is the spirit of God?* (41:38).

A book that began promisingly with humankind made in the image of God (1:26-28), after many trials and adventures ends redemptively with a portrayal of that humanity finding itself in the person of Joseph. To his story we now turn.

37:1-36. Joseph sold into slavery. The beginning the Joseph story recapitulates certain elements of the story of Cain (4:1-12), although without its unhappy outcome. Joseph's brothers *hated him* (v. 4) and *conspired to kill him* (v. 18). Strife between brothers is a motif running through the whole of Genesis.

As "helper" to the Bilhah and Zilpah tribes, Joseph, ancestor of what are territorially the two largest tribes (Manasseh and Ephraim; cf. 41:50-52) enters the story being associated with the four smallest tribes, which are immediately to the north of the Joseph tribes. These, apparently, are the brothers who hated him and conspired to kill him.

Reuben (vv. 21-22) and *Judah* (vv. 36-37)—ancestors of the two large tribes to the south of the Joseph tribes—try in different ways to save Joseph from death at the hands of the other brothers. Trouble between Joseph and his brothers in the story, then, would seem to parallel historical rivalries and relationships among the tribes of Israel.

The Hebrew phrase translated *a long robe with sleeves* (v. 3) or "a coat of many colors" (KJV) is problematic as to whether the second term means "colors," "sleeves," or something else. In the OT it occurs only here and at 2 Sam 13:18. The Hebrew word for robe, however, occurs only one other place in Genesis: in the expression *garments* [or robes] *of skins* in Gen 3:21, referring to the garments made by God for Adam and Eve after their expulsion from the garden.

Joseph's dreams (vv. 5-11) foreshadow the events to follow. The brothers' grain-sheaves bow down to Joseph's sheaf (vv. 5-8), and the sun, moon and stars bow down (vv. 9-10)—apparently portrayed in the dream either as gods, or as the animal representations among the signs of the zodiac (cf. commentary at 1:14-19). The meaning of the dreams is plain to Joseph's brothers, his father, and the reader. Since dream interpretations are from God (40:8), Joseph's eventual ascendancy over his brothers and father is determined from the beginning of the story.

The itinerary of Joseph's search for his brothers (vv. 12-17)—from Hebron in the south of Canaan to Dothan (ca. sixty mi. to the north of Jerusalem) covers the three largest tribal territories of Israel. The detail may intend to suggest Joseph or the Joseph tribes EPHRAIM and MANESSEH) as the bond between Judah in the south and the other tribes in the north.

That two different ethnic identifications (vv. 25-28, *Ishmaelites* and *Midianites*) are made of the caravaneers or traders that purchase Joseph may be due to the juxtaposition of the E and J sources. On the other hand, the shift in names could be an indication that the narrator understands them as ethnically more or less synonymous. The two groups were "half-brothers," the *Ishmaelites* being descended from Abraham through Hagar (16:15) and the *Midianites* being descended from Abraham through Keturah (25:1-2).

The brothers' deception of their father Isaac by presenting him with Joseph's blood-stained coat—to make it appear that he had been killed by a wild animal (vv. 31-35)—recalls Jacob's analogous deception of Isaac with the clothes of Esau (27:18-29).

38:1-30. Judah and Tamar. The story of Judah and Tamar would seem to be intrusive in the Joseph story. Certain motifs tend to associate it, however, with what precedes and follows it in the Joseph narrative. A comprehensive and insightful treatment of the analogies between this interpolated chapter and the Joseph story in which it is now imbedded is offered in Alter (1981, 5–12). Judah, for example, figures prominently in the Joseph narrative, at the beginning (37:26-27), in the central narrative (chap. 44), and at the end (48:8-12). The tribes Judah and Ephraim–Manasseh are to be the dominant tribes shortly before and during the period of the monarchy. It is not surprising, therefore, that Judah receives attention in this romantic novel dealing the Joseph. It is not entirely clear, however, just what Gen 38 most wants to convey concerning the patriarch Judah, the ancestor of King David.

This narrative portrays, once again, how a resourceful and determined woman finds a way to uphold the demands of tradition in the face of personal tragedy and unfair treatment at the hands of the responsible male leader of the community. The story is in four parts, skillfully woven together: vv. 1-11, Judah and his family in the region of Adullam; vv. 12-23, Tamar takes the initiative to provide a male heir for her dead husband; vv. 24-26, Judah learns of his and Tamar's misdeeds; and vv. 27-30, Tamar bears twins.

As is often the case in these narratives of Genesis, the characters are vividly drawn, in very few words, enabling hearers and readers to reflect on complex human problems in which the question of who is right and who is wrong finds no easy solution.

Adullam is a town northwest of Hebron in the territory of Judah. Settling there, Judah marries an unnamed Canaanite woman, known only as "Shua's daughter" (see v. 2). Judah is not criticized for having done so, just as Joseph will not be criticized for marrying an Egyptian (41:50). But there may be in implied criticism in the account of the conduct of Judah's sons. Judah especially will be shown to be at fault for not having followed the tradition of the levirate marriage—that is, arranging for another family member to provide an heir for a man who dies without a son (see Deut 25:5-11 for the later form of the practice, now presented as a part of the law of Moses). Judah feared the loss of his third and only remaining son, *Shelah* (v. 5), if the latter should marry this unfortunate widow.

But what is Tamar to do? Both her standing and that of her dead husband are endangered if the widow Tamar is not allowed to build up a family. To be a mother in Israel and to provide one's husband with a son are both of critical importance.

Judah's wife (still unnamed) dies, is mourned, and still Tamar remains a widow without a child. At sheep-shearing time, a time for festivities and family visits, Tamar takes matters into her own hands. Pretending to be a prostitute, she bargains with her father-in-law, lies with him, and becomes pregnant. Unwittingly Judah has done what he was unwilling to let his youngest son do, but in doing so, he has endangered the life of Tamar, not that of his son.

Tamar's pregnancy exposes her to death by burning (v. 24; stoning in Deut 22:21), but Judah, on seeing the items he gave as a pledge to the *prostitute*, acknowledges that Tamar is more in the right than he is. He did not give Tamar his third son to provide her and her dead husband with a family.

Like Rebekah, Tamar has twin sons (v. 27). Popular etymologies of the two sons probably developed to explain the prominence that the clan *Perez* was to have in Judah. From this clan King David was to come, and the Gospels trace Jesus' lineage back through this son of Judah and Tamar.

While this story fits loosely into its context within the Joseph narrative, it probably owes its place in the Joseph narrative to the importance of Judah in the story soon to be unfolded and the place that Judah will occupy alongside of the sons of Joseph in the later tribal traditions (see Gen 48–49).

39:1–40:22. Joseph's life as a prisoner in Egypt. Now the story of Joseph resumes. Ishmaelites, rather than Midianites (37:36; see 37:28), sold Joseph to *Potiphar . . . captain of the guard* (v. 1) of Pharaoh, and in Potiphar's house Joseph prospered greatly. It was the LORD who was guiding the career of Joseph, with the result that soon Joseph was the overseer of Potiphar's household and responsible for all of the goods of his Egyptian master. But trouble awaited, in the person of the wife of Potiphar—again, a woman known only through the name of her husband.

The story unfolds in five scenes: 39:1-6a, Joseph enters the household of Potiphar as a slave; 39:6b-18, Potiphar's wife tries to seduce Joseph; 39:19-23, Joseph, falsely accused, is imprisoned; 40:1-19, Joseph interprets the dreams of Pharaoh's imprisoned officials; 40:20-22, Joseph's interpretation of the two dreams proves true.

Potiphar the Egyptian discovers quickly what a treasure has fallen into his hands. Everything that Joseph does is a success, and soon Potiphar can entrust into Joseph's hands all of his affairs. The striking abilities and good fortune that had made his brothers jealous now prepares the way for Joseph to confront a new peril.

The familiar story of the efforts of Potiphar's wife to have sexual relations with Joseph and of Joseph's steadfast rejection of her advances (39:6b-18) became a classic story of virtue in the face of temptation. In the pseudepigraphical work, *The Testament of the Twelve Patriarchs*, the testament devoted to Joseph strongly underscores Joseph's patient endurance of suffering at the hands of those who were jealous of him and his untarnished moral qualities. This struggle between Joseph and Potiphar's wife greatly enhances the aura of romance that surrounds Joseph throughout Jewish history and literature. The Book of Proverbs portrays the wicked woman who seeks to entice the unwary; here a married woman is simply overwhelmed by her lust for an innocent and virtuous man who is determined, even as a slave, to be loyal to his master.

Potiphar's wife quickly recovers from her obsession with Joseph when she sees that he is adamant. Having Joseph's outer garment in her possession as Joseph flees from his encounter with her, she uses the garment as evidence that it was Joseph who tried to seduce her, thereby betraying his master. She calls him *a Hebrew* (39:14), a term used frequently as the designation of an Israelite by foreigners (see Wilson 1990 for the origin and basic meaning of the term).

Joseph, falsely accused, is imprisoned (39:19-23). Potiphar is of course enraged at Joseph's apparent betrayal and has him imprisoned in the place where state prisoners are kept. There, once more, the LORD causes all of Joseph's affairs to prosper, even though he must remain a prisoner. He becomes second in command in all of the circumstances in which he finds himself: with Potiphar first, now with the chief jailer, and soon with Pharaoh himself.

Life in the court of Pharaoh was like that in any imperial, authoritarian court—precarious! It was easy to fall out of favor, and often the return to favor occurred capriciously. In our story, a *chief cupbearer* and a *chief baker* (40:2), both probably much higher offices than the terms might suggest, come to grief and end up in prison. Their jailer is Joseph's jailer, although the *captain of the guard* (v. 3) is not identified as Potiphar. Joseph serves these high-standing officials of Pharaoh's court, and Joseph hears their dreams after each has had a dream during a single night.

In Gen 37 Joseph's own dreams are presented with such clarity that there can be no doubt of their meaning. Here too, while Joseph is tested as an interpreter of dreams, he hears dreams that do not seem to be too difficult to understand. Even the more complex dreams of Pharaoh (chap. 41) may suggest their general meaning. As an interpreter of dreams, Joseph does not appear in quite the role that his later counterpart, Daniel must fulfill. Daniel was required both to repeat the dream of his master and then interpret it (Dan 2)!

The interpretation of dreams in the ancient Near Eastern world was a part of the task of seers and prophets who were charged to assist the rulers in governance. Dreams served along with other phenomena as means by which the gifted person might gain important insight or knowledge that was not available through other means. Frequently, the interpreter of dreams would enable the ruler to see that the outcome of an impending battle was either likely to be favorable or likely to be disastrous. Or a dream could offer clues to other aspects of the future. The dream provided a window on the as yet unrealized future, giving at least a clue as to what lay in store. In our day, dreams too are avenues by which to secure insight and knowledge that is not readily available otherwise, but primarily in order to gain understanding of the past and present, not to predict the future (see Brueggemann 1982 for a detailed discussion of the importance of the dream as a clue to the whole import of the Joseph narrative).

Joseph's interpretation of the dreams of Pharaoh's out-of-favor officials centers entirely on the question whether they will be restored to favor in Pharaoh's court. He promises the chief cupbearer that he will be restored, but he must say that the chief baker is shortly to lose his life.

Very soon, Pharaoh does indeed lift *up the head*—publicly calling the attention of the court—both the chief cupbearer and the chief baker, restoring the former to office and ordering the execution of the latter. But the spared official does not carry out Joseph's plea (40:14-15) for justice; once the chief cupbearer is back in office, he gives no thought to the part that Joseph's interpretation of the dream might have played in his return to favor or to the injustice Joseph has suffered. A day will come, although well into the future, when the chief cupbearer will have occasion to remember Joseph. And all the time, the Lord is holding Joseph in readiness for great deeds yet to be accomplished.

41:1-45. Pharaoh's discovery and elevation of Joseph. The narrator now turns to the central part of the narrative: Joseph's rise to authority in Egypt, and the peaceable settlement of the people of Israel in Egypt as a result of Joseph's position, and in accordance with God's purpose all along. George Coats (1983) has pointed out how the Joseph narrative serves well to link the earlier promises of God to Abraham, Isaac, and Jacob to the tradition of oppression in Egypt and deliverance from slavery there. Joseph preceded the Israelites into slavery and rose to high rank. His descendants again fell into slavery and were brought to freedom through God's massive intervention.

This linkage is clear as the story of Pharaoh's dreams unfolds. In Egypt, a land that is the "gift of the Nile," great plenty is coming, but it will be followed by terrible privation. How is Pharaoh to handle such a future? Will he squander the goods in the time of plenty, giving no thought to the future? Or will he learn to be a prudent ruler, recognizing God's provident gifts in times of plenty and doing his own part to make those gifts available for the welfare of his whole land and people? The promise of the seven rich years and the predictions of the seven lean years offer to Pharaoh a test of leadership.

Joseph quickly says to Pharaoh that interpretation of dreams is God's business, not that of human beings. But Joseph dutifully fulfills his part in God's interpretation, being God's voice to Pharaoh. Joseph does not simply say what is about to happen; it is his task also to say how Pharaoh is to confront the coming events. Pharaoh likes what he hears, assigns Joseph to take charge of affairs in Egypt, using the prosperous years to prepare for the lean ones, and in general serving as a just ruler under Pharaoh's overall sovereignty.

The story does not fail to give Joseph all the trappings of wealth and glory that he had been denied by the action of his jealous brothers, by the false accusations of Potiphar's wife and Potiphar's uncritical acceptance of the truth of her charges, and by the ingratitude of the chief cupbearer. Joseph even receives as wife a *daughter of Potiphera* (v. 45), identified as a priest at the religious center of lower Egypt, the city of On, or Heliopolis. This daughter of a chief official of the religion of Egypt now joins the household of a descendant of Abraham, through whom the God of Israel has promised blessing to the whole world. Joseph is God's instrument in the bringing of that blessing, and so of course is *Asenath*, the Egyptian *daughter of Potiphera*. She and Joseph will rear a family that will take its place in the community destined later on to undergo oppression, gain freedom, and enter the land of the promise as Israel, the people of the covenant.

41:46-57. Egypt and the world saved from starvation. At the age of thirty years, Joseph now becomes the savior from famine of all Egypt and of many other peoples. The narrator portrays Joseph as a shrewd administrator in the time of famine, selling grain both to Egyptians and non-Egyptians. The narrator does not mention gifts from the royal granaries for the destitute, but such largesse must surely have been understood to have been a part of state policy. Later on (47:13-26), Joseph is said to have claimed all the land and all its population for Pharaoh and then to have returned it to them, reserving for Pharaoh one-fifth of the produce of the land. The narrator's attention was to portray Joseph as representing at once the best interests of Pharaoh and those of the people of Egypt.

42:1-44:34. Joseph, unrecognized, deals with his brothers. The story abruptly shifts to Canaan, where Jacob and his family are apparently still located in the region of Hebron, suffering from the same famine, which had not been confined to Egypt alone. We see that Joseph is the savior of the entire world; word of the availability of grain in Egypt is spreading to all the affected lands. And the very brothers who sold this dreamer into slavery must now appear as supplicants before him. Joseph's ability to interpret dreams had enabled him to rescue those who, despising the dreamer, had disposed of him.

Much of the remaining material in the Joseph narrative is devoted to exchanges between Joseph and his brothers. The narrator wonderfully presents Joseph's demand for the punishment of those who have wronged him, while displaying the family love that overrides his hunger to settle accounts. And in the background is the love of the patriarch Jacob for the whole family as they sort out their differences and find reconciliation.

The story unfolds in six distinct parts. Joseph recognizes his brothers but he keeps his identity hidden from them, treating them harshly and pretending to be suspicious of their intentions. The brothers are bewildered. They have constantly before them what they did to Joseph and how deeply Jacob still mourns Joseph's death. But they must have grain, or they will die, and that means that they have to do what the tyrant Joseph demands, even as they seek to reassured their aged father that he will not be required to lose yet another son.

42:1-5. Jacob sends ten sons to buy grain in Egypt. The famine has struck even in one of the richest parts of southern Canaan: the Hebron HILL COUNTRY, famous for its grapes and other fruits. Jacob hears that there is grain available for purchase in Egypt, and he thus unknowingly begins the process that will bring about reconciliation among his sons and joy to his own heart. He orders ten of his sons to go to Egypt to bring back grain, keeping the youngest, Benjamin, Joseph's full brother, with him at home.

42:6-28. Joseph meets his brothers. The first encounter of Joseph and his brothers seems marked largely by anger and resentment on Joseph's part. The narrator skillfully withholds any statement of Joseph's affection for them, his longing to see Benjamin, and above all, his hunger for reunion with his aged father. Joseph remembers past mistreatment and addresses the brothers *harshly* (v. 6). He accuses them, knowing that the charge is false, of having come down to spy out the land for some enemy of Egypt. The brothers protest their innocence, and readers are intended to recognize the irony of the governor of all Egypt being worried about the threat that these shepherds and farmers from Canaan might pose to Egypt.

The narrator shows the brothers protesting their innocence and in the process saying entirely too much: they tell Joseph that another brother of theirs is still at home with their aged and grieving father. Their father lost one son already. And so Joseph is quick to demand that one of them return and bring the youngest son, as a demonstration of their truthfulness and good faith, while all the other brothers remain in Egypt as prisoners.

After three days, Joseph allows the brothers to return home, with grain they have purchased, and with Simeon only kept in Egypt. Joseph is almost overcome as he hears Reuben speaking to the brothers about the wrong they had done to their other brother, Joseph. Reuben sees this current misfortune as a direct consequence of their having sold Joseph into slavery (v. 22).

With their grain and with their purchase money also in the sacks of grain, the brothers journey home. One brother discovers the money, and all are fearful of what that can possibly mean.

42:29-38. The brothers return to Jacob. When they arrive home they discover that *all* of the purchase money has been returned, and they are all the more mystified. What are they to do? Jacob is adamant that Benjamin will not go to Egypt; even if Simeon cannot be saved, Benjamin must not be lost also. There is

grain for a time, and Jacob and his sons know that the story has not yet reached its conclusion. And meanwhile, Joseph is in Egypt, with Simeon in prison, and Joseph must often remember the scene when Reuben spoke of the wrong that they had done to Joseph.

43:1-34. The brothers, including Benjamin, go back to Egypt. Jacob cannot maintain his resolve. Famine drives him to abandon his resolve never to part with Benjamin. Judah becomes the spokesman for the brothers, challenging Jacob to recognize the choices they face: either Benjamin goes with them to Egypt, or the brothers will not go, and there will be no grain. The narrator skillfully unfolds more of the scene between Joseph and the brothers as Judah tells of that encounter. Why had they mentioned Benjamin? Because Joseph had quizzed them in detail about their homeland, their family, and they had no choice but to mention Benjamin.

Judah pledges his own life as surety for Benjamin's safety. Judah also boldly criticizes his father for having delayed so long: they could have been and returned twice in the time that they have waited before going back to Egypt with Benjamin. Jacob relents, but carefully arranges to placate the Egyptian governor with rich gifts, with the return of the original purchase price, and with double payment for the new grain.

What follows is a story of extraordinary artistry and psychological depth. When the men arrive in Egypt, Joseph has them brought to his own house, and privately orders preparation for a great feast. The brothers are in terror; the man must be intending to punish them for having left with the money in their bags. They speak to the steward of Joseph's household and are reassured. The steward says that God must have placed the money in their bags, since he was paid in full (v. 23). He releases Simeon to them, and they all prepare for the coming feast.

The vivid description of the feast intensifies the drama. Joseph is still determined to make the brothers repentant over their mistreatment of him, but his love for them and especially for Benjamin almost overwhelms him. He greets Benjamin, and has to excuse himself as the tears come to his eyes. Once he has composed himself, the banquet proceeds, and a fivefold serving from Joseph's table is sent to Benjamin.

44:1-13. The brothers leave for Canaan but are arrested and returned to Joseph as thieves. Joseph once more arranges for the brothers to be put in the wrong. Their money is once more placed in their sacks of grain, and into Benjamin's sack is placed Joseph's silver cup that he used for divination, that is, for gaining answers about the future and the meaning of things by studying the pattern formed by wine poured onto the ground from the cup or by studying the pattern formed in the bottom of the cup by the dregs of the wine. The loss of such an important object would of course arouse the wrath of Joseph and spell doom for one accused of stealing it.

When the brothers are brought to Joseph as criminals, and when the cup is found in Benjamin's sack, Judah once again seeks to plead their cause, this time only able to confess and hope for mercy. Joseph insists that only the youngest son is to be punished. He must become a slave, but the other brothers may return to their father. And again Judah speaks, rehearsing in great detail the events concerning this son of Jacob and also what had happened to the other son. Judah asks that he be taken in place of Benjamin, so that their father will not die of grief at the loss of the youngest son. We can see here how the Joseph story fills in the character of Judah, which may help to explain the inclusion within the Joseph narrative of the account of Judah and Tamar in chap. 38.

45:1-15. The reconciliation. Judah's plea for Benjamin is too much for Joseph. Joseph has had enough of retaliation for the wrong done him, and love of family now override his toying with his brothers and his determination to teach them a lesson. Sending all of the Egyptian attendants away, Joseph identifies himself and immediately puts the question that must have been bursting to be asked: *"Is my father still alive?"* (v. 3). One can feel the anxiety in that question: has Joseph spent so much time paying back his brothers that he has forfeited the possibility of seeing his father?

The brothers are speechless, unable to believe what they are hearing, and no doubt fearful of further reprisals by this wronged brother. But Joseph reassures them, calls them closer, and provides, through the theological reading of the narrator, an explanation of the whole sweep of their life together. The brothers were jealous of Joseph (how could they not have been?) and they let their jealousy lead them into a terrible act. But God was in the act, bringing life and good out of what could only appear to be a crime against love and family. Just as Jacob's conniving against Esau and his trickery with Laban had brought blessing and wholesome consequences for Jacob's family, so the misdeeds of Jacob's sons have worked to the benefit of humankind in general and the promise of God to Israel in particular.

45:16-28. Jacob hears the news. Arrangements are quickly made to transport Jacob and his entire household from Canaan back to Egypt, where Pharaoh and Joseph stand ready to receive them and assure their protection and prosperity in the land. In the second year of the famine, Joseph sends lavish presents to Benjamin and to his father. The text notes that a parting word of Joseph to his brothers is, *"Do not quarrel along the way"* (v. 24), which could also be translated, "Do not be agitated [or: anxious] along the way" (the Heb. verb is *ragaz*). The former seems likely, since the brothers might well be tempted to shift blame from themselves to others, or they might want to take credit for having been more in the right than others. Not even Judah, whom the narrator has presented with such power and eloquence, is given a special place among the reconciled brothers. Joseph's counsel may also be intended to prevent their being jealous of Benjamin's favored treatment.

The brothers report to Jacob as a group; neither Judah nor Reuben nor the favored Benjamin appears as leader. Jacob is hard pressed to believe such good news, but the evidence convinces him, and his next concern is to make his way to Egypt to see Joseph before Jacob's day of death dawns.

46:1–47:12. Israel's Descent into Egypt. This section contains more diverse material than any treated thus far in the Joseph narrative. It opens with a remarkable THEOPHANY, an appearance of God in a night-vision to Jacob before he leaves Canaan for Egypt (46:1-4). This is followed by a brief narrative telling of the start of Jacob's journey to Egypt (46:5-7), which in turn is followed by a list of the seventy members of Jacob's family who were understood to have gone into Egypt during the time of Joseph's governorship (46:8-27). The children are identified by naming which wife of Jacob bore them: the children of Leah and Rachel, and the children of Zilpah and Bilhah. We note that Benjamin has the largest number of children (ten), once again an indication of how the youngest son was favored.

This family (actually a tribal) list is followed by the resumption of the narrative, relating the meeting of Joseph and Jacob and Joseph's preparation of his father to meet Pharaoh (46:28–12).

46:1-4. Jacob's theophany. Note that *Jacob* and *Israel* have now become alternate names for the patriarch. God's promise that Abraham's descendants will receive the divine blessing (Gen 12:1-3) has now become God's promise to Israel, the new name borne by

Jacob since his meeting with God at the Jabbok ford (Gen 32:22-32). This section gives prominence to *Beer-sheba*, closely associated with Jacob's father Isaac, and long a center of Israelite worship (see Amos 5:5). The expression *God of your father* (v. 3) is familiar from the Abraham and Isaac traditions and has already appeared in the Jacob traditions as well (see esp. Gen 28:13, 31:53, and 32:9). The meaning of the theophany is clear: Jacob is again about to leave the land of the promise; he does so only with the approval and under the explicit command of God. Canaan remains the place where the promise of God will find its realization, but Egypt, during this period, is the site where the blessing will also come to pass. Jacob also leaves with the implicit blessing of his dead father Isaac, the one from whom he once received a blessing by deceit.

46:5-27. Jacob's descendants who entered Egypt are carefully identified. The list serves the function of making clear the extent of God's blessing upon Jacob's family. Entering Egypt as the family of a single man (including children and grandchildren), Israel would return as a great multitude, preserved by God, enabled to prosper, and even to multiply in numbers during the time of oppression and enslavement.

46:28-34. Joseph and Jacob meet. Finally, Joseph and Jacob meet, embrace, and affirm their joy at being reunited. Jacob is now ready to die, he says for he has seen his lost son alive and prospering. Joseph offers instruction to his family when they meet Pharaoh: they must not speak of themselves as *shepherds* (v. 34). The instruction is puzzling, since it seems clearly not to have been followed, although Pharaoh does explicitly ask for tenders of livestock, not for shepherds, from among Jacob's family (47:6). The best explanation for the warning that they not identify themselves as shepherds but as herdsmen is suggested by Speiser (1964, 345). The popular etymology of the term HYKSOS, one of the occupiers of Egypt in the late eighteenth- and seventeenth-centuries B.C.E., was "shepherd-kings"; perhaps this is a reference to that time.

47:1-12. Jacob and Pharaoh meet. Joseph very carefully prepares for the meeting of his family with Pharaoh. He first brings the news to Pharaoh that his family has arrived, not saying that it was his, Joseph's own doing that brought them. They are settled, Joseph says, in the land of GOSHEN, apparently territory in the eastern delta region of Egypt, close to the site of later building activities in the Nineteenth Egyptian dynasty (fourteenth century and following). Then he presents five of his brothers to Pharaoh, who answer Pharaoh's

question as to their occupation with what would appear to be the forbidden answer: "We are shepherds" (v. 3). But clearly, these shepherds are not a part of the remnant of the invading Hyksos of an earlier time; they are no threat to Pharaoh or to Egypt.

Pharaoh offers them their choice of land—for example, the land where they already are settled, Goshen. He invites any specialists in livestock among them to join in the care of his own herds.

Finally, Joseph presents his father to Pharaoh. Jacob is now a very old man—according to the tradition, 130 years of age. But such an age does not compare favorably with the years of his ancestors' lives; really, Jacob says, his days have been few and hard. While this may simply be courteous and conventional speech in the Egyptian court, it may also be intended to convey the demands of a life in the service of the promise of God. After this brief but weighty exchange, Jacob joins his family in the land of Goshen, while Joseph continues to administer affairs for Pharaoh, as the famine continues.

47:13-26. Pharaoh's power over Egypt owed to Joseph. This section presents Joseph as a shrewd and almost unfeeling overlord of Egypt, seizing the opportunity presented by the famine to enrich Pharaoh and the administration of the empire at the expense of the Egyptian population at large. Joseph, on this view, could be said to have helped prepare the way for the later oppression of his own family, the Israelites in Egypt. There may, however, be another intention in this story of Joseph's impoverishing and eventually enslaving the population of Egypt. The narrative is probably reminding the Israelites that though their ancestors were subjected to slavery in Egypt, their ancestor Joseph had already, with God's blessing, dealt the Egyptians an equally severe blow. Back in the days of the famine, Joseph had demanded all their money, then all their goods, and finally their landholdings as well.

Then the story makes clear that Joseph was not just a ruthless oppressor in the service of Pharaoh. He also provided for the needs of the Egyptians, returning to them four-fifths of the goods they produced and only claiming one-fifth for Pharaoh. Even so, as Brueggemann points out (1982, 356–58), the Joseph of the narrative skirts dangerously closely to being taken in by the opportunities presented by the exercise of absolute power over the lives of others. Is Joseph going to be a faithful son of the promise made to the ancestors? Or will he be corrupted by the opportunities opened up to him by God's favor? Eventually, Joseph is seen to have remembered why he had been sent by God into Egypt: it was not for Pharaoh's sake, and not for Joseph's sake either. It was in order that God's purpose to preserve a great multitude might be realized (see 45:7-8 and 50:19-20).

47:27-31. Jacob's approaching death. The story draws toward an end. The family of Jacob, now called *Israel* regularly, settled in the region of Goshen and prospered greatly. Jacob has seventeen more years to live and reaches the age of 147 years when he realizes that his death is imminent. One thing he asks of his influential son Joseph: that he not be buried in Egypt but that he be taken back to the land of Canaan and buried with his ancestors. The tradition has in mind the cave of MACHPELAH (Gen 23), where Abraham and Sarah and Isaac and Rebekah and Leah already lie buried (see Gen 49:29-32). Rachel's tomb is elsewhere, either near Ramah in the north (see Jer 31:15-17 and 35:16-21, which may presuppose a burial site near Ramah on the way to Bethlehem), or (perhaps more probably) just north of Bethlehem at the site still identified as "Rachel's tomb." Joseph too is said to have been buried in the north, near the ancient city of Shechem (Josh 24:32). But Jacob is destined to sleep with his ancestors in the vicinity of Hebron, in the cave purchased long before by Abraham as a place to bury his wife Sarah.

48:1-22. The blessing of Ephraim and Manasseh. On Joseph's insistence that Jacob, in blessing Ephraim and Manasseh, place his right hand on the head of the younger and his left on the elder—contrary to the convention of primogeniture and to Jacob's wishes (48:13-14). What began with the stories of Ishmael and Isaac, Esau and Jacob, and even Joseph and his brothers, continues here: the rights of the first-born are superseded by the promises to the later-born.

49:1-28. Jacob's blessing of his sons. The introduction (v. 1) and long poem that follows is difficult to fit with the narrative blessing that precedes and the solemn narrative of Jacob's death that follows (see Brueggemann 1982, 365–67). Except for the important mention of the *scepter* of Judah (vv. 8-12), and the pronouncement over Joseph (vv. 22-26), the poem offers more characterizations of the tribes than it does blessings.

Jacob says of Judah, *The scepter shall not depart from Judah . . . "until he comes to whom it belongs"* (v. 10 and NRSV mg.). "To whom it belongs" is obscure in the MT, which reads "until Shiloh comes" (cf. NRSV

mg.). In this case the literal translation seems more likely the correct one. That Judah would rule in Israel "until Shiloh comes" seems to allude to the prophet Ahijah the Shilonite, who instigated Jeroboam's rebellion—which ended the rule of Judah over the Northern Kingdom (1 Kgs 11:29-31; 12:15).

The only one of the "blessings" in the poem that is indeed a pronouncement of blessing (vv. 25-26). It is also the single one that associates its recipient with God—in this case with *Shaddai* (*the Almighty*; v. 25), which is a wordplay on the Hebrew word for *breasts* in v. 25.

49:29–50:14. Death and burial of Jacob. Jacob's life is no dangling sentence. With calm and dignity the narrative reports that the patriarch assumes full responsibility for his last days and final rest. Coming at the end of the long and glorious account of Israel settling into Egypt, the story of the death of Jacob underscores and punctuates that Jacob dies as a son of promise. Although all of Egypt mourns his death Jacob did not die as an Egyptian. Jacob dies *gathered to his people* (v. 29) and is returned to Canaan (see Brueggemann 1982, 367–69).

50:15-21. The brothers are reconciled. The scene of reconciliation between Joseph and his brothers reveals the theological kernel of the whole story (and, perhaps, all of canonical Genesis; see above introduction to the Joseph stories). What some would term an irony of history is interpreted simply as God's providential care for those whom bear the promise. Following the death of Jacob the brothers of Joseph retreat to their former methods of conniving and lying: Jacob did not tell them seek forgiveness from Joseph. Joseph's response comes from genuine transformation. He knows that the evil intent (v. 20; cf. RSV) of his brothers has been redeemed by God's goodness.

50:22-26. Death and embalmment of Joseph. With the kernel of the story disclosed the narrative quickly ends. Joseph secures his brothers' oath to bring his bones out of Egypt when they return one day to Canaan. The promise is a necessary link to the narratives to follow in the OT (and is carried out, as described in Josh 24:32).

Works Cited

Alt, Albrecht. 1966. *Essays on O.T. History and Religion.*

Alter, Robert. 1981. *The Art of Biblical Narrative.*

Andrews, Stephen J. 1990. "Patriarch," MDB.

Auerbach, Erich. 1953. *Mimesis.*

Bailey, Lloyd R. 1989. *Noah: The Person and the Story in History and Tradition.*

Barrois, Georges A. 1952. "Chronology, Metrology, Etc.," IDB.

Bethge, Hans-Gebhard, et al. 1988. "On the Origin of the World," in *The Nag Hammadi Library in English*, 3rd ed., ed. Robinson.

Bjornard, Reidar B. 1990. "New Year's Festival," *MDB*.

Brown, Raymond E. 1978. *The Gospel according to John.* AncB.

Bullard, Roger A. 1990a. "Hypostasis of the Archons," MDB. 1990b. "Origin of the World, On the," MDB.

Childs, Brevard S. 1960. *Myth and Reality in the O.T.*

Christensen, Duane L. 1990. "Chronology," MDB.

Coates, George W. 1983. *Genesis, with an Introduction to Narrative Literature.*

Dahlberg, Bruce T. 1990. "Hunting," MDB.

Dalley, Stephanie. 1989. *Myths from Mesopotamia.*

Daube, David. 1969. *Studies in Biblical Law.*

Dever, William G. 1990a. "Hittites," MDB. 1990b. "Shechem," MDB.

Devries, Lamoine. 1990. "Tribes," MDB.

Gottwald, Norman K. 1985. *The Hebrew Bible: A Socio-Literary Interpretation.*

Gregory, Russell L. 1990. "Sources of the Pentateuch," MDB.

Gunkel, Hermann. 1901; repr. 1964. *The Legends of Genesis.*

Hayes, John H. 1990. "Covenant," MDB.

Heidel, Alexander. 1951; repr. 1963. *The Babylonian Genesis.* 2nd ed.

Jacobs, Joseph. 1901. "Yezer Ha-ra," EncJud.

Kierkegaard, Søren. 1954 (orig. 1841). *Fear and Trembling.*

Knight, Douglas A. 1990a. "Cosmology," MDB. 1990b. "Genre in the OT," MDB.

Lance, H. Darrell. 1989. "The Bible and Homosexuality," *ABQ* 8/2 (June): 140–51.

Laughlin, John C. H. "Canaan," MDB.

Layton, Bentley, trans. 1988. "The Hypostasis of the Archons," in *The Nag Hammadi Library in English*, 3rd ed., ed. Robinson.

Niditch, Susan. 1985. *Chaos to Cosmos: Studies in Biblical Patterns of Creation.*

Niebuhr, Reinhold. 1941. *The Nature and Destiny of Man.* Vol. 1.

Noth, Martin. 1928. *Die israelitischen Personennamen.*

O'Brien, J. Randall. 1990. "Babel, Tower of," MDB.

Oppenheim, A. Leo, trans. 1969. "The Sumerian King List," ANET.

Rad, Gerhard von. 1972. *Genesis.* 3rd ed. rev.

Redditt, Paul L. 1990. "Genealogy in the OT," MDB.

Rosenberg, David, and Harold Bloom. 1990. *The Book of J.*

Sarna, Nahum M. 1989. *Genesis.* JPSTC.

Speiser, E. A. 1969. "Akkadian Myths and Epics," ANET. 1964. *Genesis.* AncB.

Spiegel, Shalom. 1967. *The Last Trial.*

Trafton, Joseph L. 1990a. "Genesis Apocryphon," MDB. 1990b. "Jubilees, Book of," MDB.

Trible, Phyllis. 1978. *God and the Rhetoric of Sexuality.* 1984. *Texts of Terror.*

Van Seters, John. 1992. *Prologue to History: The Yahwist as Historian in Genesis.*

Vermes, G. 1987. *The Dead Sea Scrolls in English.* 3rd ed.

John Keating Wiles. 1990. "Sodom/Gomorrah/Cities of the Plain," MDB.

Wellhausen, Julius. 1885. *Prolegomena to the History of Israel.*

Westermann, Claus. 1985. *Genesis 12–36: A Commentary.*

Wilson, Johnny. 1990. "Hebrew/Habiru/Apiru," MDB.

Wintermute, O. S. 1985. "Jubilees," in *The Old Testament Pseudepigrapha*, vol. 2, ed. Charlesworth.

Wyatt, Nicolas. 1993. "The Darkness of Genesis I.2," *VT* XLIII, 4:543–54.

Exodus

John I Durham

Introduction

The Book of Exodus is the book of departure for the Bible. This is so because of its content even more than because of its narrative. Exodus presents the themes that permeate the entire canon of scripture, in both retrospect and prospect. As the second book of the TORAH, Exodus is a part of a continuing story. But as a repository of major biblical motifs, Exodus is the primary book of the OT and, in general terms, of the entire Bible.

Exodus presents the account of the birth of God's people as his people, the account of the first of his two great salvation-acts, the account of his covenant with humankind, and the account of his mercy after the first of what has become a long succession of betrayals. Above all, Exodus burns with the conviction that so undergirds the whole of OT and NT theological assumption: that God is vitally present among his people. In terms of theology, Exodus begins the Bible.

The Name of the Book of Exodus

The canonical Hebrew name of Exodus is "And these are the names" (וְאֵלֶּה שְׁמוֹת), that is, the names of the sons of Jacob, the theoretical progenitors of the twelve tribes of Israel. It was also given the name, "the book of the departure from Egypt," and it was this name, translated and abbreviated by the LXX, that has given us the English name, Exodus.

The Text of the Book of Exodus

There is no question of the availability of the original text of any OT book. The earliest textual witnesses to any part of the OT are centuries removed from any autograph, even an autograph of the "final" compilation of so composite a book as Exodus. The most a commentator can hope for is the most accurate version of the text that specialists can provide, and as scholars keep learning, that text is always a moving target.

The text of Exodus has for the most part been well preserved, owing chiefly to the fact that this book achieved what was effectively canonical status very early in the history of the growth of the OT.

The language of Exodus is classical or biblical Hebrew. For the most part it is uncomplicated and generally devoid of philological and grammatical problems. Most of Exodus is prose, either as straightforward narrative or as lists of laws and detailed sequences of cultic specification. Exodus 15:1b-18, 21 and 32:18b-e are in poetic form, and these verses are generally regarded as among the oldest parts of the book. It is also possible, at least, that some sections now rendered as prose were originally in poetic form: the Decalogue, for example, expanded in the received text from its original form as "ten words," or early recitations of the deliverance from Egypt and the sustenance in the wilderness. Later examples of such poetic originals may be found in Pss 105:24-45; 106:1-23; 136:10-16.

Composition and Compilation of the Book of Exodus

Despite the antique reference to Exodus as the second of the five "Books of Moses," MOSES cannot be defended as the author of the Exodus we know. Nor, for that matter, can any other author of Exodus be identified. The OT does not assign an author to the Book of Exodus, nor to the other four books of the Pentateuch to which Exodus is related, by content or by this title.

Tradition has assigned these five books to Moses, both because of his significant role in five of them and on the basis of such references as Deut 1:1, 2 Kgs 14:6, Ezra 6:18, 2 Chr 25:4, and Mark 12:26. This traditional view was forwarded both in early Jewish literature (PHILO, JOSEPHUS, the Talmud) and by the early Christian Church. It has had its critics almost from its inception; but it remained the dominant theory until the eighteenth century.

With the rise of what might be called modern critical study of the OT, a painstaking isolation of anachronisms, repetition, conflicting accounts, an extensive array of discrepancies, several differing conceptions of God, and at least four distinct styles of writing has led the majority of modern scholars to the view that the Pentateuch is neither a unity nor in any sense a composition of Moses.

More than a century and a half of critical study of the Pentateuch, and of Exodus within it, has led rather to the view that these five books are the product of a complex compilation of oral, written, and redactional source material. In still more recent years, this study has been further augmented by the isolation of the distinct literary forms that are recurrent not only in the Pentateuchal books but in the OT as a whole.

A combination of the results of source-research and form-analysis has suggested a theoretical literary history of the OT. The isolation and review of recurring traditions and the study of rhetorical patterns and characteristic structures have aided the understanding of what may be called the interior of the text. And the interpretation of the biblical books by the Bible has increased our appreciation of those books as works that have a life of their own, quite apart from the sources and forms that may lie behind them.

All these approaches, however, despite their obvious and contributing value, have tended to draw our attention to the *pieces* of the Book of Exodus, to what might be called the speculative Book of Exodus, and therefore away from the Book of Exodus no one can deny, the one we have in our Bibles. That Book of Exodus is being taken more seriously, and, in result, Exodus is now being read more as a whole, and as the product of a literary organization governed by a theological purpose, a purpose effectively achieved by a dramatic presentation.

The Historical Content of the Book of Exodus

The historicity of the events described in Exodus, and indeed the historicity of the persons and peoples involved in those events, is hardly to be doubted. That there was an Egyptian bondage, an exodus from it, and a special revelation at a wilderness mountain, in each of which events an extraordinary Israelite with the Egyptian name Moses is present is not to be doubted because of a lack of extrabiblical evidence.

The fact remains, however, that there is little extrabiblical information about the historical context of the events described in Exodus, and absolutely no extrabiblical corroboration for even one of them. The historical content of Exodus must therefore be described in terms of probabilities, not certainties. Once this point is understood, certain historical facts can be adduced that give support to the general background of the Exodus narrative. These facts do not however give verification to any specific details of that narrative.

The sojourn in Egypt and Joseph's rise to power are made quite plausible, for example, by either the period of HYKSOS domination (1720–1550 B.C.E.) or the rule of Akhen-aton (1370–1353 B.C.E.) in the AMARNA period (1406–1353 B.C.E.).

The rise of *a new king . . . who did not know Joseph* (1:8), and the oppression in connection with an extensive public works program in the Delta region are made credible by the rise of the Nineteenth Dynasty of Egypt and the building projects of its first two Pharaohs, Seti I and Rameses II.

The presence of a mixed group of migrant workers, mercenaries, and displaced persons known in extrabiblical sources as *habiru/'apiru* in Egypt and the ancient Near East generally during the second millennium B.C.E. lends credence to both the presence and the need of a group such as the one led by Moses.

The array of ancient Near East law codes (Ur-Nammu, 2050 B.C.E.; Eshnunna, ca. 1925 B.C.E.; Lipit-Ishtar, ca. 1875 B.C.E.; Hammurabi, ca. 1725 B.C.E.; Middle Assyrian, ca. 1400–1100 B.C.E.) and the larger body of covenantal and legal literature they represent clearly reflect the context from which some of the covenantal and legal material of Exodus is derived.

Archaeological evidence in Transjordan as well as in the central Palestinian plain confirms both a powerful Edomite presence in Transjordan and the fall of certain strategic cities in central Palestine/Canaan during the last part of the thirteenth century B.C.E. This is the very period when, in sequence to the narrative of Exodus, the Israelites would have been deflected by the Edomites, and would have fallen upon such cities as LACHISH, HAZOR, BETHEL, and DEBIR. It is also the period of the famous victory stele of Merneptah, which mentions Israel in a list of victim peoples in Palestine/Canaan.

All such evidence, however, offers confirmation only to the context and general background of Exodus. No single event in the book and no single person mentioned in its narrative is known in any extrabiblical record discovered thus far. Indeed, the question of the historicity of Exodus, a question of such acute concern to the commentators who wrote about the book in the sixty years following 1875, is the wrong question for the commentator to ask of a book so clearly and repetitiously theological and religious in its purpose. Exodus is a book about the Presence of God and the meaning of that Presence for the whole human family. To ask it to be history or biography or geography or sociology or ethnography is to misuse and therefore to misunderstand it altogether.

The Theology of the Book of Exodus

The unity of the Book of Exodus in its canonical form is a unity of theological purpose. The compilers of Exodus were intent on presenting a story of revelation and response. Every piece of the book is a deliberate statement of a single theological assertion: that God comes to his people and rescues and guides them.

The narrative sequence of Exodus, the covenantal/legal sequence, and the symbolic/liturgical sequence are each and all together expressions of this essential and central confession.

What appears at first to be an uneasy and disjointed jumble of text turns out to be, on a more careful reading, a marvelous interweaving of story sequence, requirement sequence, and memory sequence. Even the most arcane law, even the most exotic tabernacle decoration, and even the most apparently discontinuous turn of narrative all have a direct function as expressions of this central theme: God is here; God is, here.

The sequence of story, a continuation of the story of the ancestors told in Genesis, strains forward to the moment when God's Presence will be known to all his people, then describes that moment and its double aftermath. The sequence of requirement sets forth the protocols of behavior in the Presence of God, in terms of both everyday life and special-situation circumstances. The sequence of memory brings to the present the action of the sequence of story, in the acts, the spaces, and the symbols of day-to-day and special-event worship.

Exodus is of course not the sole biblical presentation of this theme, which is the theme in a way of the entire Bible. But Exodus is the first and fundamental sourcebook of the theme, and the singleness of its text is both representative of and an anticipation of what makes the Bible a whole, despite the wide diversity of its content.

For Further Study

In the *Mercer Dictionary of the Bible*: COVENANT; EXODUS; EXODUS, BOOK OF; GOD, NAMES OF; MOSES; PLAGUES; PRESENCE; RED SEA/REED SEA; TORAH.
In other sources: L. Brisman, "On the Divine Presence in Exodus," *Exodus*, ed. H. Bloom, 105–22; D. Daube, *The Exodus Pattern in the Bible*; J. Durham, *Understanding the Basic Themes of Exodus*; M. Goldberg, *Jews and Christians Getting Our Stories Straight*; M. Greenberg, *Understanding Exodus*; S. Herrmann, *Israel in Egypt*; N. M. Sarna, *Exploring Exodus*; S. Terrien, *The Elusive Presence*.

Commentary

An Outline

I. Israel in Egypt, 1:1–13:16
  A. The Family, the Oppression, the Deliverer, 1:1–2:25
  B. The Deliverer's Call, Command, and Response, 3:1–7:7
  C. Ten Wonders and the Exodus, 7:8–13:16
II. Israel in the Wilderness, 13:17–18:27
  A. The Route and the Rescue, 13:17–15:21
  B. Provision, Protection, and Complaint, 15:22–17:16
  C. Jethro, Worship, and Law, 18:1–27
III. Israel at Sinai, 19:1–40:38
  A. YHWH's Presence and Covenant, 19:1–24:18
  B. YHWH's Plan for the Spaces and Symbols of Worship, 25:1–31:18

  C. Disobedience and Its Consequences, 32:1–34:35
  D. Obedience and Its Blessing, 35:1–40:38

Israel in Egypt, 1:1–13:16

The Family, the Oppression, the Deliverer, 1:1–2:25

1:1-7. The names and the many. The beginning of the Book of Exodus presupposes the events described in Gen 38–50, whereby the family of ISRAEL came to be in EGYPT in the first place. The providential nature of their migration to and consequent prosperity in Egypt is in view. So also is the gradual unfolding of the promise to the patriarchs of a numberless progeny and a wide land to hold and to be held by such a progeny.

As Exodus opens, the progeny is present already, in great, even teeming numbers graphically suggested by the use of a verb (שָׁרַץ, 1:7) used elsewhere in the OT to describe the swarming multiplication of fish or frogs. That *seventy* (v. 5) could become so many so soon in circumstances so difficult is the first hint in Exodus of an array of miracles about to take place.

This fulfillment of the first part of the covenant promise to ABRAHAM (Gen 12:2, 15:5, 17:4-22) becomes a blessing that causes problems in Egypt and makes necessary the fulfillment of the second part, the promise of land (Gen 12:1, 15:7, 18–21, 17:8).

1:8-22. A new king and a new policy. Thus it is God's multiplication of Israel that rouses Egyptian fears and makes the family of Jacob *persona non grata* in a land that has been their home for more than four decades. The new king was the beginning of a new dynasty. Previous treaties, agreements, and obligations were null and void. Israel was an obstacle to new and grandiose building plans. Israel's growing numbers represented a threat that might just be turned into an asset.

Thus did Pharaoh attempt to deal with these numerous "Hebrews," first by the enslavement of unremitting toil in the construction of the two supply-cities, *Pithom and Rameses* (v. 11; and, according to LXX, "On, which is Heliopolis"). Incredibly, this policy had no effect on the Israelite population explosion, even when the forced labor was increased to bitter proportions, and the Egyptians "came to have a sickening dread because of the presence of the sons of Israel" (v. 12, author trans.).

So it was that the Pharaoh turned to a policy of genocide as a means of controlling the "Hebrews." He required the "Hebrew" midwives to put to death every male child and spare every female child born to his rapidly expanding Delta slave population. The term "Hebrew" is used in this narrative as an Egyptian epithet for the Israelites, and is not a name they use of themselves (cf. Gen 14:13).

Pharaoh's first method of genocide has an air of quiet conspiracy about it. The midwives could have carried out his order with some degree of secrecy, reporting stillbirths or at least a strange rash of infant deaths following birth.

The midwives, however, protected by the privacy of the circumstances Pharaoh hoped to profit by, refused to cooperate. They did so perhaps because they

too were "Hebrew," but most of all because they believed in God. When the Pharaoh called them to account, they gave him a witty retort. And Israel continued to increase in number and so in strength, and the midwives themselves were blessed with families.

Thus Pharaoh turned to open genocide, with the order that every male "Hebrew" child be cast into the Nile, an order required of every citizen of Egypt. How many Israelite boys were drowned as a result of this order, we are not told. The thrust of this narrative would suggest not many. As 1:7, 9, 12, and 20b make clear, *God* is behind the growth of Israel, and any attempt by Pharaoh or by anyone else to thwart that growth can only end in failure. *What* the result of Pharaoh's attempts will be is not in doubt; *how* that result is to be achieved provides an element of rising tension. And that tension is resolved by the arrival of the Deliverer, Moses.

2:1-10. The deliverer is born. The story of the birth of Moses is told directly and without elaboration. The fact that the parents of Moses are unnamed suggests their names were unknown in the earliest sources. In time, as the memory of Moses became more and more important, the names of his parents came to be supplied, perhaps even invented, by the priestly writers (6:20; Num 26:59; 1 Chr 23:12-13).

The sister of Moses is also unnamed here. Although MIRIAM has traditionally been assumed to be the *sister* of v. 4, she is actually called the sister of Moses only twice in the OT: in Num 26:59 and in 1 Chr 6:3. At the earliest appearance of her name, she is called the sister of AARON, and she is primarily associated with Aaron in the OT (see esp. Num 12). This fact, and the often arbitrary addition of Aaron to the Moses narratives, has led to the suggestion that both Miriam and her brother Aaron became related to Moses only in the later layers of the Moses traditions.

The essential emphasis of this birth account is presented by the manner in which this Israelite baby boy's life is preserved, and the delightful irony of Moses' rescue, nurture, and education at the expense of the very hand that sought to slay him. Indeed, the stratagem succeeds even to the extent of getting the little boy's mother onto Pharaoh's payroll, for performing the one duty she most wanted in all the world to undertake. More ironic still, the Pharaoh of Egypt and his daughter become the unwitting saviors of the Deliverer who will bring Egypt to humiliating defeat.

This account is the epitome of the folksy story at which the early sources of Genesis and Exodus excel.

It even includes a characteristically homespun—and inaccurate—name-etymology. The name Moses is Egyptian in origin, the Hebrew equivalent of an Egyptian noun meaning "son, boy-child." It occurs often in Egyptian names, as for example Tuthmose, Ahmose.

Unaware of this, the author of v. 10 turned Pharaoh's daughter into a Hebrew etymologist, and explained the name by a connection of assonance with the Hebrew verb meaning "to draw up, out" (מֹשֶׁה; cf. 2 Sam 22:17b). As Griffiths (1953, 229-31) has pointed out, Moses' Egyptian name may well present the most significant testimony of the Egyptian context of this story. It is certainly of far greater importance than the frequently mentioned parallel narratives of Sargon and other heroes exposed in infancy (Childs 1965, 109-22; Redford 1967, 209-28, has collected thirty-two such accounts).

2:11-22. The deliverer's flight and homecoming. The security of Moses' youth and upbringing thus provided for, the details of the early years are left to the reader's imagination. They are not important to the purpose of the story, which is after all not really about Moses, but about God and his coming to and for Israel.

When Moses next appears, therefore, he is a grown man, and by an instruction we are left to imagine, he is aware of his Israelite heritage and deeply concerned about the plight of his people. Thus when he comes upon an Egyptian beating one of his people, he intervenes and strikes the Egyptian a mortal blow. The same verb, "strike" (נכה), is used of the Egyptian's action and the action Moses takes. It is a verb that connotes violent and intense action, of the kind that always results in harmful, often fatal, damage (Gen 37:21; Exod 12:29; Lev 24:17, 18, 21, Num 3:13).

Despite his precaution, turning to look *this way and that* (v. 12), Moses soon learned that word of his crime was among the people. His precarious position is brought home to him vividly by one of his own people: "Who set you up as judge and jury?" (v. 14). In justified fear, Moses thus fled Egypt, under Pharaoh's sentence of death, to Midian, a land beyond Pharaoh's jurisdiction.

This flight to Midian does not appear to have been the result of a random choice. Moses escaped Pharaoh, and *settled in the land of Midian* (v. 15). The Midianites with whom Moses settled appear to have been in the main a nomadic people. Recent archaeological surveys of the area east of the Gulf of Aqaba have suggested, however, a complex and fixed-dwelling dimension of Midianite culture (Mendenhall 1992, 4:817-18). At a later period, they were at enmity with Israel (Num 22–25; Judg 6–8). They are connected, however, with the prehistory of Israel through Keturah, whom Abraham married following the death of Sarah (Gen 25:2).

One may reasonably assume that Moses had been made aware of distant family ties among the people to the east of the Egyptian Delta. If so, his connection with the family of Jethro may even be considered something of a homecoming. As Moses himself says, in explanation of the name he gives his firstborn son, Gershom ("stranger there"), *I have been an alien residing in a foreign land* (v. 22).

As the narrative makes plain, Moses has fled a foreign land with strange gods for a land made familiar by the worship there of the God of his fathers. For the first time in his life, Moses is at home among a people whose ancestors are his ancestors, and as he is shortly to find out, he is at home in the land of the God of his fathers. From a place where he did not belong, he has come to a place where he does belong. Thus the Moses-Midianite connection is a theological one, and the attention given it in this theological narrative reflects that fact.

The story of Moses' entry into the family of JETHRO is charmingly told, including as it does deft reminders of Jethro's sonless status and the high standard of ancient Near Eastern hospitality. Moses' father-in-law is called REUEL here and in Num 10:29, Hobab in Judg 4:11, and Jethro ten times (Exod 3, 4, and 18). There is confusion about Hobab in Num 10:29 and a mistaken spelling, "Jether" (Exod 4:18), but given the greater frequency of Jethro, and the fact that only that name is used with the title "priest of Midian," "Jethro" is the preferred name for the father-in-law of Moses. Despite many attempts, this names confusion remains without a satisfactory explanation.

2:23-25. The oppression in Egypt: a further note. These three verses provide an important connection with the beginning of Exodus, and the real beginning of the drama now unfolding, and an important shift in the story that opens the way to what is to come. Exod 1:1-7 list the names of the sons of the father, the grandfather and the great-grandfather who are themselves mentioned now in v. 24. The death of the Pharaoh whom Moses fled brings no letup to the suffering of enslaved Israel. And hearing their increasing cry for help, the God of Israel remembers his covenant promise to the fathers even as he is experiencing their agony (note the use of the verb "know by experience," NRSV *took notice*, in 2:25). Thus are we prepared for what now is to come.

The Deliverer's Call, Command, and Response, 3:1–7:7

3:1-22. God's arrival and Moses' call. The account of Moses' call is a composite of narrative from at least two sources. The name *Horeb*, by which the mountain of God's arrival is identified here, is the name given in two strands of tradition. The name SINAI is given to the same mountain in at least two others.

A great many proposals have been made fixing the location of this mountain, in the southern and the northern sections of the Sinai peninsula and outside the Sinai peninsula altogether, and even across the Aravah from Petra (Har Karkom, Anati 1986) and in Saudi Arabia (Davies 1979, 63-69). No firm location has so far been established. The traditional location, Jebel Musa in the southern range of mountains in the Sinai peninsula, dates from Byzantine times. The OT nowhere gives any information on this special mountain's location.

Moses was ranging far with his flock, searching, according to the Targum of Onkelos, for choice grazing for his family's flock. Suddenly, he was encountered by the Presence of God. The symbol of that Presence was a bush all aflame but strangely unconsumed.

There is no merit in the attempts to determine the species of a bush that might give the appearance of being afire, or to discover some natural phenomenon by which an illusion of a burning bush might have been impressed upon Moses. Fire is one of the recurring symbols of God's THEOPHANY in the OT. The essential element in this narrative is the real Presence of God in the place, not the flaming bush, which is but one symbol of that Presence. As the text makes clear, the bush is no more than the medium of the appearance of the messenger of God. The fascination with the bush began at least with Deut 33:16, which refers to the "kind favor of the one settled in the thornbush."

The visible manifestation of the theophany is followed immediately by an auditory one. Moses hears first his name, then special instructions, then the identification of the source of the fire and of the voice. The place has been made holy by the Presence of God, and Moses must take the precautions made necessary by the danger of the Presence before the experience can continue, lest it end prematurely and disastrously.

Once these instructions have been issued, and met, the real identity of the messenger is disclosed. As so often in the OT (Gen 18, Judg 6), the fluid interchange between symbol, representative, and God himself is suggested. The strange fire becomes God's messenger, who in turn soon becomes God himself. The moment is an electric one, and a fearful one.

Only after the authority of the speaker has been established, by the theophany and by the self-identification that Moses has heard God declare, does the call of the deliverer come. It is a pattern Moses himself is to repeat in Egypt: identification, establishment of authority, and call. Yahweh relates himself to the fulfillment of the covenant promise of progeny by referring to Israel as *my people* (v. 7). No more need be said, as Moses well knows their plight. But God, who begins to be called "YHWH" in this chapter in Exodus, refers to his people's humiliation and pain and announces his plan to "snatch them forth from the power of the Egyptians and to bring them forth from that land to a good and roomy land, to a land gushing with milk and honey" (v. 8, author trans.).

Albrecht Alt many years ago pointed out (Alt 1966, 11-15) the complex way in which early and later traditions are intermingled in Exod 3, noting the conscious attempt to identify the God known variously to the Fathers with the God of the theophany to Moses. This identification at first seems to satisfy Moses (v. 6), but is apparently judged by him to be insufficient for Israel in Egypt (v. 12).

The question, however, is not a question of identity. That has been resolved already. It is rather a question of authority. Moses is satisfied as to who the God who speaks to him is. So also, it must be assumed, will the people of Israel be satisfied, so far as the God's identity is concerned.

The crucial question is what can be done in the face of the apparently impossible difficulties in Egypt, and who will do it. The God of the Fathers, in various times and places and under various conditions, had proved himself to the Fathers. But Egypt and bondage there present a new situation. Egypt is a world power. The people of Israel in bondage are in no way the peers of their oppressors. Their situation is quite unparalleled in the history of the Fathers, who after all had to contend with local groups and local rulers, not to mention local gods.

Further, if Israel in Egypt knew the tradition of the God of the Fathers, they surely knew also that it was by his act and direction that they came there in the first place. And their very situation there seemed to discredit his ability to help, whatever his intention. The Egyptians possessed, or were possessed by, a magnificent pantheon of gods, exerting a cooperative lordship over every aspect of life and granting international influence to Egyptian power.

Moses' real questions are therefore what can be done and who is able to do it. When he is told that he is to be sent to "bring out" the people, a commission that answers his first question, he asks the second question, quite unconvinced of his own ability to carry out such an order.

The answer given to Moses is the recurrent biblical answer to the humble called to great tasks: his wisdom, his strength, his special ability are to come from the Presence with him of God (note also Judg 6:12, 16; 1 Sam 1–2; 17:41-54; Jer 1:5-10). And it is this answer, finally, that brings the dialogue to its climax and the revelation to its essential point. In effect, Moses says "So I am to go. So the God of the Fathers is with me. The people will want to know 'What is his name?'"

The literal translation of this crucial question is insufficient to suggest its real impact. Moses by his own admission will certainly have given his people in Egypt the name that satisfied him, *the God of your father* (v. 6). Thus the question מַה־שְּׁמוֹ is not one of identity but one of authority. What the people will want to know, says Moses, is what the God of the Fathers is really like; who he really is; how he can hope to accomplish the impossible.

The question Moses anticipates from Israel is the theological question the Book of Exodus is calculated to ask and to answer, and the question we may well imagine to have been in Moses' own mind in such circumstances. What is this God's credentials for what he is promising to accomplish? What is there in his reputation (see Num 6:27; Deut 12:5, 11; 14:23, 24; 16:2-6; Pss 8:1; 74:7) that lends credence to the claim inherent in his call? How, suddenly, does he expect to deal with a host of powerful Egyptian deities against whom he has for so many years apparently been ineffectual?

The question Moses poses can thus be rendered, less literally and more specifically, "What can *He* do?" (v. 13, author trans.) Only against some such understanding of the question can the significance of the much-discussed answer to it be seen. When Moses poses the question of his authority to accomplish an apparently impossible command, God replies simply,

אֶהְיֶה אֲשֶׁר אֶהְיֶה, "I am the One who always is" (v. 14). That is to say, "I am the one who really exists, whatever may be said of the gods of Egypt or any other gods."

In response to the question "What is he really like?" God replies "I really AM," and proceeds to instruct Moses, *Thus you shall say to the Israelites, "I AM has sent me to you"* (v. 14). The clue to what has been made into a very difficult formula thus lies in its essential simplicity.

Moses is to say to the people of Israel that he comes on the authority of the one who really is, the one who gets things done. And so that they may never forget the nature of the authority they will have questioned (down all the generations), God gives to Moses to give to them as his special name a name formed from the same root (היה, "to be") as the verbal form employed to explain who and how he really is, a verbal form (אֶהְיֶה) four times repeated in vv. 12, 14, the name יהוה, YHWH, NRSV's *the LORD*.

That this revelation of the name YHWH was subsequently sufficient for neither Israel nor the Egyptians is made clear in the continuation of the narrative. But that the essential meaning of the name is vindicated and that the authority sustaining it triumphs is made no less clear. Both Israel and the Egyptians come to learn that YHWH really *is*, as vv. 16-22 predict.

The key to understanding the insistent requirement that the people be permitted to go into the wilderness to sacrifice is to be found in the urgent desire of Moses, reflected in the present form of the text of Exodus for the first time at v. 12. Although Moses knew that Yahweh would be with him, he felt also the need to have the people feel at the holy mountain what he had first felt there. And their reason for going, as they are to advance it to Pharaoh, is that Yahweh has happened to them—they have encountered "the One who always IS," the "I AM."

This important name of God and this important explanation of the name are formatively influential on much of the remainder of the Bible, from the 6,823 occurrences of YHWH in the OT to the "I AM" sayings of Isa 40–55 and the Gospel of John. In a way, all the remainder of the narrative of the Book of Exodus is a proof of the truth of the name YHWH.

4:1-17. The credentials of Moses and the mouth of Moses. Convinced that YHWH means business, Moses proceeds to protest that Israel will not believe that he himself has seen such a God. On the surface, his protest is a request for authentication as the spokesman of YHWH. At a deeper level, it is a variation of the question of v. 13. The causative active form of the verb "trust" (אמן), the verb from which our word "amen" is derived, occurs five times (vv. 1, 5, 8bis, 9) in the first nine verses of this section, a vivid suggestion of Moses' concern. The Egyptians and Israel will not trust what Moses tells them, for they will have no basis for such trust.

Thus does YHWH provide three signs of Moses' authority, the first and the second of which are immediately demonstrated. Only the first and the third of the signs are actually employed in Moses' demonstration of his authority, and of course of YHWH's authority, in Egypt.

These signs leave no doubt about YHWH's authority, so Moses turns his protest to his own inadequacy, about which he has no doubt whatever. To this point, Moses has really been occupied with the question of the authority of the God who has made what seems so rash a command, and with the power of this God to support such a command.

Moses comes not for the first time to a serious consideration of his own lack of fitness for the job he is being given. His query in 3:11, at least a hint in the same direction, was answered only by reference to the gift of God's Presence. Having satisfied himself as to God's role, Moses raises now the question of his own limitation. Indeed, his protest of personal inadequacy assumes the preceding proof of YHWH's adequacy.

In what almost amounts to a correction of God, Moses states that he is not a man of words, adding in a threefold repetition that this condition is one of long standing, persistent up to the moment of their meeting, and as much in evidence as ever since. In effect, Moses says "You are clearly all that you claim. But I am the same old Moses, heavy-lipped and thick-tongued."

The answer of YHWH is properly indignant. He is the one who has put a mouth on a man, and he gives or withholds the ability to speak, to hear, to see. It is up to Moses to get on with the task, and depend in his weakness on YHWH who will be with him. This answer of course is the one Moses has already been given, and it calls forth from him his real concern: he does not want to go.

Whether the proposal that Aaron accompany Moses as his *mouth* is original to this narrative is disputed. Since the publication in 1948 of Noth's *A History of Pentateuchal Traditions* (1972), the extraneous nature of the Aaron traditions has been often recognized. As already indicated, it seems unlikely on the basis of the

text of the OT that Aaron and MIRIAM are to be considered the actual brother and sister of Moses.

Whatever the original shape of the pieces that make up the composite that is our Exodus, however, the composite in its received form has a statement of its own. And Moses' concern about his deficiencies as a speaker is treated by YHWH for what it plainly is, an excuse. YHWH promises to be "I AM" with the mouth of both Moses and Aaron, and the discussion is finished.

The postscript about the staff with which Moses is to do the signs is a further indication of the fact that it is YHWH, not Moses *or* Aaron, who is in charge.

4:18-31. The deliverer returns to Egypt. This section of the narrative of Exodus is transitional. The next stage in the dramatic proof by YHWH of his powerful Presence must necessarily take place in Egypt, and these verses move the action from Sinai to Egypt, albeit with Sinai as the ultimate destination.

Moses is not depicted here as having told JETHRO the real reason for his desire to return to Egypt, a fact that seems to be borne out by the account of 18:1-9. There is a minor difficulty in the conflict between vv. 20-26 and 18:6 that 18:2 does not fully resolve. Apparently Zipporah and Gershom went at least part of the way to Egypt with Moses, but the fact that they are never mentioned as being there, or as being on the return journey to Sinai, suggests that Moses committed his family to the care of his father-in-law prior to the final and dangerous leg of the trip into Egypt. The reference in v. 20 to "sons" seems, in the light of 2:22 and 4:25, to be at least premature at this point, and perhaps a scribal error. A second son of Moses is mentioned elsewhere in the OT only at 18:4 and by the Chronicler at 1 Chr 23:15 and 17.

The mighty "wonders" that are to be called forth by YHWH's own "firming up" of Pharaoh's heart are anticipated in YHWH's further words to Moses and perhaps also in Moses' tutelage of Aaron (v. 28), who meets Moses at the command of YHWH at Sinai. These forthcoming mighty wonders, called "signs" (אתות) in 4:8, 9, and 17 and "extraordinary deeds" (נפלאות) in 3:20, are here (v. 21) called "wondrous deeds" (מפתים) for the first time (see also 7:3, 9; 11:9, 10). They are the important proofs of YHWH's Presence in Egypt, to both the Egyptians and Israel. Verse 21 mentions the wonders Moses has been given power to do, and v. 23 mentions the climactic wonder YHWH will do, the one that will bring about Israel's release by the reluctant Pharaoh.

The strange narrative of vv. 24-26 is difficult to translate, and more difficult still to understand. A part of this difficulty is presented by the ambiguity of antecedent for the pronouns "he" and "him." Moses is not mentioned by name anywhere in these three verses (in spite of an unauthorized insertion of his name into v. 26 of earlier printings of my own translation by an anonymous gremlin-editor; see Durham 1987, 52, and cf. 53n.25a.). In v. 26, who lets whom alone?

Despite a great many learned and lengthy efforts, the passage remains a murky one. The best to be made of it is the reasonable guess that the rationale for the inclusion of these verses by the compilers of Exodus is the rite of circumcision. The Egyptians practiced a partial circumcision, one referred to in Josh 5:9 as "the disgrace of Egypt." Either according to tradition or assumption, Moses had to have this "disgrace" remedied before his arrival in Egypt as the spokesman of YHWH. Given the urgency of his journey, the act is performed vicariously on his son, so that Moses might not be incapacitated at a critical moment.

The eventual arrival in Egypt of Moses and Aaron is strangely laconic, and out of keeping with the dramatic nature of the commission and its consequences. There is good reason to think of it as a transitional synopsis, an addition to fill the gap between the last wilderness appearance and the first audience with Pharaoh. The passage presents Aaron in the best possible light, not only speaking for Moses but also doing the portentous signs for the people. Moses and Aaron confer first with the elders, and having convinced them, they represent their case to the people. The instant belief and worship in response they meet, particularly in view of Israel's subsequent paroxysms of doubting, are a further indication of the secondary nature of 4:29-31.

5:1–6:1. The first encounter with Pharaoh. In their very first encounter with Pharaoh, Moses and Aaron present, as a request transmitted directly from YHWH (*Thus says the LORD, the God of Israel* [5:1]), the need of Israel to be free to *celebrate a festival . . . in the wilderness.* Pharaoh refuses, on the grounds that he does not know any YHWH. The refusal, so stated, is a dramatic preparation for the establishment of identity and authority that the reader already knows to be coming. Pharaoh's imperious reply is also a preparation, one dripping with irony, for what is to take place: "Who is YHWH, that I should give attention to what *he* says, and so send forth Israel? I have no knowledge of YHWH, and I am not *about* to send Israel out!" (v. 2, author trans.).

The result of the first petition of Moses and Aaron is an intensification of Israel's arduous labor by a Pharaoh who thinks they have too much time on their hands if they are paying attention to such distractions, which he terms *deceptive words* (5:9), from Moses and Aaron.

When the new and onerous demands are put into effect, the people complain, and the section-leaders bring their protest directly to Pharaoh. His response is unsympathetic: *You are lazy, lazy* (v. 17). Thus do these work-bosses turn on Moses and Aaron, waiting to learn the outcome of this further audience with Pharaoh. They call upon YHWH, whose name they have apparently accepted, to judge Moses and Aaron for making them odious to Pharaoh's supervisors and so to Pharaoh himself.

Thus for the first time since Sinai, Moses doubts. Hurt by the people's accusations, he repeats them to YHWH, then asks why he was ever sent to Egypt. YHWH, he charges, has not even begun any escape for his people. This charge is a perfect preparation for a further prediction by YHWH that the promised authentication is on the way. Before he is finished, Moses will see what he is up to, and Pharaoh will send Israel out with *a mighty hand* (6:1).

6:2-13. YHWH's promise and YHWH's rescue. The compilers of Exodus have interrupted their ongoing narrative here with a sequence of material paralleling the account of 3:1–4:17. This is not the record of a second experience of call, prompted by Moses' discouragement and consequent doubt, but a parallel account of the call and commission with an emphasis on covenant instead of theophany. These verses are from the hand of the Priestly redactors, and they are set here for the practical reason that they cannot logically come after the beginning of the narrative of the wondrous deeds of YHWH.

Of particular interest are the special Priestly emphases: the introduction of the TETRAGRAMMATON (i.e., the four-letter name YHWH) in a self-confession formula, the stress upon the promises of YHWH's covenant, and a characteristic descendants-list. Unlike the Yahwistic narrators, who date the use of the name YHWH from the time of Seth (Gen 4:26), the Priestly narrators avoid using the name until it has been revealed to Moses in this experience of call and commission.

The Priestly narrators have God reveal his special name to Moses with no preparation, no theophany, in the meaning-filled self-confession, "I am YHWH." It is a basic assertion of OT theology, one about which

Zimmerli (1982, 20) has written: "All that Yahweh had to say and to declare to his people appears to be a development of the fundamental assertion, 'I am Yahweh'."

The phrase occurs with great frequency in OT passages linked especially with Priestly interests, as a declaration of the authority upon which requirement is made. Here in v. 2 it is precisely that, and the authoritative nature of the name YHWH is enhanced by its relation to the ancient title "God Almighty" (אֵל שַׁדָּי, El Shaddai), identified as the name known to the Fathers, to whom the promise of progeny and land was made as a promise of covenant. That promise was of course the promise of YHWH, whatever name was attached to it, and that promise YHWH is now about to fulfill (vv. 4, 8), and that fulfillment means rescue.

Moses' further protest of inadequacy ("the sons of Israel paid no attention to me, how is Pharaoh going to pay attention to me, especially with my stumbling speech?" v. 12, author trans.) is ignored. YHWH gives him and Aaron a direct order to get on with his commission.

6:14-27. The family line of Aaron (and Moses). The obvious dominance of Aaron in this genealogical list is a priestly attempt to establish Aaron as entirely worthy of his place in the Exodus narrative as Moses' assistant. At the same time, the genealogy—beginning with the same three sons of Jacob as does Exod 1:2 and the "Blessing of Jacob" in Gen 49:3-7—functions as another connecting link in the composite of Exodus as a whole. I have elsewhere referred to it as one of seven "sequences of memory" designed to bring to the present Israel's significant religious past (Durham 1990, 97-104).

Moses' parents are named in this section for the first time, but there is no mention of Miriam as his sister. Both Moses and Aaron are designated as descendants of Levi through Kohath to their father Amram. Aaron is referred to first (and not merely as the eldest) and at length, and Moses is only mentioned. Aaron's wife and sons (and even one of his grandsons) are named, yet there is no mention of Moses's wife and children.

The reason for this emphasis on Aaron is to be seen in the need to establish Aaron as the brother of Moses, and to trace the lineage of both of them to the priestly family of Levi within the descendancy of Jacob/Israel.

6:28–7:7. A preview of things to come. The genealogy justifying Aaron is followed by a brief summary of the call and commission of Moses as it is described in 6:2-13, and that account is resumed with a repetition (v. 30) of Moses' objection (see 6:12). YHWH then declares that he will present Moses to Pharaoh as a god (אֱלֹהִים, 7:1, not NRSV's like God) and Aaron as Moses' prophet. Even when confronted by so impressive a legation, however, YHWH predicts that Pharaoh will pay no attention, precisely because YHWH intends to "firm up" Pharaoh's mind in order to provide a cause and a setting for the ultimate proof of his Presence.

The first confrontation with Pharaoh is thus recounted in the divine prediction of how it will be. The end result of this display will be the exodus, and that will give the Egyptians (and by inference Israel) the knowledge by experience that "I am YHWH." And at the time it takes place, Moses is eighty, and Aaron, eighty-three. Thus quite handily, Exodus 6:28–7:7 sums up the narrative from 3:1 to this point in Exodus, and anticipates what is to come through 15:21.

Ten Wonders and the Exodus, 7:8–13:16

The narrative of the ten wonders that prove that YHWH is powerfully, even dominantly, present in Egypt is a skillful composite of material from three of the major tetrateuchal sources, usually designated J, E, and P. These three sources recount in common only the first wonder and the tenth. Of the others, J and E include the seventh, eighth, and ninth in sequence; J and P, the second; J alone mentions the fourth and fifth; and P alone, the third and sixth. Each source proceeds with its own vocabulary, its own formulae, its own emphases, even its own heroes (J emphasizes Moses; P, Aaron), but the three have been woven together to produce a dramatic and logically progressing account. And as intriguing as a comparison of identifiable source layers is, the composite of the Exodus we have, unified by its emphasis upon YHWH as the central figure, must remain at the center of our attention.

The relating of the first nine of the ten wonders to natural phenomena connected with the river Nile and Egypt's Delta has often been noted. Any attempt to explain these wonders as exaggerated natural events does a disservice, however, to the theological purpose of Exodus. The ten wonders are presented quite deliberately as miracles. The terms that describe them, the timing and ferocity and extent with which they fall, and above all their much-stressed role as proofs of the Presence of YHWH all assert their miraculous nature in the concept of the authors of the Book of Exodus.

The sequence of the ten wonders is a dramatic one. They move forward in an upward progression of seriousness towards their terrible climax. Pharaoh is first competitive, then aggravated, then discomfited, then dealt both fiscal and physical reverse, then finally faced with extinction, literally a fate worse than death, as in the ancient Near East sonlessness was death before death, the ultimate oblivion.

The fundamental purpose of the wonder accounts is the enhancement of the staggering implication of what appears (4:22-23) to have been the earliest wonder, and is now the tenth and most serious of them. Contrary to all past experience of and every present appearance to Israel in Egypt, it is only YHWH who really is, and YHWH who is thus alone supreme. In his Presence, the Pharaoh and all his advisers and officers and wizards, even all his magnificent pantheon of gods, are as nothing. All of them together are bested and defeated in every issue.

And the issues on which attention is focused are the very issues on which the Egyptians are supposed to have been most experienced, and so most capable of controlling. YHWH repeats with Pharaoh, and simultaneously with his people, the pattern he followed with Moses: identification, establishment of authority, and command. Pharaoh's complacent ignorance (5:2) turns first to limited respect (8:8,25), then guarded cooperation (9:27-28; 10:7-8), then fearful obedience (12:29-32).

7:8-13. The rod and the great snake. For the first time in the Exodus narrative, a request from Pharaoh for a proving wonder is anticipated. The wonder that is provided is the first of the signs given to Moses at Sinai, but it is repeated here with a significant difference. In 4:1-5, Moses' staff, thrown upon the ground, becomes a dangerous serpent (נָחָשׁ, from which Moses ran away). Here, the staff is called Aaron's, and it becomes a "terrifying snake" (תַּנִּין, translated δράκων by LXX; see Gen 1:21; Ps 74:13; Isa 27:1; Job 7:12).

This portent loses its impact when it is repeated by Pharaoh's team of wonder-workers, and this impact is only partly recovered when Aaron's staff devours all their staffs-become-reptiles.

The implication of this introductory passage thus is that weightier and more consequential portents are to be required if Pharaoh is to come to know YHWH and respect his authority. The ten wonders thus become unavoidable by Pharaoh's own recalcitrance, a recalcitrance we already know will be reinforced, when it appears to be weakening, by YHWH himself.

7:14-25. The first wonder. Each one of the first nine wonder-narratives presents an identical conclusion. In each of them, YHWH attempts to prove his Presence, to Pharaoh, to the Egyptians, and to Israel. In each of them, the Pharaoh refuses to believe, although from the sixth wonder on, YHWH is directly involved in that disbelief to the end that Israel may come to a certain belief.

The first wonder is anticipated in 4:9, where Moses is told, in the provision of a third sign for Israel, that he may dip water from the Nile onto dry ground, where it will turn to blood. In J's account of the first wonder, the entire Nile turns to blood. In P's account, every body of water in Egypt and even the water in buckets and jugs becomes blood. The term used throughout, with no qualification of any sort, is דָּם, which can only mean blood in such a context.

The report that Pharaoh's wizards duplicated the wonder wrought by Moses and Aaron creates a problem if all the water in Egypt has been turned to blood, since the wizards would be augmenting the discomforts already created by the pollution of YHWH's wonder, and without any water at that. There is an ironic touch here, in that the Pharaoh's competition with Moses and Aaron, really a competition with YHWH, makes matters worse, not better, for Egypt. The Egyptians search everywhere for potable water, for they could not drink the water of the river (v. 24). This statement is reminiscent of a text from Egypt's Middle Kingdom that refers to the water of the Nile as blood, and notes that it must be rejected "as human," despite a thirst for water (ANET 3, 441, ii 10).

8:1-15. The second wonder. The second wonder is an extraordinary abundance of frogs from the Nile. As in the account of the first wonder, the extent of this blow against Egypt is multiplied in the later version of the tradition, so that there are frogs not only in the Nile, but also in its tributaries, and even in the irrigation trenches and ponds of Egypt. The picture of frogs in beds, ovens, and mixing bowls and even leaping up onto the august persons of Pharaoh and his courtiers is characteristic of the wit of the J traditions.

Once again, Pharaoh's wizards match YHWH's feat, presumably adding still more frogs. For the first time, however, Pharaoh recognizes both the existence and the power of YHWH, and promises to let the people go if YHWH will remove the frogs. This promise is soon enough seen to be a ruse, however, for when the frogs die, Pharaoh's mind remains "firmed up," just as YHWH has predicted.

8:16-19. The third wonder. This blow of YHWH consists of a transformation of the dust of the earth, an obviously inexhaustible supply of raw material, into gnats (כִּנִּים, stinging gnats, even mosquitoes or sand flies). For the first time, Pharaoh's wizards are stumped. Unable to duplicate this wonder, they confess to Pharaoh that they are up against an act of a god (אֱלֹהִים, 8:19).

This wisdom of his wizards has no effect on Pharaoh, however, who remains as unmoved as ever. And the reader simply must by this point begin to wonder about such an extraordinarily stubborn response.

8:20-32. The fourth wonder. Some commentators have argued that the fourth wonder is only a variant version of the third. This wonder too involves insects, although a different and apparently more general term is used to designate the variety of insect: עָרֹב suggests a mixture of flying insects, hence NRSV's *swarms of flies*. There is no conclusive evidence for combining the third and fourth wonders into a single account, however.

Indeed, the best single argument for treating them as separate wonders is the fact that the compositors of Exodus did so. The two wonders are best taken as sequential, and the fourth wonder is best understood as a different, more intensive blow of YHWH. Each wonder in the sequence is more severe than the one before, as each wonder is intended to make the proof of YHWH's presence progressively more convincing.

Nothing is said in this section about the stuff whence these flying bugs come, only that they are "heavy" in number, to which adjective the Samaritan Pentateuch adds "exceedingly," and that they blanket the ground and devastate the land.

In this wonder, reference is made for the first time to the fate of the Israelites. That part of Egypt in which they are dwelling, designated for the first time in v. 22 as *the land of Goshen*, is exempt from the presence of the *swarms of flies*. This exemption is emphasized to Pharaoh as a further testimony to YHWH's authority, that the Egyptians (and obviously the "Hebrews") "may know by experience that I am YHWH." (v. 21, author trans.)

Also for the first time, Pharaoh agrees to permit the people of Israel to make their sacrifices, but with the proviso that they do so on Egyptian territory. Moses sticks adamantly by his (YHWH's) original requirement: three days' journey into the wilderness. And Pharaoh once again makes a false promise to gain relief. While there is no reminder this time of YHWH's prediction of

Pharaonic intransigence, a sense of its inevitability has been established by the recurring narrative pattern.

The protection of Israel from the insect swarm is a convincing proof of YHWH's powerful Presence to Israel, and of course it is Israel that is the real target of this sequence of proving wonders. Pharaoh learns enough to negotiate, but never enough to believe—but Pharaoh and his people are not the objects of YHWH's evangelism in Exodus.

9:1-7. The fifth wonder. A severe epidemic among Egyptian livestock comprises the fifth wonder of YHWH. Once again, the Israelites are spared the effects of the devastation, in a further proof that YHWH is in charge of events.

Protests that a reference to camels in v. 3 is an anachronism fall into the same category as questions about whether an enslaved people such as Israel in Egypt would possess herd and flock animals on any appreciable scale, and proposals of a "naturalistic" basis for the "plagues." The wonder-events are *not* "plagues," except from an Egyptian point of view, and this account is *theological* in nature as in purpose. Whether there were camels in Egypt in Moses' time or whether the epidemic suffered by the Egyptians' animals was anthrax was irrelevant to the compositors of Exodus.

This time, Pharaoh asks no relief and makes no promises, although he does send out to GOSHEN to check on conditions there. And still, as we fully expect, his mind remains "heavy and dull."

9:8-12. The sixth wonder. With the sixth wonder, Moses is instructed to alter the usual prediction of what is to come. Instead, he is to scatter towards heaven (הַשָּׁמַיְמָה in v. 8, not *in the air*, as in NRSV) double handfuls of furnace-ash (פִּיחַ כִּבְשָׁן; note Gen 19:28 and Exod 19:18) in full sight of Pharaoh. The result is a widespread and virulent pustulous condition of the skin, afflicting humans and animals alike.

Pharaoh's wizards are now completely cowed, and they withdraw from the contest, unable to stand up to Moses and Aaron and covered with boils. Pharaoh remains as immovable as ever, and for the first time in the narrative, the prediction of 4:21 is specifically described as having come to pass. Heretofore, Pharaoh has apparently been stubborn on his own. Now, YHWH is said to make Pharaoh's mind obdurate. And the reader is left with the suspicion that something of the sort has been happening all along: how else are Pharaoh's actions to be understood?

This motif, present in each of the tetrateuchal traditions, is far more than a description of YHWH's manipulation of Pharaoh as an unwilling but ultimately helpless puppet. This Pharaoh has disclaimed even any knowledge of YHWH, it is true. But YHWH's own people, the children of Abraham in Egypt, have manifested a lack of confidence in him.

YHWH, therefore, must prove his powerful Presence, and hence his authority, irrefutably. YHWH's influence on Pharaoh's stubbornness is implied from 3:19-20 forward, stated by inference in 4:21, 6:1, and 7:13, promised in 7:3-5, and now stated directly. A premature capitulation by Pharaoh would frustrate this irrefutable proof. We must not lose sight of the fact that this sequence in the narrative composite of Exodus was important to Israel's confessional worship for many years; Pss 78 and 105 are alone enough to establish such a usage.

9:13-35. The seventh wonder. The seventh wonder is a devastating hailstorm accompanied by furious lightning. It is begun with an explanation of the reason for all the wonders. YHWH tells Moses to announce to Pharaoh that his sending of such annoyance and devastation upon Egypt is to the end that they "may know by experience that there is none like me in the whole earth" (v. 14, author trans.).

For the first time, some provision is made for those Egyptians who, in contrast to their Pharaoh, are convinced. This detail is a brilliant touch, one that increases the dramatic tension of Pharaoh's recalcitrance and enhances the extent of YHWH's self-proof. Those who heed the warning instruction are spared at least the loss of the animals left to them, and at most, their own lives.

Once again, the Israelites in Goshen are wholly spared. Over the rest of Egypt, there is an awesome obliteration of all unsheltered life, human, animal, and vegetable. The poet of Ps 78:48 expands even this tradition of decimation by attributing the death of some of the Egyptian cattle to bolts of lightning.

Pharaoh is depicted not only as agreeing to let Israel go, unconditionally, but also as confessing his own sinfulness, YHWH's righteousness, and the Egyptians' collective guilt. Moses remains unconvinced (9:30), both because of YHWH's promise (4:21; 7:13, 22; 8:15; and elsewhere), and also because the sequence of mighty wonders by which YHWH is proving himself is by no means finished.

But the wonders have now for the first time brought death to the Egyptian people. The implication is full of dread. The progressive tension is intensified. A point of no return has been passed.

10:1-20. The eighth wonder. This wonder is introduced in an aside of YHWH to Moses that repeats, in direct terms, the reason for all that is happening. Specifically mentioned is the continuing obduracy of Pharaoh as the basis for the continuing and intensifying disasters, an obduracy for which YHWH takes full responsibility. Moses is reminded that he is to "recount again and again" (תְּסַפֵּר, v. 2) what YHWH has done, to his children and his grandchildren, the plainest statement to this point of the proving motive of the wonder sequence. In producing his portents among the Egyptians, YHWH says he has made a plaything of the Egyptians (cf. Num 22:29; Judg 19:25; 1 Sam 31:4) to the end that Israel may know "that I am YHWH."

In a lengthy prelude to the wonder itself, promised to be a locust-horde of unprecedented extent, Pharaoh, under pressure from his advisers, offers a compromise that is unacceptable, that the men alone be permitted to go out to worship YHWH. Moses and Aaron of course refuse, and are thrown out of the palace. Immediately, under YHWH's command, Moses sets the locust swarm in motion, and the vegetation that survived the hailstorm is quickly devoured.

Once again, when the wonder is in full progress, Pharaoh moves quickly to bring it to an end, confessing his mistake, and adding for the first time a request that his sin be "lifted away" (v. 17). The awful severity of the swarm of locusts is vividly accented by Pharaoh's desperate plea: *remove this deadly thing from me.*

Moses' prayer to YHWH brings a diverted west (or sea) wind, removing every one of the locusts brought in such number by the east wind. Once more, however, YHWH makes Pharaoh's mind obstinate, and he does not permit Israel to leave.

10:21-29. The ninth wonder. Although this wonder ostensibly causes less actual physical harm than any other single blow of YHWH against Egypt, it brings a terror more awesome in a thick, eerie darkness, *a darkness that can be felt* (v. 21). This is owing in part to a cumulative effect, and in part to an element of suspense aggravated by mystery. The Egyptians had suffered dreadfully from disasters that were visible—who could tell what the black darkness might hold?

Israel, presumably in Goshen, had light, although the implication is that it was in their homes, בְּמוֹשְׁבֹתָם, *where they lived* (v. 23).

For three days the Egyptians were in a terror of blindness in this extraordinary darkness, a cancellation of their "eternally rising sun." So Pharaoh again capitulates, with a condition, but with the weakest one thus far stated, that Israel's flocks and herds remain behind.

Moses of course refuses. YHWH "firms up" Pharaoh's mind once again, and Pharaoh's intransigence brings the negotiations to a halt. No further mention is made of the darkness, not even in a request by Pharaoh that it be removed. And Moses is expelled without the privilege of reentry, upon pain of death.

11:1-10. YHWH replaces Moses. These ten verses function as a transition sequence, providing the movement from the first nine wonders in which Moses and Aaron act as YHWH's intermediaries to the tenth wonder in which YHWH acts for himself. Indeed, from this point forward, Moses fades increasingly into the background of the action except in the narratives of rebellion in the wilderness and at Sinai. The tenth wonder is predicted, in grim detail, and the fleecing theme is introduced to suggest just how glad the Egyptians are finally to be rid of Israel. Only near the end of the section, at v. 8, is this passage linked to Pharaoh's presence. That reference suggests that death and despoilation are introduced in the angry "final" exchange between Moses and Pharaoh. *And in hot anger he left Pharaoh* (v. 8); yet again, Pharaoh's divinely-stimulated obstinacy is stated, with the sonorous repetition of a chorus in a Greek tragedy.

12:1-28. YHWH's Passover, reminder, and protection. These verses are an interruption of the story of YHWH's proof to Israel of his Presence in Egypt, but an appropriate interruption. They provide important directions for the rituals of remembrance whereby the momentous events about to take place are to be brought perpetually to the present of Israel's consciousness.

The first of these rituals, PASSOVER (vv. 1-13), probably originated in a nomadic celebration connected with flock and herd birthing in springtime. The second of them, Unleavened Bread (vv. 14-20), probably has an agricultural origin. The directions for the two celebrations are from the Priestly tradition, and therefore represent a developed application of the original intent of each, in terms of the tenth wonder and the exodus from Egypt.

Anything more than reasonable speculation about the background and time of origin of these two rituals is not possible. Certainly by the time of the compilation of Exod 12:1-20, they were time-honored in both

direction and significance. No two festivals in the ancient ritual calendar of Israel could more appropriately have commemorated the totality of YHWH's great deliverance of his people than these two, the one from the past, recalling the nomadic days of the fathers, the other from Israel's new future as a people, associated specifically with the settled, agricultural life of CANAAN. In a way, they symbolize the exodus experience in its historical totality.

The Passover may well have been connected with the Exodus from the very beginning, in part because of its apotropaic element, in part because of its nomadic character. Much as some festive features of the ancient Roman celebration of the winter solstice have been absorbed into the modern Christian celebration of Christmas, features of the Passover that predated the Exodus perhaps came with time to be expressly symbolic of it.

Subsequently, after the arrival in Canaan, the Feast of Unleavened Bread, that is, new bread from the new crop at the beginning of the harvest, was joined to the Passover ritual. The Feast of Unleavened Bread fell at the same time of year as Passover, marked a new beginning, and was naturally related through the ancient Passover requirement of unleavened bread and bitter herbs to be eaten with the paschal lamb. Joined to the Passover celebration, it became symbolic of the completion of the Exodus cycle begun in Egypt. This association was probably made early in the period of the settlement in Canaan.

The reference to the month of Passover celebration as *the beginning of months* (v. 2) is a statement of theological import as well as a specification of an agricultural CALENDAR such as the one found at GEZER. Passover marked the beginning of Israel as a people rescued by God as well as the beginning of a new undertaking of God, and thus it was an appropriate time for the start of a new year.

The marking of the doorposts and lintels of the houses in which the people of Israel were eating Passover (v. 7) is an anticipation of the protection (v. 13) Yahweh is to give them when the judgment against *all the gods of Egypt* (v. 12) falls in the tenth wonder.

The unleavened bread cakes are a keeping of remembrance, the ritual means of reminding Israel of the time, the event, and above all the rescue of YHWH's intervention on their behalf. Together with the ordered ritual of Passover, the seven days of unleavened bread were intended as a means of making the experience of exodus real to every successive generation of Israelites.

Thus also is the protection of Israel explained in this inserted sequence. It is a protection that in preparation augurs the nature of the tenth wonder, and anticipates and explains the requirement of the dedication of Israel's firstborn specified in 13:1-16. YHWH's "destroyer" is to pass throughout Egypt, including the Delta area where Israel lives, and the blood of the Passover lamb on the doorposts and lintels of Israel is the means of their protection. This act becomes another means of actualizing the past in each new present, and a further testimony of the proof of the Presence of YHWH to Israel in Egypt and so to Israel wherever they may come to be, in any period of history.

12:29-36. The tenth wonder. Thus at last the final proof of YHWH's identity and authority is presented. It has been made inevitable by Pharaoh's divinely encouraged stubbornness. It is reminiscent, at the very least, of Pharaoh's slaughter of the "Hebrews' " sons early on in the oppression (1:15-22).

As Moses had angrily predicted to Pharaoh, Egypt's firstborn, of men and cattle alike, are slain. Only one explanation is possible for Pharaoh and his subjects, and, of course for Israel, whose firstborn have been spared. YHWH, whose name and power the Egyptians and the Israelites have now come to know by experience, has struck the deadly blow. The report of it is chilling still: *there was a loud cry in Egypt, for there was not a house without someone dead* (v. 30).

Numbed and brought beyond resistance by the catastrophe, Pharaoh forgets his command ostracizing Moses (10:28-29), summons Moses and Aaron in the middle of the night and commands them to be gone as they desire, without condition. YHWH's prediction (6:1; 11:8) comes true, as the Egyptians urge Israel to leave in a hurry. The fleecing of the Egyptians so eager to be rid of these people whose God has brought them such suffering is a further fulfillment of prediction (3:21-22; 11:2). Articles of silver and gold and clothing are willingly given to the departing Israelites by their benumbed and entranced Egyptian neighbors.

12:37-51. The exodus. Thus finally does the Exodus, the saving event of such central importance in the faith of the OT, take place. The notice of it in vv. 37-39 seems anticlimactic and almost laconic. The people travelled hastily and haphazardly, ill-prepared for their journey despite (or perhaps because of) their long anticipation of it. As a result, the first leg of their journey was evidently a brief one. Neither *Rameses* nor *Succoth* can be located with any certainty (see Herrmann 1973, 23-28, and Uphill 1968, 1969), although

the narrator's intention was probably to provide a clear record of the route of Israel's departure from Egypt.

The figure 600,000 for the number of "strong men on foot" leaving Egypt with their families is generally regarded as an impossible exaggeration. Whether this number represents the male population of Israel during the monarchy, or a number that has been incorrectly transmitted or translated remains a matter of academic debate.

The period of 430 years for the sojourn in Egypt is also a number difficult to reconcile with the information we have in the OT. It is in conflict with Gen 15:13, and even more, with Gen 15:16; Exod 6:16, 18, 20 and passages in Leviticus and Numbers that imply an exodus four generations from the generation of Jacob. Like the census figure for the males in Exodus, it may be an exaggeration, even one dictated by that inflated figure.

The narrative of the Exodus itself is rounded out by a repetition of the command to keep Passover, the means by which the redemptive event is to be kept real to every successive generation of Israelites.

13:1-16. Remembering in ritual. The narrative of the tenth wonder and the Exodus it made possible is rounded out with yet another sequence of ritual instructions designed to make the story real to Israel yet to come. Because YHWH spared Israel's firstborn, of family, of flock, and of herd, those same firstborn are to be given to YHWH, either in fact or by vicarious ransom.

Reminding symbols are mentioned, albeit somewhat ambiguously here (vv. 6, 16), and the keeping of the reminding festival of unleavened bread cakes (note 12:14-20).

All this is to the end, once again, that the all-important exodus event be actualized, made a real event, to each new generation of Israelites, by keeping ritual, by symbol, and above all by personal cost. Israel has been ransomed by YHWH. YHWH commands of Israel a response.

Israel in the Wilderness, 13:17–18:27

The Route and the Rescue, 13:17–15:21

13:17–14:4. The route. The flight of Israel from Egypt appears to have been directly southeast from Succoth, although the uncertain location of the places mentioned in the account renders impossible any precise plotting of the route, either in its initial stages or later, to and from Sinai. The references in 13:17 and

14:1-3 make plain that the more direct and obvious route was divinely eliminated, and that YHWH himself determined the route Israel was to take.

Both this divine guidance and the columns of cloud and fire (13:21-22) are testimony to the divine Presence in the midst of Israel. This Presence, whose effective authority and power the Exodus narrative has to this point sought to demonstrate, becomes henceforth the essential hub around which all of the remainder of Exodus turns and from which its cultic and legal requirements stem.

The uncertainty of the identification of the place-names mentioned in the account of the Exodus make an identification of the site of the great deliverance at the sea as impossible as the fixing of the route to it. Without a doubt, the place-names were provided to do the very thing they cannot now do, because we no longer know where the places are, or were.

Two facts however emerge: (1) the initial direction of the march was set to get Israel out of Egypt and thus beyond the authority of Pharaoh by the quickest and most direct route possible; and (2) the change of direction once the border had been crossed was designed to move Israel toward the only immediate goal Moses could conceive, the mountain of YHWH's special revelation. The distinction between the crossing of the Egyptian border and the crossing of the sea is not always made, but it is nonetheless an important one.

The moment of the Exodus is noted in 12:37-38. The crossing of the Egyptian border must have occurred between *Succoth* and *Etham, on the edge of the wilderness* (13:20). The deliverance at the sea comes still later in the journey, after the departure from Etham, as 14:1-2 make plain.

By any tracking we can imagine, since the places mentioned have yet to be located, the route in which YHWH guides Moses and the Israelites is an eccentric one. The third camp of the fleeing Israelites is even a turning back, one designated by not less than four points of reference: *in front of Pi-hahiroth, between Migdol and the sea, in front of Baal-zephon* (14:2).

The reason for this maneuvering is made clear by the return, at the beginning of Exod 14, to the motif of YHWH's making obstinate the mind of Pharaoh. Pharaoh's decision to pursue Israel will be the result of more work on the part of YHWH, who is still proving his Presence to Israel.

14:5-31. The rescue. Pharaoh's pursuit of Israel is presented first of all as a decision of the Egyptian cabinet made on economic grounds: Egypt was losing an invaluable source of slave and semi-slave labor. The gathering of forces for avoiding this loss reflects their sense of its serious nature. Pharaoh gathers around himself 600 crack chariots as an attack force, to be supported by a still larger force of three-man chariots, each commanded by a שָׁלִישׁ, the "third" who coordinated the driver and the weapon wielder completing his team. Such a mode of attack is frequently attested in Egyptian battle art from the very period in which the exodus is most likely to have occurred (Yadin 1963, 86-90, 104-105). Pharaoh himself is depicted as in command of the advance force, with the support force operating as an independently commanded backup.

This extraordinary force emphasizes the hopeless plight of Israel, on foot and largely weaponless, and, at the same time, dramatizes the inevitable victory of YHWH. The dismay and panic of the people of Israel upon learning of the Egyptian pursuit is all the more understandable when it is seen as a prospect beyond which Israel believed themselves utterly removed. They are presented as having thought themselves beyond Pharaoh's authority and interest. He had, after all, sent them out. He was, they had believed, a beaten man. Yet suddenly here he was again, with a crushing, irresistible force. Their frightened expectation was death, and they longed for the slavery they had left so gladly.

Moses attempts to encourage the people with the assurance that YHWH will himself do battle on their behalf, predicting the complete removal of any threat to them of the Egyptians advancing toward them. YHWH instructs Moses to bring the staff into play once again, to manipulate the waters of the sea and to enable Israel to cross on dry ground. He adds that he is about to make Pharaoh obstinate once more, so that "the Egyptians will know by experience that I am YHWH in my winning glory for myself" (v. 18, author trans.).

Next YHWH sends the "attendant [NRSV *angel*] of God" (מַלְאַךְ הָאֱלֹהִים, v. 19; note 23:23-30) from a position of guidance before the people of Israel to one of protection behind them, also moving the daytime pillar of cloud as an obscuring cover between the encamped Israelites and the oncoming Egyptian force. As night falls, the pillar of fire, a source of light in the dark, is absent for the first time. Through the night, the two groups remained separate.

The "sea" Israel crossed the next morning, the "sea" the Egyptians were prevented from crossing remains a subject of indeterminate discussion (see Wiles

1990). A wide range of seas, rivers, and marshlands has been proposed, and "reed sea" has become a more popular translation for יַם סוּף than "Red Sea," a translation influenced by LXX and Vulgate. No location thus far suggested, however, is convincing.

The miracle of the crossing lies not in the crossing so much as in the deliverance of Israel from the forces of Pharaoh. The first part of this deliverance is the protective interposition of "God's attendant" and the pillar of cloud. The second part comes with YHWH's "confounding" or "driving to panic" the Egyptian pursuers, a divine maneuver characteristic of the HOLY WAR (Durham 1987, 336), accomplished here by YHWH's Presence looking down toward the Egyptian force and misguiding their chariots' wheels. This panic in the pursuit affords the people of Israel time for a careful crossing even as it brings the Egyptians to chaotic confusion.

The third part of the deliverance is the manipulation of the waters of the sea. This miraculous control of the waters, so obviously an echo of the creation and flood narratives of Gen 1 and 7, makes the Israelite crossing more direct and more safe, and brings disaster to the Egyptians who attempt, already in confused disarray, to follow.

Verses 30-31 are an apt summary of the events of the rescue at the sea. YHWH made the rescue. *Israel saw displayed once more, and more convincingly than ever, the great power of YHWH. And thus in awe of YHWH, Israel believed in YHWH, just as their father Abraham had in a time of testing much earlier (Gen 15:6, where the key verb, as here, is אמן).

15:1-21. Victory celebration. At least three hymns celebrating the deliverance at the sea are preserved in Exod 15. The brief song of MIRIAM (v. 21) is generally held to be the very ancient, perhaps contemporaneous kernel from which the longer song of Moses (vv. 1-12) was developed (cf. vv. 1 and 21). To these has been added another poem, celebrating the further victory of the conquest and settlement of Canaan (vv. 13-18).

A variety of dates has been proposed for the separate poems, as well as for their present arrangement. No date can be defended as certain, but the tendency in recent years has been towards an earlier date (Cross 1973, 176-78).

The hymn as it stands in Exod 15 is thus an evolved work, the oldest elements of which date from the experience at the sea, with additional lines added in a succession of decades, if not centuries. These verses are therefore neither a poetic unity nor a chronological unity. They are rather a theological unity, bound together by praise of the incomparable YHWH whose saving Presence is so undeniably real to his people.

Exodus 15:1-21 thus remains a happy combination of at least three psalms, two of which are connected directly with the climactic deliverance at the sea, and one of which is sequential to that deliverance, bridging the gap between it and the eventual settlement of the promised land. In part, at least, these verses incorporate some of the oldest poetry in the OT.

The emphasis upon YHWH's incomparability and potent Presence sung so eloquently here is in a way an excellent summarization of the whole of Exodus. YHWH, who has made the exodus necessary by the fulfillment of his promise, has himself brought it off against everything the Egyptians could do, and even against the disbelief and the objections of his own people. Having fulfilled his promise of progeny, he has carried them through every interpositioned obstacle toward the eventual fulfillment of his promise of land.

And his incomparable Presence, connected with the fathers before (v. 2) and the Temple to come (v. 17), is the basis of his ritual and covenantal expectations, woven with such skill into the exciting narrative of the Book of Exodus. Indeed, the ultimate basis of the three hymns, as of Exodus as well, is the permanent effective reign of YHWH (v. 18), who rescues his people, then protects, then establishes them. There are overtones in these lines of the celebration of a victory of YHWH much greater than his victory over Pharaoh, greater even than his victory over those who opposed Israel on the way to and in Canaan itself. The *waters* (מַיִם) and *floods* (נֹזְלִים, better "currents") of the immediate event suddenly become the "ancient deeps" (תְּהֹמֹת, vv. 5 and 8; NRSV's rendering, *floods* in v. 5 and *deeps* in v. 8, is misleading), the chaos-waters brought under control at the time of creation (Gen 1:2; Ps 93:1-4; Ezek 26:19-20; note Reymond 1958, 167–79, 182–94). And in v. 16, YHWH's people are referred to as "this people you have created" (author trans.; see also Deut 32:6; Pss 74:2; 78:54; 139:13), a further suggestion that Exod 15:1-21 celebrate YHWH, even more than his victory and his victories.

Provision, Protection, and Complaint, 15:22–17:16

15:22–17:7. YHWH provides, Israel grumbles. When Moses and the people of Israel departed from the vicinity of their sea crossing, apparently on the day of their deliverance, they headed directly for SINAI, which was for Moses the primary trysting-place with YHWH's Presence. Unfortunately, a fully satisfactory location for Sinai/Horeb has yet to be found. And the location of the various oases and stopping places *en route*, equally uncertain, leaves similarly obscure the route of travel that Moses and Israel followed.

When all the possibilities (see commentary on Exod 3:1-22, above) have been considered, the traditional location, Jebel Musa in the southern Sinai peninsula, remains most satisfactory. Thus despite the difficulties involved, particularly by conflicting OT sources, the best assumption is as direct as possible a southerly route from the crossing-place to Sinai.

The narratives of the journey to the place of YHWH's theophany to Moses, an experience he expects to be repeated for Israel (see 3:12), are moved forward through a tension of complaint and provision. Israel feels put to the test, and in return Moses and YHWH himself are put to the test.

The complaining and testing motifs occur not only in these narratives, but also in the narratives of Numbers and by allusion elsewhere in the OT (Coats 1968). They are introduced by such catchwords as *bitter* (15:23), *complained* (16:2), *fleshpots* (16:3), and *quarrel* and *test* (17:2, 7).

The text in its present arrangement presents even the cursory reader with what seems a hodgepodge of overlapping and sometimes self-contradictory narrative. The purpose of the compilers of this account is clear enough, however. They intend to make it clear that, whatever Israel's need and criticism, YHWH is more than equal to every problem, and that with each solution the effectiveness of his Presence is proven more and more. What we have in this section is a compacting of a series of stories of wilderness crises involving water, food, and hostile peoples set at an appropriate point in the narrative of the proving of YHWH's Presence with his people Israel.

The water crises are two in number, the one involving nonpotable water, the other involving a complete lack of water of any kind. Both situations are common enough to such an arid region as the Sinai peninsula, where water is very scarce and often too alkaline for consumption when it is present.

In the first instance, Moses is shown by YHWH an herb that sweetened the alkaline water (15:25). In the second, YHWH indicates to Moses a rock from which a spring gushes when Moses' rod is used to strike it (17:6). Both instances, whatever explanations may be given them, even correctly so, are plainly depicted in

Exodus as miraculous events. They are therefore a continuation of the wonders done in Egypt and in the rescue at the sea.

The point at issue in these further miracle narratives, since YHWH has abundantly proved himself powerful, is whether he is still present with his people (17:7). The question is natural enough, but it attests a lack of faith, and so the place of *the rock at Horeb* (17:6) is called *Massah and Meribah*—"Testing and Dissatisfaction" (17:7; cf. Ps 95:8-9).

According to Exod 16, there is a single food crisis which is met by the supply of two foodstuffs. Comparison of this account with Num 11 indicates that the OT gives us a tangle of traditions related to YHWH's provision of food for his people in the wilderness. The crises in Exodus occur on the way to Sinai; in Numbers they occur on the way from Sinai. Their importance, in either instance, even in the assumption that there were two sets of crises, is theological, not historical or chronological.

Exodus 16:1-12 is an introduction to YHWH's miraculous feeding of his people, and 16:13-36 then records the miracles themselves. A definite emphasis is placed on the manna (הוּא מָ, the *What is it?* [16:15]), *bread from heaven* (16:4), as the space given to its arrival, its collection and its lessons for Israel show.

The appearance of the manna in the morning, its lasting beyond one day only on the sabbath, and the arrival of the quails in the evening are miraculous keepings of YHWH's promise, to the end that the people *shall know that I am [YHWH] your God* (16:12). Here in the wilderness as in Egypt, YHWH is proving his powerful Presence. Twice in Exod 16, YHWH's *glory* is mentioned (vv. 7 and 10), and when it appears, the glory appears in a cloud in the direction of the wilderness (v. 10), that is, Sinai/Horeb.

The food crisis separates the two water crises in the present text of Exodus, and immediately following the second water crisis, there is an account of YHWH's provision of protection. *Rephidim* can no more be located in connection with this narrative (17:8-16) or the second water narrative (17:1-7) than can any of the other sites mentioned in the journey of the exodus. The Amalekites were a nomadic people whose territory included the southern NEGEB and the Sinai peninsula, and their attack upon Israel may well have been more of a defensive action than an aggressive one. There is another reference to this battle in Deut 25:17-19.

The defeat of Amalek, like the defeat of the Egyptians at the sea, is attributed directly to YHWH, although Israel this time does play more than a passive role. The mention of the rod of God, the importance of Moses' uplifted hand, and the construction of an altar commemorating the victory all emphasize YHWH's further proof of his Presence to Israel, this time through protection instead of provision.

JOSHUA appears in 17:9 for the first time. His abrupt and very brief introduction may imply the omission of additional Joshua-traditions at this point as unnecessary to the compiler's purpose. He is presented as someone we should know already.

Jethro, Worship, and Law, 18:1-27

18:1-12. Meeting Jethro. Chapter 18 has often been considered out of place in the narrative sequence of Exodus, because of the account of Deut 1:9-18, which seems to place the events of Exod 18:13-27 at the departure from Sinai, and because of Exod 18:5, which seems to refer to Israel at Sinai before the actual arrival there, recounted in Exod 19:1-2.

There is however a theological logic that overrides story logic in Exodus, as throughout the OT. The compilers of Exodus are concerned to reconnect the two branches of the family of ABRAHAM-ISAAC-JACOB/IS-RAEL *before* their experience of YHWH's Presence at his mountain. From Abraham's time, the SARAH-ISAAC-JA-COB-JOSEPH side of the family has been separate from the Hagar-Ishmael-Esau-Midian side of the family. It is important that the family be reunited *before* the events at Sinai, and thus this story of reunion is placed here, despite the fact that the long sequence dealing with the application of YHWH's laws to the needs of the people thus comes *before* those laws are actually given (Durham 1987, 240-46).

The priority given to JETHRO, both as the leader of worship despite the presence of both Moses and Aaron, and also as the instructor of Moses regarding the management of the people has given rise to an array of theories about Midianite faith and its influence on Israel. Jethro's role in this chapter hardly sustains the theory that he is a new convert, and although it is too much to claim that he introduced YHWH to Moses and the Joseph-tribes, Exod 18 clearly accords him a significant tutelary role. Elated at Moses' account of YHWH's wonders in Egypt and the exodus, he says, "Now I know for certain that YHWH is greater than all the gods" (v. 1, author trans.). And in the ensuing celebratory worship, it is Jethro who presides.

18:13-27. Leadership and Law. The account of Jethro's advice on leadership in the application of YHWH's law, and Moses' implementation of the old priest's counsel must be read alongside Deut 1:9-18. What is apparent in the content of both passages is that the situation in view is reflective of a period in history long after the time to which the two passages are assigned in the Exodus narrative.

Even so, however, there is little reason to doubt that the precedent for such a division of cases into "important" and "minor" categories, those requiring an ORACLE and those capable of settlement by extant legal precedent, may have been given to Moses by Jethro. The procedure of inquiring (דרש) the will of God in matters not provided for in extant law is based upon the theology of YHWH's Presence that appears to have originated at Sinai and that became the very basis of the theology of the Jerusalem cultus.

The principal assertion of this narrative of the beginnings of Israel's legal system is that YHWH is the source and therefore the authority of Israelite guidance in relationship. Moses is an important intermediary, as are the "able men and honest" who are called forward to represent the people and to extend Moses' wisdom and strength. But the law giver and the law definer and the law sustainer is YHWH. On such a view, there is no such thing in Israel as "secular" law. Every law, whatever its concern, is sacral, because every law, ultimately, is YHWH's.

That such a concept did not prevent abuse of the law is plain from the preaching of the prophets alone. But that it presented a high view of law, and of the motivation for obedience of law, cannot be doubted.

Israel at Sinai, 19:1–40:38

YHWH's Presence and Covenant, 19:1–24:18

19:1-25. YHWH comes to Israel. Certainly the single most important passage in the Book of Exodus is the dramatic and graphic account of the theophany on Sinai/Horeb. This is so because the THEOPHANY is the effective visible announcement of the advent of YHWH to speak to, and to be with, his people. The theophany motif is the one theme from Exodus most recurrent in the remainder of the OT, amid so many consequential motifs and traditions.

The importance of the Sinai theophany may be understood when the essential nature of the theology of the Presence of YHWH is recognized. Moses' call is predicated on such a basis. The authority Moses declares to Israel in Egypt is established by it. The sequence of wonders and the culminating victory at the sea are a direct result of it. Provision for the people in the jejune barrenness of the wilderness is guaranteed by it, as is their protection from the threatened and so threatening Amalekites. And the basis of the commandments, laws, and cultic instructions and requirements that occupy most of the rest of Exodus is, purely and simply, the immanent Presence of YHWH.

Immediately after the brief notice of Israel's arrival at Sinai, Moses received from YHWH for repetition to the people a magnificent summary of covenantal theology, often called the "eagles' wings" speech (19:4-6). These lines, probably composed for liturgical use at covenant renewal ceremonies, have been inserted here as both recital and conditional prologue to the revelation of YHWH's Presence and the giving of the law.

As such, they stand as the first of a series of insertions that form the bulk of the remainder of the Book of Exodus, insertions wonderfully woven into the narrative, and presenting the reader with a remarkably symphonic whole, but insertions all the same that interrupt the story sequence. In broad terms, the flow of that story sequence can be broadly reconstructed by a reading, *seriatim*, of the following passages: 19:1-3a, 10-19a; 20:1-21; 24:1-18; 32:1–34:35 (Durham 1990, 56–81).

Such a reading, while it makes the story of Exodus easier to follow, nevertheless does disservice to the Book of Exodus as it stands in the OT. The theological purpose of the compilers who brought Exodus to its present form is celebration and obedience. The gift of YHWH's self-revelation to Israel, with the provision, protection, and assurance that brings, is celebrated. And the gift of YHWH's guidance for living, for shaping personal lives and the national life in harmony with YHWH's intention for his people is held up as the opportunity for obedience.

All of this is summed up in vv. 4-6, which in its present location in Exodus is a passage of recollection *and* a passage of anticipation. The deliverance from Egypt is recapitulated in a moving metaphor of protective love, one developed more fully still in Deut 32:11-12. YHWH's personal direction to the mountain of his special Presence is stressed. Then the conditions of the covenant, attention to and integrity in covenantal promises are juxtapositioned against YHWH's own promises: if Israel hears him and obeys him, they will be his prized treasure, his nation of priests, his people set apart.

YHWH's theophany is anticipated, first in prediction (v. 9), then in an ordered preparation involving isola-

tion of the place of his appearance and ritual purification of the people who await it (vv. 10-13).

The description of the theophany is lean of simile, and dramatically and convincingly drawn. The violent mountain storm, along with fire and thick smoke, is a frequent accompaniment of OT theophany and therefore not to be taken as suggestive of a volcanic eruption. In the midst of the fury of this entirely unnatural storm, the loud blast of the unmusical *shophar* signals the imminent arrival of YHWH. The people are assembled by Moses. YHWH descends in the fire that accompanies his Presence (note Pss 18:7-15; 50:1-7; 97:1-5), causing the entire mountain to shake violently. The *shophar* blasts yet louder, that is nearer at hand, indicating the approach of YHWH's Presence.

YHWH has come to Israel at Sinai/Horeb, as Moses knew he would. Israel is experiencing in this special place what Moses experienced there, as he hoped they would. The way is prepared for the revelation of his expectation, his guidance, that is now to be delivered to Moses in Israel's hearing.

20:1-21. YHWH's Ten Words and Israel's fear. The TEN COMMANDMENTS in their present form have obviously been expanded from their original terse form as "ten words" of YHWH (Exod 34:28; Deut 4:13, 10:4). This expansion does not however justify the excision of the commandments from the Exodus narrative, any more than the Sinai traditions can be separated from the Exodus traditions (Durham 1970, 197–99).

The commandments in their briefest form should be assumed as a part of the Exodus narrative that begins with 19:1-19a and continues from 20:1 through v. 21, giving a sequence reading something like: "The sound of the ram's horn meanwhile was moving, and growing very strong. Then God spoke all these words, saying, 'I am YHWH, your God, who brought you forth from the land of Egypt' " (19:19a and 20:1-2b, author trans.).

The Decalogue has been transmitted with a different numbering in variant Christian and Jewish traditions, although the final number of commandments has nearly always been ten. The sequence followed here is: first commandment, v. 3; second commandment, vv. 4-6; third commandment, v. 5; fourth commandment, vv. 8-11; and fifth through tenth commandments, one verse each, vv. 12 through 17.

The Exodus Decalogue must be considered along with the parallel version of Deut 5:6-21, but contrary to an earlier view, the version in Exodus must now be thought of as the earlier OT version. Behind both versions, there lie still earlier, more terse versions, and there is no convincing reason to deny that the earliest "ten words" are to be associated with Moses.

A probable relationship in form between the Decalogue and the state treaties of the Hittites and other ancient Near Eastern peoples has been established, although the parallels must not be pressed too rigidly. The Ten Commandments follow the apodictic form of the requirements listed in such documents, and like them are begun with a prologue justifying that list of expectations.

The point of such a prologue (v. 2 and Deut 5:6) is not identification: Moses and the people of Israel would have known with whom they were dealing, as surely as the Hittite and other vassals would have known the name of the protective overlord whose strength made a covenant desirable or even necessary to them.

The point is rather a declaration of the authority that is the basis for the covenant, an authority established by experienced reality. Without this reference to such authority, the stipulation of requirements that follow would in effect be largely meaningless—a list of requirements without reason or authority and to no purpose.

The prologue to the Ten Commandments is thus to the same point as the revelation and explanation of the name YHWH at the bush aflame in the narrative of Moses' call. Here as there the question is not one of the identity of the commanding deity, but one of the authority behind the command and its implications. And here the wonders in Egypt and the Exodus rescue are cited in historical retrospect, as there in promised prospect.

In sequence, the commandments prohibit (1) the worship of other gods, assumed as a reality at least for the people; (2) the creation and use of images of any sort in worship, a commandment that is testimony to the fact that such images were made and employed in Israel's worship; (3) the profanation or vain use of YHWH's name, the equivalent of his Presence, in false covenanting, insincere swearing, or magical rites; (6) killing a fellow-member of the community in covenant with YHWH; (7) adultery; (8) theft; (9) lying or distortion of the truth that maligns persons, specifically perjury; and (10) unbridled desire for that which belongs to another, the lust to have that can lead to legal or illegal theft.

Two commandments, four and five (vv. 8-11 and v. 12) are stated not as prohibitions but as positive commands: (4) respect for the sabbath, as a special day set aside for rest and worship; and (5) appropriate esteem for parents.

The considerable expansion of commandments two, four, five and ten suggest how much trouble the people of Israel had keeping them. To the fifth commandment alone, a promise and an implied warning have been attached, an indication that this commandment may have been the most abused of them all.

The Ten Commandments not only set forth the essential priorities of life in relationship with YHWH; they also suggest in their sequence the proper arrangement of those priorities: God first, his worship next, and concern related to the human community last. The commandments must also be thought of, however, as a totality: each impinging upon all the others, and all of them together providing the general outline of Israel's covenantal obligation. The violation of any one of them by any one member of the covenantal community was a weakening of the entire group's relationship with YHWH.

The implication of the narrative of 19:1-20:21 is that the people of Israel were themselves a part of the experience of both YHWH's advent *and* his revelation of his expectation of them in covenant. 19:9 states that the people are to hear YHWH's speaking; 19:17, that Moses brought them out from the camp to encounter God; 19:21 implies the presence of the people just beyond the boundary established at the foot of the mountain; and in 20:18 the people react with fright, trembling and drawing back, and then they say to Moses, "*You* speak with us, and we promise we'll hear—but don't let God keep speaking with us, lest we die" (20:19, author trans.).

This implication is borne out by the parallel account in Deut 5:22-27 and the questions of Deut 4:32-33. It is also sustained by Moses' answer to the people's request. He seeks to allay their fear by telling them that God's coming on this momentous occasion is for their benefit, that they may have a firsthand experience of his Presence so that their joining in covenant with him may be memorable and have lasting effectiveness.

Such is certainly the result of the theophany, whether the revelation of the Decalogue be thought of as audible to the people or not, and they move some distance away, leaving Moses to venture alone into the dense cloud to encounter YHWH's Presence further.

20:22–23:33. Applying YHWH's commands. This section, which is called *the book of the covenant* in

Exod 24:7, has long been recognized as an entity in its own right. Like much of the content of Exod 20–40, it is disruptive of the story sequence into which it has been set as a part of a sequence of requirement (Durham 1990, 81–95). And like the similarly disruptive sequence of memory (Durham 1990, 97–101), it pulls apart the Exodus narrative. It does so, however, in a most appropriate way: for the sequence of requirement and the sequence of memory give a continuing present tense to a story that would otherwise not be experienced (and so believed and so heeded) by the succession of Israel's generations.

The Book of the Covenant is a mixture of requirements and regulations governing worship and "judgments," case decisions, governing what today would for the most part be called civil matters. In ancient Israel, all behavior was under religious aegis, and all law was theocratically based. Most of the judgments are casuistic in form, but alongside them are apodictic requirements that are always applicable, that require no special set of conditions to make them relevant.

The antiquity of the Book of the Covenant, once seriously doubted, has in recent years been more generally accepted, particularly in view of the parallels provided by an assortment of law codes from the second millennium B.C.E. (see introduction, above). Not surprisingly, there is material in the Book of the Covenant that reflects the settled agricultural society of life in Canaan, and there is material that reflects the nomadic life of the wilderness.

This section is thus best considered as having its origin in a premonarchial collection of laws, one perhaps even begun by Moses as an expansion and application of the Ten Commandments and as a cumulative body of precedents in judgments rendered on the "lesser cases" that Jethro had advised Moses to delegate to carefully selected "honest men." Such a collection would have had authoritative weight from its inception, and may have been circulated along with the Decalogue it was intended to apply and supplement. To it, extant laws from the oldest periods of Israel's past, new laws revealed at Sinai and in the wilderness, and laws encountered and adapted in the contact with new cultures and new situations would readily have been attracted.

The disorganization of the Book of the Covenant suggests the authoritative antiquity of some of its parts. Material on similar subjects is not always together, and there is an arbitrary and disjointed arrangement that suggests sections were added to units that already had the sanctity of long use. When the Book of Exodus was in compilation, what more logical place for this collection than between the Decalogue it was intended to supplement and the narrative of the actual ratification of the covenant it delineated in such detail?

The first sequence of laws (20:23-26) is connected with worship, and can readily be recognized as supplemental, in part, to the first two commandments. The specification that altars be earthen or of unhewn stone reflects an early period. The connection between the altars used in worship and the theology of the Presence of YHWH is strongly stressed in 20:24.

The second sequence of laws is begun (21:1-2) with an introductory statement that indicates the beginning of a collection of "judgments," that is, precedents, governing "lesser cases." This introduction governs an indeterminate number of sequences of precedents extending through 22:17.

First, there are cases that arise in connection with the ownership of slaves (21:2-11). These judgments are humanitarian in emphasis, and designed in each case to protect the familial and personal rights of the slaves in a series of situations that are certain to have been recurrent. 21:6 apparently specifies a kind of scarring or "brand" as a physical mark of the permanent attachment of a slave.

Next there are two sections dealing with harm, chiefly physical harm, willfully inflicted upon others. Cases that carry the death penalty are appropriately set first (21:12-17). A distinction is made between premeditated murder and an unplanned slaying, and a physical blow or a curse against one's parents is, along with slave-stealing, considered as heinous a crime as premeditated murder.

Cases involving injury, whether by intention or through negligence, are provided for next (21:18-36). Punishment is required, although not specified, for killing one's slave. That this punishment appears to have been less severe than in the case in which a free man is killed is owing in part to the lesser status of the slave, but more to the fact that such a killing would not in the nature of things be premeditated, as the slave was valuable and expensive property (21:21b).

If a slave should be struck and maimed (even by the loss of a tooth), he is to be freed: this action is both a reparation for the injury and a guarantee that it would not occur. If someone should be killed by a violent ox because its owner had been negligent, the owner would be subject to the death penalty, although with the right of redemption.

The fifth sequence of judgments treats instances involving thievery (22:1-4 [MT 21:37–22:3]). NRSV's reordering of these verses to 1, 3b, 4, 2, 3a is unnecessary and perhaps misleading. As Daube (1969, 74–77, 85–89) and others have pointed out, collections of legal material grow by subject more than by logical sequence.

The sixth sequence (22:5-15 [MT 22:4-14]) deals with damage or loss because of negligence. Of special interest is the provision of a ceremony (22:10-11 [MT 22:9-10]) to guarantee lack of evil intention on the part of the responsible party.

The seventh sequence (22:16-17 [MT 22:15-16]) provides for the expectation of compensation to a father whose virgin daughter has been compromised. The virgin in this context is treated not as a person, but as property valuable to her father. Thus these two judgments have been placed with other precedents governing the loss or damage of property.

With the beginning of the eighth sequence of laws (22:18-20), there is a shift to the apodictic form in the statement of the laws. This shift has often been taken to indicate a collection originally separate from the predominantly casuistic collection of 20:22–22:17. Most of the remainder of the Book of the Covenant is in apodictic form, with what appear to have been explanatory addenda in the casuistic "precedent" form here and there (22:25-27 [MT 22:24-26]; 23:4-5).

This eighth sequence specifies the death penalty for sorcery, copulation with animals, and violation of the first and second commandments of the Decalogue. The ninth sequence (22:21-27 [MT 22:20-26]) commands protective concern for the alien and the dispossessed: the widow, the orphan, and the poor.

The tenth sequence (22:28-31 [MT 27-30]) requires an appropriate respect for God and the נָשִׂיא, the leader or representative of the tribe. Specifically, in this case, the "honest man" whose job it was to help out with the lesser case decisions is probably intended. The effectiveness of YHWH's system of justice was after all dependent upon the acceptance by the people of the rightness of the oracle-decisions and the precedent-judgments. Connected with this respect are such other means of its expression as offerings from the harvest, dedication of the firstborn (by means specified elsewhere), and by rigid standards of cultic probity.

The eleventh sequence of laws (23:1-9) concerns honesty in legal matters, specifically those that involve case decisions that affect other persons. Perjury, prejudicial testimony, bending to dishonest pressure, false charges, bribery and disregard for the poor and the stranger are all strictly forbidden.

The twelfth sequence (23:10-13) is concerned with the rest of the seventh year and the seventh day. The summary statement in v. 13 probably indicates a conclusion, at some earlier point in its development, of at least a subsection of the Book of the Covenant. Verse 13 is related in theme to the first commandment, and to the beginning of the Book of the Covenant at 20:23 and to 22:28 in the tenth sequence.

The thirteenth sequence (23:14-17) is, along with Exod 34:22-23, the oldest ritual calendar in the OT, specifying as it does the three occasions in the year on which the men of Israel were to appear with gifts in the Presence of YHWH: the first harvest of grain, the harvest of the remainder of the cereal crops seven weeks later, and the final harvest of all crops in the autumn.

The fourteenth and final sequence of laws (23:18-19) lists four cultic regulations, the fourth of which occurs also in 34:26 and in Deut 14:21.

The conclusion to the Book of the Covenant (23:20-33) is a sort of epilogue, and a parallel to the beginning of the collection, at 20:22-23. It amounts to a promise-appendage similar to the conclusion of the Holiness Code in Lev 26 and the Deuteronomistic Code in Deut 28. The promises it offers, of a guiding, protecting, intervening and fighting Presence of YHWH, are in effect the reward promised for keeping the laws and the precedents just set forth.

These promises are specifically appropriate to Israel at Sinai, looking forward to the fulfillment of the ancient promise to the Fathers of land, and insecure at the prospect of encounter with unfriendly peoples. The extent of the land to be possessed is described here (23:31), as at so many places in the OT, in terms descriptive of the Davidic-Solomonic empire. And YHWH's part in the displacement of the inhabitants of the land of promise is described in the language of the HOLY WAR.

24:1-18. The covenant is made. The narrative of the making of YHWH's covenant with Israel represents a kind of "happy ending" to the Exodus story, an ideal conclusion to the story of the birth of Israel as YHWH's special people. It brings together the themes anticipated in the "eagles' wings" speech of 19:4-6, and it provides a natural point of departure for the detailed sequence of instructions for the spaces and the symbols and the arrangements for worship that follow in chaps. 25–31 and 35–40.

This "ideal" end is not however the "real" end of the Book of Exodus, as the conclusion of the Exodus narrative in chaps. 32–34 shows. It is for that reason that the covenant made here has to be remade in 34:10-28, and for that reason, in part, that Exod 24 has such a patchwork arrangement.

The making of the covenant is thus described as taking place on two levels. The first involves the people and Moses (vv. 3-8). The second involves Moses and his assistants, Aaron, Aaron's sons Nadab and Abihu, and seventy of the elders of Israel (vv. 1-2, 9-11).

The people enter into the covenant upon the instructions of Moses, who acts as the intermediary of YHWH. The Presence of YHWH is symbolized by the altar, and the symbol of ratification is the blood of the "completion-offerings" (זְבָחִים שְׁלָמִים, NRSV *offerings of well-being*), half of which is dashed upon the altar, and half upon the people.

In between these two symbolic manipulations of the blood, the Book of the Covenant, the revelation of the requirements and expectations of YHWH, is read aloud to the people by Moses. This ceremony takes place at the foot of the mountain, just beyond the appointed boundary (v. 4).

Moses and the leaders of Israel enter into this covenant, along with the people, but there is a further covenant ceremony for them as well. They are invited by YHWH to ascend Sinai/Horeb. They do so, and they experience there a theophany and share a meal of communion.

Ratification of the covenant here is at least suggested in the meal as well as in the appearance of God. Verses 10 and 11 employ different terms for the experience of Moses and his assistants: the term in v. 10 is ראה, "see, understand," and the term in v. 11 is חזה, "behold, gaze"; NRSV has *saw* and *beheld*, respectively.

What actually was seen by Moses and his companions is far from clear. The description of v. 10 is of the appearance of what lay at God's feet, not of the appearance of God himself. Even so, the experience is unique in the OT. The statement in v. 11 that the company suffered no harm (*He did not lay his hand on the chief men of the people of Israel*) is a further indication of the special nature of the experience (see also 3:20 and 9:15 for the stretching out of YHWH's hand in harm, and Ps 138:7 and Ezek 8:3 for the stretching out of YHWH's hand in beneficial action).

Immediately following the making of the covenant, Moses is commanded to come to the place of YHWH's Presence on the mountain to receive *the tablets of stone, with the law and the commandment* (v. 12) written for Israel's instruction. Precisely what was written on the tablets is ambiguous (cf. 34:1 and 34:27-28). The way is prepared, however, for the extended revelation that is to follow as YHWH is described as settling down upon the mountain in a cloud shielding his glory (כָּבוֹד), which along with שֵׁם, "name," is the equivalent of Presence, פָּנִים, in the OT.

YHWH's Plan for the Spaces and Symbols of Worship, 25:1–31:18

25:1-9 (=35:4-9). Israel's offering. The instructions for the spaces, the symbols, the personnel and the acts by which YHWH's Presence and interventions are to be called to mind are the contribution of the priestly circles. In broad summary, they are set forth in terms of instructions, 25:1–31:18, and the implementation of those instructions, 35:1–40:38, a thirteen-chapter sequence of memory (Durham 1990, 112-26).

These two sections are a near thing to a mirror image of each other, although there are differences in order and a few differences in detail. This being so, the parallels in the second of the two sections will be listed in this commentary on the first section, to avoid a needless repetition.

The raw materials for the media of Israel's worship are called for, in an instruction that makes clear that they are to be given freely by the people, by *all whose hearts prompt them* (v. 2). The materials specified are precious and semi-precious metals, yarns and fabric, skins, lumber, oil, spices, and precious and semi-precious gemstones. Only the best is to be employed in the preparations to follow.

25:10-40 (=37:1-24). The Ark, the Table, the Lampstand. These three objects are special symbols of the Presence of YHWH, and so it is appropriate that the instruction for their construction should come first in YHWH's plan. The Ark and the Table were to be made of acacia wood, a hard and durable material, which in both instances is to be overlaid with pure gold.

The Ark was to contain the "testimony" (עֵדֻת, NRSV *covenant*, 25:21), probably the tables of stone on which the "Ten Words" were recorded (on the parallel practice in the ancient Near East, see Sarna 1991, 160-61). The Table was to provide a resting-place for the Bread of the Presence, the incense, and the drink offering.

The lampstand and its accessories were to be made of one talent (approx. 75 lbs.) of pure gold, in the form of a growing tree, probably the almond tree, the "wake-up" tree of Jer 1:11-12. It was to hold seven lamps, one for the trunk of the tree and one for each of its six branches.

The Ark, the Table, and the Lampstand were each a symbolic reminder of the Presence of YHWH, and their nearness to the place of his immediate Presence dictates the material of their construction.

26:1-37 (=36:8-38). The Tabernacle. The Tabernacle was the most holy shelter of the Presence of YHWH. Its arrangement and its materials involved a gradation of movement from the most holy place, where the Ark, the special symbol of YHWH's nearness (note 26:32, and such passages as 1 Sam 4:4; 2 Kgs 19:15; Ps 80:2; and Isa 37:16), stood, to the one opening to the courtyard in front of the Tabernacle. It was also constructed to be readily portable, an indication that YHWH is a Presence in motion, not to be considered captive to a single location. This emphasis is an important one, not least in material from the Priestly source, for what it suggests about the conservative view of the Temple in Jerusalem that Jeremiah attacked so vigorously (Jer 26).

The question whether the wilderness Tabernacle really existed or is a retrojection of a Jerusalem priesthood eager to justify the Temple of Solomon (or even a reconstructed Temple) is beside the point of the description in Exodus, which has a theological point, not an historical one, in view.

27:1-21 (=38:1-7, 9-20; Lev 24:1-3). The Altar, the Courtyard, and the Light. The instructions for the altar for burnt offerings are more ambiguous than any of the instructions concerning the media of worship. It too was to be portable, and the direction that it be made of wood, albeit overlaid with copper, seems to be somewhat in conflict with its function, as also with the instructions of Exod 20:24-26. The use of copper for the altar and its accessories aids our understanding of its location, in the area farthest from the holiest space where the Ark stood.

The Courtyard that surrounded the Tabernacle and the activities in front of it was formed by an also entirely portable arrangement of columns and draperies. The space thus enclosed was 150 ft. by 75 ft., and the draperies blocked the view of any activity that did not rise higher than 7.5 ft.

The instruction for pure olive oil extracted by pounding the olives is an additional specification that only the finest substances were to be used in the place of YHWH's Presence. Such oil was nearly smokeless,

and gave off a brighter light than the easier to obtain pressed oil.

28:1-43 (=39:1-31). The Priests' clothing. The special garments to be worn by AARON and his sons are described in detail, both as to design and material, although the specifications set forth deal primarily with the vestments of Aaron, who is presented as the prototypical high priest. Provision is made for an ephod (vv.6-14) set with two stones of onyx engraved with the names of the twelve tribes of Israel, and for a kind of vest (vv. 15-30) containing a pouch for the oracular device of the sacred lot, and decorated with twelve semiprecious stones symbolizing, again, the twelve tribes.

By means of this latter garment, worn across the breast and containing the instruments of oracular decision, "Aaron" was to keep Israel before YHWH and to have Israel's judgment ever *on his heart* (v. 29) whenever he entered the Presence of YHWH.

These high-priestly vestments were completed by a robe equipped with bells (vv. 31-35), apparently for an apotropaic purpose; by a golden *rosette* (vv. 36-38) symbolizing Aaron's special status as one uniquely consecrated to YHWH's service; and by a coat, a turban, and an embroidered waistband (v. 39).

That such an elaborate array of splendid vestments represents the end of a long and cumulative evolution is more than probable. Further, this evolutionary process no doubt incorporated into the high priestly attire some elements of the king's ceremonial dress as, with time, his own role in the leadership of cultic worship decreased.

The garments to be worn by the ordinary priests (vv. 40-43) are much simpler and more practical, and are probably closer to what was actually worn by all priests on most occasions. The Hebrew idiom for ordination, "fill the hand" (NRSV *ordain*, v. 41 and in chap. 29), probably means "to complete the power of" or "to grant full authority to" the person set apart for the appointed round of sacral duties.

The vestments may be thought of as having a double significance: they were a reminder of both the priests' authority and of the source of that authority, the immanent Presence of YHWH.

29:1-46 (=Lev 8:1-36). The Priests' ordination. From the implements of cultic worship, including the apparel of the priests, the instructions are now turned to the personnel of the cult. This transition is a natural one in the present arrangement of the text of Exodus, as the description of what the priests are to wear leads directly to the directions for the consecration of the priests for sacral service.

Unlike most of the specifications of Exod 25:1–31:18, the ceremony of the ordination of Aaron and his sons is not actually carried out in Exodus, but in Lev 8. This fact, plus some inconsistencies between what is recorded about the priestly garments in chap. 28 and chap. 29, and the fact that chap. 29 contains in its final third additional material not directly connected with its central theme (vv. 38-46), suggests that chap. 29 is a collation of variant traditions about ordination, some early and some late. The chapter is closed by a summary reference to the theme underlying all the instructions in Exodus, the insistent confession that YHWH is present.

The ceremony of ordination is an elaborate one requiring extensive sacrifices and gifts and a period seven days in length. There are three stages in the ceremony: the rites of anointing, rites granting authority, and rites of setting apart (note 28:41; 29:1, 7, 9, 21, 29). The order of these rites is unclear, and they may not have been sequential but simultaneous.

The rites include ceremonial ablutions, donning the vestments, anointing with special oil, smearing the priests and sprinkling their vestments with sacrificial blood, and a communion meal in which YHWH and the ordinands are specially bound together by the manipulation of "the ram of ordination." The sacrifices include a young bull as a sin offering, and two rams—one as an offering wholly consumed before YHWH, and the other as the sacrifice of communion.

30:1-38 (30:1-10 =37:25-28; 30:17-21 =38:8). The incense altar, the atonement money, the laver for washing, and the anointing oil and the special incense. Elaborate specifications are given for the construction and placement of the altar of incense (vv. 1-10) of the inner sanctuary. This altar both symbolized and augmented the large altar of burnt offerings in the courtyard of the Tabernacle.

A special head-tax on adults (vv. 11-16), called *the atonement money* is commanded, as the means by which the financial requirements of keeping up the cult fabric may be met. There is nowhere in the OT a passage that records the fulfillment of this instruction.

The bronze laver for ceremonial ablutions (vv. 17-21), the special formula anointing oil (vv. 22-33) and the special formula incense (vv. 34-38) are ordered and precisely described. The sanctity of the oil and the incense is strongly stressed: they must never be put to any profane use. While the making of the laver is

reported (38:8), there is not in the OT any narrative of the blending of the special oil or the special incense.

31:1-18 (31:1-11 =35:10-19 and 35:30–36:1; 31:12-18 =35:1-3). The artisans and the Sabbath. The equipment of worship specified and described, the one matter yet lacking is the provision of an artisan and a capable assistant to direct the work of creating that equipment. Verses 1-11 are given to this subject, and Bezalel is designated as the man divinely endowed for the task. He is to be assisted by Oholiab; together they are to carry out the instructions of YHWH to the letter.

In the face of so much to be done, in so worthy a cause, an emphatically expanded version of the fourth commandment (vv. 12-17) provides a conclusion to the chapters of instruction, making it clear that no cause is so important as to take precedence over YHWH's specification of a day of rest.

Exodus 31:18 then serves both to close YHWH's instructions regarding the media of worship and also to anticipate the narrative section that follows immediately, in which *the two tablets of the covenant, the tablets of stone* have so important a role.

Disobedience and Its Consequences, 32:1–34:35

32:1-35. Israel's first disobedience. The account of Israel's disobedience of their covenant promises, a disobedience that comes all too soon, is the continuation of the narrative that was interrupted by the insertion of the priestly instructions regarding the media of Israel's worship in the Presence of YHWH. The interruption is a logical one, of course, as also is the continuation of the narrative describing Israel's betrayal of YHWH, *after* the instructions for worship have been given but *before* they are implemented and *before* such worship can actually take place.

The people of Israel, impatient in Moses' lengthy sojourn on the mountain and insecure because of the awesomeness of their surroundings and the uncertainty of their future, make the first of what can only have been many demands for a visible object of worship. Aaron gives in all too readily to their request, and asks for their jewelry of gold, a move strikingly parallel to Israel's own fleecing of the Egyptians.

From this gold, Aaron creates a cast and carved bull-calf, and identifies it with the power that wrought their deliverance from Egypt. The people respond with a feast, which Aaron proclaims in honor of YHWH, with sacrifices, and with wanton celebration. That the worship is the worship of YHWH is not in question.

The problem is that it is the worship of YHWH on *Israel's* terms rather than on YHWH's terms.

Thus YHWH immediately communicates to Moses what has happened, then lapses into a sharp condemnation of the people's disregard of their promise of obedience, and threatens to obliterate them. This catastrophic decimation is prevented only by the intervention of Moses, who reminds YHWH of his promise to the Fathers, and of what the Egyptians will think, if Israel has been freed only to be destroyed.

Moses heads immediately down the mountain with the tablets of stone, picking up JOSHUA on the way. When they draw near to the camp and Joshua mistakes the sound of celebration for the sound of battle, Moses replies sadly,

Not the sound of heroes exulting,
not the sound of losers lamenting,
    the sound of drunken singing
        is what I hear! (v. 18, author trans.)

Moses flies into a furious rage. He casts the stone slabs containing the commandments to the ground, breaking them. He seizes the calf, burns it, grinds it into powder, and mixing it with water, he makes the people drink it. He confronts Aaron, who blames the people, and even disavows his own role in the making of the idol: *I threw it [the gold] into the fire, and out came this calf!* (v. 24).

Moses calls the people to their covenant responsibility to YHWH on YHWH's terms. He is joined by the sons of Levi, with whom he wreaks judgment on the idolaters. How the guilty are separated from the people at large is not indicated, only that about 3,000 are put to the sword. The narrative both describes how Moses brought what had become a mob under control and glorifies the Levites as the sacerdotal tribe.

Again declaring to the people of Israel the terrible gravity of their sin, Moses returns to the Presence of YHWH, apparently on Sinai/Horeb, to intercede for them. Once in YHWH's Presence, he does not excuse the people, but asks forgiveness for them, and begs to be identified with them, even in judgment. YHWH declares that the guilty must suffer, and that the people's punishment is yet to come.

Moses is to lead the people according to the guidance of a divine emissary; for the moment, at least, the people's disobedience has so profoundly shaken YHWH's relationship to them that he is unwilling to resume his chosen place among them. And *when the day comes for [their] punishment* (v. 34), YHWH promises that he "will punish them for their sin." The punishment already meted out, having to drink their ground-up idol and losing to the sword 3,000 of their number, is not the punishment referred to in this composite Exodus narrative.

33:1-11. Israel and YHWH's Presence. What that punishment is to be, hinted at by 32:34, is now made clear. The covenant that was to have cemented the people's relationship with YHWH, and his to them, has been violated. They have been judged by him and ordered to leave Sinai/Horeb (32:34), the mountain of his Presence. And he now declares that what has happened has made it impossible for him to go himself with them: he can only send an emissary to guide them (vv. 2-3, 5, as in 32:34).

Thus do vv. 1-6 elaborate the theme of 32:34: YHWH will still keep his promise to the Fathers, but he can no longer come amongst Israel, for fear his anger will get the better of him and mean their destruction. Thus will he send a guiding emissary, in his place.

This prospect is a doleful one for the people of Israel. They realize more clearly than ever how their fortunes have been linked to YHWH's Presence in their midst. They remove, at YHWH's command, the *ornaments* (or "festive dress") that recalled their worship of the calf. This action is indicative of their depression at the prospect of their departure from YHWH's Presence and, worse still, at the prospect of his departure from them.

At this point, the narrative of disobedience and its consequences is interrupted by the insertion of a block of material dealing with the "trysting tent" (אֹהֶל מוֹעֵד, vv. 7-11) of YHWH's Presence. This material, important though it is, is completely out of place at this point in what is otherwise a tightly suspenseful account.

The compilers' purpose in placing these verses here was probably to give emphasis to the terrible isolation of the Presence of YHWH by declaring that he is no longer in the midst of encamped Israel, but outside the camp, and accessible only to Moses and his select helpers (Joshua, Aaron, Miriam and carefully picked leaders; note Num 11:16, 24-26; 12:4).

In doing so, the compilers have given us a very early tradition concerning the advent of YHWH's Presence in a tent. Indeed, this trysting tent of the Presence is not only separate from the wilderness TABERNACLE and the Ark; it very likely preceded them both, and may well be the sole tent-manifestation of the Presence in the entire wilderness period.

On such a view, the Ark would be the natural evolution in the progressive development of the theology of YHWH's Presence, and the Tabernacle, in its earliest form, a portable shrine for the Ark. The elaborate Priestly Tabernacle of chap. 26 and the ornate Priestly Ark of 25:10-22 would then be retrojections into the past of the Ark and the Tabernacle of Davidic-Solomonic times, but not retrojections without precedent.

The compilers' use of the tradition of the trysting tent to expand the theme of the departed Presence of YHWH is thus at best somewhat misplaced. And the tent may be thought of as the first post-Sinai palladium of YHWH's Presence, and so perhaps as the symbol of the fulfilled promise of 33:14.

33:12–34:9. Moses asks and YHWH answers. This continuation of the narrative of Israel's disobedience and its consequences is best read immediately following 33:6. Following YHWH's declaration of the removal of his Presence, Moses argues the total insecurity of the people he is to lead and his own total inadequacy for such a task under such conditions. His request of vv. 12-13 amounts to a rhetorical question: how does YHWH plan to accomplish his promise without granting his Presence, the very Presence that has brought every victory and every blessing the people have thus far enjoyed? YHWH's answer (v. 14) indicates some relenting. Moses presses his advantage, raising a second rhetorical question (vv. 15-16) in which he connects his own fate with that of the people he leads. Without YHWH's Presence, any further movement forward is futile, and doomed to fail. Moses' argument is incontrovertible, and YHWH agrees to his request, because *you have found favor in my sight, and I know you by name* (v. 17).

Thus encouraged, Moses asks the personal favor of a special revelation of YHWH's Presence: *Show me your glory, I pray* (v. 18). Such a request cannot of course be granted because of the danger involved (v. 20). Yet YHWH does grant Moses a special privilege: he manifests his goodness to Moses, and calls out to him his name, thus revealing to Moses as much as he can know of the essential divine self. This wondrous and mysterious experience of Moses is described, awkwardly, as a vision of where YHWH has passed (NRSV *my back*, 33:23). How else, indeed, could it be described?

YHWH's answer to this further request of Moses (34:1-9) is parallel to his response to Moses' request in 3:14-15. Here, as there, YHWH confesses the reality of his Presence by calling out his name, the name that means "the One who always is," "the I AM." There, YHWH began his story with Moses by giving him this name. Here, YHWH repeats that name, twice, then describes *how* he is "I AM" (34:6-7). Moses' response is to prostrate himself in worship. No other response would have been appropriate.

34:10-35. The covenant renewed, and Moses vindicated. Following the promise of the return of the Presence of YHWH, the logical conclusion to the whole episode of disobedience and disaster is the renewal of the covenant that Israel's idolatry had broken. There is no attempt to duplicate the dramatic narrative of chap. 24, or to list, even in summary, the conditions of relationship set forth in the TEN COMMANDMENTS. The attention here is on the sin that caused the disobedience, the embrace of divided loyalty.

Thus the commands of 34:12-26 all have to do, in one way or another, with the first commandment, *you shall have no other gods before me* (20:3). No covenant renewal ceremony is described, beyond the words of YHWH in v. 10, *I hereby make a covenant*, and the narrator's report in v. 28, "And he wrote on the tablets the words of the covenant, the ten words" (following the more literal marginal reading of NRSV).

With the covenant thus remade, Moses' leadership, rejected by the defection of the people of Israel (note 32:1), is reaffirmed by a visible sign of his special relationship with YHWH. He descends Sinai/Horeb with a shining face, the result of his close communion with the Presence of YHWH. Where his previous descent (32:15-35) was to a scene of wild idolatrous orgy, this descent meets awed and reverent respect.

This shining of Moses' face has stimulated commentators to write about cultic masks, priestly veils, radiant skin, bull-calf connections, and so on. It prompted Jerome to the famous translation *cornuta esset facies sua*, and Michelangelo Buonarroti in turn to carve horns on his *Moses*. The emphasis is really on YHWH, not Moses, as the unique use of the verb קרן, "shine," makes clear (only here, vv. 29, 30, 35). Moses has been vindicated by YHWH himself. His shining face is a reflection, no more, of the dazzling brightness of YHWH's Presence.

Obedience and Its Blessing, 35:1–40:38

As I have noted above, this section is, by and large, a mirror image of the section of instructions in 25:1–31:18. There, the directions of YHWH are given; here, they are carried out. There are a few differences in order and even a few additions here. But the major purpose of this section is to report that, after disobedience, its consequences, and covenant renewal, YHWH's instructions are finally carried out.

The parallel passages in the earlier section are as follows:

35:1-3 = 31:12-18
35:4-9 = 25:1-7
35:10-19 = 31:6-10
35:30–36:1 = 31:1-6
36:8-38 = 26:1-37
37:1-9 = 25:10-22
37:10-16 = 25:23-30
37:17-24 = 25:31-40
37:25-28 = 30:1-10
37:29 = 30:22-25, 34-36
38:1-7 = 27:1-8
38:8 = 30:17-21
38:9-20 = 27:9-18
39:1-31 = 28:1-43
39:32-43 = 31:7-11; 35:11-19

Beyond these close parallels, there are expansions and additions. A command against kindling a fire on the sabbath for domestic purposes, a prohibition that is not found elsewhere in the OT, appears in 35:3. The call for workmen is broader in 35:10-19, and the response to the call for raw materials is met with so much enthusiastic generosity that Moses has to call a halt to the giving (36:2-7).

Exodus 38:8 adds a mysterious note about the material for the base of the bronze laver, connecting it with the mirrors of certain women *who served at the entrance to the tent of meeting.* These women are not elsewhere mentioned in the OT, and the matter remains obscure.

Exodus 38:21-31 records an inventory of the gifts of metal, with large amounts listed and the notation that the inventory was taken by Ithamar (mentioned elsewhere in 6:23 and 28:1).

A final inventory of the objects made is given in 39:32-43, and the Book of Exodus is brought to a close with an account of the setting up of the Tabernacle, the arrangement and consecration of its furnishings, the cleansing of the priests, and the settling of the Glory, the Presence of YHWH, into the Tabernacle in the midst of his people Israel (40:1-38).

With that settling, the ideal of Exodus is reached. In that settling, the theology of Exodus is summarized. By that settling, the hope of Exodus is confessed.

The remainder of the story occupies all the rest of the Bible, and is still being worked out beyond it. The Presence of YHWH is still available to all who are open. The human family is still resisting the loyalty that Presence demands and deserves. YHWH's self-proclamation, "I AM YHWH your God" has become the self-proclamation of Christ: "I AM the Way, the Truth, and the Life." We have not yet come to the Promised Land, but God comes still to us, showing us still the way.

Works Cited

Alt, Albrecht. 1966. "The God of the Fathers," in *Essays on O.T. History and Religion*, 3–77.

Anati, Emmanuel. 1986. *The Mountain of God.*

Childs, B. S. 1965. "The Birth of Moses," JBL 84:109–22.

Coats, G. W. 1968. *Rebellion in the Wilderness.*

Cross, F. M., Jr. 1973. "The Song of the Sea and Canaanite Myth," in *Canaanite Myth and Hebrew Epic*, 112–44.

Daube, David. 1969. *Studies in Biblical Law.*

Davies, G. I. 1979. *The Way of the Wilderness. A Geographical Study of the Wilderness Itineraries of the Old Testament.*

Durham, John I. 1970. "Credo, Ancient Israelite," *IDBSupp* 197–99. 1987. *Exodus.* WBC. 1990. *Understanding the Basic Themes of Exodus.*

Griffiths, J. G. 1953. "The Egyptian Derivation of the Name Moses," *JNES* 12:225–31.

Herrmann, Siegfried. 1973. *Israel in Egypt.* SBT 2nd ser.

Mendenhall, G. E. 1992. "Midian," *AncBD* 4:815–18.

Noth, Martin. 1972. *A History of Pentateuchal Traditions.*

Pritchard, J. B., ed. 1969. ANET. 3rd ed.

Redford, D. B. "The Literary Motif of the Exposed Child," *Numen* 14:209–28.

Reymond, P. 1958. *L'Eau, sa Vie, et sa Signification dans L'Ancien Testament.*

Sarna, Nahum M. 1991. *The JPS Torah Commentary. Exodus.*

Uphill, E. P. 1968 and 1969. "Pithom and Raamses: Their Location and Significance," *JNES* 27:291–316 and 28:15–39.

Wiles, John Keating, "Red Sea/Reed Sea," MDB.

Yadin, Yigael. 1963. *The Art of Warfare in Biblical Lands.*

Zimmerli, W. 1982. "I Am Yahweh," in *I Am Yahweh*, 1–28.

Leviticus

James W. Watts

Introduction

Leviticus, the third book of the Pentateuch (see TORAH), usually receives less attention from readers than its neighbors, probably because it contains mostly ritual instructions and legal regulations. Yet Leviticus makes vital contributions to both the theology and the plot of the Pentateuch. Its instructions and regulations spell out the practical implications of the promise (Exod 29:42-45; 33:14) that God will live *with* the people of Israel. And its narratives, although few in number, include the fulfillment of that promise in the dedication of God's dwelling, the TENT OF MEETING or TABERNACLE, by supernatural fire (Lev 9:22-24). Thus Leviticus interprets the significance of God's COVENANT with Israel in the concrete terms of regular worship and daily life, while also illustrating the unpredictable nature of life in the presence of God.

Leviticus in Context

The Pentateuch presents itself as a continuous narrative, within which the division into five books may seem superficial. Leviticus in particular continues the setting (at Mt. Sinai) and situation (MOSES receiving divine instructions) of the latter part of Exodus.

Boundaries of the book. Nevertheless, the narrative does separate the material of Leviticus from its surroundings by several markers. Exodus concludes with the completion of the Tabernacle, which in the last scene is occupied by God's GLORY in the form of a cloud (Exod 40:34-38). Then Leviticus begins with the statement that *The LORD summoned* [or called] *Moses and spoke to him from the tent of meeting* (Lev 1:1), which establishes the Tabernacle, rather than the mountain, as the setting for the divine instructions that follow. The book concludes with several summary statements (Lev 26:46; 27:34) to the law of Sinai (i.e., all God's instructions, whether given on the mountain or in the Tabernacle pitched at its base; see the com-

mentary below). The Book of Numbers begins with a census in preparation for the people's departure from Sinai. Within the Pentateuchal narrative, therefore, the boundaries of Leviticus are marked by the completion of the Tabernacle on the one hand and the organization of the Israelite camp on the other.

Leviticus within Exodus 25–Numbers 10. Yet, the book is clearly part of a larger unit concerned with creating and preserving the divine-human community. The material in Leviticus falls into two thematic parts that generally mirror the context on either side of the book. Leviticus 1–10 describe the sacrifices and rituals conducted in the Tabernacle, whose construction and furnishings are described in Exod 25–40. Leviticus 11–27 contain, for the most part, instructions for holy living that affect all members of the Israelite camp, whose organization and features are described in Num 1–10. By analogy with modern computers, the contents of Leviticus can be thought of as the "software" for use in the "hardware" described in the surrounding material (Blum 1990, 302n.56).

Leviticus within the Pentateuch. The book's meaning, however, is shaped by an even wider narrative context. When God first encountered Moses at the burning bush, God predicted Israel would worship on that mountain (Exod 3:12). Upon their arrival at the mountain, God declared that Israel would become "a priestly kingdom and a holy nation" (Exod 19:6). Leviticus narrates the fulfillment of these promises in the inauguration of sacrificial worship in the Tabernacle (Lev 8–9). By surrounding this story with chapters of instructions on ritual worship (Lev 1–7) and holy living (Lev 11–27), the book also emphasizes that God's presence with the people, symbolized by the Tabernacle in the middle of the camp, affects most aspects of their lives. However, the story's unexpected climax—a supernatural fire consuming the sacrifices (Lev 9:24)—is a reminder that, despite the importance of ritual, living with God remains an unpredictable endeavor.

Leviticus periodically refers to events within its wider narrative context, especially the EXODUS from Egypt and the coming conquest of Canaan. But the book's narrative role within the Pentateuch is more complicated than such references to past and future events might suggest. Exodus 19–24 have already narrated the creation of the covenant community at Sinai, complete with ritual instructions (20:22-26; 23:10-19), civil and criminal laws (21:1–23:9), and sacrifices inaugurating the covenant (24:3-8). What is the purpose of going over similar ground again in Leviticus?

Obviously, the material in Exod 25–Lev 27 adds many instructional details lacking in the much shorter account of Exod 19–24. But Leviticus is more than a collection of supplemental details. It recounts the events at Sinai from a different perspective. Exodus 19–24 emphasizes the historical event of making the covenant and accepting its stipulations. Leviticus instead organizes the experiences of the people's daily lives to conform to the fact of God's presence in their midst. Where the first account points to a singular event and its historical consequences, the second points to an eternal reality—God's holiness—and its consequences for anyone who comes in contact with it.

Leviticus, together with the Tabernacle account in Exod 25–31 and 35–40, is therefore a doublet for Exod 19–24, that is, a parallel narrative of events at Sinai from a different perspective. In the establishment of the worshiping community at Sinai, the book portrays a partial restoration of the divine-human community intended at creation. It describes an orderly reality separating the distinct spheres of life, in which any invasion of one sphere by another must be isolated, lest it threaten the relationship between God and Israel that this separation makes possible. This "religious organization of reality" was summarized by Leon Wieseltier (1987, 33):

> Structure for the reception of the unstructured: this is the subject of Leviticus—indeed, of the Torah. The organization of the world for sanctity proceeded by the increasing specification of ordained structure. Cosmic differentiations (between light and darkness and so on, in Genesis) led to historical differentiations (between the children of Abraham and others, in Genesis and Exodus), which led to the differentiations of holiness (most thickly and systematically in Leviticus).

Ritual in Leviticus

Modern readers may be tempted to dismiss much of Leviticus as "meaningless ritual," but the ancient writers of this book would have found that phrase self-contradictory. It is through ritual that they create and communicate religious meaning. In Leviticus, belief cannot be divided from action. Instead, ritual action defines the symbolic meaning of Israel's relations with God, other nations, the natural world, and itself.

Offerings and Sacrifices. Offering gifts to God is a pervasive feature of ancient and modern religious observance. In an agricultural economy such as ancient Israel's, religious gifts naturally took the form of grain, fruits, and domestic animals, although their equivalent could be paid in precious metals (Lev 27). Israel, however, also believed that certain offerings were not gifts, but belonged to God by right. Offerings of *new grain* (23:16), *first fruits of . . . harvest* (23:10), firstborn animals (27:26-27), and *tithes* (27:30-33) acknowledge God's ownership of the land and the people's status as God's *tenants* (25:23).

Although gifts and tithes persist in today's religious observances, animal sacrifices do not. The practice of blood sacrifice may have arisen partly to compensate for the guilt of slaughtering animals for food (Milgrom 1991, 440–43). Priestly theology reflects such ideas in its depiction of animals and humans as originally vegetarian (Gen 1:29-30) and of a divine command allowing humans to slaughter animals for food (Gen 9:2-6). Consequently, all slaughter is sacred and must be performed as a sacrifice (Lev 17:3-4) to make atonement before God (17:11; see below on atonement). Slaughter for food thus becomes a sacrifice of well-being and the consumption of flesh a sacred meal (Lev 7:11-18).

Some of Israel's sacrifices, however, do not produce food for the worshiper or even the priests (e.g., the *burnt offering,* Lev 1). Their meaning stems from Leviticus' understanding of the relationship between God and Israel, and involves processes of purification and atonement (see below). Sacrifice preserves the conditions necessary for God's presence in Israel's midst by providing formal and repeatable means for divine-human reconciliation (Mann 1988, 121).

Blood sacrifice is an ancient religious ritual far older than the priestly theology of Leviticus, so it is unlikely that any one explanation will account for all of Israel's sacrificial practices. Nevertheless, the issue of the meaning of sacrifice must play a central role in any interpretation of Leviticus. Ritual exists to give symbolic expression to religious reality. In Leviticus, the meaning of sacrifice determines the form of its performance. In subsequent Jewish and Christian interpretation of Leviticus, the meaning of sacrifice overshadows and replaces its performance (see below).

Holy and Common, Clean and Unclean. The priests' job, according to the programmatic statement in Lev 10:10, is *to distinguish between the holy and the common, and between the unclean and the clean.* These categories pervade the theology of Leviticus and determine part of its literary structure: the sacrificial regulations in chaps. 1–7 focus on the separation of the holy from the common, and the dietary and purification laws of chaps. 11–15 classify the clean and the unclean.

The two pairs of opposites are not equivalent, but they do affect each other. God is "holy," which means that God is completely separate, different, and other than humans and the natural world, that is, the "common." People or objects that are dedicated to God's use—such as priests, the Tabernacle, and sacrifices—derive their holy status from God and are removed from common use (see HOLINESS IN THE OT).

The labels "unclean" and "clean" distinguish between people, animals, or objects on the basis of ritual purity, not hygiene. Interpreters debate the meaning of the various purity laws of Leviticus, but it is clear that the distinctions reflect the symbolic structure of Israel's world view (Douglas [1966] 1985). Israel is called to holiness by distinguishing itself from other peoples (Exod 19:5-6; Lev 18:3-5; 20:25-26), which it partly accomplishes by eating only a limited number of "clean" animals distinguished from the rest of the animal world (Lev 11) and by temporarily separating Israelites rendered "unclean" by genital discharges, diseases, etc., from contact with the holy (Lev 12–15; CLEAN/UNCLEAN).

The four categories partially overlap. What is clean may be either holy or common, and what is common may be either clean or unclean. But what is holy cannot be unclean, or vice versa. Holiness and uncleanness are dynamic; they try to expand into their static antonyms, the common and the clean (Milgrom 1991, 732). Thus in OT thought, the unclean and the holy oppose each other, and Leviticus orders Israel's world to diminish the former power and maximize the latter.

Atonement. Leviticus frequently describes the purpose of sacrifice as "atonement" (כפר). The Hebrew word ranges in meaning from the concrete notions of "rub" and "cover" through "ransom" to the more abstract "purge" and "expiate" (see ATONEMENT/EXPIATION IN THE OT; Milgrom 1991, 1079–84). Leviticus applies it not only to sacrifices for sins (chaps. 4–5, 16) but also to purification rites (e.g., after childbirth, 12:7) and to the all-purpose *burnt offering* (1:4; Wenham 1979, 57-62).

Atonement removes impediments to communion between humans and God, whether they be sin or unavoidable impurity. Through sacrificial atonement, Israelites move from an unclean to a clean state and some, the priests, from common to holy status. In Leviticus's thinking, God's residence with Israel requires a pure community surrounding a holy sanctuary. Atonement preserves the conditions necessary for a divine-human community.

The Priestly Traditions and Editors

The contents of Leviticus belong to the Priestly (P) layer of the Pentateuch. Despite considerable reevaluation in recent decades of the Documentary Hypothesis of the Pentateuch's composition, the identification and isolation of P remains virtually unchallenged. P's distinctive interests (e.g., the priesthood, the Tabernacle, rituals, holiness) and style (e.g., careful use of technical vocabulary, repetitive structure) make it the most recognizable layer in the Pentateuch (see PRIESTLY WRITERS).

Authorship. P's interest in liturgy, sacrifice, and the Tabernacle as Israel's only shrine points to its origins among the priests of the Jerusalem Temple. The narrative context of P's laws presents them as divine instructions given through Moses to the people encamped at Mt. Sinai. The Pentateuch, however, presents Mosaic Law in a threefold form consisting of instructions from the mountain top (Exod 19–40), instructions from the Tabernacle (most of Leviticus and part of Numbers), and instructions from the plains of Moab (end of Numbers and Deuteronomy). Differences in style, content, legal particulars, and theology, as well as narrative setting, distinguish the three from each other (although their boundaries do not exactly correspond to those discerned by modern interpreters; see LAW IN THE OT). Yet all three blocks are presented separately and together as the divine Torah given to Israel through Moses.

The result is a document that openly presents a variety of Israelite legal traditions as authentically representative of Mosaic law. It thereby affirms the proposition that the God who initially inspired Moses continued to inspire the development of Israel's institutions in subsequent centuries and through various groups. One of the groups claiming Mosaic legal authority consisted of the priests who formulated, elaborated, and edited the P regulations in Leviticus.

Editing. Although all of Leviticus stems from P, it nevertheless shows signs of development over time. For example, the regulations regarding sacrifices in Lev 1–7 divide into two versions. The rituals described in Lev 1:1–6:7 are portrayed in somewhat different terms in Lev 6:8–7:38. The latter passage refers to the more detailed account of the former, but also adds to it additional regulations and concerns. It seems, therefore, to be a later supplement to the instructions in Lev 1:1–6:7. Another example is the block of material in Lev 17–26, which stands out stylistically and thematically from the rest of the book. Many scholars have concluded that it was originally a separate document, the "Holiness Code," which was incorporated into the larger context of Leviticus.

A close examination of Leviticus therefore suggests that the material was not composed by a single author at one sitting, but rather developed and grew over time. Some passages show the characteristic features of oral tradition, composed and handed down by word of mouth. Others show the signs of editorial activity, which adjusted separate documents to fit side by side. Thus P seems to have been the product of a community of teachers, authors, and editors who shared the priestly outlook on Israel's history and religious institutions.

Date. Dating the composition of P is much more difficult than identifying and isolating P from the rest of the Pentateuch, and current scholarship is divided over the problem. Efforts to date P linguistically by comparing its language with that of other Hebrew texts have produced contradictory results. Attempts to place P's institutions within the history of Israel's religion have not been very convincing, aside from showing that they are not Mosaic (e.g., see TENT OF MEETING).

The most promising evidence for dating P rests on its literary relationship with the rest of the Pentateuch. Despite a number of assertions to the contrary, it still appears that P was the last layer to be added to the Pentateuch. P structures and shapes the rest of the material. P seems to consciously react to and reinterpret older non-P material in the Pentateuch.

When this literary observation is combined with the historical observation that P seems to have had no literary influence on other Hebrew literature until the postexilic period (fifth and fourth centuries B.C.E.), we can conclude that P was combined with the rest of the Pentateuch and published at this time. However, observations regarding editorial activity within Leviticus (and the rest of P) suggest that much of P's material is considerably older than this date of publication. Thus it seems that P consists of materials from preexilic as well as later times that were made part of the Pentateuch and published only in the postexilic period.

Leviticus in Jewish and Christian Interpretation

Leviticus has influenced the beliefs and practices of generations of Jews and Christians, although often in different ways. As part of scripture, the book contributes to a wide network of religious ideas. Its significance cannot be fully understood apart from that larger context.

The Old Testament. Although Leviticus directly influenced only the later OT books, many of its ideas pervade the OT literature, which develops them further. For example, Leviticus considers both ritual and ethical legislation necessary for the divine-human community. The prophetic books define the relationship between ritual and ethics more closely by arguing that without justice and mercy, sacrifice and festivals are useless (Isa 1:10-17; Jer 7:1-15; Amos 5:21-24). Again, Leviticus distinguishes between unclean and clean on ritual and symbolic grounds. Outside the Pentateuch, these terms usually describe a general religious or moral condition (e.g., 2 Sam 22:21-25; Isa 6:5-7). On a larger scale, the historical and prophetic books interpret Israel's history as the outworking of the blessings and curses in Lev 26 and Deut 28, that is, as a consequence of Israel's fidelity to or rebellion against the covenant (e.g., cf. Ezek 22 and Lev 20). Leviticus' vision of the requirements for divine-human community thus finds echoes and elaborations throughout much of the OT.

Second Temple Judaism. The Second Temple period (515 B.C.E. until 70 C.E.) witnessed the completion of the OT and the publication of a wide variety of other religious works. These extrabiblical writings develop Leviticus' ideas in a variety of ways. WISDOM LITERATURE increasingly equates the law of Moses with divine wisdom and expounds on legal texts through proverbs (Sir 24:23; on Sir 19:13-17 as an interpretation of Lev 19:17, see Kugel 1986, 91). Under Hellenistic influence, some Jewish writers allegorize the ritual legislation to signify moral and intellectual virtues: for example, parting the hoof and chewing the cud (Lev 11:3, the criteria of clean land animals) symbolize the rational virtues of ethical discrimination and thoughtfulness in the *Letter of Aristeas* (see ARISTEAS, LETTER OF; and, on Philo, see PHILO). But the anti-Hellenistic writers of the Qumran TEMPLE SCROLL also revise Pentateuchal legislation on the basis of their own ritual concerns and attack particular practices at the Jerusalem Temple (Milgrom 1991, 558–66). Thus, concern for the interpretation and application of Pentateuchal law pervades a wide variety of later Second Temple writings.

Rabbinic Judaism. Legal interpretation, called *halakhah*, plays an even more crucial role in the classical rabbinic literature (second to fifth centuries C.E.; see RABBINIC LITERATURE). Although the Mishnah's rulings rarely depend on scriptural citations, *Sifra* uses midrash (see NT USE OF THE OT) to explicate the themes of Leviticus and anchor rabbinic rulings more firmly in scripture. *Leviticus Rabbah* reinterprets Leviticus' priestly and sacrificial rules as the means to sanctify the whole people of Israel. Along with the other rabbinic writings, these texts take laws that originally addressed the conditions of Palestine and its Temple and apply them to a people without land or temple. All the people are now priests, and prayers are their sacrifices. Despite the change in conditions, the law can be obeyed and Israel made holy.

The New Testament. Concern for interpreting law spread to early Christianity as well. The NT interprets the laws of Leviticus in two different ways. On the one hand, it singles out the commandment of love for neighbor (Lev 19:18), along with love of God (Deut 6:5), as the essence of the Mosaic law (Matt 22:37-40; Mark 12:29-31; Luke 10:27; Rom 13:8-10; Gal 5:14; Jas 2:8; see LOVE IN THE NT). On the other hand, it relaxes the requirements of many Pentateuchal purity regulations (Matt 15:11; Acts 10:9-16; Rom 14:14-23) and ritual laws (Acts 15:1-35; 1 Cor 7:19; see CHURCH AND LAW). Alongside such legal discussions, the NT also interprets the law typologically (see INTERPRETATION, HISTORY OF) as foreshadowing Christ's work. Hebrews casts Jesus as the high priest on the Day of Atonement (Lev 16), who offered his own blood instead of animal sacrifices to purify from sin (Heb 9:1-14). Like Leviticus, the NT emphasizes the ideal of close communion between God and humans, but that communion is symbolized, not by the presence of the sanctuary in the middle of the camp as it is in Leviticus, but by its *absence* (Rev 21:22). This image at the end of the NT

aptly represents the conscious continuity of theme and discontinuity of practice in NT interpretations of Leviticus.

Early Christianity. Christian commentators continued to distinguish ritual laws as nonbinding on Christians, while searching every part of the OT for typological and allegorical significance. This approach was shaped on the one side by Jewish criticisms of Christians for not obeying the law and on the other by Gnostic attacks on the OT's status as Scripture. Christian interpreters defended the scriptural status of law by showing typologically how it foreshadows Christ, while also maintaining that it was completed and superseded by the new covenant. However, controversy over the status and meaning of Mosaic law marks every period of Christian history, and continues in the present.

Summary. Jewish and Christian interpretations of Leviticus have always struggled with how to apply this book's legislation to changing times and circumstances. The two communities have for the most part adopted opposite approaches to OT law: traditional Jewish interpretation usually attends to every regulation by reinterpreting them to apply to different conditions, while traditional Christian interpretation promulgates the love commandment as the essence of and replacement for all the rest. The results of either approach may seem far removed from the national and liturgical concerns that permeate the text of Leviticus. But God's people, with or without land or Tabernacle, have much to learn from a book that confronts a wilderness generation (Lev 7:38) with the ideal of a divine-human community and promises God's continuing faithfulness to their descendants in exile (Lev 26:44-45).

For Further Study

In the *Mercer Dictionary of the Bible*: BLOOD IN THE OT; COVENANT; LAW IN THE OT; LEVITICUS, BOOK OF; PRIESTLY WRITERS; TABERNACLE; TENT OF MEETING; WORSHIP IN THE OT.

In other sources: D. Damrosch, "Leviticus," in *The Literary Guide to the Bible*, 66–77; J. E. Hartley, *Leviticus*, WBC; J. L. Kugel and R. A. Greer, *Early Biblical Interpretation*; T. W. Mann, *The Book of Torah*; J. Milgrom, *Leviticus 1–16*, AncB; N. H. Snaith, *Leviticus and Numbers*, NCB; G. J. Wenham, *The Book of Leviticus*, NICOT; L. Wieseltier, "Leviticus," in *Congregation*, 27–38.

Commentary

An Outline

Regulations for Sacrifices and Offerings, 1:1–7:28

Exodus 25–31 and 35–40 narrated the building of the TABERNACLE and its furnishings, but gave few instructions as to their use. Leviticus 1–7 supplies these instructions. The sacrifices and offerings described here are the essential elements in the Tabernacle (and Temple) services. They are presupposed in the following (Lev 8–10) story of the inauguration of the priests and the Tabernacle services.

Leviticus 1:1–6:7 describes five offerings by means of divine instructions given through Moses to the people as a whole, according to headings at 1:1-2 and 4:1-2. These offerings are described again in 6:8–7:21, instructions whose intended recipients are *Aaron and his sons* (i.e., the priests) according to 6:8-9 and 24–25. Differences in style and details of the contents, together with the change of recipients, suggest that the two sets of instructions were originally distinct. Leviti-

cus 6:8–7:21, however, presupposes the elements of the preceding instructions, and Lev 7 ends with prohibitions aimed at the whole people (7:22-36). These observations indicate that the priestly instructions have been edited for their present context and are now intended for a larger audience (Hartley 1992, 94–95).

The style of Lev 1–7 illustrates all the distinctive features of P literature. The use of specialized vocabulary shows P's concern for accuracy and detail. Formulaic repetition calls attention to analogous cases, especially in Lev 1–3, but small variations prevent total redundancy in either style or contents. The results convey a sense of order and completeness in the Tabernacle service, a sense strongly reminiscent of the story of creation in Gen 1:1–2:4a—another example of P's unique literary style and theological perspective.

Introduction, 1:1-2

The phrase *the LORD summoned* marks the start of something new. In Exodus, God invariably summons or calls MOSES from Mount Sinai (Exod 3:1-4; 19:3, 20; 24:16) to hear a major new revelation. The phrase indicates the same intention here, except that now God speaks *from the tent of meeting* (אהל מועד; this is the usual term in Leviticus, although in Exodus and Numbers it is frequently called a dwelling or tabernacle, משכן). This tent, whose construction and furnishings are described in Exod 25–31, 35–40, is a mobile sanctuary of worship that can move with Israel on the journey to Canaan (see TABERNACLE; TENT OF MEETING). With only a few exceptions, it replaces Mount Sinai from this point on in the Pentateuch as the place from which God reveals the Law.

The summary command in 1:2 specifies that *offerings* (a broad term covering all gifts made to God, whether animals, grains, or precious metals) of livestock should consist of domestic animals only. This command introduces the subject that dominates chaps. 1–7, although the list of offerings also includes birds (1:14-17; 5:7-10) and grain (2:1-6; 5:11-13).

Burnt Offerings, 1:3-17

The instructions for the burnt offerings appear in three sections (vv. 3-9, 10-13, 14-17), one for each category of sacrificial animal (herd animals, flock animals, birds). Each section begins with the conditional *if*, describes the steps of the ritual in similar terms (although abbreviated in the second and third accounts), and concludes with *a burnt offering, an offering by fire of pleasing odor to the* LORD. The formulaic repetition gives the chapter a rhythmic cadence, which may reflect its origins in the priests' oral teaching of the people.

The Hebrew word עלה which is translated *burnt offering* means literally something which "goes up, ascends," presumably referring to the fire and smoke of the sacrifice. Another traditional translation is "whole offering" (REB), which points to the essential difference between this and other sacrifices: the whole animal is burnt in this offering; nothing is left to be eaten by either priests or worshipers.

The purpose of the burnt offering is not described in this chapter. Its results are merely alluded to: *acceptance* of (v. 3) and *atonement* for (v. 4) the worshiper before God. Since other offerings are described later to deal with particular sin (Lev 4:1–5:13) and restitution (5:14–6:7), the burnt offering's purpose seems to be less specific. This is confirmed by the fact that in other texts, burnt offerings are described as occurring on a variety of occasions: regular observances (Num 28–29); royal sacrifices (2 Sam 6:17-18; 1 Kgs 9:25); as accompanying prayers of petition (Ps 20:3) and thanksgiving (Ps 51:19); and celebrations of all sorts (1 Sam 6:14; Lev 12:6-8). Burnt offerings, then, seem to have been the ordinary means for smoothing the relationship between humans and God.

The burnt offering, whether cattle, sheep or goat, must be *a male without blemish* (vv. 3, 10). Both specifications emphasize this animal is to be of high value, although the option of substituting a moderately valued sheep or goat or even an inexpensive bird for the high-priced bull enables every Israelite to participate in sacrificial worship (Lev 5:7, 11). The worshipers lay hands on the animal to establish ownership of it and claim the benefits of the sacrifice for themselves (see Milgrom 1991, 150-53, and Hartley 1992, 18–20).

The worshipers are responsible for slaughtering the bulls, sheep, and goats, and helping the priest prepare them for the altar. As in all Israelite sacrifice or slaughter, the *blood* requires special treatment (cf. Gen 9:4-6; Lev 3:17; 7:22-27; 17:11). It must be drained from the carcass and offered to God, no matter what use the rest of the animal is put to.

The burning sacrifice is described as *an offering by fire of pleasing odor to the* LORD (vv. 9, 13, 17 and throughout Leviticus and P sections of Exodus and Numbers). God's pleasure at smelling the sacrifice and the resulting divine mercy towards humans is depicted in Gen 8:21. P, however, usually avoids strong anthropomorphic imagery for God, which suggests that *pleasing odor* is here simply a technical term for God's acceptance of the offering.

Grain Offerings, 2:1-16

The Hebrew word מנחה translated *grain offering* has a wide range of uses in the OT. It can refer to gifts from one person to another (Gen 32:13) or tribute paid to a king or ruler (1 Kgs 4:21). When used of offerings to God, it sometimes includes animal sacrifices as well as grain (Gen 4:3-5). Within ritual instructions, however, the word refers to offerings of grain that usually accompanied the burnt offerings of animals. The underlying notion of gift or tribute suggests that grain offerings may represent the worshipers' recognition of God's ownership of the land, an idea reinforced by the connection to first fruits in vv. 14-16.

2:1-10. Procedures. As with the burnt offerings, grain offerings should be of good quality. Hence the emphasis on *choice flour*, *oil*, and *frankincense* (a kind of INCENSE). The priest burns a *token portion* (אזכרה, often translated *memorial*) on the altar. The remainder goes to support the priests. Grain offerings can be presented in a variety of forms, so long as the quality of the ingredients remains high (vv. 4-8).

2:11-13. Leaven, honey, and salt. The reasons for prohibiting *leaven* (yeast) and *honey* (probably fruit nectar as well as honey) in grain offerings are not explained here or in other prohibitions of leaven in sacrifices (Exod 23:18; 34:25). They may be offered to God as a "first fruits" offering (v. 12, RSV for ראשית; NRSV, NJV *choice products*), but cannot be burnt on the altar. On the other hand, *the salt of the covenant* is to be included with every grain offering. Salt is a symbol of a covenant's permanence (Num 18:19; 2 Chr 13:5), so its presence in the offering reminds worshipers of the perpetual covenant between Israel and God.

2:14-16. First fruits. Israelites were expected to give to God an offering from the first harvest of the year as thanks for giving them the land (Deut 26:1-11). These *first fruits* (ראשית; בכורים in v. 12) are offered like the other grain offerings. Lev 23:9-20 associates this offering with the festivals of Unleavened Bread and Weeks.

Offerings of Well-Being, 3:1-17

Sacrifice of well-being is the NRSV and NJV rendering of זבח שלמים, elsewhere translated "sacrifice of peace offering" (KJV, RSV), "shared offering" (REB), and "fellowship offering" (NIV). The root of the crucial term is related to שָׁלוֹם *shalom* "peace, prosperity, well-being." The translations all point out the key feature of this offering: the sacrificial animal is divided between God, the priests (Lev 7:31-36), and the worshipers, and the worshipers eat the meat in a sacred meal (7:11-18). The offering of well-being is essentially a meal celebrating the relationship between God and Israel. Its performance marked many of the high points of Israel's history (Exod 24:5, 11; 2 Sam 6:17-19; 1 Kgs 8:64-65).

Like the regulations governing the burnt offering in Lev 1, Lev 3 divides into three sections (vv. 1-5, 6-11, 12-16) on the basis of the type of animal sacrificed (cattle, sheep, and goats respectively), and each part repeats the same instructions with only minor variations. The ritual follows many of the same procedures as that for burnt offerings, except that male or female animals may be used and only part of the animal (the fat and some internal organs) is burnt on the altar.

The ritual instruction to burn the fat on the altar is expanded in the chapter's conclusion (vv. 16b-17) into a prohibition against eating any fat. It is not clear why fat is added here and in 7:23-27 to the more usual dietary prohibition against blood (v. 17; cf. Gen 9:4; Lev 17:10-16; 19:26; Deut 12:16, 23; 15:23). *Fat* is used metaphorically in Gen 45:18 and Ps 81:16 for the best of something, so perhaps the reasoning is like that behind the first fruits offering: the best of the land's produce, whether vegetable or animal, belongs to God.

Sin Offerings, 4:1–5:13

Sin offering (חטאה) is sometimes translated as "purification offering" (REB), which more accurately describes its nature. Burnt offerings and guilt offerings also atone for sin (Lev 1:4; 5:16); the unique benefit of sin offerings is that they purify the sanctuary from the polluting effects of unintentional sins (4:2; 5:1-4; Milgrom 1991, 254-61). These instructions presuppose and cite previous descriptions of offerings (4:10, 26, 31; 5:10, 13).

4:3-35. Kinds of sin offerings. Lev 4 legislates the procedures to be followed for different categories of sinners: the high priest (vv. 3-12), the community as a whole (vv. 13-21), a ruler (vv. 22-26), or an ordinary person. This last category is subdivided into offerings of goats (vv. 27-31) and sheep (vv. 32-35). The first section is the longest and most explicit; subsequent sections presuppose the first (v. 21) and omit some steps. Except for the first, each section concludes with

the formula *the priest shall make atonement for them/him/you and they/he/you shall be forgiven.*

The anointed priest (הכהן המשיח, found in OT only in Lev 4 and 6) is a rare term for the high priest, who was anointed during his ordination (see below on 8:12). משיח "anointed one," transliterated as "Messiah," is normally used in the OT for the king. A *ruler* (נשיא, v. 22) is a tribal leader (Num 2:3, 5, etc.).

Sins of the high priest or whole community defile the sanctuary more than do sins by other individuals, and so require a more valuable sacrificial animal, a bull, and more thorough purification procedures. The blood is sprinkled in front of *the curtain of the sanctuary*, which separated the innermost part of the Tabernacle (the Holy of Holies), and on the *altar of fragrant incense* that stood in front of it (vv. 6-7, 17-18), rather than just on the altar of burnt offering at the Tabernacle entrance (vv. 25, 30, 34).

5:1-6. Examples of unintentional sins. Unintentional sins include acts done ignorantly, unconsciously, by accident, or even omissions due to a lack of nerve. Leviticus 5:1-4 provides examples: failure of a witness to testify in court; contact with unclean animals or humans (cf. Lev 11–15); rash oaths (Lev 19:12). Once realized, the problem is corrected by confession and a sin offering (vv. 5-6).

5:7-13. Alternative offerings for the poor. Poverty should prevent no one from making offerings, so alternative sin offerings of two birds or *one-tenth of an ephah of choice flour* (v. 11; approximately six and one-half pints) are permissible.

Guilt Offerings, 5:14–6:7

Guilt offering (אשם) is sometimes translated "reparation offering" (JB, REB). This offering is prompted by an act of *treachery* (מעל, 5:15; 6:1; NRSV's "trespass" is too weak) and accompanied by compensation for the loss plus one fifth (5:16; 6:5). Three examples of treachery form the contents of this section: misuse of God's *holy things*, i.e., anything dedicated to the sanctuary or the use of the priests (5:14-16); any violations of law (5:17-19); and acts of deceit, fraud, and robbery (6:1-7). This mixture of specific and general examples, together with the passage's failure to describe the guilt offering ritual (cf. 7:1-7) as earlier chapters have done, may indicate that it was originally separate from what precedes it. As the text now stands, however, the formulas of atonement and forgiveness (4:20, 26, 31, 35; 5:6, 10, 13, 16, 18; 6:7) unite the descriptions of the sin and guilt offerings.

Like sin offerings, guilt offerings atone for *unintentional* sins (5:15, 17). Yet the last set of offenses (6:1-3) includes flagrant acts. The OT's sacrificial system otherwise makes no provision for intentional sins. Milgrom argues, however, that heartfelt repentance and confession could reduce the severity of transgressions from flagrant to unintentional, "thereby qualifying them for sacrificial expiation" (1976, 119). Thus confession and restitution (6:4-5) are preconditions for atonement and forgiveness (6:6-7), even of willful sins.

Priest's Instructions
regarding Offerings, 6:8–7:36

God now instructs Moses to address the priests, *Aaron and his sons* (6:9, 25), rather than the whole people as in 1:2, 4:2, 7:22 and 28. The instructions cover the same five offerings discussed in 1:1–6:7, but in a different order and with particular attention to the rights and responsibilities of the priests. The phrase, *this is the ritual of* (the word translated "ritual," תורה *torah*, means "instruction, law, teaching"; see LAW IN THE OT), introduces each offering.

These differences in audience, issues, and phraseology suggest that 6:8–7:21 were originally separate from 1:1–6:7 and may have originated in the Temple as instructions for priests. In their present context, however, they supplement the earlier chapters and have been adapted to instruct the whole people, as indicated by the second person pronouns in 7:12ff., the digression on dietary prohibitions in 7:22-27, and the summation in 7:38.

6:8-30. Burnt, grain and sin offerings. Presupposing the descriptions of these offerings in chaps. 1, 2, 4–5, these instructions focus on the responsibilities (maintaining perpetual fire on the altar) and rights (to portions of the sacrifice) of the priests. Verses 19-23 describe a previously unmentioned grain offering offered daily by the high priest. Unlike ordinary grain offerings, those of priests are burned completely (v. 23); none can be eaten by priests who would otherwise be consuming what they themselves had given to God.

7:1-10. Guilt offerings. The guilt offering is described more fully than the previous three offerings, apparently to provide details omitted in 5:14–6:7.

7:11-21. Offerings of well-being. Verses 11-21 shift the address and focus from the priests to the worshipers. Most of this offering is eaten by the worshipers, so the primary concern here is with rules for its proper consumption. There are three categories of offerings of

well-being: *thanksgiving* for a specific divine act, *votive* in fulfillment of a vow, and *freewill* for general celebration.

Since lay persons as well as priests will be handling the meat, they must be as careful as priests to protect it from defilement. Failure to do so can result in the severest divine penalty known to P, being *cut off from one's kin* (vv. 20, 21), which probably means loss of offspring and perhaps loss of afterlife (Milgrom 1991, 457-60).

7:22-27. Prohibition on eating fat and blood. God now addresses all Israel explicitly. On *fat*, see comments on 3:17. Verses 22-27 limit the prohibition on eating fat to those species of animals suitable for sacrifice, *ox or sheep or goat* (v. 23), and to carrion (v. 24), implying that the fat of game animals may be eaten. The prohibition on eating blood, however, remains absolute.

7:28-36. Priest's portions of offerings of well-being. The discussion of offerings of well-being continues after the interruption of 7:22-27 by specifying that the fat belongs to God, and the breast and right thigh belong to the priests. Raising portions of the sacrifice as an *elevation offering* (vv. 30, 34) dedicates them to God (Milgrom 1991, 461–81). The rest is returned for the worshipers to eat.

Summation, 7:37-38

The sacrificial regulations conclude by listing the six priestly *rituals* or instructions of 6:8–7:36, which God gave Moses on *Mount Sinai*. At the same time, the directions on how the *people* should *bring their offerings*, found in 1:2–6:7, were given *in the wilderness of Sinai*, i.e., from the Tabernacle (1:1). Despite the Tabernacle's existence and use for divine-human communication (cf. Exod 33:7-11), the site of revelation in Leviticus sometimes reverts to the mountain (Lev 25:1; 26:46; 27:34).

Inauguration of Worship, 8:1–10:20

After seven chapters of sacrificial regulations, the narrative now resumes where it left off at the end of Exodus. Moses, having built the Tabernacle (Exod 35–40), offers the first sacrifices in it and ordains *Aaron and his sons* as priests (Lev 8). They then take over responsibility for the Tabernacle (Lev 9), and all the plans detailed in Exod 25 to Lev 7 are finally realized: the sanctuary and its rituals enable God and

Israel to live together (Exod 29:42-45). Divine fire displays the fulfillment of this promise (Lev 9:24).

Leviticus 10, however, immediately dampens the excitement of chaps. 8–9 by narrating stories of priestly disobedience and disagreement. God's presence in the sanctuary turns dangerous when taken too lightly. The center of the chapter summarizes the priests' responsibilities in terms of sobriety, discernment, and education of the people (10:8-11).

Ordination of Priests, 8:1-36

Moses acts in this chapter in accordance with *what the LORD has commanded to be done* (v. 5) in Exod 29 regarding ordination of priests. The refrain, *as the Lord commanded Moses*, echoes throughout the passage. God's instructions could not be carried out until after the Tabernacle was built (Exod 35–40) and the sacrificial regulations were given (Lev 1–7), since the priests require both to perform their duties.

The priests' vestments (vv. 7-9) symbolize their office and are to be worn when serving in the Tabernacle. Exodus 28 and 39 describe their construction in detail (see DRESS; EPHOD; URIM AND THUMMIN).

Moses consecrates both the Tabernacle and Aaron, the high priest, by anointing them with holy oil (for its composition, see Exod 30:22-33). Although oil is later sprinkled on the other priests (Lev 8:30; cf. Exod 40:15), only the high priest is anointed, as his other title, *the anointed priest* (Lev 4:3), shows. The OT uses this title, "anointed one" (מֹשִׁיחַ, often transliterated "Messiah"), more commonly for Israel's kings, who were anointed upon their accession. The act of anointing separates the recipients from common life and makes them sacred, although its implications are different for kings and for high priests (see Milgrom 1991, 553-55; ANOINT; MESSIAH/MESSIANISM).

Moses performs the sacrifices in close accord with the instructions in Exod 29, although there are some differences in order and detail. A sin offering of a bull (vv. 14-17) is followed by the sacrifice of two rams, one for a burnt offering (vv. 18-21) and the other, called the *ram of ordination* (v. 22), for an offering of well-being (vv. 22-29, 31-32). Blood is daubed on the altar and on the priests to purify them of contamination (vv. 15, 23-24), and is sprinkled together with oil on the priests and their vestments to consecrate them (i.e., make them holy; v. 30). The ordination ceremony lasts seven days, with at least some of the sacrifices repeated daily (Exod 29:35-41).

Inauguration of Worship, 9:1-24

In chap. 8, Moses acted as priest for Aaron and his sons. *On the eighth day* (v. 1), Aaron takes over and the people bring him their offerings, responding to the promise that on this first day of regular worship, *the LORD will appear to you* (vv. 4, 6).

Aaron offers the full range of required sacrifices, first for himself (vv. 8-14), then for the people (vv. 15-21). The account is abbreviated, but frequent references to Lev 1–7 (*as the LORD commanded* [v. 10]; *according to regulation* [v. 16]; *as Moses commanded* [v. 21]) make it clear that Aaron carries out faithfully every detail of the instructions.

The service ends with a blessing, perhaps that recorded for the priests' use in Num 6:24-26. Blessing is not simply the conclusion but the goal of the entire service: it is God's response to the people's worship, a statement that the divine relationship with Israel has been restored (see CURSE AND BLESSING).

This first time, however, there is a surprise ending. As promised at the beginning of the chapter, *the glory of the LORD appeared* (v. 23), probably in the form of a cloud and lightning (Exod 24:15-18; 40:34-38). Then comes the unexpected finale to this meticulously planned service: divine lightning hits the altar, devouring the already burning sacrifices. Thus human liturgy sets the stage for divine spontaneity, and the people meet God in worship.

Priestly Practice and Malpractice, 10:1-20

The same divine fire, however, destroys those who presume upon "a familiarity with the divine" (Wieseltier 1987, 33). Aaron's sons, Nadab and Abihu, bring *unholy fire* ("alien" NJV; "unauthorized" NIV; "strange" KJV; i.e., coals from a profane source instead of the altar; cf. 16:12) into the sanctuary, perhaps into the Holy of Holies *before the LORD*. A divine saying interprets their deaths as showing God's holiness and glory (v. 3), a idea found in other accounts of divine punishment (Num 20:13; Ezek 28:22; 38:16). God's separate (holy) and pure nature is revealed by intolerance for pollution of any sort.

Leviticus 10 is written artfully to balance the sudden tragedy in vv. 1-3 with another account of priestly malpractice in vv. 16-20. The latter story, however, has a very different conclusion: Aaron, who *was silent* in v. 3 and prevented from mourning in vv. 6-7, now defends the practice of his younger sons and convinces Moses that his interpretation is correct. (The problem is that the priests are supposed to eat the people's sin offering according to 6:24-30, but apparently Aaron argued that Nadab and Abihu's sin or deaths had transformed it into a burnt sin offering, like those in 8:14-17 and 9:8-11. See Milgrom 1991, 635–40.)

Furthermore, the center of the chapter contains (vv. 8-11, in a divine speech to Aaron, not Moses!) a summary of the priests' responsibilities that emphasizes sobriety in the performance of their liturgical duties, discernment in distinguishing between *the holy and the common* (specified in Lev 1–7) and between *the unclean and the clean* (specified in Lev 11–15), and the people's education in the Mosaic law. Thus the chapter as a whole emphasizes that priests should know, obey, and teach the law, and that failure to do so can result in drastic penalties; at the same time, it endorses the use of reason in the law's interpretation.

The two stories of priestly malpractice anchor instructions for disposing of corpses (which are unclean—Lev 22:4; Num 19:14-16) in the sanctuary and for the distribution of the priests' portions of the sacrifices. A five-part CHIASM therefore structures the chapter, with the narratives at the beginning and the end bracketing the two sets of instructions, which in turn surround the summary of priestly responsibilities at the center (Hartley 1992, 128-29).

Unclean and Clean, 11:1–15:33

On the categories "clean" and "unclean," see the introduction above and CLEAN/UNCLEAN.

Edible and Inedible Animals, 11:1-47

Leviticus 11 divides the animal world into five categories: land animals (vv. 2-8), water animals (9-12), birds (13-19), flying insects (20-23), and land swarmers (41-43; cf. the three categories in Deut 14). Criteria of purity and examples are provided in two cases (vv. 2-8, 20-23), but for water animals the criteria (fins and scales) appear without examples while the reverse is true of the list of unclean birds. Verses 24-40 digress into the transmission of impurity to those who touch dead animals. Along the way, the section adds another criterion for unclean land animals (v. 27) and provides examples of land swarmers (vv. 29-30) omitted from vv. 41-43.

The OT does not explain why certain animals should be considered clean and others unclean. The most credible explanation relies on anthropology to argue that the CLEAN/UNCLEAN distinction is Israel's symbolic means of structuring the world. Clean animals stay in their own sphere (land, water, air) and move in a way appropriate to that sphere (walking, swimming, flying). Unclean animals cross between the spheres and use inappropriate locomotion (Douglas [1966] 1985). Many of the unclean animals are carnivores who break the vegetarian order intended at creation (Gen 1:30; cf. 9:2-6; Carroll [1978] 1985). Israel, then, affirms God's original plan by eating only those animals whose behavior is appropriate and limited to their own sphere.

11:2-8, 26-27. Land animals. This category covers most quadrupeds, except for the reptiles and small mammals that are classified as land swarmers (vv. 29-30). Four species fail to meet the criteria of being cleft-hoofed and chewing the cud (vv. 4-7). Verse 27 adds a third criterion, walking on paws, which makes carnivores such as cats, dogs, and bears unclean and inedible for Israel.

11:9-12. Water animals. The criteria of fins and scales declares unclean all water animals except fish. The adjective *detestable* (v. 11) emphasizes the repugnance with which Israel regarded shellfish and amphibians (cf. vv. 23, 42).

11:13-19. Birds. Unclean animals of the air are named without any criterion of selection, and some cannot be identified with certainty. All those which are known seem to be carnivores or scavengers.

11:20-23. Winged insects. Insects that fly and walk mix the spheres of land and air and are unclean. It is not clear why they are described as *walking on all fours* (insects have six, eight, or more legs) nor why four kinds of grasshoppers or locusts are clean and edible (e.g., Mark 1:6).

11:24-40. Transmission of uncleanness. All carcasses, whether of unclean (v. 24) or clean (v. 39) animals, transmit impurity when they touch people or human artifacts (vv. 31-38).

11:29-30, 41-43. Land swarmers. *Swarm* describes the movement of small multilimbed creatures on the land (v. 41) or in the water (v. 10), including rodents, reptiles (vv. 29-30), and nonflying insects. All swarmers are unclean.

11:44-47. Motivation and summary. Israel should avoid unclean foods to identify with God, just as God identified with them by saving them from Egypt. *You shall be holy, for I am holy* (v. 45) is the central principle of chaps. 17-26 and links these diet laws with the rules for holy living found there.

Purification after Childbirth, 12:1-8

Leviticus 12 and 15 both treat impurity due to genital discharges and cross-references (vv. 2, 5) connect them. Since genital discharges of blood or semen convey impurity (Lev 15), the loss of blood in childbirth makes a mother unclean (Lev 12). The periods of impurity and blood purification last a total of forty days for a male child, and eighty for a female, but both require the same sacrifices (vv. 6-8). The *sin offering* purifies; it does not make restitution for particular sin, so there is no suggestion here that childbirth or sex are sinful acts. It is the loss of blood, which in the OT symbolizes life itself, that requires temporary separation and rites of purification. See further on chap. 15, below.

Growths on Skin, Clothing, and Houses, 13:1–14:57

Scaly growths on skin, clothing, and houses represented the onset of death to ancient Israelites (e.g., Num 12:12; Job 18:13). They therefore render the affected persons or objects unclean. As the parallel diagnoses and treatments for skin, clothing, and buildings show, the issue in these chapters is not contagious disease but rather ritual impurity. Scaly or peeling skin and fungal growths in cloth or house conjure up images of decomposing corpses. Such growths are therefore unclean like corpses, and contact with them conveys impurity (cf. Num 19:11-22).

13:1-46. Unclean skin growths. Seven kinds of skin growth are described together with procedures for their diagnosis (vv. 2-44). Medical identification of these skin diseases remains elusive (see LEPROSY), but one thing is clear: the traditional translation of צרעת as "leprosy" (i.e., Hansen's disease) is wrong. The priests do not perform medical treatment, but rather determine an individual's status as clean or unclean. The unclean person's appearance resembles that of a mourner, reinforcing the connection with death (vv. 45-46; cf. 10:6; Ezek 24:17, 22). Banishment of individuals or objects with persistent growths is necessary to keep the community ritually clean and protect the Tabernacle from impurity. Contagion from growths represents a more severe threat to the community in Leviticus than that from genital discharges (cf. Num 5:2-3, which ostracizes those with discharges as well as those with skin growths).

13:47-59. Growths in clothing. Mold or fungal growths on clothing are treated like skin growths. Clearly, the concern is with impurity, not disease.

14:1-32. Purification after healing. If the priest certifies that the skin has healed, the individual can be readmitted to the camp. Some of the ceremonial procedures for cleansing resemble those for consecrating priests (Lev 8–9), since both solemnize a significant change in status.

14:34-53. Growths in houses. Fungal growths in houses, such as mold, mildew, and dry rot, threaten Israel's purity as much as skin growths. Graduated measures for dealing with the problem range from a one-week quarantine to destruction of the building. The contents, however, may be removed and kept (v. 36).

Genital Discharges, 15:1-33

Semen and blood represent life in the OT. Their loss implies a loss of life. This symbolic affiliation with death characterizes all of the causes of impurity in Lev 12–15 (but not the unclean animals of chap. 11). Genital discharges therefore make a person unclean, while urinating and defecating do not (although feces must be properly disposed of, Deut 23:12-14). The issue is not sex and procreation, but their fluid byproducts. Leviticus 15 describes the impurity and purification procedures for discharges of semen, both abnormal (vv. 2-15) and normal (vv. 16-18), and of blood, normal (vv. 19-24) and abnormal (vv. 25-30).

15:2-15. Abnormal discharges of semen. Secretion of mucus (v. 3) is a symptom of gonorrhea, and renders a man unclean as long as the discharge continues. He transmits impurity to things under him, to utensils, and by touch to other people. If the secretions cease and do not recommence for a week, bathing and a small sacrifice will make him clean (vv. 13-15).

15:16-18. Normal discharges of semen. Emissions of semen, whether during sexual intercourse or not, cause impurity that requires bathing and lasts until nightfall. Normal discharges of semen or blood do not require sacrifices.

15:19-24. Normal discharges of blood. A menstruating woman is unclean *for seven days*. She transmits impurity to things under her and to those who touch her, and more severe impurity (and divine punishment according to 20:18) to a man who has intercourse with her. Unlike a gonorrheal man, however, her touch is apparently not considered contagious, probably so that she can continue to work during menstruation (cf. Num 5:2-3).

A fear of menstruating women is common in many societies around the world (for a survey, Milgrom 1991, 763-68, 948-53). Folk wisdom frequently portrays menstrual blood as having demonic power. Leviticus opposes such magical interpretations of reality, and so subordinates this fear to its system of unclean and clean, death and life. Menstrual blood, like semen, represents loss of life and is therefore unclean. Nevertheless, male anxiety about menstrual blood contributes to the lower status of WOMEN IN THE OT.

15:25-30. Abnormal discharges of blood. Women with continuous or irregular flows of blood remain unclean as long as the problem persists. Once the bleeding stops, the purification rites are the same as for gonorrheal men.

15:31-33. Motive and summary. In Leviticus, the Tabernacle is the underlying reason for distinguishing unclean from clean. God's holiness is intolerant of impurity. Since God resides with Israel, the unclean must be recognized and separated to avoid disaster.

The Day of Atonement, 16:1-34

The ritual fail-safe in Israel's system of sacrificial worship is the Day of Atonement, familiarly known by its Hebrew name *Yom Kippur*. The observances of this day atone for all impurities or sins that were overlooked by Israel throughout the year (see ATONEMENT, DAY OF; on atonement, see introduction above and ATONEMENT/EXPIATION IN THE OT).

The heading dates these instructions *after the death of the two sons of Aaron* (v. 1), i.e., after the events of chap. 10. Their appearance in chap. 16 illustrates the thematic arrangement of Leviticus: just as the inauguration of worship (chaps. 8–9) presupposed sacrificial instructions that therefore precede it (chaps. 1–7), so also these purification procedures presuppose the system of impurities detailed beforehand in chaps. 11–15.

The attention in Lev 16 is focused on the innermost part of the sanctuary and particularly on the MERCY SEAT, the golden cover on the ARK of the covenant. The Hebrew word כפרת *kapporet*, usually translated "mercy seat" or "cover," is from the same root as כפר *kippur* "cover, atonement," so the same idea identifies both the day and the place. This place is most holy, for God *appears in the cloud upon the mercy seat* (v. 2). As the locus of God's presence in Israel's midst, the ark's cover must be kept clean and holy. The rites of the Day of Atonement assure that it is.

Most of the sacrifices in Lev 16 follow the usual procedures detailed in chaps. 1–7, and serve to purify

the sanctuary from the people's sins and impurity (v. 16). Confession (v. 21) permits sacrificial atonement even for flagrant offenses (see above on 6:1-7). However, only this occasion employs a goat *for Azazel* (vv. 7-10, 20-22). The word "Azazel" is obscure and has been translated as "scapegoat," as "a rocky place," or as the proper name of a demon. The goat's role is clear, however: it *shall bear on itself all their iniquities to a barren region* (v. 22). Thus the observances of the Day of Atonement not only purify the sanctuary; they also free Israel from sin's power.

The chapter's concluding verses turn from describing the high priest's actions to addressing the people, who are to fast and rest on the Day of Atonement (vv. 29-34). Verse 29 fixes this annual observance on the tenth day of the seventh month. If the ambiguous sentence, "and he did as Yahweh had commanded Moses" (v. 34, author trans.), means that Aaron performed these instructions immediately, there is a temporal problem. This date does not fall within the month between the erection of the Tabernacle (Exod 40:2, 17) and Israel's departure from Sinai (Num 10:11)—further indication that Lev 1–16 is arranged topically rather than in narrative sequence.

The Holiness Code, 17:1–27:34

For more than a century, many scholars have identified Lev 17–26 (27) as a separate law code, usually termed "the Holiness Code." These chapters distinguish themselves by their distinctive sermonic style containing frequent self-introductions (*I am the LORD your God*), exhortations to obedience (e.g., 18:4; 19:36) and holiness (e.g., 19:2), and a preponderance of categorical (as distinct from case) laws. Such features are not unique to Lev 17–26, but they do occur here with much greater frequency than elsewhere in the Pentateuch. Recent studies have tended to dispute the unity of the Holiness Code and its separation from P (for a review of research, see Hartley 1992, 251-60).

Whatever their history, these chapters contain the rhetorical climax of Leviticus. Here religious and ethical instructions unite to describe how Israel should become holy, and thus fit for communion with a holy God. Together with the purity rules in Lev 11–15, these holiness instructions set forth standards of behavior for the whole community (see Blum 1990, 321-23). Thus the book is unified by one overarching theme: the people as well as the priests must preserve the conditions for God's residence with Israel.

Like other OT law codes, the Holiness Code begins with sacrificial regulations (Lev 17; cf. Exod 20:22-26, Deut 12). The main body of the code is in three parts: the first consists of laws governing sexual relationships (Lev 18, 20) surrounding a miscellany of ethical and ritual rules (chap. 19); the second contains priestly instructions (chaps. 21–22); and the third consists of calendar instructions (chaps. 23, 25) surrounding another miscellaneous collection (chap. 24). The code climaxes in chap. 26 with a series of blessings and curses that spell out the consequences of Israel's obedience or disobedience (cf. Deut 27–28). The book concludes with an appendix on vows and tithes (chap. 27).

Rules for Sacrifice and Slaughter, 17:1-16

The theme of blood unites the sacrificial and dietary regulations in Lev 17. Blood represents life (vv. 11, 14) and belongs to God. Therefore blood may not be eaten but must be given back to God through sacrifice.

17:3-9. Location of slaughter and sacrifice. Concerns about idolatry (v. 7) motivate these restrictions on the location of slaughter (vv. 1-7) and sacrifice (vv. 8-9). Animals suitable for sacrifice (*an ox or a lamb or a goat* v. 3; cf. v. 13 on game animals and birds) must be offered as sacrifices at Yahweh's sanctuary. Verse 4 equates slaughter apart from a proper sacrifice with murder! (On the penalty of being *cut off*, see above on 7:20.)

These rules conflict with Lev 1–4 and 22:18-25, which prohibit blemished animals from the altar although they are apparently edible, and with Deut 12:15-27, which permits nonsacrificial slaughter for food. Some commentators therefore interpret vv. 3-7 as referring only to sacrifice, not to profane slaughter. But these verses do not make that distinction, identifying all slaughter outside the Tabernacle as idolatrous sacrifices. Ancient Israelites apparently held various views on slaughter, which these discrepancies reflect (see SACRIFICE).

17:10-16. No consumption of blood. Prohibitions on eating blood appear seven times in the Pentateuch, four of those in Leviticus. Only v. 11, however, connects the blood prohibition with blood sacrifice. Leviticus identifies blood with life, so offering blood means offering the animal's life for the sake of human life (see BLOOD IN THE OT; LIFE IN THE OT; Hartley 1992, 273–77). The law reserves blood exclusively for this atoning role. The blood of nonsacrificial edible animals must be poured out on the ground (v. 13). Since animals dead of natural causes have not been properly drained of blood, eating them conveys temporary impurity (vv. 15-16).

Sexual Relationships, 18:1-30

Leviticus 18 lists prohibited sexual acts (vv. 6-23) surrounded by warnings against imitating the practices of Canaanites. The punishments for breaking these laws appear in chap. 20.

18:2-5, 24-30. Avoidance of Canaanite practices. Some ancient religions used ritual sex in attempts to ensure fertility for humans, livestock, and land. The OT, however, strips sexuality of any religious connotations, restricting it entirely to the secular realm. Leviticus 18 emphasizes this difference by explaining the Canaanites' expulsion from the land as punishment for their sexual practices, and threatening Israel with a similar fate if it imitates them (vv. 24-30).

18:6-18. Incest taboos. These examples of prohibited relations all derive from the general principle: *none of you shall approach anyone near of kin to uncover nakedness* (v. 6). The phrase *uncover nakedness* refers to sexual intercourse whether within marriage or apart from it. The speech addresses male heads of households, implicitly enjoining them not only to observe but also to enforce these laws.

18:19-23. Five offenses. Four of these prohibitions clearly concern sexual practices: intercourse with a menstruating woman, adultery, homosexual intercourse (see ADULTERY IN THE OT; HOMOSEXUALITY IN THE BIBLE), and bestiality. Menstrual blood conveys impurity (see above on 15:19-24). The other three kinds of intercourse blur the distinctions between families, between the sexes, and between humans and animals. Leviticus strives to maintain such symbolic categories (cf. above on chap. 11) because their erosion threatens Israel's communion with God. On the prohibition of MOLECH sacrifice (v. 21), see below on 20:2-5.

Rules for Holy Living, 19:1-37

Leviticus 19 contains a collection of brief commandments and longer instructions that in style and themes resemble the contents of the TEN COMMANDMENTS (Exod 20:2-17; Deut 5:6-21). As in every other OT law code religious concerns permeate the chapter, from observance of SABBATH (vv. 3, 30) and prohibitions on IDOLATRY (v. 4) through SACRIFICE regulations (vv. 5-8, 21-22; see above on chaps. 3, 5) and prohibitions on mixing animals, grain, or cloth (it blurs symbolic categories, v. 19; cf. above on chap. 11) to injunctions against ritual acts associated with Canaanite religions (vv. 26-28, 31), particularly rituals for the dead. MOURNING RITES could include shaving hair and gashing skin (Lev 21:5; Jer 7:29; 16:6), actions that may also have played a role in divination with ancestor spirits. The OT prohibits all MAGIC AND DIVINATION, because Yahweh is God (v. 28); turning for advice or help to any other spirit is idolatry.

Concern for justice also permeates Lev 19, ranging from judicial issues such as theft, fraud, perjury, and impartiality in judgment (vv. 11-13, 15-16) through honest business practices (vv. 35-36) to issues of social justice, such as prompt payment of wages (v. 13) and respect for the disabled (v. 14) and the elderly (v. 32). Through these specific examples, the chapter illustrates the central claim of justice: one standard should apply to all.

Leviticus 19, however, balances the impartiality of justice with the partiality of love. General commandments to love both the neighbor and the stranger as oneself (vv. 18, 34) are made concrete by orders to revere one's parents (v. 3), to make provision for the poor (vv. 9-10), to correct but not hate or take vengeance on a neighbor (vv. 17-18), and to treat aliens like citizens (vv. 33-34). The protection of women suggested by the injunction against forcing a daughter into prostitution (v. 29) and by the guilt offering required from men who had sex with a betrothed slave (vv. 20-22) seems minimal by current standards of morality. But in the patriarchal culture that Israel shared with all its neighbors, any limits placed on men's arbitrary power over women are welcome. The power of biblical ethics derives from the hope that the general love commandment (vv. 18, 34) will continually find expression in better concrete instructions.

Penalties for Religious and Sexual Sins, 20:1-27

The penalties prescribed in this chapter for religious and sexual offenses are extremely severe. By modern standards, only child sacrifice might qualify as a capital offense. Leviticus, however, views religious and sexual misconduct as a threat not only to the social order but also to Israel's tenure in the land (v. 22). Thus severe penalties on individuals protect the community from divine punishment.

20:2-6. Molech sacrifice and divination. Interpreters disagree on the identity of MOLECH. *Molech* was probably not the name of a god, but rather a term for child sacrifice. Genesis 22:1-14 and Judg 11:29-40 show that sacrificing children to Yahweh was not unknown

in Israel. In attacking this practice, however, Lev 18:21 and 20:2-5 turn Molech into a proper name and thus characterize the practice as idolatry. A play on the Hebrew word זרע, which means both "semen" (in the phrase translated *sexual relations* in 18:20) and *offspring* (vv. 2-4; 18:21), and the equation of idolatry with *prostituting themselves* (vv. 5, 6) probably accounts for the appearance of this prohibition in the context of sexual taboos. On *mediums and wizards* (20:6, 27), see above on 19:31.

20:9-21. Sexual offenses. The appearance of a penalty for cursing parents (v. 9) at the beginning of a list of sexual offenses indicates that the writers saw both as threatening a family's integrity. The community punishes capital offenses (vv. 9-16). Other penalties (*subject to punishment, cut off, die childless* in vv. 17-21) can be exacted only by God. From ancient Israel's perspective, the latter are probably no more lenient than the former.

20:7-8, 22-26. Motivation. Because Yahweh is Israel's God, the people must be holy. God sanctifies the people, but Israel must protect that holy status from defilement (vv. 7-8). Otherwise, history will repeat itself and the land will *vomit you out* (v. 22), as it did the Canaanites. Verses 24-26 contain the motivation for the entire priestly system: because God separated Israel from the nations, Israel must separate itself to be holy to God. All the laws of Lev 11-27 are dedicated to this end.

Rules for Priests, 21:1–22:33

Chapters 21–22 instruct the priests (21:1, 17; 22:2) regarding personal conduct and their acceptance of sacrificial animals. But the people also hear the instructions (21:8, 24; 22:18) so that they understand the priests' limitations and privileges. People and priests share the responsibility to sanctify God *among the people of Israel*, for God has sanctified them (22:32).

21:1-15. Protecting priests from impurity. Since priests come into regular contact with a holy sanctuary and holy sacrifices, they must observe special restrictions. The *anointed* high priest (v. 10), who enters the holiest areas of the Tabernacle (Lev 16), has even more restrictions placed on his activities.

Contact with corpses makes one unclean (Num 19:11). Therefore priests must avoid funerals except for close family members. (On the mourning customs prohibited in v. 5, see above on Lev 19.) Injunctions against priests marrying prostitutes (vv. 7, 14) and having daughters who are prostitutes attack the practice of sacred prostitution (see WOMEN IN THE OT; and above on 18:2-5) by arguing that, far from sanctifying the participants, such practices defile them (v. 9). The other restrictions on who priests, and especially the high priest, can marry probably involve concerns over succession to the priesthood: since the office is hereditary, care is necessary to ensure a legitimate heir.

21:16-23. Priests with physical anomalies. Physical impairments or anomalies disqualify priests from service in the sanctuary, just as "blemished" animals cannot be offered as sacrifices (22:18-25). In priestly thinking, wholeness is commensurate with holiness. Disqualification on physical grounds, however, does not make the priest unclean and therefore does not impair his livelihood (v. 22; cf. 22:4-6).

22:2-16. The priests' income. The priests' livelihood derived in part from their portion of the sacrifices (2:3, 10; 7:28-36), so it is natural that the priests' families and slaves eat them (vv. 11-13). Since the portions are holy, however, unclean persons must not touch them. Lay people (outside the priests' households) cannot infringe on the priests' rights (vv. 10, 14-16).

22:17-25. Animals with physical anomalies. Like priests (21:16-23), sacrificial animals must be *without blemish*. On the possible implications of this rule for eating blemished animals, see above on 17:3-9.

22:26-30. Three rules for sacrifices. Laws restricting slaughter involving a mother animal (or her milk) and her young (v. 28) are widespread in the Pentateuch (Exod 23:19; 34:26; Deut 14:21; 22:6) and are probably attacks on Canaanite religious practices. On eating sacrifices of well-being, see 7:15-18 and 19:5-8.

Annual Calendar, 23:1-44

Calendars of annual festivals appear five times in the Pentateuch: Exod 23:12-17; 34:18-24; Lev 23; Num 28–29; Deut 16:1-17. Exodus and Deuteronomy command Israel to observe three festivals: Unleavened Bread, Weeks, and Booths. The P writers of Leviticus and Numbers mention five, adding New Year's Day and the Day of Atonement to the other three (see FEASTS AND FESTIVALS).

23:3. Sabbath. Most of the festival calendars include commands to observe the weekly SABBATH. *Sabbath* (שבת) comes from a verb meaning "cease, rest" which aptly sums up the essence of the observance: *complete rest* (v. 3).

23:5-14. Passover. Detailed instructions for observing PASSOVER (Heb. *Pesah*) and UNLEAVENED BREAD are

contained in the Exodus story itself (Exod 12–13). Leviticus 23 focuses only on the festival's date and duration. Immediately following the feast of Unleavened Bread comes the offering of *the sheaf of the first fruits of your harvest* (v. 10). The land belongs to God, not Israel. Therefore the people cannot eat of the land's harvest until they have first offered a portion to God (v. 14).

23:15-22. Weeks. Seven weeks or fifty days later comes the festival of WEEKS (Heb. *Shavuot*; Gk. *Pentecost*, "fiftieth"), which concluded the harvest season. After the detailed instructions on offerings (vv. 17-21), v. 22 repeats almost verbatim from 19:9-10 the command to leave grain in the fields for the poor and aliens, so the produce of God's land is shared among all the people.

23:23-25. New Year's Day. The special sabbath at the beginning of the seventh month goes unnamed in vv. 23-25. From at least postexilic times, it was celebrated as New Year's Day (Heb. *Rosh Hashanah*; NEW YEAR'S FESTIVAL), despite the placing of Passover in the "beginning of months" (Exod 12:2). Ancient Israel likely had several calendars at different times, and the Talmud acknowledges four different New Year's Days in the Jewish CALENDAR (Strassfeld 1985, 96).

23:26-32. Day of Atonement. Leviticus 16 instructs the high priest how to observe the Day of Atonement (Heb. *Yom Kippur*). Here the people are told of the day's status as a *sabbath of complete rest*, threatening severe penalties for transgressors (vv. 29-30).

23:33-36, 39-43. Booths. The festival of booths or tabernacles (Heb. *Sukkot*) commemorates the wilderness wanderings of Israel's ancestors (v. 43; TABERNACLES, FESTIVAL OF). The original calendar notice about Booths (vv. 33-36) has apparently been supplemented by an appendix to the chapter (vv. 39-43) that provides more details on how the festival should be celebrated.

Miscellaneous Regulations, 24:1-23

24:2-9. Lamps and bread. The sanctuary requires regular supplies of oil and flour for the lamps and bread *before the Lord*. The instructions regarding lamp oil repeat the contents of Exod 27:20-21, but the description of the bread is more detailed than in Exodus (25:23-30; 40:23-32). Continual light represents the presence of God. The twelve loaves eaten by priests symbolize the communion of Israel's twelve tribes with their God.

24:10-23. A case of blasphemy. Aside from regular speech headings (i.e., *the LORD spoke to Moses*), this story is the only narrative in chaps. 17–27. The account is unconnected with the larger story of Israel in the books of Exodus through Numbers. It appears here because of its legal implications, and illustrates how case law arises out of concrete situations in Israel's life.

The offense occurs when a half-Israelite *blasphemed the Name in a curse* (v. 11). *The Name* refers to the divine name Yahweh (= LORD; see TETRAGRAMMATON and GOD, NAMES OF), whose use is restricted by the third commandment (Exod 20:7; cf. 22:28). The writers use this circumlocution to avoid any risk of reproducing the blasphemy themselves. Their restrained description of the incident obscures the exact nature of the crime.

Due to his parentage, the offender's legal status is uncertain and requires a *decision of the LORD* (v. 12). The ensuing divine speech upholds one standard of punishment for all (vv. 15-16, 22), so the community administers the death penalty (v. 23; on capital punishment, see above on Lev 20). The speech also advances the law of RETALIATION (*lex talionis* vv. 17-21; cf. Exod 21:22-25; Deut 19:19) which, although irrelevant to blasphemy, emphasizes the universality of law. Punishment should be proportionate to the offense, not to the status of the offender.

Sabbath Years and Jubilee, 25:1-55

Leviticus 25 promulgates a multiyear calendar of sabbath years and weeks of years. The land and its crops should rest in the seventh "sabbath" year just as humans and animals rest on the seventh day (v. 4; cf. Exod 23:10-11). God promises a bumper crop in the sixth year large enough to last until the harvests of the ninth year (vv. 20-22). Verse 18 provides the motivation to obey the fallow law: *that you may live on the land securely*. The following chapter makes clear that either Israel will allow the land to rest or else Israel will be driven off the land, which will then rest undisturbed (26:34-35).

The fiftieth year (after *seven weeks of years* [v. 8], i.e., forty-nine) is a year of release for debts, slaves, and land. The three topics are related, for in the ancient Near East, indebtedness was usually the reason for selling both one's land and oneself. (On the name *Jubilee*, see JUBILEE, YEAR OF.) The laws described in Lev 25 would have a revolutionary impact on Israel's economy: ownership of land and slaves can be transferred only temporarily and then is subject to redemption by relatives (vv. 25-33, 48-52; Ruth 4:4-6; Jer

32:6-8), prices must be set with reference to the coming Jubilee (vv. 14-17; 27:16-25), and capital cannot be accumulated because lending at interest is prohibited (vv. 35-37; Exod 22:25-27). The chapter's overriding concern is for the poor and their treatment: *you shall support them* (v. 35). This legislation prevents poverty from having permanent effects and preserves the ideal of all Israelites as God's tenants on the land (vv. 23, 38, 55).

There is, however, little evidence that Jubilee was ever more than an ideal in Israel. There is no mention of its observance in the OT, and even sabbath years seem to have been ignored in the preexilic period (2 Chr 36:21). Furthermore, Deut 15:1-18 contradicts Jubilee legislation by providing for release for debts and slaves every *seventh* year, but also for voluntary permanent slavery. Thus concern to protect the equality of Israelites before God and each other seems to have given rise to several legislative programs, but reality rarely lived up to them. The ideals of Jubilee nevertheless inspired prophetic hopes for "the year of the LORD's favor" (Isa 61:1-3).

Blessings and Curses, 26:1-46

The conclusions of ancient Near Eastern law codes and treaties usually contain lists of blessings and curses (see COVENANT; CURSE AND BLESSING), which make the consequences of obedience and disobedience clear. Such lists conclude OT law codes for the same reason (Exod 23:23-33; Lev 26; Deut 28).

26:1-2. Idolatry, sabbath, and sanctuary. This summary of the most prominent religious commands reminds readers what kind of *statutes and commandments* (v. 3) the blessings and curses presuppose. These three stipulations symbolize the whole priestly law.

26:3-13. Blessings. Prosperity (vv. 4-5, 10), security (vv. 6-8), and growth (v. 9) await those who keep the covenant stipulations. Most of all, God will live with Israel (vv. 11-12). The statement, *I will walk among you*, describes a divine-human relationship closer than any since primordial times, when God walked in the garden (Gen 3:8) and Enoch and Noah "walked with God" (Gen 5:22-24; 6:9; Blum 1990, 326). All the regulations of Leviticus aim towards this goal: recreation of the communion intended by God from the beginning.

26:14-39. Curses. Disobedience, however, will result in God's enmity. Drought, war, and plague will ravage the land and ultimately the people will be conquered and scattered "among the nations" (v. 33). There they will still be harassed by enemies (vv. 36-39). A reversal of the previous description of close communion emphasizes God's enmity: rather than *walk among you* (v. 12), God will now "walk contrary to you" (vv. 24, 28, 41, author trans.; NRSV *continue hostile*).

26:40-45. Reconciliation in exile. The exiles' confession and repentance (v. 40) will cause God to *remember in their favor the covenant* (v. 45). Remarkably, Lev 26 does not predict a return to the land. It rather emphasizes that, despite the loss of the land, Israel's covenant with God remains in force (v. 44). The result, for readers of the Pentateuch in the postexilic community, is that Leviticus identifies them with the wilderness generation with whom God made the covenant. It reminds them that the divine-human community described in this book was first experienced *outside* the land in the wilderness, and that God will preserve that covenant community regardless of location. Thus Leviticus incorporates the people's historical successes and failures, summed up in the blessings and curses, into a broader vision of God's perpetual faithfulness to Israel.

Appendix on Vows and Tithes, 27:1-34

Chapter 26 forms the rhetorical and theological conclusion to Leviticus, as the summary in 26:46 shows. The additional case laws in chap. 27 therefore come as a surprise. Verses 17-24, however, presuppose the Jubilee legislation of Lev 25, so the arrangement may owe more to legal logic than to literary considerations.

27:1-25. Assessments. Israelites consecrated people, animals, or land to Yahweh as gifts or to fulfill vows. Clean animals were sacrificed (vv. 9-10); the rest must be assessed and the equivalent paid in silver or gold (v. 25). (For earlier practices of dedicating humans to temple service or even sacrifice, see 1 Sam 1 and Judg 11:29-40.) The Jubilee year would complicate the assessment of land values (vv. 17-24; 25:13-17).

27:26-33. Exceptions. Certain people, animals, and crops already belong to God, and therefore cannot be replaced or redeemed by cash payments. The first offspring born to animals or humans belongs to God (Exod 13:2; 34:19-20), as does one-tenth (a "tithe") of the agricultural produce: clean animals must be sacrificed, the rest may be redeemed at 120% of their value (vv. 26-27, 30-33). People and property may also be *devoted to destruction* (vv. 28-29) as spoils of holy war (Josh 6:17-21) or as punishment for idolatry (Exod 22:20). The prohibition on selling or redeeming such people or property eliminates the profit motive from holy war and judicial sentencing.

27:34. Subscript. This summary statement, along with that in 26:46, encompasses all the laws from Exod 20 through Lev 27. It locates the origins of the whole corpus on *Mount Sinai*, although Leviticus' superscription describes the setting as the Tabernacle (1:1; but cf. 7:37-38 and 25:1). Since Numbers begins with preparations for Israel's departure from Sinai, the summaries in Lev 26:46 and 27:34 may not intend to distinguish the mountain from the tent. Instead, they contrast the law given in and around Mt. Sinai with law revealed later in the wilderness journey (Numbers and Deuteronomy).

Works Cited

Blum, Erhard. 1990. *Studien zur Komposition des Pentateuch.* BZAW 189.

Carroll, Michael P. 1985 (1978). "One More Time: Leviticus Revisited." *Anthropological Approaches to the Old Testament,* ed. B. Lang, 117–26.

Damrosch, David. 1987. "Leviticus." *The Literary Guide to the Bible,* ed. Alter and Kermode, 66–77.

Douglas, Mary. 1985 (1966). "The Abominations of Leviticus." *Anthropological Approaches to the Old Testament,* ed. B. Lang, 100–16.

Hartley, John E. 1992. *Leviticus.* WBC.

Kugel, James L., and Rowan A. Greer. 1986. *Early Biblical Interpretation.* LEC.

Mann, Thomas W. 1988. *The Book of Torah: the Narrative Integrity of the Pentateuch.*

Milgrom, Jacob. 1976. *Cult and Conscience.* SJLA. 1991. *Leviticus 1–16.* AncB.

Strassfeld, Michael. 1985. *The Jewish Holidays: A Guide and Commentary.*

Wenham, Gordon J. 1979. *Leviticus.* NICOT.

Wieseltier, Leon. 1987. "Leviticus." *Congregation: Contemporary Writers Read the Jewish Bible,* ed. D. Rosenberg, 27–38.

Numbers

Jack G. Partain

Introduction

The Book of Numbers stretches like a canal across a great desert, linking the narratives of the Exodus with that of the conquest of Canaan. The Book of Exodus, with its story of the LORD's great salvation of the Hebrews from Egyptian bondage—and the account of the covenant at Sinai—sets the tone for the high drama that matures in the narratives surrounding Joshua and the judges. Between those epic accounts are sandwiched the final three books of the Pentateuch. Leviticus is code or law, which has a numbing effect on the excitement that precedes it; Deuteronomy is intentionally reflective and, therefore, tends to systematize the events and interpretations of the Exodus. Nearly lost in the flow of the canon is the story of the first glimpses of the gift of a promised homeland, and the trials faced by a newborn Israel.

There is no wonder that many readers are tempted to rush through the Book of Numbers (pausing, perhaps, to enjoy the talking donkey story). Three lengthy chapters are devoted to census reports, including their fantastic totals. The story line, if one can be found, is persistently interrupted: long accounts of cultic regulations; a detailed list of offerings repeated twelve times verbatim; a description of an ordeal to expose an unfaithful wife by using water tinctured with ashes from a red heifer that had been burned; a grisly story of a zealous priest who impales on his spear an Israelite and his foreign wife; a remembrance of a day when Sheol opened up and swallowed alive a rebel and all his followers; and a report of the extermination of tens of thousands of Midianites, including women, children, and the elderly. Not, at first glance, terribly edifying reading.

Although the Book of Numbers may not be every reader's idea of religious literature, it has an important place in the Torah.

Content

The epic story that is the basic fabric of the Book of Numbers explains why the generation of Israelites who came to know Yahweh in the Exodus did not inherit the LAND God had promised them.

The Book of Numbers is set "In The Wilderness" (the Hebrew title of the book). After elaborate preparations at Mt. Sinai, including the first censuses, Israel moves toward Canaan like a great religious procession. Early complaining turns into outright rebellion when a scouting party does not give a positive report of the land Israel is to occupy. The LORD condemns the rebellious generation to wander and die in the desert. Little is said about those wanderings. Almost half the book tells of the passing of that generation and their leaders, of renewed preparations to invade Palestine, and of early successes in violently settling the east bank of the Jordan. A new generation, hardened and purified by years in the desert, stands ready for the great invasion itself.

Interspersed in this narrative are various religious plans and regulations. These materials communicate several of the priestly ideals for postexilic Israel as they reconstitute themselves the people of God, this time a holy people, with a new temple and a proper priesthood.

Structure

A glance at the suggested outline reinforces the impression that the traditions used in the Book of Numbers are diverse. Traditions from various periods in Israel's history, on a variety of topics, have been included in each section of the book by the ancient editors. The rationale for selecting and placing the various legal and cultic traditions is not easily discerned. Efforts to impose some further order on the book seem subjective. Martin Noth thought that the Mosaic tradition was used as a fabric onto which the diverse clan traditions were embroidered, giving the book its unity (1968, 4–11).

The outline is traditional, grouping the materials around three places prominent in the story: Mount Sinai, the desert (especially the oasis at Kadesh), and the Transjordan.

Authorship and Sources

Numbers is the work of priests during the Babylonian Exile. They use traditions both oral and written, from various periods of Israel's history and from diverse perspectives, giving the impression of a heterogeneous book. There is wide agreement about which materials are YAHWIST and/or ELOHIST traditions and which traditions or compositions come from the PRIEST-LY WRITERS. Over three fourths of the book may be traced to the priestly writers. Some of the poetry seems quite ancient (6:24-26; 10:35; 14:18; 21:15, 17-18). Even scholars who wish to see Mosaic compositions in the book understand Numbers, in its present form, as composite (e.g., Thompson 1970, 168).

Themes

The wilderness years that Numbers remembers were formative years in Israel's history. During that era the LORD created a people and their institutions. The creative process is recorded as less complex than it probably was. Various groups joined "Israel" in the desert, others during the invasion and settlement years. From this unpromising raw material Yahweh creates a

"holy nation" (cf. Exod 19:5-6), uniquely set apart and prepared to be his covenant society.

Some of Israel's most valued convictions are expressed in Numbers: Israel's faith and institutions are rooted in their concrete history. The LORD has chosen to bestow God's awesome Presence on and in the midst of Israel. God's Presence demands holiness of the covenant people, including uncompromising ceremonial cleanliness. Among God's gifts to the people are the land of Canaan, the law (Torah), and the Aaronite and Levitical priesthood. God's covenant loyalty to the people can be violated, but it cannot be set aside by Israel's rebellions.

All of these convictions became precious to people trying to learn the lessons of their destruction and exile, and hoping to get it right the second time around.

For Further Study

In the *Mercer Dictionary of the Bible*: ATONEMENT/EX-PIATION IN THE OT; BALAAM; CALENDAR; CONQUEST OF CANAAN; CURSE AND BLESSING; ELOHIST; HEIFER, RED; LAND; LEVI/LEVITES; MANNA; MARRIAGE IN THE OT; NUMBERS, BOOK OF; ORACLE; PRIESTLY WRITERS; PRIESTS; SOURCES OF THE PENTATEUCH; VOW IN THE OT; WEIGHTS AND MEASURES; WORSHIP IN THE OT; YAHWIST. In other sources: P. J. Budd, *Numbers*, WBC; R. de Vaux, *Ancient Israel: Its Life and Institutions*; M. Noth, *Numbers*, OTL; D. T. Olson, *The Death of the Old and the Birth of the New*.

Commentary

Preparations at Sinai to Move to Canaan, 1:1–10:10

The Book of Numbers begins where Exodus and Leviticus conclude. Israel is still camped near Sinai. Following the meeting with God and the gift of the covenant at Sinai, several kinds of preparation of the former slaves that will allow them to become the people of God have been described: the gift of the torah (instruction for covenant living), the construction of a portable sanctuary (the TABERNACLE), and the institution of Israel's religious system (the cultus), especially sacrifice (see Exod 21–40 and Leviticus).

Numbers completes the description of those preparations, beginning with a census of all able-bodied men of fighting age, and concluding with the Israelites east of the Jordan, beginning to inherit the promised LAND of Canaan.

First Census of the Tribes of Israel, 1:1-54

When readers of the Book of Numbers open the book they are in the midst of action. Like a movie-goer who comes into the theater as the projectionist begins the second reel, readers soon discover that some of the crucial events in the story have already been told.

God has rescued the Israelite people from Egypt—by means of a series of extraordinary events. Out in the Sinai desert, at "the mountain of God," the LORD was revealed to Israel and their leader, Moses. The LORD and the people have been bound together by the COVENANT. Despite eruptions of Israelite rebellion (which gave the covenant relationship an uncertain beginning), God has already shown that the divine purposes will not be deterred.

Modern readers may not be enticed by the way the Book of Numbers begins. Following the divine command to count the males able to go to war, there is a list of the twelve tribes, with the names of the headmen and their fathers; statements about the actual enrollment; a long recital of the results, tribe-by-tribe; a summary and total; and a section about the role of the Levites. The opening of the book is certainly not very exciting.

Among the several transitions that take place between the departure from Egypt and the arrival at the brink of the promised land of Canaan is Israel's transformation from a disorderly, "mixed crowd" (Exod 12:38) to an efficient fighting force. Discipline and order are the primary values that emerge during the transition narratives. If these people are to occupy Canaan they must become the army of the LORD. Thus, this census is the first in a series of preparations taken to ready the Israelites for what lies ahead—conquering Canaan and becoming a holy nation (Exod 19:5-6).

The account of the census is straightforward, but the alert reader should look for certain features of the narrative. Note the central role of Moses (along with Aaron). Moses is the sole mediator through whom Yahweh communicates with Israel. As will become obvious later, the leadership responsibility Moses carries is sometimes an odious burden to him, and an unacceptable centralizing of authority to others.

Moses receives the ORACLE of leadership not, as in the Book of Exodus on the holy mountain (Sinai), but in the recently assembled TENT OF MEETING. Exod 25–40 offers a detailed description of the construction of this portable shrine. Interest in the tent of meeting points to a central theme in Numbers, i.e., the presence of Yahweh among his people.

The Book of Numbers assumes a kind of idealized socio-political structure, even during these beginning months in the desert: all of Israel is united as a religious community made up of tribes (*the whole congregation*, v. 2), which are made up of *clans*, which are made up of *ancestral houses* (i.e., extended, patriarchal families), which are made up of individuals (with males being the ones of significance). We cannot be sure what some of the terms used referred to; meanings probably changed with time. Some terms seem to be interchangeable in this passage (v. 16).

With the list of tribes (vv. 5-15, repeated with variations in vv. 20-43) compare other lists in the OT (Judg 5; Deut 33; Gen 49; and esp. Num 26:5-50). The differences between the lists suggest that the groups themselves changed, with various tribes coming to prominence, dividing, and/or blending with others. The twelve-fold structure, however, remained the ideal through Israel's history. In this list the tribe of Levi is counted separately, as are the "Joseph tribes" (i.e., Ephraim and Manasseh, vv. 32-35).

The carefully done census reports 603,550 Israelite males, twenty years old or older, able to go to war. At the least that suggests a total population of over two million! The figure in chap. 26 is only slightly less— after thirty-eight years of desert ravages.

What is one to make of such huge numbers? Because it would take far more than the miracles of MANNA, quail, and water for two million people to live in the Sinai desert, some dismiss the totals as a fiction. The common explanation looks for another meaning for the term translated *thousand* (*eleph*). What is referred to, the explanation goes, is a small military (perhaps tribal) unit of varying size. Thus, for example, the census of Gad reports forty-five *eleph*, a total of about 650 men (assuming fourteen to fifteen men in an *eleph*).

If this explanation fits this census, the priestly editor did not know it. And the explanation misses the point (in Numbers and in Exod 12:37). God has kept his promise. He has multiplied Abraham's seed as the sand on the shore. And he can provide for this great people in a barren place. The picture of such a great host will add bleak irony to the unfavorable report brought back by the majority of those sent to spy out Canaan for invasion in chap. 13.

The Levites do not have a military role, so they are counted separately (cf. 3:1-4). They are charged with guarding, caring for, and transporting the portable shrine (*tabernacle of the covenant*, v. 50). They also prevent other non-levitical Israelites (*outsiders*, v. 51) from coming into contact with the dangerous, Holy Presence at the tabernacle. More on the Levites' duties is found in 3:21–4:49.

The Sacred Camp, 2:1-34

Following the census, we read of Israel's camp layout and order of march, organized like a solemn assembly (cf. Lev 23:33-36). The camp resembles a square, with a lead tribe on each side, with other tribes flanking the lead tribe left and right or before and behind, and with the Levites sheltering the tent of the Presence in the center.

The description reads as though it had been generated by a computer, but it is intended to convey a stirring picture of Israel at its best. Everyone is in perfect order, as God has instructed. God's Presence is at the very center of life. The holiness that characterizes God's Presence is carefully guarded. God's rule and Israel's submission to it foster solidarity among what would otherwise be a loose conglomeration of people. This formation portrays an obedient theocracy. *The Israelites did just as the LORD had commanded* (v. 34, cf. Ezek 48). The atmosphere crackles with expectation, and provides sharp contrasts with the complaints and revolts that follow.

This chapter locates *the tent of meeting*, along with *the camp of the Levites*, in *the center* of the gathered people (v. 17). In another tradition the tent of meeting was outside the camp (Exod 33:7-11). The discrepancy is beyond explanation.

Judah has the favored position (to the east, facing the entrance to the tent) and leads, a different position than that described in Gen 25:22-26. One of the Joseph tribes, Ephraim, also leads. These positions may reflect the prominence that these tribes came to have later in Israel's history.

Census and Duties of Priests and Levites, 3:1–4:49

When the first census was taken (chap. 1), the tribe of Levi was not included. Rather, the Levites were separated from the other tribes for roles related to the tabernacle (1:48-53). Those roles now are made more explicit.

3:1-4. The house of Aaron. With the formula *this is the lineage* (v. 1) the priestly writer signals that Israel's story has reached a new, significant stage. The installation of Aaron and the Levites is especially important. Aaron and his sons are *anointed priests, ordained* (3:3) to perform the various services at the *tent of meeting* (3:7), especially to offer the various sacrifices. Other Levites are *set . . . before Aaron* to serve as the priests' assistants.

3:5-39. Establishing the Levites. Yahweh instructs that the Levites now be counted (*enrolled*, v. 14). Whereas Israel was counted by tribes, Levi is to be counted by clans. Four different clusters of clans have four places in the march and camp, parallel with the four groups of tribes. Moses and Aaron, and Aaron's family have the place of honor, *in front of the tabernacle on the east* (v. 38). They also have the most sacred duties, the *rites within the sanctuary* (v. 38). The sons of Gershon have responsibility for the tabernacle, the screens, and similar furnishings (3:25-26). The sons of Kohath (i.e., the Amramite, Izharite and Hebronite clans) are entrusted with the most holy responsibility. They are in charge of the sacred equipment, *the most holy things* (4:4)—after the Aaronite priests properly stow it (v. 31; 4:5-15). The Merari clans have the least sacred task; they are responsible for the framework of the tabernacle. The census for Levi is smaller than for the other tribes, 22,000 (v. 39). Various explanations have been given for the fact that the three groups, descendants of Gershon, Kohath, and Merari, total 22,300.

3:40-51. Numbering the firstborn males. A third census is ordered to determine the number of *firstborn males of the Israelites* (v. 40). The figure arrived at, 22,273, is not easy to reconcile with a total male population over the age of thirty, given as 603,550 (cf. 1:46). Following God's great rescue in Egypt, all Israelite firstborn males were to be dedicated to the LORD. But since child sacrifice was unacceptable, the members of Levi become *substitutes* for the firstborn males (3:12, 41), one for one. For the 273 firstborn males with no Levitical substitute, money is paid (*the price of redemption*, v. 46). The counting (and substituting) of the firstborn underscores the conviction that the Levites represent all Israel in their service to God, and God to Israel.

4:1-49. Numbering the Kohathites, Gershonites, and Merarites. Three clans are set aside for service *relating to the tent of meeting* (vv. 4, 23, 30). Each of these three clans trace their lineage as *sons of Levi* (3:17). This section of the narrative provides details of the specific functions of the levitical servants in the tent of meeting.

The history of Israel's priesthood, and of the Levitical roles in particular, is complicated. After the reforms of JOSIAH in the late seventh century, and before the Babylonian Exile, the Levites saw their roles sharply curtailed (Ezek 44:10-14). What we read in Numbers seems to give expression to the ideals that animated many who shaped Judaism after the Second Temple (late sixth century and following).

Miscellaneous Laws and Observances, 5:1–8:26

Having described certain institutional or structural innovations Israel needed in order to live as the people of God (at the beginning, or during the new Exodus, which followed the Exile), the writer of Numbers lays out procedures that help insure that Israel is, at all times, a "holy nation" (Exod 19:6).

The material must be read with a lively historical and religious imagination. Basic themes (e.g., "holy," "unclean," "pure," "death," "blessing," "oath/vow," "sacrifice," "name") must be grasped and kept in mind.

The Israelite camp has been ordered in such a way that the divine Presence can take up residence in its midst. If the divine Presence resides in the midst of the camp, it is a dangerous place. Precautions must be taken to keep the camp morally and ceremonially clean.

5:1-4. Ceremonial cleanliness. Persons with skin eruptions or unusual bodily discharges are considered ceremonially unclean. Those contaminated by death, i.e., having had contact with a corpse, similarly are unholy. All such contaminations and contact are considered infected and must, therefore, be isolated—put out of the community. The reason? Because "the LORD *dwell(s) among* Israel," v. 4. Some interpreters suggest that the rationale is good community hygiene, but there is not a hint of that motive in these passages.

Leprosy probably refers to a variety of skin diseases, including but not limited to Hansen's disease.

Death is referred to as almost a substance that can contaminate a person who touches or gets close to it.

5:5-10. Broken relationships. Wrongs against fellow Israelites also disrupt relationships. In Israel, the covenant society, sins against others not only violate community; they *break . . . faith with* Yahweh. God will not tent in a community where interpersonal conflicts are left unresolved.

The provisions for restitution and reconciliation between persons set out in Lev 19 and 25 are supplemented here to include cases in which there is no *go'el* (*next of kin* advocate, v. 8).

5:11-31. Instances of adultery. Cases in which adultery is suspected (without evidence) are dealt with in a way that seems strange to many moderns. If a jealous husband suspects his wife, she is put through a ceremonial ordeal. In Israelite society wives could not accuse their husbands of adultery. Sexual intercourse with another woman was considered adultery only if the other woman was married. The accused wife (implied to be pregnant) is taken to a priest who will take her *before the LORD*, in the Holy Presence. There she will be required to drink sacred water, tinctured with dust from the sanctuary and ink from an oath. If she is innocent, nothing will happen to her; if guilty, she will suffer dropsy (?) and become infertile (or have a miscarriage).

If this seems chauvinistic—and plainly it is—the reader should remember that in most trials by ordeal the presumption is that the accused is guilty.

The ordeal is tinged with connotations of magic. Superstitious Israelites would be trapped by the ordeal, if they felt guilty. *The water of bitterness* is believed to be *the water that brings the curse* and *cause(s) bitter pain* (v. 24). But the priestly writer sees Yahweh acting by means of this ordeal. It is God who *makes your uterus drop* (v. 21).

Conflicts in a marriage are not merely a private domestic matter. Festering relationships are to be dealt with, even when there are no witnesses nor any evidence. Such disruptions, unresolved, foul community. Yahweh will not dwell where such things are ignored. The ordeal presses the LORD himself to clear the wife of guilt and forces the husband to stop his accusations . . . or vice versa.

6:1-21. Regulating the Nazirites. From time to time readers of the Bible encounter stories of men and women who have taken *the vow of a Nazirite* (v. 2). Samson is the best-known example—even though his mother made the VOW (Judg 13); Samuel is also

described as being under a Nazirite vow made by Hannah (1 Sam 1:22). This section provides the fullest details in the Bible of what a Nazirite vow involved. NAZIRITES were to separate themselves from others in the community, were expected to renew their vow if they became contaminated, and had rituals to perform once their vow had been fulfilled.

Nazirites gave themselves (or were given) to God. As a mark of their separateness, they were to abstain from wine and all intoxicants, from cutting the hair on their head, and from any contact with dead bodies. No reason is given for this choice of prohibitions. Persons under the vow who accidentally violate it—by having contact with a *corpse*, for example—were provided ways to renew the vow (vv. 9-12). In a similar way, a series of offerings and symbolic debriefing actions (e.g., shaving the head and burning the hair) are prescribed for the time when the vow has been fulfilled.

6:22-27. The Aaronite Blessing. The Aaronite Blessing is perhaps the best known text in the Book of Numbers. The blessing is poetry-like. The three lines have parallel structures, made up of three words, five words, and seven words. Many think the blessing is very ancient. The words are both a prayer for God's favor (may [understood] *the LORD bless . . .*) and a declaration that God does bless his people (*The LORD bless you . . .*). The pronoun *you* is singular.

7:1-88. Offerings from the tribes. This chapter is the longest in the Bible; some would also identify it as the most tedious. The account begins with the tribes' representatives providing transport for the tabernacle, *six covered wagons* (carts) with two oxen to pull each (v. 3). No transport is provided *the Kohathites* because they are to carry the most sacred objects (*the holy things*) *on the shoulders* (v. 9).

Verses 12-83 record a procession of tribal leaders as each presents his tribe's offering for *the dedication of the altar* (vv. 10-11), one-a-day, for twelve successive days, including even the SABBATH. All twelve offerings are exactly the same. Every detail is recounted twelve times. The effect on the modern reader is numbing; the intended effect is probably an emphasis on Israel's unanimous and lavish offering to service at the tent, laid on with meticulous care. Such mundane commitment to the priesthood and to the service at the tabernacle is an essential ingredient in Israel's preparation to be the people of God.

The account climaxes with an inventory of all that was given (vv. 84-88). The offerings are to be used in worship events and include supplies for incense and grain offerings, as well as for the burnt offerings, the sin offerings, and the well-being offerings.

The order in which the leaders present themselves differs from place to place in Numbers. A descendant of Judah leads the list here, whereas descendants of Reuben lead lists elsewhere in the book (1:5, 20; 26:5). When the encampments and the marches are mentioned, Judah leads the list (2:3; 10:14).

7:89. The LORD speaks to Moses. Once the tabernacle was properly prepared and provided for, it becomes the place where Moses goes to hear *the voice speaking to him*, i.e., where Moses receives oracles. The promise of Exod 25:22 is now realized. God speaks to his people plainly and personally. The lesson is transparent: when God's people generously support the cultus, God communicates freely with them.

The *ark of the covenant* becomes the visible symbol of Yahweh's invisible presence in the midst of his people. The LORD communicates with the people from the shrine itself, an arrangement that may stand in contrast to uncontrolled prophetic inspiration.

Sphinx-like *cherubim* were fixed to the cover of the ark, their almost-touching wings hovering over the ark. Thus, the space above the ark came to be thought of as the LORD's throne, the place where God meets with his people, *the mercy seat*.

One final task is required to put Israel's life in order before the march, i.e., setting apart the Levites themselves. Those ceremonies signal that Israel is about ready to move toward Canaan.

8:1-4. Objects of the cultus. The construction and placement of the menorah, the traditional *lampstand* with *seven lamps*, is an example of final, detailed touches given the preparation.

8:5-26. Rituals of cleansing. Elaborate ceremonies *cleanse* the Levites and separate them for a distinctive service. First, they are "de-sinned" (*the water of purification*, e.g., is a unique expression). *They shave their whole body* (symbolically ridding themselves of their old life) and wash their clothes (cf. the rituals surrounding the consecration of priests in Lev 8).

With offerings for ceremonial uncleanliness in hand, the Levites are presented in front of the tabernacle. The community itself *lay their hands on the Levites* (v. 10), designating them as representative of the entire congregation. Israel serves at the shrine vicariously through the Levites. They are presented, as it were, as Israel's *elevation offering* (vv. 13, 15). They belong to God, as substitutes for *the firstborn* (v. 16; cf. 3:44–51), and they protect Israel from the

Presence and the sacred objects in the tent of the Presence. They act as a protection, an *atonement* (v. 12), so that *there may be no plague* (v. 19).

Clearly, the Levites are being described in ways that distinguish them from Aaronite priests (cf. the consecration of priests in Lev 8). They have an important, sacred role. They are near to the people, but distinct from them. They are given to God, and he in turn gives them as *a gift to Aaron* (v. 19). Thus, their service to Israel and to God is equated with their *attendance on Aaron and his* descendants (v. 22).

Levites are only expected to serve at the tent of meeting between their twenty-fifth and fiftieth years (vv. 24-25). See the related commentary above at 4:3.

Final Preparations, 9:1–10:10

The essentials for constituting an Israel that is the LORD's holy nation, obedient in all matters to the God present in their midst, have now been described. Before Israel breaks camp at Sinai and heads for the LAND God has promised, the reader is told of three matters that anticipate their journey.

9:1-14. A Passover. Prior to the beginning of the journey Israel is instructed to observe a second PASSOVER, just as they had a year earlier on the night before they set out from Egypt. The date given for the Passover is one month earlier than the date given for developments described in chaps. 1–8 (esp. 1:1).

The festival of Passover reenacted the formative events in Israel's history. It was essential for their corporate identity. Everyone was to participate every year, without exception. The instructions recounted in Exod 12 are here presupposed.

Two specific excuses for nonparticipation are dealt with: one that could arise anywhere—ceremonial uncleanness; another that would arise once Israel was living in Palestine or the diaspora—being on a journey. Neither circumstance is a valid excuse. Provision is made for an alternate celebration a month late. Arrangements are to be made even for resident foreigners (*aliens*, v. 14) who wish to participate.

To underscore the indispensability of the Passover observance, Moses is instructed to ostracize, *cut off from the people* (execute?), anyone who did not participate.

9:15-23. The Cloud. Previous priestly themes, God's constant guidance of and the LORD's awesome Presence with the people, are here blended. The symbol of the LORD's guidance from Egypt to Sinai, a column of fire or cloud, here becomes a cloud that covered the tabernacle or an appearance of fire (v. 15), a powerful symbol of God's residence in the middle of the camp.

The emphasis is upon God's daily guidance and Israel's unfailing response—no matter how unpredictable that guidance might seem to be. The description anticipates the ways the LORD will lead Israel in the days ahead.

10:1-10. Trumpets. The instruction to shape *two silver trumpets* (v. 2) leads to a description of the community called to action by them. The trumpeters call the entire community or its leaders to an assembly at the tent's *entrance* (v. 3); they sound an alarm in time of war; and they herald great cultic occasions. Thus the LORD's rule in Israel is communicated in the concrete action of the priest-trumpeters.

The trumpets were probably straight tubes, flared at the end; not to be confused with the *shophar*, a ram's horn. Such trumpets came into common use in the Second Temple.

Days in the Desert, 10:11–21:20

Israel's story now enters a new, decisive phase, as does the Book of Numbers. Yahweh has made a covenant with Israel at Sinai. After initial disorder and rebellion the life of an orderly, obedient covenant community has been described—sometimes in meticulous detail. All is ready. At last the march toward the land promised begins.

Israel on the March to Canaan, 10:11-36

10:11-24. On the move. Eleven months after arriving at Sinai and nineteen days after the census of the tribes, Israel moves. The signal to break camp is the lifting of *the cloud from over the tabernacle* (v. 11), the cloud being a symbol of the presence of the LORD. In a different way this is described as *the command of* Yahweh *by Moses* (v. 13). Perhaps the trumpets also sounded as a signal of the command.

The description conveys a sense of large-scale but disciplined activity, as, stage by stage, according to plan, the tribes move out. The emphasis on *the tabernacle* (v. 17), the placement of the *holy things* (v. 21) at the very center, and the leadership by *the ark* (vv. 33-36), all suggest a great liturgical procession—a holy nation off on a mission.

The configuration of the camp required in chap. 2 is here adapted to a march. The Gershonites and the Merarites go ahead of the Kohathites so that the tent

will already be set up when the furniture and the ark arrive. The exact location of *the wilderness of Paran* (v. 12) in the Sinai peninsula is uncertain.

10:25-36. Offer to Hobab. The traditions dealing with Hobab and with the ark are usually considered to be quite old, probably part of the YAHWIST epic (last used by the PRIESTLY WRITERS in Exod 34).

Notice that each of these memories (v. 29 and v. 33) begin with the day of departure from Sinai and differ somewhat from the priestly version (e.g., *the ark* is some distance out in front of the march).

The point of Moses' request (*serve as eyes for us*, v. 31) is clear. This Kenite, Hobab, who presumably knows the desert and its hostile peoples, is asked to scout for Israel en route. He refuses, but seems to go anyway. *So they set out* . . . (v. 33).

That the passage, along with other passages (e.g., Judg 1:16; 4:11; 4:17), points to a close association of Kenites with Israelites during the years of the settlement seems clear. There may be a hint of a treaty.

But what is Hobab's relation to Moses? Assuming that JETHRO and Reuel refer to the same person in different traditions, the NRSV solves the riddle by taking *Moses' father-in-law* (v. 29) to refer to Reuel. But the phrase can also refer to Hobab, as in Judg 1:16, 4:11. And it may be translated "kinsman by marriage." Hobab/Jethro/Reuel is called both a *Midianite* (v. 29; cf. Exod 2:16, 18) and a *Kenite* (Judg 1:16; 4:11), groups closely associated in the OT.

Hobab's role as desert guide is not emphasized; guidance by the Presence is (vv. 33-34). The LORD's guidance is represented by *the ark of the covenant*, which is out ahead of the march (v. 33) rather than enclosed in the middle of the march (v. 21). *The cloud* of the Presence, which led Israel to Sinai and which seems to lead in 9:15-23, hovers over the march. The LORD both leads and stays with his people.

The Yahwist calls Mount Sinai the *mount of the LORD* (i.e., "the mount of Yahweh," v. 33), which is an unusual phrase ("mountain of God" in Exod 3:1).

Can the text mean that the ark traveled ahead *three days' journey* (v. 33)? The ancient Syriac version reads "one day's journey." Many think the phrase is a mistaken repetition and should be omitted.

The so-called "song of the ark" (vv. 35-36) contains lines of very ancient poetry. As quoted, it may reflect liturgical use in the Second Temple. But the song echoes a day when the LORD was thought to be enthroned on the ark and when the ark was carried into Israel's holy war battles (Josh 3–4, 1 Sam 4).

On the Way to Kadesh: Complaining, 11:1–12:16

The trek across Sinai did not go as intended. Once away from the holy mountain, the well-ordered, obedient people of God begin to complain and rebel. The abrupt change in Israel's response characterizes this entire period: one rebellion after another.

11:1-3. Murmerings. The journey has hardly begun, when the up-beat, positive mood is shattered. The *people complained* ("murmured," KJV). This paragraph introduces the complaining motif that will characterize much of the narrative that covers the next thirty-eight years.

Israel had been only three days away from Egypt on the way to Sinai when they first began to complain (Exod 15:24). In Exodus, Israel complained about genuine problems. Moses interceded. And God provided what was needed.

But in Numbers the complaining is understood differently. The grumbling is not caused by a bona fide physical need; its root cause is unfaith. Therefore, Yahweh lashes out in judgment that threatens to destroy the rebellious Israelites. Moses intercedes on their behalf, and God relents—somewhat.

God's Presence is often portrayed as *fire* (v. 3). The account gives no hint as to what phenomena might be intended.

11:4-35. Provisions. Three juxtaposed events are related in this section: the provision of quail meat, the choice of elders to share the burden of leadership with Moses, and the place of "unofficial" prophecy.

The complaint is specific: desert food. Certain riffraff (*rabble*, v. 4) incite the complaint; but soon the outcry is heard at every door in camp (v. 10): "*This manna* stuff. . . . We can't stand *to look at* it anymore. We're wasting away. Manna, manna, manna. Why can't we have some food for a change, something tasty—with *leeks* and *onions* and *garlic*? And why can't we have some real *meat to eat*?" So the people whined.

The tradition that parallels this one (Exod 16) interprets the complaint as legitimate; in response God graciously provides quail. In this telling, the complaint is tantamount to rebellion—*You have rejected the LORD* (v. 20).

The lengthy explanation about MANNA (vv. 7-9) prompts interpreters to identify it with droplets from the fruit of the Sinai shrub, *tamarix gallica*, which "bleeds" during May and June. These explanations do not fit precisely, and may miss the point.

When God instructs Moses to *consecrate* the people in readiness for a sacred occasion and to prepare to *eat meat* (v. 18), Moses expresses reservation. *The people number six hundred thousand*, he says. *Are there enough flocks and herds . . . [or] fish in the sea* (vv. 21-22) to satisfy them? The apparent hyperbole reflects Moses' exasperation. "They will eat meat—quail meat," the LORD replies, "until it comes out of their ears." (The metaphor is more literal: *You shall eat . . . for a whole month—until it comes out of your nostrils* [vv. 19-20], i.e., until it makes you nauseous.)

So, God's response to Israel's complaint—an abundance of meat—is actually a punishment. A *wind* blows in *quails from the sea* (v. 31). The Israelites seem to be in the quails' migratory path. Exhausted, the quail either fall around the camp three feet deep (the modern equivalent of *two cubits*), or they fly so low (three feet high) that they are easily taken. The meat-starved crowd harvest them by the homer full, no one gathering less than *ten homers* (v. 32), i.e., more than sixty bushels. Gorging themselves brings on some *very great plague* (v. 33) from which people died. The plague is interpreted as an act of God's judgment.

Israel's slave mentality ("Better the securities and provisions of Egypt than the risks and responsibilities of freedom and following the LORD") foreshadows an ongoing temptation in Israel's foreign policy: looking to foreign empires, especially Egypt, to save them, instead of trusting God (Isa 7–8 [esp. 8:5-8]; Jer 27).

Into the story of Israel's complaint and the LORD's answer, the writer weaves a complaint by Moses (vv. 10-15; cf. a similar tradition about Moses' leadership in Exod 18). Israel's whining is too much for Moses. From the beginning they have complained. Having sole leadership of such a crowd is a *burden* (v. 11). After all, he informs God, they are God's people, not his. He neither conceived them, nor gave them birth, nor suckled them (an interesting analogy for God's salvation; cf. Hos 11:1-9). He cannot take it any more.

Moses' complaint is legitimate. He is instructed to bring *seventy elders* to *the tent of meeting* (v. 16). There they will be anointed with some of the same *spirit* that empowers Moses to lead. Thus they can *bear the burden of the people along with* Moses (v. 17). The *spirit* is spoken of as almost a material substance that God can divide, taking *some of* it to *put on* the elders.

Beliefs integral to Israel's "theocratic ideal" are seen as present from these earliest days. The *spirit* designated Moses as God's choice to lead Israel as

Yahweh's surrogate. When that spirit was *put on* the elders, *they prophesied*, i.e., they joined in some kind of ecstatic behavior. Two elders who had been *registered* (meaning selected to serve) but who *had not gone out to the tent* (v. 26) also experienced the phenomenon or ecstasy. JOSHUA, jealous for Moses' preeminence, urged that they be silenced (vv. 28-30).

During the days of the judges and the first two kings, such ecstatic behavior was thought to be an essential qualification to lead. ANOINTing with olive oil symbolized God's "anointing" the judge or king with the divine spirit (cf. 1 Sam 10:1-13; 19:18-24). Ecstatic demonstrations are called *prophesying* (v. 27), a reminder that Hebrew prophecy had its historic roots in groups who sometimes received their messages through ecstatic trances.

Moses' reply is classic: *Would that all* of Yahweh's *people were prophets, with his spirit on them* (v. 29). Plainly, more is intended than that all would become ecstatics. In bestowing spiritual gifts, God is not limited to certain institutions or ecclesial offices. Further, if there is to be any reality to match ideals like "the people of God," or "the kingdom of God," then *all* the people must be enabled and directed by God, not just certain leaders.

12:1-16. Controversy about Moses' leadership. In these paragraphs the uniqueness and supremacy of Moses are addressed, but not without tensions. The issue is not what it first appears to be. Miriam, Moses' elder sister, and Aaron speak out (the Heb. says "she spoke") *against Moses* because of his *Cushite* wife. The reason for Miriam's objection to the woman is not part of the story. Readers are left to speculate whether the *Cushite woman* is Zipporah (cf. Exod 2:21) or another woman. Perhaps the objection is related to her non-Israelite heritage. No reason is given. Nor does it seem that the real problem is Moses' choice of a wife.

Miriam and Aaron are really objecting—so it seems—to the singularity of Moses' role in Israel. They ask: *Has the LORD spoken only through Moses* (v. 2), suggesting the questions, "What about us? Are we not also prophets?"

In the previous leadership-related incident (11:16-30), elders were drawn into the leadership and prophetic inspiration was shared with others besides Moses. Does that not suggest that all the leaders are equally special?

The aside in v. 3 asserts that Moses is not interested in gaining an advantage over others. He is *humble*; that is, he is confident and strong enough not to be drawn into his siblings' power games (since v. 3 refers to Moses in the third person, it can hardly have been written by Moses [cf. Deut 34:10-12]).

Yahweh himself intervenes. *The three* are summoned to meet at the tent, where the *pillar of cloud* appears *at the entrance* (vv. 4-5). Yahweh's *words* contrast revelation to prophets with God's communication with Moses. Prophetic revelation is opaque and indirect. It requires interpretation, and may be ambiguous. It comes through *visions* and *dreams* (v. 6), a phrase that reflects the way prophecy was understood early in the history of Israel.

But with Moses—the communication is direct and personal (*face to face*, lit. "mouth to mouth"), unambiguous (*not in riddles*), and unique (v. 8). The anthropomorphism of the Yahwist tradition is striking. Moses is allowed to see *the form of the LORD* (v. 8; cf. Exod 33:17-23 and Gen 3:8-14 in contrast to John 1:18).

The issue behind this confrontation is, of course, authority in religion: the written revelation vs. an inward revelation, *torah* vs. prophetic messages (often understood as subjective). Or, more historically, is the test of prophecy to be Moses? Or does prophecy submit to Moses?

The rebels spark Yahweh's anger. The result is immediate. Miriam is left with *leprosy* (probably not Hansen's disease). Thus, she becomes ceremonially unclean (see 5:2). A major and privileged leader is thrust outside *the camp* (v. 15). Her disgrace is complete, as though her father had *spit in her face* (v. 14) as a child, putting a curse on her. She must be ritually cleansed. No explanation is given as to why only Miriam was punished. Moses the *humble* (v. 3) man intercedes for his sister; evidently, she is healed. After Miriam's seven days of purification, *the people set out* (v. 16) again.

Reconnaissance of Canaan, 13:1-33

All the preparations have been made. Israel's army has been numbered and organized. The cultus has been put in order. The people of God have moved to the borders, ready to occupy the LAND Yahweh has promised.

But the final step is not taken—at least, not for a long time (forty years, according to the narrative). The well-known spies' story and its aftermath tell why.

The account begins positively. The LORD himself orders reconnaissance of the land, the first military move in an invasion (Cf. the Deut 1:21-22 version). And a leader from each tribe is chosen and sent—a careful reader will note that the list of leaders is different from 1:5-16, 2:3-31, and 7:12-83.

Israel remains camped at *Kadesh*, about fifty mi. south of Beersheba, in the *Paran* desert. The charge to the spies is comprehensive: check out everything, every asset, every liability. And *be bold* (v. 20). Their reconnaissance begins in mid-late July (*season of the first ripe grapes*, v. 20) and lasts "a long time" (*forty days*, v. 25).

The scouting report betrays ambivalence. To these desert seminomads, Canaan appears attractive and fertile (*flowing with milk and honey*, v. 27). The scouts brought back fruit to show. It also appears to be formidable. The people are advanced and their towns are strongly fortified.

Despite the apparent disparities, one of the spies, CALEB, called for an immediate invasion: *We are well able to overcome it* (v. 30). But the majority dissented: *they are stronger than we* (v. 31). What appears to be a contrast between seeing Canaan realistically and seeing it through rose-colored glasses is, in fact, a contrast between faith and un-faith. The majority forget their huge numbers, all their preparations in the desert, and that they are the army of Yahweh. Their low opinion of themselves wins: up against such great people *we seemed like grasshoppers* (v. 33). The two perceptions depend on the data that faith takes into consideration, as opposed to the limited data considered by faithlessness.

The enigmatic phrase, *a land that devours its inhabitants* (v. 32), seems to suggest a barren, inhospitable place—in contrast to the tradition of fertility. References to *Anakites*, vv. 28, 33, reflect Israel's lore about a GIANT race, descendants of half-god, half-human *Nephilim* (v. 33; cf. Gen 6:1-4).

The PRIESTLY WRITERS seem to be using an ancient memory in which the spying mission included only the NEGEB, the semi-desert south of HEBRON, and southern CANAAN, centered around Hebron (cf. vv. 17, 22-24, 29). To this has been added v. 21, which enlarges the mission to include all of Canaan. *Rehob near Lebohamath* (v. 21) is far to the north.

Rebellion and Condemnation, 14:1-45

With chaps. 13 and 14 the EXODUS event (indeed the Pentateuch itself) comes to a climax. The promises to the ancestors are at the point of fulfillment. The goal toward which Israel was set free from Egypt and brought into covenant at Sinai is just over the horizon.

The task for which the preparations described in the Book of Numbers should have equipped Israel is at hand. Israel has moved to the borders of the promised land. Spies have already checked it out. This is the moment in the ancient story—the moment when Israel is to "inherit" their homeland.

What was intended to be the beginning of Israel's glory, though, turns into abject shame. The climax fizzles. What was to have been a triumphal march into Canaan collapses in confusion, recriminations, failure, and condemnation.

14:1-4. A challenge. Most of the Israelites were convinced by the *unfavorable report* (13:32) brought back by a majority of the spies. "Canaan is a wonderful place, but there is no way that we can succeed in conquering it," they decided.

The report was a final straw for the easily discouraged ex-slave Israelites. People in the camp came unglued. They *raised a loud cry* and *wept* (v. 1). And they bitterly *complained*—again. Ever the victim, they blamed their leaders for liberating them. "After all we have been through, what does it come to? Our fighters will be cut to pieces. And our *wives and little ones* (v. 3) will be taken as spoils of war."

Let us choose a leader (*captain*), *and go* back where we belong, *back to Egypt* (v. 4). "Better the routines and securities of slavery than this!" The theme of the desire to return to Egypt is a common OT metaphor for apostasy (see Deut 17:16; Hos 7:11; Isa 30:1-7; 31:1-30; Jer 2:18; Ezek 17:15).

14:5-10a. The response of Moses and Aaron. *Moses and Aaron* recognize that matters have reached a critical juncture. All that God has done for Israel is on the line. They prostrate themselves in full view of *all the assembly* (v. 5). Joshua and Caleb urgently try to talk some sense into the crowd. They *tore their clothes* (v. 6), a sign of their shock and dismay at the people's disbelief. Not only is Canaan *an exceedingly good land*, they insisted (v. 7); defeating the natives will be "a piece of cake" because *the LORD is with us*. This talk of turning back is tantamount to insurrection or mutiny against Yahweh. But the irrational mob is in no mood to listen. They threaten *to stone* (v. 10) Joshua and Caleb on the spot.

Into this near-riot scene, Yahweh dramatically appears *at the tent* (v. 10). What Israel sees of his presence is *the glory*, understood as light that protects Israel from actually seeing God. The glory is sometimes associated with the column of cloud or fire (see v. 22; 16:19; Exod 16:6-7; 40:34; Ezek 11:23); it appears during times of crisis.

14:10b-38. The LORD responds. The message that God communicates through Moses is drastic: enough is enough. Yahweh has decided to *disinherit* (v. 12) and destroy these people and start over again, this time with Moses' family alone.

The root of the LORD's problem with Israel is described in two ways: they *despise* him and *they refuse to believe* (v. 11). Both phrases name an aberration of the heart and will, not just the mind only (in the NT the Gospel of John uses the phrase "believe in" in a similar manner: e.g., 3:15-16; 6:29, 47; 14:44). In his appeal to Yahweh on Israel's behalf, Moses begs God to remember the divine reputation and nature: "What will *the nations* think when you wipe out these people, and thus seem unable to do what you set out to do? Demonstrate your *power*, instead, by dealing graciously with Israel, as *you promised*" (cf. vv. 13-17; see also Exod 32:11-14; Deut 9:26-29).

The striking confession of faith about God's nature (v. 18) is probably from Israel's early worship (cf. Exod 34:6-7; Neh 9:17; Ps 103:8; Jer 32:18; Jonah 4:2). Moses appeals to God as a covenant-keeping God. The LORD is characterized by *steadfast love* (vv. 18-19), i.e., unwavering and unshakable fidelity to his covenant. God's covenant loyalty requires patience (*slow to anger*) and *forgiveness*—not only of *iniquity* (people's perverseness), but also deliberate rebellion (*transgression*). What this nature does not require is that God shield the people from the consequences of their sin, even when those consequences play out to several generations.

Throughout the passage there is a sense of corporate sin and punishment. Yahweh agrees, once again, to forgive Israel, *just as* Moses *asked* (v. 20). But he swears an oath (*as I live*) that none of Moses' rebellious generation who have seen the LORD's *glory* and the signs he *did in Egypt and the wilderness* shall so much as *see the land* their ancestors were promised (v. 23)—only *Caleb* who had a *different spirit* (see below). With that, Yahweh orders Israel to turn back and to stay in the desert.

A priestly tradition (vv. 36-38) parallels the account of the LORD's refusal. Israel's lamenting wish (14:2) will be granted; their carcasses (lit.) will litter the desert. Everyone counted in the census (chap. 1) is condemned to a life of landlessness. They and their children will be shepherds (v. 33) or ass nomads. For *forty years* they will suffer the consequences of their whorishness (*faithlessness*, v. 33), i.e., alienation (*my displeasure*, v. 34) from the LAND and the LORD.

The spies who precipitated this turn of events bear a special condemnation. They all die of some unnamed *plague*, all except Joshua and Caleb. How quickly the ten spies died is not part of the narrative.

14:39-45. The people's response. Not unexpectedly, when *Moses told* Israel what God's new plan was, consternation broke out. It is almost as if the camp, with one voice, decided, "We did not really mean what we said. Rally round. Let's do that invasion—right now!" (v. 40).

Moses tries to warn Israel that their too-late enthusiasm and obedience are actually the same old rebellion that has been their downfall from the beginning. Any fight must conform to the rules of "holy war," that is, *the ark of the covenant*, signifying that *the LORD is . . . with* them, must head the formation (v. 42). When the attack is made, both *the ark* and *Moses* stay in the camp. The outcome is inevitable. The Amalekites and Canaanites cut Israel to pieces (cf. Deut 1:41-45).

Thus the great opportunity is aborted. History turns. Not for another generation will God's purpose be realized. And Israel will always know why the people who left Egypt with such high hopes wandered in the desert until they died.

Through hindsight this turn in events may not have been all bad. A generation arose who had not known the seductions of Egypt, who were toughened by years in the desert, who could be nurtured in the Mosaic faith—a generation more ready (perhaps) than their parents to be God's covenant people.

The reader will note in chap. 14 the editor's use of at least two traditions. The older tradition features Moses alone (e.g., vv. 10b-19) and speaks only of Caleb's survival and invasion (vv. 24-25). Many think that in this tradition only the south was spied out (13:22-33) after which a Caleb group settled there.

Cultic Laws and Regulations, 15:1-41

This priestly insertion into the account gives regulations about the quantities of flour, oil, and wine that are to accompany various animal sacrifices; about first-fruit offerings of cereal grain harvests; and about what to do about unintentional and deliberate sins, with an example of the latter.

The material illustrates how Jewish law developed in response to changing situations and needs. Most agree that this material is from the hand of priestly editors, and that it is late (as suggested by the parallels with exilic prophecy, e.g., Ezek 46). These editors are anxious to emphasize their faithfulness to the Mosaic tradition (vv. 1, 17, 22-23, 35, 37).

To the reader this passage (like 5:1–8:28) may seem an incongruous intrusion because it comes immediately after the dramatic events recounted in chap. 14. But, in fact, the introduction of these regulations is a reaffirmation of faith—faith that even though Israel had revolted against God and his covenant and rejected his offer of the land, Yahweh himself remained committed to his promises. Israel would surely *come into the land* and *inhabit* it (v. 2). They would surely have agricultural produce, cereal grains, olive oil, and wine to offer God. Only adult Israel had been defeated; the LORD had not. This passage may suggest, with Amos 5:25 and Jeremiah 7:22, that the sacrificial system did not mature until Israel became farmers.

15:1-21. Sacrifices and offerings. An *offering by fire* (v. 3) may have included those sacrifices burnt and those partially burnt and/or eaten. The vivid ANTHROPOMORPHISM, *a pleasing odor for the LORD* (vv. 3, 24), recalls a time when the effect of a sacrifice was understood more literally (cf. Gen 8:21 and the parallel in the *Gilgamesh Epic*). The phrase as it appears here merely suggests that the sacrifice is acceptable.

For each kind of animal sacrificed, a *lamb*, a goat (*ram*), or a *bull*, the amount of flour (*grain*) mixed with *oil* and the amount of *wine* (vv. 4-10) are specified. The WEIGHTS AND MEASURES mentioned can only be approximated by modern standards, e.g., *one-tenth of an ephah*≈four and one-half liters, and *one-fourth of a hin*≈one and eight-tenths liters. The regulations are to apply, without discrimination, to resident aliens as well (vv. 14-15, 26; cf. 9:14).

The *donation of the bread of the land* (v. 17) refers to cakes made from the first flour ground from the first grain harvested. As with all such offerings, this one acknowledges the LORD's ownership of the land and the farmers' dependence on God's control of the natural order. Note again the renewal of the promise inherent in the phrases, *after you come . . . and throughout your generations* (vv. 18, 21).

15:22-29. Atoning for inadvertent sins. Provisions are made both for inadvertent mistakes by the whole community or their leaders in carrying out the liturgy, and for unintended mistakes made by individuals (vv. 22-29; cf. Lev 4–5). Animal sacrifices, with the accompanying grain and drink offerings, are prescribed for *atonement* (vv. 25, 27) for each offense. The gifts

that make up the sacrifice symbolize the reconciliation (at-one-ment) taking place. Covenant relations are restored.

15:30-36. Facing willful sin. No provision is made for atoning for highhanded sins, i.e., knowing, deliberate *affronts [to] the LORD* (v. 30). *Such a person shall be utterly cut off* (v. 31), having rejected the covenant community, which was in many cases tantamount to death. To be a person was to be in community.

Verses 32-36 illustrate a sin that is an affront to the LORD, a deliberate sabbath violation. The *whole congregation* is responsible for the indictment and for the execution by stoning (cf. Exod 31:14-15; 35:2).

15:37-41. Reminders for the forgetful. The old custom of attaching *fringes* to *garments* (v. 38) served as a continuous reminder that Israelites were a people of the law. The law, in turn, was a sign that they were a separated, unique (i.e., *holy*, v. 40) people.

Lest the reader forget, the motivation for obedience to the law is clearly stated in v. 41: Israel joyfully embraces the law out of gratitude for Yahweh's gracious acts on their behalf. Yahweh is their God, not as a result of their obedience, but as a result of what God did for them during the EXODUS. When the order is reversed—when the Exodus is understood as a reward for obedience—legalism or moralism results.

Revolts of Korah and Others, 16:1-50

The reader is immediately presented with another example of high-handed sin (cf. 15:30-36). Most scholars see in this section both the combination of the YAHWIST tradition with various priestly traditions, and a blending of three memories about revolts, the first led by Korah, the second led by Dathan and Abiram, and the third led by 250 lay Reubenites. It is very difficult to determine what lies behind the canonical accounts.

What is at stake is nonetheless clear. In chap. 14 we read of Israel's rejection of God's offer of the LAND. This chapter describes certain leaders' rejection of God's appointed leaders, Moses and especially Aaron and his descendants.

16:1-40. The revolts described. On its face, the rebels' complaint seems to have merit. *All the congregation are holy* (v. 3; cf. 15:40); therefore *you have gone too far when you exalt yourselves above the assembly of the LORD* (v. 3). The protesters seem to demand a democratization of leadership in general and the priesthood in particular. The ideal of a democracy seems harmonious with the conception of Israel implicit in 11:29 as a community of prophets who have the spirit of God.

Moses accuses Korah and his fellow Levites of being discontent with their place in the hierarchy, of seeking *the [Aaronite] priesthood as well* (v. 10). Dathan, Abiram and their followers reject Moses' leadership; he has not come through on his word and "lords it over" Israel, they complain.

To these challenges to the established order, Moses proposes a test. The test will show that Yahweh, not Moses and Aaron themselves, ordained Moses and Aaron's unique and supreme places. The challengers are told to act like priests, to burn incense *before the LORD* (at the TENT OF MEETING) and see if their service is acceptable to the LORD (vv. 16-18).

When the pretenders fulfill their part of the test, making sure the whole camp is present to see, Yahweh's *glory* appears, threatening to exterminate the whole crowd on the spot. Moses' intervention saves the people but not their leaders. To prove which side of the contention he is on, *the LORD creates* a creation (lit.), i.e., a singular disaster. The *ground opens its mouth and swallows them up* (v. 30). Korah, Dathan, Abiram, and their households, and all that they own fall down *alive into Sheol* (v. 33), the realm of the dead under the earth. The 250 would-be priests are consumed by fire from inside the tent as they enter to offer the incense.

Many scholars see all this as relevant to postexilic clerical conflicts, when a hierarchy was evolving (Budd 1984, 188–91). The position taken by the priestly editors is clear: *no outsider* (meaning Levite or layperson) *who is not of the descendants of Aaron* shall do priestly things (v. 40).

16:41-50. Aftershocks. When an angry crowd gathers to protest the wholesale killing of their rebellious leaders, once again God's *glory* (v. 42) appears. Again God threatens *the whole congregation* (v. 41). A plague breaks out (the nature of the pestilence is not described). Aaron is sent into the crowd, frantically to *make atonement* (v. 46, lit. "to cover," or "to protect") them from the plague). Carrying his priestly incense censer, forbidden to others, he takes his stand *between the dead and the living* (v. 48).

The point cannot be missed. Refusing to accept the supremacy of the Mosaic tradition and the Aaronite priesthood is tantamount to rebelling against Yahweh and his covenant. The punishment for such high-handed sins (cf. 15:30) is death.

Aaron's Budding Staff, 17:1-13

The lesson in chap 16 is negative. No one may act as priests in Israel except Aaron and his descendants. The point of the present passage is positive. Among all the tribes, the LORD has chosen Levi; and among the Levites, Aaron alone and supremely is to be priest.

Each tribe (*ancestral house*, v. 2) is instructed to bring the symbol of tribal authority, *the staff*, to Moses. The Hebrew text has a significant word play: the same word means "staff" and "tribe." The Levi staff is engraved with Aaron's name. That Levi is counted among the twelve tribes is unusual. All the staffs are left overnight *before the LORD* (v. 7), i.e., in front of the altar in *the tent of meeting* (v. 4). When the LORD causes only Aaron's staff to sprout and flourish, Israel takes it as a sign that Aaron is the LORD's choice as priest. The staff is stored in the shrine as a perpetual reminder of Aaron's role. The complaints are to stop. Israel recognizes that priests are essential protection; *everyone [else] who approaches the tabernacle of the LORD will die* (v. 12).

Duties and Support of Priests and Levites, 18:1-32

Following the reaffirmations of the Aaronite priesthood's role (chaps. 16–17), the priestly writer pulls together material that reaffirms the responsibility of the priests, establishes a theological rationale for the priesthood, defines the role of the Levites, and prescribes the means of support for both groups.

The priests are to protect Israel from the kind of dangers illustrated in chap. 16. Everything connected with the powerful "holiness" of God, especially the holy things at the sanctuary, is life threatening. *From now on* (6th or 5th century?) *the Israelites shall no longer approach the tent of meeting* (v. 22). Neither is any unauthorized person (*outsider*) permitted in the sanctuary (vv. 4, 7).

18:1-7. Duties of the priests and Levites. Aaron and his descendants shield Israel from the risks, serving in the tent of meeting as Israel's representative, *performing the duties of the sanctuary and . . . the altar* (v. 5). Further, they bear the responsibility if something is done incorrectly. The Levites cannot enter the shrine nor handle the sacred objects, but they serve the priests. Thus, they act as an outer buffer, protecting Israel, too. In these roles, the priests and Levites are *a gift* of Yahweh to Israel (vv. 6-7).

18:8-20. Support for the Aaronites. The rest of the chapter specifies how these clergy are to be supported.

Since they have no inheritance (*no allotment in [the] land*, v. 20), they are to receive a portion of most offerings, plus an annual tithe. The reader is not told how this corresponds with the gift of cities and pastureland to the Levites in chap. 35:1-3.

The Aaronite priests are to live off the offerings given by Israelite farmers. Normally, these offerings are in kind, animals and/or produce. Burnt offerings are burnt up completely. Only the suet and some viscera of other sacrifices were burnt; the rest was eaten. "Peace" offerings (communions, or offerings of well-being) were eaten by the worshipers, after the right thigh and breast had been reserved for the priests. After they were consecrated, i.e., made "holy of holy," (*most holy*), most gifts became the property of the priests and their families, *holy to you*, i.e., set aside exclusively (vv. 9-10). Some offerings were restricted to the officiating priests only.

The plans for upkeep of the priesthood varied through Israel's history (cf. 1 Sam 2:12-17 and Deut 14:22-29). What is required in the Book of Numbers and in later Judaism is greater than before the Exile.

18:21-32. Support for the Levites. The Levites, whose role was subordinate to the Aaronite priests, were special as well. They were to be supported by annual tithes, i.e., one-tenth of all agricultural produce (cf. Deut 14:22-29). This was their *payment for* their *service in the tent of meeting* (v. 31). They, in turn, tithe *the best* of all that is given them to the Aaronite priests (vv. 29-30).

Laws of Purification: Death, 19:1-22

In animistic societies death is often understood as a thing, almost a substance. Death, therefore is considered dangerous. It can contaminate anything that it touches (cf. 5:2-3). Touching a corpse is a powerful taboo. Since touching corpses cannot be totally avoided, such societies devise elaborate rites to cleanse the contamination by some type of ritual.

As late as the priestly writer's time, Jewish belief and practice about death seems still to have retained some such associations. Acculturation issues, i.e., how one incorporates the essence of beliefs and practices into a more sophisticated religion without adulterating that religion, continue to be crucial issues.

The mystifying rite of the *red heifer* (v. 2) has always intrigued readers. Its purpose clearly is to provide materials and rites by which persons who have touched a corpse can be detoxified. A sacrifice seems to be made; a heifer is ritually slaughtered. But no

priest does the slaughter. The sacrifice takes place away from the shrine—even *outside* the *camp* (v. 3). Every part of the animal is burned up, even *its skin* and *blood* (v. 5). The animal must be female, not male. It must be *red*. Various unusual materials are thrown on the fire (v. 6). The ashes are collected and stored. That which is to cleanse, the ashes, contaminates temporarily. And any *clean person* (vv. 18-19) may manipulate the *water for cleansing* (v. 9), not just a priest.

Israelites *who touch a corpse* (v. 13) are sternly warned and branded unclean for *seven days* (v. 14). Some of the ashes from the heifer are mixed with *running water* to make some "water of purification" (v. 17). On the third and seventh day of a person's ritual impurity, cleansing shall be effected by dashing the person with the water of purification.

Heifer is the traditional English translation, though "cow" may do as well. She must be without ritual defect and without previous service, v. 2. Why *red*? Both the heifer and the *crimson material* (v. 6, "stuff," or "*thread*") may suggest the use of blood (the seat of life) as a powerful antidote to death. Aromatic *cedarwood* and *hyssop* (NEB: "marjoram") also may have been thought to have cleansing powers (see Lev 14:4). Everyone who handles the ashes becomes temporarily unclean (vv. 7-8, 10).

In a day when the spread of deadly infection was not understood, many precautions were taken to avoid accidental contamination by death (vv. 14-16). No doubt experience had taught that death imperiled the entire community. Failure to cleanse it was taken seriously. The holiness of the community was at risk (v. 13). The penalty was isolation and thus death (vv. 13, 20). The location of these rituals just here is appropriate, following the description of so much death in chap. 14.

Last Days at Kadesh:
Moses' Sin and Edom's Blockade, 20:1-21

20:1-13. Moses' offense. Having said little about events during most of the remaining years in the desert, the writer moves to two final incidents at *Kadesh* (v. 1).

Israel's first generation was a rebellious generation. The people themselves continually complained and lacked trust (chaps. 11, 12, and 14). The priestly clans were no better; they fought over position (chaps. 16 and 17). In this section we read of the rebellious nature of Moses himself.

The priestly writer has given distinctive shape to a memory about God's giving Israel water at a place called *Meribah* (v. 13). In Exod 17:1-9 the incident is told to underscore God's providing grace. Here the account explains why Moses was not permitted to enter the promised LAND of Canaan.

The litany of whining and complaint is familiar: "Why have you (Moses) done this to us? Liberating us? Putting us at risk?" The specific quarrel (the term used has legal connotations, v. 3; see also the NRSV note at v. 13 that gives "quarrel" as a possible translation for *Meribah*) is: *no water to drink* (v. 5). When Moses and Aaron prostrate themselves at *the tent*, God grants them another theophany. Moses is told to take *the staff* (v. 8), *the one before the LORD* (v. 9), and *command the rock . . . to yield its water* (v. 8). Whether this is Moses' staff (Exod 17:5), or Aaron's budding staff (Num 17:1-11) is unclear.

Before Moses does as he is told, he makes a speech (v. 10). Is there rashness in what he says (see Ps 106:32-33)? When he strikes the rock, the congregation is given water *abundantly* (v. 11). Does Moses go beyond his mandate when he strikes the rock? When he strikes it *twice*? In the Exodus account (17:6), he is commanded to strike the rock. What he did or did not do is described as *rebellion* (v. 24; cf. 27:14). And he is told, *you shall not bring* Israel *into the land* (v. 12).

What did Moses do that was so odious? Does he claim credit for the miracle? Is that the rashness in his speech? Was he driven to exasperation by these people's impossible griping, so that his downfall is anger (see Deut 1:3; 3:26; 4:21)? The writer states the reason enigmatically: *You did not trust in me*, thus failing *to show* Yahweh's *holiness* (v. 12).

The traditions all agree that Moses did not take part in the settlement of Canaan. A reason for that is given. But nothing is said that could dislodge Moses from his central place in Jewish faith and history.

20:14-21. The message to Edom's king. With the request to *the king of Edom* (v. 14), Israel begins the move from the *Kadesh* area to the Transjordan. As part of the request to Edom, the writer includes a version of Israel's confession of faith—reciting the mighty acts of God in the Exodus. Note the use of first person pronouns by which later Israel expressed solidarity with that Exodus generation.

Israel requests and is refused passage through the area east of the ARABAH, *Edom*, along the caravan route up on the plateau, called *the Kings' Highway* (v. 17, not a constructed road, as it later would be). This incident reflects an ancient rivalry between brothers (Gen 25:19-26, the story that provides the point of departure for the subsequent struggles between ESAU and JACOB who become the eponymous ancestors for EDOM and ISRAEL). The fact that a settled and strong king controls Edom is often used as evidence in dating the Exodus. Israel must make a detour around Edom. Why Israel, off to the west of Kadesh, would request a south-north passage through Edom is not explained (cf. Deut 2:1-15; Judg 11:7-18).

March Towards Transjordan: Aaron's Death, 20:22-29

This paragraph heightens the sense of transition. The old, rebellious generation has died (or are dying off). The years in the desert at Kadesh are ending.

Israel's route and the location of *Mount Hor* (v. 22) cannot be determined. Ancient tradition put the mountain near Petra in Edom—much too far east.

When it became clear that Aaron was dying, Moses took him and his eldest son, *Eleazar*, to *the top of the mountain* (v. 28). Aaron's priestly *vestments* (see Exod 28; Lev 8:7-9) were taken from him and put on his son. Thus, continuity in the priesthood was insured, despite Aaron's rebellion (v. 24).

Aaron's death is described in ways that suggest an importance comparable with Moses'. He dies on a mountain; and he is mourned *thirty days* (v. 29), rather than the customary seven (cf. 33:38-39; Deut 10:6).

On the Way: Victory and Suffering, 21:1-20

21:1-3. Arad destroyed. The fight at *Hormah* (v. 3) seems to interrupt the sequence of events, as Israel moves east from Kadesh. The account may be another version of a Judah clan's successful settlement in the northern Negeb (see Judg 1:16-17). Recounting the incident at this juncture signals a change in Israel's fortunes. From this point, Yahweh enables a more responsive Israel to succeed. Many of the places named cannot be specifically identified (Noth 1968, 155, mentions the generality of the names). After some reverses, Israel vows complete loyalty to Yahweh. They promise to *utterly destroy* these *Canaanites* (v. 2), i.e., they put them under "the ban" and the battle is fought as a HOLY WAR. The verb *utterly destroy* and the place name *Hormah* derive from the same Hebrew root *ḥrm*.

21:4-9. The journey south. Israel moves south, not north (vv. 1-3), this time on the RED SEA/REED SEA route (?), beginning their detour around Edom. On the long journey people grow *impatient* (v. 4) once more.

Again they protest about the *miserable food* (cf. 11:4-6). The punishment for their lack of confidence in God is a plague of *poisonous* (lit. "fiery") *serpents* (v. 6). The name *seraphim* may refer to their burning bite or to their appearance (see Deut 8:15; Isa 6:2; 14:29).

When *the people* confess their sin (v. 7), Moses intercedes on their behalf. He is instructed to make an image of a *poisonous snake* (v. 8). The image is made of *bronze* (v. 9) and mounted on top of a pole. Those who look at the image are healed of their snakebites. An intimation of magic lurks under the surface (cf. 1 Sam 6:4); therefore, the episode often has been spiritualized, e.g., Wis 16:5-7 and John 3:14.

In Hezekiah's temple a bronze snake image called Nehushtan had become a magic fetish of healing to which Israel burned incense (2 Kgs 18:4). Nehushtan was attributed to Moses. Some think, instead, that the image was a Jebusite fetish incorporated into Israel's cultus (Snaith 1967, 280). Others think that the YAHWIST is accepting the Mosaic origin of the image, but making plain its original use—against any magical or cultic use (Budd 1984, 233, 235).

21:10-20. The journey north. Essentially, vv. 10-20 are an itinerary of Israel's movements after having skirted Edom. Again, the places listed cannot be identified. The itinerary ends at Mount Pisgah, east of the northern end of the DEAD SEA, with Israel poised to enter Canaan. Attempts to work out from the accounts one straightforward itinerary for Israel have been unsuccessful.

The two song fragments are inserted following catchwords: *Arnon . . . Arnon* (vv. 13, 14) and *Beer* (=well) *. . . well* (vv. 16, 17). The Hebrew text of the poetry is difficult to decipher. *The Book of the Wars of the LORD* (v. 14) is mentioned only here (cf. "the Book of Jashar," Josh 10:13; 2 Sam 1:18). The second piece of a song seems to celebrate a new well. Evidently, both songs had become traditional by the time of the composition of the Book of Numbers.

The purpose of this section seems to be to summarize Israel's advance from the borders of Moab, *the Arnon*, to those of Canaan, *the top of Pisgah*, accenting the LORD's provision on the way.

Conquests and Settling In, 21:21–36:13

Defeat of Two Kingdoms: Sihon and Og, 21:21-35

Israel's success on the battlefield, anticipated in 21:1-3, now occupies center stage. A desert-hardened generation is portrayed sweeping up the Transjordan, destroying everything in its path.

21:21-32. The defeat of Sihon. The first victim is *Sihon, king* of Jordan, between *the Arnon* and *the Jabbok* (v. 24; cf. Deut 2:26-37). The term Amorites may be a synonym for the general term Canaanites. Israel asks Sihon for passage and is refused. The wording is similar to the request put to Edom in 20:17. When Sihon tries to back up his refusal with force, *Israel put him to the sword, and took possession of his land* (v. 24). Israel's displacement is described as total: *all of the towns*, including the main site, *Heshbon, and all its villages* (v. 25). This is the first account of Israel's actually capturing territory and settling in it.

A traditional taunt song, perhaps of Amorite origin, is used to mock Heshbon in defeat, vv. 27-30 (see another version in Jer 48:45-56). "Look what has happened to Heshbon," the balladeer sings, "who once *devoured . . . Moab*, who made the Moabite god, *Chemosh*, seem a servant of Sihon." The Hebrew text of v. 30 is not fully intelligible.

The Yahwist's telling of the conquest raises, at this and subsequent points, at least two issues. First, the picture of total displacement of the Amorite natives and total control of the entire Transjordan is not easy to square with the evidence in the Book of Judges. The struggle took centuries. At first, Israel only controlled pockets of territory (cf. Judg 3:12; 10:17). Second, some of the sites mentioned were not occupied until later, e.g., Heshbon in the eighth century. A separate tradition about the conquest of an area a few mi. south of the Jabbok called *Jazer* is mentioned briefly (v. 31). *Moses* figures in this account.

21:33-35. The defeat of Og. The story of the dispossession of *Og*, the king of *Bashan* (vv. 33-35), seems to be paraphrased from Deut 3:1-7. The plateau north of the Jabbok was famous for its pasturelands and fine animals. Again, as in the case of Hormah (21:1-3), Bashan is put under the ban and *no survivor* is *left* (v. 35). Interestingly, property is not devoted to Yahweh. The point is transparent: when Israel trusts the LORD, when they obey him and the rules of holy war, they are victorious. Inheriting the promised land of Canaan has begun.

Balaam and Balak, 22:1–24:25

22:1-5. Into the Jordan valley. The conquest of the Transjordan, from the Arnon to Bashan, is complete. Israel is *camped in the plains of Moab*, i.e., in the Jordan's rift valley, poised *across the Jordan from Jericho* (v. 1) and Canaan's central highlands.

As a pause in the action, the narrator tells a fascinating story. The story of an eastern diviner, BALAAM, and a Moabite king, Balak, dramatically spotlights God's historic intentions in what is happening.

Evidently, Balaam was a common figure in near eastern folklore, like NOAH, JOB, and DANIEL. Using some of that folklore and some ancient prophetic oracles, the writer weaves a funny, satirical, enigmatic tale. And in the process he proclaims some of "the most far-reaching and positive visions of Israel's future found in the entire Pentateuch" (Ackerman 1987, 87).

The story line is easy to follow. Moab, seeing Israel's successes and numbers, hires a professional diviner with a fine reputation to put a curse on Israel. The diviner, Balaam, first refuses and then comes. Three times, elaborate preparations are made for his occult arts to work; each time Balaam blesses Israel instead. Completely exasperated, the king of Moab sends Balaam home.

Interpretations of the story have varied widely. Efforts to sort out YAHWIST and ELOHIST sources for the narrative have not been widely accepted. Discrepancies, however, are not easily papered over (e.g., God instructs Balaam to go with Balak's emissaries [22:20] but then is angry with him for going; Balaam leaves with those officials [22:21], but is accompanied by only two of his young servants [22:22]).

Is Balaam a true prophet of Yahweh or a self-serving shaman? The thrust of chaps. 22–24 is essentially positive, although at times ambivalent. But subsequent traditions portray Balaam as out for personal gain or in league with evil (see Num 25:1-18; 31:8, 16; Deut 23:3-6; Josh 13:22; 24:9-10; 29:9-10; Mic 6:5; Neh 13:2; 2 Pet 2:15-16; Jude 11; Rev 2:14).

Archaeological evidence from the sixth century suggests that Balaam was a popular figure from Transjordan. But 22:5 describes him as coming from Mesopotamia, *the land of Amon*, from a town called *Pethor*, i.e., Pitru near CARCHEMISH. His first oracle says that he was *from Aram* (23:7).

22:6-21. Negotiations. *Balak* summons Balaam to *curse this people for me* (22:6), so as to offset Israel's advantages against him. A belief in the efficacy of words in general and blessings and curses in particular lies behind the request. Because of his famous gifts as a diviner, Balaam's curses are expected to be especially effective (22:6). The representatives of the king are variously called *messengers* (22:5), *elders* (22:7), and

officials (princes, 22:8, 13, 15, 21, 35, 40). They are sent off with the customary *fees for divination in . . . hand*. Balaam will not agree to go with them until he has consulted Yahweh (22:8), which he does at nighttime—presumably through dreams (cf. 22:20, 24:1). That a Mesopotamian diviner knows *the LORD* is not explained. Note the uses of the divine name, Yahweh, and the more generic Elohim, *God*, throughout the narrative.

The answer comes: do not go. *The LORD has refused* (22:14). Nonetheless, Balak persists. This time his emissaries are *more numerous and more distinguished* (22:15). They promise *great honor* (22:17, no doubt including a large fee). If that is how it is, Balaam wonders if Yahweh *my God* might not have *more to say* to him (22:19)! This time the LORD agrees. Perhaps there is some wish-fulfillment in Balaam's dream?

22:22-24:25. The oracles of Balaam. Thus is the stage set for the popular story of Balaam's talking she-donkey. Interpreters naturally have difficulty with this story. Either they studiously avoid the talking part, or they soberly explain it, e.g., "men have sometimes sensed that God's creatures spoke to them" (Thompson 1970, 191). Israel plainly delighted in telling of the day a dumb donkey could see more clearly what God wanted than a famous Mesopotamian seer. The story is laced with irony and satire. The earnest conversation between Balaam and his donkey should not be read with a straight face.

The angel (lit., "messenger") is a manifestation *of the LORD* (v. 22) present. The angel speaking is the LORD speaking (cf. 22:35). That God is angry with Balaam for doing what he has just been told to do passes without comment. Triads are used as a literary device throughout the narrative: The angel appears three times, sacrifices are offered three times, Balaam pronounces three initial and three final oracles.

When Balaam finally sees what his beast has seen all along, the angel reveals that he (the angel) has come to Balaam as *an adversary* (Heb: "a satan"; cf. Job 1:6-9; Zech 3:1; 1 Chr 21:1) to divert him from his dangerous journey. Balaam offers to go back home, but the angel encourages him to go on, now that he has been vividly warned again to *speak only what I tell you to speak* (22:35).

When Balak and Balaam finally meet, Balak upbraids Balaam for being slow to recognize his opportunity, and Balaam responds by warning Balak that he may not get the curse he has ordered. *Do I* have the power to say just anything? (22:38) he plaintively asks. Balak pretends not to hear and prepares a great feast for everybody, 22:40.

The series of three great sacrifices, three revelations from Yahweh, and three oracles by Balaam (22:41-24:9) follows a pattern building up dramatic interest. Balaam is taken to different vantage points where he can see *part of the people of Israel* and, finally, *to the top of Peor* (23:28), where he *saw Israel camping tribe by tribe* (24:2). Each time *seven altars* are built and *seven bulls* and *seven rams* are sacrificed, presumably as part of the rites of divination. The reader recognizes that seven is a sacred number.

The first time Balaam consults Yahweh the seer is cagey: *perhaps the LORD will come to meet me* (23:3). God does *put a word in* his *mouth* (23:5). But it is not the *oracle* (a message a seer gets when he consults his god) that Balak wants. The LORD will not curse Israel, so Balaam cannot. Israel is not like other *nations*; their number is vast (23:9). The promise to the patriarchs has been fulfilled (cf. Gen 22:17, 32:12). The first oracle ends with a "so-help-me-God" oath (23:10b).

The keystone cops atmosphere increases the second time around. "What's going on?" Balak shouts. "I paid you good money. You're supposed to be cursing these people!" "What comes in is what goes out," Balaam retorts (23:12). This time Balaam does not go to a remote place (23:3, *a bare height*) to seek the oracle. "You people wait here," he instructs. "I will *meet the LORD over there*" (23:15).

The second oracle (23:18-26) reinforces the first. *God is not a human being* (v. 19, Heb. "son of man") who will *change his mind*. Yahweh, Israel's *God*, is *acclaimed as a king among them* (v. 21). God's KING-SHIP is an elemental theme in the OT. God will not abandon his people. He is raw power (*like the horns of a wild ox*, v. 22) available to them. And they are like a bloodthirsty lioness/lion that has only begun to ravage. No amount of skilful *enchantment* or *divination* can stop them (v. 23). Balaam again pleads his own inculpability: *whatever the LORD says, that is what I must do* (v. 26).

After the third series of sacrifices, Balaam did not bother to go aside *to look for omens* (24:1). Nevertheless, this time *the spirit of God came upon him*.

In the early history of Israel such spirit possession often threw people into frenzies and/or trances. It was the sign of authentic prophetic inspiration. The first verses of the oracle speak of that kind of ecstatic state. The seer *falls down* (24:4), *but with eyes uncovered,* that is, able truly to see. In this heightened state *his eye is clear* (24:3; cf. 11:25-26, 29).

The ORACLE itself describes Israel as owner of the land, a land where water is abundant and exotic plants luxuriate, a land governed by a powerful king. Like a *wild ox*, God destroys all Israel's *foes* (24:8). And a final oracle is for Israel themselves:

*Blessed is everyone who blesses you
And cursed is everyone who curses you* (24:9b).

This is the final straw for Balak. In a rage he strikes *his hands together* (24:10, a sign of contempt) and bitterly dismisses his famous seer. Before he leaves, though, Balaam defends himself with an "I told you so" reflection on what had happened. Whether Balak wants it or not, Balaam also unburdens himself of a prediction about Israel (note the repeated oracle about prophetic inspiration, 24:15-16, emphasizing the authenticity of the message). An Israelite king (*a star . . . a scepter*) shall come to power and *crush* all Israel's nearby neighbors. This may be an allusion to the conquering David and his empire, or an allusion to the northern kingdom. Balaam has finally pronounced a curse—but it falls on Moab (24:17c).

The narrative ends with three short, obscure oracles about various peoples (24:20-24). The Amalekites and the Kenites were ancient opponents of Israel who lived to the south of Judah.

It is difficult to make out whom 24:23-24 refers to. The MT is obscure. The usual guess, picking up on the mention of *Kittim* (v. 24, Cyprus), is to read the oracle as a reference to the SEA PEOPLES. Most students think the oracles themselves to be examples of early Hebrew poetry, perhaps from the tenth century. Anticlimactically, *Balaam got up and went back to his place and Balak also went his way* (24:25).

Why were this lengthy story and these oracles included by the priestly writer? The pleasures of making fun of a famous Eastern seer who could not see, and of a foreign king who could not buy a curse he wanted cannot be dismissed. But more serious purposes may be at work, too. The best of Oriental occult arts is exposed as impotent when challenged by Israel's God. God's ancient promises to Israel are reaffirmed. Yahweh controls history. Israel's historic destiny is unstoppable. Their enemies are powerless. While Balak and Balaam go through their little charade off in the heights, Israel, oblivious of what is happening, readies itself for conquest. And, ironically, the unsurpassed words of praise and promise for Israel come from the mouth of Balaam of Pethor.

The Peor Affair, 25:1-18

While Israel is poised on the plains of Moab ready to enter the promised LAND, rebellion erupts once again. And a purging is once again necessary.

For the narrative, two different memories seem to be used (cf. vv. 1-5 and vv. 6-18). Did the writer know Ps 106:28-31 and Hos 9:10? Several of the phrases are quite obscure, using words found only here. Generally, the passage is a polemic against Palestinian fertility rites and a legitimation of Phinehas' priesthood (cf. Ezra 8:2; 1 Chr 9:29; 24:3).

Israel was always attracted to the various Canaanite fertility cults. Perennially they had problems coaxing their land to produce. To the superstitious, BAAL worship seemed to lessen the insecurities of farming in such a place. More basically, the fertility rites claimed to offer ways to get the gods to do what people needed/wanted—in stark contrast to the demands of Yahwism.

25:1-5, 16-18. Prohibitions against the Moabites. *Sexual relations* with foreign women are linked with participation in a foreign cultus, which is linked to a baal. Eating and *sacrifices* are virtually synonymous (v. 2). *The LORD's anger* against this apostasy demands punishment for the leaders (v. 4 *chiefs of the people*). Exactly what the punishment was is uncertain. *The judges* who carry out the sentences are only to target guilty individuals (v. 5). The word *yoked* is used only here (vv. 3, 5; cf. Hos 9:10; Ps 106:28).

This brief treatment of the troubles at Peor concludes with an explanation why the Israelites later attack Midian (see chap. 31).

25:6-15: The example of Phinehas. The story about Phinehas assumes a correlation between *the women of Moab* (v. 1) and *a Midianite woman* (v. 6). The sin of the Israelite man, later identified as *Zimri son of Salu*, may have been marriage to a foreign woman, *Cozbi daughter of Zur* (v. 14). More likely the sin was his defiant acts during a sacred lament over Israel's sin and punishment. There is also the impression that he is guilty of some cultic action in the midst of the camp. The word play between *the tent* (v. 8) and *the belly* (v. 9)—both words are derived from the same Hebrew root—suggests a relationship between the immorality at Peor and an assault on Israel's worship. *The tent* is an inner chamber or shrine.

Phinehas proves his *zeal* (= *jealousy*) for cultic purity by running through both of them with his *spear*, thus stopping *the plague* (v. 8), but not before *twenty-four thousand* people had died. He is said to have *made atonement for the Israelites* (v. 13), that is, he "covered" their guilt so that their relations with the LORD could be good again. As a reward Phinehas is granted *a covenant of peace*, interpreted to mean *perpetual* tenure in the *priesthood* (v. 13).

A Second Census, 26:1-65

The wilderness narrative began with a census of Israel in chap. 1; it ends with another one. If the first census represented the final stage in the constitution of Israel for its mission, this census represents a re-constitution. The generation of former slaves who failed the tests of fidelity have passed off the scene. A generation disciplined in the desert is now ready to occupy the land promised their parents.

The two censuses are alike and different. Both reckon military strength, *men from twenty years old* who are *able to go to war* (v. 2). The second also looks to an apportionment of the land. The tribes are listed in the same order as before, with the exception that Manasseh comes first this time. To this list are attached lists of clan names (cf. the list in Gen 46:8-27). The totals arrived at are little different from those in chap. 3. Clan totals are not given, only the cumulative totals for each tribe (suggesting that the family-clan names have been added to the list—from Gen 46?).

Verse 4 presents a textual problem: v. 4c seems incongruous since *those who came out of Egypt* are precisely the ones *not* being counted. The large numbers reported present the same problems here as found in chap. 1. Two different criteria are put forth for deciding each tribe's apportionment of land; the size of the tribe (vv. 53-54), and the casting of lots (v. 55). Verse 56 tries to combine the two criteria.

Moses oversees the division of the land. His presence and role suggest that the allocations of tribal boundaries were based on the word of *the LORD* through Moses (v. 52). Other traditions trace the division of the land to a decision Joshua made by casting lots at Shiloh (cf. Josh 18:10).

As in the first census, a separate census is also made of the Levites (cf. 3:14–4:49). A similar total is given in both lists. The same three clan names are given in chap. 3 and v. 57, but in vv. 58-61 the list of sons is different. The Levites are not counted in the general census because they do not share in the apportionment of land. However, they do receive towns and pastureland (see 35:1-8).

The point of the second census is underscored in vv. 63-65. This census marks the end of the Exodus generation: *not one of those enrolled* in this census was old enough to be counted in the first census— *except Caleb . . . and Joshua.* A new Israel is ready.

Daughters of Zelophehad, 27:1-11

The allocation of ancestral land (anticipated by the census, chap. 26) is to be perpetual. The LAND is Yahweh's; his apportionment of it is a gracious gift. Land is not to be alienated from the family to whom it is given. Normally it is passed to the eldest son (Deut 21:15-17). When a man died leaving no sons, levirate marriage laws required the deceased's brother to take the widow as his wife and to have a son (Deut 25:5-10). If these provisions failed, the nearest kinsman was to "redeem" the land for the family (cf. Jer 32:6-15). Jubilee laws would have required sold or confiscated land to revert to the original family every fifty years (Lev 25, esp. v. 23).

The daughters of Zelophehad introduce a case of a man survived only by daughters. *Zelophehad . . . of Manasseh* died in the desert. He did nothing that would cause his family to be excluded from the allotment of land. Yet his only heirs were daughters.

The daughters contend that refusing to give them *a possession* would be tantamount to taking away their father's *name* (v. 4), i.e., causing him never to have existed. Without a sense of life after death, Hebrews believed that the perpetuation of a person's character, reputation, and name were closely linked to the land.

Here we meet case law being developed to apply the general Mosaic principles to specific situations. The daughters are granted an allotment. And a line of inheritance contingencies is worked out (vv. 8-11).

The ruling suggests that Hebrew women were not shut out of the inheritance system. However, the passage is concerned primarily with keeping the land in the family. Other contingencies would arise, as chap. 36 illustrates.

Following Snaith (1966, 126-27) some have wondered if this passage is not an explanation of why Manasseh ended up with allotments on the west bank of the Jordan, too.

Joshua's Commissioning, 27:12-23

As events move towards the invasion of Canaan proper, God communicates to Moses a sense of his imminent death. Moses is to ascend a mountain in *the Abarim range* (v. 12). Nebo also was part of this range

(cf. Deut 32:49). There he could view a panorama of the central highlands. There he would die. Moses' sin is again described in terms like those used in 20:12-13.

Moses asks that a successor be chosen and installed. In v. 16 Yahweh is addressed as *the God of the spirits of all flesh*, i.e., all humanity. Moses fears Israel's becoming leaderless, *without a shepherd*, especially as they wage war, *go out . . . come in* (v. 17).

The LORD designates *Joshua* as Israel's next leader (v. 18). Joshua has already appeared in the account, at Moses' side (11:28; cf. Exod 17:8-13; 24:13; 33:11). *The spirit* in Joshua has long marked him out. The term "spirit" suggests some extraordinary God-given abilities.

Joshua is *commissioned* in a ceremony as he stands before Eleazar, Aaron's successor. Moses lays *his hand upon* Joshua, an ancient symbol for imparting blessing. *Some of* Moses' *authority* (Heb. *hod*, "prestige," "honor," "vitality") passes to Joshua, but he is not a second Moses. God communicated with Moses directly and personally (12:6-8). Joshua must get his instruction from God via the priest, with whom the LORD will communicate his instruction by means of the sacred lots URIM AND THUMMIM, even in the conduct of war (v. 21). The precise way the priests manipulated the Urim and Thummim remains a mystery (see Exod 28:30-31; 1 Sam 14:41-42; 28:6; Ezra 2:63; Neh 7:65). The commissioning of Joshua provides a glimpse of a theocracy, with priests in control.

With the installation of Eleazar as priest (20:23-29) and Joshua as military leader, continuity is assured in Israel's government.

Laws Concerning Offerings and Festivals, 28:1–29:40

The modern reader may be tempted to spiritualize—or dismiss altogether—this detailed section of the Book of Numbers. A clear grasp of what the priestly writer is doing here is necessary to take the passage seriously. The writer draws together and systematizes various cultic regulations into a comprehensive CALENDAR of sacrifices and festivals. Materials found in Exod 29, Lev 23, and Ezek 45–56 provide a broader picture of the assumptions that undergird worship. A cultic calendar of sacrifices for the entire year is laid out: daily, at *morning* and *twilight* (28:1-8); *sabbath* (28:9-10); the new moon (28:11-15); *unleavened bread* and *passover* (28:16-25); *first fruits* or *weeks* (28:26-31); the new year, i.e., *the first day of the seventh month* (29:1-6); the day of *atonement* (29:7-11); and tabernacles (29:12-38). Passover, although a family sacrifice rather than a community-wide sacrifice, is listed for completeness. Sabbath was not a festive day for families.

Individual and shared offerings are not denigrated (29:39), but attention is focused on those sacrifices that are solely Yahweh's, *offering by fire* (28:3, 6, 8, 13, 19, 24; 29:6, 13, 36), which is burned up completely. In the case of the festivals *a sin offering,* always *a male goat* (28:15, 22; 29:5, 11, 16, 19, 22, 25, 28, 31, 34, 38), is also required. Such offerings covered offenses that would make the community ritually unclean. Thus, they are referred to several times as an *atonement.* Animal, cereal, and drink sacrifices are all specified. Quantities are stipulated and are often generous, sometimes extravagant, e.g., see the first day of tabernacles (29:12-16). The concern seems to be that Israel insure that they are fit for worship and that they dedicate themselves to costly worship.

Israel's worship calendar varied through the years. Most scholars think that this calendar represents the latest development to be found in the Pentateuch. It reflects the community's practice after the Exile.

The *sabbath* (28:9-10) was a day of rest and did not become a day of worship until after the Exile. The new moon festival evidently was significant (28:11-15; see also 1 Sam 20:5; Amos 8:4). The reasons for its importance are not known.

After the exile, the sacred *seventh month* became important and was much elaborated (29:7-11). The day of atonement (*holy convocation*) mentioned in 29:7-11, is not found in preexilic Israel. Noth suggests as a better translation for *holy convocation,* "holy proclamation" (28:18, 25-26, 29:1, 7, 12 [Noth 1968, 220]).

Laws Concerning Women's Vows, 30:1-16

The law concerning vows was clear (Lev 5:4, Deut 23:21-23). The vows should be fulfilled exactly—*a man shall not break his word* (v. 2). Failure to make good on a vow exposed a person to God's judgment. The law assumed that the person making the vow had the autonomy and the means to do what he vowed; and the law assumed the person was male.

What then about women, who would lack the independence or the resources to carry out their vows? In Israel's patriarchal society, a woman was under the authority of her father or husband. Usually, she would be dependent on her father or husband for the means to fulfill her vow. If he refused to support her in her vow, she was exposed to the danger of nonfulfillment. So, the law made the father or husband equally liable, as soon as he heard of the vow.

Provision is made for vows by a young unmarried woman (vv. 3-5) or by a married woman. The provisions for a married woman are similar to those for an unmarried one, whether she took the vow before she married (vv. 6-8) or after (vv. 10-15). Only *a widow* and *a divorced woman* could assume a vow on her own (v. 9).

Since the father or husband becomes liable, he can, when he first learns of the vow, disallow it. The vow thence becomes void, no danger to anyone. *The LORD will forgive her* (vv. 5, 8, 12). However, if he fails to act when he first hears of the vow, it stands. He becomes responsible. He cannot dawdle, vacillate, or change his mind. Vows to the LORD are to be fulfilled.

The terms "vow" and "pledge" are inclusive (v. 3). The *vow* refers to a promise to give something to God, e.g., Hannah's vow to give her son (1 Sam 1:9-11) The *pledge* refers to an oath to abstain from something for the LORD's sake, e.g., the Nazirite vows Hannah promised her son would live by (1 Sam 1:11; cf. Num 6:1-21).

Holy War Against Midian, 31:1-54

This chapter describes the last military action of Moses, how Israel would behave during and after holy war (if they were obedient), and a foretaste of the battles and victories that lay ahead. The account is so exaggerated, idealized, and stylized that one may easily dismiss it. It is probably best, with Snaith (1967, 324), to read chap. 31 as a midrash, that is, a theological reflection on an event.

The identification of Moabites and Midianites in the account of the Peor affair (25:1-18) and the instruction to *harass the Midianites,* and *defeat them* (25:16), along with the information in Josh 13:21 about the defeat of Midianite kings, become the grist for the reflection. Holy war is declared on Midian *to execute the LORD's vengeance* and to *avenge the Israelites* (vv. 2-3).

A 1,000-fighter contingent is required from each tribe, large and small, vv. 4-5. Thus, the victory is to be equally everyone's. Out ahead of the ranks of the fighters are *Phinehas,* the zealous *priest* (see 25:7-13), *the vessels of the sanctuary,* and the trumpets, v. 6. This is Yahweh's fight, and these are the symbols of his leadership. The absence of the most powerful symbol of the LORD's leadership in battle—the ark of the covenant—is not explained (cf. 10:35-36; 14:44; 1 Sam 4:4).

The destruction is massive. *Every male* Midianite is killed (v. 7), including the famous seer BALAAM. Vast numbers of women, children, animals and goods are taken *as booty* (v. 9). All the towns and villages are *burned* (v. 10). In accordance with the requirements of the "ban" of HOLY WAR, everything is "devoted" to Yahweh.

Still Moses is unsatisfied. The women who had seduced Israel into the Peor affair must not be spared. So, only females who were virgins are spared. The genocide is thorough. A strong Midianite presence in the Transjordan during the era of the judges (Judg 6–8) is curious in light of this passage.

Most of the narrative deals with the aftermath of the battle, especially with the division of the spoils taken. First, care is taken to fulfill the demands for ritual purification (vv. 7-24). All contamination caused by contact with corpses must be cleansed, including every tool and bit of clothing that may have touched a corpse (see chap. 19). This is the only OT instance of cleansing by *fire* (v. 23).

A full *inventory* is taken of the *booty captured* (vv. 25-26). The totals amaze: *sheep—675,000; oxen—72,000; donkeys—61,000;* and *virgins—32,000.* This inventory is made in order to share the goods with the priests and the Levites. Everything (including the virgins?) is divided into halves (cf. 1 Sam 30:24-25), half for *the warriors* and half for all *the congregation* (v. 27). The fighters are required to give one five-hundredth to the priests *as a tribute for the LORD* (v. 28). From the peoples' share, one-fiftieth goes *to the Levites* (v. 30). Once again, the fantastic totals are spelled out in detail (vv. 36-47).

The annihilation of Midian is accomplished without a single Israelite casualty, *not one of us is missing* (v. 49). Twelve thousand warriors wipe out a people from whom 32,000 virgins survive, 808,000 animals are taken alive—all without losing one warrior.

To express their gratitude and to cover any possible infractions of the law (*to make atonement for* themselves, v. 50) the commanders present to Moses *the LORD's offering* from the goods the warriors *found*. Various items of jewelry are mentioned (v. 50). The offering itself weighs *16,750 shekels* (v. 52; modern weight would be as much as 240 kg.). The offering becomes part of the treasure held in the shrine. It is placed in *the tent of meeting as a memorial for the Israelites before the LORD* (v. 54). Either the memorial

reminds the LORD of Israel's faithfulness and generosity; or it reminds Israel of the great victory given them by the LORD.

Thus is drawn a portrait of Israel as it should be: totally intolerant of foreign influences, obedient to the Mosaic law in every detail, and generously providing for the priesthood, the Levites, and the sanctuary itself.

Settlements in Transjordan, 32:1-42

On a first reading, chap. 32 appears to be a fairly straightforward account of a final piece of business to be cared for before Israel's thrust west into Canaan proper, i.e., the allocation of the land east of the Jordan already taken. Careful analysts of the passage agree that several traditions are present; there the agreement ends. Any literary history is, therefore, tentative (Budd 1983, 337–42).

The tribes Gad and Reuben find the plateaus east of the Jordan attractive. The good pasturelands suit these cattle keepers (v. 1). They ask agreement that they settle there. They also seek to avoid the dangers ahead, *do not make us cross the Jordan* (v. 5).

Moses adds two and two and gets nine. Overcome by a sense of *deja vu*, he assumes the worst. On the threshold of the promised land of Canaan elements within Israel are again about to rip the heart out of the people, he fears. Moses lashes out at the Reubenites and Gadites. He compares what they are doing to what the faithless spies did at Kadesh. *You brood of sinners*, he calls them, threatening them with *the LORD's anger* (v. 13). Verses 8-13 summarize chaps. 13–14, giving a deuteronomistic interpretation of those awful days.

Gad and Reuben quickly qualify their intentions. They volunteer to build themselves fortified towns where their *little ones* (families) can stay and to lead Israel's army as they conquer Canaan. *We will not return to our homes until all the Israelites have obtained their inheritance*, they pledge (v. 18). Moses agrees and requires the two tribes to take a public oath to that effect (vv. 28-32).

Verses 33-42 outline the allocation of the Transjordan by Moses to Gad, Reuben, and three clans of *the half-tribe of Manasseh*. The other half of Manasseh will settle on the west bank (cf. Josh 13:15-31; Deut 3:12-17). The inclusion of *Manasseh* seems intrusive. They settle north of the Jabbok in Bashan.

This account establishes several things: an explanation of the fact that three tribes settled outside the promised land; that Canaan proper was conquered by all twelve tribes; and that the new generation did not fail the tests of faithfulness to the LORD's purpose.

An Exodus Itinerary, 33:1-49

As a conclusion to the long Exodus narrative, the priestly writer includes a list of camp sites, a recapitulation of Israel's movements from Rameses in *Egypt* (v. 3) to the *plains of Moab* (v. 49). The itinerary is interesting for several reasons. Most of the camp sites mentioned cannot be identified today. The lists may be grouped into five phases or journeys: *Rameses* to *Sinai* (vv. 3-15), *Sinai* to *Ezion-Geber* (vv. 16-35), *Ezion-Geber* to *Kadesh* (v. 36), *Kadesh* to *Edom* (v. 37), and *Edom* through the Transjordan (vv. 41-49).

The first part of the list (vv. 5-15) parallels the itinerary laid out in the final form of Exodus 12:32–19:2, with the addition of places not otherwise known, e.g., *Dophkah* and *Alush* (vv. 12-13). The *Sinai* to *Ezion-Geber* journey is mentioned only here (cf. 10:11-12; 11:3, 34-35; 12:16). Most of the site names are unique to this list.

Only the point of departure and the terminus are listed for the Ezion-Geber-Kadesh and the Kadesh-Edom journeys. Many of the names in the Transjordan trek are unusual, too. Several places, important to the Yahwist's account of the Exodus, are not mentioned, e.g., Shur, Massah and Meribah, Taberah and Hormah. Clearly, this is a composite list. Its sources and relations to other itinerary information in the Pentateuch can only be surmised (Davies 1979).

By including these itineraries the priestly writer adds another signal to his narrative that the forty-year Exodus is ending and the day of promise is at hand. The LORD has brought Israel safely down a long, rough road.

Ideal Boundaries
of the Promised Land, 33:50–34:29

As part of the book's conclusion, and as an anticipation of the imminent occupation of Canaan, the priestly writer lays out absolutist goals for the conquest and repeats plans for the future division of Palestine among the tribes. The Mosaic origins of both are emphasized.

When they do *take possession of the land*, Israel is to receive it as a gift from Yahweh (v. 53). Note the repeated use of the word *inheritance*. The coming invasion is to be fought according to the rules of holy war: Israelites are to completely clear the country of its pagan population; particularly, they are to *destroy*

every vestige of the indigenous, idolatrous cults—*their figured stones* (idols used in manipulating gods), *their cast images* (molten idols), and *all their high places* (notorious hilltop shrines devoted to the baals). Israel is gravely warned of the consequences should they be less than thorough: the Canaanites will *trouble you in the land*, they will remain as *barbs in your eyes and thorns in your side* (v. 55). The DEUTERONOMIST/DEUTERONOMISTIC HISTORIAN was sure that many of Israel's woes could be traced to failures at this point.

The anticipated apportionment of Palestine to the various tribes is spelled out in more detail than before. Verse 54 repeats the content of 26:52-56. Chapter 34 defines *boundaries* for the Israel of the future. Sites mentioned along the northern borders are the most difficult to identify. At no time, even under DAVID and SOLOMON, did Israel actually control all of the territory delimited. The boundaries describe an ideal Israel often evoked in the OT (see Ezek 47:15-18; 48:1-2; cf. Gen 15:18; Josh 15:1-4; Judg 20:1; 1 Kgs 8:65). The LORD's promise-gift to his people will include specific geography—and spacious at that.

Further, allocation of the land to the various tribes and subtribes is to be perpetual. Although *Eleazar*, the Aaronite high priest, and *Joshua*, the military leader, along with designated leaders of the tribes (cf. this list of tribal leaders with lists in 1:5-15 and 13:4-15), will supervise the process, authority for the apportionment is seated in the revelation to Moses (*The LORD spoke to Moses*, v. 16). The parceling-out ceremonies are described in Josh 13–17, with which the writer seems acquainted.

Levitical Cities and Cities of Refuge, 35:1-34

The recital of guidelines for apportioning the land to the twelve tribes (chap 34), suggests the need to provide designated cities for Levites (vv. 1-8); this in turn leads the priestly writer to describe the provision of six of these Levitical cities as *cities of refuge* (vv. 6, 9-15); and to put forward laws related to those who take refuge in them (vv. 9-34).

As guardians and servants of the sacred precincts, the Levites were not to share in the inheritance of the land (18:24). Rather, the other tribes were to provide for them (chap. 18). But where were Levites and their livestock to live? Some traditions remembered that they lived here and there in the towns (Deut 18:1, 6). The writer of Numbers gives a different, somewhat idealized answer: forty-eight towns with over 200 acres of adjoining pastureland (v. 7) each were to be set aside for Levites to *live in* (v. 2) but not own (cf. Josh 20–21; Ezekiel 48:13-22 envisioned their all living together in one central place). There is little to suggest that this provision for Levites was actually ever implemented.

The provisions for six *cities of refuge* (vv. 6, 11, 13), respond to two ancient convictions and, perhaps, an historical development. Many ancient taboos had to do with human blood. Shedding blood (killing a person) was an awesome defilement of the land, expiated only by the death of the killer. The ancient laws of blood revenge required the closest-of-kin (Heb. *go'el*) to carry out the sentence.

Early on *a slayer* (v. 24) could take refuge at a local shrine—if he could get there (Exod 21:12-14; Deut 19). Once in the sanctuary, he took hold of the horns of the altar, thus appealing to God. These provisions for cities of refuge may reflect needs that arose following Josiah's abolishment of local shrines.

But should not *intent* (vv. 11, 15) influence what is done? And who decides guilt and intent? Numbers addresses these legal and ethical issues. The ancient law of blood revenge is not questioned. *The avenger of blood (go'el) shall execute the sentence.* But the ways the sentence is carried out are ameliorated: A clear distinction is laid down between murder and accidental killing. Murder is defined by citing several examples (vv. 16-21). Several other examples of killing *without enmity* are listed; these are not punishable (vv. 22-23).

The avenger of blood shall do nothing *until there is a trial by the congregation* (vv. 12, 24) and not only the town elders. They shall judge motive and grant asylum. The priestly writer gives interpretations that parallel deuteronomic interpretations (Deut 19).

Once given refuge, the slayer must not leave the town—on pain of exposure again to blood guilt. Only the death of the high priest can make a general amnesty possible for everyone in the town.

The congregation shall require at least two witnesses in capital cases and must not, even for accidental killings, allow a money payment (*ransom*, v. 32). The principle stands: *blood pollutes the land, and no expiation* is possible *except by the blood of the one who shed it* (v. 33.) Once again the theological reason for such laws is given: *I the LORD dwell among the Israelites* (v. 34).

Protecting Tribal Property: Women as Heirs, 36:1-13

Allocations of land to tribes and clans were to be held sacrosanct—intrinsic to the LORD's gift of the land to Israel. The case of *the daughters of Zelophehad* (27:1-11) protected a family's inheritance in the land by providing that the land of a man who died without male heirs could pass to his daughters. Now an appendix is added to Numbers that deals with a derivative case, a daughter who marries outside the tribe. Would the land become part of another tribe's inheritance (any sons would be members of their father's clan), and, eventually, would not the entire system of tribal territories be compromised (v. 3)?

It is not at all clear how v. 4 relates to the question. The Jubilee seems only to have applied to property that was sold (see Lev 25:8-34). And if it applied to this case, the Jubilee would have dealt with the problem—requiring the land to revert to the original tribe, clan, or family.

The eventuality is dealt with by requiring the women to marry within their own tribe, which they agree to and do. Thus, no *inheritance* is *transferred from one tribe to another* (v. 9).

This is yet another case illustrating the fact that the tradition was flexible, and that adaptations of the Mosaic law to on-going developments were expected.

Verse 13 concludes the section of the book describing preparations to move across *the Jordan*. It also concludes the book (cf. Lev 27:34).

Works Cited

Ackerman, James. 1987. "The Book of Numbers," *The Literary Guide to the Bible*, ed. Alter and Kermode.

Budd, Philip J. 1979. *Numbers*. WBC.

Davies, G. I. 1979. *The Way of the Wilderness*.

Noth, M. 1968. *Numbers*. OTL.

Olson, Dennis T. 1985. *The Death of the Old and the Birth of the New*.

Thompson, J. A. 1970. "Numbers," in *NBC*.

Snaith, N. H. 1966. "The Daughters of Zelophehad," *VT* 16:124–27. 1967. *Leviticus & Numbers*. NCB.

de Vaux, Roland. 1961. *Ancient Israel: Its Life and Institutions*.

Deuteronomy

John H. Tullock

Introduction

Deuteronomy is the fifth book of the TORAH or Pentateuch. The Hebrew name, "the words" (*haddebarim*), follows a Hebrew tradition of naming a book after its opening words. The English title, Deuteronomy, probably is based on the phrase "this second [or "repeated"] law" (*to deuteronomion touto*) found in the Septuagint, or LXX (Deut 17:18), the Greek translation of the Hebrew Bible. In this passage, the king is instructed to *have a copy of this law written for him in the presence of the levitical priests* (see Wright 1953, 311).

Nature of the Book

Deuteronomy is not primarily a royal book, however. Instead it is a book designed to proclaim the faith of the Israelite community. While it contains legal materials, principally in chaps. 12–26, it also is a book of exposition, structured as three sermons or addresses by MOSES (see outline).

Place of Deuteronomy in the Canon

Until the rise of modern biblical studies, Deuteronomy had traditionally been viewed as one of the five books of Moses (Genesis–Deuteronomy). As such, it does have certain affinities with the other four books, with its legal materials, its recapitulation of the Wilderness story, and its accounts of the choice of Joshua and of the death of Moses. It ends with a fitting tribute to Moses as leader of the people (Deut 34:10-12).

On the other hand, Deuteronomy also has affinities with several of the books that follow (Joshua, Judges, 1 and 2 Kings). It introduces Joshua as leader of the conquest of the land, but, more importantly, it introduces themes that are developed in the books that follow. Most notably among these are: 1) the theme of one central place for worship (see especially Deut 12:1-28), an idea brought to life in the reforms of King Josiah (640–609 B.C.E.; see 2 Kgs 22–23); 2) the theme of holy war that spoke of God's fighting for the people, the point of view from which the author of the Book of Joshua interprets the conquest of Canaan; 3) a view that Israel's history followed a pattern wherein the people would sin, judgment would come, the people would repent, and God would raise up a deliverer (see esp. Judg 2:6 to 3:6). Modern scholars refer to this interpretation of history as the "Deuteronomistic theme." This pattern is seen as recurring in the history of Israel by the writer(s) of Judges through 2 Kings, popularly known as the DEUTERONOMISTIC HISTORY.

Authorship and Date

Jewish tradition names Moses as the author of Deuteronomy, but modern scholarship has caused considerable doubt about this conclusion. For all but the most conservative interpreters, views range from those who still see a Mosaic core of materials in the book (Craigie 1976, 24–29) to those who do not give any credence to Mosaic authorship. Rather, the latter scholars see Moses only as the chief human character in a book, developed by scribes in what is called the "Deuteronomistic school." This school is credited not only with Deuteronomy but also the Deuteronomistic history (Joshua–2 Kings). Most recently, Deuteronomy has been described as a "kind of manual for future kings of Israel," similar to a type of literature found in Egyptian and Mesopotamian royal circles (Weinfeld 1991, 4; for a fuller discussion of authorship, see Christensen 1990, 211–12).

Regardless of one's view of the origins of the book, there is general agreement that at least the core of the book, chaps. 12–26, first appeared as a public document during the reign of King Josiah, serving as the basis of his reform in 622–621 B.C.E. (2 Kgs 22, 23).

Structure

Gerhard von Rad was the first scholar to propose that the book had been developed to be used in a ceremony for covenant making or covenant renewal. Later studies have tended to support his views, especially in the light of the discovery of Hittite and Assyrian treaty forms that were present in the Near East before Deuteronomy was written. Most of the elements of these treaty forms are present in Deuteronomy: an historical prologue, identifying the maker (the LORD) and specifying what he has done for the people (1-11); the stipulations as evidenced by the law code (12:1–26:15); provision for public reading (26:16-19); and a series of blessings for the proper keeping of the treaty and cursings for violations (chaps. 27–28). Until recently, the focus has been on the Hittite treaties as the model, but now the focus is on Assyrian vassal treaties as a more likely model (Weinfeld 1991, 9–13).

As an extended re-presentation of the demands of the covenant, the Book of Deuteronomy has the form of a long and complex speech of Moses to the Israelites, delivered on the plains of Moab shortly before Moses' death. The outline below seeks to preserve this feature of the book by using brief quotations from Deuteronomy to mark the divisions of the book.

For Further Study

In the *Mercer Dictionary of the Bible*: DEUTERONOMIST/DEUTERONOMISTIC HISTORIAN; DEUTERONOMY, BOOK OF.
In other sources: I. Cairns, "The Fifth Book of Moses, Called Deuteronomy," *Word and Presence*, ITC; P. C. Craigie, *Deuteronomy: Introduction*, NCIOT; A. D. H. Mayes, *Deuteronomy*, NCB; M. Weinfeld, *Deuteronomy 1–12*, AncB.

Commentary

An Outline

I. "These are the words"—On the Plains of Moab, 1:1-5
II. "The LORD our God spoke to us"—
The First Sermon of Moses, 1:6–4:40
  A. "You have stayed long enough"—
Departure from Sinai, 1:6-8
  B. "I am unable . . . to bear you"—
Organizing for Leadership, 1:9-18
  C. "We set out from Horeb"—
First Attempts at Conquest, 1:19-45
  D. "After you had stayed at Kadesh"—
Travels in Transjordan, 1:46–3:29
  E. "So now, Israel, give heed"—Conclusion to the
First Sermon of Moses and an Interlude, 4:1-43
III. "This is the law"—
The Second Sermon of Moses, 4:44–26:19; 28:1-68
  A. "These are the decrees"—
The Setting for the Sermon, 4:44-49
  B. "Moses convened all Israel"—
The Giving of the Law at Sinai, 5:1–11:32
  C. "These are the statutes
and ordinances"—12:1–25:19
  D. "When you have come into the land"—
The Concluding Rituals and an Interlude
26:1–27:26
  E. "If you will only obey the LORD your God"—
The Conclusion of the Sermon, 28:1-68
IV. "These are the words of the covenant"—
The Third Sermon of Moses, 29:1–30:20
  A. "The covenant . . . in the land of Moab"—
Renewing the Covenant, 29:1-29
  B. "When all these things happened to you"—
Blessings and Choices, 30:1-20

V. "When Moses had finished speaking"—
Moses' Final Days, 31:1-29
  A. "I am now one hundred twenty years old"—
Moses' Final Charge
to Joshua and the People, 31:1-8
  B. "Then Moses wrote down this law"—
The Ceremony of Covenant Renewal, 31:9-13
  C. "The Lord said to Moses"—
The Commissioning of Joshua, 31:14-23
  D. "When Moses finished writing"—The
Continuation of the Covenant Ceremony, 31:24-29
VI. "Then Moses recited the words of this song"—
The Song of Moses, 31:30–32:47
VII. "On that very day the LORD addressed
Moses"—Moses Views the Land, 32:48-52
VIII. "This is the blessing"—
The Blessing of Moses, 33:1-29
IX. "Then Moses went up"—
The Death of Moses, 34:1-12

"These are the words"—
On the Plains of Moab, 1:1-5

This prologue forms the setting for three sermons or addresses by Moses. The setting of this first address is twofold: geographical (vv. 1-2) and temporal (vv. 3-5). The third-person narration is typical of a later editor.

Moses speaks to the whole of the assembly (*all*) of Israel. The location is to the east and south of the Jordan and the Dead Sea, in the *land of Moab*. Most of the locations mentioned, except Moab, have not been identified at all, or if so, very tentatively. The time suggested would place this covenant-making scene just prior to the death of Moses. Indeed, Deuteronomy closes with the death and an evaluation of the ministry of Moses (chap. 34). Note, however, that the introduction is a third-person narrative reporting the events from an historical perspective.

"The LORD our God spoke to us"— The First Sermon of Moses, 1:6–4:40
"You have stayed long enough"— Departure from Sinai, 1:6-8

Moses reminds Israel of the LORD's commands to resume their journey and to begin the conquest of the land. The primary goal is the central hill country. From there they are to branch out into the surrounding areas. The ultimate boundaries are those contained in the promises to Abraham (Gen 15:18-19).

"I am unable . . . to bear you"— Organizing for Leadership, 1:9-18

This is an abbreviated version of an incident found in Exod 18. Here, however, there is no mention of Jethro, Moses's father-in-law, who according to that account suggested the plan of organization to Moses. The judges are charged with the responsibility to be fair and impartial. Only the hardest cases are to be brought to Moses. This basic pattern of organization is still to be found in judicial systems today. Note especially the phrase *the God of your ancestors* (see Gen 26:24), one of a number of old tribal names for God.

"We set out from Horeb"— First Attempts at Conquest, 1:19-45

These verses give another account of the events described in Num 13–14. When the journey from Horeb to Kadesh-barnea is completed (v. 19), Moses gives orders to prepare for the conquest (vv. 20-21). The countersuggestion by the people that spies be chosen to bring back a report on the territory to be conquered is accepted by Moses (vv. 22-25).

The spies give Moses a favorable report, but some of them report otherwise to the people; as a result, the people lose heart and are unwilling to proceed with the invasion. Their refusal brings a rebuke from Moses for their lack of faith. The gifts of the LORD God's leadership are contrasted with the people's ungratefulness and lack of faith (vv. 26-33). The LORD responds by sentencing the people to die in the wilderness, allowing only Caleb and Joshua of that generation to enter

the land (vv. 34-40). Then follows the abortive invasion that meets with defeat (vv. 41-45).

"After you had stayed at Kadesh"— Travels in Transjordan, 1:46–3:29

1:46–2:8a. Avoiding conflict with Edom. Israel journeys southward toward the Red Sea (Gulf of Aqaba), ostensibly to avoid conflict with the Edomites, traditional relatives to the Israelites through Esau, Jacob's twin (Gen 36:1). While this may reflect a tradition that some tribes encircled Edom on its eastern borders, the narrative says that they turned northward along the Arabah, the rift valley extending southward from the Dead Sea.

2:8b-25. Marching through Moab. Moab, tied to Israel by tradition through Lot, the nephew of Abraham (Gen 19:36-38), also is not to be conquered. The implication is that the LORD has given the Moabites their territory as a possession just as Canaan was given to Israel (v. 12). This is more clearly stated with regard to the Ammonites (v. 21). The doctrine of holy war, that is, that the LORD God fights for the people, is here extended to peoples other than Israel (cf. Amos 9:7). Such a blessing had not been extended to Sihon and Og, kings of the Amorites, however (vv. 24-25; 3:1-2). Deuteronomy interprets the defeat of Sihon as holy war: *The LORD our God gave him over to us* (v. 33; cf. Num 21:21-23).

2:26-37. Conflict with Sihon. Despite efforts to negotiate safe passage through the territory of Sihon, the holy war ensues with resulting devastation for the Amorites and Sihon.

3:1-11. Conflict with Bashan. A similar attitude on the part of Og, king of Bashan, brought a similar result. All that remained to mark Og's presence was his iron bed, preserved as a *museum piece* in Rabbah (NRSV note on v. 11).

3:12-22. Tribal allotments in Transjordan. Tribal territories for Reuben, Gad, and a half tribe of Manasseh were east of the Jordan River, often called Transjordan (see Num 32; Josh 13). The assurance that *it is the LORD your God who fights for you* (v. 22) is in keeping with the doctrine of holy war.

3:23-29. Moses forbidden to cross the Jordan. When Moses pleads to be allowed to cross the Jordan, he is forbidden to do so. As in Deuteronomy 1:37, the reason given is that he has to bear the brunt of the LORD's anger on behalf of the people (v. 26). This is in line with the ancient belief of corporate responsibility wherein the leader (the patriarch, or in Moses' case, a sort of surrogate patriarch for all of the people) is answerable for the sins of the people. But the reason given in Numbers 20:10-13 is that Moses' own lack of faith had caused him to lose the privilege of crossing the Jordan.

"So now, Israel, give heed"—Conclusion to the First Sermon of Moses and an Interlude, 4:1-43

4:1-8. God demands obedience. To realize their dream for a homeland, Israel has to concern itself with obeying the LORD their God. To do otherwise will bring disaster (vv. 1-4). Diligent observance of the LORD's demands will bring admiration by the nations for Israel's *wisdom and discernment* (v. 6). No other nation has such an opportunity (v. 8).

4:9-40. Learning the lessons of the wilderness days. What follows is a plea to Israel to learn the lessons of its history. Among these are: (1) There is no physical image by which the LORD is to be worshiped. This is a reminder that nothing created is to be worshiped instead of the LORD, whether an idol carved by human hands, a bird or an animal, or the heavenly bodies—sun, moon, or stars. God controls all of these creatures just as the deity has controlled Israel (vv. 9-20). (2) While the LORD has chosen Israel as a possession of the deity, this does not mean that God could not or would not punish disobedience on their part. That Moses has been forbidden to cross the Jordan should serve as a reminder *that the LORD demands absolute obedience.* Surely God would not allow the breaking of the covenant to go unpunished, especially a violation so serious as the making of idols (vv. 21-24). (3) Israel's greatest danger is the temptation to become complacent (v. 25). This could lead to the making of idols, which in turn could bring destruction and exile (v. 26). Yet, being *utterly destroyed* did not mean annihilation, since the purpose would be to stir up a desire to return to the LORD, who, in turn, would respond to the repentant people in mercy. The LORD surely would be faithful to the covenant made with the ancestors (vv. 26-31). (4) Their experiences should have taught them that the LORD their God is the only God. The themes of creation, the Sinai experience, the exodus, the leading of the ancestors and the giving of the land are evoked against a background of reminders of the LORD's wondrous powers. These reminders serve to prove that the LORD not only loved their ancestors, but that God also chose Israel because of that same love (vv. 32-37). The obvious conclusion is that *the LORD is God in heaven above and on earth beneath;*

there is no other (v. 39). This statement is closely akin to the theme of monotheism so boldly stated in Isa 40–48. It, plus the reminder that the land had been given them as a possession *as it is still today* (v. 38), supports the argument for a fairly late date for Deuteronomy since this latter quotation suggests that the conquest is a thing of the past.

4:41-43. An interlude: Moses chooses cities of refuge. Cities of refuge represent a step in the development of dealing with homicide, moving the act from the realm of family vengeance to state punishment. The punishment for a person's violent death in more primitive societies was a family matter; there was no state to act independently to determine the guilt or innocence of the one who caused the death. The three cities mentioned here probably were sites of important shrines. Shrines seemed to be neutral ground where the accused could stay while negotiations were carried out to determine guilt or innocence. Israel's oldest law code seems to envision such a role for the sanctuary (Exod 21:12-14; see also 1 Kgs 1:49-53 where Adonijah flees to the shrine until he can make a deal with Solomon). More extensive passages dealing with the cities of refuge are to be found in Deut 19:1-13; Josh 20:1-6; and Num 35:9-34.

"This is the law"—The Second Sermon of Moses, 4:44–26:19; 28:1-28

"These are the decrees"— The Setting for the Sermon, 4:44-49

The editorial introduction presents the subject matter of the sermon as *the decrees and the statutes and ordinances that Moses spoke to the Israelites* (v. 45); the site is *beyond the Jordan* (v. 46); the time is after the defeat of Kings Sihon and Og (vv. 47-49). The narrator seems be recounting events of the distant past.

"Moses convened all Israel"— The Giving of the Law at Sinai, 5:1–11:32

5:1-33. The giving of the law. What follows is a retelling of the giving of the TEN COMMANDMENTS from the perspective of the writer of Deuteronomy (v. 1a).

5:1b-5. Hear, O Israel. This call to worship introduces the sermon as a whole and the narrative about the Ten Commandments in particular. *The LORD our God made a covenant with us* (v. 2) connects *today* (v. 1b) and the past events at Horeb, emphasizing the covenant's continuing relevance. A further reminder is to be found in the assertion that *the LORD spoke with you face to face* (v. 4). These references may be taken from a ritual for a ceremony of COVENANT renewal.

5:6. I am the LORD your God. This statement identifies the LORD as covenant maker while *who brought you out of the land of Egypt* establishes the historical basis for his rights as covenant maker and giver of the commandments. Harrelson suggests the commandments are to be divided into four groups: 1–3, *God's absolute demands*; 4–5, *God's basic institutions*; 6–7, *God's fundamental personal demands*; 8–10, *God's fundamental social demands* (Harrelson 1990, 883–85).

5:7. You shall have no other gods before me. This demand for absolute loyalty on Israel's part, while not ruling out the belief in the existence of other gods, nonetheless gives Israel no choice as to where its obligations for worship lie. Such a standard eventually leads to a clear MONOTHEISM. That it was well on the way to fruition by the time Deuteronomy reached final form is strongly implied in Deuteronomy 4:39: *the LORD is God . . . there is no other* (see Ellis 1990, 581–82). Roman Catholic tradition connects this verse to 5:8-10 to form the first commandment; in Jewish usage, 5:7-10 comprise the second commandment, with 5:6, "I the LORD am your God, who brought you out of the land of Egypt," as the first commandment.

5:8-10. You shall not make for yourself an idol. The concept that the LORD could not be portrayed in any material form is a unique contribution that the religion of Israel makes to the history of religious thought (see IDOLATRY). It becomes the basis for the doctrines of God's omnipresence (the unlimited ability to be anywhere at all times) and God's omniscience (all-knowingness).

5:11. You shall not make wrongful use of the name of the LORD your God. This reflects the view that one's name summed up the essence of who one was. To misuse or abuse one's name is, in a real sense, to misuse or abuse the bearer of the name. To misuse the LORD's name would thus be abusive both to the divine power and person. Such a misuse would be involved in invoking the LORD's name to injure another person by means of a curse. That is the LORD's prerogative (see Smith 1990, 188–89).

5:12-15. Observe the sabbath day and keep it holy. This basic institution in Israelite religious life has no parallel in any other society. The emphasis in on rest, not activity (Harrelson 1990, 884). Deuteronomy sees this as the primary reason for the sabbath's existence—providing rest for self, family, servants, and animals after six days of labor. Exodus 20:11 ties it to

the LORD's rest after six days of creation. Thus, both versions emphasize rest, Exodus from the divine standpoint, Deuteronomy from the human standpoint (Tullock 1990, 779–81).

5:16. Honor your father and your mother. The second basic institution of Israelite life is the FAMILY. This commandment may also be viewed as introducing a segment on societal relationships, beginning with the most basic unit, the family. That this commandment is taken seriously is evidenced by laws in the Covenant Code providing for the death penalty for the abuse of parents (Exod 21:15, 17). The positive emphasis is on care for parents. The reward for such conduct is that *it may go well with you.* Deuteronomy has a longer version of this promise than Exodus does.

5:17. You shall not murder. MURDER is the preferred translation here since the verb is used in the prophets to imply intentional killing (Hos 4:2; Isa 1:21, cf. Judg 20:4; 1 Kgs 21:19). Life belongs to the LORD, who gives it and who alone has the right to take it. For people to assume that right is to presume upon the privileges of the LORD. When human life loses its value, human society loses its stability.

5:18. Neither shall you commit adultery. ADULTERY is viewed in this time as a violation both of one's MARRIAGE rights and of one's property rights. Wives are seen as a part of the husband's property (cf. Exod 20:17). Because of this, adultery on the wife's part probably was viewed as a more serious offense than adultery by the husband. The teachings of Jesus helped overcome this disparity (Matt 5:27-32; John 8:1-11). Beyond that, any threat to the family unit is viewed in Israel as a threat to the peace and stability of the society as a whole. Weak families mean a weak society. And adultery by the husband also weakened the family unit, while damaging another family as well.

5:19. Neither shall you steal. This is another commandment that deals with destructive elements in society. The Israelite view of the close relationship of persons to their tangible property makes theft a serious offense (cf. the story of Achan and the destruction of his property along with him, Josh 7). One's property is a means for sustaining the owner's life. To deprive a person of his/her property by theft is, in a sense, a threat to that person's continued existence.

5:20. Neither shall you bear false witness against your neighbor. The spoken word has power (Isa 55:11). Great stress is placed on truth-telling in the courts (Exod 23:1; Deut 19:15-21; 1 Kgs 22:16; Hos 4:2), especially when the lawsuit involved a neighbor (see also the story of Susanna in the Apocrypha). The damage done by lying can also threaten life. A common phrase in Israelite court procedure is the admonition to avoid shedding *innocent blood* (19:10, 13; cf. Jer 26:15). To convict a person of a capital crime on the basis of false testimony can, of course, lead to the shedding of innocent blood.

5:21. Neither shall you covet. This commandment differs from Exodus 20:17 where the order is *house . . . wife . . . slave*, etc. The order reflects the same concern for human values that appears in the sabbath commandment (5:12). In Exodus the wife is part of the property. Here she is given priority over the property. This commandment addresses the motivation that leads to the violation of the commandments listed earlier. In that sense, it is a summary commandment. The NRSV translation of the tenth commandment reflects the Roman Catholic and Lutheran traditions of dividing it into two commandments, since those traditions combine commandments one and two to form their first commandment.

5:22-27. The LORD and the people. The commandments are the LORD's gift to Israel. That they were written on stone emphasizes their permanent nature. The personal revelation of the LORD to *all the heads of your tribes and your elders* (v. 23) symbolizes the personal nature of that revelation, as well as its awe-inspiring gravity. So overwhelming is the experience that it moves the people to request that any further revelation be mediated to them through Moses (v. 27).

5:28-33. The LORD and Moses. Moses is not only to hear the *commandments, the statutes and the ordinances*, but he is also to *teach them*, so that Israel may *do them in the land that I am giving them to possess* (v. 31). He is to be mediator and teacher, both receiver and proclaimer of the will of God to the people.

6:1–11:32. An exposition of the first commandment. What follows in the next six chapters is a long expository sermon based, it seems, on the first commandment. We should note that in the Jewish tradition the first commandment is *I am the LORD your God, who brought you out of the land of Egypt, out of the house of slavery* (v. 6; Exod 20:2). In Judaism the commandment against the making of carved images is considered to be part of the commandment to worship no other gods besides the LORD. It is perhaps best to say that Deut 6:1–11:32 is an exposition of all three of these: the self-identification of the LORD as Israel's savior, the prohibition of the worship of any other deity, and the prohibition of the making of carved images. While many subjects are treated in these chapters, the underlying theme is what it means for Israel to worship the LORD only. According to these chapters, it means that Israel is to demonstrate utter loyalty and fidelity to the God of the COVENANT, the REDEEMER of Israel, the LORD.

6:1-3. This is the commandment. This phrase seems to refer to the first commandment, the basis for all the others, as well as to *the statutes and the ordinances* (v. 1). To *hear . . . and observe* are the basic requirements for blessing in the land (v. 3; 5:1), just as the LORD promised Israel's ancestors (Gen 12:1-7). If there is to be blessing, there must be reverent obedience to all that the LORD commands.

6:4-9. The great commandment. *Hear [shema], O Israel: The LORD is our God, the LORD alone.* This call for Israel's undivided loyalty to the LORD is called the SHEMA in Jewish tradition after its first word in Hebrew. This demand for undivided loyalty is the basic principle of Israelite religion. Out of that principle, all legal and religious themes and institutions flow. Israel's commitment is to be to the LORD alone. It is to be a commitment of the whole person: *with all your heart*, involving emotional as well as mental capacities; *with all your soul*, all those unique qualities that makes one a person, the essence of one's existence; *with all your might*, centering one's efforts and attention on living in total devotion to the one God who is LORD alone (vv. 4-5; cf. Mark 12:29-30). *Keep . . . recite . . . bind . . . write* all are action words suggesting practical means for maintaining the *shema* at the center of personal and family attention.

While Israelite religion is to be imageless as regards deity, it does not lack for symbols. This passage furnishes the inspiration for a number of those symbols that are found in later Judaism (vv. 6-9). The phrase *emblem on your forehead* becomes the basis for the phylactery, a small box containing verses of scripture and attached to a leather thong to tie around the arm and the head (Matt 23:5). The command *write them on the doorposts* (*mezuzot*) is the inspiration for the Mezuzah, a small box containing a bit of parchment and attached to the trim surrounding the door, showing that an observant Jewish family resides there.

6:10-19. The LORD your God you shall fear. When the people come into the land and become accustomed to its bounty, they will find it easy to become careless and become distracted, causing them to *forget the LORD* who has brought them there (vv. 10-12). For that reason, their dedicated love should be blended with profound reverence for the LORD. *Fear* here does not imply terror so much as it does a sense of awe and profound respect. Such reverence prevents idolatry (v. 13), promotes obedience and right conduct (vv. 17-18a) and will lead to Israel's inheritance of the promises God made to the ancestors (vv. 18b-19).

6:20-25. Teach the children. Jewish history has illustrated the wisdom of the principle enunciated in this passage. To preserve the family, one thing that is vital is the passing on of a sense of identity and history. That can be done most effectively as each generation assumes the responsibility to pass on the sense of family heritage and values to the next generation. This, indeed, is *for our lasting good, so as to keep us alive* (v. 24).

7:1-26. Holy land, holy people, and holy war. No teaching in Deuteronomy poses more of a moral dilemma for modern religious folk than the teaching concerning HOLY WAR. In practical terms, its objective is to allow Israel to "occupy and settle the land of God's promise with no risk of any residual heathen contamination" (Wilson 1990, 385–86). It involves carrying the exclusive worship of the LORD to its most extreme limits—by the elimination not only of other gods but also of those who worship other gods, lest their worship be a snare to lead Israel astray *to serve other gods* (v. 4). Israel is to be *a people holy to the LORD your God: the LORD your God has chosen you . . . to be his people* (v. 6). Holy war probably is best understood as part of the fabric of ancient cultures, interpreted by Israel in the light of its own understanding of God (see further, Wilson 1990, 385–86).

Ironically, in the midst of this harshest portrayal of the LORD's demands we are introduced to the most striking statement about God's choice of Israel as the people of the LORD: not because they were numerous but *because the LORD loved you and kept the oath he swore to your ancestors* (vv. 7-8). The evidence of covenant loyalty is an answering love that motivates the keeping of God's commandments, *to a thousand generations* (v. 9). If they faithfully follow God's will as revealed in the commandments and ordinances, they can confidently go forth to battle against their enemies, knowing that the LORD is going before them to give them success (vv. 12-26).

8:1-10. Obedience brings blessing. Deuteronomy alternates between the poles of positive promises and negative warnings. As the experience in the wilderness should have taught Israel, obedience brings blessing. The LORD's discipline is as the discipline of a parent (v. 5). Israel's responsibility is to "live according to his laws and have reverence for him" (v. 6b TEV).

8:11-20. Disobedience brings judgment. The plea for obedience is coupled with a warning not to forget all that the LORD has done for the people in the past (vv. 11-16). Failure to remember those lessons, coupled with disobedience, will bring judgment on Israel just as it has on other nations (vv. 17-20).

9:1-7. Why the LORD gives the land. *Hear, O Israel* (v. 1) introduces another rehearsal of the events in the wilderness. It is done so as to remind the people that neither their personal righteousness nor their past experience qualifies them to receive the gift of the land. They have no cause for self-righteousness. The land is theirs for two reasons: (1) *because of the wickedness of these nations;* and (2) so the LORD can *fulfill the promise . . . made on oath to your ancestors* (v. 5).

9:8-10:11. Recounting Israel's rebellion. What follows is Deuteronomy's most extended account of the giving of the law at Horeb: the giving of the first tablets to Moses (9:8-10); the golden calf incident, with a passing reference to Aaron's role (9:11-21, cf. Exod 32); coming to Kadesh-barnea and the failure to invade from the south (9:22-24; cf. Num 13–14); an account of Moses intervening for the people, appealing to the LORD's honor and reminding God that *they are the people of your very own possession* whom God has brought out by *great power and . . . outstretched arm* (9:29; cf. Exod 32:11-14, 31-34).

The account ends with the making of the second set of tablets. What is new here is that Moses is credited with building the ark to hold the tablets (10:1-5; cf. Exod 25:1-22). There follows an interlude with a travel narrative fragment, serving as a background for naming the Levites as bearers of the ark (10:6-9; cf. Num 33:30-38). After this, Moses once again intercedes and gets the LORD's approval to continue leading the people (10:10-11).

10:12-11:32. What does the LORD require of you? The final summation of the exposition of the first commandment begins with a restatement of the LORD's requirements: reverential awe (*fear*, see 6:13), proper conduct (*walk*), joyful devotion (*love*), humble submission (*serve . . . with . . . heart . . . and . . . soul*), and to live in keeping with God's revealed will by keeping the divine commandments. Israel is to do this for the sake of their *own well-being* (10:12-13). The LORD loved their ancestors and chose Israel to be God's own people (10:15). As the LORD who is *God of gods, and Lord of lords* (10:17), God is just and compassionate to all peoples. Israel is to exemplify that love even to aliens in the community. After all, they had been privileged to witness *great and awesome things* (10:21).

Keeping the covenant is not just a responsibility to be passed on to a future generation. Instead, this generation, on the basis of its own experiences, must live in the light of those experiences (11:1-7). Faithfulness to the covenant will be rewarded by blessing when they come into the land. Unfaithfulness, i.e., allowing themselves to be seduced into worshiping idols (11:16), will bring crop failure and famine (11:8-17). Therefore, full attention must be given to keeping and teaching the words and will of the LORD (11:18-21; see 6:5-9). Israel must be a holy people if they are to be successful in the holy war (11:22-25; chap. 7). The choice before Israel, then, is the choice between blessing that comes with obedience or the curse that will follow disobedience (11:26-28; Smith 1990, 188–89). On vv. 26-30, see comment on chap. 27.

"These are the statutes and ordinances," 12:1–25:19

The core of the second address is the Deuteronomistic Code, one of three such codes of Israelite law, the others being the Covenant Code and the Priestly Code (see Dahlberg 1990, esp. 503–07). While this particular code usually is regarded as the second oldest of the three, dating from the seventh century B.C.E., many of its laws reflect an earlier time. It is generally accepted that it was discovered during Josiah's reign and gave the theological basis for his reform (2 Kgs 22–23; Cochran 1990, 472). In general, it grows out of a settled society and advocates a more humane attitude toward less fortunate members of society, especially women and resident aliens.

12:1-28. One place to worship. A remedy that Deuteronomy proposes to combat the dangers of paganism is twofold: (1) to destroy pagan shrines (vv. 2-4); and (2) to have only one central place to worship (vv. 5-7). Both of these aims are fulfilled in JOSIAH's reform, following the finding of a document in the Temple (2 Kgs 22–23). In this single SHRINE, all SACRIFICE would be carried out (vv. 6, 11, 14). The Covenant Code provides for multiple shrines (Exod 20:24), as does an older part of the Priestly Code, known as the Holiness Code (Lev 17). As a result of the demand that all sacrifice be carried out at one central location, the code had to provide for nonpriestly slaughter of animals for food, while still maintaining the ban on eating blood (vv. 15-27, esp. vv. 23-24; Gen 9:3-4; Lev 17:10-11).

12:29–13:18. Avoiding idol worship and its advocates. A major concern of the Deuteronomistic Code was that Israel was continually being drawn to the worship of the gods of its neighbors. Coupled with the positive emphasis on total devotion to the LORD were warnings against being drawn into the worship of idols.

12:29-32. Do not worship other gods. The practices of others, whether they are social practices or religious practices, tempt Israel to *want to do the same* (12:30). The people, however, are to avoid such practices. Two examples of things to be avoided are cited: *every abhorrent thing* probably refers to cult prostitution (23:17-18), and the reference to burning *their sons and daughters* (v. 31) refers to the practice of human sacrifice, especially of children. Ample archaeological evidence of such practices has been found at ancient Carthage, a colony of the Phoenicians, where the children were sacrificed to the Phoenician god MOLECH (see Cornfeld 1976, 52; cf. Lev 18:21; 2 Kgs 23:10; Judg 11:29-40; Jer 32:35; also see Andrews 1990, 580–81 for a different interpretation of Molech).

13:1-5. The danger of false prophets. True prophets do not lead people into idolatry, no matter how spectacular their *omens or portents* (v. 1). False prophets serve only to test the sincerity of one's love for the LORD God (12:3-4). Israel is to take radical measures to rid itself of false prophets. To fail to do so would lead to idolatry (v. 5).

13:6-11. Unfaithful family members. Perhaps a more insidious threat to the health of one's religious life would be family members who try to lead others into the worship of false gods. The same radical measures are to be taken against them as against false prophets (vv. 9-11).

13:12-18. Idolatrous cities. Centers of idol worship are subject to the rules of holy war (vv. 12-16; see comments on chap. 7). Behind such radical measures as proposed by Deuteronomy are the twin convictions that: (1) the LORD God is holy, and (2) God demands an answering dedication to holy living by Israel. Anything less will not be sufficient (vv. 17-18).

14:1–15:23. Rules for holy living. In keeping with the LORD's demands, Deuteronomy sets forth specific rules for holy living. The rules cover a broad area of concern, from religious rites to be avoided to dietary taboos to humanitarian easing of religious demands.

14:1-2. Shun pagan customs. As acts of mourning, probably connected with seasonal worship, Israel's neighbors trimmed their forelocks and gashed their faces. Israel was forbidden to follow such practices (Lev 19:27-28; cf. Ezek 24:15-24; 1 Kgs 18:28).

14:3-21. Clean and unclean animals. Cleanness and uncleanness had both a physical and a religious significance. Here, an animal is clean that has *the hoof cleft in two, and chews the cud* (v. 6). A fish is clean if it *has fins and scales* (v. 9). All other fish and animals are unclean. While no clean birds are listed, unclean ones are; but no clear reason is given for the distinction, as is the case with the animals (vv. 11-20; see Eakin 1990, 159 and the commentary above on Lev 11). The ban against eating animals that die naturally did not arise out of sanitary considerations, but rather from the fact that they are not bled properly when they die. Eating flesh with blood still in it is expressly forbidden for *a people holy to the LORD your God* (v. 21). Boiling *a kid in its mother's milk* is a Canaanite religious practice and thus forbidden for Israel (v. 21).

14:22-29. The use of the tithe. Thanksgiving is an essential part of worship in early Israel. The tithe is part of that thanksgiving. It provides material support for the central sanctuary (Neh 10:35-39; Mal 3:8-10; Lev 27:30). Deuteronomy makes it clear, also, that those who bring the tithes eat a portion of them in the meals associated with the sacrifices (vv. 22-23). In light of its demand for a central sanctuary, Deuteronomy modifies the law of the tithe in two practical ways: (1) people who live too far away to bring animals or produce to the sanctuary may bring money to buy whatever is necessary for the sacrifices—*oxen, sheep, wine, strong drink, or whatever you desire* (v. 26); (2) instead of requiring the tithe to be brought annually, it can be brought *every third year* (v. 28).

15:1-18. The sabbatical year. The sabbath principle is applied to years as well as to weeks. For Deuteronomy it is, like the weekly sabbath, given for a humanitarian purpose. It is a time for the forgiveness of debts that one Israelite owes to another. Foreigners still have to pay, but the Israelite creditor has to *remit your claim on whatever any member of your community owes you* (v. 3). Lest anyone refuse to lend money as the sabbatical year approaches, there is the warning that failure to heed the cries of the needy neighbor will result in guilt being incurred. Instead, one is to *give liberally and be ungrudging*, for such liberality will bring the LORD's blessing (v. 10).

Closely related to the forgiveness of debt is the release of people who have been enslaved for debt. An Israelite can become a slave: (1) when one steals something, is caught, and cannot make the loss good

(Exod 22:1 [21:37 MT]); (2)when one becomes so poor for some reason that slavery is the only option left for survival (Lev 25:39); or (3) when children are taken from their parents in lieu of payment of a debt (2 Kgs 4:1). Not only is the slave to be freed in the sabbatical year; he or she is to be *given some of the bounty with which the LORD your God has blessed you*, as an aid in starting a new life (v. 14). The Priestly Code has no such provisions (Lev 25:40-41). While earlier laws do not provide equal treatment for female slaves, Deuteronomy does (vv. 12, 17). These actions are to be taken without complaint, since *for six years they have given you service worth the wages of hired laborers*. In addition, ungrudging compliance will cause the LORD God to *bless you in all that you do* (v. 18).

15:19-23. The sacrifice of firstborn animals. Ancient people held that the firstborn of both humans and animals had a special significance. While some other peoples sacrificed firstborn children, Israelite law provides for the redemption of such (Num 18:15; Exod 34:20; cf. Gen 22:1-19). Firstborn animals are to be taken to the central sanctuary and sacrificed, provided they have no physical deformities. Such sacrifices are joyous occasions, since the person who is offering the sacrifice eats a portion of the animal after a portion is given to the priest (v. 20; Lev 1:3-13). Defective animals are not sacrificed, but can be eaten, if they are killed in the proper way (vv. 21-23).

16:1-17. Holy days. This is Deuteronomy's version of laws for the festival days: Passover/Unleavened Bread, the Festival of Weeks, and the Festival of Booths. These regulations occupy a middle position between those found in Exodus (23:12-19 and 34:18-26), which are earlier, and those in Leviticus (chap. 23) and Numbers (chaps. 28–29), which are later.

16:1-8. Passover/Unleavened Bread. *Observe . . . by keeping the passover* (v. 1). Passover probably originated as a shepherd's festival, celebrated in the Spring (March–April), and designed to insure a successful lambing season. As a result of the exodus experience, Israel adapts it to commemorate the conviction that *the LORD your God brought you out of Egypt by night* (v. 1). The word "passover" is based on the Hebrew verb *pasach*, meaning *to pass or spring over*, and most likely has to do with the conviction of Israel that "they were *passed over* or spared by the *destroyer (death)*" (Joines 1990, 648). *You shall offer . . . at the place that the LORD will choose* (v. 2) represents a change in two important aspects: (1) previously passover was to be eaten in one's own town and essentially was a family festival (Exod 12:21-28), but now it becomes one of three major festivals celebrated at the central shrine; (2) it is combined with the festival of unleavened bread, another older festival that originated as an agricultural festival, celebrating the harvest of grain. In the Covenant Code (Exod 23:14-15), this latter festival is the first major festival of the year. Deuteronomy retains it by combining it with passover to maintain the number of three major festivals. Thus, there is *the passover sacrifice . . . from the flock and the herd* (v. 2) followed by seven days when *you shall eat unleavened bread* [*matsot*] (v. 3). The ban on offering the passover sacrifice *within any of your towns* (v. 5) is in line with Deuteronomy's emphasis on the centralization of worship. The reform of King Josiah was based on these principles and included a national celebration of the passover, the likes of which had not been kept "since the days of the judges who judged Israel" (2 Kgs 23:22). This would seem to indicate that Josiah was reviving an ancient practice (cf. Josh 5:10-11; see Kraus 1966, 51).

16:9-12. The Festival of Weeks. *Seven weeks*, that is, fifty days after the month of Abib (March–April), brings one to May–June, the time for the grain harvest that this festival celebrates. Later, it is called Pentecost (Acts 2:1), based on the Greek word for the number fifty. This is a joyous festival requiring *a freewill offering in proportion to the blessing that you have received* (v. 10). A bountiful harvest is cause for joy for all: *you . . . sons . . . daughters . . . male and female slaves . . . the Levites . . . strangers . . . orphans . . . widows* (v. 11). In short, it means that God is showing favor to Israel and that there will be enough to eat in the days ahead (Hancock 1990a, 873; 1990b, 957–58).

16:13-15. Festival of Booths. This seven-day festival comes *when you have gathered in the produce from your threshing floor and your wine press* (v. 13). It originally celebrated the fruit harvest. In later practice, it came to commemorate the wilderness experience when Israel lived in tents. Thus, the name "festival of booths" or "tabernacles." It, too, calls for general rejoicing (v. 14) and becomes "the most joyous and universal" of the major festivals (1 Kgs 8:2,65; 2 Chr 7:8; Ezek 45:23-25; Hancock 1990a, 873). The reforms of Ezra gave it an especially prominent place (Neh 8).

16:16-17. Attendance at the festivals. *All your males* were expected to attend the major festivals. They are not to appear *empty-handed*, but are *to give as they are able* as the LORD God has blessed them.

This requirement is an ideal that becomes increasingly difficult to achieve, especially after the Babylonian EXILE and the scattering of the Israelites, now called Jews, all over the Near East and the Mediterranean world. For many, to be able to journey to Jerusalem for the great festivals once in a lifetime was a major event.

16:18–17:20. Civil and religious laws. Here are found rules for the administration of justice and for the regulation of religion. The rules include the appointment of judges who will be concerned with *justice, and only justice* (16:20); how to deal with persons accused of idolatry; how to handle cases that are unusually difficult to adjudicate; and how kings are to be controlled.

16:18-20. Administration of justice. The hope for real justice always begins with the appointment of *judges and officials . . .* [who] *shall render just decisions for the people* (v. 18). Justice can be distorted in two ways: (1) by showing partiality and favoritism in its administration, and (2) by the giving and the taking of bribes, *for a bribe blinds the eyes of the wise and subverts the cause of those who are in the right* (v. 19). The preservation and promotion of justice in any society is essential for the continuing health and prosperity of the community (v. 20).

16:21-22. Avoid Canaanite customs. The *tree* or *sacred pole* could represent phallic symbols of Baal, but a more likely interpretation is that the pole was a carved representation of Asherah, "the wife/consort of the chief god of the Canaanite and Phoenician pantheons" (Vinson 1990, 68). Likewise, the tree would have the same symbolism. These, along with the *stone pillar*, are Canaanite cult objects, things that *the LORD your God hates* (v. 22).

17:1. An unworthy sacrifice. To offer an animal *that has a defect* is insulting to the LORD God because it is less than one's best and reveals an improper attitude (cf. Mal 1:7-8).

17:2-7. Penalties for pagan worship. Just as enticing one to worship idols calls for severe penalties, so also the presence of idol worship itself calls for strong measures to stamp it out in Israel (cf. 13:6-18). Imbedded in this section is a fundamental principle of Israelite jurisprudence: capital punishment cannot be carried out unless two or three persons witnessed the crime. The accused cannot be sentenced to death based on the testimony of one person alone (v. 6). Death is by stoning and the witnesses also are to lead in the execution (v. 7). This requirement, in itself, should be a deterrent to giving false testimony. See the commentary on the Book of Susanna for a later example of how this type of procedure was carried out.

17:8-13. Disposal of difficult cases. Cases too difficult for local courts to decide may be appealed to a higher court. In general, these cases are in three categories: (1) homicide cases, whether they were premeditated or unpremeditated (Exod 21:12-14; see further the comments on Deut 19:4-7); (2) civil matters, i.e., one kind of legal claim or another; or (3) physical assault (Exod 21:18-27). The higher court consists of *the levitical priests and the judge who is in office in those days* (v. 9). The priests would be those at the central sanctuary and the judge is probably a layperson (vv. 8-9; see 2 Chr 19:5-11). Their decision is to be carried out to the letter. Anyone who presumes to do otherwise is subject to the death penalty (vv. 10-13).

17:14-20. Rules for kingship. An antimonarchical bias continued to flourish in Israel long after the beginning of the monarchy. At Saul's inaugural, Samuel is said to have laid down rules for the kingship; he wrote the rules "in a book and laid it up before the LORD" (1 Sam 10:25). Such a bias undoubtedly contributed to the breakup of the kingdom at Solomon's death. Israel's kings are to be native-born: *you are not permitted to put a foreigner over you* (v. 15). *Many horses . . . many wives . . . silver and gold . . . in great quantity* all represent dangers for the king, leading to entanglements with foreign governments, too much physical pleasure, and pride, *exalting himself above the other members of the community* [or] *turning aside from the commandment* (vv. 16-20; cf. 2 Kgs 22:8).

18:1-22. Rules for proper worship. Two important categories of religious officials are the subjects of these rules—priests and prophets. Both offices have heavy responsibility. Singled out for special attention are the dangers of idolatry and of false prophecy.

18:1-8. Priests and their support. *The levitical priests, the whole tribe of Levi, shall have no allotment* refers to the fact that the Levites (LEVI/LEVITES) are, by tradition, a landless tribe, dependent upon the people for their support. At one time, they seem to have been a secular tribe who, because of their service to the LORD, were made PRIESTS (Exod 32:25-29). Yet, some passages cast doubt on this conclusion (Exod 4:14; Judg 17:7; Num 3:5-9). In later tradition, the Levites are usually spoken of more as a guild of religious workers. Tradition has it that they lost favor with the monarchy when ABIATHAR, a Levite, plotted against the

elevation of Solomon to the throne and was replaced by the priest Zadok, whose descendants then became the dominant priestly family (see Bjornard 1990a, 510–11; 1990b, 710–11). Deuteronomy's laws seem to exalt the Levites more than other codes do. Deuteronomy follows a more traditional view of the origin and function of the Levites (v. 2). Their support comes from the animals that are sacrificed (*they shall give to the priest the shoulder, . . . jowls, and the stomach*), as well as *the first fruits . . . [and] the first of the fleece of your sheep* (vv. 3-4). Since ministry is the function of the priest, he deserves the support of all the people for his service (v. 5). It should be observed that such a ministry covered more functions than strictly religious duties. The priest was also teacher, a medical practitioner, and legal expert. A Levite in *any of your towns* denotes Levites who presided over local shrines before worship was centralized during Josiah's reign (2 Kgs 23:8). While Deuteronomy decrees that they are to be allowed to function as priests in Jerusalem (vv. 6-8), it seems that, in reality, they did not do so (2 Kgs 23:9).

18:9-14. Avoiding false worship. This is yet another warning against being drawn into the worship of pagan gods. Making *a son or daughter pass through fire* (v. 10) seems to be a rite associated with the worship of MOLECH, the Ammonite deity (see 2 Kgs 16:3 where Pekah of Israel is said to have burned his son; cf. 2 Kgs 21:6; Jer 7:31; 19:5; 32:35). Israel is warned to *remain completely loyal to the LORD your God* (v. 13).

18:15-18. Respect for the LORD's prophets. While the priest is perceived as a professional who is skilled in directing communication *toward* God, prophets are known as spokespersons *for* God. Their message is not their own; it is the LORD's message. The prophet is only the messenger. Moses is seen as the prophet *par excellence* (34:10-11), the one who is the model for all other prophets. Any true prophet must be *a prophet like* Moses (v. 15). A true prophet is one to whom the LORD speaks and who, in turn, is the LORD's spokesperson (v. 18; cf. Exod 7:1). How to separate the true prophet from the false always is a continuing problem, even in modern society. Such an influential and powerful function is a magnet for charlatans. The test of the true prophet is: *If* [one] *speaks in the name of the LORD but the thing does not take place or prove true, . . . the LORD has not spoken* (v. 22; cf. Jer 28). Other tests of true prophecy also appear: those who prophesy *smooth things* (Isa 30:10) are not trustworthy, while those who have stood in God's council (Jer 23:32) have received God's true word.

19:1-21. Rules for administering justice. Several legal procedures are the subject of this section. Chief among them is the provision for cities of refuge, designed to offer temporary protection to persons who have committed homicide.

19:1-13. Cities of refuge. Here Deuteronomy gives a further elaboration of a subject introduced in 4:41-43 (see comments there). *You shall set apart three cities* in addition to those named in 4:41-43. These are to be on the west side of the Jordan (19:1-3). *This is the case of a homicide* introduces a more precise delineation between intentional and unintentional killing. Here the emphasis is on an accidental killing, illustrated by an example: an axehead comes loose from the handle, striking a bystander and killing him (v. 5; cf. Num 35:13-28 where many examples are given; see also Exod 21:12-14). The briefest of these texts dealing with places of refuge (Exod 21:12-14) is from the oldest code (Covenant) while the more elaborate discussion in Numbers is from the Priestly Code. That our passage from Deuteronomy is more detailed than Exodus but less detailed than Numbers would seem to suggest it stands between these two passages chronologically as well. *The killer may flee to one of these cities and live* reveals the purpose of the cities of refuge—to provide a chance for a fair hearing for one who is not guilty of murder. Yet there is danger, for *if the distance is too great* the killer may not be able to escape the vengeful hand of the *avenger of blood* whose *hot anger* would certainly color his sense of fairness toward one who had killed his relative accidentally (v. 6). Deuteronomy envisions that Israel's territorial expansion may necessitate the addition of *three more cities*, for a total of nine (vv. 8-10; but see Num 35:13-15 and Josh 20:7-9 where the number is six). Judgment seems to be in the hands of the elders of the killer's home city. If the elders determine that a murder has been committed, then the murderer is to be taken from the city of refuge *and handed over to the avenger of blood to be put to death* (v. 12). Here we see the beginning of the practice of the state's playing a role by judging the person who has killed someone, while still allowing the nearest of kin of the deceased to carry out the execution. This manner of dealing with murder was in vogue in Israel at least until the time of Solomon (see Solomon's belated punishment of Joab for the murder of Abner, 1 Kgs 2:28-35).

19:14. Property markers. That *your neighbor's boundary marker* is an ancient law is attested by the fact that there is reference to the same law twice in the Book of Proverbs (22:28; 23:10).

19:15-21. Rules for witnesses. *A single witness shall not suffice* introduces an expansion of the principle first laid down in 17:6 (see comment on that verse). A charge can only be sustained on the testimony of two or more witnesses (v. 15). If a malicious person deliberately gives false testimony against an innocent person, the penalty is that the assembled spectators *shall do to the false witness just as the false witness had meant to do to the other* (v. 19). Thus, the lecherous old men who were rebuffed by the heroine in the apocryphal story of Susanna accuse her of adultery. When Daniel unmasks their plot, it is they, not Susanna, who are stoned.

This passage concludes with the law of retaliation (*lex talionis*); *life for life, eye for eye, tooth for tooth*, etc. (v. 21). *Lex talionis* was a progressive step in the development of law because it adjusted the punishment to the nature of the crime. Before this development, which probably arose as the state took a more active role in law enforcement, the older law of vengeance could lead to all sorts of excessive punishment, since the avenger was the one who would determine what punishment was sufficient to satisfy the desire for vengeance (cf. Gen 4:23-24).

20:1-20. Rules for holy war. This section is a further elaboration of the rules for holy war (see comments on 7:1-26, and Wilson 1990, 385–86). The institution of holy warfare probably was no more than a cherished memory by the time the Book of Deuteronomy was completed.

20:1-9. Preparation for holy war. When Israel faces *an army*, even one that is larger than their own, in holy war, the people are not to fear, for *the LORD your God is with you* (v. 1). The basic premise of holy war is that it is the LORD God who fights for the people. The use of the priests to provide inspiration and encouragement, including the offering of special sacrifices prior to the battle, lends further emphasis to this point (vv. 2-4; cf. 1 Sam 13:8-12 where Saul, in desperation, offers the sacrifice after Samuel is delayed). The rules also provide for certain persons to be exempt from going to battle: one who has *built a new house but not dedicated it* (v. 5); one who has *planted a vineyard but not yet enjoyed its fruit* (v. 6); one who is newly betrothed but not yet married (v. 7); or anyone who is *afraid or disheartened*, since his attitude may cause *the heart of his comrades to melt like his own* (v. 8; cf. Judg 7:2-3). The warriors must have no distractions as they go into battle.

20:10-20. Prosecution of the holy war. Whether those people being attacked are allowed to sue for peace depends upon where they are located. Those outside Israel's borders are allowed to make peace and serve *at forced labor* (v. 11; cf. Josh 9 and the story of the Gibeonites). If, however, there is resistance, the men are to be killed, but *the women, the children, livestock and everything else in the town* are spoils of war. They are to be taken and used since *the LORD your God* has given them to the people (v. 14). Within the land, a different rule applies. Here, Israel *must not let anything that breathes remain alive*, lest the survivors *teach you to do all the abhorrent things that they do for their gods*, causing Israel to sin against the LORD God (vv. 16-18; cf. Josh 7; 1 Sam 15:17-23). This is not to be scorched earth warfare, however. To destroy the trees, especially fruit trees, would be self-defeating, since the people can *take food from them* (v. 19). Only non-fruit-bearing trees can be cut for the purpose of building siegeworks. The rule against cutting fruit trees such as the olive is still observed in the modern state of Israel. An olive tree that dies must stand for three years before it is cut, thus making sure it actually is dead.

21:1-23:14. Miscellaneous laws. The laws found in this section cover a variety of subjects and situations. Included are several laws designed to maintain the holiness of the land and others regulating family life on the land.

21:1-9. Bloodguilt and an unsolved murder. Because of an ancient belief that any shedding of human blood causes a ritual defilement of the land, this law addresses incidents of such ritual defilement and how to overcome the defilement. The shedding of innocent blood is one of the strongest taboos in early Israel. When a person is killed by another and the killer is known, proper punishment can be inflicted upon the guilty person, thus removing the stigma of bloodguilt (Gen 9:6; see Jer 26:1: Jeremiah plays on this fear as part of his defense in a trial for his life). This passage deals with the guilt incurred when *it is not known who struck the person down* (v. 1). The first problem is to determine what town is nearest the scene. This is to be done by measuring *the distances to the towns that are near the body* (v. 2). Then, *the elders of the town nearest the body shall take a heifer* that has never been used as a draft animal (*has not pulled in the*

yoke) to be used as a sacrifice of substitution (v. 3). The place of sacrifice is to be a valley (*wadi*) *with running water, which is neither plowed nor sown.* Here, the animal is to be killed by breaking its neck (v. 4). Nothing is said about cutting the animal's throat as is prescribed in other sacrifices, but the proclamation by the elders that *our hands did not shed this blood* (commit this murder) might seem to suggest that the animal's blood may also have been shed (v. 7; cf. Lev 1:5, 11). *The priests, the sons of Levi*, those from the central sanctuary (18:1) then *pronounce blessings in the name of the LORD*. Their decisions *in all cases of dispute and assault are final* (v. 5). At this point in the ceremony, *the elders of that town nearest the body shall wash their hands over the heifer* and declare their innocence, both as to having committed the crime and as to having witnessed its commission. All this is accompanied by a prayer to the LORD for absolution of the guilt (vv. 7-8). This done, the priests then pronounce them free from bloodguiltiness (vv. 8-9).

21:10-14. Treatment of female captives. This is a supplement to the rules of holy war. Should a beautiful non-Palestinian woman be captured some soldier may wish to take her as his wife (Num 31:18). This can be done if the prescribed rituals are observed (vv. 12-13) If the marriage does not prove satisfactory, she is to be set free, not sold to someone else as a slave. This law was undoubtedly for the purpose of cutting down on the incidence of rape in warfare, as well as emphasizing the importance of family in Israelite culture. It is in keeping with Deuteronomy's humanitarian attitude toward the less powerful members of society.

21:15-17. Status of firstborn sons. This law established the inheritance rights of firstborn sons of a man's primary wife, regardless of any change in feelings he might have toward her when he has acquired other wives (vv. 15-16). Favoritism toward a second wife and her children cannot deprive the firstborn son of the rights inherent with his position. He is to receive *a double portion* of his father's possessions: *since he is the first issue of his virility, the right of the firstborn is his* (v. 17; see Gen 25:29-34).

21:18-21. Treatment of rebellious children. This seemingly harsh law is designed to protect the sanctity and stability of the family. Not even a child of the family is allowed by disgraceful behavior to threaten the stability of the family. According to Deuteronomy, such disgraceful behavior must be dealt with by strong measures, since such behavior constitutes an evil that must be removed (vv. 18-21).

21:22-23. Burial of dead criminals. *You hang him on a tree* refers to the practice of impaling the body of an executed criminal on a sharpened upright stake. This practice was reserved for those whose crimes were especially heinous, or for one's enemies, especially pagan kings (Josh 8:29; 10:26-27; 1 Sam 31:8-10; 2 Sam 4:12). The body, moreover, is to be taken down and buried before nightfall, since the failure to do so will *defile the land that the LORD* is giving Israel. This is true because such a person is *under God's curse* (v. 23).

22:1-4. Care of lost and injured animals. Israelite law is concerned to promote mutual help among members of the community, as well as to emphasize the sacredness of property rights. *You shall not watch your neighbor's ox or sheep straying* (v. 1) introduces such a law. When a person owns only a few animals, they are an essential part of the person's livelihood. The loss of an ox, the chief means of breaking up the soil for agriculture, or of a sheep, the source of clothing as well as of meat, could be devastating for a small farmer or a shepherd whose holdings were minimal. To care for a neighbor's lost property as one would for one's own is essential for the well-being of the community. This is the practical expression of *love your neighbor as you love yourself* (Lev 19:18; cf. Mark 12:31). The same rule applies when one finds the *neighbor's donkey or ox fallen on the road . . . : you shall help to lift it up* (v. 4).

22:5. Proper dress. Since this prohibition against a woman's wearing of a man's clothing or *vice versa* is described as *abhorrent to the LORD your God* as are other Canaanite practices, this may also be a reference to transvestism or simulated sex changes practiced in Canaanite religion. It could, however, simply reflect a conservative bias against anything unusual or unnatural (see Wright 1953, 464).

22:6-7. Protection of bird life. *If you come on a bird's nest . . . you shall not take the mother* (v. 6). This is yet another instance in Israelite law of a practical ecological approach to life (cf. the prohibition of the unnecessary destruction of trees, esp. fruit trees, 20:19-20). Preservation of the female bird will insure the continued production of eggs and young, much the same as saving seed for field crops. From a practical standpoint, a continuing food supply is the best guarantee of the fulfillment of the promise that *you may live long* in the land given by the LORD (v. 7).

22:8. Proper roof construction. *When you build a new house . . . make a parapet.* This assumes a type of construction with a flat roof and an outside stairway where one can use the roof in the cool of the evening for rest and relaxation. The parapet, a wall around the four sides of the roof, protects both owner and guests—the guests from accidentally falling off the roof and the owner from bloodguilt, *if anyone should fall from it.*

22:9-11. Mixing of kinds. Prohibitions of sowing with *a second kind of seed* (v. 9), plowing *an ox and a donkey yoked together* (v. 10), or wearing clothes made of *wool and linen woven together* (v. 11) seem to arise from an Israelite belief that the LORD makes things distinctive for a purpose. To mix them is an attempt to defeat the LORD's purpose. Note the stress placed upon the different kinds of plants and animals in Gen 1:11-12, 21, 24-25.

22:12. Tassels on clothing. *You shall make tassels.* According to Num 15:39, tassels or fringes are used so that the people *will remember all the commandments of the LORD and do them.* In other words, they serve as visual reminders and thus are teaching devices. Such tassels are a prominent feature on the prayer shawls worn in synagogue services today.

22:13-30. Divorce and sexual relationships. This section is a series of case laws that pose a violation and then establish the punishment ("If this is done, the result will be this"). These laws are believed to have been taken by the writer(s) of Deuteronomy from an older source. They all deal with relations between the sexes.

Suppose a man marries a woman (22:13) introduces the case of a husband who tries to divorce his wife by falsely accusing her of not being a virgin at marriage. His real reason, however, is that after consummating the marriage (*going in to her*), he decides that *he dislikes her* (v. 13). The parents *submit the evidence of the young woman's virginity to the elders* (v. 15). This evidence is a bloody cloth, showing that when the husband first penetrated her, her hymen was ruptured and she bled on the cloth that she had under her body. The cloth is *spread out . . . before the elders of the town* (v. 17). Since they have the proof, the husband is to be fined *one hundred shekels of silver*, which is paid to the bride's father in compensation for the damage done to the bride's family. In addition, *she shall remain his wife* with no divorce allowed (v. 19). On the other hand, should the parents be unable to produce evidence of her virginity, she is to die by stoning *because she committed a disgraceful act . . . by prostituting herself in her father's house* (v. 21).

The death penalty is applied to both parties when a man is found *lying with the wife of another man* (v. 22). Regarding a virgin who is engaged and has intercourse with a man other than her intended husband, two possible situations are noted. In the first, if a man meets an engaged virgin *in the town and lies with her* and they are caught in the act, it is assumed that she had consented. The reasoning is that if she had cried for help inside a town, she would have been heard. Judgment is to be carried out in *the gate of that town* (vv. 23-24).

"In the gate" is the equivalent of our saying, in the courthouse or courtroom: the town gate, in reality, was more of a building, as a recent discovery at Tell Dan in Northern Israel has vividly illustrated. The penalty for both the man and the woman is death; she, because she consented, and he, because *he violated his neighbor's wife* (v. 24). That she is spoken of as *his neighbor's wife* shows the binding nature of betrothal or engagement in Israelite culture.

A different situation arises where a man engages in intercourse with an engaged woman in the open country. The assumption is that he raped her; therefore *only the man who lay with her shall die* (v. 25). Her innocence is assumed on the basis that *she may have cried for help but there was no one to rescue her* (v. 27).

Still another situation involves the rape of an unengaged virgin by a man who is *caught in the act* (v. 28). The rapist must pay the girl's parents *fifty shekels* (v. 29) as a bride price, a financial transaction that was part of all marriage arrangements. In a regular marriage, the amount could vary, depending upon the economic status of the families involved (see Gen 24:52-53 where Abraham's servant Eliezer pays Rebekah's family a huge sum for her). The young woman who is raped becomes the man's wife, with no divorce permitted (v. 29).

The prohibition against a man's marrying *his father's wife* (v. 30) reflects the polygamous nature of early Israelite society. The woman involved would be the man's stepmother. Such a relationship would be incestuous (27:20; Lev 18:8; 20:11).

23:1-8. Bars to membership in the assembly. *The assembly of the LORD* here refers to "a gathering of influential males" (Sutherland 1990, 70). This ban against a man whose sexual organs are mutilated probably arises from the fact that eunuchs (castrated men) were priests in pagan cults, particularly among the Canaanites (2 Kgs 9:32; Jer 34:19; but see Isa 56:4-5; Acts 8:27-38).

Since illicit sexual unions (v. 2) were so severely punished (see comments on 22:22-30), it is not surprising that a child born of such a union would be shunned. The banning of anyone who is *Ammonite or Moabite* (vv. 3-6) is justified by the fact that they are traditional enemies who *did not meet you with food and water on your journey out of Egypt* and hired BALAAM to curse Israel (see Num 22–24 on Balaam). On the other hand, the Edomites and the Egyptians are less noxious since the Edomites are kinsfolk and Egypt was Israel's home before the exodus. Egyptian influences seem to have figured strongly in the rule of Solomon, especially with regard to the wisdom tradition (Prov 22:17–24:22).

23:9-14. More rules for holy war. These rules deal with sanitary and ritual cleanness during the HOLY WAR. Early people were not aware of the dangers of a lack of proper sanitation, but would be concerned about exposed body wastes in living areas. *Any impropriety* (v. 9) is further defined in the verses that follow. *Nocturnal emission* refers to a discharge of semen, while the other references are to other normal bodily functions. For the camp to *be holy*, it must be clean, both ritually and otherwise.

23:15–25:19. Humanitarian and religious obligations. These laws highlight Deuteronomy's concern for the less fortunate members of Israelite society.

23:15-16. Treatment of escaped slaves. The phrase *slaves who have escaped to you . . . shall not be given back* seems to assume that the owner is a non-Israelite and that the slave has been mistreated, causing him to flee. The evidence that Israelite law protected an escaped slave is all the more striking in light of Law 16 in the Code of Hammurabi—a law demanding the death of anyone who harbors an escaped slave.

23:17-18. Temple prostitution. The terms for both male and female prostitutes are those that indicate that they were dedicated to a deity. Literally, they are called "holy ones," meaning "those dedicated to a special purpose." Such prostitution of both sexes was a prominent feature of fertility cults such as Baalism. The practice was strictly forbidden in Israel; in addition any financial gain from the practice was not to be given as an offering to God, for that would be *abhorrent to the LORD your God* (v. 18).

23:19-20. Loans to fellow Israelites. The matters covered here are essentially the same as those listed in 15:1-11. The kinds of interest named here (*on money, . . . on provisions, . . . on anything that is lent*) would seem to cover those things loaned to a fellow Israelite who was in need (v. 19). In other words, one does not charge interest on charitable loans. These are not business loans, but loans designed to meet a need (see Wright 1953, 472).

The permission to lend to foreigners (v. 20) provided the rationale during the Middle Ages for Christian states to permit Jews to be bankers, since Jews could make loans to Gentiles and charge interest. It also, unfortunately, became the real basis for much of the persecution of the Jews. When a ruler did not want to repay his loans, he started a pogrom or persecution, driving the Jews out of his country.

23:21-23. Vows to the LORD. The phrase *If you make a vow to the LORD* introduces a warning against foolish promises, especially dealing with acts of devotion to the LORD (v. 21). Vows are to be taken seriously, since words spoken in solemn situations were thought to carry unusual power. Thus one should speak such words carefully and carry out what is promised (v. 23; Lev 27; Acts 21:23-24).

23:24-25. Use of other's crops. To *go into your neighbor's vineyard* for the purpose of satisfying one's immediate hunger is acceptable (v. 24). Carrying off the *grapes* or *standing grain* is not (v. 25). Only the owner has the right to harvest the fruit or the grain.

24:1-5. Divorce and marriage rights. This law places the right to a divorce with the husband on the grounds that *he finds something objectionable* in the wife (v. 1). After the divorce, if the woman should become the wife of another and if he, likewise *writes her a bill of divorce* or dies, the first husband is not permitted to remarry her *after she has been defiled* (v. 4). Why this would defile her is not clear, but it is serious enough to be seen as bringing *guilt on the land* (v. 4; but see 2 Sam 3:14-15 where David insists that Michal be returned to his harem even though she is married to another). This case differs from the one treated in 22:13-19, which is designed to protect the woman from being divorced because of a false accusation (Snodgrass 1990, 218).

The holy war regulation allowing a newly married man exemption from military or related duty so that he may *be free at home one year*, is designed to assure the continuity of families. Great emphasis is placed on a man's having a son to bear his name. It is through one's sons that one continues to live, since there was no developed concept of life after death (v. 5; cf. Isa 53:8, 10; Jer 16:1-4; Job 3).

24:6. A forbidden pledge. To take away one's grinding stones, either *the mill or the upper millstone*, would deprive that person of bread, the basis of life. This would be the equivalent of *taking a life in pledge*.

24:7. A forbidden act. *Kidnaping another Israelite* in order to force that person into slavery or to sell that person to someone else as a slave is an offense that merits the death penalty.

24:8-9. Treatment of leprosy. *A leprous skin disease* may refer to various types of skin disorders, including Hansen's disease (which causes the loss of fingers and toes), as well as other skin rashes such as psoriasis (Geren 1990, 508–509). The instruction to *carefully observe whatever the levitical priests instruct you* (v. 8) seems to indicate that these levitical priests served both as religious and as medical practitioners.

24:10-15. Care for the needy. These rules dealing with the collection of debt are designed both to preserve the debtor's dignity and privacy and to minimize the person's suffering. In the first instance, when making a loan, the creditor is not allowed to invade *the house to take the pledge* or collateral. Instead, the creditor *shall wait outside*, and the debtor *brings the pledge* outside (vv. 10-11). In the second instance, while the words *the garment given you as* are not in the Hebrew text, NRSV assumes this is the meaning of the reference to sleeping *in . . . the pledge* and by the reference to the *cloak* in v. 13. Keeping a poor person's cloak overnight is seen as an act of cruelty, since the cloak is not only an article of clothing but also serves as a cover at night to keep the owner warm (cf. Amos 2:8, and King 1988, 24–25).

To *withhold wages of poor and needy laborers* (v. 14) would be a callous act. Wages are to be paid *daily before sunset*. Since the LORD is on the side of the poor and needy, one who withholds wages risks incurring guilt should the poor *cry to the LORD* about their mistreatment (24:15; cf. Matt 20:1-16).

24:16. Individual responsibility. This is Deuteronomy's modification of the ancient belief in corporate guilt or responsibility (Num 16:31-33; Josh 7:24-25; 2 Sam 21:1-9). What is stated here is more in line with Jer 31:29 and Ezek 18:1-24.

24:17-22. Care for the less fortunate. Three groups—resident aliens, orphans, and widows—are viewed as a community responsibility, since they share a common plight. Each has been deprived of family support groups. Their rights in court are not to be abridged, nor is one to *take a widow's garment in pledge* (v. 17). Since the LORD *your God redeemed* Israel from Egypt when they were still slaves, there is now a responsibility for the members of the community to share their blessings to help alleviate the sufferings of impoverished or destitute members of society. Care is extended by leaving grain in the field and fruit on the trees and vines for the needy to harvest (vv. 19-22; Lev 19:9-10; 23:22; cf. Ruth 2:1-7).

25:1-3. Corporal punishment. In the case of a judgment where *two persons have a dispute* and one is declared *to be in the wrong* (v. 1) and the wrongdoer *deserves to be flogged*, the maximum prescribed penalty is forty lashes, but may be less (vv. 2-3). In later times, the maximum number of lashes given is thirty-nine, so that if the number is miscounted, the law will not be violated by excessive punishment. Such excesses are illegal as well (2 Cor 2:6-7).

25:4. Humane treatment of animals. Proper treatment of work animals is a matter both of good business and of sound religion (cf. 22:6-7).

25:5-10. Rules for levirate marriage. *When brothers reside together. . . . Her husband's brother shall go in to her* (v. 5). The levirate marriage required a man's widow to marry his nearest male relative, here spoken of as his brother. *Brother* is to be interpreted in the context of the extended family, where the term "brother" covers a much wider range of relationships than is common in today's nuclear family. Even cousins and uncles could assume the obligations of a *brother* (Lev 25:47-49) who is called the *go'el*. Fulfilling the obligations of levirate marriage is one of three functions of the near kinsman. In addition to the obligations of levirate marriage, the *go'el* sees that his brother's murder is properly punished and that family property is redeemed so as not to be lost to the family if the present owner should need to dispose of it (see 19:6 where he is the *avenger of blood*, and Jer 32:1-15 where the redemption of property is involved). The law of the levirate marriage is designed to preserve a man's name in the event that he dies before he fathers a son to bear his name. The brother of the deceased is to marry the latter's widow. The firstborn son of that union is given the name of the dead husband (Gen 48:15-16; Ruth 4:17) While there is no punishment as such for one who refuses to assume the obligations of the levirate, there is a ceremony in the presence of the elders in which the culprit is held up to shame because *he does not build up his brother's house.* (vv. 7-10).

25:11-12. Sexual impropriety. This case law deals with a threat to a man's ability to father children (v. 11). Even though a woman would be defending her husband in this situation, seizing a man's genitals is a serious offense, calling for a severe penalty (v. 12).

25:13-16. Honest weights. This law deals with honesty in the marketplace, a universal problem. *Two kinds of weights* were used on balances to get more than an honest amount when selling or to pay less than the fair price when buying. One might also use false measures to give less than full measure when selling and to take more than honest measure when buying. The standard should be *a full and honest weight* and *a full and honest measure* (v. 15). Anything less is unacceptable (v. 16). That these practices were common in the marketplace is confirmed by archaeological discoveries from the time of the eighth-century prophets (Mic 6:10-11; Amos 8:5-6; see King 1988, 22–23).

25:17-19. Treatment of the Amalekites. Comments above on 23:1-8 provide a context for treating the issues surrounding the relationship between the Israelites and the Amalekites (also cf. Exod 17:8-15).

"When you have come into the land"—
The Concluding Rituals
and an Interlude, 26:1–27:26

The purpose of this section and the concluding exhortation of Moses in chap. 28 is to impress upon the people that the possessions they have are the gift of the LORD. They also are urged to reflect on the blessings that accrue from that gift, and the responsibilities that go with those blessings.

26:1-11. Liturgy for the firstfruits. A central element in Israel's worship is thanksgiving—thanksgiving for the land the LORD God is *giving . . . as an inheritance to possess* (v. 1) and thanksgiving for the produce that is harvested from that land (v. 2). Here the reference is to the liturgy for firstfruits, performed at the central shrine during the festival of Weeks, which celebrated the wheat harvest (16:9-12). The worshiper is to take *some of the first of all the fruit of the ground*, that is, some of each type of produce, *put it in a basket*, and take it to the central shrine (v. 2). There the worshiper is to recite a confession of faith, recalling the historical circumstances that led to Israel's possession of the LORD God's gift of the land. These circumstances include the seminomadic wanderings of the ancestors that led to the sojourn in Egypt where numerically they prospered but then became slaves (vv. 7-9); the LORD's attentiveness to their cries of distress; and their deliverance with *a mighty hand and an outstretched arm, . . . and with signs and wonders*, climaxing with the giving of the land (vv. 5-10). The use of plural pronouns throughout the confession identifies the worshiper with the community of faith, past and present. It is widely agreed by scholars that this is an old confession.

Much has been made of the failure to mention the giving of the law at Sinai. This omission could arise from the nature of the act of worship in which the confession is used. The act is designed to *celebrate with all the bounty that the LORD your God has given to you and to your house* (v. 11). Since that is the prime emphasis, rather than the giving of the law, there was no need to mention Sinai. Others argue, however, that Sinai is not mentioned because the Sinai story is from a different set of traditions, perhaps originating among Israelites who entered the land with a different set of experiences than those from whom this confession originates (see von Rad 1962, 121–28). Whatever the origin of the Deuteronomy confession, its purpose is to celebrate God's gift of the land by annually (or perhaps every seventh year—see Deut 31:9-13) bringing the first and best of the harvest as an offering to the deity.

26:12-15. Liturgy of the tithe. A similar sense of celebration also accompanied the paying of the tithe, part of which is to be eaten *in the presence of the LORD your God, you and your household rejoicing together* (14:26). It is to be paid *in the third year (which is the year of the tithe)* and its function is to provide support for *the Levites, the aliens, the orphans, and the widows, so that they may eat their fill within your towns* (v. 12). The ceremony includes an oath by the tither in which he disavows any misuse of the tithe. Indeed, it is being given *in accordance with your entire commandment that you commanded me*, a vow to the LORD that would seem to address the question of attitude or motivation (v. 13). An assurance that the tithe is ritually clean is given with three negative examples: (1) the tithe has not been eaten during a period of mourning; (2) it has not been removed (from the remainder of the produce) while the worshiper was in a state of uncleanness; and (3) it has not been used in any pagan rites for the dead (v. 14). As with the offering of the firstfruits (vv. 1-11), the tithe is an expression of worship and gratitude to the LORD who has given the land as a fulfillment of the promises made to the ancestors (v. 15).

26:16-19. Exhortation to observe the statutes and ordinances. *This very day* suggests that a COVENANT ceremony is in progress, a ceremony of covenant renewal in which the covenant will be read, followed by a recommitment to its provisions on the part of the people. This exhortation contains echoes of the *shema* (6:4-5) with its call *to observe these statutes and ordinances . . . with all your heart and with all your soul* (v. 16). The emphasis on the agreement between the LORD and the people—the LORD to be their God and they *to be* [God's] *treasured people* who are to be set *above all nations, . . . in praise and in fame and in honor*—is the kind of vow one would expect to find in a ceremony of covenant making (vv. 17-19).

27:1-26. An Interlude: The Shechem ceremony. The shift to a third person narrative in this chapter interrupts the flow of the exhortation of Moses in chap. 26 that is taken up again in chap. 28. Since chap. 27 describes what obviously is an old ceremony of covenant making, it may have been inserted here because of the suggestions of a covenant ceremony at the end of the previous chapter.

27:1-8. Instructions for building an altar to the LORD. *Moses . . . charged all the people* marks a shift from the exhortation of the sermon to a narrative about instructions for building an altar in central Palestine at Shechem (v. 1). The people are instructed to *set up large stones and cover them with plaster*, the purpose being to provide a suitable surface for writing *all the words of this law* (vv. 2-3). The practice of writing important religious matters on plaster is attested by finds at Tell Deir 'Alla, not far from where the Jabbok empties into the Jordan River (Cornfeld 1976, 55–56). These stones are to be part of an altar to be built on Mt. Ebal. It is to be an *altar of stones on which you have not used an iron tool* (v. 5). This prohibition may reflect a reaction against Canaanite religious practices, but more likely it comes from the idea that some natural sacred aura about the stone might be lost when it was worked with iron tools (Galling 1962, 1:97). In the times of the monarchy, altars of hewn stone are found as well as bronze altars used for the burning of incense (Haak 1992, 1:162–67). The sacrifices are to be *sacrifices of well-being* (see Lev 3), accompanied by a communal meal and *rejoicing before the LORD your God*. The instruction to write *all the words . . . of this law* is in keeping with a covenant ceremony (vv. 7-8).

27:9-10. The purpose of the ceremony. The purpose of the ceremony is to affirm that *this very day* Israel has become *the people of the LORD your God* (v. 9). This sense of affirmation and immediacy kept alive in the religion of Israel and later in Judaism is the cohesive force that binds the people together with a sense of history and belonging.

27:11-26. The cursing ceremony. The tribal list in vv. 12-13 is very old, as is shown by the fact that Levi and Joseph are listed as tribes (v. 12; cf. Gen 49). Later lists divide the tribe of Joseph into Ephraim and Manasseh and drop both Joseph and Levi, while still maintaining the total of twelve tribes. *Mount Gerizim* and *Mount Ebal* (vv. 12, 13), where the ceremony takes place, are mountains that stand opposite each other. Between these two mountains is the site of ancient Shechem, probably the site of the first central shrine for the Israelites.

One would expect the twelve curses (vv. 15-26) to be accompanied by twelve blessings, since both were an essential part of a ceremony of covenant making. While there are blessings given in the next chapter (28:3-6), there are only six and they are given in a somewhat different context than that of the curses found here. The expression *Amen* that accompanies each curse can be translated "Let it be so," in effect saying, "Let this fate befall us if we should commit such a crime." The first two curses closely parallel the third and fifth of the Ten Commandments: the prohibition against the making of idols (v. 15; cf. Exod 20:4-6; Deut 5:8-10) and the curse on *anyone who dishonors father or mother* (v. 16; cf. 5:16 and Exod 20:12). The former curse is directed more specifically toward one *who makes an idol or casts an image, anything abhorrent to the LORD, the work of an artisan and sets it up in secret* (v. 15). Second Isaiah and Jeremiah elaborate on this theme in their prophecies (Isa 44:9-20; Jer 10:1-16). Curses three through five are against those who violate the rights of members of the community: moving *a neighbor's boundary marker* (v. 17); misleading *a blind person on the road* (v. 18); and depriving *the alien, the orphan, and the widow* of what is their due (v. 19), reaffirming again Deuteronomy's commitment to the well-being of the community, especially as to the property rights of its members and care for those within its bounds who were weak and defenseless.

Aberrant sexual behavior is the subject of four of the curses, three of them dealing with sexual relations between relatives (incest) and one with using an animal for sexual purposes, or bestiality (v. 21). The curse on *anyone who lies with his father's wife* seems to assume that the woman is another wife other than the mother of the guilty person, although sex with one's own mother certainly would be strictly forbidden (v. 20). Relationships are more clearly defined as regards sex with one's sister; the prohibition applies whether the woman is *the daughter of his father or the daughter of his mother*. It applies as well to *anyone who lies with his mother-in-law* (vv. 22-23). Turning attention again to the broader community, the tenth curse falls on *anyone who strikes down a neighbor in secret* (v. 24). It has been suggested that the phrase *in secret*, here and in 27:15, is the key to understanding the necessity of these curses, since the crimes mentioned may not be discovered and thus escape public punishment. The power of the curse is believed to be such that punishment is inevitable (Craigie 1976, 331). The eleventh curse is double-barreled since it condemns bribe-taking and shedding *innocent blood*, two offenses that are condemned numerous times in both legal and prophetic materials (v. 25; cf. Amos 5:12; Ps 26:10; Isa 33:15; Deut 19:13; 21:9; Jer 7:6; 26:15). The final curse upon *anyone who does not uphold the words of this law by observing them* is a summary curse, covering all that has gone before, in much the same manner that *you shall not covet* seems to function for the Ten Commandments (v. 26; see comment on 5:21). Taken together, the curses emphasize the serious nature of the covenant and the solemnity with which commitments were to be made. In Israelite history, covenants were a major force in binding the community together (Hayes 1990, 177–81).

If You Will Only Obey the LORD Your God— The Conclusion of the Sermon, 28:1-68

When one reads Deut 26:16-19 and then proceeds to read the opening verses of chap. 28, it is clear that there is continuity between the two chapters interrupted by the inclusion of chap. 27.

28:1-14. Six blessings and a commentary. The introductory call to *obey the LORD your God* (28:1) and the promise that obedience will result in Israel's being set on high *above all the nations* echoes 26:19 and introduces six blessings. Since blessings are a common element in covenant ceremonies, these blessings may originally have been associated with the twelve curses of chap. 27. The first two, *Blessed . . . in the city, and blessed . . . in the field*, are comprehensive in their nature, saying, in effect, "Blessed shall you be, wherever you are." The second group of two blessings is more specific. They promise large families (*the fruit of your womb*), a necessity for the continuation of family, tribe, and people as a whole; abundant crops (*fruit of your ground*) and success in the breeding of their animals, both the larger animals (*your cattle*) and of sheep and goats (*your flocks*), all these being necessary for physical preservation and economic prosperity (v. 4). The blessing on the *basket* and the *kneading bowl* is a more intimate blessing, since these were common utensils used daily in providing for the sustenance of the family, the basket for gathering food and the kneading bowl for making bread (v. 5). As the series begins with a general blessing, so it ends with one that covers all the movements of life (*when you come in, and . . . when you go out* [v. 6]).

What then do these blessings mean? They mean the defeat of enemies, who will flee *seven ways* (in complete confusion) (v. 7). The soil will be blessed, as evidenced by the abundance of produce stored in the barns of Israelite farmers (v. 8). Most important of all, the LORD God will establish Israel *as his holy people* if they keep his commandments and *walk in his ways* (v. 9). They will thus be unique among the earth's peoples, causing the latter to be afraid of Israel when they see that Israel is *called by the name of the LORD* (v. 10). This reference reflects the ancient idea of the LORD as a god of war who leads the people to triumph over enemies in holy warfare. Prosperity in the form of numerous children, large flocks, and abundant crops, assured by plenty of rain and accompanied by blessings on *all your undertakings*, will make Israel a nation that can lend to others and not one that has to borrow (vv. 11-12). To be *at the top, and not at the bottom*, Israel must be diligent in its obedience to the LORD's commandments, not turning aside, *either to the right or to the left, following other gods to serve them* (vv. 13-14).

28:15-68. Six curses and a commentary. The six blessings are balanced by six curses as a judgment for not obeying *the LORD your God by diligently observing all his commandments and decrees* (v. 15). They are mirror images of the blessings, using precisely the same language, except that the opening words are *Cursed shall you be* (vv. 16-19). The disasters that follow the curses are to take many forms. There will be *disaster, panic, and frustration*, bringing destruction *on account of the evil of your deeds* (v. 20). This will be accompanied by a variety of maladies—pestilence ("disease after disease," TEV) afflicting the human population (vv. 21-22a) and crop failure brought on by drought and plant diseases (vv. 22b-24). They will suffer defeat at the hands of their enemies; moreover, the plagues that worked for their deliverance from Egypt will now be turned against them (vv. 25-29). None of the losses will be restored, and they will be powerless to stop the abuse (vv. 30-34). *The LORD will*

bring you . . . to a nation that neither you nor your ancestors have known would seem to refer to the conquest by the Assyrians in 721 B.C.E. (v. 36). Added to these disasters will be crop failure due to a variety of causes: locusts and other insects (vv. 38, 42); worms (v. 39); failure of olives to mature, possibly from lack of proper pollination (v. 40). The most disastrous loss will be that of *sons and daughters* who will be taken *into captivity* (v. 41), erasing hope for the future. Added to this, resident aliens will come to rule over them (vv. 43-44). Such are the disasters that Israel can expect if it fails to observe *the commandments and the decrees* that the LORD God gave (vv. 45-46).

In a further commentary on the curses in 28:47-68, images are evoked that suggest the Babylonian attack on Jerusalem (*The LORD will bring a nation from far away. . . . It shall besiege . . . your high and fortified walls* (vv. 49, 52). The desperate conditions brought on by the siege will lead to cannibalism (vv. 53-57). Such a situation is described in horrifying detail by an eyewitness to the siege of Jerusalem in Lam 4:10 (cf. Lev 26:29). The commentary ends with the suggestion that the failure to live up to the requirements of the covenant will bring a reversal of the blessing of the Exodus. Israel once more will go into exile—*The Lord will bring you back . . . to Egypt*, which here undoubtedly is a reference to the Babylonian Exile. (vv. 58-68). Thus ends the second sermon of Moses, which began with covenant making and now ends with covenant making as well.

"These are the words of the covenant"— The Third Sermon of Moses 29:1–30:20

"The Covenant . . . in the land of Moab"— Renewing the Covenant, 29:1-29

29:1. Covenant renewal. The phrase *in the land of Moab, in addition to the covenant that . . .* indicates that a ceremony of covenant renewal follows (v. 1).

29:2-9. What the LORD has done for Israel. After the identification of the LORD God as the maker of the covenant, God's power and privileges as covenant maker are given historical foundation by recounting the deity's wondrous deeds on Israel's behalf. This reminder should inspire the people to be diligent in observing *the words of this covenant, in order that you may succeed in everything that you do* (v. 9).

29:10-29. The renewal of the covenant. *You stand assembled today . . . to enter into the covenant* (vv. 10, 12). Through covenant renewal, each generation of Israel stands once again at the foot of Sinai, experiencing the awesome presence of the LORD God, hearing the story of God's wondrous deeds, committing itself afresh to the principles of the covenant. It is a covenant made not only with those *who stand here with us today . . . but also with those who are not here with us today*, that is, all future generations (vv. 14-15). The danger of idolatry is always present. It can arise from any source, like a *root sprouting poisonous and bitter growth* (29:18). It especially flourishes in the midst of complacency, *bringing disaster on moist and dry alike* (good and bad people [v. 19]). Idolaters will face the LORD's judgment, for *all the curses written in this book will descend on them, and the LORD will blot out their names from under heaven* (v. 20). The resulting disaster will be like the *destruction of Sodom and Gomorrah, Admah and Zeboiim* (v. 23; cf. Gen 19 and Hos 11:9). There are *secret things*—"divine wisdom beyond the human ken" (NOAB, note), over and beyond those things that God has revealed to Israel. This revelation is reserved only for those who *observe all the words of this law* (v. 29).

"When all these things have happened to you"— Blessings and Choices, 30:1-20

These words and what follows appear to be a reference to the Exile. The text makes clear that exile offers a fresh opportunity for the people of God to commit themselves to God's law—and live.

30:1-14. The conditions for blessings. Even the trauma of exile will not bring an end to the LORD's concern for Israel. Even there, if they will call to mind their past experiences of *the blessings and the curses that I have set before you* (v. 1), *return to the LORD your God, and . . . obey him with all your heart and . . . soul* (v. 2), the LORD's blessing will follow (v. 3).

The key words, then, are *remember*, *return*, and *obey*. *Return* is the equivalent of *repent*. It involves a radical change in direction, a turning away from one's former loyalty and giving allegiance to a new way of doing. It is evidenced by obedience. The result will be a return to the land of promise, even from the *ends of the world*. Also included is a promise that the returnees will be *more prosperous and numerous than your ancestors* (vv. 3-5).

Moreover, the LORD your God will circumcise your heart and the heart of your descendants (v. 6; cf. Jer 4:4). Circumcision originally was to be an outward sign borne by those who were set aside as the LORD's covenant people (see Gen 17:9-14). Now, the sign of the people of the LORD, borne by males and females

alike, will be changed hearts—an all-encompassing love and obedience for the LORD their God (v. 6). Their enemies will be cursed (v. 7), and their obedience will cause them to be *abundantly prosperous* in the family, the flocks, and the fields (v. 9). Total commitment on their part to *observing his commandments and decrees* (v. 10) will be answered by God's delight in prospering them, *just as he delighted in prospering your ancestors* (v. 9).

Neither is this commandment *too hard . . . nor is it too far away* (v. 11). It is not impractical—something off *in heaven*, out of human reach; nor is it on the other side of the world (30:12-13). Instead, it is an intimate, personal matter of one's inner self, *in your mouth and in your heart for you to observe* (v. 14).

30:15-20. The choices. Covenant making involves the making of choices, the choices between *life and prosperity, death and adversity* (v. 15). In every re-enactment of the covenant ceremony, Israel is urged to *choose life so that you and your descendants may live* (v. 19; cf. Josh 24:14-15). And what is life? Is it not *loving the LORD your God, obeying him, and holding fast to him* (v. 20)? Compared to following idols, there is no other viable possibility.

"When Moses had finished speaking"— Moses' Final Days, 31:1-29

"I am now one hundred twenty years old"— Moses' Final Charge to Joshua and the People, 31:1-8

You shall not cross over this Jordan (v. 2) refers to the incident at Meribah (Num 20:2-13; cf. Exod 17:1-7) where Moses was denied entry into the land for striking the rock (see 32:50-52). *The LORD your God himself will cross over before you. He will destroy these nations before you, and you shall dispossess them* (v. 3). These promises reflect the convictions of HOLY WAR: the LORD God fights for the covenant people. They, therefore, are to *be strong and bold; have no fear or dread* of the enemy, for the LORD God *will not fail you or forsake you* (v. 6). These words are especially appropriate for Joshua, the *one who will go with this people into the land* (v. 7). He, too, can expect the LORD God to lead him (vv. 8-9).

"Then Moses wrote down this law"— The Ceremony of Covenant Renewal, 31:9-13

Moses wrote down this law (31:9) reflects the tradition that Moses is the author of Deuteronomy. Writing down the provisions of a covenant was a climactic event in a covenant-making ceremony, signifying the permanence of the covenant relationship and its terms.

He *gave it to the priests . . . and to all the elders of Israel* who had the responsibility of preserving, protecting, and propagating the principles of the covenant among the people (v. 9). *Every seventh year . . . during the festival of booths* (v. 10) there is to be a ceremony of covenant renewal, in which the provisions of the covenant are read to all Israel—*men, women, and children, as well as the aliens residing in your towns* (v. 12). That this was ever carried out during the history of Israel on such a systematic basis is questionable. The uproar caused by the finding of the law book in the Temple during the reign of JOSIAH which, in turn, instituted a covenant ceremony, suggests such a ceremony was *not* being observed on a systematic basis in the period shortly before the Babylonian Exile. Some interpreters believe this provision arose only as a consequence of Josiah's reforms, but it is more likely that it is an old regulation that periodically fell into disuse, only to be revived in times of national renewal (vv. 12-13; cf. 2 Kgs 22–23; Josh 24; Neh 8).

"The LORD said to Moses"— The Commissioning of Joshua, 31:14-23

31:14-15. Joshua commissioned. *Call Joshua and present yourselves in the tent of meeting* (v. 14b). This text points to the spiritual element in the choice of leadership that was regarded as ideal. Leaders, whether they were priests, prophets, or community or national leaders like Moses and Joshua, as well as the later kings, ideally were chosen and commissioned by the LORD God. Thus the early kings, Saul and David, were anointed by a prophet as the sign of the LORD's choice of them (1 Sam 10:1; 16:12-13). The king's court on earth was considered to be organized by analogy with the heavenly court (1 Kgs 22:19-23). Here, Joshua is brought to the tent of meeting so that the LORD can *commission him* (v. 14; cf. Num 27:12-23).

31:16-22. The people after Moses. Since Moses is soon to die, the people will forget the LORD, *breaking my covenant that I have made with them* (v. 16). Moses, therefore is to write a song and *teach it to the Israelites . . . in order that this song may be a witness* to the Israelites concerning the LORD's dealings with them (vv. 19-22; see chap. 32).

31:23. A final charge to Joshua. Joshua is admonished to *be strong and bold, for you shall bring the Israelites into the land that I promised them; I will be with you* (v. 23; see the discussion above on 31:14-15).

"When Moses finished writing"— The Continuation of the Covenant Ceremony, 31:24-29

When Moses had finished writing down in a book the words of this law (v. 24), is a continuation of the covenant ceremony found in 31:9-13. *Put it beside the ark of the covenant*, that is, for preservation and keeping, so that it may *remain there as a witness against you* (v. 26). *Assemble to me all the elders . . . that I may recite these words . . . and call heaven and earth to witness against them* (v. 28). This probably takes the place of calling on the gods as witnesses, a common element in Near Eastern treaty making. In Israelite tradition the LORD God, maker of heaven and earth, swore by the divine nature that the Creator would uphold the covenant and would see that Israel upheld the covenant as well.

"Then Moses recited the words of this song"—The Song of Moses, 31:30–32:47

The song of Moses is a psalm like those found in the Book of Psalms. It contains elements of the "covenant lawsuit," a favorite literary vehicle used by the prophets to put over their messages. While the characteristic term *rib*, usually translated "contention" or "controversy," is not present, the elements of indictment and judgment are present. All that is missing is the defense that the accused would offer to refute the charges and accusations. There is general agreement that the poem is relatively old, dating at least to the period of the early monarchy.

32:1-3. The summons. *Give ear, O heavens* (v. 1) is a call for other nations or facets of the natural world to be observers when the LORD hears his lawsuit against the people; such a summons is quite common (see Isa 1:2; Mic 6:1-2). *I will proclaim the name . . . ascribe greatness to our God* (v. 3). Usually, in the prophetic versions of the lawsuit, the LORD speaks; here the poet speaks in God's behalf.

32:4-6a. The indictment. The LORD, described as *the Rock*, symbol of strength, is known for faithfulness, honesty (*without deceit*), justice, and moral integrity—*upright is he* (v. 4). In sad contrast, *his degenerate children* have dealt dishonestly with God, for they are a *perverse and crooked generation, . . . [a] foolish and senseless people* (vv. 5-6a).

32:6b-14. The evidence: The LORD's goodness. This summary statement of the problem is followed by an enlarged bill of particulars, first delineating the

LORD's loving care and keeping of the people (vv. 6b-14), followed by Israel's ungracious response to what the LORD has done (32:15-18). It is the *father, who created* Israel, who, in the beginning (*the days of old*), *apportioned the nations*, i.e., assigned each people a territory of its own *according to the number of the gods* (32:6-8). The Hebrew text here reads "the Israelites" while one Qumran manuscript and the LXX read "the gods," a reference to the heavenly court (cf. Job 1). This seems to be what is meant. While the LORD has shown divine care for all peoples (cf. Exod 19:5 and Amos 9:7), only Israel (here called Jacob) became *the LORD's own portion*, God's personal and specific people (v. 9). Because of this, God has led them through the desert (*a howling wilderness waste*), protecting them with the kind of care that an eagle gives its young. The LORD has led them into the land, given them abundant crops and healthy flocks, so that *Jacob ate his fill; Jeshurun grew fat* (vv. 10-15a). *Jeshurun*, meaning "the upright one," is used ironically since here the people are anything but upright.

32:15-18. The evidence: Israel's ingratitude. When a people is *fat, bloated, and gorged*, trouble is not long in coming. Israel *abandoned God who made him* and even went so far as to scoff *at the Rock of his salvation* (v. 15). Israel has gone after all sorts of strange gods, even sacrificing *to demons . . . to deities they had never known* (vv. 16-17). They have forgotten the God who gave them birth, forgetting who God is and whose they are (v. 18).

32:19-27. The LORD's righteous anger. Israel's callous attitude toward the LORD's blessings provoked God to righteous indignation. They are *children in whom there is no faithfulness* who follow *what is no god*; as a result, the LORD *will make them jealous with what is no people* (vv. 20-21). They have spurned the LORD's grace, exchanged faithfulness for faithlessness, turned from the true God to worship an empty symbol, a "no-god," and now will be made fools of by a nation of fools. Such perverse people are deserving of what will surely follow—*burning consumption, bitter pestilence*, attacks by wild beasts, with death stalking the streets, striking young and old alike (vv. 22-25). The LORD has even been tempted to *blot out the memory of them from humankind*, but this would give their enemies the idea that it was their doing and not the LORD's (vv. 26-27).

32:28-33. Israel is bad, but the nations are worse. Despite their advantages, Israel is *a nation void of sense*, unable to perceive the end result of their foolish ways (v. 28). Otherwise, how could they have been defeated by an enemy unless *the LORD had given them up* and allowed enemies who have no real God and who basically are fools to defeat Israel, the LORD's chosen people (vv. 30-31)? Israel has been defeated by a worthless people (vv. 32-33)!

32:34-43. The triumph of the LORD and the vindication of God's people. The time is coming when the LORD will bring things back to a state of wholeness and well-being. When the LORD says, *Vengeance is mine*, what is being said is that the LORD is the one who has the power to make things as they should be in a time when everything seems to be going wrong. Vengeance (Heb *naqam*) arises from customary law where justice was a family matter. When a family member was slain, there was no state to bring the killer to justice. The nearest of kin (*go'el*, see discussion on 25:5-10) was the avenger of blood. By executing the relative's killer, the avenger restored a balance between the two families involved. In v. 41, the term "vengeance" is used as a parallel term for "peace," or "wholeness" (*shalem*). To say that the LORD takes vengeance is a primitive way of saying that God sets things back in balance, restoring peace or wholeness.

One result of the LORD's activity against enemies will be that God *will vindicate his people*. God's compassion for them will overrule his wrath *when he sees that their power is gone, neither bond nor free remaining* (v. 36). God will then chide the enemy to call on their worthless gods to *rise up and help you, let them be your protection* (vv. 37-38)! Those false gods can do nothing, for the LORD declares that *there is no god beside me . . . and no one can deliver from my hand* (v. 39). God has taken an oath on his own honor utterly to defeat *the long-haired enemy* and *cleanse the land for his people*. For this, the LORD is due universal praise (vv. 40-43).

32:44-47. Moses sings his song. Moses recites this song to Joshua and all the people. It is to be a reminder to them that they are responsible for what they are hearing. They are diligently to observe *all the words of this law* (v. 46). That, God declares, is *no trifling matter for you, but rather your very life* (v. 47).

"On that very day the LORD addressed Moses"— Moses Views the Land, 32:48-52

This is a somewhat expanded version of an earlier passage found in Num 27:12-14. That account identifies the site as the Abarim range (Num 27:12). Here,

Deuteronomy specifies that it is from Mount Nebo in that range that the vision is to take place. In this instance, Moses is told that he cannot go in because he failed *to maintain my holiness among the Israelites* at Meribath-kadesh (32:51; see Num 27:14).

"This is the blessing"— The Blessing of Moses, 33:1-29

33:1. The blessing with which Moses . . . blessed the Israelites before his death. Deathbed blessings are a prominent feature in Israelite tradition, one of the most notable being Jacob's blessing of his sons (Gen 49). The list of tribes here differs somewhat from that of Jacob's blessing. The most notable changes are that the tribe of Simeon is missing, perhaps reflecting the historical reality of its disappearance by the time the poem was composed; and the mention of Joseph as a tribe but then, in effect, recognizing its division by the naming of Ephraim and Manasseh, the two tribes that took its place.

Modern scholars have pointed out the fact that the Deuteronomistic history (see Wells 1990, 210–11) has a similar emphasis on covenant renewal with blessings and curses at certain significant occasions—when, for example, a prominent leader passes from the scene (Joshua, Josh 24; Samuel, 1 Sam 12; Solomon, 1 Kgs 8:14, 55; Josiah, 2 Kgs 22:11-13). As Urbrock (1992, 1:760) has observed: "The theology of blessing and curse clearly pervades the Deuteronomistic History."

33:2-5. The LORD came from Sinai. Here the image is of the LORD as a triumphant warrior deity, accompanied by *myriads of holy ones; at his right a host of his own* (v. 2). The tone of this poem is similar to Hab 3, with its mention of Mount Paran, a place that cannot be located with precision. Seir is another name for Edom. The reference to *favorite among peoples* seems to be to a leader, perhaps the king, since there is mention of a king in v. 5. That it is not Moses would seem to be implied by the fact that Moses is spoken of as a figure of the past (*Moses charged us with the law* [v. 4]). *There arose a king in Jeshurun* (v. 5) may refer to Israel's king and would seem to be in keeping with the proposal that Deuteronomy was seen in some measure as a book designed to instruct the kings of Israel. Secondly, it can be interpreted as referring to the LORD as king, a concept that is common in the Psalms (Pss 95–99). Those who see Deuteronomy as having Mosaic rootage translate v. 5: "Let there be a king in Jeshurun" (Craigie 1976, 392). On Jeshurun, see comment on 32:15a.

33:6. The blessing of Reuben. *May Reuben live* suggests that this tribe, one of those assigned territory in Transjordan (Josh 22:1), faced possible extinction, since its territory was frequently under attack from Israel's enemies.

33:7. The blessing of Judah. Judah, one of the two most prominent tribes (the other was Ephraim), while not facing the possibility of extinction as is Reuben, does, nevertheless, seems to be under attack, probably from the Philistines, since this a plea to the LORD to *strengthen his hands for him, and be a help against his adversaries.*

33:8-11. The blessing of Levi. The long and laudatory blessing of Levi may be a clue to the ultimate source of this psalm of blessing. *Your Thummim, and your Urim* (v. 8; see Exod 28:30) refers to the sacred lots, or "holy dice." Since God directed how the lots fell when thrown, they were used to find divine direction in matters that could be answered by "Yes" and "No," or the choice between two possibilities (see 1 Sam 14:41-42). This placed great power and responsibility in the hands of the Levites. The blessing commends them as worthy since they passed the test at Massah and Meribah (Exod 17:1-7; Num 20:2-13). Because of their important responsibilities, they turned their backs on families (see Exod 32:25-29) and *observed your word, and kept your covenant* (v. 9). They function as teachers (*teach Jacob your ordinances*); they officiate in the worship (*place incense . . . and whole burnt offerings on your altar*). Their zeal qualifies them for the LORD's blessing upon them and upon their substance (vv. 10-11).

33:12. The blessing of Benjamin. The phrase *the beloved of the LORD* is a play on the name of Benjamin which means, "son of the right hand" or "the favored one." The right hand was the place of blessing and favor. Thus *the beloved rests between his* [the LORD's] *shoulders*, the imagery of a small boy riding on the shoulders of his father.

33:13-17. The blessing of Joseph. The blessing of Joseph, which is even longer than the blessing of Levi, gives evidence that this poem originated in Northern Israel. Ephraim is Judah's chief rival throughout the history of the Israelite kingdom. Judah is given only one verse, while Joseph (whose chief representative is Ephraim) has the longest of all the blessings. Ephraim did, in fact, possess far better territory from a strategic and an economic standpoint than did Judah. By its very nature and location, it was more likely to have had the *choice gifts of heaven above . . . choice fruits* *of the sun . . . the finest produce . . . the choice gifts of the earth,* all tangible symbols of *the favor of the one who dwells on Sinai* (vv. 13-16). That Joseph is called *the prince among his brothers* (v. 16) is indicative of the strength of the Joseph tribes as compared to their rival Judah. Joseph is a majestic bull, driving his enemies *to the ends of the earth; such are the myriads of Ephraim, such the thousands of Manasseh* (v. 17).

33:18-19. The blessing of Zebulun and Issachar. *Zebulun, in your going out* suggests that this tribe, located on the seacoast in the northern part of Israel, gains wealth from the sea. *Issachar, in your tents,* is located inland, along the Sea of Galilee. While Issachar gained wealth from the waters of the Sea of Galilee, the mention of tents indicates that its members also followed a more traditional way of life. The two are mentioned together because *they suck the affluence of the seas* (v. 19).

33:20-21. The blessing of Gad. The tribe of Gad, described as living *like a lion* (v. 20), was assigned territory in Transjordan on the tableland just north of the Dead Sea. This land included parts of the "thickets of the Jordan" (Jer 12:5), where lions were to be found in early Israel. Gad is commended here because it left its territory to assist in the conquest of the western side of the Jordan. Thus, *he came at the head of the people, he executed the justice of the LORD* (v. 21). In a word, he did his share and more (see Num 32).

33:22. The blessing of Dan. Dan, one of the smaller and weaker tribes, had already moved from its original location west of Judah to the base of Mount Hermon, in the far north.

33:23. The blessing of Naphtali. Naphtali is another tribe that was located in the region of the Sea of Galilee, one of the prime agricultural areas of the country. Thus it is *sated with favor.*

33:24-25. The blessing of Asher. Asher was located just south of the Phoenicians on the Mediterranean coast. In view of the cordial relations that Phoenicia enjoyed with various Israelite kings, Asher stood to profit more than any other Israelite tribe, given their location. The references to *oil* and to *bars of iron and bronze* possibly refer to the trade in these items that would contribute to the blessing of *the sons of Asher.*

33:26-29. Concluding words of praise. This is a brief psalm of praise to God *who rides through the heavens to your help* (v. 26). It reminds one of the lines from the song of Deborah: "the stars fought from heaven, from their courses they fought against Sisera" (Judg 5:20). *He subdues the ancient gods* refers to the fact that the conquest of a people is viewed as the conquering of their gods as well, as the parallel statement *he drove out the enemy* indicates (v. 27). The people of Israel have every reason to be happy, since they live in safety *in a land of grain and wine, where the heavens drop down dew;* their enemies are so jealous at Israel's good fortune of being a *people saved by the LORD* that they come fawning to Israel, who will tread on their backs, that is, put them in subjection (33:28-29).

"Then Moses went up"—
The Death of Moses, 34:1-12

The account of the death of Moses, along with numerous third person references to Moses in Deuteronomy, have been part of the standard arguments against the Mosaic authorship of Deuteronomy. Those who accept Moses as author would suggest that Joshua is responsible for this account, even though there is little said in tradition about Joshua as an author.

34:1a. Moses went up . . . to Mount Nebo, to the top of Pisgah. Present identifications of these mountains suggest that there is a double tradition here, since two separate mountains are named. *The LORD showed him the whole land* (v. 1). The story of Israel begins with the patriarch Abram's being told to look in all directions "for all the land that you see I will give to you and to your offspring forever." To establish his claim to it, Abram was told to "walk through the length and breadth of the land" (Gen 13:14-17). Moses' vision of the land from the mountaintop gives a kind of literary symmetry to the Pentateuch, an appropriate closure to this phase of Israel's story.

34:1b-3. Gilead . . . as far as Zoar. The sweep of Moses' vision moves first up the eastern side of the Jordan to what today is known as the Golan Heights to Mount Hermon (*Gilead as far as Dan*); then, Upper Galilee (*all Naphtali*); the central hill country from the Carmel range to just north of Jerusalem (*the land of Ephraim and Manasseh*); Judah, westward to the coastal plain and the Mediterranean Sea, and, finally, south and east to the Negev and the Jordan Rift valley and the Arabah, ending with Jericho and the Dead Sea.

34:4. The Lord said . . . .This is the land. Abraham was told, This is the land "I will give to you" (Gen 13:15), and Moses is assured that *This is the land that I swore to Abraham . . . saying, "I will give it to your descendants."* While Moses cannot enjoy the land, he can die with the assurance that he has made possible the achievement of the promise made to the ancestors.

34:5-8. Then Moses, the servant of the LORD, died. The greatness of Moses is bound up in the title *servant of the LORD* (v. 5). Like most great figures in history and literature that are remembered for their contributions to human good, the qualities of servanthood, sacrifice, and selflessness are almost always present. Whether or not we ever uncover irrefutable evidence of Moses' existence and achievements, even as a literary figure he stands for what is best and highest in human history. He is not his own; he is the LORD's servant. That *no one knows his burial place* (v. 6) contributes to the sense of awe with which tradition associates him. Like Elijah, the symbol of prophecy for Israel, who is taken up in a chariot of fire, so Moses, the liberator of his people, has a private burial by the LORD whose servant he is. *One hundred twenty years*, or three times forty, is a round number symbolizing completion or full quota. Three times that would be in keeping with the common view that righteous living leads to a long life (cf. Job 1).

34:9. Joshua . . . was full of the spirit of wisdom. The mantle now passes to Joshua *because Moses had laid his hands on him*. The mark of a great leader is to be able to train those who are left behind to build on the work that has been done. Joshua's wisdom grew out of the fact that Moses had given him on-the-job experience so that he was not thrown into the fray unprepared (Exod 17:9). Because they had confidence in him, *the Israelites obeyed him, doing as the LORD had commanded Moses.*

34:10-12. Never since has there arisen . . . a prophet like Moses. This is Moses' epitaph. He becomes the symbol of what is great about the prophets of Israel, men and women of whom the LORD has said, *I will put my words in the mouth of the prophet* [NRSV gives an alternate reading, "mouths of the prophets"] *who shall speak to them everything that I command* (18:18). A later prophet was to say of Moses, "By a prophet the LORD brought Israel up from Egypt" (Hos 12:13). The prophet stood in the council of the LORD (*the LORD knew [him] face to face* (v. 10; cf. 1 Kgs 22:19-23; Amos 3:7). Of all those prophets who stood in the council of the LORD, none had the privilege and responsibilities that Moses had: to perform *signs and wonders . . . in the land of Egypt . . . and . . . mighty deeds and . . . terrifying displays of power . . . in the sight of all Israel* (vv. 11-12). Although the stories told about Moses may have magnified his personality and accomplishments, Deuteronomy's estimate of Moses

carries credibility. Behind the Moses traditions is a towering figure—a magnificent personality, a preeminent prophet, and one *whom the LORD knew face to face* (v. 10).

Works Cited

Andrews, Stephen J. 1990. "Molech," MDB.

Bjornard, Reidar B. 1990a. "Levi/Levites," MDB. 1990b. "Priests," MDB.

Christensen, Duane L. 1990. "Deuteronomy, Book of," MDB.

Cochran, Bernard H. 1990. "Josiah," MDB.

Cornfeld, Gaalyah. 1976. *Archaeology of the Bible: Book by Book.*

Craigie, Peter C. 1976. *The Book of Deuteronomy.* NICOT.

Dahlberg, Bruce. 1990. "Law in the Old Testament," MDB.

Eakin, Frank. 1990. "Clean/Unclean," MDB.

Ellis, Judy. 1990. "Monotheism," MDB.

Galling, Kurt. 1962. "Altar," IDB.

Geren, William H. 1990. "Leprosy," MDB.

Haak, Robert A. 1992. "Altar," AncBD.

Hancock, Omer J. 1990a. "Tabernacles, Festival of," MDB. 1990b. "Weeks, Festival of," MDB.

Harrelson, Walter. 1990. "Ten Commandments," MDB.

Hayes, John H. 1990. "Covenant," MDB.

Joines, Karen R. 1990. "Passover," MDB.

King, Philip J. 1988. *Amos, Hosea, Micah—An Archaeological Commentary.*

Kraus, Hans-Joachim. 1966. *Worship in Ancient Israel. A Cultic History of the Old Testament.*

Rad, Gerhard von. 1962. *Old Testament Theology* 1.

Smith, David A. 1990. "Curse and Blessing," MDB.

Snodgrass, Klyne R. 1990. "Divorce," MDB.

Sutherland, Ray. 1990. "Assembly," MDB.

Tullock, John H. 1990. "Sabbath," MDB.

Urbrock, William J. 1992. "Blessings and Curses," AncBD.

Vinson, Richard B. 1990. "Asherah," MDB.

Weinfeld, Moshe. 1991. *Deuteronomy: 1–11.* AncB.

Weir, Jack. 1990. "Josiah," MDB.

Wells, Roy D., Jr. 1990. "Deuteronomist/Deuteronomistic Historian," MDB.

Wilson, Johnny L. 1990. "Holy War," MDB.

Wright, G. Ernest. 1953. "The Book of Deuteronomy. Introduction. Exegesis," IB.

Joshua

John C. H. Laughlin

Introduction

Some years ago the late G. Ernest Wright observed: "The gap between a popular understanding of the Book of Joshua and a [critical] understanding is so wide that one may well wonder whether it can ever be eliminated or even narrowed" (n.d.). In the years since he wrote this, the gap has only widened.

On the surface the Book of Joshua seems to recount in a straightforward manner how ISRAEL, under the leadership of JOSHUA, entered the land of CANAAN from the TRANSJORDAN, opposite JERICHO, and within a short period of time conquered the entire country, eliminating all of its inhabitants. Following this initial success, Joshua divided the land among the twelve tribes, and following a ceremony at SHECHEM, where "Israel" pledged its fealty to Yahweh, the tribes dispersed to occupy their respective allotments. Beneath this simple story line, however, lies an array of literary, historical, theological, and archaeological complexities.

Authorship

The question of the authorship of Joshua is complex and involves more than just this book. Following the pioneering work of M. Noth, it is now commonplace among most OT scholars to assign Joshua to a larger complex of writings known collectively as the Deuteronomic or Deuteronomistic History of Israel (DH). These books, in addition to Joshua, include Judges, most of 1 and 2 Samuel, and 1 and 2 Kings. This collection is called "Deuteronomic" because the theological norm presupposed by their author(s) is thought primarily to have come from the traditions now contained in the Book of Deuteronomy. It is thus incumbent upon anyone wishing to understand Joshua to the fullest extent possible to become informed about Deuteronomic methodology (see esp. Polzin 1980; Weinfeld 1972). It should also be noted that some scholars identify two Deuteronomic editions of the

book: the first completed during the time of JOSIAH (late seventh century B.C.E.), and the second following the beginning of the EXILE (598 B.C.E.).

In the following commentary, this writer will refer to the final author of Joshua simply as the Deuteronomic Redactor (DtR). Whether or not this term is thought to refer to a single individual or a school of thought representing more than one person is immaterial to this study.

Life Setting and Date

If Joshua stands at the beginning of a theological history that ends with the last king of JUDAH in captivity (2 Kgs 25:29-30), then the situation that called forth this work, as well as the other books, is the Babylonian Exile (598–539 B.C.E.). However, a distinction must be made between the final form of the book as we now have it and the original traditions, whether written or oral, from which the book is composed. Many of these traditions may be quite old and belong to Israel's historical memory. However, whatever might have been the original intent of these older traditions has now been completely superseded by the theological concerns of the DtR. In fact, it is questionable whether or not these traditions had any theological meaning before their adaptation by the final author. Thus, it will be assumed throughout this brief commentary that the original audience for whom Joshua was written was the remnant of the Israelite community in exile who had lost land and most likely hope. Ultimately, Joshua is for people in EXILE (cf. Butler 1983, xxiii–xxvii).

Literary Forms and Major Themes

The literary forms making up this book are very complex and varied. They include such things as speeches, etiologies (i.e., stories or sayings that explain and account for some custom, name, or idea), historicized cultic celebrations or liturgical stories, tribal boundary descriptions, and city lists.

One of the most innovative approaches to the literary form of this book in recent years has been the structuralist analysis of R. Polzin (1980). He has highlighted one of the major literary features of the book, the use of speeches by various characters, particularly those by God and Joshua ("reported speeches"), and has attempted to show their relationship to the direct narration of the DtR himself ("reporting speech"). By so doing Polzin demonstrates how various "voices" can be heard on the playing surface of the book. Beneath this surface, however, he hears the two major voices of the book: the voice of "authoritarian dogmatism" that claims that all of God's promises to MOSES were fulfilled by the "conquest" of Canaan by Joshua; and the voice of "critical traditionalism" (the DtR himself) that insists that this fulfillment was very ambiguous and that Mosaic laws required constant reinterpretation, modification, and application.

Since it will be seen that little in the Book of Joshua can be called "historical reality" as moderns understand that expression, Polzin's analysis has been found particularly fruitful for dealing with the theological value of Joshua. In what follows, an attempt will be made to combine some of Polzin's insights with recent historical and archaeological data to demonstrate, it is hoped, that ultimately the Book of Joshua ia a kind of "novella." It is a short story written to impress upon its intended readers or listeners that contrary to whatever they might have believed up to their present moment, Israel's existence in the land of Canaan had always been ambiguous and tenuous—made possible only by God's undeserved acts of grace and a creative and dynamic application of the laws of Moses. Only under such circumstances has God's people ever existed, then or now.

It is customary to divide the book into three major, but unequal, sections: chaps. 1–12, which treat the theme of conquest; chaps. 13–19, which describe the division of the land among the tribes; chaps. 20–24, which include several stories with which the book closes.

A Note on the Text

There are many textual variations in this book raising numerous questions concerning the history of the text. A comparison of the Hebrew (MT) with the Greek (LXX) traditions will quickly bear this out. This brief treatment will be based primarily on the MT as published in *Biblical Hebraica Stuttgartensia*. For major textual questions, the reader must refer to full-length commentaries.

For Further Study

In the *Mercer Dictionary of the Bible*: AMPHICTY-ONY/CONFEDERACY; ARCHAEOLOGY; CIRCUMCISION; CONQUEST OF CANAAN; COVENANT; DEUTERONOMIST/DEUTERONO-MISTIC HISTORY; HOLY WAR; JOSHUA; JOSHUA, BOOK OF; LEVI/LEVITES; MOSES; PALESTINE, GEOGRAPHY OF; RED SEA/REED SEA; TENT OF MEETING; WOMEN IN THE OT. In other sources: R. G. Boling, *Joshua*, AncB; J. Bright, "Joshua," IB; T. C. Butler, *Joshua*, WBC; E. M. Good, "Joshua," IDB; L. J. Greenspoon, *Textual Studies in the Book of Joshua*; M. Noth, *Das Buch Josua*; R. Polzin, *Moses and the Deuteronomist*; J. A. Soggin, *Joshua*, OTL; M. Weinfeld, *Deuteronomy and the Deuteronomic School*.

Commentary

An Outline

Introduction to the Conquest of Canaan, 1:1-18

The Commissioning of Joshua by Yahweh, 1:1-9

As mentioned in the Introduction, Polzin has shown that one of the major characteristics of the Book of Joshua is its usage of speeches, both reported and reporting (1980, 73ff.). Thus the book begins by use of a reported speech of God by which the leadership of the nation is passed from MOSES to JOSHUA (cf. Deut 31:7-8). While a royal background (Porter 1970, 102-32) has been suggested for the formula used here, these opening verses are thoroughly Deuteronomic.

1:3-4. The limits of the land. The geographical boundaries described in v. 4 include the desert to the south and east (*wilderness*), most of what was, and is, Syria to the northeast, and the Mediterranean (*the Great Sea*) to the west (*this Lebanon* is lacking in LXX). Historically, the only time Israel controlled such a large piece of real estate was during the time of David and Solomon (cf. 2 Sam 8:3-12). Whether the DtR has specifically the ancient extent of David's empire in mind or some ideal frontier, as suggested by some, is unclear. What is clear is the redactor's belief that the divine promise made to Moses (Deut 11:24) cannot be thwarted, not even by exile.

1:7-8. The thematic program of the DtR. The basic theme of the entire DH is expressed in these two verses. Israel was able to occupy the land and enjoy Yahweh's blessings when the people lived *in accordance with all the law that my servant Moses commanded you* (v. 7). The reference to *the book of the law* (v. 8) is believed by most to refer to the legal material in the Book of Deuteronomy, especially chaps. 12-26 (cf. Deut 31:9). However, as the DtR will make clear in the story he is about to tell, living "according to all the law" is no simple task but requires constant reinterpretation and adaptation.

The Commissioning of the People by Joshua, 1:10-18

Just as Joshua was prepared in a speech by Yahweh to possess the land, now the people are prepared in a speech by Joshua.

1:12-15. The Transjordanian tribes. At first reading, it seems curious that the only tribes mentioned by name here are those who historically had lived in the TRANSJORDAN and who had played an insignificant role in Israel's history. However, by referring to them directly, the DtR anticipates a problem that will require further treatment in the story (chap. 22), namely, the status of those tribes who were *of* Israel but not *in* Israel (Polzin, 134ff.).

1:16-18. Joshua's authority legitimated. The transfer of Moses' authority to Joshua is completed when the people respond. His authority will be valid only if *the LORD your God [is] with you* (v. 17). With the authority of the Davidic king destroyed by exile, the DtR reverts to a charismatic model of kingly authority (cf. Deut 17:14-17).

Preparation for the Conquest of Canaan, 2:1–5:15

Rahab and the Jericho Spies, 2:1-24

With this story of the spies sent out by Joshua the DtR begins his account of how Israel came to occupy the land of CANAAN. The literary and historical questions raised by this story are legion. Recent archaeological discoveries have seriously undermined the historicity of Israel's exploits described here (see below). What impact this undermining should or should not have on how one hears and responds to the DtR's theological themes must be left up to the individual.

Originally the story in chap. 2 may have had little to do with the city of JERICHO (cf. Boling 1982, 144). In v. 1 the spies are commanded to *Go, view the land*; and only *the land* is mentioned when they return (v. 24). The phrase *especially Jericho* (v. 1) may have been added to tie this story to that in chap. 6.

None of these historical-critical conclusions, however, explains why the DtR told this story in the first place. The answer, according to Polzin, is in the narrator's concern to show how Mosaic law was interpreted and applied in Israel's life, specifically in this case, the rules of HOLY WAR (Polzin 1980, 86ff.).

2:1-24. Rahab and the rules of holy war. According to the rules governing holy war, Israel was to "save alive nothing that breathes" (Deut 20:16 RSV). In the story of RAHAB, however, the spies, *not* God, agreed to spare her and her family for the help she gave them, ostensibly violating the ban. In chap. 7, on the other hand, ACHAN and his family are put to death for committing the same offense, i.e., violating the ban. How is one to understand what is going on here? According to Polzin, this story

> raises two hermeneutic questions for the Israelites concerning the word of God. First, how does one interpret and apply God's command to put complete trust in him while taking over the land? . . . Second, how does one interpret the Mosaic rules for holy war? (1980, 86–87)

Polzin argues that what we see here, then, is the DtR's concern "to counter an authoritarian dogmatism" by telling stories that illustrate both the conditional (Rahab) and the unconditional (Achan) aspects of the Sinai/Horeb COVENANT (1980, 87). Thus, in the immediate story, Israel is allowed to occupy a land that it does not deserve (Deut 9:4-5), while Rahab and her family are spared a death that they do deserve (at least according to the narrator's perspective!). The story of Rahab can be interpreted as a variation of the DtR's larger themes of the "justice and mercy of God vis-a-vis Israel" (1980, 88).

That a HARLOT was chosen to be the heroine of this story seems no accident. Contrary to Soggin's conclusion (1970, 39), Rahab's profession is central to the story for several reasons. First, she is said to live in the city wall (v. 15), which reflects her status as a prostitute, that is, she is portrayed as living literally on the fringes of her own society (Fewell 1992, 66). Secondly, as is commonly pointed out, by virtue of her profession, neighbors would not be made unduly suspicious by the present of men in her house, and, of course, the location of her house made it easy to dispatch the spies. But most importantly, as a prostitute, Rahab throws into bold relief the issue of "insider" vs. "outsider" that dominates the DtR's concern. In this regard, Polzin makes an interesting suggestion when he concludes that the story of Rahab is "really the story of Israel told from the point of view of a non-Israelite" (1980, 88).

The Jordan and Gilgal Traditions, 3:1–5:15

The traditions recounted here of the crossing of the JORDAN RIVER and the activity associated with GILGAL are filled with textual and literary difficulties that have led to various proposed historical reconstructions (cf. Soggin 1970, 47–67; Boling 1982, 156–58; de Vaux 1978, 598–603).). Many years ago H.-J. Kraus suggested that this complex of traditions make up a "cultic legend" (1951, 152–65). Others have called these stories a "liturgical narrative (Polzin 1980, 92) and a "sacred drama" (Soggin, 54). Whatever term one chooses to categorize this section in Joshua, it seems highly likely that as it now stands it represents a historicizing of ritual acts involving the themes of Passover and conquest. Originally this ritual reenactment may have involved only the tribe of BENJAMIN, in whose territory Gilgal was located.

By juxtaposing the themes of the crossing of the Jordan with PASSOVER (4:10) the tradition of the Exodus from Egypt has been connected with that of the entry into the land. Whether historically there was such a connection is a moot point among scholars (cf. Halpern 1983, 81–94; 1992, 89–113). This connection with Passover is strengthened by the use of the verb *'br* (to pass, passover) eight times in chap. 3 alone (vv. 1, 4, 6, 11, 14, 16).

In a very detailed literary analysis, Polzin (1980, 91–110) argues that this ritual drama is used by the biblical narrator to illustrate once again the fulfillment of God's word. Nevertheless, the story told here seems more ideal than real.

3:1-17. Crossing the Jordan. The analogies here of Moses to Joshua (v. 7), and the Reed Sea to the Jordan River (vv. 14-16) are obvious. Just as God was with Moses at the Reed Sea, now he is with Joshua, and the Jordan becomes dry land just as the sea had done (Exod 14:21c). When the literary structure of this story is appreciated, questions of its historicity become superfluous. One of the major differences, however, between the story told here and that in Exodus is the presence of the Ark of the Covenant in the former. The ARK (always a different word in Hebrew from the ark of Noah) seems originally to have been associated with war (cf. Num 10:35). Its fortunes in Israel prior to the monarchy are not clear but it was the symbol par excellence of Yahweh's presence among his people (see Boling 1982, 159; Soggin 1970, 55–56; Bailey 1990, 63).

4:1-5:1. Gilgal and the circle of stones. The importance of GILGAL in premonarchic Israel has long been noted (Miller 1990, 332), but the traditions preserved about this site in Joshua have proven to be extremely difficult to interpret. Soggin believes that the textual confusion here over the two traditions of the twelve stones makes a "more thorough study impossible" (1970, 64). Polzin's literary solution, namely that the tradition of Joshua's setting *up the twelve stones in the middle of the Jordan* (v. 9) is a DtR device to enhance the "interpretive role of Joshua" with regard to God's word seems forced (1980, 109). Furthermore, how stones set up in the middle of a river could still be seen *to this day* (v. 9) is not clear. Whatever the historical or literary solutions to these questions may be, the message to the exiles seems obvious: these stones were to be a memorial to the people of Israel forever (v. 4). Thus God's promises could not be destroyed by time nor by exile.

This episode ends with the DtR reporting the response of the inhabitants of Canaan (5:1). Polzin reminds us that as an "omniscient observer," the DtR frequently penetrates "the psychological consciousness of all his characters" (1980, 102).

5:2-15. Circumcision and a commander from Yahweh's army. The origin and meaning of CIRCUMCISION in Israel cannot be discussed here. However, the reason given in 5:4-7 why the circumcision of those born

in the wilderness could not have been done prior to the present context seems contrived at best. Perhaps it was intended to link the rite of circumcision with that of Passover, which immediately follows in this story (cf. Exod 12:48). Note that there is no hint here that the rite included infants as it ultimately would (the Priestly tradition in Gen 17 is dated by many scholars to the EXILE or later). The etymological ETIOLOGY in v. 9 for *Gilgal* is forced. But the practice of circumcision and its symbolic meaning of belonging to the family of Abraham and thus heirs to the promises God had made him, would have found receptive ears among the exiles.

The reference to rolling away the *disgrace of Egypt* (v. 9) has also elicited a variety of responses. Perhaps the most helpful is Polzin's suggestion that Josh 5:9 is the DtR's response to Deut 9:20 (1980, 111).

5:13-15. A visit from a commander of Yahweh's army. The ambiguous nature of this pericope has given rise to many interpretations. The most common suggestion is that something has fallen out of the text, because the passage seems to anticipate some sort of a command to Joshua after v. 15 (cf. Exod 3:5ff.). However, seen in the over-all context of the DtR's purpose, the ambiguity of this passage may be deliberate. God's relationship to Israel is not automatic. Just as there is a struggle to occupy the land in the Book of Joshua, there is also a struggle to understand and apply God's word (cf. Polzin 1980, 111-13).

The Conquest of Canaan, 6:1–12:24

Archaeology and the Conquest Traditions

A literal reading of the traditions contained in these chapters would force the conclusion that roughly forty years after the people left Egypt with Moses, their descendants, under the command of Joshua, marched into the land of Canaan from the desert and annihilated all of its inhabitants, beginning with the miraculous destruction of JERICHO.

This literal reading of the story was rejected many years ago for historical-critical reasons (cf. Alt 1967, 173–221). Now recent archaeological discoveries have confirmed this judgment. The issues involved here were succinctly focused by the late P. de Vaux several years ago: "The problem raised by the settlement of the Israelites in Canaan and the growth of the system of the twelve tribes is the most difficult problem in the whole history of Israel" (1978, 475; cf. Mazar 1990, 281).

There are too many issues with which to deal adequately here. The interested reader is encouraged to pursue these questions through the references given here and in the bibliographies contained in them.

Beginning in the 1920s and 1930s, two totally opposed scholarly theories were suggested to explain Israel's settlement in the land of Canaan. The most popular—and most influential in America—was the view advocated by William Foxwell Albright, who for many years taught at The Johns Hopkins University. Using the archaeological discoveries that were being made at such great Late Bronze Age Canaanite tells (a TELL is an earthen mound that frequently contains the remains of early settlements) as Tell Beit Mirsim—Albright identified it, probably erroneously, with Debir—Lachish and Bethel, Albright accepted the basic historical reliability of the opening chapters of Joshua, and created the so-called "military" model for the way in which Israel acquired the land of Canaan (1939, 11–23). Of the three basic theories discussed here, Albright's is the least satisfactory and is simply no longer viable in light of present literary, historical and archaeological knowledge.

While Albright and his students were supporting the military model, Albrecht Alt, in Germany, was approaching the problem from a different perspective altogether. Using the tools of form and traditio-historical criticism, he and his students concluded that the stories of the conquest in Joshua were for the most part etiological legends with little or no historical value (see esp. Alt 1967, 173ff.; Noth, 1958). They concluded that "Israel" emerged on the land of Canaan through the "peaceful infiltration" of pastoral groups over a long period of time. One of the major strengths of this theory is its recognition that the Israelite settlement was a long, complicated and multifaceted process. But Alt's insistence on the "nomadic" origin of these peoples has brought the theory a great deal of criticism, especially from the advocates of the third model or theory.

In 1962, George Mendenhall argued that the origin of Israel was due neither to a pan-Israelite invasion under Joshua nor to a peaceful migration of pastoral NOMADs, but to an internal revolt of indigenous Canaanites against their overlords (1962, 66–87). This theory has been expanded by Norman Gottwald (1970, 191–233) and has gained some acceptance, in part at least, by others. Based upon sophisticated social theories, this "sociological" model has raised many pertinent issues relevant to ancient Israel's emergence.

However, it too has been severely criticized both for its perceived methodological flaws and its failure to explain adequately the material culture now known to have existed in Canaan during the period under investigation (for descriptions and critiques of all of the above theories see: Dever 1990, 37–56; 1992, 27–85; Finkelstein 1988, 295–314; Halpern 1983, 47–63).

The issue at point here is the most adequate explanation for the material culture dating to Iron Age I (roughly 1200–1000 B.C.E.) that has recently come to light through archaeological discoveries in the HILL COUNTRY of Palestine (for the most up-to-date synthesis of the archaeological data see esp. Finkelstein 1988). The data include pottery forms, architectural remains (esp. the so-called "pillared buildings" and "four-room" houses), layout of sites (i.e., site plans), silos and water cisterns; they also include hundreds of Iron I sites now known through surveys to have existed during this period but that have not yet been excavated (Finkelstein 1988, 15–234). Archaeologists are not all agreed on where the people came from who built and lived in these towns and villages. Some believe they were displaced Canaanites who settled in the sparsely inhabited regions of the central hills during and following the breakup of the Late Bronze Age (Dever 1990, 37–84; 1992, 27–56; Fritz 1987, 84–100), while others have argued that the newcomers were pastoralists who were in the process of being "resedentarized" (Finkelstein 1988, 336–51; see also Finkelstein's response to Dever and Dever's response to Finkelstein in Dever 1992, 63–69; 79–82).

Many questions still remain and all conclusions are tentative and mostly likely will need modification, if not total revision, as more information is forthcoming. Nevertheless, taking into consideration all of the evidence that is currently available, especially the archaeological data, the following conclusions by Dever seem reasonable:

> The literal biblical story of an Exodus from Egypt, and a subsequent pan-Israelite conquest of Canaan, can no longer be salvaged, for all the wishful thinking in the world (1992, 84);

and:

> the inescapable conclusion . . . is that the Israelite settlement in Canaan was part of the larger transition from the Late Bronze to the Iron Age. It was a gradual, exceedingly complex process, involving social, economic, and political—as well as religious—change, with many regional variations (1990, 79).

The full implications of this emerging new synthesis for understanding the origin of the Israelite religion and its worship of the God, Yahweh, has yet to be clarified (for one effort, see McCarter, Jr. 1992, 119–36). Closer to home are the implications of this "archaeological detour" for the story told in Joshua 6:1–12:24.

Jericho and Ai, 6:1–8:29

In light of the preceding archaeological discussion, the historical problem raised by the conquest stories of JERICHO and AI can be summed up very succinctly: neither of these sites was occupied at the end of the Late Bronze Age. In fact, Ai was not occupied for over a thousand years, from its destruction in the Early Bronze Age until a small village was founded on the site in Iron Age I (Callaway 1976, 18–30). Whatever may have been the original nucleus and purpose of these stories in Joshua, the form in which we now have them appears to be a literary construct created by the DtR to serve his own theological agenda. That agenda seems to be the meaning and application of the rule of ḥerem or the ban within the context of HOLY WAR (Deut 20:16; see Polzin 1980, 113ff.).

6:1-21. The march around Jericho. The secondary literature on this well-known story is vast, but suffice it to say that while the archaeological evidence for this ancient city is ambiguous (see Kenyon, 1957), it is abundantly clear that no Late Bronze Age city of any size existed during the time most scholars would date the first appearance of the "Israelites." All rationalizations to explain this absence (e.g., rain or wind erosion, the questioning of the identification of Tel es-Sultan as Jericho, placing the event during the Middle Bronze Age) are examples of Dever's "wishful thinking." Furthermore, close literary analysis reveals that the story as we have it seems to be composed of two different traditions altogether. One version, using the popular motif of a ruse (Rahab), implies that the city was taken by normal military siege procedures. This story is picked up in 6:2, 17, 22-25 (see Coogan 1990, 19ff.) After capturing the city, Rahab and her family were spared, as agreed to, while all the other citizens, along with the city itself, were burned (6:24). It should also be noted that the mention of Jericho in Joshua 24:11 presupposes that the city was taken by military means.

The story of the miraculous fall of the city's walls would then have been added at some point in the usage of this tradition by later Israelites celebrating the "conquest." Coogan points out that there is no biblical reference to this tumbling wall story outside its present location, indicating that the story was "a local tradition incorporated only at a fairly late date into the biblical recital" (1990, 21).

6:24. The house of the Lord. This reference to *the house of the LORD* (i.e., the Temple) is obviously anachronistic and refers to the practice of bringing the booty of holy war for dedication to the God. What became a later practice in Israel is simply assumed here.

6:25-27. Joshua's curse on Jericho. This curse by *Joshua* seems to be a prophecy after the fact ("prophecy *ex eventu*") based upon the story in 1 Kgs 16:34. Curiously, in the Kings story we are told that someone ("Hiel of Bethel") other than the king built Jericho. Jericho lay in ruins from the fourteenth to the tenth-ninth centuries B.C.E. The story in Kings takes place during the reign of AHAB, an Israelite king during the ninth century. The practice of burying one's children beneath the foundation of a city was obviously viewed as an abomination by the DtR.

7:1-8:29. The story of Ai (et-Tell). Just as the story of Jericho illustrates how the rules of holy war could be ignored to spare those under the ban (Rahab and her family), the story of Ai illustrates just how complex and dynamic the interpretation and application of these rules could be. First, we are told that ACHAN and his family were destroyed for breaking the rules (7:1, 16-26). Then we are told (8:2, 27) that the rest of the Israelites were granted permission by God to do the exact same thing Achan had done! Polzin's observation is worth quoting:

> There seems to be no doubt at all that the narrative (the Ai episode) is intent upon outlining some of the possible hermeneutic situations that could arise in the continued understanding, interpretation, and application of divine commands (1980, 114–15).

8:28. A heap of ruins. The reference to *a heap of ruins* (i.e., "tell") is probably the source of the story told here, whatever the real etymology of the name "Ai" may be.

The Altar on Mount Ebal, 8:30-35

This story follows 9:2 in LXX and seems to interrupt the flow of the narrative, which continues in 9:3 in MT. Furthermore, the base of operations at this point in the story is GILGAL, not SHECHEM (cf. 9:6;10:15,43). The argument that has erupted over the claim that the remains of this altar have actually been found only serves to illustrate the extreme difficulty of identifying excavated data with biblical texts (see Zertal ·1985, 26–43; Kempinski 1986, 42–49; Rainey 1986, 66; Dever 1992, 32–34, 76–78, 84–85). The "most important feature of this narrative" (Polzin 1980, 115) is the way Joshua interprets and applies the law of Moses in his new situation (cf. Deut 11:29; 27:1-26).

The Ruse of the Gibeonites, 9:1-27

Again the DtR's preoccupation with the interpretation of the Mosaic law is clearly in view here. According to Deut 20:10-18, Israel could offer peace to a city *not* in Canaan, but all the inhabitants of Canaanite cities were to be put to death. The fact that Israel was deceived by a ruse (just as they had deceived Jericho [the Rahab episode] and Ai [8:3-8!]) does not allow them to violate their oath to spare the Gibeonites (v. 19). The situation under which GIBEON is allowed to live is analogous to Israel's: Gibeon should have been devoted to the ban, but was spared by a "covenant" made with Joshua (v. 15). ISRAEL should also have been destroyed for its unrighteousness and stubborn heart, but was spared because of a COVENANT made by God with its ancestors (Deut 9:1-29). Gibeon and Israel, then, both exist, not because they deserve to but because of sworn covenants. To people in exile the meaning of this story would be very clear: because of God's promises to their ancestors they, undeserving as they might be, once more had the possibility of becoming his people in the reoccupation of the land.

The long identification of Gibeon with the site of el-Jib, located a few miles southwest of Ai, need not be disputed. However, that Gibeon does not seem to have existed in the Late Bronze Age is another indication of the literary construct of the Book of Joshua.

The Southern Campaign, 10:1-43

There are really three episodes or stories in this chapter that have been combined: the attack against Gibeon and its miraculous deliverance (vv. 1-15); the *five kings* in the *cave of Makkedah* (vv. 16-27); and the attacks against certain cities in the southern part of CANAAN (vv. 28-43). The chapter is also filled with textual difficulties, the MT being often at variance with LXX and other versions.

10:1-15. The attack against Gibeon. This story has some connection to chap. 9, especially the first three verses. There we are told that the kings of Canaan began to unite, having heard of Israel's initial military success. Now, with Gibeon in Israel's hand (either by ruse, MT, or simply by going over to Israel's side, LXX),

and because it was a *large city* (v. 2), the kings unite at the initiative of *Adoni-zedek of Jerusalem* (v. 1; in the LXX this king is called "Adoni-bezek," as he is in Judg 1:5; are they the same person?). However, originally there must have been six kings, not five (cf. Soggin 1970, 130). *Debir*, in v. 3 is the name of a city (cf. vv. 38-39), not a person, and is not mentioned again in the accounts of the five unnamed kings (vv. 5, 16, 17, 23). Making Debir a city in v. 3 may represent a later attempt to harmonize the story with the tradition of five kings.

Whatever the solution to the ambiguities in this story, it was told by the DtR to emphasize his belief that Israel's victories were due less to its own military prowess than to God's merciful intervention (v. 11). The quotation from the Book of Jashar (vv. 12-13; cf. 2 Sam 1:18) has evoked numerous and, for the most part, meaningless attempts at rational explanation. In the first place, in context, Joshua's admonition to the sun and moon comes *after* the battle had already been won (v. 11). Thus it was a gross literalizing of this poetic verse by the biblical author (v. 13d), interpreting it to mean that the amount of daylight available for fighting was extended. In the second place, the quotation may originally have had to do with an entirely different event then the one recorded here (Soggin 1970, 122). Whatever the case may be, the story now serves the theology of the DtR: Israel succeeded only because of an act of HOLY WAR; it was God's victory, not Israel's.

10:16-27. The cave of Makkedah. The fleeing kings, no longer named, are captured in the cave, humiliated (v. 24), and killed. This story may have originated to explain a pile of stones *which remain to this very day* (v. 27; cf. v. 18). The precise location of this site in question is unknown, although Khirbet el-Qôm has been suggested (see Dever 1990, 57).

10:28-43. The southern campaign. Whether or not the traditions recorded here preserve any real historical memory is questionable. Older attempts (e.g., Albright) to identify Late Bronze Age destruction layers discovered at some of these sites with the story recorded here are untenable. Furthermore, *Eglon* (if it is Tell el-Hesi) and *Hebron* have revealed no evidence of any such destruction as described here, at least not during the Late Bronze–Iron I periods. The location of *Libnah* is still uncertain, thus its fate during this time is still unknown. The DtR's summary in vv. 40-42 again reflects the holy war construct within which Israel's conquering of the south has been placed. It may be no coincidence that the territory taken in this account closely corresponds to the reinhabited area of the returning exiles in the sixth century B.C.E.

Hazor and the Northern Campaign, 11:1-15

The excavations of the imposing site of *Hazor*, the largest Canaanite city tell in Israel, have long been used to suggest the historical credibility of the story told here in Joshua. But not only does the archaeological evidence not do this (see Finkelstein 1988, 301), the story in Judg 4–5 contradicts the version reported here. This does not detract from the use of this story by the DtR, however, which is to affirm that Joshua did all that Moses commanded him to do (v. 15). Still, as Polzin observes: "There are ways and there are ways to fulfill Moses' commands" (1980, 123). Thus, applying the ban to Hazor and to the cities of those people who joined Hazor in fighting Israel, apparently every living thing was killed (v. 11). But in the other cities, those on mounds (i.e., tells, v. 13), booty was allowed!

Conclusion of the Conquest and a List of Conquered Kings, 11:16–12:24

11:16-20. A summary of the conquest. These verses provide a DtR summary to the completion of the conquest, although v. 18 strikes a note of reality in suggesting that the process was much longer than the preceding stories might imply. That Yahweh acted to *harden their hearts* that they *might receive no mercy* (v. 20; cf. Exod 9:12; 10:1, etc.) is the capstone of a holy war mentality. This summary makes no sense, of course, in light of the current critical synthesis of modern scholarship. The implications of this conclusion for the usage of this tradition to support modern wars by some religious groups cannot be detailed here. But obviously such usage is misguided at best.

11:21-23. The Anakim and another summary statement. The story of the *Anakim* preserves an independent tradition of this legendary race of giants (cf. Num 13:32-33; Deut 1:28; 9:2). It has only a tenuous connection to the preceding stories and contradicts what has already been narrated (according to 10:36-39, Joshua had already destroyed Hebron and Debir). The date of this tradition is uncertain (Soggin thinks it is "ancient," 1970, 141), but in its present form it can date no earlier then the late tenth century since it presupposes the split of the monarchy into Judah and Israel (v. 21). The three cities mentioned where the

Anakim could not be destroyed—Gaza, Gath, and Ashdod—were all major Philistine strongholds.

This chapter concludes with another sweeping summary of the totality of Joshua's victories and prepares for the story of the distribution of the land detailed in chaps. 13–19. In its present context this summary reinforces the DtR's purpose to portray Joshua as having done *all that the LORD had spoken to Moses* (v. 23).

12:1-24. The list of conquered kings. This chapter is of unknown origin (see Boling 1982, 322) and consists of a kind of statistical summary of the preceding victories, although some of the cities listed here have not previously been mentioned. The first part (vv. 1-6) summarizes Moses' activities in the Transjordan (cf. Num 21:21-35; Deut 2:24–3:11). *The Sea of Chinneroth* and the Salt Sea (MT) mentioned in v. 3, are references to the Sea of Galilee and the DEAD SEA respectively.

The second part (vv. 8-24) recounts Joshua's victories west of the Jordan. The main importance of this list is that it mentions places conquered not included in any other version. Actually, many of these cities were not occupied and controlled by Israel until the time of David or later. There are also important textual differences in this chapter between the MT and LXX (see full-length commentaries).

The Distribution of the Land, 13:1–19:51

The boundary descriptions and city lists in these chapters have a long, complicated history. Their origin and dates are not clear, and they represent a different version of the conquest from that told in chaps. 1–12. In fact, in the past, many scholars have denied Deuteronomic authorship to these chapters. On the other hand, Polzin sees this section as being used by the DtR as an ironical exposé of the sweeping claims made by the voice of "authoritarian dogmatism" such as is found in 21:43 (Polzin 1980, 126–34). We will refer to the final author of this section simply as the "narrator" without presupposing the author's identity. None of these considerations answers questions concerning the date and function of the lists, which originally were independent of their present context. Zvi Gal, on the basis of his recent archaeological surveys of Lower Galilee, has concluded that the border descriptions and city lists for ZEBULUN, ASHER, NAPHTALI and ISSACHAR could not be any earlier than the tenth century B.C.E. (1992, 98–106). Others would date the entire list no earlier than the time of JOSIAH (late seventh century).

Furthermore, the personage of Joshua may be a secondary addition to these traditions. Not only is he introduced as the *son of Nun* (cf. 1:1), but 13:5 clearly implies that the people allotted the land themselves.

At what stage in the production of the Book of Joshua this material was added is unknown, but all indicators point to a late date. Also, whatever theology is to be found here is almost certainly the work of the final author or compiler (in addition to Polzin's comments, see Butler 1983, 144–208).

Introduction, 13:1-7

In a reported speech of Yahweh, we are told that Joshua is old, and much *land still remains to be possessed* (v. 1). This observation contrasts sharply with the summary of Joshua's efforts in 11:16-20. The speech highlights the major concern of this part of the Book of Joshua: the allotment of land to the nine and one half tribes who lived west of the Jordan. The major point of the author here seems to be that the land was given by God to the *people*, not to kings or the wealthy and powerful. Thus God's will would not be accomplished until he had given Israel *all the land that he swore to give to their ancestors* (21:43). The successful occupation of the land, based upon this reading, was conditional on the peoples' obedience to God's laws (cf. Butler 1983, 207–208).

The territories described here are more ideal then real and in most cases presuppose the kingdom of DAVID and SOLOMON. Soggin believes that vv. 2-6 are an "interpolation on the part of a redactor" (1970, 152).

The Transjordanian Tribes, 13:8-33

The actual history of the tribes who lived east of the Jordan River is complicated. Furthermore, these tribes never played a major role in Israel's history. The literary description given here reflects the sources at the disposal of the narrator, and is filled with difficulties. For details the reader should consult some full-length commentaries.

13:8-14. Introduction to the Transjordanian allotment. In a reporting speech, the narrator introduces the theological rationale guiding his usage of all the allotment traditions. REUBEN, GAD and the *half tribe of Manasseh* (v. 8), all received their land because *Moses, the servant of the LORD* gave it to them (cf. Deut 3:12-22). Only *the tribe of Levi* (v. 14) is excluded since from its ranks came priests who were scattered throughout Israel. The reference to *offerings*

by fire probably refers to the proper sacrificial functions performed by these priests (cf. Lev 10:1-3).

13:15-33. The division of the land. The historical value of the description given here is very questionable. In any event, what few sites on the list have been located and excavated (such as HESHBON and DIBON) do not seem to have been occupied and controlled by Israel before the time of David.

The Cisjordanian Tribes: Introduction, 14:1-5

In order to bring the ancient traditions of tribal allotment on line with the "official" story, this general introduction claims that the allotments were made by *the priest Eleazar, and Joshua the son of Nun* (v. 1). However, the fact that Eleazar is listed before Joshua; that Joshua is identified as the *son of Nun* again; and the fact that v. 5 claims the people allotted the land, all raise questions concerning the connection between Joshua and this tradition. But just as the Transjordanian allotments had fulfilled God's commands to Moses, the division of the land of Canaan also fulfilled divine intentions.

Caleb and Judah, 14:6–15:63

14:7-15. Caleb given Hebron. This story of CALEB's receiving HEBRON as a reward for faithfully following Yahweh during the wilderness experience (cf. Num 13:30; 14:24) is strange, given the role of Hebron during the history of Judah. Elsewhere (Judg 1:10) Judah is said to have taken Hebron. Furthermore the chronology of this tradition is also strange. Josh 13:1 implies that a long time had passed since the people of Israel accomplished their initial conquest of the land, but 14:10 suggests it had only been five years. All of this leads to the suspicion that this tradition of Caleb and Hebron was originally independent of the context in which it is now found. In any event, it is Judah, not Caleb who controlled Hebron throughout the history of the monarchy.

15:1-12. The geographical boundary of Judah. The boundaries of Judah given here are as follows: the southern border (vv. 2-4) ran roughly from the southern end of the Dead Sea westward to the Mediterranean; the eastern border was *the Dead Sea* itself (v. 5a); the northern border ran from the northern end of the Dead Sea to the Mediterranean (vv. 5b-11); and the western boundary *was the Mediterranean* (v. 12). Only in the days of the monarchy did Judah ever come close to controlling the geographical limits described here, and even then the extreme desert regions and coastal plains were not a fundamental part of the tribe's territory.

15:13-19. Another tradition about Caleb. We are told again that Caleb was given Hebron (v. 13) and that it was OTHNIEL, not Joshua (cf. 10:38-39), who took Debir. But the most interesting part of this tradition is the role of Caleb's daughter, *Achsah* (vv. 16-19). Few women figure prominently in the Book of Joshua: *Rahab* (chaps. 2, 6); the daughters of *Zelophehad* (17:3-6; see below); and *Achsah* (for an interesting perspective on all of these stories, see Fewell 1992, 63–66). Here the woman and not her husband seems to realize that in addition to land (the NEGEB is basically desert) they must have water in order to live. This story is repeated in Judg 1:12-15, though there it occurs after the death of Joshua (Judg 1:1).

15:20-63. Judah's towns and cities. Some scholars believe that the list preserved here may have come from "official archives" kept in Jerusalem. This may explain why Judah is given more attention then any of the other tribes in this listing. The reminder (v. 63) that the people of Judah did not *drive out the Jebusites* who lived in Jerusalem is one of several scattered about in this part of the Book of Joshua that again indicates the conquest was not nearly as complete as the first twelve chapters claim (cf. 13:13; 16:10; 17:12,16).

Ephraim and Manasseh, 16:1–17:18

16:1-4. General introduction. EPHRAIM and MANASSEH occupied the central HILL COUNTRY north of the tribe of BENJAMIN. Actually, for all intents and purposes, Ephraim came to dominate the northern part of the country and would become synonymous with "Israel" during the period of the Divided Monarchy (ca. 926–722 B.C.E.). The descriptions given here are sketchy and there are no extensive lists of cities and towns as in the case of Judah.

16:5-10. The territory of Ephraim. The note about the Canaanites still occupying *Gezer* (v. 10) reflects historical reality. GEZER did not become an Israelite city until the time of Solomon (cf. 1 Kgs 9:15-17).

17:1-18. Manasseh. The tradition concerning Manasseh is longer then the one about Ephraim due to the fact that two narratives have been added to the material. The first is the story of the daughters of *Zelophehad* (vv. 3-6), which interrupts the description of the allotment to Manasseh. This story is based in part on the tradition in Num 27:1-11, which arose to deal with cases where the normal male heir did not exist. In the male dominated society of ancient Israel,

women did not normally inherit family property. However, in situations where this did occur, apparently they were expected to marry within their own tribe to ensure that the property would stay within tribal bounds (cf. Num 36:1-12). Not only does this story serve to show once more how Joshua did everything *according to the commandment of the LORD* (v. 4), but also that women, not usually paid much attention to in the OT, were included in God's commands to Moses as well as the men.

17:7-13. The territory of Manasseh. The description includes those cities in the Jezreel Valley such as Megiddo and Taanach that the Canaanites controlled long after Israel settled the land (v. 12). That the Canaanites were made slaves (v. 13; cf. 9:23; 16:10) may be more literary creation than historical memory.

17:14-18. The tribe of Joseph. There seem to be two parallel traditions here (vv. 14-15; 16-18; cf. the full-length commentaries), both assuming the time when JOSEPH was one tribe, hence the editorial expansion in v. 17 (i.e., *to Ephraim and Manasseh*). The solution to this problem had already been given by the narrator by the previous allotments to these two tribes. This story also explains why Israel was unable to take the well-defended Canaanite cities located in the fertile valleys of Bethshean and Jezreel. The reference to the Canaanites's *chariots of iron* is to the metal protective plates that were attached to the chariots. That this tradition remembers the *forest* of the hill country (vv. 15, 18) may be indicative of its age, since significant deforestation rapidly occurred during the Iron Age.

The Shiloh Tradition, 18:1–19:51

18:1-10. Introduction. The location for the distribution of land to the remaining seven tribes takes place at SHILOH, not GILGAL (cf. 14:6). Shiloh was an important cult center early in Israel's history (cf. 1 Sam 2:22). Some think its appearance here is an "interpolation" (so Soggin 1970, 189; on Shiloh, see Boling 1982, 422–23). The account told here seems logically to follow 14:2, especially since this latter passage states that the tribes were to receive their inheritance by lot (cf. 14:2). Here representatives from the remaining tribes are sent out to reconnoiter the land, dividing it into seven parts. Upon returning, Joshua is said to have *cast lots* (v. 6) before Yahweh. Casting lots was supposedly an impartial way of determining God's will (cf. 1 Sam 10:19-24). The actual process by which these tribes settled this part of Canaan was far more complex then this tradition indicates.

18:11-28. Benjamin. The first lot fell to Benjamin and included the territory squeezed in between Judah and Ephraim (Joseph). Benjamin's historical importance is that it was the tribe from which SAUL came. The description of its territory given here is thought to come from a much later period.

19:1-9. Simeon. Simeon's portion is said to be within the tribe of Judah. There are few details in the Bible concerning this tribe; apparently it was quickly absorbed by Judah. According to the tradition preserved in Gen 49:5-7, Simeon, as well as Levi, were scattered throughout Israel as a result of their violent nature.

19:10-16. Zebulun. This short description of the inheritance of Zebulun is filled with textual difficulties as well as a difficult history of composition. Historically, the tribe occupied territory in central lower Galilee and is praised in the Song of Deborah (Judg 5:18a). The city of *Bethlehem* (v. 15) is not, of course, the Bethlehem in Judah, but in Galilee.

19:17-23. Issachar. Zebulun's neighbor to the southeast was the territory of Issachar. Recent archaeological surveys have shown that after the Bronze Age, this area was not occupied before the time of the Monarchy (Gal 1992, 87, 90–91; for the most recent attempt to locate the boundaries of Zebulun, Issachar, Asher and Naphtali, see Gal, 98–106). Once more, the archaeological data indicate that the settlement process was long and complicated.

19:24-31. Asher. Asher's territory is described as stretching along the Mediterranean coast from Mount Carmel in the south to the Phoenician city of Tyre in the north. According to 1 Kgs 9:10-14, Solomon gave some of this territory to Hiram, king of Tyre.

19:32-39. Naphtali. Most of the territory assigned to this tribe is in Upper Galilee but its southern border reached as far south as Issachar. The reference to *Judah on the east at the Jordan* (v. 34) is unclear.

19:40-48. Dan. The tribal history of Dan is complex; the place names listed here do not form recognizable borders. The tradition preserved here recalls the time when the Danites occupied territory west of the tribe of Benjamin. This area is the geographical context of the stories of SAMSON, a Danite (Judg 13–15). But Dan was ultimately unable to hold this area and migrated north (v. 47; cf. Judg 18:1-31). Elsewhere, the biblical evaluation of this tribe is not very positive (cf. Gen 49:17; Deut 33:22; Judg. 5:17b).

19:49-51. Joshua's personal reward and the conclusion to allotments. Unlike the preceding allotments, all of which went to tribes, an allotment is now given to Joshua *by command of the LORD*. Thus, individuals as well as nations could be blessed for faithful service. This tradition is also important because it connects Joshua with *the hill country of Ephraim* (v. 50). This chapter ends with a reference to the door of the TENT OF MEETING, even as it began (cf. 18:1).

To all of this, one might very well ask: "So what?" In what way, if any, can a modern reader of what appears to be a totally confused and confusing list of ancient borders and town lists hear "God" speaking? This question becomes more difficult when the artificiality of these traditions is appreciated. What took approximately 200 years to accomplish has been telescoped into what seems a very short period. There may be many ways to read these stories theologically (see Butler 1983, 207–208). Some would say that this material shows how Israel, when it obeyed God, was given the land.

However, the voice of "critical traditionalism" seems to be saying that despite Israel's origins, which at best were obscure; and despite its own unworthiness (see Deut 9:1-24), and despite the ambiguity in applying the laws of Moses, Yahweh had triumphed over the gods of Canaan and established his people on the land. We may never know all of the historical facts that actually occurred in this process. But for faith we know enough. For the ultimate message of the DtR seems to be that Israel was nothing less than God's miracle. For those who claim to be Israel's spiritual heirs, it is a message worth pondering.

Closing Stories, 20:1–24:33

With 19:51, the second of the two major themes running through Joshua is brought to a close. Even though the traditions making up these themes were found to be complex and varied, they were used by the biblical narrator to express his own theological concerns. In the remaining five chapters, however, no such embracing theme is discernible. These stories appear to be independent of one another (see Butler 1983, 209).

Cities of Refuge, 20:1-9

To deal with the issue of involuntary manslaughter, cities of refuge were established; three in Cisjordan and three in the Transjordan (cf. Num 35:1-15; Deut 4:41-43; 19:1-10). While the idea of sanctuary was widespread in the ancient world, setting aside entire cities for this purpose appears to be unique to Israel.

However, the date of the tradition preserved here is uncertain and there is no clear example in the OT of the practice described here (but see 1 Kgs 2). Furthermore, the reference to the *high priest* (v. 6) could only have come from the postexilic period.

Cities for the Levites, 21:1-42

The history of the Levitical priesthood cannot be traced here. The Levites appear to have been country preachers scattered throughout the tribal territory of Israel. Not having any territory of their own (cf. 13: 14, 33), they are said to have been given forty-eight cities, thus fulfilling God's command to Moses (Num 35:1-8). Included in this list are the six cities of refuge listed in the previous chapter.

Agreement over the origin, date and nature of the list given here among authorities has been in short supply. What does seem clear is that these cities would not have been in Israelite control *at the same time* prior to the eighth century B.C.E. (Boling 1982, 492–94). Note should also be made of the fact that v. 42 in LXX is much longer than it is in MT.

Editorial Conclusion, 21:43-45

The dogmatic, absolutist claim made in these verses are incomprehensible in light of the actual process by which Israel came to occupy the land of Canaan. Not only have archaeological discoveries laid to rest any notion of such a complete conquest as idealized here; other voices within the Book of Joshua itself sing a different tune, recognizing that the process was neither swift nor total (13:13; 15:63; 16:10; 17:12-13). Perhaps the most helpful suggestion has been from Polzin who interprets these verses as "irony" (1980, 130–34). The question of how God fulfilled his promises to Israel in the ambiguities that characterize the real world is as complex as it is important. But the simplistic answer of authoritative dogmatism only serves to cloud the issue, both then and in any age.

The "Show and Tell" Altar
of the Transjordanian Tribes, 22:1-34

In an almost comical story about the Transjordanian tribes, we are told of an altar that was built only for show, not sacrifice. As most commentaries point out, the story is made up of three different segments: vv. 1-6, which form the conclusion to the story begun in 1:12-18; vv. 7-8, an editorial transition to what follows; vv. 9-34, the story of the altar.

What actual episode lay behind this story is unclear. Apparently in its original version it did not include Manasseh, who is absent from vv. 25, 32, 33, and 34. Basic Deuteronomic theology allowed for the erection of an altar of sacrifice only where God's name dwelt (cf. Deut 12:11, etc.), always JERUSALEM during the time of the Davidic Monarchy. This may explain the emphasis here on the fact that the altar in this story was built only for show (vv. 23, 26, 28). It may also explain why the location of *the altar of the LORD* in v. 19 is not specified (Shiloh, Gilgal, and Shechem are options).

Beyond this, the story deals with the larger question of who constitutes the people of Israel. The term "Israel" is used in this story to the exclusion of the Transjordanian tribes (vv. 11, 12, 13, etc.). Can one be a part of "Israel" but live outside *the LORD's land*? (v. 19). This question of the connection between geographical space and religious correctness would have been of paramount concern to the exiles who were very far from *the LORD's land*.

Joshua's Farewell Address, 23:1-16

This chapter has evoked a great deal of discussion among scholars with regard to its date, authorship, and its relationship to the rest of the Book of Joshua, especially to chap. 24. It almost certainly comes late in Judah's history, if not from the EXILE itself (cf. Soggin 1970, 218–19). At one time it may have formed the conclusion to the book, though it ends on an especially pessimistic note (v. 16). Also, notably absent from this chapter is any indication as to where this speech was thought to have taken place. As Boling has pointed out (1982, 526), by giving Joshua a "farewell speech," the narrator has placed him in a select group of people within the larger DH: MOSES (Deuteronomy as a whole); SAMUEL (1 Sam 12:1-24); and DAVID (1 Kgs 2:1-9).

While Joshua admits that, while not all the nations have been subdued (v. 4), Israel will still possess the land if it is *steadfast to keep and do all that is written in the book of the law of Moses* (v. 6). The warning against mixed marriages (cf. Ezra 9:1-15), and the threat of loss of the land for transgressions against God's covenant demands, stand in stark contrast to the utopian claim already encountered (21:43-45).

Shechem and Covenant Renewal, 24:1-28

The original setting of this chapter is not clear. The LXX reads "Shiloh" both in v. 1 and v. 25 (cf. 18:1

and see Boling 1982, 533; Soggin 1972, 223). Both SHECHEM and SHILOH were important cultic centers in Israel's history. The tradition of the former was traced back to patriarchal times (Gen 12:6; 33:18-19; 35:4). Also some scholars believe that there is some connection between this chapter and Josh 8:30-35, but that assumes a basic historicity for these stories that seems most doubtful in light of the actual settlement process. More probable is the suggestion of some sort of cultic festival that was carried out here, perhaps on an annual basis that was concerned with the theme of COVENANT renewal. Thus the contents of this chapter may have been independent of its present context.

24:1-13. Introduction and the speech of Yahweh. The chapter begins much like the preceding one with the stereotyped formula of address. This is followed by a reported speech of Yahweh who recites a series of divine acts, beginning with the ancestors, performed on Israel's behalf. Notably absent from this recital is any mention of Moses and the stipulations of the Sinai covenant. According to this speech, the people of Israel were able to occupy the land of Canaan for one reason only: God's gracious acts (vv. 12-13).

24:14-28. Joshua and the people respond. It becomes obvious that Israel's becoming the people of God was not as automatic as the preceding speech by Yahweh implies when we are told that Joshua, not God, reminds them that they must choose *whom [they] will serve* (v. 15). When they respond that they will serve Yahweh because of divine acts, they are told by Joshua that they cannot serve God because of God's holiness and righteous demands (v. 19). This addition to God's words by Joshua illustrates again how, for the DtR, the history of Israel was an exercise in the interpretation, modification and application of the divine will (cf. Polzin 1980).

As has been noted more than once, the theological overlay of the Book of Joshua by the DtR is complex and easily distorted. But perhaps this much can be said. That Israel existed at all was due to God's gracious acts on Israel's behalf. But God's grace is always paradoxical: free, but not cheap. The cost to Israel was understood to be its willingness to live in covenant fidelity to the will of Yahweh. That Israel had not done so was the testimony of both the prophets and the DtR. The consequences of this failure were disastrous: exile! But hope did not die with Israel's faithlessness. Perhaps now, confronted with this failure Israel would once more face the challenge of Joshua of old and choose to serve Yahweh.

Burial Traditions, 24:29-33

The Book of Joshua closes with the three burial traditions of Joshua, Joseph and Eleazar the priest. Originally, the DtR's work probably stopped with 24:28, because he continues his story in what is now Judg 2:6. In fact it is not until Judg 2:8 that he reports the death of Joshua (cf. Judg 1:1). But at some point in the final editing of these two books, the material in Judg 1:1–2:5 was added. Since the traditions recorded in Judges already assumed the death of Joshua, the announcement of his death was appended to the book bearing his name.

Works Cited

Albright, W. F. 1939. "The Israelite Conquest of Canaan in the Light of Archaeology," *BASOR* 74:11–23.

Alt, Albrecht. 1966. *Essays on Old Testament History and Religion.*

Bailey, Lloyd. 1990. "Ark," MDB.

Boling, Robert G. 1982. *Joshua.* AncB.

Butler, Trent C. 1983. *Joshua.* WBC.

Callaway, Joseph. 1976. "Excavations at Ai (Et-Tell), 1964–1972, *BA*:18–30.

Coogan, Michael D. 1990. "Archaeology and Biblical Studies: the Book of Joshua," in *The Hebrew Bible and Its Interpreters.* Ed. W. H. Propp, B. Halpern, David Noel Freedman.

Dever, William G. 1990. *Recent Archaeological Discoveries and Biblical Research.* 1992. "How to Tell a Canaanite from an Israelite," in *The Rise of Ancient Israel.*

Fewell, Danna N. 1992. "Joshua." TWBC. Ed. Carol A. Newsom and Sharon H. Ringe.

Finkelstein, Israel. 1988. *The Archaeology of the Israelite Settlement.*

Fritz, Volkmar. 1987. "Conquest or Settlement? The Early Iron Age in Palestine," *BA*:84–100.

Gal, Zvi. 1992. *Lower Galilee during the Iron Age.*

Gottwald, Norman K. 1979. *The Tribes of Yahweh: A Sociology of the Religion of Liberated Israel, 1250–1050 B.C.E.*

Halpern, Baruch. 1983. *The Emergence of Israel in Canaan.* 1992. "The Exodus From Egypt: Myth or Reality?" in *The Rise of Ancient Israel.*

Kempinski, Aharon. 1986. "Joshua's Altar—An Iron Age I Watchtower," *BAR* (Jan/Feb): 42–49.

Kenyon, Kathleen M. 1957. *Digging up Jericho.*

Kraus, H.-J. 1965. *Worship in Israel.*

Mendenhall, George E. 1962. "The Hebrew Conquest of Palestine," *BA* 25:66–87.

McCarter, P. Kyle, Jr. et al. 1992. "The Origins of Israelite Religion," in *The Rise of Ancient Israel*.

Miller, J. Maxwell. 1990. "Gilgal," MDB.

Noth, Martin. 1960. *The History of Israel*.

Polzin, Robert. 1980. *Moses and the Deuteronomist: A Literary Study of the Deuteronomic History*.

Porter, J. Roy. 1970. "The Succession of Joshua," in *Proclamation and Presence: Old Testament Essays in Honor of Gwynne Henton Davies*. Ed. John I Durham and J. R. Porter.

Rainey, Anson F. 1986. "Zertal's Altar—A Blatant Phony," *BAR* (July/August): 66.

Soggin, J. Alberto. 1970. *Joshua*. OTL.

de Vaux, Roland. 1978. *The Early History of Israel*.

Weinfeld, Moshe. 1972. *Deuteronomy and the Deuteronomic School*.

Wright, G. Ernest. n.d. "The Conquest Theme in the Bible," unpublished.

Zertal, Adam. 1985. "Has Joshua's Altar Been Found on Mt. Ebal?" *BAR* (Jan/Feb): 26–43.

Judges

Robert C. Dunston

Introduction

The Book of Judges is the seventh book of the OT and tells the story of the tribes of Israel from the death of Joshua to the birth of Samuel. The book receives its name from the individuals who are called by God to judge Israel, specifically by saving one or more Israelite tribes from enemies. In the Hebrew canon the book appears as the second book of the Former Prophets, which indicates that the book is primarily a theological history of the period rather than an exhaustive history of the times.

The Nature of the Judge

Typically in Israel a judge was primarily charged with administering justice based on the laws of Israel (Exod 18:21-22, 1 Sam 7:15-17, 2 Chr 19:6). Yet in the Book of Judges only Deborah functions in this capacity (4:4-5).

The judges in the Book of Judges are warrior heroes who are called by God to deliver their people from oppression by enemies. Several judges are specifically referred to as deliverers (3:9, 15; 10:1; 13:5) indicating that their chief function was not legal but military. Although most of the judges are said to have "judged Israel" after their military victories, this function may indicate that they are respected figures rather than legal functionaries.

The judges came from varying backgrounds and were not connected to tribal or local government. They were understood to have been called by God in time of emergency to defeat the enemies of their people. The judges exercised authority over only a few tribes, never over all of Israel. When the enemy had been defeated they seem to have returned to normal life. The only two judges who demand lifetime appointments as authoritative leaders—Abimelech and Jephthah—are portrayed as unsavory characters (9:56-57; 11:1). The loose confederation of tribes led by tribal leaders simply did not tolerate a centralization of power.

The judges are often divided into the categories of major and minor judges based not on their stature but on the length of the material we have concerning them. Some scholars identify the major judges as military deliverers and the minor judges as legal authorities. While there may be some truth to this claim, at least one minor judge (Shamgar) was a military rather than a legal figure (3:31). The information in the text is too meager to provide a precise distinction between the function of the major and minor judges.

Authorship

Ancient Jewish tradition stated that Samuel was the author of the Book of Judges but scholars today doubt that claim. Most scholars see the book reaching its final form after centuries of collecting, editing, and revising.

The bulk of the book (3:7–16:31) probably rests on stories of tribal heroes passed down orally from generation to generation. Some aspects of these tales are quite old and may well be contemporaneous with the events (e.g., the Song of Deborah—5:1-31, Jotham's fable—9:7-15). These stories would have been collected between the tenth and seventh centuries B.C.E.

Sometime in the late seventh century B.C.E. Deuteronomic editors supplied the original collection of stories with an introduction (2:6–3:6) that recounted the death of Joshua and subsequent apostasy of the people and a story (17:1–18:31) that discussed the forced migration of the tribe of Dan. In the sixth century B.C.E. Deuteronomic editors added a prologue (1:1–2:5) detailing the tribes' failure to conquer Canaan and an epilogue recounting the near destruction of Benjamin by the other eleven tribes (19:1–21:25). The book then became an explanation and retelling of Israel's dark period between Joshua and Samuel when there was no national leader and anarchy ruled the day (cf. 21:25).

Date of Composition

The events of the time occurred before Israel had a king (18:1, 19:1, 21:25). The book further refers to the fall of Shiloh (18:31), which occurred during the time of Eli and Samuel (1 Sam 4:12-18). Thus the book cannot be any earlier than the late eleventh century B.C.E., the time of Saul. The mention of the captivity of Israel (18:30) dates the final editing of the book to the seventh or sixth century B.C.E.

Literary Structure

The final form of the book is beautifully structured. Following an explanatory introduction, the stories of three minor judges are recounted followed by the stories of two good major judges, Deborah and Gideon. The story of Gideon, who seems to be the model judge, leads into the story of Abimelech, a son of Gideon who attempts to become king by force.

Abimelech's story is the central narrative of the book and begins the account of Israel's steady decline. The mention of two minor judges is followed by a second introduction and then the story of Jephthah, who sacrifices his daughter. The stories of three final minor judges lead to the story of Samson, who selfishly squanders his ability. The two final stories of the Levite for hire and the near destruction of the tribe of Benjamin complete the tale of Israel's spiritual and moral decline.

The book thus begins in difficult times with little hope for the future. Two good judges raise the possibility that Israel might survive and prosper, but that possibility is quickly dashed by Abimelech, Jephthah, and Samson. By the end of the book one wonders if Israel will survive at all.

Much has been written concerning the cyclical pattern of disobedience-punishment-pleading-deliverance-disobedience that occurs in the book. Since Israel viewed history in linear terms rather than cyclical terms, this pattern has caused some consternation. Rather than a cyclical pattern, the book's structure indicates more of a spiral pattern. The same pattern is repeated, but each repetition moves history to a different point. Israel is never back where it started; it is typically in worse condition.

Value of the Book

Historical. The Book of Judges presents a chronological problem. If the years of service of each judge is added to the length of oppressions by enemies, the total is 410 years. According to the OT only 480 years passed from the exodus from Egypt to the laying of the foundation of Solomon's Temple (1 Kgs 6:1). Thus the sum of the years of the judges is far too long. It must be the case that some of the judges were active simultaneously. Since the judges served in differing areas and led only a few tribes, the assumption that some judges had simultaneous periods of influence is highly probable.

Still the Book of Judges provides the best information available on this period of Israel's existence (ca. 1220–1040 B.C.E.). The difficulties created by a loose confederation of tribes (sometimes referred to by the Greek term "amphictyony") feuding with one another and still attempting to conquer their portion of the land and defeat their enemies are painfully recounted. Without a strong leader like Moses or Joshua Israel certainly must have been reduced to such a state.

Cultural. The Book of Judges also supplies information regarding Israel's early culture. The Song of Deborah (5:1-31) provides an excellent example of early Israelite poetry. The individual stories provide interesting insights concerning wedding customs (14:5-18), differences in local dialects (12:6), and other aspects of Palestinian culture.

Theological. Certainly the book's greatest contribution rests in its theological teachings. Religion was simple during the period. There were many sacred spots and no strong central cultic organization or practices. Within such a religious environment people were left to their own devices and moral behavior sank to abysmal depths.

At the same time, the community of Israel was confronting Canaanite religion head-on and was being changed, both for good and ill, in the process. The notion of God's control over the universe, and especially over the processes of life and fertility, was greatly expanded, bringing both danger and promise to Israel's faith. The danger lay in the attraction presented by religious practices in which the community understood itself to be sharing the creative powers of the deity. Such practices easily became corrupt, leading to efforts to control the power and purposes of the deity and make these conform to the community's own desires. But the positive side of this confrontation was a great advance in the recognition of the range and depth and subtlety of God's control and direction of the universe and of the life and destinies of the people of the covenant. Virtually every one of the classical Yahwist's theological affirmations of early Israel was deepened and broadened through contact with Canaanite culture and religion.

During most of the period of the judges, however, this confrontation with Canaanite culture was in its early stages. And as we see, the editors of the Book of Judges severely condemned the religious practices of those who inhabit the land with Israel.

The absence of a strong faith and practice led to some of the bloodiest and most abhorrent stories in the OT. Israelite society was turned upside down. The stories show women, who were not usually viewed as the stronger individuals, triumphing in both faith and military prowess. We also see women degraded, treated as property, and terribly abused. Religion often became a crutch used in times of emergency and then

abandoned. By the end of the book it is clear that a strong form of central government led by a strong and faithful leader is desperately needed. At least this is the view of the editors of the book.

For Further Study

In the *Mercer Dictionary of the Bible*: DEUTERONO-MIST/DEUTERONOMISTIC HISTORIAN; JUDGES, BOOK OF; NAZIRITES.

R. G. Boling, *Judges*, AncB, and "Judges, Book of," AncBD; J. Gray, *Joshua, Judges, and Ruth*, rev. ed., NCB; E. J. Hamlin, *Judges,* ITC; C. F. Kraft, "Judges, Book of," IDB; G. F. Moore, *A Critical and Exegetical Commentary on Judges*, ICC; J. A. Soggin, *Judges*, OTL; P. Trible, *Texts of Terror*.

Commentary

An Outline

I. Introduction, 1:1–3:6
   A. Efforts to Occupy Canaan, 1:1–2:5
   B. Life after Joshua, 2:6–3:6
II. First Series of Judges, 3:7–8:32
   A. Othniel, 3:7-11
   B. Ehud, 3:12-30
   C. Shamgar, 3:31
   D. Deborah, 4:1–5:31
   E. Gideon, 6:1–8:32
III. Abimelech, 8:33–9:57
IV. Second Series of Judges, 10:1–16:31
   A. Tola, 10:1-2
   B. Jair, 10:3-5
   C. A Second Introduction, 10:6-16
   D. Jephthah, 10:17–12:7
   E. Ibzan, 12:8-10
   F. Elon, 12:11-12
   G. Abdah, 12:13-15
   H. Samson, 13:1–16:31
V. Epilogue, 17:1–21:25
   A. Migration of Dan, 17:1–18:31
   B. Destruction of Benjamin, 19:1–21:24
   C. Conclusion, 21:25

Introduction, 1:1–3:6

Efforts to Occupy Canaan, 1:1–2:5

With the death of Joshua Israel lost its charismatic, faithful leader and a new chapter of Israel's history began. Scholars have viewed Judg 1:1-36 as an alternate and contradictory account to the conquest of Canaan recorded in Josh 1–12. Others have assumed this passage

simply tells the story of life after Joshua. Joshua's efforts may have broken the back of Canaanite power but there would have been many pockets of strong resistance that would have continued to be a threat to Israel's existence. With Joshua gone the tribes are left to decide which one of them will first dare to attack the remaining Canaanites.

1:1-21. Struggles by Judah. The Israelites inquire of God concerning which tribe should first attack the Canaanites, and Judah is selected. God reminds Israel that the land is his but he will give it to Judah. With the help of Simeon, Judah defeats Adoni-bezek at Bezek, a city probably near Jerusalem. Adoni-bezek, who has treated his victims as mutilated dogs, is repaid in kind. His thumbs and big toes are cut off, making him unfit to rule or fight. He is then brought to Jerusalem as an example of Judah's power and resolve.

Judah then destroys Jerusalem as well as cities further south. A brief story (1:11-15) recounts how Othniel became the son-in-law of Caleb, one of the last links to Israel's faithful past. The story has a parallel in Josh 15:13-19. The Kenite relations of Moses' father-in-law move toward the south and settle with the Amalekites. Caleb takes the city of Hebron and drives out the three sons of Anak, perhaps a reference to the remnants of the legendary GIANT race of antiquity. The section ends with the failure of Judah to take the cities of the plain and the failure of Benjamin to take, or perhaps inhabit, Jerusalem.

The southern tribes led by Judah manage to take the hill country but not the coastal plain of Philistia.

Although the coastal cities are listed as conquered (1:18) the next verse mentions that they were not. The choice land has been denied the southern tribes but at least they along with Caleb and the relatives of Moses can begin to enjoy the fulfillment of their promise of land.

1:22-36. Struggles by the central and northern tribes. The Joseph tribes manage to take Bethel after an inhabitant of the city agrees to help them. As a reward for his help he and his family are spared, much as Rahab and her family had been spared by Joshua (Josh 6:25).

The remainder of the section lists cities that the central and northern tribes could not take. Here there is no concerted action by tribes to attack the Canaanites; this undoubtedly caused their failure. The coastal plain and fertile valleys are denied these tribes and they are forced to coexist with the Canaanite inhabitants of the cities. Some Canaanites are pressed into slave labor; others live alongside of Israel, providing a source of continuous temptation to Israel through intermarriage and religion. This relationship also brings cultural and religious enrichment to Israel, along with the dangers.

2:1-5. An angelic message. An ANGEL speaks to Israel at Bochim where the Israelites had apparently gathered to worship. After briefly recounting God's mighty deeds and promise, the angel accused Israel of breaking the covenant by making covenants with the inhabitants of the land and failing to destroy their worship centers. God decides to allow these non-Israelite peoples to remain in the land to fight against Israel and to tempt Israel to serve their gods. Israel responds by weeping, which explains the name of the site Bochim (Heb. "weepers"). Israel there sacrifices to God, probably in an effort to persuade him to change his mind. Apparently Israel already views religion as an emergency measure, available to reverse painful, present situations.

Life after Joshua, 2:6–3:6

The first verses (2:6-10) of the section parallel Josh 24:29-31. At the age of 110 Joshua dies and is buried in the land for which he valiantly fought. As the others of Joshua's generation die off, Israel continues to serve God, but when there are no more witnesses to God's great acts of deliverance Israel forgets God. The statement that Israel *did not know the* LORD (2:10) is painfully reminiscent of Pharaoh's remark (Exod 5:2).

The pattern of history that spirals through the book now begins. Israel abandons God and embraces the gods of the Canaanites, especially BAAL and the Astartes. In anger God abandons them leaving them powerless before their enemies. Yet God never completely abandons them. In his love he raises up judges to deliver his people from their enemies. Although the judges' military success is admirable, God's deliverance has little effect on Israel's religious life. When a judge dies, the people become more disobedient to God than before. Their disobedience provokes more punishment.

Three reasons are given to explain God's refusal to drive out the nations in Canaan. The first is as punishment for Israel's breaking of the covenant (2:2-3). The second is to test Israel to see whether or not the people will obey God, especially when circumstances are difficult (2:21-23). The final reason is to test and teach Israelites who had never experienced war (3:1-2). An earlier explanation suggests that the land would be desolate and wild beasts would multiply, if all the Canaanites were destroyed at once (Exod 23:29-30 and Deut 7:22). The common element is always obedience to God, which Israel pursues only in times of difficulty and then only in a superficial manner. Typically Israel engages in intermarriage with its neighbors and joins in the worship of their gods.

First Series of Judges, 3:7–8:32

The first series of narratives concerning judges indicates that the judges are good, faithful individuals who make a positive impact on Israel. Deborah and Gideon especially demonstrate the best in charismatic leadership.

Othniel, 3:7-11

The spiral of disobedience-punishment-pleading-deliverance-disobedience begins. Othniel serves as a prime example of what the judges will do. Israel disobeys, and God allows Cushan-rishathaim of Aram Naharaim (perhaps in Syria near the Euphrates or, more likely, in the hill country) to dominate Israel for eight years. When the people cry out to God for help, God raises up Othniel, the son-in-law of Caleb, to deliver the people. Interestingly enough, the first judge is from Judah, the tribe God called to go up against the Canaanites first (1:2). Empowered by God, Othniel removes the threat and the people enjoy forty years, one generation, of peace.

Ehud, 3:12-30

Israel again disobeys God and is tormented by King Eglon of Moab. In league with the Ammonites and Amalekites, he takes Jericho and subdues Israel for eighteen years. God raises up Ehud to overcome Moab. Although he comes from the tribe of Benjamin (Heb. "son of the right hand," cf. Gen 35:18), Ehud is left-handed, a characteristic of some of Benjamin's best warriors (cf. 20:16; 1 Chr 12:2). Left-handedness was unusual and gave the individual a distinct advantage in ancient hand-to-hand combat.

Ehud is sent with a tribute payment to Eglon. Ehud requests and receives a private audience with Eglon after delivering the tribute. When they are alone Ehud draws his double-edged sword from his right side, an unexpected location but perfect for a left-handed person, and stabs Eglon. Eglon is so fat that the entire sword including the hilt enters his stomach. His gruesome death is only the first of many in the book.

After escaping, Ehud sends out the call for assistance in Ephraim. He and his compatriots secure the fords of the Jordan River and there kill 10,000 Moabite warriors. Following this victory Israel enjoyed 80 years, two generations, of peace. Here we see that the tribe nearest to Benjamin comes to the aid of Ehud. Probably Ephraim had most to gain from the defeat of the Moabites.

Shamgar, 3:31

Shamgar is referred to as *the son of Anath.* Some scholars suggest this indicates he was from Beth-Anath in Galilee but others suggest that he was a mercenary soldier under the service or auspices of the fertility/war goddess Anat. The latter interpretation would certainly explain his prowess as a warrior using only an oxgoad.

Two problems surface with Shamgar. Although he is mentioned twice in the book (3:31; 5:6), 4:1 indicates that there was no judge between Ehud and Deborah. Some Greek manuscripts moved the mention of Shamgar after 16:31, the end of the story of Samson. Moving the mention of Shamgar to that location also alleviates the problem caused by the mention of the Philistines. Many scholars agree that the Philistines were not troublesome to Israel early in the period of the judges. If Shamgar is correctly listed, the mention of Philistines might refer to an infiltration of Israel by earlier SEA PEOPLES.

Deborah, 4:1–5:31

Deborah is one of the more fascinating judges of Israel. She is the only woman judge and was recognized by Israel as having both legal and prophetic authority and responsibility. The story of Deborah has been passed down in two forms, a prose narrative (4:1-24; 5:31b) and a poetic victory song (5:1-31a), both of which celebrate the power of God and the role of women.

4:1-24, 5:31b. Deborah and Jael. Following the death of Ehud Israel again turns from God and God again hands his people over to be oppressed. In this instance the oppressor is King Jabin of Hazor whose general is Sisera. Sisera's name is Indo-European which may indicate that he is from the Sea Peoples; it is likely, therefore that Jabin led a coalition of kings from among the Canaanites and the Sea Peoples (5:19). Sisera commands a large and highly mobile force of 900 chariots with which he is able to oppress Israel cruelly for twenty years.

Israel's savior in this time of need is Deborah, who functions as a prophet and a legal arbitrator. Like other prophets, she calls for a holy war and herself designates the leader of the Israelite forces, Barak. Barak is willing to lead the Israelite troops only if Deborah will accompany him. Although his request may be seen as a sign of weakness, he may desire to have the continuing directions from God that a prophet could provide. Deborah agrees to come but states that her presence is unnecessary. God has promised victory whether Deborah is physically with Barak or not. Deborah states that she will accompany Barak, but a woman will receive credit for the victory.

Barak musters 10,000 troops from the tribes of Naphtali and Zebulun and leads them to Mt. Tabor. Mt. Tabor dominates the east of the plain of Esdraelon and is an excellent strategic location for Israel's troops. Sisera draws up his forces to attack from the southeast. The battle is joined when Barak and his soldiers sweep down from Mt. Tabor. God throws the forces of Sisera into utter panic. Sisera flees for his life while his troops are pursued and completely destroyed.

Sisera has a particular safe haven in mind as he flees for his life. Heber, the Kenite had moved into the northern region of Canaan, separating his clan from the other Kenite clans that were related to Moses. Heber and Jabin were allies, a situation far more beneficial to Heber than to Jabin since nomads would have depended on friendly relations with the more settled population. Sisera trusts that with Heber he can find hospitality and protection. Jael, the wife of Heber, meets him and shows him the hospitality he was expecting. The warmth of the rug covering, the satisfaction of the milk, and the assumed protection combine to lull Sisera to sleep. While he sleeps, Jael picks up a hammer and drives a tent peg into his temple, through his head, and into the ground. When Barak arrives, Jael welcomes him and shows him the dead general. Deborah's prophecy that a woman would prevail may have been understood by her to refer to her winning the victory, but now that interpretation expands to include Jael's deed.

The action of Jael is difficult to understand. When she saw a defeated Sisera staggering into her camp she may have felt that the alliance between her husband and Jabin would no longer be of value. Perhaps she and her husband would do better to throw their lot in with whoever had won the victory. Since Heber was an ally of Jabin, perhaps he had been drafted into the fight as well and Jael now realized he was dead. The murder of Sisera would have avenged her husband's death. Another rationale for her action might have been the appeasement of the Israelite forces who would soon arrive. By killing Sisera she would prove herself to be sympathetic to Israel and spare the lives of herself and her clan. Or perhaps she was simply reverting to an earlier alliance more in harmony with her own views of faith and family. The Kenites, or some of them at least, are thought to have been worshipers of Israel's God (see Exod 18:10-12). Certainly her actions were based on a complex reaction to a complex series of events. Her bloody deed nevertheless remains sinister.

The victory of Deborah and Jael begins a series of attacks on Jabin that ends with his complete destruction. Israel then enjoys security and peace for forty years, one generation.

5:1-31a. The Song of Deborah. The victory song sung by Deborah and Barak is considered to be the oldest text in the OT. Scholars agree that the song is most likely contemporaneous with the victory of Deborah and Jael over Jabin's coalition.

The song celebrates the victory not as evidence of Israel's power but as evidence of the power of God. According to the song Israel was in difficult straits. Travel and trade were disrupted (v. 6) and Israel's armed might was almost non-existent (v. 8). Israel could not have won the victory by itself. God alone delivered the people.

It is interesting that according to the song more tribes were involved in the battle than Naphtali and Zebulun. Ephraim, Benjamin, and Manasseh (represented by Machir) also participate. Reuben, Gilead (representing the tribe of Gad), Dan, Asher, and an unknown group, Meroz, fail to answer the call to arms. Judah, which has played such an important role in earlier stories, is not even mentioned. The tribes that participate in the battle are those that are most threatened. The other tribes that are not threatened apparently see no reason to join in the battle. This was probably the situation throughout the time of the judges.

More information is also provided concerning how the victory was won. God destroys the forces of Sisera by using weather as a weapon. A torrential rain soaks the ground and swells the Kishon into a raging river. The heavily armored chariots are bogged down and useless. The battle plan of Sisera is worthless and the troops are easily routed.

As is to be expected, Jael is praised for her actions. The picture of the death of Sisera is somewhat different from that in the prose narrative. Here Sisera sinks and dies at Jael's feet. Perhaps Jael struck the first blow while Sisera was still standing, or perhaps he sank in exhaustion. In either case his death is still bloody.

A brief poignant moment now occurs in the song (vv. 28-30). Sisera's mother is portrayed gazing out the window wondering why her son is so late returning from battle. Those with her try to relieve her anxieties, but one gets the distinct impression that she knows that her son will not return. Sisera's mother is one in the long line of those who do not see their loved ones return from war.

The poignant moment does not last long. The song concludes with a wish that God might always be as victorious as on that day. If God will continue to act like this, his enemies will be destroyed and his friends will be blessed and preserved. The concluding statement is certainly a call to be friends with God, a call that Israel typically ignored, according to the testimony of the book.

Gideon, 6:1–8:32

The story of Gideon is the longest narrative concerning a judge who functioned as a military leader. Gideon received a variety of special revelations from God and exhibited unusual power and influence among the people. Many scholars have suggested that this man to whom the people offered kingship was the ideal judge.

6:1-10. The problem. A new round of disobedience by Israel brings a new threat. The Midianites, with assistance from the Amalekites and other groups from the east, begin a series of annual raids into Israel, destroying the produce of the fields and leaving nothing for the Israelites and their livestock to subsist upon for the next year. Even though Midian was related to Israel (Gen 25:1-6; Exod 18:1) this was not the first instance of Midianite opposition to Israel (Num 22:4-7; 25:6-18). As a nation of camel nomads, Midian was primarily involved in trade rather than agriculture and their destruction of Israelite crops implies that they did not need the provisions for themselves primarily. Their actions appear more designed to keep Israel weak and unable to participate in caravan trade. The statement that the Midianites appeared *as thick as locusts* (v. 5) when they converged upon Israel is reminiscent of one of the divine plagues against Egypt (Exod 10:4-6) and indicates that the Midianite threat is also a divine judgment.

When the people cry out to God for deliverance, they are answered by an unknown prophet. He explains the reason for the people's misfortune by briefly reciting God's gracious acts toward Israel and by stating that God expected the complete loyalty of his people. The Canaanite gods might be tolerant of the worship of other deities but Israel's God is not. The people's disobedience has caused their suffering. The prophet promises no deliverance, leaving the people to suspect that they have been abandoned by the God whom they have abandoned.

6:11-32. The selection of Gideon. Two call experiences seem to be reflected in the present narrative. The first is in vv. 11-24 and the second is in vv. 25-32. Both calls are confirmed by signs.

In vv. 11-24 an angel appears under the oak at Ophrah, apparently a site at which Gideon's father Joash inquired of Baal. Gideon is threshing the wheat in a wine press to avoid detection by the Midianites and thus save some grain for his family. The angel greets Gideon as a mighty warrior who is blessed with the presence of God. Gideon doubts God's presence with either himself or his people. The angel commissions Gideon to deliver his people from the Midianites. Gideon's protestations are reminiscent of those of Moses (Exod 4:1-17) and Jeremiah (Jer 1:6-8) and they are likewise dismissed by the angel.

Gideon requests a sign that will validate the messenger and his words and receives one. Gideon prepares a large meal of a kid and unleavened bread, which is consumed by fire when the angel touches it with his staff. The angel disappears and Gideon fears for his life because he has looked upon the face of God. God, perhaps through the angel again, reassures him and offers peace. Gideon constructs an altar to commemorate his experience and, perhaps to indicate his new allegiance to God, calls the altar *The LORD is peace* (v. 24).

The second call in vv. 25-32 begins with a feat of strength and faith by Gideon and ten of his servants and ends with the bestowing of a new name upon Gideon (cf. Gen 32:28). Acting on the instructions of God, Gideon destroys the altar of his father, constructs an altar to God, and sacrifices a bull upon it as a whole burnt offering. The next day when the townspeople discover the deed and its perpetrator, they sentence Gideon to death. Joash saves his son by cleverly arguing that if Baal is the powerful god that his worshipers claim him to be, he can defend himself. Apparently Joash has also undergone some kind of conversion to faith in God or at least has decided to step out from behind the protection of the local religion, since it seems unlikely, according to the narrative, that Joash expects Baal to retaliate by killing his son. Gideon receives the new name Jerubbaal meaning *Let Baal contend* (v. 32).

6:33-7:18. Preparation for battle. Gideon calls out to Manasseh, Asher, Zebulun, and Naphtali for troops to fight against the Midianites, and each tribe responds positively. Gideon inquires of God again, asking for a sign that success will indeed be the result of his venture. Divination before battle was typical in the ancient Near East. He asks that in the morning the dew might be on a fleece of wool but not on the hardened threshing floor. As a gift from heaven the dew is a particularly appropriate element for this heavenly sign from God. In the morning it is just as Gideon has asked which is to be expected. The fleece would naturally retain moisture as opposed to the hardened earth floor. Now Gideon asks for the reverse to occur, which would seem unlikely if not impossible. When the sign is provided, it is a convincing good omen for Gideon.

Having provided Gideon with signs of victory, God now tests Gideon and his troops. The number of Israelite troops is so great that if they win the victory they will be strongly inclined to attribute it to their own strength. To eliminate this understanding, God tells Gideon to reduce his army. Those who are afraid are allowed to return home. According to Deut 20:8, this is because fear is contagious and will dishearten all in the army, a belief that is confirmed by the fear instilled by a Midianite soldier's dream (vv. 13-14).

Still the number is too great. God commands Gideon to take the remaining men to water and let them drink. Gideon is to watch the men and divide them into two groups: those who lap like dogs and those who kneel and with cupped hands bring the water to their mouths. Those who lap number 300 and are kept as Gideon's fighting force. No reason is given to explain why those who lap are selected but the assumption is that they are simply the smallest group. Some suggest they are selected because they have such trust in God they will let God protect them while they drink in a completely vulnerable manner. Yet if the other group had been selected it could be rationalized that they were selected based on their alertness and ability to respond instantaneously to fight for God. It is futile to seek some underlying motive for selection. The point is that God can deliver Israel with either many troops or a few. Now it is up to Israel to believe.

God grants Gideon one final sign so that his courage and confidence will be strong for battle. As Gideon and his servant spy outside the Midianite camp, they hear a soldier telling a friend a dream he had. A barley cake (representing agricultural Israel) rolled into camp and knocked down the tent (representing nomadic Midian). His friend fearfully interprets this dream to mean that the small Israelite forces will unexpectedly decimate Midian. The dream and its fearful interpretation apparently spread through the Midianite camp and the Midianites are beaten before the battle begins.

A brief word must be said at this point regarding signs. In the NT signs are typically discounted (Matt 12:39; 16:1; Mark 8:11-12; Luke 11:16; John 20:29), although John records several signs performed by Jesus (cf. John 2:11; 4:54). The OT is not so antagonistic toward signs and, in fact, some are requested to ask for a sign (cf. Isa 7:10-25). It is unfair to assume that the signs Gideon receives indicate that his faith is weak. His practice of inquiring of the deity before battle is typical of his time—and God offers more signs than Gideon seeks.

7:19–8:21. The defeat of Midian. Gideon's battle plan is unusual. His 300 men are to divide into three companies and place themselves around the Midianite camp. Each soldier would carry a lighted torch covered by a pottery jar, and a horn. At Gideon's signal each man is to break his jar thus exposing the light of the torch, blow his horn, and give a battle cry. Certainly a person could not do all of this simultaneously, but the effect of these actions on a demoralized enemy camp would be and is devastating. Believing themselves to be surrounded, the Midianites are thrown into a panic and begin killing one another.

Gideon and his small force pursue the escaping Midianites and call for Ephraim to block the fords of the Jordan River so that the Midianites would be trapped. The Ephraimites do so and in the process capture and execute the two Midianite captains, Oreb and Zeeb, bringing their heads to Gideon. The Ephraimites are incensed that they were not summoned earlier, but Gideon manages to soothe their hurt feelings with flattery.

The remaining narrative of the fight against the Midianites concerns personal vengeance. When the people of Succoth and Penuel refuse to provide Gideon and his exhausted force with food, he vows to return after his victory and punish them. Gideon fulfills his threat after he captures Zebah and Zalmunna, the two kings of Midian. Gideon's desperate search for Zebah and Zalmunna is explained as his desire to avenge the deaths at their hands of his brothers, the sons of Joash and Gideon's mother. Gideon orders his firstborn son Jether to kill these two, but he is afraid and refuses. The two kings state that they should die by Gideon's hand, so he kills them and takes the ornaments from their camels.

8:22-28. An invitation to be king. The people are highly impressed with Gideon's leadership and ask him to be king but he refuses. God is to be the king of Israel and not a human being (cf. 1 Sam 8:7). This is the theologically correct answer and sets the stage for Abimelech's attempt at kingship in the next chapter.

Gideon does agree to accept a gift; he asks that the golden earrings worn by the dead Midianite soldiers be given to him. From these he makes an ephod, a priestly garment worn or displayed when consulting the deity. It is interesting that although Gideon refuses the office of king he does not refuse the trappings of power and authority that indicate his special relationship with God as a recipient of divine revelation. The ephod proves to be a snare to Israel when it is used as an idol.

8:29-32. Conclusion. Following the victory of Gideon, Israel enjoys a forty year, one generation, respite. Gideon returns to his home and fathers seventy sons (a perfect number, not necessarily the actual count of his children) from various wives. One son in particular, Abimelech, is singled out and serves to point to the following narrative. Gideon dies after enjoying a long life and is buried in the tomb of his father, a fitting reward for this man of faith.

Abimelech, 8:33–9:57

According to most scholars, the Abimelech story is the central narrative of the book. The story explores and soundly rejects kingship as a possible alternative to leadership by charismatic judges.

The name Abimelech is translated by most as "my father is *melech*" with *melech* being the name of a deity. The name can also be translated "my father is (or was) king," a name that provides a link between the Gideon and Abimelech narratives. Although Gideon did not accept kingship over his people, he certainly received high regard and respect from the people and to them may have seemed to be a king. The story of Abimelech records Abimelech's desire to retain this recognition and respect and expand upon it.

8:33–9:6. Abimelech seizes power. Upon the death of Gideon, Israel again strays from God and embraces *Baal-berith* (v. 33, Heb. "Baal of the covenant"). The remembrance of the saving deeds of God and Gideon are buried with Gideon and the people quickly embrace a new deity with a new covenant. Abimelech may be reaffirming some Israelite connection with SHECHEM, since the site was important religiously for Abraham and especially for Jacob, according to the Genesis traditions (Gen 12:1-7; 33:18–35:4; see also Josh 24). In any event, when punishment comes this time, it will not come from outside but from within.

Abimelech journeys to Shechem and offers himself, as a kinsman, to be king of Shechem rather than one of the other of Gideon's seventy sons. Apparently the people of Shechem assume that one of Gideon's sons is to rule over them and they embrace Abimelech. The lords (probably landowners) of Shechem provide Abimelech with money from the temple treasury, which Abimelech uses to hire scoundrels to help him in his bloodthirsty plan. Abimelech and his hired thugs kill seventy of his brothers (cf. 2 Kgs 10:1-7) on a single stone. The reference to the slaughter occurring on a single stone most likely suggests that the slaughter has a ritual purpose. Perhaps Abimelech intends to drain off the blood, the life (Deut 12:16, 24), of his brothers in proper cultic fashion and prevent any further trouble from them. If that is his plan,

it does not succeed. Nevertheless the lords of Shechem proclaim him king.

9:7-21. Jotham's fable. Jotham, the youngest son of Gideon, escaped the slaughter of his brothers but now comes forward to address the lords of Shechem. He begins his address with a fable. Animal and plant fables are typical in WISDOM LITERATURE and Jotham may well have borrowed his fable from wisdom circles. The parable states that those things that serve a good and useful purpose (olive tree, fig tree, vine) refuse to serve as king because they do not have the time or inclination to cease their beneficial work in order to rule. It is only the useless bramble that agrees to serve as king. Good Gideon had refused to become king but now useless Abimelech has seized kingship. JOTHAM'S FABLE finds echoes in the last words of David (2 Sam 23:1-7).

After having spoken his fable to the lords of Shechem, Jotham decries their abandonment of his father's memory and their embrace of Abimelech. If they want to be ruled by a bramble, then let them enjoy it. The lords should be warned that Abimelech will be a curse to them and them to him. Jotham then flees from the scene and the story, although his words correctly predict Abimelech's end.

9:22-57. The fall of Abimelech. Abimelech rules in Israel for three years. Certainly he does not rule all of Israel but his campaigns indicate that he rules some Canaanite and Israelite cities in central Palestine. His rule is shortened by the vengeance of God who sends an evil spirit (cf. 1 Sam 16:14; 18:10; 1 Kgs 22:21-23) to set in motion the avenging of the deaths of Gideon's seventy sons. The lords of Shechem begin to move against Abimelech, perhaps because of his failure to raise the city to glorious new heights or his involvement with his troops in matters not directly beneficial to the city. In any case, the lords of Shechem begin robbing travelers who pass through the mountain pass, thus depriving Abimelech of trade revenue.

When Gaal and his clan move in to Shechem, the lords of Shechem side with him. Zebul, the ruler of the city, warns Abimelech of the treason and Abimelech moves against the city. Gaal's boastful threats against Abimelech give way to fear when the time for battle approaches; Gaal is quickly driven out of town by Abimelech.

The next day Abimelech destroys Shechem, killing the people inside, and sowing the city with salt, a symbol of the city's perpetual desolation, a place where nothing would ever thrive again. The lords of

Shechem retreat to the stronghold of the temple of *El-berith* (v. 46, Heb. "God of the covenant"), which despite its name is not a place where the God of Israel is worshiped. Abimelech sets the stronghold on fire and burns alive the 1,000 people inside.

Abimelech then moves against Thebez and takes all but the tower. He plans to burn this tower down too but as he approaches the tower a woman drops an upper millstone on his head. An upper millstone was typically a hard stone, a foot or more in diameter, and two inches thick. The stone crushes his skull. Mortally wounded, Abimelech asks his armor bearer to kill him so that he will not be remembered as one who died at the hands of a woman (cf. 1 Sam 31:4).

When Abimelech dies the battle ceases and the people return home. Abimelech's slaughter of his seventy brothers has been avenged. Even had Abimelech lived he would have had very little of a kingdom left. His attempt at kingship meets a bloody end and prefigures the kingship of Saul.

Second Series of Judges, 10:1–16:31

The second series of narratives concerning judges does not present a single example of a good, faithful judge. The minor judges who are mentioned are distinguished only by their wealth. The two major judges, Jephthah and Samson, are distinguished by their personal failings. It becomes evident from these stories that judges are not the answer to Israel's difficulties.

Tola, 10:1-2

Tola was from the tribe of Issachar but resided in Shamir within the territory of Ephraim. He delivered Israel from some unknown enemy and then judged Israel for twenty-three years. Many scholars believe that, since the years of his influence are not rounded off, the number might reflect his precise length of service.

Jair, 10:3-5

Jair was from Gilead and judged Israel for twenty-two years. Although no information is given concerning what deeds he might have accomplished, he exerted a good deal of influence through his family. Each of his thirty sons rode a donkey, indicating wealth and prestige, and ruled over a city. The thirty cities carried on Jair's legacy even to the editor's day.

A Second Introduction, 10:6-16

The present passage likely serves as an introduction to the second half of the book. The passage picks up themes from 2:11-23 and sets the stage for Israel's descent into chaos.

The people cry out to God for help after eighteen years of oppression. God answers them by reminding them of past acts of salvation toward Israel and then stating that he will no longer save them. The people's reported response is indicative of the author's concept of their covenant with God. Trying to catch God in a loophole, the author reports, they acknowledge God's decision not to save them and ask if he will not deliver them. The words are different but the results would be the same. To the people the covenant is a legally binding document, the language of which can be manipulated to secure their self-interests. The people's subsequent repentance is probably superficial but the story concludes with God acting out of love on their behalf.

Jephthah, 10:17–12:7

The Jephthah narrative continues the trend of violence and tragedy begun with Abimelech. By the time of his death after just six years of service to Gilead, Jephthah had experienced early rejection by his half-brothers, the death of his only child, and had led in a punitive attack upon a fellow Israelite tribe. Although he is portrayed in somewhat sympathetic terms, it is difficult to applaud his actions, especially the rash and deadly dangerous vow he made that results in the death of his daughter.

10:17–11:11. The selection of Jephthah. Israel's most recent apostasy leads to persecution by the Philistines and Ammonites. Jephthah will destroy the Ammonite threat while Samson will fight the Philistines.

Jephthah the Gileadite is a son of Gilead by a prostitute. His half-brothers, the sons of Gilead's wife, later drive Jephthah away from the family because they have no intention of sharing their father's inheritance with him. Jephthah becomes head of a band of outlaws, developing quite a reputation for himself as a mighty warrior.

When the Ammonites prepare to attack Israel, Israel seeks a leader for the troops. The tribal elders of Gilead are sent to Jephthah to ask him to become the commander of the army. Jephthah reminds the elders of their previous rejection of him and then offers to lead the troops if the elders will appoint him head of Gilead. The elders have no choice but to grant him this highest tribal office.

11:12-28. An attempt at diplomacy. Rather than attack Ammon, Jephthah first tries to negotiate with them. The Ammonites demand the return of the land east of the Jordan River between the Arnon and Jabbok rivers, land that Israel had taken from them. Jephthah recounts the history of how Israel got the land (cf. Num 20:14–24:25) stressing that God had conquered both Ammon and its god Chemosh and thus by divine conquest Israel was entitled to the land. Since Chemosh could not defend his land, the Ammonites have no right to ask for it back. The Ammonites reject this argument and war becomes inevitable.

11:29-40. Jephthah's vow. As Jephthah prepares to fight against Ammon he is empowered by the spirit of God. This may indicate that, according to the tradition, Jephthah was not necessarily God's choice for deliverer but that God chose to work through the selection of the Gileadites.

Jephthah's vow is probably the most well-known feature of the narrative. If God will give him success in battle, Jephthah vows to sacrifice as a whole burnt offering whoever comes out the door of his house to meet him when he returns. While some suggest that Jephthah is thinking only of an animal sacrifice, the language indicates that the sacrifice will be human. The sacrifice will be someone who greets him, not something that ambles out the front door. The offer of a human sacrifice may be the result of a perceived state of emergency (cf. 2 Kgs 3:26-27 when a Moabite king sacrifices his firstborn) since human sacrifice is prohibited in Israel (Lev 18:21; Deut 18:10). As a nominal Israelite Jephthah may be following a Canaanite practice. In any event he is taking a calculated risk, one that ends in bitter tragedy.

When Jephthah returns home victorious, he is met by his daughter, his only child, who like other women come out to greet the victorious warrior with singing and dancing (Exod 15:20-21; 1 Sam 18:6-7). Her joyous welcome brings unbearable grief to her father. The story presents both father and daughter as persons of integrity who will not retreat from the fulfillment of the vow. The daughter asks for and is granted two months to bewail the fact that she will die childless. When she returns, her father sacrifices her.

This example of human sacrifice is one of the rare cases in the OT in which the sacrifice is not censured by God. A concluding note states that the sacrifice of Jephthah's daughter is commemorated by an annual four-day period of lamentation. Perhaps the commemoration is meant to serve as a vivid reminder to Israel that human sacrifice brings nothing but personal tragedy. It is also a testimony to this unnamed daughter of

a leader who was ready to sacrifice a child for the prize of victory in battle.

12:1-7. Conflict with Ephraim. Once again (see 8:1-3) the Ephraimites are furious that they were not summoned earlier to participate in the battle. Jephthah again tries to settle the matter through diplomacy but fails. His attack on Ephraim is successful and he sends them fleeing back toward the Jordan River. The Gileadites guard the fords and test each person who desires to cross by asking them to pronounce a word that will betray their accent. Those who pronounce the word with the Ephraimite accent are killed. In all, the tradition reports that 42,000 Ephraimites die at the hands of Jephthah's troops. Following this battle Jephthah judges Israel for six years and then dies.

Ibzan, 12:8-10

Ibzan judged Israel for seven years and lived in Bethlehem of Judah. Ibzan used his large family to cement ties with other clans and thus expand his influence. Nothing else is known of him.

Elon, 12:11-12

Elon was of the tribe of Zebulun and judged Israel for ten years. Beyond this brief note there is no information regarding his activity in Israel.

Abdon, 12:13-15

Abdon was a member of the tribe of Ephraim. He is distinguished as having forty sons and thirty grandsons, all of whom rode donkeys, indicating their wealth and position (cf. 10:3-5). He judged Israel for eight years.

Samson, 13:1–16:31

The stories of Samson's exploits have been favorite stories for centuries, and undoubtedly also were to the early Israelites. Imbued by God with prodigious strength (14:6, 19; 15:14; 16:28) and possessing a prodigious sexual appetite, Samson lived as a solitary hero engaged in his own selfish and vengeful ventures rather than as a military leader dedicated to freeing Israel from oppression. His enormous potential is never fully realized and he dies as a result of succumbing to his greatest weakness, women.

13:1-25. Samson's birth. Israelite apostasy leads to Philistine domination for forty years. Samson's tribe of Dan, which was bounded by Ephraim on the north, Benjamin on the east, Judah on the south, and Philistia on the west, would have borne the brunt of Philistine oppression.

The narrative begins with an angel announcing to the wife of Manoah, a Danite, that after years of infertility she will have a son. Typically sons born to women childless for a long time are recognized as special gifts of God and are destined to great things (Gen 17:15-16; 30:22-24; 1 Sam 1:19-20; Luke 1:13-17). The child of this nameless woman is to be no exception. He will begin the deliverance of Israel from the Philistines. The angel's words imply that Samson will not complete this deliverance, thereby hinting at the tragedy to come.

The child is to be set apart from his conception. Manoah's wife is to raise the boy as a nazirite and must immediately embrace the rules of the nazirite herself. The typical vows of the NAZIRITES are refraining from drinking alcohol, cutting the hair, and touching corpses (Num 6:1-8). To these vows the angel adds avoiding unclean foods, a strange addition, since an Israelite should avoid unclean foods anyway. The additional command may indicate significant lapses in Israel's faith and practice.

When Manoah, who was not privy to the angel's visit and words, prays for confirmation, he also receives an angelic visit and miraculous confirmation. The child is born and given the name Samson. From an early age the spirit of God begins to empower him.

14:1–15:8. Samson's doomed marriage. Samson's search for a wife leads him to a Philistine woman from Timnah. He asks his father to arrange the marriage, a typical responsibility of the father of the groom. Both his father and mother protest, wondering why he would want to marry an enemy of Israel. His request is made particularly abhorrent since he is specially dedicated to God and should refrain from contact with pagans. The marriage is divinely sanctioned, for God intends to use the events that follow to begin the divine deliverance of Israel from the Philistines.

Samson and his parents travel separately to Timnah to arrange the marriage. On the way Samson encounters a young lion and rips it apart with his bare hands, much as a person might pull cooked meat from a bone. He does not tell his parents of his action, but on his return trip to marry the woman he stops to see the carcass. A swarm of bees has invaded the carcass and produced honey. Samson scrapes the honey into his hands, eating some on the way home and giving the rest to his parents. With this action he has broken two of the vows his mother had kept for him. He has

touched a corpse and eaten unclean food. The vows his mother had kept so faithfully mean little to him.

At his seven-day wedding feast Samson probably breaks the vow to abstain from alcohol; thus, only the vow not to cut his hair is left. At the feast he propounds a RIDDLE to the guests along with a wager. Some have suggested that it was a custom for the groom to offer a riddle for the bride's family to solve. The riddle functioned not only as a game but as an indication of the groom's worthiness as a husband. Samson's riddle is impossible to solve without knowledge of his encounter with the lion and the subsequent cache of honey. The Philistine men therefore soon turn to Samson's wife to help them discover the solution to the riddle. Her constant imploring wrests the solution from Samson; in turn she tells it to the men. Samson is furious; his response to the men implies improper behavior, perhaps sexual, by the men toward his wife. Samson pays the wager by traveling to the Philistine city of Ashkelon, killing thirty men, and bringing their festal garments back. He then leaves in anger, and his wife is then given to his best man.

Many scholars suggest that Samson's marriage was a *sadiqa* marriage. This type of marriage was arranged by the groom rather than his father, which might have been necessitated by Manoah's displeasure with Samson's choice. In a *sadiqa* marriage the wife remains with her family and the husband visits her on a regular basis. Later, Samson does return to see his wife, only to be told that she has been given to another.

In his anger he captures 300 foxes (or more likely jackals), ties them together in pairs by the tails, attaches a burning torch between each pair, and sets them in the Philistine grain fields to burn the crop. The Philistines respond by burning his wife and her father. Samson then responds by killing the men who have committed the deed and then hiding out. Such bloody, personal vendettas mark the Samson narrative.

15:9–16:3. More mighty deeds. The Philistines attack Judah in an effort to find and destroy Samson. The Judeans ask Samson to allow himself to be turned over to the Philistines so that Judah might be saved. Samson agrees, is bound by two new ropes, and is brought to the Philistines. When the Philistines rush to meet him, Samson breaks the ropes as if they had been burned through. He picks up a fresh—thus not brittle—jawbone of a donkey and uses it as an effective weapon to kill 1,000 men (cf. 3:31).

The following brief poem (v. 16) is filled with wordplays. The same Hebrew word means "donkey" and "heap," thus his statement *With the jawbone of a donkey, heaps upon heaps* results in a piling up of one Hebrew word much like the bodies must have piled up. The word for "jawbone" (*lehi*) also serves as the name for the location of the event, *Ramath-lehi*.

After the fight Samson is thirsty and God refreshes him with a miraculous gift of water. The notation that Samson judged Israel for *twenty years* (15:20) may indicate the original conclusion of the Samson story. The tragic finale of Samson's life may well have been a later addition.

Again driven by his sexual appetite, Samson travels to the Philistine city of Gaza to be with a prostitute. The men of the city lie in wait for him. Believing that they have their nemesis trapped within the city walls, the men sleep. During the night Samson arises, pulls the city gate from its sockets, and—bars and all—carries it forty miles to a hill outside Hebron. Again Samson's great strength has helped him elude capture and death.

16:4-31. Samson's death. Samson's downfall comes at the hands of a woman, Delilah. The Philistine lords offer her an exorbitant reward if she can discover the secret of Samson's phenomenal strength. Samson toys with her as he gives his first two answers to her question. Fresh bowstrings and new ropes (cf. 15:13-14) are easily broken. He comes closer to the truth with his third response, since his strength is related to his hair, but weaving his hair tightly into a loom that is secured to the ground is still not enough to subdue him. Finally Delilah's coaxing forces Samson to divulge his secret. While he sleeps in Delilah's lap a man is summoned to cut off his hair. The final vow is broken, and Samson awakens with his strength completely gone. The Philistines bind him, blind him, and force him to turn the grinding mill.

While in forced labor Samson's hair grows back. When he is brought in to entertain the Philistine lords, he asks to stand between the two main pillars that support the roof. The building was filled with people, with 3,000 more sitting on the roof watching the spectacle of the defeated hero. Calling upon God for strength one last time, Samson pushes against the two pillars and the building comes crashing down. All in it and on it die.

The tragedy of Samson's life is summarized by the note that he killed more in his death than in his entire life. Samson's incredible strength made him the ultimate warrior but he squandered his abilities. His death accomplishes more than does his life. The story may be intended to underscore the need both for God's spirit, which Samson has in abundance, and God's guiding word, which Samson consistently fails even to ask for. Therein lies Samson's great failing.

Epilogue, 17:1–21:25

The two narratives of the epilogue have no introduction to tie them to the preceding sections of the book. Yet, the epilogue itself is linked together by the repetition of the observation *In those days there was no king in Israel; all the people did what was right in their own eyes* (17:6; 25:21; a similar saying occurs in 18:1 and 19:1). The two narratives are also joined by having as a main character a Levite who lives in Ephraim. In general the narratives illustrate the tragic results of Israelite faith and morals under its weak, disorganized tribal system. These two narratives complete the descent of Israel into anarchy.

Migration of Dan, 17:1–18:31

These two chapters explain how Dan moved from its assigned southern territory to its northern territory (cf. Josh 19:40-48). The narrative is difficult to place chronologically because 5:17 already seems to assume that Dan is in the north close to Asher. The narrative does logically follow the Samson story, which indicated that Dan was being hard-pressed by the Philistines.

17:1-13. Micah creates a shrine. The narrative opens with the introduction of Micah, an Ephraimite, who confesses to his mother that he had stolen 1,100 pieces of silver from her. The curse his mother had placed on the thief and the silver likely had tormented him and forced his confession. His grateful mother blesses him, which serves to neutralize the curse. She then consecrates the silver to God for the purpose of making an idol. She gives 200 pieces of the silver to a silversmith who casts an idol for her. Micah then makes an ephod and teraphim and installs his son as priest in his shrine.

Already two theological problems surface. Although all of the silver was consecrated to God, only 200 pieces are used to make an idol. Apparently the rest of the money was simply kept by the mother for her own use. In addition, the making of an idol is hardly a way to honor God (Exod 20:4-6).

Later a wandering Levite from Judah arrives and Micah employs him to serve as priest at his shrine.

Micah believes that having a shrine will bring blessing to him, but having a shrine supervised by a trained religious functionary who knows the prayers and psalms and who can consult and interpret oracles will surely make him prosper.

One interesting aspect of the text is the mention that the Levite is from Judah. Although 18:30 identifies the Levite as Jonathan, a grandson of Moses, his ancestry seems unimportant. Even as Samuel from Ephraim served as a priest for Israel, so this one who claims Judah as his home can also serve as a priest. Apparently in early Israel, religious knowledge and ability were more important criteria for selecting a priest than was ancestry.

18:1-31. Dan finds a new home. Five spies from Dan are sent north to find a new territory. On their way they stay with Micah for the night and recognize the voice of the Levite—perhaps because of his accent, or his use of prayers, or because they have met him before. The spies ask the Levite to inquire of God concerning the success of their mission. The Levite does, and the spies receive a favorable oracle.

After having spied out Laish in the north, the spies return and present a good report concerning the place to the tribe. The spies describe Laish as an unsuspecting and wealthy city, a description that agrees well with Phoenician culture. The Phoenicians were more interested in commerce and agriculture than war, so Laish would present a tempting target. The Danites send 600 soldiers with their families (18:21) to conquer the city.

On the way the Danite force stops at the home of Micah and asks the Levite to become the priest of not one family but an entire tribe. The Levite accepts the offer and accompanies the Danites, who also take the idol, ephod, and teraphim. Micah discovers his shrine and priest are gone and gives chase. In a pitiful scene he asks for the return of his homemade gods and employed priest. When the stronger Danite force threatens Micah, he returns home.

The Danites continue their journey, destroy Laish, and rebuild it as Dan. The Levite sets up the shrine, and he and his descendants serve as priests until the deportation by Assyria, probably under Tiglath-pileser III in 733 B.C.E.

Although the narrative describes how Dan settled in the north, another purpose seems to be to mock the temple constructed in Dan (1 Kgs 12:28-30). As ancestry became more important for the priesthood, it was noted that the Levite had good credentials (18:30)

but he was a priest for hire, serving his own selfish interests. Furthermore, the shrine itself was the result of thievery, a curse, greed, and death. Such a shrine could not help but produce a faithless people. In 1 Kgs 12, the shrine set up by Rehoboam at Bethel also is criticized for being under the care of unsuitable priests.

Destruction of Benjamin, 19:1–21:24

The final narrative of the book recounts the worst tale by far. The lack of hospitality shown to a Levite by the town of Gibeah in Benjamin leads to a civil war in which Benjamin is almost lost as one of the twelve tribes. The story is filled with horrible crimes and bloodthirsty vengeance. In addition to the horror of the events, interpreters have difficulty accounting for the tremendous, probably inflated, numbers of soldiers, the united action of the Israelite tribes, and Israel's action, considered not politically but theologically.

19:1-30. The rape of the Levite's concubine. The narrative begins with marital difficulty. A Levite who lives in Ephraim journeys to Bethlehem to retrieve his concubine who had left him out of anger. Apparently the Levite suitably apologizes because the reconciliation of the Levite with his concubine and her father is complete and joyful. After five days of feasting the Levite sets out late in the afternoon with his concubine, a servant, and two donkeys. As night comes the servant encourages him to spend the night in Jebus (Jerusalem). The Levite refuses because Jebus is not an Israelite city. They journey on to Gibeah in Benjamin.

Gibeah gives them a cold reception. No one shows hospitality to them until an old man from Ephraim offers to take them in. The fact that the only hospitable person in Gibeah has turned out to be a resident alien himself is not a good omen. During the night the men of the city come to the old man's house demanding to rape the Levite. The host offers his virgin daughter and the concubine instead but his offer is not accepted. The Levite pushes his concubine out the door to the men and she is raped to death. The story is reminiscent of Lot's experience in Sodom (Gen 19:1-8).

The next morning the Levite exits the house and coldly calls to his concubine to get up. When he sees that she is dead, he puts her body on one of the donkeys and takes her back to his home. He then divides her body into twelve pieces, sending one piece to the head of each tribe. Although symbolic divisions are common in the OT (cf. 1 Sam 11:7; 1 Kgs 11:29-

31), the physical division of the concubine is not necessary to summon the tribes and is used primarily to arouse the horror of the other Israelites. Such an act might be tolerated among the Canaanite nations but never should have occurred or been tolerated in Israel. The Levite seems to be acting the part of a judge in inspiring Israel to defeat its enemy, but that is all he will do. He seems bent on personal vengeance and will not lead the troops.

20:1-48. The war against Benjamin. For the first time in the book all of the Israelite tribes assemble for a common cause. The Levite recounts his story and the tribes resolve to deal with Gibeah. When Benjamin is asked to turn over the guilty ones from Gibeah, the tribe refuses, probably out of a sense of tribal solidarity. Their refusal prompts the war against Benjamin.

The eleven tribes muster 400,000 soldiers while Benjamin fields 26,000. Both numbers are extremely large and are most likely exaggerated. Of the Benjaminite forces 700 are left-handed slingers who are incredibly accurate. Benjamin was known for its left-handed warriors (3:15; 1 Chr 12:2) and their accuracy explains the heavy losses the Israelites experience on the first two days of fighting.

At Bethel, Israel inquires as to which tribe should lead the attack on Benjamin and Judah is selected (cf. 1:1-2). The first two days of the battle are victories for Benjamin with Benjamin killing 40,000 from Israel. Prayer, fasting, and sacrifices on the afternoon of the second day of battle bring a favorable oracle from God promising victory to Israel. On the third day of battle a new strategy is employed (cf. Josh 8:3-23) and Benjamin is defeated. Of the Benjaminite forces only 600 escape to hide out in the rocky wilderness. The remaining inhabitants of Benjamin, their cities, their animals, and their possessions are all destroyed. Through this destruction the evil is removed from Israel (cf. Num 16:31-33; Josh 7:24-26).

21:1-24. The restoration of Benjamin. Now that Benjamin is almost destroyed, the eleven tribes grieve that this one tribe may soon cease to exist. They have vowed not to give their daughters in marriage to any Benjaminite but to sustain the tribe, wives must be found for the 600 men who escaped.

Discussion reveals that Jabesh-gilead did not send any troops to join in the attack of Benjamin. Apparently Jabesh-gilead was as strong an ally of Benjamin at this time, as it was later (1 Sam 11:1-11; 31:11-13). Israel sends a force of 12,000 to destroy Jabesh-gilead and all of its inhabitants, excluding the virgin girls. The 400 virgin girls found in Jabesh-gilead are brought back to become wives for 400 of the Benjaminites.

Still 200 of the Benjaminites do not have wives. Israel instructs them to lie in wait in the vineyards outside Shiloh. The annual festival to God is being celebrated in Shiloh, and during the festival the virgin girls dance in the vineyards. The 200 men are each to carry off a girl for a wife. Any complaint from Shiloh will be settled by the tribes. When this is accomplished, the men of Benjamin and their new wives return home to rebuild.

The narrative of the destruction of Benjamin is perhaps the most offensive in the Bible. It is a story in which people abuse others, overreact, and think only after they have acted. It is a dreadful conclusion to the tragic period of the judges, underscoring the author's view of this lawless period.

Conclusion, 21:25

The book ends in suspense with the observations that *there was no king in Israel* and *all the people did what was right in their own eyes.* From the book as a whole it is obvious that this state of affairs cannot continue. Religion will have to be reformed and somehow standardized. A national leader will have to be appointed who has more than simple charismatic authority. The loose system could have worked, the author implies, if the people had followed God, but they did not. If the horrors are to cease, another stronger, centralized system will have to be set in place.

Ruth

Mona West

Introduction

Ruth is one of two books in the Hebrew Bible named after a woman. It is unique in the CANON of Hebrew scriptures and Israelite patriarchal society because it celebrates human friendship found in the love and devotion of one woman for another.

The Book of Ruth tells the story of two women in a man's world. One woman is an Israelite named NAOMI. The other is a Moabite named Ruth. They are women in tension with patriarchal culture. Both exist within the complex web of laws and customs of ancient Near Eastern society that define and limit their existence (see WOMEN IN THE OT). Both work out their salvation as agents of the divine, moving in and out of these laws, choosing for themselves and each other.

Not only are the women in tension with a patriarchal culture, but the story itself is in tension with the redactors and interpreters of the Hebrew Bible. The narrative exhibits a struggle between the women's story and the story of patriarchal Israel. At the end of the book readers may well wonder who will have the last say. Will it be the townswomen who pronounce a blessing on Ruth's love for Naomi? Or will it be the narrator and the final redactor who emphasize that the child *born to Naomi* is the grandfather of King David?

Ultimately, it is the interpreters of the Hebrew Bible who have the last say. Ruth has been romanticized by traditional biblical scholarship as a meek maiden in distress who is rescued by Boaz. Her only virtue is that she is the great-grandmother of King David. This predominantly white-male interpretive tradition has found itself in tension with feminist interpretations of Ruth that seek to reclaim Ruth, the woman from Moab who struggled against the odds to make a way for herself and Naomi in a foreign land.

Ruth's story is also in tension with Israel's story. Its heroine is a Moabite and the Moabites were a people who had a long history of strife with the Israelites. This story exists within the Hebrew canon as witness to the fact that even though the Hebrew Bible is the story of Israel, scripture is not monolithic in its presentation of faith. Ruth's story, embedded in the story of Israel, reminds us that God does not always play by the rules of the status quo. God comes to us in the midst of life, life that is sometimes difficult and does not follow a neat story line.

Date and Literary Form

There are two dates possible for the composition of the Book of Ruth: the period of the EXILE and during the UNITED MONARCHY. Arguments for an exilic date include: the need to explain earlier customs (4:7); emphasis on the marriage of BOAZ to a foreigner, which would be a polemic against the strict marriage laws of Ezra and Nehemiah after the exile; and the appearance in the book of certain archaic Hebrew terminology that is prominently used during the exilic period.

Those who claim an earlier date for the book counter these exilic arguments by exposing the weakness inherent in establishing a chronology for narratives based on the laws they reflect or need to explain; by claiming that there is nothing polemical about the tone of the book; and by using the same Hebrew archaisms in support of a date of composition during the united monarchy.

The literary form of the book adds to the debate. Scholars are agreed that Ruth is a Hebrew short story, but there are differences of opinion concerning the origins and development of that literary GENRE. For some, the short story developed in the postexilic period and includes examples such as Esther, Jonah, and the apocryphal Book of Judith. For others, the short story (or novelle) can be found as early as the time of Solomon (961–922 B.C.E.), with examples such as the Joseph narrative (Gen 37–50) and the Court History of David (2 Sam 9–20; 1 Kgs 1–2).

The Book of Ruth shares more stylistic and theological features with the earlier material. Like the Joseph Novelle and the Court History, Ruth foregrounds human action, while actions of the deity are backgrounded or nonexistent. The theological emphasis of these stories is that courageous and kind actions of individuals mirror the deity and provide life for the community. In contrast, selfish and violent actions do not mirror the deity and do not benefit the larger community. These comparisons, coupled with the fact that the book is set during the period of the judges (ca. 1200–1020 B.C.E.) and ends with the mention of King David (1000–961 B.C.E.), provide adequate arguments for the composition of the book during the reign of Solomon.

Place in Canon, Setting, and Purpose

Place in Canon. The Book of Ruth is found in the third division of the Hebrew CANON called the Writings. According to the most reliable Hebrew manuscripts, it is placed after Proverbs and before the Song of Solomon. Ruth is an example of the "worthy woman" described in the closing acrostic poem of Proverbs (Prov 31:10-31; cf. Ruth 3:11 where Boaz calls Ruth a *worthy woman*). Ruth's relevance to Song of Solomon is demonstrated by her example of freedom and expressiveness in human relationships, two attributes emphasized in the love poetry of the Song.

Ruth is also grouped among the Megilloth, or five festival scrolls, which are read during important Jewish religious celebrations. Ruth is read during the feast of Weeks. This festival commemorates the giving of the law on Sinai and celebrates the end of the grain harvest. The Book of Ruth is a fitting text for this Jewish observance because of its references to legal customs and its themes of harvest and famine.

Setting. Because of its setting Ruth is placed among the historical books, between Judges and 1 Samuel, in Christian Bibles. Ruth provides a balance to the lawlessness and violence exhibited in the Book of Judges, while looking toward monarchy. The editorial comment at the end of Judges—"In those days there was no king in Israel; all the people did what was right in their own eyes"—establishes a context for the beginnings of the monarchy, which will be described in 1 and 2 Samuel. Ruth provides a bridge from judges to monarchy with genealogical references to David at the end of the book.

While Ruth provides a canonical bridge from judges to monarchs, it may also provide a sociohistorical bridge. Recent sociological analyses indicate that the formative years of premonarchical Israel reflect a time when men and women enjoyed near-equal status. They would have participated "equally" in the areas of procreation, protection from enemies, and production of food as they strived to make the ideal of the COVENANT community of Yahweh a reality. Once the monarchy is established there is a certain loss of the covenant ideal and the imposition of a hierarchical/hereditary leadership structure that precludes women from equal participation in society, thereby resulting in their lowered status (see Meyers 1978 and 1983).

Purpose. Canonical placement and setting indicate that the characters of Ruth are examples of how human beings are to live responsibly toward one another in the context of covenant. Ruth, Naomi, and Boaz are exemplary characters in Israel's history. However, Ruth's actions as a foreigner and a childless widow (see WIDOW IN THE OT) stand out above the other characters. She establishes a place for herself in Israel's history and canon by making responsible choices out of love and devotion to Naomi. The book also redeems women's loss of status during the period of the monarchy by presenting the "equal participation" of Ruth in the areas of procreation, protection, and production.

Law and Narrative

There has been much debate concerning the legal material in the Book of Ruth and its relationship to the narrative. Two laws seem to be most prominent. The Levirate, which required a living brother to marry his deceased brother's widow and have a son by her (Deut 25:5-10), is alluded to by Naomi in 1:12-13 and by Boaz in 4:7-10 (see MARRIAGE IN THE OT). The *goēl* law requiring a kinsman to buy back (redeem, Heb. גאל) a relative or his land (Lev 25) is mentioned throughout the Book of Ruth, once Boaz has been introduced to the narrative. (cf. 2:20; 3:9, 12-13; 4:1, 3, 4, 6, 7). Both the Levirate and *goēl* legislations are placed in a unique context when applied to the situations of Ruth, Naomi, and Boaz.

Other laws that affect the narrative are gleaning and "spreading the skirt or cloak." In chap. 2 Ruth "happens" into the field of Boaz when she decides to take advantage of the Israelite gleaning law that provides for the poor, the orphaned, the widow, and the foreigner (Lev 19:9-10; 23:22; Deut 24:19-22). At the threshing floor in chap. 3, Ruth proposes to Boaz by using the phrase *spread your cloak over your servant* (3:9). This phrase is symbolic of marriage in Israelite tradition (Deut 22:30; 27:20; cf. Ezek 16:8).

It is important to realize that the artistry and message of Ruth are dependent on the interplay of law and narrative within the book. This artistry is lost if the book is approached as a legal treatise or test case for the laws it contains. Instead, the legal material should be viewed as a creative matrix for plot movement and character development. The laws are intentionally ambiguous in order to provide possibilities for the characters to act above and beyond what society requires of them. Laws define their identity and challenge their existence. As each character makes choices that go beyond the letter of the law, that character moves toward a more authentic existence within the narrative and Israel's society.

Ruth's choices are more astounding because she makes her way in this society and legal system as a foreigner. Not only are her actions more astounding, but they provide an example for Naomi and Boaz. Ruth inspires these Israelites to act responsibly toward her and toward each other. Without her example Naomi would have remained an empty, bitter old woman and Boaz would not have been part of the lineage of King David.

In this interplay another tension is exhibited: the creative tension between law and narrative. Law embodies the strictures of patriarchal culture that define and limit authentic existence. Narrative represents the ways in which risks must be taken and decisions made that move one toward authentic existence.

Major Themes

Themes in the Book of Ruth function in much the same way as the laws: they promote plot movement and characterization. Many themes parallel the laws found in the book; several occur in pairs. For example, the theme of redemption (see REDEMPTION IN THE OT) that dominates chaps. 2–4 is related to the duty of the *goēl*. This theme combined with its legal background provides a context for Naomi, Ruth, and Boaz to make choices concerning the letter of the law. It also provides suspense as the readers of the story wonder who will emerge as the one with the right to redeem Ruth and Naomi, Boaz, or the nearer redeemer?

Covenant kindness or *chesed* (LOVING-KINDNESS) is also related to the laws of redemption. Naomi mentions the kindness of her daughters-in-law in 1:8 as she tries to convince them to return to their homeland, Moab. More importantly, Boaz recognizes the kindness of Ruth toward Naomi when he states, *"you left your father and mother and your native land and came to*

a people that you did not know before" (2:11). Boaz also identifies a second kindness of Ruth toward Naomi that is greater than the first: *"you have not gone after young men, whether poor or rich"* (3:10).

Foreignness and familiality intertwine with the laws of gleaning, levirate, and goel as Ruth moves from a foreigner in the fields of Boaz to wife and mother in Israel. Ruth's names at different stages in the narrative reflect this movement. In chap. 1 the narrator emphasizes she is *the Moabite . . . who came back . . . from the country of Moab* (1:22). She is ambiguously referred to as *daughter* and *servant* in relation to Boaz throughout chaps. 2 and 3. She is proclaimed a *worthy woman* by Boaz in 3:11 (the same phrase used to describe Boaz in 2:1). At the end of the story she is called *wife* (4:10, 13).

The themes of emptiness/fullness and harvest/famine function on parallel levels. Emptiness/fullness describe the human realm, while harvest/famine describe the agricultural realm. Naomi goes to Moab because there is a famine in Bethlehem. Yet she leaves Bethlehem *full* because she has a husband and two sons. Once there is food in Bethlehem she returns. However, she returns *empty* because her husband and sons have died in Moab (1:21).

The emptiness/fullness of Naomi and Ruth will be worked out against the backdrop of harvest in Bethlehem. The narrator mentions in 1:22 that while Naomi and Ruth have returned from Moab empty, they have returned at the beginning of the barley harvest. This sounds a note of hope for the women's situation. Likewise, a word of caution is given at the end of chap. 2 when the narrator states that the wheat and barley harvests have ended.

Literary Structure

Each chapter in the Book of Ruth exhibits a three-part structure. The first part of each chapter introduces the choices of a particular character, which will set the stage for the choices of other characters in the middle part of that chapter. The final section of the chapter presents doubt about the outcome of the choices that have been made.

This same structure can be seen in the overall pattern of the book. Chapter 1 presents the choice of Ruth to return with Naomi. This choice sets the stage for Ruth's encounters with Boaz in the field in chap. 2 and at the threshing floor in chap. 3. Chapters 2 and 3 constitute the middle of the book in which Ruth, Boaz, and Naomi make choices that go beyond the

letter of the law. Chapter 4 deals with the consequences of their choices, with its scene at the city
gate, the blessing of the elders, and the pronouncement
of the townswomen.

For Further Study

In the *Mercer Dictionary of the Bible*: MARRIAGE IN THE
OT; MOAB/MOABITES; NAOMI; RUTH, BOOK OF; WEEKS,
FESTIVAL OF; WOMEN IN THE OT.
In other sources: J. W. H. Bos, *Ruth, Esther, Jonah*,
Knox Preaching Guides; E. F. Campbell, *Ruth*, AncB;
P. Trible, *God and the Rhetoric of Sexuality*.

Commentary

An Outline

I. Choosing between Moab and Bethlehem, 1:1-22
   A. Trouble in Moab: Elimelech Decides
      to Leave the Homeland, 1:1-5
   B. Between Moab and Bethlehem:
      Decisions about Returning, 1:6-18
   C. Arriving in Bethlehem: What Will Become
      of the Two Women?, 1:19-22
II. Choices in the Field, 2:1-23
   A. Introduction of Boaz:
      Ruth Decides to Glean, 2:1-7
   B. First Encounter: Boaz Decides to Protect;
      Ruth Continues to Glean, 2:8-16
   C. Report to Naomi: How Long
      Will This Arrangement Last?, 2:17-23
III. Choices at the Threshing Floor, 3:1-18
   A. Preparation for the Threshing Floor:
      Naomi Decides to Help, 3:1-5
   B. Second Encounter: Ruth Decides to Marry;
      Boaz Decides to Redeem, 3:6-15
   C. Report to Naomi:
      What about the Nearer Redeemer?, 3:16-18
IV. Choices at the City Gate, 4:1-22
   A. Business as Usual:
      Deciding Not to Redeem, 4:1-6
   B. Finalizing the Deal: Boaz Announces
      His Marriage to Ruth, 4:7-12
   C. The Birth of a Son:
      Who Will Have the Last Say?, 4:13-22

Choosing Between Moab and Bethlehem, 1:1-22

Trouble in Moab: Elimelech Decides to Leave the Homeland, 1:1-5

Because of famine, a man from Bethlehem decides
to move his family to the foreign land of Moab. This
choice of life soon becomes a choice of death as the
man, Elimelech, and his two sons Mahlon and Chilion
eventually die in this foreign land. Elimelech's choice
not only leads to the loss of physical life, but it leaves
his wife NAOMI with a loss of security and identity.
Naomi left Bethlehem full, now after ten years in
Moab she is empty. In a patriarchal culture a woman's
worth is measured by her husband and sons. Not only
has Naomi lost her own worth, but her two Moabite
daughters-in-law, Orpah and Ruth, have been widowed
as well.

In these few verses all the major characters of the
story have been introduced with the exception of Boaz.
The choice of Elimelech has set the stage for the
choices of Naomi, Orpah, and Ruth in the verses that
follow.

Between Moab and Bethlehem: Decisions about Returning, 1:6-18

These verses highlight the struggle of the women as
they seek to survive in a patriarchal culture. They join
together, dependent on one another for support, and
begin the long journey back to Naomi's homeland,
Bethlehem. On the way, Naomi, being the older, wiser
woman, realizes that even in their solidarity they are
three widows in a man's world. Her daughters-in-law
have a better chance for survival and acceptance if
they remain in their homeland and remarry.

Naomi is a woman conditioned by the laws of
patriarchal Israel. Through her mention of the Levirate
law (1:11-13) she claims she has nothing to offer
Orpah and Ruth: no husband, no sons. She fails to
recognize that she has herself to offer as a mother-in-
law to these two *daughters* (v. 11) who have chosen to
return with her.

Each woman is faced with a decision about returning. These decisions are made between Moab and
Bethlehem, between what seems to be the security of
homeland and the risk of foreign land. Moab is homeland for Orpah and Ruth. It is a symbol of patriarchy,
echoed in the words of Naomi to her daughters-in-law:
the only way to find security is in the house of a
husband (1:9).

Moab is foreign land to Naomi. It has been a place of death and, by patriarchal standards, a place where the security and identity of all the women have been lost. One wonders what the possibilities of life may have been had Naomi decided to stay in Moab, against the odds, joined to her two daughters-in-law.

Bethlehem is homeland for Naomi. For all of the security the homeland is supposed to offer, it is a place where Naomi returns to live out her bitterness and emptiness. As foreign land for Orpah and Ruth, Bethlehem is a place to risk life with Naomi. The risk is too great for Orpah. She is persuaded by Naomi to return to her homeland of Moab. Though her choice seems the most sensible one by patriarchal standards, it is a choice that causes her to disappear from the story.

Ruth chooses Bethlehem and Naomi. Out of love and devotion she willing changes places with her mother-in-law. In Moab Naomi is the foreign woman with no husband, no sons, no identity. In Bethlehem Ruth will be the foreign woman with no husband, no sons, no identity. It is within this context that the force of Ruth's words of commitment to Naomi are heard:

Do not press me to leave you
or to turn back from following you!
Where you go, I will go;
where you lodge, I will lodge;
your people shall be my people,
and your God my God.
Where you die, I will die—
there will I be buried.
May the Lord do thus and so to me,
and more as well,
if even death parts me from you! (vv. 16-17)

Ruth refused to accept the status quo of a male-centered society that said women were nothing without men. Instead she chose, against the odds, to commit herself totally to another woman. Truly Ruth, Naomi, and Orpah demonstrate by their choices what it means to be women in patriarchal culture, against patriarchal culture, and transforming patriarchal culture (Trible 1978, 196).

Arriving in Bethlehem:
What Will Become of the Two Women?,
1:19-22

This scene echoes the first with its themes of emptiness and fullness. After their arrival in Bethlehem Naomi makes clear her sense of loss and bitter-

ness by her response to the townswomen, *"Call me no longer Naomi* [pleasant], *call me Mara* [bitter]" (v. 20). She is still a woman who sees her own worth in terms of patriarchal society. She claims she is empty, no husband, no sons. She does not acknowledge that Ruth has returned with her. Naomi is not totally empty: there is her daughter-in-law who has taken an oath to be with her until death.

The narrator sounds a note of hope mixed with doubt in v. 22. Ruth and Naomi arrive in Bethlehem during the beginning of the barley harvest. What started as the story of a family of six has narrowed to the plight of two. What would become of these two women—the one who had chosen homeland and by implication patriarchy and the status quo, and the other who had risked the foreign land, Ruth the Moabite, who had chosen for herself and for her mother-in-law?

Choices in the Field, 2:1-23

Introduction of Boaz:
Ruth Decides to Glean, 2:1-7

BOAZ is introduced for the first time in the narrative in v. 1. The narrator emphasizes Boaz's patriarchal potential for Ruth and Naomi by stating that he is a *kinsman, a prominent rich man*, and *of the family of Elimelech*. In v. 2 Ruth decides to take advantage of the Israelite gleaning law that provided for widows and foreigners. In these two verses there is a tension between patriarchy and the women. How will Ruth and Naomi survive in Bethlehem? Patriarchy's answer is Boaz. Ruth's answer is to glean.

This tension is further displayed in Ruth's statement to Naomi and in Boaz's conversation with his foreman. Ruth claims she is going into the field to glean *behind someone in whose sight I may find favor* (v. 2). She "happens" to glean in the field of Boaz (v. 3b). Upon noticing her, Boaz asks a question only a man of his culture could: *"To whom does this young woman belong"* (v. 5)? It is a question of ownership, to which the name of a husband or father would have been a normal response. The foreman's response implies that Ruth belongs to no man. Instead, she belongs to Naomi: *"She is the Moabite who came back with Naomi from the country of Moab"* (v. 6).

Was it by chance or by design that Ruth "happened" to glean in Boaz's field? Did she have previous knowledge of Boaz? She had been married to a kinsman of his for as long as ten years in Moab (1:4). If she was not aware of Boaz as a kinsman, she at least knew (along with everyone else in town) that Boaz was a prominent rich man. She deliberately went to Boaz's field to glean, to *find favor*, to take fullest advantage of the Israelite gleaning law. Would not it make sense to glean in the field of one of the wealthiest men in town?

Ruth's choice to glean in Boaz's field is in keeping with the deliberate choice she made to return with Naomi in chap. 1, and the deliberate choices she will make throughout the book. Her choice puts her in contact with Boaz. There is some ambiguity about his relationship to Naomi and Ruth. The word used to describe him as a kinsman in v. 1 can mean "intimate friend" or "blood relative."

First Encounter: Boaz Decides to Protect; Ruth Continues to Glean, 2:8-16

As a male in Israelite society and owner of the field, Boaz offers Ruth protection from molestation as she gleans (vv. 8-9). These are the first words he speaks directly to Ruth, to which she responds, *"Why have I found favor in your sight, that you should take notice of me, when I am a foreigner?"* (v. 10) These words seem out of place given the fact that Ruth intended to find favor. She is concerned about her foreign status and wants to know *Boaz's intentions.* Ruth had hoped to find favor from an economic standpoint. She wants to know if Boaz intends anything else by his offer of protection.

Boaz makes his intentions clear. His offer of protection is out of kindness and respect. He knows of her devotion to Naomi and blesses her (vv. 11-12). Once Ruth is sure of his intentions she replies, *"May I continue to find favor in your sight, my lord, for you have comforted me and spoken kindly to your servant, even though I am not one of your servants"* (v. 13). The word Ruth uses for *servant* is from the same root as the word used to describe Boaz as *kinsman* in 2:1. Once again the language used to depict the relationship between Ruth and Boaz is multilayered and ambiguous. Ruth's words indicate that Boaz is not attempting to take advantage of her as a foreigner and a widow. Instead, he has treated her as a family member or close friend even though at this point in the story she is not. The ambiguity suggests that there is the potential for Ruth to become a family member of Boaz.

Gleaning provides the backdrop for Ruth and Boaz to make decisions that go beyond what is minimally required by the law. Ruth decides to continue gleaning in the best field in town so that she can provide food for herself and Naomi. Boaz decides to offer protection and provide special gleaning privilege to Ruth (vv. 14-16) out of kindness and respect for Ruth's devotion to Naomi.

Report to Naomi: How Long Will This Arrangement Last?, 2:17-23

When Naomi sees how much Ruth has gleaned, she asks, *"Where have you worked?"* Before Ruth can answer, Naomi proclaims, *"Blessed be the man who took notice of you"* (v. 19). Naomi's words continue to reflect her patriarchal conditioning. She assumes Ruth could not have gleaned all that she had without the help of a man. When Ruth tells her that the name of the man is Boaz, Naomi clears up any ambiguity concerning him that Ruth, or the reader, may have had. She states that the man is "near to us, one of our redeemers" (v. 20). By introducing the goel or law of redemption Naomi implies that Boaz does have a certain legal relationship to her and Ruth.

At the end of the chapter it looks as if these two women will make it in a man's world after all. Ruth had found a way to live out her commitment to Naomi: she gleaned in Boaz's field and lived with her mother-in-law (v. 23). However, the barley and wheat harvests have ended, implying that there are limits to what Ruth can do. She does not own the field. She has worked out the best arrangement she could under the circumstances, but now some other arrangement must be made.

Choices at the Threshing Floor, 3:1-18

Preparation for the Threshing Floor: Naomi Decides to Help, 3:1-5

With words reminiscent of 1:9, Naomi decides to seek security for Ruth. As a woman defined by patriarchal culture Naomi reciprocates Ruth's devotion in the only way she knows how: she instructs Ruth to make herself available to Boaz. What is Naomi's intent? Is it seduction? A romantic encounter? An attempt to jolt Boaz to action? Her intentions are ambiguous, just as the encounter itself will be. This ambiguity is echoed at the beginning of Naomi's instructions in the word she uses to relate Boaz to herself and Ruth (3:2). It is the same word from 2:1, which can mean kinsman or close friend.

Naomi's decision to act on Ruth's behalf will set the stage for the second encounter between Ruth and Boaz. On the threshing floor these two characters will make choices that place them in tension with the goel law.

Second Encounter: Ruth Decides to Marry; Boaz Decides to Redeem, 3:6-15

The encounter between Ruth and Boaz at the threshing floor is similar to their first meeting in chap. 2. In what could have been a sexual rendezvous in which Boaz has the advantage, Ruth clarifies the situation and states her intent. Like gleaning in the fields, Ruth takes advantage of the *goēl* law and proposes to Boaz by instructing him to "spread his skirt or cloak" over her because he is *next-of-kin* or *goēl*" (v. 9). Ruth repeats the words Boaz spoke to her in the field in chap. 2. The same word for *wing* in 2:12 is the word used for *cloak* in 3:9. Ruth claims that Boaz will be the means by which she and Naomi will find refuge under the wing of *the God of Israel* (cf 2:12).

Ruth's decision to marry Boaz should be seen as a business proposition in an effort to continue to take care of Naomi. The wheat and barley harvest have ended. Marriage is the alternative arrangement she suggests to Boaz. Boaz's response in v. 10 confirms the nature of the arrangement: *"This last instance of your loyalty is better than the first* [the first being choosing Naomi over Moab, cf. 2:11]*; you have not gone after young men, whether poor or rich."*

In v. 11 Boaz agrees to the marriage and decides to perform the duty of the *goēl*. He does this because Ruth is a "woman of *worth*" (RSV). This is the same word the narrator used in 2:1 (NRSV, *rich*) to describe Boaz. Could this be a turning point in the story? Has the tension between the women and patriarchy been resolved? In chap. 1 Ruth had no worth by the standards of patriarchal society. In v. 11 Ruth's worth is pronounced by Boaz (and recognized by all the people of Bethlehem) on the basis of her devotion to Naomi. The choices of Ruth have been an example for all of Bethlehem. They have spurred Naomi and Boaz to action.

Just as the narrative possibility of each character begins to come to life in this chapter, the tension of the patriarchy is reintroduced in the person of the nearer REDEEMER and the strictures of the *goēl* law. This tension is represented by the haunting repetition of the word *goēl* or *kinsman* and *next-of-kin* in vv. 12-13. Boaz states:

"Though it is true that I am a near kinsman, there is another kinsman more closely related than I.

. . . if he will act as next-of-kin for you, good. . . . If he is not willing to act as next-of-kin for you, then . . . I will act as next-of-kin for you."

At the end of v. 13 Boaz tells Ruth to *"Lie down until the morning."* This phrase has been repeated throughout the encounter between Ruth and Boaz at the threshing floor. It is indicative of the sexual tension in this chapter. Naomi was the first to introduce the possibility of a sexual encounter with her instructions in 3:1-5. She told Ruth in v. 4, *"When he lies down, observe the place where he lies; then, go and uncover his feet and lie down; and he will tell you what to do."* The narrator reiterates the possibility of sexual encounter by repeating the phrase *lie down* twice in v. 7. Then, after the marriage agreement has been made between Ruth and Boaz and Boaz instructs Ruth to *"Lie down until the morning"* (v. 13), the narrator repeats this in v. 14.

The repetition of this phrase signifies that Ruth and Boaz make their choices not only as human beings in the context of the *goēl* law, but as man and woman in the privacy of the night. While the possibility of sexual encounter exists, the reality of their previous choices would indicate that no intercourse took place at the threshing floor.

Report to Naomi: What about the Nearer Redeemer?, 3:16-18

As in chap. 2, Ruth reports the results of her encounter with Boaz to Naomi. Naomi's instructions are to wait. These instructions contrast the aggressive ones she had given Ruth at the beginning of the chapter. Ruth and Naomi wait to see what will become of the choices made on the threshing floor. They wait for Boaz to settle the matter of the nearer redeemer.

Choices at the City Gate, 4:1-22

Business as Usual: Deciding Not to Redeem, 4:1-6

What had been decided in private at the threshing floor in chap. 3 gets worked out in public at the city gate in chap. 4. In Israelite society, the city gate is the place where legal matters are settled. In contrast to the sexual overtones of the phrase *lie down*, the phrase *sit down* is repeated in 4:1-4. Boaz himself sits down at the city gate, calls to the nearer redeemer to *sit down*, then beckons to the elders to *sit down* (see vv. 1, 2, 4). The business of patriarchy takes over as the two women left waiting at the end of chap. 3 fade into the background, while decisions about their futures are worked out within the confines of the laws of Israelite society.

Boaz sets up the nearer redeemer by telling him about a parcel of land that Naomi is selling. There has been no mention of the field in the story until this point, and readers are left wondering how Boaz knows about it and why Naomi has not mentioned it. Boaz does not refer to Ruth when the field is discussed, and the tension/suspense of the *goël* from the end of chap. 3 continues with the repetition of the verb *redeem* throughout this section: *"If you will redeem it, redeem it; but if you will not, tell me, . . . for there is no one prior to you to redeem it. . . . " So he said, "I will redeem it"* (v. 4).

When the next-of-kin chooses to redeem the land (v. 4), Boaz mentions Ruth and combines the Levirate law with the duty of the *goël* (v. 5). With Ruth in the picture, the *next-of-kin* decides not to redeem the land and passes the option to Boaz. Like Orpah's choice in chap. 1, the nearer redeemer's choice represents the practical. It is indicative of the status quo, defined by the law. While neither Orpah nor the nearer redeemer is condemned for the choice made, they die to the story because they do not choose beyond what is minimally required by the law. The act of taking risks that go beyond the status quo brings life—life to the story, life to the individuals who take the risks, and life to the community.

Finalizing the Deal:
Boaz Announces His Marriage to Ruth, 4:7-12

In this section the business of the men at the city gate is extended by an explanation from the narrator concerning a legal custom of drawing off the sandal. It is associated with redemption and may be related more to sealing a business transaction than to the Levirate law (cf. Deut 25:8-10). In the context of this transaction, Boaz makes public his private arrangement with Ruth at the threshing floor (vv. 9-10). In contrast to the nearer redeemer, Boaz does more than the law requires.

The entire exchange between Boaz and the nearer redeemer has taken place in the presence of the elders (vv. 2, 4, 9). In v. 11 they speak as symbols of this society and its laws. They give voice to the tension between law and narrative in this part of the story. Will patriarchy have the last say? Will the story of these two women working out their salvation against the odds of this culture be subsumed under the legal proceedings of acquiring and exchanging fields and women? What will happen to the worth Ruth has acquired for herself, not through legal means but through her love and devotion for Naomi?

The elders speak a blessing to Boaz, *"May the LORD make the woman who is coming into your house like Rachel and Leah. . . . like . . . Tamar"* (vv. 11-12). Ruth is not mentioned by name. She is simply the woman—the woman who is valued in this society by the children she produces for the men she belongs to. The only way the elders see the worth of Boaz's woman is in light of the stories of Rachel and Leah and Tamar, women who had gone before Ruth, who struggled within this culture for identity and worth.

Rachel and Leah could not envision their worth beyond the offspring they provided for Jacob/Israel. Their situation was carried to the extreme, to the absurd, as they bargained for nights spent with the patriarch (Gen 31). Tamar, a foreigner like Ruth, worked out her own place in this society through trickery and deception (Gen 38). How will Ruth's worth measure up to these who have gone before her?

The Birth of a Son:
Who Will Have the Last Say?, 4:13-22

The struggle between patriarchy and the women's story continues as the narrator states that Boaz took Ruth as his wife, Yahweh *made her conceive, and she bore a son* (v. 13). Where is the Ruth of chaps. 1–3? The Ruth who proclaimed her devotion to Naomi, who forsook the security of homeland for foreign land, who took advantage of gleaning laws, who called Boaz to the task of redeemer, who jolted Naomi out of her complacency? Is the deal at the city gate complete?

Just when it seems the structures of patriarchal culture will win, the townswomen speak (vv. 14-17). They interrupt the narrator's words with their own pronouncement of blessing. Their blessing resolves Naomi's troubles presented in chap. 1. They identify the son who is born as a *goël*. He will restore life and happiness to Naomi who had returned from Moab empty and bitter.

Upon a first hearing, their blessing sounds no different than that of the elders. Naomi's happiness (worth) is established by a son, whom society values more than its daughters. But the townswomen go on to proclaim, *"Your daughter-in-law who loves you, who is* [worth] *more to you than seven sons, has borne him"* (v. 15). In these words the townswomen pronounce a counterblessing that reclaims the worth of Ruth in the face of patriarchy. Yes, by patriarchal standards a son will restore Naomi. But by the standards of the story, Ruth is more than seven sons. The townswomen dare to proclaim what has been obvious since the beginning of the book: Ruth *loves* Naomi. This is the only time the verb "to love" occurs in the story. It does not describe the relationship between Ruth and Boaz, nor does it describe the relationship between Boaz and Naomi. Ruth is the subject of this verb and Naomi is its direct object (Bos 1984, 58).

The townswomen continue their celebration of Ruth's love for Naomi by claiming, *"A son has been born to Naomi"* (v. 17). This counterblessing undermines the patriarchal intent of the elder's blessing to Boaz. Ruth will not be like Rachel and Leah, nor like Tamar, all of whose sons were children of patriarchy. Ruth has given Naomi a son, and it is the townswomen of Bethlehem, not Boaz, who name him *Obed* (v. 17). Indeed, this is a cultural transformation brought about by one woman joining herself to another woman in a culture that defines women through men.

As soon as the townswomen name the son, the narrator quickly adds, *He became the father of Jesse, the father of David* (v. 17). In a story that has presented the struggle of two women in culture, against culture, and transforming culture, it seems that the narrator and later redactors of the book will have the last say. In the mind of the narrator, a son has not been born to Naomi; he has been born to Boaz.

Verses 18-22 expand this notion with a later genealogical addition. The genealogy picks up where the blessing of the elders had left off: the elders' *"May your house be like the house of Perez, whom Tamar bore to Judah"* (v. 12b) leads to *Now these are the descendants of Perez . . .* (v. 18).

With this genealogy, the struggle between the women's story and patriarchy is presented to the very end of the book. Phyllis Trible has called the Book of Ruth a comedy—all's well that ends well (1978, 195)—but the closing words of the narrator and the redactor sound a note of tragedy. Who really does have the last say? The words of the narrator and the redactor serve as a reminder that throughout Israelite culture and the cultures of today women continue to work out their own salvation with courage and creativity, with their choices of love and devotion toward themselves and one another.

Works Cited

Bos, Johanna. 1984. "Out of the Shadows: Genesis 38; Judges 4:17-22; Ruth 3." *Semeia* 42:37–67.

Meyers, Carol. 1978. "The Roots of Restriction: Women in Early Israel." *BA* 41:91–103. 1983. "Procreation, Production, and Protection: Male-Female Balance in Early Israel." *JAAR* 51:569–93.

Trible, Phyllis. 1978. *God and the Rhetoric of Sexuality*.

First and Second Samuel

Carol Stuart Grizzard

Introduction

First and Second Samuel cover the beginning of Israel's experiment with the monarchy and go on to detail the lives of Saul and David, the first two kings. Manuscript evidence indicates that the book was divided into two parts in 1477 C.E. First Samuel begins with Samuel's birth in the 1070s B.C.E. and 2 Samuel ends shortly before David's death in 961 B.C.E. In the Hebrew Bible 1–2 Samuel is part of the Former Prophets (Joshua–2 Kings). This account of the nations of Israel and Judah from founding to fall is often called "the Deuteronomistic History" in recognition of its having undergone at least one editing by an individual or school taking its basic theological understanding from Deuteronomy: if the nation is faithful to God it will be blessed, but lack of faithfulness will lead to disaster (cf. Deut 6:10-15, 8:11-20).

Sources and Date

Scholars have long enjoyed dissecting 1–2 Samuel in search of sources lying behind the present text. These two books—originally one—certainly invite such explorations. Some of the most important events in 1 Samuel are told two or three times: the rejection of Eli's house (2:27-34; 3:11-14 [cf. 4:12-22]), the selection of Saul as king (9:1–10:16; 10:17-27), Saul's subsequent rejection (13:5-14; 15:1-35), the meeting between Saul and David (16:14-23; 17:31-58), the killing of Goliath (17:4-54; cf. 2 Sam 21:18-19), Saul's attempt to kill David with a spear (18:10-12; 19:9-10), David's sparing of Saul's life in the wilderness (24:1-15; 26:1-16), and Saul's death (31:1-7; cf. 2 Sam 1:1-16).

The repetition at times creates awkwardness, for example, when David enters Saul's service (1 Sam 16:14-23) and then is unknown by his master in a following story (17:55-58). Furthermore, sometimes the stories display markedly different attitudes towards the characters and the situations in which they find themselves. A comparison of 1 Sam 8:7-9 and 9:15-17 provides a clear example of different attitudes. The first story claims that God views the people's request for a king as rebellion; the second story claims that God calls Saul the ruler who will *save my people from the hand of the Philistines* (9:16).

A reasonable and popular explanation of the repetition and resulting awkwardness has been that 1–2 Samuel (esp. 1 Samuel) is an interweaving of two or more sources, each with unique theological perspectives and characterizations. The additional evidence that the Hebrew text is corrupt, containing more differences with the LXX than most OT books, makes it easier to view the books as having a long and complex history of transmission.

Julius Wellhausen, the German scholar widely recognized as a pioneer of SOURCE CRITICISM, was not the first to engage in the source-hunting enterprise. In 1878, however, he put together what was at the time the most meticulously argued statement on the subject. He found two sources in 1 Samuel, distinguishing between them based on whether they were pro- or anti-monarchical. Wellhausen assigned the first source to the period before the EXILE, while he saw the other source as exilic or postexilic. Other notable scholars such as Noth, Eissfeldt, and Gressmann followed; while many disagreed on the dates he assigned to his sources or the designation of individual verses, like Wellhausen they tended to find sources differentiated by attitude toward the monarchy. Material clustered around particular characters or specific sites and objects are also often considered to be sources (cf. Eslinger 1985, 11-37).

The search for the sources behind 1–2 Samuel may be drawing to a close; the ground has been worked and reworked to exhaustion. The source-critical enterprise nonetheless has helped readers understand the complex process through which biblical books were developed and preserved. As a method of study source criticism has also helped readers understand the many and conflicting reactions that Israel expressed at various times to its forms of government.

Some problems with the emphasis on possible sources in the books of Samuel, however, are apparent. (1) Distinguishing sources based on their attitude towards the monarchy gives the impression that the books are only about the monarchy. Noting the vast amount of material given to the kings' personal lives—rather than their reigns—indicates that the narrator is at least as much concerned with the relationships of the characters as with the political change itself.

(2) The search for sources may betray a subconciously patronizing attitude towards the original composers and audience, suggesting that they were not capable of careful editing or of noticing gaps and contradictions between sources. The assumption that modern literary skills enable us to unravel this pastiche that earlier, less sophisticated communities considered to be unified could be evidence of arrogance. A more appropriate attitude towards 1–2 Samuel would be to recognize its coherent structure, its characters that are consistent in their well-roundedness, and its use of conflicting viewpoints to achieve a subtle presentation of the issues.

(3) Most importantly, the intensive analysis 1–2 Samuel has received in the last 100 years has resulted in a literary work so fragmented that its essential coherence may be (and, indeed, has been) overlooked. By now it has become a given that the twice-told stories and apparent contradictions represent the viewpoints of multiple authors and editors spanning a period of more than 400 years. This presupposition means that readers do not have to inquire into any other reason for the repetitions and ambiguity, making it more difficult for readers to notice the depth and emphasis given to the text by its complex characterization and never-quite-identical repetitions.

Certainly a work like 1–2 Samuel was not composed overnight; research into the different traditions surrounding the pivotal characters of Samuel, Saul, and David went into its presentation. Earlier collections of stories dealing with Samuel, the ARK, the transition from the tribal confederacy to the kingship, Saul, David, and David's family may well have existed (either in oral or written form). Such stories probably circulated orally in and after the eleventh and tenth centuries B.C.E. in which they are set. Some of them may have been written as early as the late tenth century.

The books of Samuel did not assume their final form, however, until their deuteronomistic editing during or immediately after the Babylonian Exile in the sixth century. But the editors did not simply string together hitherto unrelated stories with no thought given to the effect they produced in their new context. Rather, the older traditions were assembled in such a way that they both modify and enhance each other, giving a balanced view of one of the most complicated times in the biblical period. Therefore, instead of focusing on the shadowy sources that may lie behind the text, this commentary will approach 1–2 Samuel as a finished product, dealing with it as a carefully and intentionally constructed literary work.

Primary Themes

Whatever else it may be, 1–2 Samuel is an exciting story, full of action, love, betrayal, flawed heroes, and understandable villains. This does not mean that we cannot look for historical truth or theological meaning. We find traditions describing Israel's rise to power and stability in Canaan, as well as material about both divine and human nature and the relationship between them. Nonetheless, the themes of the book are expressed through the action of a crowded plot and the interactions of complex and powerful characters. The book focuses on SAMUEL, SAUL, and DAVID, who in their own ways rise and fall in the course of this work. The relationships among these main figures and the parallels and differences in their lives reveal the narrator's agenda.

The narrator seldom intrudes on the scene, preferring to let the characters speak for themselves without necessarily endorsing what they say. This technique has the effect of quickly engaging the readers in the story, as we are called upon to decide when the characters are being honest, what their motivations are, and whether or not their decisions are wise ones. The narrator will not always make this easy for us.

The emotional impact of 1–2 Samuel is due largely to the narrator's skill in drawing the reader into the action and creating even minor characters who are vivid and complex. We are far removed from the overt issues that these stories deal with: correct procedure in sacrifice and holy warfare, the establishment of theocratic monarchy, the peculiar perils of polygamy, and so forth. This carefully woven story continues to resonate with us not because of these issues but because of the underlying themes.

Some of the main themes are the subtlety with which God works in the lives of nations (electing and speaking, but staying undramatically behind the scenes); the necessity of good leaders who will take God seriously and the difficulty in finding them; the rivalries within families and especially the tensions between fathers and sons; the difficulty of maintaining trustworthy relationships when society is changing and political and religious power are available for the taking; and perhaps most of all, the incredible potential for good and evil that is found in every human being.

Ultimately, this is a book about relationships: those between God and a nation or individuals, and those among people. None of these themes is limited to any one time or culture; it is as the characters grapple with these themes that they transcend the eleventh and tenth centuries B.C.E. and become not merely ancient Hebrews but understandable human beings. It is this universal quality that is the mark of great literature.

For Further Study

In the *Mercer Dictionary of the Bible*: ARK; DAVID; DEATH; DEUTERONOMIST/DEUTERONOMISTIC HISTORIAN; KINGSHIP; HOLINESS IN THE OT; HOLY WAR; JOTHAM'S FABLE; JUDGES, BOOK OF; LITERATURE, BIBLE AS; LOT/LOTS (CASTING OF) IN THE BIBLE; PHILISTINES; SAMUEL; SAMUEL, BOOKS OF FIRST AND SECOND; SAUL; SOURCES, LITERARY; TRIBES; UNITED MONARCHY.

In other sources: A. F. Campbell, *Of Prophets and Kings: A Late 9th-Century Document (1 Samuel 1–2 Kings 10)*; L. M. Eslinger, *Kingship of God in Crisis: A Close Reading of 1 Samuel 1–12*; B. Peckham, "The Deuteronomistic History of Saul and David," *ZAW* 97 (1985): 190–209.

Commentary

An Outline

Prologue, 1:1–2:11

Samuel Is Born, 1:1-20

As is the case with many other important biblical figures (ISAAC, JACOB, SAMSON, JOHN THE BAPTIST, JESUS), we meet Samuel's family before his birth, showing that God was involved in this life from its conception. Samuel is the leading human actor in chaps. 3 and 7–12; after that he is an authoritative but often absent figure in Saul's reign. Samuel sets David on his path to power and gives him aid at a low point in the younger man's career, but in 1 Sam 25:1 he dies (although one of Samuel's unique characteristics among OT figures is that he is granted a postmortem appearance). The fact that 1–2 Samuel is named for him rather than for David, who is center-stage far more than anyone else, emphasizes the importance of what Samuel represents: totally God-guided leadership.

This opening section has an oddly timeless quality. Except for the fact that the shrine at Shiloh is functioning, there are no clues about the chronological setting of the story. No mention is made of the national situation, the military leaders, or the Philistines (and other enemies) who were so prominent in the Book of Judges, and will be so again in the rest of 1 Samuel.

Most of this book is about the nation, but it begins with an intimate story about a family. For this reason the first chapters appear to be a prologue, introducing many of the issues dealt with later in the book.

1:1-8. Peninnah attacks Hannah. The news that Elkanah has two wives places his family in the context of the ancestral families in Genesis in which the men had more than one woman. Remembering those stories prepares us for what follows: only one wife can bear children; the other is infertile. The Genesis pattern tells us that, like Sarai and Hagar, or Leah and Rachel, the wives will compete, but that finally the barren wife will bear.

Verse 3 introduces another family. HOPHNI and PHINEHAS are referred to as *the two sons of Eli*, but Eli himself seems to need no introduction. The annual pilgrimage and miserable family banquet establish the family of Elkanah as both pious and threatened by rivalry among its members. Like Abraham and Jacob, Elkanah seems unable to make peace in his family, but he is loving if not redemptive to the weeping Hannah.

1:9-20. God helps Hannah, whom Eli misunderstands. Hannah speaks for the first time, not to Elkanah but directly to the LORD. Rachel demanded children from Jacob (Gen 30:1), but Hannah goes to God. In her heartfelt prayer she not only asks for help but also promises to God that which she most desires. If the LORD will give her a son, she will return that son to the giver, making the child a gift to both of them.

The piety of Hannah is contrasted to that of Shiloh's patriarch, who cannot even recognize prayer when he sees it. Like the onlookers in Acts 2, Eli mistakes deep communion with God for drunkenness. Eli's warmth to Hannah in v. 17 marks him as a kindly yet still oddly insensitive priest.

The LORD's act of remembering Hannah emphasizes more than power over infertility. It shows the divine initiative in vindicating and empowering one of the least valued members of a patriarchal society (cf. Elizabeth in Luke 1:24-25) without necessarily endorsing the values of that society. Just as Hannah acted independently in asking for the child and promising him to God, she and not her husband names him Samuel. There is no formal divine visitation in the story of Samuel's birth. Pronouncements were given to Hagar (Gen 16:7-14), Abraham and Sarah (Gen 18:9-15), Rebekah (Gen 25:21-23), and Samson's mother (Judg 13:25). The lack of one here gives the experience an element of ambiguity for Hannah. The narrator explicitly tells us that God answered Hannah's prayer, but no one at all tells Hannah. The requirements for the fulfillment of her private vow are simply met. Will she regard prayer and pregnancy as unrelated events rather than cause and effect?

Hannah Responds in Gratitude, 1:21–2:11

1:21-28. Samuel journeys to Eli. Our question is raised again when we find Elkanah returning to Shiloh *to pay his vow* (v. 21). The vow, of course, is Hannah's. A husband can nullify any vow made by his wife (Num 30:8-15). Elkanah allows hers to stand and accepts it as requiring a response from him, but the blessed Hannah has not yet responded to the miraculous event. Even her statement at Samuel's birth simply repeats that she *asked him of the LORD* (v. 20), not that God responded.

Verse 24 resolves any doubts the reader may have had about Hannah: she is faithful. While Elkanah accompanies Hannah and her son to Eli's shrine, the husband is not mentioned until the very end of the scene (v. 11). As was the case with the vow and the naming, Hannah takes the initiative.

2:1-11. Hannah exults. Although this trip to Shiloh could have been a mournful affair, Hannah makes it a time of remembering God's grace and exalting the LORD who has redeemed her from trouble. Her first prayer was brief and desperate, but her second is luxuriously triumphant. Like Mary in Luke 1:46-55 (a speech modeled on this one), Hannah understands that both nations and individuals—the powerful and the barren—equally need and can know the strength of God's intervention. Her prayer emphasizes God's reversal of status: the mighty, the full, and the fertile find loss, but the feeble, hungry, and barren find help. The same situation will be encountered by many other characters later in this book. Her prayer ends with the promise that God will be with the king (v. 10).

There is no king in Israel yet, but in this verse, as in so many ways, Hannah's prayer foreshadows later events of the book.

In this prologue a troubled Hannah finds solace from God, becoming more assertive and responsible as a result. In many ways she is the prototype of Israel. She appears to be of no account, but through God she is vindicated. We have observed in her an optimum relationship with God: bringing misery before the LORD in trust and responding with faithfulness and gratitude when her prayer is answered, even though there might be room to doubt that the improved conditions have been anything but fortuitous. She takes initiative and acts faithfully in this relationship. Her experience also raises the issue of qualified leadership: the priests of Shiloh are the sons of a priest with little spiritual sensitivity, which suggests trouble ahead.

Eli and Samuel:
the Old Leadership of Israel, 2:12–7:17

Shiloh under Elide Leadership, 2:12–4:1a

2:12-21. The ministry of the sons of Eli and Hannah. Our doubts about Eli are immediately justified: we are told that "the sons of Eli are sons of worthlessness" (author trans.), a striking judgment equating the incompetent, but not evil, Eli with nothingness. Leviticus 7:30-36 establishes what the priests' proper portion of the sacrifice can be, but Eli's sons take whatever they can get, not caring whether their portion is one of the prescribed parts so long as it is large.

When the sincere sacrificers try to stop them, at least to the extent of allowing the fat to be burned off first (Lev 7:3-4, 31), the priests' representative threatens them with violence. Although Eli's sons are the subject of this passage, they are not referred to by name but only as *the sons of Eli* (v. 12), emphasizing his culpability for their behavior. Eli himself is present in name but absent in fact, showing him to be negligent as both father and priest.

In contrast to Eli's sons, Hannah's is ministering before the LORD. Eli, absent but needed in the first scene, is present but not needed in the next (as was also true in his first encounter with Hannah, cf. 1:9-18), blessing the family that already has been blessed by God. Our last glimpse of Hannah shows her basking in God's continuing grace (v. 21).

2:22–4:1a. God chooses between the sons of Eli and Hannah. Eli confronts his sons feebly when forced, not reminding them of their duty to God or people but only of the danger they are courting for themselves. He is not successful because *it was the will of the LORD to kill them* (2:25). Like the frequently repeated motif of God's hardening Pharaoh's heart (Exod 4:21, 9:12, etc.) and Isaiah's calling to stop the ears, shut the eyes and dull the minds of the people (6:10), this statement is not intended to relieve anyone of the responsibility for their own actions. Eli's sons, like Pharaoh and the Judeans of Isaiah's day, commit their crimes on their own. Rather, this passage underscores both the difficulty of repentance once evil has been chosen over and over again and the inevitability of punishment for unfaithfulness. Samuel, however, grows in human and divine favor (a phrase applied to Jesus in Luke 2:52).

First Samuel 2:27-36 recounts the oracle delivered to Eli by *a man of God*. Why the priest cannot receive this oracle from God himself is by now clear. An ORACLE is an explicit foreshadowing of events, serving on one level to emphasize God's knowledge and control and on another to bind the multifaceted action of 1–2 Samuel together. We will see this pattern of oracles and signs being fulfilled again. This oracle expands on the statement of 2:25, referring to events in the near future as well as some occurring in the reigns of Saul and David (for 2:33 cf. 22:20-23; for 2:34 cf. 4:11; for 2:35 cf. 2 Sam. 8:17, 1 Kgs 2:35).

The statement in 3:2 that the uninsightful Eli is losing his sight reminds us why there is a dearth of visions: few in this time are faithful enough to have them. It is Samuel and not Eli who guards the lamp and ARK of God by night. God speaks now for the first time in the book; his first word is Samuel's name. The boy does not know the voice of the LORD, but Eli, who is not favored with direct divine discourse, is at least able to discern it when it comes to another.

We have now the third warning of destruction for the Elides. Each performs a necessary function. The first informed us (2:12-17), the second informed Eli (2:22-25), and the last informs Samuel (3:10-14). Although he is but a child, as the next leader of Israel and especially as a prophet he must know what God is doing (cf. Amos 3:7).

Israel versus the Philistines
under Elide Leadership, 4:1b–7:2

Hans Hertzberg claims that this section "has no direct connection" with what has come before (1965, 46), but it is here that we see the effect on the nation of Shiloh's leadership crisis, and it is here that the judgment on the Elides begins.

4:1b-22. Israel suffers under the Philistines. The PHILISTINES threatened Israel in the Book of Judges. They were the enemy Samson harried but did not defeat (Judg 13–16). The conflict between them and the more loosely organized Israelites provides the context for much of the action in 1 Samuel. After the loss of the first battle at Aphek, the people send to Shiloh for the Ark of the covenant. When it arrives in the custody of Hophni and Phinehas, we know from 2:27-36 that in spite of its powerful history it will not help the people now. The point is that faithfulness to God is more powerful than supernatural objects.

While many of the people of Israel have been faithful, their leaders have not; as always, the people pay for bad government. God does not fight against them but is simply absent, and they cannot defeat the enemy without divine help. The devastation of the day is shown poignantly by the fulfillment of the doom on Eli's sons and its effect on the rest of his family (cf. 2:34).

5:1–7:2. The Philistines suffer under the LORD. The Philistines could stand against Israel, but not against Israel's God. The narrator even links later Philistine priestly practice to their recognition of Dagon's subjugation to the God of Israel—a foray into the ontology of ritual that probably found more agreement in Israel than in Philistia.

The chapter ends with a comic picture of the once victorious but now panicking Philistines spreading the plague by sending the Ark rapidly through three of their five cities.

Their priests provide careful instructions on how to pacify Israel's God without forcing their own people to come close to either Ark or Israelites. Undirected cows with nursing calves left at home will naturally return to them, but these cows, protesting as articulately as cows can, head in the opposite direction to take the Ark back to Israel.

The Philistine's return of the Ark signals their awareness of God's power but not any desire to align themselves with it. According to the Hebrew text of 6:19–7:2, the Israelites of Bethshemesh look into the Ark. They do not seem to fear it as much as the Philistines do; the latter took more care not to offend the Ark's god—a god who is not even their own.

This section ends like chap. 5 with the dangerously powerful Ark being circulated in fear from city to city, but now the fearful ones are God's own people.

Israel versus the Philistines under Samuel's Leadership, 7:3-17

Samuel could not appear in the previous section describing Israel's massive loss because that is seen as the result of the flaws of the Elides. Now that they are gone, the God-called Samuel appears to provide leadership. As so often in the Book of Judges, the defeated people cry out to the LORD, who raises up a judge to lead them in repenting of their syncretism and in destroying their enemies. The use of this pattern establishes Samuel as the last and greatest of the judges.

Israel's repentance has led to the restoration of right relationship with God: exclusive worship. Now the people will be restored to what they, at least, consider to be right relationship with the Philistines: victory. They immediately look to Samuel to be their help, and like Moses in Exod 17:8-13 he intercedes for them with God during the battle.

Because of Samuel, the LORD is not absent as was the case at Aphek and so the Philistines are routed. In the first battle Israel encamped at Ebenezer, literally "stone of help," but there was no help (4:2). Now Samuel establishes a new Ebenezer in recognition of the returned help of the LORD.

This section ends with a survey of Samuel's tenure as judge of Israel (although like Eli, Samuel will serve priestly functions as well). This is not a completely happy ending, however; Samuel only achieves a stalemate with the Philistines, leaving them a strong power base from which they can again emerge to threaten God's people.

The difference in Israel's battle experience is due to the change of leadership. The old and new leaders are carefully compared, and Samuel emerges as superior in every way. Unlike the Elides, Samuel performs the sacrifices correctly, intercedes with God on the people's behalf, enables them to achieve victory, and takes pains to be aware of what happens on his watch. The stable period Israel enjoys under Samuel is scarcely summarized, however. We are not given time to see Israel at peace before the narrator catapults us into another crisis.

Samuel and Saul: the Last Judge and the First King, 8:1–12:25

This is easily the most complex section of 1 Samuel. Different understandings of the word "king," and different reactions to the possibility of having one in Israel, compete for attention while the actual individual in whom all the arguments will coalesce seems unaware of the great change his presence represents.

Israel considered the kingship twice in the Book of Judges (8:22-23; 9:1-57), but its rejection is seen positively. Even so, Judges shows that there are problems with the tribal confederacy; not all the tribes respond to Deborah's cry to fight the Canaanites in chap. 4 and 5, and the last chapters of the book show Israel degenerating into a lawless place because "there was no king in Israel" (Judg 21:25). Therefore the request for a king in 1 Samuel comes in a context of confusion.

As Gideon feared (Judg 8:22-23), a king may take God's prerogatives for his own, but it is also true that lack of strong centralized authority may result in anarchy and injustice. In a similar way, the Bible as a whole is ambiguous about government.

In the OT, many psalms extol the special relationship between God and the Davidic king, but the prophets often find those kings oppressive and unresponsive to the LORD. In the NT the evil potential of government is seen in the crucifixion of Jesus and the persecution of the church, and yet Rom 13:1 says to be "subject to the governing authorities; for there is no authority except from God."

This ambiguity is well reflected in the chapters in 1 Samuel that deal with the inauguration of the monarchy. Like most people of any nation or time, Israel had both positive and negative feelings about government—and both those reactions were grounded in realistic perceptions of it.

Samuel Disapproves of the Request for a King, 8:1-22

It is ironic that Samuel, who came to power because Eli's sons were corrupt, has equally corrupt offspring. His unorthodox attempt to establish his sons in the nonhereditary judgeship leads to the intervention of Israel's elders. In one sense they are not trying to start over with a new system; they ask Samuel, whom they have long recognized as God's chosen leader over them, to establish a different form of government. But in another sense they are making a complete break with the past. The phrase *like other nations* (v. 5), denies Israel's role as "God's treasured possession out of all the peoples . . . a priestly kingdom and a holy nation" (Exod 19:5-6) because holiness means above all being separate, distinct, and other. By requesting a king like the nations, Israel is refusing its status as God's chosen instrument in blessing the nations (cf. Gen 12:1-3).

As a God-directed leader, Samuel's initial reaction is to seek God's guidance. God is angry but will not impose the divine will on the people, a motif that permeates the Bible all the way back to Gen 3 (where human freedom is so great that all of creation is marred by it, but that freedom is nonetheless permitted). At that point God continued to deal with humanity, but not in the same way as before human decision changed the relationship.

The same thing will happen here. Samuel's warning, like that of Eli to his sons, appeals to self-interest. He does his best to dissuade the people, detailing the great financial cost of the kingship and describing an absolute monarchy similar to those of the Canaanites. The last two verses warn the people that they risk reversing their own history: they were slaves in Egypt when God heard their cry and rescued them (Exod 2:23-25), but a king will make them slaves in their own land and God will not hear their cries.

In response the people only make their request more specific. Their idea of a king is one who will *go out before us and fight our battles* (v. 20). Samuel dismisses the assembly with the political and theological issues unresolved.

God Chooses Saul Both Privately and Publicly, 9:1–10:27a

We move from the acrimonious debate of chap. 8 to a story that introduces one of the favorite themes of literature. While Saul is not in rags when we meet him, and never exactly finds riches, his story still concerns a lowly innocent who becomes great—a motif foreshadowed in Hannah's song. His rise will take place in three connected stages: the LORD will choose him in 9:26–10:27a, the people will accept him in 10:24, 27b–11:13, and finally Samuel will acquiesce in 11:14–12:25.

9:1-17. Saul journeys to Samuel, who expects him. Most biblical characters are not physically described. Saul, however, is presented as an imposing figure, one we are surprised to find searching for donkeys. He is soon discouraged; it is the servant who has the resources of knowledge and purse to enable them to continue their mission. This boy is not aware of the true status of *the man of God* (v. 7; but vv. 14 and 19 will identify him as Samuel), but Saul does not know of him at all, and so they seek out the greatest man in Israel to help them find some donkeys.

The scene shifts to the previous day, and now we find at least partial resolution of the issues left hanging at the end of chap. 8. God has chosen Saul as *ruler* (v. 17) or "designate" (the word *nagid* literally means "the one in front"), reminding us of the people's demand of 8:20. "King" (Heb. *melek*) will not be used of Saul until the people support God's choice and acclaim him so in 10:24, but this does not mean that God does not intend Saul to be king; *nagid* is used of David and other kings (cf., e.g., 2 Sam 6:21; 1 Kgs 1:35; 1 Kgs 14:7).

That this king will be anointed by God's spokesperson shows he will not be an autocratic king like the one described in chap. 8, but a theocratic one, a king under God. Like the people in 8:20, God envisions the king as being primarily a military leader. Verses 15-17 echo Exod 2:23-25 again, but unlike 8:18 that echo is positive. In Exodus, however, God responded to the people's plea by calling Moses. Because the people now make a demand, God responds with Saul. God has shifted gears to accommodate the people's decision, but the negative context of 8:7-9 still holds, reinforced by the fact that Samuel does not comment on the LORD's command. Can this young man who does not even know who Samuel is and who must borrow money from his servant compare to Moses?

9:18–10:16. Samuel privately anoints Saul. The meeting between Samuel and Saul sets the tone for their relationship. Saul is unaware of the significance of what is happening and Samuel tells him more than he wants to know without actually explaining much. Samuel honors the young man but also orders him around. Saul passively accepts both attitudes. The anointing takes place without witnesses. Samuel, in spite of his strong doubts of chap. 8, anoints Saul as *nagid* to defeat Israel's enemies, and even kisses the chosen one.

Saul does not respond at all to Samuel's speech in chap. 10. Verse 9 tells us that all the signs Samuel promised were fulfilled that day, but only the third is described. Saul receives the Spirit of the LORD in the company of charismatic prophets, unusual behavior on the part of the dutiful Saul, which surprises the people. Saul's unexpected and unnerving adventures excite no comment from him; he simply goes home. His silence may stem from disbelief or confusion; in any case, "whatever he sees fit to do" (v. 7) is nothing.

10:17-27a. God publicly chooses Saul. It is important here, as in chap. 12, to note that God acts but does not speak. Samuel continues to control events by summoning the people to Mizpah, apparently for the purpose of selecting a king by lot. He quotes God in v. 18, but v. 19 is reported as Samuel's words. Here he informs the people that they have rejected God, something God told Samuel in 8:7-8, but neither then nor later told him to tell the people. God has not said a negative word on kingship since, but Samuel is not convinced. He divides the people into clans without telling them why, but sounding as if they are to be punished.

Since this practice usually reveals transgressors (cf. Josh 7:14-15), Saul's hiding makes sense, but it means that he is passive even when being proclaimed king. He also does not seem to trust Samuel, although since Samuel has gone out of his way to be sudden and mysterious all along his caution is understandable. The lots eliminate the people until Saul is reached—God acting to reveal the chosen one to the people after Samuel's stalling. Even though Samuel obviously has doubts about this whole enterprise, he presents Saul in an entirely favorable light as God's chosen but cannot bring himself to call him either "designate" or "king."

The people, relieved by this positive outcome after Samuel's ominous opening statement and procedure, dutifully cheer God's chosen king whom they do not know. Samuel's explanation of the rights and duties of the king must include the fact that Saul will not be like kings of other nations but will be under the theocracy as represented by Samuel, which may explain why some *worthless fellows* (v. 27; cf. 2:12) grumble when all had cheered him previously. As was the case in the anointing episode, Saul simply goes home without commenting.

The People Choose Saul, 10:27b–11:13

The Ammonites provide Saul with the opportunity to show his might in warfare; this is particularly important since military power is all the people seem to really want in a king. They already shouted on his behalf, but only some followed him. The new king frustrates our expectations first by being found placidly farming, and then by responding with surprising strength to the news of the Ammonite threat, which provides his first real action in the narrative.

Saul is possessed by the Spirit (11:7) and shows that despite his earlier passivity he has power and leadership, demonstrating understanding of the theocratic nature of his kingship by calling the people out *after Saul and Samuel* (11:7). He delivers Jabesh-gilead so effectively that his enthusiastic people try to punish those who doubted him in the previous chapter, but Saul again shows his mettle by stopping the lynch party and crediting God with the victory.

Samuel Accepts the Situation, 11:14–12:25

Samuel begins to accept the situation in 11:14, referring to Saul's rule as *kingship*. However, v. 15 says that *Saul and all the Israelites*—but not Samuel—rejoice. While Samuel may feel that the chosen king has been vindicated, he still cannot celebrate. Like Moses and Joshua, Samuel has a farewell address, but unlike them he does not then depart the scene. Note that although God will support the old judge in v. 18 with *thunder and rain*, at no point is the speech presented as the words of anyone but Samuel. Here his previously unvoiced feeling of personal rejection comes to the fore (in 8:7 God identified this as the cause of Samuel's initial displeasure with the people's request).

Samuel, the man who has spent literally his whole life in service to God and Israel, has the normal human need for reassurance. He repeats the familiar idea that success depends on faithfulness, but now he adds *if both you and your king who reigns over you will follow the LORD your God* (12:14), reminding the people that they can be punished for the sins of their leaders (as they were with the Elides).

Samuel again says that the request for a king was wrong and the people, alarmed by the unseasonal thunderstorm Samuel calls on the LORD to send, agree and ask for his intercession as they have before (7:8). The storm shows God's support for Samuel and his belief that God is the true king, but God has long since responded to the people's request. Samuel, having gotten them to admit for the first time that they were wrong (and, perhaps, mollified by the fact that they still need him), reassures them of God's faithfulness and his own continued help. Saul is not even mentioned by name after 11:15, underscoring the continuing importance of Samuel in the new regime.

The kingship has been established. The people asked for it, but it is God and not they who choose Saul. They cheer him as God's chosen in 10:24 but accept him themselves in chap. 11. Samuel is slow to accept the change, trying to talk the people out of it at every turn, but his quarrel is clearly with the request and not with Saul himself. Their relationship is complex. Samuel dominates and Saul allows it, but while at times Samuel seems proud of the man he anointed, chap. 12 shows his deep unease with what Saul represents. Here we see Samuel not as a mindless automaton conveying messages from God to people, but rather as a powerful yet vulnerable human being. He has more trouble than God does in dealing with his feelings of rejection; individual emotions and ego always play a great role in affairs of religion and state.

Samuel and Saul: the Rejecting Mentor and the Abandoned Protege, 13:1–15:35

Saul's story has been about the unexpected rise of the lowly. Now it will become a story about the fall of the great. As Saul first was chosen by God, then accepted by the people, and finally by Samuel, he first will be rebuked by Samuel, then the people, and finally by God.

Saul Is Rebuked by Samuel, 13:1-15

This section is introduced by the formula that will begin the account of every king of Israel and Judah in 1–2 Kings. The corruption of the first verse in the Hebrew text—and its absence in the SEPTUAGINT—makes Saul's length of reign difficult to determine (Acts 13:21 gives the standard figure of forty years). The accepted date for the beginning of his reign is 1020 B.C.E. Saul sees his task as mainly military, and so at once begins to muster the Israelites against the Philistines, although Jonathan (not identified as Saul's son until 13:16, distancing Saul from his exploits) wins the first victory.

The Israelites respond to their king's call; all is ready except that Samuel is not present. Saul is torn between two priorities: Samuel clearly said that he would come to offer the sacrifices within a week (10:8), and as a theocratic king Saul is bound by Samuel's word. The already demoralized and outnumbered troops are leaving, however, and a king chosen primarily for military purposes cannot let the situation degenerate any further. Saul chooses to offer the sacrifices himself; Samuel appears as soon as this prerogative has been taken. Offering no explanation and paying no attention to Saul's defense, Samuel warns Saul in v. 14 that God "will choose a man after his own heart" (author trans.; the verb form may indicate future action the speaker believes to be assured) to rule Israel, although the writer says nothing about God's rejecting Saul until 15:10. Since Samuel, although obedient, was so reluctant to accept the kingship, it is certainly possible that his absence was at least subconsciously intentional to set Saul up for failure.

Saul Is Rebuked by the People, 13:16–14:52

This section contains an Israelite victory, but its purpose is to show the further degeneration of Saul's leadership.

13:16–14:23. Jonathan achieves victory over the Philistines. The Philistines, stalemated in chap. 7, are still a threatening and well-armed presence in Israel. Jonathan and his armor-bearer scout out the enemy garrison while Saul stays in the camp, unaware that anything is going on. The fact that he is accompanied by a descendant of the ineffective Elides (Eli's great-grandson, Phinehas's grandson) adds an ominous note.

14:24-52. Saul's vow leads to an unsatisfactory conclusion. Saul's vow reminds readers of the oaths in Judg 11:30-31 and 17:2, each of which accidentally endangered the speaker's child. Saul's instinct for failure is nowhere better shown than here, where he inadvertently jeopardizes his son who is also Israel's foremost warrior. The lots that brought him public acclaim (10:20-24) now bring disaster as he, torn as in chap. 13 between the practically and theologically correct, sentences Jonathan to death. The problem is not that God wants Jonathan dead but that Saul's rashness has put him in the untenable situation of either breaking the vow in which he invoked God's name or killing his son.

The people see the victory as proof that God was with Jonathan (and not with Saul?). They flocked to Saul after his first victory but refuse to follow him now, favoring a greater warrior. Unwilling to cross the people (who originally initiated the kingship and whose favor is more important now that Samuel's is lost), Saul lets his son be redeemed at the cost of his vow. While Jonathan will always trust and be faithful to his father, dying by his side in battle, this scene prepares us for problems between them. Already unnerved by the divine silence that let him know his command had been broken (vv. 37-9), Saul breaks off the war. His later victories are only summarized, ensuring that his confusion at Michmash makes the strongest impression on us.

Saul Is Rejected by the LORD, 15:1-35

15:1-9. Saul takes prisoners and booty in the battle. In spite of 13:13-15, Samuel recognizes that Saul is still chosen by the LORD and continues to deal with him on that basis. He presents his credentials, pointing out that Saul owes his throne to God as he orders him to carry out a holy war against Amalek. He is also careful to give Saul his status as king; Samuel has not previously addressed Saul by his title. *Saul and the people* (v. 9), however, save Agag and the best of Amalek's herds, destroying only the things for which

they have no use rather than consecrating all that was the enemy's to the LORD. As in 13:8-9 and 14:45, Saul is shown as being easily led by the will of the people when practicality and religious duties clash.

15:10-35. Samuel delivers the LORD's rejection of Saul. Saul has not disobeyed one of Samuel's orders as in 13:9, or gone back on his own vow as in 14:45; he has, instead, disregarded a direct word from the LORD. Samuel again shows his complexity (not to mention human orneriness) by crying out to God against the rejection of the king he never wanted in the first place and attacked in 13:13-15. Samuel is, nonetheless, as faithful in carrying out the distasteful task of rejection as he was in carrying out the distasteful task of anointing. Like Eli, Saul is blind to his situation in his pride (v. 12), in his contention that he has in fact fulfilled his task (vv. 13, 20), and most of all in his refusal to take responsibility for what the people he rules have done (vv. 15, 21). His statement that the animals are for sacrifice does not help. The claim is suspicious since v. 9 says the animals were saved for their value; and in any case Saul's orders have never included making sacrifice. His references in vv. 15 and 30 to *the LORD your God* show his lack of understanding of his own role.

Samuel's words in vv. 22-23 are an excellent example of prophetic religion (cf. Amos 5:21-24; Isa 1:11-17). They convince Saul of his sin, but while Saul the person can be forgiven, Saul the king who has failed so completely to grasp the nature of his theocratic task cannot continue to be entrusted with it. From this rejection there is no turning back. The deuteronomistic emphasis on punishment for unfaithfulness means that God's regretful rejection of it shows divine consistency rather than fickleness (v. 29). But while Samuel has had to reject the king he still has affection for the person (cf. 16:1) and concern for the nation that they lead together, and so before the people Samuel is willing to present a united front.

It is hard not to sympathize with Saul, who has the unenviable task of being a king over a people who had never had one. God, Samuel, and the people make clear that they see the king as a military leader, and Saul is gifted in that practical area. But there is more to being king than that, and it is in the theological demands of the kingship that Saul fails. As one who is "little in his own eyes" (15:17), he is always anxious to please (9:5; 11:13; 13:12; 14:45; 15:13), but this means he cannot stand up even to the people he is supposed to lead (13:8; 14:45; 15:15). The man who did not succeed in the first task we saw him undertake has neither the faithfulness nor the depth for this one.

It is also hard not to sympathize with Samuel, whose years of faithful judgeship end so abruptly but who still finds himself drawn to the man he cannot help but regard as a supplanter. The rejection seems to be a private affair between the LORD, Samuel, and Saul. The people do not know of it and those who are loyal to Saul (who will be king until he dies) are never seen as purposefully going against God's will. Only Saul and Samuel know that he is no longer God's chosen leader.

Samuel and David: the Old Judge and the Young Shepherd, 16:1-23

This short section is given equal weight with the four that have preceded it because it is so important. Chapter 16 introduces us to the major human character of 1–2 Samuel, who is also the most glamorous hero of the Bible. David's coming has been prefigured: he is the *man after [the LORD's] own heart* of 13:14, the *neighbor* of 15:28, the real anointed king of 2:10. He is more complex than any preceding character, and he will find both greater success and greater failure. Like the story of Saul, David's story begins as a rags-to-riches tale. Perhaps he, too, will suffer a reversal.

David's introduction in many ways resembles the anointing of Saul. Both rise in tandem with the previous leader's loss. The future king's appearance is appealing; so far Saul and David are the only two characters in 1 Samuel to be described physically. God reveals the chosen one to the anointing agent, who in both cases is Samuel. Both anointings take place secretly with little explanation offered. Both Saul and David receive *the spirit of the LORD* (10:6; 16:13) on the day of anointing, but neither comments in any way on what has happened to him.

One difference is important: Saul, however inadvertently, seeks Samuel out, but Samuel purposefully travels to find David. God chose Saul to make the best of a bad situation, since the people were insistent on forming a monarchy, but God's hand is in no way forced in the choosing of David. It will be years before a new king is actually needed, giving time for the selection and molding of the man after God's own heart.

Verses 6-7 show, as we have already suspected, that Samuel does not always perceive God's intentions accurately. As usual, Samuel plays his cards close to the vest, not telling anyone (including David) what is going on; perhaps he feels that Saul's knowledge of

his destiny led him to take too much initiative. At the moment that David receives the spirit, Saul loses it. Saul's credentials for the kingship were that Samuel said God had chosen him and his own possession of the spirit. After losing Samuel and spirit, Saul still has the overwhelming task of leading the nation but now he knows that he is alone and no longer qualified. Saul's behavior in the ensuing chapters resembles manic depression, but that is a modern diagnosis. To the narrator, the absence of divine guidance is sufficient cause for Saul's madness.

Saul went home after his anointing; David leaves. Whether or not he suspects that Saul's torment is connected to his own strange experience, he ministers to him. Even more than with Samuel and Saul, we find the leader who is losing status drawn to the one who is gaining it, while the supplanter is bound to the one whose place he is to take. The carefully drawn similarities between Saul and David force us to wonder if the new anointed one will make the mistakes of the old.

Saul and David: the King and His General, 17:1–19:17

David's meteoric rise to power begins in this section. Saul is seen as a frustrated, almost impotent leader, while David's youthful energy and undeniable charm capture everyone's heart—including Saul's. But his very success sows the seeds of disaster as the love-hate relationship with Saul is established.

Israel versus the Philistines under Saul's leadership, 17:1-58

17:1-11 The Israelites fear Goliath. Chapter 14 ended with a stalemate between Israel and the Philistines because of Saul's weakness (14:45-46). Chapter 17 opens with a stalemate because of Goliath's strength. He is a better physical specimen even than Saul and he is well prepared for battle. Goliath's armor and weapons (a Philistine strength, as noted in 13:19-22) are amazing. He is confident, while Saul and his men are afraid and unable to respond.

17:12-23. David journeys to Saul. Verse 12 recalls chap. 16, literally describing David's father as *an Eph-rathite of Bethlehem in Judah*. David, both shepherd and musical therapist, is still presented as his father's errand boy. The stories of Samuel and Saul also began with a journey commissioned by a parent that took them to the national leader and resulted in glory (1:24-28; 9:1-15). Verses 20-23 show David's attention to detail and his eagerness to see the action. Saul was slow to respond to his anointing; we wonder how this divinely chosen king anointed so like Saul will react to Goliath's repeated challenge.

17:24-40. David volunteers to fight. Saul will not meet Goliath himself but simply offers a prize for his death. David's character is captured in the first words attributed to him (v. 26). His first priority is personal reward and his second is the honor of God and people. His charm works on everyone except Eliab, who knows him better than anyone else and may also feel the frustration of losing the unexplained competition of the previous chapter. In spite of the necessity of ending the stalemate, Saul responds with concern when David volunteers. David's later reputation as a poet (and probably for exaggeration) is seen in vv. 34-37. His eloquent words are enough to convince the pliable Saul. Saul does his best to prepare David, but his armor only comically hampers the young man. David will meet the enemy on David's own terms, not Saul's.

17:41-58. David is victorious. The contrast between the armored Goliath and the lad with five smooth stones is an easy one to make, but David's choice of weapon in fighting one so much bigger reflects shrewdness more than naivete. He could not afford to get close to the long-armed Philistine. The more important contrast is between Saul and David. Saul met his first enemy with a huge army behind him (11:8). Now he is behind the lines while a younger man fights (cf. 14:1-15). Saul appears to put his trust in armor; David faces the enemy armed with his trust in the LORD. Goliath, stunned by a blow to his one unprotected area, subsequently is killed by his own sword. It is his good fortune that the expression "Achilles' heel" is more popular than "Goliath's forehead."

The head of Goliath could not be taken to Jerusalem until much later (v. 54; cf. 2 Sam. 5:6-7), yet v. 57 describes its immediate disposition. Saul's questioning David's identity is a sign of the increasing mental degeneration described in 16:14-23. Since David has seen this before, he is not surprised. The meeting between Samuel and Saul encapsulated their relationship (9:18–10:8); the stories of Saul's and David's also encapsulate theirs. Saul will often forget who David is and treat him as a stranger, but the greatly gifted David will respond with gentleness.

Saul Fears David's Success, 18:1–19:17

Saul's jealousy of David after his victory makes more sense when we remember that the people have consistently understood *king* as one who will *go out*

before us and fight our battles (8:19). He is also aware of what no one else but Samuel knows: the God who chose him has rejected him for another (15:28). The king who was so solicitous of David before he fought Goliath ends up trying to kill him himself after watching David effortlessly win over the people and even Saul's own family, suspecting that he may be the new anointed one.

18:1-9. David is popular. Jonathan and David form a friendship upon their first meeting that will drastically affect the outcomes of their lives, and Saul's. It is significant that we are told twice how Jonathan loves David but never how David feels (cf., however, the moving tribute from David upon learning of Jonathan's death, 2 Sam 1:19-27, esp. vv. 25b-26). The man whose first words asked about the possibility of advancement might have reasons for cultivating the king's son that have nothing to do with friendship. Jonathan gives his friend what he needs to be a successful soldier, and a success he is. The people's impudent cry in 18:7 would grate on any king's ears. One with Saul's problems could not help but be upset.

18:10-16. Saul tries to kill David I: the spear. Similar to 16:14, the *evil spirit from God* that *rushed upon Saul* (v. 10) reflects the Israelite belief that God is behind all that happens (cf. 2 Sam 24:1). The loss of the spirit is torment enough for Saul. The attempted murder is narrated matter-of-factly, perhaps reflecting how common such events were around the fragile king. It is not David but Saul who is afraid afterwards. Saul sends him away, but this only contributes to David's glory as he fulfills Israel's concept of king more than ever.

18:17-30. Saul tries to kill David II: the marriage. Saul offers Merab to David as a snare so the people will see how Saul loves their hero, but will not suspect him of complicity in his death. He does not keep his word, but when MICHAL genuinely loves David the trap is set again. Saul is clever; since most men will resist circumcision by sword, he is sure that one out of a hundred Philistines so attacked will manage to kill David, but the scheme backfires. David, like any hero, fulfills the absurd task set by the king and wins the hand of his daughter.

The offer of Merab had been private; this is a more public affair and Saul cannot back out of it, so the marriage takes place. The Bible nowhere records what Saul does with the requested marriage present. As with Jonathan, we are told twice of Michal's love for David but not of his feelings for her. Saul, who intended

David's death, is now forced to make him part of the family. David's success increases.

19:1-17. Saul tries to kill David III: the spear. This attack is almost identical to the one in chap. 18, but in this context it is more serious because two of Saul's children are involved against him. First Jonathan intercedes for David with his father, who is now serious enough to declare publically his murderous intentions. Saul swears in God's name not to harm David, but (as with the vow of 14:24) does not keep his word, pursuing David after missing him with the spear. Jonathan failed to save David through words, but Michal will save him through action. She initiates David's flight and the following coverup. David, who has grown used to Saul's rages, does not consider his situation dangerous. Michal may know that their marriage was a subtle plot against David, alerting her to the fact that her father's murderous intentions do not always express themselves in recognizable ways. David flees and Michal lies for him, although she tells her father that David forced her to help (v. 17).

David and Saul:
the Fugitive and His King, 19:18–26:25

In this section Saul is obsessed with killing David while David is forced by Saul to assemble a power base of his own. Saul is now sure that David is God's new chosen—and he is absolutely right—but his sickness prevents him from seeing that the admittedly ambitious David never threatens him. While David engages in some questionable behavior, the narrator is careful to show that David is, in fact, innocent of wrongdoing towards Saul.

One of the worst aspects of Saul's condition is that at times he remembers that he loves David only to find himself trying to kill him again. As Saul degenerates, David slowly changes from a powerless but opportunistic man to a powerful and responsible one as he makes positive relationships. Saul, who has already lost Samuel and the LORD, becomes less responsible and royal as he makes negative ones. This is shown especially in their relationships with God who, behind the scenes as always, supports David through the prophetic word and subtle action on his behalf, rather than through dramatic miracles.

David Flees from Saul, 19:18–21:15

19:18-24. Samuel and David. This is only the second meeting we are told of between Samuel and David but (as in the first) no real interaction between them is presented. Here we see God sending the spirit not upon a chosen leader or messenger but upon those who mean ill to the chosen one. Its purpose is not to illuminate but to prevent, the only time in the Bible in which this is so. In 15:35 we are told that Samuel and Saul never met again. Here they do, but since Saul is possessed by the spirit (which Samuel described in 10:6 as becoming a different person) they do not meet in any real sense of the word. Ironically, the first time Saul fell into prophetic frenzy (10:10-12) was a sign of his being chosen. Here, it is a sign of his rejection.

20:1-42. Jonathan and David. David, on the run from Saul, seeks help not from his family but from Saul's. Perhaps Eliab in 17:28-30 reflects David's family's views about him. Michal had to persuade David to go; now he wants to see how serious things really are. Jonathan believes he averted the danger in 19:6, but to reassure David he devises an elaborate plan to protect and yet help him learn the extent of his danger. Verses 13-17 show Jonathan's absolute loyalty to his friend and his belief that it is David and not he who will someday have power. His rueful statement that the LORD *has been with my father* (v. 13) may reflect his understanding that the loss of the LORD lies behind Saul's madness, yet he still claims Saul as father. The covenant of faithfulness between the friends gives Jonathan no advantage, since David is fleeing for his life. It is Jonathan, who might expect to be king, who gives all—including that expectation. Again, we are told of his love for David but not David's for him. Verse 14 asks David for *the faithful love of the LORD*, but Jonathan is the one who displays it.

Saul's surprise at David's absence reflects his continuing mental degeneration. Either he does not remember his murderous attack, or he expects David to ignore it (as he has before). Saul is angered by his son's taking another's part. Such behavior is shameful and so he responds to his opponent (as in many cultures) by insulting his mother (v. 30). The fact that he is speaking of his own wife underscores his loss of perspective. Although he does not know of the covenant of vv. 13-17, Saul speaks the truth: Jonathan's kingdom will never be established because of *the son of Jesse* (v. 31) whom Saul cannot bear to name. He attacks his son as he has twice already attacked David, since to Saul both are rebels. Jonathan tries to warn David according to the plan, but they are both in such despair that it is abandoned as the friends say farewell.

21:1-9. Ahimelech and David. After days of hiding in a field David needs food, so he manufactures a mission from Saul to deceive the priest into thinking his presence is legitimate. He is not concerned about holy bread, which is intended as a priestly portion (cf. Lev 24:5-9). Survival is his only priority. His departing on such an important mission so unprepared must confuse Ahimelech, but the king's son-in-law cannot be questioned. The presence of one of Saul's men, especially an Edomite (historically an enemy; cf. Num 20:14-21), alarms David and so he asks for a weapon. With the sword that won him the glory that enraged Saul, the fugitive takes off alone.

21:10-15. David and Achish. This account of seeking help from the enemy underscores David's desperation and ingenuity, as well as offering a note of levity in these tense chapters. Taking Goliath's sword into Philistine Gath would not be wise; perhaps David hid it when Achish's men approached. The Philistines consider him the king of Israel because he rather than Saul has led the fight against them. Their suspicion of David forces him to defend himself with wit instead of sword. Using the common ancient belief that spirits causing mental disorder can move from their host to others (cf. Mark 5:1-13), David elaborately feigns madness while on the run from a mad king. Achish's sarcastic response leads the Philistines to free the man who has killed (and circumcised) so many of them. In the words of S. Thomas Niccolls, "[David] may have been anointed with holy oil, but he often walked in slippery places. This king was not above a clownish pratfall or two" (1981, 279).

David Establishes a Base and Saul Pursues Him, 22:1–23:18

22:1-5. David and his followers. David has been a fugitive since 19:18, but once he finds a safe place near his home of Bethlehem people flock to him—not to aid him but to be aided. Some are in danger because of their relationship to him and some are in need for other reasons, but they all see David even now as one who can help them in their troubles. David proves worthy of their trust. He takes pains to insure the safety of his parents, who have roots in Moab (Ruth 1:4; 4:13-17).

Gad's warning indicates that, as David protects others, the LORD is with him as he moves into more secure Judean territory. Aside from Gad, no recognized prophetic figures deliver God's word to David in 1 Samuel (not even Samuel!). Instead, the word will come to David from some less official but no less genuine sources.

22:6-23. Saul and Ahimelech. David is aided by priest and prophet, but Saul kills the LORD's ministers. Verses 6-10 show Saul in a regal setting as he formally announces that he suspects everyone of conspiring against him and, more surprisingly, lays the blame on Jonathan rather than on the son of Jesse. The son who was almost killed by his father in the first encounter we witnessed between them has never held that incident against him, trusting him and being understanding even of his madness. It is Saul who has no love for Jonathan. Doeg, whose name was so briefly dropped in 21:7, is the only one to respond: if there is a conspiracy, Ahimelech is involved. The Edomite tells the truth. While chap. 21 did not describe the priest's inquiring of the LORD for David, Ahimelech will agree that he did (v. 15).

Saul at once sends for Ahimelech, whom we discover now to be Eli's great-grandson. The fact that Ahimelech is accompanied by all his father's house (v. 11) reminds us of the doom placed on this family in 2:31-33, warning us that this encounter will not turn out well. Ahimelech speaks boldly on David's behalf, not telling Saul of David's pretense except to say he himself has known nothing of this (v. 15). Nonetheless Saul gives the death sentence, carrying out against God's priests the holy war he did not accomplish against Amalek (cf. v. 19 to 15:3). His own battle-hardened soldiers refuse the order. Only Doeg, who is not an Israelite, is willing to slaughter the anointed priests. One survives (cf. 2:33). David admits his culpability in endangering Abiathar's family and takes his responsibility to the escaped priest seriously (cf. 2 Sam 8:17; Solomon in 1 Kgs 2:26). This represents a change for David, who has previously looked to others to solve his problems. Saul's attempt to wipe out David's "conspiracy" has only added to David's strength: he now has his own priest while Saul has murdered his.

23:1-14. The LORD and David. Although we found in the previous section that David had inquired of the LORD through Ahimelech before, here we have the first recorded encounter between them. This is the first time we have heard God speak directly to anyone but Samuel. Keilah is in southwestern Judah, not far from David's original base of Adullam but now in Philistine hands. David's men are fearful but David, trusting in the LORD as in 17:37, rescues the city. When Saul (wrongly believing that God has betrayed David and having no prophet or priest to tell him otherwise) attacks, David inquires of the LORD again. Keilah is not loyal to David but the LORD is, and so in spite of his greater numbers Saul does not capture David.

23:15-18. David and Jonathan. Here the friends meet for the last time, again to swear their loyalty. Jonathan is the first person to say explicitly that David will be king. On one level, this emphasizes Jonathan's loyalty and understanding of God's actions. Jonathan, who never acts in his own self-interest, is perhaps the only man in 1–2 Samuel who can be called "good." On another level, this statement on the lips of Saul's heir gives David's kingship some legitimation. Just as Saul has lost the prophets and priests, he has lost any relationship with his son; Jonathan will stay by him loyally but he knows his father is not only willfully wrong but doomed as well.

Encounters in the Wilderness, 23:19–26:25

Now there are two opposing armed groups in the wilderness. David's ultimate loyalty to what Saul represents as well as David's ultimate difference from him are both revealed in their encounters.

23:19-29. Saul and David. As the people of Keilah showed (23:12), Saul still commands loyalty among the people. Saul, however, sees the Ziphites' loyalty to the anointed king as *compassion* (v. 21) on him as if he were the underdog. His blessing in the LORD's name, while sincere on his part, is ironic to us since we know the LORD is with David. David really is the underdog and is close to capture when Saul is diverted by a Philistine raid (showing how Saul's obsession is distracting the army from its anti-Philistine purpose). Certainly the Philistines have no thought of saving David. His unexpected deliverance must be read in the light of the LORD's being with him in 23:14.

24:1-22. David and Saul. In the previous episode Saul had the strength; here the balance of power will shift to David even though Saul's elite troops outnumber David's men five to one. Seeing Saul's sudden vulnerability, David's men urge him to act. They cite a saying from the LORD not previously recorded—*I will give your enemy into your hand, and you shall do to him as it seems good to you* (v. 4)—although David said something much like it in 17:46-47 and God spoke a similar phrase to him in 23:4. Both of these statements referred to Philistines, but David's men generalize them to include Israelite enemies.

More significantly, we find here an echo of Samuel as he anointed Saul in 10:7; the words are different, but in each case the action is left up to God's chosen. Saul did nothing; will David do too much? No; Saul *is*

in David's hands, but he attacks only the hem of Saul's garment. There is no reason to think David knows of the incident of 15:27, but just as Saul's wild tearing of Samuel's hem led the judge to announce that the kingdom will go to a neighbor, David's cutting of Saul's hem shows the self-control of which that "neighbor" is capable—a quality Saul never had.

Since David can hardly help but think that he may be king someday, he may want to set an example of respect rather than violence towards kings in general, but he also takes Saul's status as *the LORD's anointed* (v. 10) seriously—more seriously than Saul took the similar status of the priests of Nob. That massacre has made David (but not Saul) more aware of the results of his actions.

With great emotion, David tells Saul that he is innocent of treason, but he also promises to leave the situation in God's hands. Saul repeatedly took more on himself than God had given him (cf. chaps. 13, 15), but David is the "man after God's own heart" who will let the LORD act. Both men are moved, calling each other *father* and *son*, another example of the troubled father-son relationships in this book.

Saul adds his voice to Jonathan's (23:17) in proclaiming David's coming kingdom—again, a useful point for David's supporters to make against those who remain loyal to Saul's house after his death. They briefly reach an understanding but v. 22 shows that David, who trusted Saul after several attempts on his life, will trust him no longer.

25:1-44. David and Abigail. Now, when even Saul has admitted that David should succeed him, the last righteous leader of Israel dies. The narrator does not give the expected summary of Samuel's life, perhaps because that appears in 7:13-17. In the meantime David provides for those who are loyal to him, proving again that he is capable of self-control.

It is not unusual for the poor to appeal to a rich man on a feast day, and David is still a fugitive with many mouths to feed. His request of NABAL for *whatever you have at hand* (v. 8) echoes his similarly desperate plea to Ahimelech in 21:3. Moreover, Nabal's shepherds know that he has performed a real service for them (vv. 14-17), and he offers to do the same for the shearers. Unfortunately, Nabal is a fool (which is the Heb. meaning of his name; although it may represent the narrator's judgment rather than an actual name, it alerts us as to what to expect from him). Nabal belittles the hero of Israel as an otherwise unknown escaped slave. David does not rant at the response but simply orders his men to prepare for action. His restraint in chap. 24 was in recognition of Saul's status, but he is still quick to avenge himself on others.

The clever Abigail instantly understands the danger her husband is risking and acts to save the household by responding to David's request. She treats the wilderness ruffian with incredible respect, not hesitating to sacrifice her husband's reputation to save his life. Or is it David she wants to save? Like Jonathan in 23:16-17, Abigail seems to know more about him than is apparent. She understands that he (unlike Saul) is fighting the LORD's battles. Abigail also is the third person to tell David that he will rule Israel (like Jonathan and Saul, she is not a recognized spokesperson of the LORD's). Her purpose is not to mollify him but to advise: the ruler God is sure to establish needs an unblemished reputation, and so for his own sake he must trust the LORD to handle the situation. This is the third time we have seen someone warned on the basis of their own interest (cf. 2:34-35; 8:11-18).

For the first time such a warning will be effective, since David instantly understands that Abigail's intervention is from God. Again we are reminded of the Ahimelech story: when Saul was crossed he responded with a massacre. In spite of his guilt after that and his later efforts to behave more responsibly, David would have done the same now without prophetic Abigail to prevent it. Her words are confirmed by Nabal's death by God's hand rather than David's; this chosen one allows the LORD to act on his behalf, and the LORD does. Like Hannah (1:26-28), with no revelation David sees God's hand in what could seem an ordinary event. Earlier, David won a wife from an unwilling father; now he wins one from a foolish husband (to Abigail's apparent delight; note her "hurrying" in v. 42). He also marries into nearby Jezreel, consolidating his power there as well as in Carmel. But Saul, who reneged on his promise to marry Merab to David (18:19), now takes his other daughter Michal away.

26:1-25. David and Saul. The first verse repeats 23:19 and the rest of the story is similar to chap. 24. This emphasizes that the betraying Ziphites, David's vengeful men (as represented by Abishai), and the emotional Saul have not changed since their last encounters, but David has. He is not almost captured (cf. 23:26), nor does he encounter Saul by chance (cf. 24:3). Instead, he is in control. The confusion and guilt of chap. 24 are gone. The man who referred to Saul as *father* in their previous meeting (24:11) now infiltrates

the enemy camp with only one companion, as Saul's real son once did (14:6-15), but now the enemy is Saul himself. David once used a sword against its owner (17:51), but he will not let Saul's spear be turned against him even by Abishai. From Abigail he has gained a greater faith in God's action on his behalf, understanding that Saul's destiny is God's business, and he is now willing to let God settle matters between Saul and himself.

David's speech in vv. 18-20 is not the emotional plea of 24:8-15, but a rational explanation that he cannot rectify the situation. Since he knows not God but a man (Saul himself) is behind Saul's obsessive pursuit, his only recourse is to leave the Promised Land. This decision does not come easily: in Gen 4:16 the guilty Cain goes "away from the presence of the LORD" and now the innocent David fears his exile from home will also be exile from God. He briefly hopes that Saul will not let it come to that but realizes that he cannot trust Saul's repentance; Saul will hurt him again if he has the chance. God is the real target of his final speech (vv. 23-24) as David hopes the LORD will continue to be with him even in enemy country. The two men, shouting from opposite hilltops, part forever. Saul's last word to him is a blessing, but they both know there can be no peace between them. The powerless fugitive and powerful king have traded places as even Saul sees David as a righteous man who will and should rule God's people.

David and Saul Separately against Their Enemies, 27:1–31:13

David's Fear of Saul Leads Him to the Philistines, 27:1–28:2

David knows that Saul's obsession means he must leave Israel or eventually die there because he has ruled out the possibility of anyone's harming Saul on his behalf. He does not change his Israelite allegiance even as a Philistine vassal, using his base at Ziklag to attack Israel's enemies and destroying them totally (as Saul did not with his enemy in 15:8). For his part, Achish appreciates a good fighting force and has no problem with using one that the enemy has rejected. David, who was honest with Saul but still had to leave Israel, cheerfully lies to the Philistine king about the objects of his attack. The opening paragraph of chap. 28 makes us wonder how long David can be a loyal Israelite in Gath; we see him rising as quickly in the Philistine ranks as he did in the Israelite's, seeming to agree to fight against Israel. He tells Achish *you shall know what your servant can do* (v. 2). Is this an expression of faithfulness to him or a warning that Achish does not know all now?

Saul's Fear of the Philistines Leads Him to the Medium, 28:3-25

Samuel's death notice is repeated here to emphasize Saul's isolation. Saul has killed his priests and driven David away, and the one who once spoke God's word to him is gone as well. This story is not intended to vilify or honor Saul: the weaknesses and bad judgment that cost him God's favor are evident, but so is the horror of his God-rejected situation. Neither Saul nor God is defended by the narrator for their behavior towards one another. The results of the faithlessness of the one and silence of the other are simply presented.

Saul has had his moments of trying to be a faithful king, as when he enforces the law against mediums (Lev 19:31), but in his fear when he cannot contact the LORD through any legal means he seeks out a medium against his own law. His degeneration is complete. The woman is a genuine necromancer. Unable to recognize the living Saul, she knows the dead Samuel when she sees him. This story provides a rare glimpse of early Yahwistic eschatology. The Bible has little to say about life after death; the focus is always on living as God's people in this world rather than the next.

The pathos of v. 15 is almost unbearable. While Saul's refusal to rule theocratically, his unwillingness to accept responsibility for his people, and his actions have brought him to this moment, we cannot help but feel the pain of the man who still tries desperately to reach the LORD years after there has been any word. He asks for Samuel because Samuel was the only link he ever had to God, although he cannot hope that the judge who rejected him when he was alive will have any good word for him now. Samuel confirms Saul's suspicions about David's destiny but promises Saul only total failure. He who became king to rescue Israel from the Philistines will lose army, heirs, and life to them. The fearful medium, more compassionate than Samuel, is energized by Saul's misery; forgetting her own danger she ministers to him handsomely. The night before his death, Saul is treated like a king.

The Philistine Fear of David Leads Them to Reject Him, 29:1-11

The Philistines encamp at APHEK, as they did before the disaster of 4:1-11. That reminder of the in-effective Elides, added to the picture of Saul in total collapse, makes the image of David in the company of Israel's enemies more bleak. Are there no faithful leaders for Israel?

Achish continues to trust David but the other Philistines cannot forget how he has made them suffer in the past and refuse to fight beside him now. David, meanwhile, is playing a dangerous game. Not wanting to risk Achish's trust, he protests being sent from the battle. When he says that he wants to *fight against the enemies of my lord the king* (v. 8), he is heard in one way by Achish and another by the reader. We are reassured by the knowledge that Saul is the only one David has ever referred to as *my lord the king* (cf. 26:19), and Saul's enemies are the Philistines. Achish's commanders are right. The oddly sympathetic Philistine's statement that David is *blameless in my sight as an angel of God* (v. 9) is strange coming from a pagan enemy but reinforces the concern for David's innocence that has dominated the last few chapters.

David's absence from this battle must be seen as evidence of God working behind the scenes on his behalf. Israel could forgive David's sojourn with the Philistines when Saul drove him away, but if he appeared even briefly on the wrong side in the battle in which Saul was killed, suspicion as to his true loyalties would have prevented acceptance as king.

David Is Victorious over the Amalekites, 30:1-31

David has survived the danger inherent in his Philistine vassalship only to be immediately confronted by another: Ziklag is destroyed and its civilian population taken by an enemy unknown to him. This costs him the support of his men as well. For a moment he seems as lost as he was in chap. 21. We know the additional alarming detail that the enemy are Amalekites, the same people against whom Saul fought so disastrously in chap. 15. Since David has a priest, he has the legal access to God that Saul does not, and so he (and we) are rapidly assured of his victory. Seemingly through luck David finds one who can take him to the enemy, but we know that David is not lucky but blessed by God's care. David finds the unsuspecting Amalekites and fights his first major military engagement since he was Saul's general in chaps. 18 and 19. He is no longer under Saul, but his success on the field has not changed. Although the LORD is not mentioned in the account of the battle, David understands that he has won because God is with him (v. 23). He generously shares the spoil with all his men and wisely shares it with the elders of Judah, perhaps reassuring them that in spite of his Philistine vassalship he is still a loyal Israelite at heart. David has become more responsible in his behavior towards others and more sure of the LORD's presence with him, but he is still David. His last words in 1 Samuel, like his first (17:26), look for his own advancement.

Saul Is Defeated by the Philistines, 31:1-13

While David defeats his enemies without Saul, Saul is defeated without David. The Israelites, again suffering for their leader's failures (cf. 4:10-11) as per Samuel's warning of 12:14-15, are routed by the Philistines. Saul fights a brave last stand over the bodies of Jonathan and his other sons until he is badly wounded (probably fatally) by archers; apparently the enemy did not dare get close to the king. Abimelech, the would-be king of Israel in the Book of Judges, in a similar situation successfully ordered his armor-bearer to kill him (Judg 9:54), but Saul's will not obey his command. His last order may show an awareness of what the Philistines did to Samson when they captured him (Judg 16:21-27). Since he is the king, such treatment would dishonor the nation. It is this rather than pain and death that he fears, since he entered the battle knowing that he would die (28:19).

Saul's suicide is presented not as an act of despair but of bravery; he saves the nation from shame. The Bible never calls suicide a sin. Like Saul, other biblical suicides are presented as people whose bad choices led to failure in their lives (Samson in Judg 16:28-30, Ahithophel in 2 Sam 17:23, Zimri in 1 Kgs 16:18, and Judas in Matt 27:3-5), but it is how they lived rather than how they died that is seen negatively.

The Philistines mutilate Saul, as he had known they would, but they do not get the last word. The men of JABESH-GILEAD, the city he rescued years ago on what may have been the greatest day of his life (chap. 11), when the LORD and the people and Samuel were all with him, travel at great risk into the territory of their victorious enemy to take the bodies of their king and deliverer and his sons home. Saul was a troubled man and a troubled king, but our last glimpse of him is of a mighty warrior who dies with honor and, even after death, inspires great loyalty.

Introduction to 2 Samuel

Second Samuel is the second part of the Book of Samuel, originally one volume but divided into two because of length. The sources, date, and themes of the work are discussed in the introduction to 1 Samuel.

Critics have isolated a number of sources behind 1–2 Samuel. Two of them deserve special attention: the Court History or SUCCESSION NARRATIVE (chaps. 9–20; 1 Kgs 1–2) and the appendix (chaps. 21–24; see Miller 1990, 198–99). Chapters 9–20 is generally considered to be a separate source because its focus moves from DAVID the glorious king to David the troubled man, and its intimate picture of David's domestic and court life raises the possibility it comes from an eyewitness (see Cate 1990, 859). Its vivid characterization, portrayal of family conflict, and themes are reminiscent of the J source of the Torah, which is dated to this period as well (see Gregory 1990, 850–51, and Brueggemann 1968, 156–81). It must be noted, however, that interest in David's personal life begins well before the Succession Narrative, and it can be successfully argued that the concern of chaps. 9–20 is more with David's character and its effect on Israel than with who will be king after him (Flanagan 1972, Perdue 1984).

The appendix, on the other hand, is difficult to date in both setting and composition. It contains lists, stories, and songs that belong to various periods of David's life but were not included in the body of 2 Samuel. They are placed at the end of the book immediately before his death, which is recorded in 1 Kgs 1–2.

The appendix and Court History do represent different traditions (as does the rest of the material in Samuel), but this commentary will focus on the way the editors wove them into the fabric of their work, rather than seeing them as undigested blocks of material.

First Samuel described how the faithlessness of the house of ELI resulted in loss to the PHILISTINES. SAMUEL, the last judge of Israel, was the immediate answer to this crisis. A God-guided leader, he achieved a stalemate with the Philistines, but the people ended the prevailing tribal confederacy by asking the aging Samuel for a king to bring them military victory.

Through a controversial and complicated process the nation became a theocratic monarchy under Samuel and King SAUL. Saul, a strong warrior but weak man, ultimately failed. His deterioration parallels the rise of his loved and hated general and son-in-law, David, ending with Saul's death in battle against the Philistines.

Second Samuel is the story of David, a dark and gifted man, and his relationships with God and God's people. Through the presentation of his complex character and experiences it continues to deal with the themes raised in 1 Samuel, including the necessity of God-guided leadership, the way the nation pays for its leaders' failings, the complexity and unpredictability of human nature, and, most of all, the relationships between individuals and between individuals and God. As in 1 Samuel, God takes a backstage role in choosing, advising, and speaking through prophetic figures. Nonetheless, even though the human characters seem to dominate the action, it is God's judgment that ultimately determines the outcome.

For Further Study

In the *Mercer Dictionary of the Bible*: ABNER; ABSALOM; CHRONOLOGY; DAVID; KINGSHIP; MICHAL; MEPHIBOSHETH; PHILISTINES; SAMUEL; SAMUEL, BOOKS OF FIRST AND SECOND; SAUL; SUCCESSION NARRATIVE; WOMEN IN THE OT.

In other sources: W. Brueggemann, "David and His Theologian," *CBQ* 30 (1968): 156–81; J. W. Flanagan, "Court History or Succession Document?" *JBL* 91 (1972): 172–81; L. G. Perdue, "'Is There Anyone Left of the House of Saul . . . ?' Ambiguity and the Characterization of David in the Succession Narrative," *JSOT* 30 (1984): 67–84.

Commentary

David and Saul's House:
The Difficult Transition, 1:1–5:5

First Samuel ended on a note of national defeat and solemn mourning. Second Samuel begins at that point but does not stress the crisis Israel faces or the loss of SAUL and JONATHAN. Although the elegy in chap. 1 is poignant, the focus is on the victorious and gracious figure who sings it. The people are not without gifted leadership, and this section will show how the nation recovers from Saul's loss with a stronger, wiser, and generally more able king to unify and lead them.

David Mourns the Deaths
of Saul and Jonathan, 1:1-27

We begin this chapter of ironies with David, renowned warrior of Israel, sitting in his Philistine city unaware that the PHILISTINES have killed the king of Israel and his son Jonathan—men who were not only his comrades in arms but also his in-laws. The news of the deaths of those who were once closest to David is brought by an enemy whose people he was defeating while Saul was being defeated. This Amalekite, seeking to ingratiate himself with the victor, tells a different story of Saul's death from the one found in 1 Sam 31. He denies Saul the final burst of strength and courage that saved him from a dishonorable death, taking credit for that death himself. Obviously the messenger expects David to reward Saul's killer, but David is capable of avenging the man who repeatedly tried to kill him and finally drove him into exile. The first information passed from one character to another in 2 Samuel is a self-serving half-truth, but the narrator does not alert the reader. Only by comparing this story to the previous one does the reader find the truth. Even more careful reading will be required as the text unfolds. David, who has earlier shown reluctance to harm *the LORD's anointed* (1 Sam 26:9-16), has many reasons for executing the Amalekite: genuine grief at the deaths of his king and friend, need to distance himself from any involvement in those deaths, and concern for the sanctity of *the LORD's anointed* since he himself enjoys that status (cf. 1 Sam 16).

Although David from his very first words in 1 Samuel has always had an eye to his own advancement (1 Sam 17:26), he refuses the *crown . . . and armlet* (v. 10) the Amalekite took from Saul's body to give him. Instead, he and his people mourn for Saul, Jonathan, and Israel.

The beautiful lament of vv. 17-27 closes the complex relationships David had with the dead men. Saul was his king and Jonathan his closest friend, but Saul's inability to live up to the rigorous demands of Israel's theocratic kingship, coupled with the suspicion and desire that always accompany power, ended the relationship between Saul and David. While David and Jonathan remained loyal to each other, Jonathan's faithfulness to his father separated them as well. It says much for David's character that he wants the people to remember the unstable and violent man who cost him so much (and who stood between him and the throne he had to hope God intended for him) only as a brave warrior who was generous in victory. His lament for Jonathan is more personal, stressing the loyalty Jonathan displayed towards both father and friend. In v. 26 David expresses for the first time his love for the man who was consistently his advocate against his own royal hopes, showing in his language the depth of his emotion and the importance this friendship had for him. *How the mighty have fallen!* (vv. 19, 27) is at the beginning and end of the lament. This phrase is a major motif of 1–2 Samuel: ELI, SAMUEL, and SAUL, the previous leaders of Israel, lost power in various ways. David is on the brink of his glory. Will he also fall from its heights?

David is an opportunistic man; it can hardly be supposed that he has not instantly realized that the deaths of Saul and Jonathan largely clear his way to the throne (in fact, he will begin to act on that assumption as soon as he finishes singing), but that

does not diminish the real sorrow he feels at the loss of these men who were so much to him and to Israel. Realizing that he may well benefit from their tragedy could only increase his pain.

David Becomes King over Judah, 2:1-7

In chap. 1 God was referred to distantly (1:12, 14, 16), but now through David's inquiring *of the LORD* (v. 1) God becomes the director of the action. David as the "man after God's own heart" (1 Sam 13:14) allows God to choose who is to rule rather than grasping for himself the trappings of kingship offered by the Amalekite. He has, however, done all he can to assure that the elders of his home territory of Judah will be favorably disposed to him (1 Sam 30:26-31). He chooses HEBRON, the place where ABRAHAM first gained title to part of the Promised Land (Gen 23:1-20), as the place to begin his stronghold there. The Judeans quickly anoint David as their king and the Philistines do not intervene. Probably Achish, who is unaware of how David used him (1 Sam 27:8-13) but thinks of him as a loyal vassal (1 Sam 29:6-10), believes that David will serve the Philistine cause in Judah. David, however, has other ideas. He moves to Hebron with his two wives, both of whom have ties in northern Israel, and sends messengers into the North with the double purpose of thanking those who gave Saul burial and letting them know that he is available to take Saul's place. Note that he asks God whether to move into Judah but apparently looks to Israel on his own.

David Fights for Control over Israel, 2:8–5:5

David easily becomes king of Judah, but he will have a more difficult time establishing control over the rest of Saul's kingdom. The monarchy was formed by twelve tribes, each of which had a history of independent leadership. They were united under Saul and Samuel, but Judah feels no need to continue that union. Israel gives its loyalty to Saul's family; Judah chooses to follow the strongest warrior.

2:8-17. Abner establishes Ishbaal as king of Israel. ABNER is Saul's uncle and the commander of his army. The wording of v. 8 (as well as 3:6-11) indicates that Abner is not so much supporting Ishbaal's (also called ISHBOSHETH) claim as using it to consolidate his own power. Opposing Abner is the leader of David's army, his nephew JOAB, who with his brothers Abishai and Asahel are among David's greatest warriors (8:16; 23:18, 24). When the opponents meet an attempt is made to settle their differences by twelve simultaneous single combats. Like the single combat all of the participants in this one must remember, that between David and Goliath (1 Sam 17), the result is dramatic but settles nothing. David's men win the ensuing battle.

2:18-32. Abner kills Joab's brother. Abner does not want to kill Asahel (they may well have fought together against the Philistines under Saul) and tries to push him away with the blunt end of his spear, but even this blow is fatal. Abner is able to persuade Joab not to let what is already a civil war degenerate into a feud, and both sides return home. Even though the leadership of the nation is at stake, the conflict (like many others in 1–2 Samuel) is very much a family affair.

3:1-21. Abner makes a deal with David. David's house is growing stronger and larger but there is conflict in Saul's. Verse 7 is Ishbaal's only line; it shows him to be frustrated but powerless in Abner's hands. Taking a woman understood to belong to the head of the house or kingdom is tantamount to taking that man's place (cf. Gen 35:22, 49:4); the just-mentioned AMNON, ABSALOM, and ADONIJAH will enact variations of this motif with David (13:1-14; 16:20-22; 1 Kgs 2:13-25). *Rizpah* (v. 7) is chattel here, but in 21:10-14 she is a strong character.

Abner, angry with Ishbaal and seeing David's strength, offers to make him king in the north. Now David shows a new and ultimately disastrous trait. He trusted and respected his first two wives, MICHAL and ABIGAIL, but as he moves closer to greater power he learns from the power broker ABNER to treat women differently. He requires the man who has taken Saul's concubine to give him another of Saul's women: his daughter Michal, David's first wife. Saul gave her to David as a trap although she loved him (1 Sam 18:20-29), but she saved David's life (1 Sam 19:11-17). Now without consulting her he breaks up her home, needing the connection to Saul's house to make him acceptable to the northerners who are loyal to it (notice his initial identification of her in v. 13). *Paltiel* (v. 15), the only man who has ever cared for Michal at all, is forcibly separated from her. Abner energetically prepares the north for David, cheerfully spouting Davidic claims of God's blessing that he as Saul's uncle and general must have fought against for years.

3:22-39. Joab kills Abner. In this story the characters mask their motives with dialogue but the narrative silences are more eloquent still. It introduces us to the complex relationship between David and Joab, foreshadows almost every other murder in the book, and shows the reader how difficult determining the truth of David's life will be. A close reading of the text indicates that the traitorous Abner may be the most straightforward character. The unexpected mention in v. 30 of Abishai as accomplice shows that there are at least two versions of the murder. Why is Abner killed? The narrator discounts Joab's spoken concerns about David's security and offers vengeance for Asahel as the reason for Abner's death. But this seems unreasonable; Joab gave up that cause in 2:27-28, and Abner must believe that the feud is over since he is unsuspicious of Joab.

This leads to a second possibility, that Joab kills to protect himself. Abner is commander of Ishbaal's armies just as Joab is of David's, and no king needs two commanders-in-chief. What will happen to Abner when Ishbaal's armies become David's? While David and Abner twice discuss what David is getting from Abner, it becomes increasingly obvious that no reward for Abner is ever mentioned. Shrewd Abner would never sell out Ishbaal for vengeance alone, no matter how angry he was. Probably Abner's pay is Joab's job; David will offer it to the commander of another rival Israelite army in 19:13, and Joab will kill that general because of it (20:9-10). Or is Abner's death more to David's advantage than Joab's? Once the north has been brought into line—and Abner has already done that—will David be safe with this powerful man who has already betrayed one king? Does Joab kill to benefit David against David's own wishes (as with Absalom in 18:9-15)—a third possibility? Or, fourthly, does he do David's dirty work at David's orders (as with Uriah in 11:14-21)?

The text raises all of these questions. David seems aware of the service Joab has performed, even if only after the fact. He curses Joab extravagantly but it is mere talk; Joab remains his right-hand man. Like his ostentatious mourning, it is designed to calm suspicion of his complicity in Abner's death.

It is a mark of the narrator's skill that the story can be read in any of these ways. The characters keep their own counsel, and the narrator leaves it to the reader to decide where the truth lies. As 2 Samuel progresses, finding the truth will be even more difficult and more vital. The third option above (Joab kills on his own to protect David) seems best; in 7:9 God will tell David *I have cut off all your enemies from before you,* an odd statement if David had in fact had one killed. This shows how human selfishness, greed, misplaced loyalty, and hatred (in this case Joab's) can be used to further God's ends without God creating or endorsing them (cf. the discussion of Assyria in Isa 10:5-19 or the roles played by those who betray, convict, and execute Jesus).

4:1–5:5. Ishbaal is killed; David becomes king over Israel. Abner's murder leaves Ishbaal and his army in disarray; the accidental maiming of MEPHIBOSHETH reflects their panic. It is not surprising, then, that two soldiers resolve the situation by killing Ishbaal, whom they believe cannot hold the kingdom, to win favor with the one they believe can. David, now receiving two messengers who mistakenly believe they will be rewarded for killing a Saulide, again avenges the death of the one who opposed him (cf. 1:1-16). This, along with David's reaction to Abner's death, convinces the Israelite elders that they can support him without reneging on their earlier loyalty. Like Abner in 3:18 (but presumably with more sincerity), they say that the promises God made to Saul in 1 Sam 10:1 are fulfilled in David. The elders thus join Jonathan, David's own men, Saul, and Abigail in giving David a prophetic word that he has not yet received directly himself (cf. 1 Sam 23:17; 24:4, 20; 25:30). The civil war ends with David anointed as king of all of Saul's kingdom.

In this section four people who stood between David and a throne have been killed. David's avoidance of bloodguilt has been a concern ever since 1 Sam 24, when he first had the chance to harm Saul and refused. Nabal (1 Sam 25), Saul, Abner, and Ishbaal all blocked him in some way—Jonathan, as Saul's son, did so as well—but David seems to have followed Abigail's advice and allowed God to remove his enemies (1 Sam 25:26-31). The narrator makes clear that there was suspicion about David's role in these deaths but that his behavior convinced the people of his innocence. However, it is undeniable that David has become Israel's king through treachery, even if the treachery is not his. He has been more active in the pursuit of his destiny, fighting a war to become Israel's king; we are beginning to wonder how much more he will do.

David Alone:
Consolidating Power with Ease, 5:6–9:13

This section is the culmination of David's career. With a fought-for kingdom and a new capital, David himself formally receives the promise of God's eternal support of his house. He is victorious on the field; even his potential enemies are under his control.

David Takes Jerusalem
and Defeats His Enemies, 5:6-25

The account of how Jerusalem, the city that plays such a pivotal part in the rest of the Bible, comes into Israelite hands is surprisingly brief. Once David becomes king of Israel, he moves to establish a central capital in a region not already connected with either Israel or Judah. The Jebusites taunt David with their belief that their stronghold cannot fall—a tradition that will show up again in Isa 29:5-8 and 31:4-5—but he turns their taunt on them. Through warfare the city named "City of Peace" becomes the City of David.

Verse 10 tells the reader that *the LORD was with him*; v. 12 points out that David understands his greatness is due to God's concern for Israel and not for his (i.e., David's) glory. Strangely, David's response to the perceived care of the LORD is to take more women, reminding us of his taking of Michal in 3:13-16. David may be rewarding himself, or he may merely be trying to make his bloodline even more secure. He also establishes a diplomatic tie with Tyre and defeats the Philistines, who were not concerned with his kingship in Judah but erupt in fury at his taking of Israel as well (finally realizing that he is a rival power).

David Makes Jerusalem His Capital, 6:1-23

6:1-15. The Ark comes into the city. David's first concern is to bring into Jerusalem the most sacred object known to the Hebrews: the ARK of the Covenant, understood to manifest God's presence and power (see Bailey 1990, 63–64). The Ark led the people through wandering and war during the periods of the wilderness and tribal confederacy (cf. 1 Sam 4:1–7:2). By honoring the Ark David acknowledges to God and the people his dependence on *the LORD of hosts* (v. 2). He also shows Israel that in spite of the major changes of the last few decades—the controversial move from the confederacy to the monarchy, the transition from one royal house to another, and the acquisition of a foreign city as the capital—the old traditions are still respected under the new regime.

UZZAH's death (vv. 6-11) in the midst of the festivities strikes an ominous note. Mortals approach holiness unprepared at their peril not because it is antagonistic, but because raw power is inherently dangerous (see Joines 1990, 383–84). Uzzah's intentions to prevent the Ark from tipping over are good. The statement that *the anger of the LORD was kindled against Uzzah* (v. 7) should not be read as God's punishing him, any more than a death resulting from touching an unshielded electric cable should be interpreted as punishment by electricity. The site of his death is known as *Perez-uzzah*, which means "Bursting Out Against Uzzah" (v. 8; NRSV mg.).

This divine disaster and the divine victory of 5:20 have similar names as a reminder that God's power can be fearsome as well as helpful and that even those blessed by God cannot assume that they are automatically lucky. With the proper precautions, David brings the Ark into the city. Even if he has calculated the political expediency of this move, his generosity and dancing (6:16-19) indicate that it is a personal priority as well.

6:16-23. Michal and David argue. The story of an important day in Jerusalem ends with a note about David's domestic life, a matter that received little attention in 1 Samuel but will occupy us more and more as 2 Samuel unfolds. Michal is called *the daughter of Saul* (vv. 16, 20, 23) instead of "the wife of David," reminding us that she is the only woman able to produce an heir that will unite the rival royal families. She seems eager to pick a fight, perhaps still upset over the dissolution of her marriage to Paltiel (3:15), or perhaps angry at now being only one of David's many wives. Their explosive confrontation covers etiquette, history, and theology. Verse 23 shows that the issue is never resolved, meaning that there will be no heir acceptable to both Saulide and Davidic supporters.

This strong, risk-taking woman is never mentioned again (the NRSV reading of *Merab daughter of Saul* in 21:8 is correct [cf. KJV]; Merab was Michal's sister). The young man who escaped with his life on her advice (see 1 Sam 19:11-17) has become a king who will not put up with her opinions.

The LORD Promises to Establish David's House, 7:1-29

Chapter 7 begins when David is at the pinnacle of his career. He has fulfilled both human and divine expectations of the kingship by taking care of the Philistine threat (1 Sam 8:19-20, 9:16) and has publicly acknowledged God's role by bringing the Ark into the city. Any hopes Saul's house still had have been dashed by 6:20-23.

At this crucial time in David's reign we meet NATHAN, who also appears at two other major junctures in David's life (12:1-15; 1 Kgs 1–2). God now initiates communication through an intermediary. Anonymous prophets (cf. 1 Sam 2:27-36; 10:9-13) and a few

named ones (cf. 1 Sam 22:5) earlier have spoken and acted on God's behalf, but Nathan is the first among the prophets of the kingdom who will figure so prominently in the affairs of state (and the families of the kings). Nathan, and the prophets like him that will follow, represents the charismatic leadership that is denied by the hereditary monarchy. That Nathan appears precisely at the moment that the monarchy officially becomes hereditary is significant.

God immediately shifts the meaning of *house* (vv. 4-17) from the kind of ornate structure David wants as a sign of his loyalty to the LORD to the royal dynasty that is a sign of the LORD's loyalty to him. God summarizes the historical relationship between Israel and God; while the movable Ark that manifests the divine power has been housed in various structures in its history (as at Shiloh, 1 Sam 1–4), it has never been confined in a permanent abode and will not be for another generation (vv. 6-7, 13). The gift David wants to give—a *house [for God] to live in* (v. 5)—is turned into a gift David will receive: a covenant promising an everlasting dynasty. The Mosaic covenant was conditional (Exod 19:5-6); the Davidic is not (vv. 15-16).

As was the Mosaic covenant, the Davidic covenant is based on divine rather than human faithfulness (vv. 8-9; cf. Exod 20:1-2), although verses like 5:25 indicate that God is faithful because David obediently allows God to be God. This covenant promises military defeat as punishment for human faithlessness (v. 14), but faithlessness will not lead to rejection as it did with Saul (vv. 15-16). David's house will not always be chosen for blessing and good fortune, but it will always be chosen. David's humble response mixes gratitude and inability to believe such good news; Saul's son-in-law knows better than anyone else alive that those once anointed can be rejected and suffer horribly because of it.

David Defeats His Enemies, 8:1-18

David's status as God's chosen king is reflected by his success. In war he is victorious; in peace he makes allies; and in both he gains goods to dedicate to the LORD. The reasons for his wars are not given because the narrator's purpose is to emphasize David's triumphs rather than the details surrounding them. His treatment of the Moabites, with whom he has a distant kinship and who helped him when he was a fugitive (1 Sam 22:3-4), reminds us of the quick and cruel judgment of which kings are capable. Verse 13 also strikes an odd note; here David *won a name for himself* instead of giving credit to the LORD (cf. 5:12). Verses 15-18 is a list of David's officers; 20:23-26 reflects a later period in his reign. Like a judge, David administers justice. His organization contains old faces (Joab and Abiathar [v. 17 should read "Abiathar son of Ahimelech"; see 1 Sam 22:11-23]) and new ones (Zadok, anticipated in 1 Sam 2:35, and Benaiah). Note that military and priestly duties are shared by one old and one new companion. Nowhere else are David's sons priests; later tradition will say only descendants of AARON could be priests, but earlier it was not thought unusual for the sons of the founder of a sanctuary to serve at it (cf. Judg. 17:5).

David Obtains Custody of Mephibosheth, 9:1-13

As in chap. 1, here we see David acting correctly but with a number of motives, some of which are self-serving. The events of 21:1-14 must have already occurred; David's search for *still anyone left of the house of Saul* (v. 1) implies a disaster to that house, but in the direct line only Ishbosheth has died so far in 2 Samuel. David's request harks back to his friendship with Jonathan: in 1 Sam 20:14-15 Jonathan says to him *if I die, never cut off your faithful love from my house, even if the LORD were to cut off every one of [your] enemies.* Now the LORD has done just that. The emphasis on MEPHIBOSHETH's lameness reminds us of the entangled relationships here, since he was crippled in the panic following Abner's murder in David's capital by David's general (4:4). His response in v. 8 to King David is reminiscent of David's speech to his enemy King Saul in 1 Sam 24:14-15 (v. 15 is especially noteworthy in view of the next encounter between them in 19:24-30).

Mephibosheth has reason to distrust David, who benefits from bringing him to court by having Saul's last adult male heir where he can see him. The existence of Mica (v. 12) shows that Saul's house has expanded to another generation, giving David cause for concern. Whether loyalty or paranoia is David's major motive is difficult to determine; like most people, he acts from a variety of motives, some of which even he may not know.

Now the promises and blessings of 1 Samuel have been fulfilled. David is the king who does what Saul did not (1 Sam 9:16; 10:1), whose coming was foretold (1 Sam 13:14; 15:28). More business from 1 Samuel has been finished as well: the new priest not of Eli's family has appeared (1 Sam 2:27-36) and the covenant between David and Jonathan has been

honored. The troubling relationship between David and the Philistines in 1 Sam 27-30 has also been resolved as David has defeated them. Now God has made him king, delivered him from all enemies, and endorsed his dynasty.

David is at the height of his glory, but there are warning signs: his behavior towards Michal and Mephibosheth shows him directing people's destinies for his own ends, and his taking of women in Jerusalem and killing two-thirds of the Moabites reminds us that a king may gratify all of his desires more easily than an ordinary man can.

David and His Family: Keeping Power with Difficulty, 10:1–20:26

This section, which is the heart of 2 Samuel, explores more fully David's ambiguous aspects as his disruptive family life disrupts Israel as well. In 1 Samuel there were many to assure David of his glorious destiny (23:17; 24:4, 20; 25:28-31), but he is now surrounded by those who rebuke him (Nathan in 12:1-14; his servants in 12:21; the wise woman in 14:13-14; Shimei in 16:5-8; and Joab in 12:27-28 and 19:5-7). The tendency we first noted in 3:12-16 for David to see others (esp. women) as his to dispose of as he wishes leads to a tale of personal deception and national intrigue that takes David from success to disaster, costing him sons, reputation, self-respect, and God's favor. Indeed, David almost loses the kingdom itself twice.

Notice how infrequently anyone in these narratives speaks honestly; they manipulatively distort the truth like the Amalekite of chap. 1 (and the reader must work to find the manipulations). At first David is the deceiver but he becomes the dupe as the ramifications of his betrayals close in on him. As always it is in adversity that he is at his best, displaying more character than he shows in victory.

David and Ammon, 10:1-19

Nahash of Ammon, apparently David's ally, was the brutal king Saul defeated in 1 Sam 11. Verse 2 recalls 9:1 and again we find David offering help in a way that makes his own position stronger, since at least he will solidify his relationship with Ammon, and at most he may learn something useful. Whatever David's motives may have been, he clearly has a reputation as a devious man. Joab shows his worth as a tactician and wins the first phase of the war. David, not entering the battle until the second phase, wins a great victory. This may be a retelling of the events of chap. 8 (vv. 6, 15-19 say that David was opposed by some of the same opponents mentioned in the earlier chapter), but even if that is historically so, the editors clearly intend us to read it as a separate battle. The narrative not only points out the pattern of David's questionable generosity, but it also suggests the speed with which a seemingly resolved situation (e.g., the war in chap. 8) can come undone. None of David's success is necessarily permanent.

David, Bathsheba, and Uriah, 11:1-27

11:1-5. David sends for Bathsheba. Verse 1 sets the tone for this passage: kings go to battle, but David stays home. It is a picture of David we have not seen before, the king rising from an afternoon nap while his men fight. Saul first showed himself as a mighty warrior against the Ammonites (1 Sam 11); in the course of this battle David's character will also be revealed. Robert Alter points out that the stories of David taking wives—his love stories—are set in contexts of conflict and death. Circumcising one hundred Philistines allows David to marry Michal (1 Sam 18:20-29), the death of Nabal paves the way for David to marry Abigail (1 Sam 25); and the murder of Uriah leads to Bathsheba's marriage (Alter 1981, 60–61).

David's love and death are connected. From his cool roof (which would be the highest in Jerusalem), David glimpses Bathsheba bathing. Contrary to popular representation, she is not on her roof but must be in an inner courtyard or a room of her own house. In one of the most laconic verses in the Bible David, who has sent Joab to war and sent servants for information, now sends for a woman he knows to be married to a soldier at the front and has sex with her. Uriah is doing David's job; now David will do Uriah's. The king sends at least two people to get (not ask) her; the king has power and the woman with the absent husband has none. Like Susanna, she was observed bathing privately, but unlike Susanna, Bathsheba has no advocate (Sus 1:1-64). Forms of "to send" are used twelve times in this chapter (vv. 1, 3, 4, 5, 6 [three times], 12, 14, 18, 22, 27); each time except v. 5 the sending is done by David or at his will. Bathsheba's only words in 2 Samuel fall like a judgment as she informs David about the one event he has not controlled.

11:6-27. David sends twice to Joab. The plots involving Uriah are entirely David's idea; Bathsheba does not reappear until v. 26. Because of v. 4b there is no way the child can be passed off as Uriah's, and

if the issues were not so serious vv. 6-13 would be funny as David uses adolescent innuendo (v. 8), direct pressure (v. 10), and alcohol (v. 13) to try to get Uriah to sleep with his own wife. But the Hittite is more loyal to the wartime code of conduct (cf. 1 Sam 21:4-5) than is Israel's king.

In the last two chapters we have seen David offer help but have not been sure if his motives were honest. Here we cannot misinterpret: David brings Uriah home and offers him food and drink in order to harm him and help himself. He then resorts to greater subtlety and worse betrayal, using faithful Uriah to deliver his own death sentence. He has learned from Saul, who in 1 Sam 18:20-30 tried to have David killed in war. Now David will more successfully use a war to kill someone he sees as a threat. Joab, utterly loyal to David, follows orders even at the cost of additional Israelite men. In his instructions to his messenger he mentions Abimelech, who claimed the kingship but lost the kingdom and his life because of a woman (Judg 9:50-57). The messenger, perhaps sensing the awful appropriateness of those words, does not give David a chance to utter them (although in the LXX he does). David's response in v. 25 is public relations; his musing on the randomness of death in battle could only amuse Joab, but it might reassure some who wonder if Uriah really died by chance. The many messengers involved and the fact that Uriah spent every night with David's servants mean the affair and the paternity of the child are public knowledge; suspicion over Uriah's death would be inevitable.

There is no indication that Bathsheba ever knows the truth about Uriah's death or that her lamentation is not sincere. Her relationship with David has traditionally been seen as a passionate love affair with Bathsheba as a willing if not seductive participant, but it can much more easily be read as the rape of a loyal wife. As we have seen, it is David who sends and plots and arranges murder; v. 27 (again with *David sent*) sounds as if he can hardly wait for the funeral formalities to be observed. While much of David's behavior has been open to doubt since he became king, now he is clearly wrong. Another man who was an obstacle has died conveniently, and there is no confusion as to why. Verse 27 gives us God's first sign of displeasure with his chosen king.

David and the LORD, 12:1-31

The LORD has accepted David's earlier behavior, but now the shepherd boy who learned to let God act on his behalf has become a despot who acts as if he has the right to dispose of people's lives. In keeping with the covenant of chap. 7, David does not lose the kingship but his sin will be punished *with blows inflicted by human beings* (7:14).

12:1-15a. Nathan brings the LORD's indictment to the king. 12:1-15a. God "sends" Nathan to deliver judgment to the one who "sent" others on such sorry errands. His parable involves David's emotions before the king knows what the issues really are. The story is far from an exact allegory of chap. 11, but the theme is there: a powerful man disrupts a powerless man's family by taking and destroying a loved member of it. The lamb in different ways represents both Bathsheba and Uriah. To David's credit, he is enraged at the injustice and pronounces sentence. To his further credit, he does not dispute Nathan's sudden verdict in 7. The one who in 5:12 understood that he had been given much for the sake of Israel now realizes that he has taken more than the gift entitled him to.

David's confession in v. 13 leads to forgiveness, but forgiveness does not mean that the events he set in motion by his public sin can be stopped. In questionable circumstances he once said, *The Lord pay back the one who does wickedly in accordance with his wickedness!* (3:39). The narrative ranging from 12:15 to 20:26 will show this happening as David's older sons' violent passions, like his, lead to rape and murder, costing Israel peace and David the security of the throne, and the lives of four sons (the fourth, Adonijah, does not die until 1 Kgs 2:25).

Only the death of the first is presented as a divine punishment. The rest are the inevitable result of David's behavior; God does not will Amnon's incestuous, violent desires or Absalom's ambitious and patricidal ones. The man who freely committed adultery and murder will pay through the equally free acts of his sons. Like Uriah, many who are innocent will suffer for David's sin, but others will be drawn by their own evil into the context created by David's for even greater catastrophe.

12:15b-25. The births of David and Bathsheba's children. The sentence begins at once. David's fatherly love shows in his genuine mourning in an effort to avert the death of his and Bathsheba's baby; his behavior afterwards shows his pained acceptance. His consolation of Bathsheba (v. 24) is the first evidence of tenderness towards her. The report of God's love for the subsequent child reassures us that he will not also pay for David's crime, although the natural results of David's behavior will still occur. Solomon will not even be mentioned in the rest of 2 Samuel, but in 1 Kgs 1–2 he will succeed to the throne (making it difficult to see 9–20 as a SUCCESSION NARRATIVE).

12:26-31. Joab and David defeat their enemies. We move from these stories of intimate relationships back to the larger world of national policy in which they began. David's disastrous sabbatical from the war ends at Joab's insistence; David cannot afford to lose face any further. The victory is as always a sign of God's presence with Israel, even though the statement is not specifically made here. The treasure and crown of the Ammonite kings (the probable reading of *Milcom* in v. 30) become David's and the Ammonite people are drafted into a labor force. The victorious end of this lengthy war is barely described, however; the focus is on tracing the dissolution begun in David's family.

David and His Children, 13:1–14:33

David's treatment of others creates reactions and further crimes he never intended. The connection noted earlier between David's love and death (see commentary at 11:1-5 above) now displays itself even more destructively in his children. In 1 Samuel we saw strife in father-son relationships with ELI and HOPHNI and PHINEAS, Saul and Jonathan, and Saul and David (who addressed each other with the familial terms "father" and "son"; David even refers to himself as Nabal's "son"). The father-son conflict was also implied with Samuel and his sons (1 Sam 8:1-3). The motif is emphasized more here as one son uses David to achieve incestuous rape, and another tries to kill him only to be killed by his father's men.

13:1-22. Amnon rapes Tamar. Although Amnon is David's eldest, ABSALOM is mentioned first, indicating that he is actually the pivotal character. His *beautiful sister* (v. 1) reminds us that raped Bathsheba was the last woman called "beautiful." Amnon has David's nephew Jonadab as an advisor, a man described as wise (NRSV *crafty*); perhaps his counsel is thought wise at a court where the king takes the wife of one of his men. Jonadab suggests using David's paternal concern for his son to gain access to his daughter. David duly "sends" (recall the importance of "sending" in the Bathsheba story [see commentary at 11:1-5 above]) Tamar to care for her supposedly ill brother (note how often family designations instead of names are used, emphasizing the misuse of these relationships).

Like his father with Uriah (11:13), Amnon uses food to mask betrayal. When his intentions become unmistakable Tamar does not panic but reasons with him, pointing out that a forbidden sexual relationship between them will ruin them both. It doesn't matter. The exact nature of David's taking of Bathsheba is veiled in silence, but there is no doubt that Amnon rapes Tamar. His exaggerated love for her immediately turns to exaggerated loathing. By sending her away he dooms her to an isolated life; there will always be suspicion that she was willing since she was raped in the city (cf. Deut 22:23-24, although that deals with a betrothed virgin).

Our last glimpse of this compassionate and truly wise woman shows her running from Amnon's house in a posture of mourning and abandonment. Out of her large family only Absalom cares for her. While his sons are not named in the text (they probably died young [18:18]), 14:27 says that he names his daughter after his sister who will have no child. David is angry at *all these things* (v. 21; but are "these things" the rape or David's own manipulated role in it?) but does nothing. The kindest interpretation is that he feels he cannot chastise Amnon for giving into the dangerous passions his son must know David himself has gratified, but the text says only that he does not act *because he loved [Amnon]* (v. 21). Clearly he has no such feeling for Tamar.

13:23-39. Absalom kills Amnon. Like David, Amnon uses his power to take a woman to whom he has no right. Like David, Absalom uses his to order a murder. He waits two years to kill his brother, perhaps hoping that David will avenge Tamar. When that hope fails, he uses food to mask betrayal (as did David with Uriah and Amnon with Tamar). Again a son deceives David into sending a victim to him. Although Absalom does not strike the fatal blow himself, everyone understands that he is responsible—in the same way David is responsible for Uriah's death. Jonadab (who does not seem to have warned his friend Amnon of his danger) says the murder is due to Tamar's rape.

Certainly the rape of Tamar fixed Absalom's feelings towards his brother Amnon, but like his father Absalom may be acting from multiple motives. As subsequent events indicate, Amnon's death puts Absalom first in line for the throne (David's second son Chileab may have died young; he is never mentioned after 3:3), a fact which that canny young prince cannot have overlooked. An obstacle to the throne is gone and Absalom flees to his grandfather. We are told that David mourned for his son, but not for which: the rapist or the murderer?

14:1-33. Joab brings Absalom home. Verse 19 indicates that Joab has made earlier efforts to bring Absalom back. Like Nathan (12:1-6), he resorts to a story to engage David's emotions. His coached wise woman is believable and David responds mercifully to her. When she moves the focus to restoring the unnamed Absalom, David, whom she flatters as the one *discerning good and evil* (v. 17), discerns Joab's hand. Joab's motives, like so many in 2 Samuel, are unclear here. Does he think Amnon deserved death? Does he want to restore Absalom out of concern for David?

The relationship between Joab and David is complex. David complains loudly about his violent nephew (cf. 3:39), and Joab alone at court seems totally unimpressed with David's grandeur (cf. 12:28), and yet their partnership is successful for both of them. Joab kills easily to protect himself or David, but he never attempts to seize power for himself; for his part, David obviously puts total trust in Joab's loyalty (11:14-15). Joab, apparently moved, sees the granting of his request as a sign of David's favor, but it seems more likely that David simply cannot fight against his love for his son any longer.

The *wise woman* (v. 2) reminds us of cold Jonadab in 13:3, the only other character described by this word so far in 1–2 Sam (NRSV has *crafty* in 13:3, but the Heb. is the same). There the advice of the wise led to rape and murder; perhaps it is unwise to follow wise counsel. In 14:20 David becomes the third person to be described as having wisdom. The woman means it as a compliment, but like Jonadab, this woman, and the fourth "wise" character in the book (20:16-22), his judgment has led to betrayal and death. The next "wise" character in this story is Solomon (cf. 1 Kgs 2:6, 3:12, etc.); his judgment may be questionable, too.

Like Bathsheba and Tamar, Absalom also is marked by *beauty* (v. 25), suggesting that he may not come to a good end. David is attractive but only his eyes are described by that fatal word (1 Sam 16:12), and it is his beautiful, wandering eyes that begin his troubles (11:2). After five years banished from David's presence, Absalom "sends" (again recall the importance of "sending"; see commentary at 11:1-5 above) twice for Joab, who ignores him. He then strikes at Joab, becoming the only character to cross that fearsome man until another of David's sons has him killed (1 Kgs 2:28-35). This reckless act, reminiscent of David in the wilderness, wins him reconciliation with the king; note that even the narrator does not refer to "the king" as his father.

David's Family Conflict Becomes National, 15:1–19:40

David's treatment of Bathsheba and Uriah created an environment of license and distrust that led to the rape of his daughter, one son's murder, and another's alienation. Absalom is now restored to favor, but his lack of familial address to David indicates that his earlier grievances are not resolved. His subsequent rebellion is the central event of this section, a family conflict that splits the country and splits David himself as his roles of king and father conflict.

15:1-12. Absalom revolts against his father. David's following the wise woman's advice to restore Absalom was a mistake, just as it was a mistake for Amnon to follow wise Jonadab's. There has already been reason to suspect that Absalom may have harbored kingly ambitions (in 13:27 his feast was *like a king's feast*). Now that he is again honored in Jerusalem he adds to his retinue in even more glamorous style than his father did when he became that city's king (cf. 5:13). He is the son most like his father, sharing that larger-than-life quality with the young David whom the people loved more than Saul (1 Sam 18:7, 16); perhaps that is why David cares most for him. David never attacked Saul at all, but Absalom questions David's function as judge. Casting doubts on his ability to fulfill this basic task of leadership is suggesting that he is not capable of being king. David attracted the people, but his son steals their hearts.

The man who waited two years to carry out his plot against his brother waits four to rebel against David, using the LORD in his deception. No motive is given; Absalom feels all the ambition his father did and may have convinced himself that David's inability to respond to Tamar's crisis gives him the right to pursue the kingship. Absalom begins his rebellion in Hebron, where David was first proclaimed king. Perhaps he is taking advantage of his resemblance to his father.

15:13–16:14. David flees before his son. The need for action gets through the paralysis that has gripped David since Tamar's rape, and he becomes again the decisive leader aware of his relationship to God that he was before he became king. His reaction shows the urgency of this crisis: Israel, which was never as loyal to David as the south, has followed Absalom, and by establishing his headquarters in Hebron he has annexed part of Judah as well. David abandons his capital swiftly, leaving only ten women out of all his personal and military retinue in the city he fears Absalom will soon attack. The urgency of the situation is only enhanced by the narrator's report of the many stops along the way, down in the Kidron Valley, up to the top of the Mount of Olives, stopping along the way to conduct urgent affairs.

David's reference to Absalom as *the king* (v. 19) shows his awareness that neither he nor his son is the decisive character in this conflict. He sees it as the fulfillment of 12:11, and as he did before he became king he is allowing God to decide his destiny and Israel's. Perhaps Absalom *is* the king. David has not lost faith in the covenant of chap. 7, but he knows that his behavior merits punishment, and if Absalom defeats him, it will still be his house on the throne. He states more clearly in vv. 25-26 his willingness to let the outcome depend on the LORD, who subtly responds in v. 32. Brueggemann calls David an "emancipated man" because he trusts his destiny to God out of his "enormous faith which puts him at Yahweh's disposal" even if that disposal is not David's desire (Brueggemann 1972, 18).

Although David recognizes the theological issues involved, he has not lost his savvy and realizes that on a purely human level the key factor is AHITHOPHEL's counsel. Ahithophel was one of David's advisors; why he has turned against David is not yet clear (cf. 11:3; 23:34). Even as David prays for Ahithophel's advice to be worthless his prayer is answered by Hushai's appearance, enabling him to put together a plan and a communications network (vv. 33-36). He has found loyalty in his flight, but his last two interviews on the road are not so encouraging. Ziba informs David that Mephibosheth is a traitor. The fact that Ziba brings food for David's train reminds us of how David and his sons have used food as a disguise for betrayal (11:13; 13:6, 24ff.). It is unlikely that Mephibosheth could hope to benefit from Absalom's rebellion, since Absalom spent years creating loyalty to himself, but David does not recognize Ziba's lie and promptly gives him all that he had previously granted to Mephibosheth (cf. 9:7).

David then moves from a disguised enemy to an outright one. Shimei, a Saulide, curses David as a murderer and applauds the rebellion as God's judgment for the deaths in Saul's house. He may be referring to Abner and Ishbaal (3:26-30; 4:5-8), although the events of 21:1-9 are more likely the subject here. Since the narrator has not told that story yet, the accusation is more ambiguous, in keeping with the cloud of general suspicion that has gathered over David. His response to Abishai (who offers similar counsel in 1 Sam 26:8) again shows his willingness to let God be God. David is not passive in this section (e.g., his sending of Hushai). He simply understands the extent to which his actions have made him walk the road from Jerusalem and knows God must decide if he can walk the road back.

16:15–17:23. Absalom and his counselors. Absalom now has more counselors than he needs. Ahithophel gives the first advice, telling David's son to rape David's women, and this is carried out on the spot where David first saw and sent for Bathsheba (see commentary on 3:1-21 above). David evoked God's anger for taking and using Bathsheba and her husband as he desired. The subsequent judgment of 12:11 is fulfilled because David again saw women's lives (his concubines') as his to dispose of to their detriment—they were the only ones of his household that he left in danger (15:16).

Ahithophel's next advice is also practical, brutal, and pleasing to Absalom. Hushai, hoping to buy David time, plays on Absalom's fear of his father and urges caution the young man cannot afford. He also sends David a warning before he knows whose advice Absalom will follow. Ahithophel's counsel is *as if one consulted the oracle of God* (16:23), but God frustrates it in favor of Hushai's. David may not really be *like the angel of God, discerning good and evil* (14:17), but he can discern better than the son who questioned his ability to judge. Ahithophel sees correctly that all is lost and so kills himself.

17:24–18:18. David's army defeats Absalom. The many evidences of support David has received both from God and people make him realize that Absalom has lost. He is not concerned now as a king with a kingdom, but as a father whose son is his beloved enemy. His loyal troops, not David, win the victory, but it is not dwelled on. The narrator's concern at this point is what this war means to David the father. The fleeing Absalom is caught in a tree by *his head* (18:9; not his hair as popularly told) and hangs between heaven and earth, life and death.

His father wills his life, but his father is not there. The soldier who finds him succinctly sums up the convoluted relationships and betrayals in this war. Joab, however, has no inhibitions against killing his cousin. He has many motives to choose from (grudging the burning of his fields in 14:30, unwillingness to leave a dangerous enemy alive), but it seems likely that he and his men kill Absalom because he knows what David cannot face: that his son hates him and will always be a danger to him and to his kingdom. This is borne out by Absalom's slow, careful treachery and his pleasure at Ahithophel's patricidal advice (17:1-4). The fact that Joab apparently had worked on his own to get Absalom home from banishment but then has to be coerced later to bring him into David's presence indicates that having the prince as a neighbor made him reevaluate his character (chap. 14). Perhaps part of the reason he kills Absalom is due to the responsibility he feels for bringing him and David back together.

18:19–19:8a. David receives the news of Absalom's death. David is consistently called *the king* in this section, but his questions to the messengers show him reacting as a father. Telling David of Absalom's death is described in more detail than the death itself. The exuberant Ahimaaz runs to him in spite of Joab's delegating another messenger. David assumes he brings "good news" and he does, but not to the father. Shimei was wrong: God has deemed David worthy of being King, but Absalom must pay the price. The Cushite tries to put the news in its proper context, but David can barely get to privacy before he breaks down. We have seen him grieve for an enemy's death before (1:17-27), but now he is truly broken.

Saul and Jonathan *in life and death were not divided* (1:23); David and Absalom were divided in both. In contrast to the high spirits of Ahimaaz, the soldiers who have saved David's life and kingdom sneak home in victory. Only Joab can make him see the danger of alienating the army, and he does so as bluntly as usual. David, probably not yet aware of Joab's role in Absalom's death, revives enough to greet his men. We sympathize with the bereaved father and admire the man who still loves his child in spite of the worst sort of betrayal, but we cannot help realizing that if he had loved his daughter with a tenth of the feeling he had for any of his sons this day might never have come.

19:8b-40. David and the people. There is disorganization in both Israel and Judah in dealing with the aftermath of the revolt. The title *King David* in v. 11 indicates that the public king and the personal man are again functioning as one, and he immediately begins taking care of his affairs. He makes his first overture to Judah (cf. 1 Sam 30:26-31; 2 Sam 2:1-4), adding a message giving Joab's job to his great-nephew Amasa who had headed Absalom's army (17:25). David can say he is replacing Joab to appease Absalom's followers. Like Abner, Amasa helps David enter a region that followed another king (an ominous comparison for a man taking Joab's job); David is soon restored over Judah.

On his return to Jerusalem David encounters some of those he left on his way out; these meetings indicate the toll events have taken on the king, as well as showing what he will never achieve. Absalom's revolt briefly restored David to the creative, faithful man he had once been; its end leaves him a tired old man beaten in victory. Shimei is first now as he was last before, knowing that his only chance of mercy lies in getting to David while he is rejoicing in his homecoming. As usual, Abishai urges violence, but Shimei's gamble pays off; the king promises not to take his life.

David later regrets his magnanimity; technically he does not violate his oath, but on his deathbed he will tell Solomon to kill Shimei (1 Kgs 2:8-9). This tarnishes the image of the king gracious in victory. Ziba is there as well; perhaps the wily servant knows he too needs to approach David while the king is in a good mood. Before he can speak Mephibosheth appears with proof of his innocence of Ziba's accusations (16:1-4). The narrator carefully never, now or in chap. 16, tells us who is actually telling the truth, but there are sufficient clues in the text to indicate that Jonathan's son is honest (see commentary at 15:13–16:14 above).

It is unfortunate that Mephibosheth comes immediately after Shimei; perhaps David feels that in sparing the latter he has done enough for Saul's house, or maybe the strain of carrying off a celebration based on Absalom's death is more than he can handle for long. In any case, the man who took responsibility for Mephibosheth in chap. 9 now simply divides the property between him and Ziba, not caring which is loyal and which a liar. He and Shimei are among the enmeshed relationships David has built up during his life and can no longer deal with. He seems more like himself with Barzillai (17:27-28), who is unrelated to his previous loves and hates. Barzillai sends Chimham (apparently his son [cf. 1 Kgs 2:7]) with the man whose own heir has just died rebelling against him. Barzillai, an outsider, presents a picture of contented old age surrounded by his family—something David knows he will never know.

David and Israel, 19:41–20:26

19:41–20:3. Sheba leads a second revolt against David. Repairing the division of Absalom's revolt is delayed as Israel and Judah argue over who has the best rights to the king they have both rejected. David, made king independently by north and south, ruled both without melding them into one permanent union (see Miller 1990, 198–99). Now the Israelites are threatened by David's close connection to the south while the Judeans angrily deny that they have benefitted from it. This leads to the revolt of the north led by a member of Saul's tribe (who may have a closer connection with Saul's family; 1 Sam 9:1 traces Saul's descent through one bearing a name similar to Sheba's ancestor).

David's first act on returning home is to clean up one of the most troublesome aspects of the last revolt before dealing with the next one, shutting away his concubines whom his son publicly raped as part of his claim to the throne. At the end of Absalom's story David shows no more concern for these raped women he left in harm's way than he did for the daughter he sent to her rapist at the beginning of it (13:7-21), but he does provide for their care. The rationale is that their experience with David's son makes his resumption of normal relationships with them incestuous, since the OT defines incest as sexual relations not only with blood relatives but with those relatives' partners as well (cf. Lev 18:6-18).

20:4-26. Joab kills Amasa and Sheba. David now orders his new general to take charge of the current trouble. This revolt is dangerous because it is based on loyalty to Saul's family rather than a split in David's. Amasa's unexplained tardiness forces David to resort to the sons of Zeruiah, choosing Abishai rather than Joab whom he has replaced. Nonetheless Joab kills his cousin Amasa. This murder is described in detail (while there are many battles in 1–2 Sam, the narrator always focuses much more on the smaller, more intimate scenes). By this act Joab wins back his old job; David cannot try yet another new general in the middle of a rebellion. He also can never admit that he hates Joab for killing Absalom, since by doing so Joab ended a civil war and saved both David and many troops. When he orders Joab's death as he is dying, he will have to say it is for the murders of Abner and Amasa (1 Kgs 2:5-6). With no further action by David Joab's army traps Sheba, who is betrayed and killed on the advice of the fourth person in this book characterized as "wise" (see commentary on 14:1-33). This ends the North's revolt, but it will rebel successfully against David's house in 1 Kgs 12:16-19. The section closes with another list of officials. Unlike 8:15-18, at this late date no role is given to David or his sons.

Although he has been restored, David has provided another example of the "How the mighty have fallen!" theme he articulated at the book's beginning (1:19, 27)—and for both Saul and David, the "how" is through their own choices. David handles himself well as a soldier and fugitive in 1 Samuel, but the temptations of power distract him from his intended role as the chosen king through whom God could act. This causes great suffering both for individuals and for his kingdom as a whole. Saul, who fails as a leader, is punished by seeing God choose another king and knowing that he will not found a dynasty. David, who fails most in his personal relationships, is punished by seeing those he loves turn against him. This is the penalty God gave, but the narrative shows how little God must do to punish him or anyone else (only 12:1, 24, and 17:14 directly mention God's activity). We are only too eager to do it to ourselves and to each other. It can be argued that David pays a higher price for his failures than Saul does; at least Saul dies with his sons at his side instead of trying to take his throne.

Epilogue: Other Stories about David's Reign, 21:1–24:25

The book ends with an appendix of traditions rooted in different parts of David's reign, shedding light on the material already read while continuing its themes. In four chapters it will retrace 2 Samuel, taking us from the young and glorious king restoring the kingdom after Saul's failure to the old and sinning king endangering God's people after his own. This condensed look at David prepares us for the cynical intrigue of the end of his life in 1 Kgs 1–2.

The appendix takes the form of a CHIASM. Narratives of guilt and expiation in first and sixth place surround stories and lists of David's warriors in second and fifth place. These surround the two central poems in which David summarizes his experience as king under God in third and fourth place.

Israel Endangered by Saul's Guilt, 21:1-14

This story belongs early in David's reign; there are still loose ends left by Saul and the stories of Mephibosheth (chap. 9) and Shimei (16:5-8) have yet to occur. It underscores the basic idea that people pay for the sins of their leaders (1 Sam 12:14-15). Verse 2 refers to Josh 9:3-27, but the story of Saul's slaughtering the Gibeonites is not recorded; the bloody price for it is demanded not by God but by Gibeon.

David (again involved with convenient Saulide deaths) easily sends Saul's sons to die for Saul's guilt (cf. Num 35:33), but we have seen that later he will grieve as his own son dies for his (12:15-18).

The horror of the deaths of these innocents is shown through Rizpah, who has already been used in one power play between men (3:7-11); now another disrupts her life more dreadfully. She is as silent in this story as in that one, but she is not passive. Her Antigone-like loyalty to her dead kin moves David to pity. The deaths of the Saulides do not end the famine. David responded to the Gibeonites' vengefulness, but it is not until Rizpah's faithfulness has evoked his compassion that God blesses the land again.

David's Mighty Men, 21:15-22

These stories add to the bare account of the Philistine wars in 5:17-25. Most of 1–2 Samuel stresses David's role, but here we see that Israel has many heroes. David is less the warrior than one who draws out the best in others. New images of him and Abishai are presented as the usually mighty one is rescued and the usually antagonistic one offers aid. Verse 17 gives a possible reason for 11:1. Its absence there makes David's behavior seem even worse, but here it emphasizes the warm relationship between David and his troops. Verse 19 attributes David's first dramatic success to a stranger (1 Sam 17; 1 Chr 20:5 attempts to reconcile the traditions), an assertion made easy to accept by its placement immediately after the story of David's tired dependence on his men. On the other hand, the tradition of 1 Sam 17 is much more developed and integrated into the Davidic material.

The mention of Elhanan again forces us to recognize that the truth of David's life is hard to find. That may be its purpose.

A Psalm of David, 22:1-51

This poem, along with the following poem, constitutes the center of the appendix, showing David understanding his role as God's vessel and not conscientiously but joyfully giving his LORD credit for everything. These poems move the focus away from David in two directions, emphasizing first God as the one empowering David and then David's descendants as the ones inheriting God's promise.

Verses 2-20 and 29-51 of this psalm (essentially Ps 18) are reminiscent of Hannah's song in language (cf. 1 Sam 2:2 and 22:2b-3, 32, 47) and content (the rescue of the needy and the help for the anointed one).

David's victories really belong to the mighty and sustaining LORD. But vv. 21-28 strike a jarring note by obliquely reminding us for the first time in the appendix of Bathsheba and Uriah. In all honesty, David *has* been rewarded according to his righteousness (the disasters of chaps. 13-20 are precisely that reward), but how are we to read vv. 22-24? They are not true. Their conventional piety is offensive on David's lips, as the repentant king of 12:13 would agree. Here they are subversive, reminding us that grace gives not only strength and victory but also forgiveness and the ability to continue in relationship with God.

A Psalm of David, 23:1-7

In these *last words* (v. 1) David celebrates God's working through him as the chosen one and rejoices that his house will continue to be used to provide justice to God's people. David's actual last words in the narrative will be largely directed towards revenge rather than justice (1 Kgs 2:5-9); like most of the appendix, the tradition here finds him in a more graceful moment.

David's Mighty Men, 23:8-39

The process of honoring those besides David who led to Israel's victories continues. As in 21:15-22, we find lists of names and a few exploits of warriors, here formed into the orders of *the Three* (v. 8) and *the thirty* (v. 13; the number *thirty-seven* in v. 39 is correct if Joab is added in as commander-in-chief). Credit for their victories, like David's, goes to God.

Verses 13-17 shows the young David in an intimate moment with his men. David's respect and affection for his men as well as his unwillingness to assume that any sacrifice they make for him is only his due shows how he is able to command the loyalty even of heroes and why to the end of his life he will be given loyalty in spite of his failures and reverses. This story, however, also reminds us that David did eventually think of these men's lives as his to dispose of (some of his special troops were among those killed in the plot against Uriah [11:17]), showing why he lost so much loyalty as well. One of those whose loyalty he lost was Ahithophel (15:12). This is finally explained by the mention of Bathsheba's father Eliam (11:3) in v. 34 as Ahithophel's son. Ahithophel turned against the man who raped his granddaughter and killed her husband, giving added irony to 16:20-23 since it is Bathsheba's grandfather who tells David's son to rape his women and this happens precisely where David first saw Bathsheba. Uriah's name, last in the list, brings up this episode for the third time. The king who was one with his men in 13-17 did not stay so.

Israel Endangered by David's Guilt, 24:1-25

This brings us full circle to where the appendix began: the nation pays for the sin of its king, but this time the king is David. Verse 1 says God is the tempter but 1 Chr 21:1 puts Satan in that role. The belief that God is responsible for all that happens, good and evil, is an early one (cf. Exod 4:24). By the Chronicler's time Satan rather than God was understood as the instigator of evil. David's sin in taking a (probably military) census is the one subtly brought up by 23:8-39: his belief that he controls the people's lives and may dispose of them as he will (cf. 1 Sam 8:10-18). But the people are God's, and for the king to act as if he owns them brings judgment on them all (1 Sam 12:14-15).

David repents as he did after Uriah's murder, but again the consequences of his sin must still be borne. He is willing to trust God for the punishment, just as he left the resolution of his son's revolt to the Lord. He is correct to do so, since the plague is halted through divine mercy. David then buys (rather than simply receiving) what will become the site of Solomon's Temple, linking him with an institution that will be important in the rest of the Bible and rooting it in expiation.

The appendix has clarified the material in vv. 1-20. The only person who sins in it is David (Saul's action against the Gibeonites takes place earlier). The roles of the compassionate Rizpah, the mighty and loyal men in David's service, and even the generous Araunah are stressed, while God is given the most credit for all success by David himself, the one who tries at times to take too much. David emerges from the overall narrative of 2 Samuel as an amazing character—not amazingly good or amazingly evil, but fully human. He is less a role model than an accurate picture of the heights and depths of which human nature is capable.

In his novel *God Knows*, Joseph Heller has David say at the end of his life that he has learned that "people are complete, and everybody is capable of everything" (1984, 16). This point is illustrated best in the person of David himself. He is loving and brutal, passive and decisive, generous and grasping, and faithful and betraying, acting both better and worse than we expect. His failures are not ignored or excused in the text, but neither do they wipe out his successes.

David is Israel's greatest hero, but he is remembered honestly as a man with strengths and weaknesses who proves that no one has to be perfect to be of use to God and God's people. Perhaps it is as much for his perseverance in spite of his failures before his Lord as for his flamboyant adventures that he exercised such a hold on Israel's imagination. A thousand years after his death, when Jesus rode into Jerusalem the most glorious name the people could think to call him was "Son of David!" (Matt 21:9).

Works Cited

Alter, Robert. 1981. *The Art of Biblical Narrative.*

Bailey, Lloyd R. 1990. "Ark." MDB.

Brueggemann, Walter. 1972. "On Trust and Freedom: A Study of Faith in the Succession Narrative." *Interp* 26:3–1 9.

Cate, Robert L. 1990. "Ishbosheth." MDB.

Eslinger, Lyle. 1983. "Viewpoints and Point of View in 1 Samuel 8-12." *JSOT* 26:61–76.

Flanagan, J. W. 1972. "Court History of Succession Document?" *JBL* 91: 172–81.

Gregory, Russell I. 1990. "Sources of the Pentateuch." MDB.

Heller, Joseph. 1984. *God Knows.*

Joines, Karen Randolph. 1990. "Holiness in the OT." MDB.

Hertzberg, Hans W. 1965. *I and II Samuel, a Commentary.* OTL.

Miller, J. Maxwell. 1990. "David." MDB.

Niccolls, S. Thomas. 1981. "The Comic Vision and the Stories of David." *Encounter* 42:277–83.

Perdue, L. G. 1984. "'Is There Anyone Left of the House of Saul . . . ?' Ambiguity and the Characterization of David in the Succession Narrative." *JSOT* 30: 67–84.

First and Second Kings

Thomas G. Smothers

Introduction

The Books of Kings—originally one book—conclude the section of the Hebrew Bible known as the Former Prophets (Joshua, Judges, Samuel, Kings). Kings cover the period from the last days of DAVID to the fall of Jerusalem, concluding with a hopeful note about the release of King JEHOIACHIN from prison in Babylon.

Composition

Since the pioneering work of Martin Noth, it has become customary to refer to the Former Prophets as the "Deuteronomistic History" (see DEUTERONOMIST/ DEUTERONOMISTIC HISTORIAN). Noth viewed the Deuteronomistic History as the work of a single author during the exilic age whose purpose was to explain the fall of the Hebrew kingdoms with reference to the cultic and moral ideals of the Book of Deuteronomy (see Noth 1981). Subsequent writers offered modifications of this basic view. Some posited two or three editions of Deuteronomistic History, all exilic (e.g., Smend 1971, 494–509). F. M. Cross argued for two editions of the Deuteronomistic History, one from the time of JOSIAH and the other from the exilic age (1973, 274–89). Later studies have emphasized earlier redactions or editions. Specifically with regard to the Books of Kings, André Lemaire (1986, 221–36) identified four redactions, the first three from the reigns of JEHOSHAPHAT, HEZEKIAH, and Josiah respectively, and the last from the post-exilic age, supporting the view of a long historical tradition in ISRAEL and JUDAH.

Sources

The sources utilized by the Deuteronomistic Historian (or, more likely, historians) include popular or traditional narratives, stories about prophets, and administrative archives. Three written sources are named. The *Book of the Acts of Solomon* (1 Kgs 11:41) appears to have been used sparingly; the *Book of the Annals of the Kings of Israel* (1 Kgs 14:19; 15:31; 16:5, 14, 20, 27; 22:39; 2 Kgs 1:18; 10:34; 13:8, 12; 14:15, 28; 15:11, 15, 21, 26, 31) and the *Book of the Annals of the Kings of Judah* (1 Kgs 14:29; 15:7, 23; 22:45; 2 Kgs 8:23; 12:19; 14:18; 15:6, 36; 16:19; 20:20; 21:17, 25; 23:28; 24:5) appear to have been used more extensively. Today readers of 1–2 Kings have access to literary sources from Egypt, Assyria, Babylon, and Syria-Palestine to supplement the historical data in the Books of Kings. The following commentary takes into account such extrabiblical material.

Purpose

The Books of Kings, like the other books of the Deuteronomistic History, serve a theological purpose. Overall, the Deuteronomistic History interprets the tragic history of Israel in the land of Palestine using the central tenets of the Book of Deuteronomy as guiding theological perspectives. To help explain the demise of the Israelite kingdoms and the subsequent exiles, the Books of Kings emphasize these theological concerns: the law of the central sanctuary (Deut 12); IDOLATRY and cultic deviation as COVENANT violation; the *sin of Jeroboam* (2 Kgs 3:3), that is, the establishment of alternate cultic sites and cultic practices to those in Judah and Jerusalem; and the enduring promise of David's dynasty. The role of the prophets in Israelite history is highlighted by showing how events were to be understood on the basis of the prediction-fulfillment scheme.

For Further Study

In the *Mercer Dictionary of the Bible*: CHRONOLOGY; DAVID; DEUTERONOMIST/DEUTERONOMISTIC HISTORIAN; ISRAEL; JERUSALEM; JUDAH; KINGS, BOOKS OF FIRST AND SECOND; SAMUEL; SOLOMON.

In other sources: J. Gray, *I and Kings: A Commentary*, OTL, 2nd rev. ed.; M. Haran, *Temples and Temple Service in Ancient Israel*; T. R. Hobbs, *2 Kings*, WBC; T. Ishida, ed., *Studies in the Period of David and Solomon*; B. O. Long, *1 Kings*, FOTL; R. D. Nelson, *First and Second Kings*, Interp.

Commentary

An Outline

I. Solomon's Succession to the Throne, 1 Kgs 1:1–2:46
   A. The Politics of Succession, 1:1-53
   B. Solomon's Moves to Secure Power, 2:1-46
II. The Reign of Solomon, 3:1–11:43
   A. Solomon's Wisdom and Administration, 3:1–4:34
   B. The Building and Dedication
     of the Temple, 5:1–9:25
   C. Solomon's Wealth and Wisdom, 9:26–10:29
   D. The Sins of the Kingdom Exposed, 11:1-43
III. Synchronic History of Israel and Judah,
    1 Kgs 12:1–2 Kgs 17:41
   A. Jeroboam I of Israel, 12:1–14:20
   B. Early Kings of Judah, 14:21–15:24
   C. Early Kings of Israel, 15:25–16:34
   D. Ahab and Elijah, 16:29–22:40
   E. Jehoshaphat and Ahaziah, 22:41–2 Kgs 1:18
   F. The Elisha Cycle, 2:1–8:29
   G. From Jehu to the Fall of Samaria, 9:1–17:41
IV. Judah after the Fall of Israel, 18:1–25:30

Solomon's Succession to the Throne, 1 Kgs 1:1–2:46

1 Kings 1–2 forms the conclusion to the what is now generally called the SUCCESSION NARRATIVE (also called "The Court History of David"), which begins in 2 Sam 9 (but does not include 2 Sam 21–24). All the sons of David eligible to succeed to the throne had perished except for ADONIJAH, the son of Haggith, and SOLOMON, the son of Bathsheba. The conclusion of the narrative relates how Solomon came to the throne.

The Politics of Succession, 1:1-53

The approaching death of King David precipitated the final crisis of his reign. Who would succeed him on the throne of the empire? The politicians of the court and the ever-present palace intrigue were given free rein. The chief actors in the drama were Adonijah on the one side, supported by the priest ABIATHAR and the military leader JOAB, and the prophet NATHAN and BATHSHEBA on the other side, supported by the powerful military commander BENAIAH and the priest ZADOK.

Adonijah's strategy depended on the tradition of the succession of the oldest surviving prince, while Nathan's strategy depended on his personal access to David and on the influence of Bathsheba.

1:1-4. King David's senility. The aging David's ability to inspire trust in his leadership was put to the final test. Because his circulation was poor and he could not get warm, a young woman, *Abishag*, from the village of Shunem in the valley of Jezreel, was brought to the court to minister to the king. The well-meaning strategy was unsuccessful. Although Abishag was *very beautiful* (v. 4), David was unable to have sexual relations with her. The powerful, decisive ruler who dominated the narratives of 1–2 Samuel was now viewed as lacking in the necessary vigor and virility to provide decisive leadership.

1:5-31. Political maneuvering. Adonijah, the oldest surviving son of David, seems to have taken for granted the ancient Near Eastern practice of primogeniture. Adonijah *exalted himself*, acting the part of king by assembling a chariot force, complete with men *to run before him*, and by seeking the aid of two of the most powerful and influential members of David's cabinet, *Joab* the army commander and *Abiathar* the priest from Nob. Not included in his retinue, probably because he declined their participation, were even more powerful elements: *the priest Zadok, Benaiah*, the commander of David's personal bodyguard, *the prophet Nathan*, and *Shimei and Rei*, two of David's mighty men (v. 8). Already the reader is alerted to the precariousness of Adonijah's position. His fate was sealed when *he did not invite the prophet Nathan or Benaiah or the warriors or his brother Solomon* to his sacrifice and banquet (vv. 9-10).

The prophet Nathan countered with his own plan. He suggested to Bathsheba that she inform David of Adonijah's actions and remind David of his promise to have her son Solomon succeed him as king, a promise not mentioned in any previous text. The lives of Bathsheba and Solomon were at stake, and possibly also Nathan's life (v. 21). Immediately after Bathsheba's audience with David, Nathan's presence at court was announced. The prophet recounted fully Adonijah's actions, especially the slight against Zadok, Benaiah, and Solomon, and suggested that events were running outside the king's control. In an attempt at decisive leadership, David confirmed Solomon as his successor. It is a sad picture: the once vigorous, decisive ruler now senile and susceptible to manipulation.

1:32-40. The anointing of Solomon. David gave instructions that Solomon be anointed and enthroned without delay. Solomon rode the royal mule to the spring GIHON at the eastern base of the hill of Jerusalem, where he was anointed. After the ceremony the crowd ascended the hill behind Solomon with loud shouts and music. Solomon thus became coregent with David. The Gihon spring, the main water source for Jerusalem, may have had religious associations, making it an appropriate place for an anointing ceremony (Miller 1990, 331). The site was also a suitable location for the royal procession up into the city, accompanied by the repeated shout *Long live King Solomon* (vv. 34, 39).

1:41-50. Adonijah's panic. Solomon's installation had been accomplished with such dispatch that Adonijah and his guests were still at his banquet at *En-Rogel* (cf. 1:9) when they received the news. The messenger gave an account that could only be from an eyewitness, including David's expression of gratitude to the LORD for allowing him to live to see the kingdom passed safely to his son Solomon (vv. 47-48).

Adonijah's guests fled the banquet in panic, not only because of the *fait accompli* but also because of the overwhelming support for Solomon represented by Zadok, Nathan, and Benaiah, the officer over David's bodyguard and two of its groups, *the Cherethites* (Cretans) and *Pelethites* (Philistines), mercenaries whose only allegiance was to David. Adonijah fled in fear and seized *the horns of the altar* (vv. 50-51; cf. 2:28) thus claiming divine protection at the sanctuary (according to Exod 21:12-14 one innocent of murder could claim sanctuary).

1:51-53. Solomon's response. Adonijah insisted that Solomon swear an oath that he would not slay him. Solomon refused such a guarantee, leaving Adonijah's fate to the course of events. There could be little doubt in Solomon's mind of the threat posed by Adonijah, and later events proved him right. But for the moment, perhaps fearing negative reaction from the populace if he violated Adonijah's claim of sanctuary, Solomon was satisfied with Adonijah's oath of loyalty. At least Solomon could not be accused of precipitate action on a fast-paced day filled with portentous events.

Solomon's Moves to Secure Power, 2:1-46

Although Solomon came to the throne swiftly and with formidable royal and popular support, there remained various groups and dissident persons with the potential to sow discord. David had never enjoyed the support of all the population. Some never forgave him for his perceived treatment of the house of Saul. Others were offended at his moral lapses and his cultic activities undertaken at his own initiative. The first item on Solomon's agenda was to deal with those who could oppose him and to strike fear in the hearts of others.

2:1-9. David's counsel to Solomon. Verses 2-4 are a deuteronomic insert. David's deathbed valedictory reflects deuteronomic concerns: *statutes, commandments, ordinances, testimonies, law of Moses,* and the conditional nature of the LORD's promise to perpetuate David's house (cf. Deut 17:14-20). The emphasis upon condition is contrary to the unconditional promises in 2 Sam 7:11-16, where the Davidic covenant is established.

Verses 5-9 contain David's pragmatic advice to Solomon. Personal scores remained to be settled with persons who could also be a threat to Solomon's reign. First was *Joab,* David's nephew and general of the army (see Gregory 1990, 453). David's relationship with Joab was complex. Joab's loyalty was to the person of David alone. David had often complained of his inability to control the sons of his sister Zeruiah, but Joab, Abishai, and Asahel consistently solved David's problems in such a way as to forestall immediate personal criticism of the king. Nevertheless, Joab's murder of two of David's opponents in a time of peace reflected poorly on David. In any case Joab's independence could only be a threat to Solomon, especially in light of Joab's alliance with Adonijah. Then there was *Shimei* of the house of Saul who had placed a curse on David for terminating the house of Saul through bloodshed, a charge David did not deny (v. 8; cf. 2 Sam 16:5-14). David had refused to kill Shimei then and later (2 Sam 19:16-23). But now David advised Solomon to find a way to remove the threat to the kingdom represented by Shimei.

2:10-12. The death of David. This is the first of the formulas used by the Deuteronomistic History editor to conclude the reports of the reigns of kings. However, lacking here is one other typical feature of such formulas: an evaluation of the king's reign.

2:13-25. The death of Adonijah. That Adonijah had not abandoned hope for the kingship is confirmed by his seemingly innocent request of *Bathsheba* to intercede with *Solomon* to grant him permission to marry *Abishag*, David's nurse and member of the harem. When Bathsheba acceded to his wish and made the request known to Solomon, Solomon's response was explosive, for he understood exactly Adonijah's intent. To have access to the king's harem was tantamount to making a claim on the throne. Adonijah was executed by *Benaiah*.

2:26-27. The banishment of Abiathar. During much of David's reign he was served by two priests, ABIATHAR and ZADOK. The potential for discord was always present, but David seemed unable to resolve the issue. When Abiathar supported Adonijah's claim to kingship, Solomon was free to solve the problem of priestly leadership. Abiathar's banishment *to Anathoth* is presented as fulfillment of prophecy concerning *the house of Eli* (v. 27; cf. 1 Sam 2:27-36). References to the fulfillment of prophetic oracles are a characteristic feature of the Books of Kings.

2:28-35. The death of Joab. When Joab heard of Adonijah's execution, he *fled to the tent of the LORD* and claimed sanctuary by seizing *the horns of the altar* (v. 28). At his refusal to leave sanctuary, *Benaiah* was ordered to slay him there for the bloodguilt he had brought to David's house. Benaiah was promoted to general of the army in Joab's place.

2:36-46. The death of Shimei. There remained now only the threat represented by the house of Saul in the person of *Shimei*. Solomon ordered him to reside in Jerusalem in order to keep him under surveillance, and Shimei agreed to the condition. But when two of his servants fled to Gath, Shimei left the city to reclaim them. Solomon now had his legitimate reason to remove Shimei's threat to the stability of his reign, and again Benaiah was sent to carry out the execution. Solomon was now in control of the political situation. The story of the succession was now complete.

The Reign of Solomon, 3:1–11:43

Solomon's Wisdom and Administration, 3:1–4:34

3:1-3. Introduction to Solomon's reign. The account of Solomon's reign began with two characteristic themes: international relations and the emphasis on the Temple. Solomon's treaty with Egypt was formalized by his marriage to *Pharaoh's daughter*, a move that was intended to illustrate his political power and astuteness. And yet, ironically, Solomon's history is concluded with the folly of his marriages to foreign women (see 1 Kgs 11:1-8). Since the Temple was not yet built, Solomon and the people worshiped at *the high places* in the land (v. 2), a matter of grave concern to the Deuteronomistic Historian even at this early date. The reigns of all subsequent kings of Judah up to the time of Josiah were evaluated in light of their relationship to the high places. The high places were local shrines where worship was not under central regulation.

3:4-15. Solomon's prayer for wisdom. Despite the Deuteronomistic Historian's reservations about high places, it was a fact that Solomon had an unforgettable experience at Gibeon, the great HIGH PLACE. In his dream experience Solomon asked of the LORD a receptive mind so that he might discern between good and evil in his governance. In his prayer he acknowledged God's faithfulness to David, he confessed his own inexperience, and he asked for wisdom that only the deity could grant. The LORD not only granted Solomon's request to be given understanding to render right judgments, but also gave him what he had not requested, *long life and riches* (v. 11).

Verse 14 again emphasizes the conditional nature of the promise to David's house characteristic of the Deuteronomist. Solomon became the patron of the wisdom tradition in Israel. Indeed, in the story of his reign, repeated reference is made to his wisdom.

3:16-28. The first test of Solomon's wisdom. This story of the two mothers and their babies, in which all the characters are anonymous, even the king, was utilized to show how all the people came to acknowledge Solomon's divine gift of wisdom. The classic story is a masterpiece of the storyteller's art. All the evidence in the case consisted of the contradictory claims of the two women. How could one determine the mother of the living child? The truth could be ascertained only by a stratagem. The king ordered that the living child be cut in two. The result was as he had hoped: the real mother showed her love by asking that the child be given to the other woman. And so all Israel came to acknowledge that the LORD had given Solomon wisdom to be able to render right decisions.

4:1-28 [MT 4:1–5:8]. Solomon's administration. The location of the account of Solomon's administrative organization of Israel between two passages about his wisdom, 3:4-28 and 4:29-34 (MT 5:9-14), suggests that the Deuteronomistic Historian viewed the organization as an expression of wisdom or sagacity. The account reflects use of official documents. Verses 1-6 list Solomon's cabinet at some point in his reign. The growth in the number of cabinet positions can be determined by a comparison of two lists from David's reign, 2 Sam 8:15-18 and 20:23-26, with this list. Especially significant in Solomon's cabinet was the addition of a bureaucrat who supervised *the officers*.

Solomon divided the kingdom of Israel into twelve districts (vv. 8-19), each under its officer, with all twelve officers under the supervision of *Azariah son of Nathan* (v. 5). The twelve districts sometimes approximated tribal boundaries and sometimes ignored them. Each district had to provide supplies for the court of King Solomon for one month (vv. 22-23, 27-28). The last part of v. 19 should be read "and there was one officer who was in the land," referring to the cabinet official Azariah (v. 5). The text suggests that Judah was not included in the rotation of responsibility to provide for the king (see Kallai 1986, 40–72). Ironically, while Solomon's redistricting is placed literarily in the context of passages highlighting his wisdom, such preferential treatment of Judah and the erasure of some tribal boundaries contributed to the ultimate rebellion of Israel.

Solomon's relationships to the subregions of David's empire continued (vv. 21, 24), whether through occupation or by treaty. The descriptions of Solomon's chariot forces in v. 26 probably should read "four thousand stalls and twelve thousand horsemen" (see 2 Chr 9:25; cf. 1 Kgs 10:26-29).

4:29-34 [MT 5:9-14]. Solomon's wisdom. Wisdom was regarded as a divine gift. The tradition of Solomon's extraordinary wisdom is to be accepted in the light of the long–standing international wisdom traditions to which v. 30 refers. Solomon's wisdom included the collecting of proverbs (the standard wisdom saying), as well as songs, and the making of lists of flora and fauna. Solomon became the patron of wisdom in Israel.

The Building and Dedication of the Temple, 5:1–9:25

Since the account of the building of the Temple and its dedication constitutes the bulk of the history of Solomon's reign, there can be no doubt that the Deuteronomistic Historian viewed this event as the signal act of Solomon's reign. The editorial comment at 9:25—*So he [Solomon] completed the house*—justifies viewing 5:1–9:25 as a literary unit. The account begins with two necessary features: the acquisition of building materials, especially timber, and the organization of the work force.

5:1-12. Solomon's pact with Hiram of Tyre. Solomon continued David's treaty relationship with Hiram (cf. 2 Sam 5:11-12). The phrase *had always been a friend* in v. 1 is treaty terminology. Solomon required timber, which only the mountains of Lebanon could supply. Solomon and Hiram concluded the compact, Hiram agreeing to furnish the timber and Solomon agreeing to make payment with agricultural products. Verse 12 indicates that the business arrangement was viewed in the context of a parity treaty between Solomon and Hiram.

5:13-18 [MT 5:27-32]. The labor force. Solomon raised a work force of 30,000 citizens from Israel (Canaan and Judah are not mentioned) and placed them under the command of Adoniram, the cabinet minister in charge of compulsory labor (4:6). They were to work in Lebanon for one month of every three (vv. 13-14). This treatment of Israelites became a major reason for the later division of the kingdom (11:26-28; 12:1-16). Also, there was a larger work force to quarry and dress stones in the HILL COUNTRY and to transport it to Jerusalem (vv. 15-17). Their nationality is not clear nor are the terms of their employment (unless the work force is the same as that described in 9:20-23), although it is generally held that they were also part of the corvée. The stated number of workers seems very high. An alternative is to understand the word *thousand* to have another of its senses, "unit." Thus there would have been seventy groups or units of carriers and eighty groups of quarrymen overseen by three groups of three hundred (cf. the numbers in 2 Chr 2:17-18).

6:1-7:51. The Temple and its furnishings. The construction of the Temple was begun in the fourth year of Solomon's reign and was completed in seven years. Its main features, floor plan, and furnishings and decorations were typical of contemporary temples in Syria-Palestine. Its dimensions were about ninety feet in length, thirty feet in width, and forty-five feet in height. It was also typical that sanctuaries in the ancient Near East were built according to a perceived heavenly prototype or blueprint (such as given to King Gudea in Sumer, to Moses [Exod 25:9], and to David [2 Chron 28:19]), but nothing of the kind is mentioned here.

The Temple had three main rooms: the entry hall, the central hall, and the inner sanctuary or holy of holies, the repository of the ARK of the covenant and the dimensions of which formed a perfect cube. The Temple was oriented to the east. Constructed along the outside walls on three sides were three floors of chambers. In its floor plan and decorations it would have resembled in many ways the temples in most areas of Syria-Palestine.

Solomon employed Hiram, a craftsman from Tyre, for the exacting and specialized work of casting large items in bronze, such as the two bronze pillars in front of the temple and the bronze sea (7:13-14, 40-44). These bronzes were cast in the alluvial clay east of the Jordan River.

8:1-66. The dedication of the Temple. The service of dedication was begun with the transport of the ark of the covenant, the tent of meeting, and the sacred vessels by solemn procession to the Temple. By this action Solomon intended to demonstrate the continuity of the new era and its new cultic establishment with Israel's formative past. But, as it turned out, the old religion, with its emphasis on a God who was not tied to a place and who could be with the people wherever they went and with its stress on justice for all Israel, fitted poorly the needs of a new dynastic state. The danger, often realized, was that religion would be co-opted by the state to serve its imperial political and economic goals.

It is to be noted that Solomon was the main cultic official on this occasion. He organized and directed the dedication service, he gave the blessings and the prayer, and he consecrated the middle of the Temple court where he offered the sacrifices. In ancient Near Eastern practice the king was by definition the chief priest who delegated to the priesthood the daily cultic responsibilities. If King Saul, a transition figure with no history of kingship in Israel to guide him, could be faulted for challenging priestly prerogatives (as in 1 Sam 13:5-15), Solomon makes clear his intention to be king in every sense.

Solomon addressed the audience (vv. 14-21), recounting the events leading up to the building of the Temple. The passage reflects the concerns of the Deuteronomistic editor, especially in the stress on the *name* of the LORD being resident in the Temple; the name of the LORD dwelled there (cf. v. 27). Thus the God of Israel could not be located in or restricted to any one "place," and therefore could not be limited or manipulated by cultic practices. The tension between these two ideas of the Temple's role is illustrated in the contrast between Solomon's statement in v. 13 and

the quotation in v. 16 from 2 Sam 7:5-6. The historian was anxious to negate the idea that the Temple was a guarantee of the LORD's presence among the people (cf. Jer 7).

The prayer of Solomon (vv. 22-53) begins with a recounting of the promises to the house of David. Stress is laid on the Temple as a house of prayer, and Solomon's main request was that prayers offered in this place would receive a favorable hearing in heaven. Seven typical human situations are included to represent the totality of human need (vv. 31-53). This rendition of the prayer is the product of the Deuteronomistic Historian, whose characteristic concerns are reflected throughout: for example, the conditional nature of the promises to David, the "name"-theology, and the idea that calamity is the result of sin.

8:54-66. The conclusion of the dedication service. Solomon blessed the people, asking the LORD to be present with them and ending with an admonition to purity of devotion. There followed the lavish sacrifices appropriate for such an occasion and a feast in which all could participate. The event took place at the time of the traditional Feast of Booths (TABERNACLES) in the autumn.

9:1-9. The second oracle to Solomon. Just as Solomon's reign began with a THEOPHANY (3:3-14), so now at this critical juncture there is a second divine appearance. This theophany is timed well, for it cautions the king, at a time when he might be tempted to overstep his limits, to guard his personal behavior; and it reminds him of the conditional nature of the promises to the house of David. The ORACLE itself reflects the reality of the Babylonian exile and explains ahead of time the loss of Temple and land. Ultimately Solomon failed to heed the admonition in all its terms.

9:10-14. Solomon's financial troubles. After twenty years of extensive building enterprises, Solomon's resources were so diminished that he was forced to engage in a new transaction with King Hiram of Tyre. The building program had been paid for. Now new resources were needed to keep the administration running. This time Solomon had to cede Hiram twenty Israelite towns in consideration of a large amount of cash for current expenses, a deal less than satisfactory to Hiram. The purpose of these verses is opaque unless they intend to presage the future loss of territory because of Solomon's unwise policies.

9:15-25. The account of forced labor. The account of compulsory labor in 5:13-18 seems to relate specifically to the activities relative to the building of the

Temple. Here however it is clear that Solomon's nationwide building program required a permanent levy of forced labor, which in turn required a larger group of overseers (v. 23). Verses 20-22 restrict the levy to non-Israelite residents in the land, although 5:13 claimed that Israelite citizens had been pressed into compulsory service. Excavations have recovered considerable evidence of Solomon's building and fortification program.

The *Millo* (v. 15, "filling") refers to the terraced area on the eastern slope of Jerusalem that provided space for small dwellings within the city wall. The area required periodic rebuilding.

The last statement in v. 25 is an editorial addition to indicate that the account of the building of the temple was now complete, bringing an end to the section of narratives that began at 5:1.

Solomon's Wealth and Wisdom, 9:26–10:29

These verses are to be contrasted with 3:1–4:34. Whereas Solomon initially asked for wisdom so that he might render justice for the people, and was promised wealth and reputation in addition, now Solomon employs wisdom for his own enrichment. What began with great promise now begins to founder in excess (see Walsh and Begg 1990, 167).

9:26-28, 10:11-12, 22. Solomon's sea ventures. Surrounding and embedded within the Queen of Sheba story is information about Solomon's overseas ventures. Israel had no maritime tradition. Solomon concluded business agreements with Tyre, a seafaring nation, to engage in trade in the Red Sea area and in the Mediterranean. Solomon financed the building of a fleet and provided Hiram overland access to the Gulf of Aqabah, the eastern arm of the Red Sea, while Hiram provided shipbuilding expertise and trained sailors. In addition Solomon ordered a fleet built to join Hiram's in the Mediterranean trade.

Ophir (9:28) is probably to be located in east Africa (Somalia?; see Van Beek 1962a). *Ships of Tarshish* (10:22) were large, oceangoing ships. (De Vries 1990, 820–21, surveys ships and the place of maritime ventures in the ancient Near East.) It is in the context of such international trade that the visit of the Queen of Sheba is placed.

10:1-10, 13. The queen of Sheba's visit. The kingdom of the Sabeans (Heb. *Sheba*) was located in the southwest corner of Arabia, ideally situated to command the Red Sea trade (see Van Beek 1962b). Although the Queen of Sheba was impressed with Solomon's wisdom and the splendor of the court, her visit was a trade mission (vv. 10, 13). Solomon's successful entry into the Red Sea commerce made such a visit imperative.

The story of the queen's visit serves the historian's purpose of placing Solomon's wisdom in an unfavorable light. Solomon uses the divine gift for personal aggrandizement, and it is the foreign queen who blesses the LORD and who reminds Solomon that his chief duty is to bring justice to all the people (see Walsh and Begg 1990, 167; see also Wiles 1990, 816).

10:14-25. Solomon's wealth. Solomon acquired vast wealth from international trade and from interior taxation (it is possible to read in v. 15 "from the taxes of the traders" [Ugaritic *unt*, Akk. *unuššu*]). What is remarkable is that all this wealth was for personal and secular use, none of it for the Temple. Again the historian subtly draws attention to the declining values characterizing Solomon's reign.

10:26-29. Solomon the horse trader. Aspects of these verses are unclear. What is clear is that Solomon was able financially to equip a substantial chariot force and to distribute units to fortress cities in strategic locations. The verses also suggest that Solomon regulated horse and chariot trade between Egypt and northwest Mesopotamia. *Kue* was located in Cilicia. Thus Solomon not only increased his wealth but also was able to secure military intelligence about the forces available to neighboring kingdoms.

The Sins of the Kingdom Exposed, 11:1-43

11:1-13. Solomon's moral failure. The reign that began with such great promise ended miserably. Throughout the account the historian gave hints of incipient trouble for Solomon because of certain policies. In this chapter Solomon is charged specifically with "going after other gods," a particular Deuteronomistic concern. In the LORD's two appearances to Solomon (3:5-14; 9:1-9), the king had been cautioned about the contingent nature of the promises made to the house of David, and particularly about worshiping other gods (9:6-7). Now the historian charged Solomon with allowing his foreign wives to turn away his heart to their gods, with the result that Solomon built shrines for their gods on Israelite soil. Divine judgment was severe: loss of all territory except for the patrimony of Judah. The historian has thus given a moral interpretation to what was also a political and social policy.

11:14-40. Solomon's adversaries. Although the preceding account of Solomon's reign gives little hint of internal or external opposition, this concluding section provides a more realistic picture. The account states that God raised up two adversaries against Solomon, *Hadad the Edomite* (v. 14) and *Rezon . . . [of] . . . Damascus* (vv. 23-24). Hadad had escaped the slaughter carried out by David and Joab (2 Sam 8:13-14) and had been granted sanctuary in Egypt. Rezon had survived David's campaigns against the Aramean army (2 Sam 8:3-6; 10:15-19) and had managed to become king in Damascus. Both kings posed serious threats to Solomon because Edom and Damascus were parts of the empire, although the account offers no indication of their specific actions nor any military response by Solomon.

Of more immediate consequence was the threat posed by *Jeroboam son of Nebat* (12:2), an Ephraimite who had served Solomon as an overseer of forced labor from the house of Joseph during the repair of the Millo. But the story is even more about *the prophet Ahijah* (v. 29), who, like prophets before and after him, was a kingmaker. Ahijah performed a prophetic symbolic act to deliver the oracle of God. He ripped a garment into twelve pieces, gave Jeroboam ten of the pieces, and announced that the LORD was about to rip the kingdom from Solomon's hands. The ten pieces represented the ten northern tribes of Israel, the future kingdom of Israel. Jeroboam was given the same assurance that had been given to Solomon: if he would follow the LORD, he would be given a secure dynasty like David's. When Solomon heard of it, Jeroboam had to flee to Egypt until Solomon's death. This last episode of Solomon's story thus serves as the transition to chaps. 12–14.

11:41-43. Death of Solomon. The Deuteronomistic Historian provides the typical summation to Solomon's reign. The *Book of the Acts of Solomon* (v. 41) was one of several written resources used by the historian, including official registers, memoranda, and archival materials. Solomon was succeeded in Jerusalem by *Rehoboam*, Solomon's son by Naamah of Ammon.

Synchronic History of Israel and Judah, 1 Kgs 12:1–2 Kgs 17:41

From the time of the division of the kingdom of Solomon until the fall of Samaria, the historian correlates the reign of a king of either kingdom with the reign of his counterpart. There were two kingdoms, but from the prophetic point of view, there was still one people of God. (For the evaluation formula, see commentary at 14:21–15:24.)

Jeroboam I of Israel, 12:1–14:20

12:1-25. The division of the kingdom. King David wore three crowns: the crowns of Judah, of Jerusalem, and of Israel. David's relationships with Judah and Israel differed: he had been anointed king over Judah at Hebron (2 Sam 2:4), but he became king over Israel by political agreement, a covenant (2 Sam 5:1-3). Now REHOBOAM, Solomon's successor, seeks Israel's acceptance in the same way. For David and Solomon, the service of the northern tribes had been disproportionately difficult. The elders of Judah, wise enough to understand the rightness of Israel's complaint that Israel had been neglected, advised Rehoboam to change the policy. But Rehoboam, following the insulting and obscene advice of his younger advisors, permanently alienated the northern tribes. Verse 16 includes a familiar dismissal formula (cf. 2 Sam 20:1): *What share do we have . . . ? . . . To your tents. . . . Look now to your own house.*

The cry *To your tents, O Israel!* may signal also an intention to return to the values of the distant past. But in v. 15 the historian pointed out that these events occurred according to the will of the LORD as fulfillment of Ahijah's prophecy to Jeroboam (11:29-31).

Jeroboam, who had sought asylum in Egypt, returned to Israel and was proclaimed king of Israel. To underscore that the division of the kingdom was in accord with the divine will, Shemaiah, a prophet from Judah, delivered an oracle to Rehoboam to desist from war (vv. 22-24). Jeroboam fortified two key sites, SHECHEM in the hill country and PENUEL in Transjordan, to discourage an immediate attack from Judah.

12:26-33. Jeroboam's cultic policy. For political reasons JEROBOAM I instituted cultic changes as alternatives to the Jerusalem cult: alternative sanctuaries at DAN and BETHEL, new symbols (golden bulls), encouragement of high places, a new priesthood not restricted to the Levites, and a new cultic calendar (see Bailey 1990b, 440).

The Deuteronomistic Historian condemned Jeroboam for all these changes, and in the Deuteronomistic History these became the *sin . . . of Jeroboam* (13:34; 2 Kgs 3:3; cf. 1 Kgs 15:34; 16:2, 19; etc.) according to which all the succeeding kings of Israel were judged. (See the recurring phrase *He [or king's name] did what was evil in the sight of the LORD, walking in the way of Jeroboam and in the sin that he caused*

Israel to commit [15:34] throughout the narratives of the northern kings.)

It is unlikely that Jeroboam intended the golden bulls to be worshiped as idols. The conservative population of the north would have deposed him summarily. Rather, like the ark and cherubim, the bulls were to be visible symbols of the LORD's invisible presence (see Bailey 1990a, 127). However, the historian's criticism was validated by future events when Israelites did in fact worship the golden bulls as deities.

13:1-34. Jeroboam's intransigence. Jeroboam was condemned, not for his moral failure, but for his cultic innovations. In vv. 1-5 *a man of God* from Judah prophesied the eventual profanation of the cult places by a descendant of David. The chapter concludes with Jeroboam completely undeterred, confirming his policy of appointing non-Levitic priests and placing them at the high places. For the historian the fall of Israel was now determined.

Imbedded in the chapter is the story of the two prophets (vv. 11-32). (Note that both are unnamed, but are distinguished by the designations *the man of God* [from Judah] and *the prophet* [from Israel].) Much is involved in the story: differing political commitments, differing views of the divine will, and differing prophetic traditions. *The man of God* from Judah was faithful in his proclamation of the oracle but was disqualified for his moral failure in terms of the circumstances of his mission. *The prophet* from the north lied, but he faithfully proclaimed the other prophet's disobedience. The ability of the people to determine the true prophet remained problematic throughout the remaining history of the kingdoms. In the end no one criterion could be used to determine who was a true prophet from the LORD (see also, e.g., 1 Kgs 22).

14:1-20. The end of Jeroboam's reign. The end of Jeroboam's reign was prophesied by the same prophet who prophesied his rise, AHIJAH of Shiloh. Classical prophecy arose at the same time as the monarchy in Israel and provided a corrective voice from the LORD with regard to royal policy. It is thus important to the historian to emphasize throughout the story of the kingship the crucial role of prophecy in national history, including the making and deposing of kings. Ahijah had informed Jeroboam that the longevity of his dynasty would depend on his faithfulness to the commandments of the LORD (11:38). But Jeroboam's cultic policies doomed him and all the men of his house (vv. 10-16). The immediate death of Jeroboam's infant son ABIJAH was confirmation of the initiation of

the judgment, although the historian suggests that Abijah was mercifully spared the sight of the dynasty's eventual ruin (vv. 12-13).

Early Kings of Judah, 14:21–15:24

From this point the historian provides evaluations of the reigns of the kings of Israel and Judah. The formula of evaluation typically offers the following data: (1) the name of the king, the length of the reign, synchronism with the reign of the king of the other kingdom, identification of the capital, and, for the kings of Judah, the naming of their mothers; (2) evaluations of the reigns in terms of cultic activity; and (3) accounts of the kings' deaths, references to other written sources, and the name of each successor.

14:21-31. The reign of Rehoboam. Apart from the treatment of REHOBOAM's disastrous decision related in 12:1-15, the historian highlighted three aspects of his reign. First, all Judah was condemned for cultic sins: worship at high places, use of cultic symbols and images of the Canaanite cult, and sacred prostitution. Second, mention is made of SHISHAK's invasion of the land because it resulted in the loss of the golden shields, which had a cultic use. Third, there is a brief reference to continual warfare with the north despite the prophetic restriction of 12:22-24. Also, twice it is mentioned that Rehoboam's mother was a princess of Ammon (vv. 21, 31), as though to suggest that the reader should expect nothing better from Rehoboam.

15:1-8. The reign of Abijam. Rehoboam's son and successor was Abijam (ABIJAH in 1 Chr 3:10; 2 Chr 13:1ff.), whose name means "my father is Yam," the Canaanite god of the sea. Abijam ruled but three years, but was judged a failure because he followed Rehoboam's example.

15:9-24. Good King Asa. Asa was the first of the reforming kings of Judah, receiving a qualified approval from the historian. His only listed blemish was his failure to remove the high places, a matter of particular importance in every period for the Deuteronomistic Historian. Asa went so far as to remove the queen mother from her office because of her devotion to the goddess ASHERAH. The *queen mother* was the mother of the ruling king and a very important person in the court (in this case of course it was Asa's own mother Maacah [v. 13]): compare, for example, Bathsheba after the death of David (1 Kings 2:13-25).

Asa's cultic reform may have been a part of his plan to inspire a united nationalism in the face of the threat from Baasha, the king of Israel who provocatively fortified Ramah on the border between the kingdoms. So serious was this threat that Asa made a treaty with Aram to break its prior treaty with Israel, and thus come to Judah's aid. This dependence on foreign alliances for national defense was a harbinger for the future, a policy that evoked almost universal condemnation from Israel's prophets. Subsequently Asa imposed compulsory labor for the fortification of Geba and Mizpah, perhaps only for the duration of the crisis.

Early Kings of Israel, 15:25–16:34

15:25-26, 31. Reign of Nadab. NADAB, son of Jeroboam I, reigned only two years and received failing marks from the historian.

15:27-30, 32-34; 16:1-7. Reign of Baasha. Baasha assassinated Nadab while the king was on a military campaign. Before this event Baasha's status is unknown. Baasha's first act as king was to kill all the sons of the house of Jeroboam. This was interpreted by the Deuteronomistic Historian as a fulfillment of Ahijah's prophecy: *I will cut off from Jeroboam every male* (14:10-11). This act of conspiracy and assassination was to be replayed several times in Israel's history, to the detriment of the nation's stability. The prophet Jehu credited Baasha's rise to the will of the LORD to terminate Jeroboam's dynasty, but concluded that because Baasha replicated the sin of Jeroboam, his house also would be terminated (16:1-4).

16:8-14. The reign of Elah. Elah's reign was ended in its second year by the conspiracy of Zimri, one of his military commanders. Zimri destroyed the house of Baasha, again in accordance with the prophetic word (16:1-4). However, the troops of Israel, still at the siege of Gibbethon initiated by Baasha, refused Zimri support and named Omri, the army commander, as king. Zimri's claim to the throne lasted only seven days. The army besieged the capital TIRZAH and Zimri committed suicide.

16:21-28. The reign of Omri. Omri's success against Zimri did not win him universal support. The Israelite population was divided for several years over who should succeed Elah. Omri's forces finally won, and despite the brevity of his kingship there began one of the most notable reigns among all the kings of Israel and Judah.

Omri was an able administrator. He moved the capital from the pesthole Tirzah to the virgin site of SAMARIA, thus geographically orienting the insular nation to participate fully in international relations. His dynasty lasted for a generation (forty years), and he so impressed Assyrian officials that they referred to Israel as the house of Omri (*Bit-Humri*) long after his time. Omri's defeat of Moab is recorded on the MESHA STELE (see Pritchard 1955, 320–21). The Deuteronomistic Historian's interest in Omri is virtually limited to his failure to break out of Jeroboam's mold. The historian seems vexed that such a capable ruler should be so foolish and ascribes more evil to him than to any previous ruler. Omri was succeeded by his son Ahab.

Ahab and Elijah, 16:29–22:40

The careers of AHAB and ELIJAH are so interwoven they had to be narrated together. It seems that for the Deuteronomistic Historian Ahab was the prototype of the bad king, since more space is devoted to his reign than to any other king of north or south since the division of the kingdom. Nowhere else can one see more clearly the diametrically opposite agendas of kings and prophets. The reason is clearly summarized in 16:29-34. Omri concluded a political marriage for his son with JEZEBEL, daughter of the king of Sidon, a strong-willed and evangelistic devotee of BAAL Melqart. In the historian's view, this sin exceeded even that of Jeroboam I. (Elijah's career must be understood in the light of the religious threat from Phoenicia, particularly in the struggle to determine which deity was the giver of the rains.)

17:1-24. Elijah's preparation for conflict. Elijah appears without preamble in v. 1, determined to challenge the very heart of the Baal cult: he proclaimed a drought. Baal was venerated as the giver of rain, and thus of life itself. True to the prophetic word, a drought came upon the land for three years, long enough to precipitate an agricultural crisis and to cause an embarrassing theological problem for worshipers of Baal.

The concept of the prophetic word spoken on behalf of the LORD is a major motif of these narratives. But to announce the drought was only part of Elijah's task. Ultimately he had to announce Yahweh's gift of the rain. The three events recounted in chap. 17 prepare Elijah for that crucial announcement.

Two miracle stories narrate Elijah's provisioning by the LORD in the midst of drought (17:3-7, 8-16). The God of Israel, not Baal, is presented as the sustainer of life.

In the second story, Elijah entered ZAREPHATH of Sidon, Baal's domain, where the LORD's sovereignty is affirmed in the matter of the meal and the cruse of oil. The victory of Israel's God is already presaged.

In the third story (17:17-24) the power of the God of Israel to give life to the deceased in Baal's territory is affirmed; the power of the word of the LORD is vindicated in the mouth of a non-Israelite woman (17:24).

18:1-46. The contest on Mount Carmel. Prepared and strengthened, Elijah was sent by the LORD to meet Ahab and to announce that the LORD would *send rain on the earth* (v. 1). Jezebel was already *killing off the prophets of the LORD* (v. 4). Their murder may have been interpreted as the immediate cause of the drought. Obadiah, Ahab's chamberlain, who had kept alive a hundred of the prophets, was sent by Elijah to summon Ahab.

The contest on Mount Carmel was more than a contest of wills between Elijah and Ahab, or between Elijah and Baal's prophets. It was a contest of power between the God of Israel and BAAL. The issue was, which deity actually was giver of rain and thus of life itself? At stake was the faith commitment of the people of Israel; their indecision or vacillation placed the nation's future in jeopardy.

Baal's prophets performed a rain dance (*they limped about the altar*, i.e., performed a knee-bending dance, v. 26), loudly imploring Baal to answer, while they made ritual incisions on their bodies (v. 28). This example of imitative magic produced on the skin parallel rows of incisions resembling the furrows of a plowed field ready to receive the rain, while the dripping blood was thought to cause the rain to fall. Elijah bravely ridiculed their futile efforts (v. 27).

By contrast, after preparing the altar of sacrifice, Elijah calmly prayed to the LORD to answer with fire. When the fire fell and consumed both the offering and the altar (v. 38), the people acknowledged that the LORD was God. It was a great victory, but this powerful vindication of the prophetic word produced no lasting repentance. As the rain began to fall, in exhilaration Elijah ran before Ahab back to Jezreel, apparently in the belief that Ahab was converted.

19:1-21. Elijah at Mountt Horeb. Elijah's euphoria vanished when he discovered that it was Jezebel, not Ahab, with whom he had to deal. When she threatened his life, Elijah fled in haste. Note the piling up of verbs in v. 3: *afraid, got up, fled, came, left*. Elijah deserved censure, but the LORD graciously gave him rest and food for the journey.

Elijah was headed for Mount Horeb, the site where the LORD met Moses in a theophany of fire and thunder and gave him the commandments (there called SINAI). Perhaps Elijah expected the LORD to repeat that ancient

event and thus redeem the situation. Instead, Elijah was confronted by the LORD for his cowardice. The LORD accepted no excuses. But the LORD met Elijah's expectations in a totally unexpected way, not by a traditional theophany with convulsions of nature, but in "a sound of quiet stillness" (v. 12; cf. ERV and ASV mg.; NRSV, *a sound of sheer silence*).

Elijah was being taught that the LORD was master, not just of the past, but of the future. Elijah sought the comfort of the past, but he learned that it is the future that conveys meaning (Baly 1976, 86–90). Instead of accepting Elijah's resignation of his office, the LORD gave Elijah new tasks, for example, to *anoint Hazael as king over Aram* (Syria; v. 15). HAZAEL of ARAM would be a source of great suffering for Israel. Furthermore, Elijah was to anoint JEHU as king of Israel. Jehu would terminate Omri's dynasty. Finally, Elijah was to anoint ELISHA as his prophet successor (v. 16). But Elijah was to accomplish only the last task.

20:1–22:40. Ahab's final days. The three episodes in these chapters highlight the increasing conflict between Ahab and the prophets. While Ahab's bravery and political acumen are evident—even on occasion enjoying the LORD's support—his bad decisions and moral failure are credited with hastening his end.

First Kings 20:1-43 narrate two campaigns in Ahab's ongoing struggles with Aram. When Samaria was besieged by the Arameans, Ahab showed exemplary bravery. An unnamed prophet promised victory from the LORD so that Ahab would recognize the supremacy of the LORD, and Israel won an astonishing victory. The next spring a refurbished Aramean army again attacked, and again a prophet delivered a proof oracle promising victory. Again Israel was victorious. But the victories were tarnished by Ahab's decision to spare BEN-HADAD's life and to make a treaty with him (20:31-34). Another prophet denounced this decision and predicted Ahab's death. The victorious king went home *resentful and sullen* (20:42-43).

The episode of Naboth and his vineyard is related in 21:1-29. The vineyard lay adjacent to Ahab's winter palace at Jezreel. Ahab made what appears, on the surface, to be a fair offer of purchase, but Naboth refused to sell because the property was "the inheritance of my fathers" (21:3 RSV). According to legal tradition, family property was not to be alienated permanently. The principle involved was that the land belonged to the LORD; the landholder was steward, not owner (Lev 25:23-24). Persons could not enrich themselves at the LORD's expense by selling the patrimony for monetary gain. Ahab grew sullen because Naboth was legally correct. However, Jezebel arranged a false charge to be brought against Naboth. He was executed by stoning. This judicial murder, the "shedding of innocent blood," brought immediate condemnation from Elijah. Ahab's demise is again predicted, together with editorializing by the Deuteronomistic Historian (vv. 22-26). The story functions as an explanation for Ahab's untimely demise.

The story of Naboth's vineyard calls to mind the parable of Nathan before King David (2 Sam 12). Just as David stood condemned for his moral failures as an Israelite, a son of the covenant despite his being king, so also Ahab stood condemned. Kings were subject to the *divine* claim; while they had the *power* to ignore the claims of morality and covenant, they did not have the *right* to do so. It was Elijah's task to say so and to hold the king accountable for personal misdeeds. Just as David could not commit adultery and then try to cover up the act with murder, so also Ahab and Jezebel could not confiscate the property of a citizen of Jezreel by arranging for the citizen's conviction and execution on false charges. Israel's prophets were not engaged only or primarily in a power struggle with the kings. Their struggle was for the cause of public and private righteousness.

The third episode, 22:1-40, provides the account of Ahab's final battle with Aram, this time with the collaboration of JEHOSHAPHAT of Judah. At the center is another confrontation with a prophet, MICAIAH SON OF IMLAH, who predicted that Ahab would not survive the battle. Ahab died as a result of a chance shot by an Aramean bowman.

This long story of Micaiah and King Ahab is of great value in understanding the struggle between kings and prophets. It offers insights on how prophets came to receive their messages from God, on how such messages were to be heard by the community and its leaders, and on how individual prophets managed to survive when they were out of favor with the political authorities.

While the narrative cannot be dated precisely, it probably belonged to the collection of Elijah and Elisha traditions that the Deuteronomistic Historian had available and incorporated into the Deuteronomistic History. It is thus considerably older than the late-seventh century and probably gives us reliable information on the standing of prophets at least a century earlier.

Prophets received messages through singing (see 2 Kgs 3:15) and dancing (1 Kgs 18), but they also received messages through visions like those of Micaiah—of *all Israel scattered on the mountains, like sheep that have no shepherd* (1 Kgs 22:17) or of the LORD on the throne debating with the heavenly host about Ahab and his misdeeds (1 Kgs 22:19-22). These visions, however, had to be interpreted by prophets, and the interpretations were presented along with the reports of the visions, intepretations and reports that of course could be and at times were falsified (see v. 23).

Micaiah was hated by Ahab, we are told, because he prophesied nothing favorable for Ahab (22:8); his was largely a negative witness. The hundreds of prophets who told the king exactly what he wanted to hear are clearly considered in this story to be less reliable than the one who gave a different message. But Micaiah is also ready to have his message tested by the historical outcome. If Ahab returns from battle unharmed, then the LORD has not spoken through Micaiah (v. 28), and Micaiah the prophet is a false prophet.

But there is a deeper test, suggested by the visions of Micaiah. Prophets are those who have been in the heavenly presence, have heard words and seen plans of events to be played out on earth. Jeremiah (23:22) speaks of God's "council" (Heb. *sôd*) for the prophets; Amos (3:7) affirms that *God does nothing, without revealing his secret* [or "counsel," Heb. *sôd*] *to his servants the prophets.* Yet, such visions require interpretation, human efforts to understand the divine will and state it plainly.

When prophets give such interpretation, they expose themselves to danger. Micaiah can only acquiesce, stay in prison on lean rations, and await results. Like Jeremiah, he can finally only insist, "in truth the LORD sent me to you" (Jer 26:15).

The three episodes in chaps. 20–22 stress the power of the prophetic word to determine national outcomes. (For a discussion of the extent to which prophetic opposition to the house of Omri was religious opposition to Baal of Tyre, see Hayes and Miller, 1977 403–405.)

The treatment of Ahab's reign in these chapters gives only a hint of his positive contributions. Ahab rebuilt Jericho (16:34) and fortified several cities (22:39). He was famed for his "ivory palace" (22:39) and other building projects at Samaria. The Black Obelisk of Shalmaneser III attests to Ahab's participation in the battle of Qarqar in 853 in a coalition of kings against Assyria (Pritchard 1955, 278–79).

Jehoshaphat and Ahaziah, 22:41–2 Kgs 1:18

22:41-50. Jehoshaphat's reign. The reign of JEHOSH-APHAT of Judah is evaluated in terms similar to Asa's evaluation. He is given qualified approval by the historian. What distinguished his reign was his political accommodation with Israel for common political purposes. This arrangement may hint that Jehoshaphat became a tributary to Ahab, for Ahab's daughter Athaliah was married to JEHORAM, Jehoshaphat's son. Jehoshaphat's later independence is suggested by his refusal to let Ahaziah, Ahab's successor, participate in his planned Red Sea maritime ventures (vv. 47-49).

1 Kgs 22:51–2 Kgs 1:18. Ahaziah's Reign. Ahab's successor AHAZIAH, received the typical negative evaluation from the Deuteronomistic Historian. His reign was apparently without consequence except to provide a setting for another wonder story about Elijah. An injury led Ahaziah to send messengers to the god BAAL-ZEBUB at Ekron, one of the Philistine cities (2 Kgs 1:2). *Baal-zebub*, "lord of the flies," is a deliberate distortion of Baal-zebul, "prince Baal" or "lord prince." Ahaziah's act of bypassing Yahweh to secure an oracle brought Elijah onto the scene, dressed in distinctive prophetic garb. Again the power of Yahweh through the prophetic word is determinative, and again by fire as in 1 Kgs 18 (2 Kgs 1:12).

The Elisha Cycle, 2:1–8:29

The Elisha cycle of narratives (with its completion in 13:14-21) was designed to demonstrate the power of the prophetic word and office as over against royal power. Elisha's power covered all areas, from the alleviation of personal tragedy to war policy. In a series of ten stories, most of them reminiscent of high points in Elijah's career, the historian demonstrated the centrality of the prophetic office for Israelite life. The careers of the kings of Judah and Israel were fitted into the cycle where appropriate.

2:1-25. Elisha, Elijah's successor. As commanded by the LORD (1 Kgs 19:16), Elijah designated Elisha as his successor. Elijah's prophetic commission and power were transmitted through the bestowal of his mantle (1 Kgs 19:19). Elisha had slaughtered the oxen with which he had been plowing and prepared a feast for the people, as though to indicate his entry upon a new vocation (1 Kgs 19:21). Then when Elisha saw Elijah taken up in the whirlwind, he cried out, *The chariots of Israel and its horsemen!* (v. 12). By this cryptic phrase he perhaps suggested the central role of

the prophet in Israel's life—more important than even the nation's armies.

The first test of Elisha's power confirmed the successful transfer of the prophetic office: he struck the waters of the Jordan and they parted (v. 14), just as Elijah had done (v. 8).

Guilds or associations of prophets (see v. 13: *company of prophets*; Heb. "sons of the prophets") are prominent in the Elisha cycle, as also in the Samuel stories. These were prophetic schools featuring a communal existence. When the prophets of Jericho observed Elisha's power, they placed themselves under his direction (2:15) and were sent by him on occasion to perform prophetic tasks (e.g., 9:1-10).

3:1-27. The war in Moab. Since before the time of Omri, Moab had been a vassal state to Israel. But after the death of Ahab, King Mesha of Moab saw his chance for independence and withheld the annual tribute. This account illustrates the continuing hostility between prophets and kings, although Elisha did predict victory for Israel and Judah. But the victory was not total, and Mesha ultimately succeeded in his revolt.

The events of the time are reflected in Mesha's inscription (see Pritchard 1955, 320–21, and MESHA STELE), discovered in 1868 at Dhiban. Mesha recounted the history of Moab's servitude to Israel during the reigns of Omri and Ahab, along with Mesha's successful revolt. The inscription describes Mesha's annexation of Israelite territory in the Transjordan and some of his building projects.

4:1-8:15. Stories about Elisha. The historian's preoccupation with the power of the prophetic word and with the indispensability of the prophetic office for the life of the nation is illustrated here in a series of ten stories. These stories feature prophetic activity both within and outside Israel. The prophetic power knew no national boundaries.

In the first two stories (4:1-7, 8-37) some of Elijah's feats are replayed, only this time on Israelite soil, as though to provide final confirmation of Elisha's succession to Elijah's office.

As in the first two stories, the third and fourth stories (4:38-41, 42-44) emphasize the prophet's power in the contexts of famine, want, and death.

In the fifth story (5:1-27), the emphasis is placed on the LORD's supremacy over Aram's god RIMMON. This theme is illustrated specifically in the matter of the prophet's power to provide healing for an Aramean, *that he may learn that there is a prophet in Israel*

(5:8). The story also tells, perhaps not incidentally, of the faith of a captured child, serving in the household of the warrior NAAMAN. The child believes confidently in the power of Israel's God to heal even the foreign master for whom she labors.

The sixth story, about the axhead (6:1-7), illustrates the prophet's concern for the care of his own prophetic community.

In the seventh story (6:8-23) Elisha's indispensability in time of war is highlighted. Through clairvoyance Elisha provided the means of victory so that Aramean raids into Israel were stopped temporarily. The prophet could accomplish what the king and his army could not.

The eighth story (6:24–7:20) replays the theme of the prophet's role in military victory using the schema of prophecy-fulfillment. Everything happened exactly as the prophet had predicted, followed by the death of the captain who had doubted his prediction.

The ninth story (8:1-6) is a continuation of the second story (4:8-37). The widow, whose son Elisha had restored to life, left for Philistia when famine came. During her absence her house and property had been taken by others. But the king, impressed by Elisha's great deeds for this widow, had her property restored.

The final story in the Elisha collection (8:7-15) again illustrates the prophet's power of life and death and his capacity to act in international politics. In this episode Elisha carried out the LORD's directive to Elijah to designate Hazael to be king of Aram (see 1 Kgs 19:15).

In all these narratives, the historian demonstrates that it is the prophet, the spokesman of the word of the LORD, whose acts and words are decisive, not the king's.

8:16-29. Jehoram and Ahaziah. In the last days of Elisha's ministry, JEHORAM succeeded Jehoshaphat to the throne of Judah; he in turn was succeeded by Ahaziah (or JEHOAHAZ). Neither king accomplished anything of note. Jehoram's reign was highlighted by successful revolts by Edom and Libnah. Ahaziah allied himself with Joram (also called JEHORAM) of Israel to fight the Arameans. Both Jehoram and Ahaziah are portrayed more as faithful members of the house of Omri than as kings of Judah, for in fact Jehoram was married to Athaliah, Omri's granddaughter, and she was Ahaziah's mother. The Deuteronomistic Historian condemned their reigns because they *walked in the way of the kings of Israel* (8:18; cf. 8:27).

From Jehu to the Fall of Samaria, 9:1–17:41

This section of 2 Kings provides a synchronic history of Israel and Judah from the establishment of Jehu's dynasty to the fall of Samaria, 842/1–722.

9:1–10:36. The reign of Jehu. JEHU's violent rise to power is presented as divine judgment on the house of OMRI. Elisha sent one of the prophets to anoint Jehu, a military commander, thus fulfilling the LORD's final commission to Elijah (1 Kgs 19:16). Also, no fewer than six times does the historian interpret Jehu's actions as the fulfillment of prophecy in accord with the word of the LORD (9:6, 26, 36-37; 10:10, 17, 30). Although Jehu's actions against Omri's house and against the Baal cult receive divine approval, he is still condemned for failing to turn away from *the sins of Jeroboam* (10:30-31).

After Jehu's anointing, the part of the army under his command acclaimed him king. He swiftly set out for Jezreel before the wounded king Joram (JEHORAM) could receive news of the conspiracy (9:14-16). In the confrontation of Joram and Jehu, which ironically took place on the property of NABOTH, Jehu slew the king (9:21-26) and moved immediately to slay Ahaziah (JEHOAHAZ) of Judah who had allied himself with Israel in the war against Aram (9:27-28). When Jehu entered JEZREEL, JEZEBEL tauntingly called him Zimri (9:30-31; cf. 1 Kgs 16:8-20), the murderer of Jehu's master. Jezebel was cast from the presentation window of the palace. However, her death did not mean the end of the cult of the Tyrian Baal in Israel.

Although Jehu was in command of Jezreel, the site of the winter palace, he was not yet accepted as king by the leadership of the capital city, Samaria. Tauntingly, Jehu invited the leaders to place one of Joram's sons on the throne and to let the issue be settled on the field of battle. Out of fear, the officials declined. Jehu then sent another letter with ambiguous terms: send the "heads" of the royal house to Jezreel. The officials had to decide whether to interpret "heads" literally or symbolically as "leaders." Either way they were forced into complicity with the conspiracy. They severed the heads of seventy of the men of the royal family and sent them to Jezreel (10:1-11).

With the support of religiously conservative and politically disaffected groups represented by Jehonadab the son of Rechab (cf. Jer 35), Jehu inaugurated his campaign against the cult of Baal. With cunning Jehu gathered the worshipers of Baal into the temple built by Ahab and slaughtered them, turning the sacred precincts of the *temple of Baal* into a latrine (10:18-27).

The effects of Jehu's policies lasted many years. Contact with Phoenicia was severed. Cooperation with Judah was ended. Aram was soon free to devastate a weakened and isolated Israel (10:32-33). And the rise of Assyrian power under SHALMANESER III (858–824) was a harbinger of cruel days to come. Jehu found it necessary to become tributary to Shalmaneser in 841. Jehu is portrayed on the Black Obelisk of Shalmeneser bowing in obeisance and offering tribute (see Pritchard 1955, 280).

Finally, it must be said that Jehu's religious "reform" was not permanent. Real reform had to consist of something more than the slaughter of people and the trashing of temples. (For a review of Jehu's reign and policies, see Hayes and Miller 1977, 408–14.)

11:1–12:21. Joash of Judah. The reign of JOASH is treated at considerable length for two reasons: the death of Athaliah and the renovation of the temple.

When Athaliah learned of the death of her son King Ahaziah, she moved to eliminate all the royal family because they threatened her policy of alliance with Israel. But prince Joash was hidden away until he could be proclaimed king. On the day of his coronation, Athaliah, daughter of Ahab and protector of the Baal cult in Judah, was slain, and the temple of Baal was destroyed. Thus ended the dominance of the house of Omri over the royal house of Judah. The narrator gives details of the saving of Joash from Athaliah's slaughter, the careful planning of the priest JEHOIADA, and the collaboration of portions of the temple guard. It may be that a deliberate contrast is drawn between the bloody revolution of Jehu in the north and the almost bloodless coup in Jerusalem.

With the end of the Baal cult in Jerusalem, attention was turned to the neglected temple of the LORD. Despite initial inaction due to priestly reluctance, the temple was repaired after a system of payment was agreed upon that preserved priestly income. However, the historian's approval of Joash's repair program is tempered by the notice in 12:17-18 that Joash gave up all the treasures of the temple and palace to avert an invasion by Aram. The success of his reign is further muted by the announcement of his assassination (12:20-21; see Long 1991, 145–62).

13:1–14:29. Israel and Judah under Aramean domination. These chapters are to be seen as a literary unit because of the theme of the LORD's mercy shown

to an apostate Israel (13:4-5, 23; 14:26-27; see Long 1991, 163–64).

Damascus continued to dominate Israel and Judah militarily. The army of JEHOAHAZ of Israel was so reduced that it could offer no resistance to DAMASCUS (13:7). But the LORD had mercy and raised up a deliverer (note the pattern in 13:1-5 reminiscent of the pattern in the Book of Judges). The historian seems to point to JEROBOAM II as the deliverer (14:23-29). It is also possible to see the Assyrian king Adad-nirari III (809–782) as a kind of deliverer because of his success against Damascus during these years (Pritchard 1955, 281–82).

Jehoahaz was succeeded by Jehoash (JOASH) as king of Israel. The death of Elisha occurred during his reign. The prophet's death represented the passing of an era, a fact recognized by Jehoash. No longer would the royal court be able to draw on Elisha's military intelligence. Because of the king's lack of confidence, he was able to achieve only limited success against Damascus.

AMAZIAH succeeded Joash as king in Judah. His reign was marked by a disastrous war with Israel after his suggestion of an alliance with Jehoash was insolently rejected (14:8-14). The wall of Jerusalem suffered damage and the temple and palace treasures were taken away to Samaria. In the face of an untiring Aramean foe, this was no time for such confusion. No doubt nationalistic discontent with Amaziah's lack of success figured prominently in his assassination (14:19).

JEROBOAM II (787–747) succeeded Joash as king of Israel. The prosperity of his reign was made possible largely because the Assyrian king Adad-nirari III had weakened Damascus. Jeroboam restored the northern border of Israel and gained territory east of the Jordan River. His reign was marked by stability and renewed prosperity, although its social inequities energized the prophets of the day.

15:1-38. Israel in decline. This chapter may be read as a literary unit. The reigns of five unacceptable Israelite kings are enclosed by the reigns of two good Judean kings (for a full discussion of the structure, see Long 1991, 170–72). The purpose of the literary unit seems to be to highlight the turmoil and decline of the kingdom of Israel, while the kingdom of Judah enjoyed relative stability. However, AZARIAH (UZZIAH) was struck with leprosy, making him ritually unclean. He had to live outside the capital. Azariah's son

Jotham acted as regent (v. 5) and during Jotham's regency the LORD sent REZIN of Aram and PEKAH of Israel against him, indicating hard times for Judah as a result of the advance of Assyrian power.

These waning years (ca. 750–730) were turbulent for Israel. Four of the five kings of Israel during this period were assassinated. Confusion and senseless violence reigned. With ZECHARIAH's death (v. 10), the dynasty of Jehu was terminated, having lasted four generations, as the LORD had promised (v. 12).

The main reason for Israel's unease was the growing power of Assyria, with Assyria's designs on Syria-Palestine. Assyrian power reached its zenith in the reign of TIGLATH-PILESER III (745–727). In 738 MENAHEM of Israel was forced to pay tribute to Assyria and to enter into vassalage in order to retain his throne (15:19-20). In 734–732 Tiglath-pileser directed devastating raids against northern Israel, deporting some of the population to Assyria, because of Pekah's alliance with Rezin of Aram to force Judah to join their rebellion against Assyria (15:29, 37; 16:5; Isa 9:1 [MT 8:23]). Pekah's failed policy resulted in his assassination by Hoshea (15:30; for a full treatment of Tiglath-pileser's policy, see Hayes and Miller 1977, 418–20). Israel was approaching its final hour.

16:1-20. Ahaz of Judah. The reign of AHAZ is presented as a low point in Judean history. He is portrayed by the historian as weak and indecisive, an evaluation that is strengthened by the account of Isaiah's failed attempt to inspire courage and faith in Ahaz (Isa 7).

When Rezin of Aram and Pekah of Israel besieged Jerusalem to try to force Ahaz to join their rebellion against Assyria, Ahaz appealed to Tiglath-pileser of Assyria for protection, paid him tribute and became his vassal. The Assyrian complied by devastating northern Israel (15:29) and by putting an end to the kingdom of Aram (16:9).

Although it is unlikely that Assyria normally required vassals to adopt Assyrian religion, Ahaz is presented as going out of his way to welcome the cult of Assyria. He built an altar, probably of Assyrian design, to replace the bronze altar at the Jerusalem temple. He denigrated the LORD's altar by using it for divination (v. 15). He also dismantled other cultic objects *because of the king of Assyria* (v. 18). Ahaz is condemned by the historian as an apostate king who *walked in the way of the kings of Israel* (v. 3).

17:1-41. The end of the kingdom of Israel. HOSHEA was the last of the kings of Israel. He assassinated

Pekah in order to come to the throne (15:30), perhaps because of Pekah's ill-advised attempt to throw off the Assyrian yoke. Yet Hoshea in his turn rebelled against Assyria, withholding annual tribute and seeking an alliance with Egypt (17:4). SHALMANESER V (727–722) put Hoshea in prison and besieged Samaria for three years. Shalmaneser V died in the course of the campaign, and his successor SARGON II captured the city. Sargon reported deporting 27,290 Israelites to Assyrian provinces (Pritchard 1955, 284-85).

Verses 7-20 contain the historian's theological interpretation of the fall of Israel. In a historical survey he painted a word-picture of thoroughgoing Israelite apostasy. Despite calls to repent sent by prophets (17:13), Israel pursued every sin that the Deuteronomistic Historian abominated, especially the "sins of Jeroboam" the son of Nebat (17:21-23). In 17:29 there is a forecast of Judah's fate for the same sins.

Verses 24-33 describe the theologically horrific sequel to the fall of Samaria. In accord with Assyrian policy, the conqueror deported Israelites to various places in Assyrian provinces and brought to Israel deportees from other conquered nations. With them the foreigners brought their own deities whom they worshiped alongside the God of Israel.

In 17:34b-41 there is a second theological treatment by the historian deploring the Israelite population's acceptance of the new reality. Again using historical recollection, the historian recounted the LORD's command to Israel not to worship other gods. However, even at the time of the writing of the history, the remaining Israelites continued their centuries-long habit of idolatry.

Judah after the Fall of Israel, 18:1–25:30

The Deuteronomistic Historian provided a lengthy theological interpretation for the fall of the kingdom of Israel (chap. 17). After inserting in 17:19 a literary transition to Judah's life alone, the historian details the last century and a half of Judah's political life. The historian wrote amid the ruin of the Judean state. The history is an explanation of the catastrophe. A mixed picture is presented: alternating reigns of good and bad kings (apostate Ahaz, reforming Hezekiah, apostate Manasseh, reforming Josiah), with the last few years of Judah's life taking place in an atmosphere of confusion in the face of the new foreign foe, Babylonia.

18:1-20:21. Reign of Hezekiah. The reign of HEZEKIAH was for the historian a bright spot in

Judean history despite the loss in warfare and the ensuing suffering for the population. Hezekiah is presented as a religious reformer, a king who intended to restore the territory of the kingdom of David, and as one who was unafraid to challenge the power of Assyria.

The historian's laudatory summary of Hezekiah's reign is presented in 18:1-12. In accord with 18:13 Hezekiah's reign began in 715. His policies were opposite those of his father Ahaz. Oddly, only one verse (18:4) summarizes Hezekiah's religious reforms, although the account of the removal of the high places is confirmed by the statement in 18:22 attributed to the Rabshakeh, a high Assyrian official. The removal of the high places and the resulting restriction of worship to Jerusalem were of paramount importance to the Deuteronomistic Historian. Hezekiah was the first king to accomplish this. While Hezekiah's personal religious feelings were an important factor in the reform, the political aspects must not be overlooked. His plan to restore the lost territories of David's kingdom included the development of heightened religious and nationalistic feelings. Centralization of worship could help produce unity. In the fuller account in Chronicles (2 Chr 29:1–31:21) Hezekiah appealed to Israelites in the former kingdom of Israel to celebrate PASSOVER in Jerusalem, even arranging for the Passover to be celebrated in the second month as was the custom in Israel (for a full discussion of the political factors in the reform, see Hayes and Miller 1977, 442–44). In 18:7-8 Hezekiah's rebellion against Assyria and his campaign in Philistia are noted with obvious approval.

It suited the historian's theological purpose to have the fall of Samaria occur during Hezekiah's reign (18:9-12), even though he preserves the tradition that his reign actually began in 715 (18:13). It may simply have been his purpose to contrast the hapless Hoshea's failure to preserve Samaria with Hezekiah's success in preserving Jerusalem from destruction.

A brief, but incomplete, summary of Hezekiah's revolt and the Assyrian campaigns of 701 is provided in 18:13-16. Soon after the successful Assyrian campaigns against Philistia during the ASHDOD rebellion (714–711), Hezekiah successfully campaigned against the weakened Philistine cities. Padi, king of Ekron, was delivered to Hezekiah (see Pritchard 1955, 287). When SENNACHERIB became king of Assyria in 705, he had to devote himself to military campaigns close to home. But in 701 he began a comprehensive campaign against Phoenicia, Philistia, and Judea. Sennacherib's

account of his actions against Hezekiah (Pritchard 1955, 287–88) generally agree with 2 Kgs 18:13-16. Hezekiah had to pay tribute, but the city of Jerusalem was not surrendered, nor does Sennacherib claim to have taken it.

Second Kings 18:17–19:37 appear to contain two parallel accounts of the Jerusalem siege (18:17–19:9a, 36-37; 19:9b-35), each having the same format but with different particulars and different endings. Some have thought that these parallel sections describe a later situation, perhaps ca. 690, because Tirhakah (19:9a) became king in Egypt at that time (see Bright 1981, 298–309). However, recent research has indicated that prince Tirhakah was old enough to be a military leader in 701 (Hayes and Miller 1977, 450). Thus, it may be that the parallel accounts provide in their own ways the larger story of the siege of Jerusalem in 701.

The first account in 18:17–19:9a, 36-37 includes the Rabshakeh's devastating speech, delivered in Hebrew, to the city's leaders. Hezekiah went into mourning and consulted ISAIAH, who predicted Assyrian failure. At the word of the approach of Tirhakah and the Egyptian army, Sennacherib returned to Assyria and Jerusalem was spared. The second account in 19:9b-35 gives a briefer account of the Rabshakeh's speech, includes Hezekiah's prayer, Isaiah's taunt song against Assyria, and concludes with the account of the decimation of the Assyrian army by the angel of the LORD. Parallel but differing accounts of the same event are not uncommon in the Bible. The historian apparently included both accounts, respecting his sources, in order to present a fuller picture (cf. Long 1991, 201).

In the context of the events of 705–701, Hezekiah fell ill and was told by Isaiah that he would not recover. However, Hezekiah, the Deuteronomistic Historian's paragon of virtue, prayed to the LORD and the prophetic word was reversed. Fifteen years were added to his life. It is important to note the conjunction of Hezekiah's healing and the promise of the deliverance of Jerusalem from the Assyrian attack. Whereas Ahaz had refused to ask a sign from the LORD (Isa 7:12), Hezekiah's faith in the LORD prompted him to initiate the request for a confirming sign.

Second Kings 20:12-19 give an account of MERODACH-BALADAN's embassy to Jerusalem in 703. In that year the Babylonian ruler had temporarily regained his throne while Assyria was occupied elsewhere. He sought to enlist Hezekiah in his struggle against

Assyria. Hezekiah showed his openness to the suggestion by showing the envoys all his treasures that could be contributed to the revolt effort. Isaiah was horrified by this breach of security and by Hezekiah's willingness to depend on foreign alliances for protection. The prophetic pronouncement in 20:16-18 is a chilling forecast of future reality.

The mention of the new water system built by Hezekiah in Jerusalem in preparation for the expected Assyrian attack receives confirmation in the SILOAM INSCRIPTION (see Pritchard 1955, 321). The inscription describes the circumstances of the digging of the tunnel to reroute the water from the GIHON Spring to the collecting pool of Siloam on the southern point of the hill of Ophel.

21:1-26. Manasseh and Amon. For the Deuteronomistic History historian the long reign of MANASSEH was a period of unparalleled disaster for Judah. The historian's concerns are with Manasseh's religious and social failures. There is silence about the political and international factors that must have played a role in Manasseh's policies. Manasseh revoked the reforms of Hezekiah, rebuilt the high places, thus decentralizing the cult, integrated foreign worship into the Jerusalem cult, sacrificed his son, and practiced divination (vv. 3-7). The reference to the shedding of *innocent blood* in v. 16 may apply either to child sacrifice or to judicial murder (execution of people for crimes not punishable by death).

The account of Manasseh's reign in 2 Chr 33 differs markedly from the Deuteronomistic Historian's view. According to 2 Chr 33, after Manasseh's apostasy he was taken by the Assyrians to Babylon where he prayed and repented (2 Chr 33:12-13; see the much later Prayer of Manasseh in the Apocrypha. After he returned to Jerusalem he revoked his apostate actions, with the exception of leaving the high places in place (2 Chr 33:14-17; for a positive view of Manasseh's reign, see Ahlström 1993, 730–39).

Conversely, the Deuteronomistic Historian was single-minded in his condemnation of Manasseh. In vv. 10-14 he reported the messages of anonymous prophets who announced that the fall of Judah was inevitable because of Manasseh. The fate of Samaria would be the fate of Judah. Exile awaited.

Manasseh's son Amon ruled only two years and is judged to have followed his father's policies (v. 21). He was assassinated by members of the court for reasons not clear (v. 23; for the possibilities, see Hayes and Miller 1977, 456). Whatever plans the murderers

had in mind, they were negated by the decisive action of *the people of the land* (v. 24), who installed JOSIAH, another descendant of David, on the throne. The exact identity and function of "the people of the land" is disputed. Some view them as a powerful aristocratic group interested in stability for business reasons. Others view them as the mass of the simple people, abused and downtrodden, who rose up in time of crisis to make their will known (for the views and literature, see Hayes and Miller 1977, 456–58).

22:1–23:30. The reign of Josiah. The years of Josiah's reign (640–609) were years of promise. Assyria, pressed on all sides, was in rapid decline. Egypt was stirring, but its power to intervene effectively in international affairs was not yet demonstrated. Judah had some peaceful years, and Josiah made the most of them. Like Hezekiah, Josiah formulated an integrated religious and political program to restore the glory of David's kingdom in Palestine.

The Deuteronomistic Historian's account of Josiah's reign focuses on just one year, 621. The only other year mentioned was 609, the year of Josiah's death at Megiddo (23:29-30). In 621, while the temple was being renovated (cf. 2 Kgs 12:8-16), a book of the law was discovered (23:8). When it was read to Josiah, he reacted with consternation because the provisions of the lawbook were not in force and had not been followed by his ancestors. When the prophet HULDAH was consulted, she predicted that because the stipulations of the lawbook had been ignored for so long, Jerusalem was doomed (22:15-20; cf. 21:12-15). Yet because Josiah's heart was right, Huldah predicted that he would not have to see the calamity the LORD would bring against the kingdom (22:20).

Nevertheless, Josiah prepared to place in force the provisions of the lawbook relating to cultic matters. He assembled the people and all levels of leadership and made a formal covenant to institute the laws (23:1-3).

The account of Josiah's cultic reform is found in 23:4-24. The historian emphasized the relationship of the book of the law found in the temple to Josiah's reform (in contrast to the Chronicler, who dated the beginning of Josiah's reform to 628, thereby making the book of the law unrelated to the reform).

The lawbook was Deuteronomy or some earlier version of it, because Josiah's reform actions followed closely the distinctive concerns of that book. It is not necessary to view the book as having been written in Josiah's time. Centralization of the cult was first advocated by Hezekiah. Other Judean kings had put down foreign cults and heterodox indigenous cults. But Josiah's reform movement was the perfect realization of Deuteronomy's cultic program. (For the identification of the lawbook with Deuteronomy and literature on the topic, see Hayes and Miller 1977, 461–463.)

Josiah's purpose was to restore a pure Yahwism according to the Deuteronomic model, with all worship centered at Jerusalem. Every vestige of Canaanite cult practices had to be eliminated, including deposing the idolatrous priests at the high places and removal of the cult prostitutes. The priests who served Yahweh at the high places were brought to Jerusalem for supervision. Even the observance of Passover was restricted to Jerusalem in accordance with Deut 16:1-8. However, Josiah's religious program was of a piece with his political aspirations. Because of Assyrian weakness, he moved to reassert the leadership of the house of David over the former kingdom of Israel, first by desecrating the altar at BETHEL built by JEROBOAM I, and then by moving into Philistine territory, and later by opposing Pharaoh Neco (NECHO) at MEGIDDO.

Josiah received the Deuteronomistic Historian's highest praise. He was without peer in all Judean history (23:25).

Second Kgs 23:26-27 are an addition from the last editors of the Deuteronomistic History. Events proved that even the pious reign of Josiah could not avert disaster.

23:31–24:7. Jehoahaz and Jehoiakim. The remaining years of the kingdom of Judah were chaotic, with a succession of rulers who were helpless in the face of the superior forces of Egypt and Babylon. The *people of the land* (cf. the discussion at 21:1-26, above) had chosen JEHOAHAZ to succeed his illustrious father Josiah (23:30), even though (or because?) he did not follow Josiah's policies. Pharaoh Neco deposed him because he was the popular choice, in favor of another of Josiah's sons, JEHOIAKIM. Jehoiakim laid heavy taxes on *the people of the land* in order to pay tribute to Egypt (23:35).

As a result of the impressive victory of Nebuchadnezzar (also spelled "Nebachadnezzar") of Babylon over the Egyptians in 605 at CARCHEMISH, Syria-Palestine now lay under Babylonian suzerainty. Accordingly, Jehoiakim became Nebuchadnezzar's vassal in 604. In 601 Babylon and Egypt fought a bloody, indecisive battle on the Egyptian border, and Nebuchadnezzar had to return to Babylon to refit his army. Jehoiakim seized the chance to throw off the Babylonian yoke. But bands of area soldiers, loyal to Babylon, attacked Judah and frustrated Jehoiakim's plans. Jehoiakim died a failure.

24:8–25:7. Jehoiachin and Zedekiah. JEHOIACHIN succeeded his father Jehoiakim, but he ruled only three months. In 598 Nebuchadnezzar focused attention on rebellious Jerusalem. On March 16, 597, Jerusalem surrendered. Jehoiachin was deported to Babylon, and another son of Josiah, ZEDEKIAH, was appointed by the Babylonians as king in Jerusalem. The city, though not destroyed, was despoiled. The royal family was deported along with government officials and craftsmen.

Jerusalem under Zedekiah was a hotbed of party strife. There were a pro-Egyptian party, a nationalistic independence party, a pro-Babylonian party, and probably more. Zedekiah finally declared his independence from Babylon. The Babylonian army returned, and in 587/6 destroyed Jerusalem. Zedekiah tried to escape, but he was caught, his sons were executed before his eyes, and then he was blinded and taken to Babylon.

25:8-21. Details of the destruction of Jerusalem. These verses detail the destruction of Jerusalem and the profanation of the temple. The walls of the city were destroyed, a customary practice to halt future rebellion. Larger numbers of people were exiled to Babylon after key officials had been executed at RIBLAH in Aram where Nebuchadnezzar was stationed.

25:22-26. Gedaliah the governor. GEDALIAH was a member of the famous house of Shaphan. For three generations this house had produced distinguished leaders for the government of Judah. Gedaliah himself had served with the title "Over the House" (chamberlain) in a previous administration (cf. Jer 40:5). His administrative expertise and the friendship of the family of Shaphan for the prophet Jeremiah made Gedaliah acceptable to the Babylonians for the post of governor. His policy was to inspire political peace so that the remaining population could recover. But several Judean miliary officers who had escaped the Babylonians killed Gedaliah (v. 25), resulting in a further deportation of Judeans in 582. Much of the population fled to Egypt, taking Jeremiah with them (cf. Jer 40–44 for a fuller account of these events).

25:27-30. Release of Jehoiachin. The Deuteronomistic Historian's work concludes with a modest note of hope. In 560 the Babylonians released Jehoiachin from prison, but they did not allow him to return to Judah. However, a son of David still lived, and who knew what the future might hold? Clay tablets mentioning the ration allotments for Jehoiachin, along with that of captives from Phoenicia, Egypt, and Greece, have been recovered (Pritchard 1955, 308).

Works Cited

Ahlström, Gösta. 1993. *The History of Ancient Palestine from the Palaeolithic Period to Alexander's Conquest.* JSOTsup 146.

Bailey, Lloyd R. 1990a. "Golden Calf," MDB. 1990b. "Jeroboam I," MDB.

Baly, Denis. 1976. *God and History in the Old Testament.*

Bright, John. 1981. *A History of Israel.* Third ed.

Cross, F. M. 1973. *Canaanite Myth and Hebrew Epic.*

De Vries, Lamoine. 1990. "Ship," MDB.

Gregory, Russell I. 1990. "Joab," MDB.

Hayes, John H., and J. Maxwell Miller, eds. 1977. *Israelite and Judean History.*

Kallai, Zechariah. 1986. *Historical Geography of the Bible.*

Lemaire, André. 1986. "Vers L'histoire de la Rédaction des Livres des Rois," ZAW 98:221–36.

Long, B. O. 1991. *2 Kings.* FOTL.

Miller, J. Maxwell. 1990. "Gihon," MDB.

Noth, Martin. 1981. *The Deuteronomistic History.* JSOTsup 15.

Pritchard, J. B. 1955. *Ancient Near Eastern Texts* (ANET). Second ed.

Smend, R. 1971. "Das Gesetz und die Völker," in *Probleme biblischer Theologie,* ed. H. W. Wolff.

Van Beek, Gus W. 1962a. "Ophir," IDB. 1962b. "Sabeans," IDB.

Walsh, Jerome T., and Christopher T. Begg. 1990. "1–2 Kings," NJBC.

Wiles, John Keating. 1990. "Sheba, Queen of." MDB.

First and Second Chronicles

Claude F. Mariottini

Introduction

The Books of 1–2 Chronicles were originally one book in the Hebrew Bible. The division of Chronicles into two books was made by the translators of the LXX in the second century B.C.E. The Hebrew title of the book is *dibrê hayyāmîm*, an expression meaning "the events of the days." In the LXX the book is called *Paraleipomena* or "things omitted." This title was interpreted to mean that Chronicles includes supplemental material omitted by the other historical books, mainly Samuel and Kings. The English title "Chronicles" goes back to the Vulgate; Jerome called the book "a chronicle of the whole divine history."

Position in the Canon

In the Hebrew Bible Chronicles belongs to the third division of the Hebrew CANON called the *Kethubim* or the Writings. This division is also called *Hagiographa* or Holy Writings. Chronicles is the last book in the Hebrew Bible, appearing after Ezra–Nehemiah which are also considered to be one book. In English Bibles, Chronicles is part of the historical books of the OT; it appears after 1–2 Kings and before Ezra and Nehemiah.

Content

The Books of 1–2 Chronicles may be divided into five sections.

1. First Chronicles 1–9 introduces the history of ISRAEL from ADAM to SAUL. This history is presented in the form of lists and genealogies. Some of the genealogies, however, mention the names of people who lived many years after DAVID, even the names of people living in postexilic JUDAH.

2. First Chronicles 10–29 presents the history of David's kingdom, including the preparation he made for the building of the Temple and the organization of the Levites.

3. Second Chronicles 1–9 focuses on the history of SOLOMON's kingdom. The central point of the history of Solomon's reign is the building of the Temple.

4. Second Chronicles 10:1–36:21 centers on the history of the kingdom of Judah. The history of the kings of the Northern Kingdom is largely ignored by the author of Chronicles.

5. Second Chronicles 36:22-23 is an appendix that introduces the opening section of CYRUS's decree providing for the rebuilding of the Temple in Jerusalem (see Ezra 1:1-3).

Authorship

Until recently most commentators affirmed that Chronicles and Ezra–Nehemiah formed a single work known as the Chronicler's History (Noth 1987). Several reasons were given to affirm this view: (a) The decree of Cyrus at the end of 2 Chronicles (36:22-23) appears at the beginning of Ezra (1:1-3). According to this view, the history presented in Ezra begins where 2 Chronicles ended. (b) Both Chronicles and Ezra–Nehemiah emphasize the Temple, the cult, and the work of the Levites and priests. (c) The use of genealogies and statistical records in Chronicles and Ezra–Nehemiah. (d) The similar language and common vocabulary present in Chronicles and Ezra–Nehemiah.

This view for the unity of Chronicles and Ezra–Nehemiah has been challenged recently by several authors. Japhet (1968, 330–71), although acknowledging the similarity of language, has emphasized the linguistic differences between Chronicles and Ezra–Nehemiah. A similar suggestion was made by Williamson (1982, 7). He said that an analysis of the language and style of Chronicles and Ezra–Nehemiah indicates "differences of usage between the two bodies of writing." Braun (1979, 63) has demonstrated that the emphasis on retribution and on the Davidic monarchy present in Chronicles are absent in Ezra–Nehemiah. This commentary assumes that Chronicles is a work separate from Ezra–Nehemiah. The author is unknown and will be identified as "the Chronicler." For convenience the term CHR will be used throughout the commentary to indicate the final redactor of the book. "Chronicles" will be used to refer to the two books as a unit. To refer to specific biblical passages, the abbreviations 1 Chr and 2 Chr will be used.

Date

It is difficult to ascertain a precise date for the composition of Chronicles. However, there are indications in Chronicles that point to the end of the fifth century or the beginning of the fourth century B.C.E. In 1 Chr 3:19-24 the genealogy of David is extended to the sixth generation after ZERUBBABEL. Since Zerubbabel can be dated to 520 B.C.E. (cf. Hag 1:1), the sixth generation must be dated after 400 B.C.E. Hence, the final composition for the book should be dated between 400 and 350 B.C.E.

Theology

When the CHR wrote his theological interpretation of the history of Israel, the nation had no king. The people of Israel were trying to reestablish their identity and their religious life following the return from EXILE. The purpose of Chronicles is to provide a positive view of the past and a hope for the future. A central theme that emphasizes the CHR's message is the centrality of the Temple and worship in the life of the nation. Since the Temple was at the center of the life of the postexilic community, worship served to provide continuity with the traditions of the past and a sense of identity for those who had returned from exile.

Another theme developed by the CHR is the centrality of the Davidic monarchy. David served as the model of leadership for the new Israel. In his attempt to idealize David, the CHR omits from the story of David many events that tend to tarnish David's image.

He omits the story of David's adultery with BATHSHEBA, his order to JOAB to have URIAH killed, and NATHAN's rebuke of David (2 Sam 11–12). He omits the narrative detailing ABSALOM's revolt against David (2 Sam 13–19), the rebellion of the Northern tribes under the leadership of Sheba (2 Sam 20), David's willingness to sacrifice part of Saul's family at the request of the Gibeonites (2 Sam 21:1-14), and several others. The emphasis of the CHR is David's preparation for the building of the Temple. Yahweh had chosen David and his house to lead Israel, to bless the people, and to build the Temple. David acquired the temple site, organized the temple service, and made preparations for the building of the Temple. SOLOMON also receives unconditional approval of the CHR. Solomon was designated by Yahweh to build the Temple (1 Chr 28:10; 29:1).

Another theme in Chronicles is the doctrine of RETRIBUTION. The CHR believed that the hope of Israel was dependent upon the obedience of the leaders and the people to Yahweh. The CHR correlates blessing with obedience and punishment with disobedience. When the king and the people obey the laws of Yahweh, Yahweh will bless them (1 Chr 28:8). When a leader is unfaithful he will be punished (1 Chr 10:13-14).

For Further Study

In the *Mercer Dictionary of the Bible*: CHRONICLES, FIRST AND SECOND; CHRONOLOGY; DEUTERONOMIST/DEUTERONOMISTIC HISTORIAN.

In other sources: P. R. Ackroyd, *I and II Chronicles, Ezra, Nehemiah*, TBC; R. Braun, *1 Chronicles*, WBC; E. L. Curtis and A. A. Madsen, *A Critical and Exegetical Commentary on the Books of Chronicles*, ICC; S. J. De Vries, *1 and 2 Chronicles*, FOTL; R. B. Dillard, *2 Chronicles*, WBC; S. Japhet, *I and II Chronicles*, OTL; R. W. Klein, "Chronicles, Book of 1-2," AncBD; J. M. Myers, *I Chronicles* and *II Chronicles*, AncB; H. G. M. Williamson, *1 and 2 Chronicles*, NCB.

Commentary

An Outline

Genealogies, 1:1–9:44

The purpose of the genealogies in 1 Chr 1–9 is to trace the history of the people ISRAEL from its beginning with ADAM and to serve as an introduction to the work of the CHR. The authenticity of this section has been questioned by several scholars. Noth (1987), for instance, credits only a small portion of these genealogies to the CHR. Although it is clear that several additions by different hands were included into these genealogies, the final composition is the work of the CHR.

Genealogy of the Patriarchs, 1:1-54

The patriarchal genealogies are divided into two sections, each separated by the events of the FLOOD. The first section (vv. 1-23) introduces the genealogies of the ten patriarchs who lived before the flood. The second section (vv. 24-54) introduces the genealogy of ten patriarchs who lived after the flood. The list includes the genealogies of ISHMAEL (vv. 28-31) the children of ABRAHAM by *Keturah* (vv. 32-33), and the children of ESAU (vv. 34-54). The sources of these genealogies are found in Gen 5, Num 26, and Exod 6.

1:1-4. Genealogy of Adam. The genealogy of *Adam* introduces the ten patriarchs who lived before the flood. The list also includes the sons of NOAH.

1:5-27. Genealogy of the sons of Noah. The genealogy of the sons of Noah is introduced in the reverse order from that generally found in the biblical material (see v. 4). The genealogy of JAPHETH (vv. 5-7) is given first, followed by the genealogy of *Ham* (vv. 8-16), and followed by the genealogy of SHEM (vv. 17-27). The genealogy of Shem includes the names of ten patriarchs, from the period immediately after the flood until the time of *Abraham* (vv. 24-27).

1:28-34. Genealogy of Abraham. After a brief introduction of the sons of Noah, the writer introduces the family of *Abraham*, deviating from the sources in Genesis and bypassing the genealogies of HARAN and NAHOR (Gen 11:27-29). The genealogies of the sons of Abraham are arranged according to the names of their mothers. The CHR begins with the descendants of *Ishmael*, the son of HAGAR (vv. 29-31), the Egyptian slave given as a wife to Abraham by SARAH. Then there follow the names of the sons of *Keturah* (vv. 32-33), the wife Abraham took after the death of Sarah, and then the names of Sarah's descendants (v. 34).

1:35-54. Genealogy of Esau. The genealogy of *Esau* is divided into three sections: the descendants of Esau (vv. 35-42), the *kings . . . of Edom* (vv. 43-50) and *the clans of Edom* (vv. 51-54). The five sons of Esau are introduced in v. 35; however, only the descendants of *the sons of Eliphaz* (v. 36) and of *the sons of Reuel* (v. 37) are given. *Seir* (v. 38) was the name of a mountain in Edom, south of the DEAD SEA. According to Deut 2:12, 22, the Horites were the original inhabitants of the area but they were displaced by the sons of Esau. The descendants of Seir (Gen 36:20-30) were assimilated by sons of Esau (Gen 36:8). The list of the Edomite kings (vv. 43-54) predates the establishment of kingship in Israel.

Genealogy of Judah, 2:1-55

2:1-2. The sons of Israel. After introducing the Ishmaelites and the Edomites, the writer abandons them in order to concentrate on *the sons of Israel* (Jacob). The order of the twelve sons of Israel follows the list found in Gen 35:23-26 and Exod 1:1-4 with one difference. In 1 Chronicles Dan has been moved from the ninth position to the seventh (2:2), perhaps to empha-size that Dan was adopted by RACHEL before the birth of JOSEPH and BENJAMIN. The grouping of sons into twelve follows a biblical pattern: the twelve sons of Ishmael (1:29), the twelve rulers of Edom (1:51-54), and the twelve sons of Nahor (Gen 22:20-24). The sons of Israel are enumerated according to their mothers: the sons of LEAH included REUBEN, SIMEON, LEVI, JUDAH, ISSACHAR, and ZEBULUN; the sons of Rachel include Dan (adopted before the births of Joseph and Benjamin), Joseph, and Benjamin; the sons of Bilhah include Dan and NAPHTALI; and the sons of Zilpah include GAD and ASHER.

2:3-4. The sons of Judah. Since the CHR desires to emphasize the theocratic role of David's dynasty in the life of Israel, he begins the genealogies of the sons of Jacob with the genealogy of Judah. The preeminence of the tribe of Judah in the genealogy of Jacob differs from the sources from which the information was taken (Gen 46:8-25; Num 26:5). The reference to the three sons of Judah born of a Canaanite woman may indicate the Canaanite background of the clans of Judah and the marginal relationship Judah had with the other tribes of Israel at the beginning of the confed-eracy (Deut 33:7). The name of Yahweh (*the LORD*) appears here for the first time in Chronicles. Yahweh appears as the one exacting vengeance for the wicked-ness of *Er*.

2:5-8. Genealogy of Perez and Zerah. The author accentuates the genealogy of *Perez* because he was one of the forefathers of David (Ruth 4:18). The list of *the sons of Zerah* is original to the CHR. *Achar*'s name appears as Achan in Josh 7.

2:9-41. Genealogy of Hezron. *Hezron* was the father of three sons: *Jerahmeel, Ram, and Chelubai* (v. 9). Chelubai appears as CALEB in 2:18. The genealogy of *Ram* (vv. 10-17) is presented first because he was a forefather of David. David is mentioned as being the seventh son of Jesse (v. 15, although in 2 Sam 16:10 he is listed as the eighth). The names of David's sisters do not appear in 1 Samuel. Among the sons of *Caleb* (vv. 18-24) is *Hur*, whose grandson *Bezalel* (v. 20) was selected to build the TABERNACLE in the days of Moses (Exod 31:2; 35:30). This reference to Bezalel serves to associate the tribe of Judah with the building of the tabernacle and its involvement in the cultic life of Israel. Caleb, the son of Hezron, should not be associated with Caleb, the son of Jephunneh, the Kenizzite. Caleb the Kenizzite was a member of a foreign clan that was incorporated into the tribe of Judah (4:15). The descendants of *Jerahmeel* (vv. 25-33) lived in the NEGEB, south of Beer-sheba (1 Sam 27:10). The Jerahmeelites probably were a non-Israelite tribe that was assimilated into the tribe of Judah. The CHR is the only one who identifies the Jerahmeelites as a clan of Judah. The second gene-alogy of *Caleb* (vv. 42-50a) is an addition to Caleb's genealogy listed above. The descendants of Caleb through *Hur* (vv. 50b-55) became the founders of several well-known Judean cities.

Genealogy of David, 3:1-24

3:1-9. The sons of David. The genealogy of DAVID is divided into two sections. The first section (3:1-4a), which also appears in 2 Sam 3:1-5, gives the names of the six sons of David born while he was reigning over JUDAH in HEBRON. *Daniel*, the son of ABIGAIL (v. 3) appears as Chileab in 2 Sam 3:3. According to 1 Chr 29:27 and 1 Kgs 2:11, the reign of David in Hebron was only seven years. The second section (3:4b-9) gives the names of the thirteen sons born after David moved to JERUSALEM, four of them by *Bath-shua*, the daughter of *Ammiel*. *Bath-shua* is a variation of the name BATHSHEBA. This list appears also in 2 Sam 5:13-16 and 1 Chr 14:3-7. This list of David's sons born in Jerusalem differs from the parallel passage in Samuel. *Eliphelet* (v. 6) and *Nogah* (v. 7) do not appear in Samuel. The repetition of the names *Elishama* (vv. 6, 8) and *Eliphelet* (vv. 6, 8) may indicate that the CHR used more than one list and that the present text is a conflation of duplicate lists. See the commentary on 8:29-40 and 14:3-7 for additional material on the sons of David.

3:10-16. The kings of Judah. The list names all the kings of Judah who reigned after David. Athaliah's name is not included because she was an usurper. *Azariah* (v. 12) appears in 2 Kgs 15:13 and 2 Chr 26:1 as UZZIAH. *Johanan*, the first son of *Josiah* (v. 15) does not appear in 2 Kings. It is possible that he died young. *Shallum* appears in 2 Kings as JEHOAHAZ (see Jer 22:11). Verse 15 mentions one *Zedekiah* as Josiah's son and v. 16 mentions a *Zedekiah* as Jehoi-achin's son. Which Zedekiah became king of Judah is not clear. Second Kings 24:17 declares that the Zedekiah who became king was Jehoiakim's uncle while 2 Chr 36:10 declares that Zedekiah was his brother. However, 1 Chr 3:16 says that the successor of Jehoiachin (or *Jeconiah*) was *Zedekiah his son*. Since no son named Zedekiah appears in the list of

Jehoiachin's descendants in 3:17-18, it seems clear that Josiah's son was the last king of Judah.

3:17-24. David's descendants after the Exile. This list introduces the royal line after the EXILE, covering eight generations of Davidides until approximately 400 B.C.E. *Shenazzar* has been identified with the Sheshbazzar who brought the first group of refugees from Babylon (Ezra 1:8, 11). *Zerubbabel* is presented as the son of *Pedaiah*; however, in Ezra 3:2, 8 and Neh 12:1 he is said to be the son of Shealtiel. Some have explained this discrepancy by saying that because Shealtiel had died childless, Pedaiah, by the laws of Levirate marriage, took the widow of his brother and Zerubbabel was born out of this second marriage.

Genealogy of the Tribe of Judah, 4:1-23

Chapters 4–9 present a list of the various clans and tribes of Israel, distributed according to their geographical areas in relation to JUDAH. Chapter 4 lists the southern tribes, Judah and SIMEON. Chapter 5 the Transjordanian tribes of REUBEN, GAD, and the half tribe of MANASSEH. Chapter 6 lists the tribe of LEVI; chap. 7 presents the northern tribes of ISSACHAR, BENJAMIN, NAPHTALI, the other half of the tribe of Manasseh, EPHRAIM, and ASHER. Chapter 8 lists a second genealogy of Benjamin and chap. 9 lists the inhabitants of JERUSALEM.

In the list of the descendants of *Judah* (v. 1), only *Perez* is Judah's son. *Hezron* was the son of *Perez* (2:5). Since *Hur* was the son of *Caleb* (2:19) and *Shobal* was the son of *Hur* (2:50), scholars have proposed that *Carmi* should be corrected to "Caleb, son of Hezron." Verses 5-8 continue the list begun in 2:24. Jabez's name (v. 9) is a play on a Hebrew word that means pain. His name is a reference to the pains of childbirth suffered by his mother when the child was born. Since popular ideas related the name of a person with the person's future, Jabez cries to God asking to be delivered from future evil (v. 10). OTHNIEL, the son of *Kenaz* (v. 13), was the judge who participated in the conquest of the land (Judg 1:12; 3:9, 11). *Seraiah* is unknown, but his son *Joab* was *the father of Ge-harashim*. The word *father* in v. 14 means either "the founder of" or "the leader of" Ge-harashim. The word means "Valley of the Smiths" or "Valley of the Craftsmen" (Neh 11:35).

Genealogy of the Tribe of Simeon, 4:24-43

From the earliest days of the confederation the tribe of Simeon was associated with and eventually was assimilated by Judah (cf. Josh 19:9). The list mentions five generations of the descendants of Simeon (vv. 24-27) and the towns and villages where his clans lived (vv. 28-33). It also mentions two migrations of the tribe. The first migration in the days of *Hezekiah* (vv. 34-41) displaced the Hamites and the Meunites who lived at *Gedor* (v. 39). The LXX says that the Simeonites invaded GERAR, a place located south of CANAAN (Gen 20:1). The other migration, at an unknown time, displaced the Amalekites who lived in the hill country of Seir. The statement in v. 31b may indicate that Simeon ceased to exist as an independent tribe during the reign of David. This may explain why the tribe of Simeon is not listed in the blessing of Moses in Deut 33.

Genealogies of the Transjordanian Tribes, 5:1-26

5:1-10. Reuben. REUBEN lost the right of the firstborn because he defiled the bed of his father by having sexual relations with Bilhah, Jacob's concubine (Gen 35:22; 49:4). The right of the firstborn, a double portion of the father's inheritance, was passed to JOSEPH, who received two portions of the promised land through his sons EPHRAIM and MANASSEH. Although the CHR recognizes Joseph's right of firstborn, he ascribes high honor to Judah because from him came an important Israelite leader. This statement demonstrates the writer's messianic faith in the Davidic dynasty. *Tilgath-pilneser* (vv. 6, 26) is a variant of TIGLATH-PILESER, the Assyrian king who took part of the population of the Northern Kingdom, including several Reubenite clans, into exile (2 Kgs 15:29).

5:11-17. Gad. The CHR begins the genealogy of the tribe of GAD by providing geographical information describing the places where they were settled. Detailed information about the land occupied by the tribe of Gad is found in Josh 13:24-28. Gilead is south of *Bashan*, the land north of the Jabbok River. The genealogy of Gad differs from the list found in Gen 46:16 and Num 26:15-17. The text is not clear concerning the relationship among the descendants of Gad. It seems that the genealogical list of Gad contains at least two unconnected genealogies, one beginning with *Joel* (vv. 12-13) and the other with *Abihail* (v. 14). It is possible that *Ahi* (v. 15) heads a third list; however, the text is not clear. The LXX does not consider *Shaphat* (v. 12) as a personal name and translates it "scribe," adding the title to *Janai*. Braun (1986, 69) proposes "Janai judged in Bashan." The list was composed in the eighth century, during the reign of

JEROBOAM II (ca. 750 B.C.E.). The mention of *Jotham* presupposes a co-regency with his father UZZIAH.

5:18-22. Wars of the Transjordanian tribes. It is not clear from the text whether this war of the eastern tribes against their neighbors is distinct from the one in which Reuben fought alone (v. 10). *The Hagrites* are listed as one of the enemies of Israel (Ps 83:6), although David had Hagrite soldiers in his army (1 Chr 11:38; 27:30). *Jetur* and *Naphish* (v. 19) were descendants of Ishmael (Gen 25:15). According to the CHR, the Transjordanian tribes were valiant warriors; known for their prowess in combat, they were men ready for war. The number of fighting men seems excessive, although the census of Num 1 and Num 26 may indicate that such a large army is a possibility. The immense booty may be an embellishment in order to emphasize the importance of the victory and the magnitude of the divine favor.

5:23-26. The half-tribe of Manasseh. *The half-tribe of Manasseh* settled in the fertile plain in the territory east of the Jordan, north of the YARMUK, between BASHAN and Mount Hermon. Of the three eastern tribes, Manasseh was the farthest north. The location of *Baal-hermon* (cf. Judg 3:3) is unknown. *Senir* is identified with Mount Hermon (Deut 3:9). The names of the sons of Manasseh mentioned here are different from the lists mentioned elsewhere in the OT (Num 26:29; Josh 17:2). The leaders of Manasseh were *mighty warriors* (v. 24). This title was applied to a special social class in Israel. They were owners of land who, at times of war, were called to defend it.

The clans of Manasseh were punished for their unfaithfulness to God. They, along with Gad and Reuben, were taken into exile by the Assyrians (1 Kgs 15:29). *Pul* (v. 26) was the name Tiglath-pileser used when he became King of Babylon. The exile of the Transjordanian tribes occurred as the result of the Assyrian invasion at the time of the Syro-Ephraimite war in 734 B.C.E. (2 Kgs 15:19). The names of the cities to which the eastern tribes were deported are identical to the cities to which Israel was deported at the time of the fall of Samaria in 722 B.C.E. (2 Kgs 17:6; 18:11).

Genealogy of the Tribe of Levi, 6:1-81 [MT 5:27–6:66]

6:1-15 [MT 5:27-41]. High priests. *The sons of Levi* (cf. Exod 6:16-23) were the leaders of the three great Levitical families in Israel. The purpose of this list is to trace the genealogy of the high priest through AARON and Eleazar until the EXILE. The number of high priests

who served from Eleazar to the building of the Temple was twelve. Since the construction of the Temple was begun 480 years after the Exodus (1 Kgs 6:1), it is possible the writer was presuming on twelve generations of priests from the Exodus to the Solomonic Temple, each generation averaging forty years. This ideal number may indicate that the list is not complete, since ELI and ABIATHAR, who were priests before the monarchy, are not included. Also missing are JEHOIADA (2 Chr 22:11), the high priest who served during the reign of JOASH, and URIAH (2 Kgs 16:10), the high priest who served during the reign of AHAZ. The priest who served in the Temple of Solomon (v. 10) was *Azariah*, the son of *Ahimaaz* and grandson of *Zadok* (1 Kgs 4:2). *Jehozadak*, the eleventh generation of high priests after the construction of the Temple, was the priest at the time of the Exile of Judah. His son Joshua was the first high priest after the return from Babylon (Hag 1:1). The intent of the CHR is to demonstrate the continuity of the priestly line from ZADOK until his own day.

6:16-30 [MT 6:1-15]. Levites. This list introduces the other sons and grandsons of LEVI. These Levites were not part of the priestly family but performed various tasks in the Temple. This list is derived from Num 3:27-29. *Gershom* (6:16 [MT 6:1]) also appears in the OT with the variant spelling Gershon (Exod 6:16). His line is traced for seven generations (vv. 20-21). *Kohath* was the ancestor of Aaron and the one from whom the line of high priests is traced. His son *Amminadab* (v. 22) does not appear in other lists of Kohathites. For this reason scholars have identified Amminadab with Izhar since he appears in all the genealogical lists of Kohath. Among the descendants of Kohath is *Elkanah* (v. 27), the father of SAMUEL. Some versions, following the LXX, add "and Samuel his son" at the end of v. 27 (see NIV). Since Elkanah and Samuel were from Ephraim (1 Sam 1:1), some scholars believe that the genealogy of Samuel is an addition to the genealogy of Kohath, added to explain the sacerdotal work of Samuel.

6:31-48 [MT 6:16-38]. Levitical musicians. The CHR, emphasizing the special role of music in the Temple and the role David played in the structure of Temple worship, credits David with the organization of the Levitical singers who ministered in the Temple in the CHR's own day. This organization occurred after the Ark of the Covenant was brought to Jerusalem and placed in the TABERNACLE (v. 31; cf. 1 Chr 15). The list mentions the Levitical singers by families. The

Kohathites, represented by *Heman*, were in a central place before the tabernacle. The singers from the family of *Gershom*, represented by *Asaph* were on the right side (v. 39). The sons of *Merari*, represented by *Ethan* were on the left (v. 44). In 1 Chr 16 Asaph was the leader, while Heman and Ethan (called *Jeduthun* in 9:16 and 16:41) were in charge of the music in the Temple. These three men appear in 1 Kgs 4:31 as men renowned for their wisdom. Several psalms were ascribed to them: Pss 50, 73–83 are ascribed to Asaph while Ps 88 is ascribed to Heman and Ps 89 to Ethan. In the title of Ps 77, Jeduthun seems to refer to the name of the tune of the psalm.

6:49-53 [MT 6:34-38]. Aaronic priests. While the Levites were in charge of the music in the Temple and had other duties related to the worship in the Temple, the priests were responsible for offering sacrifices upon the altar and for making atonement for the nation. The CHR again lists the genealogy of the high priests, linking the priesthood of Zadok to Aaron.

6:54-81 [MT 6:39-66]. Settlement of the Levites. The list of the Levitical cities follows, with some modifications, the list of cities mentioned in Josh 21:1-42. *The Kohathites* received thirteen cities, nine in Judah and Simeon and four in Benjamin. The omission of Simeon from the CHR's list may be an indication of the early absorption of that tribe into the tribe of Judah. The CHR only lists eleven cities, omitting Juttah (Josh 21:16) and Gibeon (Josh 21:17). The other Kohathites who were not priests received ten cities in Ephraim, Dan and Manasseh, although the CHR only mentions eight cities and does not include the tribe of Dan. The *Gershonites* received thirteen towns in Issachar, in Asher, in Naphtali, and in Transjordan in the territory of the half-tribe of Manasseh. The *Merarites* received twelve cities in Zebulun, in Reuben, and in Gad (Josh 21:40), although the CHR only mentions the names of ten of the cities. Since the Levites were dispersed among the tribes, these forty-eight cities were allotted to the Levites as their portion of the land, rather than a regular geographical allotment.

Genealogies of the Northern Tribes, 7:1-40

The CHR ends his listing of the genealogies of the tribes of Israel by introducing the tribes of the north. He omits from his list the genealogies of Zebulun (Gen 46:14) and Dan (Gen 46:23).

7:1-5. Issachar. The genealogy of ISSACHAR follows Gen 46:13 and Num 26:23-25 with minor variations in spelling the names. Tola's descendants, each designated as a *mighty warrior*, numbered 22,600. They were numbered in the census taken by David, probably the one mentioned in 2 Sam 24 and 1 Chr 21. *Uzzi*, Tola's firstborn, was also the ancestor of several leaders of the clan of Issachar. His descendants numbered 36,000. The total number of fighting men available for war from the tribe of Issachar was 87,000. This number does not represent the total of the two groups. The number may include other families not counted in the genealogy of the sons of Issachar since only the genealogies of the firstborn are provided.

7:6-12. Benjamin. The genealogy of Benjamin in the OT is a vexing problem (Mariottini 1992a). In Gen 46:21 Benjamin is said to have ten sons; Num 26:38-41 lists five; our passage lists three; and 1 Chr 8:1-2 lists five sons. Of the three sons of Benjamin mentioned here, *Bela* appears in all four genealogies, *Becher* appears only in Genesis, and *Jediael* appears only here. The genealogy of Bela appears in three places: in Num 26:39-40 he has two sons, in 1 Chr 7:7 he has five, and in 1 Chr 8:3-4 he has nine sons. None of the five sons mentioned in 1 Chr 7:7 appears in the other genealogies. Verse 12 is truncated. *Shuppim* and *Huppim* are the grandsons of Bela, if Ir is to be identified with *Iri* (v. 7). However, they have been identified with Muppim and Huppim (Gen 46:21) and with Shephupham and Hupham (Num 26:38), two sons of Benjamin. *Shuppim* and *Huppim* also appear in 1 Chr 7:15 as descendants of Manasseh. Shephupham (Shephuphan) appears in 1 Chr 8:4 as a son of Bela. These differences indicate that the CHR might have used different traditions in the reconstruction of the genealogy of Benjamin. It is also possible that vv. 6-13 might include a fragment of the genealogy of Dan since Hushim appears as Dan's son in Gen 46:23.

7:13. Naphtali. This genealogy follows, with minor variations, the genealogies of NAPHTALI found in Gen 46:24 and Num 26:48-49. BILHAH was the mother of Dan and Naphtali.

7:14-19. Manasseh. The list of the descendants of MANASSEH is fragmented and at places corrupt, and thus, difficult to interpret. According to Num 26:29 and Josh 17:1-2, Manasseh was the father of Machir, Machir the father of Gilead, and Gilead the father of Asriel. Apparently, *Asriel* entered in v. 14 by dittography. The reference to an *Aramean concubine* (v. 14) of Manasseh is evidence of the important relationship that existed between Manasseh and the Arameans.

The descendants of *Machir* formed the half-tribe of Manasseh that settled in Transjordan (Num 32:39-40). Most scholars believe that the mention of *Huppim* and *Shuppim* in v. 15 is an addition and should be deleted. They appear in Gen 46:21 as sons of Benjamin. The NIV reinterprets the text to declare that Machir "took a wife from among the Huppites and the Shuppites." The NRSV translation of v. 15 declares that *Zelophehad* was the *second* sister of Machir. But according to Num 26:3 and Josh 17:3 he was the grandson of Gilead and the great-grandson of Machir. The word *second* in v. 15 may indicate that ZELOPHEHAD is being listed as the second son of Machir, or perhaps of Manasseh. The Hebrew text as it stands is corrupt and omits the names of the first son and of the father.

7:20-29. Ephraim. This genealogy traces the line of EPHRAIM, the second son of JOSEPH, to *Joshua*, the son of *Nun* (v. 27). The genealogy differs from the list found in Num 26:35-36. The genealogy is composed of two distinct lists (vv. 20-21, 25-27), each containing the name of ten sons, separated by a narrative detailing the death of *Ezer* and *Elead* at the hands of *the people of Gath*. Gath has been associated with Gittaim (2 Sam 4:3) rather than with the Philistine city of Gath.

The conflict between the Ephraimites and the Canaanites has caused much discussion since, according to the Book of Genesis, Ephraim was born and died in Egypt. It is doubtful that the men of Gath came to Egypt to raid the cattle of the sons of Ephraim. It is possible that some of the Israelites continued to have contact with Canaan while they lived in Egypt. It is more probable, however, that this statement may reflect the fact that some groups in Canaan, who later became associated with the Israelite confederacy, may have never been part of the group living in Egypt (Japhet 1979, 205–18).

7:30-40. Asher. The genealogy of *Asher* is based in part on Gen 46:17 and Num 26:44-46. The CHR introduces the line of *Beriah* through his sons *Heber* and *Malchiel*. The source for this genealogical information is unknown and it appears only here. The number of men enrolled for service in war is 26,000. This number is small in comparison to enrollments in previous censuses and it may reflect the decline of the tribe at a later time in ISRAEL. The mention of Asher's daughter *Serah* in all three lists is unusual and may indicate an important position Serah had among the clans of Asher (Mariottini 1992b).

Genealogy of Benjamin, 8:1-40

8:1-28. Descendants of Benjamin. This is the second genealogy of Benjamin in Chronicles. For some of the problems associated with the four genealogies of Benjamin in the OT, see the commentary at 7:6-12 above. Of the five sons of Benjamin listed here, only *Bela* appears in all four genealogies. *Ashbel* fails to appear in 1 Chr 7:6-12 while *Aharah, Nohah* and *Rapha* appear only here. The difficulty in harmonizing the four genealogies is an indication that different lists were used by the CHR. Of the sons of *Bela* (vv. 3-5) listed here, the names differ from the other list found in 1 Chr 7:7. *Gera* and *Naaman* appear as children of Benjamin in Gen 46:21 and *Shephuphan* appears as a son of Benjamin in Num 26:38. *Gera* (v. 3) was probably the father of EHUD (Judg 3:15), one of the judges of Israel. If this is true, then *Abihud* should be translated "the father of Ehud" (v. 3 NRSV mg.). The descendants of Benjamin are grouped by place of residence: *Geba* (v. 6), *Moab* (vv. 8-10), *Ono* and *Lod* (vv. 11-12), *Aijalon* and *Gath* (v. 13), *Jerusalem* (v. 28) and Gibeon (v. 29). JERUSALEM, the most important city of Benjamin (Josh 18:28, but cf. Josh 15:63), became the religious center of the nation. The purpose of the second genealogy of Benjamin is to introduce the genealogy of SAUL, who would become the first king in Israel.

8:29-40. Genealogy of Saul. The genealogy of Saul is introduced by mention of *Jeiel* who *lived in Gibeon*, another important city in Benjamin. The relationship of Jeiel to any of the descendants of Benjamin listed above (8:1-28) is obscure. According to the CHR, *Ner* was *the father of Kish* and Kish the father of *Saul* (v. 33). However, in 1 Sam 14:50-51 Ner appears as Saul's uncle. Some Greek manuscripts add the name of Ner after *Baal* in v. 30 (cf. NIV), which is missing in the Hebrew text (cf. NRSV). The reading in the LXX agrees with 9:36 where Ner appears as the brother of Kish. In 1 Sam 14:51 Kish and Ner are listed as the sons of Abiel.

Baal, the son of *Jeiel*, has the same name as the Canaanite god of fertility. The name of the Canaanite deity also appears in the name of Saul's son, *Esh-baal*, "man of Baal" (8:33; 9:39), although the deuteronomistic writer changed his name to Ish-bosheth, "man of shame" (2 Sam 2:8; 4:1) and Ishvi, "man of Yahweh" (1 Sam 14:49). *Merib-baal* ("let Baal contend"), a grandson of Saul and the son of JONATHAN, also appears in the OT as MEPHIBOSHETH (2 Sam 4:4).

Genealogy of the Citizens of Jerusalem, 9:1-34

The source for the information concerning the people who returned from EXILE is Neh 11:3-19. The various groups who returned from exile are divided into four groups: the lay people, the priests, the Levites, and those who served in the Temple.

9:1-9. Political leaders. The first part of v. 1 is a concluding statement to the genealogies of the tribes of Israel in chaps. 2–8. *The Book of the Kings of Israel* (cf. 2 Chr 20:34) should not be identified with the Books of 1–2 Kings. The nature of this source mentioned by the CHR is debatable. It is possible that the CHR had access to official royal archives and census lists in reconstructing the genealogies of the tribes of Israel. The reason for the exile of the people to Babylon was *their unfaithfulness* to Yahweh. To the CHR the unfaithfulness of the people was their worship of idols and their pollution of the house of Yahweh (2 Chr 36:14).

The CHR departs from his source in Nehemiah in order to mention that some people from *Ephraim and Manasseh* also settled *in Jerusalem*. Since only people from Benjamin and Judah are listed, it is possible that the CHR is attempting to declare that the two tribes represent *all Israel* and that *all Israel* (v. 1) returned from exile and settled in Jerusalem. Three clans of Judah and four of Benjamin are listed. The numbers for each tribe, 690 for Judah and 1760 for Benjamin, differ from Neh 11:6 and 11:12-14. However, Nehemiah only lists the number of the descendants of Perez and omits the descendants of Zerah. For this reason the numbers in Chronicles cannot be compared with the numbers in Nehemiah since we do not know how the numbers were calculated. The names of the descendants of Judah and Benjamin listed in Chronicles differ considerably from the names in Nehemiah. Since the source for the two lists is unknown, it is impossible to reconcile the differences.

9:10-13. Priests. The six priestly families mentioned here appear with minor variations in Neh 11:10-14. AZARIAH appears in Nehemiah as Seraiah. Nehemiah's list seems to be more comprehensive since it contains several additional names. The number of priests in Chronicles is 1,760; it differs from Nehemiah's 1,192.

9:14-16. Levites. The list is similar to the list in Neh 11:10-17. The Levites are divided into three groups, each according to one of the three great Levitical groups: *Merari, Asaph,* and *Jeduthun.* Merari's name is omitted in Nehemiah. These Levites *lived in Jerusalem* (v. 34) and in Netophah, a nearby village.

9:17-34. Gatekeepers. The function of the gatekeepers was to protect the Temple from trespassers. There were four gatekeepers with 212 subordinates. Nehemiah 11:19 lists only the names of two gatekeepers, Akkub and Talmon, while Ezra 2:42 lists the names of six gatekeepers who returned from EXILE. The CHR identifies the chief gatekeeper as SHALLUM (v. 17); his name is omitted in Neh 11:19. However, Shallum has been identified with Meshullam, a gatekeeper whose name appears with Talmon and Akkub in Neh 12:15. Shallum was stationed at the entrance of the king's gate, the gate through which the king entered the Temple when he came from his palace (Ezek 46:1-3). The levitical descent of the gatekeepers and their identification as *Korahites* (v. 19) emphasizes their importance in the days of the CHR, but according to the CHR, their service follows a pattern that had existed from the days of the sojourn in the desert. This statement intends to declare that, although the exile created a break in the worship experience of the community, the present organization is a continuation of that which existed in the past. The CHR credits the organization of the gatekeepers to David and Samuel (v. 22). Since Samuel died before David became king and since David did not build the Temple, the statement must reflect the priestly influence of Samuel and the involvement of David in the formation of the worship of Israel at the beginning of the monarchy. The Levitical *leaders lived in Jerusalem* (v. 34) because their service was permanent. The other gatekeepers would serve from time to time since twenty-four gatekeepers (26:17-18) had to serve each day for seven days (v. 25).

In addition to being gatekeepers of the Temple, these Levites also had other duties: they were responsible for the treasury of the Temple, to watch over it at night and to open it in the morning (vv. 26-27), for the articles used in the worship service (28), for furniture and utensils used in the Temple, as well as the materials used for the offerings (v. 29). Some Levites were in charge of the preparation of breads and cakes while others were responsible for the music in the Temple. They were free from other duties and lived in Temple chambers.

Genealogy of Saul, 9:35-44

The genealogy of SAUL and the narrative about his death (10:1-14) serve as a transition to the history of

DAVID. The list is repeated here from 8:29-40 with minor differences. Kish and the first king of Israel were descendants of the Benjaminites who lived in Gibeon. The CHR's purpose is to contrast the story of Saul, the unfaithful king, with the fidelity of David, the king chosen by God.

The Reign of David, 10:1–29:30

The first nine chapters of Chronicles has served as an introduction to the history of ISRAEL. The genealogies of the tribes of Israel have also served as an introduction to the kingship of DAVID, the founder of the Davidic dynasty and the central figure of the CHR's work. The last twenty chapters are dedicated to David and his kingdom. Of these, the first twelve chapters reproduce some events and details already narrated in the Books of Samuel. The last eight chapters are original material, detailing David's organization of the Temple service and the Temple personnel.

The Death of Saul, 10:1-14

The life and death of SAUL was a tragic event in the history of Israel. Saul became king over Israel and JUDAH under difficult circumstances. He lived in the shadow of the old traditions, represented by SAMUEL and those who supported the confederation of the tribes. Saul was also confronted with a new political reality, represented by David and his charismatic movement. By omitting the events related to Saul's kingdom and by beginning the story of David with the death of Saul, the CHR is declaring that the end of Saul's kingdom came as divine judgment and that David's kingship was divinely approved and ordained by Yahweh.

The text here reproduces with few changes 1 Sam 31:1-13. The text declares that the PHILISTINES hung Saul's head in the temple of Dagon but omits the fact that they hung his body on the walls of Beth-shan (1 Sam 31:10). The text also fails to mention that the bodies of Saul and his sons were cremated (1 Sam 31:12), perhaps because it was a custom of non-Israelites. The end of Saul's kingdom is ascribed to his unfaithfulness to Yahweh (v. 14), that is, his disobedience (1 Sam 15:22-23), his visit to the medium of ENDOR (1 Sam 28) and his failure to seek Yahweh. Thus, according to the theology of RETRIBUTION developed by the CHR, the disgrace that befell Saul was a result of his unfaithfulness.

The Rise of David, 11:1–12:40

11:1-3. David, king over all Israel. The story of David's reign begins with the gathering of all Israel to anoint him king in HEBRON. The CHR omits the events related to the struggle between David and Saul, the seven-year reign over Judah in Hebron, and the civil war between the house of Saul and David (2 Sam 2–4). David is portrayed as the king elected by God and acclaimed by all the people as the true king of Israel. For this reason, all other details that are not directly related to the formation of the united theocratic kingdom is of little interest to the CHR.

11:4-9. Conquest of Jerusalem. The conquest of JERUSALEM was important to David in his effort to unite all Israel under his leadership. Jerusalem was a Canaanite enclave located between Judah and Benjamin. From a political perspective, its centrality and its neutral character made the city the ideal place for the capital of the kingdom. David subjugated the Jebusites, the original inhabitants of the city, and kept the original name of Jerusalem and ZION. The name Jerusalem appears in the correspondence of Tel-el AMARNA as *Uru-Shalim*, "Foundation of [the god] Shalem." The name Zion was a Canaanite name designating the southeast hill upon which the city was built. The name *Jebus* is related to the original inhabitants of the city. Although it is doubtful that the city was known by the name JEBUS, Jebus is used four times in the OT to designate the pre-Israelite name of Jerusalem (Josh 18:28; Judg 19:10). According to the CHR, all Israel took part in the conquest of Jerusalem, rather than the men of David only (2 Sam 5:6). JOAB, who later became commander of David's army, had a significant role in the conquest of the city (see 2 Sam. 5:8), although the details of how it was done are not clear. The term *Millo* (v. 8) probably refers to the terraces that supported buildings and other structures built on the steep ridge of the city.

11:10-47. David's men of valor. This list, taken from 2 Sam 23:8-39 with some variations, introduces the legendary men who served in David's army and who dedicated their lives to the service of the king, thus helping him to establish his kingship in Israel. The enumeration of the men of valor is not clear. The MT reads "thirty" (KJV, NRSV mg.) but some manuscripts of the LXX read *three* (NRSV). Another scribal reading (the *Qere*) reads "officers." The three great warriors (v. 12) were *Jashobeam* (v. 11, but see 2 Sam 23:8), *Eleazar* (v. 12) and Shammah (2 Sam 23:11), whose name does not appear in the text of Chronicles. Whether *Abishai* (vv. 20-21) and *Benaiah* (v. 24) should be classified with the group of three or thirty is not clear from the MT. Apparently, Abishai and Benaiah attained leadership positions among the thirty but were not counted among the three. Another possibility is to count Abishai and Benaiah as leaders of a second group of three warriors who risked their lives to bring water from *Bethelem* to David when he was hiding in *Adullam* (vv. 15-19). The names of the thirty warriors (vv. 26-41) are almost identical to the names in 2 Sam 23. The CHR adds sixteen names to the list after *Uriah the Hittite* (v. 41), beginning with *Zabad son of Ahlai*. This may indicate that the number thirty was not a firm number (the total listed in 2 Sam 23:39 is thirty-seven) or that other names were added to the list as the thirty warriors were killed in battle. The presentation of each warrior generally consists, with some variations, of three elements: his name, the name of his father, and the place of birth. The places of birth include locations in both the north and the south. The list also contains two men from Transjordan: an *Ammonite* (v. 39) and a *Moabite* (v. 49).

12:1-7 [MT 12:1-8]. Warriors from Benjamin. Chapter 12 continues the listing of the names of David's warriors. The purpose of this list is to magnify the popularity of David and to emphasize that David had the support of *all of Israel*. The twenty-three warriors from BENJAMIN came to David while he was at *Ziklag* (v. 1; cf. 1 Sam 27:1-7). David, in his attempt to escape from Saul, sought asylum in Gath with Achish, one of the leaders of the Philistines, who gave him the city of Ziklag (2 Sam 27:6), where David remained for sixteen months (Mariottini 1990b). Two of the Benjaminites who fled to David, *Ahiezer* and *Joash*, were from *Gibeah* (v. 3), the city Saul had established as the capital of his kingdom. With the mention of Saul's kinsmen, the CHR emphasizes that David's popularity had reached even the tribe of Saul. *Ishmaiah* is called a leader over *the thirty* (v. 4; see 11:20-21). This is possible because the leadership of this group of warriors probably changed periodically.

12:8-15 [MT 12:9-16]. Warriors from Gath. Eleven men from GAD joined David at the beginning of his struggles with Saul. They came to David before the arrival of the men from Benjamin, at a time when David had taken refuge in the wilderness (1 Sam 22:1). The Gadites were valiant warriors, not experts in the use of the bow and arrow, but adept in the use of the great shield and the spear. They were quick and fierce warriors (v. 8) who had demonstrated their bravery in battle (v. 15).

12:16-18 [MT 17-19]. Warriors from Benjamin and Judah. When other warriors from Benjamin and Judah came seeking David, he was afraid of betrayal (see 1 Sam 23:7-28). He questioned their intention, and *Amasai*, full of the Spirit (lit. "clothed with the Spirit"), responds to David and reassures him. Amasai's speech (v. 18) reflects the concept of prophetic inspiration. Amasai recognizes that God is with David to help him and to bless those who help David. David received them and made them part of his raiding bands.

12:19-22 [MT 12:20-23]. Warriors from Manasseh. The seven warriors from Manasseh were valiant men and expert in war. They came to David before the battle of Gilboa in which the PHILISTINES defeated the army of Israel (1 Sam 29–30). David had gone to join the Philistines in their battle against Saul, but the Philistines did not allow David to join them in their battle against Israel. When David returned to Ziklag he discovered that the Amalekites had sacked the town. The warriors from Manasseh helped David to recover what the Amalekites had taken. The CHR concludes that many more people came to join David's army, until his army became *like an army of God* (v. 22). This Hebrew expression is a superlative and means "an exceedingly great army," great in number and great in the quality of the people who had joined David in his quest for the throne of Israel.

12:23-40 [MT 24-41]. Other supporters of David. This is a list of the people who came to David at Hebron to express their support and to anoint him king over all Israel. All tribes are represented, including the tribe of Levi. The large number of men armed for battle, can be understood in different ways. Myers (1965, 98), following the proposal of Mendenhall (1958, 52–66), believes that the Hebrew word *'eleph*, translated "thousand" in English versions, means part of a tribe or a military unit. Myers translates 12:25: "The sons of Judah who bore shield and spear numbered six units with eight hundred men with military training." If this interpretation is followed, a more realistic view of the number of men prepared for war emerges. On the other hand, if the numbers are taken literally, then more than 340,000 people joined David at Hebron. As for the names of the leaders, only two are mentioned: *Jehoiada*, the leader of the Levites, may have been the father of Benaiah (2 Sam 8:8; 1 Chr 27:5). *Zadok*, a valiant young warrior, was the one who later took the place of ABIATHAR and became high priest under SOLOMON (1 Kgs 2:35). The gathering of Israel for the anointing of David was a time of great celebration and joy. The people had come to Hebron with the purpose and determination to proclaim David king over Israel. They brought provisions for the feast and contributed to the religious ceremonies that were part of David's coronation.

David's Attempt to Move the Ark, 13:1-14

The Ark of the covenant plays an important role in chaps. 13–16. The ARK had a significant place in Israel's cult because it symbolized God's presence among the people. During the days of Samuel, the PHILISTINES had captured the Ark (1 Sam 4:11) and had brought it to the house of Dagon that was located in ASHDOD (1 Sam 5:1-5). After the Philistines returned the Ark, it was kept in the house of Abinadab in *Kiriath-jearim* (v. 6; cf. 1 Sam 7:1). David's desire to bring the Ark to Jerusalem has both a political and a religious motive. With the presence of the Ark in Jerusalem David could make the city the religious center of the nation and at the same time consolidate the tribes around the ark since Yahweh, the God of Israel, was understood to be *enthroned on the cherubim* of the Ark (v. 6). For this reason David consulted with the leaders of the army and the leaders of all Israel. So, David summoned all Israel from *the Shihor of Egypt to the Lebo-Hamath* (v. 5, lit. "the entrance of Hamath"). Although this description of the extent of the land of Israel appears again in the work of the CHR (2 Chr 7:8), the description is highly idealistic, since it reflects the most extensive limits of the land of Israel. The common way for the CHR to describe the boundaries of the land is *from Beer-sheba to Dan* (1 Chr 21:2, but cf. commentary on 21:1-13, below).

The moving of the Ark was carried out with great celebration and joy before Yahweh by David and all Israel. The celebration included dances, the singing of songs, and the playing of musical instruments (v. 8). The death of *Uzzah* (vv. 9-10) marred the celebration and the enterprise ended in failure. The death of Uzzah can be explained by the fact that among the people of Israel the violation of the holy was forbidden. The people neglected the proper ritual and failed to carry the ark in the proper manner. The name *Perez-uzzah* means "the breaking forth upon Uzzah" (see v. 11). The Ark was brought to the house of *Obed-edom the Gittite*, that is, a man from Gath, where it remained for *three months.* Yahweh blessed Obed-edom and his family because of the presence of the Ark in his house. Yahweh also blessed David as a result of his desire to care for the Ark. These blessings are introduced by means of three events in the life of David narrated in chap. 14. If the Obed-edom who kept the Ark is the same individual mentioned in 1 Chr 15:18, 21, then he was granted Levitical status and became a *gatekeeper for the ark* (1 Chr 15:24; cf. commentary on 26:1-19, below).

David's Establishment in Jerusalem, 14:1–16:43

14:1-2. Embassy from Tyre. Before proceeding with the story of the Ark, the CHR introduces three important events in the life of David, although they have little chronological relationship with the ark narrative. By placing these events between David's first and second attempt to bring the Ark to Jerusalem, the CHR is intimating that the blessings David received were the results of his effort to bring the Ark to Jerusalem. The first event is the occasion when Hiram, king of Tyre, sent materials to David to help him build a palace in Jerusalem. Tyre, a Phoenician seaport city north of Israel, was known for its commercial enterprises (cf. 2 Kgs 10:11, 22). The friendship between Tyre and Israel continued even beyond the days of David. Hiram and Solomon developed many joint commercial ventures that benefitted both kings. The CHR underscores once again that Yahweh had blessed David and had exalted his kingdom for the sake of Israel. The gifts that Hiram brought were a sign of the divine blessing that Yahweh bestowed upon David and that Yahweh had confirmed David's kingship.

14:3-7. David's family. The second event is the introduction of David's sons and daughters born in Jerusalem, although only the names of the sons are given. David's large family was another evidence of Yahweh's blessing. This list is taken from 2 Sam 5:13-16 with some differences. It also agrees with the list of David's sons in 1 Chr 3:5-8, although some names are spelled differently (cf. commentary at 3:1-9 above). The CHR says that thirteen sons were born to David in Jerusalem, while the author of 2 Samuel listed eleven. *Elphelet* and *Nogah* are omitted from the list in 2 Samuel. The name *Beeliada* (v. 6) appears both in 2 Sam 16 and 1 Chr 3:8 as Eliada. Beeliada was the original name of David's son. Since the name was compounded with the name of the Canaanite god Baal, it was changed to Eliada, a name compounded with El, the Hebrew word for God.

14:8-17. Victories over the Philistines. The third event, another demonstration of Yahweh's blessing upon David, is the double victory against the PHILIS-TINES (vv. 8-12, 13-16). After the Philistines heard that David had become *king over all Israel* and had ceased being their loyal vassal, they attacked Israel. They raided the *valley of Rephaim*, located a few miles southwest of Jerusalem. The manner by which David inquired of Yahweh is not clear. Possibly he used the sacred lots, the URIM AND THUMMIM, as Saul had done (1 Sam 14:36-37, 41-42). Yahweh assured David of victory by promising to burst out against the Philistines *like a bursting flood*. The place of victory was called *Baal-perazim*, "Lord of bursting out" (v. 11; cf. NRSV mg.). The word *perazim* is related to the word *perez* in 13:11 (see also 15:13). At the time of the journey of the ark, Yahweh burst out in judgment against Israel. Now he bursts out for salvation on their behalf against their enemy. The Philistines fled in panic abandoning their gods. According to the CHR, David ordered his people to burn the idols. However 2 Sam 5:21 reads: "David and his men carried them away." The difference between the text in Samuel and the text in Chronicles reflects the CHR's effort to present David as obeying the law of Deut 7:25, which commands the burning of the images of the gods of the people of the land.

After their defeat, the Philistines raided Israel again, and again David inquires of Yahweh. By divine command David prepares an ambush against the Philistines. The sound of marching *in the tops of the balsam trees* (v. 15) refers to the movement of the wind on the leaves. This would be a sign for David and his army that Yahweh would lead them into battle and give them victory. David and his men pursue the Philistines from GIBEON to GEZER. Second Samuel 5:25 says that it was from "Geba to Gezer." This change may reflect the reading of Isa 28:21 and the fact that Gibeon was the place of one of Israel's greatest victories (Josh 10). As a result of David's victory against the Philistines, his fame spread throughout the land, another evidence of God's blessing.

15:1-29. Moving the ark. After presenting the blessings Yahweh had bestowed on David because of his faithfulness, the CHR resumes the narrative detailing the relocation of the ark from the house of Obed-edom (13:14) to Jerusalem. The narrative is based on 2 Sam 6:12-19 with several additions by the CHR. In the CHR's narrative the priests and the Levites predominate. This group, together with the commanders of

thousands and the elders of Israel, formed a liturgical procession, marked by music, sacrifices, and great celebration.

David prepared a tent to house the Ark, probably fashioned after the tabernacle of Moses, which remained in Gibeon. If David's building of houses for himself in Jerusalem (v. 1) is to be taken literally, then more than three months had passed since the Ark was left in the house of Obed-edom (13:14). Because the first attempt to move the Ark was done improperly (v. 13), David summoned the priests and the Levites and put them in charge of the relocation of the Ark. David commanded that the Levites should carry the Ark because Yahweh had given them charge of the sacred vessels of the Temple (v. 2). The priests in charge of helping transport the ark were ZADOK and ABIATHAR (v. 11). Since the priests have no direct involvement with the events related to the relocation of the Ark, their inclusion here seems secondary. The Levites, who were selected according to their families, are not mentioned in 2 Sam 6, possibly because they did not function as a religious group in the time of David. These were the Levites selected: from the house of *Kohath*, *Uriel* (6:24) with 120 assistants (v. 5); from the house of *Merari*, *Asaiah* (6:30) with 220 helpers (v. 6); from the house of *Gershon*, Joel (6:21) with 130 attendants (v. 7). Joel does not appear in the list of the family of Gershon, unless he is to be identified with *Joah* in 6:21. Two persons named Joel appear in Chronicles related to the Gershonites (cf. 23:8 and 26:22). Three other Levites from the family of Kohath are listed: *Shemaiah*, from the clan of Elizaphan (Exod 6:22) with 200 assistants (v. 8); *Eliel* from the clan of Hebron (Exod 6:18) with eighty assistants (v. 9); and *Amminadab* from the clan of Uzziel (Exod 6:18) with 112 assistants (v. 10). The total number of assistants helping the Levites was 862. The grouping of the Levites into six classes does not correspond to the usual classification used by the CHR; however, the predominance of the family of Kohath is due to the fact that they were in charge of the objects used in the sanctuary (Num 4:4-15). The priests and Levites were purified according to the proper ritual (Num 8:5-13). The ark was carried by poles inlaid with gold that were introduced into the rings of the ark (Exod 25:12-15).

David also told the leaders of the Levites to select singers to participate in the celebration. The Levites selected three singers: *Heman*, *Asaph*, and *Ethan*. On other occasions when the Levitical singers are named, Asaph generally appears first (16:5, 41; 2 Chr 5:12;

29:13-14; 35:15 but cf. 1 Chr 6:33-43). Heman, Asaph, and Ethan were selected to play the *bronze cymbals* (v. 19). Other musicians were also selected. They were grouped into three classes, according to their musical instruments. Eight musicians were appointed to play the harp according to *Alamoth* (v. 20) and six to play the lyre according to *Sheminith* (v. 21). *Alamoth* and *Sheminith* probably were musical terms; they appear in the titles of Pss 46 and 6. *Chenaniah, leader of the Levites in music* (v. 22), was in charge of leading the music because he was an expert in this area. *Berechiah* and *Elkanah* (v. 23), as well as *Obed-edom* and *Jehiah* (v. 24) were selected as *gatekeepers for the ark*. Finally, seven priests were selected to *blow trumpets before the ark* (v. 24).

The relocation of the Ark (vv. 25-29) was accomplished with a solemn ceremony that included *the elders of Israel* and the military chiefs (not mentioned in 2 Sam 6). Because David and the Levites had followed the proper procedure in handling the ark, divine favor was obtained and *God helped the Levites* (v. 26). During the march, the Levites offered seven bulls and seven rams as sacrifices. The narrative in 2 Sam 6:13 says that David himself offered the sacrifices. This change reflects the sacrificial practices in the time of the CHR. David and the Levites were dressed with linen vestments. David also wore *a linen ephod* (v. 27), the same kind of garment used by the priests. The joy of the occasion is manifested in the statement that David leaped and danced before the LORD (see 13:8). *Michal*, the daughter of Saul, *despised* David for what she took to be an indiscretion. The CHR omits the reasons for Michal's contempt for David (see 2 Sam 6:20-23). Her identification as a member of the house of Saul may indicate that the CHR is showing the disapproval of the house of Saul for David's concern for the Ark.

16:1-3. End of the ceremony. After the Ark was brought to Jerusalem and placed inside the tent David had prepared for it, sacrifices were made before Yahweh. The narrative follows 2 Sam 6:17-19. David, exercising his priestly functions (although this is attenuated in v. 2; cf. 2 Sam 6:17), offered sacrifices, blessed the people, and gave them provisions.

16:4-6. Organization of the cult. Before declaring that the people returned to their homes (2 Sam 6:19), the CHR inserts a passage into his source, describing David's organization of the ministry of the Levites before the ark in Jerusalem (vv. 4-6) and before the TABERNACLE of MOSES that was left in Gibeon (vv. 37-38;

cf. 21:29). Between these two narratives, the CHR inserts a song of thanksgiving (vv. 7-36). The work of the Levites was to minister before the Ark with prayer, music and praise. Asaph was the leader of the group. Under him was Zechariah with eight other Levites (see 15:17-18). They were responsible to play musical instruments and to blow the trumpets before the ark.

16:7-38. A song of thanksgiving. This song of thanksgiving is an anthology of several other psalms:

1 Chr 16:8-22	Psalms 105:1-15
16:23-33	96:1-13
16:34-36	106:1, 47-48

Ps 96 has no title in the MT, but according to the LXX Ps 96 was a song of David when the Temple was built after the Exile.

16:39-43. Ministry of the Levites. The ministry of the Levitical singers before the Ark was to be permanent (v. 37). Together with the singers were *Obed-edom* and *Hosah* (cf. 26:10) serving as gatekeepers, and sixty-eight assistants. Their work was to give *thanks to the LORD, for his steadfast love endures for ever* (v. 41; cf. 16:34; Ps 106:1; 107:1; 136:1). *Jeduthun*, the father of *Obed-edom* (v. 38) was one of the chief musicians (vv. 41-42). Presiding over the tabernacle of Moses in Gibeon were Zadok and several other priests. Heman and Jeduthun were in charge of the singers (15:17-22). The reason the tabernacle of Moses was in Gibeon is unknown, but the presence of the ark in Jerusalem means that during the time of David there were two legitimate sanctuaries in Israel, one in Jerusalem housing the ark of Yahweh and the other in Gibeon where the TABERNACLE was located. However, while the Levites were to offer praises and prayer before the ark (16:4), the priests were to offer burnt offerings upon the altar of Yahweh at Gibeon (v. 40). It was to the tabernacle that Solomon came offering sacrifices to God (2 Kgs 3:4; 2 Chr 1:3-6).

God's Promise to David, 17:1-27

This text is one of the most important in the OT. The covenant God established with David made clear that the CHR believed that the Davidic monarch had a role in the redemptive purposes of Yahweh. The text of chap. 17 follows closely 2 Sam 7:1-29 with some modifications that reflect the theological views of the CHR.

17:1-15. Nathan's prophecy. After David had finished building a house for himself and a tent for the ark of God (15:1), he expressed to NATHAN the desire to build a house for God. The word "house" (*bayit*) is used in the text with three different meanings. David's *house* (17:1) was the place he built for himself in Jerusalem. The *house* David desired to build for Yahweh (v. 4) was a temple to lodge the ark of God. The *house* Yahweh would build for David (v. 10b) was a dynasty, the certainty that David's kingdom would be established forever.

Nathan appeared in David's court as a PROPHET and as a political advisor to the king. David appealed to Nathan in order to discover God's will and to receive divine approval. Nathan was favorable to the present project and gave his approval. That night, Yahweh appeared to Nathan in a VISION (v. 15) and overruled the prophet, warning him that David would not build the Temple. Although no reason was given for this prohibition, the CHR will say later that the reason David could not build the Temple was because he was a man of war (22:8; 28:3). The CHR also will describe in detail how David made all the necessary preparations for the building of the Temple (chaps. 21–29). But the idea of a temple was pleasing to God. Yahweh promised that he would establish the house of David (v. 10b) and that a descendant of David would build a house for Yahweh. Although the CHR is intimating that SOLOMON was going to build the Temple (cf. 28:5-7), he is implying the perpetuity of the Davidic dynasty by his fivefold repetition of *forever* (vv. 12, 14 [twice], 23. 27). The messianic import of the CHR's words is that the stability of the Davidic dynasty was related to the presence of Yahweh in the Temple. To the CHR, the cause of Yahweh and the cause of David coincide. While 2 Sam 7:16 speaks of "your house and your kingdom," v. 14 speaks of *my house and . . . my kingdom.* The house of David is now the house of Yahweh and the kingdom of David is now the kingdom of Yahweh.

17:16-27. David's prayer. David's prayer is presented before the ark of God housed in the tent (16:1). The ark symbolized the presence of Yahweh among his people. David gave thanks to Yahweh for his promise, acknowledging that Yahweh had honored him beyond his expectations. He also expressed his confidence that Yahweh would fulfill his promise.

David's Wars, 18:1–20:8

The CHR dedicates chaps. 18–20 to describing David's wars and victories against the enemies of ISRAEL. The CHR's description of David's wars and victories affirmed David as a great military leader. These victories over Israel's neighbors helped David con-

solidate his kingdom and confirmed God's blessing upon his kingdom (see 18:6b, 13b). The spoils of war became the source of the wealth used for the construction of the Temple. A brief parenthesis in the narrative (18:14-17) provides additional information about David's court personnel.

18:1-2. Philistines and Moabites. The transitional formula *some time afterward* (v. 1) does not provide a chronological framework to date the various battles. The defeat of the PHILISTINES and the subjugation of GATH, one of the five Philistine cities (Josh 13:3), made it possible for 600 men from Gath to serve in David's army (2 Sam 15:18).

The report of Moab's defeat is subdued in the narrative. While 2 Sam 8:2 describes the massacre of two-thirds of the population, the CHR only notes that the Moabites were subjugated and were forced to pay tribute. The omission of the atrocities committed by David is part of the CHR's effort to idealize David.

18:3-11. Arameans. The Arameans formed an alliance of city-states to the north of Israel and posed a great threat to the security of David's kingdom. The conquest of *Zobah* (vv. 3-4), a city north of DAMASCUS, and the subjugation of *Damascus* (vv. 5-6) allowed David to establish garrisons in two strong Aramean states and thus greatly enlarge the borders of his kingdom. The reference to *one thousand chariots* (v. 4) is lacking in 2 Sam 8:4, while the number of horsemen (7,000) has been greatly increased from the reference in the CHR's source (700). Since the Israelites did not use chariots, David and his men incapacitated the horses, allowing only 100 to be used in the formation of an Israelite chariot corps. David brought to Jerusalem the spoils of war, gold, silver, and bronze, and dedicated them to Yahweh to be used in the construction of the Temple. In anticipation of the event, the CHR declares that *Solomon* used the *bronze* for the construction of some of the furniture of the Temple (v. 8).

King Tou of Hamath, who had been at war with *Hadadezer*, was happy that David had defeated his enemy; he sent an embassy to David headed by *his son Hadoram*. Hadoram carried a large tribute and came to congratulate David on his victory against the Arameans. David also took tribute from five of Israel's neighbors (vv. 9-10). The tribute received from these nations was dedicated to Yahweh to be used in the construction of the Temple (v. 11).

18:12-13. Edomites. The victory of Israel against the *Edomites* is credited to *Abishai* (vv. 12-13). Abishai was David's nephew, the son of Zeruiah, David's sister (2:16). However, 2 Sam 8:13 says that David made a name for himself when he killed the 18,000 Edomites, while the superscription to Ps 60 says that Joab "killed twelve thousand Edomites in the Valley of Salt." This discrepancy may reflect different traditions rather than textual corruption. The repeated assertion that David's victories were given by God (vv. 6, 13) serves to reaffirm God's promise to David that he would subdue his enemies (17:10).

18:14-17. David's officials. The list of the royal administrators is taken from 2 Sam 8:15-18. A second list appears in 2 Sam 20:23-26. *Joab*, David's nephew (2:16), was commander of the regular army. *Jehoshaphat was recorder*, an office that may reflect the function of the herald of Pharaoh. The recorder (Heb. *mazkir*) was the person responsible for the protocol in the ceremonies of the Egyptian palace. *Zadok . . . and Ahimelech . . . were priests*. Since Ahimelech had been killed by Saul and Abiathar was still the priest at the end of David's reign (2 Sam 20:25; 1 Kgs 1:7), the likely reading should have been "Abiathar, the son of Ahimelech" (McCarter 1984, 253–54). *Shavsha was [the] secretary*. He appears as Seraiah in 2 Sam 8:17 and Shisha in 1 Kgs 4:3. Shavsha was a non-Israelite name; it is possible that the different spellings of his name in the Hebrew text may be attempts to convey his name in Hebrew.

Benaiah and Jehoiada (not *Benaiah son of Jehoida*, v. 17) were in charge of the Cherethites and the Pelethites, two groups of mercenary soldiers that formed David's personal army. They were probably part of the foreign population that settled in CANAAN, known as the SEA PEOPLES. The Cherethites have been identified with the Cretans and the Pelethites with the Philistines. David's sons were *the chief officials in the service of the king* (v. 17); 2 Sam 2:18 says that they were priests. The reason for the change was that in the CHR's day, the priests came from the tribe of Levi. Since David's sons were from the tribe of Judah, the affirmation that they served as priests was incompatible with the CHR's view.

19:1-20:3. Ammonites. The story of David's war against the Ammonites and the Arameans is taken from 2 Sam 10. The war against the Ammonites occurred when the delegates David had sent to *Hanun* were humiliated (v. 4; cf. 2 Sam 10:4). Hanun prepares for war against Israel by hiring an army of Arameans. *Mesopotamia* (v. 6) is an area also known as ARAM-NA-HARAIM (NIV). According to the CHR, *Maacah* and

Zobah were paid to participate. Samuel adds Beth-rehob and Tob (2 Sam 10:6). Hanun paid *a thousand talents of silver* (about thirty-seven tons) to hire *thirty-two thousand chariots* (v. 7) and 33,000 foot soldiers (2 Sam 10:6). Confronted with the Ammonites' large army, Joab and his brother Abishai divided Israel's army into two groups, one to fight against the Arameans in the open country and the other against the Ammonites in their capital city, *Rabbah* (v. 9; cf. 20:1). The Arameans were soundly defeated and the Ammonites retreated back into the fortified city. The Ammonites brought another group of Arameans, commanded by *Shophach the commander of the army of Hadadezer* (v. 16), to reinforce their army. At this point David himself took control of the army (v. 17) to fight against the Arameans. In the battle fought at Helam (2 Sam 10:16) David completely defeated the Aramean army (v. 18) and put them under vassalage. In the final victory, David and his army killed 7,000 charioteers and 40,000 foot soldiers (v. 18); 2 Sam 10:18 says David killed 700 charioteers and 40,000 horsemen. The CHR's numbers probably are inflated in order to magnify David's victory over the enemy.

The narrative of the war against the Ammonites in 20:1-3 is taken from 2 Sam 11–12, with several omissions by the CHR. The CHR, following the pattern of omitting stories that would tend to tarnish the image of David as Israel's ideal king, omits the story of David's adultery with BATHSHEBA, David's request to Joab to have URIAH killed, and NATHAN's rebuke of the king (2 Sam 11–12). The first part of 20:1 comes from 2 Sam 11:1; the second part comes from 2 Sam 12:26.

The CHR then gives the beginning and the end of the account of David's war against the Ammonites. After David's victory he removes *the crown of Milcom from his head* (v. 2) and places it on his own head. KJV, RSV, and NIV translate *Milcom* as "their king" (but see NIV and RSV mg.). Milcom was the name of the Ammonite god who often appears in the OT as MOLECH (1 Kgs 11:5, 7). David also forced the Ammonites to work hard with instruments of iron, probably demolishing the walls of the city.

20:4-8. Philistines. The source of this information is 2 Sam 21:18-22. The CHR mentions three instances of hand to hand combat by David's soldiers against the descendants of the Rephaim, descendants of Rapha, a group of people believed to be *giants*. The NRSV uses the word *giants* to translate "Rephaim" (cf. NIV "Rephaites"). Many of the Philistine soldiers that David and his soldiers killed were descendants of

Rapha (cf. 2 Sam. 21:15-22), although only one of them was considered to be a huge man (v. 6).

The first engagement was at GEZER, identified as Gob in 2 Sam 21:18. There *Sibbecai* killed *Sippai*, a descendant of the Rephaim. In the second contest *Elhanan son of Jair killed Lahmi the brother of Goliath* (v. 5). In the third, *Jonathan*, the nephew of David, killed a man *of great size, who had six fingers on each hand, and six toes on each foot* (v. 6; see Barnett 1990, 46–51).

The statement that *Elhanan killed Lahmi the brother of Goliath* seems to be an attempt to resolve the contradiction between 1 Sam 17 in which it is said that David killed Goliath and 2 Sam 21:19 in which it is said that Elhanan killed Goliath. There are two traditions concerning the death of Goliath. The traditional passage, 1 Sam 17:41-49, says that David killed Goliath with stones (2 Sam 17:50) and with a sword (2 Sam 17:51). The second tradition says that Elhanan, a soldier in David's army, killed Goliath (2 Sam 21:19). Some scholars have said that Elhanan was David's given name and that David was his throne name (Bright 1981, 192). It is a fact that many people in the OT have two names (cf. 2 Sam 12:24-25). However, there is no evidence that David was known as Elhanan. Some scholars have said that the accomplishment of Elhanan was attached to David in order to magnify him in the eyes of Israel. Something similar is found in 1 Chr 18:12, where Abishai's victory against the Edomites is credited to David (2 Sam 8:13). The conflict the CHR found between 1 Sam 17 and 2 Sam 21:19 is not easy to solve. The CHR's attempted solution further complicates the matter without providing an adequate solution.

David's Census and God's Punishment, 21:1–22:1

21:1-13. David's Census. Chapter 21 shows that the sin of David in taking a census of Israel was the tragic occasion that caused the selection of a holy place for the location of Yahweh's Temple. The purpose of David's census was primarily for military conscription (vv. 5, 7), although it could also have been used for taxation. In the parallel narrative in 2 Sam 24:1-16, it was God who incited David to number the people. In Chronicles the action is attributed to *Satan* (v. 1). Satan appears in the OT in Job 1–2 where he is one of the sons of God who comes before God to accuse Job. He also appears in Zech 3:1-2 as a member of the heavenly court who accuses Joshua, the high priest. In Job and Zechariah the Hebrew word *satan* appears

with a definite article to emphasize his function as the "accuser." He is a being subordinated to the power of God. In 1 Chr 21 *Satan* appears as the personal name of a being who incites an individual to evil. The change made by the CHR may reflect a postexilic theological development of the concept of Satan's work.

Despite Joab's objection, David ordered a census of Israel *from Beer-sheba to Dan* (v. 2). This south-north orientation of Israel is peculiar to the CHR (see 2 Chr 30:5) and contrary to the customary north-south orientation of the OT (cf. 2 Sam 24:2) and may reflect CHR's view of the importance of the southern kingdom. The number given here, 1,100,000, differs from the 1,300,000 of 2 Sam 24:9. Although different solutions have been offered, it is possible that the discrepancy reflects the fact that the CHR says that Joab did not include Levi and Benjamin in the census.

The displeasure of God in v. 7 is omitted in 2 Sam 24. The CHR says that Yahweh *struck Israel* but this is a reference to the plague, which is not sent until v. 14. The text does not say how David discovered his action was a sin against God. The CHR emphasizes that the census was a sin (v. 3), perhaps to stress that it was a lack of trust in God. David's selection of punishment upon Israel (v. 12) was made after Gad, the seer, offered him three choices of punishment. In 2 Sam 24:11 Gad is called both a PROPHET and seer. The three years of famine here appear as seven in 2 Sam 24:13; however, the LXX agrees with Chronicles and is a preferred reading. The pestilence as the sword of Yahweh is the antithesis to the sword of the enemy.

21:14-30. The LORD's Punishment. The plague was sent by *an angel* of Yahweh (see 2 Kgs 19:35) who acted as the exterminator. With a *drawn sword*, the angel went through Israel, and 70,000 people were killed. Before the angel entered JERUSALEM, Yahweh repented. The repentance of God reflects God's change of attitude towards the punishment. With his sword stretched towards Jerusalem (v. 16), the angel of Yahweh appeared to David *by the threshing floor of Ornan the Jebusite*. Ornan appears in 2 Sam 24:16 as Araunah. The name Araunah seems to be a title, derived from the Hurrian word meaning "lord." The MT in 2 Sam 24:23 calls him a king. The vision of the angel *standing between earth and heaven, [with] a drawn sword stretched out over Jerusalem* (v. 16), caused David to pray, confessing that he alone was guilty. David pleaded that the people be spared from further punishment (v. 17). The angel commanded Gad to tell David to erect an altar on the threshing floor and dedicate it to Yahweh. David approached Ornan and offered to buy the threshing floor. The contract between David and Ornan is similar to the contract between ABRAHAM and Ephron the Hittite for the purchase of the cave of MACHPELAH (Gen 23:1-20). The price of the land, according to 2 Sam 24:24, was only fifty shekels of silver. On the other hand, the price in Chronicles is *six hundred shekels of gold* (v. 25). This discrepancy reflects the CHR's desire to magnify the importance of the site of the future temple, since the amount here is twelve times the amount in Samuel. It is also possible that the difference reflects David's purchase not only of the threshing floor, but of the whole area adjacent to the threshing floor. David built an altar for Yahweh and offered a burnt offering and a peace offering upon it. God demonstrated his acceptance of the sacrifice with two signs: *fire from heaven* (v. 26) and the cessation of the plague (v. 27). The *fire from heaven* (omitted in 2 Sam 24:25) serves the intent of the CHR, which is to underscore the importance of the altar and its divine origin. The THEOPHANY at the threshing floor and the divine approval of David's altar (24:28-25:1) serve to explain why the high place at Gibeon, where the Mosaic sanctuary was located, was abandoned and why the site at Jerusalem was selected as the place where the Temple of God and the altar of sacrifice would be built.

David's Preparations for the Temple, 22:2-19

22:1-5. General preparation. Most of chaps. 22–29 are taken from extracanonical materials, which the CHR relies on for his source of information. After the unusual events at the threshing floor, David understood that God had selected that place for the building of his house. The narrative of 2 Samuel is silent about David's plan to build the Temple. The CHR details the steps David took in preparation for the construction of the Temple. David commanded that *aliens who were residing in the land* be used as *stonecutters* to prepare the stones to be used in the building of the Temple. These *aliens* (*gerim*) were part of the Canaanite population that had lived among the Israelites (2 Chr 2:16-18). David also provided large quantities of iron, bronze, and cedar. The reason David began to make preparation for the construction of the Temple was that his son Solomon was *young and inexperienced* (v. 5).

22:6-16. Dialogue with Solomon. The CHR expresses the reason David was unable to build the Temple. In 2 Sam 7 no reason was given why David was not allowed to build the Temple. The CHR says David was disqualified because the many wars he conducted with divine approval caused him to shed much blood. His status as *a man of war* (2 Chr 28:3) disqualified him from the task of building God's house. The responsibility of building the Temple fell upon his son Solomon, *a man of peace* (v. 9). This designation plays upon the name of Solomon (a name related to the Heb. word "peace"). David's charge to Solomon (vv. 12-13) is based upon the deuteronomistic view that strict observance of the law was the condition for prosperity (Deut 26:16-19). David then enumerates the materials he has accumulated for the building of the Temple. The amount of gold (100,000 talents or 3,750 tons) and silver (1,000,000 talents or 37,500 tons) is an embellishment that allows the CHR to describe the splendor of Solomon's Temple.

22:17-19. Request for help. David exhorts the leaders of Israel to seek Yahweh and to help Solomon with the construction of the Temple. Their gratitude to God for peace and prosperity would be manifested by the construction of the sanctuary for the housing of the ark of the covenant and the holy vessels of God.

David's Organization of the Temple Personnel, 23:1–27:34

23:1-32. Organization of the Levites. The narrative of the organization of the Levites into guilds is preceded by a brief introduction (vv. 1-2) in which David proclaims before Israel, gathered in a solemn assembly, that Solomon was his chosen successor. The assembly is described in chaps. 28–29.

According to Num 4:3, the Levites came into service at the age of thirty. Later on, the age was lowered to twenty-five (Num 8:24). Because of the greater influence of the Temple in Israelite life and the need for additional personnel for Temple service, the age was lowered again to twenty. The increase in Temple personnel may reflect the needs of the Temple at the end of the monarchy or even of the age of the CHR himself. Twenty was also the age for military service for the men of the tribes of Israel (Num 1). The total number of Levites available for service was 38,000. They were divided into four groups (vv. 4-5): 24,000 Levites were dedicated for the work of the Temple, 6,000 as *officers and judges* (see 2 Chr 19:4-11), 4,000 as *gatekeepers*, and 4,000 as musicians (vv. 4-6). The Levites are listed according to the leaders of the Levitical families: the sons of *Gershon* are listed in vv. 7-11, the sons of *Kohath* in vv. 12-20, and the sons of

Merari in vv. 21-23. The genealogies of the sons of Levi differ from the genealogy in chap. 6. This may indicate that the CHR was using a list containing the names of the Levitical families of David's time or even his own time. This passage shows the subservient role of the Levites, for they were selected to serve in the Temple under *the descendants of Aaron* (v. 28). *The sons of Moses* and their descendants (v. 15) were also assigned Levitical duties. The duties of the descendants of Aaron were to consecrate the holy things, to burn the sacrifices, and to bless the people. The duties of the Levites were cleaning the Temple, preparing the bread, and assisting in the liturgy. The text describing the Levitical duties (vv. 25-32) may reflect the struggle between priests and Levites in post-exilic times, aimed at giving the priests supremacy over the ministry in the Temple (cf. Ezek 44:10-14).

24:1-31. Organization of the Priests. The priests were organized into twenty-four divisions. *Nadab* and *Abihu*, sons of Aaron, had died because of their unfaithfulness (Num 3:4); however, the CHR chose to omit the reason for their death. For this reason only two lines of priests came from Aaron, one from *Eleazar*, represented by *Zadok* and another from *Ithamar*, represented by *Ahimelech*. Since the sons of Eleazar were more numerous than the sons of Ithamar, they were divided into sixteen divisions and the sons of Ithamar into eight divisions, but each with equal standing (v. 5). The divisions were done by lots (v. 5) and the results were recorded by Shemaiah, the son of Nethanel, an unknown Levitical scribe. Most of these names (vv. 7-19) appear in Ezra 2 and Neh 12, since the names of the individuals also became the names of the divisions. Zechariah, the father of John the Baptist, is listed as being from the division of Abijah (Luke 1:5; cf. 1 Chr 24:10). Another group of Levites (vv. 20-31) were divided by lot into several divisions, perhaps twenty-four also, as suggested by v. 31. Since several names in this list do not appear in 23:6-23, it is clear that this list is a revision of the earlier list. The family of Gershon (23:7-11) is missing, probably accidentally omitted by the scribe.

25:1-31. Organization of the musicians. David also divided the Levitical singers into twenty-four divisions. David was helped by *the officers of the army* (v. 1). However, it is possible that David was helped by the leaders of the Levites (see 24:5) who were in charge of the Levites who served in the Temple (Num 8:25). The musicians were grouped around three major Levites: *Asaph, Heman,* and *Jeduthun*. Jeduthun is also known as Ethan in 15:17, 19. The ministry of the musicians was considered prophetic. *Heman* is called a *seer* in v. 5. *Asaph* is called a *seer* in 2 Chr 29:30 and *Jeduthun* in 2 Chr 35:15. This suggests that their ministry was accomplished under divine inspiration. The designation of the Temple music as prophetic associates the Temple musicians with the cultic prophets of the OT. The *sons of Asaph* formed four divisions (v. 2); the *sons of Jeduthun*, six (v. 3), and the *sons of Heman*, fourteen (vv. 4-5). Each of the twenty-four divisions had twelve men, for a total of 288 men involved in the music ministry of the Temple (v. 7).

26:1-19. Organization of the gatekeepers. The duty of the gatekeepers was to prevent unauthorized persons from entering the Temple. They were arranged into three divisions. The first division was that of the sons of *Meshelemiah* (vv. 1-3, 9), a descendant of Korah from the family of Levi (Exod 6:16, 18, 21), with a total of eighteen men (v. 9). The second division belonged to the sons of *Obed-edom* (v. 4). The identification of OBED-EDOM in Chronicles is difficult. In 13:13-14 he is a Gittite, one of the PHILISTINES that joined David's army. In 15:18 he is a gatekeeper and in 15:21 he is a musician playing the lyre. In 16:38 he appears as the son of Jeduthun and is a gatekeeper. In 26:4-8 he appears as a Levite, although the CHR does not present a Levitical genealogy for him. The statement that *God blessed him* (v. 5) is a deliberate effort to identify him with the foreigner who kept the ark (13:14). It seems that because of Obed-edom's willingness to keep the Ark of Yahweh, he and his family were accepted into Levitical service. The division of doorkeepers from the family of Obed-edom was sixty-two. This number differs from 16:38 where the number is sixty-eight. The third division was headed by *Hosah,* a descendant of *Merari* and it had thirteen men. The total number of gatekeepers was ninety-three. This number is less than the number that appears in 9:22 (212), in Neh 7:45 (138), Neh 11:19 (172) and in Ezra 2:42 (139). The difference may be explained by the fact that the need decreased with the passing of time (Braun 1968, 251) or by the fact that it began with a small number but that at a later time it had increased in number.

The assignment of each family was conducted by lot. The east gate was assigned to *Shelemiah* (the *Meshelemiah* of v. 1) and the north gate to his son *Zechariah* (v. 14). The south gate was assigned to the descendants of *Obed-edom* (v. 15) and the west gate was assigned to *Hosah* (v. 16). *Shuppim* (v. 16) should be deleted from the list since his name is irrelevant in the text and should be considered an intrusion. The meaning of the word *parbar* (v. 18 mg.) is unknown. It is generally accepted as a Persian word that the CHR used to refer to an area in the Temple precinct, thus *colonnade*.

26:20-28. Organization of the treasurers. In addition to their duties in the cult, the Levites had other duties. *Jehieli* (or *Jehiel*, cf. 23:8) and his sons (vv. 21-22) were in charge of the treasury of the Temple. This treasury included the money from freewill offerings, sacrifices, tithes, and other things dedicated to God. These Levites were descendants of *Gershon* and his son *Ladan* (or *Libni*, cf. 6:17). The reading of the NRSV, following the MT, suggests that Ahijah was in charge of the treasury of the Temple (v. 2). However, the reading of the LXX provides a better understanding of the passage: "Their fellow Levites were in charge of . . . " (cf. NIV).

Shelomoth and his relatives were in charge of all the treasury accumulated from the spoils of war (v. 21). This portion of the treasury was given by David and his warriors and by some of the great heroes of Israel's past (v. 28). These Levites were Kohathites, from the family of Amram, Moses's father. *Shebuel* (v. 24), a Gershomite, was the chief officer over all the treasuries of the Temple.

26:29-32. Appointment of the administrators. Two Kohathite families (cf. 6:18) were assigned *outside duties*. The family of Izhar was appointed to be *officers and judges* (v. 29). Of the family of Hebron, headed by *Chenaniah and his sons*, 1,700 men were assigned ministry duties to the people west of the Jordan; and 2,700 men, headed by *Jerijah* and his relatives, were assigned duties east of the Jordan, with responsibilities over the tribes of Reuben, Gad, and the half-tribe of Manasseh. It is not clear what these outside assignments entailed. Since the duties included the *work of the LORD* and the *service of the king* (v. 30), it is possible that these Levites were responsible for the administration of the Levitical cities, the collection of religious and state taxes, and the administration of justice. Jazer was one of the Levitical cities (6:81). According to the CHR, these appointments were made *in the fortieth year* of David (v. 31), his last as king.

27:1-34. Military and political leaders. Verse 1 serves as introduction to the whole chapter, although most of the terms describing the leaders apply mostly to vv. 2-15. This summary introduces the leaders of

David's army, the tribal leaders, and other officers of the court who served at the pleasure of the king.

27:1-15. Army leaders. David organized his army into twelve divisions, each headed by a chief commander. Every division consisted of 24,000 men who were on active duty for one month each year, after which they were relieved by another division. The total number of men was 288,000. It is possible to interpret these numbers in terms of military units. Since the Hebrew word *'eleph* can also be translated as "military unit," it is possible that David's army consisted of twelve divisions with twenty-four military units in each division. Under this view, the number of men serving the 288 units would be unknown. Most of the names of the twelve commanders appear with some variations in the list of David's mighty men (11:10-47).

27:16-24. Tribal leaders. The naming of twelve leaders over the tribes of Israel may indicate that David was laying the foundation for what became the twelve administrative districts of Solomon (1 Kgs 4:7-19). The listing of the tribes varies from tribal lists in Num 1 and 1 Chr 2. The tribes of GAD and ASHER are omitted from this list. To complete the number of twelve tribes, the CHR includes LEVI and divides the tribe of JOSEPH into East and West MANASSEH and EPHRAIM. The family of Aaron receives a special mention as a distinct group but it is included with the tribe of Levi. The CHR mentions David's census of Israel. The census remained incomplete because of divine displeasure (cf. 21:1-5). The CHR exonerates David from the disastrous consequences of the census by saying that he did not count anyone under twenty years of age because he believed in God's promise to Abraham (Gen 15:1-5) The blame is placed upon Joab because he did not finish numbering the people. *The Annals of King David* (v. 24) detailed the acts of David, and was part of the royal archives.

27:25-31. Administrators of the royal house. This passage portrays David as a large landowner. His estate included agricultural *fields* (v. 26), *vineyards* (v. 27), *olive and sycamore trees* (v. 28) and livestock (vv. 29-30). This list contains the names of twelve administrators who were responsible for the management of David's properties. These properties provided much of the revenue David needed to maintain the expenses of the palace. It is difficult to ascertain if David ever established a system of taxation over JUDAH and ISRAEL. Later on, Solomon imposed heavy taxation upon the nation to help him maintain the extravagances of his court.

27:32-34. Officers of the court. This list consists of several notable men who served the king as his personal advisors. *Jonathan*, David's *counselor*, is listed as his *uncle*. The Hebrew word also means a "relative"; it may refer to David's nephew mentioned in 2 Sam 21:21. *Jonathan* and *Jehiel* served as tutors to David's sons. *Hushai*'s title, *king's friend*, means a close advisor of the king. *Ahithophel* lost his position as counselor because of his part in Absalom's rebellion against David (2 Sam 15:12, 31).

David's Last Days, 28:1–29:30

This section is related to the great assembly mentioned in 23:1. The assembly was called in order to proclaim Solomon the new king and to give instructions about the Temple Solomon was to build for God. David had summoned all the leaders of Israel and, standing before them (28:2), he encouraged them to help Solomon in building the house of God.

28:1-8. David's words to the people. David declared to the people the reason he was unable to build the Temple to house the ark of the covenant (see 22:6-16), the *footstool of God* (v. 2; cf. Pss 99:5; 132:7). Because David was a warrior and a man of war, he had shed much blood. But God was not against the idea of a temple. David said that Yahweh chose Judah to be the leading tribe and from the house of Jesse he chose David himself to be king over Israel. Now he has chosen his son Solomon to continue his work. The reference to Judah and the house of Jesse may be another effort by the CHR to magnify the importance of Judah in the divine plan. Yahweh has chosen Solomon to be the next king and the builder of the Temple. Solomon would enjoy a special father-son relationship with Yahweh because of the pact established with David (2 Sam 7).

28:9-10. David's words to Solomon. According to Braun (1986, 275), David's exhortation to Solomon to *know the God of your father* (v. 9), deals with "conventional covenant terminology which exhorts Solomon to recognize Yahweh as his covenant lord and to conduct himself in accord with his stipulations." Solomon's kingdom would be established forever, provided he obeyed the commandments of Yahweh (vv. 9-10). The same dedication to the commandments of Yahweh is required of the people if they want to continue in the land Yahweh has given to them and if they want to pass this land to future generations (v. 8).

28:11-21. David's plans for the Temple. David gave Solomon the plans he had prepared for the construction of the Temple. The plans for the Temple included details for the *'ulam* or *the vestibule*, for the *hekal* or the sanctuary, and for the *debir*, the holy of holies, where the ark of the covenant was located. *The mercy seat* (v. 11) or propitiatory (*kapporet*) was the cover of the ark. On top of the cover were two cherubim. The reference to *the chariot of the cherubim* (v. 18) appears only here.

The plans also included the design for several rooms in the Temple, information about the ministry of the priests and Levites, and a summary of the gold and silver needed for the vessels to be used in the Temple. The plans David gave to Solomon were written in a document that the CHR says came directly "from the hand of Yahweh" (v. 19, author trans.). This statement indicates that according to the CHR the plans for the Temple were given to David by divine inspiration. According to priestly theology, no one could erect a temple to God without the direct approval from God. David received from Yahweh the plans for the construction of the Temple in the same way Moses received the details for the building of the tabernacle (Exod 25:9-40). The word *plan* (v. 11) in Hebrew is the same word translated "pattern" in Exod 25:40. The exhortation to Solomon (vv. 20-21) appears to be a continuation of the exhortation of v. 10. The order and the manner in which the different classes of Temple workers are presented seems to indicate that this section is a later addition to the text.

29:1-9. David's appeal for offerings. As Moses had done before (Exod 25:1-7; 35:4-9, 20-29), David made an appeal to the leaders of Israel, asking them to help Solomon build the Temple. In vv. 1 and 19, the Temple is called "a palace" (RSV; NIV: "palatial structure"). The Hebrew word was used in postexilic times; it carried the meaning of "palace" or "fortress" (NRSV mg.; cf. Neh 2:8; 7:2). Williamson (1982, 184) suggests that the CHR used the word to declare to his readers "that the kingdom ultimately belongs to God."

In order to move the leaders of Israel to offer generously to the building fund, David spoke of his own generosity. He had given the wealth of his kingdom to help the building of the Temple. In addition, he was giving his personal wealth to God: 3,000 talents (110 tons) of gold and 7,000 talents (260 tons) of silver. The word *segullah*, translated here *a treasure of my own* (v. 3), means personal or private wealth, a special possession (cf. Exod 19:5). Moved by

David's generosity, the leaders of Israel "willingly" (vv. 6, 9 NIV) gave with enthusiasm, surpassing David's offering. They gave an abundance of gold, silver, bronze, and iron to be used in the construction of the Temple. The reference to *darics* (v. 7) is anachronistic. The daric refers was a Persian gold coin minted by DARIUS I (522–485 B.C.E.). This reference to the daric is made anachronistically by the CHR as an effort to present an equivalent value to the currency of his day. The numbers are greatly exaggerated. However, the large amount given by David and the leaders and the joyful and willing response of the people clearly indicate that the CHR was expressing the majesty of the Temple, a monument worthy of the God of Israel. *Jehiel the Gershonite* and his sons were in charge of the treasury of the house of the LORD (26:21-22).

29:10-22a. David's prayer of thanksgiving. David, profoundly moved by the generosity of the people, offered to God a prayer of thanksgiving. David exalted God for his grace and glory and for his willingness to bless the people. David acknowledged that as pilgrims and sojourners on this earth, all that he and the people had given to build the Temple they had received from the hands of God. They were simply unmerited receivers of the divine abundance. The only thing David could offer as his own that might please God was *the uprightness of [his] heart* (v. 17). David asked Yahweh to preserve this same disposition in the hearts of the people. He also asked Yahweh to bless Solomon that he might obey the commandments with upright heart and that he might finish the building of the Temple (v. 19). The people blessed Yahweh on that occasion. The next day, with great gladness (v. 22a) all Israel offered a great sacrifice to God.

29:22b-30. Solomon's accession to the throne. Solomon was proclaimed king the first time at the occasion of Adonijah's attempt to seize the throne with the help of the army, an event omitted by the CHR (cf. 1 Kgs 1:32-40; 1 Chr 23:1). The reference to Zadok's being anointed is unusual since he has appeared as a priest in earlier narratives. It is possible that ZADOK was either designated as the sole high priest in Solomon's kingdom or as the successor of ABIATHAR, who had sided with ADONIJAH (1 Kgs 1:5-8). According to the CHR, Solomon had the full support of all Israel, including the support of the political and military leaders who had served under David. The CHR also asserts that Solomon had divine affirmation by saying that Yahweh magnified his reign in the sight of all Israel (cf. 2 Chr 1:1).

David's reign had lasted forty years. The CHR suggests that his seven-year reign in Hebron was over all Israel, although 2 Sam 5:5 says that he reigned seven years and six months over Judah alone. David died of old age, loved by his people, full of honors and riches, clear evidence that Yahweh had richly blessed his reign. The information about David's reign was taken by the CHR from three prophetic annals (v. 29). Although these sources have been identified with the Books of Samuel and Kings, it is also possible that the CHR used additional sources to compose his history of David's reign.

An Outline

Second Chronicles
I. The Reign of Solomon, 1:1–9:31
A. Solomon's Early Reign, 1:1-17
B. The Construction of the Temple, 2:1–5:1
C. The Dedication of the Temple, 5:2–7:10
D. God's Answer to Solomon, 7:11-22
E. The Glory of Solomon's Reign, 8:1-18
F. Solomon's Riches, 9:1-31
II. The History of the Kings of Judah, 10:1–36:21
A. The Reign of Rehoboam, 10:1–12:6
B. The Reign of Abijah, 13:1–14:1 [MT 13:1-23]
C. The Reign of Asa, 14:2–16:14 [MT 14:1–16:14]
D. The Reign of Jehoshaphat, 17:1–20:37
E. The Reign of Jehoram, 21:1-20
F. The Reign of Ahaziah, 22:1-9
G. The Reign of Athaliah, 22:10-12
H. The Reign of Joash, 23:1–24:27
I. The Reign of Amaziah, 25:1-28
J. The Reign of Uzziah, 26:1-23
K. The Reign of Jotham, 27:1-9
L. The Reign of Ahaz, 28:1-27
M. The Reign of Hezekiah, 29:1–32:33
N. The Reign of Manasseh, 33:1-20
O. The Reign of Amon, 33:21-25
P. The Reign of Josiah, 34:1–35:27
Q. The Reign of Jehoahaz, 36:1-4
R. The Reign of Jehoiakim, 36:5-8
S. The Reign of Jehoiachin, 36:9-10
T. The Reign of Zedekiah, 36:11-21
Appendix. The Decree of Cyrus, 36:22-23

The Reign of Solomon, 1:1–9:31

The story of SOLOMON as presented by the CHR is inspired by the narratives in 1 Kings. Solomon's reign is marked by the details of the construction of the Temple. This dominant theme in the Solomonic narrative is the divine fulfillment of the promise made to David and the culmination of David's work. The CHR also focuses on Solomon's wisdom and wealth but these become secondary to the CHR's major theme.

Solomon's Early Reign, 1:1-17

1:1-6. The visit to Gibeon. The establishment of the kingdom in Solomon's hand (cf. 1 Kgs 2:46b) reflects the difficulties Solomon had in winning the struggle against his brother Adonijah (1 Kgs 1:1–2:46). The same expression is used to describe the beginning of the reign of Rehoboam (12:13), Abijah (13:21), Jehoshaphat (17:1), and Jehoram (21:4). The religious focus of the CHR is evident in his declaration that Yahweh was with Solomon.

Because the CHR omits Solomon's struggle with Adonijah, the king's first act becomes his visit to the high place at Gibeon. The narrative in Chronicles differs slightly from that in 1 Kgs 3:4-15. The CHR says that Solomon went to Gibeon with the leaders and officers of Israel (cf. 1 Chr 28:1), while 1 Kings presents the visit to Gibeon as a personal pilgrimage of the new king. The CHR also says that the tent of meeting and the altar of bronze made under the direction of Moses were in Gibeon (1 Chr 16:39-40; 21:29). The Ark was in Jerusalem under the tent David had made when he brought the Ark from Kiriath-jearim (1 Chr 15:1). Solomon offered a large offering upon the bronze altar. The CHR says that Solomon *went up there to the bronze altar*, and offered sacrifices before Yahweh (v. 6). This expression, missing in 1 Kings, affirms that Solomon acted as a priest at this occasion.

1:7-13. The theophany. The THEOPHANY narrative in vv. 7-13 is an abbreviation of 1 Kgs 3:3-15. The CHR does not mention that God appeared to Solomon in a dream, although that may be intimated in v. 7. In the postexilic period dreams had fallen into disrepute because of past abuse (cf. Jer 23:23-28). Instead of power and possessions, Solomon asked for wisdom and knowledge to rule over the people. God granted him what he had asked and in addition promised to bless and prosper him with the wealth and power for which he did not ask.

1:14-18. Solomon's wealth. The accumulation of great wealth by Solomon was seen as the fulfillment of God's promise. Solomon acted as a merchant; he imported chariots from Egypt and horses from Egypt and Kue, a region in southeast Asia Minor identified with Cilicia. Solomon kept some of the horses and chariots and placed them in Jerusalem and in chariot cities he had built for them throughout Israel. Megiddo, Hazor, and Gezer have been identified as Solomon's chariot cities, but this identification has been questioned by some archaeologists. Solomon sold the horses and chariots to the kings of the Hittites and the Aramean kings (1:17 NRSV). Solomon became so rich with his commercial ventures that it was said that gold became as plentiful as the stones in the hills of Israel and the expensive cedar became as abundant as the sycamore tress found in the Shephelah, the low foothills of Judah (cf. 1 Chr 27:28).

The Construction of the Temple, 2:1–5:1

The CHR now begins emphasizing the main event of Solomon's reign, the building of the TEMPLE. So central was the Temple that most of the narrative related to Solomon's reign is given to describing the preparation, the construction, and the dedication of the Temple. The CHR also recounts the feast of dedication and the prayers and sacrifices offered at that occasion.

2:1-18 [MT 1:18–2:17]. Preparations to build the Temple. This chapter deals with Solomon's preparation for the building of the Temple and his dealings with Hiram, king of Tyre.

2:1-10 [MT 1:18–2:9]. Solomon's request to Hiram. Solomon announced his decision to build the Temple of God and his own palace. In Chronicles the building of the palace receives only secondary attention (cf. 2:12; 7:11). The Temple was to be a place for the name of Yahweh (v. 1), a place to burn incense, to make sacrifices, and to celebrate the feasts of God (v. 4). In order to build the Temple Solomon needed people who were skilled workers with metals and fabrics. Thus, Solomon sent a delegation to Tyre requesting assistance from Huram (his name appears as Hiram in Kings and in 1 Chr 14:1).

2:11-16 [MT 2:10-15]. Hiram's response. Hiram answered Solomon's request in writing, although this fact is not mentioned in Kings. His acknowledgement of Yahweh as the God who made heavens and earth is diplomatic language and does not express Hiram's faith in Yahweh. Hiram promised to send a craftsman named Hiram (1 Kgs 7:13, 40, 45) or Huram (4:11). He is also called Huramabi in 2:13 and 4:11. The final element of his name *abi* should be taken as a title, "master" (Dillard 1987, 20), a reading adopted by the NEB, "master Huram" (2:13). This Hiram was the son of a woman from Dan (2:12), although in 2 Kgs 7:14 he is listed as the son of a widow from Naphtali. The timber Solomon needed was to be sent through Joppa (v. 16) where it would be transferred to Jerusalem.

2:17-18 [MT 2:16-17]. The conscription of the workers. Solomon took a census of all the aliens within the kingdom and there were 153,600 available for forced labor (vv. 17-18; cf. 1 Kgs 9:20-23). Solomon assigned 80,000 to be stonecutters, 70,000 to be carriers and laborers, and 3,600 to be overseers over the labor force (v. 2). This figure agrees with 1 Kgs 5:13-18 where, however, the number of overseers is only 3,300. The CHR does not mention that according to 1 Kgs 5:13 Solomon also raised a levy of forced labor from among the Israelites numbering 30,000 men. The CHR emphasizes again in 2 Chr 8:7-10 (cf. 1 Kgs 9:22) that *of the people of Israel Solomon made no slaves* (8:9). However, the evidence that many Israelites were taken into forced labor appears in 1 Kgs 11:28 where Jeroboam was in charge over all the forced labor of the house of Joseph.

3:1-17. Construction of the Temple. The site where the Temple was to be built was the threshing floor of Ornan, where Yahweh had appeared to David at the occasion of the great plague (cf. 1 Chr 21:18–22:1). Ornan appears in 2 Sam 24:16 as Araunah. The site of the Temple is also called Mount Moriah. This name appears in Gen 22:2 to designate the land to which Abraham was instructed to go and offer his son Isaac as a sacrifice. The identification of the site of the Temple with Mount Moriah serves to affirm the election of the place by Yahweh. Solomon began to build the Temple on the second month of the fourth year of his reign. The NIV adds "the second day" but this reading should be considered a dittography and should be omitted. The date is April–May. The year when Solomon began to build is uncertain, since there are several chronologies for the kings of Israel. The CHR omits 1 Kgs 6:1, which places the beginning of the construction 480 years after the exodus from Egypt.

The "foundation of the Temple" (v. 3, against NRSV; cf. NIV) was sixty cubits long and twenty cubits wide. The CHR says that an old standard was used to measure the foundation. Since there were two standards of measurement in use, it is difficult to be precise about the size of the foundation. Its measurement was approximately ninety by thirty feet. The vestibule of the Temple or the *ulam* was overlaid with pure gold (v. 4). The holy place or *hekal* was paneled with cypress and overlaid with gold. The *hekal* was decorated with palm trees, chain designs, and precious stones. The significance of the chain designs is unknown. The beams, doorframes, doors, and walls were all overlaid with gold. The gold came from Parvaim, an unknown place. Cherubim were carved on the walls of the holy place. The most holy place or *debir* was thirty by thirty feet and inlaid with gold. The most holy place was

the chamber in the Temple reserved for the high priest who could enter the place only once a year (Lev 16:17). According to v. 14, a veil separated the holy place from the most holy place. This is the only place in the OT where it is said that there was a veil in the Temple. First Kgs 6:31-32 and 7:50 speak of doors separating the two chambers. It is possible that the veil was introduced in the Temple at a later time (cf. Matt 27:51), perhaps influenced by its presence in the Mosaic tabernacle (Exod 26:31-33). Two cherubim made of carved wood and overlaid with gold were in the holy of holies (v. 10). They faced the main hall and their wings touched the walls of the most holy place (vv. 10-13). At the entrance of the Temple (v. 15) there were two freestanding pillars, a feature common in other temples of the ancient Near East. The one in the south entrance of the Temple was called Jachin and the one in the north was called Boaz. The height of the pillars in v. 15 (thirty-five cubits) is different from 1 Kgs 7:15 (eighteen cubits). No satisfactory explanation has been found for this difference. It is possible that the difference is due to an error by the scribe. The pillars were decorated with interwoven chain designs and engraved pomegranates. The function and meaning of these pillars as well as the significance of their names are unknown.

4:1–5:1. The furnishings of the Temple. Solomon commissioned Hiram and the other craftsmen to make the necessary furnishings for the Temple. This section lists several items, the first of which is the altar of bronze (v. 1) where sacrifices were made (1 Kgs 8:64). The molten sea (vv. 2-6) was a basin that held 3,000 baths (17,500 gallons) of water. First Kings 7:26 says that it only held 2,000 baths. The molten sea stood on twelve bulls, divided into four groups of three, each facing a point of the compass. There were also ten smaller basins. The smaller basins were used to wash the animals for sacrifices and the molten sea was used by the priests to wash themselves. The ten gold lampstands (vv. 7-8) were made according to the specifications given by Moses (Exod 25:31-40). The ten tables were used to hold the ten gold lampstands. One hundred basins were made of gold. The purpose of these basins is unknown. They may have been used to collect the blood of the sacrifices or to make the libation offerings (Zech 9:15). There were two courts in the Temple (v. 9). They were indispensable items in the CHR's day. One of them was for the priests and the other for the people. The pots, shovels, and bowls were used to remove ashes or perhaps for the disposing of animal excrement. Solomon used so much bronze that it was not weighed. Verses 19-22 list the remaining furnishings made for use in the Temple. The CHR mentions the tables used for the showbread (Lev 24:5-9) or the bread of the Presence (Exod 25:23-30), although the CHR himself intimates that there was only one table for that purpose (13:11; 29:18).

Dedication of the Temple, 5:2–7:10

<u>5:2-12. The transfer of the Ark.</u> After Solomon had finished building the Temple and its furnishings, he assembled all Israel, the priests, and the Levites and commanded them to bring the Ark of the Covenant to the Temple. The occasion was the feast of the seventh month, the Feast of Tabernacles (Lev 23:33-36). The Levites were in charge of moving the Ark (1 Chr 15:2; cf. 1 Kgs 8:3 where it is said that the priests carried the Ark). They brought the Ark and the tent of meeting to the Temple. First Chr 16:1 says that David had prepared a tent to house the Ark, but the reference here to the tent of meeting (cf. 2 Chr 1:3) seems to indicate that the tent that was at Gibeon had been brought to Jerusalem at some time in the past, although this information is not provided. When the Ark arrived in the Temple, the priests carried it into the most holy place (*debir*) because the Levites were not allowed access into the inner sanctuary (Num 4:17-20). The Ark was placed beneath the cherubim. According to the CHR, the only content of the Ark was the two tables of the law that Moses had received at Sinai (Horeb). In the NT, Heb 9:4 says that the Ark contained a golden urn with manna and Aaron's rod. This information is not found in the OT (cf. Exod 16:33; Num 17:10). After the Ark had been placed in the Temple, the Levites, dressed in special clothing, played their instruments and in unison sang a hymn of thanksgiving to Yahweh. This song (v. 13) is repeated several times in other contexts (Pss 100:5; 106:1; 136:1). This was the same song the Levites sang before the ark as they gave thanks to Yahweh (1 Chr 16:41) and it was the same song sung at the dedication of the new Temple (Ezra 3:10-11).

<u>5:13-14. The glory of Yahweh.</u> In the midst of such solemnity, the glory of Yahweh was manifested. With the presence of the Ark in the inner sanctuary, Yahweh took possession of the house dedicated to his honor.

<u>6:1-2. Solomon's response.</u> The glory of Yahweh had filled the Temple, symbolizing his presence in the sanctuary. Solomon's words reflect the tradition that Yahweh lived in darkness (Exod 20:21). In the Temple

the inner sanctuary was constantly in darkness since the chamber where the Ark resided had no windows.

<u>6:3-11. Solomon addresses the people.</u> In Israel, it was the priest's responsibility to bless the people (Num 6:22-27). Solomon's blessing of Israel is a demonstration of the priestly role the kings at times exercised in the cult. His words to the congregation are a reaffirmation that Yahweh had chosen Jerusalem to manifest his name. *Name* appears fourteen times in this chapter to symbolize the divine presence among the people. Yahweh had also chosen David to be the leader over Israel. Since David was now dead, Solomon was the new leader. The events of that day were the fulfillment of God's promises to David.

<u>6:12-42. Solomon's prayer of dedication.</u> Solomon prayed the dedication prayer kneeling on a bronze platform prepared for this solemn occasion. Kneeling and spreading the hands toward heaven were common gestures associated with prayer. In his prayer Solomon acknowledged that Yahweh was a faithful God who "keeps the covenant and who keeps being faithful" (v. 14, author trans.). Then Solomon made several requests of Yahweh: that Yahweh keep his promise to continue David's dynasty (vv. 16-17); that he hear the supplications of the people made in the Temple (v. 21); that he arbitrate between individuals who seek divine guidance (vv. 22-23); that he forgive Israel whenever they are defeated because of sin (vv. 24-25); and that he hear the prayers of the people in times of drought and other natural disasters (vv. 26-31). Solomon also asked God to hear the prayer of aliens whenever they came to pray in the Temple (vv. 32-33); that he bless the people in times of war (vv. 34-35); and that he forgive the people whenever they sin (vv. 36-39). In 1 Kgs 8:53 Solomon's prayer ends with a reference to the Mosaic covenant. The CHR ends Solomon's prayer with a quotation from Ps 132:8-10. This quotation deals with the ark and God's promise to David. With this substitution, the CHR is clearly emphasizing that the covenant that Yahweh made with Israel culminated with David and his dynasty.

<u>7:1-11. The dedication of the Temple.</u> After Solomon finished his prayer, fire came from heaven and consumed the sacrifice (cf. 1 Chr 21:26). The fire from heaven and the presence of the glory of Yahweh in the Temple serve to legitimate the new sanctuary. Since the THEOPHANY of 7:1-3 appears to repeat the events of 5:13-14, some scholars believe that this passage is an addition to Chronicles and that it is a parallel of the first account (Dillard 1987, 36). When the people saw

the glory of Yahweh, they bowed down to the pavement in awe and sang a song of thanksgiving (cf. 5:13). The number of sacrifices offered is very high and would require many days to finish. However, since there were large numbers of people attending the dedication of the Temple, a large quantity of food was needed to feed them, thus making a large number feasible in this context. Hamath and the Brook of Egypt describe the ideal borders of Israel from north to south. According to the CHR (v. 10), the festivities, including the dedication of the Temple and the Festival of Tabernacles (or Booths), lasted twenty-two days, and on the twenty-third day Solomon sent the people home. However, 1 Kgs 8:65-66 has a different version, in which the festival only lasted seven days. The CHR attempts to explain 1 Kings by saying that both the dedication of the Temple and the celebration of the Festival of Tabernacles lasted three weeks. Verse 11 is a summary statement of Solomon's building activities, since the construction of the Temple took seven years and the construction of Solomon's palace thirteen years (1 Kgs 6:38–7:1).

God's Answer to Solomon, 7:11-22

God's answer to Solomon's prayer came at night, as it had come at Gibeon (1 Kgs 9:1-9). Yahweh had chosen the Temple to be a house of sacrifice (v. 12). He also promised to forgive the sins of the people and heal their land as Solomon had requested, provided the people meet four conditions: they must humble themselves; they must pray; they must seek God's face; and they must turn or repent from their evil ways. In turn, God promised to hear their prayer, forgive their sins, and heal their land. God's answer to Solomon expressed his desire to restore the people. This verse is a clear expression of the CHR's view of immediate retribution. To the CHR reward follows obedience and punishment follows disobedience. To the CHR reward and punishment are not delayed but are dispensed immediately. Yahweh told Solomon that if he obeyed the commandments his dynasty would last but if he disobeyed and worshiped other gods, then the people would go into exile and the exalted house he had built would be destroyed and become an object of ridicule among the nations.

The Glory of Solomon's Reign, 8:1-18

8:1-11. Solomon's political success. The CHR reverses (v. 2) the statement in Kings that Solomon gave twenty cities to Hiram in order to pay his debt (1 Kgs 9:11-13). This reversal may reflect the fact that, since Hiram did not like the cities, he returned them after Solomon paid his debt. The conquest of Hamath-zobah is not mentioned in Kings. Since David conquered Zobah (1 Chr 18:3), the CHR is saying that Solomon's empire included sections of Aramean territory, including Tadmor, the famous caravan city northeast of Damascus (v. 4). The CHR says that Solomon placed the conquered population under forced labor (cf. 1 Kgs 9:20-23). However, the statement in v. 9 that Solomon did not place the people of Israel under forced labor contradicts 1 Kgs 5:13 where it is clearly stated that a levy of forced labor was taken from all Israel (see commentary at 2 Chr 2:17-18). The number of supervisors over the forced labor was 250, which differs from 1 Kgs 9:23 (550 supervisors). The different numbers may reflect a scribal error in Chronicles. The CHR also mentions that Solomon moved the daughter of Pharaoh (cf. 1 Kgs 3:1) from the city of David to the palace he had built for her. Because she was a Gentile and a woman she could not be in contact with the places where the ark had been. This concern reflects the CHR's concern for ritual purity (cf. Lev 15:19-24).

8:12-16. Solomon's religious success. This section is an expansion of 1 Kgs 9:25. It describes the work of Solomon in the presentation of the daily sacrifices, at the weekly sabbath, at the new moon festival, and at the three annual festivals. The role Solomon played in these sacrifices is not clear. The CHR omits the fact that Solomon also offered incense, which was the duty of the sons of Aaron (2 Chr 26:16-21). But by declaring that Solomon offered these sacrifices according to the commandment of Moses, the CHR intimates that Solomon exercised an officiating capacity within the cult. Solomon also appointed the divisions of the priests and the Levites as David had commanded (1 Chr 23–26). The establishment of the sacrifices and the organization of the priests and Levites mark the completion of Solomon's major work, the building of the Temple.

8:17-18. Solomon's commercial success. Solomon's vast commercial enterprise was accomplished in partnership with Hiram, king of Tyre. 1 Kgs 9:26-27 indicates that Solomon's fleet was based at Ezion-geber and Elath (*Eloth* NRSV). With the help of Hiram's expert sailors, Solomon's servants went to Ophir from where they brought much gold. The land of Ophir is unknown (see 1 Chr 29:4). The total amount of gold was reported to be 450 talents (420 talents in 1 Kgs 9:28) or about sixteen tons.

Solomon's Riches, 9:1-31

9:1-12. The visit of the queen of Sheba. This section concludes the CHR's description of Solomon's reign. The narrative of the visit of the queen of Sheba follows 1 Kgs 10:1-13 with the addition of v. 10. Sheba has been identified with the land of the Sabeans in southwest Arabia. The Sabeans were merchants (Isa 60:6; Ezek 27:22) who dealt in frankincense and myrrh (Jer 6:20). To judge from the large gift of spices, gold, and precious stones she brought (v. 1), it is clear that trade was the main reason for her visit. Since Solomon monopolized most of the caravan routes, her spice business was deeply affected. The large gift she offered to Solomon was intended to assure that her trade would have access to the routes controlled by Solomon. According to the CHR, the reason for her visit was Solomon's wisdom and the splendor of his court. When she saw the glory of Solomon's kingdom she praised his God. Her words exalting Yahweh should be understood as the language of diplomacy and not the language of faith. At the end of the visit Solomon granted her request, which is left unmentioned.

9:13-28. Solomon's wealth and fame. The annual revenue received by the court was 666 talents of gold (twenty-five tons), in addition to income from commerce, trade, tolls, and taxation (v. 14). With this gold Solomon made hundreds of decorative shields, which he placed in the House of the Forest of Lebanon, one of the governmental buildings he built in Jerusalem made of wood from Lebanon (1 Kgs 7:2). He also made an ivory throne overlaid with gold (v. 17). Whether the back of the throne "was a calf's head" (cf. 1 Kgs 10:19; so RSV, following the LXX), "had a rounded top" (so NIV following the MT), or *was rounded in the back* is difficult to decide. The CHR avoids the problem of a possible identification of the cow's head with the golden calf of Aaron (Exod 32) and JEROBOAM I (1 Kgs 12:25-33) by saying that the throne had a *footstool* (v. 18).

Most of Solomon's gold was brought in "ships of TARSHISH" (1 Kgs 10:22). The CHR understands Tarshish to be a location (cf Jonah 1:3), perhaps a place in Spain. However, Tarshish should not be understood as a place but rather as a general designation for a seagoing ship or a type of merchant ship used on long voyages (DeVries 1990, 875). Gordon (1962) has proposed that Tarshish designates a distant place. Dillard (1987, 73) has suggested that in the days of the CHR, Tarshish was the equivalent of "going to the ends of the earth." The CHR concludes the narrative of Solomon's reign by summarizing the extent of his wealth (v. 24), his military power (v. 25) and the extent of his reign (v. 26).

9:29-31. Solomon's death. The CHR presents Solomon as a king like David who obeyed the word of God and thus fulfilled the conditions imposed by Yahweh for a successful monarchy (1 Chr 28:5-7). However, the picture that the CHR presents of Solomon is idealized. This idealization of Solomon forces the CHR to eliminate all the negative events that darkened his reign. All of the deeds of Solomon mentioned in 1 Kgs 11:1-39 are omitted by the CHR. The concluding formula for his reign is taken from 1 Kgs 11:41-43. The "Acts of Solomon" mentioned in 1 Kgs 11:41 may refer to court records, similar to the annals of the Assyrian kings. The CHR mentions three additional sources: the writings of Nathan, Ahijah, and Iddo (v. 2). Although many scholars identify these works with the book of Kings, it is possible that they refer to court records available to the CHR.

The History of the Kings of Judah, 10:1–36:21

The remainder of 2 Chronicles deals with the reign of JUDAH and the kings who sat upon the throne of David. The kings of the Northern Kingdom (ISRAEL) are not completely ignored. Some of the northern kings are mentioned, but only when they have some relationship with the kings of Judah. The CHR's emphasis on Judah and the house of David stems from his theological view. This view stresses that royal dignity was given to Judah because of David and because Yahweh had chosen Jerusalem to be his city and the Temple to be his habitation. Some Judean kings receive more attention than others. The amount of attention is directly related to the king's obedience to the word of God. Jehoshaphat, Hezekiah, and Josiah are presented as ideal kings because they were faithful to Yahweh and obedient to his words.

The Reign of Rehoboam, 10:1–12:16

The story of REHOBOAM is lengthy because it is related to the division of the kingdom and its aftermath. Chapter 10 deals with the rebellion of the ten tribes; chap. 11 deals with the events of Rehoboam's reign; and chap. 12 deals with his infidelity and punishment.

10:1-19. The division of the kingdom. After the death of Solomon, Rehoboam was declared king over Judah but needed the approval of the northern tribes to rule over all Israel. So, Rehoboam went to SHECHEM to receive the approval of the ten tribes. There, the elders of Israel, together with Jeroboam, presented their demands to Rehoboam. Jeroboam was the Ephraimite in charge of the forced labor over the house of Joseph (1 Kgs 11:26-28) who had to flee to Egypt to escape Solomon's attempt on his life (1 Kgs 11:40). The elders of the northern tribes requested that Rehoboam lift the forced labor his father Solomon had imposed upon them. Rehoboam asked for three days to consider their request. During this time he took counsel with the elders who had advised his father and they advised him to hear their request: *"If you will be kind to this people and please them, and speak good words to them, they will be your servants forever"* (v. 7). The CHR here changes the words of the elders as found in 1 Kgs 12:7. In Kings the elders ask Rehoboam to be a "servant" to the people and "serve" them. The change reflects the CHR's view that the people of the Northern Kingdom should be subjects to the house of David and not the other way around.

Rehoboam did not accept the advice of the elders who had served under his father. Instead, he took counsel with *the young men who had grown up with him* (v. 8). The expression *young men* may refer to the princes who were members of the royal court (cf. 11:22) or to inexperienced counselors who were not seasoned in the affairs of government. Their advice was to increase the burden Solomon had imposed upon them.

Rehoboam's decision was interpreted by the CHR as *a turn of affairs brought about by God* (v. 15). The division of the kingdom happened to fulfill the words that the prophet Ahijah from Shiloh had spoken concerning the split of the united kingdom after the death of Solomon (1 Kgs 11:29-39). Although the CHR does not give the words of Ahijah, his reference to Ahijah and his prophecy is an indictment of Solomon and an affirmation of the CHR's theology of retribution, that disobedience to the word of God brings immediate punishment. Since the CHR attempted to idealize Solomon, most of the blame for the division of the kingdom is placed upon Rehoboam.

The northern tribes rejected Rehoboam and the house of David by uttering a slogan voiced by Sheba (2 Sam 20:1) when he and several men from Israel rebelled against David. This song of protest had become a slogan for defiance and rebellion against the house of David (cf. 1 Sam 25:10). Rehoboam attempted to restore his control over the northern tribes by sending

Hadoram (Adoram, 1 Kgs 12:18; Adoniram, 1 Kgs 4:6), the officer in charge of the forced labor, to deal with the rebellious tribes. The people stoned him and Rehoboam had to flee in his chariot back to Jerusalem. The CHR's statement that *Israel has been in rebellion against the house of David* (v. 19) reflects his view that the true Israel has its home in Jerusalem and its king in David and his descendants.

11:1-4. Shemaiah's prophecy. Rehoboam still had visions of uniting the kingdom again by the power of the army (v. 1). He assembled an army from Judah and from Benjamin to fight against Israel. The size of Rehoboam's army was 180,000 men, a large number that may be exaggerated. However, his army was not as large as the army of Asa with 580,000 men (14:8) or the army of Uzziah with 307,500 men (26:13). Civil war was averted because the prophet Shemaiah intervened and stopped Rehoboam from fighting Jeroboam. He told the king not to fight because the division was from Yahweh. The hostility between north and south was averted temporarily but the animosity continued, for there was continual war between Rehoboam and Jeroboam (cf. 12:5). The CHR believed that *all Israel* lived in Judah and Benjamin (v. 3), as well as in the Northern Kingdom (11:13). To the CHR, the faithful people who lived in the north (cf. 11:13-17) were also part of *all Israel* since they were *kindred* (v. 4).

11:5-12. Rehoboam's fortifications. Rehoboam fortified 15 cities in Judah (the inclusion of Benjamin is to describe the limit of the Southern Kingdom) in order to protect his kingdom from foreign incursions. It is possible that these cities were built before the invasion of Shishak, king of Egypt (cf. 12:2) although some scholars have said that they were built as a result of this invasion. Recent archaeological excavations on these sites have uncovered fortifications that may be dated to the time of Rehoboam. Since these fortified cities were located in the hill country, south and west of Jerusalem, they give evidence that they were built to protect the kingdom against the Philistines in the west and Egypt in the south.

11:13-17. The migration of the Levites. This event has no parallel in 1 Kings. The religious reforms established by Jeroboam (cf. 1 Kgs 12:28-33) were seen as a denial of true Yahwism and prompted the flight of the priests and Levites to Judah (v. 13) and of the faithful people who refused to sacrifice outside of Jerusalem (v. 16). Jeroboam's reforms included several innovations that the faithful Yahwists considered apostasy (v. 15). The high places were the local sanctuaries where sacrifices were made. The satyrs were believed to be demons in the form of goats. The calves were either considered pedestals upon which Yahweh stood or direct representations of Yahweh. In the religion of the Canaanites the calves (or bulls) were symbols of fertility and part of the worship of Baal. The calves were condemned by the prophets because they became objects of worship (cf. Hos 13:2). The faithful Yahwists who migrated to Judah brought peace and security to the nation for three years (v. 17). This means that Rehoboam abandoned Yahweh in the fourth year of his reign (12:1) and that punishment came in the fifth year in the form of the Egyptian invasion.

11:18-23. Rehoboam's family. Rehoboam had a large family. His household consisted of eighteen wives, sixty concubines, twenty-eight sons, and sixty daughters. One of his wives was the daughter of Jerimoth, David's son. Since Jerimoth's name does not appear in any of David's family lists, it is possible he was the son of one of David's many concubines. Another wife was Maacah. Maacah is listed here as the mother of Abijah and the daughter of Absalom, another of David's sons. In 1 Kgs 15:10 she appears as the mother of Asa and thus as the wife of Abijah. In 13:2 she is listed as Micaiah the daughter of Uriel of Gibeah. If Maacah and Micaiah are two different forms of the same name, then the conclusion is that Maacah, the daughter of Absalom, was Rehoboam's wife and Abijah's mother and that Micaiah (or Maacah), the daughter of Uriel, was Abijah's wife and Asa's mother. Rehoboam's son Abijah was appointed *nagid*, the king designate who would succeed his father upon the throne of Judah. Rehoboam placed his sons throughout Judah and Benjamin and in the fortified cities. This wise move helped Rehoboam to extend his influence over the cities of Judah and at the same time to solidify his kingdom against possible revolt.

12:1-16. Egypt's attack on Jerusalem. The CHR does not specify what the sins of Rehoboam and the people of Judah and Benjamin (*all Israel*) were. In 7:19, forsaking Yahweh involves the acceptance and worship of foreign gods. According to 1 Kgs 14:22-24 the people promoted the worship of Asherah and the practice of sacred prostitution. The unfaithfulness of Rehoboam caused the invasion of Shishak, king of Egypt. Shishak (also known as Sheshonq) was the founder of the Twenty-Second Dynasty of Egypt. He ruled from 945–924 B.C.E. Shishak came with a large army, which included many mercenary soldiers of different ethnic backgrounds. Shishak and his army invaded Judah and, according to an inscription at Karnak detailing the invasion, he conquered more than 150 cities (ANET, 263–64). The prophet Shemaiah came to the king and his nobles in Jerusalem and announced that the invasion of Shishak was in retribution for the king's unfaithfulness. After hearing the pronouncement of the prophet, Rehoboam and the princes repented and the divine anger was subdued. Because Rehoboam and the leaders of Israel had humbled themselves before Yahweh (cf. 7:14), Jerusalem was not destroyed. According to the CHR, the people of Judah would serve Shishak for a period of time in order that they might know the true meaning of serving Yahweh. Shishak took the treasures of the Temple and of the palace. Among the booty were the decorative shields of gold Solomon had made (v. 9).

The concluding statement about Rehoboam's kingship (vv. 13-16) presents a summary of his reign. He began to reign at the age of forty-one and *reigned seventeen years in Jerusalem*. His mother was Naamah, an Ammonite, and he did what was evil in the eyes of Yahweh (cf. 1 Kgs 14:22-24). The CHR ends the narrative about Rehoboam by saying that the remainder of his acts as king were registered in the annals of the prophets Shemaiah and Iddo.

The Reign of Abijah, 13:1–14:1 [MT 13:1-23]

After the death of Rehoboam, his son ABIJAH became king. His name means "My Father is Yahweh." In 1 Kgs 14:31; 15:1, he is called Abijam, "My Father is [the sea god] Yam." Since the CHR was sympathetic with Abijah it is possible that he tried to eliminate the reference to the Canaanite god by giving Abijah a Yahwistic name. His mother's name was Micaiah, the daughter of Uriel (see commentary at 11:20, above).

The narrative about the war between Abijah and Jeroboam is unique to Chronicles; it was taken from an unknown source. The number of troops on both sides cannot be taken as an accurate number. The numbers reflect the census of Israel and Judah taken by Joab (2 Sam 24:9). The purpose is to emphasize the contrast between the two armies and the heroic struggle of Judah to achieve a great victory. Before the fight, Abijah addressed the troops of Israel from a mountain. The location of Mount Zemaraim is unknown. It was located in the hill country of EPHRAIM, probably near the city of the same name (Josh 18:22). The speech was addressed to Jeroboam and *all Israel*. Abijah's pronouncement is typical of speeches found in Chronicles. The CHR develops the speech in order to communicate his theological view to his audience. In the speech Abijah makes two important points: (1) He speaks of the perpetuity of the Davidic COVENANT (1 Chr 17) established with Israel by a covenant of salt (cf. Lev 2:13; Num 18:19). Although the precise meaning of this expression is unknown, the preservative quality of salt makes it "the ideal symbol of the perdurability of a covenant" (Milgrom 1991, 191). Jeroboam and a group of *worthless scoundrels* (v. 7; Heb. "sons of Belial/Beliar"—see 1 Sam 10:27) revolted against Rehoboam and prevailed because he was inexperienced. Williamson (1982, 253) has taken a different approach. He believes the word *defied* (v. 7) should be translated "persuaded." Hence, these *worthless scoundrels* gathered around Rehoboam to persuade him not to listen to the advice of the elders (10:8-11). Abijah appealed to the people of Israel not to resist the kingdom of Yahweh, which was present in the dynasty of David (v. 8). (2) Abijah emphasizes the legitimacy of the Aaronic priesthood and of the Levites. He said Israel followed the sins of Jeroboam when they sacrificed to the golden calves because his religious innovations were an illegitimate cult of Yahweh. Only Judah had remained faithful to God's covenant and only the sons of AARON and the Levites could offer proper sacrifices to God. The expression *do not fight against the LORD* (v. 12) was an appeal to Israel to submit to God and to the house of David. Jeroboam's response was a surprise attack. He divided his army into two groups and attacked Abijah from two sides. Confronted with the superiority of Jeroboam's army, Abijah cried out to Yahweh. The priests invoked the presence of God with the sound of trumpets and as a result Yahweh *defeated Jeroboam and all Israel before Abijah and Judah* (v. 15) because they relied upon Yahweh, the God of their fathers (v. 18). As a result of this victory, Abijah took possession of three northern cities, including BETHEL, the religious center of the Northern Kingdom. But control over Bethel did not last long because before the days of Amos (eighth century B.C.E.) the sanctuary at Bethel was again one of the most important places of worship in Israel (see Amos 7:10-17). Jeroboam did not recover from this defeat. According to the CHR, the Lord smote him and he died (v. 20), but according to 1 Kgs 15:1, 7-8, Jeroboam outlived Abijah. The CHR summarizes Abijah's reign by declaring that Yahweh blessed him with a large family and by saying that the rest of Abijah's acts were registered *in the story of the prophet Iddo* (v. 22).

The Hebrew word *midrash* (v. 22 NAB, NJB; *story* NRSV) appears only here and in 24:27. The word simply means a collection of writings that may or may not have contained some notations. Wagner has suggested that the word may refer to a historical work that was an interpretation of the CHR's source (Wagner 1978, 306). After Abijah's death the land enjoyed rest for ten years (14:1). This statement resembles the formulation found in the book of Judges describing the time of peace during and after the death of a judge.

The Reign of Asa, 14:2–16:14 [MT 14:1–16:14]

The account of Asa's reign is greatly expanded in Chronicles. The CHR dedicates a large portion of his history to the reign of Asa because of the king's effort to bring religious reforms to Judah. Because of his faithfulness to Yahweh Asa enjoyed a prosperous reign. However, the CHR does not gloss over Asa's sin—his reliance on the Aramean army rather than putting his trust in Yahweh (16:7-8).

14:1-8 [MT 14:2-7]. The early years of Asa's reign. During the early part of Asa's reign, the land enjoyed a prolonged time of peace and prosperity. This peaceful period is attributed not to Abijah's victory over Jeroboam (13:13-20) but to Asa's faithfulness to Yahweh (14:2, 6). Asa's reform probably began early in his kingdom. He removed several items associated with Canaanite religious practices. The asherim were cultic poles associated with the cult of ASHERAH, the goddess of fertility. The meaning of the Hebrew word translated *incense altars* (v. 5) is debated. Asa used the time of peace to build new fortifications around the cities of Judah. He also increased his army (cf. v. 8 with 11:1 and 13:3) and equipped it with better weapons. The statement in v. 7, that *the land is still ours* may be a way for the CHR to remind his readers that the land was lost because of disobedience to God.

14:9-15 [MT 14:8-14]. Zerah's invasion. The CHR does not give a reason for Zerah's invasion. Zerah, the Ethiopian or Cushite, has been identified as a Nubian; however this identification has been highly disputed. It is possible that Cushite was "the name of a Palestinian ethnic group" allied with the inhabitants of Gerar (v. 14; cf. De Vries 1989, 299), a city located between Gaza and Beer-sheba. The size of Zerah's army is excessive; in fact, the Hebrew can be understood differently: instead of attacking Asa *with an army of a million men* (v. 9), he attacked "with an army of thousands upon thousands" (NIV mg.). The whole narrative is infused with the terminology of holy war. Yahweh defeats Zerah's army because of Asa's prayer and his reliance upon God. Asa and his army slaughtered the enemy, plundered their cities, and returned from this great victory with the spoils of victory.

15:1-7. The sermon of Azariah. After his victory over Zerah, Asa is met by a prophet of Yahweh. The prophet *Azariah son of Oded* appears only here. His ORACLE is a sermon to Asa and the people (v. 2a) that reflects the preaching ministry of the Levites (von Rad 1966, 271). According to von Rad, the sermon is divided into three sections. The first section, "doctrine," declares that Yahweh would be with Asa and the people as long as they remained faithful to Yahweh (v. 2b). The second section, "application," uses Israel's past history, probably the period of the judges, to show that abandoning Yahweh leads to adversity and national defeat and that loyalty to Yahweh leads to blessing and victory (vv. 3-6). In the third section, "exhortation," Azariah admonishes Asa to continue his work because God will bless him.

15:8-19. Asa's religious reform. Azariah's sermon had its intended effect. Asa continued his reform (vv. 8-15), extending it to the cities he had conquered from Ephraim. There is no reference in Chronicles to Asa's having conquered these cities. As part of the reform, Asa removed the idols worshiped by the people (cf. 1 Kgs 15:12) and repaired the altar of Yahweh. In order to provide religious authority to his reform, Asa called for a solemn assembly in Jerusalem and there gathered Judah and Benjamin together with many immigrants from the Northern Kingdom. The mention in v. 9 of Simeonites living in Jerusalem as resident aliens is puzzling. Simeon was a southern tribe and from the beginning of the monarchy the Simeonites had been assimilated into Judah. It is possible that some Simeonites had to move to Jerusalem because of the military struggle against the Edomites. Asa and the people entered into a covenant in which they made promises to seek Yahweh and be faithful to him. The covenant ceremony was accompanied by great rejoicing (vv. 14-15).

As part of his reform Asa removed his grandmother Maacah (so NIV; cf. commentary at 11:18-23), the queen mother, because of her worship of Asherah. The queen mother had an important role in Israelite society; because of her position, she also had some influence on the religious life of the nation. Asa also destroyed the image of Asherah and brought some free-will gifts to the Temple that he and his father Abijah had accumulated as spoils of war. Asa however

was unable to remove the high places from Israel (cf. 1 Kgs 15:14).

16:1-6. Asa's treaty with Aram. The chronological information in v. 1 is related to 15:19. In 15:19 it is said that *there was no more war until the thirty-fifth year of the reign of Asa* (NRSV, REB, and NIV add *more* to clarify the text: "there was no *more* war").

At face value, the CHR's statement is problematic for several reasons. First, it overlooks Asa's wars against Zerah (14:9-15) and against Ephraim (15:8). Second, the CHR's chronological information contradicts several events as narrated in 1 Kgs. In 1 Kgs 15:16 it is said that "there was war between Asa and Baasha all their days." In 1 Kgs 16:8 it is said that after the death of Baasha in the twenty-sixth year of Asa, Elah began to reign over Israel. Williamson (1982, 256–57) accepts Thiele's (1965) view, followed by De Vries (1962, 580–99), that the thirty-fifth and the thirty-sixth year refer, not to Asa's reign but to the division of the monarchy. Dillard (1987, 124), however, rejects Thiele's harmonization for three reasons: it would be the only passage where a dating would be given from the division of the monarchy; because it ignores the clear statement of the text; and because it counters the CHR's theological view that retribution follows immediately after an offense. It is possible the numbers reflect a copyist's error, who misread thirty-five and thirty-six for fifteen and sixteen.

Thus, in the sixteenth year of Asa, confrontation between Asa and Baasha erupted when Baasha built a fortress at Ramah, a city located between the kingdoms of Judah and Israel, about five miles north of Jerusalem.

So intimidated was Asa by the threat posed by Baasha that he took silver and gold to make a treaty with BEN-HADAD, king of Aram, requesting him to break his alliance with Baasha. Ben-hadad accepted Asa's offer. He invaded Israel and conquered several northern cities. Baasha was forced to stop fortifying Ramah and Asa took the materials left behind and used them to build his own fortified cities.

16:7-10. Hanani's rebuke. Asa's decision to rely on Ben-hadad brought a stern rebuke from the prophet Hanani, who condemned Asa for paying tribute to a foreign king rather than relying on God. Hanani reminded Asa that in the past Yahweh gave him victory over his enemies because he had trusted God. Yahweh protects the blameless, those who devote themselves totally to God. Asa spurned the prophet's rebuke and, angry at his words, imprisoned him and the people who protested, probably some of the prophet's supporters.

16:11-14. The end of Asa's reign. The CHR concludes the story of Asa's reign by informing his readers where he found his information. The *Book of the Kings of Judah and Israel* (v. 11) should not be identified with the biblical Book of Kings but rather with one of the many sources used by the CHR. At the end of his reign Asa was struck by a severe foot disease, which the CHR does not identify. The CHR says that even in his illness Asa did not seek Yahweh but trusted the physicians. This statement should not be interpreted as an attack upon doctors. These physicians probably were involved with magic powers or pagan divinities. The CHR emphasizes that Asa trusted the physicians alone and that he did not consult Yahweh. Two years later Asa died. He was buried with much honor in a burial chamber he had prepared for himself. The fire made in his honor should not be understood as cremation but as a memorial to honor the dead king (cf. 21:19).

The Reign of Jehoshaphat, 17:1–20:37

Four chapters of Chronicles are dedicated to the reign of JEHOSHAPHAT. This extensive treatment of the reign of Jehoshaphat is because of his piety and his faithfulness to God. He is praised as a good king whose heart was firm with Yahweh. Most of the information about Jehoshaphat in Chronicles is distinctive to the CHR.

17:1-6. The establishment of Jehoshaphat's kingdom. The CHR stresses that Yahweh blessed Jehoshaphat and established his kingdom because of his faithfulness. Jehoshaphat's heart was firm in the ways of Yahweh. He closed the high places that had become centers of BAAL worship in Judah; he removed the asherim, the wooden poles used in the worship of ASHERAH, the fertility goddess; and he did not go after the Baals. As a result, God established his kingdom, Judah brought tribute, and Jehoshaphat had great riches and honor.

17:7-9. The mission of the priests and Levites. Another sign of Jehoshaphat's piety was that in the third year of his reign he sent five civil servants, eight Levites and two priests to teach the law of Yahweh in the cities of Judah (vv. 7-9). The content of the law of Yahweh is unknown. One possibility is that this Torah was an earlier form of the law of Moses.

17:10-19. Jehoshaphat's powerful kingdom. Another sign of God's blessing was that the nations around Judah, recognizing that Jehoshaphat was a powerful king, made no war against him. The Philistines paid tribute to Jehoshaphat as did the Arabian seminomadic tribes who brought a large quantity of cattle as a sign of friendship (vv. 10-11). At the same time Jehoshaphat expanded the defenses of the kingdom by organizing his army and building fortifications and store cities around Judah. The large number of soldiers in Jehoshaphat's army, larger than previous armies, demonstrates, in the CHR's perspective, the great honor Yahweh had bestowed upon him.

18:1–19:3. Jehoshaphat's alliance with Ahab. In this section, the CHR follows his source closely, taking his information almost verbatim from 1 Kgs 22. He provides an introduction (18:1-3) and a conclusion (19:1-3) in order to condemn Jehoshaphat for his alliance with *those who hate the LORD* (v. 2). Jehoshaphat became related to AHAB, king of Israel, by the marriage alliance of his son Jehoram with Athaliah, the daughter of Ahab and JEZEBEL (on Athaliah's relationship to Ahab, cf. commentary at 21:1-7). At some indefinite time (v. 2) after this event, Ahab prepared a great feast for Jehoshaphat to convince him to form an alliance against Ramoth-gilead. So strong was the CHR against this alliance that he uses a word found frequently in Deuteronomy (cf. Deut 13:6) to describe seduction into apostasy (Ackroyd 1973, 144). Verses 4-34 repeat 1 Kgs 22:4-36.

After he was invited to join Ahab against Ramoth-gilead, Jehoshaphat decided to inquire of Yahweh for divine guidance. Ahab gathered 400 prophets who as one voice guaranteed victory in battle. Jehoshaphat requests another prophet of Yahweh (18:6), implying that he was not very sure of the judgment of Ahab's prophets. While the king's messengers were on their way to bring Micaiah, the son of Imlah, to provide another oracle, Zedekiah, probably the leader of the prophets, made horns of iron to validate his conviction that Yahweh would give Ahab total victory against the Arameans. Micaiah was requested to speak an affirmative word to Ahab, and when he did the king knew that Micaiah was mocking him. Requested to speak the truth, Micaiah warns of Israel's defeat. He said that his oracle had come out of a vision of the heavenly council where he had heard God's decision.

Ahab rejected Micaiah's word, placed him in prison, and went to fight against the Arameans. Jehoshaphat went to war wearing his royal clothes and Ahab disguised himself in order not to be recognized. The king of Aram came to meet them. Jehoshaphat cried to Yahweh for help and the Aramean soldiers turned back from pursuing him. As for Ahab, he was mortally wounded by an archer who "drew his bow at a venture" (v. 33, RSV).

Ahab died as Micaiah had said and Jehoshaphat returned to Jerusalem only to be confronted by the prophet Jehu (19:1). Jehu was the son of Hanani, the prophet who had confronted Asa, Jehoshaphat's father (16:7). Jehu rebuked Jehoshaphat because he had helped the wicked and had loved those who hate Yahweh (19:2). Yet, because of his previous acts of faithfulness, Jehoshaphat was not punished (19:3).

19:4-11. Jehoshaphat's judicial reform. In order to strengthen his religious reforms Jehoshaphat extended his reform to the system of administration of justice in Judah. Some scholars have denied that this judicial reform took place in the days of Jehoshaphat, but the historicity of the reform has been strongly defended by Albright (1950, 61–82). According to the CHR, the purpose of the reform was to bring the people back to Yahweh (v. 4). Even though the CHR says that the king left his palace in Jerusalem and went throughout the kingdom again, this statement should be understood as a continuation of the teaching mission accomplished by means of his emissaries (17:7). The king went from Beer-sheba in the south to the hill country of Ephraim in the north. This south-north direction for the country represents the CHR's view of the land and departs from the traditional north-south direction.

Jehoshaphat established judges in the fortified cities of Judah to hear the people's cases. He also established a supreme court in Jerusalem comprised of Levites, priests, and the heads of Israelite families (v. 8). The supreme court had civil and religious jurisdiction over the judges of the cities concerning their interpretation of the law. Amariah, the chief priest presided over matters and cases related to God. Zebadiah, the son of Ishmael and the leader of the house of Judah, presided over matters related to the king. The Levites would serve as officials of the court, probably responsible for implementing the decisions of the court. Jehoshaphat exhorts the judges to arbitrate justly, warning them against injustice, partiality, and bribery (v. 7) and reminding them that they themselves stood under the judgment of Yahweh (v. 11).

20:1-30. Jehoshaphat's defeat of Moab and Ammon. This section is distinctive to the CHR; it is not found in Kings. The chronological introduction *after this* (v. 1) does not provide any specific reference to

time. The invaders, the Moabites, the Ammonites, and the Meunites, came from the south, from beyond the Dead Sea. According to the NRSV they are coming from Edom. However, this reading follows one Dead Sea manuscript rather than the MT. Following the MT, the text should read "from ARAM," that is, the foreign alliance that was attacking Judah at the instigation of the Arameans.

Without much time to make preparations, Jehoshaphat became afraid and set out to seek divine help. He assembled the people before the new court of the Temple and proclaimed a general fast. This new court (v. 5) may refer to an addition to the Temple constructed in the days of Jehoshaphat. The king prayed a fervent prayer (vv. 6-12). His prayer is reminiscent of Solomon's prayer at the dedication of the Temple (2 Chr 6:24-31, 34-35). Jehoshaphat's prayer affirms God's power to deliver the nation in the present (v. 6) in the same way he delivered the people in the past (v. 7), and then asks God for judgment against the enemies (vv. 8-12).

As the king and the people prayed, the Spirit of Yahweh raised Jehaziel, a Levite from the sons of ASAPH, to respond to Jehoshaphat's prayer. Jehaziel pronounced an oracle of salvation with the formula *fear not* at the beginning and at the end of the oracle (vv. 15-17). Jehaziel announced that Yahweh himself will fight for the people and give them a great victory. The enemy will come *by the ascent* [or Pass] *of Ziz* (v. 16), southwest of Tekoa, a few miles north of Engedi. Jehoshaphat and the assembly of Judah fell down before Yahweh and worshiped as the Levites praised God with a loud voice.

During the march toward the place of victory, Jehoshaphat exhorted the people to believe in God (cf. Isa 7:9) and to believe also in the prophets. The Levites joined the procession singing a hymn of thanksgiving that appears often in the Psalms (106:1; 107:1; 136:1). The intervention of Yahweh was immediate and powerful. Yahweh set an ambush against the invading army and the soldiers killed themselves. So large were the spoils of war it took the people three days to collect them. The place where God gave Judah the victory was called the Valley of Beracah, the "Valley of Blessing." The people returned to Jerusalem with great joy and much celebration. The neighbors of Israel feared Yahweh because they understood that to fight against Israel was to fight against Yahweh.

20:31-37. Jehoshaphat's last days. The CHR ends the story of Jehoshaphat with a summary of his reign.

He was thirty-five years old when he began to reign and he reigned twenty-five years. He was a faithful king although he was unable to remove all the high places in Judah (but cf. 17:6). The CHR's explanation for this failure was that the people lacked commitment to Yahweh (v. 33).

The rest of his activities *are written in the Annals of Jehu* (v. 34) and in the general history of the kings of Judah and Israel, which here is called *the Book of the Kings of Israel* (cf. 16:11).

The final note mentions Jehoshaphat's joint maritime venture with Ahaziah, king of Israel (but contrast this reference with 1 Kgs 22:48-49). The location of TARSHISH (v. 36) is unknown. Tarshish may be a designation for a distant place (cf. commentary at 9:13-28). The destruction of Jehoshaphat's fleet (v. 37) was a punishment for entering this partnership with the wicked Ahaziah. The oracle of judgment was given by Eliezer, an unknown prophet.

The Reign of Jehoram, 21:1-20

The reign of JEHORAM received only a brief treatment by the CHR. The CHR takes most of his information from 2 Kgs 17–22 but adds additional information to emphasize Jehoram's unfaithfulness.

21:1-7. The murder of Jehoram's brothers. After the death of Jehoshaphat, Jehoram, his *firstborn* (v. 3), succeeded him on the throne of Judah. In general, the king's firstborn son ascended the throne after the death of his father, but the right of succession was not automatically given to the firstborn. Solomon (cf. 3:1-9) and Rehoboam (cf.11:18-22) became kings although they were not firstborn sons. For this reason Jehoshaphat gave gifts of silver and gold to his other sons. The text mentions six sons, although two of them have the same name (v. 2). After Jehoram was established upon the throne he killed his brothers and other persons he considered disloyal or even perhaps pretenders to the throne (v. 4).

Bright (1981, 252) has proposed that Jehoram killed his brothers at the prompting of his wife Athaliah, the daughter of Ahab and Jezebel, because "she felt her own position to be insecure." Athaliah's relationship to Ahab is problematic. She is listed as the daughter of Ahab and Jezebel in 2 Kgs 8:18 and 2 Chr 21:6 and as the daughter of OMRI in 2 Kgs 8:26 and 2 Chr 22:2. NRSV and NIV interpret the Hebrew text to mean that Athaliah was a female descendant of Omri, that is, his granddaughter. Bright contends that since Ahab and Jezebel had been married only about ten years, Atha-

liah was either Ahab's daughter by a previous marriage or a younger daughter of Omri who was raised by Ahab (Bright 1981, 242).

The CHR notes the consequence of Jehoram's marriage to Athaliah, the daughter of Ahab and Jezebel (v. 6): to follow in the ways of the king of Israel means to promote the cult of Baal and to encourage worship in the high places (see v. 11). The only reason the kingdom was not destroyed was because of the covenant God had made with David promising that a son of his (i.e., a male descendant) would continue to sit upon the throne. The *lamp* (v. 7) represents the permanency of David's dynasty.

21:8-10. The revolt of Edom and Libnah. During Jehoram's reign the Edomites revolted against Judah. Although the CHR says that Jehoram defeated the Edomites (but cf. 2 Kgs 8:21), he was not able to subdue them completely. During his reign Libnah also revolted against Judah. Libnah was located in the lowlands of Judah, southwest of Jerusalem. The rebellion of Edom and Libnah came because of Jehoram's unfaithfulness and as punishment for his sins (v. 10).

21:12-15. "Elijah's" letter to Jehoram. The unfaithfulness of Jehoram prompted the prophet ELIJAH to send a letter to the king pronouncing God's judgment upon him. This letter by Elijah has been the subject of much discussion. Since the synchronism of 2 Kgs 1:17 allows for Elijah to be alive at the beginning of Jehoram's reign, some scholars accept the authenticity of the letter. Other scholars say Elijah was already dead and the letter is a midrash, a composition of the CHR. Others say that it was either a letter from the prophet *Elisha* or a prophecy of an unknown prophet placed in the mouth of the renowned prophet. Since the ministry of Elijah is completely absent from Chronicles and because the content of the letter reflects the CHR's view of immediate retribution, it seems probable that Elijah's letter is the CHR's own composition.

The letter pronounces judgment upon Jehoram for his unfaithfulness and for the murder of his brothers who, in the CHR's view, were better than Jehoram (v. 13). A plague will come upon the people and upon the king's family. The king himself will be afflicted with a serious disease of the bowels (v. 15).

21:16-20. Jehoram's death. The attack by the Philistines and the Arabs is not mentioned in Kings. The Cushites (not Ethiopians, cf. 14:9) were an ethnic group who lived in the southern part of Judah. The invasion is seen as an act of Yahweh in fulfillment of Elijah's prediction. The invaders took away Jehoram's possessions, his sons and his wives. Only Jehoahaz, also known as Ahaziah (cf. 22:1), and Athaliah escaped death at the hands of the invaders. At the end of his life Jehoram became ill with an incurable bowel disease and died in much pain. Three times the CHR emphasizes that Jehoram was not honored in his death (vv. 19-20): the people did not make a fire in his honor (cf. 16:4), he died with no one's regret, and he was not buried in the tomb of the kings. Jehoram came to the throne at the age of thirty-two and reigned in Jerusalem eight years (v. 20).

The Reign of Ahaziah, 22:1-9

The source for this material is 2 Kgs 8:25-29 with some supplemental information provided by the CHR. After the death of Jehoram, Ahaziah, also known as JEHOAHAZ (21:17) was made king. Since Ahaziah was Jehoram's youngest and only surviving son, the inhabitants of Jerusalem proclaimed him king. This unusual act may indicate an emerging crisis that demanded the urgent action of the people. Then, at a later time, Ahaziah was proclaimed king by the whole nation. The MT says that he was forty-two years old when he began to reign (v. 2) but this is incorrect for his father died at the age of forty (21:20). According to 2 Kgs 8:26 he was twenty-two at the time he ascended the throne of Judah. His mother was Athaliah, the daughter of Ahab (MT "Omri": see discussion at 21:1-7). According to the CHR, Athaliah influenced Ahaziah towards the political and religious policies of the house of Ahab *to his ruin* (v. 4). This evaluation of Ahaziah's reign implies that his impious conduct, his evil politics, and his rejection of God were the causes of his having such a brief reign. His death at the hands of Jehu was *ordained of God* (v. 7).

God had commissioned Jehu to destroy the house of Ahab (v. 7; cf. 2 Kgs 9:1-13). When Ahaziah came to visit Jehoram (*Joram*, v. 7) who was recovering in JEZREEL from a wound he had received in his fight against Hazael, king of Aram, Jehu met Ahaziah and the royal entourage and killed them. Ahaziah escaped but was soon captured, brought before Jehu and then put to death. The events related to Ahaziah's death differ from the account in 2 Kgs 9:27-28. In Kings, Ahaziah was wounded in his chariot at the ascent of Gur, near Ibleam, and died in Megiddo. The CHR says he was hiding in Samaria, was captured there, and was brought to Jehu and put to death. The author of Kings also says that his servants brought Ahaziah's body to Jerusalem and buried him in the royal tomb. The CHR

says that Jehu and his men buried him in respect for Jehoshaphat's faithfulness to God. These differences may not reflect divergent sources but supplemental information available to the CHR. The death of Ahaziah caused a political vacuum in Judah, since there was no one strong enough to succeed Ahaziah and rule over the nation (v. 9). This final statement prepares the reader for the usurpation of the throne by Athaliah.

The Reign of Athaliah, 22:10-12

Athaliah was not considered a legitimate ruler in the line of David. The CHR omits the traditional succession formula because her reign was regarded as a usurpation of the throne of David. With the lack of a designated heir to the throne after the death of Ahaziah (v. 9), Athaliah attempted to eliminate the remaining members of the royal family. The king's children who were about to be murdered (v. 11) were Ahaziah's sons and Athaliah's grandchildren. Only the infant JOASH escaped the extermination of the royal house. Joash was saved by his aunt Jehoshabeath, who hid him and his nurse in a bedroom of the palace. From there he was taken in the Temple and placed into the care of the high priest. Jehoshabeath's name appears as Jehosheba in 2 Kgs 11:2. She was the daughter of Jehoram (but possibly not of Athaliah) and the sister of Ahaziah. She was also the wife of JEHOIADA, the high priest. Curtis and Madsen (1910, 422) believe her relationship to the high priest was a mere conjecture of the CHR, but there is no reason to doubt this information. Athaliah ruled over Judah six years, the six years Joash spent hiding in the Temple.

The Reign of Joash, 23:1–24:27

23:1-11. The crowning of Joash. The narrative follows 2 Kgs 11:4-12 with some differences that reflect the theological view of the CHR. The crowning of Joash as the legitimate successor to the Davidic throne was done publicly by the assembly with the support of the Levites. In Kings most of these events occurred in secrecy. Instead of making an agreement with the captains of the Carites (2 Kgs 11:4) or Cherethites (1 Sam 30:14; 2 Sam 8:16), the mercenary army established by David, Jehoiada made a covenant with the commander of hundreds to protect the king's son. At the instigation of the military commanders and Jehoiada, the Levites and the leaders of Israelite families came to Jerusalem, and in the Temple made a covenant with Joash and declared him king. Since only the priests and the Levites could enter the Temple, Jehoiada made provisions to exclude from the Temple area those who were not Levites and priests. The Levites were divided into several groups and placed in strategic locations to ensure Joash's safety. Joash then received the crown and the testimony (v. 11 MT: '*ēdût*) as the insignias of his office and was anointed by Jehoiada and his sons. The crown was the symbol of his royalty and the testimony was the royal protocol the king received at his ascension to the throne. The Hebrew word '*ēdût* may refer to a copy of the covenant Yahweh commanded the king to make (Deut 17:18). The anointing was the pouring of oil on the head of the king to symbolize his ordination as king.

23:12-15. The death of Athaliah. The people and the Levites celebrated the coronation of Joash with the blowing of the trumpets and with musical instruments. When Athaliah saw the people running and praising the new king she came to the house of God. As she arrived there she saw the king standing by his pillar, the designated place the king occupied during worship celebrations. Athaliah tore her clothing as a sign of despair and cried, *"Treason! Treason!"* (v. 13) but no one answered her voice. Jehoiada ordered the captains of the guard to seize her. She was captured, taken outside the Temple area to the entrance of the Horse Gate, and put to death. The lack of any reference to the length of her reign is an indication that she was never considered a legitimate ruler of Judah.

23:16-21. The enthronement of Joash. As a result of the death of Athaliah, Jehoiada made an attempt at reforming the cult in order to eliminate Baal worship that was probably introduced by Athaliah. He made a covenant with the people and the king promising to remain faithful to God. Then the people destroyed the house of Baal, demolished his images, and tore down the altars dedicated to Baal. They also killed Mattan, the priest of Baal, probably according to the injunction of Deut 13:5-10. Jehoiada put the priests in charge of the Temple according to the organization established by David. He also put the Levites in charge of the security of the Temple. Then the captains of the army, the nobles of Judah, and then people of the land brought Joash from the Temple to the king's house and placed him upon the throne. The CHR mentions the rejoicing of the people over the restoration of the throne of David and the time of peace that followed the death of Athaliah (v. 21).

24:1-3. Evaluation of Joash. This section follows 2 Kgs 11:21–12:3 [MT 12:1-4] with the omission of the synchronism with Jehu and the fact that the high

places were not eliminated. Joash began to reign when he was seven years old and reigned in Jerusalem forty years. He is credited with doing what was right in the sight of Yahweh as long as Jehoiada lived. Joash's harem seems to have been limited to two wives given to him by Jehoiada. The mention of sons and daughters is a declaration of God's blessing upon Joash and an affirmation that the threat to the continuation of the dynasty was over.

24:4-14. Joash's Temple restoration. This section follows 2 Kgs 12:4-16 with several additions by the CHR. According to the CHR, the restoration of the Temple was the greatest accomplishment of Joash while Jehoiada was alive. The expression *some time afterward* (v. 4) is only a transition phrase and does not provide a precise chronological reference. However, 2 Kgs 12:6 [MT 12:7] says that by the twenty-third year of Joash the repairs were not yet completed.

Joash commanded the priests and the Levites to receive an annual collection from the people of Judah to repair the Temple, although the Levites did not handle the money (vv. 11-12). The need for reparation arose because Athaliah and her followers had plundered the Temple and used the vessels dedicated to Yahweh in the worship of Baal. The reference to Athaliah's children (v. 7) may be a reference to her followers since 22:10 intimates that she did not have more children.

Joash wanted the work done immediately. But because the Levites did not act fast enough (v. 5), the king summoned Jehoiada to inquire about the delay. The text provides no clear reason for the delay. Dillard (1987, 188) compares the CHR's version with the deuteronomistic historian's version and concludes that Joash had reallocated funds used to pay Temple personnel to be used in the repairs of the Temple (cf. 2 Kgs 12:4 [MT 12:5]). As a form of compromise, Joash commanded that a chest be made to receive the people's offerings (v. 8). According to 2 Kgs 12:9 [MT 12:10] the chest was placed "beside the altar on the right side as one entered the house of the Lord." According to the CHR, the chest was placed *outside the gate of the house of the Lord* (v. 8). The CHR's change reflects the postexilic practice that did not allow the people to enter the Temple area. This offering was similar to the Temple tax decreed by Moses in the wilderness (Exod 30:12-16; 38:25-28). The king's command was executed, a proclamation was made throughout Judah, and the people brought their money until the chest was full. The money was distributed to the people working in the restoration of the Temple and the repairs were finished. The money left over was used to make several utensils to be used in the Temple.

24:15-16. The death of Jehoiada. As long as Jehoiada lived the people were faithful to God and offered sacrifices in the Temple. This statement by the CHR serves to divide the reign of Joash into two periods: his years of faithfulness, which were coeval with the life of Jehoiada, and his years of apostasy, which began with the death of Jehoiada. The death of Jehoiada is not mentioned in Kings. Jehoiada was 130 years old when he died. To the CHR and the people in his days this was an indication that Jehoiada had lived a full and blessed life. He was buried in the city of David, in the royal tomb in recognition for the good done *in Israel, and for God and his house* (v. 16).

24:17-27. Joash's wickedness and assassination. The Deuteronomistic historian had said that "Jehoash [Joash] did what was right in the sight of the Lord all his days" (1 Kgs 12:2 [MT 12:3]). But the CHR presents a different view of Joash after the death of Jehoiada. After the death of Jehoiada, some of the officials of Judah, probably those who had supported Athaliah and who were repressed by Jehoiada, came before Joash and paid homage to him. In turn they received the king's permission to return to their idolatrous practices. The people abandoned the Temple of Yahweh to serve the asherim, the sacred poles used in the cult of Asherah, and to worship idols. This reference to the asherim may be an allusion to 2 Kgs 12:3 [MT 12:4], which notes that the high places were not removed. The wrath of God came upon Judah. Yahweh sent several unnamed prophets to warn them, but the leaders of Judah were unwilling to listen.

Among the prophets sent by Yahweh the CHR mentions Zechariah, the son of Jehoiada. Clothed by the Spirit of God (cf. Judg 6:34), Zechariah warned the people that Yahweh had forsaken them because of their idolatry. With the consent of Joash Zechariah was stoned to death in the court of the house of God. The CHR declares that by killing Zechariah Joash had not remembered the *kindness* (Heb. *hesed*, v. 22) Jehoiada had shown him. *Hesed* carries the idea of loyalty (as in REB) and faithfulness. Jesus refers to this heinous murder of Zechariah in Matt 23:35 and Luke 11:51.

The dying words of Zechariah (v. 22) soon found fulfillment. According to the retribution theology of the CHR, the punishment was not delayed. *At the end of the year* (v. 23), that is, in the spring of the next year, the time when military campaigns took place (cf. 1 Chr 20:1), the king of Aram attacked and defeated

Joash. Since the Aramean army was smaller than that of Judah (v. 24), the CHR saw the defeat of the Judean army as a visible demonstration of divine justice. The Arameans killed many Judean officials and took much booty to Damascus. Joash was left badly wounded (v. 25). Two of his servants, an Ammonite and a Moabite, conspired against him and killed him in his bed. According to the CHR, the reason for the conspiracy against Joash was the death of Zechariah (v. 25).

Joash died in disgrace. He was buried in the city of David but not in the royal tomb. To the CHR the manner of his burial was a sign of dishonor and divine displeasure. After his death his son Amaziah succeeded him. The acts of Joash are mentioned in the *Commentary [midrash] on the Book of Kings* (v. 27). On the nature of this commentary, see comments on 13:22, above. The reference that the *midrash* included many oracles against Joash indicates that the *midrash* on the Book of Kings contained prophetic materials interpreting historical events.

The Reign of Amaziah, 25:1-28

25:1-4. The Accession of Amaziah. The CHR introduces AMAZIAH by summarizing his reign over Judah. Amaziah was twenty-five years old when he began to reign and his reign lasted twenty-nine years. However, due to his probable imprisonment by the king of Israel (v. 24), his son Uzziah may have served as acting king during part of his reign (cf. Dillard 1987, 198). He was a good king at the beginning of his reign but the CHR's endorsement of Amaziah is limited (v. 2), perhaps because of his later apostasy. Upon assuming the throne Amaziah consolidated his power by killing those who had murdered his father (v. 3). He spared the children of his father's killers in obedience to the injunction in the law (Deut 24:16), which specified that innocent children should not be punished for the sins of their parents.

25:5-13. War against the Edomites. Amaziah prepares to go to war against the Edomites by taking a census of Judah, similar to the census of Jehoshaphat (2 Chr 17:14-19), conscripting 300,000 men, and organizing them under groups of 1,000 and 100. He also hired 100,000 warriors from Israel to increase and strengthen his army. However, an unnamed prophet intervened and warned Amaziah that reliance upon the men of Israel was unwise because Yahweh was not with Israel. In obedience to the words of the man of God, Amaziah discharged the mercenaries from Israel. This action was very costly because Amaziah had already paid 100 talents of silver for their services. The man of God had assured the king that Yahweh would give him back much more than what he would lose.

As a result of his obedience, Amaziah obtained a great victory against the Edomites. The army of Judah killed thousands of Edomites and took 10,000 captives and cast them from the tops of cliffs to their death. The men of Israel who were dismissed by Amaziah were very angry, probably because they would be excluded from the spoils of Edom. As an act of revenge they attacked several cities of Judah, *killed three thousand people in them, and took much booty* (v. 13).

25:14-16. The apostasy of Amaziah. After the defeat of the Edomites, Amaziah followed a custom popular in the ancient Near East and took the gods of the Edomites as spoils of war and worshiped them. He was confronted by a prophet, probably the same man of God referred to in v. 7. The prophet rebuked the king for worshiping the impotent gods of the Edomites, the same gods who were unable to save their own people. Amaziah was angry at the words of the prophet and threatened him with death. The prophet departed, but warned the king that God had determined to destroy him. The story of Amaziah's apostasy and the prophetic warning serve to explain Amaziah's defeat at Beth-shemesh (vv. 20-24) and his death at the hands of conspirators (vv. 27-28).

25:17-24. Amaziah's defeat at Beth-shemesh. Amaziah's desire to go to war against the Northern Kingdom was a result of his overconfidence after his victory against the Edomites (v. 17). It was also a desire to avenge the raid against Judean cities perpetrated by Israelite mercenaries whom Amaziah had discharged from his army. Amaziah's words to Joash (Jehoash) were an invitation to confrontation. Joash responded by ridiculing Amaziah with a fable that was similar to Jotham's fable in Judg 9:7-15. Joash's fable compared Amaziah to a little bush that dared to challenge the mighty cedar of Lebanon only to be trampled by a wild animal. Joash warned Amaziah by saying that his victory against Edom would not assure him of victory against Israel. Amaziah refused to listen to the words of the king of Israel. The CHR inserts his interpretation of the event by saying that Amaziah's refusal to listen was caused by God's desire to punish Amaziah for his worship of alien gods.

Amaziah and Joash confronted each other in BETH-SHEMESH, a city in the territory of Judah, southwest of Jerusalem. Joash defeated the Judean army, captured Amaziah and brought him back to Jerusalem, and

broke down the northern wall, from the Ephraim Gate (Neh 8:16) to the Corner Gate (Jer 31:38), the wall that protected the city against invasions from the north, and took the gold and the silver that were in the Temple. The NRSV adds that Joash also took *Obed-edom* with him (v. 24). This translation, however, does not reflect the text. The family of Obed-edom were gatekeepers and were in charge of the Temple treasury (cf. 1 Chr 26:15). The text says Joash took the silver and the gold and the vessels of the Temple "that had been in the care of Obed-edom" (v. 24 NIV). In addition, Joash took the treasures found in the palace. Amaziah was probably released in exchange for the hostages Joash took to Samaria.

25:25-28. The death of Amaziah. It is not known whether Amaziah was taken to Samaria or how long he became a prisoner of Joash. It is possible that the silver and the gold taken from the Temple, as well as the treasures from the palace and the hostages taken to Samaria, served as a ransom paid to Joash to allow Amaziah to continue as king of Judah. Dillard (1987, 202) suggests that Amaziah was not released until after Joash's death. Amaziah survived Joash by fifteen years. The CHR informs the reader that the events of Amaziah's reign were recorded *in the Book of the Kings of Judah and Israel* (v. 26; but cf. 1 Kgs 14:19). Amaziah's death occurred as the result of a conspiracy planned against him because of his apostasy from Yahweh. Amaziah fled to Lachish, a Judean city located in the Shephelah. The conspirators pursued him and killed him in Lachish. His death fulfilled the words of the prophet concerning Amaziah, that God would destroy him (v. 16). Amaziah was buried with his ancestors. While 2 Kgs 14:20 says that Amaziah was buried *in the city of David* (also v. 28), the MT of v. 28 says he was buried "in a city of Judah" (cf. "the City of Judah," NAB, NIV). This statement by the CHR seems to emphasize that Amaziah's burial in an anonymous tomb in Judah was a punishment for his apostasy (Japhet 1993, 872).

The Reign of Uzziah, 26:1-23

26:1-5. Uzziah's accession to the throne. The name of UZZIAH, king of Judah, is popularly known because of the association of his name with the call of Isaiah to the prophetic ministry (Isa 6:1). His name appears in Chronicles as Uzziah (v. 1) and as Azariah (1 Chr 3:12), although the CHR prefers to use Uzziah, perhaps to distinguish him from the high priest Azariah (26:17). The use of two names for some kings in the

OT may reflect the fact that the kings assumed a throne name at the time of their coronation. Uzziah became king at the age of sixteen with the help of the people of Judah. In light of Amaziah's capture by Joash (25:23) and since the CHR twice mentions the accession of Uzziah to the throne of Judah, it is possible that Uzziah ascended to the throne of Judah the first time as a coregent with his father at the time of Amaziah's capture. In light of the conspiracy in Jerusalem against Amaziah (25:27), it is also possible that Amaziah was killed by a conspiracy orchestrated by people in Jerusalem who opposed his return to power. Since there is no evidence that the conspirators intended to place anyone in power, it is also possible that Uzziah was aware of the conspiracy against his father.

Uzziah is presented as a good king who followed in the steps of his father Amaziah. This statement by the CHR is surprising because the author was critical of Amaziah. Since this information is drawn from 2 Kgs 15:3, it is possible that the CHR is restricting his judgment of Uzziah to the early part of his reign as he had done with Amaziah (25:2). The CHR credits Uzziah's piety to Zechariah, who taught him to walk in the fear of Yahweh. Little is known about Zechariah. A prophet named Zechariah appears in the days of Joash, king of Judah (24:20). Another Zechariah is mentioned in Is 8:3 but 2 Chr 26:5 intimates that the Zechariah who instructed Uzziah died before Isaiah became a prophet. The CHR declares that Uzziah was blessed and prospered as long as he remained faithful to God. One of Uzziah's accomplishments was the conquest and restoration of Elath, an important port on the Red Sea that was lost to Judah in the days of Jehoram (21:8-10). The rebuilding of Elath contributed to the great economic prosperity Judah enjoyed in the eighth century B.C.E.

26:6-8. Uzziah's military campaigns. During his reign, Uzziah enjoyed several military victories. The most important of these was his victory against the Philistines, for it neutralized an old foe and allowed Judah to control the trade routes that passed along the coastal highway. Gath was first conquered by David (1 Chr 18:1) and subsequently lost by Joash (2 Kgs 12:17). Uzziah also conquered Ashdod and Jabneh (Jabneel, Josh 15:11). He built cities in Ashdod and along the borders of other Philistines cities. GATH and ASHDOD were two of the five most important cities dominated by the Philistines (Josh 13:3). Later on in Jewish history, Jabneh came to be known as Jamnia and became an important center of study. Uzziah con-

quered the Arabs who lived in Gur-baal. This place is unknown; it appears only here in the OT. He also conquered the Meunites. In addition, Uzziah received tribute from the Ammonites, and as a result of these victories, his fame spread to the borders of Egypt. According to the CHR, Uzziah was able to obtain these victories because *God helped him* (v. 7).

26:9-15. Uzziah's achievements. Because of God's help, Judah, under the reign of Uzziah, flourished and became a thriving nation. The CHR lists several areas in which Uzziah was successful and prosperous. He built defensive towers in Jerusalem and outside the city in the wilderness to serve as defense outposts and storage (vv. 9-10a). He dug cisterns to help with his large herds in the Shephelah, the lower hill country located west of Jerusalem, and in the plains. He showed his love for the land by developing agriculture in the fertile lands of Judah, probably the territory around Hebron. He organized and equipped his army to defend the nation and to protect his holdings. A large army, with 307,500 trained soldiers under 2,600 commanders, was equipped with the best and most effective armaments. He also added to his army war machines capable of shooting arrows and throwing large stones. According to the CHR, because Uzziah sought Yahweh (v. 5), Yahweh blessed and prospered him greatly; he became famous and very powerful (v. 15).

26:16-21. Uzziah's sin and punishment. Uzziah's prosperity made him proud and arrogant and led him to his destruction (Prov 16:18; 18:12). His downfall came when he acted treacherously against Yahweh and the Temple. According to the CHR, Uzziah *was false to the LORD his God* (v. 16). The Hebrew word carries the idea of rebellion and unfaithfulness (see NIV). Uzziah sinned against God by entering the Temple and trying to exercise the priestly function by offering a sacrifice upon the altar of incense, an act that was the prerogative of the sons of Aaron (v. 18; cf. Exod 30:7-8). The priests defended the sanctity of the Temple forcibly. Azariah and eighty other priests confronted the king and told him that it was not proper for him to burn incense upon the altar. Uzziah, with the censer in his hand, became very angry. At this moment, the CHR says, Uzziah was struck with leprosy.

The rapidity with which Uzziah was stricken is another way of reaffirming the CHR's theology of immediate retribution. The Hebrew word for "leprosy" does not necessarily mean Hansen's disease. It is a generic term to refer to a variety of skin diseases (cf. Lev 13). This unknown disease made Uzziah unclean and excluded him from the Temple, from the palace, and from contact with other people (Lev 13:45-46). His son Jotham became coregent with his father and was in charge of the affairs of the kingdom (v. 21).

26:22-23. Uzziah's death. Uzziah was a leper until the day he died. After his death he was buried in a field adjacent the tomb of the kings. He could not be buried with his ancestors because he was unclean. After his death Jotham ascended to the throne and became sole regent.

According to the CHR, the record of Uzziah's kingdom was found in a book written by Isaiah the prophet. Many efforts have been made to identify this book with the references to Uzziah in the historical narratives found in the books of Isaiah and Kings. However, it is more probable that the CHR is referring to a different source available to him. But it is very difficult to say whether it was written by Isaiah himself.

The Reign of Jotham, 27:1-9

The CHR offers a summary of Jotham's reign that is richer in details than the parallel narrative in 2 Kgs 15:32-38. Jotham was twenty-five years old when he began to reign and he reigned sixteen years. His mother was Jerushah, daughter of ZADOK. It is possible that the reference to *Zadok* in v. 1 may indicate that Jerushah was a descendant of the Zadok who served as high priest in the days of David and Solomon. According to the CHR, Jotham was a faithful king like his father Uzziah. The CHR also commends Jotham because he did not enter the Temple of Yahweh and did not usurp the work that belonged to the priests. Jotham is portrayed in Chronicles as a faithful and prosperous king. Despite his faithfulness the people did not follow his conduct. The deuteronomistic writer says that the people continued to sacrifice and burn incense on the high places (2 Kgs 15:35).

The CHR stresses Jotham's many building activities and victories over his enemies to emphasize God's blessings. Some of these constructions were a continuation of work initiated by his father. Jotham built the upper gate (the north entrance; cf. 2 Chr 23:20) of the Temple; he fortified Ophel, the walls protecting the city, and built new settlements in the Judean hills. His subjugation of the Ammonites came probably because of their refusal to pay tribute (see 26:8). They were subjugated for three years. During this time they continued paying tribute to Jotham.

The CHR concludes the summary of Jotham's reign declaring that because of his piety he was blessed and

prosperous. He was powerful and conquered his enemies because he was firm in the ways of Yahweh. As an attempt to affirm that his reign was devoid of political problems, the CHR omits any reference to the Syro-Ephraimite war (2 Kgs 15:37), although the mention of *all his wars* (v. 7) may be a veiled reference to that conflict. After Jotham's death he was buried with his ancestors in the city of David. Jotham was succeeded on the throne by his son Ahaz.

The Reign of Ahaz, 28:1-27

28:1-4. Ahaz's Iniquity. The CHR is severe in his criticism of AHAZ. He omits any reference to Ahaz's accomplishments as king in order to emphasize his failures and his apostasy. Ahaz was twenty years old when he ascended to the throne of Judah and reigned sixteen years. Unlike David, Ahaz was unfaithful to Yahweh. The CHR compares Ahaz's iniquity to the religious practices of the kings of Israel. The wickedness of Ahaz is vividly illustrated by the CHR: Ahaz made images of BAAL, he made his son pass through the fire, and sacrificed in the high places. Passing one's son through the fire has been associated with child sacrifice, a religious practice connected with the worship of Molech, the Ammonite god. These sacrifices took place *in the valley of the son of Hinnom* (v. 3), a site southwest of Jerusalem. The Hebrew name of this place, Ge-hinnom (HINNOM, VALLEY OF) became associated with GEHENNA or HELL (see Matt 5:22). Child sacrifice was severely criticized by the prophets (Jer 7:30-31) and condemned as an abomination to Yahweh (Lev 18:21; 20:2-5; Deut 12:31).

28:5-7. Ahaz's war against Aram and Israel. The expression *Therefore the Lord his God gave him into the hand of the king of Aram* (v. 5) stresses the CHR's theology of immediate retribution. According to the CHR, the war against Aram and Israel, also known as the Syro-Ephraimite war, was part of the divine judgment on Ahaz because of his sins. The CHR presents the attacks of Aram and Israel as two separate events, although 2 Kgs 16:5-7 and Isa 7:1-6 treat the attacks on Israel as a joint effort by the Syro-Ephraimite forces.

God, through the prophet Isaiah (7:1-17), offered Ahaz an opportunity to save Judah from the agony of war. The king refused to accept the divine sign (Isa 7:12) and because of his lack of faith in Yahweh's power to save, Judah was invaded by the Arameans and Ahaz was soundly defeated. As a result, a number of Judean citizens were deported to Damascus by

Rezin, the Aramean king (2 Kgs 16:5) and many more were killed by Pekah, king of Israel.

Zichri, a soldier in the Israelite army also killed Ahaz's son and two of Ahaz's palace officials. The exile and slaughter of Judean citizens are not mentioned in 2 Kings nor Isaiah.

28:8-15. Oded's Oracle. This passage is original with the CHR. Oded was a northern prophet who lived in Samaria. Nothing is known about Oded and his ministry. He should not be identified with the father of the prophet Azariah who prophesied in the days of Asa (2 Chr 15:1). Oded met the army of Israel as they returned with the spoils of war and two hundred thousand captives (v. 8). He acknowledged that Yahweh was punishing Judah for their sins but warned that the army had abused their role as instruments of divine justice by enslaving the people. He requested the soldiers to liberate and repatriate the people of Judah because they were *kindred* to the people of Israel (v. 11). Four tribal leaders from Israel also entreated the army not to add to their sins (vv. 12-13). Oded and the tribal leaders succeeded in convincing the Israelites to allow the Judeans to return to their country. The tribal leaders fed and clothed the captives and returned them to Jericho.

This passage demonstrates the CHR's sympathy for the Northern Kingdom. Even among the sinful people of the North there were faithful people who knew how to act as brothers to the people who lived in Judah. Some of the details of this story, such as the anointing of the wounded with oil, the provision of food and drink, the carrying of the feeble on asses, and the journey to Jericho, have been compared to the parable of the Good Samaritan in Luke 10:29-37 (Spenser 1984, 317–49).

28:16-21. Ahaz's appeal to Assyria. *At that time* (v. 16) refers to the time of the Syro-Ephraimite war. The Edomites and the Philistines took advantage of the political weakness in Judah and raided several Judean cities. The Edomites invaded Judah, conquered Elath (2 Kgs 16:5) and took several people captive while the Philistines raided six cities in the Shephelah and the Negeb. Fearing further invasions, Ahaz requested help from Assyria. He raided (*plundered*) the Temple, the royal coffers, and the houses of palace official to put together the money to pay tribute to Assyria. The plundering of his officials may refer to heavy taxation imposed upon the nobles of Judah.

But because of his unfaithfulness to Yahweh (v. 19), the gifts Ahaz gave to TIGLATH-PILESER III (745–727)

were of no help (v. 21; cf. v. 16), for the Assyrian king came against him and made him a vassal (Mariottini 1990, 917–18). Ahaz is called king of Israel (v. 19) because from the perspective of the CHR the Northern Kingdom had ceased to exist. Tiglath-pileser's name appears in v. 20 as *Tilgath-pilneser*. The variation may reflect a failure to transliterate properly the Assyrian name into Hebrew (see also 1 Chr 5:6).

28:22-27. Ahaz's apostasy. The CHR provides more details of Ahaz's apostasy than his source in 2 Kgs 16:10-18. In his distress Ahaz did not turn to Yahweh but became *yet more faithless* (v. 22). He worshiped the Aramean gods because he believed they had helped the Arameans in their victory against Judah. Since the Arameans had already been conquered by the Assyrians (2 Kgs 16:9-10), it is possible that the CHR is alluding to this fact to point to Ahaz's senselessness in worshiping other gods. Ahaz's apostasy and folly became his ruin and the ruin of Judah. Second Kings 16:17 says that Ahaz removed several objects from the Temple. The CHR adds that he closed the door of the Temple and promoted the worship of other gods *in every corner of Jerusalem* (v. 24) and made high places *in every city of Judah* (v. 25). The CHR does not mention the altar made by Ahaz and placed in the Temple (2 Kgs 16:10). The words of the CHR in v. 27 do not contradict 2 Kgs 16:20. The CHR says that when Ahaz died he was buried in Jerusalem but was not placed in the royal tomb. Kings says that he was buried with his fathers in the city of David. The CHR, however makes a distinction. According to 2 Chr 21:20 and 24:25, Ahaz was buried in the city of David, but, because of his unfaithfulness, not in the royal tomb. It is possible that, like Uzziah, he was buried in the burial field that belonged to David's family (2 Chr 26:23).

The reign of Hezekiah, 29:1-32:33

The CHR is very fond of HEZEKIAH. He dedicates four chapters to recount the events related to his reign, which makes Hezekiah as important to the CHR as DAVID and SOLOMON. The CHR emphasizes the events in Hezekiah's life that demonstrate his devotion to Yahweh and to the Temple. Hezekiah is portrayed as a reformer who restored the worship of Yahweh in Judah.

29:1-2. The accession of Hezekiah. The CHR presents a very positive image of Hezekiah and his government. Four chapters are dedicated to recapitulate the events related to his reign. The CHR emphasizes Hezekiah's devotion to God and his zeal for the Temple. Special emphasis is given to Hezekiah's cleansing of the Temple and the observance of the passover. The CHR's portrayal of Hezekiah as a reformer who restored the worship of Yahweh and as an individual of profound piety makes him one of the best kings in the history of Israel (v. 2).

29:3-19. The cleansing of the Temple. Hezekiah's first act as king was to reverse the policies of his father, Ahaz, and initiate the cleansing of the Temple. This event occurred in the first month of the first year of his reign (v. 3). Hezekiah assembled the priests and the Levites in the square, east of the Temple entrance, and commanded them to open the doors of the house of God that Ahaz had closed (28:24; but see 2 Kgs 16:10-16). Hezekiah made a public confession of the sins of past generations, similar to the liturgical confessions popular in the postexilic times (v. 9 makes a reference to the Exile of Judah; cf. Dan 9:4-19; Zech 1:1-6). After Hezekiah's declaration of the nation's sins, fourteen Levites, two from each of the seven Levitical families, responded with great enthusiasm to the king's appeal. The priests and Levites sanctified themselves and began the process of removing the impurities of the Temple (v. 16). The Levites took the impurities from the Temple and threw them into the brook of Kidron, as was done in the days of Asa (15:16). The priests cleansed the inner part of the Temple because the Levites were not allowed to enter the most holy place. The process of purification of the Temple and its precincts lasted sixteen days. For eight days they purified the exterior part of the Temple and for eight days they purified the interior section of the Temple (v. 17). When the process of sanctifying the Temple was completed, the priests and the Levites reported to Hezekiah, declaring that the utensils that Ahaz had desecrated were ready to be used again.

29:20-36. The great sacrifice. After the sanctification of the Temple and the removal of the unclean things, Hezekiah and the people prepared to restore the worship of Yahweh. The king and the leaders of Judah made a special sacrifice for the sins of the kingdom, of the sanctuary, and of Judah (v. 21). Sacrifices were made in groups of seven. Seven bulls, rams, and lambs were to be sacrificed as burnt offerings and seven male goats as sin offerings. Hezekiah also made an attempt to include the Northern tribes by commanding that sacrifices be made for all Israel (v. 24).

The sacrifices were accompanied by cultic music. The Levites (v. 25) played the instruments ordered by David (cf. 23:5), and the priests played the trumpets (v. 26). Thus, with musical instruments, the singing of psalms and the worship of the people, sacrifices were offered to Yahweh.

After the burnt offerings were offered for the sins of the nation, Hezekiah exhorted the people to offer sacrifices of praise and thanksgiving. The people responded to the king's exhortation with great enthusiasm and brought their offerings to the Temple. Their gifts were so plentiful the priests could not offer them by themselves, for they were few. The Levites helped the priests with the sacrifices until more priests were ritually cleansed to assume their duties. This incident was used by the CHR to emphasize the ministry of the Levites: *the Levites were more conscientious than the priests in sanctifying themselves* (v. 34). The CHR's praise for the Levites is a veiled criticism of the priests, reflecting the conflict between Levites and priests that existed in the postexilic community.

30:1-12. The invitation to the Passover. Hezekiah, by letter (v. 1) and couriers (vv. 6, 11) invited all Israel to celebrate the Passover. This information is unique in Chronicles, since the deuteronomistic historian does not mention it. The people were unable to celebrate the Passover on the fourteenth day of the first month. It was scheduled for the fourteenth day of the second month and some of the northern tribes were invited to participate. The celebration of the Passover in the second month was celebrated according to the legislation in Num 9:1-14.

Two reasons are given by the CHR for the change of the date (v. 3). One reason was that the priests had not sanctified themselves in sufficient numbers to hold the celebration (see 29:34). The second reason was that because the people had to travel from the north, they were not able to arrive on time for the celebration. Another possibility is that since the northern tribes celebrated the Passover in the second month, Hezekiah attempted to celebrate the feast according to the customs of the northern tribes.

The emissaries of the king went through several of the northern tribes, now part of the Assyrian empire, inviting them to participate in the celebration of the Passover. One of the inducements to the remnant of the northern tribes to come to Jerusalem and celebrate Passover in the Temple was the promise that Yahweh would return the people from exile (v. 9). This promise was based on Solomon's prayer to God (1 Kgs 8:50) and God's answer to Solomon's prayer at the time of the dedication of the Temple, assuring the people of forgiveness and restoration for those who were repentant and would pray in the Temple (2.Chr 7:14-16). The expression "from Beer-sheba to Dan" (v. 5) reflects the CHR's use of the expression to designate the southern and the northern limits of the land that belonged to all Israel (cf. 1 Chr 21:2). Hezekiah's invitation to the northern tribes was met with scorn and indifference (v. 10). Only a few people from Asher, Manasseh, Zebulun (v. 11) and from Ephraim and Issachar (v. 18) came. The people of Judah responded with enthusiasm, because the hand of God was upon them (v. 10).

30:13-27. The Passover Celebration. The people came to celebrate the Passover (30:1, 2, 5) and the feast of the unleavened bread (30:12-13). Both feasts are celebrated together in Chronicles, as well as in Deut 16:1-8. Some scholars believe that the two feasts were not celebrated together until the days of Josiah. It is possible that the combination of both feasts in Chronicles may reflect the realities of the postexilic community or an effort to equate the reforms of Hezekiah with the reforms of Josiah.

The altars made by Ahaz throughout Judah (28:24) and dedicated to other gods were removed and thrown into the brook of Kidron before the passover lamb was killed (see 29:16). This incident is confirmed by the words of the Assyrian emissary sent to convey a message to the people of Jerusalem (2 Kgs 18:22). The altars for offering incense were also removed (v. 14). The priests and the Levites worked together in the presentation of the sacrifices. Many people from Judah and Israel were unclean when they ate the passover (v. 18). Hezekiah, acting as a mediator, prayed for the people and they were forgiven (vv. 19-20). The people, although unclean, were allowed to participate in the passover because of their devotion to God and the disposition of their hearts.

The celebration of the passover and the festival of unleavened bread reached its climax on the seventh day. Then the people, by unanimous accord and gladness of heart, decided to extend the celebration another seven days. Hezekiah and his leaders provided additional sacrifices for the celebration and this prompted more priests to sanctify themselves (v. 24). The elaborateness of the celebration prompted the CHR to say that no other passover had been celebrated in this manner in Israel since the dedication of the Temple in the days of Solomon (v. 26; see 2 Kgs 23:22-23). At the end of the celebration the priests blessed the people, probably with the priestly benediction mentioned in Num 6:22-27. The NRSV reads: *Then the priests and*

the Levites stood up and blessed the people (v. 27). However, the MT read that "the Levitical priests" blessed the people (cf. Deut 18:1). This translation including the Levites in the blessing of the people reflects the reading of several manuscripts and ancient translations. God's acceptance of the priests's prayer indicates the divine approval on the work of Hezekiah.

31:1-19. Hezekiah's religious reforms. The narrative concerning the reforms of Hezekiah is divided into four sections: (1) the destruction of the high places by the people (v. 1); (2) provisions for the support of the Temple ministry (vv. 2-10); (3) the reorganization of the Temple personnel (vv. 11-19); and (4) the evaluation of Hezekiah as king (vv. 20-21).

The destruction of the HIGH PLACES (see 2 Kgs 18:4) was carried out by the people after the celebration of the festival of unleavened bread. According to the CHR, the destruction of the high places was also extended to Ephraim and Manasseh. To provide for the ministry of the Temple (vv. 3-10) the king made a contribution for the burnt offering and exhorted the people to make contributions to support the ministry of the priests and Levites (v. 4) in order that they might devote themselves exclusively to the teaching of the law. The people who responded to the appeal of Hezekiah were those of Judah and those of Israel who lived in the towns of Judah. To the CHR these people formed all Israel. They responded generously to the king's appeal and brought their offerings in abundance. The offerings of the people reflect the laws of the tithe and first fruits used to support the priests and Levites (Num 18:21, 24; Deut 18:1-8).

The reorganization of the priests and Levites (v. 2) was done according to the traditions established by David and Solomon (1 Chr 23:6; 2 Chr 8:14). The priests were responsible to present the sacrifices upon the altar and the Levites were responsible to lead the liturgy of the Temple and for the maintenance and administration of the Temple. Hezekiah also ordered that chambers be built in the Temple to house the offerings dedicated to the priests and Levites (v. 11; cf. Mal 3:10). The collection lasted all summer, from the third to the seventh month, that is, from the beginning of the grain harvest to the time when fruits, grapes, and olives were harvested. Hezekiah appointed some Levites led by Conaniah and his brother Shimei, aided by ten other Levites, to oversee the collection (vv. 12-13). He also appointed Kore to supervise the freewill offerings, the tribute given to support the priests, the Levites, and their families. Kore was assisted by six other Levites who were assigned to work with him outside Jerusalem, in the Levitical cities (vv. 14-15). According to v. 17, the Levites entered their ministry in the Temple at the age of twenty. Two other references provide different information concerning the age at which the Levites entered their ministry: Num 4:3 says that they bagan their service at the age of thirty; Num 8:24 says it was twenty-five. This lowering of the age when the Levites began their ministry may reflect changes in customs or a shortage of Levites in the postexilic community (see commentary at 23:3).

The narrative concludes with an evaluation of Hezekiah's work and faithfulness (vv. 20-21). The CHR says that Hezekiah was deeply committed to the Temple. His evaluation of Hezekiah asserts that his good works came out of his obedience to the law of God. For this reason God prospered him and the work he did. Hezekiah's prosperity was another evidence for the CHR that God blesses and prospers those who are faithful and obedient.

32:1-23. Sennacherib's invasion. This chapter summarizes the events related to the Assyrian invasion under Sennacherib in 701 B.C.E. The CHR's version is based on materials founded in 2 Kgs 18:13-20:21 and Isa 36-39. In addition, the CHR used other sources that provided supplementary information on Hezekiah and his reign. The invasion of SENNACHERIB, king of Assyria, came after Hezekiah's acts of faithfulness (v. 1). This introduction by the CHR is part of his thesis that God blessed the faithfulness of Hezekiah with a great victory against the mighty Assyrian army. Politically, Hezekiah had made an attempt to declare his independence from Assyria. He broke the alliance that his father had made with Tiglath-pileser III (2 Kgs 16:7) and withheld tribute paid yearly to Assyria. This declaration of independence probably came after the death of SARGON in 705 B.C.E. With the accession of Sennacherib (705–681 B.C.E.) to the throne of Assyria, Hezekiah made preparations for war. The narrative describing the preparations for war (vv. 2-8) comes from an unknown source, since it is not found in 2 Kings. Sennacherib came against the fortified cities of Judah, believing that he could conquer them for himself (v. 1). This statement by the CHR is in marked contrast with 2 Kgs 18:13 where the deuteronomistic writer says that Sennacherib actually captured them.

The preparation for war against Assyria was accomplished in three stages. The first was the blocking up of the springs that were outside of the city (vv. 3-4). One of the springs that was protected was the Gihon (v. 30), one of the primary sources of water for Jerusalem. The second was the fortification of the walls around the city, the building of an additional wall, and the fortification of the Millo (v. 5a). The Millo were the terraces made of earth and stones built to fortify the walls of Jerusalem. The third was the equipping of the army with improved weapons (vv. 5b-6). Hezekiah also reorganized the army and appointed commanders over the militia. He then brought the people together and exhorted them to trust God and believe that Yahweh would fight for them.

Before invading Jerusalem, Sennacherib sent an embassy with a message for Hezekiah and the people of Judah, probably offering the terms for surrender. According to 2 Kgs 18:17 the embassy was composed of three high officials: the Tartan was the commander of the Assyrian army; the Rabsaris was the chief eunuch, who represented the king of Assyria, and the Rabshakeh, the cupbearer of the king who was the personal attendant of the king. Hezekiah also sent three emissaries to meet the Assyrian embassy: Eliakim was the chief of the palace, Shebna was the secretary of state and Joash was the recorder. These were the highest officials in the Judean court. The dialogue between the Assyrian envoys and the servants of Hezekiah in vv. 10-19 is a condensed version of the narrative in 2 Kgs 18:17-35. The Rabshakeh referred to Hezekiah's destruction of the altars to imply that the invasion was happening because the gods were angry with Hezekiah. The Assyrian envoy also emphasized that the gods of the conquered nations were unable to deliver their people and that Yahweh would be unable to deliver Hezekiah and those who joined him. The dialogue between the envoys of Assyria and the servants of Hezekiah was conducted in the *language of Judah* (v. 18). The language of Judah was Hebrew, also known as the language of Canaan (Isa 19:18). The envoys of Hezekiah requested that they speak in Aramaic, the language spoken by the Assyrians and the language used in diplomacy and commerce. The Assyrians refused and continued to speak in Hebrew *to frighten and terrify* (v. 18) the people (2 Chr 32:18). According to the CHR, the Assyrians blasphemed God because they compared him with the gods of the nations (v. 19).

The mention of the prayers of Hezekiah and Isaiah in v. 20 is a brief reference to the narrative of 2 Kgs 19:1-34. The CHR only mentions the prayer of Hezekiah (2 Kgs 19:15-19) and the oracle of Isaiah (2 Kgs 19:20-34) describing the deliverance of Jerusalem.

Yahweh heard Hezekiah's prayer by destroying the Assyrian army and by causing the return of Sennacherib back to Assyria and eventually his death by his own sons (2 Kgs 19:35-37). The CHR does not mention the considerable tribute of silver and gold Hezekiah paid to avert the destruction of Jerusalem (2 Kgs 18:14-16).

The salvation of Jerusalem from the Assyrian army was God's reward to Hezekiah for his faithfulness. To the CHR the defeat of the Assyrian army was clear evidence that God prospers and blesses those who are faithful to him. Faithfulness to God brought victory, prosperity, and fame to Hezekiah (v. 23).

32:24-31. Hezekiah's illness and prosperity. The narrative of Hezekiah's illness and recovery (vv. 24-26) is a brief summary of 2 Kgs 20:1-11. The CHR omits Isaiah's announcement of Hezekiah's impending death and what the prophet told him he must do to recover (cf. Isa 38:1, 21). Hezekiah recovered because he prayed to God. Yahweh gave him a sign as assurance that he would recover, but Hezekiah's heart continued full of pride. The author of 2 Kgs 20:12-19 (cf. Isa 39:1-8) declares that Hezekiah's pride consisted of the ostentatious display of his wealth and war equipment to the messengers of Merodach-baladan (cf. also Isa 39:1-8). According to 2 Kings, the Babylonian embassy came at the occasion of Hezekiah's sickness. The CHR says that they came because of the astronomical sign given to Hezekiah at the time of his illness, that is, the return of the sun upon Ahaz's dial (2 Kgs 20:10-11). Because of Hezekiah's pride, God declared his wrath upon the nation. But God's wrath would be averted because the king and the people humbled themselves before him. The judgment was postponed but not rescinded. Eventually the nation would go into exile in Babylon (Isa 39:5-8).

The CHR gives another evidence of God's blessing Hezekiah's faithfulness by giving a detailed description of the king's wealth (vv. 27-29). Hezekiah also became involved in the construction of the tunnel that would bring water from GIHON spring, outside of the walls of Jerusalem, into the city. The CHR concludes the narrative by providing a theological interpretation to Hezekiah's illness and the visit of the embassy sent by MERODACH-BALADAN. Their coming was a test of Hezekiah, to help God know what was in Hezekiah's heart and the extent of his commitment (v. 31).

32:32-33. The death of Hezekiah. The notice concerning Hezekiah's death follows the previous pattern used by the CHR. Hezekiah was a faithful king whose deeds were written down by Isaiah the prophet (v. 32). This reference to a work containing Isaiah's visions should not be identified with the canonical book that bears the name of the prophet. The CHR also stresses that Hezekiah was buried in the tomb of the kings. The reference to the "uppermost" (part/section) of the tombs of David's family (v. 33; cf. NEB, REB, NJB) may indicate a second floor of the tomb or may reflect the CHR's desire to honor Hezekiah. The translations in NRSV and NIV seem to suggest that he was buried on the hill where the tomb was located, but not necessarily in the king's tomb.

The Reign of Manasseh, 33:1-20

The CHR divides the reign of MANASSEH into two periods: the first period deals with Manasseh's apostasy (33:1-10); the second period deals with Manasseh's life after his conversion (33:11-20).

33:1-10. Manasseh's apostasy. The narrative of the first period of Manasseh's reign follows 2 Kgs 21:1-16 with a few modifications. The narrative emphasizes Manasseh's worship of other gods and the adoption of alien practices that were contrary to the religious traditions of the nation. Manasseh promoted the cult of Baal and Asherah, rebuilt the high places, fostered the worship of astral deities, the practice of sorcery and divination, the consultation of mediums and those dealing with familiar spirits, and the sacrificing of children in the *Valley of Ben-Hinnom* (v. 6; see HINNOM, VALLEY OF), south of Jerusalem, where the Topheth was. The Topheth was the place where the sacrifice of children was made. The Hebrew word for *valley of* (*gê'*) became associated with the name of the place and became GEHENNA, which in the NT became associated with the place of eternal suffering and destruction (Matt 5:22.29; Mark 9:42-48). The CHR adds that Manasseh introduced the image of an idol, which he set in the Temple, contrary to the command that God had given to David and Solomon (vv. 7-8). The CHR omits the reference to the prophetic criticism of Manasseh's evil practices (2 Kgs 21:10-15), as well as the persecution and murder of those who opposed him (2 Kgs 21:16). In the view of the CHR, Manasseh *misled Judah and the inhabitants of Jerusalem* (v. 9). As a result, the nation's sins became greater than that of the nations that Yahweh had removed from the land.

33:11-20. Manasseh's repentance. The second part of Manasseh's reign covers the period after his repentance. Because of his unfaithfulness, God punished Manasseh. His punishment came when the army commander of the Assyrian king (presumably Asshurbanipal) took Manasseh in chains to Babylon. In his distress Manasseh prayed and humbled himself before God and God returned him to his throne. *The Prayer of Manasseh* is an apocryphal book that professes to contain the prayer Manasseh offered to God at the time of his distress. His humiliation forced Manasseh to recognize that Yahweh was God (v. 13). Manasseh removed the foreign gods and the other items that had been placed in the house of God and commanded Judah to serve Yahweh.

The story of Manasseh's repentance and his religious reforms does not appear in 2 Kings. For this reason many scholars have doubted the authenticity of this story. Some believe that the CHR composed this story describing Manasseh's repentance to explain the theological problem created by the fact that an evil king reigned longer than any of the good kings. According to this view, Manasseh's punishment and repentance are intended to show that his life was not one of irrevocable apostasy. Those who accept the authenticity of the story affirm that Manasseh's repentance was short and that he returned to his evil ways. But this view is contradicted by v. 20 where the CHR's source appears to indicate that Manasseh was faithful until the end. Others say that Manasseh's repentance was genuine and that his reforms continued as long as he lived and that after his death his son Amon and the people of Judah reestablished the evil practices of Manasseh. The deuteronomistic historian, however, is adamant in his assertion that Manasseh died an evil king and that the destruction of the nation came because of the sins Manasseh committed (2 Kgs 21:10-15; 23:26-27; 24:3; cf. Jer 15:4).

The Reign of Amon, 33:21-25

The CHR's description of Amon's reign parallels the narrative in 2 Kgs 21:19-26 with a major difference. The CHR declares that Amon reverted back to the religious policies of Manasseh and made sacrifices to the images his father had made. But unlike Manasseh, Amon did not humble himself before Yahweh and thus incurred more guilt than his father. Amon was assassinated in his own palace by his servants two years after ascending the throne. The political crisis caused by this palace revolt forced the *people of the land* (v. 25) to act and secure a successor to insure continuity in the house of David. The people of the land were the property owners of Judah who acted together in times of political crisis to safeguard the

interests of the nation. Amon's assassins were killed and Josiah, Amon's son, was placed on the throne as the new king of Judah.

The Reign of Josiah, 34:1–35:27

34:1-13. The beginning of Josiah's reform. The CHR has nothing but praise for JOSIAH. Like David, Solomon, and Hezekiah before him, Josiah is presented as a faithful king who obeyed God and *did not turn aside to the right or to the left* (v. 2), but who followed the right path of God's Torah. Josiah came to the throne at the age of eight and on the eighth year of his reign he *began to seek the God of his ancestor David* (v. 3). This turning to God implies a repudiation of the gods Manasseh had assimilated into the worship of Yahweh. It also implies a repudiation of the political yoke Assyria had imposed upon Judah since the days of Hezekiah.

The deuteronomistic writer declares that Josiah's reform began in the eighteenth year of his reign with the discovery of the book of the law. The CHR says that the reform was implemented in stages and that it preceded the discovery of the book of the law. In the twelfth year of his reign, at the age of twenty, Josiah began to remove the high places, the asherim or sacred poles, and the images of false gods. Josiah also burned the bones of the priests who had served on the high places. Josiah made an effort to extend his religious reforms to several of the northern tribes (v. 6) and, according to the CHR, he was successful. In the eighteenth year of his reign Josiah began *to repair the house of the LORD his God* (v. 8), using the money deposited in the Temple. Josiah commissioned three leaders (v. 8) to take the money collected by the Levites from several northern tribes and from Judah and Benjamin to those in charge of the repair of the Temple. The CHR calls the people from the Northern tribes the *remnant of Israel* (v. 9; cf. v. 21). Josiah also put four leaders from the Levites in charge of the work on the Temple. Other Levites who were skilled musicians were in charge of the labor gangs, directing the work. It is possible that the responsibility of these musicians was to mark the rhythm of the work to facilitate the pace of the workers. The CHR emphasizes the active participation of the Levites in the restoration of the worship of Yahweh

34:14-28. The discovery of the book of the law. The account of the discovery of the law book follows the narrative of 2 Kgs 22:8-20, with some changes. The discovery of the book of the law happened while

Hilkiah the priest was receiving the money destined for the repair of the Temple. The deuteronomistic historian says that Hilkiah had found "the book of the law" (2 Kgs 22:8), while the CHR is more specific, saying that Hilkiah found *the book of the law of the LORD given through Moses* (v. 14). To the deuteronomistic writer, the book of the law found in the Temple probably was an earlier version of Deuteronomy. The deuteronomic law became the basis for the reforms of Josiah. The words used by the CHR to identify the book found in the Temple imply that he understood the book to be a form of the Pentateuch of today.

Hilkiah gave the book to SHAPHAN, an important government official who served as secretary during the reign of Josiah. Shaphan brought the book to Josiah and read it in the presence of the king. Josiah was highly distressed by the words of the book. He sent a high level delegation that included HILKIAH the priest, Shaphan and his son Ahikam, Asaiah, the personal servant of the king and Abdon, to consult HULDAH the PROPHET concerning the words in the book. (The name of Abdon appears as Achbor in 2 Kgs 22:12, 14.) Huldah was an official royal prophet who was called to validate the words of the book (Morris 1990, 394). Huldah gave an oracle of judgment against Judah, declaring that the curses written in the book would be invoked against the nation because of their sins and disobedience. She also said that Josiah would die in peace because he had heeded the words written in the book and humbled himself before God.

34:29-33. Josiah's reform. The narrative follows 2 Kgs 23:1-3. In the CHR's version of the reform, the Levites were present in the Temple convocation instead of the prophets (2 Kgs 23:2). This may reflect the CHR's own time when the Levites had assumed the function of the cultic prophets. After the delegation returned with the words of Huldah, the king and the leaders of Israel gathered in the Temple with the people. The words of the law book were read once again, this time to the whole congregation. The king stood in his designated place in the Temple (v. 31), probably by one of the two standing pillars (2 Kgs 23:3). The people, assembled in worship, made a covenant to abide by all the stipulations written in the book of the law. The people of Judah and Benjamin pledged to obey the demands of the covenant (v. 32), while the people of the north were required to worship God (v. 33). As part of this covenant Josiah removed all the abominations found in Israel (v. 33). The Deuteronomistic Historian gives detailed information of the

measures Josiah took to purge the Temple, the cult, and the nation from pagan influence (2 Kgs 23:1-20). The reforms were also extended to the northern tribes (cf. 2 Kgs 23:15-19). The CHR says that one of the results of Josiah's reform was the faithfulness of the people to God, which lasted throughout Josiah's reign.

35:1-19. The celebration of the Passover. The Deuteronomistic Historian declares that Josiah commanded the observance of the Passover festival (2 Kgs 23:21-23). The CHR elaborates on the material found in his sources and provides detailed information on the cultic preparations for the celebration of the Passover (see also 1 Esd 1:1-22). The Passover was celebrated on the first month of Nisan, in the eighteenth year of Josiah's reign (v. 19), the same year when the book of the law was found. The preparation for the celebration of the Passover includes the appointment of priests and the separation of the Levites by divisions to carry out their function *according to the word of the LORD by Moses* (v. 6). The Ark was brought back to the Temple. It was probably removed during the repairs of the Temple or hidden during the reign of Manasseh for protection. The Levites play a very important role in the celebration of the Passover. They are set apart to serve God and to assist the people in the sacrifice of the Passover lamb.

Josiah makes a generous contribution for the people (v. 7) to aid the celebration of the Passover, as Hezekiah had done (30:24). The king's officers follow his example and make a contribution for the people, the priests and the Levites (v. 8a). This is followed by the contribution of three Temple officials, including the high priest, who make a contribution for the priests (v. 8b). Hilkiah, Zechariah, and Jehiel are called *nagid* (NRSV *chief officers*, v. 8) of the house of God. This same title is given to the high priest in 1 Chr 9:1; 2 Chr 31:12. Then, six leaders of the Levites make an offering for the Levites (v. 9). The CHR gives a detailed description of the preparation of the sacrifices for the celebration of the Passover (vv. 10-15).

This section again demonstrates the increased religious influence of the Levites. They are the ones who make preparations for the priests (v. 14), for the singers, and for the gatekeepers (v. 15). The CHR emphasizes that Israelites from the north joined in the celebration of the Passover and the festival of unleavened bread. He also speaks of the uniqueness of this event, because no Passover like it had been celebrated in Israel since the days of Samuel (v. 18; cf. 1 Esd 1:20-21).

35:20-27. Josiah's death. The narrative of Josiah's death is based on 2 Kgs 23:29-30. The CHR amplifies his sources and provides additional information about events that led to Josiah's death in the plain of Megiddo. In 609 B.C.E. Neco, king of Egypt, attempted to go to CARCHEMISH to help the remainder of the Assyrian army that was being attacked by the Babylonians. To reach Carchemish, Neco had to cross land that was in Josiah's control. Josiah had successfully taken control of part of the land that had formed the Northern Kingdom and he concluded that a resurgence of Assyrian power, supported by Egyptian, would pose a threat to his autonomy. Josiah therefore attempted to stop Neco from assisting the Assyrians in their struggle with Babylon. Neco assured Josiah that his intentions against him were peaceful and declared that his actions had come as a word from God. To oppose him was to oppose God himself. Neco said to Josiah, *Cease opposing God, who is with me, so that he will not destroy you* (v. 21). Josiah refused to heed the words of Neco and went out to meet him in order to preserve the freedom of his kingdom and his independence from Assyria. In his fateful encounter with Neco, Josiah was mortally wounded and died in Jerusalem.

The death of Josiah caused a crisis of faith and confidence in Judah. The words of God in the mouth of Neco provided the CHR with an argument to explain the death of a faithful king. Josiah was killed because he did not heed the words of God spoken through Neco. Josiah's death was much lamented in Judah. Jeremiah wrote a lament to remember Josiah. This lament has not survived in written form, but Jeremiah makes several allusions to Josiah in his oracles (Jer 22:10, 15, 18). Other laments were written by poets and musicians in Israel, but these have also been lost. The *Laments* mentioned in 35:25 should not be identified with the Book of Lamentations that follows the Book of Jeremiah in English Bibles.

Josiah was buried in the tomb of the kings and all the inhabitants of Judah mourned his death. The CHR evaluates the reign of Josiah very positively by saying that his faithful deeds were performed in accordance to the law of Yahweh (v. 26).

The Reign of Jehoahaz, 36:1-4

With this chapter the CHR brings to a close his history of Judah. He emphasizes the moral and spiritual degeneracy of Judah and above all, its kings, in the last days of the nation. The CHR's source for the reign of Jehoahaz is 2 Kgs 23:30b-34. In the Hebrew Bible the name of JEHOAHAZ appears in an abbreviated form as Joahaz in vv. 2, 4. Jehoahaz was the fourth son of Josiah (cf. 1 Chr 3:15). He was also know as SHALLUM (Jer 22:11-12). It is possible that Shallum was his given name and that Jehoahaz was his throne name, the name he assumed when he became king of Judah.

Jehoahaz was placed on the throne by *the people of the land* (v. 1.; see 33:25). It is possible the other sons of Josiah were bypassed in favor of Jehoahaz because of his anti-Egyptian policies. But after three months on the throne, Jehoahaz was deposed by Neco after Neco's return from Carchemish where he had gone to aid the Assyrian army. Neco also imposed a burdensome tribute upon the people of Judah and deported Jehoahaz to Egypt where he died (cf. 2 Kgs 23:34).

The Reign of Jehoiakim, 36:5-8

Neco appointed Jehoahaz's brother Eliakim to be the new king of Judah, and changed his name to JEHOIAKIM. The act of changing his name demonstrated Neco's superiority over Jehoiakim. Jehoiakim was the second son of Josiah (1 Chr 3:15); he reigned eleven years over Israel. He was a vassal of Egypt for many years; then he became a vassal of Babylon for three years (2 Kgs 24:1). During his reign, Nebuchadnezzar, king of Babylon, attacked Jerusalem and deported some Jews to Babylon (cf. Dan 1:1). Nebuchadnezzar put Jehoiakim in chains and threatened to take him into exile, but he was not deported. Verse 7 indicates that the Babylonian king took the vessels of the Temple to Babylon and placed them in the temple of his gods (NRSV: *in his palace in Babylon*). Jehoiakim was an evil king (cf. Jer 22:13-19; 26:21-24) who abolished many of the reforms of his father and reestablished some of the religious practices Josiah had eliminated. After his death his son Jehoiachin became king in his place.

The Reign of Jehoiachin, 36:9-10

The CHR's narrative concerning JEHOIACHIN's reign is a summary of 2 Kgs 24:8-17. The CHR says that Jehoiachin was eight years old when he began to reign, but 2 Kgs 24:8 says he was eighteen. Since Nebuchadnezzar took Jehoiachin and his wives to Babylon, it is almost certain that he was eighteen rather than eight when he ascended to the throne. Jehoiachin was deported to Babylon. With him were his mother, wives, palace officials, and more than 10,000 people (2 Kgs 24:14), most of them professional people, and others associated with the government and the royal family. Archaeology has provided evidence for the deportation of Jehoiachin. Babylonian documents list the provisions given to Jehoiachin and his family in Babylon.

The Reign of Zedekiah, 36:11-21

36:11-16. The sins of the nation. After the deportation of Jehoiachin, his uncle Mattaniah became king of Judah. Mattaniah was the third son of Josiah (1 Chr 3:15) and when he became king he assumed the name of ZEDEKIAH. Zedekiah became king because Jehoiachin did not have a son old enough to assume the throne. The CHR provides a harsh judgment on Zedekiah. Zedekiah was an evil king who did not heed the words of God spoken by the prophet Jeremiah (v. 12). He was a rebellious king who violated his covenant with Nebuchadnezzar, king of Babylon (cf. Ezek 17:11-15). The CHR also passes judgment on the leaders of the nation. The priests, the nobles, and the people were accused of being unfaithful to God and of having defiled the Temple. The Temple had been polluted and desecrated by their actions. Yahweh had sent his messengers the prophets to admonish the people because God desired to forgive them and spare judgment upon his house. But the people were rebels and did not heed the message of the prophets and mocked them. When God realized that there was no evidence of repentance, he decided to punish his people. This invective by the CHR against Judah (vv. 15-17) is a summary of the religious history of Judah and provides a theological justification for the demise of the two pillars of the theocratic kingdom: the king and the Temple. The religious history of the nation comes to its final days during a crucial time in the history of the ancient Near East. To the CHR the rebellion and apostasy of Judah were the cause for the end of the monarchy, the destruction of the nation, and the deportation of the people.

36:17-21. The exile of Judah. The judgment on Judah came by means of the Chaldeans, who had become the neo-Babylonian empire after the defeat of the Assyrians in 612 B.C.E. God brought the Babylonians to Jerusalem and they killed without compassion men, women, and children, young and old alike. They also sacked the Temple and the palace and took to Babylon the vessels of the Temple and the treasures found in the palace of the king and in the houses of the nobles. The taking of the vessels of the Temple in the days of Jehoiakim (36:7), in the days of Jehoiachin (36:10) and in the days of Zedekiah (36:18) became

the tragic result of the exile of Judah. Without the Temple and *the precious vessels of the house of the LORD* (36:10), the worship of God could not continue. The return of the vessels (Ezra 1:7) marks the beginning of the spiritual and political restoration of the nation. The Babylonians destroyed the wall protecting Jerusalem, burned the Temple, the palace, and the rich houses in Jerusalem. The CHR also says that the Babylonians deported many people, without providing any specific number (see Jer 52:28-30; 2 Kgs 24:14-16). The Exile was a fulfillment of the prophetic word. Jeremiah had prophesied the destruction of Jerusalem and a seventy-year exile of the people (Jer 25:11-12; 27:7; 29:10). Because of the Exile the land would enjoy the sabbath-rest provided by the law (v. 21; see Lev 26:34-35).

Appendix
The Decree of Cyrus, 36:22-23

With this appendix to his history of Israel and Judah, which also appears in Ezra 1:1-4, the CHR announces the beginning of the restoration of Israel. Babylon fell in 539 B.C.E. and this decree was promulgated shortly thereafter. When CYRUS conquered Babylon he began a policy of repatriation of the conquered peoples to their land. Cyrus's decree allowed the return of Israel from exile and the reconstruction of the Temple and of all Jerusalem.

Jeremiah had predicted the time of the captivity. The land had enjoyed its sabbath-rest and now God was about to restore his people to their land by stirring the spirit of the king of Persia to edify the house in Jerusalem. The decree allowed those who were God's people to return under the protection of God and the blessings of the empire to establish a new beginning in the land that was the central element of the nation's existence.

The CHR thus ends his book with an optimistic conclusion, which in his theology reflects the infinite love of God for his people. The gracious God of Israel had forgiven the sinful people and is about to return them to their land, a holy and blessed land.

Works Cited

Ackroyd, Peter R. 1973. *I and II Chronicles, Ezra and Nehemiah.* TBC.

Albright, William F. 1950. "The Judicial Reform of Jehoshaphat," in *Alexander Marx Jubilee Volume,* 61–82.

Barnett, Richard D. 1990. "Six Fingers and Six Toes: Polydactylism in the Ancient World," *BAR* 16/3: 46–51.

Braun, Roddy. 1979. "Chronicles, Ezra, and Nehemiah: Theology and Literary History, VTSup 30:52–64. 1986. *1 Chronicles*. WBC.

Bright, John. 1981. *A History of Israel*. 3rd ed.

Curtis, Edward L., and Albert A. Madsen. 1910. *A Critical and Exegetical Commentary on the Books of Chronicles*. ICC.

DeVries, LaMoine. 1990. "Tarshish," MDB.

DeVries, Simon J. 1962. "Chronology in the OT," IDB. 1989. *1 and 2 Chronicles*. FOTL.

Dillard Raymond B. 1987. *2 Chronicles*. WBC.

Gordon, Cyrus H. 1962. "Tarshish," IDB.

Japhet, Sarah. 1968. "The Supposed Common Authorship of Chronicles and Ezra-Nehemiah Investigated Anew," *VT* 18:330–71. 1979. "Conquest and Settlement in Chronicles," *JBL* 98:205–18. 1993. *I & II Chronicles*. OTL.

Mariottini, Claude F. 1990a. "Tiglath-pileser," MDB. 1990b. "Ziglag," *BI* 16/4: 66–68. 1992a. "Muppim," AncBD. 1992b. "Serah," AncBD.

McCarter, P. Kyle. 1984. *II Samuel*. AncB.

Mendenhall, George E. 1958. "The Census Lists of Numbers 1 and 26," *JBL* 77:52–66.

Milgrom, Jacob. 1991. *Leviticus 1–16*. AncB.

Morris, Wilda W. (Wendy). 1990. "Huldah," MDB.

Myers, Jacob M. 1965. *1 Chronicles*. AncB.

Noth, Martin. 1987. *The Chronicler's History*.

Pritchard, James B, ed. 1955. *Ancient Near Eastern Texts Relating to the Old Testament* (ANET).

von Rad, Gerhard. 1966. "The Levitical Sermons in I and II Chronicles," in *The Problem of the Hexateuch and Other Essays*, 267–80.

Spenser, S. 1984. "2 Chronicles 28:5-15 and the Parable of the Good Samaritan," *WTJ* 46:317–49.

Thiele, E. R. 1965. *The Mysterious Numbers of the Hebrew Kings*.

Wagner, Siegfried. 1978. דָּרַשׁ *dārash*; מִדְרָשׁ *midhrāsh*, *TDOT* 3:293–307.

Williamson, H. G. M. 1982. *1 and 2 Chronicles*. NCB.

Ezra–Nehemiah

David A. Smith

Introduction

The books of Ezra and Nehemiah give a significant theological interpretation of the dangerous and uncertain early postexilic period when Israelites returning from Babylon struggled in spite of external enemies and internal disagreements to reestablish themselves in Judah. They provide a general picture of the postexilic restoration, but cannot be used to reconstruct the details and sequence of historical events because the materials are arranged for theological, not historical, purposes.

Early Jewish and Christian lists of canonical books treated Ezra and Nehemiah as a single work called Ezra. Origen in the third century referred to them as separate books, 1 Ezra and 2 Ezra. This division was followed by Jerome in the Vulgate and eventually appeared in Hebrew manuscripts and modern language translations where the books are named after their principal characters. At least two other ancient Jewish books bear the name Ezra (Gk., *Esdras*). First Esdras is a Greek work paralleling, with some rearrangements and additional materials, 2 Chr 35–36, all of Ezra, and Neh 7:38–8:12. Second Esdras is a Jewish apocalypse recounting seven visions attributed to Ezra; 2 Esdras has no other relationship to the canonical works. The books of 1 and 2 Esdras are included in the Protestant Apocrypha, but were not always viewed by Catholics as deuterocanonical. Contemporary Catholic Bibles place them among the other deuterocanonical writings.

Authorship, Sources, Purpose and Presuppositions, Date

The ancient Jewish and Christian view that Ezra was the author of Chronicles and Ezra–Nehemiah is still held by a few modern critical scholars. The majority accept common authorship of Chronicles and Ezra–Nehemiah, but not the author's identity with Ezra. They refer to the author as "the Chronicler."

Others argue for separate authorship of Chronicles and Ezra–Nehemiah on the basis of differences in language, style, and themes, and find multiple editorial layers in Ezra–Nehemiah. Their analysis cannot be taken lightly, but it still seems probable that Ezra–Nehemiah was compiled by the Chronicler or someone quite like him. In the commentary that follows this author/editor is called "the narrator."

In Chronicles this narrator chose and arranged materials from Samuel–Kings, court records, Temple records, genealogical lists and other official documents to emphasize Israel's God-directed successes in the past. The greatest of these achievements was the establishment of the Temple in Jerusalem as a sacred center in which Yahweh could be worshiped and God's Torah accepted and obeyed. This worship and obedience shaped the people of Israel into the community that Yahweh intended them to be.

In Ezra–Nehemiah the narrator emphasized that the community newly returned to Judah from Babylon had proved themselves to be the true community of faith. The author chose and arranged materials from sources similar to those used in Chronicles, giving special emphasis to two narrative collections, the "Ezra Memoirs" (Ezra 7–10 and Neh 8–10) and the "Nehemiah Memoirs" (Neh 1–7; 12:27-43; 13:4-31; see 2 Macc 2:13), to demonstrate the continuity between the successes of the past and the achievements of the leaders of the restoration: the return from EXILE as a new EXODUS; the rebuilding of the altar and the Temple; restoration of the worship of Yahweh there; rebuilding the walls of Jerusalem; and, most important of all, the acceptance of TORAH as the basis for a renewed COVENANT relationship with Yahweh.

What the narrator and his chief characters attempted and the way they went about it will be clearer for us if we consider three important dimensions of their thought.

(1) Their society was one in which moral and ritual purity separated the *holy* people from the rest of humanity. The standards of purity were clearly stated and widely known.

Israel's relationship with a holy God was maintained by keeping covenant and obeying all of God's commandments. This relationship sustained the divinely intended order of their society and of the cosmos. This sense of the necessity for purity had been heightened to exaggerations in the exilic times of crisis, when any act of impurity could be taken as threatening Israel's existence and even the existence of the world (cf. Douglas 1978, 41–57).

(2) JERUSALEM was for them the sacred center in which rituals celebrated and actualized the divine activity of creation and redemption. By postexilic times Jerusalem was viewed as a place of almost mythical power. Jerusalem clearly symbolized a divinely revealed opening into the realm of the sacred. Jerusalem was the "navel [MT; NRSV, *center*] of the earth" (Ezek 38:12), the highest mountain at the center of the world (Zech 14:10) from which flowed rivers of life-giving water (Zech 14:8 and Ezek 47; Ps 48:1-3), the heavenly city come to earth (Ezek 40:1-4), paradise (Isa 11:6-9; 32:15-20; 51:3), the cornerstone of the new creation (Isa 28:16), and the abode of God (Pss 132:13-14; 46:5).

The walls of the holy city separated this holy place from the profane (Ezek 42:20). The sanctuary in Jerusalem founded the world and dissipated chaos (2 Sam 24:15-25). Its symbols were creative and cosmic: the mountain-like altar built on the "bosom of the earth" (Ezek 43:14, author trans.), the cosmic sea, the bronze pillars, the Holy of Holies where Yahweh was enthroned.

In the midst of the exilic chaos of alien culture and power, Israel's roots still reached deep into the sacred rock of Jerusalem's holy place, "where the break in plane was symbolically assured and hence communication with the other world, the transcendent world, was ritually possible" (Eliade 1961, 45). Jerusalem was "a place that is hierophanic and therefore real, "a supremely 'creational' place" (Eliade 1974, 377). The cosmos was stable because Yahweh dwelled in Zion, and ritual recognition of that sacred presence established Israel's whole world in the midst of chaos. Jerusalem was the source of salvation, justice, and law, which are the realities in history by which mythically understood and celebrated sacred presence sanctifies the world. Jerusalem was the center where *righteous-ness* reigns so as to establish *peace*. This place, sacred above all others, infused the world with its own character as model and guarantor of present and future paradise because the presence of God there was assurance of divine universality and of human morality.

(3) Not only Jerusalem, but the entire land of ISRAEL was a special place. This land was filled with history. Things that had happened there were remembered and interpreted as having profound theological meaning, meaning that shaped the character of its people and their role in history (Brueggemann 1977, 5). There they had heard and responded to the voice of God, heard sometimes as life-directing Torah, at other times as severe prophetic rebuke, correction, and plaintiff pleas for repentance, and at other times as hopeful promises of restoration and fulfillment. This was a place to which the Messiah would come (Hag 2:23; Zech 6:9-14). This was the place that might even be reshaped by God's renewing grace and power into a paradise like that of Eden (Ezek 47:1-12).

Almost every Israelite leader of the postexilic period would have shared these ideas. Therefore, in their minds, for Israel to have a future, the exiles' return to Palestine and restoration of worship there were essential, and all measures deemed necessary to assure the purity of life lived there were justifiable.

The sources used by the narrator originated at different times, some as early as the late sixth and early fifth centuries B.C.E. and some editorial additions may date from the end of the fourth century B.C.E. or later. The major narrative dates from the early- to mid-fourth century B.C.E.

For Further Study

In the *Mercer Dictionary of the Bible*: ELECTION; CHRONICLES, FIRST AND SECOND; CYRUS; ESDRAS, FIRST; EZRA; EZRA, BOOK OF; NEHEMIAH; NEHEMIAH, BOOK OF. In other sources: P. R. Ackroyd, *Exile and Restoration; A Study of Hebrew Thought of the Sixth Century B.C.*, OTL; R. A. Bowman and C. W. Gilkey, "The Book of Ezra and the Book of Nehemiah," IB; D. J. A. Clines, *Ezra, Nehemiah, Esther*, NCB; F. C. Fensham, *The Books of Ezra and Nehemiah*, NICOT; R. W. Klein, "Ezra–Nehemiah, Books of," AncBD; J. M. Myers, *Ezra–Nehemiah*, AncB; S. Talmon, "Ezra and Nehemiah (Books and Men)," IDBsup, and "Ezra and Nehemiah," *The Literary Guide to the Bible*, 357-64; M. A. Throntveit, *Ezra–Nehemiah*; H. G. M. Williamson, *Ezra, Nehemiah*, WBC.

Commentary

Return to Jerusalem
under Sheshbazzar/Zerubbabel:
Restoration of the Community of Faith
and of Temple Worship, 1:1–6:22

Cyrus's Decree and a New Exodus, 1:1-11

1:1-4. The Cyrus decree. In the first year of his
reign over Babylon (538 B.C.E.), CYRUS issued a decree
encouraging Jews in Babylon who would to return to
Jerusalem to rebuild the Temple and encouraging those
who did not want to return to give material support to
those who did return. This decree was delivered to
Jewish communities throughout Babylon; *throughout
all his kingdom* (v. 1) does not require that the proclamation be made to everyone.

The narrator of Ezra–Nehemiah relates this decree
to a prophecy of Jeremiah, perhaps Jeremiah's poetical
oracle in 51:1-11a, which begins "I am going to stir up
a destructive wind against Babylon." The connected
prose comment in Jer 51:llb, "the LORD has stirred up
the spirit of the kings of the Medes," seems to be a
clear reference to Cyrus.

Identification with the prophecy in Jer 29:10 of a
seventy-year exile is less likely since it was given in
a context of judgment to which the exiles should be
resigned. Josephus (*Ant* 11.1-2) suggests that Cyrus
was moved by references to himself as God's chosen
destroyer of Babylon and liberator of the Jews in Isa
41, 44, and 45. While the Isaiah passages would almost certainly have been in the minds of the narrator

and his readers, Cyrus probably had no knowledge of
the Isaiah passages. His specific reference to the Jewish god, *the LORD, the God of heaven* (v. 2), indicates
a sensitivity to and respect for the religion of the Jews
consistent with statements elsewhere about the gods of
other peoples. On the Cyrus Cylinder he describes at
length the restoration of the gods of many cities and
attributes this action to the direction of Marduk, god of
Babylon (Pritchard 1955, 315–16). This sensitivity was
general and certainly not particularly slanted toward
Jewish religion. Cyrus was not a devotee of Yahweh.

Cyrus's motive in these things was political, though
doubtless influenced by the positive religious and ethical values of the Zoroastrian religion. He and his successors believed they could win the loyalty of subject
peoples by giving them some measure of self-determination and religious autonomy. The Jews, aware of
these political motivations, at the same time believed
their god had *stirred up the spirit of King Cyrus* (v. 1).

Implicit in this belief is the idea that the LORD is
sovereign not only over Israel but over all the nations.
That their god's use of Cyrus benefited not only the
Jews but all the other peoples over whom Cyrus had
authority raises a serious question about the Jews'
special relationship to God—the Jewish idea of ELEC-
TION. This question is one with which postexilic Jewish
thinkers struggled and one that must be considered in
the evaluation of certain actions of both Ezra and Nehemiah. Is Yahweh's universality one of power only, or
it is also one of love and grace?

Would the restored postexilic community be an
open community in whom "all the families of the earth
shall be blessed" (Gen 12:3) and a "light to the nations" (Isa 49:6) or would their insecurity make them
into a closed and withdrawn community?

1:5-11. A new exodus. Before the EXILE prophets
had repeatedly predicted that God would judge the unfaithfulness of his people by bringing against them
powerful kings who would carry them away into exile.
Now in contrast Cyrus is proclaimed as God's servant
who will use his power and influence to restore the
Jews in their homeland. Isaiah declared that in doing
this God was doing "a new thing" (cf. Isa 43:19). This
new thing was a new EXODUS, but one with interesting
parallels to the Exodus from Egypt. In the Exodus
from Egypt all the Israelites fled from bondage. Now
only those whose spirits were stirred by God returned.
The implication of this is, not that God limited the

participation by stirring the spirits of only a select few, but rather that only a few responded to God's stirring.

Many Jews were satisfied with life in Babylon where they really enjoyed considerable freedom even before Cyrus, and some Jews were prospering there. In the Exodus from Egypt the Israelites were encouraged to flee to an unknown but fabled land that God had prepared for them. Now the Jews are asked to return to a land known to be war-torn and desolate and probably overrun by alien peoples. Then the Pharaoh was opposed to Israel's leaving and on occasion was confirmed in that opposition by God himself who "hardened Pharaoh's heart" against Israel (see Exod 7:13; 8:15, 19, 32, etc.). Now Cyrus generously encourages and supports a return. Then the fleeing Israelites asked their Egyptian neighbors for jewelry and clothing, and their neighbors, distressed by the plague of the firstborn, let them have what they asked: "And so they plundered the Egyptians" (Exod 12:36). Now the Jews are aided with *gifts* (v. 6) of silver and gold and other goods. In addition, Cyrus returned to the Jews the vessels taken by the Babylonians from the Temple for use in the Temple the Jews were to rebuild. (In the case of other peoples, Cyrus restored the images of their gods to their original places. For the Jews, the return of the sacred vessels carried out the same intention. These holy vessels represented a very concrete objective connection between the past and the future.) Then they left Egypt to establish a community of faith and an independent nation. Now they go to reestablish a community of faith under the sovereignty of Persia.

This comparison with the Exodus intends to do more than merely contrast the past and the present. The narrator of Ezra–Nehemiah uses the Exodus motifs to stress one of his major theological concerns— the continuity between the exilic generation and the whole of the previous history of the Israelite people.

Restoration of the Community of Faith: the List of Families Who First Returned to Jerusalem, 2:1-70

Israel's vision of a new exodus greater than the Exodus from Egypt is given historical reality in a listing of exiles who returned from Babylon. This list, which also appears with some variations in Neh 7:6-73 (and in 1 Esd 5:7-46), was probably compiled from various official records of the time naming the families that settled in Judah in the early years of the restora-

tion and is intended to authenticate their lineages, a concern for cultural purity.

Lists like this, of which there are a good number in Ezra–Nehemiah, are not appealing to the modern reader. They are filled with hard-to-pronounce, strange-looking names that belong to an ancient foreign time and at first glance have little meaning, but there are a number of ways in which this list must have conveyed significant meaning to the Jews who read it in the postexilic age. The list begins by naming twelve leaders (adding Nahamani from the parallel list in Neh 7:7) and the number twelve was always a reminder of the wholeness of the Israelite people (see NUMBERS/ NUMEROLOGY).

ZERUBBABEL's name heads the list without further comment. That nothing else is said about him here is surprising, considering his royal Davidic ancestry and the rather grand messianic expectations that the prophets Haggai and Zechariah held for him (Hag 2:20-23; Zech 4:6-7, 9-10; 6:12). Nowhere in Ezra–Nehemiah is there any concern for these things. The narrator is properly wary of royalty in light of the significant failure of the preexilic monarchy. His primary concern with the Davidic dynasty focuses on its contribution to the cult. He is not concerned with the possibility of Zerubbabel's reestablishing kingship in Jerusalem, but with Zerubbabel's helping to reestablish the worship of Yahweh there.

After leaders, extended family groups are designated by their ancestral head or by their ancestral town. Then the list mentions authenticated priests, Levites, and other Temple personnel, ending by mentioning groups of persons who were unable to *prove their families or their descent* (v. 59), among whom were even some descendants of priestly families who were considered unclean and ineligible to serve as priests because they could not trace their genealogies. Only when a chief priest was chosen who could consult URIM AND THUMMIM, the objects used by the chief priest to cast lots, could they be restored to active participation in the priesthood.

These various groups are recorded as totaling 42,360 (v. 64). The same total appears in Neh 7:66 (and in 2 Esd 5:41). In all cases this total exceeds the sum of the numbers given for the various groups, and the numbers given for the various groups in the lists frequently differ. These discrepancies cannot be satisfactorily explained.

The list then adds male and female servants, male and female singers, horses, mules, camels, and donkeys. Extended families or clans of lay people, priests, Levites, and other Temple personnel, servants, singers, horses, mules, camels, and donkeys—such was the company of those who returned from exile and established themselves in their ancestral places in and around Jerusalem. This is to say that the restoration could only be accomplished by the common cooperation of everyone of all stations in the community of faith.

Early Jewish readers would have been deeply moved to find their ancestral family names or towns included here, and would take pride that they had been among those who had been willing to participate in the return and restoration. This list is an honor roll of faith, an honor roll not of the exceptional persons whose praises are in Sirach's "Hymn in Honor of Our Ancestors" (44:1–50:24) which begins, "Let us now sing the praises of famous men." The names listed here are not of "famous men," heroes bigger than life. These are the names of persons of good, devout, common stock, who in the past and now in the restoration formed the essence of the Israelite community of faith. The list also legitimized the settlement of these families in Jerusalem and the surrounding countryside.

Finally, often overlooked in the interpretation of this list is the fact that most Israelite names have meaning expressing parental hopes and expectations for the child—thanksgiving to God for the child's birth, description of the circumstances of the child's birth, description of the child's appearance, or occasionally evaluations by prophets of the circumstances of the people they addressed (cf. Hos 1:4, 6, 9; Isa 7:3, 14; 8:1). Often these names are one-sentence descriptions of God's activity. In the context of God's doing "a new thing" (cf. Isa 43:19) in the return from exile, would not readers of this list have been sensitive to meanings of names such as *Jeshua* (or Joshua; Heb. "Yahweh delivers"), *Shephatiah* (Heb. "Yahweh judges"), *Adonikam* (Heb. "the Lord has risen up"), *Hezekiah* (Heb. "Yahweh has strengthened"), *Jedaiah* (Heb. "Yahweh has known"), and *Hodaviah* (Heb. "give praise to Yahweh").

This list, which began with the naming of twelve leaders of the return and restoration calling to mind the twelve-tribe wholeness of traditional Israel, ends with all Israel settled *in their towns* (v. 70). Obviously the restoration of the community of faith was not complete, but this list of returning exiles already represents the eventual fulfillment of the restoration. The journey from Babylon was filled with danger and difficulty and

the restoration of life in a war-devastated and long-abandoned countryside would require long and hard work. The simple statement that the returning exiles *lived in Jerusalem* and *lived in their towns* (v. 70) omits any reference to the difficulties faced by those who returned (cf. Haggai and Zechariah).

In spite of these difficulties families continued to return and gave generously to the work of rebuilding the altar and the Temple and the walls of Jerusalem. These subsequent returns continue the ongoing process by which God, with this kind of faithful response, would reestablish the community of faith.

Restoration of Worship, 3:1–6:22

3:1-6. The restoration of the altar. The restoration of the altar began in *the seventh month*, the month of the New Year's celebration, the Day of Atonement, and the Feast of Booths (Tabernacles), when all the Israelites "gathered as one man to Jerusalem" (v. 1, RSV) to rebuild it. Again the narrative emphasizes the cooperation of rulers, priests, and lay people. They built the altar of natural unworked stones as prescribed in the Law of Moses (Exod 20:25), on the site of the preexilic altar that had been chosen by David on the basis of a revelation from God—continuity with preexilic Israel reaching back to the earliest times.

During the exile, the people who remained in Judah had continued to offer sacrifices on the remains of the preexilic altar (Jer 41:5). Returning leaders, however, considered themselves and their followers to be the true people of God and for them the ruined altar was unclean; worship therefore could not begin for the restored community until the new altar was built. Until it was built they felt threatened by hostile neighbors and without the protection of Yahweh. Building the altar established a center of divine presence around which those who worshiped there had sanctuary (divine protection).

Building the altar also symbolized their claim that the land of which it was the center was their land. Building an altar was a ritual repetition of the creation of the cosmos and of society. Building the altar at New Year's symbolized living in sacred time, the time when God is near and active to create and redeem. At New Year's Yahweh was celebrated as creator in two senses—the creator of heaven and earth in the beginning and the creator of Israel in the Exodus, the covenant of Sinai, and the conquest of Canaan. When the work was finished the whole of preexilic worship was renewed: regular ongoing daily worship, prescribed worship on feast days for the entire community (with the exception of the Day of Atonement, which could not properly be observed until the Temple was rebuilt), and for individuals the opportunity to make freewill offerings. But only those who had returned from exile, who were in true continuity with the past, were legitimate worshipers at this rebuilt altar.

The celebration of the Feast of Booths (TABERNACLES, FESTIVAL OF) was particularly appropriate for the circumstances of the newly resettled exiles. Booths was a festival with intertwined dimensions of meaning. It was a fall harvest festival during which people lived out in the fields in shelters constructed of branches and vines to guard the crops. There was great rejoicing over God's gifts of the fruits of the land. The exiles had not been back in Judah long enough to have planted, tended, and harvested crops, so their first Festival of Booths was a celebration of memory and anticipation.

Considering what they had endured they must have experienced great pleasure in eating and drinking the meager amounts of food and wine available to them. They had been the people who could not sing the songs of Zion in a foreign land (cf. Ps 137:3-4). Of Jerusalem, their enemies had cried, "Raze it, raze it! Down to its foundations!" (Ps 137:7, RSV). They had returned to build it again. Now they must have sung the songs of Zion with great joy. Booths also was a reminder of the postexodus days of wilderness pilgrimage when their ancestors lived in tents, a striking parallel to their own immediate past experience. Finally, Booths was a time of covenant renewal at which the community of faith recommitted itself to the covenant demands of God (cf. the discussion of Neh 8–9, below).

Worship was restored, but in a temple still in ruins, for *the foundation of the temple of the Lord was not yet laid* (v. 6).

3:7-13. Initial work on the Temple. In this account of the rebuilding of the Temple, the narrator subordinates historical and chronological concerns to a theological emphasis on the continuity between the experiences of the returned exiles and those of the preexilic community of faith.

The altar was restored soon after the exiles arrived in Judah in 538 B.C.E., but under threats from "the peoples of the lands" (3:3, RSV; NRSV, *neighboring peoples*; cf. 4:4-5), no work was done on the Temple, beyond Sheshbazzar's beginning to lay the foundation (5:14-16), until 520 B.C.E. (cf. Hag 1). The narrative in Ezra

3 gives no indication that eighteen years passed before work on the Temple itself began. Chronological gaps like this trouble those who look for a full summary history of the postexilic period. The narrator, however, is concerned with certain major, pivotal events, which he will emphasize and even rearrange in chronological sequence to suit his theological purposes.

Preparation for Temple reconstruction began with the hiring of masons and carpenters and, as in Solomon's time, the arrangement with Sidonians and Tyrenians to bring cedar trees by sea from Lebanon to Joppa. This transport would take considerable time and it was only in the second year after they turned their attention to the building of the Temple that construction actually began (v. 8).

ZERUBBABEL and JESHUA, leaders of the second return from Babylon, led in rebuilding the Temple. Jeshua was the High Priest and Zerubbabel the governor (cf. Hag 1:1; 2:2). They appointed Levites, age twenty or older, to oversee the work. The beginning age of twenty is younger than usual (cf. Num 8:23), apparently a concession to the fact that surprisingly few Levites participated in early returns from Babylon. Under Levitical leadership the work on the foundation of the Temple was soon finished (because they worked hard, but also because much of the foundation of the preexilic Temple remained).

When the foundations were completed, there was a joyous celebration like that which celebrated the construction of "the Temple of Solomon" (2 Chr 5:12-13). They praised the LORD with instrumental music and singing "according to the directions of David" (2 Chr 29:25-30). The Levites and the priests sang antiphonally, *For he is good, for his steadfast love endures forever toward Israel* (3:11). This verse of praise suggests the type of psalms of praise that would be sung in their entirety on occasions like this (e.g., Pss 100, 106, 107, 118, 136).

The people's response to the dedication was a mixture of loud weeping and shouting for joy. The old priests, Levites, and heads of households who had seen the first Temple wept. Why did they weep? Was it because they remembered the splendor of the former Temple and could not imagine this new structure rivaling that splendor, or did they weep for joy? Apparently they wept out of disappointment.

4:1-5, 24. Opposition to the rebuilding of the Temple. The Temple, however, was still not rebuilt in 520 B.C.E. (cf. Hag 1:4). Haggai blamed this delay on the people's selfishness and lack of religious commitment.

The narrator in Ezra blamed it on conflict with peoples who lived roundabout whom he called adversaries. Initially, these people do not seem to have been adversaries, but cooperative neighbors. Their offer to help in the construction of the Temple, and their reason for making this offer—their longstanding worship of Yahweh—was genuine.

Suggestions that they had ulterior motives of political or economic kind are conjectures without any real evidence to support them.

The response of the Jewish leaders did not question their worship of Yahweh or suggest that they also still worshiped the gods from their countries of origin. Their offer was rejected on the expressed grounds that the commission from Cyrus to build the Temple did not include them. Implicitly, the rejection of this offer of help is based on the returning exiles' concept of themselves as the only legitimate remnant of the preexilic community of faith.

Throughout this account of the restoration the narrator repeatedly emphasizes that the true community of faith includes only the returning exiles from the tribes of Levi, Judah, and Benjamin. No mention is made even of Jews from these three tribes who had remained in Judah during the exile. *In Israel* (v. 3) means returning exiles from these three tribes. The list in chap. 2, this rebuff of their neighbors, and the limiting of the community of faith to returning Levites, Judahites, and Benjaminites, however important for maintaining the purity of the community, suggest an emerging exclusivism that would have serious consequences for the future. The returnees' rejection of this offer to help build the Temple turned their neighbors into *adversaries* (v. 1) who took various means to hinder the Temple's construction.

4:6-23. Parenthetical account of later opposition. At this point the sequence of events becomes confusing because the narrator uses accounts of later opposition to the building of the wall of Jerusalem during the reigns of Ahasuerus (Xerxes I, 486–465 B.C.E.) and Artaxerxes I (465–424 B.C.E.) to justify the rather harsh rejection of the offer of help in Temple construction from those he designated as *adversaries* in 4:1. The narrator presents letters sent to ARTAXERXES in opposition to the building of Jerusalem's walls, and the king's responses, all in Aramaic, the official language of the PERSIAN EMPIRE. From 4:8 through 6:18 the entire narrative is in Aramaic.

Persian officials of the province *Beyond the River* (v. 10, i.e., beyond the Euphrates) wrote to Artaxerxes suggesting that the rebuilding of Jerusalem's walls was an act of rebellion like those of which Jerusalem had been guilty in the past. If the walls were rebuilt, the Jews would withhold taxes from Persia, and Persia would lose the entire province. Paid by and favored by Artaxerxes (the apparent meaning of *we share the salt of the palace*, v. 14) they felt obliged to inform Artaxerxes of this danger and assured him that if he checked *the annals of your ancestors* (v. 15, suggesting chronicles of earlier Assyrian, Babylonian, and Persian kings), he would see that the danger was real. The suggestion that the entire province would be lost is obviously an exaggeration, but the history of rebellion was confirmed by the records. Artaxerxes, therefore, ordered his officials in *Beyond the River* to stop work on the walls. The narrative continues in Aramaic but returns to the building of the Temple.

4:24–6:18. Rebuilding of the Temple continued. In 520 B.C.E. the prophets Haggai and Zechariah strongly encouraged the completion of the work on the Temple, and Zerubbabel and Jeshua began to rebuild. This activity was questioned by the Persian governor Tattenai and his associates who asked the Jews by what authority they were finishing the Temple and for a list of names of those who were doing the work. Unsatisfied with the response, they wrote to Darius to inquire about the legitimacy of the Jewish claim that the work had been authorized by Cyrus. Out of deference to Darius they also asked for a decision from him: *Let the king send us his pleasure in this matter* (5:17).

A search in Persian records verified the Jewish claim. A decree of Cyrus was found *in Ecbatana* (6:2), one of the provincial capitals of Persia, not identical with the decree of 1:2-4, but clearly authorizing the same activity. Darius, therefore, strongly affirmed support of the restoration of worship in Jerusalem, including the use of tax revenues from the province *Beyond the River* (6:6) and whatever else the priests needed for worship. He threatened severe punishment on anyone who altered his decree. His request to the Jewish God to put down all opposition is consistent with the Persian belief that Yahweh had authority over Jerusalem and Judah and with the fact that he, like Cyrus, saw restoration of Jewish life in Judah to be in his own interest.

Tattenai did as Darius ordered and the work on the Temple was completed in 516 B.C.E., the sixth year of Darius. The success of the endeavor is attributed to the interesting combination of the God of Israel, the Persian rulers Cyrus and Darius (*Artaxerxes* in 6:14 is a scribal addition, perhaps to indicate that Persian kings consistently treated Israel with justice), who commanded the work to be done, HAGGAI and ZECHARIAH who encouraged it, and the Jewish leaders and workers responsible for the actual construction. The divine command could be carried out only with the cooperation of the various human persons involved.

The service of dedication was patterned after that of Solomon (1 Kgs 8; 2 Chr 7:4-7) and the sin offering at the dedication of the restored Temple by Hezekiah (2 Chr 29:24). The sin offering of twelve male goats was made for all the tribes of Israel even though only Levi, Judah, and Benjamin were present. Here again the narrator emphasizes that the returning exiles are the true community of faith. With the Temple dedicated, the priests and the Levites were assigned their ritual responsibilities. This account of the Temple's dedication ends the Aramaic section.

The account of the rebuilding of the Temple intentionally parallels the construction of Solomon's Temple: cedars of Lebanon were imported for lumber; masons and carpenters came from Sidon and Tyre; the work began in the second month; priests and Levites oversaw the work; and the two Temples were dedicated in similar ways. These parallels demonstrate religious continuity between the postexilic community and that of their ancestors. Inevitably the returned exiles saw the smallness of their work compared to the greatness of Solomon's, and those who remembered the first Temple wept.

There is, however, another significant implied comparison. Solomon's Temple was the accomplishment of a nation in the height of its power; this Temple was built under adverse circumstances—in a war-devastated land and over against strong opposition. Its completion in spite of opposition implies that the accomplishment of the returned exiles was greater than that of Solomon; the prophet Haggai could exclaim, "The latter splendor of this house shall be greater than the former" (Hag 2:9). Its completion was the guarantee of greater things.

6:19-22. Celebration of Passover and Unleavened Bread. The first ceremony performed by the newly appointed priests and Levites was PASSOVER. The account of the restoration of worship (Ezra 3:1–6:22) gives special attention to the celebration of important feast days: Tabernacles after the dedication of the altar, Passover after the dedication of the Temple. Ritually pure priests made the Passover offering on behalf of a "pure" Israel composed of those who had

returned from exile and those from other backgrounds who *separated themselves from the pollutions of the nations of the land to worship the LORD* (v. 21).

Who these latter persons were is not clear—persons from Judah who had been in exile?, other Jews who lived in and around Jerusalem?, gentile proselytes who converted to Judaism? The circle of the community of faith has become slightly larger but still is exclusive. Any who differed in any way from the perspective of the returning exiles, whether Gentiles or Jews, were ritually polluting outsiders.

Return to Jerusalem under Ezra, 7:1–10:44

Ezra's Identity, Commission, and Response, 7:1-28

Chapter 7 begins the story of Ezra's work, supposedly based on the so-called "Ezra Memoirs."

7:1-6. Ezra's identity. Ezra (Heb. "help") is a shortened form of AZARIAH (Heb. "the LORD [has] helped"). Ezra's genealogy, though incomplete (Seraiah, listed as his father, lived about 150 years before Ezra), traces his ancestry through the high-priestly line back to Aaron. Although not a high priest himself, as a member of the high-priestly family he had the best of priestly credentials.

Ezra is also described as *a scribe skilled in the law of Moses* (v. 6). The word *skilled* originally meant "quick"—one who could write fast—but here and elsewhere defining scribe it refers to the wisdom and expertise of a highly capable official. Ezra was a student and teacher of the written Torah, the first and greatest of a class whose work became increasingly important in the postexilic period. As a skilled interpreter of the Law of Moses (the Pentateuch), he was responsible for acting upon that Law. One could not really know the Law without acting upon it. He *had set his heart to study the law of the LORD, and to do it, and to teach the statutes and ordinances in Israel* (v. 10). Artaxerxes commissioned this priest and scribe, who held the position of *the scribe of the law of the God of Heaven* (7:12), perhaps the title of a Persian official of considerable importance, to go to Jerusalem and administer the Law there.

7:7-10. Summary statement of the return to Jerusalem led by Ezra. This section is a brief introduction to Ezra's journey from Babylon to Jerusalem. The journey is treated in more detail in 8:1-36. See the text units below for commentary on the journey.

7:11-26. Ezra's commission. Ezra's commission by Artaxerxes in an official Aramaic document (vv. 12-26) is probably authentic. It authorized him to travel to Judah to reform Jewish religious and social life. That it has a certain Jewish character can be explained by the possibility that Ezra himself drafted the document. Ezra, on the highest authority, *sent by the king and his seven counselors* (v. 14), was to go to Jerusalem with any of the people of Israel who wished to accompany him, taking with them offerings for the Temple given by the king and his counselors, by the people of Babylon, and by Jews who preferred to remain in Babylon. These gifts were to be used for a major sacrificial offering on their arrival in Jerusalem. Any that remained would be used at the discretion of Ezra and his priestly colleagues as God directed them. Continuing support for the ongoing Temple services could be drawn by Ezra from the treasury of the province *Beyond the River* (v. 21).

Ezra's commission also exempted Temple personnel from Persian taxation. On arrival in Jerusalem Ezra was *to make inquiries about Judah and Jerusalem according to the law of your God, which is in your hand* (v. 14). What does the phrase *which is in your hand* mean? Did Ezra carry a scroll of the entire Pentateuch written in Babylon and now for the first time made available to Jews already in Jerusalem?

Surely the Pentateuch was already known to the Jews there (cf. v. 25). The phrase then would mean the law on which Ezra was an authority—the cultic law that had previously been the concern of the priests. With the help of judges and magistrates whom he would appoint, Ezra was to determine if the restored community understood and followed the ritual requirements and cultic practices through which Yahweh was approached and the proper observance of which maintained society. This commission to enforce the law of God was consistent with Ezra's own wishes as summarized in v. 10, wishes that Ezra may well have made known to the king and that then were incorporated into the royal decree.

7:27-28. Ezra's response. Ezra's response was twofold: first, a prayer of gratitude for the steadfast love of God's grace and then the selection of Israelite leaders to return to Jerusalem with him.

Preparations for and Return to Jerusalem, 8:1-36 (7:7-10)

8:1-14. Continuing restoration of the community of faith: the list of families who accompanied Ezra to Jerusalem. This list, which has similarities to the list in chap. 2, is not a precise census of all who returned with Ezra but is designed to demonstrate the continuity between the nation's past, present, and future. The whole of old Israel (twelve tribes) were participating in this return (descendants of the heads of *twelve* families).

The "new Exodus" was not accomplished all at once. It was an ongoing process and no stigma was attached to those who did not participate in the first return. The crucial point was that those who returned, whenever they did so, made up the ideal community of faith.

8:15-34. Preparations for departure and journey to Jerusalem. Ezra's group returned in *the seventh year of King Artaxerxes* (according to 7:7), which was either 458 B.C.E. if it was Artaxerxes I (Cross 1975, 4–18), or 428 if the seventh year should be amended to read the thirty-seventh year (Bright 1981, 391–402), or 398 if Artaxerxes is Artaxerxes II (Rowley 1965, 137–68).

Related to this question of date are those about the extent to which Ezra and Nehemiah worked together and the relationship between their reform efforts. The narrator, or an editor, associates them with one another only in a covenant renewal ceremony (Neh 8:9) and in celebrating the completion of the city wall (Neh 12:33 and 36). The nature and extent of any other relationships is pure conjecture. Whichever date is considered best, the opening phrase of chap. 7, *after this*, covers a considerable number of years. The narrator clearly does not intend a comprehensive historical account of postexilic events. He emphasizes Ezra's journey as the next important step in the ongoing process of restoration. History is understood in theological rather than chronological terms.

Before departure, Ezra's company gathered by one of the irrigation canals flowing out of the Euphrates. Thirty-eight Levites were recruited there to make this return completely representative of the tribal makeup of the restored community of faith—Judah, Benjamin, and Levi—and to make Ezra's caravan conform to the order of march through the desert in the original Exodus. Ezra proclaimed prayer and fasting for God's protection on the journey. Having refused to ask the king for the protection of soldiers and cavalry, he now made practical plans to protect his wealthy caravan. He chose twelve priests, divided the silver and gold and Temple vessels among them and made them responsible for them throughout the journey. The journey lasted about four months and must have been very difficult, covering approximately 900 miles at the rate of about nine miles per day.

8:35-36. Gratitude for a safe journey and the beginning of reformation. On arrival at Jerusalem they waited three days, apparently to rest, or perhaps to avoid a formal arrival on the Sabbath. On the fourth day the silver, gold, and vessels were weighed and everything was accounted for. Ezra and his company then sacrificed twelve bulls in gratitude for God's protection on the journey and twelve goats as a sin offering to cleanse them from the ritual defilements inevitable on such a journey.

Again the number *twelve* points to the returning exiles as the heirs and continuity of *all* Israel, all of whom had to be ritually pure.

Before beginning to teach the Law and to encourage reforms on the basis of its teachings, Ezra delivered his credentials and Artaxerxes' orders to Persian officials in the area, and these officials gave their support to the Jewish community.

Ezra's Reform:
The Problem of Mixed Marriages, 9:1–10:44

Ezra's handling of the problem of mixed marriages is introduced by the somewhat cryptic phrase *After these things had been done* (9:1). To what *these things* refers is not clear. There is an interval of more than four and one-half months between the events of chap. 8 and those of chaps. 9 and 10 (cf. 7:8-9 and 10:9). Many scholars suppose that the account of Ezra's public reading of the Law (Neh 8) originally belonged between Ezra 8 and 9.

After these things, then, would refer to this reading of the Law and the sense of guilt about mixed marriages that it prompted. However, it is difficult to explain the misplacement of this important event in a narrative that is carefully arranged to emphasize the reading and teaching of the Law as Ezra's greatest accomplishment. It seems preferable to suppose that when Ezra met with the Persian officials of the area he discussed with them the importance of determining who of the many peoples living in the region should be considered authentic Jews and, therefore, subject to the Law as administered by Ezra. If so, the question would have been raised about the legitimacy of Jews who had married non-Jewish women of the area.

Investigations into the matter would then explain the concern expressed by *the officials* (9:1) who brought that problem to Ezra's attention. These officials were probably governors of Jewish administrative districts who may well have been among those Ezra first informed about his commission from the king. They certainly would have been among the first to implement a process by which "true" Jews would be identified. In effect these officials were telling Ezra that he faced a major problem, since among those who had married foreign women were priests and Levites.

During the days of Israel's settlement in Canaan after the Exodus from Egypt, marriages between Israelites and people of certain foreign nations had been prohibited (Exod 34:16; Deut 7:1-4) because they could lead to religious syncretism and apostasy. These no longer historically relevant prohibitions forbidding intermarriage with specific people under specific circumstances were interpreted by Ezra as establishing principles that transcended their historical setting. The restrictive actions taken here and in Nehemiah are not so much a specific, legalistic application of Law as they are religiopolitical actions taken on expedient grounds with general references to the Law to support them. Here, however, the concern is more with ritual purity than with syncretism or apostasy. By marrying foreign wives, even some of those primarily responsible for ritual purity (9:2) had broken the Laws of Holiness that forbade the mixing of unlike things (Lev 19:19), making themselves impure and endangering the purity of the cultus and the community.

Surrounded by threats to their very existence, the returned exiles needed to have a clear understanding of their distinctiveness and how to maintain it. Rituals of purity defined them as the "holy" people of God and distinguished them from the rest of humanity. Indeed, the system of annual feasts and ongoing daily sacrifices was a reminder of the divine order of creation.

The round of rituals maintained a life-sustaining relationship with the sacred. Ritual purity was essential to the preservation of their world as a cosmos—a world of order, being, security, and meaning in which everything has its place. Anomalies like the unclean animals of the dietary laws of Lev 11 and the prohibited mixtures of other foodstuffs disrupted the order of things, subjecting the world to the ravages of chaos, insecurity, nonbeing, and meaninglessness. Mixed marriages, especially those of priests and Levites, would violate the system of order that the returning exiles were seeking to recover by reestablishing Jerusalem and the Temple as a sacred center. As Ezra saw it, much more was at stake here than racial purity. He believed the very existence of the *holy people* to be in jeopardy.

Ezra probably had already learned of these mixed marriages; his reaction, therefore, to this formal accusation was studied and public. In Israelite culture this did not make it any less genuine (cf. the many symbolic acts of earlier prophets, especially Jeremiah and Ezekiel). Ezra's response was extraordinary. He *sat appalled* (9:3), or, better, "horrified."

Dramatically expressing his concern, Ezra acted as though he were grieving over a death (9:3). His public action attracted a crowd to whom his confession to God of all of Israel's past sins and his denunciation of the present evil as a violation of God's steadfast love and of the responsibilities that God had assigned to the returning exiles had the effect of an accusatory sermon. He asked God what the returned exiles should expect from him, having violated their very reason for being in Jerusalem.

10:1-44. The people's reaction to Ezra's prayer. Moved by Ezra's demonstration and prayer, the people wept, and *Shecaniah*, speaking for them, confessed that marriage to foreign women was an act of faithlessness and suggested that a covenant be made with God to send away all wives and children of the mixed marriages. The words he used for *married* (v. 2, Heb. "to cause to dwell") and for *foreign women* (v. 2, Heb. "harlot") suggest that these were not to be considered authentic marriages, so it would be proper to send away these wives and their children.

With Ezra's urging, everyone agreed to Shecaniah's plan. All returned exiles were summoned with threat of serious penalty to come to Jerusalem within three days. Assembled there, they agreed to a plan implementing Shecaniah's covenant. Some time was needed to do so, but investigation by heads of families soon identified those who had married foreign women and *they sent them away with their children* (v. 44).

These are rather disturbing final words. This entire situation is strongly suggestive of exclusivism. Understanding the reasoning behind their actions does not mean that a modern reader must approve of those actions. What they did seems cruel and unjust, subordinating as it does the well-being of persons to ritual concerns. Shecaniah's suggestion that the marriages were not real marriages must have been accepted because there is no reference to the prescribed rules for divorce (Deut 24:1-2; Jer 3:8). This suggestion seems particularly calloused, and Ezra's implied acceptance of it is not admirable. The women and the children involved were real women and children. Where would they go? How would they live? To assume that measures were taken to provide for them goes beyond the evidence, which indicates that the action taken was harsh and cruel.

One factor that may have mitigated the harshness was the provision (v. 14) for the elders and judges of every town to appear with those accused of having married foreign wives as the individual cases were reviewed.

These people saw themselves as the true fulfillment of the Abrahamic covenant (Gen 12:1-3) with its promise of land and descendants. They indeed felt themselves to be the "descendants" now reclaiming "the land," thus enabling God to keep the age-old promise. This intense desire to reclaim the patriarchal promise of land and descendants limited and threatened the possibility that they could be the people through whom God would bless all humankind, the ultimate aim of the promise to Abraham.

Of course, the integrity and purity of the community of faith had to be protected in the dangerous times of postexilic restoration, but the question has to be raised: Was this the only way it could be done? Was this the cost by which Israel would preserve its identity as God's servant people to bring blessing and light to the nations? There must have been a better way.

If this is all that we knew of Ezra's work we would rightly have a low opinion of him. The narrator, however, will later describe Ezra's teaching of the Law as his greatest achievement (see Neh 8).

An Outline

Nehemiah's Return to Jerusalem: Restoration of the City Wall, 1:1–7:73a

The Book of Nehemiah opens with a first-person account of Nehemiah's distress over the situation of the Jews in Jerusalem. Most, if not all, of the first-person material throughout the book is taken from the so-called "Nehemiah's Memoirs" (see 2 Macc 2:13; cf. commentary on Ezra 7:1, above).

Report from Jerusalem and Nehemiah's Response, 1:1-11

1:1-3. Report from Jerusalem. Nehemiah's name means "the LORD has comforted," which may suggest his family's awareness of God's presence even in exile and some expectation of God's help in the future. Nehemiah was the cupbearer to King ARTAXERXES I (see 2:1) in Susa, the winter capital where the king spent most of his time. As such Nehemiah may have been a eunuch, as some (but by no means all) cupbearers

were. There is little other evidence to support the view that he was a eunuch.

He would have been skilled in choosing and serving wine, which he would taste as proof against poison before giving it to the king. Cupbearers were also expected to be congenial, helpful companions to the king. They were often in the king's confidence and were asked for counsel and advice. Nehemiah, therefore, held a position of importance with ready access to the king.

In Artaxerxes' twentieth year Jews from Judah visited Susa. They were brought to Nehemiah by his brother *Hanani* (vv. 1-2). Hanani was either from Judah or, living in Susa, had met the visiting Jews and believed they should meet with Nehemiah. Nehemiah asked them about Jews in Jerusalem, both those who had remained during the exile and those who had returned to Jerusalem from exile. They reported bad news about the devastated condition of the walls of Jerusalem. The impact on Nehemiah suggests that they were not just talking about the Babylonian destruction of the walls, but about some recent event, perhaps that referred to in Ezra 4:23 when Persian officials by order of Artaxerxes I by force stopped the Jews from rebuilding the walls and may even have destroyed what had been rebuilt.

1:4-11. Nehemiah's response. Nehemiah mourned, fasted, and prayed in distress over the conditions in Jerusalem. He felt responsibility to take action to correct the situation. That action would have to be approved and supported by Artaxerxes. Nehemiah was also distressed by the great danger of having to ask the king to overturn his own previous decree. In distress he confessed to the LORD God of heaven (v. 5) his sins and those of his people. This corporate sense of sin, the individual's sin affecting the community and the community's sins affecting all of its individuals, is characteristic of nearly all the prominent religious leaders in Israel. They felt a strong sense of identity with their people with whom they shared both responsibility and fate (cf. Isa 6:5). Nehemiah's confession echoes an established liturgical pattern of confession, reflecting his familiarity with Jewish worship. His important position in the court of Artaxerxes had not lessened his dedication to the LORD God of heaven. Private prayer is inevitably conditioned by one's experience in public prayer and worship. His prayer addressed an awesome and powerful God who is also characterized by steadfast love and faithfulness. God had punished his people with exile for failure to keep his commandments, but he had also promised to restore them and bring them back to Jerusalem where he had chosen to establish his name; that is, they would live again in Jerusalem in the presence of God. The present conditions in Jerusalem there were an indication that this fellowship of people with the divine presence had not yet been fully achieved.

Nehemiah's first petition was that God might complete the restoration of the holy city and community. His second petition was for his own success in his audience with Artaxerxes to become the instrument through whom God would grant the first petition. Here again is the emphasis on the importance of God and humans working together to accomplish God's purposes. Nehemiah's success would depend upon the cooperation of Artaxerxes and of his fellow Jews. For their cooperation he was dependent upon God.

Nehemiah's Commission from Artaxerxes and His Return to Jerusalem, 2:1-10

2:1-8. Nehemiah's commission. Any expression of Nehemiah's grief might have been misunderstood by Artaxerxes as evidence of plotting against the king since his request required Artaxerxes to revoke his previous decree, or the grief might be resented by Artaxerxes as improper behavior in a companion. Therefore, Nehemiah was careful about the way he made his request.

In this first of many critical encounters Nehemiah displayed considerable diplomatic skills that helped him succeed. In this case his success was achieved (1) by his choice of a New Year's banquet in celebration of the king's birthday or of his inaugural, a time when the king was generous in granting requests; and (2) by his putting the request in terms with which the king would have sympathy: *the city, the place of my ancestors' graves, lies waste* (v. 3). Throughout the Near East ancestral burial places were greatly respected, especially by the upper classes.

Success was also acheived (3) by avoiding any reference to Jerusalem's walls, leaving it to the king to make the connection with his previous decree concerning them, and (4) by his close relationship to the king, indicated by the king's concern when Nehemiah's face finally expresses sadness and by the king's anticipation of his request. *What do you request?* (v. 4) implies willingness to grant the request.

Nehemiah's repeated expressions of anxiety (vv. 2, 3, 4, 7) served both to emphasize his courage and his diplomatic skills and to provide occasion for crediting

God for his success: *the gracious hand of my God was upon me* (v. 8).

The interplay between Nehemiah, the king, and God throughout this scene presents again the theme that restoration of the community of faith depended upon the response to God by the Persian rulers and by the leaders in the restoration.

Nehemiah's request was granted. He was given letters guaranteeing safe passage to Judah and authority there (as governor?) to rebuild the Temple. He was also given permission to use timber from the king's forest (perhaps in Lebanon, but probably in Judah, which was more heavily forested in ancient times than now). These timbers would be used for the gates of the Temple fortress that would guard the vulnerable northern approach to the Temple mount, for the gates and towers of the city wall, and for Nehemiah's house (perhaps the restoration of his family's preexilic home).

2:9-10. Return to Jerusalem. No details are given about the journey to Jerusalem. The presence with Nehemiah of *officers of the army and cavalry* (v. 9; contrast Ezra's refusal of such protection, Ezra 8:22) guaranteed a peaceful journey. But Sanballat's and Tobiah's displeasure over Nehemiah's mission ominously foreshadowed future problems. As the narrative continues, each accomplishment is paralleled by continuing and increasing opposition.

Rebuilding the Walls, in Spite of Opposition and Economic Hardship, 2:11–6:19

Nehemiah's "memoirs" unhesitatingly depict him as a man of bold action and quick, clear, and correct decisions. Anticipating trouble, Nehemiah acted swiftly and secretly to begin the work on the walls.

2:11-16. Night inspection of the walls. Three days after arriving in Jerusalem and without revealing his plans for the city to anyone, Nehemiah and a few trusted companions inspected the walls by night. Secrecy was necessary because his opponents Sanballat and Tobiah had allies in the city, and Nehemiah did not want to betray his intention to build the walls until it was clear what that would require. They left the city by a gate overlooking the Tyropoeon Valley on the west side, moved counterclockwise along the base of the walls until they reached a point on the east side overlooking the Kidron Valley where the rubble left by the ruined walls was so extensive that they could not go farther along the base of the wall. They had to move down to the floor of the valley, and Nehemiah climbed the rubble to inspect the ruins.

How they proceeded from this point is not clear. They could have completed the circuit of the city, but there is no reference to the northern or northwestern parts of the wall. It is possible that during the three days after his arrival Nehemiah had already inspected the northern portion of the wall without anyone's knowing his purpose. Inspection of the eastern wall would have been a much more obvious activity. Nehemiah's secret inspection of the area led him to make the important decision that the rebuilt wall would be on the crest of the ridge. When this decision had been made, the inspectors either continued to finish their counterclockwise circuit of the city or they retraced their steps; probably they retraced their steps.

2:17-20. Nehemiah's presentation of his plans to the Jewish officials. When Nehemiah revealed his plans to the various officials in Jerusalem, he supported them by citing divine and royal approval (v. 18). The officials agreed to build, and Nehemiah described their decision as a commitment to the common good, that is, his success and theirs. Sanballat and Tobiah, joined now by Geshem the Arab, mocked and ridiculed this decision as an act of rebellion against Artaxerxes. These three represented a formidable opposition to Nehemiah's work.

Sanballat was governor of Samaria. He is called the Horonite, a designation of uncertain meaning, perhaps being a contemptuous term used by Nehemiah who never calls Sanballat governor. Sanballat probably was a worshiper of Yahweh (his sons' names are compounds with *yah*, the short form of Yahweh). Perhaps he was a descendant of an Israelite family not carried to exile in 722 B.C.E. Tobiah was either an Ammonite official under Persian authority or an assistant to Sanballat, probably the latter.

Geshem was ruler, under nominal Persian oversight, of considerable territory to the south and east of Judah. Nehemiah dismissed the ridicule and accusations of these formidable opponents by declaring that God would give him and his colleagues success, that they were determined to build, and that Sanballat, Tobiah and Geshem had no authority, political rights or religious rights (the phrase *historic right* [v. 20] is used frequently in association with the system of worship) in Jerusalem.

3:1-21. Work on the walls. Chapter 3 moves around the walls counterclockwise beginning with the Sheep Gate. It lists those who worked on each section of the wall and the various gates and towers included in each section. Although there are some omissions, this description provides valuable archeological and historical information. After the lines of the wall have been described, it becomes clear that Nehemiah's city was smaller than preexilic Jerusalem. It included only the eastern ridge and the Temple area. A considerable area of the preexilic city extending onto the western hill was not included. Moreover, the list of the various groups involved in the work mentions five administrative centers in Judah and their rulers. The location of these administrative centers and the listing of other place names define a province of Judah less than half the size of the preexilic kingdom of Judah. The rulers of these administrative centers were Jews, most of whom came from families who had not been in exile. Nehemiah's caution, expressed in chap. 2, was justified since the administration of the province was in the hands of officials who might have resented the intrusion of those who returned from Babylon. Memory of the earlier unpleasantness over the construction of the Temple might have raised doubts about how they would be allowed to relate to the community returned from exile. Their cooperation on the work on the wall is a credit to Nehemiah's administrative skill and, on this occasion, his openness to such people.

The groups who worked on the wall are further identified by family or profession or place of residence. All classes of the Jewish community were represented in this common task. Nehemiah had persuaded the entire community to participate, strengthening its unity. He motivated good work by assigning each group a part of the wall in which they had a vested interest. They worked on sections opposite their homes or their places of business. With such organization and cooperation the work went rapidly.

4:1-23. Work on the wall in the face of opposition. Sanballat's reaction to the work on the wall reflects a certain desperation and fear that Nehemiah might be successful. He asked his own people ridiculing questions about the work as much to bolster their morale and his own as to intimidate the Jews. His questions suggested that God was not behind the venture, that the Jews were over-optimistic about the possibility of success and that the materials being used were inadequate to build a strong wall. These questions reached the workers on the wall and discouraged them. The wall they were building *was* rough and crude compared to the earlier walls of Jerusalem. Kathleen Kenyon's excavations uncovered part of this wall, which she described as "solidly built . . . but rough" (Kenyon 1967, 111).

Nehemiah's response was an angry prayer. He interpreted these ridiculing comments as directed against God and asked God to punish Sanballat and Tobiah without mercy with the same punishment Israel had earlier received—exile and captivity. This prayer has much in common with the prayer of Hezekiah when Sennacherib threatened Jerusalem (2 Kgs 19:14-19), with the imprecatory Psalms of lament (Pss 35, 58, 59, 69, 109 and 137), and with the bitter prayers of Jeremiah's laments or "confessions" (Jer 17:18; 18:23). Nehemiah's prayer is disturbing, first, because it views God as an avenging power to be used by his people against their enemies and, second, because it reflects an attitude toward enemies that is inconsistent with better Jewish and Christian tradition. In context this view of God and this attitude toward enemies is consistent with those of the times and with the difficult situation in which Nehemiah finds himself. They are understandable, therefore, if not acceptable.

Of course it is to Nehemiah's credit that he asked God to punish his enemies rather than taking vengeance on them himself, although this might be interpreted as expediency since Nehemiah was in no position to take vengeance into his own hands. Perhaps the best thing that can be said about this prayer and others like it is that they are admirably honest. They do not pretend love for enemies when those who pray really hate enemies. Nehemiah revealed his true feelings here, made no attempt to conceal them, and presented them to God.

Something is also revealed about God here who neither carried out Nehemiah's request nor punished him for the bitter spirit with which he made it. Although difficult for all to accept, in that time and later, God is the loving father who listens to the angry ranting and raving of his children and gently but firmly encourages them to "bless those who persecute you; bless and do not curse them" (Rom 12:14) and thus to come to the better way of loving even the enemy.

Nehemiah and the people responded to the opposition of Sanballat and Tobiah by quickly raising the wall to half its height. Prayer and work was a common pattern followed by Nehemiah. Each step of progress, however, was followed by increasing opposition from Sanballat and Tobiah, supported now by Arabs, Ammonites, and Ashdodites. Now they threatened to attack the city, and the Jews responded by prayer and by guarding the city against attack.

Their opponents, though, had made a point. Disheartened workers on the wall feared that Sanballat was right and they would never be able to finish. They even began to sing a little song to that effect. Sanballat continued to threaten the city, and Jews became more and more anxious and discouraged. Repeatedly Jews from outlying villages came and asked their men who were working on the wall to return home. Nehemiah, to display his strength, stood in an exposed place along the wall and called the armed people together. He encouraged them with words like those used in holy battles of old. This perhaps forestalled any immediate attack by Sanballat, and the work on the wall continued, but under different circumstances.

Half of a select group of men personally responsible to Nehemiah worked on the wall; the other half, fully armed, guarded the city, their officers standing to direct them. These men were better armed than any of the others. The other workers were armed as appropriate to the work that they were doing. Since the workers were spread all around the city, everyone was told to listen for a trumpet call and rally to the place from which it came to drive away any attackers. Everyone was to stay in Jerusalem to work by day and guard the city by night. By this arrangement the workers from outlying villages were kept in Jerusalem. Nehemiah and his select men remained dressed and armed day and night. Nehemiah was careful to accept the full responsibility and burden of leadership.

5:1-13. Economic difficulties and their solution. Abruptly a new problem is introduced—Jews crying out against Jews about various levels of economic hardship. They brought their complaints to Nehemiah whose commission from Artaxerxes is now revealed not to be limited to rebuilding the city but to include his appointment as governor (5:14). Three groups presented experiences of the kinds of economic problems everyone was facing. The first group desperately needed food (v. 2). They were probably landless families whose meager wages were not adequate for survival. The second group were surviving only by mortgaging their lands and homes for food (v. 3). The third group had borrowed money to pay the Persian taxes on their fields and vineyards (v. 4). All were at the point of having to sell their children as laborers to other Jews. Some of their daughters had been ravished. Perhaps slave girls were expected to submit to their masters' advances. Three factors had contributed to making the difficult situation of living at the subsistence level now a desperate situation. Apparently the failure of the barley and wheat crops caused a famine (v. 3). Nehemiah's requirement that the builders not leave Jerusalem while the wall was being built left the farms understaffed at the time of harvest. Finally, some wealthy Jews had acted as moneylenders, taking advantage of the situations—*our fields and vineyards now belong to others* (v. 5). Moneylending and the enslaving of children for debts were legal (Exod 21:2-11; 22:25-27; Lev 25; Deut 15:1-18) but were to be controlled in the interest of the poor by regulations that unfortunately were seldom followed.

Legal or not, Nehemiah felt these actions were immoral. Controlling his great anger (*after thinking it over* [v. 7]) he brought public charges against *the nobles and the officials* who were taking interest from their fellow Jews. Again Nehemiah's diplomatic skill is evident. First he pointed out the absurdity of Jews selling Jews into slavery to Jews at the very time when the restored community was buying back Jews who had been sold into Gentile slavery. This was not just a matter of business; it was a violation of the family of faith to wrong their *own people* (v. 7) and their *own kin* (v. 8). Finally, he confessed that his own family and their servants had also been lending money and grain to the needy (v. 10). This behavior gave non-Israelites a misleading and embarrassing image of the Israelite community of faith and their God (v. 9).

In the presence of priests, the nobles and officials took an oath to cancel all debts. Then Nehemiah, in a manner like earlier prophets (cf. Ezek 4:1-5, 17; Jer 19:1-13), symbolically enacted a curse on all who did not keep their promises, including himself. He emptied his robe of all the objects carried in its tucks and folds and said of those who did not keep their promise, *"Thus may they be shaken out and emptied"* (v. 13).

Acts like this were understood to initiate the judgment they represented if right behavior did not continue. It was as if Nehemiah had said, "The judgment is already in effect. Be sure you do not fall under it!" Nehemiah's proposals were carried out.

5:14-19. Nehemiah's integrity as governor. Nehemiah then added a note about his integrity and financial generosity during his term as governor. He accused previous governors of abusing taxation rights for personal gain and the servants of these governors for lording it over the common people. In contrast Nehemiah rightly depicted himself as a God-fearing, dedicated, self-supporting, public servant, who with his servants worked on the wall along with the other people. He claimed no food rations from tax funds, despite the fact that he was regularly responsible for feeding large numbers of officials and visitors. He bore these expenses of office himself. Though the contrast is less dramatic, one is reminded of Jeremiah's contrast of unrighteous Jehoiakim and righteous Josiah (Jer 22:13-17). Nehemiah concludes with a brief prayer that God remember him for his service to his fellow Jews.

6:1-19. Opposition against Nehemiah's person. Work on the wall must have continued during the economic crisis, for it was soon finished except for the gates. Therefore, Sanballat and Geshem, conceding that the wall was there to stay, focused their opposition on Nehemiah's person. Four times they invited him to meet them at a village outside of Jerusalem. He refused to go. They may have had good intentions. The extensive correspondence between Tobiah and prominent nobles of Judah (vv. 17-18), including one who strongly supported Nehemiah's building program (3:6), perhaps indicates that they were hoping for a compromise, but Nehemiah did not trust them. Besides, his view of the returned exiles as *the* people of God made compromise impossible. When Sanballat sent a public letter open to anyone (was it read aloud at various places around the city?) accusing Nehemiah of ambitions that would lead to rebellion against Persia, Nehemiah denied them.

Finally, an agent of Sanballat in Jerusalem, speaking like a prophet, warned Nehemiah that his life was in danger and urged him to flee into the Temple for sanctuary. Thus he hoped to lure Nehemiah into the cultic sin of intruding into the sacred area open only to God and priests. Sanctuary was possible at the altar outside the Temple but only under certain circumstances (Exod 21:12-14), which did not include flight from a foreign enemy. It was most difficult for Nehemiah to evaluate this ruse because prophetic proclamations were always taken seriously and it was never easy to discern a true prophet from a false prophet. Nehemiah did, however, recognize the falseness of this man's prophetic claim and refused to do what he suggested.

Nehemiah's response to these attempts on his person was to ask God to judge those who had attempted to frighten him, a petition reminiscent of his earlier prayer against Sanballat and Tobiah (4:4-5) leaving retribution in the hands of God.

That the wall was finished in fifty-two days in spite of opposition is a credit to Nehemiah's strong leadership. Of course, the old wall was not completely down, the eastern wall was higher on the slope than the previous wall and, therefore, not as long, and the new wall was not of the highest standard. Even so, the wall's completion impressed the people roundabout and caused those leaders who had opposed the work to lose face (6:16).

The List of Families
Who First Returned to Jerusalem, 7:1-73a

The information treated in this section is very similar to that in Ezra 2:1-70. Refer to that sefction in the commentary on the Book of Ezra, above.

Covenant Renewal, 7:73b–9:37

The account of a great ceremony of COVENANT renewal in chaps. 8 and 9 interrupts the Nehemiah story. The obvious sequel to chap. 7 is chap. 11. This account of covenant renewal focuses on Ezra's work and is based to a large extent on the Ezra Memoirs. Nehemiah is mentioned only twice (8:9 and 10:1, probably editorial additions) and plays no prominent role. Historically this event must have taken place much earlier than the time of the wall's completion. Ezra's commission was to establish the "law of the God of heaven" (see Ezra 7, esp. v. 21) in Judah. If he returned in 458 B.C.E., he would not have waited more than ten years to do so. The narrator placed this covenant renewal account of the establishing of Law here to demonstrate that covenant obedience to the Law was essential for the continuing success of all the other accomplishments of the restored community. For him, Ezra's teaching of the Law was *the* significant achievement of the postexilic age—the climax of the restoration of sanctuary, cultus, and holy city.

Preparation for Covenant Renewal, 7:73b–8:18

This ceremony of covenant renewal based on the Law was Ezra's great achievement, the fulfillment of Artaxerxes' commission to make the Law of God the basis for Jewish life in Judah and the realization of his own sense of God-given vocation. The Law that Ezra brought with him from exile was probably the Pentateuch in more or less final form. Much of it would have been known and would have guided the lives of the earlier returnees, but it is obvious that in this covenant renewal ceremony Ezra gives new place and meaning to the Law. The Law was not just the province of the priestly class but was Torah for all the people. Law, not political authority, was to give direction to the people's lives—the rule of Law rather than the rule of women and men. Faithfulness to God, therefore, is demonstrated by faithfulness to the Law, and

obedience to the Law is not slavish legalism but willing response to divine direction.

8:1-8. Reading of the Law. At the request of the people who gathered in a large open square before the Water Gate (areas around gates were often places of public forum), Ezra read from the Law for more than six hours. Accompanied by thirteen men whose purpose is not clear, Ezra stood above the people on a wooden platform and opened the scroll; the people stood up out of respect for the Law. Ezra pronounced a benediction and the people bowed to the ground in the presence of God. Clearly, Ezra here intended to make God present to the people and the people acknowledged that presence by bowing down before divine presence. Worship in Israel always was this kind of acknowledgment of the presence of the sacred, but note here that the sacred presence was not represented by ritual nor did it occur in the Temple. The sacred was present in the reading of the Law and this presence affected all of their lives. The Law was read and explained to *all* the people—men, women and children (all who could hear with understanding [v. 2]). Only with priestly assistance could an Israelite approach God through Temple ritual, but even an understanding child could meet God in obedience to the Law.

8:9-12. A time for joy. As the people heard this formal reading and interpretation of the Law they wept because they had not adequately met its demands. This was an appropriate, but only partial and not the final, response. Ezra and the assisting Levites encouraged them not to mourn on a holy festive day. (The inclusion of Nehemiah's name here is a scribal insertion; even if Nehemiah and Ezra were contemporaries, it is extremely doubtful that Nehemiah would have taken a leader's role in this ceremony.) They should be joyful. Their response to the God who reveals himself in the Law should include remorse and confession, but should end in *the joy of the LORD* (v. 10) because the Law is also a revelation of God's grace.

The Law (i.e., the Pentateuch) is heavy with rules and regulations, but it is also a declaration of the wonderful story of *Heilsgeschichte* ("salvation history"), those acts of God that every generation relives in worship. The God who requires is the same God who forgives and saves. The requirements of the Law, therefore, can be met gladly with gratitude not because one *has* to obey, but because one freely *wants* to obey. The Law as Ezra apparently viewed it was not legalistically restrictive and punitive. It was rather an expression of divine expectations that a true community of faith would eagerly try to meet. The image of the Law left by the Pauline attacks upon it (see, e.g., Romans and Galatians) is an impression of the Law that is, for the most part, foreign to Ezra—his strict application of it in certain circumstances notwithstanding. Ezra encouraged the people to have a feast and to rejoice at this understanding of the Law, which requires them, among other things, to sit down at the same table with God and celebrate (Lev 3).

8:13-18. The Feast of Tabernacles. During further study of the Law on the following day, the people realized that it was the time for the celebration of *booths* (v. 14, also known as the Feast of Tabernacles; see TABERNACLES, FESTIVAL OF), a celebration at harvest time in joyful gratitude for the produce of the land and a reminder of the deliverance of the Israelites from Egyptian bondage—the greatest divine act in their salvation history. They prepared for and observed this celebration in a manner not equaled since the time of Joshua. As families and as a community they celebrated with *very great rejoicing* (vv. 16-17).

Covenant Renewal, 9:1-37

The day of national mourning and confession described in chap. 9 is clearly an extraordinary event and represents the climax of Ezra's work in establishing the Law in Jerusalem. It follows the reading of the Law and the celebration of Tabernacles as a solemn moment of covenant commitment to God. Limiting it to the sorrow of the people about mixed marriages (Ezra 9–10) makes it far less significant than it must have been. This so-called "great confession" is clearly the awesome confession that preceded the community's recommitment not to a part of, but to the whole of God's will (in this case, the whole of the Law) in the ceremony of covenant renewal.

9:1-3. Fasting and mourning, study and confession. The reading of the Law, the festive holy day and the celebration of Tabernacles together prepared the people of Israel for a ceremony of covenant renewal. On the twenty-fourth day of the month they fasted and gathered in Jerusalem dressed as mourners *in sackcloth, and with earth on their heads* (v. 1). Apparently some of the people of the land were allowed to participate in the celebration of Tabernacles, but now the Israelites *separated themselves from all foreigners* (v. 2) for confession of their sins. The Law's account of salvation history represents God as always faithful, but Israel was often unfaithful and, therefore, guilty under

the judgment of the Law. The way to move from guilt to rejoicing obedience to God that the Law intended is the way of confession and repentance. After a long informal study of the Law and a long period of informal individual confession (v. 3), the Levites summoned them to the formal ceremony of covenant renewal.

9:4-37. Ceremony of praise and confession. This ceremony began with a benediction acknowledging the exalted greatness of God (v. 5). Invitation to praise the God whose Law causes them to grieve because they have disobeyed it was appropriate because in the Law itself as a guide for life God has given his people every reason to praise him. Then Ezra (MT lacks *and Ezra said* [v. 6], which NRSV supplies from the LXX) prayed a long prayer of confession. This public sermonic prayer, which juxtaposes the unfaithfulness of Israel and the faithfulness of God, recites the mighty acts of God with echoes of the Psalms of community thanksgiving (cf. Ps 136). In its confession of Israel's repeated sinfulness it echoes the Psalms of community lament (cf. Ps 106). It is also quite like Ps 78, a covenant-renewal Psalm with the purpose of bringing the people to a climactic moment of confession and recommitment to God's covenant.

In ever-changing human circumstances it is necessary for the community of faith regularly to examine God's requirements of them and take the appropriate measures to see that these requirements are met and to recommit themselves in covenant to God whose covenant commitment to them is unbroken. Ezra's new emphasis on the Law inevitably required these acts of covenant renewal.

The recitation of God's mighty acts begins with praise of God as creator, the giver of life worshiped by all of nature and *the host of heaven* (v. 6, the stars?, the heavenly beings?, the heavenly powers?). This is appropriate, for in each event of covenant renewal the community of faith is being recreated. God's choice of Abraham and his promise to give him descendants and land follows. The restoration community, as Abraham's many descendants, now lives on that land as new settlers trying to protect it from all outsiders (vv. 7-8). The Exodus experience is recalled to remind the restoration community of their similar experience in return from exile. The Law given at Sinai was in essence the Mosaic Law taught them by Ezra, which they are covenanting to obey. The recitation of Israel's repeated unfaithfulness that follows is a warning to the restored community to avoid their ancestors' tendency to turn away from God in spite of his good deeds on their behalf and their pledges to be faithful to his covenant demands.

Throughout his recitation of Israel's unfaithfulness, Ezra made special note of God's righteousness (v. 8), readiness to forgive (v. 17), mercy (vv. 17, 27, 28, 31), and covenant faithfulness (vv. 17, 32). Key to the possibility of covenant renewal is the understanding of God as *ready to forgive, gracious and merciful, slow to anger and abounding in steadfast love* (v. 17; cf. 31-32; see also Exod 34:6-7). This is reminiscent of Micah's classic summary of the prophetic faith: "What does the LORD require of you but to do justice, and to love kindness, and to walk humbly with your God?" (Mic 6:8). In renewing covenant the returned exiles must humbly submit themselves to the God who in his own being, actions, and Law embodies the characteristics that he requires of his people. As best they can they are to be like God himself as his representatives. The prayer ends with a petition: *Do not treat lightly all the hardship that has come upon us* (v. 32). Ezra described them as still not fully free. They were no longer exiles in a foreign land, but they suffered under the irony of being subject to Persian masters in their own land.

This account of covenant renewal ends without any reference to the covenant requirements on Israel or to the ceremony by which the people committed themselves to keep them. These requirements had already been presented by Ezra's interpretation of the Law as relevant in constantly changing historical circumstances (cf. the discussion of Ezra 9–10 in this commentary, above). In the reading and interpretation of the Law at the time of covenant renewal, the interpretation of Law is regarded as virtually equal to Law itself (cf. 8:8). This application of the Law to the immediate situation and explanation of it in such a way that those who hear can understand its relevance was Ezra's contribution to the methodology of interpretation.

A Document of Commitment to Certain Specific Reforms, 9:38–10:39

This agreement made under Nehemiah's leadership was used here by the narrator as the conclusion to the Ezra covenant-renewal ceremony. Such an agreement to keep God's Law would be an appropriate conclusion to a ceremony of covenant renewal in which national disobedience of certain requirements of the Law had been repeatedly lamented. However, the limited focus of the commitments of this document and the absence of Ezra's name from the list of those who signed it precludes its being the climax of a covenant renewal based on an extensive reading and study of the Law like the one described in chaps. 8–9.

10:1-27. The list of witnesses. This *firm agreement* (9:38), rather than *covenant*, was signed by distinguished witnesses and each signature was verified by the signer's seal. Nehemiah's name as governor heads the list. The second name, ZEDEKIAH, interestingly, is one of those sentence names of which the LORD is the subject: *The LORD has been righteous.* This is the only use of the name in postexilic times, and although this is probably mere coincidence, Zedekiah's name here states the fundamental basis upon which all such agreements rested—the righteousness of God. The meaning of other names in the list emphasize this coincidence: AZARIAH—"the LORD has helped"; AMARIAH—"the LORD has promised"; ABIJAH—"the LORD is father," to mention only a few. The meanings of these names would not go unnoticed by postexilic readers of this document.

10:28-29. The general commitment to keep God's Law. Everyone, including women and children, pledged themselves *to walk in God's Law . . . and to observe and do all the commandments of the LORD our Lord and his ordinances and his statutes* (v. 29). But this general pledge of observance is significantly modified by the specific pledges that follow.

10:30-39. The specific pledges. To permit no more mixed marriages (v. 30; see the commentary on Ezra 9–10, above) with no reference to prior mixed marriages; to honor the SABBATH by refusing to buy merchandise from the people of the land on the Sabbath or on any holy day (v. 31a); and to observe the sabbatical year by letting the land lie fallow (cf. Lev 25:2-7; Exod 23:11) and by forgiving all debts every seventh year, which goes beyond the Law's requirements for the sabbatical year (v. 31; cf. Deut 15:1-18).

This remarkable agreement goes far beyond the temporary measures of Neh 5. The farmers and the merchants who would be disadvantaged in turn by the fallow law and by the forgiving of debts equally pledged themselves to keep laws that hitherto had never been really observed. This was a grand commitment but, unfortunately, an empty one, for there is no evidence that those who thus pledged themselves ever kept these idealistic social laws.

To pay a tax for the upkeep of the sanctuary (vv. 32-33). Darius had pledged assistance for the maintenance of the Temple and its cultus (cf. Ezra 6:9-10), but we do not know for how long. Apparently depending on this support, Jews did not give their tithes regularly, and many Levites were forced to neglect their Temple responsibilities and maintain themselves by farming (Neh 13:10). Traditionally the tithes were paid in produce, but during the Persian period Jerusalem and Judah began to develop a monetary economy. The one-third-shekel tax reflects that development. The money was for daily and seasonal offerings. Lots were cast to determine by whom the wood for the altar fires would be regularly supplied (v. 34).

To support the Temple personnel with proper offerings (vv. 35-39). The agreements made to maintain the Temple are not based on any specific laws in the Pentateuch, but were considered necessary to support a cultus prescribed by the Law these people were swearing themselves to observe.

While this particular *firm agreement* (see 9:38) is not directly related to Ezra's covenant renewal, it indirectly is the result of his sense of the meaning of the Law and of his method of interpreting the Law. For Ezra, keeping of the Law is the responsibility of everyone, not just kings and Temple personnel, and the Law is kept alive for everyone by necessary reinterpretation, modification, and addition.

The Repopulation of Jerusalem, 11:1–12:26

11:1-2. Arrangements for repopulation. After a long interruption the narrator returns to the account of the repopulation of Jerusalem begun in chap. 7. Political and religious leaders were already living in Jerusalem. What had to be decided was which lay people should live there also. The people themselves determined the procedure for making this choice. Probably using the census list that Nehemiah had found (7:5bff.), they cast lots to bring one family out of ten to live in the city. This left the choice to God, because anytime lots were cast "the decision is the LORD's alone" (Prov 16:33). *To live in the holy city Jerusaelem* (v. 1) was an awesome responsibility but also a great privilege— to live near the Temple where the presence of the Lord was felt (Pss 23, 122, 126, 128, 133). Those chosen by lot, therefore, gladly accepted the decision, in spite of the inconveniences involved in making the move. Some families even volunteered to move to the city, *and the people blessed all those who willingly offered to live in Jerusalem* (v. 2), perhaps to affirm their voluntary decisions as decisions in which God had a part. It was a matter of honor for those families who

lived in Jerusalem to have their settlement there noted in the list.

11:3–12:26. Settlement lists. By listing families from Judah and Benjamin, and priests and Levites who settled in Jerusalem and in the nearby countryside, the narrator is identifying those families deemed to be the true and faithful continuity with preexilic Israel. The presence of military terms—*valiant warriors* (11:14), *overseer* (11:9, 14, 22)—indicates that the defense of Jerusalem was an important concern in the distribution of the population. The distribution of the families living outside of Jerusalem indicates the size of the postexilic province of Judah.

The narrator attributes these lists to the *Book of the Annals* (12:23), perhaps the official Temple records— not to be confused with the canonical books of Chronicles, although the Hebrew title of both is identical. These and other lists used by the narrator have been the subject of much speculation by scholars attempting to reconstruct the history of the postexilic period. Their accuracy has been vigorously attacked and vigorously defended. Whatever their accuracy, they are important sources that must be considered in historical reconstructions of the postexilic period. This was not, however, the narrator's reason for citing them. The concern is to show continuity between the past and the present, in this case between the generation of the first return who built the Temple and that of the time of Ezra–Nehemiah. The narrator does so by pointing out the close family relationships that span both periods.

Dedication of the Walls, 12:27-43

These verses are the description of the last of many stages in the restoration of Jerusalem, achievements that the narrator sees as not of equal importance, but closely related to and dependent upon one another: an altar built in a ruined Temple (Ezra 3:1-7); a Temple built in a ruined city (Ezra 3:8–7:22); ruined walls rebuilt to protect the city (Neh 2:11–7:4); and the reading of the Law and covenant renewal (Neh 8 and 9). In a sense each of these achievements had been a meaningful ritual action by which the returned exiles reclaimed the land of promise. They had restored Jerusalem as a fit place to be the center of the sacred presence of Yahweh, and they had recommitted themselves to be the people of the promise.

Now one thing remained—to dedicate the walls. Apart from the participation of Ezra (v. 36) in the dedication of the walls, the ceremony of dedication is quite straightforward. Ezra's inclusion here, like Nehemiah's participation in the covenant-renewal ceremony (8:9), is to make the literary/theological point that the achievements of the two important postexilic leaders were complementary. Their actual participation together remains uncertain and, in the final analysis, whether their careers overlapped or not makes little difference. As the narrative reads, the significant activity of each was carried out independently of the other.

Gathering of the Levites and the Ritual Purification, 12:27-30

Levites were brought into Jerusalem from their outlying villages because the dedication ceremony was to be a joyous one with singing and instrumental music. A solemn ritual of purification preceded the celebration. Priests and Levites would have purified themselves by fasting, cleansing the body, and abstinence from sexual intercourse (cf. Num 8:7, Lev 16:28-31 for typical examples of purification). The people would have washed themselves and their clothes and would have been sprinkled with water by the priest (Exod 19:14). The wall and its gates were also purified, probably by sprinkling with water. This was an important ritual because everything involved in the dedication of the walls, especially the walls themselves, had to be separated from all impure contacts that would have jeopardized the entire enterprise of restoring Jerusalem as a sacred center. Rituals of purity celebrated the divine ordering of creation and helped maintain that order. The walls were more than just a defensive barrier. They were a symbol of sacred space separating Jerusalem from the outside, threatening and dangerous, and chaotic space. They marked Jerusalem as a *cosmos* organized and full of meaning and value, where full being could be realized in the presence of God.

The Ceremonial Procession of Dedication, 12:31-43

The purified participants formed two groups, ascended to the top of the wall and from the same starting point, probably the Valley Gate, moved in joyous celebration to the right and the to left to meet again at the Temple where they offered sacrifices and continued rejoicing. This procession ritually enclosed the city with divine security. The restoration of the altar, the Temple, the city, and the walls was complete. *The joy of Jerusalem was heard far away* (v. 43). The main narrative of the restoration ends with this climactic cry of joy, but there is a postscript.

A Summary Postscript, 12:44–13:3

In two connected passages that interrupt the first-person account from the "Nehemiah Memoirs," the narrator idealistically reflected on the entire period of the restoration. The opening phrase, *on that day* (12:44 and 13:1), should be taken as a general reference, like "at that time." From *the days of Zerubbabel* to *the days of Nehemiah* (v. 47), the returned exiles generously supported the priests and the Levites who, in turn, protected the community from dangers by rituals of purification, and this was all done as it had been done earlier in the days of David and Solomon. The restored community was, indeed, in keeping with its ancestral origins. Furthermore, they apparently continued reading the *book of Moses* regularly (13:1). Based on a reading from Deut 23:3-6, the source of the reference to BALAAM, they took further steps to separate themselves from those of foreign descent. There is no indication that these foreigners were expelled from the community, only that they were excluded from worship. This is one of the earliest accounts we have of the reading of scripture in worship as a basis for religious and social action, a pattern that becomes common later in the synagogue and the church. Would that it had been for a more worthy end.

The Reforms of Nehemiah's Second Administration, 13:4-31

The remainder of chap. 13 is taken from "Nehemiah's Memoirs." After serving as governor for approximately twelve years, Nehemiah returned to the Persian court. We do not know why nor do we know how long he remained there before he asked permission to return to Jerusalem (*After some time I asked leave of the king and returned to Jerusalem* [vv. 6-7]), where he acted with authority, apparently again as governor.

Trouble with Tobiah Again, 13:4-9

During Nehemiah's absence, Tobiah successfully established good relations with the Jews in Jerusalem. Eliashib, a priest who had charge of the storage chambers of the Temple and who was related to Tobiah, allowed Tobiah to live in one of the rooms in the storage chambers. This Eliashib could have been the high priest of 3:1, 20; 12:22; Ezra 10:6 who was related by marriage to SANBALLAT. If so, this heightens the intrigue, but it is unlikely that a high priest would have also been appointed as keeper of the storage *chambers* (v. 4). The person at fault was probably another Eliashib. Whatever their intentions were—and they may have been honorable—Nehemiah was outraged at both Eliashib and Tobiah. He personally threw Tobiah's belongings out of the storage room, which he considered to have been contaminated by the presence of a non-Jew. The sacred center, whose sanctity was of highest importance, had been defiled and it had to be ritually purified.

Measures Taken to Assure the Support of the Levites, 13:10-14

The people had not supported the Levites as they should have, and the Levites had returned to their villages to support themselves, leaving the Temple with inadequate personnel for conducting services. Nehemiah brought them back to the city. He then appointed four carefully chosen men—men of integrity representative of those to whom the stores were distributed (priests, scribes, Levites, and singers)—to oversee the equitable distribution of the Temple stores. ZADOK the scribe (v. 13), one of those who was appointed, may have been Nehemiah's secretary ZEDE-KIAH (10:1). If so, Nehemiah was placing the arrangements under his own supervision. Nehemiah prayed that God would remember him for these *good deeds* (v. 14) done for the Temple.

Actions to Insure Sabbath Observance, 13:15-22

Nehemiah strongly condemned the violation of the SABBATH by business transactions and took action to prevent these dealings. The city gates were locked and guarded by his own servants throughout the Sabbath. Merchants from the surrounding area spent the night outside of Jerusalem, creating disturbances and tempting the people in the city to clandestine transactions. Nehemiah threatened them with violence if they continued, and they ceased. Nehemiah strengthened the guard on the gates by appointing Levites to assist in preventing violation of the Sabbath. He prayed that God might remember this to his favor.

The Problem of Mixed Marriages, 13:23-29

Jewish men had married Philistine, Ammonite, and Moabite women, and their children were running around Jerusalem speaking foreign languages. Not only did these marriages, which did not conform to the accepted norm, threaten the community with the destructive contamination of impurity (cf. commentary, above, on Ezra 9); they also introduced the disruptive force of miscommunication. A common language is an important factor in the unity and security of a people struggling to maintain their identity in critical situations. Nehemiah was upset with these men: he *contended with them and cursed them and beat some of them, and pulled out their hair* (v. 25). He made them swear not to allow their sons and daughters to engage in mixed marriages, citing Solomon as an example of one who had brought evil on all Israel by marrying foreign women.

The extent to which this was a problem is indicated by the marriage of the grandson of the high priest Eliashib to the daughter of Sanballat, Nehemiah's archenemy. It was particularly inappropriate for a high priest or one in line for the high priesthood to marry a foreigner. Lev 21:14 plainly states: "He [the chief priest] shall marry a virgin of his own kin." Nehemiah banished this man. There is no indication, however, that this marriage or any of the other mixed marriages were dissolved or that their children were sent away. Nehemiah asked God to remember this priest with judgment for defiling the priesthood.

Closing Summary and Prayer, 13:30-31

Nehemiah sums up his achievements in terms of separation of the community of faith from all things foreign and making provision for all aspects of Temple worship. He asks God to remember him for good.

The one thing Nehemiah did not ask to be remembered for was the building of the wall.

Works Cited

Bright, John. 1981. *A History of Israel*. 3rd ed.

Brueggemann, Walter. 1972. *The Land*.

Cross, Frank M. 1975. "A Reconstruction of the Judean Restoration." JBL 94:4–18.

Douglas, Mary. 1978. *Purity and Danger: An Analysis of the Concepts of Pollution and Taboo*.

Eliade, Mircea. 1974. *Patterns in Comparative Religion*. 1961. *The Sacred and the Profane*.

Kenyon, Kathleen. 1967. *Jerusalem: Excavating 3,000 Years of History*.

Pritchard, James B. 1955. *Ancient Near Eastern Texts Relating to the Old Testament* (ANET).

Rowley, H. H. 1965. "The Chronological Order of Ezra and Nehemiah." In *The Servant of the Lord and Other Essays on the O.T.*, 137–68. 2nd ed.

Esther

Kandy M. Queen-Sutherland

Introduction

The Book of Esther is one of the five Megilloth or Festival Scrolls connected with the Jewish festal year. Used as the reading for the festival of PURIM, Esther comes last in the annual festal sequence following Song of Songs (Passover), Ruth (Feast of Weeks), Lamentations (Commemoration of the Destruction of the Temple on 9 Ab), and Qoheleth, i.e., Ecclesiastes (Tabernacles). Set in a Persian context, Esther is an ironic tale of intrigue and suspense that moves from a threat of genocide of the Jews to the slaughter of all their enemies. Central to the turn of events is the legendary Jewish heroine, ESTHER.

The Story

The story of Esther begins and ends with a party. The opening scene describes the Persian king Ahasuerus playing host to extended banquets for his noblemen and the inhabitants of the capital city, Susa. While tipsy with wine, Ahasuerus summons his queen to parade before the revelers. Queen Vashti refuses to appear, setting off a chain of events that culminate with Vashti being banished as queen, the proclamation of an empire-wide injunction that all wives obey their husbands, and a royal search for the next queen begun among the virgins of the land. At this point, Esther and her guardian, MORDECAI, enter the story. Both are Jews, but Esther's heritage is kept secret while Mordecai's is public knowledge. Taken into the harem of virgins, Esther quickly wins the favor of palace officials and, at the given moment, the favor of the king as well. Esther is crowned queen, insuring a comfortable life within the palace while Mordecai establishes himself outside the palace gates. From his vantage point Mordecai overhears the plans of a palace coup, and through Esther informs the King, whose life is saved from the would-be assassins.

Haman, the Agagite and leading antagonist, enters the story next through his promotion by the king to grand vizier. From this lofty position Haman commands obeisance from the people, becoming incensed when Mordecai refuses to bow to him. Haman's desire to rid himself of Mordecai escalates into a pogrom against the Jews. Mordecai seeks the aid of Esther to foil Haman's plans. At the risk of her own life Esther appears unsummoned before the king. Again winning Ahasuerus' favor, Esther hosts a series of seemingly innocent dinner parties that masterfully expose the wicked schemes of Haman. Haman is executed, the enemies of the Jews are destroyed, and Mordecai is elevated to vizier. The story ends with the celebration of Purim, a festival-party established by Queen.Esther and Mordecai to remind the generations of Jews to come of the time they were saved from their enemies.

Canonicity: A Struggle to Be Heard

The story of Esther has survived in two primary versions. In the Hebrew Bible (the Christian OT contains the same literature, although with a different arrangement) Esther is comprised of ten chapters and located in the biblical section known as the Writings. The LXX or Greek version of Esther, deriving from the late second or early first century B.C.E., contains six additional passages not found in the MT. English translations of Esther vary, with Roman Catholic Bibles (JB, NAB) integrating the MT and Greek additions, while Protestant Bibles translate the shorter Hebrew version and place the Greek Additions to Esther among the noncanonical works known as the APOCRYPHA.

Paralleling the threat of Jewish extinction in the story, the Book of Esther has itself struggled to survive. A perceived lack of religious fervor in the Hebrew version created debate over the value of the book for centuries. The story is told without any mention of God, without reference to covenant or law, without prayers and without concern for Jewish dietary laws. As heroine of the story, the Jew Esther functions apart from such Jewish traditions, accomplishing her task in a gentile world. Although popular within Judaism, the Book of Esther nevertheless struggled for canonical status. Although finally granted standing within Judaism and the Western church by the fourth-century C.E. and by the eighth century in the Eastern church, no allusions to Esther occur in the NT and few in the writings of the Church Fathers. Although the significance is debatable, Esther is the only OT book not found at Qumran.

The acceptance and interpretation of the Book of Esther have been a constant battle. Martin Luther's condemnation of the book in the sixteenth century has been reflected over and over again as Christian skeptics addressed such concerns as its overt Jewish nationalism and questionable morality. Not the least of concern is the story's heroine, Queen Esther. Male commentators have struggled with a female savior while modern women are uncomfortable with a female who sleeps her way to the Queenship and fails to question the established structures. Such skepticism perhaps reflects more on the reader than the Book of Esther, which must be appreciated on its own terms and in its own environment.

The Birth of a Tradition: Provenance, Date, Genre

The Book of Esther is at home in a Persian environment. From the opening lines delineating the boundaries of the Persian Empire (*India to Ethiopia*, 1:1) to the meting out of punishment by impalement (2:23; 5:14; 7:10), the story is colored with Persian distinctives. The repeated references to the famed Persian postal system lends plausibility to what would otherwise be considered unbelievable acts, a decree *to annihilate all Jews* (3:13) and letters allowing the Jews to defend themselves (8:10-11). That King Ahasuerus, at just the right moment, chanced to be reading from official royal diaries and discovered Mordecai's action on his behalf becomes believable in light of extrabiblical sources confirming such Persian record-keeping.

The Book of Esther claims SUSA as its setting, which places it among the Jews of the eastern Diaspora in the Persian empire. King Ahasuerus is traditionally identified as the historical Persian king Xerxes I. If this is accepted, the dating of his reign from 486 B.C.E. to 465 B.C.E. provides the earliest possible date of the book. What is known of Xerxes' reign from the Greek historian Herodotus (*History of the Persian Wars*) would seem to fit the timetable of Esther; the

events of *the third year* (1:3) occurring before Xerxes departed in an expedition against the Greeks (483–479), which would allow for the four-year interval between the deposing of Vashti and the crowning of Esther in the seventh year (Clines 1984, 260–61). Yet this observation must be tempered by the fact that historically Xerxes' queen was neither Vashti nor Esther, but Amestris. The dating of the book, therefore, is not so simple, and a range of dates from the fourth to the second centuries B.C.E. has been proposed. There is no Persian record of the events in question nor proof of Mordecai and Esther as historical personages. Indeed, striking similarities have been noted between the names of the prominent characters in the book and those of ancient Babylonian and Elamite gods: Mordecai~Marduk, Esther~Ishtar, principal Babylonian god and goddess; Haman~Humman, an Elamite god. Although undoubtedly the book is late postexilic, much more cannot be said. Should the book come from the Hellenistic era that emerged in the late fourth century B.C.E., the sympathetic view toward the ruling power reflected in the book would certainly be at odds with other books from this time period. The writings of DANIEL and 1 and 2 MACCABEES reflect a much harsher attitude toward foreign powers. During the Greek period the Jews experienced divisions among themselves as well as hostility toward their oppressors. The Book of Esther seems to address Jews familiar with life lived under foreign rulers. Whether the actual event ever occurred or Mordecai and Esther ever lived is inconsequential to the truth of the story. Any Jew from any era who had experienced what it means to be a minority in the face of a foreign power would identify with the threat of oppression and persecution found in the Book of Esther.

The presentation of Esther is in the genre of a *Diasporanovelle* (LaCocque 1990, 57). Like the JOSEPH story (Gen 37–50), DANIEL, and JUDITH, the Book of Esther is a Jewish novella that struggles with the tensions of being Jewish in a foreign land. Historical accuracy is not at issue, rather the telling of a tale that concentrates on plot and action. Characters are developed only to the extent that they enhance the plot. The interest is in presenting a tension that moves through a series of complications until it is eventually resolved.

From the outset, Esther is presented as political satire. The four main characters are caricatured through one ironic event after another. The all-powerful Persian king Ahasuerus, whose word is immutable (8:8), is characterized as a party-fool who puts down the wine bottle only long enough to issue inane decrees, even giving over an entire people to death without asking their name. Haman, as the force outside the party doors, literally rises from nowhere into the heights of power from where he looks down upon all who must bow before him. Such lofty attainment goes to his head as he becomes single-mindedly bent on ensuring that the faces of Mordecai and the Jews are literally rubbed into the ground. But Haman will be required to bestow the honor he seeks on the one he most despises, and will himself hang from the gallows he constructed for Mordecai.

Mordecai is the Jew. He lives on the outskirts of the action, yet is fully aware of even the most intimate details of the realms of power. He is wise, steadfast and within earshot of the plot. Haman may rise but Mordecai will not bow; and eventually he will attain heights denied even to Haman.

Esther is the beauty, whose sexuality wins the crown. She is virginal, secretly a Jew, obedient to Mordecai, and at the beck and call of the king. All of her qualifications fit her for pampered life in the palace. She is the most unlikely of saviors. Yet she will save her people.

Through these characters a story of excess and threatened violence unfolds. The story of Esther has a political cartoon quality about it, where the reader at times may chuckle, at other times gasp, and in the end recognize truth. Esther shows that life lived under the power of others is risky. One day you are invited to a party; the next day you could be slaughtered. Nothing is impossible. A Jewish maiden can become queen and, when the time arises, emerge a heroine. Such times must be faced with courage and the ability to live by one's wits. In the end all must face the truth that *if you keep silence at such a time as this, relief and deliverance will rise for the Jews from another quarter, but you and your father's family will perish* (4:14).

For Further Study

In the *Mercer Dictionary of the Bible*: APOCRYPHA, MODERN; APOCRYPHAL LITERATURE; ESTHER; ESTHER, ADDITIONS TO; ESTHER, BOOK OF; FEASTS AND FESTIVALS; LOT/LOTS (CASTING OF) IN THE BIBLE; MORDECAI; PERSIAN EMPIRE; PURIM.

In other sources: J. W. H. Bos, *Ruth, Esther, Jonah*; D. J. A. Clines, *Ezra, Nehemiah, Esther*, NCB, and *The Esther Scroll: The Story of the Story*, JSOTSup; M. V. Fox, *Character and Ideology in the Book of Esther*; A. LaCocque, *The Feminine Unconventional: Four Subversive Figures in Israel's Tradition*; S. A. White, "Esther," in *The Women's Bible Commentary*.

Commentary

The Disrobing of Queen Vashti, 1:1-22

The Persian Court, 1:1-9

The story of Esther opens in the Persian court of King Ahasuerus. Palace doors are thrown open to admit outside observers into the royal world of wealth and power. The grandeur of the court at SUSA testifies to the richness of the empire. Unencumbered by affairs of state, the merry king displays his majesty and greatness through a series of banquets. One hundred and eighty days—half the king's third year of reign—are given to a royal party for the recognized elite in the realm.

1:5-9. Two other banquets. Not only noblemen and people of status are treated to the delights of the kingdom. Following the six-month feast for the aristocracy, the citizenry of Susa partake of a seven-day feast where the only rule is to drink to your heart's content. Any disgruntled subject is soothed by free-flowing

wine from *golden goblets* (v. 7) as the peasantry taste the royal riches.

While the men drink the week away, Queen Vashti entertains the women. In a one-verse statement (v. 9), the queen appears without introduction and no details of the third banquet are provided. The only point of note is the location of the party, King Ahasuerus' palace. The impression is clear. Vashti may serve as hostess, but the party premises belong to the king.

Queen Vashti's Refusal to Appear, 1:10-12

The story's return to the final day of the week-long feast finds the king merry with wine. Having shown off the royal objects, the king wishes to display his royal wife. Seven royal EUNUCHs are dispatched to parade Queen Vashti through the party. Queen Vashti refuses to come. The text offers no reason for her response, prompting speculation as to what is left unsaid. Rabbis of old suggested Vashti's refusal was out of modesty, the implication being that she was to appear naked before the banqueting guests. Others see in her actions the refusal to be treated as a concubine, the women who would appear once the drinking got heavy and the wives sent home. Whatever the reason, it is private and remains with Vashti. The response of the king, like his other actions, is completely visible. No longer *merry with wine* (v. 10), anger consumes him.

The First Royal Decree, 1:13-22

Although successful at giving parties, the king's first command is a public failure. As Ahasuerus turns to his seven wise men for advice, the queen's refusal becomes a matter of national interest. What is the law in a case like this? A response by one named *Memucan* (vv. 14, 16, 21) gives a new twist to the issue, moving from legality to practical concern. By his reasoning the king and queen become representative of all husbands and wives and Vashti's disregard for Ahasuerus' command precedent for wives everywhere. Indeed a veritable uprising among the women of the land is feared. Nothing short of a royal decree can stop the perceived whispering of anarchy already underway. Vashti must be denied what she did not want, to appear before the king. The queen is to be stripped of her royal robes and all women everywhere commanded to show honor to their husbands.

One wife refuses the bidding of her husband. An "if it were my wife . . ." consultation becomes the setting for a group of partying men to ensure it won't happen to them. A scorned king influenced by wine and self-interested counselors sets the famed Persian postal system in motion with an empire-wide decree, firing off letters to every province. Like the royal banquets, the problem and its solution are exaggerated to the point of incredulity, causing one to wonder about this king and his seven wise men.

The Crowning of Esther, 2:1-23

The Gathering of Virgins, 2:1-4

With the party and its aftermath faded to the past, the memory of Vashti and her fate haunt the king. The decree's gain for other men is his loss. Lord of their homes, the king's counselors leave Ahasuerus wifeless. Again at a loss for action, the king's servants propose the solution. A beauty contest of royal proportions will determine the next queen. The men of the land have their wives but the king will have his pick of the virgins. Not surprisingly, the proposal pleases Ahasuerus.

Esther Favored by the King, 2:5-18

2:5-11. Mordecai and Esther appear at court. With the search for the new queen underway, two of the story's main characters are introduced. MORDECAI is first and foremost a Jew. His genealogy is traced to KISH, the father of SAUL, Israel's first king. He is by tradition and heritage a loyal Benjaminite, standing in the line of SHIMEI (see 2 Sam 16:5-14; 1 Kgs 2:36-46). Both his family history and personal experience speak of banishment. The tragedy of King Saul and the loss by those loyal to him are repeated in Mordecai's own story of captivity and exile.

The emphasis on Mordecai's Jewishness is contrasted with the suppression of Esther's. Her Hebrew name, *Hadassah*, gives way quickly to the Persian, *Esther* (v. 7; the name means "star"). A captive orphan, she is cousin and adopted daughter of Mordecai. The real interest in Esther, however, is her appearance. Like the other woman in the story, the banished Vashti, Esther possesses the gift of physical beauty.

The king's edict results in Esther's being taken into the palace. Quickly winning the favor of *Hegai*, the overseer of the women, Esther and her seven appointed maids advance to the head of the harem. Using language established as the ground rules for determining the contest's outcome (v. 4), the maiden pleasing the man who stands between the women and the king foreshadows the coming events. With Esther

on the inside, Mordecai begins his vigil of watching and waiting from the outside. Although separated by palace walls, the bond between the two remains as Esther follows the advice of Mordecai in keeping her heredity secret.

2:12-18. Esther wins the King's favor. An assembly-line of beautifying moves the virgins-in-waiting through the king's bedroom to the harem of experienced women. Their year-long preparation for a night with the king results in royal concubinage that may or may not be repeated based on the king's desire. Each woman is thus left waiting for the king to remember her delights.

As Esther's turn approaches, the text recalls her relation to Mordecai and emphasizes that the king's man in charge of the proceedings favors her. In the same manner she heeded Mordecai, Esther now takes Hegai's advice. That she *was admired by all who saw her* (v. 15) prepares her for the role Vashti turned down. The king loves her and makes her his queen. In the king's seventh year a fourth banquet is held. At his best when it comes to parties, Ahasuerus throws a wedding feast for Esther that spills over into favors for the rest of the land.

Mordecai and Esther Show Loyalty to the King, 2:19-23

The story shifts to Mordecai at the king's gate. Whether he is there in an official role or only loitering is unknown. From his vantage point Mordecai overhears a plot against the king and conveys the news to Esther, who reports it to Ahasuerus. The plot is thwarted and recorded in the royal Chronicles. With Esther, the unrevealed Jew, established as queen and Mordecai the Jew in place as the loyal, unrewarded servant of the king, the stage is set for the major scenes of the story.

Haman's Plot to Destroy the Jews, 3:1-15

Haman versus Mordecai, 3:1-6

3:1-2b. The advancement of Haman. The promotion of *Haman . . . the Agagite* (v. 1) is the first independent act of the king apart from banqueting. That all should bow to Haman is the king's third command; men being lord of their own homes the second (1:22), Vashti having refused the first. Like Mordecai, Haman's family tree reaches into the past to recall unsettled animosity between the two lines. Designated *the*

Agagite, Haman is the present embodiment of Saul's old enemy, Agag, king of the Amalekites, Israel's archetypal enemy (Exod 17:14-16; Deut 25:17-19). Although victorious in battle, Saul's downfall is chronicled in his conflict with King Agag (1 Sam 15:8-33).

3:2c-6. Mordecai's refusal to bow. That Mordecai refused to bow to Haman needs no explanation for an audience familiar with their respective histories. Saul and Agag's battle started on a national level yet came down to a personal duel. Mordecai and Haman face off in a one-on-one conflict that escalates into Haman's determination to destroy the Jews. Thus Mordecai becomes representative of all Jews in the same way that Ahasuerus and Vashti are used to speak generically of husbands and wives.

The Second Royal Decree, 3:7-15

3:7-11. Enlisting the King. Driven by anger (3:5) Haman begins a systematic plan to vent his wrath on Mordecai and the Jews. *In the first month* of Ahasuerus's *twelfth year* (v. 7) the fateful day for the Jews' destruction is determined by casting the lot (Akkadian "Pur"). With the twelfth month of the year, the month of Adar, singled out as the fated time, Haman seeks to enlist the aid of the king. Like the servants who brought Mordecai's behavior to his attention (3:3-4), Haman raises the Jews as a problem for Ahasuerus. Without identifying his target, Haman speaks in generalities, twisted truths, and innuendo. His characterizations, however, accurately depict Jewish life in the Diaspora. As a people scattered throughout the kingdom, Jews were distinguished by their particular religious laws. What was for the Jews a life accommodating to the tragic consequences of history is painted by Haman as conspiracy and rebellion. No evidence is given of his assertion that they disobey the king's laws. No mention is made of Mordecai. Even Haman is smart enough to know he can't argue for the destruction of a whole people because one Jew failed to bow to him.

Haman's task is to bring the king to action. Should the king fail to respond to the assertions of external threat, Haman sweetens the pot with the promise of financial gain. Where Haman intends to get the rather substantial amount goes unmentioned. Nor does the king question such an offer. By refusing the money and giving his signet ring to Haman, the king removes his own hands from the plan, yet makes possible a pogrom against a people whose name he has yet to hear.

3:12-15. Publishing the news. Once again the famed Persian postal system is put into action as the edict to destroy all the Jews is dispatched throughout the empire. On *the thirteenth day of the twlefth month* (v. 13), the people of the empire are to rise up against the Jews and wipe them from the face of the earth. No one is to be spared—not women or children, old or young—and their belongings will be for plunder. As an unlucky number for Babylonians and Persians, the thirteenth may signal that disaster awaits not only the Jews.

The slating of the day for twelve months away recalls the virgins' twelve months of beautifying before their fate was determined by their night with the king. Although death was not a threat, life in a harem of enforced barrenness was. Twelve months of preparation are thus begun as destroyer and victim are advised of the coming destruction. With the plan set in motion, Haman and the king return to their drinking. That the inhabitants of Susa are perplexed by these doings would seem a small but necessary counter to an otherwise insane affair.

Esther's Decision to Act, 4:1-17

Mordecai Responds to the News, 4:1-3

In contrast to the celebrating king and Haman, the second decree brings Mordecai to his knees. Clothing himself in the dress of grief, Mordecai appears at the king's gate publicly mourning the scheduled massacre. His actions are repeated across the empire as Jews take up the wailing cry of death.

Enlisting the Queen, 4:4-17

4:4. Esther unaware. Mordecai's behavior in the gate gains the attention of Esther's servants and is reported to her. No dialogue or questioning occurs as she dispatches clothes to the unaccepting Mordecai. Ignorant of the approaching disaster, the scene portrays Esther as a queen cloistered from the world whose servants know more than she does.

4:5-9. Esther informed. The refusal of the clothing by Mordecai prompts Esther to investigate the matter further. Dispatching *Hathach* (v. 5), a eunuch in her service, as go-between, Esther inquires of Mordecai the reasoning for his behavior. The text is silent as to how Mordecai knows the details of Haman's conversation with the king. Through Hathach, Mordecai relates his personal experience and thorough knowledge of the situation in the effort to educate Esther. A copy of the decree is sent as well so that she might see for herself the gravity of the situation. All of this is done so that Mordecai might charge Esther to act. She is to take the matter to the king, speaking to him on behalf of her people.

4:10-17. Esther decides to act. Until this point the exchange between Esther and Mordecai has been reported in narrative form only. With Mordecai's challenge of Esther to action, the narrative gives way to speech as the two struggle to a decision. Esther's immediate reaction is to remind Mordecai what everyone else knows. The king alone initiates his audiences. To appear uninvited risks possible death, and Esther, for some unknown reason, has not been summoned for some time.

Esther's fearful hesitation to risk her own life is countered by Mordecai's assertion that inaction will result in certain death for her and her family. The palace is no haven. The fate of the Jews is Esther's fate as well. The idea that deliverance might come from some other source is a vague argument without detail. Should she choose silence, not everything might be lost. This, however, is no out for Esther. Either she acts or dies. Who knows, such a time as this may be her destiny.

Queen Esther rises to the occasion. Her decision made, Esther becomes the controlling character. Now it is Mordecai who will obey her words. The Jews of Susa are to join her in a preparatory fast. Whether for life or death, Esther is committed.

Esther's Plot to Destroy Haman, 5:1–8:2

Ahasuerus and Haman on Esther's Grounds, 5:1-8

5:1-3. The robing of Queen Esther. Unlike Esther's first appearance before the king that followed intensive beautifying, the unsummoned visit reveals the haste necessitated by crisis. Fasting is her preparation and queenly garments her attire as Esther appears at the throne-room entrance. True to their respective characters, Esther wins the king's favor and he extends an exaggerated offer.

5:4-8. Invitations to dinner. Were it not so serious, the situation would be laughable. Esther risks her life. The king offers half his kingdom—all for a couple of dinner invitations! "What do you want Queen Esther?" "Can you and Haman come to dinner tonight?" (vv. 3, 4). The action is swift as Haman is fetched and the two men sit down at Esther's table. The queen knows

her king. While drinking, the affable Ahasuerus shows his bent toward excess, even to half his kingdom. A second dinner invitation stalls Esther's response to the king, who promises to grant a petition that he has not yet heard.

Haman's Self-glorification, 5:9-14

Having dined with the king and queen, Haman is full of himself. He basks in his good fortune and lauds himself before his friends and his wife. Life could not get much better except for one constant irritation, Mordecai the Jew. No mention is made of the approaching decree. Rather his audience, like the counselors of Ahasuerus in his conflict with Vashti, suggests a public solution to rid him of this embarrassment. The matter is simple for someone so close to the king. All he must do is order an eighty foot pole erected, tell the king to have Mordecai impaled, and be off to dinner. Like the duped Ahasuerus before him, Haman liked the plan.

The Robing of Mordecai, 6:1-13

The night between Esther's two dinner parties is the turning point for Mordecai and Haman. Beginning with a sleepless night for the king, one coincidence after another is strung together until Mordecai and Haman effectively change places in the story.

Unable to sleep, Ahasuerus demands to be read to from a book that happens to record Mordecai's earlier deed that saved the king's life. At the moment the king becomes concerned about Mordecai's reward, Haman enters the court. Acting according to character the spontaneous king seeks advice for his next move and the deliberate Haman responds. Only the reader is aware of the motives that drive each man. Ahasuerus needs Haman's help in honoring Mordecai while Haman must gain Ahasuerus' support to dispose of Mordecai. The conversation between the two is hypothetical in nature. Like Haman's unidentified enemy (3:8-11), the king's honoree goes unnamed. Thinking the honor is his, Haman answers with what he most desires: a public display in royal trappings. Expectedly, the king follows Haman's advice, calling upon him to execute the plan. The ironic twist comes as Mordecai is revealed to Haman as the designee. Haman's dream of grandeur becomes a living nightmare as he leads in honoring the man he most despises. Instead of Haman's gallows Mordecai is lifted upon the king's horse and cloaked in royal robes. At the end of the display, Mordecai resumes his vigil at the king's gate and

Haman, deflated, returns home disgraced. The same wife and friends who bolstered Haman's arrogance a few hours before now foretell his doom. Haman crumples before the reader's eyes as the text for the first time alludes to an indestructibility of the Jews.

A Deadly Dinner, 6:14–8:2

As the fateful words are spoken, eunuchs arrive to hurry Haman off to the second dinner. A day of eating and drinking passes into another as Ahasuerus once again asks Esther to make known her request. The gaiety of the situation changes rapidly as Esther pleads for her life and the life of her people, who still remain unnamed. Using language that recalls Haman's bribe, Esther describes their plight of being sold to destruction. For once, Ahasuerus is interested in the particulars, asking who stands behind this situation. Esther names the enemy, *this wicked Haman* (7:6). Haman shakes with fear while the angry king paces in the garden. Seeing that his fate lies with Esther, Haman turns to her. The picture of his falling upon the couch where the queen sits is related to the prophetic language spoken earlier by his wife and friends (6:13) concerning his fall before Mordecai. The king's propensity for failing to see the whole of a situation had aided Haman's cause in the past, but now works against him. The misreading of Haman's actions by Ahasuerus, coupled with information from a servant, leads to Haman's death on his own gallows. Thus the order for execution that Haman had sought from the king comes to pass, with Haman instead of Mordecai as the victim.

Esther receives Haman's house and Mordecai the king's signet ring when Mordecai's relationship to Queen Esther is revealed. Established over the house of Haman, Mordecai the Jew is publicly victorious over the enemy, Haman.

The Jews Destroy Their Enemies, 8:3–9:19

Enlisting the King, 8:3-8

Although Haman is dead, his evil plot to destroy the Jews remains in effect. Esther must approach the king again. Her ingratiating words harbor no condemnation of the king nor does he accept responsibility for the situation. He is, however, more than willing to turn matters over to Esther and Mordecai so long as they in no way alter or contradict the earlier edict. The dilemma centers on the immutable word of the king. What is written in his name and sealed with his signet cannot be revoked. True to character, the all-powerful Ahasuerus takes himself out of the picture, leaving the crisis to the ingenuity of Esther and Mordecai.

The Third Royal Decree, 8:9-14

Two months after Haman's decree to slaughter the Jews was sent out, a decree in Mordecai's words bearing the king's stamp is dispatched across the land. On the fated day of destruction all Jews are to rise to their own defense and slay the enemy. Published to Jew and non-Jew alike, the decree gives notice that the Jews will not meet the day as helpless victims. With opposing royal orders set for the same day, to attack and to defend, the question of what will actually happen looms on the horizon.

The Jews Respond to the News, 8:15-17

At the issuance of the third decree a spirit of festivity breaks out in the land. Instead of the sackcloth worn upon hearing of Haman's decree, Mordecai appears in the robes of state consistent with his change of status. The threat of doom is effectively lifted from the Jews' heads as they engage in a spontaneous feast of celebration. For many observers the quandary to side for or against the Jews is decided as they align themselves with the Jews. The stage is set for the thirteenth of Adar, some nine months away.

The Thirteenth of Adar, 9:1-19

When the day finally arrives, the Jews band together to meet the enemy head on. The ensuing battles are recalled with little or no detail, the results more significant in the tradition. The number of enemy slain (the figures total 75,800) is an intriguing element of the passage. Until this point in the story the only known enemy of the Jews is Haman—and he is long since dead. Mordecai replaces him in function, power and prestige. Although there is no physical bowing to Mordecai as was the case with Haman, an image of the mighty of the land falling before him is conveyed. The man earlier sentenced to death now elicits fear in the hearts of rulers. Just as Mordecai triumphed over Haman, the Jews triumph over their enemies. No Jewish blood is shed and the last of the house of Haman is wiped away.

Tradition recalls the occasion as a time of reversal for the Jews. Intended victims gain mastery over the attackers as Jews turn the tables on the enemy. A distinction in the tradition is made between the urban Jews and their experience within Susa proper and the rural Jews of the provinces. Two days are given to the fighting in Susa and only one in the countryside, which explains the difference in the dates of celebration between the two.

Institution of the Festival of Purim, 9:20–10:3

Mordecai's Decree, 9:20-28

Such a momentous occasion must not be forgotten. From his seat in the Persian bureaucracy Mordecai ensures the commemoration of this event by future generations of Jews. The imperial postal system carries Mordecai's letters of instruction throughout the empire, setting forth the fourteenth and fifteenth days of the month of Adar each year as festival days to recall the deliverance from their enemies. The setting aside of the two days for the celebration dispels any potential conflict among differing groups of Jews over which day shall be held in memoriam. The spirit of the celebration is to be one of rejoicing and gladness, the euphoric partying that comes when the threat of disaster is removed. It is a time for giving gifts to each other and of sharing with the poor.

By differing somewhat in detail from the extended account, the capsule retelling of the story in 9:24-25 drives home the providential nature of the event. Only Haman, the one who hatched a plot against the Jews, is addressed by name. In the Hebrew text, Esther appears as the "she" who comes before "the king," again unnamed. Three times in the two verses the Hebrew word for "plot" or "plan" occurs in noun or verbal form (חשׁב, NRSV "plot" and "devised"). But when "she" appears, the king "turns around" (Heb. שׁוּב) the evil plans so that they fall upon Haman's own head. The situation brings to mind another victim set right in a foreign court: Joseph saying to his brothers, "you planned (חשׁב) evil against me, God planned (חשׁב) it for good" (Gen. 50:20). God may not be mentioned in Esther, but Jewish tradition brings to mind divine aid in foreign places.

The festival is called PURIM, a festival of "chance." The text connects *pur* with the "lot" that was cast by Haman to determine the day of extermination for the Jews. If a Persian origin for the festival, which included the casting of lots to determine destinies, lies behind the observance, then the festival of Purim takes a Persian feast and makes it distinctively Jewish. By "chance" the Jews were to be destroyed. Then "she" appears before the king and the Jews are saved. The Jewish observance of Purim grows out of the historical experience of dispersion when Jews found themselves scattered throughout a non-Jewish world. In that world they knew the threat of destruction and the joy of victory where "chance" can be overcome by the actions of a "she," an unnamed woman, a young Jewish girl, tradition remembers as Queen Esther.

Esther's Decree, 9:29-32

Although the sending out of a letter by Esther would seem redundant after Mordecai's earlier dispatchment, the text emphasizes the establishment of a festival that is to be a part of the Jewish festal calendar for all generations to come. Stress is put on the written record, thus giving authority to the observance of a festival not established by Jewish Torah. Even more, the woman whose appearance before the king results in the salvation of her people takes her place in tradition as Queen Esther. She may have entered the palace through the king's bedroom, a beauty who found favor in his eyes, but it is as a Queen with the power and authority to speak to generations of Jews that in the final scenes she is portrayed.

The Fame of Mordecai, 10:1-3

Like the Jewish festival he inaugurated, the memory of Mordecai is committed to history. The ending of the story with the exaltation of Mordecai is the final ironic twist in a tale of unexpecteds. Haman, the archenemy, has long since passed from the scene and Mordecai, the Jew, sits at the right hand of the Persian king. Unlike Haman, Mordecai's standing in the court bodes well for Persian and Jew alike, and through the Persian Chronicles and the Jewish legend of Esther, Mordecai, the Jew, passes into history.

Works Cited

Clines, D. J. 1984. *Ezra, Nehemiah, Esther*, NCB.

LaCocque, André. 1990. *The Feminine Unconventional: Four Subversive Figures in Israel's Tradition*.

Job

Samuel E. Balentine

Introduction

In one sense the Book of Job requires little introduction. With its focus on innocent suffering, faith, and the justice of God, this book addresses universal concerns. Most persons have some personal experience with these concerns; they do not need a commentary to understand the struggle for meaning in a life broken inexplicably by pain and loss.

From another perspective, however, it is remarkable that despite the universal sympathy with this book, so little of the complexity and the candor of Job's engagement with God is appropriated by the community of faith. Too often the message of the book is reduced to a conventional slogan: the patience of Job (cf. Jas 5:11). As with all slogans, this one distorts by oversimplifying. The full picture of Job and the God before whom he presents his case is both more demanding and more honest.

Authorship, Date, and Setting

Introductions to commentaries normally address traditional questions about a book's author, its date, and its setting. The Book of Job, however, provides little or no information about such matters.

The identity of the author or authors of the book is not known. One may speculate that the author was an Israelite, perhaps someone belonging to the same intellectual tradition that produced such wisdom books as Proverbs and Ecclesiastes, but the evidence is circumstantial.

The date of the book is equally uncertain. Most would date the final composition somewhere between the seventh and fourth centuries B.C.E., although it is clear that the motif of the innocent sufferer was important in Near Eastern literature from at least the second millennium. Similarities in form and content between Job and Jeremiah (e.g., Job 3:3-10; Jer 20:14-18) and

Job and Second Isaiah (Isa 40–55), particularly with reference to the matter of innocent suffering, suggest a linkage to the exilic period. The book itself, however, provides no explicit historical information that ties it definitively to a particular period in Israelite history. Indeed, historical ambiguity is an essential aspect of the book's merit. Israel's experience of suffering, it might be argued, cannot be adequately explained by specific historical causes (cf. Penchansky 1990, 32-34).

The setting for the story in Job is also unclear. The introduction sets the action in *the land of Uz* (1:1), perhaps a reference to the region of Edom (cf. Lam 4:21), but more likely simply a general reference to a distant place somewhere east of Israel. Job himself is described as *the greatest of all the people of the east* (1:3). On balance, geographical location is unimportant for the story of Job. The world of Job is depicted instead as a "heroic world" (Habel 1985, 39), a world that cannot be identified with any specific place or time.

The name "Job" (*'iyyôb*) is curiously ambiguous. The only other reference to Job in the Hebrew Bible ranks him, along with NOAH and Danel (a legendary Canaanite king), as one of the ancient religious heroes (Ezek 14:14, 20). Within Hebrew the etymology of the word "Job" connects it with the passive participle of the verb *'āyab*, "to hate", thus "the hated one" or "the enemy." There may be a play on the words "Job" and "enemy" (*'ōyēb*) in Job 13:24. In second millennium West Semitic texts, an earlier form of the name, *'ayya-'abum*, means "Where is the (my) father?" (Pope 1965, 6).

Both of these nuances may inform the presentation of the biblical Job. He is one whose life is marked by both invocation ("Where is God?") and accusation ("You count me as your enemy"); his stance before God is that of both the suppliant and the persecuted one (cf. Janzen 1985, 34).

Composition

The Book of Job was not "authored" or "published" in the modern sense. Rather, it is a composite, a collection of parts brought together through a history of transmission. Although the major pieces of the book can be discerned rather easily, the specifics of when and how the parts were combined into a whole remain unclear.

The Frame and the Center. The frame of the book, chaps. 1–2 and 42:7-17, is a narrative about the legendary character Job. This narrative is likely based on an ancient tale that in oral or written form provides the starting point for the present book. The account is written in relatively simple prose, and utilizes a combination of speech and action to convey a coherent account of Job's suffering and restoration.

The center of the book, chaps. 3:1–42:6, consists of a lengthy series of dialogues between Job and his friends and between Job and God. These chapters are written in poetry, not prose, and are dominated by the speech of the characters, not their actions. The speeches are drawn primarily from the genrés of lament and disputation. It is likely that a later transmitter of the Job tradition utilized the existing tale of Job the righteous sufferer, and supplemented it with these dialogues to expand and elaborate on the issues of suffering and retribution.

Chapter 28. The Poem on Wisdom. Within the center of the book, chap. 28 presents a self-contained poem that differs significantly from the surrounding dialogues. It contains neither lament nor disputation; it is addressed to no one directly, and it receives no direct response from other speakers. Its subject, mining, metallurgy and the technological capacities for attaining wisdom, does not fit easily with the issues that dominate the preceding discussion between the friends. Rather, the poem presents a typical wisdom reflection on a proverbial question: "Where then does wisdom come from?" (vv. 12, 20; cf. Westermann 1981, 135-38). The poem is generally regarded as a later addition that, although intrusive, contributes nevertheless in significant ways to the overall argument of the book.

Chapters 32–37. The Elihu Speeches. The speeches of Elihu are commonly thought to be a further later addition to the poetic center. Elihu is not mentioned elsewhere in either the frame or the center of the book. His speeches appear to contribute little to the advancement of the friends' arguments against Job. They con-stitute, rather, a monologue that many scholars regard as stylistically inferior to preceding speeches. Even as a later interpolation, however, the speeches of Elihu function within the book as a whole as a dramatic interlude that prepares in significant ways for the impending appearance of God.

The Book of Job in Its Present Form

When the several parts of Job are fused together, a new whole results. The framing tale is split in two, forming a prologue (Job 1–2) and an epilogue (Job 42:7-17). The poetic center, with its additions and insertions, divides into dialogues between Job and his friends (Job 3–37) and between Job and God (Job 38:1–42:6). In this complex whole the portraits of both Job and God emerge as multidimensional.

Job's piety is portrayed as a complex fusion of both submission and rebellion (cf. Brenner 1989, 37-52; Penchansky 1990, 44-50, 78-80). In the prologue and epilogue Job exemplifies piety through his willing submission to the inscrutable decisions of God. He accepts affliction without questioning or complaining. God gives and God takes away. In this one-sided relationship with God, the correct response of faith is to worship and to remain a silent recipient of divine decrees.

In the dialogues Job insists that inexplicable misfortune puts God, not the victims, on trial. As victim, Job's piety takes on new forms. Truth and justice require that he assert his innocence, even when established religious tradition presumes his guilt. Faith requires that he hold on to God, even if God is the agent of his injustice. Thus Job curses, complains, questions, and resists *in faith*. This expression of piety insists that in the relationship with the Almighty, the human is no silent partner.

The Book of Job encourages the understanding that these are reciprocal, not opposite or contradictory, expressions of piety. Job is both reverent and rebellious, both accepting of God's mysterious ways and resistant to the notion that God cannot be questioned.

The portrait of God that emerges from this composite is also complex (cf. Penchansky 1990, 74-78; Mettinger 1992, 39-49). In the prologue and epilogue, and in the divine speeches God is wholly sovereign, wholly powerful, and unquestionably just. God afflicts and restores at will, without cause. God speaks and acts; Job listens, acknowledges, and receives. There are hints that God may be manipulated (e.g., by "the Satan") and that God can respond to human challenge with petulance (e.g., in the "whirlwind" speeches). But the primary characteristics on display in this portrait are God's majesty and God's purposive rule of the world.

The dialogues between Job and the friends offer different understandings of God's character. The friends' God is sovereign, but no longer free. In their view God's actions are determined by a rigid system of rewards and punishments. If there is guilt, God will punish; if there is innocence, God will reward appropriately. Their God is more predictable than compassionate, more consistent than gracious.

Job's understanding of God, however, is still different. Throughout the arguments with the friends, Job insists that pain and suffering force a changed perception of the divine-human relationship. To the innocent sufferer God may seem more an enemy than a companion, more an assailant than a savior, and most troubling of all, more absent than present. In Job's experience, the faithful and deserving cry for help often addresses a distant and silent God.

The reader might well wish that these portraits of both Job and God were less complex, that one view could be championed to the exclusion of others. Uniformity is indeed more manageable than diversity. The popular construal of the "patient Job" is only a small case in point. But the Book of Job resists easy solutions to ultimate questions about faith and God. That is both the problem and the invitation of the book.

For Further Study

In the *Mercer Dictionary of the Bible*: JOB; JOB, BOOK OF; JOB, TESTAMENT OF; JUSTICE/JUDGMENT; SATAN IN THE OT; SUFFERING IN THE OT; WISDOM IN THE OT; WISDOM LITERATURE.

In other sources: D. J. A. Clines, *Job 1–20*, WBC; J. L. Crenshaw, *Old Testament Wisdom: An Introduction*; C. Duquoc and C. Floristan, eds., *Job and the Silence of God*; E. M. Good, *In Turns of Tempest. A Reading of Job with a Translation*; R. Gordis, *The Book of God and Man: A Study of Job*; G. Gutiérrez, *On Job. God-Talk and the Suffering of the Innocent*; N. C. Habel, *The Book of Job*, OTL; W. L. Humphreys, "The Tragic Vision and the Book of Job," *The Tragic Vision and the Hebrew Tradition*, OBT; J. G. Janzen, *Job*, Interpretation; D. Penchansky, *The Betrayal of God: Ideological Conflict in Job*; L. G. Perdue and W. C. Gilpen, eds., *The Voice From the Whirlwind. Interpreting the Book of Job*; M. H. Pope, *Job*, AncB; H. H. Rowley, *Job*, NCB; D. Simundson, *The Message of Job*; C. Westermann, *The Structure of the Book of Job*.

Commentary

An Outline

Prologue: The Affliction of Job, 1:1–2:13

The prologue introduces the life journey of the legendary character Job. He is the model of the righteous person, exemplifying piety by his faithfulness along the journey from prosperity to affliction, from joy to pain. He seeks steadfastly to avoid *evil* (*rā '*, 1:1, 8; 2:3), yet is victimized by *evil* (*rā '*, 2:11). His stature (literally, his "greatness") is defined initially by possessions (1:3), but ultimately by pain and anguish (2:13). His journey into suffering inexplicable is decided in God's heavenly court where conversations between God and *hasatan* (1:6-12; 2:1-7a) result in calamity on earth for Job and his family (1:13-22; 2:7b-10). Job's submission to heavenly decisions beyond his knowledge and control affirms his willing commitment to a one-sided relationship with the God who both gives and takes away (1:21).

1:1-5. Job's piety. Job is presented as an exemplary model of faith. Both the beginning and ending of this initial presentation focus on his unparalleled piety. He is *blameless* and *upright*, i.e., a person of integrity and complete honesty, and he is one who *feared God* and *turned away from evil* (v. 1). He is the epitome of the righteous person as portrayed in the wisdom tradition (e.g., Prov 3:7; 16:6, 17) and in the Psalms (e.g., 25:21; 37:27). This cluster of superlatives, reinforced by its verbatim repetition in 1:8 and 2:3, makes clear the Hebraic affirmation of the essential connection between morality and piety. Further, his concern is not limited to himself but extends to his family, for whom he offers preemptive sacrifices just in case they should sin against God in their heart (v. 5).

Sandwiched between the framing descriptions of his faithfulness, vv. 2 and 3 report that Job is blessed with a full family and a contingent of servants and possessions. The numbers *seven*, *three*, and *ten* are formulaic indicators of the completeness of Job's life. The position of these verses anticipates a crucial question in the Book of Job. What is the connection between Job's piety and his prosperity? Is piety the precondition for prosperity? Or is prosperity the motivation behind one's piety?

1:6-12. First scene in heavenly court. A series of alternating scenes in heaven and on earth explore the causal connection between Job's piety and his prosperity. A heavenly council gathers to discuss God's governance of the world. Among the divine messengers present is one called *hasatan*, "the Satan". The term refers not to the devil or to Satan as known in Christianity, but to one who functions as a kind of prosecuting attorney for God (cf. Zech 3:1-2), probing the veracity of human claims for integrity and faithfulness. There is nothing in the function of this "Prosecutor/Adversary" to suggest that he is God's opponent or that his intentions are in some way evil or contrary to God's purposes. To the contrary, the dilemma posed by the Book of Job is that this one may only act in response to divine initiatives.

God initiates the discussion by asking whether in his rovings "the Satan" has considered *my servant Job* (v. 8). God affirms Job's piety with the same unqualified praise offered in v. 1, adding the assessment that *there is no one like him on the earth*. This evaluation, normally reserved as a description of God's own distinctiveness (only here, in 2:3, and in 1 Sam 10:24

with reference to humans; cf. Clines 1989, 24), heightens the portrayal of Job as righteous beyond comparison.

"The Satan" responds by questioning Job's motivation for loyalty to God. Is it not the case that Job is faithful because he is blessed? Has not God so protected him from the fires of adversity that Job's faith has never really been tested? Suffering, "the Satan" implies, will change the calculus between God and humans. Without the reward, would there be the loyalty?

God concedes that the question is worthy of consideration. Does God know already the answer or is God perhaps asking, with "the Satan," about the real possibilities of disinterested piety? The reader may find it more comfortable to presume that it is the former of these options rather than the latter, but the text itself leaves the question open. Without hesitation God hands Job over for the testing that is to decide the case. There is but one proviso: "the Satan" is to stop short of afflicting Job's person.

1:13-22. Calamity on earth. In rapid succession a series of calamities befalls Job as a consequence of the heavenly debate. Lost are *the oxen, the donkeys*, and the attendant "boys" (vv. 13-15), *the sheep* and the shepherd "boys" (v. 16), *the camels* and the caravan "boys" (v. 17). The loss of Job's family, though not explicitly stated, is indicated by the final allusion to the "children/boys" (v. 19). In all of these instances the NRSV renders the term "boys" (or "children/boys") with *the servants* (or *the young people*).

Throughout it all Job remains unquestioning and unwavering in his commitment to God. He assumes the posture of mourning and worship by falling on the ground in willing submission to the God who both gives and takes away (vv. 20-21). *In all this* Job did not sin or express contempt for God.

2:1-6. Second scene in heavenly court. A second round of discussion between God and "the Satan" repeats almost verbatim the previous debate in heaven, including God's affirmation of Job who persists in holding fast to his integrity. There is, however, one interesting addition to this scene.

Verse 3 reports that God has been *incited* by "the Satan" against Job for the purpose of destroying him *for no reason*. The verb "incite" or "provoke" (*swt*) normally carries negative connotations (cf. Deut 13:6 [MT 13:7]; Josh 15:18; 1 Sam 26:19; 2 Kgs 18:32). When used with reference to God's being provoked, the word invites consideration of God's susceptibility

to manipulation. Such consideration is further merited by the concession from God that Job's calamities are without cause (*hinnām*). The admission from God is both candid and troubling. If God acts *for no reason*, without cause, what then is the connection between human behavior and divine action?

"The Satan" heightens the challenge by suggesting that if God will permit a closer scrutiny of Job, i.e., a deeper affliction that reaches to Job's very bone and flesh, it can be shown that his integrity is lacking. Again God agrees to the proposal, offering Job into "the Satan's" hand, with only the condition that his life be spared (vv. 4-6).

2:7-10. Calamity on earth. The second round of discussions in the heavenly council effect calamity on earth similar to the first. Job has already suffered the loss of all his possessions, now he is afflicted with *loathsome sores* that cover all his body, *from the sole of his foot to the crown of his head* (v. 7). Sitting in the ashes, Job assumes the position of the mourner who feels worthless and abandoned.

The question posed by Job's wife contributes indirectly to Job's affliction. The first part of her question recalls the words of God: Are you still "holding on to your integrity" (author trans.; cf. 2:3). The second part of her question echoes the words of "the Satan:" *Curse God and die* (v. 9; cf. 1:11; 2:5; see Clines 1989, 51). Thus does she articulate the contrasting expectations of God and "the Satan" regarding Job.

The dilemma that Job faces is magnified by his wife's urging that he should curse God. The Hebrew text has the word *brk*, "bless," thus literally, "bless God. . . ." The word *brk* occurs throughout the prologue with a curious ambiguity. Sometimes it conveys its normal meaning, "bless" (1:10, 21), while in other instances it appears to have an opposite meaning, "curse" (1:5, 11; 2:5, 9). In the latter cases interpreters usually understand the word euphemistically, as a scribal substitute intended to tone down the text. If *brk* in v. 9 is read with its normal meaning "bless," rather than its presumed meaning "curse," then the wife's question takes on added significance. Can Job hold to his integrity and *bless* God? (Clines 1989, 52). Or will one commitment have to be sacrificed in order to retain the other?

Job's response hints at the quandary that he faces. On the one hand he rebukes his wife abruptly, suggesting that her option is no option. On the other hand, he moves from the positive declaration of 1:21

to an assertion now framed as a question: *Shall we receive the good at the hand of God, and not receive the bad?* (v. 10). The question is rhetorical, and yet the tremor of Job's ambiguity begins to surface (Janzen 1985, 51).

2:11-13. The arrival of the friends. Having heard of the *troubles* (*rā'*, "evil") that has fallen on Job, the three friends come to *console and comfort* (v. 11) him. The language suggests a dual intent. The verb "console" (*nwd*) means "to move back and forth," and by extension, "to show grief with," or "to identify in mourning with," by moving the head back and forth (e.g., Jer 15:5; 22:10). The form of the verb "to comfort" (*nhm*) used here means "to show sorrow/compassion," hence it conveys the friends' intent to act pastorally towards Job. The same verb, however, in a different form is the standard term for "to repent, change one's mind about." With the ensuing dialogues it will become clear that this second meaning of *nhm* is primary for the friends. Their view of consoling Job is to convince him to repent, i.e., to change his mind about the charges he will lodge against God. Only in this way can he be truly comforted.

But first, they engage in traditional acts of mourning, sitting in silence with Job for *seven days and seven nights* (v. 13). It is a gesture that both recognizes Job's great pain and at the same time isolates the friends from him, for the ritual they observe is one that treats Job as if he were already dead.

Job's Lament, 3:1-26

Job breaks the silence of pain with the voice of anguish. Pain must be spoken, even if, as these opening words of Job make clear, it drives one to curse. This speech is structured in two parts: vv. 1-10, a curse directed at the day of Job's birth and the night of his conception; and vv. 11-26, a lament that thunders a repeated question about the "Why?" of existence. From first word to last there is a steady deterioration into a bitterness of soul marked by rage and agony (v. 26).

3:1-10. Damn the day, damn the night. Job's wife had urged him to *curse God and die* (2:9). Now Job curses, not God directly, but rather the day of his birth (vv. 3-5) and the night of his conception (vv. 6-9). The intent of such cursing is to set in motion the very action the curse itself articulates. From this opening curse to Job's final summoning of God in 31:35-37, the outcome of Job's response to suffering hangs in

the balance. Will his cursing unleash the forces of his ultimate demise, as his wife anticipates? Or will Job's harangue against the heavens finally lead to the dialogue with God that he so desperately desires?

Job's curse parodies the language of Gen 1 with a series of incantations that call for a reversal of the created order (cf. Fishbane 1971, 151-67). Verse 3 sets forth the general curse of *day* and *night*, with vv. 4-5 offering an elaboration of the former ("that day, let it be darkness" [author trans.]; cf. Gen 1:1), and vv. 6-9, an extended development of the latter (*that night, let thick darkness seize it*). In sum, Job expresses a preference for darkness over light, death over life. The reason is set forth in v. 10: life outside the womb brings nothing but trouble (cf. Jer 20:18). It is a measure of Job's anguish that his death wish is more than a temporary lapse into despair. It is a recurring theme throughout his speeches (e.g., 7:15-16; 9:21; 10:1; cf. Westermann 1981, 67-70).

3:11-26. Why? why? why? Job's lament is a weaving together of both self-lament, i.e., mournful interior reflection (vv. 11-19, 24-26) and God-lament (vv. 20-23; see further Westermann 1981, 37-38). In both foci the operative word is "Why?" (vv. 11, 12, 20; also implied in vv. 16, 23). A number of Hebrew terms convey this question, but the repetition of the word *lāmmāh* in vv. 11 and 20, a word typically conveying a strong note of protest, gives to the lament a tone of angry despair.

The self-lament (vv. 11-19) expresses Job's wish that he had died at birth, for as a stillborn (v. 16) the sleep of death would offer *quiet* and *rest* (vv. 13, 17). In death there would be a levelling of all that yields inequality and oppression. Royalty (vv. 14-15) and commoner, *the wicked* and *the weary* (v. 17), *prisoners* and *the taskmaster* (v. 18), *the small and the great* (v. 19), all would be as one. But it is not so for Job (vv. 24-26). He has no *ease*, no *quiet . . . no rest*. There is only life, and from his perspective life brings only *trouble* (v. 26, *rōgez*, lit. "raging").

Job's self-lament cannot be resolved on the horizontal plane alone. Ultimately his lament is directed to God for God is the only one who can respond effectively. Thus Job hurls the "Why?" question to God (vv. 20-23). Why does God give light and life to one for whom it means only misery and bitterness? For Job life is no gift. It is a dark form of divine constriction, a "hedge" (v. 23; cf. 1:10) that God places around him to block his escape to the peace of the grave.

Dialogue between Job and His Three Friends, 4:1–27:23

First Cycle: God's Moral Governance of the World, 4:1–14:22

4:1–5:27. Eliphaz. Eliphaz' first response to Job is patient and encouraging, not accusatory. He praises Job for the instruction he has offered in the past to those who have suffered. Now Job himself must heed his own counsel (vv. 2-5). The basis for Job's *confidence* and *hope* is his own piety, his *fear of God* and his *integrity* (v. 6), virtues that Eliphaz, with God (cf. 1:8; 2:3), does not dispute.

The critical question that Eliphaz urges Job to explore is put in v. 7: *Who that was innocent has ever perished? . . . where have the upright been destroyed?* The truth to which Eliphaz summons Job is not that the innocent do not *suffer*, but that they do not ultimately *perish* in their sufferings.

The validation of this truth is drawn from two sources. First, Eliphaz' own experience and observations confirm that God sustains in the world a reliable moral connection between deed and consequence. Those who sow *iniquity* and *trouble* reap the same (vv. 8-11). Second, Eliphaz has been granted a special revelation about the nature of the human condition (vv. 12-21). There is a fundamental distinction between Creator and creature such that it is impossible for mortals of *clay* and *dust* (v. 19) ever to be wholly *righteous* and *pure* before their maker (v. 17). Even God's heavenly servants are blemished and flawed (v. 18); how much more so then a human like Job.

On the basis of these two sources of wisdom, Eliphaz concludes that Job's troubles do not place him outside the meaningful order of God's world. They are but the logical consequence of creaturely imperfection (5:1-7).

Eliphaz extends his observations on God's moral governance of the world with a hymn of praise affirming God's reliable discrimination between the innocent and the needy and their powerful, devious oppressors (5:9-16). To such a God Job should willingly entrust his cause (v. 8), even though it means submitting to a transcendent, often mysterious justice (v. 9). Before such a God the poor always have hope, because ultimately injustice will be silenced (v. 16).

Suffering is more than just an inherent necessity of the human condition. It is evidence of God's positive plan for insuring the full development of human nature. Indeed, Job should be happy for the discipline of divine reproval since it is a demonstration of God's love for him (vv. 17-27). If Job will but follow Eliphaz' counsel to seek God, he will *know* (vv. 24, 25, 27) that the God who *wounds* and *strikes* can be trusted to "bind up" and *heal* (v. 18). Job need have no *fear* (vv. 21, 22) from temporary misfortune. By life's end, when God's correcting love has achieved the intended results, Job will be restored (vv. 22-26).

6:1–7:21. Job. Job's response comprises an indictment of the friends (chap. 6) and a lament to God (chap. 7). The indictment of the friends begins and ends with an emphasis on Job's *calamity* (hawwāh, vv. 2, 30). His anguish is heavy and real (vv. 2-3). It is not the contrived imaginations of a fool, as Eliphaz had suggested (5:2-7). And it is this very anguish that keeps him honest in his assessment of the situation (vv. 28-30). The truth is that God has targeted him for destruction, without cause (v. 10), and any effort to comfort that does not acknowledge this fact is repulsive, like rotten food (vv. 4-7).

The friends, Job charges, do not admit the truth of his calamity (vv. 14-27). What despairing ones need from friends in times of crisis is loyalty (*hesed*), even if they have lost faith in *the Almighty* (v. 14; cf. NEB, NIV). Job's friends, however, are like the wadis whose water is only seasonal. When the heat comes they disappear and disappoint all who look to them for sustenance. Job has not asked them for a *gift* or a *bribe* for the judge (v. 22). He has not asked them to rescue him from the hands of the adversary. He has only expected them to stand by him, not to haggle over the worth of his friendship.

From the portrayal of false friends, Job returns once more to speak of his own misery. He compares the human condition to the life of the slave (7:1-6; cf. 3:17-19). He labors in harsh, debilitating compulsory service for the reward of an existence that is meaningless and void of hope.

In 7:7-21 Job addresses God directly for the first time. He laments that God has searched him out like a "seeing eye" (v.8) and a *watcher of humanity* (v.20). God targets him as an opponent to be terrorized and subdued (v. 14), as if he were Yamm (*Sea*) or Tannin (*Dragon*), the primordial enemies of the created order (v. 12). In the bitterness of his soul, Job cries out with anguished imperative *Let me alone* (v. 16).

Such misery turns doxology to accusation. In vv. 17-21 Job utilizes the words of Ps 8:5-6, not to praise God for humanity's exalted status, but to challenge

God for being unreasonably preoccupied with so frail an opponent as the human creature. Job asks hypothetically, *If I sin. . .* why should this be of such concern to God? Even if Job were to admit to sin, which he does not do, why should God not let the matter pass? Job's existence on earth is only brief. Surely there can be no harm to God if God suspends the assault until Job lies down in death and is no more (cf. vv. 7, 16, 21).

8:1-22. Bildad. Bildad raises for the first time the question of *justice* (*mišpāt*, vv. 1-7) and then appeals to an ancient parable to support his defense of God's reliable discrimination between the righteous and the wicked (vv. 8-19). On this basis Job can be sure that the truly upright person will not be rejected by God (vv. 21-22).

Bildad begins with a rhetorical question that makes explicit the concern that to this point has been only implied in Job's accusations: *Does God pervert* (lit., "bend," or "twist") *justice* (*mišpāt*) . . .*or the right* (*sedeq*)? (v. 3). For Bildad, the proven moral order of God's world means that God and injustice are mutually incompatible. For every consequence there is a cause, behind every misfortune a sin. If Job is innocent (a claim Bildad does not dispute), there must be a failing elsewhere. Bildad suggests the sin can be traced to Job's children. The same retributive view of justice informs Bildad's counsel. *If* Job will seek God, and *if* Job is pure and upright, *then* God will reward him with such blessings that the former days of affliction will pale by comparison (vv. 1-7).

To buttress this argument, Bildad appeals to the wisdom of the ages (vv. 8-19). He cites a parable of two plants to reiterate the respective fates of the wicked and the righteous: the *papyrus* and *reeds* (v. 11) that wither and then die for lack of water, and another unidentified plant whose shoots thrive and spread beyond the boundaries of its garden (vv. 16-19).

Finally, Bildad applies his teaching to Job, in effect answering the question he himself had posed in v. 3: *Does God pervert justice?* No, the blameless person (*tām*, v. 20; cf. 1:1, 8; 2:3) will not be rejected, and the wicked (*rěšā 'îm*, v. 22) will not survive.

9:1-10:22. Job. In his dispute with Bildad, Job takes up the question of divine justice (chap. 9), and considers the case he can make before the heavenly tribunal (10:1-17). Recognizing both the necessity and the futility of winning a verdict against the sovereign judge of the universe, Job succumbs once more to mournful lament (10:18-22).

In chap. 9 Job offers a critique of God's justice that responds to both Eliphaz and Bildad. Job 9:1-12 addresses Eliphaz' argument that human frailty makes it impossible to be righteous (*sdq*) before God (4:12-21). Job agrees that it is impossible to be *sdq* before God, but his affirmation is different, and it is made on other grounds. Job interprets *sdq* in a legal sense rather than a religious or moral sense, i.e., with reference to innocence rather than righteousness. It is true that mortals cannot be innocent before God, not because they are flawed creatures, but because in God's court "might makes right." Subverting doxological affirmations, Job charges that God uses divine powers to overturn and destroy (vv. 5-9). Such destructive force prompts bewilderment, not praise. It serves to conceal God and baffle humanity. It is a mystery that leads not to wonder and awe (v. 10; cf. 5:9), but to anxious uncertainty (vv. 10-12).

The second strophe of chap. 9 (vv. 13-24) challenges Bildad's contention that God does not pervert justice (cf. 8:3). Job charges that in God's justice there is no differentiation between the blameless and the wicked; they are both marked for destruction (v. 21). Job offers himself as a prime example of divine justice that operates "*without cause* (v. 17). Job is *innocent* (*sdq*, vv. 15, 20) and *blameless* (vv. 20, 21), yet God *mocks* (v. 23) his misfortune and forces him into the submission of the guilty as if he were the primordial chaos monster (vv. 13, 17-18). If justice is a matter of power, then who indeed can contest the verdict of the sovereign Judge?

Job ponders a number of options for his situation (vv. 25-35). He could forget his complaint and try to twist his countenance from sadness to cheerfulness, but this would not relieve his suffering or restore his innocence (vv. 27-28). He could wash himself with potent cleansing agents, but God would still submerge him in filth (vv. 30-31). Or he could appeal for an arbitrator who would lay his hand on both parties, restraining God to a fair legal process and protecting Job from unjust intimidation (vv. 33-35). In the MT v. 33 is prefaced with a negative: "There is no arbitrator." The NRSV renders the phrase *There is no umpire between us*. Other versions preface the statement with a particle suggesting a wish: "If only there were someone to arbitrate. . ." (NIV). Both translations are consistent with Job's dilemma as conveyed in the MT. He wishes for an option that he does not believe exists. Even so, it is a possibility he will continue to pursue (cf. 16:19-21; 19:23-27).

In chap. 10 Job rehearses the case he would make before God, if he only had the chance (vv. 1-17). He reviews and disputes traditional affirmations about God's purposive creation of humanity. God's own hands have fashioned individuals from the womb, knitting them together, bone and flesh, supposedly with a providential care directed towards life and love. Yet from Job's perspective God's intentions seem sinister, not benevolent. God shapes humans only to *destroy* them (v. 8). God creates humans out of *clay* only to facilitate their reduction to *dust* (v. 9). God's motive in watching over the maturation process of humans (like a cheese maker [v. 10] and a clothier [v. 11]) is to search for human flaws (vv. 10-14). If Job were guilty, he would deserve such punishment, but he is innocent (*sdq*, v. 15; cf. 9:15, 20). Now he cannot lift his head, because his shame and his affliction already pronounce him guilty. Indeed, even if he attempted to restore his integrity, God would hunt him down like a lion (v. 17).

Job closes this speech (vv. 18-22) by returning to the painful question "Why?" with which he began in chap. 3. The question is addressed to God: *Why did you bring me [out of] the womb?* (cf. 3:11). Life under God's scrutiny has become abhorrent for Job (10:1; cf. 7:16; 9:21). If he had to be born to such misery, could not God now leave him alone (v. 20; cf. 7:16, 19) so that he might pass quickly to the grave? There, in the presence of death's darkness and gloom, he might at last smile a little (NRSV *find a little comfort*).

11:1-20. Zophar. Zophar assumes the role of a teacher whose instruction is meant to enlighten Job on the matter of God's justice (vv. 1-12) and to direct him to the appropriate response (vv. 13-20).

The instruction begins with a rebuke of Job's claim to be *pure* and *clean* in God's eyes (vv. 1-6). The *secrets of wisdom* are inaccessible to human understanding. There is a surface dimension to God's ways in the world, which ordinary mortals like Job might challenge. But there is also a transcendent dimension to God's wisdom (vv. 8-9: a depth, a height, a length, a breadth) that Job cannot know and should not question (vv. 7-12). Zophar presumes to know this hidden dimension of God's justice, and affirms that on this level God most certainly does discern who is worthless and deceitful. The truth of God's unfathomable justice is that Job has received less than he deserves for his guilt (v. 6).

Zophar's counsel (vv. 13-20) is couched in the same if-then terms that Bildad offered in 8:1-7. *If* Job directs his heart to God, stretches out his hands in humble prayer, removes iniquity from his life, and does not let wickedness reside in his abode (vv. 13-14), *then* God will restore him (vv. 15-19). Whereas Bildad offered such counsel in the presumption of Job's innocence, Zophar assumes Job's need of repentance. Job's *hope* and *confidence* are conditional rewards, not inherent qualities; they are inextricably linked to his return to God (cf. Bildad's discussion of hope in 8:13-14).

12:1–14:22. Job. This complex speech brings to conclusion the first cycle of discourses between Job and the friends. A number of rhetorical themes connect the speech to Job's opening lament in chap. 3 (e.g., *trouble*, in 3:17, 26; 14:1 and *deep darkness* in 3:5; 12:22; see further Janzen 1985, 101-102), and yet the tenor of the language suggests that both Job's anguish and his resolve to protest have escalated dramatically.

The speech is a disputation, comprised of three major parts, which is directed against the friends and against God. The first unit, 12:1–13:12, contests the friends' wisdom and integrity. A crucial transition in 13:13-19 signals Job's decision to address God directly, no matter the cost. The final unit, 13:20–14:22, is Job's challenge to God.

Job disputes the friends' claim to superior wisdom. Job has wisdom of his own, equal to theirs (12:2-3; 13:1-2), and both his intellect and his experience lead him to refute their contention that God is just. Why would a truly wise being make a laughingstock of an innocent and blameless man who seeks only honest dialogue with God? Job concludes that such mockery is the product of the friends' insulation from suffering: "in the thinking of those who are at ease there is contempt for calamity" (12:5, author trans.).

Job appeals to creation itself for his knowledge of God (12:7-12). The *animals*, the *birds of the air*, the *fish of the sea*, *the earth*, all serve as teachers for those who will listen. They declare that every living creature is in the hand of God, including the innocent sufferer.

Such a declaration moves Job to a "doxology of terror" (Perdue 1991, 153), a painful praise in honor of God's destructive purposes in creation (12:13-25). *Wisdom* and "power" (*strength*) are the trademarks of God's work in the world (12:13, 16), not justice, and God uses these virtues to destroy rather than to nourish. God tears down the structures of society, without rebuilding; deprives the created order of sustenance, without replenishing; limits, overthrows, and removes the possibility of human leadership; and in general returns the created order to chaos (see esp. 12:22, 24).

In 13:1-12 Job continues his disputation against the friends by attacking their integrity. They are "lie spreaders" and "quack doctors" (v. 4, author trans.) whose so-called wisdom is as worthless as dust and crumbling clay (v. 12). With a series of rhetorical questions (vv. 7-9, 11) Job implies that the friends have spoken falsely and deceitfully for God. By defending God against Job's truth claims, they hope to curry favor with the sovereign judge. They do not realize that covering up the truth about suffering and injustice is never an adequate defense of God. If they choose to be false witnesses in the case that Job will bring against God, they run the risk of being investigated themselves.

Job 13:13-19 represents a crucial transition point in the speech as Job turns away from the friends and prepares to address God directly. He has prepared his case against God; he knows that he is *sdq*, a fact that should secure his acquittal (v. 18). But he has no misgivings about his chances against so powerful an opponent. God will slay him; he has no hope, yet he must argue his cause before the very face of God (v. 15), even if the effort destroys him (v. 14). Only in daring confrontation with God can Job salvage his integrity (v. 16).

In 13:20–14:22 Job turns with "the courage of absolute vulnerability" (Janzen 1985, 107) to address God. Two questions set the agenda for the radical dialogue with God that Job seeks: *How many are my . . . sins?* (v. 23) and *Why do you hide your face and count me as your enemy?* (v. 24). The answer to these questions requires the mutual participation of God and Job. The contribution of one partner in this relationship without the other will be inadequate for the task. Either God can present the case against Job and Job will defend himself, or Job is prepared to challenge God and await God's defense. Either way there must be dialogue. Job has derided the friends for failing to realize the legitimacy of his request for interchange with God (12:4). Surely God does not condone a stifling of honest discourse.

Having laid the groundwork for his discourse with God, Job yields once more to the realization of the futility of his quest. Mortals have no real hope of contesting God. Their lifespans are set by divine decree, and there are boundaries beyond which they must not pass (14:1-6). There may be hope (*tiqwāh*, v. 7) for a tree to bud again after it is cut down (14:7-

12), and perhaps, Job muses, there may be for humans some respite from suffering even after they descend to Sheol (14:13-17). But in truth there is no such hope (*tiqwāh*, v. 19). Mortals ultimately pass away into nothingness, like the dust of the earth that is washed away by the flood waters (14:18-22).

Second Cycle: The Place of the Wicked in a Moral World, 15:1–21:34

15:1-35. Eliphaz. Job had asked the friends to be quiet and listen to his case against God (13:13, 17). They do not cooperate. Instead they become more strident and accusatory in their approach to Job. In his second speech Eliphaz moves from exhortation (chaps. 4–5) to rebuke, reprimanding Job for his so-called *wisdom* (vv. 1-16) and lecturing him on the destiny of the *wicked* (vv. 17-35).

Eliphaz characterizes Job's speeches as a blustery sabotage of true religion (vv. 1-6). His so-called wisdom is tainted as much by his unacknowledged guilt as by his cleverness (v. 5). Job's assessment of his experience is not only inaccurate; it is dangerous. To argue with God as Job has dared to do destroys true piety (*yir 'āh, fear of God*; cf. 1:2, 8; 2:3) and diminishes contemplation of religious truths (v. 4).

To reinforce his charge Eliphaz appeals to the accumulated wisdom of the ages (vv. 7-16). Does Job propose that he has the wisdom of the Primal Human, the firstborn mortal who is privileged to God's primordial decisions (v. 7)? Does Job contend that he has stood in the divine council, where heavenly beings participate with God in the mysterious design of the cosmos (v. 8)? Even such holy ones are not entrusted with full comprehension of the divine plan (vv. 15-16); how then dare Job, a mere mortal, claim to be in the right against God (v. 14)? In his first speech Eliphaz had only briefly addressed God's treatment of the wicked (5:13-14).

In this speech the fate of the wicked is the subject of lengthy discourse (vv. 17-35). Appealing once more to the wisdom of the ancestors (vv. 17-19), Eliphaz asserts that the life of the wicked is filled with pain, terror, and deprivation (vv. 20-25). Their future is charted for a darkness and an emptiness that are unrelieved (vv. 28-31). Their final demise will come abruptly, like a vine that drops its grapes before they are ripe or an olive tree that loses its buds before they bear fruit (vv. 32-35).

The lesson for Job in this dissertation lies in recognizing the cause of the wicked person's ruin. Because they *stretched out their hands against God* and contest God as if they were a mighty warrior (vv. 25-28), they are doomed to the fortunes of an overmatched combatant. In Eliphaz' view, to challenge God is to rebel against God, and rebels, Job should note well, cannot escape the consuming justice of God (cf. v. 30).

16:1–17:16. Job. There is a disjointedness in this speech that yields a portrait of Job reeling back and forth between his disappointment in his friends (16:1-5; 17:6-10), his complaint against God (16:6-17), his hope in the midst of despair (16:18-22), and his steady descent towards death which, even if a respite from his troubles, still offers no hope for restitution (17:1-2, 11-16). The gradual diminishing of Job's direct address to God contributes to this portrait. In contrast to the lengthy address in 13:20–14:22, here Job speaks directly to God only in 16:7b-8a and 17:3-5.

Job rebukes the friends as comforters who cause trouble rather than assuage it. If he had the luxury of their freedom from suffering, perhaps he too might be content with shallow reassurance (16:1-5). The friends content themselves with the conventional position of the righteous. They look at Job's suffering and they retreat to their self-protecting theological certainties: Job is suffering; he must be godless. Job sees that there is not a truly wise person among any who insist on confirming their righteousness by denying his innocence (17:6-10).

As painful as the friends' scorn is for him, it is God who confronts Job as the real enemy (16:6-17). Eliphaz argued that it is the wicked who mount an assault against God (15:24-27). Job counters that it is God who wages war on the innocent. It is God whose teeth tear and grind the flesh like a savage beast (v. 9), who breaks and shatters (v. 12), splits open and *pours out* a person's guts without mercy (v. 13). Such ferocity against one who is gaunt and worn out (vv. 7-8) is incomprehensible. Such violence against one in whom there is no violence, whose cries to be heard are pure, is unconscionable (v. 17).

God's attack on Job is likened to murder. As when Cain murdered Abel and the spilled blood cried out to God for vengeance (Gen 4:8-10), so Job calls on the earth not to cover up the evidence of God's crimes against him (16:18-22). It is a desperate hope for a hearing that reaches to the heavens, where Job believes there is yet a *witness* who will stand in the breach between himself and God.

The identity of this witness is unclear. Is it God? If so, then Job in essence appeals to God *against* God. It

is more likely that Job is looking to a third party (cf. 9:33), perhaps a heavenly counterpart to "the Satan," whose task is to search out the good as well as the evil (Habel 1985, 274-75). Perhaps the plea should be interpreted less literally, not for some specific person as witness, but as a hope that Job's own protests of innocence would ultimately be the witness that God could not ignore (e.g., 16:20: "My own lament is my advocate with God," JB; cf. Clines 1989, 390). In either case, it is clear that Job despairs of realizing such a witness. God has attacked him. The inevitable outcome is death. Job has cried out to the earth and the heavens for a justice in which only faith can believe (cf. Janzen 1985, 125).

With this mournful hope, Job surrenders once more to the pressing reality of his impending death (17:1-2, 11-16; cf. 7:17-21; 10:18-21; 14:18-22). He manages but a brief address to God (17:3-5). Abandoned by friends, and with no discernible hope of a witness in heaven, Job offers himself as the only guarantee he has of his innocence (17:3: "take my pledge to you; for who else will give their hand on my behalf?" [author trans.]).

18:1-21. Bildad. Like Eliphaz, Bildad begins his second speech to Job with a rebuke (vv. 2-4) which in turn prepares for a lengthy lecture on the fate of the wicked in a moral universe (vv. 5-21).

Bildad chides Job for insinuating that the friends are dumb cattle (cf. 12:7). It is Job, not God, who is tearing himself apart (v. 4; cf. 16:9). Should the moral order of the *earth* be abandoned, the *rock* of God's impenetrable governance be removed from its place, all because of Job's skewed assessment of things? Bildad knows well that governing ideologies, such as the belief in retributive justice, can sustain their corporate effectiveness only if they remain indifferent to the specifics of individual complaints.

The treatise on the wicked (vv. 5-21) focuses on the certain calamity that awaits them in God's design for the world. In their *tent* (abode) light is extinguished, their stride is shortened, they fall prey to their own schemes, their vitality is consumed by affliction and death (vv. 5-13). They are torn from their *tent* and marched off to the *king of terrors* (v. 14), a reference to Mot (*Death*), the god of the underworld in Canaanite mythology (vv. 14-21). From first to last the destiny of the wicked is portrayed as the inexorable consequence of a self-regulating moral universe. There is but one reference to God in Bildad's entire lecture (v. 21), a single, pointed reminder that it is God who sanctions the system Bildad is defending (cf. Clines 1989, 413).

19:1-29. Job. For the first time since chap. 3, Job does not address God. His anguished questions *How long?* (v. 2) and *Why?* (v. 22), ostensibly intended for God's unresponsive ears, are now directed to the friends. His speech remains focused on complaint (vv. 7-20) and the hope of vindication (vv. 23-27).

Job begins, as usual, by rebuking his friends (vv. 2-6). They have tormented him and broken him apart with arguments that reach to the very center of his existence (*nepeš*, v. 2; NRSV *me*), going beyond the abuse that even "the Satan" was permitted to inflict (cf. 2:5-6). Even if he has strayed, a possibility he does not concede (v. 4; cf. 7:20), his wanderings lodge only within himself; they do not reside with the friends that they should consider themselves the real victims in this ordeal. Job is the victim, and it is none other than God who has "bent" him (v. 6: *put me in the wrong*) with a perverted display of justice (against Bildad, cf. 8:3).

Job's complaint is that he has been violated, and when he has cried out for help, neither the friends nor God proved to be agents of justice for him (vv. 7-20). On the one hand, God and the troops of heaven have laid siege to him (vv. 8-12; cf. 16:9-14). They have surrounded his fragile "tent" as if it were a mighty fortress, blocking all escape routes as if Job were the enemy. Stripped of his *glory* and *crown* (v. 9), like a king imprisoned in his own city, Job is strategically demolished on all sides, until at last every vestige of hope is destroyed (cf. 14:7-9, 14-19).

On the other hand, God has also broken down Job's network of communal support (vv. 13-20). God has alienated everyone from Job: kinsfolk and acquaintances, intimate friends and guests at his table, servants, even his wife and young children. He calls to them, but they do not answer (v. 16). They shun and abandon him like a stranger and an alien. What Job needs from all who would truly befriend him is loyalty (cf. 6:14), especially now that *the hand of God has touched* him (v. 21). What he gets from his so-called friends, instead, is the same kind of relentless abuse that he receives from God.

With no sign of help in heaven or on earth, Job reaches out to a figure called *redeemer* (vv. 23-27). He *know(s)*, i.e., he firmly believes, that his *redeemer* lives. The traditional capitalization of this word in most versions (e.g., NRSV) has influenced a decidedly Christian interpretation of Job's hope as an appeal to a divine Savior, i.e., Jesus (cf. Rouillard 1983, 8-12). The Hebrew *gō 'ēl*, however, refers to the next of kin who has the responsibility of helping a family member in danger of losing possessions (Lev 25:25-34; Jer 32:6-15),their freedom (Lev 25:47-54), or life itself (Num 35:12, 19-27; Deut 19:6, 12; Josh 20:2-5, 9).

The identity of Job's *gō 'ēl* is much debated. Interpreted within the context of Job's previous references to an *umpire* ("arbitrator," 9:33) and a "witness" (16:8), the *redeemer* would appear to be someone whom Job hopes will at last rise on earth to speak in his defense (v. 27). It is possible that Job is appealing to God, even as his enemy and his assailant, to be at the same time his defense attorney. Given the larger context, however, it is likely that Job appeals to a third party to stand in the breach between God and himself, one who would stand at his side, not as adversary, but as ally.

Job's closing words return to a condemnation of the friends (vv. 28-29). They *persecute* (or "pursue") him, aping God's misdirected aggression towards him (cf. v. 22), as if he were the cause of his own misery (v. 28: *the root of the matter is found in him*). They should be afraid, because *there is a judgment* (v. 29) when all who stand in opposition to an innocent victim will suffer the consequences.

20:1-29. Zophar. Zophar begins conventionally with a rebuke of Job and an appeal to corrective wisdom (vv. 2-5). Like the other friends in this cycle, Zophar focuses on the fate of *the wicked* in a moral universe. His thesis, argued at length in vv. 6-29, is enveloped by two summarizing statements (vv. 5, 29): whatever the apparent prosperity of *the wicked*, their ultimate inheritance is determined by God.

With Bildad (8:8) and Eliphaz (15:18-19), Zophar appeals to ancient tradition as his source of corrective wisdom (v. 4). If Job *knows* (cf. 19:25) the truth about God's moral governance of the world, then Job must *know* that the euphoric shouts and joys of *the wicked* are fleeting (v. 5).

To substantiate his argument, Zophar employs a variety of images in order to enlighten Job on the fate of the evildoer. Although their pride and loftiness may extend to *the heavens* (v. 6), their final resting place is *in the dust* of the earth (v. 11). They simply vanish into nothingness, *like their own dung* (v. 7) or a bad *dream* (v. 8), leaving no trace of their haughty existence behind them (v. 9).

Verses 12-23 center on the imagery of eating. *Wickedness* is depicted as food that, although savory and *sweet*, is poisonous and induces vomiting. The focus is on the inherent consequences of eating spoiled goods, although Zophar makes it clear that God is the true source of the sick person's misery (v. 15). The appetite that causes sickness is linked to the wicked's abuse of *the poor* (vv. 19-23). Their greed for possessions not their own will stretch their bellies to the breaking point. While the interval between ingestion, or acquisition (on this correlation see Janzen 1985, 152-53), and pain is not immediate, Job may rest assured that God has filled their stomachs with divine *fierce anger* (v. 23).

The imagery of vv. 24-29 focuses on the violent nature of the wicked's defeat. Their downfall is inevitable. If they escape weapons of *iron*, they will be struck down with arrows of *bronze* that pierce their insides. If they manage to retract the arrow, they will eviscerate themselves. If they survive even this, they will be devoured by supernatural fire, and heaven and earth will rise up against them.

21:1-34. Job. In this last speech of the second cycle, Job turns from the focus on his own suffering (chaps. 16–17, 19) to dispute directly the friends' theology of retribution. He begins (vv. 1-6) and ends (v. 34) by assailing the friends' misguided efforts to offer *consolation* (v. 1). His arguments against them are prefaced with three questions (vv. 7, 17, 28), each of which challenges some previous claim of the friends, and to which Job responds with his own contradicting witness (vv. 7-16, 17-26, 27-33). In keeping with the steady deterioration in the divine-human dialogue that has characterized this cycle of speeches, Job does not address God.

Job implores the friends to *listen carefully* to his words (v. 2) and to *look* squarely at his suffering (v. 5). If they are to speak meaningfully to his pain, they must weep with his eyes and understand calamity through his experience. If they would really look at Job, rather than only speak *at him*, they would be appalled, and his shuddering flesh would silence their empty words. Job's complaint is with God. It is God's justice, not a mortal's failings, that is called into question when an innocent person is victimized.

Job begins his counterattack by challenging Zophar's contention that the wicked enjoy only temporary prosperity (cf. 20:5-11). If Zophar is right, why then do the wicked live long and happy lives (vv. 7-12) and go to their graves in peace (v. 13)? In contrast to Job who has suffered the loss of family, home, and possessions, the wicked enjoy the blessing of children,

the security of their houses, and the fertility of their flocks. Their lives are accompanied by the music of unrestrained joy and celebration. They are confident in their powers to control their own destinies. They scoff at the idea that piety has anything to do with the rewards that one can attain in life (v. 14-15). Verse 16 may be read as an affirmation of the friends' certitude: "Indeed our prosperity is not in His hands" (Gordis 1965, 91; cf. Habel 1985, 321; Janzen 1985, 156).

Job's second challenge (vv. 17-26) centers on Bildad's claim that the *lamp of the wicked [is] put out* (cf. 18:5-6). How often, in truth, does calamity come to the wicked? In reality, it is the innocent, like Job, who are driven *like chaff* before the wind of God's anger, not the wicked (v. 18; cf. 13:25). The explanation that God's judgment is stored up for the wicked's children (v. 19) is meaningless. As far as the wicked are concerned, when persons die the question of their innocence or guilt goes to the grave with them (vv. 21-26). The silence of death mutes all questions of injustice on earth.

Job's third challenge (vv. 27-33) continues the argument against the claim that calamity befalls the wicked. The specific focus is on *the house of the* "great one" (NRSV *prince*) and the *tent [of] the wicked* (v. 28). The friends have repeatedly asserted that the houses of the wicked would not survive the destruction God has prepared for them (cf. 8:14-15; 15:28, 34; 18:15-21; 20:26-28). Job counters that *those who travel the roads* (v. 29) know better. The wicked do not receive what they deserve. Instead, their houses are spared the day of calamity, and when they die, their earthly estates are replaced by guarded memorials (v. 32).

In sum, Job turns the theology of the friends upside down. God does not cause the righteous to prosper; God does not punish the wicked. Reality affirms exactly the opposite. Theology that does not square with the facts of life is *hebel*, empty as air (v. 32; cf. the repeated use of this term in Ecclesiastes, e.g., 1:2). Worse still, when empty words of theology are foisted on the suffering, it is an act of fraud.

Third Cycle: The Breakdown of the Dialogue, 22:1–27:33

22:1-30. Eliphaz. In his last speech Eliphaz begins by posing a series of rhetorical questions designed to persuade Job of the undeniable linkage between his mortality and his sinfulness (vv. 2-5). These questions introduce two specific indictments against Job (vv. 6-

11, 12-20) and a concluding summons to repentance (vv. 21-30).

In his previous speeches Eliphaz had stressed the fundamental distinction between God and humanity: God is incomparably righteous; humanity is inherently flawed and blemished (cf. 4:17-19; 15:14-16). Now Eliphaz pushes this observation to the extreme (vv. 2-5). Can mortals do anything to profit God? Does God derive any pleasure from a person's righteousness? Is God so concerned with the piety of individuals (or, to imagine the opposite, their impiety) that God stoops to enter into a lawsuit either for or against them? The prologue has made clear that God is in fact concerned with such matters. But Eliphaz' attention here is directed towards what separates God from humanity, not towards the exploration of whatever in the divine economy might bind them together. He concentrates on what for him is a more important issue: Job's sinfulness.

His first accusation (vv. 6-11) cites a number of moral crimes of which Job is allegedly guilty. Job has oppressed the weak and the poor and favored the powerful. No evidence is offered in support of the charges, either by Eliphaz or elsewhere in the Book of Job, and the reader must therefore consider them to be false. For Eliphaz, however, the immediate need is to press ahead with the guilty verdict (vv. 10-11).

The second accusation (vv. 12-20) attributes to Job theological error. Eliphaz presumes to quote Job's views on God's transcendence, *viz.* that God is so far removed *in the heavens*, God cannot know or judge accurately the affairs of humanity on earth (vv. 12-14). Such a misinterpretation of God's mysterious otherness places Job in the company of the wicked who revel in their misdeeds while asking *What can the Almighty do to us?* (v. 17). Again, Job's guilt is determined quite apart from the evidence of his own words, which consistently affirm God's ability to see and know humanity's deeds (cf. 7:19-20; 14:3; 16:9).

For Eliphaz the solution to Job's separation from God is clear. Job must yield to God and thus secure his peace and restoration (vv. 21-30). Yielding to God means accepting a contractual relationship with the deity (cf. 8:5-7; 11:13-20). *If* Job returns to God; *if* he removes deceit from his life; *if* he learns to replace his own lesser treasures with those of greater value God has in store for him (vv. 23-25); *then* Job will be restored. He will have pleasure in God (v. 26); his prayers will be answered (v. 27); and he will be rescued from the fate that awaits the wicked (vv. 29-30).

23:1–24:25. Job. Job abandons the failed dialogue with the friends and withdraws to the kind of interior reflection that characterized his words in chap. 3 (cf. Janzen 1985, 164–65). He longs for the presence of the absent God, with both confidence (23:3-7) and fear (23:8-16). His hope, however, begins and ends with lament (23:2, 17).

For Job, God's absence is the causal link to the injustices of *the wicked*. They freely abuse the poor and the powerless, and God pays no attention (24:1-12). They work their evil ways by day and by night (24:13-17). Job knows the argument that they will not finally succeed (24:18-20), but the evidence is that their success is assured by none other than God (24:21-25).

Eliphaz had summoned Job to submission before God. In his view, when one suffers, the only proper response is to pray for forgiveness (cf. 22:21-30). But when Job stretches out his hand in prayer it is heavy with a groaning that will not yield, and in his piety he offers rebellion and defiance (23:2: "my complaint is defiant" [cf. NRSV mg.]).

Job's compelling hope and lingering fear is that he might yet find God. On the one hand he eagerly awaits the encounter, because he remains confident that in God's presence an upright person (*yāšār*, v. 7; cf. 1:1) will be given the chance to argue without impunity. God would not use divine power to prosecute Job, but would pay attention to a just cause (23:3-7).

On the other hand, Job searches the far corners of the world, but God remains ever hidden (23:8-9). Job persists in believing that if he could find God's hiding place, his claim to be innocent would be vindicated (23:10-12). Yet in hiddenness, God retains exclusive control over divine decisions. "God is one" (23:13, NRSV *he stands alone*), and in this absolute oneness, God's desires effect decisions that are irrevocable (23:13-14). Before such overwhelming power, Job is terrified. The "face" from which he seeks justice (23:4; literally, "to his face"), is the "face" that strikes fear in the one who seeks a fair trial (23:15-16).

From the lament about the hiddenness of God, Job turns to the consequences of the absence of divine justice for the righteous and the wicked. Why do those who know God never see God's days of judgment? (24:1) When the timetable for the realization of justice on earth is as hidden as God, then injustice rules without restraint. The wicked snatch and seize at will. Like wild asses they prey on the defenseless, stripping them of the basic necessities of life. Victims are left to die, their only resource a wounded cry for help to a God who does not see that anything is wrong (24:2-12).

When there is no timetable for the execution of divine justice, then the governing cycles of the world are reversed. The wicked rebel against the light and embrace darkness as their accomplice in crime. Day's light is shut out; darkness of night beckons evildoers to their missions (24:13-17).

The relation of 24:18-25 to the speech as a whole is disputed. Because the content of these verses, particularly vv. 18-20, appears to contradict Job's position elsewhere, a number of commentators suggest that they comprise part of the missing speech of Zophar in the third cycle (cf. Pope 1965, 168-74; Rowley 1970, 210-13; Habel 1985, 358). If Job is the speaker, the verses likely represent a quotation of the friends' position (cf. Gordis 1978, 533; Janzen 1985, 169).

25:1-6. Bildad. In the final speeches of cycle three (chaps. 25–27) the steady alternating exchange between Job and the friends ends. Bildad's speech is disproportionately short (25:2-6); Job's response is long (chaps. 26–27), and in several places inconsistent with his previous positions (26:5-14; 27:13-24); and Zophar's final speech appears to be missing altogether. Many scholars attempt to restore order to these chapters by rearranging the text in order to lengthen Bildad's speech (by adding 26:5-14) and to reconstruct Zophar's speech (from 27:13-24; e.g., Pope 1965; Gordis 1978; Habel 1985). The option favored here, however, is to interpret the disarray of the text as a clue that the dialogue between Job and the friends has broken down (Janzen 1985, 171-86; cf. Good 1990, 281-90).

Bildad's words in 25:2-6 return to themes that have been well rehearsed in previous speeches. God is incomparably powerful, making peace in the cosmos with "awesome dominion" (NRSV dominion and fear, vv. 2-3; Gordis 1978, 274). If the luminescence of the moon and the stars cannot match the purity of God, how can a mere mortal, a maggot, a worm, expect to measure up? (vv. 4-6).

26:1-14. Job. To Bildad's affirmation of God's power, Job responds sarcastically by asking how such a claim can offer any comfort to him (vv. 2-4). He does not dispute his powerlessness and vulnerability before God. But how can a defense of God's incontestable power be construed as "help" or "assistance" or even "counsel" to one innocently victimized by God's prowess? What can possibly be the inspiration for such words?

Verses 5-14 comprise a hymn about divine power. On the surface they appear to be an elaboration on the theme of God's "awe" and "dominion" that is consistent with Bildad's argument in 25:2-6 (cf. Habel 1985, 370-75). Thus these verses are often reassigned as the completion of Bildad's speech. Yet the present configuration of the text attributes the words to Job and thus invites us to interpret them as indicative of his impatience with arguments he has heard already too often.

Job too can affirm God's control over the cosmos, but from his perspective divine dominion elicits cowed submission, not adoration and reverence (cf. Good 1990, 285). The "shades of the dead writhe" before God's power (v. 5, author trans.); Sheol—and its parallel identification, Abaddon—are exposed (v. 6). The heavenly canopy yields to God's stretching and hanging and wrapping and circumscribing (vv. 7-10). The pillars of heaven "tremble" (v. 11), and the primordial opponents of God are smitten and defeated (v. 12-13). Indeed, such evidences of God's complete subjugation of the cosmos are but a whisper compared to the thunder of God's limitless power (vv. 13-14).

27:1-23. Job again. On the heels of his paean to God's dominating power, Job pauses, as if awaiting the retort of Zophar (note the modified introduction to the speech in v. 1). The text preserves no response from Zophar, and the third cycle is brought to conclusion with Job continuing to push his own position. He begins with an oath of innocence (vv. 2-6), followed by a curse against his enemy (vv. 7-12). Verses 13-23 conclude the speech with a description of the destiny of the wicked.

Job swears to his innocence by taking an oath on "the life of God" (vv. 2-6, author trans.). The oath is a potential self-curse that calls on God to bring down on him unspoken calamity if what he swears is not true. It is a "catalytic action" (Habel 1985, 380) designed to force a response from the one whose name has been invoked. Paradoxically, Job swears by the life of the one who has denied him justice and embittered his soul. Thus even in this act of desperation, Job remains true to his sense that God is both enemy and ally. The substance of the oath (vv. 4-6) asserts that if Job is guilty of falsehood or deceit, may God be vindicated and Job's punishment be as God decrees. But until his guilt is established, Job will not relinquish his claim to integrity and righteousness.

Job follows his oath with a curse upon his enemy (vv. 7-12). While in vv. 11-12 the address is to you (pl.), presumably meaning the friends, the reference to enemy in v. 7 is singular. The logical referent is God whom Job has repeatedly claimed was his real adversary (cf. 13:24; 16:9; 19:11). In his imprecation Job calls for his enemy (God, and to the extent that they side with God, the friends) to be accorded the same treatment as the wicked. With astonishing audacity Job dares to imagine that if his adversary could know the hopelessness of one whose cries for justice are not heard, then perhaps at last the way would be open to a fair resolution of his case.

Verses 13-23 describe the fate of the wicked in a fashion very similar to the speeches of the friends in cycle two. Because an affirmation of the wicked's downfall seems so out of character for Job, these verses are often reassigned to Zophar as his missing speech in the third cycle. The only attribution in the chapter, however, names Job as the speaker. If we follow this clue, then it is suggestive to imagine that Job has grown so weary of hearing the standard line on the punishment of the wicked that he preempts Zophar's anticipated tired rendition by delivering the speech himself (cf. Janzen 1985, 185-86).

Meditation on Wisdom, 28:1-28

This hymn on the inaccessibility of wisdom has been the focus of enormous scholarly scrutiny, but as yet there is no real consensus on important questions. Who is the speaker, Job, one of the friends, or God? Who is the author of the poem, and is the author the same one responsible for the rest of the book? Does the poem date to the earliest stages of the book, or is it an independent and later insertion? And what is the function of the poem in the Book of Job? To each of these questions there are multiple answers and speculations.

In the absence of consensus on the poem's authorship and date, it is wise to concentrate on its function in the present context. And lacking any definitive indication of a change in speaker, it is plausible to attribute the poem to the last mentioned speaker in the book, viz., Job.

The poem serves as a fitting end to the dialogue between Job and the friends, and a key transition towards what will be explored in the rest of the book. As a closure to the dialogues, the poem ends with a reaffirmation of the importance of the *fear of the Lord* and turning away *from evil* (v. 28), virtues the prologue has repeatedly assigned to Job (cf. 1:1, 8; 2:3). These virtues are then further identified as the

key to wisdom and understanding. But if the poem serves to reaffirm Job's piety, it also challenges the simple identification of piety with justice. Job *fears God* and *turns away from evil* (1:8), yet Job is suffering. Clearly there must be more to come before a critical challenge to the traditional understanding of wisdom's rewards can be resolved.

The poem divides into three major sections, vv. 1-14, 15-22, and 23-28, each of which explores the *place* of wisdom (vv. 1, 6, 12, 20, 23) and the *path* (or "way," vv. 7-8, 13, 23) towards its acquisition (cf. Habel 1985, 392-94). Two questions provide the refrain that guides the search for wisdom (vv. 12, 20) and points in the direction of the right answer: God understands the "way" and knows the "place" of wisdom (v. 23).

28:1-14. Wisdom's inaccessibility. The poem begins with an affirmation (vv. 1-6) but ends with a question that negates the possibilities of finding wisdom (vv. 12-14). There is a *mine* (lit., a "coming out place") and a *place* where the earth hides its precious metals of *silver, gold, iron,* and *copper* (vv. 1-2). Although the path to these precious stones cannot be discerned by the sharpest vision of any *bird* or the rovings of even the mightiest of beasts (vv. 7-8), the ingenuity of human miners can achieve relative success (vv. 1-6, 9-11). Miners can open shafts, suspend themselves in the bowels of earth's deep darkness, overturn mountains by their roots, and cut channels to reveal precious things ordinary eyes can never behold.

But even with such skills, mortals cannot discern the *place* of *wisdom* (vv. 12-14). They may know the way to the depths of the earth, but when they arrive at the end of their probe, they hear the primordial sources of the watery abyss say, wisdom is not here.

28:15-22. Wisdom's incomparable value. A catalogue of thirteen precious materials is listed in vv. 15-19. Before each item there is a negative particle (seven times), indicating that whatever the value of this particular treasure, it cannot equal the greater worth of wisdom.

If wisdom cannot be found through human ingenuity, and if it cannot be acquired through buying and selling precious commodities, where then is wisdom to be found? (vv. 20-22). Once more the question introduces a negative response. Wisdom is not only inaccessible and incomparable; it is also hidden. Even *Abaddon* (i.e., *Sheol,* cf. 26:6) and Death (*māwet,* an allusion to the Canaanite God Mot, the god of the underworld; cf. 18:13) have only hearsay knowledge of this most prized possession.

28:23-28. The way to wisdom. The final section offers the answer to the questions posed by the refrains of vv. 12 and 20. God *understands* and *knows* the *way* (or "path") to wisdom. Surprisingly, this answer does not affirm that wisdom is an inherent attribute of God. Rather, just as mortals "dig out" (*hqr*, 28:3) the treasures hidden in the depths of the earth, so God "digs out" (*hqr*, v. 27; NRSV *searches out*) wisdom as the primordial ordering principle of the world. In the act of weighing the wind, measuring the waters of the cosmos, decreeing the limits of rain and thunder, God searches out and establishes the place of wisdom in governing the whole of the created order. Thus wisdom both precedes God (cf. Prov 8:22-31) and is employed by God in the primordial creative act.

God attains wisdom through direct experience. Mortals, however, possess wisdom only derivatively. God alone discloses ('*mr*, v. 28, "say") what the *deep*, *the sea*, *Abaddon*, and *Death* can never make known ('*mr*, vv. 14, 22, "say"). Wisdom as revealed by God consists not in striving for hidden knowledge, but in piety, specifically in *fearing God* and in *turning away from evil*, the very qualities that, according to God, define Job (cf. 1:8; 2:3).

The reader knows from the prologue that, by God's definition, Job is unfailingly innocent. Now the reader is instructed to understand that, by God's definition, Job is a recipient of the divine gift of wisdom. Job is innocent and wise, yet besieged by God. God is unassailably righteous and unfathomably wise. Given these truths that the book has brought to the fore, what is to be the relationship between God and this suffering servant? The dialogue with the friends over this dilemma has ended. But the dialogue that will push the dilemma to its farthest extremes is yet to begin.

Job's Summation, 29:1–31:40

Job closes the dialogues as he began them, in internal deliberation. But much has transpired since Job's opening soliloquy. In chap. 3 his pain had driven him to despair of life and to long for the relief of death. In these closing chapters Job refuses to relinquish the truth about either his integrity (chap. 29) or his pain (chap. 30). Integrity and pain are now forged into a renewed oath of innocence (chap. 31; cf. 27:2-6) that challenges God to appear at last for the trial which Job has sought (cf. 23:3-7).

Declaration of Past Integrity, 29:1-25

29:1-10. Past status. Job opens with a declaration that reaffirms his past status with God (vv. 2-6) and in the community (vv. 7-10). He remembers his "autumn days" when he enjoyed both the presence and the friendship of God (v. 4). Under the "lamp" and the "light" of God's protection and sustenance, Job experienced the blessing of children all around (v. 5) and prosperity abundant (v. 6). His honored status was acknowledged by the community. When Job took his place at the city gate to adjudicate the disputes of his peers, they would rise in recognition of his stature, and their words would cease in willing submission to his authority (vv. 7-10).

29:11-17. Administration of justice. His recognized authority was confirmed in his administration of justice in the community (vv. 11-17). Every ear that heard of Job's decisions blessed him, and every eye that witnessed his counsel encouraged him. Contrary to Eliphaz's charge (cf. 22:6-11), Job never failed to respond to the cries of the needy and the disenfranchised. His justice was directed specifically to those who are vulnerable to abuse: *the poor*, *the orphan*, *the widow* (vv. 12-13), *the blind*, *the lame* (v. 15). Even the cause of those whom Job did not know was investigated (v. 16). Indeed, Job did not merely dispense justice, he embodied it, clothing himself with *righteousness* (*sdq*), so that *justice* (*mišpāt*) was like his *robe* and his *turban* (v. 14).

29:18-20. Hope. His devotion to justice became a reason for hope. He had thought that he would be granted the blessing of dying in his nest, and like the immortal *phoenix* (on this imagery see Gordis 1978, 320-21), his honored reputation (NRSV *glory*) would be ever secure.

29:21-25. Leadership and compassion. Job's position in the community was tied not only to his administration of justice. It was also the result of his unfailing compassion and concern for his neighbors' general welfare. The community looked to him with the same need they had for the spring rains. Job smiled upon them with favor. Even when they would not believe, they could not extinguish the guiding light of his countenance. Rather than abandon them to their own resources, Job chose their course for them. *Like a king among his troops* (v. 25), Job was their leader and their comforter.

Job's declaration of integrity serves in the interest of more than just self-flattery. It also continues indirectly his challenge to God. Job asserts with unmitigated confidence that he has been the ideal judge. He has heard the cries of those who look to him for justice, and he has responded by breaking the strangle-hold of the wicked on their helpless prey. Can God claim as much? Job has faithfully presided over the welfare of those entrusted to him, providing for their needs and comforting them when they mourn. Can God claim to have offered the same faithfulness to those who look to the heavens for their guidance and consolation? Job has been both judge and king for his community. Who will be judge and king for Job?

Acknowledgment of Present Misery, 30:1-31

30:1-8. Public scorn. If once Job had been among the honored of society (chap.29), now he is the object of public scorn. To add insult to injury, those who now find him contemptible are themselves outcasts of society. They are compared to animals who, driven out from their community, live in caves and bray in the bushes. Job refers to them as the children of the "foolish" and the "nameless" (v. 8). As fools (nābāl), they share the moral and religious blindness (cf. Ps 14:1) attributed to Job's wife (cf. 2:10). As nameless ones, they have no identity, no recognized value in society.

30:9-15. Public hostility. The perspective shifts from the character of Job's antagonists to their actions. Job is the "butt of their jokes" (v. 9), like one ostracized from the community and spit upon whenever he breaches the strictures of their alienation. Not content with ridicule, these opponents add all-out attack (vv. 12-15). With the efficiency of an army they build roads for the siege, they break through Job's defenses, and they put him to rout. Such abuse is possible, Job charges, because God has in fact loosened his "cord" (perhaps "tent cord," cf. 4:21; perhaps bowstring [as NRSV]; cf. Ps 11:2), leaving him defenseless before his attackers (v. 11).

30:16-19. God, the assailant. Job's real enemy, however, is God. Days of affliction take hold of Job, and pain chews on his bones throughout the night without relief, but it is God who seizes him with power beyond resistance (v. 18, reading God as the implied subject; cf. Pope 1965, 195). God has flung him into the mud, and he has been reduced to nothingness, like dust and ashes (v. 19).

The phrase dust and ashes recalls Job's previous posture of mourning (2:8). On that occasion Job accepted his suffering as the incomprehensible consequence of God's sovereignty. Now his assignment to dust and ashes is interpreted as an act of divine violence, as senseless as the wanton abuse heaped on him by the rogues of society. Job will make one further reference to his position in dust and ashes (42:6), a final response to the nothingness that defines his life.

30:20-31. Cry for justice. These verses focus on Job's cry for justice (šw ', vv. 20, 24, 28). Job cries to God (vv. 20-23), but there is no answer. God has become the cruel one (v. 21: 'akzār), raging against him with the same ferocity attributed to Leviathan, the primordial monster ('akzār; cf. 41:10 [MT 41:2]). In contrast to God's cruelty, Job recalls his own compassion for those who cried for help in a time of need (vv. 24-27). Now Job cries for justice in the assembly, but his cries are as futile as the doleful sounds of jackals . . . ostriches (vv. 24-28). In a world where cries for justice go unheeded both by God and the sanctioned system, evil replaces good, darkness preempts light (v. 26), and instruments for happy occasions accompany mourning and weeping (v. 31; cf. 21:12).

Oaths of Innocence, 31:1-40

31:1-4. Declaration of covenant fidelity. Job's declaration of innocence derives from the covenant he has made with his eyes (v. 1). It is a covenant pledge that Job has sworn to avoid even the appearance of wrongdoing. He will not even look on a virgin, though to do so would in itself be no crime. His decision to master not only his actions but also his attitudes was based on his conviction that there is indeed a fixed destiny for the wicked. The rhetorical questions of vv. 3-4 both state this conviction and hint at Job's uncertainty about whether it continues to apply.

31:5-34, 38-40. Oaths of innocence. In support of his assertion of innocence, Job lists a catalogue of sins from which he insists he is free. The exact number of sins that he disavows is difficult to determine (proposals range from eleven to sixteen), in part because a variety of different literary forms are mixed together throughout the list: questions (vv. 14-15); statements (vv. 6, 11-12, 18, 23, 28, 30, 32); and self-imprecations.

The imprecations proper follow two patterns. The traditional form consists of an "if (not)" ('im) phrase (protasis), which presents a crime or sin, followed by a "result" clause (apodosis), which stipulates the punishment expected. In other words, "If I have done A . . . then let B happen to me." This pattern is followed in vv. 7-8, 9-10, 21-22, and 38-40. A variation of the traditional pattern has an "if" clause without the "result" clause. In these cases the conditional statement about sin/crime is assumed to be false. Thus the incomplete statement "If I have done A . . . " is an emphatic way of saying "I have *not* done A." This pattern is more frequent in Job's speech, occurring in vv. 5, 13, 16-17, 19-20, 24, 25, 26-27, 29, 31, 33-34.

The sins stipulated in these two patterns cover a wide range of both actions (e.g., adultery, vv. 9-10; withholding food from the poor, vv. 16-17; exploiting the land, vv. 38-40) and attitudes (e.g., rejoicing in the calamity of others, v. 29; hypocrisy, v. 33). Interlaced with these disclaimers of sin are a number of personal statements that express Job's abhorrence of the sins he is denying (v. 11), his intimate friendships with the disadvantaged whom he insists he has not abused (v. 18), and his understanding that his ethical purity is fundamentally an extension of his relationship with God (vv. 6, 14-15, 23).

Job's oaths of innocence portray him as the epitome of the ethical person. While the prologue affirms that Job is *blameless and upright, one fearing God and turning away from evil* (1:1, 8; 2:3), this summation of his innocence defines in concrete ways how these virtues manifest themselves in Job's life.

31:35-37. Final plea. Job affixes his signature to these oaths of innocence with a final plea that God will address his case in court (vv. 35-37). His plea begins with the formula "Oh, that" (*mi yitten*), an expression used more frequently in Job than in any other book. It is an expression that introduces Job's most important hopes (e.g., 6:8; 14:13; 19:23; 23:3; 29:2; cf. Habel 1985, 347). In this final plea Job's hope is that God, his *adversary* at law (*'îš rîb*, v. 35; Habel 1985, 438), will not only hear and answer him, but will also submit to the court a written document.

The content of this document is not specified. It may constitute a formal indictment (Gordis 1978, 355; Fohrer 1974, 3) or a writ of acquittal (Pope, 1965, 209; Habel 1985, 439). This document Job will wear as a "paper crown" (Habel 1985, 439) when he at last meets God in court. He will come with his own self-assertion of innocence and with this formal attestation, which will either exonerate him or be proven once and for all as an empty indictment.

He will address *the Almighty*, not as the guilty one who must relinquish all arguments before an inscrutable judge (as the friends would have him do), but as *a prince* (v. 37; cf. 29:11-17, 21-25) whose royal status emboldens him to approach God as an equal (cf. Good 1990, 316; Perdue 1991, 193). Although God may

number all his steps (v. 4), Job will assume a joint responsibility for "numbering" (*spr*; NRSV *give an account*) his own steps before the God who sits in judgment over him. As a measure of his courage in demanding this appearance before God, Job places these strong statements within the context of the self-imprecations that have defined the center of his speech. *If* Job does not/cannot approach God (cf. v. 36, *'im lō '*, lit. "If I do not...") as one who has joint responsibility for accounting for his ways, *then* may he suffer the consequences that God has in store for him.

Speeches of Elihu, 32:1–37:24

Introduction of Elihu, the "Answerer," 32:1-22

32:1-5. Introduction. With Job's words ended, the narrative anticipates the long-awaited answer from God. An answer is offered in chaps. 32–37, but it comes from Elihu, not from God. The speeches commence with a lengthy "throat-clearing introduction" (Good 1990, 321). Not until 33:1 will Elihu address Job directly.

Although the introduction provides more information about Elihu than has been given about the other friends, it is not really family credentials that define him. It is his anger (four times in vv. 2-5) and his concern with the *answer* (three times in vv. 1, 3, 5) that must be obtained in the case against Job. Ten of the sixty occurrences of the root *answer* in Job appear in this chapter (cf. Habel 1985, 445). Elihu is angry with Job because Job thought himself more righteous than God (v. 2). Elihu is angry with the friends because they could offer no convincing answers to Job, thus making it appear God, not Job, was guilty (vv. 3, 4).

32:6-10. Elihu's claim to knowledge. Elihu commences with an admission of the discrepancy between his youth and the age of the friends. Normally, with many years comes wisdom. But upon listening to the friends, Elihu concludes that wisdom and understanding are not synonymous with advanced age. It is rather the spirit, *the breath of the Almighty* (v. 8), within a person that discloses understanding. Elihu claims to possess this spirit (cf. v. 18). He will speak; the imperative to listen now falls to others (v. 10).

32:11-16. Elihu's impatience. These verses begin and end with a reference to Elihu's "waiting" futilely for the friends' wisdom. Elihu has listened to their *words* and their *wise sayings* (v. 11), and he has found them lacking. The friends do not have the necessary wisdom to serve as the "arbiter" of Job's case (v. 12, *mōkiāh*; NRSV *one that confutes*). When Job had sought someone to arbitrate, he had envisioned someone who would lay hands on both God and himself in order to facilitate a fair and just legal proceeding (cf. 9:33). What Elihu intends, however, is one who will answer Job (v. 12b; cf. 14, 15, 16), that is, prove him wrong.

32:17-22. Elihu's compulsion to speak. Elihu describes himself as so full of *spirit* (or "wind," v. 18; cf. v. 8) that his belly is bloated. The only relief is to belch forth words. Such enthusiasm for speaking, however, identifies him more closely with the fool than the wise person. Ironically, belching forth windy words is precisely the criticism that Eliphaz used to challenge Job's claim to wisdom (cf. 15:2). That Elihu claims a status he will not demonstrate is further indicated by his pretended impartiality (vv. 21-22). Despite his assertion, his speech thus far is replete with references to his undisguised anger at the friends and at Job, and his conclusion that neither has any answer that is worth listening to.

The Case against Job, 33:1-33

33:1-7. The challenge to Job. Elihu reasserts his legitimacy as Job's "Answerer" (vv. 3-4), and challenges Job to enter into a disputation with him. He summons Job to prepare his case and take his stand *before him* (v. 5). Job had summoned God to appear in court to hear the case he had prepared, and had challenged God to speak so that Job might refute the charges against him (cf. 13:17-28). Now Elihu presumes to stand in for God, and at the same time he reverses the ground rules for the confrontation Job has sought. Elihu will issue the summons to Job to appear in court; Elihu will be the prosecutor (and judge), Job the defendant.

33:8-13. The charges against Job. Elihu cites two charges that Job has levelled against God: Job is innocent, yet God treats him as an enemy (vv. 8-11); and God does not answer Job (vv. 12-13). Elihu counters that *in this* Job is not right, and as refutation he states simply that God is greater than humans (v. 12; the issue of God's justice will be addressed more fully in chaps. 34–37). The focal point of Elihu's challenge is Job's accusation that God does not answer him (v. 13; cf. 9:2-4).

33:14-30. Defense of God's answering. Elihu offers a lengthy defense of God's multiple ways of answering people, even if they do not discern what God is saying. First, God speaks through dreams that warn against pride and seek to turn people from their misdeeds (vv. 15-18). Second, God speaks through pain and suffering (vv. 19-22) that serve to "chasten" (*hûkah*) and put one on trial (*ryb*, v. 19; NRSV *with continual strife*). Further, for those tested by suffering, there is an *angel* (lit. "messenger," *mal'āk*), an "interpreter" (NRSV *mediator*, *mēlîs*), who gives instructions about morality (v. 23), and obtains for the afflicted a ransom and a restoration (vv. 23-26).

These multiple ways of divine communication are framed by an ascending numeration (v. 14, *in one way, and in two*; v. 29, *twice, three times*), which serves to emphasize God's persistence in seeking to speak to people (cf. Good 1990, 324). The purpose of God's efforts is to redeem humanity *from the Pit*, that is, from death (v. 30; cf. vv. 18, 24, 28).

33:31-33. Summation. Elihu extends an apparent invitation to Job to respond. But it is more instruction than invitation. Three times he orders Job to *listen* or *pay heed* to him; twice the instruction is *be silent*. Although Job is given an opening, it is a small one, and it closes quickly as Elihu makes it clear that *he* will address the issue of what is Job's "right" (*sdq*, v. 32).

Defense of God's Justice, 34:1–35:16

The superscriptions at 34:1 and 35:1 introduce these chapters as two separate speeches of Elihu. In terms of their content, however, these chapters share a common concern: the defense of God's justice. In chap. 34 the focus is on Job's charge that he is innocent and that God is in the wrong. Chapter 35 centers on Job's claim that whether he is innocent or guilty, it makes no difference to God. Elihu disputes these charges with lengthy and often entangled theological argumentation, and concludes that in both accusations Job has spoken *without knowledge* (34:35; 35:16).

34:1-9. Summons. Elihu opens with a summons to his peers, the wise and learned ones (vv. 2, 10, 34), to heed his words. Together they will choose what constitutes *justice* (*mišpāt*) and what is *good* (*tôb*) or "legally defensible" (Habel 1985, 481). To put the matter before this tribunal, Elihu cites two of Job's allegations against God (vv. 5-9): Job is innocent, and yet God has denied him justice (*mišpāt*; vv. 5-6); and there is no profit in being in God's favor (v. 9).

Elihu's prejudice in making the case against Job, however, is only thinly disguised. His representation of Job's position borders on being caricature rather than quotation. The first citation seems to be a reference to Job's argument in 27:2, although in Job's mouth the charge is set within the context of an "if-then" self-imprecation. The citation in v. 9 connects with several places in Job's argument (cf. 9:22; 21:7-12); however, the words that Elihu uses are closer to what Eliphaz has said (22:2; cf. Gordis 1978, 244; Good 1990, 142). Adding further to the impression that Elihu is anything but impartial is the insertion in vv. 7-8 of unsubstantiated allegations against Job.

34:10-30. Defense of God's justice. God is not wrong (v. 10), Elihu announces, and God does not pervert the cause of justice (*mišpāt*, v. 12). Two virtues of the divine judge, justice (v. 11) and incomparable power (vv. 13-15), become the center of Elihu's defense in vv. 16-30.

God is both "just" (*sdq*) and powerful (*kabbîr*, v. 17; NRSV *righteous, mighty*). God is certainly just, because God sees all the deeds of humans and faithfully enacts the justice of retribution where it is needed (vv. 21-22, 25-28). And God is just as certainly a judge with inscrutable power, because God's decisions do not require/permit the consultation of others (vv. 23-24). Who will say that God is wrong? When God is absent, who will be able to discern anything different? (v. 29).

34:31-37. Summons to confession. It is Job who must reassess his position, not Elihu, and the court awaits his response. Once more the invitation for Job to speak is more formal than substantive (cf. 33:31-33). As Elihu rushes on to say, the verdict against Job is already in (vv. 34-37). The intelligent and the wise in Elihu's audience will certainly have already concluded that Job's accusations are *without knowledge* (34:35; 35:16).

35:1-4. The advantages and disadvantages of piety. Elihu rehearses Job's position on the advantages and disadvantages of piety. Again Elihu's representation of Job's words is skewed. Job had not argued that he was "more righteous than God" (v. 2, author trans.); rather, he had asked rhetorically (and despairingly), *How can a mortal be just before God?* (9:2). It is Eliphaz who comes closest to the words Elihu assigns to Job (cf. 4:17). And Job had not asked specifically, "How does it benefit you, what do I gain if I avoid sin?" (v. 3, author trans.). It is Eliphaz who uses the language that Elihu cites, and he does so to deny that Job's righteousness makes any difference to God (22:2-4).

35:5-16. Defense of God's relationship with humanity. Elihu offers two observations concerning God's relationship with humanity. First, he appeals to God's transcendence (vv. 5-8). As high as the heavens and the clouds are above the earth, so God is above any-

thing that humans do or do not do in their creaturely ways. God is not affected personally by any individual's actions for good or evil. Goodness and evil redound to the virtue or the disgrace of humans, but God gains or loses nothing either way.

Secondly, Elihu explores the allegation that divine transcendence masks God's sinister silence (vv. 9-13). That some cry out to God for relief but receive no answer does not constitute evidence against God's concern for humanity. The truth of divine silence is that human entreaties are often unauthentic. God will not reward deceit masquerading as piety. On what ground then does Job dare equate God's silence with injustice? Job's arguments are empty and his accusations against God are *without knowledge* (vv. 14-16).

A Second Defense of God's Justice: The Majesty and Order of Creation, 36:1–37:24

36:1-15. The pedagogy of divine affliction. Elihu returns to the theme of God's incomparable power (cf. 34:10-30). God is *mighty* (*kabbîr*, twice in v. 5), a virtue that he equates with divine justice (vv. 5-15). God governs by giving death to the wicked and justice (*mišpāt*) to the oppressed. If some are *bound in fetters* and *caught in the cords of affliction* (v. 8), it is only the corrective discipline of God who seeks to instruct them about the error of their ways (cf. 33:19-22). Espousing the same kind of contractual relationship with God that the friends have advanced (cf. 8:4-7; 11:13-20; 22:21-30), Elihu contends that the afflicted are afforded two options: *if* they listen and serve God, they can complete their lives in prosperity and pleasantness; *if not*, they will die in ignorance (vv. 11-12).

36:16-25. Warning and summons. It is these two options that Job has before him. Elihu suggests that Job is tilting toward the latter rather than the former (vv. 16-21). He is obsessed with his case and his pursuit of justice, as if by the strength of his own efforts he could remedy his distress. Elihu warns that such misplaced passion will turn Job toward evil, not toward God.

It is to God that Job is summoned (vv. 22-25). It is God who is exalted in power; God who has no peer either as teacher or as judge. Before such incontestable power, the proper response is submission (cf. 36:11 *'ābad, serve*) and praise, not rebellion.

36:26–37:13. Praise of God's cosmic governance. The praise of which Elihu speaks is defined in terms of the majesty and order of God's creation. The testimony to God's governance is *in rain* (vv. 27-29), and in the thunder and *the lightning* (36:30–37:4) through which God both judges the people and sustains the created order. It is in the winter storms, the snow, the rains, the frost, which serve as signs for all to see, humans and animals alike, that God is at work regulating the habitable world in keeping with divine purposes (vv. 5-13).

37:14-22. Closing challenge. Elihu addresses Job with a series of questions that seek his compliance with the praise he has modelled. Does Job know how to bring forth the lightning or how to balance the clouds in the sky? Can Job stretch out the heavens? The certain answer to these questions is "No." If Job would consider the wondrous witness to God's control of the world, he would realize that his pretensions toward equality with God are ridiculous.

37:23-24. Summation. Elihu returns to the themes he has emphasized: God's power, justice, and righteousness. To these he adds the affirmation, consistent with Job's own charge, that God remains inaccessible to humans. For Elihu, as for the friends, these virtues summon mortals like Job to fear or reverence (*yir'eh*, v. 24).

Fear and reverence do indeed characterize Job, according to the prologue (cf. 1:1, 8; 2:3); however, with the conclusion of the dialogues, it is clear that the friends define these qualities very differently than Job. The debate has ended, but the resolution concerning the true definition of piety before God is still pending.

Dialogue between Job and God, 38:1–42:6

God's First Address: The Order of the Cosmos, 38:1–40:2

38:1-3. God's appearance and summons. The God who addresses Job is now called "the LORD" (Heb. YHWH), rather than *Shaddai* or *El*, the names used throughout the dialogues with the friends. On the one hand, the encounter with YHWH indicates that Job, like Moses at Sinai, will be granted a personal appearance of God. On the other hand, the imagery accompanying this revelation of presence suggests that YHWH confronts Job with the force of one who comes to do battle. Before the one who speaks with hurricane-force winds, Job is to "gird his loins like a hero," that is, he is to prepare like a warrior for the encounter that is coming. The hopelessness of Job's position, however, is apparent from the outset. In the contest that looms

ahead, the one who is *without knowledge* (v. 2) is summoned to "give knowledge" (v. 3; NRSV *declare*).

The agenda for YHWH's initial confrontation with Job is set with the first question (v. 2). Job had charged that God's design, or purpose, for the world was chaotic and destructive (12:13-25; cf. 9:5-9; 10:8-14). YHWH rebuts this accusation by asking, *Who is this who in ignorance has cast darkness over divine intentions?* The question centers not on Job's identity, but on his pretense to having a knowledge commensurate with God's about the purpose of the world (cf. Good 1990, 343). Thus Job is summoned, not to receive answers (cf. 13:22), but to be interrogated.

38:4-38. The design of the physical world. With a rhetorical sweep across the far regions of the universe, YHWH summons Job to consider the divine plan for the world: *the foundation of the earth* (vv. 4-7); the waters of the sea (vv. 8-11); the *morning* light (vv. 12-15); the watery depths of the netherworld (vv. 16-18); light and darkness (vv. 19-21); the meteorological mysteries of heaven (snow and hail, vv. 22-25; rain, vv. 25-27; dew, frost, and ice, vv. 28-30); the constellations (vv. 31-33); and *the clouds* (vv. 34-38). YHWH questions not only whether Job was present at the beginning of creation (vv. 4-7, 8-11) but also whether Job can demonstrate power over and knowledge of the intricacies of the created order. The intended, yet unspoken, answer to these questions is "No, I cannot," "No, I do not know."

It is clear from this survey of the complexities of the world that God's perspective on order differs from that of the friends and Job. The world is stable, secured by divinely established foundations (v. 4), *measurements* (v. 5), boundaries (vv. 8, 10), places (vv. 12, 19), times (v. 23), and *ordinances* (v. 33). Within this order, the forces of chaos and evil are controlled, but not eliminated (vv. 8-11; 12-15). Light and darkness, good and evil, regularity and randomness, are held together in unyielding tension (cf. Habel 1985, 534; Good 1990, 348). In the midst of such precision and ambiguity, the created order both celebrates (v. 7) and submits (e.g., v. 35) to the divine plan.

38:39–39:30. The design of the animal kingdom. Five groups of animals are cited, along with the characteristics of each that bind them to God: *the lion* and *the raven* and their need for food (38:39-41); *the mountain goats* and *the calving . . . deer* and their reproductive cycles (39:1-4); *the wild ass* and *the wild ox* and their freedom from domestication (39:5-12); *the ostrich* and *the horse* and their speed (39:13-25); and *the hawk* and *the eagle* and the wisdom by which they soar to the heights (39:26-30).

In the animal world, as in the physical world, God embraces disparity within a divine symbiosis. There are *wisdom* (39:26) and stupidity (39:17), courage (39:22) and timidity (39:1-4), domestication (39:19-25) and wildness (e.g., 39:5-8). And within the whole there is an acknowledged dependency on God (38:41) and a submission to the authority of the master designer (39:9).

Again God questions both Job's knowledge of this design and his power over its details. Again the answers expected are "No, I do not know," and "No, I cannot display such power."

40:1-2. Closing summons. God ends this defense of the world's design by resuming the opening challenge to Job. Will the one who is bringing suit against *the Almighty* "instruct" (the verb may also mean "chastise") God in the ways of the world? The time has come for the one who would argue with God (*môkîah*; cf. 13:3, 15) to answer.

Job's First Response: *I Am . . . Small*, 40:3-5

Job's response to God's lengthy discourse is not to join with creation in submission and celebration, but to retreat to silence. His opening words are curiously ambiguous. The translation, *I am . . . small* is often interpreted as an indication that Job has been humbled, and therefore, in recognition of his insignificance, he will not attempt to instruct the creator of the world (e.g., Rowley 1970, 326; Gordis 1978, 466).

The verb employed here, however, may just as easily convey complaint rather than confession (e.g., Habel 1985, 549). To be *small* is to be "trivial," "of little weight," or in a more disparaging sense, "to be held in contempt" by another person. When interpreted as complaint, Job's response is consonant with his previous posture toward God. Job has repeatedly complained that he is no match for God's incontestable power (e.g., 12:13-25). He may now be understood to complain further that since his encounter with God has only proven that God despises him, there is no point in proceeding with a mock dialogue.

Whether an indication of defiance or humility, Job's response is certainly not a simple "I have sinned" or "I am wrong," as the friends and Elihu have prescribed. Job claps his hand to his mouth in amazement at what he has beheld in this encounter with God (cf. 21:5; 29:9). He has had his say. God has interrogated him into silence. From Job's perspective, there is little point in proceeding further.

God's Second Address: The Just Governance of the Cosmos, 40:6–41:34 (MT 41:26)

40:6-14. The summons to govern like God. Once more from the whirlwind, YHWH summons Job to prepare for confrontive interrogation (vv. 7-8). The issue is no longer the design of the cosmos but instead its governance. The initial question states the matter in stark either-or terms: "Will you annul my justice (*mišpāt*), make me guilty in order that you may be innocent?" The question implies that Job has understood justice to require a clean differentiation between guilt and innocence. If Job is innocent, as he claims, then God must be guilty. The friends share this assumption about justice; however, in Job's case they interpret the situation differently: If God is innocent, as they insist, then Job must be guilty. The question that YHWH now puts to Job (and we may assume to the friends as well) focuses on this latter assumption. In order for there to be justice, must there be a guilty party and an innocent one, a wrong that is countered by a right, evil that can be, and is, clearly separated from good?

From the question about guilt and innocence, YHWH turns to a second question that sets the issue of justice within the context of power (vv. 9-14). Can Job match God's power, can he exert authority comparable to God's own *arm* and *voice*? God summons Job to clothe himself in the regalia of a king and administer the justice that he claims is God's responsibility. He is invited to unleash his anger on the wicked, to humble them, subdue them, and trample them where they stand. Having intervened directly to judge them, he is to complete the swift processes of justice by delivering them to the netherworld where they will be bound forever. If Job can execute his own standard of justice on *all* the world's wicked (cf. vv. 11, 12), then YHWH will acknowledge Job's authority, and concede that indeed Job's own right hand has won a victory.

Is this a sarcastic invitation on God's part, a rhetorical taunting of Job's presumption of royal status (29:21-25; cf. Janzen 1985, 244), or a serious offer to recognize Job's authority? Is it a concession from God that stamping out wickedness in the world is indeed a difficult and unfinished agenda, even for God (cf. Brenner 1981, 133)? Is the whole scenario merely hypothetical (cf. Good 1990, 358)? The tone of God's speech is unclear. Yet within the context of the remainder of the address, there is little doubt that in the matter of power, God has no equal.

40:15-24. Behemoth. The remainder of God's address focuses on the creatures *Behemoth* (40:15-24) and *Leviathan* (41:1-34 [MT 40:25-41:26]), mythical monsters of the land and sea who symbolize the primordial forces of chaos and evil. *Behemoth*, like Job, is one of God's creatures (v. 15), and hence shares with Job a common status before the creator of the world (cf. Habel 1985, 565). What distinguishes this creature from Job, however, is its power (vv. 16-19) and its dominion over the forces of nature (vv. 20-24). With bones like *tubes of bronze* and limbs like *bars of iron* (v. 18), *Behemoth* reigns supreme in the kingdom of the wild. The mountains bring forth tribute (v. 20), the mighty Jordan gushes toward its mouth (v. 23).

But even *Behemoth*, with all its power and dominion, is no match for God. God is creator; *Behemoth*, the creature (v. 15). God and God alone dares to bring the sword against the mighty Behemoth (v. 19). And it is God who subjugates and controls this otherwise unstoppable monster (v. 24).

41:1-34 (MT 40:25-41:26). Leviathan. *Leviathan*, like *Behemoth*, is a creature of strength and ferocity that is beyond the control of humans like Job (vv. 1-11). One cannot fish for it or hunt it. One cannot domesticate it as a servant or play with it as a pet. Those who might try to capture this monster of the deep would be undone by the mere sight of it.

The remainder of the address details the terrible and awesome characteristics of *Leviathan* (vv. 12-32). Its skin is covered with impenetrable rows of shields, like a warrior's armor (vv. 13-17). It sneezes fire and spews forth smoke like a boiling pot (vv. 18-21). It is hard like rock, immovable by external force (vv. 22-24), yet when it rouses itself up, even the gods tremble in fear (v. 25). No weapons can prevail against it (vv. 26-29). It resides in the primeval deep, and thrashes about leaving a wake in its trail (vv. 30-32). In sum, *Leviathan is a creature without fear*, a king in his own realm (vv. 33-34).

Throughout these descriptions of *Behemoth* and *Leviathan* there is no mention of justice, no explicit linkage of God's treatment of these representatives of chaos with the requirements of justice that God has urged Job to demonstrate (cf. 40:11-14). Job is invited to look and listen. What is he to learn from the lessons of *Behemoth* and *Leviathan* about God's justice? The forces of evil are part of the world God has made. God

has power sufficient to combat them, to subjugate and control them, but God does not eliminate them.

Job's Second Response: "I Relent," 42:1-6

42:1-2. Concession and complaint. Job begins where God left off, with the matter of divine power (v. 2). He concedes that God indeed has the power to do everything, that no plan God proposes is impossible (*bsr*). In his concession, however, there remains the hint of complaint.

The word used in 38:2 to describe God's plan, or design, is *'esāh* . The word Job uses is *mĕzimmāh*, which may refer both to good and righteous purposes and to evil schemes (e.g., Job 21:27; Jer 11:15; Pss 10:2; 21:11). That Job perhaps tilts toward the latter meaning—God's schemes—is suggested by the close parallels between this verse and Gen 11:6 (cf. Perdue 1991, 234-35). In Gen 11 it is humans who plot against the heavens, evoking from God the response: "nothing they plan (*zmm*) to do will be impossible (*bsr*) for them." In addition to using the same root word for plan, or scheme, that occurs in Job 42:2, Gen 11:6 also uses the very same verb for "to be impossible" (*bsr*). In Gen 11:6 it is God who complains that humans seek to determine their own destinies by scheming against the heavens. Job concedes—complains—that God has the power to plan, or scheme, against humans with devious purposes that are not dissimilar to those on display at Babel.

42:3-6. Concession and relinquishment. Job continues by quoting portions of God's previous challenge to him: *Who is this that hides counsel without knowledge?* (v. 3a, cf. 38:2); *I will question you, and you shall declare to me* (v. 4b, cf. 38:3b=40:7b). Job responds to the first of these challenges by conceding that he is the one who has spoken of things he did not understand, of "wondrous things" he could not comprehend (cf. 5:9; 9:10; 37:5, 14). Job was also challenged to "declare" to God what he would. To this challenge Job turns in vv. 4-5.

Job acknowledges that something has changed since he first launched his quest to find God. To the knowledge of God that he had gained through hearing, he is now privileged to add the insight of personal encounter. He has seen God, an experience he shares with only a select few in Hebraic faith (e.g., Moses, Exod 3:1-6; 24:9-11; 33:23). That God has granted Job a direct revelation of the divine presence is a vindication of Job's integrity, for the godless cannot expect a personal audience with the deity (cf. 13:16).

So Job has been specially prepared for a response that will reflect his new experience with God.

Job's final words represent the crux of the book. It is a frustration in the extreme that the response remains unclear despite enormous scholarly efforts to penetrate its ambiguity. What is clear is that the conventional translation *I despise myself* (v. 6) misses the mark. The verb *m 's* is active, not reflexive. In the Hebrew Bible it occurs both with and without a direct object. With an object it has the meaning "despise" or "reject" (e.g., Amos 5:21: "I despise your festivals"; Hos 4:6: "you have rejected knowledge"). Without an object the meaning is "protest" (e.g., Job 34:33: "Should he pay back on your terms because you protest?").

In 42:6 the verb *m 's* is not followed by an object, hence a plausible translation would be "I protest." A number of scholars have argued that an object should be supplied for the verb. Two proposals merit consideration: "I reject/despise the *case* against God" (Habel 1985, 576); and "I reject/despise *God*" (Curtis 1979, 503). Whether Job is merely giving up his case, or, more radically, giving up on God, he is not simply agreeing that he is guilty as charged.

The meaning of Job's declaration is further dependent on the interpretation of v. 6b. The traditional translation—*repent in dust and ashes*—has encouraged the understanding that at long last Job confesses his sins and assumes the posture of penitence. Not only does this interpretation contradict every other affirmation of Job's innocence in the book, including the affirmations of God in the prologue, it also depends on a misreading of the Hebrew text. The Hebrew is "repent of (i.e., concerning [*'al*]) dust and ashes." The expression suggests that Job changes his mind about his position as mourner and relinquishes his litigation against God.

What is left unspoken is what Job would say to God now that he has decided to proceed no further with protest and lamentation. If the text had continued Job's response beyond v. 6, would his next words offer praise (cf. Patrick 1976, 369-71; Perdue 1991, 236-37)? Would he give up his isolation as a sufferer and return to the community prepared to accept suffering as an inevitable part of God's inscrutable design for the world (cf. Habel 1985, 582-83)? Would he remain defiant to the end, giving up on God and rejecting the religious system that enthrones God on the misery of innocent sufferers (cf. Curtis 1979, 503; Good 1990, 378)?

One comes to the end of Job's declaration with these questions still awaiting a definitive answer. Perhaps in the ambiguity of the responses *I am . . . small* and "I relent" there remains yet a further invitation, one directed to the recipients of this anguished testimony to the difficulty of life in relationship with God (cf. Janzen 1985, 258). What does it mean to be faithful to God in the midst of inexplicable pain? The friends argue that it means to submit to God and confess sin. Job insists, before the friends and before God, that he will deny neither his pain nor his innocence. God has spoken of the design of the cosmos and its intricate governance, but has neither affirmed nor denied that Job has been wronged.

There is one scene in this drama yet to come. In the epilogue God will have a further word to speak to the situation. It is this word that provides a final clue to understanding what has preceded.

Epilogue: The Restoration of Job, 42:7-17

42:7-9. God's verdict. The epilogue returns the story to the opening scene where God is assessing human character and dispensing judgment from on high. Two divine verdicts are offered here. The first is a judgment *against* the friends to whom God now speaks in anger. The second is a judgment *for* Job whom God identifies four times as *my servant*. The basis for God's judgment in each case is that Job, not the friends, has spoken truth. The term *truth* (*někônāh*, vv. 7, 8) points to that which is correct, not merely in an intellectual sense, but with reference to facts that are established and consistent with reality.

What is striking in this verdict is that it focuses on the truth *about God*. In the prologue Job affirms that God is the sovereign dispenser of both good and evil (2:10). Before this one who both *gives* and *takes away* (1:21) Job bows in willing submission. In the dialogues Job insists, against the conventional views of the friends, that God is often an enemy, whose inexplicable absence is not only unjust but also destructive. Job has spoken truth about God.

For Job, God is both present and absent, and true piety, therefore, is by necessity a risky combination of devotion and confrontation. God's verdict is that only the prayers of one who speaks truth like Job will be effective against the "foolishness" (NRSV *folly*) of those who, like the friends (v. 8), and his wife (cf. 2:10), champion a less honest understanding of God.

42:10-17. The restoration of Job's fortunes and family. Following Job's intercession for others, God restores both his fortunes and his family. A central part of his restoration, however, is effected by the community of *brothers and sisters and* "friends" (v. 11) who gather round to impart solidarity and companionship. It is they who finally extend to Job the "consolation" and "comfort" that Eliphaz, Bildad, and Zophar could not, or would not, offer (cf. 2:11). They comfort him for *all the evil that God has brought upon him*, not with words or theology, but with active communion. They offer fellowship through the sharing of a meal, and they demonstrate their compassion with tangible gifts that contribute to Job's material needs.

And so it was, the narrative concludes (vv. 16-17), that Job lived and died. The one introduced as *blameless* and *upright* (1:1) departs life *full of days* (v. 16). For all who will be instructed by his journey from the ash heap to the communion table of family and friends, the expression *full of days* becomes an invitation to a larger understanding of what it means to be in relationship with God.

Works Cited

Brenner, A. 1989. "Job the Pious? The Characterization of Job in the Narrative Framework of the Book," JSOT 43, 37–52. 1981. "God's Answer to Job," VT 31, 129–37.

Clines, D. J. A. 1989. *Job 1–20*, WBC.

Curtis, J. B. 1979. "On Job's Response to Yahweh," JBL 98:497–511.

Fishbane, M. 1971. "Jer. 4 and Job 3: A Rediscovered Use of the Creation Pattern," VT 21:151–67.

Fohrer, G. 1974. "The Righteous Man in Job 31," *Essays in Old Testament Ethics (J. Philip Hyatt, In Memoriam)*, ed. J. L. Crenshaw and J. T. Willis.

Good, E. M. 1990. *In Turns of Tempest. A Reading of Job with a Translation.*

Gordis, R. 1965. *The Book of God and Man: A Study of Job*. 1978. *The Book of Job: Commentary, New Translation, Special Studies.*

Habel, N. C. 1985. *The Book of Job*, OTL.

Janzen, J. G. 1985. *Job*, Interpretation.

Mettinger, T. N. D. 1992. "The God of Job: Avenger, Tyrant, or Victor?" *The Voice From the Whirlwind. Interpreting the Book of Job*, ed. L. G. Perdue and W. C. Gilpen.

Patrick, D. 1976. "The Translation of Job 42.6," VT 26:369–71.

Penchansky, D. 1990. *The Betrayal of God: Ideological Conflict in Job.*

Perdue, L. G. 1991. *Wisdom in Revolt, Metaphorical Theology in the Book of Job.*

Pope, M. L. 1965. *Job. Introduction, Translation, and Notes*, AncB.

Rouillard, P. 1983. "The Figure of Job in the Liturgy: Indignation, Resignation, or Silence," *Concilium* 169.

Rowley, H. H. 1970. *Job*, NCB.

Westermann, C. 1981. *The Structure of the Book of Job. A Form-Critical Analysis.*

Psalms

Marvin E. Tate

Introduction

Understanding the Psalter requires some awareness of the literary and historical contexts that shape it. The history of research of the Book of Psalms and its interpretation, however, is unfinished work. This introduction is supplemented by a selected bibliography that may guide further study.

Terminology

Three designations are commonly used for the Psalms. The Hebrew title *t̊hillim* means "songs of praise" or "hymns." Not all of the psalms are "songs of praise," thus the title probably represents a stage in Israel's past when the psalms were used as a general hymnal, suitable for all occasions.

Two other terms appear in the Book of Psalms. The Hebrew word *mizmor*, fifty-seven times as a title for individual psalms, means a "song that may be accompanied by stringed instruments." *T̊philloth* ("prayers") appears at the end of Ps 72: *The prayers of David son of Jesse are ended.* "Prayers" is an appropriate title for the collection, even though not all of the psalms are specifically prayers.

Two other titles, derived from Greek manuscripts, are well known in English: "Psalms," from a Greek word that meant "playing a stringed instrument," is found in *Codex Vaticanus*; and "Psalter," which also refers to a stringed instrument, is found in *Codex Alexandrinus*. *Codex Sinaiticus* lacks a title for the collection, but has "psalms of David" at the end. The oldest Hebrew manuscripts have no title for the whole book.

Titles of the Psalms

Superscriptions (i.e., titles) appear on 116 of the 150 psalms in the Hebrew Psalter including eighty-seven of the first 100. In addition to the titles, the term *selah* occurs seventy-one times (cf. Hab 3:3, 9, 13). The ancient Greek translations provided all of the psalms with titles except Pss 1 and 2 (see Pietersma 1980, 213–26).

Such a large number of titles would seem to offer assistance in interpretating the psalms. Unfortunately, this is true only to a limited degree. The titles are ancient (how old is uncertain), but they are still later additions and, therefore, give little information about the original meaning and use of the psalms to which they are attached.

Some psalm headings refer to the literary form of a psalm and contain various notes on its rendering, for example, the general terms for "psalm" (*mizmor*), "song" (*shir*), and "prayer" (*t̊phillah*). These represent early attempts to classify the psalms according to their literary-cultic types.

Many titles contain technical notes relating to the occasion and method of recitation, for example, *to the leader: with stringed instruments* (e.g., Ps 4), *to the leader: for the flutes* (e.g. Ps 5), and so forth. Some of the instructions are relatively clear, such as *with stringed instruments* (e.g. Ps 4), *a song for the dedication of the temple* (Ps 30), *for the memorial offering* (Ps 38), *for the Sabbath Day* (Ps 92), or *a prayer of one afflicted . . .* (Ps 102). Other titles remain conjectural at best, such as "according to a silent dove of distant ones" (Ps 56, author trans).

Such titles are commonly assumed to refer to the tune names used when the psalm was sung or chanted, but proof is lacking. In some cases, the parts of the titles that suggest technical performance matters may have originally been postscripts for preceding psalms and incorporated into the superscriptions of following psalms by later copyists (cf. Pss 3/4; 17/18; 87/88; 108/109; 138/139; 148/149). The most obvious case in support of the theory is found in Pss 87/88 (see comment on Ps 88). The postscripts at the end of the psalms in Hab 3, Ps 72, and the end of a Dead Sea

Scroll text of Ps 145 (*11QPs^a* adds "this is for a memorial") provide important data for this interpretation.

Other titles identify psalms with a person or group of persons. The most common of these is DAVID (seventy-three psalms), ASAPH (twelve psalms), and the Sons of KORAH (eleven psalms). SOLOMON (two psalms), Heman, Ethan, and MOSES (one each) also occur. Traditionally it was assumed that the names were of the authors of the psalms. Today, however, it is generally recognized that the titles provide little or no certain indication of authorship (e.g., David would hardly have written Ps 18:49-50). There is no certainty about the meaning of the "of" in such titles as "a psalm of David." The Hebrew construction is a flexible one that can mean "for" or "in relation to" as well as "of." Therefore, "of" may refer to the collection to which the psalm belongs or to its use.

One text from the caves of Qumran (where the DEAD SEA SCROLLS were found) credits David with 4,050 psalms, while a letter from the Nestorian Patriarch Timotheus I in the eighth century C.E. refers to a discovery of scrolls near Jericho including more than 200 psalms of David—compared with seventy-three in MT. The Davidization of the Psalms is also reflected in the increased number of Davidic titles in the LXX (e.g., Pss 33, 42, 43, 67, 91, 93–100, 104). The Davidization of the Psalms was accompanied by an increased emphasis on the tradition of Davidic authorship.

The matter of authorship in postexilic Israelite life is without clear resolution. However, it is highly probable that authorship became more crucial as texts became more authoritative and fixed as scripture. Throughout the history of usage, the traditional authority of texts required supplementation by reference to authorship by persons endowed by God. Thus the *11QPs^a* prose insert on David's composition of psalms concludes with: "All these he spoke in prophecy which was given him from the presence of the Most High." David's authorship of Psalms (as was Moses' of the Pentateuch) was elevated to the status of "prophecy" (Kugel 1986, 134–36).

Few biblical writings have any definite indication of authorship. Such anonymity may be disturbing to the modern reader. The psalms, however, come from a different world. Ancient people generally had a sense of history that lacked precision (by modern standards). Before the Hellenistic period, at least, readers had relatively little interest in the actual personalities of authors, except when the content of texts became authoritative (or canonical) as scripture, relatively

fixed in text forms, and no longer subject to being freely modified (when texts became "fixed" new "noncanonical" compositions emerged).

When personalities were linked to written material, it was done either by naming the individual writings after the principal character found in them (e.g., the Pentateuch was ascribed to Moses) or by assigning songs or recitations to famous people in particular situations. For example, a psalm is put in the mouth of Hezekiah in Isa 38:1-20 (which is missing from the parallel account in the Books of Kings) and David appoints a thanksgiving song in 1 Chr 16:7-36 to be sung by Asaph and his brother (which is made up of material from Pss 96, 105, 106).

A similar process probably lies behind the headings of several psalms that contain references to the details of some historical situations in the career of David (see Pss 3, 7, 18, 34, 51, 52, 54, 56, 57, 59, 60, 63, 142). The historical value of these notes must be decided in each case on its own merits. The only value of such headings is to show what situations ancient Jewish scribal commentators thought to be appropriate for them.

One of the best-known words in the Psalter is SELAH, a scribal notation found seventy-one times in Psalms (and three times in Habakkuk). While there is widespread agreement that the term marked an interlude or interruption in the recitation of the psalm, its exact meaning is uncertain. Perhaps the best conjecture is the one that interprets it as marking a pause during the recitation of the psalms when the congregation fell prostrate in homage and submission to God, probably with shouts of praise. The action may have been signalled by trumpet blasts from the priests, and the recitation by the people of a refrain such as "Praise the Lord, for he is good; for his steadfast love endures forever." Another approach is to think of a "recitative" or "cantillation" in the pause that recalled a major story or tradition in Israel's history. Frequently, the *selah* seems to serve as an intensifier coming just before some climactic statement or between such statements.

The Collections of the Psalter

The present Hebrew Psalter is composed of 150 psalms. The numbering of these psalms is not as fixed as it may seem at first. There is a marked variation between Protestant translations and those of the Roman Catholic and Orthodox traditions. The variations arise at Pss 9–10 (separate in Protestant translations; as one psalm in others); Pss 114–115 (113 in Catholic translations); Ps 116 (114–115 in Catholic translations); and 147 (146–147 in Catholic translations). These differences develop from following the Hebrew texts on the one hand (Protestant) and the Greek and Latin texts (Roman Catholic and Orthodox) on the other. There are other cases where the present numbering of separate psalms is doubtful (see the commentary on Pss 9–10, 32–33, 42–43, 70–71, 117, 150), while other separate psalms may be composed of originally independent units (see Pss 19, 40, 108, 144). Psalm 14 is essentially the same as Ps 53; and Ps 70 repeats the conclusion of Ps 40. Thus the numbering of the psalms must not be considered immutable.

The number 150 as the total of psalms in the Psalter is subject to some variation also. The Greek-text SEPTUAGINT version of the Psalter contains 151 psalms. Psalm 151 (known also in Latin and Syriac translations) has been described as a kind of poetic *midrash* on 1 Sam 16:11-13, and the text of the psalm in Hebrew has recently become known from a psalms manuscript from Cave 11 at Qumran on the Dead Sea *(11QPsᵃ)*. The Syriac Psalter contained 155 psalms (of which 154 and 155 also appear in *11QPsᵃ*). The psalms scroll from Qumran has been dated to the first half of the first century C.E.

The Psalter is, of course, a collection of psalms. In the present state of the Hebrew Psalter there are five books or divisions: 1–41, 42–72, 73–89, 90–106, 107–150. Each one of the first four books ends with a similar section of praise or doxology: 41:13; 72:18-19 (to which v. 20 has been added); 89:52; 106:48. The fifth book closes with five psalms that are characterized by a tenfold *Praise the LORD* ("Hallelujah!") and ends with Ps 150, which contains a thirteenfold praise of Yahweh. While this division of the Psalter is deliberate, the exact purpose of the editors is disputed. The fivefold division corresponds to the fivefold division of the Pentateuch (the TORAH) and becomes, in a way, the response of Israel to the Torah of Moses.

The exact date of the present arrangement of the Psalter is not known. It probably should be placed in the postexilic period of Israel's history, and may be as late as the first century C.E. The Psalter contains several earlier collections of psalms that have been taken up into the present arrangement. For example, there is a change in the dominant usage of the name of God in Pss 42–83. The name "Yahweh" (read as LORD in most English translations), is usual in Pss 1–41, while "Elohim" ("God" in English translations) predominates in 42–83; "Yahweh" appears again in most cases in 84–150. There can be little doubt that an Elohistic collection (that cuts across present divisions) was made at some point. This conclusion is strengthened by the obvious substitution of "Elohim" for "Yahweh" in such places as Pss 43:4; 45:7; 50:7; 53. This collection may have originated from circles in postexilic Israel when the reluctance to pronounce the divine name *Yahweh* led to the substitution of *Elohim*, before the practice began (common later) of pronouncing Yahweh as *adonai* ("Lord").

The note attached to the end of Ps 72 (*The prayers of David son of Jesse are ended*) probably marked the end of an earlier collection. The reader will notice that in the first book of the Psalter (1–41) only four psalms (1, 2, 10, 33) are without a title, while all the others are ascribed to David. Since Pss 1 and 2 are introductory psalms (Ps 2 was probably interpreted as a Davidic psalm when placed in its present position because of its references to the king) and Ps 10 belongs to Ps 9, only Ps 33 is a real exception. It may be that Ps 33 should be linked with Ps 32 (cf. 32:11 and 33:1) or it may be that Ps 33 was placed in its present position to mark the end of some prior collection. In other sections of the Psalter the Davidic psalms are grouped together (51–65, 68–70, 108–110, 138–145), although some are isolated (86, 101, 103, 122, 124, 131). The obvious conclusion is that there was a Davidic collection (or collections) of the psalms at some earlier date.

As noted above, the significance of the preposition "for" or "to" David in the titles is uncertain. It probably indicates psalms that were originally intended (or later so interpreted) for the use of the Davidic king, or were designed to evoke memories of David and his career in the minds of those who read or heard the psalms. David would have been considered to be the speaker in the psalms. After the end of the monarchy (if not before), such psalms were "democratized" and used by ordinary people, while retaining their Davidic associations. In the course of time, conventional idiom associated *all* the psalms with David, similar to the association of *all* the Torah with Moses, and *all* the wisdom works with Solomon.

There are some indications Pss 90–150 may have been compiled from four smaller collections: 90–104 (with 105–107 added); 108–110 (with 111–118 added); 120–134 (the Songs of Ascent or Pilgrimage with 135–136 added); 138–145 (to which the concluding five-psalm doxology of 146–150 was attached). Finally, the royal psalms (2, 20, 21, 45, 72, 89, 101,

110, 132) are now scattered through the Psalter. They probably formed a separate collection in preexilic Israel and their positions in the present Psalter are not accidental.

The history of the Psalter is still impossible to formulate in precise detail, but there is some measure of agreement on its general outline. There is no reason to doubt POETRY was used by the Israelites from the earliest periods of their history, some of which may have been indigenous, while much was borrowed from neighbors. The content of the present psalms, indicates that most of them come from the time in Israel's history when life was centered in the Temple in Jerusalem.

It is difficult to date any psalm within narrow limits; direct historical statements are few. The psalms were probably developed at the worship centers of the Israelite tribes after their settlement in Palestine, although we cannot be certain that we have any of these psalms in the present Psalter. The establishment of the monarchy and center of worship in Jerusalem by David undoubtedly brought a new stimulus for the writing and collecting of psalms and prayers. We cannot be sure which psalms belong to the early period of the monarchy, but such a dating cannot be ruled out for several (e.g., 2, 18, 29, 110, 132).

The establishment of rival centers of worship in BETHEL and Dan by JEROBOAM I must have brought about the production and collection of psalms from this source. We may have some of these psalms in the present Psalter (e.g., Ps 68), but no one can be absolutely sure. Some of the psalms must have been written in the postexilic community that was centered in Jerusalem, and that community preserved and arranged the Psalter in the present order. It was once assumed by many biblical critics that a good number of the psalms were as late as the Maccabean period (second–first century B.C.E.), but the view has little support in present scholarship.

The Poetry of the Psalms

Modern translations distinguish by form poetic from prose sections. The reader will see at once that the psalms are poetic. A full understanding of them involves an awareness of the basic formal and stylistic features of Hebrew POETRY. The most important of these features is the use of what is called PARALLELISM. In its simplest form parallelism is the supplementation of one short line (colon) by another that either essentially repeats the meaning of the first line or adds to it: "This is true, and so is this" (e.g., see Pss 2:1; 3:1;

5:1; 24:1). However, there are many variations and expansions of this pattern. There are also rhythmic patterns ("meter") in Hebrew verse. These are rarely without some irregularity and are frequently read in different ways by different readers. The poets seem to have exercised great freedom with rhythmical (metrical) patterns. The poetry of the OT also displays a wide array of sound patterns, stylistic features, structuring devices (such as the CHIASM, INCLUSIO, and theme words), and the literary arrangement of texts to form strophes (see Ps 107) or other sections.

Another form of poetry found in the Psalter is that of the "alphabetic" or "acrostic" type. These poems have successive lines, verses, or stanzas that begin with the letters of the Hebrew alphabet in order. The alphabetic design in Pss 9–10, 25, 34, 37, 11, 112, 119, and 145 cannot be carried over into translation, but it is helpful for the reader to be aware of this poetic formation.

The poetry of the OT is not confined to the Psalter. The Israelites were a people who, like other peoples, loved songs and singing. It is true that the OT does not contain a great deal of what we would call "secular" songs or poems, but there is evidence that the Israelites knew and used such songs on many occasions. Prophets used the forms, and even the words, of various kinds of songs (see Amos 5:1-2 [cf. 6:5]; Isa 5:1-7; 23:15-16; 37:22). And there is the example of the well-known song that greeted David when he returned from his exploits against the Philistines (1 Sam 18:6-7). The presence in the Psalter of an essentially "secular" poem for the wedding of the king (Ps 45) is significant, as are the many references to musical instruments and activities in the psalms (e.g., Ps 150). In terms of what may be called "cultic" poetry (having to do with worship), there are extensive sections elsewhere in the OT (e.g., Gen 48:1-28; Exod 15:1-18, 21; Deut 32:1-43; 33; Judg 5; 1 Sam 2:1-10; 2 Sam 1:19-27; 22:1-51 [=Ps 18]; 23:1-7; Isa 38:9-20; Jonah 2; Hab 3; Jer 15:13-21). The Book of Lamentations and the Song of Songs also contain collections of poetry.

The Classification of the Psalms

The collections of the Psalter show evidence that one of the factors in their formation is the similarity of psalms according to type. Most of the Davidic psalms are lamentations or prayers closely associated with complaint and lament. The close linking of Ps 93 to 95–99 is related to the fact that they deal with the kingship of Yahweh. Another example is the section formed by Pss 146–150, marked by the use of *Praise the LORD!* The titles give indications of attempts by the early Jewish communities to classify the psalms (see above). The church continued with various classifications of the psalms. The best known of the Christian classifications is that of the seven "Penitential Psalms" (6; 32; 38; 51; 102; 130; 143) and the classification of the Royal Psalms (2, 20, 21, 45, 72, 110, 132) as "Messianic."

In the early stages of the development of modern critical study, the Psalter did not receive the same measure of attention as the Pentateuch, but in time biblical scholars also came to apply the methods of historical-criticism to it. The first stage of this study was concentrated (1) on discovering the most suitable historical context for the composition of each psalm, assuming that each was the result of the literary activity of a single individual poet, (2) and on reducing the present form of the psalms (where necessary) to an authentic nucleus assumed to have been written by a poet out of personal experience.

The historical-critical approach has, however, been mostly superseded by the form-critical approach. Form-critical study does not begin with the assumption that each psalm represents the literary activity of an individual poet writing out of personal experience in a given historical context, although it does not exclude the validity of personal experience. Instead it begins with comparative study of the psalms with one another (and with poetry outside the OT) in order to ascertain common features of structure, style, and content within certain groups of psalms. Beyond the form, form criticism seeks to discover a *Sitz im Leben* ("situation-in-life") that could have elicited the form in question. These situations can be historical, but they normally belong to the basic affairs of life: birth, death, marriage, sickness, disaster, legal proceedings, war, harvests, and so forth. Form criticism also seeks to understand how the literary unit ("form") passed from one generation to another in the course of history, a process that sometimes involved changes of the *Sitz im Leben* from the original, plus expansion or modifications of the original unit.

The legacy of the investigation of psalm types or categories from Hermann Gunkel (1929 and 1933) has had wide acceptance by interpreters of the Psalms in the twentieth century. Gunkel (1929) defined five main types of psalms: hymns, communal laments, royal psalms, individual laments, and individual songs of thanksgiving. He also recognized other categories, and four are of special note: songs of pilgrimage, communal songs of thanksgiving, wisdom poetry, and liturgies. He made allowance for the difficulty of defining some psalms in any of these categories because of a mixture of types and set forth a type called "mixed poems" (actually, quite a number of psalms).

The changes in method and result have been considerable, but the framework of his analysis has been remarkably durable. The discussion that follows is limited to three broad classifications: psalms of lament, psalms of praise, and other types of psalms. The third, of course, is not a form-critical category, but only an umbrella designation for a variety of psalm types.

Psalms of Lament

These psalms are found in individual forms (the speaker is a first-person "I") and communal forms (the speaker is a plural "we"). The individual lament is the most numerous type in the Psalter (e.g., Pss 3, 4, 5, 6, 7, 13, 17, 143). The laments are prayers addressed to God concerning complaints, lamentations, and frequently enemies. God is addressed directly (typically, "Hear O God" or "My God, my God") with complaint about distressful conditions. Petitions to God for divine action is an expected feature, especially for action relating to enemies (enemies are not normally addressed directly). These psalms may contain appeals to God, which seek a favorable hearing for the prayer, and there is a tendency for them to move toward praise. In most cases the speaker seeks grounds for praising God, and vows of praise, contingent on a favorable response to the prayer, may occur.

Psalms of Praise

This broad category encompasses psalms designated by Gunkel as thanksgiving psalms as well as those known as hymns. A category of such scope includes great diversity. Thanksgiving-praise (Claus Westermann's [1981] "declarative praise") is marked by direct address to Yahweh and a testimony element of proclamatory and exhortative speech directed toward the people who may be listening to the praise (e.g., Pss 18:46-50; 22:22-31; 30:4-5; 34:9-22; 66:15-20; 107:43). The more "descriptive praise" (Westermann's [1981] term for the general hymns) features a summons to praise, or a call to worship, addressed to varied groups (e.g., 33:1, *O you righteous*; 113:1, *O servants of the LORD*; 148:2, *all his angels . . . all his host*—vastly extended to include all creation). The summons may be elaborated, of course, in terms of how, when, and where to praise Yahweh (e.g., Pss 113:1-3; 149:1-3). The praise poetry is replete with reasons for the praise: personal experience of deliverance, works of creation, saving works, and the goodness and glory of the divine nature.

The individual poetry of thanksgiving-praise is focused more closely on personal help and deliverance (e.g., Pss 18, 30, 116, 118), sometimes recalling the prayers of complaint directed to God before the deliverance. The more descriptive praise has a tendency to focus on the qualities of God and the works of creation and establishment of the earth and heavenly bodies (e.g., Pss 33, 93, 113, 136). However, the saving acts of Yahweh in making Israel his people are not neglected (e.g., Pss 98, 114, 135). Alternative expressions of praise, such as praise wishes and blessings, may be found (e.g., Pss 19; 85:6; 103:1-2; 104:34). Despite the fact that commentators have struggled to devise adequate classification systems (including those of Gunkel) for the wide diversity of praise poetry, no consensus has emerged. The poetry has a high degree of mixing (e.g., elements of thanksgiving and descriptive praise are usually blended, and praise elements may be found in laments).

Other Types

A goodly number of psalms do not fit the standard categories very well. Among these is one of Gunkel's categories called "royal psalms," psalms that appear to have content focused on the kingship in ancient Israel, especially dealing with the Davidic kings in Jerusalem. The commonly accepted royal psalms are Pss 2, 18, 20, 21, 45, 72, 89, 101, 110, 132, 144. Some scholars, however, argue that this list should be expanded to include many more psalms. A small group of psalms are usually called "historical psalms" (Pss 78, 105, 106, 135, 136), though by genre these psalms are properly praise poems or hymns. Psalms 15 and 24 are commonly referred to as entrance liturgies to worship. Psalms 1, 19, and 119 (an alphabetic psalm) are centered on the praise of Yahweh's *torah*. While major efforts to establish a category of "wisdom psalms" or "didactive poetry" (Kraus 1988, 58–60) have met with only limited acceptance, there is wide agreement that Pss 37 and 73 may be treated as such.

The Relationship of Psalms to Life Situations

As noted above, one facet of form-critical analysis has been to seek a *Sitz im Leben* or situation-in-life for literary units. In the twentieth century, scholars have devoted much time and effort to this task as related to the Psalms, with mixed results. Sigmund Mowinckel has been the most influential scholar in this regard, arguing for the direct relatedness of psalms to cultic (organized worship) rites and ceremonies. In Mowinckel's approach many psalms are considered to have been designed and produced to accompany liturgical actions, and it has been assumed that these actions can be recovered, in large measure, from the psalms themselves. This cult-functional approach centered on preexilic Israelite worship, especially in the Temple in Jerusalem and in the context of the autumnal festivals (chiefly the Festival of Tabernacles in the OT). Mowinckel (1962) argued for an Enthronement Festival celebrating the victory of Yahweh over chaos and his enthronement as the divine king. Others have emphasized New Year festivals, covenant renewal ceremonies, and Zion-Davidic king celebrations.

The autumn festival has not been the sole concern of scholars. In regard to the laments, it has been argued at length that they arose out of sacral judicial procedures in the sanctuaries, especially the Temple in Jerusalem. A number of the laments (e.g., Pss 3, 4, 5, 6, 17, 26, 27, 54, 55, 57, 59, 63) have been interpreted as prayers for those who would flee to a sanctuary for asylum and deliverance from enemies who were falsely accusing them. In some cases, it has been argued, they were intended to be inscribed (perhaps on the wall or on a SCROLL) or engraved on a stele which was placed in the sanctuary (cf. Exod 22:8-9; Deut 17:8-13; 19:15-21; 1 Kgs 8:31-32). Some laments have been assumed to be prayers of sick persons who would go to the temple for purification and healing (e.g., Pss 6, 38, 39, 62, 69, 88).

Recent interpretations of the Psalms have seen a departure from the cult-functional approach defined exclusively in terms of the major Israelite festivals and the Temple. One of the factors involved has been the emphasis on the literary art of biblical narrative and biblical poetry, with a tendency to read a psalm in terms of its own context and structure, with diminished interest in its situation-in-life or situation-in-worship. The forced reading of some psalms in the cult-functional approach has also been a factor. The reconstruction of worship situations assumed to be directly related to a psalm is a highly subjective endeavor that inspires confidence only in the general features of the liturgies and rituals postulated. The reflection of cultic traditions and practices in psalm texts can hardly be doubted, but this does not necessitate the detailed reconstruction of an actual worship situation and the assumption that a given psalm was composed for that particular situation—either purely cultic or historical.

Increased recognition of the composite nature of psalms and the use of mixed and traditional material in a given psalm is found in recent work on the Psalter. Along with this has come heightened appreciation of scribal psalm writing (e.g., see Mowinckel's discussion of "learned psalmography" [1951, 104–25]) and the long-continued tradition of such in postexilic Israel, including the Qumran community and early Christian communities (e.g., see the poems of praise attributed to MARY and ZECHARIAH in Luke 1–2). The dating of psalms is as slippery as ever, but scholars seem more willing to eschew the early dating of a psalm in its present form because it may contain some material that is quite old.

Continuing sociological analysis of community life in the ancient world and the study of ritual texts from the ancient Near East have led to a broader understanding of the probable nature of the Israelite cult and the relationship of psalms to it. For example, it is unlikely that sick people would normally have been taken to a temple for healing. The Israelite priests were involved to some extent with certain illnesses (e.g., skin diseases, Lev 13–14; Deut 24:8), but were not responsible for the actual treatment of illness. When well again, a sick person would go to a temple for purification and thanksgiving ceremonies. The care and treatment of the sick took place in homes or at special places for healing (e.g., see 1 Kgs 8:37-40; 2 Kgs 1:2-8; 20:1-11; Job 2:7-8; 2 Chr 26:21; Mark 2:1-12; John 5:2-3). Some psalms were probably used as prayers by persons in such home or healing-place contexts, perhaps assisted by a ritual expert, not a priest but someone trained to help people engage in prayers and healing rites (Gerstenberger, 1988). Scholars involved in such sociological analysis stress the importance of individual participation in primary groups (such as families, groups of friends, and communities of common interests) and avoid the tendency to think of prayer and worship as either purely individual or else wholly corporate (as in the great festivals and official worship of the temples).

For Further Study

In the *Mercer Dictionary of the Bible*: CULTS; DEAD SEA SCROLLS; DISEASE AND HEALING; ESCHATOLOGY IN THE OT; FEASTS AND FESTIVALS; HYMNS/CREEDS; MASKIL; MUSIC/MUSICAL INSTRUMENTS; ORACLE; PARALLELISM; POETRY; PRAYER/THANKSGIVING IN THE OT; PSALMS, BOOK OF; RESURRECTION IN THE OT; RIGHTEOUSNESS IN THE OT; SALVATION IN THE OT; SOUL IN THE OT; TEMPLE/TEMPLES; TESTIMONY; THEOPHANY; UGARIT, RAS; WISDOM IN THE OT; WISDOM LITERATURE; WORSHIP IN THE OT; WRATH OF GOD.

In other sources: A. A. Anderson, *The Book of Psalms*, NCB; L. Allen, *Psalms 101–150*, WBC; B. Anderson, *Out of the Depths*; W. H. Bellinger, Jr., *Psalms: Reading and Studying the Book of Praise*; P. C. Craige, *Psalms 1–50*, WBC; M. Dahood, *Psalms 1–50, Psalms 51–100, Psalms 101–150* AncB; M. Tate, *Psalms 51–100*, WBC; A. Weiser, *The Psalms*, OTL; C. Westermann, *Praise and Lament in the Psalms*.

Commentary

Book One. Psalms 1–41

Psalm 1

Psalm 1 belongs in a general way to the WISDOM LITERATURE of the OT. It is one of several psalms in the Psalter that show features of poetry like that in the Book of Proverbs. The reward of *the righteous* and the punishment of *the wicked* is a major theme in both the Wisdom and Deuteronomic teachings in the OT.

Verses 1-3 tell of the blessedness of *the righteous* person (v. 6), who is first defined in a negative way (v. 1): as one who does not walk in the counsel of *the wicked*, does not follow the ways of *sinners*, and does not sit with the *scoffers*. The verbs indicate a habitual or regular way of doing things; that is, *the righteous* have a daily course of life separate from *the wicked* (cf. Ps 26:4-5).

The exact identity of *the wicked* is a problem throughout the Psalter. However, it is most probable that the reference here is to those who are recognized as despisers of the TORAH of Yahweh. They are characterized by hostility to godliness and to the righteous behavior of the *torah*-keeping community. The righteous make the correct negative judgments by not doing certain things.

The positive side of the picture presents the *delight* of the righteous person *in the law* [Heb. *torah*] *of the Lord* (v. 2), the good fortune of the one whose *delight* is centered in those teachings that reveal the merciful will and power of Yahweh. In this context, the verb *meditate* denotes the low murmur of reading aloud to one's self. The kind of life that results for the righteous person is compared with a tree that does not fail in leaf or productivity because it is "deeply rooted" and its water supply is constant (v. 3), free from the withering of drought. The comparison occurs elsewhere in the OT (Amos 2:9; Jer 11:19; 17:7-8; Ezek 17:5-6; Pss 52:8; 92:13-15), and appears also in non-Israelite wisdom literature.

The metaphor of a green and productive tree is a common one for strength and well-being. The use of the "tree of life" for Wisdom in Prov 3:18 (cf. Prov 15:4) is especially significant for Ps 1 with its wisdom-*torah* characteristics (cf. Gen 2:9; 3:22). Those comforted in Zion will be called "trees of righteousness, the planting of Yahweh, to display his glory" (Isa 61:3). The "streams of water" (v. 3) is derived from an expression that refers to artificial watercourses through which a controlled supply of water is provided. The result is abundant and perennial fruitfulness. The last statement of v. 3 is a key one: the righteous person is able to carry through to a successful result all he or she endeavors to do (cf. Josh 1:8).

The wicked lack the stability and nourishment of the righteous (vv. 4-5). They are compared to the *chaff* that is blown away from the threshing floor by the wind (cf. Ps 35:5; Job 21:18; Isa 17:13; Hos 13:3). They lack the security of the righteous.

The judgment (v. 5) poses a problem. Most commentators do not believe that the final, eschatological judgment is intended here, although it is the common meaning of later Jewish and Christian interpreters. Some understand the idea as that of divine judgment in general; every act by which Yahweh separates between the righteous and the wicked and shows his ruling power in the world (Sarna 1993, 45). A more probable interpretation seeks the background for *the judgment* here in passages such as Pss 5:4-7; 15:1; 24:3. The questions of 15:1 and 24:3 are answered negatively: the wicked will *not* stand in the holy place of judgment. In the background are actual cultic rituals by which those whose conduct did not conform with the *torah* of the congregation were excluded from worship at the holy places.

The congregation of the righteous (v. 5) is the fellowship of those who are permitted to praise God at the sanctuary (Pss 111:1; 118:19-20), perhaps *the great congregation* at Zion (see Pss 35:18; 40:9-10). However, in the present psalm such an actual cultic situation may not be intended. Indeed, it seems more probable the verse has an eschatological thrust looking beyond the cultic present to the ultimate judgment of God, and to a purified congregation of the righteous in which sinners will be unable to participate.

Verse 6 concludes the psalm by setting forth in summary fashion the ways of the righteous and the wicked. To be known by Yahweh means to be in an intimate relationship with God. Intimacy with God is the real source of the blessedness (or happiness) with which the psalm begins, a word that expresses an exclamation regarding the well-being of an individual: "Oh, how well-off is that person!" (cf. Pss 112:1; 128:2; Matt 5:3-12). The death-way of the wicked lacks the "rightness" that produces such good fortune. Psalm 1 calls for faith in God's ways for the righteous, and confidence that those ways bring pleasure and fruitfulness.

The meaning of the word *torah* (*the law*) in this psalm continues to be a subject of discussion. There is no reference to any body of literature in Ps 1, or in other *torah* psalmic material (Pss 19:7-14; 119:1-176; 37:31; 40:8; 78:1, 5, 10; 89:30; 94:12; 105:45). Therefore it is likely that in the Psalter *torah* should be read as "instruction," "teaching," or "guidance," which is the fundamental meaning of the word (cf. the *torah* in the "heart" or "inward being" in Pss 37:31 and 40:8; see commentary on Ps 119).

In subsequent readings there can be little doubt that *torah* was understood as the Torah, a defined body of law and narratives. In the course of time, the Torah came to be identified especially with its core material in the canonical form of the Pentateuch. However, even when Torah was basically the Pentateuch it was at the same time a composite entity. The Pentateuch itself is not composed of legal formulations alone, but contains extensive narrative and poetic sections (both story and commandments). Further, the prophetic literature was associated with Torah (including Joshua, Judges, Samuel, and Kings), and in time the concept of an oral Torah derived from Moses was authoritative along with the written Torah. Indeed, *torah* has never been a simple, clearly identified entity.

Finally, the arrangement of the Psalter with Ps 1 as introduction to the whole collection must indicate that in some sense the Psalms are also Torah (McCann 1993b). The Psalter is also a *torah* worthy of continual delight and meditation, a "tree of life" that never fails to yield fruit and whose leaves never wither.

Psalm 2

This is a royal psalm, paired with Ps 1 at the beginning of the Psalter as a powerful affirmation of the sovereignty of Yahweh. In the course of the postexilic history of Israel the royal psalms came to be interpreted messianically, as referring to a future Messiah who would come to rule over Israel. Psalm 2 was so considered and is applied to Christ in the NT (Acts 4:25-28; 13:33; Heb 1:5). A proper understanding of the royal psalms, however, must begin with their place in the context of Israelite kingship. In the case of this psalm, most commentators have interpreted it as belonging to the enthronement and coronation of a king of JUDAH in JERUSALEM, possibly DAVID himself. However, rebellion and the threat of attack may be equally as probable as royal coronation. It is possible the psalm was repeated on periodic occasions when the establishment of the Davidic dynasty would have been celebrated or when the Israelites were threatened by enemies.

It is strange that the psalm has no title. The title may have been lost when Ps 1 was prefixed to the whole collection but it is more probable that Ps 2 was left untitled and added as a sort of messianic prelude to the Davidic collection of Pss 3–41.

A tense scene of rebellion by earthly nations and kings *against the LORD and his anointed* is introduced in vv. 1-3 by a question that expresses astonishment that these hostile forces would dare risk an insurrection. The same verb used for vocally expressed meditation (Heb. *hgh*) on *torah* in Ps 1:2 is used for the rebellious mutterings of kings and nations who *conspire* and *plot* [Heb. *hgh*] . . . *against the LORD and his anointed* (Ps 2:1). However, their efforts are *in vain* because a rebellion against the "anointed one"—the king in Jerusalem (1 Sam 2:10; 35; 12:3; 5; Pss 18:51; 20:7; 28:8; 89:39; 52; 132:10; 17; etc.)—is a rebellion against the power of Yahweh himself. Verse 3 expresses the desire of the hostile kings for complete autonomy.

It becomes clear in vv. 4-6 why the poet thinks the insurrection is such a futile venture. Yahweh surveys the scene from heaven and *laughs . . . in derision*, unintimidated by the hostile counsels and plots of the kings (cf. Pss 37:13; 59:8). God is not remote and indifferent toward those who challenge his purpose in history; he will speak to them with terrifying fury. Verse 6 contains the divine word: Yahweh, himself, has established his king (*my king*) on Zion, his holy hill (*my holy hill*).

In vv. 7-9 the speaker changes and the king tells of his commission by Yahweh to reign with potential power over the nations of the earth. It was by *decree* of Yahweh that he had obtained his authorized status. The "decree" reflects the practice of using some documentary record or protocol of the king's legitimate right to the throne. In Egypt the protocol seems to have contained the Pharaoh's coronation names and the affirmation of his divine sonship and power. There probably was a similar custom in Israel (cf. 2 Kgs 11:12).

The thrust of the king's testimony in vv. 7-9 is twofold. First, he declares that his reign is legitimate. He is no usurper who has seized the throne by force or fraud, or even merely because he is a king's son. The kingship in Israel was never purely hereditary; there was always some need for a charismatic legitimation. The king had to become a *son* of Yahweh as well as a *son* of David.

However, the "sonship" of the king did not represent an actual divine begetting—as the literal wording of v. 7 would indicate, and as is found in texts referring to kings from Egypt and Mesopotamia. The OT "sonship" (see 2 Sam 7:13; 1 Chr 28:6; Ps 89:27-28) represents adoption (cf. Gen 15:2; 30:3; 50:23) rather than begetting in the literal sense, that is, the king was either physically or mentally begotten, but begotten by a decree that expressed the word of Yahweh (cf. the creative speaking of God in Gen 1). By decree the king becomes the heir and representative of the sovereignty of Yahweh.

Second, the king declares that his divinely granted status has endowed him with tremendous potential power. He has been granted the privilege of prayer which opens up unlimited possibilities (v. 8). Such privilege enhances the status of the king on the one hand, but it shows his dependence on Yahweh on the other. Great dominion is to be obtained as the gift of the heavenly king (*and I will make*). Further, the king is promised the potential of great power in dealing with alien nations (v. 9; read as "You can smash them . . . you can shatter them . . . " [author trans.]).

Verse 9 also reflects an Egyptian practice in relation to kingship. In the Egyptian ritual of coronation, the extensive power of the king was demonstrated by the smashing of earthenware bottles that bore the names of foreign peoples, or by the symbolical destruction of four pillars that represented the four cardinal points of the heavens. Similar language was applied to the conquests of Mesopotamian kings.

In vv. 10-12 an ultimatum is directed to the hostile rulers: serve Yahweh or experience the quick and sure judgment of divine wrath (cf. v. 5). The psalm does not close with this warning but with a blessing (*Happy are all who*) that frames Ps 2 with Ps 1 (cf. 1:1). These verses make it clear that the rebellion of the earthly kings is really against Yahweh, even though the immediate target may be the king in Jerusalem.

Thus, the rulers are not directed to serve the honor of the Davidic king.

A great scope of sovereignty is attached to the Davidic kings in the royal psalms (see Pss 2:8; 18:44-48; 71:8-11; 17; 89:27-29; 36-37; 110), which seems to be out of harmony with the historical realities of their modest kingdoms. How could such grandiose concepts have been taken seriously?

First, there is considerable use of "court-language" in these psalms. The Israelites adopted a good deal of the language and ideology of kingship from their neighbors, along with the institution itself.

Second, the Israelite concept of kingship was modeled on the reign of David, who did eventually rule over an extensive empire that for a time held an important role in ancient Near Eastern affairs. In subsequent generations the extent of the kingdom was diminished but the language of the Davidic reign remained fixed and finally was projected into the future as a hope.

Third, it is important to remember that the dominion of the Davidic king is a conferred one, transferred to him by virtue of his election or adoption to the office of king. However, the dominion transferred was not the dominion of David his father; but the dominion of Yahweh. To Yahweh as creator and Lord of the world belong *the nations* (Ps 82:8) and *the ends of the earth* (Pss 24:1-2; 47:3; 9; 89:12; Isa 6:3). This became the *heritage* (Ps 2:8) of the Davidic king. The really determining factor was not the geographic extent of the Davidic kingdom, but the entire redemptive purpose of Yahweh's choice of Israel.

Fourth, it is also significant that the power and dominion of the king are expressed primarily as potentialities. It is nowhere claimed that the conditions described currently prevailed. The channels for their fulfillment were, however, open to the king (and to the people) through the king's special relationship with Yahweh.

Taken together, then, Pss 1 and 2 constitute a prologue to the canonical Psalter. The two psalms are linked by the INCLUSIO formed by the "blessed" (or *happy*) in Ps 1:1 and Ps 2:12. This linkage is strengthened by the use of the verb *hgh* in 1:2 (*meditate*) and in 2:1 (*plot*, lit. "mutter"). In Ps 1 the "murmuring" aloud in meditation on *torah* is positive; in Ps 2 the "murmuring" becomes "muttering" by the nations and their kings in rebellion against Yahweh and his anointed, and such "muttering" is *in vain* ("empty") because it arouses the wrath of God. The wicked in Ps 1 will *perish* (v. 6) and so will those in Ps 2 who conspire against Yahweh in (v. 11). Thus in a fashion like that of the WISDOM LITERATURE (cf. Prov 10-15) there is a contrast between *the righteous* and *the wicked* in these psalms: Psalm 1 is individual and Ps 2 is corporate (McCann 1993b, 41–42). The summation of the message of both psalms is found at the end of Ps 2:12: *Happy are all who take refuge in him* (i.e., in Yahweh)—the fundamental message of the Psalter.

The kingship ideology in Ps 2 has attracted much attention, but in its canonical function as part of the prologue to the Psalter we should concentrate on the sovereignty of God (McCann 1993b, 42), linked of course with the Davidic kingship exercised *on Zion* (v. 6). The ultimate reign belongs to Yahweh, not to the earthly potentialities of the king. The *king on Zion* represents "an extension of Yahweh's reign into the murky world of human politics" (Levenson 1986, 48).

Psalm 89 contains the same high kingship ideology as Ps 2 (although in different words), but emphatically confronts the seeming failure of Yahweh to keep his commitment to the Davidic dynasty (Ps 89:38-51), a failure that was a major part of the theological crises emerging from the EXILE after 587 B.C.E.

Books four and five function to respond to the unanswered question of Ps 89:46: *How long, O LORD? Will you hide yourself forever?* Part of the answer is found also in Ps 2: Yahweh reigns and is not intimidated by the world powers and he still intends to maintain his commitment to his *king on Zion*.

If faithful Israelites cannot forget Zion (Ps 137:5), surely Yahweh will not do so. The emphasis on Zion is a major one in the Psalms (see commentary on Pss 42–50, and the summary of book five at the end of Ps 150). However, the royal psalms leave the matter of the kingship open and without resolution. Expectantly, not in despair, the reader of the Psalms is led toward saying, "How long, O Yahweh, until you reign through your king on Mt. Zion?" Thus the prologue of the Psalter points toward the future and calls for faith.

Psalm 3

This psalm belongs among the laments, but notes of trust also are strong. The title contributes little directly to interpretation. It does illustrate the practice of assigning psalms (and speeches) to prominent people in especially dangerous or climactic moments.

The suppliant begins with a cry to Yahweh (vv. 1-2) that is characteristic of the laments, and expresses the greatness of the speaker's distress and danger. The

mention of *foes* (or "enemies") is not uncommon in the laments and presents a special problem (see commentary on Ps 7). The suppliant is beset by foes who taunt the speaker by saying that *no help* from God can be expected.

The mood changes abruptly in vv. 3-6 from lament to confidence. The *but you* (v. 3) is a strong beginning of a statement of confidence, which is grounded in Yahweh, who is my *shield, my glory*, and the lifter of *my head* for the speaker. The last term may reflect the freedom of an accused person to lift up the head after prostration on the floor before charges of guilt hurled in the gate by adversaries. Verse 4 may indicate that the psalm was designed originally for a king (see Ps 18:6). Three statements of confidence follow one another: the certainty of being heard in prayer (v. 4); the security of sleeping and waking in the sustaining providence of God (v. 5); the freedom from fear, even when the situation seems impossible (v. 6).

Petitions for divine help appear with great force in v. 7. *Rise up* echoes the ancient invocation of the ark (Num 10:35). The references to *the cheeks* and *teeth* are in harmony with the language of the individual laments where frequent mention of the mouth, throat, lips, and teeth is made (Pss 5:10; 10:7; 31:19; 52:4; 57:5; 59:8; 140:4). The psalm closes with a positive note of confidence and blessing (v. 8). We could read this verse as relinquishment of the situation to the power of God. It also indicates that the individual laments must not be considered as purely private poetry. Concern for the people of the covenant community is included: *may your blessing be on your people!*

Psalm 4

Psalm 4 is best treated as an individual lament with such a preponderance of confidence that it becomes a song of trust. The situation of the suppliant is not defined in detail, although the general condition is stated. Yahweh has shown the speaker grace and lifted him or her out of the constrictions of distress into a new freedom. Nevertheless, the suppliant is experiencing vicious attacks from foes (v. 2), and finds many who are discouraged and discontented in their faith (v. 6).

Verse 1 appeals to God, based on past reception of help. *Distress* carries the idea of being restricted to narrow limits, pressed in on and deprived of freedom. God's intervention had relieved this terrible pressure.

The suppliant turns immediately to the opponents who are, apparently, men of influence (vv. 2-5). The *you people* suggests outstanding people rather than the ordinary numbers of the community. Thus the psalm reflects the abuse and oppression of the POOR by rich and influential people. One particularly dangerous weapon used by the rich was the false accusation of social or ritual crimes—charges that could result in the loss of property and life unless refuted (e.g., Nabob in 1 Kgs 21). The psalm represents a situation in which such false charges have been repudiated, in part at least, by a trial, but in which the speaker is still abused and slandered by foes. The affirmative judgment already given (vv. 1, 3) is cited, and the adversaries are warned to stop their opposition and bring themselves into right relationship with Yahweh (vv. 4-5). Verse 4 can be rendered in connection with v. 5 as: "Tremble, and do not continue to sin; think about it upon your beds, and be silent" (author trans.).

Verse 5 may point to a worship context, possibly in the sanctuary where charges against the suppliant have been heard. The person involved is admonished to go to the sanctuary and *offer right sacrifices*. The sacrifices must be *right*, not misused for malicious endeavors as they were on occasion. Verse 5 also provides a succinct summary of the basic nature of worship in Israel. The cult was always essential and, therefore, the sacrifices must be "right," that is, they should conform to the regulations stipulated for the covenant people. Sacrifices also must be accompanied by trust in Yahweh. The poles of obedience and reverence were to be held together in worship.

The speaker (vv. 6-8) addresses those in the congregation who are spiritually discouraged. Verse 6 includes a direct quotation from them. The suppliant's testimony of inner peace and strength is the confession that a "glad heart" is greater than rich harvests (v. 7). Despite the slanderous attacks from false accusers, the speaker is able to sleep well (v. 8). The suppliant's sleep (the accused and accusers may be passing a night together in the SANCTUARY [see Ps 17]) is not disturbed by fears of the future (cf. Isa 50:8-9).

Psalm 5

This individual lament is a prayer for deliverance from the charges of enemies. The speaker, despite accusations of wrongdoing, has gained admittance to a temple area in order to plead a personal case before Yahweh and the temple priests. The speaker prays and prepares to receive some revelation of innocence.

In the style of the laments, the suppliant prays that Yahweh will heed a cry for help (v. 1). *My King and my God* (v. 2) is a fixed formula that seems to have

been used often (cf. Pss 44:4; 68:24; 74:12; 84:3). The suppliant has a case to be judged by Yahweh and waits for a verdict with the coming of morning, which probably reflects the custom of an accused person passing a night in a SANCTUARY while waiting for vindication (see Ps 17).

There is no word for "sacrifice" in the text (cf. v. 3 RSV), which literally reads, "I prepare for you." The word "prepare" can denote the preparation of a sacrifice (see Gen 22:9; Lev 1:8, 12), explaining the addition of "sacrifice" in some English translations. The verb that follows (*and watch*) indicates a worshiper waiting for a divine response. Such waiting may accompany sacrifice (Num 24:3; cf. Gen 15:7-18), but the verb is most commonly used of the prophets waiting for a revelation (Hab 2:1; Mic 7:7). When "watching" is combined with the word "prepare" the meaning also can refer to the preparation of words and speeches (Job 32:14; 33:5; 37:19; Ps 50:21). Thus it may be that "presenting one's case" (v. 3) and waiting for some indication of the divine verdict is a better reading of the text than "preparing a sacrifice."

The suppliant gains confidence from the privilege of worship in the temple (vv. 4-8), while the boastful evildoers are denied access to Yahweh's presence. *Stand before* (v. 5) is used of the assembly of the covenant people before Yahweh (Josh 24:1; 1 Sam 10:19). *The boastful* are denied participation in the assembly (cf. Ps 15:1-5). The speaker is one of *the righteous* (v. 12) who is permitted access to the divine presence by means of the *steadfast love* of Yahweh (v. 7). The *steadfast love* (*hesed*) of Yahweh refers to the force of will to remain committed to obligations—enduring loyalty and love. The suppliant disavows any arrogance in approaching worship (v. 7) being one who knows the need for protection and instruction (v. 8).

A charge against the enemies and a prayer for their destruction are found in vv. 9-10. A bright and joyful comparison in the mood is found in vv. 11-12 as the speaker urges all who take refuge in Yahweh to rejoice in the providential care they receive, praying that those who love the divine name (vv. 11-12) will rejoice because Yahweh will keep them safe.

Psalm 6

This individual lament includes a plea in the first part (vv. 1-5) with an abrupt change to confidence and answered prayer in the last part (vv. 8-10). Psalm 6 was first among the penitential psalms of the ancient church (others were Pss 32, 38, 51, 102, 130, 143).

The psalm begins with the agonizing prayer of a person under great suffering (vv. 1-5). The exact reason for the prayer is not given although sickness easily is suggested. The suppliant prays for release from the rebuke and wrath of Yahweh (cf. Pss 27:9; 90:7; Jer 10:10; Job 9:5; 17:1). The speaker knows the torment of the chastisement of God, although the reasons for the punishment are not specified. The speaker is *languishing* (v. 2), which indicates that the vitality and strength of life are draining away (cf. Ps 37:2; Job 14:2; 18:16). The speaker's *bones* (which equals "body"; see Pss 35:9-10; 42:10; Jer 20:9) are "troubled" (RSV) or, perhaps (with slight text changes) we should understand them as decayed or weakened.

The continuation of the prayer in vv. 4-5 emphasizes what commentators call "motivations" or reasons God should hear and answer a prayer. Two are given. The first is an appeal to Yahweh's *steadfast love*, the loyal-love (*hesed*) that transcends the weaknesses and failure of Israel. The second appeal (v. 5) is based on the inability of the dead to participate in worship (cf. Ps 88:11; Isa 38:18). If Yahweh expects to receive the praise of his people, he must keep them out of SHEOL.

A further description of the speaker's condition is given in vv. 6-7. Suffering is accompanied by moaning and the flowing of copious tears, and the speaker's situation is aggravated by the presence of foes (vv. 7-8). The change of mood from v. 7 to v. 8 is remarkable. The suppliant declares that the prayer to Yahweh has been heard, and the *workers of evil* (v. 8; see Ps 7) are summarily bidden to leave.

Psalm 7

The context of this individual lament is revealed in vv. 1-2. The suppliant has fled from unidentified pursuers to Yahweh's presence (cf. Ps 11:1), although the *refuge* may be metaphorical rather than cultic. The speaker feels like one being torn apart and dragged away by a lion (v. 2). The opening statements are followed by a protestation of innocence.

After the affirmation of innocence (vv. 3-5), the suppliant appeals to Yahweh to arise in anger against the enemies and "wake up" for judgment (vv. 6-8; on God awakening from sleep, see commentary on Ps 44). The prayer is a bold one—almost a challenge—that brings the suppliant to the brink of irreverence.

The terse, sharp idiom of these verses communicates the speaker's deep feelings and great agitation. *Awake, O my God* (v. 6) is derived from an ancient cry that signaled the movement of the ark of the cove-

nant (see Num 10:35-36; Ps 68:1); it was a battle cry (adapted to liturgical poetry) for Yahweh to arise against enemies. Thus, the prayer is directed to the great leader and judge (i.e., the LORD) of the nations who comes to the throne above the ark in the Temple. The speaker appeals a personal case to the judge of *the peoples* of the earth (v. 8), on the basis of *righteousness* and *integrity*, boldly urging Yahweh to *judge me*.

The end of the wicked and the establishment of the righteous is sought (vv. 9-11) and an appeal is made to God who knows the inner mind and heart of human beings (cf. 17:3; Jer 17:10), and who can establish genuine judgment. The suppliant changes to affirmations of confidence in vv. 10-11. Verse 11 is uncertain, but may refer to God's attitude toward the wicked.

Verses 12-16 are clearly separated from the preceding verses, and from v. 17, which is a vow of thanksgiving and praise. They may have been added later as comment. A problem concerning the subject arises in vv. 12-13. The RSV assumes that God (not mentioned in the MT) is the subject, and the text is corrected and translated accordingly. It may be, however, that the subject is the enemy who is pictured preparing deadly weapons for battle. Thus the translation of vv. 12-13 would be

If the enemy does not repent, but whets his sword,
  bends and strings his bow,
he has prepared weapons of death against himself,
  making his arrows glowing hot. (author trans.)

The action of the enemies is described with a striking succession of verbs related to childbirth (v. 14), which is an ironic use of the ideas of conception and birth blessing. The entire passage stresses the teaching that the wicked suffer their own wickedness as judgment. Sinfulness judges itself. The *pit* which is dug for others becomes a trap for the digger (v. 15), who suffers the boomerang effect of ungodly conduct. To the person who lacks spiritual sensitivity, the fate of the wicked seems to be but a part of the paradox of life or the irony of existence. Those who have faith perceive the providential judgment of God.

This psalm is a suitable context for discussing two matters that often occur in the interpretation of the laments. The first of these is the protestation of innocence (vv. 3-5). The statements lack contrition and exhibit a deplorable self-righteousness on the part of the suppliant. In the case of Ps 7 the problem is not great because the vigorous declarations are clearly aimed at specific charges made against the accused—who emphatically denies them. Further, the speaker does not claim a general perfection and freedom from all faults. The claims are more sweeping in passages such as Pss 17:1-5; 26:1-6; Job 31, where they sound like declarations of absolute rightness before Yahweh. How should such passages be understood?

An answer begins with the recognition of cultic formulae used by worshipers to declare their fitness to participate in the worshiping fellowship on the basis of having fulfilled its requirements. An example of the use of such formulae is found in Deut 26:13-15, which contains statements to be used by the Israelite at a tithe-offering ceremony. The gate liturgies or formulae found in Pss 15 and 24 are closely related; they stipulate the requirements laid upon a worshiper who seeks to enter the sanctuary and participate in the ceremonies. Persons who declare themselves to have met the requirements are "righteous," that is, they are in a right relation with Yahweh and the people. Thus, the suppliant in v. 8 asks for judgment *according to my righteousness*. Remember that RIGHTEOUSNESS IN THE OT is neither a virtue or work of merit, nor a legalistic concept. Instead it refers to rightness of attitude and relationship.

Nevertheless, this is hardly an adequate explanation for the wide-ranging claims of innocence and virtue that are affirmed in passages like Ps 7. The relatively simple affirmations of cultic righteousness may become generalized statements of moral perfection. There are at least two roots to this development. First, never in Israelite worship was there a middle way between the "righteous" and the "wicked." A person was either one or the other. Israelite theology did not allow for a "fringe" member!

Another angle acknowledges the didactic design of liturgies and formulae. The confessions of innocence were intended to challenge and to instruct the worshipers in facets of life and devotion that made an ideal righteous person. The didactic features must have become stronger when the psalms were no longer used in specific cultic situations and were interpreted as scripture.

The second subject that needs attention is that of "the enemies" referred to in many psalms. Foes are described in manifold ways. If Pss 3–7 alone are surveyed a considerable list will result: *my foes*, and those who *are rising against me* (3:1); *ten thousands of people who have set themselves against me all around* (3:6); *the wicked* (3:7); *the boastful* and *evildoers* (5:5), and so forth. Such a listing could be extended

throughout both the individual and communal laments. While such psalms are generalized descriptions that never specifically identify an adversary, the descriptive language is vivid, intense, and carries powerful emotional content.

Scholars have advanced several theories about the identity of the enemies. One interpretation understands the enemy as self-righteous neighbors or former friends who interpret the sufferings of the accused (especially in illness or economic distress) as a retribution for former sin. In other cases the enemies are seen as rich, powerful, arrogant, and oppressive members of society who take advantage of poor and humble folk.

Others emphasize the role of the enemies as false accusers, whose accusations necessitate the flight of the accused to a sanctuary where the charges could be laid before the priests (and before God) in order to secure a judgment that would release the accused (see above). A variation of this situation would occur in cases of sickness. The enemies may have had no direct connection with the illness, but they aggravated the condition of the sick person with charges of guilt, and with whispers and taunts of being forsaken by God. Many psalms probably contain references to such false accusers (e.g., Pss 3, 4, 5, 7, 17, 57, 59, 143).

Another theory is concerned with the *evildoers* or *workers of evil* found in the psalms (e.g., 5:5; 6:8; 14:4; 28:3). The word translated "evil" (*awen*) carries the idea of "power." In this usage, the power would be devoted to destructive and antisocial objectives. The power of the spoken word is particularly significant, thus it is assumed that the *workers of evil* are "sorcerers" or "cursers" who hurled their abusive words and curses at others with traumatic results. It is not necessary, however, to assume that such "sorcerers" were professional MAGICIANS or practitioners of the occult. The "sorcerer" could have been anyone who made use of cursing or condemning words, especially in community gossip. A person suffering from such attacks would use suitable laments and prayers provided by priests or some other liturgists. In addition to the prayers, some type of purificatory ritual, with a sacrifice and offering, was probably used to insure the suppliant's proper relationship to God and to nullify the effects of the *workers of evil*. The sick person, family, friends, and members of the community also would participate in the ceremonies.

Another important theory begins with the fact that some references to enemies identify them as foreigners. This is true in the community laments of the people, and in the royal psalms (e.g., Pss 44:9-16; 54:3-11; 18; 79:1-7; 89:22-23). The enemies of the king and of Israel are also the enemies of Yahweh (e.g., Pss 2; 18:3; 21:8-12; 66:3; 83:2-8; 89:10; 42; 52; 92:9; 110:1; 2; 132:18) although domestic enemies also may be included. Some references in the individual laments point in the same direction (e.g., Pss 9:5; 43:1-2; 54:3 [reading "strangers"]; 56:7; 59:5). Such psalms were originally intended for the use of the king although they were also recited by ordinary Israelites in subsequent usage. There is some logic in the conclusion that since "enemies" refers to foreigners in many places, the same meaning may be given to its use in other places. The analysis, however, must not be taken too far.

Such generalization is not confined to the descriptions of "enemies." It is found also in the descriptions of the condition of the worshipers. Repeated and varied accounts of distressing situations are found in the laments. Specific diagnoses of the speakers' troubles elude the interpreter again and again. This is less the case with the "we" laments, where there are fairly clear indications of attack from external foes (e.g., Pss 44, 74, 79, 80). The situation is far more difficult in the individual laments.

Two psalms (42–43 as a single psalm and 137) show that separation from Zion is the cause of lamentation. Others are characterized by such expressions as *I am weary* (Pss 6:6; 69:3), *my groaning* (Pss 22:1; 32:3); *my bones are out of joint* (Ps 22:14), *my eye wastes away* (Ps 31:9); and *my spirit faints* (Pss 77:3; 143:4). Even relatively precise passages such as Ps 38:3-8 permit no firm conclusions. The prayers of the suppliants do not help either. Such terms as "deliver me," "be gracious unto me," "forsake me not," or "save me" do not add greatly to the diagnosis.

Generalization indicates that psalms were composed for the common use of worshipers in ceremonies of different types. General formulae that could be used on many occasions had to be used. An example is found in the title of Ps 102: "A prayer for one afflicted, whenever one is faint and pours out complaint before Yahweh," a title that means the psalm is suitable for anyone in the condition described.

This judgment is no denial of the authenticity of the experiences described in the psalms. After all, professional poets and writers are among the most sensitive and perceptive of human beings. The mark of great writers is that they are able to transcend their own experiences and become fully "human." The cultic nature of the psalms enhances their power and has contributed immeasurably to their unique place in Jewish and Christian devotion.

Psalm 8

This is a hymn of praise that glorifies God the Creator whose handiwork is visible both in the heavens and in humanity. The major emphasis is not on the acts of creation themselves, but rather on the lordship of Yahweh over creation. It is God's "name" that is *majestic* in all the earth; it is God' *glory* that is "chanted" (RSV) above the heavens; it is the work of God's "hands" (*fingers*) that has been given over to the dominion of human beings.

There are problems in the translation of the invocation (vv. 1-2) that cannot yet be solved with assurance. The "chanted" of the RSV is uncertain, but it is possible that it should be understood in the sense of "recite in antiphonal song," referring to praise being sung by celestial beings (cf. Isa 6:3; 1 Kgs 22:19; Job 1:6; 38:7). A change of vowels (and reading the first two words in the Hebrew text as one) yields the translation: "O let me chant your glory above the heavens, with a mouth of babes and infants." The meaning, then, would be that the worshiper wishes to join in the heavenly chorus of praise even though his or her own voice would be like the babble of an infant in such exalted company. Although such a reading is attractive, however, it is conjecture.

The NRSV (also NIV; cf. NAB) *You have set your glory above the heavens* (v. 1c), is linked to v. 2, which seems awkward. The RSV of v. 2 assumes that the chanting of Yahweh's glory is done "by the mouth of babes and infants" (i.e., by the weakest members of humanity). Commentators have noted that a child has the capacity (often lacking in adults) to surrender to the great and glorious without repressive inhibitions. Childlike language may voice the praise of God in a manner worthy of the celestial chorus.

I prefer to treat v. 2 as a separate sentence with a period at the end of v. 1 (NRSV's two sentences in v. 1 seems less likely to me). The recitation (not *set*) of the heavenly glory is done by celestial beings (v. 1c). The meaning of v. 2 is pointed toward an earthly context. The praise of weak and mortal human beings is used by God to construct a *bulwark* against dangerous *foes* (cf. 1 Cor 1:27; 29; Matt 21:16). The weakness of human beings who trust in Yahweh is used as a fortress of strength against evil foes. *Founded a bulwark* (or "strength") seems strange; the NIV reflects the Greek text (cited in Matt 21:16) that reads "perfected [or prepared] praise." This eases the expression in v. 2: "From the mouth of babes and infants you have ordained praise." However, the Greek text is probably an interpretation of the Hebrew and indicates that the meaning is a "bulwark of praise": that is, foes and avengers cannot break through the praise of God that flows forth both in heaven and on earth.

There may be a thought pattern in the psalm, beginning above the heavens (v. 1) and moving to the earth (v. 2). Again, there is an upward look to the heavens (v. 3) followed by a consideration of humanity (v. 4). The pattern continues in the following verses. The exalted status of humanity is declared in v. 5 while the earthly role of humanity is established in vv. 6–8. The psalm opens in the plural person but a solo voice begins in v. 3. Verse 9 is a repetition of v. 1a.

The solo voice marvels at the wonders of the heavens, which are *the work of [Yahweh's] fingers* (v. 3). A night scene is indicated since there is no mention of the sun. There is no praise of the heavens as such; it is *your heavens, the work of your fingers, the moon and the stars that you have established.* The Creator, not the creation, is glorified. In v. 4, the comparison is not between humanity and the creation, but between humanity and the Creator. What are finite human beings in comparison with the glorious One whose praise is sung in the heavens and on earth and whose handiwork the moon and the stars show forth? Both terms for humanity in v. 4 point to a mortal and earthbound status. Human beings are mundane creatures, afflicted by transience and death. Yet, they have been the object of the concern of God, who is *mindful* of them and visits them both in salvation and in judgment.

Yahweh's care for humanity is grounded in creation itself (v. 5). Humanity has been made by Yahweh to be a *little lower than God*, that is, a "little less" than divine (Heb. *elohim*; "angels" in LXX). This is the place for humans in the universe, their "slot" in the cosmic order. Human beings do not belong among the celestial beings of the heavenly court, but they are given an exalted status and crowned with the *glory and honor* that belongs to God (cf. Pss 29:1; 104:1). The same terms are also used of kings (cf. Ps 21:5), and the role of humanity in creation is expressed in terms of royal ideology (cf. Gen 1).

The verses that follow (vv. 6–8) expound the status of humanity in the arena of human action in the world. Humanity has been given dominion over the works of God's hands, and *all things* have been put *under his feet*—placed under human power. No other animal threatens human dominion (vv. 7-8), because all other classes of animal life are subordinate to humanity.

The psalm closes with a repetition of the doxology of v. 1a, because it is the glory of Yahweh that is praised. Modern readers may miss the point. The exalted status of humanity in vv. 3-8 is often seen as separate from the glory of God. Such is not the case with the psalmist. The glory of Yahweh overshadows all other beings and things. Both the world and humanity are subordinate to the Creator. The real significance of human beings consists in their relationship to God's majesty and to God's *mindfulness* of them. The true glory of humanity is to live as God's creatures whose status is a given one.

Psalms 9–10

These two psalms belong together. They are printed as one psalm in Greek texts, and are linked by the acrostic principle, meaning that successive verses begin with words that begin with successive letters of the Hebrew alphabet (other examples of the acrostic style are Pss 25; 34; 37; 111; 112; 119; 145; Prov 31:10-31; Lam 1–4; Nah 1:2-11). Other evidence that Pss 9–10 should be treated as a single work include (1) Psalm 10 has no title, the only such psalm in Pss 3–41 except for Ps 33 (which may be read with Ps 32); (2) the *selah* occurs at the end of Ps 9, whereas elsewhere it appears in the body of psalms rather than at the end; (3) common language and form also join the two psalms; and (4) the two psalms together form a considerably extended and modified individual lament and thanksgiving.

The psalm begins with a thanksgiving vow (9:1-2), which occurs more normally at the end of a supplication. The speaker vows to praise Yahweh for all his *wonderful deeds* and declares an intention to testify of them to others. The "wonderful deeds" are explained in vv. 3-6: the grateful worshiper has been delivered from enemies by the righteous judgment of Yahweh. The exact nature of the judgment is not explicitly given, although vv. 5-6 indicate that the defeat of foreign foes was involved. If we think of a king (like DAVID) reciting this psalm, the context is probably that of victory in war. If an ordinary Israelite is the speaker, the reference is more probably to the judgment the suppliant has received, possibly at a SANCTUARY.

In 9:7-8 the horizon widens to include the whole world and all times. Yahweh is the king and the judge of the peoples of the world, whom he judges with justice and equity. Possibly a historical event lies behind vv. 5-8, but it is more probable these verses are drawn from festival worship when Yahweh's universal power and kingship were celebrated (cf. Pss 24:1; 8-9; 47:6-7; 96:10-14; 98:9; 1 Sam 2:10; Acts 17:31; Lev 20:11-15). The power of Yahweh, so strongly stated in vv. 5-8, is available for the oppressed and for all who seek a place of security in times of trouble (9:9–10).

In 9:11-12 an invitation to sing the praises of Yahweh is directed to the congregation and correlates with vv. 1-2. Verse 12 reminds the worshipers of an aspect of Yahweh's attitude that often is found repeatedly in the OT, namely God's mindfulness of the oppressed and afflicted, whose cries he never forgets.

In 9:13-14 the psalm swings back to the personal situation of the worshiper. The speaker is confident that Yahweh will lift him or her *up from the gates of death* (cf. 107:18; Matt 16:18), and that he or she may recount the praises of Yahweh in the *gates of daughter Zion* (i.e., the Temple).

The word *daughter* refers to the people of Zion as a unit (cf. the "daughters of Egypt," Jer 46:24; and Isa 22:4; Jer 44:11; Lam 4:10). The translation should be either "the One who will lift me up from the gates of death" or "O One who lifts me up from the gates of death!" The judgment of Yahweh is especially manifest in the ways nations and the wicked fall by their own pits and devices: in nets made for others, that is, *in the work of their own hands* (9:15-16).

Yahweh's praise is set forth in the powerful affirmations of 9:17-18. *The wicked shall depart to Sheol* where they belong (v. 17). Verses 19-20 express both confidence and strong pleading for judgment of the wicked peoples: *Let the nations know that they are only human* (cf. Pss 8:4; 90:3; 103:15-16).

Psalm 10:1-11 begins with an introduction that is typical of the complaints, and expresses the speaker's concern with the apparent remoteness of God. Why does God seem to hide *in times of trouble?* Verses 2-11 give a detailed picture of the situation that results when arrogantly wicked members of society are allowed to have their unrestrained way.

The evildoers care only for themselves and seek their own profit and security. They counsel their own hearts to have assurance in their self-gained prosperity (v. 6). The poor always suffer most from the wickedness of the godless (vv. 9-11).

In the closing section (10:12-18), the worshiper prays to Yahweh and implores him to arise to meet the needs of the afflicted. The bases for the appeal are set forth in v. 14. "Arise, O Yahweh" (v. 12) is a regular cultic formula (Num 10:35-36; Pss 3:5; 7:6; 17:13; 74:22; 132:8). The language of this passage contains a polarity between petition and statements of confidence, ending with the positive assertions of vv. 17-18.

Psalm 11

This psalm is one of trust and confidence, closely associated with the laments. The speaker addresses a demoralizing crisis of faith. The situation of the worshiper is described as one who takes refuge with Yahweh (possibly in a place of worship) from the persecution of enemies. The victim expects to find security and vindication with Yahweh. There are some, however, who counsel the speaker to flee to the mountains. However appropriate such advice may be at some times, the speaker rejects flight and chooses to rely on the power and righteousness of Yahweh (vv. 1-2).

The speaker quotes what appears to be a proverbial saying (v. 1; cf. Ps 55:6). The saying incorporates the message of unidentified counsellors, who add to their admonition a description of the dangerous situation (v. 2) in which the enemies of the speaker have prepared a deadly ambush by night.

Another proverbial saying is found in v. 3: *If the foundations are destroyed, what can the righteous do?* It means that the righteous have no basis for effective action if the very foundations of justice and religion are destroyed.

The real foundation of the worshiper's faith is Yahweh's righteous judgment (vv. 4-7). Yahweh makes no mistakes in his assessment of people (v. 4c); the statement that "his eyelids test" (RSV) refers to the movement of the eyelids when the eyes are focused for close scrutiny. The righteous judgments of Yahweh will bring terrible punishment to the wicked (v. 6). On the other hand, the upright ones will have the privilege of seeing the *face* of Yahweh (v. 7), that is they will experience God's presence, possibly with some reference to a theophanic appearance.

Verse 4ab express a paradoxical tenet of the faith of Israel. Yahweh is both in heaven and in the Temple (cf. the prayer of Solomon at the dedication of the Temple [1 Kgs 8:27-30; 12–13]). In the ancient world there was a strong tendency to identify an earthly temple with its heavenly counterpart because they shared the same qualities. The presence of Yahweh in the Temple on Zion does not indicate God's absence from the heavenly throne. The two merge into one reality and the Temple links heaven and earth.

Psalm 12

This psalm is a lament, but it is not clear whether it is individual or communal. It has some of the characteristics of a liturgy. In any case, its emphasis is on *the promises of the LORD* (v. 6) that are pure and reliable, even in a prevailing context of moral degeneration and spiritual bankruptcy.

A faithless situation is described in vv. 1-4. The godly people have vanished from human society (cf. Mic 7). Lying and *flattering lips* (v. 2; lit. "lips of smooth things") mark the decadence of the time. The flatterers and liars boast of their power (v. 4) because they know the effectiveness of "smooth talk" in deception and fraudulent manipulation. Their deceitful behavior arises from a *double heart* (v. 2), an idiom that designates the opposite of the "one heart" (cf. Jer 32:39; Ezek 11:19; 1 Chr, 12:39; Acts 4:32) that is found in a mature unity of will, thought, and feeling. Such "double-heartedness" tears the fabric of society and destroys the basis for fellowship. No challenge to the godly person exceeds that of a *generation* (v. 7) characterized by double hearts and smooth lips.

The worshiper(s) pray for deliverance from this sorry plight (v. 3). The reply is put in the form of a prophetic ORACLE (v. 5) that quotes Yahweh's response (cf. Ps 91:14-16; Isa 33:10). He will arise *now* to intervene on the part of the poor and needy.

The last part of v. 5 has an uncertain text. A hymnic element in v. 6 stresses the purity of the promises of Yahweh: there is no double-heartedness here! Verse 7 may be translated: "You, O Lord, will keep them [i.e., the promises of v. 6]; You will guard us ever from this evil generation." Translated in this way, it becomes a statement of confidence. In this case, v. 8 should be understood with the force of "even though on every side the wicked prowl." Yahweh's protective care will be adequate even for such a degenerate time.

Psalm 13

This psalm has been described as a model individual lament (Gunkel 1929). It contains, in brief form, the major elements of the laments, and its depth of emotion is rarely exceeded in the Psalter.

A fourfold *How long?* adds great force to the complaint that opens the psalm (vv. 1-2). The problem of the speaker is revealed as a terrible sense of godforsakenness that is almost unendurable (cf. Ps 22:1-2). Yahweh's face seems hidden (v. 1); enemies rise against the speaker (v. 2); and the suppliant dreads the potential cry of victory and rejoicing from the adversaries (v. 4).

From lament the speaker turns to petition in vv. 3-4. The prayer seeks to span the gap that separates the worshiper from Yahweh, and to reestablish the communion that had been broken. The speaker complains of the nearness of death and expresses a desperate need for a response from Yahweh (v. 3) because the light of his eyes is about to go out in death (cf. 1 Sam 14:27; 29; Lam 5:17; Pss 6:7; 38:10). Verses 3c-4 contain what is sometimes called a "motivation"—a prayer statement that gives the rationale for God's granting the requests of a worshiper. Motivations are varied in content, and they add extra force and urgency to the prayers.

The mood of the psalm changes abruptly from lament and prayer to confidence and a vow of praise (vv. 5-6). The speaker anticipates rejoicing in forthcoming deliverance and being able to sing the praises of Yahweh. These verses strengthen the petitions in v. 3 that form the heart of the psalm.

Psalm 14

Psalm 14 is identical with Ps 53 except for some textual changes. However, the messages of the psalms are different and should not be dealt with as merely the product of textual corruption or editorial changes.

Psalm 14 usually has been considered as a mixed type, almost in a class by itself. However, the psalm seems to fit the genre of prophetic-judgment speech, with two of its main features being (1) a lament or complaint by a speaker regarding social conditions and (2) either the citation of or reference to a speech by God. The social complaint is clear in vv. 1-3, and it is possible that v. 4 (or even vv. 4-7) forms a speech by Yahweh, although it seems more probable that these verses are written as from a PROPHET who reproaches evildoers in a taunting style. The psalm is converted into a prayer by the wish expressed in v. 7.

An abrupt statement introduces the situation and interprets its cause: a corrupt society where the fool says, *"There is no God"* (v. 1, lit. "absence of a god") and *no one . . . does good* (lit. "absence of one doing good"). *No God* does not refer to theoretical atheism, but to a practical atheism that may be paraphrased "God is not here." *Fools* have formulated judgment in their *hearts* (or minds). Such persons may not speak of it with their lips, but at the volitional power center of life they act as if God is absent.

The *fool* is designated by one of several terms used in the OT. *Nabal*, used here, represents the condition that is neither the result of inexperience and lack of education (the *pethi*) nor that of a brutish, stupid, and barbarous manner. The *nabal* is not stupid but rather one with a stubborn will and deliberate disregard of spirituality. By conventional standards the *nabal* may have been judged anything but a fool.

Yahweh is portrayed as looking *down from heaven* upon the activities of human beings (v. 2). This seems to refer to his role as the king-judge of the world and of all mankind (cf. Pss 2:4; 7:7; 9:7-8; 11:4; 33:13-14; 102:18-20). The focus of the divine scrutiny falls on the shockingly complete depravity of human beings (v. 3). They have all *gone astray* "together."

Verse 4 returns to the *evildoers* (the *corrupt* of v. 1) and expresses divine amazement at the thoughtless conduct of human beings who do not know the true nature of their way of life, The *no God* people *eat up* their neighbors (*my people*) as casually as people eat bread, unconcerned by thoughts of God's presence.

The judgment of God will not fail "the generation of the righteous" (i.e., those who are true to their relationship with Yahweh [v. 5]). The *there* of v. 5 is strongly emphasized: it may refer to the place where the evildoers try to carry out their foolish deeds against the people of Yahweh—the arena of their actions will be the place they will know the terror of judgment. More probable, however, the reading for *there* is in the sense of "that being so" or "then."

Verse 6 follows with the affirmation that Yahweh is the *refuge* of *the poor* whose *plans* are caused to fail by the evildoers who devour them in arrogant disrespect for the divine will (v. 4).

Verse 7 expresses a prayer in the form of an ardent wish for the deliverance of Israel by Yahweh coming forth from Zion to restore the fortunes of his people (cf. Amos 9:14; Hos 6:11; Joel 4:1; Jer 31:23; 33:7; 11; 26: Job 42:10). Such a deliverance would change the situation in vv. 1-6. Then Jacob-Israel would *rejoice* and *be glad*, and humankind would know that evil efforts to manage the world in defiance of God will finally fail.

Psalm 15

This psalm reflects the form of a "liturgy of entry" into a holy place or temple. Psalm 15 is not necessarily an actual admission liturgy; it may have been used in school and family teaching to express norms and ethical standard of the community.

The questions in v. 1 reflect those asked by approaching worshipers. The use of the word *tent* rather than "temple" is probably an archaism (cf. Ps 61:4; Isa 33:20) that kept alive the old tradition of the tent-SANCTUARY of Yahweh—here shifted to Mount Zion the *holy hill* (cf. Pss 2:6; 3:4; 43:3; 48:2). Possibly, however, there was a tent-shrine or tabernacle in the Temple itself, which would have eased the fusion of the two concepts. The terms "sojourn" and "dwell" (RSV) reflect the old practice of providing camping space in the sanctuary area for pilgrims. The worshipers wished to receive the privilege of being guests of Yahweh and of enjoying the benefits of divine hospitality (cf. Pss 65:4; 84:4).

A general statement of entrance requirements appears in v. 2, while vv. 3-5 explain it. Nothing is said of ritual requirements—such as purity rites and sacrificial correctness—since the essence of OT theology focuses on obedience in ethical relationships rather than ritual correctness. Obedience is better than offering sacrifices (1 Sam 15:22), although sacrifices had great significance (see Ps 4:5).

Verse 2 describes a trustworthy, mature person whose *heart* (mind) is a source of *truth*. Such persons "do righteousness" (*do what is right*) by behaving in a manner that sustains healthy relationships, both in the community and in worship.

Of the statements in vv. 3-5, two should receive special note. The "reprobate" (*the wicked*) is to be *despised* (v. 4a). The "reprobate" is one who is rejected and barred from worship because of behavior.

Verse 5a is startling for modern readers, but it reflects the laws that prohibited changing interest to fellow Israelites (cf. Exod 22:25; Deut 23:19; Lev 25:36). The Israelites attempted to eliminate the very high and destructive interest rates common in ancient times.

Psalm 16

Translators have had difficulty with this psalm, probably because it originated in the northern kingdom and its language contains elements of northern Israelite Hebrew (Rendsburg 1990, 29–30). It belongs to the psalms of confidence, those that affirm trust in God.

The opening petition is brief and changes quickly into testimony (vv. 1-2). In v. 3 the term for *the holy ones* can be understood either as the people of Israel who are especially devoted to Yahweh, or the priests. The more general reference to devout worshipers is better. In v. 4, the speaker refuses to be associated with the practice of IDOLATRY.

There is a THANKSGIVING addressed to God (vv. 5-6), a testimony of the happiness of communion with God, and a declaration of the assurance of victory over death in vv. 5-11. A remarkable use of the terminology of the allocation of the land of Canaan to the Israelite tribes occurs in vv. 5-6 (cf. Josh 13:23; 14:4; 17:5; Num 18:21-24; Deut 4:21), used here of the thanksgiving of an Israelite who has experienced a prerogative like that of the Levitical priests: *The LORD is my chosen portion and my cup* (see Deut 10:8-9; Num 18:20). The *cup* points to an intimate association with Yahweh. The conjecture has been advanced that there was a "festival cup" that was passed among those dining together at a feast. To drink from a common cup bound those participating in peace and fellowship.

Verses 7-8 also express a close relationship with Yahweh. It is Yahweh who *gives . . . counsel* that was received intuitively at night (*my heart* is lit. "my kidneys," a designation of the seat of inner feeling and emotion). The content of the *counsel* is not explicitly stated, but is probably included in v. 11. The speaker has been "caused to know" *the path of life* and has experienced a renewed measure of the *fullness of joy* and *pleasures* found in the presence of Yahweh. Even the thought of death cannot disturb the resulting joy and security (vv. 9-10).

Verses 9-10 contain no doctrine of a resurrection or any development of the idea of life after death. But v. 10 should not be reduced to only confidence that Yahweh would spare the speaker a premature death. The central point is that communion with Yahweh leads one onto a *path of life* that cannot end in death. Yahweh's inexhaustible resources for life will not be surrendered to SHEOL. So far as the speaker is concerned, the future holds nothing but life (cf. Ps 73). The Greek text of vv. 8-10 is used in Acts 2:24-28 to support the resurrection of Jesus.

Psalm 17

Psalm 17 is an individual lament in which the speaker makes a strong claim of innocence (vv. 3-5). Although the setting is vague, the psalm would have been suitable for varied contexts: one falsely accused seeking vindication in the temple; a king confronted by rebels and/or foreign foes; or a prayer of a person of faith oppressed by the wicked.

The opening verses (1-2) contain a prayer for Yahweh to grant judgment and *vindication*. The opening prayer is followed by an assertion of innocence (vv. 3-5). The speaker asserts a purity from guilt under vigor-

ous testing (cf. Ps 7). The mention of *night* (v. 3) may indicate that the psalm reflects the practice an accused person spending a night in the *sanctuary* in order to receive an *oracle* or other indication of Yahweh's decision. The night was considered to be especially favorable for receiving a divine message (e.g., JACOB at BETHEL [Gen 28:10-17], SAMUEL at SHILOH [1 Sam 3:2-14], SOLOMON at GIBEON [1 Kgs 3:4-15], and GIDEON at ophrah [Judg 6:25-27]). Night also heightens the expectation of help and deliverance that comes in the morning (Pss 3:5; 4:8; 5:3; 16:7; 59:16; 143:8).

Assertions of innocence were designed to refute specific charges against the accused, charges that would have excluded them from communion with Yahweh. The declarations of innocence were not intended to be used in a boastful way. The language in declarations of innocence is standardized and reflects an ideal of the righteous person. The confessions of innocence also are testimony to the boldness and forthrightness of Israelite prayer. The very prospect of such prayer was calculated to produce repentance.

After the declaration of innocence, the psalm moves into a prayer (vv. 6-9), and on to a description of the conduct of deadly adversaries (vv. 10-12). The torment felt by the speaker explodes with the powerful petitions found in vv. 13-14. With the ancient battle cry of Israel over the ARK—*Rise up, O Lord . . . !* (cf. Num 10:35-36)—the speaker prays for Yahweh's deliverance from enemies. Verse 14a is a strong expression of the desire for judgment upon the children of the wicked (see Ps 58). Verse 14b refers to a mysterious "food of wrath" that is stored up for the wicked and their posterity (the meaning of this part of the verse is very uncertain).

Verse 15 reflects the confidence of the speaker who is sure of a meeting with Yahweh where the divine face will be seen *in righteousness* (i.e., with vindication and deliverance). Some interpreters think *when I awake* refers to awaking from the sleep of death in a resurrection, but it is more probable the verse reflects an expected deliverance, in a sanctuary, that the speaker anticipates receiving at dawn (cf. v. 3). The worship background may possibly go back to a vigil in the sanctuary with worshipers waiting for a solar THEO-PHANY at dawn (when the light of the sun rising over the Mount of Olives shined into the Temple, enhanced by the gold plating of many objects in the interior). In time the actual rite of the theophany faded, while the imagery remained as figurative speech for God's face and presence (cf. Pss 4:8; 89:15; 90:8; 119:135).

Psalm 18

This psalm, which also appears in 2 Sam 22 with some changes of detail, is a royal thanksgiving psalm. The psalm is "royal" because it was intended to be spoken by a Davidic king. Some scholars question the unity of the psalm, but when it is interpreted from a traditio-historical perspective the difficulties largely disappear. The psalm apparently had a long history in the traditions of Israel, through which it was modified, especially the addition of the victory song in vv. 31-45. The powerful theophanic description in vv. 7-15 seems inserted into the main frame of the psalm, found in vv. 1-6, 16-19.

Commentators have dated Ps 18 as early as the tenth-century B.C.E. (some even to the time and authorship of DAVID himself). Others, however, date it to later periods, particularly the period of HEZEKIAH (727–698 B.C.E.) and JOSIAH (640–609 B.C.E.). There can be no certainty about a specific date.

18:1-3. The context. Some scholars have argued that, regardless of later usage in the cult, it was prepared for a king on the occasion of some historical deliverance. Others maintain that it refers to the conflict and suffering experienced by the king in a ritual humiliation, and the deliverance that it is supposed was part of the autumn festival (Tabernacles) in preexilic Israel. The hypothesis of the humiliation of the king in the Israelite cult is plausible, but it is supported by very little evidence. The psalm invites the reader to think of a king, especially of David, as the speaker (note the superscription).

The opening testimony of love for Yahweh (vv. 1-3) is unusual in the OT. These verses contain a treasury of metaphors that describe attributes of Yahweh; strength and action are the qualities most evident. The king has available a great source of energy and power (and when the psalm became "democratized" they were available to ordinary worshipers). Yahweh has *saved* the king from his *enemies* (v. 3).

18:4-24. Thanksgiving. Verses 4-24 is a long THANKSGIVING. The conditions that prevailed when the king was delivered are described in vv. 4-5, 16-19. The "waves of death" (v. 4) had threatened to overwhelm and carry down the speaker to the primeval deep of death. Such language (reminiscent of mythological texts from the ancient Near East) apparently is applied to the threat posed to the king (and the nation) by enemies (vv. 16-19, 37-42). Those who interpret the psalm in a purely cultic context see a cultic drama in

which the king has been attacked by his *enemies* (representative of the enemies of Israel) before he cried out to Yahweh and was delivered.

In any case, the king called out to Yahweh, who heard his voice in the heavenly temple (v. 6). Yahweh's response to the prayer of the king is a thunderous, earthshaking theophanic intervention (vv. 7-15). This passage is heavy with the imagery of a thunderstorm used as the instrument of divine action (cf. Pss 29; 97; 114). The description of the theophany is closely related to those that refer to Yahweh's coming to SINAI and those of his going forth to save his people in war (see Exod 19:16-24; Deut 33:2; Judg 5:4-5; 1 Kgs 19:9-18; Pss 50:1-6; 68:7-8; Isa 30:27-28; Hab 3:3-15). The king is delivered from his distress into a new freedom (vv. 16-18), which is not of his own doing. The repeated emphasis on divine action—*he reached, he took me, he drew me out, he delivered me, he brought me out*—is noteworthy.

The testimony of the king continues in vv. 20-24, emphasizing that his deliverance has been a vindication of his *righteousness* (his "right-relatedness" to Yahweh). This passage is very similar to the protestations of innocence in the laments (cf. Ps 7:3-5), except that it is put into the form of a testimony, a common motif for thanksgiving psalms. These verses should not be read as making a claim to a general sinless perfection. They constitute an affirmation of faith and a testimony of the salvation received from Yahweh.

18:25-30. Testimony. The king continues the testimony in hymnic terms (vv. 25-30). He declares that human behavior does matter to God, whose response is appropriate to the attitudes manifest towards him. In v. 27 what is true for an individual is applied to the people: the king knows that he, alone, has not been saved but as one of the company of *humble people* who have taken refuge with Yahweh.

18:31-50. God's strength. The second part of the psalm begins in the third person plural (*our God*), which can be either an opening verse spoken by the congregation, or by the king praising Yahweh before the congregation and identifying himself with them in loyalty to Yahweh. The verses that follow tell of the charismatic equipment and training Yahweh has given to the king (vv. 32-36). A graphic picture of victory in battle follows (vv. 37-42). The victory of the king (either cultic or historical) was complete, and afterwards he was made *head of the nations* (v. 43) and served by foreigners who, cringing before him, cease their opposition to him (vv. 44-45; cf. Ps 2).

Verses 46-50 contain closing sections of praise and thanksgiving. Again, Yahweh is lauded for the triumphs he gave the king over his enemies. Verse 50 establishes the connection of the psalm with *David and his descendants*.

Psalm 19

Two separate and independent units compose this psalm (vv. 1-6 and vv. 7-14). The units differ in subject, language, and poetic meter. The first unit is hymnic praise of Yahweh's glory in creation; the second unit praises the *torah* (cf. Pss 1; 119). The originally separate units have been deliberately bound together; the resulting combination ought to be interpreted as a whole. The link that binds them is theological: Yahweh's will and action.

19:1-6. God in creation. The *glory* and *handiwork* of God in creation is praised in vv. 1-4b. The testimony of creation is a perpetual one, *day to day* and *night to night*. Yet the testimony is given without speech, words, or voice. The "silent eloquence" (Kirkpatrick 1901) of their witness goes out to the ends of the earth. These verses mock the beliefs of many in ancient Egypt and Mesopotamia, where there was a tendency to identify the heavens, as well as the forces of nature, with deities. For the Yahweh worshiper, however, the FIRMAMENT was a witness of the handiwork of God.

Verses 4c-6 refer to the course of the sun across the heavens, and recall numerous examples of ancient Near Eastern praise of the sun-god. However, vv. 4c-6 is not a hymn to the sun, since there is no summons to praise or any direct access. By juxtaposition, these verses praise the God whose handiwork is displayed in the heavens (v. 1). A small change in the text of "in them" (NRSV mg.) of v. 4c results in the reading "in the sea." However, the change is unnecessary and the "in them" provides a connection between vv. 1-4b and 4c-6. The *tent for the sun* is set *in the heavens* (vv. 1, 6). The note of comprehensiveness in vv. 3-4 appears again in v. 6c. Both the glory of God and the heat of the sun pervade the whole world.

19:7-14. The will of Yahweh. The second unit, vv. 7-14, is concerned with the *torah* of Yahweh. With an abruptness similar to v. 1, the psalmist begins the description of the "*torah* of Yahweh" in v. 7. A series of terms for *torah* are used (vv. 7-9), along with repeated praise of its effects. Its comparative value is stated in v. 10; v. 11 is the speaker's own testimony, a joyful affirmation of the goodness and greatness of

the *torah*, which is the revealed will of Yahweh (note that LORD is used repeatedly in vv. 7-14 while not at all in vv. 1-6).

The mood of the psalm changes quickly to that of prayer in vv. 12-14. *Meditation* on the *torah* leads to awareness of one's own inner needs. The prayer expresses a consciousness of the liability of all people to sin, for there are those *hidden faults* no one avoids. Verse 13 addresses the rebellious and proud will that so easily rises to usurp the behavior of human beings. This verse may have in view the provision of the *torah* for the atonement for sins of inadvertence (Lev 4–5; Num 15:22-29) while lacking any provision for a sacrifice for sins with a "high hand" (Num 15:30-31).

In the closing verse, acceptance of prayer by Yahweh is sought. The word translated *be acceptable* is used in cultic regulations for proper sacrifices (cf. Lev 1:3-4). Perhaps the prayer is offered here as a substitute for sacrifice (see Pss 40:6-8; 141:2).

It seems that the poet wished to bring together creation and *torah* as the two great works of Yahweh. In its present form, Ps 19 probably originated in those Israelite theological circles associated with WISDOM LITERATURE. Elements of wisdom vocabulary are found in vv. 7-11, and the cosmological view of vv. 1-6 is that of the fixed, stable, and silent universe of wisdom theology. The stability of creation was matched by the certainty and dependability of the *torah*.

From another angle, the poet wanted to bring such "natural theology" as that in vv. 1-6 into subordination to the revealed will of Yahweh. The heavens silently tell the glory of God, but only the *torah* restores life, rejoices the heart, and enlightens the eyes. The will of Yahweh for the people is not in speech or knowledge of the heavens (v. 3); it is in *torah*. A person may contemplate the handiwork of God in the heavens, but a person becomes a *servant* (v. 11) who can speak of God as *my redeemer* (v. 14) only by the *torah*.

Psalm 20

This royal psalm in the form of a prayer for the king has two main parts: a prayer for the king (vv. 1-5, although the king is not mentioned until v. 9), and the assurance that the prayer has been heard (vv. 6-8). Verse 9 is a concluding exclamatory statement that recapitulates the main idea of the psalm. The people pray for the king in vv. 1-5. An individual speaks (v. 6) and affirms that Yahweh will answer the prayers for *his anointed*, the king. The solo voice is not identified, but may be a priest. The group joins in the affirmation in vv. 7-9. Verse 7 sets forth the basic faith of Israel when confronted by the powers of the world. The heart of this faith is the confidence that the ultimate decisions of history do not depend on the might of military armaments (see Ps 33:16-17). Israel's power lies in the privilege of pronouncing (RSV, "boast of") the name of Yahweh (cf. Ps 118:10-12).

The occasion for the recitation of this psalm was probably a day of prayer for the king prior to an engagement in war. The ceremonies would have included prayer and sacrifices (see v. 3; cf. 1 Kgs 8:44-45; 1 Sam 7:9; 13:9-12; 2 Chr 20).

Psalm 21

This royal psalm contains three different types of literary material: vv. 1-7 is a thanksgiving; vv. 8-12 is an affirmation addressed to the king; v. 13 is a short prayer similar to those found in the laments of the people (cf. Pss 44:23; 74:22; 79:9). The mixture of literary types points to a liturgical character of the psalm with change of speakers, probably priests or other liturgists.

The psalm is usually considered to be a thanksgiving after a king's victory in battle, intentionally paired with Ps 20. That conclusion is doubtful since the victory in vv. 8-12 seems to be in the future. It is more likely that the psalm's context is in the festival rituals centering around the Davidic king. The welfare of the nation depended upon the welfare of the king.

The first section (vv. 1-7) opens with praise to Yahweh for answering the king's prayer. The general nature of the prayer and its answer are found in vv. 4-5. The exalted language was used of kingship (cf. 2 Sam 7:13-16; 23:3-5; 1 Chr 18:6; Pss 2; 61:6-7; 72:15-17; 89:19-37).

The king has been given *life* (v. 4) that will endure *forever and ever*, a Hebrew idiom that carries the connotation of "many years" of indefinite duration, plus the blessing of vitality (cf. Pss 2, 110). The phrase is probably an honorary attribution (Neh 2:3; Dan 2:4).

Verses 8-12 is an affirmation (or perhaps an ORACLE) addressed to the king, declaring that he will be victorious over his enemies. The victory will not be that of the king alone, however, because an annihilating fire will go out from Yahweh and engulf his foes (vv. 9-10; cf. Exod 24:17; Deut 4:3; 9:3). Yahweh is Israel's "devouring fire" (v. 9) the one who defends the king and his people. The psalm closes with a brief prayer and vow of praise by the congregation (v. 13).

Psalm 22

By form this psalm is a combination of individual complaint and thanksgiving (v. 22-31). The marked change of mood after v. 21 is a common characteristic of the laments. The shift in mood can be explained either by spiritual and psychological changes in the worshiper, by some ORACLE or cultic act carried out in response to the first part of the psalm, or more easily by assuming that there is a time span between vv. 1-21 (or 1-21a, NRSV) and the thanksgiving ceremony assumed in vv. 22-31. If there is a temporal change, the agonizing prayer in vv. 1-21 is recalled after divine relief of the sufferer's distress; thus the psalm takes its orientation from its second part.

The psalm is deeply embedded in Christian tradition because Jesus quotes the first line of v. 1 from the cross (Matt 27:46; Mark 15:34). The long tradition of Christological exegesis is appropriate, but the psalm in its OT setting is not a prophecy of Jesus, regardless of how significant the Gospel writers' use of v. 1 may be. Psalm 22 is a prayer of complaint, which expresses the agony of great suffering and plumbs the depths of the human experience until it rejoices in the divine deliverance. In the latter part, the psalm celebrates a triumphant faith that has overcome the terrible sense of godforsakenness that dominates the first part of the psalm.

The context of the lament (vv. 1-21) is not certain. The language is to a degree that of the conventional complaint (a lament), but the dimensions of the suffering seem to exceed the distress of an ordinary worshiper. Possibly the psalmist had a king in mind, even if the psalm was later "democratized" and placed in common cultic use. The condition of the suppliant also is not clear. There are striking descriptions of adversaries (vv. 6b, 7, 8, 12, 13, 16, 17b, 18), but illness appears in vv. 14, 15, 17a. There may be no opposition between the two views, however, if we think of the enemies as those who mock the speaker as one godforsaken on the basis of the suffering from physical misfortune.

The sense of being abandoned by God is poured out in the repeated cries of vv. 1-2. The cries of despair are addressed to *my God*, a personal God, and could come from a king. The cries may also recall the worship of families or other small groups. There is no loss of faith, only the incomprehensible remoteness of God. Despite the importunity of the prayer there is no answer (v. 2). *Groaning* (v. 1) is a translation of a word commonly used of the roar of a lion (Isa 5:29), but when applied to human beings it is a wail of pain and anguish.

In vv. 3-5 the mood shifts to the first statement of confidence. Yahweh is addressed as *holy* and *enthroned on the praises of Israel*. This strange phrase is similar to "enthroned on the cherubim" in Pss 80:1 and 99:1, a reference to the ARK of the covenant. The expression reflects the concept, known elsewhere in ancient Near Eastern religions, of a deity whose throne is supported above the earth by the loyalty and praise of his subjects. The faith of the ancestors is recalled in vv. 4-5. The individual finds comfort by identification with the sacred history of the people.

Overwhelmed by suffering, which is aggravated by the taunts of adversaries, the speaker again falls into despondency (vv. 6-8). The speaker is so despised and mocked by the people that there is a loss of a sense of human status. The validity of the speaker's commitment to Yahweh also is scornfully questioned by the adversaries (vv. 7-8; cf. Matt 27:42-43).

Again the attention of the worshiper turns to the acts of God, but this time to God's involvement in personal existence (vv. 9-11). The speaker has been a child of God since birth, and now prays (v. 11) to the God on whom he is totally dependent.

The pilgrimage through suffering and doubt does not end, however, with v. 11. Emotional turbulence arises again in the lengthy complaint found in vv. 12-18, which extends the complaint in vv. 6-8. The descriptions of the suppliant's condition are extreme and show that death is near (v. 15, *you [are about to] lay me in the dust of death*). Indeed, the enemies are so sure of impending death that they have already divided the victim's clothing among themselves (v. 18).

In vv. 19-21, there is a return to prayer and to the sense of God-remoteness that was dominant at the beginning of the psalm. Probably the last word in v. 21 (see RSV mg. and NRSV mg.) represents the sudden turning point in the psalm. The prayer is broken off abruptly with "You have answered me!" (NRSV mg.). If this is correct, a sudden realization of contact with God breaks into the speaker's consciousness.

There is a change of mood and a shift of context in vv. 22-31. The suppliant expresses a determination to bear testimony to *the congregation* (lit. "my brothers") of worshipers at the sanctuary (v. 22). The speaker also invites the assembled worshipers to join in praise (v. 23). Yahweh has been exceedingly gracious to the suppliant, as to all who cry out to him (v. 24). The praise of suppliant will be accompanied by the fulfill-

ment of vows, probably with offerings (v. 25). Some interpreters think v. 26 indicates a communal meal, to be shared by the rejoicing person with the poor.

A remarkably extended view concludes the psalm (vv. 27-31). The suppliant turns attention from the immediate context in Israel to include *all the families of the nations*. In a VISION of the future, a vast panorama of people will prostrate themselves in worship before Yahweh. The central verse (v. 28) asserts that sovereign kingship belongs to Yahweh, for God is the ruler of the nations.

Verse 29 is difficult to translate. The general thrust of vv. 29-31, however, seems clear: not even death will stop the testimony of praise (cf. 6:5; 88:10-12). It is doubtful that v. 29 conveys an idea of resurrection, but the limitations of death are broken. The psalm closes with an abrupt cry of triumph: *he has done it.* The completeness of Yahweh's great deliverance will be proclaimed from generation to generation. The terrible forsakenness of vv. 2 and 11 is replaced by the joyful praise of those who have been delivered.

Psalm 23

This best-known psalm is a declaration of trust, and implies an audience for the speaker, who directly addresses God (v. 5). The speaker testifies to a close relationship with Yahweh (*my shepherd* is possessive). The psalm uses three images: shepherd (v. 1), guide-protector (vv. 3-4), and host (v. 5). The metaphors of the psalm are held together by three elements: (1) they are associated with kingship; (2) they are used elsewhere for Yahweh; and (3) the name Yahweh (LORD) in vv. 1 and 6 forms an INCLUSIO that binds the parts together.

The psalm is very personal, but may have been designed as a confessional prayer for worship, perhaps for a thanksgiving-praise service. The first three verses contain a concentration of verbs and figures of speech that evoke images of security and well-being. *Shepherd* is a universal figure, associated with both the care of sheep and the function of kings.

The shepherd is also the guide-protector who directs the sheep to a secure camp near water (the emphasis is not on the stillness of the water but the security and comfort of the site) and protects those whom he leads with rod and staff—symbols of kingship—even when they pass through "the valley of death." Verse 4 is sometimes read as "the valley of deep darkness" or as *through the darkest valley*, carrying the idea of great danger and the nearness of death.

Thus the speaker can declare that there is no "lack" in Yahweh's providing for his people (v. 1), and no fear as he guides them through the times of terrible distress (v. 4). The divine presence (*you are with me*) guarantees safety. Yahweh leads his people in "paths of righteousness" (v. 3 KJV, RSV, NIV), that is, in those ways that go where they are supposed to go (one does not get lost on such paths) and those that are beneficial. He restores and fortifies the vigor and vitality of his flock (v. 3, *restores my soul*; cf. Ps 19:7; Lam 1:11; 16; 19).

The restoring of the *soul* in v. 3 is matched by the metaphor of the host (v. 5) who prepares a safe and abundant table, and extends hospitality despite the presence of enemies (cf. Ps 78:19). Yahweh as host provides a place of life and comfort for his guests. The background of this image includes the protection that is required for the host to extend to a guest. The guest is well cared for by the host in v. 5: the table is prepared, the guest's head is anointed with oil, and a cup filled to the brim is provided. The *presence of my enemies* (v. 5) indicates that enemies watch impotent to do any harm, while the speaker is blessed by the protective hospitality of Yahweh.

The change of metaphor from shepherd and guide to that of host is not surprising when it is remembered that *shepherd* is kingship language. Kings have great houses and entertain favored guests with lavish hospitality. Further, the shepherd in this case is Yahweh; and it is customary for reigning deities to have "houses" (temples) in which they dwell. The setting of vv. 5-6 is that of the Temple, a place where the worshiper feels safe and well supplied with food and drink (as those who attend the festivals). The idea of defeated enemies looking on while a victorious deity prepares tables for its soldiers is found in the Canaanite accounts of the goddess Anat at Ugarit (cf. Ps 27:6).

Follow me (v. 6) is too weak for the verb that means "to pursue" or "to chase." *Goodness* and "enduring-love" (a better translation than *mercy* or "kindness" [NRSV mg.]) will pursue the speaker *all the days of my life* (cf. the pursuit of the wicked by tempest and hurricane in Ps 83:15). The pursuit by enemies is terminated and replaced by being chased by Yahweh's fidelity and love.

The last part of v. 6 expresses confidence that the longing of pilgrims participating in the festivals at the Temple for permanent residence there will be fulfilled (cf. Pss 15:1; 27:4-6; 36:7-9; 52:8-9; 61:4; 65:4; 84; 92:12-13). The literal "I shall return to the house of Yahweh" probably means "I will be a regular guest in the house of Yahweh," that is, it will always be "home" for me. Verse 6 expresses a close and enduring contact with the divine presence. Indeed, *the house of the LORD* here may include the idea of "the household of Yahweh" in a broader sense—even to the land of Israel and the company of Yahweh's people.

Psalm 24

This hymn of praise opens with a declaration of Yahweh's cosmic ownership of the peopled and fertile earth and of his establishment of it on the *seas* and the *rivers*, which recalls the concept of the bringing forth of an ordered world out of the unruly forces of chaos. The COSMOLOGY is that of an established world founded above the primordial seas and rivers below it (see Gen 1:6; 7:11; Exod 20:4; Deut 33:13; Pss 18:15; 77:16-20; 93:1-4; 95:3-5; 104:5-9; 136:6; Job 38:4-11). Yahweh has given the world its stability but the reader is also reminded that the raging floods flow beneath the surface of earth and are always a potential threat.

The rest of this psalm has a liturgical aspect that recalls processions of worshipers going to Zion (and the Temple) for festivals. Verses 2-6 have been described as an "entrance liturgy" (cf. Ps 15), recalling the instruction and encouragement exchanged by pilgrims as they approach the Temple. The question-answer-promise format sets forth the nature of those who are worthy to come to the holy place of Yahweh and *seek the face of . . . God* (v. 6).

The last part of the psalm (vv. 7-10) also has a liturgical character with the question–answer form. These verses suggest a procession into Jerusalem and the Temple area. The assumption of a cultic ceremony involving the movement of the ARK of the covenant into the inner area of the Temple as a part of the celebration of the kingship of Yahweh is rather widely held. Heralds of the king address the gates and doors as a prelude to the entrance of the victorious monarch.

The cry to the gates to *lift up your heads* (vv. 7, 9) has been the subject of considerable difference of opinion. Is it simply the poetically exaggerated language of worship because even the highest gates and doors would be too low for the King of Glory? Are they the gates of the heavenly abode of Yahweh? (Sarna 1993, 133–34). Does the cry reflect the destruction of the Temple in 587 B.C.E. (see Lam 2:9) and, therefore, represent a call for its rebuilding?

The most likely interpretation is that the *heads* do not refer to the gates but to the people on the towers of the gates who are depicted as expectedly waiting for the return of a king from battle. The gate towers are personified as those who wait, bent over in fear, for the return of the king. The situation envisioned is that of Yahweh, the divine warrior, returning victorious after going forth to battle against the forces of evil and death that threatened the land and the world. Verses 1-2 announce success. Yahweh of Hosts is described in v. 8 as *strong and mighty . . . mighty in battle*." For *the LORD [Yahweh] of Hosts*, see 1 Sam 1:3; 4:3-4; 2 Sam 6:2; Pss 80:4; 7; 14; 19; 84:1; 3; 8; 12; 89:8; and LORD OF HOSTS; cf. 2 Kgs 19:15; Ps 80:1. *Hosts* refers to the heavenly armies that are led by Yahweh, who *is the King of glory*.

Psalm 25

This individual lament is in an alphabetic, or acrostic, form (i.e., each verse begins with a successive letter of the Hebrew alphabet). This form does not lend itself to a smooth logical development of thought, and accounts for a degree of literary "stiffness" in the POETRY of the psalm.

The exact context of the psalm is impossible to determine. There are references to the presence of violent enemies (vv. 2, 19) and statements of innocence (vv. 15, 21), which may indicate that the poet had in mind the situation of a person who seeks vindication from false charges by going to the SANCTUARY in order to plead a case before Yahweh. The most interesting element in the psalm is the prayer for forgiveness of sin (vv. 6-7, 11).

The opening verses (vv. 1-3) express a prayer to Yahweh. Verse 3 may be read as a statement rather than a petition: "Yea, no one of those who put their hope in you will be put to shame / but those who are treacherous without cause will be put to shame" (author trans.). Such conviction provides the basis for the prayer in vv. 1-2.

The prayer continues in vv. 4-7, as the suppliant seeks divine instruction. The terms *ways, paths,* and *truth* are all similar to the term *torah* (law), and refer to Yahweh's will for the people. In vv. 6-7 the prayer becomes petition for the forgiveness of personal sin.

A short hymn-like section interrupts the prayer in vv. 8-10. These verses lay a theological foundation for the prayer as they describe the ways of Yahweh with *sinners* and *the humble*. The prayer resumes (vv. 11-22) with a renewed plea for pardon from guilt (v. 11). Verses 12-15 contain statements of confidence about the condition of the person who "fears Yahweh" and

express the posture of the speaker toward Yahweh. Verse 22 is a prayer for all Israel attached to the end of the lament.

Psalm 26

The dominant features of this individual lament are confidence and certainty. Imperative petitions for acquittal and vindication dominate vv. 1-2, buttressed by a confidence in personal faith and unwavering loyalty.

The opening of the psalm is followed by a declaration of innocence (vv. 4-7) that also describes the ritual actions of the accused (vv. 6-7). Washing hands was a rite that publicly proclaimed purity (see Deut 21:6; Ps 73:13; Matt 27:24). To *go around your altar* may refer to joining a solemn procession during which the worshipers chanted the great acts of Yahweh. The sanctuary proper was not open to lay persons; only priests and Levites could enter it. The courts were accessible to non-priests, however, and the altar was located in one of them. The speaker's love of the Temple is expressed in v. 8, and petitions are renewed in vv. 9-11. The speaker contrasts hands washed *in innocence* (v. 6) with hands *full of bribes* (v. 10).

Verse 12 is a closing statement of certainty. The metaphor of the foot, in one form or another, is frequently found in the Psalter (see Pss 31:8; 40:2; 56:13; 66:9; 73:2).

Psalm 27

The sharply defined break in mood and language between vv. 6 and 7 has led some commentators to treat this psalm as composed of two independent and unrelated parts. On that analysis, vv. 1-6 is a song of trust that expresses a powerful and steady faith in Yahweh and vv. 7-14 is the lament of one who is in great distress.

The contrast between vv. 1-6 and vv. 7-13 should not be exaggerated because there is considerable correspondence between the two sections. The statements of vv. 1-6 may be read as presupposing a context of danger and distress. Psalm 27 may reflect, but is not necessarily directly related to, the experience of an Israelite pilgrim going for festival worship who is attacked by enemies (probably false accusers) while some distance from the Temple. Verses 1-6 may be read in the context of danger and distress where the speaker is nonetheless sure that security and vindication will be found at the holy place (vv. 4-6, 13).

The prayer of vv. 7-12, then, is that offered by the persecuted pilgrim after arrival at the sanctuary. The speaker prays in the presence of the congregation and, probably, before threatening *false witnesses* (v. 12). At the close of the prayer, a word of encouragement is given to the speaker by a priest (v. 14).

Psalm 28

This psalm belongs to the individual laments, but the situation that lies behind the speaker's prayer is not very clear. There is a reference to *the wicked . . . who are workers of evil* (v. 3), and the prayer is made toward, not in, the inner part of a SANCTUARY, probably the Temple in Jerusalem.

The opening call in vv. 1-2 is directed to Yahweh as the suppliant's hands are lifted *toward your most holy sanctuary* (v. 2; NRSV mg.: "your innermost sanctuary"). The speaker probably should be thought of as a worshiper in an outer court of the Temple. The term *debir* (*sanctuary*) in v. 2 refers to the Holy of Holies (Heb 9:3) where the ark of the covenant was kept (cf. 1 Kgs 6:16-19; 8:6; 24-30). The ark was the locus of Yahweh's appearing to his people (cf. 1 Sam 4:4; 2 Sam 6:2; Exod 25:22).

For *my Rock* (v. 1a), see Pss 19:14; 31:2; 92:16; 94:22; Deut 32:15; 30; 31. A silent response from Yahweh to prayer is equal to a death sentence (v. 1b).

The speaker pleads not to be destroyed in the judgment of *the wicked* (vv. 3-5) whose judgment is prayed for (vv. 4-5). The speaker seeks to disassociate from the wicked who *do not regard the works of* Yahweh, who treat lightly the saving acts of God.

The mood changes to a hymnic testimony of thanksgiving in vv. 6-7. The individual praise of vv. 6-7 broadens to include the whole people of Yahweh in vv. 8-9, with special mention of the king (*his anointed*). The confession of v. 8 becomes an intercessory prayer for the people in v. 9.

Psalm 29

Psalm 29 is a hymn that glorifies Yahweh's power and majesty. There are significant parallels between this psalm and Ugaritic poetry (which incorporates much of Canaanite religious understanding). The hymn probably was modified for Israelite theological purposes from a Ugaritic prototype. For example, it has been observed that BAAL, the name of a major Canaanite deity and one associated with thunderstorms, can be substituted for Yahweh (LORD) in the psalm with an improvement of the poetry, especially in terms of alliteration and rhyme with the sounds *b*, *l*, and *ah* (Holladay 1993, 21-2).

Verses 1-2 are a prelude or overture that is set in the heavenly court of Yahweh. The *heavenly beings* are more accurately the "sons of gods" (cf. Pss 82:1; 89:6; 7; 97:7), members of the celestial court where they worship and serve Yahweh (see commentary on Ps 82). The assembly of the gods, a rather common idea in the world of Israel's day, has become the court of Yahweh. The divine beings are divested of their status as deities and reduced in rank to that of servants of Yahweh.

In holy splendor (v. 2) is a doubtful translation. It can be "bow down before Yahweh in holy attire" (in suitable garments) or "bow down before Yahweh when the Holy One appears." The first translation is better for the poetic parallelism, but the entire context of the psalm can be cited in favor of the idea of the second, which would indicate a THEOPHANY.

Verses 3-9 describe a thunderstorm, understood as a manifestation of Yahweh's POWER and GLORY. It is a poem that links the power of the thunderstorm (one of the most awe-inspiring releases of energy experienced on this planet) with Yahweh. Distant thunder as it rolls in over the waters of the sea and gathering cloud masses (cf. 1 Kgs 18:44) is suggested by vv. 3-4. The "voice of Yahweh" expresses the thunder and power of the storm, which seems to reach a climax in v. 4. If *voice* is translated as "roar," v. 4 may be read as follows: "The roar of Yahweh—powerful! The roar of Yahweh—awesome!"

The full fury of the storm breaks over the land (vv. 5-7). The great trees of *Lebanon* go down, while the mountains themselves shake and quiver until they seem to move like jumping young animals (v. 6). *Sirion* in v. 6 refers to Mount Hermon (cf. Deut 3:9).

Verse 7 is much shorter than the other verses. It possibly belongs with *the God of glory thunders* (v. 3), which seems isolated in its present context. Or the line may be read as a part of v. 8, forming three colons to correlate with the tricolon in v. 3. On the other hand, the poetic irregularity may be deliberately intended to emphasize the climax of the storm in *flashes . . . of fire* that issue forth from the voice of Yahweh.

The movement of the storm into the wilderness is described in vv. 8-9. The mention of *the wilderness of Kadesh* first marks the general southern border of Palestine as Lebanon (vv. 5-6) marks the north. Second, the wilderness was associated with the great formative events in Israel's religion. There Yahweh had appeared both to deliver and to judge. Third, thunderstorms, while they have destructive aspects, were above all the bringer of the rain that broke long dry seasons and restored fertility to the land. The fertility aspect is taken a step further in v. 9 if *causes the oaks to whirl* is translated "makes the hinds to calve" (RSV mg.; cf. NRSV mg.), referencing the premature calving of deer.

The isolated third colon of v. 9 (*and in his temple all say, "Glory!"*) does not seem to fit into its present context very well because one half of a colon stands alone without a counterpart (also in vv. 3b and 7). However, v. 9c should be read as the conclusion of vv. 3-9, and it picks up the "glory" theme of the praise of Yahweh in the heavenly temple called for in vv. 1-2. In fact, vv. 3-9 may be read as a series of five tricolons (vv. 3abc; 4ab-5a; 5b-6ab; 7-8ab; 9abc).

The *heavenly beings* in vv. 1-2 are summoned to praise Yahweh, but they do not do so expressly until 9c, after they have seen the mighty display of divine power in vv. 3a-9b. Thus vv. 1-9 of this psalm seem to leave out the human community reciting the psalm. However, there may be a double reference in 9c to both the heavenly temple and the earthly temple. The coming of the rain and the breaking of the dry season seems to have been a major feature of the Tabernacles festival (cf. Zech 14:16-19). Thus the statement may have a deliberately double sense. The praise on earth joins with that in heaven, with a kind of synergistic merger of the heavenly and earthly dwelling places of Yahweh as found in some psalm references (see Pss 11:4; 48:2). The Temple in Jerusalem is the earthly form of the heavenly temple.

Verses 10-11 form a postlude and benediction. Above the raging storm, Yahweh *sits enthroned* over the tumultuous scene on earth. He is enthroned above *the flood*, which refers directly to the downpour of rain that follows an initial line of thunderstorms, but which also alludes to the primordial FLOOD that must be overcome for ordered life to exist (see Gen 6:17; 7:6; 7; 10; 17; 9:11). Behind this term is the connotation of the great chaotic flood that had to be controlled in the creative process. Yahweh is master of the chaotic powers that threaten the ordered universe; he can cause them to flood the earth or to subside.

The psalm closes with a prayer to Yahweh in v. 11, indirectly expressed in a wish form. Yahweh is implored to *bless his people with peace*. This is the last word in the psalm and the translation "peace" is only partially suitable, because the word is *shalom*, which refers to a condition of wholeness, health, and prosperity—a positive situation rather than the absence of war and calamity that is conveyed by the modern term

"peace." Yahweh's supreme blessing bestowed on people is *shalom* (cf. John 20:19; 21), which is the opposite of the *flood* (*mabbul*) in v. 10.

Psalm 29 is the classic example of what has been called the "Canaanite Connection" in the study of the Psalms (Kugel 1986, 119–21). Actually, the connection might be more broadly expressed as the "Ancient Near East Connection." These terms refer to resemblances, sometimes involving the same words and styles, between the POETRY of the Psalms and compositions from Mesopotamia, Palestine-Syria, and Egypt. The most extensively discussed of these "connections" are those between the poetic material from Ugarit and the Bible. Ugaritic poetic style and language are very close to that found in much biblical poetry. The diction of the Ugaritic texts has been incorporated into texts of the psalms, and in many cases remained unrecognized by later scribal copyists.

Psalm 30

This individual thanksgiving psalm expresses praise to God from an individual who received deliverance. The psalm seems especially appropriate for one who has been healed from illness (vv. 2-3). The illness is described as bringing the person to the brink of death (vv. 3, 9); the recovery is described with joyous language. The psalm probably was written for recitation at a ceremony and festive meal for a circle of family and friends called together to rejoice over an experience of deliverance and healing. The psalm may be very old. The title, which is later than the psalm, associates it with the dedication of the Temple, probably the dedication of the second Temple in the time of EZRA (see Ezra 6:16-18; Neh 12: 27-43). The psalm may also be inclusive of the Hanukkah celebration (see DEDICATION, FEAST OF) of the restoration of the Temple in 165 B.C.E.

In vv. 1-3, Yahweh is praised because he has *drawn . . . up* the suffering person from SHEOL and prevented the triumphal rejoicing of personal foes. Note the four verbs in vv. 1-3b: "drawn up," "healed," "brought up my life (soul)," "restored to life." Verse 3 does not mean a resurrection from the dead is intended. The reference is to a condition fraught with the qualities of SHEOL, a condition in which the speaker had joined the company of those who were ready to descend to *the Pit* (a synonym for *Sheol*).

In vv. 4-5, the restored person calls on the *faithful ones* of Yahweh to join in the praise and thanksgiving.

A general basis for such praise is given in v. 5. It affirms the conviction that the joy that God gives exceeds his wrath (cf. Isa 54:7-8).

In vv. 6-7, the speaker recalls presuffering prosperity and (false) confidence. This comfortable situation was devastated when Yahweh hid his face (vs. 7). Then the speaker recalls how he had cried out to Yahweh from a suddenly desperate situation (vv. 8-10). Among those ready to go down to *the Pit* (v. 3), the speaker pleaded with Yahweh not to be allowed to pass into the profitless and praiseless condition of Sheol (v. 9). The worshiper who is cut away from praise dies (cf. Isa 38:19).

Psalm 31

This psalm is a composite prayer that incorporates elements of trust, thanksgiving, and complaint. The situation reflected in the psalm is that of a person who has suffered for a long time from illness (vv. 9-10), accompanied by the abuse and scorn of enemies (vv. 4, 11, 18, 20), but whose trust in God remains strong (v. 14). The speaker recites the prayer in the presence of a group of people of like faith.

Verses 1-5 reflect the faith of a person who has "taken refuge" with Yahweh (v. 1). The statements of the security that Yahweh provides are blended with petitions (vv. 1b-3c). Verses 3b-4a may be read as statements rather than petitions: "You lead me and guide me as befits your name. You free me from the net laid for me, for You are my stronghold" (NJV). Following that reading, vv. 3-5 form a unit composed of statements of confidence.

The first part of the psalm closes with a testimony of deliverance (vv. 6-8) that differs considerably from vv. 9-13. The latter verses are a complaint, using language that is typical of individual laments. The sufferer's personal distress has been augmented by the attacks and plots of neighbors and adversaries (vv. 11, 13), and total ruin seems imminent (vv. 10, 12).

Statements of confidence return in vv. 14a, b, 15a, corresponding to v. 1a. They are prelude to further petitions in vv. 15-18. *Do not let me (ever) be put to shame* (vv. 1 and 17) links the two sections that express confidence in God. In vv. 19-22, the speaker voices praise and thanksgiving. The supplicant has experienced the abundance of Yahweh's *goodness* and *steadfast love*. Prayers have been heard and the sense of estrangement from Yahweh (v. 22) is no more.

In vv. 23-24, the thanksgiving becomes an exhortation addressed to the *saints* or *faithful*, meaning those who are faithful worshipers of Yahweh. The Hebrew *hasidim* ("saints") is derived from *hesed* ("steadfast love") and refers to the loyalty and devotion directed toward the keeping of a relationship.

Psalm 32

This was the favorite psalm of the early Christian scholar Augustine. It is one of the seven penitential psalms of the ancient church (Pss 6, 32, 38, 51, 102, 130, 143). Modern scholars classify Ps 32 as an individual thanksgiving combined with some elements of wisdom poetry, instead of listing it among the penitential psalms. The psalm assumes an experience of forgiveness and deliverance in the past that has become the subject of grateful testimony to a congregation at the SANCTUARY, or to a similar group.

The happy state of the forgiven person is expressed (vv. 1-2) in language hardly surpassed in the Bible. The "happiness" (cf. Ps 1) of the forgiven person permits a look back on the agony of past experience.

Verses 1-2 contain a concentration of OT terms for SIN. TRANSGRESSION conveys the idea of willful disobedience and rebellion against the divine purpose. It has been called the OT's most profound word for sin.

Sin translates the most common Hebrew word for sin in the OT. The basic idea is of missing the mark of the thing aimed at, failure.

Iniquity indicates an action or omission of action that produces some twisting effect or deviation from the straight. It carries the idea of distortion and warping of character and of relationships.

The word translated *deceit* bears undertones of self-deception and unwillingness to honestly assume responsibility for one's actions.

The terminology of sin is matched by the terminology of forgiveness. To be *forgiven* is to have a burden lifted away so that it no longer interferes with one's freedom of action. When sin is *covered* it is treated in such a way that the offense is no longer seen as the subject of judgment. In this context it is God who has "covered" the sin. If a person has *no iniquity* imputed he is no longer held guilty.

Verses 3-4 express the distress that had developed in the worshiper before confession and forgiveness relieved the condition. The hand of God *was heavy*—as it always is for the unforgiven. Relief came to the speaker when sin was confessed to Yahweh (v. 5). *Then* (i.e., after the confession) the speaker received forgiveness. Honesty before God is an essential prerequisite for a satisfactory relationship.

There seems to be a dual address in vv. 6-7, which are directed both to God (as prayer) and to the congregation (as teaching).

The vocabulary used in vv. 8-11 is either that of the wisdom traditions or very similar to them. The determination of the speaker in v. 8 is uncertain. The verse may be understood as a message from God, or it may be treated as instruction by the speaker in the main part of the psalm. It seems more probable that God is the speaker.

A parable-like saying is found in v. 9, which is a warning against stubborn, mulish behavior. The plural form of the command indicates the speaker wants to admonish the group addressed to be open to the instruction referred to in v. 9. Verse 10 is a general statement that contrasts the ways of *the wicked* with *those who trust in the LORD*. A hymn-like call to praise concludes the psalm (v. 11).

Psalm 33

This communal hymn falls into three main divisions: vv. 1-3, 4-19, and 20-22. The main division (vv. 4-19) also divides into three sections: vv. 4-9 (the creative word of Yahweh), vv. 10-12 (the enduring counsel of Yahweh), and vv. 13-19 (the rule of Yahweh from his heavenly throne). The twenty-two verses correspond to the number of letters in the Hebrew alphabet, but there is no acrostic structure. The psalm probably was designed to be sung in festivals and for worship contexts (including the SYNAGOGUE).

33:1-3. Call to worship. The "righteous ones" of the congregation are urged to praise Yahweh with musical instruments and *a new song*.

What is the meaning of the *new song* in v. 3? The term also appears in Pss 40:3; 98:1; 144:9; 149:1; Isa 42:10; Rev 5:9; 14:3. In its most direct sense, a "new song" would have been a new composition for a new occasion of worship, possibly referring to the psalm itself. Note that "new" things are appropriate for worship (1 Sam 6:7; 2 Sam 6:3). Such a psalm will celebrate the "new" things Yahweh does, such as the "ever-newness" of Yahweh, whose mercies are "new every morning" (Lam 3:23). A *new song* reflects new experience (cf. Ps 40:3) and anticipates a new future.

33:4-19. The word, counsel, and rule of Yahweh. This is the main part of the hymn. The *for* of vv. 4 and 9 is characteristic of the hymns and points to the reasons for praising Yahweh. The first *for* emphasizes the power of Yahweh's *word*, which is linked to creation in vv. 6-9 (cf. Gen 1). In vv. 10-13, the emphasis

shifts from *the word* of Yahweh to the *counsel* of Yahweh that guides history. Yahweh created by *the word* but rules history by divine *counsel*. The counsel of Yahweh survives the catastrophes of history that brings even the greatest *nations to nothing*.

The hymn is expanded in vv. 13-19 by stanzas that center around the "eye" of Yahweh. Nothing that happens on earth escapes the scrutiny of Yahweh, who *looks down* upon it. God's eye is on everything that happens, but especially *on those who fear him* and *on those who hope in his steadfast love* (v. 18). A better translation might be "those who wait for his steadfast love" (i.e., those who wait with hope).

33:20-22. A testimony. In vv. 20-22, the trust of the congregation is sung in testimony and supplication as the hymn closes. The last verse looks to the future and prays that Yahweh's response may meet the hope the congregation projects toward him (lit. "as we wait for you"; cf. vv. 1-3, 18; 31:24).

Psalm 34

This is an acrostic psalm (cf. Ps 9) of the individual thanksgiving type. In vv. 1-10, Yahweh is praised in the worship services of the community. The praise lauds Yahweh's past acts of deliverance and the unfailing goodness of God's providential care. Verses 11-22 are written in the style of the instructions given by wisdom teachers to their students. The general theme of these verses is the fear of Yahweh.

In the hymnic section, the speaker has a good message for *the humble* (v. 2); they can rejoice when they hear it, and join with the speaker to magnify Yahweh and *exalt his name* (v. 3). In this context, the "humble" are those who *take refuge* with Yahweh (v. 8), those who *fear Yahweh* (vv. 7, 9), and those who are *his holy ones* (v. 9)—those who have been willing to be set apart by devotion and commitment to God (cf. Ps 16:3), but not necessarily priests.

In vv. 4-10, the speaker recounts personal experience of deliverance and exhorts others to enter into a relationship of trust with Yahweh. Yahweh had responded to a quest for divine help (v. 4). *This poor soul* of v. 6 can refer either to the speaker or to one of those who in like manner had received help from Yahweh. Exhortations are found in vv. 8-10.

The reference in v. 7 to the *angel of the LORD* recalls old traditions (cf. Gen 16:7; 21:17; 32:1; 2; Exod 14:19; Josh 5:14; Zech 9:8; Ps 103:20). Although the verbs *taste and see* in v. 8 are metaphorical for judgment and discernment (cf. Prov 31:18), the verse reminds the reader that spiritual experience also involves the physical senses (cf. Heb 6:5; 1 Pet. 2:3).

Verses 11-22 are in the wisdom style, and *the fear of the LORD* is advocated as the key to the good life (v. 12). *The fear of the LORD* links the first part of the psalm (vv. 7, 9) with the latter part (v. 11). The "fear of God" is an expression that combines meanings of reverence for God's sovereignty over life, obedience of the divine will, and commitment to the divinely ordained ways of life.

The focus shifts in vv. 15-22 to an emphasis on *the righteous*, who are given well-being by Yahweh (vv. 15, 17, 19-20). In this context, *the righteous* are those identified by several expressions: the humble, those who fear Yahweh, Yahweh's holy ones, *the broken-hearted* and those *crushed in spirit* (v. 18; cf. Ps 51:17), those *who take refuge* with Yahweh (vv. 8, 22; see Pss 5:11; 7:1; 11:1; 16:1; 25:20; 31:1, 19; 37:40; 57:1; 64:10; 71:1; 118:9; 141:8; 144:2; Isa 14:32; 30:2; 57:13; Nah 1:7), and the *servants* of Yahweh (v. 22). As in Ps 25:22, v. 22 is added beyond the alphabetical order followed in the previous verses and begins with the word for "redeem" or "deliver"; Yahweh *redeems his servants . . . those who take refuge in him*, which contrasts with the fate of *the wicked* in v. 21.

Psalm 35

This long psalm has a multiplex lament-complaint character. It begins with a series of petitions directed to Yahweh (vv. 1-3). The speaker implores Yahweh for help and deliverance, concluding with a request for a divine declaration: *"I am your salvation"* (v. 3c).

In vv. 4-8, a series of imprecatory wishes relating to the suppliant's enemies are directed to Yahweh. Imprecatory wishes are designed to counter EVIL schemes and actions of foes and strengthen the speaker and the speaker's group against the foes.

The speaker moves to a vow of rejoicing and praise in v. 10. Seven imprecations appear in vv. 4-6, 8, matched by seven petitions in vv. 17-25. *All my bones* (v. 10) is an idiom for the whole human being, thus the whole self will be put into the TESTIMONY.

In vv. 11-16, the complaint returns to evil *witnesses* who seek to falsely accuse the speaker. The speaker had attempted to comfort them in illness (v. 13) and had shared their suffering in true sympathy (vv. 13-14), but his own *stumbling* (illness? economic misfortune? loss of popular favor?) brought no reciprocity on their part. They had gathered about like wild animals

eager for the kill (vv. 15-16). Petitions for divine redress, and another vow of praise follow in vv. 17-18.

More petitions follow in vv. 19-25, with an imprecatory wish in v. 26, matched by a wish that those who desire the speaker's vindication would be able to *shout for joy* and praise (v. 27). The psalm closes with a vow of praise (v. 28). On the concept of God waking from sleep (v. 23), see commentary on Ps 44.

Psalm 36

None of the major categories of psalm classification exactly fit this psalm and, therefore, it is frequently identified as a mixed-type psalm. Verses 1-4 are often treated as derived from wisdom teaching, and indeed their descriptive language is similar to that found in WISDOM LITERATURE. Actually, however, vv. 1-4 compose a description of godless people more commonly found in the prophetic literature (e.g., see Isa 59:4-8; Mic 2:1-2; 3:3-4; 7:2-6). Verse 1 begins literally as "an oracle of transgression to the wicked," possibly a parody of an ORACLE form, and means that the message heard by the sinner is that of sin rather than a message from God. Another option is to take the "message" or "oracle" as an independent word serving as the title of the verses that follow. In any case, the description of the wicked serves as a complaint in the psalm.

Verses 5-9 have the qualities of a hymn that praises Yahweh for his great loyal-love and righteousness. Those who participate in Temple worship (vv. 7-8) have access to the great abundance of feasting and drink that Yahweh gives. Yahweh is the *fountain of life* and the giver of light (v. 9). Without the light-giving presence of Yahweh, human beings would be like the earth without the sun (Weiser 1962).

In vv. 10-12 the psalm becomes a prayer. The reference to *the foot* (v. 11) alludes to the custom of conquering kings placing a foot on the neck of defeated opponents. The concluding statement (v. 12) refers to vv. 1-4 and expresses the certainty of vindication.

Psalm 37

If any psalm should be properly classified as a wisdom psalm, Ps 37 should be it. It is acrostic in form and strongly didactic in content. The success of *the wicked* and the seeming triumph of the evil ones are major concerns. The acrostic form causes a certain rigidity in the psalm and it becomes, to a degree, similar to the collections of wise sayings in the Book of Proverbs.

In vv. 1-11, counsels of calm faith are directed to those who *fret* over the well-being of *the wicked*. There is a twofold concern. First, there is no need to allow inner attitudes toward evil to dominate one's life. The restraint of anger and emotion can be accomplished by trusting in Yahweh. Second, the well-being of *the wicked* is of short duration (v. 10). The ultimate victory belongs to *those who wait* for Yahweh (v. 9). *Those who wait for the LORD*, who are *the meek, shall inherit the land* (vv. 9 and 11). *The meek* (cf. Matt 5:5) were originally those who were "overcome with want" (poverty stricken), but in time the word came to represent "the poor in spirit," meaning those who knew and accepted their dependency on God.

Verses 12-22 tell some of the dreadful things *the wicked* can do. They *plot against the righteous* and kill *the poor and needy* (vv. 12, 14). This, however, is not the whole story, for *the wicked* will receive retribution corresponding to their deeds. The weapons of the wicked will be turned back against them (v. 15), so that the *little* of *the righteous* is better than *the abundance* of *the wicked* (v. 16). The godly person errs when begrudging the wicked rich their abundance, for the godly should know that such wealth brings more liabilities than assets. The ultimate judgment of the person who trusts in wealth is found in v. 21: perpetual debt (read v. 21 as in RSV: "cannot pay back").

Verses 23-26 include the personal testimony of the teacher in vv. 25-26 (also in vv. 35-36). The first premise is that the providential care of Yahweh misses no one (v. 23). The wicked as well as the righteous must reckon with God. No person can fall out of his hand (v. 24). Second, the duration of the wicked is short. They may have their day, but their judgment comes quickly (vv. 13, 20). Further, while the teacher generalizes in v. 25, it is testimony out of personal experience and not intended to establish a comprehensive ideal of righteousness and rewards.

The dominant note in vv. 27-40 is the providential power of Yahweh that gives victory to the righteous. Yahweh *loves justice* (v. 28), that is, God is devoted to keeping the relationships of society in the right order so that the righteous can live securely in the land. Yahweh will not abandon to the power of *the wicked* those who are faithful to him (vv. 28, 33, 39-40).

Psalm 38

The traditional seven penitential psalms (Pss 6; 32; 51; 102; 130; 143) included this lament. The lament is marked by the confession of the suppliant's *sin* (vv. 3, 4, 18) and by expressions of anguish. The physical condition of the sufferer is given more specific description than is common in the laments. It is possible the disease described is leprosy (or a leprosy-like disease), and reflects the situation discussed in Lev 13:1-46.

In vv. 1-2, the opening cry for help states the conviction that the condition of the sufferer is the result of Yahweh's *wrath*, assuming that bodily suffering is the discipline of Yahweh. In vv. 3-10, the condition of the suppliant is described and declared to be the result of a merger of divine wrath and personal *sin* (v. 3). The burden of the speaker's iniquities adds to the suffering of the illness (v. 4).

The spiritual and physical suffering is greatly aggravated by the speaker's loneliness (v. 11; cf. Pss 88:8; 18; Job 19:14; 15; Lam 1:2) and by vicious attacks from enemies (v. 12). Nevertheless, the suffering has been accepted without loud and angry protest (vv. 13-14a; cf. the "servant" in Isa 50:4-6; 53). The speaker continues to pray and expects an answer from Yahweh (vv. 15-16), having confessed *sin* (v. 18) and protesting that foes are punishing goodness with evil (v. 20). A concluding prayer for help closes the psalm (vv. 21-22) and emphasizes the urgency of the speaker's distress.

Psalm 39

This psalm has some close relations with the preceding one. It is less of a lament, however, and more of a prayer of reflection on experience. A condition of severe illness may be indicated, a condition that is augmented in its gravity by the scornful charges of those who oppose the suppliant.

In vv. 1-3, the psalm begins in an unusual manner with a TESTIMONY of the suppliant's experience. The speaker had struggled with the agony of a distressful condition, and had resolved to endure the suffering silently rather than lash out at *the wicked* and encourage them (vv. 1-2). The burning distress grew worse, however, and now has forced the suppliant to speak (v. 3).

The brevity of human existence is stated repeatedly in vv. 4-6. Life is as fleeting as a *breath*; human beings pass away from it like the going of a *shadow*. The evaluation of the status of humankind in this psalm is at an extreme polarity from that in Ps 8:5-8.

In vv. 7-11 the personal condition of the suppliant comes into clearer focus. The speaker commits his entire future to Yahweh (v. 7) and prays for deliverance *from . . . transgressions* (v. 8) and for the removal of a *stroke* (v. 10) from Yahweh. The speaker knows that the divine punishment is for sin, but does not want this to provide an opportunity for the scornful abuse of fools (v. 8).

In v. 9 the speaker again reverts to an attitude of silent submission, helpless before the power of Yahweh. The blows of Yahweh's hand (v. 10) reduce those whom he punishes until all that is human is *a mere breath* (v. 11—see v. 5; also in vv. 5 and 6, *as/for nothing*).

In the closing prayer (vv. 12-13) the speaker prays that Yahweh will not allow death to take him. Verse 12 is a confession of humanity's true relationship to God. Humans live before God as do sojourners on the land. The terms *guest* and *alien* may also convey the position of a worshiper in the sanctuary (Ps 15:1).

The prayer in v. 13 reverses the usual petition for Yahweh's attention (e.g., Pss 13:4; 25:16-18; 59:4; 139:23-24). In this case, however, the supplicant knows he is suffering under the wrath of God and prays for alleviation before death (cf. Job 7:19; 10:20-22; 14:6).

Psalm 39 differs from most laments in the absence of any statement of confidence or of the certainty of answered prayer.

Psalm 40

Two divisions make up this psalm (vv. 1-10 and 11-17) suggesting that two originally independent units have been combined. The appearance of 40:13-17, with a few variations, in Ps 70 supports this suggestion. Verses 1-10 is a thanksgiving psalm that was written for individual use, while vv. 13-16 are composed of petitions and complaints, with a closing verse of confidence (v. 17). Verses 11-12 provide the transition linking the two units. The usual order in the Psalms is for thanksgiving to follow lament, but the reversed order, as here, appears elsewhere (see Pss 27, 44, 89).

In vv. 1-2, the worshiper recalls with forceful metaphors an experience of deliverance by Yahweh. Verse 1a may be read as "I waited intensely for Yahweh," that is, for Yahweh's help. The exact nature of the situation is not given. The . . . *pit* (v. 2) suggests the realm of the dead (SHEOL), and it is possible that the poet recalls a nearly fatal illness.

In v. 3, the delivered one declares that Yahweh has charismatically endowed *a new song* (cf. Pss 33:3; 96:1; 98:1; 144:9; 139:1; Isa 42:10) that is identified as a *song of praise to our God*. Its purpose is evangelistic and didactic (v. 3cd). The *new song* is one that

sets forth the new work of God. New songs are required because God is always doing new things (see Lam 3:22-23).

The "beatitude" form (*Happy are those . . .* , v. 4; see Pss 1:1; 2:12; 32:1; 2; 34:8, etc.) is used for statements of general truth or the good fortune of those so described. The speaker gives a testimony that is conscious of the congregation (see *our God* and *us* [vv. 3, 5]). One of the characteristic tendencies of the individual thanksgiving psalm is a shift towards the instruction of others, acknowledging that thanksgiving is communal.

The poet seems to incorporate into the psalm a negative judgment of the sacrificial cult (vv. 6-8) in words similar to other OT passages (cf., e.g., 1 Sam 15:22; Amos 5:21-27; Hos 6:6; 8:11-14; Isa 1:10-17). The intention behind the negative judgments is directed toward "sacrifices of righteousness" or *right sacrifices* (Ps 51:19) those made properly by persons who are devoted to the will of God and whose behavior reflects the divine will. Acceptable sacrifices are those offered with *broken spirit* and *contrite heart* (Ps 51:17).

What is meant by *in the scroll of the book it is written of me* (v. 7)? One view suggests a reference to Yahweh's "record scroll" mentioned in other contexts (see Pss 56:8; 69:28; 87:6; 139:16; Dan 7:10; 10:21; Mal 3:16). If so in this case, what is written on the scroll is found in v. 8. More likely, however, *the scroll* is the *torah* (law), and the prepositional phrase at the end of the line means "for me."

This reading is in keeping with v. 6b (*you have given me an open ear*: lit., "you have dug ears for me"), which means that the speaker has been "gifted to hear and understand the will of the LORD" (Gerstenberger 1988, 171).

This reading also is consistent with v. 8 where the speaker declares that "your *torah* (law) is within my inner being (intestines)." The speaker offers himself as a living sacrifice, with the *torah* of Yahweh assimilated into personal life.

In vv. 9-10, the speaker declares that the obligation of testimony and praise has been carried out: *I have not concealed your steadfast love and your faithfulness from the great congregation* (v. 10c). The confession has been made despite the *evils . . . without number* that *have encompassed* the speaker (v. 12). The speaker identifies with the *poor and needy* (v. 17; cf. 35:10; 37:14) who love the salvation of God (v. 16) and who do not waste the glad news of Yahweh's faithfulness and salvation.

Psalm 41

This psalm is best read as a thanksgiving psalm intended for recitation following an answer to prayer. There is, however, the peculiarity of the presence of a long lament (vv. 4-10) in place of the more commonly seen narration of past troubles and sufferings. The final verse is generally recognized as the closing statement of the first division of the Psalter and, therefore, it was probably not originally included in the psalm.

The introduction is phrased in the "beatitude" formula (*Happy are those . . .*) that expresses congratulations to those who are concerned for the *poor* (LXX, "poor and needy"). The verbal form for *consider* implies careful thought and action rather than mere attention. That these verses are a prayer addressed to Yahweh is clear by the *you* in vv. 2c and 3b.

"Blessed is he who considers the poor!" (v. 1 RSV) is unique among the beatitude-like statements of the Psalter. Normally the beatitudes refer to one's behavior towards God. Concern for the poor was deeply planted both in Israel's worship and wisdom teaching (see Pss 35:13-14; 72:4; 12-14; Prov 14:31; 19:17).

In vv. 4-10, the speaker quotes the prayer of lament that was directed to Yahweh before it was answered. The description of the actions of the enemies is unusually detailed (vv. 4-9). They speak maliciously against a sick person, anticipating the coming of death with no sympathy. Their comfort is devoid of any real significance (*empty words*). They spread disturbing reports abroad in whispering campaigns. The enemies include a close friend of the sick person (v. 9).

A closing confession of gratitude is spoken to God in vv. 11-12. The speaker is grateful for healing and deliverance, which has thwarted a triumph of the enemies and vindicated his integrity (v. 12). The last word of the speaker is an affirmation of having been established in the *presence* of Yahweh *forever*.

In the psalm's present arrangement, v. 13 is intended for a family group or a congregation, and marks the end of book one.

Summary of Book One

By the superscriptions throughout, book one is certainly a Davidic collection. Only Pss 10 and 33 lack a Davidic title, and these are tucked under the Davidic umbrella by close connections with preceding and following psalms. We may assume book one was read as if DAVID, or a person like him, were the speaker.

The psalms in this collection were judged to be representative of David's faith and charisma.

The postscript in Ps 2:12 (*Happy are all who take refuge in him*) links Ps 2 both to Ps 1 and to the collection that follows. Also note that Ps 41 begins *Happy are those who consider the poor*, recalling the beatitudes of 1:1 and 2:12. Seybold (1990, 146) says the beatitude in Ps 2:12 refers to all "who are able to find their way to the kind of faith which is demonstrated by the king who speaks in Ps 2:10-12a." The speech in Ps 2 is a confident affirmation of the power of Yahweh to deal with kings and nations.

The prologue in Ps 2 and the general character of book one point to the provenance of this collection, in its present form, in a community or communities facing "the disorienting reality of foreign domination" (McCann 1993a, 104) and the continuing threat of the loss of trust and assurance in God's power and purpose for Israel.

Especially in such a community context, the strong and numerous individual laments easily lead to the conclusion that lament/complaint is the major component of book one (e.g., Pss 3–7, 12, 13, 17, and the extraordinarily powerful lament in 22:1-21, as well as 35, 36, 31, 35, 38). Testimonies of trust, thanksgiving, and praise, however, compose an equal or larger part of Pss 3–41 (Pss 8; 9:1-12; 11; 15; 16:5-11; 18; 19; 20:6-8; 21; 22:22-37; 23; 24; 27; 29; 30; 32; 33; 34; 37; 40; 41). Some psalms are mixed but on the whole they give positive testimony (14, 16, 36, 39). The confidence and praise in the laments is not to be overlooked. Thus, despite strong elements of lament, book one is actually focused on faith and praise.

The thesis that book one focuses on faith and praise is substantiated by the language. For example, the verb *hsh*, "take refuge," is important (that it occurs in Ps 2:12 is significant). The use of the *hsh* in affirmative statements is found in Pss 7:1; 11:1; 16:1; 18:2; 25:30; 31:1 (other forms are found in 5:11; 18:30; 34:22; 37:40; and the noun *mhsh*, "refuge," is used in 14:6). The verb expresses faith in the protective care of Yahweh, despite unfavorable circumstances. Seybold (1990, 145) argues for a "creedal intention" in the usage of *hsh* in the Psalms, meaning that the statements in which the verb appears set forth affirmations of faith directed both to God and to other persons.

The verb *bth*, "trust," is closely related to *hsh*, and is found in varied forms in Pss 4:5; 9:10; 13:5; 21:7; 22:4; 5; 25:2; 26:1; 27:3; 28:7; 31:6; 14; 32:10; 33:21; 37:3; 5; 40:3; 41:9. Seybold (1990, 145) argues that *bth* is less dynamic and active than is *hsh*, indicating a state of feeling secure, and lacking the "creedal tone" of "take refuge." However, I fail to see that this is the case. The verb "trust" seems as "creedally intentional" as the verb "take refuge." Both verbs are used in statements affirming active faith that are intended to promote faith in others.

Thus book one in its present form is primarily intended for the encouragement of those who might waver in their commitment to Yahweh, designed to focus the mind on faith, and crafted to emphasize the life-giving function of divine instruction (Pss 15; 19; 24; 37). In the language of Ps 1, book one is *torah* (cf. Pss 37:31; 40:8).

Book Two. Psalms 42–72

Psalms 42–43

These two psalms should be read as one. The repetition of the refrain in 42:5, 11, and 43:5 points to Ps 43 as the third strophe of one psalm. Further, Ps 43 is one of only two psalms in book two that lacks a superscription (the other is Ps 71). There is also a close connection of thought between the two psalms (see 42:9 and 43:2).

Psalms 42–43 form a lament composed of three stanzas and a refrain (42:5, 11; 43:5). The speaker appears to be a devout worshiper living in the far north of Israel, and is unable (either because of oppression by enemies or illness) to join pilgrims to the festivals at a central place of worship. In the present form of the Psalter the worship center would certainly be Jerusalem, but in the original design of the psalm the place may have been in the northern kingdom of Israel, perhaps the SANCTUARY at Dan. The psalm reflects an experience typical of the Israelite exiles who were cut off from the joy of festivals, for whatever reason and in whatever place.

The opening words of the psalm (42:1-4) express a passion for worship. The image is of a thirsty, timid deer tortured by thirst and vainly seeking water in the dried up wadis of an arid region. The speaker also is terribly thirsty, even though he lives among the cataracts that roar down the slopes of Mount Hermon to form the Jordan river (42:7). The speaker's thirst is *for God* (42:2). The suffering of thirst is augmented by the taunts of people around the poet: *"Where is your God?"* (42:3; see Pss 79:10; 115:2; Joel 2:17).

The suppliant remembers participation in the processions into the Temple and the *shouts and songs of thanksgiving* (42:4) of a great festival. There were no questions then about the reality of God!

The refrain first appears in 42:5, and the suppliant speaks in a kind of personal dialogue. In the inner self (*soul*) the speaker is depressed like a groaning and grieving mourner. In the manner of a priest who delivers an ORACLE of deliverance and encouragement to a lamenting worshiper, the speaker counsels himself: *Hope in God*.

The lament resumes (42:6-11) as the suppliant remembers God in the present situation of remoteness from worship, and feels overwhelmed by the roaring waves of the surging deep—the *t'hom* (42:7). The water seems like the waves of a great flood to the speaker because it represents separation from the worship of Yahweh in the festivals. Psalm 42:8 may be read as a statement of confidence, despite the thunderous *waves and . . . billows* (42:7). On the other hand, it can be read as a supplicatory wish:

> By day may Yahweh grant his steadfast love,
>   so that at night his song will be with me,
>   a prayer to the God of my life (author trans.),

The taunting of adversaries is again a concern (42:9-10) and the refrain reappears (42:11). The taunting of enemies is like "murder in my bones" (i.e., a shocking, bruising trauma).

In the final stanza (43:1-5) the suppliant prays for vindication from the attacks of ungodly and deceitful people, imploring God to send out *light and . . . truth* as agents from the heavenly council to ensure safe passage to the *holy hill* in order to approach the altar and join in the worship. The refrain (43:5) closes the psalm with a note of hope.

My help in 42:5, 11, and 43:5 is too weak. The expression (lit. "the salvation of my face") means something like "my deliverer" or "my personal savior."

(For discussion of the *Korahites* titles and collection, see the end of Ps 49.)

Psalm 44

This psalm is a communal lament designed for the use of Israelite congregations on occasions of disaster, such as war or other calamities (cf. 2 Chr 20:5-19; Joel 1:13-14; 2:15-17). In Ps 44, the armies of Israel appear to have been defeated in battle (v. 10), many being killed and taken as prisoners (v. 11). Israel has received the scorn of her neighbors (vv. 14-16); Yahweh no longer gives his people victory (vv. 4, 9). The people have been *broken* (or crushed) in a *haunt of jackals* (v. 19). A better reading is "crushed us into a place of jackals" (i.e., a place where the jackals live; see Jer 9:11; 10:32; Isa 13:22; 34:13). The proposed reading is supported by the parallel in v. 19b. The nation now dwells desolate in *deep darkness* or in "the shadow of death" (cf. Ps 23:4—the same word is used in 23:4 and 44:19).

A long tradition holds that this psalm was composed during the time of the Maccabean Wars (second century B.C.E.), but that is doubtful. Other dates have been assigned to the psalm, including preexilic ones.

The psalm begins with a hymnic narration (vv. 1-3) by the congregation of the sacred history they had received. They had been told of the victories of Yahweh *in the days of old*, when he won the land of CANAAN for them (cf. Deut 4:37-39; 8:17-18; 9:4-6). The ancestors of Israel had been faithful in passing on the history to new generations (see Exod 12:26; Deut 6:20; Josh 4:6; 21).

The opening statements are supplemented by declarations of trust (vv. 4-8). Note the change of person in these lines: a lone voice speaks. The verses may have been intended for recitation by the king, or a priest, or a precentor who was leading the congregation in lamentation, but in any case the solo speaker personifies the nation and declares that Yahweh is the King who gives triumph over Israel's foes.

A complaint (vv. 9-16) describes the terrible condition of Israel. The situation contrasts sharply with the glories of the sacred history in vv. 1-8. The complaint lays an intolerable present before Yahweh, juxtaposed with the victories of previous times.

Verses 17-22 correspond closely to the protestations of innocence in the individual laments (see Ps 7). The people declare that they have not behaved in a manner that justifies their plight. The theological background of this passage should be sought in the Book of Deuteronomy and the Deuteronomistic History (Joshua–2 Kings; see DEUTERONOMIST/DEUTERONOMISTIC HISTORIAN) where the oppression of Israel is caused by the breaking the COVENANT with Yahweh. The statement here, however, rejects Deuteronomic theology and postulates another cause (v. 22): *because of you* (i.e., God). Yahweh is held responsible for the present calamity of Israel: *You have sold your people for a trifle* (v. 12). They claim that they have neither violated the covenant nor forgotten the name of their God, but suffer because of their faithfulness to the covenant (vv. 17-19). The suffering of innocent people was the great theological problem of Israel after 587 B.C.E.

The closing petitions (vv. 23-26) are agitated and boldly anthropomorphic. God is addressed with calls to wake up and rise up for the help of his people: "Help us and redeem us for the sake of your loyal-love" (v. 26).

The language of a "wake-up call" for Yahweh (see Pss 7:6; 35:22-24; 59:5; 78:65; 80:2; Isa 51:9-11; Zech 2:13 [17]) seems to be grounded in the notion of a "sleeping deity" found in ancient Near Eastern literature. The concepts of a deity resting in leisure (*otiositas*) and that of a sleeping god are primarily motifs of divine sovereignty and not those of idle, distracted, or tired gods. Sleeping in peace was a prerogative of a sovereign god. If other gods, or human beings, disturbed the rest of such a deity, they were considered to be in rebellion against the divine rule; they challenged a symbol of divine authority. Thus the call for Yahweh to wake up and come to the help of his sorely troubled people symbolized two things. (1) It acknowledged Yahweh's absolute sovereignty as the divine king. (2) The situation is so bad that he can no longer rest and sleep; the disorder that now rages must be put down again if God is to sleep in peace (and for the people to rest with God).

Psalm 45

The speaker in this royal wedding poem identifies himself as a professional writer (*a ready scribe* or "an expert scribe"). The first part of the psalm (vv. 1-9) is addressed to the king. The speaker, probably a court poet or prophet, begins with enthusiasm, "bubbling over" within and with a tongue prepared to pour forth words like the pen of a skilled scribe (cf. Job 32:17-20). The king is praised with exalted language (cf. Pss 2, 72, 89, 110, 132): he is *handsome*, victorious in war, fluent in speech, and *blessed . . . forever* by God (v. 2). He is a superlative warrior, who goes forth in the cause of truth and justice for the poor (assuming that is what v. 4 means). He is dressed in royal robes and exudes a fragrant aroma of *myrrh and aloes and cassia* (vv. 7-8). He dwells in pleasant and luxurious surroundings (v. 8).

Verses 6-7 assign an extremely elevated status to the king. It seems best to stay close to the Hebrew text and read *Your throne, O god, endures forever and ever* (v. 6). In this way the king is addressed as an *elohim* or a god. However, it is most probable that something less than the full status of deity is intended here (any theory of kingly apotheosis would be alien to the OT context).

In vv. 10-12a, the poet addresses the bride. He advises her to forget her people and her father's house and to give herself wholly to the king she is to marry. She is addressed as a "daughter of Tyre" in v. 12 (NRSV requests a different interpretation). The wedding procession of the princess into the palace is described in vv. 12b-15, and the king is addressed with promises for the future in vv. 16-17.

Why is a psalm about the marriage of a king in the canon (Kraus 1988, 457)? Jewish interpretations solve the problem by reading the psalm as about David, or his messianic son and eschatological Israel. Christian tradition follows by reading the psalm in terms of the marriage of Christ and the church (cf. Heb 1:8-9). These views merit respect and contain valid content.

A historical-critical analysis of the psalm, however, works with a different approach. First, we should try to read the psalm in terms of a history of interpretation in ancient Israel. Perhaps it was composed for a royal wedding in the northern kingdom (traditionally supposed to be that of AHAB and JEZEBEL), and later adapted for the monarchy in Judah (possibly for HEZE-KIAH). In post-monarchial contexts the psalm would be read with the sense of the union of Zion–Israel as the bride of Yahweh, a union that will cause the King's name (i.e., Yahweh's name) *to be celebrated "in all generations* and praised forever by the peoples (v. 17). Thus the Christian extension to the marriage of Christ and the church was in line with the psalm's tradition history. The psalm is implicitly messianic, but not explicitly so.

The speaker in this psalm praises a king who loves *righteousness* and hates *wickedness* (v. 7) and defends the cause of truth and justice (v. 4). In this regard, the psalm may be compared with Pss 72 and 101. These psalms express the high ideals of Israelite kingship and have a message for public servants in every age. The royal throne, which represents the divine kingship of God on earth, is intended to promote and establish stability and justice in society.

Psalm 46

This psalm is famous in its own right and has been made more so by Martin Luther's great hymn "A Mighty Fortress Is Our God," which is based upon it. The general classification of the psalm is as a hymn of confidence, of the song-of-Zion type (see Pss 48, 76, 84, 87, 122). The psalm has been connected in much interpretation with the deliverance of Jerusalem from the invasion of SENNACHERIB in 701 B.C.E. (2 Kgs 18:13-19; 37), although there is no proof to support the tradition. It may have been a hymn prepared for recitation during the great religious festivals of preexilic Israel, but the specific festival context is uncertain. Since the autumn festival (Tabernacles) was the most important one in preexilic Israel, it is probable Ps 46 represents some of its major themes (e.g., the supply of water). The general tenor of the psalm seems to fit better in exilic and postexilic Israel, when the people felt threatened by the uproar of the nations and by the foreboding return of chaos.

The psalm consists of three stanzas (vv. 1-3, 4-7, 8-11) with a refrain (vv. 7, 11). There is no refrain after the first stanza in the present text, but one may originally have been there. Some translators, therefore, insert a duplicate of vv. 7, 11 into the text after v. 3.

Verses 1-3 contain a powerful affirmation of trust. The community (note the communal *we* and *us* throughout) shows an awareness of God's help in the past (v. 1b). Confidence in God's care allows for the renunciation of fear (vv. 2-3), even in the face of changes that threaten the dissolution of the created order. The expressions of vv. 2, 3 represent those forces that lie beyond the control of human beings. They do not shatter, however, the refuge that God provides.

The mood and scene change from the shaking, roaring turbulence of vv. 2-3 to a peaceful picture of Zion, *the city of God*, secure in the midst of the raging nations of history, and rejoicing because of her streams of a river (vv. 4-7). Jerusalem is not built on a river; this picture probably arises out of the application to Zion of ideas of the Garden of Eden (see Gen 2:10-14; Isa 33:20-22; Ezek 47:1-2; Joel 3:18; Zech 14:8; Rev 22:1-2). The raging waters of the primordial flood in v. 3 are transformed in v. 4 into a river that gives joy to the city. The archetypal river becomes streams which make *the city of God* a place of gladness.

The real security of Zion is God's presence (v. 5). His power will manifest itself at the darkest hour, which is just before the dawn (v. 5). The onslaught of the nations, which surges against the city of God (Zion) like the waves of the cosmic sea (v. 6), will be broken by the thundering voice of God from *the holy habitation of the Most High* (v. 4, God's heavenly dwelling place). God is identified in v. 7 and 11 as *the God of Jacob* and "Yahweh of Hosts" (see Ps 24).

The invitation to the congregation in v. 8 has led some interpreters to think that some ritual-dramatic presentation of the pictures described in vv. 1-7 was given in the cult.

The sight that greets those who respond to the invitation in v. 8 is, at first, a dreadful one of the desolation of a battlefield (vv. 8, 9) with broken bows, spears cut to pieces, and burning vehicles (*shields* follows LXX and some Ugaritic evidence for the use of the word that normally means "cart" or "wagon" [see Dahood 1966, 280]; if *shields* is correct it refers to wooden frames covered with oiled leather). Yahweh passes through the nations and leaves desolate battlefields behind. The objective of the destruction of armaments by Yahweh is world peace (Mic 4:3), which is what the community needs so badly. The nations are summoned to desist (*be still*) from their militant ventures and acknowledge the power of Yahweh (v. 10). The psalm is framed by statements of confidence in the refuge and help offered by Yahweh (vv. 1-2 and 11; "God" is equal to Yahweh in this psalm).

Psalm 47

This is a hymn that praises the kingship of Yahweh (see Pss 93; 95–99). Such psalms are frequently referred to as "Enthronement Psalms." Yahweh is the one "enthroned" as the Divine King, not the Davidic king in Jerusalem.

The term "Enthronement Psalms" originated out of the hypothesis that there was a periodic celebration and re-enactment on Mount Zion of Yahweh's coming to the throne. It is assumed that this was ritually dramatized by the carrying of the ARK (above which was considered to be the place where Yahweh was revealed) in a procession into the city and up to the Temple (see 2 Sam 6; 1 Kgs 8:1-11).

Some scholars associate an enthronement ritual with the autumn festival (Tabernacles), but "enthronement" should not be read as excluding the kingship of Yahweh that always exists. He *is* King (v. 8) but he also *becomes* king in ritual reenactment and in a new realization of divine sovereignty over the powers of evil and disorder that are continually active in history and nature. The celebration of the divine kingship also had a future thrust toward a fuller coming of Yahweh's sovereignty (see Zech 14:9).

An exhortative summons to "all the peoples" (vv. 1-4) to join in hand clapping and shouting out exclamations of joy to God opens the hymn (cf. v. 6). The celebration of Yahweh's kingship in enthronement psalms shows many parallels with kingship in Israel. Shouting and trumpet blowing (v. 5) were parts of the demonstrations that greeted a newly anointed king in Israel (see 1 Sam 10:24; 2 Sam 15:10; 1 Kgs 1:34; 39;

40; 2 Kgs 9:13; 11:12). The *peoples* of v. 1 may have originally referred to the pilgrims who had gathered from various places for the festival (cf. v. 9).

Yahweh is the *great king* who has given Israel wide dominion over *subdued peoples* (vv. 2-4). He is identified as *the Most High* (v. 2, Heb. *Elyon*), overlord of heaven and earth, a title that appears to have been used in Jerusalem before David's conquest and only subsequently applied to Yahweh (Gen 14:17-24). Verses 2-5 have the character of a victory song and make this psalm a communal hymn.

Verse 5 almost certainly refers to the carrying up of the ARK of the covenant to the Temple in a procession, rather than a return of Yahweh to his heavenly abode, although the actions are not mutually exclusive. The going up of Yahweh's ark was accompanied by enthusiastic songs and praises by the people. He is praised as *the king of all the earth* (vv. 6-7).

Some interpreters read vv. 8-9 to refer to the future (i.e., eschatological) consummation of Yahweh's kingship. The first part of v. 9 is understood by others (as in NRSV): *The princes of the peoples gather as the people of the God of Abraham*. Thus, "the gathering" is interpreted as fulfillment of the promise made to Abraham (Gen 12:3) and a realization of statements by the prophets that anticipated the joining of the gentiles with the people of God (Isa 19:23-25; 49:6; 56:6-7; Zech 8:20-23; cf. Matt 8:11). The gentiles become part of the people of the God of Abraham.

An interpretation that includes gentiles as part of *the people of the God of Abraham* is doubtful. It would be unique indeed for the title "the people of the God of Abraham" to apply to gentiles (although Egyptians are called "my people" in Isa 19:25 and gentiles are included among God's people in Rom 9:24). It seems more plausible to conjecture that a "with" has fallen out of the text of v. 9. In this case, the princes of the nations gather *with* the Israelites; not *as* Israelites.

The reader is invited to ponder a manifestation of God that is not yet. The historical background (as in vv. 2-4) probably lies in the actuality of the kingdom of DAVID and SOLOMON. The conquests of David were extended over a number of non-Israelite peoples (vv. 3-4). It was according to the customs of the ancient world that captive people should gather with their conquerors to pay homage to the god (in this case, Yahweh) who had subdued them. In the course of Israel's history, the historical actuality in the psalm faded and an eschatological reinterpretation emerged.

We should note that the enthronement psalms lack the royal ideology of the Davidic monarchy. The community in Pss 46, 47, and 48 has no earthly king to rule and defend it: *God is in the midst of the city; it shall not be moved* (Ps 46:5). Thus, in these psalms we probably are dealing with postexilic liturgies that "jubilantly recall the history of Israel's election by Yahweh . . . and glory in his supreme, as yet unrealized, power over all the earth" (Gerstenberger 1988, 198).

Psalm 48

This psalm is a hymn that praises the glories of Zion, the City of Yahweh (see Pss 46, 76, 84, 87, 122). As in the case of Pss 46 and 47, some interpreters argue that the psalm can be traced to the deliverance of Jerusalem from the Assyrians in 701 B.C.E. If so, Ps 48 is a testimony of the peril from which the city was saved. Some details, however, seem inappropriate for a deliverance context (e.g., *the ships of Tarshish* in v. 7 and *the kings* of v. 4). The origin of the psalm in the northern sanctuary of Dan has also been proposed. The psalm probably originated in cultic use, rather than from a specific historical situation. In its present form the psalm describes a worship experience on Mount Zion, such as would have been experienced by pilgrims to an Israelite festival. This does not exclude all historical and eschatological significance, but it does point to the main angle of interpretation.

The beauty and significance of Mount Zion is praised in vv. 1-3. The psalm opens with a shout of praise declaring the greatness of Yahweh (v. 1). Supremely *the city of the great King* and *the city of our God*, Zion belongs to Yahweh and is *his holy mountain*. The passage borrows heavily from Canaanite descriptions of Mount Zaphon (or "North"), which is the mountain of BAAL in the Ras Shamra texts. These descriptions developed from Jebel al-Agra (called *Mons Casius* by the Romans) near Ugarit, a mountain whose height dominates northern Syria, that served as a Canaanite version of Mount Olympus.

The idea of Zion *in the far north* is impossible geographically, and Zaphon should not be read as an actual place name in the psalm. Mount Zion is declared to be the real mountain of the gods (Zaphon was the place of the assembly of the gods; see Isa 14:13-14; Ezek 28:14; 16). A reading of the last part of v. 1 as "Mount Zion, the summit of Zaphon, city of the Great King" fuses the concept of Zion with that of Zaphon, the home of the creator god El. The only god who really matters, however, has his city on Mount Zion: Yahweh, *the great King* (the only use of this title for God in the Hebrew Bible).

The significance of Yahweh's presence in Jerusalem has been manifest in the way that attacks against the city have broken up (vv. 4-8). Assembled kings fled in panic at the mere sight of *it* (v. 5)—apparently Zion, where Yahweh had made himself known as *a sure defense* (v. 3). The confusion and fear of the kings is like the anguish of women in travail (v. 6). The strange reference to *the ships of Tarshish* (v. 7) seems originally to have been the deep-sea vessels used in the Mediterranean trade from Phoenician seaports to the port of Tartessas in Spain, or Sardinia (and may further indicate a northern origin for the psalm). In the present usage they become a metaphor for pride, destroyed by an *east wind* (see 1 Kgs 10:22; Isa 2:16; Ezek 27:25; 27:26; Isa 27:8; also Jonah 1:3).

There is an eyewitness quality about these verses that is very striking. Something has been *seen* and *heard* in Jerusalem (v. 8). It was *there* (v. 6) that the attack of the kings was thwarted. Verse 9 indicates the scene of action is the Temple area. A ritual portrayal of Yahweh's defense of Zion may have been acted out during festival times.

In vv. 9-11, the worshipers tell how they comprehended Yahweh's praise and power through worship in the Temple. The right hand of Yahweh is *filled with victory* (v. 10; cf. 118:15-16). Verse 10 makes it clear that Yahweh's power and presence are not confined to Zion; his name and powerful right hand reach out to *the ends of the earth*.

In vv. 13-14, the congregation is exhorted to begin a procession (or perhaps, a tour) about Mount Zion, and to note carefully the outstanding features of the city. Such a procession would have had at least a twofold objective. First, the pilgrims (many of whom had come from *the ends of the earth*, v. 10) could be reassured that the city was safe under the protective care of Yahweh. Second, the procession would recall the salvation-history that had centered in Jerusalem, and equip the pilgrims to pass it on *to the next generation* (v. 13).

The RSV and NRSV translation of the last statement of v. 14 hides some of its force: "He will lead us against (or over) Death." However, the translations may be correct if the two words "over death" are read as one word "eternally" or *forever* (cf. v. 8). Regardless of the translation, these words speak of confidence that the power of death will not prevail over Zion.

Psalm 49

This psalm is frequently classified as a meditative wisdom psalm, and it has some affinities with Pss 37 and 73. The speaker struggles with the problem of the well-being of the wicked versus the suffering of the righteous. The distribution of wealth in the world follows a seemingly unfair pattern. The wicked gain more than their share and persecute the righteous who have less than their due. The main concern of the speaker is not an analysis of the problem, however, but the one solution of death that levels out all inequalities. The rich person and the poor person approach death on level ground. Life should be lived on the basis of this fact.

The speaker begins (vv. 1-4) in the manner of the prophets, but with a vocabulary more like the WISDOM LITERATURE. Unlike the prophets, he brings no word from God, but he speaks of *wisdom* (v. 3) and the *meditation of my heart* (cf. Ps 1:2) that will be recited to the accompaniment of music (v. 4).

Next, the speaker meditates on the features of the *riddle* referred to in v. 4. Death is a universal experience from which no person finds a *ransom* (v. 7). There is no exit by which a person can evade "the pit" (v. 9, NRSV mg.). *The wise* and the *fool* alike perish and leave their wealth behind (v. 10).

The recapitulation of the analysis of vv. 5-12 in vv. 13-14 adds a comment on the futile confidence of human beings in their wealth and achievements. In reality they live like a flock of sheep, shepherded by *Death* and bound for SHEOL (v. 14, although this verse is uncertain in part)—a striking contrast to Yahweh as shepherd of his people (cf. Ps 23).

An abrupt contrast is interjected at v. 15. The speaker of vv. 1-2 declares that *God will ransom my soul* (i.e., "me") out of *the power of Sheol*, an act that lies beyond the capacity of any human wealth and wisdom (vv. 7-12).

The basic meaning of this "boldly confessional statement" (Brueggemann 1984, 109) is probably that of assurance of God's power to take the person out of "the hand of Sheol" (i.e., protection from the conditions that endanger life), but we should not narrow the meaning too strictly.

Verses 16-20 have the didactic form of instruction, as the speaker exhorts and teaches a group of people who seem to be both cowered and tempted by the wealthy who surround them—especially tempted as poor people to adopt the values and way of life of the

rich: *Do not be afraid when some become rich, when the wealth of their houses increases* (v. 16).

Verse 20 closes the psalm and functions as a refrain with v. 12. The NRSV reads the two verses as the same, but the Hebrew text (and other ancient versions) read *cannot abide* (or "will not last long") in v. 12 and "do not understand" in v. 20: "Mortals in pomp do not understand."

The "Korahite" collection. Psalm 49 is the last of a collection of Korahite psalms in book two (Pss 42–49; but Korahite psalms are also in 84–85, 87–88). The Korahites appear to have been temple singers and functionaries (e.g., Exod 6:21-24; Num 16:31-35; 26:28; 1 Chr 6:22; 2 Chr 20:19), who were probably active in both preexilic and postexilic times, eventually, at least, related to Jerusalem and the Temple.

Psalm 50

This psalm is a "liturgical sermon" (Gerstenberger 1988, 210), which is closely related to Pss 81 and 95. These three psalms have a sermonic style of admonition and instruction, plus content similar to oracles in the prophetic literature (vv. 7-23) without, however, the use of the messenger formula ("Thus says Yahweh") common in prophetic literature.

The first part of the psalm (vv. 1-6) is a report of a THEOPHANY in which God comes out of silence to give a great summons that resounds in the heavens above and on the earth: *"Gather to me my faithful ones, who made a covenant with me by sacrifice"* (v. 5). The *sacrifice* alludes to Exod 24:5-8 (note also Gen 15:8-20; Jer 34:18; for another theophanic summons to judgment, see Mic 1:2-7 and cf. Joel 2:16-17; Isa 48:14-16). The speaker describes the coming of Yahweh to a meeting with his "covenanters," in which he will be *the judge* (v. 6) who deals with *his people* (v. 4), against whom he has charges that are spelled out in vv. 7-23. The heavens and the earth are summoned as the covenant witnesses of the behavior of the people.

The theophany with its stress on the "coming" of God to his people is an important element of Israelite religion (see Pss 18:7-19; 68:7-8; 50:1-6). The God of Israel was not permanently fixed on some far-off SINAI or other sacred mountain, nor in heaven, nor only present in a past history of events. A renewed experience of the divine "coming" was one of the major aspects of Israelite worship.

In vv. 7-23, divine discourse (God is present as the speaker) is used for instruction and impeachment of the people for religious practices without proper ethical prerequisites. They are not reproved for any failure to provide suitable sacrifices (vv. 7-8), but for their thinking that God has need of their sacrifices. If God were hungry, he could help himself to the cattle and goats of the world without dependence on human resources: *for the world and all that is in it is mine* (v. 12). This psalm should not be read as a rejection of sacrifices as such. True sacrifices of thanksgiving— which involved the sacrifice of an animal, a fellowship meal, and a renewal of covenant (v. 5)—are proper and honor God (vv. 14, 23). Those who make these sacrifices "fix" or "set" their ways so that the salvation of God may be experienced.

The style of preaching found in Pss 50, 81, 95 finds its closest counterpart in Levitical preaching in Deuteronomy and Chronicles (see Kraus 1988, 490; Gerstenberger 1988, 207; Tate 1990, 321). The Levitical preachers were probably priests who exercised a prophetic-type function in the postexilic festivals, especially the Festival of Booths (Tabernacles). These psalms were possibly part of covenant-renewal liturgies, but may have been used in other contexts as well.

The title of Ps 50 is worthy of note, as well as its placement in book two of the Psalter. In book two this is the only psalm ascribed to ASAPH (a traditional singer and liturgical expert whose descendants were among the personnel of the postexilic temple; see Ezra 2:41; 3:10; 2 Chr 35:15; a collection of eleven consecutive Asaph psalms is found in Pss 73–83). Psalm 50 seems to have been detached from the Asaph collection in Pss 73–83 and placed before Ps 51 because of its emphasis on Zion (see v. 2). It concludes a run of Korahite psalms (42–49) that have the divine presence on Zion as their central focus. For further discussion of the psalms of Asaph, see the commentary on Ps 83.

Psalm 51

This is the best known of the traditional seven penitential psalms of the ancient church (also Pss 6, 32, 38, 102, 130, 143). It is an individual lament that probes deeply into sin and forgiveness. The psalm assumes a worshiper who bears a crushing sense of guilt, and whose culpability has already been made clear. There is some indication of illness (v. 8), but the main concern is with spiritual restoration. Although not all of the historical notes in the psalms superscriptions are appropriate, the note here, referring to DAVID and NATHAN, is apt.

In vv. 1-2, the suppliant prays to God for mercy and cleansing from sin. As in Ps 32:1-2, the vocabu-

lary of sin and forgiveness is prominent in these verses. The terms *blot out my transgressions* (cf. Num 5:23; Isa 43:25; Ps 109:14) and *wash me thoroughly* are very strong, and both are related to cultic acts of purification.

The confession of sin in vv. 3-6 is strongly personal and direct: *For I know my transgressions. . . . Against you, you alone, have I sinned.* The speaker is continually aware of sin and realizes that acts of sin against other people are actually sins against God.

The supplicant confesses that the judgment of God is deserved (v. 4) because of involvement in a sinful nature from conception onwards (v. 5). Verse 5 does not refer to a concept of sinfulness attached to sexual intercourse, but to the human condition in which every person is conceived and born. Sins are inherent in character, they are not freak events (Kidner 1975a, 190) that merit no response from God. The language is hyperbolic and should not be taken literally. The interpretation of v. 6 remains obscure, but the most common interpretation is: *You desire truth in the inward being; / therefore teach me wisdom in my secret heart.* This interpretation links v. 6 with vv. 7-12 (Tate 1990, 3, 6, 20 offers an alternative reading).

In vv. 7-12 the prayer that follows the lament uses language borrowed from ritual procedures. The supplicant prays for a word of *joy and gladness* (v. 8), which may refer to a hoped for ORACLE of forgiveness and promise of salvation from God (to be delivered by the priest). The consciousness of the true nature of human sinfulness is evident in vv. 10-12. Forgiveness really involves a new creation, a radical change of inner being that makes a new relationship possible (v. 10). It also includes a regenerative process. The supplicant, having confessed lifelong sinfulness (vv. 3-5), now prays for a new beginning. Such a new status can be achieved only by the *holy spirit* of God (v. 11), for *the joy of . . . salvation* is only God's to bestow (v. 12).

In vv. 13-17 the prayer of vv. 7-12 is followed by a vow by the supplicant to teach sinners the *ways* of God (v. 13), and to praise him for his salvation (v. 14). The nature of the deliverance sought in v. 14a is uncertain. Perhaps the reference to *bloodshed* is to the death of uninstructed sinners (v. 14; cf. Ezek 3:18-21; 33:7-9). Many scholars interpret the word as a reference to the supplicant's own death, and as a prayer for continued life in order to praise God. They may be correct. The numerous references to "bloodguiltiness" on the part of David (see 1 Sam 25:26; 31; 33; 2 Sam 1:16; 3:28) suggests that either the original writer, or a later reviser, wrote the phrase with David in mind (as the title suggests). It is also possible that the expression is simply hyperbole for "deadly guilt."

The attitude toward sacrifice in vv. 16-17 is similar to that in Ps 40:6. The sacrifice that God wants most is a living sacrifice of a life with pride and rebelliousness broken before the divine will; God is not willing to accept any other kind. Verses 18-19 seem to look forward to the rebuilding of Jerusalem and were probably added in the exilic or postexilic periods. The reviser seems to have interpreted the "I" of the psalm as the nation, most probably reflecting the experience of the Babylonian exile. The denial of the validity of sacrifice in v. 16 was considered to be a temporal one that applied to the limited period shortly before and during the EXILE. The highly personal and individualistic expression in the psalm does not negate the significance of corporate religious experience. The context for the most personal and private religious experience is in the worshiping community. Further, the lament and prayer of vv. 1-17 prepare the worshiper in mind and spirit for sacrificial rituals. It was not, therefore, an act of theological violence to adapt the psalm for recitation in the postexilic rituals of the Temple.

One of the interesting features of this psalm is the threefold work of the spirit of God in vv. 10-12. The "steadfast spirit" (NRSV mg.) in v. 10 provides enduring strength; the *holy spirit* in v. 11 marks and activates the empowering presence of God; the *willing Spirit* in v. 12 gives sustaining energy to a person freed from the bondage of guilt which makes possible steadfast and willing commitment to God.

Psalm 52

Commentators disagree about the classification of this psalm, but it seems best to read it as a prophetic judgment speech, or if not actually a speech of judgment then like one (for such speeches, see Isa 22:15-19; Jer 20:3-6; 28:12-16). The prophetic judgment speeches have varied features, but two common ones are an accusation, and an announcement of judgment. An accusation of a rich, haughty, deceitful person is found in vv. 1-4. The essential charge is in v. 3: *You love evil more than good*. The announcement of judgment in vv. 5-7 is expressed in strong language. The contrast between the righteous and the wicked is a motif commonly found in the WISDOM LITERATURE.

A contrast to the judgment on the boastful person of vv. 1-7 is found in vv. 8-9. The style is that of the thanksgiving psalms: testimony by one who has experienced the help of God and now voices a thanksgiving in the presence of the "godly", that is, *the faithful* in the congregation. The person who has been expelled from the Temple (if that is the correct interpretation) lacks the blessing of participation in worship. The reader will easily relate the *green olive tree* (v. 8) that grows in the Temple—a figure of the blessing of worship—and the tree *by streams of water* in Ps 1:3 that is a symbol for the blessing of the person who is devoted to *torah*. The purpose of this psalm is to encourage the faithful in a community under stress to be faithful to God.

The title of this psalm is the first of a run of four with the expression *a Maskil of David*. The Heb. *maskil* is found in a total of thirteen psalm inscriptions (32, 42, 44, 45, 52, 53, 54, 55, 74, 78, 88, 89, and 142) plus in Ps 47:7 (translated *psalm*). *Maskil* probably indicates a psalm judged to be artistically devised and productive of thought and meditation (note the title of Ps 32 and the use of the verb from *maskil* in 32:8: *I will instruct you and teach you the way you should go*). These psalms invite reflection. Second Chronicles 30:22 refers to a group of Levites spoken to by King Hezekiah as *Maskilim*, who have "good understanding as to Yahweh." This may indicate that the *maskil* psalms were the work of a group of liturgical specialists in the Temple. It is interesting that the four *maskil* psalms in 52–55 are followed by five *miktam* psalms in 56–60.

Psalm 53

This psalm is usually treated as a slightly different version of Ps 14, perhaps the result of textual corruption. Each is a discrete entity, however, even though they are versions of the same psalm. Both psalms belong to the genre of prophetic speech, at least in a general sense. Therefore Ps 53 is closely related to Ps 52 and Ps 14. Verses 4-5, however, seem to indicate a prophetic-like taunt or mocking speech (e.g., Num 21:27-30; Isa 14:4-20; Ezek 28:2-10; 12-19).

In Ps 53 the *fools* are understood as foreigners, not Israelites as in Ps 14. The *fools* are foreigners who think they can attack Zion and destroy the people of Yahweh (retaining the Hebrew text "for God scattered the bones of your besieger[s]" in v. 5). The people have been put to shame because they have failed to trust God to deliver them. The psalm seems to appeal for faithfulness on the basis of God's past performance. Future deliverance and restoration is anticipated in v. 6. For vv. 1-3, see the commentary on Ps 14.

Psalm 54

This psalm follows the general style of a lament. There is a cry for help (vv. 1-2), followed by a complaint (v. 3). As usual in the laments, the references to the *enemies* (v. 5) lack preciseness, but v. 3c may indicate that they were Israelites. In any case, the suppliant expresses a sense of deadly danger.

The NRSV reads vv. 4-5 as statements of confidence based on faith in God. This may be correct, but it is better to read these verses as petitions:

Surely, O God, my helper,
O Lord, the sustainer of my life,
   let evil turn back onto my slanderers;
   in your faithfulness put an end to them!
                (author trans.)

A vow and anticipated testimony of victory follows easily in vv. 6-7. The name of God is emphasized in this psalm (see vv. 1 and 6), which represents his presence and availability to those who know and use that name in prayer and praise.

Psalm 55

This psalm is a lament or complaint of the individual type, but it also has mixed elements. Textual uncertainties and changes from the singular to plural in references to *adversaries* (vv. 12-13, 15, 20-21, 23) add difficulty to interpretation. The adversary is described in vv. 12-14 and vv. 20-21 as a friend and companion who has turned against the suppliant. The foe is described in the language of hostile enemies (vv. 9-11 and vv. 15, 16-19). The theme of trouble because of the treacherous actions of a friend holds the psalm together, and is a type of attacks by enemies in general (see esp. v. 15).

The psalm is a mixture of prayer, complaint, and declarations of confidence, found in a natural sequence: prayer (vv. 1-2a), complaint (vv. 2b-8), prayer and complaint (vv. 9-11), complaint (vv. 12-15), declarations of confidence (vv. 16-19), complaint (vv. 202-1), and declarations of confidence (vv. 22-23). The title is identical with Ps 54 (except the historical note added in Ps 54), which probably indicates that later scribal interpreters read them together. If Pss 54–55 are read together, the historical note in the title of Ps 54 applies to both psalms. The psalms have some parallels in content and the declarations of confidence in 55:22-23 follow well the ending of Ps 54.

Psalm 56

This individual lament is a prayer for deliverance from personal enemies. Problems in the text and the uncertainty of the speaker's situation make interpretation difficult. Lament because of the oppression of enemies is found in vv. 1-2, 5-6ab. Verses 3-4, 8-11, are statements of trust in God; vv. 6c–7 express prayer for the judgment of God. A vow to render thank-offerings to God for the deliverance experienced appears in vv. 12-13.

The use of language that applies to military enemies (vv. 1-2) may suggest a general or king as the suppliant, but the statements in vv. 5-6ab and v. 9 seem to preclude it. The enemies are in the community; it therefore is better to think of an ordinary suppliant to whom the language of king and military leader is applied.

The lament closes with thanksgiving for deliverance from death and for continued life. The speaker has no doubt of God's attention during times of distress (v. 8). Regardless of the circumstances, the speaker has a basic certainty: *This I know, that God is for me* (v. 9). The repeated use of the *word* of God (vv. 3-4, 10-11) constitutes two foci around which the psalm is constructed. The *word* of God the speaker is determined to praise probably refers to the promises of God, but could also indicate an expected word from God.

The "Miktam" collection. The title of this psalm contains the term *Miktam*, which is found in the titles of five other psalms: 16, 57, 58, 59, 60. The meaning of the word is not certain, but its form suggests it means "written" or "inscribed." The psalms designated as *miktam* may have been "letter-prayers," written to God and placed in the Temple (cf. Hezekiah's prayer in Isa 38:9; possibly the word in Jer 2:22 usually translated as "stain" should be read as "inscribed": "your guilt is inscribed before me" [Craigie 1983, 154]). The six *miktam* psalms all seem to reflect a time of crisis, which is in keeping with the prayer of Hezekiah in Isa 38. The use of "letter-prayers" seems to have been a feature of ancient Near Eastern religions. Psalms 56–60 form a core near the center of book two of the Psalter.

Psalm 57

This psalm is a lament-prayer of the individual type, with two distinct parts. Verses 1-4, 6 have the content of lament, and vv. 7-10 is thanksgiving (substantially the same as Ps 108:1-4, and v. 10 is similar to Ps 36:5). The psalm is held together by a refrain in vv. 5 and 11 (= Ps 108:5).

A cry for help, directed to God (v. 1) is followed by statements of confidence (vv. 2-3). The speaker has taken refuge under the protective *wings* of God (v. 1)—possibly in the Temple, although this does not rule out the figurative, spiritual significance of the term. The expression *I will take refuge* is equal to "I place my trust in," so the line can be rendered: "In the shadow of your wings I place my trust." *In the shadow of your wings* suggests the wings of the cherubim over the ARK in the Temple, and the wings that bear the throne of God.

God will send forth *his steadfast love and his faithfulness* (v. 3) as agents from heaven (cf. Ps 43:4). The situation of the speaker is described in v. 4 as like that of Daniel in a den of lions (Dan 6:16-24), but these lions are human beings who wait to attack with their sword-sharp tongues.

Verse 5 is a hymnic refrain that is repeated in v. 11. The transition to thanksgiving is made in v. 6, where it is declared that the suppliant's adversaries have fallen into their own ditch (cf. Pss 7:15; 9:15).

A joyful song of thanksgiving and praise forms the last part of the psalm (vv. 7-11), verses also found in Ps 108:1-5 with minor changes. The speaker experiences an inner "steadfastness" of heart. HEART in biblical language usually refers to the mind and the will of a person. Verse 10, along with the refrain in vv. 5 and 11, reflects the ancient Near Eastern idea of the huge stature of deities, whose *steadfast love* and *faithfulness* ("reliability" or "truth") extends into the clouds and the heavens.

Psalm 58

This psalm has characteristics of the laments, but it is most similar in form to prophetic judgment speech as found in Pss 14, 52, 53, and 55. The psalm's primary purpose is to strengthen *the righteous* (vv. 10-11) against *the wicked* (vv. 3-5).

The psalm opens with a prophetic type of condemnation of "mighty ones" (usually read as "mighty lords" [NRSV mg.] or as *gods*) because of their failure to conduct human affairs correctly (vv. 1-2). If *gods* are rebuked in vv. 1-2, the psalm may be read as an attack on pagan deities who have responsibility for the conduct of human affairs (see Deut 32:8-9; Ps 82).

An earlier version of the psalm may have been a judgment speech against divine beings who had failed to establish justice and order in human affairs, but in the present version of the psalm it seems more likely that the "mighty ones" (reflecting a slight change in the Hebrew text) refers to the leaders of society.

The terrible consequences of the failure of the "mighty ones" is described in vv. 3-5—the sinful condition of society (cf. Gen 6:1-8) and the class to which the "mighty ones" belong. The sinful propensity of *the wicked* (cf. Pss 36:1-4; 10:3-11) goes back to *the womb* (cf. Ps 51:3-5). They are so completely evil that they are like deaf cobras that cannot be charmed for the removal of their venom (vv. 4-5).

The prayer in vv. 6-11 is not exceeded in its violence by any other prayer in the Psalter. The NRSV sufficiently conveys its fury. Psalm 58, therefore, provides a good example of the type of material in the Psalms that raises ethical problems for the modern reader. Should such psalms be allowed to remain in the canon of the church? Do they not foster attitudes of vengeance and violence that violate all the standards of proper attitude and behavior? What shall we say to these questions?

First, we should not attempt to evade the issue by resorting to spiritualizing or allegorical interpretations, although such approaches are valuable in the larger picture of biblical interpretation. Further, any reductionist approach—a method that simply eliminates from the canon and liturgy those portions of the Bible that are found to be offensive—should be resisted. Selective reading of scripture has its place (see Holladay 1993, 304–15), but it suffers from the constant danger of excessive subjectivity and the tendency of theologians to import foreign elements into basic biblical understanding.

The Israelite commitment to Yahweh resulted in a remarkable freedom of worship. In the sanctuaries of Israel, men and women were free to speak, to pray, to confess, to sing, to shout, to dance, even to curse their enemies—and, above all, to praise God. They were also liable to receive oracles of judgment that laid on them unavoidable demands. In such honest worship there was no need to disguise one's true feelings. Israel's worship as it appears in the Book of Psalms has a childlike adulthood about it. God is real and present, and his people know it.

Further, the nature of the "enemies" must be considered when evaluating the imprecations in the psalms (on the "enemies," see also the commentary on Ps 7). The "enemies" were both the foes and adversaries of the suppliants and the enemies of Yahweh. Only rarely does the suppliant pray for the power for personal vindication through personal acts of vengeance against enemies (see, e.g., Ps 41:10; 52:6-7; 62:3). The speakers in the Psalms usually pray that Yahweh will judge and punish. The imprecations may be vengeful at times, but they are not prayers *for* vengeance.

The character of the "enemies" as presented in Psalms reveals a profound awareness of the actuality and depth of human wickedness. Indeed, the "enemies" are more than human (as in Ps 58) because they are allied with cosmic beings and forces that threaten the very order of creation and lie beyond the power of humans. The imprecatory fury of sections like Ps 58:6-11 is not aimed primarily at wicked, weak mortals who stand on the same ground with the suppliants, but at foes and forces that threaten the created natural, historical, and moral orders of Yahweh and his people.

Psalm 59

This psalm is an individual lament with the usual themes expressed forcefully, although there seem to be communal elements in vv. 5, 6-8, and 11-15.

The psalm opens with a prayer for deliverance from enemies who threaten the life of the suppliant, but for no reason on the speaker's part (vv. 1-4a). The enemies are described in vv. 6-7 and 14-15 as *dogs . . . prowling* who howl and snarl as they roam about for food. The prayers in vv. 4b-5; 11-13 are almost as furious as those in Ps 58:6-11.

For the idea of God waking from sleep, see comment on Ps 44. Statements of trust are found in vv. 8-10 and a vow of praise appears in vv. 16-17.

The psalm may have been designed for a king as the speaker, possibly DAVID himself, although the speaker could also be a priest or other leader. In time, any individual could use the psalm as a prayer for deliverance from a dire situation. The title indicates that later circles in Israelite history read the psalm as being a prayer of David (which is true of many psalms). The scribal historical note sets the psalm in a crisis context in the life of David and is probably derived from an exegesis of the accounts of David in 1 Sam 19 and 24.

Psalm 60

All interpretations of this psalm are problematic, but it appears to be a prayer of communal complaint. There is a mood of humiliating defeat as the people bring their laments and prayers to God. Attempts have been made to fit this psalm into a historical context; the superscription assigns it to a situation in the career of David (see 2 Sam 8; 1 Chr 18). Other suggestions

have ranged from David's time to the time of the MACCABEES. Verse 9 may indicate that some campaign against Edom was the occasion, but provides no definite clue as to date. The psalm probably had a long history in the traditions of Israel. The psalm's concern with Edom points to the exilic and postexilic periods as the psalm's basic provenance.

The complaint is marked by the fact that it emphasizes the suffering of the people as the direct result of divine action (cf. Ps 44). The action of God is ascribed cosmic features (v. 2) usually associated with theophanies (see Pss 18:6-15). In this case it is a THEOPHANY of judgment. Interpretation of v. 4 is uncertain. It may mean *a banner* has been set up to warn farmers and others in outlying areas to flee to a fortified city before it is too late. However, in this case the refuge has failed and the people have suffered *hard things* (v. 3).

The prayer of the people, with its emphasis on an answer, is given in v. 5. The answer is received in the sanctuary in the form of an ORACLE, that would have been spoken by a priest or prophet (the oracle in v. 6-8 is also found in Ps 108:7-9). The oracle itself is probably not original to the psalm, but was one already used in worship and inserted here. Its main point is Yahweh's ownership of the land of Canaan, which he gave to the Israelites. The geography of the psalm reflects the Davidic empire.

A solo voice prays with questions that express concern over a campaign against Edom, and suggest that the speaker is a king or leader of the army (v. 9). It is possible, however, that Yahweh is the speaker (Gerstenberger 1988, 241), summoning Israel to take part in his triumph. The congregation responds in vv. 10-12, moving from a lament in v. 10, to a petition in v. 11, to a statement of potential victory. Verse 12 could read "With God we could do valiantly, he could tread down our foes" or, "With God we can do valiantly. . . . " Despite defeat, the people know that God's power to save is intact and essential. All human help is vain. The prayer represents a struggle for faith.

Psalm 61

This psalm is an individual lament that is concerned with the security found by those who take refuge in the protective care of God. It is possible the lament is that of a king whose testimony (v. 5) is followed by a congregational prayer for him (vv. 6-7). It seems more probable, however, that the psalm is a pilgrim's prayer spoken far away from the Temple (*from the ends of the earth* [v. 2]).

The speaker knows *the heritage of those who fear your name* (v. 5), and expresses a wish in v. 4 to continue forever to dwell *in your tent* and *find refuge under the shelter of your wings* (on the *tent*, see Ps 15:1; 27:4-5; Isa 33:20). Goulder (1990, 152) calls attention to the concentration of leitmotifs and other features in this psalm that also are found in Pss 51–71: *refuge, rock, fortress* (NEB, REB, "strong tower") in 59:9, 16, 17; 62:2, 6, 7, 8; 71:3, 7; shelter under the divine *wings* in 57:1 and 63:7; (the Temple on) *Zion* in 52:8; 53:6; 63:2; 65:1; 68:24, 29; *vows* of *praise* in 52:9; 56:12; 65:1; 66:13; 69:30-31; 71:8, 14-15, 17-18, 24; reference to the king in 64:11 and possibly in 65:4; the divine agents *steadfast love* and truth (*faithfulness*) sent to protect the speaker in 57:3, 10 (*steadfast love* and *strength* in 59:9-10, 16-17). Clearly these are basic concepts in this set of psalms.

The prayer for the king would not have been out of order for preexilic Israelites visiting Jerusalem for one of the festivals or because of some urgent personal reason. In the later periods when there was no king, it is probable that the prayer for the king became a messianic prayer for a future king. Note the divine agents who are to guard the king in v. 7: *steadfast love and faithfulness*, the same as found in Ps 57:3. Verses 2c-3 is an excellent example of prayer. The vows in vv. 5 and 8 are not defined, but we may surmise that they are a response of the speaker to a divine deliverance from a threatening situation (see Ps 56:12-13).

Psalm 62

This psalm is usually treated as a song of trust, and an affirmation of faith in God. It may be more properly classified as testimony and instruction. The prayer element is minimal, lacking any direct address to God until the last verse, and the speaker assumes a human audience. Verses 1-2 express a basic affirmation of trust in God. The assurance expressed has come about through a struggle (cf. Pss 73, 131). The opening word (*alone* or "surely") expresses assurance despite outward circumstances to the contrary. The Hebrew particle for "surely" or "even so" occurs six times in this psalm (vv. 1, 2, 4, 5, 6, and 9) and gives it a "nevertheless" quality—*power belongs to God* (v. 11) regardless of commonly perceived appearances. The speaker has seen through the veil of human riches and power.

In v. 3 the speaker addresses enemies directly, which does not happen often in the Psalms (see note on Ps 58). Ordinarily speakers talk to God *about* their enemies. In v. 4, however, the speaker talks about the enemies to an audience. The enemies are described as hypocrites: blessing with their mouths while cursing inwardly. A testimony of confidence in God follows (vv. 5-7).

In vv. 8-12, the speaker turns to the audience and instructs them as a wise teacher. On the basis of personal experience the speaker exhorts all who listen to trust God (v. 8), because their own achievements can provide no dependable and enduring base for confidence (vv. 9-10; cf. Jer 17:5-8). In the ultimate balance of things human glory is ephemeral. It is foolish to set one's heart on riches, even when they increase (v. 10). The speaker has firsthand knowledge, for God has "spoken" once, even twice (vv. 11-12). The *once . . . twice* formula is found in the WISDOM LITERATURE (see Prov 6:16; 30:15, 21; Amos 1:3; etc.). In this case, however, the *once . . . twice* may refer to *power* (or strength) and the *steadfast love* that belongs to God (v. 11c-12a).

Psalm 63

This psalm is usually considered to be a song of trust and praise recited by a worshiper who has participated in a worship experience in the sanctuary (v. 2). The speaker is now assured that those who seek to destroy him (vv. 9-10) will suffer the wrath of divine judgment. The mention of *the king* in v. 11 seems unrelated to the preceding verses (cf. Ps 61:6-7), but it is probable that affirmation of, and prayer for, the king was a regular part of Israelite worship. The life of the nation and well-being of individuals were inseparably linked to the kings.

In vv. 1-4, the desire of the suppliant for an experience of the nearness of God is strongly expressed (v. 1; cf. Ps 42–43). A burning thirst for the divine presence characterizes the speaker's life; it is a thirst that has been satisfied in the sanctuary (v. 2). A lifelong vow of praise is made in v. 4.

In vv. 5-8, the speaker continues to praise God for the richness and power of the communion experience. Verses 6-7 possibly allude to the practice of spending a night in the area of the sanctuary in order to await a word from God at dawn. *In the shadow of your wings* refers to the protective presence of God, and may allude to the ARK in the Temple and to the cherubim whose wings were extended over it (1 Kgs 6:23-29; 8:6-7). This psalm is unusual in its degree of emphasis on the intimate relationship between the speaker and God: *My soul is satisfied. . . . My soul clings to you* (vv. 5, 8).

Verses 9-11 include a prophecy of the coming judgment of the adversaries followed by an affirmation of the well-being of the king and *all who swear by him*. *Him* can refer to either the king or God; it is difficult to decide which is intended because there is support for both interpretations (see Deut 6:13; 10:20; Isa 65:16; 1 Sam 17:55; 25:26; 2 Sam 11:11; 15:21).

The historical note attached to the Davidic title is the last of eight such notes in book two (Pss 51, 52, 54, 56, 57, 59, 60, 63). The historical notes are probably scribal additions that assign the reading of certain psalms to life situations in the career of David. These notes seem to be artfully constructed on the basis of wordplays and general associations of content with the Davidic accounts in the books of Samuel and Chronicles. They have little or no value for the actual history of David, but they are helpful in understanding later interpretation of the psalms. Since there are only thirteen psalms with historical notes in the Psalter, the appearance of eight of them in sequence is striking and may be a clue to the intention and use of book two (see the summary that follows the commentary on Ps 72). The effect of the Davidic notes provides a context for them as prayers of David. Individuals could identify with David and the stories about him, and thus make the prayers their own.

Psalm 64

This psalm belongs to the individual laments; perhaps more specifically it is a prayer for protection. The first part (vv. 1-6) is composed of a prayer to God for deliverance from the plots and schemes of evildoers who threaten the life of the speaker. Because the text is difficult to read, the exegesis is tentative at several points. The adversaries seem to make special use of their tongues and words (v. 3). Perhaps curses and deadly accusations are indicated. The speaker complains of the threat of ambush (v. 4).

In vv. 7-9, there is a "certainty of hearing" passage. The verbs should be translated as future tense, or as characteristic present tense (as in REB): "God will shoot an arrow at them unexpectedly and suddenly they will be wounded." The punishment of the wicked will result directly from their own behavior (v. 8). Verse 11 is a closing statement of encouragement of the righteous and the upright.

The key statement in this psalm is the passing comment in v. 6: *For the human heart and mind are deep*. The devious and corrupt nature of the human heart (mind) defies logical explanation, being both sinister and deadly as well as hidden from normal scrutiny.

Psalm 65

This is a psalm of praise with a variety of stylistic features, such as the beatitude form (*Happy are those*) and the extended length of v. 4. Opinions of commentators about the situation behind the psalm vary. The most common position is that the psalm was designed for a harvest festival, when God was praised for the bounty that he had bestowed on crops and people (esp. appropriate for a praise service after the end of a drought). It has also been read as a prayer for rain, by reminding God of past blessings of rain and fertility (vv. 9-13).

Verses 1-4 praise the God who is present on Mount Zion and who "hears prayer." Further, God forgives sins (vv. 2-3), which is a need of *all flesh*. Verse 4 adds a note on the happiness of those who have access to the nearness of God in Temple worship. The worshipers are permitted to share in the "goodness" of God's house, (i.e., in the joyful fellowship and all the blessings that flow from Zion). This means more than sharing in the sacrificial banquets; a share in the "goodness" of God in a broader sense is intended.

Verse 4 uses the language of priests who are "chosen" and "brought near" to God (see Num 16:5; cf. Jer 30:21; Zech 3:7). The language here should be understood to include all worshipers who "come near" to God at the Temple; they share the priestly privilege. Although v. 4ab uses the singular ("Happy is the one . . . he will dwell in your courts"), the meaning is collective (as v. 4de indicate).

In the pivotal verses 5-8, the great acts of God are praised. With awe-inspiring deeds of deliverance, God has made himself known to the ends of the earth. The God who hears prayer in Zion is the master of the world, who sets the mountains in place, and who controls the chaotic forces of the universe and of history (v. 7). The inhabitants of the whole earth are awed by God's *signs* (v. 8).

In vv. 9-13 the praise of God continues with an emphasis on the giving of rain and fertility. The "land" (v. 9; better than *earth*) receives water from the *river of God* (really an irrigation canal as in Ps 1:3) that *is full of water* and is the source of rain cascading in a downpour for the grain and the pastures (see Ps 46:4; Isa 33:21; Joel 4:18; Ezek 47; Zech 14:8). The hills and valleys become verdant and all of nature is awakened to abundant life to shout and sing the praise of God (vv. 11-13). Because this description seems to fit the Palestinian spring better than the autumn, some interpreters assume the psalm was intended for a spring festival (either Passover or Weeks).

Psalm 66

The three sections of this psalm (vv. 1-7, 8-12, 13-20) all have praise-thanksgiving content. The original speaker may have been a king, but that is not required for the use of the psalm in the present collection. The psalm has a liturgical character and was probably designed for use in thanksgiving ceremonies led by the king in preexilic Israel. In later usage the speaker could be anyone speaking for the congregation.

The psalm begins with a typical call to praise God, directed to *all the earth* (vv. 1, 4). A song suitable for such praise is given in vv. 3-4. The awesome power of the divine deeds will send the people of the earth to their knees, singing praises to the name of God.

A second summons is found in v. 5; a summons to *come and see* the awesome deeds of God. The deeds recall the deliverance of the Israelites from the Egyptians at *the sea* (v. 6; Exod 14:21; 15:19), and perhaps the crossing of the Jordan (Josh 3) as well (*the river*, although never elsewhere used of the Jordan). The summons in v. 5 and *there* in v. 6 is similar to the language of Pss 46:8 and 48:4-8, leading some commentators to conclude that some the of worshipers were being urged to see a cultic ritual that reenacted the ancient events. This may be, but *there* is subject to different interpretations (see Tate 1990, 146, 149), and may simply refer to the place where those summoned in v. 5 would assemble: "Come and see . . . there let us rejoice in him!" The place of assembly would almost certainly have been primarily the Temple. In more general usage, the *come and see* of v. 5 may mean basically to become acquainted with and to understand the works of God.

Two probable merisms in vv. 6 and 12 (a merism cites extreme or contrasting examples in order to be comprehensive, such as "from A to Z"). The *river* in v. 6a may be another term for *the sea* and the two words stress the great dimensions of the divine deeds. The same thing is probably true of *through fire and through water* (v. 12), meaning all manner of testings and trials. Verses 6 and 12 join vv. 1–7 and 8–12. The deliverance of God described in vv. 10-12 has not been easy for the Israelites, but he has kept them *among the living* (v. 9) and brought them out to abundance (v. 12).

Verses 13-20 constitute an individual thanksgiving section setting forth the fulfillment of vows (vv. 13-15) and the testimony of a speaker (vv. 16-20). The speaker summons all those *who fear God* (v. 16), that is, all true and serious worshipers. The speaker refers to vows made in a time of great trouble (cf. Pss 22:25; 61:8; 116:18; Jonah 2:10). Verse 20 is a closure for the entire psalm, picking up the *bless our God* of v. 8.

"Songs (of David)." Pss 66 and 67 do not refer to David in their titles. Pss 51–71—except 66, 67, and 71—refer to David. Ps 71 should be read with Ps 70, which leaves 66 and 67. The scribal interpreters who supplied the titles probably intended for Pss 66 and 67 to be covered by the Davidic references in the titles of Pss 65 and 68, forming a small collection (or run) of psalms in Pss 65–68.

Psalm 67

Usually classified as a thanksgiving psalm, especially designed for a good harvest, Ps 67 is more nearly a prayer for continued blessing. It may have been used during the festival of Tabernacles as a prayer of thanksgiving for the harvest (v. 6). If so, it shows considerable connection to Ps 65. This psalm functions well as the closing prayer of a festival or worship service. The Jewish use of the psalm at the end of SABBATH is appropriate as well.

Verse 1 adapts the priestly blessing of Num 6:24-26 into a prayer for God's blessing and presence. The motivation for such blessing is so the *way* and *saving power* of God may be known *among all nations* (v. 2).

The prayer becomes praise in v. 3—5—actually a short hymn with a refrain at the beginning and end. What God does in Israel becomes a testimony to the whole world because the lordship of God over history is not confined to Israel. God judges and guides all nations (v. 4). This is a prayer for the inclusion of the nations in praising God's blessings.

The thanksgiving of vv. 6-7 refers to the blessing that is prayed for in v. 1. The nations can see how God has blessed Israel.

The *increase* of *the earth* (v. 6) is a word that refers to the harvest that God gives in fulfillment of his promise (Lev 26:4; Deut 11:17; 32:22; Judg 6:4; Ps 85:12). It need not, however, refer to the final harvest of the year but to growing grain and other crops (cf. Ps 78:46). Verse 7 is a prayer for the continuation of the process of blessing that begins in v. 6. For a survey of the comprehensive range of divine blessing, see Deut 28:1-6.

Psalm 68

This psalm is exceedingly complex. The difficult text is matched by a style that oscillates from one form of speech to another, and by historical and geographical allusions that elude positive identification. These problems have led some commentators to consider the psalm as a collection of poetic pieces, perhaps incipits (beginnings of independent poems) rather loosely joined together in an anthology with little or no inner relationship. Others are more constructive and, despite the psalm's "disconnectedness," consider it as a liturgical collection designed for use in the communal worship of the festivals. Identifying the psalm as a liturgical collection seems the better option.

The context of the psalm seems to be that of a procession entering the Temple (vv. 24-27). The exact nature of the festival intended is a matter of considerable debate among scholars, although it is highly probable this psalm was used during the autumn festival of Tabernacles.

Apart from a liturgical unity, the psalm has a fair degree of internal consistency and literary structure. In terms of genre, the psalm is a supplicatory, hymnic prayer designed to exalt the victories of Yahweh and seek further victories and blessings from him. The concentration on God and praiseworthy divine deeds transforms the disconnectedness of the psalm into a poetic, theological display of the saving works of God.

The prelude (vv. 1-2) is an adaptation of the ancient cultic cry that signaled the movement of the ARK of the covenant (Num 10:35-36). The verses are appropriate as an invocation to begin a procession, and may have been so used when the people and the ark started toward the SANCTUARY. The petitions in vv. 2c-3 express the familiar contrast between *the wicked* and *the righteous* (cf. Ps 1).

In vv. 4-6 a hymnic section praises God who blesses the needy while he leaves those who rebel against him to perish in the desert (v. 6). *Who rides upon the clouds* (v. 4) represents a small textual change from the "who rides through the deserts" (NRSV etc. mg.) of the Hebrew text. The validity of this widely accepted correction is debatable. It does bring the expression into harmony with v. 33, but the context of the desert in vv. 4-6 and vv. 7-10 may point to God's presence with his people during the wilderness wanderings and the settlement of Canaan. However, the giving of rain (vv. 8-9) is more easily linked with the idea of the "Cloud Rider" (cf. NJB).

The hymn continues (vv. 7-10) with allusions to major events in the early history of Israel: the EXODUS from Egypt and the passage through the wilderness. There is a close relationship between these verses and the Song of Deborah in Judg 5:4-5. The motifs of the THEOPHANY (see Ps 18:6-15) and the giving of rain are blended. The literal expression "this Sinai" in v. 8 is uncertain; the interpretation represented in the NRSV (*the God of Sinai*) may be correct. Another interpretation reads the phrase with the force of a divine name: "Him of Sinai" or "The Sinai One." In any case, this section recapitulates in hymnic form the providential care by which God (now understood as Yahweh) brought his people to dwell in the land of Canaan and provided the rain that made life possible. In Canaanite worship, BAAL was the great rain giver, but for Israel Yahweh poured out the rain and restored his languishing *heritage* (v. 9)—the land of Canaan where the Israelites lived.

An abrupt transition into a new section (vv. 11-14) recalls the victory of the Israelites over Sisera (Judg 5:16, 28-30). The interpretation of these verses is plagued by several uncertain details. *Wings of a dove covered with silver* may refer to booty captured in war, but perhaps more probably it refers to the release of colorful messenger doves to signal a victory in war. The location of *Zalmon* (v. 14) is uncertain. It may have been a mountain in the area of Shechem (see Judg 9:48). The mention of *snow* (v. 14) has been explained in varied ways; perhaps it recalls a meteorological phenomenon that occurred in connection with a victory over enemies of the Israelite tribes. However, it is probable that the imagery in this section is more poetic than historical.

Verses 15-18 glorify the "high mountain" that Yahweh has chosen as a dwelling place. In the present context it is clear Zion is intended. The mighty mountains *of Bashan* (vv. 15-16) are taunted for their envy of Yahweh's choice of Zion. Some scholars, however, suspect that the original reference of these verses was not to Zion, but to a sacred place of worship in northern Israel (possibly Mount Tabor). The ascent to the high holy place was made by Yahweh as a mighty warrior, returning with his armies from a great victory (vv. 17-18). It seems more probable that *Sinai* (v. 17) should be read as a divine name ("the Lord is among them, Sinai in holiness" or "among the holy ones"; cf. v. 8), but the emendation followed by the NRSV is popular. In any case, the main point of these verses in that of a "change of mountains" in Israel from Sinai to

Zion (Deut 33:2). Yahweh, long associated with Sinai, has now made Zion his abode.

In vv. 19-23, the congregation sings the praises of Yahweh, who continually sustains the people and gives them victory over their enemies. There is no escape from divine power (v. 22; cf. Amos 9:3). *Bathe your feet in blood* (v. 23) perhaps should be read "shake the blood off your feet," meaning to stamp the blood of battle from the feet.

Verses 24-27 give a description of a procession into the sanctuary. A solo voice, perhaps one of the singers, excitedly points to various groups in the procession. The "fountain of Israel" can refer to the starting place of the procession (perhaps the spring Gihon at Jerusalem), or the text may be modified to read "assembly" or "convocation" of Israel, which agrees better with the *congregation* of the preceding line.

Four tribes are mentioned in v. 27. There is no clear reason these four are named. Among the more probable reasons are: (1) the tribes named are representative of all the tribes; (2) dependence on the song of Deborah (see Judg 5:18) led to the mention of *Zebulon* and *Naphtali*, while *Judah* and *Benjamin* are added because they are so closely associated with the monarchy and Jerusalem; and (3) the psalm was originally used in a northern cult center especially associated with *Zebulon*, *Naphatali* and *Benjamin*, to which *Judah* was added after the psalm was adapted for use in Jerusalem.

In vv. 28-31, a prayer is directed to God for continued manifestation of his strength and power in defeating the hostile forces of Israel's enemies. If there is a historical referent in v. 30, it is probably Egypt. In any case, these are types of powerful forces subdued by Yahweh.

A hymn in vv. 32-35 summons all the *kingdoms of the earth* to praise Yahweh, who is described as the one "who rides in the heavens" with a voice of thunder (cf. Ps 29). This powerful, majestic God of the heavens gives power to the people from the (heavenly) sanctuary.

The closing statement, *Blessed be God!* (v. 35), serves both as the end of Ps 68 and as the end of the run of pss 65–68 (see commentary on Ps 66). It summarizes a major thrust of all these psalms, since all four focus attention on the powerful deeds of God, the *God of our salvation* (Pss 65:5; cf. 68:19, 20).

Two broad movements seem to characterize Ps 68: (1) a theophanic emphasis on God's rising up and coming forth to defeat enemies and provide for his people; and (2) an emphasis on Yahweh's role as the divine warrior who *gives power and strength to his people* (v. 35). He is *awesome in . . . his sanctuary* because he is the victorious divine warrior. Two aspects of the psalm are held together by two uses of the name "Yahweh" in vv. 16 (*LORD*) and 20 (*GOD*). The coming God and the abiding God are the same; both give power and strength to the people.

Psalm 69

This is an individual lament in which the speaker complains bitterly about the attacks of enemies and prays for their punishment. The speaker claims to be a servant of God (v. 17) whose zeal for the house of God (v. 9) has provoked humiliating and deadly opposition. This psalm is noted for its graphic language and its frequent use in the NT (e.g., Matt 27:34; Mark 15:26; Luke 23:36; John 2:17; 15:25; 19:28-29; Acts 1:20; Rom 11:9-10; Rev 16:1). The speaker's *zeal for your house* in v. 9 leads many interpreters to find a context for the psalm in the time of HAGGAI and ZECHARIAH and the rebuilding of the Temple in Jerusalem (see also vv. 35-36; Ezra 4:1-5, 23-24; 5:2-3; Neh 4:1-5). The zeal of a devoted servant of Yahweh for the Temple could have been true, however, throughout a long span of Israel's history.

Some parts of the psalm suggest a context of sickness, intensified by callous treatment by members of the speaker's community (vv. 19-21). In fact, the language of the psalm is general enough to cover almost any situation of severe distress on the part of a devoted servant of God (cf. Ps 102). The psalm probably emerged in the exilic or postexilic periods and likely was used in ceremonies of fasting and penitence. In such usage the speaker would have been a priest or other representative of the community.

Psalm 69 contains three major sections: vv. 1-13b; a parallel section (vv. 13c-29); and a vow to praise God and a hymn of praise conclude the psalm (vv. 30-36). The heart of the psalm is in vv. 16-18. Yahweh is implored to answer the speaker's prayer on the basis of *steadfast love* and not to *hide your face from your servant*. The hidden face of God is an expression of divine wrath, the negative counterpart of God turning his face toward those in distress in order to help them (cf. Pss 13:1; 3 22:24). The hidden face of God means separation from his attention and care (cf. Ps 51:9 where the hidden face is positive because God's face is hidden from the speaker's guilt). The prayer of the speaker in this psalm is bold and forthright, in which folly and wrongdoing are freely admitted (v. 5), and there is no false modesty about the basic character of the speaker (vv. 6-9). The heinous actions of the enemies are put forward in stark detail (vv. 19-29).

Psalm 70

The psalm is a lament, a prayer for deliverance. It is nearly identical with Ps 40:13-17. Psalm 40 probably depends on Ps 70, but this is uncertain since (1) Ps 70 could be a detached section of Ps 40 or (2) both could be versions of common poetic content.

Psalm 71

Psalm 71 should be read with Ps 70 as a single unit. The two psalms were probably juxtaposed to form a unit because of liturgical use. Perhaps the two psalms were read together to form two units of about the same length.

The two units of Pss 69 and 70–71 form a frame with Pss 61–64 around the "victory songs" in Pss 65–68 (incidentally composing a run of ten psalms, 61 to 70–71, that matches the ten-psalms run of 51–60).

The speaker in Ps 71, and by extension in Ps 70, speaks from the perspective of maturity looking ahead to old age (vv. 9, 17-18). The speaker manifests a serenity often lacking in the young, the product of a long memory of God's faithfulness.

The structure of Pss 70–71 can be analyzed as follows: 70:1-6 is an urgent appeal for help against those who seek to hurt the speaker (the language is dominated by entreaty for God to hasten to help); 71:1-4 begins with an affirmation of trust and moves to petitions for protection and deliverance; 71:5-11 sets forth the main complaint of the speaker, juxtaposed against a life of trust and dependence on God from birth (vv. 5-6); 71:13-18 includes petition and a vow of praise (vv. 14-16); 71:19-24 contains another vow of praise (multiple).

Verse 12 may be read with either the preceding or following section; it is the key verse that functions as the center of the compound psalm formed by Pss 70 and 71.

The speaker could not keep the vow unless God heeds the prayers—it would be physically impossible; the dead cannot praise Yahweh (see Ps 115:17). The vows are explicitly conditional, but implicitly they are expressions of faith because they represent the speaker's dependence on God. The petitioners in such prayers and vows expect to be answered and they are prepared to deliver on their vows.

Psalm 72

This is a royal psalm that expresses prayer for God's blessing on the king. The superscription ascribes the psalm to SOLOMON (cf. Ps 127). A postscript refers to the prayers of David, suggesting that later scribal interpreters read it as a prayer of David for Solomon.

The petition in v. 1. is followed by prayer for a favorable reign of the king (vv. 2-7), in two stanzas (vv. 2-4, 5-7). The reference to the *king's son* (v. 1) may indicate that the poet has the coronation of a new king in mind. The phrase may mean no more, however, than that the king is the scion of the royal family. The petitions for the king give helpful insight into the Israelite conception of the role and significance of kingship. The king sustains the right order of life in the nation. The emphasis is on the words for *justice* and *righteousness*. Special attention is given to the king's defense of the *poor* and *needy* (v. 4). The total welfare of the nation is bound up with the monarch's reign. Thus the king needs the charismatic endowment of divine qualities for his task (v. 1). The king is dependent on Yahweh and responsible to God for the conduct of his reign. The people are Yahweh's people (v. 2); the king is Yahweh's agent.

The prayer continues in vv. 8-12 with wishes for a wide and victorious dominion (cf. Ps 2). God is asked to give the king a universal hegemony that will sway the kings of far-distant places, who will bring him tribute and fall down before him in homage so that he draws together the world. *The River* (v. 8) is not the Euphrates but the cosmic stream that waters Zion and flows out to bring fruitfulness to the land (Ps 46:4; Ezek 47; Zech 9:10). The dimensions of the reign that are envisaged become, therefore, almost cosmic.

Verses 12-14 return to the theme of vv. 2 and 4, stressing the king's role as the helper of the weak and the poor. Of course, this also is the role of Yahweh (Pss 116:15; 146:6-10). The prayer resumes in vv. 15-17 with a plea for long life for the king and for the prosperity of his reign that he, like Abraham (Gen 12:1-3), may become a source of blessing and model for all nations (v. 17). The prosperity of the king's reign will be a fulfillment of the promises of God to the ancestors of Israel.

Verses 18-19 constitute a doxology that has been added to the closing psalm of Book Two of the Psalter. Verse 20 is an editorial note, now attached to this psalm, that probably marked the end of an earlier collection of Davidic psalms.

Summary of Book Two

Two major sections make up book two of the Psalter. The first section (Pss 42–50) centers around the role of Zion in the life of the people of Yahweh. The second section (Pss 51–72) may be called the Prayers of David (see Goulder 1990). The combination of the Korahite psalms, plus one Asaph psalm (Ps 50), with the Prayers of David may seem odd at first. Psalms 42–43 and 44, however, establish an exilic context for both the Korahite psalms (in their present setting) and for the rest of book two (McCann 1993a, 102–103).

The perspective of the speakers in book two is set by Ps 44:11: *You have made us like sheep for slaughter, and have scattered us among the nations.* The individual speaker in Pss 42–43 becomes an example for the community (42:5, 11; 43:5). Psalms 42–43 and 44 form the prologue to Pss 45–50 that sets forward the continued place of Zion in the life of Israel and indirectly keeps the royal hope alive in Ps 45.

Thus in book two Yahweh's abiding presence on Zion is a fundamental focus: *Out of Zion, the perfection of beauty, God shines forth* (Ps 50:2). Zion remained as a fundamental element of Israelite theology in the exilic and postexilic period. The monarch was gone and EXILE had become a permanent way of life, but Zion remained, the Temple was rebuilt, and from there Yahweh comes and calls out: *"Gather to me my faithful ones, who made a covenant with me by sacrifice!"* (Ps 50:5). Yahweh refuses ordinary sacrifices (Ps 50:8-13), but seeks sacrifices of genuine thanksgiving and the faithful keeping of vows (50:14; 23). Indeed, *The sacrifice acceptable to God is a broken spirit; a broken and contrite heart, O God, you will not despise* (Ps 51:17).

The *broken and contrite heart* mingled with praise and thanksgiving is set forth in the powerful Prayers of David in Pss 51–71. These are prayers for a people whose history has imposed on them great hurt, but who rise up out of their guilt, and agony to present their case to God and to vow commitment and praise if he will answer. They have found their mentor in David and the stories of the crises in his life (see the historical notes in the titles of Pss 51–64). In him they found a mixture of iron and clay that reflected their own spiritual condition.

The ancient promises given to David (see Ps 89) are not dealt with explicitly in book two, but two psalms implicitly point to the possible future reality of the promises. Ps 45 revels in the glory of a king who is blessed by God and who fights victoriously for the cause of truth and justice. Such a king will have his name *celebrated in all generations* and be praised by the peoples forever (v. 17). Psalm 72 closes book two with a prayer for Solomon, who represents David's future. David left behind much unfinished business (see 1 Kgs 1–2 and Chronicles 1–2), including the building of the Temple on Zion.

Book two ends with a benediction (Ps 72:18-19) that focuses all eyes on the *blessed* and *glorious name* of Yahweh, the God of Israel, *who alone does wondrous things. . . . may his glory fill the whole earth.*

Book Three. Psalms 73–89

Psalm 73

Form critics have had a difficult time deciding on the proper classification of this psalm. It seems sufficient to say that it is a testimony of the thanksgiving type that also has the form of a reflection. Its content, therefore, is similar to the WISDOM LITERATURE, which has led to its common designation as a wisdom psalm. The psalm assumes the speaker is addressing a group of listeners, who could be almost any group in worship, community, or family contexts.

The literary structure of the psalm divides rather nicely into eight parts, with two major parallel sections: vv. 2-16 (2-3, 4-12, 13-16) and vv. 18-28 (18-20, 21-26, 27-28); v. 17 serves as a pivot between the parallel sections and v. 1 is a prologue. The reading of v. 1 as "Truly God is good to Israel / to those who are pure in heart" (RSV mg.) is better than *Truly God is good to the upright* (RSV and NRSV). The short colon in v. 1b is the result of ellipsis in which *truly God is good* in the first colon are double-duty words and are understood in the second colon but without direct expression. Ellipsis is common in the poetry of the Psalms (Dahood, 1970, 429–39).

The speaker has a message for the Israelite community and his own experience embodies the life of Israel. The parallel colon makes it clear, however, that the primary audience in Israel is *those who are pure in heart* (i.e., those whose devotion to God is pure and makes them fit for worship [cf. Isa 1:15-16]). Verse 1 also sets forth a thesis that will be tested in this psalm (and indeed throughout book three of the Psalter): God may be good to those who are pure in heart, but is he really good to Israel?

This psalm is marked by the forceful use of the Hebrew particle *'ak* (vv. 1, 13, and 18), which has the force of indicating a condition that is contrary to what is normally expected: a "yes, but" construction (the particle can also mean "surely" or "truly"; note its sixfold usage in Ps 62). This construction has led commentators to label Ps 73 as "The Great Nevertheless." This is especially evident in vv. 18-19, where *the wicked* whose prosperous and arrogant ways had produced such envy in the speaker that he reached the brink of spiritual disaster (vv. 2-3, 4-12, 13-16) are perceived to be themselves standing on slippery ground with no enduring security.

The outward demeanor of the wicked seems strong and vibrant with successful life, but appearances are deceptive: "The LORD does not see as mortals see; they look on the outward appearance, but the LORD looks on the heart" (1 Sam 16:7). The real power of the wicked is their ability to evoke jealous envy in the righteous. Incidentally, *heart* (the volitional center of being, the mind) is used six times in this psalm (vv. 1, 7, 13, 21, 26 twice) and is a major emphasis.

The speaker in Ps 73 testifies to a liberating reorientation of understanding, a breakthrough that occurred in the SANCTUARY (v. 17). We are not told how the new way of thinking happened, but the results are dramatic.

First, as already observed above, there is a reorientation of understanding toward the wicked (vv. 18-20). The veil of invincibility is taken away from them and their true future is perceived.

Second, there is a reorientation of the speaker's own self (vv. 21-22): acceptance of the stupid bitterness of a heart ruled by envy (v. 3).

Third, there is a new orientation toward the presence of God, in which the speaker now realizes that God's presence and guidance is continuous, even when human flesh and heart are spent (vv. 23-26).

Fourth, the speaker has a new orientation towards the future, which will not be ruled by the wealthy and arrogant who are so much envied. The speaker's "strength" and *portion* ("heritage," as in land that belongs to a family) is secure and a glorious reception by God awaits (vv. 24-26). On the basis of the new orientation, the speaker affirms traditional faith in Yahweh in vv. 27-28.

The title of this psalm attributes it to ASAPH. It is the first in a run of Asaph psalms that extends through Ps 83 (see comments on Ps 50 and on the Asaph psalms at the end of commentary on Ps 83).

Psalm 74

This is a communal complaint that describes the grief and dismay following a destruction of the Temple on Mount Zion (vv. 3, 4-8). The date is uncertain. Some commentators read the psalm in the context of the profanation of the Temple by Antiochus Epiphanes IV (175–163 B.C.E.). Others relate it to the destruction of 587 B.C.E. The psalm may have originated in preexilic times in a northern context (Rendsburg 1990, 69–71), and later transferred to Jerusalem. In its present form the psalm clearly applies to *Mount Zion* (v. 2) and Jerusalem.

The opening cry for help (vv. 1-3) pleads for God to remember Zion, and to bring to an end the terrible godforsakenness of his people. There is a sense of an unbearably long duration of calamity, which may indicate that the psalm was written some time after the attack on the sanctuary to which it refers (v. 3). Verse 2 recalls the sacred history of Zion and the worshiping *congregation* of Israel. The place where Yahweh dwelt is now in ruins.

In vv. 4-11, the enemies of Israel have invaded the *holy place* (lit. "meeting place"), where they have carried out brutal devastation. The exact meaning of the *emblems* or "signs" in v. 4b is uncertain. The reference can be either to religious or military symbols (cf. Num 2:2) or to both. Verses 5-6 are uncertain, but the NRSV translation conveys the general sense. Verse 8 indicates the destruction was not confined to the Temple but included all the sacred sites in the land. In this distressing situation, there are no "signs" (v. 9) that Yahweh is about to intervene and redeem his people. There is no PROPHET (see Lam 2:9; Ezek 7:2-6; 1 Macc. 4:46; 9:27; 14:4) who knows the duration of the ruined condition. Yahweh's hand is "held back" from smiting the foe and comforting his people (v. 11).

A hymnic passage probably intended for a solo voice (vv. 12-17; see esp. v. 12) follows the complaints and petitions of the previous verses. God is addressed as *my King* and as the salvation-worker. The great acts of God in the past are recalled: his triumph over the monster of chaos, his control of the waters, and the order that he fixed in the natural world. If he broke the power of chaotic forces then, why not now? *The heads of Leviathan* (v. 14; see LEVIATHAN) is an allusion to the seven-headed monster Lotan that was crushed by the god BAAL. The poet has borrowed some of the imagery of the Canaanites to describe the power of Yahweh.

The petition of the people is resumed in vv. 18-23. Repeated supplications for divine intervention and deliverance are made. *Your dove* of v. 19 refers to Israel's defenselessness before the violence that spreads throughout the land. *The dark places of the land* (v. 20) may refer to places where Israelites fled to protect themselves from the invaders. Yahweh is implored to keep his covenant commitments (vv. 20-23).

Psalm 75

Frequently designated as a communal thanksgiving, this psalm has more of a prophetic-didactic nature, and is a prophetic exhortation. The speaker could be a king, but more likely we should think of a PROPHET or other leader. The communal nature of the thanksgiving-praise in v. 1 indicates that the psalm is set in a public worship context.

The presence of Yahweh is invoked by the use of his name in recalling his wondrous deeds of the past, which would include his judgments on *the wicked* (vv. 3-4). Perhaps we should read at the end of v. 1: "Your name is brought near as they [the people] tell of your wondrous deeds" (cf. REB).

In vv. 2-5, an ORACLE received from God is related—probably by a prophet or priest. God is coming for judgment. He is identified in v. 3 as the one who maintains the stability of the earth. This is followed by a warning to the foes of Israel who might dare to attack, the meaning of *lift up your horn* (vv. 4-5).

A commentary on the oracle follows (vv. 6-8), spoken by an unidentified speaker, but probably by a prophet or other leader. Those who boast and *lift up [their] horn* against Yahweh will have to drink from a cup of judgment (v. 8; cf. Ps 60:3; Jer 25:15-16; Isa 51:17, 22; Ezek 23:31-34; Hab 2:16; Zech 12:2; etc.). The concept of the cup of judgment may have been borrowed from the custom of an ordeal involving drinking from a cup (see Num 5:11-28).

The cup may also reflect the festival cup passed around by members of the fellowship who participated in communal meals during the festivals (see Pss 16:5; 116:13; Jer 16:7; 1 Cor 10:16). Ironically, this is a cup of fellowship for *the wicked*, and they will drink it *down to the dregs*.

The certainty of divine intervention is the basis for the joy and praise which closes the psalm (vv. 9-10). *The horns of the wicked [will be] cut off* while *the horns of the righteous shall be exalted*. Verse 10 is a short oracle, corresponding to the oracle in vv. 2-5.

Psalm 76

Traditionally understood as one of the Songs of Zion, this psalm is a hymn of praise. It has some of the characteristics of Pss 46, 47, and 48 (see also Pss 84, 87, and 122). The psalm may have been written for, or in commemoration of, a historical event. The defeat of SENNACHERIB in 701 B.C.E. (2 Kgs 19 and Isa 37) and David's defeat of the Philistines (2 Sam 17-25) are two possible events behind the psalm. The psalm has the generalized language of cultic poetry and it celebrates the kingship of Yahweh (although it is not specifically mentioned). The reality of Yahweh's power for those who wait and trust is the main point developed in the psalm.

The first part of the psalm (vv. 1-6) recalls the revelation of Yahweh to Judah that focuses on the history of Judah and Zion, specifically the Davidic tradition of the conquest of Jerusalem and the establishment of Yahweh's sanctuary there. *Salem* (v. 2) is an old designation for Jerusalem (Gen 14:18), which also is reminiscent of the term *shalom* (peace, salvation, well-being). The dwelling-place of Yahweh is intended to be a city of peace and salvation (cf. Ps 46:9; Hos 2:18; Isa 2:4; 11:9), thus the implements of war are smashed by dazzling displays of sovereign power. The language of Yahweh's breaking *the weapons of war* (v. 3) is similar to Ps 46 (see also Hos 1:4; 2:18; Jer 49:35; Mic 5:9-13; Zech 9:10). Yahweh destroys both the weapons of the enemies of Israel and the weapons of Israel. Yahweh is Israel's sole warrior, defender, and the peacemaker among the nations. Compare the emphatic *there* in v. 3 with Pss 46:8-9; 48:4-8; 66:5-7.

Verses 7-12 exalt the role of Yahweh as judge of the earth. Human powers are immobilized before the irresistible force of God's wrath. Let the mighty ones of this world prepare their gifts and homage for Yahweh! Let *the oppressed of the earth* (v. 9) rejoice and praise God for the liberating judgment of the Terrible One (*the one who is awesome*, v. 11)! The redeeming purpose of God will not be thwarted by the wrath of the wicked; *human wrath* will praise him (v. 10).

Psalm 77

This psalm begins with a lament that conveys the acute distress of a speaker (vv. 1-3) who is suffering from a severe sense of godforsakenness (vv. 7-10) that causes soul-torment day and night (vv. 2-4). The present situation is contrasted with that in the past (v. 5).

There is a vagueness about the nature of the trouble that has beset the speaker, but it seems best to assume it is not a personal calamity so much as it is the condition of the people of Israel.

The general historical context is most probably that of the exilic or postexilic period of Israel's history (at least for the psalm in its present setting; it may have been a northern psalm originally) when doubt of Yahweh's *steadfast love* (*hesed*) and *promises* (v. 8) was prevalent. The personal crisis of faith has arisen out of the national crisis of Israel.

Verse 10 has been given different renderings and interpretations, but it seems best to interpret it in the sense of the preceding verses—God's providential power no longer seems to be effective.

In the second part of the psalm (vv. 11-20) the speaker recalls the wonderful deeds of Yahweh. These verses, however, do not represent a shift of mood from lament and complaint to praise. The words are full of praise, but the mood is that of the perplexed and painful reflection in vv. 1-11.

The point is that a God of such great power and wondrous deeds should be able to duplicate such power and deeds in the present. The speaker meditates on the inscrutable ways of God that were so great in the past, but seemingly are so impotent in the present. Yahweh's powerful *right hand . . . has changed* (v. 10) and no longer effects the deliverance and defense of his people (cf. v. 15).

This psalm is "a prayer of unanswered lament" (Tate 1990, 275). The speaker's hand is stretched out in unwearying prayer, but God's hand no longer has its power—and there is no *hand of Moses and Aaron* (v. 20) to lead the people. In vv. 16-19 the EXODUS event is portrayed in terms of the ancient idea of the deity battle against the chaos-force represented by the sea (cf. Pss 66:6-7; 74:13-14; 89:9-10; 93:3-4; 114:3, 5).

Perhaps the last clause of v. 19 contains a veiled hope: *Your way was through the sea . . . yet your footprints were unseen* (or, "your trail was not recognized"). The rule of God leaves no visible trace in normal human events, although it was manifest in crashing thunder, flashing lightnings, swirling winds, and the wild turbulence of the raging sea.

Psalm 78

Psalm 78 is ordinarily grouped with Pss 105, 106, 135, and 136; together they are designated "historical psalms." They use a poetic form of narrative storytelling in order to recite Yahweh's deeds in Israel's history. Psalm 78 has, by form, elements of the thanksgiving psalms and the hymns. In addition, the influence of wisdom poetry appears in vv. 1-3.

The place of this type of psalm in the worship of the Israelites is not certain. It may have been used, however, in ceremonies for the renewal of the COVE-NANT between Yahweh and Israel. Such a usage is supported by the liturgy of the feast of the renewal of the covenant of the sect of Qumran. In this liturgy, a recapitulation of the great saving deeds of God was given by the priests and followed by an account of the "sins of Israel" given by the Levites. The congregation then confessed its own sins and those of its ancestors and affirmed its commitment to God (cf. Josh 24:1-28; Deut 29:1-31:13; 2 Kgs 23:1-3; Neh 8:13-9:38).

In its present form Ps 78 reflects the preaching style of the Levites in 1–2 Chronicles, and may come from the period after the Babylonian EXILE. However, the historical retrospect of the psalm reaches a climax with the reign of DAVID, leading some interpreters to date it as early as the tenth century B.C.E. An early date seems unlikely, although use may have been made of very ancient traditions that extend back into the early history of Israel. Despite the lack of reference in the psalm to the destruction of the Temple in Jerusalem, a postexilic date should not be ruled out, although any dating is speculative. If a preexilic date is preferred, the time of the reform of HEZEKIAH (late 700s B.C.E.) would be a good guess.

Psalm 78 was not intended as a mere recital of a series of events in Israel's history. Rather, it aims to show how God has worked in that history, and to probe the mystery both of the divine providence and of the persistent APOSTASY of Israel. The opening verses indicate that the sacred history is a "parable"—the translation of the Hebrew word *mashal* (more commonly PROVERB). This word has a wide range of meaning, but in its most fundamental form it is used for the expression of relationships between things, or between persons, that are difficult to grasp or are obscure. The user of a *mashal* aims at pungent, sometimes ironic, statements of what has been called "capsulated wisdom" that need to be taught and interpreted. The *dark saying* (v. 2) or RIDDLE has a similar function. In brief, it may be said that both the *mashal* and the "dark saying" seek to express the deeper aspects of that which may appear to be simple and superficial. Thus, the history of Israel is known (v. 3), but without interpretation its meaning may remain hidden from new generations. The didactic nature intended for the psalm is made clear in vv. 1-8 by the repeated emphasis on causing the children to know about *the glorious deeds of [Yahweh]* (v. 4, 5, 6) so they will *not forget the works of God* (v. 7) and follow the *rebellious* ways of *their ancestors* (v. 8).

The historical allusion of vv. 9-11 is uncertain. It could refer to the failure of the Ephraimites to drive out the Canaanites (Num 14:1-10; Judg 1:22-36), or even to the defeat of Saul on Mount Gilboa, or to the fall of Samaria in 722 B.C.E., or to some otherwise unrecorded tradition. In any case, the Israelites "forgot" the wonderful acts of God and did not keep the *torah* of the covenant.

Verses 12-32 contain a recitation of God's wonderful acts in caring for his people in the EXODUS from Egypt and the wilderness wanderings. This recitation includes the "riddle" of Israel's response: the rebellious sinfulness that matched the mighty acts step by step and aroused the wrath of God. Despite the doubt and lack of faith, God continued to bless the Israelites with food.

The enigma of Israel's history is continued in a sequel (vv. 33-39). Under the wrathful judgment of God, the Israelites sought for God and repented, but their repentance was *not steadfast*. Even though God was compassionate and patient, Israel was "not faithful to his covenant" (vv. 37-39). Neither miracles nor mercy was sufficient for the sinful heart of Israel.

The historical summary continues in a second recital in vv. 40-64 with a recitation of the *signs* in Egypt (i.e., the PLAGUES). The account of the plagues differs from that in Exod 7–12 both in number and in details. There seems to have been varied forms of the accounts until later, and the tradition varied from place to place. The plagues were followed by the leading forth of the Israelites from Egypt (v. 54). The story of the conquest and settlement is greatly abbreviated in vv. 54-55 and linked with Mount Zion (*the mountain* of v. 54).

The sad summary of Israel's sinful response to God's gracious acts continues in vv. 56-64. Rebellion and IDOLATRY again aroused the full wrath of God (v. 59; cf. v. 38) and he abandoned Shiloh to the sword and to captivity (vv. 60-64). The destruction of the temple at Shiloh (1 Sam 1:9) is mentioned elsewhere in the OT only in Jer 7:12-14; 26:6; the defeat of the Israelites by the Philistines (which probably included the destruction of Shiloh) is found in 1 Sam 4:1–7:2. *Power* and *glory* in v. 61 refer to the ARK of the covenant that was captured by the Philistines (cf. Ps 132:8).

The sequel to the recital of history in vv. 40-64 is found in vv. 65-72, which corresponds to the sequel in vv. 33-39. The severe judgment of God seemed to mean the end of Israel. But God *awoke as from sleep* like a strong man arousing from intoxication (a very bold portrayal of God; cf. 2 Kgs 18:27), and he put his adversaries to rout (vv. 65-66). Afterwards, he rejected the tribes of northern Israel (v. 67) and chose the tribe of Judah, David, and Mount Zion.

Psalm 79

This communal lament has as its context an invasion and destruction of Jerusalem and the sacking of the Temple (but the particular situation is, like that of Ps 74, difficult to establish). Psalm 79 has been dated to the Maccabean period, but this seems improbable (cf. 1 Macc 7:17). The disaster of 587 B.C.E. provides a better context, although it is possible that some unknown catastrophe after 500 B.C.E., or even some disaster prior to 587 B.C.E., lies behind it.

A complaint (vv. 1-4) describes the disaster of an invasion of Jerusalem and its ruin. The enemy is not identified, but if the date of the calamity is 587 B.C.E., the Babylonian army was responsible.

The prayer of the people (vv. 5-12) reveals their deeper concern about the wrath of Yahweh, which they understand to be at work in the terrible events described in vv. 1-4. They confess the sinfulness of their past (v. 8), but pray that the compassion of God will meet them with speedy salvation. The force of the prayer conveys the agony the people experience. The congregation prays for God to help them for the glory of his name. God's servants have had their blood poured out, God's name has been mocked and derided by Israel's neighbors, and God's Temple has been ravished (v. 1). The reputation of God is at stake; let him listen to *the groans of the prisoners* who are doomed to die unless he acts (v. 11).

The closing verse expresses the congregation's hope and vow of praise for the future. Despite the appalling disaster that has come upon them, they are still the flock of the great shepherd and prepared to pay their vows of thanksgiving.

Psalm 80

This is a communal lament that verbalizes the prayer of the people in the midst of a disastrous historical situation. Good arguments have been advanced for dating Ps 80 in one of two periods: (1) the period preceding the fall of the Northern Kingdom,

732–722 B.C.E. and (2) the reign of JOSIAH, 640–609 B.C.E. The former is supported by the superscription of the psalm in the LXX, which contains a reference to the Assyrians. Of these two, probability leans toward the period of Josiah and JEREMIAH, at least for parts of the psalm. The present psalm also may be a scribal composition from the postexilic period that utilizes older preexilic Ephraimite traditions and content.

The opening prayer (vv. 1-3) is directed to the *Shepherd of Israel* (see Pss 23:1; 78:52; Gen 48:15; 49:24; also Exod 15:13) who leads and cares for the people. The reference to *Joseph* suggests the northern tribes of Israel. The *Shepherd of Israel* is further identified as the one who is *enthroned upon the cherubim* (or the Cherubim-enthroned-One), which relates to the ARK of the covenant and goes back at least to SHILOH (see 1 Sam 4:4; 2 Sam 6:2; Ps 99:1). God is asked to *shine forth* (Exod 24:10; Deut 33:2; Num 6:24-26; Ps 50:2; 67:1; 94:1) in salvation to EPHRAIM, BENJAMIN, and MANASSEH—tribes that belonged to the Northern Kingdom, although Benjamin is sometimes grouped with Judah. The mention of the three tribes possibly points to the period when the district of Galilee was under Assyrian domination, but before 721 B.C.E. when Samaria fell. Verse 3 is a refrain that is repeated in vv. 7 and 19. It uses the ancient term for Yahweh: "Yahweh of Hosts" (*O LORD God of hosts*, v. 19, here with the addition of *elohim*) associated with the ark (see Ps 24 and LORD OF HOSTS).

The prayer of complaint (vv. 4-13) indicates the situation that has come to pass for the people: the language suggests prolonged suffering. The general picture would fit well the period after 722 B.C.E., but, as previously noted, an actual historical referent is secondary. Israel is compared to a *vine* (vv. 8-13) that Yahweh brought out of Egypt and planted (cf. Exod 15:17) in ground prepared for it (i.e., in Palestine). Growing in this ground, it grew large, but now Yahweh has broken down the walls that protected it from exploitation by those who passed by and from the ravages of wild animals (cf. Isa 5:1-7; Hos 10:1; Jer 2:21; Matt 21:33-43; John 15:1-11). Yahweh has allowed a terrible catastrophe to come to the people; the great vine and its vineyard has been ravaged by wild boars (originally, perhaps, the Assyrians).

The prayer continues (vv. 14-19) with the plea that Yahweh will again be the vine dresser who cares for the vine (Israel) that he planted. God is reminded that Israel's enemies have burned the vineyard and cut down his vine. There is some uncertainty about the

meaning of v. 17. The reference to *the one at your right hand* may be a play on the name Benjamin (which means "son of the right hand") and be a special prayer for that tribe, or it may be a reference to the king (cf. 110:1). It refers more probably to the *stock* and "son" (Israel) in v. 15 (obscured by the NRSV; see Tate 1990, 304, 307, 315).

Verses 14-19 continue with a vow of fidelity and loyalty to God: "We will never be backsliders again!" (v. 18). Verse 19 repeats v. 3, and closes the psalm (v. 14 is a variant of vv. 3 and 19). The prayer assumes the ravagers of the vineyard would perish (v. 16) if Yahweh turned his face toward the vineyard and beheld its destruction.

Psalm 81

This psalm falls into two distinct parts: vv. 1-5b and 5c-16. The first part begins in a hymnic fashion, while the second part is a prophetic ORACLE. Treating the two parts separately, however, is not necessary. The psalms often contain bits and pieces that are shaped into whole compositions.

Psalm 81 is clearly associated with one of the festivals of Israel. Both OT evidence and Jewish tradition agree that the Feast of Tabernacles is most likely, although its use at the PASSOVER in postexilic Israel cannot be ruled out entirely. It has also been argued that the autumn festival (Tabernacles) was a feast of COVENANT renewal and that this psalm was associated with the ceremonies; the suggestion is possible, but not certain. The date of the psalm cannot be fixed any better than many other psalms, but it is possible that its origin was in the period of Israel's history before the monarchy when the tribal groups gathered annually at a cultic center for festivals (SHECHEM, SHILOH, BETHEL—since Jerusalem was not an Israelite city before the days of David). The close association of Ps 81 with Pss 50 and 95 is widely accepted—all of them seem to be festal psalms. Also, all three are marked by the presence of ORACLE material in which God speaks directly.

The hymnic opening (vv. 1-5a) is a call to praise God with "shouts of joy" and with songs and music. It reminds us that the festivals, while solemn, were also occasions of great joy—and exceedingly noisy! The large assemblies of the people echoed with the festival shouts, while trumpets sounded their commanding blasts and other musical instruments added to the volume of sound. The interpretation of v. 3 raises considerable debate. The blowing of the trumpet at the *new* moon, the first of the month, is provided for in Num 10:10. The reference here, however, is more probably to the special occasion at the beginning of the seventh month referred to in Lev 23:24 and Num 29:1.

The words for trumpet vary. The primitive *shofar*— the horn of a ram, goat, or cow, and primarily an instrument for giving signals—is used here. This word is found in the Pentateuch only once (Lev 25:9) where it is associated with the tenth day of the seventh month, the Day of Atonement. The word used in Num 10:10 seems to refer to a metal, therefore a more sophisticated instrument, while the word in Lev 23:24 and Num 29:1 is a general term for giving a signal without specific indication of the instrument (but the *shofar* was probably used as in Lev 25:9). The *shofar* along with the trumpet is indicated in Ps 98:6.

A further problem arises in connection with *the full moon, on our festal day*. Since Tabernacles begins with the "full moon" (fifteenth day of the seventh month, Tishri) it is assumed the reference is to the beginning day of that festival (Lev 23:33-36; Num 29:12), but some interpreters argue that all of the references in v. 3 refer to the same day, a New Year's day. An alternative interpretation may be best (Kraus 1989, 149): the *shofar* was blown twice, at the beginning of the festival period (*new moon*) and at the beginning of Booths (*full moon*), that is, on the first day of the seventh month (Lev 23:24) and on the first day of Tabernacles (the fifteenth day), a period that includes the Day of Atonement.

Verses 4-5b stress that the festival celebration was established in Israel by divine decree and associated with the experience of the Israelites in the EXODUS from Egypt (see also, v. 10). *Joseph* may be a synonym for all of Israel, but it has special reference to the Israelites who were in Egypt. The purpose of the festival is to serve as a "testimony" (better than *decree* in v. 5a) to Israel of Yahweh's great saving acts in bringing her out of Egypt (see Lev 23:42-43; cf. Deut 16:3).

A solo voice delivers a prophetic oracle to the people in vv. 5c-16. Verse 5c is difficult (lit. "a lip I know not I hear"), but is best understood as referring to the reception of an oracle by a prophet or priest. The message has been received from God; it is not one *known* to the speaker in terms of personal experience. Verse 10 (*Open your mouth wide, and I will fill it*) seems to follow v. 5c, and the colons have been separated in a kind of "envelope" construction for the insertion of vv. 6-9, which contains the message of the oracle.

The oracle itself recalls Yahweh's redemptive act of deliverance from slavery in Egypt and the situation at the sacred mountain in the wilderness when Yahweh made his covenant *torah* known. The *secret place of thunder* (v. 7) recalls the THEOPHANY of Yahweh in the thunderstorm (Exod 19:16-19; Pss 18:7-15; 77:18; 104:7; Isa 29:6). The testing at *the waters of Meribah* (v. 7) alludes to Exod 17:1-7; Num 20:1-13 (cf. 95:7-11)—but the situation is reversed here: the people do not "test" God, but he "tests" them!

The understanding of vv. 6-7 depends upon close attention to the changes in tense and person in the Hebrew text (obscured in the NRSV). Verse 6 should read: *I relieved [his] shoulder of the burden; [his] hands were freed from the basket.* The "his" refers to Joseph in the preceding verse, and to the generation that had undergone slavery in Egypt. However, in v. 7 the pronoun changes to a collective *you*, that is, to the festival congregation now being addressed as the people of the exodus generation had been addressed in the wilderness (for a striking illustration of a similar change of person, see Deut 26:5-11). The interval of history is removed, as it were, and theologically the people are once more before Yahweh in the wilderness.

In vv. 13-16, it is interesting to note that God vows to defeat the enemies of his people and care for them with abundance (v. 16; cf. Deut 32:13-14) if they will listen to him and walk in his ways (v. 13). Vows of individuals or groups (e.g., Pss 79:13; 80:18) to praise and serve God on the condition that he will do what is asked of him are more common. In this case, God vows to respond to Israel's affirmative acts.

Psalm 82

This important psalm has sparked considerable controversy among interpreters. One controversial point has been the identity of *the gods* (vv. 1 and 6). One interpretation assumes they are human judges who have failed in their responsibilities. This view follows the Targum and cites such passages as Exod 21:6; 22:7-8; 28; 1 Sam 2:25. Another interpretation considers them to be kings of earthly nations who are judged because of their corrupt ways. There may be truth in both interpretations, since the function of the judge and king (often the same) was to mediate the divine will and to act as an agent of God (cf. Deut 1:17). The references cited for the interpretation of *gods* as judges, however, can be more properly understood as referring to deity. If kings or judges were intended, v. 7 seems strange indeed.

It is much more probable that *gods* refers to divine beings, and, thus the psalm must be interpreted against the background of a heavenly assembly over which Yahweh presides (see Pss 29:1; 58:1; 89:5-7; 103:20-21; 148:2; 1 Kgs 22:19-22; Job 1:6-12; 2:1-6; Dan. 7:9-10). This is in line with ancient Jewish interpretation that "gods" refers to angels who failed to carry out their authorized functions properly. Behind this interpretation is the concept that the nations were allotted to individual gods, who were responsible for their proper administration (see Deut 32:8; 29:25-26; Isa 24:21; Dan. 10:13, 20-21; Eccl 17:17). This concept makes use of the ideas pertaining to the assembly of the gods prevalent in the thought of the ancient world.

Psalm 82 is related to the Canaanite poetry from Ugarit. Therefore, it is best to deal with Ps 82 as an effect, a brief dramatic scene "in the affairs of the assembly of the gods" (Miller 1986, 121).

The charge against *the gods* is found in vv. 2-5; they have failed to defend the rights of *the weak* and poor within their territories, while showing partiality to *the wicked*. They stumble about so much in their ignorance and darkness that the very *foundations of the earth are shaken* (v. 5). Their failure threatens a return to the chaos from which the world has been delivered. This must be read against the arbitrary and often capricious activity of the gods in the pagan myths. Such gods provided no stable order of life for either divine or human life, and no consistent standard for human behavior. In Ps 82, the divine world is rendered impotent and the gods are sentenced to die as mortals do.

The judgment of Yahweh relegates the gods to the status of ordinary human mortality (vv. 6-7). They had been given a higher status (v. 6; the *I say* should be read as "I said" indicating divine appointment), but by their failure they have forfeited it. Yahweh, who alone is the giver of life, is left alone in his sovereignty. He is the only one who is able to rule the earth, thus the prayer in v. 8. *All the nations* belong to God, and the congregation prays that he will take possession. The assembly of the gods has become an assize; Yahweh alone is vindicated. But the earth is bereft of divine administration unless Yahweh himself rises to judge.

This psalm reflects part of the theological process of the Israelites confronting the worship of various deities in the cultures among which they lived. The gods were overcome by their reduction to a rank subordinate to Yahweh and deprived of their prerogatives and powers. They became no-gods. The psalm also attempts to explain the presence of EVIL in human exis-

tence. Evil conditions continue because the divine beings responsible for the administration of the nations tolerate it. A cosmic aspect is given to the presence of evil in the world. The failure of justice in the world is rooted in the necessity of a judgment of the gods by Yahweh. The psalm should not be read, however, as relieving human beings of their responsibilities.

Psalm 83

The historical situation that produced this lament of the people cannot be determined exactly despite the several references to particular nations, places, and events. Attempts have been made to relate the psalm to the Assyrian threat of the eighth century B.C.E., but we do not know of any coalition of nations against Israel such as the one given (and Syria is not mentioned). A specific historical situation, therefore, may not have been in the poet's mind, and the psalm is worked out on the broad flow of Israelite traditions. The list of nations may be a more or less standard recitation of the enemies of Israel. The speaker is not identified, but we can think of an Israelite leader praying for the nation.

After the urgent petitions to God (v. 1) their basis is laid out (vv. 2-8). The nations are in commotion as they conspire together to obliterate Israel. ASSYRIA is the great power that lies behind the hostile actions of Israel's immediate neighbors. The Assyrians are described as *the strong arm of the children of Lot.* *Children of Lot* refers to the Moabites and Ammonites (Gen 19:36-38; Deut 2:9, 19) who are supported by the Assyrians in their endeavors against Israel.

Verses 9-18 contain extended petitions for deliverance from enemies. The conspiracy against Israel is actually against Yahweh (cf. vv. 4-5). Therefore, this prayer is for swift and certain judgment aimed at bringing the enemies to seek the name of Yahweh. The events referred to in vv. 9-12 reflect the destruction of the Canaanites by DEBORAH and BARAK (Judg 4–5) and the rout of the Midianites by GIDEON (Judg 7–8). Yahweh is implored to mightily act again as he did in the history of Israel, so that he alone may be exalted *over all the earth* (v. 18).

"Psalms of Asaph." Psalm 83 is the last of eleven consecutive psalms (73–83) associated by their titles with ASAPH. (Psalm 50 is also an Asaph psalm.) Some features of these psalms show a fair degree of commonality (helpfully summarized by Day, *Psalms*, 118): concern with divine judgment; appeals to Yahweh's mighty deeds in the past; more allusions to Israel as a

flock and Yahweh as its shepherd than in all the rest of the Psalter (Pss 74:1; 77:20; 78:52; 70-72; 79:13; 80:1); relatively high number of references to the northern tribes, especially to Joseph (Pss 77:15; 78:9; 67; 80:1; 81:5) who is mentioned elsewhere in the Psalter only in Ps 105:17; and (added to Day's list) attention to the condition and significance of Zion-Jerusalem (Pss 50:2; 74:2; 76:2; 78:68; 79:1; 3). The arguments for an original northern Israelite provenance for these psalms has been revived and extended by Rendsburg (1990, 73–81) and it seems plausible to accept his conclusion. In their present forms and setting, however, the psalms are clearly centered on Jerusalem and Zion.

"Elohistic Collection." Psalm 83 also marks the end of the section of the Psalter frequently called the Elohistic Collection (Pss 42–83) because of the frequency of the use of *elohim* as a name for Yahweh. (*Yahweh* [LORD] occurs 272 times in Pss 1–41 and *elohim* (*God*) fifteen times; in Pss 42–83 *elohim* occurs 200 times versus forty-three times for *Yahweh*.) The change of Yahweh to Elohim seems to have been deliberate in many cases (e.g., cf. Pss 14 and 53; 40:13-17 and 70), but no one knows for sure why Pss 42–83 were so treated. These psalms probably functioned as a separate Psalter at some time in the history of Israel. The use of *elohim*, as in the case of the widespread use of *adonai* (*Lord*), was probably to avoid the divine name Yahweh except in very important contexts, and may indicate that Pss 42–83 were intended for the teaching of the laity in postexilic Israelite communities.

Psalm 84

This hymn (with mixed elements) praises Zion and the temple of Yahweh with its joys of worship. It would have been appropriate for pilgrims making their way to Jerusalem for participation in the festivals, especially Tabernacles, which was associated with the coming of the rains in the autumn (see v. 6). The psalm has features similar to other Songs of Zion (e.g., Ps 48), the Songs of Ascents (120–134), and Pss 42–43. The viewpoint of the speaker in the psalm is that of a pilgrim on the way to Zion (v. 7). Perhaps, the *dwelling place* of Yahweh has come into view (v. 1), and the pilgrim describes the longing of mind and heart for the joy of worship in the Temple (v. 2).

The pilgrim recalls the blessedness of those (priests and others) who have the privilege of abiding in the Temple (vv. 3-4), like the birds that nest in the Temple

courts. Also blessed are pilgrims who make their way through difficult journeys to Zion (vv. 5-7) and those who have their heart set on *the highways to Zion* (although this involves correction of the text in v. 5).

The *valley of Baca* (v. 6) is unknown. *Baca* refers to a species of tree (2 Sam 5:23) that grows in dry soil and the word is also related to weeping. *Valley of baca* has been translated "valley of weeping." It is better to think of an arid territory, perhaps even a place name, that becomes a valley of springs as the pilgrims pass through it. The strength of the pilgrims is constantly renewed until they appear before God in Zion (v. 7).

A prayer is interjected in vv. 8-9. The pilgrim prays for *our shield* and *your anointed*, perhaps terms for the king. If so, these terms point to a preexilic date for this part of the psalm at least, and to the significance of the king in the festival. In postexilic times, however, when there was no monarchy, these terms would have referred to the HIGH PRIEST in Jerusalem.

In the last section of the psalm (vv. 10-12), the pilgrim returns to the theme of the blessings of worship at Zion. There is no *elsewhere* (v. 10) in the Hebrew text, but it seems required. It may be that the psalmist meant "at home." *Doorkeeper* may refer to a temple servant charged with menial duties, but more probably refers to a pilgrim suppliant who waits at the doors of the Temple to be admitted to the holy precincts (see Ps 15). The pilgrim would rather be an entrance-seeking worshiper, a humble pilgrim who has given up much to beg permission to enter the sanctuary of Yahweh, than to dwell among those whose attitude and conduct cut them off from access to the holy place.

The speaker is confident Yahweh will respond favorably to the upright (v. 11). *No good thing* is withheld from the righteous person; true blessing is not found among the wicked. The truly blessed person (cf. Ps 1) is the one who trusts Yahweh (v. 12) and longs for his courts.

Psalm 85

Usually classified as a national lament, this psalm is assumed to reflect harvest festivals. An argument can be made for dating the psalm to the period after 538 B.C.E. when some of the Israelites returned to Palestine from the Babylonian EXILE. The economic and spiritual depression of this period, as reflected in the Books of Haggai, Zechariah, and Malachi, contrast strongly with the exalted hopes of Isa 40–55. In this interpretation, the great restoring acts of Yahweh in vv. 1-3 refer to the restoration from the Babylonian exile, and the speaker in the psalm seeks an extension of these saving acts in the future.

Verses 1-3 look back to Yahweh's acts when he restored the fortunes of Israel and forgave their sins. Deliverance from exile probably is meant (see also Ps 126) in an immediate sense, but Exod 32–34 may be in the background. These verses form the basis for the petitions in vv. 4-7, which contain the passionate prayer of the people for a restoration. The gracious acts of vv. 1-3 have not continued in full effectiveness and the people again feel themselves to be under the burden of divine wrath. Further revival of life is needed (cf. Isa 59:9-15; Hag 1:5-6; Zech 1:12). Their great need is for Yahweh to *show* (i.e., demonstrate in action) his *steadfast love* and grant his deliverance or *salvation* (v. 7).

In vv. 8-13 it is frequently assumed that the voice of a PROPHET or priest follows the prayer of the congregation with an ORACLE of comfort and assurance. It is not necessary, however, to conclude that there is a change of speakers. The speaker of vv. 1-7 may continue with a reflective message of assurance and encouragement.

Note the personification in vv. 10-11 of the great characteristics of Yahweh as divine agents: *steadfast love . . . faithfulness . . . righteousness and peace* (*shalom*)—as well as *glory* in v. 9 (representing the powerful presence of Yahweh). The description of physical and spiritual well-being culminates in bountiful supplies for human needs through the coordinated endeavors of these agents (vv. 10-12). In v. 13, *righteousness will go before* Yahweh as a herald before the visit of a king to his land (cf. Isa 40:3-5; 46:13; 58:8; 62:11).

Psalm 86

Little of the suppliant's personal situation can be gathered from this individual lament. Adding to the difficulty of establishing the precise situations, a prevalent problem in most laments, is the fact that this one is heavily dependent on other passages from the Psalter and the OT. Its date cannot be fixed exactly, but it probably belongs to the postexilic period of Israel's history (at least in its present setting).

In vv. 1-7 the speaker prays for a hearing by Yahweh. A series of statements beginning with *for*, and interspersed with the petitions, indicate motivation for the hearing desired. The speaker claims to be *poor and needy*, but one who trusts in Yahweh as a person and as a servant. The *devoted* ("godly") servant places a

claim on Yahweh's goodness and *steadfast love*. The *for* statements change from being statements about the suppliant to statements about God as the prayer moves to a basis of firm trust in God.

In vv. 8-13, the prayer and lament become a hymn-like expression of praise and thanksgiving. The incomparable God will receive the homage of all nations (cf. Pss 22:27-28; 65:2; 66:4; 8; 67:1-7; Isa 45:22-23; 66:23). He is the worker of *wondrous things*, and no works like his are found among the nations and their gods. The certainty and confidence of the speaker lead to a prayer for instruction as a disciple (v. 11) and to a vow of praise and testimony of deliverance in vv. 12-13.

The lament and prayers of vv. 1-7 are renewed in vv. 14-17. Enemies oppress the speaker (vv. 14), but their presence does not destroy his confidence in Yahweh. The *sign* requested in v. 17 refers to some sort of favorable indication of divine action, perhaps an ORACLE or a token of healing from illness.

Psalm 87

This is a hymn of the "Songs of Zion" type, praising Zion as the city founded and loved by Yahweh, whose citizens are especially recorded in God's census records of the world (v. 6; cf. Pss 56:8; 69:28; 139:16; Isa 4:3).

The meaning of vv. 4-6 is not entirely clear, but it is best to interpret these verses as meaning that all those who "know Yahweh" belong to Zion in a spiritual sense. For Zion is the mother city (*this one was born there*) of all God's children regardless of where they live (cf. Phil. 3:20; Gal 4:26; Rev 21). God is depicted as keeping a birth register, and Zion becomes the birthplace of the nations (v. 6). The background of this action is found in the practice of kings declaring that conquered foreign peoples now belong to the royal realm of the conquering country (Tate 1990, 385–93). In the case of Ps 87, Yahweh has decided to make Zion the universal birthplace of the world (translate v. 5b "Everyone was born in her [Zion]", and read v. 6b read as a performative statement of Yahweh that establishes the Zion birthright of the peoples). Even hostile peoples nearby and those far away are included (v. 4). "It is a bold picture—Yahweh taking inventory of the peoples of the world, all of them his . . . and giving everyone a birth certificate marked 'Zion'" (Durham 1971, 350).

The psalm reflects the exuberant mood of Jerusalem when pilgrims gathered for festivals from many "dwelling places" (v. 2) both in Judah and in other lands to praise Yahweh and to renew their devotion to him. This is evident in v. 7, where the psalmist's attention falls on the *singers and dancers* who participate in the festival celebrations, perhaps including the foreigners in vv. 4-6. *All my springs* (or fountains) in v. 7 is a metaphor for the source of life and blessing (Ps 36:9; Isa 12:3; Joel 3:18).

Psalm 88

This individual lament has been called "the saddest psalm in the Psalter" (Kirkpatrick 1901) and described as without "a single ray of comfort or hope" (Weiser 1962, 586). The shift of mood from lamentation and petition to that of confident testimony, which is found in some laments, is missing. Some interpreters postulate that a sequel of certainty and assurance has been lost from the psalm, but there is no proof to support the conjecture. As it stands, the speaker clings to God in passionate lament and petition, despite the fact of having been swept near death by a flood of divine wrath.

The psalm begins with direct address to God and moves quickly to complaint focused on unanswered prayer, prayer directed day and night to God (vv. 1-2). The condition of the speaker is graphically presented as one near death (v. 3). The supplicant is already reckoned with the dead, who are remembered no more and cut off from the powerful aid of God's hand (vv. 4-6). *Forsaken among the dead* (v. 5), is read better as the "free among the dead" KJV, in the ironic sense of being "set free" (i.e., already judged by family and community as dead and thus relieved of the normal obligations of life).

The wrath of God *lies heavy* upon the speaker (v. 7), although there is no confession of sin in the psalm. Like JOB (Job 19:13-19), the speaker charges God with causing companions to turn away as from a *thing of horror* (v. 8). The praiseless quality of death is emphasized in vv. 10-12 where the rhetorical questions call for negative answers. *Abaddon* (v. 11) is a synonym for SHEOL (see v. 3), the realm of the dead.

The complaint resumes (vv. 13-18) after being interrupted by the rhetorical questions of vv. 10-12. The condition described is that of a person shunned by God (the speaker assumes this, vv. 13-14) and friends: "afflicted and near to death from youth" (v. 15) and attacked by *terrors* (v. 15) and *dread assaults* (v.16)—agents of divine destruction let loose by the wrath of God. Thus, although different words are used,

the theme of divine wrath is renewed (cf. v. 7). The last word of this terrible psalm is *darkness*; the dreadful darkness of the Pit of death from which there is no exit.

Psalm 88 is a bold prayer of protest that creates a verbal lifeline between ebbing human life and God who gives and saves life. Anger and protest are forms of energy for resistance and modes of connectedness to God. The psalm assumes God can still speak and act and thus seeks to forge a solidarity with God in suffering. The psalm also assumes the deadly silence of God will not last forever, even if it seems so.

A conflation of collections. The title of Ps 88 is strangely compounded: "a song, a psalm of the Korahites, to the leader according to *mahalath leannoth* [probably a tune or chanting pattern], a *maskil* [possibly a well-written and strongly expressed psalm] of Heman the Ezrahite." The solution may lie in scribal conflation of an original postscript for Ps 87 with the superscription of Ps 88. The postscript of Ps 87 may have read: "A song, a psalm of the Korahites. For the leader: according to *mahalath leannoth*," leaving "A *maskil* of Heman the Ezrahite" as the title of Ps 88. Possibly the postscript to Ps 87 marked the end of a small collection of Korahite psalms (Pss 84, 85, 87) and called the reader's attention to the addition of two Ezrahite psalms (Pss 88 and 89). The Ezrahite psalms are attributed to two different scribes, Heman and Ethan, who appear in lists of scribal singers associated with KORAH and ASAPH (see 1 Chr 6:33-48; 15:17; 19); The postexilic scribal interpreters would have had no difficulty in linking Asaph, Korahite, and Ezrahite psalms, and this may account for the conflation. The Asaph collection in Pss 73–83 is supplemented by the Korahite and Ezrahite psalms, all likely to have originated in scribal circles.

Note that Ps 86 is the only Davidic psalm in book three of the Psalter. It may be where it is simply because it is suitable for the context, but it also serves to provide Davidic authority for book three. Taken with Ps 89 (which deals with the Davidic covenant), Ps 86 makes a frame around Pss 87 and 88, thereby forming a closing to book three.

Psalm 89

This long psalm is usually classified as a royal lament. Verses 1-18 are identified properly as a hymn (in two parts: 1-4, 5-18), and vv. 19-37 (along with vv. 3-4) compose a divine ORACLE that recounts the divine election of and the promises made to David. The last part of the psalm (vv. 38-51) is a lament over the disaster that has come to the king and to the nation and the failure of Yahweh to keep the promises he made. The key to the interpretation of the psalm in its present form is the prayer in vv. 38-51.

The psalm addresses the problem of unfulfilled promises and expectations relating to the monarchy of David "Where is your former steadfast love, O Lord?—(Those promises) you promised on oath to David?" (v. 49, author trans.). The psalm also asks why the *enemies* of Yahweh (v. 51) have been allowed to overcome and mock his *anointed* with impunity.

Interpreters have sought a specific historical context for Ps 89, but there is no consensus. Major suggestions include the time of REHOBOAM, the crisis during the reign of ahaz of Judah (735–34 B.C.E.), and the time of JEHOIACHIN after the Babylonian attack on Jerusalem in 597 B.C.E. A postexilic date seems more likely (see Tate 1990, 416–17). The speaker in vv. 39-51 may be one of the faithful servants of Yahweh (v. 51), pious folk who sought to maintain their faith during the bleak period after 515 B.C.E.

In vv. 1-4, a solo voice (priest or prophet), begins the hymn with an announcement of intention to proclaim the *steadfast love* and *faithfulness* of Yahweh. The faithfulness of Yahweh is especially manifest in the COVENANT with David, a covenant that embodies the promise of a perpetual dynasty (vv. 3-4; cf. 2 Sam 7). The Davidic covenant should be as lasting as the *steadfast love* of Yahweh himself (cf. Isa 55:3).

The hymn proper (vv. 5-18) opens with a call to the members of the divine *assembly* to praise the wonders of Yahweh (on the heavenly *assembly*, see Ps 82 and COUNCIL, HEAVENLY). Yahweh is presented as the incomparable God who rules the raging sea and brings the chaotic forces of the universe into created order.

Rahab (v. 10) is a name for the primeval chaos monster, also known as LEVIATHAN (cf. Ps 74:12-17; Isa 27:1). *Tabor and Hermon* (v. 12) are mountains in northern Israel, which could indicate that this part of the psalm originated in north Israel—but this is not certain. Both mountains were sites of Canaanite worship in pre-Israelite times, but it is now declared that they praise the name of Yahweh.

The people who know the festal shout (v. 15; cf. 1 Sam 4:5; 6; 2 Chr 15:14; Pss 27:6; 33:3; 47:5) of praise to Yahweh, and who have experienced his glory and strength in their behalf are blessed people. The significance of the king in the life of the people is indicated by the language of v. 18.

In vv. 19-37, a prophetic revelation or oracle recalls the covenant Yahweh made with David and the promises that were included (already set forth briefly in vv. 3-4). The key concept in this passage is that of the enduring faithfulness with which the throne of David was established (see vv. 24, 28, 29, 36-37). The scope of David's dominion is given cosmic dimensions (see v. 25 where the *sea* and *rivers* refer to the primeval waters). David is designated as the son of Yahweh (by adoption) who cries *my Father* (vv. 26-27), and who is the most exalted of the kings of the earth (on the scope of the reign of the Davidic king, see Ps 2). Nevertheless, the Davidic king is subject to the covenant *torah* of Israel (vv. 30-34), although the word of promise will not be broken (vv. 34-35). Yahweh will punish the descendants of David who do not keep his commandments, but God affirms his intention to maintain the dynasty.

The change of mood and style that begins with v. 38 is drastic. The language is emphatic and strong as the charge is made that despite the solemn promises of the past, Yahweh has *renounced the covenant with your servant* (v. 39). The king has suffered a humiliating defeat while his foes have been exalted. The strongholds of the nation have been invaded and ruined (v. 40). His reign has been discredited and brought to shame. The lament changes to prayer in vv. 46-51, with the speaker crying out *How long, O [Yahweh]? Will you hide yourself forever?* (v. 46). Pleas for God to remember the finite nature of human life are found in vv. 47-48; these verses seem to intensify the complaint that Israelites cannot be separated from the frailty and finitude of all humanity, and that Yahweh's actions relating to David call into question his purpose for all human beings.

Yahweh is reminded again (v. 49) of his oath of faithfulness made to David, which is not now in evidence (vv. 50-51). The hurt and anger are not resolved. The speaker "can only lift his hands to God in prayer . . . and lay before him the problems which his own thinking and reasoning are unable to master."

Summary of Book Three

The blessing of Yahweh (Ps 89:52) marks the end of book three. The placement of Ps 89 in the canonical arrangement of the psalms seems significant. The emphasis in Ps 89 on the failed covenant with David is an appropriate finale for book three, which is marked by communal laments and complaints. The collection is rather clearly from the postexilic period, reflecting on the sad development of events after 597 B.C.E.

As noted in the commentary on Ps 73, book three begins with the thesis: "Truly God is good to Israel, to those who are pure in heart" (Ps 73:1, author trans.). The psalms that follow test the thesis. Is Yahweh really good to Israel and to those who are pure in heart? The answer seems to be affirmative for individuals who are "pure in heart" (i.e., fully devoted to Yahweh). Psalm 73:21-28 contains forceful affirmations of the presence and care of God: *But for me it is good to be near God; I have made the LORD God my refuge* (73:28).

This personal faith and satisfaction in the presence of Yahweh is expressed elsewhere in book three (see Pss 75:69; 84:1-12; 86:5-7; 8-13, 15, 17). The personal faith expressed in these psalms constitutes an example both for individual Israelites and for the community as a whole. J. Clinton McCann (1993a, 96) argues that Ps 73 sets the tone for all of book three with a reorientation of insight into the actual nature of things in the world, and the closing expression of hope (1993a, 96). Individuals are given grounds for confidence that reorientation and a sense of powerful solidarity with God are possible.

Book three surfaces a major problem of faith that may be put in the form of a question: Is individual faith and experience of the divine presence enough when the whole enterprise of saving history seems to have failed? Thus Ps 78 is at the heart of book three, with its explanation of the "riddle" of Israel's history with Yahweh (see commentary on Ps 78). What about the *glorious deeds of the LORD . . . and the wonders that he has done* (78:4)? Clearly, the communal aspects of Yahweh's saving work are endangered, as the repeated use of communal laments indicates (Pss 74, 79, 80, 83, 85). Psalm 89 culminates in the charge that Yahweh has defaulted on his commitment to the Davidic dynasty. As a result, individual faith is brought to the brink of failure by the collapse of the communal framework of salvation, and the individual is plunged from the victory of faith in Ps 73 to the nadir of depression and darkness in Ps 88.

Book three, therefore, presents a struggle for a viable faith and asks if it is possible for faith to live while wild boars ravage the vineyard of Yahweh (Ps 80:13) and there is no evidence that God intends to keep his solemn commitment to David (Ps 89). Is personal faith sufficient when the nation and all its institutions are gone? The high triumph of Ps 73 descends to the deep depression of Pss 88–89. Between these psalms the depths of faith's struggle are plumbed.

Psalm 81 is an anomaly in book three, with significantly different content in two instances. First, it begins with a summons to praise, which is characteristic of the hymns: *Sing aloud to God our strength, shout for joy. . . .* Second, it contains a lament on the part of God, who mourns over the people and longs for them to listen to him so he can bless them again (vv. 6-16). God also identifies himself as *I, [Yahweh], am . . . your God who brought you up out of the land of Egypt* (v. 10; cf. Exod 20:1). Lament and complaint do not belong to Israel alone; Yahweh also has disappointment, grief, and frustration. Psalm 81 seems to set a boundary for the protest of book three and provides a counterpoint for the rest of the collection. As Israel grieves and struggles for faith, it is wise to remember how the people have wounded the heart of God, and how God suffers with the people.

Book Four. Psalms 90–106

Psalm 90

Psalm 90 is the first psalm of book four and the only psalm attributed to Moses. For discussion of these matters, see the summary following the commentary on Ps 106.

Most commentators treat this psalm as having two major divisions: vv. 1-12 and 13-17. The structure seems somewhat more complicated, however, since v. 4 seems to follow v. 2 more closely than it does v. 3, and thus forms an envelope around v. 3, which in turn relates closely with vv. 5-10. Within vv. 5-10, v. 8 is in an envelope formed by vv. 7 and 9, followed by an envelope containing v. 11 formed by vv. 10 and 12, while vv. 9 and 12 frame both v. 10 and v. 11. The *anger* and *wrath* of God in v. 11 is paralleled by the *wrath* in vv. 7 and 9. Verse 11 also relates to vv. 13-15, and vv. 13 and 16-17 frame vv. 14-15.

The content of the psalm seems a character as intricate as its form. Verses 1-2 express affirmations of God, while vv. 3-11 deal with the conditions of human finitude under divine wrath, ending with the petition in v. 12. The petitions in vv. 13-17 are direct and in the common language of laments. The psalm as a whole is a communal prayer composed of reflection, complaint, and petitions. The content of the psalm points to long-lasting communal distress: *Make us glad as many days as you have afflicted us, and as many years as we have seen evil* (v. 15). The conditions of immediate distress that seems to characterize the communal laments in Pss 44, 74, and 79 are missing in Ps 90, which suggests it is a literary composition belonging to scribal psalmography in postexilic Israel.

Psalm 90 is well known for its treatment of the transitory condition of human life (vv. 1-6) in which Israel fully participates (vv. 7-12). The *servants* of Yahweh (vv. 13, 16) have experienced the full measure of human finitude. They know the fragile nature of human endeavors, thus they pray to experience the favor of God, to have an awareness of what he is doing in the world, and for the establishment of the work of their hands (v. 17). They pray that their work may have a place of significance and importance and for deliverance from meaninglessness.

Psalm 91

This psalm should be read with Ps 90. The scribal placement of the psalm is probably not incidental: the lament and petition of Ps 90 finds its counterpart of bold faith, confidence, and safety in Ps 91. The two psalms together and with Ps 95 seem to form an INCLUSIO around Pss 92–94. Psalm 91 has the character of instruction and exhortation, and it has been described as a sermonette of encouragement (Stuhlmueller 1983, 73).

Verse 1 should be read as a thematic statement: "Whoever dwells under the protection of the Most High will abide in the shelter (shadow) of the Almighty" (author trans.). Verses 3-13 are in the form of direct address to an unidentified person, and spoken by an individual person of faith who offers testimony and encouragement. The person addressed could be anyone willing and privileged to dwell under the shelter of Yahweh. The speaker does not argue the case for the security of those under the protection of Yahweh but declares it.

The references in vv. 5-6 are probably to the fear of unseen powers that exercised such a tenacious grip on so many in the ancient world. *The arrow that flies by day* is the missile of dreaded demonic power, whether exercised by divine or human beings. Further, the poet may have in mind sickness and sunstroke (vv. 5b and 6b), which were often thought to be the result of supernatural forces. In the hot sunlight of the Middle East, sunstroke can strike with fearful suddenness like arrows shot from ambush (cf. 2 Kgs 4:8-37; Exod 11:4-7; 12:29-30; Isa 37:37; Pss 121:6; God himself is the archer in Ps 38:2; Lam 3:13; Job 6:4). Lightning

also strikes suddenly and *the arrows* could be a synonym for "flashes of lightning" (Pss 18:14; 77:18).

The fourfold danger in vv. 5-6 that alternates between darkness and light is probably a merism (see commentary on Ps 66:6, 12). The ministering *angels* of Yahweh (vv. 11-13) are set over against the destructive demons of the night and day (cf. Ps 34:7; Exod 23:20; Tob 5–12; Bar 6:6). The wings of the Almighty are over all (v. 4). Verses 7-8 depict a battle-like scene, but the addressee is assured of personal safety. The plagues of vv. 5-6 may be understood as causing the carnage.

The psalm concludes with an ORACLE (vv. 14-16). Note the change of person from *you* in vv. 1-13 to *he* and the *I* of Yahweh in vv. 14-16. The oracle is a message of assurance and a promise of long life and well-being to those who cling to Yahweh and who *know* his name. (cf. the oracle in Ps 95:7d-11).

Psalm 92

This psalm combines the characteristics of a hymn with the form of an individual thanksgiving. Such psalms were designed for recitation in the company of other worshipers, and are marked by testimonial elements intended for both speaker and audience.

The singer declares the goodness of praising Yahweh throughout each day. The reason for such comprehensive praise is stated in v. 4: *You, O LORD, have made me glad by your work*. Verses 5-9 praise the mystery and power of Yahweh, attributes that a *dullard cannot* properly appreciate. Among Yahweh's thoughts that *the stupid cannot understand* is the doomed condition of the wicked who temporarily seem so prosperous (cf. Pss 73:21-22; 94:8).

The worshiper praises Yahweh for deliverance from the power of enemies (vv. 10-11). The speaker has been given the horn of an ox (a symbol of strength) and supplied with fresh oil, which may refer to a priestly anointing for healing (Lev 14:10-20), or to another ritual act. The meaning of the verb is not clear, but it may refer to horns rubbed with oil and, thus, gleaming with strength and virility (Tate 1990, 467). After the personal testimony of vv. 10-11, general statements about the blessedness of the righteous are given in vv. 12-15 (cf. Ps 1).

The righteous are compared to healthy, growing trees planted in the Temple courts. Whether the poet had in mind trees that actually grew in the Temple courts is secondary to the emphasis on the life-giving power of Yahweh (cf. references that link the source of water and life to the Temple area, e.g., Ps 46:4; Ezek 47:1-12; Isa 33:20-21; Zech 14:8; Rev 22:1-2).

The title prescribes this psalm as "for the sabbath day," the only psalm with this rubric, and it is so used in Jewish tradition. The psalm contains nothing that is specifically sabbatical, but it is reasonable to think that there were reasons for its selection. Themes in the psalm that relate to sabbath observance include creation (v. 4; cf. Gen 2:1-3; Exod 20:11; 31:17), thanksgiving for Yahweh's *steadfast love* (v. 2) and great works (the name Yahweh is repeated seven times in this psalm), and the thriving of the righteous (vv. 12-15)—the Sabbath was an expression of social morality and concern for the whole community (see Deut 5:14-15; Isa 56:1-2; Ezek 22:6-8).

Psalm 93

This short hymn belongs to the so-called Enthronement Psalms of Yahweh (Pss 47, 93, 96–99) that praise the kingship of Yahweh. They are marked by the use of the phrase "Yahweh (the LORD) reigns" and other references to the divine kingship. Enthronement Psalms were appropriate for any occasion when the worshiping congregation desired to praise the reign of Yahweh, but the autumn festival (Feast of Tabernacles) was their most specific context.

However the expression "the LORD reigns" is translated (see Ps 47:8), the emphasis is on Yahweh and his reign. The description of divine kingship borrows from the language used of earthly kings, but the scope of praise surpasses that of human kings. Yahweh's reign is based on cosmic victories over great forces, such as the surging floods and roaring seas, that constantly threaten creation. The *floods* may also be historicized references to hostile human powers. The verbs should be read as past tense in vv. 3-4, but the cosmologic victory of Yahweh is not purely a past event. In the last verse of the psalm attention passes from the thought of Yahweh as the conquering creator to the exceeding dependability of the decrees of the divine King and to the holiness that belongs to Yahweh's "house" (or temple).

Psalm 94

This psalm is difficult to classify according to literary types. Verses 1-7 have the form of a communal lament that reflects a disaster that has come to the nation. *Evildoers* crush and afflict the people with arrogant boasting, and disregard the prospect of any effective intervention by Yahweh (v. 7; cf. Pss 10:11; 14:1;

59:7). The *evildoers* are not specifically identified, but they seem to be Israelites of influence rather than foreigners (v. 20). An address in the style of the wisdom teachers is found in vv. 8-15. The speakers in v. 7 are the *dullest of the people* and *fools* (v. 8; cf. Ps 92:6). By the use of rhetorical questions they are called to common sense about the ways of Yahweh (vv. 9-11). In the language of the wise ones, the truly *happy* or "blessed" person (v. 12; cf. Ps 1) is defined as the one who is disciplined and instructed from the *torah* of Yahweh. Verse 14 refers to the situation described in v. 5, and makes a division of the psalm into two independent parts—vv. 1-11 and vv. 12-23—improbable. The people are assured that Yahweh will not forsake his heritage.

The last part of the psalm (vv. 16-23) expresses the thankful testimony of one who has received the help of Yahweh. The speaker is one who had been very near to *the land of silence* (v. 17; a designation for SHEOL), but who had been saved by the *steadfast love* of Yahweh (v. 18). The *consolations* of Yahweh revive the speaker's inner being when trouble becomes a burden (v. 19). The worshiper has found relief from the oppressive reality of corrupt and wicked rulers who constantly threaten the life of the righteousness (vv. 20-23). *Wicked rulers* (v. 20) is literally "throne," so v. 20a should read "Can a throne of destruction be allied with you?" (cf. Ps 122:5). The saving and vindicating might of Yahweh is greater than the iniquity of the wicked (vv. 22-23).

The basic nature of this psalm appears to lie in vv. 8-15 and 22-23, which have the nature of communal instruction. The genre of Ps 94 seems, therefore, to be liturgical instruction for those whose faith is sorely tried (cf. Pss 91:112). The psalm's placement between Pss 93 and 95–99 "creates a counterpoint to the surrounding enthronement hymns by asking in effect that Yahweh exercise his rule of judging the wicked" (Kselman and Barré 1990, 542). The opening petitions (vv. 1-3) address Yahweh in language that denotes kingship (e.g., *O Judge of the Earth*; see Tate 1990, 489–90). Theophanic language (*shine forth*, v. 1; *rise up*, v. 2) is used in the appeals for imminent divine action. The basic message of this psalm is that there is accountability for wicked oppressors (vv. 20-21, 23); the righteous will win (vv. 12-15).

Vengeance/Vindication. The translation of the word *neqamot* (root *nqm*; used of God twice in v. 1) as *vengeance* is unfortunate. In contemporary English, "vengeance" conveys the idea of "revenge" or "getting even." The Hebrew root *nqm* is generally used in a positive sense in the OT and takes its basic meaning from judicial practice. The action involved is commonly that which rectifies wrongdoing or a lack of justice, and is especially concerned for those in need. In Ps 94, Yahweh is not implored to act in "vengeance" in the sense of getting revenge on his enemies; he is asked to judge the earth, rendering to the arrogant wicked what they deserve because they disregard the rights of vulnerable people (v. 6) and *crush your people* (v. 5). "Vindication" is better here than "vengeance" (Holladay 1993, 321). The plea is addressed to the sovereign God to put things right on earth by vindicating those crushed by their oppressors, and by establishing justice (vv. 14-15).

Psalm 95

This psalm is similar in form to Pss 50 and 81. It falls into two parts: vv. 1-7c compose a hymn that celebrates the kingship of Yahweh and vv. 7d-11 form a prophetic ORACLE that warns the people against stubborn disobedience. Commentators commonly speak of the liturgical nature of this psalm, and it is probable that it was shaped by liturgical practice. Perhaps a procession of worshipers entering the Temple area for worship at one of the Jerusalem festivals is the original setting of Ps 95.

The worshipers encourage one another to go into the Temple courts and into the presence of Yahweh in vv. 1-2. The poet may have had in mind the movement of the worshipers into the sanctuary in vv. 3-5. In v. 6 the people have arrived in the holy area and are summoned to assume the postures of worship. Verse 7a-c is an affirmation of Yahweh by the worshipers; it parallels the statements in v. 3 and forms a frame around vv. 4-6. The *great king above all gods* (v. 3) is declared by the speakers in v. 7 to be *our God*, the shepherd of the people.

The voice of a prophet or other speaker, such as a levitical priest, is then heard bringing an oracle of Yahweh to the people. This is, however, no *shalom* (peace) oracle such as that in Ps 85:8-13 or Ps 91:14-16. This oracle warns the people about disobedience. It lays the claims of Yahweh on the people—as do the oracles in Pss 50 and 81, and the historical Pss 78 and 105–16. The Israelites of *today* (note the emphasis in v. 7d) are reminded of the obdurate disobedience of their fathers at *Meribah* ("testing") and at *Massah* ("strife") in the wilderness (cf. Exod 17:107; Num 20:1-13; Ps 81:7) and of the consequent refusal of permission to enter into the *rest* of the promised land (Deut 12:9). The prophet seeks a different response from the present generation (cf. Heb 3:7-4:13).

Psalm 96

This is another of the hymns that praise the kingship of Yahweh. The LORD is praised as the mighty creator, who is *to be revered above all gods*" (v. 4). All people of the earth are summoned to praise Yahweh (vv. 7-9); the physical universe also is called upon to exult and rejoice because "The LORD reigns!" (vv. 10-12). By contrast with Yahweh, *the gods of [other] peoples are idols* or "things of nought" (v. 5; cf. Ps 97:7; Isa 40:18-26; 41:23-24; 44:6-8; 46:5-8). Unlike the impotent gods of other peoples, *honor, majesty, strength*, and *beauty* attend the ways and worship of Yahweh (v. 6). The psalm closes with an affirmation of the coming of Yahweh for worldwide judgeship (vv. 10-13).

All of creation is summoned to greet the manifestation of Yahweh's kingship with gladness and praise, including *the trees of the forest* (v. 12; cf. Isa 55:12). The psalm is set in the worship of the Temple (vv. 8-9; on *in holy splendor*, see Ps 29:2). Verse 6 refers to *his sanctuary* while *strength and beauty* may have reference to the ARK of the covenant (see Ps 78:60-61; 1 Chr 16:27). *Honor and majesty* are descriptive of the attributes of divine royalty (cf. Pss 8:2; 104:1; 11:3; 148:13; 1 Chr 29:11, 25; Jer 48;18; Dan 11:21; Hab 3:3; Zech 6:13). Verses 7-9 use the same language as Ps 29:1-2 (*Ascribe to the LORD*), except that the summons to praise is directed to the peoples of the earth rather than to divine beings.

Two things are worthy of special note in regard to this psalm. First, it has a "missionary" character (Kselman and Barré 1990, 542), calling on the people of Yahweh to declare his glory and marvelous works to all the peoples (v.3). The nations are called to worship Yahweh (vv. 7-9), and the summons is expanded to all creation (vv. 10-13).

Second, the call to sing a *new song* to Yahweh (v. 1) is an expression found elsewhere (see Pss 33:3; 40:3; 98:1; 144:9; 149:1; Isa 42:10). In the most direct sense a "new song" probably refers to a song that is new for each festival occasion. In this regard, a "new song" is analogous to new objects used in some rituals (see 1 Sam 6:7; 2 Sam 6:3). A "new song" would celebrate the new acts of Yahweh, anticipating new works of deliverance and redemption (see Isa 42:10; 43:18-19; 48:6-7; Lam 3:22-23).

Psalm 97

Like Pss 96, 98, and 99, this hymn praises the kingship of Yahweh. After the initial summons to worship (v. 1), a description of a theophanic manifestation of Yahweh is given (vv. 2-5), accompanied by a mixture of thunderstorm and earthquake imagery. Lightning flashes illumine the world, the earth writhes before the coming presence, and *the mountains melt like wax* before the fiery coming of Yahweh (characteristic elements of theophanic descriptions; see Exod 19:16-20; 24:10, 16-17; Deut 5:4; 9:10, 15; Pss 18:8-16; 50:3; Hab 3:3-12). Theophanic language is highly metaphorical and it should not be read as literally descriptive or as history. The throne of Yahweh, surrounded by clouds and thick darkness, rests on a foundation of *righteousness and justice* (v. 2).

The theophanic manifestation of Yahweh described in vv. 1-5 differs from other theophanic descriptions in that this is an appearance to the whole world (note the framing of vv. 1-5 by the word *earth* in v. 1 and *all the earth* in v. 5), while elsewhere such appearances are primarily for the covenant people of Israel (cf. Exod 19:16-25; Judg 5:4-5; Pss 18:7-15; 50:1-3). All the peoples will see his glory (v. 6; cf. Isa 40:5; 52:10), not just Zion and "the daughters of Judah" (see Ps 48:11). His glorious appearing will bring shame to all the worshipers of images and idols (v. 7; cf. Isa 42:17; 45:16; Jer 10:14).

A question arises about the time of the action presented in vv. 1-9. The action in v. 6 can be read as completed: "The heavens have proclaimed his righteousness and all the peoples have seen his glory." The text probably has a future expectation in mind (though not necessarily the distant future) viewed as already complete. The position is the same as that in Isa 40:5, that is, anticipation in the near future of a great new revelation of Yahweh's "glory"—his power and might in delivering his people and in judgment over all peoples. The anticipated coming may have been celebrated as completed in the cultic ceremonials of the festivals (cf. "for he has come" of 96:13 [NRSV, *for he is coming*]). Psalms such as these were possibly recited in connection with the movement of the ARK into the Temple, a kind of enthronement ceremony for Yahweh. The cry "Yahweh reigns" greeted those coming to the throne of a king. This would not mean, however, that there was any time when Yahweh did not reign, but the ritual acclamation of his newly begun reign should not be ruled out. The rituals were designed to link the worshiper with both the past and the future.

Verses 6-8 describe the response to the THEOPHANY (vv. 2-5), which centered on the "putting to shame" (i.e., a humiliating loss of face for all those who worship images of "mere idols" [v. 7]). This is followed in vv. 10-12 with a description of the kind of righteous and just rule exercised by Yahweh. The righteous can rejoice, because Yahweh guards the faithful.

Psalm 98

The psalm belongs to the hymns that celebrate the kingship of Yahweh (esp. Pss 47; 95; 96–99). It has much in common with Ps 96. Like the other "enthronement hymns" of Yahweh, Ps 98 was probably used in the worship of the festivals, particularly, the Festival of Booths (Tabernacles) in the autumn. The congregation is exhorted to sing *a new song* (cf. Ps 96:1) to Yahweh (v. 1) that corresponds to the "newness" of the *marvelous things* that Yahweh has done, and to the triumph that he has made known *in the sight of the nations* (vv. 2-3). Yahweh's great act of "salvation" (a key idea in vv. 1-3) is defined in terms of his having *remembered his steadfast love . . . [for] Israel* (v. 3; cf. Isa 40:5; 52:10).

A question of the time of the action arises because the verbs seem to represent completed action. It would be a mistake to push the time factor too far, however, because the verbs can be read as referring to the future (completed action in future time); in the language of the cult, time becomes secondary to theological conviction and testimony. The future actuality is even now laid hold of by the worshiping community. The psalm looks back to the past (v. 3) and recalls the salvation-history of Israel, which it then projects toward its ultimate consummation (v. 9). In keeping with the grand vision, *all the earth* (v. 4) and the forces of nature (vv. 7-8) are summoned to praise Yahweh *the King* along with the cultic community whose presence is indicated in vv. 5-6. Yahweh in coming to judge the earth with *righteousness and . . . equity* (v. 9).

Psalm 99

This psalm, like Pss 47, 93, 95–98, belongs to the hymns that celebrate the kingship of Yahweh and are marked by the phrase "the LORD reigns" (v. 1), but it is different from Pss 96, 97, and 98. A refrain (probably designed to be sung by a choir or the congregation) is especially noticeable in this psalm (vv. 3, 5, 9). The refrain emphasizes the holiness of Yahweh:

Holy is he! The psalm also differs from 96–98 in that it does not have the same degree of parallelism to Deutero-Isaiah, and it is less universal in scope.

Yahweh is identified as: (1) the one who *sits enthroned upon the cherubim* (the reference is to the ARK, which was conceived of as the throne of Yahweh; see 1 Sam 4:4; 2 Sam 6:2; 2 Kgs 19:15; 1 Chr 13:6; Pss 80:2; Isa 57:16; "between the cherubs" was the place of Yahweh's meeting with Israel: Exod 25:10-22; 37:7-9); (2) as the one who is *great in Zion* and *exalted over all the peoples* (v. 2); (3) as the *Mighty King* (v. 4) who loves justice. The peoples of the earth are exhorted to *worship at his footstool* (v. 5). The *footstool* can refer to Zion (Isa 60:13; Ezek 43:7) or to the whole earth (Isa 66:1; Matt 5:35), but more probably here to the ark, above which Yahweh is invisibly enthroned (Ps 132:7; 1 Chr 28:2).

In vv. 6-8, the poet turns to the salvation-history of Israel and recalls the names of MOSES, AARON, and SAMUEL who had served in important ways as intercessors between Israel and Yahweh, and as mediators of the COVENANT, as well as priest-prophets. The reference to the *pillar of cloud* (v. 7) goes back to the revelation of Yahweh to Moses in association with the travels in the wilderness (Exod 33:9; Num 12:5). The ark and the tent traditions were originally separate, but combined in later traditions (see 1 Kgs 8:6, 10-11).

The mention of Samuel in relation to *the pillar of cloud* is strange since there is no specific mention in the extant traditions of such experiences for him. The reference may be simply parenthetical in v. 6 ("Moses and Aaron among his priests—and yes, Samuel too—were among those who called on his name").

The psalm closes in vv. 8-9 with a strong emphasis on Yahweh as *a forgiving God*, although one who punishes wrongdoing: "Yet you called them to account for their misdeeds" (REB). The KJV's "though thou tookest vengeance of their inventions" hardly has meaning any longer and also uses the word "vengeance" for the Hebrew verb *nqm*. This word when used of Yahweh usually refers to "vindication" or the establishment of justice rather than the "vengeance" in relation to personal enemies (see above, Ps 94). In the case of v. 8, it means Yahweh deals appropriately with wrongdoing, even that of people like Moses, Aaron, and Samuel.

Psalm 100

This short hymn that praises Yahweh concludes the series of kingship psalms in 93, 95–99. It has some similarities to Ps 95: a call for shouts of joy and thanksgiving (the noun for *thanksgiving* in v. 4 appears elsewhere in book four only in Ps 95:2a) and the liturgical *come* and *enter* (vv. 2, 4; cf. 95:6). Both psalms also emphasize the close relationship of Yahweh with the people. Psalm 100 suggests a worship setting, probably in festival contexts when people came to sanctuaries to worship (v. 4).

The psalm contains a sevenfold summons to give praise and homage to Yahweh and thus forms a suitable sequel to the psalms that exalt the kingship of Yahweh (Pss 96–99; see Tate 1990, 535–36). Its universal scope (*all the earth* in v. 1) also relates well to the exaltation psalms.

The repeated calls to praise and homage are supplemented by two important statements in vv. 3 and 5. The NRSV adopts a reading that yields *and we are his* in v. 3 (giving the alternate "and not we ourselves" in mg.). A preferred reading is: "He (Yahweh) made us and we are indeed his people and the flock he shepherds (or the flock of his pasture)." Compare the entire statement to Pss 79:13 and 95:5a, 6-7. The second statement (v. 5) declares that "Yahweh is good" and that *his steadfast love* and *faithfulness* never fail.

Verse 5 is a formulaic saying found repeatedly in contexts praising Yahweh (e.g., Pss 106:1; 107:1; 118:1; 129; 136:1; 1 Chr 16:34; 2 Chr 5:13; 7:3; Jer 33:11). Verse 5 seems to be the fullest form of this saying in the OT, including aspects of goodness, steadfast love, and faithfulness.

Psalm 101

This psalm is commonly considered to belong to the royal psalms (Pss 2, 20, 21, 45, 72, 89, 110, 132) and classified as a "loyalty–affirmation" or vow of intention for an Israelite king. It was intended, perhaps, for recitation at a coronation by the new king, who declares his intention to rule properly in the COVENANT made by Yahweh with DAVID (cf. 2 Sam 23:1-7; Pss 89:19-37; 132:11-12). Another view, but improbable, considers the psalm as a kind of royal "protestation of innocence" (cf. Ps 7) recited by the king as a part of a ritual of humiliation carried out as a component of the autumnal festival in preexilic Israel.

Commentators may have been too quick to assume that this is a royal psalm, and that the speaker throughout the psalm is intended to be a king. First, it is not necessary to assume that the speaker in vv. 1-5 must be a king. The speaker could be any devoted Israelite leader or citizen concerned about the spiritual condition and the welfare of the community. The NRSV *When shall I attain it?* obscures the question of complaint in v. 2 that reads "O when will you come to me?"—when will my faithful behavior be rewarded and those who act as in vv. 3b-5 be corrected? (Translate NRSV's *I will destroy* in v. 5 as "I will reduce to silence.") Second, the speaker in vv. 6-8 may be God, with the verses forming a divine ORACLE (cf. Ps 32:3-5, 8-9; 1 Kgs 9:3-7; Kselman and Barré 1990, 543). In this case, *my house* (v. 7) refers to the Temple. This reading seems better in the present context in book four of the Psalter.

Reading the psalm this way does not nullify its centuries-old interpretation as "The Prince's Psalm" or "The Mirror for Magistrates." It still sets forth high ethical standards for rulers and ordinary citizens alike. Even if vv. 6-8 are read as the words of Yahweh, they call leaders toward actions compatible with divine ways. In the ideology of ancient kingship, the king was God's representative on earth and charged with manifesting qualities pleasing to God.

Psalm 102

This is one of the seven penitential psalms of the church (Pss 6, 32, 38, 51, 102, 130, 143), although it has little direct expression of penitence. Modern scholars classify it with the lament-complaints, but note additional elements. Similarities of style and content suggest it belongs to a common context with a group of other psalms: Pss 22, 35, 38, 40, 69, 70, 71 (see Tate 1990, 204–05). Verses 12-22 are hymn-like.

According to the title, the speaker in this psalm can be anyone who is *afflicted . . . faint and pleading before the LORD*, which seems to be appropriate. Interpreters frequently read the psalm as the prayer of an acutely ill person, but it could also be the prayer of anyone in severe distress. The similes and metaphors of the psalm should not be read as directly descriptive of physical conditions (e.g., the speaker would hardly actually *eat ashes like bread*, v. 9).

In vv. 1-11, the speaker appeals to Yahweh to hear a complaint and to respond to an affliction that has grown desperate. As usual in the laments, the situation is graphically described but no precise diagnosis is possible. In any case, the speaker is taunted by *enemies* because of an overly distressed condition (v. 8). The complaints of the speaker resemble those of JOB: *lonely* (vv. 6-7), tormented by the realization of the extreme finitude of human existence (vv. 3, 11), and contending that suffering is the result of God's anger

and punishment (v. 10), although the speaker gives no reason for the divine wrath (Allen 1983, 14).

In vv. 12-22, the suppliant turns with an emphatic *But you, O LORD* from personal calamity to consider Yahweh and the condition of Zion. Appeal is made to Yahweh in the traditional cult language of the hymns that praise him as *enthroned forever* (v. 12) and as the one who built *Zion* (v. 16). Zion is the place where Yahweh has appeared *in his glory* and where he has heard the prayers of the people (v. 17). In vv. 18-22, the lament becomes assurance that Yahweh will favor Zion again (cf. v. 13), for the ruins of the Temple remain precious to the servants of Yahweh (cf. v. 14). The suppliant's concern is with the future (v. 18), recalling the history of Zion as a basis for the expectation of future acts of Yahweh (vv. 21-22).

The lament returns in vv. 23-24, followed by a fragment of a hymn that praises the enduring sureness of Yahweh as creator (vv. 25-28). Verse 28 looks to the future that is secure for the people of Yahweh despite the present distressing circumstances. In a manner similar to Ps 90, the psalm contrasts human finitude and brevity of life with the eternity of God.

Psalm 103

As great personal testimony of thankful praise, Ps 103 has contributed significantly to the devotion of the people of faith. It is a personal thanksgiving psalm that becomes a hymn of praise, framed by a personal note: *Bless the LORD, O my soul!* (vv. 1, 35). The change from the singular form of the thanksgiving (vv. 1-5) to the plural form of the hymn (vv. 6-14) may reflect the use of the psalm in congregational worship; if so, vv. 6-14 would be recited by the congregation in response to the individual thanksgiving.

In vv. 1-5, the speaker engages in a intrapersonal dialogue, calling upon *my soul* (i.e., myself) to *bless* Yahweh. *Bless* in this context means to praise. Participial forms are used in vv. 3-5 to recall the *benefits* of Yahweh. The successive use of the verbs encompasses the whole of a person's life experience (Westermann 1989, 239). The reference to *the eagle* (v. 5) is similar to its use in Isa 40:31. The long-lived eagle—it molts and renews its feathers annually—is used as an example of the vigor and renewal of life.

Verses 6-14 recall the acts of Yahweh in Israel's salvation-history. The emphasis in these verses is on the merciful and gracious ways that Yahweh deals with his people, not in terms of proportionate measure for their sin, but as God remembers their finitude and acts toward them as a father acts toward the children he loves (cf. Hos 11:1; Exod 4:22; Isa 1:2; Mal 1:6).

Verses 8-10 (cf. Exod 34:6) are key verses. Yahweh's love is greater than his wrath—a doctrine that is verified in the history of the people and in the speaker's personal experience. The GRACE of God abounds more than human sin. Grace is the biblical message of salvation; it is the thrust upward to life and joy. The ephemeral frame of humanity could never endure without the constant sustaining power of Yahweh's providential care. Humanity's finitude is described in vv. 15-16 in a manner similar to Isa 40:6-8 (see also Ps 90:5-6; Job 14:1-2; Isa 51:12). Human transitoriness and vulnerability are contrasted with the *everlasting* value of Yahweh's *steadfast love* and *righteousness* (v. 17), which is for *those who keep his covenant and remember to do his commandments* (v. 18). Human achievements (*place*, v. 16) are soon forgotten, but the *steadfast love* of Yahweh endures.

The conclusion (vv. 19-22) is a song of praise in which the heavenly beings and all creation are urged to praise Yahweh. His is the universal kingdom (cf. Ps 148), over which he reigns on his *established . . . throne*. The psalm closes (vv. 20-22) with nearly the same language as in vv. 1-2, except the self-summons to praise God at the beginning of the psalm now "broadens out to embrace the whole creation" (Westermann 1989, 243): "Bless the LORD, all created things" (v. 22a REB).

Psalm 104

This hymn was written to be sung by an individual (note the first-person singular in vv. 1, 33, 35) who praises God as creator of the heavens and the earth. The psalm reflects the influence of Near East literature contemporary with the history of Israel. Parallels with the "Hymn to the Sun" of the Egyptian Pharaoh Amenhotep IV (AKHENATON, 1377–1360 B.C.E.) are especially close. Any direct literary dependence, however, is unlikely. The same observations are true with regard to Gen 1, to which the psalm has considerable parallel (see Allen 1983, 29-31). The poet drew from a large body of traditional sources and the broad genre of creation accounts in the history of Israel's worship. There is nothing to indicate exactly the psalm's cultic context, but the themes of creation and the lordship of Yahweh must have been prominent in the Festival of Tabernacles (Booths) that included concern with the harvest, the coming new year, and the indispensable

rains. Booths would have been an appropriate time to sing about God's creative works. Israelites may also have used the psalm on other occasions.

The psalm opens (vv. 1-4) with the same statement that closed Ps 103. *Bless the LORD, O my soul* may have been added to link the two psalms. In any case they may be read together in the context of book four. Yahweh is praised in exalted language (vv. 1-4): he covers himself with a *garment* of light, which is the source of life and joy (cf. Exod 3:2; Isa 60:1; John 1:5; 1 John 1:5; 1 Tim. 6:16; Rev 21:23). The language is similar to that used to describe theophanic appearances of God (see 18:7-15; 97:1-5; Exod 19:16-19; Hab 3:3-6). The idea of Yahweh riding on the clouds (v, 3) may have a Ugaritic background (see Ps 68:4, 33). The forces of nature are the messengers and ministers of Yahweh (v. 4).

The establishment of *the earth* is presented in vv. 5-13. Yahweh put the earth on its foundations (cf. Job 38:69; Ps 24:1-2). In its primeval condition it was covered with the waters of the great deep (the *t*hom*; cf. Gen 1:2)—waters that covered the mountains (v. 6; cf. Gen 7:19-20). The ordered world resulted when God gave a thunderous shout and the water dispersed to be held within immutable bounds (vv. 7-9).

The description of the creative process continues in vv. 10-13 with provision for springs and streams of water. Animal life (including the birds) appears (vv. 11-12), and Yahweh enriches the earth with *the fruit of [his] work* (v. 13). From his heavenly chambers (*lofty abode* of v. 13 is the same as *chambers* of v. 3) God sends the rain (a major feature in the worship of the Feast of Tabernacles; see Zech 14:16-19). The role of God as creator merges into the role of sustainer of the world. As sustainer, God uses the primordial enemy of terrestrial life (the flood) as life-giving sustenance for the creatures that live on earth (Allen 1983, 33). Waters come from two sources: springs that flow up from below and rain that pours down from the heavenly abode.

Verses 14-23 form the third strophe of the psalm, and continues the description of the divine provisions for life on earth. Verses 14-15 present a compact version of the agricultural year (Kselman and Barré 1990, 544); provisions for the trees, birds, and other wild creatures are described in vv. 16-18. The seasons and the days are marked off and the rhythm of life is maintained (vv. 19-23). The whole ecological organism of the cosmos lives in the ordered patterns created and sustained by God (vv. 21-23, 27-30).

In the fourth strophe (vv. 24-30), v. 24 breaks the context with an exclamation of wonder at the *manifold . . . works* of God and the wisdom with which he has made them (cf. Prov 3:19; 8:22-31), with special attention given to *the sea* and its inhabitants (vv. 25-26). They, too, are under the absolute control of Yahweh. That the poet is concerned with more than the creative works of God once accomplished is clear in vv. 27-30 where the text affirms the continuation of creation. Without the divine breath of life all would be death and dust (vv. 29-30). Yahweh is the great provider and renewer as well as the great creator.

The common distinction between God as creator and God as sustainer/provider/renewer is not theologically valid unless creation is restricted to origination in an absolute beginning. The creative work of God is never "finished" and is manifest in the sustaining and renewing of life as well as in its beginning.

The psalm concludes (vv. 31-35) with a prayer for the continuation of the glory of Yahweh and for the elimination from the earth of two sources of discord and destruction: *sinners* and *the wicked* (v. 35). The ideal is for all of creation and all creatures to praise Yahweh so Yahweh's rejoicing in his creation may be responded to by the creation rejoicing in his works.

In the prayer *May my meditation be pleasing to him* (v. 34), *meditation* may be understood as "poem" or "poetry" and the verse indicates that the individual worshiper is aware of reciting—if not composing—a psalm of praise as an act of worship.

Psalm 105

The psalm is another of the historical hymns (closely related to Pss 78 and 106) that recapitulate the salvation-history of Israel. Commonly it is assumed that Ps 105 was composed for use at one of the major festivals, perhaps in connection with ceremonies of covenant renewal (see vv. 7-11). Verses 1-15 are quoted in 1 Chr 16 (together with Pss 96:1-13; 106:1; 47-48) in connection with the narration of David's moving the ARK to Zion.

With repeated imperatives, the fellowship is urged in vv. 1-6 to remember and to praise the wonderful works of Yahweh. Those who *seek the LORD* are encouraged. The term "seekers of Yahweh" suggests pilgrims who attend a festival or other ceremonies at a SANCTUARY, but should not be restricted to such people. They are exhorted to seek his presence continually, not only in periodic journeys to the sanctuary. The congregation is addressed as descendants of

ABRAHAM and JACOB, who were the recipients of the COVENANT and its promises (v. 6).

In vv. 7-25, the historical survey begins with the period of Israel's ancestors and the Abrahamic covenant with its promise of CANAAN as an inheritance. The life of the ancestors as seminomadic wanderers is described in vv. 12-15 and includes an account of JOSEPH and the migration to Egypt (vv. 16-25). The details vary from the accounts in Genesis, but the general pattern is the same. The result of Jacob's sojourn as a resident alien in Egypt was that God made his people to be exceedingly fruitful and "too numerous for their oppressors" (v. 24, Dahood 1968, 59).

MOSES and the EXODUS from Egypt is the subject of vv. 26-42. Moses and AARON were the leaders sent by Yahweh as the agents of the PLAGUES on the Egyptians (vv. 26-36; cf. the plagues in Ps 78:43-51 and Exod 7-12). In a very emphatic way, the actions of deliverance are said to be the direct deeds of Yahweh (see the repeated *he*, referring to Yahweh, in vv. 28-42). Moses and Aaron disappear from the picture (and there is no account of the Sinai covenant). All these great deeds of deliverance were done because *Yahweh remembered his holy promise [to] Abraham* (v. 42, reading the *and* in RSV and NRSV as "to"). Verse 42 forms an INCLUSIO with vv. 8-10 and frames all verses in between.

The closing section (vv. 43-45) refers to the triumphant exodus of the people from Egypt (v. 43) and to the gift of the LAND (cf. v. 11). The final verse states the covenantal obligation of obedience that all of this places upon the covenant people: salvation-history should lead to obedience and faithfulness.

Psalm 106

This psalm is a combination hymn and communal lament. Its content places it among the historical psalms (Pss 78, 105, 106, 135, 136). The sober mood emphasizes Israel's continual guilt, and is contrasted against the much more positive mood of Ps 105. In this respect, Ps 106 is more closely related to Ps 78 than to Ps 105; in the present arrangement of the Psalter, however, Ps 106 is clearly intended to be read with 105. The "Hallelujahs" (*Praise the LORD*) at the end of Ps 104 (which really belongs with the beginning of 105), at the end of Ps 105, and at the beginning and end of Ps 106 further support the intended relationship between Pss 105 and 106. These are the first appearances of the HALLELUJAH formula in the Psalter.

Verses 27 and 47 indicate that this psalm in its present form originated after the Babylonian EXILE in 587 B.C.E. Some interpreters link it (and Ps 105) with a covenant renewal ceremony assumed to have been a regular feature of preexilic worship. That may be correct, but the covenant renewal liturgies were more probably used in worship at the second Temple after 515 B.C.E. Verses 47-48 are also found in 1 Chr 16:35-36, and the provenance of the psalm is almost certainly exilic or postexilic.

After an opening call to praise Yahweh (vv. 1-3), a lamenting confession begins. A solo speaker voices a personal prayer (vv. 4-5) and the sin-history of the people (vv. 6-46). The speaker is not identified, but we may think of a priest or devoted Israelite leader speaking for the community. The speaker implores Yahweh for the privilege of personal participation in the joy of a renewed well-being of the people.

The sins of the ancestors began *in Egypt* (v. 7). Even in the Exodus itself there was rebellion and the characteristic *they did not remember*. God continued to perform redemptive acts, despite the rebelliousness of the people, until they believed his words and sang his praises (vv. 8-12).

The people soon forgot the wonders of the Exodus and the chain of rebellion and disbelief extends with the recall of six episodes of sin: (1) their *wanton craving in the wilderness* (v. 14; see Num 11:1-35; Exod 15:22–17:7); (2) their jealousy of Moses and the rebellion of *Dathan and . . . Abiram* (v. 17; see Num 16; Deut 11:6); (3) the making of the golden calf (v. 19; see Exod 32:1-35; Deut 9:8-21); (4) the unbelief in response to the report of the spies (vv. 24-27; see Num 13–14); (5) the participation in Moabite worship (vv. 28-31; see Num 25:1-18; Exod 34:15); and (6) the rebellion at *Meribah* (vv. 32-33; see Exod 17:1-7; Num 20:1-13; Pss 81:7; 95:8). After the wilderness experience, the people failed to exterminate the Canaanites and their practices (vv. 34-39; see Deut 7:2; 16; 20:16-18; Judg 1:21–2:5), and continued their disobedience during the time of the judges (vv. 40-46).

The recall in vv. 40-46 goes beyond the period of the judges and actually summarizes the whole history of Israel. Despite the long extension of Israel's rebelliousness, Yahweh continued to hear their prayers and respond in mercy and deliverance to their distress (vv. 41-46). *He remembered his covenant* and acted toward them on the basis *of his steadfast love*, causing those *who held them captive* to treat them with kindness (vv. 45-46; cf. 1 Kgs 8:50).

In v. 47, the people pray that Yahweh will gather them from among the nations where they are scattered, in order that they may more properly give thanks to him (cf. v. 1).

Ps 106 has been called a "judgment doxology" (von Rad, 1962, 357–58), that seeks to "bring to an end a chapter of history, and to set one's sights on a new beginning" (Seybald 1990, 159). Verse 48 is the doxology that closes book four of the Psalter, and probably did not belong to the original psalms (it is found, however, in 1 Chr 16:35).

Summary of Book Four

Ps 106 ends book four of the Psalter. If book three is especially concerned with the tension between personal faith and the seeming failure of the historical salvation-enterprise, it is appropriate to ask how book four responds to the unresolved dilemma. At least three answers emerge.

First, the extraordinary emphasis on the universal kingship of Yahweh responds to the loss of the Davidic kingship for Israel. The Davidic dynasty is gone, but the *great God . . . great King above all gods* (Ps 95:3) reigns. The Israelites are called to sing *a new song* (Pss 96:1; 98:1) praising the great King because he is not finished with doing new things. He will yet *judge the world with righteousness, and the peoples with equity* (Ps 98:9).

Second, book four seems to be a Moses book, suggesting a shift of authority from DAVID to MOSES (see Tate 1990, xxvi-xxvii, 418). The first psalm in book four (Ps 90) is ascribed to Moses in its title, and Moses is referred to by name in Pss 105:26; 106:16, 23, 32. Also, the wilderness accounts are prominent in Pss 95 and 106. In the case of Ps 106, the speaker is clearly identified in v. 47 as one who is experiencing the "wilderness" again in the form of EXILE. The psalms of book four suggest that the faith of Israelites should be grounded in premonarchical, Mosaic traditions; Moses himself proclaimed the divine kingship of Yahweh (Exod 15:18). The new generation of the postexilic communities should not harden their hearts and test Yahweh as the Israelites did in the wilderness (Ps 95:8-11).

Third, individual faith can rest on the assurance Yahweh has not abandoned his salvation-enterprise with Israel. If I am correct about Ps 101, this seems to be the message in vv. 6-8: Yahweh will purify his elect faithful and rid the land of the wicked, so that the divine name may be declared with praise in

Zion/Jerusalem when the peoples and kingdoms gather to worship Yahweh (cf. Ps 102:21-22). The servants of Yahweh may also live secure in the powerful presence of their God (Ps 102:25-28).

Psalms 105–106 are designed to revive faith in Yahweh's enterprise with Israel. The end of the Davidic monarchy is not the end of salvation-history. Faith must be grounded in both the individual and the communal work of God.

Book Five. Psalms 107–150

Psalm 107

Psalm 107 falls into two main divisions, each of which belongs in a different literary classification. The first part (vv. 1-32) is a communal thanksgiving; the second (vv. 33-43) is part of a hymn that has been added to the first section. A popular interpretation of the psalm places it against the background of a festival that attracted groups of pilgrims (they may even have been captives returning from the EXILE). Various segments of the festival participants are called upon to offer their thanksgiving sacrifices, and to give their testimony of the benefits which they have received from Yahweh (vv. 22, 32). The psalm in its present form probably dates from the postexilic period (see v. 3), but it may have an earlier history, with vv. 2-3 and vv. 33-43 added to an individual thanksgiving psalm to make it appropriate for a postexilic communal thanksgiving (Allen 1983, 62–5).

The first division (vv. 1-32) opens with a call to give thanks to Yahweh (v. 1). The *redeemed from trouble*—those who have received special benefits and are prepared to sacrifice (cf. Lev 7:11-15)—are addressed and called to testify. The groups reported in vv. 4-32 are introduced with a threefold form: a description of the trouble the group experienced; a report of their petition to God (*then they cried to the LORD*) and his deliverance from their afflictions; and a summons to thanksgiving which forms a refrain and may indicate some sort of antiphonal recitation of the psalm (vv. 8-9, 15-16, 21-22, 31-32). The groups are (1) desert wanderers who had suffered hunger and thirst, until Yahweh relieved their distress and led them to a city (vv. 4-7); (2) prisoners who rebelled against God and suffered punishment for it until Yahweh gave them their freedom (vv. 10-14); (3) those who were sick until the word of Yahweh went forth and healed them (vv. 17-20); and (4) seafarers who were in danger of losing their lives in a storm until Yahweh quieted the sea and brought them to their port (vv. 23-30). All of these must be considered as poetic expressions of various types of situations in which God's help is powerfully experienced.

The hymnic section (vv. 33-43) praises Yahweh both for his compassionate care for those who are in need and for the thoroughness with which he punishes the wicked. His power over the natural world (both the cultivated land and the wilderness) is complete as he responds to the behavior of human beings (vv. 33-35). The hymn constitutes a suitable response by the congregation to the sacrifices and testimonies of those who have been benefitted, especially Jews who had made their way back to their homeland by what they considered to be the goodness and power of Yahweh. The psalm is not limited to Jews, however—the refrain in vv. 8, 15, and 21 continually acknowledge *his wonderful works to humankind*.

Psalm 108

This is a composite psalm formed from Pss 57:7-11 (vv. 1-5) and 60:5-12 (vv. 6-13). For the exposition of the verses see the commentary on Pss 57 and 60.

The reasons for the combination of Pss 57:7-11 and 60:5-12 into a new psalm are not certain. It may be, however, that the postexilic Israelite communities continued to have their hope framed by the boundaries of the promised land with *Shechem* and *Succoth* (v. 7), representing God's claim to the whole land (Allen 1983, 69). Edom became the archetypical enemy of Israel in the exilic and postexilic periods (see Obad; Isa 63). The "grim beginning" (Allen 1983, 69) of Ps 60 is replaced with the positive assurance of Ps 57:7-11. In this manner Ps 108 becomes a "believing prayer" for postexilic communities for the God of old—who is still their God—to manifest a theophanic demonstration of his love and power. The key verses are 5-6: *Be exalted, O God . . . let your glory be over all the earth . . . so that those whom you love may be rescued.*

This psalm is a good example of the use of older material in a new context, a method of composition probably used in many psalms, although we often lack earlier contexts to demonstrate it. New demands and pastoral needs brought about the creative reuse of older content (Stuhlmueller 1983, 125).

Psalm 109

This individual complaint is best known for the severity of the imprecations in vv. 6-19. It seems best to interpret these verses, however, not as the words of the speaker in vv. 1-5 and 20-31, but as curses direct-ed toward the speaker by accusers (as in NRSV, cf. RSV). The enemies of the speaker are referred to in the plural in vv. 1-5, the singular is used in vv. 6-19, and the plural returns in vv. 20-31. Thus it is probable that the suppliant quotes the charges that have been made against him (see v. 28 that refers to the cursing on the part of enemies). The situation seems to be that the speaker, under furious attack from enemies (an attack declared to be without cause and, ironically, in re-sponse to love, vv. 3-5), brings the charges made before Yahweh (cf. HEZEKIAH and the Assyrian letter in 2 Kgs 19:14-19). The accuser (lit., a *satan* [see SATAN IN THE OT]) stands at the speaker's right hand (v. 6); but the speaker is sure that Yahweh stands *at the right hand of the needy* in order to save (v. 31), and the speaker places himself among the *needy* (vv. 22-25). Having presented the charges of the accusers, the speaker turns to Yahweh and implores him for deliverance (vv. 21, 26-29).

The charges made by the enemies of the speaker (vv. 6-19) are violent and designed to crush the defendant's answer with their overwhelming force. The translations are mostly self-explanatory and require little comment. Verse 8b possibly should read "take his office" rather than "seize his goods" (RSV) and may indicate that the accused is a person of some *position* (NRSV) and responsibility (cf. Acts 1:20). The person attacked is accused of being himself one who loves to curse others; the accusers pray that the curses will cling to the attacked like a garment with terrible effects (vv. 12-19). If the interpretation indicated above is correct, v. 20 should read: "This is the work (i.e., the curses quoted in the preceding verses) of my accusers (*satans*)"; or, if the verse is read as it stands in the NRSV, it means the suppliant prays that the curses of the accusers be returned upon them by Yahweh. Verse 20 recalls vv. 2-3.

Psalm 110

This royal psalm has been the focus of much attention and dispute. In traditional Christian interpre-tation it has been interpreted as messianic and Christo-logical (see Matt 22:41-45; 26:64; Acts 2:34; Col 3:1; 1 Pet 3:22; Heb 1:3, 13; 5:6; 7:1; 8:1; 10:12-13). But there can be little doubt that the original reference of the psalm was to the Davidic king in preexilic Israel. It was later given a messianic interpretation, which is the background of Jesus' use of the psalm (Mark 12:35-37 and par.; see Pss 2 and 132). For a full treat-ment of the psalm in the NT, see Hay (1973). The occa-sion for the recitation of the psalm could have been the enthronement of a king, or possibly an autumnal festival when the COVENANT with the Davidic dynasty was renewed. The first is more probable. Indeed, it is possible the psalm was composed for the enthronement of DAVID himself.

The psalm begins with an ORACLE from Yahweh with reference to the king (*my lord*). The language is that of the prophets (lit. "oracle [utterance] of Yahweh to my lord"), and the speaker should be thought of as a court PROPHET. The message of the oracle is that of a command of Yahweh granting the king authority and honor at Yahweh's right hand (cf. Ps 45:9; 1 Kgs 2:19; Matt 20:21). The king shares the throne with Yahweh, but his authority remains delegated and not absolute. The second part of the message is a promise to the king of victory over his enemies: *until I make your enemies your footstool* (v. 1b; cf. Josh 10:24; 1 Kgs 5:3; 1 Cor 15:25).

The prophetic address continues in v. 2, but the words are those of the prophet, not of Yahweh. The prophet expands the oracle with a statement that may be interpreted either as a prediction ("Your mighty rod—Yahweh is going to send it forth from Zion") or a wish ("Let Yahweh send forth your mighty rod from Zion"). The first seems preferable. The prophet con-cludes v. 2 with an exhortation for the king to exercise the power granted him over his enemies.

Verse 3 is the most uncertain verse in the psalm. One approach is to consider it a reference to the willingness of the people to serve the king in times of war (cf. Judg 5:23). We may therefore read the verse as an assurance to the king that his strength and re-sources will remain fresh and adequate. The *dew*, especially significant in the dry climate of Palestine, marks the invigorated life of a new day. Some ritual in which the people offered themselves as willing ser-vants of the king as part of the enthronement cere-mony may be in mind.

In v. 4, a second oracle is addressed to the king: Yahweh has sworn a divine oath which will not be broken, affirming that the king has a perpetual priest-hood *according to the order of Melchizedek*. Identify-ing the king with the priesthood is unusual, although there is evidence kings functioned in priestly roles (see 1 Sam 13:9; 2 Sam 6:12-19; 8:18; 15:12; 1 Kgs 1:9; 8:14; 55-56; 62-63; 9:25; 10:19; 12:32; 16:12-15).

The reference to MELCHIZEDEK is to be understood in terms of Gen 14:18-20, where Melchizedek, who is identified as the "king of Salem" (i.e., Jerusalem; cf. Ps 76:2), blesses Abram (Abraham) and in turn Abram gives him a tithe. It may be that v. 4 refers historically to David and his successors acquiring the priest-king status of former Jebusite kings of Jerusalem, which in time became an accepted role for Israelite kings. The assignment of the king to a priesthood of *the order of Melchizedek* avoided giving the king an Aaronite or Levitical priesthood, and thus distinguished him from ordinary priests. Of course, the transfer of an ancient tradition of authority as king-priest to the Davidic kings enhanced their status.

The style changes again in vv. 5-7 to that of prophetic explanation that interprets and expands the oracle. The king is assured of the protecting power of Yahweh (called *Lord, adonai*—i.e., not LORD—in v. 5, the same term as used for the king in v. 1), who is at the king's right hand (cf. v. 1; Ps 109:31). *The day of his wrath* (v. 5) and the great victories and judgment of Yahweh relate well to passages that deal with the "Day of Yahweh" (see Amos 5:18-20; Zeph 1:14-18; 2:3). The language is violent, but not unexpected in divine warrior passages. The concept is marked by expectation of Yahweh's victories in battle and the judgment of the nations.

Like v. 3, v. 7 is the subject of varied interpretations. If it is assumed that Yahweh is the subject (as in vv. 5-6), then (1) he may be thought of as the divine warrior who executes judgment among the nations, and refreshes his strength from streams as he pursues his enemies or (2) it possibly means that Yahweh "on the way" drinks from the stream (of blood) that flows from his conquered foes and lifts his head in victory. If the king is the subject, the verse refers (1) to the renewing of his strength as he pursues his enemies or (2) to a ritual act in which he drinks from the sacred river (probably the Gihon Spring at Jerusalem; see 1 Kgs 1:9; 38-40; 45) as a part of an enthronement ceremony. If the latter is correct, he symbolically partakes of the stream of life (which literally was so when Jerusalem had to depend upon the spring for its water supply). See Ps 46 and Ezek 47.

Psalm 111

Each succeeding line of this psalm begins with a successive letter of the Hebrew alphabet (other acrostic formations are found in Pss 9–10, 25, 34, 37, 112, 119, 145). This style of writing may seem stiff, but it is a form of literary artistry that merits our appreciation even if it does appear disjointed. The psalm has

characteristics both of a hymn (vv. 1a, 2-9), and of a thanksgiving psalm (v. 1), and it concludes with a wisdom saying (v. 10). The basic theme is that of the "works of Yahweh" (vv. 2, 3, 4, 6, 7). These *works* demonstrate both the majesty and power of Yahweh (v. 3) and the gracious and merciful ways in which he has cared for his people (vv. 4-9). The closing verse has the didactic quality of the WISDOM LITERATURE (cf. Prov 1:7; 9:10; Job 28:28), and sets forth the "fear of Yahweh" as the sound basis for wisdom and successful living. Reverence for God is the foundation for abundant living.

The psalm may have come from the postexilic period, aimed perhaps at the kind of tepid religion that is reflected in the books of Haggai and Malachi—religion that had settled into ritual with lethargic commitment. As such it may be a meditation on Exod 34:5-7 (Allen 1983, 90).

Psalm 112

This psalm is commonly designated a wisdom psalm. The points it develops include fear of Yahweh, delight in divine commandment, contrast of the righteous with the wicked, and the act-consequence sequence (or reward and retribution). It also begins with the congratulatory formula *Happy are those who fear the LORD* (cf. Pss 1; 32; 84; 119:1-2). Like Ps 111, it is an acrostic poem; the two psalms share common themes and key words and should be read together (see Allen 1983, 95). Psalms 111, 112, and 113 are also joined together by the use of the HALLELUJAH (*Praise the LORD*) in Pss 111:1; 112:1; 113:1, 9 (although Ps 113 is traditionally related to the Talmudic "Egyptian Hallel" formed by Pss 113–118; see commentary on Ps 114). Psalm 111 praises the works of Yahweh and Ps 112 praises the blessed condition of those who fear Yahweh, continuing a subject begun in 111:10: "The opening beatitude creates the perspective of the whole psalm" (Allen 1983, 97).

The psalm requires little comment beyond its translation. We are reminded in v. 1 that *fear* and *delight* are not antithetical in religious experience. The Bible claims that reverence for God is the real source of joy. Further, this verse equates the one who fears Yahweh with the one who delights in God's commandments. Those who fear God take him seriously and devote themselves to his will. The RSV translates v. 4 with "light" as the subject and adds "LORD" to the text: "Light rises in the darkness for the upright; the

LORD is gracious. . . . " The NRSV reads "those who fear Yahweh" (v. 1) as the subject: *They* [those who fear Yahweh] *rise in the darkness as a light for the upright.* Either reading is acceptable, but the NRSV seems better.

In v. 7-8, the *firm* and *steady* heart of the God-fearer is stressed. *Heart* refers to the inner being—the mind and will of a person. The words for *firm* and *steady* are both passive and represent qualities which are given and received (i.e., the heart is made to be firm and steady). The firm, steady heart is the inner power from Yahweh that relieves one of fear and offers calmness in the face of adversaries. In v. 10 the condition of *the wicked* is contrasted with that of the one who fears Yahweh. The angry gnashing of the teeth of the wicked as they see the success of the righteous (vv. 6-9) contrasts with the righteous looking in triumph over their foes (cf. Ps 54:9).

Psalm 113

This hymn is the first in the collection known in the Jewish liturgical tradition as the "Hallel" or the "Egyptian Hallel" (to distinguish it from Ps 136, which was called the "Great Hallel"). Hallel means praise and is derived from the *hallᵉlu-yah* ("Praise the LORD"; see HALLELUJAH) that is dominant in these psalms. The collection is used in Jewish festivals (except New Year and the Day of Atonement), and in the family celebration of PASSOVER. Pss 113–114 are sung before the Passover Seder meal and 115–118 afterwards (cf. Matt 26:30; Mark 14:26). Psalm 113 was designed for congregational worship, and it contains good examples of the basic elements of the hymn form.

In vv. 1-4, after the initial *Hallelujah*, the congregation (addressed as "servants of Yahweh") is urged to praise the "name of Yahweh." The "name of Yahweh" (three times in vv. 1-3; Yahweh occurs in each of the first five verses) is a concept that denotes divine presence. The summons to praise encompasses all of time and the whole earth (vv. 2-3; cf. 8:1). Yahweh is exalted above all else (v. 4).

In v. 5-9 a rhetorical question is used to introduce six causative participle constructions that affirm the incomparability of Yahweh. He is incomparable both in his exalted status and in his compassion for the *poor* and *needy*. The biblical idiom is so well known in our culture that it is easy to forget that in the ancient myths human beings were considered to be the menial servants of the gods—and on occasion the beneficiaries of their favors—but not the great subject of the

actions of the deity. Perhaps, nothing in OT theology is more significant than the constant reiteration of God's preferential option for the lowly, the sick, the captive, the oppressed, and the poor and needy. The almighty king is the savior of the helpless. There may be no finer passage anywhere in the OT than vv. 5-9. Cf. Ps 113 with the "Song of Hannah" in 1 Sam 2:2-8, and with the MAGNIFICAT in Luke 1:46-55.

Psalm 114

The liturgical tradition of JUDAISM associates this psalm with the PASSOVER. It is a short thanksgiving hymn that recounts Israel's history from the EXODUS to the crossing of the Jordan. The psalm seems incomplete, as if it were a section from a longer hymn. Clearly, it should be read with Ps 113, and also may be read with Ps 115 as well. Psalms 114 and 115 are framed by the *hallelujahs* at the end of Ps 113 and the end of Ps 115.

The psalm begins with the exodus from Egypt and the establishment of *Judah* and *Israel*. Judah and Israel in v. 2 could be interpreted to refer to the divided kingdoms, but it is better to read the two names as synonymous. The verse presupposes the fall of the Northern Kingdom and assumes that Judah is the heir of all that was "Israel."

In vv. 3-8, the poet recalls both the crossing of the sea following the exodus from Egypt and the crossing of the Jordan. The language in vv. 4, 6 is that of storm and THEOPHANY (cf. Exod 19:16-19; Pss 18; 29:6; Hab 3:6). The reactions of the natural order are in response to the theophanic appearances of Yahweh (v. 7). The sea flees away, the Jordan turns back, the mountains and hills shake and skip before the divine coming (vv. 5-6). Verse 8 recalls Yahweh's provision of water during the wilderness wanderings (Exod 17:6-7; Num 20:8-13; Deut 8:15; Pss 78:15-16; 20; 107:35). Note the move to present time in vv. 5-8. The events of Israel's salvation-history are entered, as it were, and participated in by subsequent generations of worshipers (cf. Deut 26:5-11).

Psalm 115

The SEPTUAGINT joins Pss 114 and 115 as one psalm; they may be read together even though they have different content. As noted above, Pss 113–118 form the traditional Jewish "Hallel," and when recited at PASSOVER Pss 113–114 are chanted before the meal and Pss 115–118 afterwards. Psalm 115 is probably a prayer of Jews living among foreigners in EXILE (after 587 B.C.E.) and tempted to abandon their faith in Yahweh. Its liturgical nature is widely recognized, although one cannot be certain about the exact assignment of parts to different groups. One possibility suggests the people (vv. 1-2); Levitical priests (vv. 3-8); solo worship leader (vv. 9-11); people (vv. 12-13); Levitical priests (vv. 14-15); and people vv. (16-18).

The psalm affirms that Yahweh reigns in the heavenly realm (vv. 3, 16) and that human endeavors are possible because God allows them. Yahweh has the power to confer blessing, without which life is impossible (vv. 15-16). The Israelites, therefore, are urged to *trust* Yahweh (note the threefold use of the verb in vv. 9-11). The gentiles worship many gods represented as idols, but those idols are only human constructions and are as impotent as the gods they represent (vv. 4-8).

The gentiles taunt the "fearers of Yahweh" (v. 11) with the question *"Where is their god?"* (v. 2). The answer is: *Our God is in the heavens; he does whatever he pleases* (v. 3).

We are given an idea of the composition of the congregation in vv. 9-11: lay Israelites, priests, and "fearers of Yahweh." The last designation may possibly refer to non-Israelites who worship Yahweh, but it more probably seems to be an inclusive term for the whole group, *both small and great* (v. 13).

The worshiping group concludes the psalm with a hymn of praise (vv. 16-18). The heavens belong to Yahweh, not to a pantheon of gods and goddesses. So does the earth. The dead do not praise Yahweh (cf. Pss 6:5; 30:9; 88:4-5; 10-12; Isa 38:18), but the people of Yahweh vow to praise him without limit (vv. 17-18).

Psalm 116

In this thanksgiving psalm, which a worshiper recites in the presence of the congregation (vv. 18-19) as testimony, the speaker tells how Yahweh heard his prayers and delivered him from a situation of "death" (vv. 3-11). The condition from which the speaker has been released is not clearly defined. The speaker testifies that Yahweh saves *the simple* (v. 6), meaning those who cannot help themselves but who are open to trust and instruction.

Apparently, vv. 10-11 recall a time when the worshiper was depressed and despaired of finding any good in life (the LXX divides this psalm into two psalms: vv. 1-9 and vv. 10-19). But faith in God had brought the speaker through that difficult period, he now considers what kind of grateful response should be made to Yahweh (v. 12). *The cup of salvation* (v. 13) must refer to some ritual act, which may have had its ultimate origin in the ordeal of drinking "holy water" to determine innocence or guilt ("trial by ordeal"; cf. Num 5:11-28). In the present reference we should think instead of something like a "festival cup" that was passed among the participants at the communal meals that accompanied thanksgiving sacrifices (see Lev 7:11-18; Deut 32:38; cf. Pss 11:6; 16:5; 23:5). The lifting up of the cup to Yahweh may have been a special ritual gesture of thanksgiving, shared with others. The vows are paid and the sacrifices are offered in the presence of the assembled people in the Temple (vv. 17-19. The gratitude of the worshiper finds expression both in cultic ritual and in the joyful affirmation of personal relationship to God (v. 16). Verse 15 declares that the death of his devoted ones is *precious* in Yahweh's sight (i.e., not something that he allows to happen without concern and grief). The Hallelujah rings out at the end of the psalm.

Psalm 117

This is the shortest of all the psalms, a brief hymn that is probably not even a complete composition. It may be read either with Ps 116 or Ps 118, and also forms a pivot between Pss 115–116 and Ps 118. It is suitable as a brief opening call to worship and was doubtless so used in Israelite practice. The basic elements of a major type of the hymn form are found in it. The form can be analyzed by asking questions: Who is to be praised? Yahweh. Who is to praise Yahweh? *All . . . nations* (i.e., all peoples). Why is Yahweh to be praised? *For* is the characteristic word that introduces the answer to this question, which here focuses on *his steadfast love . . . and the faithfulness* God shows toward the people Israel. Other questions that apply to the hymn (Where is Yahweh to be praised? How is Yahweh to be praised?) are not answered in this brief poem. The psalm emphasizes the universal dominion of Yahweh and the enduring faithfulness that he demonstrates in his relationship with his people. The formula for opening a hymn may be repeated at the end, as is true here.

Psalm 118

This is the last psalm of the "Hallel" collection (Pss 113–118) used at PASSOVER meals (see commentary on Pss 113, 115). According to other Jewish traditions it belonged to the festival of Tabernacles, and it has features that point toward that context (*tents* in v. 15; a *festal procession*, possibly carrying *branches* in v. 27; *this is the day* in v. 24 [cf. Ps 81:4]; also *light* in v. 27). Beyond this it may have had other liturgical usage, including use in victory celebrations.

The setting of the psalm and the identity of the speakers in it have fostered considerable debate. The psalm is a thanksgiving composition that begins with a communal summons to praise in vv. 1-4, is followed by an individual thanksgiving in vv. 5-21, returns to communal speech in vv. 22-27, and then reverts to individual speech in vv. 28-29.

At least one commentator has argued that three groups are represented by different speakers in vv. 5-19: the falsely accused (vv. 5-7), travelers (vv. 10-14), and the sick (vv. 17-19). It seems more probable that one speaker is assumed for all of vv. 5-21 and that the voice is that of a king (or other leader), who, beset by enemies, has won a victory by the power of Yahweh (vv. 10-18). In the present Psalter this psalm has been "democratized" (perhaps it always was) and any individual can identify with the speakers and situation in the text.

If this represents the correct history of the psalm, the democratization was aided by two factors: (1) the king embodied the life of the nation and spoke for every Israelite and (2) there is some indication the central section (vv. 5-21) reflects the "Song at the Sea" attributed to MOSES in Exod 15 (Hammer 1991, 491–92; cf. v. 14 with Exod 15:2 and vv. 15-16 with Exod 15:6). This may indicate that Moses, represented by a worship leader, was thought of as the speaker addressing the people in a new situation. Israel may again be in mortal peril, but it need not fear because *[Yahweh's] steadfast love endures forever* (vv. 1, 29).

The psalm may have been used in actual thanksgiving rites of the Temple (Allen 1983, 124–25). On the other hand, it may be a purely literary composition that invites the reader-hearer to participate by imagination in a communal thanksgiving service centered around the victory of a leader.

The opening call to thanksgiving (vv. 1-4) has an antiphonal quality. Three groups of festival participants are called upon to respond with the liturgical formula *"His steadfast love endures forever"* (cf. Pss 106:1; 107:1; 136:1-26; Jer 33:11). The three are the same as those in Ps 115:9-11. They represent the people, the priesthood, and the "fearers of Yahweh," possibly non-Israelites who worship Yahweh (cf. 135:19-21) but more probably "fearers of Yahweh" is a comprehensive term for the whole community of faith.

The *I* of vv. 5-21 was probably intended to represent a king or other worship leader. The speaker recalls the lament brought before Yahweh before he heard the prayer and delivered the speaker from *distress* (vv. 5-9). The speaker continues in a recital of the situation that prevailed before Yahweh helped (vv. 10-14). Fighting in the name of Yahweh and by divine help the speaker gained victory, and recalls the cheers and rejoicing of those *in the tents of the righteous* at the victory of Yahweh's *right hand* (v. 15; cf. Ps 110:1, 5). The speaker resumes the recital (vv. 17-18) with a testimony of continued survival, despite rigorous discipline by the LORD. The speaker is now a living testimony of the saving deeds of Yahweh.

In vv. 19-20, the poet visualizes the king leading a procession of worshipers as he approaches the gates of the Temple courts and asks for admittance (v. 19), speaking for the people. Verse 20 represents the response of a priest or gatekeeper (cf. Pss 15 and 24). The speaker affirms an intention to offer thanksgiving (v. 21); the people, or a choir, then sing of the marvelous nature of the divine deliverance (vv. 22-25).

The stone that the builders rejected (v. 22) has now been made the most important one—either an end-stone which links two walls at right angles or the top-stone which completes a structure (cf. Zech 4:7). (This verse is given Christological significance in the NT: see Mark 12:10 and par.; Acts 4:11; Eph 2:20; 1 Pet 2:7].) The reference to *the day* (v. 24) points to the festival occasion when Yahweh's work is revealed in fullness, the day of victory and thankful praise.

The prayer in v. 25 is well known because of its use in the Festival of Tabernacles and in the NT (Matt 21:9). The NT "Hosanna" is derived from the *Save us [Heb. hoshianna], we beseech you*. This call upon Yahweh for deliverance should be understood as a call for continued deliverance in the future (Hammer, 494).

In v. 26, a blessing is pronounced on the procession of worshipers as they enters the Temple. *Light* (v. 27) reflects the priestly benediction of Num 6:24-26, and possibly the ceremony of "lights" in the later Jewish celebration of Tabernacles. The Festival of Tabernacles also had a ceremony in which worshipers encircled the altar while carrying palm, myrtle, and willow branches. Such a ceremony probably is indicated here by the liturgical instruction given in v. 27b (see Lev 23:40) although the exact nature of the ritual is not clear.

A solo voice closes the psalm with a vow of praise in v. 28 and a call to the congregation in v. 29 that repeats v. 1.

Psalm 119

This enormous composition is in the form of an alphabetic acrostic (cf. Pss 9-10; 25; 34; 37; 11; 112; 145). Each of its twenty-two sections (each eight verses long) corresponds to a successive letter of the Hebrew alphabet, and each line within a section begins with the letter that marks that section. The acrostic form is useful for extended and repeated treatment of a single subject; in this case it is the TORAH.

In this psalm, the wonders of the life-giving *torah* and the glory of Yahweh—the giver of glory—is the constant focus of the speaker's attention. At least eight different *torah* words are used (*torah* is generally translated "law", but has a broader meaning, not exclusively related to the written *Torah*; see commentary on Ps 19): *law* (v. 1, etc.), *decrees* (v. 2, etc.), *precepts* (v. 4, etc.), *commandments* (v. 6, etc.), *ordinances* (v. 7, etc.), *statutes* (v. 5, etc.), *word* (v. 9, etc.), and *promise* (v. 38, etc.); if *way(s)* (v. 3, etc.) and *faithfulness* (v. 90) are counted, there are ten such synonyms. Eight or more words for *torah* are used in each stanza, and one of the ten words is used in each verse except four (vv. 122, 132, 149, 156). Each of these words has its own shade of meaning, but in this psalm they all refer to the revealed will of Yahweh in *torah*.

The attitude of the speaker towards the *torah* is one of grateful praise. It is a source of *wondrous things* (v. 18), something in which those who fear Yahweh may *delight* continually (e.g., vv. 16, 77, 174). The *torah is sweeter than honey* (v. 103) and loved *more than gold* (v. 127). Unchanging in its dependability (v. 142), it is a source of *light* (v. 105) and those who love it have a great *shalom* (*peace*, v. 165). Yahweh is the source of the *torah* (note the repeated *your law*, etc.; v. 72 refers to *the law of your mouth*).

Psalm 119 manifests a mixture of literary types. In addition to the hymnic and wisdom elements, some sections have a distinctly lament character (vv. 81-88; 105-128; 145-176). The speaker seems to reflect a context in which there is considerable affliction and persecution, while clinging to *torah* in defiance and hope (v. 23). The speaker is confident that Yahweh is near and that the divine commandments are reliable (v. 151). The briefness of this commentary and the repetitive length of the psalm exclude any detailed treatment. Fortunately, the translations are clear and self-explanatory in most cases. Attention should be given especially to vv. 10-11, 17, 19, 34-40, 73, 75-77, 89-96, 97, 103, 105, 125, 127, 135, 160, 165, 171-172.

The speaker in Ps 119 is not specifically identified, but the language of the prayers and petitions points toward a deeply pious person of faith and commitment, who is designated repeatedly as a *servant* of God (*your servant*, vv. 17, 23, 38, 49, 65, 76, 84, 123, 124, 125, 135, 140, 176) and as a *companion of all who fear you* (i.e., God; v. 63). An extensive argument has been advanced to identify the speaker as a king, or alternatively that the content was written from the perspective of a king, perhaps King JEHOIACHIM of Judah during the EXILE (Soll 1991). However, even if this is the case, faithful Israelites could identify with the language and experience of a king (as with DAVID) so that the king's prayer could become that of any devoted Israelite. From another perspective, while the psalm lacks explicit language to identify the speaker as a sage or teacher, nevertheless the closest exemplar may well be Ben Sira (Sirach) in the Book of Ecclesiasticus, who was also devoted to *torah* (see, e.g., Sir 1:26; 2:15-18; 6:37; 15:1-8; 24:23-29). The psalm is an awesome expression of comprehensive faith and devotion.

Psalm 120

This psalm is often interpreted as a lament, a view adopted by the RSV and NRSV. It may be better to treat it as an individual thanksgiving psalm, translating v. 1: "In my distress I cried to the LORD, and he answered me" (cf. REB, NAB, and esp. NJB; see Kraus 1989). Verse 2 would then recall the petition the speaker prayed before the prayer was answered. This view is the more natural one (cf. Ps 30:8-10).

The answer of the suppliant's prayer is not stated explicitly, but the context of the *Songs of Ascents* (see below) gives an implicit answer in the ability of the suppliant to go on pilgrimage and leave behind the condition described in vv. 5-7.

Verses 3-4 are not entirely clear, but it seems best to understand them as a curse directed toward enemies who had attacked the speaker with *lying lips* and a *deceitful tongue* (v. 2). The formula of oath or curse lies behind the language of v. 3: "May God do so to you, and more also, if . . . " (see 1 Sam 3:17; 14:44; 20:13). The punishment that the persecuted one thought appropriate for the enemies is found in v. 4. The wood of *the broom tree* was noted for its intense and long-lasting heat when burned. Since the tongue is compared with an arrow (cf. Pss 7:13-14; 11:2; 57:4; 64:3), it is likely the poet had in mind the destruction of the enemies with their own weapons (i.e., that they receive what they proposed to give to others).

Verses 5-7 indicate that the speaker lives (or better, did live) among a hostile and contentious people, who make peaceful desires difficult to sustain. The geographical references in v. 5 are probably figurative and perhaps descriptive of the hostile character of the people among whom the supplicant lived. The locations of the nomadic tribes of *Meshech* and *Kedar* are separated by too much distance for anyone to live among both groups at the same time (see Gen 10:2; Ezek 27:13; 32:26-27; 38:3; 39:1). Meshech is located to the north of Palestine, perhaps in the area of the Black Sea. Genesis 25:13, Isa 42:11, etc. locate the Bedouin tribe of Kedar in the desert south of Damascus and east of Israel.

This is the first of a series of psalms known as the Songs of Ascents or Pilgrim Songs (120–134). These psalms have traditionally been understood as a collection of psalms sung by pilgrims on their way to festivals in Jerusalem. Thus Ps 120 has been interpreted as the thanksgiving of an Israelite living in a foreign land, possibly in exile, who is now on pilgrimage to Zion. The misery of exile is left behind as the pilgrim moves toward Zion (for further comment on the Songs of Ascent, see Ps 134).

Psalm 121

The change of speaker in v. 3 of this short psalm is an interesting point in its interpretation. There is some sort of dialogue in the psalm, but the identity of the speakers is not clear. Perhaps the speaker is communing with himself on a journey toward Jerusalem and the hills of Zion in a manner similar to the monologues in Ps 42–43. However, it may be best to postulate two speakers, possibly a priest (vv. 3-8) and a pilgrim (vv. 1-2)—or possibly two pilgrims. If this is the case, the setting may belong to the departure of a pilgrim from a home community for a pilgrimage to Zion, or a departure from Jerusalem for home at the end of a festival. It has been suggested that the dialogue is between a father and his son, which is quite possible and cannot be entirely ruled out.

The hills of v. 1 can refer either to the hills of Jerusalem or hills on the pilgrim's journey. Yahweh is the source of help and strength in any case. The KJV prejudices the case for the hills or mountains as the source of help by following the LXX and translating: "I will lift up mine eyes unto the hills, from whence cometh my help." However, it is better to read as (1) "I lift up my eyes . . . [to see] where my help is to come from" (Allen 1983, 150) which leaves the matter open—my

help may come from the mountains of heaven where Yahweh dwells (Ps 123:1) or from his dwelling on Zion (cf. Ps 20:2-3); or (2) "I lift up my eyes . . . from where will my help come?" (author trans.)—in this case the hills are hostile and full of danger, and the question is answered by v. 2. However we read, the source of help is not the hills, but Yahweh.

Verses 3-8 responds to the pilgrims' affirmation of faith in v. 2. The message of vv. 3-8 can be summarized around these statements: (1) the creator is able to protect and is available for the pilgrim. (2) Yahweh is the nonslumbering keeper of Israel. Unlike the gods found in a HIGH PLACE (see 1 Kgs 18:27), Yahweh is never absent or sleeping when his people are in trouble. The pilgrim can entrust the keeping of his *going out and . . . coming in* (v. 8) to him.

For discussion of divine sleeping, see commentary on Ps 44. In the case of v. 4 the converse of the sovereign sleep of deity is presupposed, that is, in some circumstances the ability to conquer sleep (considered to be a form of death) was a mark of divine power. In the Gilgamesh Epic from Mesopotamia, Gilgamesh is unable to attain immortality by remaining awake for six days and seven nights, a confirmation of his mortal and human status.

Psalm 122

This "Song of Zion" (see Pss 46–48, 76, 84, 87, 137) is written for a pilgrim who, having come to Jerusalem for a festival (probably Tabernacles), has arrived in the city, or is ready to depart from it for home. Arrival rather than departure seems to be the better choice. Verses 1-2 recall the pleasure of an invitation to go to Zion for a festival. *Jerusalem* is praised in vv. 3-5 as the pilgrimage city of the tribes who go up to worship as decreed (vv. 3-4; cf. Exod 23:17; Deut 16:16). It is the city of *judgment* and the place where the throne of the Davidic king is situated (v. 5). Verses 6-9 is a prayer for the city of Jerusalem. A priest or other leader may speak in vv. 6-7; the festival goer responds in vv. 8-9.

Psalm 123

This is a lament, possibly offered by an individual, a king, or worship leader, but more probably by a pilgrim who is on the way to Jerusalem and festival time, and who speaks for the community. The situation in vv. 3-4 fits the postexilic period when Israelites were under the pressure of living in hostile environments, although such evidence can never be definite.

The people have suffered for a long time from the contempt and scorn of those who oppress them. The prayer is directed to the heavenly King (vv. 1-2), whose servants intently watch his hand for a gesture of favor. The individual in v. 1 and the people in v. 2 look up to Yahweh in complete dependence.

Psalm 124

This is a short, but forceful, communal thanksgiving of a group of people for deliverance from a situation that had threatened their life. The poet may have had some particular historical event in mind, or the psalm may reflect Yahweh's manifold acts of deliverance in the salvation-history of Israel.

The translation of the psalm is reasonably clear and requires little comment. It is sufficient here to call attention to the fact that the one who gives *help* (v. 8) is the same as in Ps 121:2: the maker of *heaven and earth*.

The graphic descriptive language of the psalm used to describe the situation from which the group has been delivered is characteristic of the laments and presents the full force of the distress. The group commends their testimony to all Israel: *let Israel now say* (v. 1). Perhaps we should think of a group of pilgrims on their way to Jerusalem who consider their experience representative of that of the nation (cf. Ps 107).

Psalm 125

This is a communal psalm of confidence that affirms the nation's trust in Yahweh and prays for his continued favor. Verse 3 indicates that Israel is under the domination of a foreign power, or possibly of apostate Israelites (v. 5; cf. Isa 56:9–57:13). The context seems to be that of the postexilic period when the circles of *the righteous* (v. 3) were under the pressure of a pagan environment and the threat of alien culture, and when many defected. The righteous ones are being assured that they will inherit the land even though they are temporarily dispossessed (cf. Isa 57:13; 60:21; 65:9). They are called upon to trust that Yahweh controls the future and to reject the ways of those who yield to the pressures of their cultural environment.

The security of those who trust in Yahweh is declared to be like that of Mount Zion, immutably chosen and protected by the divine presence (vv. 1-2; cf. Ps 34:7; Zech 2:5). The actual geographical situation of Jerusalem is reflected in v. 2, since the city is lower than the surrounding hills (cf. Ps 48:1-2). The prayer in vv. 4-5 contains a warning to those who

apostatize from the ways of goodness and uprightness, ways that mark those who are loyal to Yahweh.

Psalm 126

It seems best to interpret this psalm in relation to Ps 85 (see commentary there). The tense of the verbs is a problem. Verses 1-3 can be interpreted as referring to the future, looking forward to the completed fulfillment of the prayer in v. 4, but it is better to treat them as looking back to a wonderful restoration of the fortunes of Zion. It seems probable that the great changing event that is recalled is the restoration of Israel after the surrender of Babylon to CYRUS in 539 B.C.E. An objection may be raised with regard to v. 4. If the fortunes of Zion have already been restored, why does the congregation continue to pray that they will be restored? The answer is found in the condition that prevailed after the first stages of the restoration. A great event had occurred (Babylon had fallen, CYRUS had come to power, and some Israelites had returned), but the full measure of the prophetic promises was lacking. The prayer in v. 4 looks forward to the full manifestation of the glory of Yahweh (cf. Isa 59:9-15).

The *watercourses in the Negeb* of v. 4 recalls the fullness and transformed nature of the wadis when the usually dry NEGEB receives rain. They literally become streams of life in an arid semidesert. Verse 5 may be read as a continuation of the prayer, as in the NRSV, but it is better to read it with v. 6 as positive statements of comfort and assurance in response to the prayer in v. 4. The sowing with tears (v. 5) could allude to customs of weeping for the dead fertility god in Canaanite religion in order to insure the germination of the seed and the growth of corps. The origin of this custom is found in belief that the god of fertility died in the dry season when no vegetation was growing, and that he must be brought back to life through rituals that included weeping because of his death. But here it is most likely a proverbial saying that incorporates a maxim of life: the disappointed sorrow of the people will be changed to joy (cf. Ps 30:5; Job 16:20). Verse 6 expands on the proverb in v. 5.

Psalm 127

The theme that ties the separate parts of this psalm together is that of the dependence of every human endeavor on the purpose and favor of God. The psalm has the characteristics of the wisdom sayings (such as those found in the Book of Proverbs) and this may account, in part at least, for the ascription of it to

SOLOMON. Commentators typically read the psalm as composed of two parts (vv. 1-2 and vv. 3-5) that are different and only loosely related. Actually, however, the psalm deals with four activities: house building, protection of a town, daily work, and the blessing of offspring.

House in v. 1 has the double connotation of a dwelling place and of a household or family. The latter relates well to vv. 3-5, and frames the activity of dwellers in a town in vv. 1b-2. "The house that Yahweh builds includes the sons who are the subject of vv. 3-5" (Kselman and Barré 1990, 548).

The futility of godless toil is expounded in vv. 1-2. No amount of rising early and going to bed late and working in *anxious toil* (v. 2) will compensate for the absence of the protection of God (*anxious toil* is better read as "hard work"). The effort to build is *in vain* unless God's blessing rests upon it. The *for he gives sleep to his beloved* of v. 2 has produced different interpretations. Some (e.g., Kraus 1989, 452) suppose that an "in" or "during" should be understood, with the resulting idea that while others may wear themselves out in hard and incessant work, Yahweh "provides for his beloved *during* sleep" (NRSV mg.). However, the blessing of sleep itself is not insignificant, particularly for toilers who know little except exhaustion, and so it is probably better to retain "he gives sleep" and read the "beloved" as plural "his loved ones." The laborer, the watcher, the toiler of long hours—they are all dependent on the favor of Yahweh.

The domestic blessings of the family is the subject of vv. 3-5. The land is not the only *heritage* of Yahweh. Children are a heritage too. They are like the arrows of a warrior, and offer security *in the gate* (v. 5). The gate was the place where legal hearings were held and local administrative matters were decided. One's reputation and so one's situation depended to a large degree on one's status in the gate (cf. Job 29:7-10). Children as the gift of Yahweh secured the existence of the family as well as its prestige.

Psalm 128

Like Ps 127, this is a wisdom psalm in the form of a blessing on the Yahweh-fearer. It probably developed out of the priestly benediction pronounced during the worship of a festival (see. vv. 5-6). The person who fears Yahweh will be one who enjoys *the fruit of [personal] labor* (i.e., endeavors will not result in loss or frustration [v. 2]). This is a blessing of the first-rank importance for happy living. Such a person will know the domestic happiness of a wife who *like a fruitful vine* produces children, who in turn sit about the table *like olive shoots* (v. 3).

The benediction in vv. 5-6 is only loosely attached to vv. 1-4 by the association of the idea of the blessing of children in v. 6. Zion is the earthly source of Yahweh's blessing. Ps 128 is closely related to Ps 127 (note *happy* in 127:5 and v. 1, and the blessing of children in both psalms). The formal blessing in vv. 5-6 is appropriate for a pilgrim at the festivals in Jerusalem, with families actually in attendance at times (see Deut 14:26 and 1 Sam 1).

Psalm 129

This psalm is difficult to classify. The best explanation may be that it is an adaptation of an earlier individual lament of one who had suffered for a prolonged time (vv. 1a, 2-4) and who had asked for judgment (vv. 6-8) on those who attacked "and scored my back with scourges " (v. 3 REB). The revision of the psalm to fit a context like that of the Songs of Ascent (Pss 120–134) is seen in the addition of *let Israel now say* (v. 1) and the identity of the enemies as those *who hate Zion* (v. 5), plus a closing greeting at the end of v. 8. Now the individual experience has been transferred to the whole nation—personal experience has merged with that of Israel.

Like the long furrows left by plowman on the land, the back of Israel bears the indelible stripes of those whose lashes have left their marks. But the congregation also recalls that Yahweh has been faithful and has cut loose the cords by which wicked oppressors bound them. In this freedom the pilgrim goes to Jerusalem to worship. A prayer for the destruction of the enemies of Zion is found in vv. 5-8—petitions that they may be shamed, repulsed (v. 5), and become like the grass that grows accidentally on housetops and withers quickly from lack of rootage and water (vv. 6-7). Such vegetation will never produce a harvest worthy of the blessing of passersby (v. 8). The last line of v. 8 may be a closing blessing by the priests on the congregation.

Psalm 130

This psalm is usually read as a lament of an individual in which a suppliant cries out to Yahweh for deliverance from a present predicament. This may very well be the case, and Ps 130 is one of the traditional seven penitential psalms in Christian tradition (Pss 6, 32, 38, 51, 102, 130, and 143). However, it is quite possible to read this psalm as a thanksgiving, an especially appropriate reading in the context of the festival participation of speakers in the Songs of Ascent (Pss 120–134). In this case read the verbs in vv. 1 and 5 (v. 6 has no verb in Hebrew and takes its tense from v. 5) in past tense: "Out of the depths I cried to you, O LORD! . . . I waited for the LORD . . . and in his word I hoped. My soul waited for the LORD." If this is correct, the psalm recalls blessings already received. The prayer that the worshiper prayed before deliverance is in vv. 2-4. The exhortation to Israel (the congregation) in v. 7 fits poorly in a lament, but it is appropriate for a thanksgiving. Read as thanksgiving, the psalm becomes a testimony of one delivered from *the depths* (v. 1), although the deliverance is not explicitly stated.

However, the traditional reading of this psalm as a penitential lament has a long and moving history among people of faith (e.g., McCann 1993b, 87). The message of the psalm is not significantly changed if it is read as lament, which vv. 2-4 are in any case. If the traditional reading is retained, vv. 5-6 become statements of confidence in the present, expressing assurance that waiting in hope and anticipation for divine action will not be disappointed.

The depths (v. 1) is a metaphor for mental and physical anguish and disaster, reflecting the waters of the cosmic deep (cf. Ps 69:2; 14-15; Isa 51:10; Ezek 27:34), but it is a metaphor suitable for any great distress, such as that in Ps 69 or of an exile living amid contempt and scorn as in Ps 123. From *the depths* the suppliant cried out to Yahweh. The expected answer to the rhetorical question in v. 3 is "No one"; no one has any standing before God on the basis of a sinless life. A relationship may exist, but it is based on God's forgiveness (v. 4). The *that you may be revered* indicates the reverence and willingness to obey that results from the experience of God's forgiveness. Such fear is the fruit of love; it is the "right fear" of John Bunyan's *The Pilgrim's Progress* that reminds us that forgiveness opens up new involvement and obligations in terms of God's will and removes our ability to calculate the cost of our own involvement.

Such a prayer leads to the kind of relinquishment and expectant waiting that is expressed in vv. 5-6. The worshiper's whole being was (or is) "toward God" (*for the LORD*, v. 6a). Like a watchman who expectantly anticipates the dawn, the worshiper waits for the word of Yahweh. We are not told that a word is received and there is a measure of unresolved tension in the psalm. As in Ps 120, we may have an implicit deliver-

ance manifest in the context of a pilgrim able to go to Zion for festivals. In any case, the worshiper is able to exhort the congregation in vv. 7-8 to join in the "hope directed toward the LORD." It is Yahweh who will redeem Israel from iniquity (v. 8). The hope of the speaker is pointed toward a fellowship of the forgiven, for *with the LORD there is steadfast love, and . . . great power to redeem* (v. 7).

Psalm 131

This brief psalm of trust (cf. Pss 16, 23, 62) is one of the finest expressions of humble faith in the Bible. The words require little comment, but meditation upon them may impart something of the full confidence and honest self-appraisal before God that makes for healthy and abundant living. The psalm speaks of a maturity and balance that permits the relinquishment of proud ambitions for the satisfaction of communion with God. Further, the psalm avers that "submissive reliance leaves one free of anxiety," the anxiety that results from the futile attempts to be self-sufficient or of trying to be equal with God (Brueggemann 1984, 49). Verse 3 (a liturgical addition) closes the psalm and binds it to Ps 130 (note *O Israel, hope in the LORD!* in 130:7). Verses 1-2 may have been written by (or for) a woman (cf. NRSV translation; Holladay 1993, 40).

Psalm 132

This is a royal psalm (see Pss 2, 20, 21, 72, 89, 110) insofar as it has to do with Israelite kingship. It commemorates David's bringing the ARK of the covenant to Jerusalem, the Davidic covenant, and Yahweh's choice of Zion as his *resting place forever* (v. 14). There are liturgical features in the psalm, and it may have been designed originally for use in connection with the cultic re-enactment of the bringing of the ark to Jerusalem (see 2 Sam 6) and the founding of the Davidic dynasty (cf. 2 Sam 7). A reenactment probably took place during the autumnal festival (see 1 Kgs 8:2). Note the use of some verses from this psalm in 2 Chr 6:41-42, although in slightly altered form.

The first part of the psalm (vv. 1-10) is a prayer beseeching Yahweh to remember DAVID and his zeal for finding a dwelling place for Yahweh (cf. 1 Kgs 8:13; 2 Sam 7:1-3). The finding of the ark by David and his entourage is recalled in v. 6, which names the places where they went to look for the ark. *Ephrathah* may refer to BETHLEHEM, the hometown of David, or to SHILOH in EPHRAIM, where the ark was once kept. *The fields of Jaar* is a poetic designation of KIRIATH-

JEARIM where the ark had been kept until David moved it. Having discovered the ark, the traditional processional summons is given in v. 7 (cf. 122:1). The *footstool* (v. 7) can be either the Temple or the ark, but probably the ark. The procession with the ark is begun with vv. 8-10. *Rise up, O LORD* is the ancient cry pronounced wherever the ark was moved (see Num 10:35; cf. Pss 7:6; 9:19; 10:12; 17:13). Verse 10 indicates this psalm was used as a prayer for a Davidic king, and not by David himself.

The second part of the psalm (vv. 11-19) sets forth the Davidic COVENANT and Yahweh's choice of Zion. The oath of Yahweh regarding the continuation of his dynasty is recalled (see 2 Sam 7; 23:5; Ps 89). Verse 12 qualifies the commitment of Yahweh by making the obedience of David's sons prerequisite for the promise in v. 11. To what do *my covenant and my decrees* in v. 12 refer? They are probably references to the SINAI covenant and the covenant-law of the Yahweh-Israel relationship. It is possible, of course, that they refer to the covenant of Yahweh with David and the stipulations regarding kingship (see Ps 89:3-4; 28; 1 Sam 10:25). (For *my decrees* see the commentary on Ps 2, although it is doubtful the term in 132:12 is the same as the *decree* in 2:7; a relationship to 1 Sam 10:25 is much more likely.)

Yahweh's choice of Zion and his promises to it is the subject of vv. 13-16. The last two verses (vv. 17-18) emphasize that Zion is also the place of the Davidic dynasty, where Yahweh will cause *a horn* to grow and *a lamp* to burn for the Davidic king. The *horn* is a symbol of power and victory and the *lamp* is a symbol of the king's presence before God (note Exod 27:20-21; 1 Kgs 11:36; 2 Sam 21:17). Verse 18 contrasts the *disgrace* that clothes the kings' enemies with his splendid, gleaming crown.

Psalm 132 may be a psalm from preexilic times, possibly quite early in the monarchy but probably no earlier than the period of JOSIAH (Allen 1983, 208–09). One suspects v. 12 is a later addition (after the failure of the monarchy) to give a conditional nature to the Davidic covenant. The conditional promises to the Davidic dynasty, however, may have been understood as such from the beginning of the monarchy, even when the language was explicitly unconditional (cf. Isa 7:1-9; 28:14-22; 1 Kgs 2:3-4; 9:4-5; for Zion, 1 Kgs 6:11-13). In any case, Ps 132 in its present context was almost certainly read differently than in preexilic Israel. Verse 12 now serves to give a reason for the fall of the monarchy and vv. 17-18 are directed toward

a future, messianic hope; the *horn to sprout up for David* will emerge from a now-dead dynasty.

The position of this psalm in the Songs of Ascent is probably due to its emphasis on Zion; David's role is secondary except in terms of messianic promise (Allen 1983, 211; cf. Acts 2:30; 7:46). The monarchy was gone, but pilgrims still made their way to Zion for the festivals and the renewal of their faith. The ark itself does not seem to have been physically present in the Temple after 515 B.C.E. (see Jer 3:16), but the traditions regarding it were doubtless still important.

Psalm 133

The RSV and NRSV follow some text traditions and omit the "to David" (or "Davidic") from the title of this psalm. If the "Davidic" is retained, the psalm is linked to Ps 131 by title. Also note that both psalms are short, both end with the same expression (*forevermore*), and both utilize the language of domestic tranquility; in addition Pss 131 and 133 frame Ps 132.

The opening verse of Ps 133 praises the harmony and well-being of an extended family (cf. Deut 25:5), but in its present context it probably refers to the celebration of the festivals at Zion (see the *for there* in v. 3b). The celebrants were all *kindred* during the times they spent together on Mount Zion, a fellowship described as *good and pleasant* (v. 1). The crowds in the holy city epitomized the nation, bound together as it were not only by race but by covenant relationship with God (Allen 1983, 215).

Two word pictures describe the goodness of the unity experienced at Zion. The first is that of the fragrant oil used in the consecration of AARON as high priest (cf. Exod 29:7; 21; Lev 8:12), which was poured on his head and ran down over the collar of his robes. The oil signified peace, health, joy, and the grace of God (Pss 23:5; 45:7-8; Exod 30:22-33).

The second word picture is that of the *dew of Hermon* (v. 3) that falls on the "mountains of Zion" (Mount Zion). The *dew of Hermon* is a heavy dew like that which falls on Mount Hermon, a mountain in the north of Palestine, more than 9,000 feet high, and known as an abundant source of water (one of its modern names means "the snow mountain"; cf. Ps 42:6-7). In the dry climate of Palestine, a heavy dew was both a pleasant experience in the early morning of a hot day and important for growing dry-season crops. "Dew" was proverbial for refreshment and life (Gen 27:28; Deut 33:28; Hos 14:5; Mic 5:7; Isa 26:19; Zech 8:12; Job 29:19; cf. Ps 110:3).

Mount Zion is the place of divine blessing, the source of life *forevermore* (v. 3). *Hermon* is a larger mountain than Zion and renowned for being the dwelling place of gods and the location of ritual centers (cf. Josh 11:17; 1 Chr 5:23), but Zion is the source of everlasting life—a greater blessing than any offered by Mount Hermon. The emphasis on Zion in this psalm ties it closely with Ps 132:13-16 and focuses attention on the experience of the divine presence attached to that place. Allen (1983, 215) notes that this emphasis prepares the way for the conception of a heavenly counterpart in NT traditions (Heb 12:22-24; 13:14-16; cf. Gal 4:26; Rev 14:1)."

Psalm 134

This very short hymn and priestly blessing closes the series of psalms known as the Songs of Ascent. A night ceremony was an important part of the festival of Tabernacles in later times, and very probably earlier as well (cf. Isa 30:29). A night ceremony marking the end of the festival is probably assumed by this psalm. The picture is that of a festival congregation (*servants of the LORD* [v. 1] is not restricted to the priests and the Levites; see Pss 34:22; 79:2; 86:1-4, 16; etc.) standing before Yahweh in the Temple (cf. Deut 10:8; 18:7; 1 Chr 23:30; 2 Chr 29:11). Those who stand before Yahweh are especially the priests, but ordinary people are referred to in Deut 19:17; Jer 7:10; Ps 135:2, 14. They are exhorted by the priests to praise Yahweh and to lift up their hands toward the holy place; probably the area of the Temple where the ark was kept (cf. Ps 28:2).

Verse 3 is the blessing of the priests pronounced at the end of the ceremony introduced by vv. 1-2. The blessing is appropriate for pilgrim celebrants preparing to leave for home. One suspects this psalm is only part of a liturgy for a major service of farewell.

"Songs of Ascent" (Pss 120–134). One salient feature of the Songs of Ascent is their concentration on Zion (explicitly in Pss 125, 126, 128, 129, 132–134; Ps 122 mentions Jerusalem). Zion remained, indeed probably became more so, the center of the religious world for Israelites in the postexilic period. Even living far from Jerusalem as permanent exiles, Israelites always longed for Zion; in far off Babylonia they sang

> If I forget you, O Jerusalem,
> let my right hand wither!
> Let my tongue cling to the roof of my mouth,

> if I do not remember you,
> if I do not set Jerusalem
> above my highest joy. (Ps 137:5-6)

From Pss 120–134 we can gain something of the joys and hopes of devoted Israelites whenever they were able to go to Zion at festival time. Memories and traditions nurtured their faith wherever they lived. Zion was the home for which they longed, hoped, and prayed.

Psalm 135

This is a HALLELUJAH hymn with a rather standard, though expanded, literary form: summons to praise God (vv. 1-3); grounds for the praise (vv. 4-5); explication of the action and greatness of Yahweh (vv. 4-5) set forth in a recital of divine deeds in creation and history (vv. 6-12); a hymnic element that resumes vv. 1-3 (vv. 13-14); a treatment of idols (almost the same as Ps 115:3-8) that magnifies the power of Yahweh by contrast (vv. 15-18); repeated summons to praise God and a closing Hallelujah, verses (19-20) that with vv. 1-3 form a frame for the psalm.

This psalm seems very formulaic and dependent on traditional elements in its composition. The recitation of history in vv. 8-12 is selective, focusing on three deeds: the PLAGUES on Egypt (vv. 8-9), victory over kings and foreign nations (vv. 10-11), and the gift of a LAND for Israel (v. 12). Other great deeds are missing: the deliverance from the Egyptians at the sea, Sinai (Horeb) and the events there, and the wanderings in the wilderness. The purpose of the psalm is not that of a complete recital of God's saving history, but the setting forth of his power vis-à-vis other gods and their idols. The implied community in this psalm (almost certainly actual Israelite communities of the postexilic era) is tempted to doubt the power of Yahweh and turn to other divine sources of power. The psalm also sets forth a classic example of the triangular relationship between Yahweh, Israel, and the land (Allen 1983, 228). The *servants of the LORD* (v. 1; see Ps 134:1) might be prone to doubt the divine intention while living under the domination of world powers who "know not Yahweh." Verse 14 is the answer of Ps 135.

Psalm 136

The twenty-six occurrences of the refrain *for his steadfast love endures forever* is the most distinctive feature of this psalm. It is a communal thanksgiving (beginning and ending with the verb *hodu*, "give thanks") in which Yahweh is praised for his deeds in creation and in Israel's salvation-history. The refrain was an intended congregational response to each verse of the psalm prayer. After the opening summons to thanksgiving (vv. 1-3), the main part of the psalm recalls Yahweh's acts of creation (vv. 4-9); the EXODUS from Egypt (vv. 10-15); Yahweh's providential care of the Israelites in the wilderness (vv. 16-20); and the gift of the LAND as Israel's heritage (vv. 21-22). In vv. 23-25, Yahweh is praised as the great deliverer and sustainer, who remembered and rescued, and who is the one continuously providing nourishment for all creatures (Pss 104:27-30; 145:15; 147:9).

The cultic context of the psalm seems likely to have been the autumnal Feast of Tabernacles, as is the case of Ps 135, but there are those who advocate the PASSOVER, which may have been true in postexilic Israel. The exact festival cannot be determined. Note the psalm begins (vv. 1-9) with the universal work of God and shifts to Israel (vv. 10-24; Israel is mentioned specifically in vv. 11, 14, and 22; *his people* in v. 16), then returns to the universal scope of God's work (vv. 25-26). In vv. 23-24, the community identifies with the history given in third person and past tense in vv. 11-22: *who remembered us in our low estate* (v. 23). The enduring love of Yahweh is manifest in all his works in creation and in history.

In Jewish tradition, Ps 136 is often known as "The Great Hallel" (see Ps 113 for the "Hallel" or "The Egyptian Hallel"). Some modern interpreters (see Allen 1983, 219) treat Pss 135–136 as a supplement to the Songs of Ascent (Pss 120–134). Psalm 135, as well as Ps 136, is a SABBATH psalm (except for the sabbath before New Year) in Jewish usage, and Ps 136 was attached to "The Egyptian Hallel" (Pss 113–118) on the eighth day of PASSOVER.

Psalm 137

This is an unusual psalm in the sense of its specificity of location: *By the rivers of Babylon* (v. 1). In vv. 1-4, the psalm looks back to the fall of Jerusalem in 587 B.C.E. and recalls the EXILE of Israelites to Babylonia. Jerusalem is addressed in the present in vv. 5-6. The speaker may well be one who has survived the burden of the years in Babylon, and who has returned to Jerusalem where conditions are still bad and arouse the memories expressed in the psalm. The poem expresses the unforgettable devotion of the exiles to Jerusalem and recalls their great reluctance to sing the

Temple songs in a pagan land. It was not considered proper to sing the *songs of Zion* (v. 3) in a foreign and unholy context (cf. Amos 7:17; Ezek 4:13).

The Israelites were captives who wept for Zion "by the waters of Babylon." The "waters" or "streams" refer to the irrigation canals that were common in Mesopotamia (cf. Ezek 1:1; 3:15). The psalm itself looks back on the experiences of the exiles, although Babylon seems still to be in existence (v. 8); the description could, however, refer to the situation after 539 B.C.E. when Babylon surrendered to CYRUS without being destroyed. In any case, the psalm probably emerged from the context of ceremonies of lamentation and fasting that were conducted in Palestine during and after the exile (see Jer 41:5; Zech 7:1-7). It also is possible the psalm recalls similar ceremonies of lamentation in Babylon on the part of the exiles (see 1 Kgs 8:46-53).

Verse 3 recalls the tormenting request of their Babylonian captors. *The songs of Zion* probably refer to those psalms that celebrate Yahweh's choice of Zion and his promise concerning the city's future (e.g., Pss 46, 76, 84, 87), promises that seemed irreparably broken to the exiles. They rejected the taunting request of their captors (v. 4), but at the same time they could never forget Jerusalem, still their *highest joy* (vv. 5-6).

Two imprecations are found in vv. 7-9. The day of Jerusalem's destruction is recalled along with the unrestrained hatred and glee with which *the Edomites* encouraged the devastation by the Babylonians (cf. Obad 11-15; Ezek 25:12-14; 35:1-15). The violence of the imprecation against Babylon is severe (cf. Ps 79:10-13; Lam 1:20-22; 3:64-66). Isaiah 13:16 uses similar language for judgment of the Babylonians, and indicates that Babylon had become archetypical of a world power and that the violent language of judgment had become somewhat conventional (see also Jer 50-51).

Psalm 137 represents one pole of the Israelite attitude toward the exile. Jeremiah and Ezekiel express considerably different attitudes. It was in Babylonia, at possibly the same place alluded to in Ps 137:1, that Ezekiel encountered the glory of Yahweh and received his commission to prophecy (see Ezek 1:3-48; 3:22-27). Psalm 137 expresses the grief of exiles, whose "bittersweet memories" of Zion are a daily torment (Allen 1983, 241–42). Theirs is the passion of a people who have been overwhelmed by the injustice of events beyond their control. They live by remembering, which can be traumatic but also healing. Forgetting is a way of death; God's remembering is essential (v. 7).

Psalm 138

This individual thanksgiving psalm has a Davidic title and is the first of eight Davidic psalms (138–145), a collection that seems to be the actual ending of book five, since Pss 146–150 form a separate collection. The LXX of Ps 138 adds "of Haggai and Zechariah" to the title, indicating that an earlier psalm was edited (or reread) for use in the postexilic period. The speaker appears to be either some distance away from the Temple (v. 2; see Dan. 6:10), or in the actual Temple courts (cf. Ps 5:7).

The psalm expresses the praise of a person who has been delivered from great distress (v. 3), and is now confident of ongoing life and protection even *in the midst of trouble* (v. 7).

One point of interpretation concerns the clause *before the gods I sing your praise* (v. 1). The psalmist seems to be thinking of the gods of pagan peoples and rulers, which the worshiper does not hesitate to defy by singing Yahweh's praise. The expression also can be read as a reference to the heavenly assembly of divine beings around the throne of Yahweh (see Ps 82). The LXX reads as "before the angels" which supports the second understanding (cf. 1 Cor 4:9; 11:10; Eph 3:10; Rev 3:5; 14:10). A third reading of the phrase understands the term *elohim* in the sense of "strong (god-like) persons" (cf. the Syriac translation "kings" and the Aramaic Targum "judges"). It seems best to understand *the gods* as in either the first or second sense, probably the first, rather than the third (see v. 4). In the postexilic context of the psalm, at least in its present position in the Psalter, the first interpretation fits well. Yahweh alone has power, despite the claims of worldly powers—an important point for a devout person far from the Temple in Jerusalem.

There is a change in the thought pattern in vv. 4-6 from individual worship to a future, universal worship of Yahweh (cf. 22:27-31). Then *the kings of the earth* will praise Yahweh, who is the Lord of the whole world and of all history.

The singer's own experience is cited (vv. 7-8) as an example of Yahweh's regard for the lowly. The one to whom all the kings of the earth should pay homage has saved the speaker. The confidence in vv. 7-8 is similar to that in Ps 23. The colon at the end of v. 8 (*Do not forsake the work of your hands*) is a brief closing prayer for Israel and the divine purposes for Yahweh's people.

Psalm 139

This psalm is well known in the Christian tradition where it has been quoted especially by theologians developing the concepts of the omnipresence and omniscience of God. The literary form of the psalm is somewhat difficult to determine, but it seems best to consider it a lament in the form of a prayer of deliverance from enemies. The situation of the worshiper is revealed in vv. 19-24, where the suppliant speaks of *wicked* and *bloodthirsty* enemies of God. The psalm assumes the suppliant is pleading a case before Yahweh, having been falsely accused by theses enemies, and is praying for vindication by Yahweh on the basis of divine knowledge of the speaker's personal life. The speaker maintains that the creator knows him completely, and that there are no grounds for identity with the enemies (v. 22, "I hate them without stopping / they are my enemies" [author trans.]).

Verses 1-18 have much the same force as the protestations of innocence found in some laments (see Pss 7:3-5; 8:1-11; 17:3-5; 26:1-3; 44:20-22; Jer 12:3; Job 31). This psalm is the prayer of a person who bases a case on the omniscience and omnipresence of God in relation to the true and faithful quality of personal inner life.

The suppliant confesses in vv. 1-6 that God has omniscient knowledge of his life; no part of it is hidden from the divine scrutiny (vv. 2-4). Such knowledge lies beyond human capacity (v. 6). The attitude of the suppliant is reciting these verses in different from that of JOB (Job 7:11-21). Job complains that he is receiving too much attention from God and asks for a respite, but the suppliant in this psalm finds confidence in the affirmation that God has such complete and pervasive personal knowledge of his life (cf. 1 Kgs 8:39; 1 Sam 2:3). This speaker does not want to flee from the inescapable presence of God.

The omnipresence of God is described in vv. 7-12. A series of hypothetical statements are used to express the ever-present reality of God. The farthest extremities of the universe provide no refuge from the divine presence and power. There is no darkness black enough to hide one from the creator of both darkness and light.

The suppliant declares praise of God's wonderful work in the creation of the speaker himself (vv. 13-18). This is the basis of God's intimate knowledge of the speaker's life and existence (cf. Pss 33:13-17; 94:8-11).

Verse 15 is rather strange. It can be a poetical reference to the human womb, or it can be a reference to the idea of Mother Earth and the concept of a human being's derivation from the ground (cf. Gen 2:7). In any case, even the fetal stage of human life does not lie beyond the sight and control of God (v. 16). The meaning of v. 16bcd is uncertain; I prefer to read it with the Hebrew marginal text as "and on your scroll all of them (the days of the fetus) were written, (all) the days were formed, and one among them for it (to be born)." However, the most common reading given is that the days of the speaker's life were "fashioned" (or "planned") even before birth and written on the divine scroll (cf. Isa 49:1; Jer 1:5; Pss 56:8; 69:28; Exod 32:32). In any case, no rigid, theoretical predestination is intended. The emphasis is on the absolute and comprehensive nature of God's knowledge and purpose (cf. Jer 1:5; Isa 42:9; Job 14:5). Again, there is an expression of reverent astonishment at the extent of the divine knowledge (vv. 17-18; cf. vv. 1-6).

Verses 23-24 with vv. 1-3 form a frame for the psalm: God's past searching out of the speaker is supplemented by petition for God to continue the process.

This psalm may be classified in the broad category of lament, but it is also an affirmation of faith in Yahweh despite the widespread APOSTASY surrounding the speaker. The psalm was a reminder to exiles of Yahweh's omniscience and omnipresence, welcomed by the speaker but of no comfort for those who hated Yahweh (v. 21). The speaker affirms a way of life devoted to Yahweh in v. 24. Idolatry was a major issue in exilic and postexilic communities.

Psalm 140

This is an individual lament with unusually sharp descriptions of the actions of the suppliant's enemies. The speaker has been seriously threatened by violent, crafty, and arrogantly effective foes (vv. 1-5), and turns to Yahweh with a prayer for deliverance and vindication (vv. 6-11). The depiction of the social situation in this psalm fits with other descriptions of the early postexilic period (see Isa 56:9–57:13; 59:1–15), even if the psalm itself originated at a much earlier date. (Rendsburg [1990, 95-102] argues for a northern origin for Pss 140 and 141, on the basis of linguistic evidence.)

The petitions for judgment, in the form of imprecations against the enemies (vv. 9–11), are severe (see the commentary on Ps 58). The closing two verses are a fine expression of confidence in Yahweh. In the laments, the suppliants often associate themselves with the *needy* (RSV "afflicted") and *poor* as well as with *the righteous* (v. 12). The imprecations against the evildoers who plague the speaker and the community rest on the faith that Yahweh sustains the cause of the poor and needy. Verse 13 begins with the Hebrew particle *'ak*, which indicates that the following statements are true despite overt circumstances to the contrary (see Pss 62, 73). Thus, v. 13 continues and strengthens the affirmations of v. 12.

Psalm 141

The text of this individual lament presents some problems (see RSV and NRSV mg.), but the attitude of the suppliant is much less imprecatory than in Ps 140. Here the speaker is more concerned with inner conditions and preservation from temptation and evil. The speaker prays that his prayer may be acceptable to Yahweh (vv. 1-2). Verse 2 may recall the use of prayer with the evening sacrifice at the Temple (cf. Exod 29:39-41; Num 28:4-8b; Isa 1:13; Jer 41:5; Neh 13:5, 9), but here there is a spiritualization of the sacrifices in which the prayer itself becomes a sacrifice (cf. Pss 40, 50).

In vv. 3-4, the suppliant prays to be guarded and restrained so as not accept compromises of principle and yield to the temptation of keeping company with *the wicked*. The lure of the wicked is similar to that in Ps 73, namely, the well-being of the wicked versus the distress of the righteous.

Verses 5-6 pose some difficulties and their meaning must be considered tentative (see Allen 1983, 269–71), but the speaker seems to be affirming that it is better to be smitten by the righteous one (Yahweh) and be disciplined by his steadfast love, than to live in style with the wicked (cf. Prov 27:6). The NRSV follows LXX in v. 5, *the oil of the wicked*. The LXX is possibly a better text, but "head" or "choice" is supported by 11QPsª, as is "fine oil." Accepting the Qumran text it is possible to read vs. 5:

Let the Righteous One Yahweh strike me,
    the One who is Steadfast Love,
    let him discipline me;
my head will not refuse such fine oil!
My prayer will continue to be
    against their [the wicked in v. 4] evil deeds.

Verse 6 expresses confidence that when "their judges" (not in NRSV) are condemned (or destroyed) they will hear with understanding the words of the speaker—words they now refuse to heed. Verse 7 seems to be a complaint about the present terrible condition of the speaker's community (read with the MT: "Our bones are scattered at the mouth of Sheol").

Verses 8-10 express the concentration of the speaker on Yahweh and supplication for safekeeping. Verse 10 is a prayer that the wicked experience the consequences of their actions designed to harm others, and is an example of the act-consequence sequence found in a number of places (e.g., Prov 1:18; 26:27; 28:10; 29:6, 23; Pss 7:14-17; 9:16; 38:8; 57:7). The idea behind these statements seems to be that God's faithfulness provides that the built-in consequences of actions are maintained.

Psalm 142

In this individual lament the suppliant cries out to Yahweh for help in dealing with persecution. The NRSV translation needs little comment. The appeal to Yahweh is found in vv. 1-3b. The condition of the suppliant is described in vv. 3c-4. Petitions for deliverance form the last part of the psalm (vv. 5-7). The solitary and forsaken condition of the suppliant (v. 4) is similar to that of JOB (19:13-22; Pss 22:11; 38:11). There is no advocate or helping friend at his *right hand* (v. 4) in the present situation (cf. Pss 16:8; 109:31; 110:5; 121:5)—"No one cares about me!" Such loneliness is one of the most distressing of all human emotions. *Prison* (v. 7) is probably figurative (cf. Ps 88:8; Lam 3:7); however, a literal meaning cannot be ruled out because the poet may have had in mind the condition of a persecuted prisoner, who is near death. Dahood (1970, 316) describes this psalm as "the lament of an Israelite on his deathbed."

Psalm 143

The suppliant in this individual lament has been persecuted by *enemies* (vv. 3, 9, 12). Now in peril of death (vv. 3, 7, 11), the speaker turns to Yahweh and prays for the preservation of an endangered life. In the opening plea (vv. 1-2), the speaker appeals to the *faithfulness* and *righteousness* of Yahweh, but does not follow this appeal with a protestation of innocence (cf. Pss 7:3-5, 8; Job 27:6), but with a further plea that God will *not enter into judgment with your servant.* The basis for the second plea is the universal condition of humanity: *for no one living is righteous before you*

(cf. Ps 130:3; Job 4:17; 9:2; 15:14; 25:4; Gal 2:16). None can gain vindication before God on the basis of their own strength and merit. Verse 2 is not intended as an excuse, but as a confession that no one can lay a claim on God that will gain salvation.

The suppliant's condition is described in vv. 3-6. As in most laments, it is impossible to define the exact circumstances. This person, however, is in a condition that already approximates death, languishing in darkness and perishing *like a parched land.* Nevertheless, the speaker can meditate on the great acts of Yahweh in the past (v. 5) and pray with urgent trust (vv. 6-8). *In the morning* (v. 8) may point to the cultic situation in which a suppliant hopes for divine guidance at dawn (see Pss 5, 17). The suppliant prays for instruction in the will of God (v. 8) and to be taught and led to perform it (v. 10). The speaker prays as a servant of Yahweh whose life and well-being depend on God's *righteousness* (delivering power) and *steadfast love.*

The seven penitential psalms of the church (Pss 6, 32, 38, 51, 102, 130, 143) concluded with this lament. The closing statement of the speaker, *for I am your servant,* is the basis for the prayer that precedes.

Psalm 144

A Davidic psalm, indicated both by its title and by an explicit reference to *David* (v. 10). The psalm has a recognizably canto literary character, making use of material found in other psalms and combining different types of psalm elements in vv. 1-11 and vv. 12-15. The relationship to Ps 18 seems especially close (cf. Ps 18:2; 9; 14; 16; 47 and Ps 144:1-2; 5; 6; 7). The content of vv. 12-15 expresses family-community ideas of well-being and prosperity, content that seems to have no formal relation to vv. 1-11 and that constitutes the speech of one who either prays for the nation or expresses the results of a fulfillment of the prayer in v. 11. The disparity of the parts of the psalm probably reflects the reuse of Davidic-kingship prayer by the postexilic Israelite community. The Davidic tradition is recalled and reused for a community which needs to identify with David and Yahweh's great intervention for him. The monarchy is a thing of the distant past, but the traditions of David live on.

The language of v. 2c seems a bit out of place: *subdues the peoples under me* (NRSV "peoples" is probably to be preferred to the Hebrew "my people" and is supported by some ms. evidence and Ps 18:48). The repeated references to requests to be delivered from the power (*hand*) of foreigners (vv. 7 and 11) points to Israel under the domination of foreign powers after 587 B.C.E. A king as the speaker is not required; rather the Israelite community is praying a king's prayer for Yahweh to "subdue peoples" again (as he had done for David) and break the grip of foreign powers.

The prayer in vv. 1-11 is especially pertinent because of vv. 3-4, which express the finitude and weakness of mortal human beings (cf. Pss 8:4; 90:5-6; 146:3-4), a condition felt acutely by the communities of the exilic and postexilic eras. The community longs for a theophanic intervention by Yahweh to set it free from the *mighty waters* of oppressive domination and the *hand of aliens* (vv. 5-7). The community would delight to take up the vow of the king to praise God for such deliverance (vv. 9-10; translate v. 10b with past tense, "the one who rescued David, his servant"). The Davidic king from the past speaks for the community in v. 11 (the "right hand of falsehood" in vv. 8 and 11 indicates those who swear oaths false or break them, or both—people who cannot be trusted because they break their commitments).

Verses 12-15 may be read as prayer, but this is not certain. It is easier to read these verses as statements descriptive of the people, and the conditions that would result from the deliverance prayed for in v. 11 (v. 12 begins with a relative pronoun, probably added to the text to relate what follows to v. 11, and it can be read as "in order that" or "so that our sons . . . "). The superb description of a healthy and strong community in vv. 12-14 is applicable to every age (disregard the *no exile* in v. 14 and read, "no cry of distress in our public places"). Verse 15 refers to the good conditions of vv. 12-14: "How well-off are the people for whom this would be so!" (for the *happy* or "blessed" of v. 15 see, e.g., Pss 1:1; 34:8; 84:4; 5; 15; 112:1; 127:5; 128:1).

Psalm 145

The skilled use of the alphabetic-acrostic form of poetry marks this hymn. Each verse begins with a successive letter of the Hebrew alphabet (the letter *nun*, missing from MT, is supplied by 11QPs[a], LXX, and Syriac, and appears as v. 13cd in RSV and NRSV). The psalm has some similarities with Ps 111. Psalm 145 weaves together declarations of praise in first person (vv. 1-2, 5-6, 21) with praise in third person (vv. 3, 7-9, 12, 14, 17-20) and praise directed to Yahweh in second person, *your works*, etc. (vv. 4, 7, 10-11, 13, 15-16), providing an intricate poetic structure. The individual speaker seems to be meditating on the praise found in the third person sections (v. 5) and addressing God with praise in the second person verses. Calls to praise alternate with grounds for praise.

In general, the psalm divides into two major sections: vv. 1-9, praise of the might and power of Yahweh (v. 3), and vv. 10-20 praise the kingship of Yahweh (vv. 10-13), including the faithfulness and integrity with which God works. Yahweh's loyal-love provides for the whole creation: *You open your hand, satisfying the desire of every living thing* (v. 16). Yahweh's faithfulness and justice holds together the creation, which depends on his open hand (cf. Ps 104:27-30). The just and reliable ways of Yahweh are especially evident to those who love him, fear him, and call upon him (vv. 17-26). The royal power of Yahweh is used to care for the needy. On the other hand, *the wicked* can expect destruction (v. 20b). Verse 21 closes the psalm with a vow of praise on the part of the speaker and a summons to *all flesh* to *bless his holy name forever and ever* ("all" also is found in the Hebrew text of vv. 2, 9, 10, 13, 14, 15, 16, 17, 18, 20, and 21).

"Of David." Psalm 145 is the last psalm attributed to DAVID in a series of eight psalms (138–145), and in the Book of Psalms. The LXX has Ps 151, which is said to be a genuine but supernumerary Davidic psalm. Psalm 151 is found also (with some different content) in the Qumran scroll 11QPs[a]. Psalm 151 is a poetic account of how the young shepherd David came to be the ruler of Israel, and is a midrash on 1 Sam 16:1-13 (the David and Goliath narrative). It attempts to describe what Yahweh saw in David's heart (1 Sam 16:7) that led to the anointing by Samuel and David's rise to power. (See "Psalm 151" in MCB, below.)

Psalm 145 has had extensive usage in both Jewish and Christian liturgies. In Jewish settings the psalm may be recited daily in the synagogues for morning, noon, and evening prayers. In one liturgical tradition it is called *Ashrei* ("Blessed") because its recitation is preceded by Pss 84:5(4) and 144:15. In Christian usage v. 2 is included in the "Te Deum," a hymn of praise. Verses 10, 15-16 are used in grace before meals.

Book five terminus? Psalm 145 may be considered as the last psalm of book five of the Hebrew Psalter, since Pss 146–150 form a final set for the Psalter as a whole (Holladay 1993, 80). If this is true the Psalter begins and ends with psalms attributed to David (Pss 3–41 and 138–145). In book five, the Davidic Pss 108–110 and Pss 138–145 bracket Pss 111–137. Psalm

107 constitutes a bridge between books four and five, picking up the gathering of the exiles in Ps 106:4 (MT 107:2-3). Psalm 118 begins and ends with the *O give thanks to the LORD, for he is good* (also used in Pss 104:1; 105:1 and 107:1) and with Ps 107 brackets Pss 108–117. Psalms 108–119 consist of the Davidic Pss 108–110, plus two Hallelujah psalms (111 and 112), and introduce the "Egyptian Hallel" collection in Pss 113–118.

The centerpiece of book five is the massive work of Ps 119, which precedes the "Songs of Ascent" (Pss 120–134). Psalm 119 is a gigantic affirmation of the well-being of those "who walk in the *torah* of Yahweh" (119:1-3). Psalms 135–136 form a supplement to the Songs of Ascent in Pss 120–134 and also bracket back to Pss 111–118 with their "Hallelujah" (*Praise the LORD*) and *O give thanks* beginnings. Psalm 137 stands alone to remind the reader that the setting of book five is the experience of EXILE, with powerful remembrance of Zion-Jerusalem and the dreadful oppression of foreign captors. As noted above, book five moves to its proper conclusion with the Davidic collection in Pss 138–145. This collection is a "little Psalter" in itself, containing the "great notes" of the Psalms: lament and complaint addressed to Yahweh about evildoers and other enemies and praise-thanksgiving-confidence directed toward Yahweh:

> *My mouth will speak the praise of the LORD,*
> *and all flesh will bless his holy name*
> *forever and ever.* (Ps 145:21; cf. 138:1)

Psalm 146

An individual speaker voices praise of Yahweh in this hymn, with a somewhat unusual warning against putting trust in human beings (vv. 3-4). This element is more germane to a thanksgiving psalm, as is the *Happy are those* statement in v. 5, but thanksgiving is a form of praise and the elements are frequently mixed (cf. *Happy is* declaration in Ps 33:12). This psalm brings together praise of God as creator (vv. 1-6) with praise of God as redeemer who delivers the oppressed and cares for the needy (vv. 7-9). Verse 10 declares the everlasting reign of Yahweh, the God of Zion.

The psalm opens with a singer vowing to praise Yahweh *all my life long*. Turning from personal commitment to the listeners in vv. 3-4, the speaker warns them of the futility of trusting in human power and position (read *princes* in v. 3 as "those of influence and power"). On the other hand, the helper of human beings is God; the person who puts hope in the plans and purpose of the creator is in a condition of true happiness (vv. 5-7). The security of those who do trust God is not founded upon mortals, but upon Yahweh who has and continues to demonstrate his power to save (vv. 7-9). The hymn calls for full confidence in God and full dependence upon him.

There are few, if any statements in the OT that exceed vv. 6-9 in describing the basic nature of Yahweh (cf. Ps 113:4-9). He is not described with static concepts or attributes, but with participial constructions that are characteristic of the hymns and of Israelite theology. Yahweh is a God who acts, and is, therefore, known through actions. It has been noted (Weiser 1962) that each case where Yahweh demonstrates his efficacy involves situations where human power falls short. Human beings for whom God is dead are without hope. However, those who put their trust in Yahweh are to be congratulated (v. 5); their confidence and hope will not be disappointed.

Psalm 146 is the first of a series of five HALLELUJAH psalms that form a collection that closes the Psalter. Each of these psalms is formed by "Hallelujah" (*Praise the LORD*) at the beginning and end; a tenfold use can hardly be accidental. In addition, the verb *halel* ("praise") is used in its plural imperative form (*praise you . . .*) ten times in Ps 150 and eight times in Ps 148, plus two imperfect forms that serve the same purpose for a total of ten. These five psalms (Pss 146–150) form a final doxology of praise, a jubilate that climaxes in Ps 150:6: *Let everything that breathes praise the LORD!*

Psalm 147

The second of the Hallelujah hymns stresses one main theme: the creation power and providential care of Yahweh for those who *fear him* and *hope in his steadfast love* (v. 11). His power and sustaining care are demonstrated in the natural order (vv. 4-5, 7-9, 15-18) and in the salvation-history of Israel (vv. 2, 12-13, 19-20). The date of the psalm's origin is rather clearly postexilic (v. 2). Perhaps it originated with the rebuilding of the Temple in the time of HAGGAI and ZECHARIAH or with the work of NEHEMIAH (445 B.C.E.) in rebuilding the walls of Jerusalem (vv. 12-13). The LXX divides it into two psalms (vv. 1-11 and vv. 12-20) and gives to both titles that refer to Haggai and Zechariah. Indeed, the psalm seems to be "stitched together" (Stuhlmueller 1988, 493).

The connection of Yahweh's tremendous power in creation with his tender providential care of Israel is the dominant feature of vv. 1-6. Both RSV and NRSV obscure the PARALLELISM of v. 1, which is retained in NIV: "How good it is to sing praises to our God, / how pleasant and fitting to praise him!" (cf. REB). Verse 2 seems to refer to the rebuilding of Jerusalem and the return of exiles after 538 B.C.E. A striking contrast is found in v. 6: Yahweh is the one who restores the humble (or, meek), but he is also the one who *casts the wicked to the ground*. This is the God who *builds up Jerusalem* and *gathers the outcasts of Israel* (v. 2; cf. Ps 102:16).

A new section begins with v. 7 and Yahweh is praised for the way in which he sustains the natural order of the world (cf. Ps 104:14-23; 27-30). This section concludes with the declaration that Yahweh takes pleasure only in *those who fear him* and who depend upon *his steadfast love* (vv. 10-11).

Yahweh's blessing of Israel is praised in vv. 12-20. Israel's status as the people of Yahweh results in many blessings, but the one above all is the gift of the *word* (vv. 15-20). Yahweh's *word* of *command* (vv. 15 and 18) sets in motion the natural processes of the land (vv. 16-18) that sustain life on the earth. *The waters flow* before his *word* and *wind* (spirit). Yahweh's creating and controlling *word* (vv. 15-18, cf. Ps 33:6-7; Isa 55:10-11) has also been given to Israel in the *statutes and ordinances* of Yahweh (vv. 19-20). This is Israel's peculiar privilege, which is shared with no other nation (cf. Deut 4:7-8; Acts 14:16). The *statutes and ordinances* (synonyms for *torah* or "law") are the expressions of the divine will, which have been given for Israel's guidance as the covenant people.

Psalm 148

This is a superb hymn of praise. Its style shows the influence of the type of writing that enumerated lists of the various features of the heavens and the earth, a style found in the teaching of the Egyptian wise man Amenemope (fl. ca. 11th c. B.C.E.) and reflected in Job 38 (cf. Pss 33, 104). The psalm itself divides into two main parts. Verses 1-6 summon the heavenly host to praise Yahweh for his work of creation (v. 5). As in Ps 19, the heavenly bodies are treated as parts of Yahweh's creation. The view of the universe is common to the ancient Near east and reflected in several OT passages (see Gen 1; Ps 104). Yahweh not only created the heavens and the heavenly bodies, but he fixed their relative positions and functions (v. 6).

He is both creator and sustainer of his creation (see Gen 8:22; Hos 2:21-22; Jer 31:35-36; 33:25; Job 28:23-26; 38:8-38; Ps 135:7; etc.).

In vv. 7-14, the praise of Yahweh is summoned *from the earth*. Again, God's absolute command of the forces of nature is affirmed. The summons to the natural world (vv. 7-10) becomes a summons to *all peoples . . . of the earth* (vv. 11-12). The reason for Yahweh's praise is the exalted status of his *name* and *glory* (v. 13). A final testimony (v. 14) points to a festival congregation of devoted and loyal people. Yahweh has *raised up a horn* for them (i.e., given them strength and victory). He has provided them with a *praise*, or a hymn, that recounts his marvelous acts of creation and salvation history.

The praise of God called for by this psalm is marked by its comprehensive scope. Leslie Allen (1983, 316) notes how the word "all" (it appears ten times) in this psalm "rings out in a striving for totality of praise." Praising God sets off a chain reaction that continues without end, generating its own energy as it spreads.

Psalm 149

The fourth of the five HALLELUJAH Psalms (146, 147, 148, 149, 150) that close the Psalter is a hymn that is marked by a strong warlike character. A long tradition of interpretation links the psalm to a victory of the Israelites in the postexilic period, most commonly related to the events of Maccabean times. The general language of the psalm, however, provides little evidence for such an interpretation. Another interpretation reads the psalm as an eschatological depiction of the triumph of God's cause and future victory over his foes. This approach also seems forced onto the more natural interpretation of the psalm. It is easier to understand the basic orientation of the psalm in terms of a cultic situation, and the most reasonable hypothesis is to assume that it reflects the festival context of Tabernacles, and participation in the celebration by the assembled worshipers in its ceremonies.

The people are urged to praise Yahweh in vv. 1-4. They are to *sing . . . a new song* (cf. Pss 33:3; 96:1; 98:1; 144:9) *in the assembly of the [covenant] faithful* (v. 1). A *new song* is one appropriate for the occasion, one that expresses the new reality of the worship experience as it also revives the spirit of the people. The singing is to be accompanied with music and dancing, for Yahweh has been gracious to his people and has given them salvation (*victory*, v. 4). *The humble* (v. 4) refers to the assembled worshipers. The songs of joy and *high praises of God* are already in their mouths and throats, ready for use.

The *assembly of the faithful* are urged to execute judgment on the enemies of God in v. 5-9 (the translation of *nqm* as *vengeance* [v. 7] should be dropped; see commentary on Ps 94:1). The background here is probably that of a ritual battle drama in which the enemies of Yahweh and of Zion, led by their kings, are routed, defeated, and judged (see Ps 2, 46, 48). Verse 5 refers to the reclining of the worshipers during the festival, probably, during a night that preceded the ritual combat in the morning of the following day. In the Jewish traditions of the Festival of Tabernacles as found in the Mishnah, there is a record of a night ceremony with torches carried by the people while they sang songs and praises and the Levites played various musical instruments. These celebrations continued until the cockcrow of dawn. This later ceremony probably preserved elements of earlier ones.

There is a history of unfortunate Christian interpretation of this psalm. It has been used more than once to justify participation in war and the taking of revenge on enemies, who were conveniently classified as the "enemies of God." Verse 9 declares that it is *glory for all his faithful ones* to carry out the *judgment* of Yahweh. The *judgment* of God is not executed by Christians by means of a sword, but with a cross.

Walter Brueggemann (1984, 27) says that psalms of praise like Pss 146–148 can be used as a form of social control by entrenched people of power. Thus it is important that in the midst of the exalted praise of Pss 146–150 there is in Ps 149 a statement of "sobering realism" (Brueggemann 1984, 166). Praise keeps at least one foot firmly planted in the messy reality of this world. Yahweh is praised in this psalm because: (1) he *takes pleasure* in the welfare of his people and exalts *the humble with victory* (v. 4) and (2) he executes judgment on the nations, which rebounds to the glory of his faithful people (vv. 7-9). As noted above, *vengeance* in v. 7 should be disregarded and understood as the vindication of the faithful and the imposition of order on the nations in accord with the divine will (regarding *nqm*, mistranslated "vengeance," see commentary on Ps 94).

Psalm 150

The last psalm of the Hebrew Psalter, and the last of the five Hallelujah psalms, is marked by the repeated use of the imperative form of "praise" (see above

on Ps 146). The tenfold use of the imperative form of the verb *halel* is augmented by the use of the imperfect form in v. 6, plus the HALLELUJAH at the beginning and end of the psalm, for a total of thirteen times. Jewish tradition was aware, of course, of the symbolism of the number ten (e.g., the Decalogue or "ten words"; Exod 34:38; Deut 4:13) as well as of thirteen (the thirteen times God speaks in Gen 1 and the thirteen divine attributes in Exod 34:6-7 [Stuhlmueller 1988, 494]).

The psalm emphasizes the place of music and musical instruments in Israelite worship, but the details and exact use of the various instruments is difficult to fix. The *trumpet* mentioned is the *shofar*, the ram's horn used for signals as well as for praise (cf. Josh 6:4-5; Judg 3:27; 1 Kgs 1:34; 39; Isa 18:3; Pss 47:5; 81:3; 98:6). Stringed, wind, and percussion instruments are also listed. The enumeration of the instruments includes those more closely associated with priests (*trumpet . . . lute and harp*) and those of more secular relationship. All of them are called into the service of the divine praise. Priest and laity, indeed *everything that breathes*, is exhorted to praise Yahweh. Praising God is the goal of all life, of every living thing. Psalms 146–150 tell us that "the proper mode of existence for humankind and all creation is relatedness to God" (McCann 1993b, 56), and praise is indispensable for that mode. Praise of God is the breath of life. A closing Hallelujah ends the psalm, the Hallelujah collection that began with Ps 146, book five, and the canonical Psalter.

Summary of Book Five

To focus on the basic message of book five is a daunting task. Book five is the largest of the five books of the Psalter and highly varied. Any attempt to systematize the content of so diverse a collection should be approached cautiously.

First, a setting in postexilic Israelite communities seems rather clear. In this regard, Book five belongs to the same general context as book four: note that Ps 106:47 closes with a plea for divine salvation and for the people to be "gathered" from among the nations. The same verb for "gathered" is used in Ps 107:3a:

> *gathered in from the lands,*
> *from the east and from the west,*
> *from the north and from the south.*

This same idea of "gathering" exiles (although with a different verb) is found in Ps 147:2.

A number of passages indicate exilic contexts (e.g., see Pss 118:12-14; 120:5-6; 126:1-6; 129:1-2; 130:5-8). A powerful and direct testimony of postexilic ethos in provided by the placement of Ps 137 ("How could we sing Yahweh's song on foreign soil?") between the Songs of Ascent (Pss 120–134 plus a supplement in Pss 135–136) and the Davidic collection in Pss 138–145.

In some cases the psalms and psalm content may be quite old, but the collection itself is quite late and older psalms have been reread in new contexts. Thus it is not surprising that these psalms declare that Yahweh will provide and protect his people, and that they sometimes contain appeals for the continuation of such divine help. The expressions of "help" are too numerous and varied to cite here. It is sufficient to note that Yahweh is the great "Helper" of his people: *He is their help and their shield* (Ps 115:9, 10, 11); "Our help is in the name of Yahweh, Maker of heaven and earth" (Ps 124:8; see also Ps 146:5-6). The affirmation of Yahweh's faithful, upholding work also is set forth in an excellent way in Ps 145:13-20.

Second, no reader can miss the emphasis on praise in book five that begins with Ps 107. Lament, complaint, and pain are not absent, of course, but praise overcomes lament, and the collection moves toward the crescendo of the five "Hallelujah psalms" in Pss 146–150. Praise is the lifeblood of faith and worship. Israelites far from their homeland, sometimes oppressed, and always in danger of being intimidated by the power and wealth of the nations, found strength to persevere and overcome in the praise of Yahweh's mighty works.

> Praise the LORD. . . .
> Put not trust in princes or in any mortal,
>   for they have no power to save. . . .
> The LORD your God, O Zion, will reign forever.
>   (Ps 146:1, 3, 10, author trans.)

The speaker in Ps 145 (which actually closes book five) vows:

> *My mouth will speak the praise of the LORD,*
>   *and all flesh will bless his holy name*
>   *forever and ever.* (145:21)

Third, the basic theme of book five seems to be set in Ps 107:1:

> *O give thanks to the LORD, for he is good;*
>   *for his steadfast love endures forever.*

Book five tests whether or not these declarations are true and affirms how they are true.

The affirmation that *he is good* is repeated in Ps 118:1, 29 (the beginning and end of the psalm), 135:3, and 136:1. Yahweh is addressed directly in Ps 119:68—*You are good and do good*—and he is asked to *let your good spirit lead* the speaker in 143:10. The judgments of Yahweh are said to be *good* in Ps 119:39 (cf. 119:66). The *abundant goodness* of Yahweh is declared in Ps 145:7 and Yahweh is said to be *good to all* with his compassion extended to *all that he has made* in v. 9 of the same psalm.

Likewise, the references to the *steadfast love* of Yahweh are especially numerous and striking in book five, appearing sixty times (twenty-six times in Ps 136 alone). Yahweh's *steadfast love* is described as *higher than the heavens* while his *faithfulness reaches to the clouds* (Ps 108:4); thirty-three times his *steadfast love* is said to *endure forever* (Ps 107:1; five times in Ps 118; twenty-six times in Ps 136; 138:8; elsewhere in the OT in Ps 106:1; 1 Chr 16:34; 41; 2 Chr 5:13; 7:3; 6; 20:21; Ezra 3:11). Rather clearly book five was intended to assure postexilic Israelite communities that the *steadfast love* of Yahweh, so powerfully demonstrated in the past (e.g., Pss 106:7-8; 107:8, 15, 21, 136), was still extended to them.

Fourth, the book emphasizes the continuing significance of Zion (Jerusalem) for all who worship Yahweh. Israelites dispersed to the far corners of the known world could still anticipate the actual experience of pilgrimage to the joyous festivals at Zion (cf. Songs of Ascent in Pss 120–34). For those who could not go and had to remain at home, the reports and testimonies of those who did would have been good news (cf. Ps 48). Zion was still the chosen place of Yahweh's habitation (Ps 132:13-14), still the center of the world, theologically speaking, and a place of paradise on earth. Zion was still a place fundamentally different from the rest of the world, *perfection of beauty*, whence God shined forth into the world (Ps 50:2), and where pilgrims drank from *the river of your delights* and from the *fountain of life* (Ps 36:7-9; cf. Pss 122; 132:15-17). From Zion the blessing of Yahweh, *maker of heaven and earth*, went forth (Ps 134:3), and in time Zion would dominate the world (Isa 2:2-4; Mic 4:1-5).

Finally, what of Ps 119? This huge psalm, a psalter in itself, is enigmatic and is indeed a challenge. As noted in the commentary on Pss 1 and 2, it has been suggested that Ps 119 closed an earlier collection of the Psalms, forming a Torah-Psalter. The last appearance of *torah* in the present Psalter is in Ps 119:174, an observation that may or may not be significant. I suggest that Ps 119 is placed in its present position in order to link book five with an earlier Torah-Psalter. It is also possible that Ps 119 was placed after Ps 105 in an earlier collection, as a prelude to Ps 106 and as the end of book four (Ps 105 ends with the expected outcome of the saving history of Yahweh as *that they might keep his statutes and observe his [torah]*, v. 45; Ps 106 laments the failure of the Israelites to do so).

In any case, the present position of Ps 119 may be suggestive. It follows the Hallelujah-thanksgiving-praise series in Pss 111–118, which centers around the deliverance of Israel from Egypt in Pss 113–115 and is placed immediately before the Songs of Ascent in Pss 120–134 (plus Pss 135–136 that appears to be a supplement) with their strong emphasis on Zion. although *torah* does not appear in connection with Zion anywhere in book five, the juxtaposition of the great Torah-psalm (Ps 119) is suggestive of the declarations that Yahweh's *torah* will go forth from Zion (Isa 3:2; Mic 4:2).

Regardless of validity of these matters of shaping and arrangement in the Psalter, *torah* and praise belong together (as in Ps 19). Those who are blessed "to walk in the *torah* of Yahweh" (119:1) are those for whom the praise of God is natural. They are ready for the summons of the Hallelujahs of book five and convert the whole of the Psalter into *t^ehillim* ("praises"), its Hebrew title, and a primal expression of faith.

Works Cited

Allen, Leslie. 1983. *Psalms 101–150*. WBC.

Bos, Johanna W. H. 1993. "Psalm 87," *Inter* 47:285.

Brueggemann, Walter. 1984. *The Message of the Psalms*.

Craigie, Peter C. 1983. *Psalms 1–50*. WBC.

Dahood, Mitchell. 1966. *Psalms 1–50*. AncB. 1968. *Psalms 51–100* AncB. 1970. *Psalms 101–150*. AncB.

Durham, John I. 1971. "Psalms" in BBC.

Gerstenberger, Erhard S. 1988. *Psalms*. Part 1. FOTL.

Goulder, Michael. 1982. *The Psalms of the Sons of Korah*. JSOTSup. 1990. *The Prayers of David*. JSOTSup.

Gunkel, Hermann. 1929/1968. *Die Psalmen*. 1933/1966. *Einleitung in die Psalmen*.

Hammer, Reuven. 1991. "Two Liturgical Psalms: Salvation and Thanksgiving," *Judaism* 40:491–92.

Hay, D. M. 1973. *Glory at the Right Hand: Psalm 110 in Early Christianity*. SBLMS.

Holladay, William L. 1993. *The Psalms through Three Thousand Years*.

Kidner, Derek. 1975a. *Psalms 1–7*. 1975b. *Psalms 73–150*.

Kirkpatrick, A. F. 1891–1901. *The Book of Psalms*. The Cambridge Bible for Schools and Colleges.

Kraus, Hans-Joachim. 1988. *Psalms 1–59*. 1989. *Psalms 60–150*.

Kselman, John S., and Michael L. Barré. 1990. "Psalms" in *NJBC*.

Kugel, James L. 1986. "Topics in the History of the Spirituality of the Psalms" in *Jewish Spirituality*, 113–44.

Leslie, Elmer A. 1949. *The Psalms: Translated and Interpreted in the Light of Hebrew Life and Worship*.

Levenson, Jon. 1986. "The Jerusalem Temple in Devotional and Visionary Experience," in *Jewish Spirituality*, 32–61.

McCann, J. Clinton, ed. 1993a. *The Shape and Shaping of the Psalter*. JSOTSupp. 1993b. *A Theological Introduction to the Book of Psalms*.

Miller, Patrick D., Jr. 1986. *Interpreting the Psalms*.

Mowinckel, Sigmund. 1951. *The Psalms in Israel's Worship*.

Pietersma, Albert. 1980. "David in the Greek Psalms." VT 30:213–26.

Rad, Gerhard von. 1962. *O.T. Theology*. Vol. 1.

Rendsburg, Gary A. 1990. *Linguistic Evidence for the Northern Origin of Selected Psalms*. SBLMS 43.

Sarna, Nahum M. 1993. *Songs of the Heart. An Introduction to the Book of the Psalms*.

Seybold, Klaus. 1990. *Introducing the Psalms*.

Soll, Will. 1991. *Psalm 119: Matrix, Form, and Setting*. CBQMS.

Spurgeon, C. H. 1874–1892/1966. *The Treasury of David*.

Stuhlmueller, Carroll. 1983. *Psalms 1* and *Psalms 2*. O.T. Message 21, 22. 1988. "Psalms" in *HBC*.

Tate, Marvin E. 1990. *Psalms 51–100*. WBC.

Westermann, Claus. 1989. *The Living Psalms*.

Weiser, Artur. 1959/1962. *The Psalms*. OTL.

Proverbs

David Penchansky

Introduction

Modern Western society divides into political parties, religions, and even competing factions within religions. In this same manner, ancient Israel breaks into distinct and often competing social groupings. These groupings were both political and religious, although the Israelite would not have understood the distinction. Scholars today call the educated class the sages, or the wise ones. These sages wrote Proverbs, as well as other biblical books. In the same way the voice of one conservative radio commentator does not represent the thinking of an entire country, so the sages must be understood as one voice among many in their culture.

Sages argued with each other. They took positions on controversial issues both among themselves and in opposition to other parties of power within Israel. The Book of Proverbs contains some of these controversies. Although the culture of the sage was often at odds with that of other groups in Israel, among themselves they usually reached a consensus, a standard of wisdom acceptable to the community of the Wise. This consensus is most clearly exemplified by faith in the fundamental orderliness and reasonableness of the universe, a complete confidence that "God smiled on the just and sent transgressors straight to hell" (Hassler 1990, 16), and that following the elders' advice brings life and blessing.

A few questioned the eternal verities. In scripture, readers see imprints of discussion between the dominant group of sages and these questioners. Traces of their doubt or skepticism remain in the text. Thus, although the writings maintain the dominant position, doubt became canonized as it played a role in the discussions that eventually produced Proverbs.

Scholars characterize the book as part of the corpus known as WISDOM LITERATURE. Wisdom literature features two chief concerns: first, an attempt to draw insight from careful observation of the world; second, an effort carefully to assemble and preserve the accumulated insights of previous generations of sages and elders. Proverbs offers instruction in some of the more practical aspects of wisdom. It tells how to get along in life. Much of the book instructs the young student on how one should conduct oneself as an official of the royal court.

The disagreements among the sages derive from the two sources of wisdom mentioned above. The scientific-like observations made by the individual sage often conflict with the appeal to the traditions, the accumulated insights of society. The two differing stances typify the chief concerns of wisdom. First, and most common in Proverbs, is a supreme confidence, a certitude about the ways of the world and about the correct means of advancement in the world. Second, one finds sacred doubt, the questioning of society's truths. Proverbs is the actual arena for this conflict, containing both positions.

Authorship

The ancient collectors of this material ascribed most of it to the fabled King SOLOMON. In Proverbs, the significance of authorship lies not in the question of the origin of the material, but in its authority. When one attributes words to a figure who looms as large in Israel's history as Solomon, who has such a reputation for wisdom in the tradition of Israel, one enables the literature ascribed to him to seem much more persuasive.

Names arise in the book to which no significant tradition is connected, names such as *Lemuel* (31:1, 4) and *Agur* (30:1). Perhaps they were famous at some point in the past, but such information is no longer available to a contemporary reader. The various "authors" cited do suggest a boundary between the particular collections. Most collections begin with the ascription by name to a particular figure or group. Such ascriptions contribute little to our understanding of individual proverbs or individual collections of proverbs, but they do give an air of authority to the statements that follow. These statements claim to be written by men who have a reputation in Israel for wisdom and for access to the upper reaches of power.

Tribal Wisdom. Historical evidence exists for the identification of three distinct purveyors of Wisdom. The earliest form of Wisdom was transmitted orally—presumably never written down—and passed on from parents to children. This early form of Wisdom is commonly called Tribal Wisdom because it reflects an agricultural and pastoral world, offering advice to farmers and the keepers of livestock. These texts provide a raw, common-sense approach to daily life. There is much in Proverbs that brings to the forefront the economic reality of this world of commerce, a world of false weights and measures, of failed crops and livestock.

This accumulated wisdom likely formed into collections, and was enshrined in writing, localized either by clan, family, tribe or even region. These collections of tribal wisdom no longer exist in any "pure" form, but are incorporated into larger collections that originate in a different cultural setting.

Royal Wisdom. Scholars of wisdom literature locate a second type of wisdom found in schools and the royal courts of Israel and Judah. The schools were probably coextensive with the royal court. They functioned to train the children of the bureaucratic functionaries (the "Princes") to take their roles of middle-management leadership in Israel.

In Israel a distinctive class of individuals known as "sages" emerged; they were the teachers and leaders of the "schools." The sages were a cultural elite who defined the intellectual, scientific and aesthetic standards of the Israelite aristocratic society. They taught the children, including those of the royal family; they became advisors to the king and were often the chief foreign policy strategists and economic planners.

It would appear that the sages used the early collections of the accumulated wisdom of the ways of the royal court, combined with older collected sapiential reflections—the Tribal Wisdom—not as a guidebook for the sages themselves (presumably they had internalized these directions) but as a kind of drill book for Israelite youth.

This type of wisdom produces advice that is much more cautious and reserved than what is found among the tribal elders. The writings urged extreme care when navigating the dangerous world of royal politics, in which supporting the wrong faction could lead to one's execution. The advice is cautious and state-supportive. The Wise advised the prospective royal functionaries to keep their mouths shut and to listen to their elders, while making their way up the administrative ladder.

Philosophical Wisdom. The sages produced another type of literature, as well, called Philosophical Wisdom. Although this type of Wisdom is most commonly associated with the Books of Job and Ecclesiastes, it also finds a place in the Book of Proverbs. This literature reflects upon the deep issues of life, the problems of evil and innocent suffering, for instance, or the absence and the darkness of God.

Structure

Proverbs, as it has appeared in versions for the last twenty centuries, divides into several different collections, with some overlap. Each collection can be distinguished by a noted and obvious prologue that introduces what follows and distinguishes it from what came before. To a lesser degree, the collections appear to divide on the basis of genre or style. A new collection is often characterized by a new type of literature.

The first collection, 1:1–9:18, is one of the most philosophical. It begins, *The proverbs of Solomon, son of David, king of Israel*, and consists of lengthy poems on the importance of following the elders' advice. Most notably, two strong women appear in this collection, often designated Dame Folly and Dame Wisdom. Each in her own way contrives to seduce a sexually innocent young man.

The second collection, 10:1–22:16, is the lengthiest and, according to many, the oldest collection in the book. It begins with the ascription, *The proverbs of Solomon*. It mainly consists of short pithy sayings, most akin to what we think of by the English word PROVERB. The Hebrew word has a much wider range of meaning, including parable, riddle, and fable. Short proverbs, like compressed pills of accumulated wisdom, are sometimes collected according to similarity of topic; more commonly, however, they are strung together quite randomly.

The remaining collections are briefer and will be grouped as follows: the third (22:17–24:22) is introduced by the phrase *The words of the wise*. Included with this section is a small group of proverbs introduced by the words: *These also are sayings of the wise* (24:23-34). The fourth, traced to *the officials of King Hezekiah* who served as copyists, is found in

25:1–29:27. The fifth, *the words of Agur* (30:1-33) and *the words of King Lemuel* (31:1-9), will be handled together, along with a lengthy acrostic poem about the *capable wife* (31:10-31). The commentary, therefore, will divide into five unequal sections.

In the outline and commentary the material is arranged topically within the several sections of the book. Readers should read through the indicated sections first and then turn to the discussion of the topics. In this way readers will gain a clearer picture of the social world of the Wise and also a better understanding of their counsel to their age and to any age.

In the outline readers will find references to the most important texts in the relevant sections of the Book of Proverbs dealing with the subject listed.

For Further Study

In the *Mercer Dictionary of the Bible*: ORACLE; PROVERB; PROVERBS, BOOK OF; RIDDLE; SOLOMON; WISDOM IN THE OT; WISDOM LITERATURE.
In other sources: S. H. Blank, "Proverbs, Book of," IDB; J. Crenshaw, *Old Testament Wisdom, Prolegomena to the Study of Wisdom*, "Proverbs, Book of," AncBD, and *Wisdom in the Old Testament*; C. R. Fontaine, "Proverbs," HBC; T. P. McCreesh, "Proverbs," NJBC; R. Murphy, *The Tree of Life*; G. von Rad, *Wisdom in Israel*; R. N. Whybray, "Proverbs, Book of." IDBSup.

Commentary

An Outline

The First Collection: Dame Wisdom and Dame Folly, 1:1–9:18

Introduction, 1:1-6

For the attribution of the collection to King SOLOMON, see the introduction. Verses 2-6 express the purpose of the book, explaining the results for the diligent listener, the one who obeys these words, and what is to be gained from the study of wisdom. The passage introduces the first collection, 1:1–9:18, although it could have been written later to introduce the entire Book of Proverbs. The section functions to explain the reason for the writing that follows. It claims: "What I am about to say is important—it ought to be attended to very carefully."

Note that very little in this opening section speaks of the kind of life the sage leads, nor does it indicate why someone would want to live a life according to wisdom. The catalogue of benefits for the one who listens to these words consists of synonyms. Interpreters have attempted to develop fine points of distinction among the terms, but they are better treated as synonyms.

The whole might be summarized, "Read this and be wise," or perhaps more properly, "Learn this and know what the wise ones are talking about." The Book of Proverbs is an introduction to a particular kind of technical discussion or discourse used by an interpretive community. We here meet groups of people with shared language and values, for whom various words and descriptions mean the same thing. Skillful and knowledgeable use of these words makes a separation between those who use them and those who do not. It is as though the reader is presented with a codebook for entrance into the community of the wise. Those who enter will know *the words of the wise and their riddles* (v. 6).

The Fear of the LORD, 1:7

In a few texts we are presented with a particular activity that is identified as the beginning of wisdom. In this section, the first one occurs in 1:7 (and again in 9:10), where the text ascribes the honor of the first place to *the fear of the LORD* (see also Ps 111:10 for the same expression). In 4:7, the first thing is to simply *Get wisdom*. The word *beginning* implies primacy, either in importance, or foundationally, or temporally. That is, "Before you can gain any wisdom, you must do this first."

Fear implies a kind of relationship to superior power. One never fears (using this Hebrew word) anything that lacks authority over others. But beyond that, the particular content remains to be defined, it is defined in various ways. We are told that *the fear of the LORD* is "to hate evil" (8:13), or that it consists of *instruction in wisdom* (15:33). The results of this fear are wonderful. The fear of the Lord *prolongs life* (10:27); (gives) *strong confidence* (14:26); and *is a fountain of life* (14:27). We learn that it is better to have *a little* with this fear than to be fantastically wealthy (15:16). It enables one to avoid evil (16:6). It brings success.

We might therefore conclude regarding these words, first, that wisdom is a language, a discourse by which to understand the world. This discourse is mastered only through careful attention to the teachings of the wisdom tradition, and the teachings of the established sages. Second, fear characterizes this movement. Wisdom is not a secular notion in Proverbs. It admonishes its members to maintain a vague and undefined attitude of piety toward the Israelite God, promising success to all who do so.

Two Strong Women Woo the Hapless Youth, 7:1–9:18

There are three voices present in this series of long, somewhat related poems. First there is the voice of the parent, identified as father or mother. The entire passage (1:8–9:18) can be understood as the voice of this parent, giving important counsel to a child. This parent presents the child with an allegorical story of a youth torn between two conflicting desires. One voice entices the youth to participate in wickedness. This voice comes first in caricature. An evil gang entices the innocent young person to go out on a raid to steal someone's wealth. This gang seeks among themselves consciously and willfully to excel one another in evil (4:16).

The parental voice admonishes the youth to avoid such people because their way leads to a terrible, painful death. The cartoon-like way the gang is depicted leaves readers without a clue as to their identity. We are not likely to know anyone so utterly evil and destructive.

Although the *loose woman* (2:16-19) is patently dangerous, the description of her is sexually enticing. She is a sexual fantasy, like Mrs. Robinson in the film *The Graduate*: older, experienced, taking charge. It is all the poor young fool can do to keep out of her clutches, for she tempts him with a night of pleasure that, without her, no one can possibly discover. But the youth *goes like an ox to the slaughter* (7:22). In an earlier poem on this *loose woman*, we are told that to follow her causes one to lose honor (5:9), lose wealth (5:10), and to become sick in old age (5:11) and regretful (5:12).

Finally, we hear the voice of Dame Wisdom, who cries in the street, seeking to bring her charges to her home. Our first contact with her (1:20) is more prophetic and didactic than seductive. But in chapter five (vv. 15-20) we encounter dame wisdom in an openly erotic appeal to marital fidelity, the fountain serving as a vaginal image. *May her breasts satisfy you at all times; may you be intoxicated always by her love* (5:19). Such texts function simultaneously on two levels, first to persuade the youth against the erotic appeal of the dangerous and forbidden, that is, to demystify cheating on one's spouse; and second as an exhortation to a life married to wisdom.

Although we will encounter wise women in subsequent collections, we have in this section the fullest and most suggestive figure of Dame Wisdom, who looks more like a wisdom goddess than a virtuous Israelite woman (chap. 8). This lyrical poem divides into three sections. The first (8:1-21) corresponds to the seductive story of Dame Folly, the woman who seduces a young student, inviting him to a secret encounter in her house after her husband had gone away (7:6-20). In contrast, Dame Wisdom persuades her charges by means of a public invitation to a feast. Her proclamation reminds one of Second Isaiah crying out in Yahweh's voice,

Ho, everyone who thirsts, come to the waters;
and you that have no money, come, buy and eat!

(Isa 55:1)

We also think of the great nobleman who invited all the poor and dispossessed to his feast, because those of his own class refused to attend (Matt 22:1-10).

Dame Wisdom invites all the simple. The sages classified many stages and kinds of ignorance that prevented one from understanding the wise. "Simple" is the most innocent kind of stupidity. Here they are the directionless, those without rudder who blunder through life with no idea of what is going on. If only they will eat at Wisdom's table they will gain life! She has prepared for them as carefully as the adulterous woman (Dame Folly) prepared her bedchamber (chap. 7). Here we do not have that wanton sexuality, but rather a coy invitation nonetheless. The reader is left with anxiety as to which woman the simple person will choose to follow.

In the next section of the poem (8:22-31) we encounter an ancient biblical text in which an entirely different religious sensibility bursts in, like a shaft of a different-colored light. The language is beautiful, even touching, but the picture of the divine realm that is disclosed must have alienated many Israelites. It alienates many modern interpreters as well. Wisdom is depicted as a little girl, divinely begotten, the first creation in all the universe. She sits at the feet of the divine creator and delights in his presence. Her power somehow focused YHWH's creative energy, it seems, enabling him to produce the world. The creative activity of these two bears similarities to what is termed a theogony, where a male and a female deity procreate and produce the world.

But the words *daily his delight, rejoicing before him always* (8:30) remain an undiminished burst of joy, maintaining its intensity over the centuries. It was joy that brought the universe into being, not power. Such a message continues to stir the reader, whether one regards Dame Wisdom here as a polytheistic vestige of an old non-Israelite tale, or a symbolical device representing an idea. She sits at God's feet as either *a master worker* or "little child" (NRSV mg.) depending on the way the Hebrew is translated.

She is not the mature woman waiting at her banquet hall for the simple to come. Rather, we note her childhood. When she was a child, the firstborn of YHWH, she played at his feet. And there is no one in creation with primacy over her. The author of the Epistle to the Colossians described the Christ using similar terms, "The firstborn of all creation . . . in him all things . . . were created, . . . through him were all things made" (Col 1:15-16). Had the gender not been changed, one would naturally think that the author was describing the same divine, supernatural person. One may wonder how such a figure got past the late Israelite and Rabbinical censors. Perhaps there were no censors, and the picture of God in late postexilic or early Hellenistic times was far more diverse and perplexing than we usually imagine.

The Israelites thought deeply and developed varied answers to the ultimate questions. Somehow, the late Israelite period brought these differing perspectives together into single works that others read as unitary. The diverse perspectives of Proverbs provide one example. The sages and editors collected in a single book many conflicting ways of answering the same questions.

The final section of this extended poem (8:32–9:18) draws the contrast more explicitly, describing again Dame Wisdom preparing her table for the simple, while Dame Folly sits at the door of her house and invites the simple to stolen water and secret bread. Augustine, the fifth century theologian, reflected upon the added attraction that the word "stolen" contributes to the value of the item. For him, stolen apples carried their appeal into his old age. Folly knows this about people instinctively. The invitations differ so profoundly that the narrative clarifies for the innocent student the immensity of the moral choice that she or he inescapably confronts.

Thus, this extended narrative (chaps. 8–9) exerts a hortatory, persuasive influence. It functions as a sermon does in some modern religious meetings. The sermon lays out a decision in the starkest contrast, with the speaker depicting one choice as unmistakably superior. In the biblical poem the writer shows great skill in depicting the evil choice in persuasive and attractive terms. But what is the choice? The student who chooses Dame Wisdom chooses a certain way to look at the world, choosing at the same time a certain group of people who share these common beliefs. In modern terms we might describe them as distinct interest group within a society.

In religious terms, the sages shared many of the same symbols with the rest of Israel, but they invested these symbols with dramatically different meanings. They also employed different ways of arguing in favor of those meanings. The sages argued, for example, in favor of the law of retribution from a different perspective than did the prophets. Dame Wisdom, then, functions as the personification of this group, the community of wisdom, and also at the same time, as a manifestation of their understanding of and approach to the divine realm. The poem reveals their theology. For some modern Christians, the virgin Mary functions similarly.

This woman, the personification of wisdom, appears later writings as well. She inspires sages such as Ben Sira, the authors of the Wisdom of Solomon, and of the wisdom poem in Baruch, and she is widely believed to have strongly influenced the Hellenistic notion of the *logos* in Jewish philosophy and in the Gospel of John. Such a powerful symbol, while not competing with descriptions of the Israelite God, powerfully tempers the radical MONOTHEISM of later Jewish and Christian theology. Dame Wisdom challenges later interpreters to widen their notions of divine influence and spiritual insight.

The Law of Retribution, 1:18-19

This collection vehemently teaches what is commonly called the law of retribution. The maxims depict the wicked as destined for a terrible fate (1:18–19, 31). Concerning the foreign, strange, or loose woman, *her way leads down to death* (2:18). The good, on the other hand, enjoy rich rewards for their righteousness (2:21). Therefore, the youth is exhorted by the wise parental figures to *trust in the LORD with all your heart* (3:5), which will result in *healing for your flesh* (3:8). Wisdom *will exalt you* (4:8), *place on your head a fair garland* (4:9) and grant you life (4:22) and *healing* (3:8; 4:22). Therefore, being wise involves both *trust*

in the LORD (3:5) and giving generously in support of cultic sacrifice (3:9), with the result being full barns and full vats of wine (3:10).

We are told that following Dame Folly leads to horrible destruction but following the path of wisdom (as now described) leads to financial reward (3:10). Following wisdom also leads to a happy life, for *her income is better than silver, and her revenue better than gold* (3:14), and security (3:23). The confidence in God's governance of the world is undiminished in this wisdom collection:

The LORD's curse is on the house of the wicked
but he blesses the abode of the righteous (3:33).

The Ethical Inscriptions, 3:27-30

In the third chapter we find the first truly ethical teaching in Proverbs, the first hint that wisdom is found in just action. The object of this attention is not specified: *to whom it is due* (v. 27), or more specifically, *your neighbor* (v. 28). These texts refer to specific situations in which a person (here no longer a youth) holds a position of power and is thus able to exercise authority over another. The sage is exhorted not to withhold money (v. 28) or security (v. 29); neither should the sage withhold peace (v. 30) from one who has not harmed him.

Keep Your Heart, 4:23

This passage speaks well to the modern condition, but it is difficult to articulate. *Keep your heart* (see also 4:24-26) seems to refer to strictly controlled speech and behavior. It also has an internal sense, that from which speech and behavior proceeds. The Hebrew term *leb* usually refers more to the thinking processes than to the emotions. *Keep your heart* might then suggest the importance of controlling one's thoughts.

The second part of the verse appears not to represent an elaborate anthropology—i.e., different "humors" pulsing out of the circulatory muscle—but is rather a poetic way of saying, "The heart is very important." Mental discipline provides a key to success.

One must not rest on laurels of privilege, but work hard at internal discipline or control. The old tell the young to exert discipline toward the mastery of an internal skill. It is one thing to have available the accumulated wisdom of previous generations, even to assent to its reliability. It is quite another to employ these insights in the practical living of life.

The Second Collection: The Proverbs of Solomon, 10:1–22:16

This section has a common style that reflects PARAL-LELISM or parallel couplets, and common concerns (see below), but does not have any discernible structure that is distinctive. If one rearranged these proverbs in a random order, that would not appreciably change the impact of the whole. The section is only delineated by an introductory phrase, *The proverbs of Solomon* (10:1), and by a dramatic shift in style after 22:16, which suggests the probability that the collection ends there. Besides that, there is no development of themes from beginning to end, and no significant thematic or topical arrangement, although there are occasional clusters of two or three couplets with similar topics. Therefore, the passages within this collection will be interpreted topically.

Parenting, 10:1

As with references to mothers and fathers in the first collection (1:1–9:18), here too there remains an ambiguity as to whether the references are to biological parents raising their children or to teachers in the schools. In the case of this collection, the writer probably intends actual parents. This is indicated by references to inheritance and by the intense way that the happiness of the parents is bound up with the success of the child.

The collection makes three separate points regarding the complex relationship between parent and child: (1) A child's character not only reflects upon the character of the parents; it also determines the ultimate happiness of the parents (v. 1). (2) Children should listen to the advice of their parents. Children who reject their parents and parental counsel suffer destruction (20:20). Note the following typical statements: *A fool despises a parent's instruction* (15:5), or, most blatantly: *the one who hates a rebuke will die* (15:10). (3) The sage exhorts the parents to discipline their children, including physical punishment (13:24).

This advice opens up into a general exhortation (similar to the statements in the first collection) to obey instruction and advice from elders. The collection glorifies the dignity and wisdom inherent in old age: *the beauty of the aged is their gray hair* (20:29; cf. 19:20). Proverbs 10:1; 13:1, 24; 15:20; 19:13, 18, 26-27; 20:20; 22:6; 22:15 also exhibit further instances of parental instruction.

Riches and Poverty, 10:2, 16; 11:4; 18:9-11

Whereas the collection presents a single consistent, strongly authoritarian position regarding parenting, the notion of wealth and its lack appears to be a point of significant controversy among the sages. Virtually every societal attitude towards the accumulation of property can be gleaned from the text.

The messages are given to the upper classes and consist of various exhortations to live responsibly with wealth and to understand the role of wealth in society; even so, there is no unanimity. The following positions may be isolated.

(1) Wealth without righteousness will not endure. *Treasures gained by wickedness do not profit, but righteousness delivers from death* (10:2). See also, for example, 10:16; 11:4, 18, 28; 16:8, 16, 19; 17:1; 19:1; 22:1-2.

(2) The righteous will be or become wealthy, while the wicked are invariably poor (10:3). See also 12:27; 13:6, 18, 22-23; 19:10.

(3) Poverty is a result of laziness, get-rich-quick schemes and devotion to pleasure rather than diligent hard work. *The lazy person does not plow in season; harvest comes, and there is nothing to be found* (20:4). See also 10:4, 5, 26; 11:16b; 12:11-12, 24, 27; 13:4, 11; 14:23; 15:19; 18:9-11; 19:15, 24; 20:13, 21; 21:5, 17, 25; 22:13.

(4) Riches are good in that they provide security. Poverty produces a miserable existence. Therefore, it is much better to be rich. *The wealth of the rich is their fortress; the poverty of the poor is their ruin* (10:15). *The poor are disliked even by their neighbors, but the rich have many friends* (14:20). See also 15:15; 18:23; 19:4, 7; 22:7.

(5) It is the sacred responsibility of the rich to care for the poor through generosity and fairness. *Those who oppress the poor insult their Maker, but those who are kind to the needy honor him* (14:31). See also 11:24-26; 19:17; 21:13; 22:9, 16.

(6) There is a bare suggestion that poverty might in fact be the result of injustice in society and not the laziness of the poor themselves. *The field of the poor may yield much food, but it is swept away through injustice* (13:23).

The Speech of the Wise and Foolish, 18:21; 14:5, 25; 16:23-30

Death and life are in the power of the tongue; and those who love it will eat its fruits (18:21). The question that greatly troubled the sage concerned the power and proper use of speech. If we were to over-simplify and divide into two neat categories (a common practice in wisdom literature itself), we might ask, "What are the characteristics of the speech of the wise?" and "What are the characteristics of the speech of the foolish and/or the wicked?" Approached in this way, the material in this section of Proverbs yields the following results.

The speech of the wise is characterized by: (1) Truthfulness. There is no willful effort on the part of the speaker to create the wrong impression. *A faithful witness does not lie* (14:5). *A truthful witness saves lives, but one who utters lies is a betrayer* (14:25).

(2) Aptness. Their words are not spoken thoughtlessly, at an inopportune time. *To make an apt answer is a joy to anyone, and a word in season, how good it is!* (15:23).

(3) Health. Words of the righteous bring healing, both to the speaker and to the community. Wise speakers, through their speech, defuse conflict and promote reconciliation. *The mouth of the righteous is a fountain of life* . . . (10:11a). *The lips of the righteous feed many* . . . (10:21a). *The words of the mouth are deep waters; the fountain of wisdom is a gushing stream* (18:4; see also 12:6).

(4) Kindness. The speech of the wise does not seek the destruction of another individual through desire for personal gain or spite. More positively, wise speech is a source of life to the community. *A soft answer turns away wrath* (15:1a).

(5) Pleasantness. Such speech is pleasant to listen to, aesthetically pleasing, and thereby persuasive.

The mind of the wise makes their speech judicious, and adds persuasiveness to their lips.
Pleasant words are like a honeycomb, sweetness to the soul and health to the body (16:23-24).

Wicked or foolish speech, in contrast, might be described as: (1) desiring to conceal and deceive, fundamentally untrustworthy. *The mouth of the wicked conceals violence* (10:6). *One who winks the eyes plans perverse things; one who compresses the lips brings evil to pass* (16:30).

(2) The intention of evil speech is the unlawful gain of the speaker, often achieved through the promotion of violence. *The getting of treasures by a lying tongue is a fleeting vapor and a snare of death* (21:6).

(3) Wicked speech leads to destruction. It leads, first, to the violent destruction of others through the intention of the speaker. *The babbling of a fool brings ruin near* (10:14b; see also 11:9; 16:27). But ultimately, wicked speech leads to the destruction of those who speak it. *The evil are ensnared by the transgression of their lips* (12:13a).

Although godly speech is prescribed in this section of Proverbs, one must also note the importance of godly silence. A wise person, according to Proverbs is one who speaks seldom. *Whoever belittles another lacks sense, but an intelligent person remains silent. . . . one who is trustworthy in spirit keeps a confidence* (11:12-13). See also 12:23a; 14:17, 29-30; 15:18; 16:32; 17:27-28; 19:11, 19.

In our world of pundits, where we pay experts dearly to speak their knowledge in every conceivable forum, this notion of the silent sage might seem unusual. However, according to the Egyptian model, which was very influential on Israelite wisdom, silence bespeaks a confidence and self-mastery seldom seen in our society.

Sacrifice and Worship, 15:8, 29

It has often been noted that references to "cult," that is, to outward, ritualized, communal religious observances, are sparse in the wisdom literature in general and in Proverbs in particular. The unique "secular" concerns of the sages might perhaps have caused this surprising omission in the literature of an ancient people for whom sacrifice and offering were central. The few references to cult in this section of Proverbs would seem to suggest that, for the sage, purity of purpose and motive were far more important than getting the forms and rituals exactly right (15:8; 15:29; 21:3, 27). In this, the sages agreed with the Israelite prophets throughout the biblical period, who were appalled at the moral laxity of worshipers, those who sang heartily to YHWH and offered expensive sacrifice, while oppressing the poor and the powerless (see for instance Amos 5:21-24). It is interesting to note that these two groups in Israel, whose concerns coincide infrequently, here take up a common cause for justice within the Israelite community.

Also, the writer admonishes the student to be prudent, thoughtful and reflective in worship, as in all other aspects of life. *It is a snare for one to say rashly, "It is holy," and begin to reflect only after making a vow* (20:25).

The Law of Retribution, 11:3-8, 21

The authors of this collection seem to have little difficulty with the notion that evildoers will suffer in their wickedness, while the righteous will be rewarded. What interests us here are the various ways that the punishments and rewards are meted out. That all get exactly what they deserve is never questioned! First, the wicked are thought to suffer punishment in the present, that is, during their lifetimes (11:31; 12:21; 17:13).

Second, punishment will also come at some time in the future, although the notion of some eternal punishment in the afterlife is not present in Proverbs. In the future, the reputation of the wicked will be blotted out (10:7), their hopes will be dashed (11:7), and they and their house will suffer trouble and death (10:25). See also 11:19; 12:21; 17:13. The sufferings of the wicked are caused by their own foolish choices (11:3-8; 11:27; 14:32a). But sometimes the wrath and condemnation of an enforcing deity will destroy the wicked: *Those who devise evil [YHWH] condemns* (12:2; see also 11:21a).

The arguments in this section are so strenuous and insistent that one can only suspect that they are in reaction to a deeply perceived threat to the law of retribution within the sapiential community. The future orientation of most of the punishments implies that at the present time the wicked appear to prosper. Further, there are strong rhetorical flourishes seeking to comfort those deeply troubled by the present state of affairs. *Be assured, the wicked will not go unpunished* (11:21, emphasis added).

Finally, there is a bare hint at more troubling details, the acknowledgement that the actual situation is not as it appears in this confident collection. It seems evident that, in fact, the evil are doing quite nicely. The teacher is desperate to assure that the present sweetness of the evil behavior is only temporary. *Bread gained by deceit is sweet*, we are told, *but afterward the mouth will be full of gravel* (20:17, emphasis added). It remains for the later sections of Proverbs to grapple more fully with this incomplete and misleading doctrine, and for the books of Job and Ecclesiastes to demolish it completely.

Commerce, 11:1-4; 16:11

Characteristic of Proverbs are some very secular comments on conduct in the arena of commerce. For the most part, they are ethically driven. Then, as now, there were ample opportunities to cheat and be cheated when exchanging objects of value. Two areas of trade are highlighted in this section. In the first, the sages focus on honesty. The second is more complex, dealing with issues such as power, naivete, and the consequences of foolish economic choices.

(1) False balances. Before the invention of MONEY (probably around 700 B.C.E.) the exchange of commodities (barter) was replaced by a system of WEIGHTS AND MEASURES of useful and/or precious metals. Their value was determined by balance against fixed weights. It would be relatively easy—and no doubt was common practice—for a merchant to possess two sets of stones, one (heavier) for when he was buying and another (lighter) for selling. Thus he would pay less for purchases, but get higher payment for goods offered for sale. The authors of Proverbs strongly condemned this practice (11:1; see also 16:11, 20:10 and 20:23). The seriousness of the theological explanation for such an economic injunction (*abomination to the LORD* [11:1]) indicates how dependent ancient peoples were on trust to maintain the continuance of the economic system.

Ultimately, these admonitions were not successful. The invention of stamped metal coins, which assured both the purity and the weight of the pieces, replaced balances of weights, because coins were more difficult to counterfeit. The governments themselves then asserted the accuracy of the metallic value objects. In any case, the Bible places responsibility upon the merchant to maintain scrupulous standards; it does not endorse the Latin proverb *caveat emptor* ("Let the buyer beware!").

(2) Frequently, when buyers did not have sufficient value to procure needed commodities they would offer something of value as pledge or surety. Presumably, if at some appointed time the buyer was not able to redeem this pledged object, it would revert to the seller in lieu of the agreed purchase price. For instance, if an individual desired to buy a donkey at the agreed price of three shekels (a unit of weight) of silver, but did not have the silver, the buyer might offer a milk cow as surety until the debt was paid. If after the agreed time, the purchaser did not have the silver, the cow would revert to the one who had made the loan.

The buyer might further complicate the situation by asking a friend to provide the surety. It is here that the sages step in and offer their advice. From their perspective, providing surety for a neighbor or a stranger is the height of foolishness and self-destruction (11:15;

17:18). The language is strong. The writers characterize such dealings as trouble-causing and senseless, but no reason is given. It should be obvious, however, that such economic transactions produce division and hostility within the community.

The sages go one step further and suggest that anyone foolish enough to engage in this kind of economic suicide is "fair game." *Take the garment of one who has given surety for a stranger; seize the pledge given as surety for foreigners* (20:16). The ethical injunctions of caring for the poor and powerless seem not to apply in such situations. It is "found" money, and the person who suffers such loss clearly deserves to lose everything.

We may note some other general points about commerce in Proverbs. There is a category of proverbs that appears simply to observe economic behavior without comment, without judgment. These Proverbs have a faintly ironical and humorous slant on the vagaries of human nature, as if to say, "Aren't we silly, the ways we do things?" Note the following examples: *Some pretend to be rich, yet have nothing; others pretend to be poor, yet have great wealth* (13:7); *"Bad, bad," says the buyer, then goes away and boasts* (20:14; see also 16:26, 18:17).

Court Politics, 16:10, 15

We have already observed that the sages served as counselors to the royal household, serving as part of the palace bureaucracy. This collection within the larger works of the sages contains much advice as to how such royal officials are to regard the king and conduct themselves in the royal court. Such proverbs reflect the ambiguous relationship that Israelites had with their monarchs. On the one hand, they regarded them as the full representatives of God on earth, viewing them much as Egyptians and Babylonians regarded their monarchs (16:10, 15; 20:8). But on the other, the king was subject to YHWH who was the only true king over all Israel (21:1). Therefore, the sages enjoin the king to scrupulous honesty (17:7). The king's limitations required that he surround himself with loyal and intelligent counselors. Only then could he rule his kingdom successfully (15:22; see also 11:14; 20:18). The king's counselors, therefore, were exhorted to serve the king with diligence, loyalty and wisdom.

Ancient Near Eastern kings were enormously powerful; as a result, they were served and approached with great care (19:12; 20:2). Bribes have always been used to gain the ear of the well-connected, and to sway the king and officials towards a particular policy. Moderns call the practice "lobbying." The sages are ambivalent about the morality of bribing one's way to the inner sanctums of power. Its effectiveness is not in question! (18:16; see also 17:8, where a bribe is called *a magic stone*, and 19:6; 21:14). Only one verse raises an ethical objection: *those who hate bribes will live* (15:27).

The picture of the royal court, confirmed in much of the historical material in the Bible, is of a place fraught with danger and intrigue, where choosing the wrong side of an argument could mean imprisonment or execution. It was a place where the king, whether selfishly accumulating wealth and power or diligent to provide for the needs of his people, found himself in an extraordinarily lonely position. Sages looking out for the king's interest were therefore regarded as of the highest value (15:22; see also 11:14; 20:18).

Women and Wives, 12:4; 21:19

More will be said about the role of women in Proverbs when we examine subsequent sections. Here, the picture is clearly prejudicial against women. For the most part, in this section women are regarded as appendages and decorations for their husbands, either for good or ill. *A good wife is the crown of her husband, but she who brings shame is like rottenness in his bones* (12:4; see also 18:22; 19:13). Further, stereotypically, the sages regard women as prone to nagging and quarrelling to get their way, inflicting great misery upon their husbands: *A wife's quarreling is a continual dripping of rain* (19:13b; see also 21:9, 19).

Modern readers may be pleased to note the relative importance given to a woman's character and intelligence over her appearance: *The wise woman builds her house* (14:1); *A gracious woman gets honor* (11:16). But such a sentiment is framed in the most highly charged and offensive terms in one pronouncement: *Like a gold ring in a pig's snout is a beautiful woman without sense* (11:22). Although the comical image of swine jewelry effectively gets the message across, the association of this animal, regarded in Israel as highly unclean, with an unworthy woman is nothing less than abusive language.

We must ask exactly how a woman might be judged *without sense*. Are we speaking of women preoccupied with trivialities and superficialities, preferring the comforts of wealth over the just treatment of the poor? Amos described such women as the "cows of Bashan," who lie on their couches and ask their husbands to bring them drink (Amos 4:1). Or are we rather speaking of strong women who demand justice from their husbands, and for this reason are regarded as *contentious and fretful* (21:19)?

Individual Human Emotions, 13:12; 14:13

Some parts of Proverbs, as we have seen, are deeply grounded in the times in which they were produced, whether for good or ill. They share the prejudices and the common sense of an era that we have come to regard as unenlightened. Characteristic of the Israelite mentality is the notion of group ethos. Ancient peoples in general did not regard the individual as supremely important in relation to the desires and activities of the community. In modern Western society, individuals and their fulfillment are everything, it sometimes seems.

Even so, the insights of Proverbs on the complexities of *individual* emotional life are remarkable! There is a recognition that separate human persons have deep and important inner experiences that shape who they are. Such emotions work at profound levels, both to heal and to destroy. As one might imagine, the poetry that contains such insights is many times more complex than the average proverbial couplet in this section of Proverbs. A number of insights are gleaned from an examination of these passages: (1) Profound inner emotions are caused by outer developments, for example, by news that either fulfills expectations or dashes them! (13:12,17; see also 12:25).

(2) Emotions, by their very nature, will either heal or destroy the inner self. Their effect on the body is worse than physical illness. (18:14; 17:22; see 15:13b).

(3) Emotions, the way we truly feel inside, can never be fully shared with another: *The heart knows its own bitterness, and no stranger shares its joy* (14:10).

(4) Emotions, important as they are, are difficult to pin down. Can we ever really know exactly how we feel, or exactly what others are feeling? The sages wisely note the fundamental ambivalence of the world of human emotions: *Even in laughter the heart is sad, and the end of joy is grief* (14:13). Feelings are important, powerful, and yet impossible to understand.

Theology and the Mystery of the Divine, 15:3, 11; 21:1

We have already spoken of the "secular" nature of wisdom and of Proverbs in particular. Further, we have noted the relative inattention to cultic concerns on the part of the wise persons who assembled this collection.

But there is a profound piety at the very heart of these reflections and in the sapiential sensibility as such. Proverbs bespeaks a profound sense of divine mystery. It displays a strong recognition that God is so wholly other as to be unapproachable and—more importantly—incomprehensible. Surprisingly, those supreme representatives of the intellectual tradition in Israel recognize the limitations of human wisdom. Perhaps this is the source of their sadness, their disappointment with the circumstances and possibilities of life.

The sages make many claims about their God; we note the following assertions: (1) YHWH has unique and total insight into all aspects of the human psyche; for this reason the deity can effectively evaluate humans and refine their character (15:3, 11; 16:2; 17:3; 20:12, 27; 21:2).

(2) YHWH controls all things. This belief has three implications for the sage. First, it diminishes the importance of human intention and efforts (16:1; see also 16:9; 19:21; 20:24; 21:30-31.) Second, even the destructive side of creation is attributed to divine activity (16:4). Third, this divine control provides a basis for divination, telling the future through the operation of sacred LOTS, something like flipping a coin (16:33).

Further, divine control of the human will provides a key theological understanding of the courtier's ways with a king. The sage must recognize that the will of the king is not absolute: *The king's heart is a stream of water in the hand of the LORD; he turns it wherever he will* (21:1). Therefore, the sage must focus on conforming to the discerned will of the divine king rather than to that of the human king.

(3) The sage must depend upon God, considering the deity's power and control over all things. Faith characterizes the inner life of the sage (16:3). Note the tension between the notion of God's control and the importance of faith. Looked at in one way, it does not matter what one does, for God is in control and will do whatever the deity wills. But some texts indicate that God's control requires human response by commitment to God's ways (16:3).

(4) *The rich and the poor have this in common: the LORD is the maker of them all* (22:2). This text implies an important ethical injunction that has enormous implications for the personal life of the sage, who is identified with the richer classes. This verse implies that the high and the low, the rich and the poor, the powerful and the dispossessed are not greatly different in the eyes of this God; accordingly, they *should* not treat each other as if the differences were significant.

Certainly, many or perhaps most sages did not follow this injunction; even so, the idea presents itself, and the truly wise must act accordingly.

Therefore humility is enjoined. Pride and arrogance are not characteristic of the sage. And in true and consistent retributive fashion, the haughty are declared to be doomed by means of some unspecified moment of great reversal (16:5). Mary reflects a similar confidence in her joyful song, the MAGNIFICAT: "He has scattered the proud in the thoughts of their hearts. He has brought down the powerful from their thrones, and lifted up the lowly" (Luke 1:51-52; see also the Song of Hannah, 1 Sam 2:1-10).

The Third Collection:
The Words of the Wise, 22:17–24:34

The Poor, 22:22-23; 24:10-12

The student is commanded not to rob the poor because YHWH pleads their cause. This section of Proverbs is more pious than the earlier sections. It claims an active role for God in enforcing the demands of wisdom. Yet it appeals to a sense of enlightened self-interest. One may not oppress the poor because they have a very powerful protector who will avenge injustice (22:22-23). A second passage (24:10-12) takes another tack. One is obligated not only to *avoid* taking advantage of the weak, but also to *rescue* those oppressed by others (*those taken away to death*). If one fails to help the powerless who are in danger of imminent destruction, God will know. God will exact a price because of one's failure to intervene to help the weak and the oppressed.

Anger, 22:24-25

Avoid a person whose emotions and behavior are uncontrolled, one who is capable of breaking out unpredictably against others. Avoid them and do not be like them. Such behavior is regarded as a snare or a means by which others might gain advantage over one, one's goals and even one's life, one's family and property. Also, in a more spiritual sense, such behavior hinders one's development as a full human being.

Pledges, 22:26-27

This passage offers greater detail about the consequences of such foolish action. Those who make foolish pledges will soon be sleeping on the floor, having lost their bed.

Ancient Landmarks, 22:28; 23:10

The sages commend the importance of a social conscience. One must not remove a neighbor's landmark. See the discussion above, on the treatment of the poor. The warrant is the same here. The redeemer is strong and will come to the owner's defense. The terms used in this case are legal: the "redeemer" is the "next of kin" (Heb. *go'el*); the case at law is a "complaint," (Heb. *rib*). The arena has shifted from robbing the poor and crushing the afflicted at the gate to moving the ancient landmarks. Someone, presumably a wealthy landowner, desires a neighboring field owned by a poorer family, which field is described as *fields of orphans* (23:10). In Israelite thought, a child missing only one parent was regarded as an orphan. The wealthy landowner moves the landmarks at night in order to include a choice field as part of his property, taking it from the poor family. The notion of legality, which would normally work in favor of the wealthy and well-connected landowner, works, in this schema, in favor of the widow and her children. She has a powerful *go'el* (redeemer) working on her behalf. The sage does not need to say that the *go'el* is YHWH.

We enjoy accounts of a great reversal. The poor, for whom the legal system usually does not work, in this case find themselves to be the most powerful. Their defender (God) equalizes all inequities.

Work Ethic, 22:29

The term "work ethic" is not used in the Bible. Rather, the sages speak of those who are skillful in their work, who apply themselves with diligence to the tasks at hand. The skilful person serves kings and not common people. There is a strong sense of class distinction in this verse, a distinction also found elsewhere in Proverbs. The sages imply that it is better to serve kings than commoners, implying also that those who serve the common people are the less skillful, while the ones who are worthy to serve kings are the more skillful.

Such a distinction may be understandable and simply a commonplace. But there is also an ethic here that is troubling. Working for the poor and disenfranchised is not regarded as a worthy occupation for a skilful worker. Such a view is the exact opposite of the idea found elsewhere that one honors God by helping the poor (14:31; 11:24-26; 19:17; 21:13; 22:9, 16). The mandate that gives preference to the poor, although occasionally present in Proverbs, does not dominate.

To articulate the position most frequently expressed in Proverbs: the ruling elite deserve the best, and everyone else receives the leftovers.

Riches are ephemeral (23:4-5), and people who are rich often lose their wealth in sudden and unexpected ways. The sages imply that the pursuit of wisdom has more enduring value. Being rich is not criticized here, but rather the sages attack the notion that one must make great efforts in order to become rich. Such effort does not often succeed. Some people pursue wealth with unalloyed zeal and yet remain poor. Others, through no effort of their own, have riches thrust upon them. The patriarch Job, for instance, lost his wealth suddenly, although he did nothing to deserve his sudden poverty. He regained it just as easily.

In the light of this passage, then, how might we regard riches? The diligent worker will not necessarily become rich, but will become well-connected. Riches are not worth pursuing, because they are easily lost. The implication is that one must pursue things that are not so easily lost. A similar sentiment finds expression in the NT: "Do not store up for yourselves treasures on earth, . . . but store up treasures for yourself in heaven" (Matt 6:19-21).

Taking Care of Business, 24:27

This passage advises putting one's own comfort, security and well living last, after one has taken care of necessary business, that is those things that when neglected cause an entire enterprise to collapse. This sentiment represents "Tribal Wisdom" (see introduction), the wisdom that comes from small agricultural communities. However, it has been included in this collection characterized as primarily "Royal Wisdom" because its counsel was recognized as applicable within the royal courts even to individuals who never worked in a field.

Story of a Lazy Man, 24:32-34

This is a more lengthy reflection than we have seen in the second or the third collection. It is a little story or parable based on observation. Again it is agricultural and probably originates among the tribes. A lazy man's field is overgrown and in disrepair. The sage infers that the man's laziness caused his poverty. The last line further implies that just a *little* laziness causes a great deal of poverty. There is a significant contrast between the *little sleep* and the *little slumber*, and the *little folding of the hands to rest*, on the one hand, and

poverty, which comes swiftly and destructively like a marauding army.

Poverty is depicted as an aggressive conquering force, waiting for any sign of weakness to sweep in with destruction. Only through constant diligence may one keep away the marauding hordes of poverty. The sages picture life as fraught with extreme insecurity and threat. Such is the life of an agricultural community: it is totally dependent on the chaotic forces of nature, forces over which the community has no control.

Courtly Behavior, 23:1-3, 6-8

Do not give free reign to your appetite when in the presence of royalty, the sage warns, not because it will create a bad impression, but because such fare is *deceptive food* (v. 3). Do not trust the king's friendship. Here we find a very cynical view of the court. One who depends upon the king's generosity and patronage will regret it for the king serves only himself. Those who live for the "perks" that come from access to the centers of power will regret the trouble that is sure to come.

The sages here do not emphasize manners. Rather, they describe the court as a very dangerous setting. Trust no one! It is a very negative view of the monarchy, written for the benefit of those who will actually work for the monarchy, and written by those who have ample experience of how kings behave.

In 23:6-8 we have an interesting variation on the previous passage. Again the advice is, *Do not eat*. In this case, however, the dangerous hosts are not royalty but *the stingy*. In the first passage there is no reference to the consequences of eating with a ruler, but only a warning that the situation is dangerous. In the second passage, the consequences are graphically recorded: *You will vomit up the little you have eaten, and you will waste your pleasant words* (v. 8). The food is "wasted," that is, vomited out. It affords no nourishment, and it provides minimal pleasure. And the pleasant words too are wasted, presumably because *the stingy* are unable to appreciate or are unwilling properly to applaud the pleasant speech.

It remains to discuss the relationship between these two passages. They are placed moderately close in the collection, and they offer comment upon each other. Together, these writings are remarkably antiestablishment, antiauthority, and antiwealth. Their tone is considerably different from what we find in the previous collections. Although warnings about the dangers of wealth and its responsible use might be found in the earlier collections, here these points are made much more forcefully.

This third collection of Proverbs develops a powerful theological critique of its society. It tends to be more pious, using theological justifications to support the advice: Don't do this, or you will suffer divine punishment. Further, this collection expresses hostility towards the avenues leading to wealth and power.

Proverbs 24:21-22 seeks to bridge the tension discussed above, between the power of the king and the power of YHWH, although it does not do so successfully. It urges fear of *both* the king and YHWH. It bases its argument on practical and self-serving considerations. Fear these kings, the earthly and the divine king, not because they are worthy of respect, loyalty and obedience, but rather because they are both capable of destroying you. This is a continuation of the advice to put a knife to one's throat when in the presence of a king. The point is clear: if you don't, the king will put a knife to *your* throat! The passage diminishes YHWH. YHWH rules and deserves to be respected only because he is brutal and vicious and may destroy you. YHWH is a dangerous and unpredictable king, an evil monarch. If you don't do things exactly right the deity will see that you are killed. Surely there are better reasons to devote oneself to God.

Legal Behavior, 24:23b-29

The sage urges honesty in the legal courts. First, this text speaks against those who unfairly favor the guilty, presumably because they are friends, or because they have been offered bribes. The sages condemn class loyalty (taking care of friends) when it interferes with others' rights.

In 24:17-20 the legal system is not at issue, but rather a circumstance in which one's enemy experiences a misfortune, presumably not as a result of any effort on the part of the sage's student. We are told, "Don't be happy about it." If God's anger is diverted towards *you* rather than your enemy, your enemy's suffering will be reduced, and you will lose the satisfaction of seeing your opponent suffer.

The consequence of favoring the wicked in the legal system is that *you . . . will be cursed by peoples, abhorred by nations* (v. 24). Cursing has much more serious overtones then a stained reputation. YHWH fulfills the curse by visiting destruction upon those who violate the moral order. Rather, the sage commands that the powerful person *rebuke the wicked* (v. 25).

The person who stands against corruption will enjoy delight and *good blessing*.

Child Rearing and Parenthood, 23:13-14, 22-25

Here we find advice regarding child rearing, addressed first to the parents and then to the children. The message to the parents, repeating what has been said in the second collection, urges corporal punishment as a means to enforce parental authority. The sage tells the parents that such punishment will not result in the death of the child. There must have been some people who condemned corporal punishment. They might have suggested that physical discipline results in injury, and proposed alternate means of discipline. The sage here argues, however, that if you discipline your children physically you will save their lives.

The advice to the children (23:22-25) corresponds to the advice given previously to the parents, who have been told to assert their control over their children. Parents who do not discipline the young, harm or even kill their children. The advice to the children in *this* passage is to submit to the discipline (in this case discipline refers to the wisdom of the parents). The physical threat is not present here, but rather the promise that if the children obey, they will make their father and mother glad. The parents are told to discipline their children in order to save their (the children's) lives, while the children are told to submit to the parents' discipline because it will make the parents happy.

In all these child rearing passages, one finds an unspoken assumption that the well-being of society depends upon the maintenance of the rigid hierarchy between parents and children, and by extension, between those older ones who support the social order (and are in turn supported by that order) and the younger members of society. Probably, this injunction is directed toward those who are being groomed to take over the reins of power. The weak must be protected by the paternal efforts of those in power. If young people want to advance, they must be taught to respect the institutions of society, such as the schools, the temples, and the royal court.

Envy, 23:17

When the righteous were tempted to envy sinners, it was because the "righteous" were not doing as well the wicked. That is the only reason why sinful behavior would seem attractive. Envying sinners contrasts with continuing in the fear of the LORD. We are told not to envy the wicked because (in what seems like a tautology) they are so bad that *their minds devise violence, and their lips talk of mischief* (24:2).

Wine, 23:29-35

Why are certain kinds of immoderate behaviors strongly forbidden to the budding sage? Part of the reason relates to the work ethic, as we have seen above. Simple observation will suggest that those who indulge their appetites do not have the energy or motivation to make their way in a world that requires hard work and persistence if one is to achieve success.

In this passage the sages compose a funny story in order to ridicule unacceptable behavior. A drunken person has lost complete control, but he does not have the slightest idea of his present condition. "Why would anyone want to be like that?" the teacher implies. The student is urged not to envy the wicked. Here the pleasure-seeking style of the libertine appears at the outset very attractive, but it quickly results in disaster.

Strange Woman, 23:26-28

Here are further warnings against the danger of consorting with loose women. Two words are used, referring to different aspects of what is regarded as the same problem. The prostitute, one who sells her body, and the adulterous person, one who is unfaithful to her husband, are here lumped together (although the social dynamics of each is quite different). They pose a similar danger to the student. The sage argues that one must never associate with such wicked women for to do so can only result in harm.

Importance of Wisdom, 23:22-25; 24:3-7

The child is urged to obey the parent, regarded as the source and fount of wisdom. Further, the parent provides the reason and incentive for pursuing wisdom. The student (son) should buy wisdom in order to make the parents glad. In this instance, the metaphor is commercial. Wisdom is regarded as a valuable commodity, one that should be purchased at any cost, and never sold for any other commodity. One finds similar themes in several NT passages, (e.g., the pearl of great price, Matt 13:45-46; the treasure in the field, Matt 13:44; see also Matt 16:26). Each of these texts also uses some kind of commercial metaphor. There are many things that one may "purchase" in this life at the price of one's character, or one's soul. When persons make such a purchase, thereby sacrificing their charac-

ter, the soul shrinks. Rather, one should spend all of one's personal capital to gain "wisdom."

Such efforts of elders to control the young contributed continuity and stability to the structures of society. Elders gained insight through living their lives actively self-reflective and aware. Usually, it is wise to pay careful heed to the counsel of the more experienced in society. We expect children to learn from their parents, a process that need not cease when an individual reaches maturity.

In 24:3-7 the claim is made that wisdom brings blessings, here understood to include the building and establishment of houses and the accumulation of wealth. Further, the writer claims that wisdom is *better* than strength. By contrast, much contemporary thinking regards wisdom as stable, something homogenized and warmed over. Contemporary psychological analyses hardly ever use the term. But the sages understood wisdom as a significant element in society. They preferred wisdom to the accumulation of military might. Though they were not anti-military, the sages believed that their insight gleaned through wisdom was the most important aspect of military preparedness. In the historical narratives, sages often made the difference between military victory or disastrous defeat (e.g., Ahithophel and Hushai, 2 Sam 16:14–17:23).

The sages declare wisdom to be too high for fools. In the gate, fools do not speak with authority. Be wise, we are told, because fools contribute little to the common good. No one respects them. In the villages and rural communities the elders delivered legal decisions at the gate; in the more urbanized situations, judgment was rendered by the king or the king's representatives. Fools have no authority, no weight in such environments.

In 24:13-14 the sage leaves the commercial and legal metaphors, employing instead a metaphor of eating. Wisdom is like honey, sweet, pleasant, pleasurable. Just as the body delights in honey, the soul takes delight in wisdom. And in the last analysis, the sage reminds us, those who commit themselves to wisdom have a future, while those who don't, have their hope cut off.

Law of Retribution, 24:15-16

In 24:15-16 the sage affirms strongly the doctrine of divine retribution on the unjust and reward for the righteous, despite the many chaotic, random disasters of life. Righteous people fall seven times and rise again, unlike the wicked. The sage is arguing that the righteous recover from such blows more consistently and more rapidly than will the wicked.

The Fourth Collection:
Other Proverbs of Solomon, 25:1–29:27

The maxims here are collected in larger units, usually made up of four or five related proverbs arranged according to similar concerns, structure or vocabulary.

The Mystery of God, 25:2; 27:1

Proverbs 25:2 compares God and the king, but not in the same way as in the previous collections, which saw the king and God as nearly the same. They are both a source of life, and both hold the power of life and death over their subjects. They both rule. They both exercise power with dangerous, unpredictable force. But in this collection the king and the deity contend over control of information. God remains hidden and conceals the divine plan. Therefore, an individual can have no access to the future. The king, however, in order to rule effectively, must uncover the concealed layers of information hidden by God in the world. In this conception, the king is not God, does not function as God, and is not to confuse his role with divine functions.

In 27:1, the sage, in a very sober and practical way, recognizes the limitations of wisdom: even with wisdom and careful observation, one cannot know the future.

Court Politics, 25:4-5; 29:12

The material in this collection regarding politics can be divided into two sub-topics: The first surveys advice to the king and observations concerning the nature of kingship and rule. The second contains advice to the royal counselor and observations concerning the role of the royal counselor.

The king is given strong and practical advice about the way he is to conduct his rule. The proverbs warn him regarding the limitations of his authority and of his critical need for sound moral principles and honest advice so that he might accomplish the true aims of the state. He must strive to create a just and happy kingdom. The sages urge the king (or potential king) to surround himself with wise counselors. The writer compares wicked counselors to *the dross* that the metalsmith must remove when refining the silver (25:4-5). Conversely, a king who is surrounded by courtiers who tell him only what he wants to hear will surely pervert justice (29:12).

An "intelligent" king should expect to rule firmly, but will share his responsibility and authority with no one. The proverbs opt for strong, centralized government, something akin to the Davidic monarchy (28:2). An intelligent king promotes justice and righteousness in the kingdom (28:12, 15-16, 28; 29:2, 16). He must not oppress the poor (28:3; 29:14) or make *heavy exactions* (29:4). Although a wise king possesses absolute power, he must use that power to defend the weak, the poor, and the powerless. One who so rules causes the people to rejoice and find security (28:12).

Wise counselors must dedicate themselves to promoting such qualities of intelligence in the king. Such a counselor is humble, lacking obvious ambition (25:6-7), exercising persuasion with careful and courteous talk, and not exerting undue pressure (25:15). Wise counselors must treat fellow courtiers shrewdly and with suspicion. They are not to *give way* (25:26) before the wicked, and should mistrust those who compete with them for the king's attention (26:25; see 26:23-28). These passages paint a picture of the royal court as a struggle between the honest counselors who seek to steer the king toward just and unselfish practices that benefit the people, and manipulative flatterers who seek to win the king's attention through lies, telling the king only what he wants to hear.

The sages are careful to recognize both the limitations of the king and their own limitations. Justice, it is recognized, comes ultimately not from the king but from YHWH (29:26). The sage need not fear losing the king's ear to flatterers, because ultimately the divine presence in the kingdom will steer things in the right direction. Finally, we are given an enigmatic statement: *Where there is no prophecy, the people cast off restraint, but happy are those who keep the law* (29:18). "Prophecy," or more properly "vision," the communication of the divine will through direct revelation, seems to run exactly counter to the impulse of the sages who emphasize observation and critical reflection. The sages here acknowledge that other sources of information remain vital for the continuance of the work of the kingdom.

"Prophecy" restrains the people. The sages recognize that *their* type of information, while acceptable within the higher courts of royal power, does not function well in the popular realm (although the writer of Ecclesiastes probably saw things differently). "Vision" is necessary to mobilize the people to support the royal house and the king's initiatives. Clearly an examination of the written history of the kingdoms of Israel and Judah would demonstrate that the people were more likely to be swayed by prophets who claimed supernatural inspiration than by the sober advice of a wise person. For the sages, however, this would not be a problem in a well-balanced society that recognizes the need for many categories of persuasion.

Prophecy is juxtaposed with keeping the law, which again is a source of authority that differs from that of the sages. *Torah* or "law" has many meanings, but often is understood, as here, to represent the authority of the priests. The sages, wise in the extreme, recognize once again the limitations of their own efforts; they see their need to share authority with the other institutions of power in Israel. They should not seek to dominate the king by excluding those who do not share their outlook and method for understanding the divine will.

Legal Behavior, 25:7b-10

This section contains two comments about the legal system in Israel. The first one advises that one avoid excessive litigation. The advice here is based on the eventuality that one may not have all the information in the case so that, if additional information comes out subsequently, one will look foolish. Secondly, it is not fitting or seemly to air one's neighbor's secrets in public. It is far better for the offended party to take care of things privately and avoid a public scene. Again, to disobey this advice results in public shame, not for one's opponent but for oneself. Similar counsel appears in Matt 5:25; 18:15-17, and 1 Cor 6:1-8.

The second legal pronouncement, although couched in the form of advice, seems to comment on actual provisions found in the Torah itself. It refers to the individual carrying "bloodguilt" (BLOOD IN THE OT is a powerful symbol). In the ancient Near Eastern legal codes, such an individual must be avenged by the family or the community of the murdered victim. The sages command that no help or assistance be offered to such a fugitive. They are to be hounded until they are killed, and thus balance and harmony will be restored in the land (28:17).

Speech, 25:13, 25; 26:20-21; 29:19-20

The sages contrast wise speech to both speech that is ineffective and speech that is damaging. Wise and positive speech accomplishes its intention and provides health to the community. Another kind of speech does not do damage but has no real or no significant effect. A third kind of speech has an effect, but it is a damaging effect; it creates divisions within the community. These three must be distinguished if one is to understand the Israelite philosophy of rhetoric.

Positive speech is described as aesthetically pleasing (*apples of gold in a setting of silver* [25:11], a stunning image of beauty!), bringing refreshment, fruitfulness and agricultural abundance (25:13, 25).

Ineffective speech consists of words that accomplish little. The promise of a gift undelivered is compared to *clouds and wind without rain* (25:14). Words of rebuke to a servant are wasted words (29:19-20). The writer regards servants (slaves) as naturally lazy. They resist cooperation with their masters. To treat them as responsible human beings, that is, to tell them what is required in a simple and respectful manner, has no effect. Rather, the words must be accompanied by action, presumably with the threat or actual deliverance of physical punishment. This expresses the sentiment of wealthy members of society who feel that "the help" are fundamentally unreliable and must be dealt with as recalcitrant children. Words to such individuals have no effect, and are thus pointless and wasted.

In 26:2 we see how far the wise sometimes go in breaking with what they considered to be credulity or superstition. Many in the ancient world believed that words uttered in sacred curses or blessings took on a magical power that broke free and acted independently of any intention of the speaker. Because of such a concept of CURSE AND BLESSING extraordinary care must be used in choosing words, considering the damage they might do. The third commandment refers to this: "You shall not make wrongful use of the name of the LORD your God, for the LORD will not acquit anyone who misuses his name" (Exod 20:7). Use of the sacred name of God to empower a curse was forbidden, for the power of the divine name was simply too dangerous to unleash.

Contrary to this understanding, the sage here asserts that an ill directed curse remains ineffective. It *goes nowhere* (26:2). This is consistent with the sages' attitude that internal intentions hold more weight than external actions. In a similar way, we are told that cultic actions have no meaning unless accompanied by the correct internal attitude (15:8, 29; 21:3, 27).

This attitude of disparagement of ritual is seductive; it accords well with the contemporary Western notion that considers ritual and symbolic activity to be of little real importance. Only that which is done with intellectual understanding and proper emotional attitude has any value. For example, the ritual of marriage is often regarded as invalid if the two people find out later that they were not "in love," or if they are no longer "in love." One must affirm, however, that the sages are writing at a time when there might have been excessive emphasis on getting the exact ritual correct, without regard to internal attitudes or understanding. We might identify our culture as taking the opposite extreme. Therefore, the sage's counsel to our own day might well be to give greater weight to ritual than our society tends to give.

As for damaging speech, there are many words that, although neither wise nor just, are all too effective in that they tear apart the community that God has established. Such words are compared to *a war club, a sword, or a sharp arrow* (25:18), depicting a violent attack of one person on the neighbor. Such words destroy like a fire (26:20-21). Their effect is sure (25:23). Damaging speech ruins the community.

We are reminded of the many ways that speech might wound and divide. The last includes *false witness* (25:18; see also 26:28), *backbiting* (25:23), meddling in another's quarrel (26:17), malicious, deceptive joking (26:18-19), *whispering* (26:20-21 probably referring to concealed, malicious gossip), flattery (29:5), scoffing (29:8), *hasty . . . speech* (29:20), all of them examples of damaging speech.

Why does hurtful talk find such ready practitioners in the Israelite community? The writer suggests a powerful psychological explanation: *The words of a whisperer are like delicious morsels; they go down into the inner parts of the body* (26:22). Inexplicably, it feels good to tear down another person.

Social Advice, 25:16; 27:7

Here we have assembled the various maxims regarding human behavior. Two subcategories emerge that are uniquely characteristic of the wisdom point of view. The first has to do with appetite and self-control. The image of *honey* appears frequently. Sometimes it refers to the food itself. These comments provide some insight into the ways of appetite and physical well-being. In a world in which natural sweetness was not commonly available except in the form of fruit, honey when discovered was consumed enthusiastically. It caused Samson to willingly plunge his hands into the dead carcass of a lion, thereby defiling himself and

breaking his vow (Judg 14:8-9). The possibility of excess was likely. The sage is warned to curb the appetite for sweets as well as other appetites indulged into excess.

Further, if one is full, honey loses its appeal. If one is starving, even the bitter appears sweet. In either case, one's judgment is skewed by appetite; appetite renders judgment unreliable. Honey also functions as a symbol for honor, reputation or standing in the community (25:27). Eating too much honey is compared with seeking too much honor. The passage enjoins humility in other contexts as well (27:2; 29:1).

Thus self-control becomes a ruling principle (25:28). Self-control counteracts the deceptive nature of appetite. It enables one to respect the boundaries of social relationships, not presuming on another's hospitality (25:17). Sages control their appetites, thereby not grabbing inappropriately for reputation, for gratification of appetite for food, or taking advantage of neighbors.

The second category of social advice is that which enjoins support for the institutions of power, and expects one's social behavior to submit to and uphold these institutions (27:8, 10; 28:24). The sages who assembled this collection highly valued the institutions of home, friendship, parents. These social constructions that hold a society together are valued highly in this collection.

Finally, the fundamental division between two groups within Israel is encouraged and maintained: *The unjust are an abomination to the righteous, but the upright are an abomination to the wicked* (29:27). The wicked, presumably those who oppose the institutions of Israel, are declared outsiders in the community, and eternal enmity is observed and commanded.

The Behavior of Fools, 25:19; 26:6, 10-11

Proverbs frequently create an imaginary group, seemingly recognizable in the constructed world of the sages but not quite so obvious in the actual lived world—a group known as or characterized as "fools." Fools possess exactly the opposite qualities of those that the sages find admirable. Fools are recognized as a terrible pain to those who depend upon them (25:19; 26:6, 10), persons not worthy of honor (26:1, 8), sluggards who only accomplish something when beaten (26:3), individuals not worthy of engaging in any kind of serious discourse:

> *Do not answer fools according to their folly,*
> *or you will be a fool yourself.*

Answer fools according to their folly,
or they will be wise in their own eyes (26:4-5).

Although these two passages appear to contradict one another, in either case the notion is that fools are not capable of serious conversation. Fools also are incapable of wise communication, that is, they do not know how to communicate by using the categories of wisdom (26:7, 9), and finally, they are incapable of changing (26:11).

Other passages, not in this particular cluster of descriptions, build on the description of the fool. These references point out that the anger of fools is dangerous (27:3), that they do not know enough even to escape from danger (27:12), and that they make a mess out of the legal system (29:9).

As bad as the condemnation of fools appears, this cluster of negative descriptions is marshalled to support a different point that the sage is making. As bad as the fool appears to be, there is one quality commonly found in the sage that is even worse. This is the point the writer wants to make:

Do you see persons wise in their own eyes?
There is more hope for fools than for them (26:12).

The writer describes two kinds of fools, the second less obviously so, because they appear to be wise. A self-confident, independent sage is *a greater fool* than the hapless figure described in the preceding verses. This is an admirable moment of self-criticism on the part of the sages. In 28:26, walking in wisdom is contrasted with trusting one's own wits. Presumably, the sage expects the wise person to depend on wisdom that is external, either in the tradition or from some invisible divine source, rather than wisdom that proceeds only from raw, self-contained intellect.

The Fifth Collection: The Words of Agur and Lemuel, 30:1–31:31

Because of the unique nature of this section, I will treat its material differently. Section five consists of three lengthy, coherent poems that are very philosophical and literary. They are Philosophical or Theological Wisdom (see introduction) and have much in common with the other samples of philosophical wisdom, including the poems about Dame Wisdom and Dame Folly in the first section, as well as the Books of Job and Ecclesiastes. *The words of Agur* (30:1-33), *The words of King Lemuel* (31:1-9), which include a distinct literary piece, and the Song of the Capable Wife (31:10-31), will be treated in order, since they represent coherent treatises.

The Words of Agur, 30:1-33

There exists no independent attestation regarding Agur. Although the name occurs in the ancient Near East, there is no figure with that name recorded in the Hebrew Bible. He must remain an anonymous scribe, although his profound reflections deserve our careful attention.

He introduces his thoughts as an ORACLE, *hammassa'* (often translated "the burden of . . ."), and also by the formula *thus says* (*ne'um*; more literally "utterance of . . ."). Both terms in Hebrew are standard, almost stereotypical introductions to prophetic speech. But the utterance here is not ascribed to YHWH as is customary in prophetic speech, or even to the king (often messengers would assume the prophetic formula when they delivered messages from the king). Instead, the utterance is attributed to *the man* (*hageber*). There is no clear precedent for this use of prophetic formulas; it creates an entirely unique space for the discourse that follows, one that is decidedly at home in the wisdom tradition. The utterance here is not from God, or from God's representatives, but is from the camp of mortality, from *the man*.

As we read on, we will note that this utterance is world-weary, from an individual who has given up on the normal sources of authority and information. He despairs of the entire wisdom enterprise, and finds himself in a deep pit of hopelessness and ennui. *I am weary, O God . . . Surely I am too stupid to be human . . . I have not learned wisdom* (vv. 1-3). Although he has identified himself as *the man*, in the next few verses he distances himself from normal human capabilities; these are no longer available to him. *I do not have human understanding* (v. 2).

Following his declaration of ignorance and inability, he asks a series of rhetorical questions, the answer to which is obviously "God." *Who has ascended to heaven and come down? . . . Who has established all the ends of the earth?* (v. 4). Agur does not know the answer, but he challenges the reader to answer the question. The tone mocks the presumption of the readers who think that they do know the answers. The questions are reminiscent of the questions that YHWH asks Job in the frightening climax to that book (Job 38–41). In Job, the questions are framed, "Can you do these things?" Of course, these questions silence Job, for only God can do these things and Job knows it.

But here, the speaker denies even the ability of anyone to know who can do such magnificent deeds.

The following verses do not share the cynical tone of the opening lines. From a historical perspective, we might suggest that these subsequent verses originate from a different source, and were simply added here to fill out the collection. That certainly remains a possibility, but the placement of what follows after such a painful introduction, skews the reading and compels us to question the confident statements we find.

These positive words began as follows: *Every word of God proves true; he is a shield to those who take refuge in him* (v. 5). But has not Agur just told us how unavailable such a word might be in the world *he* inhabits? This weary sage does not even attempt to find such a word, but speaks from the heart of his own limited, damaged human experience. One might then understand this confident pronouncement as one half of a dialogue opposed to the cynicism of Agur. Here an individual finds refuge in God's word and expresses supreme confidence in the ability to remain true and unchanging through all the exigencies of life. Who then are we to believe, given this confluence of conflicting voices?

The tension here embodied expresses the struggles of faith in the wisdom enterprise. Wisdom, committed to the reliability of observation, looks upon the pain of the world, the stupidity and cruelty of humans, and despairs. In response, the pious believer declares confidence in what God has spoken, warning the intellectual regarding the danger of adding to the divine words. With ruthless honesty and confidence in the reader's ability to navigate this theological swamp, the sages place both expressions side by side. We must assert that both are expressions of faith, although we must enlarge our idea of faith in order to include both of them.

What follows in the Agur collection fits somewhere in between the two other pronouncements. The speaker recognizes the fundamental limitations of the human perspective. Poverty and riches both may turn a person away from God. The rich may deny YHWH, while the poor may profane God's name through violation of the moral order (theft). What is left is a kind of moderation, a safe mean where it may be possible to serve the LORD. The speaker makes two requests: the first, for deliverance from falsehood, and the second, for economic moderation. Both requests are characteristic of a sage who is committed to integrity in speech and mastery of appetites.

Not all proverbial statements affirm this notion of economic moderation. Some are rather supportive of rich people, regarding them as the uniquely blessed of the Lord. Here, however, riches are seen not as a blessing but rather as a snare that can drive someone from the divine path.

One finds here a unique sensitivity to the struggles faced by the poor, struggles that place them in moral dilemmas. The rich remain blissfully unaware of such dilemmas, according to this portrayal. Put very simply, issues of survival can easily overshadow efforts to "do the right thing."

In vv. 10-14 we have a list of various activities that are regarded as wicked. They include slander of a servant, cursing of parents, moral hypocrisy, and the oppression of the poor. It might be significant that the litany of negative behaviors concludes with a pronouncement concerning the poor, which relates this passage to the previous one (vv. 7-9). The first in the list of bad behaviors deals with persons who are marginalized by their profession, the servants; the last speaks of those who *devour the poor . . . [and] the needy* (v. 14).

Such a structure is called a CHIASM, where the beginning and the end of the poem reflect similar concerns, while the middle provides some comment on the whole. In this case, the frame speaks of subservient individuals oppressed by the rulers, of the poor devoured by the rich, while the middle verses refer to the moral hypocrisy of the proud. We note a profound criticism of the moral wickedness of the rich who, while *pure in their own eyes . . . are not cleansed of their filthiness* (v. 12). Perhaps throughout we are presented with a single sin, a boastful pride that shows no regard for those less powerful.

How can we relate any of these statements to the disillusioned pronouncements of the sage Agur? Perhaps we cannot. But a few connections appear possible. First, throughout most of these early poems of the chapter we note a profound disappointment in and distrust of the social structures of ancient Israelite society, which traditionally had regarded the rich as rightfully in first place, not only in power, but also in moral and spiritual blessedness. Historically, the sages tended to come from this group of the elite, and in their professional efforts they normally would support the structures that maintained this social division.

Agur has despaired of the wisdom enterprise. In the prayer that follows (vv. 7-9), the sage asks the LORD to keep him from riches because (contrary to the conventional wisdom) they breed forgetfulness of divine priorities. Poverty is regarded here not as a punishment but rather as a state that compels desperate measures for survival.

Finally, a picture of society is created in which the servants and the poor are oppressed horribly by the lofty, those who devour the weak and the powerless. The writer offers a twofold societal criticism, first, of the rich, and second, of the institution of the sages who are produced by the ruling class and in turn support its hold on power in society.

There follows a series of numerical proverbs that come close to pure natural observation without comment or wider application. They are similar in structure to v. 7 (*Two things I ask of you . . .*) but unlike v. 7 seem to contain no moral judgment.

It is difficult to determine whether the whole point of the numerical series found in vv. 18-19 is contained in the final item, or whether the list lacks any logical or literary arrangement. What does the sage mean exactly by *too wonderful for me*? Certainly there is an admission, present in the early statements of Agur, that there are some things that even the wisest sage cannot figure out, no matter how long and complex one's observation may have been. Scientific understanding of snakes or eagles does not in any way make the observations of their behavior any less wonderful. The last item, *the way of a man with a girl*, speaks of the mystery of romance. What makes men act the way they do? The sages shake their heads and confess bewilderment.

This last example, from the human community rather than from the world of nature, is meant to correspond to the others, but what qualities create this correspondence? What do the three descriptions have in common? In each case, a kind of movement appeared to have no external motive force—the movement seems to happen by itself. Romance and sexual attraction partake of this mysterious movement. It must also be pointed out that the last item functions as a kind of punchline, and in its original context it probably evoked laughter.

In v. 20, a powerful image describes the adulteress. Every time this woman appears in Proverbs the allusion is to Dame Folly. The image of sexual seduction communicated through eating makes this connection more intense. The woman wipes her mouth and cravenly claims her innocence. How better to express the cold and calculating picture of unrepentant evil? The verse seems to hang loose in this final collection,

connected to nothing. Who is this woman? Is it simply a warning to the student against compromising his commitment to wisdom because of a hedonistic devotion to sexual experience? Or is it rather part of the teacher's continuing polemic against false doctrine and the teachers of such doctrine? We must suspend judgment until we get to the final poem in the collection, which deals with the *capable wife* (31:10).

What kinds of things make the earth tremble? The answer is given in vv. 21-23. Earthquakes shake the very foundations of a community, and in this case the writer challenges not physical structures but the very social fabric that maintains the human communal web. Trembling is negative, a fear at things shaken that were always believed stable and secure. Slaves will become kings. Fools will no longer be poor, but rather *glutted with food* (v. 22), and a maid will usurp her mistress. In each case relations between the classes break down, and that causes the sage to tremble with dread. The song of Mary in the NT regards the same reversal but with great joy. She sings:

He has brought down the powerful from their thrones,
    and lifted up the lowly;
he has filled the hungry with good things,
    and sent the rich away empty (Luke 1:52-53).

See also the Song of Hannah: "He raises up the poor from the dust . . . to make them sit with princes and inherit a seat of honor" (1 Sam 2:8). In these verses in Proverbs however, that same reversal becomes a cause for terror and insecurity.

How does the reference to *an unloved woman when she gets a husband* (v. 23) fit the context? There appears to be a sense of appropriateness that certain women by virtue of their station deserve to remain lonely, and if such a woman finds companionship, it too threatens the communal ethos. What a mean-spirited series of pronouncements we find here! This writer acknowledges the same moral and intellectual collapse as Agur had portrayed in the first four verses. This person reacts differently, regarding the rise of the banished classes with horror, as a threat to the desirable status quo.

In vv. 24-28, the writer offers a list of things small but wise, all occurring in nature. We might want to find allegorical significance in the observations regarding the ants, the badgers, the locusts and the lizards, but the meaning is plain, more transparent than the sense of the preceding numerical series. The weak and the powerless, by virtue of their unique gifts and abilities, are able to compensate for their lack of power and thereby accomplish great things. These verses constitute a direct attack on the effectiveness and meaningfulness of the social order that is designed to keep people in their proper place. A lizard's place, for instance, is not in the king's palace, and yet, in spite of its seeming defenselessness, it frequents the domain of the royal family. In a similar fashion, the poor can move from their place to the place of privilege.

The next passage, vv. 29-31, by itself might express approval for the stately stride of the lion, the rooster, and the king, but juxtaposed with the earlier series, these descriptions take on a more mocking, ironic tone. Although we might admire the lion, the description of the king follows the image of a strutting rooster, thus allowing the possibility of its farcical intent. Lizards find access to king's houses, the social order is mocked (or reversed as in the previous series [vv. 21-23]) and so the strutting of the rooster/king takes on a rather comic or ludicrous aspect.

We conclude that these various passages in the chapter did not originate from a single hand. They represent different political and theological perspectives, frequently at odds with each other. However, when placed together, they take on a significance that none of them would have by itself. Agur begins the collection with his world-weary attitude, despairing of the ability of wisdom to solve humanity's problems or to answer humanity's questions. He raises significant doubts about the social and political structures that supported the institution of the sages. Therefore the later passages, which alternately support or question those social structures, come to be understood in the context of the original questions raised by Agur. The chapter, read as a whole, creates the impression of a world in turmoil, its stability shaken to the core. It remains for the reader to determine the possibilities of the new world that might yet be created.

The Words of King Lemuel, 31:1-9

Although these words are placed in the mouth of a king, a masculine figure, they claim to originate with the king's mother: *An oracle that his mother taught him* (v. 1). The queen mother advises the young monarch about life. The pronouncement takes the form of a series of prohibitions regarding behavior considered inappropriate to a king. They are introduced with a resounding threefold No!: *No, my son! No, son of my womb! No, son of my vows!* (v. 2). Stronger language can hardly be imagined.

The first prohibition is a warning once more, against the predatory woman who will rob the strength of a young man. How ironic that this warning against women comes from the mouth of a well-placed feminine figure. Were women ever as dangerous and soul-destroying as those portrayed in the Book of Proverbs? Although claiming to be a woman's admonition, must we characterize the text as typical patriarchal propaganda?

Or might this warning, like many others, be a warning against a rival theological perspective, personified here as the ravenous woman, frequently appearing as an alternate rendering of Dame Folly. The warning does not stand alone, however, but is first in a series. Kings must not consort with strange women; kings should not drink wine. The warrant for the command concerning women is that such women will rob the king of his strength and destroy him. Strong drink causes kings to forget their decrees and *pervert the rights of all the afflicted* (v. 5). Strong drink is dangerous because under its influence the king might not protect the poor, which is his chief responsibility!

The themes of strong drink and poverty are then treated from a different perspective. *Give strong drink to one who is perishing* (v. 6), but not to a king. A king should not drink because it will cloud his moral judgment. Poor persons should drink to forget their misery. Lemuel's mother again directs the discourse towards the king, giving him strong advice regarding his treatment of the poor.

Speak out for those who cannot speak,
 for the rights of all the destitute.
Speak out, judge righteously,
 defend the rights of the poor and needy (vv. 8-9).

The Capable Wife, 31:10-31

What follows in the chapter functions as the counterpart to the warning against the ravenous woman in 31:3. Lemuel's mother speaks of a *capable wife* (v. 10). What qualities make her so capable, so desirable to her husband, qualities that are *far more precious than jewels*? There are many passages throughout Proverbs that picture women who cause their husband misery. We have reflected upon some of the implications of these passages and what they say concerning the roles of women in the ancient world. Here we have their opposite figure.

How is she described? Why is she so good? Her efforts bring economic advantages to her husband and her family. She trades in fibers (v. 13), she imports necessities for her household (v. 14), and she works hard and long hours to direct and provide for them (v. 15). She increases her holdings and wields considerable economic power, acting with considerable autonomy.

The second section (vv. 17-24) regards specifically her manual labor. *She girds herself with strength* (v. 17). *She puts her hands to the distaff* (v. 19). *She makes herself coverings* (v. 22). It is mentioned that *she opens her hand to the poor, and reaches out her hands to the needy* (v. 20). We have here an example of an attitude common in this final collection of Proverbs. Strength and authority always bring with them responsibility to provide for the needs of the poor. "Survival of the fittest" does not function in this economy of the wise.

The third section of the poem about the capable wife (vv. 25-31) addresses the reputation of the woman and her husband, first in the community and then in the smaller family unit. *Her husband is known in the city gates, taking his seat among the elders of the land* (v. 23). Presumably, the husband has time to engage in civic activities because his wife cares for the more "material" needs of the household. Frequently, this passage has been regarded as one that empowers women more than most others in the Bible. However, the division of the labor, which here gives the woman a surprising degree of authority, nonetheless places the husband in the superior position.

The sage continues the description: those who surround the woman recognize and admire her qualities. *Her children rise up and call her happy; her husband too, and he praises her* (v. 28). Her husband compliments her: *Many women have done excellently, but you surpass them all* (v. 29). Finally, the woman's speech is marked by wisdom: *She opens her mouth with wisdom, and the teaching of kindness is on her tongue* (v. 26, lit. "a *torah* of steadfast love"). Note that wisdom here is associated with kindness.

We find, therefore, that women are capable of wisdom and of exercising significant economic freedom within the constraints of the ancient society. Therefore, at the close of the entire book, we confront once again the essential paradox at the heart of the wisdom enterprise: wisdom liberates; it opens up the possibilities of being human regardless of gender or economic status. But on the other hand, wisdom takes on the shape of the social structures in which it finds itself, and thereby assumes traditional prejudices that have always oppressed the powerless.

At the conclusion of this study, therefore, we are left with the necessity of making our own choice. *We may listen* to wisdom when it liberates, when it challenges us to break the boundaries and chains that hurt and restrict human potential. *We may listen* when the wisdom tradition protects us from accepting every trend or fashion that seems exciting and new but ultimately damages. But we will need to *reject* the teachings of the sages when they maintain and support the oppressive social structures that continue to plague our culture. So wisdom ultimately demands the exercise of *our* wisdom—as it always has.

Work Cited

Hassler, Jon. 1990. *North of Hope.*

Ecclesiastes

James L. Crenshaw

Introduction

Ecclesiastes is possibly the strangest book in the Bible. Its author, who bears the unusual name Qoheleth, considers life futile, even absurd. He questions the advantage of virtuous conduct and identifies death as the culprit. Nevertheless, he urges youth to seize the moment and to enjoy the positive things God has bestowed on humankind, reminding them of unwelcome days yet to come.

The author presents his reflections arising from close scrutiny, the ego remaining dominant throughout the book. Both form and content link his thoughts with Proverbs, Job, Sirach, Wisdom of Solomon, and a few of the Psalms (e.g., 49, 73, 37, 34). Modern interpreters label these works WISDOM LITERATURE, yet Ecclesiastes alone denies the power of wisdom to benefit human existence.

Authorship

The author identifies himself as *Qoheleth* (1:1; NRSV, *Teacher*), a feminine form construed as masculine, and claims to have been a ruler in Jerusalem (1:12). A colophon in 1:1 makes the claim specific, linking the book with Solomon. A major literary unit, 1:12–2:26, purports to be a royal testament, an experiment so grand that it recalls the Deuteronomistic portrayal of Solomon's vast wealth and achievements. Other parts of Ecclesiastes are written from the perspective of a subject rather than a king, and Qoheleth observes that oppression of the weak is a fact of life.

The language of the book indicates a considerably later period than the tenth century, confirming modern scholars' skepticism about the historicity of Solomonic authorship. Clearly, the author wished to alert readers to the literary fiction at work. Why else would he have referred to Solomon's kingship as a past event (1:12), a curiosity that prompted a later rabbinic suggestion that the king was deposed?

Like many books in the Bible, Ecclesiastes has been submitted to editorial activity. Qoheleth's teachings consist of 1:12–12:8, with possible glosses in 2:26; 3:17; 8:12-13 which contradict his understanding of divine judgment. A superscription (1:1) and two epilogues (12:9-12, 13-14) refer to Qoheleth in third-person narrative (vv. 9-10, perhaps also in v. 11, *one shepherd*: Solomon) and introduce traditional piety at odds with Qoheleth's views.

A thematic statement in 1:2 recurs in 12:8 and forms an inclusion for his teachings. It may derive from Qoheleth, or it may represent an astute editorial summary of his thoughts.

Contradictions in the book have evoked several different explanations. Some early Christian commentators suggested that the author employed a Greek device, diatribe, to emphasize the dialogic nature of reality. Qoheleth thus entered into debate with himself or with imagined disputants. Some modern critics think he cites opponents' views, without any indication of quoting, which he then proceeds to challenge in toto or in part.

Other interpreters consider Qoheleth's teachings a sort of notebook with entries from different periods and circumstances, hence contradictory in character. Still others distinguish between the author and his persona, while stressing both Qoheleth's honesty and life's ambiguities that led to opposing conclusions.

In short, Qoheleth describes life, which seldom accommodates the desire for tidiness. Some interpreters suggest the modern concern for consistency did not apply to ancient logic. However one understands the contradictions in the book, the fact stands that more than one author is responsible for its final form.

Historical Context

Like Proverbs and Job, Ecclesiastes lacks historical references that would enable critics to ascertain its date of composition. To be sure, a few allusions (4:13-16; 8:2-4; 9:13-15; 10:16-17) have seduced interpreters into considerable speculation, but such effort has borne little if any fruit.

The story of a poor person who emerged from prison to rule the land was a literary topos, recalling the Joseph episode, and the same goes for the ambiguous anecdote about a little city that was rescued (might have been spared?) by a poor wise man who was forgotten. The reference to a king may actually connote any local Persian authority. Two Persian loan words, *pardes* (garden) and *pitgam* (decree) occur in the book, and the Aramaizing language most resembles that of other biblical books from the transitional period before rabbinic Hebrew came to prominence.

Qoheleth seems to have fallen under minimal Hellenistic influence, but nothing suggests that he lived during or after the momentous events of the Maccabean revolt in the second century. His emphasis on entrepreneurial enterprises, wealth, mercantile ventures, and investments fits into the age reflected by the remarkable Zenon business records from Egypt which describe the economic situation in Syria-Palestine. A mid-third-century date for Qoheleth is therefore likely. Fragments of 5:13-17; 6:3-8; and 7:7-9 discovered at Qumran and dating from the middle of the second century B.C.E. do not permit a date for Qoheleth much later than the third century.

Ecclesiastes was probably written in JERUSALEM, although a few interpreters opt for EGYPT or PHOENICIA as place of origin. Certain features indicate a Judean environment: the references to clouds and rain (11:3; 12:2), a farmer's preoccupation with changes of the wind (1:6; 11:4), use of wells and cisterns (12:6), the almond tree (12:5), and mention of temple and sacrifice (5:1; 9:2).

Style and Structure

Qoheleth's style is rich in literary forms. Besides the reflection based on personal observation (I saw, I said, I turned, I considered, I know, I concluded) and royal fiction, he drew on traditional wisdom. One finds short sayings, admonitions, exemplary story, parable, antitheses, better sayings, statements of existence (there is . . .), lists, and autobiographical narratives. His special antitheses, variously described as polar opposites or *zwar/aber* statements (yes . . . but), engage the mind by recognizing relative truths.

Use of preferred phrases, refrains, and special words hammers away at resistance to the content of Qoheleth's teaching. Life is futile, indeed absurd; all effort amounts to chasing after or feeding on (shepherding) the wind; there is nothing better than to enjoy life. Favorite expressions (under the sun) and words (futile, toil, work, profit, chance, time, gift, portion, death, evil, good, etc.) echo through the corridors of the mind.

Neither the structure nor the form of discourse is clear. The lines between poetry and prose have thus far eluded critics, who cannot agree as to which of these best characterizes the book. Similar controversy surrounds the attempt to identify a structure.

Most interpreters agree that Qoheleth's teachings are enclosed by a colophon and by one or two epilogues, while poems prominently featuring nature's rhythm (1:4-11) precede and conclude (11:7–12:7) his insights. Beyond these indications of structure, scholars have identified formal linkages (refrains; polar expressions) and have sought the book's structure in its content (a palindrome or mirror image; unity of tone and spirit). Perhaps part of the difficulty derives from the inadequacy of the Hebrew language to convey abstract philosophical observations of the sort Qoheleth wished to advance.

Theology

Interpreters are divided over the nature of Qoheleth's teachings. Some critics think he champions the cause of joy and protects divine freedom. Others argue that Qoheleth announces the bankruptcy of wisdom with respect to its mastery of life and its faith in divine benevolence. Whether the ambiguity rests in the text or in its readers, the fact remains that Qoheleth's teachings continue to fascinate moderns and to compel them to ask the same questions he did more than two millennia ago.

Given the presence of death's shadow, does life have any purpose? Enjoyment, when possible, certainly seemed an appropriate response to Qoheleth, but was it sufficient to offset the terrible silence or indifference of God? Qoheleth's oft-mentioned divine gift softened the concept only if human beings controlled this good, which they did not. Chance determined everything, irrespective of worth. Such a message, however accurate, offers little basis for joy, even while encouraging efforts to live as fully as possible before old age and death put an end to all hope.

For Further Study

In the *Mercer Dictionary of the Bible*: ECCLESIASTES, BOOK OF; WISDOM IN THE OT; WISDOM LITERATURE. In other sources: J. L. Crenshaw, *Ecclesiastes*, OTL; *Old Testament Wisdom*; and "Qoheleth in Current Research," *HAR* 7 (1984):41–56; M. V. Fox, *Qohelet and his Contradictions*; R. Gordis, *Koheleth—the Man and his World*; A. Lauha, *Kohelet*, BZAW; J. A. Loader, *Polar Structures in the Book of Qohelet*; N. Lohfink, *Kohelet*, DNEB; R. Murphy, *Ecclesiastes*, WBC; G. Ogden, *Qoheleth*; G. von Rad, *Wisdom in Israel*; C. F. Whitley, *Koheleth*; R. N. Whybray, *Ecclesiastes*, NCB.

Commentary

An Outline

I. Introductory Framework, 1:1-11
  A. A Colophon, 1:1
  B. Thematic Statement, 1:2-3
  C. Nothing New under the Sun, 1:4-11
II. Qoheleth's Teachings Enclosed
by the Envelope Structure, 1:12–11:6
  A. A Royal Experiment, 1:12–2:26
  B. Events and Their Times, 3:1-15
  C. The Tears of the Oppressed, 3:16–4:3
  D. Some Proverbial Insights, 4:4-6
  E. Advantages of Companionship, 4:7-12
  F. The Fickle Crowd, 4:13-16
  G. Religious Duties, 5:1-9 [MT 4:17–5:8]
  H. The Disappointments of Wealth,
    5:10–6:9 [MT 5:9–6:9]
  I. A Transitional Unit, 6:10-12
  J. A Collection of Proverbs, 7:1-14
  K. On Moderation, 7:15-22
  L. Seeking and Finding, 7:23-29
  M. Rulers and Subjects, 8:1-9
  N. The Mystery of Divine Activity, 8:10-17
  O. Death's Shadow, 9:1-10
  P. Time and Chance, 9:11-12
  Q. Wasted Wisdom, 9:13-18
  R. Another Collection of Proverbs, 10:1-20
  S. The Element of Risk, 11:1-6
III. Concluding Framework, 11:7–12:14
  A. Youth and Old Age, 11:7–12:7
  B. Thematic Statement, 12:8
  C. Two Epilogues, 12:9-14

Introductory Framework, 1:1-11

A Colophon, 1:1

As in so many biblical texts (e.g., Prov 1:1; 30:1; Amos 1:1; Jer 1:1), an editor identifies the author. The name Qoheleth, otherwise unattested outside this book, occurs seven times (1:1, 2, 12; 7:27; 12:8, 9, 10), twice with a definite article (7:27; 12:8). The participle form indicates a function, like similar terms for a scribe and binder of gazelles in Ezra 2:55, 57 and Neh 7:59, respectively. In light of the reference to Davidic lineage, the verb *qahal* (to assemble) may allude to Solomon's actions recorded in 1 Kgs 8:1-2, and by extension to his assembling of wives and proverbs.

Alternatively, the name Qoheleth is taken to be a personal name, a pen name, and an acronym. The name is also explained as haranguer, as in a diatribe, and as a personification of sayings in the way wisdom and folly were personified in Prov 8 and 9. In the Latin Vulgate, Jerome equated the Greek translation of the word *ecclesiastes* with an official function of speaking in an assembly, which gave rise to Luther's "Der Prediger" and English renderings such as "the Preacher" (NRSV, *the Teacher*).

Thematic Statement, 1:2-3

A thematic statement and its elaboration set the tone of the book. The expression, often translated "vanity of vanities," is a superlative, meaning the ultimate futility—like "Song of Songs," the most excellent song. The word *hebel* (NRSV, *vanity*), which Qoheleth uses thirty-eight times, expresses brevity and insubstantiality, ephemeral like breath and a nonentity like idols. The repetition underlines the absurdity of everything, as does the question, which functions as negation. One achieves nothing from toil on earth.

Nothing New under the Sun, 1:4-11

A remarkable poem leads into Qoheleth's royal experiment and increases the irony of such endeavor. Some critics think Qoheleth borrowed the poem, which uses several stylistic devices to maximum effect—*generations* with respect to the heavenly bodies and human beings, *goes* as a euphemism for death, withholding of the subject *wind* until the latest possible moment, achieving a sense of totality by referring to the four compass points, and imitating life's monotony by dull repetition. Movements in nature and society have no discernible results except to exhaust the participants; the glorious sun (god) pants, like his steed, and the everflowing rivers do not make any permanent difference in the depth of the sea. In society ceaseless speech, ears eager to hear, and insatiable eyes engage in a frustrated search for something new. Forgetfulness alone provides an illusion of novelty, and the human wish to be remembered is declared to have no basis in reality.

Qoheleth's Teachings Enclosed by the Envelope Structure, 1:12–11:6

A Royal Experiment, 1:12–2:26

1:12-18. Qoheleth's conclusions. Qoheleth claims to have been *king . . . in Jerusalem* (v. 12), and boasts about surpassing all previous rulers there. Both comments expose the author's literary fiction, for neither actually applies to SOLOMON, although the tradition about his exceptional wisdom gave rise to the remark here.

Qoheleth assesses life as an unpleasant preoccupation and shepherding (or chasing) the wind. Two proverbs reinforce his point. The first saying asserts that the crooked (back?) cannot be straightened and what is missing cannot be counted. Ancient educators in Egypt used the former notion differently; they insisted that carpenters could indeed straighten a crooked stick and that teachers could educate reluctant students. Qoheleth sets the proverb in the context of divine determinism, which none could alter. The second proverb also derives from an educational context. It acknowledges the unwelcome aspects of increased knowledge.

2:1-11. Pleasure examined. The purpose of the royal fiction becomes evident in this section, for only a king had the means and the power to put pleasure to the ultimate test. A curious feature of this text is Qoheleth's insistence that his intellect remained in control, which arguably skewed the results, but one must not forget that a wise man speaks here. Qoheleth examines pleasure and dismisses it as futile; is this a commentary on his subsequent admonitions to enjoy life? Here he calls pleasure a profitless endeavor. The other royal activities are typical in the ancient Near East. The king built monuments to his greatness—houses, vineyards, gardens, parks—and acquired unlimited possessions, precious metals—gold and silver—and slaves for sexual pleasure. He did what he desired, in the end concluding that the entire experiment only highlighted life's futility and profitlessness, indeed reinforced the image of chasing the wind.

2:12-23. The life of the intellect. Now Qoheleth puts wisdom to the test and concedes that it is relatively superior to stupidity. He uses a proverb to make this point: the eyes of intelligent people are open, whereas ignorant people walk in darkness. Ancient Sumerian teachers referred to their school as the place to which students came with closed eyes and from which they departed with open eyes. Qoheleth notes, however, that a common end awaits the wise and the fool, making all his own efforts to be wise wasted energy. Death cancels all supposed benefits, and short memories exacerbate matters. Such unpleasant thoughts prompt Qoheleth to reach the astonishing conclusion, at least for a sage, that he *hated life* (v. 17).

His subsequent remarks take up another irksome reality, one connected with the earlier observation about death's leveling power. No one can be certain that the person who inherits will act intelligently, thus the one slight comfort for those who cannot take their possessions with them is effectively canceled.

2:24-26. What then? Qoheleth concludes that nothing is better than the ordinary pleasures of eating, drinking, and working. One need not be a king to enjoy these things; however, Qoheleth observes that God determines who can find such joy. The language lacks moral connotations; the one who pleases God simply means "the lucky person," and the sinner is "the unlucky person." Of course, such arbitrary treatment of human beings occurs in an absurd universe where people feed on the wind.

Events and Their Times, 3:1-15

3:1-9. A list of times. In form, this brief section resembles Prov 30:11-14 and 18-19, where the words "generation" and "way" unite short lists of related things. Qoheleth uses a poem, which some interpreters think antedates him, to demonstrate life's profitlessness. The chiastic form sets vv. 1-8 off from Qoheleth's concluding question; v. 1 refers to birth and death, whereas v. 8 mentions love and hate, war and peace.

Fourteen antitheses appear here, each introduced by the word *time.* The rhythm is noteworthy, and in several instances the first and third verb are related, as are the second and fourth (e.g., weeping and laughing, mourning and dancing). This practice favors an erotic understanding of "casting stones" (NRSV, *throw*) as some rabbinic interpreters recognized. Other explanations for this image appeal to counting procedures in commerce, agricultural efforts to clear land for tilling, and mythological concepts for repopulating the earth after a flood. The poem spans the course of human events, beginning on the personal level and ending in the public domain.

3:10-15. God's relationship to time. This section begins positively, only to end on a somber note. God made everything appropriate for its occasion and concealed something within the human intellect—perhaps a sense of mystery or a yearning for eternity—but rendered the gift useless. The word translated frequently as "eternity" (v. 11, ASV, RSV, NJV, TLB, NIV, NKJV, NASV; NRSV, REB, *a sense of past and future*) means "hiddenness" if vocalized differently, which makes sense of futile searching from A to Z (by astrologers claiming to know the times?). The divine purpose is said to be educative—to instill fear in human beings, a curious idea when juxtaposed alongside the image of God chasing past events (cf. Sir 5:3).

The Tears of the Oppressed, 3:16–4:3

3:16-22. A single fate for human beings and animals. The prevalence of injustice provokes an explanation: that God has surely fixed a time for judging deeds—if the principle behind 3:1-8 holds true.

Qoheleth ventures still another justification for divine inactivity, the posing of a test to show people that they do not differ essentially from beasts. They breathe the same air and then die, returning to dust (cf. Gen 3:9; Job 10:9; 34:15). With this observation Qoheleth rejects the emerging belief in survival after death as more substantial than a shadowy existence in SHEOL. The *who knows . . . ?* (v. 21) functions as a strong denial: no one knows what happens to human breath at death. This ignorance again prompts Qoheleth to urge enjoyment in toil.

4:1-3. Undried tears. Qoheleth witnessed oppression and looked in vain for comforters. The repetition of the pitiful words "and there was none to comfort them" may indicate how deeply Qoheleth felt their pain. If the observer were really King Solomon, he could punish offenders promptly; instead, Qoheleth notes that power belonged to the oppressors. He thinks of the unborn as luckier than the living and the dead, for they are spared such sights.

Some Proverbial Insights, 4:4-6

Qoheleth views envy as an invigorating passion that forces people to waste time competing for nothing. One can never know the result of an action, for a fool remains idle and lives off accumulated fat or has ample food in spite of laziness. The final aphorism seems to imply that a morsel is preferable to the ceaseless struggle for something more.

Advantages of Companionship, 4:7-12

An observation about the absurd striving to accumulate wealth by one who has no dependents gives rise to a rare concession that something is better than the much-prized individualism of sages. In companions one finds a measure of security against robbers, accidental falls, and the night's chill. Qoheleth clinches the point with an aphorism about the strength of a threefold cord, a saying also current in ancient MESOPOTAMIA. The ego remains supreme in this acknowledgment that companions make life more comfortable and safe, for Qoheleth thinks about what others can do for him. The same heightened ego had come to expression in the royal experiment, which frequently uses the words "for myself."

The Fickle Crowd, 4:13-16

The section echoes the JOSEPH story, although somewhat erratically. The praise of youth contrasts markedly with earlier wisdom and may signify Greek influence. Older attitudes to the poor often implied fault, a laziness that contributed to poverty. That understanding necessarily followed from the optimistic claim that good people mastered their lives by using wisdom and therefore earned wealth, honor, progeny, and longevity. A poor but wise youth was almost an anomaly, but so was much of what Qoheleth taught. Wise counselors worked closely with Egyptian kings, and DAVID is said to have had two advisors, Ahithophel and HUSHAI. A king who refused to take advice, or one who heeded foolish counsel, was headed for disaster. In Qoheleth's anecdote, the youth supplanted the king and was subsequently replaced, it seems, amply demonstrating the fickleness of society.

Religious Duties, 5:1-9 [MT 4:17–5:8]

5:1-7. Prayer, dreams, and vows. This section advises against rash speech in the holy place, presumably the TEMPLE. Qoheleth thinks of a great distance separating worshipers and God, both spatially and essentially. Fear is the appropriate attitude for human beings, who should speak sparingly lest the sacrifice of fools (insincere praise?) prompt an angry reaction from on high. Qoheleth's distrust of religious dreams was more consistent than SIRACH's, perhaps owing to the necessity of interpreting them. The advice against reneging on religious vows echoes Deut 23:21, but Qoheleth goes further when advising against the taking of vows in the first place. The term for unwitting offenses (v. 6, *mistake*) is a technical expression in biblical legal codes. The *messenger* is either a priestly emissary or the death angel, which Egyptian wisdom also mentions.

5:8-9. A hierarchy of responsibility. Qoheleth probably alludes to the complex Persian system of officials in Judah, which complicated matters greatly when one endeavored to locate blame for injustice. The prophetic outcry on behalf of victims has made no impression on Qoheleth, who merely registers awareness that such cruelty happens and none can put a stop to it. Does he think of God as ultimately at fault? The obscure comment about the advantage of a king with fields may imply that even a corrupt monarch at least keeps a semblance of order (contrast Judg 19–21).

The Disappointments of Wealth, 5:10–6:9 [MT 5:9–6:9]

5:10-12. Money's unwelcome companions. The third century witnessed a rise in acquisitiveness and the resultant disparity between rich and poor. Fortunes were won and lost overnight, particularly those resulting from investments at sea. Qoheleth observes that money never brings satisfaction, for people invariably want more. Furthermore, increased holdings require additional laborers, who inflate expenditures, and add to one's worry about loss through an ill-advised venture or robbery. Perhaps Qoheleth refers to sleeplessness resulting from overeating, a problem seldom affecting day laborers who fall asleep from exhaustion.

5:13-20. An object lesson. Qoheleth is moved by an instance in which a man loses everything as a result of a bad venture, although that man has a son who hopes to inherit the wealth. Both father and son will depart empty-handed; the allusion to the sentiment otherwise expressed in Job 1:21 can hardly be missed. Neither the man's toil nor his resentment made any appreciable difference. Qoheleth concludes that people should accept their lot as God dispenses it, knowing that they will little remember the joys with which God occupies their minds (or afflicts them with thoughts of how things ought to be). This section introduces the notion of DARKNESS, which will come to prominence in 11:7–12:7. The present reference seems to suggest a miserly lifestyle in which the person is too stingy to light a lamp during evening meals (v. 17).

6:1-9. Divine irony. Qoheleth recognizes the irony in circumstances where individuals prosper mightily but lack the ability to enjoy such largess. The usual signs of divine approval often deceive, for someone may have numerous children and lengthy existence without the honor associated with a proper burial. Qoheleth sees that one's ability to enjoy life and one's burial depend on others, God in the first instance and people in the second. He considers a stillborn luckier than a person who has a long life but lacks power to enjoy it, for an untimely birth quickly attained rest (cf. Job 3:11-19).

A Transitional Unit, 6:10-12

The mention of the first human creature, ADAM, in a context denying anything new is nicely ironical. Qoheleth seems to refer to JOB who multiplied words in the colossal struggle with one more powerful than he. The principal aim of ancient wisdom has been summed up in the words "what is good for men and women?" By denying that anyone can actually know the answer, Qoheleth calls into question the fundamental premise of the sages. In doing so he returns to the earlier notion, often repeated, that life is futile. He also introduces a new image, that of a lengthening shadow. Many interpreters think these three rhetorical questions bring the first half of the book to a close.

A Collection of Proverbs, 7:1-14

Ancient sages tried to weigh the relative merits of various things, often using "better proverbs" to state their findings. This unit effectively uses alliteration, for example, in the Hebrew words for *name* and oil (*ointment*), *thorns*, *pot*, and *laughter* (v. 6). Qoheleth indicates a preference for life's darker features; he chooses death over birth, the house of mourning over one of feasting, sorrow over laughter. Nevertheless, he values wisdom more than folly, comparing the advantage of knowledge to that of wealth, which offers a measure of security. Once more he quotes the traditional saying about the impossibility of straightening out what God *has made crooked* (v. 13). This time it is introduced by an invitation to examine God's work. In v. 14 Qoheleth repeats the earlier observation (3:11) that God has concealed the future from humankind.

On Moderation, 7:15-22

An instance of gross injustice—wicked persons who prosper and virtuous people who perish—leads to Qoheleth's radical conclusion that one should not try to be a model of piety, like legendary Job, or for that matter a master villain. Presumably, Qoheleth fears that either extreme might call God's attention to the person and bring misfortune. At least one critic thinks this section has nothing to do with moderation but attacks self-righteousness. Another interpreter compares its teaching to the Chinese concept of a median way instead of the more obvious Greek parallel.

Seeking and Finding, 7:23-29

This section emphasizes the limits imposed on human knowledge, an insight familiar to earlier sages. It also focuses that limitation precisely where some older proverbs do: on the mystery of eros. In the Book of Proverbs the foreign woman—by action or by nationality—constituted a threat to young men. Qoheleth appears to generalize that threat to include all women. He may cite a popular aphorism with which he disagrees, or he may simply relativize its point by indicating that men are only 1/1,000th more reliable than women. The text probably plays on Solomon's reputation for having a thousand wives and concubines, and it thereby offers a subtle clue to the meaning of "the Qoheleth" (v. 27, *the Teacher*). He gathers women in search of the *sum* (profit?) but ends up with a huge zero, nay a minus, for evil women are *more bitter than death* (v. 26; or stronger than death, like love in Cant 8:6).

Rulers and Subjects, 8:1-9

This unit begins by citing an obscure saying that praises the perspicacity of the wise, which may allude to the previous mystery about women, then moves on to treat an equally potent threat. Qoheleth cautions those who come in contact with rulers to keep a safe distance when unpleasant matters come up, for kings do as they please. Royal power as depicted in 1 Esd 4:1-12 is eclipsed by that of woman (1 Esd 4:13-32). Qoheleth mentions death as the power to which everyone must submit, kings and women (cf. 1 Esd 4:37). This advice about conduct before rulers does not seem to be aimed at courtiers, like the "men of Hezekiah" (Prov 25:1, RSV) who probably disappeared in Judah with the collapse of the monarchy.

The Mystery of Divine Activity, 8:10-17

Qoheleth reports on a particularly galling incident involving evil persons whose guilt was hidden even in death. Praise instead of rebuke accompanied their burial. Delay in divine judgment encourages such con-

duct. Without warning, the text suddenly affirms God's justice in the face of contradictory evidence (vv. 12-13). Many interpreters consider this statement out of character and attribute it to a later editor, particularly since vv. 14-15 go on to talk about the absence of divine justice as grounds for seeking pleasure.

Qoheleth has no patience with sages who claim to have access to the truth about what God is doing. For them a single response suffices: they are mistaken. This sharp attack may be directed against emerging apocalyptic movements and their leaders, the sort of mantic wisdom reflected in the Book of Daniel.

Death's Shadow, 9:1-10

This section lumps all people together in a common fate; it makes no difference whether they have been good or bad. Such a state of affairs strikes Qoheleth as indication that one cannot determine whether God's disposition toward human beings is favorable or unfavorable. Qoheleth employs a powerful rhetorical device to suggest death: he simply breaks off the sentence in the middle—like life itself. The traditional saying that *a living dog is better than a dead lion* (v. 4) probably derives from another setting, one justifying marriage to a person of lower social status. Here the saying reeks with irony: if the only advantage that the living possess over the dead is the knowledge that they must die, then the "hope" is hollow to the core.

Qoheleth's counsel in v. 7 is liberating to persons who possess a scrupulous conscience, but it probably only means that if one can do something then it follows that God has approved the action. The advice in vv. 8-10 resembles Siduri's counsel to Gilgamesh ("Death is decreed for mortals, eternal life is reserved for the gods"), although one need not think of direct literary influence. Qoheleth's syntax—"a woman you love"—is unusual if *wife* (as in KJV–NRSV) is intended.

Time and Chance, 9:11-12

In Qoheleth's opinion, chance governs human lives. The outcome of actions has no direct correlation with the effort expended. Such a view stands in opposition to older wisdom, which insisted that by careful mastery of the passions and by wise action, human beings could assure certain desirable consequences. According to the Book of Proverbs danger certainly existed, but one could escape its clutches by taking care. Qoheleth abandons such optimism, for he thinks none can avert disaster, which falls unexpectedly like a fishnet.

Wasted Wisdom, 9:13-18

An example illustrates society's low estimate of wisdom. The incident may be hypothetical. When a mighty ruler attacked a tiny village, a poor wise man saved it but was promptly forgotten, or he might have saved the city had anyone thought to consult him. Qoheleth still considers wisdom superior to force, although he concedes that one wicked person can cause considerable harm.

Another Collection of Proverbs, 10:1-20

Such unassimilated sayings as these frustrate all attempts to discover a consistent structure in the book. A few words in these sayings occur elsewhere in Qoheleth's thought, but much of the material would be equally at home in the Book of Proverbs. The sayings give voice to the ancient tendency to attribute moral connotations to right and left, express dismay when reversals occur within society (slaves riding horses, princes walking), alert those who do domestic chores to some inherent dangers, and praise eloquence (a frequent subject in ancient wisdom). The final warning against useless curses has a parallel in Egyptian wisdom (v. 20).

The Element of Risk, 11:1-6

Qoheleth recognizes that life always carries risk, whether in commercial ventures or in agricultural pursuits. He advises action despite the danger and warns against a cautious attitude that paralyzes one. The advice to throw bread on the water, which has a parallel in the Egyptian *Instructions of 'Onkhsheshonqy* (19.10), probably refers to mercantile investments. Qoheleth notes that the mystery of life does not surrender to human investigation any more than does God's activity, so people should sow seed at opportune times.

Concluding Framework, 11:7–12:14

Youth and Old Age, 11:7–12:7

This exquisite poem describes the collapse of a house during a storm as a symbol of a wasting human body. The verbs *remember* and *rejoice* and the nouns *darkness* and *light* unite the poem, which juxtaposes youth and old age. Three times the word *before* points beyond the formula to unwelcome occurrences culminating in death. The domestic images for death are not exactly clear, but they refer to the breaking of a cord that holds a lamp and the shattering of a pitcher as a result of a faulty pulley at the well. A puff of dust and the release of God's breath signal the end and evoke Qoheleth's solemn remark that both have returned to their source. The translation *creator* in 12:1 does not fit the context. The unusual word may allude to one's wife ("well" in Prov 5:15-19) and grave. The warning of divine *judgment* in 11:9 also seems strange; it may be a gloss.

Thematic Statement, 12:8

This verse serves as an inclusion with 1:2.

Two Epilogues, 12:9-14

Two editors comment on Qoheleth's teachings. The first, vv. 9-12, speaks admiringly of his honesty, trustworthiness, and aesthetic sense. This editor identifies Qoheleth as a sage who taught the people, not just young boys, and concedes that his words were at times demanding, indeed exhausting. The second editor submits Qoheleth's radical teachings to traditional piety: fear God and keep the commandments, for a judgment day is coming (vv. 13-14).

Song of Solomon

Mona West

Introduction

Song of Solomon is unique in all the literature of the Hebrew Bible. It contains erotic poetry that celebrates human love and the joy of sex. Neither of these, in the Song, leads to marriage or procreation. There is no mention of God or of any event of Israel's salvation history. The primary speaker of the poems is a woman, who is free to express sexuality and mutuality in advances toward the male beloved.

Early Jewish and Christian interpretations allegorized and spiritualized the Song, stripping the book of its sensual, bodily focus. Currently, theologians are reaffirming the book's emphasis on the erotic. In an age when we as human beings feel alienated from the world, God, each other, and our own bodies, Song of Songs can help us celebrate our sexual selves and rejoice in our physical bodies.

The lovers in the Song show us the goodness of sex without shame, domination, or alienation. The poetry of the Song challenges us to embrace and encounter God and the world with the same senses and passion used in sexual intercourse.

Authorship and Date

The opening verse, along with the references of 3:7-11 and 8:11-12, indicate King SOLOMON may have been the book's author. However, it is unlikely he actually wrote the poems found in the Song. Because he was known for his poetic compositions (1 Kgs 4:32-33) and his love of women (1 Kgs 11:3), Solomon was associated with the book's composition.

In reality the majority of the poems are spoken by a woman. One commentator has noted, "the protagonist in the Song is the only unmediated female voice in scripture" (Weems 1992, 156). One must not rule out the possibility that the author(s) may have been female. Even so, her identity remains anonymous.

The timeless nature of love poetry makes it difficult to assign a specific date to the book. The nature of some of the poetry would indicate a time in Israel's history (postexilic) when lovers were compelled to affirm their right to love whomever they chose regardless of class, ethnicity (1:5-6; 6:13), or societal or family approval (5:7; 8:1-4, 8-9).

History of Interpretation

While there is no scholarly consensus on how to construe the Song, interpretations generally fall into one of two categories: a unified work with intentional design, or an anthology of independent poems.

Dominant interpretive theories that assume some type of unity include: (1) an allegory of God's relationship to Israel (Jewish) and Christ's relationship to the Church (Christian), (2) a drama with two or three characters and a chorus, (3) a liturgy celebrating the sacred marriage of a fertility god and goddess, (4) a cycle of wedding songs sung during the wedding feast.

Anthological readings of the Song will vary concerning the number of poems found within the book, the criteria used to delineate the poetic units, and the relationship of the poems to one another. Scholars who view the Song as a collection of independent poems are willing to admit some "surface structure" based on the repetition of key words (e.g., lilies, stags, and *gazelles* in 2:1, 2, 7, 9, 16, 17), refrains (*I adjure you* . . . in 2:7; 3:5; 5:8; 8:4), and characters (*daughters of Jerusalem* in 1:5; 2:7; 3:5, 10; 5:8, 9; 6:1; 8:4). This "surface structure" could be the result of skillful editing and/or the recurrence of stock phrases used in the love poetry of ancient Israel.

More recently, feminists have offered their interpretation of the Song. Emphases include: the possibility of female authorship; positive cultural reflection of the role of women (assertive, sexual without the strictures of patriarchal marriage or procreation); mention of the mother's house and the mother as images of the woman's autonomy in lovemaking.

Literary Unity

The outline and commentary that follow are attempts to preserve the independent nature of the poems. However, readers encounter the Song as a "book" of the Bible and its repetitions invite efforts to group the poems into meaningful subunits.

Thirty-three distinct poetic units are identified in the outline (but not all of the units receive extended treatment). The criteria used for determining these poetic units were: a change in speaker, tone, content, or context; repetition of words, phrases and refrains; a general sense of an ending or beginning.

These units can be grouped into five categories. The categories are an effort to aid the reader by assigning labels that indicate how the poems function within the book.

Poems of *description* can be of the lover (the woman) or the beloved (the man). They are physical descriptions of beauty, incorporating a variety of images, usually made by one lover of the other. However, there is one instance in which a group of people describe the woman (7:1-5). Other descriptions include the power of love (8:6-7) and Solomon's marriage processional (3:6-11).

The *wasf* is the most distinctive poem of description. It is a type of Arabic poetry that describes parts of the female or male body beginning from top to bottom (head to feet), or the reverse. Images from nature, architecture, and the military are used to create a sensory (most often visual) picture of the lover or the beloved. The *wasf* can be found in 4:1-7; 5:10-16; 6:4-10; 7:1-5.

Encounter poems depict the sexual meetings of the lovers. These can be present (1:12-14; 5:1) or past (2:4-7). Often their lovemaking is depicted with imagery of eating and drinking (2:4-7; 5:1).

In *seeking* poems lovers search for one another in the contexts of pastures (1:7-8) and city streets (3:1-5; 5:2-8). Sometimes the lovers find one another; sometimes they do not. Another type of seeking occurs in 8:1-4 when the woman seeks the approval of her love by society.

Related to seeking and encounter, poems of *beckoning* are made by both male and female. Often desire is expressed and lovemaking is described (2:8-15; 4:8-11). In one instance a group beckons the woman (6:13).

Poems of *affirmation* fall into three subcategories: self affirmation (1:5-6; 8:10); mutual affirmation (1:15-17; 2:1-3); general statement of affirmation (6:1-3; 7:10-13; 8:11-12). Affirmation poems usually occur within the context of objection (1:5-6) or competition (6:1-3).

The polemical tone of the book may be yet another way to make sense of the individual poems. Much of the poetry seems to focus on the lovers' right to their relationship regardless of societal and family pressures. This polemic provides an organizing principle for reading the poems as part of a larger whole.

When society will not affirm the lovers' relationship because of race, class, and sex-role stereotypes, the lovers' affirm each other with descriptions of beauty and lovemaking (1:5-6, 9-11, 12-14, 15-17; 5:2-8, 9-16; 8:1-4, 5, 6-7). The woman continues to assert her right to love when family members attempt to discourage her (1:5-6, 7-8; 8:8-9, 10). The fact that the lovers are continually seeking and beckoning one another in hopes of lovemaking indicates their determination to be together whatever the cost (1:7-8; 2:8-15; 3:1-5; 4:8-11, 16; 5:2-8; 8:13-14).

Related to the argumentative tone of these poems is the theme of barriers: barriers that prevent or threaten love; barriers that invite or protect love. Race, class and family would be barriers that prevent love (see above). Barriers that provide an opportunity for love are the countryside (2:8-15); the beloved's chambers and banqueting house (1:2-4; 2:4-7); the mother's house (3:1-4).

For Further Study

In the *Mercer Dictionary of the Bible*: FEMINIST HERMENEUTICS; LOVE IN THE NT; LOVE IN THE OT; SOLOMON; POETRY; SONG OF SONGS; WOMEN IN THE NT; WOMEN IN THE OT.

In other sources: A. Brenner, *The Song of Songs*; M. Falk, *Love Lyrics from the Bible: A Translation and Literary Study of The Song of Songs;* M. D. Goulder, *The Song of Fourteen Songs*; M. H. Pope, *Song of Songs*, AncB; P. Trible, *God and the Rhetoric of Sexuality*.

Commentary

An Outline

Introduction, 1:1-4

Title, 1:1

The book's title in the Hebrew Bible comes from the phrase in 1:1 which is translated, *The Song of Songs*. This phrase can be rendered in a number of ways, including "A song made up of many songs," and "The most sublime or best song." Because the book has traditionally been associated with SOLOMON, the title, "Song of Solomon," will occur in some English translations.

Encounter, 1:2-4

The first poem serves as an introduction. It is a poem of encounter but contains imagery and themes that are repeated throughout the book: physical love (kiss), sensual imagery (wine, oil, fragrance), the presence of others (maidens), barriers that protect love (beloved's chambers).

Love that Transcends Class and Race, 1:5-17

The woman's self-affirmation in 1:5-6 is the first indication that not all is well with the love expressed in the Song. The identity of the woman is uncertain. She is different from the *daughters of Jerusalem* (v. 5) in two ways. Her skin is dark as a result of working in the fields, which may indicate her lower socioeconomic status. (Her darkness implies the fairer skin of the *daughters of Jerusalem* who stayed indoors.) There is also the possibility that her skin color may denote a different ethnic background than the Jerusalem daughters. The claims she makes about herself are not apologetic, but boastful: *I am black and beautiful* (v. 5).

The woman is also different in that she is experienced sexually. She indicates her brothers were angry because she had not kept her vineyard (vines and vineyards are symbols for lovemaking throughout the Song, cf. 2:15; 7:12). Her remarks to the daughters of Jerusalem elsewhere in the Song are words of advice from an experienced lover to the unexperienced (2:7):

I adjure you, O daughters of Jerusalem,
  by the gazelles or the wild does;
do not stir up or awaken love until it is ready!

The poems that follow in the remainder of this section indicate that regardless of the strictures of class, race, family, or societal norms lovers will continue to seek out one another and claim their right to relationship. While the daughters of Jerusalem may stare and brothers may be angry, lovers mutually affirm the beauty of their love and are content with each other (vv. 15-17).

Love in Springtime, 2:1-17

Images of flowers, fruit, and animals are interwoven in the poems of this section as the lovers single out one another for encounter and speak of their love as a banquet. The woman claims that she is one flower among many, yet the man claims her for his own (vv. 1-2, 16). Likewise, out of all the trees of the wood, the woman claims the man for her own (v. 3). Their encounter is described as a banquet at which they feast on the fruit of love (vv. 3-6).

In vv. 8-15 the woman recalls a spring visit by her beloved. The beloved is described as *a gazelle or young stag* who invokes the rite of spring in his beckoning of the female lover. In the midst of the beauty and promise of spring, a note of caution still surrounds the lovers with a reference to *the foxes that ruin the vineyards* of their love.

The section closes with a statement of affirmation in which the images of *lilies, gazelle, stag,* and *mountains* are repeated (vv. 16-17).

Love's Couches, 3:1-11

In dream or reality the woman puts herself at considerable risk seeking the beloved in the city streets in the middle of the night. The search climaxes in lovemaking with advice to the *daughters of Jerusalem* concerning the hazards of this kind of meeting (vv. 1-5).

Juxtaposed to the nighttime lovemaking of the woman and man is the description of Solomon's marriage processional (vv. 6-11). King Solomon is symbol for the double standards the lovers face in overcoming the barriers to their love. Solomon, the king associated with class structure in Israel. Solomon, who had many foreign women, sanctioned by marriage, but how many for love and how many for political expediency?

The juxtaposition is carried further with the images of two couches for love: the lovers' secret rendezvous in the chamber of the house of the woman's mother, presumably upon a couch or bed (cf. v. 1); Solomon's marriage processional, which consists of a fortified couch (v. 7) whose interior is *inlaid with love* (v. 10).

Description and Desire, 4:1–5:1

Poems of description and beckoning alternate as the man and woman express their desire for one another, which culminates in an encounter of lovemaking. The *wasf* is used by the man to describe the woman in 4:1-7. To the modern reader it may not seem complimen-

tary to compare one's hair to a *flock of goats moving down the slopes*, or one's teeth to a *flock of shorn ewes that have come up from the washing, all of which bear twins, and not one of them is bereaved* (v. 2). However, the visual image is striking if the graceful, curved, flowing, movement of goats coming down a mountain from a distance is considered for the hair. Likewise, ewes shorn smooth and washed white, evenly matched, none broken, are fitting imagery for healthy white teeth in a society that did not know about fluoride or preventative dentistry.

The words *sister* and *bride* in 4:8, 9, 10, 11, 12 and 5:1 are not to be taken literally. *Sister* was a term of endearment used in Egyptian love poetry (Falk 1982, 122). Here the words are metaphors for the love relationship. The words may also be an allusion to the boundaries of acceptability against which the lovers struggle.

In vv. 12-15 the woman is described as a locked garden and sealed fountain, indicating her fidelity, or her inaccessibility. The images of garden and fountain also allude to the woman's sexuality and fecundity. The woman invokes the north and south winds to blow the fragrance of her garden abroad, beckoning her beloved to *come to his garden and eat its choicest fruits* (v. 16). In 5:1 the beloved comes to his garden, eats his honeycomb, and drinks his wine and milk.

Dialogue with Jerusalem's Daughters, 5:2–6:3

The seeking poem of 5:2-8 is parallel to 3:1-5. Both take place at night with a thin line between dream and reality. In chap. 3 the woman had gone in search of her beloved; in chap. 5 the beloved comes to her. The scene is suggestive, the language titillating.

The beloved knocks on the woman's door in the middle of the night and says, *"Open to me, my sister, my love . . . , for my head is wet with dew . . ."* (5:2).

The woman claims, *My beloved thrust his hand into the opening, and my inmost being yearned for him* (5:4).

She is slow in her response and finds the beloved gone when she finally opens the door. As in chap. 3, she searches for him in the city streets. By contrast with chap. 3, she is beaten by the sentinels of the city (cf. 5:7 and 3:3) and does not find her beloved. (This may indicate societal objection to her assertiveness.) As in 3:5, *the daughters of Jerusalem* are adjured; this time, however, she says, *If you find my beloved, tell him this: I am faint with love* (5:8).

This variation on the repeated refrain to the daughters of Jerusalem leads to a dialogue. In 6:9 the daughters ask the woman why her beloved is so special that she entreats them in this way. She responds to their question with a *wasf* in which she describes her beloved with images of precious metals and stones (vv. 10-16).

After this description, the daughters are interested in searching for the beloved, too. The poetry takes on a competitive tone when the woman replies with a statement of affirmation: *I am my beloved's and he is mine* (v. 3a).

Description and Encounter, 6:4-12

The dialogue with the daughters of Jerusalem is followed by a *wasf* in which the man describes the woman (vv. 4-10). It is essentially the same *wasf* found in 4:1-7, framed by the phrase, *terrible as an army of banners* vv. 4, 10). The phrase denotes the awesomeness of gazing upon the lover.

The encounter in vv. 11-12 presents some difficulties. The speaker of the poem is ambiguous and the Hebrew in v. 12 is virtually untranslatable (Falk 1982, 126). Since the man has been speaking in the previous poem, it is assumed that he is the one recalling this encounter. The word translated *prince* could be rendered "princely people." The whole line seems to be alluding to the ecstasy of lovemaking.

The Dance of the Shulammite, 6:13–7:13

A crowd beckons the woman at the beginning of this group of poems. The designation, *Shulammite*, is uncertain. It probably refers to the woman's distinctiveness (cf. 1:5-8). There is a hint of voyeurism when the crowd pleads, *Return . . . that we may look upon you*, to which she replies, *Why should you look upon the Shulammite, as upon a dance before two armies?* (6:13; MT 7:1). The meaning of this last phrase is debatable, but the earlier context of competition (6:4-12), as well as the alternating descriptions that follow (7:1-5; 7:6-9), indicate that the woman dances before two parties, a crowd and her beloved.

The crowd describes the woman and her dance with a *wasf* (vv. 1-5). This *wasf* differs from the others in that it starts with the feet and moves upward. It is also complete. (The others describe only half of the body, the upper torso.)

The man, in turn, describes the woman and expresses his desire for her (vv. 6-9).

Just as the woman's description of her beloved and the dialogue with the daughters of Jerusalem (5:9-16; 6:1-3) ended with a statement of affirmation, *I am my beloved's and he is mine* (6:3), so too, *the dance before two armies* and alternating descriptions (6:13; 7:1-5; 7:6-9) culminate in the statement of affirmation found in 7:10-13.

The Triumph of Love, 8:1-14

Themes from previous poems are repeated in this last section of the Song: longing for approval (vv. 1-4); the mother and the mother's house (vv. 1, 2, 5); the *daughters of Jerusalem* (v. 4); encounter under a fruit tree (v. 5); the disapproving brothers (vv. 8-9); King Solomon (vv. 11, 12); vineyards and gardens (vv. 11, 12, 13).

In the midst of all these images that recall the struggles of lovers, there is a strong statement and description of the power of love. It is strong as death, fierce as the grave, unquenchable, without price (vv. 6-7).

The Song has an open ending of mutual beckoning (vv. 13-14) indicating the triumph of love. In the face of whatever adversity, lovers will continue to listen for one another's voice, bounding unfettered upon mountains of spices.

Works Cited

Falk, Marcia. 1982. *Love Lyrics from the Bible: A Translation and Literary Study of the Song of Songs.*

Weems, Renita J. 1992. "Song of Songs" in *The Women's Bible Commentary.*

Isaiah

John D. W. Watts

Introduction

The Vision of Isaiah

Isaiah is the first of the Latter Prophets, as Isaiah, Jeremiah, Ezekiel, and the Book of the Twelve are called in the Jewish Bible. The canonical material identified as "the Prophets" is primarily concerned with portions of the history of Israel, and with the prophets' interpretation in light of the confession that God shapes history. Christian readers often overlook the continuity among the Prophets because the biblical books have been rearranged. The Former Prophets—Joshua, Judges, 1–2 Samuel, and 1–2 Kings—are broken by the insertion of the Book of Ruth, and separated from their companions, the Latter Prophets, by the insertion of the Writings. Remembering the Book of Isaiah in its canonical setting in the Jewish Bible is a helpful point of departure in any attempt to understand this rich and diverse work.

Isaiah and the Other Prophets

Each of the prophetic books in the OT relates in a specific way to the fall of JERUSALEM in 587/6 B.C.E. and the end of the monarchy which that event symbolized. The Former Prophets (Joshua–2 Kings, excluding Ruth which belongs with the Writings) lead up to that event and end with it. Jeremiah and Ezekiel focus narrowly on the decades before the fall and a brief period afterward. Isaiah and the Book of the Twelve take a wider view, surveying the 150 years before and the 150 years after Jerusalem's fall.

In addition, three of the prophetic books focus on the rebuilding of the Temple in Jerusalem as a goal. Ezekiel's vision of the new Temple is told in Ezek 40–48. Isaiah anticipates it in Isa 2 and describes its fulfillment in Isa 66. The Book of the Twelve places the prophecy of a new Temple in the center—Mic 4—and then portrays life in the new Temple in the Book of Malachi.

Parallels. Isaiah 2 and Mic 4 use nearly identical passages to portray the prophecy of the new Temple. Isaiah includes a narrative of SENNACHERIB's siege of Jerusalem in Hezekiah's time at the midpoint of the book, Isa 36:1-39:8, apparently making direct use of 2 Kgs 19–20.

Unique features. Isaiah uses a chronological sequence in its structure that has much more in common with the Former Prophets and Ezekiel than Jeremiah o the Book of the Twelve. God's control of historical events to achieve divine goals with the people is the driving impetus of the narrative. The use of the title *the Holy One of Israel* (1:4, and twenty-four more times through chap. 60), appears as a distinctive name for God, portraying the sovereign grace of God toward his people in a grander style than is found in any of the other prophets. Only Exodus, in portraying God's use of PHARAOH to accomplish his will with Israel, makes as great a claim to God's use of sovereign power as is found in Isaiah's portrayal of God's use of Assyrian and Persian powers to accomplish the divine will for Israel.

The Book of Isaiah presents a broad interpretation of the history of JUDAH and Jerusalem from the eighth to the fifth centuries B.C.E., guided by God's firm hand.

Authorship

The author, or authors, of the book are unknown. Jewish tradition understood the reference to the PROPHET in the superscriptions (1:1; 2:1 and 13:1) as indications of authorship. Attention to the person ISAIAH certainly suggests that this is a book about the prophet Isaiah, known to us otherwise only through the account in 2 Kgs 19–20. The existence of an apocryphal book, *The Martyrdom and Ascension of Isaiah*, is ample evidence that the figure of Isaiah had an enduring place in Jewish traditions. The superscriptions in 2:1 and

13:1 claim that prophecies of a future temple and the destruction of Babylon also belong to *Isaiah son of Amoz* from 1:1.

Modern critical scholarship has trouble ascribing authorship of the entire book to an eighth century prophet because the work of chaps. 40–66 so clearly relates to persons and events of the sixth and fifth centuries. The apparent periodization of the material in the Book of Isaiah led to the division of the book into First, Second, and Third Isaiah.

The difficulty of crediting an eighth-century author with so broad an interpretation of history is removed if the phrase *of Isaiah* (1:1) is understood as more than an author's signature (these issues are also treated below in the commentary on the superscriptions). The author or authors remain unknown.

Unity

If the claim for eighth-century authorship is eliminated, no strong reason remains to deny unity to the book. Chapters 1–2 at the beginning and 65–66 at the end form an INCLUSIO around the historical development in the book. The use of the name *the Holy One of Israel* for God continues throughout the book. The plot, which portrays God's decree of destruction in chap. 6, is balanced by his reversal of that fate in chap. 40. Taken together, these three points open the possibility of reading the book as a coherent whole.

Possible Life Settings

The book was intended to confess to its earliest readers the providence of God that had guided Israel through the judgment of EXILE to the rebuilding of the Temple and the new existence of the Jewish people after the Exile. Early Christians read Isaiah to support their messianic interpretation of the life of Jesus. Modern readers rightly see the Book of Isaiah as an important feature in the Bible; they may read the book both as a witness of God's work in Israel's history that led to the beginnings of JUDAISM and as a significant confession of the purpose of God that led to the coming of Jesus his son. This commentary will do some of both, but will primarily try to help the modern reader see what the first readers of Isaiah would have understood from its magnificent vision and verse.

Literary Form

Isaiah, like most prophetic literature, is composed primarily in poetic speeches. They are not speeches by a prophet but are presented like a drama in speeches by God and/or by some beings like angels (1:2 refers to *heavens* and *earth*). The book also has speeches by someone like a prophet (e.g., chap. 6) and choral speeches by groups of people (e.g., 32:9-20). There are also narratives about the prophet and kings (e.g., 7:1-14; 20:1-6; 36:1-39:8). Taking 1:1 as a superscription for the whole literary work encourages the reader to see it as "a Vision." Perhaps the highly dramatic arrangement of speeches for God and other speakers in the book is best characterized by this term. The book is a VISION in the literary sense of a work that includes both audible and visual imagery.

Date

Since the final chapters of the Book of Isaiah do portray the fulfillment of the Vision in the building of the new Temple in Jerusalem, the likely date for completion of the Vision should fall somewhere near the time of EZRA and NEHEMIAH in the fifth century B.C.E. But many parts of the Vision show signs of belonging to a long period of tradition and of prior use, perhaps going back to the time of the prophet himself.

The Prophet Isaiah

The prophet Isaiah is credited with crucial material in the book. The superscription in 2:1 calls attention to the Vision of the future temple as belonging to Isaiah. The narrative of chaps. 7–8 places his intervention at the turning point of AHAZ's reign. Similarly, the superscription in 13:1 credits the prophet with anticipating the failure of Babylon under MERODACH-BALADAN. The narrative in chap. 20 places Isaiah at a crucial point in HEZEKIAH's reign, a claim supported by chaps. 36–39. The Vision of Isaiah is based on these actions and messages from the prophet Isaiah. The book builds around his work, and a picture of God's work over three centuries in the life of Judah and the exiles.

Historical Background

The Near East forms a land bridge between the great civilizations of Egypt in the south, Mesopotamia in the northeast, and Asia Minor in the northwest. The area is bounded by the Mediterranean Sea to the west. In the ancient world, Egyptian and Aegean shipping brought commerce and occasional invasions to the area. The desert lay on the eastern border. Invaders such as the Midianites or Arabs could enter the land from that side.

Egypt controlled the land during the second millennium B.C.E., repelling invaders such as the Hittites out of Asia Minor, the Amorites out of Mesopotamia, and the Aegean Philistines. But substantial elements from each of these peoples settled in the land. Israel was one of the peoples that settled in the land under the larger controlling influence of Egypt.

In the ninth and eighth centuries B.C.E. Mesopotamian nations became very aggressive and cast aspiring eyes on CANAAN. The dominant nation of that period was ASSYRIA, with its capital at Nineveh on the upper Tigris river. Assyria pushed its campaigns into northern Palestine in the ninth and first half of the eighth centuries B.C.E. About 740 B.C.E. TIGLATH-PILEZER began a series of invasions that eventually won him control of Palestine. Later Assyrian kings would conquer Egypt as well. Assyria continued to be the ascendant power in Palestine until the collapse of Nineveh in 612 B.C.E. and the final defeat of the remnants of its armies in 605 B.C.E.

Babylon under Nebuchadnezzar (or NEBUCHADREZZAR) inherited control of Palestine. Nebuchadnezzar invaded Palestine and threatened Jerusalem in 598 B.C.E. and effectively reduced the nation to a puppet state by installing ZEDEKIAH as king. When Zedekiah began to resist Babylonian control, Nebuchanezzar returned and sacked the city, taking many Judeans into exile.

The PERSIAN EMPIRE succeeded to power in Babylon and Palestine by 540 B.C.E. Under the Persians successive returns of exiles to Palestine were allowed; the returning exiles restored Jerusalem and rebuilt its Temple. They continued to have control of Palestine until the invasions of ALEXANDER the Great in 330 B.C.E.

The Book of Isaiah covers a period that begins with the Assyrian invasions of the Near East in the latter half of the eighth century, and ends with efforts at restoration that continued well into the Persian period. Between those points of beginning and ending the book also offers a significant glimpse of exilic fears and hopes.

For Further Study

In the *Mercer Dictionary of the Bible*: ASSYRIA; BABYLONIAN EMPIRE; CYRUS; EXILE; ISAIAH; ISAIAH, BOOK OF; ORACLE; POETRY; PROPHET; MESSIAH/MESSIANISM; NEBUCHADREZZAR; PERSIAN EMPIRE; TEMPLE/TEMPLES; VISION.

In other sources: P. H. Kelley, "Isaiah," BBC; C. R. North, "Isaiah," IDB; G. L. Robinson and R. K. Harrison, "Isaiah," ISBE; J. M. Ward, "Isaiah," IDBSupp; J. D. W. Watts, *Isaiah 1–33*, *Isaiah 34–66*, WBC, and *Isaiah*, UBT.

Commentary

An Outline

The Superscription, 1:1
I. The Vision of the Age of Uzziah, 1:2–6:13
   A. In the Hall of the King of Heaven, 1:2–2:4
   B. The Day of the LORD, 2:5-22
   C. Jerusalem's Travail, 3:1–4:6
   D. Israel's Funeral Dirge, 5:1-30
   E. In God's Throne-room, 6:1-13
II. The Vision of the Age of Ahaz, 7:1–14:32
   A. Sons and Signs, 7:1–9:7 [MT 7:1–9:6]
   B. A Word against Jacob, 9:8–10:23 [MT 9:7–10:23]
   C. Do Not Fear, You Jerusalemites, 10:24–12:6
   D. Burden: Babylon, 13:1–14:32
III. The Vision of the Age of Hezekiah, 15:1–22:25
   A. Burden: Moab, 15:1–16:14
   B. Burdens: Damascus and Egypt, 17:1–20:6
   C. Four Ambiguous Burdens, 21:1–22:14
   D. Shebna Is Dismissed, 22:15-25
IV. The Vision of the Age of Manasseh, 23:1–27:13
   A. Tyre Is Ordered to Respond, 23:1-7
   B. The LORD Planned This against Tyre, 23:8-10
   C. The LORD's Hand over the Sea, 23:11-18
   D. The LORD Is Devastating the Land, 24:1-20
   E. The LORD Judges Armies and Kings, 24:21-22
   F. The LORD of Hosts Reigns, 24:23–25:5
   [Key Verse: The Banquet of the LORD of Hosts, 25:6]
   F'. The LORD Destroys Death Forever, 25:7-9
   E'. The LORD Judges Moab, 25:10–26:20
   D'. The LORD to Judge the Inhabitants
      of the Land, 26:21
   C'. The LORD Judges Leviathan, 27:1-11
   B'. The LORD Will Thresh
      and Gather Israel, 27:12-13
V. The Vision of the Age of Josiah, 28:1–33:24
   A. Disaster because of Expansion, 28:1-29
   B. Disaster through Political Relations, 29:1-24
   C. Disaster from Self-Help in Rebellion, 30:1-33
   D. Disaster because of False Faith
      in Egypt, 31:1–32:20
   E. God Vows to Punish the Tyrant, 33:1-24
VI. The Vision of the Age of Zedekiah, 34:1–39:8
   A. Edom's Curse—Judah's Renewal, 34:1–35:10
   B. The Assyrian's Speech, 36:1-22
   C. From Hearsay to Knowledge, 37:1-20
   D. Isaiah's Response from the LORD, 37:21-38
   E. Hezekiah's Illness, 38:1-22
   F. Hezekiah's Mistake, 39:1-8
VII. The Vision of the Age of Jehoiachin in Exile,
     40:1–44:23
   A. Prologue: In the Hall of Voices, 40:1-9
   B. Like a Shepherd, 40:10-31
   C. Israel is the LORD's Servant, 41:1-20
   D. The Trial Continues, 41:21–42:12
   E. Hear, You Deaf!, 42:13–43:21
   F. Remember These, Jacob!, 43:22–44:23

VIII. The Vision of the Age of Cyrus, 44:24–48:22
   A. The LORD Introduces Cyrus, 44:24–45:13
   B. Righteousness and Strength
      Are in the LORD, 45:14-25
   C. Bel Bows . . . the LORD's Purpose Stands, 46:1-13
   D. Sit in the Dust, Babylon!, 47:1-15
   E. Move out from Babylon!, 48:1-22
IX. The Vision of the Age of Darius, 49:1–57:21
   A. The Servant of Rulers, 49:1–50:3
   B. A Student's Tongue, 50:4–51:8
   C. Awake! Put on Strength!, 51:9–52:12
   D. Restoration Pains in Jerusalem, 52:13–54:17b
   E. A House of Prayer for All Peoples, 54:17c–56:8
   F. Rebellion, but Healing, 56:9–57:21
X. The Vision of the Age of Artaxerxes, 58:1–66:24
   A. The LORD's Kind of Fast, 58:1-14
   B. Troubled Times in Judah, 59:1-15a
   C. The LORD Decides to Act, 59:15b-21
   D. Zion's Day Dawns, 60:1-22
   E. The LORD's Agents Bless Jerusalem, 61:1-11
   F. A New Name for Jerusalem, 62:1-7
   G. An Oath and an Apparition, 62:8–63:6
   H. A Sermon and Prayers
      (with Interruptions), 63:7–64:12
   I. The LORD Deals with Opponents, 65:1-16
   J. The LORD's Great Day:
      A New Jerusalem, 65:17–66:24

This outline follows traditional breaks in the text except at two points: (1) The death of AHAZ (14:28) suggests a break in a manner similar to the death of UZZIAH (6:1). For that reason the section on Ahaz is extended from the end of chap. 12 to include chaps. 13 and 14.

(2) The sentence, *There is no peace, says my God, for the wicked* (57:21) has a parallel at 48:22, and is similar in tone to 66:24. Therefore, they are taken as internal marks that set the divisions of the text in chaps. 40–66.

The Superscription, 1:1

The opening phrase of the Book of Isaiah, *The vision of Isaiah*, suggests that the entire book is written as a VISION. The whole work is clearly related to a man named *Isaiah*, who is identified as a *son of Amoz*, but it need not be narrowly considered as a designation of the author. The issue of authorship involves a number of problems, especially the evidence that the book describes things that happen over a span of centuries. No one person could have recounted all of them.

The *vision* narrates several events from the life of Isaiah of JERUSALEM (chaps. 7–8, 20, 36–39). That prophet's name also is repeated in headings over chaps. 2 and 13. From chap. 40 on, however, it is clear that an era other than the one experienced by *Isaiah son of Amoz* has dawned.

Judah is the tribal district in which the city of Jerusalem is found. After the rebellion of JEROBOAM against the son of SOLOMON the twelve tribes of Israel were divided. Only JUDAH and BENJAMIN remained under a Davidic king in Jerusalem. During the reign of Uzziah—and, of course, before—the northern kingdom of Israel remained intact, with its capital in SAMARIA. But, while Ahaz was king in Judah, Samaria fell to the Assyrians (722/1 B.C.E.) and lost its national identity.

Judah and Jerusalem continued to exist for almost a century and a half under Davidic kings, although they were vassals of the Assyrians or the Babylonians throughout that period. Under the Persians Jerusalem is rebuilt as a temple city, using its own laws, but having no national existence. The people of Judah and Jerusalem were scattered over the empire.

The superscription notes that Isaiah prophesied over Judah and Jerusalem during the reigns of four Judaean kings: UZZIAH, Jotham, AHAZ, and HEZEKIAH. Uzziah had a long reign in the eighth century B.C.E. His death year is noted in 6:1. Jotham apparently overlapped the reigns of his father, Uzziah (they shared a co-regency during Uzziah's last years of rule), and son, Ahaz. Hezekiah succeeded Ahaz. Despite the reference in the superscription, no part of the Book of Isaiah can be placed during the reign of either Uzziah or Jotham. Isaiah of Jerusalem appears to have been prominent in the days of Ahaz and Hezekiah.

Ahaz was already king during the war with Syria and Israel (734 B.C.E.) as told in chap. 7. He survived the Assyrian invasions that followed. His death is noted in 14:28. Hezekiah lived and worked during the last decades of the eighth century and the first decade of the seventh. He was involved in two wars with ASSYRIA. Stories about Hezekiah are found in chaps. 20 and 36–39.

During this period Judah was a tiny kingdom, long separated from the northern tribes that constituted the kingdom of Israel. As the result of Assyrian invasions, the Kingdom of Israel came to an end during the reign of Ahaz, but Judah survived as a semi-independent entity.

The Vision of the Age of Uzziah, 1:2–6:13

The first section of the book contains a series of oracles that establish the relationships between God and Israel, and between God and Judah (and Jerusalem). This section also interprets what God's intentions toward Israel and Judah are in that period, and for the foreseeable future. Israel's (i.e., the Northern Kingdom's) fate is sealed. Although Jerusalem is also charged with many sins, an opening is left for repentance and future restoration. Generations will pass before the hoped for repentance and restoration becomes a reality.

In the Hall of the King of Heaven, 1:2–2:4

God is the principal speaker throughout this section, which has three divisions. God speaks first to Israel, which either may refer to the Northern Kingdom or to the entire elect people. Here *Israel* first has the broader meaning of all of the descendants of ABRAHAM. The second meaning refers to the political unit, the Northern Kingdom.

A second division concentrates on Judah and Jerusalem, while a third looks to the hope of a distant future.

1:2-7. A disappointed father. Heavenly witnesses are called to hear God's complaint against his children, i.e., Israel. Rebellion and lack of knowledge are the charges. The first is a wrong against authority; the second rejects the intimacy of accepting the closeness of family.

The nation is addressed. Its troubles are interpreted as punishment from God intended to lead it to repentance. All in vain. The nation is doomed.

1:8-20 Jerusalem's status. The political and military events of the mid-eighth century swept past Jerusalem, leaving it the isolated exception as other countries lost their sovereignty to become Assyrian provinces. Jerusalem's special circumstance is interpreted as the LORD's work.

Before Jerusalem can claim some special merit that led to this situation, the LORD addresses them. Neither the Temple nor its vain sacrifices, offered without the required concern for justice and right, have protected Jerusalem. The LORD's will, however, offers them a chance to repent and learn how to please God. Nothing else can account for their good fortune. What God wants from them in return is clear: *learn to do good, seek justice, rescue the oppressed, defend the orphan, plead for the widow* (v. 17).

Jerusalem's options are made equally clear in the LORD's invitation to dialogue (vv. 18-20). Grace and cleansing are possible. Jerusalem's options turn on the choice between being *willing and obedient* (v. 19) or the city may *refuse and rebel* (v. 20).

1:21-31. Jerusalem's fate. The LORD recognizes how degenerate the city has become (vv. 21-23). This requires God's judgment that will serve to burn out the evil (vv. 24-25) before restoration and regeneration can take place. The theme of redemption, which simultaneously requires elimination of the evil and the rebellious (vv. 27-31), continues throughout the book, with particular application in chaps. 65–66.

2:1-4 God's goal. The Book of Isaiah is oriented toward a future goal, one defined in this paragraph, but only achieved in chap. 66. The goal is not a new nation, but a new temple with its worshiping people who come from all over the world. The vision is attributed directly to *Isaiah son of Amoz* (v. 1), although it also appears in Mic 4.

The goal of a multinational congregation at worship defines more exactly than any other passage of Isaiah the change the LORD intends for Judah and Jerusalem—indeed for all Israel—from being a nation among the nations (cf. 1 Sam 8:4-22) to becoming a people gathered in worship before the LORD. Jerusalem is to become a Temple city, not a political capital.

The *days to come* (v. 2) are pictured in the book in the last two chapters. The *mountain of the LORD's house* is Zion. After many years of humiliation, the Temple and its place will be exalted and attractive, so much so that *the nations will stream to it*. Isaiah 66:18-21 anticipates the fulfillment of this vision.

The purpose of their pilgrimage to the Temple is spelled out in v. 3. They come to be taught God's ways. Then the second great characteristic of postexilic JUDAISM is named. It turns on *instruction* and the *word of the LORD*. It is not the presence of the Davidic king or even of the Aaronic priests, but the opportunity to learn about the word of God and experience his presence that draws the pilgrims.

God's judgment over the nations is asserted, with resultant peace. There is no reference to a restoration of the monarchy. Isaiah does not foresee a future messianic political leader. He does, however, envision God's continued assertion of authority over the nations, as the rest of the book will amply show.

The Day of the LORD, 2:5-22

2:5-9. Israel's rejection. The passage begins with an invitation for Israel to join the pilgrimage. But the rest of the passage gives reasons why they cannot. The usual English translation does not make sense. The explanation is that the first word of v. 6 has been mistranslated. The word in Hebrew can be translated *for* (as in the NRSV), or it may be translated "but." In this context "but" is preferred. Israel is denied access to the pilgrimage and clear reasons for that are given.

The passage looks back to 1:2-7 and repeats the same negative assessment. Israel has permanently forsaken the ways of God and of their ancestors. Apostasy, greed, and militarism, as well as idolatry, have brought them to their current state. The entire people have been *humbled* (v. 9). The LORD is urged not to forgive them.

2:10-22. The LORD's day. This passage is a classic description of the great and terrible Day of the LORD. The Day of the LORD is predominantly judgment against pride and everything haughty and lifted up. These attitudes are the ultimate symbols of rebellion against the authority and lordship of God. In that day the LORD alone will be exalted (v. 17).

The Day, with its expression of God's power, marks the end of IDOLATRY. The idols have proved to be without power to protect or to deflect the LORD's wrath.

The final exhortation is directed to God. The imperative in 2:9 had urged the deity, *Do not forgive them* (meaning the house of Jacob). At the end of this passage (v. 22) God is urged, *Turn away from mortals . . . for of what account are they?* The rest of the Book of Isaiah shows how God ignores this plea. In judgment and in salvation the LORD continues to care for mortals, including those in Israel.

Jerusalem's Travail, 3:1–4:6

Following oracles against Israel, the pendulum of attention swings back to Jerusalem. But the pronouncements are connected to the previous paragraphs by the words *For now* (3:1, RSV "For, behold").

3:1-12. Loss of support. One tends to forget how much of life is dependent upon networks of support. The LORD announces here that Jerusalem's life-support system shall be removed. Leadership and civil government are among the things removed, resulting in chaos.

3:13-15. Leaders at the bar of justice. The LORD stands in judgment over the peoples. The docket includes the elders and princes of his own people. They are accused of *devour[ing] the vineyard* (v. 14). The image is of a steward who had responsibility for a vineyard. Within the image, the vineyard represents the city and its people. Evidence is presented: *the spoil of the poor is in your houses* (v. 14); and the LORD's outrage is expressed: *What do you mean by crushing my people?* (v. 15).

3:16–4:1. The women of Jerusalem. The fashions and manners of the capital's women are held up to ridicule; these are then contrasted with the women's situation when the city has fallen to an invader and the men have been lost in battle. The list of cosmetics and jewelry is one of the most complete in ancient literature. Modern readers should recognize the sharp male-female role dichotomy as indicative of the ancient world.

4:2-6. The branch of the LORD. Interpretation of this passage has turned on the phrase, *the branch of the LORD* (v. 2). The Targum gave it a distinctively messianic interpretation, a perspective that has dominated commentary down through the Middle Ages. But early translations like the LXX did not turn on a messianic perspective. In the context of Isaiah, *the branch of the LORD* is parallel to *the fruit of the land* (v. 2) and refers to the LORD's plans and purposes. They will flourish *on that day* (v. 2) and Israel's survivors will take pride and glory in them.

Survivors of the population of Jerusalem will be held in high esteem in the period after the catastrophic events will have purged away Jerusalem's guilt. Mount Zion will stand protected by the special care of the LORD. The prophecy is parallel to 2:2-4 and envisions a glorious future for Jerusalem beyond the judgment.

Israel's Funeral Dirge, 5:1-30

Now the pendulum swings back to attention on Israel. Six times *Ah* (vv. 8, 11, 18, 20, 21, 22; RSV, "woe" in each case) introduces laments over the deceased after a song mourns her death and before an announcement of the coming disaster.

5:1-7. My friend's song for his vineyard. The use of *vineyard* as a symbol for Israel was anticipated in 3:14. The song itself (vv. 1-2) is a love song, perhaps like that sung at a wedding. But it is not a happy song. It is more like a tragedy.

The effort is pictured as the making of a vineyard using the most intensive effort and the best plants. But without success. In vv. 3-6 the owner of the vineyard takes up the song, addressing the people of Jerusalem and Judah. They are invited to join him in deciding what to do about the failed venture. What else could he have done? Now he decides to destroy it.

Only in v. 7 does the real meaning of the song emerge. The owner (or is it the bridegroom?) is the LORD. The vineyard is the house of Israel. The plantings are the people of Judah. The bad fruit is the social injustice evident in the land.

5:8-25. Lamentable acts and their consequences. Six times in this passage the word *Ah* (vv. 8, 11, 18, 20, 21, 22) appears. The *Ah*s mourn the announced death of the Northern Kingdom, of its people, and of men from Judah. Each instance of the word singles out a group who will suffer from the invasion and the exile.

Four speeches begin with *therefore* (vv. 13, 14, 24, 25) and describe the judgments that result. The first such judgment takes the form of an oath that is overheard (vv. 9-10). Verse 13 lists exile and hunger, v. 14 lists the number who die, while v. 13 harks back to 2:9. In contrast to the humiliation of the people, the LORD will be exalted and proved righteous by the events.

Verse 24 sees judgment as a fire sweeping the land because the people have rejected instruction and despised the word of God. He is called *the Holy One of Israel*. This name or title appears often in Isaiah. Verse 25 is the last *therefore*, describing the anger of the LORD as an earthquake. The section ends with the note that God's anger is not finished.

5:26-30. God summons a distant nation. God's punishment of Israel has been pictured in many forms. This passage turns to the historical judgment through invading armies that will hold center stage through Isaiah. God's initiative in the matter is stressed even as the swift and eager response of the armies are pictured. They are awesome in power and skill. The future for the land, meaning Canaan, is dark.

In God's Throne-room, 6:1-13

6:1-8. The vision. Someone, not identified but presumably the prophet, tells of a VISION that came the year King Uzziah died. The vision of the LORD presents the heavenly throne, attended by beings called SERAPHIM who each have six wings (these attendants appear in every picture of the LORD on the throne, but they have different names each time).

The solemnity of the occasion and the awesome character of the place are intoned in the *Holy, Holy, Holy* (v. 3). God is identified as the LORD of Hosts. This name is used regularly of God, especially in the prophets. *Hosts* literally means "the armies." It appears to be a military title. *Earth* may also be translated "land." The full range of territory affected by the vision is *full of his glory*. The solemnity is emphasized by the shaking and the smoke.

In this setting the narrator is overcome and fears for his life. But an attendant touches his lips with a live coal and pronounces him fit for attendance on the LORD. The LORD is calling for someone to be his messenger and he volunteers.

6:9-13. The message. Instructions are short and direct. A message is to be delivered to this people. In context this can only be the people of Israel and Judah.

The message is strange. No matter how much they listen, they will never understand. They are commanded not to understand. It is not the LORD's intention that they repent and be healed. The Hebrew text states this as a command. The Greek translation simply states a consequence. Later in Isaiah (43:8) there is reference to these blind, but they have eyes. In the NT Jesus explains the difficulty in understanding his parables by referring to these verses (Mark 4:12 and par.). God's decree of judgment is not reversible for this generation.

The protest, *How long?* (v. 11) evokes the response, not in terms of time, but of effect. Total destruction is decreed. It will be repeated until final. Nothing of the tree will remain. The message concludes with the enigmatic words, *The holy seed is its stump* (v. 13). Despite total destruction, can there be hope? If so, it lies in the stump that remains. This is not interpreted here. In the context of Isaiah, *its stump* must refer to the scattered exiles or the ruins of Jerusalem. In a later era, Christians looking to a horizon beyond those available in the days of Isaiah, have sought here a hint of the coming Messiah, as they have in Gen 3:15 (the so-called "protoevangelium").

The first section covering the reign of Uzziah ends with a picture of doom on Israel and severe threat to Jerusalem for the foreseeable future.

The Vision of the Age of Ahaz, 7:1–14:32

The age of AHAZ witnesses the precarious survival of Judah and its king at a time when Assyrian inva-

sions subjugate all the kingdoms to the north, including Aram and Israel. According to the Book of Isaiah, Judah is spared when God, through the prophet, orders Ahaz not to resist, but to wait out the events to come.

Sons and Signs, 7:1–9:7 [MT 7:1–9:6]

This section is composed of a series of narratives and speeches in which sons and signs are prominent. It begins by introducing Isaiah and his son, *Shear-jashub* (7:3). The name is significant; readers of English versions (e.g., NRSV, RSV, NIV) must look to the margin for the translation, "a remnant shall return." The narrative continues by introducing the current Davidic ruler of Jerusalem, Ahaz the son of Jotham, for whom the name of Isaiah's son is a meaningful sign (see below, 7:1-9).

Associated with sign of *Shear-jashub* is a comment about *the two smoldering stumps of firebrands* (7:4). Isaiah explains these two images as representing the kings of *Aram* (Syria) and *Ephraim* (Israel), and their kingdoms. The image suggests these last independent rulers and their kingdoms are in their final days.

In the next scene, Ahaz is offered a sign for himself. When he refuses, it is given anyway. A new son will be born whose childhood will mark the time of fulfillment for the previous sign (7:10-16).

The coming Assyrian invasion is announced in figurative language but without signs (7:16-25). But the invasions are confirmed by the name of another of Isaiah's sons, *Maher-shalal-hash-baz* (8:1, again translated in the margin: "The spoil speeds, the prey hastens"). This sign, too, refers to the time in which the previous announcements would take place.

Further figurative language describes the Assyrian invasions and the confusion in Jerusalem related to them. Then Isaiah announces his retirement from public life and commands the conservation of his teachings among his disciples. But he and his sons remain, even in retirement (and later in the publication of the book), to be *signs and portents in Israel from the LORD of hosts* (8:18).

One further passage deals with a son who is a sign (9:1-7 [MT 8:23–9:6]). In the reign of Ahaz, a day with little or no hope or glory, a son is born. Is it the one anticipated in 7:14? Clearly, he is greeted with all the royal pomp and promise that an heir to David's throne deserves.

7:1-9. The sons of Jotham and Isaiah. The various speeches and prose portrayals of the previous chapters are followed by historical narrative for the first time in the book. The narrative describes a confrontation—on divine command—between the prophet Isaiah and the newly crowned King Ahaz. The kingdom faces a critical moment. The kings of Aram and Israel invaded Judah to persuade it to join in revolt against ASSYRIA. They were too much for Judah, had already occupied most of its territory, and now laid siege to Jerusalem to force a change in government to comply with their plans (cf. 2 Chron 28:5-21).

The first son to be named is *Ahaz son of Jotham son of Uzziah, king of Judah* (v. 1). The threat against him is *the son of Tabeel* (v. 6) who is being promoted to be the successor of Ahaz by the enemy kings. The LORD sends Isaiah and his son to meet Ahaz. This son's name carries the LORD's message for Jerusalem and for Ahaz: "A remnant shall return" (NRSV mg.). The child's name is Jerusalem's decreed fate: devastation will leave only a remnant, but that remnant will survive. Isaiah's name means "the LORD will save." His son's name defines that salvation more precisely.

In light of the message in these names Ahaz is commanded to ignore the threat from the neighboring kings. Their revolt will not succeed. The two kings are themselves symbols of the near end of their kingdoms. Ahaz is challenged: *If you do not stand firm in faith, you shall not stand at all* (v. 9). The verbs are plural. They apply both to the king and to the entire kingdom of Judah.

7:10-16. The LORD's sign—a son. The LORD has the prophet offer Ahaz a sign to strengthen his faith. Ahaz refuses the sign with the excuse that he doesn't want to *test* (v. 12; the Hebrew word also means "to tempt") God. Ahaz has a technical point: according to Deut 6:16 putting "the LORD your God to the test" is forbidden. But there are other OT instances where testing is an approved activity resulting in a sign from God (cf. Judg 6:36-40; 1 Sam 2:34; 10:7). Perhaps the motivation behind the "testing" is also important to consider.

In the case of Ahaz, a sign is offered without his seeking it. A designated, though not identified, *young woman* (v. 14; the LXX uses a specific word for "virgin") conceives and bears a son. She names her son *Immanuel*, which means "God with us" (NRSV mg.). The name of the child would seem to be a good indication that God's presence and providence are obvious when he was born. But the sign goes on to say that by the time the child is old enough to make moral judgments his diet will be of *curds and honey* (v. 15), which would indicate a prosperous period. Finally the purpose of the entire sign is revealed: by

the time the child is grown, the countries of Israel and Aram will lie deserted (v. 16).

Christian interpretation of these verses has taken a different turn. The LXX translated the Hebrew *almah* "young woman" of 7:14 with a Greek word, *parthenos*, meaning "a virgin." Matthew 1:22-23 refers to this verse—from the LXX—in the account of the birth of Jesus, thus providing a foundation for the confession of Jesus' "virgin birth." The likelihood that the child foreseen in 7:14 is a royal child, because of a linkage to the Davidic king, makes the subsequent Christian messianic interpretation appropriate.

7:17-25. The Assyrian invasions. The significant historical events during the reign of Ahaz were not the conspiracies of his neighbors, but the serious efforts of Assyria to absorb the Palestinian kingdoms into its own growing empire. The emphasis in the Book of Isaiah, however, is not the Assyrian campaigns. Rather, it is the assertion that the LORD is bringing about this turn of events. The LORD has ordered the invasions and the LORD has decreed the devastation of the land of Canaan. Such assertions fulfill the convictions of 6:11.

The result of the invasions is seen in the destruction of the agricultural economy. Cultivated fields revert to wilderness, forcing survivors to eat a subsistence diet. Food will be available to those who have a goat to give milk and bees to produce honey. The *curds and honey* of 7:15 (associated with prosperity) now is reinterpreted to be the diet of a deprived people—a survival diet (v. 22).

8:1-4. Swift plunder, hastening booty. This entire chapter is a first-person account, following the style of chap. 6, in which the prophet Isaiah is the speaker. The words *Belonging to Maher-shalal-hash-baz* (v. 1; NRSV mg. offers the translation: "The spoil speeds, the prey hastens") are written on a bulletin board (the meaning of the *large tablet*) according to the LORD's command. The words, and the writing of them, are witnessed by *reliable witness* (v. 2). Then the prophet's wife conceives a child. When he is born, he is named *Maher-shalal-hash-baz* (v. 3). This child, then, becomes a walking bulletin board, a testimony to the LORD's word of judgment against Aram and Israel (v. 4). For a second time the coming destruction of Aram (*Damascus*) and Israel (*Samaria*) is indicated.

8:5-10. The waters of Shiloah. The phrase *waters of Shiloah* (v. 6) refers to water used for irrigation, in contrast to a flowing stream or a rushing torrent. It is used here to characterize the peace policies of Ahaz that accept the necessity of Assyrian sovereignty. There was no place for rebellion in that policy. *This people* (v. 6) echoes the covenant identity of 1:3b, the ones who are destined for destruction and exile (6:9-10). They reject Ahaz' policy, which is God's will. *Melt in fear* (v. 6) is a conjecture. A better translation would be "a joy to." Undoubtedly the popular favor that the policies of the kings enjoyed in Israel was a joy to both of them.

The coming Assyrian invasions to quell the rebellious activities of Israel and Aram are described as a rising flood, a contrast to the irrigation *waters of Shiloah*. They will draw Judah into the consequences of their folly.

Immanuel (v. 8) means "God with us." It either can be understood as a prayer, "Oh, God be with us!" or as an affirmation, "God is with us." In v. 8 it appears as a prayer; in vv. 9-10, which stress the immutability of God's decreed fate, it is an affirmation.

8:11-15. The LORD is your fear. The prophet's sense of inspiration is conveyed in the phrase *his hand was strong upon me* (v. 11). Ezekiel uses similar language to express the weight of the spirit's presence. But it is the word of the LORD that is important, not the experience of the spirit. It is a warning not to follow *this people*'s (v. 11; cf. 8:6) way.

This way is further defined as a *conspiracy* or problem, and a *fear* (v. 12). The people have their attention on the situation around them; the prophet is warned to concentrate on the LORD. If he wants to think of God in that way, as *holy* and *a fear*, that is all right. For indeed God will become both to the dynasties of Israel and the Jerusalemites.

Is it possible for God himself to become *a rock one stumbles over* (v. 14; RSV "a stone of offense") to his people? The implication here, with all the ambiguities of language, is that the people understand God's ways as the problem. Through that way of thinking, many will be offended and fall away. Others will be trapped and taken captive.

It is all too true that, when God's ways are clearly and correctly seen, many people find them offensive and intolerable. It was seen as so in 6:9-10. In the NT Jesus offers a beatitude for those who are not offended by his ways (Matt 11:6), and Paul recognizes that the message of the cross was scandalous—"a stumbling block"—to unbelieving Jews.

8:16-18. Binding up the testimony. The words are expressions of despair as well as strong statements of hope. The LORD is hiding his face from the house of Jacob. This is the cause for Isaiah to withdraw. He is sealing his testimony among his followers.

But there is no reason to despair. He will hope in and wait for the LORD. The realism of prophecy that recognizes God's negative judgment upon a generation does not eliminate the strong prophetic sense of God's ultimate good will toward the people. Isaiah's ministry has transformed him and his children into *signs and portents* (v. 18) of the LORD's anger and judgment on Israel. Even after withdrawing, the LORD still dwells in Zion.

8:19-22. Attention to instruction and testimony. This paragraph (although the NRSV does not show a paragraph break, it should) describes the way people in times of crisis tend to turn to various superstitions for guidance. The key phrase is clearly *for* (or *to*) *teaching and instruction* (v. 20). The NRSV ignores the verse division and attaches the phrase to the preceding sentence. But it can also be understood as an answer to the implied question that asks approval of the activity. It says: No! Instead one should turn to Torah and Wisdom.

Persons who turn to such superstitions have no hope and can only end up in disillusioned anger and despair.

9:1-7 [MT 8:23–9:6]. To us a son is born. The tenses of the verbs in translation make it difficult to make sense of this passage. The verbs in translation are not correlated to the Hebrew tenses at all. The passage begins by insisting that present anguish need not indicate future gloom. It suggests a difference between the former times and the latter times. The entire Book of Isaiah deals with the idea of the two eras: the former times of judgment, exile, and distress, the latter times of restoration, rebuilding, of rediscovery of the LORD's presence.

These contrasts move throughout the passage. The distressing condition of the border areas in the north of Canaan will be reversed. Darkness will be replaced by bright daylight. God will increase the people and their joy will know no bounds. Oppression will have been removed. The clothing of warriors will be destroyed because it has no current purpose.

The guarantee of all the preceding statements of reversal is the news that a child has been born to us. Every birth is a sign of hope and future, but this is no ordinary child. He is a royal child with divine promise. His birth anticipates a period of peace, with prosperity to follow.

His names are auspicious: *Wonderful Counselor, Mighty God, Everlasting Father, Prince of Peace* (v. 6). Certainly this is no ordinary child. His authority will expand and carry the promise of *endless peace* (v. 7). He will reign on the *throne of David* (v. 7). So he is clearly a royal heir who brings the promise of peace, prosperity, and longevity. The magnificent picture comes to a close with the assurance that *the LORD of Hosts will do this* (v. 7). Perhaps it should be translated as a prayer that the LORD will bring this to pass.

The obvious question is: "Who was this child?" The context would lead the interpreter to look to the promise of 7:14 and ask whether this refers to the next king of Judah. In that case this would be a description of the birth ceremonies of Hezekiah. Ahaz' ability to hold the tiny kingdom together through the crisis of the Assyrian invasions meant that Judah would be able to crown a new king at the right time, a privilege denied to Aram and Israel in the course of events. The passage is not framed as a promise but as a joyous recognition of a current event.

The royal hope that these verses express is a legitimate part of OT messianic theology found in 2 Sam 7:12-14 and royal Psalms like Pss 2, 72, and 89, and elsewhere. But such blatant messianism is not at home in the Book of Isaiah, which has pronounced judgment on the kingdoms, including Judah, and looks beyond them. Isaiah's future, as seen in chaps. 40–66, does not have a place for king or nationhood. But the Book of Isaiah does allow the opposition, with its claim to a royal future, to be heard here and in 10:34–12:6 (see Watts 1985, 135).

Christians have laid hold of the divine elements in the names and their royal setting to find messianic significance in this passage. But Christian messianism has the same difficulty applying these words to Jesus of Nazareth that we do in relating them to the message of the Book of Isaiah. They would identify Jesus as a political messiah who would reestablish the Kingdom of David, which he refused to do. So Christians have applied the vision of the future king to Christ's second coming.

A Word against Jacob, 9:8–10:23 [MT 9:7–10:23]

This section concentrates on an interpretation of God's work through the historical events of that period. It contains three smaller units. The first offers a prophetic interpretation of events in Israel. The second looks at Assyria as God's instrument. The third is an exposition of the name of Isaiah's first son.

9:8–10:4. History from a prophet's viewpoint. The mood and viewpoint change dramatically, returning to that attitude last heard in chap. 5. In these paragraphs there is no resistance to God such as was found in the previous section. The dialogue is more detached, like that of the heavenly observers. The company of mourners that begin "speaking" in 10:1 recalls a similar development in chap. 5. The *Ah* in 10:1 seems to reflect the series of *ah* statements that ended in 5:8-24. Thus, the theme and mood of chap. 5 are revived.

The events are founded on a word sent by God against Israel. All the people knew that it was from the LORD, but they insisted their current plight was only a temporary disaster that they could overcome. They would build a better future (9:8-10).

The LORD met this false hope by raising *adversaries against* the people (v. 11). The political troubles are interpreted as God's way of punishing Israel. The punishment included pressures from the Aramaeans and the Philistines—but that was not the end. God's wrath continues, as shown in the repetition of the phrase *his anger has not turned away*. This refrain first appeared in 5:25, and is used four more times in this passage (9:12, 17, 21; 10:4) to indicate God's attitude. The repetition also serves to explain the tumultuous times (9:11-12).

The people did not heed the LORD, so their leaders were cut off (9:13-17). Wickedness burns in the land, but the wrath of the LORD burns hotter. The people become self-destructive, consuming each other (9:18-21). Through all this, the book asserts, God's punishment works on.

The *Ah* (v. 1; RSV, "woe") turns against those who practice injustice, from the legislators to the perpetrators of oppression who ignore the needs of the poor and of widows. They are asked what they hope to do in the day of *punishment* and *calamity* (v. 3) to come. How will they hope to avoid death or imprisonment? Of course, they have no answer. Their kind of corruption has no appeal to the military conqueror to come who is already gorged with booty. But God's anger still burns (10:1-4).

The passage gives a prophet's view of the events of the 734–721 B.C.E. in the recurrent invasions of the Assyrians, and the attendant political chaos that followed. Modern readers must wonder how a prophet would write the history of our generation?

10:5-19. Assyria, rod of my anger. ASSYRIA became the preeminent world power after the middle of the eighth century B.C.E. This country with its capital, Nineveh, on the upper Tigris river, took control of Mesopotamia to give it a base approximately as large as modern Iraq. With fairly strong neighbors on the east and north, it turned its attention westward toward Palestine, and eventually against Egypt. Assyria's great leaders, TIGLATH-PILESER III (745–727 B.C.E.), SHALMA-NESER V (727–722 B.C.E.), SARGON II (722–705 B.C.E.), and SENNACHERIB (705–681 B.C.E.), all took part in invasions of Palestine during Isaiah's lifetime. Assyria's dominance of the region continued until near the end of the seventh century.

Significant political units in the region exist at four levels. The big powers who were potential super powers or empires included Egypt, Assyria, Babylonia, Persia, and later the Hellenistic empires and Rome. Secondly, there had been powers whose armies roamed widely, taking booty and sometimes leaving one of their own as king. The Hittites, Mittani, and Midianites fit this category. A third level was that of smaller states, often built on ethnic majorities. Judah, Israel, Aram, Moab, Edom, the Philistines, and Phoenicia belonged to this category. A final significant unit was the city. Cities were often the most durable political unit, preceding the development of states and often surviving their destruction. Babylon, Damascus, Tyre, and Jerusalem belonged to this category.

Assyria was introduced in the vision of 7:17 as the real power to fear because the LORD is bringing them into the land. In 10:5-19 Assyria is personalized and characterized. First the LORD makes clear that the Assyrian is his instrument, *the rod of my anger* (v. 5). Assyria is being sent *against a godless nation* (v. 6, i.e., Israel), a people upon whom the LORD's wrath is being poured. Assyria will utterly destroy and despoil them.

Before anyone can complain, the passage recognizes that the Assyrians are unaware of their divine motivation. They are intent on conquest and empire. Samaria and Jerusalem are just two more cities to add to the list of Assyrian conquests.

Then there is also recognition that criticism of Assyria for its arrogance and boasting (recall 2:10-22!) is justified. The LORD promises to deal with that as soon as Assyria has finished its assigned task in relation to Mount Zion and Jerusalem. The Assyrian's boasts are exemplified in the king's boasts that he has accomplished all his conquests *by the strength of [his] own hand* (v. 13). He has determined new boundaries, stolen national treasures, and destroyed the champions of the peoples. He did all this just as the farmer takes eggs from a sitting hen—without protest of any kind (v. 14).

The discrepancy between the LORD's claim to have sent the Assyrian and the king's boast of self-determination evokes a protest. *Shall the ax vaunt itself over the one who wields it?* (v. 15). Is Assyria an instrument of divine intention, or a self-motivated conqueror? *The LORD of hosts* (v. 16) will settle that issue by *a wasting sickness* among the conqueror's soldiers. Is this dysentery? And does this refer to Sennacherib's sudden lifting of his siege of Jerusalem in 701 B.C.E. (see 37:36)? *His glory* will be undermined as if a fire burned it up. How fleeting and precarious is political glory! The Assyrian Empire did in fact deteriorate and fall from within, not from any military challenge from without, much as the USSR has in our time. *His stout warriors* (v. 16) is literally "his fat ones" and may refer to all who have profited from Assyrian rule.

The light of Israel (v. 17) is a divine title (see Pss 27:1 and 36:10). *His Holy One* means Israel's God as in The Holy One of Israel. God's move to reverse the Assyrian's fortune will be swift and devastating. There will be nothing left. The speed with which a great power's authority, power, and glory can dissipate is always surprising, but it is documented in history again and again.

The effect of this pericope is to emphasize that Assyria is God's chosen instrument for this time, but only for this time and purpose. Assyria will also be judged and found wanting in its time. It is only the authority and power of God that lasts. This is small comfort for Judah when it must face another century of Assyrian power, but it is the basis for continued faith in God and hope for the future. Nonetheless, Assyria's role as God's instrument certainly is the basis for the readers of the book to recognize how God works in history. A sovereign God can use the great powers of the world for the LORD's own purposes, without losing sight of the commitments made to Israel—in the broad sense of the name—and of the deity's future goals.

10:20-23. Only a remnant. When all this happens, there will be a remnant of survivors, but only a remnant. They will not all have been destroyed, even when the invasions have taken their terrible toll. The remnant will include some from Israel and from Judah.

The surviving remnant will no longer depend on the oppressors for their hope and welfare, as eighth century Israel did depend on political saviors by pitting one power against another. Instead they *will lean on the LORD, the Holy One of Israel, in truth* (v. 20).

To an exilic audience hope that *a remnant will return* (v. 21) might, at first glance, promise a return of exiles to Judah, but here the statement clearly means repentance in turning to the LORD. The real goal of God's work in Israel, according to the Book of Isaiah, is the spiritual renewal of the people. That was their sin in chap. 1; it will be their salvation in chap. 66.

The remnant theme is developed in terms of Genesis and the Patriarchs. The word that begins this is the use of *Jacob.* The term *mighty God* (v. 21, an echo of "God Almighty" from Gen 17:1; 35:11?) presents God as a warrior. And the reminder of the promise to Abraham that his seed should be *like the sand of the sea* (v. 22; cf. Gen 32:12) is a reminder of the way Israel had been promised a future of expansion and growth.

Now the promises are contrasted with the current fate: *destruction is decreed* (v. 22) and God is going to make a full end in the land of Canaan to the two kingdoms—kindgoms that are the high-water mark of growth and development in terms of the patriarchal promises. Now the future will be based on only a tiny remnant. This paragraph is a concise statement of Isaiah's vision of judgment that permeates chaps. 1–39.

Do Not Fear, You Jerusalemites, 10:24–12:6

In contrast to the decreed destruction of Israel, Jerusalem is called to faith and hope. This section returns to the theme from 10:12 and develops it in a complex literary structure—a CHIASM—that can be understood as an arch that has its center in 11:3b-4:

A—Very soon my anger will turn
    against the Assyrians, 10:24-25
  B—The LORD will whip them
    in the way of Egypt, 10:26-27
    C—He marches on Zion and waves
      at Jerusalem, 10:28-32
      D—The LORD is cutting trees
        in Lebanon, 10:33-34
        E—The shoot from Jesse's root, 11:1
          F—The Spirit of the LORD
            rests on him, 11:2
            G—The Fear of the LORD
              —his delight, 11:3a
Keystone: The LORD's righteousness
        and justice, 11:3b-4

G'—Righteousness his belt,
  11:5-8
F'—Knowledge of LORD
  in all the land, 11:9
E'—The root of Jesse, a banner
  to the nations, 11:10
D'—The LORD will recover refugees
  and restore the kingdom, 11:11-14
C'—The LORD will dry up the sea, 11:15-16
B'—You will sing in that day, 12:1-2
A'—And you will drink from the well
  of salvation, 12:3-6

<u>10:24-27. The LORD's anger against Assyria.</u> Assyria will not destroy Jerusalem. The invasions that would destroy the political structure of Canaan would not destroy the city. It would survive the loss of kingdoms and allies.

The reference is then to Israel's experience in Egypt. The Israelite slaves were not destroyed. Assyria will not be able to do that anymore than Egypt was able to destroy the Israelite slaves. When the time of the LORD's wrath is past, Jerusalem's salvation will be like that when Moses led Israel of old against enemies in the wilderness or raised the LORD's staff over the sea. The power to save, which began Israel's life in Egypt, will still be there. No matter how great the burden of oppression by the Assyrian looks in this moment, Jerusalem's future is held in a greater, more powerful hand.

The use of references to the Torah is interesting here. First, Israel's fate in the destruction of Canaan (10:21-23) is contrasted with the promises to Abraham in Genesis. Then Jerusalem's hope is pictured in terms of the Exodus and the journey through the wilderness in Exodus and Numbers (two obvious examples are the allusions to the water from the rock at Horeb [Exod 17:6], and the crossing of the sea [Exod 14:16]). This prophetic literature is clearly using the Torah to make its point.

<u>10:27d-32. God's march of conquest.</u> The subject of these verses is not clear. *He* (v. 27d) is often thought to be the Assyrians. But the passage has many similarities with 63:1-6 and suits the tradition of the LORD's march on Canaan (cf. Judg 5:4-5 and Ps 68:8-9). The tradition of the LORD's march suggests that this pericope, like the ones before and after it, has the LORD as its subject.

What is the point of the march? The context suggests that it should be positive to Jerusalem. There is terror in the villages, but not in Jerusalem. *He will shake his fist* (v. 32) is literally "he will wave his hand." The words are neutral as to intent. A slight emendation would make it read "he will enlarge Zion" (Watts 1985, 161).

10:33-34. The divine forester. God is pictured in many ways in Isaiah. He was a builder of vineyards in chap. 5. Here he is pictured as a forester whose tasks include trimming trees and choosing those that are to be cut down. The forests of Lebanon were the most beautiful of that part of the world, but those magnificent trees also often represent mighty rulers.

11:1-10. The shoot of Jesse and the LORD's righteousness. This beautiful poem combines two brief statements about Davidic kings (vv. 1-3a and 10) with a longer section that deals with how the LORD judges the poor and helpless with righteousness in a way that produces a city without violence. The entire passage joins the announcement in 10:33 about the work of the LORD.

While the divine forester is going about his business, *a shoot comes out from the stump of Jesse* (v. 1). In other words, a child grows up in the royal palace in Jerusalem. The passage seems to be taking up where 9:7 left off. This child is imbued with every spiritual gift. Apparently the promise inherent in his royal names (see 9:6 for the catalog) is being borne out in his character.

The gifts are fitting for a prince. There is *wisdom and understanding, the spirit of counsel and might, the spirit of knowledge and the fear of the LORD* (v. 2). The last quality is his special delight—he is a pious and religious lad. All of these qualities are thought of as gifts of the divine spirit bestowed on him.

The next paragraph turns to the qualities of the LORD who merits the fear and devotion of the prince. He judges *with righteousness* the poor and the meek of the land. He punishes by *the rod of his mouth* (v. 4), that is, by his words. And these are effective in curbing the wicked. *Righteousness . . . and faithfulness* (v. 5) are the characteristics of his life.

When such a divine ruler is in charge, the quality of life is also perfect. There is no violence or need for fear. All the elements of nature or society work together without friction. His edict is: *they will not hurt or destroy in all my holy mountain.* The concomitant results for the land around the city are stated: *for the land (earth) will be full of the knowledge of the LORD as the waters cover the sea* (v. 9). Recall that Israel's paramount sin in 1:3 was lack of knowledge of God!

Then the passage reintroduces the royal prince. On the day that this reign of God in Jerusalem is accomplished the royal prince will stand as a signal to the peoples. He will be the sign that the LORD does in fact rule there. He will have representatives from those people seeking audience with him as they did with Solomon, his ancestor. And his court will be glorious in every way.

11:11-16. The LORD's second deliverance. *On that day* (v. 11), like the references in 10:20 and 11:10, refers to the LORD's actions that were announced in 10:12 and 33. Note that this section makes no reference to a king who will serve as the LORD's instrument. Instead it is the LORD alone who acts. *A second time* seems to put the anticipated action of deliverance in a parallel relationship to the Exodus. The LORD will . . . *recover the remnant . . . of his people* as he did in bringing up Israel out of Egypt. This time they are brought back from several nations and regions.

Verses 12-14 describe how the LORD goes about the recovering action. A *signal* is raised. Those brought back are *the dispersed of Judah*. The old rivalry between Judah and Ephraim will be overcome. Together they will conquer the neighboring peoples as David had done. Obadiah 17-21 contains a parallel portrayal.

Verses 15-16 describe God's action in broad symbolic terms. *The tongue of the sea of Egypt* is another reminder of the Exodus. It also signals the elimination of the southern boundary of Canaan. *The River* usually refers to the Euphrates, the northern boundary of Davidic Israel, and signals the removal of a fixed northern boundary. With these natural boundaries destroyed, the new nation can expand in both directions. But the passage in v. 16 draws a different implication from these miracles. They remove the barriers to return. Highways from Assyria will be open for the return of God's people *as there was for Israel when they came up from Egypt*. The return, then, is portrayed as a second Exodus.

12:1-6. Hymns for that day. The future held open for Jerusalem requires praise and thanks. The first hymn (vv. 1-2) gives thanks for the LORD's mercy and comfort after judgment, and confesses the LORD as Savior.

The second hymn (vv. 4b-6) proclaims the continuation of this state of living in *salvation* (v. 3). The worship includes thanksgiving, calling on the name of the LORD, proclaiming his deeds to the nations. Praises are commanded *for he has done gloriously* (cf. Exod

15:1). Joy is appropriate for Zion *for great in your midst is the Holy One of Israel.*

This section, including 9:1-7 and 10:24–12:6, presents some of the best examples of Zion theology and praise. Only the Zion Psalms and the Royal Psalms are comparable. They present a program of salvation in which Zion—and its Davidic king—play key roles, in which the restoration of the glories of the UNITED MONARCHY is the goal. It shouts that the power of the LORD that brought Israel out of Egypt is adequate to accomplish salvation. The Vision is glorious and is solidly based on traditions of the Exodus and of Zion.

But the question arises: What does all this have to do with the Vision of Isaiah (cf. 1:1)? It has some relation to the message of 37:30-35 (= 2 Kgs 19:30-34), but it does not conform to the message of chap. 6, nor to the overall direction of the book. It does not fit the picture of 2:1-4. There is nothing in chaps. 40–66 indicating the conclusion anticipated by the Zion theology as found here. These chapters are an anomaly in the book. They reflect the kind of ideology of Zion that was put forward by Jeremiah's opponents in the last days of Jerusalem's siege at the hands of Nebuchadnezzar and Babylon. They probably must be seen as the voice of Isaiah's opposition who expected Hezekiah to be their Messiah who would accomplish all these things. The following chapters show how thoroughly wrong they were.

Burden: Babylon, 13:1–14:32

This section brings the period of Ahaz to a close (cf. 14:28), and introduces the LORD's action against Babylon and the Philistines. Babylon's history during these days gets little attention, but chap. 39 (= 2 Kgs 20:1-11) provides a clue in the name of MERODACH-BALADAN, who conquered and held Babylon from 720 until 710, and again in 703 B.C.E. He sought to organize rebellion among the client states of Assyria in Mesopotamia and Palestine. Babylon under the rule of Merodach-baladan is the one against which these passages speak.

These events, Babylon's successful rebellion against Assyria and its attempt to draw the Philistines and other states into the rebellion, are interpreted as major threats to the LORD's plan to use Assyria in Palestine. The chapters announce God's war against Merodach-baladan and against the Philistines. Samaria has recently fallen to the Assyrians. Ahaz's reign is drawing to a close. Hezekiah's reign will get caught up in the events related to the destruction of Babylon (cf. 21:1-10; 39:1-8).

13:1-22. The Day of the LORD against Babylon. Chapter 13 has the first superscription since chap. 2. Each of these superscriptions uses the name *Isaiah son of Amoz.* The final editors of the book thought it important that these two chapters (the vision of the mountain of the LORD's house and the subjugation of Babylon) be related to Isaiah, the prophet in Jerusalem. Chapter 39 also ties Isaiah to a word about Babylon, but that is the Babylon of the Exile.

The LORD is assembling a huge army *to destroy the whole earth* (v. 5). The destruction is identified as *the day of the LORD* (v. 6), taking up the theme from chap. 2. The same theme appears later in the line *I will put an end to the pride of the arrogant* (v. 11). This poem is one of the most graphic descriptions of the anticipated day of the LORD to be found anywhere.

The poem takes on historical details when it refers to *the Medes* (v. 17) as a major enemy recruited against Babylon. The destruction will be so thorough that Babylon will be like Sodom and Gomorrah. The prediction also claims that Babylon will be so thoroughly destroyed that it will never rise again.

14:1-21 Israel's taunt of the fallen king. This section interrupts the description of the day of the LORD to portray God's compassion and care for Israel. They will again be chosen (elected) and placed in their own land. Nations will help them and serve them. They will rule over those who had oppressed them. Here again is an alternative vision, not centered in Zion but in Israel. But it also is one of conquest and power. The ultimate picture in the Book of Isaiah will confirm the help of nations in return. It will not support the picture of conquest and power.

The passage then looks beyond the *pain and turmoil and the hard service* (v. 3), which are usually code words for the exile, to a day when they will *sing a taunt against the king of Babylon.* Within the narrow context of Isa 1–39 this must refer to Merodach-baladan. Verse 3 also would point exilic and postexilic readers to a double meaning that would include Nebuchadnezzar, the destroyer of Jerusalem. The theme of the world power of this king is more appropriate to Nebuchadnezzar than to Merodach-baladan. The arrogance and pride that are to be brought low are exemplified here. The mighty ruler of the earth is dead and all the world is relieved. He is ushered into the realm of the dead.

In v. 12 the king of Babylon is called *Day Star, Son of Dawn.* The hyperbole of the poem expresses the ambition of emperors to have themselves considered divine. His ambition was limitless. But even emperors must die. The desecrated corpse looks so harmless. One wonders how he could have conquered nations. He is denied a proper burial and tomb. His family is condemned to join him.

Behind the poem there seems to lie an older poem. *Day Star* is *helel* in Hebrew, which is rendered as "Lucifer" in Latin. The Latin rendering explains why the poem has sometimes been taken to depict the fall of Satan from heaven after an unsuccessful revolt against the LORD. Whatever the background and possible applications of the older poem may be, here it has been historicized to portray the death and disgrace of the mighty king of Babylon. Israel is called to join in taunting the mighty oppressor who is now dead and harmless.

14:22-27. Conclusion of the Day of the LORD. These verses conclude the great picture in chap. 13 of the day of the LORD against Babylon. They contain three short but distinct messages. The first asserts that the object of God's wrath is Babylon, not the king. It is a declaration of absolute destruction. The words parallel 13:17-22. The second passage (vv. 24-25) is an oath by the LORD that Assyria will, at the right time, be banished from Palestine. It echoes 10:7 and parallels 13:9-16. The third passage (vv. 26-27) claims that the LORD has a strategy for all his actions. It parallels the verses 13:6-8 and claims that the announcements of destruction over Babylon and the ultimate elimination of Assyria are the LORD's plan for the land (of Canaan) and its nations. It further claims that the LORD's decrees are immutable. No one can deter God. The idea that God's plan determines the course of history is taught in the Book of Isaiah more fully than anywhere else in the Bible.

14:28-32. Burden over the Philistines. The chronology of this period is confused. The year King Ahaz died is probably 718 B.C.E., sixteen years after 735–34 when he assumed the throne (2 Kgs 16:1) or 715 B.C.E., fourteen years before 701 B.C.E. (2 Kgs 18:13) or 728 B.C.E., four years before 724 B.C.E., when Shalmaneser marched on Samaria. The more likely date is 718 B.C.E.

An *oracle* (v. 28) is a prophecy directed against a foreign land. But this is not the kind where kings of the nations are made to bow to Zion's king. Rather it shows how the LORD moves against nations that resist his will. Philistia in rebellion against Assyria has acted against God's plan. The passage is a lesson for Judah and Jerusalem, teaching the futility of resisting God's signals.

The rod that *is broken* (v. 29) may refer to the death of Shalmaneser, the Assyrian emperor. There was a rebellion in Palestine at the time of his death. Ahaz followed his usual policy and continued to be loyal to Assyria. Philistine cities joined the rebellion. *The snake* must also be Shalmaneser. *The adder* and the *flying fiery serpent* would then represent Sargon who put down the rebellion in 718 and 714 B.C.E.

Assyria restores order to the countryside, while the LORD exacts his own punishment from the rebels. The funeral lament is sung over Philistia, which joins Babylon in defeat and destruction.

Verse 32 concludes the section. An embassy from abroad waits for an answer. But what is the question? And what nation wants to know? The context suggests that the occasion for the embassy's presence is the death of Ahaz. The question is whether there will be a smooth succession to the throne. The answer is: The LORD is Zion's foundation. Not SARGON, not alliances, not armed rebellion—but the LORD. It is interesting that Hezekiah's name is not mentioned. *His people* is the term used for Israel (as "the elect ones"). Israel's future rests with Jerusalem. This is the theme of the entire Vision, and this is the message for exilic Israel as well. The city is and will be a secure refuge.

The Vision of the Age of Hezekiah, 15:1–22:25

That HEZEKIAH is the king through this section is conjectured from the listing of the death of *Ahaz* in 14:28, the historical notice of *Sargon's* invasion of *Ashdod* in 20:1, and the references to *Shebna* and *Eliakim,* in 22:15 and 20, who are ministers in Hezekiah's government. Of particular significance is the fact that Hezekiah's name is never mentioned, although he is listed among the kings in 1:1.

Burden: Moab, 15:1–16:14

This passage appears to react to an attack by some group out of the desert to the east upon Judah's neighbor to the east, Moab. The country is devastated. Refugees push toward Judah and leaders ask for assistance.

A description of the devastation opens the passage (15:1-4), followed by a sympathetic response (15:5), apparently from someone in Judah, and a further description of the devastation (15:6-9). The passage ends (15:9b) with a word, apparently from the LORD, indicating that this is the first of several acts of judgment on Moab.

Moab prepares a delegation to ask Judah to act on its behalf. They ask for advice or direction. They ask for Judah to extend its shadow, that is, to declare that this invasion is a threat that Judah interprets as a threat to its own interests as well. They ask that the border be opened for refugees.

Isaiah 15:4b-5 interprets these events as an opportunity for the Jerusalem monarchy to extend its authority over Moab again. A chorus (15:6-8) exults that Moab's pride has finally caught up with it. Someone expresses grief over the events, but without conviction (vv. 9 and 11). The LORD notes that this is his doing (v. 10). Moab will be worn out with this effort, so that it is actually no longer able to pray. And the LORD declares that within three years Moab's population will be reduced to an insignificant remnant. With the decimation of Moab the circle closes around Judah.

Burdens: Damascus and Egypt, 17:1–20:6

This passage should be interpreted as a self-contained unit. The setting is Jerusalem, which is portrayed as the one entity that has a choice as to the future. Aram and Israel do not have choices. The differences between the choices of Judah compared to those of Aram and Israel are depicted in the outline below; Judah is the subject from D to D'.

These four chapters form one symmetrical whole that climaxes with the bringing of gifts to the LORD in Zion (18:7). The section is characterized by *in that day* passages, with variations *in that time* (18:7) and *in the year* (20:1). The outline is again in the form of a CHIASM (what follows is author's trans.):

A—Behold! Damascus and Ephraim lie ruined!, 17:1-3
  B—On that day Jacob's glory
  will be leftovers, 17:4-6
    C—On that day one looks to his Maker, 17:7-8
      D—On that day you (fem. sing.)
      forgot God, your Savior, 17:9-11
        E—Woe! Raging of the nations, 17:12-14
          F—Woe! Go, swift messenger, 18:1-2
            G—Peoples see:
            The LORD is silent, 18:3-6
Keystone: At that time gifts to the LORD in Zion, 18:7
            G'—Behold! The LORD coming
            to Egypt, 19:1-15

          F'—In that day Judah will be a terror
          to Egypt, 19:16-17
        E'—In that day five Egyptian cities
        speak Canaanite, 19:18
      D'—In that day an altar to the LORD
      in Egypt, 19:19-22
    C'—In that day a highway:Egypt and Assyria
    worship together, 19:23
  B'—In that day Israel will be third
  to Egypt and Assyria, 19:24-25
A'—In the year Sargon came to Ashdod,
the LORD spoke to Isaiah 20:1-6

The letters B, D, G, and G' mark the planting and harvest imagery that is used in key places. The letters G and G' are also speeches from the LORD, the only ones in the passage, aside from the instructions to Isaiah in chap. 20. Because they are from the LORD they have special significance.

17:1-8. Israel's position. Damascus and Ephraim have suffered from the invasions and are no longer viable political units. The passage ends with the call for all to seek *their Maker* (v. 7) and not to seek things *their own fingers have made* (v. 8), such as sanctuaries or idols. Both Aram and Israel are only remnants of their former selves. IDOLATRY is often used to bolster the pride and power of the rich and powerful. When neither riches nor power remain, one must seek divine reality, not just symbols of human ambition.

17:9-14. Focus on Jerusalem. In view of the disasters visited on its neighbors, it appears that Jerusalem has not remembered the God of its salvation (*the Rock of your refuge* [v. 10]). The planting pictured in vv. 10b-11 is probably a pagan rite to an unidentified deity. Verses 12-14 seem to present the terror evoked by the pagan rites, a terror that has no substance.

18:1-7. Messengers from Ethiopia. Egypt is divided into three distinct parts. Its Pharaohs tend to represent one of them. The Ethiopian portion is making a bid to replace the leadership exercised by the princes of the Delta. The messengers are apparently seeking the aid of Assyria and are sent on their way by Jerusalem.

The LORD will not interfere, but simply observe the developments. When the political developments mature, Assyria will send messengers and gifts to Jerusalem, probably as a bribe to secure their loyalty in protecting Assyria's flanks during an invasion of Egypt.

19:1-17. The LORD's invasion of Egypt. God will incite internal turmoil in Egypt and turn the country over to a hard master, a fierce king. This is probably the same Ethiopian referred to in chap. 17. The LORD has decided to determine the matter. God uses internal social unrest, natural disasters, and confused political advice to achieve that end.

The Egyptians are terrified because of the LORD's intervention in their affairs. Because they identify the LORD with Judah, their fear relates to Judah, too. Verse 17 has been a problem for translators. The Hebrew word translated *will become a terror* occurs only here in the Bible. The Greek translation made of it "a terrifying object." The Latin identified it with the word for"festival" and translated "will be in festival mood." NRSV has, with most English translations, followed the Greek. Perhaps both senses play a role.

The internal revolt in Egypt has weakened the country to the extent that even a small country like Judah must be respected. The festival referred to must be PASSOVER. The LORD's involvement in events raises the specter of a repetition of the disasters of the time of the EXODUS. Judah can be a factor here. But only as it cooperates with the LORD's plan involving Ethiopia and Assyria.

19:18-25. The LORD's intervention in Egypt. Four vignettes are developed, beginning with the phrase *on that day* (vv. 18, 19, 23, 24). The first reflects growing Canaanite influence seen in five cities that speak a Canaanite tongue similar to Hebrew and *swear allegiance to the LORD* as all the small nations of Canaan did under David and Solomon. The name of the city is in dispute because of a textual problem caused by two Hebrew letters that look very much alike. The versions differed on them from earliest times. One translation is *City of the Sun.* Another is "the city of destruction."

Then the worship of the LORD in Egypt is pictured (vv. 19- 22). There will be an altar to the LORD and a pillar as a monument to the LORD's saving powers. The LORD will be revealed to the Egyptians so that they worship God with sacrifices and offerings. They will make religious vows and fulfill them, and the relation to the LORD through judgment and repentance will be in effect for them.

A highway will allow full relations between Assyria and Egypt. Presumably the relations will include commerce, but the key binding feature will be common worship. Israel, too, will exist alongside these great powers, serving as *a blessing in the midst of the earth* (v. 24). This great land that stretches from Assyria to Egypt will be a blessing that the LORD has blessed. The key to this whole passage is this blessing from the LORD. A political and religious balance has

been achieved that merits the LORD's blessing. The blessing is spoken on all three countries: *Blessed be Egypt my people* (v. 25). The reference to Egypt with a term usually reserved for Israel is significant. *Assyria the work of my hand* reflects the same view of Assyria, as the LORD's instrument, that has been typical of the book. *Israel my heritage* shows the same relation that is usual in the Pentateuch in which Israel is the LORD's portion, the current generation being the direct descendant of the LORD's chosen.

What a beautiful vision of hope and peace! It is presented as the LORD's vision of what could be. Peace did not come in this way, however; the major thrust of the book turns toward another vision that corresponds to the historical developments. This is the second picture of an alternate vision of the future that God could happily support. The first was that of the ideal monarchy in chaps. 11-12. Genesis 2–3 had already shown that God sometimes is forced by human intransigence and sin to change plans. So here the course of events turns back to the previous plan envisioned in chap. 2: the Temple lifted high.

20:1-6. A walking prophetic sign. Instead of performing the mediatorial service of linking Ethiopia with Assyria, apparently Hezekiah chose to join the Philistine cities in an alliance with the princes of lower Egypt against Assyria. Sargon answered the challenge by a campaign in 712 B.C.E. that resulted in the capture of Ashdod. The LORD registered his disapproval of this course of action on Hezekiah's part through Isaiah the prophet. He was told to take off his clothes and his sandals and to walk about *naked and barefoot for three years as a sign . . . against Egypt and Ethiopia* (v. 4). The LORD's vision of a truce had foundered. In a conflict situation the LORD still backed Assyria, and Hezekiah had chosen the wrong side.

Four Ambiguous Burdens, 21:1–22:14

21:1-10. First burden: a swampland. Babylon is the focus of this ORACLE. Some background to understand Judah's relation to Babylon in the last quarter of the eighth century B.C.E. is needed (see chaps 13-14). Judah seems to have been impressed by MERODACH-BALA-DAN's ability to hold power in Babylon from 721 to 710 B.C.E. His control also may have influenced Merodach-Baladan to join the Philistine rebellion. When Babylon was finally retaken by SARGON in 710, Merodach-Baladan escaped, fleeing into the marshlands to the south, which was his traditional home. When Sargon died in 705, Merodach-Baladan took Babylon again, only to be ousted again, this time by SENNACHE-RIB in 703 B.C.E. Either of the occasions when the Assyrians conquered Babylon could fit this chapter, but the latter would fit the connection with chap. 22.

The prophet reports his vision of treachery and violence. *Elam* and *Media* (v. 2) have apparently been summoned to aid Assyria in an attack. The news is emotionally difficult for the prophet. The officers prepare for battle. The visionary is told to post a lookout for messengers; he finally reports someone coming. The message is terse: *Fallen, fallen is Babylon* (v. 9). Babylon's claim to fame and power lay in the favor of its idol god, the very symbol of empire, yet *all the images of her gods lie shattered on the ground*. The picture of Babylon's failure is complete.

This message is taken as a message from the LORD and is devastating to Judah because it had raised its hopes in light of Babylon's example.

21:11-12. Second burden; silence. The Hebrew word is *dumah* means "silence." The Greek translation inserted "Edom," but the term is probably intended to remain ambiguous and mysterious. Also mysterious is the watchman who answers the sensible question, *What of the night?* with a non-answer: *Morning comes, and also the night. If you will inquire, enquire; come back again* (vv. 11-12).

21:13-15. Third burden; in the wasteland. The peoples named here are in Arabia. They are urged to prepare to deal with the persons fleeing from the path of conquest. Within a year the power of Arabian tribes will come to an end.

22:1-14. Fourth burden; the valley of vision. This terrible vision is of the Day of the LORD, and Judah is the victim. Judah has failed to fight and its military leaders have fled. In this ignominious situation many helpless persons are massacred. *Elam* and *Kir* (v. 6) are undoubtedly mercenaries in the service of Assyria. *The covering of Judah* (v. 8) is the circle of fortified cities intended to defend the city of Jerusalem.

Defensive measures for Jerusalem are described in vv. 8b-11. *The House of the Forest* must have been an armory. The issue of a water supply is vital in times of siege. JERUSALEM's water supply was outside its walls and vulnerable to attack, hence the rush to collect water in pools within the city (the SILOAM INSCRIPTION reflects the importance of the water supply in times of battle). But v. 11 makes the LORD's point: *But you did not look to him who did it, or have regard for him who planned it long ago*. In all the feverish military preparation the leaders gave no thought to God's

intentions for the attack or to his plans either for Jerusalem or for this historical moment.

So the LORD reveals his intentions. He calls for mourning, but instead they feasted with the happy-go-lucky attitude: *Let us eat and drink, for tomorrow we die* (v. 13). The LORD finds this failure to take seriously the terrible condition of the city to be unforgivable.

Shebna Is Dismissed, 22:15-25

Finally the section moves to naming names of those responsible for the fiasco of Judah's near destruction. Strangely, Hezekiah's name does not occur. Instead, his ministers are the objects of blame and punishment.

Shebna . . . master of the household (v. 15), or prime minister, is arraigned first. He is accused of misusing his office. A specific offense lies in preparing a mausoleum for his own tomb that has all the grandeur of a royal tomb. The LORD is about to dislodge him violently and have him exiled because he is a disgrace to his master's house. Isaiah 22:8-9 should also be seen as accusations against Shebna. His administration had left the little kingdom militarily unprepared.

Eliakim son of Hilkiah (v. 20) will succeed Shebna. The passage describes the duties of the prime minister. He has a special *robe* and *sash*. His authority makes him like *a father to the inhabitants of Jerusalem and to the house of Judah* (v. 21). He holds *the key to the house of David* (v. 22), probably meaning that he serves as steward to the royal house and its estates. Such authority is almost absolute. God promises security and honor for Eliakim and for his entire extended family. But on the Day of the LORD foreseen in this chapter, he too will be cut down and will die.

The elevation of Eliakim brings the passages related to the age of Hezekiah to an end. Whereas the age of Ahaz had briefly brought the hope that the Davidic monarchy might provide the salvation that Israel needed, the age of Hezekiah brought hope that changing political conditions in Egypt and Assyria might make an opening for a new age of peace and blessing. Neither materialized. In the Book of Isaiah the age of Hezekiah is seen as a period of disappointment for things that might have been.

The Vision of the Age of Manasseh, 23:1–27:13

Assyrian power peaked in the half century following SENNACHERIB's siege of Jerusalem. Judah was the abject vassal of ASSYRIA, a spectator of history, rather than a participant. The brunt of Assyria's aggression in this period was borne by EGYPT and especially its Phoenician allies TYRE AND SIDON.

The Vision deals with this period in the bright colors of an end of an age. The clash of the world powers, Assyria and Egypt, is pictured with an appropriate sense of ultimate doom. But the Vision chooses precisely this age to assert the LORD's sovereignty and to deal with the impersonal issues of blessing and curse that determine so much of the course of life.

An outline of the section is again a CHIASM with the center at 25:6 and references to the fate of Tyre providing the outer frame. The whole is introduced by a section on Tyre that has no corresponding element at the end. All of this section contains responses to the fall of Tyre, in the same way the city itself is commanded to respond in the first section. The responses are noted in the chiastic arrangement below.

A—Tyre is ordered to respond, 23:1-7
   B—The LORD planned this against Tyre,
      23:8-10 (response of the sailors, 23:10)
      C—The LORD's hand over the sea, 23:11-18
      (responses from sailors and prophets, 23:12b-18)
         D—The LORD is devastating the land,
            24:1-20 (responses, 24:4-20)
            E—The LORD judges armies and kings,
               24:21-22 (responses, 24:22)
               F—The LORD of Hosts reigns,
                  24:23-25:5 (individual responses,
                  25:1-5)
Keystone: The LORD of Hosts's banquet, 25:6
               F'—The LORD destroys death
                  forever, 25:7-9 (Jerusalem's
                  response, 25:9)
               E'—The LORD judges Moab,
                 25:10–26:20 (Judah's response, 26:1-20)
            D'—The LORD judges the inhabitants
               of the land, 26:21
         C'—The LORD judges Leviathan,
            27:1-11 (the LORD's response, 27:2-5)
   B'—Israel will take root and the LORD
     will gather Israel, 27:12-13

On the rising steps of the chiastic ladder, Tyre and the land (of Canaan) are called to respond. On the descending steps JERUSALEM, JUDAH, and ISRAEL respond. We note the frame of *seventy years* provided for the act (23:17). Various primary sections show the LORD's response to the fall of Tyre. In this section the entire

land of Canaan, all the cities or city-states, and even the sea, which in this period was becoming the channel of commerce and power, come under the authority of Assyria, "the rod of the LORD's anger."

Tyre Is Ordered to Respond, 23:1-7

The passage is called an *oracle concerning Tyre* (v. 1), the impressive Phoenician city that, with Sidon, had dominated shipping and commerce on the coast of CANAAN during all of Israel's history in Canaan. But now Tyre has been destroyed.

The inhabitants of the city are called to respond. *Ships of Tarshish* (v. 2) were great freighters that were a mark of Tyre's commercial power around the Mediterranean Sea. *Inhabitants of the coast* included Sidon, Philistine cities like ASHDOD to the south, and coastal cities to the north. Sidon is addressed as a type of alter ego to Tyre. All of Tyre's trading partners are called to join the mourning for the destruction of this ancient commercial power.

The LORD Planned This against Tyre, 23:8-10

This passage returns to the theme that plays such a great part in the Vision. *Who planned this?* (v. 8). Tyre had seemed to be untouchable to the currents of history. Its commercial influence and riches had so often put it beyond the destructive tides of history. The answer comes: *The LORD of Hosts has planned it* (v. 9), but why? The answer corresponds to the theme of the day of the LORD in chap. 2: to bring down pride and glory.

Sailors have to respond in a practical way. Tyre is no longer a safe or desirable harbor. They must turn back to their own ports.

The LORD's Hand over the Sea, 23:11-18

The universal authority and dominion of the LORD has been demonstrated. Not only has he *given command concerning Canaan* (v. 11), which led to the destruction of kingdoms and their fortresses. He has also stretched his hand over the sea, which was the element that Tyre ruled with its fleets and commercial influence. So Tyre was no longer exempt from the fate of other Canaanite cities. It had to flee to Cyprus with what was left of its riches.

Verse 13 introduces the Chaldeans (i.e., Babylon), disturbing many interpreters. The NRSV reads as though Babylon destroyed Tyre; however, the Hebrew reads: "See the land of the Chaldeans! This was the people who no longer existed! Assyria assigned them to the wild beasts" (Watts 1985, 301). The destruction of Babylon has played a large role in the Vision. Here it is used as a parallel to that of Tyre.

The ships of Tyre are again called to mourning. But then the passage recognizes that Tyre will rise from its ashes to ply its trade again. *At the end of seventy years* (v. 17), it, like a prostitute who resumes her trade, will lure its trading partners again. It will make profits, as before. But this happens because of the LORD's decision. *Visit* may also mean "decide the fate of." Tyre is restored as profitable again because of the LORD's decision and on the LORD's terms. Its profits will be dedicated to the LORD *and for those who live in the presence of the LORD* (v. 18).

Perhaps the image of the LORD's visit is a foreshadowing of 60:4-16? An earlier king of Tyre provided both expertise and workers to build Solomon's Temple (see 1 Kgs 5:1-10). The profits of Tyre will make possible the restoration of the Temple and its services in proper style.

The LORD Is Devastating the Land, 24:1-20

The same Hebrew word can mean both "the earth" and "the land." "The land" has been the translation consistently used in the Book of Isaiah so far; there is no reason to change now (as the NRSV does in v. 1). Chapter 24 refers to the devastations wrought in the land of Canaan, not on the entire world. The previous chapter had narrowly looked at the effect of the fall of Tyre on the city and its interests. Now the Vision turns to the situation in the hinterlands that reach from the Euphrates through Lebanon, the coastlands and the highlands of Palestine to the border of Egypt in the south. *Twists its surface* (v. 1) could refer to earthquakes. *Scatter its inhabitants* could describe the results of many causes.

The devastation happens to everyone of all layers of society. The LORD's decree calls for the land to *be utterly laid waste* (v. 3). The image continues the decree enunciated in 6:11-12. The fulfillment of the LORD's command is a withered and dried up land.

Verse 5-7 shift the imagery. Instead of the personal commands of God the picture is of violated statutes and a broken covenant that "pollutes" the land. The pollution produces *a curse* that *devours* the land. The *inhabitants suffer for their guilt*. Such an impersonal view of sin, and its consequences, is very different from the personal judgment of God. Both views are evident throughout the OT. The results for the land are the same as for individuals.

The things that make for good living are gone. *The city of chaos* is the theme of vv. 10-12. It can also be translated "a desolate city." References to a city are repeated in 25:2-5, 26:1-6, and 27:10-11, yet the identity of the city remains ambiguous. Certainly the CITY is a counterpoint to the LAND. Both are significantly involved in the destruction. Cities have been prominent in the Vision—Jerusalem, Babylon, and Damascus among them—but the meaning here must go far beyond the destruction of a specific city.

The development of cities and city-states had been a particular phenomenon of the historical period of Israel's presence in Canaan. The Vision is signaling the end of that era (Watts 1985, 318–19). With the rise of the great empires, cities and city states in Palestine would never have the importance and power that they had before. These chapters mark the end of an age. Life would eventually be restored to the area, but things would never return to the previous way of life.

Verse 13 describes the situation in the land and *among the nations* as like that of an olive tree when the harvest is finished. Bare, without leaves or fruit, it can only await another season to restore its beauty, glory, and life.

Verse 14-16 respond to the devastation differently. There is joy and praise of the LORD. The locations of these responses are very exact. *From the west, in the east, in the coastlands of the sea*, from the extremities of the land come sounds of praise. Persons in these areas recognize the hand of the LORD in the turmoil. They see it as just RETRIBUTION. Perhaps they even stand to gain from the Assyrian actions.

But a single voice recognizes the terrors of the situation and the total chaos in the area. The situation appears hopeless. All the natural order is endangered. That is the meaning of the sentence: *for the windows of heaven are opened and the foundations of the earth tremble*. The description of the situation is similar to that of the great flood in Genesis. The utter ruin of the land (*earth* in NRSV) is expressed in vv. 19-20 where the word occurs four times. The fall is related to its sins through the words *its transgressions*. The description is of judgment, not mere happenstance.

The LORD Judges Armies and Kings, 24:21-22

The dominant word in this section is *punish*; it occurs at the beginning and the end. The LORD is the subject. As noted above (see commentary at 23:17) the Hebrew word may also mean "decide the fate of," which fits here. The translation *heaven* goes beyond the usual meanings of this word. Here it means "height." A literal translation would be "the army of the heights in the heights." *Earth* is the word that refers to "tillable land." In contrast to "heights" it would mean "lowlands." So the verse should read: "In that day, the LORD will decide the fate of the army of the highland in the highland, and of the kings of the lowland in the lowland" (author trans.). In Palestine the mountainous highlands and the lowlands together include everything. This is another picture that includes everything in the land.

The response foresees them all gathered as prisoners of war, to be held many days before this judgment takes place. Not only the cities and the kingdoms are to be destroyed completely, but the armies and the kings that used them are to come to an end. The new era will have none of the terror of marauding armies sweeping across the land that had characterized the previous thousand years and more.

The LORD of Hosts Reigns, 24:23–25:5

With this passage the section approaches a climax. The greatness of the moment and the occasion is indicated by the cry concerning the sun and the moon. The stupendous announcement is that "the LORD of hosts reigns on Mount Zion." The present tense fits better than a future (cf. the NRSV *The LORD of hosts will reign on Mount Zion* [24:23]).

The importance of this announcement cannot be exaggerated. All the land lies in ruins. The cities are waste. Tyre's influence and commerce are gone. But the LORD's kingship, instead of being destroyed with all the rest, is actually enhanced. Is this what 24:14-16a had glimpsed?

Since the royal scene is set in Jerusalem the courtiers are called *elders*. The scene in 6:1-8 had called the heavenly courtiers *seraphim*, but both scenes stress the *glory* that surrounds the throne. God's reign and his glory are evident in times of judgment as well as those of victory.

This is the second of three throne-room scenes in the Vision. The one in chap. 6 had declared the edict of a devastated land. That has been fulfilled in chap. 24 after the final loss in the conquest of Tyre. Now it is time for a new edict and a new direction. The Vision takes the reader back into the throne-room of God to hear it. This one, however, is not in heaven; it is in Jerusalem.

A song of praise and thanks adorns the scene. It is sung by individuals, each of whom confesses faith and devotion to the LORD. The first singer confesses faith because the LORD has done *wonderful things* (25:1). Specifically, the song recognizes that God had planned what has been done: the destruction of *the city*. This is the second of the passages that speak of cities and their destruction. Now the destruction is accomplished as previously announced; for that, God has received recognition and glory.

God also is perceived to be *a refuge to the poor* (v. 4). Rather than simply reflecting the power structures of that day, the LORD is seen to have opposed *the ruthless* (v. 5) in the cause of the weak and needy. God has been victorious and that is cause for praise.

Key Verse:
The Banquet of the LORD of Hosts, 25:6

The reason for the royal session in Jerusalem is revealed. The LORD has prepared a banquet *for all peoples* who are all to be witnesses to what he has already done and what he is about to do. This is the second element of a royal trilogy. The first (24:23) had portrayed the LORD'S appearance on the Jerusalem throne in glory before the elders. This one announces a banquet for all peoples. Note that these are not kings of nations. The kings are now gone, but the *peoples* remain.

The LORD Destroys Death Forever, 25:7-9

Now the third element of the royal trilogy announces a heroic deed. It will bring about an end to the long chain of vengeance and curse that has plagued the land and its peoples in all the military incursions, especially for the previous one to two hundred years. The heroic deed will end the reign of *death* in the land.

A curse was said to "devour the land" in 24:6; now the LORD *will swallow up death forever* (v. 7). Death is *the shroud* or sheet that covers all the peoples and nations. But the banquet has been called to announce that this fearful curse is being destroyed. The LORD alone has the power to destroy the destroyer (cf. Rev 20:13-14).

Two parallels to death are also to be removed. *Tears* are to be wiped from *all faces* (v. 8). The inevitable mourning and grief that accompanies death will be banished. *Disgrace*, or reproach, refers to actions worthy of such blood-guilt. *Disgrace* is a synonym of guilt and contamination (cf. 24:5-6); it, too, will be removed from all the land. The new decree wipes the slate clean and allows for new life and new joy in the land.

The response to such an action reveals the meaning of true faith in times of trouble. The response is a cry of recognition: *This is our God* (v. 9). The confession is a recognition that salvation and deliverance, especially from death, can only come from God. *We have waited for him* (v. 10), the peoples say. Their response is the best reply of faith. Waiting on the LORD is the frequent piety of the Psalmists. Those who wait experience *salvation*.

Such a *salvation* calls for joy and gladness, in sharp contrast to the weeping and mourning throughout the land. Jerusalem's hope in the LORD can be crowned by joy.

The LORD Judges Moab, 25:10–26:20

On the descending ladder of the chiasm, this passage balances the judgment on kings and armies in 24:21-22. *This mountain* (25:10) is Mount Zion. The LORD's hand on the mountain refers to the re-establishment of the LORD's sovereignty there as described in 24:23–25:9. When that happens, Moab must be returned to a place of subservience.

The imagery is drawn from the farm where a manure pit is kept near the barn. Manure is layered with straw. In time all of the mixture will be spread on the fields as fertilizer. So Moab will be trodden down like straw in the manure pit. Their resistance to the defeat and humiliation will be in vain. Fortifications will be leveled.

A song to be sung by Judah gives the response to the judgment of Moab (26:1-20). The song is a pilgrim song to be sung by Judaean pilgrims as they approach Jerusalem. Although the song is a response to the judgment of Moab, it still reflects the period of the fall of Tyre. The song strikes a festive note, but the pall of war still hangs over the land.

A strong city (i.e., Jerusalem, 26:1) stands in contrast to *the city of chaos* of 24:10 (cf. 24:12 and 25:2). *The gates* are those of Jerusalem. *The righteous nation that keeps faith* refers to the pilgrims approaching the city. *Peace* in a time when war is all around is difficult to keep, even if it is only peace of mind. But *steadfast mind* and *trust* can make that possible. So the pilgrims exhort all who will hear: *Trust in the LORD forever* (26:4).

In 26:5-6 the dialogue resumes the theme of the destroyed city. The *lofty city* recalls the earlier words about the high and the mighty (2:11-18) and the great king who would be reduced to SHEOL (14:11). The city is accused of oppressing the poor.

The song of the pilgrims goes on, alternating pious proclamations of faith with cynical observations of an evil time that cannot change. The shifting emphasis is the very sort of thing that one would expect in the period when Judah is helpless, with war swirling all around for well over half a century.

Verses 7-9 are words of faith and piety contrasted with a cynical view of the ways of the wicked in vv. 10-11a. Verses 11b-13 issue a call for God to act with divinely righteous zeal while protesting that the faith of Judah never wavered. Verse 14 disconsolately wails that *the dead do not live*, seeming to deny the efficacy of the LORD's decree in 25:7. Nonetheless, v. 15 insists that what the LORD has done has been for the good of the nation.

The two themes are combined in a confessional stanza in vv. 16-18. Verse 19 returns to the positive view with an affirmation *your dead shall live*, but v. 20 recognizes that the LORD's wrath is still dominant. The people are called to hide themselves for a little while more.

The LORD to Judge the Inhabitants of the Land, 26:21

This verse announces another action on God's part. He is moving out from *his place*, which could be either the heavenly dwelling or the Temple in Jerusalem. *Punish* is again the word that may mean "determine the fate of" (see commentary at 23:17 and 24:21-22). The action is against *the inhabitants of the land*. The reason is explained: *their iniquity*. Midway the verse turns to the other theme of this chapter: the dead. The land will be forced to show where its dead are buried. The earth will no longer hide the bodies of those that died.

The LORD Judges Leviathan, 27:1-11

The announcement of this new act of God is in v. 1. *Punish* repeats the word for "decide the fate of" (see above). And the decision is to *kill him*.

The LORD's sword is described as *cruel . . . great and strong*. *Leviathan* is called the *fleeing serpent, . . . the twisting serpent, the dragon that is in the sea*. LEVIATHAN is one of the names used in ancient Near Eastern literature for the monster of chaos, but it can also be used as a figure for historical enemies (e.g., Ezek 29:1-16; 32:2-8; Hab 3:1-9). In the same way that *son of Dawn* was used in 14:12 for the King of Babylon, here Leviathan is intended to have an historical reference. It probably is to be understood to stand for Assyria or the Assyrian king. Assyria is having its fate decided; it will be destroyed.

Verses 2-5 give the LORD's response to this turn of events. The prophet returns to the motif of Israel as a *vineyard* (cf. chap. 5) that the LORD guards. This time God is without wrath. God will fight against the *thorns and briers* until Israel comes to *cling to him*. The theme is: *Let it make peace with me.*

Verse 6 is the first of two announcements at the end of this long passage that began at 23:1. It tells of Israel's taking root and prospering in the land. The second announcement, treated below, is found in 27:12-13; both speak of Israel's fate.

Between the two announcements come questions and responses. The first question concerns Israel (v. 7). The questioner recognizes the judgment just made on Assyria and asks whether the same fate befell Israel. The answer (vv. 8-11) rehearses the reasons for judgment that led to *expulsion* and *exile*. It is necessary for *the guilt of Jacob to be expiated* (v. 9). Their sins and idolatries had led to the terrible events of the past century. These in turn had led to abandoned cities and an empty countryside. The Israelites are characterized as a people *without understanding*. The reader is reminded of 1:3. It was this lack that caused God's loss of favor toward them. But now the favor has returned under the new conditions.

The LORD Will Thresh and Gather Israel, 27:12-13

Now the second announcement is offered; it is aware of the existence of a Diaspora of the exiles who are still reckoned as people of Israel. Whether they are in the land of Assyria or in the land of Egypt, they are still recognized as God's people. They will be summoned to come and worship the LORD on the holy mount at Jerusalem. Here again is the theme of *worship on the holy mountain* (cf. 2:2-4).

This section has marked the end of Assyria's usefulness to God as the "rod of his anger." His wrath had achieved its full result. The land was empty and accursed. Hence, with the picture of another scene in God's throne-room a series of events is announced that will bring this dreadful era to an end. Assyria will be destroyed. Israel will be restored in the land and invited to pilgrimage from without.

The Vision of the Age of Josiah, 28:1–33:24

This section assumes an historical background of the reigns of JOSIAH and JEHOIAKIM. The Assyrian Empire is weakening, while Egypt, Babylon and Media jockey for position in the race to succeed Assyria as the world power of that day. Judah is living through the final phase of existence under the judgment pronounced on it more than a century before.

Each of the sub-sections begins with "woe" (as in RSV; NRSV has *ah*) in a kind of funeral litany that denies Judah any real sense of renewal or new chance in that era. The brief surge of new life under Josiah is not the real answer to Judah's fate. The section will continue to depict true hope to be in the LORD's support of Zion as a city of worship, in his promise of grace and the outpouring of his spirit, just as previous sections have done.

The five "woes" here are parallel to the five "woes" for Israel in chaps. 5 and 10. The scenes about Jerusalem are parallel to those in chaps. 2, 4, and 66. But there is a contrast to chap. 11. No Davidic heir appears in this section.

References to Assyria in this section describe its imminent fall (30:31; 31:8). References to Egypt portray the eagerness of some parties in Jerusalem to ally themselves with Egypt against Assyria (30:2; 31:1).

Disaster because of Expansion, 28:1-29

The section is composed of three parts. The first is a doleful review. The second is a reminder of Zion's role in God's plan. The third teaches God's strategy for his people.

28:1-13. Woe, Ephraim's drunkards. The central motif of this passage is the metaphor of drunkenness as applied to Israel. It contrasts the bumbling and repulsive ineptness of *people*, *priest*, and *prophet* (vv. 1, 3-4, 7-8) with the decisiveness (v. 2), determined compassion (vv. 5-6) and patience (vv. 9-10) of the LORD in working with them.

The passage fits the period when Josiah reoccupied much of the territory of Israel and probably aroused hopes that the days of David's glory might be repeated.

Garland may refer to a city on a hill, such as SAMARIA had been. Pride and glory are contrasted with a *fading flower*, depicting the former and present state of the great city. Drunkenness is the metaphor for the inept bumbling of Israel's leaders a century before. No one now mourns the events that led to their earlier disaster.

One who is mighty and strong (v. 2) refers to the Assyrian emperor, SHALMANESER, who besieged Samaria or to SARGON II, who captured the city and took its people into exile. Through these events *the LORD of hosts* received glory and was exalted among the remnant who had suffered under the kings. But then the leaders of the remnant also reeled with wine (vv. 5-8).

The passage scoffs at any attempt by these drunkards to teach or explain anything. They are like children learning the alphabet, repeating the letters. But the passage insists that the LORD could use even those worthless teachers to teach some truth, to accomplish something. They repeated literally precepts and lines (vv. 10, 13), but the result was the breakup, capture and exile of the kingdom and its people. What had begun in v. 10 as mumbling incompetence is changed by the LORD in v. 13 into an authentic word of judgment.

Note the relation of v. 12 with Exod 33:13-14. *Rest* implies dwelling and the security needed for that. This is Israel's rest as paralleled in Deut 12:9; Isa 30:15 and Ps 95:11. The same sovereign LORD acts toward Israel in the time of the Assyrian invasions as he had acted in bringing the people into the land of Canaan under Joshua. The original offer of rest had been conditioned upon Israel's willingness to listen to God and his law. The same condition applied to the eighth century. Israel had failed to meet that condition.

28:14-22. Scoffers in Jerusalem. Attention turns from affairs in old Israel to current events in Jerusalem. Crucial actions by the LORD are about to take place (vv. 16, 21). The leaders posit their *covenant with death* (v. 15) as their reason for holding back. This may refer to their treaty obligation to Assyria in a time of growing Egyptian strength. *The overwhelming scourge* may refer to the Scythian invaders who broke through the Assyrian defenses in the north. *Lies* and *falsehood* apply to a treaty partner, perhaps Egypt. It is hard to believe that anyone in Jerusalem really thought good could come from the confused political situation of the period; the verses display such incredulity.

In v. 16 the LORD answers the argument of political necessity that is put forward as an excuse for this action. He repudiates the idea that the old values can no longer be held. He affirms what he is willing to do in his commitment to Zion. The *cornerstone* or *foundation stone* in Zion may refer either to the Temple or to the Davidic king. What God is doing in Zion is the key to understanding the history of that time. Isaiah 2:1-3 and chap. 66 suggest that the building of the Temple in Zion is the theme of the Vision. The Temple is to continue to be the symbol of the LORD's reign and authority. The believer is encouraged to exercise patience while waiting for the LORD to complete the work.

God commits himself to *justice . . . and righteousness* (v. 17) as the standards by which to measure right and wrong. Policies based on practical politics and personal advancement are not to be trusted.

The message that their self-serving *covenant* (v. 18; see, also, v. 15) is going to be swept away is bound to bring terror to the city. The figure of *the bed* and the *covering* being *too short* and *too narrow* (v. 20) applies to the inadequacies of treaty alignments made with Egypt. These left no room for Judah to accommodate itself to Babylon's rise to power or to the LORD's new moves.

Mount Perazim (v. 21) is not clearly located in the OT, but "Baal-perazim" appears in 2 Sam 5:20 where David defeats the Philistines. The announcement that *the LORD will rise up* implies that God is going to war. Earlier in the OT this meant that the deity would fight for Israel against their enemies, but in Isaiah the LORD's work is that of raising up the Assyrians against Israel. That Jerusalem should cry out, *strange is his deed! . . . alien is his work!* is understandable. They believed that God's proper role lay in saving and supporting Israel. The Vision of Isaiah argues repeatedly that the people were blind, uncomprehending, and unbelieving to this "other work" of God, the work that the prophet announced as God's being responsible for the Assyrian invasions. In the people's eyes their understanding of what God should be doing was contradicted by such a claim.

The last speech urges Jerusalem not to scoff at this word from God. *Your bonds* (v. 22) refers to the political alliances. Prudence and restraint are needed to keep a bad situation from getting worse.

28:23-29. The LORD's strategy: a parable. The prophet employs a parable as a teaching tool, using the experience of farmers. Farmers need to work differently in different seasons and times. They do not confuse the times and seasons, or allow one task to make them overlook another. The scoffers and speechmakers among the people would argue that God's ways are always the same and consistent. The parable defends the prophetic view that God acts in history in ways that fit the times to achieve divine goals.

The story is a parable because it is told as an analogy for another truth. God's strategy for history is wonderful and will succeed. Jerusalem's leaders need to seek instruction from God concerning their plans, just as farmers learn from God when to plant and to reap. And God's strategy is to be trusted, as farmers trust God's instruction about sowing.

God's strategy in the Vision is not pictured as ideal plans fixed in eternity. It refers to the LORD's decisions in specific historical situations. God's success implies prudence that issues finally in success and salvation.

Disaster through Political Relations, 29:1-24

This section consists of three parts. "Woe, Ariel" (29:1-8; NRSV begins *Ah, Ariel, Ariel*) mourns for Jerusalem, which now must be attacked and humbled. "Like a Dream" (29:9-14) describes the fulfillment of the task assigned in 6:11-13 as a terrible nightmare that will be perceived, after it has happened, merely as a dream. "Woe, you schemers" (29:15-24) is directed against the plotters in Jerusalem; it sees new opportunity for Jacob.

29:1-8. Woe, Ariel. This part is a very compact and careful construction relating imagery from a royal Zion festival to the realistic siege of the walls of Jerusalem by the horde of nations. This is developed around three motifs: *Ariel* (vv. 1, 2, 7), the siege or *distress* (vv. 2, 7, 8), and the horde or *multitude* (vv. 5, 7, 8).

The drama of the festival demonstrates the dependence of the city on God. Zion exists by the decree and power of the LORD God. If that is understood in the festival drama, then it is equally true for historical reality. Once the LORD has decided Zion's fate, the oppressing nations will no longer be a factor. Chapters 36–39 are parallel in meaning. The prophetic oracle there serves the same purpose that reference to the festival does here.

Jerusalem was besieged several times in history: In Ahaz's reign (chap. 7, which was 734 B.C.E.), Sennacherib's siege (chaps. 22 and 36–37, which was 701 B.C.E.), and Nebuchadnezzar's sieges (in 598 and 587 B.C.E.). The usual form of a siege account has the LORD defending the city, but here the situation is reversed. The LORD lays siege to the city. This literary inversion portrays a ritual humiliation of the city that is carried to the very point of death.

Ariel may mean "lioness of God," "God's champion or hero," or "the altar-hearth of El." It is certainly applied to Jerusalem. The implication is that although Jerusalem is a city founded by God in ancient Jebusite times, and although David himself claimed the city, the LORD is forced now to fight against it.

Deep from the earth in v. 4 seems to refer to the world of the dead. After being besieged, Ariel will descend into the land of the dead, becoming like a ghost. If the experience humbles Jerusalem to the point of deathly helplessness, the nations around the city are a part of the dust of that deathlike, unreal experience.

The LORD is the only reality. He alone has decisive power. After he has acted, all other threats will be like a dream only partly remembered. This passage, like chap. 7, calls attention away from the immediate historical threat to the underlying reality of God's purpose and action.

By referring to the ancient ritual of humiliation through ordeal, which preceded the "deciding of the fate," this passage interprets Jerusalem's military difficulty as God's humiliation of the city, which must precede his decision about its fate. The LORD's sovereign decisions and his salvation—these are the realities, the only decisive factors that Jerusalem needs to consider.

29:9-14. Like a dream. This passage picks up the theme of the drunken stupor from chap. 28, and from 6:9-10 the theme of blindness caused by God. It also resumes the theme of insincere worship found in the first chapter of the book.

The festival crowds still move through the city, but they walk as though they are asleep. This stupor is from God, as was predicted in 6:9-11. The prophets, leaders and seers are all affected by it.

The *vision of all this*, which has been revealed by the book, of God's strategy, of what God is doing and why, is something the people are unable to see. Having a revelation or a Bible is of no use if the people's lack of faith keeps it *sealed* (v. 11).

The LORD distances himself from *this people* (v. 14). Their religion is only verbal, lacking heart, mind, and will. This affects the character of their worship. *Their worship* (v. 13) means their attitude in worship. It should be inspired by awe, by deep respect for the Holy One. Instead, worship had become a human command that is taught and recited without moving the will.

Because of this, God must intervene with *amazing things* (v. 14) to restore the sense of the holy and awesome presence of the LORD. Because he is intervening directly, ordinary wisdom and teaching can no longer correctly advise what God will do.

29:15-24. Woe, you schemers. This passage has three parts and a conclusion. Woe to planners, who plan without God (vv. 15-16). God's reversal is near (vv. 17-21). The LORD announces a new opportunity for Israel (vv. 22-23). And then even *those who err in spirit* can understand (v. 24).

All who think they can dig deep to escape God's scrutiny are mistaken. In the LORD's plan things will soon be reversed. The *deaf*, the *blind*, the *meek*, and the humble have suffered much in a world that honors power and cunning. But the day will come when God changes the rules to work to their advantage.

God is clearly identified: God of *the house of Jacob, who redeemed Abraham*. The message is about Israel. God expects the sight of surviving *children* among them, after all the terrible things that have happened, to lead them to see these acts as the *work of [God's] hands*, as products of miraculous preservation. This may bring understanding to their leaders again.

Disaster from Self-Help in Rebellion, 30:1-33

This passage brings to a head the struggle between God and the Judean leaders, who are determined to follow their own plans. The first part (vv. 1-18) contrasts God's acts with the policies of Judah's leaders. The second part (vv. 19-26) repeats the doctrine of hope in God, ignoring the terrible plight of their country. The third part (vv. 27-33) presents the religious exercise of cultic prophecy that promises God's salvation no matter what the people are doing.

30:1-18. Woe, rebellious children. God distances himself from Judah and its plans. Pharaoh's promises of protection will prove to be a sham. The historical setting is before the fall of Assyria but after Egypt had begun actively to conspire in Palestinian politics. This would apply to almost any period of Josiah's reign.

The complaint of *rebellious children* picks up a theme from chap. 1. The rebellion takes the form of *a plan* (v. 1). The LORD has a plan for Israel, but the political leaders have another. In Ashurbanipal's late reign and in the reigns of his successors, Assyria became less aggressive and strict. Psamtik I (Psammeticus I), Pharaoh of Egypt, became correspondingly more aggressive and powerful. Jerusalem's leaders were determined to play the game of power politics,

pitting one superpower against the one they thought they would take its place.

Their prediction proved to be false. It was a misjudgment. Egypt's power in Palestine was short-lived. Babylon, not Egypt, was destined to succeed Assyria. Babylon's power would last only half a century, so those who depend on Egypt will be shamed.

Rahab (v. 7) is the name of a mythical monster that rules chaos. Here Egypt is called "Rahab" only to be doomed to inactivity. The LORD's word makes it a harmless dragon who breathes fire but is, in fact, innocuous.

The LORD wants his accusation to be written down for a later day. In a sense, this is exactly what the Vision of Isaiah does. It bears witness to Israel's and Jerusalem's unwillingness to heed the LORD's instruction through these twelve generations.

They tried to still the voices of the prophets (v. 10), but the LORD's judgment condemns them for rejecting his word. *Oppression and deceit* (v. 12; Heb. "a perverse tyrant") must refer to Egypt's Pharaoh. The judgment speech uses the metaphor of a masonry wall that bulges in the middle (v. 13). When it falls nothing of any consequence will be left.

God's plan called for retreat and quiet patience, for heroic restraint and waiting. But the activists in the palace could not wait. They saw in the crumbling Assyrian power an unparalleled opportunity. But their plans were short-lived, fixed on the immediate goal of relative autonomy for a brief generation. Josiah's reign lasted from 640 to 609 B.C.E. That slight glory was bought with the price of Jerusalem's destruction by the Babylonians in 598 and 587 B.C.E.

The activists tried to flee, presumably toward Egypt. But their pursuers were faster. So now the LORD's mercy must make way for justice. The phrase *rise up to show mercy* (v. 18) contains an inner tension. "Rise up" usually describes the LORD's rising to do battle with his enemies. Here it is joined to showing mercy. The LORD has to take a violent course of action because Israel refused the quiet course that God had planned, for he is a God of justice. The final line is a sigh over what might have been: *Blessed are all those who wait for him!* Judah under Josiah was not willing to wait.

30:19-26. Hope from the teachers. This little homily on assurance and hope is presented in a style like that of the teaching of the Wise (reflected throughout the WISDOM LITERATURE). It addresses the pilgrims in Jerusalem.

The pilgrims in Zion are called to forget the hard times of the past. They are assured God will hear their prayers and help them. They are reminded of Israel's trials in the wilderness. *Bread of adversity* and *water of affliction* (v. 20) are provisions for prisoners. The bad times are pictured as a prison sentence from God. *Your Teacher* is a unique name for God. It could also be translated "your instructor." *Will not hide himself anymore* (v. 20) recognizes periods when God's guiding, instructing presence has not been sensed so clearly. This text promises that this will no longer be true. In 45:15 God is called *a God who hides himself*. The OT understands that God's presence with his people is not simply a fact of existence, presumed to be universal and constant. It is a gracious and deliberate gift offered by God. It is to be recognized and welcomed as such. In JUDAISM, from EZRA on, the Torah was the teacher of the people. In the Vision of Isaiah teaching is done by the instructing, guiding presence of the LORD. Seeing God and hearing his voice as instruction are understood to be the ways of knowing and experiencing his presence.

God's words are like those of a shepherd, spoken from *behind* (v. 21), keeping his flock on the path. The presence of the Teacher makes the getting rid of all traces of idols urgent. The role of idols is to represent a god's presence. The true presence of God among his people removes all reason or excuse for artificial symbols.

Palestinian agriculture is totally dependent on rain. The LORD claims to be able to give or withhold the life-giving rain. *Brooks* on the heights suggests abundance of water. *Great slaughter* (v. 25) and towers falling present a scene of war and destruction. The effect of *the sun* and *the moon* (v. 26) is to be felt on the great day. Moderns would be appalled at the thought of a seven-fold increase of the sun's heat and light. The intention is to represent the participation of the cosmos, which is also a part of the LORD's realm.

The LORD's healing will apply to his people's wounds, even to those that his punishment had caused. The idea of God's punishing and also healing is also found in Deut 32:39, Job 5:18 and Hos 6:1.

30:27-33. A theophany. This passage invites the reader to envision God's approach as in 26:21, 40:10, 66:15 and other OT passages. The use of *the name of the LORD* (v. 27) in such a vision is unique.

We are then called upon to see a list of anatomical features attributed to God:

the name of the LORD	coming from a distance
anger (or nose)	burning
liver	raging
lips	full of indignation
tongue	a devouring fire
breath	like a stream
	to sift the nations
	a bridle for the peoples

A holy festival is the setting. A pilgrimage to Jerusalem is indicated by going *to the mountain of the LORD* (v. 29). The goal of the trip is shown in the *Rock of Israel*. On that festive occasion the LORD will reveal himself in power.

The historical reality that is portrayed is the downfall of Assyria and its king. The funeral pyre for the king has long been ready. *The breath of the LORD . . . kindles it* (v. 33) signals the reversal of the LORD's attitude toward Assyria as portrayed in chaps. 7–10. That nation has performed its assigned task and is now to be turned aside.

The collapse of the Assyrian empire began with its gradual weakening soon after mid-century. Nineveh fell to a combined Babylonian and Median force in 612 B.C.E. and the retreating armies finally fell in Haran in 609 B.C.E. under Babylonian attack, just before an Egyptian column of troops could arrive. A major battle at CARCHEMISH between Egypt and Babylon followed, which put Palestine under Babylonian rule for the following decades.

Disaster because of False Faith in Egypt, 31:1–32:20

The section presents criticism of the parties who called for using help from Egypt to gain independence from Assyria. Such political scheming ignores God's determination of events like those portrayed earlier in the book. The first passage (31:1-9) engages leaders who prefer human dependence on alliances to dependence on an alliance with God. The second passage (32:1-8) teaches a lesson in civic righteousness. The third passage (32:9-20) engages a group of women, contrasting their prosperity with the devastation to come *in little more than a year* (32:10).

31:1-9. Against depending on Egypt. The passage mourns the determination expressed by some of the political leaders to seek military help from Egypt against Assyria. The passage insists that God will be the determinative factor in rescuing Jerusalem and in bringing Assyria down. It calls for Jerusalem to recognize God's control, turn to the LORD, put aside their idols, and wait for the deliverance of God.

32:1-8. A lesson. This is a very different passage, cast in the form of a dialogue between a teacher and students. It begins with a supposition: *See, a king will reign in righteousness*. If one may assume a righteous king, what else will happen? All the wonderful conditions of a righteous reign will result. Especially, it would be true that there would no longer be any confusion about values. No more confusion about who is a fool and who is noble, who is a villain and who is honorable. The ambiguity that surrounds the political process would be put aside. Israelites of that day had the same problem in judging their political leaders that we have today.

32:9-20. Dialogue with women. A group of women are warned that disasters are about to disrupt their pleasant way of life. They cannot conceive of their fields being destroyed. The warning continues, including warnings of the loss of palaces and cities.

The women express their faith (v. 15-16) that an ideal justice will come upon them, even beyond any troubles that come. They feel secure in the belief that *the effect of righteousness will be peace* (v. 17), but the warning is repeated.

God Vows to Punish the Tyrant, 33:1-24.

In this section the Vision approaches a critical point as violence increases and God prepares to intervene. In the first passage (33:1-6) expectation of imminent violence brings reactions from individuals and from a chorus. The second passage (33:7-12) portrays a worsening situation. The last passage (33:13-24) portrays the LORD's intervention. Persons near and far are challenged to assess the event and recognize what the results of God's intervention will be.

33:1-6. Ah, you destroyer. Verse 1 addresses a *destroyer*, announcing his destruction. Assyria is probably the intended figure. The phrase *when you have ceased to destroy* recalls the prediction in 10:12, *When the LORD has finished all his work . . . he will punish the arrogant boasting of the king of Assyria*. Assyria's task as seen from the book itself is to be a destroyer. Now that task is complete and it will itself be destroyed.

A group that says *we wait for you* (v. 2) pleads for mercy. A voice addresses God, recognizing God's approach in the sounds of battle. God is exalted in Zion, and the faith is voiced that God will use these times. The real *stability* (v. 6) for such times is to be found only in God. Then the gifts from God are listed. All of them in Hebrew are related to *the LORD*: saving acts of the LORD, *wisdom* of the LORD, *knowledge* of the LORD, and *the fear of the LORD*.

33:7-12. The LORD rises up. Apparently efforts for peace have failed and the land prepares for the worst. The LORD announces that the time has come for divine intervention. The plans of the human advisors will be nothing more than *chaff* and *stubble* (v. 11); modern readers would say "they were only paper." Because of their wrong judgments, peoples are going to be burnt up.

33:13-24. Who can survive the fire? This passage takes seriously the announcement that the war, with the LORD as its impetus, is about to sweep over them. They ask, Who can survive?

Verses 15-16 provide an answer. A way of life, according to the things that God has taught, gives promise of survival. The rest of the passage portrays the results of the LORD's intervention. The counter and weigher who had collected the tribute due the emperor (v. 18) for so long are gone. The foreign officials, symbols of the tyranny that had oppressed them also are gone.

Zion appears as a very different kind of city: like a tent, but a permanent tent. The LORD will be their king. The contrast to Egypt or Assyria could be implied with *a place . . . no galley with oars can pass* (v. 21), as they might on the Nile or the Tigris rivers. The LORD is confessed as judge and king.

The NRSV has understood v. 23a in nautical terms, but the words can also mean "a measured portion," or "a lot," referring to fields. This would make the verse refer to the fields that are assigned to peasants and to permits to do business in the towns. These had been restricted under the empire. But the fall of Assyria makes land reform and business reform possible. The foreigners can no longer enforce their authority or defend their flag. Hometown people will get their share of things that foreigners had dominated for over a century. Even the lame will get their share.

The sick will participate and there will be a general amnesty for past crimes.

The Vision of the Age of Zedekiah, 34:1–39:8

This part differs from the preceding ones. It begins with a long treatment of Edom's curse and Judah's renewal (34:1–35:10). The rest of the section is a series of readings from 2 Kgs 18–20 with an added poem,

Hezekiah's Psalm (38:9-20). All this fills the place in the book where one would expect a treatment of the destruction of Jerusalem and the beginning of Judah's exile. Instead, the Vision presents the largest block of prose in the book, narrative borrowed from 2 Kings and specifically dated to a time contemporary with chap. 22. The enigma of the missing details of Judah's fall dominates the interpretation of this section.

Exilic Israel read the HEZEKIAH stories even as their recent experiences, that had turned out so differently, were still fresh in their memories. In 701 B.C.E. the royal house survived in Jerusalem. In 586 B.C.E. the only survivor was JEHOIACHIN, who was a prisoner in Babylon at the time. In 701 the villagers and towns-folk who had fled to Jerusalem were released to return to their homes. In 586 many of them began the long march into EXILE. Near 701 the portent of a Babylonian peril was spoken by Isaiah. In 586 it became grim reality.

The readings present a reverse image of what happened. In this negative image the entire terrible period is brought vividly to mind.

A brief history of the period would have to include the following events. In 605 B.C.E. Nebuchadnezzar, Babylon's king, having defeated Assyria and then Egypt, marched into Palestine to establish his sovereignty over the territory. He gained Jehoiakim's pledge of loyalty, in spite of the Judean king's original loyalty to Egypt.

In 598 B.C.E. Nebuchadnezzar returned to confront JEHOIAKIM, who had been conspiring with Egypt. Rather than face him, Jehoiakim abdicated in favor of his son Jehoiachin who was seized and taken hostage to Babylon along with a number of Jerusalem's leaders and their families. Subsequently ZEDEKIAH was placed on the throne. By 587 he was also in trouble. This time Nebuchadnezzar destroyed the city and killed Zedekiah and his sons. A large proportion of the people were taken into exile.

Edom's Curse—Judah's Renewal, 34:1–35:10

A single theme binds these chapters together: God's vengeance against Edom (34:8 and 35:4), which is seen as an everlasting decision (34:16-17). The form is a "day of the LORD" prophecy. The outline is concentric:

A—The LORD's day of wrath on all nations, 34:1-4
  B—Vengeance and ban on Edom
      for Zion's sake, 34:5-8

    C—Edom to be burned and deserted, 34:9-15
Keystone: The LORD's decision,
              recorded and perpetual, 34:16-17
    C'—Wilderness and Arabah—
          glad and renewed, 35:1-2
  B'—The LORD's action—
        salvation for Israel, 35:3-4
A'—Festival in Zion again for pilgrims, 35:5-10

Judah's wars with Edom had a long history that reached a peak when Edom supported Babylon in its siege of Jerusalem in 586 B.C.E. Neither the Books of Kings nor the Books of Chronicles recount Edom's alliance with Babylon, but the Book of Obadiah and other passages in the OT clearly indicate it. These chapters imply that Edom impeded the travel of pilgrims through its territory.

Four sentences that begin with *for* claim certain rights for the LORD: the right to anger (34:2), the right to his sword (34:5), the right to a sacrifice (34:6b), and the right to a day of vengeance (34:8).

The LORD's judgment on Edom is interrelated with the salvation of Jerusalem. By pushing Edom back, southern and southeastern Judah regain access to favored lands and to water from which they had been cut off. Pilgrims regain rights of passage to Jerusalem.

The picture of the desolate country contains, among other words, one that requires comment: *Lilith* (34:14). This is the only place in the OT where she is mentioned, unless some suggested emendation to 2:18 and Job 18:15 be accepted. The word is similar to the Hebrew word for "night," but a demon by this name was well known in Mesopotamia. Judaism used the name and Christian demonism picked it up as well. Mention of it here in Isaiah only intends to describe the utter desolation that is to come.

Chapter 35 then turns to a reversal of that sad state when all nature will respond to the approaching glory of the LORD by bursting into life. The weak and sick pilgrims are urged to continue in order to be part of it. The reversal in nature is mirrored by a reversal in personal fortunes (vv. 5-6). A highway for the pilgrims will be opened so that the LORD's ransomed may travel on it to come to Zion with rejoicing that knows no bounds.

The Assyrian's Speech, 36:1-22

This chapter is a reading from 2 Kgs 18:13-37. 36:1-3. Jerusalem 701 B.C.E. The dates of HEZE-KIAH's reign are disputed. Biblical evidence is contradictory, but the year of SENNACHERIB's siege of Jerusalem is not, thanks to Assyrian records. The year is 701 B.C.E.; Hezekiah had been in rebellion since the beginning of Sennacherib's reign in 705 B.C.E. He had joined the rebellion of Babylon's MERODACH-BALADAN at that time. But Babylon had been subdued in 703 B.C.E. Now, two years later, it is Jerusalem's turn.

Hezekiah had prepared the outer defenses of Jerusalem as a circle of fortified towns. These fortifications had been overrun. Assyria's main objective was against Egypt. The foray against Jerusalem was a side trip from the headquarters at the Philistine city of Lachish. *Rabshakeh* (v. 2) is apparently a title for a high military official.

Jerusalem's WATER SYSTEMS consisted of springs and pools outside the walls that flowed through conduits into the city. The *Fuller's Field* (v. 2; see 7:3) is the place where people came to wash their clothes. The army was so close to the city that the general could stand this near the city, well within earshot of the people on the walls.

Three officials of Hezekiah's court are sent out to talk to him. The names of two of them are known from chap. 22, but their positions are reversed. There *Shebna* is the higher official, *Eliakim* is his successor.

36:4-10. The general's first speech. This is a very remarkable speech. The hearers of the speech within the narrative itself are the people on the wall in 701 B.C.E. 2 Kings has used the same setting for the context in narrative, but the Book of Isaiah gives it a very different context in the generation of Jews in Jerusalem at, or shortly after, the fall of Jerusalem in 587 B.C.E. They faced—or had faced—a very similar situation. For them the voice might well have been Nebuchadnezzar's.

The speech attacks the confidence of the besieged city that help will be forthcoming. The speaker invites them to negotiate a settlement. The Rabshakeh questions (v. 5) the basis of the residents of Jerusalem's will to resist. He attacks the idea that Egypt will help and offers to arm their troops if they will join his cause. He scorns any ideas that the LORD will help, with the reminder that Hezekiah had destroyed the LORD's altars outside the city in Judah. He closes with the suggestion that the LORD had sent Sennacherib against Jerusalem in the first place.

That the Rabshakeh was using all this as psychological warfare is obvious. But the Book of Isaiah's use of this narrative has another meaning. It has already said the same thing about TIGLATH-PILEZER in

7:17-20. The idea that the LORD was using the Assyrians now places Hezekiah's responses in an entirely different light than they have in 2 Kings.

36:11-12. Protest and response. Hezekiah's officials recognize the negative effect that this speech could have on the listening people; accordingly, they ask the Rabshakeh to speak in Aramaic, the language of the Empire. The request underscores the fact that he had been speaking in Hebrew. Northern Israel had been an Assyrian province for about twenty years, so officials of the occupying power are able to use the language.

The general refuses, insisting that his message is not only for the ears of the king; it should be heard by all. After all, they are the ones risking death by continued resistance.

36:13-20. The general's second speech. The general again speaks for the king and tries to discredit Hezekiah, who had been urging the people to rely on the LORD. Then the general makes his offer. If the people surrender they can all go back to their own villages and eat their own food until arrangements are made for transport to their place of exile in another country.

He discounts any chance for survival otherwise, citing Assyrian victories over many peoples. He claims that none of their gods were able to deliver them from his power and surely the LORD will not be any more able to do so.

36:21-22. No response. The delegation had been given no instructions to answer the general. So they remained silent and went back into the city.

From Hearsay to Knowledge, 37:1-20

37:1-4. Hezekiah's reaction. Hezekiah reacts with extreme grief and anguish. He went into the Temple, but sent his delegation to Isaiah. They ask for a word from God to respond to the mocking blasphemy of the general.

37:5-7. Isaiah's response. Isaiah admonishes them not to be afraid. The prophet then tells them that God promises to rid them of the army by inspiring a rumor that will cause the king to return to Babylon, where he will commit suicide. Other descriptions of the way the LORD will send the king away are found in vv. 28-29 and 36-38.

37:8-13. The general's renewed message. Having had no success in persuading Jerusalem to surrender, the general rejoins the main army. He finds them *fighting against Libnah* (v. 8). An intelligence report lets him know that a major Egyptian force under *King Tirhakah* is marching to meet him.

He is anxious to wrap up the loose ends of his campaign against Jerusalem, so he renews his communication with Hezekiah by letter. His strategy is to shake Hezekiah's faith in God. He again refers to Assyria's victories over other cities and their gods, implying that the LORD can do no better for Jerusalem.

37:14-20. Hezekiah's prayer. When the letter arrives, Hezekiah goes to the Temple and spreads it before the LORD. His prayer is majestic and remarkable.

The address is three-fold. *LORD of Hosts* (v. 16) uses the name for God employed in relation to divine kingship over all the nations; it is a military title. *Hosts* means armies and refers to the heavenly armies. *God of Israel* refers to the LORD's covenant relation to the people through ABRAHAM and MOSES. *Enthroned above the cherubim* places the LORD in the Holy of Holies of the Temple over the Ark of the Covenant.

The prayer begins with a confession that the LORD alone is God. In all the kingdoms of the land there is no other living God. The address closes with the confession that the LORD is creator of heaven and earth.

The prayer begs God to see what is going on and to hear the mocking words of Sennacherib. Hezekiah asks the LORD to recognize the personal challenge to God's own being that is contained in the words of the challenger.

Hezekiah recognizes, and asks God to recognize, the truth in the Assyrian's words. Sennacherib's claim to victories over many nations is no empty boast. His removal of their gods, replacing them with the gods of Assyria, had actually happened. The confession reveals utter helplessness on Hezekiah's part.

The prayer moves to its point: Hezekiah appeals to the LORD to show his unity with Judah and its people, to save them from the Assyrians. This would make all the nations of the land know that he alone is the LORD. The God of Judah bows to no king or emperor.

Isaiah's Response from the LORD, 37:21-38

37:21-29. The LORD's word for Hezekiah. Isaiah brings an answer to the prayer. The first word from the LORD had been a short ORACLE in the usual form of the prophets as we know them in the Books of Kings, but this one belongs to the longer poetic forms that are found in the Book of Isaiah.

The word begins with the messenger formula, *thus says* (v. 21). God is identified by one of the titles Hezekiah used, *the LORD, the God of Israel*. God is responding in his role of the COVENANT God of Israel.

The subject of the prayer is acknowledged, then God's word concerning SENNACHERIB is relayed.

First Jerusalem's proud disdain is described; then the point of the general's speech is recognized as a direct insult to God because of the Rabshakeh's claims. This is an act of pride and haughty arrogance toward the LORD (see chap. 2).

God's reply is a reminder that it is he who determines the fate of nations and kings, and that long in advance. God was responsible for the Assyrian successes (as suggested in chaps. 7 and 10). The LORD then reminds Hezekiah that God is well aware of all of Sennacherib's words and thoughts. Nothing is secret from God. So now the LORD will dominate and humiliate him. God will put *a hook in [his] nose*, like a farmer who tames a bull, and put *a bit in [his] mouth* (v. 29). The LORD will turn the Assyrian king around and send him back where he came from.

37:30-32. The LORD's sign for Jerusalem. The words turn to address Hezekiah. He is given a sign, just as Ahaz was offered a sign (cf. chap. 7): *This year eat what grows of itself* (v. 30). It is probably too late for farmers to plant their fields for this year. They will have to eat whatever has come up on its own. The *second year* will not be much better. But, by the *third year*, the normal planting and reaping will occur and the land will be back to normal.

The word turns to the implications of this promise in a broader sense. Judah itself is just a surviving remnant of God's people. Israel has already gone into EXILE. And the group that returns to the villages from the besieged city had certainly suffered its losses, too. But this group will be reestablished on the land and will enjoy its fruits again.

The reestablishment of Judah is accomplished by the direct intervention of *the LORD of Hosts* (v. 32). This is that second title for God that Hezekiah used.

37:33-38. The LORD sends the Assyrians home. The style reverts to prose narrative. A third description of what happened to the Assyrian army is given (cf. 37:7 and 29). The LORD's *angel* (v. 36) annihilated the army, 185,000 of them in a night. Understandably the king withdrew.

He lived in Nineveh, but was assassinated by his sons as he worshiped in his temple. The sons fled. Esar-haddon, another son, ruled in his place. The historical note is correct. Esarhaddon did succeed Sennacherib in 681 B.C.E. after he had been assassinated by two older sons who then had to flee.

Hezekiah's Illness, 38:1-22

38:1-8. Hezekiah becomes ill. The prophet declares Hezekiah's illness to be terminal. The prayer that follows is the second one in the longer narrative.

This prayer is a prayer for remembrance. The king claims to have walked before God *in faithfulness* (v. 3). He speaks of living *with a whole heart*, and *having done what is good in [God's] sight*—a picture of Hezekiah that the dueteronomistic historian of the Books of Kings portrays. Then the king weeps.

Isaiah is then instructed to give God's answer to the prayer. God is identified as *the God of your ancestor David* (v. 5). God is prepared to answer the king in line with his promise in 2 Sam 7:13-16. He is dealing with David's ancestor with a mercy given for David's sake.

God has heard the king's prayer and seen his contrition. The LORD answers by adding fifteen years to his life. Then the LORD renews the promise to deliver him and the city from the king of Assyria. Again the contrast with the events in 587 B.C.E. is evident: on the latter occasion both the city and the king with his family were destroyed.

The LORD offers a sign that a reprieve will happen. He promises to make the shadow cast by the sundial built by Ahaz go back ten steps. The narrative then confirms that the sundial did back up.

38:9-20. Hezekiah's prayer. This Psalm with a superscription identifying it as from Hezekiah on the occasion of his recovery is inserted here. It is not found in Kings.

The Psalm is built around a meditation on the king's expected death (vv. 10-14), followed by thoughts after his healing (vv. 15-17). Verses 18-20 form a conclusion.

The mourning over approaching death culminates in a prayer for the LORD to be his security. The Psalm is a liturgical thanksgiving for personal healing like several in the Psalms.

38:21-22. Hezekiah's recovery. The narrative does not actually say that Hezekiah recovered, but that is implied. The story ends with the recognition that Isaiah had ordered a healing poultice for the boil, and that Hezekiah had asked for a *sign*.

Hezekiah's Mistake, 39:1-8

This incident is dated by the reference to *Merodach-baladan . . . of Babylon* (v. 1). This means that it happened prior to Sennacherib's campaign, which is narrated in chaps. 36–37. MERODACH-BALADAN was dislodged from Babylon by 703 B.C.E. An earlier date would also be more plausible for Hezekiah, since he would have had little treasure to show after the 701 siege.

After Hezekiah's illness and recovery, he receives messengers from Babylon. He welcomes them and conducts them on a tour of his armory and *treasure house*. He is obviously proud of his treasure and his armed strength.

The prophet thinks that Hezekiah is less than wise in showing off in front of the Babylonians. Hezekiah was a vassal of the Assyrian king. Babylon was probably in rebellion at this time. This kind of reception could well be seen as encouraging the rebellion, if not actually joining it. Hezekiah's answer seems unbelievably naive.

Isaiah presents the LORD's word that in days to come the entire Davidic family and their wealth will be carried into Babylon. Even some of his sons will become *eunuchs* and servants to the kings of Babylon. A later generation, hearing this read, would identify the fulfillment of this prophecy in what happened to Jehoiakim in 598 B.C.E. (cf. 2 Kgs 24:10-16). The Babylon of that day was a very different Babylon, but the prophecy fit.

Hezekiah's response is remarkably sanguine. He has hoped to win peace and security for his own days, even if that costs his successors the throne and their freedom.

This chapter, although it is exactly like that in 2 Kings, functions in the Book of Isaiah to sketch in the fall of Jerusalem and the exile imposed by the Babylonians. The chapter sets the stage for the following scenes.

The Vision of the Age of Jehoiachin in Exile, 40:1–44:23

The generation of the EXILE still falls under Babylonian rule. Most of the people who once lived in Judah are scattered over the Near East. Only a tiny group survives among the ruins in Jerusalem.

This section announces a pivotal change in God's strategy. It is counterpart to chap. 6. The era in which Israel was fated for destruction has come to an end; a new day of grace and blessing is decreed. The central theme for the section is Israel's new calling, which will be symbolized in the restoration of Jerusalem.

In order to distinguish this section, when chaps. 1–39 were considered to have been written in the eighth century, historical critical scholarship referred to chaps. 40–48 as "Second Isaiah" and claimed that they were written during the Exile. When the entire Book of Isaiah is thought of as having been written in the fifth century—the perspective of this commentary—such a distinction is no longer necessary (see Introduction).

Nonetheless, the recognition that the earlier chapters are understood to fall under the judgment notice of chap. 6 underscores the importance of recognizing the bright new vision of God's grace for Israel that is announced after the fall of Jerusalem.

Prologue:
In the Hall of Voices, 40:1-9

The context of this scene is apparently the same throne room described in chap. 6. The announcement of judgment (see commentary at 6:9-13 above) has already been made. Here only the reactions to the announcement are heard.

The announcement is repeated: *Comfort! Comfort my people!* (v. 1). The command comes from God and is directed to Jerusalem as a notice that all the penalty anticipated in chap. 6 has now been paid. The account is completely closed.

Now voices fill the throne room. To fulfill the command to be comforted, preparations must be made for the divine visit. A royal road must be built for the appearance that is expected.

One voice commands *Cry!* But another responds in confusion, *What shall I cry?* And the question is supported by the observation that *all people are grass* (v. 6), implying that they are hardly worth the effort. The first voice responds that the motivation for their message comes from God's command, not an evaluation of the stability of the people because *the word of our God will stand forever* (v. 8).

Like a Shepherd, 40:10-31

God's announced return to his city is described to be like that of a conquering king taking charge of a city. The LORD comes in power, bringing rewards. The royal motif of v. 10 is expanded to include images of a shepherd in v. 11. God's rewards include food and nurture, protection and direction.

The announcement of God's return is met with skepticism, not only in the heavenly council (40:6b), but also in Israel (v. 27). The speeches beginning in v. 12 take on a defensive tone, explaining how God can and will accomplish a return to Jerusalem.

God is great enough to create the worlds and the heavens. The Creator does not rely on someone else for direction and instruction in matters of justice. The LORD moves among the nations as a sovereign God, greater than all of the peoples of the earth.

The challenge continues in v. 18. The skeptics are scorned because they could find nothing or no one to compare with God. No idol is sufficient. They are asked why they do not know. The LORD controls the heavens and history; nothing and no one stands above God. Again the skeptics are challenged to look up at the stars and ask: *Who created these?* (v. 26).

Then Israel is addressed directly (v. 27). Who is Israel at this time? The people of the Northern Kingdom had been scattered over Assyrian territory almost two hundred years before. Judeans were in exile in Babylonia, in Egypt, and a few were still near the ruins of Jerusalem in Palestine. It is no wonder that Israel should be confused about its own identity, not to mention its relation to the LORD.

These people could legitimately wonder what their *way* (v. 27) under God was, or what rights they possessed. This section is addressed to confused Israel, assuring them of God's continued interest in them. It suggests that they may discover their identity as a people in their relation to the LORD. God has not forgotten or abandoned them or the divine hope for them.

Verse 28 reminds the people that the LORD is the Creator whose goals and purposes have persisted from the beginning of time. God's patience and strength are undiminished. The LORD's strength is given to *the faint* and *the powerless.* Lacking these is no excuse for lack of faith. Then the persons who are eligible to be part of the new Israel are identified: *those who wait for the LORD.* This wording will appear several more times in the book.

Those who wait for the LORD (v. 31) can participate in the LORD's renewed activities. This verse is one of the most encouraging confessions found in all of scripture.

Israel Is the LORD's Servant, 41:1-20

The scene continues. The LORD assembles the peoples of Palestine. The *coastlines* (v. 1) are the habitations of the Philistines and the Phoenicians. *The ends of the earth* (v. 5) should probably be translated "the borders of the land" and refer to the areas that mark the outer border of CANAAN. The groups are summoned to hear the LORD's case: the claim that he is acting faithfully with Israel.

The LORD's evidence is the approach of a new military power in *the east* (v. 2). The historical background for this scene is the status quo that has held firm in the region since the fall of Assyria. Three powers vied to be Assyria's heir. Media agreed with Babylon that it would concentrate on territory to the east and north of Mesopotamia while Babylon could concentrate on Palestine and Egypt. Babylon had used this agreement to consolidate its power in those areas. It defeated Egyptian armies and occupied Palestine, finally destroying Jerusalem and taking Judeans into exile in the process. However, after the death of Nebuchadnezzar, Babylon became complacent and soft.

Meanwhile, Media had expanded its power eastward almost to India and westward into Asia Minor, and after half a century of that arrangement was restless to press on to greater things. There was news of a young prince from a Persian tribe who experienced a spectacular rise and led a combined Median-Persian empire in a series of victories that stripped away Babylon's defenses in the east and the north. These are the historical developments to which vv. 2-3 point.

The LORD asks the rhetorical question: *Who has . . . done this?* Verse 4 provides the answer: *I, the LORD, have done this; I have called the generations from the beginning.* The LORD is not only the creator of heavens and earth, but claims to be the LORD of all history as well.

The coastlands have seen the events that have reshaped the region. They are afraid and prepare for the inevitable as only an idolater can. But from Israel something different is expected. Israel is reminded of who it is, from whom it has come, and what its relation to the LORD is. Israel is the LORD's servant, especially chosen. Israel comes from Abraham, and is the fulfillment of God's promise to God's friend.

Israel is reminded that God has taken it *from the ends of the earth* calling it to be the LORD's *servant* (v. 8). Then comes the most important part: Israel has been *chosen . . . and not cast . . . off* (v. 9). Israel must not interpret the actions that brought an end to the kingdoms, destroyed Jerusalem, and scattered the peoples as abrogating God's special relation to the children of Abraham. The LORD still considers them to be God's people and the heirs of the promises to Abraham.

If Israel is indeed still God's people, and if indeed the LORD is the one bringing the invader *from the east,* they should have nothing to fear. God assures them that *I am with you* and that *I am your God.* Further, the LORD promises to help them with a *victorious right hand* (v. 10). The promise apparently means that the victorious invader will be a benefit to Israel.

Verses 11-13 deal with Israel's problems with groups that hate them and persecute them. Those enemies will disappear when it becomes evident that the LORD protects Israel.

Verses 14-16 contrast the way Israel thinks of itself, as a *worm* or an *insect,* with the power of God. The *Redeemer is the Holy One of Israel,* a title for God that is typical in the Book of Isaiah. It combines the majestic idea of the Holy One with the identification with Israel that makes God so personal and near.

God is going to make Israel an instrument capable of threshing mountains. The role of the nation will be important and great, and the people will rejoice in the LORD.

Verses 17-20 consider the situation Israel faces in terms of being *poor and needy,* with no resources. They face the need of water, a constant worry in Palestine, especially now that the land has been in ruins and uncultivated for so long. Then the passage becomes a reminder of an old theme in the Bible: God is the source of rain and of the life it brings. God promises to provide the water needed to make the land bloom again. The restoration of the land will be a testimony that God has acted again.

The Trial Continues, 41:21–42:12

The coastlands and the borderlands continue to serve as witnesses. The case against Israel continues to identify idolatry as the main cause for its blindness and unwillingness to assume the role for which it has been prepared, and to which it is called.

In vv. 21-24 the LORD's advocate speaks, challenging the idols. The LORD picks up the argument in vv. 25-29, asserting again that God is sovereign.

In 42:1-4 the LORD presents the *servant,* designated to implement justice, the result of the LORD's verdict, first among *the nations* and then in the land (NRSV *the earth*) where the *coastlands wait for* his instructions (the servant role is assigned to CYRUS in chaps. 44 and 45). The servant will avoid ostentation and arrogance; his patient persistence will succeed.

42:5-7 identifies the LORD as creator of heavens and earth and sustainer of the life of all people, before the passage returns to address the servant, defining his role. The servant is to be *a covenant to the people, a light to the nations.* He is to enlighten and to free captive peoples.

42:6-7 appears to address those who stand by. The LORD claims his victory, implies that Cyrus is the fulfillment of his prediction (cf. chaps. 44–45), and now looks ahead to new things. The servants of the LORD have been shown to be Israel and Cyrus. Each of them has a distinct task in separate spheres.

42:10-12 is a hymn calling on the witnesses, coastlands and borderlands, to join in praising the LORD. Under David all these countries had been under the rule of the LORD. Now they are called to worship God, but the relation is religious, not political.

Hear, You Deaf!, 42:13–43:21

The passage is a unit with five major parts; once again the form is chiastic (cf. the commentary at 10:24–12:4; 17:1–20:6; 23:1–27:13, above):

A—A presentation concerning Israel
    and what is happening to her, 42:13-25
    B—A speech promising salvation to Israel, 43:1-7
Keystone: A trial speech against idols, 43:8-13
    B'—A speech promising salvation
      to Israel, 43:14-15
A'—A closing argument, 43:16-21

Isaiah 42:13-17 introduces the LORD as *a soldier* roused to action without violent results. God the soldier *will lead the blind* (v. 16) in new directions. Perhaps *the blind* represent Israel. The LORD's work will shame all of those people who trust in idols.

Isaiah 42:18-22 appeals to the deaf servants to heed the LORD's servant. This must be an allusion to Cyrus, but Israel is too bruised and broken to respond.

Isaiah 42:23-25 identifies the LORD as the one who turned Israel over to those who preyed on them because of their sins.

Isaiah 43:1-7 identifies the LORD as the one who made Israel in the first place. The passage twice calls on Israel not to fear (vv. 1, 5). First Israel belongs to the LORD who is the savior. Then God is with Israel and will return its sons and daughters from far places because they have been formed for God's glory.

Isaiah 43:8-13 proposes a contest. The people *who are blind, yet have eyes* must refer to Israel. They are summoned to the contest. On one side are the nations. They are challenged to bring witness concerning anyone among them who predicted the coming of Cyrus. Then Israel is summoned to witness that the LORD has predicted the coming of Cyrus and has used him to save the people. The LORD alone is worthy to be God.

Isaiah 43:14-15 claims that the LORD has sent Cyrus to Babylon for Israel's sake. Therefore the LORD deserves to be known as Israel's king.

Isaiah 43:16-21 refers first to the EXODUS and God's victory there, then it calls attention to the *new thing* (v. 19) that the LORD is about to do. This time God will lead the people through the wilderness instead of the sea. They are God's own people, created by the LORD in order that they can declare praise to the Creator.

Remember These, Jacob!, 43:22–44:23

Isaiah 43:22-28 is a judgment speech against Israel. The nation has worshiped other gods, but the LORD forgave those sins. God has not abandoned Israel, even though, from its first ancestor (probably Jacob) on, the nation has sinned. Because of these sins God has given Israel over to punishment.

Isaiah 44:1-5 announces a decision in the judgment. It begins with a confirmation that Israel is God's servant—*hear, O Jacob my servant, Israel whom I have chosen.* A decision has been reached in the heavenly council. The LORD will bring new life: water on the parched land, spirit on the new generation. A revival of hope is in store for Israel.

Isaiah 44:6-8 is the third speech by the LORD in this section. It begins with the herald's introduction and ends with the admission of the witnesses. The heart of it is the LORD's claim to be the unique and dominant factor in all that is happening on Israel's behalf. He alone is God.

Isaiah 44:9-20 is a dialogue that makes fun of makers of idols. It breaks the series of speeches by the LORD with an almost comic relief.

Isaiah 44:21-23 reiterates the LORD's announcement that Israel is his servant, that its sins have been removed. God calls Israel to return to him, now that redemption is achieved. Verse 23 closes the section with a call to *heavens* and *earth* to recognize with praise the great event of the LORD's act of redemption with praise.

The Vision of the Age of Cyrus, 44:24–48:22

Cyrus leads a Persian army to Babylon in 739 B.C.E. fulfilling the LORD's words in 41:2-3 and 42:1-4, 6-7. The city is opened to him and he occupies it without a battle, thereby falling heir to the Babylonian empire.

This part of the Vision introduces Cyrus to Israel as the LORD's servant, interprets his role as it relates to Israel's in restoring Jerusalem, rebuilding the Temple and freeing the captives. The LORD urges Israel to accept the plan and insists that Israel is still God's chosen servant.

Babylon's humiliation in having idols moved through the streets is described as a part of the submission to an invader. A final scene describes preparations for an expedition from Babylon to Jerusalem that may be the one described in Ezra 1:8 under the leadership of Sheshbbazzar.

The LORD Introduces Cyrus, 44:24–45:13

The setting is still in the heavenly court, but a new cycle of themes begins with attention on CYRUS. The speeches are in hymnic style, but the tone of disputation is still there. This passage is a bridge between the EXILE and the return to Jerusalem. The themes of redemption, creation, ridicule of idolatry, fulfillment of prophecy, and the rehabilitation of Jerusalem are continued. The role of Cyrus now turns to the subjects that will dominate the rest of the book: the restoration of Jerusalem and the Temple.

44:24-28. To Israel. The LORD introduces himself as Israel's *Redeemer*, and also the creator of all that exists. God is also the one who fulfills valid prophecy, the one who can make prophesied events come to pass. As Creator the LORD is in control of all nature. The point of the introduction is clear: God is the one who has called Cyrus to rebuild Jerusalem.

45:1-7. To Cyrus. The LORD addresses *his anointed* one who has been led to victory after victory. God has chosen him to *subdue nations . . . and kings*. The LORD has gone ahead of Cyrus's armies, smoothing his way and giving his enemies' treasures into his hand. God has done all this so Cyrus may know the LORD and know he is being blessed for Israel's sake.

45:8-13. To Israel. The LORD asserts again his position as Creator and claims the right to determine Israel's way. God threatens anyone who questions the deity's right to shape history. As Creator of the world the LORD claims the right to decide that Cyrus will rebuild Jerusalem.

Righteousness and Strength Are in the LORD, 45:14-25

This passage takes the form of a dialogue between the LORD and Cyrus. The emperor is promised success in his campaign against Egypt. Cyrus is amazed and confesses surprise at Israel's good fortune. He congratulates Israel.

The LORD repeats his claims and his intentions (vv. 18c-19). Cyrus calls refugees of the nations of Palestine to assemble. The LORD tells them to recognize that he has brought this about.

Cyrus calls for the borderlands to recognize him, pay tribute, and avoid military action. The LORD adds his support, legitimatizing Cyrus's right to rule the region. Cyrus proclaims that everyone must submit to him, since the LORD has approved him. Someone observes that Cyrus cannot be stopped and that Israel will be protected.

Bel Bows . . . the LORD's Purpose Stands, 46:1-13

The fall of Babylon to Persia was a most humiliating defeat to its gods, as it was to the rulers. Idols had been moved about to protect them during the war. Their helplessness was obvious.

On the other hand, exilic Israel's fortunes have been enhanced. The LORD claims credit for this turn of events. God has cared for Israel in the time of need.

The LORD calls on Israel to remember the *former things* (v. 9), undoubtedly referring to the centuries that have passed, with their heavy weight of invasion and judgment. The LORD then announces again the decision to put salvation in Zion. Jerusalem is the chosen instrument for these latter times.

Sit in the Dust, Babylon!, 47:1-15

The LORD addresses conquered Babylon in a sarcastic and taunting tone, similar to that found in chap. 14. The address begins with a metaphor: the princess has become a slave. A choral section follows, expressing Israel's recognition of God and the judgment that falls over Babylon.

A taunt that notes the reversal of fortunes follows. Babylon is accused here in the same way its king was accused in chap. 14 of having failed to recognize the LORD's hand in all the events.

Babylon had trusted in its oracles and charms. But those in their demonic nature turned back against her and brought about her doom. The last verses mock Babylon's helplessness.

Move out from Babylon!, 48:1-22

Israel is summoned to listen to the LORD's speeches. The people are recognized as bearing the name, descending from Judah, and worshiping in the LORD's name. But they have been hypocrites, not worshiping sincerely. They are summoned to hear two speeches of the LORD.

48:3-11. The LORD's first speech. The LORD repeats the previous claims that have foretold the events. But Israel has been deaf, rebellious, and unreliable. The people must still be refined (cf. 1:25).

48:12-20. Dialogue with a chosen leader. The LORD repeats his claims as Creator. A leader picks up the call to Israel in v. 14, calling on Israel to gather, recognize the LORD's fulfillment, and listen.

The LORD repeats that God is the one who has brought Cyrus to power and that it had been announced openly. The leader then claims that the LORD has sent him and granted him the divine spirit. He cites the LORD's presence and promise to accompany them on the way.

The LORD's "if only" speech maintains that none of this exile and return would have been necessary if only Israel had obeyed from the beginning.

The leader calls for the people to move out from Babylon. He calls ahead for Canaan to know: *The LORD has redeemed his servant Jacob!* (v. 20).

The final verses (21-22) signal a distinction between two kinds of Israelites. God's providence watches over those who take up the pilgrimage. But those who are adversaries of God and the group that rally to him shall have *no peace*.

The Vision of the Age of Darius, 49:1–57:21

The Book of Ezra refers to three great Persian emperors who proclaimed or confirmed an order to build the Temple in Jerusalem. CYRUS issued the decree. DARIUS confirmed the decree for ZERUBBABEL. This commentary suggests that Isa 49–57 should be read against the background of the generation of Darius (522–486 B.C.E.)

The Servant of Rulers, 49:1–50:3

49:1-21. A light to nations. The opening speech, the first part of which (vv. 1-6) is often treated by scholars as the second of the "servant songs," is addressed to *coastlands* and *peoples from far away*. These may well be the nations in Palestine along the coast and in the interior. The speaker identifies himself as *Israel* (v. 3). He recites his testimony to having been called by the LORD before birth. The calling was to be the LORD's servant *in whom he will be glori-*

fied (v. 3). But it had not worked out that way; God knows why not.

A second voice answers with a similar testimony to having been called of the LORD. But his task is *to bring Jacob back to him* (v. 5). In contrast to the first voice, this one testifies that he has been honored in the LORD's sight and received his strength from God. Cyrus received a similar command in 45:13; here the command is renewed to Darius to fulfill what Cyrus had not completed.

The commission is enlarged to include becoming *a light to nations* (v. 6). Darius has become the LORD's instrument to extend his salvation *to the end of the earth*. *Earth* may also be translated "land"; if so it refers to the farthest extent of the land of Canaan, that is, to all Palestine.

A second ORACLE is recited in v. 7. The speaker of v. 5 is now described. He is one *deeply despised, abhorred by the nations, the slave of rulers*. Darius had been a lowly aide to emperor Cambyses, with no royal status, no position in line for the throne.

The oracle proclaims that recognition and status await him because *of the LORD . . . who has chosen him* (v. 7). Darius's success in establishing his throne and authority over the Empire is attributed to being chosen by the LORD. Darius in fact did gain complete control of the government in all the parts of the existing empire and then proceeded to enlarge it to become the largest empire known to that time.

A second oracle (vv. 8-12) gives the LORD's speech. This is a favorable time, a time of salvation in which God addresses Darius. The LORD has protected Darius and gives him *as a covenant of people*. Darius becomes the way the LORD expresses his faithful relation to the people *to establish the land* of Canaan for them. They will be assigned portions they may cultivate.

Darius's assignment includes freeing the exiled prisoners so that they can return. The LORD will care for them on the way as he did for those that came out of Egypt. Everything will be done to facilitate their return. They will come from far away, and from all directions. The land that is named in v. 12, *Syene*, is unknown. Some have thought it referred to China, others to a city on the Egyptian border.

Verse 13 begins with an address to *heavens and . . . earth*, as in 1:2. They are called to rejoice because the LORD *has comforted his people* (cf. 40:1, 10).

In v. 14 Zion enters the conversation. Zion complains, as Israel had done in v. 4, that *the LORD has forsaken and forgotten me*. The LORD protests that this is not so. He tells of growth and buildings, of increased population and prosperity, all proof that Zion has not been abandoned.

49:22–50:3. Even the captives of a tyrant. The LORD continues with an oracle to the effect that he will use the rulers of nations to rescue Jerusalem. When it happens, Jerusalem will know that the LORD is God. Then the book picks up a theme from 40:31 concerning *those who wait for the LORD.* The theme will appear repeatedly to the end of the book. Those who wait will not be put to shame; they will be vindicated.

Zion is still skeptical. *Can prey be taken from the mighty? Can the captives of a tyrant be rescued?* (v. 24). They have become convinced of the kind of power and absolute authority that the great empires possessed and used. They do not believe anyone, even God, can overcome that. The people of Zion have missed the point of these chapters. The emperors have been made God's servants. The LORD will not act against them, but use them to do his will.

The LORD answers that rescue is possible—and will be done. When it is done, not only Zion, but *all flesh shall know* that God has done it and that Israel and Zion enjoy God's special favor.

In 50:1 the LORD addresses Zion concerning the complaint that it had been abandoned. God asks for proof that Zion had been deserted. God did not do it. Zion was sold as a slave, but its own sinfulness was the cause. It was the people who had abandoned God, and who did not respond when the LORD called.

Then God protests that the divine strength and abilities are as secure as ever. The LORD can deliver or redeem. The language returns to the argument of chaps. 40–41 that God has clothed *the heavens* (v. 3). If the LORD can *clothe the heavens*, surely salvation from tyrants is also possible.

A Student's Tongue, 50:4–51:8

Verses 4-9 are thought to be one of the "servant songs" of Isaiah 40–55, but the passage does not speak of a "servant." Servant language appears outside the unit in v. 10. The first person speech is from a self-described *teacher.* He has been trained and disciplined for the task of *sustaining the weary with a word.*

The teacher is also a pacifist who accepts abuse rather than striking back. He claims the LORD's support and urges his adversaries to confront him. The teacher is confident that the LORD will vindicate him.

Who is this person? Who are his adversaries? This teacher and leader in the age of Darius should be one that represents the LORD's cause in restoring Jerusalem. The Books of Haggai and Zechariah are set in this period. The prophets and and also the priest, Joshua, support the leadership of ZERUBBABEL in efforts to rebuild the Temple. Ezra 3 tells of Zerubbabel's actions in beginning the Temple. Ezra 4:1-4 speaks of adversaries who managed to frustrate the efforts and delay completion for a long time. Perhaps Isaiah's suffering teacher-leader portrays the role of Zerubbabel.

A strong and authoritative voice claiming to represent the servant (Darius) calls for trust in the LORD. He promises to suppress the agitators. He rallies those who *pursue righteousness, [and] . . . seek the LORD* (51:1). They are urged to remember what God did for Abraham. They are reminded of God's promise now to *comfort Zion.*

A strong speech closes the section. It is addressed to *my people.* The speech could be understood as spoken by the LORD, yet a number of features, such as *my justice for a light to the peoples* (v. 4), echo the words to the servant in 49:6, a servant whom we identified as Darius. If this is Darius's speech, too, then it is one in which he appeals to the religious traditions and faith of the people in Jerusalem. He claims that his power and authority are being recognized in Palestine and that this established order is to be permanent. He then calls on them to trust his commission to rebuild the city and the Temple.

Awake! Put on Strength!, 51:9–52:12

51:9–52:2. Celebrate deliverance. Choral exhortations and the LORD's own words respond to the political challenge uttered in the preceding section. The combination of the words of the chorus and the words of the LORD recognize the events as the LORD's work, comparable to the work in creation when *Rahab, . . . the dragon* (v. 9) was destroyed. The returning Judaeans are called the LORD's ransomed ones. They return with joy and singing.

The LORD is identified as the one who *comforts you* (v. 12). Then God addresses the fears of the people; whom they fear is not identified. Perhaps it is the same adversary who persecuted the teacher in 50:4-9. The adversary is certainly *only a human being who fades like grass,* as the voice in 40:6 said. Fear can only come because they have forgotten the LORD under the oppression of that time. But relief is promised for the oppressed, for the LORD who redeems them is the same.

This LORD who stirs up the storms at sea is the same one who has *put my words in your mouth* (v. 16). Israel's and Zion's great treasure is the word of God, which they are to proclaim and confess. This is their calling, as it was for the teacher in 50:4. The LORD has *hidden them in the shadow of his hand.* Israel complained of being hidden in 49:2. But even as he hid them, the LORD had assured Zion: *You are my people.*

The people of Zion are called to rouse themselves from the stupor caused by the events of the past generations when the city was destroyed and left in ruins. Now the LORD promises an end to that. The cup *of staggering* (v. 17) is the fate that caused the destruction of Jerusalem. Now it is being passed on to the oppressors who have walked on them during the time of their humiliation (v. 23).

Jerusalem is called to celebrate its deliverance. The city is no longer a captive, no longer a prey to any alien who chose to enter it.

52:3-12. The messenger who announces peace. The LORD announces his presence in Zion and compares it to the divine appearance in Egypt to deliver the Israelites centuries before. Just as at that time Israel came to recognize who the LORD was both through appearance and action, so this generation will come to know God through the events of the day.

There is a joyous recognition of the approach of messengers who come to proclaim peace. This *peace* is much more than the cessation of war. It announces a coming health and wholeness for the city. This *peace* is nothing less than salvation for the ruined city. The messengers who were ordered sent in 40:1, 9-11 have finally arrived.

The message they bring is found in vv. 9-10. The people in Zion are to rejoice *for the LORD has comforted his people.* The arm God *bares* represents the Persian emperors and their commitment to rebuild the Temple. God's presence in history will become clear to all the surrounding peoples who will see the rebuilding as the salvation of Israel's God.

Verses 11-12 renew the call to *Depart*, first heard earlier in 48:20. The call is for priests and Levites to return, being careful to purify themselves for the travel so that they can be ready to serve on the sacred grounds when they arrive. But they must go with dignity. This is not a backdoor escape. The LORD, the God of Israel, will both lead them and protect their flanks as they travel.

Restoration Pains in Jerusalem, 52:13–54:17b

52:13–53:12. The punishment that made us whole. A number of themes that have been introduced in earlier passages come to a crisis and conclusion in this passage. The LORD's exclamation: *See, my servant prospers, is exalted, is very high* (52:13) opens the section. Two servants were introduced in chap 49. One was Israel; the other we identified as DARIUS, later successor to CYRUS, the servant of chap 45. It seems more likely that this acclamation greets Darius's success in establishing himself as emperor. Verses 14-15 fulfill the announcement in 49:7. The success of the servant is unexpected and the rulers are astonished.

The first verse of chap. 53 presents another incredible report. This is often interpreted as a reference to the servant of the previous verses but that is not necessarily the case. I take it to refer to another person, one who also grew up without promise of great things. He was despised, a man of pains. There is an echo here of the persecuted teacher of 50:4-8, but now a chorus recognizes that the blows he received were their fault. He had carried the burden on their behalf. They had earlier thought this one to be punished by God. Now they recognize that it was their rebellions that caused his suffering. Because he was punished, they were exonerated. Everyone confesses his own part in the guilt but recognizes that for some unexplained reason the LORD had laid on him the iniquity of them all.

In v. 7 the address changes. It is no longer a chorus. Someone speaks of the afflicted person. He is compared to *a lamb that is led to the slaughter.* The persecution led to his death. *He was cut off from the land of the living* by no fault of his own. It happened because of *the rebellion of my people.* Here is that phrase again: *my people.* It occurred in 51:4 where it could have been spoken by the LORD or by Darius. I chose Darius then. If this is Darius speaking here, he is recognizing Zerubbabel's innocence.

But in v. 10 he recognizes the LORD's hand in what has happened. He sees the death *as an offering for sin* through which Zerubbabel will succeed as he never could have in life. *Through him the will of the LORD shall prosper.*

In v. 11 it is difficult to determine to whom the pronouns refer. Suppose we read it as a speech from the LORD: "Out of Zerubbabel's anguish, Darius will see. He will be satisfied. In knowing (about) Zerubbabel, my Servant (Darius) becomes a righteous one for many and will forgive their wrongs."

This passage is ambiguous in many ways and this proposed reconstruction is only one of many ways to view the original meaning of the passage. What is clear is that someone has been killed and the people confess that much of the fault was their own. This person died in their stead. Then this is understood to have been God's will through which a redemption was achieved for the people. The death is perceived as a sort of human sacrifice through which good things came for the people because God accepted it that way.

The NT has used the interpretation of a vicarious sacrifice as a model in explaining the death of Jesus on the cross (Luke 22:37; Matt 27:57-60; Acts 8:32-33). Few modern readers can read these words in Isaiah without hearing the music of Handel's *Messiah* throbbing in the background.

Verse 12 announces the rehabilitation of the name and rights of the one who had died because he had allowed himself to be executed and in so doing he bore the sin of many.

54:1-17b. *Sing, O barren one!* This chapter returns to the call for celebration and joy. Jerusalem is addressed. The barrenness refers to the years of lying in ruins since the destruction of the city over sixty years before. Now the growth of the city will be unbelievably rapid. Jerusalem will have to spread out on all sides to accommodate the increase.

The city must not be afraid. All the changes are due to God's work. The LORD is called both *Maker* and *husband* (v. 5). The God of the whole earth is the redeemer of Jerusalem. What a tremendous thought! Our personal God, who answers our prayers, is the Creator of all things, the LORD of all.

Zion is being called to resume her position after having been *like a wife forsaken* (v. 6), one who has been *cast off*. The LORD recognizes that briefly she has been abandoned; he has hidden his face. But now God moves toward reconciliation, showing compassion and everlasting love. He will gather Zion to himself again.

The LORD swears that this abandonment will not happen again. As in Noah's time, judgment came. But God swore never to send a flood again. The mountains might disappear, but God's *steadfast love shall not* be removed again (v. 10). His compassion is Zion's again.

Zion's restoration is happening. The walls and towers will be built in fine stones. All the children are to be taught by the LORD. The city's future is secure. Anyone striving against Zion cannot claim support from the LORD. God claims to be the creator of power, even the power to destroy, but nothing that is fashioned to be used against Zion will succeed.

A House of Prayer for All Peoples, 54:17c–56:8

This passage announces a great invitation to the LORD's house of prayer. It anticipates the soon completion of the goal announced in 2:4. In 54:17c this hope for completion is announced as *the heritage of the servants of the LORD*. For the first time "servants" occurs in the plural. It refers to the congregation of individual Israelites who choose to worship the LORD. The change is significant, recognizing that not all Israelites want to belong to the Israel of God.

With that in mind the call goes out to assemble all those who choose to serve the LORD. What is offered has no price. It is nothing less than an *everlasting covenant* (v. 3). God's love for David is legendary; now that same love is offered to anyone who will come to God.

David had been called to be *a witness to the peoples* (v. 4). Now the new Israel will understate the task that the Davidic kings used to have. Now the gathered Israel of covenant faith *will call nations that [they] do not know* (v. 5) and they will run to them. They will come because the LORD their God has glorified them. The world of Jewish proselytes comes into view.

The great invitation continues in classic words: *Seek the LORD while he may be found* (v. 6). Even the wicked are called to repent, with the promise of abundant pardon. God declares that divine thoughts are different from human thoughts. His grace is of a sort unknown to human reason. It is higher and greater.

God speaks of the efficacy of his *word* (v. 11). It will accomplish the mission given to it. A symbol of all this will be the evidences that God has led his people back to their land. All nature will be glad. Its flowering will be *a memorial, an everlasting sign* (v. 13).

God has expectations for this new people. *Justice and right conduct are the order of the day, for salvation will come; deliverance will be revealed* (56:1). An additional sign of blessing is the keeping of SABBATH. The prophetic emphasis on justice and the priestly emphasis on Sabbath are included and blended.

This is to be an inclusive fellowship. The law normally excluded foreigners. Ezra 10 demanded that all foreign wives be divorced and excluded. Yet there are many signs in the law codes that efforts were made to include foreign bond servants in some of the worship forms. But 56:3 calls on foreigners who have joined themselves to the LORD to have no reason to feel separate or threatened.

Another group that was traditionally excluded were EUNUCHs (see Lev 21:20-21; Deut 23:1). They, too, are urged to feel welcome if they keep sabbath, choose the things that please the LORD, and keep covenant. They have no chance of having children to perpetuate their names. But the LORD will give them both *a monument and a name, better than sons or daughters* (v. 5).

The foreigners who answer the invitation, minister to the LORD, love his name, become his servants, keep sabbath and covenant, will be brought to the holy mountain. The words echo the vision of 2:2-4. They may rejoice in God's house, which is here called his *house of prayer* (v. 7). Burnt offerings and sacrifices will be accepted from them. It will be called *a house of prayer for all peoples.*

The section ends by saying that God's efforts to bring in foreigners and eunuchs will reach out to gather still others to join them. One is reminded of Jesus' parable about the wedding feast (Matt 22).

Rebellion, but Healing, 56:9–57:21

56:9–57:13. The dark side of Jerusalem. The positive and joyful tone of the preceding chapters is interrupted by a very negative and violent section. Not everything is right about Jerusalem.

The watchmen and shepherds are *blind* (56:10) and drunken (56:12). They are unable or unwilling to defend the people from the wild animals. The watchmen are called dogs who are blind and silent. They have great appetites. The shepherds are more concerned with drinking than with shepherding.

This state of affairs puts righteous people at risk. They perish and no one takes note. *Taken away* (57:1) must mean taken to prison. Apparently the innocent are jailed for standing up to the violent ones. God promises that things will be corrected for the righteous when peace comes.

The harsh words that follow are directed to the wicked who obviously have not answered the invitation. Verses 3-5 are addressed to a masculine group. They are called *children of a sorceress, . . . offspring of an adulterer and a whore.* Their mocking ways and lustful behavior, even including the slaughter of children, are castigated.

In v. 6 the address changes to a feminine singular, apparently addressed to pagan Jerusalem. She is both

pagan and carnal. And her philandering ways are chronicled.

Verse 11 questions the reasons for such conduct. Who could they have feared so much that they forgot the LORD? God's silence meant that they had no reason to plead that they were terrified of him. God will recognize all their rights and their works, but these do not help. Let their idols help them in their distress. The paragraph ends on a positive note of promise, however, that *whoever takes refuge in [God] . . . shall possess the land* (v. 11). The ancient promise of the land (cf. Gen 12:1-3) echoes here. More importantly, those who flee to the LORD will *inherit [God's] holy mountain.* A place in the assembly in God's presence will be their lot.

57:14-21. I will heal them. The pendulum swings back to a positive word. Verse 14 picks up the practical instructions for the returning group from 48:20 and 52:11-12. The building project is a highway for the pilgrims and returnees as in 40:3-4.

Verse 15 announces that the LORD has taken up his dwelling in the Temple in Jerusalem. God is introduced as *the high and lofty one*, a description fitting for the one who will inhabit *the high and holy place* (v. 15). *Who inhabits eternity* is literally "one who dwells on and on." The language here is similar to that in Pss 33:21, 103:1, and 145:21.

But God is not only to be understood in terms of the Temple's Holy of Holies. The LORD also wants to be known as the spirit who dwells with the contrite and humble in spirit (v. 15), presumably wherever they are. The reason for God's indwelling presence is to revive the spirits and hearts of those who seek him.

Verses 16-18 is a concise apologetic for the way God has acted toward Israel. It begins with the insistence that God will not always be *angry* and accusing, else the spirits and the souls that he has created would grow faint and die. This is an admission that God has been angry and accusing toward the people.

The LORD explains this anger in terms of the *wicked covetousness* of the people. In anger God struck them. This image refers to the historical judgments against Israel through invasions and the judgments through droughts and earthquakes. God says *I hid* from the people, a reference to God's being absent from the Temple when it was destroyed and not answering prayers. The people had complained that God had abandoned them. God says that was true because he was angry with them on account of their sins.

The most disheartening thing to God was that the people kept turning back to their own ways, the conduct that had occasioned divine wrath in the first place. God's frustration in dealing with a people who do not learn from punishment is recounted throughout the book.

In v. 18 the gospel, the good news, comes. God has *seen their ways* of sin and always falling back into rebellion. In spite of that the LORD has determined to *heal them*. The healing process has three stages. God will *lead them* into a way of life fitting for his presence. This may include leading them on the return to Jerusalem.

The second is *repaying them with comfort*. Chap. 40 began with the announcement that God had ordered comfort for his people. This is strengthening of spirit and soul, as v. 15 has said. It includes providing the necessities for their restoration, including the building of the Temple.

The third provision is *creating* for *their mourners* the words that will bring life and hope. "Creating" is the strongest word for God's action that one can use. *The fruit of the lips* is a flowery term for "words." Those words of comfort and restoration are: *Peace, peace, to the far and the near, says the LORD*. What could be better to enunciate the good news that God has determined to *heal them*.

Verses 20-21 give the other side of the hard-earned knowledge that comes from experience. Not all Israel belong to the contrite and the humble, or to those who answer the invitation given in chap. 55 and in many other places. The book has shown repeatedly the dark side of Israel's being. *The wicked* remain. The word can also be translated "the adversaries." They remain stubbornly adverse to everything God stands for. They are restless and unable to achieve the stillness that characterizes the humble and the contrite. They cannot "wait for the LORD." And their restlessness stirs up the ugly *mire* and *mud* of their inner beings.

The peace God proclaims for the humble and contrite of Israel cannot come to these adversaries. *There is no peace, says my God, for the wicked*. This closing refrain repeats that of 48:22. The final verses of the book will be a variation on this theme.

The Vision of the Age of Artaxerxes, 58:1–66:24

At the end of the reign of Xerxes conditions in Palestine deteriorated. The government had lost control and lawless bands roamed the countryside. When ARTA-XERXES took the throne, hope for improvement brought calls for reform in Jerusalem. When stable Persian control was reestablished, the city and the Temple were rebuilt under EZRA and NEHEMIAH.

The LORD's Kind of Fast, 58:1-14

Chapter 58 begins with the LORD's command (vv. 1-2) to announce to his people *their rebellion*. The recipients of this announcement are to be God's people, *the house of Jacob*. The language is reminiscent of chap.1. Although the. northern kingdom has long since been destroyed and Judah has also been exiled, God is thinking of the remaining and returning people as the children of Israel, as the LORD's people.

They are religious and want to do right. Yet they must be deemed rebellious and sinful. Things haven't changed much since chap. 1. But this discrepancy between religious intention and perceived rebellion cries out for definition and explanation.

The people in Judah respond with a complaint (v. 3ab). They ask why their religious observances and fasts, particularly, have not gotten a favorable response from God. They think of fasting and prostrating themselves in prayer as things that will elicit the kinds of responses from God that they want.

God's command in v. 2 recognizes that these rebellious people are in fact a religious people. The answers to their questions begin with critiques of their fasts. The motivation for fasting is that they *serve their own interests* (v. 3) or find pleasure in fasting. Another reason, *[you] oppress all your workers*, uses an obscure Hebrew word related to a word meaning "be hurt, or be in pain." The ancient versions and NRSV have understood it to refer to oppression of workers.

A second answer (v. 4) points out that their fasting has led to contention and fighting. Such fasting is clearly not what God wants. Fasting became a common practice in the hard days of EXILE (cf. Lev. 23:26-32; Jer 36:9), but the prophets have frequently objected that God's requirements are not fasting from food, but kindness and justice (Mic 6:6-8; Jas 1:27).

Then the LORD speaks to the issue, defining the kind of fast or religious expression that God would choose (vv. 5-7). The LORD first asks whether self-denigration or groveling is what he wants, implying that it is not.

Verse 6 describes an exercise that promotes freedom that is a worthwhile activity, from God's point of view, or service that responds to the needs of the hungry, the homeless, the naked. That is true service that honors God. *To hide yourself from your own kin* (v. 7) must mean failure to perform the common decencies toward members of one's own family, such as caring for the elderly or ignoring an orphaned cousin, and so forth. One doing service to God doesn't fail to do those things.

That kind of worship and service brings beneficent response from God. When God's people act like that, all kinds of good things can happen (vv. 8-9). Light, healing and vindication will be the characteristics of their time. God's glory will be their protection. Then comes the real answer to the question in v. 2: *Then you shall call, and the LORD will answer* (v. 9).

Verses 9b-12 expand on the type of worship actions that will being God's blessings. They define the kind of community actions that will make the restorations that are being undertaken in Jerusalem a success.

Verses 13-14 relate these to SABBATH observance. The implication is that special fasts are really not necessary. The opportunities to keep Sabbath allow the people to worship in ways that please God. A major objection to the people's actions in this chapter involves *serving their own interests* (vv. 3, 13a, 13c).

Proper service is clearly that which serves God's interests and the needs of others.

Troubled Times in Judah, 59:1-15a

The chapter describes disturbed conditions in Judah. It first speaks from the objective viewpoint of outsiders (vv. 1-8), and then has insiders confessing their relation to the situation. It speaks of the evils:

in general	as *iniquities* (vv. 2, 12b)
	sins (vv. 2b, 12a)
	evil (v. 15a)
specifically as	violent deeds (vv. 3a, 6b, 7)
	lying speech (vv. 3b, 4b, 13b)
	mischief (vv. 4a, 5, 6a, 7b, 13b)
what is lacking	*righteousness* (vv. 4a, 9a, 14a)
	honesty, or truth (vv. 4, 14a, 15)
	peace, or wholeness (vv. 8a, 8b)
	justice (vv. 8a, 9a, 11b, 14a)
	salvation (vv. 1, 11b)
results	rebellion (vv. 12, 13a)
	oppression (v. 13)
	insurrection (v. 13)

The situation is bad. There is no real government and therefore no peace, justice, or protection from violence. Yet the scene does not blame the outsiders for

the troubles. It points its finger at the Judeans themselves. They blame God. But no one of them takes responsibility for action. The scene equates the chaotic conditions with religious sins and turning away from God.

The LORD Decides to Act, 59:15b-21

The first part of this section narrates the LORD's displeasure and response. If vv. 16b-17 are to be understood as we have understood chaps. 44–45 and 49, these must refer to the LORD's raising up a third Persian emperor to restore his people and his city. In this case it would be ARTAXERXES I. The chapter identifies the LORD's intention with Artaxerxes's military intervention in vv. 19-20.

In v. 21 the LORD addresses Artaxerxes, renewing God's covenant with Israel with the promise that his spirit will be on the Persian. His *words* are those spoken first to CYRUS and renewed to DARIUS, as related in the Book of Ezra.

Against this historical background, vv. 15b-20 described the way Artaxerxes enters Palestine as the LORD's instrument to correct the conditions portrayed in the last two chapters. Verses 18-19 indicate the Phoenician and Philistine territories that draw the primary attention of the Persians. V. 20 contrasts the way the invasion will impact Jerusalem, or at least those in Judah who turn away from rebellion.

Zion's Day Dawns, 60:1-22

The chapter builds upon chaps. 40 and 54. Jerusalem's good news is about to become reality. It is a time when light replaces darkness, when people come to Zion from everywhere (vv. 1-5a), and its poverty is to be replaced by riches (vv. 5b-9). Foreigners help to rebuild the city and contribute to sacrificial offerings (v. 10).

The scene is described from another viewpoint in Ezra 7 and Neh 2. The key terms for the city is that it is to be *glorified* (vv. 7b, 9, 13, 19, 21). The riches of the nations are gathered to build the Temple, the walls, and the gates.

The government's authority in the city is reestablished. Peace and order reign. This brings order and safety and the rights of Jews once again to own land (v. 21a). This implies Persian authority to uphold Jerusalem's position (v. 12) and bring relief from oppressive neighbors (v. 14).

The LORD's plan is to use Persian wealth and power to accomplish his purpose. When Artaxerxes re-establishes Persian authority in Jerusalem, the LORD's presence, city, and Temple can flourish. What the Emperor dedicates to the LORD, the LORD gives to Jerusalem. These include:

permission for Jews to travel (vv. 3-4; Ezra 7:13)

support for rebuilding the Temple and the city (vv. 6-7, 11, 17; Ezra 7:15-16, 21; Neh 2:8-9, 13)

support for operating the Temple (vv. 3-4, 9; Ezra 7:23, 26)

threat of imperial reprisal for injury (vv. 12, 14; Ezra 7:23, 26)

rights granted to administer the city under the Torah (Ezra 7:25) and the rights of inheritance (vv. 18, 21).

Light is a major theme in the chapter (vv. 1-3, 5a, 19-20). The idea of beautifying or glorifying the Temple and the city dominates the heart of the chapter (vv. 7b, 8, 9, 13, and 21). The call to rejoice appears in vv. 5a, 15b, 22.

The LORD's Agents Bless Jerusalem, 61:1-11

The Spirit of the LORD God again assumes an important role in the chapters (as in 42:1 and 59:21). Verses 1-3 are like the "servant song" of 50:4-11. Jesus quotes it in Luke 4:16-20; the words pick up the theme of joy from chap. 40.

A solitary person speaks in Jerusalem of the LORD's calling. His task is to *bring good news to the oppressed* (v. 1). The consistent understanding of the prophetic calling relates to the poor and the oppressed. The announcement is of liberty and of release.

The message is all contained in the announcement of *the year of the LORD's favor* (v. 2). This sounds like the Year of Jubilee in Lev. 25. It refers to a time when the land holdings will be reassigned and renewed for all the villagers. *Provide* (v. 3) can be translated "assign" and refer exactly to that.

Judeans, whether returnees or survivors in Jerusalem, fit the description of the oppressed, the captives, the mourners. The time first envisioned in chap. 40 has arrived when all things shall be turned around, with blessing in place of sorrow.

The great reversal in their fortunes is described in v. 3, when they are called *oaks of righteousness* (what a contrast to the stump in 6:13!). Planted by the LORD *to display his glory*. The practical effect is to change the ruined city into a thriving, beautiful city.

Israel's specific calling will be service as *priests of the LORD*. Other peoples can perform the other tasks that are needed. Israel is the servant to worship the

LORD. The other roles as rulers can be assigned to the Persian authorities. Supporting roles can well be filled by others. But ministry in the LORD's house must be handled primarily by Israel.

In v. 7 the NRSV's *because* is an unnecessary addition. The verse announces that apportionments of land to till will now be doubled. Joy will now be their permanent lot.

The LORD announces his love of justice and his promise to continue to support the people. God promises to them an *everlasting covenant*. Their very existence will be a testimony among the nations that they are *a people whom God has blessed. People* is originally "a seed," reminiscent again of 6:13.

Verses 10-11 have another individual speak, rejoicing in God's gifts of *salvation* and *righteousness*. The speaker could be seen as Israel. But if the second servant, the Persian ruler is also a part of these concluding chapters, it might be he who speaks. In that case *righteousness* might better be understood as legitimacy. By his part in the restoration of Jerusalem he establishes his legitimate place in Palestine before the nations. And this is a gift from the LORD who called him for this role from the beginning.

A New Name for Jerusalem, 62:1-7

With this chapter the Vision moves toward its completion. The opening verses are a speech that convey an angry determination. The speaker purports to speak for Zion. But who is the speaker? If this were the LORD or the prophet speaking on his behalf, one would expect a continuation of the tone of the previous two chapters.

But the tone and content are different. They are directed against the LORD's silence or inaction. The speaker must be different, perhaps a leader in Jerusalem. He is leading a demonstration in the city against the LORD's announced policy of having an open city that depends on the Persian forces for its defense. The LORD does not speak until v. 8.

The scene creates a tension in the drama. It is opposed to the views of chaps. 60–61, even of the entire Vision to this point. It is true that the speech calls for salvation and righteousness for the city as in other passages. But these are sought for the city in its own right, whereas they had been granted through the Persian emperor who was called to restore, rebuild, and protect the city.

This speech calls for Jerusalem to defend itself (v. 6). The city wants to be closed off from groups around it, in contrast to the Vision's hope for a city open to worshipers and artisans from all nations. The speech pleads for blessings and riches, but it is unrealistic in spurning the aid offered by its neighbors. This policy and plea will also dominate the next two chapters.

An Oath and An Apparition, 62:8–63:6

This scene answers the challenge of 62:1-7 in two ways. First the LORD reviews the situation: the security already provided (vv. 8-9) and the ongoing work on roads that will make travel possible (v. 10). It is known in Palestine that Zion has a powerful patron (vv. 11:a-d); and everyone knows that the restoration is funded and that Jerusalem's functioning sanctuary is a reality.

The LORD does not respond to the speech, but renews the pledge that Jerusalem will not be pillaged again (v. 8). Then the section returns to a summons to go out and begin the work. Announcement should be made to Jerusalem that the author of its salvation is on the way. This returns to the emphasis on the Persian ruler's plans for Jerusalem's restoration. The new city will have wonderful names when it is recognized that the LORD has accomplished this through his chosen vessels.

The second answer is portrayed. A terrible blood-stained figure appears from Edom. *Bozrah* is a major town in that direction. The figure is a soldier who is challenged (63:1-6). He claims to have authority and ample strength to protect the city, put down rebellion, and make the territory safe again. He tells of a battle (vv. 3-6) in which he fought without support from the peoples (i.e., without support from the Persian vassals in the area).

The two answers to the complaints in 62:1-7 demonstrate that the LORD is using Persian military force (63:1-6) to protect and secure the work of restoration (62:8-11). The LORD is in control, even when it takes an application of force to keep things on track.

A Sermon and Prayers
(with Interruptions), 63:7–64:12

The passage consists of a recital (63:7-14 and 64:4-9) broken by a series of interruptions (63:15–64:3, 10-12). The scene is like a preacher who has his sermon or liturgy interrupted by some of his hearers who insist on shouting questions and taunts at God during the service.

The recital is in the form of a sermon like those found in Deut 4–11 and some Psalms. It is unique,

however, in using a number of new and different words and themes. It chronicles God's compassionate acts toward Israel in the past ages (vv. 7-9).

But, then it notes that they rebelled (v. 10). God's mercy in the age that follows is in terms of remembering the previous acts and the Israel that was (vv. 11-14). Remembering is a major act of worship and theological reflection. This recital is positive throughout. It recognizes periods of affliction but insists that God shared these with his people and eventually saved them.

The interruptions turn the scene into an occasion for accusations against God and for sectarian complaint. In some of them the perspective changes from portraying God as being at work in history to God who comes down from heaven (63:15a and 64:1-3). The concern for the welfare of all Jerusalem turns into appeals on behalf of segments of the community.

The setting for the entire scene is the same as that of 62:1-7, when there was an appeal for continuous prayer for the safety of Jerusalem. The levitical preacher recites God's saving acts as reminders that can provide a basis for repentance and forgiveness that is acceptable to God. But the crowd is in no mood for such spiritual sermons. It breaks into loud prayers that contain complaints, claims, and demands stating their own sectarian views. They demonstrated how divided the Jerusalem of that day was. There were Zadokite priests, and there were Israelites who were not Judean. There also were militant activists who wanted military respect. These are the evident signs of disunity and rivalry in which each group poses its claim to be God's people.

The preacher is able to resume his sermon in 64:4-9. He proclaims that there has been no God other than the LORD among them throughout this period (vv. 4-5a). Then he appeals to God who despite his justified anger toward them is still their father. He appeals for him to still regard them as his people. The sermon attempts to be inclusive and unifying.

One last protest points to the charred embers of the city (here as in Neh 1:3 much too recent to have been the destruction of 587 B.C.E.) and asks how God can restrain himself from action on their behalf.

The LORD Deals with Opponents, 65:1-16

This passage is composed of a series of speeches by the LORD dealing with enemies, the people within Israel that continue to rebel against God and resist God's course of action. It contains three major speeches and three edicts, with a closing speech interpreting the meaning of separation. The setting is that of the heavenly court.

The LORD's opening speech addresses the court about God's rebellious people (vv. 1-6). God reviews his patience and willingness to receive them, but points out how the LORD received from them provocation through pagan acts and stubborn unwillingness to turn back to God. Now God will have to act.

The first edict is directed to Israel in the second person (NRSV's emendation is wrong). Israel is to be punished for their heathen worship (v. 7). The second edict (v. 8) mitigates the first so that not all of them will be destroyed.

A second speech (vv. 9-10) promises hope for God's *chosen*. They will have descendants who dwell in Canaan, a people *who have sought me*.

A third speech is directed to the sinners who, in contrast, *forsake the LORD* (vv. 11-12). They are destined for slaughter. The reason is clear: they refused to answer God's call.

A third formal edict (vv. 13-15a) defines their fate. In contrast to God's chosen servants who have responded to him, these will be hungry, thirsty, shamed, pained, anguished, and cursed.

A final section (vv. 15b-16) interprets the separation. God's separated people will receive a new name. God will be called *the God of faithfulness*. God and the new people will close the door on the past.

The LORD's Great Day:
A New Jerusalem, 65:17–66:24

The outer limits of this section are marked in the beginning by the phrase *For I* in v. 17. The Hebrew is much more dramatic "Behold me creating!" The passage ends in 66:5 after describing the contrast between groups in the new city: one who *trembles at God's word*, and another that hates them for that reason.

The passage is structured around two formal edicts. The first (vv. 24-25) announces: *Before they call I will answer*. The second (66:1-2a) is a question about the kind of house they intend to build for God.

These are framed by speeches from the LORD. Verses 17-23 describe the new creation. The second (66:2b-5) states his rejection of the old priestly ways and his installation of a more directly spiritual form of worship.

The historical background for this scene fits the period after EZRA and NEHEMIAH have returned. The interactions are between Zadokite priests who still wield authority over all sacrifice and the Temple area. The Vision opposes both the view that the sacred area should be limited to the Temple and the view that worship is primarily a matter of sacrifice. It also disputes the views that one priestly family should have exclusive privileges in Jerusalem. This sets the Vision at odds with Leviticus and with Malachi. The Vision is much more at home with the kind of broad participation in worship pictured in Neh 12:27- 47 through songs, prayers, and processions. It argues that the entire city, not just the Temple, comprises the LORD's sacred mountain.

This debate is understandable in the 5th century. The application of 66:1-3 can be even more clearly defined. Nehemiah was determined to build the city's walls before turning to repairs of the Temple (Neh 2–6). People in Jerusalem as well as their neighbors opposed this (Neh 4 and 6). The policy from the time of Zerubbabel on had been to concentrate only on the Temple. The Vision supports Nehemiah but also goes well beyond him. It sees the entire city as sacred, a place for Jews and other worshipers from all the known world to gather, worship, and be taught God's word.

65:17-25. See the LORD creating. The LORD calls for all to look at what he is doing at Jerusalem as an awesome act of creation. He wants it to be seen in terms like the creation of heavens and earth. But these are new. It is a new order, to be sharply distinguished from the old order.

A series of sharp contrasts is listed in vv. 19b-25:

No more	but
cry of distress	rejoice
an infant who *lives a few days*	one who dies at a hundred
a person dying prematurely	one hundred—
	an early age to die
build and another live there	build and live there
plant for another to eat	plant and eat their fruit
work for nothing	be like a tree
bear children for terror	wear out their things
receive answers to prayer	before they call,
	God answers
constant violence	no harm or destruction
	in all God's mountain

This is to be a place and time of *joy and . . . delight* (v. 18). The temporary relations of life and its arbitrary changes will be gone. Life will be stable and prosperous. God's presence will be clear and constant. It will be a period of peace and there will be no hurt or destruction.

That is God's vision and hope for his new work. It parallels the original vision for creation in Gen 2. But, like that one, it then had to turn to a more realistic experience of life as it is. This comes in chap. 66.

66:1-5. What kind of house? From the vision of new heavens and a new earth, the LORD turns his attention to a proposed building for God in the city. The LORD cannot be concerned about a house separate from the city. God's real attention is devoted *to the humble and contrite who trembles at his word.*

The LORD repudiates sacrificial worship. He describes this as a self-chosen way. The reason is clear. It did not come about in answer to God's call. The people chose what was evil in his sight.

A series of sacrifices recognized in Torah is said to be like some that are prohibited (v. 3):

Acceptable in Torah	Unacceptable
slaughtering an ox	striking a person (Lev. 24:17-21;
(Lev. 17:3-4)	Deut 19:6; 27:24-25)
sacrificing a lamb	breaking a dog's neck
(Lev 14:10-24)	(Exod 34:20 of a donkey)
a cereal offering	swine's blood (Lev. 11:7; Deut 14:8;
(Lev. 2:1, 13)	Isa 65:4; 66:17)
frankincense	an idol
(Lev. 2:2,16;6:8)	

Then the LORD addresses the party to which he is partial, *you who tremble at his word.* He encourages them to believe that those who hate and deride them will be *put to shame.*

66:6-24. The LORD confirms the servants in the new city. The Vision ends as it began with a scene in the heavenly court room of God. But all the speeches relate to the happenings in Jerusalem. The speeches relate to the worship and the attitudes of the worshipers rather than to any historical events.

This scene brings closure for three openings earlier in the book: the city on a mountain to which all the peoples flow (2:1-4) is fulfilled in vv. 18-20, the good news for Jerusalem (40:1-9) is fulfilled in this scene, and the promises of restoration for the city in chaps. 45, 49, 54, and especially chaps. 60–62, are picked up and closed here. It is a grand finale.

66:6. Disturbance noted. Someone takes note of noise offstage, as it were. It is an *uproar* from a city, from a Temple. It is identified as *the voice of the*

LORD. Then one can tell from the words and the tone that the LORD is dealing with his enemies. His patience with the adversaries has come to an end.

66:7-14. Like a birth. These verses use birth and child imagery to describe the appearance of the new city. It has come so suddenly! Everyone is surprised. *Yet as soon as Zion was in labor she delivered her children.* EZRA and NEHEMIAH had accomplished more in a few years than everyone before them had accomplished in decades. The destruction of 587 B.C.E. had left scars on the city that were not removed until Nehemiah rebuilt the walls. He completed his work in a short two years. The metaphor picks up the words from 49:20-21.

The children of Zion are the new covenant community there, the faithful servants of the LORD. These might also be the new inhabitants for the city that Neh 11 speaks of.

The LORD describes the stages of birth. God is the midwife. The process must be carried out. In chap. 40 the LORD had initiated the process. Now it has come full term.

Everyone who loves Jerusalem and who has mourned over the city is called to rejoice. Mourning for Jerusalem had been a preoccupation for a long time. Isaiah 60:20, 61:2-3, and the Book of Lamentations witness to the extent of the mourning. But to mourn now is to indicate a lack of faith in God's plans. Rejoicing with the city is also a theme in the Psalms (26:8; 122:6; 137:6).

The child imagery continues. The people of the dispersion are invited to draw nourishment from Jerusalem's restoration. The city will give them a focus for their faith and hope. They can make pilgrimages to the city. They can take satisfaction and consolation from knowing that Jerusalem is functioning again.

Prosperity renders the Heb. *shalom*, meaning "peace" (and much more). The *wealth of nations* continues the picture in chaps. 60 and 61 of the city's prosperity supported by the contribution from foreigners. Then the child imagery continues. Jerusalem nurtures the faithful as a mother nurtures a baby.

Jerusalem will be comforted by the LORD. When they see they can rejoice. They can know, as the nations know, that the LORD is active on behalf of his city. This is accomplished by separating the fate of *his servants* from that of *his enemies.* The separation described in chap. 65 is now complete.

66:15-18a. The LORD is coming in anger. The verses build on the thought of the LORD's indignation on his enemies. The LORD appears here as the Divine Warrior to execute judgment with the sword. The imagery here is very old in Israel (see also Jer 4:13; Ps 68:17 and Hab 3:8). Fire appears in many others scenes of judgment in the book.

Verse 17 describes pagan rites again. These must be brought to an end. In v. 18 *their* has a clear antecedent in v. 17. The Hebrew lacks a verb, but the two words show God's concern for the sins through their actions and their intentions.

66:18b-21. The LORD will gather. The LORD's coming has another focus more pertinent to the goal of this Vision. God will move to fulfill the rest of the picture in 2:2-4 by gathering people from all nations and tongues to come and see his glory in the new city.

The sign God will establish is the last of a series. In 7:14 the sign was a child to be born. In 19:20 it was a monument on Egypt's border. In 55:13 it was the return and the land's renewal. This sign will be in the nations. The *survivors* are those who remain in the dispersion. They will be sent out to the nations.

These ancient missionaries may include some of those who survive in Jerusalem. The Vision has so far focused on the peoples in Palestine. But now it looks far away. *Tarshish* is a distant port, perhaps as far away as Spain or the Black Sea. *Pul* may be in Africa and *Lud* is in Asia Minor. *Tubal* may be in Asia Minor. *Javan* is Greece. These are ancient names and must be intended symbolically.

They are to go to all those who have not heard or seen. They are to declare the LORD's glory among the nations.

A second task will be for the believers in the diaspora to bring the brothers in faith and covenant to Jerusalem to share in this experience. They will constitute *an offering to the LORD* that is seen as far more acceptable than the ox or the lamb of 66:3. The vision of 2:2-4 is coming true. The effort to transport pilgrims joins the efforts of those who restore the city—and all will be blessed.

The LORD promises that *from them*, the pilgrims from the diaspora, the LORD will choose Levites and priests. The new openness in the city will not reserve the positions of service and leadership for some special group (cf. 56:3-8). The Temple will become *a house of prayer for all nations* (56:7).

66:22-24. Last words. The verse refers back to 65:17 and the new creation in order to promise permanence and security in the LORD. The cycle of worship, both monthly and weekly, for all who will come is permanent. It will continue.

But the dark side is also still apparent. God's judgment on those who stubbornly rebel will be painfully visible to the worshipers as they leave the city.

Work Cited

Watts, John D. W. 1985. *Isaiah 1–33*. WBC; 1987. *Isaiah 34-66*. WBC.

Jeremiah

Leo G. Perdue

Introduction

The Book of Jeremiah is one of the three "major prophets" (major in terms of length; that is, Isaiah, Jeremiah, and Ezekiel) that, together with the "minor prophets" (Book of the Twelve), comprise the latter prophets (nĕbî'îm 'ahărōnîm) in the OT. The many complex problems present in interpreting this fascinating book include literary composition and authorship, the differences between the MT, that is, the Hebrew, and the LXX, that is, the SEPTUAGINT, and identifying the historical settings in which the various materials may be located.

Literary Composition and Authorship

Like most other prophetic books, the Book of Jeremiah was not written by a single author, but rather is a collection of various types of materials that were transmitted orally at first, then written down and edited over an extended period of time. This entire process may have taken some two centuries to complete. These materials include various types of prophetic sayings, normally in poetry, that may derive from Jeremiah himself. In the collection and transmission of these sayings, the prophet's disciples and later editors continued to add to the corpus additional prophetic sayings, prose sermons, narratives about the prophet's life and the people of Judah and Jerusalem, wisdom texts, and different kinds of psalms (hymns, laments, and thanksgivings). The final composition of Jeremiah, which began at the end of the seventh century B.C.E., more than likely was not completed until the fifth century B.C.E.

The narrative in chap. 36 may provide some interesting insight into the composition of the book. This chapter refers to two scrolls (vv. 1-31, 32), dictated by the prophet to Baruch, his disciple and scribe. The first scroll (vv. 1-31) contained the oracles of Jeremiah from the time of King Josiah (640–609 B.C.E.) to the battle of CARCHEMISH (605 B.C.E.). The contents of the first scroll are not specified, but they may have included the call of the prophet (1:3-10), the oracles of judgment, especially those concerning the *evil from the north* (4:6; in this commentary the phrase "foe from the north" is used—see the outline for chaps. 4–10), and the laments (interspersed throughout 11:18–20:18). When the scroll was read to King Jehoiakim, he responded by destroying it and ordering the arrest of Jeremiah and Baruch. Later, Jeremiah dictated a second scroll that included the contents of the first scroll, together with *many similar words* (36:32). This allowed for the inclusion of other materials from the prophet's later life and from disciples and editors over two centuries.

Whatever the precise contents of these two scrolls may have been, it is clear that several collections of materials were edited and then later combined into larger literary sources. These collections, at times identified by an editorial introduction, include the judgment oracles concerning the "foe from the north" (eleven oracles scattered throughout chaps. 4–10), the "laments" (found among the poems in chaps. 11–20), oracles concerning the royal house of Judah (21:11–23:8), oracles concerning the prophets (23:9-40), the so-called "Book of Consolation" (chaps. 30–31), and "oracles against the foreign nations" (chaps. 46–51). Chapter 52 is largely borrowed from 2 Kgs 24:18–25:30.

Jeremiah contains three major literary sources, conveniently designated A, B, and C. Poetic oracles of judgment (Source A) are found primarily in the first twenty-five chapters. Many scholars attribute these oracles to the historical Jeremiah. Prose narratives about the life and times of Jeremiah (Source B) are found primarily in chaps. 26–45. Prose speeches (Source C) that often embellish and elaborate on shorter poetic oracles are embedded throughout the first forty-five chapters. The literary style and theology of the prose materials, including both narratives and sermons, are quite similar to what one finds in the Book of Deuteronomy and the Deuteronomistic History (Joshua, Judges, Samuel, and Kings). Consequently, the prose texts most likely are attributable to deuteronomic scribes who produced two major editions of Jeremiah, the first completed by the sixth century and the second during the fifth century B.C.E. These scribes sought to enable Jeremiah to speak to later exilic and postexilic communities of Jews long after he had died. The first edition is reflected in the LXX that preserves the short text of Jeremiah, and the second is represented by the MT, or long text.

Two major collections of materials in Jeremiah, not usually placed in one of these three sources, are the oracles about the future (the "Book of Consolation," chaps. 30–31) and a collection of oracles against foreign nations (chaps. 46–51). The authorship of these two collections is debated, although it is conceivable that several oracles in each may have been uttered by Jeremiah. The others were added by later prophets who sought to have Jeremiah speak to events of the exilic and early postexilic periods.

The Text of Jeremiah

The MT of Jeremiah contains about 2,700 more words than the text preserved by the LXX. This makes the MT of Jeremiah approximately one-eighth longer than its Greek counterpart. For example, several extensive sections of Jeremiah present in the MT are absent in the LXX: 33:14-26; 39:4-13; 51:44b-49a; and 52:27b-30. Furthermore, the MT and LXX differ in the arrangement of materials, the most notable being the location of the "oracles against the foreign nations" (chaps. 46–51). This collection appears in the LXX in the middle of the book (i.e., 25:13a of the MT). Based on the content of chap. 25, the LXX's location is likely original.

The long (MT) and short (LXX) texts are represented by the manuscript fragments of Jeremiah in Hebrew found at Qumran. This underscores the fluidity of the Jeremiah tradition, prior to the finalization of the canonical text sometime during the transition to the early common era. It is unlikely that the LXX presents an intentionally abbreviated text. Rather, the two texts probably represent two stages of the deuteronomic redaction of Jeremiah. Both versions continued to circulate in different scribal circles until the canonization of the OT in the first century, C.E.

The Historical Setting

Jeremiah, his disciples, and the scribes who shaped his tradition, beginning with BARUCH, lived during a tumultuous period of history that witnessed a significant transformation in the nature and fortunes of the Jewish community. The prose narratives and sermons (1:2, 25:3) trace the call of the prophet (found in 1:3-10) to the *thirteenth year* of King Josiah (627 B.C.E.) and further indicate that he was active during the latter part of this king's reign (640–609 B.C.E.). This date for the call, marking the beginning of his prophetic activity, was an important one in the history of Judah, the southern kingdom. In 627 B.C.E. the last strong king of the Assyrians, Asshurbanapal, died, resulting in revolution throughout the Assyrian empire. The assaults by the Babylonians and Medes led to the overthrow of the Assyrians. Nineveh, the capital, fell in 612 B.C.E. and the surviving remnant of Assyrian forces, located at Harran, was defeated in 610/9 B.C.E. When Nebuchadrezzar, commander of the Babylonian forces, defeated the Egyptians at the battle of Carchemish in 605 B.C.E., Babylon soon became the heir to much of the former Assyrian empire in MESOPOTAMIA and Canaan. When the Babylonian king Nabopolassar died a short time later, NEBUCHADREZZAR became king (605/4–562 B.C.E.). Babylonian suzerainty lasted until 539 B.C.E. when the Persians defeated the Babylonians at Opis and then entered the city of Babylon without resistance. The Persians subsumed the former empire within their expanding domain.

Josiah participated in the general uprising against the Assyrians in 627 B.C.E. and liberated Judah from a tyrannical government that had held the nation in subjugation since 735 B.C.E. During the intervening years between the collapse of Assyrian control and the reconfiguration of power in the ancient Near East, Judah enjoyed a short-lived period of independence (627–609 B.C.E.). Five years later (622 B.C.E.), Josiah led a religious reform inspired by the discovery of "the book of the law" in the Temple. This law was probably an earlier form of what became the Book of Deuteronomy. The reform aimed at the centralization of official religious worship in Jerusalem and the elimination of pagan religions in Judah and the expanding territory under its control. Josiah's political design may have been to recreate the Davidic empire, an ill-fated objective that failed when he led his army into battle against the Egyptian forces under NECHO II (610–595 B.C.E.) at MEGIDDO in 609 B.C.E. Josiah died, and his soldiers were routed by the Egyptians, apparently on their way to aid the Assyrian forces resisting the advance of the Babylonians.

Following the death of Josiah, Judah came under Egyptian control until the battle of Carchemish (605 B.C.E.) that culminated in a Babylonian victory. Jehoiakim, ruling Judah at the time, soon transferred allegiance to the Babylonians. A series of Judahite kings followed Josiah to the throne: Jehoahaz (609 B.C.E.), Jehoiakim (609–598 B.C.E.), Jehoiachin (598–97 B.C.E.), and Zedekiah (597–587 B.C.E.). Jehoiakim rebelled against the Babylonians, leading to the first exile in 597 B.C.E. Zedekiah, succumbing to anti-Babylonian pressures, also rebelled, a decision that led to the destruction of Jerusalem and the Temple, the end of the monarchy, and the second exile in 587 B.C.E. Nebuchadrezzar appointed Gedaliah, a member of the prominent family of Shaphan (Josiah's royal secretary), as governor of Judah, although a group of assassins led by ISHMAEL, a descendant of the royal line, murdered the governor shortly after he had assumed the reigns of government. A third deportation to Babylon may have taken place in 582 B.C.E.

With the former leaders of Judah among the deportees to Babylon, the conditions of those remaining in the land were quite difficult. However, the biblical materials provide little information about life during this period (587–538 B.C.E.). There also is very little information about the Jewish community in Babylon during this same time. It appears that the exiles lived in Jewish communities and attempted to carry out some form of worship of Yahweh. Their captivity ended with the Persian conquest of Babylonia in 539 B.C.E. A year later, the Persian king, Cyrus, issued an edict allowing those Jews who so desired to return to their homeland.

Jeremiah's Life as a Prophet

The life of Jeremiah and indeed the lives of his later disciples and the scribes responsible for shaping his prophetic tradition interfaced with the larger public events in the life of Judah before 587 B.C.E. and the later Jewish community that survived the Babylonian onslaught. The prose materials date his call to 627 B.C.E., that most auspicious time when revolution against the Assyrians was widespread (chap. 1). It may be that the poetic materials probably deriving from Jeremiah himself suggest a later date for the call, perhaps 609 B.C.E. when Josiah died at Megiddo. If so, then 627 B.C.E. could have been the birth date of the prophet. In any event, it is very difficult to associate much of the prophet's own sayings with the events during the lifetime of Josiah. If the prophet were active this early, his ministry would have been largely limited to the area around Anathoth in the tribe of Benjamin in the old territory of the former Northern Kingdom, that is, Israel, for this is where the prophet was born and raised. It is likely that he would have been a supporter of the religious reforms of Josiah, although he probably would have been skeptical about the rising nationalism developing from the king's political ambitions. If the oracles concerning the "foe from the north" (see chaps. 4–10) were uttered during this early period, it is little wonder that his prophecy about an enemy to the north, not identified as the Babylonians until the battle of CARCHEMISH, coming to destroy Judah would have met with either serious opposition or biting ridicule. With the tragedy at Megiddo, however, the prophet soon moved his sphere of activity to Jerusalem where he continued to prophesy doom for the nation, unless there was an abandonment of nationalistic ambitions and a wholesale repentance resulting in returning to Yahweh (see chaps. 2; 3:1–4:4; and 7:1–8:3). During the torrents of national disaster, Jeremiah continued to preach to the people of Jerusalem and the royal house that they should be peaceful servants of the Babylonian king. This message not only led to the official persecution of the prophet on occasion (see chaps. 26 and 36), but eventually fell on deaf ears as first one rebellion and then another met with disaster. Jeremiah's struggles with external persecution and inward doubt in the faithfulness of Yahweh are reflected in the "Laments" found throughout 11:18–20:18. Jeremiah's harsh criticism of both the ruling kings, save for Josiah, and the city of Jerusalem is found in the collection, "Concerning the Royal House of Judah" (21:11–23:8).

Following the sacking of JERUSALEM in 587 B.C.E., Nebuchadrezzar, pleased with Jeremiah's pacifism, offered him the option of going to Babylon or of staying in Mizpah where Gedaliah's government was being set up. The prophet chose to remain behind to help in the rebuilding of the nation. It may have been that Jeremiah then began to speak of hope for the future, envisioning a restoration of Jewish life in Judah and the old territory of Israel at some undetermined time (see chaps. 30–31). However, following the assassination of Gedaliah, a group of Jewish refugees who fled to Egypt forced Jeremiah to accompany them. There he disappears from history.

The tradition of Jeremiah did not die with him. Disciples and editors continued to shape the tradition by adding prose speeches and narratives and a variety of later oracles (e.g., most of the oracles against foreign nations, chaps. 46–51), allowing his prophetic voice to address several groups of survivors of the Babylonian conquest in their own time: those who went into exile in Babylon and Egypt and those who remained in the former territories of Judah and Israel. Indeed, through their activity, they shaped a narrative and preaching tradition that enabled the prophet to address the exiles, those who were left behind, and their successors who faced the challenges of rebuilding national life primarily in and around Jerusalem during the early Persian period.

One of the more intriguing aspects of Jeremiah in the prose tradition is his presentation as the prophet like Moses (cf. Deut 18:15-22). In the passage in Deuteronomy, Moses addresses liberated Israel, assembled in the plains of Moab immediately prior to their entrance into the land of Canaan. He speaks of a future prophet whom the people should heed. In the prose tradition, the deuteronomic scribes make a concerted effort to present Jeremiah as this Mosaic prophet who speaks of new covenant, an inward law, and judgment to a people awaiting and then experiencing liberation from another captivity. Like Moses in Deuteronomy, Jeremiah offers God's redemption to those who are offered the decision for life or death. Life may be chosen by repenting of sins, entering into a new covenant with Yahweh, and living according to the law inscribed on their hearts. Following the Deuteronomic pattern of retributive justice, this Jeremiah blames the destruction of Jerusalem and the Temple, the burning of the palace and the captivity of kings, and the exile on disobedience to the Mosaic covenant, a disobedience that permeated the entire nation, from its political and religious leaders to the people themselves. By returning to the covenant, the nation would be reborn in Judah as the people of God and its institutions, from kingship to temple, would be restored.

The social location of Jeremiah is the tribal, agrarian tradition that was especially nurtured in the towns and villages of the northern state of Israel and, to a lesser extent, the hill country of Judah. In contrast to the monarchic tradition flourishing in the royal cities of Judah, the rural areas tended to favor a tribal society of extended families who cultivated their own farms and practiced a form of social justice that was based on the ideals of kinsmanship, care for the neighbor, and charity towards the poor, including the levite, widow, orphan, and stranger. During the period of the judges (ca. 1200 to 1000 B.C.E.), the political and judicial system inclined towards a system of village elders for local matters and tribal elders for internal and external matters affecting the tribes. A loose-knit federation of tribes was favored as the political system necessary for dealing with tribal disputes and military threats from the outside. Even after the establishment of the monarchy and Solomon's attempt to subvert the tribal tradition by overt pressure, it continued as an active expression of social, political, and religious life. Theologically, the traditions of exodus, wilderness wandering, taking of the land of Canaan, and the covenant were nurtured in these rural enclaves. A strong antipathy developed towards kings and the royal tradition cultivated in Jerusalem and to a lesser extent in other cities and towns in Judah. The royal tradition emphasized dynastic rule (the house of David), established royal boundaries that ignored tribal domains, centralized rule and judicial oversight in the hands of the monarchy, placed national religious institutions including the Temple under the control of the royal house, favored the expansion of aristocratic land holdings, placed economic institutions, including agricultural markets and trade, under monarchial authority, and gave the kings the important powers of control over the military, conscription for both military service and work gangs, and taxation.

Jeremiah was born in Anathoth, a small levitical town less than three mi. north of Jerusalem, but situated in the hill country of Benjamin, once a northern tribe. This village was home to a family of levitical priests who traced their ancestry back to Abiathar, one of David's chief priests who fell into disfavor with Solomon by supporting the royal pretensions of the king's half-brother, Adonijah. After consolidating power in his hands, Solomon took care of his political opponents, including Abiathar whom he exiled to Anathoth. This denied to Abiathar and his descendants any participation in the royal cult in Jerusalem and the Temple eventually constructed by Solomon. More than likely, the deuteronomic traditions were originally nurtured in the northern towns and villages like Anathoth. When the Northern Kingdom fell in 722 B.C.E. to the Assyrians, numerous refugees fled south to Judah, with some establishing a ghetto of northern Israelites on the western hill of Jerusalem. One of the descendants of these northern refugees was

Huldah the prophet who perhaps was Jeremiah's aunt (cf. Jer 32:7 and 2 Kgs 22:14). She was the prophet consulted by Josiah when the law book was discovered in the Temple (see 2 Kgs 22:14-20), a text that was likely an earlier form of the Book of Deuteronomy.

A descendant of the levitical, priestly family of Abiathar, Jeremiah was nurtured in the tribal tradition of his ancestors. Subsequently, the social and religious values of the older Mosaic covenant, reformulated by the deuteronomists, played a formative role in shaping his religious and social views. This background also helps to explain Jeremiah's hostile attitude towards the Davidic monarchy, with the exception of Josiah who pursued a vigorous religious reform according to the guidelines of a proto-deuteronomic text, and his virulent attack on the Jerusalem Temple (chaps. 7 and 26). This double edged criticism had deep roots in a tradition strongly opposed to royal pretensions and tyranny. It may have been that Josiah's reform gave the disenfranchised levites the role of priests in the Temple in Jerusalem. This may explain the hostility directed against Jeremiah by his own family and the people of Anathoth when he preached judgment against nation, monarchy, and Temple. Even though he commanded the respect of King Zedekiah, for the most part Jeremiah was a peripheral prophet who lived on the outer edges of power in the Judahite state. Indeed, his association with Baruch may have been developed in part because of the scribe's political connections at court. When Jeremiah spoke of a new social and religious order residing at some distance in the future, he gave no place to kingship and Temple. His deuteronomic editors lessened the severity of this glaring omission by pointing to the reemergence of kingship and the levitical priesthood in the time of restoration.

The Theology of Jeremiah

To understand the theology of Jeremiah, one must begin by recognizing that the different materials collected together to form the book paint different portraits of the man and vary the contents of his message. Consequently, there is not one prophet with a coherent, unified theology, but several prophets with differently nuanced messages.

The first portrait of Jeremiah is found in Source A (see above, "Literary Composition and Authorship") and the "Book of Consolation" (chaps. 30-31). Here Jeremiah is a prophet of judgment who announces the impending doom of Judah and Jerusalem at the hands of a northern enemy because of religious apostasy and

the establishment of treaties with foreign nations. Jeremiah does offer the possibility of redemption, but only if the nation abandons foreign gods and treaties with other countries and returns to the Mosaic covenant and a sole dependence on Yahweh. This does not mean political freedom, for Jeremiah preaches that Judah must bow the knee to the newly emerging power that he identifies by 605 B.C.E. as the Babylonians and their king, Nebuchadrezzar. Even though Judah—and especially its leaders—refuse to repent, the disaster promised by the prophet comes, not from an angry God bent on vengeance, but a suffering deity who agonizes over and mourns the destruction of his people.

After the fall of Jerusalem, the destruction of the Temple, the end of the monarchy, and the exile to Babylon, the prophet begins to articulate a theology of hope for the future, grounded in divine compassion that will lead to new acts of divine redemption. Yahweh will reconstitute the people of God by bringing together once again Israel and Judah. The theological traditions on which the prophet draws both for judgment and promise are those of exodus, divine sustenance in the Sinai wilderness, and the Mosaic covenant. These older traditions of faith that Israel before the Babylonian conquest of 587 B.C.E. had violated hold out the promise of divine redemption in the future. The traditions of the promise to David (e.g., 2 Sam 7 and Ps 89) concerning a royal dynasty and Jerusalem (also called Zion) as the city of God, symbolized by the Solomonic Temple, are not expressions of faith for this Jeremiah. Indeed, he is most critical of these traditions, for they embody not the proper expression of religious faith and piety, but rather the corrupt tyranny of many kings and a formal religion more concerned with sacrifice than with justice. Indeed, Jeremiah characterizes dependence on Temple theology and its view of a deity who dwells in its precincts and defends Jerusalem against attack as *a lie* (see esp. chaps. 28–29). In this view of Jeremiah and his message, the "I" of the prophet often merges with the character and being of God. The line between prophet and deity, while not eliminated completely, is often blurred. The personality of Jeremiah, both his rationality and emotions, often blends with that of Yahweh.

A second portrait of Jeremiah emerges in the laments (see 11:18–20:18), which, while different, does have points of connection with Source A and the "Book of Consolation." These confessions, borrowing heavily from the form and content of the laments in the Psalter and the Book of Lamentations, present the inner struggles of the prophet and his conflict with Yahweh. Here the prophet accuses God of injustice and deceit, complains of humiliation and persecution endured because of his prophetic activity, demands vindication for his abused integrity, and cries out for vengeance against his enemies. If read as private prayers, they depict the inward turmoil of prophetic existence that bears the burden of judgment and alienation. At one point the darkness of despair that enshrouds the prophet leads him to curse his birth, negating the tradition of his call that tells of Yahweh's formation of him in the womb for the purpose of becoming a *prophet to the nations* (1:5). If read as a community lament in which Jeremiah voices the grief and pain of Judah, then the prophet utters the people's pain, questioning of divine justice, lack of trust in the faithfulness of God, insistence on vindication, and call for vengeance against their enemies. Jeremiah's role would be, then, more of a prophetic intercessor than an individual struggling with personal questions of faith and existence. In either case, Yahweh responds, at least to the first several laments, promising, not cheap grace, but divine support to endure even more difficulties that lay ahead. Indeed, when Jeremiah (Judah?) abandons God, the promise of acceptance remains intact, but only if repentance occurs. However, the last lament (20:14-18) ends rather shockingly with the prophet cursing his birth and wishing he had never been born. To this God makes no response. The laments emphasize the agony that comes at times to those who seek to embody prophetic existence. It is a life that at times becomes almost unbearable torment.

A third portrait of Jeremiah is present in the prose tradition. In the prose speeches, following the style of paraenetic addresses common to Deuteronomy and the Deuteronomistic History, Jeremiah is a preacher of the law who argues that all history is under the control of Yahweh who administers retributive justice. This means that, because of the violation of the Mosaic covenant, God is bringing disaster upon his own people. The catastrophe of 587 B.C.E. is interpreted as God's punishment of Judah for the sins of its leaders and people. Speaking to a people in exile who hope to return to their homeland, this prophet offers them the alternative of salvation or judgment. The choice belongs to them. Yahweh is powerful, gracious, and ready to save, but they must return to him in trusting faith and ready obedience to the law.

While the prose narratives present the same portrait, they also indicate how the divine word of the prophet is implemented in both his life and the life of the nation. There is a correspondence between word and deed, message and life. The word by which the prophet suffered eventually became the word that brought life to the exiles. This is not yet a doctrine of vicarious or redemptive suffering, but it comes very close. Here one finds biography and history shaped by prophetic preaching. Jeremiah becomes the model of faithful preaching and action to be emulated by those seeking a proper relationship with God.

One other depiction of Jeremiah and his message is found in the "Oracles against the Foreign Nations" (chaps. 46–51). The time for judgment against wicked nations and especially the evil empire of the Babylonians is at hand. This Jeremiah announces divine judgment against the foreign nations who had caused Judah to suffer: Egypt, Philistia, the Transjordanian states, Damascus, the Arab tribes of Kedar and Hazor, Elam, and Babylon all fall beneath the hammer of divine punishment. More than likely, the prophet has in mind both the Medes and Persians as the new instrument of divine judgment. But it is especially Babylon, earlier the instrument of divine judgment, that now is the recipient of the harshest condemnation. Babylon will be utterly destroyed. This harshness towards the foreign nations is ameliorated by the qualification that God will give some of them a future. This Jeremiah preaches judgment and divine vengeance against Judah's enemies that allow for the redemption of the Jewish captives. Indeed, it is out of the destruction of the nations that a new Israel may be built.

For Further Study

In the *Mercer Dictionary of the Bible*: BABYLONIAN EMPIRE; BARUCH; CARCHEMISH; CURSE AND BLESSING; DEUTERONOMIST/DEUTERONOMISTIC HISTORIAN; EXILE; GEDALIAH; JEREMIAH; JEREMIAH, BOOK OF; JERUSALEM; JOSIAH; KINGSHIP; NEBUCHADREZZAR; ORACLE; PROPHET; SOURCES OF THE PENTATEUCH; ZEDEKIAH.

In other sources: J. Bright, *Jeremiah*, AncB; W. Brueggemann, *To Pluck Up, to Tear Down: A Commentary on the Book of Jeremiah 1–25* and *To Build, to Plant: A Commentary on Jeremiah 26–52*, ITC; R. P. Carroll, *Jeremiah*, OTL; S. Herrmann, *Jeremia*, BKAT; W. Holladay, *Jeremiah*, Herm; J. P. Hyatt, "The Book of Jeremiah," *IB*; W. McKane, *Jeremiah*, ICC; E. W. Nicholson, *Preaching to the Exiles*; K. O'Connor, *The Confessions of Jeremiah*, SBLDS; L. G. Perdue and B. W. Kovacs, *A Prophet to the Nations*; P. Trible, *God and the Rhetoric of Sexuality*.

Commentary

An Outline

Superscription, 1:1-3

The superscription of the book, written by a deuteronomic redactor, follows a typical pattern for prophetic books: the title (*the words of Jeremiah*), personal background (*son of Hilkiah, of the priests who were in the land of Benjamin*), reception of the revelation (*to whom the word of the LORD came*), the subject of the revelation (in Jeremiah's case 1:4-10 identifies the subject as *the nations*), and the date (vv. 2-3). For other examples of prophetic superscriptions, see Isa 1:1; Amos 1:1; Mic 1:1; Zeph 1:1.

Anathoth, located at modern Ras el Kharuba, was a levitical town in the tribal territory of Benjamin, less than three mi. northeast of Jerusalem. The *priests* of v. 1 included the descendants of Abiathar, one of David's chief priests, whom Solomon exiled upon the death of his father. Abiathar had supported Adonijah's claim to the throne over Solomon. Hilkiah is not an uncommon name. While the chief priest of Josiah who figured prominently in the deuteronomic reformation was named Hilkiah (2 Kgs 22:4-14), it is doubtful he is to be identified with the priest who was Jeremiah's father. Except for his profession as a priest, Jeremiah's father is otherwise unknown (see the introduction). The superscription dates Jeremiah's prophetic activity from the thirteenth year of the reign of King Josiah (640–609 B.C.E.), that is, 627 B.C.E., through the reign of King Jehoiakim (609–598 B.C.E.), to the end of the eleventh year of the reign of King Zedekiah (597–587 B.C.E.) *until the captivity of Jerusalem in the fifth month* (v. 3, which would be 587 B.C.E.). Thus, Jeremiah prophesied from 627 to 587 B.C.E. However, the prose tradition presents Jeremiah as active until some time after the assassination of Gedaliah in 586 B.C.E. (see 40:7–44:30).

The Call and Initial Visions of Jeremiah, 1:4-19

1:4-10. The call of the prophet. The opening chapter contains the call of Jeremiah (1:4-10), two initial visions (1:11-14), and two prose additions: the first interprets the second vision in more detail (1:15-16), while the second speaks of Yahweh's concluding exhortation to the prophet (1:17-19). Chapter 1 offers an overture to the entire book by introducing the sounds of important themes, motifs, and words that will be played time and again throughout the subsequent chapters. The date of Jeremiah's call is debated (see introduction). It is clear that the prose tradition dates the prophet's call to the thirteenth year of the reign of King Josiah, that is, 627 B.C.E. (cf. 1:2, 25:3). This early date would make the prophet active during the reign of Josiah and a witness to his political ambitions. Jeremiah would also have been aware of, if not an actual participant in, the comprehensive religious reform of Josiah (see 3:6; 36:2). The major problem with the early dating is the difficulty of locating any of the prophet's poetic sayings in Josiah's reign. One solution to this problem has been to argue that 627 B.C.E. is the birth date of the prophet who believed he had been appointed to be a prophet by Yahweh before

he was born (1:5). The poetic tradition may implicitly support this later date. Jeremiah's call, then, would correspond with the death of Josiah in 609 B.C.E., motivating the prophet to move to Jerusalem to begin his prophetic activity.

Jeremiah's call follows the first of two forms of prophetic calls: the encounter with (the word of) Yahweh (cf. Exod 3:1–4:17; Judg 6:11-27; 1 Sam 3); and the vision of Yahweh in the heavenly court (cf. 1 Kgs 22:19-23; Isa 40:1-11; and Ezek 1:1–3:11). The first literary pattern consists of the following parts: the divine confrontation (*Now the word of the LORD came to me*, v. 4), introductory word (*Before I formed you in the womb I knew you, and before your were born I consecrated you*, v. 5a), commission (*I appointed you a prophet to the nations*, v. 5b), objection (*Ah, Lord GOD! Truly I do not know how to speak, for I am only a boy*, v. 6), reassurance (*Do not say, "I am only a boy"; for you shall go to all to whom I send you, and you shall speak whatever I command you. Do not be afraid of them, for I am with you to deliver you, says the LORD* vv. 7-8), and sign (*Then the LORD put out his hand and touched my mouth; and the LORD said to me, "Now I have put my words in your mouth. See, today I appoint you over nations and over kingdoms, to pluck up and to pull down, to destroy and to overthrow, to build and to plant,"* vv. 9-10). The form and content of Jeremiah's call closely parallel those of Moses (Exod 3:1–4.17), indicating that the tradition presents Jeremiah as the "prophet like Moses" (see Deut 18:15-22). It is unlikely that the call of Jeremiah was a personal experience. More probably his call, as well as prophetic calls in general, was set within a liturgical service that commissioned certain individuals for this role.

Yahweh predestined Jeremiah to the prophetic role, "consecrating" (v. 5, literally: "setting aside for divine service") and appointing him to be a *prophet to the nations* (v. 5; see "Oracles Against the Nations," chaps. 46–51). The call picks up the theology of Yahweh's creating of humans in the womb, nourishing them through gestation, assisting in the birthing process, and nurturing them after birth (see Gen 2:4b-25; Job 3; 10; Ps 139:13-16). In his final lament, Jeremiah curses his birth, thus negating his call (20:14-18).

Ah, Lord GOD (v. 6) introduces a complaint or accusation against God (see Josh 7:6-9; Jer 4:10; 14:13; 32:17; Ezek 4:14; 9:8; 11:13; 20:49). *I do not know how to speak* refers to the primary role of the prophet as a spokesperson for God (see Exod 4:10-12). The

Hebrew word for "boy" may refer to a child, adolescent, or young man. It normally refers to a male who is unmarried. The presence of this word in Jeremiah's call brings to mind the call of another "prophet like Moses," the lad Samuel (see 1 Sam 3).

Yahweh reassures the prophet of divine presence and redemption: *I am with you to deliver you* (v. 8); but this is a promise that Jeremiah in his laments comes to doubt (see the laments in 11:18–20:18). Yahweh's touching and placing divine words in the mouth of Jeremiah also draws from the imagery of the "prophet like Moses" in Deut 18:15-22 (cf. Jer 15:19). God appoints Jeremiah, not kings, over nations to determine their destiny by the proclamation of the divine word that shapes human history. The word will be both destructive (*to pluck up and to pull down, to destroy and to overthrow* [v. 10]; see the oracles of judgment in chaps. 2–25) and redemptive (*to build and to plant* [v. 10]; see the oracles of salvation in the "Book of Consolation" in chaps. 30–31).

1:11-14. Initial visions. Reports of visions in the prophetic corpus contain an introduction in which the prophet sees something, a description of what is seen, a dialogue between Yahweh and the prophet, and Yahweh's explanation of the meaning of the vision (see Jer 24; Amos 7:1–9:4). These two visions of Jeremiah follow this general pattern. The first vision (vv. 11-12) is built around a word play between *a branch of an almond* (*šāqēd*) and *watching* (*šōqēd*). Yahweh's interpretation, *I am watching over my word to perform it*, emphasizes God's firm intention to enact the content of the prophetic word. The second vision, the *boiling pot* (v. 13), mentions for the first time the imagery of destruction *from the north* (see the "Foe from the North" oracles in chaps. 4–10).

1:15-16. Interpretation of the second vision. The second vision is expanded by a deuteronomic scribe who explains to an exilic or postexilic audience that the Babylonian conquest of Jerusalem and Judah was divine punishment for breaking the Mosaic covenant by worshiping other gods and practicing idolatry.

1:17-19. Exhortation to Jeremiah. A second redactional addition contains the encouragement offered by Yahweh to Jeremiah to persevere in his efforts in spite of strong opposition from his enemies, specified as the leaders of Judah: *kings of Judah, its princes, its priests, and the people of the land* (v. 18; the last phrase is a social term for male land owners who possessed considerable political power). Unlike the city of Jerusalem with walls that were eventually breached,

Jeremiah is to be impregnable: *a fortified city, an iron pillar, a bronze wall* (see 15:20), because Yahweh will be present with him (see 1:8).

Israel's Political and Religious Disloyalty, 2:1-37

Chapter 2 is an elaborate poem consisting of several oracles united by the theme of Israel's and Judah's religious apostasy and political disloyalty to Yahweh and the covenant. The elaborate literary structure consists of the following poems: Israel's faithfulness as a young bride (vv. 1-3), religious apostasy—Baal worship (vv. 4-13), political disloyalty—alliances with Assyria and Egypt (vv. 14-19), religious apostasy—Baal worship (vv. 20-28), political disloyalty—alliance with Egypt (vv. 29-37). This literary pattern has the following sequence of poems: A, B, C, B1, C1.

The literary form of the poetic oracles in chap. 2 is the prophetic "law-suit" (*rîb*, see 2:9), consisting of the following parts: heaven and earth are called upon as witnesses, the defendant is summoned to hear the charges, the indictment is presented, rhetorical questions with obvious answers make up part of the diatribe against the defendant, Yahweh's merciful acts on behalf of the accused are remembered, and finally the defendant is judged guilty and sentenced. In the trial, Yahweh serves as both the plaintiff and the judge (see Isa 5:1-7; Hos 9:10-13; 13:4-8; Mic 6:1-8).

If the early date of Jeremiah's call (i.e., 627 B.C.E.) is historically accurate, then one would place these oracles in the first period of Jeremiah's ministry, prior to his move to Jerusalem in 609 B.C.E. Within an environment of a growing nationalism, stimulated by Josiah's early successes, Jeremiah utters oracles of judgment against Israel and Judah that draw upon the theology and language of another prophet from the North, Hosea. Like Hosea, Jeremiah also spoke of Israel as a young bride and the wilderness as a honeymoon period prior to entrance into the land of Canaan (chap. 3). He too condemned Israel for religious and political apostasy in images of a faithless bride and a disobedient child.

2:1-3. Israel's faithfulness as a young bride. The prose introduction (*The word of the Lord . . . Jerusalem*, vv. 1-2) is inserted by deuteronomic redactors who have Jeremiah speak the oracles of the poem *in the hearing of Jerusalem* (v. 2). Following the imagery of Hosea (chap. 2), Jeremiah describes the beginnings of Yahweh's relationship with Israel in the wilderness of Sinai as a marriage of newlyweds. This depiction of the wilderness experience, which follows the exodus from Egypt, strongly contrasts with the theme of murmuring and rebellion in the Books of Exodus and Numbers (cf. Exod 15:22–Num 36:13). For Jeremiah, Israel was a faithful bride "devoted" (*hesed*, love or loyalty) to her marriage to Yahweh. The metaphor of *a bride* for Israel's relationship to God is a common one (see Hos 2; Isa 49:18; 61:10; 62:5).

The prophet then uses priestly metaphors to characterize Israel's relationship with God. Israel is described as *holy* to Yahweh, meaning "to be set apart or consecrated for divine service" (cf. Jer 1:5), and as the *first fruits of his harvest*, that is, the initial and best yield of the harvest of crops that also was holy or set apart as an offering to Yahweh (Exod 23:19; 34:26; Deut 26:2, 10). The unauthorized eating of this sacred gift led to defilement and punishment. The prophet indicates, then, that those nations who mistreated Israel met with disaster.

2:4-13. Religious apostasy and the worship of Baal. The mood now changes when Jeremiah issues an indictment of Israel's faithlessness. This relationship of newlyweds deteriorated after Israel's entrance into the land of Canaan. In spite of Yahweh's bringing Israel out of Egyptian slavery, guiding and sustaining her in the Sinai wilderness, and giving her the land of Canaan, Israel became unfaithful by worshiping the Canaanite god Baal (literally "husband") and idols (*worthless things*, v. 5, and *things that do not profit*, v. 8; cf. Deut 32:21; 1 Kgs 16:13; Jer 8:19; 10:8; 14:22). Using priestly language, Jeremiah speaks of Israel's defiling or polluting the land with wicked actions. Those who led Israel's apostasy were priests, rulers, and prophets. This act of changing deities (exchanging its *glory*, v. 11, literally, "divine manifestation or presence") is unparalleled, says the prophet, even among pagan nations. Mentioned specifically are Cyprus, an island and center of trade lying in the eastern Mediterranean that is approximately sixty mi. west of the Phoenician coast, and Kedar, a confederation of Arab tribes that controlled eastern trade routes through Arabia. Jeremiah calls on the heavens as witnesses to Israel's disloyalty to respond in shock.

2:14-19. Political disloyalty—alliances with Assyria and Egypt. Israel's faithlessness is manifested not only by following after other gods. Jeremiah also indicts Israel for refusing to depend on the power of Yahweh and seeking to make alliances with Egypt and Assyria.

Israel was liberated by Yahweh from Egyptian slavery to experience freedom in a new land. While not a slave to be bought and sold, Israel has become the plunder of nations. The Assyrians (*lions*, v. 15) and Egyptians (*the people of Memphis and Tahpanhes*, v. 16) both have inflicted terrible destruction on Israel. Even so, instead of turning to God for redemption, Israel goes to the very nations who had ravaged it to seek political alliances that surely will fail. In the hope for political survival and even independence, Judah attempted to strengthen its position by means of military alliances. *Memphis*, a former capital of Egypt, is located on the Nile about fifteen mi. to the south of modern Cairo. *Tahpanhes* is modern Tel Defenneh, near Lake Menzaleh in the northeastern delta region. King Psammetichus of Egypt (664–610 B.C.E.) established a garrison there for Greek mercenaries to defend Egypt's borders against Assyrian attacks. These two cities would have been places where royal diplomats would have gone to attempt to work out political and military alliances. It would be natural then for refugees from Judah to flee to these cities in the aftermath of the Babylonian destruction of the nation (43:7-9; 44:1).

In this oracle, Jeremiah may be alluding to the desires of some advisors within Josiah's government, if not also the king himself, to establish an alliance with the Egyptians and the Assyrians to stop the advance of the Babylonians. If this effort were attempted, it certainly backfired. The Egyptians routed the Israelites at Megiddo, and Josiah was killed.

2:20-28. Religious apostasy—Baal worship. Jeremiah now returns to his indictment of Israel's religious apostasy. He speaks of the former faithful bride becoming a whore who, having broken her marriage vows and throwing off all restraint, offers herself *on every high hill and under every green tree* (v. 20). These are images of fertility religion practiced at a HIGH PLACE or sanctuary located on forested hills. Asherah, an earth mother goddess in Canaanite religion, was represented by a sprouting tree, while Baal's presence was depicted in the form of a free standing stone called a *massebâ*. Jeremiah changes the images in v. 27, perhaps for ironic effect. These gods, whose number Judah has greatly multiplied, do not have the power to redeem in difficult times (see 10:1-16; Isa 40:18-20; 41:5-7, 21-29; 44:6-20; 46; Pss 115; 135).

Images used to depict Israel's faithlessness include those of a whore, an ox that breaks its yoke, a vine that becomes wild, a stain even lye and soap will not wash off, the lust of a young camel, and a wild ass in heat. Again, Judah's leaders are the culprits in this apostasy: kings, officials, priests, prophets (see 1:18).

2:29-37. Political disloyalty—alliance with Egypt. It is ironic, says Jeremiah, that Israel "complains against God" (literally, seeks to indict God), since the people, not their LORD, have been unfaithful. Israel has forsaken her marriage to God and forgotten she was a bride. Although women could not legally divorce their husbands in Israel, Israel has abandoned God, claiming *We are free, we will come to you* (i.e., God) *no more* (v. 31). Even Yahweh's warnings in his causing the death of Israel's disobedient children have not led her to return to him.

Israel's abandonment of Yahweh for other gods and political powers, coupled with her injustice, including the death of the innocent poor, will lead to her shame at the hands of one of the very nations with whom alliances were sought. As Assyria before, so now Egypt will humiliate Israel. Josiah died at Megiddo in 609 B.C.E. at the hand of the Egyptians, led by Necho II, and Judah came for a brief time within the orbit of Egyptian rule, until King Jehoiakim shifted his allegiance to the Babylonians after the battle of CARCHEMISH (see introduction).

Sermon on Repentance, 3:1–4:4

The sermon on repentance is also a collection of oracles, only in this case, they exhort Israel to *return* (v. 1, Heb. *šûb*) to Yahweh (i.e., "repent"). The Hebrew word *šûb* ("return," "repent") occurs sixteen times in this sermon. The collection begins with a lawsuit (*rib*) that uses the law concerning marriage and divorce as an analogy for describing Yahweh's relationship to Israel as a faithless wife who has many lovers (3:1-5). The prophetic genre called a "summons to repentance" shapes the three interior poetic oracles: 3:12-13; 14, 19-20; and 21-23 (cf. Amos 5:4-7, 14-15; Hos 14:2). The concluding oracle, 4:1-5, offers the alternative ("either-or") of repentance leading to blessing or persistence in evil and destruction. The conditional formulation of the initial two verses and the emphasis on "return" echo the beginning poem in 3:1-5, thus serving as an INCLUSIO for the whole. The "summonses to repentance" are placed between the first oracle, a law-suit that intends to condemn and punish, and the fifth and final oracle that holds out the condition of blessing for a people who would truly repent. In following Hosea, Jeremiah depicts Yahweh as both father and husband and Israel (as well as Judah) as an adulterous wife and faithless children.

The poetic sections include: vv. 1-5 (the adulterous wife and the faithless child), vv. 12-13 (the adulterous

wife), vv. 14, 19-20 (faithless children and adulterous wife), vv. 21-23 (faithless children), and 4:1-4 (faithless Israel exhorted to repent). The poetic call to repentance is addressed to both Israel and Judah. If the early date for the call is historical, this poem consists of oracles most likely issued during the early stage of Jeremiah's activity when Josiah had defeated the Assyrian and Scythian garrisons and moved into the northern territory to reestablish the empire of David. The audience of these sermons would then be both Israelites who continued to live in the former northern kingdom and some who migrated south as well as the people of Judah and Jerusalem.

Deuteronomic editors inserted into this poetic collection three prose speeches: 3:6-11, 15-18, and 24-25. Allowing the prophet to address an exilic or early postexilic audience, the first prose sermon notes that Israel and Judah are guilty, that Israel (the northern territories) did not return to Yahweh, her husband, and that Israel's *false sister* (v. 7, i.e., "faithless sister") Judah did not learn from Yahweh's divorce of Israel, but also had *played the whore* (v. 6) to become even more guilty than her sister.

The second prose speech addresses the future: Yahweh will raise up faithful *shepherds* (v. 15, i.e., rulers), *the ark of the covenant* (lost or destroyed in the Babylonian destruction of Jerusalem) will not be missed or replaced, Jerusalem will become Yahweh's *throne* (v. 17) to which the foreign nations shall come, and Israel and Judah will be reunited. The last prose speech is a confession of sin uttered by a repenting nation that is the prerequisite for salvation.

3:1-5. The adulterous wife and disobedient child. Israel is characterized as both a faithless wife and rebellious child. Jeremiah uses the same deuteronomic legislation concerning divorce (Deut 24:1-4) that influenced Hosea to speak of Yahweh's return to faithless Israel. In the deuteronomic law, a husband could not remarry his divorced wife, even if her second husband died or divorced her. Jeremiah's two rhetorical questions have rather obvious answers. Yes, the land would be polluted by the violation of this law. And yes, a repentant Israel, having become a prostitute, could return to her divine husband. This second yes is rather shocking, for God would do what the law would not allow a husband to do: take a faithless, divorced wife back. This is Jeremiah's understanding of divine grace: even a faithless Israel could repent and expect God to take her back. The notion that unethical behavior "pollutes" the land, that is, profanes its holiness, is not an uncommon idea in priestly religion (see Lev 19:29; Num 35:33-34). This pollution, caused by Israel's religious harlotry, had led to Yahweh's punishment of withholding rain to water the soil, resulting in crop failure and drought. Jeremiah's reference to Israel's having *the forehead of a whore* (v. 3) may indicate that prostitutes wore a phylactery or cord around their heads.

3:6-11. A prose commentary on 3:1-5. This prose commentary, fashioned in a question and answer style, was written by deuteronomic editors who place at least the opening oracle in 3:1-5, if not the entire collection of 3:1–4:4, in the reign of King Josiah. As is often typical of prose speeches, elements of a poetic speech are picked up, elaborated, and made more specific in terms of time and place. In this prose speech, Yahweh asks Jeremiah if he has seen the harlotry of faithless Israel who has engaged in Canaanite fertility religion. Israel did not return and was divorced by Yahweh, that is, sent into Assyrian exile. Yahweh then notes that *her false sister Judah* (v. 7), failed to learn from Israel's experience and also became a whore, pursuing false gods. Judah also failed to return to Yahweh, who regards Israel as less guilty than Judah, presumably because Judah should have learned from the example of her older sister and did not. This commentary is written primarily to explain that religious apostasy was the occasion for the tragic events that occurred in the time preceding and including the Babylonian exile.

3:12-13. Israel as an adulterous wife. A prose introduction provides the recipient of this oracle: Israel, the territory to the north of Judah. This first summons to repentance is directed to Israel as a faithless, disobedient wife who has committed adultery with multiple partners. Even so, Yahweh exhorts his faithless wife to confess her sins and return, for he is *merciful* (v. 12, Heb. *hasid*), that is, loyal to the marriage (i.e., covenant). It is divine mercy that is the basis for Yahweh's grace and forgiveness.

3:14, 19-20. Israel as faithless children and an adulterous wife. This second summons to repentance may have been addressed to Israelites from the former Northern Kingdom who are invited to return to Zion (Jerusalem) in Judah and become part of the new people of God. If the event is located in the reign of Josiah, then the prophet sees the opportunity to reincorporate remnants of Israelites into the religious community of the greater Israel being fashioned by Josiah. Indeed, Israelite refugees had moved south following the Assyrian destruction of the Northern Kingdom in 722 B.C.E. Jeremiah would not necessarily have in mind, however, physical relocation of refugees or political reunification. He would have in mind the bringing together of Israelites and Judahites in the common worship of Yahweh.

3:15-18. The new future. This is the second prose speech inserted into the collection by deuteronomic editors. More than likely it serves as a commentary on 3:14 that points towards the future return of Israelites in the northern territory, at least spiritually and religiously, to Zion. The prose speech uses this as the occasion to address the future, following the Babylonian conquest and the exile of the leaders of Jerusalem to Babylon. *Shepherds* (v. 15, a metaphor for "kings"; see Jer 10:21; 22:22; 23:1-4; 25:34-38; Ps 78:70-72; Isa 44:28; Ezek 34:1-10; Nah 3:18; Zech 10:3; 11:4-17), obedient to Yahweh, will care for those returning from captivity. After the return from exile, the population, devastated by conquest, will increase. The *ark of the covenant* (v. 16) in the Temple, stolen or destroyed during the taking of Jerusalem and the razing of the Temple, will neither be replaced or missed. First placed in the TENT OF MEETING (2 Sam 6:17), the ark was a chest containing the two tablets of the law (Deut 10:2, 5) and possibly the sacred lots (URIM AND THUMMIM, Judg 20:27; 1 Sam 14:17-18). David's placing of the ark in Jerusalem was done to symbolize the unification of the empire, especially North and South (cf. 2 Sam 6). After the construction of the Temple, Solomon placed the ark in the holy of holies (1 Kgs 8:4-7). Here it was regarded as an empty throne, guarded by two cherubim (2 Kgs 19:15). The primary theological meaning of the ark was the symbolizing of divine presence on an empty throne (cf. Exod 25:10-22; Deut 10:8). In this prose speech, however, Jerusalem in the new age will itself be called the *throne of the LORD* (v. 17).

In expanding the universal character of this eschatological vision, the speech promises that all nations will come to Jerusalem, having rejected their own stubbornness and iniquity. Finally, the remnants of Israel and Judah, having finished their languishing in exile, will be reunited and then will return from the "north country" (cf. Isa 40–55). Jerusalem will then become the center of a world kingdom ruled by God.

3:21-23. Israel as faithless children. The third summons to repentance also was addressed to Israel. *Hills* and *mountains* (v. 23) were important locations for shrines and temples. These sacred sites are sometimes identified as "high places" (*bāmâ*, 1 Kgs 14:23).

Orgies refer to fertility rites involving sacred prostitution, a central feature of Canaanite religion. Fertility rites were believed to secure the fecundity of flocks and people, as well as bountiful crops.

3:24-25. A confession of sin. This is the third and final prose speech inserted into this collection by deuteronomic redactors. It is shaped in the form of a liturgical confession of sin and placed in the mouth of the exilic or postexilic community. It provides the paradigmatic response that the prophet has urged the community to make. While the earlier generations of Israel, including those addressed by the prophet himself, had failed to repent, now this generation of exilic or postexilic Jews makes the proper confession of sin and does repent. The confession thus serves as the ritual response to the prophet's summons to repentance.

4:1-4. Call to repentance. The final poetic oracle in 3:1–4:4 opens with three conditional clauses that lay out the requirements for Israel to experience blessing. The conditions are as follows: they are to return to Yahweh, remove the trappings of idolatry and fertility worship (*abominations*, v. 1, see Deut 29:17; Jer 7:30; 13:27; 16:18), and *swear "As the LORD lives!" in truth, in justice, and in uprightness* (v. 2). Swearing in the name of Yahweh or by the life of the Almighty is common to oaths in the OT. This means that Yahweh becomes the guarantor of the oath, making sure it is truthful and its conditions fulfilled. Yahweh would punish those who swore falsely. The violation of oaths secured by ritual swearing is one way of taking Yahweh's name in vain (cf. Exod 20:7; Lev 19:12). While there were a variety of oaths in the OT, the type to which Jeremiah is alluding most likely is the oath taken within the context of covenant renewal ceremonies in which the community swears to follow the stipulations of the covenant (cf. Gen 26:28). The conditional clauses echo the initial line of the opening poem in the collection (3:1-5), thus providing an INCLUSIO for the entire unit.

The reference to blessing is also important. A "blessing" is a ritual pronouncement, usually by God through a priest, that secures well-being and enhances life for the recipient. The mentioning of *nations shall be blessed* (v. 2)—alternatively "shall bless themselves"—echoes the promise to Abraham in Gen 12:1-3. The promise of Yahweh to Abraham includes being the ancestor of a great nation, a great name, being blessed, and becoming the conduit of divine blessing to the nations. In the last regard, Yahweh promises to bless any who bless Abraham and curse those who

curse him and through him "all the families of the earth shall be blessed" (or "shall bless themselves"). Jeremiah appears to be referring to this significant text and indicates that a faithful Israel will again become the means by which the nations shall be blessed. Swearing and blessing are both examples of language that has the power to effectuate its contents, because Yahweh is associated with them both. In the admonition of v. 4, Jeremiah uses the language of circumcision to refer, not to the ritual removal of the foreskin of the male penis as a covenantal sign of being a descendant of Abraham (cf. Gen 17:9-14; Lev 12:1-5), but rather to the act of repentance and submission to Yahweh's will.

The Foe from the North (I), 4:5–6:30

Oracles of judgment united by the theme of the "Foe from the North" are found throughout chaps. 4–10. Prophetic judgment oracles generally have a common pattern, beginning with a commission or appeal for attention (e.g., 5:20-21), followed by a description of the situation (often introduced by *says the LORD*; e.g., 5:22-28), and a prediction of disaster (e.g., 5:29), and ending with a concluding characterization (5:30-31).

It is likely that the oracular poems dealing with a "Foe from the North" were compiled as a separate collection before later editors worked the collection into the expanding Jeremiah tradition. The theme figures prominently in eleven different sections: 4:5-31; 5:1-9; 5:10-17; 5:20-31; 6:1-8; 6:9-15; 6:16-30; 8:4-13; 8:14–9:11; 9:17-22; 10:17-25. Deuteronomic redactors added to the collection the following prose speeches and comments: 4:9-12, 27; 5:18-19; 7:1-8:3; 9:12-16; and 9:23-26.

The poetic oracles of judgment about a northern foe most likely would have been delivered by Jeremiah during the reign of Josiah, if the early date for the call is historical. These dire warnings of coming destruction would have directly opposed the rampant nationalism associated with King Josiah's early successes in driving out both the Assyrian garrisons and their Scythian mercenaries and moving into the northern Israelite territories to reclaim them for the Judahite state. Another possibility for their deliverance would have been shortly after the prophet's coming to Jerusalem following the death of Josiah in 609 B.C.E., but before the battle of CARCHEMISH in 605 B.C.E. The oracles would still be powerful warnings in later political efforts at independence that eventually culminated in the destruction of Judah and Jerusalem in 587 B.C.E. and the exile of leaders to Babylonian captivity.

Nowhere in these poetic oracles does the prophet clearly identify the northern foe. The identification of the foe as the Babylonians is made by the deuteronomic redactors in the prose tradition (25:8-14). Jeremiah's strong sense of coming destruction from the North offers a warning to political leaders in Judah who continued to work for an independent state, free of foreign control. After the battle of Carchemish in 605 B.C.E., there is little doubt about the threat the Babylonians posed to the state of Judah. King Jehoiakim's transfer of allegiance to Babylonia from the Egyptians was a move of expediency, but eventually he and then Zedekiah led rebellions that produced disastrous consequences (see introduction).

The prose additions once more redirect Jeremiah's message to exilic and early postexilic audiences who were challenged to come to grips with both the destruction of Judah, Jerusalem, and the Temple and also the exile and the harsh conditions they faced once more in and around Jerusalem following the return to their homeland. These insertions modify the grim announcements of total devastation by allowing for survivors who would become the nucleus to rebuild the future. The speeches and comments also provide the theological explanation that the destruction and exile were divine punishment for disobedience to the covenant of Moses. Finally, the prose speeches promise that the uncircumcised foreign nations and Jews who are not circumcised in the heart will face divine punishment.

4:5-31. The threat from the North. This first section is directed against Judah and Jerusalem. A northern enemy is stirring and threatens destruction. In a macabre poem of striking beauty and sadness, Jeremiah likens this impending destruction to the return of chaos prior to creation. The literary structure of the sections consists of three oracles of judgment and two interludes containing the reactions of the prophet to the terrible destruction: judgment oracle (vv. 5-8), interlude (vv. 9-12), judgment oracle (vv. 13-18), interlude (vv. 19-26), and judgment oracle (vv. 28-31).

The first judgment oracle (vv. 5-8) warns people in the countryside to take refuge in the fortified cities, for Yahweh is *bringing evil from the north, and a great destruction*. The land and cities will be destroyed. The prophet then tells the people to don *sackcloth, lament and wail*, that is, to participate in rites of lamentation that are designed to appease Yahweh's anger, to stop the devastation, and to move him to defend Jerusalem against the invader (cf. Psalms of Lament: Pss 44; 60; 74; 79; 80; 83; 89;123; 125; and 144).

In the initial interlude (vv. 9-12), a prose insertion by the deuteronomic editors, the leaders are *appalled and . . . astounded* over the invasion. Then, like Moses (cf. Ex 32:30-34), Jeremiah begins to intercede on the people's and Jerusalem's behalf, even accusing Yahweh of deceiving them by causing devastation instead of carrying out his promise of well-being (cf. 1 Kgs 22:13-28). *Ah, Lord GOD* (v. 10; see note on 1:6). Then Yahweh speaks that he is bringing judgment, like a fierce desert wind.

In the second judgment oracle (vv. 13-18), Jeremiah describes the next stage of the invasion: their laying siege to the walled cities (vv. 16-17). Jeremiah explains this has happened as a result of the nation's rebellion. He urges Jerusalem once more to repent in the hope that the city might be saved.

The anguish of God is now felt by Jeremiah in the second interlude (vv. 19-26), for he sees the devastation wrought by the invading army. Jeremiah then utters a beautiful although terrifying poem in vv. 23-26 that likens the deadly invasion to a reversal of creation. Drawing on depictions of creation in various biblical texts, but especially Gen 1–2, Jeremiah describes the land after the invasion as *waste and void* (see Gen 1:2), the vanishing of light from heaven (see Gen 1:3-5), the earthquakes that shake the mountains that were considered in ancient cosmology as pillars that support the cosmos, the absence of human population (see Gen 2:5), the flying away of the birds of the air (see Gen 1:20), and the fruitful land becoming a desert (Gen 2:4b-9). The softening of the scene of total devastation is brought about by the insertion of a prose commentary in v. 27 where Yahweh promises *I will not make a full end*.

The final judgment oracle (vv. 28-31) describes the lamentation of *earth* and *the heavens*, the two spheres of creation (see Gen 1:1; 2:1, 4) who were surviving witnesses to the destruction of the nation. Zion (i.e., Jerusalem) is now personified as a woman. Like Jezebel (2 Kgs 9:30-37), Zion dresses and paints herself like a willing prostitute to offer herself to the invaders in the vain hope of escaping destruction, but even this act of desperation does not succeed (see 3:2-3).

5:1-9. In quest of a righteous person. This oracle of judgment also belongs to the collection dealing with the "Foe from the North." Jeremiah tells the audience, most likely the inhabitants of Jerusalem, to search through the city streets and squares to find one righteous person. This compares to Abraham's intercession with Yahweh to save Sodom and Gomorrah for the sake of the righteous (see Gen 18:22-33). Even though the citizens swear an oath, most likely an oath of commitment to the covenant (cf. the discussion concerning 4:2), they are lying. Both the rich and the poor had forgotten the law and their knowledge of Yahweh. Neither divine punishment nor reward has brought about allegiance and faithfulness to God through covenant obedience. The worship of false gods and adultery, both prohibited by the ten commandments (Exod 20:1-17), are mentioned specifically as sins the people have committed against God.

5:10-17. The destruction of the vineyard. This oracle of judgment takes up the metaphor of Israel and Judah as a vineyard that has grown wild and now is to be destroyed. Even *the prophets are nothing but wind* (v. 13), a word play on the Hebrew word *ruah* ("spirit," "wind," "breath") that is a source of divine inspiration (see Num 27:18; 2 Kgs 2:15; Isa 29:10). For Jeremiah these false prophets have prophesied only well-being, believing that Yahweh will not bring punishment (see 5:30-31; 6:14; 23:9-40; 28). By contrast, Jeremiah is to utter words becoming a burning fire in his mouth that will devour the people of Israel and Judah. These words are the words of judgment about the northern enemy who is described as *an ancient nation* (v. 15), speaking a foreign language not known and understood by the people, who will consume their harvest and flocks, kill their children, and destroy their fortified cities.

5:18-19. The destruction is not total. The deuteronomic editors insert a prose speech at this point to make the depiction of destruction less grim. Yahweh promises he will not make a total end of Israel and Judah. Even so, the destruction of the nation followed by exile will occur because of Israel's serving other gods.

5:20-31. Judgment against sinful Israel and Judah. In this oracle of judgment, Jeremiah contrasts the power of Yahweh as the creator who is able to control the great powers of chaos with the stubbornness and rebelliousness of Judah. *The sea* (*yām*) is often personified as the ruler of chaos or of the seas in Canaanite myth. Yam fought with Baal, the god of fertility, for lordship over the earth (also see Job 38:8-11; Ps 74:12-14). Even Yahweh's providential care for creation through the sending of the rains does not evoke in them the "fear of God," that is, the faithful response of

religious piety. Their injustice has led to their enrichment, while they abuse the rights and needs of the destitute, including orphans. A concluding observation points to prophets as guilty of false prophecy. Most likely they have spoken only of well-being and prosperity, a message followed by the priests.

6:1-8. The northern invader approaches. The advance of the northern foe is picked up again in this oracle of judgment. Now they are approaching Jerusalem. Jeremiah exhorts his fellow Benjaminites who have sought protection within the walls of Jerusalem to flee the city before it is taken. Watchmen from *Tekoa* (twelve mi. south) and *Beth-haccherem* (Ramet Rahel?, two mi. south) send signals to Jerusalem warning them of the approaching army. Now the attack against the city is launched, not at night to take advantage of stealth aided by darkness, but at noon, during the bright light of day. The military measures of assaulting a city are described. Jeremiah, at the conclusion of the oracle, returns from the terrible vision of future destruction to the present to warn the city to mend its ways or face the prospects of becoming *a desolation, an uninhabited land* (v. 8).

6:9-15. Jeremiah's warnings are ignored. This judgment oracle, a part of the collection dealing with the "Foe from the North," describes the pouring out of Yahweh's wrath upon all groups within the nation: children, young men, married couples, and the old. All will be victims. The injustice of the nation is pervasive, but those especially guilty are the leaders who should be responsible for ethical guidance: the prophets and the priests. However, even these religious leaders have deceived the nation, falsely promising *Peace, peace* (v. 14). They too will be among the victims at the time of disaster.

6:16-30. Forsaking the *ancient paths*. This judgment oracle also speaks of the northern foe and the terrible destruction that they are bringing against Zion (i.e., Jerusalem). Jeremiah exhorts the people to stand at the crossroads to look for the *ancient paths* that should be followed to avoid the coming devastation. These paths are the covenant of Moses and its teaching of life. However, the people are characterized as having rejected this exhortation, choosing instead disobedience. Because Yahweh's teachings and warnings have gone unheeded, he rejects the nation's sacrifices and gifts (cf. Hos 9:4). *Frankincense . . . from Sheba* (v. 20) is a fragrant gum resin from Boswellian trees growing in South Arabia, northeastern Africa, and India for use as perfume (Cant 3:6; 4:6, 14) and incense (Exod 30:34-38). *Sweet cane* was ·used for anointing oil in priestly ritual (Exod 30:23). *Burnt offerings* and *sacrifices* cover in general the different animal sacrifices offered in worship (see Lev 1–7).

The military power of the foe is once more depicted (vv. 22-23). The people's response in vv. 24-25 is one of helplessness in the face of such a powerful enemy. Jeremiah tells them to initiate rites of lamentation, for the enemy suddenly will appear (v. 26). In vv. 27-30 Jeremiah is likened to a metal-smith, who, having examined the mettle of the people, that is, their religious character, determines them to be *rejected silver,* that is, metal either not containing enough silver or having too many impurities to use for jewelry and decorations (see Job 23.10; Zech 13.9).

The Temple Sermon, 7:1–8:3

Inserted within the larger collection concerning the "Foe from the North" is a prose speech composed by deuteronomic redactors that breaks down into the following components: the Temple sermon (7:1-15), pagan worship (7:16-20), disobedience and rejection of sacrificial ritual (7:21-29), *the high place of Topheth* (7:30-34), and the disinterment of the bodies of the dead (8:1-3). This lengthy speech explains to an exilic or postexilic audience that the destruction of Judah and the exile resulted from pagan worship and disobedience to the stipulations of the Mosaic covenant.

7:1-15. The Temple sermon. Chapter 26 summarizes this sermon and then adds a description of the trial of Jeremiah that follows. According to 26:1-2, this deuteronomic speech occurs in the year of King Jehoiakim's accession to the throne of Judah (609 B.C.E.). Jehoiakim was placed on the throne by Necho II when Judah became a vassal nation to the Egyptians (see introduction), following the death of Josiah at Megiddo and the rout of his army by Egyptian forces. The *people of the land* (male land owners in Judah, cf. 1:18) anointed Jehoahaz, a son of Josiah but younger than his brother Jehoiakim, as the next king. However, Necho II, for unknown reasons, removed Jehoahaz and exiled him to Egypt. Jehoahaz had only sat on the throne of his father, Josiah, for three months before being deposed (see 22:10-12; Shallum is the birth name of Jehoahaz). Subsequently, Jehoiakim did not enjoy either prophetic anointing or the endorsement of the tribal leaders who included the male land owners.

Pilgrims have come to Jerusalem to worship Yahweh. The specific type of worship is not given, although it more than likely would have been one of the pilgrimage festivals, perhaps the Festival of Booths, a seven day festival held in September–October to give thanks for the fall harvest and to remember God's guidance of Israel during the wandering through the Sinai wilderness following the exodus (Lev 23:39-43). According to 1 Kgs 8, Solomon dedicated the Temple during this festival, while Deut 31:10-11 states that the law was to be read every seven years during the occasion of the manumission of slaves.

In the introduction (vv. 1-2), Jeremiah is told to stand in *the gate of the LORD's house* (Jerusalem Temple) and address the pilgrims who are coming to worship. Then follow two exhortations (vv. 3-4 and 5-8). In the first, Jeremiah admonishes the audience to act with moral integrity so that Yahweh either may dwell in their midst or will allow them to dwell in the land, that is, not go into exile. The Hebrew in v. 3b may be read in two ways: "let me dwell with you" (i.e., divine presence in the Temple), or "I will let you dwell" (i.e., not go into exile). If the first translation is followed, then the argument is that a God of justice and holiness may dwell only in the midst of a moral and holy community (cf. Isa 6:5). The second translation emphasizes that a failure to practice justice will result in exile. But in either case, Jeremiah then admonishes the pilgrims not to trust in these *deceptive words* (*šeqer*, "lie, falsehood"), *the temple of the LORD* (v. 4, repeated twice more for emphasis). What Jeremiah denies is not that God dwells in some fashion in the Temple, that is, is present with the community in Jerusalem, or that the Temple belongs to Yahweh. Rather, what he is disputing is the theology of the inviolability of Jerusalem; in other words, God will defend Zion against the attack of its enemies, regardless of obedience to the covenant (see Pss 46; 48; 76; Isa 31:4-5). For Jeremiah, obedience to the covenant, including especially the moral commands of the law, and not the Temple and its theology of an invincible Jerusalem, is the one hope for the city and its inhabitants to avoid devastation. In the second exhortation (vv. 5-8), Jeremiah makes the clear connection between the people's continuing to dwell in the land and obedience to the law. For legislation designed to care for *the alien, the orphan, and the widow* (v. 6), see Deut 10:18-19; 24:17-22; 27:19. The alien is a foreigner residing in Judah (or Israel). In Deuteronomy, the spirit of which is captured in this speech, the care for the destitute who are especially subject to abuse derives theologically from Israel's remembrance of its experience as slaves in Egypt, prior to the Exodus.

In vv. 9-11, Jeremiah then refers to five of the TEN COMMANDMENTS (Exod 20:1-17; Deut 5:6-21) that the nation violates. Jeremiah emphasizes that ethical behavior as defined by the law cannot be separated from religious observance. Indeed, it is ludicrous for worshipers to believe that they can violate the moral stipulations of the law and still expect Yahweh's protection. Having set forth his accusations, Jeremiah then issues in vv. 12-15 his threat. He does so by recalling the destruction of the temple at Shiloh, a town located some eighteen mi. north of Jerusalem (modern Khirbet Seilun). This town served as the seat of the Levitical priesthood and was an important religious center during the period of the Judges (Josh 21:1-2; Judg 21:19; 1 Sam 1:3, 9). However, it was destroyed, probably by the Philistines in the eleventh century B.C.E. (see Jer 26:6-9). In like manner, Yahweh promises he will destroy Jerusalem and its Temple, and he will take the population into exile, just as he did to the northern kingdom (*offspring of Ephraim*, v. 15) at the time of the Assyrian conquest in 722 B.C.E.

7:16-20. Pagan worship. One of the more interesting points is Yahweh's forbidding Jeremiah to intercede to save the people, seeing that intercession on behalf of people to God is a primary task of prophets (see 11:14; 15:1; Exod 32:30-34; Amos 7–9). The reason is the religious apostasy of entire families in Jerusalem and other towns. The *queen of heaven* is the Assyro-Babylonian goddess, Ishtar, an astral goddess of both war and fertility (see 44:15-30). Yahweh's wrath will issue forth in the destruction of the entire land, including both the human population and animals, fruit trees, and crops.

7:21-29. Rejection of sacrifice. The pilgrims gathered in Jerusalem to worship are told to do a thing that was forbidden by law: eat the flesh of burnt offerings. The flesh of this sacrifice was to be consumed by fire, signifying it was reserved for God (see Lev 1). Then Jeremiah makes an astonishing claim: Yahweh did not command Israel to establish the sacrificial cult at the time of the exodus, but rather commanded them to be obedient to the law, that is, the moral imperatives of the covenant. The prophet appears to reject the entire sacrificial system as a human invention. Yahweh has sought to speak to his people through the prophets, but without success. Verses 27-29 warn the prophet that no one would listen to his speech. Verse 29 is a poetic fragment of a judgment oracle, presumably from Jeremiah, that is embedded within the prose. The exhortation, *cut off*

your hair (v. 29), refers to part of the ritual of lamentation that the people are to pursue, because they have been rejected by Yahweh (cf. 16:6; Mic 1:16).

7:30-34. High place of Topheth. Jeremiah then condemns the people of Judah for carrying out religious pagan rites even in the Temple (see 2 Kgs 21–23) and for building a pagan high place (sanctuary), Topheth (from an Aramaic word meaning "fireplace"; cf. 2 Kgs 23:10), located in the Valley of the son of Hinnom that was to the west and south of the walls of Jerusalem. The valley was the site of idolatrous practices that included the sacrifice of children (see 19:5; 32:35; 2 Chr 28:3; 33:6). It is possible that the commandment requiring the giving of the first-born to Yahweh (Exod 22:29-30) was at times interpreted to mean child sacrifice, a view Jeremiah counters (see Lev 18:21). However, in the future, this high place and this valley will be known for another horror: the piling up of corpses too numerous to bury.

8:1-3. Disinterment of the dead. The prophet presents a gruesome prediction of the disinterment of the corpses of the population of Jerusalem and its leaders who will perish in the fall of the city. These corpses will be laid out before the astral deities to whom they had looked for life and protection (i.e., the sun, moon, and host of heaven; see Deut 4:19; 17:3; and 2 Kgs 23:5). Jeremiah may be alluding to the Assyrian practice of disinterring the corpses of leaders of a vassal nation that had broken a treaty. Also compare Josiah's desecration of tombs at the sanctuary of Bethel (2 Kgs 23:16).

The Foe from the North (II), 8:4–10:25

Once more the theme of the "Foe from the North" reappears (see 4:5–6:30) in the following poetic oracles of judgment: 8:4-13; 8:14–9:11; 9:17-22; and 10:17-25. Prose speeches are inserted by deuteronomic editors in 9:12-16 and 9:23-26. There is also a poetic diatribe against idol worship (10:1-16) that includes a prose insertion (10:11).

8:4-13. Judgment against people and leaders. In this judgment oracle, Jeremiah indicts the people for refusing to repent and contrasts their lack of knowledge of the revealed law with species of fowl who instinctively know the natural order of the seasons (vv. 4-7). He then announces judgment against the religious leaders for falsely construing the law (scribes, prophets, and priests, vv. 8-13).

Jeremiah's prophetic *word* (v. 9) conflicts with the written law only because the sages (*the wise*) who have the responsibility for interpreting it rightly have made it into a lie, that is, they have offered a false meaning. Sages in Jeremiah's time served the two great national institutions: court and Temple. Royal sages or scribes were members of the monarchic bureaucracy that had the task of governing according to the will of the king, while Temple scribes wrote cultic legislation, interpreted priestly law, and taught the nation God's torah. Sages were often at odds with prophets over discerning and understanding the divine will (see 18:18; Isa 3:1-4; 30:1-5; 31:1-3; Obad 8). The sages understood wisdom to be a divine gift developed through study that gave them the insight into the order of creation, understood as justice, and through this order an understanding of the nature and will of God. By ruling in conformity with the order of the world, kings were believed to govern wisely and well, producing peace and well-being for their nation. Individuals were taught that obedience to wisdom, implemented in life, also led to well being and success. Jeremiah's complaint against the sages is that they have wrongly construed the law to mean there will be peace and well-being for the nation, failing to recognize that judgment is coming.

8:14–9:26. Lamenting the coming destruction. Several prophetic speeches are woven into this long poem: 8:14-17 (the people resigned to their doom); 8:18–9:3 (an interlude describing God's anguish over the suffering of his people); 9:4-9 (the neighbor's deceit); and 9:10-22 (three exhortations to lament over imminent destruction).

In 8:14-17 the people flee into the fortified cities for protection from the invaders, recognizing that the peace they had been promised by their leaders was an illusion. The reference to *Dan* in v. 16 points to the presence of the enemy near this city located on the northern border of Israel. The quaking of the land in v. 16 reflects not only the thunderous sounds of a mighty cavalry but also the chaos tradition that describes the shaking of an unstable cosmos at the approach of divine judgment (see Hab 3). Once more the prophet experiences divine suffering because of the destruction that is soon to engulf his people (8:18–9:3). The false security in the presence of the Temple and the presumed inviolability of Jerusalem because of Yahweh's presence is contrasted with Yahweh's anger seething against his people because of their idolatry (v. 19; cf. 7:1–8:3). The "daughter of my people" (v. 21, RSV; NRSV, *my poor people*, is a metaphor for Jerusalem) has suffered such a grievous

wound that even the *balm in Gilead* (v. 22), the resin or gum of the balsam tree used to heal wounds, and their physicians are unable to offer healing.

The deceit of the neighbor and brother is underscored in 9:4-9, a deceit that is so pervasive that it has corrupted the nation with lies and treachery. In 9:10-11, 17-19, 20-22, the prophet issues three exhortations to the inhabitants of Jerusalem, professional mourners, and the women of the city to lament the death of the cosmos and the destruction of Jerusalem occasioned by the invasion. *The mourning women* and *the skilled women* (9:17) are professional mourners paid to weep during a funeral or over destruction of a city (see 22:18-19; Lam). In ancient Near Eastern fertility religions, female mourners engaged in cultic lamentations designed to aid fertility gods in rising from the dead in order to bring new life after a season of languishing in the underworld. Thus, lamentation in these settings was a prelude to life. But not so for Jeremiah, for the invader's destruction is so great the cosmos has been laid waste. There is only death without the promise of life. Verses 21-22 allude to the Canaanite deity Mot ("Death") who in mythology kills his nemesis Baal, the god of fertility, and brings him into the underworld.

Jeremiah 9:12-16 and 9:23-26 are two deuteronomic prose additions interpreting the destruction of the country as due to disobedience to the law, reassuring the exiles of God's covenant love and justice, and promising future punishment of "uncircumcised" pagan nations and Jews who are uncircumcised in their hearts. *Those with shaven temples* (v. 26) are Arabs who engage in the cutting of hair as a religious ritual (see 25:23, 49:32).

10:1-16. An idol satire. Idol satires, like this one, are especially common to Second Isaiah (Isa 40:18-20; 41:6-7; 44:9-20). Jeremiah describes the fashioning of an idol by humans and then lampoons its obvious deficiencies: it cannot speak, walk, breathe, and do good or evil. Only fools worship idols. By contrast, Yahweh is unparalleled in greatness and inspires legitimate fear. He is the creator of the world and providential overseer of cosmos and history.

In v. 9 *Tarshish* is mentioned as the source for silver, although it continues to be an unidentified seaport apparently famous for being a great trading center (see 1 Kgs 10:22; Isa 23:1, 14; 60:9; Ezek 27:25). *Uphaz* has not been identified, although it could be a corruption for Ophir, a place well known for its gold (1 Kgs 9:28). Verse 11 is a prose addition in Aramaic, the only occurrence of this language in Jeremiah. It promises destruction of false gods who did not create the heavens and the earth.

10:17-25. The final siege. This oracle is the last one in the collection dealing with the "Foe from the North." The siege against the cities will not be lifted. The inhabitants of these cities are told to prepare for exile. Once more Zion (i.e., Jerusalem), depicted as a mother who has lost her children, laments her suffering and grievous wound. She castigates *the shepherds* (v. 21, a metaphor for the kings) who, because they did not seek and follow divine guidance (*inquire of the LORD*), have scattered their flocks (see *Rachel . . . weeping for her children* in 31:15-22). In v. 22, there is a warning of the approach of the foe from the north country. Finally, in vv. 23-25 Jeremiah prays for divine mercy towards himself, since he, like all humans, is sinful. It may be that the prophet uses the "I" of the prayer to represent the nation, a not uncommon practice in OT prayers (see laments in the Psalter). In any case, in v. 25 he then offers intercession for Jacob (i.e., Israel) by asking for divine punishment of the foreign nations who do not know God and have destroyed his people. This intercessory prayer, in accordance with the role of the prophet like Moses, comes too late to save Israel from the northern foe (cf. the "Oracles against the Foreign Nations" in chaps. 46–51).

The Broken Covenant, 11:1-17

This prose speech, composed by deuteronomic editors, renders judgment against Judah and the people of Jerusalem for violating the covenant of Moses. The language of the chapter and its theology are strongly reminiscent of Deuteronomy. Examples of deuteronomic language include *cursed be anyone who does not heed the words of this covenant* (v. 3; cf. Deut 27:26); *when I brought them out of the land of Egypt, from the iron-smelter* (v. 3; see Deut 4:20); *that I may perform the oath that I swore to your ancestors* (v. 5; see Deut 7:8; 8:18; 9.5); *a land flowing with milk and honey* (v. 5; see Deut 6:3; 11:9; 26:9, 15; 27:3); *as at this day* (v. 5; cf. Deut 2:30; 4:20, 38; 6:24; 8:18; 10:15; 29:28). Also following a deuteronomic theological tradition is the explanation that the destruction of Judah and Jerusalem and the Babylonian exile came as a result of the violation of the covenant. Once again the prophet is not allowed to intercede for Judah and Jerusalem in order to divert Yahweh's punishment (v. 14; see 7:16; Exod 32:30-32).

Jeremiah's Laments (Confessions), 11:18–20:18

The poetic and prose materials in 11:18–20:18 are various in nature and include laments, judgment oracles, biographical narratives, and oracles of salvation. However, laments are the major literary form. Jeremiah utters some seven laments (11:18-23; 12:1-6; 15:10-21; 17:14-18; 18:18-23; 20:7-13; and 20:14-18) that follow a typical two part pattern: the prophet's complaint and Yahweh's response. A fragment of a lament describes the conversion of pagan nations in 16:19-21, while sections of two thanksgiving psalms, a genre that serves as a response to laments, are inserted in 17:12-13 and 20:13. Yahweh also utters laments (12:7-13 and 14:17-18), while the people of Jerusalem offer up two of their own (14:1-10 and 14:19-22). Two prose additions speak of Yahweh's prohibiting Jeremiah from offering intercessory prayers on behalf of the people (i.e., laments; 14:11-12 and 16:1-13), while another comments that even if intercessions were offered by the great prophets, Moses and Samuel, the nation's punishment would not be averted (15:1-4).

As a literary form, laments are a common genre in the Psalter (e.g., Pss 3, 4, 5, 6, 7, 9–10, etc.). Yet they are also present in other biblical books, including, e.g., the Book of Job (cf. e.g., chaps. 3 and 29–30). Laments are characterized by a recurring pattern. In full blown examples, one finds the following: invocation, complaint (description of suffering, reproachful questions addressed to God), plea for help, condemnation or cursing of enemies, affirmation of confidence, confession of sins, acknowledgment of divine response, and such hymnic elements as praise of God and blessings. Announcements of salvation by a worship official (priest or cult prophet) or thanksgiving psalms are usually considered the proper response to a lament.

Jeremiah's laments (confessions) are unique in prophetic literature and have received a variety of different interpretations. They may be understood as issuing from the historical prophet's own religious experiences of doubt, persecution, and suffering. Taken in this way they provide a look at the interiority of the prophet. If they are prayers of the historical Jeremiah, these prayers could be placed in any period of his life. However, the laments also may be viewed as expressing corporate experience, and thus are more stereotypical and formal than personal and private. Perhaps Jeremiah is speaking at times as the representative of the nation in both its struggles with God and its reactions to suffering. A combination of these two views stresses that the prophet as intercessor expresses at times his own struggles and at other times those of the community to which he preaches. Finally, there is the question of whether these laments are the words of the historical Jeremiah or prayers that are placed on his lips by later editors who, along with their own religious communities, struggle with important questions of faith, authentic existence, and human suffering.

The laments of Jeremiah are placed in their literary context to interact with various other materials, including especially judgment oracles, both poetic and prose: 13:1-11, 12-14; 13:15-17, 18-19, 20-27; 14:13-16; 15:1-9; 16:16-18, 21; and 17:1-4. The setting presupposed by the judgment oracles appears usually to be the siege of Jerusalem and an imminent exile (thus either 597 or 587 B.C.E.). Biographical narratives are also present for the first time and provide illustrations of both the struggles of the prophet that lead to the laments and the context out of which the oracles of judgment/salvation issue. These narratives include 18:1-12 (the potter and the clay), the broken earthenware jug (19:1-15), and the persecution of Jeremiah by Pashhur (20:1-6).

Finally, two types of prose speeches are present in these chapters: the promise of salvation (12:14-17 and 16:14-15; cf. chaps. 30–31), and an "either-or" sermon on the sabbath that offers the choice between salvation and punishment (17:19-27).

11:18-23. The first lament. Jeremiah's initial lament consists of a poetic complaint to God by the prophet (vv. 18-20) and a prose response by Yahweh (vv. 21-23). Jeremiah complains of being an innocent victim (*gentle lamb*, v. 19) of a plot against his life. He quotes or at least summarizes the words of his opponents who are plotting not only to kill him, but also to destroy even the last traces of his memory: *his name will no longer be remembered*. While belief in life after death did not come to expression in the OT until several centuries after Jeremiah (cf. Dan 12:2-3), there was the hope to continue to exist through one's descendants and through their memory of the deceased (cf. Gen 12:2; Eccl 1:16; 7:1). Looking to God for protection, the prophet asks for divine punishment of his persecutors. This call for vengeance is a common feature of laments (cf. Pss 3:7; 7:6).

In Yahweh's prose response, the enemies of Jeremiah are identified specifically as *the people of Anathoth* (v. 21), that is, his own family and neighbors. This response is likely added by the deuteronomic redactors who typically attempt to make references and events in poetic texts more clear. The reason for persecution of Jeremiah by *the people of Anathoth* is not stated, although Yahweh does issue a promise of judgment against them.

12:1-6. The second lament. In this lament, Jeremiah raises one of the most critical theological questions in the book: the question of the justice of God. Verse 1a may be translated: "Righteous are you, O LORD; nevertheless, I shall bring charges against you." It may be that the prophet begins his complaint with a confession of divine justice but then moves to a lawsuit. Indeed, the standard confession is the legal basis for the suit. Jeremiah makes clear that it must be God who supports the wicked and enables them to prosper. It is interesting to note that when Jeremiah brings this legal charge, God is both defendant and judge.

Once more God responds (vv. 5-6), but not with soothing words of promised salvation or with a reasoned defense of divine justice. Rather, God informs the prophet that his present persecution is only going to intensify and warns him that his own brothers from his father's house are those who seek to do him harm.

12:7-13. Yahweh's lament. Now God utters his own lament in which he grieves over his having given *the beloved of my heart into the hands of her enemies* (v. 7). Judah is destroyed by invaders, but in the last line Yahweh promises to take vengeance against them. This is an interesting display of the inner turmoil of the passion of God who carries out a terrible judgment against Judah, and yet laments for his people; who brings the invaders to effectuate divine judgment, and yet promises they will meet with their own punishment.

12:14-17. Judgment against Judah's neighbors. A prose promise of salvation added by deuteronomic editors comments on the lament in 12:7-13. Judah is promised that as a result of divine compassion God will bring them home after the exile. Judah's neighbors who have been its enemies are also offered salvation, but only if they convert to the worship of Yahweh (see 30:10-11).

13:1-11. The linen waistcloth. This prose narrative tells the story of a symbolic action that illustrates the message of the prophet (see also chaps. 19 and 32). The typical pattern of symbolic actions of prophets has three parts: God commands the prophet to perform a symbolic act, the narrative describes the completion of the act, and then an explanation of the act is provided. In this narrative, the action centers on a linen waistcloth. A waistcloth was an undergarment covering the middle portion of the body. The material from which the waistcloth was made is linen, also used for various types of clothing, sheets, curtains, and burial shrouds. All garments worn by priests were made of linen (Lev 16:4), but there is no suggestion here of some connection with priestly apparel.

The Euphrates and the Tigris were the two major rivers (hence, the word Mesopotamia, a Greek term meaning "in the midst of rivers") in Babylonia. It is doubtful that the prophet made the journey to Mesopotamia twice; this would have been a journey of at least 400 miles one way. Instead of the Euphrates (Heb. *pĕrātâ* or *pĕrāt*), an alternative reading is Parah, modern Khirbet Farah, located about eight km. northeast of Jerusalem. However, it is more likely that the journey, like the larger narrative, is a symbolic action, not to be taken literally. Indeed, the event may have been created by deuteronomic editors seeking to illustrate Jeremiah's judgment against his people. In any event, the spoiled waistcloth illustrates the sinful corruption of Israel and Judah.

13:12-14: The symbolism of the wine-jars. This prose speech, coming from the hands of deuteronomic editors, takes the form of a promise of judgment against both the leaders of Judah (kings, priests, and prophets) and the inhabitants of Jerusalem. Jeremiah apparently quotes a popular proverb, *every wine-jar should be filled with wine* (v. 12), to which the audience responds that they know this saying. Jeremiah then makes the application: the leaders and the inhabitants of Jerusalem will be filled with wine from the wine-jar and become drunk, an image either of stupor that inhibits their making wise decisions or of a "cup of wrath" from which they are made to drink (see 25:15-29).

13:15-27. Exile. Three poetic oracles addressing the exile either of 597 or 587 B.C.E. are shaped into a larger poem that describes the tragedy of captivity. In the first oracle (vv. 15-17), Jeremiah calls the people to repentance. The expression, *give glory to the LORD* (v. 16), refers to a doxology uttered by a person found guilty of a crime. The doxology praises the God of justice, and its utterance indicates that the judgment has been fair, even when the verdict is guilty (see Josh 7:16–21; 2 Chr 30:8). Images of chaos are used to describe the effects of impending judgment: *darkness, twilight, gloom*, and *deep darkness* (cf. Job 3). Since the nation is guilty, it should utter a doxology, repent,

and hope for a reprieve. Otherwise the prophet will grieve for the departing captives.

The second oracle is one of judgment and addresses a *king and queen mother* who have been deposed (vv. 18-19). *The king and queen mother* would be Jehoiachin and Nehushta, if 597 B.C.E. is the time in question (2 Kgs 24:8-17). If it is 587 B.C.E., the identities of the two would be Zedekiah and Hamutal (2 Kgs 24:18-20). In Judah, the *queen mother* was the mother of the ruling king and not one of his wives. This position had significant political influence (see 1 Kgs 2:19; 15:13; 2 Kgs 8:26; 11:1-3). The *Negeb* was the southern part of Judah. While a hot and arid region, the Negeb at the time was dotted with villages that were engaged in agriculture and with fortresses to protect both Judah from the south and the several trade routes through the area. For Jeremiah, even Judah's more remote towns will be emptied of its people in the coming invasion and exile.

The third oracle is a law-suit that attributes the ravages of exile to religious apostasy (vv. 20-27). *Those who come from the north* are again mentioned as the ones who bring destruction (see chaps. 4–10). Judah, like a prostitute who has shared her favors with false gods, will be raped by the invaders. Yahweh will lift up her skirts over her face, exposing her nakedness. In v. 23, the prophet asks two rhetorical questions to emphasize that a corrupt nation cannot change its ways. Ethiopian refers to an inhabitant of Cush, a country located south of Egypt.

14:1-10. The lament of the people. The first section provides a poetic description of the devastation of a lengthy drought (vv. 1-6). The people of Judah and Jerusalem engage in a lamentation, but to no apparent avail. The second section (vv. 7-9) contains the lament of the people in which they acknowledge their sins and ask for Yahweh to deliver them. The reproach of God in vv. 8-9 is common in laments of accusation. In v. 10 Yahweh responds, not with an oracle of salvation, but rather with an announcement of his rejection of their plea due to their continuing wickedness.

14:11-12. Jeremiah may not intercede. In a prose speech from deuteronomic editors, Yahweh forbids Jeremiah from engaging in intercessory prayer on the people's behalf (see 7:16; 15:1; 16:5-9). In following up v. 10, the prose speech emphasizes that Yahweh will not accept the people's petition and sacrifices, for he intends to bring judgment against them (6:20; 7:21-29).

14:13-16. Lying prophets. In spite of this commandment against intercession, Jeremiah still voices his protest (*Ah, Lord GOD*, v. 13; see 1:6). The point raised by the prophet is the deceit of those prophets who have prophesied peace and not destruction (see 23:9-40; 28). Jeremiah may be implying that Yahweh has sent them to deceive (cf. 1 Kgs 22). In any case, God denies that he has sent these lying prophets, for they are speaking the illusions of their own invention. The very prophets who deny that Yahweh will send famine and a sword against his people will themselves, along with those who listen to them, be victims of the same judgment. These victims will suffer the onerous curse of not being buried (see 7:29–8:3).

14:17-18. Yahweh's second lament. God again laments over the destruction of his *virgin daughter*, the city of Jerusalem (see 12:7-13). Prophet and priest are once more singled out as the cause of the disaster that is coming.

14:19-22. The people lament again. The people of Judah and Zion (i.e., Jerusalem) once again express an accusatory lament reproaching God for the devastation they are experiencing. They confess their sinfulness and ask God to save them. The throne of Yahweh (v. 21) in this context is either Jerusalem (see 3:17) or the Temple (see 17:12; Ezek 43:7).

15:1-4. Intercession cannot divert destruction. In the language of a deuteronomic prose speech, Yahweh contends that Moses (Exod 32:11-14, 30-34; Num 14:13-19) and Samuel (1 Sam 12:17-18) could not be successful in interceding on Judah's behalf. Yahweh still would not change the decision to bring judgment against the nation (see 7:16; 14:11-12; 16:5-9). In the prose tradition, Jeremiah becomes a deuteronomic prophet, one like Moses (Deut 18:15-22). Manasseh reigned over Judah for forty-five years (687/86–642 B.C.E.) as a loyal Assyrian vassal. The deuteronomic editors of 2 Kings blame him for the eventual destruction of Jerusalem and the exile of Judah, because of his leading the people into religious apostasy (2 Kgs 21:1-18). According to deuteronomic justice, the destruction of Judah and the exile were at least in part the result of the sins of the ancestors.

15:5-9. The announcement of Jerusalem's end. This judgment oracle announces the final destruction of Jerusalem, using the image of winnowing the chaff from the grain (see 51:2; Isa 21:10). Earlier disasters did not cause the people to change their evil ways. The bearing of seven children is a sign of divine blessing of the womb (Ruth 4:15; 1 Sam 2:5). The mother of seven faints, because of the loss of her children.

15:10-21. Jeremiah's third lament. (see note on 11:18-23). This lament follows what has been the usual pattern: complaint by the prophet (vv. 15-18) and Yahweh's response (vv. 19-21). However, deuteronomic scribes added a prose lamentation and response in vv. 10-14. Jeremiah utters a lament to his mother, telling her he wishes he had never been born. The reason: he has become the object of cursing. One should remember that God determined before his birth that he would be a prophet (see 1:5). In the last lament, Jeremiah curses his birth, wishing he had been aborted (20:14-18). A *man of strife and contention* (v. 10) refers to Jeremiah's being both the object of persecution involving at times legal action against him (see chap. 26; 36:20-26; 37:11–38:13) and the mediator of Yahweh's lawsuit against the nation (see 2:1-37). Even his own family sought to destroy him (11:21-23). The Hebrew word for "curse" (*qillēl*) refers to both verbal abuse (Eccl 7:21-22) as well as physical harm (Gen 8:21). Curses were considered to have the potency to harm the person against whom they are directed.

In the response to this prose complaint, Yahweh takes responsibility for Jeremiah's suffering, although he argues that he has intervened in the prophet's life *for good* (v. 11). This probably means Yahweh has protected him from his enemies (cf. 1:8). Even so, persecution builds the prophet's character, making him fit to endure the great sufferings inflicted by the northern invader (see 1:17-19). Yahweh then announces, probably to Judah, that it will be plundered and forced into exile (vv. 13-14).

In this complaint (vv. 15-18), Jeremiah states he has "eaten Yahweh's words," a graphic metaphor for his having received the prophetic message given to him by God (1:9; see Isa 55:1-11; Ezek 2:8–3:3). *I am called by your name* (v. 16): Jeremiah's name means "Yahweh exalts." While he rejoiced in the call and reception of the divine word, his prophetic ministry has led to alienation and an often burdensome life. *Weight of your hand* (v. 17) is a rather common metaphor for prophetic inspiration (see 1 Kgs 18:46; 2 Kgs 3:15; Isa 8:11; Ezek 1:3; 3:14). Jeremiah concludes his lament with a rather harsh indictment of God. The prophet uses two related metaphors for Yahweh: *deceitful brook* and *waters that fail* (v. 18). These metaphors oppose Yahweh's affirmation of being a *fountain of living water* (2:13) and denial of being *a wilderness to Israel* (2:31).

Yahweh's response in vv. 19-21 implies that Jeremiah has relinquished his role as a prophet. Three times Yahweh uses the term *turn back* (v. 19, Heb. *šûb*), recalling the sermon on repentance in 3:1–4:4. "To stand before the Lord" refers either to a messenger who stands before the king, waiting for the royal proclamation, or to one who offers intercession in a ritual setting or a law court. The language of v. 20 echoes that of 1:18-19 (the conclusion of the call), while the promise to redeem the prophet from the wicked reflects 1:8.

16:1-13. The symbolism of Jeremiah's lack of family. In this deuteronomic prose sermon, Yahweh prohibits the prophet from marrying and having a family. This prohibition helps to illustrate Yahweh's coming judgment that will afflict families. Those who die by means of disease, famine, and the sword will not be buried. Rather their corpses will be consumed by birds and wild animals. Once more Jeremiah is commanded by Yahweh not to lament on behalf of the people, for their punishment is inevitable (7:16; 14:11-12; 15:1). Their ancestors and they have committed religious apostasy, and this is the basis for understanding why they have suffered.

The *house of mourning* in v. 5 is a room or hall in a house where a funerary banquet is held (see Amos 6:7). *Gashing* and *shaving* (v. 6) the head were prohibited funerary practices associated with pagan worship (Lev 19:28; 21:5; Deut 14:1). The question and answer form recurs throughout the prose tradition (5:19; 13:12-14; 15:1-4; 22:8-9).

16:14-15. The future return from exile. This prose sermon of salvation promises that in the future a new confession will replace the one centering on the exodus from Egypt. The confession will focus on the new act of God's liberation, this one the return from Babylonian captivity. Confessions like these were central to religious faith and worship. Jeremiah 23:7-8 almost exactly duplicates this passage.

16:16-21. The fishers and hunters of Judah. The prose sermon that left off with v. 13 now continues and speaks of fishermen and hunters who will seek out the people of Judah in every conceivable place. These fishermen and hunters are likely the Egyptians (Isa 19:5-10) and Babylonians (Lam 4:18-19.). Verses 19-20 are a part of a lament that expresses faith in God and a universal recognition by the nations of his lordship (see Ps 2; Isa 2:3 = Mic 4:2). Verse 21 continues v. 18, stating that with this punishment Judah will finally know Yahweh.

17:1-4. Judah's sin. This prose sermon announces judgment against Judah for practicing fertility religion. The reference to *an iron pen; with a diamond point* (v. 1) suggests an engraving instrument used to incise characters on stone. The point more likely was a hard stone, possibly emery, and not diamond. The ten commandments were engraved on tablets of stone (Exod 31:18; 32:16). In this case the sin of Judah is to be incised on the tablet of their heart and the altar's horn (cf. Job 19:24). This text in v. 1 is similar to 31:31-34 that speaks of writing the law on the heart. The image points to the embodiment of either sin or of the commandments (31:31-34). Altars had *horns*, that is, projections from their four corners (Exod 27:2) on which the blood of sacrificial animals was smeared (Lev 4:7). People seeking asylum would grab hold of the altar's horns (1 Kgs 1:50-51; 2:28-34). Tablets were made of stone, metal, or wood.

Sacred poles (v. 2, *'ăshērâ*) were either carved wood (Judg 6:25) or living trees (Deut 16:21) that represented the Canaanite fertility goddess, Asherah (see 1 Kgs 15:13; 18:19; 2 Kgs 21:7; 23:4; Mic 5:13-14).

17:5-11. A collection of wisdom. Inserted at this point is a collection of wisdom sayings, most likely originating with sages like the ones who wrote and collected the wisdom texts of Job, Proverbs, and Ecclesiastes. Jeremiah 17 contains a wisdom poem (vv. 5-8), a rhetorical question (v. 9), a first person proverb (v. 10), and a comparative proverb (v. 11). The editors or compilers of Deuteronomy, the deuteronomistic history (Joshua through Second Kings), and Jeremiah may have been scribes raised in the wisdom tradition passed down in scribal schools.

The poem consists of two strophes (vv. 5-6; 7-8) and is reminiscent of the one that begins the Psalter (Ps 1). While the psalm stresses that the study of the law results in blessing, the poem in Jeremiah emphasizes trusting in Yahweh in contrast to self-reliance or trusting in mere human beings. The imagery of the *tree planted by water* (v. 8) in both texts calls to mind the "tree of life," a common wisdom motif originating in myths of the ancient Near East dealing with paradise (see Gen 2:9; 3:22; Prov 3:13-18). The sages believed that wise behavior led to well-being in life. Rhetorical questions (v. 9) are queries that have obvious answers (see "the voice from the whirlwind" in Job 38–41; and Amos 3:3-8). The mind and the will are associated with the heart in the OT (Prov 14:10; 16:9, 23; 25:3). Yahweh has the ability to discern even the thoughts of people and to requite each person according to his/her deeds (see Pss 7:10; 17:3; 139:14; Jer 20:12). Comparative proverbs (v. 11) are sayings in which two things are compared in order to discover an underlying unity or an element held in common. This saying underscores the theory of retributive justice by an analogy or comparison from nature.

17:12-13. The praise of Yahweh and the ark. This text is a hymnic fragment in praise of Yahweh and the sacred ark (i.e., the *throne*, v. 12). The ark was an empty throne placed in the holy of holies of the Temple to signify divine presence (see note on 3:16).

17:14-18. Jeremiah's fourth lament. (see note on 11:18-23). For the first time in the sequence of Jeremiah's lament, there is no response from Yahweh. Jeremiah turns to the divine physician for healing and salvation, two areas often related in the OT (see Pss 6; 41:4; 147:3). Jeremiah denies he has pressured Yahweh to send disaster, but notes that the delay has led to skepticism that he speaks the truth. He has played the role of earnest intercessor, hoping to delay Yahweh's judgment so that Judah and Jerusalem may finally repent and avert the promised disaster. However, the prophet continues to press Yahweh to destroy his (Jeremiah's) enemies.

17:19-27. Honoring the sabbath. This deuteronomic prose speech assumes the form of "either-or" and exhorts Judah to honor the sabbath day. The decision the people make will be either life or death, blessing or punishment. Recurring seven times in this speech, *the sabbath* was the seventh day of the week and was observed as both a day of rest and of worship (see Exod 16:23; 20:8-11; 23:12; 31:12-17; Lev 23:3; Deut 5:12-15). In priestly theology (cf. Gen 2:1-4a; Exod 20:8-11), the emphasis was placed on the place of the seventh day in the temporal order of creation: by remembering the sabbath and keeping it holy (i.e., separating it from the work days of the week as a day of rest and religious observance), creation would be blessed and life enhanced. In deuteronomic theology (cf. Deut 5:12-15), the day was a time of rest and remembrance of Egyptian slavery and exodus liberation. The observance of the sabbath was an important commandment of the Mosaic covenant (also see Amos 8:5; Neh 13:15-22). The prose speech in Jeremiah on one hand explains that the judgment of disaster against Judah and Jerusalem was due, at least in part, to violating the sabbath commandment. On the other hand, the speech offers hope to the exilic and postexilic communities that the monarchy and the kingdom will be restored, if the sabbath is observed.

Jeremiah stands *in the People's Gate* (v. 19), one of the entryways to the Temple, and delivers the speech. *The Shephelah* (v. 26) refers to the low hills between the coastal plain and the central hill country to the east. Most biblical references are to the "Shephelah of Judah." For *the Negeb* (v. 26), see the note on 13:18-19.

18:1-12. The potter and the clay. This deuteronomic prose narrative combines a symbolic act with a promise of judgment (see 13:1-11). In the story, Yahweh directs Jeremiah to go to a potter's house where he will obtain a divine message. Jeremiah then observes a potter fail in making the first vessel, but later succeed in shaping the clay into another type of vessel. Yahweh then issues a promise of judgment in which he is the divine potter shaping nations for destruction or salvation depending on whether or not they repent. Yahweh announces he is *a potter shaping evil against* Judah and Jerusalem, but will alter this plan if they will repent of their evil ways (v. 11). Thus, the people of Judah and Jerusalem are given a choice to determine their own fate. Verse 12 quotes the people who in defiance declare they will follow their own plans and their own stubborn will.

The pottery industry was a significant one in ancient Israel. Villages and cities normally had their pottery workshops. Pottery-making required important skills that could be significantly enhanced by artistic creativity. Pottery in ancient Israel was shaped by hand according to a variety of methods: attaching clay to the inside of a basket that was then fired to harden the new vessel; shaping clay in the palm of one hand with the other hand; piecing clay strips around a base; and connecting lengths of clay with slip (clay mixed with water). The most advanced procedure was the use of a potter's wheel. One hand or foot turned the wheel, with the free hand or hands used to shape the clay moving on the platform. While some vessels were sun-dried, most were hardened by means of firing. Artistic enhancements included incisions, painting, and burnishing (polishing the slip which coated the dried pottery before firing).

The metaphor of God as the divine potter who created humanity (Gen 2:7) and determined the destinies of people and nations (Isa 29:16; 64:8) is an important one in the OT. However, the image does not convey a strict view of the divine determination of destiny. As is the case in the speech, humans still possess the freedom to be able, within the limitations of their humanity, to participate in creating their futures. In v. 12, it is the stubborn refusal of the people to repent that leads to their punishment.

18:13-17. The folly of idolatry. Jeremiah engages in another lawsuit against Israel, this time for idolatry. Because of this sin, Yahweh convicts Israel of sin and announces judgment. The oracle is quite similar to the lawsuit in chap. 2. One possible historical setting is Josiah's move into the northern territory of the former state of Israel to bring it back under Judahite control. Jeremiah argues that Israel will be scattered like the wind, an image of the devastation to be brought by the northern enemy.

The *snow of Lebanon* and *crags of Sirion* (v. 14) allude to the range of mountains north of Israel that extends northward for another 100 mi. Sirion is also called Mt. Hermon, a mountain with three peaks that rises some 9,230 ft. above sea level (Deut 3:9; 4:48). The charge that *my people have forgotten me* (v. 15) or that they perish for a lack of knowledge is a common one in Jeremiah (cf. 2:32; 13:24-25). *Delusion* refers to idols (see Ps 31:6; Jonah 2:8). Jeremiah picks up again the image of *ancient roads* to refer to the traditional religion of Yahweh worship that Israel has left in order to take other paths, that is, those of pagan idolatry (see 6:16). The *wind from the east* (v. 17, also known as "sirocco") is a strong hot wind that blows in from the desert carrying dust particles (see Exod 10:13; 14:21; Ps 48:7; Jonah 4:8).

18:18-23. Jeremiah's fifth lament. (See note on 11:18-23). The fifth lament of the prophet returns to the theme of his enemies plotting against his life. The prose introduction (v. 18) is added in order to make more explicit the identity of Jeremiah's opponents. His enemies are the religious leaders of Judah who make their case for removing the prophet for laudable reasons. They wish to preserve the priestly instruction (the law), the counsel of *the wise* (or sages), and the prophetic word (see 8:8). These were the three forms of divine revelation that were believed to provide proper knowledge of God and the divine will for the nation. The priests are probably the chief priestly officials of the nation, *the wise* were either royal counsellors to kings or interpreters of the priestly law, and the prophets were so-called court prophets who prophesied peace and prosperity.

In the poetic lament, Jeremiah contends that he had in times past offered intercession even in behalf of his enemies (see 4:10, 19-22; cf. 14:11-12; 15:1; 16:5-9 where Jeremiah was forbidden to intercede). But now it is time, argues the prophet, for Yahweh to cause them to perish. This call for vengeance against his enemies, including even their families, is common in the laments (see 11:18-23; 12:6; 15:15; Pss 3:7; 5:4-10; 7:6). Once more Yahweh does not respond to this lament.

19:1-15. The broken jug. This prose narrative, written by deuteronomic redactors, is another symbolic action connected with a prose judgment speech (see 13:1-11). Yahweh tells the prophet to purchase *an earthenware jug* (v. 1) from a potter (see 18:1-12), *take some of the elders and some of the senior priests . . . to the valley of the son of Hinnom* (see 7:31 and note), and prophesy the destruction of Jerusalem. The judgment speech is to be reinforced by the breaking of the jug. Jeremiah then returns to the Temple and announces that Yahweh will bring evil against Jerusalem and its surrounding towns (v. 15).

The Potsherd Gate (v. 2), perhaps another name for "the Dung Gate" (Neh 2:13; 3:13-14; 12:31), may have been located in the south wall of Jerusalem. The groups and Jeremiah would have exited the gate through which the refuse of Jerusalem was taken for disposal in the garbage dump located in the Hinnom valley. This valley was also the general location of altars to false gods where various idolatrous practices, including child sacrifice, were carried on (see 7:30–8:3 and note). Eating the flesh of one's children, and of one's neighbors (vv. 6-9; cf. 2 Kgs 6:24-31; Lam 4:10), was a curse for disobedience to the covenant (Lev 26:29; Deut 28:53; Isa 9:20; 49:26; Zech 11:9).

Smashing pottery (vv. 10-13) was a ritual act designed to destroy one's enemies (see Ps 2:9). In Egyptian execration texts, the names of the king's enemies were written on pieces of pottery, and then curses against the enemies were recited while the pottery was smashed.

20:1-6. Pashhur's public punishment of Jeremiah. In this prose narrative, *Pashhur*, a priest and *chief officer* of the Temple, is in charge of the Temple police responsible for order in the Temple precinct. Because Jeremiah was in the court of the Temple (19:14-15) when he preached against the city of Jerusalem, Pashhur arrests him, has him beaten, and then puts him in stocks located in the upper Benjamin Gate that led to the Temple. A day later, when Pashhur releases the prophet, Jeremiah utters a judgment speech against Judah, Jerusalem, and Pashhur (vv. 3-6). The prophet tells Pashhur that his name will be changed to *"Terror-all-around"* (v. 3, cf. 6:25; 20:10). NAMES in the OT often bore a meaning that spoke of peoples' character or destiny. In this case, Pashhur's new name refers to the northern foe who will surround the city in siege (hence, "Terror-all-around"), destroy it, and take its survivors into exile, a fate that Pashhur and his family will share (see chap. 28; and Amos 7:10-17). Jeremiah tells Pashhur that he will die in captivity and be buried there, along with his friends.

20:7-13. Jeremiah's sixth lament. (See note on 11:18-23). Jeremiah's sixth lament is found in vv. 7-12 and is followed by a fragment of a thanksgiving psalm in v. 13. *Enticed*, occurring twice in v. 7, means both to deceive and to seduce. The connotation of deception echoes the motif of Yahweh's sending lying spirits to inspire prophets to "entice" Ahab to wage battle and then fall at Ramoth-gilead (1 Kgs 22:19-23). The same word means "to seduce" a virgin in Exod 22:16-17 (MT 22:15-16). In Hos 2:14 (MT 2:16) Yahweh will "seduce" Israel in bringing her back to the wilderness in order to renew the romance with this faithless wife. *Overpowered* (v. 7) is a term that on occasion refers to rape (e. g., Amnon's rape of Tamar in 2 Sam 13:14). The deuteronomic law sentences to death a man who "overpowers" a betrothed virgin in the open countryside (Deut 22:25-27). The woman is spared, since no one can hear her when she "cries out" (see Jer 20:8). Jeremiah complains that Yahweh has "seduced" and then "raped" him, and although he cries out no one rescues him. Even when he decides to keep silent (cf. 15:19-21), the compulsion is so great to speak that he must. Jeremiah's enemies also use the language of seduction and rape in their plotting to do him harm (v. 10).

Verse 13 expresses a worshiper's testimony and exhortation to a community to praise Yahweh, affirming that he redeems *the needy* from those who work evil. Thanksgivings are usually given as a response to a lament, either in anticipation of salvation or its experience (see note on 17:12-13).

20:14-18. Jeremiah's seventh lament. (See note on 11:18-23). In this concluding lament, at least in the editorial sequencing, Jeremiah curses the day of his birth (cf. Job 3). For other curses, see 11:1-17; 17:5-8. Curses were designed to harm those against whom they are uttered. They contrast with blessings that are to effectuate well-being and life for their intended subjects. By cursing his birth, Jeremiah wishes to destroy his own life, not just wish that he were dead. The curse is also an assault on creation theology in the OT, in that God is active in conception, cares for the

fetus, and helps in the birthing process (see note on 1:5). Jeremiah's curse against his birth (cf. 15:10) is also a rejection of his call. In the OT, birth, and especially the birth of a son, was considered good news to be celebrated (cf. Ruth 4:13-17). The comparison of the one who announced to Jeremiah's father the good news of the birth of a son is cursed by the prophet to be like the two cities Yahweh *overthrew without pity* (i.e., Sodom and Gomorrah; see Gen 19; Isa 1:9-10; 3:9; Jer 23:14; Amos 4:11; Zeph 2:9). The prophet wishes his mother had resorted to ABORTION so that he would never have drawn breath.

Concerning Zedekiah and Jerusalem, 21:1-10

This narrative and the accompanying oracles appear to be an alternative rendition of 37:1-10. Perhaps it was placed in its present location because of the reference to another Pashhur in the preceding narrative (20:1-6) and because the collection of oracles that follow in 21:11–23:8 have the same theme of warning and judgment against the kings and the city of Jerusalem. In any case, the narrative provides the framework for oracles of judgment against King Zedekiah and Jerusalem and for a promise of conditional salvation for the inhabitants of the city.

A prose narrative, originating in the exile or early post-exile, provides the setting for two oracles of the prophet. *King Zedekiah* (597–587 B.C.E.) sends two people to Jeremiah to obtain a word from Yahweh concerning NEBUCHADREZZAR's invasion. This would be perhaps 588 B.C.E., sometime after Zedekiah has rebelled against the Babylonians. In vv. 3-7, Jeremiah utters an oracle indicating that the city will fall into the hands of Nebuchadrezzar and that Zedekiah, his servants, and the people of the city will be struck down by the sword. However, to the inhabitants of Jerusalem Jeremiah offers the alternative of remaining in the city and dying or surrendering to the Babylonians and saving their lives. The city shall be burned with fire (vv. 8-10). Also compare 34:1-7, which contains another warning to Zedekiah.

Nebuchadrezzar replaced Jehoiachin (598–97 B.C.E.) with his uncle, Zedekiah, another son of Josiah, after the first Babylonian conquest of Jerusalem in 597 B.C.E. Jehoiachin had been on the throne only three months, following the death of his father Jehoiakim who, so it seems, died in the siege. Although a faithful vassal to Nebuchadrezzar at first, Zedekiah yielded to anti-Babylonian pressure at court and rebelled. This foolish action led to the destruction of Jerusalem and the second exile in 587 B.C.E. Nebuchadrezzar killed Zedekiah's family, blinded him, and took him captive to Babylon (2 Kgs 24:18–25.7).

This *Pashhur* (v. 1), not to be identified with the person of the same name in 20:1-6, was the *son of Malchiah*, a prince who owned the cistern in which Jeremiah was imprisoned (38:6), and possibly a son of King Zedekiah (38:1). *Zephaniah* was the priestly overseer of the Temple who refused to rebuke Jeremiah for his announcement to the exiles in 597 B.C.E. that their captivity would be a long one. Nebuchadrezzar executed Zephaniah at Riblah after the fall of Jerusalem in 587 B.C.E. (52:24-27).

Zedekiah sent the two emissaries to Jeremiah to persuade him to *inquire of the LORD*, that is, to ask for an oracle (10:21; 37:2). The king hoped for a *wonderful deed* (v. 2, "deeds" in Heb.), that is, mighty acts of redemption, that would defeat Nebuchadrezzar and save the city of Jerusalem (cf. Exod 3:20; Pss 9:1; 26:7; 86:10). "Mighty deeds" in Israelite faith included acts of redemption such as the exodus from Egypt, victory at the Red Sea, guidance in the Sinai wilderness, and the taking of the land of Canaan. Zedekiah hopes that Yahweh will perform a similar act of deliverance.

However, according to Jeremiah (vv. 2-7), Yahweh will not protect the city, in spite of the strong belief in Judahite confession that he defends the city against all enemies (cf. Pss 46; 48; 76; Isa 31:4-5). On the contrary, Yahweh himself is fighting against the city and will destroy it. Even the son of David, in this case Zedekiah, will not enjoy Yahweh's protection. Royal theology in Jerusalem was grounded in the belief that Yahweh entered into a perpetual covenant with the house of David, meaning that he would defend the monarchy against its enemies (see 2 Sam 7; Pss 2; 18; 20; 21; 45; 72; 89; and 110).

In vv. 8-10, Jeremiah addresses an oracle of conditional salvation to the inhabitants of the city of Jerusalem. The prophet uses a covenantal formula found elsewhere only in Deut 30:15, 19: *I am setting before you the way of life and the way of death.* This "either-or" formulation offers life to those who leave the city and surrender *to the Chaldeans* (i.e., Babylonians).

Concerning the Kings of Judah and Jerusalem, 21:11–23:8

This collection of poetic oracles and prose speeches about the *house of David* (21:12) and the city of Jerusalem more than likely represents a later form of a once

independent collection. The deuteronomic editors shaped it into its present form, added speeches and comments that made the references more specific, and enabled the poetic Jeremiah to speak to later generations. The recurring motifs are *house* (dynasty and palace) and (cedars of) *Lebanon* (representing the city of Jerusalem, palace, and Temple). The references to Lebanon recall that cedars of Lebanon were used to build both the palace and Temple (1 Kgs 5–7; 9:10-28). The general oracles addressed to the Davidic dynasty (*house of David*) are 21:11-12 (poetry), 22:1-5 (prose), and 22:6-7 (poetry), while the poetic oracles concerning individual kings are 22:10 (Jehoahaz = Shallum), 22:13-19 (Jehoiakim), and 22:28-30 (Jehoiachin = Coniah). The prose sermons that deal with specific kings are 22:11-12 (Jehoahaz) and 22:24-27 (Jehoiachin).

It is interesting to note that Jeremiah does not address directly two kings: Josiah and Zedekiah. Josiah is indirectly mentioned in 22:10, 11, and 15-16, while an allusion may be made to Zedekiah in word plays on *righteous Branch* and *the LORD is our righteousness* in 23:5-6 (the name "Zedekiah" means "Yahweh is my righteousness"). Jeremiah 23:1-8 also contains prose speeches that broach the future: the promise of *shepherds* (i.e., kings) who will rule faithfully, and a *righteous Branch* who will rule according to wisdom and justice. The oracles and speeches in the rest of the collection pertain to Jerusalem (Lebanon): 21:13-14 (poetry), 22:8-9 (prose), and 22:20-23 (poetry).

In this collection, Jeremiah takes on the twin pillars of royal theology in Jerusalem: the promise to David and Zion (i.e., Jerusalem) as the city of God. The strong criticism of both the kings and Jerusalem (the location of palace and Temple) is in line with Jeremiah's blaming of the leadership as primarily responsible for the religious and political apostasy of the nation. While Jeremiah may not have been opposed in principle to the existence of the dynasty and Temple, these institutions and their theological understandings did not play a decisive role in his own religious views. Later prose speeches written by the deuteronomic editors attributed to the prophet the view that both kingship and Temple would play an important role in the future restoration (23:1-8; 30:9; 33:14-26). However, it is doubtful if this adaptation of the words of the prophet accurately reflects his own views.

21:11-14. General oracles against the house of David and Jerusalem. Two poetic oracles introduce the larger collection: a warning to kings to rule justly (vv.

11-12), and a judgment against Jerusalem (vv. 13-14). Assuming the form of an admonition, Jeremiah issues a warning to kings to practice social justice (see Isa 1:16-17; 56:1; Ezek 45:9; Amos 5:4b, 14-15). The imperative, *execute justice* (v. 12), recurs in 22:3, 15, and 23:5 and provides a major theme for the entire collection. Jeremiah stresses that it is the implementation of justice in social life that guarantees the continuation of the monarchy and the nation. He never refers to God's eternal covenant with the *house of David* (cf. 2 Sam 7 and Ps 89) that guarantees rule to the descendants of David. The deuteronomic formulation of the Davidic covenant (2 Sam 7), does promise punishment of kings who strayed from the Mosaic law, but does not allow for the end of the monarchy. Justice, for which the king is primarily responsible, brings well-being to the nation (Ps 72).

The initial oracle against the *inhabitant of the valley* (v. 13) (better translated: "one enthroned over the valley") includes a threat in v. 13 (see 23:30-32; 50:31; 51:25) and announcement of judgment in v. 14. The *inhabitant of the valley* refers to Jerusalem (cf. 22:23). The word "inhabitant" is a feminine participle and agrees in gender with the Hebrew word for "city," a feminine noun. Jerusalem is not called a *rock of the plain* (v. 13) elsewhere in the OT, although some thirty-three times God is called the "rock," usually describing divine strength and support (see Deut 32; Isa 17:10; Pss 31:3; 62:7; 71:3).

This image of *rock of the plain* may be a parody of Jerusalem that considers itself impregnable because of its fortifications, Davidic king, and Temple housing the powerful God who will defend the city against forces of chaos and human invaders (Pss 46; 48; 76; Isa 31:4-5). *Forest* (v. 14; "of Lebanon" is understood) may be a term for either the palace (see 22:14; 1 Kgs 7:2-12; 10:17, 21; Isa 22:8) or the Temple (1 Kgs 6:9-36), since Solomon purchased cedar wood from Lebanon to construct both of them. In either case, Jeremiah announces a *fire* will burn down this *forest* of Lebanon (cf. 22:7).

22:1-5. A warning to kings of Judah. The deuteronomic redactors compose and insert into this collection a prose speech that makes the oracle against the kings in 21:11-12 more specific. Jeremiah is told to *go down to the house of the king of Judah* (i.e., to go down from the Temple to the palace) and address the king. Written in the conditional "either-or" style, this speech tells the reigning king that the implementation of justice, not only for the victim who has been robbed but

also for the alien, orphan, and the widow (see Deut 16:11, 14; 24:19-21; and the note on 7:6), will enable the monarchy and the nation to endure. But if not, this *house* (either the monarchy or the palace) will become a *desolation*. The term, "desolation" is used to characterize the ruins of cities (Lev 26:31; Isa 44:26; Jer 25:18; 27:17; 44:2, 6).

To underscore the certainty of the warning, Yahweh swears by his own name. Oaths in the OT were often accompanied by swearing in the name of Yahweh to stress that the OATH maker was entering into an agreement with God to perform a certain activity. Consequently, oaths were serious pledges that were expected to be carried out (Ps 15:4; Lev 5:1-4). Curses, whether stated or implied, were usually a part of oath taking (Ruth 1:17; 1 Sam 3:17; 1 Kgs 2:23). In this context (22:5), Yahweh will make the dynasty (or palace) a desolation, if the royal house does not practice justice. This sermon explains that royal injustice was the cause of the destruction of Jerusalem, the end of the monarchy, the fall of the nation of Judah, and the Babylonian captivity (cf. the blame placed on kings in 1 and 2 Kings by deuteronomic editors).

22:6-7. Judgment against the royal palace. The language of this poetic oracle of judgment is similar to the one directed against the *inhabitant of the valley* in 21:13-14 (*cedars* and *fire* = *fire in its forest*). However, the prose introduction in v. 6 indicates it was addressed to the house of the king of Judah, that is, the dynasty of the Davidic monarchy. And masculine language is primarily used, including male pronouns. Masculine language fits the monarchy rather well. At the end of v. 6, the Hebrew noun "cities" is modified by a feminine participle. This suggests that the plural "cities" originally may have been a singular. If so, the NRSV translation is correct: *an uninhabited city*. While the palace or dynasty may have been addressed by this oracle, the close relationship between the Davidic monarchy and the City of David (i.e., Jerusalem) even to the point of merging identities is clear in this collection.

The oracle compares the house of the king of Judah to *Gilead* (v. 6), a territory located in the Transjordan between Bashan and Moab, and to the *summit of Lebanon*. Both regions contained thick forests, especially on their mountain ranges. Solomon's palace was called a forest, because it was constructed of cedars from Lebanon (1 Kgs 7:1-12; see note on 21:13-14).

22:8-9. Commentary on Jerusalem's destruction. The deuteronomic editors compose and insert a prose commentary on vv. 6-7 in the form of a question and answer in order to explain why Jerusalem and the palace were destroyed. When foreigners pass by and see the ruined city and wonder why, the answer to be given is that the city has violated the covenant and worshiped other gods (see 5:19; 9:12-16; 13:12-14; 15:1-4; 16:10-13; Deut 29:22-28; and 1 Kgs 9:8-9).

22:10-12. Concerning Josiah and Jehoahaz (Shallum). This part of the collection contains a fragment of a poetic oracle (v. 10) concerning two unidentified males (one dead and the other in exile) and a prose speech (vv. 11-12) by the deuteronomic editors that specifically identifies the person exiled as *Shallum* (i.e., King Jehoahaz).

Verse 10 admonishes an audience, presumably the citizens of Jerusalem, not to continue lamenting *for him who is dead*, presumably King Josiah who perished in 609 B.C.E. during the battle against the Egyptians at Megiddo (2 Kgs 23:28-30). The lament over this popular king would have been even greater, because with his death Judahite independence, enjoyed since 627 B.C.E., came to an abrupt end. The hopes for the restoration of the Davidic empire also died with Josiah.

Instead of lamenting for Josiah, the people are exhorted to grieve for one who has been taken into exile. More than likely this would have been Jehoahaz, a son of Josiah chosen by the *people of the land* (male land owners, cf. 1:18). Rather, the people should lament the exile of Jehoahaz (609 B.C.E.) who was chosen to reign in Josiah's stead. Jehoahaz, condemned by the deuteronomic editors of 2 Kgs as "doing evil in the sight of the LORD," was to reign for only three months. Necho II, King of Egypt, replaced him with another son of Josiah, Jehoiakim (2 Kgs 23:30-34). Jehoahaz was taken to Egypt where the Books of Kings says he died. Consequently, Jeremiah seeks to put an end to any popular speculation that one day this son of Josiah would return and claim the throne.

The deuteronomic editors make clear in their prose speech that follows (vv. 11-12) that the one who has gone into exile and will die there is Shallum, the birth name of King Jehoahaz (see 1 Chron 3:15; Ezek 19:2-4). Kings in Israel had two names: a birth name and then a name given at the time of coronation and installation.

22:13-19. Against King Jehoiakim. Jeremiah's harshest oracle against members of the royal lineage was directed against King Jehoiakim (609-598 B.C.E.). Necho II replaced Jehoahaz (cf. 22:10-12) with his older brother Jehoiakim. Jehoiakim's birth name was Eliakim (2 Kgs 23:34). Jehoiakim came to the throne without the popular support of the *people of the land* (cf. 1:18) and without any stated anointing by priests or prophets. Following the Babylonian victory over the Egyptians at CARCHEMISH in 605 B.C.E., Jehoiakim quickly switched his allegiance to Nebuchadrezzar II. Seeking Judahite independence, Jehoiakim decided after serving the Babylonians for three years to rebel, a foolhardy action that led to a Babylonian invasion culminating in the surrender of Jerusalem and the first exile in 597 B.C.E. Jehoiakim's heavy taxation, mainly necessitated by the demands for tribute by the Egyptians, is singled out for mention in 2 Kings (see 2 Kgs 23:34–24:7). He too is condemned by the deuteronomic editors of the Books of Kings as one who "did what was evil in the sight of the LORD." The death of Jehoiakim occurred in 598 B.C.E. during the Babylonian siege of Jerusalem, although the exact circumstances of his passing remain unclear. Second Kings simply notes that Jehoiakim "slept with his ancestors" and was succeeded by his son Jehoiachin. Second Chronicles 36:6 states that he was placed in chains to be transported to Babylon by Nebuchadrezzar. Jeremiah suggests an ignominious death for the king: he would die without a proper burial and funeral (22:18-19; 36:30).

The speech against Jehoiakim in 22:13-19 is a poetic judgment oracle with a prose insertion by the deuteronomic editors in v. 18a to specify Jehoiakim as the person addressed. The term *alas* (or "woe," "ah") in v. 18 originates in the funeral lament and is used on occasion by the prophets to announce the demise of the audience (see Isa 10:5; 17:12; 28:1; Amos 5:18; 6:1; Hab 2:6, 9, 12, 15, 19). The lengthy indictment of the king centers on Jehoiakim's injustice, particularly the use of unremunerated labor in the building of a palace or a renovation of an old one (vv. 13-17). Solomon also used uncompensated labor in the building of royal projects (see 1 Kgs 5:13-18; 9:15-22). The use of cedar recalls the wood that Solomon had purchased for the building of the palace and Temple. The palace of Jehoiakim was painted *with vermilion* (v. 14), that is, red ocher. Jeremiah contrasts Jehoiakim, described in the images of the great tyrant Solomon (cf. 1 Kgs 3–11), with Josiah who practiced social justice. Jehoiakim also is condemned for stealing (v. 17, *dishonest gain*), most likely heavy taxation and refusing to compensate workers, and *shedding innocent blood* (cf. 2 Kgs 24:4). *Shedding innocent blood* is one of the twelve curses associated with violating the Mosaic covenant. It especially refers to the corruption of the legal process when judges were bribed to condemn innocent people (Deut 27:25).

Jeremiah's judgment (vv. 18-19) speaks of the death of Jehoiakim who will be denied a royal funeral with full honors. The references to *brother, sister, lord* (father), and *majesty* suggest either the stereotypical language of funeral songs, adapted to the occasion, or the symbolism of the king fulfilling various family roles on behalf of his people. Jehoiakim's burial will be like that of *a donkey* who dies in the city and then is dragged through the city gate to a garbage dump to rot in the open (the Valley of Hinnom? see 36:30). The denial of burial was a horrible fate (see 8:1-3; Deut 28:26).

22:20-23. Judgment of Jerusalem. Once again Jeremiah directs a judgment oracle against the "inhabitant of Lebanon," the city of Jerusalem. The city is personified as a woman, addressed in feminine language (cf. 21:13-14), and told to go to the mountains and lament (see Jephthah's daughter who weeps over her fate in Judg 11:37-38, and Rachel weeping for the children she lost, Jer 31:15-22). Jerusalem has been an adulterous woman with many lovers; an inclination to fornication has accompanied her since her youth (see 2:2; Ezek 16:22, 43, 60; Hos 2.17). She is called upon to lament her approaching humiliation (see 4:8; 9:17-22; 14:1-10). The three mountainous areas where she is to wail over her imminent destruction are *Lebanon, Bashan,* and *Abarim,* respectively north, northeast, and southeast of Israel. Jerusalem's lovers may be either false deities (Hos 2) or allies (Ezek 23:5, 9) who promised her support. These lovers and their kings (*shepherds*), as well as the rulers of Jerusalem, shall go into exile (see 2:8; 3:15; 23:1-4).

22:24-30. Against King Jehoiachin (Coniah). The judgment against the next king, Coniah (i.e., Jehoiachin), comprises two parts. The first part is a prose speech in vv. 24-27, written by deuteronomic editors who wish to give more specific information about Coniah in vv. 28-30. Coniah was the birth name of King Jehoiachin who came to the throne most likely during the last weeks of the siege of Jerusalem in 597 B.C.E., succeeding his father Jehoiakim, who died in mysterious circumstances. Jehoiachin ruled for only three months before Nebuchadrezzar deported him to Babylon (2 Kgs 24:6-17) and replaced him with Zedekiah, his uncle and another son of Josiah. While Jehoiachin died in exile, speculation about his possible

return to the throne (cf. 28:4) and the recognition of his continuing authority by some of the people of Judah gave his successor, Zedekiah, added difficulty in ruling. The Jewish community in exile calculated their calendar by reference to Jehoiachin's captivity (e.g., Ezek 1:2), while Babylonian texts continued to call Jehoiachin "King of Judah" after his exile and even indicate he received a pension from Nebuchadrezzar. Inscriptions on jar handles from the period demonstrate that royal property belonged to Jehoiachin, not Zedekiah. Second Kings fuels this speculation by ending with the report that Jehoiachin, in the thirty-seventh year of his captivity (560 B.C.E.), was released from prison by "Evil-merodach of Babylon" (2 Kgs 25:27; "Amel-Marduk" is the Babylonian name), given a place of honor above the other exiled kings, and provided with food from the king's table and a regular allowance.

However, the deuteronomic speech, like Jeremiah's that follows, emphasizes that Jehoiachin will die in exile and will not return home. Indeed, Jeremiah predicted the exiled king would never return home. *As I live* (v. 24) introduces an oath (see notes on 4:2 and 22:5) to underscore that Yahweh will not allow Jehoiachin to return home. The reference to Jehoiachin as the *signet ring* in v. 24 is to the authority of the king as Yahweh's representative. The bearer of the signet ring was authorized to press clay seals on official documents with the king's stamp. Zerubbabel, a descendant of David, is called Yahweh's "signet ring" in Hag 2:20-23, thus stimulating messianic expectations.

The second part of this section about Coniah is Jeremiah's judgment speech (vv. 28-30) which dispels any hope that Jehoiachin will rule again in Judah. He has been taken away into exile, along with his children, and will never return. The same is true of his offspring. It is as though Jehoiachin were childless (actually, he had seven sons, 1 Chr 3:17-18). Neither he nor one of his sons shall come to the throne of David.

23:1-8. Sermons of future hope. The concluding section of the collection concerning the House of Judah and Jerusalem is written by deuteronomic editors who compose three prose speeches that address the future. The first speech (vv. 1-4) uses images of the "woe oracle" (see note on 22:13-19) to place the blame for the disasters that befell Judah and Jerusalem on the kings (*shepherds*), and then promises the future return from exile when the people will have new rulers. The language of being "fruitful and multiplying" echoes Yahweh's promises to Abraham and Jacob whose descendants would be many, inherit a land, and become a mighty nation (Gen 17:1-8, 20; 28:3; 48:4). Thus a judgment speech is followed by one of salvation.

The second speech focuses on the *righteous Branch*, a descendant of David whom Yahweh will raise up to be a just and wise king (vv. 5-6). This speech is repeated in 33:15-16. It is an example of the messianic hope that a future king would rule wisely and righteously and enable Judah and Jerusalem to prosper (cf. Isa 9:1-6; 11:1-9). The word "branch" is a messianic title in Zech 3:8, 4:12, and 6:12 that refers to Zerubbabel, a descendant of David who some thought might reestablish the Davidic monarchy during the early Persian period following the return from captivity (cf. Hag 2:20-23). The deuteronomic editors may be alluding to Zerubbabel in this speech.

The name of the future ruler is in Hebrew *yhwh sidqēnû*, meaning "the LORD (Yahweh) is our righteousness" (or "our legitimate [ruler]"). This is a wordplay on the name of Zedekiah, the last king of Judah. His name means "righteous or legitimate one (ruler) of the LORD (Yahweh)." Nebuchadrezzar gave him the regnal name Zedekiah when appointing him to reign as king in place of Jehoiachin. Zedekiah's birth name was Mattaniah (2 Kgs 24:17). Nebuchadrezzar may have chosen the regnal name to emphasize that Zedekiah, not Jehoiachin or any other pretender to the throne, was the legitimate king (cf. note on 22:24-30). While Jeremiah did not question Zedekiah's right to rule, many looked to Jehoiachin as the legitimate king. The deuteronomic editors may be suggesting that in the future the new king will convey in his name the faith of the community: "Yahweh is our righteousness or legitimate (ruler)." Thus, it is Yahweh who is the true king.

The third and final speech indicates that in the future the return from Babylonian captivity will surpass the exodus from Egypt in importance in religious confession (vv. 7-8). This speech is a promise of salvation that holds out the hope of the return from the north country. The centrality of exodus liberation in Israelite and Jewish faith is seen in its prominence in the ancient confessions found in Deut 26:5-9; Josh 24; Pss 78; 105; 106; 135; 136; and Neh 9. It is especially Second Isaiah who speaks of a "new exodus" from Babylonian captivity that will be even greater and more glorious than the liberation from Egypt (cf., e.g., Isa 43:15-21; 51:9-11).

Concerning the Prophets, 23:9-40

A collection of prophetic oracles and speeches about false prophets follows the one about kings and Jerusalem. For a narrative about a prophet of good fortune, see the one about Hananiah in chap. 28. The collection consists of three parts: a section of poetic oracles (vv. 9-22, except for vv. 16-17), a lengthy prose speech and commentary in vv. 23-32, and a commentary on the meaning of *the burden of the LORD* (vv. 33-40).

The first section divides into the following parts: the wickedness that priest and prophet share (vv. 9-12), an oracle of judgment against the false prophets of both Samaria and Jerusalem (vv. 13-15), a warning in deuteronomic prose not to listen to the false prophets (vv. 16-17), rhetorical questions and a vision report about the failure of the false prophets to see the coming judgment of Yahweh (vv. 18-20), and a rejection of false prophets (vv. 21-22). The second section is a sermon stating Yahweh's opposition to false prophets (vv. 23-32). The third section, as previously noted, presents a commentary on the meaning of the expression *the burden of the LORD* (vv. 33-40).

One of the great difficulties that confronted not just Jeremiah but also ancient Israel and early Judaism throughout their history was the problem posed by false prophets (see Ezek 13). How to distinguish between true and false prophets continued to be a perennial problem (e.g., see 1 Kgs 13; 22; Jer 28). Even the effort represented by Deut 18:15-22 to distinguish true from false prophets was not especially pragmatic and helpful: false prophets prophesied in the name of false gods, falsely represented themselves as speaking in the name of Yahweh, and foretold events that did not transpire. In chap. 23 Jeremiah presents his own tests: false prophets were immoral, speak sometimes in the name of Baal, see visions and dreams of their own mind, prophesy good fortune and not disaster, tell lies, and have not *stood in the council of the LORD* (v. 18). Yet what of false prophets who spoke in the name of Yahweh and at times even predicted disaster? What of those times when "true" prophets spoke of good fortune?

23:9-12. The wickedness of priest and prophet. The first oracle expresses judgment against priest and prophet. Verse 9 uses images of lamentation (see note on 11:18-23) to describe the state of inspiration when a prophet receives a divine revelation (see 4:19-21;

1 Sam 10:1-13; 19:23-24). Jeremiah likens it to trembling and shaking *like a drunkard*. These religious leaders will be punished.

23:13-15. Against the prophets of Samaria and Jerusalem. This oracle announces judgment against the prophets and Jerusalem. While the prophets of Samaria are indicted for deceiving the people and for prophesying in the name of Baal (see 1 Kgs 18:25-29 for a description of the activities of Baal prophets), the prophets of Jerusalem are worse, for they are adulterous liars who support the wicked. The people and country have become *like Sodom* and *Gomorrah*, two cities renowned for their evil (see Gen 18–19; Isa 1:10; and the note on Jer 5:1; also see 20:16; 50:40).

23:16-17. A warning about false prophets. This deuteronomic speech is a warning not to listen to false prophets who speak visions of their own minds and not the word of Yahweh. Especially emphasized is the content of false prophecy that promises well-being.

23:18-22. False prophets cannot see Yahweh's judgment. This oracle distinguishes between the true prophet like Jeremiah *who has stood in the council of the LORD* (vv. 18, 22) to receive the divine message and the false prophet who has not. The "council of Yahweh" is an assembly of divine beings in the royal court of heaven over which Yahweh presides (1 Kgs 22:19-23; Job 1–2; Pss 82; 89:7; Isa 6:1-8). This is the place where Yahweh issues his decrees concerning the fate of nations and people. Had false prophets truly stood in this council, they would have perceived that Yahweh's judgment was one of disaster and not salvation. The *storm of the LORD* in vv. 19-20 (repeated in 30:23-24) describes a theophany in which Yahweh comes to do battle against evil and then, following victory, sentences the wicked to destruction (see 25:32; Job 38:1; 40:6; Hab 3). Prophets ran in the sense that they were messengers of Yahweh who carried his decrees to speak to the audiences he chose.

23:23-32. Yahweh's rejection of false prophets. This prose judgment speech uses a series of rhetorical questions to indicate that the ever-present Yahweh is able to know that the false prophets have preached lies in his name. They dream their own concocted dreams, lie, and deceive. Yahweh denies he has sent them, and instead is "against them," that is, is entering into judgment against them.

23:33-40. The burden of Yahweh. The final section of this collection on false prophets focuses on the enigmatic expression, *the burden of the LORD*. Using a question and answer format (cf. 5:19; 9:12-16; 13:12-14; 15:1-4; 16:10-13; and 22:8-9), Jeremiah identifies the people, their priests, and their prophets as the *burden of the LORD*, and he indicates that they shall be punished. The commentary focuses on the word *burden* (*maśśā'*), that also means "oracle" (see Nah 1:1; Hab 1:1; Mal 1:1). When Jeremiah is asked for a *maśśā'* (i.e., "oracle") from Yahweh, he is to respond: "You are the *maśśā'* (i.e., *burden*) of the LORD." Further, the *maśśā'* ("oracle") is now simply everyone's own word, not a divine revelation. The multiplying of false oracles claiming to be from Yahweh results in corrupting the true word.

The Baskets of Figs, 24:1-10

This prophetic vision report (see 1:11-14, 15-16; Amos 7:1–9:4) has the following structure: introduction (*The LORD showed me . . .* ; v. 1), description (v. 2), dialogue (v. 3), and interpretation (vv. 4-10). The deuteronomic redactors place the narrative in the period after the first exile in 597 B.C.E. According to the deuteronomic editors, the first exiles were the *good figs* (v. 2), that is, the group chosen by Yahweh to build a new future for Judah after the return from Babylonian captivity. Jehoiachin would have been included in this group. The emphasis on Yahweh's giving them a heart to know him describes the transformation of the will and character that will occur among this group (see also 31:33-34; 32:39; Deut 29:4). The covenant language, *they shall be my people and I will be their God* (v. 7), occurs elsewhere in 7:23; 11:4; 30:22; 31:1, 33; and 32:38.

On the other hand, the *bad figs* (v. 2) were those left behind in Jerusalem following the exile, including especially Zedekiah and his officials, and those who were in Egypt. The latter would have included Jehoahaz and his entourage. Because Jeremiah had earlier spoken of Jehoiachin's dying in exile (22:24-30), it is unlikely that this narrative reflects the views of the prophet himself. The narrative would best be seen as religious propaganda used to enhance the claims of the first exiles in 597 B.C.E., including Jehoiachin and his officials, to be those who would be the true remnant around whom a new future would be built (see 28:3-4; 2 Kgs 25:27-30). This view of Yahweh especially favoring the exiles is found also in Ezra and Nehemiah in the fifth and fourth centuries B.C.E. On *return* (v. 7) see notes on 3:1–4:4. This text anticipates the new covenant passage in 31:31-34.

Judgment against the Nations, 25:1-38

25:1-14. The Babylonian captivity. This prose speech is composed by the deuteronomic editors to conclude and summarize the content of Jeremiah's speeches from the beginning of his prophetic activity (627 B.C.E., *the thirteenth year of King Josiah*, v. 3) to *the fourth year of Jehoiakim* (v. 1, which coincides with the date of the battle of CARCHEMISH, 605 B.C.E.; see chap. 36).

The sermon issues a call to repent in vv. 5-6 (see the summons to repentance in 3:1–4:4; 18:11), then quickly moves to an announcement of judgment because of Judah's and Jerusalem's lack of repentance. The refusal to listen to Jeremiah compares to the general lack of receptivity of prophets sent by Yahweh to call his people to repentance. The judgment is the coming of the *tribes of the north* (v. 9; see chaps. 4–10, the "Foe from the North"), now specifically identified as Nebuchadrezzar and the Babylonians. Nebuchadrezzar is called Yahweh's *servant* (v. 9), emphasizing that this foreign king's triumph over Judah is due to his carrying out the will of God (cf. Second Isaiah who calls Cyrus the Persian king the "anointed" of Yahweh, 45:1-7).

However, *after seventy years* (v. 12), Babylon will receive the punishment of God. Even they will become slaves to *many nations and great kings* (v. 14; cf. chaps. 50–51). This period of "seventy years" may be a rounded number for the period of time from 605 B.C.E. (the battle of Carchemish) to 539 B.C.E. (the conquest of Babylonia by the Persians). In Zech 1:12 the period of seventy years begins with the destruction of the Temple (587 B.C.E.) and concludes with its rebuilding (516/15 B.C.E.). Seventy may also suggest the normal life-span (Ps 90:10). *This book* in v. 13 may refer to the first or more likely the second scroll (see chap. 36; and introduction).

25:15-29. The cup of wrath. Serving as the original introduction to the "Oracles against the Nations" in chaps. 46–51, this prose narrative describes a symbolic action in which Jeremiah receives from Yahweh's hand the *cup . . . of wrath* (v. 15) and makes the nations listed drink and become drunk (see 13:1-11, 12-14; 18:1-12; 19:1-15). Drinking from a cup is a frequent image of punishment in the Bible (49:12; 51:7; Pss 11:6; 75:8; Isa 51:17, 22; Lam 4:21; Ezek 23:31-34; Hab 2:15-16; Rev 14:10; 16:19; 17:4; and 18:6). In the LXX, the "Oracles against the Nations" in 46–51 follow 25:13a. Judgment oracles against foreign nations are found in other prophetic texts (see Isa 13–23; Ezek 25–32; and Amos 1:3–2:3).

The nations listed in this passage roughly parallel those in chaps. 46–51. *Mixed people* (v. 20) refers to people of various cultural and ethnic identities who comprise a larger political grouping. Uz is an area in the desert east of Israel, possibly to be found in *Edom. Ashkelon, Gaza, Ekron,* and *Ashdod* are Philistine cities located on the southern Coastal Plain. *Edom, Moab,* and *Ammon* are the countries in the Transjordan, located to the east of Israel. *Coastland across the sea* (v. 22) refers to islands and coastal areas in the Mediterranean settled by the Phoenicians. *Dedan* and *Tema* are tribes in northwest Arabia. The location of *Buz* is unknown. *Elam* and *Media* are located in what is now western Iran. *Zimri*'s location is unknown. Hebrew letters are substituted in reverse alphabetical order to refer to Babylon as *Sheshach* (see 51:41). While all the nations listed are threatened by Babylonia, ultimately it too shall drink from the same cup.

25:30-38. Judgment against the nations. This poetic oracle of judgment continues the theme of the preceding section (25:15-29) by announcing that Yahweh is bringing disaster against the foreign nations. The section breaks down into two parts: an announcement of *judgment* (vv. 30-32) and a call to *shepherds* (i.e., kings and rulers) to lamentation (vv. 34-38; see 4:8; 13:18-19; and Joel 1:13-14). Verse 33 is a prose insertion that describes the cosmic devastation caused by Yahweh's judgment and the lack of funeral laments and burial for those slain (see 8:2; 9:22; 16:4).

The Trial of Jeremiah, 26:1-24

The deuteronomic narratives in chaps. 26–45 point to the actualization of the prophetic word in the life of the prophet. They show the correspondence of word and life. Jeremiah 26:1–29:32 contains three episodes in the life of Jeremiah that illustrate his conflict with the priests and the prophets (see 23:9-40). The first episode involves the trial that followed the Temple sermon (see notes on 7:1-15). The prose sermon is abbreviated in 26:1-6, with the rest of the chapter devoted to narrating Jeremiah's trial for his life.

26:1-6. The Temple sermon summarized. Chapter 7 is the first mention of Jeremiah's Temple sermon. The heading of this chapter dates the sermon and trial that follows to *the beginning* of Jehoiakim's reign (609 B.C.E.). When Josiah died in battle against the Egyptians at Megiddo in 609 B.C.E., his son Jehoahaz succeeded him to the throne. However, the reign of

Jehoahaz was short-lived (only three months), for Necho II deposed him and put Jehoiakim on the throne. Jehoahaz was exiled to Egypt (see notes on chap. 22). The *beginning of the reign* probably means the king's "accession year." One possibility for a specific setting for the sermon is Jehoiakim's coronation during the New Year's festivities in early autumn, perhaps in association with the Festival of Tabernacles, when large crowds would be in Jerusalem and coming to the Temple. The sermon is a conditional one, offering the possibility of salvation in return for repentance. Otherwise, Jerusalem will become a curse among the nations and the Temple will suffer the fate of the one at Shiloh (see notes on 7:1-15).

26:7-24. The trial of Jeremiah. Jeremiah's sermon sounded treasonous to the priests, the prophets, and all the people assembled in the Temple court. They tell him that he must die. Hearing the noise because their offices were nearby (see chap. 36), the officials of Judah came from the palace and took the seat of judgment located at the entry of the New Gate of the Temple. The location of this gate is unknown.

In vv. 12-15, Jeremiah defends himself by claiming to be a prophet, mentioning once more the possibility of salvation in return for repentance, and then warning the officials and the crowd that his execution would bring innocent blood upon the city. The officials and the people tell the priests and the prophets that Jeremiah is innocent, for he has spoken in Yahweh's name. Deuteronomy stipulated death for prophets who spoke in the name of a false god or falsely claimed to speak a word in Yahweh's name. In the latter case, the only test for authenticity was whether the prophecy came to pass (18:15-22), but it is clear that the officials and people believed Jeremiah.

Some of the elders of the land, perhaps leaders among the *people of the land* (male land owners, cf. 1:18), defend Jeremiah by referring to earlier precedents of prophets who spoke against Jerusalem. They first mention Micah's prophecy against Jerusalem (Mic 3:12) during Hezekiah's rebellion against Assyrian rule (Hezekiah, 715–687/6 B.C.E.). They indicate that Hezekiah did not bring Micah to trial to punish him. The elders then mention the story of Uriah's execution, although this may have been added to the narrative at a later time. Uriah was executed by the wicked ruler Jehoiakim for speaking similar oracles of judgment against Judah and Jerusalem. Unlike good King Hezekiah, Jehoiakim has Uriah executed. Finally, Ahikam supported Jeremiah, and he was not handed over for execution. Ahikam was an officer who served Josiah (2 Kgs 22:12, 14). His father, Shaphan, was Josiah's secretary who was involved in reporting the discovery of the law in the Temple to the king. According to the story, this law became the basis for Josiah's reforms. Ahikam also was among the entourage who consulted the prophet Huldah after the discovery of the law (2 Kgs 22). Ahikam was the father of Gedaliah, the governor of Judah after the fall of Jerusalem who was later assassinated (Jer 40–41). The association between Jeremiah and the family of Shaphan was a long and important one.

Submission to Babylon, 27:1–29:32

The second and third episodes in the life of Jeremiah that illustrate his conflict with the priests and the prophets are found in chaps. 27–29. Jeremiah's prophetic word and the actualization of that word in life in the deuteronomic narratives throughout chaps. 26–45 reach a level of heightened tension in the conflict with other religious leaders also claiming divinely given authority for their views. In chaps. 27–28, Jeremiah opposes the efforts at court to persuade King Zedekiah (597–587 B.C.E.) to rebel against the Babylonians. And in chap. 29 Jeremiah confronts by means of correspondence similar revolutionary efforts spurred on by certain religious leaders of the exiles taken to Babylonia in 597 B.C.E. Some of the Jewish exiles in Babylon, incited by nationalistic prophets, were involved in the conspiracy against Babylonia brewing at home in Jerusalem (chap. 29). The date for these confrontations between certain religious leaders and Jeremiah was probably 594/593 B.C.E. (see 28:1) when emissaries from Edom, Moab, Ammon, Tyre, and Sidon met in Jerusalem to plan revolution against the Babylonian empire. Hananiah, a prophet, predicts the breaking of the yoke of the Babylonian king and that within two years Jehoiachin, the other exiles, and the sacred vessels of the Temple, taken away by Nebuchadrezzar in 597 B.C.E., would return to Jerusalem. In the royal court, some of the conspirators looked to Egypt for help, especially with the accession of their new king, Psammetichus II (594–589 B.C.E.). Jeremiah opposed rebellion, arguing that Judah's only hope was to remain a vassal to the Babylonians. For Jeremiah, those prophets and other leaders who promised a successful rebellion were wrong and, if followed, would lead Judah down the path to destruction. Jeremiah advised the exiles in Babylon to settle down and rebuild their lives, for it would be seventy years before the restoration. Zedekiah decided not to rebel, at least on this occasion. However, under increasing pressure he eventually changed his mind and revolted, a disastrous decision that led to the destruction of Jerusalem and the major exile in 587 B.C.E.

27:1-22. The yoke of Babylon. This prose text, written by deuteronomic editors, centers on a symbolic act of Jeremiah: the fashioning and wearing of a yoke that is interpreted to mean that Judah should continue to submit to Babylonian rule (see 13:1-11; 16:1-13; 18:1-12; 19:1-15; and 24:1-10). Jeremiah preaches some three sermons: one is addressed to the envoys of foreign kings (vv. 3-11), another is directed at King Zedekiah (vv. 12-15), and the third has as its audience priests and people (vv. 16-22).

The superscription in v. 1 dates the events in chaps. 27–29 *in the beginning of the reign of Zedekiah* (597 B.C.E.), but this date does not fit the chronology of the period. While most Hebrew manuscripts read, "in the beginning of the reign of King Jehoiakim," it is likely this reading reflects a scribal error. In 28:1, the error is repeated (*the beginning of the reign of King Zedekiah*), although it is corrected in the following phrase: *in the fifth month of the fourth year.* This second date is far more likely, since the events described in chaps. 27–29 would correspond well with the fourth year of Zedekiah (594/93 B.C.E.; see 28:1).

In v. 2 Yahweh tells Jeremiah to make a *yoke of straps and bars, and put them on your neck.* This is the type of yoke that would be placed on two oxen to pull a heavy load. Normally, yokes had a crossbar with nooses made of leather, rope, or wood that would be fitted around the necks of the oxen. Attached to the crossbar would be a wooden shaft for pulling the load (see Deut 21:3; 1 Sam 6:7; 11:5; 1 Kgs 19:19). The yoke is attached to two oxen to pull a heavy load. As is the case here, yokes are at times symbolic of submission to a greater power (cf. 1 Kgs 12:1-11).

Jeremiah is then told to wear the yoke and address the envoys sent by the kings of Edom, Moab, Ammon, Tyre, and Sidon to persuade Zedekiah to join in revolution against the Babylonians. The message contains a warning that Yahweh, who controls the destiny of creation and nations, has given Nebuchadrezzar, his servant (see 25:9), rulership over their nations. The nation that refuses to serve him will face devastation. The religious leaders of the foreign nations who are attempting to persuade their rulers to revolt and promising success are prophesying lies.

The prediction in v. 7 was not fulfilled, at least literally, since the last king of the Babylonian Empire was Nabonidus (556–539 B.C.E.), the fourth king to succeed Nebuchadrezzar. Also, Nabonidus was not a descendant of Nebuchadrezzar. The reference appears to be to Nebuchadrezzar, Nabonidus, and the latter's son Belshazzar (see Dan 5.2). While Belshazzar did not become king of Babylonia, he did serve as a viceroy who filled in for his father when he was absent from Babylon.

In vv. 12-15, Jeremiah delivers to King Zedekiah almost the same warning issued to the foreign rulers through their emissaries in vv. 3-10: do not believe the prophets who are encouraging him to revolt against the Babylonians. They too are prophesying lies. Zedekiah is told to submit to the yoke of Nebuchadrezzar or face destruction. The lying prophets are the subject of the oracles in 23:9-40, and Jeremiah encounters several deceitful prophets in chaps. 28–29 (Hananiah in chap. 28, and Ahab and Zedekiah in chap. 29).

In vv. 16-22, Jeremiah warns the priests and the people not to listen to the prophets who are prophesying that the sacred vessels of the Temple, carried to Babylon in 597 B.C.E. will be returned. Jeremiah calls this prediction a lie and announces that such talk will lead to the devastation of Jerusalem. Indeed, Jeremiah predicts that the sacred objects that remained after 597 B.C.E. also will be taken away to Babylon, there to remain until Yahweh decides to return them. Among the items that Jeremiah lists as destined for eventual removal to Babylon were two bronze, free-standing *pillars* (Jachin and Boaz) at the entrance of the Temple (1 Kgs 7:15-22) and the *sea*, a very large basin standing approximately ten feet in height, made out of bronze, and located perhaps at the entrance to the Temple and before the altar (1 Kgs 7:23-26). The basin may have held approximately 12,000 gallons of liquid. According to 2 Kgs 25:13 and 16, the Babylonians broke the pillars and the basin into pieces and transported them to Babylon in 587 B.C.E. Also destined for Babylon were the *stands*, ornamented bronze wagons that formed the basis for the ten lavers or wash basins in the Temple (see 1 Kgs 7:27-39). These specific items and other Temple vessels would be taken to Babylon (see 2 Kgs 25:13-17). Jeremiah would be willing to concede his prophetic opponents are true prophets, if they are able to intercede with Yahweh to keep these sacred items of the Temple from being taken to Babylon.

28:1-17. Jeremiah's conflict with the prophet Hananiah. The oracles concerning the false prophets stirring up revolution in chap. 27 become more specific in chaps. 28–29 when Jeremiah enters into conflict with several prophets: Hananiah, Ahab, Zedekiah, and Shemaiah. In chap. 28 Jeremiah contends with *Hananiah*. The date provided in the deuteronomic narrative for this controversy poses a problem. The NRSV accurately translates the Hebrew: *at the beginning of the reign of King Zedekiah of Judah, in the fifth month of the fourth year* (v. 1). This is obviously contradictory, for the *beginning* would be 597 B.C.E., while the *fourth year* would be 594/593 B.C.E. The LXX leaves out the reference to the beginning of Zedekiah's reign and reads "in the fourth year of Zedekiah king of Judah, in the fifth month." The LXX must relate the correct date.

Hananiah, whose name means "Yahweh has been gracious," came *from Gibeon*, modern el-Jib, five and a half mi. northwest of Jerusalem. It contained a great high place where Solomon prayed for wisdom (1 Kgs 3:4-15). Hananiah was a revolutionary prophet who uttered an oracle of salvation: the yoke of Babylon has been broken and within two years Yahweh will return to Jerusalem King Jehoiachin, the exiles of 597 B.C.E., and the sacred vessels taken from the Temple. Hananiah, speaking in the name of Yahweh, announces that God has *broken the yoke of the king of Babylon* (v. 2). To counter the prophecy, Jeremiah, wearing the yoke that symbolizes submission to Babylon (see chap. 27), opposes Hananiah and his oracle of salvation. In doing so, Jeremiah refers to earlier prophets whose messages were filled with disaster, contrasting these with the good news of salvation announced by Hananiah. This is one of the criteria used by Jeremiah earlier to distinguish between true and false prophets: false prophets usually prophesied good fortune, while true ones normally announced judgment (23:17). Jeremiah then uses the criterion of fulfillment in Deut. 18:15-22—when a prediction comes true, then the prophet is proven to be a true prophet.

Hananiah performs his own symbolic act by taking Jeremiah's yoke and breaking it, proclaiming at the same time that Yahweh *will break the yoke of King Nebuchadrezzar of Babylon from the neck of all the nations within two years* (v. 11), that is, the Babylonian empire will soon fall. Jeremiah leaves, only to return to face Hananiah at a later time. In this confrontation, Jeremiah announces Yahweh has replaced the wooden yoke broken by Hananiah with an iron one, signifying that all the nations of the Babylonian empire

will be forced to wear it. Jeremiah then utters an oracle of judgment against Hananiah, predicting that within the year he will die for speaking rebellion against Yahweh. The narrative concludes with the statement that Hananiah died *in that same year* (v. 17).

29:1-32. Jeremiah's letters to the Babylonian captives. This deuteronomic prose narrative describes the third incident in the life of Jeremiah involving conflict with the priests and prophets. Prophets living among the exiles taken to Babylon in 597 B.C.E. also were predicting a quick return to Judah. Jeremiah attempted to oppose this sedition by sending a letter (vv. 1-23) to the exiles *by the hand of Elasah . . . and Gemariah* (v. 3). Elasah was *the son of Shaphan*, probably the same Shaphan who served as secretary to King Josiah (2 Kgs 22–23), and therefore the brother of Ahikam who intervened on behalf of Jeremiah during his trial following the Temple sermon (26:24). Gemariah was *the son of Hilkiah*, probably the chief priest of Josiah who was involved in the discovery of the book of the law that became the basis of the reform (see 2 Kgs 22–23). This indicates that Jeremiah was supported by two very powerful families involved in the religious reform of Josiah. In the first letter, Jeremiah states his opposition to the false hopes that deceitful prophets are raising in predicting an early return. Two prophets condemned by Jeremiah by name are *Ahab son of Kolaiah and Zedekiah son of Maaseiah* (v. 21). He prophesies they will be executed and their names will become part of a common curse. The Babylonians would have executed them for sedition, although Jeremiah says it is because they have *committed adultery* (v. 23) and prophesied lies in Yahweh's name (see 23:9-22). Jeremiah tells the exiles not to expect an early return, but rather to settle down in the land and even pray on behalf of Babylon.

This was a rather radical exhortation, seeing that it could be misconstrued as treason. Jeremiah adds that God will bring the captives home, but not for *seventy years* (vv. 10-14; see 25:11; 27:7). Indeed, Yahweh will carry out a judgment of disaster and exile against Jerusalem and the reigning king (vv. 16-20). Verses 16-20 are similar to chap. 24, the vision of figs, and do not sound very much like Jeremiah. Absent in the LXX, these verses were a later insertion in the prose tradition, seeking to favor the exiles of 597 B.C.E. over those who had remained behind.

In vv. 24-32, Jeremiah confronts by letter another false prophet, *Shemaiah of Nehelam*. Shemaiah had written a letter to the new overseer of the Temple, the priest Zephaniah (see 21:1; 37:3; 52:24-27), questioning why he had not rebuked Jeremiah and put him in stocks (cf. 20:1-6) for being a *madman who plays the prophet* and for telling the exiles to settle down, seeing that the exile will be a long one. Learning of the contents of Shemaiah's letter, Jeremiah writes the exiles telling them that Yahweh has decreed that neither Shemaiah nor his descendants would witness the future time of release.

The Book of Consolation, 30:1–31:40

The Book of Consolation is a largely self-contained collection that consists of oracles in both poetry and prose that address the future restoration of both Israel and Judah. More than likely, this collection existed as a separate unit before the addition of later oracles by Jeremiah's disciples and the deuteronomic insertions of prose speeches. The deuteronomic editors would have been responsible for inserting the collection into the growing tradition.

These chapters contain the following materials: a general introduction that specifies the nature of the collection and its recipients, Israel and Judah (30:1-4); a poetic oracle that laments the Day of Yahweh (30:5-7); a prose oracle of salvation that promises the removal of the yoke of Babylon and the restoration of the house of David (30:8-9); a poetic oracle concerning the salvation of Jacob (30:10-11); a poetic oracle of salvation describing the restoration of Jerusalem (vv. 12-17); a poetic oracle of salvation that speaks of the restoration of Jacob (i.e., Israel, 30:18-22); a poetic oracle describing a theophany (30:23-24); a prose covenant formula (31:1); a poetic oracle of salvation describing the redemption of Israel and the return to Zion (31:2-6); a poetic oracle celebrating Israel's return (31:7-9); a poetic oracle in which Israel praises Yahweh for salvation (31:10-14); a poem promising a weeping Rachel the future restoration of her children (31:15-22); a prose oracle promising the restoration of fortunes in Judah (31:23-26); a prose oracle promising the repopulation of Israel and Judah (31:27-30); a prose oracle that promises a new covenant (31:31-34); a poetic oracle comparing Israel's future with the continuing order of creation (31:35-37); and a prose oracle promising Jerusalem will be rebuilt and purified (31:38-40).

Which of these oracles may have come from the historical Jeremiah is not easy to determine. It is doubtful that any of the prose oracles were original with the prophet, although it is possible that they at times

captured and developed his thinking. In addition, it is difficult to attempt to date these oracles with any real success. The most likely oracles to have come from Jeremiah are those in 30:5-7, 12-15; 31:2-6; and 31:15-22. Two time periods would be possible for these oracles: the early date of Jeremiah's ministry (627–605 B.C.E.) and the period shortly after the fall of Jerusalem in 587 B.C.E. The second possibility is the more likely. This would have been the time between Gedaliah's appointment as governor and his assassination (40:7–41:18; 2 Kgs 25:22-26). The later oracles would come from the exilic and early postexilic periods.

The most frequent literary form in this collection is the "prophecy of salvation" that consists of the following: the appeal for attention and/or the introductory messenger formula (e.g., *Thus says the LORD* [Yahweh]), the description of the present situation, the prediction of salvation, a final characterization either of God or of the message, and the concluding messenger formula (*says the LORD* [Yahweh]).

30:1-4. General introduction. The deuteronomic editors were responsible for writing this introduction to the collection of oracles of salvation in chaps. 30–31. The oracles address at times Israel, at times Judah, and at times both.

30:5-7. The day of the Lord. The "day of the LORD" is a time of Yahweh's judgment, either against the nations or against Israel or Judah (cf. Isa 2:12-21; Amos 5:18-20; and Zeph 1:14-18). Using rhetorical questions that have obvious answers, this poetic oracle makes use of the language of lament when Jeremiah describes the rituals of lamentation that people are pursuing because of the day of Yahweh's judgment (cf. the laments in 11:18–20:18). However, the last line of v. 7 indicates that Jacob (Israel) will be rescued from the terrible day. Thus, what sounds at first like a judgment oracle referring to lamentation is transformed, at least in the editing of the oracle to fit the collection, into a prophecy of salvation.

30:8-9. The removal of the yoke of Babylon and the restoration of the Davidic monarchy. This prose oracle of salvation promises that the yoke of Babylon will be removed and that no longer will he (Nebuchadrezzar) be Yahweh's servant (see chaps. 27–28). In addition, the oracle promises the restoration of the Davidic monarchy (23:5-6; 33:14-26; Ezek 34:24; and Hos 3:5). In the collection of oracles concerning the house of David (21:11–23:8), Jeremiah was especially critical of kings. Indeed, the historical Jeremiah more than likely did not anticipate the restoration of the monarchy. But this was not the case in the deutero-nomic tradition that regarded the restoration of the institution as vital to the future (cf. 23:1-6).

30:10-11. The salvation of Israel. This poetic oracle of salvation is repeated with minor variation in 46:27-28. The language and content are patterned after Second Isaiah (see Isa 41:8-14; 43:1-5). Second Isaiah does refer to Israel (Jacob) as the servant of the LORD (cf. 49:3).

30:12-17. The restoration of Jerusalem. In this poetic oracle, the divine physician will heal an incurably wounded Zion (Jerusalem; see 15:18) and will punish her enemies who have devoured her. Zion's distress and lamentation are described in similar terms to 4:31; 8:18-21; and 9:17-19. In her distress, Zion's lovers (here probably her allies) have forsaken her. Perhaps the reference is to the Egyptians who withdrew before the Babylonian advance (37:5).

30:18-22. The restoration of Jacob. This poetic ora-cle of salvation promises Yahweh's restoration of Isra-el, the rebuilding of *the city* (Jerusalem most likely), the joyous thanksgiving of those who have returned, their increase in population, and the appearance of their own prince who *shall approach* (v. 21) Yahweh. This ruler shall be an Israelite, not a foreigner (see Deut 17:15). To "approach" Yahweh was normally a priestly prerogative (see Exod 29:4, 8; 40:12, 14; Lev 7:35). Compare Ezekiel's prince in 46:1-18. The oracle concludes with the repetition of the covenant formula (24:7; 31:1).

30:23-24. The storm of Yahweh. This poem de-scribing a theophanic storm is a repetition of 23:19-20. The earlier setting is the collection of oracles dealing with false prophets. Part of a judgment oracle, these verses in this context suggest that Yahweh will destroy the wicked as a part of the restoration of Israel and Judah in the future.

31:1. The covenant formula. This verse repeats the covenant formula found earlier in 24:7 and 30:22.

31:2-6. Yahweh's everlasting love. This poetic ora-cle of salvation grounds Israel's future redemption in the everlasting love of Yahweh. According to the prose introduction and images in the poem itself, the prophet addresses the Northern Kingdom (*Israel, mountains of Samaria*, and *hill country of Ephraim*). Jeremiah draws on the wilderness tradition once more (2:2-3; Hos 2), this time to indicate that the redemption of Israel ex-perienced in the wilderness following liberation from Egyptian slavery (*found grace in the wilderness*, v. 2) will be experienced in the future because of the ever-lasting love and faithfulness of Yahweh. In Hosea and Jeremiah, the wilderness was a period of intimacy between Yahweh and Israel. However, both also spoke of the entrance into Canaan as a line of demarcation between Israel's faithfulness and unfaithfulness. In the present context, Jeremiah assures Israel that God's everlasting love has not diminished, but rather is the basis for her future redemption and rebuilding. One day both Israel and Judah will be reunited and will worship Yahweh in Zion (Jerusalem).

31:7-9. Joy over Israel's return. In this oracle of salvation, the call is extended to sing in joyous celebra-tion on Jacob's (Israel's) behalf, asking God to redeem the remnant of Israel. Then Yahweh announces his intention to redeem Israelites from all the countries to which they have gone. The redeemed will include even the blind and the lame, those with child, and those in labor. In v. 9 Yahweh is called *father*, a common metaphor to depict God in the OT (see especially Hos 11:1; Jer 3:19; 31:20). The *firstborn* son was privi-leged in Israelite society, receiving a double share of the father's estate, the paternal blessing, and the posi-tion of familial authority after his demise. Here Israel is Yahweh's *firstborn*, an expression of election (cf. Exod 4:22).

31:10-14. The joy of returning exiles. This poetic oracle of salvation speaks of Yahweh's future redemp-tion of Israel and the exiles coming to Zion to praise him for the gifts of bountiful crops and productive herds. The lamentation of despair in a time of judg-ment and destitution will turn into an unending period of joyous praise and unlimited bounty. In this oracle, Yahweh is presented as the savior who, like the next of kin, "redeems" (v. 11) Israel from the powerful oppressor (see the redeemer and law of redemption in Lev 25:25; also see Yahweh as redeemer in Exod 15:13).

31:15-22: Rachel's weeping for her children. This poem of five strophes is replete with feminine imagery: Rachel cries for her children (v. 15), Yahweh consoles her (vv. 16-17), Ephraim (Israel) confesses (vv. 18-19), Yahweh has a mother's compassion on Ephraim (v. 20), and Jeremiah exhorts virgin Israel to return (vv. 21-22).

In biblical narratives about Israel's ancestors (cf. Gen 25–35), Rachel was the more favored wife of Jacob (Israel) and the mother of Joseph and Benjamin. Joseph had two sons, Ephraim and Manasseh. Ephraim is the name for the large tribe in the North that be-came synonymous with Israel. Along with her sister

Leah and their handmaidens, Rachel is one of the matriarchs of the nation. According to 1 Sam 10:2, Rachel was buried in the tribal territory of Benjamin, thus to the north of Jerusalem. This poem suggests the specific burial place was Ramah, approximately five mi. north of Jerusalem (modern er-Ram) and a staging area for the deportation of exiles to Babylon (40:1, 4). For an alternative location for Rachel's burial place, see Gen 35:16-20; 48:7; and Matt 2:18. In v. 15 of the poem, the dead Rachel is heard weeping over her dead and exiled children.

The verb in the last line of the poem is subject to many translations and interpretations: "a woman protects a man," "the woman woos the man," "the woman sets out to find her husband again," "the woman must encompass the man with devotion," "a woman is turned into a man," "a woman (Israel?) embraces the man (Yahweh?)," "a woman is pregnant with a male." Two meanings seem likely. One, Virgin Israel is the woman who is pregnant and will bear a son (a posterity). This is in contrast with Rachel whose children are dead or exiled. Two, the man, Ephraim, is "embraced" by the women who are mentioned in the poem (Rachel, the nurturing Yahweh, and Virgin Israel). Phyllis Trible argues for the latter meaning on the basis of the rhetorical structure of the poem: the male Ephraim is surrounded by women or feminine images of the larger poem that support and sustain him. She offers the translation: "female surrounds man."

31:23-26. Judah's restoration. This prose oracle of salvation points to the restoration of worship in the Temple in Jerusalem and the resettlement of the land of Judah and its towns. People again will utter a blessing for Zion. In v. 26, Jeremiah awakens from his dream of the future restoration.

31:27-30. The repopulation of Israel and Judah. In the future time, Yahweh will rebuild the nation (cf. the language of 1:10). In this time of new beginning, no longer will people suffer for the sins of their parents, but rather will receive punishment for their own misdeeds. This doctrine of individual responsibility, probably influenced by the prophet Ezekiel (see esp. chap. 18), replaces the teaching of corporate guilt where later generations inherit the punishment for the crimes and sins of their ancestors (cf. Exod 20:5-6). The land of Israel and Judah will be repopulated with people and herds (Ezek 36:9-11).

31:31-34. The new covenant. This prose oracle of salvation promises a new covenant for the restored community that will not be breached by a sinful peo-ple. The old covenant established at Sinai had been violated, but the new covenant will continue because the law will be written on the human heart, and not just on tablets of stone. This metaphor indicates that the character of the people will be transformed by their embodiment of the teachings of the law. They will no longer need a teacher to tell them the content of the law, but rather they will know instinctively the will of God. Further, in this new age, Yahweh will not only forgive their sins but also will forget them. The fact that the teaching of the law will no longer be required is a remarkable assertion for Deuteronomic teachers to affirm.

The language in v. 33, *I will make,* reads literally "I will cut." "Cutting a covenant" reflects the ritual practice of sacrificing animals, cutting the larger carcasses in half, and then walking between the slaughtered animals (34:18; Gen 15:7-21). In the Genesis passage, Yahweh's presence is represented by taking a smoking fire pot and a flaming torch and walking between the sacrifices.

31:35-37. Israel's unlimited future. This is a poetic oracle of salvation that praises God as the creator who orders and sustains the cosmos (cf. Pss 19, 33, and 104). Jeremiah compares the power of God to create and sustain the cosmos with his ability to recreate and then sustain a new Israel. As the cosmos will continue into perpetuity, so then will Israel. This combination of creation and redemption theology is developed especially by Second Isaiah (see Isa 40:12, 26; 42:5; 44:24; 45:7, 18; 54:10).

31:38-40. The rebuilding and purification of Jerusalem. This prose oracle promises the rebuilding of Jerusalem, the expansion of its precincts, and the purification of the areas that have been desecrated by death (see Zech 14:10-11). The passage mentions several boundaries of Jerusalem: *the tower of Hananel* located in the northeast (Neh 3:1), *the Corner Gate* found in the northwest (2 Kgs 14:13), the southern boundary of Hinnom (7:31-32), the eastern boundary of Kidron (2 Kgs 23:4, 6), and the *Horse Gate* situated in the southeast corner (Neh 3:28). *Gareb* and *Goah* are unknown. The valley of the dead most likely alludes to the valley of Hinnom, the location of child sacrifice (see 7:31-32; 19:2, 6; 32:35; 2 Kgs 23:10).

The Field of Anathoth, 32:1-44

Once more Jeremiah is told to engage in a symbolic action that will enhance his prophetic message (see notes on 13:1-11). And as is true for all the prose narratives in chaps. 26–45, there is a correspondence of the life and word of the prophet. The structure of the narrative divides into four parts: Jeremiah's arrest (32:1-5), the purchase of the field at Anathoth (32:6-15), the prayer of Jeremiah (32:16-25), and Yahweh's response (32:26-44). This narrative continues the theme of future restoration in chaps. 30–31.

32:1-5. Jeremiah's imprisonment. This deuteronomic prose narrative is placed in the context of Nebuchadrezzar's siege of Jerusalem, in the tenth year of the reign of King Zedekiah (588 B.C.E.). Jeremiah had been imprisoned in the court of the guard in the royal palace. When the prophet had attempted to go to Anathoth during a temporary lifting of the siege of the city, he was accused of deserting to the enemy and placed under arrest (see 37:11-21). Zedekiah accused Jeremiah of giving aid and comfort to the enemy by prophesying that Yahweh was giving the city of Jerusalem into the hands of the Babylonians and that the king would be taken captive. For another accusation of prophetic treason, see Amos 7:10-17.

32:6-15. The purchase of the field at Anathoth. Yahweh tells Jeremiah that his cousin would come to the court of the guard and ask him to purchase his field at Anathoth. The *right of redemption* (v. 7) refers to the responsibility that the next of kin had to "redeem" the property of an impoverished relative in order to keep it within the family (see Lev 25:25-28). The purchase price of seventeen shekels of silver (about seven oz.) refers to weight, not coins. Coins were probably not used until the Persian period (beginning in 539 B.C.E.). The original deed of purchase was rolled up and sealed, while the open copy remained unsealed for easy reference. Baruch, Jeremiah's secretary and companion (see chaps. 36 and 45), was given the deed and witnesses signed it. Both copies of the deed were then placed in a jar for preservation. Then Jeremiah prophesied that in the future restoration, property (houses, fields, and vineyards) would once again be bought. This purchase of a field, occurring at the time of siege, emphasizes the prophet's faith in Yahweh's promise of a future restoration.

32:16-25. A prayer of Jeremiah. Jeremiah then offers a prayer of confession that begins by praising Yahweh for being the creator who directs history. Yahweh's great deeds of salvation, the exodus from Egypt and the gift of the land of Canaan, are also the basis for praise. These acts of salvation are contrasted with Israel's disobedience to the law. The prayer explains that disobedience is the reason for the siege and the

imminent fall of Jerusalem to the Babylonians. For a similar prayer of confession and intercession on behalf of a sinful people, see Neh 9:6-37. For hymns that recount great acts of salvation see Pss 78, 105, 106, 135, and 136.

32:26-44. Yahweh's response. Yahweh responds to Jeremiah's prayer by outlining the sins of the people as the basis for the fall of Jerusalem. Israel's history has been one of disobedience (see Ezek 20:1-32). Yet, Yahweh also promises that the exiles will return home and the covenant will be renewed (see 31:31-34). Once again fields will be bought in the land, a future reality that is underscored by Jeremiah's purchase of the field in Anathoth.

Promises Concerning the Future Restoration, 33:1-26

Continuing the theme of salvation in chaps. 30–32, this chapter consists of several prose speeches that address future restoration.

33:1-9. Judah and Israel will be rebuilt. Still under arrest in the court of the guard (see 32:1-3), Jeremiah prophesies that the Babylonians will succeed in taking the city of Jerusalem and cause great slaughter. However, the speech then turns to salvation: Judah and Israel will be rebuilt as before, the sins of the people will be forgiven, and the name of Jerusalem will be synonymous with joy and praise.

33:10-13. Promises of salvation. The first prose speech (vv. 10-11) announces the return of joyous song and thanksgiving in the future restoration (contrast 7:34). Thank offerings and thanksgiving psalms were delivered by individuals and communities who were the recipients of divine salvation (see Lev 7:11-18; Ps 107). Verse 11b is taken from Ps 136:1, an antiphonal thanksgiving psalm that praises God for creation and great deeds of salvation on Israel's behalf, including the exodus from Egypt, the defeat of Pharaoh and his army at the Red Sea, guidance through the Sinai wilderness, victory over the kings of Canaan, and the gift of the land of Israel.

The second prose speech (vv. 12-13) promises that the desolate land will once again have pastures, flocks, and shepherds.

33:14-26. Davidic rulers and levitical priests. This prose sermon, absent in the LXX, expands upon the one in 23:5-6. Jeremiah promises the restoration of two institutions: the Davidic monarchy and the Levitical priesthood. Yahweh will raise up a *righteous Branch* who will *execute justice and righteousness* (v. 15; cf.

21:11–23:8; Hag 1:1; 2:23; Zech 4:11-14; 6:9-13). While this sermon may be speaking of an individual who will one day come to the throne, the promise is that the dynasty of David will continue. The covenant of David in 2 Sam 7 that contains Yahweh's promise of a perpetual dynasty is as sure as the divine covenant with day and night that sustains the temporal order of creation (cf. Gen 8:22). The divine covenant with the Levitical priesthood also insures that they will continue to serve, and their role will include the priestly prerogative of offering sacrifices (see the roles given to the Levitical priesthood in Deut 18:1-8). The offspring of the two families that appear to be rejected by Yahweh, Jacob (Israel) and David, are promised divine mercy and the restoration of their fortunes. This promise is as good as God's covenant with creation.

Judgment against Jerusalem and the Broken Covenant, 34:1–35:19

34:1-7. Warning to Zedekiah. This prose sermon, placed in the context of the Babylonian siege of Jerusalem (588 B.C.E.), announces to King Zedekiah that Jerusalem will fall to the Babylonians and he will be taken captive. However, the king is promised that he will die a peaceful death and have a proper funeral (contrast Jehoiakim in 22:18-19). According to other texts, Zedekiah was blinded and exiled to Babylon where he died in prison (39:7; 52:8-11; 2 Kgs 25:5-7). The ritual of burning spices was part of a royal funeral (2 Chr 16:14; 21:19). Verse 7 mentions that at the time of this speech only two fortified cities in addition to Jerusalem had not yet been conquered: LACHISH and Azekah. Lachish is modern Tell ed-Duweir, located thirty mi. southwest of Jerusalem, while Azekah is modern Tell ez-Zahariyeh, situated to the northeast of Lachish. The fourth letter of the Lachish ostraca, composed just before the fall of Jerusalem, mentions that Hoshaiah, an official in an outpost to the north of Lachish, writes Yaosh, the military commander of Lachish: "We are looking for the signals of Lachish, according to all the indications my Lord has given, because we do not see Azekah."

34:8-22. The release of slaves and the broken covenant. This prose narrative relates an incident during the siege of Jerusalem (588 B.C.E.). In the effort to obtain Yahweh's help against the Babylonians, King Zedekiah enters into covenant with the people of Jerusalem to release their Hebrew slaves. This action would bring them into accord with the requirements of Deut 15 that Hebrew slaves are to be set free in the seventh year, unless the slave does not want to leave. In that case, the slave will be a slave for life. In sending forth the released slave, Deut 15 specifies that released slaves should be given provisions for their sustenance by their former owners. The theological basis for this release is the exodus: Israelites are to remember that they once were slaves in Egypt and Yahweh redeemed them.

However, the people of Jerusalem broke their covenant and took back their slaves when Nebuchadrezzar lifted the siege in order to meet an advancing Egyptian army (37:6-15). Jeremiah then utters a prose speech that refers to Deut 15 and condemns the people for taking back their slaves. Yahweh is going to grant a release to the citizens of Jerusalem (v. 17), a release to destruction. They will be like the calf cut in two in the covenant ceremony (see Gen 15:7-21; Jer 31:33).

35:1-19. The faithfulness of the Rechabites. According to v. 1, this narrative describes an event in the life of Jeremiah that occurred sometime during the reign of King Jehoiakim (609–598 B.C.E.). The location of this narrative in the Book of Jeremiah serves to contrast the faithfulness of the Rechabites with the faithlessness of the people of Jerusalem who broke their covenant and took back their released slaves (34:8-22). The Rechabites were a religious sect founded by Jonadab, the son of Rechab, during the reign of Jehu (842–815 B.C.E.). Jonadab supported Jehu in the slaughter accompanying the revolt against the dynasty of Omri (2 Kgs 10:15-28). This sect was distinguished by the following practices: abstaining from wine, living as nomads in tents, and refusing to settle down to farm the land. They believed that the practice of Yahweh religion was better suited to a nomadic life. Indeed, they considered agricultural life, including the drinking of wine produced from vineyards, to be a corrupting influence in the direction of Canaanite fertility religion. The Rechabites had come to Jerusalem to seek refuge from the Babylonian army.

Jeremiah uses the Rechabites as an example of faithfulness to religious beliefs. In contrast to their devotion to religious principles, the people of Jerusalem and Judah have been disobedient to Yahweh. While disaster will overtake them, Jeremiah promises that Jonadab will continue to have descendants *to stand before* (v. 19) Yahweh. "To stand before Yahweh" is an expression that refers to priestly service. While the Rechabites were not priests, their religious zeal is likened to divine service.

The Scrolls of Baruch, 36:1-32

This narrative provides important insight into the lcomposition of the Book of Jeremiah, at least as seen through the eyes of the deuteronomic editors. The story begins in the *fourth year of King Jehoiakim* (605 B.C.E.), the very same year that Nebuchadrezzar defeated the Egyptians at CARCHEMISH (see introduction). In essence, the narrative tells about the origins of two scrolls written down by Baruch at the dictation of Jeremiah.

36:1-3. Jeremiah commanded to write down his oracles. The contents of the first scroll consisted of the prophecies of Jeremiah from the time of his call (627 B.C.E.) to the fourth year of Jehoiakim's reign (605 B.C.E.). The description of these prophecies suggests they were largely oracles of judgment. Jeremiah's scribe and companion, Baruch son of Neriah, appeared to be a royal scribe with powerful political connections (36:32; see chaps. 32 and 45). He was a member of an important Judahite family. Seraiah, his brother, was a minister to King Zedekiah (51:59). Archaeological excavations in the City of David have yielded scribal seals belonging to these two brothers. Baruch's seal reads: "to/from Baruch // son of Neriah // the scribe."

36:4-10. Baruch's reading of the scroll in the Temple. Jeremiah had been barred from the Temple precinct, perhaps because of the Temple sermon (see chaps. 7 and 26). Following the writing of the first scroll, Baruch read it aloud *in the chamber of Gemariah* (v. 10), the son of Shaphan, in the fifth year of Jehoiakim's reign (604 B.C.E.). The chamber was located in the New Gate entrance into the Temple, thus allowing the people who had assembled in the sacred precincts during a fast day to hear him. Public fasts were observed during times of national difficulty or threat (see 2 Chr 20:3; Ezra 8:21-23; Neh 1:4-11). The threat more than likely was posed by Nebuchadrezzar's army advancing into the Philistine plain and conquering Ashkelon in 604 B.C.E. Shortly thereafter, Jehoiakim decided to shift his allegiance from Egypt to Nebuchadrezzar. A fast would have been a most auspicious occasion for the people to hear Jeremiah's oracles of judgment, especially those dealing with the "Foe from the North." Jeremiah's scroll is to be read in the hope that the people of Judah will repent, be forgiven, and avoid the judgment that Yahweh is planning to bring against them (see 3:1–4:4).

36:11-19. Baruch reads the scroll before the royal officials. When Gemariah's son hears the contents of the scroll, he informs the royal officials sitting in the secretary's chamber in the palace. Baruch was then summoned to the secretary's chamber and directed to read it again.

36:20-26. Jehoiakim burns the scroll. After the officials warned Baruch to go into hiding along with Jeremiah, the king's secretary, Elishama, reported the words of the scroll to King Jehoiakim. When the scroll is brought and read to the king, he responded by cutting the scroll into strips and placing them in the fire burning in the brazier. The king then ordered Baruch's and Jeremiah's arrest, but they were in hiding. This response to Jeremiah's prophecy is in sharp contrast to Josiah's when he hears the Book of the Law read. Josiah lamented, inquired of Huldah the prophet to obtain a word from Yahweh, declared a day of covenant making, swore along with the people to follow the law, and began a major religious reformation (2 Kgs 22–23).

36:27-32. Baruch writes a second scroll. Yahweh later tells Jeremiah to dictate his prophecies to Baruch once again. The contents of the second scroll included those of the first, but the narrative notes at the end that *many similar words were added to them* (v. 32). This allows for the addition of other oracles from Jeremiah as well as from later disciples and redactors. Jeremiah also utters a judgment oracle against Jehoiakim, saying he would have neither a successor to sit on David's throne nor a burial. Rather his dead body would be exposed to the elements (cf. 22:13-19).

As noted in the introduction, these two scrolls are difficult to reconstruct. However, the first scroll probably included at least the call (1:4-10), some of the poetic oracles of judgment, especially those concerning the "Foe from the North" (see chaps. 4–10), and possibly the laments (see 11:18–20:18). The second scroll and the additional words added to it probably refer to the larger book, or at least much of its contents.

Jeremiah's Encounters with Zedekiah, 37:1–38:28

Chapters 37–45 set forth the "passion history" of Jeremiah. Composed by the Deuteronomic editors, this largely continuous story points to the relationship between the prophetic word and the life of the prophet. The prophet's life participates in the suffering occasioned by the word of judgment.

These deuteronomic prose narratives in chaps. 37–38 describe Jeremiah's encounters with King Zedekiah in 588 B.C.E., shortly before the fall of Jerusalem to the Babylonians (cf. 34:1-7). Once more the narrative reflects the confluence of prophetic word and life.

37:1-10. The Egyptian advance and Nebuchadrezzar's lifting of the siege. In order to meet the threat of an advancing Egyptian army, Nebuchadrezzar lifted the siege against Jerusalem (see 34:21). The Egyptian king was Hophra (589–570 B.C.E.) who only a short time before had ascended to the throne (see 44:30). Zedekiah's rebellion against the Babylonians was based in part on his anticipation of Egyptian support (cf. Ezek 17:15) and the hope that other states in Canaan would join in the rebellion (cf. chap. 27). How many states in Canaan actually did rebel is unclear, although apparently not very many. It is the case that Tyre and Ammon revolted along with Judah, but it is doubtful that other states joined in revolt. Edom eventually sided with the Babylonians. The Egyptian army was quickly repelled, and the siege was resumed.

During this interlude, Zedekiah sends his envoys to ask Jeremiah to make intercession for the city to save it from destruction (see 21:1-10). Jeremiah responds that the Babylonians will return and destroy Jerusalem.

37:11-15. Jeremiah arrested for desertion. While the siege was lifted, Jeremiah attempts to leave Jerusalem to go to Benjamin to receive his "portion," that is, his share of his family's property. This is probably not directly connected to the prophet's redemption of his cousin's field in chap. 32. In any event, Jeremiah is arrested and accused of deserting to the Babylonians. He is beaten and put in prison.

37:16-21. Zedekiah's secret audience with Jeremiah. Once again Zedekiah attempts to receive a favorable word of Yahweh from the prophet. Jeremiah tells him that he shall be delivered into the hand of the king of Babylon. Yet the prophet does plead successfully with the king to be transferred from the prison located in the house of Jonathan the secretary to the court of the guard. There the king provides him a ration of bread until the bread is gone as the siege intensifies.

38:1-13. Jeremiah imprisoned in a cistern. Jeremiah's prophecy that those who surrender will save their lives is considered treason by his enemies, including those officials who were pro-Egyptian and supportive of the rebellion. These officials, conspiring to kill Jeremiah, cast him into a muddy, but waterless cistern. The charge of treason against Jeremiah is similar to a charge in letter six of the Lachish letters against some officials in Jerusalem (see note on 34:7).

Ebed-melech the Ethiopian (v. 7), who was either a eunuch or palace official (*sārîs*), intercedes for Jere-

miah with King Zedekiah. The king directs him to remove Jeremiah from the cistern. Later, Jeremiah promises Ebed-melech that he would survive the destruction of Jerusalem (39:15-18).

38:14-28. Zedekiah's last consultation with Jeremiah. Zedekiah meets for the last time with Jeremiah in a private conference held at *the third entrance* of the Temple. Jeremiah warns the king to surrender in order to save the city and himself. If not, the city will be burned and Zedekiah will not escape with his life. Zedekiah's fear of the officials at court is clear.

The Fall of Jerusalem, 39:1–40:6

39:1-10. The fall of the city. These verses are a more succinct version of 52:4-16 (see 2 Kgs 25:1-12). The dates for the beginning of the siege and the fall of the city are given in reference to the regnal years of King Zedekiah. The siege commenced in late 589 or early 588 B.C.E. with the city falling in 587 B.C.E. When the city is taken, the Babylonian officials meet in the middle gate. Their names and titles are Nergal-sharezer the Simmagir, Nebushazban the chief court official, and Nergal-sharezer the Rab-mag. Simmagir and Rab-mag are titles of Babylonian offices. Nergal-sharezer the Rabmag (see v. 13) was Nergalsharusur (Neriglissar). He was Nebuchadrezzar's son-in-law who became king of Babylon in 560 B.C.E. and ruled until 556 B.C.E.

Zedekiah attempts to escape the city, but is captured and brought to Nebuchadrezzar at Riblah in Hamath. Riblah was a fortified city in the Beqaa Valley in Lebanon that guarded the highway between Egypt and Mesopotamia. Nebuchadrezzar orders Zedekiah to witness the execution of his sons, blinds the Judahite king, and sends him to Babylon in chains (cf. 52:8-11; 2 Kgs 25:5-7). According to 52:11, Zedekiah died in a Babylonian prison. The city is burned, its walls are broken down, and its inhabitants are exiled.

39:11-14. Nebuchadrezzar's protection of Jeremiah. See 40:1-6. Nebuchadrezzar orders the captain of his guard to treat Jeremiah well and to allow him to determine his own future. This good treatment of Jeremiah was probably due to the prophet's opposition to the rebellion and to his insistence that the officials and people surrender to the Babylonians, once the rebellion had begun.

39:15-18. The salvation of Ebed-melech. Prior to Jerusalem's fall, Jeremiah promises Ebed-melech, the Ethiopian who had saved him from the cistern (38:7-13), that his life will be spared, because he trusted in

Yahweh. The people Ebed-melech fears are probably not the Babylonians, but rather the officials who sought Jeremiah's life and had him thrown into the cistern (38:1-6).

40:1-6. Jeremiah chooses to remain with Gedaliah at Mizpah. This is a somewhat different version of Jeremiah's good treatment at the hands of the Babylonians than the one in 39:11-14. In this version, Jeremiah had been taken with the other exiles to Ramah, a staging area for transporting the captives to Babylon. It is interesting to note that Nebuzaradan, the captain of the guard and a Babylonian, speaks an oracle of Yahweh to Jeremiah, explaining that Yahweh made an end of the city because of its evil. The Babylonian official allows Jeremiah to choose his own future. Jeremiah chose to remain behind and to dwell at Mizpah with the newly appointed governor, Gedaliah.

The Governorship of Gedaliah, 40:7–41:18

This section compares to 2 Kgs 25:22-26. Following the Babylonian conquest of 587 B.C.E., the Davidic monarchy and the royal state of Judah came to an end. Judah was incorporated into the provincial system of the Babylonian empire. The devastation of the country, the destruction of the former capital along with the Temple, and the execution or deportation of many of the leaders and officials left those who remained in the Babylonian colony enormous challenges to rebuild the future. Nebuchadrezzar appointed Gedaliah, a member of the prominent family of Shaphan (cf. 26:24 and 2 Kgs 22–23), to be governor. He set up his provincial government in Mizpah, perhaps modern Tell en-Nasbeh, located on the border between Benjamin and Judah and some eight mi. north of Jerusalem. He attempted to convince those who remained behind to rebuild their lives and to submit to Babylonian rule. How long Gedaliah was governor is not known, although he was assassinated by rebels, an action that may have led to a third exile in 582 B.C.E. (52:30). Ishmael, a member of the house of David who conspired with Baalis, king of the Ammonites, to resist Babylonian rule, and his small group of rebels assassinated Gedaliah, killed his Jewish supporters at Mizpah, and wiped out the Babylonian garrison located there. The survivors of Mizpah, including Jeremiah, were taken captive with the intent of going to Ammon. Intercepted by Johanan, a Judahite military commander and ally of Gedaliah, Ishmael escaped with a small band of eight men to Ammon. Fearing Babylonian reprisal for Ishmael's deeds, Johanan and his forces decided to seek refuge in Egypt, taking an unwilling Jeremiah with them.

40:7-12. Gedaliah as governor. Gedaliah's rule as governor was short-lived. He exhorted the survivors of the Babylonian destruction who remained in Judah to settle down, rebuild the country, and serve the Babylonians.

40:13-41:3. Gedaliah's assassination. Although warned by Johanan of the assassination plot of Baalis, king of the Ammonites, and Ishmael, Gedaliah refused to believe the report. Ishmael carries out the plot, murdering Gedaliah, his Jewish supporters at Mizpah, and the Babylonian soldiers stationed there.

41:4-10. Ishmael's slaughter of pilgrims. On the day after the slaughter, a group of pilgrims arrive at Mizpah on their way to participate in a fast at the Temple in Jerusalem. Ishmael and his cohorts slaughter all but ten of them and cast their corpses into a cistern. He then takes the survivors of the slaughter at Mizpah, including Jeremiah (cf. 42:2), with him on his journey towards Ammon.

41:11-18. Johanan's victory over Ishmael. The military commander, Johanan, intercepts Ishmael and his party at the *great pool . . . in Gibeon* (v. 12; cf. 2 Sam 2:13). While the captives are freed, Ishmael makes good his escape to Ammon. Johanan and his party, fearing the Babylonians response to the slaughter at Mizpah, decide to go to Egypt. They stop at Geruth Chimham (an inn?) near Bethlehem.

The Flight to Egypt, 42:1–43:7

This prose account narrates the details of the decision of Johanan's party to flee to Egypt, in spite of Jeremiah's opposition to the plan. The prophet and Baruch are forced to accompany them to Egypt.

42:1-6. Jeremiah asked to intercede with Yahweh. Unsure of their future, Johanan's group asks Jeremiah to intercede with Yahweh in their behalf and to obtain a divine word to tell them what they should do. Jeremiah agrees, but warns them he will speak forthrightly what Yahweh tells him. The people swear that they will follow the divine directive.

42:7-22. Yahweh's reply. After ten days, Jeremiah receives Yahweh's instructions. The prophet delivers a prose sermon that takes the form of a promise coupled with a warning. They should remain in the land and thereby receive God's blessings, including protection from the king of Babylon. However, should they disobey by going to Egypt, they will suffer many disasters and die in Egypt, without a survivor.

43:1-7. The flight to Egypt. The people deny that Jeremiah has spoken the word of Yahweh, thus categorizing him as a deceitful prophet (cf. 23:9-40; Deut 18:15-22), and contend that he has taken the advice of Baruch whom they charge with plotting to turn them over to the Babylonians. The group decides to reject Jeremiah's word and to flee to Egypt, taking Jeremiah and Baruch with them. They arrive in Tahpanhes in Egypt (see note on 2:16).

Jeremiah in Egypt, 43:8–44:30

This narrative contains Jeremiah's two prose sermons of Jeremiah: the first is an announcement of judgment against Egypt (43:8-13) and the second is directed against the Jewish refugees in Egypt (44:1-30). This negative indictment of the Jewish community in Egypt demonstrates that the deuteronomic editors considered them to be apostate Jews who had no claim to being the people of Yahweh.

43:8-13. Egypt is no safe haven from Nebuchadrez-zar. Jeremiah is instructed by Yahweh to engage in a symbolic act (see 13:1-11; 16:1-13; 18:1-12; 19:1-15; 27:1-22; and 32:1-44) and then to deliver an accompanying oracle that indicate Nebuchadrezzar will invade Egypt and cause great devastation, including the taking of Tahpanhes. Jeremiah indicates that even Egypt is not a safe haven for Jewish refugees. Nebuchadrezzar (Yahweh's "servant," cf. 25:9, 27:6) did invade Egypt during the reign of Amasis in 568/67 B.C.E. (cf. 46:13-26). Verse 11 generally repeats 15:2. Jeremiah notes that in this invasion the temples of Egypt will be burned and the Egyptian gods will be carried away. Among the cities and temples that will be devastated, Jeremiah mentions in particular Heliopolis (modern Tell Hisn and Matariyeh) which was the center for the worship of Re, the Egyptian sun god, and noted for its obelisks (four-sided, granite pillars with pyramidal tops).

44:1-14. Condemnation of the Jews in Egypt. Jeremiah's second prose sermon begins with a reminder of Yahweh's devastation of Jerusalem and Judah because of their *wickedness* (v. 3), in particular their serving other gods and refusing to repent. Then the prophet condemns the Jewish refugees, including those who desire to come to Egypt and those already residing there, for abandoning their homeland in Judah and for pagan worship. In addition to the one in Tahpanhes (2:16; 43:7), other Jewish settlements in Egypt include

Migdol, Memphis, and the land of Pathros. Migdol may be modern Tell el-Heir, located in northern Egypt (46:14). Memphis was a former capital of Egypt located on the west bank of the Nile River, some fifteen mi. south of Cairo. The land of Pathros is Upper Egypt. They also will experience devastation at Yahweh's hand, and most will not survive or return home to Judah.

44:15-19. The stubborn refusal to listen. The Jewish refugees refuse to listen to Jeremiah, announcing that they will continue their pagan worship of the queen of heaven (see note on 7:18). They argue that when their ancestors in Judah and Jerusalem worshiped her they prospered. The refugees contend that their cessation of worshiping her led to their hardships.

44:20-30. The continuation of Jeremiah's condemnation of the Jews in Egypt. Jeremiah continues his sermon of judgment, indicating that Yahweh will destroy most of the Jewish refugees with only a few to escape to return to Judah. The sign that this judgment will come to pass is Yahweh's deliverance of Pharaoh Hophra (Aphries) *into the hands of his enemies* (v. 30; cf. 37:5). Hophra (589–570 B.C.E.) was assassinated by Amasis (570–526 B.C.E.), a court official who had ruled as co-regent for three years.

Oracle of Salvation concerning Baruch, 45:1-5

Jeremiah addresses a prose sermon of salvation to his secretary and companion, Baruch (see notes on chaps. 32 and 36). The sermon is situated in 605 B.C.E. when Jeremiah dictated the first scroll to him (see notes on chap. 36). Baruch offered up his own lament to which Yahweh responds through the prophet (cf. the laments in 11:18–20:18). Baruch is promised that in the coming period of destruction his life will be spared. It is not clear what *great things* (v. 5) Baruch desired for himself. He did have important political contacts in the government, perhaps indicating he was an important official himself. For the language of *break down what I have built, and pluck up what I have planted* (v. 4), see 1:10; 18:7-9; 24:6.

Oracles against the Foreign Nations, 46:1–51:64

46:1. Superscription. The last major collection of oracles in Jeremiah is the collection of "Oracles against the Foreign Nations," so named because of the superscription in 46:1 (cf. Isa 13–23 and Ezek 25–32). The LXX places this collection after 25:13a, a more likely original position. Why the oracles were relocated to this part of the book and when this occurred are not known. The authorship of this collection and its individual oracles, most of which are poetic, is a matter of debate, although certain oracles may have come from the historical Jeremiah (e.g., the oracle against Egypt in 46:2-12). However, it is likely that most of these oracles were added by later prophets and editors.

46:2-26. Against Egypt. Two oracles of judgment are uttered against Egypt. The first concerns the Egyptian defeat at CARCHEMISH (vv. 2-12), and the second signals the approach of Nebuchadrezzar (vv. 13-26). The prose superscription, inserted by a later editor, dates the first oracle of judgment to the fourth year of King Jehoiakim's reign, that is, 605 B.C.E. when Nebuchadrezzar defeated Necho II and the Egyptians at the battle of Carchemish. The vivid language describing the battle calls to mind the images of war associated with the "Foe from the North" (cf. chaps. 4–10). Three Egyptian allies are mentioned: Ethiopia, Put (probably a region in Libya), and Ludim (a group of people either in North Africa or Asia Minor).

The prose introduction (v. 13) to the second oracle of judgment against Egypt has Jeremiah predicting Nebuchadrezzar's invasion of Egypt in 568/567 B.C.E. (see note on 43:8-13; and Ezek 29:19-21). Apis was an Egyptian fertility deity worshiped in Memphis as a sacred bull. The prose addition in vv. 25-26 explains that Yahweh's judgment through Nebuchadrezzar was against Egypt, its kings, and its gods. The one deity specified is Amon, an Egyptian sun god whose cultic center was Thebes. The addition concludes by promising that Egypt will once again be inhabited *as in the days of old* (v. 26).

46:27-28. Salvation for Israel. This promise of salvation reduplicates 30:10-11 (see note). Israel in exile is promised a return home after a period of punishment. The foreign nations among whom the exiles are living will come to an end. This reference to the foreign nations is the likely reason this fragment of a salvation oracle is placed here.

47:1-7. Against the Philistines. The prose introduction in v. 1 places the oracle against the Philistines in the period shortly before an unidentified Pharaoh attacked the city of Gaza. One possibility for a specific historical location is offered by the Greek historian Herodotus (2.159) who writes that Necho II conquered Kadytis (Gaza) following his victory at Megiddo (609

B.C.E.). Yet, from the content of the oracle itself (especially the *waters rising out of the north* (v. 2) and the reference to Ashkelon), a better historical location would be Nebuchadrezzar's successful campaign against Philistia in 604 B.C.E., following the battle of Carchemish in 605 B.C.E. Nebuchadrezzar conquered Ashkelon in 604 B.C.E. In any case, Tyre and Sidon, two Phoenician cities, are mentioned in v. 4, suggesting that they were allied with the Philistines as Nebuchadrezzar made his entrance into the Coastal Plain of Israel. Caphtor is the island of Crete, one of the places from which the Philistines came (see Amos 9:7). For the association of the Anakim with the Philistines (v. 4), see Josh 11:21-22. The Anakim were supposed to be a race of giants (Deut 2:10-11).

48:1-47. Against Moab. This chapter contains several judgment oracles against Moab, one of the Transjordan countries to the east of Israel. Throughout the history of Israel and Judah, Moab was usually an enemy, receiving at times prophetic condemnation (Isa 15–16; Zeph 2:8–11). According to 2 Kgs 24:2, Moab raided Judahite territory following Jehoiakim's rebellion against Nebuchadrezzar. While Moab participated in conspiratorial talks against Babylonian rule in 595 or 594 B.C.E. (27:1-22), it is unlikely that the nation joined in the actual rebellion. The oracles indicate significant borrowing from Isa 15–16. These oracles may anticipate a future destruction of Moab by Nebuchadrezzar.

The first oracle (vv. 1-10) is a lament over the destruction caused by Nebuchadrezzar's advance against Moab. Nebo and Kiriathaim are cities in Moab, the former likely modern Khirbet Mekhayyet located five mi. to the southwest of Heshban (Isa 15:2). Kiriathaim probably was located near modern el-Qereiyat, five and a half mi. northwest of Dibon (Ezek 25:9). Heshbon (modern Heshban) was located in the north of Moab. Horonaim was a city in Moab, while Luhith, a Moabite city, was located at the south end of the Dead Sea. Chemosh was the national god of the Moabites (1 Kgs 11:7). Verse 10 offers a double curse that in its context is directed against those who do not carry out the slaughter against Moab.

The second oracle announces judgment against Moab (vv. 11-17) and begins by noting the country's good fortune in not suffering devastation, heretofore. But this soon shall change when an invader comes to destroy the country and bring down its ruling house. The prose announcement of judgment in vv. 12-13 indicates that at the time of Moab's destruction, it will be ashamed of Chemosh, its national deity, even as Israel was ashamed of Bethel. The city of Bethel, the location of a royal sanctuary of the Northern Kingdom, was criticized for the infiltration of pagan worship and political apostasy from the house of David ruling in the south (1 Kgs 12:25-33; Amos 7:10-17).

Verse 18-28 contain a taunt uttered against destroyed Moab. Dibon (modern Dhiban) was a Moabite city on the King's Highway some thirteen mi. east of the Dead Sea (Isa 15:2, 9). Aroer was a fortress (modern Khirbet Ara'ir) on the Arnon River that cuts through Moab from the east and empties into the Dead Sea. The prose insertion in vv. 21-24 contains a list of several towns and cities in Moab that had been the recipients of judgment. Verses 26-27, also in prose, explain that arrogant Moab who had taunted Israel during the latter's time of destruction is now the object of derision from other nations.

Verses 29-39 express a lament over fallen Moab (cf. the laments in 11:18–20:18). Yahweh, the destroyer of Moab, now laments over the country (cf. God's lament in 14:17-18). The capital city of Moab was Kir-heres (modern el-Kerak; see Isa 15:1), located approximately eleven mi. east of the Dead Sea. Sibmah is perhaps modern Qurn el-Kibsh, some five mi. southwest of Heshban. Jazer was another Moabite city located perhaps to the west of Amman. Added to the end of the poetic lament (vv. 29-33) is a prose lament of Yahweh over the destruction of Moab (vv. 34-39).

Verses 40-44 contain a poetic judgment oracle against Moab that depicts the invader in images of an eagle. The reason for Moab's destruction is its arrogance.

Missing in the LXX, vv. 45-47 speak of the reversal of fortunes of destroyed Moab. Yahweh will restore the nation in the future. This stereotypical language of the restoration of a country's fortunes occurs at the end of several units detailing the destruction of the foreign nations (e.g., 49:6, 49:39). Sihon was an Amorite king defeated by Israel during its journey toward Canaan (Num 21:21-30; Deut 2:24-37; and Judg 11:18-22).

49:1-6. Against Ammon. Located in the Transjordan that is east of Israel, Ammon was Israel's perpetual enemy. The Ammonites participated with the Babylonians in the attack on Judah following Jehoiakim's revolt (2 Kgs 24:2). They also were participants in the conspiratorial talks against Babylonia (Jer 27:3) and decided to revolt (Ezek 21:18-23). Ammon continued to struggle against the Babylonians after Jerusalem had

fallen in 587 B.C.E. Ammon's king supported Ishmael, the member of the royal house of Judah who assassinated Gedaliah (see chap. 41). Eventually Nebuchadrezzar brought an end to the state.

The poetic judgment oracle in 49:1-6 announces the coming destruction of Ammon. In vv. 3-5, the prophet calls on the cities of Heshbon and Rabbah to begin rituals of lamentation (cf. 6:26; 9:10; 9:17-22). The prose verse, added at the end (v. 6) and promising the restoration of the Ammonites, is absent in the LXX (cf. 48:47).

Ammon had occupied the territory of the Israelite tribe of Gad in the Transjordan (Judg 10:6–12:6; 2 Sam 12:26-31). Milcom was the national deity of Ammon (see 1 Kgs 11:5, 33). Rabbah (modern Amman) was the capital of Ammon (see Ezek 25:5; Amos 1:14). Heshbon (see comments on 48:1-10) may have fallen into Ammonite hands. The word "Ai" means "ruin" (Tell), and thus may refer to Rabbah mentioned in the next line.

49:7-22. Against Edom. According to the patriarchal traditions, Esau was the twin brother of Jacob (Israel) and the ancestor of the nation of Edom (Esau; see Gen 25:19-28). Located to the south and east of Israel, Edom was a hated enemy of Israel, often the object of condemnation (see Ps 137; Isa 11:14; 34:5-17; Ezek 35; Amos 1:6, 9, 11; 2:1; Obad; Mal 1:2-5). Folded into Nebuchadrezzar's empire not too long after the battle of Carchemish, Edom participated with the Babylonians in the conquest of Jerusalem in 587 B.C.E. and rejoiced over the fall of the city (Ps 137:7; Lam 4:21-22; Obad 10-16). After 587 B.C.E. Edom took control of southern Judah with Hebron as their capital (Lam 4:21-22; Ezek 25:12-14).

This poetic oracle of judgment is largely shaped by Obadiah. Compare vv. 14-16 to Obad 1-4, and vv. 9-10a to Obad 5-6. Edom was especially famous for its wisdom. Teman was an important city located in central Edom, while Bozrah was the major city in northern Edom (see Isa 34:6; Amos 1:12). Dedan was a country located in northwest Arabia (see Ezek 25:13).

Two prose insertions are made in this oracle. Verses 12-13 refer to the cup of wrath first mentioned in 25:15-38. In vv. 17-22 the destruction of Edom is compared to that of Sodom and Gomorrah (see note on 20:16).

49:23-27. Against Damascus. This brief judgment oracle is issued against Damascus, the capital of Syria (see 1 Kgs 11:24; 15:18; 19:15; 20:34; 2 Kgs 8:7, 9; 16:10-12; Isa 7:8). The city was conquered by the

Assyrians in 733/32 B.C.E. and made into the center of a region ruled by various foreign empires. Little is known of Damascus after the Assyrian conquest. Damascus is not listed among the foreign nations in 25:18-26, suggesting that the oracle is quite late.

Prior to the taking of Damascus, the Assyrians conquered the cities of Arpad in 740 B.C.E. and Hamath in 738 B.C.E. (see 2 Kgs 18:34; 19:13; Isa 10:9; 36:19; 37:13). Arpad (Tell Erfad), located some twenty-five mi. north of Aleppo, was a city in northern Syria, while Hamath (modern Hama) was a Syrian city located on the Orontes River between Damascus and Aleppo. Verse 27 is borrowed from Amos 1:4.

49:28-33. Against Kedar and Hazor. The Arabian tribes of Kedar and Hazor now receive from Jeremiah a poetic judgment oracle (see 25:23-24). Kedar controlled the trade route from Arabia to the Fertile Crescent (2:10-11; Isa 21:16-17; Ezek 27:21). They were apparently conquered by Nebuchadrezzar. Hazor is an unknown site in the Arabian desert, also possibly conquered by Nebuchadrezzar. For *shaven temples*, see note on 9:26.

49:34-39. Against Elam. This prose oracle, dated to the beginning of the reign of Zedekiah in 597 B.C.E., reflects Nebuchadrezzar's conquest of Elam. Elam was a country located east of the Tigris River and had its capital at Susa. The conquest occurred in 597 B.C.E. Earlier, Elam had been conquered by the Assyrians and became an ally in the Assyrian invasion of Israel (see Isa 11:11; 21:2; 22:6).

50:1-51:58. Against Babylon. The largest number of oracles in the collection of "Oracles Against the Foreign Nations" is directed towards Babylon (see chaps. 24, 25, and 29). The authorship of these oracles, both poetic and prose, is a subject of debate. When the historical Jeremiah mentions Babylon prior to 587 B.C.E., he speaks favorably of them. They are the instrument of Yahweh in bringing judgment against Israel and Judah, and Nebuchadrezzar II is the "servant" of Yahweh. Jeremiah tells the people of Judah and Jerusalem that they should submit to Babylonian rule. In the prose tradition, Jeremiah tells the exiles of 597 B.C.E. who are living in Babylon not to expect an early return, but rather to settle down, build homes, raise families, and pray for the welfare of Babylonia (chap. 29). Nebuchadrezzar sees to it that Jeremiah is treated well after the fall of the city (39:11-14; 40:1-6).

It is possible, of course, that after the fall of Jerusalem in 587 B.C.E. Jeremiah altered his views concerning Babylon, asserting that in the future the empire will face Yahweh's wrath and be destroyed. However, it is more reasonable to think that these oracles against Babylon came from later prophets of the exile (cf. Second Isaiah) who predicted the fall of the evil empire, making it possible for the exiles to return home. The Persians and Medes conquered the Babylonian empire. Cyrus, the Persian king, allowed the Jews in exile to return home in 538 B.C.E. (Ezra 1:1-4).

50:1. Superscription. (see Hag 1:1; Mal 1:1). The superscription notes that the following collection consists of Jeremiah's oracles concerning Babylon.

50:2-3. Judgment from the north. In his poetic oracle of judgment, the prophet tells his audience to announce the fall of Babylon. Bel is one of the names of Marduk, the major god of Babylonia worshiped as creator and determiner of destinies. Merodach is the biblical name for Marduk. The language of the "foe from the north" (see chaps. 4–10) is now used to speak of the enemies of Babylon: the Medes and the Persians.

50:4-5. The return of Israel and Judah. This brief prose sermon portrays the return of Israel and Judah to Zion (Jerusalem) as a pilgrimage. United, they will both enter into an everlasting covenant that shall never be forgotten (cf. chaps. 30–31).

50:6-7. Israel's shepherds. In this prose oracle, Yahweh announces that the shepherds of Judah (i.e., their kings; cf. 23:1-4) have led them astray.

50:8-10. Exhortation to flee Babylon. The prophet warns people, probably the Jewish exiles, to flee Babylon in expectation of the attack of nations from the north (see chaps. 4–10; and 50:3).

50:11-16. The invaders are commanded to attack. In this poetic oracle of judgment, Mother Babylon (cf. Mother Jerusalem in 10:20) shall be shamed, because her children have plundered Judah. Yahweh commands the invaders to attack the city. Historically speaking, Babylon was not taken by force and destroyed. The city surrendered to the armies of Persia, led by Gobryas.

50:17-20. The Restoration of Israel. This prose speech tells of Israel's destruction, first by the Assyrians and then by the Babylonians. While Babylon will be punished, Israel will be redeemed and restored to its land. Israel's and Judah's sins will be forgiven.

50:21-32. Yahweh fights against Babylon. This oracle describes Yahweh's assault against Babylon. "Double rebellion" (*Merathaim*) is a word play on the name of southern Babylonia, while "punishment"

(*Pekod*) is a word play on an east Babylonian tribe named *Puqudu*. Two prose additions are inserted. Verse 28 speaks of Jewish refugees from Babylon coming home to Zion to declare Yahweh's vengeance, including his vengeance for his Temple. Verses 29-30, also in prose, tell the invading army to lay siege to the city and let none escape. Verses 31-32 present Yahweh's invective against Babylon, promising the arrogant city that it will fall. A self-exalted pride is the basis for Babylonia's judgment (see Ezek 28).

50:33-34. Yahweh will give rest to Israel and Judah. In this prose sermon, Yahweh promises to redeem the oppressed people of Israel and Judah.

50:35-38. A sword against the Babylonians. The sword will destroy the Babylonians.

50:39-40. A deserted city fit only for wild animals. Only wild animals shall inhabit Babylon, a city that never again will have a human population.

50:41-43. Invaders from the north country. In images similar to the "Foe from the North" in chaps. 4–10, Babylon the once mighty and feared northern foe is now terrified at the approach of its own foe from the North.

50:44-46. Yahweh will conquer Babylon. Yahweh promises the fall of Babylon and the appointment of a new shepherd of his choosing to rule over it.

51:1-4. The winnowing of Babylon. Yahweh will send a destructive wind to winnow Babylon like grain.

51:5-10. Israel and Judah are not forsaken. Israel and Judah have not been abandoned by Yahweh. The Jewish inhabitants of Babylon are warned to flee and escape the wrath that Yahweh is bringing.

51:11-19. Prepare for Yahweh's attack. Yahweh gives the command to the defenders of Babylon to prepare for the invasion (identified in the prose insertion as the Medes) to attack the city. Yahweh as the creator of the world and the one who commands the elements is contrasted with lifeless, worthless idols. Verses 15-19 are taken from 10:12-16. Media, located in modern northwest Iran, was a separate empire that helped overthrow the Assyrians at the end of the seventh century B.C.E. It became a Persian province in 549 B.C.E. and participated in the defeat of the Babylonians (see Isa 13:17).

51:20-23. Persia is Yahweh's hammer. These words appear to be addressed to Cyrus, described as the hammer used by Yahweh to smash nations (cf. Isa 41:2-3).

51:24. Yahweh's repayment of Babylon. Yahweh announces repayment against Babylon for their evil doings in Jerusalem.

51:25-26. Yahweh is against Babylon. Babylon, called a *destroying mountain*, will be levelled with no stone being reused for building other structures.

51:27-33. The nations war against Babylon. Nations are summoned to wage war against Babylon. Ararat (Urartu) refers to people inhabiting a region near Lake Van (southeast Turkey and northwest Iran); Minni (Mannaya) refers to people who lived in an area south of Lake Urmia in modern northern Iraq; and Ashkenaz likely refers to an Indo-European people who lived near modern Armenia, identified as the Scythians by Herodotus.

51:34-40. Jerusalem will be revenged. The inhabitants of Jerusalem who suffered so much at the hand of Nebuchadrezzar call for revenge. Yahweh responds that he will take vengeance on their behalf.

51:41-49. Babylon has fallen. Sheshach is a cipher for Babylon. The city has fallen, and the Jewish survivors are admonished to flee the destruction.

51:50-58. The sounds of Babylon's destruction. The Jewish exiles are to remember Jerusalem. They confess their guilt. Babylon will be destroyed. Even now the sounds of its destruction can be heard.

51:59-64. Jeremiah's prophecies against Babylon are taken to the exiles. This narrative is an etymology that seeks to explain the origins of the collection of oracles against Babylon. According to this story, Jeremiah wrote down these oracles and had Seraiah take them to Babylon. He is to read the scroll aloud, remind Yahweh of his promised destruction of Babylon, and then attach to it a stone weight and cast it into the Euphrates. This symbolic act is to be accompanied by the announcement that Babylon likewise shall sink. The date given is the fourth year of the reign of King Zedekiah (593 B.C.E.). Seraiah was Baruch's brother (see 32:12).

Historical Appendix, 52:1-34

Most of this chapter is taken from 2 Kgs 24:18–25:30. The chapter, coupled with 39:1-10, narrates the story of Zedekiah's rebellion against the Babylonians, the fall of Jerusalem, and the exile. Written by deuteronomic editors, this material does end on a note of hopeful anticipation resulting from Jehoiachin's release from a Babylonian prison (vv. 31-34).

52:1-3. The reign of Zedekiah. The introduction provides a succinct summary of Zedekiah's reign. His wickedness is said to be the basis for what happened to Jerusalem. This is the standard deuteronomic assessment of the reigns of most kings in Israel and Judah.

52:4-11. The fall of Jerusalem. These verses describe the siege and fall of Jerusalem along with the capture, torture, and exile of Zedekiah.

52:12-16. The burning of Jerusalem and the exile. Nebuzaradan, the captain of Nebuchadrezzar's guard, burns the city of Jerusalem and takes the captives into exile.

52:17-23. The spoils of the Temple. These verses list the booty stolen from the Temple.

52:24-27. The execution of high officials and priests. The chief priest, Seraiah (see 36:26), and the second priest, Zephaniah (see 21:1; 29:24-32), are executed at Riblah along with important military leaders, royal advisers, and leaders of the *people of the land*.

52:28-30. The lists of exiles for three deportations. The number of exiles from three deportations is given (597, 587, 582 B.C.E.).

52:31-34. King Jehoiachin released from prison. Evil-merodach (Amel-Marduk, 562–560 B.C.E.) releases Jehoiachin, the king of Judah exiled in 597 B.C.E. He was honored above other exiled kings, allowed to eat daily at the Babylonian king's table, and given a royal allowance. This release occurred in the thirty-seventh year of his captivity (560 B.C.E.). Amel-Marduk, the son and successor of Nebuchadrezzar, was overthrown by his brother-in-law, Neriglissar. The release of the king from prison must have given some hope to the Babylonian exiles about a future restoration.

The account of the chjange of fortunes for Jehoiachin, taken from the end of 2 Kings and thus the ending of the "Former Prophets," is a way by which the Deuteronomic editors of Jeremiah and the Deuteronomistic History (Joshua–2 Kings) affirm that God has not abandoned the exiles. Indeed, the editors hope that even kingship will be restored. In addition, Jehoiachin's release indicates that life even in exile can be good (see chap. 29).

Lamentations

Mona West

Introduction

The Book of Lamentations is a series of five poems that describe with graphic detail the siege of JERUSALEM by the Babylonians in 587 B.C.E. The poems offer one of the few sources of information concerning Israel's life during the Babylonian EXILE. The poetry immediately engages its audience, gives voice to the devastation of the city, and provides a vehicle for the expression of grief. For all its wealth of information and emotion, Lamentations tends to be a book that is unfamiliar to most readers of the Hebrew Bible.

Authorship and Date

Tradition has assigned the authorship of Lamentations to the prophet JEREMIAH. Reasons for Jeremianic authorship include Jeremiah's use of the lament form (2 Chr 35:25) and his prophecy of the destruction of Jerusalem (Jer 9:10-11; 27:1-22; 28:1-17). Modern biblical scholarship has concluded that the vocabulary, style, and theology of Lamentations point to an author other than Jeremiah. In all likelihood the author of Lamentations was an anonymous poet who was an eyewitness to the events described.

The events described in Lamentations are associated with the final destruction of Jerusalem, the capital city of the southern kingdom, JUDAH, in 587 B.C.E. The Babylonian king, NEBUCHADREZZAR, broke down the walls surrounding the city, burned homes, the Temple, and the palace. There was mass execution and deportation of the city's inhabitants (2 Kgs 25).

Literary Form

It is significant that the author chooses poetry over narrative to convey the horror of the Babylonian destruction of Jerusalem. This choice exemplifies what has been identified as the twofold purpose of Hebrew poetry: (1) to transmit tradition; (2) to effect an immediate dialogue between the audience and the form and content of the poems (Lichtenstein 1984, 120). The poetry of Lamentations achieves the first purpose by its use of lament, which is Israel's traditional response to crisis. The second purpose is achieved through the poems' articulation of the suffering experienced by the inhabitants of the city.

Influence of the psalms of lament. The language of individual and communal lament is found in the poems of Lamentations. Some of the formal elements of the lament that the author uses are: address to God (1:11c; 2:20; 5:1); complaint or description of situation (1:1-11b; 2:1-10; 4:1-16); statement of trust (3:22-24, 55-60); petition (5:19-22); words of assurance (3:55-63).

The "vow of praise," a significant part of the lament form, marks a shift in mood from a "minor key" of sorrow to a "major key" of hope and trust in the LORD. It is glaringly absent from the Book of Lamentations, indicating that the author and the people were urgently in need of expressing the full scope of their grief and may have been wavering in their confidence in the LORD. Other elements of the psalms of lament that are present in the Book of Lamentations are mention of the enemy (1:2, 5-10; 2:22; 3:46, 52; 4:17-19) and a plea for vindication of the sufferer (1:21-22; 3:64-66; see 4:22).

The use of the acrostic. Another striking formal feature of the poems of Lamentations is the acrostic. Chapters 1–4 are complete acrostics, each strophe beginning with a successive letter of the Hebrew alphabet. Chapter 5 is not acrostic, but mimics the form by containing twenty-two lines (the same number of letters in the Hebrew alphabet). Chapter 3 is a triple acrostic: each strophe uses the same letter of the Hebrew alphabet three times before moving on to the next strophe and the next letter of the alphabet. The acrostic form functions in Lamentations by expressing the totality and completeness of the destruction of Jerusalem while offering some sense of order amid the chaos of the experience.

Narrative Movement of the Poems

The acrostic form assures that each poem in Lamentations can stand on its own as a unit. However, the repetition of vocabulary and key themes suggests a connectedness from poem to poem. This narrative movement is further indicated by the alternating speaking voices of the poet, *daughter Zion* (1:6; 2:1, 4, 8, 10, 13, 18; 4:22), and the community. Each poem, except for the last, is an antiphonal weaving of the first person singular and plural among descriptions of the city. This weaving is indicative of the poet's experience of the devastation of Jerusalem on an individual and corporate level. Through personal identification with *daughter Zion* the poet moves from the stance of a horrified observer (chaps. 1, 2, 4), to an individual sufferer (chap. 3), to a member of the suffering community (chap. 5).

The rhetoric of comfort. The search for comfort is a major theme in the poems of Lamentations. After the destruction of the city, the Temple, the monarchy, prophet, priest and people, all that is left is language. It is this language that seeks to comfort the inhabitants of Jerusalem. The language of comfort can be found especially in chaps. 1 and 2 where both the poet and *daughter Zion* claim *there is no one to comfort* (1:2, 17, 21). This language is heightened by references to "looking/seeing" and "weeping eyes" (1:2, 8-12, 16, 20; 2:11, 20; 3:48-51; 4:17; 5:1, 17) as God, enemies, and all who pass by are called upon to acknowledge the suffering of *daughter Zion.*

"Rhetoric" refers to the ways in which the particular language (discourse) of Lamentations is constructed in order to describe a certain reality or achieve a certain effect. Often the language will function on a variety of levels engaging author and audience. The rhetoric of comfort functions on at least two levels in the Book of Lamentations. On one level the poems describe the destruction of Jerusalem, calling on the LORD, enemies, and passersby to "look" and "see," to acknowledge the suffering. On another level, the rhetoric of comfort found in the poems is calling the people of Jerusalem to look and see, to acknowledge their own suffering (cf. 1:7). This second level of looking requires moving beyond rote recital of traditional deuteronomic (1:5, 8, 14, 18, 20, 22; 2:14) and wisdom (3:25-39) explanations of suffering. Tradition alone cannot comfort. Instead, each person must incorporate with these traditional explanations his or her own personal experience of suffering. This type of

looking allows each inhabitant of Jerusalem to relinquish the stance of horrified observer and to embrace the reality of personal sinfulness and suffering. Only then can each stand in solidarity with the suffering community. Only then can true grieving and comfort begin.

The poet embodies this second level of looking, which moves one from observer, to suffering individual, to member of the suffering community. In the first two poems the author describes the devastation of Jerusalem in the images of a worthless woman and a worthless place. By the end of the second poem the poet will move beyond description to an emotional outburst concerning the suffering of *daughter Zion* (2:11-19). In chap. 3 the poet is identified as the one who is experiencing the suffering. Through the claim, *I am one who has seen affliction* (3:1) the author stands in solidarity with *daughter Zion* by accepting affliction as a personal reality. This identification with *daughter Zion* opens the poet's eyes to look beyond a mere description of suffering and the traditional explanations for it and to visualize the only statement of hope found in the book (3:19-24).

Only after having "seen" at this level is the poet able to speak for the first time in the plural as a member of the suffering community (3:40-47). It is this level of seeing that is reflected in the poet's words of 3:48-51:

> My eyes flow with rivers of tears
> > because of the destruction of my people.
> My eyes will flow without ceasing,
> > without respite,
> until the LORD from heaven
> > looks down and sees.
> My eyes cause me grief
> > at the fate of all the young women in my city.

Because of the identification of the poet's own suffering with *daughter Zion*'s, it becomes possible to look and see even when the LORD will not. What the poet sees is not only the worthless woman of chap. 1, but the fate of *all the young women* in the city (3:51). Through the poet's identification with *daughter Zion* the suffering of one has become the suffering of many.

In the fourth poem the poet describes *daughter Zion* as a worthless place using some of the same themes and vocabulary found in poems one and two. The description is different, however, than those of the first two poems because it ends with a lament of the community (4:17-20). The transformation of the poet into a member of the suffering community is confirmed in the fifth poem, which contains no description or shifting from first person singular to first person plural. The entire poem is a communal lament recapitulating the themes of the preceding poems, which also have been transformed. Instead of describing Zion as a worthless woman, the poet proclaims as a member of the suffering community, *we have become orphans, . . . our mothers are like widows* (5:3); *woe to us, for we have sinned!* (5:16); *because of these things our eyes have grown dim* (5:17).

For Further Study

In the *Mercer Dictionary of the Bible*: AB, NINTH OF; EXILE; JEREMIAH; LAMENTATIONS, BOOK OF; POETRY; SUFFERING IN THE OT.

In other sources: N. K. Gottwald, *Studies in the Book of Lamentations*, and "Lamentations," *HBC* 646–51; D. Hillers, *Lamentations,* AncB; W. F. Lanahan, "The Speaking Voices in the Book of Lamentations," *JBL* 93 (1974): 41–49.

Commentary

An Outline

I. Daughter Zion as a Worthless Woman, 1:1-22
  A. Jerusalem as a Widow
     and a Shamed Woman, 1:1-11b
  B. Daughter Zion Laments, 1:11c-22
II. Daughter Zion as a Worthless Place, 2:1-22
  A. Jerusalem's Places Torn Down, 2:1-10
  B. Emotional Outburst
     concerning Daughter Zion, 2:11-19
  C. Daughter Zion Laments, 2:20-22
III. Identification with Daughter Zion, 3:1-66
  A. Soliloquy of Affliction, 3:1-24
  B. Wisdom's Response to Suffering, 3:25-39
  C. Solidarity with the Suffering Community, 3:40-51
  D. Offering of Personal Lament, 3:52-66
IV. Daughter Zion as a Worthless Community, 4:1-22
  A. Reversal of the Hierarchies of Society, 4:1-16
  B. The Community Laments, 4:17-22
V. Catharsis of Grief, 5:1-22

Daughter Zion as a Worthless Woman, 1:1-22

Jerusalem as a Widow and a Shamed Woman, 1:1-11b

This is the first of three descriptive passages in Lamentations concerning *daughter Zion* (cf. 2:1-10; 4:1-16). In each, Jerusalem's former glory (worth) is reversed to worthlessness. Here the poet personifies the city as a woman. The worth of a woman in Israelite society was measured by her function within two roles: unmarried virgin or child-producing wife. In order to communicate the tragic reversal of the place of the city among the nations, the poet uses images antithetical to these acceptable roles. As fertile wife Jerusalem had many offspring; now she is *like a widow* (v.

1), *her children have gone away* (v. 5). As faithful wife she once had a place of honor, but because of her unfaithfulness she wanders among her lovers *with tears on her cheeks* (v. 2). Because of her sinfulness she has been exposed (nakedness) and shamed; all who look on are appalled (vv. 8-9). Even in her vulnerable state she is violated, as enemies *stretch out their hands over all her precious things* (v. 10).

The poet's images reflect the preaching of the Hebrew prophets in which Zion, or Jerusalem, (as well as other cities) is sometimes personified as a woman (Isa 51:17; Ezek 16). Female imagery is often used in the prophetic tradition to speak of the rebellion and punishment of the inhabitants of Jerusalem: harlotry (Jer 4:30); violated women (Isa 13:16; Ezek 19:7; Zech 14:2); shamed women (Jer 13:22, 26, 50:12; Nah 3:5); widowhood (Isa 9:17, 47:8-9; Jer 18:21).

In addition, the poet will use other metaphors and images to describe the reversal of the fortunes of Jerusalem (a worthless place in poem two and a worthless society in poem four). These images will incorporate male and female as well as all sectors of society (infants, mothers, high officials, warriors, priests, kings, the affluent, even the prophets themselves). While there is little word of consolation in Lamentations, female imagery is also used in the prophetic tradition to speak of Jerusalem as a city of future comfort (Isa 66:10-13) and a symbol of restoration (Isa 49:14-18; 54:1).

The theme of comfort is mentioned twice in 1:1-11b. The poet claims that *daughter Zion* has *no one to comfort her* (v. 2), there is *none to comfort her* (v. 9). The poet *sees* the empty city and describes her as a widow, surrounding nations *have seen* Zion's nakedness and are appalled, the enemy *sees* Zion's vulnerability and takes advantage. All who surround her cannot help but *look and see*. In contrast the LORD does not see and Jerusalem herself *turns her face away* (v. 8).

Daughter Zion Laments, 1:11c-22

There is a shift from description to first person singular as *daughter Zion* laments her worthlessness and calls upon the LORD, as well as those who pass by, to *look and see* (vv. 11c-12, 20). As she looks for comfort, *daughter Zion* repeats what had been said about her earlier: *For these things I weep; my eyes flow with tears; for a comforter is far from me* (v. 16; cf. 1:2). The poet will interrupt Zion's lament at this point to proclaim again, *there is no one to comfort her* (v. 17). Zion laments that not even her former lovers will lend comfort (v. 21).

Zion confesses her sin using such traditional deuteronomic formulations as: *The Lord is in the right, for I have rebelled against his word* (v. 18); *My heart is wrung within me for I have been very rebellious* (v. 20); *You have dealt with me because of my transgressions* (v. 22). These words of repentance sound hollow on the lips of Zion. Truly she weeps. Her suffering is real. Yet there is no sense of resolution at the end of this lament. Zion has brought her case before the LORD, and there still has not been found one to comfort.

Daughter Zion
as a Worthless Place, 2:1-22

Jerusalem's Places Torn Down, 2:1-10

Verse 1 sets the tone for the description of *daughter Zion* as a worthless place. Her reversal is from high to low. In anger, the LORD has *humiliated daughter Zion*. Throughout this section, verbs that connote downward movement are coupled with nouns describing the places of Jerusalem. The LORD *has destroyed . . . all the dwellings of Jacob; in his wrath he has broken down the strongholds of daughter Judah; he has brought down to the ground in dishonor the kingdom and its rulers* (v. 2). *He has cut down in fierce anger all the might of Israel* (v. 3). *He has destroyed all of [Israel's] palaces*, and *strongholds* lie in ruins (v. 5). *He has broken down his booth* (v. 6).

This flinging down is completed with reference to the levelling of the outer structures of the city itself and with the repetition of the word *ground* (2, 9, 10bis, 11, 21). The wall lies in ruins, *and rampart and*

wall lament (v. 8). *Her gates have sunk into the ground* (v. 9). *The elders of daughter Zion sit on the ground . . . the young girls of Jerusalem have bowed their heads to the ground* (v. 10).

Emotional Outburst
concerning Daughter Zion, 2:11-19

Up until this point the poet has remained a horrified observer of Jerusalem's reversals. Now the author speaks in the first person with a level of emotion that echoes *daughter Zion's* lament in poem one. The poet proclaims in 2:1, *My eyes are spent with weeping; my stomach churns; my bile is poured out on the ground* (cf. 1:16, 20). After stating in poem one that there is none to comfort *daughter Zion*, the poet then cries out, *What can I say for you . . . to what can I liken you, that I may comfort you?* (v. 13). Here the purpose of the poet and of the five poems is stated in a moment of intense identification with Zion and her people: The purpose is consolation for *daughter Zion* and her people.

What can I say . . . ? This question reflects the poet's attempt throughout the book to give voice to the suffering of *daughter Zion. To what compare you . . . to what can I liken you?* (v. 13). The poet uses personification, metaphor, simile, and comparative analogy in order to name what is seen, to describe the horror of Jerusalem. This naming is an attempt to move both poet and the community beyond that horror to the grieving process and eventually to comfort. *That I may comfort you* (v. 13). This is the turning point of the book. It has been stated by the poet and *daughter Zion* that there is none to comfort. When former lovers, enemies, passersby, tradition, even the LORD, fail to comfort Zion, the poet steps forward. The attempt to comfort *daughter Zion* is at its most intense in poem three where the poet will totally identify with the suffering of the city and be transformed by it.

Daughter Zion Laments, 2:20-22

At the end of this emotional outburst the poet calls on *daughter Zion* to *cry aloud to the Lord* (v. 18); *arise, cry out in the night* (v. 19). Zion responds with a lament that calls on the LORD to *look* and *consider* (v. 20). She speaks as the widow of poem one. Offspring are lost as a result of cannibalism (v. 20). In his anger the LORD has killed her young women and young men (v. 21). Those whom she had borne and reared have been destroyed (v. 22).

Identification
with Daughter Zion, 3:1-66

Soliloquy of Affliction, 3:1-24

The poet's attempt to comfort *daughter Zion* reaches its climax in vv. 1-24 with the resumption of the first person singular pronoun from poem two (it is also at this point that the acrostic form becomes more complex and detailed). The poet's choice of the Hebrew word גֶּבֶר for "man" in 3:1 is significant. The term denotes "strong man"; it is repeated throughout poem three. "I am the strong man who has seen affliction" (v. 1, author trans.). "It is good for a strong man to bear the yoke in youth" (v. 27, author trans.). "The right of a strong man is perverted in the presence of the Most High" (v. 35, author trans.). "Why does a living man complain, a strong man because of the punishment of his sins" (v. 39, author trans.)?

"Strong man" is used in the Hebrew Bible to distinguish a man from the "women, children, and noncombatants whom he is to defend" (Brown, Driver, Briggs 1980, 150). Indeed, the poet has sought to defend *daughter Zion* and in his description of her devastation has remained distinct from her. However, in seeking to comfort Zion the poet becomes the one who is afflicted, and in that moment a new meaning is assigned to the term. The poet recognizes that it is not just *daughter Zion* who bears the yoke of the LORD's chastisement (1:14), but it is also good for the גֶּבֶר to *bear the yoke* (v. 27). Widow Zion has been shamed in the presence of the nations, and now the question is asked, "Can a strong man's right be perverted in the presence of the Most High" (v. 35, author trans.)? Like *daughter Zion* the גֶּבֶר complains because of sin (v. 39).

Not only does this term undergo a change in poem three, but the poet also is transformed into an individual sufferer through this identification with *daughter Zion*. The author is the one who has seen affliction and now is afflicted personally. In language reminiscent of Job, the poet speaks out as one who has been attacked by God (vv. 3, 5, 10-13), walled up and chained (v. 7), and robbed of peace (v. 17). (Job also searched for comfort, a mediator, an umpire, someone to arbitrate between God and himself.) It is only when the poet can lament this personal reversal that hope is at its strongest in the book (vv. 18-24).

Wisdom's Response to Suffering, 3:25-39

After such an intense experience of personal suffering, responses from Israel's wisdom traditions provide an interlude before the poet is finally transformed into a member of the suffering community. The responses in 3:25-39 are similar to the "advice" given by Job's friends, thus continuing the Joban theme found in Lam 3:1-24. One should be patient in the midst of suffering (Lam 3:25-26; cf. Job 4:5). Suffering is part of the human condition (vv. 27-30; cf. Job 4:17-19; 5:6-7). The LORD chastens those whom he loves (vv. 31-33; cf. Job 5:17-18). Does God pervert justice (vv. 34-39; cf. Job 8:1-7)?

Solidarity with the Suffering Community, 3:40-51

This section marks the poet's transformation into a member of the suffering community. It is a weaving of first person plural (vv. 40-47) with first person singular (vv. 48-51). It is also the first time that the first person plural pronoun is used in the Book of Lamentations. As a result of identifying himself as the one who has been afflicted (3:1-24), the poet now is able to stand in solidarity with the suffering community. The author knows from personal experience within the community the absence of God's gaze and comfort (vv. 43-44). Now it is no longer *daughter Zion* who laments her shame and loss of honor; the poet, along with the entire community, laments, *You have made us filth and rubbish among the peoples* (v. 45).

In the midst of solidarity with the suffering community the poet speaks in the first person singular to proclaim a seeing that is on a level different from the one found in the first two poems. The poet's eyes flow with *rivers of tears* because of the destruction of the people. These eyes will *flow without ceasing* until God looks and sees (vv. 48-50). The poet is able to see that the suffering of *daughter Zion* is not only one person's suffering but the suffering of many, and because of this level of seeing the poet can grieve (v. 51).

Offering of Personal Lament, 3:52-66

The poet had called on *daughter Zion* to cry aloud to God in 2:18-19 and now, as a member of the suffering community, offers an individual, personal lament. It is a remembrance of a previous time when the poet called upon the LORD and the LORD responded. Within the structure of the Book of Lamentations, the poet's individual lament parallels the personal laments of *daughter Zion* found at the end of poems one and two. This lament also functions as a literary inclusion within the transformational third poem by paralleling the soliloquy of vv. 1-24 with its elements of hope stated in the first person singular.

Daughter Zion
as a Worthless Community, 4:1-22

Reversal of the Heirarchies of Society, 4:1-16

Now in solidarity with the daughter of Zion, the poet is able to describe *daughter Zion* as a worthless community. The author articulates the reversal of the hierarchies of Zion's society by using comparative analogy and simile. Children who were once worth their weight in fine gold have become *as earthen pots* (v. 2). The well-to-do *perish in the streets* and *cling to ash heaps* (v. 5). Princes were *purer than snow, whiter than milk . . . , but now their visage is blacker than soot* (vv. 7-8). Prophet and priest have become defiled (vv. 13-15). There is no favor extended to the elders (v. 16). Themes from previous poems are mentioned again in this description of the community: hunger (vv. 3-5, 9); cannibalism (v. 10); the LORD's wrath (v. 11).

The Community Laments, 4:17-22

In keeping with the first three poems, the fourth poem ends with a lament. Verses 17-20 are a communal lament in which the theme of looking is repeated as the poet and the community complain, *Our eyes failed, ever watching vainly for help* (v. 17). The reversal of the hierarchies of Israelite society is complete with the loss of the king in v. 20. The poet's voice dominates vv. 21-22 as Edom and Zion are addressed. There is a glimmer of hope when the poet states, *The punishment of your iniquity, O daughter Zion, is accomplished; he will keep you in exile no longer* (v. 22).

Catharsis of Grief, 5:1-22

This is the only poem in the Book of Lamentations that does not contain alternating voices. The entire poem is a communal lament. Structurally, this lament parallels the laments that have ended each of the previous poems. Poems one and two ended with a lament by *daughter Zion*. Pivotal poem three ended with a personal lament of the poet. Poem four ended with a community lament that was concluded by words of address from the poet. In poem five there is no individual voice because there has occurred a total identification with the suffering community.

Themes from previous poems are repeated in the plural of solidarity as the *community* laments *We have become orphans, fatherless; our mothers are like widows* (v. 3). *With a yoke on our necks we are hard driven* (v. 5). The worthlessness of the community is lamented in vv. 11-16 with the conclusion, *Woe to us, for we have sinned! Because of this our hearts are sick, because of these things our eyes have grown dim* (vv. 16b-17).

As a community lament, this poem bears witness to the gradual transformation of the poet and any individual of the community who has dared to look into the experiential level of personal suffering. Yet the book seems to end on a troubling note. The LORD has not seen nor comforted. There is the thought that perhaps the LORD has *utterly rejected* the community and is angry with them *beyond measure* (v. 22). There is however an underlying element of hope within the community itself. Before they can receive comfort from the LORD they must become comfort for one another. By embracing personal sinfulness and suffering each is able to enter into solidarity with the suffering community and create a space that prepares them for receiving the LORD's comfort.

Works Cited

Brown, Francis, Samuel R. Driver, and Charles A. Briggs. 1980. *The New Brown, Driver, Briggs, Gesenius Hebrew Lexicon, with an Appendix Containing the Biblical Aramaic.*

Lichtenstein, Murray H. 1984. "Biblical Poetry," *Back to the Sources.* Barry W. Holtz, ed.

Ezekiel

Joel F. Drinkard, Jr.

Introduction

The Book of Ezekiel stands in English Bibles (as in the Hebrew Bible) as the last of the Great Prophets, so called due to their size. It is the shortest of the three, and, in terms of the historical setting of the PROPHET whose name the book bears, the latest of the three.

The Person

Although the OT gives more biographical information on EZEKIEL than on any other prophet, there is still relatively little precise information, certainly not enough to piece together any full biography.

The name Ezekiel (יְחֶזְקֵאל) means "God (El) will strengthen" or "May God strengthen." The name has been interpreted as a note of hope to a people in exile.

Ezekiel's father was named Buzi, and apparently both were priests. Ezekiel's priestly role is evident throughout the book in his great concern with holiness, the defilement of the Temple, CLEAN/UNCLEAN, Torah, and in his many references to the legal codes, especially the Holiness Code.

Ezekiel was among the leaders of Judah deported to Babylonia in the first EXILE of 597 B.C.E. (Brownlee 1986 holds a different view; see the Setting, below). There he lived among a contingent of the exiles at an unknown site Tel Abib on the banks of the Chebar River, usually identified with a major irrigation canal that ran from Babylon past Nippur to Erech. He apparently lived out his life in Babylonia.

Ezekiel was married. He records the sickness and death of his wife while in Babylonia (24:15-18), but no reference is made to children.

One of the most intriguing, and most debated, issues concerning Ezekiel is his personality and the likelihood of physical and/or personality disorders. The strange behavior associated with Ezekiel (muteness, lying on one side and then on the other for 390 days, trembling as he takes food) are described in the book as his being overwhelmed by God's spirit as he began his ministry and as he experienced later visions. The interpretation most scholars today assume, and as will be followed here, is that these symptoms are to be related to the prophetic experience: they relate to the ecstatic state the prophet experiences in his calling and in his vision-messages. Therefore, no attempt to psychologize or diagnose will be made; instead the behaviors will be treated theologically.

The Setting

The book opens with a reference to *the thirtieth year* (1:1). Some scholars relate that to the thirtieth year of the Exile and suggest that was the date some edition of the Book of Ezekiel was completed. If the date refers to the Exile, it is the latest date in the book and would correspond approximately to 567 B.C.E. However, it seems better to take the reference to the thirtieth year as referring to the prophet's age when he had the call experience of chap. 1. Such a date would place Ezekiel's birth near 623 B.C.E.

Ezekiel's childhood and early teen years would have been under the reign of the reformer King JOSIAH, whose sweeping religious reforms began about the time of Ezekiel's birth. If his father was a priest, Ezekiel and his family must have been profoundly influenced by those reforms.

Ezekiel lived in a time of great political change. The Assyrian Empire was on the wane. Josiah's reforms were possible largely because of Assyrian weakness. Nineveh fell in 612 B.C.E. to a coalition of the Babylonians and others. Egypt now exerted more authority in Syria/Palestine. In 609 B.C.E. Pharaoh Necho of Egypt marched northward through Judah in support of a remnant of the Assyrian army attempting to form a state in the upper Euphrates valley. On that march, Necho was opposed by the Judean King Josiah, who was killed in battle at MEGIDDO. Interim King

JEHOAHAZ was deposed by Necho three months later and a pro-Egyptian king, JEHOIAKIM, was placed on the throne.

Quite soon it became clear that Babylon was now the major political force throughout Mesopotamia. After the battle of CARCHEMISH in 605 B.C.E., Babylonian forces led by the crown prince, and soon-to-be-king, NEBUCHADREZZAR pursued Necho and his Egyptian forces back through Syria/Palestine to the border of Egypt. Judah now became a vassal of Babylon. Several of the small states of Syria/Palestine revolted against Babylon during the next six to eight years, resulting in Babylonian incursions into the region. Jehoiakim revolted against Babylon in 598 B.C.E.; he died or was assassinated late that year and was replaced by his son Jehoiachin. Jerusalem fell to Nebuchadrezzar early in 597 B.C.E. after a short siege; Jehoiachin, the queen mother, and many of the leading royal, military and administrative officials were taken captive to Babylonia. The Babylonian Chronicle places the number of exiles at 3,000. The OT adds to this number 1,000 craftsmen and 7,000 soldiers. Heavy tribute was also exacted as part of the punishment. Ezekiel was among the captives.

As the Book of Ezekiel makes clear, this initial deportation did not end the intrigue in Judah, nor the suffering. ZEDEKIAH, the puppet-king placed on the throne by Nebuchadrezzar, also revolted against Babylon, expecting to receive Egyptian aid. The aid never materialized; retribution was swift and thorough. Judah was again invaded and besieged; the siege of Jerusalem lasted approximately eighteen months. When it fell, Jerusalem was devastated and burned; the Temple was destroyed. The second deportation of 587 B.C.E. brought additional captives to Babylonia. Date formulas within the book place the call of Ezekiel in the fifth year of captivity, about 593 B.C.E. Most of these formulas refer to the years of Jehoiachin's captivity, suggesting that Ezekiel and the Babylonian exiles considered Jehoiachin still to be the legitimate ruler of Judah.

The last date formula in the book (assuming the thirtieth year refers to Ezekiel's age as suggested above) mentions the twenty-seventh year of exile, approximately 571. B.C.E. If this formula lies close to the end of Ezekiel's ministry, then that ministry spanned a period of at least twenty-two years. Also, if Ezekiel was thirty years old when the call experience took place, he would have been about twenty-five at the time of his exile, and about fifty-two at the time of the last dated message.

The book has no reference to the overthrow of the Babylonian Empire by the Persians in 539 B.C.E., nor any reference to the restoration of the exiles in 538 B.C.E. This suggests a relatively short time frame for the composition and initial editing of the book. It is, of course, possible and even likely that the editorial-redactional work continued over a longer period.

The geographical setting of the book is taken to be Babylonia. The principal location is an otherwise unknown site, Tel Abib, on the banks of the River Chebar. The river itself is usually identified with the *naru kabari*, "great river," mentioned in inscriptions from Nippur. That river was actually a major irrigation canal that ran from Babylon southward past Nippur and Erech and then rejoined the Euphrates. That location, along with the "plain" or "valley" associated with it, is the site of several of Ezekiel's visions. The great detail with which he recounts events and places in Judah, particularly Jerusalem, has suggested to some scholars that Ezekiel traveled back and forth to Judah, or that he had a prior prophetic ministry in Jerusalem, or that the entire ministry was set in Judah, and only redactionally placed in Babylon (see Brownlee 1986, xxiii–xxv). This commentary will follow the most commonly accepted view, that Ezekiel's prophetic ministry was located in Babylon and that he was taken there as an exile in 597 B.C.E.

The exiles themselves apparently were not living in extreme circumstances. There is no evidence of duress, of concentration camps or prisoner-of-war internment. Apparently the exiles enjoyed freedom of movement and the possibility of practicing their occupations. They were free to build homes and plant gardens; they even had some communication with the Judean community back home. The exiles may have had an easier time than many of the ones left behind in war-torn and decimated Judah, especially after 587 B.C.E.

The Book of a Community

That the Book of Ezekiel, like other books of the OT, underwent editorial-redactional processes is clear. The third person introduction of 1:1-3, followed by a first person work, and the use of catchwords to collect originally diverse materials together, and the larger process of grouping together oracles of judgment against Jerusalem and Judah, oracles of judgment against foreign nations, and oracles of hope, all point to an editorial-redactional process. The recognition of such a process does not indicate responsibility for the process. The issue of who is responsible for this process, and when it was completed, is still unresolved after over a century of vigorous debate. Many scholars hold that Ezekiel himself, or a disciple, was responsible for most of the editorial work. Some, although a minority, maintain that Ezekiel was responsible for virtually none of the book. Without debating the merits, this commentary will follow the former position.

The book itself, after the extended call vision of chaps. 1:1–3:15, has a broad outline found in a number of the OT prophets: (1) oracles of judgment against Israel-Judah; (2) oracles of judgment against foreign nations; (3) oracles of hope and restoration. Similar patterns may be found, though not necessarily to the same degree, or in the same order, in Amos, Isaiah, and Jeremiah. It may be that these messages were the expected content of a prophetic ministry.

In Ezekiel these broad divisions form an outline. In addition, much of the attempt to date the material in the oracles (using Ezekiel's own date formulas where appropriate) relates the material as follows:

(1) Chapters 1–24, oracles of judgment against Judah and Jerusalem, are mostly dated before the fall of Jerusalem in 587 B.C.E. The judgment proclaimed is precisely the kind experienced in the invasions and exiles of 597 B.C.E. and 587 B.C.E. Having himself experienced the siege warfare of 597 and remembering the defeat and death of Josiah in 609 B.C.E., Ezekiel could well be expected to anticipate similar devastation and judgment on the people for their sins. And knowing firsthand the might of the Babylonians, he would naturally depict them as the instruments God would use again in that judgment.

(2) Chapters 25–32, the oracles against foreign nations, are mostly dated after 587 B.C.E. The context of the oracles against the nations presupposes that Jerusalem has already fallen. The judgment spoken against the nations is based largely on those nations' response to the fall of Judah and Jerusalem. Some took delight in Judah's plight; others took advantage of Judah's defeat to expand their borders; and still others offered no aid to Judah, or aided the Babylonians in the assault against Judah. Because of their response, they too will be judged.

(3) Chapters 33–48, the oracles of hope and restoration, are also dated after 587 B.C.E. They likewise presuppose that Judah and Jerusalem have fallen. However, these chapters maintain that judgment is not the final word God has, even for a rebellious people. If they will repent, God may restore both people and land. There is yet a future hope.

One should not be too strong in asserting the independence of the divisions of the Book of Ezekiel. Clear links serve to tie together the sections and the book as a whole. Indeed, it may be argued that the Book of Ezekiel displays more literary unity than any other of the great prophetic collections. Here are a few of these links: the departure of the glory of chaps. 8–11 is paralleled by its return in chaps. 40–48, especially chap. 43. Furthermore, the glory in those sections picks up the references to the glory in the inaugural vision of chaps. 1–3. Even more broadly, the destruction of Jerusalem described in many of the oracles of chaps. 1–24 is paralleled by the restoration hope of chaps. 40–48. The sixth chapter speaks of devastation of the mountains of Judah because of idolatrous worship practices; chap. 36 describes the transformation of those same mountains in preparation for the restoration. The commission to be a watchman in 3:16-21 is paralleled by an oracle concerning watchmen in 33:1-9. Likewise the message on individual responsibility in chap. 18, with its cry that the individual who sins will be judged for his or her own sins, is paralleled by a call to individual repentance with the promise of forgiveness in 33:10-20. Thus the book exhibits many examples of literary unity or coherence.

The Book of Ezekiel has many of the literary elements found in other prophetic books. Especially prevalent are the visions, allegories, symbolic prophetic acts, and autobiographical material. Unlike the literature of most of the preexilic prophets, the material in Ezekiel is predominantly prose. Ezekiel has fewer of the short oracles; the book is noted for its extended visions and metaphors. Typical Ezekielian phrases include the prophetic proof formula *that you may know that I am the LORD* (e.g., 20:20), *O mortal* (e.g., 2:1; KJV, RSV, "son of man" = "human being"), *set your face* (e.g., 4:3), and *the glory of the LORD* (e.g., 1:28) as the symbol of the LORD's presence.

Even in his use of the genre of preexilic prophets, Ezekiel serves as a transition toward postexilic prophetism. The movement is away from oracles and more toward the allegories. His concern with priestly matters of holiness, cleanness, and purity becomes a major concern of the postexilic community. His extended visions include elements that seem to be precursors of apocalyptic.

Theology

Ezekiel's theology centers around a God who is intimately involved with the people. The prophet declares God's judgment on the people due to their sins, and that judgment is devastating—the total destruction of the nation and its religious institutions. But this God also offers restoration if the people will repent. And in that glorious restored community God will be ever-present with them (48:35; *Yahweh-shammah, The LORD is There*, is the name of the restored city).

According to Ezekiel, Israel's and Judah's history had been one filled with sin; the people were entirely rebellious. Not only was the society sinful, but especially was the people's cultic (religious) life—and this was especially abhorrent to God. Thus judgment was certain and thorough. The fall of the nation and the destruction of the Temple were the direct result of the people's rebelliousness. Nevertheless, judgment was not the last word to Israel-Judah. The prophet also issues a call to repentance. This call if heeded could not avert the judgment that was pronounced. But it could lead to a restoration. Repentance alone would not bring deliverance. Just as judgment came from God, so also restoration must come from God. But the prophet announces that if the people truly repent, the LORD will graciously offer restoration just as surely as God had earlier brought judgment.

Another major theological concern of Ezekiel's is that of individual accountability or responsibility. Both nations and individuals fall under God's law. Just as surely as rebellious nations will be judged, so also will rebellious individuals be judged. And the judgment is based on that individual's actions. No person is to be held accountable for the actions of another, not for a parent's action nor for a child's action. One is accountable only for oneself. Likewise, repentance is an individual matter. The case law principle (if a person does this, then the result or judgment is this) is held to be applicable. And the Deuteronomic principle is the basis for the actions of God: If you obey, you will live long in the land; but if you disobey, you will be exiled and die outside the land.

Again it must be stated that the book closes on a note of restoration. The final word is one of future hope. As terrible as the judgment for the peoples' sins was, and as rebellious as they had been to deserve such judgment, restoration was still a possibility. And if they would indeed repent, the future would become reality. That was a promise.

For Further Study

In the *Mercer Dictionary of the Bible*: BABYLONIAN EMPIRE; EXILE; EZEKIEL; EZEKIEL, BOOK OF; JERUSALEM; NEBUCHADREZZAR; PROPHECY; PROPHET; ORACLE; SYMBOL; TEMPLE/TEMPLES; THEOPHANY; VISION; ZEDEKIAH.

In other sources: L. C. Allen, *Ezekiel 20–48*, WBC; W. H. Brownlee, *Ezekiel 1–19*, WBC; K. W. Carley, *Ezekiel among the Prophets*, SBT; G. A. Cooke, *A Critical and Exegetical Commentary on the Book of Ezekiel*, ICC; W. Eichrodt, *Ezekiel*, OTL; M. Greenberg, *Ezekiel 1–20*, AncB; R. M. Hall, *Ezekiel*, FOTL; J. D. Levenson, *Theology of the Program of Restoration of Ezekiel 40–48*, HSM; D. M. G. Stalker, *Ezekiel*, TBC; J. B. Taylor, *Ezekiel*, TOTC; B. Vawter and L. J. Hoppe, *A New Heart: Ezekiel*, ITC; J. W. Wevers, *Ezekiel*, NCB; R. R. Wilson, "Ezekiel," HBC, 652–94; W. Zimmerli, *Ezekiel*, Herm.

Commentary

An Outline

The Book of Ezekiel may be divided most simply into three sections following the extended call of 1:1–3:15. These divisions are: messages of judgment against Jerusalem and Judah (3:16–24:27); oracles against foreign nations (chaps. 25–32); and oracles of hope and consolation (chaps. 33–48).

The book begins with the prophet's call and commission. Many OT prophets had a call experience (cf. Amos 7, Isa 6, Jer 1), but none is reported so thoroughly and extensively as is Ezekiel's.

Ezekiel's Call and Commission, 1:1–3:15

Introduction, 1:1-3

This brief introduction gives vital information concerning Ezekiel: his father's name, Buzi, his vocation as priest, his situation as an exile in Babylonia near the River Chebar. The second and third verses are among the only third person materials in the book; unlike most of the OT prophets, Ezekiel is written primarily in first person.

1:1. In the thirtieth year. As discussed in the introduction, this date formula is taken as Ezekiel's age at his call. The date formula in v. 2 relates the time to political events with which the reader would be familiar (the fifth year of King Jehoiachin's exile, 593 B.C.E.).

1:3. And the hand of the LORD was on him there. This is one of the phrases used frequently in Ezekiel to describe the experience with God, usually related to a vision or its aftermath.

The Chariot-Throne Vision, 1:4-28

The VISION begins with the description of a natural phenomenon, a thunderstorm with heavy lightning, before it moves to the supernatural realm. Throughout the vision are recurrent references to the sights and sounds of the thunderstorm. Three major images are combined in the vision: the thunderstorm, the chariot-throne attended by the living creatures, and the glory of the LORD. The vision progresses as that which is at a distance draws ever closer, disclosing more and more details. It reaches its climax with *the appearance of the likeness of the glory* (v. 28).

1:4. The storm wind out of the north. North was one of the locations mentioned as the LORD's abode (see Isa 14:13). Mount Zion/Jerusalem as God's abode is even said symbolically to be in the far north (Ps 48:2). So the storm is to be understood as coming from God; indeed God is present in the midst of this storm. The use of storm, cloud, lightning, and fire imagery is common in OT theophanies (e.g., Ps 29), and plays a major role as a symbol of God's presence and guidance in the wilderness by means of the pillar of cloud and the pillar of fire. Cloud and fire serve both to reveal and to conceal God. Both symbolize the divine presence, but surround and conceal the fullness of God, which no one could experience.

1:5-14. The four living creatures. The living creatures are clearly related to the cherubim that were over the ARK (1 Sam 4:4) and the seraphs of Isaiah's vision (Isa 6:2-6). Both are understood as attendants of the deity. The iconography of the cherubim was undoubtedly intended to depict those attendants with God enthroned above them and the ark. Ezek 10:20-22 specifically relates the living creatures to the cherubim on the ark of the covenant. Such part-human, part-animal, part-bird imagery is well known from MESOPOTAMIA. The gates of Mesopotamian cities and the throne rooms of palaces were often decorated with such beings, who were the attendants of the Mesopotamian deities also. The rabbis understood the four faces of the living creatures as representing the most exalted of all creation (humans), and the most exalted of the birds, domestic animals, and wild animals. The number four represents completeness or wholeness.

The burning coals and torches moving to and fro (v. 13) are reminiscent of Isaiah's call (Isa 6:6) and Abraham's THEOPHANY with the burning fire pot (Gen 15:17) respectively.

1:15-21. The wheeled chariot. Although the chariot-throne itself is not described, its wheels are. The image of the ark as a chariot-throne is shared by 1 Chr 28:18. Related images are those of the chariots and horses of the LORD (2 Kgs 11:17) and the LORD as a rider of the clouds or heavens or winds (Pss 68:4, 33; 104:3). The wheels are specifically related to the cherubim of the ark in Ezek 10:2-20.

1:22-25. The dome. Above the chariot-throne, Ezekiel sees a dome (רקיע), the same word as used in Gen 1 for the dome of heaven that separates the waters above from the waters below. Here the dome separates the throne of God from the realm where Ezekiel and the living creatures are. God's throne is above this dome or platform. Similarly a pavement separated God from Moses and the elders (Exod 24:10). The dome is transparent; Ezekiel can see into the realm above it.

Now Ezekiel also hears sounds; the noise of the living creatures' wings is *like the sound of mighty waters* (v. 24); and from above the dome he hears *a voice* (v. 25).

1:26-28. The appearance of the glory of the LORD. The climax of Ezekiel's vision is the description of *the glory of the LORD* (v. 28). First there is something like a throne with a human-like form seated upon it. Surrounding this human-like form was something like fire and the colors of the rainbow in its splendor. Ezekiel goes to great lengths to say that the vision is indescribable. Qualifiers are added to virtually every phrase in the vision. He does not say that God *had* a human form, only that he saw something *like* a human form— likewise he saw *something like . . . living creatures* (1:5) and *something like a wheel within a wheel* (1:16). Nor does he say that he saw God; instead he says, *This was the appearance of the likeness of the glory of the LORD* (1:28).

Ezekiel's response to this vision of God's glory was to fall on his face (cf. Gen 17:3; Exod 3:6). Then he heard the sound of someone speaking to him.

Commission to Go to a Rebellious People, 2:1-7

2:1. O mortal. Most often translated as SON OF MAN (KJV, RSV), בן־אדם denotes one who is human in contrast to the divine speaker. The phrase occurs nearly ninety times in Ezekiel, almost always as a title for the prophet in the visions and messages he receives from God. It later became a messianic title, as it is in the NT, although even there it, along with another messianic title, SON OF GOD, may point to the human and divine aspects of the messiah respectively.

2:1-2. Stand up! Although Ezekiel had fallen on his face at *the appearance of the likeness of the glory* (1:28), he is now told to stand, and a spirit brings him to his feet. Whether from internal or external motivation (i.e., is it his spirit or God's?) he obeys.

2:3-7. The audience. The message to the prophet identifies the audience to whom he is to speak. In this call experience Ezekiel, unlike Jeremiah, is commissioned only to Israel and not to other nations. This limited commission is made even more definite in chap. 3 below.

Israel is called a *rebellious house* (v. 7), and this rebellion is dated from the time of the ancestors. Again somewhat in contrast to Hosea and Jeremiah, Ezekiel finds no period of obedience in Israel's history. All of them were *rebels, ancestors* (v. 3) and *descendants* (v. 4) to the present day (v. 3).

To this rebellious house, Ezekiel is commissioned with the prophetic message, *Thus says the Lord GOD* (v. 4). His message is clearly from God and directed to Israel. Ezekiel's task is to proclaim the message; it is not necessarily to bring change and repentance. Whether they hear or reject the word (vv. 5, 7), Ezekiel is to speak that word. As in the later sentinel passages (3:16-21; 33:1-20), Ezekiel's task is to sound the alarm of the Lord's message, and to do so as convincingly as possible. But the response is in the hearers' hands. Already the theme of individual accountability (cf. chap. 18) enters the message.

Another formula introduced in these verses is the prophetic recognition or proof saying (*they shall know that . . .* [v. 5]). By the words he speaks and the signs he does, the people will be aware that Ezekiel is indeed the LORD's prophet. Like Jeremiah, Ezekiel is told not to be afraid of those to whom he speaks.

The Scroll Containing the Message, 2:8–3:3

2:8-10. A taste of woe. The prophet is now told not to be like the rebellious people, but to be obedient, to consume what he sees. Again there is a shift in senses from sound back to sight, and even to taste (v. 8). Ezekiel sees an outstretched hand holding a scroll with writing on both sides. Written on the scroll are words of lamentation, mourning and woe, the initial message Ezekiel is to bring. Although some scholars would argue that Ezekiel's message was only one of judgment and that later disciples or editors added the message of hope, that is too much to read from this passage. Certainly in this first call experience his

message is to be judgmental. But this awareness does not preclude other messages given later in his ministry.

3:1-3. God's sweet word. Obediently, Ezekiel takes and eats the scroll. He accepts by this action the prophetic commission and commits himself to proclaim God's message to Israel. The sweetness of the scroll (cf. Jer 15:16) should not be interpreted as any delight Ezekiel felt in delivering his judgmental message. Indeed, he is bitter and angry over that message (3:14). But the scroll is sweet because it is God's word.

Explanation of the Call
and Ezekiel's Response, 3:4-15

3:4-11. The commission. Three aspects of the commission receive attention in these verses: the people Ezekiel will address, their response, and Ezekiel's empowerment for the people's negative response. Sound is now the dominant sense mode again.

3:4-6. Ezekiel's own people. These verses give renewed emphasis concerning the intended audience: Ezekiel's mission is to his own people. The task would be easier if he were sent to a foreign people. Certainly their difficult language would present a barrier, but at least they would listen!

3:7. Israel's rebelliousness. Israel has a stubborn and rebellious nature that has not changed. They will not listen to Ezekiel. The warning implied in 2:5-7 is made explicit. Just like so many of the prophets before him (Amos 7, Isa 6, Jer 1), Ezekiel is to proclaim the message, but should not expect a positive hearing.

3:8-9. Ezekiel empowered by God. If the people have hard heads and stubborn hearts, God has made Ezekiel's face and head harder than theirs; God has fortified or strengthened (חזק) Ezekiel, a play on his name (יחזקאל, "God will strengthen"). Similarly God strengthened Jeremiah (Jer 1:17-19) and his servant (Isa 50:7).

3:10-11. The commission repeated. After the assurance of empowerment, Ezekiel is reminded again of the task: speak to the exiles, *Thus says the Lord GOD*.

3:12-15. The close of the vision and Ezekiel's response. The vision closes with Ezekiel being lifted up and the LORD's glory also rising. Ezekiel is returned to his people, the exiles by the River Chebar. It is not that he had been physically removed from them, but in his prophetic vision he had been transported into God's presence. Now he is transported back to the realm of human existence.

Ezekiel is not happy with the task and the message he is to bring. He has *bitterness* (v. 14) and anger, but

God's hand was on him strongly. A clear wordplay is present between Ezekiel's bitterness (מר) and the people's rebelliousness (מרי). Ezekiel is not rebellious, but he does not easily embrace his commission. Ezekiel expresses the same feelings as Jeremiah in several of his confessions (Jer 15:16-18; 20:7-9, 14-18). He returns to his regular life among the exiles, but is too *stunned* (v. 15, RSV "overwhelmed") by the message to speak for seven days. The Hebrew indicates another probable wordplay between different significances of שמם: the prophet is *stunned*, the people are to be *devastated, ravaged, desolate*. The latter usage is common to both Jeremiah and Ezekiel.

Messages of Judgment against Jerusalem and Judah, 3:16–24:27

Ezekiel's call experience leads directly into a series of messages against Jerusalem, Judah-Israel. These messages are partly spoken and partly symbolic actions enacting the judgment God is bringing against the people.

The Prophet as Sentinel, 3:16-21

A transition paragraph ties the call experience to the messages—the description of the prophet as a sentinel. A temporal clause, *at the end of seven days* (v. 16), connects this paragraph with the conclusion of the call experience. There Ezekiel was too stunned to speak for seven days. After that time the LORD again speaks to him.

The job of the sentinel is to stand watch and sound the alarm when danger appears. Ezekiel's role as prophet is described as that type of watchman for the nation. Here, however, the primary thrust of the passage is on the responsibility of the prophet to give warning. If the sentinel fails to warn, he will be held accountable for the judgment that befalls the nation—they must be warned in order to respond. But if he faithfully warns, then the people are accountable for their response, whether they heed the warning or not (cf. chaps. 18 [individual responsibility] and 33 [sentinel image again]).

The Muted Prophet, 3:22-27

Again the prophet feels the hand of the LORD upon him, taking him *out into the valley* (or "plain," v. 22). Again he encounters the glory of the LORD. Strangely, this sentinel prophet is now made mute (אלם, "bound, silenced") by God, so that he cannot warn the people (v. 26). He is told that he will be able to speak only when God opens his mouth and removes his muteness (v. 27). Also he will be *bound* (אסר, "tied, bound, imprisoned") with *cords* (v. 25); his mobility will be limited by some means, so that he cannot go freely among the people. This limitation of mobility may indicate a physical restriction placed on the prophet, or it may be symbolic of the lack of mobility that results from siege warfare.

Many commentators take these two "bindings" to refer to serious illness such as a stroke, but the binding may not have been an actual physical disability. Certainly the actions that follow in chaps. 4 and 5 are interpreted as having symbolic meaning, and probably actual cords were used visually to indicate the binding. The muteness is clearly connected with 24:25-27, which speaks of Ezekiel's silence being ended at the news of the fall of Jerusalem (see also 33:21-22). Such muteness may refer to silence in terms of public pronouncements, broken only when the prophet is given a specific word of the LORD. In effect, the people are left virtually without a prophet. The muteness begins with the beginning of the oracles of judgment; its removal is reported at the close of the oracles of judgment.

Four Symbolic Action Messages and an Interpretation, 4:1–5:17

Following directly upon the previous message, the prophet is given four symbolic actions to carry out (4:1–5:4). These four actions are followed by an interpretation (5:5-17) explaining the significance of the actions. No specific word is given that Ezekiel actually carried out the actions, but that is implied. For the most part, the actions are self-explanatory. No interpretation is required. However, the interpretation given makes the meaning more explicit for Jerusalem and the nation.

4:1-3. The first action: portraying siege warfare on a brick. Ezekiel is to take a large building brick, such as might be used in the construction of a house or city wall, and draw on it a depiction of Jerusalem surrounded by *siegeworks*. He himself is symbolically to press the siege against the city with an iron griddle or baking pan. The very stuff of city and household walls is used to depict their destruction in Jerusalem. The iron pan placed on the hot coals to cook its contents indicates the heat of the siege set against the people. Ezekiel sets his face against the city, but it is the LORD who presses the siege. Ezekiel represents God's actions; God is behind the siege, not the Babylonians.

The purpose of the action is to serve as a sign (v. 3), a warning that takes on some of the essence of the judgment signified.

4:4-8. The second action: lying on one side and then the other. Ezekiel is to lie 390 days on his left side followed by forty days on his right side. These time periods are explained as representing the years of bearing the punishment of Israel and Judah respectively, a day for a year. Is the prophet suffering vicariously for his people? He certainly is symbolically bearing their guilt and punishment. However, if the prophet represents the LORD, as was the case in the previous paragraph, the message would be that God has been bearing the sin of the people for all this time.

The time periods have produced many interpretations, none fully satisfactory. The LXX has 190 days rather than MT 390. But that date still presents as many difficulties. The forty years of Judah's sin, guilt, and punishment could relate to the forty years of wandering in the wilderness for the people's sin at Sinai. Forty years could also represent a generation in general terms. Might the 390 years represent an approximate period from the establishment of the monarchy or the building of the Temple to the EXILE of 597 B.C.E. or 587 B.C.E.? Such a figure would fit well Ezekiel's understanding that the people had never been faithful, but continually rebellious and sinful.

As he lies first on the one side and then the other, Ezekiel is to continue facing the siege depiction on the brick and to prophesy against Jerusalem. He is to have his arm bared, representing the LORD's arm outstretched against the people. The imagery reverses the expectations of the people who thought the LORD would bare the divine arm against Israel's enemies. Now Israel is the enemy!

The cords mentioned earlier (3:25) are again mentioned. The prophet is to be bound in cords so that he cannot move from one side to the other until the symbolic demonstration is completed. One can easily visualize Ezekiel taking his position each day, entwined with cords, lying on one side, facing the brick depicting the siege, and having one arm bared, prophesying against Israel and Jerusalem as God gave a word, and silent the rest of the time.

4:9-17. The third action: siege famine portrayed. In keeping with the siege imagery of the previous two prophetic actions, Ezekiel is to prepare and eat a multigrain bread for food. Unlike the previous two actions where the prophet represents God and God's actions, here the prophet clearly depicts the people and what

will happen to them. The combination of grains and the small quantity (usually figured at only about eight ozs. per day), indicate the famine-like conditions of siege and exile. Likewise the small quantity of water (taken to be just over a pint) indicates the rigors of siege. Normally bread was prepared of flour from a single kind of grain and was eaten with other vegetables. Here only bread is available.

When commanded to bake this bread in the sight of his fellow exiles using *human dung* for fuel (v. 12), Ezekiel protests. In the midst of siege, human dung might be the only fuel available, but the thought is too much for Ezekiel. He is a priest; use of human dung would defile him and the food. He compares eating bread baked in that manner with eating *carrion flesh*. So God relents, having made the point in the command itself; Ezekiel may use cow dung to bake his bread.

The final paragraph of the chapter (vv. 16-17) amplifies and repeats the main imagery of the action. The staff of bread, the food supply, of Jerusalem is going to be broken. The people will eat with anxiety and dread; they will drink with appallment (שממון). Because of the famine they will be appalled (שמם) at one another and they will waste away (מקק). The last word returns to Ezekiel's remark that he had never eaten carrion; now the people will virtually become carrion.

5:1-4. The fourth action: shaving the head and beard, and dividing the hair. Ezekiel is to shave his head and beard, often a sign of mourning, but also a sign of disgrace and punishment. In this case, the latter seems more likely. Ezekiel again represents the people themselves. What happens to him (the disgrace and punishment), and to his hair (being cut off and destroyed) is precisely the judgment to come upon the people. One third of the people will die in the siege (apparently of pestilence and famine) just as one third of the hair is burned. One third of the people will die by the sword just as one third of the hair is cut in pieces with a sword. The last third of the people will be scattered in exile as the last third of the hair is scattered by the wind. A few hairs are taken and bound up in the hem of the prophet's garment, but even some of these are burned in fire. These few remaining hairs represent the remnant that will be preserved. Like the previous actions, this one maintains the imagery of siege warfare and judgment to come on the people.

5:5-17. Interpretation of the prophetic actions. Two components make up the interpretation found in these verses: the reason for God's judgment and a description of that judgment.

5:5. This is Jerusalem. This phrase clearly identifies the city that is the subject of the four symbolic actions as Jerusalem. This had been stated at the beginning of the actions (4:1) and repeated throughout them; it is now mentioned again emphatically lest any hearer miss the subject of God's judgment. Jerusalem is described as being the center of the nations, an *omphalos* (= navel, center of the earth) metaphor. The Hebrew concept emphasizes God's election choice of Jerusalem, with the concomitant responsibility of the people to do God's bidding.

Unfortunately, Jerusalem has not fulfilled its responsibility. Instead it has *rebelled*, disobeying God's *ordinances* and *statutes* (v. 6). Indeed, it has become worse than any of the nations around it; they lacked the advantage of knowing God's laws and expectations, but Jerusalem knew them and refused to heed them. Instead, it followed the practices of the other nations. As a result, the LORD will bring *judgments* (v. 8) on the people.

5:9-12. Sins of the people. The specific sins of the people are called *abominations* (v. 9), most often a reference to proscribed religious or cultic acts such as child sacrifice, idolatry, witchcraft, and the like. God's intended action is so striking that God has never done anything like it before and will never do so again (v. 9). The famine will be so severe during the judgment that cannibalism will occur; parents will eat their children and children, their parents (v. 10).

The nature of the people's sins is clarified somewhat in v. 11. The people have defiled the sanctuary with their *detestable things* (usually a reference to idolatry and idolatrous practices) and their *abominations* (v. 11). So repugnant are their actions to God that God swears by the divine life itself to have no pity on them. Verse 12 repeats the judgment of the fourth prophetic action: one third each will fall by pestilence or famine, by sword, or be scattered in exile.

5:13-17. God's anger. The LORD's anger will be furious against the people. The enormity of judgment matches the enormity of their sinfulness. But God's anger is not forever. After bringing judgment, God will be satisfied (v. 13, "ease oneself, be comforted, have compassion"). Whether this indicates that God's anger is satisfied, or that God takes compassion on his people, there is an indication of an end to the anger and judgment. Nevertheless, the emphasis in this passage is on the judgment rather than its completion. But

when God has completed or spent the divine anger, the people *shall know* (v. 13) that the LORD is the one who has done it—another example of a prophetic proof statement. Specifically, they will know that the LORD in divine *jealousy* (or better, "zeal"), has spoken (דבר) and done this. The verb indicates both a spoken word and a deed carried out. With this understanding, one can immediately see that both God's spoken word and action deed are not only intertwined, but in many respects are one and the same. The spoken word becomes the deed.

At least five words are used to describe the devastation of the people and its results. They will become a *desolation* (v. 14), an object of mocking or a *mockery*, a *taunt*, a *warning*, and a *horror* (v. 15). Most of these words are identical with words JEREMIAH used to describe the devastation of the people. The words describe the results of military defeat and the disparagement of the conquered by the victors. Likewise, the people become an example, a warning to others not to rebel. The threefold judgments of famine, pestilence and sword are typical of siege warfare, and are also found in Jeremiah. The threefold statement *I the LORD have spoken* (vv. 13, 15, 17) serves to emphasize that this ORACLE is not from the prophet; it is God speaking. When this devastation comes, the people are to remember that it comes not from the Babylonians or any other political or military force; it comes from the LORD! Further, the repetition serves to highlight the word-deed aspect of the oracle: the spoken word is as good as done.

Oracles against Israel, 6:1–7:27

6:1-10. Against the mountainous high places. The oracle is directed specifically against *the mountains* and *hills* although *ravines* and *valleys* are also mentioned. Judgment is spoken against the high places in particular. These *high places* (v. 3) were cultic sites that were used in the worship of Canaanite and other pagan deities. The Deuteronomist speaks of those who worship "on every high hill and under every green tree" (see Jer 3:6) suggesting open air sites, some found in groves of trees. Other passages relate the worship of Asherah to trees and wooden poles planted like trees. Certainly the prophet is speaking against similar worship practices. This people was practicing a syncretistic religion that worshiped the LORD and pagan deities both. Such was an abomination to God. To be destroyed are all the accessories of worship: idols, altars, incense stands, and the HIGH PLACE itself. The people will be slain alongside the idols. The *high places* will be torn down, desecrated, and defiled by the presence of corpses and bones. The depiction is apparently that of people worshiping their pagan deities even as the invading army comes through. The army destroys the site and kills the people. The dead remain unburied. For a similar action by a reformer king, see the report of Josiah's deeds (2 Kgs 23:4-20).

Verses 8-10 return to the remnant themes. Some will be spared and scattered in exile. Those who are spared are to remember how God was crushed by their rebelliousness and idolatry. This recognition will cause them to loathe themselves for their actions and abominable practices.

Where the previous chapter depicted the shame or disgrace committed upon the exiles (5:1), this passage indicates the shame they feel because of their actions. It will also remind them that God did not warn them about coming disaster for nought. These verses also serve as a transition from the oracle against the mountains to the oracle against abominations.

6:11-14. Against the abominations of Israel. The prophet is commanded to clap his hands and stamp his foot, applauding God's action of judgment on the abominations of the people. It is not that Ezekiel (or God) delights in bringing judgment, but that the judgment is correct for the circumstance. A stubborn and rebellious people who have refused all correction, all warning, must now face God's anger.

The judgment itself is described as the threefold *sword*, *famine*, and *pestilence*. All will fall victim to God's judgment, those nearby and those far away alike. The destruction of the high places and slaughter of the worshipers relates this paragraph to 6:1-7. A full description of the location of these high places is given: *on every high hill, on all the mountain tops, under every green tree, and under every leafy oak* (v. 13). The totality of devastation covers the whole land. The phrase *from the wilderness to Riblah* (v. 14) compares with Amos 6:14, "from Lebo-hamath to the Wadi Arabah," as descriptive of the whole land (see also Ezek 47:13-20 for similar boundaries of the restored land). *Riblah* is also noteworthy for the fact that in 587 B.C.E. it was the location of Nebuchadrezzar's headquarters where ZEDEKIAH was brought after the fall of Jerusalem. There his sons were killed before his eyes, and he was blinded for his rebellion.

7:1-27. Poetic oracles. Unlike most of the book, this chapter is predominantly poetry; the poetry addresses imminent judgment. Terse cries punctuate the oracles, resembling the cries of alarm of a sentinel: *An end! The end has come* (vv. 1, 6); *Disaster after disaster! See, it comes* (v. 5); *Your doom has come/gone out* (vv. 7, 10); *The time has come* (vv. 7, 12); *the day is/draws near* (vv. 7, 12); *See, the day! See, it comes!* (v. 10). The warnings have been sounded; now the battle is being joined.

7:1-4. An announcement of judgment. This oracle is addressed against *the land* (v. 2) relating it to chap. 6 and the oracle against the *mountains. The land* becomes the symbol of the people. In vv. 3 and 4, God shifts speech to address the people directly: *Now the end is upon you.* Judgment is brought against their *ways*, their practices, and their *abominations.* The judgment is simply called *the end*, although later paragraphs in the chapter clarify that military defeat in siege warfare is the means of this end. God warns that he will not spare nor pity the people. The result of this ultimate judgment will be that they *shall know that I am the LORD* (v. 4). The judgment will finally prove that God is God and that God vindicates the divine commands and promises.

7:5-9. A second announcement of judgment. This oracle builds on the previous one and increases the level of intensity. There is a repetition of terminology: *the end has come* (v. 6). But more is added now: *Disaster after disaster . . . comes* (v. 5). In a wordplay Ezekiel says the *end* (קֵץ) has *awakened* (קִיץ) against the people. The cry is one of doom.

Ezekiel then introduces two of the cultic terms familiar to his hearers. He says *the time* has come and *the day* is near (v. 7). The people would naturally have thought the time referred to one of the sacred times, the holy times and seasons of their CALENDAR. Further, the day would refer to the day of the LORD's appearing, the Day of the LORD, when God would vindicate the people and defeat all their enemies. Both terms were common in the worship practices. But, as in Amos, Ezekiel states that the *time* and *day* will not be a day of celebration and shouting; it will be tumult and panic of battle. God is coming, but coming to attack rather than to defend the people of God.

Verses 8b-9 repeat almost verbatim vv. 3b-4. This repetition intensifies God's resolve. The mood of doom is made more pervasive. The prophetic proof formula is also repeated, with one addition: now the people will know that it is the LORD who strikes. They are to remember that the army of the Babylonians is not bringing disaster and doom upon them; the LORD is bringing it.

7:10-13. A third announcement of judgment. In the previous judgment oracle, reference was made to the time and the day. In increasing intensity, this paragraph focuses on those concepts. Now that day has arrived. And instead of a day of worship and celebration, a day of rejoicing and reveling, it will be a day of defeat and disaster. The blossoming rod (v. 10) would remind the hearer of Aaron's budding rod (Num 17: 5, 8), a sign to the murmuring Hebrews of God's presence and election of Aaron to be priest. But here the rod is one of *pride* (v. 10), *violence*, and *wickedness* (v. 11). It will indicate judgment and not election; the people of Israel are the rebels here. The vocabulary of this paragraph is very reminiscent of Amos, especially Amos 8 and 9 with references to buying and selling, mourning and celebrating, and none remaining. *It shall not be revoked* (v. 13), referring to the vision of judgment, is clearly similar to Amos's repeated formula: "For three transgressions . . . and for four, I will not revoke the punishment" (the phrase appears eight times in Amos 1-2). The last phrase, *they cannot maintain* (חזק, "strengthen") *their lives* (v. 13), is another play on Ezekiel's name. God strengthens (the Hebrew meaning of Ezekiel); but the people cannot strengthen their own lives by themselves.

7:14-19. The battle and its results. The alarm has sounded; the battle should have been joined—but no one has gone out to do battle. Why? Because God has already brought down divine wrath upon them. The phrase is virtually identical with the last phrase of v. 12, tying the two paragraphs together and building to a climax. The addition here is that the wrath is specified as *my* (i.e., God's) *wrath* (v. 14). The outcome of God's wrath is devastating: those outside the city die by the sword, and those inside die of pestilence and famine. The description of the people in vv. 17-18 could reflect the ravages of famine and pestilence, or it could indicate the terror at defeat and the mandated submission to an enemy. Silver and gold are flung into the streets, useless. Either the people recognize that their money cannot save them nor buy them food (there was no food to be bought because of the siege), or the invading army ransacks and pillages, tossing prized possessions into the streets as booty. No bribery can save the inhabitants now.

7:20-27. The Temple pillaged. Verses 20-24 describe the desecration of the Temple by the invading army. It is called a *beautiful ornament* and *treasured place*; it will be profaned and plundered, because there the people made and placed their *abominable images*

and *detestable things*. The judgment has moved to the very center of Israel's existence. From the invasion of the land to the siege of Jerusalem, now to the desecration and destruction of the Temple, this chapter has brought every aspect of life under judgment.

They *seek peace* (v. 25), but there is none. The people probably are not seeking a military truce to surrender; they are seeking God's peace and comfort in the Temple—but there is none. Ezekiel takes up a proverbial saying, also cited by Jeremiah (Jer 18:18), that the people keep seeking vision from the prophet, instruction from the priest, and counsel from the elders. But it is all in vain; no response is forthcoming. God will deal with the people according to their own ways; the LORD will mete out to them the same kind of justice they have been practicing. The chapter ends with another proof formula: *And they shall know that I am the LORD* (v. 27).

The Temple Vision, 8:1–11:25

The Temple vision, like the chariot-throne vision of chaps. 1–3, is a unit. In this vision, Ezekiel is transported to the Temple in Jerusalem where he witnesses the abominable, idolatrous practices of the people. He also sees six executioners killing the inhabitants of the city. He then sees the departure of God's glory from that place paving the way for its destruction. But God is not destroyed; God is the one bringing the destruction. This destruction falls heavy on those who had considered themselves as God's favored ones and had thought of the exiles as those under special judgment. Instead, the exiles are described as the remnant who will restore Israel.

8:1-6. An abomination in Jerusalem. The date formula at the beginning of this paragraph sets the time frame a year and two months after the initial call experience. The elders of the people in exile with Ezekiel are gathered at his house when the LORD's hand is upon him and he is transported in a vision to Jerusalem to the northern gateway of the inner court of the Temple, *to the seat of the image of jealousy* (v. 3). The glory of the LORD was there, in the Temple, just as it had been in his vision in the valley.

The *image of jealousy* was an idol, probably of Asherah the Canaanite goddess, which had been set up in the temple courtyard. Such abominable worship practices by the people were driving God from the Temple, but even greater abominations were being practiced.

8:7-13. A second abomination. Then Ezekiel was told to dig through a hole in a wall, and there he saw seventy elders of the people worshiping all kinds of creeping and unclean animals in the dark. The worship of serpents was associated with the Asherah cult, as well as other Canaanite and Egyptian cults. The fact that this worship was taking place in the dark suggests an association with underworld deities. Perhaps the most appalling aspect of all was that the elders of Israel, the people's leaders, were participating in such abominable activities. And they are saying, *the LORD does not see us, the LORD has forsaken the land* (v. 12). When the leaders have so lost their faith, what will become of the people? But even greater abominations awaited Ezekiel.

8:14-15. A third abomination. Ezekiel is moved again, this time to the north gate of the Temple. There he sees women *weeping for Tammuz*. The cult of TAMMUZ, also known as Dumuzi and Adonis, was a Mesopotamian cult of a dying and rising god. Tammuz was a vegetation god who died each summer in the great heat and drought. His adherents would hold a midsummer festival of mourning for him. With the intervention of his consort Inanna/Ishtar, he is brought back to life with the fall and winter rains. The new vegetation of winter and spring indicates his rising. The practice of this Mesopotamian cult was also taking place within the Temple precincts. But still greater abominations were taking place.

8:16-18. A fourth abomination. Ezekiel is brought to the door of the Temple itself. There between the Temple and the altar were twenty-five men facing eastward, away from the Temple, bowing down in worship of the sun. Solar worship was common in the ancient Near East, whether as Shamash, Shipish, Marduk, or one of the Egyptian solar deities. More appalling than the worship of the particular deity is the location of this worship in front of the Temple. And the worshipers, perhaps priests because of the location, turn their backs to God rather than their faces—the worst offense of all.

Because of all their abominations, and especially because they have themselves desecrated the Temple, God will now act: the LORD *will act in wrath*; his *eye will not spare*, nor will he *have pity* (v. 18; cf. 5:11).

9:1-11. Jerusalem's execution. This chapter follows directly on chap. 8. The last line of that chapter is linked with a similar catchword phrase to this chapter. God will not listen to the people of Jerusalem even

though *they cry in* his *hearing with a loud voice* (8:18). Now God *cried in* Ezekiel's *hearing with a loud voice* (9:1).

9:1-2. Summoning the executioners. Six executioners are summoned, each with his destroying weapon or war club in his hand. A seventh individual dressed in linen and carrying a writing case is in their midst. They stand beside the bronze altar, the altar of burnt offerings (1 Kgs 8:64).

9:3-7. Sending the executioners out. First the one in linen is sent out to place a mark on the foreheads of those who lament the abominations committed in the Temple. At least a remnant will be spared from the executioners. Then the other six are sent out to kill everyone not marked. No one is to be spared, not man nor woman nor child. The instructions given to the executioners are exactly what God has previously said of himself, *your eye shall not spare, and you shall show no pity* (v. 5). These executioners are reminiscent of the Passover at the Exodus when the LORD destroyed all the firstborn of Egypt; there all with a mark on their houses rather than their foreheads were spared (Exod 12). This execution begins at the sanctuary with the elders, apparently the same ones involved in sun worship.

9:8-11. Ezekiel's intercession. Ezekiel is left alone in the Temple, surrounded by the ones slain. He cries out to God, *Will you destroy all who remain of Israel?* (v. 8). Ezekiel may have a forehead harder than flint to deal with the rebellious people, but his heart is touched by this slaughter. God's response, however, gives little occasion for hope. God speaks of the great guilt, the bloodshed and perversity of the people. Again God responds that his eye will not spare, nor will he have pity. He will simply bring down their own deeds upon their heads. The judgment is clearly that of individual accountability. No direct mention is made of those spared. The last verse does remind readers of those spared, however: the individual dressed in linen returns and states that he has done just as God commanded.

10:1-22. Departure of the glory. Accompanying the slaughter of the people is the departure of the LORD's glory from the Temple prior to its destruction. The elders had said the LORD had forsaken the land (8:12; 9:9); now, in fact, the LORD was departing. The land would be godforsaken indeed. In this chapter the glory moves from over the ark of the covenant in the holy of holies (although the ark is never mentioned by name, but is clearly indicated throughout by references to *the cherubim*), to the threshold of the Temple, and then to the east gate of the Temple courtyard.

10:1-8. Scattering coals. The individual in linen is instructed to take *burning coals* from the altar under *the cherubim* and scatter them over the city. As he enters the Temple building, the theophanic cloud fills the inner court and the glory moves from over the cherubim to the threshold. One of the cherubim takes coals from the fire within the wheelwork of the chariot-throne and gives the coals to the individual in linen, and he goes out to scatter the coals.

10:9-17, 20-22. Cherubim and chariot-throne. In these two paragraphs the cherubim and the chariot-throne, which are clearly associated with the ark of the covenant in the Temple, are identified as the cherubim and chariot-throne of Ezekiel's inaugural vision by the River Chebar. The importance is two-fold. Not only are Ezekiel's two visions interrelated by the identity, but also the LORD, who was believed by many to reside only in the Jerusalem Temple, is shown to be with Ezekiel and the exiles in Babylonia as well. The glory of the LORD, that symbol of the LORD's presence, is not limited to the land of Israel.

10:18-19. From threshold to gate. Once again the cherubim and the glory of the LORD move. This time they move from the threshold of the Temple to the east gate. The tension mounts as it becomes evident that the glory of the LORD is departing from the Temple by stages: from the inner sanctuary to the threshold and then to the eastern gate. But the chapter closes before the departure is finalized.

11:1-25. Another view of the destruction. This chapter presents another view of the judgment God has brought on Jerusalem. Ezekiel is brought to the east gate of the Temple, the same location where, according to chap. 10, the glory of the LORD had paused.

11:1-4. Wicked counselors. Here Ezekiel sees a group of twenty-five men against whom he is to prophesy. The sin of these individuals is that they *devise iniquity* and *give wicked counsel* (v. 2). They claim to be ones under special protection of God: they are the select meat in the pot, and Jerusalem is the pot. The implication drawn later in the chapter is that the exiles must be considered by them to be the refuse who have been cast off.

11:5-12. The prophet speaks. God's spirit falls upon Ezekiel and he prophesies against the men. Those who have been slain are the select meat; these men will be removed from the pot. God will bring the sword on them, and give them into the hands of foreigners. Twice it is said that God will judge them at the border of Israel, a probable reference to Riblah of 6:14 where NEBUCHADREZZAR set up his camp during the final siege of Jerusalem.

11:13. The prophet intercedes. In his vision, Ezekiel sees one of the men die even as he prophesies. And similarly to 9:8, he intercedes for the people, *will you make a full end of the remnant of Israel?* The question suggests that the ones still in the land were considered to be the remnant, just as their comment about the meat and the pot implied.

11:14-21. Hope for the exiles. This paragraph interprets for Ezekiel the reality that the exiles were not in captivity because they were most guilty. Those remaining in the land assumed that the divine inheritance had been given to them. Now God tells Ezekiel that the exiles will be gathered and the land will be given to them. When the exiles return to the land there will be renewal. They will remove all the idolatrous images and practices from the worship (v. 18), and God will remove their stony heart and *give them a heart of flesh*. They will also have *one heart, and . . . a new spirit* (v. 19). As a result they will be obedient to God. This covenant renewal has God's promise, *they shall be my people, and I will be their God* (v. 20). However, should any follow after the former idolatrous practices, they will be held accountable. The promises are repeated in the later part of the book, the section of hope and restoration, in 36:24-27 and 37:21-28. The paragraph closes with the prophetic messenger formula, lest any think Ezekiel himself was responsible for the words.

11:22-25. The vision concluded. The cherubim then rise up and the glory of the LORD moves away from the Temple. It moves from the midst of the city to the mountain east of the city, where it stops. Here the vision is concluded and Ezekiel is brought back to the exiles in Babylonia. He then tells them of his vision.

Two Symbolic Action Messages and the Imminence of Judgment, 12:1-28

In a scene somewhat reminiscent of chaps. 4–5, Ezekiel is once more told to act out a message. His actions will depict symbolically the judgment God is speaking to the people of Jerusalem and Judah.

12:1-7. An exile's baggage. Ezekiel is commanded to gather together baggage as an exile would. Only a few necessary belongings could be taken, only what one could carry easily, for the way would be difficult, and there would be no one to help carry heavy burdens. As instructed, Ezekiel gathered his baggage by day. Then by night he dug through the wall and went out the hole, just as one fleeing from imminent invasion might try to escape. He also covered his face so that he would not see the land.

The message is two-fold. The oracles to this point have all indicated the imminent judgment on Jerusalem. But, not only were the people in Jerusalem a rebellious people; even those in exile with Ezekiel did not believe these oracles. They too were a rebellious people who had *eyes to see* and *ears to hear*, but did neither (v. 2). Therefore, this message is enacted for their benefit so that perhaps they will understand.

12:8-16. An interpretation. The next morning Ezekiel is told to explain his actions to his fellow exiles. The focus of the oracle is the king of Judah—here called *the prince in Jerusalem* (v. 10). He will try to flee captivity with an escape from Jerusalem. But he will be caught and brought to Babylon where he will die in captivity. All his supporters will be killed or dispersed. A few will survive to tell of their sins in the place where they are exiled.

12:17-20. Eating and drinking with trembling. The prophet is told to eat and drink with quaking, fear and trembling, for the people of Jerusalem will live in similar fear and dread. Again a judgment of devastation and desolation for Jerusalem is given.

12:21-28. Certainty of swift judgment. In response to a proverbial saying that prophetic visions and oracles were not being fulfilled in the present time, God instructs Ezekiel to tell the people that these visions and prophecies would take place very soon, in their days. Further, there would be no more flattering words of false prophets. God guarantees that he will both speak and fulfill the word, and that very soon.

A second oracle responds to another proverb, that visions and prophesies were for distant future days. Here again the warning (or assurance) is given that these words are for the present; they will not be delayed.

Oracles against False Prophecy and Idolatry, 13:1-14:23

These two chapters speak judgment against groups of leaders among the people, against male and female prophets who speak falsely, and against idolatrous elders. If the officials to whom the people turn for guidance are misleading, there is little hope for the people. But more to the point, these leaders are giving the people what they want, and telling them what they want to hear.

13:1-16. False prophecy. The charge against these false prophets is threefold: that they *prophesy out of their own imagination* (v. 2); *follow their own spirit* (v. 3) rather than God's spirit (cf. 3:12, 14, 24 and often); and *envision falsehood and lying divination* (v. 6). While the exact content of the false prophecies cannot be ascertained, it may well have been the *flattering divination* mentioned in 12:24. Such a message would be similar to Jeremiah's complaint against ones who prophesy "Peace, peace" when there is no peace (v. 10, cf., e.g., Jer 14:13, 7:1-15). Nor may one discover whether these *senseless prophets* (v. 3) were deliberately bringing false messages, or actually believed the content of their own messages to come from God. In either case, Ezekiel speaks God's judgment on the content: *they say "Says the LORD," when the LORD has not sent them* (v. 6). Further, these false prophets have not been building up the nation; their influence has been destructive in the long run. If their message was a pleasing message of reassurance, it gave the people a false assurance rather than calling them to repent and respond to the LORD's warning.

Because of their false messages, God has set himself against these false prophets; they will not endure in places of leadership. Ezekiel compares them and their message to whitewash painted on a wall in place of proper plaster. The whitewashed wall looks fine to the casual observer, and all is well in fair weather. But when the rains and storms come, the whitewash offers no protection to the mudbrick wall; it has not sealed the pores like plaster, so the wall collapses. So it will be with the messages of these false prophets. False assurance will be of no help in the day of judgment. The wall and those depending on the wall for protection will all fall in that day. The false prophets will fall as does the wall.

13:17-23. Women who prophesy falsely. Along with the condemnation of male false prophets, is a special word for the women who prophesy falsely. These are women who prophesy, but they are never specifically called prophets or prophetesses. Therefore these women are often designated as sorceresses or witches (Taylor 1969, 123). Nevertheless, they are designated similarly to the male prophets, *who prophesy out of their own imagination* (v. 17, cf. v. 2). The purpose of the *bands* for wrists and full length *veils* (v. 18) is not known. Usually some magical function is ascribed to these objects. Like the false prophets, these deceiving women discourage the righteous and encourage the wicked. They are accused, not only for their false practices, but also because they do not lead the wicked to turn from their ways. They are sentinels who have been false (3:16-21; 33:1-20). The outcome is clear: the magic will prove ineffective and the people will be delivered from such false practices. In addition the outcome will be another proof that God is the LORD.

14:1-11. Idolatrous elders. Ezekiel was visited by *certain elders of Israel* (v. 1), apparently seeking an oracle. These were among the elders in exile living near Ezekiel. Because of their idolatrous practices, no oracle is forthcoming from the LORD through Ezekiel. Instead, the LORD promises to answer (ענה) them directly (v. 4), a word used with double meaning in the prophets, either responding positively (Hos 2:21-22; Isa 49:8), or of bringing judgment (Hos 5:5, 7:10; Isa 3:9). The idolatrous acts are not specified, whether they are taken from Babylonian cultic practices, or practices of the sort Ezekiel was shown in Jerusalem (see chap. 8).

The call to all the people, including the elders, is to repent (שוב, "turn, return, repent"), to *turn away from . . . idols* and abominable practices (v. 6). This is the classic call of the prophets for repentance; the double use of the verb in two linguistic stems is common for emphasis. If anyone continues to practice idolatry and seeks an oracle from God, that person will be cut off, completely ostracized and accursed. Furthermore, the prophet who gives an oracle to such a person will receive the same judgment. Any true prophet would know that idolatrous practices were an abomination to God, and would know that God would not condone them. Therefore to offer an oracle is to become as guilty as the one practicing idolatry.

14:12-23. Even the righteous will save only themselves. The situation is so bad that even persons who were the epitome of righteousness would save only themselves. The emphasis is only on individual accountability. Each person will be held responsible for his or her own actions and judged on that basis. Unlike the intercession for Sodom and Gomorrah, where ABRAHAM bargained with God, such that even ten righteous ones would have sufficed to save the cities (Gen 18), here no surplus of righteousness in one individual can help another. Even more in contrast with both the story of NOAH and Sodom and Gomorrah, God states specifically that not even the families of righteous ones would be spared because of that indi-

vidual's righteousness (vv. 16, 18, 20). The principle is that of individual accountability as prescribed more fully in chap. 18 below.

In case the oracle might have seemed too theoretical for the hearers, the point is made more explicit. God is ready to send against Jerusalem sword, wild animals, famine and pestilence. Hardly anyone will survive. Those who do survive will recount the sins of Jerusalem that have caused this judgment. Then the exiles will understand why Jerusalem had to be destroyed.

Four Allegories, 15:1–17:24

15:1-8. The allegory of the vine. The vine becomes an image of judgment for Ezekiel. In a manner similar to the parable of the vineyard in Isa 5, Ezekiel uses what was a popular positive metaphor concerning the people and turns it into judgment. The continued use of the vine metaphor may be seen from Jotham's fable (Judg 9) to Jesus' teachings (John 15). The vine was prized for its produce of grapes and wine (Num 13 in the spying of the land) and was a symbol of God's blessing. But Ezekiel reminds his readers that the wood of the vine has no practical use. Indeed he describes Jerusalem as a vine that has been burned once and is now charred and less than useless. Further, the vine will now be completely consumed. A burned, charred vine produces no fruit. This vine is burned from both ends, root and branch; it is good only as fuel, but since it is half-burned, it is scarcely even valuable as fuel.

16:1-63. The allegory of Jerusalem as a prostitute. This allegory has six scenes or paragraphs describing Jerusalem. Beginning with God's mercy extended to an exposed infant, Jerusalem's story is told. God rescued, provided for and gave his covenant to her. She was false to that covenant and thus judgment is certain. But beyond judgment, restoration is possible.

16:1-7. Jerusalem, an infant exposed at birth. Jerusalem's parentage is given; her mother was Hittite, her father Amorite. This mixed-breed baby, born in the land of Canaan, was abandoned at birth. She was unceremoniously thrown out and left to die, unclean, unwashed, and naked. But the LORD came along, saw her, and gave her life. No descent from the gods is claimed for Jerusalem and Israel; they are the offspring of the land of Canaan. Both Amorites and Hittites are said to inhabit Canaan. From the very beginning, her existence was dependent on God's grace. But for the LORD, she would surely have died. She grew and developed into a beautiful young woman; but was still naked, unprotected.

16:8-14. Jerusalem and the marriage covenant with God. When Jerusalem reached marriageable age, God entered into covenant relationship with her. The spreading of the cloak over Jerusalem (v. 8) was a sign of marriage pledge (Ruth 3) as well as providing cover for her nakedness and protection. Following the metaphor of the previous paragraph, God then washes, cleanses, anoints Jerusalem and provides her with the finest attire and jewelry. The result was that Jerusalem's fame and beauty both grew. But one is reminded that her fame and beauty come from the splendor or majesty that God had bestowed. Again the emphasis is on what God has made of Jerusalem; by herself, she would still be unclean, unwashed, and naked.

16:15-34. Jerusalem as a prostitute. In imagery well known from Hosea (e.g., Hos 2:9) and Jeremiah (e.g., Jer 2–3), Ezekiel describes Jerusalem's adulterous activities—playing the whore to shrines she made to pagan deities—giving to these false gods the gifts of food, clothing, oil and drink that the LORD had provided for her. She even offered her children in child sacrifice, an abomination Jeremiah also condemns (Jer 7; 19). But most of all she was unfaithful to the LORD and forgot all God's provision and sustenance for her.

The passion of Ezekiel's language is clear from the repeated appearance of the verb *play the whore* (זנה, seven occurrences in this paragraph) and the noun *whorings* (תזנות, eight occurrences in this paragraph) as well as the participle *adulterous* (נאף). In the legal codes adultery and prostitution were punishable by death (Lev 20:10; Deut 22:20-21). So also was playing the whore after other gods (Lev 20:1-6; Exod 34:15-16). Jerusalem stands convicted of a capital crime.

The people were guilty of liaisons with Egypt, Assyria and Chaldea (Babylon). In God's sight, political alliances showed the same lack of faith in the deity as did religious syncretism. To be involved in a political alliance with a foreign nation meant acknowledging the power of that nation's gods, and probable involvement with the religious cults of that nation. Clearly the *platforms* and *lofty places* mentioned in vv. 24, 31, 39 were related to foreign cults.

Ezekiel accuses Jerusalem of being worse than common whores. Whores receive payment or gifts for their prostitution. But Israel paid others rather than receiving payment for her prostitution.

16:35-43. Judgment on Jerusalem for her prostitution. Here Jerusalem is directly addressed as a whore.

The sentence of one caught in prostitution is to be exacted against her—death. All her lovers, all those foreign nations whose deities she had worshiped and with whom she had entered into political alliances will turn on her and destroy her. She will be left naked and destitute, just as she was when God first found her.

16:44-58. Jerusalem like her sisters, Samaria and Sodom. Going back to the original allegory of Jerusalem having a Hittite mother and an Amorite father, Ezekiel now adds two sisters to the family. The *elder* sister (literally "big") is Samaria, the *younger* (literally "small") is Sodom. The major point of comparison is that both these cities and their *daughters* (i.e., villages) have been destroyed because of their wickedness. Sodom was a well-known byword for God's judgment on wickedness; here the wickedness is not caring for the poor and needy, and practicing abominations. Samaria, the capital of Israel, had been destroyed over a century prior to Ezekiel's time; it had been the subject of prophetic outcry for its wickedness (Amos and Hosea). Yet Ezekiel says that, by comparison with Jerusalem, those two cities were righteous. The implication is clear—Jerusalem will suffer the same fate as her two "sisters." Jerusalem's sin is so bad that were God to restore all three, Samaria and Sodom would be consoled that their sins were not as great as Jerusalem's. No longer would Sodom be a byword of wickedness; now Jerusalem would replace Sodom.

16:59-63. Threat and promise. This last paragraph of the chapter begins with a renewed word of judgment. God will deal with Jerusalem according to her deeds; she will be held accountable (cf. chap. 18). But then beyond the certain judgment comes a ray of hope demonstrating God's grace. Despite the fact that Jerusalem has broken covenant with him, God will remember the covenant (v. 8), and will re-establish with Jerusalem an *everlasting covenant* (v. 60; see also 36:22-32 and 37:24-38). Jerusalem, though forgiven, will remember her sins and be ashamed. Even though she was more wicked than Samaria or Sodom, those two cities will be placed under her dominion by God's grace. She will then know that she indeed exists only because of God's mercy and grace, certainly not due to her own merits.

17:1-21. Allegory of two eagles, cedar, and vine. Ezekiel is told to use the form of *riddle* or *allegory* (v. 1; the Heb. for *allegory* could also mean "proverb" or "parable") in speaking to Israel. Nevertheless, just as in some of the parables of Jesus (e.g., Matt 13; Mark 4), the allegory is followed by an explicit interpretation. This interpretation relates to a specific set of events in Judah's recent history as Ezekiel speaks. The *great eagle*, Nebuchadrezzar, came to the Lebanon (Jerusalem, perhaps specifically the palace, one portion of which was called "the House of the Forest of Lebanon" [1 Kgs 7:2]), and took *the topmost* shoot of the cedar (the king, Jehoiachin) to *a land of trade* (Babylon). In place of that topmost shoot, he planted a seed that became a vine with branches and foliage (Zedekiah, whom Nebuchadrezzar placed on the throne). Surely no hearer could miss the implication in vv. 1-6 that this vine was far inferior to the cedar.

The second *great eagle* is the Pharaoh of Egypt, Hophra. Zedekiah renounced vassalage to Babylon and turned to Egypt for assistance. Such a policy reflected the Judean court politics, which included both pro-Egypt and pro-Babylon factions. In the allegory, this shift of policy is described as the vine being transplanted. But the transplant will be unsuccessful, the vine will only be weakened so that an east wind (another reference to Babylon) will cause it to wither.

The explanation makes clear that Egypt will provide no aid. When the siege is set against Jerusalem, Egypt will not help; Jerusalem will fall. Zedekiah will not escape; he will be brought to Babylon in captivity.

17:22-24. Allegory of the sprig from the topmost cedar. The final allegory of this section presents another message of future hope. The same image of the cedar found in the previous allegory is present here. However, it is *the Lord GOD* himself, not a foreign ruler, who takes and plants a *sprig* from the topmost of the cedar. The sprig will be planted *on a high and lofty mountain, on the mountain height of Israel* (vv. 22-23), a clear reference to Jerusalem (cf. Isa 2:2-4, Mic 4:1-4). This restored ruler will prosper *and become a noble cedar* (v. 23). This image of a future ruler may be compared with Isa 11:1. The result envisioned in v. 24 indicates that this restoration will cause all nations (*trees*) to know that God is the LORD. Further, the restoration will result in a reversal, the high and mighty will be brought low while the lowly will be elevated (1 Sam 2:1-10, Luke 1:46-55); the green tree will dry up and the dry tree will blossom forth.

Individual Accountability, 18:1-32

Although this chapter begins with a *proverb* (v. 2, the same word translated as "allegory" in 17:2), it is not allegorical. The proverbial saying simply serves as the point of departure for a discourse on individual accountability.

18:1-3. A proverb rebutted. The proverb suggests that the younger generation suffers for the sins of the older generation. The proverb itself is also mentioned in Jeremiah (Jer 31:29-30). Both prophets speak of the termination of this proverb. One must acknowledge that in some instances this proverb seems to hold true. Lam 5:7 reflects the expression of the proverb. Many politicians today argue that our generation has mortgaged our children's future by amassing an enormous national debt. In addition, some interpreters of Scripture would point to "crack babies"—those born with drug addiction—and babies born HIV-positive as proof of the proverb. Nevertheless, the thrust of this discourse is to disprove the proverb. Each individual will be held accountable before God for his or her actions and only for his or her actions. Examples may on the surface seem to support the proverb, but ultimately they will not stand.

18:4. Each individual is accountable. The major premise is stated in v. 4: *all lives are mine . . . . it is only the person who sins that shall die.* God's justice here is consistent with the Deuteronomic paradigm: obedience results in blessing and life, disobedience results in curse and death.

18:5-18. Three cases. These verses present three cases set over three generations that illustrate the premise. The individual representing the first generation is completely righteous; that person will live. The acts of this person are noteworthy: he practices no idolatry, adultery, oppression, robbery, charges no interest on loans. Positively he gives to the needy, executes justice and obeys the statutes and ordinances of God.

Apart from the reference to idolatry, the specific actions mentioned are all from the realm of interpersonal relationships rather than from the realm of religious acts. No mention is made of the sacrificial system or tithing. What this individual does in relationship to other people is primary (cf. Mic 6:6-8).

The second case presents a son of the first individual. This man is the opposite of the father. He commits all the wicked acts his father avoided and does none of the righteous acts. The judgment is that he will surely die for his actions. The third case, a son of the second man, again presents a reversal. This man sees the sins of his father and does not do them. Instead he does righteously. He will live.

18:19-20. Summary and premise restated. Parents will not be held responsible for the sins of their children, nor will children be held accountable for the sins of their parents. Each person will be accountable for, and only for, his or her own sins.

18:21-24. Previous actions do not replace current actions. What about the person who changes? Do previous actions preclude any change in God's response to an individual? No. If a wicked person repents and turns from wickedness, that person will live. Further, if a righteous person turns to iniquity, that person will die. This paragraph offers hope to anyone who repents, but a warning against turning to wickedness.

18:25-29. Is the LORD's way unfair? Israel was accusing God of being unfair. God reverses the question back on Israel: Is it not rather that Israel's way is unfair? If one who has been righteous turns and becomes wicked, that person will die for his or her wicked acts. That is justice in action. If a wicked person repents and turns from the wickedness, that person will live. That is God's grace and mercy in action. Nothing is unfair, unless one accuses God of being unfair by being merciful and forgiving.

18:30-32. A warning and a renewed call to repentance. The chapter closes with the statement of God's justice: God will judge every one in Israel according to each individual's ways. This warning is followed by a renewed call to repentance. God does not seek to condemn anyone. The call is to turn, to repent and to live. If one would repent, God would give *a new heart and a new spirit* (v. 31; see also 36:22-32). Such a renewal is itself a grace gift of God.

Although we generally refer to this entire chapter as a message concerning individual responsibility, and the major examples of the chapter do reflect accountability, we must note that the chapter is addressed to the whole people. The opening proverb (vv. 1-4) is a proverb *concerning the land of Israel* (v. 2). The final two paragraphs (vv. 25-32) also address the entire nation, *house of Israel* (vv. 25, 29, 30, 31). Ezekiel is making clear that larger entities than the individual are also held accountable for corporate sins. The whole *house of Israel* is accountable for its transgressions.

Two Laments, 19:1-14

This chapter is called a lament in the INCLUSIO (i.e., the use of the same term at the beginning and end of a literary unit) found in vv. 1 and 14. Furthermore, most of the lines of the poem are in the 3+2 *qinah* rhythm of the lament. The laments themselves are allegorical.

19:1-9. Lament of the lioness bereft of two cubs. The image of lion is associated with Judah (Gen 49:9-

10), so the lioness therefore represents the nation Israel/Judah. This lioness raises up two cubs, each of which becomes a strong predator, and each of which is ultimately captured and taken captive, the one to Egypt and the other to Babylon. Usually these two cubs are associated with Jehoahaz and Jehoiachin who were taken captive to those lands. But neither of those kings ruled long (approx. three months each); nor was either a strong predator. It seems preferable to see these two cubs as strong rulers such as JOSIAH and JEHOIAKIM or as symbols for the royal throne representing no specific person. The ending of the first lament has the land without a lion's voice—without a ruler.

19:10-14. Lament for a burned vine. Ezekiel returns to the vine image (see chap. 17) as descriptive of the nation. The vine prospers; its strongest stem becomes a ruler towering high. But then the stem is plucked up and cast down; it withers and is burned. The fire consumes branches and fruit so that no strong stem remains. Again the nation is left without a ruler. This second lament probably depicts Zedekiah as the strong stem, although as above no person need necessarily be intended. In both instances the lament is less for the ruler who is removed than for the nation that remains. The lament is over the lack of a ruler; the land is left leaderless.

Past, Present, and Future, 20:1-44

This chapter opens with a date formula, *the seventh year*, *the fifth month*, and *the tenth day of the month* (v. 1). The date would place the oracle in 591 B.C.E., about eleven months later than the date set in chap. 8. Some of the elders in captivity had come to Ezekiel's house to receive an oracle. They receive an oracle, but not what they anticipate. Following a lengthy review of Israel's history (vv. 5-29), a brief application to the present situation is given (vv. 30-32), followed by an oracle speaking both judgment and hope (vv. 33-44).

20:1-4. Context for the oracle. Both the date and the context are set in these verses. The elders come to Ezekiel, seeking an oracle. The specific elements of their request are not mentioned. However, the LORD makes clear that the deity will not give an oracle based on their desires or expectations. The oracle presented reminds the elders of the *abominations of their ancestors* (v. 4). Note however that the oracle does not indicate that their present condition in exile is due to the sins of the ancestors; such would be antithetical to much of Ezekiel's teaching concerning individual accountability (see chap. 18).

20:5-29. Retelling Israel's history. Ezekiel retells Israel's history, mentioning four periods of its early history, each indicating the utter sinfulness of the nation. Not even in its earliest period was Israel faithful to the LORD. Unlike Hosea (Hos 2:15 [2:17 MT]) and Jeremiah (Jer 2:23) who point to Israel's early period in the wilderness as a period of faithfulness to the LORD, Ezekiel paints even that period as one of rebellion and sinfulness. Never was Israel pure and faithful. All through its history, only God's grace has sustained the people.

20:5-9. Israel's election. Israel's election by the LORD is set in Egypt. The only call upon the people was to cast off idolatry and serve only the LORD. But even there they were not faithful; they continued their idolatry. God considered bringing judgment on Israel in Egypt, but did not. Instead, God remained faithful to the divine promise and brought Israel out of Egypt.

20:10-17. God's statutes. In the wilderness, God gave Israel statutes and laws so that they might know how to live obediently. God gave them sabbath to be a sign of covenant between the nation and himself. Despite all this, the people continued to rebel against God, disobeying his laws and profaning his sabbaths. Although God did judge that generation, and did not permit them to enter the land, God did not totally destroy the nation. The children were spared.

20:18-26. Like parent, like child. The children themselves were commanded to follow God's ordinances and statutes and to keep his sabbaths. But, like their parents, they also rebelled against God. God considered destroying them in the wilderness, but again refrained. Yet God held out the possibility of eventual exile and dispersion in judgment for their sins.

The statutes that were *not good* and the ordinances by which Israel *could not live* (v. 25) are usually understood to refer to God's requirement that the firstborn males be presented to the deity (see Exod 22:29b-30 [MT 22:28b-29]). Apparently, Ezekiel is saying that the people were being tested: would they actually engage in human sacrifice, or would they understand that God was calling for an act of dedication and devotion of what was dearest and most valuable to them?

20:27-29. Continuing in sin. Once in the promised land the younger generation continued their sinful ways. They began following the Canaanite worship practices, making offerings to the baals and other pagan deities.

20:30-32. Application to the present. The present generation is no different from the past ones. They are still practicing the same sins, and still rebelling against God. Therefore, God will not be consulted by them as they desire. Verse 32 points to one possible request the elders made, to be permitted to worship the LORD using stone and wood images. (Perhaps the request went something like this: "Our children see all the Babylonian children worshiping images of their gods Marduk and Nebo. Let us make similar images of the LORD so that our children will have something concrete to worship, and therefore will not begin worshiping those false gods.") Never will God permit such worship.

20:33-44. Judgment and restoration, threat and promise. God's response to this continued sinfulness is one of judgment. The full measure of judgment, which God so far has withheld, will now be brought to bear. God will bring his wrath against all opponents, those in the land and those in exile. All rebels will be purged away. Those who wish to serve idols may do so, but they will not be able to claim that they are worshiping God.

Further, God will restore the faithful to Israel and Zion. No longer will the profane worship there; instead, Zion will be a place of obedience. The LORD will reign as king, and God's faithful will serve him there.

Fire and Sword,
20:45–21:32 (MT 21:1-37)

The motif of judgment found in the previous paragraph continues in this section. Here the judgment is unabated and no mention of restoration or hope is included (unless vv. 30-32 offer a prelude to hope; see below).

20:45–21:7 (MT 21:1-12). Fire and sword against Israel. The image of a devouring fire as a symbol of destruction by warfare was well-known to the prophets. AMOS, ISAIAH and JEREMIAH used the same imagery (e.g., Amos 1:4, 7, 10; Isa 1:7, 5:24; Jer 3:4, 5:14-17). Ezekiel speaks judgment against the south-land from a fire kindled by the LORD. But the hearers do not understand; they say that Ezekiel is just *a maker of allegories* (20:49). Thus the second oracle is given to interpret the first. In the second message, the land is specified as Jerusalem and Israel. The image shifts from fire to the sword. No one could misunderstand the relationship between the sword and warfare as the means of God's retribution. The devastation of this judgment will fall on all equally, both on the *righteous and wicked* (v. 4). Ezekiel further is commanded to *moan* (v. 6) as he delivers this message. The moan is to be that of one who has just received news of terrible tragedy: the tragedy to come upon Jerusalem when it falls.

21:8-17 (MT 13-22). Song of the sword. This poetic oracle is probably based on a song of a sword known to the hearers. Some commentators suggest that a dance with a sword accompanied the song (Taylor 1969, 162). The image portrayed is striking and clearly evokes the picture of destruction whether an actual sword was used or not. The repeated phrases of the sword's being *sharpened* (vv. 9, 10, 11), *polished* (vv. 9, 11) *flashing* (vv. 10, 15), and *slaughter* (vv. 10, 15) add intensity to the scene. Because Israel has refused discipline (v. 10), the most severe sentence possible will now befall the people: the sword of warfare.

21:18-32 (MT 23-37). Sword of the king of Babylon. A further explanation of the judgment against the nation is given. Specifically, God will use the sword of the king of Babylon as his agent. Ezekiel is told to mark out two roads for the Babylonians to follow, one leading to Rabbah, the capital of the Ammonites, and the other leading to Jerusalem. The king casts lots to decide which to attack first, and the lot falls to Jerusalem. The oracle continues to say that Jerusalem may indeed fall first, but ultimately both will be taken.

Verses 24-27 state that Jerusalem's sins, and especially those of its ruler, its *prince* (v. 25), have brought this siege. *Turban, crown* (v. 26), and all symbols of power and prestige will be gone. The fortified city will become *a ruin* (v. 27). The threefold repetition of the word indicates the greatest intensity possible (cf. the threefold "holy, holy, holy, is the LORD of hosts" in Isa 6:3).

The one *whose right it* (i.e., Jerusalem) *is* (v. 27) could refer to Nebuchadrezzar, to whom God has given the city because of its wickedness, or to Jehoiachin, whom many of the exiles considered still to be the rightful ruler of Israel, or to a future messianic ruler. The text does not clarify the issue.

An oracle against the Ammonites follows in vv. 28-32. The oracle began (vv. 19-20) with the king of Babylon at the crossroads. He moved first against Jerusalem. Now he moves against the Ammonites also. The sword of warfare is to destroy the Ammonites as well as the Israelites. They should not assume they have been spared just because Nebuchadrezzar moved first against Israel.

Interpretations of vv. 30-32 vary. They could refer to the judgment against the Ammonites. But the words *Return it* (the sword) *to its sheath* (v. 30) are strange. Normally that would indicate an end of the warfare.

Some commentators take this as a reference to judgment falling upon Babylon itself: that after God uses Babylon as his agent of judgment on Israel, God will turn the sword on Babylon also (so Stalker 1968, 183, and Allen 1990, 28; cf. Jer 25; Isa 10).

Judgment against the Bloody City, 22:1-31

22:1-16. Jerusalem the city of bloodshed. The sins of Jerusalem are related to bloodshed. The sacrificial system, where animals were slaughtered to make atonement for sins, has been abused. The people have continued their sacrifices, but to pagan gods and idols. Further, in their interpersonal relationships the leaders and citizens have abused those lacking protection, thus shedding innocent blood. A catalog of sins is listed in vv. 7-12: dishonoring parents, oppressing foreigners, orphans and widows, profaning sacred times and places; engaging in slander, adultery, and extortion; charging interest and practicing bribery. All these sins point to the ultimate sin: *you have forgotten me, says the Lord GOD* (v. 12). The judgment spoken for these sins is exile and dispersion (v. 15).

22:17-22. Smelting Israel. The image shifts to one of smelting ore to remove the dross or slag from the pure metal. Israel has become like pure metal mixed with dross. Worse yet, Ezekiel describes the nation as the dross. When melted in the smelting furnace, the slag floats to the top of the pure metal and is removed by the smelter. Similarly, God will refine the people to remove all impurities. But more slag is present here than pure metal. The remnant of pure metal will be small.

22:23-31. Like leaders, like people. All the people are guilty of similar sins: the *princes* (v. 25), the *priests* (v. 26), the *officials* (v. 27), the *prophets* (v. 28), and the *people* (v. 29). Priests and prophets have profaned God's teachings and sacred institutions; they have taught lies. Princes and officials have oppressed and destroyed people for gain. All the people have done similarly. God sought for one to stand in the breach like Moses (Ps 106:23; cf. Ezek 14:14), to intercede so that God might not destroy, but none was found. The whole people were utterly corrupt. Therefore God speaks absolute judgment on the people.

Allegory of the Two Sisters: Oholah and Oholibah, 23:1-49

23:1-4. The two sisters introduced. In this allegory, the two nations Israel and Judah are represented by their capitals SAMARIA and JERUSALEM. Oholah (אָהֳלָה, "her tent[-shrine]") is Samaria, and Oholibah (אָהֳלִיבָה, "my tent[-shrine] is in her") is Jerusalem. The names are usually interpreted as referring to the Northern Kingdom's illegitimate sanctuaries—she has her own tent shrine, but it is not the LORD's—in contrast to Judah's legitimate sanctuary—my (the LORD's) tent is in her. These two nations are depicted as sisters in Egypt, perhaps indicating something of their original separateness prior to the United Kingdom of DAVID and SOLOMON. More importantly, both are depicted as prostituting themselves while in Egypt. This is no depiction of a pure, innocent Israel in its early history. Even in earliest times they prostituted themselves to other lovers than the LORD (see 20:5-29).

23:5-10. The elder sister: Oholah, Samaria. That Samaria is called the elder (v. 4, lit. "the greater") need not speak of antiquity. The Northern Kingdom was certainly the larger, more populous, and, probably, more prosperous of the two. But Oholah sought other lovers than the LORD (cf. Hos 2). She went after political alliances with Assyria, and practiced the idolatry of the foreign nations. For these sins she was destroyed and became a byword.

23:11-21. The younger sister: Oholibah, Jerusalem. Surely one would expect that when Oholibah saw the judgment on her own elder sister she would learn and turn from her own sinfulness. Yet the very opposite was the case. Oholibah was even worse in her sins than her sister. Not only did she prostitute herself with political alliances and religious practices of the Assyrians; she also went after the Chaldeans, Babylonians, and Egyptians. Not content with one lover, Oholibah spurned one after another, turning to more adulteries. God's response was to turn in disgust from her (v. 18). The very strong sexual language of the passage was intended to incense hearers with the strongest disgust, precisely what God felt about the people's sins.

23:22-35. Consequences of Oholibah's actions. Just as the elder sister, Oholah, was destroyed for her sins, so also Oholibah would pay for her sins. The LORD, whom she had spurned, would rouse other spurned lovers to come against her: the Babylonians, and all the Chaldeans, Pekod and Shoa and Koa (probably tribal groups from the area north and east of Babylon and Assyria, so Allen 1990, 50, and Taylor 1969, 174), and all the Assyrians (v. 23). Although these nations would be the destroyers, it is the LORD who directs and brings them. God uses them as instruments of divine judgment, even letting them judge the nation

according to their ordinances (v. 24). The result will be devastation, destruction, disgrace and death.

Using the metaphor of the cup also known to Jeremiah (Jer 25, 49), Ezekiel speaks of Jerusalem's drinking from the cup of her sister. The cup will bring drunkenness and sorrow, horror and desolation (v. 33). The final verse of the paragraph reiterates the cause of this terrible judgment and the resulting accountability: because you have forgotten me (i.e., the LORD) and cast me behind your back, therefore bear the consequences (v. 35).

23:36-49. Trial, sentence and execution of the two sisters. These verses depict a court scene where the two sisters, Oholah and Oholibah, are charged, brought to trial, convicted, sentenced and executed. The charges are stated: adultery (worship of other gods), sacrifice to other gods, child sacrifice, defiling the sanctuary, profaning sabbath (vv. 37-39). Their political alliances with foreign powers are described in terms of a prostitute serving a banquet for her lover (vv. 40-44). The judges declare the two defendants guilty as charged. The sentence is execution. They will be stoned, cut down with the sword, their children killed, and their houses burned (v. 47). Stoning was the legal sentence for adultery (Lev 20:2, 10). The remainder of the judgments clearly depict the results of warfare on the land. Samaria had been destroyed by warfare over a century earlier. Yet the two sisters are placed together in guilt and in punishment. Jerusalem was about to suffer the fate of her elder sister.

Fall of Jerusalem Announced, and the Death of Ezekiel's Wife, 24:1-27

24:1-2. The date. A new date formula is given: the ninth year, the tenth month, the tenth day of the month (v. 1). Ezekiel is told to record this date precisely, for this is the very day the king of Babylon had laid siege to Jerusalem (v. 2). This date is traditionally set as January 15, 588 B.C.E. The same date is mentioned in 2 Kgs 25:1 and Jer 52:4. Zech 8:19 may refer to the same date as a fast day for the postexilic community.

24:3-14. Allegory of the rusty pot. The allegory begins with the description of a pot filled with choice pieces of meat and set to boiling. Although the pot could represent a common household pot, it seems more likely that Ezekiel has in mind the pots used in the sanctuary for cooking the meat of sacrifices.

The pot is now identified as being the bloody city (see 22:2), and is a pot with rust inside it. Further, the pot is filled with blood. A rusty pot would be considered unclean or polluted. And meat with blood remaining in it was also unclean (Lev 17:10-14). Thus, whether the meat was for consumption or a sacrifice, clearly it was improperly prepared. Allowing the blood to remain in the meat for either use was an affront to God; the life was considered to be in the blood, so the blood was to be treated properly. Since the people have shed blood and done so openly, God will now bring judgment on them.

The pot becomes a symbol of God's judgment. God himself will heap up the logs, kindle the fire and cook the meat (v. 10). Further, God will heat the fire so hot that the copper of the pot will glow and the rust will be burned away (v. 11). Yet even this action does not remove all the rust (v. 13). So God's judgment will be unsparing and unrelenting (v. 14), a clear indication of the fall of Jerusalem in 587 B.C.E.

24:15-24. The death of Ezekiel's wife. God also told Ezekiel that his wife would die and that he was not to mourn her death. He could *sigh, but not aloud* (v. 17), and was to carry out none of the normal mourning rites. He reported this oracle to the people in the morning, and that night his wife died. When the people asked why Ezekiel was behaving in this manner, he interpreted his behavior as due to God's actions. God was about to destroy Israel's beloved: Jerusalem, the Temple and the people. Those in exile were not to mourn aloud the destruction or loss of family there. The command not to mourn aloud and publicly may be intended to affirm the justice of God's judgment. It may also be designed, in part, to avoid giving satisfaction to Israel's enemies. And indeed, the exiles may be intended to draw hope and consolation from this command. Exiles may yet return to the land of promise.

24:25-27. Muteness to be removed. The prophet was silenced in 3:25-27. He was told that he would speak only when the word of the LORD came upon him. Such silence probably referred only to public or prophetic proclamations. However, now he is told that when a survivor of the fall of Jerusalem brings news of its fall, he will no longer be mute. Once again he will be able to prophesy and intercede freely. Perhaps the removal of the muteness is intended to mark the transition in the prophecy from judgment to hope and restoration. This passage is related to 33:21-22, which also reports the removal of the muteness. The muteness was announced at the beginning of the oracles of judgment against Jerusalem/Judah; the report of its impending removal closes the oracles of judgment. The

muteness of the prophet serves almost as an INCLUSIO for those oracles. The muteness is removed near the beginning of the messages of hope and restoration (see below, 33:21-22).

Oracles against the Nations, 25:1–32:32

This section serves as a transition from judgment to hope. The ultimate judgment against Jerusalem has been spoken. The final siege has been laid. Only the fall of the city itself remains. But God's justice reaches all peoples. The same justice that is meted out to Israel and Judah will also be meted out to the nations. This unit describes oracles of judgment on foreign nations. Further, the judgment meted out against foreign nations may be seen as the first step in the restoration of Israel. Among the charges against these nations is that they profited from or made light of the fall of Jerusalem/Judah. Such charges place the oracles in a context after 587 B.C.E. and may justify their incorporation at this juncture in the book. The number seven plays an important role in these oracles. Seven nations are judged in these oracles: the Ammonites, Moab, Edom, Philistia, Tyre, Sidon and Egypt. The seventh nation, Egypt, has seven separate oracles directed against it. And the seventh oracle mentions seven nations who have been destroyed and are in SHEOL.

Oracle against the Ammonites, 25:1-7

The Ammonites are condemned for expressing glee over the fall of Jerusalem: the sanctuary being profaned, the land made desolate, and the people going into exile. The judgment is that people from the east, tent dwellers and camel owners, will inhabit the land. The reference is to the displacement of the Ammonites by nomadic peoples from the desert to the east.

Oracle against Moab, 25:8-11

The Moabites said that Judah was like all other nations, not recognizing Israel as God's chosen. So Moab will suffer the same fate as the Ammonites; it will be occupied by tent dwellers from the eastern desert regions.

Oracle against Edom, 25:12-14

The Edomites are accused of *taking vengeance* (v. 12) against Judah, of taking part in the fall of Jerusalem, or perhaps invading and occupying part of Judah after the fall. Ps 137:7 and the Book of Obadiah reflect the bitterness the postexilic Israelites felt toward the

Edomites. The judgment against the Edomites will come at the hand of Israel rather than another group.

Oracle against Philistia, 25:15-17

The Philistines are also accused of taking vengeance on Judah at its fall. The judgment against Philistia mentions no human agent: God himself will exact the sentence.

Oracles against Tyre, 26:1–28:19

Four separate but intertwined oracles make up the judgment against Tyre. Unlike the previous oracles in chap. 25, the material against Tyre begins with a date formula. It is set *in the eleventh year, on the first day of the month* (v. 1). No month is mentioned; however, many commentators suggest that it was the eleventh month (so Zimmerli 1983, 33; Stalker 1968, 209; and Taylor 1969, 190; each follows Albright 1932, 93). Such a date would place the oracles early in 586 B.C.E., shortly after the fall of Jerusalem, which Jer 52:12 places in the fifth month.

26:1-6. Tyre's glee and punishment. Much like the oracles against Ammon, Moab, Edom and Philistia, this brief oracle accuses Tyre of taking glee and seeking profit from the fall of Jerusalem. The judgment is that Tyre, that mighty island state, will be buffeted and destroyed by nations, as a raging stormy sea buffets and destroys an island.

26:7-14. Nebuchadrezzar will destroy Tyre. Building on the previous section, this paragraph identifies Nebuchadrezzar, the Babylonian king, as the one who will destroy Tyre. The siege, breaching of the walls, and plunder of the city are depicted. Tyre will be left like a *bare rock* (v. 14) never to be rebuilt. The image here is that of a barren rocky island standing uninhabited in the ocean. The same words (צחיח סלע) were used in 24:7-8 of the blood of Jerusalem's sacrifices, left exposed for all to see. So too will Tyre be exposed.

26:15-18. Mourning over Tyre. Other maritime powers and their rulers are depicted as mourning and lamenting the fall of Tyre. Tyre was such an important sea power at this time that its demise would have impact across the Mediterranean world. Especially would that impact be felt along the Syro-Palestinian coast since Tyre was the major seafaring power there.

26:19-21. Tyre brought down to Sheol. The destruction of Tyre is to be absolute and final. Tyre will be brought down to *the Pit* (v. 20), a synonym for Sheol, the abode of the dead. It will exist no longer, unlike Israel, which will at least have some survivors.

27:1-36. The great ship Tyre. In this allegory, Tyre, both an island-state and a great maritime power, is depicted as a ship.

27:1-11. The ship described in its perfection. The phrase *perfect in beauty* (vv. 3, 4, 11) forms an inclusio marking off this section. The ship is described as being built of the finest components. The craftsmen who built it were the most skilled available. The oarsmen, pilots, artisans, and warriors on the ship were also the best of their trades. This ship-state was the finest possible—it was unsinkable. One thinks immediately of the "unsinkable" *Titanic*.

27:12-25a. The merchandise on the ship. The double reference to Tarshish (vv. 12, 25a) forms an inclusio for this section. Within this paragraph is a catalog of the varied merchandise and items of trade the ship Tyre carried. Tyre was the main center of Phoenician trade during this period. It stood at a crossroads linking overland trade from Mesopotamia, Asia Minor, Syria-Palestine, and the Arabian peninsula with sea trade from Egypt, North Africa, Greece, Rome, Tarshish (=Spain?), and the Mediterranean islands. Goods from all parts of the Near Eastern world flowed through its port. This catalog of merchandise suggests the extent of the city's trade and influence. It is also an important inventory of economic activity characteristic of this general period.

27:25b-36. Sinking of the ship. This magnificent ship, filled with every kind of merchandise, set sail into the sea. A great east wind arose and wrecked the ship, causing it to sink. All was lost at sea: the ship, its merchandise, its crew and passengers. All the lands around are horrified at the collapse of the great ship, Tyre. The reference to the east wind undoubtedly refers to Nebuchadrezzar and his army coming from the east against Tyre. Again the fall of Tyre is depicted as leaving no survivors.

28:1-10. The pride of the king of Tyre. As in several oracles against Judah/Israel, this message is directed against the ruler of Tyre. The ruler considered himself a god (vv. 2, 6, 9), sitting on the throne of gods. This claim is not one of descent from the gods, but a statement of arrogance and pride. It is less directed toward a particular ruler than to the king as representative of the nation. Yet this claim will be shown unfounded; this *god* will be shown to be a mere mortal (vv. 2, 9).

Both the wisdom and the wealth of this ruler/state are acknowledged (vv. 3-5). But the pride engendered by this wealth and wisdom will bring forth destruction. Foreigners will come against this king/state and slay it.

The ruler/state will go down to the Pit, to Sheol, and die. Even worse, Tyre will die a disgraceful, dishonorable death—the death of the uncircumcised (v. 10).

28:11-19. Lament over the king of Tyre. This lament over the king of Tyre uses imagery from the Eden tradition to show how great was the fall of Tyre. Like the original humans, Tyre "had it all." Tyre was in Eden (עֵדֶן, "delight, luxury"). He was perfect in wisdom and beauty. Every precious stone was his (each of those mentioned was found on the high priest's breastplate [Exod 28:17-20]). But like the first human couple, this ruler was brought down by pride (v. 17). He became corrupted by all his possessions; he sinned, and committed violence. Therefore, like that first human couple, the king of Tyre was cast down and driven out (v. 16); he was consumed with fire, and completely destroyed (vv. 18-19).

Oracle against Sidon, 28:20-23

Sidon was another of the Phoenician city-states, usually under the influence of the larger and stronger Tyre to its north. Although Sidon is not charged with any specific sins, it too will be judged and destroyed. The same warfare that destroys Tyre will destroy Sidon.

Restoration of Israel, 28:24-26

These few verses mark the first indication of restoration for Israel within the oracles against foreign nations. No longer will these nearest neighbors of Israel serve as a *thorn* and a *brier* (v. 24) to the people. God promises to gather the scattered of Israel safely and securely; they will build houses and plant vineyards in their land. Their safety and security are assured by God's judgment on the neighboring nations.

Oracles against Egypt, 29:1–32:32

Seven oracles make up the condemnation of Egypt. This material begins with a date formula, *the tenth year, the tenth month, the twelfth day of the month* (29:1), early in 587 B.C.E. if the traditional dates are accepted.

29:1-16. Brief oracles against Egypt. The first oracle is actually a pair of metaphors followed by a prediction of Egypt's fall.

29:1-6a. Pharaoh the dragon (crocodile). Pharaoh is described as a *great dragon* (v. 3). This metaphor could refer to the mythical sea monster or dragon as the NRSV understands or to the crocodiles that inhabit the waters of the Nile (Zimmerli 1983, 111–12;

Vawter and Hoppe 1991, 137). The dragon image would bring to mind LEVIATHAN and chaos combat with God. The Egyptians themselves prayed that Pharaoh would be a crocodile to their enemies. Either is an apt image. Like the king of Tyre, Pharaoh is depicted as claiming deity: *My Nile is my own; I made it for myself* (v. 3). For such a claim, God threatens to destroy the dragon (crocodile) and all the fish of the channels. The fish refer either to the people of Egypt or its army. Egypt's death will be disgraceful—exposure without proper burial.

29:6b-9a. Egypt, a reed staff for Israel. Egypt was a land of reeds, especially well-known for its papyrus reeds. But when Israel turned to Egypt for assistance after rebelling against Babylon, Egypt's assistance was as helpful as a reed staff. A staff was often used by shepherds to defend themselves from wild animals, or to help a sheep that had fallen into a hole. It was also used to steady and support oneself in uncertain terrain. Egypt proved to be a reed staff, a flimsy stalk that broke the first time one tried to lean on it. Because of this lack of support, God will judge Egypt.

29:9b-16. Mighty Egypt will become lowliest of nations. Reference is again made to Pharaoh's claim to have made the Nile. God threatens to make all Egypt desolate and waste for forty years. In a surprising development and unlike the other nations that are to be destroyed completely, Egypt is to be restored somewhat after a period of forty years. Forty years may indicate a full generation; it was the period of wilderness wandering for the Hebrews, during which time the entire generation from Egypt died. After the forty years of exile, Egypt will be returned to its land, but will be the lowliest of nations, never again to rule or exalt itself. This sentence is related directly to Egypt's lack of aid to Judah when Judah turned to it.

29:17-21. Egypt given to Nebuchadrezzar instead of Tyre. This brief oracle has the latest date formula found in the book, *the twenty-seventh year, the first month, the first day of the month* (v. 17). The date would be 571 B.C.E. The oracle substitutes Egypt as booty for Nebuchadrezzar in place of Tyre. Ezekiel had prophesied the fall of Tyre to Nebuchadrezzar (26:7). And Nebuchadrezzar had brought armies against Tyre and had besieged the city. But after thirteen years of siege Nebuchadrezzar was still unable to capture it; apparently a negotiated settlement took place under the terms of which Tyre acknowledged Babylonian supremacy but maintained self-rule. Since the Babylonians did not thus get the spoils of Tyre, they are now given Egypt to despoil instead. Also, this event will vindicate Ezekiel and his oracles to the people of Israel, since the previous oracle had not been fulfilled.

30:1-19. The Day of the LORD against Egypt. The emphasis of this entire oracle is on the Day of the LORD concept. Very similar to the way in which the Day of the Lord was depicted against Israel earlier (7:10-12), it is now described against Egypt. The popular expectation of the Day of the LORD was that it would be a day of Israel's vindication and God's judgment on its enemies. That is precisely the way the Day of the LORD is described in this pericope. While Israel's vindication is not mentioned, its enemies, Egypt, and *the nations* (v. 3) are all destroyed by the LORD.

30:1-5. Alas for the day. The oracle begins with a cry of despair. Ezekiel here raises the cry of the citizens of Egypt. Just as Israel had lamented with despair over God's judgment, so now does Egypt.

30:6-9. Egypt and its allies will all fall. The destruction and devastation that befalls Egypt will also fall upon all its allies. The allies will be destroyed by the sword and lie desolate and waste. God's judgment will reach as far south as Ethiopia.

30:10-12. Nebuchadrezzar to be the agent of destruction. Again Ezekiel's prophecy is specific in indicating that Nebuchadrezzar will be the human agent the LORD uses to bring down Egypt. The result will be devastation.

30:13-19. All Egypt to be destroyed. This section gives a catalog of the principal cities of Egypt, all of which are to be destroyed. The list includes political and religious centers of Upper and Lower Egypt. All Egypt will come to know the LORD.

30:20-26. Breaking the arm of Pharaoh. This oracle is dated to *the eleventh year, the first month, the seventh day* (v. 20), sometime in 587 B.C.E. The oracle speaks of the arm (זרוע, often "might, power") of Pharaoh being broken and not healing. Most likely, this oracle refers to the abortive movement of Egyptian forces against Nebuchadrezzar in 588 B.C.E. in response to a request by Zedekiah (Jer 37). The result was a brief respite from siege for Jerusalem. However, after minor engagements, the Egyptian army retreated back to Egypt. That retreat is described here as the broken arm. The oracle further says that both Pharaoh's arms will be broken; Pharaoh and Egypt will fall, and the Egyptians will be exiled.

31:1-18. Allegory of the cedar, fall of Assyria and Pharaoh. The date formula, *the eleventh year . . . the*

third month . . . the first day of the month (v. 1), places this oracle in 588 B.C.E. just a couple of months later than the previous oracle.

31:1-9. Assyria like a cedar of Lebanon. Egypt is asked with what it would compare its greatness. The Assyrians? Assyria is described as a great cedar of Lebanon, tall, full of branches, and filled with birds' nests. Earlier in chap. 17, the king of Judah was described as a cedar of Lebanon. This tree, Assyria, was like the trees of Eden in beauty (cf. 28:11-14). But all the hearers knew what must follow: Assyria had been destroyed more than two decades previously. The greatest empire known to that part of the world had ceased to exist.

31:10-17. The cedar cut down, cast to Sheol. That tall, magnificent and proud cedar was cut down. Foreigners felled it. Where the mighty cedar once stood now only broken branches and a trunk remain. The mighty nation was sent down to Sheol with all its allies.

31:18. Pharaoh's fate is the same. In a single verse application is made to Pharaoh. He can expect no better treatment than Assyria. Egypt also will be brought down to Sheol, and will lie with the unclean foreigners. Perhaps the linkage of Egypt with Assyria recalls that Pharaoh Necho was allied with the remnants of the Assyrians when he marched through Judah and killed King Josiah in 609 B.C.E.

32:1-16. Lament for the dragon (crocodile). This oracle is dated to *the twelfth year . . . the twelfth month . . . the first day of the month* (v. 1), March 585 B.C.E. Much of it is in the *qinah* or lamentation rhythm. Pharaoh considers himself to be a lion, king of beasts. In reality he is a dragon (crocodile) who will be captured, killed, and thrown out into the open countryside for wild animals and birds to feast upon. The land will be filled with Egypt's blood; even the skies will be darkened as from a great sandstorm. The destruction will come at the hand of the Babylonians. Livestock and people alike will be killed and only desolation will remain.

32:17-32. Egypt in Sheol with the foreign nations. The date formula places this oracle prior to the previous one by about eleven months. Nevertheless, the content clearly makes this oracle the climax to the oracles against Egypt, and to the oracles against foreign nations as a whole. The *qinah* lament meter continues in the first half of this oracle. Egypt is mourned as it goes down to Sheol. It dwells there with the other foreign nations that have been destroyed. A total of seven nations are listed as being in Sheol: Egypt, Assyria, Elam, Meshech, Tubal, Edom, and Sidon. Great powers and lesser groups—all suffer the same fate; all are judged by God for their actions and all are destroyed.

The one surprising element in the oracles against foreign nations is the omission of Babylon among the nations. In many of the oracles Babylon serves as the instrument of God's judgment. Perhaps for political reasons Ezekiel omitted Babylon since he was living among the exiles there, or perhaps there was the hope that Babylon would also be the agent to bring about Israel's restoration. In any case Babylon escapes the strong denunciation of the other nations. It should be mentioned that the Book of Jeremiah includes oracles against Babylon. There the oracles against Babylon are placed at the very end of the oracles against the nations (see Jer 50–51).

Messages of Hope and Restoration, 33:1–48:35

The third and final major section of the Book of Ezekiel represents a shift in the content of his messages after the fall of Jerusalem. The judgment that had been proclaimed on Israel/Judah for its sins is an accomplished fact. The foreign nations have received similar messages of judgment based on their actions. But God is not finished with the elect people. The judgment on Israel, while necessary, is not final. If the remnant who remain, those in exile and those in the land, will repent and turn back to God, there still is hope. Had God not said that their God took no delight in the death of sinners? Had the LORD not said that God would rather the wicked turn from their sins so they might be delivered and live?

One might expect such a message of hope to be received gladly. However, apparently that was not the case. Just as the people had refused to heed the warning the prophet had previously given, now they have lost all hope and refuse to hear his words of hope. As we know, there *were* faithful exiles and faithful Israelites in Judah; Ezekiel describes a general refusal to heed the prophet's call to repentance.

The Prophet as Sentinel Revisited, 33:1-20

This opening oracle of the messages of hope has many parallels with 3:16-21. It serves both as a transition to the messages of hope and a link to the oracles of judgment. The message of individual accountability is stressed in the passage. The prophet as sentinel is accountable for bringing the message God gives him, both words of warning and words of consolation. The warning of the prophet need not be seen only as a prelude to judgment; the warnings also included a call to repentance with a promise of life for those who repented. The repetition of that message should offer hope to the hearers. God takes no pleasure in the death of the wicked; the LORD would much prefer that the wicked turn from their sin and live. But God will be just. The wicked will die; the righteous will live. If one who has been righteous turns to wickedness, that one will die. If one who has been wicked repents and returns to God, that one will live. That simple formula is how God's justice operates, whether on a personal or a communal or national level.

Report of Fall of Jerusalem; Muteness Removed, 33:21-22

The Book of Ezekiel opened with the call experience of the prophet, followed by an oracle of the prophet as sentinel. The prophet was then made mute, except when he spoke words of judgment against Jerusalem/Judah. In the previous paragraph, the prophet as sentinel has been revisited. Now follows the report of the fall of Jerusalem (see 24:26-27) and the removal of the prophet's muteness. The stark words of the survivor, *The city has fallen* (v. 21), mark the end of judgment. The fall of the city now allows the proclamation of restoration. So long as the city remained uncaptured, messages of restoration would hold little meaning. But once the city has fallen and lies in ruins, the message of restoration offers hope for the future.

Oracle concerning Those Remaining in the Land, 33:23-29

Those who survived yet another exile and remained in the land, the ones Jeremiah calls the poorest people of the land, vinedressers and tillers of the soil (Jer 52:16), were assuming they were the inheritors of the land. Because they remained, they must be the righteous remnant. Ezekiel proclaims that they are guilty of the same sins as those who have been exiled or killed. They too will be destroyed and the land will be left a desolation and a waste.

The Entertainer, 33:30-33

A prophet's lot was never an easy one. Ezekiel was now receiving a measure of respect as a prophet of God. He had proclaimed the fall of Jerusalem and Jerusalem had fallen. Yet this brief oracle addressed to

Ezekiel makes clear that the people, or at least many of them, had not truly understood his message nor obeyed it. They heard the words, but they did not repent and act on those words. They were still concerned only about their own individual well-being. Now that he was proclaiming a message of hope and restoration, they gladly received his words. But to them the prophet was just an entertainer, *a singer of love songs*, with *a beautiful voice*, and who *plays well on an instrument* (v. 32). How tragic that they hear, but do not act on those words, for the restoration was based on accountability and repentance. But every generation has more who *hear* than who *do*. When finally the restoration becomes reality as did the fall, then the people will know a prophet has been in their midst!

The Shepherds, the Ideal Shepherd, and the Sheep, 34:1-31

34:1-6. Israel's shepherd-rulers. The prophets used the metaphor of shepherd for the rulers of the nation (see Jer 23, 1 Kgs 22:17). The image depicts the care, protection and leadership expected of the rulers. As in Jeremiah, Ezekiel decries the violence of these shepherd-rulers. They have fed on the sheep rather than caring for them. Because the sheep have in reality had no shepherd, they have become scattered.

34:7-10. The LORD against the shepherds. Because the shepherds have abandoned their responsibility, because they have not protected the flock nor cared for it, the LORD himself will intervene. God will rescue the sheep from their false shepherds. The vivid image of rescuing the sheep from the mouth of the shepherds shows the shepherds as they actually are: ravening animals who feed on the flock.

34:11-16. The LORD as shepherd. Now the LORD himself will become the shepherd-ruler of the people. Using imagery well known from Psalms (especially Pss 23; 95:7; 100:3) Ezekiel describes God's actions. God will rescue and gather the scattered sheep, will feed them, making them lie down in rich pastures, and will especially minister to the injured and weak.

34:17-22. God judges between the sheep. Even among the sheep, there are strong and weak. The stronger were bulling their way over the weaker, taking the best of the pasture, and trampling down the rest, getting to the water hole first and fouling it before the weaker could drink. God will intervene on behalf of the weaker ones. The LORD will give all the people equal justice, the weak and the strong, the powerful and those without advocate.

34:23-24. One shepherd. When God has rescued and restored the flock, *one shepherd* (v. 23) will lead them. The fact that one shepherd is specified indicates Ezekiel's vision of a single restored nation, Israel, rather than a divided monarchy.

This shepherd is identified as *my servant David* (v. 23); he will be a king of the Davidic line. He will be a servant ruler, one who does God's bidding. The covenant will be restored for *the LORD will be their God* (v. 24). The Davidic ruler is not called king, but *prince* (v. 24). He will not "lord it over the people." Further, he will be *prince among them*, that is, he will be one with them rather than over them (see also Jer 31:21).

34:25-31. Covenant of peace. This restoration will result in a covenant of peace. Under this covenant all will live securely and peacefully. Wild animals will be banished. No longer will Israel be enslaved or plundered. Their existence will be one of idyllic bliss and blessing. The Lord will be their God; the people will be God's people and the sheep of God's pasture.

Desolation of Edom, 35:1-15

The desolation of Edom (*Mount Seir*) is the focus of this chapter. The word root שׁמם, "to make desolate" or "desolation," occurs ten times in the chapter. Edom had been briefly mentioned in an earlier oracle (25:12-14), but is here treated in more detail. The preference for the term *Mount Seir* in this oracle may parallel the references to *the mountains of Israel* in this chapter and in the next.

Following the introduction of the oracle in vv. 1-2, the substance of the judgment is presented in poetic form in vv. 3-4. The fifth verse presents the charge against Edom introduced by *because* (יען). Verse 6 moves to the judgment introduced by *therefore* (לכן). The ultimate result is given in v. 9, *Then you shall know that I am the LORD*.

Exactly the same pattern occurs in vv. 10-15: v. 10 presents the charge again, introduced by *because*; v. 11 presents the judgment introduced by *therefore*; and v. 15 closes with the result *Then they shall know that I am the LORD*.

The two sets of charges and judgment are parallel. Edom is charged with invading Judah at the time of the fall of Judah and Jerusalem to Babylon; Edom does so in order to expand its borders, *cherish[ing] an ancient enmity* (v. 5). The enmity may refer to that between Esau and Jacob (Gen 28:41), or to more recent strife as mentioned in Amos 1:11-12. The invading of Judah's territory by Edom is mentioned in Obad 10-14.

The *two nations* (v. 10) refers to Israel and Judah. Perhaps it was feared that Edom's incursions into the Negev, the southern portion of Judah, would extend also into the territory of the Northern Kingdom as well. Continued Edomite presence in the Negev is shown by the region's name in later Hellenistic and Roman times: Idumea.

The judgment spoken in the poetic oracle, and in the prose expansions of the oracle as well, is desolation. Mount Seir, and all Edom, will become desolate. As Judah was made desolate, so shall Edom.

Restoration of the Mountains
of Israel, 36:1-15

This oracle concerning the restoration of the mountains of Israel has two major points of reference previously in Ezekiel: the desolation of *Mount Seir* in the previous chapter, and the desolation of the same mountains of Israel in chap. 6. This chapter serves as a counterpoint to each of those two oracles. Chapter 6 spoke of a desolation that would come upon the mountains of Israel, and that desolation came with the fall of Judah and Jerusalem in 587 B.C.E. However, that destruction was not the end of the story. This chapter proclaims the restoration of those mountains. Similarly, Edom, which had enlarged and enriched itself when Judah fell, is to be made desolate while Israel is to be restored. In each point-counterpoint pair there is desolation and restoration.

The same structural elements that were found in chap. 35 also occur here: *because* (יען, vv. 2, 3, 6, 13), *therefore* (לכן, vv. 3, 4, 5, 6, 7, 14), and *Then you shall know that I am the LORD* (v. 12). However, in this oracle the elements do not list charges and judgment. Instead, the elements list the afflictions the land has already suffered and offer a word of comfort and consolation.

This message is the undoing of judgment on the mountains of Israel. Now the judgment will fall on the other nations (vv. 5, 7), and especially Edom (v. 5). But for the mountains of Israel, there will come restoration, renewed agriculture (v. 9), rebuilding and repopulation (v. 10) by humans and by domestic animals (v. 11). They will *increase and be fruitful* (v. 11), a clear reference to God's command in creation (Gen 1:22, 28). In this restoration, God *will do more good* to the mountains *than ever before* (v. 11). The land will become fruitful like Eden. With the restoration,

the land will be populated by the LORD's people, Israel, as their inheritance (v. 12).

Restoration of the People
of Israel, 36:16-38

Not only are the mountains of Israel to be restored; so also are the people. But the restoration of the people is not just a return of the same sinful people to the land. The people are to be transformed as certainly as the mountains, from a desolate waste of a people into a new, fruitful people.

Ezekiel does not mince words in describing the peoples' sins. They have been exiled, but they fully deserved it. They had defiled the land with their sins, and accordingly they were exiled from it (vv. 16-19). Even in exile they continued to profane the LORD's name (vv. 20-21).

When God restores the people, it will not be for their sake, but for the sake of God's holy name (vv. 22-24, 32). The result of this restoration will not be to glorify the people of Israel, but to glorify God's holy name and to cause the nations to know that God is the LORD (v. 23).

The people themselves will be transformed and restored. The transformation is an inner one brought about by God, who will cleanse all their uncleanness (v. 25) and give the people *a new heart*, and *a new spirit* (v. 26; cf. Ps 51:10 [51:12 MT] and Jer 31:31-34). The new heart will not be like the old stony one, stubborn and unmoving, but will be *a heart of flesh* (v. 26), warm and soft and obedient (v. 27). The new spirit will be God's spirit (v. 27) within them.

When the people are transformed, they will recognize their former sinful ways and despise themselves for those practices (v. 31). That the transformation had not yet taken place for Ezekiel's hearers is evident from the injunction in v. 32: *Be ashamed and dismayed for your ways.*

Once this inner transformation occurs, the people will again live in the land of promise and the covenant relationship will be restored: *you shall be my people, and I will be your God* (v. 28). The land is also transformed in that it will become fruitful and never again blighted with famine (vv. 29-30). Likewise, along with restored agriculture will come the rebuilding of towns and desolate places (vv. 33-36). And the population will increase like the flocks that formerly filled the lands (vv. 37-38). Passers-by will say that the land, once desolate, has become like the garden of Eden (v. 35).

The Valley of Dry Bones, 37:1-14

Ezekiel is taken by the hand and *spirit of the LORD* out to a valley filled with dry bones. No location is indicated. The valley may be a visionary one. If the scene is not visionary but a real one, then the valley was apparently the site of a major catastrophe, such as a calamitous battle. So great was the disaster that the bodies of the dead were left unburied, a horrible fate to any Hebrew. Further, touching such bones would mean being unclean for seven days (Num 19:16-18). As a priest, Ezekiel was not to come near any corpse except for the body of some member of his immediate family. Here he is put in the midst of innumerable dead. There is no doubt that these people were dead. All flesh had decayed; the bones were very dry, bleached white.

Ezekiel is asked: *Mortal, can these bones live?* (v. 3). The question seems absurd. These bones are the very epitome of death and desolation; these are no "warm bodies"; these are dried, bleached bones left behind even by the scavenging animals. Though they are very numerous, there is no life in them. Ezekiel's response, *O LORD God, you know* (v. 3), probably means "LORD, you surely know there is no life in them." Ezekiel has more to learn!

Ezekiel is then commanded to prophesy to these dead, dry bones, that breath come into them and that they live (vv. 4-5). Ezekiel prophesies as commanded: the bones form into their skeletons, and then sinew and flesh and skin appear on them (vv. 7-8). Ezekiel prophesies again to them and breath comes into them and they come alive (vv. 9-10).

The climax of the episode explains what the bones represent. Israel in exile was describing itself as being like bones dried up, dead, without hope, completely cut off (v. 12). But to a hopeless people, God has a message of hope: "I am going to bring you back from the dead." This people, this nation would live again and would return to its land. A God who can restore life to dry bones can also gather people from nations where they have been scattered and restore them to their land.

The Two Sticks:
A Symbolic Action, 37:15-28

Ezekiel is told to take two sticks, one representing *Judah*, and the other representing *Joseph*—also called *Ephraim*—and to *join them* (v. 17; Heb., "bring near") as one in his hand. This action clearly symbolizes the reunification of the former Northern and Southern Kingdoms. The restoration envisioned by Ezekiel is not limited to survivors of 597 B.C.E and 587 B.C.E. from the fall of Jerusalem and Judah. In addition, the survivors of the earlier fall of the Northern Kingdom, or their descendants, will also be brought into this restored nation. In the restored nation there will be one kingdom, never again to be divided, and one king. Further, this restored nation will be cleansed from its idolatries and apostasies (v. 23) and the covenant will be restored: *they shall be my people and I will be their God* (v. 23).

The one king will be a Davidic ruler who will shepherd them; and all will be obedient to God. The land will be theirs forever. The covenant will be *a covenant of peace* and *an everlasting covenant* (v. 26). God will place the divine sanctuary, God's dwelling place, the place of God's very presence, in their midst forever. To ones in exile, many of whom had been eyewitnesses to the destruction of the Temple, this is a powerful message of hope, a message that will be elaborated in chaps. 40–48. In the restored land there will be one nation, one people, one ruler, one covenant, and one God over all who will dwell in the midst of the people.

The Gog Oracles, 38:1–39:29

These oracles break into the flow of the text that would otherwise move from the hopeful message of restoration in chap. 37 to the vision of the restored land and community in chaps. 40–48. They serve to reinforce God's resolve to restore Israel in its place permanently. God could and did use a foe from the north such as Assyria or Babylonia to bring judgment on the people for their sins. But could it happen again? What about some great military power in the future? Could such a power thwart God's promise of restoration? What would become of the eternal covenant of peace (see 37:26)? These oracles address such a possibility. The oracles fit in this context to reinforce the hope expressed in chap. 37, affirming that such desolation as the nation had suffered will never happen again.

38:1-13. Gog, his armies, and the plan. The identity of *Gog of the land of Magog, chief prince of Meshech and Tubal* (v. 2) is unknown. Some commentators relate him to a seventh century ruler of Lydia in Asia Minor known to the Greeks as Gyges, and to the Assyrians as Gugu (see Allen 1990, 204). Others suggest that the oracle was intended against Babylon, but is deliberately put in cryptic style since Ezekiel was himself an exile in Babylonia (Wells 1990, 284). Perhaps the identity of Gog was as mysterious to the original hearers as it is to us today (see Vawter and Hoppe 1991, 175). Clearly, the identity and homeland of Gog are not primary in the oracles; what is important is his power and the real threat his armies pose for a restored Israel. As with Assyria and Babylonia, God is the one who leads these armies out. But unlike other armies who wreak God's judgment on Israel, these armies will themselves be destroyed in a show of God's power. This destruction is foreshadowed in the description of the call of Gog and his armies: *I will turn you around and put hooks into your jaws; and I will lead you out* (v. 4). Gog is treated just like the dragon (crocodile) Egypt (29:4) and will suffer the same fate—death.

But before the destruction of Gog is described, we see him throwing all his might against God's land and God's people. Only by this action will it be known that God will keep the divine covenant of peace with Israel. So the armies are gathered. From every direction they advance against the mountains of Israel, the restored nation. Amos depicts a similar assembly of Philistines and Egyptians against the mountains of Samaria (Amos 3:9-11). The plan is to fall upon this peaceful people, this people of unwalled villages without gates or bars (v. 11) to plunder, despoil, and lay waste (vv. 12-13). The contrast between the people of Israel, who dwell in peace and security, and this advancing, powerful army is striking. Why do the people not act to defend themselves? Because the LORD dwells in their midst and their trust is in God, not in weapons or walls for defense.

38:14-23. The battle and its outcome. The stage is set for the battle. The invading hordes are ready; the land lies defenseless before them. Then a critical question is raised by the LORD:

Are you he of whom I spoke in former days by my servants the prophets of Israel, who in those days prophesied for years that I would bring you against them? (v. 17).

Many commentators follow LXX and Vulgate and take this as a statement rather than a question: "You are he of whom I spoke" (so Zimmerli 1983, 288, 312; Allen 1990, 198, 201, 206). But if one retains the question, as in MT, the passage reinforces God's promise of an eternal covenant of peace. *No*, this Gog is *not* the one about whom the earlier prophets spoke (see v. 17). For the earlier prophets had spoken of one who was God's instrument of judgment on the people for their sins. That judgment has come. This scene follows restoration and forgiveness when the eternal covenant of peace has already been restored. The LORD has brought up Gog, not to judge Israel, but to judge Gog and to let all nations know that the LORD is God and that God has a covenant with the restored people.

The results are devastating—against Gog. The LORD's presence produces great shaking and quaking and upheaval in the land, as in an earthquake. Then God brings all the dreadful plagues against Gog: sword, pestilence, bloodshed, rain, hailstones, fire and sulfur (vv. 21-22). The result will be that the nations will know God is the LORD (v. 23).

39:1-20. Death and burial of Gog and his army. This chapter begins with words almost identical to those that open chap. 38. This repetition is one of many parallels between the two chapters. Both speak God's judgment against Gog. When God brings Gog against the mountains of Israel, Gog and all his forces will fall (vv. 4-5); they will be given as prey to the carnivorous birds and wild animals (v. 4). Magog, Gog's land, will be burned (v. 6). God will not permit the divine name to be profaned by any opponent (vv. 7-8).

So numerous will be the weapons left by the destroyed army that the people of Israel will use them as firewood for seven years (vv. 9-10). Now, instead of being despoiled and plundered by the weapons, Israel will despoil and plunder the weapons Gog's army brought with it.

Gog and all his forces will be buried there in Israel, in a valley to be called the *Valley of Travelers* (עברים, "ones passing through" or "ones passing away, perishing") or the *Valley of Hamon-gog* (i.e., the Horde of Gog [v. 11]). All those fallen will be buried to cleanse the land; so many must be buried that the burial will take seven months (vv. 12-16).

In a parallel description of the end of Gog and his forces, one that picks up on the imagery of v. 4, all birds of prey and wild animals are assembled for a great feast (v. 17). They feast on the flesh and blood of the fallen forces of the invading army (v. 18). This gory banquet is the sacrificial feast the LORD is preparing on the mountains of Israel. That which Gog and his forces planned for the people of Israel, a slaughter, is what becomes of them. It is God's vindication on enemies, on any who would attack God's restored people and land.

39:21-29. Recapitulation and hope. When Israel was exiled, it was because of its sins against God. When Gog and his forces are destroyed, it will be due to their presumption in attacking God's people. But just as God can bring exile and judgment, so also can God in mercy bring restoration. God's promise to Israel is that they can hope in that mercy. They need never fear any human armies of Gog or any other despot. God will gather all the exiles of Israel, leaving none behind; God will bring them into their own land where they will live securely with none to make them afraid. Such is the hope for Israel's future, if they will but trust God.

The New Temple, 40:1–42:20

The nine chapters from 40 to 48 are a unit that describes the new Temple in the restored land, new worship regulations, and a new allotment of the land. The unit begins with a visionary experience similar to that reported in chaps. 8–11 where the prophet is taken to Jerusalem and into the Temple. In many regards this whole unit becomes the reversal of the judgment of chaps. 8–11. In those earlier chapters Ezekiel was shown many abominable practices that led to the departure of God's glory and the giving up of the city for destruction. In chaps. 40–48 there is the description of a new Temple, followed by the return of God's glory, new cultic practices that are according to God's commands, and the permanent blessing God's indwelling presence affords. These chapters from Ezekiel influenced the author of the TEMPLE SCROLL, the largest of the manuscripts found at Qumran.

40:1-4. An introduction. The account begins with a date formula, the tenth day of the first month of the twenty-fifth year of exile, approximately April 573 B.C.E. This date is also the fourteenth year after the destruction of Jerusalem. Ezekiel is brought in a vision to Jerusalem and is presented with a new Temple structure. He is to measure and report this structure to the exiles.

40:5-47. The outer and inner courts of the Temple. Ezekiel enters the outer court of the Temple through the eastern gate. There are three gates to the outer court, one each on the north, south and east. The outer wall forms a square; there is no gate on the western side because the Temple building adjoins the wall. The gates are identical in size and have side rooms or chambers in them. In addition, there are chambers along the length of the north, east and south walls of the outer court. Another wall separates the outer court

from the inner court. Three gateways lead from the outer to the inner court.

The Temple and its courtyards have an east-west orientation. The east gate is the primary entrance into the outer and inner courtyards. The entrance to the Temple building itself is on the east.

Special mention is made of the area where the sacrificial animals are slaughtered and prepared for offering; this act takes place in a chamber in the vestibule of the north gateway that leads into the inner court (vv. 38-43). Mention is also made of two groups of priests and their chambers. Those simply called the priests have charge of the Temple and have chambers on the north side of the inner court (v. 45); they will later be called simply the Levites. The Zadokite priests have charge of the altar and have chambers on the south side of the inner court nearer the altar (v. 46). These Zadokite priests only *may come near to the LORD to minister to him* (v. 46). Thus a hierarchy of priests is indicated.

40:48–41:4. The vestibule, nave and inner sanctuary. Considering all the detail of measurement for the courtyards, the Temple building itself is described in very cursory fashion. Like the Solomonic Temple, this one has three primary parts: the vestibule or porch, the nave, and the inner sanctuary, here called *the most holy place* (v. 4). It is interesting to note that Ezekiel is brought into the nave, which priests could enter, but only his visionary guide enters and measures the most holy place. This understanding of holiness and restricted boundaries is like that of Lev 17 where only the high priest may enter the most holy place, and then only on the Day of Atonement after proper preparation.

41:5-26. Further description of the Temple and adjacent buildings. The exterior of the Temple was three stories high and had chambers on both sides. The whole Temple structure was on a raised platform above the inner court. There was also a Temple yard surrounding the Temple and on the west side a building whose function is not described. The nave and vestibule were decorated with paneling having cherubim and palm trees on them. There was also a table resembling a wooden altar in the nave in front of the most holy place (vv. 21-22).

42:1-14. The priests' chambers. The priests' chambers lay along the north and south wall of the inner court. They filled much of the area of the inner court immediately north and south of the Temple building itself. Here the Zadokite priests were to eat the most holy offerings. Also in these chambers the most holy offerings were to be deposited, and here the priests were to leave the clothing they wore into the nave before they went into the outer court. That clothing was too holy to wear when they went into an area open to the people in general (see below, 44:15-31).

42:15-20. Final measurements, purpose of enclosure wall. The outer measurements of the Temple enclosure wall are made: the enclosure is 500 cubits square. The purpose of the enclosure wall is made clear: it separates the common from the holy. Only that which is holy may enter the Temple courts. Greater holiness is necessary to enter the inner precincts, and only the priests may enter the vestibule and nave of the Temple. The most holy place was the dwelling place of the LORD himself. Without discussing each measurement individually, one can note that each move inward from outside the Temple enclosure ultimately to the most holy place involves moving into increasingly smaller spaces and increasingly elevated spaces. The inner court is smaller than the outer court; it is also raised above the outer court. Likewise the Temple building sits on a raised platform. Even the altar in the inner court sits on a raised platform. In the case of the Temple building, the entryways become increasingly smaller as one moves from the vestibule to the nave and to the most holy place. The elevation, the smaller space, and the increasingly limited access all were indicators of increasing sacredness.

Return of the Glory of the LORD, 43:1-12

Following the completion of the measurements of the Temple, Ezekiel is brought to the east gate of the Temple compound. There he sees the glory of the LORD returning from the east. Ezekiel makes clear that the vision he sees is the same glory that he saw by the River Chebar in his call experience and the same as the departing and destroying vision he had seen in chaps. 8–11. The LORD's glory enters the Temple courtyard through the eastern gate, and as Ezekiel himself is brought to the inner courtyard, the LORD's glory fills the Temple building.

Ezekiel hears the LORD's voice proclaiming that this place, the Temple, is God's throne and footstool from which God will dwell with the people of God forever (v. 7). The people are to abandon their idolatry (v. 9) and their burial practices of burying persons, especially the kings, too close to the sacred precincts (vv. 7-9). Such practices were defiling God's name.

Then Ezekiel is commanded to relate all the Temple plan to the people. They are to repent of their iniquities. Then they are to follow all the plan and ordinances of the Temple. The return of the LORD's glory completes the reversal of God's judgment given in chaps. 8–11. The return of the glory is the return of blessing and life. The same God who judged the people for their sins now offers restoration and blessing to a transformed and repentant people. This future hope is still based on repentance, but it is a glorious hope if they will only repent. The restoration is not merely a return to the former condition; it is a return to a new Temple, new worship practices, and an eternal presence.

Consecration of the Altar, 43:13-27

Once the glory of the LORD has returned, the Temple can be consecrated and the practices of worship can begin. Ezekiel begins with the altar of burnt offerings, the focal point of atonement and worship. The altar is first described and its dimensions given (vv. 13-17). Only the Zadokite priests are permitted to offer sacrifices on the altar (v. 19); they are to consecrate the altar by offering the appropriate sin offerings and burnt offerings for the altar for a period of seven days. On the first day a bull for a sin offering is sacrificed. Some of its blood is put on the horns of the altar, the corners of the ledges, and along the rim. The sacrificed animal is burned outside the sacred precinct (vv. 18-21). On the second through the seventh days a goat, a bull, and a ram are offered as burnt offerings (vv. 22-26). At the end of the seven days, the altar will be purified and consecrated, and the people may bring their burnt offerings and offerings of well-being; then God will accept the people and their offerings (v. 27).

East Gate of Temple Closed Permanently, 44:1-3

Ezekiel is taken back to the eastern gate of the sanctuary—referring to the entire Temple enclosure, not just the Temple building—and finds that the gate is shut. The LORD says that it is to remain shut. The reason is twofold: since the LORD entered this gate it has great holiness attached to it and no one else is holy enough to pass through the gate; and, secondly, in a symbolic sense, the closed gate indicates that the LORD will remain permanently within the sanctuary. In this passage the glory of the LORD is identified with the LORD himself, for previously it was the LORD's glory that was said to have entered the Temple by the eastern gate (43:1-4).

Although no one may enter or leave by the eastern gate, the prince is permitted to eat a meal in the LORD's presence within the chambers or vestibule of the gate (v. 3). But he is to enter the gate area from the outer court and leave the same way.

Ordinances concerning the Priests, 44:4-31

44:4-9. Exclusion of foreigners from sanctuary. No foreigners (i.e, non-Jews, uncircumcised) are to be admitted to the sanctuary in this new Temple. The only reference to foreigners being admitted to the Solomonic Temple is the Carite guards mentioned in 2 Kgs 11 who, as palace guards, also had duties around the sacred precinct. This exclusivism seems to contrast other restoration ideals that envision the nations as flowing up to the mountain/house of the LORD (Isa 2:2; Mic 4:1,2); even Ezekiel would allot foreigners living in the land a portion of the land (47:22-23). This exclusivism is noted in the Herodian Temple by the historian Josephus who mentions a sign written in Greek and Latin forbidding foreigners entry into the inner courts under threat of death. The apostle Paul was accused of bringing an uncircumcised gentile into the Temple (see Acts 21:27-29).

44:10-14. Responsibilities of the Levites. The Levites' duties as mentioned in 40:45 are expanded here. Because the Levites went after idolatry at some time, they are not to come into the most sacred precincts nor handle the sacred offerings. They are to have charge of the Temple; they are to stand before the people and minister to them; they are to slaughter the burnt offering and sacrifices of the people. But the Levites are not to offer the sacred portions nor minister before the LORD, nor enter the most sacred precincts. The idolatry of which they are accused may have been the worship in the rural shrines and sanctuaries prior to Josiah's reform, which centralized all worship at the Temple in Jerusalem (2 Kgs 23:8-9). Clearly, Ezekiel has the Levites in a lesser role than the Zadokite priests, although he still recognizes them as having a legitimate role in the Temple.

44:15-31. Responsibilities of the Zadokite priests. In this section, only the Zadokites are considered as true priests. They are the ones who come into God's presence and minister at the table and handle the most sacred offerings on the altar. This is because they did not go astray as the people of Israel did, nor did they commit the idolatry of the Levites. They are to wear

special clothes made entirely of linen while they are within the inner court and Temple. They are to change clothes before they go into the outer court among the people because of the holiness of the clothes worn in the inner court. Holy things have been set apart for God; such holiness could be dangerous to the common person who had not made proper preparation to handle that which was set apart.

Other regulations for the priests included directions concerning cutting the hair, abstinence from wine when entering the inner court, and marriage. The priests were not to marry a widow or divorced woman (unless the widow had been married to a priest). They were to marry only ones who were full Israelites.

They were responsible for teaching the people the difference between the holy and the common, the clean and the unclean. Some of the regulations involved teaching the people by example. The priests were also to serve as judges, deciding cases on the basis of God's justice. They were responsible for the proper observation of festivals, holy days, and sabbaths. The priests were not to defile themselves by going near or touching a dead person; only for their immediate family were they to so defile themselves. Then they had to undergo ritual purification before they could function as priest again.

The priests were to have no inheritance of the land: the LORD himself was their inheritance. They were to have the grain offerings, the sin offerings, the guilt offerings, all devoted things (things consecrated to God that could not be redeemed), the first or best of the first fruits, and even the first of the dough. These offerings were to supply their needs and to replace an inheritance of land. Finally, the priests were prohibited from eating any meat of an animal that died of natural causes or was killed by other animals.

Property for Sanctuary, Priests, Levites, City, and Prince, 45:1-9

In the restored land, there is to be a redistribution of the tribal inheritance. Each tribe will receive an equal inheritance (see below, 47:13–48:29). Surrounding the sanctuary itself will be portions of land reserved for the homes of the priests and the Levites. This entire tract is a holy district. The sanctuary itself, the most holy land, is to be flanked on all sides by the priests' land. Next comes the Levites' land. The city of Jerusalem has a tract adjacent to the holy district. The portion allotted to the prince extends the width of the holy district and the city's district; in length it runs from the western to the eastern border of the land. The purpose of this allotment to the prince is to limit his holdings. No longer will he be able to dispossess people of their inheritance and enlarge his own holdings. The purpose of enumerating these allotments at this point is to show how the land, like the Temple grounds, is set in varying degrees of holiness, from the common land of the tribal allotments to the most holy portion where the sanctuary sits (cf. chaps. 40–42 above).

Weights and Measures, 45:10-12

Along with a redistribution of the land was to come a standardization of WEIGHTS AND MEASURES. Furthermore, the people are exhorted to use honest weights and measures in their transactions. Practices in daily life, in trade and commerce, were as important to God as worship practices.

Offerings and Festivals, 45:13–46:15

A new schedule of offerings is indicated in this section. Of the wheat and barley, one-sixtieth is to be given; of the oil, one one-hundredth; and of the sheep, one two-hundredth. No mention is made of other products. These offerings are for grain offerings, burnt offerings and offerings of well-being to make atonement for the people. All the people, from the prince down, were responsible for bringing these offerings of their produce. The prince had special responsibility to provide certain sacrifices at the festivals and sabbaths. He also provides leadership at certain of the festivals, by his sacrifices representing the whole people. Whether these sacrifices provided by the prince came from taxation of the people or from his own holdings is not indicated.

Three festivals are mentioned in this calendar of festivals, though they do not directly parallel the other priestly calendars. New Year's Day is here a Spring Festival along with Passover, unlike the more familiar Fall New Year's Day. The New Year's Day ritual is intended as a purification for the sanctuary. This purification is followed on the seventh day (or if the LXX is followed, on the first day of the seventh month) by an additional purification ritual. By these rituals, the Temple was preserved from any uncleanness caused by those who had unwittingly sinned and thus polluted the Temple.

Even the movements of the people are prescribed in this section (46:9-10). The prince may enter into the vestibule of the inner court for certain sacrifices and festivals; the people may only come to the gateway of the inner court. This indicates that the prince had a measure of holiness beyond that of the people—he could come more closely into the LORD's presence. In general, the descriptions of the offerings and festivals are intended to suggest the orderliness of the worship. Prescribed sacrifices and festivals were to be observed at fixed times, and certain movement in and out of the Temple areas was permitted at fixed times. Everything was to be done in a proper and orderly fashion.

The Prince's Property, 46:16-18

A further reference is made to the prince's holdings (see 45:7-9). Here the regulations deal with inheritance rather than the extent of the holdings. Three principles are set out in these regulations. (1) The prince may bequeath to his children portions of land for their permanent inheritance. (2) The prince may grant tracts of his property to his officials; however, this property will revert to the prince at the *year of liberty* (v. 17), either at the end of seven years when slaves were freed, or at the year of jubilee, the fiftieth year. This regulation prevents later generations of the royal family from being impoverished by a lack of land holdings. (3) The prince is not to dispossess any of the people of their inheritance or build up his holdings, or provide additional holdings for his children.

Two Cooking Areas, 46:19-24

The preparation, cooking and baking of the holy offerings, those reserved for the priests' use, was to take place in a section of the inner court west of the priests' quarters. In this manner the holiness of the offerings could be preserved. Presumably these offerings were also to be consumed within the inner court. In the corners of the outer court were four additional food preparation areas. Here the Levites were to prepare the sacrifices of the people. This food was consumed as a communal meal by the worshipers and their families and the Levites. These sacrifices were not considered as filled with holiness, and therefore did not represent the same danger of transmitting that holiness to the people.

River of Water from the Temple, 47:1-12

Ezekiel is brought back to the entrance into the Temple. Here he is shown water flowing out from under the threshold of the Temple and just south of the altar. The water flowed eastward and under the eastern wall of the Temple enclosure, south of the eastern gate. The volume of water increases as Ezekiel is led eastward. One thousand cubits away from the Temple (about 1,500 ft.) it is ankle deep; after another 1,000 cubits it is knee deep; yet another 1,000 cubits and it is waist deep; a final 1,000 cubits is measured and the water is so deep that Ezekiel cannot cross it; one would have to swim across it.

This great river flows eastward down to the Dead Sea. Its waters will change the Dead Sea into fresh water filled with all kinds of fish and water life. As in 37:1-14, that which is dead will be restored to full life. In chap. 37 it is dead bones that live again, symbolic of a hopeless people; here it is a barren wilderness and a dead sea that are restored. People and land are both restored by God's blessing. The banks of this river will be filled with every kind of tree. The leaves will not wilt or fall from these trees, and they will bear fresh fruit every month. The fruit will be for food and the leaves for healing.

The image is one of paradise. Eden's four rivers are replaced with one flowing from God's sanctuary. There are trees here, just as there were in Eden. The paradisal blessing of this river seems comparable to that of the Tree of Life in the garden of Eden. Ps 46:4 apparently refers to the same tradition of a river flowing out of the Temple, as do the postexilic prophecies of Zechariah (14:8) and Joel (3:18 [MT 4:18]) and the NT Book of Revelation (22:1).

Boundaries of the Land and Tribal Allotments, 47:13–48:29

The borders of the restored land are given, beginning at the north and then moving east, south, and west. The northern borders cannot be identified with certainty. Most scholars consider the borders to be comparable to those of classical Canaan, modern Palestine and southern Syria. The northern border is often placed in the vicinity of, or just north of, Tyre (see Allen 1990, 280–81) and runs eastward from the Mediterranean Sea to the territory of Damascus. The east border runs between Hauran (roughly comparable to Bashan) and Damascus, and then follows the Jordan River to the south end of the Dead Sea. The border then runs southwest to Meribath-Kadesh (Kadesh Barnea) and then northwest to the Wadi of Egypt,

south of Philistia. The Mediterranean Sea forms the western border.

The tribal allotments are to be equal in size (47:14), each one a roughly rectangular strip from the Mediterranean Sea to the Jordan River (or border of Hauran north of the Sea of Galilee). There were to be twelve allotments, ten tribes each receiving one allotment, Levi receiving no property allotment, but receiving the offerings for maintaining the Temple, and the Joseph half-tribes of Ephraim and Manasseh each receiving a full allotment. Even those foreigners who reside in the land are to receive an inheritance. They are to be treated like citizens in terms of land allotments; they receive the same portion as any Israelite family in the tribal territory in which they live.

The tribal locations do not fully match those of Joshua (Josh 13–19). Dan is still the northernmost (as it was following the migration recorded in Judg 18). Benjamin and Judah still are closest to Jerusalem, though in reverse order. Emphasis is placed on the equal size of the tribal allotments rather than location.

Gates of the City and its Name, 48:30-35

The city itself will be square; it will have twelve gates, three on a side. Each of the gates will be named for one of the twelve tribes. The city will have a new name from that time forward. It will be called *Yahweh-shammah, The LORD is There* (v. 35). The new name represents the promise of God's eternal presence within the city as surely as the closed eastern gate (44:1-2) depicts God's eternal presence within the sanctuary.

Works Cited

Albright, W. F. 1932. "The Seal of Eliakim and the Latest Preexilic History of Judah, with Some Observations on Ezekiel." *JBL* 51:77–106.

Allen, Leslie C. 1990. *Ezekiel 20–48*. WBC.

Brownlee, William H. 1986. *Ezekiel 1–19*. WBC.

Stalker, D. M. G. 1968. *Ezekiel*. TBC.

Taylor, John B. 1969. *Ezekiel*. TOTC.

Vawter, Bruce, and Leslie J. Hoppe. 1991. *A New Heart: A Commentary on the Book of Ezekiel*. ITC.

Wells, Roy D., Jr. 1990. "Ezekiel, Book of." MDB 283–84.

Zimmerli, Walther. 1979, 1983. *Ezekiel 1, 2*. Herm.

Daniel

Mitchell G. Reddish

Introduction

The Book of Daniel is one of the most enigmatic books in the Bible. Filled with visions, strange beasts, and angels, Daniel has often seemed to be an esoteric writing that has little relevance for the modern world. Understood in its historical and literary contexts, however, the book contains a powerful message of hope, encouragement, and faithfulness. Through the centuries Daniel has continued to inspire and challenge its readers with its emphasis on the sovereignty of God and the ultimate vindication of the righteous. The book has also produced some memorable images: the statue with feet of clay, the three men in the fiery furnace, the handwriting on the wall, Daniel in the lions' den, and the four beasts from the sea. Furthermore, its ideas of the SON OF MAN and individual resurrection have had a profound impact on JUDAISM and even more so on Christianity.

Literary Form

The LXX and the Vulgate place Daniel among the Prophets; the MT, however, considers it a part of the Writings. Modern critical scholars understand the book not as prophetic literature but as the only complete example in the Hebrew Bible of an apocalypse, a specific genre of literature that became popular in Judaism from the second century B.C.E. to the first century C.E.

The first six chapters contain stories of Daniel and his three friends in Babylon during the EXILE. These stories set the narrative context for the visions in the latter half of the book. According to form-critical studies, these stories are classified as court legends or court tales, whose purpose was not to provide historical information but to exhort and edify their readers.

The most apocalyptic section of Daniel is the last half, chaps. 7–12, which contains four eschatological visions received by Daniel and explained to him by angels. These visions correspond to the type of apocalypses classified as historical apocalypses because they contain summaries of historical events cast in the form of predictions of future happenings. The use of these *ex eventu* "prophecies" is a literary technique of many apocalyptic writers. The writer claims to be a famous person from the past who predicts major events yet to come. By presenting the past as future, the writer gains credibility and authority. If what is prophesied has proven true so far, then the reader likely assumes that events in the future will also occur as predicted.

Structure and Unity

The Book of Daniel divides easily into two major sections. Chapters 1–6, written in third person, contain six folk tales about DANIEL and his three friends in Babylonian Exile. Chapters 7–12, written in first person, contain Daniel's four apocalyptic visions and their interpretations. The two halves of the book are interlocked, however, in several ways.

First, the internal chronologies of the two sections overlap. The first six chapters refer to events in the reigns of Nebuchadnezzar (NEBUCHADREZZAR), BELSHAZZAR, and DARIUS the Mede. The visions of the last six chapters begin not after the supposed time of Darius but during the reign of Belshazzar and continue through the periods of Darius and CYRUS of Persia. (See "Date and Occasion," below, regarding difficulties with these chronologies.)

Second, the variation in languages in which Daniel was originally written helps tie the work together. Like the chronologies, the language shifts do not coincide with the break between chaps. 6 and 7. Chapters 1–2:4a and chaps. 8–12 are written in Hebrew; the center section (2:4b–7:28) is written in Aramaic.

Third, the contents of the chapters bind the work together. In a general way, the purpose of the tales and of the visions is the same: to encourage faithfulness to God in times of difficulty and to offer assurance of God's sovereignty.

Date and Occasion

The book presents itself as originating during the Babylonian Exile of the sixth century B.C.E., written by a pious Jew named Daniel who was among the Jewish people deported to Babylon. As early as the second century C.E., however, critics noted problems with this view. A major difficulty concerns historical problems or inaccuracies in the book, one of which is found in the opening verse of the book. The text describes the siege of Jerusalem as occurring during *the third year of the reign of Jehoiakim*, which would be 606 B.C.E. The first siege by Nebuchadnezzar, however, did not occur until 597. The author later describes Belshazzar as the son and successor to the throne of Nebuchadnezzar (5:2). Belshazzar was in reality the son of NABONIDUS, a later king, and was never officially the king but ruled only as viceroy during his father's absences. Even more problematic is the author's reference to *Darius the Mede* (5:31) as the successor to the neo-Babylonian kingdom. Babylon was captured by Cyrus of Persia, not Darius. Furthermore, Darius was Persian, not Median, and succeeded Cyrus rather than preceded him.

Much of the historical information presented in the visions, often in veiled form, is accurate and detailed. The focus of these reports is the reign of Antiochus IV Epiphanes, ruler of Syria 175–164 B.C.E., and persecutor of the Jews in Palestine. The historical information becomes inaccurate again when describing the circumstances of the death of Antiochus. The combination of inaccurate information about the exilic period and detailed descriptions of events leading to and occurring during the reign of Antiochus points to a date of composition for Daniel during the second century B.C.E. The author is aware of the persecution by Antiochus and the desecration of the Jerusalem Temple (167 B.C.E.) but is unaware of the death of Antiochus or the rededication of the Temple by the MACCABEES (164 B.C.E.). The work can then be dated more closely between 165 and 164 B.C.E.

The purpose of the book was to give encouragement and hope to the Jews in Palestine during the second century B.C.E. The tales in chaps. 1–6 are older materials that were reworked and used by the author of Daniel. They betray no knowledge of Antiochus or his persecution. Persian and Hellenistic influences in the tales point to the third century B.C.E. as a likely date for their composition. These tales set the narrative context for the apocalyptic visions, provide information on the legendary figure Daniel, and serve as example stories and didactic material for the readers of Daniel.

Authorship

The identity of the author is unknown. As with almost all Jewish apocalypses, the Book of Daniel is pseudonymous. The purported author Daniel was a legendary figure known for his wisdom and righteousness (Ezek 14:14, 20; 28:3), perhaps derived from the fourteenth century B.C.E. Ugaritic legend of Dnil, a wise judge. Since Daniel was apparently not as well known as other persons to whom pseudonymous works were attributed, the author of the book precedes Daniel's apocalyptic visions with tales that demonstrate Daniel's wisdom and righteousness. Interest in the folk hero Daniel continued beyond the stories contained in the Hebrew Bible, as evidenced by the stories of SUSANNA and BEL AND THE DRAGON (contained in the Greek texts but not the MT of Daniel) and by references to Daniel in some of the manuscripts of the DEAD SEA SCROLLS.

The actual author of the book probably was a Jew of the second century who was apparently one of the *wise*, or *maskilim*, mentioned in 11:33-35 and 12:3. The *maskilim* were committed to righteousness and loyalty to God. They were revered by the masses as pious examples and teachers. These descriptions also fit the Hasidim, a pious sect in Palestine who rejected the Hellenizing measures of Antiochus and were strict in their faithfulness to Jewish law and customs. If the term *maskilim* is another designation for the Hasidim, as some scholars have argued, then the author of Daniel held to a more pacifist stance than did many of the Hasidim.

The author of Daniel certainly calls for resistance to the ways of Antiochus, but not for violent resistance. The Hasidim, on the other hand, joined forces with the Maccabees in the early years of the armed conflict with Antiochus (see 1 Macc 2:42-48). The author of Daniel views such efforts as only *a little help* (11:34) against the monstrous evil of Antiochus. Human efforts will fail. The only solution to the dilemma facing author and readers lay in supernatural intervention, the ending of the present world order, and the establishment of God's eternal kingdom. The task of God's people was to remain faithful, as Daniel and his three friends had done. As God had delivered them, so God would also deliver the faithful of every age, if not in this life, then in the age to come (12:1).

Language

The bilingual aspect of the Book of Daniel is puzzling. Why is the material in 2:4b–7:28 written in Aramaic and the material in 1:1–2:4a and 8:1–12:13 written in Hebrew? No completely satisfactory solution has been proposed. Most scholars agree that the tales in chaps. 2–6 were originally written in Aramaic. Some have argued that the entire work was originally written in Aramaic and then portions were later translated into Hebrew, possibly for religious or patriotic reasons.

Another plausible explanation for the bilingualism is as follows: (1) Chaps. 1–6 were originally written in Aramaic during the third century. (2) In the second century, chaps. 7–12 were written. Chap. 7 was written in Aramaic to tie the tales and visions together; chaps. 8–12 were written in Hebrew due to the author's nationalistic pride or desire to use "sacred" language. (3) When the tales and the visions were joined,

1:1–2:4a was translated into Hebrew in order to form a literary inclusion with the end of the book (4a is a natural break because the Chaldeans' speech would have been in Aramaic). (Collins, 1984b, 29-32.)

For Further Study

In the *Mercer Dictionary of the Bible*: APOCALYPTIC LITERATURE; BABYLONIAN EMPIRE; BEL AND THE DRAGON; CYRUS; DANIEL; DANIEL, BOOK OF; EXILE; HELLENISTIC WORLD; MACCABEES; MENE, MENE, TEKEL, PARSIN; NEBUCHADREZZAR; NUMBERS/NUMEROLOGY; PERSIAN EMPIRE; VISION.

In other sources: J. J. Collins, *The Apocalyptic Imagination*; *Daniel, First Maccabees, Second Maccabees*; and *Daniel, with an Introduction to Apocalyptic Literature*, FOTL; J. E. Goldingay, *Daniel*, WBC; L. F. Hartman and A. A. Di Lella, *The Book of Daniel*, AncB; A. Lacocque, *The Book of Daniel* and *Daniel in His Time*; N. W. Porteous, *Daniel*, OTL; W. S. Towner, *Daniel*, Interp.

Commentary

An Outline

I. Tales from the Exile 1:1–6:28
   A. Daniel and His Three Friends, 1:1-21
   B. Nebuchadnezzar's First Dream, 2:1-49
   C. Three Men in the Fiery Furnace, 3:1-30
   D. Nebuchadnezzar's Second Dream and Madness, 4:1-37
   E. Belshazzar's Arrogance and Punishment, 5:1-31
   F. Daniel in the Lion's Den, 6:1-28
II. Visions of the Future, 7:1–12:13
   A. The Four Beasts from the Sea, 7:1-28
   B. The Ram and the Male Goat, 8:1-27
   C. The Seventy Weeks of Years, 9:1-27
   D. The Last Days, 10:1–12:13

Tales from the Exile 1:1–6:28

Daniel and His Three Friends, 1:1-21

1:1-7. The setting. The opening verses set the supposed historical context for the book and introduce the main characters. Nebuchadnezzar, king of Babylon 605–562 B.C.E., has captured Jerusalem and deported many of its leading citizens. The statement that the siege of Jerusalem occurred *in the third year of the reign of King Jehoiakim* (v. 1) is inaccurate. This and other historical inaccuracies in the book are insignifi-

cant, however. The author's intent is to place Daniel and his friends in the king's court during the Exile.

Chapter 1 was possibly created as an introduction to the entire book, or more likely as an introduction to the other tales. (The benevolent attitude toward the foreign kings argues for a date of composition prior to the time of Antiochus.) Only in this introductory story do Daniel and his three friends appear together. (There is one exception in chap. 2. The role of the three youths in that story, however, is minor and probably secondary to the original tale.) The mention of the Temple vessels that were taken from Jerusalem prepares for the story in chap. 5. Daniel's ability to interpret dreams and visions sets the stage for his role in the subsequent tales.

1:8-17. Refusing royal rations. How the king's *food and wine* would defile Daniel and his three friends is not explained. Perhaps the story is intended to reflect the keeping of the food laws of the Torah, a practice that grew in importance during the time of Antiochus. Perhaps the young men feared that the food had been offered to idols. Or perhaps to accept the king's delicacies was to capitulate too much to the gentile culture. For whatever reason, Daniel and his friends refuse to compromise their beliefs while in the court of the gentile king. Instead, they propose a trial period during which they are fed only *vegetables . . . and water* (v. 12). The success of the test vindicates not only them but also their faith in God.

1:18-21. Health and more. Along with robust health, God grants Daniel and his friends knowledge and wisdom. Particularly significant for the remainder of the episodes is the statement that Daniel is given *insight into all visions and dreams* (1:17). The superiority of the four young men is recognized by Nebuchadnezzar, who grants them a position in his court. Here and elsewhere in the tales, strong similarities between the JOSEPH stories in Genesis and the Daniel stories are evident: young men in a foreign court, emphasis on wisdom and dream interpretation, change of names, and elevation to an important position in the court.

The larger issue addressed in this tale, aside from dietary scruples, is the question, "Can a person remain true to his or her faith in a hostile or secular environment?" That question was a serious one for Jews living in the Diaspora. For the earliest readers of Daniel, confronted with the physical threats of Antiochus and the religious encroachments of Hellenization, the question was of utmost importance. Through the example of Daniel and his friends the author illustrates that faithfulness to the laws of God is possible even in a difficult setting.

Nebuchadnezzar's First Dream, 2:1-49

2:1-11. A troubled king. The setting of the second tale is supposedly during *the second year* of Nebuchadnezzar. According to 1:5, 18, however, Daniel and his friends have already been in the royal court for at least three years. This inconsistency supports the contention that these were originally separate tales.

Bothered by a troubling dream, the king calls for his court sages to explain it to him. The exaggerated nature of the king's challenge heightens the drama of the tale. Not only must the sages interpret the dream, they must also reveal the dream itself. The key to the tale is in v. 11, when the king's wise men reply that no one except the gods can reveal such secrets to the king. Since the gods of the sages do not reveal the dream and its interpretation to the sages, then their gods must be weak and ineffective.

2:12-30. The king's rage. Furious over the failure of the wise men, the king orders them killed. Daniel intervenes in the situation and offers to interpret the dream for the king. Daniel's prayer of thanksgiving to God, as well as his statement to the king, emphasizes that the source of the wisdom displayed by Daniel is

the God of heaven (v. 18) and not Daniel himself. Reminiscent of the Joseph episode in Gen 41, the message of the story is that the God of Daniel is superior to the gods of the court sages.

2:31-45. The dream made clear. The king's dream draws on imagery familiar in the ancient world. Greek and Persian writers portrayed the generations of humanity or the reigns of kings as various metals. In his interpretation Daniel identifies only the first kingdom—the gold signifies the neo-Babylonian kingdom of Nebuchadnezzar. The other three kingdoms are the Median, Persian, and Greek. In actuality, a Median kingdom did not exist as a major Near Eastern power between the time of the neo-Babylonian and Persian powers, as the author of the tales indicated (cf. 5:31–6:1).

Verse 43 interprets the mixture of iron and clay as signifying intermarriage, likely a reference to the intermarriages between the Seleucids and the Ptolemies (possibly a later addition to the tale).

The final kingdom, the stone cut by no human hands that becomes a great mountain, is the eternal kingdom established by God. Although this kingdom is an earthly kingdom, the text is ambiguous about its further identity. Jewish readers would certainly have understood this symbol as a reference to Israel.

2:46-49. Promotions. In response to Daniel's feat, the king "worships" him and promotes him and his three friends. Nebuchadnezzar's exclamation summarizes the message of this tale: *Truly, your God is God of gods and Lord of kings and a revealer of mysteries* (v. 47).

Three Men in the Fiery Furnace, 3:1-30

3:1-7. The king's demands. Daniel is absent from this tale. The protagonists are his three companions. The late date of this story is evidenced by the Persian titles of the officials and the Greek names of some of the musical instruments. Huge statues of gods or rulers were not uncommon in the ancient world. The text is ambiguous concerning the likeness of the colossal golden statue of this tale (approx. ninety ft. high). Apparently the image was that of either Nebuchadnezzar or, more likely, a Babylonian god (presumably Bel-Marduk).

3:8-18. Faithful refusal. As court officials, *Shadrach, Meshach, and Abednego* (v. 12) were conspicuous in their refusal to obey the king's command that everyone worship the golden statue. Their reply to the king is a classic statement of uncompromising religious faith. They believed that God would save them from this threat. Even if God does not rescue them, however, they will not abandon their trust in God. These words would have been especially meaningful during the persecution by Antiochus when many faithful Jews were *not* delivered from torture and death (cf. 2 Macc 6–7).

3:19-30. Punishment and salvation. The dramatic effect of the tale is heightened by the command to heat the furnace *seven times more than was customary* (v. 19). The furnace, or kiln, was a large structure with an opening at the top and one at ground level.

(The Greek texts of Daniel add, after v. 23, a passage known as the Prayer of Azariah and the Song of the Three Young Men. "Azariah" is the Hebrew name of Abednego. This addition contains Azariah's prayer for deliverance, a brief report on the young men while in the furnace, and their song of thanksgiving to God for deliverance. These additions to the Greek text are also treated in this commentary.)

After the men are thrown into the furnace, Nebuchadnezzar is astonished. Looking through the ground-level door, he sees four men, not three in the furnace. The fourth individual, described as having *the appearance of a god* (v. 25), is an *angel* (v. 28), a sign of divine intervention. God has not abandoned Shadrach, Meshach, and Abednego but is with them in their fiery ordeal. Their rescue is described in exaggerated terms: *the hair of their heads was not singed, their tunics were not harmed, and not even the smell of fire came from them* (v. 27). Amazed by the power of the God of the Jews, Nebuchadnezzar decrees that no one is to speak against this God. The question that the king raised earlier, *Who is the god that will deliver you out of my hands?* (v. 15), he now answers himself.

Few biblical stories have been as popular as this tale of Shadrach, Meshach, and Abednego. It is a story about the God of Israel who is more powerful than Nebuchadnezzar or any of his gods. It is a story of religious persecution and divine deliverance. More important, it is a story of a religious faith that does not surrender, a faith that endures even in the face of martyrdom.

Nebuchadnezzar's Second Dream and Madness, 4:1-37

4:1-8. Another dream. The fourth tale is cast in the form of a written decree, an epistle, from Nebuchadnezzar. The events of the tale explain why the king is offering praise to the God of Israel. Nebuchadnezzar

had had a strange and frightening dream. As was the case earlier, his court sages were unable to interpret the dream. Once again Daniel provides the interpretation.

4:9-18. A contest. In the case of the first dream (chap. 2), the king refused to disclose its contents. He asked that his sages reveal to him both the dream and its interpretation. This aspect of the story intensified the contest between Daniel and the court sages. With the second dream, the element of competition between Daniel and the king's wise men is present, but is a minor part of the tale. The king readily divulges the contents of the dream. In this fourth tale, the interpretation of the dream is the major concern.

In his dream the king saw a massive tree that reached to heaven and provided shade, nesting, and food for all the animals of the earth. This tree is the mythological cosmic tree, located in the center of the earth. References to it can be found in myths of several ancient cultures. Ezekiel adapts the myth to describe the arrogance and downfall of Egypt (chap. 31). In this dream the tree represents the king.

The king's dream continues with the appearance of a *holy watcher* (v. 13), an angel. This term for a heavenly being is used extensively in certain pseudepigraphal works, such as *1 Enoch*, *Jubilees*, and the *Testaments of the Twelve Patriarchs*. The watcher orders the great tree to be cut down. The imagery undergoes a strange shift in v. 16. Instead of a tree, the fallen ruler is described as a human and his mind is now changed into the mind of an animal. This situation must last for *seven times* (v. 16), perhaps meaning seven years.

4:19-27. An interpretation. Daniel tells the king that the mighty tree represents Nebuchadnezzar and his great kingdom. As the tree in the vision was cut down, so the king shall lose his kingdom. He shall become like a wild animal, living in the open and eating grass for food. The affliction foretold by Daniel is a form of insanity known as zoanthropy in which a person believes he or she is an animal and acts accordingly. This ailment would befall Nebuchadnezzar because of his pride and arrogance. Once he has repented, he shall regain his kingdom. Daniel offers the king a way to avoid the disaster of his dream: he should act *with righteousness, . . . with mercy to the oppressed* (v. 27).

4:28-37. Advice ignored. Daniel's advice is ignored, however, and the judgment of the dream is fulfilled. The event that brings about the punishment is the king's boasting. Nebuchadnezzar fails to recognize that his reign and his accomplishments are transitory; true power and majesty belong to God. After the allotted time, Nebuchadnezzar comes to his senses, recognizes the sovereignty of God, and offers praises to God. The king then receives again his sanity and his kingdom from God. The purpose of this tale is to assert that the God of Israel is the sovereign of the universe, the one who *is able to bring low those who walk in pride* (v. 37).

This story is apparently an adaptation of a tradition about Nabonidus, the last king of Babylon. Ancient inscriptions report that Nabonidus left Babylon for ten years and stayed in the city of Tema. A fragmentary manuscript discovered at Qumran, known as the *Prayer of Nabonidus*, presents in first-person form Nabonidus's description of his seclusion at Tema for seven years. While there he is afflicted with an evil ulcer, from which he is finally delivered by a Jewish exorcist who is one of the exiles. After his healing, Nabonidus confesses that he had been guilty of idolatry. The similarities to the tale in Daniel are obvious. Both the Daniel tale and the *Prayer of Nabonidus* are likely variations on popular traditions about Nabonidus.

Belshazzar's Arrogance and Punishment, 5:1-31

5:1-12. Handwriting on the wall. In the fifth tale, Nebuchadnezzar is no longer the king. Instead, Belshazzar, said to be his son, is king. (The historical problem with this statement has already been mentioned above: see "Date and Occasion.") The setting is a great festival in which Belshazzar becomes intoxicated. In an act of arrogance and sacrilege, Belshazzar orders that the Temple vessels that had been brought from Jerusalem when the city was destroyed be brought to him. Belshazzar and his guests drink from the vessels and offer libations to their gods from them.

The sacrilege of Belshazzar leads to the famous scene in which Belshazzar literally "sees the handwriting on the wall." The fingers of a hand mysteriously appear and begin writing a message on the wall. Visibly shaken, Belshazzar calls for his court sages and offers a reward to anyone who can read the message on the wall or interpret it for the king. As in the earlier tales, the king's wise men are helpless.

The queen (v. 10) is apparently the queen mother, since she dares to approach the king uninvited, a practice that was forbidden to the king's wives. She informs Belshazzar that there is a person in the kingdom *endowed with a spirit of the holy gods* (v. 11) who can interpret the message for him.

5:13-31. Words of judgment. Belshazzar, who is unfamiliar with Daniel and his ability, offers Daniel a high reward (the third-highest position in the kingdom) if he can solve the riddle that has so terrified the king. Daniel boldly delivers a scathing denunciation of Belshazzar by comparing him to Nebuchadnezzar.

In a retelling of the events of chap. 4, Daniel describes how the mighty Nebuchadnezzar was brought low because of his arrogance and then regained his sanity and his kingdom because he came to realize that God is sovereign over the universe. Belshazzar, however, has not learned this lesson, even though he knew the experience of Nebuchadnezzar. Arrogance and idolatry, instead of humility and worship of God, characterize Belshazzar. Daniel's words are a ringing indictment: *You have praised the gods of silver and gold, of bronze, iron, wood, and stone, which do not see or hear or know; but the God in whose power is your very breath, and to whom belong all your ways, you have not honored* (v. 23).

Daniel then reads and interprets the Aramaic words written on the wall: MENE, MENE, TEKEL, and PARSIN (v. 25). The words are words of judgment against Belshazzar. The original meaning of these words is unclear. Most scholars agree the words are nouns, referring to weights or coins (the mina, the shekel, and the half-mina; the mina was equal to about sixty shekels). This saying was perhaps a popular wordplay describing certain kings or kingdoms and their relative worth.

Whatever the saying's original meaning, Daniel gives it a new interpretation built upon puns of the Aramaic words. The three words are treated as verbs meaning *numbered*, *weighed*, and *divided*. Applied to Belshazzar, the cryptic message foretells the impending loss of Belshazzar's kingdom to the Medes and Persians.

According to the tale, the prediction of Daniel comes true that very night when Belshazzar is killed and Darius the Mede takes over the neo-Babylonian empire. Although Cyrus of Persia was the actual conqueror of Babylon and history knows of no "Darius the Mede," the story in Daniel perhaps contains echoes of historical traditions. The Greek historians Herodotus (*Hist* 1.191) and Xenophon (*Cyr* 7.5) say that the capture of Babylon occurred while a feast was being held. Furthermore, Xenophon adds that the capture occurred at night. Also, Persia did later have a king named Darius—three, in fact.

Like the other tales in Daniel, this story of Belshazzar is a fictionalized account. But its status as fiction does not lessen the importance of its message. It is a graphic portrayal of the folly of human arrogance, pride, and insolence. God is ruler of the universe, not kings, or queens, or presidents, or generals. All worldly powers are ultimately subservient to the God who controls history. For Jews in the Diaspora, and especially for Jews suffering under Antiochus, that message would have been a powerful encouragement to faithfulness.

Daniel in the Lion's Den, 6:1-28

6:1-9. A familiar story. One of the best-known tales from the book, the story of Daniel in the lion's den, is set during the fictional reign of Darius the Mede, supposed successor to Belshazzar. The plot and intention of this story have much in common with the story of the three young men in the fiery furnace (chap. 3).

Daniel is given an important position in the Persian kingdom. He is appointed one of three presidents who oversee the 120 satrapies, or provinces, in the kingdom. (The later Darius I was responsible for organizing the Persian kingdom into satrapies. Ancient sources disagree concerning the number of these satrapies.) Each satrapy was administered for the king by an individual called a satrap. Daniel's abilities are recognized by the king who plans to appoint Daniel as chief over the other presidents and the satraps. Jealous of Daniel, they seek a way to thwart his success.

Daniel is such a righteous man and honorable servant of the king that his enemies must conspire to use his religious beliefs against him. The plotters convince the king to sign an irrevocable decree forbidding anyone to pray to any god or human for thirty days, except to the king. The men know that Daniel, the faithful Jew, will not be able to keep this new decree. The idea that a law of the Medes and the Persians could not be altered or revoked, while found also in Esther (1:19, 8:8), is poorly supported in other ancient sources.

6:10-18. Piety brings trouble. Because he is a pious individual, Daniel ignores the decree and continues his habit of privately praying *three times a day* (v. 10) to God. The practice of praying toward Jerusalem is mentioned already in 1 Kgs 8:44, 48. Daniel does not flaunt his faith nor does he court martyrdom. He simply perseveres quietly because he knows that the decrees of humanity do not negate the claims of God.

The story presents Darius as an unwilling participant in the scheme. He does not want to throw Daniel to the lions, but the irrevocable *law of the Medes and*

Persians (v. 12) forces his hand. Darius is powerless to save Daniel, but he recognizes that Daniel's God may be able to deliver him. Accordingly, he offers a prayer on Daniel's behalf. Daniel is thrown to the lions, the den is sealed, and the king returns to his palace where he spends a sleepless night in worry over Daniel.

6:19-24. Saved from harm. At dawn the king rushes to the lions' den and cries out to Daniel, asking if his God had been able to save him. As was the case with Daniel's friends in the furnace, Daniel is unharmed. Because Daniel was blameless before God and the king and because he had trusted in God (vv. 22-23), God had sent an angel to close the mouths of the lions so they could not harm him. In retaliation for the unsuccessful plot against Daniel, the king orders that the men who had schemed against Daniel, along with their wives and children, be thrown to the lions. This gruesome justice (even vengeance) is in keeping with several passages in the Hebrew Bible (Deut 19:16-21; Num 16:25-33; Esth 7:10; 9:13-14).

6:25-28. Praise for the God of Israel. The last of the folk tales about Daniel ends on a jubilant note: a gentile king praises the God of Israel. Darius, like Nebuchadnezzar in chap. 3, issues a proclamation to all peoples in which he recognizes the sovereignty and power of this God who has miraculously delivered the faithful.

The six tales in Daniel served several purposes: (1) They were example stories, demonstrating how Jews in the Diaspora were to live. (2) They were calls to faithful endurance, urging the Jewish people not to give up on their faith. (3) They were also stories of encouragement, reminding the Jews that God and not Nebuchadnezzar or Belshazzar was in control of history. When read during the time of Antiochus Epiphanes, the stories continued to function in these ways, but with a greater intensity, for the situation had become more desperate for the Jewish people. (4) Finally, as a part of the larger work of Daniel, the tales also serve to set the narrative framework for the visions of Daniel, found in chaps. 7–12.

Visions of the Future, 7:1–12:13

The second half of Daniel is much different from the first half. The second half contains no court tales of contests, intrigues, or miraculous deliverances. As opposed to the first half in which Daniel is described in the third person, the second half is written as a first-person account from Daniel. Daniel is now not the interpreter of dreams, but the recipient. In place of human interpreters, Daniel's visions require angelic interpreters.

Daniel's three friends do not appear in the second half. Furthermore, a different worldview pervades the second half. Gentile rulers are no longer simply misguided, arrogant, or foolish; they do not regret their wrongful acts and offer praise to the God of Israel. Instead, gentile rulers are evil monsters, agents of chaos and destruction. The world has become a place of terror where justice and divine retribution no longer occur. The faithful are not encouraged to live exemplary lives in hopes that a beneficent gentile ruler will value and reward them. Hope lies in the future, when God will intervene to bring about the defeat of evil.

The Four Beasts from the Sea, 7:1-28

7:1-8. Vision at night. Daniel's first VISION occurs one night during the reign of Belshazzar. (These visions do not follow the tales in chronological order, but begin a new chronology that overlaps the former.) Daniel sees *four great beasts* arising from *the sea* (v. 2), an ancient mythological symbol for chaos, the untamed portion of creation that is opposed to the order and control of God. These beasts, like the various metals in the statue of chap. 2, represent four kings or kingdoms. In keeping with the vision in chap. 2, these four kingdoms would be the neo-Babylonian, the Median, the Persian, and the Greek. (The author's choice of *a lion* [v. 4], *a bear* [v. 5], *a leopard* [v. 6], and a *fourth beast . . . different from all the beasts that preceded it* [v. 7] may be based on Hos 13:7-8.) The *little* horn (v. 8) on the fourth beast is Antiochus Epiphanes, the persecutor of the Jews (175–164 B.C.E.), who attained his power by driving out several other claimants to the throne. The *mouth speaking arrogantly* (v. 8) is an appropriate description for one who issued decrees outlawing the practice of Judaism (cf. 1 Macc 1:54-61; 2 Macc 6:1-11). The *ten horns* (v. 7) that precede the little horn represent Hellenistic rulers, although scholars disagree concerning the identification of the ten.

To understand the beasts as referring to the four kingdoms is correct, but not adequate. These beasts are horrifying creatures, unlike any actual animal. Arising out of the primeval chaos, they are agents of evil. They represent a power that is larger than life. By using this imagery, the author is asserting that the struggle in which he and his readers are engaged is no mundane skirmish. They are involved in a cosmic struggle that is as old as creation itself—order versus chaos, God versus the forces of evil. Such an understanding elevates and gives new meaning to their sufferings and to the struggles in which they are involved.

7:9-14. The vision changes. The setting is now not the earth, but the heavenly throne room. Daniel sees God, *the Ancient One* (v. 13; Aramaic: "one like an ancient of days"), seated on a throne that is like a chariot with wheels of fire (cf. Ezek 1 and 10). The white clothing and white hair symbolize God's purity and glory. The white hair indicates also God's longevity. Flowing out from the chariot are streams of fire (cf. *1 Enoch* 14:19).

The scene is one of judgment, with God and the heavenly court in session. The heavenly books are opened and the judgment begins. Ancient Near Eastern traditions (including biblical traditions) refer to at least three types of heavenly books: those that contain all the deeds of each person by which people are judged, those that are a register of the heavenly inhabitants (the "book of life"), and those that contain the future course of world events. The first type seems to fit the present context.

The fourth beast, containing the arrogant little horn, is destroyed by fire. The other three beasts, whose evil does not equal that of the fourth, lose their power but have their lives prolonged for a brief period.

Daniel then sees the arrival of a new figure, *one like a human being* (v. 13), who comes with the clouds. The Aramaic phrase translates literally as "one like a SON OF MAN." God gives to this human-like figure everlasting and universal dominion. Who is this "son of man" figure? The answer to that question is one of the largest enigmas of the entire book. Some interpreters have seen him as the messiah. He does function as God's chosen and is granted sovereignty of this new kingdom, but he is never called God's anointed (messiah) and is not described as a Davidic ruler, the traditional messianic view. Is he an angel? His *coming with the clouds of heaven* seems to support that identification. Additional support for this identification comes from the later uses of *one . . . having the appearance of a man, man,* or *one in human form* (lit., "having the likeness of the sons of men") to describe angelic figures (see 8:15; 9:21; 10:16, 18). Since Michael is the angel who is described as the protector of Israel (12:1), the identification of this figure with Michael is most plausible.

This solution to the problem is only partially satisfactory, however. Later in this chapter the recipient of this new kingdom is not the son of man figure, but *the holy ones of the Most High* (vv. 18, 22) or *the people of the holy ones of the Most High* (v. 27). Who are these "holy ones" and what is their relationship with the son of man figure? In the Hebrew Bible "holy ones" is usually a designation for angels, but the term can also be applied to humans. In chap. 4 of Daniel, the *holy ones* (4:17) are certainly angels. That is probably their identification here as well.

In the present vision the connection between these holy ones and the faithful Jews who are persecuted under Antiochus is obvious (see v. 21). What is the key for understanding this confusing vision in which the human-like figure, the holy ones, and the faithful Jews seem to be identical, yet separate?

The worldview of Daniel presupposes that events in the heavenly world have their counterparts on earth. The struggle between Antiochus and the faithful is a cosmic struggle in which the angels are engaged also. This idea is more clearly present in chap. 10–12. John J. Collins cites a text from Qumran in which a similar idea is found. The passage from the WAR SCROLL says that God "will raise up the kingdom of Michael in the midst of the gods, and the realm of Israel in the midst of all flesh" (1QM 17:7-8; Collins 1984a, 84). When the text in Daniel states that Michael, the *one like a human being* (v. 13), the guardian angel of Israel, receives the kingdom it is saying that the faithful people of God receive the kingdom.

7:15-28. An interpretation. Puzzled and terrified by what he has seen, Daniel approaches one of the angels and asks for an interpretation of the vision. Verses 19-22 recount the major elements of the vision, after which the angel interprets the vision for Daniel. As in the vision, the focus of the interpretation is on the fourth kingdom, specifically the "little horn" of the fourth kingdom.

Verse 25 lists the atrocities of Antiochus: blasphemy, violence, and changing religious regulations and observances (cf. 2 Macc 6:1-11). Although Antiochus will be initially successful, his reign of terror will last only a short while, *for a time, two times, and half a time*, that is, three and a half years. (The duration of Antiochus' persecution was very close to this prediction, roughly 167–164 B.C.E. The statement, however, is likely only a figurative expression for a short period of time.) Then Antiochus will come under divine judgment and will be destroyed. God will then establish a new kingdom, an everlasting kingdom, which will be ruled by the faithful.

This vision offered hope to an oppressed people. To all appearances, Antiochus seemed in control of Israel's history. His persecution seemed endless. The vision asserts otherwise, however. It claims that Antiochus's day of reckoning will come, and soon. The faithful must endure a short while longer, but ultimately God will render judgment against Antiochus and all other tyrants. Then God's faithful will share in a new kingdom.

The Ram and the Male Goat, 8:1-27

8:1-14. Another vision. The second vision begins by locating Daniel in Susa, the winter residence of the Persian kings. Like Ezekiel when he received his first vision, Daniel is standing by a river when this vision appears to him. He sees a powerful ram with two horns who overpowers all the other beasts and has complete dominion. A challenger appears from the west in the form of a male goat with a single horn between its eyes. The male goat defeats the ram, but eventually its great horn is broken. In place of this horn, four prominent horns appear.

As the interpretation by the angel in the last half of the chapter makes clear, the ram with the two horns is a symbol for the Medo-Persian Empire. The male goat is the Greek kingdom begun by Alexander the Great, the great horn that is broken. At Alexander's death in 323 B.C.E. his kingdom was divided among his generals. The four prominent kingdoms that resulted from this breakup were Macedonia and Greece, Asia Minor, Syria and the Mesopotamian region, and Egypt. The ram and male goat were chosen to symbolize these powers because of their astrological associations in the ancient world. The ram was the zodiac sign (Aries) for Persia; the goat was the sign (Capricorn) for Syria, the kingdom over which the Seleucids (the family of Antiochus Epiphanes) would rule.

Verses 9-14 describe the emergence of Antiochus, the little horn. *The beautiful land* (v. 9) is a reference to Palestine, which had come under Seleucid control in 198 B.C.E., and against which Antiochus initiated stringent measures. His arrogance is so great that he reaches even to the heavens and casts down *some of the host and some of the stars* (v. 10) and tramples them.

The activity of Antiochus is not a minor, unimportant event. It is an assault on heaven itself. In the ancient world stars were often viewed as being supernatural beings. Antiochus's struggle is also seen as an attack on God. The act of Antiochus that is singled out in this passage is his desecration of the Jerusalem Temple, God's sanctuary. In December 167 Antiochus established inside the Temple an altar for the worship of Zeus Olympius. Sacrifices and offerings to the God of Israel ceased; in their place were offerings to Zeus. This event is the *transgression that makes desolate* that the angel of v. 13 asks about. In response to the question of how long this desecration will last, another angel replies that its duration will be 2,300 evenings and mornings (1,150 days), a figure similar to, though slightly less than, the three and a half years of 7:25.

8:15-27. An interpretation. As with the vision in chap. 7, Daniel does not understand this vision and asks for an interpretation. *A human voice* (v. 16, a heavenly being speaking human language) calls for the angel *Gabriel* to interpret the vision to Daniel. Daniel's bewilderment is understandable, for this vision concerns *the time of the end* (v. 17).

Through his interpretation, Gabriel assures Daniel that the arrogant little horn will be defeated, but *not by human hands* (v. 25). The Book of Daniel does not call for violent resistance to Antiochus. Such matters can be resolved only by divine intervention. The command to *seal up the vision* (v. 26) is a common motif in APOCALYPTIC LITERATURE. The message of the vision is not for Daniel's time, but for the future (the time of Antiochus). This technique serves to explain why this revelation, supposedly received during the time of Daniel in the sixth century, was not known until the second century. The message had been "sealed up" for the appropriate time.

The Seventy Weeks of Years, 9:1-27

9:1-19. Interpreting Jeremiah. Set in the fictitious reign of Darius the Mede, chap. 9 deals not with a vision (although the angel in 9:23 speaks of a *vision*) but with the interpretation (and novel application) of a biblical passage mediated to Daniel by an angel.

Daniel is perplexed by statements in Jeremiah (25:11, 12; 29:10) that the Jewish Exile will last seventy years. (In actuality, exiles began returning from Babylonia after about fifty years.) Having Daniel raise the issue of the seventy years is only a means of introducing the text from Jeremiah so it can be reapplied to the time of Antiochus.

Daniel prays to God, confessing the sins of the Jewish people and asking for mercy. The prayer reflects standard Deuteronomistic theology: Jerusalem deserves what has happened to it because of the sinfulness of the Jewish people. Daniel does not deny the people's guilt, but instead entreats God to show mercy on Jerusalem. This prayer is possibly a traditional prayer that the author of Daniel has incorporated here.

9:20-27. Angelic assistance. *Gabriel* (v. 21), the angel who appeared to Daniel in chap. 8, comes once again to provide an interpretation of the text to Daniel. The seventy years are in actuality seventy weeks of years, or 490 years. This application of the text from Jeremiah is probably inspired by the idea of the year of jubilee, described in Lev 25. The jubilee year followed a period of seven "weeks of years" (Lev 25:8), or forty-nine years. The emphasis of the jubilee year was "liberty throughout the land" (Lev 25:10). In the angel's periodization of history, the first seven weeks (forty-nine years) covers the period of the exile, ending with the coming of an anointed prince (either Zerubbabel or Joshua; cf. Zech 4:14). The exact referent of *the time when the word went out* (v. 25) is uncertain. Perhaps it applies to the time of Jeremiah's prophecies about the exile and restoration of the Jewish nation.

Following the first seven weeks is a period of sixty-two weeks of years that culminate in the destruction of Jerusalem and its Temple by *the prince*, obviously Antiochus. This begins the last week in the scheme. The anointed one who is cut off (v. 26) is a reference to the removal in 175 of Onias III as high priest or to his murder in 171 B.C.E. Neither Jerusalem nor the Temple was actually destroyed, but many *desolations* (v. 26) did occur, including the *abomination that desolates* (v. 27), the offering of sacrifices to Zeus in the Temple.

Nevertheless, as fearful as the reign of Antiochus is, it shall not last forever. The angel decrees that this despot shall rule only for one week (seven years). At that time, God will bring an end to "the desolator."

The author and the author's readers were living in the last half of the last week of history, according to the timetable presented here. The message of this chapter is that Antiochus's time is limited. Through this reapplication of Jeremiah's prediction, the author encourages all readers to endure in their faith. Antiochus's end is decreed. The time is set. They must remain faithful and wait.

The Last Days, 10:1–12:13

10:1–11:1. Conflict in heaven and on earth. This final section of the book is the longest. It is set in the reign of *Cyrus of Persia* (10:1), who supposedly follows Darius the Mede.

Daniel is mourning and fasting, perhaps in preparation for receiving a vision, since fasting is often associated with revelation. Daniel sees a figure, described in terms reminiscent of Ezekiel's description of God in his first vision (Ezek 1:26-28). Although not identified, this figure is probably Gabriel, who had appeared to Daniel in the two previous chapters.

Gabriel tells Daniel that God had heard his words when he first sought understanding (the beginning of the fast, three weeks prior; see 10:2). The angel had been deterred in coming to Daniel, however, due to conflict in heaven with the patron angel of Persia. He was able to come now only because the angel Michael had come to his assistance. Soon he must return and continue the struggle against the angel of Persia; he expects to be opposed also by the patron angel of Greece.

As seen already in chaps. 7 and 8, talk of heavenly conflict is a way of describing earthly conflict. When foreign nations fight against Israel, their gods (or, as here, patron angels) are understood as fighting against the LORD, the God of Israel. Chapter 11 describes in detail the earthly effects of this cosmic conflict, which are inscribed already in the heavenly *book of truth* (v. 21).

11:2-39. A review. This section is a thinly veiled review of history in the form of *ex eventu* prophecy. Anyone well-versed in the history of the Mediterranean world during the Hellenistic period can easily discern the historical referents. Verses 3-4 describe Alexander the Great and the breakup of his kingdom. The kings of the south described in the following verses are the Ptolemies. The kings of the north are the Seleucids. The major figures depicted in these verses are:

Ptolemy I Lagi—*king of the south* (v. 5)
Seleucus I Nicator—*one of his officers* (v. 5)
Antiochus II Theos (a Seleucid) married to Bernice, daughter of Ptolemy II Philadelphus (v. 6)
Ptolemy III Euergetes—*a branch* (vv. 7-9)
Seleucus II Callinicus—*king of the north* (vv. 7-9)
Seleucus III Ceraunus—one of the sons (v. 10)
Antiochus III—one of the sons and *king of the north* (vv. 10-19)
Ptolemy IV Philopator—*king of the south* (vv. 11-12)
Ptolemy V Epiphanes—*king of the south* married to Cleopatra, daughter of Antiochus III (vv. 14-17)

Seleucus IV Philopator—the one who *shall arise* (v. 20)
Antiochus IV Epiphanes—the *contemptible person* (vv. 21-39)
Onias III, high priest—the *prince of the covenant* (v. 22)
Ptolemy VI—*king of the south* (vv. 25-27)
the Romans—*ships of Kittim* (v. 30)

The primary concern of this section is Antiochus Epiphanes, with whom the majority of the material deals. Verses 30-35 recount his campaign against Judaism, his desecration of the Jerusalem Temple, and his persecution of the faithful Jews.

The wise among the people (v. 33) is likely the group to which the author of Daniel belongs. The *little help* (v. 34) possibly refers to the Maccabees, who led an armed revolt against the forces of Antiochus. Although the Maccabees were ultimately successful, the author of Daniel (who is apparently writing prior to the success of the Maccabees) does not see them as the solution to the crisis. In the author's understanding, deliverance will come only by God's hands and at *the time appointed* (v. 35). Human efforts against Antiochus are futile, because *he shall prosper until the period of wrath is completed, for what is determined shall be done* (v. 36).

11:40-45. Events to come. The description of Antiochus shifts in v. 40 from a rather detailed, accurate review of history to erroneous predictions of events yet to occur. This shift is a clear indication that the author of Daniel actually wrote after the events of v. 39 but before the events of vv. 40-45. The events described in vv. 40-45 did not occur (another war with Ptolemy VI, the capture of Libya, Egypt, and Ethiopia by Antiochus, and the death of Antiochus along the coastal route during one of his military campaigns).

12:1-4. Close of the age. These verses bring to an end the revelation that began in chap. 10. They describe the consummation of the present age and the rewards and punishments that follow. After the death of Antiochus, Michael, the guardian prince of Israel, will bring the present age to an end. Although a time of great distress and trouble will precede the end, the faithful Jews, those whose names are inscribed in the heavenly book of life, will be delivered.

The author gives few details about the events of the end. He does introduce, however, an important idea into biblical eschatology: the concept of resurrection. Verse 2 is the only undisputed text in the Hebrew

Bible that mentions individual resurrection. The resurrection envisioned by the author of this passage is apparently a limited resurrection. *Many . . . shall awake*, some for reward of everlasting life, some for punishment. Those who are resurrected for reward include *the wise*, who have led *many to righteousness* (v. 3) through their teachings and their examples. They will *shine like the stars forever and ever* (v. 3), apparently meaning they will join the hosts of angels.

For Daniel to divulge the message that he has received would be premature, because the revelation is intended for the end times. For this reason the angel tells Daniel to *keep the words secret and the book sealed* (v. 4; cf. 8:26).

12:5-13. How long? The final verses of the book are intended to answer the question, *How long shall it be until the end* (v. 6) will come? Two angelic figures appear at the river where Daniel and Gabriel are. One asks Gabriel (*the man clothed in linen* [v. 7]), *How long?* Gabriel's answer (three and a half years) is in agreement with the prediction in 7:25. Once more the importance of secrecy is urged upon Daniel. Verses 11 and 12, which give different answers, are problematic. They are possibly later additions to the text. After the three and a half years of 7:25 and 12:7 (as well as the 1,150 days of 8:14) had passed and the end had not yet arrived, a pious Jew added the prediction of 1,290 days. Shortly thereafter, an even later prediction of 1,335 days was added.

The Book of Daniel ends with a promise to Daniel that he will share in the resurrection that awaits God's faithful at the end of time. As the differing figures attest, the value of the visions in Daniel lies not in the accuracy of their timetables. Rather, their enduring message is that the God of Israel is the God of history. Ultimately the kingdom of God shall prevail over all earthly tyrants and political powers.

Works Cited

Collins, John J. 1984a. *The Apocalyptic Imagination.*
1984b. *Daniel, with an Introduction to Apocalyptic Literature.* FOTL.

Hosea

Jeffrey S. Rogers

Introduction

Hosea is frequently designated "the prophet of love." Indeed, no book in the Bible depicts God's love for God's people more winsomely. But it is also the case that the language and imagery that this book uses to express God's relations with the people of God's affection are often as violent as they are tender, and as oppressive as they are profound.

The violence, especially that directed toward women and children, is patently offensive to anyone who is sensitive to the real physical, psychological, and social consequences of such acts. The threat of public humiliation and death for a wife and mother (Hos 2:3-10 [MT 2:5-12]), a prayer calling for miscarriage (9:14), and a proclamation that the divine will is to be fulfilled when *their little ones shall be dashed in pieces, and their pregnant women ripped open* (13:16) are hardly words one would expect from a "prophet of love."

The greatest challenge in interpreting this small book is to do justice to it without doing ourselves and others injustice, and vice versa. But its explicit violence and overt sexuality, its depiction of treachery in domestic politics and duplicity in foreign policy, and its experience with self-centered and self-serving religion contribute to making Hosea read as one of the most contemporary of all the books in the canon. It gives offense to many modern readers precisely because it is too much a mirror on our own present in addition to being a window on ancient Israel's history.

Historical Setting

The Book of Hosea can be assigned with confidence to roughly 750–725 B.C.E., in the Northern Kingdom of ISRAEL. Some portions of the book point to the stable, prosperous years at the close of the reign of JEROBOAM II (786–746 B.C.E.). For instance, Hos 10:1 speaks of a nation experiencing increased agricultural production (and religious building projects as a result),

and 12:8 is familiar with the considerable commercial successes of this period.

Other passages reflect the stormy domestic and international developments that overtook the Northern Kingdom soon after Jeroboam II's death. Hosea 1:4 anticipates the demise of the dynasty of JEHU, and Hos 8:4 depicts the political machinations surrounding the assassinations of four Israelite kings between 746 B.C.E. and 732 B.C.E.

Several passages (e.g., 5:8-14; 7:8-17) reflect the turbulent years of the so-called Syro-Ephraimite conflict (736–732 B.C.E.) in which Israel and JUDAH became bitter enemies over the northern kingdom's anti-Assyrian political and military maneuvering. The end of Israel's existence is portrayed in 13:15-16 which portends the inevitable and brutal Assyrian onslaught. There are no passages in the book that depict the fall of SAMARIA in 722/1 B.C.E. as an accomplished fact.

A few brief portions of the book probably derive from a later period, as copyists in Judah attempted to ensure that the timely message of this thoroughly northern document would not be lost on southern audiences. However, it is a mistake to assume, as some commentators have, that an Israelite prophet who frequently criticized developments in Israel's relations with Assyria and Egypt would seldom or never have spoken of Judah in his oracles.

Religious Setting

This PROPHET is clearly engaged in a struggle for the heart of the nation. As typically portrayed, Hosea represents authentic, moral Israelite religion ("Yahwism") embattled against the expanding powers of foreign, immoral Canaanite religion ("Baalism"). This typical portrayal rests on several faulty assumptions.

First, "Israelite" and "Canaanite" are not mutually exclusive terms in the history of religion. Ancient Israelite religion is essentially "a subset of Canaanite religion" (Coogan, 1987, 115). Evidence of obvious similarities in texts and materials testify to "Israel's *continuity* with her religious world" (Miller 1985, 207–208; emphasis added). The typical portrayal misrepresents the complexity of the interrelation of "Israelite" and "Canaanite" religion.

Second, there was considerable diversity within ancient Israel's religion. The remarkable inscriptions from KUNTILLET 'AJRŪD that refer to "Yahweh and his Asherah" and to "Yahweh of Samaria" and "Yahweh of Tenan" are simply the most striking of many indications of the multiformity of Israelite religion. Even Hosea acknowledged that the "Baalism" that he condemned was ancestral among the Israelites, that is, it began with the ancestors prior to entry into the promised land (Hos 9:11; cf. Josh 24:14). The typical portrayal's assumption of a homogeneous religious "orthodoxy" in Israel is contrary to the biblical and archaeological evidence.

Third, despite the prevalent sexual imagery in Hosea, it is not at all certain that "sexual orgies" (Hos 4:18) were central and pervasive in Canaanite (and Israelite) religious practice. In particular, the assumption of widespread "cultic prostitution" has little direct evidence to support it. To take the sexual imagery of prophetic polemics as a reliable description of Canaanite religion is to mistake a caricature for a portrait. Thus, the typical portrayal of Canaanite religion as an immoral "fertility religion" is a misleading oversimplification of a rich and complex religious system.

The central issue in the Book of Hosea, then, is not a conflict between "Canaanite" and "Israelite" belief and practice, but a struggle between ancient and competing *Israelite* traditions of belief and practice within a larger Canaanite framework. Furthermore, the prevalent cultic and sexual allusions in this book are employed by the prophet in the service of a comprehensive indictment that addresses much wider domestic and international issues in which Israel's very existence is at stake.

Message

The Book of Hosea offers no reactionary "back-to-Moses" program. It is striking that although Hosea knows and uses traditions associated with exodus, wilderness, and Decalogue, Moses is referred to only once, and then as an anonymous *prophet* (Hos 12:3). Hosea champions a sophisticated and profound conservatism in addressing the ills of a nation torn by competing interests and conflicting ideologies.

Domestic affairs—political, social, and religious—are in disarray (4:2; 7:3-7; 10:3, 13; 12:8). Foreign policy is flighty and fickle (7:8-11; 8:8-10; 12:1). Clearly, the violent attempts at "final solutions" in the previous century—Jezebel's pogrom against prophets of Yahweh (1 Kings 18:13), Elijah's wholesale slaughter of prophets of Baal (1 Kgs 18:40), and Jehu's massacre of worshipers of BAAL (2 Kgs 10:18-28)—brought neither peace nor integrity to the Northern Kingdom.

The proclamation of Hosea presents a creative, indeed, an inspired alternative to narrow-minded and reactionary factionalism that inevitably hastens the demise of the very thing it tries desperately to preserve. Hosea puts forward a remarkable synthesis that preserves competing ancient traditions of belief and practice by charting a mediating course between thoroughgoing Baalism and rabidly exclusivistic Yahwism. He combines the Baalistic categories of divine marriage, dying and rising, and the revelatory capacity of nature with Yahwism's historic traditions and covenantal principles.

Hosea draws on these competing traditions to proclaim that the essential character and activity of God are not revealed in deterministic processes (in nature or history) or in tribalistic exclusivism but in God's passionate relationship with persons and the world such that God does not fail to judge obstinateness, faithlessness, and injustice and yet heals disloyalty, loves without constraint, and turns from anger. Furthermore, according to Hosea, this God expects the same character and activity from all who would say, "I do," to the divine invitation to relationship.

Perhaps the best way to hear the full range of the message of this remarkable little book is to begin reading the text (and commentary) at Hos 4:1. After becoming thoroughly familiar with chaps. 4–14, the reader can then appreciate the most famous part of the book, chaps. 1–3, for what it is: an overture that highlights (very) few themes and motifs in a major dramatic work.

For Further Study

In the *Mercer Dictionary of the Bible*: ADULTRY IN THE OT; BAAL; FAMILY; HARLOT; HOSEA; HOSEA, BOOK OF; ISRAEL; JEROBOAM II; MARRIAGE IN THE OT; NAMES; ORACLE; PROPHET.

In other sources: P. Bird, "'To Play the Harlot': An Inquiry into an OT Metaphor," in *Gender and Difference in Ancient Israel*, ed. P. L. Day, 75–94; J. Blenkinsopp, *A History of Prophecy in Israel*; F. M. Cross, *Canaanite Myth and Hebrew Epic*; P. D. Miller et al., eds., *Ancient Israelite Religion*; J. Rogers, "Women in the Hands of an Abusive God?" in *Interpreting Hosea for Preaching and Teaching*; C. L. Seow, "Hosea, Book of," *AncBD*; G. A. Yee, "Hosea," *TWBC*.

Commentary

An Outline

Editorial Superscription, 1:1
I. Overture: Yahweh's Wife—Israel, 1:2–3:5
  A. Hosea's Family as Signs, 1:2–2:1 [MT 1:2–2:3]
  B. Yahweh's Marriage Dissolved and Restored, 2:2-23 [MT 2:4-25]
  C. Recapitulation, 3:1-5
II. Main Section: Impending Desolation, 4:1–9:17
  A. Indictment, 4:1–5:7
  B. First Alarm, 5:8–7:16
  C. Second Alarm, 8:1–9:17
III. Conclusion: Retrospect and Prospect, 10:1–14:9 [MT 10:1–14:10]
  A. From Egypt to Exile and Back, 10:1–11:11
  B. Ephraim's Bitter Offense, 11:12–13:14 [MT 12:1–13:14]
  C. Death and Rebirth of Israel, 13:1–14:9 [MT 13:1–14:10]

Editorial Superscription, 1:1

The relation of this verse to the book as a whole is problematic because it gives priority to southern kings and makes no reference to northern kings after JEROBOAM II. In its present form, it is certainly a product of Judean editing.

Overture:
Yahweh's Wife—Israel, 1:2–3:5

The metaphor of marriage and family, applied to the deity, is a conception typical of Canaanite religion: the deity (e.g., BAAL) has a consort (in Baal's case, Anat or sometimes Astarte or Asherah), and their relationship is essential to fertility, productivity and prosperity in the world.

According to the overture of the Book of Hosea, Yahweh also has a partner, indeed a wife, Israel; and the well-being of the world is dependent on their relationship (see, negatively, 2:3, 9, 12 and 4:2; positively, 2;18, 21-22). When Hosea presents Yahweh as the male partner in a marriage and then ascribes to the deity marital vows of a distinctively covenantal charac-

ter (see 2:19-20), the prophet has produced a remarkable synthesis of Baalistic and Yahwistic traditions.

Hosea's Family as Signs, 1:2–2:1 [MT 1:2–2:3]

1:2-9. Signs of judgment. Four commands of Yahweh and the interpretation of each (vv. 2, 4, 6, 9) depict Hosea's spouse and three children as dramatic signs of God's dissatisfaction with God's people.

Hosea's marriage to Gomer, representing the relationship of Yahweh to Israel, has been the subject of considerable debate, as has the nature of Gomer's *whoredom* (v. 2), representing Israel's *forsaking the LORD.* Chapter 2 associates Gomer's promiscuity with misunderstanding agricultural produce as gifts of the Canaanite deity BAAL (2:5, 8, 12-3), but Hosea employs the imagery of promiscuity and adultery to express Israel's inconstancy in many different areas of the nation's life (e.g., domestic affairs, 7:3-4; foreign policy, 8:9). The image of the wayward wife never appears outside the overture.

The children's names symbolize Yahweh's intention toward Israel and Israel's condition in relation to Yahweh. The place-name *Jezreel* (v. 4) is employed to announce the end of the dynasty of JEHU (of which Jeroboam II's son ZECHARIAH was the last member) which began with a bloodbath when Jehu overthrew the dynasty of King Omri in the preceding century. A daughter named "Not-pitied" (v. 6, mrg.) and a son named "Not-my-people" (v. 9, mrg.) are signs of Israel's estrangement from God.

It is remarkable that Hosea would speak negatively of the radically anti-baalist Jehu (v. 4) whose purge of worshipers of Baal in 2 Kgs 12:18-28 was praised in 2 Kgs 12:30—unless, of course, radical anti-Baalism was not consistent with Hosea's vision of what was necessary for Israel to be healed of its inconstancy.

1:10–2:1. Signs of salvation. In this loosely connected section, the children's symbolic names are transposed into signs of salvation and are related to one of the great themes of Israel's salvation history: the repeated promises to the ancestors of innumerable progeny and the possession of the land (Gen 13:14-17; 17:4-8; 26:2-5; 28:13-14; 35:11-12). "Not-my-people" becomes innumerable *Children of the living God* (v. 10), *My-people* again (2:1). *Jezreel* becomes a sign of the political reunification of Israel and Judah and their possession of the land (v. 11). "Not-pitied" is once again "Pitied" (2:1). Judgment has not been avoided; but as is the case throughout this book, judgment is not God's final word or act.

Yahweh's Marriage Dissolved and Restored 2:2-23

2:2-5 Dissolution. On grounds of infidelity, God's relationship with Israel is effectively dissolved in v. 2: *she is not my wife, and I am not her husband*. This statement is an obvious play on the reversal of the formula, "I will take you as my people, and I will be your God" (Exod 6:7), which appears in Hos 1:9: *you are not my people and I am not your God*. The children are also rejected, on account of their mother's infidelity (v. 5). The spouse is threatened with public humiliation (2:10) and death (v. 3) for seeking sustenance from other providers (*lovers*, v. 5).

The imagery of domination and degradation of a woman in this chapter—and the next—is neither redemptive nor prophetic in the modern world, and the portrayal of God as a husband who metes out physical punishment (even to death) on a wife is among numerous offensive images for the deity contained in this book (e.g., God is like *maggots* and *rottenness*, 5:12; a slayer of children, 9:12, 16; a *wild animal* ripping open, devouring, and mangling, 13:8). The prophet's attention-getting image of God as a cuckolded and enraged male is no more constitutive of the divine nature than is the imagery of maggots, rottenness, and so on.

2:6-13 Punishment. The punishment threatened in 2:3 is detailed in vv. 6-13. Confinement and futility (vv. 6-7), agricultural failure (vv. 9, 12), exposure (vv. 9-10; see Sanderson 1992, 219–20), the removal of *mirth* (v. 11), and devouring animals (v. 12) are the deity's response to Israel's waywardness. This catalogue of punishments has striking parallels among traditional maledictions and treaty curses (see Deut 28; Lev 26; Hillers 1964). Although this passage focuses on Baalism as Israel's failure, similar indictments for misplaced trust recur in political and economic contexts (5:13; 10:13-14; 12:8-9), as does the sequence of debasement and death (5:9, 11-12; 7:11-13; 13:15-16).

2:14-23 Restoration. The tone of the chapter changes dramatically in v. 14. The language is quite sugges-tive, as the Hebrew verb translated *allure* appears also in Exod 22:16: "When a man *seduces* a virgin who is not engaged to be married, and lies with her" (emphasis added). Seductive, tender speech (v. 14) will result in willing responsiveness on Israel's part (v. 15). As in chap. 1, reconciliation follows judgment (see Rogers 1993).

The courtship of vv. 14-15 ends in v. 16, where the relationship previously dissolved is reconstituted by Yahweh whom Israel will call "my marriage partner" (*My husband*) instead of "my master" (*My Baal*). Although Yahweh rejects being called *Baal*, the Baalistic marital imagery remains intact. In the verses that follow, the Yahwistic category of *covenant* (v. 18) defines the marriage relationship.

Yahweh's threefold commitment to Israel, *I will take you as my wife* (vv. 19-20), evokes a legal conclusion of a marriage contract (Mays 1969, 50) in obvious contrast to the beginning of the chapter (2:2). The substance of Yahweh's commitment is portrayed in terminology associated with covenant: *righteousness, justice, steadfast love, mercy,* and *faithfulness*. Remarkably, Yahweh promises to Israel precisely what Israel had failed to deliver to Yahweh.

A double entendre closes this section in v. 20: *and you shall know the LORD*. The metaphorical progression is obvious: courtship (vv. 14-15), betrothal (vv. 19-20), and consummation (v. 20; on *know* in the OT as a euphemism for sexual intercourse, see TDOT 5:464). "Knowing the LORD" expresses above all comprehensive fidelity to covenantal principles and behaviors, but both senses of the double entendre are central to the prophet's message.

The essence of fidelity to the covenant is an intimate and passionate relationship with the God who invites, even seduces, people into willing and faithful partnership.

The children are also restored to their former status, as is clear in the transformation of their names from signs of alienation to signs of renewed relation (vv. 21-23).

Recapitulation 3:1-5

Considerable effort has been expended on attempts to explain the relation of these verses to chap. 1, but the closer thematic connection is to chap. 2 (Wolff 1974, 59). Hosea (representing God) pursues a promiscuous spouse (representing the people, v. 1) who will experience deprivation but will eventually return (vv. 3-5).

The statement in v. 1, *the LORD loves the people of Israel, though they turn to other gods*, is sometimes taken as the thematic center of the entire book. However, the rhetorical discontinuity in this verse is that the LORD *loves the people*, but *the people love raisin cakes*. These baked goods are associated elsewhere with pagan worship (Isa 16:7; Jer 7:18), but David distributed the same delicacy as part of the celebration of the arrival of the ark of Yahweh in Jerusalem (2 Sam 6:19). The cakes themselves were not a problem. But the misplaced love for them instead of for Yahweh and the turning to other gods are both symptomatic of a common religious disorder: an obsession with the external and material benefits of religion rather than devotion to the relationships, principles, and behaviors that are its source and substance.

Main Section:
Impending Desolation, 4:1–9:17

Indictment, 4:1–5:7

In 4:1–5:7 a number of smaller units are organized into a scathing indictment of all *the inhabitants of the land* (4:1): people (4:1, 6, 8-9, 12, 14), priest (4:4, 9; 5:1), prophet (4:5), and ruling officials and royal court (5:1). The section is framed by a primary and comprehensive failing: there is *no knowledge of God in the land* (4:1); *they do not know the LORD* (5:4). The indictment closes with the announcement of the withdrawal of the divine presence (5:6), a catastrophic development, in light of Moses' response to Yahweh at Sinai:

If your presence will not go, do not carry us up from here. For how shall it be known that I have found favor in your sight, I and your people, unless you go with us? In this way, we shall be distinct, I and your people, from every people on the face of the earth (Exod 33:15-16).

It is Yahweh's presence that constitutes Israel's well-being and identity as a people, but now *he has withdrawn from them* (5:6).

4:1-3. Yahweh's case against Israel. The opening salvo in this segment is a typical prophetic call to the *people* to *Hear the word of the LORD* (v. 1a; cf. Amos 7:16; Isa 1:10; Jer 2:4). This form of speech identifies the prophet as a spokesperson (or "messenger") of Yahweh, and it introduces not only this section but the entire collection at least through the end of the climactic chap. 9 (see commentary on 9:10-17). The proceed-ings are reminiscent of a courtroom scene with an indictment (v. 1b), an accusation (v. 2), and a sentence (v. 3).

The accusation includes nine elements. The first three, *no faithfulness or loyalty, and no knowledge of God* (v. 1), constitute a comprehensive complaint against Israel for failing to live all aspects of its life according to covenantal principles and behaviors. As the remainder of the book makes abundantly clear, there can be no authentic relationship with Yahweh that is not also a relationship with neighbor, at home and abroad.

But Israel's foreign policy plays one potential ally off against another: *they call to Egypt* at the same time that they *go to Assyria* (7:11; see 12:1); *they bargain with the nations* (8:10). Above all, *falsehood and violence* characterize their international affairs (12:1). On the domestic front, they make contracts they do not fulfill, *so litigation springs up like poisonous weeds* (10:4). Unscrupulous business practices (e.g., the use of *false balances*) are exacerbated by self-righteous exoneration (12:7-8). Governmental officials delight in *wickedness* and *treachery* (7:3). According to the first three elements of the accusation, Israel has no integrity in any of its dealings.

The next five elements (v. 2a) correspond to specific prohibitions in the Decalogue, which is presented in Exod 20:1-17 (and Deut 5:6-21) as the stipulations of a covenant with Yahweh. The five cited here all address acts involving interpersonal relationships. *Swearing* is a violation of the injunction against "wrongful use of the name of the LORD your God" (Exod 20:7) in treaties, contracts, oaths, etc. (cf. Hos 10:4). *Lying* violates the prohibition against false statements against one's neighbor (Exod 20:16; cf. Hos 10:13; 11:12).

The ninth and final element is best paraphrased, "capital crimes abound." *Bloodshed* here is employed in the sense of "bloodguilt" (Wolff 1974, 18; see NRSV's *crimes* in 12:15 and "bloodguilt" in Exod 22:1 for the same Heb. word).

According to v. 3, the consequences of Israel's violation of the terms of its relationship with Yahweh are catastrophic, not only for Israel but also for the entire created order. In the Book of Hosea, then, right relationship with God is not principally a private and personal religious affair; it is inevitably a matter of the greatest social, political, economic, and even ecological consequence.

4:4-5:2. Failure of Israel's leadership. The shortcomings of the people are cited (4:6, 8, 12, 14), but ultimately it is Israel's leaders who are responsible for the people's well-being. *Priest* (4:4; 5:1), *prophet* (4:5), ruling officials (*house of Israel*, 5:1; see Micah 3:1, 9), and royal court (*house of the king*, 5:1) are designated as responsible parties in Israel's failure. They have been to the people *a snare, a net,* and *a pit dug deep* (5:1-2) and will by no means escape judgment. The operant principle is illustrated in 4:13b-14: God will not punish dependents in the family (*daughters* and *daughters-in-law*) while the heads of the family (*the men*) are themselves irresponsible.

Cultic language abounds, including references to sacrifices (4:8, 13, 14, 19), divination (4:12), incense (NRSV, *offerings*, 4:13), cultic centers (*tops of the mountains, hills,* and woodland shrines, 4:13; *Gilgal* and Bethel—derogatorily referred to as "house of wickedness" instead of "house of God", 4:15; *Mizpah* and *Tabor*, 5:1), and *idols* (4:17). Sexual language is pervasive (promiscuity, 4:10-15; *adultery*, 4:13-14; prostitution, 4:14; *sexual orgies* and *lewdness*, 4:18). Whatever literal basis the latter language may have, it is above all a polemical metaphor in Hosea. The former—that is, the corruption of worship—is but one example of the failure of people and leadership alike.

5:3-7. Withdrawal of divine presence. The indictment closes with a recapitulation of motifs and themes appearing previously in this section (lack of knowledge, promiscuity, stumbling, sacrifices and divination, children). The climax of the section arrives in v. 6 with the announcement of the withdrawal of Yahweh's presence from Israel: *they will not find him; he has withdrawn from them.* It is set up by the antitheses of Yahweh's knowing Israel (v. 3) but Israel's not knowing Yahweh (v. 4) and Israel's way not being hidden from Yahweh (v. 3) but Yahweh's being hidden from Israel (v. 6). Just as Israel has *forsaken* Yahweh (4:10, 12), Yahweh has now forsaken Israel.

First Alarm, 5:8–7:16

Beginning with an alarm (5:8) on account of the impending desolation of Ephraim (5:9, 11), this section is framed by depictions of Yahweh as the bringer of destruction and death (5:12-14; 7:12-14) and by Ephraim's ineffectual cries for help (5:15–6:6; 7:14). At the center is an accusatory litany on the *corruption of Ephraim* (7:1), especially its leadership (*priests*, 6:9; *king*, 7:3; and *officials*, 7:3, 5, 16). Both domestic (6:7–7:7) and foreign affairs (5:13; 7:8-11, 16) are featured as areas in which Ephraim has failed to exhibit the covenantal behaviors of *steadfast love* ("unfailing

loyalty to one's commitments" or "faithfulness in action," Sakenfeld 1985) and *knowledge of God* (6:6; see commentary on 2:20). This section is a pointed illustration of both the rationale for and the consequences of Yahweh's withdrawal from Israel, which was the climax of the preceding section.

5:8-15. Desolation and death. After the alarm (v. 8) and declaration of Ephraim's desolation (vv. 9-11), Yahweh is portrayed in deathly imagery (*like maggots* and *rottenness* in a *wound*, vv. 12-13; *like a lion* that tears its prey and carries it off, v. 14). Israel's demise is imminent and inevitable.

In contrast to the previous section, which featured cultic affairs as the arena of Ephraim's inconstancy, this one focuses on politics. Ephraim has sought healing and a cure for its problems by turning to *Assyria* and appealing *to the great king* (v. 13), a common title for the monarch in Assyrian documents. Verse 15 closes this part of the larger section by reaffirming Yahweh's withdrawal from Israel; but it also indicates that Yahweh's absence will last only *until they acknowledge their guilt and seek my face.*

6:1-3. Plea to be raised up. Introduced at the end of 5:15 (*they will beg my favor*), the impassioned prayer of vv. 1-3 begins with Israel's summons to itself to *return to the LORD* (v. 1). To return implies turning away from sin and turning to Yahweh, in other words, authentic repentance. The prayer acknowledges that what the people have suffered is the judgment of Yahweh (*it is he who has torn; he has struck down*), and it expresses confidence in Yahweh's mercy and grace after wrath (*he will heal us; he will bind us up*).

The second verse of the prayer confesses that Yahweh will give us life (NRSV, *revive us*) and *raise us up* so that *we may live* in his presence (NRSV, *before him*). Israel trusts that its return to Yahweh will result in a return of Yahweh to Israel. Because Israel has turned to *know the LORD* (v. 3) and thereby rectified its principal shortcoming according to the indictment of 4:1-5:7, Yahweh will surely once again "appear" among Israel: *he will come to us.*

The imagery of v. 3 (*as sure as the dawn; like the spring rains*) is both beautiful and essentially Baalistic. The sequence of death (5:12-15) followed by new life (v. 2) associated with the spring rains and the reappearance of the deity is a decidedly Baalistic complex.

6:4-6. Yahweh's response. The prayer of 6:1-3 is ineffectual. Yahweh's immediate response in vv. 4-6 is even more impassioned than the plea: *What shall I do with you . . . ? What shall I do with you . . . ?*

Your love is like a morning cloud, like the dew that goes early away. The people want Yahweh to be as the life-giving spring rains to them, but they are to Yahweh as a cloud in the morning that promises rain but does not deliver. They are as dew that dries up.

There is no indication that the prayer is rejected because it is couched in Baalistic categories (dying, rising, reappearing, and raining). In fact, the response takes up the rain imagery and employs it with reference to the people. The crux of the response is that the people's professed repentance is just one more example of their inconstancy. According to Yahweh's response, a statement of repentance is not necessarily any more indicative of *steadfast love* and *knowledge of God* than *sacrifice, burnt offerings* (v. 6).

What, then, can Israel do to satisfy Yahweh's demand for *steadfast love* and *knowledge of God*? A direct and explicit answer to that question is given in a later dying and rising sequence in chaps. 13–14. For now, the focus remains on documenting the *corruption of Ephraim* (7:1).

6:7–7:10. The corruption of Ephraim. Three independent units catalogue Ephraim's failures. The first (6:7-10) concerns domestic affairs. The focus is on cultic (or at least priestly) abuses. The second (6:11–7:7) also addresses the domestic scene, though the focus shifts from priests to *the king* (7:3, 5, 7) and *officials* (7:3, 5) who revel in the *wickedness* and *treachery* that surround them (7:3). Of particular interest is the assertion that Yahweh would, in fact, turn to *restore the fortunes* of the people and to *heal Israel* (6:11b; 7:1; cf. 5:13), but the *corruption of Ephraim* and the *wicked deeds of Samaria* are too great.

The third and shortest unit (7:8-10) takes up the issue of international relations, which are featured in the next segment. The final verse of the unit reaffirms the negative assessment of Israel's plea in 6:1-3: *they do not return to the LORD their God, or seek him, for all of this* (7:10).

7:11-16. Destruction to them. In keeping with the opening segment of this section (5:8-15), destruction and death are the result of Ephraim's failures, both political (vv. 11, 16) and cultic (v. 14).

Because of their flightiness in international affairs, Yahweh will cast a net over them and *bring them down like birds*. The dramatic center of this segment is v. 13 in which appears the first of only two woe-oracles in the book. *Destruction* is decreed (cf. 5:9). In keeping with 6:11–7:1, Yahweh *would redeem them*,

but their duplicity alienates them from their only real source of salvation (v. 13).

The cries and ritual acts of repentance that Yahweh sees (e.g., 6:1-3) are motivated by material concerns (*for grain and wine*, v. 14). Despite the deity's past acts of nurture and provision, *they plot evil* against Yahweh (v. 15). The blow of judgment specified at the end falls principally on the leadership whose duplicity has no doubt come to light in Egypt or Assyria (see v. 11): *their officials shall fall by the sword* (v. 16). This limited blow stands in stark contrast to the conclusion of the next section.

Second Alarm, 8:1–9:17

As did the last section, this one begins with an alarm and Israel's ineffectual cry to God (8:1-2) and ends with destruction and death (9:10-17). The parts of this section are intricately related (e.g., *my God* at the beginning in 8:2; at the end in 9:17; and in the climactic unit in 9:8). Political and cultic sins (8:4-14) are followed by their respective consequences (9:1-4), all of which pales by comparison with the rejection of the prophet (9:5-9) and the corresponding rejection of Ephraim (9:10-17).

8:1-14. Political and cultic sins. The initial alarm and cry (v. 2b) in the first unit are fragmentary and desperate (contrast 5:8 and 6:1-3). The truncated alarm does not even include a verb: "to your lips a trumpet!" The abrupt plea, *My God, we—Israel—know you!* (v. 2) contributes to a picture of Israel in full retreat before its enemies (v. 3b). The expression *house of the LORD* frames the first two segments of the larger section (v. 1; 9:15) and appears only here in the book. It refers to *the land of the LORD* (9:3) rather than to a temple (see Wolff 1974, 137).

According to the next unit (vv. 4-6) Israel's politics (v. 4a) and worship (vv. 4b-6) are both anathema to Yahweh. The reference to *kings* and *princes* set up without Yahweh's approval (v. 4) asserts Yahweh's right to sovereignty over political affairs.

The *calf of Samaria* (v. 6), is problematic, since the official temple of Baal in SAMARIA (built by AHAB, 1 Kgs 16:32) was destroyed by JEHU in the previous century and furthermore did not contain such an image, according to the evidence of 2 Kgs 10:26-27. According to Hos 10:5, the calf before which the people of Samaria worshiped was at BETHEL (Wolff 1974, 140). Bethel was a "royal sanctuary" (Amos 7:13), one of two containing bull images set up by

JEROBOAM I as a northern alternative to the Temple in Jerusalem (1 Kgs 12:26-29).

Calf imagery had an ancient and storied (and not always negative) past in Israelite religion (see CALF, GOLDEN). The calves themselves were not worshiped as a deity (despite the polemical intimations of Hos 10:5 and 13:2). Rather, they served the same purpose as the ARK of Yahweh and the winged cherubim of the Jerusalem Temple, which were pedestals above which the invisible presence of God was enthroned and thus were pre-eminent symbols of the divine presence. The rejection of the calf symbolizes the rejection of Bethel and its cult as a sacred site that mediated the presence of Yahweh to the people (cf. Hos 4:15; 10:5, 15).

The focus in the third unit (vv. 7-10) is international affairs. Imagery drawn from nature and agriculture (v. 7) makes clear that Israel's duplicitous foreign policy will result in futility. Rather than being Yahweh's "treasured possession out of all the peoples" (Exod 19:5; cf. Deut 7:6), Israel is *among the nations as a useless vessel* (v. 8). The image of alien *lovers* with whom Ephraim *has bargained* expresses the nation's political inconstancy. The appeal to ASSYRIA (v. 9) will result in the *burden* of foreign domination (v. 10).

The fourth unit (vv. 11-14) highlights the cult once again. The accusation here might or might not involve worshiping other gods. Either way, the prophet sees the problem as a cultic innovation departing from the *instructions* (or "laws") that Yahweh provided (v. 12). Expanding sacrificial activity would have resulted in considerable economic benefit, especially for priests and for those who had the resources to make many *choice sacrifices*, since priest and worshiper shared the *flesh*. Again, the prophet attacks an appetite for material benefits of religious activity rather than a genuine devotion to God (cf. the love for *raisin cakes* in 3:1).

A related failing is in view at the close of this unit (v. 14) where Israel and Judah are condemned for having *forgotten* their *Maker* when they attempt to provide for themselves luxury (*palaces*) and security (*fortified cities*).

9:1-4. Political and cultic consequences. An introduction (v. 1) addresses Israel in the second-person singular with a prohibition of celebration (v. 1a) followed by a blanket accusation (v. 1b) in the language of promiscuity typical of Hosea. The *threshing floors* are a logical location of Israel's "prostitution," since these open, public places served as sites for cultic activity (e.g., 2 Sam 24:18-25) and even for international coalitioning (1 Kgs 22:10), among other activities.

With a shift to third-person plural and the theme of futility the focus moves to political and economic consequences of Israel's sin. Loss of the produce of the land (v. 2) escalates into loss of the land itself in v. 3 (Yahweh's land, not Israel's; cf. *house of the LORD*, 8:1 and 9:4). The political catastrophe is also a religious disaster, since expulsion from the house of the LORD means alienation from Yahweh's presence and the reversal of the first element in God's great salvation-history promise to Israel's ancestors (see commentary on 1:10-11).

The *unclean food* (v. 3) of exile results in the complete collapse of the cult (v. 4a). The people's alienation from Yahweh is now complete, not only because eating unclean food makes people defiled (v. 4) before Yahweh but also because their drink offerings and sacrifices (v. 4) were always to be taken from the very best stock that the people had for themselves. Reduced to eating unclean food, they have nothing to offer which can please Yahweh.

9:5-9. Rejection of the prophetic word. Alternating between second- and third-person discourse, these rather unassuming verses are not only the catalyst for the vituperative close of this section (9:10-17); they are also the dramatic climax of the book.

This segment opens with a bitterly ironic question: *What will you do?* One would expect the *day of the appointed festival, the day of the festival of the LORD* (v. 5), to be a day of celebration of God's gracious acts on Israel's behalf.

A joyful autumnal harvest festival was probably the setting for the original proclamation (see Wolff 1974, 153), a context that would significantly heighten the offense to the audience that such words as these would give. Israel has nothing for which to rejoice (9:1), because the *days of punishment* and *recompense have come* (v. 7). The futility motif returns in v. 6 with an intensification of the reversal of the promise of the land: even those who *escape destruction* will die in *Egypt*.

Then, for the first time in the book we hear clearly and in the audience's own words how the proclamation of Hosea was received: he was condemned as *a fool* and *mad* (v. 7). The aphoristic reply—great sin makes for great animosity—reflects the people's anger back on themselves, but the ominous import of the next two verses cannot be underestimated. The prophet has been true to his task as a *sentinel* who keeps watch and announces the approach of good and bad alike (thus the alarms of 5:8; 8:1). But his service has been met with threats to his person (*a fowler's snare is on all his ways*) and open *hostility* to his message (v. 8).

The invocation of GIBEAH associated with "profound corruption" recalls the brutal and horrifying events of Judg 19–20, about which it was said, "Such a thing has not happened or been seen since the day that the Israelites came up from the land of Egypt until this day" (Judg 19:30). By its explicit rejection of the prophetic proclamation, Hosea's audience has irredeemably compounded its guilt.

The climax of the book is here, because the Israel whom Hosea addressed has not only disregarded Yahweh's instructions or law (8:1, 12; cf. 4:6), but it has also now rejected the corrective and *redemptive word of the LORD* (4:1) that Yahweh has put "in the mouth of the prophet" (Deut 18:18). Of the one "who does not heed the words that the prophet shall speak in my name," says Yahweh, "I myself will hold accountable" (Deut 18:19). Indeed, *he will remember their iniquity, he will punish their sins* (v. 9). It is one thing to err in one's ways; it is another thing entirely to reject with open hostility the salvation available through correction. Israel has now done both.

9:10-17. Rejection of Ephraim. And so the Book of Hosea reaches its thematic nadir in a brutal and horrifying segment of its own. Now added to the loss of the land and the cult (9:3-4) is the loss of fertility and the slaughter of children, marking the reversal of the second element in the great promise to the ancestors (see commentary on 1:10-11). Associated with the loss of fertility is the loss of divine presence (vv. 11-12; see commentary on 5:6).

The first of two units (vv. 10-14) opens with a brief historical precis (v. 10). Until the reference to *the days of Gibeah* in the preceding unit (9:9), Hos 4–11 focused exclusively on "current events"—present shortcomings of the people and their leaders. In v. 10, however, the book begins to take up a retrospective approach in which present ills and judgments are intertwined with failures of the past. With the loss of promise assured, Israel's salvation-history begins to "pass before its eyes" as a history of ignominy.

Despite the potential for good fruit that Yahweh saw in them (v. 10a), the people became *detestable* even before they entered the land of promise (v. 10b; see Num 25:1-18). Recollection of past failure is juxtaposed with present judgment (vv. 11-14) highlighting the loss of fertility (v. 11b) and the utter futility of it should it occur (vv. 12a, 13b, 16b).

The association of the loss of fecundity and fertility with the absence of the deity (the departure of *glory* in v. 11a; cf. the departure of the presence of Yahweh in 1 Sam 4:21-22; Ezek 10:18-19; 11:22-23) is a typically Canaanite motif. Here, the flight of *Ephraim's glory* refers with bitter irony to the loss of divine presence when the preeminent symbol of it at Bethel, the golden calf, is removed by the Assyrians (cf. 10:5-6; see commentary on 8:6).

The second of the two woe-oracles in the book plays on Israel's misconception by pointing out the departure that really will be devastating: *Woe to them indeed when I depart from them!* (v. 12). The two woes are a matching pair that reflect the character of the respective sections of the book in which they occur. The first pronounces woe for Israel's departure from Yahweh (7:13), and the second pronounces woe for Yahweh's departure from Israel.

The vicious prayer of the prophet at the end of this unit, with its repeated *give them!* (v. 14) requesting miscarriage and *dry breasts* in Israel, is indicative of Hosea's personal and emotional response to the opposition and threats of his audience evident in 9:7-8 (cf. Jer 11:20b; 12:3b; 15:15a; 17:18; 18:21-23; 20:12b).

The second unit (vv. 15-17) begins with an extremely brief reference to GILGAL (v. 15; the Heb. text says only "all their evil at Gilgal"). The sequence Peor-Gilgal in vv. 10, 15 can hardly be accidental. The apostasy at Peor occurred "While Israel was staying at Shittim" (Num 25:1), the last camp in the trans-Jordan. Gilgal was Israel's first camp in the promised land (Josh 5:19). Hosea 9:15 is probably best understood when translated: "All their evil was (i.e., remained with them) at Gilgal; even there I hated them." Exile from the land—being driven *out of my house* (v. 15; see commentary on 8:1)—is thus artfully juxtaposed with the traditions of the entry into it. According to Hosea, Israel did not begin with a "clean slate" in the promised land. They *became detestable* at Peor (v. 9) and have only become more so ever since.

The recapitulation of the reversal of the promises of progeny (v. 16) and land (v. 17) lends an ultimate finality to the close of the unit and the larger section. In fact, there is an even more comprehensive closure here that reinforces the climactic rejection of Hosea's proclamation (9:5-9). The prophetic summons with which the indictment began, *Hear* (*šimě'û*) *the word of the LORD, O people of Israel* (4:1), was in the end ineffectual: *they have not listened* (v. 17, *lō'šāmě'û*). Those who were addressed as *the inhabitants of the land* (4:1) now *shall become wanderers among the nations* (v. 17).

Conclusion: Retrospect and Prospect, 10:1–14:9 [MT 10:1–14:10]

From Egypt to Exile and Back, 10:1–11:11

After the dramatic climax of the book in the preceding section, the denouement begins in this section with a brief sketch of Israel's past and present that portrays the coming judgment as a necessary and inevitable response to a people who *are bent on turning away* (11:7).

But because of the passionate nature of Yahweh's character and of Yahweh's love for Israel, wrath and judgment are not Israel's only prospect. After a remarkable soliloquy revealing the depth and power of the emotional struggle within the deity's own self (11:8-9), for the first time in chaps. 4–14 comes the clear indication that destruction is not God's only intention for Israel (11:10-11).

10:1-15. End of cult and king. The loss of the land entails the loss the two principal institutions that connected the people to Yahweh in monarchical Israel: the cult and the king. The first unit (vv. 1-8) begins by reflecting on the destruction of the most prominent features of Israel's religious building programs (*altars* and sacred *pillars*, vv. 1-2). Those who contributed to them no doubt considered these expansion programs to be grand expressions of their devotion to God, but Yahweh saw them as one more indication of self-centeredness and sinfulness (v. 2; cf. 4:7-9; 8:11).

The absence of a king does not appear particularly disconcerting to the people (v. 3; a human king or the "divine king"—Yahweh—may be in view here), but they will *mourn* when the *calf* from the sanctuary at Bethel (v. 5, *Beth-aven*; see commentary on 4:15) is *carried to Assyria* as part of the spoils of the conquest of Israel (vv. 5-6).

The unit closes with the people bereft of king and cult (vv. 7-8) and crying out for their own destruction as the only relief available to them (v. 8).

The second unit (vv. 9-15) is less reflective and more accusatory. It begins by invoking the sin of Gibeah (see commentary on 9:9) which resulted in a devastating internecine war with eleven tribes of Israel aligned against Benjamin to punish it. This time, however, it is Yahweh who *will come against the wayward people to punish them* (v. 10). The instrument of Yahweh's wrath will be *nations . . . gathered against*

them. The middle verses in this unit employ similar agricultural imagery to make three very different points. In v. 11 the coming change in Ephraim's life is expressed as the difference between the relatively easy existence of a *heifer that loved to thresh* (Wolff 1974, 185 points to the frisking heifer of Jer 50:11 and the provision for feeding in Deut 25:4) and the laborious work to *break the ground.*

In v. 12 the admonitions to *sow . . . righteousness* and *reap steadfast love* are attached to an exhortation to *seek the LORD*, the first time in the Book of Hosea that such an explicit call to covenantal behavior occurs. As previously (6:3), the hoped-for coming of the deity is associated with the arrival of "spring rains" (Andersen and Freedman 1980, 568), a typically Canaanite complex.

The prophet is calling the people to do the antithesis of what they have been doing: they have *plowed wickedness* and *reaped injustice* (v. 13a). Furthermore, their self-centered religion has been accompanied by a self-reliant militarism that will contribute to their downfall (vv. 13b-14). The final verse invokes the demise of *Bethel* and the *king* together (v. 15) and thus recapitulates the two central concerns of the unit.

11:1-7. From Egypt to exile. This segment presents the briefest synopsis of the span of Israel's history with Yahweh as presented in the book to this point: *called out of Egypt* (vv. 1-2) and condemned to *return* there (v. 5). In the most poignant imagery in the entire book, Israel is depicted in the first unit (vv. 1-4) as a child *loved* (v. 1) and nurtured (vv. 3-4) by God, despite the child's waywardness. Thus, God's love for Israel never was dependent on Israel's right behavior (v. 2) or conscious recognition of God's saving (v. 3) and sustaining activity (v. 4). God's love is the sole basis for Israel's relationship with God.

Israel's *return to the land of Egypt* (and/or exile to Assyria) comes not because Israel transgressed, but because *they have refused to return to me* (v. 5) when the error of their ways was called to their attention by the prophet (see commentary on 9:7-9; cf. Deut 18:19). The text of v. 7b is extremely difficult and highly disputed; but NRSV's rendering, *To the Most High they call, but he does not raise them up at all* is a vast improvement over RSV and KJV. As rendered, this verse recapitulates Yahweh's refusal to respond favorably to the people's cries recounted in 6:1-3 and 8:2.

11:8-11. And back. This segment suggests for the first time in chaps. 4–11 that judgment is not God's final word (cf. 1:10–2:1; 2:14-23; 3:5).

The passionate soliloquy of God in vv. 8-9 depicting an agonizing struggle in the deity's own *heart* (v. 9) is the most sophisticated theological achievement in the book. On the one hand, it employs the anthropomorphic image of a God whose *heart recoils within* and whose *compassion grows warm and tender* (v. 8). At the same time it declares that God is *no mortal* at all (11:9); and thus it affirms that any depiction of God in human terms, however revelatory, is ultimately insufficient as a depiction of holiness itself (*the Holy One*). This striking unit simultaneously confirms and subverts both the language of the prophetic proclamation and the entire enterprise of Christian theology.

Because the *Holy One* "acts" (a metaphor with essentially anthropomorphic underpinnings) in a manner consistent solely with the nature of holiness itself (i.e., independently of the actions of others; see Wolff 1974, 202), it is God's determination to *return them to their homes* after the execution of judgment (v. 11). Thus, in 10:11-12 imagery that was previously employed to express the destructive intent of the deity—*the LORD, who roars like a lion* (cf. 5:14; 13:7-8) and the people like *birds* (cf. 7:11-12)—is now transposed into salvation imagery. The closing formula, *says the LORD* (or "saying of Yahweh"; v. 11), appears only here in chaps. 4–11 and not only marks the end of a unit but also authorizes this new and remarkable word in the book.

Ephraim's Bitter Offense, 11:12–13:14 [MT 12:1–13:14]

This relatively brief section appears at first glance to have no particular connection to what precedes it. However, it develops the theme of the rejection of prophetic proclamation which is the *bitter offense* (12:14) of Ephraim.

11:12–12:9. The roots of rejection. Although the speaker who is surrounded by *lies* and *deceit* (v. 12) is conventionally understood to be Yahweh (see Andersen and Freedman 1980, 600–601), Wolff has argued quite cogently that it is the prophet (1974, 208–209). Elsewhere in Hosea, *lies* appears as terminology for a wrong against other people (see commentary on 4:2; cf. 7:3—NRSV, *treachery*; 10:13). The otherwise sudden and incongruous introduction of *the prophets* to whom Yahweh spoke in 12:10, 13 makes perfect sense if the "me" of v. 12 is Hosea rather than Yahweh. The slander and the *hostility* faced by the prophet (9:7b-8), here called *lies* and *deceit*, are characteristic of Ephraim in all its dealings (*they multiply*

falsehood and violence, 12:1), even with the superpowers Assyria and Egypt.

Two units revealing Israel's character explain "the betrayal of the word of Yahweh spoken through his prophet" (Wolff 1974, 209). The first (12:2-6) reaches back to the eponymous ancestor, Jacob. The intended punishment of *Jacob* (i.e., Israel *according to his ways* and *according to his deeds* (12:2) with which this unit begins forms an INCLUSIO with the impending return to wilderness-wandering at the end of the second unit (12:9b).

Jacob (=Israel) has been a supplanter from the first (12:3). From the beginning he has attempted to wrest all he could from God (and anyone else with whom he dealt; see 12:12) by force of might or wit. He has always trusted in his own *manhood* or "strength" (the word is translated *wealth* in the next unit, 12:8).

The faithful alternative, expressed in the first explicit prophetic call to *return* in the entire book, is to *hold fast to love and justice, and wait continually for your God* (12:6). The first two terms emphasize integrity in social relations. *Love* here is unfailing loyalty to all one's commitments (NRSV typically uses "steadfast love" for this Heb. term); *justice* is action that puts the well-being of neighbor and community on the same plane as that of self. The concluding exhortation to live in expectant anticipation of God's blessing and deliverance stands in marked contrast to Jacob in 12:3-4 (and Israel throughout the book). Inconstancy, self-centeredness, and a proclivity for attempting to seize the reins of control from God is a character flaw in Jacob-Israel from the outset, according to the prophet's testimony.

The second unit (12:7-9) employs the imagery of commerce. In addition to the deceitful business practice of using *false balances* (fraudulent weights and measures; see Lev 19:35-36; Prov 11:1; 20:23), there is an obvious play on words, as well, since the term *trader* here is "Canaan" (12:7). *Ephraim* (12:8) so thoroughly *mixes himself with the peoples* (6:8) that he is indistinguishable in character from those around him.

As did the ancestor Jacob, Ephraim revels in his *wealth* (or "strength"; see 12:3, *manhood*) which he pronounces to be honest *gain* because *no offense has been found in him* (12:8). There is clear dramatic irony here, since the reader knows what Ephraim appears not to know in his self-righteous claim concerning his practices: the offense has indeed *been found* by Yahweh. In translation an artful juxtaposition appears in

Ephraim's self-adulatory *I am rich* (12:8) and Yahweh's auto-kerygmatic (but!) *I am the LORD your God* (12:9) which introduces the judgment in which Ephraim will lose all that he has gained.

In addition to the theme of rebellious self-reliance, there are several allusive ties in this unit to the rejection of prophetic proclamation. The *false balances* (12:7a) are, literally, balances of *deceit*, the same term which was used synonymously with *lies* in 11:12 expressing the response to the prophet's message. The associated terminology of oppression (12:7b), though typically employed in economic and social contexts (see Amos 4:1; Jer 7:6; 22:3), also appears quite suggestively in Amos 3:9 in a context in which rejection of Yahweh's prophets (and the concomitant judgment) is at the fore (Amos 2:11-16; 3:1-8).

The final phrase invoking the *appointed festival* (12:9b) reprises the opening of the climactic unit in which the rejection of Hosea's proclamation is taken up (9:5-9), and the tent-dwelling recapitulates the rejection of Ephraim for not having *listened* to God speaking through the prophet: *they shall become wanderers* (9:17).

12:10-14. Bitter offense. As Israel's rejection of the prophet has been shown to be consistent with its historic pattern of behavior, so too Yahweh's working through prophets is seen to be of considerable antiquity. The variety of prophetic activity is considerable: they hear, as Yahweh "speaks" to them; they see *visions* that Yahweh gives them; they are agents of *destruction* that Yahweh brings (v. 10); they are instruments of deliverance that Yahweh works; and they are ministers of Yahweh's protection or oversight of Israel (implicit in the passive verb *was guarded* is a concluding phrase, "by Yahweh" v. 13).

Israel, in the meantime, has paid no attention to prophets, so involved has it been in its self-interest at cultic centers such as in Gilead and at Gilgal, which will not escape *destruction* (v. 11).

Moses is obviously the prophet by whom *the LORD brought Israel up from Egypt* (v. 13a). The synonymously parallel reference in v. 13b may also be to MOSES (Wolff 1974, 216), or it may be to a second eminent prophet (Andersen and Freedman 1980, 621). If so, the most likely candidate is SAMUEL. Jeremiah identifies the pair by name in the context of a condemnation of Judah: "Though Moses and Samuel stood before me, yet my heart would not turn toward this people. Send them out of my sight, and let them go!" (15:1).

The *bitter offense* of Ephraim (v. 14), then, is the rejection of the prophet through whom Yahweh would deliver and protect Israel (v. 13) but through whom now Yahweh will *pay him back* for *his crimes* and *his insults* (v. 14; cf. *bring destruction*, v. 10). The term translated *bitter offense* involves a play on the root of the previously repeated *deceit* (see 11:12; 12:7) and thus ties the beginning, middle, and end of the section together.

Death and Rebirth of Israel, 13:1–14:9 [MT 13:1–14:10]

At the close of the collection comes a promise of healing, love, and fruitfulness (14:4-8) after the brutal and horrifying destruction that Israel will experience (13:7-16). After having rejected previous pleas (see 6:1-3; 8:2), Yahweh will in the end respond favorably to a plea (14:2-3) that the prophet instructs the people to take to Yahweh. Thus, rebirth comes with accepting the prophetic instruction.

Remarkably, the imagery of new life with Yahweh is drawn exclusively from the language of fertility and fecundity—in other words, from the rich matrix of the Canaanite religious thought-world.

13:1-3. Ephraim's death. The introductory segment raises up Ephraim's *guilt through Baal* and the death that results (v. 1). Past *guilt* (v. 1), present *sinning* (v. 2), and future futility (v. 3) encapsulate Hosea's perspective on the history of Israel's relationship with Yahweh.

13:4-16. The blast from the LORD. The first unit (vv. 4-8) of this violent and troubling section begins with Yahweh's own interpretation of Israel's salvation history. *God* and *savior* to Israel *ever since the land of Egypt* (v. 4) and provider *in the wilderness*, Yahweh has watched as the people became *satisfied, and their heart was proud; therefore they forgot me* (v. 6). Here the people's physical and material satiation and their arrogant self-centeredness are presented as the cause of their loss of knowledge of God. That this all-important concept is at issue here is clearer in the Hebrew text with its juxtaposition of *you know no God but me* in v. 4 with "I knew (NRSV, *fed*; see mrg.) you" *in the wilderness* in v. 5 (cf. 5:3-4). The unit closes with stunning and terrifying animal imagery depicting Yahweh's coming in judgment that will inevitably result in Israel's death (vv. 7-8).

The next four brief units (vv. 9-11, 12-13, 14, 15-16) elaborate on this death. The blunt *I will destroy you, O Israel* of v. 9 colors all that follows down to the final *Compassion is hidden from my eyes* in v. 14. There is no political solution this time; *king* and *rulers* can offer no hope of salvation (vv. 10-11).

The *iniquity* and *sin* which is *bound up* and *kept in store* is more than picturesque speech (so Mays 1969, 180). Andersen and Freedman propose the secreting of idols for safekeeping (1980, 637–38). However, it is quite suggestive that in response to the rejection of his proclamation concerning the Syro-Ephraimite conflict, Hosea's southern contemporary Isaiah ordered that his prediction be "bound up" and "sealed" until such time that it had come to pass, whereupon it could be opened and he vindicated as a "true" prophet of Yahweh (Isa 8:16; Roberts 1992, 214).

So, too, with Hosea's prediction of deportation from the land (9:3-6), which was met with slander and *hostility* (9:7-8). It has been recorded, sealed, and stored until the time that Yahweh *will remember their iniquity* and *will punish their sins* (9:9; note the same word pair as in v. 12). Then the prophet who was attacked as a *fool* and *mad* (9:9) will be exonerated (a life-and-death matter for a prophet; see Deut 18:20-22).

The *childbirth* imagery of the next verse, with its emphasis on knowing *the proper time*, further illustrates Ephraim's rejection of the prophetic word, as one of the essential tasks of the prophet throughout the ancient Near East was to reveal the "times" (see Roberts 1988, 212). Ephraim, however, is *unwise* and has failed to *present himself* when the opportunity for life was offered by Yahweh through the corrective proclamation of the prophet.

The first two rhetorical questions of v. 14 are reminiscent of the internal struggle of Yahweh in 11:8 in which God's *compassion* for Israel won out over *fierce anger* (vv. 8-9). Here, however, Yahweh calls out impatiently for *Death* to bring on its *plagues* and for *Sheol* to deliver its *destruction*. This time, *Compassion is hidden* from Yahweh's eyes (v. 14; cf. v. 9).

Although for a time Ephraim may flourish, *a blast from the LORD* is coming (v. 15). In 16 the *sword*, previously wielded against duplicitous envoys (*officials*, 7:16) and then raging in surrounding *cities* (11:6), now comes to the heart of the Northern Kingdom, *Samaria*. The historical correlate of the thematic nadir of the collection (9:10-17) is reached here with the anticipated slaughter of innocents in the destruction of Samaria.

14:1-9. Return and rebirth. For only the second time in the book, the explicit prophetic call to *return* appears in vv. 1-2a (cf. 12:6). But far more important

than the call itself is the model prayer that follows it (vv. 2b-3) as the "words to take with you," i.e., as the appropriate verbal expression of authentic repentance.

The model prayer begins with an acknowledgment of sin in the request that *guilt* be taken away. The entreaty that Yahweh *accept that which is good* does not refer to the words being offered here. This often repeated interpretation reflects an anti-sacrificial bias foreign to Hosea. The good here is an acceptable sacrifice or offering (see the priestly discrimination between "good" and "bad" for votary offerings in Num 27:10, 14, 33) without which no Israelite was to appear before Yahweh (Exod 23:15; 34:20).

Hosea's animosity toward the cult as practiced in his day should not be misinterpreted as a call for life without tangible offerings to Yahweh. The prophet himself cited just such an existence as one of the horrors of exile (9:4).

The third element, *the fruit of our lips*, refers to the vows of renunciation that follow. But here, too, words are not all that is involved: it includes the fulfillment in action of what the words have promised. Words (like sacrifices) have been offered before and were rejected as insufficient (see 6:1-3; 8:2).

Authentic repentance requires the renunciation of self-sufficiency and self-centeredness. Israel's attempt to manufacture security through political coalitioning (with Assyria), militarism (*riding upon horses*), and cultic innovation (*work of our hands*) was a denial of the sovereignty and sufficiency of God. The final element (*the orphan*) reinforces the necessary shift from self-centeredness to concern for the vulnerable. It also brings the book full circle, as the verb translated *finds mercy* is from the same Hebrew root as the name of Hosea's daughter, *Lo-ruhamah*, "Not pitied" (1:6), who is renamed *Ruhamah*, "Pitied" (2:1).

In contrast to the previous occasions of Israel's appeal, Yahweh responds immediately with a promise to *heal* and to *love them* without constraint (v. 4). Renewed relationship with Yahweh comes when Israel finally accepts prophetic instruction. However, even on the other side of judgment and repentance, Israel's character is no different—*disloyalty* remains. Yahweh has chosen to do what Israel could not do for itself—effect healing—not because Israel now deserves it, but because Yahweh's *anger has turned from them*.

In rich botanical imagery (with a particular emphasis on the fruitfulness of Lebanon; vv. 5, 6, 7), vv. 5-8 employs language and imagery common in love songs (see Wolff 1974, 234–38) to characterize new life with

Yahweh. Sumptuous sensory images abound (sight, smell, taste) to communicate safety, security, and well-being. There is salvation here, but no hint of "salvation history." In fact, the Israel earlier condemned for its penchant for enjoying the *shade* of trees (4:13) is now offered the "shade" (NRSV *shadow*, v. 7; the Heb. term is identical) of Yahweh, who is depicted as an *evergreen* tree (v. 8).

Remarkably, the God who repeatedly reminded Israel, *I am the LORD your God from the land of Egypt* (12:9; 13:4; cf. 11:1; 12:13), says in the end, *I am like an evergreen cypress* (v. 8). For this great prophet, then, Yahweh the God of Israel remains every bit as authentically revealed in the nature and agriculture of Canaan as in the historical traditions of Israel.

The last verse in the book employs the language of wisdom literature, an international idiom in the ancient Near East. In contrast to the superscription (1:1), which directs the reader's attention to the specific historical context of the preaching of Hosea, this postscript points to the universal applicability of the message of the book.

Works Cited

Andersen, F. L., and D. N. Freedman. 1980. *Hosea.* AncB.

Coogan, M. D. 1987. "Canaanite Origins and Lineage: Reflections on the Religion of Ancient Israel," *Ancient Israelite Religion*, 115–24.

Hillers, D. R. 1964. *Treaty-Curses and the Old Testament Prophets.*

Mays, J. L. 1969. *Hosea.* OTL.

Miller, P. D. 1985. "Israelite Religion," *The Hebrew Bible and Its Modern Interpreters*, ed. D. A. Knight and G. M. Tucker, 201–37.

Rogers, J. S. 1993. "Women in the Hands of an Abusive God? The Trouble with Hosea 2." *Interpreting Hosea for Preaching and Teaching*, ed. C. P. Staton, Jr., 21–30.

Sakenfeld, K. D. 1985. *Faithfulness in Action.*

Sanderson, J. E. 1992. "Nahum," *The Women's Bible Commentary*, ed. C. A. Newsome and S. H. Ringe, 217–21.

Wolff, H. W. 1974. *Hosea.* Herm.

Joel

Margaret Dee Bratcher

Introduction

The Book of Joel, the second in the collection of twelve prophetic books known as the Book of the Twelve, announces the coming of the Day of Yahweh, the Day of the LORD, as a day of judgment and salvation for JUDAH and JERUSALEM in the wake of a devastating infestation of locusts. This proclamation is the most extensive depiction of the Day of Yahweh in the OT.

In its interpretation of the natural disaster brought on by the locusts, the Book of Joel contributes a distinctive understanding of the acts of Yahweh within history and nature. In addition, its employment of other biblical writings provides a remarkable example of the continued transmission and application of the language of Israel's faith into new settings and time periods.

Date and Place in the Canon

A common feature of the prophetic literature is a superscription placed at the beginning of each book. These superscriptions usually identify briefly the prophet whose message follows and provide other pertinent information, such as the people to whom the message is directed, the time period in which it is given, and perhaps even the substance of the message itself. Usually the prophetic books also contain concrete references to events and people that help to date them.

The Book of Joel, however, lacks any chronological reference in its superscription as well as any specific references to events or people. In the absence of such indications of time period, OT scholars up to the beginning of the nineteenth century usually maintained that Joel was a preexilic PROPHET because of the book's place in the CANON between the eighth-century prophets HOSEA and AMOS.

The dating of Joel in recent OT scholarship depends more on allusions in the text that suggest a time period and on certain features of style and content rather than the book's place in the canon. For example, Joel assumes the postexilic rebuilding of the Temple in 515 B.C.E. and the walls of Jerusalem in 445 B.C.E. (see 1:9, 14, 16; 2:7, 9, 17; 3:18). The depiction of Judah as a well-organized religious community under the leadership of the priesthood and elders suggests a date after the reforms of EZRA and NEHEMIAH (see 1:2, 9, 13-14; 2:14, 16-17, 19), and references to Judah's neighbors seem to describe the geopolitical scene in the late Persian period, before the conquest of ALEXANDER (see 3:4, 6, 17, 19).

Moreover, Hebrew terms and expressions are used in Joel that appear elsewhere only in later OT books (see Wolff 1977, 10–11; Thompson 1956, 731–32 for a detailed list). The book shows a dependence on the thought of other prophets, including notably the late prophets OBADIAH (v. 17; see Joel 2:32) and MALACHI (3:2; 4:5; see Joel 2:11, 31).

These examples suggest that Joel must be dated sometime after the reforms of Ezra and Nehemiah and before the Hellenistic conquest of Judah, most likely the first half of the fourth century B.C.E. or the end of the fifth century B.C.E.

The related issue of the arrangement of the Book of the Twelve in the canon is a difficult question to resolve, but several factors appear to have influenced the arrangement of the books. For example, when a book's superscription contains information that locates it in a particular time period, the book is placed in approximate chronological order. For example, Hosea, Amos, JONAH, and MICAH are all identified with persons or events in the eighth century B.C.E.

As a result of the arguments above about the date of Joel, the rationale for the position of Joel in the canon now seems to be the connection between its themes and those of other books, rather than the date of its message. That is, the language of Joel 2:31 and

3:16, 18, 19 concerning the Day of Yahweh closely resembles the beginning of Amos. Most likely, then, Joel was placed before Amos as an introduction to Amos's proclamation of the coming of the Day of Yahweh against Judah and its neighbors. The arrangement of the Greek collection of the Twelve supports this proposal, since it appears to be more interested in chronology than the Hebrew and places Joel later in its collection (see Wolff 1977, 3–5 for a fuller discussion of these issues).

The Structure and Unity of Joel

The three chapters in the Book of Joel (1) lament the coming of a locust plague, (2) announce the Day of Yahweh as a comprehensive disaster for Judah and Jerusalem, and (3) promise a future salvation. A major issue in the study of the book is how these chapters relate to each other and whether they indicate any compositional unity.

Joel 2:17-18 is usually considered the midpoint of the book, for there the tone of the book turns from judgment and destruction for Judah to the proclamation of salvation for Yahweh's people. The book is also usually judged to be a unified work by a single author, with perhaps some minor materials added by a later editor, indicated by the continuity of themes and language throughout the book (see Wolff 1977, and Childs 1979 for discussion of the arguments).

Joel 2:27-28, however, has also been understood as the midpoint in the book, a turn from history to eschatology. That is, prior to this point the message of Joel has been directed at the agricultural crisis caused by the locusts, interpreting it as the Day of Yahweh in judgment on Judah and as a sign of the coming, eschatological Day of Yahweh. After 2:27 the focus of Joel is entirely on the coming eschatological battle between Yahweh and his enemies, which will result in Israel's ultimate vindication and Yahweh's exaltation, and references to the locusts and the present distress of Judah disappear (a view first stated by Bernhard Duhm in 1911).

Recent efforts to understand and articulate the structure and unity of Joel suggest that chap. 3 represents additional oracles added to a lament about a locust invasion and Yahweh's response to that lament in 1:5–2:27, but that these materials have been edited in such a way as to give internal coherence to the entire book (Hiebert 1992, 874).

The primary discussion of the coherence of the book comes from Hans Walter Wolff, who points out that the materials after the midpoint in 2:17-18 correspond inversely to those that precede it. That is, 1:14-20, a lament over destroyed harvest and pastures in the aftermath of the locusts, is reversed by the promise of abundance in 2:21-27. The announcement of coming judgment against Jerusalem and Judah in 2:1-11 is reversed in 3:1-3, 9-17 by their vindication over their enemies. The call to repentance in 2:12-17 is reversed by the promise of the pouring out of the spirit in 2:28-32 (Wolff 1977, 7).

Theme and Style

The primary theme of Joel is the coming of the Day of the LORD, the Day of Yahweh. Although the term itself, "Day of the LORD," appears in the OT only sixteen times (five times in Joel alone), the earliest instance of which is Amos 5:18, 20, the concept is found in at least twenty other contexts and is very ancient. It denotes a decisive event of Yahweh's activity, understood first in Israel's thinking as Yahweh's giving victory to Israel over its enemies, but understood later as Yahweh's own judgment upon Israel. The language that describes the Day of Yahweh derives most likely from the traditions of holy war and from descriptions of THEOPHANY, God's appearance to the people in their acts of worship or in times of danger. For example, descriptions of the Day of Yahweh typically depict Yahweh's leading his army into battle against his enemies to overturn them; they also frequently portray the response of creation, heaven and earth, at the coming of Yahweh.

The Book of Joel reflects the last stage in Israel's understanding of the Day of the LORD: it is a day of both judgment and salvation for ISRAEL. In Joel, the day comes in the natural disasters of locust plague and drought that devastate the land and call the people to return to Yahweh (1:15; 2:1, 11). The day comes in the cosmic eschatological battle between Yahweh and his enemies that results in Israel's final deliverance (2:31; 3:14).

The book continues to describe the Day of Yahweh in the language of HOLY WAR and theophany and repeatedly draws on earlier traditions through its quotation and paraphrase of those materials. For example, the description of the locusts as an invading army both calls to mind the Exodus plague of locusts and prepares for their identification with the Day of Yahweh. The book thereby exhibits a fine depth of shading in its portrayal of the Day of Yahweh. At once a present devastating infestation of locusts evokes the locust plague of the Exodus and portends the coming final battle between Yahweh and the hordes of his enemies. The crisis in nature is understood as an omen for the Day of Yahweh, both ancient acts of Yahweh and future ones.

This concern for the past, present, and future acts of Yahweh is an explicit part of the purpose of Joel: the events described within the book, without parallel in Israel's experience (1:2; 2:2), become a lesson for the generations of Israel to come (1:3), so that they may know that their LORD is God, *and there is no other* (2:27). Yahweh transforms judgment into sal-

vation; the people of Yahweh are returned to their God, and Yahweh alone is acknowledged and exalted as the one true God.

For Further Study

In the *Mercer Dictionary of the Bible*: ESCHATOLOGY IN THE OT; JOEL, BOOK OF; JUDGMENT, DAY OF; ORACLE; PROPHET; VISION.
In other sources: B. S. Childs. *Introduction to the OT as Scripture.*; J. Limburg. *Hosea–Micah*. Interp; H. W. Wolff. *Joel and Amos*. Herm.

Commentary

An Outline

I. Superscription, 1:1
II. The Locust Plague, 1:2-4
III. A Call to Lamentation, 1:5–2:17
   A. Affected Groups, 1:5-14
   B. Lamenting the People's Distress, 1:15-20
   C. The Day of the LORD, 2:1-11
   D. Call to Repentance, 2:12-17
IV. Promises of Salvation, 2:18–3:21 [MT 2:18–4:21]
   A. Devastation Reversed, 2:18-27
   B. The Spirit Poured Out, 2:28-29 [MT 2:28–3:2]
   C. Further Oracles of Salvation, 2:30–3:21 [MT 3:3–4:21]

Superscription, 1:1

The superscription of the Book of Joel is similar to the beginnings of the prophetic books HOSEA, MICAH, ZEPHANIAH, and JONAH in describing the book as *the word of the LORD that came to* the PROPHET. The assertion is a claim that the message of the book derives from Yahweh, not the prophet himself. These are Yahweh's words for his people.

The name Joel means "Yahweh is God" and is attested in the OT most frequently in writings from the postexilic period (for example, the Chronicler's History). The name of Joel's father, *Pethuel*, is otherwise unattested in the OT, and its meaning is uncertain.

The Locust Plague, 1:2-4

Verses 2-3 call the people of JUDAH and JERUSALEM to attention and emphatically assert the purpose of the book: an extraordinary crisis has befallen the people, and they are to tell its story for generations to come. The exhortation to make this present event known to the future introduces a fundamental idea in Joel: events

may teach lessons not only to those who experience them but also to those who live in their aftermath.

The phrase *hear . . . give ear* is a typical call to receive instruction. The address to the *elders* and *inhabitants of the land* (v. 2) is an address to the community of Yahweh's people in Judah and Jerusalem and their leaders.

A rhetorical question highlights the singular circumstances of this crisis: *Has such a thing happened?* The people are to compare this crisis with their own experiences of trouble and with the experiences of earlier generations; implicit within the question is the answer that nothing compares with this crisis. The crisis, then, is so extraordinary that it holds greater meaning for Israel than some chance occurrence of trouble. This event will be instructive for generations long to come.

One generation is to hand the story on to the next in an unbroken line of tradition. Of the numerous references to the next generations in the OT, the most emphatic is the one found here, to the fourth generation, the generation of great grandchildren. To live to see great grandchildren effectively marks the longest length of a person's life in the OT. The prophet thus commends the retelling of these events into the farthest reaches of the future one may envision.

Verse 4 makes clear what kind of crisis has come upon the people: a swarm of locusts has thoroughly devastated the land. The repeated statement that the remains left by one swarm of locusts is eaten by the next dramatizes the complete destruction of the land. The locusts have left nothing. The terminology for the locusts, *cutting . . . swarming . . . hopping . . . destroying,* is usually understood as descriptive of the developmental stages in the lifespan of the common desert locust, although some interpreters understand it as a description of successive waves of invasions (see Thompson 1956, 737; Wolff 1977, 27–28; Hiebert 1992, 876).

A Call to Lamentation, 1:5–2:17

This section of the book is a lament in response to the locust plague. References throughout the section to the drying up of the harvest suggest the presence of drought conditions in addition to the locust infestation. The section may be subdivided into 1:5-14, a call to lament in the aftermath of the locusts; 1:15-20, the lament of the community and prophet; 2:1-11, a description of the Day of the LORD, understood as foreshadowed in the plague; and 2:12-17, another call to the people for prayer and fasting.

Affected Groups, 1:5-14

These verses call the people to cry their lament to Yahweh in time of distress. The unit consists of four calls to lament, in vv. 5-7, 8-10, 11-12, and 13-14, addressed to the groups most affected by the crisis. The basic pattern of each call is an introductory line of address consisting of imperatives, in which the second imperative is *wail*, and vocatives of address. A statement of the reason for the lament and description of the situation of distress follow. Verses 8-10 differ from this structure, perhaps due to faulty transmission of the text. The rearrangement of the stanza, with v. 9b preceding v. 8, suggests the original order.

1:5-7. Drunkards and wine-drinkers. The *drunkards* and *wine-drinkers* (v. 5) are wakened to the crisis of the complete destruction of the vineyards. The locusts are likened to an invading nation, *powerful and innumerable* (v. 6), a depiction that prefigures the description of the army of *the day of the LORD* in 2:1-11. Their force, which strips clean vine and branch, is compared to *the fangs of a lioness* (v. 6), a common OT image for fierce, destructive power. The use of the first person, *my vines* and *my branches* (v. 7), evokes the direct language of the prophets in speaking for Yahweh and reminds the audience of whose interests are ultimately involved: Yahweh is the owner of these vineyards.

1:8-10. Grain and drink offerings lost. The second call to lament is for the loss of the grain offering and drink offering. In the devastation of the fields, the grain, wine, and oil that provide the grain and drink offerings are lost. Such a loss calls forth the mourning

of the priests, the ministers of the altar, whose responsibility it is to offer sacrifices, for the crisis threatens the very worship of Yahweh. Moreover, the recitation of the series *grain . . . wine . . . oil* recalls the classic harvest of the land in OT tradition, where the land is recognized as the gift of Yahweh and the harvest as the sign of his blessing. The loss of these, then, signifies the loss of Yahweh's blessing and the coming of his judgment, evoking the mourning of the land itself. The comparison of lamenting like a virgin in sackcloth (an onomatopoeic word from the Heb. *saq*) for the husband of her youth refers to dressing in garments of mourning like a young woman whose bridegroom has been killed. It is the announcement that all the joy and hope of the future are cut off.

1:11-12. The disgrace of farmers and vine-dressers. Those who work the land, *farmers* and *vine-dressers*, face the ruin of their harvest. The call to lament in v. 11, *be dismayed* or *be ashamed*, probably refers to the disgrace of the farmers at the loss of Yahweh's favor, indicated by the devastation of the harvest. The joy of the people at the gift of Yahweh's blessing is dried up and becomes shame.

1:13-14. Instructions to the priests. The final call to lament instructs the priests to dress themselves in sackcloth, lament, and call a fast for the community. These activities are the community's responses in worship to the catastrophe that they have experienced.

Lamenting the People's Distress, 1:15-20

This unit laments the people's distress and announces the coming of the Day of Yahweh (v. 15). The swath of destruction cut through the land by the locust invasion makes clear that the Day of Yahweh is near and that it comes as destruction from Yahweh. Word play between *destruction* (*shōd*) and *the Almighty* (*Shaddai*) helps to evoke the terror of the approaching judgment of the LORD.

Verses 16-18 confirm the proclamation about the significance of the community's crisis. The rhetorical questions in v. 16 provide the ground for the announcement of the Day of Yahweh. The loss of the harvest and the threat to the sacrifices of the Temple service signal its coming, and illustrations of the ruined condition of the land follow in vv. 17 and 18. Seed has shriveled in the soil and granaries have fallen to ruins because they have stood empty. The grazing animals, large and small, suffer from lack of pasture. The effects of both locusts and drought are suggested in these verses.

Verses 19-20 express the prophet's lament, *to you, O LORD, I cry*, and report the animals' lament for the loss of pasture.

The Day of the LORD, 2:1-11

This section describes the approaching Day of Yahweh, which has been introduced in 1:15. The unit begins with a cry of alarm raised to warn of the threat of armed attack. A description of the approaching army, the army of Yahweh, follows in three paragraphs: vv. 3-5, 6-9, and 10-11. The vivid imagery used here to describe the army of the Day of Yahweh is consistent with both the descriptions of the locusts of chap. 1, whose invasion has served as a sign of the coming day, and the customary depictions of the Day of Yahweh found in holy war traditions. The prophet Joel thereby points away from the present crisis to its real meaning, the coming of Yahweh in judgment.

2:1-2. A cry of alarm. The unit begins with the call to *blow the trumpet* and *sound the alarm*. The purpose of the alarm is to warn Jerusalem (*Zion . . . my holy mountain*) of the approaching threat of the Day of Yahweh. The trumpet is the *shophar*, or ram's horn, used in Israel in several contexts: to signal danger at an approaching army, to sound a battle cry, as well as to call the community to religious ceremonies. The *shophar* also appears in texts that describe the presence and activity of Yahweh himself, such as the coming of Yahweh as judge in Ps 98:6-9 and the coming of the Day of Yahweh in Zeph 1:14-16.

The description of the Day of the LORD as *a day of darkness and gloom, a day of clouds and thick darkness* (v. 2), derives from Amos 5:18, 20, the earliest reference to the term "the day of Yahweh" (a description followed by Zeph 1:15; see Deut 4:11, 5:22-23 and Ps 97:2 for similar phenomena accompanying Yahweh's presence or coming, but not specifically the Day of Yahweh).

Verse 2b makes explicit what the Day of Yahweh means: the coming of a *great and powerful army* (Heb. *'am rab we'āsûm*, "great and powerful people"). The phrase recalls both 1:6, the description of the locusts as *a nation . . . powerful and innumerable*, and also the army of the Day of the LORD in Isa 13:4, an important passage on the Day of Yahweh (*'am rab*; NRSV "great multitude"). That *their like has never been from of old, nor will be again after them in ages to come* represents the unique instance of this force over the farthest extent of time, from memory past to the future ahead. The description intensifies the distinc-

tiveness of the locust invasion in 1:2 and also evokes the description of the locust plague in the Exodus tradition (Exod 10:14-15). Those forces, so distinctive then, will be overshadowed by comparison with the coming Day of Yahweh.

The translation *like blackness spread upon the mountains* (v. 2b) is without textual witness, but is suggested by the references to the darkness of the day in v. 2a and the blackening of the land caused by the Exodus locusts in Exod 10:14. The MT vocalization reads "like dawn spread upon the mountains" (so NIV, KJV), which may refer to the shining of light upon the locust wings (Wolff 1977, 43).

2:3. Devastation. Verse 3 describes the effect of this army: the complete, fiery devastation of the land. The reference to *fire . . . in front of them and behind them a flame* may echo Pss 97:3 and 50:3 in their portrayal of the coming of Yahweh as a devouring fire. The contrast between the land as like the garden of Eden before their coming and as a wilderness afterward is not only a poetic description of the contrast between verdant growth before and charred stubble afterward, but also a reversal of the prophetic image of salvation describing the end of the Exile, when Yahweh would turn the land from wilderness into a new Eden (Ezek 36:35; Isa 51:3). It serves, therefore, as a stark proclamation of judgment upon Jerusalem and Judah.

2:4-9. A charging army. In vv. 4-5, the army is pictured as a cavalry of horses and chariots charging upon the mountains (see Judg 6:5, 7:12; Jer 46:23, 51:27; Nah 3:16-17; Job 39:20; Rev 9:7 for similar metaphors). The scene conveys both their devastating power and number (*powerful army drawn up for battle*) and the tumultuous noise with which they invade (*as with the rumbling of chariots* and *like the crackling of a flame of fire devouring the stubble*).

In vv. 6-9 the army is compared with infantry advancing on a city, overrunning its defenses and unstoppable. The paragraph begins with a reminder of the tragedy wrought by such an onslaught—*peoples are in anguish, all faces grow pale*. The remaining phrases in the stanza emphasize the power of the attacking forces and explain why there is such terror and suffering. The army invades the city, advancing in line and overpowering all the city's defenses as they scale the walls and enter people's homes. No place is safe from violation.

2:10-11. Cosmic results. The prophet reaches the climactic description concerning the attack in vv. 10-

11: Even *the earth quakes* and *the heavens tremble* before this host, and *the sun and the moon are darkened*, for Yahweh is *at the head of his army*. The shaking of the cosmos is a motif found in THEOPHANY accounts in the OT (Judg 5:4; Pss 18:8, 68:9, 77:19) and in connection with the coming of the Day of Yahweh (Isa 13:13; Ezek 38:19-20). The approach of the army is experienced throughout creation precisely *because* Yahweh is at its head. Moreover, the note of alarm sounded with the trembling of the people in v. 1 at the approach of an army is intensified here with the trembling of the heavens at the approach of Yahweh himself and the impossibility of escape. The uttering of Yahweh's voice is a familiar prophetic expression for the unleashing of Yahweh's judgment (see Amos 1:2).

An INCLUSIO formed by the repetition in v. 11 of *the day of the LORD* from 2:1 ends the paragraph. The repetition reinforces how very imminent is Yahweh's coming and how terrible is the predicament of his people. Who can endure it?

Call to Repentance, 2:12-17

This unit is a call to repentance, divided into two sections. Verses 12-14 assert the need for sincere, inward repentance and probe the possibility of Yahweh's relenting. Verses 15-17 provide direction for the expression of repentance in the rituals of worship.

2:12-14. Return to the LORD. Two calls for the people to return to Yahweh appear here, one prescribing what the people must do and the other reminding them of the source of their hope, Yahweh's compassionate nature and actions.

The people are called to return, or repent (Heb. *shūv*), in the traditional prophetic understanding of repentance, as an entire reordering of priorities (see Amos 4:6-11; Hos 3:5; 14:2; Jer 3:10; 24:7). The call to return with one's heart, which is in Hebrew the center of the will, is a call to turn toward Yahweh exercising the very center of the self's power to choose its way, establish its priorities, and fix its loyalties. *Fasting, with weeping, and with mourning* (v. 12) are accompanying signs of repentance. *Rend your hearts and not your clothing* (v. 13) is a play on the ritual act of mourning—the tearing of one's garments before putting on sackcloth. The prophet thus enjoins a sincere, inward experience of sorrow, repentance, and recommitment to Yahweh.

The reason for hope in Yahweh's relenting from judgment is found in v. 13: *the LORD . . . is gracious*

and merciful, slow to anger, and abounding in steadfast love. The prophet repeats a traditional confession of faith that describes the gracious, compassionate character of Yahweh (see Exod 34:6-7; Neh 9:17, 31; Ps 86:15 et al.). The phrase *relents from punishing* (v. 13) applies the confession to the community's crisis; the hope for Israel is that a compassionate Yahweh will turn from his punishment. Rather than the scorched earth described in 2:3, then, Yahweh would *leave a blessing behind him* (v. 14); that is, the land would be revitalized so that the *grain offering* and *drink offering* may be brought forth from it and given to Yahweh.

2:15-17. Call to worship. The call to *blow the trumpet* (v. 15) repeats the call of 2:1, but whereas then it sounded an alarm because of a threat, now it calls the people to repentant worship in response to that threat. The command to *sanctify a fast, call a solemn assembly* indicates what religious rites are to be performed in response to the call to repentance. Three groups within the community are summoned specifically: the old, the young, and the newly married. These are ones who were frequently excused from participation in the services, but just as the coming of the Day of Yahweh will allow no one to escape, so this call to repentance must involve everyone in the community, without exception.

Verse 17 instructs the priests to ask Yahweh to spare his people; the reason is an appeal to Yahweh's own righteousness and majesty. Common in the prophets (see e.g., Ezek 20), this appeal links the fortunes of Israel with the nation's understanding of the sovereignty of Yahweh: for Yahweh to preserve Israel is to show his sovereignty to the nations. Their welfare reflects back upon the nations' estimation of Yahweh.

Promises of Salvation, 2:18–3:21 [MT 2:18–4:21]

This section contains Yahweh's response to the people's prayer, addressing both the present crisis and also the larger threat of the Day of Yahweh. The message of comfort and hope promised by Yahweh's response in 2:18-27 is further extended by short oracles of salvation in 2:28-29 (MT 3:1-2) and 2:30-32 (MT 3:3-5). A longer oracle against the nations in 3:1-21 (MT 4:1-21) concludes the section.

Devastation Reversed, 2:18-27

2:18. An introduction. The acts that follow are because Yahweh *became jealous for his land and had pity on his people*. Yahweh's jealousy is his "saving zeal," as in Ezek 39:25, Zech 1:14, 8:2; and Zeph 1:18. The Day of Yahweh becomes a Day of Yahweh's compassionate, zealous salvation for his land and people.

2:19-20. A promise. These verses promise the turning of lamentation into harvest joy and the removal of danger, for Yahweh will replenish the *grain, wine, and oil*" (cf. 1:10, 16) and destroy the threatening army. The army is at once the locust horde and the army of the Day of Yahweh; in addition, the description *northern army* alludes to the enemy brought by Yahweh according to the proclamation of earlier prophets (see Jer 1:14-15; 4:6; 6:1, 22; Ezek 38:6, 15; 39:2).

2:21-27. The LORD's deliverance. These verses expand the assurance of Yahweh's deliverance in the present agricultural crisis, reversing point by point the lament of 1:16-20 with the promise of full granaries, pastures, and rain. Land, people, and animals had once mourned, but now they are called to rejoice at Yahweh's salvation. Verse 27, the climax in this proclamation of salvation, speaks to the larger theological issue of Israel's relationship to Yahweh: Israel will acknowledge and experience the presence of Yahweh in its midst and his exaltation as the one true God.

The Spirit Poured Out, 2:28-29 [MT 2:28–3:2]

Once the present, imminent crises have been deflected, vv. 28-29 announce the pouring out of Yahweh's spirit. In the past, the Spirit had been given only to certain people, commissioned with special tasks: judges, kings, and above all in Joel's day, the prophets. The pouring out of Yahweh's Spirit here, however, depicts the entire nation as a community of inspired prophets. *Prophesy*, *dreams*, and *visions* are parallel terms for prophetic inspiration. The references to young and old, male and female, and slave and free in v. 29 encompass the entire community. These human divisions and distinctions are rendered void by the coming of the Spirit, for all will share the presence of Yahweh. *All flesh*, all weak mortality, therefore, will be transformed by the ultimate saving action, the very presence of Yahweh poured out upon all of the people.

Further Oracles of Salvation, 2:30–3:21 [MT 3:3–4:21]

The Book of Joel concludes with a pair of oracles. The first oracle (2:30-32 [MT 3:3-5]) is an announcement of salvation for the people of Yahweh. The second oracle (3:1-21 [MT 4:1-12]) is an extended pronouncement directed toward *all the nations* (3:2).

2:30-32. The day of salvation. This oracle proclaims the coming Day of Yahweh as a day of salvation for Yahweh's people. *Blood and fire and columns of smoke* are signs, or portents, on earth that precede the coming day; they refer to the devastating effects of warfare. The darkening of the sun and reddening of the moon portend the coming day in the heavens. The promise of salvation is for *everyone who calls upon the name of the LORD*, that is, those who worship Yahweh; and the promise of escape is for all those threatened with no escape from the judgment of 2:3, 11—if they turn to Yahweh in faithful worship.

3:1-21. An oracle against the nations. The Book of Joel closes with a lengthy proclamation directed against Judah's enemies and exalting the power and actions of Yahweh in Judah's behalf. The oracle has four subunits: vv. 1-3, 4-8, 9-17, and 18-21.

Verses 1-3 make clear that the day of salvation for Judah and Jerusalem means Yahweh's judgment on the nations. The *valley of Jehoshaphat*, the place of judgment, appears only here in the OT. It is a symbolic name, meaning "Yahweh judges," and expresses a play on words with the reference to judgment which follows it (Heb. *shāphat*, "to judge"). The provocation for this judgment is the EXILE, the dispersion of Judah. Although the Exile occurred years ago, Israel still struggles to reestablish itself in the land, and the agony and humiliation that Israel experienced have not faded with the passing of time. The bitterness of Jerusalem's destruction and of the exile are grimly captured in the image of the selling of Israel's children to hire prostitutes and to purchase drink.

Verses 4-8 are an oracle against foreign nations, a frequent element in the prophetic literature. The oracle is against *Philistia* and the Phoenician cities of *Tyre and Sidon* (v. 4). For their crimes against Judah, plundering wealth and selling people into slavery (see Amos 1:6, 9; Ezek 27:13), they will experience a similar fate, the selling of their own sons and daughters. Such correspondence between a crime and its punishment is frequent in the OT, especially in Deuteronomy and the prophets. The pattern affirms the justice inherent in Yahweh's actions and relates it to the outworkings of human choices to do evil. *The Sabeans* (v. 8) are the people of Sheba in southern Arabia.

A call to arms and a description of the final judgment are found in vv. 9-17. The call for the nations to prepare for war and to present themselves at Yahweh's judgment opens the section (vv. 9-12). The impact of the call is dramatized in the inversion of the promise of salvation found in Isa 2:4 and Mic 4:3: tools of peace are to be converted into weapons of war.

The description of Yahweh's judgment follows in vv. 13-15. It is likened to a harvest: *put in the sickle . . . go in, tread. The harvest is ripe*, the *winepress is full*, and the *vats overflow* offer parallel imagery for the excessive wickedness of the nations. The phrase *valley of decision* in place of the valley of Jehoshaphat points specifically to the verdict, the final judgment awaiting the nations. The paragraph closes with an echo of 2:10, affirming the cosmic ramifications of the events.

Verses 16-17 appear as a coda to the announced judgment, moving attention to the fundamental meaning of these events. Verse 16 quotes Amos 1:2, announcing the sending forth of Yahweh's judgment like a lion's roar. The impact is felt in the shaking of the cosmos, but its outcome is the security of Yahweh's people in Jerusalem, for Yahweh dwells with them there. The promises of v. 17, that Israel will *know* that Yahweh dwells with them and will protect them, recall the assurances of 2:27; these promises address the ultimate concerns of Yahweh's people.

Finally, vv. 18-21 convey a similar promise. In that day, the land will produce abundantly and the watercourses flow plentifully. The reference to the fountain flowing from the Temple is akin to the stream in Ezek 47:1-12 (see also Zech 14:8): it signals the marvelous abundance of the land as a result of Yahweh's dwelling there. Yahweh's presence in the Temple, in the land, and among the people gives them life and security and results in the destruction of their enemies.

Works Cited

Childs, Brevard S. 1979. *Introduction to the Old Testament as Scripture*.

Hiebert, Theodore. 1992. "Book of Joel." AncBD.

Thompson, John A. 1956. "Joel. Introduction and Exegesis." IB.

Wolff, Hans Walter. 1977. *Joel and Amos*. Herm.

Amos

John C. Shelley

Introduction

In the Hebrew Bible, Amos is the third member of the "Book of the Twelve," a collection sometimes bearing the misleading title "the minor prophets." Except for its relative brevity there is nothing "minor" about Amos. This little book has generated a major corpus of secondary literature and has exerted extraordinary influence in shaping modern notions of human rights and social justice. Many will recall the stirring oratory of Martin Luther King, Jr., challenging the forces of segregation with Amos's powerful rhetoric: *But let justice roll down like waters, and righteousness like an everflowing stream* (5:24).

Author

Except for a brief quotation (of 8:10a) in Tob 2:6 and a passing reference in 2 Esdr 1:39, AMOS is not mentioned in the Bible outside the book that bears his name. He is widely viewed as the first of the classical or "writing" prophets, but he himself refuses the appellation of *prophet* (7:14). He is identified only as one found *among the shepherds of Tekoa* (1:1) and as *a herdsman, and a dresser of sycamore trees* (7:14). This identification has led to the popular image of Amos as a poor, uneducated common laborer commissioned by God to challenge the rich and powerful. Yet it is difficult to believe that a simple, untutored shepherd could have penned such dramatic poetry and prose or that such a person could even have commanded an audience in BETHEL. It seems likely that Amos was a person of some standing, more like a cattle rancher than a common shepherd. In fact, the terms translated *shepherd* and *herdsman* in the NRSV are not the usual Hebrew terms for shepherd, and in 2 Kgs 3:4 the latter is rendered "sheep breeder." In addition to his remarkable passion for justice, Amos was blessed with a keen intellect, a thorough familiarity with literary genres and techniques, an astute knowledge of national and international politics, and a poet's genius for creating pictures with words.

Setting

Amos prophesied during the reign of JEROBOAM II (786–746 B.C.E.). Given scant attention by the Deuteronomist (2 Kgs 14:23-29), Jeroboam's reign of forty-one years was marked by economic and territorial expansion, military resurgence, and religious revival. The leading economic indicators pointed to stability, growth, and prosperity, traditional "signs" of God's favor. The sanctuaries at Bethel and other shrines were thronged with worshipers. For Amos, however, things were not what they seemed. The booming economy was fueled by exploitation of the poor, and its actual beneficiaries were few—the king, the royal court, government bureaucrats, wealthy land owners. Israel was becoming two distinct societies, an ever-widening gap separating rich and poor.

The premonarchical traditions that protected the poor, the widows, and the orphans, and that governed the use and transfer of land were being eroded. The lavish lifestyles of the few depended upon wine and olives for export, inciting the wealthy to acquire more and more land. But that demanded a disregard for the tradition of the *nahala*, the affirmation that tribal lands belonged to YHWH and therefore could not be sold in perpetuity (Lev 25:23). Jezebel's ploy to gain control of Naboth's vineyard a century earlier (1 Kgs 21:1-29) had become common stuff in Amos's time.

The situation addressed by Amos is similar to that found today in many third world countries: The richest arable land is owned by a few wealthy families and used to grow export crops (coffee, tea, bananas, etc.), while the poor are left to subsist on the remaining scraps. As landholdings accumulated in the hands of a few, the poor became more and more vulnerable to exploitation, often finding their children sold into slavery to pay family debts (2 Kgs 4:1-7). Israel had finally discovered the "ways of the king" (1 Sam 8:10-18).

Interpretation of Amos

The modern interpreter of Amos is confronted with several problems. For one, there is little doubt that Amos has been subject to editing in both the pre- and postexilic periods, although the extent of such interpolation and its specific occurrences in Amos are widely debated. One should not assume, however, that editorial changes and additions are necessarily contaminants that must be excised to get back to the pure message of Amos. For one thing, historical judgments distinguishing Amos from his editors are risky business and can never be made with certainty. But more importantly, such changes and additions, which may indeed be in some tension with what Amos said, are neither arbitrary nor narrowly orthodox. Rather, as a good wine enhances the flavor of a good meal, such interpolations often bring to light meanings hidden to a purely historical approach. The interpreter, therefore, must be prepared to move back and forth between at least two fronts: the message of the historical Amos and the message of the book as it stands. Generally speaking, the former task emphasizes the historical-critical method, while the latter depends more heavily on literary approaches. Both are necessary to see and enjoy the full richness of Amos.

Two additional problems facing the interpreter of Amos are closely related. The first lies in the fact that Amos contains an unusual number of unique words and grammatical constructions (the technical term for such constructions is *hapax legomena*), that is, words and constructions not found elsewhere in the Bible or in the literature of the ancient Near East. One must use imagination to envision the possibilities Amos may have had in mind.

The second problem involves Amos's poetic genius. Amos is not a theologian or philosopher who constructs a carefully reasoned argument. He is an artist who paints pictures with words. To understand Amos it is imperative to grasp the image or picture and then construct meaning by the process of analogy.

For Further Study

In the *Mercer Dictionary of the Bible*: AMOS; AMOS, BOOK OF; BAAL; BETHEL; CHRONOLOGY; GILGAL; ISRAEL; ORACLE; POETRY; PROPHET; RELIGIONS OF THE ANCIENT NEAR EAST; SAMARIA; VISION.

In other sources: P. Hanson, *The People Called*; H. Marks, "The Twelve Prophets," in *The Literary Guide to the Bible*, ed. R. Alter and F. Kermode; J. L. Mays, *Amos*, OTL; S. Paul, *Amos*, Herm; S. N. Rosenbaum, *Amos of Israel*; J. D. Smart, "Amos," IDB; J. D. W. Watts, *Vision and Prophecy in Amos*; H. W. Wolff, *Joel and Amos*, Herm.

Commentary

An Outline

I. Superscription and Epigraph, 1:1-2
  A. Superscription, 1:1
  B. Epigraph, 1:2
II. A Sermon against the Nations, 1:3–2:16
  A. The Crimes of Israel's Neighboring Enemies, 1:3–2:3
  B. Judah's Idolatry, 2:4-5
  C. Israel's Social Injustice, 2:6-16
III. Israel's Sinfulness and God's Punishment, 3:1–6:14
  A. Election to Punishment, 3:1-15
  B. Excessive Luxury, Sinful Piety, Unheeded Warnings, 4:1-13
  C. Requiem for a Fallen Maiden, 5:1-17
  D. Delusions of Grandeur, 5:18–6:14

IV. Prophetic Vision: Judgment, Irony, and a New Beginning 7:1–9:15
  A. Three Visions: Locusts, Fire, a Plumb line, 7:1-9
  B. A Confrontation of Authorities, 7:10-17
  C. Visions of the End, 8:1–9:6
  D. No Immunity for Israel, 9:7-10
  E. A New Beginning, 9:11-15

Superscription and Epigraph, 1:1-2

Superscription, 1:1

The superscription is the most complete of any of the prophetic books, giving Amos's occupation, hometown, and historical era (see "Introduction"). The reference to the *words* that Amos *saw* indicates the visionary character of prophetic experience (cf. 7:1-9;

8:1-3; 9:1-4). The *earthquake* must have been one of unusual magnitude, for it was recalled centuries later by Zechariah (14:4-5). That the earthquake is mentioned here probably means it was seen as partial fulfillment of Amos's prophecies (e.g., 9:1).

Epigraph, 1:2

Although often ascribed to a later Judean editor, this verse functions both as an epigraph to the entire book and as a prologue to the Sermon against the Nations (1:3–2:16). The theme of the passage is thoroughly fitting for a Judean called to prophesy in the northern kingdom of Israel. The word of YHWH, which comes to Amos in Jerusalem, reaches to Carmel and beyond. The "roaring lion" as a metaphor for the voice of God appears again in 3:8 and is common enough in the Bible and the literature of the ancient Near East. The "roar" signals judgment, as the voice of God withers the pastures and dries up the lush and fertile slopes of Mount Carmel. The epigraph sets the tone for what follows.

A Sermon against the Nations, 1:3–2:16

Oracles against foreign nations were standard fare for the court prophets of ancient Israel. Such oracles typically functioned as political propaganda, arousing support for the king's wars and diverting attention from domestic ills. Here Amos adapts this prophetic form for his own purposes, engaging the attention of his hearers with attacks on Israel's enemies (1:3–2:5) and then startling and probably rankling them with an abrupt shift to the crimes of Israel (2:6-16).

Some scholars have questioned, on formal and historical grounds, the authenticity of the oracles against Tyre, Edom, and Judah. Literary considerations, however, support the authenticity of all eight oracles. In the ancient world the number seven was the typological symbol for completeness and finality. Amos's audience, therefore, likely expected the climax, and the conclusion, of the sermon to come with the seventh member of the series, the attack on Judah (2:4-5). The hearers were then totally unprepared when Amos suddenly launched a prophecy against Israel. Amos uses a similar technique in 3:3-8; elsewhere also he betrays a decided penchant for sequences of seven (e.g., 2:6-8, 14-16; 4:6-12; 5:8-9; 9:1-4) and for unexpected conclusions (e.g., 3:1-2; 5:18-20, 21-24; 8:1-3).

The oracles follow a similar pattern, each beginning with *Thus says the LORD*, a phrase that accentuates the Hebrew understanding of prophet (*nabi*) as a messenger of YHWH. This is immediately followed by a graduated number saying: *For three transgressions . . . and for four, I will not revoke the punishment.* Such sayings are common in the literature of the Bible and the ancient Near East and typically are used in two ways: (1) to indicate an indefinite or approximate number or (2) if followed by a list of specific items (e.g., transgressions), to single out for emphasis the member that corresponds to the second number in the saying (in the present case, *four*). But Amos's use is not typical. He does not follow each saying with a specified list of crimes, nor does he seem to mean an indefinite or approximate number. Given that *three*, like the number seven, was a typological number for wholeness in the ancient world, it is likely that the combination of *three* and *four* suggests both completeness and finality. A complete and final transgression, therefore, would mean the most heinous of crimes, "the most vile, abominable, and despicable of all, thereby causing God to intervene directly and execute punishment" (Paul 1991, 29). Those are in fact the very things Amos singles out for attention.

Transgression (REB; NJB, "crime") in this context suggests revolt, the refusal to acknowledge authority. These heinous crimes against humanity are understood as a revolt against God. Here Amos, perhaps for the first time in Hebrew history, renders explicit the MONOTHEISM of the Sinai Covenant. YHWH, the God of Judah and Israel, is also the sovereign of all nations.

The Crimes of Israel's Neighboring Enemies, 1:3–2:3

The first seven oracles, slightly more than half the sermon, are directed against the seven nations that shared Israel's borders. The first three—Aram (Syria), Philistia, and Phoenicia—are indicated metonymically by their major cities: *Damascus* (1:3), *Gaza* (1:6), and *Tyre* (1:9), respectively. Israel enjoyed little in common with these three, but did share strong ethnic ties with Edom (Gen 36:1-43), with Ammon and Moab (Gen 19:30-38), and especially Judah, with whom it also shared the covenantal traditions of Yahwism. Yet, except for brief alliances, none had been a model neighbor. Relationships fractured by a long history of violence simmered in suspicion and mistrust. No doubt Amos's hearers in BETHEL shivered with nationalistic fervor and self-righteous glee as he announced the terrible consuming fire that God had decreed as punishment for the unspeakable crimes against humanity perpetrated by Israel's enemies.

The transgressions cited in the first six oracles are vicious crimes: brutalizing inhabitants and the land with a scorched earth policy (1:3), developing and maintaining a slave trade with Edom (1:6, 9), pursuing one's brother without respite (1:11), ripping open the wombs of pregnant women in Gilead in search of more land (1:13), burning the bones of a neighboring king to acquire lime for use in building construction (2:1). There seems little doubt that Amos is referring to actual historical events, but these are now lost to us. It may be significant that the crime charged to Moab (2:1-3) involves neither Israel nor Judah. Amos leaves no doubt that a crime against Edom is just as despicable as a crime committed against Israel or Judah.

In all cases the punishment is a consuming fire. In Amos 7:4 fire is a metaphor for scorching heat and drought, but here it is a harbinger of war and total destruction. In 1:4-5, for example, in describing the punishment of Damascus, Amos paints a vivid picture of battle in the ancient Near East: enemy forces set fire to the city; they break the bars of the gate and rush in upon the defenseless population; they block the escape routes, even for the king, and slaughter those who are trapped; they take the survivors into exile. Details vary in the succeeding oracles but the result is the same: devastation, exile, death.

Judah's Idolatry, 2:4-5

The ORACLE against Judah begins like the others, a tacit signal that even God's chosen are not exempt from judgment. The charges are nonspecific but clearly relate to violations of the COVENANT, *the law of the LORD*. The emphasis is probably on IDOLATRY since *led astray* almost always refers to the worship of false gods. Yet, as the message of Amos unfolds, it becomes clear that faithfulness to the covenant is not simply a matter of renouncing pagan deities and offering sacrifices only to YHWH. The true worship of YHWH is unconditionally fused with justice and righteousness in personal relationships and in the social sphere (e.g., 5:21-24).

Israel's Social Injustice, 2:6-16

As with Judah the covenant does not grant Israel immunity from prosecution but becomes the actual basis for judgment. Precisely because Israel is God's chosen, the standards will be more strict and the community will be punished for all its iniquities (3:2). 2:6-8. Crimes of Israel. Instead of one transgression, Amos lists seven, the sum of all the others com-

bined. Yet the crimes of Israel are of a different order. They are not the atrocities perpetrated against the enemy in the heat of a military campaign, nor are they simple idolatry. Scholars disagree about specific nuances of interpretation, but there is little disagreement about the central charge: Israel is guilty of oppressing and exploiting the poor and vulnerable among its own people.

The crimes are allusions to the Book of the Covenant (Exod 20:22–23:33). *They sell the righteous for silver* (v. 6) may refer to bribes paid to judges to rule against an innocent party, but more likely it refers to the poor being forced into slavery for debts they cannot pay. In either case, it is suggested that the legal system is being subverted in violation of Exod 23:6. *They sell . . . the needy for a pair of sandals* (v. 6) suggests that debts are called in and mortgages foreclosed even for the most paltry sums, again resulting in bonded slavery for the debtor and perhaps a claim against the debtor's land. *They who trample the head of the poor into the dust of the earth, and push the afflicted out of the way* (v. 7) point to gross violations of basic rights.

Father and son go in to the same girl (v. 7) is often understood as referring to sacred prostitution connected with the worship of BAAL and other fertility gods. But given the other crimes that Amos mentions, it seems more likely that the phrase refers to father and son taking advantage of a slave or indentured servant (Exod 21:7-11).

So that my holy name is profaned (v. 7) may refer to the immediately preceding crime, but it is likely a reference to all the crimes mentioned thus far. It is not just sexual misconduct that profanes the name of God but the exploitation of the poor and vulnerable.

The two crimes listed in v. 8 give a picture of people worshiping in their sanctuaries with garments taken in pledge (in violation of Exod 22:25-27) and wine purchased with fines imposed. The worshipers profane YHWH's name because they see no incongruity between their worship and their immoral treatment of their fellow human beings.

2:9-11. Care of YHWH. The focus shifts from what Israel has done to what YHWH has done for Israel. Amos reminds his hearers of the conquest of the Amorites (v. 9), the escape from Egypt and the wandering in the wilderness that preceded the conquest (v. 10), the gift of prophets and nazirites (v. 11). This summary of YHWH's great deeds may well carry an allusion to the preface of the TEN COMMANDMENTS

(Exod 20:1), setting Israel's obligations within the context of YHWH's gracious initiative in delivering Israel from bondage in Egypt.

2:12. No respect. Israel has failed to respect the NAZIRITE vows and has refused to heed the message of the prophets (2:12). Therefore, like its neighbors, Israel will be punished.

2:13-16. Judgment. YHWH makes war on Israel. The metaphor of an overloaded cart that makes ruts in the soft earth perhaps suggests that Israel will be ground into the earth just as it has done to the poor (2:7). In vv. 14-16 a picture of terror is drawn such that even the swift and powerful armies of Israel cannot stand up against YHWH (just as the Amorites could not). The archers, the foot soldiers, the cavalry—even *those who are stout of heart* (REB, NJB, "the bravest of warriors")—will flee in terror.

Israel's Sinfulness and God's Punishment, 3:1–6:14

This second major section of Amos does not have the literary unity of chaps. 1–2, although there is unmistakable thematic coherence. Many commentators find three collections of oracles here, each beginning with *Hear this word* (3:1, 4:1, 5:1).

Election to Punishment, 3:1-15

3:1-2. Election. The chapter and verse divisions are both a blessing and a curse. They give order to the text and provide a most helpful standard of reference, but they often obscure important literary connections within the text. For example, should vv. 1-2 be seen only as the beginning of a new section? Or might it also function as a concluding coda for the Sermon against the Nations, an exclamation point sealing the case against Israel?

In any case Amos here invokes the theme of ELECTION (e.g., Exod 19:3-6) but with jarring irony reverses the traditional logic. Election is not for salvation but for punishment. *Known* is to be understood relationally, not cognitively. There is obvious tension between v. 2a and the universalism reflected in 9:7, and one cannot be certain whether Amos is here affirming that Israel is indeed God's chosen or whether he is satirizing the view of election held by his contemporaries. In either case, Israel does not have moral license to mistreat the poor.

3:3-8. A familiar pattern. These six verses are a carefully crafted unit following the same 7/8 structure of the Sermon against the Nations. It begins with a

sequence that builds to an apparent climax with the seventh member, which is then transcended by the surprise introduction of an eighth member. Amos snatches the attention of his audience with a series of rhetorical questions dealing with obvious instances of cause and effect, something like "Is the Pope Catholic?" or "Is the sky blue?" Most problematic is v. 3: the NRSV (*Do two walk together unless they have made an appointment?*) suggests too much precalculation or preplanning. The REB is better: "Do two people travel together unless they have so agreed?"

Amos's choice of images—a lion hunting prey, a bird caught in a snare, disaster befalling a city—carry veiled allusions to the judgment that is to come upon Israel. The sixth and seventh members of the sequence (v. 6) shift the frame of reference to the human world, and in v. 6b the name of YHWH is introduced for the first time. The audience is captured and Amos presses his point: given the fact that God does call prophets and reveals the divine secrets to them (cf. 2:11), then who can refuse to prophesy when God has so commanded? This is, clearly, Amos's defense of his calling, possibly in response to criticism and charges that he not be taken seriously (7:10-12). But it is also a defense of all other prophets whose voices have gone unheeded (2:12b). If the world is indeed structured by precise sequences of cause and effect, then how can one deny the prophets a hearing?

3:9-11. Questioning protection. Note the recurring use of *strongholds*, the walled cities or fortresses that shielded the rich and powerful. The setting is in court as Amos summons the strongholds of *Ashdod* (a Philistine city) and Egypt to bear witness to the *tumults* and *oppression* in SAMARIA. The real addressee, of course, is the accused, the aristocracy of Israel whose strongholds have been built and maintained by *violence and robbery*. The sentence, to be carried out by an anonymous adversary, reflects the justice of *lex talionis* (Exod 21:23-25): Israel's own strongholds shall be plundered. As is the case in several oracles of Amos, there is clever wordplay in the Hebrew that is lost in English.

3:12. Judgment. Although likely reflecting a separate oracle, v. 12 serves in the present context to expand the judgment against Israel announced in 3:11. The image of a shepherd snatching *two legs, or a piece of an ear* from the mouth of a lion probably alludes to Exod 22:13: shepherds were not held responsible for a sheep mangled by wild beasts if they could produce acceptable evidence. The salvaging of *two legs* and/or *a piece of an ear* does not suggest that a remnant will be saved (cf. 5:15); it testifies to total destruction. The precise image intended in the last part of the verse is uncertain; but given the parallel with the shepherd, the NRSV certainly captures the essential meaning with *corner of a couch and part of a bed.*

3:13-15. Destruction. This oracle, which further details the destruction of Samaria announced in 3:11, includes the first mention of BETHEL. Literally the "house of the god El," Bethel had long been a sacred place and became increasingly important during the period of the divided kingdom. It seems strange to *punish the altars of Bethel*, but the meaning probably relates to the use of the altar for sanctuary or asylum (Exod 21:12-14; 1 Kgs 1:50-53; 2:28-34). In other words, the altar will provide no refuge. Probably the meaning is even broader, for altar is a metonym for religious ritual (cf. 5:4-5). The recurring references to *house* in v. 15 suggest excessive luxury—two residences, lavishly decorated, etc. These shall come to an end.

Excessive Luxury, Sinful Piety, Unheeded Warnings, 4:1-13

4:1-3. The folly of coveteousness. Bashan was a territory east of Galilee noted for its agricultural riches (cf. Deut 32:14; Ps 22:12; Ezek 39:18). *Cows of Bashan* is a striking metaphor, therefore, for excessive luxury. Although an interesting case has been made for a fertility cult whose deity is symbolized by a bull of Bashan (see Rosenbaum 1990, 57), the phrase probably refers to the rich women of Samaria. The women *oppress the poor* and *crush the needy*, not directly, but through their insatiable appetite for luxury and leisure. Their sin is not simply collaboration with injustice but an unchecked covetousness that both initiates and maintains the war against the poor. The image is certainly chauvinistic, but it does point to the connection between covetousness (Exod 20:17) and injustice. Covetousness is decidedly not restricted to the women alone.

The punishment is announced in v. 2a in the form of an oath. *The time is surely coming* probably has something of an eschatological bearing, suggesting radical disjunction between this age and the next. The key terms in v. 2b (NRSV, *hooks* and *fishhooks*; REB, "shields" and "fish-baskets") are difficult to decipher. The most literal meanings are "shields" and "pots," respectively, but both terms can also mean "thorns" and, by extension, "hooks." If Amos is continuing the

metaphor of cattle, the reference may be to harpoon-like devices that double as cattle prods or perhaps as hooks used to drag a carcass (Mays 1969, 72–73). If he is switching metaphors, Amos probably means the wire baskets and pots used both to catch and transport fish (Paul 1991, 130–35).

Another lexical difficulty arises in v. 3. The first clause is relatively clear, suggesting numerous breaches in the city wall through which the inhabitants can be carried straight out, with no need for detours. The difficulty is with *Harmon*, an unknown term. It is obviously a place, but does it designate a geographical area or a specific location? Is it a place of death or a place of exile? Should it be emended to read "Hermon" (i.e., Mount Hermon) which is located in Bashan? The REB rendering "dunghill" is an interesting guess.

4:4-5. A parody. In a bitter parody of Israelite worship Amos attacks religion that has become a tool of self-interest and the occasion for evading God's commandments. BETHEL and GILGAL were sanctuaries with long and venerable histories, and Amos assumes the posture of a cultic official welcoming the pilgrims to the shrine. But again Amos surprises, and certainly infuriates, his hearers with a jarring conclusion: *Come to Bethel—and transgress; to Gilgal—and multiply transgression! Transgression* is the same term used repeatedly in the opening Sermon against the Nations (1:3–2:16). The point is not subtle: the worship of God has itself become rebellion. The rituals of offering, established to atone for human sin and thereby restore the relationship between God and human beings, have themselves become occasions for sin. Amos anticipates the tireless warnings of Reinhold Niebuhr that it is precisely in their worship that human beings are most powerfully assailed by temptation.

It is difficult to identify precisely the sacrifices and offerings that Amos mentions, but there are noticeable similarities with Lev 7:11-18 and Deut 12:6. More important is his use of second person pronouns—*your sacrifices, your tithes, for so you love to do*—which suggest that worship has become a means of addressing Israel's own agenda instead of attending to God's desires and demands. In violation of the third commandment (Exod 20:7), religion has been co-opted for selfish ends. As Amaziah protests to Amos (7:13), Bethel has become *the king's sanctuary, a temple of the kingdom*; but to Amos that means that it is no longer YHWH's.

It is possible to read this and similar passages (e.g., 5:21-24) as Amos's total repudiation of the cult, a reduction of religion to ethics like that of the philosopher Immanuel Kant. It is more likely, however, that Amos did not attack the cult per se but a theology that failed to acknowledge the connection between those worship practices and YHWH's demands for justice and righteousness. Both the Hebrew Bible and the NT are adamant that faithfulness to God cannot be separated from responsibility to one's neighbor.

4:6-13. Reversal. In an ironic reversal of tradition, Amos reminds his hearers of seven calamities that God has visited upon Israel. The irony is especially apparent when seen in connection both with YHWH's gracious acts of deliverance (highlighted in 2:9-12), and the description of rebellious piety described in vv. 4-5. It was expected that faithfulness to the covenant would bring good and prosperous times and that disobedience would bring misfortune. The calamities, therefore, should have been a warning that things were not right, but the warnings went unheeded. Now, like the Pharaoh whose heart was hardened, Israel has no more opportunity to repent.

In describing the seven calamities Amos again draws upon his genius for image-making. Famine is described as *cleanness of teeth* (v. 6). The effects of drought are portrayed in the figure of a dehydrated person staggering from town to town in search of water (v. 8). Military disaster is captured in the stench of rotting flesh (human and animal) that burns the nostrils (v. 10b). The earthquake and the resulting conflagration recall the destruction of Sodom and Gomorrah (v. 11). The other calamities are less vivid but no less destructive: *blight and mildew* (v. 9a), locusts (v. 9b), and *pestilence* (v. 10a). The sequence is punctuated five times by an unsettling refrain: *yet you did not return to me, says the LORD* (vv. 6, 8, 9, 10, 11).

In v. 12 Amos shifts from past to future. This is another example of a sequence apparently climaxing with the seventh member (the earthquake reminiscent of Sodom and Gomorrah in v. 11), only to be followed by an eighth. The eighth calamity is not described, except that it involves a face to face meeting with God. Seven warnings were enough. God will now meet Israel face to face. The lack of description is probably deliberate, for the unknown is always more terrifying than what is known.

The doxology in v. 13 is the first of three in Amos (see also 5:8-9; 9:5-6), all of which may derive from the same hymn. There is no reason to challenge the broad consensus that these are later additions to the book, but it is quite remarkable how well the first and third doxologies fit the context. The THEOPHANY described here (v. 13) is a suitable epilogue to the final warning of v. 12: *Prepare to meet your God, O Israel!* Israel must prepare to meet YHWH, the God of hosts, who creates the mountains and who is manifest in the wind and clouds of a morning thunderstorm. The clouds darken the sky and hide the mountain peaks.

Requiem for a Fallen Maiden, 5:1-17

The first seventeen verses of chap. 5 appear at first glance to be a random collection of oracles. However, recent studies (e.g., Paul 1991, 157–81) have shown convincingly that this passage is a composite collection of oracles arranged precisely in a CHIASM, a repetition in reverse order. Assuming that the doxology of 5:8-9 is an interpolation, the passage can be diagrammed as follows.

> A 5:1-3, Requiem for a fallen Israel
>   B 5:4-6, Seek YHWH and live
>   C 5:7, 10-13, An evil time
>   B' 5:14-15, Seek good and not evil
> A' 5:16-17, Requiem for a fallen Israel

5:1-3. Requiem for a fallen Israel. The word of the prophet in v. 2 is a carefully constructed elegy in the meter of Israel's funeral dirges. Written in present perfect tense, it is a dramatic and electrifying presentation of what is yet future. Israel's funeral is pictured as that of a young maiden, still a virgin, who is raped, beaten, and left to die by an invading army. The tragedy occurs on her own land, where help would be expected, perhaps even by YHWH (see 1 Sam 2:8; Hos 6:2; Amos 9:11), but there is *no one to raise her up*. The image of military disaster continues with the word of the *Lord GOD* in v. 3: casualties will total ninety percent of those who march out to fight. Like Ebenezer Scrooge encountering his own tombstone, Amos's audience must have been terrified to hear their own obituary (Mays 1969, 84). For Amos himself it must have been a moment of unbearable sorrow (cf. 6:6).

5:4-6. Seek YHWH and live. There is still hope that disaster may be averted. But everything hinges on Israel's response to YHWH's invitation. The NRSV rendering of *seek me* (v. 4) seems misleading here since what is meant is something like "make your way to me" (REB) or "turn to me." The invitation must have been baffling to Amos's hearers, especially when coupled with the negative imperatives regarding *Bethel, Gilgal,* and *Beer-sheba.* No doubt they thought they *were* turning to YHWH by offering sacrifices at these prominent sanctuaries. The invitation is repeated in v. 6 and followed by the judgment for disobedience, the fire that signals the devastation of war.

This passage continues Amos's assault upon the cult. Just as YHWH is not to be found in ritual (4:4-5), neither is the deity found in "holy places." Amos thus reiterates a biblical theme that culminates in Stephen's speech in Acts: "Yet the Most High does not dwell in houses made with human hands" (Acts 7:48). Amos does not indicate here just where YHWH is to be found, but the answer comes in 5:14-15: YHWH is to be found in doing good and establishing justice.

5:8-9. Doxology. This, the second of the doxologies (cf. 4:13; 9:5-6), quite obviously interrupts the flow between 5:7 and 5:10 (the REB is surely correct in linking 5:7 directly with 5:10-13). Internally, the doxology has problems of its own. For example, the closing line of v. 8, *the LORD* (YHWH) *is his name,* fits much better at the end of v. 9. The meaning is relatively clear, however, praising YHWH both as lord of nature (v. 8) and as lord of the nations (v. 9). As the one who controls the stars and the sun as well as the rains, YHWH is the sovereign of time. As an interpolation, the doxology may have been inserted here to suggest reasons why YHWH is not found in the sanctuaries (5:4-5). As the Creator of the world and the sovereign of time and the nations, YHWH cannot be confined to "holy places."

5:7, 10-13. An evil time. This passage marks the middle term in the chiasm. Coming on the heels of 5:6, it details evidence that Israel has not turned to YHWH. The passage as a whole assumes a setting in Israel's courts of justice, the proceedings of which took place *in the gate* (v. 10; 5:15). The courts were established to administer justice (e.g., Exod 23:1-9), but Amos charges that they have been corrupted, with the assistance of the "judges" themselves, to serve the interests of the rich and powerful.

The terms JUSTICE and RIGHTEOUSNESS (v. 7) also appear together in 5:24 and 6:12. The terms are closely related but not identical. *Righteousness* is the broader term; it describes the will of YHWH, especially as that will ought to be manifest in the relationships of a given community or society. *Justice* has a narrower legal focus, the process by which righteousness is restored to the community.

Israel is guilty both of unrighteousness and injustice. The poor have been brutally mistreated, trampled upon with heavy taxes (v. 11). They turn to the courts seeking justice; but they are hated for filing charges and telling the truth (v. 10), and they are bullied and ignored by the courts (v. 12). Note the irony of the punishment in v. 11 (having built houses and planted vineyards with money extorted from the poor, they will enjoy neither) and the despair of v. 13.

5:14-15. Seek good and not evil. The chiastic parallel to 5:4-6, this passage answers the question as to where YHWH is to be found. To *seek the LORD and live* (5:6) means *to seek good and not evil* (v. 14). YHWH, and therefore life, is not to be found in the holy places or in the formality of worship, but in turning and devoting oneself wholly to what is *good.* The closing phrase of v. 14, *just as you have said,* indicates that Amos is quoting from his hearers who have insisted all along that "YHWH is with us." Seek good and YHWH *will be with you* (v. 14). But Israel must change its ways, establishing justice instead of tearing it down. The reticence of v. 15b, *it may be,* declares that God's graciousness cannot be presumed upon; God cannot be manipulated for selfish ends.

5:16-17. Requiem for a fallen Israel. These verses return to the elegy with which the unit began. The wailing includes every aspect of society: the city dwellers, the farmers, the professional mourners (*those skilled in lamentation*). Even the vineyards, normally a place of celebration, are invaded with scenes of mourning (v. 17). *I will pass through the midst of you* may allude to the death angel of Exod 12:12, 23.

Delusions of Grandeur, 5:18–6:14

5:18-20. A powerful image. The *day of the LORD* makes its earliest appearance in biblical literature in the words of Amos, but there can be little doubt that it already functioned as a powerful image in the popular ideology of Israel. Scholars are divided on the precise origins of the concept, but the meaning is clear. The *day of the LORD* referred to that future time when God would intervene decisively on Israel's behalf and destroy her enemies. For Israel, the reign of JEROBOAM II was filled with signs of God's favor and hence pointed to God's continuing presence in Israel. Amos attacks this popular notion with two rhetorical questions (vv. 18, 20) that envelop a vivid description of catastrophe from which there is no final escape (v. 19; cf. 2:13-16).

5:21-24. Questioning the popular. Returning to the theme of 4:4-5, Amos contradicts the popular view of religious ceremony, leaving no doubt that ritual is not YHWH's concern. The *solemn assemblies* (v. 21) are the lavish ceremonies that marked holiday festivals and sought help in times of trouble. *I will not accept them* means, literally, "I will not smell them." Thus the cumulative image of vv. 22-23 is God's holding the nose, shutting the eyes, and closing the ears to Israel's ceremonies. The reason is that God is concerned about *justice* and *righteousness* (v. 24). The image of an *everflowing stream* is especially powerful in a country crisscrossed with so many wadis, the dry riverbeds that carry water only during a storm.

5:25-27. Another question. This passage, which many scholars regard as a later addition, is more intricately connected to 5:21-24 than first appearances suggest. The rhetorical question is intended to show that during Israel's wilderness experience YHWH was known through justice and righteousness and not through the ritual of sacrifice (cf. Jer 7:22-23). It seems that Amos looks back to the wilderness wanderings as the golden age of Israel, while the Israelites look with nostalgia to the time of DAVID and SOLOMON. *Sakkuth* and *Kaiwan* designate Mesopotamian deities, whose effigies are taken up as part of a solemn procession. The bitter irony is that the procession of worshipers and their idols is driven into exile by none other than YHWH, the God of hosts. *Beyond Damascus* (v. 27) is understood by many as a veiled reference to ASSYRIA, but Paul (1991, 198) sees this as a second irony, namely, that exile will take Israel even farther than its military conquests.

6:1-7. Affliction for the comfortable. In graphic terms, Amos describes the lavish self-indulgence and cockiness of Israel's leaders. *Notables* (v. 1; REB, "men of mark") is possibly a self-designation used by those who thought of themselves as the "first families" in *the first of the nations* (v. 1). *Calneh, Hamath,* and *Gath* were wealthy commercial centers that once boasted of their invincibility before going down to defeat. The rhetorical questions of vv. 2-3 thus serve to warn the notables of their delusion of grandeur. The *evil day* (v. 3) is probably identical to the *day of the LORD* (5:18). The point of v. 3 seems to be that deliberate disregard for the approaching day of judgment is causally linked to the violent exploitation of the poor.

The feast depicted in vv. 4-6a may be a description of a *marzeah*, a religious and social fraternity of the wealthy. In any case the picture is one of obscene

extravagance: the guests recline on expensive furniture; they enjoy the choicest cuts of meat while being serenaded with music; they gulp their wine from widemouthed bowls and garnish themselves with the finest perfumes. In the social sphere such self-indulgence eventually leads to apathy, the inability to grieve and show compassion to those who suffer. The oracle ends on a note of irony: the *notables of the first of the nations* (v. 1) will be *the first to go into exile* (v. 7).

6:8-11. Judgment. YHWH's oath suggests the irrevocability of the judgment to come. YHWH's anger is directed at the *pride of Jacob* (v. 8), Israel's cocky arrogance, and quite possibly a nationalistic slogan used by the Israelites themselves (cf. Ps 47:4). In 6:9-10 the scene shifts to a specific household, although the precise circumstances are not clear. Perhaps Amos intends a devastating plague from which there is no escape. Those responsible for disposing of the bodies (REB, "a relative and an embalmer") fear even to mention the name of YHWH, lest they too suffer the same fate. The *great house* and the *little house* (v. 11) are a composite symbol for Israel.

6:12-14. Disastrous consequences. The rhetorical questions of v. 12a indicate the disastrous consequences that occur when the natural order is violated. One would be a fool to run one's horse over the rocks or attempt to plow the sea (or perhaps the rocks) with oxen. Yet the perversion of justice and righteousness is just as foolish (v. 12b). *Lo-debar* and *Karnaim* were towns conquered by Jeroboam II in an earlier campaign (see 2 Kgs 14:25). Amos's sarcasm is evident in the literal meaning of *Lo-debar*: (REB, "nothing"). The boast of v. 13b is likely a quotation from the Israelites themselves. Hence the irony of v. 14 in which YHWH, *the God of hosts*, speaks of the deity's own military plans.

Prophetic Vision: Judgment, Irony, and a New Beginning, 7:1–9:15

The third major section of Amos features five visions (7:1-3, 4-6, 7-9; 8:1-3; 9:1-4), but it also includes a narrative account of Amos's confrontation with Amaziah (7:10-17), additional oracles of judgment (8:4-14; 9:7-10), a doxology (9:5-6), and a prophecy of hope (9:11-15). The five visions are probably the most intensely studied, and the most passionately debated, sections of the book.

Visions were commonly understood in the ancient world as a means of divine communication and hence the source of a prophet's message. Partly because of the prominence of VISION in the call of Isaiah (Isa 6:1-13), it has often been assumed that the five visions of Amos relate specifically to his call and thus precede the other oracles in the book. But there is nothing thematic about the visions that warrants this conclusion. Furthermore, the visions portray Amos as already having assumed the mantle of a prophet (Paul 1991, 222–25). The five visions bear striking similarities, but it is the subtle differences that provide the key to their interpretation.

Three Visions: Locusts, Fire, and a Plumb line, 7:1-9

7:1-3. Locusts. Amos has no difficulty understanding the first two visions, the *locusts* and the *shower of fire* (7:4). The *time of the latter growth* (v. 1) refers to the period in the spring just after the vegetable crops have sprouted. The grain crops are planted earlier (cf. the "winter wheat" crops in the United States), and although showing signs of maturity by spring, they are not ready for harvest. Thus the *locusts* attack at a particularly vulnerable time, destroying both the grain and the vegetable crops. The meaning of *the king's mowings* is not certain but likely refers to a share of the harvest demanded by the king.

Amos assumes the mantle of the prophet in interceding for Israel. *He is so small* (v. 2) refers simply to Israel's vulnerability, its inability to survive such a catastrophe. Making no appeal to the covenant and relying entirely upon God's mercy, Amos asks for a complete pardon. God does not grant the pardon but does offer a temporary reprieve (Paul 1991, 229), patiently extending the deadline for repentance.

7:4-6. Fire. The *shower of fire* is a scorching heat wave with cosmic consequences. In Hebrew cosmology the *great deep* is the cosmic aquifier that supplies all springs and rivers. When it dries up, everything becomes desert. Again Amos intercedes, but this time the petition is not to pardon but only to *cease* (v. 5).

7:7-9. Plumb line. Visions three and four are puzzling for Amos, rendering him speechless. Instead of a scene of destruction he "sees" ordinary objects (v. 7, *plumb line*; 8:1, *summer fruit*), which he can identify but the meaning of which he is unable to decipher. He is in a sense stripped of his role as intercessor and is given a message to proclaim to the people. The *plumb line* is a metaphor for the COVENANT, the standard by which Israel (*my people Israel*) was created. But now as God takes the measure of Israel's moral rectitude, the people are found to be grossly aslant. Hence the

prophecy of judgment. The *high places of Isaac* (v. 9) is a pejorative reference to the various sanctuaries of Israel and Judah (see 2 Kgs 17:7-18), intimating the worship of idols.

A Confrontation of Authorities, 7:10-17

The encounter between Amos and Amaziah is in essence a confrontation between YHWH and JEROBOAM II. The issue is one of authority. Whom does Israel serve? YHWH or Jeroboam? Bethel has become *the king's sanctuary . . . a temple of the kingdom* (v. 13). It bows to the king's authority and thus serves the interests of the state. Having been squeezed out of the sanctuary, YHWH must now assert divine authority from outside. God does so through Amos, a reluctant outsider.

7:10-13. Amaziah speaks. Amaziah has no doubt about whom he serves. He reports Amos as a dangerous conspirator who must be silenced lest his words incite rebellion. He seems not to consider that Amos might indeed be a true prophet of YHWH. As reported, the message to Jeroboam includes only those themes that relate directly to the king, suggesting that Amaziah has deliberately concealed Amos's prophecies against the high places and sanctuaries, since these are his own concern.

Amaziah's words to Amos are not in themselves mocking or disrespectful and may even indicate an eagerness to be rid of Amos without further confrontation. A *seer* (Heb. *roeh*) is practically synonymous with "prophet" (Heb. *nabi*), although more directly related to visionary experience. The *king's sanctuary* (v. 13) refers to the fact that shortly after the division of the kingdom, Bethel had been designated an official sanctuary of the northern kingdom. The move was intended to break the ties to the sanctuary in Jerusalem that remained in Judah. The tragedy is that the king's authority has replaced the authority of YHWH. YHWH is forced to speak from the outside.

7:14-15. Amos responds. Amos's opening response to Amaziah is one of the most perplexing statements in the book. It is clear that Amos was not a *prophet's son* (v. 14), that is, a member of a prophetic guild. But what does Amos mean when he insists that he is not a *prophet* (Heb. *nabi*)? One reading, followed by the REB, sees this statement in the past tense: "I was no prophet, nor was I a prophet's son." The point is that he was not a prophet until he was called by God to prophesy to Israel (v. 15). A second reading understands *prophet* here to refer to one of the professional cultic prophets. These professionals were paid by the royal court and were expected to serve the interests of the king. The point of this second reading is that Amos speaks as an outsider and not as one of the professionals retained by the king. In either case, especially in view of 2:12, Amos surely identified with that line of prophets like Elijah who spoke from outside the cult and the royal court.

7:16-17. Judgment on Amaziah. This is the only oracle in the entire book directed to an individual. Since Amaziah has sought to stifle the prophecy of Amos (cf. 2:12), the punishment will be especially severe. The reference to an *unclean land* (v. 17) is surely ironic, since it means the forfeiture of Amaziah's vocation. The one who has tried to silence Amos will himself be silenced.

Visions of the End, 8:1–9:6

8:1-3. Summer fruit. The fourth vision is very similar to the third, but now the judgment is extended to the nation as a whole. *Summer fruit* refers to fresh tree-ripened fruit, probably figs, harvested in late summer and normally a sign of celebration. But in a dramatic play on words the image of *summer fruit* (Heb. *qayitz*) is transmuted into a symbol for Israel's imminent *end* (Heb. *qētz*). The cause of the catastrophe is unspecified, but the results are graphically depicted in v. 3. The command to *be silent* recalls 6:10 and may indicate a fear that speaking will invoke further disaster.

8:4-8. Concern for the poor. This oracle is directed at the merchants who exploit the poor and needy with deceitful business practices and even traffic in the slave trade. Israel observed a lunar calendar and attached special significance to the monthly observance of the festival of the *new moon*. The festival was observed with sumptuous feasts and accompanied by sacrifices (cf. 1 Sam 20:5). As with sabbath observance, the festival of the new moon demanded the suspension of all business dealings. The merchants, eager to resume their dishonest wheeling and dealing, protest these "blue laws" even as they piously observe the festivals (v. 5a).

The *ephah* was a dry measure that corresponded to something like our modern bushel. The *shekel* here is not a unit of currency, but a unit of weight used to determine the amount of payment (usually in silver). The images in v. 6a recall the selling of debtors into slavery in 2:6, only here the focus is on those who buy the slaves.

YHWH's judgment is pronounced in vv. 7-8 in the form of an irrevocable oath. *Their deeds* refer to the deceitful and inhumane practices of the merchants just mentioned (vv. 5-6). The remarkable rise and fall of the NILE River, an annual occurrence now known to be caused by the tilt of the earth's axis, was widely considered an ancient wonder. Here it depicts the upheavals of a horrendous earthquake.

8:9-10. Day of judgment. *That day*, the day of judgment, is here compared to a solar eclipse at high noon. In the ancient world, eclipses, solar and lunar, were almost universally regarded as portents of disaster. Even for sophisticated moderns a solar eclipse sends chills down the spine. The darkness recalls Amos's earlier words about *the day of the LORD* (5:18-20). Again the precise nature of the calamity is not spelled out, but it will bring a reversal of the festive air that pervades the current life of the rich and powerful. Donning sackcloth and shaving the head were traditional expressions of mourning. The pain of that *bitter day* can only be likened to the death of an only child.

8:11-14. The absence of YHWH. The two preceding oracles portray disaster in terms of the destructive presence of God. Here the disaster is just the opposite, *a famine . . . of hearing the words of the LORD*, the complete absence of YHWH. YHWH has been present to Israel, but not in the way Israel thought. YHWH was not in the worship at Bethel and Gilgal but in the words of the prophet. Failing to heed the prophet, Israel is left on its own without divine guidance. The futile search for divine guidance is pictured in v. 12 using verbs that suggest a staggering and unsteady gait. *From sea to sea* probably means "from the Mediterranean to the Dead Sea." *From north to east* seems a bit strange and one would expect something like "from north to south." The omission of any reference to the south may be deliberate, suggesting obliquely that the famine will not extend to Judah.

While vv. 13-14 was originally a separate oracle, it adds to the sense of futility expressed in vv. 11-12. In YHWH's absence the people turn to other gods; but these gods, like mirages in the desert, cannot slake the thirst for YHWH's word and presence. It was a widespread custom in the ancient world to invoke the deity to guarantee one's credibility.

There are serious difficulties regarding the exact identity of the gods in v. 14, but the essential point is not hard to see: The indictment falls upon those who swear by—and in effect, worship—the gods of Bethel,

Dan, and Beer-sheba. Bethel, of course, was the principal sanctuary of Samaria, and Dan and Beer-sheba defined the northern and southern boundaries of the early tribal league and the united monarchy (Judg 20:1; 1 Sam 3:20; 1 Kgs 4:25). Hence the specific mention of these three sanctuaries is a symbolic way of designating all sanctuaries of Israel and Judah. According to an early tradition, the name *Beer-sheba* was related to the swearing of an oath (Gen 21:25-31).

9:1-4. Earthquake. The fifth vision is the most despairing of all. Amos glimpses YHWH standing by the altar (cf. Isa 6:1-5), probably the altar at Bethel during a festival when the sanctuary is crowded with worshipers. It is not clear to whom the order is given to *strike the capitals* (the prophet? the heavenly hosts?), but the image is an earthquake that topples the massive stone columns of the sanctuary and virtually annihilates the assembled worshipers. The message is another variation on a theme: there is no salvation in the cult at Bethel. YHWH's presence there is not a saving presence.

The remainder of the vision (vv. 1b-4) reiterates another theme of Amos: God's omnipresence renders impossible the escape of those who survive the initial assault. God is sovereign throughout the cosmos, from the depths of Sheol to the highest reaches of heaven. In a dramatic reversal of images Amos pictures God's hand snatching the people from Sheol, only this time for destruction. God's sovereignty also extends throughout the earth, from the dense forests on the top of Mount Carmel to the bottom of the sea and into all alien lands. Even deportation to a foreign land is no means of escape. The *eyes* of God (v. 4b) typically suggest God's favor; here they suggest a destructive gaze.

9:5-6. Hymn of praise. In context, on the heels of 9:1-4, this hymn of praise extolling the power of the Creator becomes in effect a hymn of judgment, affirming the power of YHWH to carry out the punishment. At God's mere touch the earth "heaves" (REB) and quivers like a liquid, rising and falling like the Nile (cf. 8:8). The picture of the cosmos in v. 6 is strikingly similar to that of Gen 1, a firmament or vault setting the boundaries of the earth.

No Immunity for Israel, 9:7-10

9:7. God's Sovereignty. Two rhetorical questions push the theme of God's universal sovereignty in a radical direction. The first question compares Israel to the Ethiopians, the biblical Cushites who lived at the periphery of the known world. The suggestion is that no nation has special claim upon God's favor. The second question compares Israel to its closest neighbors, declaring that both the Philistines and Arameans were also beneficiaries of an exodus experience. Thus Israel's tradition of exodus is no guarantee of immunity from judgment.

9:8. Sinful kingdom. Interpretative difficulties abound in v. 8. Is *the sinful kingdom* a generic reference—that is, does it refer to any nation that sins? Or does it refer specifically to Israel, who is so obviously singled out in the book? If the former, the exception clause of v. 8c would seem to reintroduce Israel's special status in that it is the recipient of God's mercy in a way other nations are not. Understandably, many commentators have come to view v. 8c as a later addition. If, however, the reference is specifically to Israel as *the sinful kingdom*, the intended contrast is between *kingdom* and *the house of Jacob*, that is, between Israel as a political entity (e.g., a nation) and Israel as a people. In this case, it is the nation that will be destroyed, but a remnant may survive, even if in exile.

9:9-10. Judgment. The latter interpretation seems supported by the image of sifting in v. 9. It is not clear just what kind of *sieve* is intended, but the focus is on the separation of the wheat and the chaff, an analogy for the separation of the righteous from the sinners. The judgment seems to be specifically on the sinners, those who are so arrogant or cocky as to claim, *"Evil shall not overtake or meet us"* (v. 10). The quotation is almost certainly a statement that Amos has heard from his opponents.

A New Beginning, 9:11-15

The two oracles in vv. 11-15 give the Book of Amos a stunning and startling conclusion. The unqualified and unconditional announcement that God will restore *the booth of David that is fallen* (v. 11) seems a radical departure from the terrible judgments and qualified hopes of the previous oracles. Yet, while it is quite likely that these verses were penned by an unknown postexilic author, they devise a fitting conclusion to the book, reminding the reader that God does not punish simply for the sake of punishment. "The prophet's chastisement is meant to serve as a transitional stage to a period of future restoration, at least for the surviving remnant" (Paul 1991, 289). Judgment is not the whole of the prophetic word, nor is it the final word.

9:11-12. Restoration. Elsewhere in Amos (8:3, 9, 13) *that day* signals impending judgment; here it proclaims a time of restoration. The *booth of David* (v. 11) is an unusual construction that has elicited several different interpretations. The specific images in v. 11b suggest the restoration of a walled city, leading many commentators to see this as a reference to the fall of Jerusalem in 587/6. Other scholars see it referring to the division of the kingdom after the death of Solomon and/or to the bleak and precarious state of affairs that existed throughout much of the era of the divided kingdom. In either case the restoration is conceived in terms of a return to the era of David. *All the nations who are called by my name* (v. 12) is likely a reference to the neighboring states that were conquered and ruled by David. These are the same nations charged with heinous crimes in 1:3–2:3. They are included in the restoration as well as Israel and Judah.

9:13-15. Salvation. The announcement of unconditional salvation continues. In contrast to the drought and famine of earlier oracles, v. 13 pictures a time of optimal agricultural conditions and abundant harvest. Normally, the growing season was from November to May, which meant a wait of six months between the harvest and the next planting. But now conditions will be such that planting will begin before the harvest is gathered, and the grape harvest will be so abundant that treading will not be completed until the new seed is sown. The image of mountains dripping with wine both recalls the earlier vision of a "land flowing with milk and honey" (Exod 3:17) and symbolizes for some early Christians the coming of the messianic age (John 2:1-11).

The promises of restoration in v. 14 signal the undoing of the curses in 5:11. Similarly, the promise of v. 15 reverses the judgment of exile that figures so prominently in the book. Like a tree carefully planted and cared for, Israel will never again be uprooted. The land, the original gift of Yahweh, will be unconditionally returned (Wolff 1977, 354).

Works Cited

Mays, James L. 1969. *Amos. A Commentary*. OTL.

Paul, Shalom M. 1991. *Amos. A Commentary on the Book of Amos*. Herm.

Wolff, Hans Walter. 1977. *Joel and Amos. A Commentary on the Books of the Prophets Joel and Amos*.

Obadiah

Cecil P. Staton, Jr.

Introduction

Only twenty-one verses in length, the Book of Obadiah is the shortest book in the OT. This interesting but often overlooked book is a collection of brief prophetic utterances that hurl both words of judgment toward Edom, Israel's enemy (and relative—see Gen 25:19-34; 27:1–28:9) to the southeast (vv. 1-14, 15b), and words of hope toward ISRAEL (vv. 15a, 16-21).

Frequently criticized for a retributive spirit and a narrow nationalism, Obadiah suffers from a neglect few portions of scripture can rival. To its credit the book offers the student of scripture a unique glimpse into a period of Israel's history about which we know all too little. Although Obadiah is not likely to attain the status of a much-loved biblical text, when viewed against the backdrop of its original setting an appreciation for Obadiah may be recovered.

The Book of Obadiah served as a "word from God" for a particularly difficult moment in Israel's history— a word with surprising contemporary relevance. Obadiah declares the terrible consequences for those who participate in cruel and inhuman oppression of neighbors or stand idly by while others do so (vv. 1-14, 15b). Moreover the prophet offers the promise of a future in YHWH's kingdom for those who suffer under the enormous burden of oppression (vv. 15a, 16-21).

The Prophet

Almost nothing is known of the person Obadiah, whose name means "servant of Yahweh" (a name shared by twelve different individuals in the OT). What little can be learned of Obadiah and his ministry must be deduced from the few details revealed in the collection of prophetic utterances that bear his name.

Date

Much of the limited scholarly attention given to Obadiah has focused on two central issues: the literary unity of the book and its setting in Israel's history (see Childs 1979, 412–13).

Whereas the first section of the book (vv. 1-14, 15b) generally employs the second person singular form of speech, the second part (vv. 15a, 16-21) utilizes the second person plural. On this basis it is generally accepted that vv. 15a and 15b were reversed at some point during the transmission of the text. Although some interpreters discern signs of a complicated and lengthy process of literary development (see Wolff 1986, 21, 37f.), in its present form the text reflects a careful organization around both subject (Edom and Israel) and message (judgment and hope). Those interested in pursuing the literary unity or history of exegesis are referred to the larger commentaries, especially Wolff.

Fortunately several significant clues in the text of Obadiah offer assistance to the interpreter searching for both a plausible date and a life setting for the prophet's work.

Evidence pointing to a possible date for Obadiah's ministry is found in vv. 11-14. The pronouncement against Edom recalls *the day* (nine times) when foreigners entered the gates of Jerusalem and deported the people of Judah. The Edomites, though relatives and neighbors of the Jews, gloatingly looked on during this disaster and ultimately participated in looting Judah's resources. They further contributed to Judah's downfall by betraying the survivors of the catastrophe to their enemy (vv. 11-14). These verses can refer only to the events surrounding the destruction of JERUSALEM during the Babylonian conquest of 587/6 B.C.E.

The question of date may also be enhanced by the fact that Obad 1b-5 closely parallels Jer 49:9, 12-15 (in the Hebrew Bible three-fourths of the words are exactly parallel). Did the prophetic tradition *concerning Edom* (v. 1b) originate with Obadiah, or Jeremiah, or did both rely upon a common prophetic tradition?

Jeremiah's ministry dates from 627 to sometime after 587/6 when he probably died in Egypt. The material in the Book of Jeremiah therefore was collected and edited initially in the years following the destruction of Jerusalem, or during the early exilic period. A review of Obadiah's use of the material (see Wolff 1986, 38–42) suggests that the prophet is adopting a traditional prophetic announcement of judgment which he expounds upon and applies to a new situation. In the aftermath of the destruction of Jerusalem in 587/6 B.C.E., Obadiah announces both a word of judgment for Israel's old enemy, the Edomites, and a word of hope for the survivors who now face an uncertain future.

Possible Life Setting

Zechariah 7:3-6 and 8:18-23 suggest that sometime after 587/6 annual services were held to commemorate the fall of Jerusalem and the destruction of the Temple. The form of Obadiah itself—a word of judgment for Israel's enemies followed by a word of hope for Israel—offers the possibility of an example of the kind of preaching that was heard in these services of lamentation.

Edom is addressed first (vv. 1-14, 15b). Its betrayal of family and neighbor is described poetically and an indictment is offered. Obadiah announces Yahweh's sentence: *As you have done, it shall be done to you; your deeds shall return on your own head* (v. 15b). Edom will learn firsthand the tribulation experienced by Israel. The second section addresses Israel. All the nations shall taste the cup of Yahweh's wrath from which Israel has already drunk. A similar fate awaits all who seek to thwart God and God's people. The prophet announces the good news that the Edoms of this world will not be ultimately successful. The future of God's people is with Yahweh who will reign over all: *the kingdom shall be the LORD's* (v. 21).

The role of the prophetic individual who stands behind this brief collection is in many ways that of the modern-day preacher. Obadiah takes a text and applies it to his own setting and time. Obadiah reveals a minister reaching back into the prophetic traditions of his people in order to bring an important message to his hearers. Perhaps Obadiah functioned as a cult prophet in the aftermath of the destruction of Jerusalem (Wolff 1986, 19). He served as Yahweh's spokesperson at a particularly difficult moment when the dejected people of God needed the assurance that their enemies would reap the consequences of their tragic actions and that Yahweh was still in control of their future.

It is also likely that Obadiah's words continued to be used in the postexilic age when the Jews returned to their ancestral homeland. For those who later faced new problems and challenges that threatened their future, Edom became symbolic of all powers that seek to thwart God's purposes and God's people. Obadiah's assurance that Yahweh would ultimately reign over all would have become words of enormous hope and strength for later generations of Jews who faced the difficult postexilic period.

For Further Study

In the *Mercer Dictionary of the Bible*: BABYLONIAN EMPIRE; EDOM/EDOMITES/IDUMAEA; ESAU; EXILE; JACOB; JEREMIAH; JEREMIAH, BOOK OF; JERUSALEM; JUDAH, KINGDOM OF; JUSTICE/JUDGMENT; OBADIAH; OBADIAH, BOOK OF; PALESTINE, GEOGRAPHY OF; PROPHET; VISION.
In other sources: B. S. Childs, "Obadiah," in *Introduction to the Old Testament as Scripture*; J. Limburg, *Hosea–Micah*, Interp; H. W. Wolff, *Obadiah and Jonah*, Herm.

Commentary

An Outline

Superscription, 1a

Verse 1a, the briefest of OT prophetic superscriptions, identifies the oracles that follow as *the vision of Obadiah* (cf. Isa 1:1; Nah 1:1). The word *vision* is a derivative of the Hebrew word *hazah*, "to see," from which the word *hozeh*, "seer," also originates (see 1 Sam 9:9). In its oldest usage "vision" probably refers to the divine communication received during the ecstatic state of the prophet while under divine inspiration (translated "prophetic frenzy" in the NRSV; cf. 1

Sam 19:18-24). In time the word "vision" became a technical term for prophetic communication and here identifies what follows as prophetic utterances.

The Consequences of Betrayal and Pride, 1b-14, 15b

The Humbling of Edom, 1b-10

Verse 1b identifies the subject of Obadiah's vision. What follows is a word from *the Lord GOD concerning Edom*. A knowledge of Edom's relationship with Israel is crucial for understanding Obadiah. Edom is addressed in vv. 1-15. Verses 16-21 are addressed to Judah. Even here, however, the dominant subject is the ultimate triumph over Edom.

The territory of ancient Edom, located southwest of Israel, extended for some 100 mi. between the River Zered and the Gulf of Aqaba. The OT portrays a long history of enmity between Israel and Edom. The Edomites began settling this territory as early as 1300 B.C.E., or just before the arrival of Israelite tribes in Palestine. Notable biblical references to this ongoing hostility include the struggle of the twins in Rebekah's womb (JACOB and ESAU), which became symbolic of the struggle between Israel and Edom (Gen 25:19-34); the Israelite confrontation with the king of Edom during the Exodus (Deut 2:1-8; cf. Num 21:4); the Edomite conflict with King Saul (1 Sam 14:47); and David's eventual conquest and subjugation of the Edomites (2 Sam 8:13-14; see Kelm, 232–33 for a more complete review of the biblical witness).

Nothing was remembered with more enmity, however, than Edom's conduct at the time of the fall of Jerusalem in 587/6 B.C.E. Obadiah's severe words concerning Edom are reflected in similar texts from other sixth- and fifth-century writers (cf. Ps 137:7; Isa 34:5-7; 63:1-6; Lam 4:21-22; Ezek 25:12-14; 35:1-15; Mal 1:2-4). Nowhere is this recalled more vividly, however, than in the brief Book of Obadiah.

1b-4. Pride goeth before the fall. Obadiah chooses as the launching point for his sermon a text pregnant with meaning for his people. He borrows a text from the prophetic tradition that announces the humbling of Edom (cf. Jer 49:9, 14-16). The text begins with a familiar call to arms: *Rise up! Let us rise against it for battle* (v. 1b). The nations are coming together to bring low the one nation that lives *in the clefts of the rocks* and *in the heights* (v. 3; on the habitations of the Edomites see Kelm 1990, 232–33 and Fry 1990, 679). With fateful pride Edom asked, *Who will bring me*

down to the ground? (v. 3). Obadiah wastes no time in announcing Yahweh's judgment for such an arrogant people. Edom's proud heart has deceived him: *I will bring you down, says the LORD* (v. 4).

5-10. The pillager is now the pillaged. In these verses the prophet speaks of future events as if they had already occurred, a common form of prophetic speech sometimes called the "prophetic future" tense. The prophet envisages a future when *Esau* (v. 6, Jacob's twin and father of the Edomites) is pillaged in the same manner as Edom pillaged Jacob. Moreover, unlike those robbers who take only what they desire, Edom's plunderers will take it all: *How you have been destroyed!* (v. 5). Edom will find no refuge with its allies (v. 7). Its legendary wisdom and the renowned strength of its warriors will not be enough to stand against the ravages of this enemy (vv. 8-9). Why? It is all *for the slaughter and violence done to your brother Jacob* (v. 10).

The Indictment against Edom, 11-14

The most detailed description of Edom's conduct at the time of Jerusalem's fall in 587/6 B.C.E. appears in vv. 11-14. *On that day*, indelibly written upon the collective memory of Israel, Edom committed the most horrendous of atrocities. The first act mentioned is perhaps the worst. Initially Edom *stood aside* (v. 11). Edom became a bystander to a horrible act of injustice. It watched as *strangers* (i.e., Babylon) entered Jerusalem's gates and carried off its resources (v. 11). The guilt of the one who stands idly by while such injustices occur before one's very eyes is clear: *you too were like one of them* (v. 11). By its actions or lack of them Edom became just as guilty as those perpetrating the crime.

Unfortunately it did not stop there. Afterwards Edom *gloated*, even *rejoiced*, over Judah's misfortune (v. 12). Edom shoved it in Judah's face—poured salt into their wounds. Edom entered the gates of Jerusalem and gloated over Judah's disaster on the day of their calamity. It gets worse! Apparently Edom joined in the looting of Jerusalem's resources and even cut off those attempting to flee and delivered them to their captors (vv. 13-14). What could Edom expect in return for its betrayal of family and neighbor in the day of their greatest need?

The Obvious Conclusion, 15b

There is but one conclusion to this sad description of the ultimate betrayal. Obadiah declares, *As you have done, it shall be done to you; your deeds shall return on your own head.* The Christian is reminded here of Jesus' words on the night of his betrayal, "for all who take the sword will perish by the sword" (Matt 26:52), or the words of Paul, "for you reap whatever you sow" (Gal 6:7). Perhaps more significant for the one who stands idly by while harm comes to another are Jesus' words from Matt 25:40, 45: "just as you did it to one of the least of these who are members of my family, you did it to me . . . just as you did not do it to one of the least of these, you did not do it to me."

The Day of Yahweh is Near, 15a, 16-21

Hope for Mount Zion and the House of Jacob, 15a, 16-21a

Beginning with vv. 15a, 16-21 the *you* is no longer Edom (second person sing.), but now Israel during the exile—and the Jews of the postexilic age—and, still later, other people of faith longing for a word of hope while languishing under enormous oppression (second person pl.).

This section is linked to the first in significant ways. Although the prophet's words are now addressed to a different audience, Edom is still the major focus. Israel now receives the news that there *is* a future for the house of Jacob; all the nations hostile to Yahweh and his people and especially Edom (Esau) will be subjugated.

The two sections are also tied together by the use of the word *day*. In the first section *the day* that Edom *stood aside* (v. 11) was contrasted with *the day* of Edom's demise (v. 8). In fact *day* appears nine times in vv. 11-14 alone. This must now be contrasted with *the day of the LORD*, which will be a day of judgment for all the nations (v. 15a; cf. Joel 2).

As Israel has *drunk* the cup of Yahweh's punishment in the events of 587/6 B.C.E., so now the nations must also drink, even *gulp down* their penalty (v. 16; cf. Ps 75:8; Isa 51:22-23; Jer 51:7; see Limburg 1988, 133–34). Yet some will escape, and gather on Mount Zion, the holy residence of Yahweh's presence. The house of Jacob shall become the possessor rather than the dispossessed (v. 17).

From *all the nations* (v. 15) the focus of v. 18 returns specifically to Edom. Esau is now but stubble to be consumed by the fires of the people of God. The authority for this action is nothing less than the word of Yahweh, *for the LORD has spoken.*

Verses 19-20 describe the full extent of the new territorial possessions of the formerly *dispossessed* (v. 17). Israel will inhabit its former territory as well as that of its enemies Edom and PHOENICIA. Borders will be extended in the north as far as ZAREPHATH and in the south into *the Negeb* (v. 19; see Hopkins 1990 for details on geography). One final jab at Edom occurs in 21a. Proud *Mount Esau* will now be ruled from *Mount Zion*, geographically a far less notable mountain. Theologically, however, there is no higher place than this. Israel will once again dominate Edom—politically and theologically.

The Obvious Conclusion, 21b

Following a survey of the rugged terrain of the little Book of Obadiah the student of scripture may be inclined to join the chorus of criticism advanced by those who find here a retributive spirit and a narrow nationalism. One may very well conclude that Obadiah deserves the neglect it receives.

Yet when viewed against the backdrop of its original setting a greater appreciation for Obadiah is possible. On the surface the modern reader is inclined to find what Wolff describes as "pure, primitive hate." Wolff is surely correct, however, when he writes:

> But anyone who is prepared to enter imaginatively into the historical hour in which these sayings were written discovers a wretched people in a ruined city, in dire need of comfort. It is only if we try to picture the service of mourning in the rubble of Jerusalem after the days of catastrophe in 587 that we can begin to understand the proclamation of the prophetic spokesman (Wolff 1986, 22).

The fact is that the Book of Obadiah is included in the canon of scripture embraced by people of faith, both Jews and Christians. Surely this is because history is filled with many stories of "Edoms" and "Israels" in both national and interpersonal relationships. Obadiah's message was a "word from God" for a particularly difficult moment in the history of the people of God, yet a moment that has recurred more than once since these words were spoken.

Obadiah declares the terrible consequences for those who participate in cruel and inhuman oppression of neighbors or stand idly by while others do (vv. 1-14, 15b). Moreover the prophet offers the promise of a future in Yahweh's kingdom for those who suffer under the enormous burden of oppression (vv. 15a, 16-

21). This prophet joins the chorus of the larger biblical witness in announcing the good news all sufferers long to hear, *the kingdom shall be the LORD's* (v. 21).

Works Cited

Childs, Brevard S. 1979. "Obadiah," in *Introduction to the Old Testament as Scripture*.

Fry, Virgil. 1990. "Petra," MDB.

Hopkins, David D. 1990. "Palestine, Geography of," MDB.

Kelm, George L. 1989. "Edom/Edomites/Idumaea," MDB.

Limburg, James. 1988. *Hosea–Micah*, Interp.

Wolff, Hans Walter. 1986. *Obadiah and Jonah, A Commentary*. Herm.

Jonah

Kenneth M. Craig, Jr.

Introduction

No one doubts that Jonah, the fifth in a collection of twelve short prophetic books, is unique. The author focuses on the actions of the prophet rather than on his prophecy. Jonah's proclamation to Nineveh in 3:4 consists of only five words in the Hebrew. Outside the book, JONAH is mentioned only in 2 Kgs 14:25, a verse that refers to the prophet's home town of Gath-hepher, a city of modest size identified with Khirbet Ez-Zurra three miles northeast of Nazareth. In the Book of Jonah, the PROPHET is commissioned to set out for Nineveh, the capital of the ancient Assyrian empire. From an Israelite perspective, ASSYRIA was synonymous with oppression and domination.

Authorship

The book never identifies its author. Like SAMUEL and other famous characters of the Hebrew Bible, Jonah never claims to have written the book that bears his name. Arguments for and against the eighth century prophet as author are discussed in *MDB* (see JONAH, BOOK OF). The wide range of possible dates (see below) cautions against assigning a specific author and time of composition.

Date

The date of the Book of Jonah is difficult to determine. The time of the prophet mentioned in 2 Kings (ca. 780 B.C.E.) is not necessarily the time of composition. It may be that the story makes more sense before the fall of Nineveh (612 B.C.E.), but a date after this time is also possible since Nineveh could have been subject to judgment after 612. The reference to *the king of Nineveh* (instead of to "the king of Assyria") in 3:6 clouds the issue since Assyrian records never use the title. If the last two chapters allude to Jer 18 and Joel 2, a postexilic date is likely. References to Persian customs such as domestic animals participating in mourning ceremonies (3:8), and the mention of *the king and his nobles* together (3:7) may suggest a date during the Persian period (550–330 B.C.E.). The use of nonbiblical sea motifs ("great fish," "being swallowed," "vomited up") makes a date in the early Hellenistic period (330–200 B.C.E.) possible. According to Sir 49:10 the Book of Jonah (included in the reference to "Twelve Prophets") was known by 200 B.C.E. This range of dates and the lack of compelling evidence for any one period lead to the general observation that the book was written sometime between 750 and 250 B.C.E.

Literary Form and Primary Themes

Virtually every imaginable genre or genre-like label has been applied to the book including didactic tale, short story, satire, sermon, fable, myth, folk tale, allegory, parable, midrash, legend, *erzählte Dogmatik* ("narrated dogmatics"), and sensational didactic historical narrative (Trible 1963, 126–77; Craig 1989, 24–33). The appearance of so many labels for the Book of Jonah suggests that George Landes is correct in calling attention to the literary category of *mashal*. This type of writing does not refer to a specific literary form but rather to the way multiple forms are shaped to serve a specific didactic purpose (Landes 1978, 137–58). The writer is not a systematic theologian, but the story does touch on a number of important theological themes. These themes include: justice, mercy, repentance, creation, the encompassing nature of God's love, and the free nature of God's compassion. An additional theme may be described as the relationship between Creator and creature. In the scene outside Nineveh, the LORD asks the prophet: *Is it right for you to be angry about the bush?* (4:9). This rebuke is reminiscent of the LORD's response to Job from the whirlwind in Job 38–41.

For Further Study

In the Mercer Dictionary of the Bible: ASSYRIA; JONAH; JONAH, BOOK OF; POETRY; PROPHET.
In other sources: J. S. Ackerman, "Jonah," *The Literary Guide to the Bible*, ed. R. Alter and F. Kermode; L. Allen, *The Books of Joel, Obadiah, Jonah, and Micah*, NICOT; K. M. Craig, Jr., *A Poetics of Jonah*;

G. M. Landes, "Jonah: A Mashal?," in *Israelite Wisdom: Theological and Literary Essays in Honor of Samuel Terrien*, and "The Kerygma of the Book of Jonah: The Contextual Interpretation of the Jonah Psalm," *Int* 21 (1967): 3–31; J. H. Sasson, *Jonah*, AncB; D. Stuart, *Hosea–Jonah*, WBC; P. L. Trible, "Studies in the Book of Jonah," Ph.D. diss., Columbia University, 1963; H. W. Wolff, *Obadiah and Jonah*, Herm.

Commentary

An Outline

I. Jonah's Call, Disobedience, and Adventures, 1:1-16
  A. Jonah Resists the Commission, 1:1-3
  B. The Storm at Sea, 1:4-5
  C. Jonah Is Singled Out, 1:6-16
II. The LORD Rescues Jonah, 1:17–2:10 (MT 2:1-11)
  A. The Fish Swallows Jonah, 1:17–2:2a (MT 2:1-3a)
  B. Jonah Prays, 2:2b-9 (MT 2:3b-10)
  C. Return to Dry Land, 2:10 (MT 2:11)
III. Jonah in Nineveh, 3:1-10
  A. A Re-Commission, 3:1-3a
  B. Proclamation and Repentance, 3:3b-10
IV. Conversation between Jonah and the LORD, 4:1-11
  A. Jonah's Complaint, 4:1-3
  B. The LORD's Response, 4:4-11

Jonah's Call, Disobedience, and Adventures, 1:1-16

Jonah Resists the Commission, 1:1-3

The brief introduction alludes to 2 Kgs 14:25 where "Jonah son of Amittai," is also mentioned. The divine commission in v. 2 is presented with familiar words also reminiscent of language from Kings: "Arise, go to Zarephath" (1 Kgs 17:9, RSV). Prophets were not ordinarily summoned to travel long distances to deliver a message. They usually spoke against foreign nations (Ezek 27–32; Isa 13,15–19; Jer 46–51; Amos 1–2:3; Obad; Nah 1–3), but rarely traveled to them. The content of the message is not told to the reader until chap. 3. Jonah, like MOSES, ISAIAH, and JEREMIAH before him, is reluctant. Unlike other prophets, however, Jonah protests with his feet instead of with words. In a blatant act of disobedience, he heads for Tarshish, a city usually identified with southwest Spain. The focus on action in v. 3 (*set out, flee, went down, found, paid, went, go*) indicates the extreme measures to which Jonah goes in order to resist the LORD's call. The introduction sets the fast-paced tempo for this story.

The Storm at Sea, 1:4-5

Jonah soon learns of the LORD's power. The emphasis in v. 4 is on a chain reaction set in motion by the LORD. The LORD causes a wind, which causes a storm, which causes the ship to virtually break up. The passage also introduces key words (*throwing, hurling, the sea*, and *fear*) that will be developed in the remainder of the chapter. In v. 5 the author contrasts the sailors who cry out to their gods and hurl the cargo overboard with Jonah who falls asleep.

Jonah Is Singled Out, 1:6-16

The captain of the sailors comes to Jonah, wakes him up, and instructs him to *get up* and *call* (v. 6). These commanding words are the same two words that the LORD spoke to Jonah in 1:2. In an effort to find the cause of their problems, the sailors then cast lots that determine Jonah's guilt. Thus far in the story (1:1-8a), Jonah's speech has not been quoted by the narrator. This portrayal of a laconic prophet is reinforced when we notice that Jonah responds in the first chapter only when he is asked questions (1:8, 11). As soon as the lots determine Jonah's guilt, the sailors bombard him with a series of questions (v. 8). Since nationality and religion were inextricably tied together in the ancient Near East, the sailors ask about his nationality in an attempt to discover which god is responsible for this disaster. Jonah responds by telling them that he is *a Hebrew* who worships *the LORD, the God of heaven, who made the sea and the dry land* (v. 9). This statement is charged with irony. If he fears God who made the sea and dry land, what does he hope to accomplish by fleeing? After the men consider their options, Jonah responds by advising them to pick him up and throw him into the sea. One notices an acceleration in the action and emotions in the first chapter: *the mariners were afraid* (1:5); *the men were even more afraid* (v.

10); *then the men feared the LORD even more* (v. 16). The crescendo effect is also accomplished in the description of the storm at sea: *such a mighty storm came upon the sea* (1:4); *the sea was growing more and more tempestuous* (v. 11); *the sea grew more and more stormy against them* (v. 13). Surprisingly, Jonah's disobedience produces some significant results. In v. 14 the sailors cry out and address the LORD by invoking God's intimate name, and in v. 16 they offer a sacrifice and make vows.

The LORD Rescues Jonah, 1:17–2:10 (MT 2:1-11)

The Fish Swallows Jonah, 1:17–2:2a (MT 2:1-3a)

The LORD continues to assume a commanding role by providing a fish that swallows Jonah. While some interpreters emphasize the fish as punishment motif, it may also be properly understood as a shelter for the drowning prophet. The author reports that Jonah *prayed to the LORD his God* (2:1 [MT 2:2]). Praying or crying out to God emerges as a central issue in this story (1:5; 1:6b; 1:14; 2:2-9 [MT 2:3-10]; 3:8; 4:2-3). Once again, in the opening verses of this chapter, we focus on the action between the two principal characters, Jonah and the LORD. The great fish, which will later be echoed in Matt 12:40, refers to any large fish.

Jonah Prays, 2:2b-9 (MT 2:3b-10)

Jonah finally calls out to the LORD, as the captain and sailors had begged him to before (1:6; 1:14). Four standard elements of the Thanksgiving Psalm type are found in Jonah's poetic prayer: reports of answered prayer, personal crisis, divine rescue, and a vow of praise. Numerous parallels exist between Jonah's prayer from the belly of the fish and prayers from the Psalter. In fact, the prayer that Jonah offers consists almost entirely of phrases from Psalms. The distinguishing feature of the Jonah psalm is that it is spoken by one person in a specific context. With these words, the author establishes that Jonah is in fact *a Hebrew* who worships *the LORD . . . who made the sea and the dry land* (1:9). This pastiche also highlights the prophet's frenzied mental state. The psalm is connected by recurring words and motifs. For many years it was regarded as an extraneous or arbitrary addition, but a number of clues suggests that it is intimately connected to the surrounding prose narrative. For example, Jonah's two verbal formulations of prayer (vv. 2-9 [MT 2:3-10] and 4:2-3) share three key words: (a) חַסְדָּם, *their true loyalty* (v. 8 [MT 2:9]); *steadfast love* (4:2);

(b) חַיִּי, *my life* (v. 6 [MT 2:7]); *to live* (4:3); (c) נֶפֶשׁ, *me* (v. 5 [MT 2:6]); *my life* (4:3) (Allen 1976, 198–99). The prayer uttered from the belly of the fish also displays thematic similarities to the action and words of the previous chapter. In the opening scene, Jonah's descent began when he went down to Joppa. Jonah also went down into the ship (1:3) and continued to descend into its recesses (1:5). Even the sailors' activity reinforces this movement. They cast lots that "fall" to Jonah (1:7) and then finally throw him overboard (1:15). This descent motif continues in the first half of the psalm, and is reversed beginning in v. 6b [MT 2:7b] when Jonah recounts that the LORD brought him up *from the Pit.* The prophet's concluding remarks at the end of the prayer in v. 9 [MT 2:10] may remind the reader of the sailors' action at the end of the previous scene (1:16).

Return to Dry Land, 2:10 (MT 2:11)

The fish responds to the LORD's command and *spews Jonah out upon the dry land.* The specific location of Jonah's place on land is not mentioned. With Jonah out of the water, the story returns to prose. The prophet's plan to flee from the LORD was unsuccessful. The first half of the story concludes.

Jonah in Nineveh, 3:1-10

A Re-Commission, 3:1-3a

This brief passage serves resumptive and transitional functions. The commission is repeated word for word (3:2a=1:2a) in the Hebrew. The parallel between the two scenes ends, however, when we learn that this time Jonah sets out for Nineveh *according to the word of the LORD* (v. 3a). Like the wind, sea, and fish before him, Jonah now bends to the will of the LORD. A sense of mystery surrounds the proclamation itself. What is it? Will the city be punished, destroyed, or spared?

Proclamation and Repentance, 3:3b-10

When this scene begins, Jonah is (finally) in Nineveh. His message to the Ninevites, *Forty days more, and Nineveh shall be overthrown!* (v. 4), is somewhat open-ended. Do his words suggest that the Ninevites have reason to hope that they may be spared if they repent? No conditions are attached to the proclamation, and the prophet says nothing about what could or should be done. The message to the Ninevites contains the only words that the prophet will speak in the third chapter. In the midst of foreigners, Jonah is, once again, laconic.

After the proclamation, the author focuses on the events in Nineveh. Jonah fades to the background. The prophet's words stir the Ninevites, and the overall effect of the proclamation is reported in v. 5. The people *believed God . . . proclaimed a fast, and . . . put on sackcloth*. These elements of threat and/or disaster followed by acts of penitence and eventual divine intervention (vv. 4b-10) are part of a pattern found in several portions of the Hebrew Bible (1 Sam 7:3-14; 2 Sam 24; Ezra 8:21-23; Esth 3:7–4:17; Joel 1:1–2:27). The Hebrew word for *fast* (צום) implies abstention from food as well as accompanying mourning and repentance. The focus on religious activity is made from three angles: the response of the people, the king's reaction, followed by the king's official decree (which virtually mirrors the response that the people had already made). The encompassing nature of the decree includes even animals who, along with humans, are to be covered with sackcloth (v. 8). Such actions by the foreigners have a good effect once again for *God changed his mind . . . and he did not do it* (v. 10; cf. 1:16; Joel 2:12-14 and Jer 18:7-10).

Conversation between Jonah and the LORD, 4:1-11

Jonah's Complaint, 4:1-3

The first verses of chap. 4 signal a drastic turn of events. As the LORD's anger ceases, Jonah's begins. Once again, Jonah prays. He begins by focusing on himself *What I said while I was still in my own country . . . I fled . . . for I knew* (v. 2a, emphasis added) and concludes by describing God in traditional language in v. 2b (cf. Exod 34:6; Num 14:18; Pss 86:15; 103:8; 145:8; Nah 1:3; Neh 9:17). Jonah's prayer in v. 2 contrasts with his earlier praise and thanksgiving (2:9 [MT 2:10]). The words of this second prayer also reveal that the author has kept information from the readers or listeners until this opportune moment. At this late stage, Jonah says, *Is this not what I said . . . at the beginning* (v. 2)? The request that his life be taken from him in v. 3 is reminiscent of Elijah's prayer in 1 Kgs 19:4.

The LORD's Response, 4:4-11

The LORD quickly challenges Jonah's right to be angry by asking an incisive rhetorical question in v. 4. Verse 5 may be viewed as a flashback, or it may re-

flect Jonah's expectation that something might yet happen in the city of Nineveh. Just as Jonah in the initial part of the story did not respond to the LORD with words, he, once again, displays a defiant attitude with actions (v. 5).

Beginning in v. 6, the LORD launches a game by sending a shade plant that causes Jonah to become *very happy*. God then appoints *a worm* and prepares *a sultry east wind* (vv. 7-8). Jonah asks a second time that his life be taken from him (v. 8). When God's rhetorical question comes to Jonah once again (v. 9), the first clause is repeated verbatim and then an additional phrase is added (*Is it right for you to be angry about the bush?*). The prophet's anger has surfaced because of the shade that was lost over his head. Jonah insists in the strongest possible words that the bush is important to him. He loves it. He is "extremely happy" about it (v. 6), and when it withers, he is furious (v. 9). The prophet is so mad that the thought of death seems better than the idea of living without the plant! This game is intended as an object lesson to teach Jonah something about the inconsistency of his own position compared with God's. The LORD's final words to the prophet (vv. 10-11) focus on the word "concern." Jonah is concerned about the plant because he lost the shade it provided. The LORD is concerned about the people and animals of Nineveh. Jonah and the audience are left with the profound rhetorical question at the end of the book. Despite the many harrowing experiences, no human or animal loses its life in the story. The prophet's emotions that had previously been emphasized starting with the first verse in chap. 4 (rage, disappointment, extraordinary happiness, frustration) are now summarily contrasted with the compassion that the LORD feels for all of creation.

Works Cited

Allen, L. 1976. *The Books of Joel, Obadiah, Jonah, and Micah*. NICOT.

Craig, K. M. 1989. "The Poetics of the Book of Jonah: Toward an Understanding of Narrative Strategy," Ph.D. diss., Southern Baptist Theological Seminary.

Landes, G. M. 1978. "Jonah: A Mashal?" in *Israelite Wisdom: Theological and Literary Essays in Honor of Samuel Terrien*.

Trible, P. L. 1963. "Studies in the Book of Jonah," Ph.D. diss., Columbia University.

Micah

Jerome F. D. Creach

Introduction

The Book of Micah is a collection of prophetic sayings reportedly spoken by Micah, an eighth-century PROPHET from *Moresheth* (1:1). The content of the book is similar to that of other prophetic works of the same period. Both AMOS and Micah emphasize social justice (Mic 2:1-2, 8-9; 3:9-10; 6:11-12; Amos 2:6-8; 4:1; 5:10-12; 8:4-6). Micah and ISAIAH have one common passage (Mic 4:1-3=Isa 2:2-4) and numerous other thematically similar texts (Mic 1:8~Isa 20:3; Mic 2:6~Isa 30:9-10; Mic 3:1-3~Isa 5:20; Mic 5:4~Isa 40:11). These analogous passages are the reason Micah is sometimes described as "Amos *redivivus*" or "Isaiah in miniature."

Despite its many shared ideas, Micah stands alone with at least two distinctive features that prevent the work from being read as merely a condensed derivative of these larger contemporary collections. First, Micah is the only prophetic work from the eighth century to include a prediction of the fall of JERUSALEM (3:9-12). This inflammatory speech against Judah's capital was so shocking that JEREMIAH was arrested for proclaiming an similar message nearly 100 years later (Jer 26:1-9). In the ensuing trial Jeremiah was successfully defended because of an appeal to the earlier prediction of Micah (Jer 26:16-19). Second, the book foretells the birth of an Israelite ruler, reminiscent of DAVID, who hails from BETHLEHEM (5:2). The NT identifies this regent as Jesus (see Matt 2:6; also see the debate in John 7:40-43 that contains the same understanding, although ironically spoken in ignorance by Jesus' opponents). Thus, the Book of Micah makes a unique contribution to the prophetic tradition of ancient Israel and provides the early Christian church with a central claim concerning the birth of Jesus, confessed to be the MESSIAH. The Christian claims notwithstanding, Micah deserves to be examined on its own merit and for its distinctive contribution to Israelite prophecy and OT thought in general.

The Prophet

Apart from the brief biographical sketch of Micah in 1:1, the only information known about the prophet's social status or prophetic vocation is that implied in the prophetic utterances of the man. The prophet Micah (the name means "who is like YHWH?") is identified by his town of origin, *Moresheth* (1:1). This name probably refers to Moresheth-Gath, a settlement about twenty-four mi. southwest of Jerusalem. The prophet's provincial identification implies that Micah was not part of the ruling class of Jerusalem. Indeed, he distances himself from the corrupt practices of the professional prophets, priests, and rulers of the capital city (see Mic 3:5-8). This explains why Micah was described in relation to a locality rather than by reference to his father (cf. Hos 1:1; Isa 1:1) or by his sense of a "call" to be a prophet (cf. Amos 1:1; Jer 1:1; Ezek 1:1) (Wolff 1990, 6–7). Micah spoke as an outsider, uttering a cry for "justice" (מִשְׁפָּט) for those oppressed in Judah by the Jerusalem elite (Mic 2:1-2).

Micah proclaimed YHWH's message *in the days of Kings Jotham, Ahaz, and Hezekiah of Judah* (1:1), that is, between 750 and 687 B.C.E. During this turbulent period in Israel's history ASSYRIA established control over Syria-Palestine. After repeated rebellions against the Assyrian yoke, the Northern Kingdom and its capital, SAMARIA, were finally decimated in 722 by the powerful Assyrian army. The Assyrian threat forced the Southern Kingdom into a state of vassalage, but Judah survived as an independent political entity. Micah makes reference to these events (1:6-9), with the apparent implication that Assyria is YHWH's instrument of judgment on Israel and Judah, although he never mentions Assyria directly, as Isaiah did (10:5).

Scholars generally limit material original to Micah to chaps. 1–3, excluding 1:1, 2:12-13, and brief editorial additions. Some other passages, however, may be debated because they seem to correlate with an eighth century context (e.g., 5:2-6 [MT 5:1-5]). Still other passages appear anachronistic (e.g., 7:11-13) because they assume an exilic setting in which the people hope for the restoration of Zion. The authentic words of Micah tell that the prophet protested against the unjust seizure of land by wealthy citizens (2:2) and the mercenary motives of prophets, priests, and judges (3:1-3, 5-6a, 9-11). Micah identified himself as one *filled with power, with the spirit of the LORD, and with justice and might, to declare to Jacob his transgression and to Israel his sin* (3:8). In other words, Micah saw himself as one called to uncover the wrongful acts of the nation's leaders. As punishment for their deeds, the capitals of Israel (Samaria) and Judah (Jerusalem) would be destroyed.

The Form of the Book of Micah

The Book of Micah is not merely a group of disjointed oracles haphazardly ordered in the work's final form. In fact, the book's organization assists in the interpretation of individual units. Micah contains two fairly distinct sections: 1:2–5:15 and 6:1–7:20 with 1:1 as an introduction. Both divisions open with the imperative *Hear* (שִׁמְעוּ), which introduces a juridical setting. In 1:2–5:15 the audience is the *earth, and all that is in it* (1:2). In this universal context the prophet declares that YHWH will come in THEOPHANY to wreak destruction upon the earth because of the transgressions of Israel and Judah (1:3-7).

Chapters 2–3 indicate the reason for the devastation as the failure of the nation's leaders. The pivotal point in this first section then comes with the prediction that Jerusalem will be razed (3:9-12). In stark contrast, chaps. 4–5 present hope for restoration. However, chaps. 1–3 and 4–5 are connected by the emphasis on Zion, its destruction (3:12) and subsequent rebirth (4:1-4). The phrases, *the mountain of the house* (3:12) and *the mountain of the LORD's house* (4:1) provide an unmistakable link between the two sections.

As a unit, chaps. 1–5 contrast the failed human leadership in Israel (3:1-7) with the righteous rule of YHWH (4:7b). After YHWH metes out punishment to his people (1:6-16; 3:12), he will re-establish them under the domain of a powerful shepherd king from Bethlehem (5:2-6 [MT 5:1-5]). Israel will be characterized by perfect trust in YHWH (5:7-9). Then the nation will be protected from all its foes (5:10-15).

Chapters 6–7 mirror the development of chaps. 1–5. Micah 6:1-2 introduces a *controversy* (רִיב) between the LORD and his people. These two chapters emphasize God's covenant faithfulness on the one hand (6:4-5) and the wicked perversion of justice by his people on the other hand (6:10-12). The climactic point is evident, however, in 7:1-7 when the personified city of Jerusalem confesses the sins of its leaders and declares trust in YHWH alone (v. 7). YHWH is called to *shepherd [the] people* (7:14).

The book closes with the assurance that YHWH will pardon Israel for its sins (7:18-20). Thus, like chaps. 1–5, chaps. 6–7 highlight YHWH's governance of Israel after the nation has been punished for its transgressions. Both sections of the book reverberate with the themes of justice (or lack thereof) and God's kingship. Under the sovereignty of YHWH the oppressed of the land are able to dwell secure (4:4) and those who suffered from the unfaithfulness of Israel's rulers are revivified (4:6-7; 7:11-12).

The Formation of the Book of Micah

The question of the book's formation, or redactional history, is very difficult and any conclusions will be hypothetical. However, three general stages of growth seem evident. First, the book began with a core of oracles that originated with the prophet Micah in the eighth century B.C.E. These sayings can be located only in chaps. 1–3 with certainty. Second, editors added brief statements approximately one century later in order to reapply Micah's words to the time of the reforms of King JOSIAH and the Babylonian crisis (e.g., 5:10-15 [MT 5:9-14]). Finally, in the exilic and postexilic periods, sections were added to round out the bleak picture of destruction with a more complete word of hope for the revitalization of Zion and of the people who lived there (e.g., 4:6-7).

For Further Study

In the *Mercer Dictionary of the Bible*: ASSYRIA; CHRONOLOGY; ISAIAH; ISAIAH, BOOK OF; JEREMIAH; JEREMIAH, BOOK OF; JERUSALEM; MICAH; MICAH, BOOK OF; ORACLE; PROPHET. In other sources: D. G. Hagstrom, *The Coherence of the Book of Micah: A Literary Analysis*; D. R. Hillers, *Micah*, Herm; K. Koch, *The Prophets*, 1:573–74; J. L. Mays, "Justice: Perspectives from the Prophetic Tradition," *Int* 37/1 (1983): 5–17, and *Micah*, OTL; H. W. Wolff, *Micah*.

Commentary

An Outline

Superscription, 1:1

The opening verse of the Book of Micah has a form much like the introduction to other prophetic books (e.g., Isa 1:1; 2:1; Jer 1:1-3; Hos 1:1; Joel 1:1; Amos 1:1). The fact that Micah's work is dated with a list of Southern kings indicates that the prophet spoke primarily to Judah (the reference to *Samaria* is probably influenced by the emphasis on the Northern capital in 1:5-7).

YHWH's Court Case against All the Earth, 1:2–5:15 (MT 1:2–5:14)

Punishment of Two Capital Cities, 1:2-16

1:2-7. Announcement of controversy and judgment. This passage is set in the heavenly council where YHWH reigns as judge. The imperative, *listen, O earth* (v. 2), indicates that YHWH is concerned with establishing justice in the whole cosmos. However, the focus quickly moves to the iniquities of a single nation, ISRAEL. Because of the transgressions of Samaria and the idolatry of Jerusalem, God is about to come *out of his place* (v. 3, indicating the Temple), in an awesome theophany that will shake the foundations of the earth.

1:8-9. Lament of the prophet. As a sign of mourning, the prophet will *go barefoot and naked* (v. 8) to presage the shameful condition of capture and deportation (cf. Isa 20:3). Verse 9 probably refers to the Assyrian presence in Judah in the late eighth century B.C.E.

1:10-16. Roll-call of cities facing destruction. This is one of the most difficult passages in the book to comprehend. Most scholars think the town names are part of a word play. For example, in v. 10 the word, *dust* (עָפָר) is clearly a play on the place name, *Beth-leaphrah* (בֵּית לְעַפְרָה). However, since such a pun does not exist in every case, scholars must amend the MT to make the theory work. The most certain proposal for the passage is that the cities listed were in danger of Assyrian invasion, or perhaps had already been decimated by SENNACHERIB (701 B.C.E.), when the ORACLE was spoken. The mention of baldness (v. 16) refers to a rite of mourning that was practiced on the occasion of military defeat.

Crimes and Punishment of Israel's Leaders, 2:1–3:12

2:1-5. Seizure of land and its consequences. This first specific indictment addresses wealthy landowners who, probably through foreclosure on loans, obtain the property of less powerful individuals. Such action is repugnant for two reasons. First, those implicated seized the estates of others because they coveted them (v. 2), in violation of the tenth commandment (Exod 20:17a, b). Second, in ancient Israel ownership of land determined identity and the benefits of citizenship. Thus, the loss of property stripped an individual of dignity and social standing. During the eighth century B.C.E. an ever-widening gap between rich and poor highlighted the results of this practice. For such greed and disobedience, these land owners will lose the *fields* (vv. 2, 4) they took. Verse 4 probably refers to a postexilic redistribution of land from which these profiteers would be excluded.

2:6-11. False preaching and false prosperity. This unit reveals much about the reception of Micah's proclamation. Like Amos (7:12-13), Micah is told, *do not preach* (v. 6). The ensuing message of doom angered Judah's authorities because it was an affront to their theology and social position. They could not conceive of their nation's being destroyed, nor could they accept the charge that their activity was unacceptable to YHWH. However, Micah identified these opponents with the perpetrators of injustice in 2:1-5. They were capitalists (to employ a modern term) who dispossessed women and children in order to build their own estates (Mays 1983, 9). The victims are defended and described as the *peaceful, . . . those who pass by trustingly,* and those who do not consider war (v. 8). These terms portray people who are innocent, rely upon

YHWH, and have no power to oppress others. Micah's opponents, on the other hand, are not upright (v. 7).

2:12-13. Gathering and deportation. Most scholars read this passage as a hopeful promise of return from dispersion (like 4:6-7). However, it is difficult to accept such an idea when the unit sits in the midst of overt declarations of punishment. One solution is to read these verses as an oracle of doom. The ambiguity of v. 13 makes such a reading viable. Indeed, breaking through a gate probably should be understood as a negative action. Thus, the fact that YHWH breaches the entrance to the sheepfold (a metaphor for city) may mean that YHWH will lead an invading army to take Judah away into exile (Mays 1976, 73–76).

3:1-4. The abuse of power and the LORD's reaction. The imperative, *listen* (v. 1), harks back to the court setting at the beginning of the book (1:2). Here, however, the command is addressed to the defendants, not the witnesses in the case. *Heads of Jacob and rulers of the house of Israel* (v. 1) are synonymous expressions that Micah uses to describe the Jerusalem officials responsible for establishing justice (see 3:9). The prophet argues they are committed to their own avaricious desire for gain more than to the founding of an equitable society. The graphic image of cannibalism communicates the offensive nature of their feeding off the people entrusted to their care (cf. Hos 4:8).

3:5-8. Prostitution of the prophetic office. Continuing the catalogue of sins of Israel's leaders, Micah's attention shifts to the prophets, the ones responsible for relaying the word of YHWH to the people. The official prophets of Jerusalem prophesy solely for monetary reward. They speak favorably for those who pay for their services; they *declare war* (v. 5) on those who refuse, that is, they show hostility (see 2:8). Therefore, the LORD will remove all revelation from these false seers. In contrast to their unfaithfulness, Micah declares his message to be truly the word of YHWH, untainted by bribes and physical rewards (v. 8).

3:9-12. Summary indictment of leaders. In this decisive passage of the first section of the book, the expression *hear this* (v. 9) signals a concluding oracle of judgment (see 1:2; 3:1). The imperative is a sweeping address to all of Israel's leaders: rulers, chiefs, priests, and prophets. All of the groups are charged again with perverting their professions, bringing injustice upon God's people. To assure themselves, they declare, *Surely the Lord is with us* (v. 11), as if to anticipate Micah's prediction of destruction for Jerusalem. Their belief in Zion's impregnability is understandable. Jerusa-

lem was thought to be a place of supreme beauty (Ps 48:2 [MT 48:3]), a city founded by YHWH (Ps 87:1-3 [MT 87:1-2]), a place YHWH protected as a warrior king (Pss 46, 48). Yet, the corruption of Israel's ruling classes would bring YHWH's wrath; a conquering army would devastate the capital (v. 12). Undoubtedly Micah thought of Assyria as the conqueror; thus, this prediction did not come to pass. However, a later tradition (Jer 26:16-19) indicates that the city was spared because of the repentance of HEZEKIAH. The prediction later materialized in 587 B.C.E. when the Babylonians defeated and destroyed the city.

Superiority of Reconstructed Zion, 4:1–5:6 (MT 4:1–5:5)

4:1-5. Zion as a center of world government and peace. This unit is the beginning of a larger section emphasizing the restoration of Zion (4:2, 7, 8, 10, 11, 13). The placement of this passage after 3:9-12 apparently is intended to show the failure of Israel's rulers, and consequently the downfall of the city they established with bloodshed. Micah 4:1-5 indicates that the city will prosper in a time to come, dominated by YHWH's just rule. As Mays states, "the promise of peace is founded on a prior promise that the reign of YHWH shall become the center of order for all peoples" (Mays 1976, 93). Indeed, *in days to come* (v. 1) when Zion is governed by YHWH's *instruction* (v. 2, תּוֹרָה), this city shall be the place where all nations will find peace and security. Such a glorious vision is hard to image within history as we know it. Yet the text indicates no knowledge of a period outside the temporal historical realm. Many interpreters concede, however, that 4:1-5 can only occur when the limits of the present time are transcended.

4:6-7. Renewed life under YHWH's kingship. The opening words, *in that day* (v. 6), connect this unit to 4:1-5. Logically, this section follows the more general prediction of Zion's recovery, adding the specific promise that the people of Israel will return from dispersion. The promise is not for renewed political strength in the traditional sense. Rather, the sole characteristic of these people is that they live under the kingship of YHWH.

4:8. The new Zion, a royal capital. Here the prophet portrays Zion as a secure dwelling for the *flock* of YHWH. The term *tower* (מִגְדַּל), refers to part of the defensive structure of a city wall. Also, *hill* (עֹפֶל) is associated with a place of lookout (see Isa 32:14). This city, which houses the remnant, the prophet proclaims, shall regain royal power and standing. The nature of the renewed kingdom, however, is unclear.

4:9–5:6 [MT 4:9–5:5]. The birth pangs of Zion. This conclusion of the *Zion* section (4:1–5:6 [MT 4:1–5:5]) features three units united by the introductory *now*. Each of these sayings describes a present, threatening situation followed by a promise of rescue by YHWH. The first set of verses (vv. 9-10) likens Zion's troubles to the travail of a woman whose labor pains (a metaphor for the Babylonian exile) will soon end. The second unit (vv. 11-13) gives a kind of theology of military and political world events, similar to Isaiah (e.g., Isa 19:16-17). Specifically, Micah assures the people of Zion that YHWH has a plan for the eventual destruction of the nations that currently are destroying their land. The final *now* saying (5:1-6 [MT 4:14–5:5]) promises a ruler, following the model of David, who will lead Israel to peace. The statement, *when she who is in labor has brought forth* (5:3 [MT 5:2]) is probably another metaphor for the groaning of exile (see 4:9-10). After the return from Babylon, the "new David" (the fruit of the exile?) will defend Israel from *Assyria* (v. 6), perhaps a generic symbol for any foe from the north (cf. Ezra 6:22). The third person singular verb in MT, *rescue* (v. 6, הִצִּיל), probably refers to the action of the ruler from Bethlehem.

The Faithful Remnant, 5:7-15 (MT 5:6-14)

5:7-9 [MT 5:6-8]. Dependence upon YHWH. The comparison of Israel to *dew* and *showers* is a promise that the remnant will be characterized by its dependence on YHWH (v. 7). Because they *wait* for YHWH (that is, "trust in" or "depend on"), the Israelites will be empowered to dominate the surrounding nations (vv. 8-9).

5:10-15 [MT 5:9-14]). Purification of Israel's relationship to YHWH. The final saying of the first section of the book describes an eschatological event in which YHWH will remove all objects that garner Israel's trust and devotion. YHWH insisted that his people not rely upon military might (e.g., Ps 44:6). Also, Israel was prohibited from setting up any image of the deity (Exod 20:4).

YHWH's Controversy with His People, 6:1–7:20

Requirements of Covenant Loyalty, 6:1-8

Like Mic 1:2, the opening of the book's second section introduces a court case between YHWH and his people with the imperative, *hear* (v. 1). In this section the prophet broaches the problem of covenant faithfulness. YHWH addresses the rebellious Israelites (v. 3) with a reminder of several key events in their foundational story (vv. 4-5). The effect is a heightened sense of YHWH's steadfastness to the covenant agreement with Israel. Following this summary, a representative of the people proposes increasingly drastic ritual acts meant to assuage their guilt and reestablish proper relationship with God (vv. 6-7). The list begins with common burnt offerings but extends to the more unusual act of child sacrifice. This catalogue of ritual acts prepares for the prophetic voice of v. 8, *what does the Lord require of you but to do justice, and to love kindness, and to walk humbly with your God?* Herein lies the key to covenant faithfulness (cf. Ps 50; Amos 5:24; Hos 2:19-20; 6:6; Isa 7:9; 30:15). The call for justice connects well with Micah's criticism of Israel's leaders (see 3:9-11).

Jerusalem's Sins and YHWH's Intolerance, 6:9-16

YHWH again (see 6:1) opens a controversy, this time against *the city* of Jerusalem (v. 9). The capital's inhabitants are guilty of dishonest business practices, a failure to *do justice* (6:8), and following the example of the dynasty of King OMRI in IDOLATRY (2 Kgs 10:18; 21:3). Therefore, YHWH declares, the city will be destroyed. This prediction is roughly parallel to 3:9-12 in the first major section of the book.

Despair over Ubiquitous Evil, 7:1-6

The speaker of 7:1-6 may be the city of Jerusalem personified. Like chaps. 2–3 this unit exposes the profligate leaders of Judah (vv. 3-4). Unfaithfulness runs so deep that not even the closest friend, relative, or spouse can be trusted.

Confession and Assurance of Pardon, 7:7-20

The Book of Micah ends with a liturgical piece that sums up many of the major themes of the whole work. Verse 7 responds to the widespread unrighteousness in the land (7:1-6) with a resolve to *wait for the God of my salvation* (v. 7). In form the verse is similar to so-called "psalms of confidence" (cf. Ps 52:8-9 [MT 52:10-11]); thematically, the line is related to Micah's description of the righteous remnant in 5:7. Verses 8-10 treat the threat to Zion or to God's people posed by enemies, a major concern of the book (1:15-16; 3:12; 4:10, 11-13; 5:5-6). The speaker recognizes the sins of the nation (v. 9) and their consequences; however, he or she also looks forward to a time when YHWH's wrath will abate and Israel's enemies will be punished (cf. 4:5–5:6 [MT 4:5–5:5]). This hope takes on more specificity in vv. 11-13. Here the address to Jerusalem looks forward to NEHEMIAH's rebuilding of the city (445–433 B.C.E.). Continuing the concern for vindication among the nations, vv. 14-17 call on YHWH to *shepherd* the people while putting the nations to shame. The shepherd image in the ancient Near East is a royal metaphor; thus, these verses request YHWH to lead Israel as king (cf. 4:7). Finally, the book closes with an assurance of pardon from YHWH (7:18-20). Thus, Micah opened with a portrait of YHWH's anger being displayed in theophany and now concludes with the assertion that he *will cast all our sins into the depths of the sea* (v. 19).

Works Cited

Mays, James L. 1983. "Justice: Perspectives from the Prophetic Tradition," *Int* 37/1:5–17. 1976. *Micah*. OTL.

Nahum

William P. Steeger

Introduction

Midway into the last half of the seventh-century B.C.E., the PROPHET Nahum raised his hymns of Yahweh's greatness and thundered his taunts over Nineveh's fall. ASSYRIA's cruelty and power had swept through the ancient Near East oblivious of the legacy of God's love and call to repentance left by the prophet JONAH a century and a half before (see 2 Kgs 14:25). His messages, often couched in outstanding POETRY, proclaimed doom to Assyria's capital, hope to struggling Judah, and promised restoration to outcast ISRAEL. Nahum's intricate weaving of the threads of Yahweh's love amidst the awesome tapestry of his wrath, provided assurance to the faithful that Yahweh is sovereign of history.

Nahum's prophecy is the seventh in the "Book of the Twelve," or minor prophets, coming just before HABAKKUK. Although following Jonah in the LXX, Nahum comes after MICAH in the MT. The ministry of Nahum probably is much broader than the handful of poetic oracles preserved in this book might suggest. Although the heart of his message focuses on the sure destruction of Nineveh and the justice of Yahweh that will not let sin go unpunished, Nahum knows of the coming restoration of all Israel, the follies of IDOLATRY and immorality, and the importance of social responsibility. He is not simply a partisan prophet blasting a world super power. Nahum's message encompasses the very character of Yahweh. God's justice and judgment are applied in a universal fairness. No nation is exempt from God's standards of righteousness. Like the prophets before him (cf. Amos 1–2), Nahum proclaims Yahweh's judgment and vindication upon foreign powers.

Authorship

This prophecy presents the message of Nahum, mentioned only here in 1:1 (the Nahum listed in Luke 3:25 most certainly refers to another individual by the same name in the ancestry of Jesus). Although the name is found in nonbiblical sources, little is known about this prophet. Nahum means "comforted," or "consoled," and is possibly a shortened version of the common biblical name NEHEMIAH. He is called the Elkoshite, although the exact location of *Elkosh* is unknown. Some have suggested a location on the TIGRIS (modern Elkush), or in GALILEE (ancient CAPERNAUM, i.e., "village of Nahum," a frequent proposal), or one of three sites in JUDAH. Current scholarship favors one of the southern locations, since by the time of the composition of Nahum the northern Kingdom was already in exile. However, the specific mention of *the LORD is restoring the majesty of Jacob, as well as the majesty of Israel* (2:2) lends credence to a possible Galilean site. Nahum's general familiarity with Nineveh conforms to the common knowledge of his day and does not require the manufacture of theories that place his family in exile in Assyria prior to his proposed return to Judah.

Date

Although no exact date is given in the superscription, internal evidence provides a framework within the mid-seventh century B.C.E. Mention of the fall of the Egyptian city of *Thebes* (663 B.C.E.) in 3:8 and the anticipation of the destruction of Nineveh (612 B.C.E.) provide terminal points of reference. Those suggesting a date after the fall of Nineveh usually understand the prophecy as a cultic liturgy. For the most part, contemporary scholarship has not accepted this view. The prophet's constant assurance of Nineveh's coming destruction, in order to calm the fears of an oppressed Judah, seems highly unlikely after the fall of Nineveh. Nahum's discussion of the prowess and strength of Assyria mandates a time prior to the death of Assyria's greatest king, ASSHURBANAPAL (668–627 B.C.E.). Assyria declined rapidly following his death. Silence regarding the growing menace of Babylon (rebelling against Assyria around 625 B.C.E.) further strengthens this dating. During the reign of MANASSEH (667/6–673 B.C.E.) Judah felt the heaviest Assyrian hand. Under JOSIAH's rule (640–609 B.C.E.) Judah experienced some relief from Assyrian oppression. The resurgence of Thebes in the last quarter of the seventh-century would make the illustration of 3:8 weak and meaningless if the prophecy is dated to that period. A date in the third quarter of the seventh-century seems most likely.

Literary Form

The superscription (1:1) calls the prophecy an *oracle* (lit. "burden," as in KJV). Although not always associated with judgment, as here in Nahum, the ORACLE form is well known in prophetic writing. Nahum uses an abundance of literary devices and forms. The rhetorical question is common throughout his prophecy. Rich metaphors and similes, drawn from nature and history, appear in each dramatic poem and punctuate all the prose. The opening hymn of praise flows quickly into a courtroom scene where alternating decrees of judgment and acquittal are pronounced upon Nineveh and Judah. The second chapter invites the reader to smell the smoke and see the flames in the vivid descriptions of battle and the terrifying pictures of a city under siege. Irony brackets the limping meter of lament in the dramatic funeral dirge that sweeps the prophecy to a dynamic conclusion in chap. 3.

Most scholarly attention has focused on the puzzling form of the opening hymn. The presence and extent of a purported alphabetic acrostic is the issue. Such acrostic poems are well known in scripture (cf. Pss 111; 112; 119; Lam 1; 2; 3; 4). Since the last century, many suggested that 1:2-8 forms such an acrostic, although only about half of the full alphabet is recognizable. Elaborate reconstruction of the text is necessary to identify a complete alphabetic acrostic (all without manuscript evidence) and efforts to present the first half of the alphabet (*aleph* through *kaph*) require textual emendations in at least four of the eleven lines of this poem (some critics continue the acrostic through *mem*; see below.) While many contemporary scholars argue for an acrostic structure, the fact remains that the poem as presented in the MT is completely comprehensible and the possible acrostic form was not suspected until late in the last century. The function, form, and extent of such an acrostic fragment will be debated for years to come.

For Further Study

In the *Mercer Dictionary of the Bible*: ASSYRIA; JONAH, BOOK OF; LORD OF HOSTS; NAHUM; NAHUM, BOOK OF; ORACLE; POETRY; PROPHET.

In other sources: D. W. Baker, *Nahum, Habakkuk, Zephaniah*, TOTC; E. R. Daglish, "Nahum," BBC; R. D. Patterson, *Nahum, Habakkuk, Zephaniah*, WEC; J. J. M. Roberts, *Nahum, Habakkuk, and Zephaniah*, OTL; R. L. Smith, *Micah–Malachi*, WBC.

Commentary

An Outline

Superscription, 1:1
I. A Hymn to the Sovereign Lord, 1:2-15 [MT 1:2–2:1]
   A. Lord of Wrath and Love: General, 1:2-8
   B. Lord of Wrath and Love:
      Specific, 1:9-15 [MT 1:9–2:1]
II. An Oracle of Nineveh's Fall Assured,
   2:1-13 [MT 2:2-14]
   A. A Call to Arms, 2:1-2 [MT 2:2-3]
   B. Nineveh's Siege Described, 2:3-5 [MT 2:4-6]
   C. Nineveh's People Displaced, 2:6-9 [MT 2:7-10]
   D. Nineveh's Greatness Destroyed,
      2:10-13 [MT 2:11-14]
III. A Taunt Song on Nineveh's Fall Secured, 3:1-19
   A. Nineveh: City of Bloodshed, 3:1-7
   B. Nineveh: Like All the Nations, 3:8-15
   C. Nineveh: Mortally Wounded, 3:16-19

Superscription, 1:1

The superscription explains the formal nature of Nahum's message as an *oracle* (lit. "burden" as in KJV) and is a common expression for God's revelation to the prophets. The term calls attention to the serious nature of the message and often describes a note of impending judgment (note, e.g., the play upon the word "oracle" in Jer 23:33-38.) The word *book* does not preclude an oral delivery of these sermons but does call attention to the written form they soon assumed. The term *vision* also is frequent in prophetic literature (Hab 1:1; Amos 1:1; Mic 1:1; Obad 1:1) and emphasizes the dynamic impact of God's message upon the prophet. Nahum's vivid language paints graphic pictures of Nineveh's fall, giving full meaning to the visual theme developed throughout the book.

For the meaning of *Nahum of Elkosh* see the introduction above.

A Hymn to the Sovereign Lord, 1:2-15 [MT 1:2–2:1]

Lord of Wrath and Love: General, 1:2-8

This majestic poem describes Yahweh in alternating pictures of wrath and love. Like the two sides of a coin, both are needed to describe divine nature. Some modern scholarship finds portions of an alphabetic acrostic in vv. 2- 8 (others include v. 9, see below). The poem does not mention Nineveh by name, causing some commentators to suggest that Nahum has selected a previously prepared poem for the introduction of his book. Details, however, in the actual wording of the hymn (see v. 8) may focus on the doomed city. Adopting an acrostic structure for this hymn necessitates a forced and fragmented use of the present text. The awesome sovereignty of Yahweh unfolds as follows:

א: *A jealous and avenging God is the LORD* (v. 2);

ב: *His way is in the whirlwind and storm* (v. 3b);

ג: *He rebukes the sea and makes it dry* (v. 4);

(ד: is missing);

ה: *The mountains quake before him,*
    and the hills melt; (v. 5a);

ו: *the earth heaves before him* (v. 5b);

ז: *Who can stand before his indignation?* (v. 6a);

ח: *His wrath is poured out like fire* (v. 6b);

ט: *The LORD is good* (v. 7a);

י: *he protects those who take refuge in him* (v. 7b);

כ: *He will make a full end of his adversaries* (v. 8).

Making v. 9 a part of the acrostic requires reversing the present order of the lines. The vision of Yahweh's majesty as evidenced in nature is a familiar theme (cf. Pss 18; 29; Hab 3) and often associated with the salvation history passages of the OT.

1:2. God of vengeance. The opening lines of the poem declare Yahweh's jealous and avenging nature. Alliteration in the Hebrew text and the stair-step repetition of key related words (*jealous, avenging, vengeance*) heighten the forcefulness of the message. Calling attention to *jealous* emphasizes God's serious dealings with sin. The terms *vengeance* and *avenging* reflect a Hebrew verbal root that is basic to biblical theology, appearing seventy times in the OT. Divine vengeance is set in the context of God's MERCY and must be understood in light of JUSTICE and HOLINESS. Both the OT and the NT balance God's wrath against sin

with divine mercy and redemption from sin. Wrath is necessary for mercy to be meaningful. Vengeance is under God's control alone (Lev 19:18; Deut 32:35-41). The day of the Lord's vengeance is an important theme in other prophets (Isa 38:8; 61:2; 63:1-6). This hymn shows the balance in God's nature by noting that *The LORD is slow to anger* (1:3), and *The LORD is good, a stronghold in a day of trouble; he protects those who take refuge in him* (1:7).

1:3-6. God of patience and power. The majestic power of God is evidenced in nature (vv. 3b-6). References in v. 4 to God's drying the sea and the rivers point to the mighty acts of God in Israel's redemptive history (cf. Pss 18:7-19; 106:9; 114; Isa 50:2; Hab 3:8). *Bashan, Carmel,* and *Lebanon* (v. 4) were known as exceptionally fertile territories. Many see these references and those to *the mountains* (v. 5) as challenges to Canaanite mythology. Yahweh, not BAAL or any foreign god, controls the forces of nature and moves them toward divine ends. From this vivid picture of *whirlwind, storm,* earthquake, and drought (vv. 3-5), Nahum assures Judah that Yahweh is sovereign over nature and history.

1:7-8. God of goodness and justice. Following the penetrating questions of 1:6, the surety of God's coming wrath is pronounced. Yet in the midst of this vision of vengeance, God reaches out to embrace and protect the people *who take refuge in him* (v. 7). The goodness of God is one of the most common OT themes. This great promise has brought hope and comfort to countless of God's people living in a violent and oppressive world. The arrangement of the words of the text is debated but the meaning of the passage is clear. The awful fate of the enemy is contrasted to the protection and refuge afforded *those who take refuge in him.* Nahum's hymn echoes the themes of Ps 46. God's justice is certain. No evil can outrun divine vengeance. The slowness of God's anger (v. 3) is no indication of the speed and certainty of holy wrath (v. 8). Some commentators see in the opening line of v. 8 a reference to the actual fall of Nineveh, which was accompanied by a flooding of the Tigris.

Lord of Wrath and Love: Specific, 1:9-15 [MT 1:9–2:1]

The hymn now turns from the general proclamation of God's wrath and love to the specific verdict given in a formal legal suit. The prophet alternates pronouncements of judgment and salvation upon Assyria and Judah, respectively.

1:9-11. Judgment against Nineveh. Nineveh's foolish plots against the LORD will bring certain destruction. There will be no recovery from this fall. Indeed, following Nineveh's fall in 612 B.C.E., a small remnant, under the leadership of Asshur-uballit II, fled to HARAN and established a capital. There they were finally overrun in 609 B.C.E. Assyria was gone from the pages of history. Nahum questions Nineveh directly (v. 9): *Why do you plot against the LORD?* Some include this verse in the proposed acrostic (see introduction above). The total destruction pictured in v. 10 is clear, although the passage is difficult and provides a variety of scholarly opinion. Many evil kings have gone out from Nineveh over the years (the *you* of v. 11 should be understood collectively).

1:12-13. Comfort to Judah. Beginning with the familiar prophetic cry of authority, Nahum proclaims comfort to Judah in the destruction of Assyria (v. 12a) and the promise of relief from his judgment (v. 12b). Like the prophet ISAIAH, Nahum understands the oppression of Judah by Assyria as God's judgment upon the people (Isa 10:5). The promises of relief and release are certain (v. 13).

1:14. Judgment against Nineveh. Once again the prophet addresses Nineveh directly, proclaiming their sure and permanent defeat (see above 1:9-11). In the mindset of the ancient Near East, the power of a nation's gods determined the power of a nation. Yahweh declares the gods and nation of Assyria defeated and worthless.

1:15 [MT 2:1]. Call to rejoicing. The familiar ring of this messianic cry of good news (cf. Isa 52:7) is a fitting conclusion to Nahum's hymn in praise of God's majesty. News of the destruction of Nineveh and the collapse of the Assyrian Empire will be welcome words of *peace* to Judah. Nahum uses such a time of rejoicing to admonish God's people to religious faithfulness (*fulfill your vows*) and offer assurance of Nineveh's permanent defeat.

An Oracle of Nineveh's Fall Assured, 2:1-13 [MT 2:2-14]

The poems that conclude the Book of Nahum are vivid descriptions of battle and detailed explanations of defeat. Although some claim that the name of God is not mentioned in the poems, *the LORD* is clearly in view in Israel's restoration (v. 2:2) and the *LORD of hosts* (v. 13; 3:5) is the subject of the frequent use of the first person pronoun that follows. The English translation and MT are one verse out of line throughout

chap. 2 (see above on 1:15). The vivid description of battle does not necessitate a date after 612 B.C.E. since battle scenes were a part of Judah's national experience.

A Call to Arms, 2:1-2 [MT 2:2-3]

This passage forms a transition to the battle scene that follows. As in the preceding verses, Nahum first addresses Assyria and then Judah. In biting satire he charges Nineveh to prepare for battle. The *shatterer* (v. 1; lit. "attacker," or "scatterer") has come and no preparation can stay the flood of Yahweh's wrath even if they *collect all [their] strength*. Although Medes, Babylonians, and Scythians compose the besieging army, it is Yahweh, the LORD OF HOSTS, who has come up against Nineveh. Just as God's actions assure the defeat of Assyria (v. 1), they also secure the restoration of Israel (v. 2). A reunited Israel is in view. Judah has been the focus of the preceding verses of comfort and hope, but here the scattered Northern Kingdom (with its many *ruined . . . branches* is the subject. The vine is a well known OT picture of Israel (cf. Isa 5:1-7). The restoration of a united Israel is a frequent prophetic theme (cf. Ezek 37:15-23; Amos 9:11; Zech 10:6-12).

Nineveh's Siege Described, 2:3-5 [MT 2:4-6]

The three stanzas of this poem of Nineveh's defeat (vv. 3-5; 6-9; 10-13) form one of the classic descriptions of battle. Each phrase succinctly captures the full flavor of the city's siege. The *red* (v. 3) may refer to the splendor of the uniform of the Medes (as reported by Xenophon) and the colorful array of the Babylonian army (cf. Ezek 23:14-15). The bright metal fittings of the racing chariots flash in the sunlight. The NRSV reads *the chargers prance* (v. 3), but there is no need to emend the text. The Hebrew "the cypresses are made to quiver" can easily be understood as spears or other instruments of war made from wood. As the battle intensifies the chariots race through the streets of Nineveh (v. 4) and officers stumble through the confusion as they seek to man the weakening wall (v. 5). The term *mantelet* (Heb. "protector") probably refers to the temporary covering of shields raised by the besieging soldiers at the foot of the city wall.

Nineveh's People Displaced, 2:6-9 [MT 2:7-10]

In one profoundly simple verse the fall of the great city is etched permanently into world history (v. 6). Descriptions of the dislocation of people and the plundering of property consume the remainder of the stanza. The *river gates* (v. 6) may be a figurative expression for the invading armies. The suggestion that the fall of Nineveh was aided by the flooding Tigris overflowing the adjoining canals and crumbling the city's defenses, causing the palace to tremble (lit. "melt"), is tempting. The nonbiblical supporting evidence (the Babylonian Chronicle) is deficient at this point. As Assyria has treated its captives, so its cruelty returns upon its own head. The population is enslaved and deported (v. 7). The phrase *it is decreed* (v. 7) is an attempt to translate an uncertain Hebrew expression (*huzzab*). Some suggest that the term is a symbolic name for the city, or is related to a deity (in which case the last phrase may refer to the deity's female slaves being taken captive). The city is clearly identified in the midst of this poem as Nineveh. The mighty army of Assyria (here compared to *a pool* of water no longer held back by secure banks) is routed. Even the command to *Halt!* (v. 8) can not cause its fleeing soldiers to return and protect the city's treasures from the spoilers. Centuries of looting and tribute-taking made Nineveh a wealthy storehouse of the ancient Near East. *There is no end of treasure! An abundance of every precious thing!* (v. 9).

Nineveh's Greatness Destroyed, 2:10-13 [MT 2:11-14]

As the previous stanza began with a profoundly simple statement of Nineveh's fall, so this stanza begins with a simple word play. David Baker observes, "The progressive stages of intensifying dereliction are indicated by three Hebrew words, each adding one syllable to the preceding word, i.e., *buqa, mebuqa, mebullaqa*" (1988, 35). This stanza is known as the taunt proper. Following the initial cry of devastation, the stunned survivors stand trembling as the looted city crumbles around them (v. 10). A lions' den is the closing metaphor of this taunt and *What became of the lions' den . . . ?* (v. 11) is the startling reality of Nineveh's plight. Centuries of plunder and bringing home the spoil have proved fruitless. The Assyrian lion is defeated and devastated. The taunt is brought to a formal conclusion with the powerful pronouncement of Yahweh, *See, I am against you, says the Lord of hosts* (v. 13). Although some see this passage as transitional, it is climactic. God calls attention to the divine nature (lit. "behold me"). The focus is *the LORD of hosts*. With this declaration, Nahum pulls the varying threads of his poem to a grand conclusion and

unites the picture of the battle's fury with the metaphor of the lions' den.

A Taunt Song on Nineveh's Fall Secured, 3:1-19

This final poem (possibly a collection of poems) represents the finest of Israel's battle songs. The short crisp phrases press home each vivid picture. The speed of conquest and the depth of sin are graphically portrayed. Nahum explains the reasons for Nineveh's fall. As it lived by the sword so it will die by the sword (cf. Matt 26:52b). This taunt song follows the classic prophetic form of a woe oracle found frequently in the OT (cf. Isa 5:8-15; 10:1-4; Hab 2:6-20; Zeph 3:1-8).

The NRSV is not consistent in translating the Heb. הוֹי. The Hebrew word for "woe" is אוֹי; הוֹי is rightly translated by several terms, chiefly "Ah!," "Alas!," etc. The first word of v. 1 translated *Ah!* is the same as those found in Hab 2:6, 9, 12, 15, and 19 translated "Alas," and is a key to the proper recognition and understanding of this literary form.

Nineveh: City of Bloodshed, 3:1-7

The term *Ah!* or "woe" is a powerful expression of pending doom found in formal laments for the dead. The lament (*qina*) meter is used here, adding to the heightened tension and gloom. *Bloodshed, deceit, booty,* and *plunder* (v. 1) beautifully describe the foundations of Assyrian society. Built upon the spoils of conquest and fed by the fuel of tribute and plunder, Nineveh is aptly described. The rapid staccato expressions of vv. 3-4 paint pictures of battle reminiscent of the poem above (2:3-10 [MT 2:4-11]). From the initial charge (as the *crack of the whip* is heard) to the agony of defeat (as the *piles of dead, heaps of corpses, dead bodies without end* are stumbled over), Nahum's poem outlines the conquest. Reasons for Nineveh's fall are enumerated in a metaphor of a greedy harlot who *enslaves nations through her debaucheries* (v. 4). The harlot metaphor is well known in prophetic literature of both testaments (cf. Isa 1:21; 23:16; Ezek 16; 23; Hos 5:4; Rev 17–18).

The stanza races to a climax in v. 5, where *the LORD of hosts* declares: *I am against you*. The humiliation pronounced upon Nineveh is reminiscent of other prophetic judgments (cf. Isa 47:3; Jer 13:22; Ezek 16:37-39; Hos 2:3, 9; Amos 4:2-3; Mic 1:11). Made a spectacle to the nations, Nineveh will be pelted with *filth* and treated *with contempt* (v. 6). There will be no one to mourn its passing or comfort the grieving exiles. Once again the city is mentioned by name (v. 7, as in 2:8).

Nineveh: Like All the Nations, 3:8-15

Nineveh is no less vulnerable than the surrounding nations. In a biting reminder, Nahum recalls the fall of mighty *Thebes* (Heb. *No-amon*). This ancient city spread majestically on both sides of the NILE and boasted grand temples, courts, and imperial luxury. The impressive temple ruins of Luxor and Karnak are ample testimony to the greatness and grandeur of Thebes. Protected by the Nile and its canals, strengthened by alliances with Ethiopia, Put and Libya, Thebes still was not secure. Shall Nineveh fare better? Certainly not! In another of Nahum's rhetorical questions, Assyria is humiliated again (vv. 8-9). The same afflictions Assyria hurled upon Thebes would return to haunt Nineveh: exile, captivity, infanticide, slavery, and chains (v. 10). The vivid list reads like Assyria's own conquering cruelties. Just as Thebes fell to the onslaught of ASSHURBANAPAL in 663 B.C.E. (see introduction), so also Nineveh was doomed.

As the battle rages, Nineveh's mighty defenders will appear *drunken* and run into *hiding* (v. 11), but no refuge will be found (the only refuge is in *the LORD*, 1:7). The ring of fortresses surrounding the city will be useless. Like a fig tree laden with ripe fruit, a mere shaking will bring them all down into the mouth of the enemy (v. 12). The demoralized troops are like *women in your midst* and the battered defenses stand as open gates to the invading armies (v. 13). In harsh satire Nahum calls once again for the majestic city to prepare for war (v. 14; cf. 2:1). The irony is evident. *Draw water for the siege*, he cries, but the flooding waters of the Tigris aided Nineveh's demise. *Strengthen your forts*, he urges, but the surrounding fortresses fell like ripened figs. *Trample the clay, tread the mortar, take hold of the brick mold!* he pleads, but the defenses are already breached (v. 14). The *fire* and *sword* are coming. Like a plague of locusts settling on a field of green and leaving it brown and barren, nothing will remain of Nineveh. Nahum makes one final call to arms: *Multiply yourselves like the locust* (v. 15). Not even superior numbers can avert Assyria's coming disaster.

Nineveh: Mortally Wounded, 3:16-19

Nahum's final stanza ridicules the fickle Assyrian merchants, the self-serving military, the opportunist scribes, the slumbering rulers, the complacent nobility, and the destitute masses. The *merchants* had grown more numerous than *the stars of the heavens* and are known in some detail from the trade records of the ancient Near East. These businessmen are fair-weather friends, swarming on Nineveh like locusts to enjoy the treasures sparkling in the summer sun. However, they soon shed their skin and fly away to greener pastures (v. 16). The military (*guards*) and *scribes* are like grasshoppers and locusts who huddle together for common warmth on a cold day but quickly fly away when the sun comes up (v. 17). The scribes may have served a special function associated with Assyrian military recruitment practices.

Nahum addresses the king of Assyria directly in his final condemning charge. The term *shepherds* often serves as a metaphor for leaders in the OT (cf. Jer 17:16; Ezek 34; Zech 10:2-3). The Assyrian king is advised that his leaders and *nobles* are sleeping on the job, oblivious of the precarious condition of the sheep (citizens) *scattered on the mountains* (v. 18). The *people* are deserted: without economic support, protection, leadership, or example. Assyria's wound is fatal! There is no cure for its hurt. Instead of expected sympathy, comfort, or mourning, comes only the clapping of hands and rejoicing at Nineveh's helpless estate. The empire's *endless cruelty* showed mercy to none (v. 19). In return, Nineveh's passing will be a time of celebration.

Within a generation Assyria was gone from the pages of history. Nahum's prophecy was complete. For Judah the moment is not a time of gloating but a time of recognizing God's vindication of evil. Sin is punished. With the closing phrases comes a reminder for Judah to heed a similar warning. Scarcely half a century beyond Nahum's taunt, Judah too would hear the sobering message of God through Ezekiel: "prophesy against the shepherds of Israel" (Ezek 34:2ff.). God's justice is sure. Each nation and individual is measured against no earthly standard but called to conform to God's righteousness alone and to find *refuge in him* (1:7).

Work Cited

Baker, David W. 1988. *Nahum, Habakkuk, Zephaniah: An Introduction and Commentary*.

Habakkuk

William P. Steeger

Introduction

Habakkuk's prophecy stands unique among the prophetic books called the Minor Prophets or the Book of the Twelve and is as relevant today as it was in the crisis period of the late sixth century B.C.E. Where other prophets focused on the LORD's word to ISRAEL, HABAKKUK carried the burden of the oppressed of his people to the LORD. The autobiographical style provides a fresh and forceful approach. The PROPHET delivered his burden to the people of Judah in an unusual format. He shared the doubts and questionings of his heart and reported the response these met from the LORD. This theodicy, i.e., a questioning of God's justice and actions, begins with Habakkuk's prayers. The prophet decried the injustice rampant in Judah and questioned God's apparent lack of concern for the innocent. After Habakkuk's three queries, God challenges this limited view of history and divine sovereignty. He declares that the wicked will meet an appropriate end but the righteous live by trusting in God's control of history and waiting for the completion of his ultimate purposes. The prophet evaluates the LORD's ORACLE that *the righteous live by their faith* (2:4), and concludes with a vision of Yahweh's sovereign majesty as he marches to deliver his people throughout history.

Authorship

Few scholars still challenge the traditional authorship of Habakkuk, although little is known of the prophet apart from this book. Conjecture regarding the meaning of his name ranges from an Assyrian word for a plant to Luther's suggestion of "embrace" (based on 2 Kgs 4:16). The liturgical references surrounding the concluding hymn of the prophecy (3:1, 19) suggest that Habakkuk served in the Temple or was from a priestly family. The apocryphal book BEL AND THE DRAGON reports his ministry to DANIEL.

Date

The exact date of the prophecy depends upon internal critical judgments: (1) the problem of structure and unity of the book, (2) the canonical form of the prophecy, (3) various social and political issues, (4) and textual evidence (including the DEAD SEA SCROLLS). Suggestions for dating this prophecy range from the eighth through the second century B.C.E. Contemporary scholarship favors the late sixth century B.C.E. Some writers prefer a date during the wicked reign of MANASSEH (686–643 B.C.E.), or during the reign of JOSIAH (prior to the reforms of 621 B.C.E.). The evidence best supports a time during the reign of JEHOIAKIM (609–598 B.C.E.) and can be sharpened even further.

The Egyptian army defeated Judah and killed King Josiah (609 B.C.E.). After three months, Pharaoh Necho dethroned Jehoahaz (Josiah's son and successor) and exiled him to Egypt, placing a subservient Jehoiakim on Judah's throne. The neo-Babylonians (Chaldeans) were an expanding threat in the collapsing ruins of the Assyrian Empire and defeated Egypt at Carchemish (605 B.C.E.). In 1:5-6 *the Chaldeans* are mentioned as if the invasion was still in the future and the astonishment mentioned in v. 5 requires a date prior to 605 B.C.E. The reference in 3:2 to *in our own time revive it* (or "let him live") and in 3:13 to *to save your anointed*, may indicate Habakkuk's call for the return of JEHOAHAZ from Egyptian exile (or the placing of a new Davidic king on the throne). This dictates a date closer to 609 B.C.E.

Literary Form

Modern scholarship affirms the unity of the book but suggests a variety of settings and possible backgrounds. The dialogue form of the prophecy graphically portrays the prophet as an intermediary. He was not performing a cultic rite, but engaged in dynamic dialogue with God. This resembles more the debate and actions of court life, or elders at the city gate, than the formality of the Temple cult. Habakkuk adopted the "prophetic I" and presented the revelation he received in autobiographical form. The various sections of his prophecy move from this dramatic dialogue to oracle, taunt-song (woe oracle), prayer, hymn of praise, and vow of commitment.

For Further Study

In the *Mercer Dictionary of the Bible*: HABAKKUK; HABAKKUK, BOOK OF; NEBUCHADREZZAR; ORACLE; POETRY; PROPHET; VISION.

In other sources: D. W. Baker, *Nahum, Habakkuk, Zephaniah*, TOTC; D. D. Garland, "Habakkuk," BBC; D. M. Lloyd-Jones, *From Fear to Faith*; R. D. Patterson, *Nahum, Habakkuk, Zephaniah*, WEC; J. J. M. Roberts, *Nahum, Habakkuk, and Zephaniah*, OTL.

Commentary

An Outline

I. Dialogue with God, 1:1–2:5
  A. Superscription, 1:1
  B. Prayer and Response, 1:2–2:5
II. Questions from Life, 2:6-20
III. Solutions for the Faithful, 3:1-19
  A. Superscription, 3:1
  B. Prayer of Faith, 3:2-19a
  C. Postscription, 3:19b

Dialogue with God, 1:1–2:5

Superscription, 1:1

The opening verse calls Habakkuk's entire prophecy an *oracle* (lit. "burden," as in KJV), a common expression for God's revelation to the prophets, emphasizing the deep concern placed upon their hearts. The verb *saw* is rarely used with *oracle* (see Isa 13:1; however the element of VISION and references to "seeing" the word of the LORD are frequent in prophetic literature; cf. Nah 1:1; Amos 1:1; Mic 1:1; Obad 1) and emphasizes the dynamic impact of God's message upon the prophet. This visual theme is developed throughout the prophecy: *Why do you make me see wrong-doing and look at trouble?* (1:3); *Write the vision, make it plain on tablets, so that a runner may read it* (2:2); and most distinctively in the powerful theophanic vision of the LORD's march through history in the prayer-hymn of 3:3-15.

Prayer and Response, 1:2–2:5

1:2-4. Habakkuk's lament. The prophet's first prayer arises from his encounter with the corruption and injustice prevalent during the reign of JEHOIAKIM. Many identify *the wicked* in v. 4 with *the Chaldeans* introduced in 1:6. However, such an interpretation contradicts the surprise element of the response in 1:5-11.

The complaint raised is similar to the liturgical laments in many of the psalms and the theme of much of Jeremiah's preaching dating to the same period. Habakkuk has cried to the LORD repeatedly and now questions why God has ignored his prayers and failed to respond to the needs of the innocent. The word *save* (v. 2) is a cry for a redeemer. This is a key theme in Habakkuk and linked to the *anointed* mentioned in 3:13 (see also the introduction). Why does God tarry? Why does the promised redeemer not come and deal with the *violence* and *wrong-doing*?

The words used to describe the *violence*, *strife*, and *contention* Habakkuk saw are strong expressions, reflecting the utter degradation of the times (cf. 2 Kgs 23:34–24:7; 2 Chr 36:4-8). The people of JUDAH suffered under the heavy hand of Jehoiakim as he struggled to exact taxes sufficient to meet the demands of the Egyptian tribute and his own extravagant life style (see Jer 22:13-19). The revival and reform program of JOSIAH collapsed. The corruption, perversity, and utter wickedness experienced during the reign of MANASSEH (2 Kgs 21:1-18; 2 Chr 33:1-20) returned. The imposition of Egyptian (and later Babylonian) religious influences added to the complexities and problems caused by the revival of Canaanite Baalism. The greed and exploitation of this perverse age prostituted the justice and judgment characteristic of God's holiness (the model for Judah's legal structure).

1:5-11. The LORD's reply. The LORD responds to Habakkuk's questions of his justice and concern in the most unexpected way in this powerful oracle. As if to say "you haven't seen anything yet," the LORD challenges the prophet to gaze beyond the limits of the confines of Judah (and beyond the limits of his own imagination) and be astonished at what the LORD is doing in the nations near and far (v. 5).

The groundwork for the message of faith (2:4) is laid. The Chaldean threat seemed unbelievable, for they would not become a menacing world power until after the defeat of the Egyptians (605 B.C.E.). The sovereign creator of the universe is not limited to the regions of Judah to accomplish divine purposes. God has roused *the Chaldeans* (v. 6) and is using them as instruments of judgment. The person of faith lives in the understanding that the LORD controls history. Even *that fierce and impetuous nation* (v. 6, i.e., *the Chaldeans*) falls under God's scepter.

Graphic metaphors punctuate the description of *the Chaldeans*. This dreaded and fearsome nation is a tool in the hand of the sovereign LORD, used to bring judgment upon many nations and the wicked of Habakkuk's Judah. Three strophes explain their preparation (vv. 5-6), their power (vv. 7-8), and their purpose (vv. 9-11). Each verse sweeps over the hearer pounding home a message of fear and dread. *The Chaldeans* are a law unto themselves (v. 7) whose cavalry, like *leopards* and *wolves*, comes swooping into history to devour its prey like swift eagles (v. 8). This passage races toward a climax as the army, like a mighty desert sand storm (v. 9), scoffs at kings and builds earthen ramparts to breach the fortresses where cowering rulers await defeat (v. 10). Their goal is to glory in their might and make their own strength (military machine) their god (v. 11).

1:12-17. Habakkuk's lament. The abruptness and boldness of his first prayer met an unexpected answer. Habakkuk now uses a more flattering technique of challenging God's justice. How could a holy and righteous God allow the wicked to encompass the righteous? How could he use such an idolatrous force as the Chaldeans to discipline and punish? These questions form the heart of Habakkuk's cry. The first three verses of this lament (12-14) focus on the LORD, while the last three (vv. 15-17) depict the Chaldean enemy.

The lament opens with two questions (v. 12). The first flows from God's eternity and the second from the expected salvation and preservation of the people. The NRSV departs from the MT (following an ancient Jewish scribal correction) in translating *You shall not die* instead of "We shall not die" (see NRSV mg.). The better reading is "Shall we not die?" This phrase is a question introduced by the interrogative particle serving both queries. The OT frequently applies the names and metaphors for God used here. The questions of v. 13 emphasize Habakkuk's dissatisfaction with God's earlier response. The people of the world are like *fish of the sea* (v. 14) and the Chaldeans have developed a war machine with nets, seines, and fishing gear capable of vast destruction. Will the Chaldean army devastate the world unchecked?

2:1. Habakkuk's wait. The prophet expected a response from God. The silence was deafening. Perhaps the community demanded an explanation from Habakkuk. The MT reads "I will answer" (not the *he will answer* of the NRSV) suggesting such a challenge. Habakkuk stationed himself at his watchpost awaiting what God would say *to* him (lit. "in"), seeking the equipping and opportunity to serve as God's spokesman. The concept of the "watchman prophet" is well known (Isa 21:8; Jer 6:17; Ezek 3:17; 33:2-3). The stationing of Habakkuk on the *rampart* suggests a city under siege. (Some suggest a tower in an open field or vineyard, others even the Temple, but the Hebrew word is used to describe a fortified town.) As God's messenger to a desperate age, the besieged prophet needed a fresh word from the LORD for life's most perplexing questions.

2:2-5. The LORD's reply. The long awaited response finally comes. Verses 2-4 provide initial instructions for the preserving of the oracle. Habakkuk must *write the vision* clearly *on tablets* (v. 2) so anyone running past may read it. God's revelation may be long in arriving but it will surely come. Some suggest the vision in question was already given in 1:5-11. However the location of the oracle and the threefold reference in the NT (Rom 1:17; Gal 3:11; Heb 10:38-39) surely affirm vv. 4-5 as the vision to be written. These verses contrast the wicked and the righteous. The former are proud, wealthy, and arrogant. Their greed is never satiated. The righteous live by their faith (v. 4).

The Hebrew noun is better translated "faithfulness" and conveys the idea of a stance of faith that is "secure," "firm," or "steady" (Exod 17:12 provides a beautiful illustration of this identical word: "Moses' hands were steady"). Persons of faith flesh out their faithfulness in deeds of righteousness (cf. Isa 1:17; Mic 6:8; Jas 1:27), thereby demonstrating that they have a firm and steady trust in God's judgment and actions. The NT's use of v. 4 continued this line of thinking. Persons of faith look at life through a long view of history. One cannot see the world properly from the bottom of a well. Persons of faith look at God's mighty acts of salvation through the vast stretches of time and cling steadily to the LORD. They know that God has acted faithfully in the past and can be trusted to deliver his people once again. Individuals may walk through dark valleys and nations pass through periods of grave despair, but God comes in salvation to those who live by faith and patiently wait for his deliverance.

Questions from Life, 2:6-20

In these five three-verse taunt songs the classic prophetic form of "woe oracle" (each indicated in the NRSV by *alas*, vv. 6, 9, 12, 15, 19) is used (cf. Isa 5:8-25; 10:1-14; Nah 3:1-7; Zeph 3:1-8). This passage also belongs to a class of prophecies known as "oracles against foreign nations." God speaks these oracles, although Habakkuk may be placing the cry of woe in the mouth of the nations oppressed by Babylon. The prophet is also recalling the exploitation of his own people at the hands of local tyrants (the abuses common in numerous ages). Many of these stanzas reflect atrocities perpetrated during the reign of Jehoiakim and form a protest and cry for radical social change. Judah needs a redeemer. The prophecy rushes toward the cry for such a deliverer and the theophany of chap. 3, where the record of precisely such deliverance is recounted in praise.

2:6-8. Woe to exploiters and plunderers. The object of the taunt and *mocking riddles* (v. 6) is translated *such people* and *them* in NRSV (lit. "him"). The immediate reference is to the *proud* (2:4) but may be broadened to include the Babylonians and the wicked of Judah discussed in the previous chapter. God proclaims that all exploiters shall be repaid like the plundering Babylonians who will suffer a similar fate at the hands of their victims. The references to *goods taken in pledge* and *your own creditors* (vv. 6, 7; cf. Amos 2:8) refers to the injustice within Judah (cf. 1:3-4). Babylon is amassing a great debt at the expense of *human bloodshed, and violence to the earth, to cities and all who live in them* (v. 8). That debt will be repaid in kind.

2:9-11. Woe to self-seekers. These verses denounce the splendors of ancient Babylon and promise that kingdoms built on ill-gotten gain must fall. The details of this stanza reflect a similar taunt song in Jer 22:13-19, where that prophet castigated Jehoiakim for building a lofty palace during a time of grave international crisis. Perhaps Habakkuk is speaking to the same situation. The righteous were abused and pressed into service without wages and the people exploited by taxation and conscription to meet the avarice of a tyrant. Habakkuk's song shares the same pain and echoes again the cry of despair in 1:3-4.

2:12-14. Woe to false kings. God denounces abusive and wicked kings, whether NEBUCHADREZZAR is enhancing the grandeur of Babylon or Jehoiakim beautifying the city of Jerusalem. Habakkuk's barb in v. 13 resembles Jeremiah's attack on Nebuchadrezzar in Jer 51:58. God's kingdom is coming. Like a mighty river of justice flowing from his throne, the glory of the LORD will sweep away the hatred and debris of scurrilous kingdoms and bring the justice and righteousness of the knowledge of the LORD. In v. 14, Habakkuk echoes the refrain of Isa 11:9.

2:15-17. Woe to oppressors. Habakkuk contrasts *the glory of the LORD* (2:14) with the glory turned into shame of abusive tyrants (twice in v. 16). Nebuchadrezzar and Jehoiakim may both be in view, for the *violence done to Lebanon* (v. 17) may refer equally well to Jehoiakim's excessive building material demands and to Nebuchadrezzar's raids. These oppressors are likened to exploitative neighbors who intoxicate others to abuse them. The expression *stagger* (v. 16) in the received Hebrew text is "be uncircumcised," referring to the debauching acts of pagan surroundings. This may favor the Judean setting rather than the Babylonian. The *cup in the LORD's right hand* (v. 16) is a familiar biblical reference to God's firm and decisive judgment (Ps 75:8; Isa 51:17; Jer 25:15-17; 49:12; 51:7; Ezek 23:31-34).

2:18-20. Woe to idolaters. The final stanza of woe attacks the foolishness of idolatry, whether the proud statues of Babylon and its mighty war machine (cf. 1:16) or the reintroduction of Canaanite worship under Jehoiakim. The conclusion (v. 20) serves a dual purpose of contrasting idolatry with the LORD's sovereignty (similar to the function of 2:14) and forms a powerful climax to the entire taunt song. This is an excellent backdrop for the majesty of the LORD's theophany in chap. 3. The prophet does have a response to those demanding answers from him (cf. 2:1). The LORD is sovereign (*in his holy temple*, v. 20); let there be *silence*! A vividly clear answer meets Habakkuk's questions of God's justice: Be still! The LORD is in control!

Solutions for the Faithful, 3:1-19

Superscription, 3:1

While Habakkuk's prayer is written in a formal liturgical style (reflected in the technical expressions included in the introduction and conclusion, 3:1, 19b), an intensely personal tone is evident throughout the hymn (cf. 3:2, 16-19a). Some scholars rejected the poem (3:2-19a) as an integral part of Habakkuk's prophecy. The discovery of the Qumran commentary (*pesher*), without comments on this section, seemed to confirm the suspicion. Further evaluation has reversed that conclusion and most scholars now support the unity of Habakkuk. Superscriptions to Pss 146–148 in the LXX indicate that other prophets (HAGGAI and ZECHARIAH) recorded prayers also. The term "prayer" occurs as the title for the entire collection of Davidic psalms concluding in 72:20 and is also found in the titles of Pss 17; 86; 90; 102; 142. *Shigionoth* is a technical term for an emotional or enthusiastic song. Further liturgical elements are evident in the use of *selah* (vv. 3, 9, 13) and the final reference to *choirmaster* and *stringed instruments* (v. 19).

Prayer of Faith, 3:2-19a

3:2. Confession and cry for mercy. Habakkuk's emotional prayer anticipates the great hymn of praise that follows. *I stand in awe* (lit. "afraid") is the formal attitude of worship in the OT. This is reverence and awe that leads to a life of obedience and service. *Revive it* may also be translated "let him live," a possible cry for restoration of the rightful king (see v. 13 *save your anointed*) or a cry for the redeemer to come and perform God's work of salvation and deliverance in Habakkuk's tragic age. This portion of the prayer concludes with a plea for mercy and sets the stage for the majestic theophany of vv. 3-15, a rehearsal of the LORD's many past deeds of mercy.

3:3-15. Hymn of praise for God's presence in history. This majestic hymn recounts the story of "salvation history" and the LORD's deliverance in ages past. The poetry is difficult and often reminiscent of similar ancient songs (cf. Deut 33; Judg 5). It is one of the greatest poems in a long line of passages that form a nearly creedal recitation of the LORD's love, mercy, and deliverance (cf. Deut 6:20-25; 26:1-11; Josh 24:2-

13; Judg 6:8-10; 1 Sam 12: 6-12; Pss 68:7-14; 74:12-17; 78:12-72; 104; 105; 106; 114; 136; Isa 43:15-18; 48:20-22; 51:9-11; Jer 2:6-8; 23:7-8; 32:17-24; etc.). Many of these passages end in personal testimony or strong affirmations of faith in God as Redeemer. Flowing through biblical narrative in many forms, these majestic songs burst into narrative portions, form small or large sections of psalms, punctuate the messages of prophets, and become the structure for dramatic passages (sermons, poems, and narrative) in the NT (Acts 7:2-50; 13:17-25; Eph 1:3-14; Heb 11) where Jesus is presented as the ultimate anointed one to bring the promised deliverance.

God challenged Habakkuk to live by faith (2:4). The prophet's recitation of the mighty acts of the LORD in this poem reminds him of God's faithfulness to his people and bolsters that faith for the coming Babylonian crisis. Habakkuk ransacks history, filling his poem with fleeting references to numerous historical events in Israel's journey to the promised land. The poem becomes metaphorical of the prophet's personal pilgrimage from perplexing and handicapping fear to power and victorious faith in the LORD of history.

Some scholars suggest two poems (vv. 3-7/8 and 7/8-15). The first describes the LORD's triumphal march in front of his people as he leads them out of the wilderness into the promised land. The second poem extols the deliverance from Egypt. The possible reference to creation and the jumping from one moment in history to another suggest that the prophet, overwhelmed at the LORD's majesty, is recalling many of the lessons from the past at once. The poem is singular, a unit of vast diversity.

The THEOPHANY begins in *Teman* and *Paran* (v. 3), the southern trans-Jordanian regions through which Israel passed on their trek to Canaan (cf. Deut 33:1-2; Judg 5:4). God is described in great splendor with rays of his glory emanating from him like those of the sun. His march shakes the earth and scatters the mountains (cf. Ps 114; Nah 1:2-8). The mention of *Cushan* and *Midian* (v. 7) may refer to portions of the Exodus experience or events in the days of Gideon (Judg 6–8).

The moon stood still (v. 11) probably refers to Joshua's battle at the valley of Aijalon, where another ancient poem records that "the sun stood still, and the moon stopped" (Josh 10:12-14). Verse 8 focuses on the crossing of the sea (Exod 14) and the Jordan River (Josh 3–4).

Interpretation suggestions for the *anointed* in v. 13 range from Moses, David, a later Davidic king, and the Messiah, to the nation Israel. Certainly an individual is in view. A Davidic king or the Messiah seems most appropriate. The emphasis throughout this hymn is on deliverance.

3:16-19a. Commitment and vow of trust. Exhausted from wrestling with God and overcome by the vision of God's mighty acts of salvation in history, Habakkuk's weak knees and quivering lips now give way to a calm assurance that sweeps over his limp body (v. 16). The person of faith can stand in the day of trouble. Let the Babylonians come! Let them destroy houses, fields, and flocks. The righteous person will find strength in the LORD, not the artificial props of any materialistic society (v. 17-19a). The theophanic vision has brought a long view of history to the prophet. He can now look beyond immediate calamity to see the ultimate victory of the sovereign LORD of history. The difficult questions and nearly blasphemous accusations of 1:2-4 have melted into the peaceful assurance of the person of faith. Habakkuk's own experience (*my salvation* v. 18) stands as a powerful testimony to the truth of the central oracle of 2:4.

Postscript, 3:19b

Liturgical instructions bring the prophecy to a conclusion. Some argue that the traditional titles found in the Book of Psalms may not be headings for the psalms that follow but colophons for the psalms that precede such references. This passage supports such suggestions. The reference to *my stringed instruments* may suggest the prophet's formal connection to the Temple.

Zephaniah

John Joseph Owens

Introduction

The Book of Zephaniah is the ninth segment of the book known as "The Twelve" (Prophets). It forms a link between Habakkuk (a liturgy attacking the religious syncretism of the times) and Haggai (a champion of the reform of the worship of the LORD). Modern interpreters have so isolated the individual units of "The Twelve" that they have deprived students of signs of the unity of this great book of prophecy.

The three final sections of "The Twelve," for example, begin in the same way: "An Oracle (of) the word of the LORD" (Zech 9:1; 12:1; Mal 1:1). This phrase suggests that what follows, or perhaps what precedes, marks a distinct literary unity. Readers should be alert to the signs erected for them by the original writer and editors.

Author, Date, and Setting

ZEPHANIAH (650–625 B.C.E.) was a contemporary of HABAKKUK. The name "Zephaniah" means "Yahweh has treasured (hidden)." The three letters of the name, Z, P, and N, are also the three consonants in the Hebrew word "north." This may be coincidental or it may be a clever punning device of the author: giving the prophet a name that underscores the influence of the Northern Kingdom (ISRAEL) over JUDAH in that day.

The Assyrians from the north has exerted superiority over Palestine for a long period. They had captured SAMARIA (North Israel) in 722 B.C.E. They laid siege to Jerusalem (Judah) ca. 701 B.C.E. and captured forty-six of the fortified cities of Judah. Kings MANASSEH (687–642 B.C.E.) and AMON (642–640 B.C.E.) of Judah were practically vassals of the Assyrian superpower.

The opening verse of the book gives an unusual four-generation heritage, instead of a one- or two-generation heritage. The fourth generation name is HEZEKIAH. It is not possible to be certain of the identity of this Hezekiah, but the name strongly suggests that Zephaniah was of royal heritage. King Hezekiah of Judah (727–698 B.C.E.) ruled in the time of Isaiah. Isaiah was an influential prophet during Hezekiah's rule. Zephaniah re-asserted the teaching of Isaiah after more than seventy years of extreme Assyrian influence upon Judah. Just as AMOS, HOSEA, ISAIAH, and MICAH had been raised up during the time of the dissolution of the Kingdom of Israel, so God raised up NAHUM, Habakkuk, JEREMIAH, and Zephaniah in the final century of the state of Judah.

The ministry of Zephaniah is set *during the reign of Josiah* (639–608 B.C.E.). Zephaniah 1:2-6 describe an impending destruction, probably to be associated with the Scythian invasion of Palestine, ca. 627 B.C.E. Other interpreters refer this devastation to the coming breakup of the Assyrian empire, ca. 612 B.C.E.

The prophet's style is direct, forceful, and vigorous. His figures of speech are concrete and clear. The literary style is the *qinah* meter, a mournful, melancholy, or plaintive poem, often used as a funeral song or a lament for the dead. The *qinah* meter is a five-beat line of POETRY, generally divided as 3 + 2 or 2 + 3 accented syllables. The opening message of the book well fits this literary style. Like the opening oracle of the Book of Isaiah, the Book of Zephaniah opens with the assertion that Israel is so sinful that complete annihilation is well deserved.

For Further Study

In the *Mercer Dictionary of the Bible:* CHRONOLOGY; ORACLE; POETRY; PROPHET; ZEPHANIAH; ZEPHANIAH, BOOK OF; VISION.

In other sources: T. P. Wahl, "Zephaniah," *The New Jerome Biblical Commentary*, 255–58; "Zephaniah, Book of," *Nelson's Illustrated Bible Dictionary*, 1121–22.

Commentary

An Outline

Superscription, 1:1

As noted above, the four-generation genealogy given for Zephaniah, tracing his lineage back to Hezekiah, may be intended to place the prophet within the royal house of Judah, descendants of King DAVID. As in the case of Isaiah, Zephaniah's royal family connections do not prevent him from speaking out against Judah's leaders and against the corrupt capital city.

God's Cosmic Judgment, 1:2-6

In 722 B.C.E. the Assyrian army came from the north and destroyed the Northern Kingdom (Isa 10:5-6). The Southern Kingdom became very self-righteous. Their interpretation of the world scene was that their neighbors deserved God's condemnation. In contrast, since they had the temple, they were God's *only* people; they were secure. Instead of being warned by the prophet, they were guilty of perpetual backsliding (Jer 8:5). The prophet had a difficult task of changing a people, a nation, its leaders, and its individual members.

Yahweh *will sweep away everything* (v. 2). This would also include the self-righteous remnant of God's people. The people of Judah deserved condemnation because they had so enraged the LORD as to cause the threat of world-wide destruction. Judah's misinterpretation of God's action is part of the reason for the universal threat.

Judah and the world are interrelated, *I will sweep away everything* (v. 2). This includes beast, birds, and sea animals (v. 3) as well as humanity throughout the world. Pursuant to the abolition of Israel in 722 B.C.E. by the Assyrian horde, Judah had mental fantasies about their exaltation, importance, and uniqueness within God's plans. Yahweh's oracle moves from the cosmic vista to the self-exalted citizens of Judah. The reason for such universal destruction is outlined in vv. 4-6. Isaiah had expressed his disgust at those who claimed to be God's exclusive people: "They have forsaken the Lord, they have spurned the Holy One of Israel" (Isa 1:4). He condemns their syncretism: *all who dress themselves in foreign attire* (v. 8). Even though Yahweh was their Lord, Zephaniah points out that there were idolatrous priests who followed BAAL (a Canaanite deity), those who prostrate themselves to the hosts of heaven (an Assyrian god), and those who swear by Milcom (god of the Ammonites).

The Day of the LORD, 1:7–3:13

The central idea in the Book of Zephaniah is the "Day of Yahweh."

Against Judah, 1:7-13

The day of Yahweh was for them a day of exclusive exaltation, rather than a day of mourning and repentance for their sins.

1:7-9. They copy Assyria. The LORD dashes their hopes by accusing them of seeking to appease the foreigners and the foreign gods. The officials and the king's family appeared in Assyrian habits.

Also Judah was guilty of leaping *over the thresholds* (v. 9). This is a rare expression. It could be a reference to their making unusual entry for the purpose of robbing the poor. It may have reference to the manner in which the priests entered the place of worship to avoid contamination by proximity to the various gods. The prophet points out the violence and unjust dealings of the officials and royal family.

1:10-11. No business dealings. *The Fish Gate, . . . the Second Quarter, . . . the hills*, and *the Mortar* will be different by virtue of the loud moans. This moaning was brought on by the elimination of the traders and merchants.

1:12-13. Power confused. It is strangely common that mortals who attain a position of authority or power assume that they bring power to the position. In reality the position offers, even to the second-rate person, any authority available. Persons of inferior ability have a tendency to be complacent.

Zephaniah agrees with Mal 2:17 in portraying the human community as suggesting that God does not act in human affairs. All of Judah shall be shown that God is a definite part of their lives, whether they cooperate with him or not. No element can be hidden from God's light.

Against the Whole Earth, 1:14-19

Even though Judah's view of the Day of Yahweh was of a day of exaltation, Zephaniah enlarges the people's vision.

1:14-16. The great day is imminent and coming quickly. It is close enough to be seen and heard. This brings bitterness and anguish, not praise and compliment.

1:17-18. The great day is upon all the earth. The cause of all this terror is that persons *have sinned against the LORD*. The writer includes *the whole earth*.

Even when the Day of Yahweh is portrayed as terror, there is hope. For God is a redeeming God. This does not invalidate, but rather confirms, God as one who is interested in and involved with the entire created order.

God's Offer of Hope, 2:1-15

2:1-4. The imperative for Judah. Just as the prophet had pled with Judah to *be silent* (1:7), he urges this *shameless nation* to *seek the Lord . . . righteousness . . . [and] humility*. These are commands. The people's only hope was to eradicate their shame and become the *humble of the land*. Then perhaps they could escape the fury of the judgment. Even the long-time settlers of their land (the prophet mentions four of the five main Philistine strongholds) will be decimated.

2:5-15. Woe to the nations. The extent of God's wrath is shown in 2:5–3:8.

2:5-11. The nations with whom they were involved are singled out by name and description. If they seek the LORD, Judah could still win victory over the PHILIS-TINES, ASHKELON, MOAB, and AMMON. The promise to which Judah clung so tenaciously, *restore their fortunes* (v. 7), is extended to these nations. Just as the threat is for the whole world, so also is the promise.

2:12-15. The remote nations. God's hands reach to the far south, Cush or ETHIOPIA. But he will extend his power to the north (*zaphon*) and destroy ASSYRIA. This was spoken before 612 B.C.E., when Nineveh was destroyed. Nineveh had ruled from 747–612 B.C.E., exalting notions of its worldwide authority and power. Prosperity would be turned into derision.

Against Jerusalem, 3:1-7

Verses 1-2 identify the aim of the message. Woe to the *soiled, defiled, oppressing city* refers to Jerusalem.

The officials, judges, prophets, and priests are the ones who were doing the opposite of what their trust dictated. They had assumed that they were the source of their nations's pride. But they were the cause of the nations's downfall.

Nations had been brought low (v. 6) in the hope that Judah would take warning.

Hope for All Nations, 3:8

Once more hope is explained: *wait for me*. God will gather all nations and judge them. The reality of sin dictates that *all the earth will be consumed* unless the imperatives are followed, that is, *be silent* (1:7), and *gather together* (2:1).

Hope and the Day of the LORD, 3:9-13

Then and *on that day* are the imperative connectors. Based on the power and presence of God, hope can be reality. All the world will be given a purified way of expression to the end that all of them may worship the LORD. This does not downgrade Judah. There will always be a remnant who are characterized by humility (v. 12). These are they who seek refuge in God.

God's Restoration of Zion, 3:14-20

The changed congregation shall seek refuge in God's name. The remnant of Israel are the ones referred to as *daughter Zion*. They will have the stigma removed. *On that day* reminds us that the evil has been removed, the thoughts are purified, condemnation is no longer. God is very active within their world. Within the day of the LORD, there is purification. The prophet's point is that those who are silent (submissive) to the LORD, who wait for him, who rejoice in him will be preserved. These will have the presence of the warrior Yahweh, the grounds for their joy and singing. In the day of the LORD, God will punish the guilty, change the negative to positive, unify all humankind (instead of isolating or dividing).

The prophet concludes his prophecy with the sixth century promise to *restore their fortunes* (v. 20). This is the promise for many nations, including Judah (and Israel). This promise is found repeatedly in Jeremiah, one of Zephaniah's contemporaries: 29:14, 30:3, 31:23. 32:44, 33:7, 26. These passages and Ezek 39:25 involve Judah (including Israel). Jeremiah 46:26 and Ezek 29:14 give a promise to EGYPT. Ezekiel 16:53 even makes a promise to SODOM and SAMARIA. Jeremiah 48:47 includes Moab, Jer 49:6 includes Ammon, and Jer 49:39 includes Elam with the same Hebrew terms as used in the promises to Judah (including Israel). This term appears in only eight other places (three in the Prophets and once each in Deuteronomy, Psalms, Job, and Lamentations). Whereas Judah had misinterpreted the promises to apply all the good things to itself and all the bad things to its enemies, the Day of the Lord will be to punish sin in all nations (including Judah), to bring out the humility and lowliness of all nations to turn these repentant ones to God, to give grounds for joy and exultation, and to reward with restoration and glory all those who think his way and call on his name.

Haggai

Jon L. Berquist

Introduction

This lesser known PROPHET delivered a message in a time of crisis, during August through December of 520 B.C.E., while Jerusalem, which was now a small colony within the vast PERSIAN EMPIRE, was experiencing great turmoil and uncertainty. HAGGAI was politically astute, and his utterances conveyed a theological interpretation of contemporary events in Jerusalem.

Prophecy under the Persian Empire

The Persian Empire had allowed the return of exiled populations, including the Jews, as early as 539 B.C.E., but most of the Jews chose not to return. Instead, they stayed in Babylonia, the homeland of their parents and grandparents. The return from EXILE was a slow process of immigration over decades. Near Jerusalem, a Jewish culture had maintained itself after the devastation of the land in 587 B.C.E., and these natives resented and resisted the influx of immigrants from Babylonia (see Neh 5:1-13).

The Persian Empire showed little concern with its western border, including Jerusalem, until Persia's third emperor, DARIUS, took the throne in early 521 B.C.E. Darius intended to capture Egypt. At the time of Haggai's prophecies, Darius's army was approaching Jerusalem on its way to conquer Egypt. This army lived off the land through which it passed, presenting an economic drain on the surrounding territories. In preparation, the Persian Empire built administrative facilities at state expense along the path. Jerusalem was one of the sites slated for an administrative complex, which became Jerusalem's Second Temple. Built during 520–515 B.C.E., this temple served the political administrative needs of the Persian Empire and its lo-cal colonial government (cf. Neh 13:6-9), as well as the religious needs of the Jerusalemites. Haggai's prophecies encouraged the construction of this temple and persuaded the people not to fear the approaching army.

The Setting of the Book of Haggai

Haggai's prophecies reflect the early phases of temple construction, in which he argued against various reasons for delay in building. This collection of oracles might have originally reminded the people of the necessity of temple construction. Once these oracles were placed within an editorial framework of precise dates, the character of the book changed. The book in its current form may have functioned as a historical reminiscence of the support of prophet, priest, governor, and people for the temple construction. Perhaps such a compilation would have been part of the liturgy at the dedication of the new temple in 515 B.C.E., although such a notion must remain speculative.

For Further Study

In the *Mercer Dictionary of the Bible*: DARIUS; EXILE; HAGGAI; HAGGAI, BOOK OF; ORACLE; PERSIAN EMPIRE; PROPHET; ZERUBBABEL.

In other sources: R. J. Coggins, *Haggai, Zechariah, Malachi*; P. D. Hanson, *Dawn of Apocalyptic*; C. L. Meyers and E. M. Meyers, *Haggai, Zechariah 1–8*, AncB; D. L. Petersen, *Haggai and Zechariah 1–8*, OTL; D. L. Smith, *Religion of the Landless*; H. W. Wolff, *Haggai*; E. M. Yamauchi, *Persia and the Bible*.

Commentary

An Outline

I. The Call to Build the Second Temple, 1:1-15
  A. Introduction, 1:1
  B. Current Failings, 1:2-6
  C. Protection against Disaster, 1:7-11
  D. God's Presence with the Builders, 1:12-15
II. Promises for the Second Temple, 2:1-23
  A. Wealth and Glory, 2:1-9
  B. The Communicability of Holiness, 2:10-14
  C. Blessing instead of Lack, 2:15-19
  D. Zerubbabel's Protection, 2:20-23

The Call to Build the Second Temple, 1:1-15

Introduction, 1:1

The introduction refers to the second year of the reign of DARIUS, the third ruler of the PERSIAN EMPIRE. This date formula also indicates the book's orientation. These prophecies connect the life of the religious community around Jerusalem to the larger world, especially the world of Persian imperial politics. In addition to Haggai and the emperor, Darius, two others play significant roles in these prophecies: Joshua the high priest (see Zech 3:1-10 and EZRA 3:1-13) and ZERUBBABEL the governor (see Zech 4:1-14 and Ezra 4:1-5). Thus Haggai's concerns are at the intersection of religion and politics within Jerusalem.

Current Failings, 1:2-6

Haggai's first prophetic statement moves directly to the root of the people's problem, and only then describes its economic symptoms. Haggai offers a theological perspective on the people's experiences. Because the people have failed to build a temple for God, they suffer deprivation.

1:2-4. Time to build. The people of Jerusalem have refrained from constructing a temple, claiming that the time was not yet right. Haggai disagrees; God charges the people with living too well. This provides the first clue into the audience's economic condition. These Jerusalemites have not been suffering economically in the past.

1:5-6. Economic disaster. Through Haggai, God directs these people to "set their hearts upon their paths" (the import of *concern* . . . in v. 5; see also 1:7; 2:15, 18 [twice]—that is, to decide future activity based on consideration of current events. Haggai argues for a decision in favor of temple construction because of the current economy. The frustrating futility of agriculture in v. 6 refers to the inability to keep what the people produce. Taxation seems to be the material problem, possibly reflecting an imperial tax upon the populace of Jerusalem to feed the Persian army as it marched to Egypt. Haggai understands temple construction as the proper response to this economic crisis. If the Persian army was the chief temporal concern, then adherence to a Persian policy of temple construction would allow for future prosperity. Haggai interprets the source of the difficulties as God, who also will solve the problems once the people build a proper temple.

Protection against Disaster, 1:7-11

Once again, God calls the people to decisive action. They should immediately begin the work of temple construction. The prophet repeats that construction is the solution to economic deprivation (v. 9). Here the text states clearly that the reason for the current lack is God's displeasure at the lack of a temple.

God's Presence with the Builders, 1:12-15

Haggai is one of the few prophets in the Hebrew Bible who meets immediate success and receives credit in the scriptural records.

1:12. Statement of success. Zerubbabel the governor and *Joshua . . . the high priest*, plus all the people of Jerusalem, obeyed God and Haggai and started construction, after appropriate worship.

1:13-15. Statement of God's presence. Construction began twenty-three days after Haggai's first message. The temple project is much more than human politics; it is the working of God's spirit (cf. Zech 4:6).

Promises for the Second Temple, 2:1-23

Wealth and Glory, 2:1-9

Haggai's prophetic activity resumed about a month after the beginning of temple construction (v. 1). The project was underway, but the prophet knew that there would be opportunities to delay, and so he offered words of persistent encouragement.

2:1-3. The diminished Temple. This message comes to all the people, but the leaders Zerubbabel and Joshua receive special mention. The new construction hardly compares with the grandeur of the old temple, which had been built with Solomon's wealth and which had expanded with three and a half centuries of use. However, the size and the stature of the new temple are not the point; its *existence* is the essential issue.

2:4-5. Be strong. The two leaders receive personalized messages: *Take courage*. The strength leads to a second command: *work*! God repeats the assurance of the spirit's presence (cf. 1:13-14). Since the EXODUS from Egypt, God has agreed to bring the people into Jerusalem and center them around a temple. This is not an innovation, forced upon the Jerusalemites from outside by their imperial masters; the construction of the temple has been part of God's plan since forming the people into a nation. Thus, there should be no fear.

2:6-7. Shaking the earth. God will soon shake all creation. The term *shake* refers to an earthquake, but is probably not literal; the term can connote other natural or human-made calamities. The noisy marching of the huge Persian army could well suggest an earthquake. This approaching threat would provide ample cause for alarm and fear. The prophet encouraged the people to remain steadfast in their project. The coming forces will only work for the benefit of the new temple and thus also for the people who participate in its construction. Through Persia's approach, God will fill the temple with glory.

2:8-9. Glory and peace. God owns *the silver* and *the gold*, and presumably God will choose to place the silver and gold of other nations in the temple itself. In this way, the glory of the second Temple will be greater than that of the first Temple. Glory and wealth go hand in hand. God then offers a further promise: the new temple will encompass peace. Peace also exists within this military and economic framework. The army comes not as aggressor, but as a harmless, stabilizing force. *Peace* refers to more than the avoidance of war, though that is certainly at issue here; *peace* indicates a time of security and *prosperity* for all persons, and the passing of the Persian army will bring this condition to all the people of Jerusalem.

The Communicability of Holiness, 2:10-14

The construction of the temple at Persian behest and the presence of these foreigners in large numbers created several religious problems. At stake was the purity of the temple. Only a ritual cleanliness gave the temple the ability to atone for the people. Would the Persian involvement render the temple unclean, and thus useless for Jerusalem's faithful? Would the Persians be able to use this temple for their own benefit, to win God's favor for themselves?

2:10-11. Introduction. This ORACLE occurred exactly three months after the beginning of construction (1:15). Like the previous unit (2:1-9), it came at a time when temple construction was in jeopardy. Haggai offered divine words to encourage that the construction proceed without interruption. In this case, Haggai conducted the prophecy in a question-and-answer format with the priests, who strongly encouraged the construction of a temple.

2:12. The first question. If a priest carries something holy, and then touches something that is not holy, does the holiness transfer from the holy object to the other? The answer is *No*. Holiness does not spread. If the priests offer unclean sacrifices or touch the offerings of pagans, such as the Persians, there can be no benefit gained for these foreigners. The holiness of the temple itself does not make everything offered therein holy; one must still offer right sacrifices. There is no indication that the holy object, or the priest or the temple itself, becomes unclean through this contact. Instead, neither holiness nor uncleanness is communicable. Impurity cannot endanger the holy, and the impure receive no benefit from their contact with the holy. The Jews are safe from the Persians, and the Persians shall receive no benefit.

2:13-14. The second question. The next question concerns persons who have become impure through the touching of a corpse. This may well refer to the Persian soldiers. Because these persons are unclean, their offerings are unclean. Once more, there is no indication that the other holy objects, the priests, or the temple itself become unclean through this contact. Haggai and the priests formulated a theology of holiness that protected the Jews against the Persians while still maintaining the possibility of operating a pure temple in the midst of a foreign occupation. Haggai then provided a summary: everything that this nation touches is defiled. This is not a condemnation of Jewish worship; Haggai uses the term *nation* in reference to Persia or other world powers. Haggai's interest in the religious effects of occupation is consistent with the themes found throughout the book.

Blessing instead of Lack, 2:15-19

Haggai's next-to-last oracle returns to the need for decisive action in building the temple in order to solve the economic problems. Obedience to God, as expressed in the construction of the temple desired by the Persian Empire, will bring an end to the suffering of the people.

2:15-17. Severe lack. Before the temple construction began, there was economic hardship. Again, the difficulty was the overtaxation of Jerusalem to finance the passing Persian army. Anyone who wished to draw from the stores of food and wine could take only a fraction of what was there; the rest was reserved for the soldiers. Haggai interprets this as God's reaction against the people for their refusal to build previously.

2:18-19. Blessing. This climax to the oracle repeats the earlier date, three months after the beginning of construction (2:10). The time to build is *now*, on this very day. Haggai encouraged construction by showing the people that they possess the resources for their future. There was still grain in the storage silos, and some of the trees were still yielding. Haggai assures the people that these goods will remain, and that now—since construction has begun—God will bless them. The signs of blessing were not manna from heaven, but the tools with which to build in partnership with God. God's blessing to the people would come as a response to their faithfulness.

Zerubbabel's Protection, 2:20-23

Haggai's last oracle turns from the religious and economic issues of the previous unit to military concerns. The approaching Persian army brings fear into the hearts of Jerusalemites. Thus, the prophet assures them of safety, if they follow the dictates of their governor, Zerubbabel.

2:20-22. Turning aside chariots. This final oracle occurs on the same day as the previous ones (2:10-19). The shift is both a switch of audience from the people as a whole to their leader, *Zerubbabel*, and a movement of topic from internal to external political realities. God's message is that the heavens and earth soon will shake, repeating a message of hope and expecta-

tion (2:6-7). Here, the oracle continues and gains specificity:

> I am causing the heavens and the earth to quake.
> I will turn aside the throne of the kingdoms,
>   and I will exterminate the strength
>   of the kingdoms of the nations.
> I will turn aside the chariotry and its riders,
>   and the horses and their riders will go down,
>   each by the sword of the other.
>   (vv. 21b-22, author trans.)

When the earth shakes from the army's near passage, God promises that the Persian forces will not attack Jerusalem, but will turn away from that city and go down to Egypt. This was the intention of the Persian Empire, and it presumably had been announced, at least to the Persian governor, Zerubbabel. The army's intended target was Egypt, not Jerusalem, even though the last army of that size so close to Jerusalem had brought it destruction and exile in 587 B.C.E. Haggai expects that these two huge armies, from Persia and Egypt, would clash mightily and destroy each other in Egypt, leaving Jerusalem to enjoy an era of peace without any external pressure. Such was not the case; Egypt surrendered to Persia immediately and crowned the Persian Emperor Darius as the Egyptian Pharaoh. Haggai's prophecy remains, however, because its promise of safety to Jerusalem was fulfilled.

2:23. God's choice of Zerubbabel. God declares a special choice of *Zerubbabel*, who becomes the privileged leader on the day that the Persian army passes around Jerusalem. Zerubbabel becomes *like* God's *signet ring*, an indication that God will use Zerubbabel for God's own tasks. The previous use of the "signet ring" image was negative, when Judah's king, JEHOIACHIN, was compared to a signet ring cast off from God's finger (Jer 22:24). Now, Zerubbabel was God's chosen one to fulfill the role left vacant by the true kings. Zerubbabel protects Jerusalem from Persian harm, and God protects Zerubbabel as a chosen leader.

Zechariah

Jon L. Berquist

Introduction

Zechariah's prophecies are remarkable in their variety. ZECHARIAH walks through visions accompanied by an ANGEL who interprets the viewed symbolism. The PROPHET utters oracles of a restored and peaceful community. The harsh visions near the end of the book are close to the APOCALYPTIC LITERATURE found among noncanonical works.

Authorship

The variety of the book is so striking that most scholars perceive multiple authors. Chapters 1–8 are the work of a prophet of the late sixth century, whose name is given as *Zechariah son of Berechiah* (1:1, 7). Despite the differences in form between the visions and the oracles in these eight chapters, the thematic connections among this material are very strong, and there is no reason to assume alternative authorship for parts of these chapters. However, the material changes sharply with chaps. 9–14, which seem to be a group of oracles from one or more visionaries in a time much later than Zechariah.

Historical Setting of Zechariah ben-Berechiah

The Book of Zechariah dates Zechariah son of Berechiah's prophecies to 520–518 B.C.E., mostly after the prophecies of his contemporary, HAGGAI. Certainly, there are strong connections in the historical situation between these two prophets. Both were concerned with the construction of the Temple, which the PERSIAN EMPIRE had funded and which, according to the two prophets, God supported. Both prophets were very sensitive to the religious issues of constructing a new society that included the natives in the Jerusalem area and the immigrants from Babylonia whose families were returning after seven decades of EXILE. Both assured the people that the approaching army under the command of DARIUS, emperor of Persia, did not intend to destroy JERUSALEM, but to pass nearby on its way to conquer EGYPT.

Despite these thematic similarities between Haggai and Zechariah, Zech 1–8 forms a very different expression of these concerns than Haggai 1–2. Zechariah experienced God through visions and reported what he saw, along with some interpretive comments provided by an accompanying angel. These visions occurred while the Persian Empire's army was marching through the surrounding territory. In chaps. 1 and 6, Zechariah assured the community that the army offered no threat, because God controlled international events. Zechariah 1 and 7 frame the book's concern that safety requires obedience to the prophetic word and to Jerusalem's leadership. Zechariah 8 offers an idyllic portrait of life in the wake of Persia's army.

Historical Setting of the Later Additions

The later additions (chaps. 9–14) are very difficult to date. Although there are connections among the various oracles, there is little evidence that these oracles derive from the same person or even from the same period. The material probably dates from the fifth and/or fourth centuries B.C.E., composed by persons familiar with the themes and perspectives of Zech 1–8. There may be a separation between chaps. 9–11 and chaps. 12–14. Certainly, the outlook becomes increasingly negative closer to the end of the book.

The writers of these later additions experienced life in a fundamentally different way than Zechariah did. Whereas the prophet lived in a time of hope even in the face of danger, these later writers doubted their own present and future. They were very much concerned with the problems among the leadership, including governmental corruption. Zechariah lived in a time of international peace (as long as the people maintained loyalty to Persia), but the later writers felt profound insecurity. They envisioned the need for

God's violent intervention to save them from destruction. This may reflect a time in the later Persian Empire, when the empire's attention turned away from the Palestine area, allowing social fragmentation. Under the mounting pressures of these times, these writers added their own fears and their yearnings for power and revenge.

For Further Study

In the *Mercer Dictionary of the Bible*: APOCALYPTIC LITERATURE; EXILE; PERSIAN EMPIRE; PROPHET; ORACLE; VISION; ZECHARIAH; ZECHARIAH, BOOK OF.

In other sources: R. J. Coggins, *Haggai, Zechariah, Malachi*; C. L. Meyers and E. M. Meyers, *Haggai, Zechariah 1–8*, AncB; D. L. Petersen, *Haggai and Zechariah 1–8*, OTL; D. L. Petersen, "Zechariah," HBC 747–52; E. M. Yamauchi, *Persia and the Bible*.

Commentary

An Outline

Visions and Oracles of Zechariah, 1:1–8:23

Introduction, 1:1-6

The thematic introduction to the prophecies of Zechariah begins with a date formula placing the prophecy in October or November 520 B.C.E., toward the end of Darius's second year as Persian emperor. Zechariah begins his prophecy just before Haggai's last recorded ORACLE. According to Ezra 5:1 and 6:14, HAGGAI and ZECHARIAH worked together.

The introduction provides a summary statement with DEUTERONOMISTIC overtones, interpreting the EXILE as a result of the people's violation of God's law. Zechariah states that the people repented (v. 6), recognizing that they had deserved God's punishment.

Horses and Horns, 1:7-21 [MT 1:7–2:4]

Many of Zechariah's prophecies appear in the form of VISION reports. Often, an angel accompanies Zechariah to explain the symbolic visions. Zechariah 1:7 dates the first visions to the middle of February, 519 B.C.E., during the Jerusalem Temple construction.

1:7-17. First vision of the horses. Zechariah sees four horses who report to God that they have investigated all the world. At this time, the Persian army was marching toward Jerusalem, but the prophet proclaims that there is no cause for alarm here; all is at peace.

God intends to return to Jerusalem, after an absence of seventy years during the exile. God's absence from Jerusalem reflects the notion that God required a temple; thus, the Temple construction project is at the forefront of Zechariah's prophecy. When the construction is finished and God once more inhabits Jerusalem, then there will be prosperity.

1:18-21. Vision of the four horns. Zechariah sees horns, which symbolize the nations and armies (principally, Babylonia) that destroyed Jerusalem in 587 B.C.E. The ANGEL explains that craftspersons have arrived to scare off the horns and to prevent destruction. These craftspersons build the Temple; their presence shows the loyalty to God's desire and to the Persian Empire that will keep Jerusalem safe.

Jerusalem, 2:1-13 [MT 2:5-17]

This section of Zechariah focuses on Jerusalem's future. God's chosen city will once more be the center of life, especially the life of faith. The city will remain undefended, except by God's own power in Jerusalem's center. The exiled Jews will all return.

2:1-5. A city without walls. Zechariah watches the measuring of the city under construction. The angel declares that the new city will have no walls. The angel claims that the population will be too large to be contained; this indefensibility accords with Persian policy that colonies not fortify themselves. God promises to be *a wall of fire* around the city, offering it all needed protection without constructing physical barriers. Again, Persian policy and divine command coalesce.

2:6-13. Call to come to Jerusalem. Those Jews *from . . . the north*, that is, from Babylonia, are invited to immigrate to Jerusalem. When they arrive at the Temple's completion, God will live in the people's midst, and Jerusalem will be protected and blessed.

Joshua and Zerubbabel, 3:1–4:14

In the next two chapters Zechariah turns attention to leadership in Jerusalem. Both *the high priest* (3:1) and the governor deal directly with the Temple, and the holders of each office were Persian-born Jews. Both would have been charged with enforcing Persian policy in Jerusalem. Zechariah supports a sharing of powers between these two officials, although he deals with each in distinct ways. Many scholars have envisioned a dyarchy that collapses into a rule by the high priest after the removal of Zerubbabel, but there is insufficient evidence for such a view.

3:1-10. Joshua, the high priest. Zechariah observes Joshua, the high priest, standing in the presence of God and Satan. Satan opposes Joshua, but God supports the priest, forgives his sins, and provides him with new, expensive garments. An angel repeats God's promise to give Joshua control of the Temple, since God intends to bring a day of purity and prosperity to the land through Joshua (v. 9). This vision provides unflagging support to Joshua, equating submission to this Persian-appointed priest's authority with God's plan and identifying any political opposition to Joshua with the work of the Accuser, Satan.

4:1-14. The Temple and Zerubbabel. In this vision, Zechariah examines the Temple furnishings that symbolize God's protection of Jerusalem's inhabitants. In large part, this protection comes through the governor, Zerubbabel, whose work is described in an oddly inserted section (vv. 6-10a). Zerubbabel began the Temple construction, and God firmly supports his completion of the project (v. 9). In this vision's hyperbole, Zerubbabel levels mountains and brings the people to rejoicing. The Temple construction proceeds *not by might nor by power, but by [God's] spirit* (v. 6). The military might of Persia and its economic power are not the real reasons for the Temple; they are

only God's agents. This section concludes with the statement that there are two—presumably Joshua (chap. 3) and Zerubbabel (chap. 4)—who serve God in a special way.

Destroying Wickedness, 5:1-11

The power of the completed Temple to destroy evil is an important theme for Zechariah. The prophet senses the disasters that had befallen the people through the exile and recognizes the extent of impurity that must be eradicated. Thus, Zechariah envisions the removal of iniquity itself from Jerusalem.

5:1-4. The flying scroll. Zechariah sees a scroll flying throughout the land, searching out thieves and liars. Wherever the scroll finds such a sinner, it enters the house and destroys it with fire. Perhaps this indicates an attempt to purge those who were withholding from the Temple project.

5:5-11. Wickedness in a basket. Zechariah now gazes upon a large basket, which contains the iniquity of Jerusalem. This wickedness is sent through the air to Babylonia, where a house or temple will be built for it. This is a powerful image of deliverance, as God removes the source of sin from the people. It may critique pagan Babylonian religions, claiming that such practices are so contrary to the true worship of God that they would construct shrines to sin itself. There may also be more concrete political overtones, perhaps pointing toward a policy of deportation for those who opposed Temple construction and who thus were, in Zechariah's eyes, wicked.

Safety and Government, 6:1-15

Zechariah's political concerns reappear in both the international and the local arenas. The prophet sees horses once more that represent God's involvement in international affairs, and then God oversees the crowning of Joshua for his role in Temple construction.

6:1-8. Second vision of the horses. This vision is not identical to that of 1:7-17, but shares many of the same details and certainly the same concerns. These horses have matching chariots, and they examine the four corners of the earth on God's behalf. They report that there is safety to the north. Once more, Zechariah reaffirms that the Persian army presents no danger.

6:9-15. Joshua's crown. This passage oddly envisions the crowning and enthronement of a priest, rather than a king. This oddity, along with the text's mention of *two* crowns, has caused many scholars to wonder if an earlier version of this story included Zerubbabel, but the branch symbolism has already been connected to Joshua, and both of these leaders have legitimate roles in the Temple construction. There is no reason to read a rejection of Zerubbabel into this emphasis on Joshua. Both are God's agents in Temple construction; Zechariah refers to the harmony between temple and throne (6:13). A unified leadership structure that extends into Persia is envisioned and valued for its effectiveness in bringing prosperity and respect to the colony.

Fasting Laws and Visions of Community, 7:1–8:23

These final two chapters of Zechariah's prophecies are dated to December, 518 B.C.E. Temple construction continues, but there is international stability. The Persian army has passed by Jerusalem; God has ensured the city's safety as promised through the prophets. Zechariah's concerns now turn to thoughts of how the members of the community can live together in a lasting peace.

7:1-14. Fasting laws. Zechariah intervenes in a priestly discussion about the fasts of the fifth and seventh months. Zechariah attacks the people, charging that their fasting was never a truly religious act (vv. 4-7). Instead, God calls the people to social justice as the true religion. Because the people failed to listen to the earlier prophets' message, they suffered the EXILE. The fasts mourning that exile would be useless unless the people first addressed the problems behind it, through a new commitment to social justice. Zechariah answered the fasting question in 8:18-23.

8:1-17. Visions of community. In this section, the prophet reports seven sayings of God. God first acknowledges intensity of emotion for Zion (v. 2), and then states plans to return to Jerusalem, bringing truth and holiness (v. 3). The city will be a place of idyllic peace, where the eldest and the youngest share the streets together (vv. 4-5). In the central statement, God declares how amazing all of this seems—even to God (v. 6). The fifth saying promises the immigration of Jews from throughout the world to live in Jerusalem in right relationship with God (vv. 7-8). God then encourages the Temple construction and promises blessings of fertility upon completion (vv. 9-13; cf. Hag 2:1-5, 15-19). The final statement supplies a vital summary of Israel's traditional morality: speak truth, give true justice, do not plan evil, do not love lies. This simple and powerful moral code forms the basis for God's good community of faith (vv. 14-17).

8:18-23. Fasts of joy. Zechariah now answers the questions about fasting (7:1-14). All fasts should become times of celebration, not mourning. Then, people from throughout the world will flock to Jerusalem because of God's obvious presence. Because of the ideals of community presented in 8:1-17, the city has become an attractive place to the nations, who see God's goodness made manifest in the daily life of God's own people.

God's Protection for Judah, 9:1–11:17

At this point, the nature of the prophetic material changes. No longer are there visions and oracles from the peace of 520–518 B.C.E. Instead, these three chapters reflect a time of fear and promise that God will protect Jerusalem from severe threats.

God the Watchful Defender, 9:1-8

This first oracle promises God's protection through the divine destruction of Israel's neighbors. Now that God is keeping watch, there will be no destruction for Jerusalem.

Zion's Joyous Salvation, 9:9-17

This vision of striking beauty depicts God's joyful salvation of Jerusalem. Jerusalem receives its king, *riding on a donkey* (v. 9), and then God takes away all implements of war from Israel and extends a peaceful rule throughout the world. God will free Israel's prisoners and restore Israel's losses. But struggle is not over; Zion will attack Greece. This prophecy derives from a later time, when Greece had begun to overshadow Persia's influence in the region. Still, Israel maintained its loyalty to Persia and envisioned a struggle against the pagan Greeks. God will lead the battle, fighting on Israel's behalf, and will rescue the Israelites.

Anger against the Shepherds, 10:1-5

The prophet rails against poor leadership. It is the LORD, not any other god, who brings rain in its season; thus those who seek truth from idols and diviners mislead themselves. With these kinds of leaders, the people are like sheep without a shepherd. God promises to destroy those shepherds and leaders who have failed their task.

Strength for Judah, 10:6-12

God will provide strength for Judah. Survivors will return from throughout the world, and there will be overpopulation. Despite the crowding, everyone will have enough to eat, and the boundaries of the land will expand. Assyria and Egypt will give up their captives, and the evil nations will be destroyed.

Destruction for Lebanon, 11:1-3

Fire will destroy the strength of Lebanon and the northern stretches of the JORDAN. This oracle directs attention to the problematic shepherds, whom God also destroys.

Two Shepherds, 11:4-17

As a sign-act, the prophet shepherds the flock that has been marked for slaughter. This flock's shepherds have concerned themselves only with profit and wealth. When the prophet takes over the shepherding, using staffs called Grace and Union (*Favor* and *Unity* in NRSV), three of these evil shepherds are forced from office. The prophet tires of caring for the sheep and destroys the staffs, symbolizing God's rejection of the people despite God's own promises. The owners of the flock pay the prophet *thirty shekels of silver* (v. 12), which are then flung into the potter's field. This sign act, taken by the gospels as a symbol of Judas (Matt 27:3-10, which inaccurately cites Jeremiah), demonstrates the desire of the wealthy to pay off God for the abandonment of the oppressed. However, God raises up another worthless, evil shepherd to oppress the people; God then curses this shepherd. This confusing allegory tells of Israel's history, throughout which leaders oppressed the people, despite God's desires to heal them.

Apocalyptic Visions of Destruction, 12:1–14:21

In the final three chapters of the Book of Zechariah, the text becomes more apocalyptic. The severity of the visions and the deep despair of the people are undeniable. Salvation for Jerusalem will be achieved only at the fearsome price of destruction for the rest of the world.

Judah the Destroyer, 12:1-9

In this ORACLE, Jerusalem comes under siege by many strong nations, but God remains watchful over Judah. Because of their faith, God enables the leaders of Jerusalem to destroy the besieging nations. God's strengthening of the people will be so great that even the poorest will be as rich as DAVID, and David's house will be like God.

Weeping for God, 12:10-14

In that day of deliverance, the inhabitants of Jerusalem will realize their sin and will pray to God for forgiveness. All will recognize that they have injured God through their disobedience, and they will weep because of this sin. Their crying will be like that at JOSIAH's death at the battle of MEGIDDO, that horrific battle that became a symbol of utterly demoralizing defeat (2 Kgs 23:29-30; cf. Rev 16:16, where God reverses that defeat). The penitent weeping will be shared by representatives of Jerusalem's political, prophetic, and priestly groups.

Purification, 13:1-6

In response to the weeping, God prepares a fountain that will remove sin for all the inhabitants of Jerusalem. The purification will bring an end to two types of religious practices that this visionary abhors: idolatry and prophecy. All idols will cease from the land, and the remaining prophets will deny their prior work. This passage derives from a Jerusalem faction that disparaged the possibility of receiving true words from God through prophecy.

Destruction for the Sheep, 13:7-9

In a passage reminiscent of the remnant thought of earlier prophets (Isa 10:20-23; Ezek 5), this visionary declares that God will bring destruction among the people. Firstly, God will destroy the shepherd. Then, two-thirds of the people will perish. God will refine and purify the remaining third, so that in the end they will respond to God, and claim intimate connection between God and themselves.

The Future Day of Battle, 14:1-21

The book's concluding vision presents a cataclysmic vision of God's rescue. God brings the nations to destroy Jerusalem, and they succeed in exiling half the population. Then God appears to defend the chosen city. The *Mount of Olives* (v. 4) splits into a huge valley to allow escape; on that day, nature ceases its normal processes (vv. 6-8). Jerusalem remains eternally safe, but the surrounding countryside is devastated. The nations that had fought Jerusalem suffer from horrible plagues, along with their livestock. All the survivors of the nations are forced to join in the worship of God, who destroyed them, lest they face drought. Canaanites, Israel's ancient enemies, will suffer complete genocide.

This stark vision demonstrates the depths of despair that these Jerusalemites experience. The desire for revenge overwhelms them, and they celebrate a God who brings destruction. Even worship becomes sullied through its compulsory nature; God threatens other nations to join in false celebration. The older visions of the nations flocking to Jerusalem in joy and desire to know God (8:20-23) are reversed; the nations worship their destroyer out of fear. Surely this reflects a time in Jerusalem's life when their own sense of disaster had brought bitterness.

Malachi

Jon L. Berquist

Introduction

Malachi is the last book in the canon of the Protestant OT. Although Malachi is probably not the last written of the Prophets, it reflects one of the last recorded impulses of Israelite prophecy, centuries after the better-known prophets. Malachi deals with the vital question of cooperation between priests and laity as together they serve God in the context of the early Second Temple period.

Authorship

This book has been traditionally attributed to a PROPHET named MALACHI, but "Malachi" means "my messenger." It is quite likely Malachi was not a person's name, but a title taken by this prophetic messenger of God. The book lacks a prophetic call narrative, genealogical information, biographical data, and any unambiguous note of the prophet's social location, affirming a sense of anonymity. The prophet's name and past are not important. This prophet could be anyone, and speaks not to kings and rulers but to common people, calling them to repentance and to the fullness of faith.

Historical Setting

The Book of Malachi is extraordinarily difficult to date. There are no references to specific rulers or persons. Early in this century, several scholars argued for a late date for the book, perhaps as late as the Maccabean period, but these arguments have been generally rejected. Other dates have ranged as early as 605 B.C.E. Typically, scholars dated the book by its references to intermarriage and divorce (2:10-16). Since EZRA and NEHEMIAH also mention these social problems, it is tempting to date Malachi near them, in the second half of the fifth century B.C.E. However, Malachi's marriage and divorce passage is a metaphorical discussion of the worship of other gods, and so there is no clear connection to Ezra and Nehemiah.

Malachi discusses a decrease in the seriousness accorded to the temple offerings. This may correspond to certain political realignments in the first half of the fifth century B.C.E., during the time of the PERSIAN EMPIRE. Under the reign of the emperor DARIUS, the Persian Empire built the Second Temple in Jerusalem (see the commentary on HAGGAI and ZECHARIAH). Xerxes replaced Darius as emperor in 486 B.C.E., and Xerxes redirected funding away from provincial temples. The decrease in imperial funding for local temples may have created the specific crisis that faced Malachi: the people of Jerusalem needed to raise more funds to pay for their own temple worship. Some people did not want to pay for full worship, but thought that God would still accept less costly worship. Malachi argues that God would accept only the best worship, faithful to the oldest traditions. The prophet then encouraged priests and laity to rise to the challenge together.

Form

Malachi uses a distinctive form in its prophecy. The book's six main units are organized into sets of questions and answers. Typically, the unit begins with a categorical statement by God, followed by a reactive rhetorical question by the people. This allows God, through the prophet, to expound upon the issue at hand. At times, the question-answer format is repeated within a unit (1:6-7; 2:7-8). These six units are framed by an introductory phrase (1:1) and by two endings (4:4-6), all of which are probably later additions.

For Further Study

In the *Mercer Dictionary of the Bible*: EXILE; MALACHI; MALACHI, BOOK OF; ORACLE; PERSIAN EMPIRE; PROPHET; WORSHIP IN THE OT.

In other sources: J. L. Berquist, "The Social Setting of Malachi," *BTB* 19 (1989); R. J. Coggins, *Haggai, Zechariah, Malachi*; B. Glazier-McDonald, *Malachi:*

The Divine Messenger, SBLDS; J. M. O'Brien, *Priests and Levites in Malachi*, SBLDS.

Commentary

An Outline

Introduction, 1:1

The brief introduction identifies the book as an ORACLE, similar to the introductory statements in Zech 9:1 and 12:1. "Malachi" may be a title, meaning "[God's] messenger." No temporal information is given. *Israel* in this postexilic time refers not to a nation, but to a people.

God's Love for Jacob, 1:2-5

The first unit begins with a categorical statement of God's love for Israel. Immediately, the people ask God for proof. God compares Israel with its enemy, Edom, the descendants of Esau (Gen 36). Although Israel's ancestor, Jacob, was Esau's brother, the peoples derived from these siblings have met different ends. Because God loved Israel and hated Edom, Edom is doomed to permanent devastation; all their attempts at rebuilding will fail. But Israel has God's blessings for reconstruction. If Israel rebuilds itself, God will respond.

This states clearly the essential theme of Malachi. The prophet calls the people to rebuild themselves and

their society, with the assurance that God will support their actions and will not frustrate their work. There is no indication that God will rebuild Israel, but that Israel has the ability—and the call—to rebuild itself.

Problems with the Sacrifices, 1:6–2:9

Unacceptable Offerings, 1:6-14

After the unconditionally positive statement in 1:2-5, the shift to indictment in vv. 6-14 seems severe. Nevertheless, it shares the same intention: God's people can rebuild themselves into a community of proper worship. Malachi argues against those who would block true worship.

1:6-8. The priests' defilement. The priests have not given God the due respect, because they have sacrificed unacceptable animals. Malachi affirms the ancient priestly codes that the priests should know: crippled and diseased animals should not be offered to God (Lev 22:17-25). Malachi presses the point further: the priests would not dare to deliver such defective animals to the governor (probably for payment in taxes, although possibly for some state-sponsored religious ceremony). They should give God at least the same level of respect.

1:9-11. A worldwide God. In angry rhetorical flourish, the prophet expounds on the scope of God's concerns. God has plans larger than Jerusalem. In this striking departure from ancient priestly traditions of the temple as the *only* place of God's presence, the prophet reflects the reality of the postexilic period, in which the worship of God was spreading throughout the Persian Empire. This also portrays Malachi's bias toward the laity, who can worship in places other than the Jerusalem temple.

1:12-14. A curse. The prophet closes the first half of this unit with a condemnation of the laity. God curses those who have the resources to bring unblemished animals but who hoard their wealth. There is never condemnation for the poor who lack the ability to give pure animals, here or elsewhere in the Hebrew Bible (Lev 5:7-13; 14:21-22; 27:8). Malachi sees both priests and laity as responsible for the quality of worship in the temple.

Covenant for the Priests, 2:1-9

The subject returns to the priests in this unit's second half. The priests have offered inadequate sacrifices (1:7-8); now the prophet calls them to live by their own highest standards. The challenge criticizes the priests in light of priestly tradition.

2:1-3. Curses. The priests risk curses because of their activity, turning their attempts to bring blessing to the people into cursing, if they refuse to listen to the prophetic warnings. The curses here are conditional; there are still opportunities for avoiding them.

2:4-9. The covenant with Levi. Despite the priests' failings, they can return to the covenant of LEVI. This covenant is otherwise unknown in the Hebrew Bible, but there is a clear reference to Moses' blessing of Levi (Deut 33:8-11), in which three elements appear: rejection of partiality (Deut 33:9; cf. Mal 2:9), teaching the Torah of God to all (Deut 33:10a; cf. Mal 2:6-7), and correct worship (Deut 33:10b-11a; cf. Mal 1:7-8). The priests must establish the right relationship with the laity, through impartiality, effective teaching, and proper worship. Even though the priests have stumbled from the ideal and caused others to stumble, the priests can still be faithful.

A Marriage Metaphor, 2:10-16

The Rejection of God, 2:10-12

Malachi's third unit emphasizes the need for unified faithfulness among all the followers of God. Many interpretations of 2:10-16 have attempted literal treatments of the marriage images, but the text itself does not support such use of the metaphors. Literal interpretations force themselves into the inconsistency of desiring the end of wrong marriages (v. 11) and also rejecting divorce (2:15-16), which Israel's governors favored in subsequent years (Ezra 9–10; Neh 13:23-28). This inconsistency demonstrates Malachi's intention to use the marriage language symbolically to describe the relationship between the people and God, reflecting the same prophetic concerns as the rest of the book.

Although all the people share common parentage in God, divisions have shattered proper relationships among God's people (v. 10b). In addition to these damaging divisions, some of the people have used the temple to worship other deities (v. 11). Malachi's solution is simple but drastic: excommunication for those who reject the worship of God (v. 12).

Godly Offspring, 2:13-16

The marriage metaphor shifts in Mal 2:13-14, which describes God as the deserted wife of one's youth. Even though the people approach God in tears, God the spurned spouse is hesitant and wary. God desires a productive relationship, like that between spouses (v. 15). This requires a relationship that precludes attraction to other deities. The separation that God condemns (v. 16) is not human divorce but separation from God.

A Day of Judgment, 2:17–3:5

Wearying God, 2:17

Through their complaints, the people have tired God. They have asserted that God rewards the evil and that God's justice is absent. Both are such fundamental misunderstandings of God's activity that they deny the possibilities for relationship between God and humans. Belief in God's presence and morality is essential to the faithful life.

God's Messenger, 3:1-4

God promises future decisive action that will remove the misconceptions of those who have wearied God. First, a messenger will appear, and then God will arrive in the temple. God's presence within the temple will purify the people, including the Levites; God will again accept sacrifices. Malachi understands this as a return to a much earlier condition.

Justice, 3:5

God proves the divine justice by listing those guilty ones who will suffer judgment. This list, like many others throughout the Hebrew Bible, focuses on the protection for society's weakest. God's judgment also convicts those who practice the kind of unreality that wearies God, especially those who practice magic and who lie in court.

Tithes and Offerings, 3:6-12

Call to Repentance, 3:6-7

Malachi's fifth unit begins with a call to repentance. In light of the future divine action discussed in the previous unit, the people should return to God. God affirms the divine constancy, by which the people have not been destroyed, despite their intransigence. The people ask what kind of return God desires.

Tithes, Offerings, and Blessings, 3:8-12

God responds that the people should return by ceasing to rob God. They should reinstate the full practices of tithes and offerings. These two terms appear together only here. The tithe is the temple tax paid to the Levites, their only source of income (Num 18:20-30); the offering, a general term, usually refers to sacrifices presented in worship. This command would mandate full payment of wages to the temple staff, as well as the presentation of right sacrifices for worship. Again, laity and priests appear in partnership, with the laity responsible for funding right worship.

Once priests and laity cooperate, God's faithfulness will be made manifest. The blessings of heaven will overflow, but they will not remove the need for human activity. This is not a *quid pro quo* in which God's blessings rain down upon the people as fecund rewards for right action. Instead, the people work together with God. Partnership is the ideal. God will prevent the insects from devouring the produce (v. 11), but the people are still responsible for planting and harvesting. Human effort meets divine effort, and together the produce reaches the table in such abundance that the nations call the people blessed (v. 12).

Those who Fear the LORD, 3:13–4:3

A Time for Repentance, 3:13-18

Malachi's final unit repeats the call for REPENTANCE. At the beginning, Malachi returns attention to the people's negative statements about God, but then the possibilities for healing and the consequences of rejection become clear.

3:13-15. Charges against God. The people have charged God with injustice. Certainly, the wicked do not receive their due in the short term, but these accusations distort the reality of God (cf. 2:17). These statements caused discouragement; the people no longer find any benefit in serving God. Perhaps the temple worship is the primary service envisioned here, but certainly the issue is larger.

3:16-18. A scroll of remembrance. A narrative note interrupts the prophetic dialogue. The faithful discuss together, and the LORD responds to these who fear the LORD, honor God's name, and serve the LORD. A scroll records the meeting, and God declares that these faithful ones will be God's treasured possession, to be spared on the day of God's action (v. 17). At that point, the argument shifts once more. Earlier, Malachi

depicted a rejected group (3:5); in vv. 16-17, a group that God accepts completely. For Malachi these form the righteous and the wicked, but neither is the audience for Malachi's speaking. Both the righteous and wicked appear only in third-person statements, but Malachi tells a separate audience that, in the day when God acts, "if you return, you will see the difference between the righteous one and the wicked one, between the one who serves God and the one who does not serve God" (v. 18, author trans.).

The audience consists of those who are not completely right but who are also not completely wrong. This middle group receives the call to repentance. They have not rejected God through their lack of belief, but they have not fully accepted God's intentions for the world. Malachi calls them forward to a day when the distinctions between the righteous and the wicked, in the present so vague, will be perfectly clear; this vision of future decisive action encourages present repentance.

A Day of Judgment, 4:1-3

Malachi's vision of God's future action includes a day of utter destruction for all the wicked. The faithful will receive healing through brilliant righteousness, in which God's intended order will be restored (v. 2). They will leap like calves released from stalls of captivity, and in this freedom they will trample the wicked, completing the destruction begun in the wicked's rejection of God.

Conclusion, 4:4-6

Moses, 4:4

Two endings were added to the book later, perhaps as a summary to the entire Book of the Twelve. The first ending is a call to obey the law of MOSES. Certainly, amid later concerns about possible conflicts between the Law and the Prophets, such a verse concluded the Prophets with the affirmation that there was no inconsistency between these parts of the canon.

Elijah, 4:5-6

The second ending has become important in later religious traditions. In JUDAISM, this forms the basis for the expectation of Elijah's return at Passover, at which a vacant chair is set at the table in anticipation. Within Christian tradition, the expectation of ELIJAH as a forerunner appears in the interpretations of JOHN THE BAPTIST (Luke 1:17; cf. John 1:21).

Tobit

Richard A. Spencer

Introduction

The Book of Tobit is an ancient novel about a righteous and merciful man who experiences natural misfortunes, including the loss of his sight. It is also about an innocent woman, Sarah, whose life is plagued by a demon named Asmodeus, who has killed her seven husbands on their wedding nights. Most of all the book is about God's gracious help given to these two unfortunate people, which links their families in blessing.

Although its story is set in ASSYRIA in the eighth century B.C.E., the book was written by an anonymous Jew of the diaspora about 200 B.C.E., perhaps in EGYPT or MESOPOTAMIA. It was perhaps written in Aramaic first, then translated into Hebrew and Greek. Considered apocryphal by Protestants, it was held to be canonical by Augustine, Ambrose, the Council of Hippo (393), and the Council of Trent (1547) (Rost 1971, 61; Nowell 1990, 568). The text on which the NRSV relies is that represented by Codex Sinaiticus, one of three Greek recensions (the second is represented by Vaticanus and Alexandrinus, and the third by some later minuscule mss.).

Source Materials

The author borrowed from famous legendary materials, widely known folklore motifs, and biblical types. Among the legendary source materials are the stories of Ahikar (or AHIQAR) and the "Grateful Dead." The ancient story of Ahikar, dating from at least the fifth century B.C.E., tells of a man who became a famous counselor to SENNACHERIB and ESARHADDON. He adopted his nephew NADAB to succeed him. Nadab forged Ahikar's signature on some treasonous documents, causing the king to order Ahikar's death. He was saved from death by the servant who was sent to execute him, although it was widely thought that he was dead. Later, a crisis arose between Egypt and Assyria that threatened war. The king of Egypt proposed a joint project of building a castle in the air. The Assyrian king, wishing for Ahikar's help, was told that the counselor was alive. Ahikar was restored and put in charge of this impossible project that was designed to embarrass and offend the Assyrians.

Ahikar trained eagles to lift boys into the air. From there the boys called for the Egyptians to bring up bricks. Since this was impossible, the responsibility for the project's failure fell on the Egyptians. When Ahikar returned, having saved the honor of his country, Sennacherib honored him and put Nadab to death. Ahikar is mentioned in 1:21-22 and 14:10.

The ancient folk-legend of the "Grateful Dead" also is source material for Tobit. In that legend a wealthy man, seeing others abusing the body of someone who died in debt to them, rescued and buried the body. He later became poor and was advised by a slave to marry a woman with a rich father. The woman had married five husbands already, but each was killed by a serpent on his wedding night. He married her and on his wedding night the slave killed the serpent and revealed that he was the spirit of the dead man whom he had rescued (Dancy 1972, 2–10).

The proverbial language of the wisdom tradition is reflected in the advice given by Tobit (4:6-20) and Raphael (12:6-10). Tobit's hymn of praise (chap. 13) is similar to the songs found in second Isaiah (Isa 40–55). Throughout the book prayers are offered that resemble those in Psalms and that recite biblical moments. The motif of a quest to change one's fortune and the linking of magical practices with conservative Jewish observance of the Law of Moses make this story pure fiction, an ancient novel.

Theology and Teaching

The Book of Tobit stresses family devotion and piety. Piety or righteousness is expressed principally in almsgiving, but also in prayer and fasting. A theology of retribution pervades the work (do good and God blesses you; do evil and God punishes you) as well as a fondness for prayer and a call to open honoring of God. An interesting aspect of the book is the conjoining of obedience to the Law and utter confidence in the prophetic word with magical therapeutic rituals and a developed angelology. The point of the story is that God works out good for his faithful people.

For Further Study

In the *Mercer Dictionary of the Bible*: AHIQAR; ANGEL; APOCRYPHAL LITERATURE; FEASTS AND FES-TIVALS; TEMPLE/TEMPLES; TESTAMENTS, APOCRYPHAL; TESTAMENTS OF THE TWELVE PATRIARCHS; TOBIT; TOBIT, BOOK OF.

In other sources: J. C. Dancy. *The Shorter Books of the Apocrypha.* G. W. E. Nickelsburg, *Jewish Writings of the Second Temple Period*, ed. M. E. Stone, 40–46; I. Nowell, "Tobit," *NJBC*; N. R. Petersen, "Tobit," *The Books of the Bible* 2:35-42; D. C. Simpson, "Tobit," *APOT*; A. Wikgren, "Tobit, Book of," *IDB*; F. Zimmerman, *The Book of Tobit.*

Commentary

An Outline

Preface, 1:1-2

The story is set in a specific place and time, although it is legendary, to add realism to the fantastic story that will ensue. The name *Tobit*, a Greek spelling of the Hebrew name that means "God is my good," reveals the main theme. Reference to *Shalmaneser*, who conquered Israel and took the Jews captive in 722 B.C.E., sets the time of the story.

The Distress of Tobit and Sarah, 1:3–3:17

Two stories of misfortune are told in sequence with the slenderest of connections (*On the same day . . . it happened that*, 3:7). At the end of this section, however, the stories merge. The separate misfortunes of Tobit and Sarah eventually result in common blessings. Their stories show God working in diverse situations to effect rescue for his people. Tobit tells his story in first person while Sarah's is told in third person. His story of devotion in crisis is at first a tragic tale: a pious and devoted man having lost his home, family, and eyesight, prepares to die.

The Piety of Tobit the Exile, 1:3-22

The genuinely righteous life involves *acts of charity* (v. 3; see 14:8-9). Tobit's were directed toward his fellow exiles in ASSYRIA. Verses 4-15 flash back to Tobit's life before exile and up to the narrative time of v. 3. The excursus is framed with the theme *I performed many acts of charity for my kindred and my people* (vv. 3, 16).

Before his day, JUDAH and ISRAEL had divided (ca. 922 B.C.E.) and JEROBOAM led the Northern Kingdom into idolatry by erecting at Dan and BETHEL two golden calves as items of worship, thereby supplanting the Temple and the ark of the covenant in Jerusalem (1 Kgs 12:28-29). Although Tobit's tribe of NAPHTALI accepted the new places and means of worship, he resisted. He *alone* (the Greek word is unusual and perhaps emphatic) kept true to God's *everlasting decree* by worshiping in the Jerusalem Temple. He gave three tenths of his earnings rather than three payments of a single tithe.

Women have a role in this story. For example, Tobit's grandmother *Deborah* was his instructor in the Law and Sarah is Tobit's companion in misery and blessing. Nevertheless, women are viewed as extensions of their male counterparts or patrons.

Tobiel is Tobit's father, according to v. 1; but in v. 8 the Greek has *Hananiel*. The confusion of names is complicated; the point is that he was an orphan. In one compact verse Tobit grows up, marries, fathers a child, announces the theme of marriage among one's own people, and introduces his son Tobias, one of the principal characters of the story (v. 9).

In exile Tobit's unique devotion to God (v. 12) resulted in his prosperity. At an earlier time he had deposited an enormous sum of money with Gabael (1:14 has *Gabriel*, although from 4:1 he is called *Gabael*). No justification is given for the trust he had in this minor figure in the story. When the kingship fell to SENNACHERIB (ca. 705 B.C.E.), Tobit had to depart and leave the money behind in Media.

By repeating in v. 16 the refrain of v. 3 Tobit concludes his flashback. His acts of kindness mark him as a caring person and help to define "piety." Burying the unburied dead (vv. 17ff.) put Tobit's life at risk, for he defied the government. His merciful actions toward the dead showed respect for the biblical precept of honor of all dead people, and protected his people's bodies from public disgrace (Zimmerman 1958, 51). Shalmaneser's cruelty to the Jews is recorded in Isa 36 and 2 Kgs 18:13–19:37.

Although Tobit went into hiding and fled when he was betrayed, his fate improved under a new ruler, *Esarhaddon* (680–669 B.C.E.), when his nephew *Ahikar*, elevated to a high position, secured his return to Nineveh. Ahikar's reappointment (v. 22) may simply mean that although he had served as counsellor to one king (Sennacherib) his service under another (Esarhaddon) was not automatic, but represented a second confirmation. More likely, however, this reflects Ahikar's reinstatement after his fall from royal favor. By making Ahikar *a close relative* of Tobit, the author locates Tobit in royal circles, even though he is an exile.

Tobit Loses His Sight, 2:1-14

Chapter 2 begins with a hopeful scene. Tobit returns to Nineveh during better days. His family is restored to him and they celebrate Pentecost, during which slaves, Levites, strangers, orphans, and widows were invited to a feast (cf. Deut 16:9-11). Tobit sends Tobias out to *bring whatever poor person you may find of our people* (v. 2). Tobias reports that an Israelite *has been murdered* by strangulation and lies unburied. We know from 1:17 that Tobit's moral sensitivity to this grievous insult to the Jewish people would move him to bury the man. He keeps the body hidden until after dark for safety's sake (in 1:18 he said he buried the dead *secretly*). Afterward he *washed* himself

because, according to Jewish law, touching the dead made one ritually unclean for seven days (Num 19:11). The "biblical" word of prophecy about mourning (v. 6) adds pathos to the scene. Tobit's pity is described simply and powerfully: *and I wept* (v. 6). This is the first of many occurrences of weeping in the book (2:6; 3:1, 10; 5:18; 6:1; 7:6, 7, 8 bis, 16; 9:6; 10:4, 7; 11:9, 14).

Having become unclean, he washes again and sleeps *by the wall of the courtyard* (v. 9). An ironic consequence of his following the letter and spirit of the Law is that he is blinded by sparrow droppings that fall on his eyes that night. His frequent and futile visits to physicians remind us of the story of the woman with the issue of blood (Mark 5:25-26). As the *four years* of his blindness stretched on, Tobit became resigned to it as permanent. Even though he was pious and merciful Tobit was not immune to the misfortunes of nature and society (see Dancy 1972, 22).

2:11-14. Trouble at home. Anna (whose name means "full of grace") has to earn wages for the family. This causes tension and Tobit begins to treat her with self-pitying suspicion; he does not believe her when she tells the truth. Her response cuts to the quick; she cynically asks what good all his merciful deeds have done them.

His Prayer for Death, 3:1-6

Tobit begins to lose heart and to weep again. He prays to God for mercy (vv. 2-5), but also expresses his acceptance of the theology of retribution. He confesses God's uprightness and the sins both of himself and his people. In his depression and hopelessness he asks God to let him die (v. 6). There are many parallels to Job's story here. What he longs for is not peace and heaven but the cessation of his miseries and *the eternal home* (v. 6).

Sarah's Misfortune and Averted Suicide, 3:7-10

Sarah is presented much more briefly than is Tobit. The narrative changes from first person to third person and shifts to the distant city of Ecbatana. The only link between the crisis of Tobit and that of Sarah that is about to be narrated is that Tobit's prayer for death and Sarah's contemplation of suicide occurred *on the same day*. This shows that it is not the people, places, or events that link the two characters but the work of God. The names of the personalities serve as sign posts for the story: *Raguel* means "Friend of God"; *Sarah* means "Princess"; *Asmodeus* means "One who destroys." Sarah is under siege by the demon who inhabits her bridal chamber. She becomes despondent when one of her maids curses her for beating them in her distress. This curse initiates Sarah's contemplation of suicide.

As Tobit has wept over his situation, so now Sarah weeps over her own (v. 10). She decides to hang herself but does not go through with it. Her ethical reasoning is typically Hebraic—she is concerned for the well-being of her father. A radical individualism was not part of the ancient Hebrew and Jewish mentality. She resolves, as did Tobit, to ask God to put an end to her troubles. As her story progresses, she shows increasing similarities to Tobit that help the reader to anticipate a merging of their fates.

Her Prayer for Death, 3:11-15

In a gesture reminiscent of DANIEL, Sarah raises her hands, faces toward Jerusalem (see Dan 6:10), and offers a prayer that is almost as long as the narrative that has introduced her. Her prayer is unlike Tobit's, in that she quickly makes her request to die. There is no retribution theology here, for she says, *I am innocent . . . I have not disgraced my name* (vv. 14-15). She prays out of misery, not guilt.

Sarah's claim that her father has *no . . . other kindred* (v. 15) is problematic, for she later marries Tobias because he is her relative. Perhaps her despair and her being a distant relative to Tobias are the causes of this complaint. Despair and depression often obliterate hope.

The Merging of the Fortunes of Tobit and Sarah, 3:16-17

God's miraculous answer to Tobit's and Sarah's prayers simultaneously is dramatized by an INCLUSIO framing v. 16 with the words *at that same time*. Raphael, the angel of God sent to help them, must have been familiar to the readers as an angel, for he is simply called Raphael here and not called an angel until 5:4.

The writer puts the cure of Tobit's and Sarah's dilemmas in the form of a CHIASM: the blindness of Tobit is narrated (A), then the crisis of Sarah (B); but her remedy (B') will precede his (A'). Another literary feature is used here also, the motif of light and darkness. Tobit's cure means he can *see God's light*. By this image, the story intends to teach theology and

faith, and not simply to entertain. "At the same time" (v. 17) links the two characters and their fates.

Tobias Journeys to Media, 4:1–12:22

Tobias's Departure, 4:1–5:17a

4:1-2. The reason for the journey. God had heard and answered Tobit's prayer although Tobit did not know it. He makes final preparation for death. Recalling the ten talents in Media, he plans to send Tobias to retrieve them. It is strange Tobit did not remember the money earlier, when Anna had to go to work.

4:3-21. Tobit's fatherly advice on living. Drawing on the wisdom tradition and on the story of Ahikar, the writer now delivers one of the book's two main blocks of wisdom teaching (see 12:6-10). The advice of v. 10 that *almsgiving delivers from death* is proved for the author by the life of Ahikar (see 14:10). In this type of deathbed exhortation known as a "testament," one advised his children or followers to avoid his vices and pronounced a blessing on his heirs (see the TESTAMENTS OF THE TWELVE PATRIARCHS, John 14–17 and Heb 11:21-22). Verse 6 shows retribution theology: prosperity comes to those who live truly. While sincerity should underlie acts of mercy and kindness (v. 7), retribution theology also has an eye to personal benefit for pious living (vv. 7, 9, 10, 14). Tobit reemphasizes the teaching of marriage within the family (v. 12) with historical precedent (NOAH, ABRAHAM, ISAAC, JACOB). He expresses the hope of many ancient Jews, that they *will inherit the land* (v. 12; see Ps 37:3, 9, 11, 22, 29, 34, and Jesus' beatitude that "the meek . . . will inherit the earth," Matt 5:5). Tobit counsels Tobias to *love your kindred* and to marry within the family (v. 13).

The guideline of reciprocal behavior in v. 15 is made into the positive "golden" rule later by Jesus (Matt 7:12). Not only mercy but generosity must mark real acts of piety (v. 16). The advice of v. 17 may refer to the gentile practice of giving food to the bereaved or even of holding banquets for the deceased. It distinguishes the righteous from sinners. Tobit calls his final admonitions *commandments* because he is earnest about their observance.

At the end of his testament Tobit returns to the silver talents in Media. The financial situation of the family is serious, for the word which Tobit uses for *become poor* (v. 21) in Greek means to be destitute or resourceless. Tobit does not believe that they are rich because of the silver, but that they have great wealth if they reverence God, since God is free to do as he *chooses* (see v. 19). He believes that piety before God must precede all else.

5:1-3. Tobias's response to his father. Tobias is eager to obey his father (v. 1); but he is also ready to get the money. The security of the deposit is based on a *bond*. This word probably means that each party had a copy or receipt of the transaction and that Gabael's was in two parts—one to be kept by Gabael and one to be put inside the bags with the silver as an invoice (Zimmerman 1958, 72–73). Tobit sends his son to find a *trustworthy* companion and to get the money (v. 3).

5:4-8. Raphael the guide. The narrator tells the reader what is unknown to Tobias—that his companion is an angel. This guide later (v. 13) gives his name as Azariah, by which he goes until his self-disclosure in 12:11-15. Ancient novels were not concerned with literary truthfulness: Raphael lies about his family, experience and knowledge and withholds truth from his "employer." By contact with pagan religions, Jewish angelology had now developed to the point that angels could appear as people, carry on conversations, and even use magic to do God's work.

5:9-17a. Raphael's job interview. Raphael's attitude of hope contrasts with Tobit's despair (v. 10). His foreknowledge of Tobit's cure stated in his encouragement (*Take courage; the time is near for God to heal you*, v. 10) ought to arouse suspicions, but it appears to be lost on Tobit who turns directly to business. In their conversation, Raphael gives a series of symbolic names: his own means "God helps"; his so-called father's name, Hananiah, means "God is merciful"; Nathan means "He (God) gives"; Shemeliah means "God hears." (see Nowell 1990, 570). The hopeful names and fortuitous discovery of so many mutual acquaintances should encourage Tobit to see that God is at work in this venture. Ironically, he cannot recognize that Raphael's words of encouragement (v. 16) already guarantee what he prays for as the two depart (v. 17).

A Farewell Scene, 5:17b–6:1a

It is now Anna's turn to weep (v. 18). By *the staff of our hand* she probably means one on whom they depend (Zimmerman 1958, 77). What she means by *ransom* is unclear but she may mean that she prefers to let the money stay in Media if it will "buy" her son's safety. Tobit calls her his *sister* (v. 21; see also 7:15; 8:4), probably a term of endearment like the term "brother," which the men use for each other. His encouragement works, for she stops weeping (6:1a).

The Journey, 6:1b–9:6

6:1b-9. A strange medical fish story. The dog (Tobias's pet?) has no function in the story, except to reappear when Tobias returns home (11:4). This may be the remnants of an earlier version of a quest folktale used by the author. Many stories of fish with surprising contents circulated in the ancient world. This tale is more natural, for the anatomy of the fish, not its peculiar contents, is the "gift" the fish gives. Raphael says that the *gall, heart, and liver* are good as medicine. The point of the story is God's unforeseen provision for his people.

6:10-18. Raphael instructs Tobias about Sarah. Raphael's coaching must be quite a shock to Tobias who set out to retrieve Tobit's money, not to obtain a wife. Raphael appears to know all about the family situation of Tobias and Raguel, yet his omniscience arouses no suspicion on the part of Tobias. Sarah would be a fine catch for Tobias, because she is *sensible, brave, and very beautiful* (v. 12). The rapier edge of Jewish legalism intrudes into even this happy circumstance: Raguel's refusal would mean the *penalty of death* (v. 13). This penalty, not found in the OT, may be a rabbinical teaching.

We do not know how Tobias heard of the curse on the girl (v. 14), but his statement gives us full information about her situation (vv. 14-15). As a pious son, Tobias fears not for himself but for what his death would do to his parents.

Raphael describes the marriage as a fulfillment of Tobit's orders and Tobias accepts it as such. The angel also gives instruction on how to use the fish heart and liver to drive off the demon by their odor. Alongside the magical rite Tobias and Sarah are to pray to God for aid (v. 18). The marriage, presented as God's will ordained before creation (see 7:11), will benefit both bride and groom: Tobias *will save her* (i.e., from her curse) and she *will go with* Tobias (to his home to perpetuate their family). Tobias loves her *very much*, even though he has never seen her. Raphael was apparently a very successful matchmaker.

7:1-9a. The reception at Raguel's home. The journey to Media ends at Raguel's house in Ecbatana, indicating that it is God's work and not money that truly blesses. The travelers are invited inside without Raguel's knowing who they are and they call one another *brother* before any formal introduction. Raphael's answer (v. 5) that Tobit is *in good health* is hard to understand, since in v. 7 Raguel refers to Tobit's blindness as the *most miserable of calamities*. All three members of the host family weep.

7:9b-16. Tobias's proposal and their wedding. The travelers *bathed* themselves and *washed* their hands in ceremonial cleansing before eating (see Mark 7:1-12). Raguel's offer of Sarah to Tobias is surprising—perhaps he has realized that Tobias is the only eligible relative (although we must infer that; it is only stated *after* the offer). Raguel's injunction to *Eat and drink, and be merry tonight* (v. 10) is more than hospitality, for he fears that Tobias will die that night. Raguel is not hopeless, because his words *the Lord will act on behalf of you both* (v. 11) are a Hebraism that means God will deal mercifully or beneficially with them (see 1 Sam 14:6; Zimmerman 1958, 88). His hope is mixed with dread, for on the wedding night he digs a grave for Tobias (8:9), and when Tobias does not die he thanks God that it did not turn out as he expected (8:16).

Raguel repeats his belief in the foreordination of the marriage (v. 11). By this marriage Tobias obeys his father's injunction to marry within the family. Raguel sends for Sarah and Edna, who dined apart from the men, and confirms the marriage contract in writing. Preparation of the wedding room causes Edna to weep, probably because she fears another death. She advises Sarah twice to *take courage*.

8:1-9a. The wedding night. Tobias performs the exorcism as Raphael had directed and at the smell of burning fish parts the demon flees *to the remotest parts of Egypt* (v. 3) where Raphael secures him hand and foot. The Jews thought of the desert as the home of the demons.

The narrative here is awkward. The parents appear to be present during the exorcism, but between the exorcism and v. 4 the demon and Raphael go all the way to Egypt. Also, if Raguel were present, why does he dig a grave (vv. 9ff.)? Ancient magical tales were not concerned with narrative perfection.

Tobias follows Raphael's instruction (6:18) and prays specifically for God's *mercy and safety*. The prayer is quite "biblical," being both a blessing and a recitation of the creation of ADAM and EVE. Tobias requests that his rightful and pure marriage be blessed by God.

8:9b-18. God preserves the newlyweds. Raguel's fears overcome his hope, for he digs Tobias's grave, anticipating his death. In a manner reminiscent of fairy tales Edna sends her maid to the bedchamber to see if Tobias is alive or dead. Strangely, the maid shows no

emotion and *informs* the parents that all is well. Raguel offers thanksgiving for God's mercy and covers up his pessimism by having the grave filled in.

8:19-21. A prolonged wedding celebration. In his joy, which had eluded him seven times before, Raguel prepares an abundant feast and a two-week celebration (twice as long as the Jewish law prescribed: Gen 29:27; Judg 14:12). Part of the significance of marriage and childbirth in antiquity was that it provided for the protection and transmission of property. Raguel rejoices at having an heir and elaborates on the union of the two branches of the family.

9:1-6. Raphael brings Gabael to the celebration. The purpose of the journey is not yet fulfilled, for Tobit's bond has not been acquired. Tobias sends Raphael to get the money and to bring Gabael to Ecbatana to the wedding celebration. Tobias feels obligated not to leave (v. 2) but obligated also to fulfill his father's charge. Gabael is a trustworthy man, for the investment had *their seals intact* (v. 5). When Gabael sees Tobias he weeps with joy (v. 6). The purpose of the journey is now fulfilled.

Tobias Returns Home with Sarah, 10:1–11:18

10:1-7a. Tobit and Anna fear for Tobias. In a sudden shift of tone the author turns from the joyous wedding to the anxious homefront. The fourteen-day celebration has delayed Tobias, causing Tobit to rationalize the delay. *To worry* in Greek means "to be grieved." When Anna begins to fear that Tobias has died Tobit tells her to *stop worrying*. In a realistic characterization of human passions the writer has Anna turn on the would-be comforter and say, *Be quiet yourself!* Anna's watchfulness, which belies her conclusion that Tobias is dead, is also a pathetic touch.

10:7b-13. Tobias begins his return journey. After the interlude of anxiety at Nineveh the author returns to the scene at Ecbatana. Tobias is a dutiful and honorable youth—willing to be bound to the lengthy celebration, but as soon as it is over, eager to return to his father. Both Raguel and Edna bless the couple and state their anticipation of grandchildren. In the farewell the parties restate the solidity of family ties.

11:1-15. Tobias and Raphael arrive before Sarah and heal Tobit's eyes. The writer tells only of the end of Tobias's return journey. Raphael wants to see Tobit's healing before Sarah arrives, perhaps for the sake of Tobit, or for Sarah, or both. He reminds Tobias of the curative fish gall. The dog mentioned at the beginning of the journey (6:2) is with them. In light of her earlier emotions, Anna's reaction when she first sees Tobias is strangely subdued. The procedure for curing Tobit's blindness is repeated by Raphael, except that earlier (6:9) an additional procedure was mentioned—blowing upon the scales or films on the patient's eyes. When Tobias provides the cure, however (v. 11), he does blow on Tobit's eyes.

The portraiture once again rises to its earlier level with v. 9. Anna's weeping and blind Tobit's stumbling offer real pathos. The exorcism and healing miracles include an injunction to *take courage* (v. 11). The point seems to be that they should trust God in the midst of discouraging circumstances. The cure seems almost forced upon Tobit; but it works and he weeps. A prayer of thanksgiving follows, as usual. With his sight restored Tobit can now see fully the blessings that have come to him.

11:16-18. A time for rejoicing. The amazement of the people at Tobit's health confirms the healing miracles. Tobit blesses Sarah, affirms the family relations and four times refers to her as his daughter. The writer hyperbolically says that all the Jews of Nineveh rejoiced that day (v. 17). The regular seven-day wedding celebration is held in Nineveh with Ahikar and his nephew NADAB present. Perhaps the writer wanted to demonstrate that Ahikar was Tobit's *close relative* (1:22). At this point almost all of the story is complete: Tobit sees, Sarah's curse is lifted, the money in trust has been recovered, the travelers have returned home safely, and two sets of worrying parents are happy. Even the dog has come home. Therefore what follows in the Book of Tobit is complementary to the story—the explanation of God's mercy (12:1-22), a grand finale of prayer (13:1-17), and a fitting conclusion to the whole (14:1-15). One matter remains unresolved that must be settled first.

The Conclusion of Raphael's Work, 12:1-22

12:1-5. Father and son attempt to pay the companion. The only unfulfilled action in the story is the remuneration of the *brother* who was hired to go with Tobias (5:10-17a). Tobit and Tobias, men of honor and generosity, determine to pay *the man* and to give him *as a bonus* one-half of all they brought back. The accomplishments of Raphael are summarized tersely and the offer is made to the hired man (vv. 1-5). Folklore scholars see in this generous offering a trace of the tale of the "Grateful Dead."

12:6-10. Raphael gives wise counsel. The guide does not accept the offer but offers his employers wise advice. First, he advises them to recognize and honor God publicly (vv. 6-7a). Secondly, he gives wisdom teachings on doing good and its benefit (vv. 7b-10). He encourages them mostly to almsgiving with righteousness, but also to prayer and fasting. A traditional definition of Jewish righteousness included these three components of almsgiving, prayer, and fasting (see Matt 6:1-18 where Jesus taught *piety* by instruction on almsgiving, prayer, and fasting). Raphael's wise teaching is quite similar to Tobit's (4:3-21), both holding that *almsgiving saves from death*. Piety and ethics are inextricably conjoined in the mind of the writer.

12:11-22. He reveals himself and ascends. Raphael follows his own counsel by honoring God publicly and reveals that all along he, as angel of the Lord, has been at work before God for their aid. In the OT angels do not play nearly so great a role as this. Angelology was introduced into Judaism during the Babylonian Exile by association with pagan religions. Among the many similarities this story has to the Book of Job is the idea that God tests his favorites (the testing being done to Job through Satan, to Tobit through the angel Raphael, v. 14).

Beginning with v. 16, Raphael's self-disclosure and ascension are quite similar to the stories of Jesus' transfiguration, resurrection, and ascension. D. C. Simpson (1913, 1:234n.) noted these similarities: *Do not be afraid* (v. 17; cf. Matt 28:5, 10); *peace be with you* (v. 17; cf. Luke 24:36); *you were watching me* (v. 19; cf. Luke 24:37, 39); *I . . . did not eat* (v. 19; cf. Luke 24:43); *I am ascending to him who sent me* (v. 20; cf. John 20:17, 21; 16:5); *write down* (v. 20; cf. John 20:30; 21:25; Rev 1:11); *he ascended* (v. 20; cf. Eph 4:9); *they stood up, and could see him no more* (v. 21; cf. Acts 21:9, 10); *an angel of God had appeared to them* (v. 22; cf. 1 Tim 3:16). In this revelation the father and son are only "seconds" on the stage. The focus has shifted to Raphael.

Tobit's Prayer of Praise, 13:1-17

13:1-7. Song for the exiles. At the end of Raphael's self-disclosure Tobit and Tobias *kept blessing God and singing his praises* (12:22). Chapter 13, which has no connection to the rest of the narrative of Tobit, records Tobit's praise. First Tobit gives a word of encouragement to the exiled Jews. While his song does not fit the preceding narrative, there are some continuities. Tobit has learned that God *afflicts, and he shows mercy* (v. 2), that as all the events of his life were overseen by God, so *there is nothing that can escape his hand* (v. 2). He has believed in a theology of retribution, that *He will afflict you for your iniquities* (v. 5). He has shown openly his pious devotion to God and has been advised by Raphael to honor God openly (v. 6). Most of all, in spite of all the weeping he and his family have done, he has learned to take courage in his God, for *he will turn to you* (v. 6). As an exile himself, Tobit declares his resolve to honor his God openly (v. 7).

13:8-17. Song for Jerusalem. Tobit now holds out to Jerusalem the saving activity of God that he and his family have known and that he proposes for the exiles. Retribution theology is still present (*he afflicted you for the deeds of your hands*, v. 9), but the same hope in God's mercy is also present (*but [God] will again have mercy*, v. 9). He calls upon Jerusalem to honor God openly (v. 10). The language and content of v. 11 resemble Isa 60. In v. 16 Tobit prophesies the rebuilding of the Temple (*tent* of v. 10) with precious stones (influenced by Isa 54:11-12).

Tobit's Legacy, 14:1-15

The Book of Tobit closes with a description of the conclusion of Tobit's life and the continuing blessings his life produced. The writer gives something of an obituary of Tobit and his final testament (earlier in the story Tobit had given what he thought would be his testament since he expected to die then).

The Obituary of Tobit, 14:1-2

At the end of a story that began with Tobit's distress and is filled with weeping, the author says he *died in peace*, aged and honored. Tobit did not forget God after his healing but continued to live a kind and merciful life and to honor God openly.

The Testament of Tobit, 14:3-11a

In 4:3-21 Tobit summoned his son Tobias for the purpose of giving to him what he thought would be his last legacy and testament. But his life was to be longer and more blessed than he could know. The author now gives Tobit's last testament. This time he calls for *Tobias and the seven sons of Tobias* (seven, a perfect number, indicates his perfect blessedness in the matter of progeny, so significant to ancient Jews). He advises Tobias to heed the prophetic warning of NAHUM regarding the destruction of Nineveh. Six times in one verse (v. 4) Tobit states his utter confidence in the fulfillment of the prophets' words. It was easy for the writer to portray Tobit's having such confidence, for by his own time those prophecies had been fulfilled, all except one: that through Israel all nations would *be converted and worship God in truth . . . abandon their idols . . . [and] praise the eternal God* (vv. 6-7). Tobit concludes his testament with his hope for the gathering in of exiled Jews to Jerusalem. He enjoins his successors to continue the aspects of mercy that marked his own life—almsgiving and open honoring of God (vv. 8-9).

Finally Tobit returns to the point at which he began his testament. Tobit warns Tobias and his family to flee Nineveh when Tobit and Anna die. In his final exhortation to almsgiving as a true expression of piety Tobit summarizes the story of Ahikar as his paradigm (v. 10).

Conclusion, 14:11b-15

The writer concludes his tale by showing that even Tobit's testament was fulfilled. Tobias obeyed his father, honored his parents at their death, and moved to Ecbatana. This made possible an additional family reunion of Sarah with her parents, who can now see the grandchildren they anticipated. Tobias's familial devotion is stressed. The prosperity that came to him witnesses once again to the writer's theology of retribution.

Works Cited

Dancy, J. C. 1972. *The Shorter Books of the Apocrypha.*

Nowell, I. 1990. "Tobit." *NJBC.*

Rost, Leonhard. 1971. *Judaism Outside the Hebrew Canon.*

Simpson, D. C. 1913. "Tobit," in *APOT.*

Zimmerman, Frank. 1958. *The Book of Tobit.*

Judith

Thomas O. Hall, Jr.

Introduction

Judith is a historical novella in which the chief character Judith (Heb. "Jew" [fem.]), a devout widow from Bethulia (Heb. virgin), kills the commander of the allied Assyrian army and saves JERUSALEM, the Temple, and the Jewish people. She and her exploits are reminiscent of other Hebrew women who helped to deliver Israel, for example, DEBORAH (Judg 4:4-10), Jael (Judg 4:17-22), an unnamed woman of Thebez (Judg 9:50-57), and ESTHER.

Date and Authorship

An unknown author wrote the book between 165 B.C.E., when Judas Maccabeus led in cleansing the Temple, and the end of the first century C.E. when the book is mentioned by Clement of Rome.

Some have attempted to date it as early as the Persian period because of Persian expressions employed by the writer. (From 539 B.C.E. until Alexander the Great, the Jews lived under the suzerainty of the Persians. Undoubtedly Persian expressions would survive in the vocabulary in the same way that Zoroastrian religious influences remained in JUDAISM.)

If the author drew on the story of the defeat of the Syrian Greek general Nicanor and the displaying of his head in Jerusalem, the story would have been written between 161 B.C.E. and the fall of the Temple, 70 C.E.

Internal evidence does not clearly establish whether the writer lived in Palestine or the diaspora.

Canonicity

Why Judith was not included in the OT canon is open to conjecture; arguments are inconclusive. The question is intensified by the fact that Esther, which without its apocryphal additions is not an obviously religious book, was included although the name of God is not even used. Judith on the other hand is extremely religious, extolling piety, rigorous observance of religious rituals, prayer, and faith.

The early church, whose OT was the LXX, accorded Judith recognition among the sacred books, and the Jews in Alexandria for whom the LXX was translated probably accepted it in the same light. Most scholars believe it to have been written in Hebrew, but when the Council of Jamnia convened ca. 90 C.E. the Greek translation probably was the only one known to the participants. At least Origen, less than a hundred years after the close of the council, stated that no Hebrew text was known to exist (Enslin and Zeitlin 1972, 43).

Among the reasons given for the exclusion of Judith from the Jewish canon is the uneasiness over the conversion of Achior the Ammonite (14:10), in spite of the fact that Deut 23:4 forbade the admission of Moabites and Ammonites to the Israelite assembly. In addition, a first century C.E. ruling demanded that following circumcision a proselyte also be baptized; Achior, however, was only circumcised. Zeitlin (Enslin and Zeitlin 1972, 24) states that these were sufficient reasons for Judith's exclusion.

Toni Craven (1983, 117-18) argues convincingly that the novella was excluded because Judith, the heroine, was such a strong, dominant female character. The fact that the book is nonhistorical should also be considered a possible reason for its exclusion.

In the early church only a few voices, including some Eastern leaders (Metzger 1957, 179), were raised against the canonicity of the Apocrypha, including Judith. Jerome included Judith in the Vulgate although he claimed to have translated it from a Chaldean text. Jerome's translation is considerably briefer than the LXX but there is no compelling evidence that the "Chaldean" text was the original Hebrew. Since Jerome the books of the Jewish Apocrypha have been interspersed, in supposed historical order, in Catholic Bibles, accorded canonical status, and called deuterocanonical. Judith is placed between Tobit and Esther. Although there were some who had earlier expressed opposition to its inclusion, since Luther the Apocrypha has not been considered canonical in Protestant circles.

For Further Study

In the *Mercer Dictionary of the Bible:* APOCRYPHAL LITERATURE; JUDITH, BOOK OF; MACCABEES; NEBUCHADREZZAR; RED SEA/REED SEA; SAMARITANS; WOMEN IN THE OLD TESTAMENT.
In other sources: B. Bayer, "The Book of Judith in the Arts," *EncJud*; L. H. Brockington, *A Critical Introduction to the Apocrypha*; R. H. Charles, ed., *APOT*; T. Craven, *Artistry and Faith in the Book of Judith*,

SBLDS; J. C. Dancy, *The Shorter Books of the Apocrypha*; R. C. Denton, *TheApocrypha, Bridge of the Testaments*; M. J. Dresden, "Ecbatana," *IDB*; M. S. Enslin and S. Zeitlin, *The Book of Judith*; B. M. Metzger, *An Introduction to the Apocrypha*; W. O. E. Oesterly, *An Introduction to the Books of the Apocrypha*; C. F. Pfeiffer, *Between the Testaments*; R. H. Pfeiffer, *History of New Testament Times, with an Introduction to the Apocrypha*; E. Purdie, *The Story of Judith in German and English Literature*; C. C. Torrey, *The Apocryphal Literature*; P. Winter, "The Book of Judith," *IDB*.

Commentary

An Outline

Assyria's War against the Jews, 1:1–7:32

Nebuchadnezzar's Defeat of Arphaxad, 1:1-16

Nebuchadnezzar II reigned over the Babylonian Empire from 605 until 562 B.C.E. and never was king of Assyria. Nor was his capital Nineveh; it had been destroyed by his father Nabopolasar in 612 B.C.E. He undoubtedly represents Antiochus IV Epiphanes, who polluted the Temple in 168 B.C.E. For a Jewish audience Nineveh was a good choice to represent a ruthless power. There is no evidence that such a Median king fortified and ruled from Ecbatana, located in present Iran. These references plus other inexact historical and geographical data alerted Jewish readers to the fact that the author did not intend to present the following story as factual.

1:7-12. Eastern and western powers respond to Nebuchadnezzar. The nations of the east come to meet Nebuchadnezzar probably in peace and join his forces as allies. They are not described as defeated along with Arphaxad or subsequently punished as were a vast number of western nations from Persia to Ethiopia who refused Nebuchadnezzar's summons. They treat his ambassadors with disdain because they consider Nebuchadnezzar no more than their equal, an ordinary man (Enslin and Zeitlin 1972, 63). This is a stunning rebuke if Nebuchadnezzar represents Antiochus IV Epiphanes whose honorific title, Epiphanes, means "manifest," understood as "God manifest."

1:13-16. Arphaxad killed. To rest and refresh his troops, Nebuchadnezzar gives a banquet that lasts one hundred twenty days. This seems extremely prolonged but it was not as lengthy as one the Persian king, Ahasuerus, gave for his subordinate leaders. The banquet lasted one hundred eighty days, followed by seven additional days for the common people of Susa (Esth 1:3-5).

Holofernes to Subdue Western Nations, 2:1–3:10

Holofernes (2:4), commander-in-chief of Nebuchadnezzar's army, serves as his surrogate villain. There is no other reference to a person by this name serving Nebuchadnezzar. There was a military leader named Holofernes from Asia Minor who fought the Egyptians in the mid fourth century B.C.E. (Dancy 1972, 78).

The vastness of the Assyrian army, one hundred twenty thousand infantry and twelve thousand cavalry, is not unusual in ancient biblical and secular references. The route of the army, which marched three hundred miles in three days (2:21), is impossible to reconstruct. The writer does not concentrate on historical or geographical accuracy but on the psychological affect of the Assyrian juggernaut of pillage and slaughter which spread paralyzing fear.

The cities along the coast (2:28) send envoys to Holofernes, calling themselves *slaves* (3:4) of Nebuchadnezzar, and offering to surrender unconditionally. This is meant to contrast vividly with the following story of Jewish resistance.

Holofernes chooses auxiliary troops (3:6) from those who had capitulated, thus increasing his forces by fifty thousand infantry (7:2). The destruction of their sanctuaries, *sacred groves* and *gods* (3:8) and the statement that only Nebuchadnezzar would be worshipped as deity reminded the Jews of Antiochus IV Epiphanes and other Syrian rulers who had insisted on their own deification.

Because of its history as a battlefield, the vicinity of Esdraelon, OT Jezreel (3:9), was well chosen as a setting for the showdown struggle between an evil secular power and God's covenant people.

Only the Jews Refuse to Surrender, 4:1–7:32

4:1-15. The Judeans prepare to resist the Assyrians. The reference to the recent return of the Jews from captivity (v. 3) is strange indeed. It was the Persian king, CYRUS the Great, who allowed them to return to their ancestral home in 538 B.C.E. The setting of the Judith narrative is in the eighteenth year of Nebuchadnezzar (587 B.C.E.), who carried them to Babylon in 587/6 B.C.E. The cleansing of the Temple, its vessels, and the altar (v. 3) better describes the time of Judas Maccabeus when he led his people in such an event in 165 B.C.E. Samaria's (v. 4) inclusion among the cities warned by Jerusalem seems unusual. After the end of the Babylonian captivity until NT times mutual animosity prevailed between Jews and SAMARITANS.

Joakim, the *high priest* (v. 6), is not known to have served in Jerusalem during Maccabean times but a high priest by that name is alluded to in Neh 12:10. This seems insufficient evidence for dating the book's events during the Persian suzerainty. *The senate* (v. 8) is a council of elders and is a term used especially of the *sanhedrin* in the NT. The term also appears in 1 Macc 12:6 and 2 Macc 1:10. The identity of Bethulia (v. 6), the geographical focal point of the remaining narrative, is uncertain, although C. C. Torrey (1963, 91) claims that it had been long established as a pseudonym for the Samaritan city of SHECHEM. He argues strongly that the use of the word Shechem would have been offensive to the Jews but this position is militated

against by the fact that Samaria had already been warned by the forces in Jerusalem (v. 4). Although there are narrow passes in the hill country of Judea the reference to passes "only wide enough for two men" is the author's way of emphasizing their strategic importance in controlling the invasion route to Jerusalem (v. 7).

The author shows the intensity of the peoples' penance by references to their dressing in sackcloth, not only themselves but even the livestock and the altar (v. 12). Throughout the OT the wearing of sackcloth and the spreading of ashes on the head indicate intense emotion.

5:1-24. Holofernes seeks reason for Jewish defiance. Holofernes addresses the leaders of his auxiliary troops from Moab, Ammon, and the Philistine coastal plain as Canaanites (vv. 2-3). This is, of course, inaccurate but not surprising coming from the mouth of an Assyrian leader who shows only limited knowledge of the whole area. The Moabites and Ammonites did in fact join forces with the Babylonians when Nebuchadnezzar destroyed Jerusalem in 587 (2 Kgs 25:8-21). Holofernes's question (vv. 3b-4) as to the source of the Jewish strength emphasizes military power. The storyteller possibly uses this to highlight his belief that Jewish strength is in faithfulness to their God. The Ammonite leader Achior, apparently a literary invention, gives a generally accurate biblical account of Jewish history from UR of the Chaldees to the return from the EXILE (vv. 5-19).

The writer indicates that the Israelites crossed the Red Sea (v. 13), which is the same as the LXX rendition of Exod 13:18; however, the Hebrew of the later passage reads "Sea of Reeds."

Achior's warning not to attack unless the Judeans have been guilty of sin against their God (vv. 20-21) is certainly in harmony with the preexilic prophets who depicted Israel's defeats as a result of apostasy from their God. The Assyrian boast that they will not be afraid of the Israelites who cannot field a sufficient army shows they still miss the point. The struggle will not be decided by superior military strength (vv. 23-24). Achior does not serve an essential role in the plot unless it is to contrast this knowledgeable gentile who became a proselyte with the weak faith of Bethulia and its three male leaders.

6:1-21. Holofernes delivers Achior to Bethulia. Holofernes's address further sets the stage for confrontation between the God of Israel and Nebuchadnezzar, whom Holofernes claims is the only god. Although

Achior and his mercenaries (v. 2) are Ammonites, they are referred to as Ephraimites in the LXX and some other translations, for example, NEB. This is probably a sarcastic allusion to their being actually loyal to the Jews.

Bethulia's magistrates and inhabitants readily accept at face value Achior's rehearsal of what had happened in Holofernes's council (vv. 14-17). Only in a fictional account would he have escaped careful questioning. Historical identification of the magistrates is impossible. The most significant statement about them is that the chief magistrate, Uzziah, is from the tribe of Simeon (v. 15), which later is identified as the same tribe as that of Judith (9:2).

That the feast given for the elders (vv. 20-21) is literally a drinking party (Enslin and Zeitlin 1972, 100) should cause readers no problem. The drinking of wine was such a regular part of dining that the phrase is probably just a synonym for a feast. One might more naturally wonder how they could feast during such a depressing episode.

7:1-18. The Assyrians and allies besiege Bethulia. After effective use of psychological warfare by parading his army, now increased by fifty thousand mercenaries (v. 2), in the plain below Bethulia, Holofernes seizes the springs which supply the city's water. The reader undoubtedly wonders why Bethulia's water source is twice captured; first by Holofernes's forces (v. 7) and later by the Moabites (v. 17) after they and their Edomite cohorts (vv. 8-17) convince Holofernes that this would be good military strategy.

The Edomites are by tradition descendants of Esau, Jacob's twin brother. Being closely related did not make them friends with the Jews. They were known later as Idumeans and were conquered by John Hyrcanus, and forcefully converted to Judaism. The Herods of NT times were Idumeans.

7:19-32. Inhabitants of Bethulia insist upon surrender. After thirty-four days with water almost gone the city's inhabitants upbraid their leaders for not surrendering. Even if the city were sacked and the citizens taken into slavery they would at least be alive! This reminds one of the Sea of Reeds episode when the disheartened Israelites blamed Moses for leading them into the wilderness to die (Exod 14:10-12). The cry that they were being punished for the sins of their fathers (v. 28) is antithetical to Jeremiah's assertion that henceforth the person will die for his own wrongdoing (Jer 31:29-30). Uzziah's promise to heed their wish if deliverance does not come within five days is

further proof of his depiction as essentially weak (vv. 30-31). A later reference shows he hoped that rain would fill their cisterns (8:31) even though rain would have been unusual at harvest time (4:5), which came at the end of the October to April rainy season.

Judith Decapitates Holofernes 8:1–13:20

Judith Reproves Elders for Testing God, 8:1-31

8:1-8. Beautiful, virtuous widow Judith introduced. After informing his readers that Judith had heard about the inhabitants' outrageous upbraiding of their rulers (7:23-32) the narrator describes her in a long, parenthetical excursus. Judith, the feminine form of the word "Jew," could very well stand for the ideal Jewish woman (cf. Prov 31:10-31). Her genealogy is rather long and historically confusing (v. 1). Obviously its purpose was to show that she was descended from Simeon whom, for some unclear reason, she desired to rehabilitate (Gen 34; 49:1-6), but his name is left out of the ancestral list. Her piety is highlighted by the fact that she remained unmarried after her husband's death, continuously wore mourning clothes and sackcloth, and voluntarily fasted during each day—except special days and festivals when it was forbidden (vv. 4-6). Further, she has erected a structure on the roof of her house for pious meditation (v. 5). Her widow's lot was atypical inasmuch as she had inherited wealth from her deceased husband (v. 7). This status could well have been considered as proof of her godliness. Her piety and meditation did not keep her from taking a personal interest in her estate (v. 7) nor in the affairs of the city. As the long introduction 1:1–7:32 leads up to the main story, so this excursus sets the stage for Judith's dramatic acts.

8:9-31. Judith chides Bethulia's leaders. Judith's unusual standing in the community, probably enhanced by her piety and possibly by her wealth, is clearly evidenced by the fact that she could summon the leaders to her rooftop tent (vv. 10, 36). The maid (9:10) was a favorite slave (16:23) who was steward over Judith's possessions and her companion in the daring foray into the Assyrian camp (10:11).

Judith claims the oath given by Uzziah to surrender in five days unless God intervened is *not right* (v. 11) for two reasons. The leaders were testing God, forbidden in Deut 6:14, and putting themselves above (NRSV, *in the place of*) God (v. 12). Her disdain for this foolish action is revealed when she exclaims, *you will never learn anything* (v. 13). Her point is that God tests people and not vice versa. God cannot be coerced to do humans' will.

In the most profound part (vv. 18-27) of her speech Judith gives a clear rationale for the nation's current suffering. It could not be for worshipping gods made with hands that had caused the Exile, for none of her contemporary Israelites were guilty of such practices (vv. 18-20). Thus, she claims, all suffering is not due to sin, citing examples from Israel's history—Abraham (Gen 22), Isaac (Gen 24), and Jacob (Gen 27)—whose suffering was more intense than their present suffering. She suggests God sends suffering to discipline his people, not to destroy them but to strengthen and mature them (v. 27).

The weak Uzziah, who professes to agree with Judith, shows he still does not understand what Judith has said (vv. 11-27) by pleading with her to pray for rain (v. 31).

Judith Announces a Secret Plan for Deliverance, 8:32-36

The NRSV, as opposed to several other translations, correctly indicates that Judith considers her secret project as being already underway when she admonishes the leaders not to *try to find out what I am doing* (9:34).

Judith Intercedes with God, 9:1-14

The more natural order would have been for Judith to reveal her sackcloth, put ashes on her head, and then to prostrate herself (lit. "to fall on her face") (v. 1). Prostration was a normal posture for prayer. Incense (v. 2) symbolizes prayer rising to God.

Judith's allusion to her ancestor Simeon amounts to an interesting attempt to restore honor to him and his brother Levi, who by falsehood, treachery, and violence avenged Shechem's rape of their sister Dinah (Gen 34:1-29). Jacob was critical of his sons who had made him odious to the inhabitants of the land (Gen 34:30, 49:5-7). Judith is here exonerating Simeon to such a degree that in retrospect he seems to have done God's work (vv. 2-6). Perhaps this is the author's way of justifying Judith's deceit and violence in slaying Holofernes. Or, does it reflect her fear that she, a widow, might suffer the fate of the virgin Dinah (Dancy 1972, 102)? The elements of the rape of Dinah (v. 2) are arranged in dramatic order; thus, the NRSV is justified in correcting the LXX "loosed her womb" to read *virgin's clothing*. The NEB correction to "virgin's veil" is also logical. What the Assyrians purported to do to

the sanctuary, the tabernacle, and the altar (v. 8) closely parallels the rape of Dinah (v. 2).

Judith's prayer that God give efficacy to her proposed deceit has raised questions of moral propriety, but the reader should bear in mind the moral standards of the time. The question might also be asked if a skillful military strategist had won a great victory by deceiving the enemy, would this cause the same kind of moral outrage? What then is the difference if a lone widow uses similar tactics to accomplish the same end? Mt. Zion (v. 13) represents Jerusalem. To be killed by *the hand of a woman* was a disgrace (cf. Judg 9:54) but an honor for the woman (cf. Judg 5:24).

Judith Taken to Holofernes, 10:1–12:20

10:1-10. Judith prepares to go to the Assyrian camp. Judith changes her mourning clothes and dresses in such finery that she could entice any man who saw her. The author obviously was not concerned about the extreme drought when he stated that Judith *bathed her body in water* (v. 3). She takes her own rations and vessels in order that she not be polluted by unclean food or vessels. This sounds pharisaical but by itself is not adequate to prove that the author was a Pharisee or "proto-Pharisee." Enslin and Zeitlin (1972, 130) are correct in stating that Judith was giving an "amen" (v. 8) when in response to the farewell blessing of the elders she *bowed down to God*.

The men of the city, not just those at the gate, unable to take their eyes off her, watch until Judith passed through the valley below (v. 10). The author evidently had forgotten it was night (8:33)!

10:11–11:4. Judith captured by enemy soldiers and taken to Holofernes. Smitten by her beauty, the soldiers, upon hearing the purpose of her appearance, usher Judith to Holofernes, who befriends her. The narrator's sense of humor is revealed when he notes that a hundred men (11:17) accompany two lone females. There is no indication any soldiers objected to this additional duty!

The canopy (10:21) over Holofernes's bed was a net to keep out insects. The richness of the captain's tent is suggested when the canopy is described as being woven with purple, gold, and precious stones and by the fact that silver lamps were carried before him (10:22). These are destined to be part of the spoils received by Judith (15:11).

11:5-23. With flattering words Judith deceitfully explains her mission. Judith explains that Achior is correct but adds that Bethulia is about to sin against God, which will allow Holofernes to conquer them easily. Thus the battle of deceit between the two antagonists begins. Judith seeks to win his confidence so that she can destroy him, all the while that he seeks to seduce her (12:16). Bethulia's decision to consume the livestock would not be sinful in itself, but to devour the animal parts the priestly laws had forbidden them to eat, for example, any fat or blood (Lev 3:6-17), would be disobedient to God. The reference that *the first fruits of the grain and the tithes of the wine and oil* (v. 13) are untouchable by nonpriests cannot be taken literally because those who were tempted to consume them were the farmers who had produced these commodities. This is best interpreted as a hyperbole meaning "hands off" as far as lay use was concerned. If the inhabitants of Jerusalem (v. 14) were already doing these forbidden acts why would their sins not be sufficient cause for divine punishment? Strangely, Holofernes does not note this but is willing to wait for Bethulia to sin against God.

Judith's statement that God has sent her to accomplish wondrous things (v. 16) has a double meaning and is intended to deceive, having one meaning for Holofernes and the reverse for the narrator's hearers. Judith's request to go to the valley to pray (v. 17) serves several functions. Holofernes thinks it is so that she can receive God's message as to when to attack. In reality the purpose of her nightly sojourns is to establish this regular routine in the minds of the soldiers and thus facilitate her final escape. Judith's bath following her prayers is to remind the readers of her punctilious observance of religious ritual.

Holofernes's statement, *your God shall be my God* (v. 23) should best be interpreted as a rhetorical literary device of this master storyteller. It is comparable to such comments repeatedly made by Nebuchadnezzar (Dan 2:47; 3:28, 29; 4:37). At any rate hearers (or readers) would hardly take seriously such a remark made by one who has claimed that Nebuchadnezzar alone is God (6:2, 4) and whom they recognize as engaged in a contest of deceit.

12:1-9. Judith is Holofernes's guest for three days. During this time Judith sleeps in her own tent and carefully attends to proper religious ritual. Her assurances that her own food will not be depleted *before the Lord carries out . . . what he has determined*, (v. 4) is another example of doublespeak. Holofernes interprets it to mean that his victory will soon be assured, while Judith means that his destruction is

near. The camp (v. 7) is the one earlier established by Holofernes to guard Bethulia's water source (7:7, 17). Before the Romans came (63 B.C.E.) the Jews divided the night into three watches (Enslin and Zeitlin 1972, 145); thus she went to the valley to pray close to 2 a.m. when the morning watch began (v. 5). This is an indication that the work dates before the end of the Hasmonean dynasty.

12:10-20. Judith accepts Holofernes's invitation to a banquet. *Bagoas* (v. 11) is a Persian name meaning "eunuch." Eunuchs were in charge of the royal harem but some of them held high rank at court.

When Judith expresses delight in doing whatever Holofernes wishes, the author indicates that she discerns the banquet's true purpose, which is to seduce her, and is in line with the continual deception of the commander (vv. 4, 6). Judith's lying down (v. 16) has no significance except to indicate what was customary at meals. Her claim that this was the greatest day of her life (v. 18) is another example of the regular use of double entendre.

Judith Kills Holofernes and Flees to Bethulia, 13:1-20

13:1-10a. Judith beheads Holofernes. This passage, especially v. 8, is the core of the story. *When evening came* (v. 1) is a correct translation but "when it grew late" (NEB) better correlates with the fact that the servants immediately went to bed because the banquet had been prolonged. *Dead drunk* is correctly and picturesquely rendered by Zeitlin as "fair swimming in wine." (Enslin and Zeitlin 1972, 151). *Jerusalem* (v. 4) stands for the whole people of Israel. *Now . . . is the time* (12:5) contrasts with the five days arbitrarily set by Uzziah (7:30). The insult of being slain by a woman is heightened when the deed is done with the warrior's own sword. The instrument is a short Persian sword that necessitated the two strokes. The canopy, probably made of gauze (v. 9), was taken by Judith as further proof that she had killed the commander (v. 15). Assuming it was finely woven the canopy could easily be placed in the food bag along with Holofernes's head (v. 10a) since their food supply had been reduced by three days use.

13:10b-20. Judith and her servant return to Bethulia. The phrase *circled around the valley* (v. 10b) indicates their route avoided the spring and the soldiers guarding it. The narrator probably anticipates the auditors' unverbalized questions when Judith asserts that only her face had lured Holofernes to destruction and she had not been shamed (v. 16) as had been Dinah (Gen 34:2). Rather than *For your praise* (v. 19), some texts read "For your hope." If this alternate reading, which seems to fit the context, is adopted it refers to Judith's hope that God would not forsake his faithful people (Enslin and Zeitlin 1972, 156). In Hebrew the word *heart* (19:19) has the same function "mind" does in Greek and modern psychology.

The Jews Defeat the Assyrians, 14:1–15:13

Judith Devises a Battle Plan, 14:1-10

The summoning of Achior is out of place both logically and chronologically (vv. 5-10) and should follow 13:16. He alone of those in Bethulia could verify that the decapitated head belonged to Holofernes. Jerome appears to have recognized this material in the Vulgate (Dancy 1972, 120). For a discussion of Achior's conversion, see Introduction, "canonicity." If Judith should be dated during the Maccabean period *remaining so to this day* (v. 10) refers to Achior rather than to his descendants.

The hanging of Holofernes's head on the city wall was done to inspire Bethulia's army (v. 1). The beheading of vanquished enemies is not unknown in the OT, for example, David severed Goliath's head (1 Sam 17:51); the head of Ishbaal was delivered to David (2 Sam 4:8); Saul's head was displayed in the Philistine temple of Dagon (1 Chr 10:10); and a wise woman of Abel had the rebel Sheba's head thrown over the wall to besiegers (2 Sam 20:21, 22). A more nearly contemporary story (1 Macc 7:39-48; 2 Macc 15:20-37) relates how the Greek general Nicanor's head was displayed by Judas from the citadel in Jerusalem. Nicanor's contemptuous attitude toward the Jewish religion, including the Temple, is similar to that of Holofernes.

The *Assyrian outpost* (v. 2) is the contingent of soldiers guarding the springs that had supplied Bethulia's water.

Leaderless Assyrians Flee, 14:11–15:13

14:11-18. Bagoas discovers the headless body of Holofernes. The Assyrian use of *slaves* (v. 13) in a derogatory sense is a literary preparation for Bagoas's statement the *slaves have tricked us* (v. 18). This would have brought a chuckle from Jewish hearers. The plural *slaves* (v. 18) could grammatically refer to Judith and her maid, but since the verse goes on to specify that one Hebrew woman has brought disgrace

on King Nebuchadnezzar, the reference probably denotes the Hebrew nation.

14:19–15:7. All Israel devastates the fleeing Assyrians. As the news of Holofernes's death spreads from the leaders to the common soldiers, fear spreads throughout the army, which abandons all military discipline and flees pell-mell. *Who had camped in the hills* (15:3) refers to the Moabites, Edomites, and Ammonites who were stationed to watch from the mountains around Bethulia (7:13, 18).

The magnitude and length of the ensuing rout is suggested by the fact that soldiers came from Jerusalem, forty miles away, and from Gilead twenty miles to the east. The carnage extended even to Damascus almost 100 miles to the northeast (15:5). *The rest of the people of Bethulia* refers to the city's noncombatant (15:6) inhabitants.

15:8-13. The Israelites continue to loot the Assyrian camp and celebrate victory. The Assyrian wealth is highlighted by the plundering of the camp for thirty days (v. 11). The victory dance performed by the women has historical precedents, for example, the dances of Miriam (Exod 15:20-21) and of the women who greeted Saul and David when they returned from defeating the Philistines (1 Sam 18:6-8).

The ivy-wreathed wands (v. 12) and the olive wreaths (v. 13) show Greek influence. The worshippers of Bacchus carried wands, with a pine cone on one end, and wrapped with ivy and vine leaves. There is no Bacchic implication in this reference.

Judith's Hymn of Thanksgiving, 15:14–16:20

There has been much conjecture as to whether this hymn was an earlier composition that became the basis for the preceding historical novella or if the author composed it as a fitting conclusion. The fact that this hymn has some similarities to the Song of Deborah (Judg 5), which many believe to be older than the parallel prose account (Judg 4), conceivably has caused some to date the Judith hymn prior to the preceding prose account. The surprising reference to the Persians and Medes (16:10) cannot be used to date the book in the Persian period inasmuch as it has been demonstrated that the author's account is historically inaccurate.

All the people loudly sang this song (15:14) probably indicates it is sung antiphonally. Judith speaks (16:2-5), the people respond (16:6-10), and Judith concludes (16:11-17). *Sons of the Titans* and *tall giants* are in synonymous parallel lines, thus mean the same thing (16:6). The term *Titan* is, of course, drawn from Greek mythology but the LXX translators use it simply to refer to the Rephaim, giant inhabitants of early Canaan.

Verse 16 should not be considered a condemnation of religious ritual, which Judith practiced regularly, but as a significant counterweight. Ritual, which can become formality, is not all that is required. *Fear of the Lord* (16:16) is a common biblical concept meaning reverential awe and obedience.

One verse (16:17) out of the entire book does not provide adequate evidence for a doctrine of everlasting punishment after death.

Judith's Venerated Last Days, 16:21-25

This is a most appropriate conclusion, emphasizing Judith's continued fame and faithfulness. Her lasting widowhood (v. 22) seems to reflect the author's view that it was an indication of her piety but from OT precedent one could have expected she would have been rewarded with a family. Her longevity (v. 23) can best be seen as a reward for her virtuous life. It seems forced to suggest that her long life of one hundred five

years is a cryptic reference to the Maccabean domination that lasted from 168 B.C.E. until 63 B.C.E. (Enslin and Zeitlin 1972, 181). Judith's distribution of property to her in-laws was according to the pentateuchal law of inheritance in such cases (Num 27:5-11), but there is no corresponding rule given for a widow's gift of property to her own kin.

The Vulgate adds an additional verse to this paragraph to the effect that a festival commemorated Judith's notable deed (Dancy 1972, 126).

Works Cited

Craven, Toni. 1983. *Artistry and Faith in the Book of Judith.*

Dancy, J. C. 1972. *The Shorter Books of the Apocrypha.*

Enslin, Morton S., and Solomon Zeitlin. 1972. *The Book of Judith.*

Metzger, Bruce M. 1957. *An Introduction to the Apocrypha.*

Torrey, Charles C. 1963. *The Apocryphal Literature, a Brief Introduction.*

Additions to Esther

Kandy M. Queen-Sutherland

Introduction

The Additions to Esther are passages in the Greek OT, the SEPTUAGINT, that are not part of the Book of Esther in the Hebrew Bible (MT). Classified by Protestants as apocryphal (i.e., noncanonical), the Additions to Esther are omitted from Jewish Bibles and if included in Protestant versions are grouped with other apocryphal writings between the OT and NT or after the two (e.g., RSV, NEB). Catholic Bibles treat the material as deuterocanonical, placing the Additions to Esther with the MT (e.g., JB).

The six additions comprise 107 verses. In the fourth century C.E. Jerome began a tradition with the Vulgate that separated the additions from their LXX location, placing them at the end of the Hebrew Esther. Some versions (e.g., KJV, NEB, REB, NRSV) number the additions as chaps. 10–16 following Esth 10:3. An alternative designation (e.g., NAB, TEV) employs the letters A–F, with a different numbering of verses. This commentary, while refering to the individual additions as A–F, follows the NRSV in its numbering of chapters and verses.

The Six Additions

A = 11:2–12:6. The section includes an introduction of MORDECAI, his world-shattering dream, and the thwarting of a conspiracy against the king.

B = 13:1-7. The section includes a royal letter ordering the enactment of Haman's plot to destroy the Jews.

C = 13:8–14:19. The section includes the prayers of Mordecai and ESTHER.

D = 15:1-16. The section describes Esther's unannounced appearance before the king.

E = 16:1-24. The section includes a royal letter denouncing Haman and ordering help for the Jews.

F = 10:4–11:1. The section includes an interpretation of Mordecai's dream and a colophon authenticating the Book of Esther.

Provenance and Date of the Additions

The final verse in Additions to Esther (11:1) is a colophon with bibliographic information pertaining to the origin and transmission of the text. The text is said to have been translated from Hebrew into Greek in Jerusalem by Lysimachus, a resident of the city. It was then carried to Egypt in the fourth year of the reign of Ptolemy and Cleopatra (ca. 114 B.C.E.) Although the inscription is designed to attest to the text's genuineness, speculation remains as to the provenance and dating of the several additions.

The 114 B.C.E. date is regarded by many as a plausible date for the actual composition of the additions themselves. Since there was more than one ruling Egyptian pair bearing the names Ptolemy and Cleopatra, other dates are possible (e.g., ca. 77 or 48 B.C.E.). Variances in style and emphases within the additions indicate differing origins. The additions survive only in Greek, yet four (A, C, D, F) show evidence of an earlier Hebrew or Aramaic stage. The remaining two (B, E) are distinguished by Greek rhetorical style. These observations suggest that the four semitic additions originated in Palestine, the other two in the Greek speaking world of the Jewish diaspora (e.g., the home of the LXX, Alexandria, Egypt). All are regarded as Jewish with antigentile sentiments discernible in the opening and closing additions (A, F).

The Effect of the Additions

A reader of the Hebrew Esther is impressed by a plot that moves from one coincidental event after another. Mordecai, a Jew, saves King Ahasuerus' life but is not rewarded (Esth 2:21-23). When Haman, the prime minister, feels powerful enough to bring about Mordecai's death (5:9-14), the king passes a sleepless night and discovers in the royal annals that Mordecai has never been honored for saving the king's life (6:1-3). The king seeks advice about the proper means of decoration from Haman, who mistakenly assumes he will be the designee (6:6-9). Other examples abound. The piling up of coincidences in the Hebrew Esther is such that an "I can't believe it" response is coupled with a "there's got to be someone or something behind all this" conviction.

What the Hebrew version leaves unspoken, the Greek Esther makes plain. From the opening dream of addition A to its interpretation in addition F, God is the unmistakable force behind the story. Any concern for the absence of specific reference to God in the MT, a critique often made, is canceled by more than fifty direct references to God in Additions to Esther. When the king cannot sleep, the cause is God (6:1). When Esther risks her life appearing unannounced before the king to plead for the Jews, it is God who *changed the spirit of the king to gentleness* (15:8). The final speech of Mordecai (addition F) makes the action of God in the entire story explicit: *These things have come from God* (10:4); *The Lord has saved his people* (10:9); *And God remembered his people and vindicated his inheritance* (10:12).

Although Mordecai's confession is not surprising, such words in the mouth of a Persian king are noteworthy. Addition E, the royal letter counteracting Haman's plot to destroy the Jews, has Ahasuerus interpreting the execution of Haman as divine punishment: *for God, who rules over all things, has speedily inflicted on him the punishment that he deserved* (16:18). The events of the thirteenth day of Adar are, according to the king, in the hands of God, *for God, who rules over all things, has made this day to be a joy for his chosen people instead of a day of destruction for them* (16:21). In the words of a pious Jew or a pagan king, the Greek Esther gives voice to the reality of God in the story.

For critics of the Hebrew account, the characterization of the Jews within the story is an equally redeemable feature. Void of references to covenant, law, or concern for Jewish dietary regulations, the Hebrew Esther was vulnerable to attack for centuries. The two extended prayers that make up addition C counter such thought. Not only Mordecai and Esther, but *the whole righteous nation . . . cried out to God* (11:9-10). While both the Hebrew and Greek versions speak of Mordecai warning Esther not to reveal her Jewish identity, the Greek text adds the instruction *to fear God and keep his laws* (2:20). Indeed any question of Esther's

morality is handled by her "I've been a good Jewish girl" prayer of confession (14:16-18).

Although the six additions are the most prominent variances between the LXX and MT, revisions or omissions of text occur throughout. The intrusion of the explicitly religious elements in the LXX is often regarded as the key for understanding the purpose of the Additions to Esther, the judgment being that the Hebrew text was considered deficient in this area. Such reasoning assumes that for God to be present, God must be mentioned. In reality, the strength of the Hebrew text lies in the unstated. When one's fate seems to rest in the hands of a "wino king" and a power-crazed henchman, the salvation of a nation can be attributed to only one source, named or unnamed.

The spelling out of the involvement of God in these affairs in Additions to Esther may be more than the transformation of an irreligious story into a religious one. The work of David Clines (1984, 168–74) suggests that the reworking of the Hebrew text results in the Additions to Esther sharing closer affinities with its postexilic canonical counterparts: EZRA, NEHEMIAH, and DANIEL.

Clines sees the specific references to the actions of God at critical junctures in the Greek Esther story to parallel similar interventions of God reported in the " 'Persian histories' of Ezra and Nehemiah" (169). The prayers of Mordecai and Esther parallel prayers in Ezra, Nehemiah, and Daniel (Ezra 9:6-15; Neh 1:5-11; 9:6-37; Dan 9:4-19), exemplifying appropriate behavior for pious Jews in questionable times (171). The dream-interpretation motif of additions A and F in the LXX version of Esther conforms with Daniel where the meaning of history is also revealed through such a pattern. Like Daniel, Additions to Esther presents the threatening conflict at the heart of the story on a cosmic level (cf. Add Esth 11:7 with Dan 6:27 [171–72]).

Clines draws connections between the royal letters in additions B and E and foreign documentary material incorporated in Ezra and Daniel; each attesting to the "impact of the truth of the Jewish religion upon outsiders, neighbors and overlords" (173). The distancing of the Greek text from its Hebrew original occasioned by the additions and revisions had the effect of creating a work more closely aligned with Ezra, Nehemiah, and Daniel, its nearest counterparts in the Hebrew canon (174).

While the additions may result in a work more compatible in style with other Jewish writings of the postexilic period, the question of intentionality remains. The purpose the additional material and re-workings was intended to serve can only be guessed at, the originators themselves lost to history. Interestingly enough, it is the Hebrew Esther that survived the canonization process within Judaism and Christianity. The question is, what do the Additions to Esther add to the story?

For Further Study

In the *Mercer Dictionary of the Bible*: APOCRYPHAL LITERATURE; ARTAXERXES; DANIEL; ESTHER; ESTHER, ADDITIONS TO; ESTHER, BOOK OF; EZRA; MORDECAI; NEHEMIAH; PERSIAN EMPIRE; SEPTUAGINT; WOMEN IN THE OLD TESTAMENT.

In other sources: D. J. A. Clines, *The Esther Scroll: The Story of the Story*, JSOTSup; C. A. Moore, *Daniel, Esther, and Jeremiah: The Additions*, AncB; and "Esther, Additions to," AncBD.

Commentary

An Outline

I. Addition A. The Framing of the Esther Story, 11:2–12:6
   A. Mordecai and His Dream, 11:2-12
   B. Mordecai Saves the King, 12:1-6
II. Addition B. The First Royal Letter, 13:1-7
III. Addition C. Prayers for Deliverance, 13:8–14:19
   A. Mordecai's Prayer, 13:8-18
   B. Esther's Prayer, 14:1-19
IV. Addition D. Esther's Appearance before the King, 15:1-16
V. Addition E. The Second Royal Letter, 16:1-24
VI. Addition F. The Closing Frame 10:4–11:1
   A. Mordecai's Dream Interpreted, 10:4-13
   B. Colophon, 11:1

Addition A.
The Framing of the Esther Story,
11:2–12:6

Mordecai and His Dream, 11:2-12

Additions A and F function as opening and closing frames for the Hebrew Esther's story of deliverance of the Jews from their enemies. The events that are to occur are revealed beforehand in a dream to MORDECAI (11:5-11) and interpreted by him once the dream's events have come to pass (10:4-13); the story of the Hebrew Esther is the enactment of the dream in between. Textual position alone could establish addition A and addition F as brackets for the MT, in the dream-fulfillment-interpretation scheme, but the content of the two literally surrounds the story.

Addition A opens with a date one full year before the Hebrew story (cf. "the second year" of ARTAXERXES [Gk. = Heb. Ahasuerus] in 11:2 with 1:3) with the introduction of Mordecai and the dream. Like the Hebrew story, the Greek version opens in the courts of the Persian king; Mordecai is said to serve there (11:3). A distinction, however, is immediately clear. While the MT begins with the power and pomp of the Persian king, the Greek begins with a Jew, a dream, and the one who will bring it to pass. Apocalyptic images of mythological dragons and catastrophic upheavals on a cosmic level signal war, the nations of the world rising up against the righteous nation. In the midst of threatened chaos, the righteous cry out to God. A small stream suddenly becomes a mighty river. Darkness turns to light. The reversal of fortune for the oppressed is none other than the work of God. Whatever is to happen will be *what God had determined to do* (11:12). Mordecai is left pondering.

Mordecai Saves the King, 12:1-6

The second part of addition A relates an event paralleled in the Hebrew Esther at a later point in the story. Characteristic of the Greek text, details are added that are left unanswered in the MT. Mordecai learns of an assassination plot against the king, advising him of such. Two eunuchs confess and are executed. Both the king and Mordecai record the events. Mordecai is rewarded for his act of loyalty and serves at court.

The characterization of Mordecai in the Additions to Esther differs radically from the Hebrew. In the MT the introduction of Mordecai occurs at the point where Esther enters the story. The family tree is recounted, Mordecai's connection to Esther revealed, and the fact that Mordecai, for whatever reason, hangs out at the king's gate (Esth 2:5-20). When he learns of a plot against the king in this context (Esth 2:21-23), he advises Esther who, in turn, warns the king. The event is recorded in the annals but Mordecai goes unrewarded, a lapse crucial to the unfolding of the rest of the Hebrew story. In the Hebrew version Mordecai is the outsider looking in until the tables are turned through the twisted irony of the plot. In the Greek Esther, Mordecai begins on the inside. He is a person of position within the royal court and in that context draws the enmity of another court player, Haman son of Hammedatha. The territory of the one (Haman) is threatened by the other (Mordecai) and Haman determines to put an end to it. Both Mordecai and his people are to be destroyed (12:5-6).

Addition B.
The First Royal Letter, 13:1-7

Addition B is presented as the body of a letter that decrees the coming destruction of the Jews, placed between vv. 13 and 14 in chap. 3 of the Hebrew text. It reads like a letter written by King Artaxerxes to the subjects of his empire. Haman, however, is the actual composer. Unless it is an authentic Persian document (highly unlikely, cf. e.g., stylistic differences with Ezra 4:17-22; 6:3-12; 7:12-26), the real author is a Jew. The irony of content and author cannot be missed!

The letter presents Artaxerxes as the gentle conqueror of the known world who wants nothing more than the safety and security of his subjects. Second only to the king, Haman is noted for his kindness and sound judgment. It is he who recognizes the threat of a certain people who insist on living according to their own traditions and laws. They stand in opposition to Persian judgment, jeopardizing the unity and stability of the empire. The solution is total annihilation of this people. No one is to be spared—neither woman nor child. The date is set for the thirteenth of Adar. Only then will the Persian government be secure.

Addition C.
Prayers for Deliverance, 13:8–14:19

Mordecai's Prayer, 13:8-18

With Esther's agreement to petition the king on the Jews' behalf secured (Esth 4:1-17), Mordecai directs his own petition to God. The prayer is stated in form and content consistent with other biblical prayers with several points noteworthy. First, any attention that the Hebrew text directs to the actions of Mordecai and Esther with regard to the outcome of the story, the prayer of Mordecai lays at the feet of the Lord (Gk. κύριος, occurring nine times). The Lord is the king and creator of the universe who has redeemed Israel in the past and can so again. Whatever happens is up to God. Secondly, any question concerning Mordecai's

refusal to bow to Haman, stated without reason in the Hebrew Esther and given as cause for Haman's vengeance against the Jews (Esth 3:2-6), is answered here. Mordecai asserts his own innocence, his actions being the pure intention to honor no one but God. Whatever blame might be placed on Mordecai is removed while responsibility for what lies ahead is placed on God.

Esther's Prayer, 14:1-19

In 14:1-19, Esther is driven by fear to her knees. Her prayer asserts the power of God, the sin of the Jews, and Esther's own abhorrence of her situation. Whatever her present life may look like on the outside, on the inside she has remained a good Jew. She is faithful to the law and despises her life in the gentile court. In this moment of both personal and national crisis, Esther turns to God, who alone can save Israel and Esther from her fear.

The portrayal of Esther in the Greek account is distressing. Without question the Additions to Esther raise the figure of Mordecai in the story while repressing the role of Esther as heroine, so prominent in the Hebrew text. Although this in itself is disturbing, the real problem is the way Esther is victimized in the prayer. On the surface her avowals of being a faithful Jew are commendable. Questions concerning her moral character, having slept her way to the queenship, are answered by her own repugnance at her state. These issues, however, are addressed at the expense of Esther herself who becomes a joyless pawn prostituted in a pagan's bed. Queen Esther of the Hebrew text has no dignity here, only fear and self-loathing.

Addition D.
Esther's Appearance before the King, 15:1-16

Addition D provides the color commentary to the lackluster description, given the gravity of the situation, of Esther's unsummoned appearance before the king in 5:1-2. Though radiant with beauty, Esther is weak with fear; the king is terrifying in all his royal splendor. He is angry. She faints. God changes the king's spirit to gentleness and he rushes to the fallen queen. She need not have been concerned. The law of death to unwelcome visitors did not apply to her—a little piece of information that could have spared Esther a few sleepless nights! As in the prayer (14:1-19), the reader encounters a weakened Esther who survives in a role of the fainting female saved by God and a man made gentle by God. Lost is the Esther of the Hebrew story who by her own cunning and wit saved not only herself but the lives of her people.

Addition E.
The Second Royal Letter, 16:1-24

Addition E purports to be the second royal letter sent throughout the empire under the auspices of the king. With Haman dead and King Artaxerxes publicly siding with Mordecai and Esther the addition, placed after 8:12 in the Hebrew text, inserts a farcical note into otherwise somber events. The purpose of the letter is to cancel out the plans of Haman to destroy the Jews. The orders by which this will be accomplished come at the end of a rambling excuse that the kind-hearted Persians were hoodwinked by a foreigner but will try to do better in the future.

Extravagant enactments and caricatures of the story's principles make the letter implausible as an authentic Persian document. Haman is the vilest of villains. He abused the favored status bestowed on him by his hosts to seek the destruction of the Jews. This was part of an overall one-man plot to weaken the Persian empire, making them easy prey for the Greeks (Macedonians).

Mordecai, the dictator of the letter, has the king speak of him (i.e., Mordecai) as *our savior and perpetual benefactor* and Esther as the *blameless partner of our kingdom* (16:13). It was Artaxerxes' own goodness that made him susceptible to the evil Haman. All shall now be set right. The Jews are none other than *children of the living God* (16:16). Since Haman and his household have been hanged at the city gate (16:18 conflicting with 9:6-14), God's judgment on him, everyone will be well advised not to follow Haman's murderous plans.

The immutable word of the king, central to the resolving of the crisis in the Hebrew story (Esth 8:8), is not an issue here. Nor is the festival of celebration to commemorate the Jews' victory over their enemies a purely Jewish occasion. All are ordered to observe the day, Jew and non-Jew alike. Any failure to comply will result in such destruction that even wildlife will find the region intolerable.

Addition F.
The Closing Frame, 10:4–11:1

Mordecai's Dream Interpreted, 10:4-13

Addition F is the closing bracket for the Greek version of the Esther story. As in addition A Mordecai dominates the scene, interpreting his initial dream through the events that followed. Esther is the stream that became a river, Haman and himself the dragons. The "nations" proved to be Jewish enemies who sought their destruction. God heard the cry of Israel, rescuing them from evil. The interpretation, like the dream, is brief, raising questions as to the interrelatedness of its parts. An overall impact is accomplished, however, as Mordecai, Haman, and Esther, the story's key characters, are overshadowed by the wonders of God. The casting of lots to determine a nation's fate assigned to Haman in 3:7, is the action of God in Additions to Esther. Once again God chooses Israel. Adar fourteenth and fifteenth is to be observed with joy and gladness for all time to come.

Colophon, 11:1

The colophon in 11:1 is an appendage similar to notations a Greek librarian might make regarding the provenance of a text. The text is said to have been brought to Egypt by Dositheus, who claimed to be a priest and Levite. He and his son claimed the text to be authentic. On this note, the letter about Purim closes. Like Mordecai remembering his dream, readers of the text are left pondering.

Work Cited

Clines, D. J. A. 1984. *The Esther Scroll: The Story of the Story*, JSOTSup.

Wisdom of Solomon

John Keating Wiles

Introduction

The Wisdom of Solomon is a *logos protreptikos* or exhortatory discourse, a genre commonly used in the Hellenistic age to urge a particular manner of life. Wedding philosophy and rhetoric, protreptic legitimates its recommendations by demonstrating their justice, practicality, and attractiveness. The Wisdom of Solomon is committed to its recommended manner of life, however, because of its accordance with the will of God. Rhetoric and philosophy serve that prior devotion. Though acquaintance with and exploitation of Hellenistic philosophies is evident, Wisdom is content to show that its recommended life is not contrary to sound philosophical knowledge but is its fulfillment. The book advances its argument primarily with rhetoric rather than philosophy, and it incorporates numerous smaller genres, including kingship tract, aretalogy, prayer, diatribe, comparison, imagined speech, (pseudo)-autobiography, and midrash.

The most important of these for understanding Wisdom is the kingship tract. Kingship tracts had developed in the classical period as instruction from philosophers to royalty. In the conviction that a wise ruler was a good ruler, kingship tracts sketched philosophers' views of what was wise, good, true, and fitting for a king embodying the human ideal. The address to royalty later became a convention of Hellenistic tracts outlining philosophers' views of the ideal human life, views applicable to persons as humans (Reese 1970, 90–121; Winston 1979, 18–20).

Background

The protreptic presupposes an environment where Hellenistic philosophical traditions flourished. The life urged by Wisdom presupposes an environment where JUDAISM had taken root, and the manifold interpretive traditions of Jewish scriptures in the book indicate a flourishing Judaism. Among these is the employment of Isis ideology to enrich the traditional figure of personified wisdom. Patronage of the Isis cult by the Ptolemaic (and Roman) rulers of Egypt occasioned its revival in the late Hellenistic period there (Kloppenberg 1982, 62), and most commentators have looked to Alexandria for the composition of Wisdom.

The composition of Wisdom of Solomon has been dated from ca. 220 B.C.E. through ca. 50 C.E. with the greater likelihood falling toward the latter end of that range. Winston is persuasive in his argument that 14:16-20 points most easily toward the age of Augustus (27 B.C.E.–14 C.E.) or later. His insistence that the reign of Gaius Caligula (37–41 C.E.) is "the likeliest setting" because the rage of 5:16-23 "could only be called forth by a desperate historical situation" (Winston 1979, 20–23) is less convincing. The passage reflects scriptural rhetoric more than international political developments.

Hellenistic influence together with creative devotion to definitive Jewish traditions (monotheism, the ELECTION of ISRAEL, the Law) implies a group conversant with Jewish and Hellenistic literature and culture. The recommendation to love *righteousness* understood as wholehearted devotion to the Lord (1:1) evinces a faithful Jewish writer. Use of Hellenistic forms, artful Greek language, and exploitation of Hellenistic scientific, mythological, and philosophical knowledge served a two-fold function. Internally, it assured Jews that their heritage was not obsolete. Externally, the borrowings showed how faithful Jews could communicate in the idiom of the intellectual and political elite (Kloppenberg 1982, 82–84; Reese 1970, 146–52).

Significance

The Wisdom of Solomon is a testimony to the religious and intellectual vitality and creativity of Judaism in the cosmopolitan environment of Alexandria. The course followed by Judaism following 70 C.E. rendered its long term significance for Jews worthless, but its adaptation of Hellenistic idiom to a Jewish heritage assured its importance for Christianity. Preserved in the Greek-speaking Christians' Bible, it was used in their liturgies (cf. Cabaniss 1956; Hennig 1952). Its theological worth was established by Alexandrian theologians, Wis 7:25-26 proving fertile in the articulation of christological views. While Gnostic theologians were fond of launching their speculations from Prov 8:22 and appear not to have used Wis at all, Alexandrian theologians countered using Wis 7:25-26 as the norm to which they could safely assimilate other passages (Grant 1966, 464–72). These verses figured regularly in the theological ferment of the fourth century stretching from the prelude to Nicea (325 C.E.) to the Council of Constantinople (381 C.E.) (cf. Hanson 1988, passim).

For Further Study

In the *Mercer Dictionary of the Bible*: APOCRYPHAL LITERATURE; HELLENISTIC WORLD; NUMBERS/NUMEROLOGY; ROMAN EMPIRE; SOLOMON; SOLOMON, WISDOM OF; WISDOM LITERATURE.

In other sources: E. G. Clarke, *The Wisdom of Solomon*; J. A. F. Gregg, *The Wisdom of Solomon*; J. M. Reese, *Hellenistic Influence on the Book of Wisdom and Its Consequences*; "Plan and Structure in the Book of Wisdom," *CBQ* 27 (1965) 391–99; and *The Book of Wisdom, Song of Songs*; J. Reider, *The Book of Wisdom*; D. Winston, *The Wisdom of Solomon*.

Commentary

An Outline

I. The Book of Righteousness and Life, 1:1–6:21
   A. Exhortation to Righteousness, 1:1-15
   B. Speech of the Wicked, 1:16–2:24
   C. Triumph of the Righteous, 3:1–5:1
   D. Speech of the Wicked, 5:2-23
   E. Exhortation to Wisdom, 6:1-21
II. The Book of Wisdom, 6:22–10:21
   A. The Guide's Pledge and Invitation, 6:22-25
   B. "Solomon's" Quest for Wisdom, 7:1–8:21
   C. "Solomon's" Prayer, 9:1-18
   D. Wisdom, the Deliverer, 10:1-21
III. The Book of Salvation and History, 11:1–19:22
   A. Israel Compared to Egypt, 11:1-14
   B. God's Universal Justice and Mercy, 11:15–12:27
   C. Humanity's General Folly, 13:1–15:19
   D. Israel Compared to Egypt, 16:1–19:22

The Book of Righteousness and Life, 1:1–6:21

Exhortation to Righteousness, 1:1-15

The two parts of the opening exhortation set the agenda for the book with their focus on righteousness (vv. 1-10) and life in creation (vv. 11-15). Creation sustains righteousness; unrighteousness invites death.

1:1-10. Exhortation to "rulers." Although a literary convention, the address in v. 1a poses the issue of power. The well-educated Jewish population of Alexandria was tempted to imagine that power was accessible by assimilation, but our author promises that life-sustaining power is available to the righteous. Verse 1bc unfolds the implications of the command to *love righteousness* in terms of whole-hearted devotion to *the Lord* signalling uncompromising commitment to the God of Israel. Verse 2 encourages this quest by promising the Lord's care for those who are neither presumptuous nor distrustful.

The remainder draws connections between wisdom and righteousness. Although not identical, they belong together. The two-sided claim is made that twisted ways of thinking alienate one from God, while a pious life renders one approachable by wisdom (vv. 3-5). Wisdom, although beneficent, takes speech seriously, and unrighteous persons court judgment by their thoughtless, lawless, and ungrateful estimate of human beings' lot in creation (vv. 6-10).

1:11-15. Warning against injudicious speech. Because both speech and behavior can be self-destructive, the exhortation closes with a warning. Human beings *invite death* (vv. 11-12), but the Creator is anti-death, and creation is healthful and sustaining (vv. 13-14). The exhortation is closed by an INCLUSIO (*righteousness*, vv. 1, 15) linking the issues of life and righteousness: righteousness is not prey to death.

Speech of the Wicked, 1:16–2:24

In this imagined speech (2:1b-20) our author shows how the unrighteous *summoned death*. The speech is framed by an introduction (1:16–2:1a) and concluding reflection (2:21-24; cf. the inclusio on *belong to his company*, 1:16d, 2:24b) subverting the speech.

1:16–2:1a. Introduction. Those whom the writer opposes are denominated the *ungodly* and are described as persons who had *made a covenant with [death]* (cf. Isa 28:15). Their worthiness of death will be substantiated by the rehearsal of their crooked thinking (2:1a; cf. 1:3a).

2:1b-20. Speech. The speech itself falls into five parts. First, the ungodly murmur over the brevity and futility of human life (vv. 1b-5), a complaint reminiscent of portions of Job and Ecclesiastes. The echo of Ecclesiastes is reinforced by the second part of the speech (vv. 6-9) issuing the *carpe diem*, but the third part (vv. 10-12a) moves in a drastically different direction. Moving from the familiar *carpe diem* to the sinister invitation to enjoy life at the expense of *the righteous poor*, attention focuses on righteousness, power, law, and weakness (v. 11). Their speech expresses the constant accompaniment of self-seeking lawlessness masquerading as judicial authority (see v. 20): might makes right. They determine to use their power against the weak righteous person (v. 12a). The fourth part (vv. 12b-16) turns to a description of the righteous person, and it becomes clear that the controversy in The Wisdom of Solomon is primarily an intramural conflict between a faithful and progressive piety (Di Lella 1966, 146–54), and thorough-going assimilation. The righteous accuses the ungodly of *sins against the law* and their *training*, while personally claiming to have *knowledge of God* and to be *child [or servant] of the Lord* (v. 13). In the final part (vv. 17-20), the ungodly announce their intention to *test* the righteous person by means of verbal harassment, physical torture, and judicial murder.

2:21-24. Concluding reflection. The author notes their shortsightedness. Their lack of knowledge did not reckon on God's creation of humankind with *incorruption* (*aphtharsia*, v. 23). *Incorruption*, to be distinguished from *immortality* (*athanasia*), was a technical term in Epicurean philosophy referring to a special power of the gods rendering them immune to the disintegration of their atoms. According to this book, humankind, although created mortal, was originally granted *incorruption*, which should have prevented personal disintegration (Murphy-O'Connor 1976, 31–37). God's creation, however, was distorted by the invasion of death. Having already claimed that death is *invited* by human words and deeds (1:16), the writer now adds that death found access by means of *the devil's envy* (v. 24).

Triumph of the Righteous, 3:1–5:1

The Book of Righteousness and Life (1:1–6:21) reaches its central focus here. Marking this section at the beginning and end by claims that the righteous finally emerge from their trials unscathed (3:1; 5:1), the author characterizes the destinies of the righteous and the ungodly (3:1–4:6), addresses the problem of longevity and theodicy (4:7-15), and affirms the hidden but enduring power of the righteous (4:16–5:1).

3:1-9. The destiny of the righteous. The Wisdom of Solomon declares that the righteous are actually in the care of God where no harm can befall them. Only to fools do they *seem to have died* (v. 2). Their hope is *immortal* (v. 4) because of their unswerving pursuit of righteousness, itself *immortal* (1:15). Although they suffer, that is a *testing* from God (contrast 2:17, 19), a test they pass (vv. 5-7). The outcome is power (v. 8). What the ungodly thought accessible through assimilation is promised to those who remain devoted to the God of Israel.

3:10–4:6. The destiny of the ungodly. The characterization of the destiny of the ungodly opens by announcing the thesis of the just desserts of the wicked (3:10-11). This will be elaborated in the treatment of God's universal justice and mercy and human folly (11:15–15:19) in the Book of Salvation and History (11:1–19:22). Here, the thesis is concretized as infertility (3:12–4:6). The ungodly suffer infertility and the premature death of their heirs. Their longevity turns out to be unproductive (3:12-13a, 16-19; 4:3-6). Infertility also touches the righteous, but, in their case, human and divine recognition of their virtue sustains their memory (3:13b-15; 4:1-2; cf. 3:4; 1:15).

4:7-15. Longevity and theodicy. Given the universal appreciation of longevity, premature death of the righteous poses questions concerning the life-sustaining, death-averting value of righteousness. In response our writer reiterates the restfulness of the righteous in death (v. 7; cf. 3:3b). This is legitimated by proverbial formulations of the asymmetry between age and wisdom (vv. 8-9), a theme reminiscent of Elihu (Job 32:6-9). The example of Enoch's departure further contradicts facile correlation between premature death and the alleged futility of virtue (vv. 10-15). This resort to historical example anticipates the historical surveys utilized in the poem of Wisdom, the Deliverer (10:1-21), and the comparisons of Israel and Egypt in the Book of Salvation and History (11:1-14; 16:1–19:22).

4:16–5:1. The enduring power of the righteous. The issue of power surfaces again in the closing verses of this central section of the Book of Righteousness and Life. The power of the righteous is manifest in their condemnation of the ungodly (v. 16; cf. 3:8). The royal overtones of this power are reinforced by aligning the ungodly with the nations of Ps 2 (Wis 4:18b-20). Given their secure defense by the God of Ps 2, the righteous have good reason to *stand with great confidence* (Wis 5:1).

Speech of the Wicked, 5:2-23

Like its earlier counterpart (1:16–2:24), this speech is framed by remarks of the author (vv. 2-3, 15-23). Here, the framing remarks do not subvert the speech. The wicked align themselves with the thesis of the book, and this self-subversion frees the author to portray the psychological condition of the wicked (vv. 2-3) and to promise life to the righteous (vv. 15-23).

5:2-3. The psychological condition of the wicked. The recognition by the wicked of the triumph of the righteous fills them with fear, amazement, penitence, and anxiety.

5:4-14. The speech of the wicked. This speech, like the last, falls into five parts. First (vv. 4-7), the ungodly reprise their mockery of the righteous, but now they proceed to acknowledge that they were the ones who were misguided. With this they align themselves with their earlier evaluation (cf. v. 6 and 2:21) and confirm the characterization of their speech as penitential (5:3a). The second part (5:8-12) has them reaffirm their thesis of the transiency of human pleasures (cf. 2:1b-5), but here the commonplace bespeaks regret over wasted life rather than self-justification. After elaborating the evanescence of their arrogance and wealth in five similes (vv. 9-12), the fourth part (v. 13) has the wicked confess their lack of virtue (cf. 4:1). The final part (v. 14) is a traditional characterization of the destiny of the ungodly. It is perfectly aligned with the view of the book, but it should be punctuated as part of the speech of the wicked (*contra* NRSV). By placing these words in the mouth of the wicked, the writer completes the portrait of the wicked *speak[ing] . . . in repentance.*

5:15-23. Promise to the righteous. The author is now free to shift attention to the destiny of the righteous. Where 2:22 had simply mentioned the *wages* (*misthos*) of the righteous as unknown and unhoped for by the ungodly, their *reward* (*misthos*) is here elaborated in the language of royal accoutrements and

divine care and protection (v. 16). Note that the eternal life promised is not a necessary outcome of their "nature." It is a work of God. The work of God in this gift of eternal life is emphasized by the following sketch of the divine warrior (vv. 17-20a; cf. Isa 59:16-19). This traditional pattern drawn from Jewish scriptures is combined with the parallel picture of creation as a warrior against the foes of God (vv. 17b, 20b-23b; cf. Judg 5:20-21). The final couplet (v. 23cd) warns of the ecological and socio-political consequences of *lawlessness* and *evil-doing*.

Exhortation to Wisdom, 6:1-21

Just as the Book of Righteousness and Life opened with an exhortation to righteousness (1:1-15), so it closes with an exhortation to wisdom. This exhortation achieves the following: integration into the ongoing discourse flowing out of chap. 5, anticipation of the Book of Wisdom (6:22–10:21), linkage of the first two major sections of the entire book, and closure of the Book of Righteousness and Life.

6:1-11. Summons to be instructed. Following immediately upon the warning of socio-political disruption in 5:23d, vv. 1-2 resume the conventional address to rulers. This resumption of political language integrates this exhortation into the ongoing discourse. The summonses are undergirded with motives (vv. 3, 6-7) and warnings (vv. 5, 8) together with an indictment (v. 4). The claim that all political power is given by God (v. 3) reduces kings to servants (v. 4). Having been proven untrustworthy executors of God's will, they are threatened with disaster from the personal appearing of their divine sovereign (vv. 4-5). Verses 6-8 assert that the powerful, those with the wherewithal to effect various choices, are held to strict account for their action, while the powerless, those whose effective choices are more restricted, are granted mercy. This apparent disproportion is grounded in the oneness of the Creator. Verses 9-11 resume the address to rulers. These words are proffered as a guide to wisdom, a prophylaxis against future malfeasance, and a safeguard for the future.

6:12-16. Personification of Wisdom. By the time Wisdom of Solomon was written, personification of Wisdom as a desirable and beneficent woman had a long and honorable heritage in Jewish literature (cf. Prov 8). These verses present the first clear example of the personification of Wisdom in the book, thereby anticipating what will be the norm in the second major division of the book (6:22–10:21). By placing this anticipation before the final closure of the Book of Righteousness and Life, these verses rhetorically bind the first two sections together.

6:17-21. Final exhortation. Having briefly adverted to a speculative portrait of Wisdom, this final exhortation reclaims the quotidian turf of practicality. Verses 17-20 utilize a *sorites* in which the final term of one clause is taken up as the starting point of the succeeding one. Enclosing the *sorites* itself in an INCLUSIO on the word *desire* (vv. 17, 20), the figure advances from *instruction* to *love of [instruction]*, from *love* to *keeping of her laws*, from *heeding laws* to the *assurance of incorruption* (*aphtharsia*, v. 18, NRSV *immortality*; cf. 2:23), and finally from *incorruption* to proximity to God (v. 19). Thus the writer has wedded the quest for wisdom to God's primal design for humanity. The inclusio, which wraps itself around the *sorites* reinvokes royal dimensions (v. 20). Addressing rulers one last time (v. 21; cf. 1:1; 6:1-2, 9, 11), the Book of Righteousness and Life closes. Those who want what rulers typically want (thrones and scepters) should *honor wisdom*. If they do so, it is promised they shall reign forever, recalling the promise of eternal life already declared to the righteous, a promise accompanied by their investment with royal insignia (5:15-16). The book thereby encourages the relatively weak audience, the righteous, with the subtext that they, not the relatively more powerful elite, are the actual recipients of God's promise of life.

The Book of Wisdom, 6:22–10:21

The Guide's Pledge and Invitation, 6:22-25

In 6:22 the implied author speaks in first person for the first time. This predominates throughout chaps. 7–9. Third person speech will most commonly refer to personified Wisdom in these chapters as well as chap. 10. Second person speech in these chapters, rather than being plural as in 1:1–6:21, will be singular and will be set aside for address to God in prayer.

Whereas 6:17-20 had spoken of practical wisdom that could be approached through instruction and obedience to its laws, the anticipatory personification of Wisdom in 6:12-16 had spoken of a contemplative approach, a religious quest in confidence of her personal disclosure. Success with such an approach is rendered more likely if assisted by a guide who has already trod the path. In the opening of the Book of Wisdom, therefore, the implied author offers to serve as

guide. The offer includes a pledge of clarity in presentation (v. 22abcd) and personal honesty and healthy disinterestedness (vv. 22e-23). This is followed by a proverbial formulation of the importance of sages and kings in the world order (v. 24) thereby hinting that the guide is a wise ruler, the embodiment of ideal humankind.

"Solomon's" Quest for Wisdom, 7:1–8:21

It is only in this section and the next that the implied author assumes the persona of SOLOMON. Even here, the speech is anonymous; acquaintance with the traditions rooted in 1 Kgs 3:3-28; 4:29-34; 10:1-10, 13, 23-25 is necessary to discern the assumed identity. Within "Solomon's" speech readers are treated to autobiography (7:1-14; 8:2-21), wish (7:15-16), and curriculum and praise of Wisdom (7:17–8:1).

7:1-14. "Solomon's" autobiography. In the opening of his autobiography (vv. 1-6), "Solomon" insists on his common humanity. This is the obverse of the royal status bestowed on the righteous: "Solomon," the paradigmatic figure of the wise and righteous king, is *mortal, like everyone else* (v. 1). Several features of Hellenistic anthropology are evident. Most remarkable is the assumption of a ten month gestation period for humans, a commonplace of Greek and Roman writers, whereas Talmudic sources speak of a nine month gestation (Reese 1970, 9). Recognizing his own weakness, "Solomon" prayed, and God gave him wisdom (v. 7). "Solomon's" preference for Wisdom above all earthly goods (vv. 8-9) echoes traditional figures (Prov 3:14-15; Job 28:15-19), but v. 10 adds distinctive features in preferring Wisdom over *health*, *beauty*, and *light*. Verse 7 has already indicated that "Solomon's" prayer for Wisdom was answered affirmatively, but v. 11 adds that *all good things* came in the bargain. Verses 12-14 narrate "Solomon's" happy reception of Wisdom with her gifts. Only this received gift, not any merits of "Solomon's" own nature, qualifies him to offer his instructive words to other sincere seekers.

7:15-16. Wish for eloquence. Even the gift of Wisdom, however, is not enough, for she herself serves at the pleasure of God. Hence, Solomon wishes for God to grant eloquence in offering his teaching (v. 15ab). This is motivated by the claim that God is the ultimate guide, corrector, protector, and source of Wisdom herself and sages together with their thought, speech, and skill (vv. 15c-16; throughout 6:22-10:21 *Wisdom* is personified and should be capitalized, *contra* NRSV).

7:17–8:1. Curriculum and praise of Wisdom. God gave "Solomon" mastery of an encyclopedic curriculum (vv. 17-22a). Comparison with 1 Kgs 4:32-33 intimates the wider world in which this generation of sages pursued their vocation. Sirach 39:1-11 offers an earlier presentation of a sage's proficiencies in the Hellenistic context. Comparison of Wis 7:17-22a with the more traditional Ben Sira (Di Lella 1966, 139–46) shows how much pious Jews could glean from the intellectual advances of Hellenism and one way they could be harnessed to the monotheistic constraints and energies of JUDAISM. The relationship between God and personified Wisdom is finessed by introducing this list as the gifts of God (v. 17) and closing it with the claim that *Wisdom, the fashioner of all things, taught me* (v. 22a).

Following this transition to personified Wisdom, vv. 22b–8:1 hymn her excellencies. The praise lists twenty-one (3 x 7) adjectives describing the *spirit that is in her* (vv. 22b-23); besides betraying numerological motives the list is artfully enclosed in an INCLUSIO keyed on *intelligent* (vv. 22b, 23e). "Solomon's" praise then returns to poetry describing Wisdom's relationship to God (vv. 24-26) and proceeds to praise her beneficence toward humans, making some *in every generation . . . friends of God and prophets* (v. 27, cf. v. 14). Intimate association with Wisdom renders one loved by God (v. 28). Wisdom's excellencies exceed sun, stars, and light itself, for while light is succeeded by night, Wisdom continually *prevails* against evil.

8:2-21. "Solomon's" autobiography resumed. "Solomon" declares his passionate resolve to enjoy Wisdom's companionship (v. 2). His form of expression here together with that used in the second declaration (v. 9a), which uses "the ordinary term for 'spouse'" (*symbiōsin* [NRSV *live with*], Reese 1970, 41, n. 45), confirms the erotic inclinations hinted in 7:28. Between the declarations of his resolve in vv. 2 and 9, "Solomon" again praises her (vv. 3-8). Following the astonishing claim that Wisdom *lives with* (*symbiōsin*) God is a series of conditional sentences presenting Wisdom as the distributor of human desires (vv. 5, 6, 7, 8). The most remarkable of these lines are v. 7cd identifying the four cardinal virtues of the Greek ethical ideal (*self-control, prudence, justice,* and *courage*) as the products of Wisdom's labors. The importance of this identification is strengthened by the first line of the verse proposing association with Wisdom as a worthy goal for *anyone [who] loves righteousness* (v. 7a; cf. 1:1).

Following his second declaration of resolve to associate with Wisdom (v. 9a), "Solomon" details the benefits that shall accrue to him (vv. 9b-18). In the listing he reinforces the link between association with Wisdom and righteousness. Both vv. 13 and 17c count *immortality* (*athanasia*) among Wisdom's benefits. Thereby a major burden of the Book of Righteousness and Life (1:–6:21)—pursuit of righteousness answered by the divine gift of immortality—is complemented by the terms of the Book of Wisdom (6:22–10:21): intimate companionship with Wisdom leads to immortality.

Because "Solomon's" autobiography (7:1-14; 8:2-21) is a narrative, 8:19-20 mark a pivotal point on a developmental path from conception and infancy (7:1-4) to youth. Therefore, the doctrine of the preexistence of souls is better not invoked to explain these verses. One might argue that the writer here adopts wholesale a Greek body/soul dualism over against the embodied unity of human personhood more typical of Hebrew anthropology, but it is probably more discerning to see here an effort to adapt the insights of Greek psychology to the Hebrew anthropological inheritance. The developmental stage here articulated does not refer to the entrance of a preexistent soul into a body. Were that the intended meaning the writer should have used the Greek idiom *eiserchomai eis* (cf. 1:4; 10:16) instead of the unprefixed verb + preposition *erchomai eis*. Instead, the text is pointing to that developmental stage in which the animating, noncorporeal factor of human selfhood, the *soul*, exercises effective and harmonious governance of the human personality expressed in its corporeal extension, the *body*. The writer is speaking of a fully human phenomenon: healthy integration of human personality in both "inner" and "outer" dimensions (cf. Reese 1970, 80–86). "Solomon's" insistence that even at such an advanced stage of natural human development, one cannot *possess Wisdom unless God [give] her* (v. 21a) underlines the necessity of divine grace for human beatitude. "Solomon's" only distinguishing grace was his recognition of whose gift Wisdom in fact was (v. 21b).

"Solomon's" Prayer, 9:1-18

Apart from its primary focus—"Solomon" requests wisdom—this rendition of "Solomon's" prayer is quite different from its precursors in 1 Kgs 3:6-9 and 2 Chron 1:8-10. It falls into five parts. Verses 1-3, invoking God with hymnic phraseology, prepare the way for the first petition in v. 4. This is followed by motives (vv. 5-9) that are themselves followed by a renewal of the petition (v. 10) and more motives (vv. 11-18).

9:1-3. Hymnic invocation. God is invoked as the ancestral deity and *Lord of mercy* who is also the Creator of all humankind (vv. 1-2a). The tension between God as the God of a particular people and God as the universal God of all peoples will be an important burden of the last major section of the book (11:1–19:22). Here, although God's universality is acknowledged, petition is made to the ancestral deity. Verses 2b-3 elaborate the creation of humankind for the role of God's vice regent (cf. Gen 1:26-28; Ps 8:5-8). The royal dimensions of humankind's status universalize the address of the book (1:1; 6:1, 21).

9:4. Petition. "Solomon's" first petition is that God give him Wisdom who *sits beside* (cf. 6:14) *[God's]* throne. The obverse of the request for Wisdom is that "Solomon" not be excluded from God's *servants*.

9:5-9. Motives. The first motives in "Solomon's" prayer include implicit appeals for sympathy on the basis of common human frailties (vv. 5-6) and God's historically peculiar relationship with "Solomon" (vv. 7-8). The reference to human frailty in v. 5 is completely traditional, but that in v. 6 is more distinctively characteristic of our writer: even one who is *perfect*, meeting the ideal of 8:19-20, requires God's gift of Wisdom in order to amount to anything. These motives conclude by reiterating Wisdom's significance. Her primeval association with God acquaints her with God's desires and will (v. 9).

9:10. Petition renewed. This renewal of the original petition doubles the lines devoted to Wisdom's place in God's presence (v. 10ab), and requests that she toil alongside "Solomon" in order that he may discern *what is pleasing* to God (v. 10cd). This coheres with "Solomon's" claim that Wisdom's labors result in the cardinal virtues (8:7).

9:11-18. Motives. The final motives incorporate another statement of Wisdom's excellence as a guide to what pleases God (v. 11) and the salutary consequences for "Solomon" (v. 12). These themes are repeated (vv. 14-16b) within a frame of rhetorical questions on human inadequacy (vv. 13, 16c-17). Verse 15 especially reveals our author's view of the human predicament: bodily corruptibility (*phtharton*, NRSV *perishable*). This is not of God's design, and it is precisely by attending to the norms of wisdom that one is assured of incorruptibility (cf. 2:23; 6:18). The final lines of "Solomon's" prayer universalize the salutary

work of Wisdom by pointing out that people *were saved by Wisdom*. This first usage of this verb *to save* (*sōzō*) in the book signals a turning point.

Wisdom, the Deliverer, 10:1-21

This poem, lauding the historical acts of Wisdom, the Deliverer, may be of independent origin, but it meets an important need in the design of the book. Tracing the history of salvation from ADAM through MOSES, it elaborates the theme of Wisdom as agent of historical salvation (cf. 9:18c). That theme will dominate the remainder of the book, although it will be presented as the work of God rather than Wisdom. Following its first appearance in 9:18c, the verb *to save* will reappear in 10:4; 14:4; 16:7; and 18:5. This poem effecting the transition to salvation ideology favors the synonym *to rescue* (*hryomai*, vv. 6, 9, 13, 15).

By supplying the subject *Wisdom* at 11:1 and adding the marginal note *she*, NRSV leads one to read 11:1ff. as the conclusion of this poem. The poem's final line, however, is 10:21. The poet designated the subject with the feminine pronoun *she* (*hautē*, 10:1, 5, 6, 10, 13, 15) and only later clarified the antecedent as *Wisdom* (vv. 4, 8, 9, 21). NRSV correctly supplies marginal notes (vv. 1, 5, 6, 13). The placement of this poem on the heels of 9:18c weakens the effectiveness of its opening and closing devices, but it originally began with the emphatic pronoun *she* (v. 1) and closed with the fully stabilized identity of Wisdom (v. 21; cf. Reese 1965, 392). Wisdom 11:1, however, does not use the emphatic feminine pronoun. It opens with a simple third person singular verb the subject of which could be masculine, feminine, or neuter. The nearest and most likely subject is the neuter plural *works* producing a translation, *their works prospered in the hand of a holy prophet.*

Three further observations are in order. First, the thesis of the poem is declared in the single line of v. 9. Wisdom delivers her servants from toilsome, meaning-threatening difficulties. Second, the poet invokes the dominant motifs of both the Book of Righteousness and Life and the Book of Wisdom. Wisdom is presented as the agent of salvation within history, and those who are saved are *the righteous* (vv. 4, 5, 6, 10, 13, 20; cf. 3:1–5:1, 15). Finally, just as the closing unit of the Book of Righteousness and Life anticipated the personification of Wisdom (6:12-16) characteristic of the Book of Wisdom, so the Book of Wisdom does not close without anticipating the theme of Israel's salvation history that will dominate the Book of Salvation and History.

The Book of Salvation and History, 11:1–19:22

Israel Compared to Egypt, 11:1-14

Following an introductory rehearsal of Israel's wilderness guidance (vv. 1-3) is the first of seven comparisons drawn between ISRAEL and EGYPT (vv. 4-14). Verses 1-3 establish the environment for the remainder of the book: Israel's defining history under Moses' guidance demonstrates creation's righteousness sustaining inclination. These verses also draw links to earlier material. Deliverance from adversaries (v. 3) *by the hands of a holy prophet* (v. 1) echoes 2:18b; Israel's traverse *through an uninhabited wilderness* (v. 2a) contrasts the parallel experience of the ungodly (cf. 5:7b; Reese 1965, 397).

The first comparison turns on Israel's and Egypt's experiences of thirst. When Israel experienced thirst, their cries were favorably answered (v. 4). An important statement of the writer's thesis is set out in v. 5: the polarity of creation is such that natural phenomena function punitively for the wicked and beneficently for the righteous. This comparison also draws connections of empathy between Israelites and Egyptians (vv. 8-9). The experience of thirst enabled Israel to appreciate the suffering of their enemies' justly deserved punishments. Psychological insight is evident in the remark on the Egyptians' *twofold grief* (v. 12). Not only suffering immediate discomfort when their water was polluted with blood (vv. 6-7a), they also experienced the humiliating recognition of their miscalculations when finally *they finally felt thirst in a different way from the righteous* (v. 14c). The first comparison closes with an INCLUSIO on *thirst* (cf. v. 4a).

God's Universal Justice and Mercy, 11:15–12:27

Theodicy is the subject of the remainder of chap. 11 and all of chap. 12. The issue is raised by the contrasting destinies of the righteous and wicked together with a monotheistic insistence that both are equally creatures accountable to God. The discussion proceeds by stating the thesis of the perfect "fit" between sin and its penalty, a correspondence grounded in God's creative power and orderly will (11:15-20). God's freedom and power as creator predispose God toward mercy (11:21–12:2), and this is illustrated by reflection on God's treatment of the Canaanites (12:3-11). Historical illustration is then laid aside in favor of a more general doxological theodicy (12:12-22). Finally, return is made to the "fit" between sin and penalty demonstrated by Egypt's experience (12:23-27).

11:15-20. Correspondence of sin and penalty. Upon the basis Egypt's theriomorphic religious traditions, the writer rationalizes the plagues of frogs, gnats, flies, and locusts (Exod 8–10), all *irrational creatures* (v. 15). The plagues were not outbreaks of irrational divine anger. They were intended pedagogically (v. 16). God was capable of creating new beasts or destroying the wicked in more direct ways (vv. 17-20c), but commitment to orderliness prevailed (v. 20d).

11:21–12:2. God's inclination toward mercy. This commitment to orderliness manifests itself in God's self-restraint. Although God's power beggars the magnitude of creation (vv. 21-22), its very certainty sustains a divine readiness for mercy, because God's power assures a universe of divine options. The human importance of this divine power which sustains mercy is the continued possibility for repentance (v. 23). The spark that ignites this mercy and receptivity to human repentance is God's love *for all things that exist* (v. 24a), and that is evident in the simple fact that things exist and have life (vv. 24b-26). Indeed, the single factor preventing the dissolution of things is the presence of God's *incorruptible* (*aphtharton*, 12:1; NRSV *immortal*) *spirit*. Conceived and nourished by God's power, mercy, and love is the divine pedagogical program. God's program disciplines with patience, making use of the very items *through which [people] sin*, in order that they may be liberated from wickedness for trust in the Lord (12:2; cf. 1:1-2).

12:3-11. The example of the Canaanites. The tradition of Israel's struggle with the Canaanites is offered as an historical proof of God's patience. Most remarkable in this description of the Canaanites is the accusation that they engaged in cannibalism (vv. 3-7). Such claims could perhaps be made on the basis of exaggerated deductions from anti-Canaanite polemic in Jewish scriptures, but more likely the rhetoric has been influenced by Greek tragedies involving child murder and cannibalism. This probably represents an attempt to associate some of the more aesthetically alluring features of Hellenism with the dangers posed to ancient Israel by Canaanite religious practices (Gill 1965, 386).

12:12-22. Doxological theodicy. Having followed the theodic strategies of theological discussion and demonstration from history, the author resorts to doxology and confession. God is accountable to no higher court of appeal (vv. 12-14). Traditional praise of God's righteous governance is reaffirmed, followed by reiteration of God's power which disposes toward divine forbearance (vv. 15-18). The lessons drawn from such praise are that God's patience toward non-Israelites compared with *strictness* toward Israel is a token of election and that Israelites may themselves be charitable in their judgments and may expect mercy when they are judged (vv. 19-22).

12:23-27. Correspondence of sin and penalty. This discourse on God's universal justice and mercy concludes by returning to the opening theme illustrated by Egypt's horrific experience of *those creatures that they had thought to be gods* (v. 27b). Then Egypt recognized that the one *they had refused to know* was none other than *the true God* (v. 27c). Therefore, the rightness of their judgment was indisputable.

Humanity's General Folly, 13:1–15:19

The writer next turns to discuss the general folly of humankind: idolatry. Opening with a feint mitigation of nature worship (13:1-9), the discourse proceeds to a long treatment of the despicable practice of idol worship (13:10–14:11). The author then treats the origin and consequences of IDOLATRY (14:12-31). Finally, true worship of the true God is compared with idolaters' destructive service of their false gods (15:1-19).

13:1-9. Nature and the knowledge of God. The shortcoming of nature worship is that people devote themselves to elements of the creation rather than the Creator, their Lord (vv. 1-4). Such missteps are tentatively mitigated because of the beauty of God's creation (vv. 6-7), but the mitigation does not prevail for if people were competent to search creation successfully in the first place, it would be inexcusable for them not to have found *the Lord of these things* (vv. 8-9).

13:10–14:11. The folly of idolatry. Worshipers of idols are more foolish and inexcusable yet, for they do not worship things made by God but *works of human hands* (13:10). This fundamental critique of idolatry is followed by a rendition of the woodcutter's tale (13:11-19; cf. Isa 44:9-20). Most remarkable in this stock satire are the interior view of the woodcutter's knowledge that the image *cannot help itself* (13:16) and the list of the worshiper's petitions versus the idol's incompetencies (14:17-19). The text next points to the folly of sailors' expecting help and succor from something weaker than the wooden ship carrying them

(14:1-5). And yet, there is a proper righteousness that comes of wood. At the time of the flood, *the hope of the world took refuge on a raft* (14:6b). The atomistic exegesis characteristic of antiquity allowed patristic interpreters to read 14:7 as a prophecy of Jesus' cross. The concluding verses of this treatment of the wretchedness of idolatry announce the destruction of both idol makers and idols (14:8-11).

14:12-31. The origin and consequences of idolatry. The notion of idols was already a departure from God's design for life (vv. 12-14). Our author offers three possible scenarios for the entry of idols into human history: parental grief (vv. 15-16), political flattery (v. 17), and aesthetic ambition (vv. 18-20). The perceptive proviso is added in v. 21 that images are most alluring when people are in *bondage to misfortune or royal authority*. The fundamental consequence of idolatry is a loss of the proper human passion for truth; people who worship idols insist upon *calling such great evils peace* (v. 22; cf. Farley 1990, 194–205). Since it was never a part of God's design (v. 27; cf. vv. 12-14), apathy toward truth issues in chaos both social (vv. 23-26) and religious (vv. 28-29). In the orderly creation of the ordering Creator, departures into idolatry can only end in disaster (vv. 30-31).

15:1-19. True worship compared to false. In contrast to the general folly of humanity, Israel has been preserved from the worship of idols. Although Israel may sin, her recognition of God's power will preserve her from idolatry (v. 2a), *the beginning of fornication*, the *corruption of life*, and *the beginning and cause and end of every evil* (14:12, 27). The dynamics of divine power, human praise (v. 1), and divine acknowledgement (v. 2b) issue in the striking thesis of 15:3. Obedient fellowship with God who is kind, true, patient, and merciful (v. 1; cf. Exod 34:6) is *righteousness*, and the lived recognition of God's power (contrast idols' impotence) is the *root* from which *immortality* grows (cf. Murphy 1963). This knowledge of God and God's power, knowledge grounded in praise, has been Israel's protection against idolatry (vv. 4-6).

Finally, the text returns to the discussion of idolaters. Makers and worshipers of clay images (vv. 7-13) are more miserably misguided than are those of wooden idols (13:11–14:11), for they make them only for financial gain and they know that they profit from sin (vv. 12-13). Worst of all idolaters, however, are *all the enemies who opposed [Israel]* (v. 14b). Not only do they worship dead fabrications of mortal humans who are themselves better than the idols before which they bow down (vv. 15-17), they even worship strange, irrational, ugly beasts (vv. 18-19). With this polemic reprise of Egypt's theriomorphic traditions (cf. 11:15), the writer is ready to resume comparisons between Israel and Egypt.

Israel Compared to Egypt, 16:1–19:22

The remaining comparisons include strange animals (16:1-4), poisonous animals (16:5-14), transformation of nature (16:15-29), darkness and light (17:1–18:4), unbelief and fidelity to the Law (18:5-25), and the sea as grave and birth-place (19:1-17). The Book of Salvation and History is rounded off with a summary conclusion (19:18-21) balancing its introductory lines (11:1-3), and the whole book itself is capped with a laudatory formulation of the Lord's ever dependable care for Israel (19:22). Although the many interpretive traditions utilized in these chapters are intriguing, the distinctive contributions lie elsewhere. They are best seen in the central comparison of the experiences of the transformation of nature (16:15-29) with its morality lesson (vv. 24-29) and in the section on darkness and light (17:1–18:4) with its acute analysis of fear (17:11-19).

Wisdom 16:24-29 appends a brief morality lesson to the comparison of Israel's and Egypt's experiences of the transformation of nature (16:15-23). The thesis is declared in v. 24. Creation serves God who made it. Its elements stretch their capacities to punish the unrighteous and ease off their normal predictability for the good of the righteous. Negotiating the strait between mechanistic views of nature and interventionist views of God's work in the world, the author assumes a dynamic creation. Creation is a *minister* or *servant* (cf. 6:4) in God's governance of the universal kingdom of righteousness. As creation, it has independent standing in the presence of its Maker and is entrusted with relative "autonomy" in executing the policy directives of its King. This dynamic, righteousness sustaining, beneficent view of creation is present throughout the book (cf. 1:14; 5:17-23; 16:17c; 18:8; 19:6, 18-21). Here, the author goes on to say that creation comes to the aid of supplicants so that they may learn the truth of the deuteronomic interpretation of manna (vv. 25-26; cf. Deut 8:3), to add a halachic interpretation in favor of regular prayer at dawn (vv. 27-28), and to close the lesson with an image of ingrates' disintegrating hopes (v. 29).

Finally, in the middle of its long description of the Egyptians' discomfiture during the plague of darkness (17:2-21) the writer inserts a striking analysis of fear (17:11-13). The author maintains that *wickedness* is *cowardly* (contrast *courage* coming to those who *love righteousness* in 8:7) and stands self-condemned. Persons in the grip and practice of evil are troubled by their consciences and exaggerate the difficulties they encounter. Fear itself is a treasonous surrender of the aids available in sound reasoning (v. 12, cf. v. 15b). Once this internal betrayal is enacted, thereby weakening the self, one's expectation of things to come prefers ignorance to knowledge of what causes the torment. Thus driven by the nameless fears of the darkness, whatever the Egyptians encountered *paralyzed them with terror* (v. 19e). Because of the internal subversion in which fear is rooted, however, they were finally more burdensome to themselves than was the darkness that was merely the occasion of their terror (v. 21c).

Works Cited

Cabaniss, A. 1956. "Wisdom 18:14: An Early Christmas Text." VC 10:97–102.

Di Lella, A. A. 1966. "Conservative and Progressive Theology: Sirach and Wisdom." CBQ 28:139–54.

Farley, Edward. 1990. *Good and Evil: Interpreting a Human Condition.*

Gill, D. 1965. "Greek Sources of Wisdom XII:3–7." VT 15:386.

Grant, R. M. 1966. "The Book of Wisdom at Alexandria: Reflections on the History of the Canon and Theology." *Studia Patristica* 7:462–72.

Hanson, R. P. C. 1988. *The Search for the Christian Doctrine of God: The Arian Controversy 318–381.*

Hennig, J. 1952. "The Book of Wisdom in the Liturgy." CBQ 14:233–36.

Kloppenberg, John S. 1982. "Isis and Sophia in the Book of Wisdom." HTR 75: 57–84.

Murphy, Roland E. 1963. "'To know your might is the root of immortality' (Wis 15:3)." CBQ 25:88–93.

Murphy-O'Connor, Jerome. 1976. "Christological Anthropology in Phil 2:6-11." RB 83:25–50.

Reese, James M. 1965. "Plan and Structure of the Book of Wisdom." CBQ 27: 391–99. 1970. *Hellenistic Influence on the Book of Wisdom and Its Consequences.*

Winston, David. 1979. *The Wisdom of Solomon: A New Translation with Introduction and Commentary.* AncB.

Sirach
(Ecclesiasticus)
Max Gray Rogers

Introduction

Sirach is the longest and likely the earliest work in the Apocrypha, the only book in this group with its author identified by name. Roman Catholics regard it as deuterocanonical and consider it, together with the remainder of the Apocrypha (excluding 1 and 2 Esdras and the Prayer of Manasseh) to be part of the OT. By the end of the first century C.E. leading rabbis excluded this book from the Hebrew Bible. Martin Luther, following their lead, excluded Sirach—along with the other books of the Apocrypha—from the OT canon.

Sirach has appeared under various names. Greek manuscripts entitled the work, Wisdom of Jesus the son of Sirach. The Hebrew text in 50:27 is usually corrected to give the author's name as Jeshua (Jesus in Gk.), son of Eleazar, son of Sira. The work itself has been described as Words of (Heb. text), Proverbs of (Jerome), Book of or Instruction of (Talmud) Ben Sira. Latin manuscripts entitle the work Ecclesiasticus, "ecclesiastical (church) book." The author's name is either given as Ben Sira (Heb.) or simply as Sirach (Gk.).

The traditional title in English translations is Ecclesiasticus (so KJV), but modern American practice is to refer to the book as Sirach.

Authorship, Date, and Setting

Ben Sira resided in Jerusalem (50:27) where he practiced his profession as scribe and teacher. He devoted himself to the study of the Law, the Prophets, and other writings highly regarded within JUDAISM. His students were most likely young Jewish males from well-to-do families. He urged the unlearned to avail themselves of his *house of instruction* (51:23).

The time frame generally proposed for this work is reinforced by the author's description of the High Priest Simon (or Simeon) whose performance during Temple rituals Ben Sira considered majestic (50:1-21). This reference is thought to identify the High Priest Simon II (219–196), son of Johanan (*Onias* in some Greek mss.). If this is correct, it would indicate that Ben Sira published his work (at least the second part of it) after 196 B.C.E. since 50:1c seems to indicate that Simon was then deceased.

No mention is made by Ben Sira of the turbulent times that ensued with the reign of Antiochus IV Epiphanes (175–164). He seems unaware that Simon II's son Jason purchased the high priesthood from Antiochus IV in 174 B.C.E., and thus displaced his own brother Onias III from his rightful succession to that Zadokite post—an outrage that contributed directly to the Maccabean revolt. There is broad consensus that Ben Sira published his work between 196 and 180 B.C.E. He likely died before 175 B.C.E.

Earliest Greek Translation

The earliest Greek translation of this work was made by the grandson of Ben Sira. A prologue was provided in which the grandson described his grandfather Jesus as one who had devoted his life to the study of the scripture. For the first time we have a direct reference made to the Prophets (*nebi'im*) as a literary entity within scripture. A further word of explanation was offered as to how the grandfather's proficiency in these studies had led him to contribute something of his own for the benefit of those who desired to live according to the law.

In the second of the three Greek sentences that comprise the prologue, the grandson begs the reader's indulgence for any imperfections in translation. Acknowledging the difficulties in translating from the Hebrew, he noted that even the Law and the Prophets in (Gk.) translation differed substantially from the original. The translations mentioned here by the grandson almost certainly refer to writings translated within the LXX that differ substantially from the later MT.

The conclusion of the prologue is most informative concerning the time of the grandson's arrival in Egypt, the thirty-eighth year of the reign of King Euergetes. Since the earlier of two Egyptian kings known as Euergetes reigned fewer than thirty-eight years, the King in question was likely Ptolemy VII Physkon Euergetes II who began to reign jointly with his brother Ptolemy VI Philometor (181–146) in 170 and died in 117 B.C.E. The thirty-eighth year of his reign would have been 132 B.C.E.

Upon his arrival in Egypt, the grandson apparently discovered the work of his grandfather in Hebrew and set about translating it into Greek. He likely published his translation together with the prologue sometime after 117 B.C.E.

Composition

The format of Ben Sira's work has been discussed at length. Despite an obvious lack of organization, various patterns or divisions have been proposed for the book's fifty-one chapters. One such proposal holds that the work consists of two parts (chaps. 1–23 and 24–50) which were published separately. Each part begins with an extensive hymn to wisdom (1:1-20 and 24:1-33).

The Book of Proverbs begins with similar instruction devoted to wisdom (Prov 1–9) and concludes with an alphabetic acrostic (Prov. 31:10-31) as does Sirach (51:13-30).

It is argued here that if the "Hymn in Honor of Our Ancestors" (44:1–50:24) can be considered a conclusion to the combined work, rather than belonging only to the second part, and the hymn in 42:15–43:33 can be seen as an introduction to that hymn, then the two parts of the combined work each conclude with instruction concerning women (23:22-27 and 42:9-14). This is fitting since Ben Sira seems to have regarded women as the most serious threat to achieving the good life.

Text

Since 1896, portions of six Hebrew manuscripts (A–F) of Sirach have been recovered from the Genizah of the Ezra Synagogue in Old Cairo. These manuscripts were produced by Qaraite copyists after 800 C.E. (Di Lella, 1987, 569). The leaves found in the Cairo Genizah are thought to date from the eleventh and twelfth centuries C.E. More recently the caves of Qumran have revealed additional Hebrew fragments.

Perhaps the most important of recent discoveries have been twenty-six fragments in Hebrew (found at Masada in 1964 by Y. Yadin) from a scroll dating to the early first century B.C.E. (Di Lella 1987, 53). This scroll, copied within a century of the publication of Ben Sira's work, confirms the accuracy of Hebrew manuscripts A–F in general and manuscript B in particular.

The Greek translation of Ben Sira's grandson is the version that overall continues to be regarded as the most authentic despite errors in copying and other literary and translation flaws. The book's inclusion within the LXX is indicative of its status among the sacred writings of Greek-speaking Jews.

For Further Study

In the *Mercer Dictionary of the Bible*: APOCRYPHAL LITERATURE; HELLENISTIC WORLD; MACCABEES; PROVERBS, BOOK OF; SCRIBE IN THE NEW TESTAMENT; SCRIBE IN THE O.T.; WISDOM LITERATURE.

In other sources: G. H. Box and W. O. E. Oesterley, "The Book of Sirach" in *APOT*; J. L. Crenshaw, *Old Testament Wisdom: An Introduction*; A. A. Di Lella, "Wisdom of Ben Sira." AncBD; Ahmed Osman, *Stranger in the Valley of the Kings*; G. von Rad, *Wisdom in Israel*; J. A. Sanders, *The Psalms Scroll of Qumran Cave 11*; P. W. Skehan and A. A. Di Lella, *The Wisdom of Ben Sira*, AncB; Y. Yadin, *The Ben Sira Scroll from Masada*.

Commentary

An Outline

I. Prologue
II. Book One, 1:1–23:27
  A. Hymn to Wisdom, 1:1-20
  B. Instruction and Proverbs, 1:22–23:27
III. Book Two, 24:1–42:14
  A. Hymn to Wisdom, 24:1-34
  B. Instruction and Proverbs, 25:1–42:14
IV. Three Hymns of Praise, 42:15–50:24
  A. Praise of the Works of the Lord, 42:15–43:33
  B. Praise of Famous Men, Our Ancestors, 44:1–49:16
  C. Praise of Simon Son of Onias, 50:1-24
  D. Addenda, 50:25-29
V. Three Appendixes, 51:1-30
  A. A Psalm of Thanksgiving, 51:1-12
  B. A Litany, 51:12 i-xvi
  C. An Acrostic Poem, 51:13-30

Prologue

The grandson of Ben Sira not only described his grandfather's commitment to Jewish scripture, he revealed much about his own pursuit of instruction and wisdom. In identifying the writings worthy of special praise, he named *the Law and the Prophets and the others* (i.e., "books of our ancestors"; see NRSV mg., 1:1). This statement both affirmed the primary role of the Law (*Torah*) and introduced the hitherto unmentioned collection, the Prophets (*Nebi'im*).

It is quite likely that some of these "other books" were later included in the Writings (*Kethubhim*) that became the third division of the Hebrew Bible by the end of the first century C.E.

Book One, 1:1–23:27

Hymn to Wisdom, 1:1-20

1:1-10. Origin of Wisdom. The opening hymn proclaims that all wisdom comes from the Lord and remains the Lord's prerogative forever. The sands of the sea, the span of eternity, the depth of the abyss are joined by the equally unfathomable wisdom whose existence preceded creation.

1:11-20. Fear of the Lord. The fullness, the crown and the root of wisdom are each identified as the fear of the Lord. Numbered among its gifts are longevity and a happy life.

Instruction and Proverbs, 1:22–23:27

1:22-30. Virtues and vices. As anger produces ruin, so patience produces prudence. Only by observing the commandments in trust and humility can wisdom be gained from the Lord.

2:1-17. Patience. The role of misfortune in the lives of those who serve the Lord is explained as a testing to be endured patiently with trust and hope. Given the frustration prevalent among Jews of that day who suffered oppression at the hands of a succession of foreign powers, this material is strategically placed in terms of its importance.

3:1-16. Filial responsibility. Since the family life of that time reflected the social stature of the father, it was important that the father not be demeaned by the unruly behavior of his children. The severity of the injunction here is best seen in v. 7 where children are enjoined to serve *parents as their masters*. Those who honor their father will have hidden treasure, joy in their own children, and atonement for their sins. Indeed, their prayers will be heard and their lives will be long. The latter is the only promise attached to a commandment in the Decalogue (Exod 20:12; Deut 5:16).

3:17-24. Humility. Dependence upon God should move one to humility in all human affairs. The Lord is glorified by those who are humble. For things beyond our strength we should not search. One should be content with what is revealed in the law and not pursue the speculations of Greek philosophy.

3:25-29. Obstinacy. Obstinacy is counterproductive. It does not heed the lessons of knowledge. It prefers instead the course of danger with its risks of destruction. The obstinate heart piles mistake upon mistake, sin upon sin. For the wise, wisdom is a joy.

3:30–4:10. Almsgiving. Chapter 3 illustrates Ben Sira's tendency to combine topics virtually at random. Having addressed such subjects as the honoring of parents, humility, and obstinacy, his last two lines of the chapter introduce the theme of almsgiving which extends into the beginning of chap. 4.

Since alms will atone for sins, one should respond to the poor, the needy, the hungry, and the oppressed generously and without delay. The disadvantaged have not been rejected by the Lord; they may only be in the process of being tested. Live an exemplary life. No negative stigma is attached to wealth, but the wealthy should redress the needs of the disadvantaged.

4:11-19. Wisdom's instruction. Those who love Wisdom, who seek her and obey her shall receive the love and favor of the Lord. Nevertheless, Wisdom warns her children that she will torment them with tests and trials. Only to those who demonstrate their trustworthiness will Wisdom reveal her secrets.

4:20-31. The importance of being humane. Do not be ashamed of who you are. Feelings of shame felt for one's sins attest to one's nobility. Unwarranted partiality shows poor judgment and is demeaning.

Wisdom is conveyed through speech. Do not humor fools or curry favor with the powerful. Above all, stand for truth, and the Lord will stand with you. Let your speech match your deeds. Never abuse your authority. Let your generosity toward others exceed your expectations of them.

5:1-8. Overconfidence. Neither wealth nor strength should warrant a sense of self-sufficiency. Do not assume that punishment delayed is punishment escaped. God acts in good time.

5:9–6:1. Propriety of speech. Be quick to listen but patient in response. Speak from knowledge; but without knowledge, cover your mouth. Speech can produce both glory and disgrace. Condemnation is the lot of the *double-tongued* (v. 14).

6:2-4. Crush of passion. Uncontrolled passion destroys its possessor and fills one's enemies with sheer delight.

6:5-17. Friendship. This topic is addressed in a lucid and pragmatic fashion. Words of warmth are conducive to friendship. Be friendly to all, but confide in none until you have tested them thoroughly as Wisdom tests her suitors. Fear of the Lord makes for firm friendship.

6:18-37. Wisdom in full panoply. Discipline is essential in the search for wisdom. It is reflected in patience and endurance. The discipline of the plow produces the harvest. Access to wisdom is ultimately gained through commitment. Search it out and keep its ways, and wisdom's yoke will become for you a golden ornament.

Only those who apply themselves can become wise. Seek those elders who are wise. Hang upon their every word. Let your delight be in the Law of the Lord; and upon this law meditate unceasingly (cf. Ps 1:2). Then the wisdom you desire will be yours.

7:1-36. Maxims for the wise. Chapter 7 is a random collection of maxims ranging from iniquity to caring for cattle, from laborious work to the raising of daughters, from offerings and sacrifices to the value of a good wife. Twice in this chapter direct reference is made to the ultimate fate of human beings (v. 17b and v. 36a). In v. 17 that end is described as *worms*. One who remembers the end of life *will never sin* (v. 36).

8:1-19. Thou shalt not. Consideration is given to how one might relate to a broad spectrum of persons. Discretion is clearly the better part of wisdom. Do not strive against the rich or powerful, incite the garrulous, or consort with the senseless. Do not demean repentant sinners, the aged, or the dead; these circumstances apply to all readers. Do not dismiss the discourse of sages or the elderly. You can learn much from them. Do not lend or pledge what you cannot afford to lose.

Activities to be avoided: taking judges to court; travelling with reckless persons who will place your life at risk; contending with quick-tempered individuals who think nothing of bloodshed and who will strike you down; taking counsel with fools who cannot keep a secret; and sharing secrets with strangers. Do not open your heart to anyone.

9:1-9. The company of women. The risk of jealousy is that it may produce what it fears most. Do not become so enslaved to a woman that she can trample you. Avoid the *loose woman* (prostitute), lest you be enticed by her charm. Do not be fascinated by the *singing girl* (prostitute) who attracts attention with her songs. Avoid virgins at all costs; they can prove expensive. Do not even frequent parts of the city where prostitutes await. Do not become fascinated by the beauty of a woman who is not yours. Many have perished in such flames. Never eat and drink with a married woman, lest you be drawn into ruin.

9:10-16. On choosing companions. Old friends are to be preferred to new ones as old wine is preferred to new. Do not envy the prosperity of sinners; their demise will surely come. Distance yourself from anyone who has the authority to kill you (kings, governors, etc.). Be discerning among your neighbors and converse with the wise. Have the upright for table companions and exult only over the fear of the Lord.

9:17–10:5. The wise ruler. Like a craftsman whose skill is seen in his work, the skill of the ruler is measured by his words. The quality of rule is determined at the top. The sagacity of a judge is reflected in his ministers. The citizens of a city reflect the character of their ruler. All sovereignty is in the hands of the Lord.

10:6-18. Beware of pride. The fruits of pride are anger, arrogance, and injustice. How presumptuous can *dust and ashes* (v. 9) be? The king today is dead tomorrow. In death, worms are our portion. Withdrawal from God is the beginning of pride. The proud are uprooted to make way for the lowly. This is the fate of nations as well as individuals.

10:19–11:1. The role of honor. Honor is attached to whoever fears the Lord, poor or rich. Honor ranks above social standing.

Do not boast of your own wisdom, especially when you are in need. It is better to labor and have plenty than to be boastful and lack even bread.

Humility does not exclude self-esteem. Persons are judged in part by the level of their self-esteem. How can those who condemn themselves be justified? How can those who disgrace themselves be honored?

Wealth is enhanced less by honor than is poverty. By the same token wealth is also diminished less by dishonor than is poverty. Thus those in poverty have more to gain from honor and more to lose from dishonor.

11:2-6. Appearances can be deceiving. Wisdom lifts the poor to the level of princes. Appearance is no grounds for praise; clothing is no cause for derision. The motives of the Lord are unknown to humankind. Those least likely are often exalted; those of renown are brought low.

11:7-9. Act not in haste. Investigate thoroughly before finding fault. Consider carefully before rendering judgment. Do not answer before hearing; do not interrupt when someone else is talking. Never involve yourself in the disputes of others, especially sinners.

11:10-13. Paradox of prosperity. There is no guarantee that those who labor relentlessly will acquire wealth commensurate with their labor. There is no restriction that renders those less inclined or less able to toil incapable of achieving extraordinarily good fortune. Such results can only be attributed to the Lord. Nevertheless one is advised not to multiply life's activities needlessly. Busyness in and of itself is a mistake rather than a solution.

11:14-19. The Lord giveth—both good and evil. Good and evil, poverty and wealth, life and death all come mysteriously from the Lord. Ben Sira nevertheless remains confident that the godly enjoy God's favor. A person may become rich through careful management and greed. Yet there is no assurance that one will live long enough to enjoy the fruit of one's labors. Death is ever close at hand, ready to disperse hard-earned wealth.

11:20-28. Redressing imbalance. Devote yourself to your assigned duty. Grow old in your work. Do not trouble yourself about the prosperity of sinners. Trust in the Lord. Fortunes can be easily reversed. Only the fool boasts of self-sufficiency.

Ben Sira lived at a time when it was commonly held that death led to the dim, gray domain of SHEOL. He knew of no afterlife in which the imbalance between reward and suffering could be redressed. That problem could be solved only within the span of a lifetime.

Ben Sira believed that retribution would be achieved in this life, if only in its waning moments. A few moments of adversity at the end would erase a lifetime of ill-gained delights. Conversely, a few moments of happiness at the end would nullify a lifetime of adversity. Therefore he could write: *Call no one happy before his death* (v. 28a). We will be known by how we die.

The intensity of Ben Sira's treatment of this issue reflects the extent of the growing concern with the doctrine of retribution. Consequently, following Ben Sira, it became necessary to posit the existence of an afterlife in order that the concept of retribution might be vindicated.

11:29-34. Your home is your castle. In v. 8:19a Ben Sira warned his reader: *Do not reveal your thoughts to anyone.* In v. 29 these words are echoed: Do not open your home to everyone. There are many who will harm you and your possessions if given the opportunity. The stranger who will disturb you and alienate you from your family may be a reference to someone who would alienate you from your Jewish heritage.

12:1-7. Give to the needy, but.... One is enjoined to give alms speedily, generously, and cheerfully, (3:30–4:6), *but do not give to the ungodly.* Since God hates sinners and punishes the ungodly, we should do no less. For good rendered to the ungodly, you will receive twice the evil in return. Give only to the devout, to the one who is good.

12:8-18. Never trust your enemy. Adversity is the true catalyst of friendship. Wickedness is as endemic to your enemy as corrosion is to copper or tarnish, to a polished surface. With deviousness and duplicity, he will plot your downfall.

13:1–14:2. Richer is better. Although Ben Sira views wealth favorably, he has many unfavorable things to say about the wealthy. The rich are the natural predators of the poor. To avoid being exploited, the poor must be ever vigilant. The wealthy enjoy an insurmountable advantage; they can add insult to injury. The poor can only apologize for being poor.

As there can never be peace between the wolf and the lamb, there can never be peace between rich and poor. The poor are pasture for the rich, detested by the rich. The rich are respected for their wealth; the poor are demeaned because of their poverty. Despite his disparaging comments about the wealthy, Ben Sira does not denounce wealth per se. Only ill-gotten wealth is condemned. The wise are enjoined to acquire wealth in order to enjoy the good life.

14:3-19. Health and wealth and the time to enjoy them. Wealth is wasted on misers and the greedy. Those who withhold from themselves the advantages of their affluence will only provide for others what they were unwilling to enjoy themselves. None are more abusive than those who begrudge themselves. Never satisfied with what they have, they are victims of their own greed.

Be generous with your friends before you die. Do not deprive yourself of the choice portion. Death does not tarry; there are no luxuries in Sheol. All works, like their makers, will pass away.

14:20–15:10. Wisdom and its blessings. The one who pursues Wisdom considers its ways, searches out its paths, lies in wait for it, peers in its window, listens at its doorways, and attaches a tent to its walls.

To such a one who fears the Lord and has mastered the law, Wisdom will respond as a mother and a bride. Wisdom will nourish the one who fears with food and drink. Wisdom also will provide sustenance for honor, eloquence, and the joy of an imperishable name. For fools and sinners, it is not so.

15:11-20. Free to choose. Do not blame God for moral failures. God does not promote despised things. The Lord has no need of sinners. From the beginning, God created human beings free to choose between good and evil, life and death. No human act escapes God's attention. No sinful act will escape redress.

16:1-4. Quality, not quantity. Children are a blessing only if they fear the Lord. One such child is better than a thousand ungodly offspring. To die childless is preferable to having worthless children. A city founded upon one person's intelligence can be destroyed by one lawless clan.

16:5-23. Lessons of history. History is replete with examples of such rebellious activities and of God's wrathful response. Ben Sira cites the GIANTS of old (Gen 6:4), the inhabitants of Sodom (Gen 19), the Canaanites, and the 600,000 Israelites in the desert (Num 14), all of whom perished as a result of their rebellion against the Lord.

Never assume that God is unaware of human deeds. Among the countless inhabitants of the earth no one goes unnoticed. The heavens above, the earth below and the abyss in between quake at the mere presence of the deity. Only a senseless person thinks that God's justice is remote.

16:24–17:14. The created order. In creating the earth, celestial mechanics were carefully fashioned. The Lord then blessed the earth and covered its face with living creatures; unto it they must all return.

Out of the earth *the Lord created human beings* (v. 1); but to it they must return. The Lord numbered their days and gave them dominion over every earthly thing. The Lord clothed them with strength like his own, and made them in his own image. The Lord put the fear of humans in every other living creature. Reason, speech, and sight are theirs; humans also possess hearing and a discerning mind. God gave them knowledge of understanding, showing them good and evil. The grandeur of creation instilled fear in them, that they may praise God's holy name. Humans received knowledge and a law of life as their inheritance. The Lord made an everlasting covenant with them and gave them the commandments to guide them in their relations to others.

17:15-24. The compassionate judge. The Lord has chosen rulers for each nation, but has reserved Israel as God's own possession. The Lord observes Israel's every act, seeing all their iniquities. The giving of alms is cherished by the Lord who will respond in kind. Those who forsake their sins will be received with compassion.

17:25-32. A plea renewed. It is never too late for the living to repent and praise the Most High. Only the dead are denied this privilege. The mercy of the Lord is exemplified in forgiveness received by those who repent. If the highest hosts of heaven are accountable, how much more so those who are only dust and ashes.

18:1-14. What indeed is humanity? What indeed is humanity? Of what use? These questions echo the concerns raised in Ps 8 and Job 14. Instead of destroying human hope—as Job asserted (14:19)—God recognizes the wretchedness and frustration resulting from the mortal nature of the human predicament. Thus the Lord responds toward all humanity with compassion and forgiveness.

18:15-18. A cheerful giver. The spirit of charity should not be diminished by harsh speech. A kind word can mean more than a gift. A gift given grudgingly brings grief to the recipient.

18:19-21. Be prepared. Thorough preparation can mitigate a mistaken action even if it cannot prevent it.

18:22-26. Importance of being earnest. Once vows are made, it is important that they be honored promptly. Never make a vow if you lack sufficient means. If the Lord is involved in a vow not honored, the Lord is embarrassed. Remember hunger in a time of plenty, poverty in a time of wealth. Circumstances can change quickly. Take nothing for granted.

18:27-29. A self-portrait of Ben Sira. The wise are circumspect in all things, rising above wrongdoing. Steeped in the virtues of wisdom, they should proclaim its praise. Schooled in wisdom's rhetoric, they should bring forth worthy proverbs.

18:30–19:4. Control over self. A life given to lust will make you a laughingstock to your enemies. Do not indulge in luxury you cannot afford. Do not impoverish yourself by feasting on borrowed money. One who fails to manage resources responsibly will have nothing. Wine and women entice even men of understanding. Decay and worms will be their lot.

19:5-12. Control over tongue. One who delights in evil will be destroyed by it. Never repeat what you are told, and you will have no regrets. Repeat nothing to friend or foe, unless remaining silent would be sinful. Whatever you hear should die with you. The urge to repeat what is heard is as irresistible as pain at childbirth. Foolish gossip is as unbearable as an arrow lodged in the thigh.

19:13-17. Control over impulse. Inquire before accusing. Take no action until facts are ascertained. Remember that slips can be made unintentionally. Let your response be in accord with the law of the Most High.

19:20-30. All knowledge is not wisdom. Ben Sira opens this section with a familiar maxim capturing the key principle of his teaching: *The whole of wisdom is fear of the Lord* (v. 20a). Of ancillary importance is the thought: *In all wisdom there is the fulfillment of the law* (v. 20b). The acknowledgment that appearances do not reveal the inner workings of an evil mind contrasts sharply with the naive assumption that a people are known by their attire, laughter, and walk. Perceiving the true intent of a human mind is an adventure in uncertainty.

20:1-8. To speak or not to speak. Silence is preferable to inappropriate speech. Timely silence actually enhances speech. Reasons for silence can include having nothing to say, realizing that silence is appropriate, or simply biding one's time. The wise will keep silent until the proper moment, but a bragging fool is unaware of the proper moment. The excessive talker is detested, but one who speaks presumptuously is hated.

20:9-17. Much that glitters may be fool's gold. Personal fortune is often a matter of perspective. Advantages can come out of adversity. Yet some gains may result in losses. The cheapest price may prove to be the most expensive cost. A gift from a fool is the most worthless of all.

20:18-20. Importance of discretion. A slip of the foot is preferable to a slip of the tongue. This frequently accounts for the downfall of the wicked. Coarse persons and coarse tales are constantly on the lips of the ignorant. Even a PROVERB loses its savor when recited by a fool.

20:21-23. Fates worse than poverty. One who is constrained from sinning through poverty need have no regrets when taking rest. Another can be embarrassed to death, or effect self-destruction by his senseless expression. Yet another out of embarrassment makes promises to a friend that cannot be fulfilled, and so makes an enemy for no good reason.

20:24-26. Stigma of lying. Lying leaves a stigma upon the liar. It is the hallmark of ignorance, more despicable than thievery. A liar's lot is dishonor; shame is his constant companion.

20:27-31. Proverbial sayings. A reputation is cultivated through words as a harvest is enhanced through the soil. Those who please persons of influence can atone for wrongdoing. Gifts and presents can blind the eyes as a muzzle silences the mouth. Those who hide their folly are preferable to those who hide their wisdom.

21:1-10. Wages of sin. The SERPENT is a familiar image for sin. Unlike in the narrative in Gen 3, here the serpent has the teeth of a lion and bites its prey. All iniquity is like a two-edged sword; the injury it inflicts cannot be healed. Building one's house with another's money is like gathering stones (instead of wood) for the winter. The wicked are described collectively as a bundle of fibers fit for a blazing fire (imagery confined to earthly life). The road of smooth stones that leads to SHEOL (Hades) does not suggest that a different end awaits the repentant. It is likely, however, that sinners will reach that pit sooner rather than later.

21:11-14. A living spring. Some acumen is required in order that learning might occur. There is a dimension of acumen, however, that produces bitterness. Knowledge flows forth from wisdom *like a life-giving spring* (v. 13). The mind of a fool is a broken vessel that *can hold no knowledge* (v. 14).

21:15-17. Intelligent speech. A prudent person appreciates a wise saying and expands upon it. A fool dislikes such a saying and dismisses it. Unlike foolish chatter, intelligent speech *is sought in the assembly* (v. 17) and cherished in retrospect.

21:18-21. Value of education. To the fool knowledge is words without meaning. Education fetters the ignorant, hand and foot; it adorns the sensible person like a priceless ornament.

21:22-24. Discretion. A discreet person enters only when invited and respects the privacy of a home.

21:25-28. Imprudent speech. The imprudent speak of things that do not concern them. Fools' minds are in their mouths; but the mouths of the wise reflects their minds. When an ungodly person curses an adversary (possibly a Jew), the curse recoils upon himself (Gen 12:3). Slanderers defame themselves and are hated in the community.

22:1-2. A slothful person. In one of his most graphic metaphors, Ben Sira describes the slothful person as a filthy stone (used to clean away fecal matter) and a dunghill, which if touched, will cause one to shake it off his hand.

22:3-6. Some thoughts about daughters. An ignorant son is a disgrace to his father; but a daughter is a complete loss. A sensible daughter will find a husband for herself, but one who is disgraceful brings grief to the father who obviously failed to raise her properly. A brazen woman disgraces father and husband and is hated by both. A woman's worth is measured in terms of how she affects the reputations of father and husband. She herself has no reputation to be considered. Ben Sira's embarrassing thoughts about daughters will reappear at 26:10-12 and 42:9-14.

22:9-18. Fools, fools, everywhere. Instructing a fool is as futile as gluing a broken pot, or awakening a sleeper out of a deep sleep—who can only ask, "What was that?" *Weep for the dead* (v. 11) for light has failed them. Weep for fools for understanding has failed them. Weep less for the dead for they are at rest; *the life of the fool is worse than death* (v. 11). Mourning for the dead lasts seven days; for the fool it lasts an entire life.

Avoid witless people and you will not be wearied by their senselessness. The only burden heavier than lead is a fool. Sand, salt, and iron are all less oppressive than stupidity.

Wooden joists connecting masonry walls are not loosened in an earthquake. Nor is a position reached after careful consideration abandoned during a crisis. An idea based on sensible thinking stands apart like a plaster relief on a smooth wall. Small stones atop an elevated surface cannot resist the wind. Neither can an uncertain position foolishly arrived at resist the power of fear.

22:19-22. Resiliency of friendship. The topic of friendship is again addressed (cf. 6:5-17), reflecting upon the enduring qualities of this relationship. Only the most extreme and offensive breach of decorum can sever this bond.

22:23-26. A risk worth taking. The self-serving dimension of friendship is clearly evidenced here. The goal of friendship seems to be sharing in a friend's prosperity and inheritance. It is reassuring to know that if you should suffer harm for sheltering a friend, that friend will bring suspicion upon himself. Verse 24 appears to be displaced in its present position.

22:27–23:6. An acknowledgment of inadequacy. This confession acknowledges many human tendencies that can thoroughly discredit one in the eyes of the community. It is coupled with an impassioned plea for deliverance from these weaknesses.

23:7-15. Discipline the tongue. Do not indulge in oaths or the frequent use of God's name. These two practices are fraught with the danger of personal degradation as well as the affliction of one's household. Do not use coarse or foul language; it is unbecoming to the descendants of Jacob. Remember your parental instruction and behave accordingly lest you be devastated by bad habits.

23:16-27. Sexual misconduct. This numerical proverb is built upon the number three. Described here are three kinds of misconduct involving insatiable sexual desire, incest, and adultery. The perpetrators of such conduct assume that discretion will keep their behavior hidden from their peers. They fail to realize that no amount of discretion can conceal their actions from the all-seeing eyes of God.

Although stoning is not mentioned, punishment in a public place is indicated. Perhaps stoning had given way to the whip.

The female involved is presumed to be married. The three sins of the adulteress are against God, her husband, and her children. Interestingly enough, no mention is made of the adulterer's wife or children.

Book Two, 24:1–42:14

Hymn to Wisdom, 24:1-34

24:1-7. Origin and scope of Wisdom. In the prologue (vv. 1-2), before the heavenly court, Wisdom heralds her own glory. Having come forth from the mouth of God, she covered the primeval deep like a mist before God's first creative word. (Gen 1:2). Having dwelt in the highest heavens (the realm of God), her throne stood in a pillar of cloud (reminiscent of Exodus). Alone, she encompassed the vault of heaven and the depths of the abyss. She has claimed almost every major attribute of God. Small wonder that Wisdom is identified with virtually every visual manifestation of God in the Hebrew Bible. Where indeed shall she reside?

24:8-12. Jerusalem—where else? Wisdom reveals that God directed her to dwell in Israel. Affirming once more that she was created *in the beginning* (v.9) and for all time, Wisdom cites ministrations *in the holy tent* (v. 10) (prototype of the Temple) as a basis in Zion. Wisdom's domain was Jerusalem, the Lord's own portion.

24:13-17. Self-portrait. To the stature of the cedar with the elegance of the cypress and the grace of the palm tree grew Wisdom. As lovely as the rose, as fair as the olive, and as lofty as the plane tree she grew. With an aromatic fragrance like myrrh and incense, Wisdom abundantly flowers into fruit.

24:19-22. Sweeter than honey. Wisdom invites her suitors to feast on her fruits and drink, assuring them that insatiable hunger and unquenchable thirst will be theirs. The memory of Wisdom is *sweeter than honey* (v. 20); and those who embrace her will remain free from sin.

24:23-29. The principal manifestation of Wisdom. This hymn culminates in the identification of Wisdom with the Law inherited through Moses. The bountifulness of this Law is compared to the great rivers of the known world at flood tide. As the first human did not fully comprehend Wisdom, neither will the last. So vast and profound are Wisdom's thoughts.

24:30-34. A word from the author. This section constitutes a prefatory note to what was originally the second volume of Ben Sira's work (24:1–50:29). Here he describes how his initial attempt at compiling a body of instruction proved to be so productive that a second volume was required. Once again Ben Sira will bring forth instruction in the manner of prophecy for the benefit of future generations.

Instruction and Proverbs, 25:1–42:14

25:1-2. Pleasures and aversions. The first of two numerical proverbs describes pleasure in what is atypical: agreement among siblings, friendship among neighbors, and harmony within marriage. The second detests inconsistency that has no basis for practice: paupers who boast, the rich who lie, and the elderly who commit adultery.

25:3-6. A bounty in old age. What is harvested in old age was planted in youth. Sound judgment, understanding, and wise counsel consist simply of wisdom acquired in youth brought to fruition.

25:7-11. Beatitudes. The numerical format is used to introduce ten beatitudes, nine of which are general in nature. The tenth however constitutes Ben Sira's strongest statement thus far on behalf of the fear of the Lord, which he declares surpasses everything else including wisdom.

25:13-15. How many wives? The only thing worse than having one wife is having two or more. The wrath and vengeance that multiple wives direct toward each other is more than any husband can endure.

25:16-26. Woman's iniquity. The wickedness of a woman defies description. Beware of her beauty and her wealth. The lot of a kept husband is resentment and disgrace.

The fervor of Ben Sira's denunciation may reach its peak in v. 24 where sin is traced initially to a woman; and because of her we all die. Though some hold that the reference here is to the evil wife, it is more likely Eve whom Ben Sira has in mind. Later Jewish thought held that sin and death entered the world through the first human (*adham*). This is also seen in the NT (Rom 5:12-19; 1 Cor 15:22; cf. 1 Tim 2:14).

The evil wife who refuses to submit to her husband's instructions should be divorced.

26:1-4. A belated beatitude. Following the lengthy recitation of the sins of the evil wife, a scant four verses is all Ben Sira needs to sum up the blessing of a good wife. Rich or poor, her husband's life will be lengthened and made peaceful. A good wife is granted to one who fears the Lord.

26:5-9. More iniquity. This numerical saying cites three causes of fear: slander (gossip) in the city, a gathering mob, and false accusation. Having offered this diversion, Ben Sira continues with a fourth fear: jealous and wicked wives. A public scene between two jealous wives of the same husband is followed by yet another litany including the imagery of chafing yokes, drunkenness, and the unmistakable appearance of the unchaste wife.

26:10-12. Like mother, like daughter. With this description of the headstrong daughter (Di Lella argues for "unruly wife"), Ben Sira makes a blanket indictment against the presumed promiscuity of headstrong women that is exceeded in venom only by the obscene and offensive imagery in which it is couched.

26:13-18. A brief respite. Perhaps in an effort to redress intemperate remarks just made about women, Ben Sira here reflects upon the good wife—her charm, silence, modesty, and beauty from her lovely face to her *shapely legs and steadfast feet* (v. 18).

26:19-27. A late addition. Regarded as a late addition, this material is found in late Greek and Syriac texts. It is presumed to have been translated from the Hebrew although no Hebrew text of this material has been discovered.

26:28. Ironies that cause grief. This numerical saying notes three human conditions that are truly lamentable: a warrior trapped in poverty, intelligent persons treated with contempt, and a person who forsakes righteousness for sin. The Lord will prepare the latter for the sword.

26:29–27:3. Ill-gotten gains. Desire for gain is irresistible. Those seeking wealth will overlook their own sinful behavior. The marketplace is inseparable from sin. Only steadfastness in the fear of the Lord can preserve the vendor.

27:4-7. The test of speech. Through your speech you shall be known. Conversation exposes the substance and character of a person as a sieve reveals debris, a kiln points up flaws in a pot, and fruit discloses the quality of a tree.

27:8-10. A matter of retribution. Those who practice justice and honesty shall attain them. Evil awaits those who pursue it.

27:11-15. The language of fools. The conversation of the godly is praiseworthy; but that of the fool is offensive. Coarse and abusive language frequently results in public spectacles, strife, and bloodshed.

27:16-21. Importance of confidence. Nothing destroys friendship more quickly or permanently than violation of confidence. Physical wounds will heal, and abuse can be reconciled; but no friend can forgive the betrayal of a secret.

27:22-27. The absence of trust. Those who ingratiate themselves to you only to discredit you in your absence are not to be trusted. Ben Sira admits that he hates such persons more than all others. Those who practice such treachery are inevitably the victims of their own schemes.

27:28–28:1. Vengeance belongs to the Lord. Those who contribute to the misfortune of others or who rejoice in such misfortune will experience the Lord's vengeance. No sin is overlooked.

28:2-7. The blessing of forgiveness. Forgiveness is as beautiful as it is necessary. If we cannot forgive others such as ourselves, how can we expect to be forgiven? Ben Sira applies the commandments of Lev 19:17-18 to enjoin his readers against harboring enmity and anger toward their neighbors.

28:8-12. The tragedy of strife. Avoid strife and lessen the likelihood of sin. Directly proportional to obstinacy is strife, to strength is anger, and to wealth is wrath. The mouth is an instrument that either promotes strife or quells it.

28:13-26. Scabbard the tongue. The tongue is a destructive weapon. It has destroyed cities, overthrown ruling houses, and scattered nations. Even virtuous women have been defamed. A slanderer (a third tongue that can come between spouses, friends and others) injures both the victim and those who believe the slander. Victims of the tongue are more numerous than those of the sword.

Blessed are those who have been spared from the tongue of the slanderer. Contrary to Ben Sira, the godly frequently suffer most from slander, for example, the virtuous women who have been driven from their homes. The ungodly may be more vulnerable to slander than the godly; but both suffer its pain.

Guard your mouth as carefully as you guard your property. Weigh your words with the same precision with which you weigh your gold and silver.

29:1-7. Borrowing and lending. Lending to a needy member of the community is an admirable deed that complies with the law (Deut 15:7-11). The borrower must in turn respond responsibly. The promises and terms of repayment must be honored. Those who borrow not intending to repay are not only guilty of robbery, but they cause potential lenders to refuse their aid out of fear of being defrauded.

29:8-13. The giving of alms is twice blessed. Respond quickly to those in need. The alms you give are never lost. The treasure you acquire from the Lord by giving will deliver you from every disaster and foe.

29:14-20. The dilemma of surety. Providing surety (a pledge to be liable for a debt) is as dangerous as it is commendable. In fact the risks far outweigh the rewards. After citing the pitfalls involved, Ben Sira advises (over against the repeated warnings in Proverbs) that we go surety for a neighbor, but only within our means.

29:21-28. What price dignity? Those who sponge off the largess of others pay a price for that privilege. A guest is constantly at the mercy of the host. The menial chores, the demeaning treatment, and the daily anxiety that a more *honored guest* (v. 27) might require your quarters are too great a price to pay for being tolerated at the home of an affluent host.

It is far better to curtail your life-style to the basic necessities that fall within your own means. The independence you gain contributes immeasurably to your sense of personal dignity. They are also rich who have few needs.

30:1-6. The many faces of love. Very strict discipline of sons is urged by Ben Sira. The successful father can fashion his son in his own image. The well-disciplined son will remain a source of pride—the bane of his father's enemies and a boon to his father's friends.

30:7-13. Spare the rod at your own peril. Failure to impose adequate discipline over a son will be a source of unending grief. Who among us has not indulged our children, played with them, laughed with them, and encouraged their individual growth? For Ben Sira these are unthinkable mistakes. The severity of his proposed tactics was not uncharacteristic of the ancient Near East.

30:14-25. Health is wealth. Health and well-being are our most precious possessions. Good foods that are so vital for nourishment must be eaten. Those whose loss of health is the result of divine punishment are denied even the pleasures of good food.

Insofar as possible, avoid stress. Focus upon those aspects of life that promote joy. Sorrow, jealousy, and anger only serve to shorten life. Happiness further enhances the benefits derived from a good meal.

In all extant Greek manuscripts, 30:25–33:13a is placed after 33:13b–36:16a. Old Latin has the correct order of these verses (Di Lella 1987, 56).

31:1-11. Ambiguity surrounding wealth. Ben Sira approaches the riddle of rich and poor with mixed feelings. He is aware that both are frequently responsible for their respective states. Yet he believes riches and poverty can be visited on us by the Lord. Although he personally prefers wealth and advocates the quest for it, he knows all too well the evil that can result.

The ideal for Ben Sira is the wealthy person who has not sinned in acquiring his wealth. For this person wealth is not an end in itself but rather a means toward a productive, charitable, and exemplary life that the community will celebrate.

31:12–32:13. Moderation in all things. What more revealing moment is there in a person's life than when he is seated before a delicious meal? Ben Sira offers careful instruction for table etiquette in proper company. His directions are as thoughtful as they are appropriate. A guest who embarrasses himself or his host will not be invited again.

Practical advice is offered concerning discomforts from overeating. Disturbances of sleep, nausea, and colic can all be avoided. The self-disciplined individual knows when the need for food has been satisfied.

Wine-drinking should not be considered a test of virility. When misused, wine can destroy both health and reputation. Yet Ben Sira readily declares that wine is the very life of human beings: What is life without wine? He wisely advises that one not reprove or reproach a neighbor while he is enjoying his wine since to do so will only be counterproductive (31:31).

If you are named master of the feast, remember that you can best play that role by being a servant to the guests.

The elderly are urged to speak but admonished to do so with care. They should not interrupt the music and entertainment. Wise words, like precious jewels, are enhanced by a proper setting (32:6).

Younger guests are enjoined to speak only when asked and then no more than twice. The importance of brevity in one's choice of words is comparable to the respect shown to one's superiors. All are advised that a timely departure is much to be preferred to either a prolonged stay or bombastic speech.

32:14–33:6. Confidence in the Law. Ben Sira is concerned here for survival in a world filled with uncertainties. The focus of his instruction is reflected in vv. 18-23 where he stresses the importance of a deliberative approach to decisions. Consider thoughtful suggestions; simplify any course of action you pursue; do not make the same mistake twice; do not be overconfident when travelling through unexplored terrain; always be alert to your surroundings; and be confident in your decisions.

In attempting to reach any decision, never lose sight of the importance of the Law. Observing the Law and fearing the Lord are the surest guides for successfully implementing the above directives. Ben Sira's assurance that no evil will befall one who fears the Lord may well say more about his confidence in the fear of the Lord than it says about the reality of the human situation.

33:7-15. For every thing, an opposite. Ben Sira reflects upon an early observation of ancient philosophy: for every single thing there is an opposite. The mystery in which this was earlier regarded is explained here as originating in the wisdom of God. It is the Lord who distinguishes between the favored and the unfavored, the exalted and the ordinary, the blessed and the cursed, good and evil, life and death, the sinner and the godly, male and female. Although Ben Sira does not specifically mention man and woman here, there can be little doubt that this rationale lay behind his negative view of women.

33:16-19. Ben Sira on Ben Sira. Our teacher reflects here upon his understanding of his own role in the study of wisdom. He is the last (the most recent) to come along as a picker and gleaner in the vineyard of the Lord. Verse 18 is almost verbatim with 24:34. He concludes by exhorting the congregational leaders: *pay heed* (v. 19)!

33:20-24. Control of financial destiny. Never allow another to gain control over your financial well-being. One who possesses such power can control your life. Let your heirs inherit when you die. Note the absence of any reference to daughters.

33:25-33. Living with slavery. The views expressed here reflect a social institution fully accepted in Ben Sira's time. The advice offered is entirely practical. The initial comparison with beasts of burden is later tempered by acknowledging the slave's personhood.

If your means limit you to only one slave, value your investment. Kindness will inspire loyalty whereas cruelty will cause your slave to flee resulting in financial loss. Deuteronomy 23:15-16 forbids returning an escaped slave to the master.

34:1-8. Dreams and visions. Ben Sira leaves no doubt as to his opinion of dreams and the like. All such phenomena are without substance and are deceiving. Mindful of his own tradition, he allows for a single exception in v. 6a, namely, those visions sent by God. Wisdom alone is more than sufficient for fulfilling the law.

34:9-13. Travel is a broadening experience. Travel itself is a learning experience. One sees and hears more than can be described. One also acquires certain skills that not only alleviate the minor discomforts and inconveniences of travel, but can actually save one's life in time of danger.

34:14-20. A favorite refrain. Ben Sira never tires of extolling the many blessings of the fear of the Lord. This was obviously one of his most comforting and reassuring convictions.

34:21-31. Unacceptable sacrifices. Ben Sira compiles a list of practices and conditions that render a sacrifice offensive to God. Offerings that are blemished, ill-gotten, or stolen are unacceptable as is any sacrifice offered by the ungodly. Wealth acquired at the expense of a neighbor or an employee is repugnant to the Lord. Sacrificing what has been stolen from the poor is doubly offensive.

Sincere repentance for one's sins is the most pleasing offering one can make to the Lord.

35:1-26. Efficacy of sacrifice and prayer. The Law requires offerings and sacrifices. Indeed, one is commanded to sacrifice regularly and generously. Offerings should be made with *a cheerful face* (v. 11) and a glad heart. Despite assurances that God remains impartial even toward the poor, Ben Sira proceeds to describe those whose prayers and circumstances will elicit an immediate and impassioned response. The passion and ire of God are readily provoked against multitudes and nations. Yet the Lord's own people will rejoice in his mercy. Quite clearly the level of passion to which Ben Sira builds here carries over directly into the prayer that follows (36:1-22).

36:1-22. Deliverance delayed. In the wake of the many assurances professed above, Ben Sira cannot escape the realization that Israel's present circumstances in no way bear out the substance of his promises. He is profoundly moved by this and offers this impassioned lament.

Ben Sira pleads for God to act directly and forcefully using signs and wonders to destroy Israel's enemies and return to the nation its original inheritance (possession of its land), remembering Jerusalem, God's dwelling place and fulfilling *prophecies spoken in your name* (v. 20). The depth of Ben Sira's faith in this prayer is matched only by the intensity of his frustration, living as he did under the yoke of Seleucid oppression and its Hellenistic influence.

36:23-31. Discerning tastes. As the discerning individual prefers certain foods and exercises certain judgments in selecting companions, so also does the discerning male in choosing a wife. Ben Sira readily acknowledges that some girls are preferable to others, although he does not extend this sense of discernment in selecting a mate to females (v. 26).

After acknowledging such attractive feminine qualities as beauty, humility, and personal support, Ben Sira is not reluctant to recommend marriage, noting that a man who has *no wife* is likely to *become a fugitive and a wanderer* (v. 30).

37:1-6. The risks of friendship. Although many will claim to be a friend, few will prove worthy. Ben Sira blames this upon the evil inclination whose existence he laments. One should not only remain loyal in time of crisis, but should also be willing to share one's good fortune with a friend.

37:7-15. Beware of counselors. Counselors, like all others, are primarily self-serving. Especially avoid those who are suspicious or *jealous of you* (v. 10). Ben Sira's list of those whose advice one would never seek is as humorous as it is profound. Since there is no guarantee that even the most promising candidate will suffice, you should rely upon your own judgment. Who is more concerned about your well-being than you? As in all matters, you should seek God's guidance.

37:16-31. Wisdom applied. The mind is the basis of all behavior: the evil committed by the fool, that results in death, and the good done by the wise, leading to life.

Ben Sira is aware that there are those who are widely regarded as wise, but whose lives do not reflect all the advantages that are attributed to the truly wise. There are degrees of cleverness that do not measure up to genuine wisdom. The person who is truly wise will be recognized as such and honored by the community. The fruit of his labors and good sense will endure, not only within his own limited life span, but throughout the life of Israel whose existence will continue forever. Thus a good reputation is assured forever.

A basic application of wisdom can begin with something as rudimentary as the foods we eat. Learn what is good for you and avoid what is not. Eat in moderation, for wisdom so applied can prolong your life.

38:1-15. The role of the physician. Ben Sira offers a spirited defense of physicians and their profession on the basis of human intelligence and medicines, both of which are gifts of the Lord. He recognizes the efficacy of prayer, repentance, and sacrifice for illnesses that are inflicted by God. Nevertheless, do not be without the services of a physician. The Lord created the physicians, and they depend upon the Lord in their diagnosis and treatment. Those who reject physicians also reject the Lord.

38:16-23. A practical approach to mourning. Mourning is an indispensable part of the death experience. One or two days should suffice, however; then grief should be put aside lest it bring about your own death. Ben Sira sounds a note of finality in asserting that beyond death there is nothing further to be done for the deceased. Death is a fate that awaits us all: mine today; yours tomorrow. Once the dead are at rest, there is no point in dwelling upon their death. Take comfort that their ordeal is over (v. 23).

38:24–39:11. The noblest profession. Ben Sira compares the profession of the scribe with the leading crafts and trades of his day. The wisdom of the scribe can only be acquired with time and energy that are not drained away by other activities resulting in physical exhaustion. Leisure is essential to scholarly endeavor.

The descriptions of the other crafts and trades are presented in sympathetic and appreciative manner. Cities cannot exist without the labor of these artisans. Yet in making policy, rendering judgments, or giving counsel in the public assembly, even master artisans have no role to play.

The scribe devotes his life to the study of the law, the wisdom of antiquity, prophecies, sayings of the famous, parables, and proverbs. His extensive preparation and devotion to learning are augmented by foreign travel, dealings with rulers, and service among the renowned.

Always mindful of his dependence upon the Lord for his wisdom, the scribe's reputation will carry far and wide and his praise will be unending.

39:12-35. In praise of creation. A growing tendency on the part of Ben Sira as he moves through this second part (24:1–42:14) is to fashion his thoughts within larger themes and with greater sensitivity to theological development. He is obviously dealing with issues that were current in his time that could not be readily ignored if the sufficiency of wisdom and the law were to remain above challenge.

Accordingly, the Deuteronomic doctrine of retribution, which held that all injustice in this world would be redressed before the deaths of its perpetrators, was undoubtedly under attack. Ben Sira affirms the goodness of creation and argues therefore that God's actions cannot be questioned. All that exists was created, appointed, and commanded by God with God's purpose in mind. There is no dimension of earthly existence where this is not the case.

Nevertheless, evil exists, and it constantly impacts upon human life. Unable to deny the presence of evil, Ben Sira has no choice but to include it within his overall scheme. He relegates evil to the vengeance of the destructive forces of nature, assuring his reader that this arrangement is quite sufficient to maintain the balance of retribution.

The ten *basic necessities of human life* (v. 26) were created for the godly. Since it cannot be denied that sinners also have their share of these goods, (and sometimes a disproportionate share at that) Ben Sira hastens to reassure his readers that even these goods will *turn into evils* (v. 27) in the hands of sinners.

Ben Sira concludes by declaring that he has long been convinced of all this and has now put it in writing. This emphasis is intended to attest to the validity of his thesis: all things prove good in their appointed time. Let us praise and *bless the name of the Lord* (v. 35).

40:1–41:13. The human plight. Human existence is burdened with a heavy lifelong yoke of labor, perplexity, fear, and anxiety. This affliction is visited upon every human being by God regardless of status in life. This burden is experienced through anger, envy, frustration, and unrest. Life is lived amid the fear of death. The struggles of day become the visions of night. All creatures are the victims of misfortune and death; and sinners, *seven times more* so.

Although Ben Sira is aware that neither the righteous nor the wicked are exempt from the ravages of suffering, he can only conclude that this fate was intended for the wicked. He blames the wicked for the flood (Gen 6:5-7, 11-13) without offering an explanation for why the righteous also perished. Are the numbers of the wicked so great that the righteous are to be seen as insignificant by comparison? His only effort at resolving this question is to declare that what derives from the earth remains with the earth, and what comes from above (the breath of life, from God) returns to God.

Perhaps aware of the unsatisfactory nature of his treatment of this issue, Ben Sira next offers reassurance that bribery, injustice, and unjust wealth will not last, but good faith, kindness, and almsgiving will endure forever (40:12-17).

The somber tone of this section is lifted slightly by a somewhat superficial list of ten unrelated proverbs, each of which purports to describe a more desirable human condition. All of this culminates in the fear of the Lord which is to be desired beyond *any glory* (40:27).

A life reduced to begging appalls Ben Sira. Even though he has acknowledged that wealth and poverty are assigned by God (11:14b), he cannot accept the indignity and loss of personal esteem that begging entails. *Better to die than to beg* (v. 28). Although the intelligent will protect themselves against this practice, the shameless have no scruples against it.

In a rather dispassionate appraisal of death, Ben Sira acknowledges that for those at peace in their prosperity and still vigorous in health, death is a bitter thought. For those in need and *failing in strength*, and for the aged who fear the world around them, death is readily welcomed. His advice to all is not to fear death. It is the decree of the Lord for all flesh. Whether death comes early or late, SHEOL (Hades) requires no explanations (41:1-4).

Ben Sira is vehement in his denunciation of those Jews who have adopted the lifestyle and values of the Greeks. Some Jews even renounced their faith in pursuit of Hellenistic culture. Such sinners leave a legacy of perpetual disgrace to their offspring. Their own calamity is assured; the memory of them is a curse. Their lot is destruction (41:5-10).

Although the human body and human life are of brief duration, a virtuous name will endure forever. Perhaps Ben Sira is saying that a life nobly lived can ultimately triumph over the worst of the human predicament.

41:14–42:8. The roles of shame. Ben Sira offers here a practical list of both acceptable and unacceptable actions that if carefully followed will demonstrate not only the caliber of one's training but insure broad approval. Both lists are as profound as they are practical. The list of acceptable actions is well grounded in the basics of doing business and managing financial affairs.

42:9-14. The father of a daughter. The worst fears a father can entertain about his daughter are succinctly summarized here. Over the lifetime of the daughter, from the father's house to the husband's house, no possibility of sin and disgrace is overlooked. None of this, however, reflects upon the daughter. It is the father who constantly risks becoming a *laughingstock* before his enemies and being put *to shame in public gatherings* (v. 11).

The concluding proverb (v. 14) is perhaps the most demeaning indictment of womanhood found in this book. As unfortunate as this is, it reflects the sentiment of the times.

See the introduction ("Composition") for some thoughts concerning the conclusion of this second part of the work.

Three Hymns of Praise, 42:15–50:24

Praise of the Works of the Lord, 42:15–43:33

This hymn of praise to the Lord of creation begins as a declaration of what its poet has seen and contains some of the most remarkable insights and imagery to be found in this work. Creation is replete with the glory of the Lord. This is seen in the sun whose heat and light proclaim the blessing of day, in the moon, that beacon in the night that denotes the change of seasons, and in the feast days of the lunar calendar. It is true for the glittering array of a starry night, for the brightly arched shaft of a RAINBOW. All of these are the handiwork of the Most High.

The forces of nature in their incomparable beauty carry out God's judgments by both rebuking and refreshing the earth. The grandeur of the Lord defies description.

Praise of Famous Men, Our Ancestors, 44:1–49:16

44:1-15. Prelude. The introduction to this hymn of praise is characterized by both tranquility and ambiguity. These great men had apportioned to them the glory of the Lord. Apart from a single reference to *valor* (v. 3b) the range of their activities included: ruling, intelligent counsel, prophetic oracles, knowledge of traditional lore, wise instruction, musical composition, writing in verse, being endowed with wealth, and peacefully domiciled. What a stark contrast this represents when compared with the precarious, if not violent, state of affairs that characterized so much of Israel's existence.

Ambiguity is reflected in the latter portion of the prelude (vv. 9-15) where it is acknowledged that over against those ancestors who left behind a name, there are indeed those whose memory has perished as if they had never been born. Having said this, it is quickly noted that these forgotten ones were also *godly men*. This gives rise to a sequence of ideas which builds upon the righteous deeds of those forgotten ones: their wealth, the inheritance of their children's children, the dedication of their descendants to the covenants, their continuing offspring, their irrepressible glory—all of

which leads up to the assertion that even the names of the forgotten will also live on as the people proclaim their wisdom and the congregation celebrates their praise.

44:16. Enoch. Although present in Greek and Hebrew manuscripts, this text is absent in Syriac and Hebrew fragments from Masada. Some regard this verse as a late insertion resulting from Enoch's reputation for having been taken up bodily into heaven by the Lord.

44:17-23a. Noah and the patriarchs. Assuming that Enoch was a late insertion, Ben Sira's list of heroes begins with NOAH, the principal figure following the FLOOD. In a somewhat nostalgic and uncritical fashion the list moves quickly to ABRAHAM, ISAAC, JACOB, and the twelve tribes.

While acknowledging Abraham's role as a father of nations and God's promise of a numerous offspring that would cover the earth, Ben Sira perhaps inadvertently observes that the law was already known to Abraham, thus predating Moses. The same assurance and blessing is in turn extended to Isaac, Jacob, and the twelve tribes.

44:23b–45:5. Moses. The appearance of MOSES leaves no doubt as to the favor with which Ben Sira regarded him. The description of Moses, however, is as superficial as it is idealistic. Moses is afforded the distinction of being the recipient of *the law of life and knowledge* (45:5) that he might impart God's decrees to Israel.

45:6-26. Aaron and Phinehas. Moses is greatly overshadowed by the description of AARON. The elaborate trappings with which Aaron's attire is described exceed even the description afforded Simon (50:1-24). With a slight variation in language Aaron and Simon are each described in their *glorious robe . . . clothed . . . in perfect splendor* (45:7c-8a, cf. 50:11).

The extent of the material devoted to Aaron is almost four times that devoted to Moses, indicative of the importance Ben Sira attributed to the priesthood. PHINEHAS, the grandson of Aaron, is accorded as much coverage in the hymn as is Moses. In his zeal to preserve the priesthood for the descendants of Aaron, Ben Sira draws an analogy with the succession of the Davidic line to the throne: only the descendants of Aaron shall ascend to the priesthood. This section on the priesthood concludes with a benediction (45:26) in which wisdom is sought for the priest so that he may judge with justice and that Israel's prosperity and glory may endure forever.

46:1-12. Joshua and the judges. In a passage reminiscent of the praise of Moses, JOSHUA son of Nun is celebrated for his military prowess in *the wars of the Lord* (v.3). Joshua and CALEB are lauded as the only two spies sent to the promised land who urged the people move in and occupy that land.

The judges are dealt with collectively and anonymously. Not one name is mentioned. The expression of praise registered here indicates that Ben Sira either knew little about them or considered their contributions of no real consequence.

46:13-20. Samuel. Although SAMUEL's initial role in the tradition may have been that of a judge, Ben Sira identifies him primarily as a prophet. Through the witch of Endor, Samuel's ghost prophesied the deaths of Saul and his sons at the hands of the Philistines (1 Sam 28:19).

47:1-11. David. Samuel's successor as prophet, NATHAN, serves to introduce the section dealing with DAVID, which appears to be closer to the Books of Chronicles than to the Books of Samuel. Scandals in David's personal and family life are ignored. This dimension is dismissed with the assurance that his sins were taken away (v. 11a).

47:12-25. Solomon. Ben Sira's treatment of SOLOMON more closely reflects the interpretation of the Books of Kings than does his treatment of David. Solomon began his reign doing what pleased the Lord and he prospered accordingly. Largely through his marriages to foreign wives Solomon stained his honor and corrupted his family line. His misdeeds prepared the scene for the division of the kingdom. Despite Solomon's folly the Lord's commitment to David saved the family line.

Ben Sira is specific in identifying the policy of Solomon's son REHOBOAM as the cause of the revolt. He is equally candid in describing JEROBOAM's role in Israel's sin of establishing a separate monarchy. It is quite likely that neither the name of Rehoboam nor that of Jeroboam actually appeared in Ben Sira's earliest draft. However, both names now appear in all extant texts (Di Lella 1987, 530–31).

48:1-16. Elijah and Elisha. Rehoboam's folly and Jeroboam's sin provide a transition for a brief comment concerning the increasing sinfulness within the Northern Kingdom of ISRAEL (47:23d-25), followed by accounts of the ministries of two northern prophets, ELIJAH and ELISHA. In each instance a catalogue of their respective wondrous deeds is concluded with the unusual circumstances surrounding their deaths. Despite these signs and wonders the people of Israel pursued their sinful ways until they were scattered throughout the earth (v. 15cd).

48:17-25. Hezekiah and Isaiah. In Judah the throne was still occupied by Davidic rulers, some of whom did what was right while others sinned. The first of two kings singled out for attention is HEZEKIAH. The major focus is on the Assyrian siege of Jerusalem. The Lord struck the Assyrian camp through his angel (Gk.) or with a plague (Heb.) and the siege quickly ended.

The flattering tribute offered to Hezekiah in v. 22 is for the most part taken from 2 Kgs 18:3. Ben Sira neglects to point out the foolish acts of Hezekiah recounted in 2 Kgs 18–20.

ISAIAH's role is described primarily in connection with Hezekiah whose life he is said to have prolonged by fifteen years. The reference to hidden things and revealing what would occur until the end of time clearly indicate that Ben Sira attributed the entire corpus of the book to Isaiah of Jerusalem.

49:1-7. Josiah. The second king of Judah mentioned by Ben Sira is JOSIAH. The treatment of Josiah is long on verbiage but short on substance. Only in one verse (v. 2) does Ben Sira make any reference at all to Josiah's cleansing of the Temple and his instigation of the Deuteronomic Reform. It is possible that the significance of Josiah's reform was simply lost on Ben Sira.

Of all the kings of JUDAH, Ben Sira identifies only three who were not great sinners: David, Hezekiah, and Josiah. Judah came to an end (v. 4) when its power and glory were given over to an unnamed adversary that burned Jerusalem and made its streets desolate. JEREMIAH is mentioned for having foretold Judah's destruction as well as for having been mistreated by Judean kings.

49:8-16. Other worthy figures. EZEKIEL is remembered only for the vision in which he attempted to capture the appearance of the likeness of the glory of the Lord (v. 8). Even within this one verse, the reference to the chariot of the cherubim is a figure of speech not found in the Book of Ezekiel but rather in 1 Chr 28:18 and other later traditions with which Ben Sira seems to have been more familiar.

In Ezek 14:14, 20, three worthies of antiquity are mentioned: NOAH, Dan'el and JOB. Noah appeared at the outset of this hymn (44:17-18). Job is afforded a single verse (v. 9) in which he is said to have held fast to righteousness. The third worthy, Dan'el, is of Canaanite tradition and not to be confused with the biblical

Book of Daniel, which had not been written in the time of Ben Sira.

Reference to the Twelve Prophets in v. 10 reproduces a line already used in praise of the judges: *May their bones send forth new life from where they lie* (46:12a). In light of the fact that Ben Sira seemed to know very little about the judges, it seems reasonable to draw a similar conclusion about his knowledge of the Twelve. His comment to the effect that the Twelve comforted the people of Jacob likely reflects rabbinic tradition that the Twelve were books of consolation.

ZERUBBABEL and Jeshua, son of Jozadak, rebuilt the temple and restored the altar which destined them for everlasting glory. The imagery of the signet ring that is applied to Zerubbabel is accumulative; beginning with Jer 22:24, it acquires messianic overtones in Hag 2:23.

NEHEMIAH is celebrated for having erected the walls and gates of Jerusalem and having secured the city.

Perhaps Ben Sira realized he had neglected a significant segment of primordial history. He suddenly reverts from what has been an orderly chronology from Noah to Nehemiah to a brief three-verse section dealing with five antediluvian figures plus JOSEPH. The entry concerning Enoch (v. 14) appears to be more authentic than the earlier entry in v. 16. Enoch's claim to fame consists of the statement in Gen 5:24, which the rabbis interpreted to mean that Enoch had avoided death and been taken directly into heaven. He was the first to have such a claim made on his behalf.

The parallel structure of vv. 14 and 15 is apparent as Joseph is introduced as being unlike anyone else ever born. Joseph is cited for having his bones [body] carried from EGYPT to CANAAN for burial at SHECHEM. There is reason to suspect however that Joseph's body to this day remains in Egypt in the Cairo Museum, (Osman 1988).

Shem (v. 16) is the first son of Noah and the progenitor of the Semites, the family of nations from which Israel is descended. With the murder of Abel and the virtual banishment of Cain, Seth became the one descendant of Adam through whom all subsequent lineage is traced. Enosh is the son of Seth next listed in the genealogy. Seth and Enosh are first mentioned in Gen 4:26 where it is said that at that time human beings first began to invoke the name of the LORD (YHWH). These two are then mentioned in Gen 5:3; 4, 6-11 following the priestly tradition's pronouncement that Adam was created in the likeness of God (Gen

5:1) and that Seth was created in the likeness and image of Adam (Gen 5:3).

At this point Ben Sira has little recourse other than to acknowledge Adam's primary role in this succession. Di Lella has noted that this is the first time Adam is idealized in Jewish literature (1987, 545).

Notable omissions. Ben Sira's list of ancestors is almost as remarkable for some of its omissions as it is for the names it included. Since David was one of Ben Sira's favorite figures, the omission of Saul is understandable. Saul is best remembered for the tragic qualities of his life and rule that cannot be considered exemplary for Ben Sira's generation.

Despite the lengthy description of the priesthood of Aaron and Phinehas, Ben Sira did not include either ABIATHAR or ZADOK, the priests of David. This seems unusual in light of the significance attributed to Zadok in Ezekiel (40:46; 43:19; 44:15; 48:11). In Ezra 7:1-5, Zadok is identified in the lineage of Phinehas and Aaron. Zadok is mentioned in a litany reminiscent of Ps 136, which is placed between 51:12 and 13 in one Hebrew text but not in the Greek or Syriac. Its authenticity is questionable.

The most glaring omission within this list of ancestors is that of EZRA. Does Ben Sira not credit Ezra with introducing the Torah in Jerusalem? What does Ben Sira's mentioning of Nehemiah while ignoring Ezra indicate about the relationship of these two figures or their traditions?

Given his low regard for women in general it is not surprising that Ben Sira includes no women in his list of ancestors.

Praise of Simon, Son of Johanan (Gk. *Onias*), 50:1-24

In what is virtually an appendix to his list of ancestors, Ben Sira offers a eulogy on behalf of the High Priest Simon II, son of Johanan. Simon had obviously made a profound impression upon Ben Sira. The latter had likely known Simon and had certainly observed him presiding over ceremonies celebrating either the Day of Atonement, *Yom Kippur* or the daily whole-offering. The pageantry of Temple rituals had a lasting effect upon Ben Sira that served to reinforce his conviction that only in the person of the high priest of Aaron vouchsafed through the covenant of Phinehas, could the traditions of Judaism properly function. It was Ben Sira's prayer that the perpetuity of this priestly office continue indefinitely through Simon's descendants.

Addenda, 50:25-29

50:25-26. A note of invective. By way of summing up his thoughts on various and sundry topics, Ben Sira informs his readers that there are certain peoples whom he detests. First are the Edomites or Idumeans (Seir) for their treacherous support of the Babylonians following the fall of Jerusalem in 587 B.C.E. (Ps 137:7-9; Ezek 25:12-14; 35; Obad).

Second are the PHILISTINES, a component of the Aegean Sea People, who destroyed Egyptian and Canaanite sites along the southwestern Canaanite coast until they were defeated at the Egyptian border by Ramses III in the mid-twelfth century B.C.E. They remained a dominant factor in the area for 150 years until defeated by David. Despite Ben Sira's dislike of them, the Philistines contributed a rich cultural, military, and maritime heritage to the area.

Third, and the most detestable of all, were the SA-MARITANS (Shechem) who were *not even a people* (50:25).

50:27-29. A postscript. The author identifies himself by name and in succinct fashion describes his task assuring those who seriously pursue his teachings that they shall be both wise and equal to anything they might encounter.

Three Appendixes, 51:1-30

A Psalm of Thanksgiving, 51:1-12

Chapter 51, which bears the Greek title "Prayer of Jesus son of Sirach," is comprised of three components. The first (51:1-12) appears to be the prayer to which the other two elements may have been added.

A Litany, 51:12i-xvi

The second part (following 51:12) consists of a litany of thanksgiving that is found in only one He-

brew text (Manuscript B) but is missing in the older Greek and Syriac texts. Modeled after the refrain of Ps 136, its opening verse echoes the opening words of Ps 136 and several other psalms (106:1; 107:1; 118:1). In light of certain expressions that appear nowhere else in this book, as well as the arrangement of this material, it is unlikely that this litany originated with Ben Sira.

An Acrostic Poem, 51:13-30

The third part of this chapter is an acrostic poem (each verse begins with a regular sequence of the letters of the Hebrew alphabet) that offers an auto-biographical account of the poet's search for wisdom.

The authenticity of the first and third parts of this chapter have also been challenged as has that of part two. This is based on the postscript found in 50:27-29 that seems to serve as a fitting conclusion to the book. Unlike part two, the other two components are found in all the major manuscripts (Hebrew, Greek, Syriac, Latin). The Greek and Latin versions contain the title identifying the chapter as a prayer of Jesus ben Sirach. The autobiographical poem in part three has also been found in a manuscript discovered at Qumran dating from the first century C.E. (11QPs^a). Thus there is a greater likelihood that parts one and three may have been from the hand of Ben Sira.

A finale following 51:30 exists only in Hebrew and with variations in Syriac. It is thought to have been added after Ben Sira's death.

Works Cited

Osman, Ahmed. 1988. *Stranger in the Valley of the Kings.*

von Rad, G. 1972. *Wisdom in Israel.*

Skehan, P. W., and A. A. Di Lella. 1987. *The Wisdom of Ben Sira.* AncB.

A. A. Di Lella. 1992. "The Wisdom of Ben Sira," AncBD.

Baruch and the Letter of Jeremiah

Kenneth M. Craig, Jr.

Introduction

The Book of Baruch and the Letter of Jeremiah exist in different locations in various manuscripts and versions. In the LXX they are separated by the Book of Lamentations. In Syriac manuscripts and in the Vulgate, the Letter appears as the sixth chapter of Baruch. Therefore, some English Bibles, such as the KJV, NEB, RSV, and NRSV enumerate the verses of the Letter as chap. 6 of the Book of Baruch. In this commentary, the Book of Baruch and the Letter of Jeremiah are discussed jointly, and in each section issues related to the Book are discussed before those of the Letter.

Although no Hebrew text survives, most experts agree that the first two major sections of the Book of Baruch, 1:15–3:8 (prose) and 3:9–4:4 (poetry), were originally written in Hebrew. The third section, 4:5–5:9 (also written in poetry), is less Hebraic in style and may have been originally composed in Greek. The entire book does survive in Greek, and various ancient versions are based upon it (Latin, Syriac, Coptic, Armenian, Ethiopic, and Arabic). It appears in most early copies of the LXX (but not in Codex Sinaiticus), and in most Greek manuscripts it appears between Jeremiah and Lamentations. No fragments of Baruch have been identified from the Qumran caves, although a Greek version of the Letter has been found there (Moore 1992, 701). The Book of Baruch was often quoted by the early church fathers, but the later church, both Protestant and Catholic, has virtually ignored it.

Based in part on Jer 10:1-15, the Letter of Jeremiah is an exhortation to the Jews in Babylon on the subject of idols. It is stylistically and thematically unrelated to the five chapters which form the Book of Baruch. Working from such texts as Jer 10:1-15 and Jer 21, the author of the Letter of Jeremiah writes what he alleges is another epistle of Jeremiah to the exiles in Babylon. Quite apart from the superscription in v. 1, however, no textual clues suggest that the deuterocanonical composition is from the hand of JEREMIAH. In fact, one finds no formal features that would suggest the composition is a letter.

Authorship

The Book of Baruch purports to have been written by *Baruch son of Neriah* (1:1) during the Babylonian captivity. According to biblical tradition, Baruch son of Neriah never reached Babylon (Mendels 1992, 618). The Book may have been written in the diaspora, but composition within Israel is also possible. Most scholars agree that it is a pseudonymous work written by multiple authors. In the words of Carey Moore, the ancient authors may have intended "to increase the book's authority by attributing it to the eminent and long dead scribe" (1992, 698). The evidence for multiple authorship has been well summarized by Dancy (1972a, 170–72).

The precise compositional relationship among the three major sections of Baruch (1:1–3:8, 3:9–4:4, and 4:5–5:9) remains unclear. Because of virtual unanimity among scholars that the first two sections were originally composed in Hebrew and the final section in Greek, it would follow that the final section was added to 1:1–3:8 and 3:9–4:4 sometime after the first two were translated into Greek.

The Letter of Jeremiah appears also to be a pseudonymous writing. In the preface to his commentary on Jeremiah, Jerome admits that the early church recognized it as such (Dancy 1972b, 197). Internal evidence also supports the claim that the author was writing under the name of Jeremiah. Language and images reflect biblical passages that were written after the time of Jeremiah (Deut 4:27-28; Isa 44:9-20; 46:5-7; Pss 115:3-8; 135:6-7, 15-17). In terms of its literary and theological content, the Letter lacks the Book of Jeremiah's literary quality and religious depth. The Letter exists in Greek (but not in Hebrew), and a small fragment of the Greek has been found in Qumran cave 7. Certain characteristics of language and style do, however, suggest that the so-called letter was first written in Hebrew (or Aramaic). For example, several incoherent expressions in the Greek may be explained as mistranslations of an earlier Hebrew text. Like so many books of the Bible, it is difficult to determine the precise place of composition. The author's familiarity with Babylonian religion may indicate that it originated in Mesopotamia.

Date

The Book of Baruch opens with a statement in vv. 1-4 that Baruch read his book in the hearing of Jeconiah, the deposed king of Judah (also called Jehoiachin in 2 Kgs 24:15), in Babylon in the fifth year after the fall of Jerusalem (the fall was in 587/6 B.C.E.; presumably the reading of Baruch, then, was 582/1 B.C.E.). The book makes no reference to historical events after the sixth century B.C.E., and the ideas expressed throughout were a major concern among Jews for centuries. The internal evidence does not point decisively to a specific time of composition. For these reasons, the book's date remains uncertain.

It has been dated variously between the sixth century B.C.E. and 135 C.E., and the possible dates have been well discussed by Mendels (1992, 619–20). It is unlikely that the book was written as early as the sixth century B.C.E., however, because 1:15–3:8 is modelled on a prayer from Dan 9, which dates from ca. 165 B.C.E. The book does depend upon late biblical works such as Deutero-Isaiah, Daniel, Job, and Sirach, and for this reason many experts assign a date sometime after 250 B.C.E. If the book were written as late as the fall of Jerusalem in 70 C.E. or afterward, Nebuchadnezzar and his son Belshazzar may represent the Roman emperor Vespasian and his son Titus who captured Jerusalem.

The opening chapter of the Letter of Jeremiah alludes to the captivity of the Jews as lasting for *seven generations* (v. 3). Second Maccabees 2:1-3 alludes to the Letter, and may indicate a date of the second or first century B.C.E. Such a date appears to be confirmed by the Letter itself, if by "generation" (v. 3) the author has in mind the characteristic number of forty years. But an earlier date of the fourth century B.C.E. is also possible because the Letter's message would have then been especially relevant throughout the diaspora as well as in Israel itself.

Literary Form and Primary Themes

The Book of Baruch stands out among the deutero-canonical books as the only one based on a model of OT prophecy. The religious fervor of the classical prophets is evident at times, and the Book's sections are linked by the twin themes of EXILE and return. The Book does bear some literary affinity with the prophetic Book of Jeremiah (see the discussion in Nickelsburg 1984, 142–44). H. Thackeray has argued that the Book of Baruch was part of the prescribed liturgy of the synagogue for the Jewish New Year, and J. A. Goldstein has suggested that it reflects the situation of the Jews of Judah under Seleucid rule in 163 B.C.E. (Moore 1992, 702).

If the so-called Letter of Jeremiah does not follow an epistolary form, as mentioned above, what is its form? The author is concerned that a meaningless form of faith has been substituted for the religion of the prophets. He writes an impassioned plea, an exhortation or sermon based on a verse from the canonical Jeremiah. This verse, Jer 11:10, describes a situation wherein Jews participate in idol worship. Taking his cue from this text, the author of the Letter of Jeremiah expounds upon the folly of worshiping gods of wood, silver, and gold. Contrary to the arguments of the heathens, idols are not what the gentiles suppose or claim. The Letter was thus written to discourage Jews from worshiping false gods in a foreign land.

In addition to the introduction (vv. 1-7), the Letter contains ten sections of unequal length: vv. 8-16, 17-23, 24-29, 30-40a, 40b-44, 45-52, 53-56, 57-65, 66-69, and 70-73. A slightly varying refrain concludes each of these sections and recalls vv. 4-5 from the introduction. Verse 23 is typical of the refrain that varies slightly from stanza to stanza: *From this you will know that they are not gods; so do not fear them.*

The so-called Letter is characterized by a satiric tone, and its form is based in part on Jer 29:1-23, a letter written to the Jews who had been exiled to Babylon in 597 B.C.E. The lack of a logical progression in thought or argument may suggest a haphazard composition, but the Letter is more accurately described as "a thread of images, not of arguments" (Dancy 1972, 199). The sermon against idolatry is intended for the Jews of the diaspora, and the references, especially to the worship of Bel and Tammuz, suggest a Babylonian context. One finds no references to Egyptian and Greek customs.

For Further Study

In the *Mercer Dictionary of the Bible*: APOCRYPHAL LITERATURE; BARUCH; IDOLATRY; JEREMIAH; JEREMIAH, BOOK OF; JEREMIAH, LETTER OF; LAMENTATIONS, BOOK OF; WISDOM IN THE OT; WISDOM LITERATURE.

In other sources: R. H. Charles, "Baruch," *EncBri*, 11th ed., 5:453–54; J. C. Dancy, *The Shorter Books of the Apocrypha*, CBC; A. Fitzgerald, "Baruch," JBC;

J. A. Goldstein, "The Apocryphal Book of I Baruch," *Jubilee Volume of the American Academy for Jewish Research Proceedings* 46–47 (1979–1980): 179–99; B. Metzger, *An Introduction to the Apocrypha*; C. A. Moore, *Daniel, Esther, and Jeremiah: The Additions*, AncB; G. W. E. Nickelsburg, 1984. "Baruch," in *Jewish Writings of the Second Temple Period*, CRINT; H. B. Swete, "Baruch" and "Epistle of Jeremiah," in *The O.T. in Greek according to the Septuagint 3*; E. Tov, *The Book of Baruch also Called I Baruch*.

Commentary

An Outline

Baruch
I. Narrative Introduction, 1:1-14
II. Prayer of Confession, 1:15–3:8
III. Praise of Wisdom, 3:9–4:4
IV. Psalm of Hope, 4:5–5:9

Narrative Introduction, 1:1-14

The book opens with statements of purpose and circumstances of composition, and the speaker attributes the words to Baruch. Baruch reads the book to Jeconiah (or JEHOIACHIN), son of JEHOIAKIM, king of JUDAH and to a general assembly of the diaspora. Four major points are addressed to Jews of Jerusalem. First, money sent by diaspora Jews is to be used for purchasing sacrifices for the altar in Jerusalem. Second, the Jews of Jerusalem are asked to pray for King Nebuchadnezzar and his son Belshazzar that *their days on earth may be like the days of heaven* (v. 11). Third, Jerusalemites should pray for the Jews of the diaspora. Fourth, the Letter should be used by the Jews of Jerusalem as a liturgy in the Temple during feasts and festivals.

The introduction leaves the reader with a number of questions. The reference to composition in *the fifth year* (v. 2) is awkward. To what does this fifth year refer? The location of *the river Sud* in v. 4 is unknown. Verse 11 identifies *Belshazzar* (rather than NABONIDUS) as the son of Nebuchadnezzar. This introduction also shows evidence of being translated from a nonextant Hebrew text.

Prayer of Confession, 1:15–3:8

The exiles address their fellow Jews in Jerusalem and acknowledge reasons for present difficulties. The prayer resembles prayers found in Ezra 9:6-15; Neh 1:5-11; 9:6-37; Dan 9:4-19, and consists of a corporate confession of sin and a petition that God will withdraw God's wrath and allow the exiles to return home. The theme follows the logic of Deut 28–32, and the language is reminiscent of Deuteronomy and Jeremiah.

1:15–2:30. Confession of past sins. The Jews of Israel confess. They speak in a collective voice, and in this review of history the nation's disobedience is highlighted. They declare that the people of Judah and of Jerusalem have turned against the TORAH, beginning at the time of EXODUS and lasting *until today* (1:19). Because of their transgressions they were punished as MOSES had predicted (Deut 28–32). They continued to turn away from God when they worshiped other gods, and then they were finally dispersed among the nations.

In 2:1-30a one finds once again a confession of past sins against the Torah. A summary of Jeremiah's words (Jer 25:8-11 and Jer 27:11-12) appears as three expressions: God asks the people to serve the Babylonian king (v. 21); the Israelites ignore God's words (v. 24); and the people are then punished by exile and the destruction of the Temple (vv. 25-26). The passage also contains a reminder of God's words spoken through the prophets.

A prayer for divine mercy begins at 2:11 and is reminiscent of the traditional laments and supplications from books such as Deuteronomy, Jeremiah, and Daniel.

2:31-35. God will return. Although Israel is a stubborn people, the prayer reflects the view that the people will repent. As a result, God will bring them to their land once again and renew the covenant with them. The encouraging words of return to the promised land are accompanied by the promise: *and I will never again remove my people Israel from the land that I have given them* (v. 35b).

3:1-8. Prayer for salvation. The section ends with a prayer for mercy coupled with a confession of past sins. The prayer is one that God had anticipated (vv. 7-8; cf. 2:31-33), and the petitioner concludes with an explicit request for return.

Praise of Wisdom, 3:9–4:4

The author shifts from prose to poetry in 3:9. In this passage, which celebrates Wisdom, the author draws from Prov 2:4, Job 28:12-38 and Sir 24 and asks about Wisdom:

> Learn where there is Wisdom,
>   where there is strength,
>   where there is understanding,
> so that you may at the same time discern
>   where there is length of days, and life,
>   where there is light for the eyes, and peace.
> Who has found her place? (3:14-15a).

The discovery of Wisdom is the major idea of the section, and is based on Job 28:12-28.

The first major sections (1:1-14 and 1:15–3:8) contain a mosaic of biblical passages, but the poem praising Wisdom is based on a pattern of logical argument. The deuterocanonical book Wisdom of Solomon also figures prominently in this praise of Wisdom poem (Wis 9:4a; 9:18b; 9:10). The opening strophe admonishes hearers to discover that Wisdom is the source of strength and life (3:14). The following three strophes (3:15-19, 20-23, 24-28) list those who have *not* found Wisdom. In the next strophe, 3:29-37, the poet mentions that God alone found the way to Wisdom and shared it with Israel. The final strophe (4:1-4) identifies Wisdom with Torah.

Wisdom is not to be found among the rulers of nations, the rich, the young, the people in Canaan or in Teman. God also did not choose the GIANTS to be the bearers of Wisdom; they perished because they lacked Wisdom (3:22, 26-28). God possesses Wisdom and God alone shares it with the people (3:32-37). Thus true Wisdom is hidden from the world and it cannot be searched out. God, who knows all things and commands the light and stars, encompasses Wisdom and has given Wisdom to Israel in the form of an everlasting Torah. The Israelites experienced calamities because they forsook God, the fountain of Wisdom. The section ends on a felicitous note: *Happy are we, O Israel, for we know what is pleasing to God* (4:4).

Five themes are expressed: EXILE is the result of the people's abandonment of Wisdom; no human being can discover Wisdom; Wisdom is as old as creation itself; God bestowed the gift of Wisdom on Israel; and Wisdom is identified with Torah (Harrelson 1992, 158).

This section differs from the previous material in Baruch in several respects. The author writes in poetry; virtually ignores the prophetic view, as reflected, for example, in the Book of Jeremiah; focuses on Torah as Wisdom; prefers the word "God" rather than "Lord"; and depends on the language of Job.

Psalm of Hope, 4:5–5:9

In a psalm of hope, the author resolves the dilemma with which the book began. Exile will end; sorrow will turn to joy; prayer will be answered. The psalm recalls past action and provides an optimistic picture for the future. This section contains themes and language of Deuteronomy, Deutero-Isaiah (i.e., Isa 40–55), and Lamentations.

4:5-29. Psalm to Jerusalem's children. Like the opening to the second part of Isaiah (chap. 40), the author introduces a song of hope to Jerusalem's children. Verses 5, 21, and 27 reiterate the refrain, *Take courage*—the equivalent of "Be of good cheer." Jerusalem is here portrayed as a grieving widow bereft of her children. She utters a lament over them (vv. 9-29). This lament shares affinities with the themes of Lamentations and ends with words of hope and comfort:

> For the one who brought these calamities upon you
>   will bring you everlasting joy with your salvation
>   (v. 29).

Mother Zion here recounts her grief to her neighbors. She then addresses her children in stanzas that begin with the words *take courage* (vv. 21-26, 27-29). The verses contrast past calamity with future salvation. While it is true that the people are in diaspora and Zion is deserted, these conditions will change. The people will return to Jerusalem, and Jerusalem will regain its glory.

4:30–5:9. Psalm to Mother Jerusalem. In the light of the promise of salvation, the author addresses four strophes to Jerusalem herself (4:30-35, 36-37; 5:1-4, 5-9). Each begins with an imperative for action in the unfolding drama of salvation. The tone of the prayer shifts to an expression of renewed hope. Jerusalem is encouraged to rejoice because her children will be led back to her from captivity. The city will be reestablished forever, and enemies will be humbled in the dust. The final lines reflect a tone of optimism.

An Outline

Introduction, 1-7

The narrative introduction is modeled on Jer 29:1, but this deuterocanonical letter gives the impression of having been written just before the exiles were taken to Babylon (v. 1). The reference to *gods made of silver and gold and wood, which people carry on their shoulders* (v. 4), may refer to the Babylonian New Year procession.

Ten Stanzas, 8-73

By means of repetition IDOLATRY is condemned in a series of ten stanzas. The claim that idols are not gods is drawn from multiple observations about those things that idols cannot do. In a parallel theme the author condemns certain cultic practices such as prostitution (v. 43), scandalous actions of the priests (vv. 10, 33), and so forth.

First stanza, 8-16

In the first stanza one finds a description of idols bearing royal attire. The reference to *prostitutes* (v. 11) is most likely to temple prostitutes. Cultic prostitution was common from Babylon to Greece. Deuteronomy 23:17 expressly forbids Israelite women from becoming temple prostitutes. Adopting a sarcastic tone, the writer points out that while the idols are dressed as kings in purple they do not have the power to protect their faces from dust or their clothes from moths (vv. 13-15).

Second stanza, 17-23

The author continues the theme of the idols' helplessness and adds to it the notion of uselessness. Although these idols are covered with gold or silver, their hearts are made of wood and thus *are eaten away when crawling creatures from the earth devour them* (v. 20). The idols have faces but are unable to see the smoke that comes from the temple sacrifices and blackens their faces (v. 21). The reference to *cats* in v. 22 is unique in biblical literature.

Third stanza, 24-29

The gold mentioned in v. 24 may actually be a gold substitute because it tarnishes. Without breath (v. 25) and unable to move (v. 27), these idols are lifeless. If one *falls to the ground* someone must set it upright because *it cannot move itself*. Those who bring gifts to the idols are placing them *before the dead* (v. 27). The author indicts the priests who sell the sacrifices and *use the money themselves* (v. 28).

Fourth stanza, 30-40a

Idols are unable to repay good or evil. In gloomy rituals resembling those of a funeral, the priests sit, tear their clothes, and shave their heads and beards. Such actions are forbidden according to Lev 21:10-11. These acts of mourning are reminiscent of those mentioned in Ezek 8:14 for the god Tammuz. These wooden gods overlaid with gold and silver are not unlike the *stones from the mountain* (v. 39). They take no pity on widows nor do good to orphans (v. 38).

Fifth stanza, 40b-44

The Chaldeans reveal that their gods are useless. They continually petition them to do what they have no power to bring about. They pray to Bel *as though Bel were able to understand* (v. 40).

Sixth stanza, 45-52

In the sixth stanza the author continues the theme of the uselessness of idols by pointing out that *they are made by carpenters and goldsmiths* (v. 45). They are things manufactured. They appear only as artisans would have them appear. *They cannot save themselves from war or calamity* (v. 49). During times of disaster, priests must hide them to avert their destruction (cf. Rachel's concealment of the teraphim in Gen 31:34-35).

Seventh stanza, 53-56

Rain was a sign of God's renewed favor for the people (1 Kgs 8:35-36). The prophet Jeremiah had posed a rhetorical question, "Can any idols of the nations bring rain?" (14:22). Perhaps inspired by that verse, the author of the Letter highlights the uselessness of idols: *they cannot set up a king over a country or give rain to people* (v. 53).

Eighth stanza, 57-65

False gods cannot defend *themselves from thieves or robbers* (v. 57). In contrast to fire and heavenly phenomena (vv. 60-63), idols lack such spectacular appearance and power. They cannot *decide a case* (v. 64) as the true God can (Exod 18:19; Ps 43:1).

Ninth stanza, 66-69

The image of helpless idols continues in the ninth stanza. Idols *can neither curse nor bless kings* (v. 66). They also *cannot show signs in the heavens* (v. 67), as the superstitious Babylonians held they could.

Tenth stanza, 70-73

In the final stanza idols are compared with the *scarecrow*, a *thorn bush*, and *a corpse*. The concluding verse reminds the reader of a major theme of the Letter: *better, therefore, is someone upright who has no idols; such a person will be far above reproach* (v. 73).

Works Cited

John C. Dancy. 1972a. "The Book of Baruch." In *The Shorter Books of the Apocrypha*. CBC. 1972b. "A Letter of Jeremiah." Ibid.

Walter Harrelson. 1992. "Wisdom Hidden and Revealed According to Baruch (Baruch 3.9–4.4)." In *Priests, Prophets, and Scribes: Essays on the Formation and Heritage of Second Temple Judaism in Honour of Joseph Blenkinsopp*. JSOTSup 149.

Doron Mendels. 1992. "Baruch, Book of." AncBD.

C. A. Moore. 1992. "Jeremiah, Additions to." AncBD.

George W. E. Nickelsburg. 1984. "Baruch." In *Jewish Writings of the Second Temple Period*. CRINT.

Additions to Daniel
(The Prayer of Azariah and the Song of the Three Jews, Susanna, and Bel and the Dragon)
Richard A. Spencer

Introduction

DANIEL was the subject of many legends during the last centuries B.C.E., as, for example, fragments from the DEAD SEA caves attest. The Greek text of the Book of Daniel contains three additions that were widely accepted in the early church, but were removed by Protestants during the Reformation, although complete editions of the Authorized Version included them.

The setting of the stories is the Babylonian EXILE, but their actual backdrop is probably the persecution of the Jews by Antiochus IV Epiphanes (175–163 B.C.E.). They teach that God cares for and will rescue the pious.

The original language of these materials may have been Hebrew or Aramaic, although Susanna may have been written in Greek. They are preserved in two Greek traditions, the LXX version (ca. 100 B.C.E.), and the more literal translation by Theodotion (second century C.E.). The NRSV follows the text of Theodotion.

The Prayer of Azariah and the Song of the Three Jews

This addition, placed between Dan 3:23 and 3:24, expands the story of Shadrach, Meshach, and Abednego who were thrown into the fiery furnace by King Nebuchadnezzar. It stresses the piety of the men and the power of God. The Prayer of Azariah (vv. 3-22) and the Song of the Three Jews (vv. 29-68) are linked to the Book of Daniel by two narrative sections (vv. 1-2, 23-28), which were probably written in Aramaic since their context in the Book of Daniel (2:4b–7:28) is in Aramaic.

The prayer and the song, probably written in Hebrew, do not address the situation in which the martyrs find themselves, except for the concluding verses (66-68). Azariah's prayer is not a plea for deliverance from the furnace but a national psalm of lament, similar to Pss 44, 74, 79, and 80. The song is made up of two parts, a doxology (vv. 29-34) and a hymn in which the youths invoke all creation to bless the Lord (vv. 35-68).

Susanna

In some Greek copies of Daniel Susanna comes before chap. 1, but in other Greek manuscripts and in the Latin Vulgate, it follows Dan 12 (as chap. 13). It may have been placed first because in v. 45 Daniel is referred to as a young lad and because the addition ends with the words "and from that day onward Daniel had a great reputation among the people" (v. 64), which serves as a good introduction to Daniel.

This addition tells of a young Jewish woman and two elders who attempt to seduce her. Because she refuses their advances, they have her condemned to death on a charge of adultery. Her prayer to God is answered by Daniel's cross-examination of the elders, whose contradictory testimonies lead to their own deaths. The story is unique in that the rescue is from evil Jewish leaders, not from pagans. This leads some scholars to think it may have been written as a Pharisaic polemic against the SADDUCEES, who for a while controlled the law courts and allowed abuses of testimony that the PHARISEES later tried to correct (ca. 95–80 B.C.E.).

Bel and the Dragon

This addition, composed of two separate episodes, is designated in the Greek text of Daniel and in the Vulgate as chap. 14 (13 if Susanna is set before Dan 1). These tales pit Daniel against CYRUS, king of the Persians, to whom Daniel is a most illustrious companion. They juxtapose pagan idolatry and the worship of Daniel's God.

In the first story Daniel exposes the deceptions of the prophets of Bel and causes the pagan temple and priests to be destroyed. In the second, Daniel, compelled by Cyrus to worship a giant serpent (Greek *drakōn*), challenges the king to let him try to kill this "immortal" god. Daniel succeeds and exposes the serpent's unworthiness. The Babylonians revolt, compelling Cyrus to persecute Daniel. God provides for his survival by miraculously bringing HABAKKUK from JERUSALEM with food. When Cyrus finds Daniel alive after seven days he praises God and executes the persecutors.

For Further Study

In the *Mercer Dictionary of the Bible*: APOCRYPHAL LITERATURE; AZARIAH, PRAYER OF; BEL AND THE DRAGON; CYRUS; DANIEL; DANIEL, BOOK OF; EXILE; IDOLATRY; JUDAISM; NEBUCHADREZZAR; SUSANNA. In other sources: R. H. Charles, ed., *APOT*; A. A. Di Lella, "Daniel," IDBSupp; S. B. Frost, "Daniel," IDB; L. F. Hartman and A. A. Di Lella, "Daniel" *NJBC*; S. B. Hoenig, "Bel and the Dragon," IDB; "Song of the Three Young Men," IDB, and "Susanna," IDB B. M. Metzger, *An Introduction to the Apocrypha*; C. A. Moore, *Daniel, Esther, and Jeremiah: the Additions*, AncB; W. S. Towner, "Daniel and Additions to Daniel," *The Books of the Bible* 1:333–47.

Commentary

An Outline

Prayer of Azariah and Song of the Three Jews
I. The Prayer of Azariah, 1-22
A. Narrative Introduction, 1-2
B. Azariah's Prayer, 3-22
II. The Song of the Three Jews, 23-68
A. Narrative Introduction, 23-28
B. Doxology of the Ruling God, 29-34
C. Song of Praise, 35-68

The Prayer of Azariah, 1-22

Narrative Introduction, 1-2

Daniel 3:23 says "Shadrach, Meshach, and Abednego fell bound into the fiery furnace" (RSV), but in 3:25 Nebuchadnezzar professes to see "four men" walking about in the furnace, one of whom looks like a god. *They* (v. 1) refers to the youths, called here by their Hebrew names (Hananiah, Mishael, Azariah) rather than their Babylonian names (see Dan 1:7). These verses link the prayer Azariah is about to utter with the narrative context by showing the youths alive and offering praise to God. *Azariah* (Abednego), whose name means "Yahweh has helped," voices the prayer.

Azariah's Prayer, 3-22

This "blessing" does not fit the context very well, for it does not refer to Azariah's situation. He does not pray for deliverance or mention the fire or the king. Rather, he confesses the sins of his people (odd, because it was not Azariah's sin but his faithfulness that got him into the furnace), confesses God's rightful judgment in his treatment of the Jews, and utters a plea for mercy and deliverance of his people.

Antiochus IV Epiphanes tried by the fiercest means to eradicate JUDAISM. Under this *unjust king* (v. 9) some Jews turned away from their faith, adopted Greek ways, and became *a shame and a reproach* (v. 10; see 1 Macc 1:11-64). Azariah pleads for God's help for his people and recognizes that their security exists in God's constant *covenant* (vv. 11-13).

That *a contrite heart and a humble spirit* (v. 16) might replace sacrifices and offerings was an insight of the Jewish tradition later adopted by PAUL. Genuine prayer seeks not the benefit of the person praying (although that is surely part of the petition here, vv. 20-21), but the glory of God (v. 22). This prayer encourages the readers to be faithful as were these youths, so that God will save them in their crisis.

The Song of the Three Jews, 23-68

Narrative Introduction, 23-28

The king's servants who threw the three young men into the furnace and who were killed by the heat (Dan 3:23) here stoke up the fire—evidence of a rather awkward insertion. Heating up the furnace dramatizes Nebuchadnezzar's attempt to crush the faith of the young men, the miraculous sustaining work of God, and the king's praise of God (Dan 3:29–4:3). To speak of *the angel of the Lord* (v. 26) is a reverent way of saying that God was with them. He not only saved the youths; he also relieved them by creating a moist breeze (v. 27).

Doxology of the Ruling God, 29-34

Their unison song is more elaborate than Azariah's prayer. It has two parts: a doxology (29-34) addressed to God and a song of praise (35-68) addressed to God's creations. After each pronouncement that God is blessed comes the repeated refrain that God is to be praised and exalted forever (vv. 29-34).

Song of Praise, 35-68

This song or prayer of praise gives thanks for God, for his presence in his Temple, and for his kingdom. Its repeated refrain is worded much more uniformly than the refrain in the preceding doxology. The youths say *sing praise to him and highly exalt him forever* more than thirty times. This form of praise imitates the model of Ps 136 which repeats the words *for his steadfast love endures forever* twenty-six times. The content of the song is very similar to Ps 148, a hymn that calls upon all creation to praise God.

The focus of the prayer starts with the widest expanse and narrows to the three youths themselves.

They call upon all the works of the Lord (v. 35), the various components of creation (vv. 36-51), the earth itself (v. 52), the things and creatures of the earth (vv. 53-59), the people of the earth (v. 60), God's own people Israel (v. 61), that people designated in different categories (vv. 62-65), and finally themselves (v. 66). Their song climaxes with an appeal to *all who worship the Lord* to praise him (v. 68).

Powers of the Lord (v. 39) may mean Israelite armies, angelic hosts, or celestial bodies. *Spirits and souls of the righteous* (v. 64) refers not to the dead but the living, since the context is an appeal to the living (Bennett 1913, 636). The *holy and humble in heart* (v. 65) contrast with the Jewish sinners of Azariah's prayer who were *a shame and a reproach* (v. 10).

The two parts of this addition have quite different tones. Azariah's prayer speaks of apostasy and cruel punishments. The prayer of the three youths is exuberant, confident, and victorious (v. 66). This difference may be accounted for if the former emerged during the rule of Antiochus IV Epiphanes and the latter after his death when life improved for the Jews (Metzger 1957, 104).

An Outline

> **Susanna**
>
> I. Introduction, 1-4
> II. Two Lecherous Judges, 5-14
> III. The Assault on Susanna's Virtue, 15-27
> IV. The "Trial" of Susanna, 28-43
> V. The Conviction of the Judges, 44-62
> VI. Conclusion, 63-64

Introduction, 1-4

Susanna is extolled as a Jewish woman of virtue and courage. Yet her story is told from the male point of view: her husband is introduced first and she is said to *go into her husband's garden to walk* (v. 7); the last word of praise for Susanna identifies her as her father's daughter and her husband's wife (v. 63). The symbolism of the name Susanna, "Lily," gives the theme of innocence under assault. Identifying her as being *a very beautiful woman* (v. 2) probably rationalizes, from a male point of view, the advances of the elders. As *one who feared the Lord* Susanna upheld Jewish traditions, particularly regarding home and

family. Although Joakim was an exile he became *very rich* (v. 4; see Jer 29:5; 2 Esdr 3:1-2).

Two Lecherous Judges, 5-14

Ancient Jews believed that the two evil elders in this story were the lying prophets whom JEREMIAH mentioned (Jer 29:21-23), probably an incorrect assessment since there are many dissimilarities. The writer records a prophecy about two judges that cannot be found anywhere else. The irony of this episode is that judges were supposed to honor God and serve the people (cf. Jesus' parable about an unfit judge, Luke 18:1-8).

7-12. The elders both desire Susanna. Each man is guilty of desire unchecked by conscience. Susanna's innocence contrasts with their deliberate disregard for *Heaven* (i.e., God). *Overwhelmed with passion for her* means they were sick with love for her. Lust had overcome them. The Greek says plainly that their desire was to have sex with her (v. 11). Whatever shame they felt is mentioned not to elicit sympathy for them but to indicate that they knew they were in the wrong.

13-14. The collusion of the wicked judges. The meeting of the judges on their way to seduce Susanna has features similar to Roman comedies. Their lies—neither really intended to go home for lunch—catch up with their wretched behavior. Having begun independently, they join forces against Susanna.

The Assault on Susanna's Virtue, 15-27

15-21. The judges catch Susanna unawares. The calculating behavior of the respected leaders contrasts with the respectable behavior of Susanna. They *ran to her* to force her into compliance. Their approach is coarse, cruel, and selfish—tacky and insensitive. She was to be their sex object or to pay with her life. Cloaked by their privileged positions they try to force her into adultery (v. 21). They had the legal ability and the credibility of the people to condemn her if she refused.

22-27. Susanna's response and its results. Susanna knows that she was *completely trapped* (lit., "restrained all about me"). If she were convicted of adultery, death by stoning would result (Lev 20:10, Deut 22:22; see also Ezek 16:38-40). She fears God more than the men and refuses the elders, forcing them to carry out their plot. At the end of the scene Susanna stands virtuous but suspected by the entire community, with the elders in control.

The "Trial" of Susanna, 28-43

28-33. Tried in her own home. On the next day Susanna is put on trial and the judges attempt to have her put to death. The sickness of lust has changed to the madness of vengeance. Susanna's friends and family are with her, although little is said about their support. In fact, nothing is said about Joakim's attitude about the charges or his support for his chaste wife. In v. 31 Susanna's beauty and refinement contrast with the judges' disgraceful manner. Some manuscripts say she was not only *unveiled* but stripped to the waist or even stripped entirely—both customs were practiced in ancient JUDAISM (Ezek 16:37-39; Hos 2:3, 10; Talmud Sotah 1.5). The judges want to view the woman's privacy and, by disgracing her at the outset of her "hearing," turn the crowd against her as though she were a disgraceful person.

34-41. The lies of the judges. The judges now serve as witnesses. The Law of Moses prescribed that witnesses lay hands upon the head of the accused in a case that leads to stoning (Lev 24:14). Touching and testimony would be followed by the ritual of stoning as prescribed in Deut 17:5-7. Execution had to be justified by the evidence of two witnesses.

Susanna *looked up toward Heaven* (v. 35), whereas the judges had *turned their eyes from looking to Heav-en* (v. 9), showing how wicked the trial and these witnesses were. Verse 41b indicates the unquestioned authority of the office the evil judges held. They thought they could escape because of the fear the people had for their divine office.

42-43. Susanna calls upon the Lord. Bereft of all human rescue before the tribunal of "holy justice," Susanna calls upon God. Her cry, not for delivery but a complaint of injustice at the hands of liars, assumes that God is omniscient and not swayed by liars.

The Conviction of the Judges, 44-62

In the ritual for stoning, as the victim was led to execution anyone could protest the sentence by coming forth and giving the reasons (*Sanh* 6.1.2.; see Kay 1913, 650). God arouses *the holy spirit* of DANIEL to speak up in behalf of Susanna. Youth is contrasted with age, for Daniel confronts the people and the elders. His protest is based not on factual evidence or improper procedure but on moral grounds: *I want no part in shedding this woman's blood* (v. 46).

At the outset of his speech where one usually seeks to gain the goodwill of the audience, Daniel asks, *Are you such fools . . . ?* (v. 48). By *fools*, he may mean those who turn away from or ignore God (see Ps 94:8), as the evil judges had done. Moreover, the situation is life-threatening. This may make Daniel's verbal assault understandable (see Moore 1977, 109).

The characters are not the final concern of the author: Susanna has a rather low profile by comparison with her anonymous accusers and Daniel is not introduced until v. 45. The central concern is seen in the words *without examination* (v. 48): "justice" based on falsehood is evil.

Daniel knows that the men have lied, even though he was not a witness. God must have given him this knowledge by inspiration (v. 45). Technically, this appears weak, for Daniel prejudges the men without examination.

The request of the other elders is probably sarcastic (*Come, sit among us and inform us,* v. 50). Daniel is sometimes deferred to by non-Jews because of his divine, holy spirit (see Dan 2:46-49; 4:9). Here his own elders give place to him. Daniel seizes his opportunity and calls for the witnesses to be separated and examined individually.

52-55. Cross-examination of the first witness. According to the standards of jurisprudence and rhetorical practice, Daniel treats the first witness unfairly. Without evidence he criticizes the judge for a career of evil pronouncements. As a story that teaches the value of investigation and cross-examination, it makes its point. At the center of the contradiction is a play on Greek words (vv. 54-55): since the lying witness said the crime took place under a *mastic tree* (Gk. *schinos*) God's sentence is for the angel of the Lord to *cut* him (Gk. *schisei*) in two.

56-59. Cross-examination of the second witness. Daniel berates the second witness as an *offspring of Canaan*, one who has surrendered to pagan ways. The contrast between the *daughters of Israel* who have been perverted by pagan people and the *daughter of Judah* is problematic, for in v. 48 Daniel referred kindly to Susanna as a *daughter of Israel*. Here it is not complimentary.

The cross-examination actually begins in v. 58. The second witness contradicts the first, saying that the adultery took place under the *evergreen oak* (Gk. *prinos*). The judgment on the liar plays on the words: the angel of the Lord will *split* (Gk. *prisai*) the witness in two. These wordplays lead some scholars to hold that Susanna was written originally in Greek.

The cross-examinations could be much simpler, but the expansions reflect the moral outrage of the writer and his audience. The root problem in this "trial" of Susanna and its outcome is not just inadequate procedure but evil (which is usually associated with pagan ways) and the absence of fear of God among the Jews. Daniel is the divinely appointed corrector of this evil. The story encourages the Jews to remain steadfast and to be like Susanna and Daniel.

60-62. Community response. The people approve of Daniel's wise actions. The Law was not annulled because of wicked judges, for they received precisely what it required of false witnesses (Deut 19:16-21)—the same pitiless sentence of death they sought for Susanna.

Conclusion, 63-64

The final two verses report the doxologies offered to God by the parents and husband of Susanna—and *all her relatives*—because of her courage and purity. Daniel, too, is acknowledged as having *a great reputation among the people*.

An Outline

> **Bel and the Dragon**
>
> I. Introduction, 1-2
> II. Daniel Destroys Bel, the Idol, 3-22
> III. Daniel Kills the Dragon, 23-27
> IV. Daniel's Trial in the Lions' Den, 28-42

Introduction, 1-2

This story is set in the reign of the Persian king CYRUS (550–530 B.C.E.) whom the Jews thought of as the Lord's "anointed" or Messiah, because he allowed them to return to JUDAH in 538 B.C.E. (Isa 45:1). DANIEL is the king's personal *companion*, perhaps a court counsel. Because of their relationship, the king *asks* Daniel about his not worshiping Bel (v. 4) rather than *commanding him*, as a subject, to worship the idol.

Daniel Destroys Bel, the Idol, 3-22

Bel, a short form of BAAL, or Bel-Marduk, the principal Babylonian god, was worshiped by the people and required massive daily provisions of food and drink. Their gods made an important difference between Cyrus and Daniel: the king *went every day to* worship it [Bel]. But Daniel worshiped his own God (v. 4).

A dialogue between Cyrus and Daniel eventuates in a life-and-death contest. The dialogue begins with a confrontational question by the king (v. 6). He is convinced by the daily consumption of foods and drink that Bel is alive. Daniel's response insults the king's god and his character: within and without, the idol is only man-made materials (v. 7).

Pagan belief in idols was a laughing matter to the Jews, and Daniel's laughter speaks for them, but the laughter stirs the king's anger (v. 8). Daniel laughs twice at the worship of Bel (vv. 7, 19) and the king is angered twice, once at the blasphemous challenge to the worship of Bel that Daniel gives, and once at the deception of the priests (vv. 8, 21). Cyrus is the political power figure, but Daniel is more in control, spiritually, than the great king.

8-14a. The king's angry challenge. The king wants proof and warns his priests that if they do not confess that someone besides Bel has been eating the enormous amounts of food, he will kill them (if they make such a confession he probably will kill them anyway). If they prove that Bel eats, then Daniel has blasphemed and must die. Daniel's composure and confidence in God are expressed in his ready compliance with the terms of the challenge (v. 9b).

The priests, planning to remove the food secretly as they always do, try to influence the king by letting him set out the food and seal the door while they are outside. Making it appear that they have laid no trap (v. 11), they turn the challenge back upon the king (v. 12). The confidence they pretend to have in Bel is actually trust in their own deceptions (v. 13).

14b-22. Daniel's brilliant exposure of the priests. When the priests finish arranging their exhibits, Daniel takes action laying a trap for the priests (v. 14b). The next morning when the temple is opened and the foods are gone Cyrus praises Bel for his integrity (v. 18). Daniel laughs at the king's faith and restrains him from entering the temple until Cyrus can see the many footprints on the dusty floor. The king, now more angered than before and set on vengeance, forces the truth from the priests and has them and their families killed. Daniel's victory is dramatized by the surrender of the image of Bel to him (Cyrus could have simply had it torn down) and by Daniel's destruction of the temple.

Daniel Kills the Dragon, 23-27

The *dragon* (Gk. *drakōn*) was probably a huge live serpent the Babylonians worshiped as a god. A second confrontation after vv. 1-22 seems almost incredible. Both stories set IDOLATRY over against the God of Daniel and both use food as a test (Bel seems to eat but cannot, the serpent is killed by eating). Daniel is commanded to worship the serpent (v. 24) but he confesses God as the living God (i.e., the one who is active and powerful) and he proposes to kill the dragon. The king is as compliant to Daniel's proposal (*I give you permission*, v. 26) as Daniel's response was to Cyrus' challenge to the priests (*Let it be done as you have said*, v. 9). Cyrus believes the serpent is immortal and cannot be killed. Daniel makes a toxic potion into cakes, which rip open the serpent as he digests them. Daniel exults over the corpse and exposes the god's unworthiness.

Daniel's Trial in the Lions' Den, 28-42

The Babylonians revolt over Daniel's victories and subject him to persecution. The people turn against Cyrus and complain that he *has become a Jew* (v. 28). Historically, this is most improbable; literarily, though, it is like other events in the Book of Daniel in which Nebuchadnezzar sides with Daniel and his God. The revolt polarizes the king and his people and perpetuates the theme of idolatry versus faithfulness.

Cyrus, who now twice has found that idolatry is wrong, must surrender Daniel to the mob (v. 30). Daniel is thrown to the lions once again (vv. 31-42; see Dan 6:16-24), this time for six days instead of one night.

33-39. God uses Habakkuk. God preserves Daniel miraculously by bringing HABAKKUK from JERUSALEM with food. The prophet protests that he is not up to the challenge (v. 35), which means that God, not the prophet, is the deliverer. In a manner reminiscent of EZEKIEL's experience (Ezek 8:3ff.), Habakkuk is taken by his hair to Babylonia. God does not rescue Daniel out of the pit but provides for him within the pit. The teaching of this addition is summarized in v. 38: in times of trial, when surrender to idolatry is tempting, God remembers and does not forsake those who love him.

40-42. Cyrus releases Daniel. Cyrus discovers Daniel alive and well and praises God more greatly than he did his own god Bel (v. 18). The best he could say of Bel was that he had no deceits in him; now he claims there is no other besides Daniel's God. The instant punishment of Daniel's persecutors seals the teaching of faith superior to idolatry.

Works Cited

Bennett, W. H. 1913. "Prayer of Azariah and Song of the Three Children," APOT.

Davies, Witton. 1913. "Bel and the Dragon," APOT.

Kay, D. M. 1913. "Susanna," APOT.

Hartman, Louis F. and Alexander A. Di Lella. 1990. "Daniel." NJBC.

Metzger, Bruce. 1957. *Introduction to the Apocrypha.*

Moore, Carey A. 1977. *Daniel, Esther, and Jeremiah: the Additions.* AncB.

First Maccabees

Richard A. Spencer

Introduction

First Maccabees is a history of the Jews under Seleucid rule (175–134 B.C.E.). Along with 2 Maccabees it is the best available source for the Maccabean era. The two books, written by different authors, offer different details on the same era (2 Maccabees covers 175–160 B.C.E.), and have different points of view. Their greatest difference is the enthusiastic praise of the Maccabees in 1 Maccabees and the more critical attitude toward them in 2 Maccabees.

This is a history of the Maccabean heroes—Mattathias and his family—who are portrayed as the salvation of JUDAISM in a critical age. Since the fate of Judea revolved around those men, this history is arranged according to their successive leadership. The writer depicts the revolutionaries as savior figures, praising each for his unique leadership or courage: *Judas* in 3:3-9; 9:10, 29; *Eleazar* in 6:43-47; *Jonathan* in 9:29-30; *Simon* in 13:4-6; 14:4-15; John Hyrcanus in 16:6. In addition, he praises the entire family (2:1ff.; 5:63). They are idealized for their piety, reverence, and their successes, which the writer believes were due to their zeal for the law.

The straightforward historical narration is complemented by a testament of Mattathias and a number of poetic passages (1:24b-28; 1:36-40; 2:7-14; 3:3-9, 45; 14:4-15). It also contains biblical elements such as laments, OT quotations, prayers like those of the psalmists, deliberate allusions to the OT (2:26), the practice of *cherem* (see chap. 5), an editor's conceit like that of the kingly chronicles (9:22; 16:23-24), and even the use of terminology for Judas that makes him look like a MOSES-figure (5:63). These features depict the Maccabean struggle as a continuation of the righteous zeal of their forebears.

The writer includes foreign treaties with the MACCABEES and official documents. Letters and speeches by high governmental and royal figures play a significant role here. The informed use the writer makes of these materials might suggest that he was present for many of the events narrated.

The work is important for biblical study because it is a primary historical document for the Second Temple period. It documents the emergence of heroic types that endured for centuries to come, types by which other messianic figures would be judged. It discloses the hopes and values of the Jews that continued into the first century of the common era. The high regard that the Maccabees commanded can be seen in the continued practice of naming Jewish boys after them: Matthew, Judas, John(athan), Sim(e)on. First Maccabees gives us a first-hand glimpse of the origins of the major parties of Judaism in Jesus' day—the PHARISEES, SADDUCEES, and the ESSENES. Finally, it shows us the source of the courageous spirit of Jewish nationalism that lasted until the end of Palestinian Judaism in 135 C.E.

Date and Authorship

The writer is unknown, but his sympathies and opinions are clear. He opposes the Hellenists and supports the Maccabees. He has a hatred for both the gentiles who oppressed the Jews and for apostate Jews. Because he refers the reader to chronicles of the deeds of John Hyrcanus, which were probably written after his reign (134–104 B.C.E.; see 16:23-24), and because he praises the Romans in chap. 8, he must have written after 104 but before 63 B.C.E. when the Romans conquered the Jews and ended Hasmonean (Maccabean) rule. Approximately 100 B.C.E. is a fair estimate. Originally 1 Maccabees was written in Hebrew or Aramaic and later translated into Greek. No Hebrew or Aramaic copies or fragments have survived.

Theological Perspective

This work teaches that God punishes his people *en masse* for the sins of part of the people and that he used a non-Jew (Antiochus IV) as his instrument of punishment. It also teaches that by zealous attention to the law and by attempts to purify Israel, his people can turn away his anger. The Maccabees were the saviors of Judaism because they accomplished just that. The writer's view is retrospective. He looks back to a former time of greater righteousness and holds that such a time has been revived by his heroes. At the same time he accepts the new situation in which religion and politics have merged.

For Further Study

In the *Mercer Dictionary of the Bible*: APOCRYPHAL LITERATURE; CIRCUMCISION; FEASTS AND FESTIVALS; HELLENISTIC WORLD; JUDAISM; MACCABEES; MACCABEES, FIRST; MACCABEES, SECOND; ROMAN EMPIRE.

In other sources: H. W. Attridge, "Historiography," *Jewish Writings of the Second Temple Period*, ed. M. E. Stone, 157–84; John R. Bartlett, *The First and Second Books of the Maccabees*; W. H. Brownlee, "Maccabees, Books of," IDB; R. Doran, "I and II Maccabees," *The Books of the Bible* 2:93–114; J. A. Goldstein, *I Maccabees*, AncB; N. J. McEleney, "1–2 Maccabees," NJBC; W. O. E. Oesterley, "The First Book of Maccabees," APOT.

Commentary

An Outline

I. Hellenization, A Crisis for Judaism, 1:1-64
  A. Alexander and His Successors, 1:1-10
  B. Some Jews Accept Greek Ways, 1:11-15
  C. Antiochus Brings Horror to the Jews, 1:16-40
  D. Religious Persecution of the Jews Begins, 1:41-64
II. Mattathias Starts the Maccabean Revolt, 2:1-70
  A. The Family of Mattathias, 2:1-14
  B. The Precipitating Event, 2:15-28
  C. Slaughter of the Pious
    and Jewish Response, 2:29-41
  D. The Hasideans Join Mattathias, 2:42-48
  E. Mattathias's Testament, 2:49-70
III. Judas Maccabeus Delivers the Jews, 3:1–9:22
  A. Judas a Praiseworthy Successor, 3:1-26
  B. Judas's Most Notable Deeds, 3:27–4:61
  C. More Battles for the Maccabees, 5:1-68
  D. Antiochus IV Dies, 6:1-17
  E. Attack on the Citadel; Battle of Beth-zur, 6:18-63
  F. A New King and His New High Priest, 7:1-25
  G. Judas Defeats Nicanor, 7:26-50
  H. Treaty with the Romans, 8:1-32
  I. Judas Dies in Battle, 9:1-22
IV. Jonathan Extends Jewish Successes, 9:23–12:53
  A. The Continued Fight with Bacchides, 9:23-73
  B. Jonathan Joins Alexander Balas, 10:1-66
  C. Jonathan and Simon Defeat Apollonius, 10:67-89
  D. Ptolemy the Aggressor;
    Demetrius the Winner, 11:1-19
  E. Concessions Gained from Demetrius II, 11:20-37
  F. Changing International Relations, 11:38-74
  G. Alliances with Romans
    and Spartans, 12:1-23
  H. Jonathan's and Simon's Successes, 12:24-38

I. Jonathan Betrayed and Captured, 12:39-53
V. Simon Secures Jewish Independence, 13:1–16:24
  A. Simon Succeeds Jonathan, 13:1-30
  B. Simon's Accomplishments, 13:31–14:49
  C. Antiochus VII Wages War on Trypho, 15:1-14
  D. Alliance with Rome, Continued, 15:15-24
  E. The Treachery of Antiochus VII, 15:25-36
  F. War with Antiochus VII Begins, 15:37-41
VI. John Hyrcanus Continues the Dynasty, 16:1-24

Hellenization,
A Crisis for Judaism, 1:1-64

Alexander and His Successors, 1:1-10

In a one-chapter preamble the writer summarizes how JUDAISM's greatest crisis came about—Greek rule in Judea. Verses 1-10 give his précis of 158 years of history and reveal his tone and perspective. Although ALEXANDER the Great was responsible for bringing Greek ways to Judea, the writer treats him with respect, perhaps because he deposed kings (a characteristic of the Romans whom he praises in chap. 8). Alexander's conquests began among the *Kittim*, a people who occupied the coastlands of Greece and Crete. After much success, his *heart was lifted up*, that is, he allowed himself to be worshiped as a god, a trait abhorred by the Jews (see Dan 11:12; Ezek 28:2, 5).

This evil was enlarged when on his deathbed Alexander divided his kingdom among the Diadochoi, the generals who succeeded him. These successors (the Ptolemies and especially the Seleucids) put Judaism to a severe test. The writer grows angry when he begins to speak of these dynasties and the kings they created. He exaggerates, for not *all* but only five of the Greek leaders who succeeded Alexander *put on crowns*. Their rule was the cause of *many evils* (v. 9b). The worst of the royal lot was Antiochus IV (175–164), who assumed the title *Epiphanes*, meaning "the manifest god," but whom his enemies called *Epimanes*, meaning "the insane." He was the *sinful root* (v. 10) of the Jews' problems. He had spent twelve years in Rome, taken there as a hostage under terms of the Romans when they defeated his father at Magnesia (190 B.C.E.).

Some Jews Accept Greek Ways, 1:11-15

The crisis at hand was from without (Seleucid oppression) and from within (the Hellenists, Jews who adopted pagan ways). The writer calls the apostates "renegades" and "lawless" (Gk. *paranomoi* 1:11, 34; 10:61; 11:21; *anomoi* 2:44; 3:5, 6; 7:5; 9:23, 58; 10:61; 11:25; 14:14) and "scoundrels" (*loimoi* 10:61; 15:3, 21). They opposed the Maccabeans and hated their nation (11:21). Their greatest evil was that they departed from the Law of Moses. Further details of their apostasy, which include the buying of the high priesthood, are found in 2 Macc 4:7-22. These Hellenists were influential, for many followed them (see 1:52). The writer calls their association with pagan ways a *covenant*, to indicate that they departed from the heart of the law.

The motive of the renegades was self-interest, to prevent further *disaster*. Since 538 B.C.E. when the Jews returned from EXILE, they did not accept the ways of or marry gentiles. The actions of the Hellenists spelled the end of this rule of pious orthodoxy. Their leader was Jason, the brother of the high priest Onias, according to 2 Macc 4. By building a gymnasium, where young men trained naked, and by the Jews' undergoing a surgical removal of the *marks of circumcision*, which distinguished them from the Greeks, the Hellenists turned the holy city into a Greek city and rejected the covenant of Abraham. The writer's tone in v. 15b shows his contempt for the Hellenists.

Antiochus Brings Horror to the Jews, 1:16-40

1:16-19. Antiochus conquers Egypt. Motivated by the despicable desire *to become king*, Antiochus invaded Egypt with a huge force. Failing to capture Alexandria, he returned north and punished Judea, perhaps because of his incomplete success in Egypt.

1:20-24a. Antiochus robs the Temple. In 169 B.C.E., he stripped the Temple of its valuables, probably to compensate for the tribute that the high priest Menelaus owed him, and to pay his troops, since he was not officially at war with Judea (Bartlett 1973, 24). The writer declares that Antiochus acted *arrogantly*. He mentions arrogance again in v. 24, cites arrogance as Mattathias's main complaint on his deathbed (2:49), and refers to the Hellenists as *the arrogant* (2:47). In this way he links the Hellenists and the beastly king. The *hidden treasures* may have been 1800 talents (see 2 Macc 5:21).

1:24b-28. Poems of lament. The writer's dirge on the times laments matters that have not been told in the narrative—bloodshed, the threat of war, the loss of joy that shake the young bride and bridegroom. He uses commonplaces instead of specific events for his lament. He enlarges the complaint to personify the land, which *trembled*. He seems to have at his disposal an array of resources, including Hebrew poetry (see above, Introduction).

1:29-35. Further plundering of Jerusalem. Two years later Antiochus sent to Judea a chief tribute collector (Apollonius, according to 2 Macc 5:24) to harass the people. A characteristic of the Syrians that the writer abhors is duplicity, such as Apollonius exhibited (in 7:10 the writer will refer again to the enemy's *peaceable but treacherous words*). JERUSALEM was burned, Jews were killed, and women and children were taken captive. The Seleucids welded their grip by building a *citadel* or high place overlooking the Temple and the city. They stationed sympathetic Hellenists, "renegades," there to oversee their fellow Jews.

1:36-40. A poem on the sanctuary. This poem is a lament for the despoiled sanctuary reminiscent of the psalms of lament. It is filled with pathetic touches that contrast innocence with guilt: the sanctuary and innocent people of Jerusalem, her offspring and children, her feasts, honor, SABBATH, glory, and exaltation are contrasted with the citadel's "ambush," the evil adversary, the shedding of blood, defilement, estrangement, forsaking, desolation, mourning, reproach, contempt, and dishonor. In sum, the lament says that everything beautiful has been ruined.

Religious Persecution of the Jews Begins, 1:41-64

1:41-50. Antiochus consolidates his realm. To forge his kingdom's diverse peoples and religions into one dynasty and to prevent dissension, Antiochus imposed

Hellenism everywhere. His power is portrayed by the fact that he completed his goal primarily through letters. The Jews were a problem to him, though. He demanded that they cease their religious practices. To make them *forget the law* he imposed the death penalty for violations of his decree (v. 50). In his mercilessness he withdrew concessions to the Jews that his own father had granted.

1:51-53. Summary of affairs. To test their loyalty Antiochus forced his subjects to sacrifice swine to Zeus. Many people complied (perhaps out of fear, but also because some Jews approved of the new ways). The writer distinguishes these apostates from *Israel*, the true covenant people, who had to flee and hide.

1:54-61. The desolating sacrilege. Antiochus struck at the heart of JUDAISM when on 15 Kislev (December) 167 B.C.E. he had an altar to Zeus erected on the altar of burnt offering in the Temple, an act that came to be referred to for centuries as the *desolating sacrilege* or abomination of desolation. Copies of the Law were burned or shredded, possession of books of the Law or obedience to the Law were made capital offenses (so the Jews were prohibited from observing SABBATH or circumcising their boys). *Month after month* means that the overseers made monthly inspections and tests of loyalty throughout the countryside. The cruelties of vv. 60-61 show Antiochus's heinous fanaticism.

1:62-64. Conclusion. The writer summarizes that even though many apostatized, others kept the law at the greatest cost to themselves. Nevertheless, God punished Israel. The writer believes that God used the king to punish them for their sin. This did not absolve Antiochus for his deeds. His arrogance led to his own downfall.

Mattathias Starts the Maccabean Revolt, 2:1-70

The writer now turns from his preamble of misery, sin, and punishment to the purpose of his work—extolling the heroic Maccabees and celebrating their leadership in resurgent faithfulness to the law that turned away God's anger from Israel (3:8).

The Family of Mattathias, 2:1-14

2:1-6. The Hasmonean family. Mattathias, the elder priest, had moved to *Modein* (about seventeen mi. northwest of Jerusalem) perhaps when the true people

of God had to flee and hide (see 1:53). His family name was Hasmon, so he and his successors are sometimes called the Hasmoneans. The title *Maccabeus*, "the hammerer," seems to have been given first to Judas because of his swift guerrilla attacks on the Syrians. The entire family later came to be known as the Maccabees.

2:7-13. Mattathias's lament. Mattathias, a man of deep piety, lamented for the fate of the people and the holy city. His lament is directly focused on the events previously narrated, unlike the lament of 1:24b-28. He bemoaned the desecration of the Temple and the despair of the people. He wept for the city as for a woman seized as war booty and dishonored, whose children have been killed, who is stripped of adornment and made a slave.

2:14. The family's grief. The lament of Mattathias is shared by the family as they engage in customary acts of mourning and grief.

The Precipitating Event, 2:15-28

2:15-22. Mattathias put to the test. The Syrian officer appealed to Mattathias to comply with the king's decree. He used flattery, an appeal to self-interest, and finally bribery. He offered him the privilege of being a *Friend of the king*, that is, one of the king's associates who were classed according to the measure of their support. Mattathias loudly announced his refusal to commit apostasy and his commitment to the covenant and the law.

2:23-26. Mattathias's holy outrage. In a scene that the author reminds us is just like one played out long ago (PHINEHAS, see Num 25:6-15), Mattathias killed an apostate Jew, to cleanse Israel of its evil. His murder of the man and the king's officer were from *righteous anger* and *zeal for the law*.

2:27-28. Mattathias's revolution. His forming a revolutionary corps is interpreted from a religious point of view—his followers are called to be *zealous for the law*. Their flight solidified their new forces and showed the certainty of coming Syrian recrimination.

Slaughter of the Pious and Jewish Response, 2:29-41

Many people fled to the hills to escape Antiochus's response to this affront. They fled in mass with their families and livestock (which indicates that they left in fear, not to go train for war). One thousand of the fugitives were slaughtered on a SABBATH (vv. 32-38) because they refused to fight and defend themselves on the holy day. The response of Mattathias and his followers to this was to propose a new principle—to put life above religion.

The Hasideans Join Mattathias, 2:42-48

The "pious" or "holy" men, *Hasideans*, had religious, not political or civil concerns. They came to see, however, that unless they fought they would become extinct; so they joined the revolutionaries. Later, they would separate from the Hasmoneans (7:12ff.) because they wanted religious freedom only, but the Hasmoneans held that without political freedom, religious freedom could not be guaranteed. *Mighty warriors* describes their dedication to the fight, not their skill in warfare. Carrying on Mattathias's righteous vengeance by killing Hellenists and aggressively reasserting the practices of the law, they were the salvation of JUDAISM (v. 48). The Jews were now fighting a civil war as well as an international one. The Hasideans are generally considered to be the forebears of the ESSENES and the PHARISEES—both of whom were utterly devoted to the law and neither of which was politically inclined.

Mattathias's Testament, 2:49-70

An ancient "testament" was a deathbed exhortation by a venerated sage to his sons or followers. In it he might encourage his successors to avoid his own vices, emulate his virtues, follow examples of great heroes of the past, and accept wise counsel. *Arrogance* (the characteristic of Antiochus IV and the defining quality of the apostates) came to Mattathias's mind first. It was the attitude opposite to piety and devotion to the law. At least four times Mattathias encouraged his sons to uphold the law (vv. 50, 64, 67, 68). With a litany of praise for past heroes who faced trials and dangers and who were blessed because of their devotion to God, Mattathias encouraged his sons to be fearless and to die protecting the covenant. He appointed Judas to be their leader (v. 66). Judas's being *a mighty warrior from his youth* (v. 66) is the opinion of the writer and hardly a historical statement from Mattathias, whose death came only a year after the desolating sacrilege (166 B.C.E.). A family of priests would not be trained from youth as mighty warriors.

Judas Maccabeus
Delivers the Jews, 3:1–9:22

Judas a Praiseworthy Successor, 3:1-26

3:1-2. Introduction of Judas Maccabeus. The writer now narrates the successes of the sons of Mattathias, beginning with the hero who secured for the family its nickname and who is remembered for regaining and restoring the Temple (celebrated in the feast called Hanukkah). The transition of power to Judas stands in stark contrast to Alexander's transfer of power on his deathbed and the rival dynasties that it caused. Perhaps the writer wants us to compare gentile arrogance with Jewish devotion to God's purpose.

3:3-9. Hymn of celebration of Judas. In a poem of praise showing that Judas heeded his father's advice and became a successful hero, Judas is lauded with the similes of a giant, a lion, and a lion's cub. He is praised for punishing the Hellenists, making *Jacob glad*, that is, honoring the ancestral faith, and for turning God's wrath away from Israel. The language of v. 9 makes Judas appear to be a savior. As time passed the Maccabees were depicted increasingly as the saviors of the Jews, creating a legacy that lasted for centuries. Later deliverers, including Jesus, would be measured against the Maccabees.

3:10-12. Judas defeats the Samaritans. *Apollonius*, governor of Samaria and Judas's first opponent in war, was defeated summarily. The brief narration defines the character of Judas for the reader—one expects that he will continue to show himself forceful and successful. Taking Apollonius' *sword* was a way of showing that Judas usurped the power of his enemy and never lost it again . . . another feature of the author's characterization of the hero.

3:13-26. Judas routs Seron at Beth-horon. Judas's second opponent, *Seron*, was motivated by a desire to make a name for himself—an ambition that later would cause ruin for two Jewish leaders (5:55-61). The writer abhors this selfish motive, and relates it closely to arrogance. Seron was assisted by some Hellenists, *godless men*. Judas was at war not only with the Syrians but also with the apostates among his own people. He calmed the fears of his outnumbered and hungry troops with maxims (vv. 18-19) and with his confidence that their cause was more excellent than *insolence and lawlessness*. JOSEPHUS says that the battle was won because the Jews forced the Romans into a constricted pass and assaulted them from high ground.

By circumlocutions for God, which avoid too frequent use of the divine name ("Heaven," vv. 18-19; "He himself," v. 22), the writer expresses his own reverence (as well as Judas's). The purpose of the story is to report the fame that immediately came to Judas and his growing reputation as a warrior (vv. 25-26).

Judas's Most Notable Deeds, 3:27–4:61

3:27-31. Antiochus's financial difficulties. Antiochus needed money to pay tribute to the Romans and to pay his troops in advance (v. 28). He had inadequate resources because of the Jews' failure to pay tribute and because of his own extravagance (v. 30). In *Persia* he could *collect the revenues*, probably by plundering as he did elsewhere.

3:32-37. Lysias appointed to destroy Judah. In 165 B.C.E. Antiochus entrusted the war, his nine-year-old son Antiochus Eupator, and one-half his forces to Lysias, *a distinguished man of royal lineage*, during his absence. Lysias was commissioned to eradicate Israel and to distribute the Jews' land by lot.

3:38–4:35. Judas defeats Lysias at Emmaus and Beth-horon. Lysias delegated the destructive mission to Ptolemy, Gorgias and Nicanor, who engaged Judas at Emmaus (3:38–4:25) and Beth-zur (4:26-35). The writer alludes to a practice that benefitted from ancient warfare, the slave trade (v. 41).

Judas sought to rescue the people and the sanctuary (v. 43). This prepares us for his greatest accomplishment, the rededication of the Temple (4:36-61). His piety is reflected in his choice of a *place of prayer* to prepare his troops for battle. The writer contrasts the Jewish resource (*the book of the law*) with the Greek resource (*the likenesses of their gods*, v. 48). The actual preparation for battle (vv. 54ff.) involved the dismissing of some men according to the regulations for holy war (Deut 20:5-9). Judas inspired the remaining men not to long for victory but to be totally committed (vv. 58-59). His humble trust in God (v. 60) contrasts with the arrogance of his enemy.

Guided by the apostate Jews from the citadel, Gorgias tried to attack Judas before dawn. Judas, desiring to glorify God (v. 11), exhorted his outnumbered and under-equipped men with the recollection of God's Red Sea deliverance. He defeated Nicanor and frightened away Gorgias. After the flight of the enemy, Judas's troops began *to plunder the camp* (v. 23). While Antiochus had to plunder the east for money, Judas's troops found *great riches* in their own land. Judas is depicted again as a savior: *Israel had a great deliverance that day* (Gk. *soteria*, lit. "salvation," v. 25).

The Syrians who escaped informed Lysias of this defeat (v. 26). One year later (164 B.C.E.) Lysias engaged Judas at Beth- zur. Faced this time with overwhelming numbers, Judas prayed a war prayer (vv. 30-33) reminding God of his help to David and Jonathan, who were similarly outnumbered, and concluded with his usual primary concern—not the victory of his troops but the victory of God's honor (v. 33). Lysias fled from the *boldness* or courage of Judas's troops.

4:36-61. Judas rededicates the Temple. One of the most famous events in Jewish life is recorded here. After three years of fighting, the Jews regained, cleansed and rededicated the Temple. The feast that celebrates this is known as Hanukkah (or the Feast of Dedication or the Feast of Lights). The writer elaborates on the ruin of the Temple (v. 38) to accentuate the extent of loss and gain. The troops engaged in ritual lamentation (vv. 39-40). Soldiers were dispatched to keep the citadel garrison preoccupied. The unclean stones used to make the altar to Zeus on top of the altar of burnt offering were removed and the stones of the altar itself, which was now unclean, were removed *until a prophet should come*. The Jews believed prophecy had died out (see also 9:27; 14:41) and since no prophet could give them guidance, the stones were set aside.

The rededication took place exactly three years after the desolating sacrilege. The Temple was decorated with *golden crowns and small shields* (v. 57). The shields may emulate Solomon's work (1 Kgs 10:16-17); but decoration of a temple with crowns and shields was common after a battle among the Greeks also. The most important result of the affair was that the disgrace was removed (v. 58). Judas's sagacity matched his piety, for he stationed guards to protect their gains (vv. 60-61).

More Battles for the Maccabees, 5:1-68

Soon, other non-Jewish neighbors took over where the Syrians left off and Judas faced war on many fronts. The central theme of this chapter, however, is not the constant battles but the saving quality of the family of Judas (see vv. 55-62). These were not battles of aggression by Judas but of defense against anti-Jewish actions of the gentiles. His response to attacks on the Jews was decisive and successful. He brought many Jews who were vulnerable to such attacks back to Judea (vv. 23, 45). When he vowed the enemies' *complete destruction* (v. 5), he was following Joshua's HOLY WAR practice of *cherem*, that is, devoting to the Lord for destruction a conquered land and its people (Judg 6:17; see McEleney 1990, 430; see also 1 Sam 15:8—Saul's complete destruction of the Amalekites). In this chapter Judas leads in the slaughter and plunder of the tribe of the *Baeans* (v. 5), and the cities of *Bozrah* (v. 28), *Maapha* (v. 35), *Carnaim* (v. 44), *Ephron* (v. 46; see v. 51), *Hebron* (v. 65), and *Azotus* (v. 68).

The writer portrays Judas as the sole source of hope in the face of ubiquitous attempts to annihilate the Jews. After Judas called *a great assembly* (v. 16) to plan the rescue of besieged Jews, most of the forces went out to rescue these victims—led by Simon into Galilee and by Jonathan and Judas into Gilead. The rest, under the leadership of Joseph and Azariah, were left to guard Judea and were commanded not to battle the gentiles until the Maccabees returned. In their conquest of cities and liberation of the Jews the Maccabees were welcomed as saviors, before whom the enemy fled at the dreaded name *Maccabeus* (v. 34). The battles and victories were so numerous that the writer makes a cluster of them in v. 36.

In his decisive battle against *Timothy* at *Carnaim* (vv. 40-44) Judas appeared to know the mind of his enemy and to defeat him psychologically by not allowing anyone to encamp at the river—which Timothy would have taken as a sign of the Jews' fear. Judas showed no respect for the gentile belief that a god's temple should afford sanctuary (v. 43), because to him the gods and their cultus were obscene. The summaries in this chapter praise the Maccabees: vv. 23, 36, 44b, 51b, 54, 63-64, 68. Simon and Judas are hailed as conquering heroes who dedicated their victories to God. The writer uses a formula, *the man Judas* (v. 63), which emphasized Moses' greatness in the OT (see Exod 11:3; 32:1; Num 12:3), perhaps to associate the two great leaders.

An interlude about Joseph and Azariah breaks the narrative of praise of the Maccabees, but serves in its own way to perpetuate that praise (vv. 55-62). These men had several failings: first, they were jealous of the Maccabean victories and motivated to *make a name for [them]selves* (v. 57); secondly, they disobeyed their orders and attacked the gentiles (vv. 57, 61).

Their story sets in bold relief the Maccabean successes that came because of right motives and piety. The writer reveals his bias when he explains *they did not belong to the family of those men through whom deliverance was given to Israel* (v. 62). After this

interlude the author praises the Maccabees without restraint (vv. 63-64) and concludes this chapter with another litany of victories for Judas. Verse 67 is problematic. It may be out of place and belong with the previous interlude. The priests who die are blamed for their own death, and Judas remains faultless. 2 Macc 12:38ff. says they died because they concealed under their tunics sacred tokens they took from the idols in temples at Jamnia.

Antiochus IV Dies, 6:1-17

6:1-4. Antiochus IV fails to capture Elymais. The king, who has been out of the picture since 3:22-37 when he went to Persia to get revenues, loses his battle for Elymais and its wealth in four short verses. The blunt report of failure contrasts starkly with the chapter-long paean of Judas's successes that precedes it. The historical data of this failed attempt, the date of Antiochus's death, and its location are given differently by this writer, 2 Maccabees and Polybius. Our author's point is primarily religious, not historical.

6:5-17. Antiochus dies in despair. Antiochus's *great disappointment* (v. 4) was accentuated when he learned of Judas's successes (vv. 8-9). His *deep disappointment* (lit. "grief," v. 9) may have been insanity as Polybius tells it or sickness as 2 Macc 9:5 says. The writer depicts a remorseful deathbed scene that shows the instability of the king, who said he was *kind and beloved* in his power (v. 11). That does not agree with the writer's depiction of his rule. The sources disagree over the date of his death: 1 Macc says it took place after the rededication of the Temple while 2 Macc puts it before. Antiochus blamed his death on the desolating sacrilege (vv. 7, 12-13).

It seems to be poetic justice that the pagan tyrant's demise resulted from his attempt to destroy the Jews and their God. As he lay dying, Antiochus charged Philip to rear his son Antiochus V, whom he had earlier committed to Lysias (3:33). These men would eventually battle for rule.

Attack on the Citadel; Battle of Beth-zur, 6:18-63

After a year of respite from war (163 B.C.E.) Judas besieged the citadel. Under attack, some of the Syrians and Hellenists (*the ungodly Israelites*, v. 21) escaped and informed the new king of their loss. They convinced him that he would be the real loser if he did not defeat Judas. The outcome was a second battle at

Beth-zur (vv. 28-54). For the battle, the Syrians enraged their living "tanks," the elephants, by getting
them drunk. The Syrians were much better equipped
for battle than were the Jews. The splendor of the
army is depicted with epic images (v. 39). Judas's
brother Eleazar showed his singular courage but lost
his life in the bargain (vv. 43-47), and the Jews retreated before superior forces.

The battle of Beth-zur proved difficult for the Jews,
who lacked adequate provisions because it occurred
during a year for leaving the fields unworked. Jerusalem was in peril of falling again. Syrian internal conflict saved the Jews. Philip had come from Persia to
Syria and was trying to seize control. Lysias called off
the siege of Jerusalem to go and stabilize his rule and
sued for peace with the Jews, granting them religious
freedom (vv. 55-63). Judas made the mistake of letting
Lysias enter Jerusalem. When he saw the fortifications
of the Jews, he broke his pact and had the walls torn
down before he left for Syria. Still, Jerusalem was no
longer under siege.

A New King and His New High Priest, 7:1-25

Syrian instability resulted in the murder of King
Antiochus V Eupator. Evil resurged and crested with
the installation of a Hellenist, Alcimus, as the HIGH
PRIEST.

7:1-4. Demetrius seizes the kingship. When Antiochus III lost a battle with the Romans in 190 B.C.E.,
they demanded that he provide hostages from his
family to be kept in Rome as an incentive not to attack
Rome again. Demetrius I, who had been the lawful
heir to the throne years earlier when his brother Antiochus IV became king, had been held hostage in Rome
but escaped with some of his supporters in 162 B.C.E.
He returned to Syria, began to rule, and had Lysias
and Antiochus V Eupator killed to eliminate opposition. His new rule put an end to peace between the
Jews and Syria.

7:5-7. Alcimus becomes high priest. With Demetrius's appointment of a Hellenizing supporter *Alcimus* as
high priest, the Syrians again intruded into the religion
of the Jews. This was a time of the resurgence of *the
renegade and godless men of Israel* (v. 5). Alcimus's
group accused Judas of plunder and aggression and
called for his punishment.

7:8-18. The treachery of Bacchides. Demetrius I
selected a trusted official, Bacchides from Mesopotamia, to help Alcimus keep Judea under control. The
Maccabees were wary of the *peaceable but treacher-*

ous words (v. 10) of these men. The Hasideans,
though, who were prone to trust a high priest, wanted
to make peace with the new leadership. Alcimus, not
trusting these former supporters of the Hasmoneans,
had sixty of them killed. The writer offers a psalm of
lament (Ps 79:2-3). The murder revealed the duplicity
of the new priest and the Hellenizers (v. 18).

7:19-25. Judas's defeat of Alcimus. Bacchides
continued to exterminate his enemies. A reversal of
terms occurred when, thinking things to be under
control, he left Alcimus in charge and returned to
Syria to see the king. Alcimus had to fight to retain
his office, which shows how political it had become
(v. 21). The Hellenizers, not the Syrians, were now in
charge of persecuting the faithful Jews, and they were
even keener than the gentiles in their work. It was no
time for compromise. Those who had deserted to
Bacchides might be killed out of suspicion (v. 19) but
they were also in peril of Judas's vengeance (v. 24).
Alcimus petitioned the king for aid.

Judas Defeats Nicanor, 7:26-50

A fellow escapee from Rome with Demetrius,
Nicanor, was now dispatched *to destroy the people*. He
had been defeated by Judas previously (3:38ff.) and
therefore he *detested Israel*. He used the trick of
peaceable messages for his treachery, but was detected
immediately. Second Maccabees implies that Nicanor
and Judas were friends, a surprising notion not mentioned here. Nicanor was met in Jerusalem by priests
who sought to placate him with a show of sacrifices
offered on behalf of the king. He *spoke arrogantly* to
them and defiled them (one interpretation is that he
spat on them) and threatened to destroy the Temple
unless Judas were handed over to him. The priests
now prayed for Nicanor's defeat and the protection of
the Temple. Judas offered a prayer for battle, recalling
Hezekiah's prayer for rescue from the Assyrians and
the success of that prayer (see 2 Kgs 19:15-19, 35).

In swift defeat, Nicanor's troops threw down their
arms and fled (a behavior exhibited earlier by other
gentiles, 5:43). Throughout, the author portrays the
enemy as cowardly, in panic, pursued in disorderly
retreat. Judas's pursuit of the enemy resulted in their
annihilation and the murder of Nicanor, whose head
and arm were displayed in Jerusalem as tokens of
revenge on the enemy (vv. 46-47). For centuries after
this the Jews celebrated a "Nicanor Day" on which
they were not permitted to weep.

Treaty with the Romans, 8:1-32

8:1-16. Praise of the Romans. With the Syrians again threatening, Judas sought alliance with the Romans, whose power in the Mediterranean was growing fast. This would both strengthen him against the Seleucids and perhaps prevent having Rome as another enemy. The first part of this chapter prepares for the alliance by explaining how Rome came to be a great force (somewhat similar to 1:1-10 that detailed the growth of Greek power). The conquests and powers of the Romans are listed and the virtues of the victors recited: very strong, favorable to alliances, ready to befriend allies, brave, planning and patient, subduing kings. This last quality was especially appealing to Judas (and the writer). Rome had enslaved her Greek and eastern opponents and retained that control even until the writer's own day (v. 10). His praise that the Romans *have kept friendship* (v. 12) would not hold true for long. A few decades after the writing of this book the Romans subdued Judea (63 B.C.E.). The details about the senate, their meeting times and one-man rule are not correct; but the writer is praising a people whose government and situation seemed to him ideal and he eulogizes rather than analyzes their situation.

8:17-32. Peace embassy to Rome. Judas had a fail-proof plan—to make alliance with Rome against Syria. Since Demetrius I had escaped from Rome as a hostage, Rome would surely side with Judas against him. The full text of the Roman treaty is introduced and said to be confirmed by letter and bronze tablets (vv. 22-32). The treaty is similar to other ancient Roman treaties, except for vv. 31-32, which are the writer's own addendum. It is ironic that the narrative leads the reader to hope that the Jews have a trustworthy ally, when the next chapter indicates that during the Jewish-Syrian war the Romans, who had promised to assist the Jews against Syria, played no part at all. In short, the treaty failed. The resulting picture shows the Jews confronting the world alone.

Judas Dies in Battle, 9:1-22

9:1-10. Demetrius attacks Judas again. The king sent Bacchides and Alcimus a second time to destroy Judas. They set their forces strategically for battle. The 22,000 Syrian troops vastly outnumbered Judas's 3,000, which were quickly reduced to 800 by desertion. Judas showed unique courage. Though he could see that the battle would be lost, he announced his true Maccabean resolve to die in battle rather than to flee and be dishonored (v. 10).

9:11-22. Judas's death and burial. The writer describes the engagement in classic historical fashion with descriptions of military contingents. He draws a verbal picture of the uneven match by listing the Seleucid companies, slingers, archers, army, chief warriors, Bacchides on the right wing, and a phalanx flanked by two companies that advanced to trumpet signals, but stating simply that Judas's handful of men *also blew their trumpets* (v. 12). The limited success of Judas's men and the assertion that it took all day for the 22,000 to defeat 800 appears more like a nationalist's proud apology of honorable defeat than objective truth. The writer gives the heroic conflict "biblical" coloration by saying *the earth was shaken* (v. 13; see David's hymn of victory over the PHILISTINES, 2 Sam 22:8). The terse conclusion of v. 17 reads more like the expected result of this conflict. The leadership of Judas is emphasized succinctly (v. 18). His death is not dwelled on, for the family's devotion was not to their own fame but to God's glory and the writer respects that.

At Judas's death the battle ceased, for his men fled. The fact that his brothers were allowed to acquire his body indicates that Bacchides, having attained his goal of victory, did not perpetrate further horrors on his enemy. The lament for Judas calls him a *savior of Israel* (v. 21), a term reminiscent of the judges (OTHNIEL, Judg 3:9; an unknown deliverer, 2 Kgs 13:5). The heroic deeds of Judas are concluded with a statement in the "biblical" style of the kings (v. 22; see also 16:23-24). It is not as successful as its prototype, though, for it states ironically that *the rest of the acts of Judas . . . have not been recorded.*

Jonathan Extends Jewish Successes, 9:23–12:53

The story of Jonathan begins with worsened conditions but shows him eventually gaining a peace with Bacchides. A few surprising turns enliven his era: Jonathan sided with Alexander Balas, the pretended son of Antiochus IV, in order to defeat Demetrius. In turn, he was made a high priest and governor; but at last he was betrayed and captured.

The Continued Fight with Bacchides, 9:23-73

9:23-27. The situation worsens. The writer gives his usual analysis of the worsened political situation: *renegades* and *wrongdoers* emerged. Hellenists persecuted the faithful with renewed vigor, with Bacchides as their sponsor. The fate of Judea was again in peril.

9:28-31. Jonathan appointed leader. When Mattathias was dying he appointed Judas as his successor (2:66). After the death of Judas, his followers acclaimed Jonathan as Judas's successor. The transition provides the author the opportunity to praise Judas's uniqueness, as he records the people saying of the fallen leader that *there has been no one like him* (v. 29). Jonathan was now granted both an office and a commission, as *ruler and leader*.

9:32-49. Jonathan beset by Bacchides. The power of the Syrians and the diminished status of the revolutionaries caused Jonathan to flee to the wilderness from the murderous Bacchides. He sent his brother John to the Nabateans to hide their belongings there, but on the journey he was killed by an Arab clan and their equipment was seized. They recovered some goods and avenged the death of John by attacking a huge wedding procession of that clan, killing many. With an effective rhetorical twist the writer confirms the reversal of the situation (v. 41).

Bacchides laid a trap for Jonathan—again on a SABBATH. He surrounded the revolutionaries and forced them to retreat by swimming across the Jordan River. The enemy did not pursue, perhaps to pick up the spoils of the wedding Jonathan had to abandon (McEleney 1990, 434). The body count of v. 49 sounds inflated.

9:50-73. Jonathan defeats Bacchides. Bacchides turned his energies to fortifying Judea and holding sons of noble families hostage. Alcimus gave tangible form to the Syrian-gentile presence by removing the walls in the Temple that had been built in the time of Haggai and Zechariah and that served to separate Jews from gentiles. The author seems to imply that Alcimus's stroke and death were punishment for tampering with the prophets' work. The results of his death were that the high priesthood was vacant and the Hellenist party without its strong leader. Bacchides retreated and the Jews enjoyed two years of peace.

The Hellenists pleaded for Bacchides to return and capture Jonathan but Jonathan and his men spoiled the planned onslaught. He defeated Bacchides tactically: he left the towns and killed some nearby supporters of Bacchides (vv. 65-66), drawing him away from his *machines of war*, which Simon and his men then burned. Bacchides was defeated, took revenge by killing many of *the renegades* who had advised him, and planned to return to Syria. Jonathan seized the

moment and sued for peace. This was the end of Bacchides' work in Judea. For five years there was peace, during which Jonathan functioned as a judge in Israel and punished the Hellenists.

Jonathan Joins Alexander Balas, 10:1-66

Internal affairs in Syria caused great changes for the Jews. About 152 B.C.E. *Alexander Epiphanes*, called Alexander Balas, appeared in *Ptolemais* (Acco or Acre) and claimed to be the son of Antiochus IV, and therefore the rightful king. Many of the neighboring kings who wanted to see Demetrius deposed supported Alexander Balas. Looking for support, Demetrius courted Jonathan by making concessions to the Jews. Alexander Balas responded by offering Jonathan the high priesthood and status as *king's Friend* (v. 20). Demetrius countered by offering considerable reprieves and benefits to the Jews in a letter directed not to Jonathan but to the Jews. At Alexander's wedding to Cleopatra III, the daughter of Ptolemy VI, the king honored Jonathan publicly as one of his *chief Friends* and made him *general and governor of the province* (v. 65). The honor was in recognition of his support for Alexander and in return for rich gifts that Jonathan gave the king (which brought Jonathan a flurry of criticism that the king suppressed).

10:1-21. The Jews are courted by two kings. The conflict between rival kings in Syria appeared to be headed for battle, (which would occur later, vv. 48ff.). First, though, the writer gives detailed attention to the attempts of each to gain the support of the Jews. The crafty Jews exploited the advances of desperate kings. The *peaceable words* of Demetrius's letter did not persuade the Jews who remembered his cruelties (vv. 7-8, 46). The writer is intriguingly silent about Jonathan's response to Demetrius's proposal. He does not say whether Jonathan agreed, only that he built up his fortifications. That the Syrians and the Hellenizers in the strongholds fled (vv. 12f.) when Jonathan was allowed *to recruit troops* (v. 8) shows that they feared that Demetrius's favor of them had changed and that they were in danger for having supported Jonathan (i.e., that he had now become an ally of Demetrius).

Alexander Balas's bid for support included the appointment of Jonathan as high priest. The hereditary office had been a political reward for friendship since the time of Antiochus IV. While the writer of 1 Maccabees does not criticize this, nor record objection to it, a number of scholars maintain that some Hasideans who disapproved of the pagan appointment broke with the Hasmoneans, departed into the Judean wilderness, and founded the Qumran sect of the Essenes in protest.

10:22-47. Demetrius bids again for alliance. By depicting Demetrius as weak and frustrated the writer makes the Jews look stronger. In a letter the king detailed astonishing offers in turn for their support, including freedom from taxes, tributes, the surrender of the citadel, release of all Jewish captives, religious liberty, opportunities for civil service, benefits for the Temple, and the rebuilding of the walls of Jerusalem. It was too good a gift from too evil a man. The Jews refused him and sided with Alexander who was *the first* to seek their alliance (v. 47). The Greek word for "first," *archegos*, does not mean his offer was the first one made but it was the leading, that is, better, offer.

10:48-50. Defeat of Demetrius. The writer finishes off Demetrius by a terse description of the battle we have anticipated since v. 2. The attitude of the Jews toward Demetrius is obviously his own as well.

10:51-66. Alexander makes alliance with Ptolemy VI. A royal marriage between Alexander Balas and the daughter of the king in Egypt was an ancient kind of peace treaty. At the wedding at *Ptolemais* Jonathan's gifts to the two kings elicited criticism from the Hellenists (*malcontents . . . renegades*, v. 61) who felt betrayed by this new alliance. Both religious and civil honors now had been bestowed on Jonathan—a further blurring of the unique identity of the Jewish faith. This was a greater degree of self rule than was enjoyed by the Jews earlier, but still self rule was a gift offered at the pleasure of the Seleucids.

Jonathan and Simon Defeat Apollonius, 10:67-89

The kingship of Syria was contested again, this time by Alexander and the son of Demetrius, Demetrius II, who appointed Apollonius as governor of Lebanon and Palestine. Apollonius challenged Jonathan militarily at *Jamnia* and *Joppa*. The Hasmoneans were no longer unskilled rebels but leaders of a reinforced and trained army. Jonathan and Simon joined forces and took Joppa quickly. The Maccabees routed the Syrians and performed *cherem* on Azotus and its temple. Alexander rewarded Jonathan by elevating him to the highest rank of the king's friends, *King's Kinsmen*.

Ptolemy the Aggressor; Demetrius the Winner, 11:1-19

The peace by marriage between Ptolemy VI and Alexander Balas was broken by the former's greed for some of the latter's kingdom. Again the writer depicts the gentiles as duplicitous, using false but *peaceable words* (v. 2). Ptolemy invaded Syria and fortified the cities he entered as his own, appealed to Demetrius for alliance and betrayed his son-in-law. Ptolemy assumed Alexander's kingship and routed him in battle. The fugitive Alexander was killed by his Arab host. Because of his death and the contemporaneous death of Ptolemy, Demetrius II assumed the kingship ca. 145 B.C.E. by default and married Cleopatra III.

Concessions Gained from Demetrius II, 11:20-37

Jonathan seized the moment to conquer the citadel, but was betrayed in his effort by Hellenists. Demetrius II called a conference at Ptolemais that Jonathan attended. Favors and honors were again bestowed on Jonathan, though it was not really honor but angry diplomacy that sparked the benefaction (see v. 22). The writer includes a letter detailing the concessions to corroborate his story.

Changing International Relations, 11:38-74

Because it was a time of relaxed tensions (see vv. 38, 52, *the land was quiet before him*) Demetrius dismissed the nationals in his army. They revolted against him for this. *Trypho* (v. 39) had changed allegiances several times—from Demetrius I to Alexander Balas, to Ptolemy VI, and now to Demetrius II. His self-serving now reached its height. He attempted to install Antiochus VI, son of Alexander Balas, as boy-king in whose stead he himself would reign. Jonathan took advantage of the civil turmoil in Syria and asked for removal of Seleucid troops from the citadel and Judean strongholds. In turn he promised to assist Demetrius II with keeping his throne. Jonathan kept his part of the alliance by sending troops into Syria to put down an internal revolt, but the king only responded to Jonathan with threats.

Trypho gathered Demetrius's disgruntled troops and turned them against him, securing the throne for Antiochus, who granted honors including the high priesthood to Jonathan. Jonathan, with the Syrian army now as his ally, began to strengthen his grip on his own land.

The engagement of Jonathan with the forces of Demetrius in Galilee gives the writer the opportunity to celebrate Jonathan's piety and courage in his victory over the enemy.

Alliances with Romans and Spartans, 12:1-23

A digression on treaties with Rome and Sparta illustrates the international standing of the Jewish people under the Maccabees. Jonathan sought to solidify his people's security by making an alliance with the Spartans who had not been a part of the Achaean League that was defeated by the Romans in 146 B.C.E. and by renewing their alliance with Rome. The letter to the Spartans is an exhibition of diplomacy. Many of the regular features of ancient political alliances are in evidence there, but the disclaimer for needing aid because of the people's *help that comes from Heaven* (v. 15) is uniquely Jewish. The letter purporting to have been from the Spartans to the high priest claims a common heritage for both Spartans and Jews—perhaps a psychological or diplomatic more than an historical fact.

Jonathan's and Simon's Successes, 12:24-38

In these verses the writer extols the wisdom, courage and military ability of Simon, perhaps in preparation for his taking the Maccabean leadership very soon. Jonathan acted on his secured power and fortified his positions and isolated the citadel so as to topple resistance there.

Jonathan Betrayed and Captured, 12:39-53

Trypho, who had ruled as regent in behalf of Antiochus VI, now decided to seize the throne for himself, but feared that Jonathan would defend the king. Pretending to be peaceable he convinced Jonathan to dismiss his troops and come to Ptolemais for peace discussions. Jonathan made the mistake of trusting him. This is ironic, for the writer has led us to know that peaceable words from these tyrants were deceptive. In an ambush Jonathan's men were killed and he was taken hostage. The writer interprets the aftermath of the capture of Jonathan in his usual way—when the gentiles saw an opening, they determined to destroy Israel (v. 53).

Simon Secures
Jewish Independence, 13:1–16:24

In this section the writer narrates Simon's appointment as leader of the Hasmonean Dynasty after the death of Jonathan, and Simon's accomplishments. He describes it as a high water mark for Jewish nationalism, tells of Simon's alliance with Spartans and Romans, his war with Antiochus VII, and eventually his death and the succession of John Hyrcanus.

Simon Succeeds Jonathan, 13:1-30

13:1-11. Simon appointed leader. The writer turns directly to recite the qualities of Simon who took charge in the absence of his brother. Simon announced *I alone am left* (v. 4) and showed the courage and resolve of the Maccabees. Because of his courage the people spontaneously elected him leader. He fortified Jerusalem and occupied Joppa as a hedge against Trypho.

13:12-24. Trypho kills Jonathan. Trypho offered to release Jonathan for ransom—much money and two of his sons as hostages to prevent future Jewish attacks on Syria (a tactic the Seleucids had learned from the Romans by sad experience in the time of Antiochus III the Great). The writer absolves Simon of guilt in reporting his compliance with the terms (vv. 17-20) and charges it to his discretion. A snowfall turned Trypho away and prevented his confrontation with Simon. In retaliation, Trypho killed Jonathan.

13:25-30. Simon inters Jonathan at Modein. Just how Simon secured the remains of Jonathan is not stated. Reference to Jonathan's *bones* may indicate some delay of time, though it may be only a figure of speech. The monument for the Maccabees described here was said to have been extant until at least the fourth century C.E., according to EUSEBIUS (McEleney 1990, 438).

Simon's Accomplishments, 13:31–14:49

This passage offers unrestrained praise of Simon. He supported Trypho's opponent Demetrius, in return for which Judea was relieved of all taxes and granted virtually full political independence in 142 B.C.E. He seized *Gazara* (Gaza), captured and cleansed the Hellenists' citadel in Jerusalem and ushered in a new era of peace.

13:31-40. Simon sues for peace with Demetrius II. Trypho put to death the boy-king for whom he was regent and ruled on his own, so Simon joined Trypho's opponent, Demetrius II. The writer illustrates Simon's prestige by saying that while he asked Demetrius only for financial relief, the king granted much more—appointment as high priest, release from tribute, forgiving of grants made to Jews, cancellation of taxes, and enlargement of political and religious privileges.

13:41-42. Greater independence for the Jews. The political situation for the Jews marked a new day from which public and official records were to be dated. Perhaps from the writer's point of view Gazara and the citadel, which still remained to be taken, were "mop-up" operations of small concern by comparison with these new successes.

13:43-53. Simon routs all resistance. After his military conquest of Gazara Simon performed no *cherem*, no slaughter of renegades. He offered a peaceable agreement conditioned upon the renegades' departure and his repopulation of the city with his own supporters. The citadel inhabitants were starved out, but they secured peace from Simon on asking for it. Since the time of Antiochus IV the citadel had been a Syrian stronghold in Jerusalem. The day of its cleansing was made an annual day of festival. As a link to the last of the Maccabean heroes, the writer introduces John Hyrcanus (Simon's son) in v. 53.

14:1-3. The end of Demetrius II. In a short space the writer gives the essential details to show how internal strife in Syria led to the elimination of Demetrius II from the life of Judea. In effect, Demetrius II was now out of the way.

14:4-15. Poem praising Simon. Judas and Simon are the writer's favorite Maccabees. He recalls Mattathias's particular praise of them in his testament (see 2:65-66) and offers a poem in praise of Judas (3:3-9). Here he presents a poem in praise of Simon. These poems of praise parallel each other and signal the beginning and the end of the leadership of Mattathias's sons. The poem depicts a peaceful, almost idyllic era and is filled with allusions to OT terminology, as if a grand old age were renewed. Simon's unique accomplishment was that he *did away with all the renegades and outlaws* (v. 14). It is interesting to note that the author has no praise for Jonathan comparable to that for Judas and Simon, perhaps because of his diplomatic involvement with Seleucid and Ptolemaic kings or because he was not a remarkable military leader (Bartlett 1973, 181).

14:16-24. Renewed alliances with Sparta and Rome. The gentiles now take the initiative in seeking renewed alliance with the Jews because of their independence. The Roman alliance is cited briefly (vv. 17-19) while the Spartan letter is recollected at length. One thousand minas was probably the worth, not the *weight* (v. 24), of the shield sent to Rome.

14:25-49. Simon honored by the people. There follows a resolution of gratitude for Simon. Though he was praised as an individual, his fame was as an individual member of the glorious Hasmonean family

(v. 26). The eulogy repeats many of the events of chap. 13. Some new features appear in vv. 41-43: his right to appoint officials, and the writing of all contracts in his name (perhaps this refers to the dating of documents according to the chronology of his reign, 13:42). Simon's wearing royal attire (v. 43) marked a new level of Jewish acceptance of gentile symbolism for a high priest and national leader. His office appeared to be absolute (vv. 44-45). The writer concludes with the official endorsement of Simon's powers (vv. 46-49).

Antiochus VII Wages War on Trypho, 15:1-14

After focusing on Simon for almost a chapter, the writer turns back to affairs in Syria. With Demetrius II out of the way (14:1-3) Trypho could exercise his power. But Antiochus VII, the son of Demetrius I and brother of Demetrius II, attempted to gain the kingship. He married Cleopatra III, his brother's wife, and made war on Trypho. This king is a clear example of gentile treachery and duplicity. He wrote to Simon (vv. 1-9) declaring his intent to claim his own kingdom and stating his complete approval of Jewish independence. He also mentioned expanding the Jews' privileges and promised future benefits. His generosity, however, was only a trick to gain Simon's support; he reversed his stance quickly when he gained power (15:25ff.). With a massive army and naval support Antiochus attacked Trypho and his army, decimated by desertion, and surrounded them at Dor on the coast.

Alliance with Rome, Continued, 15:15-24

This material, which reports the return of the embassy that Simon had sent to Rome to renew their alliance, would have come more naturally after 14:24. It breaks into the story of Antiochus and serves no purpose except to make the reader sympathetic for the Jews by showing that they, who were about to be betrayed by the Syrians, were strongly supported by a major and respected people, the Romans. The role of Simon in making this alliance with Rome and the personal affirmation of him repeated several times in the Romans' letter (15:16-21) also add pathos to the narrative by painting Simon (soon to be killed by his own son-in-law) as an honored and recognized leader. That the letter of support was sent to numerous kings and free peoples stresses the international standing of the Jews.

The Treachery of Antiochus VII, 15:25-36

15:25-31. Antiochus refuses alliance with Simon. The story returns to Antiochus's assault on Trypho. Whether he launched an attack *for the second time* or "on the second day," (as some mss. have it) is uncertain; but the writer himself now returns a second time to the assault on Trypho. Simon was apparently deceived by Antiochus's offer of support, and did not realize that the king intended to recapture Judea. He offered military and financial backing that Antiochus VII refused (though Josephus records that he accepted it) and *broke all the agreements he formerly had made with Simon* (v. 27). He dispatched *Athenobius* to Simon to demand that the Jews either surrender to him Joppa, Gazara and the citadel or to remit to him one thousand talents of silver.

15:32-36. The Syrians threaten war. When the ambassador came to Jerusalem, he confronted Simon with extortion, the surrender of hard-won cities, or war. The astonishment of the Syrians at the wealth of the Jews (vv. 32, 36) indicates that they had underestimated their resources and status. The narrative depicts the courtly grandeur of the newly independent Jews. Simon refused Antiochus's terms and offered to pay only a tenth of the amount demanded. A counteroffer is incredible, but perhaps the amount was intended to insult the king, which it did. War ensued.

War with Antiochus VII Begins, 15:37-41

Simon recedes from the narration at this point and his son John Hyrcanus I enters. He and his brother Judas engaged the Syrians, though John had the higher profile in the war. The writer returns to Antiochus's assault on Trypho. The king pursued his enemy (whose fate is not reported here, but who was either killed by the king's army or killed himself as other historians indicate), and left *Cendebeus* in charge of the war to secure the coastal regions. The events of the war are reminiscent of the horrible times before Simon's successes (vv. 40-41).

John Hyrcanus Continues the Dynasty, 16:1-24

16:1-3. Simon appoints his successors. With this transition we observe the fourth appointment. The dying Mattathias had appointed Judas; the friends of Judas acclaimed Jonathan their leader; the people appointed Simon in the absence of his captive brother;

now Simon appoints John Hyrcanus and Judas to take the lead because he has grown too old to serve. This appointment contains a recitation of the heroic commitment of Simon and his predecessors and their saving efforts (*we have delivered Israel many times*, v. 2). Simon reverently avoided the use of God's name, as did his predecessors (*by Heaven's mercy . . . the help that comes from Heaven*, v. 3). He commissioned his sons to a holy task and prayed for divine aid to them in their task.

16:4-10. John Hyrcanus defeats Cendebeus. John now not only had the sanction of his father to respond to the assaults of Cendebeus; he was free to make his own response as leader. The author seems to bring the stories of the Maccabean heroes full circle by mentioning that John's men encamped at *Modein* (v. 4), where his grandfather Mattathias had initiated the Jewish revolt (2:15-26). The two armies met at the Sorek River. The Jewish army was reluctant to engage the enemy. John Hyrcanus, displaying unique courage, crossed the river first and inspired his troops to follow (v. 6). The result was a forceful and resolute victory for John. The whole affair of Antiochus's threats and the war is submerged with a victorious statement that John Hyrcanus *then returned to Judea safely* (v. 10).

16:11-17. Simon and his sons betrayed with hospitality. The theme of treachery reaches a climax with the murder of Simon and two of his sons. It is ironic that the treachery hidden beneath peaceable overtures that destroyed Simon came not from the gentiles, (from whom the reader would expect such behavior) but from within the Maccabean family. Simon had given JERICHO and the land north of the DEAD SEA to Ptolemy, his son-in-law, as a wedding gift. But Ptolemy wanted greater power that could come only by removing the ruling Maccabees. So he plotted their death. In 134 B.C.E. Simon and two of his sons visited Ptolemy, who had them killed. His *great treachery* and returning *evil for good* (v. 17) remind us of the renegades and the Syrians. In saying of Ptolemy that *His heart was lifted up* (v. 13), the writer comes full circle. He used the same idiom, which describes arrogance and pride, to refer to Alexander the Great at the beginning of his history (1:3).

16:18-22. John Hyrcanus escapes Ptolemy's treachery. Ptolemy reported his act to Antiochus VII and encouraged the king to join in the overthrow of the Maccabean Dynasty at this crucial moment. He must have planned to be made the Syrians' local ruler or governor. First Maccabees says nothing about the king's response. Ptolemy's plot was ruined when John Hyrcanus learned of it and killed the assassins.

16:23-24. Summary statement. In an anticlimactic way 1 Maccabees comes to an end without telling us the outcome of Ptolemy. For those details we have to turn to JOSEPHUS who says that John Hyrcanus attacked Ptolemy and that he escaped. The writer leaves us in no doubt, though, that the Maccabean Dynasty was still in place and unshaken. In a summary reminiscent of the history of the kings (2 Kgs 14:28-29; also see above, 9:22) he refers us to sources for the further deeds and accomplishments of John Hyrcanus. The effect of this reference to abundantly documented feats is to imply that there is much more that could be said about this leader (a rhetorical figure which causes the hearer/reader to think that what has been said is only a small part of a much larger story). The writer has made his point—the heroic family served their God with devotion and piety and were the salvation of JUDAISM in their time.

Works Cited

Bartlett, John R. 1973. *The First and Second Books of the Maccabees*.

McEleney, N. J. 1990. "1–2 Maccabees." NJBC.

Second Maccabees

Calvin Mercer

Introduction

The books of 1 and 2 Maccabees constitute testimony, by different writers and with varying degrees of historical reliability, to the second century B.C.E. severe persecution of the Jews and the resulting victorious rebellion known as the Maccabean revolt. Both books, along with 3 and 4 Maccabees, were widely read by and inspiring to early Christians who often identified with Jewish suffering. Second Maccabees, long neglected by scholars due to its propagandistic nature, is the object of a minor revival of scholarly interest.

Relation to 1, 3, and 4 Maccabees

First and Second Maccabees are concerned with the Jewish struggle for liberation from Syrian, or Seleucid, kings, although the books approach their subject with somewhat different purposes and sometimes focus on different time periods. First Maccabees, making the attempt to recount military and political history, traces a forty year period from the ascension of the Syrian oppressor Antiochus IV (Epiphanes) in 176 B.C.E. and the rise of the famed Hasmonean family ("Maccabean" refers to the earliest members who started the revolt), to the assassination of the Jewish revolutionary Simon. A major concern of 1 Maccabees is the rise and legitimacy of the Hasmonean dynasty.

Second Maccabees, generally considered less historical in nature, or more theological as the case may be, although there are exceptions, uses as its historical context Jewish life in JERUSALEM during the reigns of the Seleucid kings Seleucus IV, Antiochus IV Epiphanes, and Antiochus V Eupator. It covers a period before and just after the 167 B.C.E. outbreak of the Maccabean Revolt. With the exception of Judas Maccabeus, 2 Maccabees does not hold the Hasmonean family in very high regard; its concern is with the safety and sanctity of Jerusalem and its holy Temple.

The following are parallel passages in, respectively, 1 and 2 Maccabees: 1:10 || 4:7; 1:20-54 || 5:1-20 and 6:1-3; 3:38-40 || 8:9-11; 4:14-25 || 8:22-25; 4:28-29 || 11:1-5; 6:1-4 || 9:1-3; 6:16 || 9:28-29 and 11:17-26; 4:52-55 || 10:3-9; 5:9-62 || 10:14-38 and 12:2-45; 6:19-63 ||.13:1-26; 7:1-5 || 14:1-2; 7:25 || 14:4-7; 7:43-49 || 15:28-36.

Although carrying the same name, 3 and 4 Maccabees are largely removed from the historical events that gave rise to the first two books. There is some similarity in style and content between 3 Maccabees, a romance set in the context of Egypt's Ptolemy IV Philopator (king from 221–204 B.C.E.) and his threatened persecution of Jews, and 2 Maccabees; however, similarity is probably not sufficient to conclude direct knowledge either way. Second and Fourth Maccabees are clearly closer, with similar themes and some stories told in both books; 4 Maccabees, a first century philosophical discourse, probably used 2 Maccabees, especially the martyrdom stories in 6:18–7:42.

Authorship and Date

The unknown writer probably penned his work before 124 B.C.E., the date of the first letter prefixed to the text and the latest year cited in the book, and certainly before 63 B.C.E., when the Roman general Pompey conquered Jerusalem, a most significant event not mentioned in the text (see 15:37). The latest event mentioned in 2 Maccabees is the death of Nicanor (15:20-36), which occurred in 160 or 161 B.C.E., the earliest date for the book.

The book, with possible exception of the two introductory letters that contain numerous semitisms, was written in good Greek style, using a wide vocabulary. Nontraditional Jewish notions and the Greek style have led some to suggest an origin outside Jerusalem, perhaps Alexandria; however, the author's zeal for the Temple makes Jerusalem a good possibility. Even if the book was composed by a Jerusalem writer, some stories could have originated elsewhere.

Sources

By his admission (2:19-31), the writer abridges a five-volume historical narrative by an otherwise unknown Jason of Cyrene, North Africa, and is, therefore, commonly referred to as the "epitomist." In a somewhat self-serving—and probably accurate—preface (he refers to his *toil . . . sweat, and loss of sleep*, vv. 26-27), he says his intent is to *condense* Jason's work in order to *please those who wish to read, to make it easy for those who are inclined to memorize, and to profit all readers* (see Doran 1981, 77–84 for a good discussion of this statement).

One of the more intriguing—and hazardous—critical tasks is uncovering the author's actual use of his principal source. Even though it was not uncommon for ancient writers, in order to gain authority, to base their work on a purported ancient worthy, most commentators agree that on this point the epitomist's preface is accurate. Determining specifically how closely the epitomist followed Jason's actual wording (and identifying Jason's sources, as some try to do) is problematic.

In addition to the primary source of Jason, two letters (1:1–2:18), supposedly written from Palestinian Jews to encourage the Jews in Egypt, are attached, perhaps by a later editor, to the beginning of the book. Whether the epitomist knew 1 Maccabees or both books drew on a common source, such as a biography of Judas Maccabeus, is uncertain. While many other sources are mentioned, most of which may have been contained in Jason's volumes, 2 Maccabees, apart from the introductory letters, is generally considered a unified piece. For detailed discussion of and elaborate hypotheses on source-critical matters, see Goldstein 1983 and Schunk 1954.

In this commentary, 2 Maccabees (except for the two prefixed letters) is considered the work of the epitomist, even when he is using a source; so the use of "epitomist" with reference to a particular passage does not necessarily imply that we are reading the words of the abridger rather than his source.

Message

Second Maccabees is an example of pathetic history, that is, writing that sensationalizes events and personalities in order to make its points by playing on the reader's emotions. The epitomist tells a good story. This kind of "history" writing would never meet the canons of modern historiography. A bias toward histo-

ry as an accurate record of past events has unfortunately resulted in relative neglect of this work. Beyond the concerns of reconstructing history, strictly understood, study of the epitomist is of value in providing insight into the nature of ancient propaganda, and a better understanding of the tensions, concerns, and ideologies of the Jewish people during an important period of their history.

As alluded to above, the holy city of Jerusalem and especially its holy Temple (e.g., 2:19, 22; 3:12; 5:15-21; 14:31; 15:18) are of major concern to the epitomist. Looking at recent history (and at his sources), the epitomist saw that the oppression under the Seleucid kings had been severe and the revolt overthrowing that yoke had been remarkably successful. Why did God allow his people to suffer and his Temple to be desecrated and why did God then come to the aid of his people and save the Temple? The epitomist felt it was important for his audience to understand the answers to these questions so they would never again find themselves in similar circumstances.

Reiterating the Deuteronomistic theology—the central confession of the DEUTERONOMISTIC HISTORIAN— the epitomist asserts that these sufferings were caused by the people's sins and served as (disciplinary?) punishment (e.g., 4:7-26, 47, 50; 6:12-16; 7:32; 10:4; 12:40-42; 15:32-33). Often, the cause of the suffering is traced specifically to Jewish traitors (see comment on 3:4-8). As in the Deuteronomistic scheme, repentance and prayer will elicit the saving activity of God, usually in the form of assistance in battle. Whatever the odds, victory is certain with God on one's side (e.g., 8:18, 36; 11:13). Often the assistance comes in the form of miraculous divine warriors, who arrive at crucial points to turn the tide (see comment on 3:24-35). The epitomist, however, does not fully share the apocalyptic outlook of the author of DANIEL, a book also written during the Maccabean period. The epitomist ends his work not with a new age firmly in place, but rather with God's people currently in control, a situation that can change if they revert to unfaithfulness.

Just as God helps his people, so he punishes evildoers, Jew and pagan. The epitomist is especially interested in showing that punishment is an exact retribution for the evil deed(s) (see comment on 4:30-38). Sometimes the evildoer will eventually acknowledge God's power in a conversion of sorts (e.g., 3:40-45; 8:34-36).

Of particular interest for study of doctrinal development has been the epitomist's presentation of relatively novel religious ideas that eventually found their way into Christianity. These notions include prayer for the dead, resurrection, and the atoning blood of martyrs (see comment on 7:7-19; 12:39-45). Bodily resurrection, with the restoration of injured body parts, is an appropriate divine response to the sufferings of the martyrs (see comment on 6:18-23).

Courage in the face of oppression, sacrifice even of one's life for what is right, justifiable violence, and justice ultimately prevailing are all themes that contemporary liberation theologians, interested in biblical perspectives, might find useful.

For Further Study

In the *Mercer Dictionary of the Bible*: APOCRYPHAL LITERATURE; DANIEL, BOOK OF; FEASTS AND FESTIVALS; HELLENISTIC WORLD; MACCABEES; MACCABEES, FIRST; MACCABEES, SECOND; MACCABEES, THIRD;

MACCABEES, FOURTH; ROMAN EMPIRE; RESURRECTION IN THE NT; RESURRECTION IN THE OT.

In other sources: F. M. Abel, *Les Livres des Maccabees*; J. R. Barlett, *The First and Second Books of the Maccabees*, CB; W. H. Brownlee, "Maccabees, Books of," IDB; J. J. Collins, *Daniel, First Maccabees, Second Maccabees*; R. Doran, *Temple Propaganda: The Purpose and Character of 2 Maccabees*; J. Efron, *Studies on the Hasmonean Period*; J. Goldstein, *II Maccabees*, AncB; D. J. Harrington, *The Maccabean Revolt: Anatomy of a Biblical Revolution*; J. Kampen, *The Hasideans and the Origin of Pharisaism: A Study in 1 and 2 Maccabees*; G. Nickelsburg, *Resurrection, Immortality, and Eternal Life in Intertestamental Judaism*; L. Schiffman, "2 Maccabees," HBC; K. D. Schunck, *Die Quellen des I. und II. Makkabäerbuches*; A. P. Spilly, *First Maccabees, Second Maccabees*; S. Tedesche, *The Second Book of Maccabees*.

Commentary

An Outline

I. Prefixed Letters, 1:1–2:18
  A. Letter to the Jews of Egypt, 1:1-9
  B. Second Letter to the Jews of Egypt, 1:10–2:18
II. Prologue, 2:19-32
III. God's Protection of the Temple, 3:1–4:6
  A. Simon's Evil Plot, 3:1-8
  B. The Temple Is Saved, 3:9–4:6
IV. Apostasy, 4:7-50
  A. Jason's Sin, 4:7-22
  B. Menelaus's sin, 4:23-50
V. God's Punishment, 5:1–7:42
  A. The Persecutions of Antiochus IV, 5:1–6:17
  B. Martyrdom of Eleazar, 6:18-31
  C. Martyrdom of the Seven Brothers
    and Their Mother, 7:1-42
VI. God's Deliverance, 8:1–15:36
  A. Early Victories by Judas, 8:1-36
  B. Death of Antiochus IV, 9:1-29
  C. Purification of the Temple, 10:1-9
  D. Later Victories by Judas, 10:10–13:26
  E. The Last Great Battle, 14:1–15:36
VII. Epilogue, 15:37-39

Prefixed Letters, 1:1–2:18

Letter to the Jews of Egypt, 1:1-9

While there has been debate about the number of letters (one to three), a consensus has emerged, perhaps prematurely, at two. The letters are not integral to the work and were likely prefixed by a later hand.

The first letter, written to the substantial Jewish community in Egypt, generally provides encouragement to maintain the traditional faith. The epitomist's dates are based on the year the Seleucid dynasty came to power (312 B.C.E.). The year 188 (v. 9) is 124 B.C.E. This is a festal letter in genre, a type of which there are several ancient examples, written to diaspora Jews with advice on correct ways to observe upcoming holidays. In this letter there is perhaps a subtle suggestion that the Egyptian Jews have been lax in their devotion and behavior.

In making reference to an earlier letter (v. 7), written in 143 B.C.E., our letter reminds readers of earlier trials experienced by the Jerusalem and Judean Jews during the rule of Antiochus IV Epiphanes. Significantly, Antiochus IV is not mentioned; the cause of the oppression is traced to Jason, who became high priest in 175 B.C.E., and is charged with apostasy (see 4:7-26). Theologically, the suffering is a result of Jewish sin (see under "Message," above), and the relief provided by God is a result of Jewish repentance.

Finally, the letter details proper observance of Hanukkah, a festival celebrating the restoration of Temple worship by Judas Maccabeus in 164 B.C.E. Because of possible similarities with the Festival of Booths (or Tabernacles) (cf. 10:6), celebrated at the end of harvest and on no fixed date, Hanukkah is referred to as the *festival of booths in the month of Chislev* (v. 9).

Second Letter to the Jews of Egypt, 1:10–2:18

The second prefixed letter, a rambling and much longer epistle, is also festal in type, designed to provide theological and "historical" reasons for keeping the eight-day Hanukkah festival. Second Maccabees 1:19–2:15 contains legendary material supporting the letter's intent but which can easily be viewed as an insertion; hence the scholarly discussion about the number of letters.

1:10. Greeting. The *senate* was a council presided over by the high priest; it later evolved into what is called the SANHEDRIN. *Judas* would be Judas Maccabeus, hero of the revolt. *Aristobulus*, obviously a leading citizen of the Jewish community in Egypt, was known as a philosopher who dedicated a book, now lost, to an Egyptian king, probably Ptolemy VI (180–145 B.C.E.), who was possibly a student of the philosopher. Undated, the letter is usually read (at 1:18 and 2:16) as claiming to be written just before the purification of the temple in 164 B.C.E. Goldstein (1983, 157–67) argues that the letter is a forgery written in 103/2 B.C.E.

1:11-17. Fate of Antiochus IV. *Nanea* (v. 13) was a Syrian goddess who can also be identified with Anahita (Persian), Artemis or Aphrodite (Greek), and Venus (Roman). Marriage of royalty to a goddess was a known Mesopotamian rite that, not incidentally, entailed receipt of a dowry (i.e., temple treasures). On Antiochus IV Epiphanes, see comment on 5:7-17.

The account of Antiochus's fate conflicts with information known from other sources (e.g., 1 Macc 6:1-16), including 9:1-29. Despite this fact, the epitomist, even if he did not prefix the letter, would have certainly relished the vivid description of the evil king's death. He would also have agreed fully with the theological import of the account, namely God's saving of his people (v. 11) and judgment on evildoers (v. 17), even when the evildoers seem *irresistible* (v. 13).

1:18. Festival day. The author encourages his readers to keep Hanukkah "as" (certainly understood and attested to by some ancient mss.) they would Booths, celebrated for eight days, a point of some apparent interest (2:12). The Festival of Fire is otherwise unknown, at least in these terms. The author's confusion of NEHEMIAH with ZERUBBABEL, who rebuilt the Temple (Ezra 3:1-13), is echoed by later writers. The point is that there is good precedent for Hanukkah.

1:19–2:15. "Festival" of fire. Here a series of probably legendary stories are utilized to support celebration of Hanukkah. Noticeably prominent in the materi-

al are references to fire (vv. 1:19, 20, 22, 32, 33; 2:1, 10). Fire was sacred (see 1:34) in old Persia, the soil out of which grew the Zoroastrian religion with its fire temples and movement of fire from place to place, and Persian influence on our letter is a good possibility. Fire, often used among Jews as a symbol of purification, and light play an important role in the Hanukkah celebration, sometimes called the Festival of Lights and that includes lighting lamps (1 Macc 4:50) in the Temple and the menorah in family gatherings.

Persia (v. 19) is an anachronism for Babylonia. The *thick liquid* (v. 20; see also v. 36 where the author's etymology is flawed) is certainly petroleum, which was known as early as the Sumerians. The identification of *Jonathan* (v. 23) is uncertain.

Repentant prayer (vv. 24-29, perhaps a model prayer for the Jews of Egypt) is a crucial ingredient in the process of achieving *rescue* (v. 25) by God and punishment of the oppressors (v. 28). Miracles (as in vv. 31-34) sometimes authenticated divine favor and, in this case, underscores the divine origin of the fire in the second Temple.

The Nehemiah story prompted the telling of a legend about JEREMIAH, which also carries the theme of the fire not being extinguished during the EXILE. Likewise, the Jeremiah story reminded the writer of a SOLOMON legend that could be marshaled as additional precedent for the Festival of Fire. The purpose of 2:9-12 is apparently to argue for a Hanukkah celebration of eight days (cf. the seven days of 2 Chr 7:9, 1 Kgs 8:65). The MOSES quote (2:11), not found in the TORAH, is awkward here, perhaps due to a defective text.

The closing comment in this material (vv. 13-15) is an interesting bibliographic note (see also 2:1) and, unfortunately, one for which the references are not otherwise known. It is possible that *founded a library* is some allusion to the canonization of the Pentateuch and other books. It is also possible that the author's several references to authoritative texts (vv. 1, 4, 13, 14) is a fraudulent way of legitimizing his accounts, although his offer to share the books (v. 15) seems genuine.

2:16-18. Conclusion. The letter's conclusion, following the long excursus, picks up the thought from 1:18 and reminds the readers of the importance of keeping the holy days.

Prologue, 2:19-32

2:19-22. Preview. Here the epitomist, in a fashion typical of Greek histories, provides the reader with a preview giving some of the highlights of Jason's work (see 2:23). Epiphanes, which means "God manifest" and was Antiochus IV's self-designation, is set over against true *epiphaneiai* (*appearances*) from God (on the *appearances* see comment on 3:24-35). Chapters 8–9 recount Judas's wars against Antiochus IV (176–165 B.C.E.) and chaps. 10–13 are about the wars against *Eupator* (165–162 B.C.E.). No mention is made here of the battles recounted in chaps. 14–15 against Demetrius I (162–150 B.C.E.). The epitomist provides the first known use of the term *Judaism*, here set over against *barbarian hordes*.

The themes of Temple purification, victory against the odds (i.e., *few in number*), and God's favor toward his people, all found later in the book, are stressed here.

2:23-32. Condensed Version. On *Jason* and other aspects of the prologue, see "Sources" in the Introduction.

God's Protection of the Temple, 3:1–4:6

Simon's Evil Plot, 3:1-8

3:1-3. When all was well. *Seleucus* IV Philopator, the son of Antiochus III, reigned from 187–175 B.C.E. Apparently the events of 3:4–4:6 take place during his reign (cf. Dan 11:20). The faithfulness of Onias III, a hero of the epitomist, is the reason for the peace in Jerusalem, just as the unfaithfulness of Simon will bring trouble.

3:4-8. Simon's mischief. *Simon* administered the Temple affairs under the direction of high priest Onias III. Considered by the epitomist the instigator of the current troubling affair, Simon enlisted Apollonius, the provincial governor, in the plot to steal the Temple treasures, an act considered sacrilege by the Jews. Eventually King Seleucus IV commissions Heliodorus, who we know from other sources later assassinated Seleucus IV, to play the role of agent in the underhanded attempt to plunder the Temple (cf. 4 Macc 4:6). This mischief is the first of three attacks on the Temple in 2 Maccabees.

Crucial in the thinking of the epitomist is that, despite the fact that pagans were important agents in this evil affair, a Jew, *Simon, of the tribe of Benjamin*, was the sinful source of the threat to the Temple. Simon is the first of several Jewish traitors, including *Jason* (4:7-22; 5:5-10), *Menelaus* (4:23-50; 13:8), and *Alci-*

mus (14:3-13; 26-27), whose stories are told by the epitomist. In the cases of Jason and Menelaus the traitors are punished with a judgment befitting their crime.

The Temple Is Saved, 3:9–4:6

3:9-14a. Threat to the Temple. Despite whatever truth there might be to Simon's claim (v. 6) that the money could legitimately be taken by the king, the epitomist clearly believes (v. 12) such action would violate the Temple. The significant role of the Temple in his thinking is evident in v. 12.

3:14b-23. Prayers of the people. Imminent violation of the Temple elicits prayer and petition from the people. The rich drama and detailed description of the response by the high priest and the people is a good example of the epitomist's sensational style, clearly designed to evoke the reader's emotion.

3:24-34. Defeat of Heliodorus. The drama continues, here with a vivid account of the spectacular and supernatural attack on the evil Heliodorus, the first example of an *appearance from heaven* mentioned in the prologue (2:21). Flashy celestial warriors miraculously appearing just in time to assist the righteous and win the victory, common in ancient accounts of warfare (although not in 1 Macc), is prominent in the epitomist's scheme of things (e.g., 2:21; 5:1-4; 10:29-31; 11:6-12; cf. Judg 5:20; Josh 5:13; Zech 9:14-16; 3 Macc 2:21-23; 4 Macc 4:10). The legendary account is of no value in determining what really happened to turn Heliodorus and his men back.

The notion of a deity defending his temple from those who would defile it is common in the ancient Near East and Greece. In our case, literary analysis suggests that the epitomist has woven together two accounts, both of which have parallels in Greek literature. In one account (vv. 24-25, 29-30) a single mighty warrior rides up and swiftly strikes the villain Heliodorus to the ground. The second account (vv. 26-28, 31-35) relates how two men (angels?), apparent only to Heliodorus, beat him continuously while his bodyguards stand by helplessly.

3:35-40. Conversion of Heliodorus. Following the miraculous intervention by God's agents and Onias III's successful sacrifice for the fallen villain's recovery, Heliodorus exhibits a remarkable change of heart in a fairy tale-like ending (cf. 8:34-36; 9:12-18).

4:1-6. Epilogue. The epitomist describes how the propaganda efforts of the evil Jew Simon continued, although to no avail.

Apostasy, 4:7-50

Jason's Sin, 4:7-22

The evidence is that Antiochus IV Epiphanes ("god manifest," which suggests something about his ego), whom the Jews called Epimanes ("madman"), promulgated a most severe persecution for the purpose of stamping out the Jewish religion. First Maccabees provides our best and most vivid account (e.g., 1:10-64). The epitomist, however, does not portray Antiochus IV in overly mean terms, as he was certainly capable of doing. Rather, Antiochus IV and other Seleucid kings are depicted as typical Hellenistic rulers who support Greek culture and readily take bribes.

The epitomist lays the blame for the severe persecutions on Jason, who *obtained the high priesthood by corruption* (v. 8). Not one with moderate views about key Jewish leaders, our author condemns in strong language (v. 13) Jason, who was the polar opposite of his brother Onias III and who (according to JOSEPHUS, *Ant* 12.5.1) had given up his Hebrew name Joshua to take a Greek name. Other Jewish traitors in the book, to whom he can be compared, are Simon, Menelaus, and Alcimus (see comment on 3:4-8).

It is Jason, not Antiochus IV, who is responsible for *Hellenization* (a term first used by the epitomist), that is, shifting the people *over to the Greek way of life* (v. 10). The intent was to reconstitute Jerusalem as a Greek city called ANTIOCH (vv. 9, 19). This *extreme of Hellenization* (v. 13) included establishment of a *gymnasium* (v. 10), a Greek institution devoted to educational, cultural, and athletic training. Here privileged Jewish lads, wearing the broad-brimmed *Greek hat* (v. 12) for protection from the sun and otherwise probably naked, engaged in wrestling, discus throwing, and other sports, neglecting, of course, the traditions of Israel (v. 14). The degree of success which the Hellenization policies achieved is suggested by the reference to the priests being diverted from their sacred duties by the activities in the gymnasium (v. 14).

The disasters suffered by the people are due to the sins of Jason (v. 13) and those Jews who followed in his ways (v. 16). The moral of the story is stated in v. 17.

In connection with his political and military activities, Antiochus IV visited Jerusalem and was welcomed by Jason and other Greek sympathizers (vv. 18-22). *Triremes* (v. 20) were a type of warship.

Menelaus's Sin, 4:23-50

4:23-29. Menelaus steals the high priesthood. True to his pattern of locating the source of trouble to Jews, the epitomist roundly condemns *Menelaus*, the unscrupulous usurper of the high priesthood (v. 25; see also 4:47, 50 and comment under "Message" in the Introduction). Also as a reflection of his notion of divine retribution for sin, the epitomist describes the "eye for an eye" punishment which Jason received (v. 26; see comment on 3:4-8). The reference to *Crates* (v. 29) is abrupt and probably reflects the unevenness that sometimes results from the epitomist's proce of abridgment.

4:30-38. Menelaus has Onias III murdered. Giving cities to a *concubine* (v. 30), as a way of providing them with income, was a common practice of kings.

In an echo of an earlier offense (3:9-14a), Menelaus violates the Temple, not a minor infraction for the epitomist. The situation brings forth from hiding the legitimate high priest, Onias III, who is promptly murdered by Menelaus's agent, *Andronicus*, known only in 2 Maccabees. Amazingly, even considering the epitomist's moderate opinions about the Seleucid kings, Antiochus IV is depicted as grieving for the slain priest (v. 37). The murderer Andronicus is repaid *with the punishment he deserved* (v. 38). In a strict application of *lex talionis* (the old law of "an eye for an eye"), the epitomist delights in illustrating how evildoers are punished in accordance with their evil actions (cf. 5:10; 7:36; 8:33-36; 9:5-6, 28; 13:6-8; 14:32-33; 15:32). The epitomist's account of the death of Onias III, perhaps alluded to in Daniel 9:26, is contradicted by other sources (e.g., Josephus, *BJ* 1.1.1; 7.10.2).

4:39-50. Menelaus remains as high priest. The *Mishnah* (*Sanh* 9.6) states that a person stealing a temple vessel should be killed by anyone finding him. *Lysimachus*, Menelaus's brother who had been left in charge (v. 39), was killed by a mob for his acts of sacrilege.

The *senate* (see comment on 1:10) unsuccessfully attempted to "prosecute" Menelaus for his many transgressions. The Scythians (v. 47) were infamous for their brutality. *Ptolemy* was one of the king's governors (see 6:8; 8:8). The account of Menelaus ends with wickedness growing, a preview of things to come.

God's Punishment, 5:1–7:42

The Persecutions of Antiochus IV, 5:1–6:17

5:1-4. Celestial warriors. The apparition (see comment on 3:24-35), here a sign of some impending significant event, provides a good picture of the threatened *second invasion* (probably 169 B.C.E., see 1 Macc 1:16-20) of Antiochus IV; the Jews, as usual, pray that they will have the victory.

5:5-10. Jason's miserable end. Jason (see 4:7-22), again condemned by the epitomist (vv. 8-10), is unsuccessful in the coup. His evil actions return as his own punishment (v. 10), a favorite theme of the epitomist (see comment on 4:30-38).

5:11-20. Desecration of the Temple. The number of Jews said to be massacred by Antiochus IV (v. 14) is perhaps exaggerated, but, even so, the massacre is not considered by the epitomist as horrifying as the desecration of *the most holy temple in all the world* (v. 15).

The epitomist, consistent with his earlier interpretations (see comments on 4:7-17 and 4:23-29), shifts the blame from Antiochus IV to Menelaus. Antiochus IV came to Jerusalem because he thought the Jews were in rebellion (v. 11) and was *guided by Menelaus* (v. 15) through the Temple. There are wide textual variations in v. 16, but the epitomist probably means that Menelaus, *with his polluted hands*, gave the holy vessels to Antiochus IV.

In a theological sidebar (vv. 17-20), the epitomist explains that the pagan king Antiochus IV is but a tool in the hand of God (cf. Heliodorus in 3:9-35) who, fully in control of all events, is temporarily disciplining his sinful children.

5:21-26. Additional massacres. *Andronicus* (v. 23) is not the same as in 4:31-38, if the account of his death there is correct.

5:27. Judas Maccabeus. Unobtrusively, but with a clear interjection of hope, the epitomist introduces his great hero, Judas, surname Maccabeus, of the Hasmonean family and leader of the famous guerrilla-type Maccabean revolt. The *nine others* likely include his brothers and his father Mattathias, not mentioned by the epitomist but prominent in 1 Maccabees at the beginning of the revolt. Unlike 1 Maccabees, the epitomist has no interest in the Hasmonean dynasty; his concern is with Judas's protection of Jerusalem and the holy Temple.

6:1-6. Forced Hellenization. The tempo increases as Antiochus IV initiates a policy requiring the Jews to abandon their religion and turn to Greek gods and ways (see 1 Macc 1:41-50). The temple in *Gerizim* (v. 2), near SHECHEM, refers to the temple of the SAMARITANS, half-breed Jews considered by the Seleucid rulers in the same light as other Jews. The *abominable offerings that were forbidden by the laws* of vv. 5-6 may refer to swine (cf. 1 Macc 1:47). This action is probably the "abomination that desolates" of Daniel 8:13; 9:27; 11:31; 12:11.

6:7-11. The first martyrdoms. The Jews were required to participate in the festival of the pagan wine deity Dionysus. This festival typically included sensual dancing by the ivy-clad (ivy being a symbol of Dionysus), probably intoxicated, worshipers. In a preview of things to come, the epitomist provides an uncharacteristically brief, but vivid, account of the killing of two women who had circumcised their children (1 Macc 1:60). Others, who hid in a cave in order to keep the Sabbath, were burned (1 Macc 2:29-37). *Ptolemy* (v. 8) is probably the same as in 4:45-46 and 8:8.

6:12-17. Theological digression. In this brief theodicy, which can be seen as both comment on the previous atrocities (5:21-26; 6:1-11) and prologue to the upcoming stories, the epitomist again (cf. 5:17-20) explains for his readers the deeper religious meaning behind the events he describes. Contrary to those who might interpret the people's suffering as an indication that God is in some sense evil, the epitomist argues that it is, in fact, the *great kindness* of God (v. 13) that makes for the immediate and, indeed, gracious discipline of his children. Despite the severity of the sufferings, the underlying reality is that God never leaves his people (v. 16) and the final word will always be one of hope and salvation (cf. Isa 54:7-8; Ps 94:12-15).

Martyrdom of Eleazar, 6:18-31

6:18-23. The saint's refusal to give in. Here is the first of two back-to-back martyrdom stories (cf. the martyrdom of Razis in 14:37-46 and the probable allusion in 1 Macc 1:62-63) for which 2 Maccabees is most famous. The vivid description, even in this introductory and summary statement, presents the epitomist at his best. The Eleazar story, along with the martyrdom of the brothers and their mother, occupies center stage in 4 Maccabees (5:1–18:24) and is there given with greater drama, more gruesome detail, and some disagreement in particulars. That author almost certainly used our book as a source.

The present accounts of martyrdom are significant in being our earliest elaborate stories of Jewish martyrs, which stories undoubtedly provided the pattern later authors utilized. As the genre developed, martyrdom stories became very popular in Jewish and especially Christian circles.

Goldstein (1983, 282–86), who contrasts Eleazar the martyr with Mattathias the rebel (1 Macc 2:1-28), discusses the usual features of martyrdom stories: possession of characteristics (e.g., long life) signaling God's favor, willing acceptance of torture and faith to death rather than committing an act the pagans would consider trivial, dialogue between the martyr and the oppressors, graphic description of torture, record of both the anger and admiration of the persecutors, and depiction of the martyr as an example to be followed.

Given that these legends are written in the traditional type of martyr stories, what, if any, historical core lies behind them cannot be determined. Since there were certainly martyrs during this period in Jewish history, the stories can be understood, at least, as a kind of historical fiction.

Eleazar's faithfulness is total; because it might negatively influence others, he refuses even to opt for a strategy of technical adherence to the law that would save his life (vv. 21-23), a response that the rabbinic tradition later interpreted as required in such circumstances (cf. 1 Cor 8:1-13).

Beauty and long life (v. 18) were considered signs of God's blessing. Eating pork, a central prohibition in Israel's legal tradition (e.g., Lev 11:7; Deut 14:8; cf. Exod 34:15), was apparently a prominent issue in the struggle against Hellenism (cf. 7:1).

6:24-28a. The saint's speech. In a manner similar to Greek writers, the epitomist reports, or perhaps composes, the final words of Eleazar, who, like the Greek philosopher, approaches death fearlessly. On the parallels between the deaths of Eleazar and Socrates, see Goldstein (1983, 285).

There is a strong hint (v. 26) of survival after death; the doctrine of resurrection is more clearly expressed in 7:1-42.

6:28b-30. Death and final words. The *rack* was a torture device, probably some structure to which he was tied, perhaps stretched, and beaten. *Fear* is here best understood as deep reverence or awe.

6:31. An example to follow. The purpose of the story, indeed, one purpose of the book, is to encourage

readers to follow the fine examples of faithful Jews, heroes of the epitomist. *Courage* (Gk. *aretē*) is the word usually translated "virtue" in the Greek writers.

Martyrdom of the Seven Brothers and Their Mother, 7:1-42

7:1-6. First brother's death. This story of the martyrdom of the seven brothers was very popular with the early church fathers. Embedded with interesting theological ideas, the story provided Jews and Christians with an interpretation that gave meaning to the terrible violence they sometimes experienced, and, importantly, encouragement in the face of this maltreatment. On the characteristics of martyrdom legends, see comment on 6:18-23.

That there were *seven* brothers is not accidental, given the symbolic role of this number among ancient peoples. The barbaric practice of scalping (v. 4) was apparently well known. The Scythians were said also to take off the skin from the whole body and remove the nails. The Moses reference (v. 6) is to the well-known poem in Deut 32, specifically v. 36.

The prominence of Antiochus IV in the story suggests it may have originated from Antioch.

7:7-19. Death of brothers two through six. The epitomist used the accounts to inspire his readers and to communicate, through words placed in the mouths of the martyrs, religious ideas, some of which were new, or relatively new. Verses 9, 11, and 14 (see also the mother's words in 7:23) supply a clear statement of the doctrine of resurrection of the dead (cf. 6:26; 14:46). Resurrection provided hope for the suffering pious that they would be the recipients of specific, physical manifestations of justice. Just as those who perpetrated the evil would be repaid in kind (see comment on 4:30-38), so those who lost body parts would have them restored (vv. 10-11). For an excellent study of the development of resurrection and related ideas in this period, see Nicklesburg (1972).

Antiochus IV is clearly insulted with the reference to God as *King of the universe* (v. 9), and his own awful death, conveyed in 9:5-28, is here predicted (v. 17).

7:20-23. The mother's response and speech. In typical patriarchal religion, the image, role, and status of women were secondary to men in the domains of family, government, and religion. Here, however, the mother is presented as a faithful, courageous, and even shrewd martyr whose actions rival those of her sons and Eleazar. She encouraged her sons in the *language of their ancestors* (v. 21), that is, in Hebrew, not understood by the tormentors (cf. 7:27).

7:24-42. Death of the seventh son and the mother. The youngest son's speech, the longest one, sums up many of the ideas previously articulated in chap. 7. It also makes clear that Jewish suffering is a result of Jewish sin (v. 32; see comment under "Message" in the Introduction) and has the purpose of *discipline* in order to bring God and his people back into proper relationship (v. 33). None of this, however, means that their oppressor, Antiochus IV, will escape his own deserved punishment (vv. 34-36).

Since the patristic period, v. 28 has been seen as a clear expression of the idea of *creatio ex nihilo*, creation out of nothing. Some critical scholars see ambiguity in the language (*ouk ex ontōn*). In any case, if the idea is here present it is the first expression in Jewish texts and was probably borrowed, perhaps indirectly, from Greek philosophers. Although the connection is unclear, creation out of nothing, if it is found here, seems to be used to support the notion of resurrection (Goldstein 1983, 308–11).

The fact of the mother's death is stated, but without amplification. Later writers, who could not resist embellishing a brief account of her death, report that she threw herself into the fire (4 Macc 17:1), jumped off a roof (Talmud: *Gittin* 57), and died on the bodies of her sons (*Josippon* 68, ca. 953).

The epitomist's comment in v. 42 suggests he suspects that the audience's capacity for reading about such *extreme tortures* may be exhausted. For the remainder of the book he provides accounts of God's deliverance of the Jews.

God's Deliverance, 8:1–15:36

Early Victories by Judas, 8:1–36

8:1-4. Prayer for victory. The epitomist shifts the focus from graphic accounts of the behavior of Jewish traitors and the courage and death of individual faithful Jews, to the victorious struggle of Jewish resistance forces. Judas, the hero of the second half of the book, takes center stage and the wrath of the Lord turns to mercy (8:5).

In the overall structure of the book, the prayers and sacrifices recorded earlier provide the necessary backdrop for the favor of God and the victories about to be described. However, within the second half of the book, the epitomist will still periodically point to the prayers of the people. The battles constitute holy war, fought and won as an act of God.

Notice in the prayer the prominence given to the *temple* (v. 2) and the *city* (v. 3; see also v. 17).

8:5-20. Getting ready for battle. Judas's strategy of guerrilla warfare, understandable in light of being outnumbered and out equipped, is evident from the description in vv. 6-7.

Philip (v. 8), appointed by Antiochus IV as governor of Jerusalem, enlists *Ptolemy* (same as 4:45-46; 6:8; 1 Macc 3:38) to help respond to the threat. The key player for the opposition becomes the general Nicanor (v. 9; cf. 1 Macc 3:38–4:25 where Gorgias plays the major role).

Curiously, the odds against Judas are better in our account than in 1 Maccabees. The opposing army, *no fewer than twenty thousand* (v. 9), compares to the 47,000 of 1 Macc 3:39. Judas's *six thousand* (v. 17), which has perhaps been strengthened with recruits (cf. 8:1 with 8:13-14), compares to only 3,000 in 1 Macc 3:6. Ancient writers were prone to exaggerate troop numbers. On v. 13, compare 1 Macc 3:56.

Judas, the heroic mighty warrior, is also depicted in a role reminiscent of a priest (cf. Deut 20:1-9), and is able to rally his men, convincing them that with God on their side victory is certain (cf. 8:36; 11:13). Relief for the Temple and for Jerusalem (as in 8:2-3) is a major motivation for the troops (v. 17). The reference in v. 19 is to 2 Kgs 19:35 (cf. 1 Macc 4:9). In v. 20 it is unclear which war is referred to when God's army fights against the mercenary Galatians of Asia Minor.

8:21-33. Victories over the enemy. *Joseph* (v. 22, also 10:19) is called John in 1 Macc 2:1, although there may be some confusion on the number of brothers as well. In accord with the principle expressed in 1 Macc 2:29-41, the epitomist gives a religious reason for the termination of Judas's pursuit in v. 26 (cf. 12:31-32, 38; 15:1); 1 Macc 4:16-18 gives a tactical reason. In v. 28 the spoils of victory are shared with the families of the martyrs portrayed in the first half of the book. On the *watchword* (v. 23), compare 13:15, and on the *common supplication* (v. 29), see above on 8:1-4.

The account of the victories over *Timothy and Bacchides* (vv. 30-33), two generals not earlier introduced, appears inserted by the epitomist into the Nicanor account. The number of enemy forces was often exaggerated by ancient writers and the epitomist, or his source, seems especially fond of the number 20,000 (cf. 10:17, 23, 31).

8:34-36. Humiliation of the enemy. Like Androni-cus (4:38), Jason (5:7-10), and Callisthenes (8:33) earlier and Antiochus IV in the next section (chap. 9), Nicanor's evil boomerangs on him. In a final note to the account, the one who would make slaves of the Jews (making slaves of the losers in war was common) now is *like a runaway slave* (v. 35, see comment on 4:30-38). Like Heliodorus earlier (3:35-40), Nicanor is humbled before God.

Death of Antiochus IV, 9:1-29

9:1-4. Antiochus's boast. Sections 9:1-29 and 10:1-8 may have been reversed at some point in the book's history. Hints of disarrangement are the statement in 10:9 and a reversed order in 1 Macc 4:36-61 and 6:1-17. Because the present sequence follows that suggested in the prefixed letter (1:10–2:18, esp. 1:11-18), it has been suggested that the order was changed by the same hand that attached the letter.

The words attributed to Antiochus IV (v. 4b) would stir the passions of readers and heighten the tension inherent in the story.

On Antiochus IV see comment on 5:7-17. *Persepolis*, near present day Shiraz, was the capital of Persia; Ecbatana, to the northwest of Persepolis, was the capital of the old Median Kingdom. Other ancient sources name Elymais as the city of the king's attempted plunder (cf. 1 Macc 6:1-4).

9:5-11. Antiochus's illness. Ancient sources disagree over the specific illness (e.g., insanity, leprosy) which plagued Antiochus IV. The epitomist's major concerns were two. First, he wanted to point out that the evil king suffered, *justly*, in like measure to the suffering he had caused others (vv. 5-6; see comment on 4:30-38). He who had *superhuman arrogance* was *brought down to earth* (v. 8). Second, the epitomist wanted to portray graphically the king's suffering, and this he did in typically fine fashion. The Greeks also loved to depict the punishment of the mortal who contends with the gods (see citations in Goldstein 1983, 260, 353–54), and death by worms was a favorite of Greek and Jewish writers.

9:12-18. Antiochus's "conversion." This radical change of heart, to the point of wanting to *become a Jew* (v. 17), is possible, but certainly improbable. Portraying villains as having such drastic transformations in the face of God's power seems to be a theme of the epitomist (cf. Heliodorus in 3:35-40 and Nicanor in 8:34-36). Perhaps the epitomist is influenced here by the account of Nebuchadnezzar in Daniel 4:28-37.

9:19-27. The letter. The letter is presented as the king's correspondence to loyal Jewish subjects, informing them of his sickness (with no mention of God's role), applauding them for their support of his policies, and encouraging them to support his son. The letter's authenticity has been seriously questioned. It does not at all match the style of Hellenistic royal letters. It certainly does not easily fit its description as *supplication* (v. 18).

My father (v. 23) is a reference to Antiochus III who placed his son Seleucus (later designated "IV") as coregent and heir from 189–187 B.C.E.

9:28-29. Antiochus's death. In a final note, the epitomist again asserts that the evil king *endured the more intense suffering, such as he had inflicted on others* (see comment on 4:30-38). Antiochus IV died in 164 B.C.E. (cf. the account here with 1:11-17).

Purification of the Temple, 10:1-9

On the possible confusion of sequence between this section and the death of Antiochus IV (9:1-29), see the comment on 9:1-4.

Certainly the purification of the Temple is a definite high point for the epitomist. While he is remarkably restrained in his report of it, the simple brevity of the account, given everything that has gone before, is potent. On the *incense, lamps,* and *bread of the Presence* (v. 3), see Exod 25:30; 30:7-8. Later rabbinic tradition embellished the story with a legend about how the Maccabean warriors found only enough oil to light the lamps, but miraculously, the fire burned for eight days.

The epitomist's theology of sin surfaces in v. 4 with a report that the people prayed *if they should ever sin*, their *discipline* would be tempered by God's patience with his people. The point is that the trials reported in the book resulted from sin (see comment under "Message" in the Introduction).

The eight-day celebration, according to the epitomist, apparently derived from the seven day celebration of the Festival of Booths, followed by a day of solemn assembly (Num 29:12-39). On the similarity between the Festival of Booths and the Festival of Purification, compare 1:9.

Because Hanukkah was not a festival prescribed in the Bible, a new decree was needed (v. 8).

Later Victories by Judas, 10:10–13:26

To call this large section "filler" might be extreme; however, while interesting at points, it is clearly anticlimactic. In the epitomist's mind, the fundamental prize, the Temple, has been won back. It is conceivable that the epitomist is now for the most part drawing rather mechanically, and probably without careful regard for chronology, on his source (i.e., Jason) in order to complete his "history" (see 2:32; 10:10b). The thrust of these accounts is that the Maccabean warriors are an unstoppable group of soldiers, *invincible because the mighty God fought on their side* (11:13) and miraculously assisted in battle at key points by celestial fighters.

10:10-13. Antiochus V and Ptolemy Macron. Antiochus V Eupator, *son of that ungodly man* (Antiochus IV) (v. 10), reigned, beginning at nine years old, from 164–162 B.C.E. *Lysias* (v. 11), probably not actually appointed by Antiochus V (see 1 Macc 3:32-33), shows up later (11:1-15) in opposition to the Jews.

10:14-23. Victory over the Idumeans. *Gorgias* (v. 14, see 8:9) became governor following Ptolemy's suicide (10:13). *Idumeans* (v. 15) is another name for Edomites. On the number killed by Judas (v. 17), see comment on 8:21-33; a later writer, Josippon, says it was 8,000. Even at this late victorious stage in the struggle, Jewish traitors surface (vv. 20-22), and are, appropriately and swiftly, dealt with.

10:24-38. Victory over Timothy. Timothy, who is killed in this episode (v. 37), is either the first of two opponents by this name (see 12:2) or the accounts are confused. The appearance of the divine warriors to aid the Jews (vv. 29-31) is common in the epitomist (see comment on 3:24-35). On the number of enemy soldiers killed, see comment on 8:21-33.

11:1-12. Victory over Lysias. This engagement at *Beth-zur* (v. 5), twenty miles south of Jerusalem, occurred in 165 B.C.E., before the purification of the Temple, and is out of order here (cf. 1 Macc 4:26-35). Chapter 11 should probably be placed after chap. 9. On the *good angel* (v. 6) and the *horseman* (v. 8) see comment on 3:24-35.

11:13-38. Peace treaty letters. There are fairly good reasons to view these four letters as authentic. Their order, dating, and authenticity are discussed at length by Goldstein (1983, 406–28).

In the letter to the *people of the Jews* (vv. 16-21), reference to the Maccabean hero Judas is noticeably absent. The correspondence may have been targeted to a Jewish group in sympathy with a quick (premature, according to the Maccabees) ending to the war, perhaps resulting from the designs of Menelaus (see vv. 29, 32). The historical background may be one in which pious Jews who want religious freedom are distinguished from the more nationalistic Maccabean revolutionaries who want religious and political freedom (see comment on 14:6).

Brother (v. 22) is not meant literally. Antiochus IV was worshipped as deity during his lifetime and so is referred to as *gone on to the gods* (v. 23).

Menelaus (v. 29) apparently went to Antioch after the purification of the Temple and his deposition. Notice that the king still considers Menelaus a Jewish leader (v. 32). The first and third letters are dated 164 B.C.E. (vv. 21, 33).

12:1-38. Various victories by Judas. This chapter should probably come after chap. 10 (see comment on 11:1-12).

In rapid-fire succession, the epitomist sketches the amazing success of the Maccabean patriots against numerous enemies and unfavorable odds. In this holy war, they win victory *with God's help* (v. 11; cf. 13:13), *by the will of God* (v. 16), and by calling on *the Sovereign who with power shatters the might of his enemies* (v. 28; cf. v. 36b). If the numbers could be trusted, which they cannot, Judas and his holy warriors killed at least 90,000 of the enemy (vv. 19, 23, 26, 28), not counting the *untold numbers* (v. 16) who were *slaughtered* (v. 16), *massacred* (v. 6), or otherwise defeated (vv. 9, 11). The *manifestation* in v. 22 may be another instance of the divine apparition so common in the epitomist's accounts (see comment on 3:24-35). Notice how the warriors interrupt their military activity to celebrate the *festival of weeks*, also called *Pentecost* (vv. 31-32), and the *Sabbath* (v. 38; cf. 8:25-26; 15:1).

The *Toubiani* (v. 17) were Jews from Tob (Judg 11:3; 1 Macc 5:13), located just west of Bozrah and near the headwaters of River Yarmuk.

12:39-45. Burial of the dead. This section, occasioned by the epitomist's account of Judas's burying their dead, is theologically rich.

First, there is the doctrine, now familiar in 2 Maccabees, that Jewish sin brings judgment from God (see comment under "Message" in Introduction). Jewish soldiers fell because they were wearing pagan amulets, *which the law forbids* (vv. 40, 42; see Deut 7:25-26). They should know by now that sin cannot be hidden from God (v. 41; cf. 13:21).

Despite the sin of these Jews, they had fallen in service to God and this fact was sufficient to insure that they would be rewarded with resurrection (v. 45). The notion of slain Jews rising from the dead is most clearly expressed in the martyrdom stories of 6:18–7:42.

Sinners will not be resurrected; holy martyrs will (7:14). In such unambiguous cases the outcome is sure, but not so with the soldiers in question. That these Jewish soldiers (1) died in God's service and deserve resurrection and yet (2) broke the law and merit punishment constitutes a theological problem here "solved" by the notion of prayer *for the dead* (v. 44) and *atonement for the dead* (v. 45; cf. v. 43). This section is the first statement of this doctrine that came to play an important role in both Judaism and Christianity, especially in the Roman Catholic and Eastern Orthodox traditions. Whether the teaching originated with the epitomist or his source is uncertain; its use in this context is certainly understandable.

13:1-26. Victory over Antiochus V. The events in this chapter, dated 163 B.C.E. (v. 1), are reported, with variation, in 1 Macc 6:18-54. Since Antiochus V is a child (see comment on 10:10-13) the attribution of adult emotions and actions (e.g., vv. 4, 9, 18, 22) should not be read literally. Lysias, *his guardian* (v. 1), is probably the authority behind the throne.

This chapter continues to project themes found in previous accounts of military "history" (e.g., 12:1-3). Against the odds (vv. 1-2), the holy warriors, with God's help (vv. 10, 12, 13, 15, 17), win victory over the evildoers. On the *watchword* (v. 15), cf. 8:23.

The law of RETRIBUTION, now familiar in 2 Maccabees (see comment on 4:30-38), surfaces in the report of the death of Menelaus, a Jewish traitor from earlier in the book (4:23-50). Guilty of *sins against the altar*, he *met his death in ashes* (v. 8), a form of execution traced to the Persians.

The Last Great Battle, 14:1–15:36

The epitomist ends his work grandiloquently, drawing out the account of the last battle (in his account), telling the story in the dramatic, pathetic style most characteristic of the first half of the book. The themes that run through the previous accounts of Maccabean military exploits (see comments on 10:10–13:26 and 13:1-26) are also found here. The major characters are Alcimus, Nicanor, Razis, and Judas. This section is roughly paralleled in 1 Macc 7.

14:1-10. The traitor Alcimus. The date (vv. 1, 4) is apparently 161 B.C.E., during the reign of Demetrius I Soter, who was on the throne from 162–150 B.C.E. *Tripolis* (v. 1) was north of Sidon.

Alcimus is one of several Jewish traitors whose story is told in 2 Maccabees, although, unlike Jason and Menelaus (see comment on 3:4-8), his fate is never reported. Although Alcimus is mentioned in other sources (1 Maccabees, Josephus), his speech (vv. 6-10), on literary grounds, is judged a composition of the epitomist. The wicked priest Alcimus and his detestable speech provide a striking contrast to the pious Razis (14:37-46).

The Hebrew or Aramaic *Hasideans* (v. 6; cf. 1 Macc 2:42; 7:13), usually translated "pious" or "saints," refers to a group whose origins and exact purpose is unknown. Although far from certain, it is possible that they were distinguished from the Maccabees by the former's primary interest in religious freedom, as opposed to the religious *and* nationalistic concerns of the latter (cf. 11:16-21). There is evidence that the Hasideans and Maccabees were later rivals for the high priesthood. The Jewish sects of the PHARISEES and ESSENES may have their origins in the Hasideans.

14:11-25. Nicanor makes peace with Judas. *Dessau* (v. 16) is probably Adasa, six miles north of Jerusalem.

Given the ill-will and harsh fighting that has gone on before, the description of Judas agreeing to a covenant (v. 20) and settling down to marry and have children (v. 25) seems somewhat out of character. However, apparently, as we shall see, the ever cautious (v. 22) Judas was not lured into complacency by whatever pact he made. Nicanor's sincerity is questionable, especially given his later actions and (if it is the same person) the sinister motives attributed to him in 1 Macc 7:26-30.

14:26-36. Nicanor breaks the treaty. Alcimus, a villain in this story along with Nicanor, is portrayed as provoking the unfortunate developments. Judas, here shrewd and always equal to the challenge, outsmarts Nicanor. Events quickly accelerate to extreme crisis and high drama, when Nicanor swears to level the temple and institute worship of the pagan god Dionysus (v. 33). All the effort and successes recorded up to this point in the book are now at risk of being undone. Immediately, the threat is faced by the holy priests who call upon God to *keep undefiled forever this house that has been so recently purified* (v. 36).

14:37-46. Martyrdom of Razis. This story, and especially the description of Razis's suicide (vv. 41-46), rivals in theatrics and gruesome detail the martyrdom stories in 6:18–7:42. This is the epitomist at his best; while the story is not essential to its context, it serves the epitomist's purpose well. There are admonitions (in the rabbinic literature) and stories (e.g., MASADA) about pious Jews taking their own life in such threatening circumstances. Again, as in the earlier martyrdoms (6:26; 7:7-19), the certain hope of resurrection is present.

15:1-19. Preparing for battle. Nicanor was knowledgeable enough about Jewish traditions to plan an attack on the Sabbath, *a day of rest* for the Jews (v. 1, cf. 8:25-26; 12:31-32, 38). The status and motives of the *Jews who were compelled to follow him* (v. 2) are unknown. *Thrice-accursed* (v. 3) is the same title given to one named Nicanor in 8:34, although it is not certain that the same person is being referred to.

With skill and charismatic persuasion, and as he had before previous battles (see 8:16-20), Judas provides leadership that arouses the troops, this time for the final challenge reported in the book. Saving the Temple was the primary motivation for action (vv. 17-18). The *law and the prophets* (v. 9) refers to the two parts of the Hebrew Bible that were viewed as scripture at this time, the Writings having yet to be canonized. Judas's vision of Onias in the Temple (vv. 12-16) recalls the events of 3:9–4:6; the reference to the revered prophet JEREMIAH, also praying for the victory (vv. 14-15), is all the more encouraging. Whether the epitomist understands the *golden sword* (v. 15, cf. the gold instruments of war in 3:25; 5:2) literally or figuratively is less important than the point being made, which is that God is on their side.

15:20-36. The end of Nicanor. As the armies meet, Judas offers up a final prayer (cf. 1 Macc 7:40-42), recalling the well-known, greatly loved, and inspiring story of how God miraculously saved Jerusalem from the Assyrian king SENNACHERIB (v. 22; see 2 Kgs 19:35). *Elephants* (v. 20) were often used, as modern tanks, to open enemy lines.

As expected, and once again despite all odds, the holy warriors with God's help defeat the enemy and save the Temple (vv. 25-27).

Dramatically and with clear regard to the law of retribution (see comment on 4:30-38), the epitomist describes how the evil Nicanor's head and arm is cut off and displayed by the victors (vv. 28-35).

The holiday (v. 36) was eventually superseded by Hanukkah and PURIM. Perhaps Purim is called *the day before Mordecai's day* in order to parallel the accomplishment of Judas with that of MORDECAI (cf. Esth 8:9-12; 9:12, 16)

Epilogue, 15:37-39

The epitomist ends his work in fairy-tale fashion, suggesting that the hero Judas and his holy warrior patriots won Jewish independence. We learn from 1 Macc 9–13 (whose author does not view the victory over Nicanor as having the significance that the epitomist attributes to it) that the struggle continued, with Judas dying in battle and his brothers picking up the mantle.

Verse 37 strongly suggests the book was written before 63 B.C.E. when the Roman general Pompey conquered Jerusalem. *Harmful to drink wine alone* (v. 39a) refers to the routine practice of cutting strong pure wine. *Delights the ears* (v. 39b) refers to the ancient practice of hearing books read or reading aloud to oneself.

Works Cited

Doran, R. 1981. *Temple Propaganda: The Purpose and Character of 2 Maccabees*, CBQMS.

Goldstein, J. 1983. *II Maccabees*, AncB.

Nickelsburg, G. W. E. 1972. *Resurrection, Immortality, and Eternal Life in Intertestamental Judaism*.

Schunck, K. D. 1954. *Die Quellen des I. und II. Makkabäerbuches*.

First Esdras

Edd Rowell

Introduction

In modern versions the Ezra/Esdras writings include Ezra-Nehemiah in the Hebrew Bible and 1–2 Esdras among the Apocrypha. The title relates to EZRA, the priest/scribe who became a "second Moses" for his leadership in Israel's postexilic restoration, the "prophet" who restored to Israel "the books" lost during the EXILE (2 Esd 1:1; 14:37-48). "Ezra" transliterates the Heb. אֶזְרָא; "Esdras" follows the Gk. Ἔσδρας.

Place in Scripture

First Esdras appears in the LXX between Paraleipomena ("leftovers" = Chronicles) and 2 Esdras (= Ezra-Nehemiah). Early during the Christian era, the Apocrypha materials were fenced out of the Hebrew Bible, yet JOSEPHUS used 1 Esdras as a source for his *Antiquities*, and it was freely cited in the early church. Jerome called it Third Esdras and relegated it to an appendix following the NT. The Council of Trent (1546) ruled 1–2 Esdras and other works noncanonical, yet the Vulgate continued to append 1–2 (as 3–4) Esdras, "lest they perish altogether." First Esdras appears in no modern Catholic English version, however. For Orthodox churches it is deuterocanonical.

In the Bishops' Bible (1568) and through the RSV, 1 Esdras appeared in Protestant editions as first among the Apocrypha, until TEV then NRSV subdivided apocryphal and deuterocanonical books to reflect that the canonical status of these writings varies among Christians. The TEV and NRSV divisions of Apocrypha revert to a Vulgate-like order, with 1 Esdras and others in subordinate positions. In NEB and REB, 1 Esdras remains "first among Apocrypha" and between the OT and NT as in the KJV, ERV, and RSV.

The current status of 1 Esdras remains mixed. For Jews it is of course "outside," a "midrash in which the facts are warped to suit the purpose of the writer" (UJEnc). The Vulgate still appends 1 Esdras, yet for Catholics it remains noncanonical. Protestant views vary widely, from scornful dismissal to viewing 1 Esdras as almost, but never quite, canonical. At the least, 1 Esdras is a variant text by means of which to evaluate especially Ezra, if only by contrast. (Catholic scholars even note its text is sometimes better than Ezra's: see, e.g., Ezra 1:6g in NJB.)

Contents

On the surface, 1 Esdras is an alternate version of Ezra, with pieces from Chronicles and Nehemiah prefixed and appended; 3:1–5:6 is unique.

First Esdras recounts JUDAH's history from JOSIAH's reforms to the postexilic covenant renewal led by Ezra, that is, from ca. 621 to 458 or 398 (?) B.C.E. This "history" emphasizes the centrality of Torah and Temple, ZERUBBABEL's leadership, and Ezra's preeminence among the rebuilders of Jerusalem. The following synopsis shows canonical relationships.

1 Esdras	2 Chronicles, Ezra, Nehemiah
1:1-22 ‖	2 Chr 35:1-19
1:23-24 ‖	2 Chr 35:19a-d (LXX only)
1:25-58 ‖	2 Chr 35:20–36:21
2:1-15 ‖	2 Chr 36:22-23 ‖ Ezra 1:1-11
2:16-30 ‖	Ezra 4:7-24
3:1–5:6 ‖	[*Ant* 11.3.2-10]
5:7-46 ‖	Ezra 2:1-70
5:47-73 ‖	Ezra 3:1–4:5, 24
6:1–7:15 ‖	Ezra 5:1–6:22
8:1–9:36 ‖	Ezra 7:1–10:44
9:37-55 ‖	Neh 7:73–8:12

Sources, Purpose, and Date

The relationship of 1 Esdras with its canonical parallels is perplexing. Views regarding the provenance of 1 Esdras are as diverse as theories about the origin of the synoptic Gospels, and as hotly contested. Possible solutions include *at least* the following. (1) Ezra-Nehemiah and 1 Esdras are from different originals. (2) They are divergent versions of a common original. (3) Ezra-Nehemiah is an edited, expanded version of 1 Esdras. (4) First Esdras is an edited extract from Ezra-Nehemiah with additions.

Because of its abrupt beginning and sentence-fragment ending, some scholars (esp. Torrey 1945ab) conclude that 1 Esdras is only part of an original from which the beginning and ending have been lost. This may suggest the narrative was *deliberately* curtailed in order to focus on the Temple and cult from the last PASSOVER before its destruction to the restoration of Temple and cult under Ezra (Eissfeldt 1965, 575), thus emphasizing continuity between the ancient and restored Temple/cult (Attridge 1984, 160).

That Josephus used 1 Esdras in his *Antiquities* (ca. 90 C.E.) indicates *some kind* of established authority, suggesting a date generations if not centuries earlier. Text comparison suggests second-century B.C.E. Greek, and if Esdras is a translation of a Hebrew or Aramaic original, an even earlier date may be indicated.

A plausible date of composition or compilation, then, is mid-second century B.C.E., probably before 150. This date suggests that the purpose of 1 Esdras somehow served the developing Temple-centered and Torah-focused JUDAISM of the mid- to late-Hellenistic Period.

First Esdras belongs to the postexilic literary tradition of Chronicles-Ezra-Nehemiah, still conveniently labeled the "Chronicler." In common with Chronicles-Ezra-Nehemiah, 1 Esdras is interpreted history, a dramatic presentation calling postexilic Jews back to their destiny. Esdras, like Chronicles-Ezra-Nehemiah, not only recounts the past but uses that retelling for a particular present purpose. It is important then to distinguish "the past events recounted and the present occasion for recounting those events" (Bain 1990, 146).

Yet 1 Esdras remains problematic for interpretation largely because the occasion for its writing can be determined no more closely than the general period of postexilic, developing Judaism.

For Further Study

In the *Mercer Dictionary of the Bible*: APOCRYPHAL LITERATURE; CHRONICLES, FIRST AND SECOND; ESDRAS, FIRST; EZRA; EZRA, BOOK OF; EZRA, FOURTH; EZRA, FIFTH AND SIXTH; JUDAISM; NEHEMIAH; NEHEMIAH, BOOK OF.

In other sources: R. J. Coggins and M. A. Knibb, *The First and Second Books of Esdras*, CBC; J. Myers, *I & II Esdras*, AncB; E. Schuller, "1 Esdras," *WmBC*.

Commentary

An Outline

I. Cult Renewal and Disaster, 1:1-58
   A. Josiah Reinstitutes Passover, 1:1-24
   B. Josiah Dies, Judah Falls, and the Temple is Destroyed, 1:25-58
II. Return, Restoration, 2:1-7:15
   A. Cyrus Orders Rebuilding Jerusalem, 2:1-15
   B. Opposition to Rebuilding, 2:16-30
   C. Truth Triumphant, 3:1-4:63
   D. Exiles' "Second Return," and Census, 5:1-46
   E. Cult Restored but Rebuilding Postponed, 5:47-73
   F. Temple Restored, Rededicated, 6:1-7:15
III. "After these things," 8:1-9:55
   A. "To look into matters," 8:1-9:36
   B. "Ezra . . . brought the law," 9:37-55

Cult Renewal and Disaster, 1:1-58

Josiah Reinstitutes Passover, 1:1-24

Josiah's PASSOVER was the climax of his reforms sparked by the rediscovery of "the book" in the Temple (2 Kgs 22:8ff.; 2 Chr 34:14ff.). Upon reading "the book"—an early version of Deuteronomy?—Josiah vowed to "perform the words" written therein (2 Kgs 23:3; 2 Chr 34:31). Some of those words (cf. Deut 16:1-8) concerned Israel's most important annual festival—Passover, which was to be celebrated "at the place that the LORD your God will choose . . . only there" (Deut 16:6).

Second Kgs 23:21 says Josiah's Passover was according to "the book," and 1 Esdras begins with the notice that the site was *Jerusalem . . . in the temple of the Lord* (vv. 1-2), the LORD's chosen dwelling place.

Earlier, Passover had been a "pilgrim and sanctuary feast" (Joines 1990, 649) as celebrated by Joshua at

GILGAL (cf. Josh 5:10-11) in a cultic-community manner that may have carried over into the period of the judges. Passover lost some of its "pilgrim and sanctuary" emphasis until Josiah reinstituted it according to "the book." Not since Samuel (1:20) or at least the judges (2 Kgs 23:22) had it been so.

Esdras's emphasis on "the book," cult, and sanctuary, then, begins appropriately with notice of the reinstitution of Passover—"by the book" (1:6).

The piece of theodicy in 1:23-24 is not unique. In the LXX (not MT or English versions) the apology in 2 Kgs 23:24-27 also appears in 2 Chr 35, between vv. 19 and 20; 1:23-24 appears to be a variant that likewise attempts to explain why Judah suffered defeat and exile despite Josiah-led reforms: "The wickedness of the nation was so ingrained and persistent that Josiah's good deeds were insufficient to alter its headlong plunge to disaster" (Myers 1974, 28).

Josiah Dies, Judah Falls, and the Temple Is Destroyed, 1:25-58

According to the popular doctrine of RETRIBUTION, Josiah should have lived long and prospered. Likewise, Judah, in the process of national repentance and sweeping reforms, should have been victorious over gentile foes. Yet Josiah died before age forty (2 Kgs 22:1 =2 Chr 34:1), and Judah was overrun by first one foe, then another. While 1:23-24 presents a general apology for such an outcome, v. 28 offers a more specific reason for Josiah's and Judah's downfall: Josiah ignored the word of the prophet. Despite Josiah's previous righteousness, then, his going against the prophet cost him his life, thus upholding both divine retribution and the prophet's word. The lesson would not have been missed by postexilic Jews.

Succeeding Judean kings were no more than puppets of Egypt, then Babylon. The inevitable result of Judah's decline was the indiscriminate slaughter of Judeans, the looting and trashing of the Temple, and exile for the survivors. To scoff at the prophet's word (v. 51) was to court disaster.

To *keep sabbath* (v. 58) refers to the Torah requirement that even *the land* was to "observe a sabbath for the LORD" (Lev 25:1), that is, the land was to rest fallow for one year in seven. Jeremiah (25:11) prophesied that when Babylon overran Judah, the land would become for seventy years "a ruin and a waste." Both the Chronicler and Esdras apparently interpreted this as making up for sabbaths previously missed or ignored, thus also fulfilling Lev 26:34-35.

Return, Restoration, 2:1–7:15

Cyrus Orders Rebuilding Jerusalem, 2:1-15

The first year of Cyrus (2:1), 538 B.C.E., dates the decree quoted in vv. 3-7; *that the word . . . might be accomplished* relates it to prophecy fulfillment (e.g., Jer 24:6; 29:10-14). Excepting the sanctuary *vessels* inventory summary (2:13-14), this text unit is almost identical in 1 Esdras and Ezra (1:1-11). The inventory may have been to emphasize continuity between pre- and postexilic temples. The decree states that CYRUS would build *a house in Jerusalem* for Israel's God (2:4), thus explaining the exiles' return (2:5).

Opposition to Rebuilding, 2:16-30

Here 1 Esdras seemingly "stands history on its head" (Torrey 1945a, 44, 50) with events in reverse order. He mentions ARTAXERXES (465–424 B.C.E.; 2:16-30), then DARIUS (522–486 B.C.E.; 3:1–5:6), and back to Cyrus (538–530 B.C.E.; 5:7-73). Furthermore, 1 Esdras has Darius giving Zerubbabel permission to return to Jerusalem (3:1ff.), but then has Zerubbabel returning during Cyrus's reign (cf. 5:70-73). Such seeming confusion leads to charges of "chronological incompetence" (Shürer 1986, 709), a common, facile conclusion. It is all too easy to focus on problems and miss or misconstrue the intent of the text. Esdras's purpose seems obviously *not* chronological, although that recognition does not guarantee right interpretation.

The purpose for immediately referring to the opposition of some *in Samaria and other places* (v. 16) may have been simply to explain why the rebuilding was delayed until the time of Darius (2:30; 5:73–6:1).

Those in opposition were not exclusively SAMARITANS (2:16, 25). Both Ezra 4:4 and 1 Esd 5:72 refer to the opposition as the *peoples of the land* who had remained in or migrated to Judah and environs—as pointedly distinguished from exile returnees. Later, 1 Esdras reports that these *peoples of the land* asked permission to share in the rebuilding of Jerusalem, but were refused (5:68ff.). The end result was of course a permanent rift between Jews and Samaritans. Economic, political, or religious reasons for opposition to the rebuilding ostensibly explain the division between Jew and Samaritan and the Ezra-led exclusion of the *people of the land*. Whether in fact such a division occurred then and for those reasons is uncertain.

For 1 Esdras the opposition at least explained the twenty-year delay in rebuilding, and that may have been the only purpose for mentioning an exchange of letters between the resident Palestinians and the king. The king was persuaded the returnees were politically unstable, and he stopped the rebuilding program.

Truth Triumphant, 3:1–4:63

The adaptation of this apparently popular story demonstrates the midrashic character of 1 Esdras—that it is a dramatic presentation of history for a purpose. While the story appears nowhere else in the Bible, certain elements link it closely to other postexilic scriptures. Darius's banquet (3:1ff.) is very like that of Ahasuerus/Xerxes (Esth 1:1ff.; cf. Dan 5:1ff.). Darius's nervous alertness or insomnia (3:3) recalls that Ahasuerus/Xerxes also had trouble sleeping (Esth 6:1)—opportunity for a wise hero to offer help and thus win the king's favor, a story element at least as ancient as JOSEPH and PHARAOH. The *three young men* recall Daniel's friends (Dan 1:6-7; 2:17; 3:8ff.). A master storyteller, the author perhaps "baptized" this tale with such recognizable elements to make it more palatable and understandable to his audience.

(It has been observed—perhaps correctly so—that in the original form of this piece of Near East folklore "the argument in favor of women [i.e., not truth] formed the climax." So this was originally "a popular statement from a male perspective of the relationship between the sexes" [Schuller 1992, 236].)

Esdras scarcely identifies *Darius*, leaving room for much speculation, including even that he was Daniel's enigmatic "Darius the Mede" (Dan 5:31). That 1 Esdras does not specifically identify Darius rather suggests Esdras's readers would assume Darius I.

There were probably some twenty-odd *satrapies*, not 127 (3:2; cf. Esth 1:1; 8:9; Add Esth 1:1; 16:1; 120 in Dan 6:1; cf. *Ant* 10.11.4); but these twenty-odd satrapies were divided into many smaller parts, as the fifty states are divided into counties or parishes.

The king's troubled sleep (3:1) sets the stage for the contest from which a hero would emerge. Like Joseph earlier—and ESTHER, MORDECAI, and DANIEL later—Zerubbabel wins the contest with his answer to the question of *what one thing is strongest* (3:5): *truth is . . . stronger than all things* (4:33-41). (Augustine saw this as probably prophesying Christ who in the gospels is depicted as the Truth: *CivDei* 18.36.)

For his answer, Darius grants Zerubbabel, *the wisest*, whatever he wishes. Zerubbabel asks that Darius *fulfill the vow* to rebuild Jerusalem and the Temple and to return all the Temple *vessels. Vowed to the King of*

heaven with your own lips (4:46) strongly identifies with the previous Cyrus episode (2:3ff.). Indeed, a likely historical kernel is that Cyrus directed some exiles to return to Jerusalem and rebuild, and that Darius later confirmed and supported Cyrus's wishes.

Interpreters complain that Darius surely did not support Zerubbabel to the heroic extent depicted here. The point is, the exiles did return, a heroic leader did emerge, and—according to 1 Esdras—it all happened because *truth* was strongest and did prevail.

TRUTH was more than mere factual accuracy or even knowledge or understanding. Among truth's many attributes are especially firmness and dependability (4:38); but in the OT truth is essentially an attribute of God, the *will* of God. The exiles' return led by a heroic figure, the subsequent rebuilding program, and reestablishment of the cult—all this, then, is God's will, according to plan, on schedule (4:58-60).

First Esdras could have come right out and said that; that Esdras dressed the lesson in a great story probably means hearers listened better and remembered more. It is little wonder some scholars suggest 1 Esdras has survived *only* because of this story.

The most famous line from 1 Esdras is the last clause of 4:41 in its Vulgate form: "Great is truth, and it prevails." Esdras, however, did not coin this phrase: Ptahhotep (ca. 2400 B.C.E.), for example, Egyptian teacher and textbook author, wrote as his first maxim: "Truth is great and its effectiveness endures."

Exiles' "Second" Return, and Census, 5:1-46

With Darius's blessing and authorization letters in hand (4:47ff.), Zerubbabel organized a return to Jerusalem (4:61). The list of returnees is essentially the same as in Ezra 2:1-70 and Neh 7:6-73, most differences being explained as variations in translation. Nehemiah 7:5 suggests the list is from an already existing census of returnees. The core of the original list may have been a census conducted by the Persians.

Both 1 Esd 5:8 and Neh 7:7 list twelve leaders against Ezra's eleven, but all agree that Zerubbabel and Jeshua were the two main coleaders in the postexilic restoration of Jerusalem. Jeshua is named before Zerubbabel only three times (5:5, 48 || Ezra 3:2) but the parallel texts concern the restoration of the cult, thus suggesting Jeshua was, in that area at least, more prominent than Zerubbabel.

(The priest was *Jeshua* in Aramaic, *Joshua* in Heb., and *Jesus* in Gk. NRSV follows Ezra-Nehemiah in rendering the Gk. *Jesus* as *Jeshua*; TEV has *Joshua*.)

The genealogy of 5:5 is confused by the inexplicable addition of *Joakim son of* (cf. 1 Chr 3:19). TEV (cf. Torrey 1945b, 404) sees this as an error in transmission: the Greek mistranslated the Heb. ויקם בו, and perhaps should read "Joshua, son of Jozadok and grandson of Seraiah. *He was accompanied by Zerubbabel*" (TEV) or "Jeshua . . . and Zerubbabel *rose up with him*" (cf. esp. 2:8; see also NEB).

Cult Restored but Rebuilding Postponed, 5:47-73

The chronology remains a problem: in Ezra 3 this episode occurred during Cyrus's reign (ca. 538 B.C.E.) while in 1 Esdras the events are during Darius's time (ca. 520). It is possible that events of the first return (chap. 2) and the second have run together in the storyteller's mind. It is also possible Zerubbabel and Jeshua had to start from scratch following the aborted first attempt at restoration, thus explaining the repetition. At any rate, the declaration again is prominent that worship was renewed *in accordance with* Torah, God's instructions (5:49; cf. 1:6, 11).

Again, chronological confusion disrupts the text: presumably Jeshua and Zerubbabel operated during Darius's time, but in 5:55, 71, 73, the author refers this episode to Cyrus's reign. The writer seems to have his characters in the wrong time frame. Yet in 4:46 Zerubbabel petitions *Darius* to fulfill his *vow . . . vowed to the King of heaven with your own lips*. On the surface there appears to be no antecedent to this *vow*. But *the king* indeed had made such a vow in the person of Darius's predecessor Cyrus (2:1ff.), a vow the king had proclaimed and *written down* (2:2; cf. 5:55; 6:23ff.). Even during Darius's reign, Zerubbabel and Jeshua were building a house for the *Lord of Israel*, indeed *as Cyrus, the king . . . commanded* (5:71).

Such a midrashic interpretation, however, does not remove the chronological confusion, which is no less perplexing in Ezra 3:1–4:5, 24. The confusion may have resulted from efforts to telescope into a more manageable story a series of events that in fact began during Cyrus's reign (539–530) but were only resolved much later during Darius's time (522–486). Esdras's report of the work stoppage (5:66-73), for example, telescopes an event during Cyrus's reign into the time of Darius, and puts his hero Zerubbabel in the thick of it, from beginning to end. Had historical accuracy been desirable, it might have been more accurate to say Zerubbabel completed what Sheshbazzar began, as in fact 1 Esdras later points out (6:18-20).

Temple Restored, Rededicated, 6:1–7:15

With Jeshua's and Zerubbabel's continuing leadership and with the moral support of the prophets Haggai and Zechariah, the exiles resumed work on the Temple in 520/19 B.C.E. (6:1) and completed it in 516/15 (7:5). Again there was opposition to the Jewish resettlement of Jerusalem and Judah, this time from Syria. This opposition came as a diplomatic inquiry to Darius while the work continued (6:6). Darius confirmed that Cyrus had ordered the Temple rebuilt at Persia's expense and the previously removed Temple furnishings returned (6:23-26). So it was indeed in compliance with Cyrus's command that the rebuilding had begun and was continued even through the administration of more than one succeeding king.

First Esdras's epic of restoration climaxes with the same theme with which it began—the celebration of Passover/Unleavened Bread (7:10ff.; cf. 1:1ff.). Again, the book emphasizes that worship in the restored Temple was according to *the book of Moses* (7:6, 9: cf. 1:6), an emphasis that anticipates Esdras's concluding narrative regarding Ezra.

"After these things," 8:1–9:55

The rest of 1 Esdras focuses on the postexilic mission of Ezra who became for Judaism a "second Moses." Ezra's story as related here corresponds closely to parallel accounts (Ezra 7:1–10:4; Neh 7:73–8:12).

Except for 5:8, 40, Esdras ignores Nehemiah the person altogether (as 2 Macc 1:18–2:15 and Sir 49:11-13 ignore Ezra). At least that must be the conclusion if Neh 1–7 was part of a larger text from which Esdras was excerpted. Verse 9:37a—perhaps a variant of Neh 7:73a—may support the theory that 1 Esdras is an extract of Ezra-Nehemiah: that is, 1 Esdras extracted most of Ezra, then skipped Neh 1–7 and picked up with Neh 7:73. It is as reasonable, however, to suppose Neh 1–7 was inserted into the Ezra account. Nevertheless, 9:37a points up the difficulty of deciding the provenance of the Ezra/Esdras writings.

"To look into matters," 8:1–9:36

The transition from 7:15 to 8:1 seems abrupt. *After these things* may signify passage of many years, depending on which *Artaxerxes* was *king of the Persians* at the time. The obvious conclusion is that it was Artaxerxes I, ca. 465–424 B.C.E., thus dating Ezra's entry (8:6) ca. 458. This seems likely here since 1 Esdras appears to consider Cyrus, Darius, and Artaxerxes as more or less contemporaries—at least for Esdras's storytelling purposes (see esp. 7:4). But the chronology of this period is very problematical, including not only whether Ezra should be dated ca. 458 or ca. 398 but also whether Ezra or Nehemiah came first.

Yet, the transition from 7:15 to 8:1 may not be so abrupt as it seems. All that preceded in 1 Esdras—Josiah's by-the-book reforms and the postexilic restoration of both worship site and liturgy in Jerusalem—was prelude to and preparation for the Ezra-led cult and covenant renewal.

Ezra was Artaxerxes' emissary to Judah, with powers to investigate and encourage or change the theocratic structures in Judah. A significant and characteristic part of Ezra's mission was the reform he led regarding racially mixed marriages. Marrying outside one's race apparently had become accepted during the Exile, but it was not widespread if the list in 9:18-35 is actually representative. With the strict promotion of Torah—at the heart of which was a certain ethnic exclusivism—it became a serious problem for Judeans who, following the Exile, began to stress racial purity with a vengeance. Ezra's involvement (9:36) in "purifying the strain" is fitting for the "father of Judaism," and representative of his work of reestablishing the integrity of Israel's cultic life.

"Ezra . . . brought the law," 9:37-55

Ezra's reading of *the law* before the people recalls of course both Josiah the reformer (2 Kgs 23:2) and Moses the lawgiver (Exod 19:7). The implication is that the reading resulted in repentance and covenant renewal just as had occurred during Josiah's time and originally with Moses (Exod 19:8ff.). The mission of Ezra, then, results in racial, cultic, and covenant renewal all in accordance with *the law of Moses*, which was reintroduced to Israel by Ezra *the priest and reader of the law* (8:9).

The last phrase of 1 Esdras—*and they came together*—is routinely considered a sentence fragment (see Neh 8:13) indicating some text has been lost. This suggests that 1 Esdras originally continued with at least an account of the celebration of Booths (=Tabernacles), as also related in Neh 8:13ff. The case is thus made that the rest of the 1 Esdras scroll beyond 9:55c has been lost. Another possibility of course is that 1 Esdras is complete and Neh 8:13ff. is an expansion of the original. Following KJV and ERV, for example, Goodspeed's translation of 1 Esdras concludes:

And they went off to eat and drink and enjoy themselves, and to give portions to those who had none, and to hold a great celebration, for they had been inspired by the words which they had been taught, *and for which they had come together* (1 Esdras 9:54-55 AT).

Works Cited

Douglas Bain. 1990. "Chronicles, First and Second." MDB.

Harold W. Attridge. 1984. "Historiography: 1 Esdras," *Jewish Writings of the Second Temple Period*, ed. Michael E. Stone, 157–60.

Otto Eissfeldt. 1965. *The O.T. An Introduction.*

Karen R. Joines. 1990. "Passover." MDB.

Jacob M. Myers. 1974. *I & II Esdras.* AncB.

Eileen M. Schuller. 1992. "The Apocrypha. 1 Esdras." *The Women's Bible Commentary (WmBC)*, ed. Carol A. Newsom and Sharon H. Ringe, 236.

Emil Schürer. 1986. *The History of the Jewish People in the Age of Jesus Christ.* Rev. ed.

Charles C. Torrey. 1945a. *The Apocryphal Literature. A Brief Introduction.* 1945b. "A Revised View of First Esdras," *Ginzberg Jubilee Volume*, 395–410.

Prayer of Manasseh

Joseph L. Trafton

Introduction

One of the most beautiful pieces in all APOCRYPHAL LITERATURE, the Prayer of Manasseh is a short prayer of confession for individual sin reminiscent of Ps 51, which the author undoubtedly knew well. Probably composed to fill the gap left by the reference to Manasseh's prayer in 2 Chr 33:18-19, it is a powerful expression of trust in the forgiving mercy of God and in the efficacy of heartfelt REPENTANCE.

Authorship

The prayer is attributed to MANASSEH, who ruled JUDAH for fifty-five years from ca. 687–642 B.C.E. The writer of 2 Kings viewed Manasseh's reign as wicked beyond measure (2 Kgs 21:1-18). The Chronicler, however, noted that while captive to the Assyrians in Babylon, Manasseh prayed a prayer of repentance to God, who restored Manasseh to his kingship (2 Chr 33:11-13). The Chronicler noted further that Manasseh's prayer was recorded in the "Chronicles of the Seers" (2 Chr 33:19), a document that is now lost. There is no reason to believe that the Prayer of Manasseh comes from the hand of Manasseh himself. An unknown Jew probably composed the Prayer of Manasseh to replace the lost prayer. Whether the original language was Hebrew (or Aramaic) or Greek is uncertain. It is extant in Greek, Syriac, and Latin.

Date

The Prayer of Manasseh was probably composed prior to the destruction of Jerusalem in 70 C.E.

Influence

Although a beautiful example of Jewish piety at the turn of the era, the Prayer of Manasseh has had its greatest impact not upon JUDAISM, but upon Christianity. Two early Christian books of ecclesiastical instruction, the *Didascalia* (third century) and the *Apostolic Constitutions* (fourth century), contain it. A number of early biblical manuscripts, including Codex Alexandrinus (fifth century), place it among the odes, or liturgical canticles. Eventually the Greek Orthodox Church received the prayer as canonical, and the Roman Catholic Church placed it in an appendix following the NT. Most early Protestant translations of the Bible included the prayer in the Apocrypha, and one, the widely used Geneva Bible, even placed it between 2 Chronicles and Ezra, with the label "apocryphe."

For Further Study

In the *Mercer Dictionary of the Bible*: APOCRYPHAL LITERATURE; JUDAISM; MANASSEH; MANASSEH, PRAYER OF; REPENTANCE.
In other sources: J. H. Charlesworth, "Prayer of Manasseh," *OTP*; D. J. Harrington, "Prayer of Manasseh," HBC; R. K. Harrison, *Introduction to the Old Testament*; B. M. Metzger, *An Introduction to the Apocrypha*; H. E. Ryle, "The Prayer of Manasses," *APOT*; C. C. Torrey, *The Apocryphal Literature: A Brief Introduction*; G. Vermes and M. Goodman, "The Prayer of Manasseh," *The History of the Jewish People in the Age of Jesus Christ*, ed. E. Schürer, rev. and ed. G. Vermes, F. Millar, and M. Goodman, 3/2:730–33; A. Wikgren, "Manasseh, Prayer of," IDB.

Commentary

An Outline

I. Invocation of Praise to God, 1-7
   A. God of the Ancestors, 1
   B. God of Creation, 2-5
   C. God of Mercy, 6-7
II. Confession of Sin, 8-10
   A. Acknowledgment of Sin, 8-9a
   B. Effect of Sin, 9b-10
III. Prayer for Forgiveness, 11-15
   A. Expression of Humility, 11
   B. Entreaty to God, 12-13
   C. Expression of Confidence in God's Mercy, 14-15a
   D. Concluding Doxology, 15b

Invocation of Praise to God, 1-7

Manasseh begins by invoking God as God of the ancestors (v. 1), of creation (vv. 2-5), and of mercy (vv. 6-7).

God of the Ancestors, 1

The OT representation of God as God *of Abraham and Isaac and Jacob* (Exod 3:15-16; 4:5; 1 Chr 29:18; cf. Acts 3:13) highlights the historic roots of God's covenantal relationship with Israel. The addition *and of their righteous offspring* anticipates the sharp contrast the author will develop in v. 8 between the righteous and sinners.

God of Creation, 2-5

Manasseh follows an allusion to Gen 1 with a traditional concern for God's shackling of *the sea*, specifically *the deep* (cf. Job 38:8-11; Ps 104:6-9), which was often viewed as the home of God's enemies (Ps 74:13-14; Isa 51:9-10; cf. Rev 9:1-11; 11:7; 17:8). This depiction of God's power sets the stage for the introduction of *sinners*, who can scarcely stand up to God's *wrath*.

God of Mercy, 6-7

Yet alongside of God's wrath is his *immeasurable* and *unsearchable mercy*, which the author sets forth in classic OT terms (Exod 34:6; Ps 103:8; 145:8-9; Joel 2:13; Jonah 4:2). In v. 7b, missing from the early Greek mss. but probably part of the original prayer, Manasseh affirms that one aspect of God's mercy is the provision that *sinners* might repent and *be saved* (cf. TGad 5:7).

Confession of Sin, 8-10

The affirmation in v. 7b provides the basis for the confidence that enables Manasseh to offer his own confession. He acknowledges both the multitude of his sins (vv. 8-9a) and their effect upon him (v. 10).

Acknowledgment of Sin, 8-9a

Manasseh highlights his own need for repentance by first acknowledging that *the righteous* do not need to repent (cf. Luke 5:32; 15:7). The mention of *Abraham and Isaac and Jacob* (cf. v. 1) as not having sinned *against you*, although striking in itself, furthers the dichotomy between the *God of the righteous* and his own, on the one hand, and Manasseh, as a representative *sinner*, on the other. Indeed, Manasseh reckons his *sins* as beyond measure (cf. 1 Tim 1:15)

Effect of Sin, 9b-10

Manasseh focuses on the humbling effect of his *sins*: he acknowledges that he is *not worthy* (cf. Luke 15:19, 21) *to look up and see* (cf. Luke 18:13) *the height of heaven*—i.e., God (cf. Isa 38:14; Ps 123:1). His general confession that he has *done what is evil in your sight* (cf. Ps 51:4) is bracketed by allusions to his being *weighted down with many an iron fetter*—i.e., being led away in chains by the Assyrians (cf. 2 Chr 33:11), provoking God's *wrath* (cf. 2 Chr 33:6), and *setting up abominations*—i.e., idols (cf. 2 Chr 33:3-5, 7; 2 Kgs 21:3-5, 7).

Prayer for Forgiveness, 11-15

Manasseh's confession of his sin prepares the way for the emotional and literary climax of the document: the prayer for forgiveness. After a beautifully picturesque expression of humility (v. 11), Manasseh entreats God for forgiveness (vv. 12-13) and expresses confidence in God's mercy (vv. 14-15a).

Expression of Humility, 11

Manasseh boldly combines two images for worship (*I bend the knee*) and sincerity (*of my heart*; cf. Joel 2:13; Rom 2:29) in seeking God's *kindness*.

Entreaty to God, 12-13

Bluntly acknowledging his sin (cf. Ps 51:3-4), Manasseh asks for forgiveness and the diversion of God's wrath (cf. 5; Ps 51:9; Luke 18:13). He recognizes that the *God of the righteous* (v. 8) is also *the God of those who repent. The depths of the earth* is not so much a place of torment as a place of isolation—i.e., the farthest point from God (cf. Ps 88:4-6; Isa 44:23; Eph 4:9).

Expression of Confidence in God's Mercy, 14-15a

Manasseh expresses his confidence that the God who has appointed repentance for sinners (cf. v. 7b) will indeed act in accordance with his *great mercy*. In response, Manasseh will *praise* God *continually* (cf. Ps 51:15). According to 2 Chr 33:15-17, Manasseh, following God's reinstatement of him as king, removed the foreign gods from Jerusalem and restored the worship of the God of Israel.

Concluding Doxology, 15b

The prayer concludes with an affirmation of the eternal *glory* of God, who is praised by *all the host of heaven* (cf. 2 Chr 18:18; Luke 2:13; Rev 4–5).

Psalm 151

Joseph L. Trafton

Introduction

While the traditional Hebrew OT Psalter is numbered at 150 psalms, most manuscripts of the LXX contain an additional psalm that is designated in a superscription as falling "outside the number" (i.e., of 150). This psalm, which is attributed to DAVID and narrated in the first person, is called Psalm 151. Through a brief recounting of David's anointing by SAMUEL and subsequent victory over Goliath, the psalm celebrates what God has accomplished through the one who, although *small among my brothers* (v. 1a), *took away disgrace from the people of Israel* (v. 7b).

Composition

Psalm 151 is choppy and, in places, difficult to understand. Particularly confusing is the narrator's question and answer in 3. The discovery of a DEAD SEA SCROLLS psalter (11QPsᵃ) in 1956 shed important light on the compositional history of Psalm 151. The Qumran Psalms Scroll contains forty psalms from the traditional Hebrew Psalter as well as eight noncanonical psalms. One of these additional psalms (151A) is apparently a longer version of Ps 151:1-5, while Ps 151:6-7 is similar to the beginning of a *second* psalm (151B), most of which is lost. Thus, Psalm 151 seems to be a conflation and condensation of two Hebrew psalms. The commentary below will focus on the Greek Psalm 151, both in its present form and as the end result of an editing process.

Date

Psalms 151A and 151B were probably composed no later than the third century B.C.E. Sometime before the third century C.E. an editor combined these two psalms into the Greek Psalm 151.

Authorship

The ascription of psalms to David is common in Jewish literature. The superscriptions of seventy-three of the 150 psalms in the Hebrew OT attribute those psalms to David. The Qumran Psalms Scroll contains a prose supplement that numbers David's compositions at 4,050–3,600 psalms and 450 songs. There is no reason to believe that David actually wrote either Psalm 151A or Psalm 151B. The writer who edited them into Psalm 151 is unknown.

Influence

Psalm 151 is found in a number of ancient versions of the Bible. In particular, some Syriac manuscripts contain five extra psalms, the first corresponding to Psalm 151 and the others numbered as Psalms 152 to 155. Although neither Protestants nor Roman Catholics view Psalm 151 as canonical, both the Greek Orthodox Church and the Russian Orthodox Church accept it as authoritative.

For Further Study

In the *Mercer Dictionary of the Bible*: ANOINT; APOCRYPHAL LITERATURE; DAVID; PSALMS, APOCRYPHAL.
In other sources: J. H. Charlesworth and J. A. Sanders, "Psalm 151," *OTP* 2:612–15; D. J. Harrington, "Psalm 151," HBC; J. A. Sanders, *The Dead Sea Psalms Scroll*; G. Vermes, "Apocryphal Psalms," *The History of the Jewish People in the Age of Jesus Christ*, ed. E. Schürer, rev. and ed. G. Vermes, F. Millar, and M. Goodman, 3.1:188–92.

Commentary

An Outline

> I. God's Choice of David, 1-5
> II. David's Victory over the Philistine, 6-7

God's Choice of David, 1-5

The psalm begins with a brief, first-person account of DAVID's selection and anointing by SAMUEL (1 Sam 16:1-13). The author includes the following elements from the OT narrative: David as the *youngest* of the *brothers* (v. 1; 1 Sam 16:11; cf. 17:14), his task of tending his *father's sheep* (vv. 1, 4; 1 Sam 16:11), his being taken *from* the *sheep* (v. 4; 1 Sam 16:11-12; cf. Ps 78:70-71) and *anointed* by the Lord's *messenger* (v. 4; 1 Sam 16:13; cf. Ps 89:20), and the Lord's displeasure with his *brothers* despite their outward appearance (v. 5; 1 Sam 16:7-10). There is also a mention of David's musical abilities (v. 2; cf. 1 Sam 16:18, 23).

One of the Syriac manuscripts includes in 1 a reference to David's killing of a lion and a wolf (cf. 1 Sam 17:34-37), but this is probably a secondary addition under the influence of Psalms 152 and 153 (the fourth and fifth apocryphal Syriac psalms). The author departs from the OT story by adding a rather obscure question in v. 3a: *And who will tell my Lord?* The answer, given in v. 3b, is that *the Lord . . . hears*, and what he hears presumably includes David, who with his musical gifts has composed this psalm. Verse 3 then seems to justify the composition of this psalm: it is a psalm glorifying God for what God has accomplished through David.

More important are the Greek alterations of the original Hebrew psalm. In v. 1c the editor has combined two lines concerning David's role as *shepherd*, thus destroying the synonymous parallelism in the Hebrew. In addition, the Greek has omitted from v. 2 two lines that make explicit David's intention in using his musical gifts to give *glory* to God.

The editor has left out four more lines (151A: v. 3) that state that the "mountains [and] hills do not witness to" God, but David does. The difficult question and answer in 3 in the Greek is actually a condensation of four lines into two. The Hebrew (151A: v. 4) is more clear:

> Who can proclaim and who can bespeak
> and who can recount the deeds of the Lord?

The answer:

> Everything has God seen
> everything has he heard and he has heeded,
> (including, apparently) the trees and the flock,
> which have elevated David's "words" and "works."
> (151A: v. 3cd, author trans.)

In v. 4a the Greek uses one line to speak of the coming of God's *messenger*, thereby condensing two lines in the Hebrew (151A: v. 5ab), which name "Samuel," God's "prophet." The editor further has abbreviated the description of David's brothers from four lines (151A: vv. 5cd-6ab) down to one (v. 5a) and has changed God's response from not choosing them (151A: v. 6c) to not being pleased with them (v. 5b).

Finally, the Greek has altered the end of the psalm. The Hebrew closes with two lines about Samuel calling and anointing David (151A: v. 7ab) and two lines specifying the significance of this event (151A: v. 7cd). The editor has placed the first pair *before* the description of the brothers and has omitted the second pair altogether. The Hebrew builds to a powerful and ironic climax: the one who was "smaller than my brothers" (151A: v. 1a) becomes "ruler over the people of his covenant" (151A: v. 7d). The Greek leaves the reader to infer the significance of David's having been *anointed* with *oil* (v. 4b) and ends the entire section with a negative comment about David's *brothers* (v. 5a).

David's Victory over the Philistine, 6-7

The editor moves from David's anointing by Samuel to a very brief account of his defeat of Goliath (1 Sam 17:4-51). He neither mentions Goliath by name (although Goliath is named in the superscription) nor calls him a Philistine (so the Heb.: 151B: v. 1). He simply labels him "the foreigner" (v. 6, author trans.; *contra* NRSV), perhaps to make the psalm more generally applicable at the time when it was edited. From the OT narrative the author includes Goliath's cursing of David *by his idols* (v. 6; 1 Sam 17:43: *gods*) and David's taking of Goliath's *sword* and beheading him (v. 7; 1 Sam 17:51). Strikingly absent is any mention of David's slaying of the giant with a sling, although some of the later versions (e.g., Old Latin, Arabic, Ethiopic) include this part of the story. The psalm ends on the note that through his defeat of the foreigner David *took away disgrace from the people of Israel* (v. 7b).

Third Maccabees

Edd Rowell

Introduction

Third Maccabees seems to have nothing to do with the MACCABEES. It opens with the Battle of Raphia (217 B.C.E.), fifty years before the Maccabean Revolt, and almost immediately leaves Palestine to focus exclusively on pre-Maccabean events in Egypt. Yet language, style, and even specific episodes are similar in 2 and 3 Maccabees. These books also share a common theme—persecution of or severe attempts to "Hellenize" the Jews, and their eventual vindication.

Since the main protagonist is the Egyptian ruler Ptolemy IV Philopator (r. 221–203 B.C.E.), 3 Maccabees might more aptly be entitled "Ptolemaica." Indeed, a reference by Pseudo-Athanasius can be read as "the Maccabean books and [the] Ptolemaica," and Byzantine historian George Syncellus suggested that 3 Maccabees and the *Letter of Aristeas* were together called "Ptolemaica" (see Schürer 1986, 3.1.540–41). Yet both Pseudo-Athanasius and Syncellus were late (eighth–ninth century C.E.), and may represent only belated efforts to "correct" the 3 Maccabees "misnomer."

Third Maccabees has been characterized as a "romance" or "romantic fiction" (Schürer 1986, 537), a "historical novel with a religious message" (Collins 1993, 1753), or "pathetic history" in the classical Greek tradition (Nickelsburg 1984, 80). It also has been designated as a "festival legend" (Eissfeldt 1965, 582), an etiological tale depicting the origins of a religious festival (see 6:36). The ambiguity of its origins precludes any certainty regarding the circumstances that motivated its author(s). Third Maccabees is preserved for us in the so-called "longer canon," however, not because of its romantic, etiological, or historical contribution, but because of its theological ideas.

Origin, Source, Date

Third Maccabees interprets history theologically. A main idea is that God's purposes are being worked out in history. Among several subthemes are God's choice of the Jews (a *holy people*, 2:6), the ultimate authority of Torah (*the law of God*, 7:10, 12), and the God-ordained and exclusive sanctity of the Temple (with the Temple-centered cult; cf. 2:9, 16).

The text itself (e.g., 4:21) suggests that the immediate specific purpose of 3 Maccabees was to respond to some attack on the integrity of God's chosen people— the Jews—in the context of ongoing attempts to Hellenize (or Romanize) the Jews, to make them loyal subjects of the culture and government then in power. (Such a culture-change of course would require the Jews to compromise their calling to be God's peculiar people, and thus to desert their ethnic, cultural, and religious exclusiveness.) Whatever the specific historical event that prompted its writing, the lesson of 3 Maccabees' theological reading of previous history would have been clear: "God remains faithful to his chosen people, to bless and preserve them throughout the vicissitudes of their experiences" (Constantelos 1991, AP285, and see AP292, 4:21n).

While 3 Maccabees is interpreted history, it does not follow that it disregards facts. The episodes that structure the story of 3 Maccabees are historical. The Battle of Raphia was one of several encounters between the Ptolemies of Egypt and the Seleucids of Syria. The portrayal of Philopator as a sometime jealous enemy, sometime reluctant friend of the Jews fits the known facts. The depiction of the prejudicial treatment of diaspora Jews in Ptolemaic Egypt is accurate, although some events mentioned probably did not occur during Philopator's reign. The author apparently collected several pieces of historical tradition that together make an impressive story to support the idea that, in general, God is working out his purposes in history and that, specifically, God will do for his chosen people as well in the future as in the past.

It is evident that 3 Maccabees was written long after Philopator. Third Macc 6:6, for example, reflects a knowledge not just of DANIEL but of later Greek additions (cf. PrAzar 23-27). Close similarities of language and style with 2 Maccabees and the *Letter of Aristeas* suggest it originated no earlier than very late second century B.C.E. The possibility that 3 Maccabees was familiar with LXX ESTHER would date it well into the first century B.C.E.

Other considerations help date 3 Maccabees. It likely was written in Greek by an Alexandrian Jew, and was addressed primarily to Alexandrian Jews. What precipitated 3 Maccabees, then, may have been a specific chain of events affecting Jews in Alexandria. (Philo estimated that, by the first century C.E., one million of the world's almost eight million Jews lived in Egypt, mostly in Alexandria and Cyrene. Philo's numbers may be inflated, but there was a substantial colony of Jews in Egypt, noticeable by their very numbers and thus vulnerable to discrimination by Egyptian nationals.)

A possible clue regarding the time frame is the rare word in 2:28 (*laographia*, *registration*), especially since it may be defined as *a registration involving poll tax* (2:28). A poll tax was reinstituted in 24 B.C.E. by Augustus when Egypt became a Roman province. Yet the Romans were generally tolerant toward Jews, probably at first because the Jews had favored Julius Caesar over Pompey in the civil war (48 B.C.E.). Augustus (r. 31 B.C.E.–14 C.E.) favored the Jews in many ways, exempting them from taxation during sabbatical years and allowing them wide latitude in local affairs, allowances not generally granted other "foreigners." Augustus even permitted diaspora Jews to send money to support the Temple in Jerusalem. Claudius (r. 41–54 C.E.) later intervened on behalf of diaspora Jews, especially in Alexandria, when their civil rights and personal safety were threatened by nationals.

A glaring Roman exception was Caligula (r. 37–41 C.E.), the demented emperor who delighted in torture, who elevated his favorite horse to the office of consul, and who seemed to regard claims of his divinity with utmost seriousness.

In 37–38 C.E., in Alexandria, perhaps encouraged by Caligula's friend AGRIPPA I who was visiting from Palestine, an anti-Jewish faction complained to Caligula that the "foreigner" Jews had refused to place images of the emperor in their synagogues. They demanded that Jewish rights be revoked. The situation is like that described in 3 Macc 2, where *registration* (e.g., vv. 28-30, determining citizen status, assessing

for taxes) and the state religion are prominent elements. One clear implication of 3 Macc 2 is that Jews enjoyed some kind of special status even in a land where they were immigrants. That special status was in jeopardy. The Jews were accused of disloyalty because they ignored the state religion. In order to maintain citizenship status, the Jews had to adopt the state religion—in effect, they had to cease to be Jews.

The parallels are obvious between the attack on Alexandrian Jews in Caligula's time and the earlier episode in Ptolemaic Egypt as related in 3 Maccabees. Philopator, who fancied himself descended from Dionysus, aptly represents the divine pretender Caligula, with no need for caricature either way. An important parallel regards the question of citizenship: Would the Jews be allowed to remain Jews, or must they, to survive, participate in the state religion?

There had been small enclaves of Jews in Egypt for centuries, but during his Palestine campaigns Ptolemy I Soter (r. 323–285 B.C.E.) had resettled thousands of captive Jews in Egypt. The Jewish community enjoyed a degree of self-government though they were never full citizens, ostensibly because they would not participate in the state religion. There were tensions between these "foreigners," their Greek neighbors, and the Egyptian nationals, tensions that from time to time worsened for one reason or another. Philopator's attempt to enter the Temple, followed by his jealous attacks on the Jews, was one memorable episode.

Then, under Rome and Caligula another crisis occurred, reminding at least one Alexandrian Jew of certain episodes of recent history. This poet-novelist-prophet then wove together several stories of recent memory to demonstrate that even in such a critical present time his fellow Jews could and should remain confident: this too would pass and God's people would emerge intact.

That some such scenario explains the provenance of 3 Maccabees is strongly supported by another parallel that ties together not only Caligula and the Ptolemies but also Caligula and the Maccabees.

Upon hearing that they refused to install his image in their places of worship, Caligula severely attacked the Jews of Alexandria. Such refusals in other places prompted Caligula to issue an imperial decree that his image be installed in the Jerusalem Temple itself (*Ant* 18.8.2; *BJ* 2.10.1-5). This abomination never occurred because the order was successfully avoided by Agrippa in Jerusalem until Caligula, a sick and mad old man at age twenty-nine, was assassinated by his own guards.

Antiochus IV Epiphanes had installed a cultic image and altar in the Temple, and commanded the Jews to worship him there (167 B.C.E.). The parallel with Caligula's attempt to desecrate the Temple is obvious. The connection with Philopator's earlier attempt to violate the Temple with his profane presence would be apparent to an Alexandrian Jew. The episode was part of Jewish tradition. Antiochus's "abomination that desolates" (Dan 11:31; 12:11) was the single focal event, the flash point, that precipitated the Maccabean Revolt.

It is quite possible, then, that the experience of the Egyptian Jews during the infamous reign of Caligula explains why and for whom 3 Maccabees was written as well as why it was given its name.

Place in Scripture

Third Maccabees originally appeared in some LXX manuscripts, and later was included in editions of the Peshitta (Syriac) and in most Armenian versions. Since it was composed as late as the first century C.E., it was probably never related to the Hebrew Bible; hence it is absent from the Vulgate.

The Peshitta and Armenian versions belong to what became the Eastern Orthodox division of the church while the Vulgate relates to the Western church. Since earliest times, then, 3 Maccabees has been among the scriptures of the Eastern church (although only deuterocanonical) but has always been outside the Catholic canon. Hence Protestant Bibles—which follow the Western tradition—exclude 3 Maccabees. (The Catholic Church assigns 3 Maccabees to OT Apocrypha; Protestants generally relegate 3 Maccabees to the so-called Pseudepigrapha.)

Third Maccabees did not appear in English versions until the expanded edition of RSV (1977). It was then included in NRSV (1990/1991), but appears in no other English version; otherwise it occurs only in collections of extracanonical texts such as APOT and OTP. Consequently, 3 Maccabees remains little known among Western Bible students. Even among the Eastern Orthodox, 3 Maccabees is rarely mentioned. The book has had little influence, religious or otherwise.

Given its lesser canonical status, 3 Maccabees may be little regarded. Yet it helps develop a portrait of the postexilic JUDAISM from which rabbinic Judaism emerged and that was the background—if not the matrix—from which Christianity emerged.

Contents

Third Maccabees has been dismissed as "a fantastic novel [that] can make very little claim to literature, [whose style] is mouthy and declamatory [and whose plot] is artificial and forced" (NCE 1967, 397a). Indeed, the style is bombastic (Eissfeldt 1964, 582) and "abounds in rhetorical repetitions and exaggerations" (Anderson 1985, 510). This, however, only supports the conclusion that 3 Maccabees is a historical novel/romance in the classical Greek style.

The *New Oxford Annotated Bible* (NRSV) rightly observes that 3 Maccabees is composed according to the familiar principles of concentric parallelism (see outline, below). The story moves purposefully from Ptolemy's threat against the very essence of Jewishness (Law-Temple-Cult) to his eventual defense of the Jews. The climax is the threat against the Jews and their Jewishness posed by the "registration," which the Jews could survive only by ceasing to be Jews.

The main lesson of 3 Maccabees is succinctly stated in 4:21: God acts in history on behalf of the Jews (cf. 2:21; 6:29; 7:22).

For Further Study

In the *Mercer Dictionary of the Bible*: APOCRYPHAL LITERATURE; HELLENISTIC WORLD; MACCABEES; MACCABEES, FIRST; MACCABEES, SECOND; MACCABEES, THIRD.
In other sources: H. Anderson, "3 Maccabees," OTP; M. Hadas, *The Third and Fourth Books of Maccabees*; G. W. E. Nickelsburg, "3 Maccabees," *Jewish Literature between the Bible and Mishnah*.

Commentary

An Outline

A   Ptolemy Threatens the Jewish "Holy Place," 1:1-29
B   Simon Intercedes; God Intervenes, 2:1-24
C   Philopator Seeks Vengeance on the Jews, 2:25–4:15
D   God Intervenes and Thwarts
    Philopator's Pogrom, 4:16-21
C' Philopator Renews Efforts to Destroy the Jews, 5:1-51
B' Eleazar Intercedes; God Intervenes, 6:1-29
A' Philopator Restores the Jews;
    the Jews Celebrate, 6:30–7:23

Ptolemy Threatens
the Jewish "Holy Place," 1:1-29

1:1-7. Battle of Raphia. The abruptness with which 3 Maccabees begins suggests something is missing (see also on 2:25). But if so, how much and whether by accident or design is now impossible to tell.

At the Battle of Raphia, Philopator defeats Antiochus III (r. 223–187 B.C.E.) to regain Palestinian territories. This was only one among many battles over these border and trade-route territories. Here, Raphia places Philopator at the Palestinian border whence he may conveniently call on his Jewish *subjects* in their capital, Jerusalem.

1:8-29. Ptolemy presumptuously invades the Temple. Following his victory at Raphia, a Jewish delegation visits Philopator, perhaps to acknowledge his restored rule and to pay tribute. Philopator reciprocates with a visit to Jerusalem, where he pays homage to the God of his subjects at their Temple, as perhaps ALEXANDER had done (*Ant.* 11.8.5). Entering the outer courts, Philopator is impressed with the architecture and furnishings, and intrigued by restrictions regarding entrance to the inner spaces of the Temple. Either curiosity or assertiveness and then imperial arrogance (vv. 13-15) prompts him to attempt to enter *the sanctuary* (v. 10; KJV, "the most holy place"; Gk. and RSV, "holy of holies"; see Heb 9:3).

Supreme God (v. 9; Gk. "the greatest god") as an appellation for God occurs in 1:9, 16; 3:11; 4:16; 5:24; 7:22; and in 2 Macc 3:36. Compare the fairly common Greek epithet for the gods *megasthenēs*, "of great strength," and the Hebrew *el elyon*, "god most high" or simply "most high."

The place (vv. 9, 23) and *the holy place* (2:14; NRSV has added *holy* in vv. 9, 23) stand here as elsewhere in the OT (see Lev 6, 16) for "the Temple," not just the inner court.

Sanctuary (see above) here (v. 10) is the "inner sanctuary [or] most holy place" (1 Kgs 6:16) as also in 2:1, 18, and often in 2 Maccabees (see esp. 15:17).

Philopater's attempt *to enter the sanctuary* (v. 10) parallels Heliodorus's attempt to invade the Temple treasury (2 Macc 3; "Apollonius" in 4 Macc 3–4), especially as regards the reaction of the priests and the *young women* (v. 18; 2 Macc 3:19). Some Jews determine to *take arms and die* (v. 23) for the law that proscribed entrance to the sanctuary (cf. Mattathias's resolve to defend the sanctuary against violation: 1 Macc 2:19-28; see also 3:21 and cf. 2 Macc 8:21).

Philopator's attempt *to enter the sanctuary* (v. 10) is an attack on the very core of their existence, and the Jews are terrified of the destruction such an invasion would portend. Their genuine terror—which modern readers superficially might relegate to primitive superstition—is a critical dramatic element.

Simon Intercedes; God Intervenes, 2:1-24

Finally, *the high priest* (Simon II, ca. 219–196) prays, asking God, not directly to stop Philopator, but not to punish the Jews for Philopator's transgression. The prayer is in classic postexilic Jewish form with a rehearsal of God's attributes and the history of salvation followed by confession and a plea for mercy (see Ezra's prayer in Ezra 9:6-15 and Neh 9:6-37). It was a *lawful supplication* (v. 21), that is, "by the book."

God was bound to hear a proper prayer, so God *scourged* Philopator till he lay in a *paralyzed* heap (vv. 21-22). But Philopator recovers; he has not committed a capital offense, but only threatened to do so. Philopator remains unrepentant and vengeful toward the Jews, however, like PHARAOH of the hardened heart.

Philopator Seeks Vengeance
on the Jews, 2:25–4:15

2:25-33. Philopator orders a registration. Still smarting from his rebuff at the Temple, Philopator seeks revenge on the Jews in Egypt. Jewish resistance and his own growing anger intensifies Philopator's aims from mere *public disgrace* (2:27) to a full-fledged pogrom of *shameful death* (3:25).

At first Philopator's was an in-kind revenge: he had been shamed by the Jews; now he would publicly disgrace the Jews by reducing them to the status of serfs.

Verse 28 in NRSV is confused. We may read: "Those who do not worship *our* gods cannot worship *their* god; and all these Jews must be registered (by the state) and will be reduced to the status of slaves" (cf. Hadas 1953, APOT, and OTP).

The implication is that Egyptian Jews heretofore had been at least to some extent exempted from Egyptian registration (regular tax assessment?), perhaps in deference to their own registration (Exod. 30:11-16).

Much discussion has centered on the word *laographia* (*registration*) in v. 28, which occurs only here in scripture. The usual word for "registration" is *apographé*, as here (vv. 29, 32; 4:14-15, 17 [*census*]; 6:34, 38; 7:22) and in the NT (Luke 2:1, 2, 3, 5; Acts 5:37); indeed, this is the usual word in the Egyptian papyri and for the Roman "registration." The occurrence of *laographia* in v. 28 appears to be an aberration, especially since the usual *apographia* occurs immediately (v. 29) and exclusively thereafter. To decide questions regarding 3 Maccabees on the basis of this single occurrence of *laographia* is at best risky.

This registration probably did involve some kind of *poll tax*, especially since v. 31 alludes to the Jewish "poll tax" for maintaining the Temple in Jerusalem. (In v. 28, *involving poll tax*—though probably correct—is an interpretive addition by both RSV and NRSV.)

We may paraphrase the rather difficult v. 31: "Some Jews readily submitted to Philopator's demands, thinking they might as well pay taxes to maintain Dionysus's temple as to pay taxes to maintain the Temple and the priests in far-off Jerusalem; besides, supporting the local religion would help secure their standing with Philopator."

Most Jews, however, resisted Philopator's attempts to force them to join the syncretistic masses, and they ostracized the few who did give in (vv. 32-33).

The *companions and comrades* were not in fact *previously mentioned* (v. 25). This suggests either that some text is missing or that our author slavishly followed some source. (Slavishly following some source could also explain the aberrant *laographia* in v. 28.)

Their former limited status (v. 29) evidently refers to a previous time of discrimination, perhaps specifically prior to the liberation of the Jews by Ptolemy II Philadelphus (r. 285–246; see *EpArist* 16–27).

3:1–4:15. Philopator's revenge escalates to holocaust proportions. *This situation*—the resistance of *the majority* (2:32) exacerbated by rumors against them (v. 2)—enrages Philopator, and he orders the annihilation of *all* Egyptian Jews (v. 25). The *rumor* against the Jews represents them as unfit and even hostile citizens because of their *separateness* (v. 4; see esp. Esth 3:8 and Add Esth 13:4-5). In his letter of indictment against the Jews (vv. 12-29), Philopator appears convinced by the rumors that the Jews are *ill-disposed toward us in every way* (v. 24), and this becomes his rationale for ordering their destruction. Philopator includes in his indictment any who shelter the Jews (vv. 27, 29), while promising rewards for any who help identify either Jews or those who shelter them (v. 28). It was a sweeping judgment, then, calling not only for the destruction of the Jews but for removal of any sympathy for them.

The description of the herding of the Jews toward Alexandria and the resulting suffering of both old and young (4:1-10) is excessive prose and illustrates why the style of 3 Maccabees has been characterized as bombastic. Whether this particular episode is historically accurate or not, however, the description could scarcely be overdone of a people's *incessant mourning, lamentation, and tearful cries* (4:3; see Esth 4:1-3) on their way to wholesale extermination preceded by ignominious torture (4:14). The account may well be a classic example of "pathetic history."

Schedia (4:11, modern Kom al-Jizah), a town at the Canopic mouth of the Nile, three miles east of Alexandria, was connected to Alexandria by a roadway and a canal; it was the most convenient port of entry to Alexandria for those arriving from the Egyptian interior. The *hippodrome* or racecourse into which the Jews were herded was to the east, outside the Canopic Gate.

God Intervenes and Thwarts Philopator's Pogrom, 4:16-21

After forty days (v. 15), Philopator's clerks say they are forced to suspend the registration of the Jews *because of their immense number* (v. 17). There were so many Jews that the supply of *paper and . . . pens* to record the registration had been completely exhausted. (This was "a remarkable enough miracle, but perhaps not an absurd touch in a country whose administration involved such huge masses of paperwork" [Hadas 1953].) Third Maccabees interprets theologically: *this* (v. 21), that is, the miraculous disruption of the registration, was the doing of God, the one who continues to watch over the Jews (cf. 2:21).

Philopator Renews Efforts
to Destroy the Jews, 5:1-51

Philopator is unmoved by the remarkable frustration of his attempts to humiliate and then to annihilate the Jews. His *overpowering anger and wrath* (v. 1) remain unabated. In fact, his rage against the Jews intensifies with each setback—most reminiscent of the earlier EXODUS drama in Egypt, which also involved the Jews and Egypt's ruler. But 3 Maccabees compares Philopator to a more recent tyrant, and one of Greek memory: *Phalaris*, tyrant of Acragas/Agrigentum in Sicily (ca. 570–555 B.C.E.). Phalaris's ingenious cruelty was legendary: he was said to have enjoyed roasting alive his enemies in a large bull-shaped brazier. Philopator, 3 Maccabees tells us, has become even more cruel than Phalaris (vv. 20, 42). So he renews his efforts to get revenge on the Jews by enlisting Hermon and his elephants, and orders the elephants driven into the hippodrome to trample the Jews incarcerated there.

This is high romance, of course, and probably would have been recognized as such by the first readers of 3 Maccabees.

It may also be intended that *Hermon* (v. 1) remind the reader of Haman, the Jews' enemy in Esther. Like Haman, Hermon apparently suffered the very destruction he planned for the Jews, 6:21; cf. Esth 7:9-10.

Of course 500 is a fantastic number of elephants: with his "ten thousands of infantry and his thousands of calvary," we are told, Lysias had only eighty elephants at Beth-zur (2 Macc 11:4; cf. 13:2), and, according to Polybius, Philopator had only seventy-three at Raphia.

It may be objected that intoxicating the elephants (vv. 2-4) makes little sense, but stimulants were indeed sometimes given to elephants prior to battle (see 1 Macc 6:34).

Two times Hermon musters the elephants for the task at hand. Both times the Jews are spared by the remarkable inaction of Philopator. First, Philopator is overcome by sleep (vv. 11-12); the second time, he is beset by *incomprehension* and *forgetfulness* (vv. 27-28) to the point that he even turns on Hermon (vv. 31-33.). Both these events, 3 Maccabees points out, were initiated by *God who rules over all things* (v. 28).

Eleazar Intercedes; God Intervenes, 6:1-29

Philopator, like Pharaoh of old, keeps coming back at the Jews; he is now determined to see their *universal* annihilation (5:42-43). But again a hero emerges to intercede for the Jews: *Eleazar*, whose very name ("God has helped") supports the theme that God helps his chosen people. Eleazar was a familiar hero's name, probably reminding readers of the martyr of 2 Macc 6:18-31 and 4 Macc 5:1–7:23. But readers might especially think of Mattathias's son (1 Macc 2:5) who turned the tide of battle at Beth-zur by killing the Syrians' lead elephant (1 Macc 6:43-44; cf. 2 Macc 13:15).

(In his thanksgiving, Eleazar remembers *the three companions in Babylon* [v. 6], obviously referring to Dan 3:13-30. But the detail regarding *moistening the fiery furnace* [v. 6] is lacking in Daniel and is paralleled only by the "moist wind" in Pr Azar 27, a later addition to Daniel.)

Like Simon before him (2:2-20), Eleazar prays a proper Jewish prayer. God is bound to hear. Just as the elephants are about to charge, God himself dispatches *two glorious angels of fearful aspect* (v. 18) to confront the charging elephants. The sudden appearance of the angels confuses and terrifies the elephants, who turn back upon their own keepers and drivers, trampling and destroying them (vv. 19-21).

In the face of the intervention of the *almighty and living God* (v. 28), Philopator has a complete reversal of attitude toward the Jews. He now looks upon the Jews as—*from the beginning*—the best friends Egypt ever had (vv. 25-26; contrast 3:24).

So Philopator turns upon his own *friends* (v. 23; cf. 5:36ff.; see 2:25-26), loudly proclaiming that they are to blame for various atrocities against the Jews. (In Esther and Daniel, the friends of the king, his advisers and counselors, are to blame for attacks on the Jews.) Finally, Philopator orders the Jews released and reinstated.

JOSEPHUS (*Against Apion* 5) recounts a similar incident, including the herding together of the Jews in one place, bound and exposed before the elephants, the drugging of the elephants, and the turning of the elephants to trample their own drivers. The details of the two narratives are so close that they seem unmistakably related. The major difference is that the Ptolemy using elephants in 3 Maccabees is Philopator; in Josephus, it is "Physco(n)" (Ptolemy VIII, r. 145–116 B.C.E.). It may be best to regard this episode as a piece of general Jewish lore that was adapted by both 3 Maccabees and Josephus for their interpretive histories. The vindication of the Jews in the face of tyrants using elephants was not unknown (see above on Eleazar).

Another common element in the stories is that both suggest the deliverance was occasion for establishing an ongoing festival, unnamed but not unlike the Feast of PURIM or "Mordecai's day" (2 Macc 15:36), celebrating the similar deliverance recounted in Esther: *because of the deliverance that had come to them through God* (v. 36 || Josephus, *CAp* 5).

Philopator Restores the Jews; the Jews Celebrate, 6:30–7:23

Upon Philopator's initiative, the Jews celebrate their deliverance (much to the consternation of their previous persecutors, v. 34), and establish an annual festival to commemorate their deliverance (v. 36).

Philopator formalizes his changed attitude toward the Jews in a letter on their behalf (7:1-9). The letter is in response to their *petition for dismissal* (6:40), and is to inform all Egyptian authorities that the Jews are vindicated and should not be hindered in any way from returning home. This of course rescinds Philopator's previous letter (3:11-30).

Before scattering to their homes, the Jews petition Philopator for permission to punish the apostates among them (see 2:31), according to the *law of God* (7:10; see Deut 13:6-18).

(Under foreign domination, the Jews were often given wide latitude in managing their daily affairs; capital punishment, however, could be executed only by the civil authorities—see John 18:31.)

With Philopator's permission, then, the Jews executed *more than three hundred men* (7:15; cf. Esth 9:15), publicly and shamefully—that is, as public examples (7:14).

The Jews are also returned to their former privileged status, indeed even more privileged than before (7:21). Their property, apparently confiscated as part of the *registration*, was returned, an indication that all things—even the despised registration—had worked out for the good of the Jews. (That property was recovered *in accordance with the registration*, 7:22, suggests the registration indeed involved assessment for tax purposes.) So 3 Maccabees can conclude that God continues to protect and defend his people, the Jews.

Some commentators see in this section as many as four separate festival celebrations: 6:30-41; 7:13-15; 7:17-18; 7:19-20. This extended festival narrative suggests that at least one purpose of 3 Maccabees may have been to explain a major Purim-like festival celebrated by the Jews in Egypt (cf. esp. Esth 9:16-32).

Ptolemais (7:17)—there were several cities so named, from Syria to Lower Egypt—may have been the port (modern Barce) in Cyrenaica. Cyrenaica, the western boundary of Ptolemaic Egypt, was largely populated by Greek-speaking Jews, settled there by the Ptolemies. The Cyrenian Jews enjoyed a high level of citizenship, due probably to their contribution as export merchants. A major export was silphium, a now-extinct plant from which both spices and medicine were extracted. That Jews from the important Jewish colony at Cyrenaica were transported to Alexandria for Philopator's registration pogrom explains mention of the *sea* in 7:20. That the silphium plant was an important product of Cyrenaica, exported worldwide through the port at Ptolemais, may explain the otherwise obscure *rose-bearing* of 7:17.

Works Cited

Hugh Anderson. 1985. "3 Maccabees," OTP.

"Bible, Canon, Apocrypha of the O.T." 1967. NCE.

John J. Collins. 1988. "3 Maccabees," HBC. 1993. "3 Maccabees," HCSB.

Demetrios J. Constantelos and John Breck. 1991. "3 Maccabees," NOAB.

Otto Eissfeldt. 1965. *The O.T.: An Introduction.*

C. W. Emmet. 1913. "The Third Book of Maccabees," APOT.

Moses Hadas. 1953. *The Third and Fourth Books of Maccabees.*

G. W. E. Nickelsburg. 1984. "3 Maccabees." *Jewish Writings of the Second Temple Period*, ed. Michael E. Stone, 80–84.

Leonhard Rost. 1976. *Judaism Outside the Hebrew Canon.*

Emil Schürer. 1986. *The History of the Jewish People in the Age of Jesus Christ.* Rev. ed.

Second Esdras

Joseph L. Trafton

Introduction

Second Esdras is one of the finest examples of apocalyptic (from the Greek word *apokalypsis*, "revelation") literature. APOCALYPTIC LITERATURE purports to contain information that has been revealed to the author by God, either directly or through a messenger, usually an ANGEL. As it stands, 2 Esdras is a composite document. The heart of the book is a Jewish apocalypse (chaps. 3–14) commonly designated as 4 Ezra. To the beginning is prefixed a small Christian apocalypse (chaps. 1–2) typically called 5 Ezra. To the end is appended a collection of oracles of judgment (chaps. 15–16) commonly called 6 Ezra. The book purports to be written by the OT figure EZRA; the actual authors are unknown. Second Esdras is extant in its entirety only in Latin.

Fourth Ezra

Fourth Ezra was probably composed in Hebrew or Aramaic by a Palestinian Jew at the end of the first century C.E. It was translated into Greek not long afterward. It is extant in Latin, Syriac, Ethiopic, Georgian, Arabic (two versions), Armenian, and Coptic—all translated from the Greek—and in several other versions based on the Latin. Fourth Ezra consists of a series of seven visions. The first three have a similar structure: Ezra, troubled, raises a series of complaints about God's justice; an angel appears and replies to Ezra's complaints, both questioning Ezra and answering Ezra's further questions as he goes along. The next three begin with Ezra having a VISION (of a woman, an eagle and a lion, and a man from the sea, respectively); the angel then interprets the dream for Ezra. The final vision focuses on God's charge to Ezra to write down what God reveals to him.

Like the Apocalypse of Baruch, with which it is closely related, 4 Ezra was written in response to the destruction of JERUSALEM by the Romans in 70 C.E. Fourth Ezra centers around the theme of God's justice in the light of the devastating defeat of his people ISRA-EL by a godless nation, an event with which the author was struggling to come to grips. It includes significant discussions on the nature of sin and its connection with ADAM, the limitations of human understanding, the signs of the end, the final judgment, the intermediate state between death and the final judgment, the destruction of the Roman empire, and the coming MESSIAH. Both in its overall orientation and in many of its details, 4 Ezra contains a number of striking parallels to the Book of Revelation, with which it is contemporary. Indeed, more than perhaps any other ancient writing, 4 Ezra enables the modern reader to penetrate the bewildering conceptual world out of which Revelation arose.

Fifth Ezra

Fifth Ezra was prefixed to Greek 4 Ezra sometime before the middle of the second century C.E. Fifth Ezra records Ezra's call by God, which culminates in a vision of a great multitude surrounding the Son of God. Its theme is God's rejection of Israel because of its sins and election of a new people—the (gentile) Church—to replace it. Fifth Ezra was probably composed in Greek by a Christian in order to counter the overall pessimism of 4 Ezra by focusing on the blessings that will come to those who follow the SON OF GOD.

Sixth Ezra

Around the middle of the third century C.E., another Christian composed 6 Ezra in Greek and appended it to the combined 5 Ezra–4 Ezra. Sixth Ezra consists of a series of judgment oracles culminating in various exhortations to God's people to flee sin and trust in God. Its twin themes are God's punishment of unbelievers and his deliverance of his persecuted elect. Sixth Ezra was probably added to the book during a time of widespread persecution to soften the basic pessimism of the book's core.

Influence

Although composed by a Jew, 4 Ezra owes its preservation not to Jews but to Christians, who translated it into various languages and edited it into what came to be called 2 Esdras. Second Esdras enjoyed a broad popularity in the church for centuries. For example, Ezra's prayer in 8:20-36, often called the Confession of Ezra, was widely used in the liturgy of the church. Eventually the Roman Catholic Church placed 2 Esdras in an appendix following the NT. Most early Protestant translations of the Bible included the book in the Apocrypha. Perhaps the most unusual impact of 2 Esdras was its role in the discovery of the New World: Christopher Columbus used 2 Esdr 6:42, a passage that was understood to imply that sixth-sevenths of the earth's surface is covered by land, to solicit support for his voyage, arguing that the distance from Europe westward to the Indies was less than it was believed to be.

For Further Study

In the *Mercer Dictionary of the Bible*: ANGEL; APOCRYPHAL LITERATURE; APOCALYPTIC LITERATURE; DANIEL; ESDRAS, FIRST; EZRA; EZRA, FOURTH; EZRA, FIFTH AND SIXTH; PERSIAN EMPIRE; REVELATION, BOOK OF; ROMAN EMPIRE; VISION. In other sources: G. H. Box, "4 Ezra," *APOT*; R. J. Coggins and M. A. Knibb, *The First and Second Books of Esdras*, CBC; H. Duensing, "The Fifth and Sixth Books of Esra," *N.T. Apocrypha*, ed. E. Hennecke and W. Schneemelcher; B. M. Metzger "Fourth Ezra," *OTP*; and *An Introduction to the Apocrypha*; J. M. Myers, *I and II Esdras*, AncB; G. W. E. Nickelsburg, *Jewish Literature between the Bible and the Mishnah*; W. O. E. Oesterley, *II Esdras*; G. N. Stanton, "5 Ezra and Matthean Christianity in the Second Century," JTS 28 (1977): 67–83; M. E. Stone, *Fourth Ezra*, Herm.; M. E. Stone and T. A. Bergen, "Second Esdras," HBC; G. Vermes, "The Fourth Book of Ezra," *The History of the Jewish People in the Age of Jesus Christ*, ed. E. Schürer, rev. and ed. G. Vermes et al., 3.1:294–306; T. W. Willett, *Eschatology in the Theodicies of 2 Baruch and 4 Ezra*.

Commentary

An Outline

Introduction (5 Ezra), 1:1–2:48

The Christian introduction to the otherwise Jewish core (3:1–14:48) of 2 Esdras contains Ezra's call and subsequent vision of a great multitude and focuses on God's replacement of Israel with the church.

Preamble, 1:1-3

The preamble introduces the "author" *Ezra*, who is called a *prophet* (v. 1; cf. 12:42); his priestly genealogy (cf. Ezra 7:1-5; 1 Esdr 8:1-2); the place of his writing: *the country of the Medes* (v. 3)—i.e., the eastern part of the PERSIAN EMPIRE—and the time of his writing: *in the reign of Artaxerxes* (v. 3)—either ARTAXERXES I (465–425 B.C.E.) or Artaxerxes II (404–359). In the OT Ezra is identified as a priest (Neh 8:9) and a scribe (Ezra 7:6; Neh 8:1), but not a PROPHET. He is active during the reign of Artaxerxes (Ezra 7:1), but his activity centers around Jerusalem (Ezra 7:9).

Ezra's Call, 1:4–2:32

The word of the Lord comes to Ezra (1:4; cf. , e.g., Jer 1:2; Ezek 6:1; Hos 1:1; Joel 1:1). He receives a commission to bring a message of judgment to Israel (1:4-11), a summary of what he is to say (1:12-37), a second commission to bring a message of hope to a new people (1:38–2:14), and a second summary of what he is to say (2:15-32).

1:4-11. Ezra's call to Israel. God commissions Ezra to *declare to my people their evil deeds* (v. 5). Israel has *forgotten me* (1:6, 14), *offered sacrifices to strange gods* (1:6), and *not obeyed my law* (v. 8), despite the *great benefits* God has *bestowed* on them (vv. 9-11).

1:12-23. Israel's indifference to God's past acts. God summarizes the *great wonders* (v. 14) he has done for Israel in the EXODUS, during the wandering in the wilderness, and in bringing them into the promised land. Yet Israel still complains (v. 16). For *manna* as *the bread of angels*, cf. Ps 78:24-25; Wis 16:20.

1:24-32. God's rejection of Israel. God will *turn to other nations* and *give them my name* (v. 24); he will *forsake* Israel and *show* it *no mercy* (v. 25); he will *not listen to* Israel (v. 26); he will *cast* Israel *out from my presence* (v. 30) and *turn my face* away (v. 31). But Israel's wounds are self-inflicted: because *you have . . . killed my servants the prophets* (v. 32; cf. 1:26), says the Lord, *you have forsaken yourselves* (v. 27). This section contains several echoes of Matt 23:29-39.

1:33-37. God's election of a new people. God *will give* Israel's *houses to a people that will come* (v. 35). That these people have not *heard* God (v. 35), have been *shown no signs* by God (v. 35), and *have seen no prophets* (v. 36) identifies them as gentiles. That they are described as coming in the future (v. 35) and as those who *do not see me with bodily eyes* (v. 37—probably an allusion to John 20:29) further identifies them as Christians (cf. 2:42-48). Unlike Israel, the new people will believe and obey God (vv. 35, 37).

1:38-40. God shows Ezra the new people. That the new people will be given *Abraham . . . Malachi* (vv. 39-40) shows that God has rejected the Jews, not the Jewish heritage (i.e., in the OT).

2:1-7. God informs Ezra of Israel's coming destruction. *The mother who bore* Israel (i.e., Jerusalem, or Zion—cf. 9:38–10:27; Isa 54:1; Jer 50:12, 1 Bar 4:5–5:9; Gal 4:26) mourns over Israel's fate (vv. 2-4). Because of Israel's sins, *their mother* will be brought *to ruin* (Jerusalem was destroyed by the Romans in 70 C.E.), her children will *be scattered among the nations,* and *their names* will *be blotted out from the earth* (vv. 6-7).

2:8-9. Warning to Assyria. *Assyria*, probably a cryptic reference to Rome, will not escape God's judgment.

2:10-14. Ezra's call to God's new people. God commissions Ezra to *tell my people* (v. 10) of the blessings God is about to bestow upon them, instead of upon Israel. They will be given *the kingdom of Jerusalem* (v. 10—an expression not found in the Bible), *everlasting habitations* (v. 11; cf. 2:37; Luke 16:9), and *the tree of life* (v. 12; cf. 8:52; Gen 2:9; 1 Enoch 24:4–25:7; 2 Enoch 8:3; Rev 2:7; 22:2, 14).

2:15-32. God's message to the "new" mother. God now addresses the *mother* (vv. 15, 17, 30) of his new people—i.e., the Church. He assures her of her ELECTION (vv. 15, 17) and protection (vv. 18-19, 26-29). She in turn is to exhort her children to good works (vv. 20-23). There is a strong emphasis on *resurrection* (vv. 16, 23, 31). The *twelve trees loaded with various fruits* (v. 18) is perhaps an allusion to the tree of life bearing twelve kinds of fruit in Rev 22:2; the *seven mighty mountains* (v. 19) to the seven mountains of precious stones in 1 Enoch 18:6; 24:2.

The New People of God, 2:33-48

Ezra addresses (vv. 33-41) and then has a vision of (vv. 42-48) the new people of God.

2:33-41. Ezra's address to the nations. After a futile attempt to speak to *Israel*, Ezra turns to the *nations* (vv. 33-34). They are encouraged and exhorted (vv. 34-38). The *shepherd* who is *close at hand* (v. 34) is Jesus Christ (cf. John 10:11, 14; Heb 13:20; 1 Pet 2:25; 5:4). Several expressions are reminiscent of Revelation—e.g., *those who have been sealed* (v. 38; cf. Rev 7:3-8), *clothed in white* (v. 40; cf. Rev 3:5; 7:13, 14), and *the number of your children*, which *is now complete* (v. 41; cf. 2:38, 40; Rev 6:11). Again there is a reference to resurrection (v. 39).

2:42-48. Ezra's vision of a great multitude. Ezra sees *on Mount Zion* (cf. Rev 14:1) *a great multitude,* beyond *number, praising the Lord with song* (v. 42; cf. Rev 7:9-10), and *a young man of great stature . . . more exalted than they* (v. 43; cf. Hermas, Sim 9:6:1), who is placing *a crown on the head of each of them* (v. 43; cf. Sim 8:2:1; 2 Tim 4:8; Jas 1:12; 1 Pet 5:4; Rev 2:10). *An angel* (v. 44) identifies the multitude, who are further said to *receive palms* (cf. Rev 7:9), as *they who have put off mortal clothing and have put on the immortal* (cf. 1 Cor 15:53-54)—i.e., resurrected Christians—who *have confessed the name of God* (v. 45). He identifies the *young man* as *the Son of God*—i.e., Jesus Christ—*whom they confessed in the world* (v. 47). The Introduction closes with the angel charging Ezra to *tell . . . the wonders of God that you have seen* (v. 48).

The Seven Visions (4 Ezra), 3:1–14:48

The Jewish core of 2 Esdras consists of seven visions. The first three, which have a similar structure, center around Ezra's complaint to God concerning the gentile destruction of Jerusalem and subsequent exile of Israel. God sends the angel Uriel to respond to Ezra's questions, although not always answering them directly, and to reveal to Ezra aspects of the end of the age and the final judgment. The next three relate actual visions given to Ezra of a woman in mourning—i.e., Jerusalem; an eagle and a lion—representing the ROMAN EMPIRE and the MESSIAH; and a man coming up from the sea—representing the Messiah. In the final vision, Ezra is divinely inspired to write the OT and the secret, apocryphal books.

The First Vision, 3:1–5:20

Ezra raises questions about God's justice (3:1-36). The angel Uriel comes to him and instructs him on the limitations of human understanding (4:1-21) and the end of the age (4:22–5:20).

3:1-3. Ezra's consternation. The composition of the book is ostensibly set *in Babylon* (v. 1), i.e., during the Babylonian EXILE. *The thirtieth year after the destruction of the city* (3:1)—Jerusalem—by Nebuchadnezzar would be 557 B.C.E. This expression, which is taken from Ezek 1:1, may well be a clue to the approximate date of the book: thirty years after the destruction of Jerusalem by the Romans would be 100 C.E.

Salathiel (v. 1) is the Greek form of the Hebrew Shealtiel. Shealtiel was the father of ZERUBBABEL (Ezra 3:2; Neh 12:1), one of the leaders of the first wave of returning exiles to Jerusalem following the decree of CYRUS in 538 B.C.E. (Ezra 1–2). The date of 557 B.C.E. is therefore appropriate for Shealtiel but not for *Ezra* (who is never called Shealtiel in the OT), who lived at least one hundred years later. The identification of Shealtiel with Ezra—*I, Salathiel, who am also called Ezra* (v. 1)—is therefore an artificial device probably intended to place Ezra in the proper time period for writing a book dealing with the destruction of Jerusalem. *Troubled* at *the desolation of Zion and the wealth of those who lived in Babylon* (vv. 1-2), Ezra speaks *anxious words to the Most High* (v. 3).

3:4-27. Ezra's analysis of the human condition. Ezra begins by surveying human history up to his time. He speaks of *Adam* (vv. 4-8), *the flood* (vv. 9-11), the patriarchs (vv. 12-16), the Exodus and the giving of *the law* (vv. 17-19), the subsequent decline of Israel (vv. 20-22), *David* (vv. 23-24), and the further decline of the people resulting in the destruction of *your city*—i.e., Jerusalem (vv. 25-27).

Ezra emphasizes that Adam's sin has had a profound, negative effect on all of humanity (4:30; 7:11, 116, 118; cf. Rom 5:12-21; 1 Cor 15:21-22). First, after his transgression, God *appointed death for him and for his descendants* (v. 7; cf. 3:10). Second, Adam's *disease*—i.e., being *burdened with an evil heart*—has become *permanent* in *all who were descended from him* (v. 21-22). *The evil heart* leads all—even those who have been given the law—into transgression (vv. 22, 25-26; cf. Sir 15:14-17, where there is greater emphasis on a person's free choice). Ezra stresses further God's role in choosing not to restrain human sin: *You did not hinder them* (v. 8); *you did not take away their evil heart* (v. 20). Thus, the human predicament is grim: Adam's transgression has resulted in an inner tendency to sin that humans cannot overcome and about which God does nothing.

3:28-36. Ezra's complaint. Ezra thus raises his complaint to God: why has God allowed *Babylon* to gain *dominion over Zion* (v. 28; cf. Hab 1)? Perhaps it is because *the deeds of those who inhabit Babylon* are *better* (vv. 28, 31); yet Ezra's own observations have been otherwise (vv. 29, 33). Indeed, Ezra has not found any nation that has kept God's *commandments* better than *Israel* (vv. 32-36). Yet other *nations . . . abound in wealth* (v. 33). Why has God *spared those who act wickedly and . . . destroyed your people* (v. 30)? And why has God not *shown to anyone how your way may be comprehended* (v. 31)? It is precisely such comprehension that Ezra seeks.

4:1-21. The limitations of human understanding. God sends to Ezra the *angel Uriel*, who is not mentioned in the OT but appears in later Jewish literature (e.g., 1 Enoch 9:1; Life 48). He proposes to answer a question that Ezra has not asked—*why the heart is evil* (v. 4)—if Ezra is able to *solve one* of *three problems* (vv. 3-4). Ezra fails (vv. 5-6). The angel, noting Ezra's inability to *answer* questions concerning *things that you have experienced* (vv. 7-9), asks, *how then can your mind comprehend the way of the Most High* (vv. 10-11; cf. John 3:12)? Ezra's response is one of dismay: *It would have been better for us not to be here than . . . to suffer and not understand* (v. 12). The angel then tells Ezra a parable about a *war* between *a forest of trees* and *the sea* (vv. 13-18): there is a proper sphere of human understanding, but it is limited to *what is on earth* (vv. 19-22).

4:22-25. Ezra's objection. Ezra objects that he has not asked *about the ways above* (v. 23), but about earthly events. He wishes to know *why Israel has been given over to the Gentiles in disgrace* (vv. 23-25).

4:26-52. The nearness of the end. The angel answers that *the age is hurrying swiftly to its end* (v. 26). It is an age *full of sadness and infirmities* (v. 27) due to all of the *ungodliness* that has resulted from *a grain of evil seed sown in Adam's heart from the beginning* (v. 30). Therefore, the vindication of *the righteous* lies beyond this age, not in it (v. 27). To Ezra's question, *How long?* (v. 33), asked also by *the souls of the righteous in their chambers* (v. 35; cf., Rev 6:9-10)—i.e., the righteous dead—the angel answers, *when the number of those like yourselves is completed* (vv. 36-37; cf. 2:41; Rev 6:11). God's time can neither be hurried (vv. 34, 37) nor delayed (vv. 38-43). Ezra asks *whether more time has come than has passed* (vv. 44-46). The angel shows him *a parable* of *a flaming furnace* and *a heavy and violent rain* (vv. 47-49): the point is that *the quantity that passed* is *far greater* (v. 50; cf. 5:51-52; 14:10-12). But the angel is unable to tell Ezra whether he *shall live until those days* (vv. 51-52).

Noteworthy in this section are the image of the end as harvest (vv. 28-32, 35, 39; cf. Joel 3:13; Matt 13:24-30; Rev 14:14-20); a reference to the archangel Jeremiel, like Uriel unknown to the OT (v. 36; cf. 1 Enoch 20:8: Remiel; ApocBar 55:3: Ramael); and the anticipation of resurrection from *the chambers in Hades*—i.e., the realm of the dead (vv. 41-42; cf. John 5:28-29; Rev 1:18-19; 20:12-13).

5:1-13. The signs of the last days. The angel describes for Ezra the signs that will precede the end (cf. 6:11-28; Matt 24:4-31; Mark 13:5-27; Luke 17:22-37; 21:8-28). It will be a time of *great terror* (v. 1), characterized by the increase of *unrighteousness* (vv. 2, 10); the desolation of *the land that you now see ruling* (v. 3)—i.e., the Roman empire; cosmic disasters (vv. 4-5; cf. Rev 6:12-15); the *reign of* one *whom those who inhabit the earth do not expect* (vv. 6-7; cf. Rev 13); unusual occurrences in nature (vv. 6-9); the disappearance of *reason, wisdom,* and *righteousness* (vv. 9-11); and human futility (v. 12). The angel then instructs Ezra to prepare to *hear yet greater things*: he is to *pray, weep,* and *fast for seven days* (v. 13).

5:14-20. Ezra's response. Ezra awakes from his vision deeply *troubled,* but the angel strengthens him (vv. 14-15). Ezra is chastised by *Phaltiel, a chief of the people* who is otherwise unknown to the OT, for forsaking his role of leadership over the people (vv. 16-18). But Ezra sends Phaltiel away and prepares himself in accordance with Uriel's instructions (vv. 19-20).

The Second Vision, 5:21–6:35

Ezra again raises questions about God's justice (5:21-30). The angel again comes to him and instructs him on the limitations of human understanding (5:31-40), the successive generations (5:41-55), and the end of the age (5:56–6:35).

5:21-22. Ezra's consternation. *After seven days* (cf. 5:13) Ezra is once again troubled (cf. 3:2) and begins to speak to God.

5:23-30. Ezra's complaint. After affirming the uniqueness of Israel before God (vv. 23-27)—*this people, whom you have loved* and to whom *you have given the law* (v. 27)—Ezra again raises his complaint of Israel's destruction by the heathen: *why have you handed the one over to the many* (vv. 28-29; cf. 3:28-36)? Ezra is even so bold as to propose that God *should* have *punished* Israel *at your own hands* (v. 30), rather than at the hands of *those who opposed your promises* (v. 29).

5:31-40. The limitations of human understanding. Once again the angel comes to Ezra (vv. 31-32). Ezra's response in v. 34 encapsulates the experience of the author of 4 Ezra: *Every hour I suffer agonies of heart, while I strive to understand the way of the Most High and to search out some part of his judgments.* The angel's response is blunt: *You cannot* (v. 35). As Ezra again despairs over being born (v. 35; cf. 4:12), the angel once again reveals to him the limitations of human understanding (vv. 36-40; cf. 4:3-21): *you cannot discover my judgment, or the goal of the love that I have promised to my people* (v. 40).

5:41-55. The successive generations. Ezra inquires as to whether those *who are alive at the end* will have some sort of advantage over preceding generations (v. 41; cf. 1 Thes 4:15-17). The angel responds that all will be treated equally (v. 42). To Ezra's question as to why God did not simplify matters by creating all *at one time* (v. 43), the angel replies that there are limitations to the number that *the creation* can *sustain at one time*; God's plan entails a series of successive generations (vv. 44-49). Ezra asks how old *our mother*— i.e., the earth—is (v. 50). The angel gives the odd answer that the steady decrease over generations in people's *stature*—apparently a reference to the Nephilim of Gen 6:4 (often understood to have been GIANTS—cf. 1 Enoch 6-7)—is indicative of *a creation that already is aging and passing the strength of youth* (vv. 51-55; cf. 4:44-50; 14:10-12).

5:56–6:10. The end of the age. Ezra inquires of the agent *through whom* God will usher in the end (v. 56). The angel responds that God needs no help: just as the creation was effected by God *alone and not through another* (contrast John 1:3; Col 1:15-16; Heb 1:2), so also *the end shall come through* God *alone and not through another* (vv. 1-6). The angel further uses the images of ESAU—*the end of this age*—and JACOB—*the beginning of the age that follows* (cf. 8:52)—to inform Ezra that the coming age of glory will follow immediately upon the present corrupt age (vv. 7-10).

6:11-34. The signs of the end. In response to Ezra's request for the *signs* of the end, the angel commands him to *rise to your feet* and prepare for the ground to be *shaken*, as *the foundations of the earth will tremble and be shaken, for they know that their end must be changed* (vv. 11-16). After Ezra rises, *a voice like the sound of mighty waters* (v. 17; cf. Rev 1:15; 14:2; 19:6) tells him of the *coming* of *the days* of judgment (vv. 18-19; cf. 5:1-13). The *signs* of the end will be that *the books*—i.e., the heavenly books containing the record of human deeds (cf. Dan 7:10; 1 Enoch 90:20; ApocBar 24:1; TAbr 12:7-12; ApocZeph 7:1-7; Rev 20:12)—*shall be opened* (v. 20); there will be unusual occurrences in nature (vv. 21–22, 24); *the trumpet shall sound* (v. 23; cf. 1 Cor 15:52; 1 Thes 4:16); and *war* will break out among *friends* (v. 24).

But there is hope, for *whoever remains after* these events *shall be saved* (v. 25; cf. Matt 24:13). Then *they shall see those who were taken up . . . and have not tasted death* (v. 26; cf. 8:19; 14:9)—i.e., Enoch (Gen 5:24) and Elijah (2 Kgs 2:11-12); *the evil heart of the earth's inhabitants* (cf. 3:21, 26) *shall be changed* (v. 26); and the present triumph of iniquity over righteousness will be reversed (vv. 27-28). As *the place where* Ezra is *standing* begins to shake (v. 29), the angel instructs Ezra to *pray . . . and fast again for seven days* (v. 31). Ezra is warned against being so concerned over *the former times* that he be unprepared for *the last times* (v. 34).

6:35. Ezra's response. Ezra obeys the angel. *The three weeks* probably assumes a seven day fast prior to the first vision.

The Third Vision, 6:36–9:26

Ezra again raises questions about God's justice (6:36-59). The angel again comes to him and instructs him on the final judgment, the small number to be saved, and the intermediate state between death and judgment (7:1–8:3). After Ezra pleads for God's mercy for his people (8:4-62), the angel instructs him on the signs of the end and the small number to be saved (8:63–9:26).

6:36-37. Ezra's consternation. *On the eighth night* (cf. 6:31) Ezra is once again *troubled* (cf. 3:2; 5:21) and begins to speak to God.

6:38-56. God's work in creation. Ezra begins by re-telling God's activities on each of the six days of creation (cf. Gen 1). Ezra expands the work on the fifth day to include the creation of *Behemoth* and *Leviathan*, two primeval monsters seen as ruling the land and the sea respectively (vv. 49-52; cf. Job 40:15–41:34; 1 Enoch 60:7-10). They are being *kept* by God to be food at the eschatological banquet (v. 52; cf. ApocBar 29:4; Ps 74:14; Isa 27:1). Ezra ends his review of the creation story with the creation of *Adam*, from whom have come *the people whom you have chosen* (v. 54; cf. 3:10, 21, 26), for whom God *created this world* (v. 55), and *the other nations*, who *are nothing* (v. 56).

6:57-59. Ezra's complaint. Ezra raises his concern to God: why have *your people*—i.e., Israel—been *given into* the *hands* of *these nations* (vv. 57-58; cf. 3:28-36; 5:28-30)? Why does God's people *not possess our world as an inheritance* (v. 59)? Ezra adds one final question: *how long will this be so* (v. 59)?

7:1-16. The narrow path. The angel responds by giving Ezra two illustrations: a *wide sea* with a *narrow entrance* (vv. 3-5) and a *city full of all good things* approachable only by a *narrow path lying between fire and deep water* (vv. 6-9). The point is that *the entrances of this world*—i.e., the paths leading to *the greater world*—are few and evil, full of dangers and involved in great hardships* (vv. 10-13; cf. Matt 7:13-14; Luke 13:24). Thus is Israel's plight, but it is a necessary one: *unless the living pass through the difficult and futile experiences, they can never receive those things that have been reserved for them* (v. 14; cf. vv. 9, 11). What is striking about the angel's response is that there is no mention of Israel's sin; rather, the troubles of this world are blamed on the fact that *Adam transgressed my statutes* (v. 11; cf. 7:116, 118; 3:21; 4:30). The angel chastises Ezra to be more concerned with *what is to come* (7:16).

7:17-25. The standard of the law. Ezra observes that although both *the righteous* and *the wicked* suffer hardship, the latter *will never see the easier* days (vv. 17-18). The angel replies that the wicked have been warned *what they should do to live, and what they should observe to avoid punishment* (v. 21). *The law is God's standard for acceptable human behavior* (v. 20); one disregards it at one's own risk (vv. 22-24). It is obedience to the law, not the mere possession of it, that qualifies one to inherit God's promises (v. 25).

7:26-44. The coming judgment. The angel informs Ezra of what will take place after *the signs* previously revealed (cf. 5:1-13; 6:18-28). *The city that now is not seen*—i.e., Jerusalem—*shall appear* (v. 26; cf. 8:52; 10:27, 44, 54; 13:36; ApocBar 4:3; Rev 2:12; 21:2–22:5). *The land that now is hidden*—i.e., paradise—*will be disclosed* (v. 26; cf. 7:36, 123; 8:52). *My son* (cf. 13:32, 37, 52; 14:9) *the Messiah shall be revealed*, shall *remain* for a *four hundred* year period of rejoicing (v. 28; cf. Rev 20:4-6), and *shall die*, along with *all who draw human breath* (v. 29). There will be *primeval silence for seven days*, after which the new world *shall be roused*, the old world *shall perish* (vv. 30-31), and the resurrection shall take place (v. 32, 37; cf. 4:41-42). Then *only judgment shall remain* (vv. 34-35). *The Most High* will sit upon *the seat of judgment* (v. 33) and will show to the resurrected *nations the pit of torment*, which is *furnace of hell*, and *the place of rest*, which is *the paradise of delight* (vv. 36-38; cf. Matt 25:31-46; Luke 16:23-28; Rev 19:20; 20:14-15). The judgment *will last as though for a week of years* (v. 43)—i.e., seven years.

The explicit designation of *the Messiah* as *my son*, the mention of him dying, and the reference to a *four hundred* year messianic period are both striking and without parallel in prechristian Jewish literature. One should note that this section is not about a messianic "reign" as such; the only thing *the Messiah* does here is die (cf. 12:32-34; 13:25-38).

The section 7:36-105 is absent from standard editions of the Latin Vulgate but is present in several of the other ancient versions. It was probably deliberately removed in the ninth century C.E. for dogmatic reasons—i.e., because it contains a denial of the value of prayers for the dead (vv. 102-05).

7:45-61. The small number to be saved. Ezra bemoans the fact that the universality of sin, caused by the *evil heart* that *has grown up in us* and *has alienated us from God* (v. 46, 48; cf. 3:21-22, 26), means that *the world to come will bring delight to few, but torments to many* (vv. 47-48). The angel replies that just as the most *precious stones* are those that are most *rare* (vv. 52-58), so also God *will rejoice over the few who shall be saved* (vv. 60-61).

7:62-74. Judgment and the human mind. Once again Ezra laments the very existence of humanity (vv. 62-63; cf. 4:12; 5:35). Now, however, his concern is that humans know too much: *we are tormented . . . we perish and we know it* (v. 64). *The wild animals* are better off, because *they do not know* their fate (vv. 65-66). What good is it for humans, who *are full of sins*, to know *that we shall be preserved alive but cruelly tormented* (vv. 67-68)? Ezra muses that *perhaps it would have been better for us* if there were no *judgment* at all (v. 69): salvation is unobtainable; torment is certain. The angel replies that the human mind is precisely what makes humans responsible for their actions: *though they had understanding, they committed iniquity; and though they received the commandments, they did not keep them* (vv. 71-72; cf. Rom 1:18-32). Humans have chosen their fate (v. 73). Now there remains *the judgment* that God *foreordained* by preparing before he *made the world the things that pertain to judgment*—i.e., (according to rabbinic tradition) paradise and hell (vv. 70, 74).

7:75-101. The intermediate state between death and judgment. Ezra asks whether upon death the torment comes *at once* or whether there is a period of *rest until those times come when you will renew the creation* (v. 75). The angel prefaces his response by assuring Ezra that he will not be *among those who are tormented* (v. 76); rather, Ezra has *a treasure of works stored up with the Most High* (v. 77; cf. 8:33, 36; ApocBar 14:12; Matt 6:19-20).

The angel then teaches Ezra about the *seven ways* of the *spirits* of those *who have despised* God's *law* (vv. 78-87) and the *seven orders* of those who *laboriously served the Most High that they might keep the law of the Lawgiver perfectly* (vv. 88-99). The first group *shall immediately wander about in torments, always grieving and sad* (v. 80). They shall be aware of both *the reward* of the righteous (vv. 83, 85; cf. Luke 16:23) and *the torment* they will receive when they are *judged in the last times* (vv. 83, 87). And they will realize that it is too late to do anything about it (v. 82). *The righteous* will have *great joy* (vv. 91, 96, 98) and *rest* (vv. 91, 95) as they look forward to *the glory waiting for them in the last days* (vv. 95, 96), when they shall *shine like the sun* (v. 97; cf. 7:125; 1 Enoch 104:2; ApocBar 51:3, 10; Matt 13:43) and *see the face of him whom they served in life* (v. 98; cf. Rev 22:4). They will also *see the perplexity of the ungodly* (v. 93). To Ezra's question concerning how much *time the souls* will have *to see* these things (v. 100), the angel replies that they will have *freedom for seven days* after death, following which *they shall be gathered in their habitations* to await the resurrection (v. 101).

7:102-15. Prayer for the ungodly on the day of judgment. Ezra asks whether it will be possible *on the day of judgment* for *the righteous to intercede for the ungodly* (vv. 102-03). The angel answers in the negative: *no one shall ever pray for another on that day . . . all shall bear their own righteousness and unrighteousness* (vv. 104-05). To Ezra's objection that OT figures sometimes prayed for others (vv. 106-11), the angel replies that prayer *for the weak* is possible only in *this present world* (v. 112); at *the day of judgment*, which *will be the end of this age and the beginning of the immortal age to come* (v. 113), *mercy* and condemnation will be final (v. 113-15).

7:116-31. The fate of humanity. Again Ezra laments the existence of humanity (cf. 7:62-63), this time focusing on the creation of *Adam*; if only *the earth had not produced Adam, or . . . had restrained him from sinning* (v. 116). Ezra views Adam's fall as affecting all of humanity; *the fall was not yours alone, but ours also who are your descendants* (v. 118; cf. 3:21-22, 26; 4:30; 7:11; Rom 5:12-21; 1 Cor 15:21-22). *What good* are the promises then, when *we have done deeds that bring death* (v. 117, 119-26)? The angel replies that life is a *contest*: one is either *defeated* or emerges *victorious* (v. 127-28). Since humans are responsible for their own fate (v. 127-30; cf. 7:72), *joy over those to whom salvation is assured* overshadows any *grief* over the *destruction* of the rest (v. 131).

7:132–8:3. The mercy of God. Ezra acknowledges God as *merciful* (v. 132), *gracious* (v. 133), *patient* (v. 134), *bountiful* (v. 135), *abundant in compassion* (v. 136-37), *the giver* who can relieve people of their *iniquities* (v. 138), and *the judge* who shall *pardon* and *blot out . . . sins* (v. 139). The angel responds by telling Ezra *a parable* of *a large amount of clay from which* comes *only a little . . . gold* (v. 2). The point is that *many have been created, but only a few shall be saved* (v. 3; cf. 8:1; Matt 22:14).

8:4-41. Ezra's prayer for mercy for sinners. After surveying the marvelous work of God in creating and sustaining human life (v. 8-13), Ezra asks *to what purpose* humanity was *made*, if God *will suddenly and quickly destroy* it in judgment (v. 14)? Ezra proposes to *speak out*—not on behalf of *all humankind*, but *about Israel, for whom I am sad* (v. 15-19). His *prayer, before he was taken up* (v. 19; cf. 6:26; 14:9—

there is no known Jewish tradition that Ezra did not die), begins with an affirmation of the majesty and power of God (v. 20-23). Ezra then moves to a series of requests (v. 26-30) that have a single point—i.e., that God will *not look upon the sins of your people* (v. 26). Ezra confesses that *we and our ancestors have passed our lives in ways that bring death* (v. 31). He acknowledges that in theory *the righteous, who have many works laid up with you, shall receive their reward in consequence of their own deeds* (v. 33). But he points out that in fact *there is no one who has not done wrong* (v. 35; cf. Rom 3:9-18, 23). Therefore, Ezra asks that God be *merciful to those who have no store of good works* (v. 36; cf. 8:32; Eph 2:8-9; Tit 3:4-7).

The angel responds by ignoring Ezra's plea: what Ezra has *spoken* is partially correct, but not in the way in which Ezra had hoped (v. 37). God will indeed *not concern* himself about the sinners, but not because he will be merciful to them: he will simply be unconcerned with their impending *destruction* because he *will rejoice* in the *salvation* of the *righteous* (v. 38-39). The angel uses an example of a *farmer* sowing *seeds* (cf. Matt 13:1-8) to affirm that *not all will be saved* (v. 41; cf. 8:3).

8:42-62. Ezra again pleads for mercy. Continuing the angel's analogy of the farmer, Ezra objects that *people, who . . . are called your own image*, are more important than *seed* (v. 42-44) and again pleads for *mercy* for *your people* (v. 45). The angel replies that Ezra does not understand God's plan for *the future* or his *love* for his *creation* (v. 46-47). He further chastises Ezra for comparing himself *to the unrighteous* (v. 47; cf. 7:76-77): because Ezra has *humbled* himself, he *will receive the greatest glory* (v. 48-50; cf. Matt 23:12; Luke 18:14). Ezra should be concerned not with the unrighteous, but with *those who are like yourself* (v. 51; cf. 14:9), who shall inherit *paradise* (cf. 7:36, 123), *the tree of life* (cf. 2:12), *the age to come* (cf. 6:9), *plenty, a city* (cf. 7:26; 8:52; 10:27, 44, 54; 13:36), *rest* (cf. 7:91, 95), *goodness*, and *wisdom* (v. 52-54). *The Most High did not intend that anyone should be destroyed* (v. 59), but *the great number of those who perish* (v. 55) have chosen to defile God and *his law* (v. 56-58, 60). They shall receive *thirst and torment* (v. 59): God's *judgment is now drawing near* (v. 61).

8:63–9:13. The signs of the end. Ezra asks *when the signs that you will do in the last days* will take place (v. 63). The angel replies that certain *signs*—i.e., earthquakes, tumult of peoples, intrigues of nations, wavering of leaders, confusion of princes (v. 3; cf. Matt 24:6-7)—will signal that *the Most High is about to visit the world* (v. 1-2; cf. Matt 24:33)—i.e., in judgment. Some *will be able to escape the dangers* because of *their works* or their *faith*: they *will see my salvation* (v. 7-8). The rest, who refused to take advantage of their *opportunity of repentance, shall live in torments* (v. 9-12). Ezra is encouraged *not to be curious about how the ungodly will be punished*, but about *how the righteous will be saved* (v. 13).

9:14-25. The small number to be saved. Ezra again laments the small number *who will be saved* (v. 14-16). The angel responds by affirming God's grace: seeing that sin had placed his *earth in peril* (v. 18-20), God decided to *spare some*, albeit a small number, whom he is determined to save and perfect (v. 21-22). The angel then instructs Ezra to *go into a field of flowers* and spend *seven days* eating *only flowers* and praying (v. 23-25).

9:26. Ezra's response. Ezra obeys the angel and goes to a field *called Ardat*, the meaning of which is unknown.

The Fourth Vision, 9:27–10:59

Ezra meditates on the abiding glory of the law over against the punishment of Israel (9:27-37). He then has a vision of a woman in mourning (9:38–10:27a) that is interpreted for him by the angel Uriel (v. 27b-59).

9:27-28. Ezra's consternation. *After seven days* (cf. 9:23) Ezra is once again *troubled* (cf. 3:2; 5:21; 6:36) and begins to speak to God.

9:27-37. Ezra's complaint. After meditating on God's giving of the *law* to Israel and Israel's subsequent disobedience and punishment by God (v. 29-33), Ezra notes that *the general rule* is that when something contained in a vessel is *destroyed*, the vessel remains (v. 34-35). With Israel, however, the reverse has occurred: Israel has been destroyed, yet, *the law . . . survives in its glory* (vv. 35-37). Ezra's implied question is: Could God have not preserved Israel as well?

9:38–10:27a. Ezra's vision of a woman in mourning. This time the angel does not come immediately to Ezra; instead he encounters *a woman . . . mourning and weeping with a loud voice . . . deeply grieved at heart* (v. 38). Ezra asks *why* she is *weeping* (v. 40). When she asks to be *let alone* (v. 41), he repeats his question (v. 42). So the woman tells her tragic tale: *barren for thirty years*, she *prayed to the Most High night and day* (v. 43-44). At last she bore a son, raised

him, and arranged his *marriage* (vv. 45-47). But on his wedding night *he fell down and died* (v. 1). After receiving consolation from her *neighbors*, the woman *fled to this field*, where she intends to remain *until I die* (vv. 2-4). *In anger* (v. 5) Ezra rebukes the woman. *Mourning* is indeed *most appropriate, for Zion, the mother of us all, is in deep grief and distress* (vv. 7-8, 10). Indeed, Zion's grief is much greater than the woman's (vv. 6, 9, 11). The woman's mourning is selfish (vv. 12-14): she must *keep your sorrow to yourself, and bear bravely the troubles that have come upon you* (v. 15), hoping for the birth of another *son* (vv. 16-17). But the woman is adamant: *I will die here* (v. 18). Through a graphic description of the aftermath of the destruction of Jerusalem and the Temple (vv. 21-23), Ezra again tries to get the woman to see that her *great sadness* is nothing compared to *the adversities of Zion* (vv. 20, 24). But *while* Ezra is still *talking to her* (v. 25), the woman is transformed into *a city . . . being built* with *huge foundations* (vv. 25-27a).

10:27b-37. Ezra's response. Terrified, Ezra cries out for *the angel Uriel* (v. 28). *The angel* comes and, finding Ezra *lying there like a corpse*, raises him up (cf. Dan 8:18; 10:9-10; Rev 1:17) and asks, *why are you troubled* (vv. 29-31)? Ezra replies that he feels *abandoned* by the angel and is *unable to explain what . . . I saw* (v. 32). He begs for *an explanation of this bewildering vision* (vv. 34-37).

10:38-59a. The interpretation of the vision. Since God has seen Ezra's *righteous conduct* and continual sorrow *over Zion*, the angel agrees to explain to Ezra *the interpretation* of his *vision* (vv. 38-43). *The woman . . . is Zion* (v. 44)—i.e., the heavenly Jerusalem. The *son* she *bore* is the earthly *Jerusalem*, which has experienced *misfortune* and *destruction* (vv. 46-48). Because Ezra is *sincerely grieved and profoundly distressed for her*, God *has shown you the brilliance of her glory* through the transformation of the woman into the city (vv. 50-54; cf. Rev 21:2-22:5). The angel invites Ezra to enter and *see* the city's *splendor* and *vastness* (vv. 55-57). Ezra is to *remain here* on the following night, and he will see *in . . . dream visions* what the Most High will do to those who inhabit the earth in the last days (vv. 58-59a).

10:59b. Ezra's response. Ezra obeys the angel's instructions.

The Fifth Vision, 11:1–12:51

Ezra has a vision of an eagle and a lion (11:1–12:3a), which the angel interprets for him in terms of the Roman Empire and the Messiah's judgment upon it (12:3b-51).

11:1-35. Ezra's vision of an eagle. *On the second night* Ezra has *a dream* of *an eagle rising from the sea* (v. 1; cf. Dan 7:1-3; Rev 13:1). The appearance of the eagle is grotesque: It has *twelve feathered wings and three heads* (v. 1; cf. Rev 13:1), *the middle head . . . larger then the other heads* (v. 4). There are an additional *eight* (v. 11) *opposing wings,* which are *puny* (v. 3). The eagle flies and reigns *over the* entire *earth* (vv. 5-6; cf. Rev 13:2-4) and has a *voice* that speaks *from the middle of its body* (v. 10). *The twelve wings and two* of the *little wings* (v. 22) rise up to rule *over all of the earth* one at a time (vv. 7-21), after which they disappear (vv. 13-14, 18-20, 22-23). The second rules the longest (vv. 15-17). Some of the other wings disappear *suddenly* or do not rule at all (vv. 20-21). *Two* of the remaining *six little wings* separate and remain *under the head that was on the right side* (v. 24). Of the remaining four, two—*set up* one at a time to rule—disappear *suddenly* (vv. 25-27). The last *two, while . . . planning between themselves to reign together,* are *devoured* by *the middle head* (vv. 28-31), which gains *control of the whole earth* with *greater power over the world than all of the wings that had gone before*; then it disappears *suddenly* (vv. 32-33). As the final *two heads* rule *over the earth,* Ezra sees *the head on the right side devour the one on the left* (vv. 34-35).

11:36-46. The lion addresses the eagle. Ezra then sees *a lion roused from the forest, roaring* (v. 37). The lion, as God's spokesman, identifies *the eagle* as the last of *the four beasts that I made to reign in my world so that the end of my times might come through them* (vv. 37-39; cf. Dan 7:2-8, 17-27). Describing the eagle's rule as one characterized by *great terror, grievous oppression, deceit,* and *insolence* (vv. 40-43), the lion announces that God's *ages have reached completion* (v. 44): The *eagle* is about to *disappear, so that the whole earth . . . may hope for the judgment and mercy of him who made it* (vv. 45-46).

12:1-3a. The end of the eagle. The lion's words come to pass: Ezra sees *the remaining head* disappear; *the two wings set up a brief,* tumultuous *reign* before they disappear; and *the whole body of the eagle* burns.

12:3b-9. Ezra's response. Awakening *in great perplexity of mind and great fear* (13:3b), Ezra asks God to *show* him *the interpretation and meaning of this terrifying vision* (13:7-8).

12:10-30. The interpretation of the eagle. The angel (cf. 12:51) interprets *the vision* for Ezra (v. 10), just as in Rev 17:9-14 the angel interprets for John the vision of the beast in Rev 13. But just as the interpretation in Rev 17 of Rev 13 is highly cryptic and open to various understandings, so also is the interpretation of Ezra's vision (for an excellent survey of interpretations, see Myers 1974, 299–302). A common—and plausible—understanding will be followed here.

Ezra's vision is interpreted in terms of Daniel's *vision* of four beasts rising out of the sea (Dan 7:2-8), which represented for Daniel four kingdoms. *The eagle . . . is the fourth* beast (v. 11), but now *explained* differently (v. 12)—for Daniel it was the Greeks, for Ezra the Romans. The *twelve wings* are *twelve kings* (vv. 14, 16), probably the twelve Caesars of the Roman historian Suetonius: Julius Caesar, Octavius Augustus, Tiberius, Gaius Caligula, Claudius, Nero, Galba, Otho, Vitellius, Vespasian, Titus, and Domitian. *The second,* Augustus (27 B.C.E.–14 C.E.), reigned longer than any of the others (v. 15). The *voice from the midst of its body* represents *great struggles in the midst of the kingdom* when *it shall be in danger of falling*; yet it shall *regain its former power* (vv. 17-18).

This is probably a reference to the struggle for power at the end of the Julian-Claudian line of emperors—i.e., at the death of Nero in 68 C.E.—when three emperors—Galba (68–69 C.E.), Otho (69 C.E.), and Vitellius (69 C.E.)—ruled briefly before Vespasian (69–79 C.E.) consolidated his authority. The *eight little wings* are *eight kings whose times shall be short and their years swift* (vv. 19-21), and who are probably governors and generals whose identity cannot be ascertained. The *three heads* are *three kings who shall rise up* in *the last days* of the kingdom (vv. 22-25). These are probably the three Flavian emperors—Vespasian (69–79 C.E.), Titus (79–81 C.E.), and Domitian (81–96 C.E.)—with the vision probably dating near the end of Domitian's reign (cf. 3:1).

The *one who shall die in his bed* (v. 26) is probably Vespasian, who suffered a serious plague at the end of his life. Of the remaining two, *the sword of one shall devour* the other, *but he also shall fall by the sword* (vv. 27-28). According to tradition, Domitian conspired in Titus's death, and he himself was later assassinated. Finally, *the two little wings passing over to the head* are *kept for the eagle's end* (vv. 29-30). These cannot be identified; presumably they lay in the author's future.

12:31-39. The interpretation of the lion. *The lion* is *the Messiah* (vv. 31-32; cf. 7:28-29), who is further identified as *kept until the end of days* (v. 32; cf. 7:28; 13:25–26; 1 Enoch 48:6; 62:7; ApocBar 29:3) and as *from the offspring of David* (v. 32; cf. 3:23; PssSol 17:21; Matt 1:1; Rev 5:5; 22:16). His task is twofold. First, he will pronounce *judgment* on *them*—i.e., the Roman empire—and *destroy them* (vv. 32-33). Second, *he will set free the remnant of my people*—i.e., the Jews—and *make them joyful until the end comes* (v. 34; cf. 7:28). As Ezra *alone* is *worthy to learn these secrets of the Most High*, he is ordered to *write all these things . . . in a book* and *put it in a hidden place* (vv. 36-37). He can *teach them*, but only *to the wise* (v. 38; cf. 14:6, 26, 46; Dan 12:4, 9). Ezra is then instructed to *wait here seven days more* (v. 39).

12:40-45. The people's concern over Ezra's absence. When Ezra does not return after *seven days, all* the people come out to find him (v. 40; cf. 5:16-19). They fear that Ezra, *alone left* out of *all the prophets*, has forsaken them (vv. 41-45).

12:56-51. Ezra's response. Ezra assures the people that God *has not forgotten you* and that he himself has not *forsaken you*: he has merely *come to this place to pray on account of the desolation of Zion, and to seek mercy on account of the humiliation of our sanctuary* (vv. 47-48). After sending them home, Ezra remains *in the field seven days as commanded* (vv. 49-51).

The Sixth Vision, 13:1-58

Ezra has a vision of a man from the sea, an innumerable multitude desiring (and failing) to conquer him, and a peaceable multitude (vv. 1-20a), which the angel interprets for him in terms of the Messianic judgment of the ungodly and the salvation of faithful Israel, including the "lost" tribes (vv. 20b-58).

13:1-13a. Ezra's vision of a man from the sea. *After seven days* (cf. 12:39) Ezra has *a dream* (v. 1) of *something like the figure of a man* (cf. Dan 7:13; Rev 1:13) coming *up out of the heart of the sea* (v. 3; cf. 11:1). The man flies *with the clouds of heaven* (v. 3; cf. Dan 7:13; Rev 1:7), and everything trembles before him (vv. 3-4). Ezra then sees *an innumerable multitude of people . . . gathered together from the four winds of heaven to make war against the man* (v. 5; cf. Rev 16:14-16; 19:19). After the man carves out *for himself a great mountain* and flies *up on to it* (vv. 6-7), the multitude attack (v. 8). The man *neither lifted his hand nor held a spear or any weapon of war* (v. 9); rather he sends forth *from his mouth . . . lips . . . and tongue*

a stream of fire . . . a flaming breath . . . and a storm of sparks (v. 10; cf. Rev 19:15), that utterly burn up *the onrushing multitude* (v. 11; cf. Rev 19:21). After descending *the mountain the man* calls *to himself another multitude that was peaceable, some . . . joyful, some sorrowful, some . . . bound, and some . . . bringing others as offerings* (vv. 12-13a; cf. Isa 66:20; PssSol 17:31).

13:13b-20a. Ezra's response. *In great terror* Ezra awakes and asks God to *show* him *the interpretation of this dream* (vv. 13b-15). He acknowledges that while *the last days* will be a time of *great dangers and much distress*, it is better to experience them than die before they arrive (vv. 16-20a).

13:20b-24. The angel's response. *He* (v. 20b)—presumably the angel—explains to Ezra why it is better to experience the last days: God *will protect those who fall into peril*, provided that they *have works and faith* (vv. 22-23). *Therefore . . . those who are left are more blessed than those who have died* (v. 24; cf. 1 Thes 4:15-17).

13:25-50. The interpretation of the vision. The angel then reveals to Ezra *the interpretation of the vision* (v. 25). The *man* is *he whom the Most High has been keeping for many ages* (v. 26; cf. 12:32), further identified as *my Son* (vv. 32, 37, 52; cf. 7:28; 14:9)—i.e., the Messiah. The *innumerable multitude* are those who, after plotting against one another in the last *days*, will join together against the Messiah when he is *revealed* (vv. 29-34). *The mountain* is *Mount Zion*—i.e., the new Jerusalem—where the Messiah will stand (vv. 35-36; cf. 7:26; 10:27, 44-54). *The storm, fire*, and *flames* represent the judgments that the Messiah will mete out upon the ungodly according to the standard of *the law* (vv. 37-38).

The *peaceable multitude* represent *the nine* (other mss. read *ten* or *nine and a half*) *tribes*. Speculation among Jews on the fate of the (ten) "lost" tribes of the northern kingdom of Israel that were taken into exile by the Assyrians in 721 B.C.E. (v. 40; cf. 2 Kgs 17:5-6, 24-34) was common during the prechristian period. The answer given here is that *they formed* a *plan* to *go to a more distant region, where no human beings had ever lived* (hence, no one presently knows where they are), somewhere beyond *the Euphrates river* to a *country . . . called Azareth* (Heb. for "another land"; cf. Deut 29:27), where they will live *until the last times* (vv. 41-46; cf. ApocBar 77:19, 22; 78:1-2). At that time God will lead them back to Jerusalem in a new Exodus (vv. 46-47; cf. Isa 11:15-16). Then they, together with the other faithful Jews (cf. 13:23) *will be saved* (vv. 48-50). Thus it is that the Messiah will *deliver* God's *creation and . . . direct those who are left* (v. 26).

13:51-56. The hiddenness of God's plan. To Ezra's question as to *why the man* comes *up from the heart of the sea* (v. 51), the angel replies that knowledge of the Messiah, like knowledge of *what is in the depths of the sea* is impossible apart from God's revelation (vv. 52-53). Ezra *alone* is worthy of such enlightenment (vv. 43-56). The angel concludes by telling Ezra that he will reveal more *after three more days* (v. 56).

13:57-58. Ezra's response. Ezra gets up, praises God for his *wonders* and his sovereignty, and waits *in the field three days* (vv. 57-58).

The Seventh Vision, 14:1-48

God tells Ezra to prepare to depart this life (vv. 1-18). After Ezra asks for an anointing so that he can rewrite the law, which has been burned (vv. 20-22), God grants his request, and Ezra writes the entire OT and the "seventy" secret apocryphal books (vv. 23-48).

14:1-18. Ezra's commission to write. *On the third day* (cf. 13:56) God speaks to Ezra *out of a bush* (v. 1; cf. Exod 3:4). The implied parallel between Ezra and *Moses* is made explicit as God briefly recounts his call of Moses, the Exodus, and his revelation to Moses *on Mount Sinai* of *many wondrous things*, including the *secrets of the times and . . . the end of times* (vv. 3-6). God *commanded* Moses to *publish* some things—i.e., the Pentateuch—*openly* and to *keep* other things—i.e., apocalyptic writings, such as Jubilees and the Assumption of Moses, both of which are attributed to Moses—*secret* (vv. 5-6).

Ezra will receive a similar command (vv. 26, 45-46), but for now he is told to *lay up in your heart the signs . . . the dreams . . . and the interpretations* (vv. 7-8). He is to prepare himself to *be taken up* (cf. 6:28; 8:19), where he *shall live with my Son* (cf. 7:28; 13:32, 37, 52) *and with those who are like you* (cf. 8:51), *until the times are ended* (v. 9), by renouncing *the life that is corruptible* and by reproving, comforting, and instructing the people (vv. 13-15). The end is fast approaching: *nine* and a *half* of the *twelve parts* (cf. ApocBar 53-68) of the present *age have already passed* (vv. 10-12; cf. 4:44-50; 5:51-52), and *the eagle* (cf. 11) *is already hurrying to come* (v. 18). As the age hastens to its end, *evils worse than those that you have now seen happen* (v. 16) *shall . . . be increased* (v. 17).

14:19-22. Ezra's request. Ezra expresses his concern for *those who will be born* after his departure: with *your law . . . burned*—i.e., in the destruction of Jerusalem—*who will warn* them (vv. 20-21)? He therefore asks that God anoint him with *the holy spirit* (cf. Isa 11:2; Wis 9:17; PssSol 17:37) that he might rewrite *your law, so that people may be able to find the path* (v. 22).

14:23-26. God's reply. God tells Ezra to *go and . . . tell* the people *not to seek you for forty days* and then to return to the field with *many writing tablets* and *five* scribes (vv. 23-25). As in the case of Moses, *some things* that God reveals to Ezra will be made *public*, and others will be delivered *in secret to the wise* (v. 26).

14:27-36. Ezra's speech to the people. After gathering *all the people together* (v. 27), Ezra reminds them that their present exile is a result of their having *transgressed the law of life* (vv. 28-33). He exhorts them to *rule over your minds and discipline your hearts* so that *after death you shall obtain mercy* at *the judgment* (vv. 34-35). But for now, *no one* is to *seek* him *for forty days* (v. 36).

14:37-44. Ezra dictates what God reveals to him. Returning *to the field* with *the five men* (v. 37), Ezra is given *a full cup* to drink by God (vv. 38-39; cf. Ezek 3:1-3; Rev 10:8-10). After drinking it, *my heart poured forth understanding . . . and my mouth was opened and was no longer closed* (vv. 40-41). *The five men* write all that Ezra dictates *using characters that they did not know* (v. 42), which is apparently a reference to the tradition that Ezra invented the (modern) square Hebrew script. In all, *ninety-four books were written* (v. 44).

14:45-47. God's direction concerning what Ezra has written. God tells Ezra to *make public the twenty-four books that you wrote first* (v. 45; cf. 14:6), but to *keep the seventy that were written last* for *the wise among your people* (vv. 46-57; cf. 12:37-38; 14:6; Dan 12:4, 9). *Twenty-four* is the number of the books in the Hebrew canon, the twelve minor prophets being counted as one book, as are 1–2 Samuel, 1–2 Kings, 1–2 Chronicles, and Ezra–Nehemiah, respectively. *Seventy* represents the vast number of secret, apocalyptic—i.e., apocryphal—books, such as 4 Ezra itself, which are not in the Hebrew canon. Ezra is therefore given credit for having written (by divine inspiration) the entire OT as well as the apocryphal books. Perhaps more importantly, for the author of 4 Ezra and other apocalyptic writers, the apocryphal books are presented as having not only the same inspiration, and hence authority, as the canonical writings, but indeed a higher value, since they are reserved for the wise.

14:48. Ezra's response. Ezra does as he is instructed. While the Latin text ends here, perhaps as a result of the later addition of chaps. 15–16 to the earlier core of chaps. 3–14, other early versions add a reference to Ezra's being *caught up, and taken to the place of those who are like him* (cf. 6:26; 8:19; 14:9).

Appendix (6 Ezra), 15:1-16:78

The Christian appendix to the Jewish core (3:1–14:48) consists of a series of oracles affirming that God will punish the wicked and deliver his persecuted elect.

God's Commission to Ezra, 15:1-4

God charges Ezra to *speak* and to *cause . . . to be written on paper the words of the prophecy* God will give him (vv. 1-2). He is not to *fear plots* or to *be troubled by unbelief* (v. 3). God's assurance to Ezra—*for all unbelievers shall die in their unbelief* (v. 4)—is one of the main themes of the appendix.

The Coming Judgment, 15:5–16:34

God speaks of what he is about to bring upon the world: the avenging of the righteous martyrs (15:5-27); warfare (15:28-45); woes to Asia (15:46-63) and to Babylon, Asia, Egypt, and Syria (16:1-17); and calamities (16:18-34).

15:5-27. God's avenging of the righteous martyrs. God will bring *evils upon the world* (v. 5); He *will be silent no longer* (v. 8). Although the world's sins are sometimes mentioned in general terms—e. g., *iniquity* (v. 6), *harmful doings* (v. 6), *ungodly acts* (v. 8), *wicked practices* (v. 8), *sin* (vv. 24, 27), not obeying God's *commandments* (v. 24), and polluting God's *sanctuary* (v. 25)—the recurring theme throughout the appendix is that the wicked have persecuted and martyred God's *elect*, whose *blood cries out to* God (cf. Gen 4:10; Rev 6:9-10) and whom God *will surely avenge* (vv. 8-10, 21-22, 52-53, 56; 16:68-73). God's *calamities* (v. 27) will include famine (vv. 5, 13), war (vv. 15, 20), and anarchy (vv. 16-19). God promises a new Exodus: he will strike *Egypt*—probably a cryptic reference to Rome—with plagues and will lead *my people* out *with a mighty hand* (vv. 10-12). There may well be an allusion here to the terrible famine and plague that Alexandria suffered during the reign of Gallienus (260–68 C.E.).

15:28-45. The coming warfare. There will be a great warfare, *appearing from the east* (v. 28; cf. Rev 16:12). *The nations of the dragons of Arabia* (v. 29) probably depict a loose confederation of peoples from the North Arabian desert. *The Carmonians* (v. 30) are those from Carmonia (Kirman), the southern province of the Parthian empire. Together they shall attack *the land of the Assyrians* (vv. 30, 33)—i.e., the Roman province of Syria—and then move on to *Babylon* (v. 43)—i.e, Rome—which they shall *blot out* (vv. 43-45; cf. Rev 17:16). The carnage will be so great that *there shall be blood from the sword as high as a horse's belly* (v. 35; cf. Rev 14:20). The destruction of Babylon shall be mourned by all *who are around it* (v. 44; cf. Rev 18:9-20). This section probably reflects the military campaigns of the Persian King Shapur I (240-73 C.E.) upon Syria and into Asia. After an initial series of stunning successes against the Roman forces, Shapur was eventually defeated. For a reconstruction of how the details of the vision relate to these events, see Myers 1974, 349–51.

15:46-63. Woe to Asia. Asia, likened to a *prostitute* (vv. 47, 51, 55; cf. Rev 17:1-5) because of its association with Babylon (vv. 46-48), will receive God's punishment. As before (vv. 5-27), its overarching sin is that of persecution: it has *killed my chosen people continually* (v. 53; cf. 15:56; Rev 17:6). Again, for the historical background of this section, see Myers 1974, 351–52.

16:1-17. Woe to Babylon, Asia, Egypt, and Syria. The *destruction* of Babylon, Asia, Egypt, and Syria— i.e., the Roman Empire—is *at hand* (vv. 1-2). No one will be able to turn back God's *calamities* (vv. 5, 8); they will run their course *over the earth* (vv. 14, 16).

16:18-34. The coming calamities. God sends *famine and plague, tribulation and anguish* for disciplinary reasons—i.e., *as scourges for the correction of humankind* (v. 19)—yet they have no such effect: humans *will not turn from their iniquities* (v. 20; cf. Rev 9:20-21; 16:9, 11). Thus, *the calamities* will come at a time least expected, when *people will imagine that peace is assured for them* (v. 21; cf. 1 Thes 5:3). The devastation will be severe.

Exhortations to God's People, 16:35-78

The book concludes with God warning his people of the nearness of the calamities (vv. 35-39), exhorting them to be like strangers on the earth (vv. 40-52) and to cease from sin (vv. 53-67), warning them of the coming persecution (vv. 68-73), and assuring them of his deliverance (vv. 74-78).

16:35-39. The nearness of the calamities. God warns his *servants* (v. 35) that *the calamities draw near* (vv. 37, 39). They will come *upon the earth* like the *pains* of *a pregnant woman when the time of her delivery draws near* (vv. 38-39; cf. 1 Thes 5:3).

16:40-52. Exhortation to be like strangers. God's *people* are to *prepare to be like strangers on the earth* (v. 40; cf. Heb 11:13; 13:14; 1 Pet 2:11). They are to be ready to set aside everyday activities (vv. 41-44; cf. 1 Cor 7:29-31), which will be carried out *in vain* when God comes in judgment (vv. 45-47). Indeed, *iniquity will be removed from the earth* (v. 51). But then will follow the *reign* of *righteousness* (v. 52).

16:53-67. Exhortation to cease from sin. It is useless to deny that one has *sinned* (v. 53), for *the Lord certainly knows everything that people do* (v. 54). God, who created all things (vv. 55-61; cf. Job 38:4-38), *knows your imaginations and what you think in your hearts* (v. 63). Those who *want to hide their sins* (v. 63) will be made *a public spectacle* (v. 64; cf. Luke 12:2-3). Therefore, one must *fear God* and *cease from . . . sins* (v. 67).

16:68-73. The coming persecution. God warns *those who fear the Lord* (v. 70) of *the burning wrath of a great multitude* (v. 68)—i.e., a widespread persecution (v. 70). Specifics of the persecution include forcing the *elect to eat what was sacrificed to idols* (v. 68; cf. 2 Macc 6:7-9, 21; 4 Macc 5:2; Acts 15:20; 21:25; 1 Cor 8:1-13; 10:14-33; Rev 2:14, 20), holding them *in derision and contempt* (v. 69; cf. Heb 10:33), plundering *their goods* (v. 72; cf. Heb 10:34), and driving *them out of house and home* (v. 73). This section might be an allusion to the persecution of Christians by the Emperor Decius in 250 C.E.

16:74-78. The promise of God's deliverance. God assures the *elect* that although *the days of tribulation are at hand, I will deliver you from them* (v. 74). Therefore, the elect are commanded neither to *fear* nor to *doubt* (v. 75; cf. 1 Pet 5:7). Yet they must take care not to be *overwhelmed by their iniquities* (vv. 76-77).

Work Cited

Myers, J. M. 1974. *I and II Esdras*. AncB.

Fourth Maccabees

Edd Rowell

Introduction

Protestants count 4 Maccabees among the Pseudepigrapha; for Roman Catholics it is apocryphal; it appears in the Bible only of Greek Orthodox Christians, but even there as an appendix. The book does not appear on any canonical or even deuterocanonical list. The RSV appended 4 Maccabees to its expanded edition (1977), so it also appears in NRSV. It appears in no other modern version.

Augustine might have considered the book canonical. He said the church accepts "the Books of the Maccabees because they record the great and heroic sufferings of certain martyrs who, before Christ's coming, fought even unto death to keep God's law and bore for it appalling persecution" (*CivDei* 18.36). Augustine's description recalls especially, probably even specifically, this last of the "Maccabees" books.

At an early date, 4 Maccabees appeared with some Josephus manuscripts and was mistakenly credited to Josephus by Eusebius (*EccHist* 3.10.6) and Jerome (*DeVir* 13). Both knew it as "On the Sovereignty of Reason," after the thesis statement in 1:1. In the two great Greek manuscripts Sinaiticus and Alexandrinus (Vaticanus lacks all four Maccabees) and in the even earlier Syriac Peshitta, it is entitled "Fourth Book of the Maccabees (and Their Mother)."

Although 4 Maccabees originated in the Jewish Diaspora, there is little evidence of its use among the Jews. Christians, however, over the centuries regarded 4 Maccabees most favorably.

The early church eagerly accepted 4 Maccabees and saw the Maccabean martyrs as Christian protomartyrs. Heb 12:1-2 (cf. 4 Macc 17:9-10) may be the earliest literary allusion. Both Origen (ca. 185–254) and Cyprian (ca. 200–258) pointed to the Maccabean martyrs as examples of heroism. Gregory of Nazianzus (330–389) honored the martyrs in a grand speech ("In Praise of the Maccabeans") that was essentially a paraphrase of 4 Maccabees. Gregory said that Eleazar (4 Macc 5:4–7:23) was the firstfruits of those martyrs who suffered before Christ just as Stephen was for those who suffered after Christ. Ambrose's (339–397) *De Jacob et vita beata* is virtually a transcript of 4 Maccabees. In 1517, the year Luther nailed his theses to the church door, Erasmus prepared a paraphrase of 4 Maccabees, perhaps in anticipation of persecutions to come.

The perennial appeal of 4 Maccabees was due no doubt to its dramatic recounting of the great and heroic sufferings of certain martyrs. The importance of martyrs to the early church can scarcely be overstated. Indeed, veneration of the martyrs became a Christian subcult, with its own heroes, holy days (martyrdom anniversaries), and devotional literature. At first, Christians looked to Jewish martyrs for inspiration and encouragement. Most prominent among those Jewish precursors were the Maccabean-era martyrs, eulogized especially in 4 Maccabees. Fourth Maccabees was probably the first piece of martyrology adopted by Christians. (The mid-second-century *Martyrdom of Polycarp* evidently was the first *Christian* piece of martyrology [see Trafton 1990, 699].)

Despite its lesser status in the canon, 4 Maccabees was popular in the early church and is still a well-regarded devotional text among Greek Orthodox Christians.

Date and Authorship

It is no longer possible to determine where 4 Maccabees was written. Theories abound. If there is any consensus, it is only that 4 Maccabees is a product of Diaspora Judaism, and is at least related to the Jewish-Hellenistic apologists of Egypt.

Contents suggest 4 Maccabees may have originated in the mid-first century. In 2 Macc 3:5 Apollonius is "governor of Coelesyria and Phoenicia," a correct designation of that district under Seleucus IV (187–175 B.C.E.). Under the Romans at least part of Cilicia was attached to Syria to make up the district called SYRIA AND CILICIA. So when 4 Macc 4:2 designates Apollonius as *governor of Syria, Phoenicia, and Cilicia*, it suggests that the book belongs to the period during which Syria (with Phoenicia) and Cilicia comprised a Roman province (ca. 39 B.C.E–72 C.E.).

Since 4 Maccabees concerns the suffering of the Jews under Antiochus Epiphanes, its recounting of the Maccabean martyrdoms may have been for the sake of Jews in Alexandria who were in similar circumstances under the emperor Caligula (r. 37–41), specifically during 37/38 (see Rowell 1994). Thus, 4 Maccabees was quite possibly composed approximately mid-first century, contemporaneously with the writings of Paul.

The theory that 4 Maccabees was composed later as a grand panegyric to be delivered at a dedication of memorials to the martyrs in Antioch seems less likely, although it may indeed have been *edited* for such use or perhaps for use at the annual Feast of Dedication (see esp. 1:10; 3:19).

Regarding the author we know no more than that he was apparently a well-educated Diaspora Jew, steeped in Hellenistic learning but also well grounded in the faith of his ancestors. He may well have been an Alexandrian (or even Cyrenian) Jew who was probably at least acquainted with PHILO. In fact, while Philo was in Rome (ca. 38 C.E.) pleading the case of the Jews in Alexandria, the author of 4 Maccabees may have been in Egypt putting together this apology of the martyrs to encourage those very Jews for whom Philo was pleading. At any rate, our author was quite likely a contemporary of both Jesus and Paul.

Form and Content

Fourth Maccabees has been characterized as a "combination of Greek form and Jewish content" (Eissfeldt 1965, 614)—like Philo's writings, which harmonized Jewish law with Greek philosophy but never diminished the superiority of Torah. It is, as for the Diaspora generally, Jewish wine in Greek wineskins.

Fourth Maccabees is cast in the form of philosophical discourse, a formal treatise whose theme is that devout reason is sovereign over the emotions (1:1, 13). It explains and "proves" (1:7-8) that theme in typical Greek rhetorical fashion (see outline, below). The fundamental framework is pure Stoic ethics: reason rules the passions. The content is faithfully Jewish: the subject is *devout reason,* that is, reason based in *wisdom,* which is the unde tanding of *divine and human matters and [their] causes,* which in turn is grounded in the law, *by which we learn divine matters reverently and human affairs to our advantage* (1:15-17). That is, the norm and foundation of this *sovereign reason* is the law or Torah. In fact, "reason" and "the law" are virtually interchangeable in 4 Maccabees.

Fourth Maccabees is thus a strong apology for Judaism: not only should the religion of the Jews—specifically the law—be considered as *wisdom,* but as superior wisdom.

(In the very turns of phrase used to describe the law and its source and influence, 4 Maccabees suggests acquaintance with the influential Stoic philosopher Posidonius [ca. 135–51 B.C.E.], who said that the only source and origin of law—*which is king of all things human and divine*—is in the will of God. See the summary in Hadas 1959, 108–109.)

But the bulk of 4 Maccabees is the story of the martyrs (3:19–18:19), perhaps an expansion of the narrative in 2 Macc 6:12–7:42.

Regarding content, then, 4 Maccabees is a philosophical treatise in which the martyr stories constitute the "proofs," but it was the martyr stories, not the philosophical exposition, that claimed the attention of Christians.

For Further Study

In the *Mercer Dictionary of the Bible*: APOCRYPHAL LITERATURE; MACCABEES, FOURTH; MACCABEES, SECOND . In other sources: H. Anderson, "4 Maccabees," OTP; J. R. Bartlett, "The Books of the Maccabees," OComB; M. Hadas, "Aretalogies and Martyrdoms," in *Hellenistic Culture: Fusion and Diffusion*, and *The Third and Fourth Books of Maccabees*.

Commentary

An Outline

Prologue, 1:1–3:18

Such martyrdom accounts as appear in 4 Maccabees are typical of the hero narrative called aretalogy, a popular narrative form perfected by the Greeks and copied to extremes by the Romans. An aretalogy often concluded with an account of the remarkable circumstances (actual or invented) of a hero's death. The ultimate heroic deed after all is how one faces death: heroes face death heroically, indeed as martyrs of *virtue* (=*aretae*, 1:8 and often in 4 Maccabees). An aretalogy memorialized the heroic dead, but was also intended to encourage the hearers toward virtuous and heroic living.

The aretalogical section of 4 Maccabees, while it does comprise the bulk of the text (3:19–17:6), is nevertheless a component element of the main form, a *diatribe* or *treatise* to be presented aloud, a lecture or speech. The diatribe was perfected by the Cynics and Stoics. It was a favorite literary form, for example, of PHILO (sometimes called "the Hebrew Plato") and of Epictetus the Stoic master (ca. 55–135).

Besides its basic structure as a logical discourse designed to persuade, a diatribe routinely includes the dramatic element of imaginary dialogue in which questions are asked or objections interjected and answered. (Diatribe earned its later bad reputation by the fact that the answers characteristically ridiculed the question or questioner.) Interjected questions from imaginary opponents mark the introductory sections of 4 Maccabees: *Some might perhaps ask* . . . (1:5) and *How is it then, one might say* . . . (2:24). Indeed, in its basic structure 4 Maccabees is an exemplary diatribe.

Introduction: Thesis and Plan, 1:1-12

In excellent didactic style, the author states his subject and explains how he will discuss it. The thesis is that *devout reason is sovereign over the emotions* (v. 1). This he intends to *prove*, especially with examples of the Maccabean martyrs (vv. 7-8). First he restates his thesis (v. 12) by discussing its component parts (1:13-14).

The arresting term *devout reason* is explained by the author in 1:15-17: devout reason is that which prefers *wisdom*, the *knowledge of divine and human matters*, which is learned by means of *the law*, which is, of course, Torah, the expression of God's will. This combination of Hebrew piety and Greek philosophy is nowhere more explicit than in 1:17: *we learn divine matters reverently and human affairs to our advantage*.

Devout (or "pious" or "religious") *reason* may sound harsh to our post-Enlightenment ears, but for the ancients human wisdom was not possible apart from a dutiful or pious attitude toward the divine.

Devout reason complements or enhances the *virtues* and controls the *emotions* (vv. 2-6). The reference is especially to the four cardinal *virtues* (or *kinds of wisdom*, 1:18) of the Platonists and Stoics: (1) *rational judgment* (prudence), (2) *self-control* (temperance), (3) *justice*, and (4) *courage* (vv. 2-4). These appear often in Philo and in wisdom literature in general (e.g., Wis 8:7). For some Stoics, *virtue* was the only real good; for 4 Maccabees, it was worth dying for (v. 8).

Emotions might better be translated "passions," in the sense of mental sensibilities, attitudes, or even "natural" inclinations (cf. 1 John 2:16; 1 Pet 4:2-3). Uncontrolled, the "passions" hinder the "virtues," so the passions must be controlled. The passions can be controlled by *devout reason* (cf. 3:17-18). Fourth Maccabees proposes to demonstrate the truth of this with the story of the martyrs (vv. 7-12).

(Beware that *on this anniversary* [v. 10] is the RSV and NRSV translators' *interpretation* of the Greek phrase "at this time"—cf. 3:19.)

Thesis Exposition, 1:13–3:18

This section may be subdivided into 1:13-30a, in which the theme is restated and terms are redefined, and 1:30b–3:18, in which well-known examples are cited from scripture (and related specifically to the law) to indicate that Torah-instructed reason indeed *rules the emotions* (1:30a, 35; 2:6, 9c, 15, 24; 3:5).

1:13-30a. Our inquiry. First, this *reason* is the *wisdom* that issues from *education in the law* (vv. 15-17). It is of four *kinds* (v. 18), that is, it issues in the four cardinal virtues mentioned above, among which *rational judgment* or prudence is most important (v. 19; see 1:2).

The *emotions* or passions over which reason rules are of two basic *types* (or spring from two sources): all *emotions* are *offshoots* of either *pleasure* or *pain* (vv. 20-30). *Rational judgment*, informed by the law, results in a *self-control* (v. 30b) that acts as a *sacred governor* (2:20) over all the emotions and issues in a virtuous life.

Examples are given of emotions controlled by law-informed reason: desire for food (1:30b-35), sexual desire (2:1-6b), greed (2:6c-9), even the prejudiced preference for home and family and against outsiders (2:10-14), and the *more violent* passion of *lust for power* (2:15-20)—*more violent* of course because it encompasses all the rest. Experiences of some of the ancestors are cited as proofs: Joseph controlled his *sexual desire* (2:2-3); Moses and Jacob overcame *anger* (2:17-19); and David would not give in to a powerful *irrational* thirst (3:6-18).

Verses 2:24–3:5 again (see 1:5-6) refute the objection that reason cannot control *its own emotions*, such as *forgetfulness and ignorance*: reason instead governs the passions of the whole person. Reason can rule the emotions but it cannot *uproot* and/or *eradicate* them, that is, it cannot remove them from our awareness or memory. In fact—as 4 Maccabees surely implies (e.g., 2:21)—it is not even desirable to do away with the emotions (as some Stoics would do). The emotions are God-given and thus good. A desire for food is a good thing; sexual desire is good; family devotion is good; and so forth. It is when either one or more such emotions become extreme and dominant that they become evil. The answer of course is *control* over these emotions, which reason instructed by the law is able to do for us.

1:30b–3:18. Jewish vs. Greek. The tension inherent in this "Jewish wine in Greek wineskins" is apparent in 4 Maccabees' reference to emotions of the *body* and of the *soul*. The distinction is most explicit in 1:20, 26-27, 28, but especially 1:32. Of course the severe distinction between *body* and *soul* is a Greek distinction, not Hebrew. That our author catalogs emotions as belonging to either *body* or *soul* (1:26-27) is evidence of his Greek education; that he does not set the two in opposition but rather uses them as simply two sides of the same thing bespeaks his Hebrew heritage. He is, like his probable contemporary Paul, a paradigm of Hebrew wine in Greek wineskins.

Some commentators (e.g., Hadas 1953, 157n.1) find it problematic that 3:1-5 identifies certain emotions (*desire, anger, malice*)—which seem more mental than physical—as being *of the body* (v. 1). Yet in v. 3 anger belongs to the "soul" (APOT, OTP, Hadas; NRSV *mind*). The use of "body" and "soul" (not, we should note, "flesh" and "spirit") here (3:1, 3) seems rather to be the quite natural confluence of more or less interchangeable terms. By either "body" or "soul" (physical or mental, outer or inner), the author of 4 Maccabees—Hebrew that he was—meant the *whole person*.

Thesis "Proofs," 3:19–17:6

At the conclusion of his exposition our author restates his thesis: the reason-controlled mind (*temperate mind*) can control even the strongest passions (3:17-18). Then he announces some stories (*narrative demonstration*, 3:19) to "prove" his point.

The present occasion (3:19) may refer simply to the first time 4 Maccabees was read publicly or to some special occasion (*anniversary*? 1:10) at which it was the "keynote speech." There is now no way to ascertain what *present occasion* is meant. Indeed, it may mean only "*at this time* in the course of our narrative."

An Occasion for Proofs, 3:19–5:3

This section is prologue to the martyr stories that comprise the rest of the book. It sets the scene during the reign of the infamous Antiochus IV Epiphanes and concludes that this was indeed an occasion for proving the thesis that even the most frenzied of passions—the fear of torture and painful death—can be controlled by law-informed reason.

This section appears to be an abbreviated version of the historical narrative in 2 Macc 3:1–6:17; of course, it may be based on another source in common or not with 2 Maccabees (see also 1 Macc 1:20-64 regarding esp. Antiochus).

Regarding details of the intrigues of Onias and Simon see the comments of Mercer (1994) on 2 Macc 3:1–4:6. Here, note that 4 Maccabees emphasizes that the cause of the *various disasters* that destroyed the *profound peace* was the eruption of the more violent emotion of lust for power, which of course is what drove Simon to attempt to unseat Onias as high priest. Fourth Maccabees will show that law-informed reason can govern even the most violent emotions. On the other hand, when one allows passion to control one's life, reason and law are forgotten and disaster replaces the peace and prosperity of law and reason.

Fourth Maccabees (3:20) has Seleucus I Nicanor (r. 305–281) where Seleucus IV Philopator (r. 187–175) should be, and compounds the error by naming Antiochus as Seleucus IV's son (4:15). Seleucus IV was in fact Antiochus's older brother and both were sons of Antiochus III (the Great, r. 223–187). Fourth Maccabees also has Apollonius attempting to plunder the temple (4:4-14); in 2 Macc 3:7 Heliodorus is dispatched by Seleucus to do so. In these apparent errors the author may be telescoping the facts, he may simply have inferior sources, or he may be streamlining his narrative by discarding distracting details.

In the survey of events leading up to the persecutions under Antiochus, 4 Maccabees emphasizes that this "heavy disaster" (2 Macc 4:16) is a direct result of the Jews' *complete violation of the law* (4 Macc 4:19). Even before Antiochus instituted his most severe demands (4:26) many Jews had followed the puppet-priest Jason and had embraced Hellenism (cf. 4:15-20 and especially 2 Macc 4:13-15). *Divine justice* was insulted and disaster was bound to follow (4:21; 2 Macc 4:16-17). The Jews forsook the law, and they in turn were given up to be disciplined by Antiochus and his maniacal anti-Jewish pogrom (4:21).

The discipline fit the sin: the sin was heinous; the discipline was severe. But according to 2 Macc 6:12-17 persecution under Antiochus indeed was meant to discipline, not destroy, and in fact was the result of the mercy of God who, in any case, would never forsake his people (Isa 54:7-8; Ps 94:12-13).

4:21–5:3. The present occasion. Antiochus demanded that those Jews who had not followed Jason into apostasy renounce the Jewish law on pain of death (4:23). Some still were willing to die rather than abandon the law, and Antiochus added torture to the death penalty (4:24–5:3). At this point the martyrs take center stage.

Martyr Proofs (a "Martyrology"), 5:4–17:6

The martyrdoms of Eleazar and of the seven brothers are related in generally similar fashion. The mother's martyrdom is unique, befitting her special status. The narrative cycles of Eleazar and the seven brothers include (1) Antiochus's offer of exoneration in return for submission (5:5-13; 8:3-14); (2) the victim's continuing refusal to apostatize (5:14-30; 9:1-9); (3) torture to force submission (6:1-25; chaps. 9–12 passim); (4) last words and death (6:26-30a; chaps. 9–12 passim); and (5) a rhetorical conclusion consisting of

a eulogy and (philosophical) interpretation (6:30b–7:23; 13:1–14:10). The two narratives differ in length and the interjection of a rational argument—in true diatribe style—into the brothers' narrative (8:15-26).

5:4–7:23. Eleazar (2 Macc 6:18-31). Eleazar (=Lazarus), "God has helped," was a proud and historic name (esp. in Numbers; in 2 Macc 8:23 the name becomes a motto for the Jewish armies). Here Eleazar may be not an actual person but a narrative character who represents aged and pious Jews (cf. 3 Macc 6:1) who suffered torture and death rather than abandon the law—that is, *like a true Eleazar* (6:5).

More than fifty times 4 Maccabees refers to Antiochus as a *tyrant* (e.g., 5:1, 14). *Tyrant* was generally negative and referred to a ruler who gained and/or kept his kingship by force, that is, illegitimately; in the LXX the term is used almost exclusively of Antiochus. The repetitive use of the term for Antiochus (while referring, e.g., to David and Seleucus as *king*, 3:6; 4:3) emphasizes the innocence of the law-abiding martyrs at the mercy of lawbreaking persecutors.

The general term *defiling foods* (4:26) is for Eleazar specified as *pork* (5:2-3). While it was prominent among prohibited foods (Lev 11:7-8; Deut 14:8), it was probably because of its abundance and popularity (cf. 5:8-9) that *pork* became for the Jews a ready symbol of uncleanness. Eating pork was tantamount to idolatry: it defied the law and thus God himself (cf. 5:19-21).

The exchanges between Eleazar and Antiochus (5:5-38) and between Eleazar and his would-be friends (6:12-23) point up their contrasting "philosophies," the contrast between what Paul called—in almost *déjà vu* circumstances—the "wisdom of this world/age" and the "wisdom/foolishness of God" (1 Cor 1:18-25). It is also a contrast between *religion* (θρησκεία, 5:7, 13) and *piety* (εὐσέβεια, 5:18, 31), a contrast that is somewhat obscured in 6:22 by the translation of εὐσέβεια as *religion*.

Of course, religion or cult has to do with outward appearances while piety or reverence toward God has to do with inner disposition, attitude, or mind-set. Antiochus advises Eleazar that it is irrational, unreasonable, or unphilosophical to insist on strict adherence to religious observances at the cost of life itself (5:5-13). What is involved is more than outward appearances, Eleazar responds; to disregard the law in part, even to save one's own life, is to despise the whole of the law and to defy God who gave it (5:14-38)—also, we may note, a common Stoic principle.

Eleazar's response includes especially a defense of *our philosophy* (5:22-24). *Our philosophy*, Eleazar insists, does for us what philosophy is supposed to do: it teaches us the cardinal virtues of temperance (*self-control*), *courage, justice*, and, ultimately, *piety* or *proper reverence* toward God. Note that for Eleazar the *highest virtue* (*rational judgment* = prudence, 1:2) has become *piety* or *proper reverence* toward God (5:24). For 4 Maccabees this *devout reason* (1:1), *rational judgment*, or *piety* is not only the highest virtue; it is the best philosophy.

Eleazar's would-be saviors counsel him to be reasonable and save himself by eating the false pork that they will provide (6:12-15). Eleazar refuses, pointing out that by even the appearance of evil he would *become a pattern of impiety to the young* and a *laughingstock* to his persecutors (6:19-21). Death was preferable (6:22-23).

Eleazar's suffering and his concern that his life be an example of piety for the young and a frustration to his persecutors (6:18-21) recall the tragic figures of Greek philosophy who were held up as heroes to be emulated. Yet Eleazar also is remarkably reminiscent of the Suffering Servant of Isa 40–55. The *burning torments* (6:27) of Eleazar's suffering described in such lurid detail (6:1-11, 24-26), recall the catalog of sufferings of the Servant in Isa 53:4-12. Both Eleazar and the Servant were seen as victims of a "perversion of justice" (Isa 53:8). But, most pointedly, Eleazar's dying prayer recalls certain lines of the Servant hymn in Isa 52:13–53:12: *let our punishment suffice for* [*your people*] . . . *take my life in exchange for theirs* (6:28-29; cf. esp. Isa 53:4-6).

(Of course the Servant and Eleazar are thereby also identified with the pivotal figures of Moses [Exod 32:32] and David [2 Sam 24:17] whose self-offerings prefigure that of the Servant, Eleazar, and Jesus in the best Hebrew tradition of substitionary atonement.)

This idea of "vicarious sacrifice" or "substitutionary atonement" is a key concept in 4 Maccabees (see esp. 1:11; 17:21-22).

As developed in Isa 40–55, the Suffering Servant is corporate Israel, "God's servant in the world, required to uphold God's Torah . . . faithful to God despite the mistreatment endured" (Harrelson 1990, 812), with whom Eleazar repeatedly identifies (*we . . . our*, 5:16, 25; 6:17-22, 28). Later, Jesus is identified with Isaiah's Servant and his mission is interpreted in terms of substitutionary atonement or ransom (Mark 10:45 and par.; Rom 5:6-9). It is possible, then, to see Eleazar as a transitional figure between the corporate Suffering Servant and the individual Christ.

Finally, Eleazar's eventual exaltation (17:20; 18:23) recalls that of the Servant (Isa 53:12) and may prefigure that of Christ (Phil 2:5-11).

Eleazar's ultimate defense was his freedom of conscience. His statement in 5:38 recalls especially the advice of Epictetus: "Will the tyrant chain you by the leg? Will he remove your head? But one thing he can neither enslave nor take away: your character, your will" (*Discourses* 1.18.17; author trans.).

6:31–7:23. Proof indeed. The episode concludes with the affirmation that mastery of *devout reason* over all kinds of emotions is indeed *proved* by Eleazar (6:31-35). Chapter 7 enlarges on this conclusion by likening Eleazar to a *pilot* on a ship who successfully steers a course through stormy seas (7:1-3)—a familiar figure in Greek literature, and repeated in 13:6-7 and 15:31-32.

The subsequent figure of a fortified city that survives a fierce siege (of emotions, 7:4-5) was popular among the Stoics and recalls a saying of the Cynic Antisthenes as quoted by Diogenes: "Prudence is a secure fortress. . . . We should enclose [our lives] with impregnable reason" (Diogenes Laertius, *Lives* 6.13; author trans.).

With the Stoics, 4 Maccabees agrees that not everyone is like the venerable Eleazar, not everyone is prudent (7:17, 23). Nevertheless, everyone who is wholeheartedly pious, like Eleazar and the patriarchs before him, can exercise complete self-control (7:18-22). Eleazar, 4 Maccabees insists, is our proof.

8:1–14:10. Seven brothers (2 Macc 7:1-39). Eleazar represents *advanced age* (5:4); the seven brothers are among the *very young* (8:1). Even these very young, with the aid of *devout reason*, are able to exercise self-control, in stark contrast to Antiochus who is at the mercy of a *violent rage* (8:1-2).

As with all martyrs, God favors the brothers. God's favor of Eleazar was marked by his advanced age, learning, wisdom, and leadership (5:4). The sign of God's favor of the brothers was that they were *handsome, modest, noble, and accomplished* (8:3).

(Antiochus's infatuation with the seven brothers [8:4-5] may have homosexual overtones, which further emphasizes the contrast between the law-abiding Jews and the out-of-control tyrant.)

First by trying to "reason" with them (8:5-11), then by showing the awful instruments of torture (8:12-14), Antiochus attempts to turn the youths to the *Greek way of life*. Neither inducements nor threats can turn the brothers, however, and their refusal to be persuaded effectively *nullified his tyranny* (8:15; cf. 5:38; see also 1:11; 11:24-26).

As an example of how *not* to do it (but perhaps as some less-stalwart Jews had responded) 4 Maccabees imagines a response of easy reason and excuses (8:16-26). The basic premise is that God will excuse slight transgressions in the face of fearsome threats (8:22, 25; cf. 5:13), a false argument already eloquently answered by Eleazar (5:16-38).

But the seven brothers, *with one voice together, as from one mind* (8:29), that is, like a Greek chorus (cf. 8:4), refused Antiochus's demands, and with pious reason like that of Eleazar from whom they—unlike Antiochus (9:5)—had learned (9:1-9). (In 2 Macc 7:2 one brother speaks for all.)

The ensuing torture and death of all seven brothers is narrated in gruesome detail, so gruesome that 4 Maccabees has been chided for preposterous exaggeration. The author may indeed be guilty of overdoing the "special effects" of his drama. But we must not be so shocked as to deny the extent of evil and cruelty for either Maccabean times or our own. A little history can quickly disabuse us of the delusion that human beings could not possibly be so inhumane. The inhumanities in 4 Maccabees seem tame when compared, for example, to those of Phalaris, the tyrant of Sicily who delighted in roasting alive his victims (see Rowell 1994 on 3 Macc 5:20), or of the savage Scythians (cf. 10:7) who skinned their victims *slowly* in order to prolong the agony. To conclude that even Antiochus the tyrant could not be so cruel is to be as deluded as many were during the Nazi era—until mutilated corpses stacked by hundreds and thousands behind the walls of the death camps came to light.

Nevertheless, compared to the account in 2 Maccabees, on which 4 Maccabees may be dependent though different in details, the expanded account in 4 Maccabees seems to be intentionally declamatory. This is to be expected of a diatribe intended to persuade.

The seven brothers are tortured and killed by age or family rank, from the eldest to the youngest. The response of the eldest at the crucial moment of decision is the same for all seven: "Do to me your worst. You cannot force me to recant" (9:17-18; cf. 9:7; 10:4 mg.). This recalls of course the basic Stoic principle that no matter what may be done to one's person, the character or will of one who lives by devout reason is impregnable (cf. 5:38).

12:1-19. Last in line. The death of the youngest brother concludes the episode on a note of high drama. The tyrant's *strong compassion* (12:2; cf. 8:10—this was his last chance at the boys) is the controlling passion. The king calls in the mother to help persuade the youngest boy: this was her last chance also, or so the tyrant must have reasoned.

The mother spoke to the boy *in the Hebrew language* (12:7), suggesting either the sacredness or the intimacy of her words or both. That the tyrant misperceived both her intentions and the boy's perhaps is to suggest he did not know the sacred language.

The mother's speech is not given but promised for *a little later*. This *later* may be 16:15-23 (but see the setting) or possibly 18:6-19, yet neither of those later speeches seems to fit here.

Apparently deceived into thinking he is about to recant, the tyrant releases the boy who runs to the nearest *brazier* where he gives instead a defiant speech that is a summary statement for all the brothers. Then *he flung himself* into the flames (12:19), as his mother does herself later (17:1). Both the Stoics and the Jews could resort to suicide in such impossible circumstances. (Cf. the mass suicide of the Jews at Masada when capture by the Romans was inevitable—an episode that also prominently involved an *Eleazar* and in which their enemies took no pleasure: see BJ 7.8.6–7.9.2.)

13:1-14:10. A chorus of proofs. Finally, 4 Maccabees concludes that the sevenfold martyrdom of the brothers is, like Eleazar's, proof of *the sovereignty of right reason over emotion* (13:5). The content and imagery of this section closely parallels 6:31-7:23 regarding Eleazar. Compare especially the opening paragraphs of both conclusions, 13:1-5 and 6:31-35; and note the repetition of harbor-fortress imagery, 7:1-5 and 13:6-7.

The brothers were grounded in *right reason* by virtue of both their training (13:24) and their heritage (13:12)—and see below, 18:6-19—but in the final analysis it was their piety or devotion to God by which they overcame their most vital passions (13:27: *for the sake of religion* is literally "by means of [their] piety/reverence toward God").

14:11-17:6. The mother of proofs. The mother's martyrdom is barely mentioned in 2 Macc 7:41; in 4 Maccabees it is the climactic episode of the author's *narrative demonstration* (3:19) or "proofs." Perhaps in a frenzy of political correctness, both RSV and NRSV obscure the emphasis on the phrase *mind of a woman* by either ignoring or misplacing the emphatic enclitic γε (*ge*). We should beware of overemphasis, but 4 Maccabees is in fact emphatic: <u>even</u> *the mind of a woman*, who indeed is not just a woman but a *mother*, as of course the paradigm here and elsewhere—Abraham—was not just a man but a father. Fourth Maccabees apparently intends a sharp contrast between the aged Eleazar, the youthful brothers, and *even* a woman.

Yet the emphasis seems to be not on gender but on parenthood. If Eleazar puts his life's reputation and example on the line, if the seven brothers stake the open promise of their young lives, the mother, like Abraham before her, offers not only herself but the life of (all) her progeny. (The gender emphasis may be strongest in the fact that there is no mention of daughters, only sons.) The mother's sacrifice was not just different in kind but in extent. She sacrificed more, much more.

The mother's suffering was in standing by while every one of her children was brutally tortured and killed. Her suffering was greater than even Abraham's because ostensibly mothers are more devoted to their children than fathers and this mother was more devoted than any other (15:4-7). But she was more loyal to piety or devout reason (*religion*, 15:3); she had the *mind* of Abraham (14:20) and *a man's courage* (15:23—another "even-a-woman" allusion). She was thus able to control the strongest of human passions, not just the passion for one's own life but the passion of a mother for the life of her children.

"If you have not been amazed up to now," 4 Maccabees seems to say, "let me tell you about the mother" (14:11-12).

16:1–17:6. It must be admitted. Again, the episode is concluded with a restatement of the theme and the observation that its proof is in the narrative just recounted (16:1). We may also compare the opening paragraph of the concluding statement (cf. 16:1-4 with 6:31-35; 13:1-5), and note the recurring nautical imagery: *flood . . . emotions, violent winds,* and *wintry storms* (15:32).

Finally, her heroic suffering is ended when the mother, as her youngest before her, throws herself into the flames (17:1). Her martyrdom, 4 Maccabees concludes, was the capstone on the heroic martyrdom of her sons (17:3—*roof on the pillars of your sons*). She and they are like the lesser lights (*moon* and *stars*) before God who is of course the greater light. The allusion to wisdom here—"a reflection of eternal light," "a

mirror of the working of God" (Wis 7:26, e.g.,)—seems obvious. And the designation of the sons as *pillars* invites comparison to the obscure "seven pillars" of Wisdom's house (Prov 9:1), for which allegorical interpretations are legion.

Summary Conclusion and Exhortation, 17:7–18:24

This final section of 4 Maccabees seems to consist of three distinct pieces: (1) a general summary of the meaning of the martyrdoms (17:7–18:5); (2) a contemplative aside (in the mother's words) regarding heritage and training (18:6-19); and (3) a final benedictory summary paragraph (18:20-24).

17:7–18:5. What martyrdom hath wrought. This section recounts the effects of the martyrdoms—realized and anticipated—on the martyrs themselves, on the tyrant and his henchmen, and on those to whom this martyrology is addressed.

If it were possible (17:7) could be in the sense of "permitted" with reference to the prohibition against images of any kind (Exod 20:4). Elaborate frescoes at DURA-EUROPOS suggest rather that, at least during some periods, paintings were very much in vogue. The phrase is then simply to introduce the reference to an imagined painting of the dramatic scenes just described and now summarily rehearsed.

Like the description of a painting, the imagined epitaph (17:9-10) was a rhetorical device and neither proves nor disproves that 4 Maccabees was an address delivered at a dedication of some martyrs' tombs (see introduction above).

For the martyrs it has been an (athletic) *contest* to test their faithfulness (*endurance*). The prize was *immortality*. The martyrs won the prize (17:11-16; cf. esp. 6:10-11).

In winning immortality and honor for themselves, the martyrs became an *atoning sacrifice* (v. 22) by which the nation was *purified* and ransomed from the effects of sin (v. 21). *Peace* (wholeness, right relationships—not necessarily the absence of conflict) was thereby restored and the enemies of the people were frustrated (18:4).

(*Through the blood* and *atoning sacrifice* [v. 22] points esp. to Rom 3:25, but any direct relationship is only supposition.)

Remarkably, 4 Maccabees says that Antiochus was so impressed by the courage of the martyrs that he held them up as examples to his soldiers (17:23-24). But the main effect on the tyrant and his associates was punishment both here and hereafter (18:5, 22). (Both reward and retribution are key themes in 4 Maccabees.) In the meantime, Antiochus gave up on the Israelites and attacked the Persians (18:5—which action, incidentally, precipitated his defeat and death, 1 Macc 6:16).

The brief but pointed exhortation in 18:1-2 is one of the few times the author addresses his hearers directly (cf. 1:1, 7, 30b; 3:19). His exhortation is plain: "Go, thou, and do likewise."

18:6-19. Remember whence you came (see 13:12). This contemplation, in the mouth of the mother, may seem obtrusive and out of place. It could be the speech promised in 12:7, but does not really seem to fit there. It rather seems like an authentic oratorical device—a quiet reminder of basic truths (*principles*, v. 6) inserted for good effect between a dramatic conclusion statement and a final summary and benediction.

The basis of all this, the mother's words suggest, is Jewish heritage and training in the home: your mother nurtured you, your father taught you. The passage is filled with allusions to scripture, suggesting a grounding in both Torah and the Prophets. The final allusion (v. 19) is to Deut 32:39 and 30:20, that (1) recognizes God's sovereignty over all creation and that (2) states that this recognition (reverence toward God) is life's fulfillment (*your life and the length of your days*).

18:20-24. Benediction. *Bitter . . . yet not bitter* aptly sums up the martyrology—like naming the day of crucifixion *Good* Friday.

Pierced the pupils is a detail not previously mentioned. The author is declamatory—or at least exuberant—to the end.

The doxology (v. 24) was common for Jewish literature (Psalms, 3 Maccabees, Prayer of Azariah, Tobit) and for Christian literature (esp. the NT letters). For one thing, the doxology marks this *most philosophical* discourse (1:1) as religious (pious, devout) and not just philosophical.

Works Cited

Eissfeldt, Otto. 1965. *The Old Testament: An Introduction.*

Hadas, Moses. 1953. *The Third and Fourth Books of Maccabees*; 1959. *Hellenistic Culture. Fusion and Diffusion.*

Harrelson, Walter. 1990. "Servant." MDB.

Mercer, Calvin. 1994. "Second Maccabees." MCB.

Rowell, Edd. 1994. "Third Maccabees." MCB.

Trafton, Joseph. 1990. "Polycarp, Martyrdom of." MDB.

Matthew

Stephenson Humphries-Brooks

Introduction

Christians approach Matthew as a catechetical manual, as a source book for homily, and as a guide to faith and practice within contemporary Christian communities. Scholars use Matthew as a historical text that informs us about Jesus of Nazareth, the structure of faith of an early Christian author, and/or the faith and practice of an early Christian community of the Mediterranean world in the first century C.E. Moreover, the Matthean depiction of Jesus influences the development of ethical and legal systems in Western culture.

In the following commentary the process of investigation and interpretation begins and ends with the text. Matthew prompts significant questions for a contemporary critical audience broadly conceived.

The Text of the Gospel of Matthew

The Plot of Matthew. We tend to read Matthew as containing an organized series of episodes about Jesus. We find a "plot" of his life complete with complication, climax, and denouement. The series of episodes implies some causal relationship from one event to the next. For example the information that Jesus is adopted into the Davidic royal line by Joseph (1:1-21) helps us to make sense of the visit of the MAGI and the attempt by HEROD to destroy the one born *king of the Jews* (2:1-18).

The plot of Matthew does not directly violate normal historical expectations. In general the sequence of the plot of Matthew conforms to causal and temporal sequence, that is, no events occur out of their normal order. We can easily summarize the plot of Matthew: Jesus is born and adopted into the royal line of Israel. He escapes a murderous plot by a rival king. He is baptized and immediately tempted by Satan. He begins a career of preaching the arrival of the kingdom of heaven. He teaches, performs miracles, recruits disciples. The religious leaders become his enemies. He arrives in the capital city and one of his own disciples betrays him. He is tried and put to death by crucifixion for blasphemy and political sedition. He is buried and resurrected.

Characters and Characterization in Matthew. The episodes that form the plot of Matthew focus on the actions of JESUS, who is the main character. The text depicts Jesus by commentary from the narrator, by Jesus' actions, by commentary from other characters, and finally and most importantly by what Jesus says. The picture that emerges of Jesus is that he is the SON OF GOD, the SON OF MAN. During the process of his story he also becomes invested with all authority and power, a claim the narrator makes for him implicitly by calling him *Emmanuel, . . . God-with-us* (1:23). Jesus himself explicitly claims such power after the resurrection (28:18).

The development of the divine power and authority of Jesus throughout his life occurs in conjunction with a downward trend in Jesus' mundane fortunes. Initially, Jesus appears as a claimant to the throne of David. He is a legitimate threat to Herod and the rulers of Jerusalem. As an adult he takes up residence as a free householder of an urban area, CAPERNAUM (4:13; 9:1). His disciples, also, are depicted as free householders. Contrary to this depiction, Jesus identifies himself as homeless (8:20). At the CRUCIFIXION the text avoids referring to MARY as his mother and names instead only his brothers as her sons, thereby emphasizing his homelessness (27:56; cf. 13:55). At the same time Jesus becomes not only the preacher and teacher of the kingdom of heaven, but also its chief citizen. Ironically, he is crucified as *King of the Jews* (27:37) the same title under which Herod seeks his death. Jesus, therefore, is not depicted as Christ or Messiah in historical terms.

We are led by the Gospel to evaluate other characters according to Jesus' actions and words. With regard to social status as understood in the ancient

Mediterranean world three major types of characters appear: powerful urban elites; the free of the cities; women, children, and other supplicants. Repeatedly characters of different status interact in specific episodes. Matthew contains episodes interwoven into the plot to show how characters with lower status displace those with higher status as more dependable witnesses to the kingdom of heaven. Those characters associated with the urban elite oppose Jesus. They are not part of the kingdom of heaven. The disciples remain ambiguous as to their future faithfulness to Jesus. Only women, children, and other supplicants, those of the lowest status according to mundane social-historical perception, appear as faithful witnesses to Jesus (Humphries-Brooks 1991).

The treatment of other characters and character groups is consistent with the treatment of Jesus in the plot of the Gospel. Only as a homeless and marginal person does Jesus become fully empowered; only homeless and marginal people fully perceive and act on the faith that arrives with the kingdom of heaven.

The Speeches of Jesus. The text begins with a carefully plotted series of episodes associated with the birth and early career of Jesus (1:1–5:1). Similarly the conclusion to the Gospel (26:1b–28:20) contains a carefully recounted series of episodes concerning the PASSION, death, and resurrection of Jesus.

In the midsection of Matthew, however, narrative plot becomes less significant as attention shifts to speeches and PARABLES (5:1–26:1a). These serve several functions in the context of the plot of Matthew: 1. They focus attention on the character and person of Jesus; 2. They make the "once-upon-a-time" ministry of Jesus contemporary with every new performance of the text; 3. They describe the kingdom of heaven; 4. Therefore, they provide the vantage point from which all characters and episodes in Matthew are to be judged. We cannot fully understand Matthew by merely understanding the causal sequence of Jesus' life. Rather, we must perceive Matthew as a whole and use information provided in the speeches of Jesus to interpret the activity of those characters described by the plot.

The author asks us by this arrangement of the narrative to pay less attention to the continuous unrolling of the life of Jesus, and more attention to associations in the narrative that reveal the kingdom of heaven. The work must be read as layers, or perceived like a building, "architectonically" (Davies 1964, 14). We become, therefore, actively involved with the text

as we construct meaning from it. This perception makes it impossible to read or interpret according to one-dimensional thematic- or plot-oriented outlines. In this commentary, we follow the text as it shifts from plot to speech. The divisions proposed by the outline and commentary are governed by a concern to describe the reading experience for us as a critical contemporary audience. Such divisions do not necessarily reconstruct the experience of the text for the original ancient audience, nor do they attempt to recover the conscious intent of the author who probably did not compose according to an outline.

By disrupting our attention from plot, the speeches and parables of Jesus present a view of the kingdom of heaven as disruptive to perception of the historical world. They invite us, as they invited the ancient audience of the Matthean community, to see the presence of the kingdom of heaven in the world.

Major Themes in Matthew

Based on this analysis the single underlying and organizing theme of the Gospel of Matthew is the arrival of the kingdom of heaven in history and its effect on normal experience. Matthew makes apparent that the mystery of the kingdom of heaven is not limited to or encapsulated by the person of Jesus, but requires a discernment of God's will from the perspective of the kingdom proclaimed by Jesus. In the final analysis, Matthew is not a christological or ecclesiological document, but a *theological* one; its focus is on God.

The kingdom of heaven becomes the major term used to describe the power of God on earth in Matthew. It possesses its own justice, a justice that is unique in terms of politics, ethics, economics, and status orientation. The kingdom of heaven comes into conflict with the historical world familiar to us and represented in the plot of the Gospel as well.

The totality of Matthew exposes a world fractured and restructured by conflict and struggle between the kingdom of heaven and the kingdoms of the world. Clearly those kingdoms are claimed by the power of EVIL represented by a variety of titles including "Satan," "the Devil," "Beelzebul," and "the Evil One." Matthew assumes that the world possessed by evil powers can only be overcome by the intervention of God independent of normal human individuals, institutions, and political structures. God's intervention takes on real political form in the life and teaching of Jesus, which bears witness to and invites discernment of the kingdom of heaven and the battle currently engaged.

The conclusion to that conflict will be one of judgment and the removal of evil from the world by God.

Therefore, the kingdom of heaven always takes its bearings from God's end to time rather than from the discernment of God's purposes through past events. The value of persons in its justice is based upon God's righteousness that includes a balance between GRACE and judgment. Matthew depicts God's righteousness at odds with normal political existence because such human justice is in the control of evil.

The worldview of Matthew accords with views expressed in early Christian and Jewish APOCALYPTIC LITERATURE. It has its roots in the prophetic tradition of JUDAISM and in modes of thought that come from a combination of traditional Hebrew culture with Hellenistic thought. Unlike the Jewish and Christian apocalyptic tradition out of which it arises, however, Matthew abandons the view of God as divine warrior who opposes the institutionalized violence of oppressive regimes with invasions of heavenly death-dealing hosts. Consistently, Jesus in Matthew resists the use of violence to combat violence. Rather, the antidote to death in Matthew comes in the resurrection of Jesus by God.

The Composition of the Author

The Gospel of Matthew recounts the significant events of Jesus' life in such a way that those who read it know that these events are not regarded by the author as fictions or fabrications. One of the most popular genres of the ancient world is biography. Ancient biographers seek to reveal to their audiences the essential truth about a person through actions and speech (Talbert 1988). But further, by encountering the truth about a particular person, the audience becomes educated into the universal truths that inform action in the world. An ancient audience, therefore, anticipates that Matthew will educate them not only about the person, Jesus, but through him about their own appropriate action in the world.

The accurate depiction of historical event remains of paramount importance for most modern biographers. For the ancient biographer, including the author of Matthew, the unveiling of truth that cannot be contained in the merely historical is of paramount importance. After all history is mere appearance: biography lays bare essence not otherwise apparent. Therefore, Matthew contains only a selection of the events of Jesus' life told in such a way as to effect a change in the audience. The following commentary is guided by the thesis that the author of Matthew constructs a biography because it most effectively educates the church community into the way of life that characterizes the kingdom of heaven. As such, Matthew, even though it may not prove to be historical in the modern sense, may not be regarded as fiction. For the author and for the original audience, witness to the kingdom of heaven in the life of Jesus is not entertainment, but a matter of life and death.

The author uses both direct quotations from and allusions to the scriptures of Judaism (after about 150 C.E. Christians refer to these as the "Old Testament"), particularly the divisions known as the Law and the Prophets. On at least twenty-two occasions Matthew contains direct quotations from the Prophets. In seventeen of these instances the quotation is introduced by a formula, for example, *All this took place to fulfill*. Additional quotations from and allusions especially to the Law may be found throughout Matthew (see Brown 1977, Gundry 1967, and Stendahl 1968).

While citations from the Jewish scriptures appear in Matthew, at no point does the text explicitly cite or give evidence of other early Christian writings. This may mean that at the time Matthew was composed, no other Gospels were regarded as "scripture" by the author or the Matthean community. Most scholars think, however, that the author knew at least two early Christian writings. One, the Gospel of Mark, provided the majority of the episodes and their arrangement for the author. The second, a collection of sayings of Jesus at least partially in written form provided the sayings and parables found both in Matthew and Luke. Scholars refer to this source as Q.

In addition to these two sources of information the author has access to a broad assortment of traditions handed on within the community for which Matthew was written. These may have included narratives about Jesus, such as the birth account, sayings of Jesus, and parables not otherwise attested in the Gospels. Generally, such material is referred to as "M" by scholars and may have been in both oral and written form (see Brooks 1987).

The familiarity with the Jewish scriptures demonstrated from the text of Matthew allows us to suppose that those writings, particularly the Law and the Prophets, had a significant literary influence on the author and the Matthean community. Furthermore, the adoption of a popular genre, biography, known to all Greek-speaking audiences of the Mediterranean world indicates that the author and community live and work within the broader culture of their day. The Gospel of

Matthew is a hybrid of diverse cultural traditions focused through the inspired creative genius of an individual.

The author carefully and subtly arranges and uses the sources and traditions available from the history of the church community for which Matthew was written. In that sense, to the extent that we read Matthew as a self-contained textual world, we are subject to the intent of the author. We also, because we bring to the text our own preconceptions and perceptions, may see implications in the text that the author did not consciously intend. To that extent we participate in the revelatory superfluity of the text. The commentary will be guided by both aspects of the text. We shall, however, remain within the confines of the text by seeking to interpret only that which may be found in Matthew. To offer a critical interpretation means to offer an interpretation that accounts for the text as written, not as we wish it.

From about the middle of the second century onward, major churches thought that the Gospel of Matthew was written by MATTHEW, a disciple of Jesus. The sources that report this opinion, however, are suspect and we do not know the identity of the author of the Gospel. Since we do not know who the author is, in our commentary we will simply speak of "the author" and of the book by its shortened traditional title "Matthew." The story of the call of the tax collector in 9:9 refers to the man by the name *Matthew*. Since the parallel passage in Mark 2:13-14 calls the tax collector "Levi" this passage may indicate a conscious change on the part of the author that shows that the disciple Matthew played an important role in the founding of the community.

Speculation on the personal history of the author depends exclusively on the interpretation of implicit and perhaps tenuous evidence in the text itself. It has been suggested that the author was a converted Jewish RABBI or scribe, or that the author was a non-Jewish convert to a Jewish-Christian community, or that the author was a member of a "school" of scribes within a Jewish-Christian community.

While almost all recent scholarship refers to the author as "he," we can be no more sure of the gender of the author than of the author's name. Many women in the Mediterranean basin of the first century possessed the education necessary to write the Greek found in Matthew. We know from other early Christian writings that women occupied high places in early Christian communities. The Gospel itself indicates the consistent and faithful witness of key women to Jesus. Such a motif in the Gospel leads us to suspect that women played important roles in the formation and transmission of the Matthean tradition. There is no secure historical means to determine the gender of the anonymous or pseudonymous author of a NT book from its content.

Internal evidence makes it probable that Matthew was written after the destruction of the Temple of Jerusalem in 70 C.E. Matt 22:7 apparently contains an allusion to this event. IGNATIUS, writing between 110 and 115 C.E. is the first writer to quote Matthew. Other less-clear indications may help us to further limit the date of composition. Matthew's use of Mark may be helpful. Mark (according to most scholars) was composed no earlier than 67 C.E. Some time must have elapsed during which Mark was used by and commented on in the community of Matthew. The modifications to Mark noticeable by a comparison with Matthew would indicate some significant duration of use and commentary within the community, perhaps by a scribal school. Further, as we shall see below, the history of the community implied by the text would indicate a separation of the community from the synagogues of its city that would best fit in the decade between 90 and 100. These considerations would suggest that Matthew was composed sometime between 90 and 105 C.E.

The Matthean Community

Perhaps no other question has exercised recent interpreters so much as the question of the social, historical, and religious configuration of the community of Matthew. We shall summarize here the view that emerges from and informs the following commentary (see Kingsbury 1988, 147–60).

The Greek of Matthew indicates that the community was most likely urban. While at times the Greek of the text is semitic in flavor or style, there is little indication that the audience was bilingual, knowing both Greek, the *lingua franca* of the Mediterranean world, and Aramaic, the language of rural Syria and Palestine. The semitic nature of the Greek would fit well, however, with the Greek spoken and written by residents of a major city of the eastern Mediterranean, such as Antioch in Syria. When we add to the linguistic observations the evidence from Ignatius of Antioch who first quotes the Gospel, then a good working hypothesis is that the community of Matthew was to be found in Antioch of Syria (modern Antakya, Turkey) in the last decade of the first century.

The community was relatively well-off and enjoyed material prosperity. Jesus and the disciples are characterized as ministering to cities and being resident householders in cities. The word "city" is used no fewer than twenty-six times in Matthew. The text also refers to a wider variety and larger amounts of money than those that occur in Mark or Luke (Kingsbury 1988, 152-3).

The religious configuration of the community remains problematic, probably not least because our understanding of ethnic relationships, of which religion is a part, remains fragmentary for the ancient Mediterranean world. We may venture the following suggestions.

The community for which the author writes is Jewish with regard to its authoritative scripture. We know from Jewish documents of the third to sixth centuries that early the Law or Torah: (Genesis–Deuteronomy) and the Prophets (Joshua–Kings [excluding Ruth]) were recognized as canonical.

Matthew also shows high regard for the Temple in Jerusalem (5:23-24; 23:16-21). Further, we detect no animosity toward the Temple cultus per se, although appropriate Temple worship and use is advocated. Therefore, with regard to the religious institution of the Temple, Matthew seems to represent some segment of Judaism in the first century.

The author portrays the PHARISEES as a powerful religious elite in control of the synagogues. The text of Matthew constantly refers to "their" synagogues in a pejorative sense. The corresponding institution ordained by Jesus is not "our" SYNAGOGUE but rather the *ekklēsia* (gathering, community). Further, the community may not use synagogue titles of respect for each other (23:8-12). Finally, 10:16-23 and 23:34-36 indicate the strong possibility that the some members of the community or their predecessors have suffered persecution at the hands of synagogue authorities. Such considerations indicate that the community of Matthew does not associate with the Jewish synagogues of its city.

Furthermore, the community recruits members who are not originally from Judaism, that is, "gentiles." The resurrected Lord sends the disciples out to all of humanity or the *nations* (28:16-20). There may be other references in the text to non-Jewish proselytes within the community as well (e.g., 6:7-8; 23:15). We may conclude that the community of Matthew was composed of Jewish-Christians and their gentile converts who had a positive regard for the Jewish scriptures and Temple, while constituting themselves outside of the local synagogue(s) of their city (see Brown 1983). The community had its own means of internal organization including provisions for the reception of new members.

From the perspective of the study of religions, a community that both identifies with a dominant established tradition and separates itself from other institutions representative of that tradition may be considered a sect. As the commentary explores, this sect holds to specific beliefs about its founder, Jesus. With regard to its adherence to the person of Jesus Christ, then, this Jewish sect may also be called CHRISTIAN.

The text contains few indications about the terms used within the community for community members. The term "Christian" does not occur. Nor does the text ever refer to the community as the "New" or "True" Israel. Terms of equality dominate, however. Jesus speaks of "brothers," "children," and "little ones" when referring to members of the community. We may suspect, however, that two groups are recognized as given special gifts by God: prophets and teachers (scribes [Kingsbury, 1988, 158]). While these two groups probably possess specific gifts appreciated by the community, they are not associated with special church office or privilege.

There are indications that some from these groups are trying to assert hierarchical preeminence at the time of the publication of the Gospel. They do this by invoking traditions about the preeminence of PETER and THE TWELVE. Matthew was written in part as a corrective to these tendencies. It reasserts the egalitarian tradition of the community and denies the sanction of Jesus to those who would assert authoritative doctrinal or interpretative power over the community members. The commentary explores the religious perspective of the author and the sect from which the author and text emerge and to which it speaks.

The author sought to bear witness to the events of Jesus Christ and by the composition of the Gospel to give the audience a perspective that would inform the faith and practice of their religious community. The text, therefore, gives evidence of both perceptions the author had of the intended original audience and conventions operating at an unconscious level. These perceptions and conventions interest us because we wish to understand and be informed by the beliefs and practices of our ancient forebears.

Having begun with the text of the Gospel of Matthew, however, we consider also the appropriation of this faith into our own historical moment. This happens first and foremost because we take seriously the claim of the Gospel to bear witness to Jesus Christ and his revelatory value for the real world. We undertake, therefore, to understand the faith to which the Gospel of Matthew bears witness and to ask how we might responsibly receive and understand the meaning of the Gospel text for our own lives.

Theologically, therefore, we will accept as our interpretative starting point the claim of Matthew that God has manifested God's self in the life of Jesus of Nazareth and ask what that might say to our own historical moment.

For Further Study

In the *Mercer Dictionary of the Bible*: DEMON IN THE NT; GOSPEL; GOSPELS, CRITICAL STUDY OF; JOHN THE BAPTIST; KINGDOM OF GOD; MATTHEW; MATTHEW, BOOK OF; MIRACLE STORY; PASSION NARRATIVE; Q; REDACTION; RESURRECTION IN THE NT; RHETORICAL CRITICISM; SCRIBE IN THE NT; SLAUGHTER OF THE INNOCENTS; SON OF GOD; SON OF MAN; SYNOPTIC PROBLEM; TEMPTATION OF JESUS; TRANSFIGURATION.

In other sources: J. C. Anderson, "Matthew: Gender and Reading," *Semeia* 28 (1983): 3-27; H. D. Betz, *Essays on the Sermon on the Mount*; R. E. Brown and J. P. Meier, *Antioch and Rome*; W. D. Davies and D. Allison, *A Critical and Exegetical Commentary on the Gospel according to Saint Matthew*, ICC; D. Garland, *Reading Matthew: A Literary and Theological Commentary on the First Gospel*, Reading in the New Testament Series; D. R. A. Hare, *Matthew*, Interp; D. Harrington, *The Gospel of Matthew*, SacPag 1; J. D. Kingsbury, *Matthew As Story*, 2d ed; A.-J. Levine, *The Social and Ethnic Dimensions of Matthean Salvation History: "Go nowhere among the Gentiles . . . " (Matt. 10:5b)*, Studies in the Bible and Early Christianity 14; U. Luz, *Matthew 1–7: A Commentary*; J. P. Meier, *The Vision of Matthew. Christ, Church, and Morality in the First Gospel*; D. Patte, *The Gospel According to Matthew: A Structural Commentary on Matthew's Faith*; D. Senior, *The Passion of Jesus in the Gospel of Matthew* and *What Are they Saying about Matthew?*; F. Stagg, *Matthew*, BBC.

Commentary

The following outline indicates shifts between plot and speech and provides a guide to the dominant strategies for reading the text. The heading of each section comes directly from the text itself. The outline may be read, therefore, as a summary of and guide for the reading of the Gospel. Within the major divisions of plot and speech, the outline and commentary try to emulate the structure and language of Matthew as closely as practical and possible. Such an organization will allow for easy reference to the text of Matthew as we proceed. An outline, however, may be used only as a constructive entry point into the text for our generation of readers. The commentary seeks to open up new interpretations, not offer the final word or closure on previous ones.

The commentary presumes that our discussion will proceed with the Gospel of Matthew open before us so that we may hear the voice of the author constantly correcting and informing us as part of the interpretative enterprise.

An Outline

I. Plot: The Book of the Birth of Jesus Christ, 1:1–5:1
  A. An Account of the Genealogy
     of Jesus the Messiah, 1:1-17
  B. The Birth of Jesus the Messiah
     Took Place, 1:18-25
  C. In the Time of King Herod,
     Wise Men Came, 2:1-25
  D. John the Baptist Appeared, 3:1-17
  E. Jesus Was Led Up by the Spirit
     to Be Tempted by the Devil, 4:1-11
  F. Now When Jesus Heard
     That John Had Been Arrested, 4:12–5:1
II. Speech: Jesus Began to Speak,
     and Taught Them, 5:2–7:27
  A. Then He Began to Speak 5:2-16
  B. Do Not Think That
     I Have Come to Abolish, 5:17-48
  C. Beware of Practicing Your Righteousness, 6:1-34
  D. Do Not Judge, 7:1-23
  E. Everyone then Who Hears, 7:24-27
III. Plot: When Jesus Had Finished
     Saying These Things, 7:28–10:4
  A. The Crowds Were Astounded, 7:28-29

Plot: The Book
of the Birth of Jesus Christ, 1:1–5:1

The first sentence of Matthew is ambiguous as to the intention of the book and immediately gives us clues to the multidimensionality of meanings in the Gospel (see Brown 1977, 45-232 for a thorough treatment of the Matthean infancy narrative). The translation, "A book of the birth of Jesus Christ," presents a literal rendering of the Greek into English. Does the phrase refer to the entire Gospel, or only to the first section ending at 2:23, or should we understand the phrase to refer only to 1:1-18 and accept the more restrictive interpretation offered by the NRSV? The translation offered by the NRSV also raises the question of how to understand the use of the term *christos* in Matthew. Should we understand this title to be a general surname for Jesus or does it bear the specific political implications associated with the Davidic monarchy? As we read this section, we become aware of the multilayered conflict between the kingdoms of the world and the kingdom of heaven. It establishes the major themes that will be further developed as the Gospel proceeds.

An Account of the Genealogy of Jesus the Messiah, 1:1-17

The genealogy introduces Jesus as the Messiah who comes from the line of DAVID and ABRAHAM. The Greek *christos* rendered by the NRSV according to its Hebrew/Aramaic equivalent as *Messiah* means "anointed" in reference to the king of Israel. While "Christ" becomes the surname of Jesus in Christianity quite early, it retains its reference to political power. The narrator uses the term as a proper name for Jesus only here and in 1:18 (see also 1:17). The genealogy establishes that Jesus is the legitimate, albeit adopted, heir to David's throne (v. 16). The genealogy points out the historical claim that Jesus is a royal, messianic figure who, like David, might establish rule over Israel.

The genealogy also establishes a tie between Jesus and non-Israelite proselytes. It begins with Abraham. He is the ancestor of all of Israel and therefore of David. He also is the first convert to the God of Israel and may be seen as the patron of all proselytes.

Furthermore, the genealogy refers specifically to four ancestral women. *Tamar* (v. 3) is regarded as an Aramean in some traditions (Jub 41:1). *Rahab* and *Ruth* (v. 5) are non-Israelites who marry into Israel. And in v. 6, *Uriah*, a Hittite, is named to identify *Bathsheba*, the mother of *Solomon*, thereby emphasizing her relationship to non-Israel.

In addition to the concern with non-Israelites the presence of these particular women in a patrilineal genealogy points to the faithfulness of God to justice for the marginal. TAMAR must seduce her father-in-law Judah in the disguise of a prostitute as a means of gaining justice under the rule of levirate marriage (Gen 38:26). RAHAB, a prostitute, hides the spies of Israel from the king of Jericho. She expresses faith in the God of Israel (Josh 2:12; see 6:17-25). RUTH and NAOMI gain social justice from the patriarchy of Bethlehem by deftly reminding the next-of-kin of the obligations to justice that go along with property possession in Israel (Ruth 3:1–4:6). They gain security over against the greed of a patriarchally organized society that would condemn them to penury. Finally, BATHSHEBA is taken

by David in an adulterous union (1 Sam 11:1– 12:25). The story shows her as powerless in the face of the king's lust. David, God's anointed, is alone responsible for the adultery and murder that results. Later, she presses for Solomon's inheritance of the throne.

Each of these women either explicitly or tacitly express their faith in God. In the cases of Tamar and Bathsheba the direct injustice of patriarch and king comes to the fore. These common elements coupled with the absence of the more well-known royal mothers, for example, Sarah, Rebecca, or Rachel, indicate that the genealogy is designed to persuade the reader that sexual relations as preferred by patriarchal society frequently do not serve the purposes of the God of justice. We may look for faithfulness and righteousness to emerge not from the political and ethical center that stands for correct order but from the chaotic and questionable fringes.

The Birth of Jesus the Messiah Took Place, 1:18-25

1:18-19. His mother Mary had been engaged. These verses provide a narrative transition to a carefully written scene of a dream annunciation to JOSEPH. Joseph is a *righteous man* (v. 19). These words may refer to his piety in legal observance. They also align Joseph with the characterization of Jesus (3:15) and children of the kingdom of heaven elsewhere in the Gospel (see especially 5:20 and 6:33). Furthermore, such terms and Joseph's characterization accord with the appropriate behavior of a member of the messianic lineage as depicted in Isa 9:6-7.

1:20-21. An angel of the Lord appeared. In the dream annunciation Joseph is clearly instructed about the circumstances of Jesus' conception and as to Joseph's future action in adopting Jesus as his legal heir. Jewish law, similar to both Greek and Roman law, provided that by naming the child the father claimed all the rights and duties of legal paternity. Joseph does as he is instructed and thereby becomes the first character in the Gospel to be shown to fulfill the will of God.

1:22-23. All this took place to fulfill. The text introduces a quotation from a prophet with the phrase *All this took place to fulfill*. The following quotation comes from Isa 7:14. A Greek form of the text is quoted which has the term VIRGIN rather than the Hebrew form which has a word meaning any young woman who has reached puberty. The Hebrew text makes no comment on the previous sexual activity of the woman. By introducing this reading, the author directs attention to the unusual nature of the conception of Jesus.

By the placement of this scene after the genealogy, the author provides a new perspective that distances Jesus from the royal lineage of Messiah. At the end of the genealogy the author sets the stage by referring to Joseph as *the husband of Mary,* rather than as Jesus' father. The author also suggestively refers to the one *called the Messiah* (1:16). This designation proves inadequate for Jesus. In 1:23 the citation designates Jesus not as Messiah, but as *Emmanuel.* At least a portion of the original audience must not have understood Hebrew, since the author explains the meaning of the name as *God with us.*

The presentation of the genealogy and adoption of Jesus in Matthew serves several functions. It shows the unusual relationship of Jesus to the royal household of David. It links Jesus with the tradition of incorporation of non-Israelites into Israel. God works in unusual ways in order to extend the message of Israel's God to non-Israelites. It reminds us of stories about God's dealing with Israel for the sake of God's justice in behalf of the marginal outside of the social and political structures controlled by the patriarchy.

The genealogy also focuses attention on women as bearers of faith. The virginal conception along with the presence of the four women in the genealogy emphasizes God's power manifested through faith for the sake of God's justice and righteousness. Women of abused status bear in their bodies the signs of faith that come into the world from God. The virginal conception disjoins Jesus from the normal royal patrilineage.

In the Time of King Herod,
Wise Men Came, 2:1-25

2:1-12, 16-18. He was frightened. The interaction of characters in these episodes constitutes a major means by which the text forms the audience's judgment about Jesus and the world into which he is born. The text depicts Herod along with the entire city of Jerusalem as frightened at the announcement of the birth of Jesus, who is the only character identified as *King of the Jews* in Matthew. The *chief priests and scribes of the people* (v. 4) are the male religious and political leaders who reside in Jerusalem and who have power to advise Herod. They use their education to deduce, by scriptural interpretation, that the Messiah comes from BETHLEHEM. Finally, this information is used by Herod as the basis for his attempt to murder

Jesus which results in the murder of all children in and around Bethlehem (v. 16). The combination of political power and scriptural interpretation results in the annihilation of innocent children who have no power in this world of the urban political elite. There are no records of Herod's murder of the children in Bethlehem outside of this text.

The wise men remind us that Jesus even as a child draws foreigners, non-Israel, to himself. The idea of wise men, magi, or astrologers from the East, perhaps priests of Zoroastrianism or Mithraism, has particular appeal to the Greek-speaking Mediterranean audience of the first century, who tend to regard things Eastern with both fascination and fear. Abraham was also from the East (Gen 12:4).

2:13-15. An angel of the Lord appeared to Joseph. The dream of Joseph and the departure to Egypt align Joseph with the patriarch Joseph who also descended into Egypt and was noted for his dreams and interpretations (Gen 37:1–47:28). Jesus escapes the plot of a murderous king, reminiscent of the plot by PHARAOH to kill the male children of the Israelites (Exod 1:22). Clearly the story of the descent into Egypt and return is shaped by a desire to align the story of Jesus with Jewish tradition of the EXODUS from Egypt.

2:19-23. When Herod died. The concluding verses provide the motivation for the removal to Nazareth and also provide yet another scene of the opposition of the political rulers of Jerusalem to Jesus. By the conclusion of this section, those associated with the powerful elites of Jerusalem are characters not to be trusted; indeed, they are intent on the destruction of Jesus.

Furthermore, the author aligns Jesus in important ways with the common history of Israel both in terms of explicit commentary by the prophets and in terms of story reminiscent of important events in Israelite history. The action of Archelaus is perfectly understandable as the response of earthly kings to an earthly threat to their throne from David's heir. The virginal conception and angelic appearances indicate that the point at issue is to understand Jesus from the perspective of God and not in normal political and social terms. Joseph adopts God's perspective and becomes the father who protects and nurtures rather than owning his family.

John the Baptist Appeared, 3:1-17

3:1-12. Repent for the kingdom of heaven has come near. John the Baptist looks and acts like ELIJAH or ELISHA. Both prophets are noteworthy for their opposition to the royal household of AHAB. Both function as warriors in behalf of the God of Israel (1 Kings 17–21; 2 Kings 1–13). John announces judgment not based on ethnic identity, as the PHARISEES and SADDUCEES suppose, but according to action by those who follow God's will. Admission into the kingdom of heaven does not depend on ethnic identity or religious status. The kingdom of heaven as judgment arrives in the ministry of John and will continue into Jesus' ministry. The kingdom of heaven invades the world for the purpose of judgment.

3:13-17. Jesus came from Galilee to be baptized by John. John preaches the arrival of the kingdom of heaven. The term *kingdom of heaven* indicates the actualizing of the foreshadowing in birth and dreams in the previous sections. Jesus by his baptism associates with a kingdom configured differently from the kingdom of Herod.

Verse 15 epitomizes the content of the previous verses: the kingdom of heaven contains righteousness or justice. Here, Jesus shows himself as servant of the righteousness that belongs to the kingdom of heaven. His character arises out of the will of God. His behavior provides the antinomic and determinative opposite to that of the Pharisees and Sadducees. In the same way that the events of Jesus' birth have been shown to fulfill the will of God expressed in the prophets, the action of Jesus as an adult also fulfills God's will.

The text may imply that Jesus' baptism is one of repentance (v. 6). God approves of his action by announcing Jesus' sonship. Jesus correctly perceives the kingdom of heaven and its justice. Here the text introduces for the first time Jesus' own awareness of his divine sonship by virtue of a visionary experience from the heavens and direct communication by a voice.

Jesus Was Led Up by the Spirit to Be Tempted by the Devil, 4:1-11

The scene bears similarities to the wanderings of Israel in the DESERT recounted in Exodus, Numbers, and Deuteronomy. Unlike Israel, however, Jesus successfully resists temptation to sin and indicates clearly the nature of his ministry and proclamation (Meier 1979, 59–62).

The temptation occurs in three scenes culminating dramatically in the temptation to possess universal political power (4:3-4, 5-7, 8-11). In each scene *the devil* speaks first followed by a quotation of Jesus from the Law (Deut 8:3; 6:16; 6:13 at vv. 4, 7, 10). The devil is shown to be a powerful and intelligent individual learned in techniques of scriptural argumentation.

In the final scene, vv. 8-10, Satan asserts that he owns the kingdoms of the world. Jesus does not dispute the point, but rather responds with a quotation from the Law that places the issue on the theological grounds of the lordship of God. Two points emerge from this scene. First, evil powers possess and control the mundane political process. Second, the coming of the kingdom of heaven means that a new politics arrives, one overseen by God. We meet here a view derived from Jewish apocalyptic perspectives as found for example in Isaiah 56–66, Zechariah, Daniel, and 1 Enoch (Hanson 1979). The underlying view is one of a world in antinomic conflict (see Martyn 1985).

The scene opens up a multi-dimensional drama being worked out in the life of Jesus. What appeared to be a political power play between the urban elite of Herod's household and the adopted son of David is the universal struggle between the kingdoms of the world ruled by Satan and the kingdom of heaven. The two dimensions mutually inform and interact with each other throughout Matthew.

Now When Jesus Heard That John Had Been Arrested, 4:12–5:1

4:12-17. He made his home in Capernaum. Jesus resettles to CAPERNAUM as a householder. The citation in vv. 15-16 refers to the same prophetic context as the citation in 1:23 (Isa 9:1-2) and reconfirms Jesus' status as God-with-us. It also emphasizes that Jesus' ministry begins both in traditional Israelite tribal territory (Zebulun, Naphtali) and among non-Israelite peoples (*Galilee of the Gentiles*, v. 15). The ministry is set amidst ethnic diversity. Within this context, Jesus begins the same proclamation as John (3:2). This episode is framed by the notation of John's arrest and the repetition of his preaching. Such framing suggests that the ministry and destiny of John serves as a model for the ministry and destiny of Jesus.

4:18-22. He saw two brothers. The following episode illustrates the immediate fulfillment of the citation of v. 15. Jesus recruits his first followers. They are depicted as male Israelite householders like himself. The Greek names PETER, ANDREW, JAMES, and JOHN show by comparison with the name ZEBEDEE, the father of James and John, the cultural diversity of the generation who will constitute the disciples.

4:23–5:1. Jesus went throughout Galilee. The third episode illustrates the PROPHECY of 4:16. Jesus' actions define him not as a mundane political revolutionary, but as witness to and embodiment of a kingdom whose concern is healing and *good news of the kingdom* (v. 23). For the first time in Matthew we encounter the term "gospel" (NRSV mg.). In 9:35 and 24:14, as here, it is the *good news of the kingdom*. Good news, the preaching of Jesus (and John?) therefore belongs to the kingdom of heaven. According to the prophecy of v. 16, this gospel means the elimination of death. The place names imply that Jesus' activity attracts not only Israelites but also non-Israelites as well. Both *Syria* (v. 24) and the *Decapolis* (v. 25) are composed of non-Israelite territory and non-Jewish populations. From the beginning of his ministry Jesus heals and preaches to both Jewish and gentile crowds.

Matthew 5:1 may be read either as the first verse of the next literary section or as the conclusion to the previous plot section. Since we are organizing our commentary according to shifts in reading strategy, 5:1 is the last plot notation until 7:28-29. These two inclusive sentences establish for the reader that Jesus speaks both to the disciples and the crowds. Hence the content of the following speech is directed at a universal and multicultural audience. The teaching may be read as representative of Jesus' proclamation. Unlike the preaching of 4:23, the following teaching takes place outside of the confines of the synagogue.

Speech: Jesus Began to Speak, and Taught Them, 5:2–7:27

Explicitly, the SERMON ON THE MOUNT focuses attention on the content of the kingdom of heaven with emphasis on the righteousness that belongs to that kingdom (5:20; 6:1; 6:34). Implicitly, the speech also reveals more to us about the character of Jesus and his relationship to the kingdom of heaven.

The sermon on the mount introduces a new literary technique that is used throughout the Matthean speeches and parables. The narrated story that frames the sermon consistently occurs in the past tense, while the speech itself is stated in the present tense as direct discourse. Because the speech takes up considerable space, our temporal orientation becomes dehistoricized. We experience the sermon as the direct address of Jesus to us. By this technique the text of Matthew invites the reader to take up Jesus' perspective as definitive.

Then He Began to Speak, 5:2-16

5:2-12. Blessed are the poor in spirit. The form of these verses corresponds closely with blessings found in the wisdom writings of JUDAISM (cf. Pss 1:1; 32:1;

41:1; 119:1-2; 128:1; Sir 25:7-11). They have distinct characteristics that mark them, however, as peculiar to the tradition about Jesus. First, vv. 4, 5, 6, 7, 8, and 9 contain a statement of reward in the future in their result clause. By comparison, vv. 3, 10, and 11, which refer to the kingdom of heaven as reward, are present tense. It becomes apparent that these blessings are set in a time that is different from and yet impinges upon the current historical moment. The kingdom of heaven is a present possession and a future reward for God's children. These blessings then, are eschatological and apocalyptic in nature.

Each of the BEATITUDES represents the reality of the kingdom of heaven as opposed to the normal experience of historical reality. The first clause of each beatitude mentions a group of people who, in the ancient world, are not considered at the center of political, religious, or social power. By completing the list with two beatitudes concerning persecution, Jesus makes it clear that these blessings describe the destiny of God's children within the kingdoms of the world. Their comfort is and will be in the kingdom of heaven (v. 12). The beatitudes define the kingdom of heaven from the perspective of God's future.

The time and content of the kingdom flows backwards from an assured future into the oppressive kingdoms of the present. This backward flow may be seen as the epistemological crux of interpretation for understanding the kingdom of heaven in Matthew.

5:13-16. You are the salt of the earth. The concluding verses to this section summarize the current status of God's children and imply a subtle warning about the results of failure to fulfill that status by the negative comparisons involved. Verse 16 also identifies the work of the children of God with that described for Jesus by 4:16.

Do Not Think That I Have Come to Abolish, 5:17-48

5:17-20. I have come not to abolish but to fulfill. Jesus in v. 17 adopts self-consciously the perspective given by the narrator of the Gospel when citing prophetic passages and when constructing scenes alluding to the Law or Prophets. The following commandments are to be read as expressing the apocalyptic-eschatological filling up of canonical tradition. Verse 17 implies a polemic against a group of opponents that holds that Jesus is guilty of the abolition of God's will as expressed in the Law. Based on v. 20 we may suspect that the group is the scribes and Pharisees. In response to this position, Jesus does not argue, he asserts. He at no point in the subsequent commandments submits his judgment to the structures of scriptural exegesis.

Verse 18 suggests that the Law has a temporal limit at the juncture of the ending of heaven and earth. Jesus later confirms that this temporal limit will be reached (24:35). What transcends the temporal limits of history, however, are the words of Jesus. In this sense they displace the Law, regarded by significant portions of first-century Judaism as eternal. In Matthew the Law may be conceived as limited and bounded by history and therefore subject to the evil powers that are brought to light by the arrival of the kingdom of heaven.

Verse 19 poses the most perplexing problem for interpretation in this paragraph. The reference of *these* is not absolutely clear. It may refer backward to the commandments of the Law indicated by the phrase *not one letter, not one stroke* (v. 18), but that reading is grammatically difficult since no plural noun occurs in the phrase. Or, alternatively, it may refer forward to the subsequent commands of 5:21–7:27. This second reference, while not a common construction, is grammatically possible and may make the best sense of the composition of the speech as a whole.

Jesus uses a form that suggests a curse and a blessing for those who break or keep these commands. The blessing is enhanced status in the kingdom of heaven. The curse is not exclusion from the kingdom, as we might expect, but simply a lower status in the kingdom. If this verse refers to the commands of Jesus, then v. 19 makes clear that the following commands are not entrance requirements but the characteristics of children of God already in the kingdom.

Verse 20 provides a polemical summation and perhaps an indication of the opponent group envisioned by the statement of v. 17. The verse calls to mind 3:7 where the Pharisees were first introduced as those who appeal to their ethnic identity as a means of ensuring their acceptability to God as children of Abraham. Here they are apparently a group who possess some form of recognizable "righteousness" or "justice" that is insufficient for entry into the kingdom of heaven. Verses 17-20 establish a clear division between the presentation of the commands of Jesus and the interpretation of the Law by the Pharisees. The character of this excessive righteousness becomes the focus of the remainder of the speech.

5:21-48. You have heard that it was said. In this section five statements use an antithetical formula on

the pattern of 5:21 (Brooks 1987, 74–7). In addition, 5:31 contains a shortened form of the formula that functions to relate the saying on DIVORCE to the previous antithesis on ADULTERY. The saying on divorce occurs as a subpoint to the broader structure of this section. Each of these antitheses is composed of three elements: (1) the thesis, *You have heard that it was said*; (2) a scriptural citation or paraphrase; (3) the antithesis, *But I say to you*. The phrase *to those of ancient times* in the theses of vv. 21 and 33 refers to those who received the written Law on Sinai. The citation of scripture from the Law that follows each thesis in (2), supports this identification.

Since the formula refers to the scene of the giving of the Law on Sinai, then we should recall that scene. In Exodus Moses acts as the spokesperson between God and the people. Exodus 20:1 makes clear that the DECALOGUE is spoken by God.

The implication of Jesus' claim is contained in the third part of each saying. *But, I say to you* shows that he is the originator of what follows. By referring to written Law, rather than ORAL TRADITION or a rabbi's opinion, Jesus emphasizes his identification with God and his independence from the confines of the institutions of normal religion. Official teachers teach with the support of group authority, sanctioned by official and historical institutions, and seek to interpret canonical texts harmoniously. Jesus, on the other hand, appeals to no group authority, has the support of the tradition of no official historical institutions, and interprets the Mosaic Law antithetically.

In three of the sayings that follow this pattern, the antitheses on MURDER, adultery, and love of neighbor, Jesus extends and radicalizes existing interpretation of the Law. In the remaining three, on divorce, oaths, and talion, he utters new commands that may be seen by those outside the kingdom to revoke the plain meaning of canonical Law (Meier 1976, 131–61). Jesus as God-with-us takes his bearings not from Sinai but from the future of the kingdom that is now present. He further commands fellow members of the kingdom to do likewise. Fulfillment for the Gospel of Matthew means perception of the righteousness of God from the perspective of God's future, not the historical past.

Beware of Practicing Your Righteousness, 6:1-34

6:1. For you have no reward. Jesus continues the theme of righteousness begun in 5:20. Unfortunately, this connection is blurred in the NRSV translation *prac-- ticing your piety*. The Greek word is the same word translated as *righteousness* in 3:15, 5:20, and 6:34. The Gospel makes no distinction between what we might call acts of piety and other ethical acts.

6:2-18. So whenever you give alms. Jesus discusses almsgiving, PRAYER, and FASTING. Jesus' teaching alters significantly but does not preclude public worship. He offers specific restrictions and a theological principle: that which can be understood as rewardable by public acclaim should be avoided. Matthew 6:2-18 is unique to Jewish and Christian documents of the first century in its designation of God as *your Father who sees in secret.* The inclusion of these teachings here may be motivated out of a polemic against what the author regards as inappropriate worship forms within the community. The attempt seems to be to separate the community's worship from synagogual practice and from non-Jewish types of worship habits being brought into the community by gentiles (vv. 7-8). Jesus' injunctions prohibit the assignment of status to members of the community by virtue of their financial donations, laudatory prayers, or works of pious observance. Thereby, this teaching on righteousness implies social equality between all children of God. Any judgments on individual righteousness are left only to God.

6:19-21. Do not store up treasure on earth. Jesus completes the description of God's righteousness begun antithetically in vv. 1-18. This saying describes the dualism between heaven and earth that determines the allegiance of the heart based upon the storing of treasure.

6:22-23. The eye is the lamp of the body. Jesus describes an interaction between LIGHT and DARKNESS that can result in failure to see. These verses also unify physical and moral perception (Betz 1985, 85). Hence we cannot talk about a physical and spiritual dualism because the kingdom of heaven as indicated by Jesus' speech in Matthew regards the material, physical cosmos as coextensive with the spiritual cosmos. Division occurs not along spiritual/physical lines but along the lines demarcated by light-darkness, good-evil.

6:24. No one can serve two masters. Jesus contrasts two figures as competing lords: God and Mammon (Gk.). Mammon, that is, *wealth*, is depicted as a lord who rules over the things of the earth and (by parallel relation with v. 23) associates with evil and darkness. A person's place within the realm of one lord determines allegiance and the truth of perception.

6:25-34. Do not worry about your life. Jesus concludes with a more precise discussion of this interactive dualism. Verse 25 centers attention on the authority of Jesus, who describes the world as it is to true sight.

Verses 26-32 describe first the created order as apparent to usual mundane perception. By the use of the terminology *his righteousness*, v. 33 makes explicit the connection between the kingdom of God and the righteousness of God. In order for God's righteousness and God's kingdom to be realities that are sought, they must not only be possessions of God but also available for possession by others. Therefore, *his righteousness* indicates that one is to seek both the kingdom and the righteousness that belong to God and comes as a gift from God, the Lord who grants true sight.

The guarantee that follows in v. 34 is not based on the theological idea of the continuity of God with creation, but rather on the radical discontinuity between God and the world, which is in the possession of evil powers. Verse 34 presupposes that the outcome of the confrontation has already occurred in God's future, or kingdom of heaven. It presumes that this confrontation issues in the final victory of God. Once again is visible the remarkable truth that time flows from future to present in the text of Matthew. The righteousness of God is thus both the presupposition and end for the disciple.

The apocalyptic instruction given through Jesus becomes a powerful education. It does not provide the terms of admission into God's rule. Rather it draws the disciple more deeply into the mystery of the kingdom which is a new creation by God and in which the disciple is found. Jesus describes the boundary line between God's kingdom and the kingdom of evil that rules the world. The world thinks possessions and the reduction of anxieties about material security are prime issues in life. The children of the kingdom of God know what lord they serve and recognize that the righteousness that comes from God is their only pursuit. They are guaranteed on the basis of the power-infused authority of Jesus as God-with-us that they will find this righteousness. They are free from the anxieties of this world (see further Humphries-Brooks 1989).

Do Not Judge, 7:1-23

7:1-6. For with the judgment you make you will be judged. Jesus warns against judgment of another within the community. "Brother" is used regularly in Matthew to indicate other members of the community. The Greek word need not refer only to males and the NRSV uses the word *neighbor*. Jesus advises self inspection for HYPOCRISY.

Verse 6 indicates that as readily as Jesus prohibits judging for the sake of exclusion or hierarchy, he also enjoins care over the dispensation of those things that belong to God's kingdom to those incapable of appropriating them. There seems to be an ideological distinction here that may refer to problems of mission. Verses 1-5 refer to intracommunity relationships while v. 6 refers to relationships with those of the outside. It may also refer to those within the community who in the past have proven unworthy or unteachable from the perspective established by Jesus in the Gospel.

7:7-14. Ask and it will be given you. By comparing the positive behavior of broken humanity with God's infinite grace, the saying promises the resolution of judgment between good and evil in the future of God out of which and to which the kingdom of heaven moves. The community must wait in anticipation of that final fulfillment guided by the rule of mutual care embodied in v. 12.

Taken alone, the statement *in everything do to others as you would have them do to you; for this is the law and the prophets,* would miss the reference in the text of the sermon to the inbreaking of the kingdom of heaven, which Jesus claims is the fulfillment of the Law and the Prophets (5:17). The fulfillment is not salvation built out of the ethical systems of the past somehow summarized in a wise saying like v. 12, but rather it is grace that comes from the future into the present as apocalyptic-eschatological event.

7:13-14. Enter through the narrow gate. Verse 12 is situated between the grace of God artfully referred to by a short narrative in vv. 7-11 and the judgment of God clearly demarcated by the saying on the narrow gate in vv. 13-14. This tension reflects a fundamental theological insight in Matthew. The Gospel of Matthew represents throughout its text the problems of life as a child of the kingdom between the CRUCIFIXION and the PAROUSIA. At stake is the child's education to the insight that privilege and status come not from human will or action but only from God.

7:15-23. Beware of false prophets. Jesus warns against false prophets who appeal to his name as a means of validating their mighty words and works. These warnings indicate the probability that the Matthean community experienced divisions created by some type of early preachers and miracle workers. Verse 20 reminds the audience of the charge of John the Baptist in 3:8 to the Pharisees and Sadducees.

Apparently, these false prophets are to be understood as a phenomenon parallel to the religious leaders of Jesus' day. They are hypocrites when tested against the content of the commands of Jesus that provide the greater righteousness referred to by 5:20. Jesus, however, remains consistent in his advice. Warning is given, the audience is to recognize them when they come (v. 20). They are to be known by tests of orthopraxy, not orthodoxy, but no action against such individuals is to be taken.

Everyone Then Who Hears, 7:24-27

The concluding simile emphasizes the urgency of the sermon. The speech takes on the significance of life and death. The idea of foundation upon rock will be later exploited by Jesus in 16:13-23 in response to the confession of Simon Peter.

The sermon on the mount becomes the perspective by which all subsequent and previous narrative should be judged. Further, the text is so structured here and throughout the sermon as to press upon the audience the urgency to interpret their own personal and corporate histories from the same perspective. In short, the text presumes that its readers are children of God, members of the kingdom of heaven.

Plot: When Jesus Had Finished Saying These Things, 7:28–10:4

Both Israelites and non-Israelites emerge from the crowds as the supplicants of Jesus. By the end of the section, however, the crowds are narrowly conceived of as Israelite. This careful description of the narrowing of Jesus' ministry exclusively to Israel provides the setting for the speech of 10:5-42 and the plot of chaps. 11–12.

The arrangement of episodes in this section also follows a careful pattern of three sets of three miracle stories divided by three sections that describe Jesus' disciples (Meier 1979, 67–73). The content of each episode shows unnamed supplicants as better examples of faith than the disciples. Careful attention to the details of these miracles demonstrates that the speech or behavior of the supplicant frequently reveals to Jesus the faith of the individual and provides the opportunity for the exercise of Jesus' power.

The Crowds Were Astounded, 7:28-29

Jesus has *authority*. The underlying Greek concept more closely relates to what we might call directed, intelligent power. It is power appropriate to God-with-us (cf. 1:23). The word will be repeated again at the conclusion of the Gospel (28:16).

The crowds have been present all along to hear the sermon. The description of the kingdom provided by Jesus is presented not only to the disciples but to all. Verse 29 compares the speech of Jesus to that of normal human traditioners. The term *their scribes* implies that the crowds are part of Israel's institutions. Nevertheless, the following miracle stories include non-Israelite supplicants who emerge from the crowds.

When Jesus Had Come Down from the Mountain, 8:1-17

This section is composed of three healings: the leper, the centurion's slave, and the mother-in-law of Peter. The stories highlight the faith of the supplicants. The clearest pattern occurs in the healing of the centurion's slave. In vv. 9-13 the text depicts in detail the faith of the centurion by direct speech. The status of the centurion as non-Israel and the status of the ill slave give precise detail to the text and evoke Jesus' amazement. The plot shows Jesus as being educated into the will of God with regard to non-Israelites and slaves. The character, Jesus, perceives the faith of the centurion by his speech.

The centurion, like the leper before him, addresses Jesus as "Lord." Based upon what we have learned from the discussion of lordship in 6:19-34 as well as the use of this term of Jesus only in a confessional sense throughout the whole of the Gospel, we may understand that the use of the term is a sign of faith. The scene shows Jesus applying the perception of the kingdom of heaven to actual events within his ministry.

While the account of the healing of Peter's mother-in-law is not as detailed as the accounts of the two other healings, we may infer that Jesus perceives faith in her, or (on the pattern of the slave) in her behalf.

Now When Jesus Saw Great Crowds, 8:18-22

The kingdom overturns obligations of property and paternity, two of the most revered institutions of the ancient Jewish and non-Jewish world. Jesus addresses the scribe in v. 19, thereby tying the verse to the scribes in 7:29. Further, a disciple, which one we are not told, is given the even more severe injunction in v. 22. We are left not knowing the reaction of either character. We may presume that the disciple is also involved in the following episode.

Jesus himself denies his own status and identifies here for the first time with the homeless and fatherless,

that is, those unprotected by the normal social and religious structures of the day. He implies that his disciples must do the same.

And When He Got into the Boat, 8:23–9:8

8:23-27. A windstorm arose on the sea. The miracle of the stilling of the storm provides important contrasts with the previous set of miracles. Unlike the supplicants, the disciples do not emerge from the crowd. Since we do not know the decision reached by the disciple in the previous episode, we cannot yet judge whether Jesus' disciples, like himself, will renounce their status as free householders. Identical to the leper and the centurion, they address Jesus as "Lord." But their address is interpreted by Jesus to mean that they are of *little faith*. Surprisingly Jesus finds faith in great measure among the nameless with little or no status, while the faith of his disciples by comparison is untrustworthy and meager. By asking about the nature of the humanity of Jesus in v. 27, the disciples provide the question which will be answered by the two subsequent miracles. Each depicts more fully the nature of faith and the person of Jesus and his authority.

8:28-34. Two demoniacs met him. The element of faith seems missing altogether in the story of the Gadarene demoniacs. But the demoniacs place this story on a different footing from the others by addressing Jesus as SON OF GOD, the first humans to do so in the Gospel. This story boldly depicts a direct exorcistic battle between the Son of God and the demonic realm. It is therefore an appropriate story here because it prepares for the claim to power by Jesus in the subsequent story.

Unlike the parallel story in Mark, two demoniacs rather than one are mentioned. The text may be constructed in this way under the influence of the Jewish legal provision that requires two witnesses to any act (Deut 19:15). The witness to the Son of God recognizes him by non-human power. In this case, those enslaved to evil recognize their liberator, but fear him as conqueror.

In the ancient understanding, different sorts of demons lived in different places. Some lived in water, others in the air, or on land. All were regarded as striving for power over some host creature. The demons, by asking to be allowed to go into the SWINE, seek to trick Jesus into allowing them to continue their lives. They do not fool Jesus, however. The story might well have elicited humor from the Matthean community if a significant portion were ethnically

Jewish and therefore regarded the swine as unclean animals.

The text leaves it to the reader to surmise the townspeople's motivation for asking Jesus to leave. One possible motive that is consistent with the Matthean view of material possession would be that they feared further property destruction. The sanity of two demoniacs is less important than a herd of swine to these people. They do not recognize the presence of God and God's righteousness and do not seek it. The fact that this event occurs in the DECAPOLIS, a collection of non-Jewish cities, also may serve to emphasize that not all mission to the gentiles was necessarily successful. It may constitute part of Jesus' motivation for limiting the mission to Israel in 10:5.

9:1-8. Some people were carrying a paralyzed man. The contrast between the supplicants and the disciples continues in the last miracle of this trio, the healing of the paralytic (9:2-8). The supplicants form the model for faith as opposed to the anti-model provided by the disciples.

Jesus recognizes the faith of the paralytic's friends and heals him. The faith of a group of unknowns becomes the positive model to which we may compare the faith of the disciples. The story also becomes the occasion for Jesus to initiate a dispute with the scribes. Verse 5 makes clear that Jesus has provoked his opponents into an error of theological judgment by forgiving the man's sins. God in the healings of Jesus makes whole a created order broken and diseased by sin, an instrument of evil. Healing is the grace of God expressed through the SON OF MAN as a sign that the power of evil is coming to an end.

As Jesus Was Walking Along, He Saw Matthew, 9:9-17

9:9-13. He got up and followed him. By singling out the tax gatherer by name, the Gospel directs attention to the fact that the kingdom is composed of sinners. Sinners, or the unrighteous are, therefore, those who exceed the righteousness of the PHARISEES (5:20). The author repeatedly ironizes the religious self-consciousness of this group thereby exposing the claim to religious status as part of condemnable hypocrisy.

9:14-17. The disciples of John came to him. The disciples of John concur with the Pharisees in the religious observance of FASTING. Jesus interprets fasting as mourning the unrighteous state of the world prior to the coming of the day of the Lord. The conclusion of Matthew promises Jesus' presence to the end of the

age (28:20). Verse 15 indicates, therefore, that the children of the kingdom continually experience the presence of the bridegroom so that signs of mourning such as fasting are inappropriate. This verse adds to the understanding of religious observance begun in 6:1-18 and may suggest that even the type of fasting envisioned by 6:16-18 is unnecessary. The apocalyptic-eschatological context of the audience is the time after the crucifixion and before the coming of the Son of Man to judge, but the wedding feast continues in its celebration because Jesus remains with his community (see also 18:20).

Viewed from the perspective indicated by v. 15, the *both* of v. 17 refers to the *new wine* and *fresh wineskins*. Jesus indicates the radical disjuncture of the kingdom with religious forms that precede it or oppose it historically.

While He Was Saying These Things, 9:18-34

9:18-26. A leader came in and knelt before him. The placement of the story of the woman with hemorrhages within the story of the leader's daughter highlights the contrast of the faith of the woman with the unfaith of the crowds (vv. 22, 25). Matthew lets us infer that Jesus *seeing her* recognizes her faith and comments on it. The Greek text of Matthew does not contain *of the synagogue* (v. 18). The author probably did not intend for this civic leader to be understood as part of that institution. This accords with the overall characterization of Jesus' ministry as moving outside of the confines of traditional synagogue authority and with a general antipathy to the synagogue. The reading of the NRSV in v. 18 seems to be an unfortunate confusion of the Matthean story with the similar story in Mark 5:36.

9:27-31. Two blind men followed him. The idea of seeing as an essential metaphor for faith continues in the story of *the two blind men*. Here Jesus perceives their faith by direct question (v. 28).

9:32-34. A demoniac was brought to him. The following miracle indicates the division that Jesus creates within Israel. It fulfills to some degree the apocalyptic statement of 9:17. The crowds are amazed, while the Pharisees explicitly assign his power to the realm of evil.

Then Jesus Went about All the Cities and Villages, 9:35–10:4

The division described narratively in 9:32-34 now receives direct comment by Jesus in vv. 35-38 and is followed by his own reaction to the situation of a divided Israel in 10:1-4. The two scenes are written in such a way as to relate closely to each other, therefore, we have chosen to include 10:1-4 as the conclusion to the previous plot narrative.

Matthew 9:35 restates 4:23 and acts as an inclusionary summation but unlike 4:23 focusses exclusively on Israel. The text adds the observation that the crowds have no leadership (v. 36). The gathering opposition of the synagogue authorities summarized by their indictment of Jesus in the previous episode shows that they have an unsound eye and cannot discern the kingdom. Therefore, Jesus directly addresses this problem discovered within Israel by summoning THE TWELVE for the first time (10:1-4).

Speech:
These Twelve Jesus Sent Out, 10:5-42

Go Nowhere among the Gentiles, 10:5-15

Jesus' ministry as depicted from 4:23 has included both Israel and non-Israel. The sending of the disciples exclusively to Israel is in response to Jesus' discovery of the blindness of its leaders not to a preordained plan of salvation first to Israel and then to non-Israel.

The specific nature of the mission spelled out in vv. 7-8 corresponds precisely to the ministry of Jesus depicted in 4:23–9:35. The disciple reproduces what has been learned observing the master. The prohibition of accepting payment (vv. 8b-10) demands ministry in identification with the homeless SON OF MAN (8:20). Finally, this ministry carries with it both grace and judgment as indicated by vv. 13-15.

See, I Am Sending You out like Sheep, 10:16-23

From v. 16 onward the speech takes on significance beyond the events narrated in the text of the Gospel. Jesus foretells judicial action at the synagogue level and trial by non-Israelite leaders (vv. 17-20). Within the text, however, the disciples are never so treated. Therefore, we may suspect that this prediction applies to some time after the crucifixion and prior to the PAROUSIA. The Matthean community either knows of those who have undergone persecution or anticipates it. Such a mission results in the direct dissolution of family ties.

The limitation of the time frame of the mission to Israelite cities in v. 23 to the time prior to the coming of the Son of Man may indicate that the mission to Israel continues even in the time of the Matthean community. The coming of the Son of Man is clearly described in Matt 24 and that arrival is different from the beginning of the end time that arrives with the CRUCIFIXION and resurrection of Jesus.

A Disciple Is Not above the Teacher, 10:24-42

10:24-25. If they have called the master Beelzebul. These verses continue the shift of focus for the audience begun by the mention of the Son of Man in v. 23. The reference to *Beelzebul* shows that the conflict with the Pharisees in history is nothing other than a portion of the world-encompassing conflict between the kingdom of heaven and the kingdoms of the world (see 9:34; 12:24). Therefore, the trials depicted in 10:17-23 should be reread not only in reference to the particular politics of sectarianism in the ancient world, but also as a sign of the apocalyptic conflict initiated by the preaching of Jesus and the ministry of his disciples.

10:26-31. Have no fear of them. The following verses depict from various angles the reality of this apocalyptic conflict. An alternative translation of the beginning of this verse reads, "Do not fear them, for there is nothing hidden that will not be *apocalypsed*." The following verses direct attention to appropriate allegiance during the apocalyptic hour. Hope is grounded in the justice and mercy of God as the juxtaposition of judgment and grace makes clear in vv. 28-31; Jesus provides images of God as both righteous judge and caring parent.

10:32-38. Everyone who acknowledges me. Jesus relates the problem of the disintegration of households in normal historical existence to the creation of a new family in the kingdom of heaven. The conflict initiated by the arrival of the kingdom results in both death to normal patriarchal structures and death for the individual. The series begins in v. 35 with relationship to the father and concludes in a manner consistent with the teaching in 9:21-22. The image of cross-bearing in v. 38 results in the conundrum of v. 39. The problem of this paradoxical teaching can be solved only by applying what we learn from the whole of Matthew. Jesus shows that the disciple must identify with Jesus' own destiny in terms of crucifixion and resurrection. The antinomic opposition to death is life given from God.

10:40-42. Whoever welcomes you. Jesus discusses reward as a paradoxical concept. It refers both to the reward of God within God's kingdom as well as the destiny of the prophets and the righteous placed at the mercy of the kingdoms of the world (see 23:29-39). Children of the kingdom cannot avoid the conflict. The conclusion in v. 42 introduces the idea that the emissaries of Jesus have in their OBEDIENCE the sanction of the judgment of the kingdom. It also directs attention to *these little ones.* The reference must be to those supplicants seeking healing from the disciples with the same faith as the supplicants in Matt 8-9. Hence, the rule of justice employed by Jesus as God-with-us (cf. 1:23) in the apocalyptic moment is one of service to those who are at the margins and have no advocate, save God.

Plot and Speech: Now When Jesus Had Finished, 11:1–12:50

With this section the text fully manifests the ambiguity between plot and speech narration in the Gospel of Matthew. Two major movements of plot can be discerned: (1) Jesus teaches and preaches *in their cities* (11:1-30); (2) Jesus disputes with the Pharisees (12:1-50). The activity of Jesus combined with dialogue and brief speeches indicates that the gospel comes to the nation Israel and that both its people and its leaders reject it. The urban mission of Jesus within Israel fails.

The text directs us to perceive within these historical events the confrontation with the kingdom of evil brought about by Jesus. The confrontation becomes apparent through Jesus' interpretation of event. With this section, the strategy of speeches enters into the middle of the strategy of plot in the same way as the kingdom moves into the world. Literary pattern represents world palingenesis (Wilder 1982, 34).

He Went on to Teach, 11:1-30.

11:1-6. He went on to proclaim in their cities. John sends disciples to Jesus to determine if he is the Messiah. Jesus does not affirm the title but answers by a recapitulation of his ministry (vv. 4-6). The language of Jesus echoes Isa 61:1-2, a passage that refers to a prophetic, not messianic, anointing and ministry. The conclusion in v. 6 establishes the basis for reproach and judgment against the cities and against the Pharisees in the following episodes. We are not told of John's reaction to Jesus' reply, rather this episode provides the opportunity for the speech of Jesus that follows.

11:7-30. Jesus began to speak to the crowds. These verses comprise one extended speech by Jesus addressed to the urban Israelite crowds (vv. 7, 20). The first section (vv. 7-19) serves to differentiate the ministry of Jesus from that of John. Verse 11 appears to consign John to the mundane historical plane and to separate him to some degree from those in the kingdom of heaven. Notwithstanding this indication, however, vv. 12-14 show that he is the initiator of the presence of the kingdom of heaven in the historical world and the recipient of the first attacks of violence by those who serve the kingdoms of the world. We should read v. 12 in the context of the arrest, imprisonment, and eventual beheading of John by Herod, who belongs to the urban power elite reckoned throughout Matthew as servants of evil (3:12; 11:2; 14:1-12). Verse 12 interprets the two-level battle observable in the realm of mundane historical existence interpenetrated by the powers of evil aligned against the power of God. In this context, v. 14 indicates that John is a new type of emissary not to be confused with the *prophets and the law* (v. 13).

Verses 16-19 conclude this first section by interpreting the crowds as like children whose whims cannot be satisfied. In the illustration religious and cultural practices related to weddings and funerals are invoked (Jeremias 1972, 160–62). Even though John adopts the perspective that the arrival of the kingdom is a time of repentance and mourning, while Jesus adopts the perspective of the wedding feast, neither the judgment nor the grace of God is acceptable to the crowds.

Therefore, Jesus condemns the cities for their lack of repentance in vv. 20-24. Following this general condemnation Jesus makes clear that only the least powerful of status groups receive the apocalypsis of God. The word translated by the NRSV as *infants* should better be understood from context as the direct antonym to the *wise and intelligent* (v. 25), that is, uneducated and naive. Along with v. 27 this passage makes clear what has been implicit throughout the ministry of Jesus: those who manifest faith to Jesus do so by the gift of God's gracious will and Jesus responds by revealing God to the faith that comes from God.

The idea of education links vv. 28-30 with the preceding section. Jesus addresses the uneducated and naive and offers them a particular education that results in rest. Jesus does not characterize the apocalyptic-eschatological message of the kingdom as difficult or impossible.

Jesus Went through the Grainfields on the Sabbath, 12:1-50

12:1-14. His disciples began to pluck heads of grain. After the aside to those chosen from among the least, we view the unfaith and condemnation of the greatest, the leadership represented by the Pharisees. In two scenes they initiate disputes over proper SABBATH observance (12:1-8; 9-14). In each case Jesus invokes an emergency situation to claim the overturning of mundane sabbath observance as the will of God. The emergency alluded to in these stories is the arrival of the kingdom of heaven. The Pharisees, on the other hand, remain on the side of historical perception with the result that they make plans to kill Jesus.

12:15-21. Many crowds followed him. The narrator interrupts the disputes with the Pharisees with a citation of Isa 42:1-4. The quotation shows that the future of the kingdom of heaven lies with the gentiles. The interruption recalls earlier sections of Matthew that imply that non-Israel is included in the mission of Jesus. In this regard it may well be that v. 15 refers to "many" who follow him (instead of *many crowds*) and that we are to understand this as a reference to predominantly non-Israelite groups. Reliable ancient manuscripts do not contain the word "crowds," which in this section of Matthew has been used to refer to Israelites. Verse 16, therefore, indicates that during this special period of Jesus' ministry, the mission to non-Israel should remain secret.

12:22-45. By Beelzebul this fellow casts out demons. The concluding episode in this series of disputes with the Pharisees exposes once and for all their allegiance to and determination by the powers of evil. Jesus responds to their accusation by an extended speech (vv. 25-45). Jesus is in the business of destroying the kingdom of Satan (vv. 25-28). Underlying the story of the strong man bound (v. 29) is an apocalyptic perspective of the world possessed by evil powers. Jesus interprets his role as miracle worker as robbing those powers of their control over human beings. The Pharisees oppose such activity as impious because it violates the sabbath. By refusing to recognize the power of God in the action of Jesus, religious leaders judge themselves. By accusing Jesus, the Pharisees reveal their true origin. Such misnaming of powers is unforgivable (vv. 32; 33-37).

Verses 38-45 pronounce the eschatological judgment of the Son of Man against the Pharisees. The sign of Jonah indicates the time between the death and resurrection of Jesus. It also links Jesus in his death to the Son of Man, who will judge. The references to Nineveh and the queen of the South enhance the theme of the discovery of faith among non-Israel and women begun in the genealogy.

The story of the unclean spirit indicates that those whose origin is in the power of evil rather than in God, condemn themselves to a descending cycle of absorption into the realm of Satan (vv. 43-45). What begins as religious propriety may end in acts of evil. The religious leaders are this type of person. They oppose Jesus on the historical and religious plane and in doing so dwell more and more radically and enslave themselves more and more surely to the kingdom of Satan until there is no escape. Their plot to kill Jesus referred to in 12:14 is only the historical manifestation of the power that controls their lives and destiny.

The speech concludes with positive instructions about Jesus' own household (vv. 46-50). By the use of terminology derived from family relationships, Jesus throughout Matthew develops a model of the community of the kingdom of heaven that is both similar to and distinct from patriarchal families. The will of God determines the reality of family relationships rather than allegiances based on blood or ethnic ties. Consistently in Matthew all status markers normal in human society are transcended or negated by participation in the kingdom of heaven.

Speech: He Told Them Many Things in Parables, 13:1-52

Two small movements of plot divide this speech into four episodes in which Jesus' speech is directly addressed to two different character groups (Bauer 1988, 131). In addition, the four episodes are interrupted by a citation of scripture by the narrator. The integration of plot with speech represents the permeation of the current historical process by the kingdom of heaven. Matthew 13:52 states the purpose of the speech: to train scribes for the kingdom of heaven. As we explore this speech, therefore, we need to be aware that here we have evidence of the process of training for the kingdom as well as its content.

A Sower Went out to Sow, 13:1-9

The scene of the first parable by Jesus in Matthew links it closely with the preceding narrative. Jesus addresses the parable to the crowds. Given the previous section of narrative, the setting implies that these crowds are predominantly Israelite. The emphasis of the parable seems to fall on the miraculous production of the seed (v. 8).

Why Do You Speak to Them in Parables?, 13:10-23

13:10-17. To you it has been given. The PARABLES divide the disciples from the crowds. Israel has been judged first by the miracle-working activity of Jesus and now is being judged by the parables. The judgment of parable-telling comes in revealing the fact of nonperception of the kingdom of heaven (v. 13). Further, Jesus himself interprets this judgment as a fulfillment of the prophetic judgment of Isa 6:9-10, a prophecy that specifically indicts the rulers and people of Jerusalem for their refusal to repent. The parables act as an eschatological sealing of the consciousness of the people for judgment by God.

13:18-23. Hear the parable of the sower. While the parable appears to emphasize the miraculous gift of an excessive harvest, Jesus provides to the disciples a specific key to interpret the parable at a deeper level: the different types of soils represent different types of people and their response to the word. In each case the opposition to the word is connected to the kingdom of Satan. Verse 19 connects it to the *evil one* himself. Verse 20 connects it to persecution; the source of persecution is not only human institutions but also the lord served by those institutions. Verse 22, which identifies the cares and wealth of the world as the seduction away from the word, may be read with reference to 6:24 and understood to indicate that wealth is under the control of Mammon (cf. 6:24), a servant of the *evil one* as well.

According to Jesus, the key to understanding the parable is the ability to see a two-level conflict in the present moment. The conflict on the surface may appear to be a historical one: normal worldly cares, greed, and persecution destroy one's attention to the word of salvation to humans. But more, all of these are weapons in the struggle of the kingdom of the evil one against the incoming kingdom of heaven. This understanding cannot be deduced from the parable itself, which emphasizes the miraculous growth of the kingdom, but only from the proper perspective provided by Jesus to those to whom the secrets of the kingdom have already been given. The trained scribe adopts the apocalyptic perspective of Jesus in order to properly interpret the parables at all levels.

He Put before Them Another Parable, 13:24-34

Jesus addresses the three parables that follow the interpretation to the crowds once more (v. 34). Since they are addressed to the crowds composed of urban Israel who are being judged by the parables, no interpretation of these parables is provided. We shall wait to offer an interpretation of these parables from Jesus' perspective when the text returns to these parables at v. 36.

This Was to Fulfill 13:35

The narrator interrupts the development of the parable speech of Jesus with an interpretative citation of prophetic scripture. The citation comes from Ps 78:2 and is traditionally attributed to ASAPH who according to 2 Chr 29:30 was a seer or prophet. According to Ps 78:2-4 the parable reveals what previously has been hidden. In Matthew, Jesus uses parables on the one side to judge the crowds and on the other to instruct the disciples and through them all members of the kingdom of heaven.

Then He Left the Crowds, 13:36-52

13:36-43. Explain to us the parable. Jesus explains in allegorical fashion the parable of 13:24-30. The key to interpretation remains an apocalyptic-eschatological perspective. Judgment is reserved for the Son of Man who is both the sower of good seed and the judge at the end of the age. The interpretation of Jesus makes clear that his ministry to Israel as the Son of Man forms the basis for justice in the final time. The justice of God assigns proper place to those found as children of the kingdom or children of the evil one at the end time.

13:31-32. The kingdom of heaven is like a mustard seed. At this point we return to the earlier parables (13:24-34), since we now have a pattern of interpretation established by the presentation of the text. While Jesus himself does not provide an interpretation, the text presumes that we can provide one based upon the method of Jesus. The parable of the mustard seed, therefore, may be interpreted as referring to the planting of the kingdom of heaven through the ministry of Jesus. The result is an unexpected home for the homeless (v. 32).

13:33. The kingdom of heaven is like yeast. The parable of the leaven breaks the pattern of its group of parables since planting is not involved. Jesus is compared to a woman, or perhaps the female character is God. The emphasis falls on the miracle of leavening. The image indicates the active nature of God's kingdom through Jesus. As the depiction of the miracles of Jesus in Matthew makes clear, the kingdom of heaven is not simply beset and beleaguered by the Evil One and its children, it also is in the business of claiming territory for itself.

13:44-45. The kingdom of heaven is like treasure. This pair of parables emphasizes the inherent and almost irrational value of the kingdom; the emphasis in both falls on the activity of the individual in selling all that he has for the sake of the treasure of the kingdom. Jesus provides a parabolic expression of the activity he advocated in 6:19-34. The theme will be further developed in 19:16-29.

13:47-50. The kingdom of heaven is like a net. The final parable of the speech returns to the theme of eschatological judgment already emphasized by the parables of the sower and the weeds among wheat. Here, presumably since Jesus is speaking only to the disciples and through them to the audience, parable and apocalyptic-eschatological interpretation occur together.

13:51-52. Have you understood all this? The parable discourse concludes with a dialogue between Jesus and the disciples. Verse 52 marks the purpose of the discourse as the training of scribes for the kingdom of heaven. The simile invites an apocalyptic-eschatological reading, first, because of its place within the parable chapter. The reversal of normal historical sequence in the phrase *what is new and what is old* points in the same direction. The perspective induced by the speeches of Matt 13 begins with the new: the inbreaking of the kingdom of God into the world. God's arrival creates a division within humanity through the parables of Jesus. Humans are being judged by the ministry of Jesus who is already the coming Son of Man. From the Matthean perspective, the division of humanity occurs for the first time in the life of Jesus. The final process of judgment will not be complete until some point in the historical future.

Plot and Speech: When Jesus Had Finished These Parables, 13:53–17:27

The plot focuses on the reaction to Jesus' person and message on the part of three groups of characters: crowds, Pharisees, and disciples.

He Came to His Hometown, 13:53-58

NAZARETH rejects Jesus and on the basis of this lack of faith he performs no miracle (v. 58). The story implies that the rejection comes out of the towns-people's association with the synagogue. They seek to understand Jesus as part of a human household, com-posed of his mother and brothers (v. 55). By depending on a social perspective, the people of Jesus' hometown become offended at him. According to Jesus, national identity, ethnicity, and association with family prohibits the perception generated by God's kingdom (v. 57). After this episode, Jesus moves outside of normal social and religious institutions for the proclamation of his message.

Herod the Ruler Heard about Jesus, 14:1-12

HEROD the ruler along with his wife Herodias brings about the death of JOHN THE BAPTIST. Herodias's daughter, unnamed by the narrator, has no real power vis-à-vis her mother. She is both an object of her stepfather's lust and the means to accomplish Herodias's murderous intent. The story does not portray the daughter as culpable for her actions. She extends the Matthean theme of the victimization of children begun in the infancy narrative. The text exposes the stupidity of male pride and the false valuing of personal status by showing Herod's adherence to a frivolous oath (see 5:37) and acquiescence to her unjust request so as to preserve his personal power in the eyes of those assembled. Among the kings of the world, children, especially female children, become tools instead of persons.

Jesus Withdrew to a Deserted Place, 14:13-21

The miracle of the feeding of the five thousand and the walking on the water occur together in all four Gospels. The association probably was influenced by the similar stories about MOSES, ELIJAH, and ELISHA found in the Jewish scriptures. Matthew, however, contains its own peculiar emphases. The focus in each story becomes the disciples and their faith.

Whereas previous miracles have emphasized the marginality of the supplicants, this miracle by its setting depicts the advent of the kingdom as outside of the cities, synagogues, and households of Israel. The enactment of the feeding miracle before the crowds reflects compassion. The crowds' eagerness to follow Jesus and the presence among them of the sick implies that Jesus recognizes faith from their action.

The disciples and their response become the focus by virtue of their request of Jesus. The disciples reflect a lack of faith since they judge according to mundane historical needs and satisfaction of those needs (cf. Patte, 209-11). Jesus' blessing directed toward the heavens draws attention to the power of God expressed through the miracle.

Jesus Made the Disciples
Get into the Boat, 14:22-36

The first scene depicts Jesus walking on the water to the disciples who as a group fail to recognize him and take him to be a ghost. The motif of their lack of discernment implicit in the previous story becomes explicit.

Peter acts both as an individual and as a representative of the Twelve. Jesus recognizes and emphasizes his lack of faith (v. 31). His behavior remains consistent with the previous behavior of the disciples in a similar situation at 8:26. The author depicts Peter throughout the Gospel as undependable and doubting.

The Pharisees and Scribes
Came from Jerusalem, 15:1-20

Jesus condemns the PHARISEES for substituting their will for God's will. Jesus regards their interpretation as opposed to God's commandments. Verses 6-9 indicate that such a tradition is a human, not divine, institution and imply that their tradition antithetically opposes the word of God. For Jesus the word of God means the will of God revealed to be righteous and just in the eschatological time of Jesus' ministry. The function of the parable like those of Matt 13 must be to judge the crowd.

Beginning with v. 12, Jesus interprets the parable of 15:11. The scene shows that the disciples have not understood the speech of Matt 13, nor have they understood the actions of Jesus. They as yet lack faith that comes from the perspective of the kingdom. In Matthew faith and understanding appear to be two aspects of the same gift from God.

Jesus Left That Place
and Went Away to Tyre and Sidon, 15:21-39

15:21-28. A Canaanite woman started shouting. The use of Canaanite rather than SYROPHONECIAN as in Mark 7:26 emphasizes that the woman comes from an ethnicity traditionally an enemy of Israel worthy of extermination (see Josh 12:20). The story of the Canaanite woman shows that Jesus himself can initially fail to perceive faith and thereby refuse access to the kingdom to those to whom he was sent. Jesus, an Israelite man, allows himself to be duped by the appearance of this supplicant as a woman and a non-Israelite.

Jesus refuses to hear her petition and strives to silence her by ignoring her (v. 23a). But the woman demands a hearing for her daughter's need. The disciples become upset at her noisy importunity and plead for Jesus to *send her away* (v. 23b). The male householders strive to silence the supplicating woman and assign her to the margins.

At v. 24 Jesus finally engages in conversation with her after reiterating his statement of mission in the same words as 10:5. Matthew depicts Jesus' earlier mission up to that point as universal. During that mission Jesus recognizes and heals women supplicants from Israel as well as men of both Israel and non-Israel (Matt 8–9). Here, for the first time, Jesus confronts a non-Israelite woman.

Jesus' journey to TYRE AND SIDON indicates an intention to transcend the borders of the Israelite homeland with his mission. Therefore, on the basis of the previous behavior of Jesus and the development of plot in this section, we might anticipate that here Jesus himself will move beyond the ethnic and national boundaries imposed since 10:5. Such a return would confirm the earlier indications in Matthew of a universal mission.

The speech and action of Jesus do not accord with either his own actions or speeches elsewhere and therefore disconfirms our expectations. The woman, however, proves to be a better theologian than Jesus. She willingly identifies her utter abasement as a crumb-lapping dog and refers to the "Lords' table" from which she begs scraps. This phrase is usually translated as *masters' table* thereby referring to the people of Israel who are also understood as the *children* in Jesus' response of v. 26. Such a reading is difficult within the larger context of Matthew since the narrative previously condemned the people and leadership of Israel as unrepentant.

The woman appears, at one level, to argue a truism—dogs eat crumbs from their masters' table. At a second level, however, the woman's statement implies a confession of faith. In Matthew the singular *Lord* occurs as a confessional title used by supplicants of Jesus. Jesus recognizes in this title the presence of faith. The woman uses this form of supplication in vv. 22, 25, 27. By using the plural the woman shows that she recognizes not only Jesus but also God as her lord. She understands the table as the table of the final banquet presided over by God and the SON OF MAN, that includes all despite accidents of ethnicity. Her interpretation accords with Jesus' own interpretation of the faith of the centurion in 8:10-13. Her understanding can come only from God.

Jesus pronounces her faith and heals her daughter. The author does not shrink from showing Jesus as learning from a woman of an inappropriate ethnicity. Both status as woman and as non-Israel are highlighted in order to show the apocalyptic faith that comes from the kingdom of heaven and that destroys all historical claims to prerogatives within the kingdom. Even Jesus in this Gospel can be educated by such faith.

15:29-39. He passed along the Sea of Galilee. The following episodes show Jesus re-initiating a self-conscious ministry to gentiles after the education by the woman (cf. Gundry 1982, 317–22). Galilee has already been associated with the gentiles in 4:13-18. The healing ministry and the feeding miracle apparently take place on the eastern shore of the Sea of Galilee in the general area of the DECAPOLIS. *Magadan* (v. 39) is on the western shore. The sentence *And they praised the God of Israel* (v. 31) indicates clearly that the crowds are non-Israel. Jesus fulfills the prophecy of Isa 61:1-2 specifically for a non-Israelite crowd. The miracle of the feeding of the four thousand contrasts with the earlier feeding of the five thousand performed for a predominantly Israelite crowd.

The Pharisees and Sadducees Test Jesus, 16:1-12

Within the plot of Matthew this episode repeats in an abbreviated form the episode found in 12:38-42. Therefore, the episode offers another opportunity for Jesus to condemn the religious leadership. He does so as the Son of Man who will die. Implied is the eschatological perception that the crucifixion and resurrection of Jesus function not only to include children in the kingdom of heaven, but also to judge. Matthew presents Jesus as Son of Man who judges: first, during his historical ministry to the cities of Israel; second, by his death and resurrection; and third, in his PAROUSIA. Such a rich conceptualization of the Son of Man indicates the fluidity with which the author discerns the movement of time and event along spatial axes. The future of God erupts in Matthean narrative where God wills it regardless of the clocks of historical causality. Such thought here and elsewhere proves disorienting to those of us accustomed to narratives that express a worldview that privileges historical sequence and causality. The disciples represent the historical viewpoint as well. They lack faith (v. 8) and perception (v. 11). They finally gain some understanding (v. 12).

Jesus Asked His Disciples about the Son of Man, 16:13–17:23

The previous episodes introduce an extended section composed of three episodes in which Jesus directly teaches the disciples about his person and destiny. Jesus connects the titles, Son of God and Son of Man. Peter and the other disciples with him fail to understand Jesus. Ultimately, they are pronounced faithless. Ironically as Jesus reveals himself fully to them the disciples' own lack of faith becomes apparent.

16:13-27. You are the Messiah. To Peter, first, and then later to all of his disciples, Jesus gives power of interpretation and adjudication (16:19 and 18:18). This development is surprising, since PETER and THE TWELVE have yet to be shown to be trustworthy.

Peter—whom Jesus calls *rock* (for the foundation of the community in the eschatological moment)—is given power to *bind* and *loose*, which is understood to be the power to interpret the kingdom of heaven on earth. He is the chief scribe in a school of scribes.

In what sense Peter or Peter's confession constitutes the *rock* on which the community is built remains ambiguous in the text. The ambiguity may be due to the fact that the following scene de-centers and uproots Peter and his tradition from any claim to authoritative hegemony over the Matthean community.

The bestowal of authority is followed immediately by the condemnation of Peter (vv. 21-23). The juxtaposition creates ironic tension. In v. 23 Jesus places Peter in the same relationship to the kingdom of heaven as the powerful urban elites. He is to be found with Satan aligned against God. As elsewhere in Matthew, Jesus knows this not by superhuman insight but by what Peter says. Peter expresses misperception—the wrong epistemology—in v. 22. The condemnation of Peter indicates that the confession of v. 16 is only partial and inadequate from the viewpoint of Jesus and the author. Indeed it is dangerous. Jesus is not the Messiah that Peter would like, the David who will restore Israel to its national independence, but rather he is the Son of God and Son of Man who judges and who dies for the entire world. Peter seeks the kingdom of humans dominated by the evil one and opposed to the kingdom of heaven whose agent is God-with-us. Peter is christologically, theologically, and politically in error.

17:1-21. Jesus took with him Peter and James and his brother John. The section demonstrates who Jesus is and the disciples' failure to understand his identity as the Son of God who is also the Son of Man who will suffer. This failure of perception results in their condemnation as *faithless and perverse* (v. 17).

The implicit comparison between Jesus and MOSES and ELIJAH established in the miracles of the feeding and the walking on the water becomes explicit here. In addition the themes of the lack of faith and understanding of Peter and the other disciples continue. Peter wants to engage in a building program (v. 4) rather than listen and must be silenced from heaven by the same words heard at Jesus' baptism. Jesus supersedes the authority of Moses and Elijah. Their appearances here may represent the impending end of time. Both were regarded by some segments of Judaism as returning from heaven in the final days prior to the DAY OF THE LORD (cf. Mal 4).

As in the previous section, a warning about the earthly destiny of the Son of Man follows direct revelation from God about who Jesus is as the Son of God (v. 9). The disciples again indicate their lack of insight because they ask about Elijah, rather than addressing the more apparent issue of the identity and destiny of Jesus (vv. 10-12).

Verses 14-21 conclude this section and focus attention on the disciples' lack of faith. Jesus condemns them as a group in terms almost identical to the condemnation of the Pharisees and Sadducees in 16:4. Supplicants, however, have faith. The disciples cannot heal because of their little faith (v. 21).

17:22-23. As they were gathering in Galilee, Jesus said. These verses contain a concluding teaching about the Son of Man in Galilee. They provide an inclusion with 16:13 in which Jesus answers his own question of his identity and destiny. Furthermore, the episode is written so that when we come to the gathering of the eleven disciples in Galilee after the resurrection (28:16-20) we will be immediately reminded of the disciples and their distress at Jesus' prophecy. As is shown in the teaching about the Son of Man who must suffer and die, the disciples lack the faith to understand Jesus and his destiny. The faithless disciples gathered in Galilee are greatly distressed. Later in Galilee some will doubt (28:17).

The Children Are Free, 17:24-27

The episode singles out Peter. Jesus frees the children of the kingdom from religious obligation and sees the Temple tax as imposed by the kings of the earth. A historical problem is addressed, as well as the true origin and allegiance within the kingdom. The miracle places the provision in the hands of God and conforms to the teaching on Mammon in 6:19-34. Hence the plot of Matthew provides concrete examples of the principles articulated in the speeches of Jesus that describe the constitution and politics of the kingdom.

Verse 27 makes clear that violent resistance must not be the course of action for the child. To refuse to pay would align Jesus with political seditionists that might use the power of Mammon withheld from the Temple officials for the purpose of bringing down the kings of the world. Implicit here is the theological and political principle that the means can never justify ends. The use of worldly power necessarily brings enslavement to the powers of the world.

Speech: Who Is the Greatest in the Kingdom of Heaven? 18:1-35

Matthew 13:52–17:27 contains little or no plot advancement. Therefore, the movement to the fourth extended speech by Jesus fuses without disruption into the preceding section. The immediately preceding episode provides an excellent introduction to the speech since it highlights children as free within the kingdom and the world. Literarily, the speech represents an artistic use of both dialogue and parable. It is organized into two parts. The first answers, *Who is the greatest in the kingdom of heaven?* (vv. 1-5). The second explores the question of how the *little ones* are to be treated (vv. 6-35). The weight of the speech rests on the last point. Thereby, Jesus shifts the attention of the audience from rank in the kingdom to service and relationship within the community or *ekklēsia*.

Matthew infuses ecclesiology with theology. Unlike the narrative section that precedes it, direct reflection on the person of Jesus, christology, is absent or at best only implied in the fact that he is the speaker. Rather, the entire focus is on the kingdom of heaven, the master who deploys it, and the relationship of the children of that kingdom in their historical gathering to one another. In this speech Jesus teaches about living in mundane human community as children of God. Politics becomes focussed through ethics.

He Called a Child, 18:1-5

Jesus presents for the first time an expanded teaching on the understanding of status within the kingdom. While Jesus has used diminutive terms such as "children," "little ones," and "naive ones" in prior contexts, he here presents a coherent view.

In Matthew children are characters of the lowest and most vulnerable status. They never speak in Matthew. Herod murders them. Those who are healed are healed at the request of adults of higher status. If we understand the daughter of Herodias to be still a child, then we must also recognize sexual abuse implied as an aspect of children's status in Matthew. No children, except Jesus himself, receive names in Matthew.

This representation accords well with the place of children in the ancient world. While there is some evidence for the romanticization of children in the art and literature of Hellenistic culture, such ideas appear to have had little effect on the treatment of children. Infanticide, for example, was advocated by many moral philosophers as a means of eliminating unwanted or handicapped children. How common the practice was, we have no way of knowing. Similar to our society, children in the ancient world have minimal civil rights and remain completely under the domination of their fathers. Children are regarded as naive, uneducated, and foolish. No philosopher or wise man would seek to emulate them. Jesus appears to be unique in the ancient world in his valuation of children as exemplars for the life of a community.

These points should help reveal to us the uncomfortable irony that the ancient audience would likely feel at this episode. The disciples are free male householders who receive the instruction of Jesus. They should be the wise and pious models of the kingdom. Jesus instructs them to become like the child. The aspiration to humility runs opposite to the desire for knowledge and maturity. The kingdom of heaven requires the direct reversal of status aspirations.

If You Put a Stumbling Block before One of These, 18:6-35

Jesus constructs an answer to a question not asked by the disciples. By this rhetorical device he shifts attention to the question of relationships within the kingdom of heaven and its specific historical manifestation, the community. These verses fall into three sections: vv. 6-9; 10-14; 15-35. The extensive discussion of the last section indicates the emphasis of the speech that moves from the general conceptuality of the kingdom to the specifics of individual religious communities. As we interpret these verses we should remember that the teaching of vv. 2-5 shows that we should presuppose a community in which all members have the status of children and therefore no hierarchical roles may be assigned.

18:6-9. Woe to the world. Jesus warns against being the cause of temptation to other members of the kingdom in graphic terms of eschatological judgment.

18:10-14. Take care. Jesus offers the positive alternative to this negative behavior. The shepherd's behavior in the parable beginning in v. 12 constitutes foolishness. By leaving the ninety-nine on the mountain he endangers his entire livelihood. Seen from the perspective of the kingdom, however, the shepherd represents God's care for the lost.

18:15-35. If another sins against you. The third section follows logically and forcefully on these first two principles. Verses 15-20 apply in a practical case the principle enunciated by the parable. The reader of the English text has the disadvantage of a language that makes no formal distinction between you (pl.) and you (sing.). In Greek, however, there is a clear distinction. Verses 15-17 in Greek use you (sing.). Hence, they should be read as referring to the behavior of the one wronged toward the one doing the wrong. The conclusion of the process in v. 17 allows for the entire community to be brought together to settle the dispute. The outcome of the process, should it not result in reconciliation, is that the sinner be regarded as a gentile *tax collector*. Given the depiction of these groups in Matthew as those most likely to hear the message of the gospel then the offended party is being instructed to consider the sinning community member as a mission field for the gospel. Matthew provides no basis for the practice of excommunication or exclusion from the community by a hierarchical collegium, group of elders, or those who appeal to the traditional lineage of the apostles (cf. Thompson 1970).

Verses 19-20 support this interpretation. They return to the use of the you (pl.) in reference to the disciples and/or the community envisioned as the audience of the speech. This "you" group is the group described earlier in v. 4 as having the status of children. Hence, claim to status privilege would remove one from the presence of either the Father or Jesus and withhold divine sanction for the decision of the community. Verse 20 indicates the presence of Jesus as God-with-us (cf. 1:23) to guarantee the status-free structure of the community. In this context, Jesus bestows anew the privilege of judgment and interpretation earlier granted to Peter. This time, however, the unity of the speech makes it clear that such privilege depends upon the perception by the disciple of her/his own dependence on God and equal status before God with all other members of the community. The view of the historical church that emerges from Matt 18 therefore is a congregation of equals whose access to God and Jesus depends upon their continued affirmation of their nonhierarchical, noncentric status.

Peter presses the teaching further. Does he genuinely desire a mathematics of GRACE? If so, then he adopts a casuistic stance already condemned by Jesus in the Pharisees. He displays a behavior appropriate only to the leadership of their synagogues, not to the leadership of the community. The parable that Jesus tells to conclude this speech indicates the theological basis of equality among all children in the kingdom. It should be read according to the apocalyptic-eschatological method taught in Matt 13. From the perspective of God's judgment, the child of the kingdom should extend to those sinning against itself the same mercy extended by God to the child, otherwise it condemns itself to the judgment of God. The child of the kingdom must be merciful, as God is merciful, must be perfect as God is perfect, or it transgresses the delicate balance between grace and justice advocated so eloquently by Jesus. Such a balance can be seen only from the eschatological perspective of God's future coming in the Son of Man, whose apocalypse is now in Jesus.

Plot and Speech:
When Jesus Had Finished
Saying These Things, 19:1-29

In the following episodes Jesus eliminates claims to special religious and social privileges claimed through Israelite custom and law by the male heads of households.

Some Pharisees Came to Test Him, 19:1-12.

19:1-9. Is it lawful for a man to divorce? Jesus protects women from invidious impoverishment by males and conforms to the overall concern of the text for the marginal. The scene applies the apocalyptic-eschatological perspective to the problem of DIVORCE. Jesus concerns himself only with the practice of men unilaterally divorcing their wives as provided by Mosaic Law. He does not discuss the relatively modern phenomenon of a mutual decision to dissolve a household.

By combining quotations from Gen 1:27 and 2:24, Jesus reveals the intention of God at creation to be for males to leave their family and property for their wives. This matrilocality constitutes the opposite of property relationships of the first century. The law that allows for divorce was given by Moses, not God, be-

cause of the formation of patriarchal marriages after the advent of SIN. Even within the current patrilocal practice, a man who has undertaken responsibility for a household may not abandon it, according to Jesus. Male householder property rights that include possession of their wives come not from God, but from humans.

Only in the case of *unchastity* (v. 9) may men unilaterally dissolve their marriages. The exception is obscure since the Greek word used refers to almost any sort of undesirable sexual activity. It may refer to marriages discovered to be incestuous by first-century Judaism but allowable in the non-Jewish world (see 5:31; Meier 1976, 147–50; Baltensweiler 1967, 88–100). Therefore, the exception might refer particularly to problems among non-Jewish proselytes within the Matthean community.

19:10-12. It is better not to marry. The disciples apparently find the elimination of their privileges in marriage so harsh as to be almost unbearable. Jesus, having eliminated the preeminent place of the Israelite male as disposer of household property including women, further indicates that maleness is not essential for inclusion within God's kingdom. Infertile, phallically disempowered males may be as blessed by God as others. Such a teaching contradicts directly the prescriptions of the Law that refuse a EUNUCH access to the congregation of Israel (Deut 23:1). Such prescriptions reserve full righteousness before God only for "normal" phallically capable males. Jesus aligns himself, rather, with the prophetic tradition of Isaiah that foresees the eschatological time as a time when eunuchs will enter the congregation of Israel (Isa 56:3-5). Jesus sees that time as now. Therefore, women and nonmales hold as high a position of privilege in the kingdom as males.

Then Little Children
Were Being Brought to Him, 19:13-15

The immediately preceding episode shows the disciples to be fixed on their own privilege as male householders so as to exclude the marginal. In this episode, in spite of the instruction of Matt 18, they still are unable to accept and act upon the kingdom as proclaimed by Jesus. Therefore, he must instruct them again in speech that eloquently testifies to God's concern for the powerless. "Suffer the little children to come unto me and forbid them not for of such is the Kingdom of heaven" (KJV). By its forceful simplicity the theological and social radicality of this verse eludes its appropriation by the original readers and by all subsequent readers of Matthew.

What Good Deed Must I
Do to Have Eternal Life?, 19:16-29

The third episode concludes a consideration of the situation of the male householder in the kingdom of heaven. Two conversations occur: one, between Jesus and a young man (vv. 16-22); the second, between Jesus and the disciples led by Peter (vv. 23-29).

19:16-22. Why do you ask? In the first conversation, the dispersal of material wealth for the poor is placed at the end of a discussion of righteousness according to the Law. Jesus' statement in v. 21 epitomizes the demand of God given through Moses in Deut 15:4-5. This scripture describes the sabbatical year of the remission of debts in Israel. God guarantees that there will be no poor "if only you will obey the Lord your God by diligently observing this entire commandment that I command you today" (see also Lev 25). In the historical field, the keeping of the Law, as indicated by the claim of vv. 18-20, must include the elimination of the poor in Israel. The continued presence of the poor should be regarded as a sign of the unrighteousness of those who have possessions. The young man cannot go this far (v. 22).

19:23-29. It will be hard for a rich man. More than the historical field emerges here. The teaching of 6:19-34 illuminates the underlying cause of the young man's failure as being in the lordship of Mammon. Only the powerful lordship of God can overcome economic investiture. The disciples recognize that the problem exists not only for the extremely wealthy but for householders such as themselves (v. 25). Their reply to the teaching parallels their response in 19:10. They resist applying the perspective of the kingdom to their own status.

Peter seeks to identify himself and his brother disciples with the homelessness of Jesus (v. 27). Nevertheless he remains fixated on hierarchical privilege ensured by eschatological reward. Jesus' answer deftly avoids promising material hierarchy by leaving unspecified the nature of the hundredfold reward (v. 29; cf. Mark 10:30).

Verse 28 seems to promise the power of judgment to the apostles at the PAROUSIA. The immediate context strongly circumscribes understanding this verse as guaranteeing privilege. The parable that follows (20:1-16) further arrests the plot and opens a window into the organization of the kingdom as a uniform field in-

fused by God's justice and grace. Should we not also read irony here, since the disciples are given power over only the judgment of Israel patriarchally arranged in tribes. This patriarchy is no longer valid in the kingdom in which only the Son of Man exercises universal judgment (Matt 24–25).

Speech: But Many Who Are First
Will Be Last, 19:30–20:16

The parable compares the kingdom of heaven to a *householder who.* According to the interpretative perspective taught in Matt 13, we should understand the householder either to be God or Jesus as the Son of Man/Son of God. Jesus draws on prophetic teaching tradition by reference to the figure of the *vineyard* as a figure of Israel's relationship to God (Isa 5).

The householder promises those hired at nine o'clock to pay *whatever is just* (v. 4). The question of righteousness thereby becomes the focus of the parable. Verse 8 provides the setting for the conflict with which the parable ends. It provides those hired first with the opportunity to see the act of payment. This act of payment defines within the plot of the parable what is just.

No hierarchy of merit exists among the workers at the conclusion of the parable. Jesus depicts economic relationships within the kingdom of heaven as a uniform field of power whose nature is utterly nonhierarchical. The choice implied in v. 13 is whether or not to remain in the harvest field.

Verse 15, "Am I not allowed to do what I want with what is mine? Or is your eye evil because I am good?" (author trans.) refers to teaching by Jesus found in 6:23 where the same phrase *your eye is evil* denotes a connection between physical sight and moral judgment. The author ends the parable with a question about the appropriate judgment to be made.

In v. 16 Jesus echoes 19:30. In what way did the last become first and the first last? Clearly, it was not in the reward granted: all are equal. Rather, v. 16 forces us to reread v. 8, to stand with those hired first, and to decide about the justice of the kingdom of heaven.

The last receive their wages for the day. A *denarias* constitutes the amount necessary to sustain a worker and family for one day. According to the theological economy of the Gospel of Matthew, physical sustenance is guaranteed by God in the kingdom of heaven. Matthew 6:19-33 indicates that more than this causes anxiety that emanates not from God, but from the kingdom of Satan. The first hired, along with the disciples and the audience of the Gospel, are invited to see the justice of God, and choose.

Plot: While Jesus Was Going Up to Jerusalem, 20:17–21:27

The Son of Man Will Be Handed Over, 20:17-28

20:17-19. They will condemn him to death. The episode begins with Jesus' prediction of his death and resurrection as the Son of Man and concludes with his interpretation of his death as a servant, the Son of Man, who gives his life for many. Jesus emphasizes the complicity of both the chief priests and scribes along with the Roman ruler in v. 19. The elite of Jerusalem who sought to kill Jesus as a child will accomplish their intention shortly. The prediction of the resurrection completes the prediction theologically and in parallel with v. 28 shows the result of the service of the Son of Man. In Matthew, the crucifixion and resurrection are always held together as one event of salvific significance.

20:20-23. The mother of the sons of Zebedee came. The reference to the rulers in v. 25 reminds us of the historical plane infused by evil powers. The action of the mother of the Zebedee brothers coincides with this historical emphasis by presuming that there will remain a hierarchical organization in the kingdom. Her presence here indicates perhaps the presence of those other than the male disciple band during the ministry of Jesus. She will reappear in the narrative at the foot of the cross. She, unlike her sons who abandon Jesus prior to his death, learns the meaning of kingdom and service.

20:24-28. When the ten heard it they were angry. The disciples also are in grave danger of hoping for a hierarchy in the kingdom of heaven that mirrors the hierarchy in the kingdoms of the world. Jesus predicts a nonhierarchical, noncentered system with no special privileges afforded to the disciples except service and death. Here the historical destiny of the Son of Man becomes the epistemological key for the disciples to understand the destiny of the children of the kingdom.

As They Were Leaving Jericho, 20:29-34

Two blind supplicants emerge from the crowds and form an ironic counterpoint to the blindness of the disciples in the previous scene. The last healing before entering Jerusalem emphasizes that these two suppli-cants, unlike the inhabitants and rulers of Jerusalem, see and follow Jesus. They not only form a counterpoint to the blindness of the disciples, but they also function as witnesses against the city of Jerusalem.

When They Had Come near Jerusalem, 21:1-27

21:1-17. You will find a donkey tied and a colt. The quotation from Zech 9:9 has shaped the emphasis in vv. 2 and 7 that *two* animals are brought and ridden. The image evoked by the text makes Jesus into a sort of circus rider. We may doubt whether an ancient author intended to propose a difficult if not impossible physical act. Rather, concern to show the precise fulfillment of prophecy may override more mundane considerations.

The literal fulfillment of the prophecy results in the perception of Jesus as the Davidic Messiah by the crowds (v. 9). Zechariah's prophecy, however, refers not to the triumphal entry of the Davidic monarch but rather to the arrival of the Lord God at the endtime (Zech 9:14-17). Using ZECHARIAH, the narrator makes clear that the crowds misunderstand Jesus' entry as a messianic act. The crowds also misunderstand him to be a PROPHET (v. 11). Rather, the entry into Jerusalem constitutes the final arrival of God in power to usher in the endtime.

Verses 12-17 continue to characterize Jesus as the arrival of God in the Temple. He claims rulership over his Temple both by his words and action (vv. 12-13). He heals in the Temple as a sign of the presence of God. Verses 15-16 emphasize the objection of the Temple leadership to the cries of *children*. Jesus' response taken from Ps 8:2 identifies himself as God. The entry into Jerusalem and cleansing of the Temple constitute the episodes in which Jesus' status as God-with-us in the eschatological time becomes fully apparent. Jesus by action and scriptural reference proclaims who he is.

21:18-22. He was hungry. The withering of the FIG TREE functions within the plot of this section as a sign of the impending judgment against Jerusalem. It also provides another opportunity for the disciples to perceive faith. The disciples are challenged to faith by the sight of the tree.

21:23-27. By what authority? Jesus forces the urban elites to choose between the sources of John's authority. They refuse because of political considerations. Jesus' argument implies that since John is the lesser of the two, if they do not understand John, they cannot understand him.

Speech:
What Do You Think?, 21:28–22:14

The previous episodes have made clear that Jesus is God. The continued BLINDNESS of the rulers of Jerusalem results, therefore, in the following three parables of judgment. Not since the parables of Matt 13 has Jesus developed an extended speech composed of parables and interpretation. Three parables occur: two sons (21:28-31a); vineyard (21:33-41); and wedding banquet (22:1-14).

The first two parables receive immediate interpretations. The parable of the two sons receives a direct interpretation by Jesus that judges the chief priests and elders of the people for their failure to respond to the way of righteousness proclaimed by John (21:31b-32; 3:7-10). Jesus provides an interpretation to the second parable by scriptural citation. This parable of the vineyard understood from an allegorical eschatological-apocalyptic perspective refers proplepticly to Jesus' own death. The reaction of the chief priests and Pharisees in vv. 45-46 makes this interpretation apparent.

The final parable of the wedding feast contains within it elements that specify it as an ALLEGORY of apocalyptic judgment. Therefore, it is not followed by an interpretation. In v. 7 the rage of the king involves a destruction of the city of the murderers and probably refers to the actual destruction of Jerusalem in 70 C.E. Verses 11-14 recount the judgment against those within the banquet indicating that those within the kingdom are also liable to judgment.

The section builds to a forceful conclusion. The parables refer allegorically to the judgment of God that has already arrived. The author expects the audience to see the judgment of God against the urban ruling elite of Jerusalem for the rejection of John the Baptist and for the death of Jesus in the destruction of Jerusalem in 70. At some future date the judgment of God will be completed, including judgment of members of the kingdom. The same understanding of God's justice in the final days will be restated in the final speech of Jesus in Matt 23-26.

Plot and Speech:
Then the Pharisees Went
and Plotted to Entrap Him, 22:15-46

The return to plot in this section shows three arguments in which Jesus silences the PHARISEES and SADDUCEES.

Is It Lawful to Pay Taxes
to the Emperor, or Not?, 22:15-22

In the first episode the Pharisees seek to entrap Jesus as a political seditionist. His reply operates at two levels. First, it affirms that economic systems rely on the political authority for their daily functioning. Therefore, taxes belong to that authority. On a second level, however, the response relativizes such political authority. The coin bears the emperor's image. The unspoken question of theological importance therefore would be, what bears the image of God? According to Gen 1:27, humans, male and female, bear God's image. Jesus' response implicitly lays the claim of God to humanity as God's own. The answer fits with the Matthean view that the kingdoms of the world are under the sway of the evil one who controls Mammon. Political claims over human beings are contrary to the will of God who by creation confirms God's Lordship over humanity. In a real sense, Jesus' answer is seditious. Governments regularly claim power over human lives and bodies.

Some Sadducees Came to Him, Saying
There Is No Resurrection, 22:23-33

The episode of the Sadducees' challenge to the idea of resurrection accords with the depiction of JOSEPHUS, a Jewish historian of the first century, of the Sadducean sect (*BJ* 2.164–66). They deny the resurrection from the dead based on the fact that it is not recorded in the Pentateuch, the only scripture that they hold as authoritative. Jesus interprets Exod 3:6, a central confessional passage in the Pentateuch, from within his power as God to refer to the resurrection. The Sadducees are silenced.

When the Pharisees Heard
That He Had Silenced the Sadducees, 22:34-46

The final episode of silencing of Jesus' opponents occurs in two parts: vv. 34-39 and vv. 41-46. In the first the Pharisees receive an answer directly from the Law (Deut 6:5; Lev 19:18). Jesus' interpretation remains clearly within the traditions of Judaism.

Jesus then turns the tables on the Pharisees and asks for their own interpretation. The quotation comes from a psalm attributed to David (Ps 110:1). Jesus regards David as the speaker, therefore, the implication is that David refers both to God (the first Lord) and also to the Messiah (the second Lord). Therefore, David adopts the same theological position as we noted of the Canaanite woman in Matt 14.. The Messiah must be regarded as prior to, not descended from, David. From the perspective of Matthean christology, the conundrum presented by Jesus can be resolved only by seeing Jesus as God-with-us.

Speech: Then Jesus Said to the Crowds and to His Disciples, 23:1–26:1

The speech blends almost without seam into the preceding narrative and emphasizes in discourse form what has already been portrayed through emplotment. The Matthean literary technique shows the full leavening of the historical with the mythopoeic. The kingdom of heaven interprets and alters the causality of history through the action and speech of God-with-us.

We should avoid the tendency to fragment this speech into discreet components. Rather, its literary organization functions within the world of the text to describe the judgment of various political-religious groups and institutions. Like the parables found in 21:28–22:14, the speech also refers to events known to the Matthean community. That referentiality serves to guide possible interpretations of the text.

The Scribes and the Pharisees Sit on Moses' Seat, 23:1-36

Jesus condemns the leaders of the SYNAGOGUE who interpret Mosaic Law. He accuses them both of improper action and improper interpretation of the Law (vv. 2-28). The community should avoid titles of respect and hierarchy adopted from the synagogue (vv. 8-12). Such hypocrisy, Jesus implies, results in unbelief that leads to murder of the righteous emissaries of God, both in the past and in the future (vv. 29-36). The future emissaries include prophets, sages, and scribes sent by Jesus who will be persecuted and killed by the religious institutions led by the Pharisees (v. 34). Such behavior results in bloodguilt that will be judged within a generation (v. 36).

Jerusalem, Jerusalem, the City That Kills the Prophets, 23:37–24:26

Jesus associates the Pharisees and scribes of the synagogues with the guilt of the city of Jerusalem. The condemnation of Jerusalem provides a transition to the prophecy of the judgment of the Temple (24:1-28). Jesus dwells on the details of some form of military campaign against the city emphasizing that this aspect of judgment (while necessary) is not the coming of the Son of Man or Messiah (vv. 5-8; 15-26). Jesus' viewpoint conforms closely to the view of the Hebrew prophets who understand the judgment of God to come upon the unrighteousness of Israel/Judah particularly by foreign military action against Jerusalem. God uses mundane historical power to God's own purposes of justice.

The destruction of the Temple and Jerusalem will be accompanied by persecution and by false prophets (vv. 9-14). Jesus counsels endurance to the end including active continuation of his own ministry beyond the confines of Israel to the whole world. Only upon the completion of this universal mission will the end come.

After the Suffering, 24:27-35

Jesus briefly describes the coming of the Son of Man to gather the children of the kingdom. Here the theological perspective moves beyond prophetic conceptualities like those of the previous section to apocalyptic-eschatological modes of thought. The endtime is not conceived in a messianic fashion as the reconstruction of mundane political structures through the power of a righteous king supported by God. Rather, the entire cosmos is involved (v. 29) in an event that obliterates historical reality and continuity (v. 35). Jesus provides no details except the enigmatic statement that all will take place before *this generation* passes away (v. 34). The reference may be to those who read the Gospel, rather than to the disciples per se.

But about That Day and Hour No One Knows, 24:36–25:30

The section of sayings that follows continues the emphasis on avoiding idle speculation and begins a call to watchful attentiveness. Jesus warns against counting days and hours implying that such preoccupation distracts from watchful, faithful attentiveness (vv. 36-44). The issue is so important that Jesus tells three parables illustrating the principle. Each parable addresses the community of believers. Each grows in length and intensity. Failure results in expulsion from the kingdom (25:30).

When the Son of Man Comes, 25:31-46

Jesus depicts the final universal judgment by the Son of Man. The metaphor of the sheep and the goats is used; nevertheless, this section is not a parable but a direct vision of the final judgment. The principle of judgment invoked by the Son of Man is to identify the presence of Jesus with supplicants, the marginal, indicated by the *least of these*. The Gospel shows this group to be the women, children, and other supplicants among whom faith is consistently found in the Gospel. The idea of the Son of Man hidden among these is consistent with the idea of God as one who sees in secret (6:1-18). The result of failure to perceive the presence of God in the marginal, silent ones including the homeless, imprisoned, and sick is eternal punishment (v. 46).

When Jesus Had Finished
Saying All These Things, 26:1

Only with the concluding transitional sentence do we recognize the full importance of this section. It concludes the sayings of Jesus in Matthew. It announces the arrival of the judgment of God through the Son of Man in the world.

The concluding formula asks the reader to reconsider the entirety of the preceding section in the terms of the total context of Matthew. We must not read this text as a bifurcation of salvation-history into an "us-them" perspective on God's actions with Israel first and then Christianity. Rather, the text makes the radical claim that holds institutions accountable for their historical refusal of the gospel of the kingdom. It portrays a universal people of God composed of both Jews and non-Jews whose response to the kingdom determines, individually and not ethnically, their destiny in the judgment of God's day.

Matthew identifies the enemies of Jesus as the leadership and people specifically and historically aligned with the kingdoms of the world. The text portrays their judgment already to have been accomplished by the destruction of their city and shrine of ethnic, political, and religious identity. Such a portrayal arises as a prophetic vision from within the traditions of Judaism, not as an externally imposed historical analysis. For Matthew the judgment falls not on Jews as a family (Gk. *genos)* or race (Gk. *ethnos)*, but upon the leaders of national religious institutions. This leadership has opposed the arrival of the kingdom from the birth of its proclaimer and Lord. For the Matthean community this judgment begins with the crucifixion of the Son of Man and ends with the destruction of Jerusalem by the Romans in 70.

Matthew also portrays a universal judgment of the world at some indefinite and incalculable time. This judgment will separate evildoers from the children of the kingdom based upon their faithful action toward the marginalized among whom Jesus dwells. The insis-

tence that faith comes first and foremost from the least is raised to the principle of eschatological justice. Both the mercy of God and the righteousness of God cohere in the scene of final judgment.

Matthew reserves for the community the strongest warning to watchfulness in three parables. Failure in preparation may lead even the most well-intentioned into outer darkness. If we ask what the members of the community are to engage themselves in while watchfully waiting, these parables integrate with the prediction that the proclamation of the gospel must go first to the world. The community in word and deed bears witness to the kingdom of which they are a part. Members cannot smugly await final salvation while the world tears itself asunder.

Therefore, the final speech of Jesus locates its anticipated audience between the destruction of Jerusalem in 70 and the manifestation of the Son of Man at the final judgment. We should not make the mistake of associating the apocalyptic-eschatological viewpoint of the text as indicating an expectation of the chronologically imminent return of the Son of Man. Matthew ties the judgment directly to the witness-bearing mission of the community. Historically seen the chronological duration of that witness is of no consequence to the urgency of an apocalyptic-eschatological expectation of the kairotic imminence of the kingdom of heaven. The mercy and righteousness of God are always and everywhere imminent. The vision of God's grace and justice cannot be limited by historical causation.

Plot: The Son of Man Will Be Handed Over to Be Crucified, 26:2–28:20

Each section of the PASSION NARRATIVE contains episodes that allow the audience to view the actions of various characters or character groups in relationship to Jesus. Their faithfulness, doubt, or opposition becomes apparent as they respond to the unfolding of Jesus' faithfulness to the will of God as he suffers, dies, and is resurrected.

The Passover Is Coming, 26:2-16

26:2. The Son of Man will be handed over. The Gospel of Matthew portrays Jesus, especially in his passion, to be aligned with the events that befall him. These are the last things and they are overseen by the will of God. The disciples are reminded once again of the impending death by crucifixion of the Son of Man.

26:3-5. They conspired to arrest Jesus. *The chief priests and elders of the people* previously in collusion with Herod were unsuccessful in destroying the child Jesus (2:4). Now they will be successful in collusion with PILATE, but not before Jesus has completed his mission. Their plot is left incomplete for the moment since they require stealth.

26:6-13. A woman came to him. The episode returns to the disciple band and provides a contrast between the faith of the marginal and the little faith of the inner circle. *Simon the leper* (v. 6) does not appear elsewhere in the Gospel of Matthew, but he recalls the leper healed by Jesus at the beginning of his ministry (8:1-4). An unnamed woman shows that she has understanding superior to the disciples concerning the person and destiny of Jesus. They should apply the understanding given by Jesus previously that he is about to die (most recently at 26:2 and also at 16:21; 17:22-23; 20:17-19). No prediction to the woman occurs in Matthew. The text allows the inference that she has this knowledge by divine will. In addition Jesus links her act inextricably with the proclamation of *this good news* (v. 13).

26:14-16. One of the twelve went to the chief priests. With the action of Judas, the plot to arrest and kill Jesus is completed. By inserting the anointing at Bethany between the two episodes of plotting, Matthew allows reflection on the disciples' lack of faith in perceiving the divine will and on the collusion of one of their band with the opposition. Among the Gospels, only Matthew develops the story of JUDAS and does so as one of a pair of negative examples of discipleship. The other is PETER. Money motivates Judas.

On the First Day of Unleavened Bread, 26:17-75.

26:17-19. My time is near. Jesus shows his alignment with God's will and control over his destiny by directing the preparations for his last Passover with his disciples. In identifying *my time* Jesus in Matthew uses the Greek word *kairos* rather than *chronos* indicating thereby a time of fulfillment and new beginning (Senior 1985, 60).

26:20-30. One of you will betray me. Jesus shows for the first time that he knows that he will be betrayed. Judas reveals himself to Jesus as the betrayer. In a typical Passover meal of the first century, all of the disciples are likely to have dipped their hand into the same bowl. The notation in v. 23, therefore, only indicates that Jesus knew that one of the Twelve would betray him, not which one.

Even in the face of this knowledge and with Judas presumably still present Jesus interprets his own death

for his disciples using the bread and cup as parabolic symbol. In Matthew no specific interpretation of the bread as body is given, rather the interpretation of the cup as *blood of the covenant, which is poured out for many for the forgiveness of sins* (v. 28) stands as interpretation of the entire symbolic act. By declaring this act an interpretation of his impending death, Jesus combines the ideas of the covenant-making sacrifice with the image of the sin offering also found in Jewish ritual and tradition. The combined force of the religious symbol contextualized into the life of Jesus, God-with-us (cf. 1:23), remains a mystery that transcends sacrificial or covenantal religious symbolization and interpretation.

Jesus adds to this complex religious experience by making the celebration of his death a promise of the final banquet within the coming kingdom of heaven. The performance of this parable in the midst of the twelve disciples in spite of their unfaith and even betrayal holds open the promise of forgiveness. Set within the action of Peter and Judas, the words of Jesus take on particular poignancy. The use of the plural *you* in v. 29 may well imply that even the betrayer will be found in the kingdom.

26:30-35. You will all become deserters. In the face of the promise of v. 29, Jesus predicts the desertion of all of the disciples (v. 31). This is followed by a denial by Peter and all of the disciples who emphasize their willingness to die with Jesus. While Peter is depicted as an individual disciple, the text makes us aware that his behavior characterizes the disciples as a group.

26:36-56. Sit here while I pray. Such characterization continues into the next episode in GETHSEMANE (vv. 36-46). The disciples, Peter and the sons of Zebedee are especially mentioned, are unable to watch and pray with Jesus. Jesus' admonition to *stay awake and pray* (v. 41) associates this episode with his previous instruction on the coming of the Son of Man (24:36-25:30) and further develops the implication that his death means the eschatological coming of the Son of Man. Verse 46 directly links the fate of Jesus with the fate of the Son of Man.

The narrator reminds us that Judas is *one of the twelve* yet again at his arrival in v. 47. In this episode, Judas aligns himself not only with the power of money but also with the power of violence to which Jesus has been opposed throughout Matthew. This alignment even afflicts the disciple band, presumably one of which (v. 51) initiates armed resistance against the arresting officials. Jesus repudiates the use of violence to protect his life and mission (Senior 1985, 86). He remains consistent with his own teaching throughout the Gospel. Additionally, he repudiates the traditional Jewish and Christian anticipation of the intervention of Yahweh God as a warrior in behalf of the righteous. Such an understanding is deeply embedded in the Hebrew traditions of the EXODUS (e.g., Exod 14-15) and is heightened in the apocalyptic traditions of Isaiah, Zechariah, and Daniel. While 26:52-54 closely parallels Rev 13:10, the overarching apocalyptic vision expressed in Matthew clearly refuses the solution of divine warfare advocated by the apocalyptic tradition of the Book of Revelation. Jesus, while recognizing the warrior aspect of God, declares such a solution to be aside from the will of the Father (vv. 52-56). The Matthean depiction of the crucifixion remains consistent with such a vision. For the Matthean apocalyptic view, directly informed as it is by the suffering of the Son of Man who is God-with-us, the antidote to the structured and legal power of political violence is not retributive violence. Both are rooted in evil. The antinomic opposition to death is resurrection, not death and blood, however justified, in return.

26:57-75. Those took him to Caiaphas. The final episode of the section recounts an interrogation at the house of the high priest, CAIAPHAS. The procedure was not a normal judiciary procedure of the SANHEDRIN according to what we know of such procedures in the first century. Caiaphas swears an oath in order to get Jesus to speak, contrary to the teaching of Jesus (5:33-37). Jesus answers by declaring the immediate arrival of the Son of Man. The scene shows that the end of the age and the PASSION of Jesus are considered as one event by Matthew. Matthew does not locate the coming of the Son of Man purely at the end of history, but sees the end of history as already present in the historical moment of Jesus' passion. Such a view strains narration, dependent as it is on sequential reading.

The actions of Peter invite comparison with those of the HIGH PRIEST since they follow immediately and conclude the scene. Peter, questioned three times, denies knowledge of Jesus concluding with an OATH in v. 74. By this action Peter aligns himself against Jesus and with the same power that informs the oath-taking actions of Jesus' opponents. He is portrayed in the narrative as in grave danger of joining them in their opposition. His weeping at the remembrance of Jesus' prediction is left ambiguous by the narrator. It should not be taken as showing more than an emotional response to his own failure (cf. Senior 1985, 95–102).

When Morning Came, 27:1-56

27:1-10. Judas repented. While Peter's weeping remains opaque, the conclusion to the story of Judas reveals more about Judas' inner motivations. The episode of Judas interrupts the movement from the high priest's house to the trial by Pilate. The scene stresses the guilt of the religious leadership and the innocence of Jesus, as well as Jesus' obedience to God's will indicated by a citation of prophecy (cf. Kingsbury 1988, 88).

Judas sees his error in the condemnation of Jesus and declares that Jesus is innocent. Judas declares his sin (v. 4). The narrator states that Judas, *repented.* By returning the money he acts on that new perception. The word translated *repented* (v. 3) also occurs in the parable of the two sons in 21:29, 32 to indicate the change of mind of the first son who later is judged to do the will of the father. Typically the author uses a different Greek word to mean "repent" (3:2, 8, 11; 4:17; 11:20, 21; 12:41). Judas indicates his frame of mind both by what he says and what he does.

The suicide of Judas constitutes an antitype to the innocent death of Jesus who also is "hung" in crucifixion. Both may be seen as condemned to a death under the curse of the Law according to Deut 21:23. The portrayal remains ambiguous, however, since Judas is the only disciple to "change his mind." While he is not present to witness the resurrection, we are only left to wonder whether his doubt was removed by what he saw (v. 3). No other disciple is portrayed as recognizing the innocence of Jesus and acting to ameliorate his own denial.

27:11-26. Jesus stood before the governor. The charge before Pilate shifts to political sedition. Pilate completes the work begun by Herod and eliminates the adopted Davidic heir. While the opponents of Jesus believe him to be *King of the Jews*, Jesus himself will not confirm their viewpoint. The ascent of Jesus to messianic kingship in Matthew is a result of his opponents' charges. His descent to identity with marginal and homeless people comes through his own fulfillment of the roles of SON OF MAN and SON OF GOD according to the righteousness of the kingdom. Only Jesus of all the male characters in the Gospel succeeds in this self-emptying (cf. Phil 2:5-11). Such emptying earns him the condemnation of the leaders.

Counterpoint to Pilate's behavior is that of his wife (v. 19). She affirms the innocence of Jesus at his trial. She knows his innocence from a dream. In Matthew the only other dreams mentioned occur to Joseph and the magi in the infancy narrative. Her dream is a revelation of divine will to which Pilate will not listen. The unnamed woman knows the truth.

The action of the crowds in vv. 24-25 has been used in the history of Christian interpretation to condemn Jews as "Christ killers." Such a view exceeds the text and misses the viewpoint of Matthew, rooted as it is in Israelite prophetic tradition. In this climactic scene, the Gospel makes clear that Jerusalem, its leaders and people, reject Jesus. The author crafts this scene in accord with what we have already observed in Matt 23–25. The destruction of Jerusalem by the Romans in 70 constitutes for the author the judgment of God against Jerusalem, its rulers and people, in retribution for the crucifixion of Jesus as the Son of Man, Son of God, the unrecognized God-with-us (cf. 1:23). The event coincides rather precisely with a "generation" if we accept ca. 30 C.E. as the death date of Jesus. In Jewish tradition forty years usually is regarded as a generation (see Senior 1985, 116–22).

The Gospel indicates a continuing mission to all in 28:16-20 as well as perhaps to any cities of Israel remaining post-70 (see 10:23); it does not depict a salvation-historical rejection of Israel or of the Jews by God. It does not even depict condemnation for all of Israel for the crucifixion of Jesus. Rather the condemnation remains specific.

27:27-30. The soldiers took Jesus. Matthew depicts with great care and circumspection the brutal torture of Jesus by the Praetorian guards. The episode shows the control Pilate has over the crucifixion and emphasizes the political nature of Jesus' condemnation. The title *King of the Jews* is emphasized; other titles are excluded. Herod's fear of political sedition by a messiah culminates in Rome's derision of the same pretender.

27:32-44. This is Jesus, King of the Jews. The text shows Jesus as the legal heir to David's throne, therefore, the ruling elite correctly see him as a historical threat. We know, however, that the threat to the mundane order runs deeper because Jesus is not the Davidic Messiah of historical anticipation, but rather is the Son of Man, Son of God, God-with-us who undercuts and robs the kingdoms of the world of their power rooted in violence, death, and injustice. Jesus is a threat because in his person and proclamation he embodies the lordship of God and God's kingdom. The ruling center rightly seeks to kill him in order to preserve their power undergirded by the evil whose face takes shape in hypocrisy and violence. These percep-

tions come to the fore in the taunts of the bandits, religious leaders, and bystanders. They combine traditional titles of the Davidic monarch and deride Jesus as Son of God and King of Israel.

27:45-54. Darkness came over the whole land. Five responses to Jesus' death occur. First, the earth responds with darkness. Second, Jesus responds with the theological question of abandonment to the power of death. Third, the bystanders respond by seeking to drug him and provide more time for their jeers. Fourth, God responds by initiating the turn of the ages, opening the tombs. Fifth, the CENTURION responds by the affirmation of Jesus' divine sonship.

The climax of the plot of Matthew occurs in this scene. Jesus' own cry and death raise the question of God's response and dependability. Jesus' statement of mind in his final moment reveals the pernicious evil of death. God's resurrection prolepticly indicated in vv. 52-53 is the cause for recognizing Jesus' emptying on the CROSS transformed into life for all by God's will. Death is not further education for Jesus, but rather is regarded in the text as annihilating even his perception of relationship to the God to whom his life bears witness. In Jesus' death the kingdom of God arrives in power to liberate from death those who have fallen asleep. The answer to Jesus' question is the resurrection from God.

27:55-56. Many women were also there. The women followers of Jesus receive introduction. They, parallel to THE TWELVE, have followed him from Galilee. They also witnessed the events narrated previously in Jesus' life. Two are named. Mary Magdalene does not appear previously in Matthew. The second Mary almost certainly is the mother of Jesus (see 13:55; Gundry 1982, 579). She is not named as his mother in order to preserve the emphasis in the text on Jesus as a homeless and householdless person. These two women provide consistent witness to the life, death, burial, and resurrection of Jesus. Mary, the mother, can bear witness to his identity from birth.

When It Was Evening, 27:57-66

Two episodes contrast faithful followers with the opponents. Missing are the eleven disciples. In v. 57 JOSEPH of Arimathea, *a rich man* and *a disciple*, is said to have provided for Jesus' burial. He apparently was drawn through the eye of the needle by God (19:23-26). Unlike the Twelve who had left everything (19:27) Joseph aligns himself as a marginal follower of Jesus, as do the two Marys who watch the tomb.

In opposition to the faithfulness of Joseph and the Marys, the political and religious opponents post their own guard. The text by this juxtaposition emphasizes the difference between centralized violent guarded authority and marginal faithful watchfulness.

After the Sabbath, 28:1-15

Two episodes emphasize the resurrection of Jesus as part of the eschatological turn of the ages and the proper response to the event. The Marys are consistent witnesses to the biography of Jesus on the historical plane. Also to them comes the revelation of God's resurrection of Jesus (vv. 2-3). The angelic messenger sends the women to re-include the eleven who have denied Jesus (vv. 5-7). The eleven will see him in Galilee. The Marys see him immediately: *Suddenly Jesus met them and said, 'Greetings!' And they came to him, took hold of his feet, and worshipped him* (v. 9). Their response to the resurrection provides a model with which we may compare subsequent responses.

The response of the chief priests to the account of the guards provides a negative foil to the Marys. They use the power of money to silence the news of the resurrection. Their disinformation continues to deceive the Jews to the author's own day. This deception may be emphasized here because it has a negative impact on a continuation of a mission to JUDAISM by the Matthean community.

Now the Eleven Disciples
Went to Galilee, 28:16-20

The final scene of Matthew opens the story of Jesus as God-with-us (cf. 1:23) into an all-powerful future. It also leaves open the future of the eleven and with them the orientation of the audience of the Gospel.

The appearance to the eleven completes the episode begun with the appearance to the women and should be read as a third response to the resurrection. We understand that the women faithfully fulfilled their mission. The response of the eleven also directly parallels that of the women, *when they saw him, they worshipped him, but some doubted* (v. 17; emphasis added). This verse is constructed so as to continue the irony that has attended the characterization of the disciples throughout the narrative. The only character said to doubt previously in the plot is Peter (14:31). The verse also reminds us of the pattern of each episode of *little faith* on the part of the disciples (8:26; 14:31; 16:8; 17:20) and each episode of faith and

worship on the part of the marginalized. The disciples have never been shown to be effective interpreters, teachers, or missionaries within the text. The text, therefore, will not allow for the conclusion that in 28:19 the authority of Jesus is transferred to the disciples. Nor does it clearly rehabilitate them as faithful apostles after their abandonment of Jesus.

The scene as written subverts and destroys any claim by the disciples and/or their institutional heirs to patriarchal or hierarchical authority over gentiles, women, children, or other supplicants within the community. The text remains true in its emplotment and characterization to a vision of the kingdom of heaven that de-centers, de-marginalizes, and in short abandons all -archic, -centric structures with their attendant systems of status.

The audience and not the disciples becomes *scribes trained for the kingdom* (13:52). The work involved in the commission of 28:19-20 is left to those who accept the role and education provided them by Matthew. They behave not like the disciples, but like the faithful of the margins.

Nevertheless, the eleven are not assimilated to the character of the Pharisees . They are left as ironic example. The commission does not transfer Jesus' authority to them. Rather, Jesus remains with them (v. 20), while reserving his own complete power to himself to the end of the age. His story may not be closed by any but God's power expressed through Emmanuel, God-with-us (cf. 1:23).

Works Cited

Baltensweiler, H. 1967. *Die Ehe im Neue Testament*.

Bauer, David R. 1988. *The Structure of Matthew's Gospel: A Study in Literary Design*. Bible and Literature series 15.

Betz, Hans Dieter. 1985. "Matthew 6.22-23 and Ancient Theories of Vision," in *Essays on the Sermon on the Mount*, 71–87.

Brooks, Stephenson H. 1987. *Matthew's Community: The Evidence of His Special Sayings Material*. JSNTSup 16. (*See also* Humphries-Brooks, Stephenson.)

Brown, Raymond E. 1977. *The Birth of the Messiah*. 1983. "Not Jewish Christianity and Gentile Christianity but Types of Jewish/Gentile Christianity," *CBQ* 45:74–79.

Davies, W. D. 1964. *The Setting of the Sermon on the Mount*.

Gundry, Robert H. 1967. *The Use of the Old Testament in St. Matthew's Gospel, with Special Reference to the Messianic Hope.* 1982. *Matthew: A Commentary on His Literary and Theological Art.*

Hanson, Paul D. 1979. *The Dawn of Apocalyptic.* Rev. ed.

Humphries-Brooks, Stephenson. 1989. "Apocalyptic Paraenesis in Matthew 6:19-34," in *Apocalyptic and the New Testament. Essays in Honor of J. Louis Martyn,* ed. Joel Marcus and Marion L. Soards, 95–112. JSNTSupp 24. 1991. "Indicators of Social Organization and Status in Matthew's Gospel," SBLSP 30:31–49.

Jeremias, Joachim. 1972. *The Parables of Jesus.* Second ed.

Kingsbury, Jack Dean. 1988. *Matthew As Story.* Second ed.

Martyn, J. Louis. 1985. "Apocalyptic Antinomies in Paul's Letter to the Galatians," *NTS* 31:410–24.

Meier, John P. 1976. *Law and History in Matthew's Gospel. A Redactional Study of Matt 5:17-48.* AnBib 71. 1979. *The Vision of Matthew: Christ, Church and Morality in the First Gospel.*

Patte, Daniel. 1987. *The Gospel according to Matthew: A Structural Commentary on Matthew's Faith.*

Senior, Donald. 1985. *The Passion of Jesus in the Gospel of Matthew.*

Stendahl, Krister. 1968. *The School of St. Matthew and Its Use of the Old Testament.* Second ed.

Talbert, Charles H. 1988. "Once Again: Gospel Genre," *Semeia* 43:53–73.

Thompson, William G. 1970. *Matthew's Advice to a Divided Community. Matt 17:22–18:35.* AnBib 44.

Wilder, Amos Niven. 1982. *Jesus' Parables and the War of Myths: Essays on Imagination in Scripture,* ed. James Breech.

Mark

Sharyn E. Dowd

Introduction

Of the more than twenty extant gospels, Mark is one of the four that was finally included in the CANON of the early church. Its traditional title "The Gospel according to Mark" did not come from the hand of the author, but was added to a copy of the manuscript during the second century C.E. The name and gender of the author, the date and place of composition, and the intended audience are all unknown.

Mark in Context

Before Mark there was no genre of literature known as "gospel," a term that means "good news." The author of Mark (another term for the author in this commentary is "the evangelist") was not inventing a new genre, but writing a biography of Jesus. Like many ancient biographies, Mark was written not to provide a list of facts about Jesus of Nazareth, but to interpret the significance of the life, death, and resurrection of *Jesus Christ, the Son of God* (1:1). Thus, this biography is a kind of narrative theology. It proclaims Christian faith in the form of a story.

Mark is a popular ancient biography. That is, it was not stuffy elite literature written in elevated language, but a lively story written in a popular style that was easy to read, much like paperback novels today. Of course, the author did not invent the stories; they had been handed down through preaching and teaching in the early Christian communities. What the evangelist did was to arrange the material in its present order and retell the story of Jesus so those who heard the story read aloud would understand how committing themselves to Jesus and his way would affect their lives.

Books were expensive in the ancient world, and not everyone could read, even if books had been easily accessible. It is likely that the Gospel of Mark was intended to be read aloud and heard by an audience of gathered Christians, rather than read privately by one person.

The structure of Mark is distinguished by various kinds of repetition. Repetition is useful in helping the listening audience keep track of the story. For example, in 3:10 the audience hears that people could be healed by touching Jesus. In 5:24b-34 an example is given of a woman who actually was healed by touching Jesus' clothes. Then in 6:56 the audience is reminded again that even touching Jesus' clothes was enough to bring healing to people. Repetition reinforces the point.

Other kinds of repetition found in Mark are the INCLUSIO and the CHIASM. The inclusio is simply a frame. The same information or phrase that begins a unit of material is repeated at the end. This A-B-A form is familiar to us because of its use in many musical compositions.

The chiasm is similar except that the repetition is more extensive. Not only do the first and last parts match each other, but the second and next-to-last also match, and so on. Chiastic structures can be as short as a sentence (*The sabbath was made for humankind, and not humankind for the sabbath*, 2:27), or as long as several pages. These patterns of repetition and other literary devices were used by ancient authors to indicate where thought units began and ended. The chapter divisions now found in the NT were added in the thirteenth century C.E. and often do not reflect the actual literary shape of the text.

Some ancient authors did not like for the sections of a work to be joined end to end like blocks in a row. They preferred that the sections overlap, like links in a chain. The author of Mark was one such author. That is why the outline that begins this commentary may look strange to modern eyes. The reader will notice that one section begins at a point before the end of the previous section. These "hinges" or "hooks" in the structure of the Gospel will be pointed out in the outline and in the commentary.

Mark is a popular biography written from the pre-suppositions of the apocalyptic worldview, so although it is not an apocalypse like the Book of Revelation, it is in a sense apocalyptic literature. The evangelist believed that in the ministry of Jesus, God's kingdom or reign was breaking into history. The resurrection of Jesus was the beginning of the end. Soon the forces of Satan would be defeated for good and Jesus would return for his *elect*, or "chosen ones" (13:27). The apocalyptic presuppositions of the Gospel of Mark are the reason for the prevalence of conflict and even the language of warfare in the story. Jesus is the divine warrior who does battle with the enemies of God who afflict God's creation with illness, demonic possession, and temptation.

Mark is a popular biography written from within an apocalyptic worldview with a feeling of urgency. Therefore, the author uses every means available to persuade the Christians who hear the story to remain faithful. Two of these means are Jewish scriptural interpretation techniques and Hellenistic rhetorical techniques.

Even though God has done something radically new in Jesus, the evangelist is certain that everything about Jesus is in perfect continuity with the way that God has dealt with people in the past. Everything in the Gospel of Mark is interpreted in terms of the way it fits in with the OT. The author's favorite OT books seem to be Isaiah, Daniel, and the Psalms, although others are used as well to help explain the meaning of Jesus' story.

In ancient Greek schools pupils like the author of Mark learned rhetorical techniques, that is, appropriate ways of proving a point or persuading an audience. Studying how the NT writers used these techniques and adapted them to suit their material is called RHETORICAL CRITICISM. Some of these techniques will be discussed in the commentary.

The Gospel of Mark can be very helpful to the church today not only because of *what* it tells us about the theological significance of what God has done in Christ, but also because of *how* it combines a variety of cultural and literary traditions into an intricate and interesting whole in the service of that good news.

This commentary is intended as a reading guide to the Gospel of Mark. It has been deliberately written in such a way that it will make no sense to the reader who does not have a Bible open alongside the commentary. No commentary can be a substitute for the Bible itself.

For Further Study

In the *Mercer Dictionary of the Bible*: APOCALYPTIC LITERATURE; APOCRYPHAL GOSPELS; DISCIPLE/DISCIPLESHIP; ESCHATOLOGY IN THE NT; GENRE, CONCEPT OF; GENRE, GOSPEL; GOSPEL; GOSPELS, CRITICAL STUDY OF; INCLUSIO; KINGDOM OF GOD; MARK, GOSPEL OF; MARK, LONG ENDING OF; RHETORICAL CRITICISM; SON OF GOD; SON OF MAN; SYNOPTIC PROBLEM; TWELVE, THE; WOMEN IN THE NT; WORSHIP IN THE NT.

In other sources: W. Harrington, *Mark*; E. S. Malbon, "Narrative Criticism: How Does the Story Mean?" *Mark and Method*, ed. Anderson and Moore, 23–49.

Commentary

An Outline

Prologue, 1:1-15

The prologue is held together by a frame or INCLU-
SIO in 1:1-3 and 1:14-15. Both ends of the inclusio
contain the word *good news* (εὐαγγέλιον) followed by
an ambiguous prepositional phrase (good news
of/about Jesus Christ, v. 1; good news of/about God,
v. 14). Although there are a number of scriptural allusions in the prologue, the author of Mark names only
Isaiah (v. 2). This makes it clear that the evangelist is
interpreting the story of Jesus in terms of the theology
of Isaiah, particularly the portion often called Deutero-
Isaiah (chaps. 40–55).

Jesus' announcement in v. 15 echoes the prophetic
promise that the time of slavery and bondage is filled
up and the time of God's favor is on the way (Isa
40:1; 49:8). The good news is that God reigns (Isa
52:7). This message is first announced by a voice crying in the wilderness, *Prepare the way of the Lord!* (v.
3; Isa 40:3 LXX). Thus, the ministry of Jesus is interpreted as a new exodus from bondage into freedom,
like the new exodus from exile announced by Isaiah.

But the audience of Mark will soon learn that like
Isaiah, Jesus speaks to people who have deaf ears and
hardened hearts. He enacts God's liberating power in
the presence of people whose eyes see only dimly or
not at all (4:12; 8:17-18; Isa 6:9).

Within the frame provided by vv. 1-3 and vv. 14-
15, there are three smaller units, each of which emphasizes the activity of the Spirit in connection with the
ministry of Jesus: vv. 4-8, 9-11, 12-13. The frame and
the inner sections are knit together by repeated words
and phrases: *messenger(s)* (1:2, 13); *in the wilderness*
(1:3, 4, 12); *baptize/baptizer/baptism* (1:4, 5, 8, 9);
Jordan (1:5, 9); *son* (1:1, 11); *proclaim* (1:7, 14); *re-
pent/repentance* (1:4, 15).

John Announces the One
Who Will Baptize in the Spirit, 1:4-8

In this unit John the baptizer announces that although he immerses in water, the coming stronger one
will immerse in the Holy Spirit. This will be necessary, the audience may surmise, because John's water
baptism does not effect the reversal of mindset (μετά-
νοια, usually translated "repentance") to which he calls
the inhabitants of Judea. Although they confess their
sins, the narrative is silent about any change of mind
and heart. That there is none is made evident by the
blindness, deafness, and hardness of heart with which
Jesus' message is greeted in the subsequent narrative.
Only the transforming baptism in the Holy Spirit,
promised but not narrated in the Gospel of Mark, will
effect a change to God's way of thinking (8:33) and
result in bold witness (13:11).

In this first appearance in the story, John wears the
costume of ELIJAH (v. 6; 2 Kgs 1:8). This identifies him
as the forerunner promised in Mal 3:1; 4:5 (v. 2; 9:11-
12) and prepares for his persecution by a scheming
queen (6:17-29; 9:13).

Jesus Is Baptized in the Spirit, 1:9-11

The baptism scene establishes Jesus' God-given
identity for the information of the audience of the Gospel. In Mark, John does not share Jesus' vision of the
descending Spirit (v. 10; cf. John 1:32), nor does the
voice from heaven make a public announcement (cf.
Matt 3:17). Thus, only Jesus and the audience understand that Jesus' baptism legitimates him as PROPHET,
servant, and anointed royal SON OF GOD. The bystanders at the story level see only a country boy from Gali-

lee joining in the mass confession and baptism in the Jordan River.

It does not occur to the author of Mark, as it does to the author of Matthew, that Jesus' baptism as one of the crowd requires the explanation that Jesus had no sins to confess (cf. Matt 3:14-15). On the contrary, the Markan Jesus identifies with the sin of his people even as he accepts his call to the prophetic vocation (Isa 6:5). In this way, the baptism prefigures the passion: "He was counted among the lawless" (Isa 53:12 LXX).

Sight (v. 10) is reinforced by hearing (v. 11). The voice from heaven, like the narrator (vv. 2-3), quotes scripture; again the evangelist emphasizes the continuity between the good news and the old, old story of God's self-revelation in the past. The heavenly voice quotes a combination of Ps 2:7 ("You are my son"—God's word to the Davidic ruler) and Isa 42:1b ("my chosen, in whom my soul delights"—God's word to the servant).

But there is another, more disturbing element: the word *beloved* (v. 11) which comes not from the psalmist nor from the prophet but from Gen 22:2. This is the story about a brush with death of another "beloved son"—Isaac. For Jesus there will be no ram in the thicket; he will give his life to redeem others (10:45).

The Spirit Thrusts Jesus into Battle with Satan, 1:12-13

Here the narrator introduces the conflict that will drive the plot of the Gospel: the cosmic conflict between Jesus, God's agent, and Satan, leader of the resistance to God's reign. Later in the Gospel, Satan will be identified with Beelzebul, the chief of the demons (3:22-27). The exorcisms, which will begin in 1:21-27, will demonstrate that Jesus was the victor in this desert encounter.

In ancient thought, human beings who could remain unharmed in the presence of wild animals were believed to be the recipients of divine favor and protection; Romulus, the founder of Rome, was believed to have been saved from starvation by a wolf. In the Israelite wisdom traditions, it was the righteous sage who was protected against wild animals (Ps 91:11-13). According to Isa 11:6-9, all humanity will be at peace with the animals in the reign of God, when "a shoot shall come out from the stump of Jesse" upon whom "the spirit of the Lord shall rest" (11:1-2). Thus, the narrative logic is complete when, immediately after the wilderness testing scene, the Markan Jesus announces that God's reign is imminent (1:14-15).

Ministry in Galilee and in Gentile Territory, 1:14–8:30

The first major section of the Gospel is an interpretation of the in-breaking reign of God in Jesus' ministry of teaching, exorcism, healing, and forgiveness. The section begins with Jesus' initial proclamation of God's reign in 1:14-15 and concludes with Peter's identification of Jesus as the one anointed to bring in God's reign (8:27-30).

The portrait of Jesus presented by the evangelist combines elements of the OT prophetic traditions, Davidic kingship motifs, and Hellenistic understandings of the wandering teacher/philosopher and his band of followers. This enabled both gentiles and Jews in the audience to grasp the significance of Jesus and his revelation of God.

Paradigmatic Beginning of Jesus' Ministry, 1:14–3:12

The section 1:14–8:30 is made up of three overlapping subsections: 1:14–3:12, 3:7–6:30, and 6:14–8:30. These develop the audience's understanding of Jesus progressively, beginning with a paradigmatic depiction of the various aspects of his ministry in 1:14–3:12. This subsection may be outlined as follows: Introductory summary of Jesus' message (1:14-15); Calling the first disciples (1:16-20); Jesus' power over illness and demonic oppression (1:21-45); Jesus' authority to forgive sins and interpret scripture (2:1–3:6); Concluding summary of Jesus' healings and exorcisms (3:7-12).

1:14-15. Introductory summary of Jesus' message. Returning to Galilee after his baptism and encounter with Satan in the Judean desert, Jesus begins to proclaim "the good message of God" (τὸ εὐαγγέλιον τοῦ θεοῦ, v. 14). The deliberate ambiguity informs the audience that God's message, proclaimed by Jesus, originates with God and is a message about God. Specifically, it is a message about the kingdom of God, that is, God's reign or sovereignty, which has come near (ἤγγικεν).

This is an eschatological message, because, although God is the rightful sovereign over all creation, God's sovereignty is presently contested by evil and its human agents. In Jesus' ministry the reign of God that will soon be fully present is experienced in a preliminary way by those who encounter Jesus. His teaching and ministry of power prefigure the final defeat of all opposition to God's sovereignty and show what life will be like when God reigns unopposed (Boring 1987, 131).

The appropriate response to this proclamation is repentance and trust (v. 15). The two are related; only the one who trusts that God, and not evil, is ultimately in control is prepared to undergo the change of mindset and attitude signified by the imperative *Repent!* Those who persist in holding a human outlook rather than adopting God's view of reality (8:33b) are not ready to trust the good news that God reigns.

1:16-20. Calling the first disciples. The author of Mark does not narrate the call of each individual named in the list of disciples (3:16-19). The call story at the beginning of the Galilean ministry is meant to characterize the summons to all disciples: they are to follow Jesus, who will cause them to fish for people (v. 17).

In this story the Markan Jesus does not behave in the way that was most typical of rabbis or philosophers in antiquity. Jewish rabbis and most pagan philosophers did not recruit followers. Rather, those who wanted to learn sought out a teacher and requested permission to become a disciple. However, the Greek writer Diogenes Laertius repeats two call stories that are similar to the story in Mark 1:16-20.

In one story the philosopher Socrates encounters Xenophon in an alley and asks him where various kinds of food can be bought. Xenophon answers correctly. Socrates then asks where people can become good and honorable. When Xenophon does not know the answer, Socrates says to him, "Then follow me and learn."

The second story concerns Zeno, the founder of Stoicism. He is portrayed as sitting in a book shop reading Xenophon's biography of Socrates. Impressed with the life of the great philosopher, Zeno asks where men like Socrates might be found. At that moment Crates, a disciple of Socrates was passing by, so the bookseller pointed to him and said to Zeno, "Follow that man." Zeno then became Crates' disciple.

The similarities with the Markan call story are: (1) people are engaged in the daily activities of life with no thought of seeking a teacher; (2) a teacher suddenly attracts their attention; (3) there is an imperative summons to "follow"; and (4) they respond by becoming disciples.

It is likely that the author of Mark chose this model over the more common one in which the student seeks a teacher because this summons/response pattern conforms more closely with the theology of the OT. In the

OT God takes the initiative, calling into a covenant relationship people who are going about their business with no thought of being called by God. This is true of Abraham (Gen 12:1-4), Jacob (Gen 28:10-17), Moses (Exod 3:1-6), and Israel as a people (Deut 6:21-25).

The initiative of God is also an important feature of prophetic call stories (Amos 7:14-15; Jer 1:5). Isaiah speaks of Israel as "called" by God (42:6; 49:1). The Markan Jesus calls disciples in a way that conforms to the biblical understanding of the way God relates to the chosen people.

The specific promise of the Markan Jesus is that those who had been catching fish would now catch human beings (v. 17). Again the evangelist is drawing upon a metaphor that would have been familiar to both the Jewish and the gentile members of his audience. The analogy of fishing was used in the Israelite wisdom tradition as well as in Greek educational philosophy to speak about the way in which people were lured by the bait of the teacher's ideas and thus were prevented from wasting their lives in meaningless pursuits.

Greeks hoped to be caught in the nets of the gods rather than being snared by the evil spirits that were also out fishing for people. The Hebrew prophets spoke of Israel's enemies as God's fishers, gathering in the people of Israel for judgment—a judgment designed to lead to their repentance and return to covenant faithfulness (Ezek 17:19-21; Jer 16:16). So when Jesus' disciples go out to heal and to preach that people should repent (6:12) they are fulfilling Jesus' promise that they will become fishers for people.

1:21-45. Healings and exorcisms. This section and the one that follows it are both organized in the literary form of the chiasm, sometimes called a "concentric" or "ring" composition:

A Jesus makes a demon "go out from" a man.
    Jesus contrasted with the scribes, 21-27
    B Jesus' reputation goes from a synagogue
        into "all Galilee," 28
        C Simon's mother-in-law
           is healed by Jesus, 29-31
           D Summary: healings and exorcisms,
               Jesus' identity, 32-34
        C' Simon interrupts Jesus' prayer, 35-38
    B' Jesus goes into synagogues in "all Galilee," 39
A' Jesus makes leprosy "go off of" a man.
    Jesus contrasted with the priests, 40-45.

The parallel elements will be considered together.

In A (vv. 21-27) Jesus casts a demon out of a man in the Capernaum synagogue. The response of the people is noteworthy. They exclaim, *What is this? A new teaching—with authority! He commands even the unclean spirits, and they obey him.* In this way the evangelist makes the point that Jesus' teaching includes not only what he says, but also what he does. His teaching and his healings and exorcisms form a unified whole. One is not more normative than the other.

In A' (vv. 40-45) the disease the Bible calls LEPROSY seems to have been thought of as demonic in character, at least in an early stage of the transmission of this story. Three elements in the story are more characteristic of exorcism stories than of healing stories: (1) Jesus' anger in v. 41 (see note *n* in the NRSV) and in v. 43; (2) the verb "cast out" (ἐξέβαλεν) in v. 43; (3) the report of the result of Jesus' action in v. 42 (*Immediately the leprosy left him*; cf. v. 26: "it [the demon] went out of him").

In both stories Jesus' authority and power are contrasted with those of the religious establishment. He has authority that they do not have and he can make a leper clean, whereas they can only give official recognition to the cure that has already taken place.

The hostility toward Jesus that becomes explicit in 2:1–3:6 is prepared for by these two stories. Jesus' behavior disrupts the established lines of teaching authority and the traditional ways of dealing with uncleanness. He should have become ritually unclean when he touched the leper; instead, the leper became clean. Because healing leprosy was understood as something that only God could do (2 Kgs 5:7) this story makes it clear that Jesus' power and authority are not his but God's. As *the Holy One of God* he has indeed *come to destroy* the demons and illnesses that afflict humankind (1:24). But he will be persecuted because his authority comes from God and not from the religious establishment.

In B (v. 28) Jesus' reputation goes out *throughout the surrounding region of Galilee.* This notice prepares for B' (v. 39), when Jesus himself goes into synagogues *throughout Galilee.*

Simon, the first disciple Jesus called (v. 16), plays a role in both C (vv. 29-31) and C' (vv. 35-38). In vv. 29-31 the Markan Jesus heals Simon's mother-in-law. She responds by "serving" (v. 31). It is customary in a healing story for the last element in the story to constitute some kind of proof that the person has indeed been restored to health. But in this story, the nameless woman's service has another point; it is the mark of a true follower of Jesus, as James and John will be reminded in 10:45.

Simon appears again in C' (vv. 35-38), where he and his companions seek Jesus, who has slipped out of CAPERNAUM before dawn to pray. Like so many sincere activists in today's churches, Simon sees no point in wasting time in prayer when there are hurting people back in Capernaum to be helped. The contrast in the story is between Simon's human-centered concerns and Jesus' focus on God as the source of his direction and his power to heal. Jesus is not lacking in compassion, but he demonstrates the importance of putting priority on the discovery and the doing of God's will. In this case, his assignment is not to continue healing people in Capernaum, but to move out into other areas.

The central part of the chiasm (vv. 32-34) sums up the healing and exorcistic activity of Jesus, which the individual stories are intended to illustrate. Jesus attracts large numbers of the sick and demon-possessed and restores them to wholeness. Here for the first time the evangelist introduces a theme that will become increasingly problematic as the story progresses: the issue of Jesus' identity: *He would not permit the demons to speak, because they knew him* (v. 34).

Indeed the demons do know him; the one in v. 24 knows that he is *the Holy One of God* and that he has *come to destroy* the demons. The disciples, however, do not do as well as the demons; they puzzle over Jesus' identity and fail to understand him despite their close association and private instruction. Indeed, the last words on the lips of any disciple in the Gospel are "I don't know the person of whom you are speaking" (14:71, author trans.).

Since the audience of the Gospel has been fully informed about Jesus' identity since 1:1, the disciples' confusion and Jesus' puzzling commands to silence create a tension and expectation that contribute to the movement of the narrative.

By the end of the section Jesus' fame has spread so widely that he *could no longer go into a town openly* (v. 45) without being overwhelmed by the numbers of people coming to him.

2:1–3:6. Controversies. The previous section demonstrated Jesus' authority and power over demons and illness—an authority that was superior to that of the religious establishment. In this section, which is also arranged chiastically, the author of Mark tells five controversy stories which demonstrate Jesus' authority to forgive sins and to interpret scripture in nontraditional ways.

Jesus' authority to forgive sins is linked by the evangelist with his specific concern for sinners, rather than for righteous people who seek no forgiveness. According to Mark, protecting and enforcing religious law is not the focus of Jesus' ministry. Jesus and his followers, past and present, serve a God who is interested in reconciling sinners, feeding the hungry, and healing the sick.

This focus puts Jesus in conflict with religious people whose power depends upon identifying and ostracizing sinners. At first their opposition is limited to private criticism (2:6), but by the end of the section they are plotting to destroy Jesus (3:6).

It is important to note that the author of Mark does not criticize Jews or Jewish leaders as such. That is to say, Mark does not sanction anti-Semitism. Rather, like the OT prophets, the evangelist points out that God's reign runs counter to the claims of all who attempt to preempt God's sovereign authority, even those who claim to represent God. The section may be outlined as follows (Dewey 1980):

A Healing of paralytic. Controversy plus healing
   [call of Levi (2:13-16) echoes 1:16-20
   and prepares for 2:15-17], 2:1-12
  B Controversy over eating. Jesus and his disciples
    eat with the wrong people, 2:15-17
   C Controversy over fasting (not eating), 2:18-22
  B' Controversy over eating. Jesus' disciples acquire
    food in the wrong way, 2:23-28
A' Healing of withered hand.
   Controversy plus healing, 3:1-6

The parallel passages will be discussed together.

A (2:1-12) and A' (3:1-6) lay the groundwork for the two trials of Jesus and establish his innocence ahead of time. In 2:7 the scribes accuse Jesus of blasphemy (cf. 14:64) because he exercises God's prerogative to forgive sins. They are correct that only God can do this, but they miss the point. The audience realizes that Jesus is not blaspheming because his authority comes from God.

It is not illegal on the SABBATH to command a person to stand up in the SYNAGOGUE and stretch out his hand (3:1-5). Jesus has done nothing wrong (cf. 15:14). His opponents are the guilty ones because they plot to commit murder, which is not legal on any day of the week. Jesus saves life (3:4); for this he will die.

B (2:15-17) and B' (2:23-28) emphasize God's initiative toward human beings. The community whose life is centered on fellowship with Jesus is a communi-ty of sinners and their religious practice represents God's provision for their benefit, not their attempt to please God.

The call of Levi (2:13-16) is important preparation for the controversy over eating with sinners because tax collectors (publicans) were not only regarded as dishonest, but were also despised as collaborators with the Roman overlords. Revolutionary groups who might have applauded Jesus' association with the poor peasants would have been appalled by his association with the running dogs of Roman imperialism.

But the Markan Jesus is not captive to ideological categories. The only requirement for his company is to understand oneself as a sinner—no better than the lowest form of human being one can imagine. "If you don't consider yourself to be in that category," the Gospel writer says, "then don't count yourself among the associates of Jesus."

If the point of Christian community is *not* to avoid sinners, then the point of sabbath observance is *not* to be religious, but rather to meet human need. *The sabbath was made for humankind, not humankind for the sabbath* (2:27). Furthermore, Jesus, the Son of Man, is lord even over the sabbath and over the scriptures, which he interprets to prove his point: David broke religious laws to feed his hungry troops (1 Sam 21:1-6). The Gospel writer cites David's act during the days of ABIATHAR, which poses a problem for careful readers of the Bible.

Right in the center of the chiastic structure is the controversy over fasting (2:18-22). In an oblique reference to the CRUCIFIXION, the Markan Jesus speaks of a time when he (the bridegroom) will be *taken away* (v. 20). That will be the time for fasting.

The discussion about fasting leads into a pair of sayings on the relationship between the old and the new. The good news that Jesus brings is by its very nature disruptive of old patterns. New and flexible structures are necessary, because the fermentation of the gospel will soon destroy containers that are rigid and fragile.

Taken together, 1:21-45 and 2:1–3:6 present a complete overview of Jesus' ministry, which the evangelist regards as normative for the church in his own day. The church is about the business of teaching, healing, casting out demons, building a community of sinners, and meeting human needs. Jesus' authority to interpret scripture overrides that of the old establishment and creates new wineskins flexible enough to allow for the gospel's disruptive bubbling.

But it is not a cheap victory. It will cost Jesus his life and it will cost his followers every shred of security and self-righteousness.

3:7-12. Conclusion. The large section 1:14–3:12, which establishes the basic pattern of Jesus' ministry, concludes with a summary in 3:7-12. The return to the sea with the disciples (3:7) forms an INCLUSIO with the original calling of the disciples by the sea (1:16).

There Jesus had promised to make the former fishermen into fishers for people. Here the audience learns that Jesus himself is a successful people-fisher; not only has he attracted crowds from Galilee, but people have come from long distances after hearing about him.

The summary reemphasizes Jesus' ministry of healing and exorcism and reminds the audience that although the demons knew Jesus' true identity as Son of God, Jesus did not permit them to make him known to others.

Extension of Jesus' Ministry and Intensification of Conflict, 3:7–6:30

3:7-12. Introduction. This summary serves not only to conclude the previous section, but also to introduce places and ideas that will be important in the second and third major sections of the ministry in Galilee and gentile territory.

The crowd that follows Jesus includes people from Galilee, Judea, Jerusalem (which is in Judea), Idumea (home territory of the Herodians), the territory east of the Jordan River, and the region around TYRE AND SIDON (Phoenicia). Information that sick people were pressing around Jesus attempting to touch him prepares for the story of the hemorrhaging woman (5:25-34).

The mention of Tyre and Sidon prepares for Jesus' visit there in 7:24-30 and explains to the audience why the SYROPHOENICIAN woman expected Jesus to be able to exorcise her daughter. According to Mark, gentile followers of Jesus had spread the word in their home territory about the miracles they had seen in Galilee.

The boat that will become the platform for Jesus' teaching in 4:1 and the means by which he himself ventures into gentile territory in 5:1 is introduced in 3:9. The material in 3:13–6:30 may be outlined as follows:

A Disciples appointed ("sent out ones,"
   sent out, 3:14), 3:13-19
B Misinterpretation by family
   and religious leaders, 3:20-35

C Jesus' words and deeds heard and seen
   but not always understood, 4:1–5:43
  1. Jesus' words (collection of parables),
     4:1-34
  2. Jesus' deeds (collection of miracle
     stories), 4:35–5:43
B' Misinterpretation by associates in home town,
   6:1-6
A' Disciples *sent out* ("sent out ones," 6:30), 6:7-13

3:13-19. Disciples appointed. As Baptist translator Helen Barrett Montgomery points out, the word translated "apostle" in most English Bibles actually means "missionary" or "one sent out" (1924, Mark 3:14, n. 1). Thus the material in 3:13–6:30 is framed by an emphasis on Christian mission (3:13-19 and 6:7-13, 30).

But the author of Mark is careful to make clear that mission *follows* a period of developing a relationship with Jesus:

And he appointed twelve (whom he also named missionaries) in order that
  (1) they might be with him and in order that
  (2) he might commission them
    (a) to proclaim and
    (b) to have authority to cast out the demons
and he appointed the twelve (author trans.).

In the ancient world it was thought that a disciple could not properly carry out the instructions of the teacher without first spending a great deal of time in the teacher's presence. The Gospel of Mark applies this insight to Christian formation.

The active ministry of the disciples is patterned after that of Jesus himself: proclamation (cf. 1:14) and spiritual warfare (cf. 1:21-27, 34, 39; 3:11-12), speech and action. Neither is optional and one may not be substituted for the other. It is worth noting that the authority of the disciples extends only to demons. They are given no authority over other followers of Jesus.

In Mark, THE TWELVE named in chap. 3 do not constitute an inside group of disciples who have special privileges. The size of the group called "disciples" or "followers" of Jesus varies from scene to scene in Mark, and includes, besides the twelve named here, Levi (2:14), *many* tax collectors and sinners (2:15), Mary Magdalene, Mary the mother of James and Joses, Salome (15:40), Bartimaeus (10:52), and the Gethsemane "streaker" (14:51). The greatest privilege bestowed in the Gospel seems to be the gift of "the mystery of the reign of God" (4:11 author trans.), and that gift is said to have been given to a group larger than the twelve. Thus, "twelve" should be understood as symbolic of the new people of God; the number corresponds to the twelve tribes of Israel in the OT. It does not delineate an exclusive group.

3:20-35. Misinterpretation by family and religious leaders. In this unit, a controversy with the scribes is framed by the misunderstanding of Jesus by his family of origin and their replacement by "those who do the will of God" (author trans.). Since the controversy involves two charges by opponents, to which Jesus responds in reverse order, the result is a chiastic structure (Robbins 1989, 172, n. 27):

A Jesus' family comes to seize him, 20-21
  B Accusation 1: He has Beelzebul, 22a
    C Accusation 2: By the prince of demons
      he casts out demons, 22b
    C' Refutation 2: Satan would not
      cast out demons, 23-27
  B' Refutation 1: Saying Jesus has an unclean spirit
    is blasphemy, 28-30
A' Jesus' true family consists of those
  who do the will of God, 31-35

In 3:21, members of Jesus' family respond to the crowds that he is attracting by coming out to seize him because in their opinion Jesus is out of his mind (ἐξέστη, lit. "standing outside [himself]"). In 3:31, however, the evangelist turns the tables; now the family is standing outside (ἔξω στήκοντες) by contrast with those who are seated around Jesus on the inside.

The Markan Jesus explains that his kin are not those who are related to him by blood, but those who are related to him by sharing his purpose: doing the will of God. The message to the audience is twofold: (1) Sometimes even one's own relatives will think one crazy for doing the will of God; (2) Those whose relatives misunderstand their Christian commitment find a new family in the Christian community, just as Jesus did (cf. 10:29-30).

When the scribes accuse Jesus of having Beelzebul and of using that demon's power to perform exorcisms, the audience would have understood that they were accusing Jesus of practicing magic. Magicians were believed to have gained control of spirits that they could call upon to do their bidding. Spells and incantations were used to force the gods and spirits to do the will of the magician or witch who was casting the spell.

When an ancient miracle worker was accused of practicing magic, his defense often was to claim that he had not used incantations, but had prayed. He was not, after all, a magician trying to force the gods to do his will, but a pious person who did only the will of the gods. So when the author of Mark portrays Jesus and his followers as those who "do the will of God" he is relying upon a commonly accepted line of argument to make his point.

Further, the Markan Jesus responds to his opponents by pointing out that it would be inconsistent for Satan, the ruler of demons, to allow his power to be used to cast out demons. Finally, the audience is reminded of the real source of Jesus' power—the Holy Spirit that came into him at his baptism (1:8, 10). The scribes' false attribution of the work of the Holy Spirit to Satan is not an innocent mistake. It is an unpardonable sin.

As the scene closes Jesus and his associates are inside and those who misunderstand and oppose him are standing outside. This contrast between insiders and outsiders, which seems so clear-cut in this passage, will become increasingly problematic as the story progresses.

4:1-34. Jesus' words (parables). The parable chapter is the first of only two long speeches by the Markan Jesus. The other is the apocalyptic discourse in chap. 13. In fact, both speeches are primarily about eschatology. In chap. 4 the author of Mark combines PARABLES and sayings from the Jesus tradition to explain why the proclamation of God's reign is meeting with resistance and to assure the audience that despite the present apparent lack of progress, God's reign will eventually burst forth in amazing fruitfulness.

A secondary and related concern of chaps. 4 and 13 is a warning against apostasy. This is regarded by the evangelist as a danger even for those who have experienced God's grace mediated through Jesus.

The author of Mark has arranged the material into a carefully constructed chiastic arrangement (Marcus 1986, 221):

A Narrative introduction, 1-2
  B Seed parable (public teaching), 3-9
    C Statement about hiddenness
      (private teaching), 10-12
      D Allegorical explanation of parable
        (private teaching), 13-20
    C' Statements about revelation
      (private teaching), 21-25
  B' Seed parables (public teaching), 26-29, 30-32
A' Narrative conclusion, 33-34

According to this arrangement, all three seed parables are addressed to the crowd that assembles in 4:1 and is left behind in 4:36. This public teaching frames the private teaching to "those around him with the twelve" (v. 10, author trans.). The private teaching, while it picks up the agricultural images of the parable in the allegorical explanation (vv. 13-20), also introduces images drawn from domestic life: lamp, basket, bed, lampstand, house, and measure (vv. 21-25).

Agricultural images were commonly used by Hellenistic writers to teach lessons about education and improvement of character. They were used in the OT and in apocalyptic Judaism to teach about God's will and God's coming reign. The Markan Jesus combines these emphases, but alters the images to suit his purposes.

The seed parables (vv. 3-9, 26-29, 30-32) make three points:

(1) The ultimate success of God's reign is inevitable, despite present appearances to the contrary. Although much seed falls on unproductive soil, the good soil will yield a harvest abundant beyond all imagination.

(2) God's reign is the result of what God does, not the result of what human beings do. All the farmer has to do is sow the seed. Everything else is outside his control. This is a marked contrast with Hellenistic emphases upon the importance of human effort in producing a good "harvest," but it coincides with the apocalyptic idea that in the drama of history God is the primary actor and human beings merely respond to God's initiative.

(3) God's reign is inclusive, but not imperialistic. The parable of the mustard seed speaks of God's reign as a plant with large branches that shelter the birds of the air. In Dan 4:10-17 the BABYLONIAN EMPIRE is portrayed as a large tree; in Ezek 31:3-14 the same image is used for ASSYRIA. The author of Ezek 17:22-24 regards that image as appropriate for the glorious Messianic kingdom that was expected after the humiliation of the exile. But the Markan story deflates all this grandiosity by comparing God's reign, not to a mighty cedar, but to a humble mustard bush. It doesn't look like much, but it provides shelter for all who flock to it (Waetjen 1989, 108–109).

The sayings on hiddenness and revelation (vv. 10-12, 21-25) have presented a challenge to interpreters over the centuries. In the Markan context, three points are being made:

(1) Just as Isaiah's words were meant to prevent understanding and repentance, so Jesus' parables prevent understanding and repentance by those "outside" who oppose God's reign (vv. 10-12).

(2) Concealment is not the last word. *There is nothing hidden, except to be disclosed; nor is anything secret, except to come to light* (v. 22).

(3) Those who have been "given the secret of God's reign" (v. 11, author trans.) had better not be complacent. They need to pay attention to the insight they have (v. 24). This includes not only the disciples in the story, but the audience of the Gospel as well.

The central emphasis of the passage falls on the allegorical interpretation of the first seed parable. The Markan Jesus says that understanding this parable is critically important for understanding all the parables (v. 13).

The parable itself pointed to the ultimate success of God's reign. The interpretation explains why the present circumstances are so difficult and why so much seed fails to bear fruit. The explanation is a typically apocalyptic one: God's reign is temporarily opposed by Satan and his forces.

In the first case, Satan snatches away the word before it takes root. This is a reference to people who, although they hear the message, do not even begin as followers of Jesus.

The second and third cases are about people who begin as followers of Jesus, but fail to follow through in discipleship. Some are unable to withstand *when trouble or persecution arises on account of the word* (v. 17) and some are distracted by the concerns of the present age (an apocalyptic term), the seductive power of wealth, and the desire for "things" other than the "things of God" (8:33, author trans.). APOSTASY, according to Mark, can be a response either to difficulties or to comfortable circumstances.

When Christians encounter opposition and persecution, or when they see converts lost to the seductive addictions of increased ease and affluence, they are not to be discouraged. This is all part of the ministry to which they are called. Their part is to keep sowing. The rest is up to God.

4:35–5:43. Jesus' deeds (miracle stories). The unit of parables is followed by a unit of miracle stories. Like the parables, the miracles proclaim the reign of God and are a source of misunderstanding for some. Jesus' words are heard, but not understood; his deeds are seen, but not perceived (cf. 4:12).

The miracle stories are grouped in two pairs:

A Conquest of demonic storm, 4:35-41

Setting: on the sea, on the way to gentile territory

Beneficiaries: male disciples
Level of threat: the disciples fear
   that they are about to die
A' Conquest of demons in GERASA, 5:1-20
   Setting: near the sea, in gentile territory
   Beneficiary: male gentile
   Level of threat: the demoniac lives among the dead
B Healing of hemorrhaging woman, 5:24b-34
   Setting: Jewish territory
   Beneficiary: female; ritually unclean;
     ill for 12 years
   Level of threat: she is in the process of dying
     (life is draining away)
B' Raising of Jairus' daughter, 5:21-24a, 35-43
   Setting: Jewish territory
   Beneficiary: female; ritually unclean corpse;
     twelve years old
   Level of threat: she is already dead
     when Jesus arrives

The confidence that God's unlimited power is at work in Jesus is called "faith" in these miracle stories (5:34). The evangelist puts them here not merely to record Jesus' past activity, but to encourage those who hear the stories to resist paralyzing fear (4:40; 5:36) and to maintain confidence in God's power to overcome evil, sickness, and death.

In the first pair of stories Jesus' role as divine warrior against evil is emphasized. The storm that Jesus and his disciples encounter on the Sea of Galilee is interpreted in the narrative as an attempt by demonic forces to keep Jesus from invading gentile territory (5:1-20). In order to make sense of the Markan Jesus' movements back and forth across the sea, the reader should consult a map of the area (MBD, plate 23). Jesus "rebukes" the storm (4:39) in the same way that he addresses the demons (1:25, 3:12). Like the demons, *the wind and the sea obey him* (4:41). The sea represents the forces of chaos and death, over which Jesus, the life-bringer, exercises control.

But the disciples are still in the dark, asking, "Who then is this?" The demons know, the audience knows, but even those who have been given the mystery of the reign of God fail to perceive the meaning in what they see.

Having resisted the onslaught of the sea demons, Jesus lands in gentile territory and immediately encounters more demons in a militant mood. A whole legion of them are tormenting a man whose days of living death are passed *among the tombs and on the*

mountains (5:5). Like Pharoah's army, however, these enemy troops rush into the sea and are drowned (5:13). Again the victory goes to the divine warrior. Chaos becomes order and wholeness (5:15).

But again Jesus' saving power is seen by blind eyes. The Gerasenes see the loss of the pigs and send Jesus away. Before he goes, he commissions the former demoniac to tell *how much the Lord has done* for him (5:19). The man's response has two effects: (1) By preaching (κηρύσσειν, cf. 1:14, 3:14), he does what disciples are supposed to do. He becomes one who makes the deeds of the Lord "known . . . among the nations" (Isa 12:4); (2) His proclamation equates the merciful activity of the Lord with the ministry of Jesus (5:20). The answer to the disciples' question, "Who then is this?" is "Jesus is the Lord."

In the second pair of stories the setting shifts from gentile to Jewish territory and the emphasis shifts from cosmic combat to healing, but the boundary-crossing character of Jesus' ministry is still apparent. Having crossed geographical boundaries to release a gentile from bondage, Jesus now crosses traditional purity boundaries to restore life to two suffering women.

Neither woman is ritually "clean" when Jesus encounters her. According to Torah, vaginal bleeding renders a woman unclean (Lev 5:19-30) and all corpses are unclean (Num 19:11-21). In these stories the theme first sounded in the cleansing of the leper (1:40-45) is repeated. Although Jesus should have become unclean by touching the bleeding woman and the dead girl, exactly the opposite happens. His touch restores both women to health and to states of ritual purity.

Both Jairus and the bleeding woman are portrayed positively as having faith in Jesus' healing power. Jairus is called upon to "keep on believing" (5:36, author trans.) for an even greater miracle than healing after his daughter is pronounced dead before Jesus' arrival.

Jairus is a leader of the synagogue—a religious and social insider. He has a right to ask for help and he does so directly, but not arrogantly. Rather than flaunting his social and religious status, he humbles himself (5:22-23), an attitude that Jesus will praise in 9:35, 10:41-45.

The anonymous woman, by contrast, has been a religious and social outsider for twelve years, experiencing neither the worship of God nor human embrace. She has no right to jeopardize Jesus' ritual status by touching him. However, she refuses to be defined by her situation and takes bold action on the basis of what she has heard about Jesus (5:27; cf. 3:10).

Whereas the parables emphasize assurance of the *final* victory of God's reign, this unit of MIRACLE STORIES promises *present* help for those who call on Jesus with confidence in his power.

6:1-6. Misinterpretation by associates in hometown. This second instance of misinterpretation of Jesus' miracle-working activity by intimate associates corresponds to 3:20-35 in Mark's chiastic outline of 3:13–6:30. Like the scribes (3:22), the people of Nazareth raise questions about the source of Jesus' power and wisdom. They recognize that Jesus is doing miraculous things and that he has been given extraordinary wisdom (v. 3), but they do not see in these phenomena the inbreaking of the reign of God. They do not admit that God is the source of Jesus' power.

They point to Jesus' ordinary occupation; he is a carpenter, not a scribe or a rabbi. He does not come from a traditional family; they call him *son of Mary* (v. 3) rather than the traditional "son of Joseph" (cf. Luke 4:22; John 6:42). The hometown boy is getting something from somewhere, but where? No one suggests God.

The evangelist comments, *they took offense at him* (ἐσκανδαλίζοντο ἐν αὐτῷ). This phrase can mean two things in Mark. In 4:17; 9:42-47; and 14:27 it means to be caused to abandon allegiance to Jesus after beginning as a disciple. Here, however, it is used of nonfollowers and means that the people of Nazareth were prevented from becoming Jesus' disciples.

The people of Nazareth are like the seed that fell beside the path: they never take root at all. Their opinions of who Jesus is prevent their seeing God at work in his miracles. Jesus is amazed by their unbelief.

In the miracle stories (4:35–5:43), to "have faith" means to have confidence in Jesus' power. Here the evangelist expands the definition beyond that. To recognize that Jesus has power is not enough; it is necessary to recognize that Jesus' power and wisdom come from God, and from no other source.

The conclusion of this scene is strangely paradoxical. The evangelist says that *[Jesus] could do no deed of power there* and then says *he laid his hands on a few sick people and cured them* (v. 5). The reason for this odd sentence is that the author of Mark wants to summarize his complex view of the relationship between faith and miracles.

On the one hand, confidence in Jesus' power (faith) is basic if the Christian community expects to experience that power in its life and ministry (5:34, 36; 9:23; 10:52). On the other hand, there are no absolute conditions that can limit God's freedom to act in sovereign power. Even when faith is inadequate, grace may extend miraculous help (4:35-41; 6:5; 9:24-27).

The Markan Jesus summarizes the misunderstanding of Nazareth with a traditional proverb: *Prophets are not without honor, except in their hometown, and among their own kin, and in their own house* (v. 4). Many Christians have found it so.

6:7-13, 30. Disciples sent out. The large section 3:13–6:30 concludes with Jesus' sending out of the disciples to do the ministry to which he had appointed them at the beginning of the section (3:13-19). Having now been with Jesus (3:14b) and observed his ministry of word (4:1-34) and deed (4:35–5:43), the disciples are ready to be sent out in pairs to proclaim repentance and to exercise Jesus' authority over the demonic spirits. They also bring God's healing to the sick.

There is no hint here of the kind of dispensationalist understanding of miracle that came to characterize the church in later generations. The author of Mark believes that Jesus' followers are to replicate his ministry. They do not do this alone, but with others. There are no superstars or lone rangers.

Finally the evangelist stresses accountability. Mark 6:30 is not merely a narrative conclusion. It suggests that disciples will give an account of their faithfulness to the one who sent them out.

In Mark 6:8-11 the Gospel writer sets out instructions for missionaries. They are allowed to have a walking stick and a pair of sandals, which are all they need to get from one place to another. They are not allowed to carry bread, money, a begging bag, or an extra tunic. For the necessities of life they will have to depend on God and God's people. Like the Israelites who lived from one day's supply of manna to the next, they are radically dependent on God's providential care.

The rejection that missionaries encounter is not regarded as a surprising development, but as an expected outcome. The response is to be neither discouragement nor vindictive reprisal, but continued ministry elsewhere. The result is not the problem of the sowers. All they have to do is sow.

Jesus' Ministry Removes Barriers between Jews and Gentiles, 6:14–8:30

This third and final subsection of 1:14–8:30 picks up and expands the theme of the inclusion of the gentiles that was introduced in 5:1-20. The section is framed by identical speculations about Jesus' identity:

Is he John the baptizer reincarnated? Is he Elijah, the forerunner of the Messiah? Is he some other prophet? (6:14-16; 8:27-30).

In chap. 6 the question of Jesus' identity is left hanging, but the question of whether his opponents will succeed in destroying him (3:6, 3:19) is clarified in a chilling flashback. The execution of John the baptizer suggests that the prospects are grim for those who run afoul of Herod and his partisans.

Beginning at 6:31, Jesus feeds and heals first Jews (6:31-56) and then gentiles (7:24–8:10). Between the ministry to Jews and the ministry to gentiles, a discussion with Pharisees over the proper understanding of religious defilement (7:1-23) prepares for the move to the gentiles in 7:24.

The section closes with summaries illustrating the failure by Jesus' opponents (8:11-13) and by his disciples (8:14-21) to perceive the significance of his ministry. The arrival at Bethsaida in 8:22 marks the end of the sea crossings that began in 4:35; the story of the blind man healed in two stages (8:22-26) prepares for the discipleship section 8:22–10:52, which ends with the only other healing of blindness in Mark (10:46-52).

6:14-29. Death of John the baptizer. The execution of John the baptizer by Herod Antipas is confirmed by Josephus (*Ant* 18.5.2), who understood it as an attempt to prevent John's organizing a political revolution. Mark's macabre interpretation of the episode is designed to foreshadow the passion of Jesus and perhaps also to suggest future suffering for his followers, who have just been sent out on their first assignment.

It is important to notice the artistry of this story, which is one of the more obvious of the Markan "sandwiched" narratives. The story is told between the sending of the disciples in vv. 7-13 and their return in v. 30. After the disciples have been sent out, the narrator informs the audience that "King Herod heard of it, for Jesus' name had become known."

Herod's participation in the speculation about Jesus' identity prepares for the narrative flashback of vv. 17-29. Herod's own conclusion is that Jesus' power is due to the fact that he is a reincarnation of the executed prophet. This failure to identify God as the source of Jesus' power has already been labeled "unbelief" by the evangelist (6:1-6).

The Markan account of the circumstances leading to John's death is the longest and most melodramatic that has been preserved. It is also replete with OT allusions. By calling Herod the tetrarch a "king" and by making John's criticism of Herod's immoral marriage

(Lev 18:16, 20:21) the reason for his imprisonment, the evangelist identifies John with the long line of prophets who rebuked kings (1 Sam 15:17-29; 2 Sam 12:1-15; 2 Kgs 20:16-18; Jer 38:14-23) and of martyrs who upheld the law in the face of royal opposition (2 Macc 6:18–7:42; 4 Macc 5–18).

The primary prophet that the author of Mark has in mind, however, is Elijah, with whom he identifies John elsewhere in the Gospel (1:6-7; 9:11-13). In this story Herodias plays Jezebel to John's Elijah. But whereas Jezebel was unsuccessful in eliminating Elijah, Herodias succeeds in destroying John.

The involvement of the young daughter is a particularly chilling detail. Textual variants make it uncertain whether the evangelist regards her as the daughter of Herodias only, or also of Herod (see NRSV v. 22, mrg). Commentators usually assume that the dance was erotic, although this is likewise uncertain. What is plain, however, is that she is put by the evangelist into the same age group as Jairus's twelve-year-old daughter. The same word (κοράσιον) is used for both. One little daughter is restored to life; one participates in a grisly murder. It is the child who adds the detail of the platter. John's head is the final course in this macabre banquet (Anderson 1992).

John's headless body is claimed by his disciples and laid in a tomb. When Jesus' time for burial comes, however, his disciples will be nowhere to be found.

6:30-56. Ministry to Jews. This section has three parts: the feeding miracle (vv. 31-44), the sea-walking story (vv. 45-52), and a series of healings (vv. 53-56). The first and third take place on the western side of the Sea of Galilee, that is, in Jewish territory. The three-part series opens and closes with references to the crowds that surround Jesus and the disciples (v. 31 [cf. 3:19]; vv. 54-56).

In the first of two feeding miracles in the Gospel, Jesus is portrayed as the faithful shepherd promised to Israel in the prophetic and APOCALYPTIC LITERATURE (Ezek 34:23; Jer 23:4; PssSol 17:40). Because both Moses (Exod 3:1) and David (1 Sam 16:11) had been shepherds, the shepherd became a metaphor for the religious and political leaders of Israel and also for Yahweh, Israel's ultimately faithful shepherd.

The prophets criticized Israel's leaders for being irresponsible shepherds (Isa 56:11-12; Jer 23:1-2; Ezek 34:1-10), or for leaving the people unprotected, without a shepherd (Ezek 34:5; cf. Num 27:17; 1 Kgs 22:17; cf. Isa 53:6). Through the prophets, Yahweh promised to replace the unworthy shepherds, either by shepherding the people himself, or by raising up a faithful shepherd, usually a Davidic leader (Ezek 34:11-16; Jer 23:3-6; Isa 40:11; 49:9b-10).

By invoking these images in v. 34, the author of Mark proclaims the good news that the eschatological shepherd has arrived to provide for the needs of God's people. As their shepherd, Jesus teaches the crowds (v. 34b), provides them with food (v. 42; cf. Ezek 34:2, 8; Isa 40:11; Ps 23:2), and heals their sick and injured (vv. 53-56; cf. Ezek 34:4). There is also an implicit criticism of the religious leaders who oppose Jesus; they are the irresponsible shepherds condemned by the prophets.

The desert setting of the feeding miracle (vv. 34-35) reminds the audience of the Isaian theme of the New Exodus (Mark 1:3) and of God's miraculous provision of manna during the original Exodus. Both this story and its gentile counterpart (8:1-10) foreshadow the last meal Jesus will share with his disciples. There, as in the feeding stories, Jesus takes bread, pronounces a thanksgiving or a blessing, breaks the bread, and gives it to his disciples (14:22). Not only is the hunger of the crowd satisfied, but the leftovers fill twelve large baskets typically used by Jews for carrying loads. The number twelve further reinforces the Jewish cultural setting. Interestingly enough, the disciples, who have just returned from a mission on which they were forbidden to take bread (v. 8), manage, when pressed, to produce five loaves and two fish (v. 38).

After the feeding the Markan Jesus sends the disciples across the sea toward Bethsaida on the *other side* (v. 45), that is, in gentile territory. Jesus dismisses the crowd and, like Moses and Elijah before him, retires to the mountain to meet with God.

It soon becomes apparent, however, that without Jesus' leadership the disciples are not going to make it to gentile territory; again they are meeting with opposition, as in 4:35-41. Seeing this, the Markan Jesus again demonstrates his superiority over the hostile sea power by striding across the sea (vv. 47-52), an activity attributed to God in Job 9:8 and Isa 43:16. His intent was to walk ahead of them—to guide them, like a good shepherd, to their destination. However, the disciples do not recognize him and cry out in fear.

Continuing the imagery of the New Exodus, the narrator has Jesus identify himself with the self-designation of Yahweh, "I am" (Exod 3:14, Isa 41:4, 43:10-11). Thus the author of Mark provides the audience with a defintive answer to the question raised by the disciples in the previous sea-rescue story: *Who then is*

this? (4:41). The promise of deliverance is reinforced by an echo of Deutero-Isaiah's *Do not be afraid* (v. 50; cf. Isa 43:10, 43; 45:18; 51:2). Sadly, none of this clarifies things for the disciples, who remain "utterly astounded."

Their astonishment reveals that they have missed the exodus allusions completely. They *did not understand about the loaves* (v. 52—the renewal of provision in the wilderness), or about Jesus' being the eschatological shepherd who takes care of his own, or about the way being made for God's people through the sea and the desert, or about Jesus' revelation of the character of God and God's reign in his person and ministry.

Worse yet, the narrator informs the audience that, like Jesus' opponents (3:5) and *those outside* (4:10-12, alluding to Isa 6:9-10) their hearts have been hardened. Despite their having been chosen and sent out on a successful mission, despite their having just participated in Jesus' own miraculous ministry, the disciples seem to be in danger of becoming outsiders. The narrator leaves the audience no room for complacency.

The trip to gentile territory aborted, Jesus and the disciples disembark at Gennesaret on the Jewish shore and are immediately surrounded by people seeking healing (vv. 53-55). As their shepherd, it is Jesus' responsibility to heal them (Ezek 34:4) and he does so. Echoing 3:10 and 5:24b-34, the narrator reports that people were healed merely by touching Jesus' clothes (v. 56).

This series of three episodes repeats the pattern seen throughout the Gospel in which Jesus' ministry has three components: teaching, healing, and domination of the demonic powers. The pervasive image throughout this series is the Jewish expectation of the eschatological shepherd who will feed, heal, and lead his flock to safety through watery chaos and threatening wilderness. The next section of the Gospel redefines membership in this eschatological flock.

7:1-23. Redefinition of clean/unclean. Coming immediately after the teaching, feeding, and healing of the Jewish crowds, this section prepares for the mission to the gentiles by challenging the understanding of defilement represented as that of the religious establishment and by asserting Jesus' authority to replace ritual boundaries with ethical ones. The Markan Jesus does not eliminate the notion of impurity; rather, he redefines it.

The literary structure follows the pattern set in 3:20–4:34: a controversy with authorities from Jerusalem is followed by a parable and its private interpretation to the inquiring disciples. The controversy (7:1-13) appears to be over the validity of the oral law. At a deeper level, it is about the way in which human sinfulness uses religion as a way of avoiding confrontation with God.

The parable (vv. 14-15) and its interpretation (vv. 17-23) deny the polluting character of nonkosher foods and insist that impurity is caused by behaviors that destroy human community. That this material was understood by some early readers as a literary parallel to the parables in chap. 4 is indicated by the addition of v. 16: "Let anyone with ears to hear listen," which is a scribal attempt to achieve conformity with 4:9, 23.

Whether or not one must perform ritual hand rinsing before eating (vv. 1-5) must not have been a burning issue for Christians at the time the gospel was written, since the evangelist finds it necessary to explain the practice in a long parenthesis (vv. 3-4). The religious leaders want to know why Jesus' disciples do not observe the oral traditions *of the elders* prescribing such cleansing rituals (v. 5). Jesus' answer is given in chiastic form (Gundry 1993, 349):

A Biblical citation from the prophets
  (Isa 29:13, LXX) with application, 7:6-7
  B Accusation: *You abandon the commandment
    of God and hold to human tradition*, 7:8
  B' Accusation: *You have a fine way of rejecting
    the commandment of God in order to keep
    your tradition*, 7:9
A' Biblical citation from the law of Moses
  (Exod 20:12; 21:17) with application, 7:10-13

The Markan Jesus asserts that the oral tradition was not, as its proponents thought, a way of guaranteeing faithfulness to God's will by building a fence around Torah. Instead, people had found a way to put religion to their own use; a veneer of religion covered a complete reversal of God's explicit commandment. Instead of honoring mother and father by providing for them, the subject of Jesus' illustration uses a religious vow to put the resources the parents need out of their reach.

Since the evangelist has to explain the meaning of *corban* (v. 11) and the handwashing issue to the audience, it is unlikely that he is attacking Jewish practices familiar to and controversial among Christians or defending Christians against Jewish opponents. Rather, the author may be critiquing the tendency within the Christian community itself to prefer the practice of religion over obedience to God. Human traditions and lip

service substitute for wholehearted self-surrender, as Isaiah said so well.

The parable about inside and outside (vv. 14-15) and its interpretation (vv. 17-23) complete the unit. The Markan Jesus begins as he did in 4:3 by addressing the crowd with the command, *Listen!* What follows is a change of subject from the previous discussion. There the issue was *how* one might eat; here it is *what* one may eat. The parable demands an explanation since the *word of God* so important to Jesus in v. 13 explicitly forbids the ingestion of foods that *defile* a person. Furthermore, the second claim of the parable seems to contradict Torah, which teaches that defecation does not defile the defecator (Gundry 1993, 354-55). Again, as in chap. 4, the disciples' question provides the opportunity for the evangelist to explain to the audience.

Everything turns upon an assumption that is not stated directly until v. 21, but ultimately derives from the Isaiah quotation: it is the human heart that is the locus of purity and defilement. What goes in through one's lips and down into one's stomach cannot defile because (as Torah teaches) its evacuation into the latrine does not cause impurity in the person. That which does not involve the heart does not pollute. But although what comes out of the intestines does not pollute, what comes out of the heart certainly does.

Lists of vices like the one in v. 21 are common in Hellenistic discussions of ethics (cf. Epictetus, *Diss* 2.16.45) and appear frequently in the NT (Rom 1:29-31; 1 Cor 6:9-10; Gal 5:19-21; Eph 5:5; Rev 21:8; 22:15). Everything on Mark's list is destructive of human relationships and is condemned by the OT. The Markan Jesus thus does not deny the authority of scripture, but he does revoke the food laws in favor of Isaiah's emphasis on the importance of the attitude of the heart toward God. In the evangelist's view, devotion to God results in right relationships with other human beings.

To make sure the audience does not miss the point, the author points out parenthetically that in this statement, Jesus "made all foods clean" (author trans.). Again Jesus is seen to speak *as one having authority* by contrast with the scribes (1:22). Having made all foods clean in this section, the Markan Jesus proceeds in 7:24-30 to make all persons clean as well.

7:24–8:9. Ministry to gentiles. Like 6:31-56, which described Jesus' ministry to Jews, this section consists of three stories: exorcism of a Syrophoenician woman's daughter (vv. 24-30), restoration of hearing and speech to a man (vv. 31-37), and the feeding of 4,000 in the DECAPOLIS (8:1-9). Whereas the first panel *began* with a feeding miracle, this panel *ends* with one. Both sections witness to Jesus' power to heal disease and to defeat demonic powers.

The transition from the previous material in 7:1-23 is marked by a change of setting. Jesus goes alone into Phoenicia, not to preach or to heal, but to escape (v. 24). His vacation is cut short, however, by an "uppity" woman who invades his private space with a request for help (Wahlberg 1975, 13). The narrator has prepared the audience for this story by making certain that there were people from Tyre and Sidon present in 3:7-12 to benefit from Jesus' healings and exorcisms; the audience is to understand that the woman has "heard about him" from other gentiles who have encountered the power of Jesus.

The evangelist's description of the woman specifies the three ways in which she is unworthy to make demands on Jesus: She is female, a Greek (probably meaning "pagan" by religion), and a Syrophoenician by race. Like the Jewish father Jairus, this pagan mother bows at Jesus' feet and makes her request. She wants her daughter whole.

The Markan Jesus responds with the mission strategy that everyone knew was the right one: Jew first, then gentile (Isaiah; Luke–Acts; Rom 1:16; 2:9-10). It isn't right, he says, to take the bread from the table of the descendants (τέκνων, v. 27) and toss it out (βαλεῖν) to the dogs. Like any Palestinian Jew, the Markan Jesus is portrayed as thinking that all urban dogs are scavengers who run wild in the streets; Jews did not have house dogs. It would be unthinkable to deprive the descendants of Abraham of their due in order to minister to gentile dogs.

The woman responds out of a different cultural context. For her it is not a matter of sequence but of simultaneity. "In our culture," she explains, "the children (παιδίων, v. 28) and the house dogs eat at the same time" (Dufton 1989, 417). By changing the cultural context, the woman appeals to the experience of her people; they were receiving the benefits of Jesus' ministry before he ever left Galilee. They went to him before he came to them. There is enough healing for everyone all at the same time. No one need be deprived or made to wait.

By replacing the word for descendants (implying those entitled to an inheritance, 12:19) with the word Jesus will later use to describe those who are included *despite* their lack of status (9:37, 10:14), the woman completes her rhetorical coup and wins the argument

(Grimes 1991). The woman's effective sermon (λόγος, cf. 2:2, 4:33) achieves its goal; the unclean spirit leaves her daughter. Having made clean all foods in the previous section, the Markan Jesus now makes clean all races and peoples. It is worth noting that according to Mark, this anonymous woman won a place at the table not merely for her daughter, but for every gentile Christian who reads these words.

Mark next displays his lack of interest in geography by having Jesus travel north to Sidon in order to arrive in the region of the Decapolis, southeast of Phoenicia on the eastern (gentile) side of the Sea of Galilee. Here Jesus heals a deaf man, one who, although he has ears, cannot hear (8:18, cf. 4:9, 12, 23). This suggests that the spiritual deafness Jesus continues to encounter may ultimately be overcome as well.

Having made it possible for the man to hear and also to speak, Jesus promptly commands him and the witnesses to the miracle to keep silent, but to no avail. Like the Jewish leper, these gentiles ignore Jesus' instructions and proclaim (κηρύσσειν, 1:45, 7:36) his mighty works. Their words echo Gen 1:31 LXX and Isa 35:5-6. In the Gospel of Mark, even the gentiles quote the Law and the Prophets to announce the good news of God's eschatological reign.

There is no change of scene at the beginning of the story of the feeding of the 4,000; the gentile setting of 7:31-37 remains the same. What has changed is the cast of characters; the disciples have rejoined Jesus after missing every previous encounter with gentiles. Sadly, they have learned nothing from their earlier experience and repeat their despairing question, *How can one feed these people with bread here in the desert?* (8:4). Although the audience might have forgiven them for not expecting a miracle the first time, this time their dismay is inexcusable.

Jesus, however, is unperturbed by the disciples' anxiety about scarcity and again lays claim to their meager supplies. The Syrophoenician woman turns out to be right after all. When everything the disciples have is given to Jesus, he transforms it into enough to feed the whole crowd of undeserving gentiles without depriving the disciples at all. They collect enough leftovers to fill seven baskets large enough to hold a man (σπυρίς, 8:8, Acts 9:25).

This story brings the third subsection of 6:31–8:9 around to where it began—with the feeding of the 5,000 in 6:31-44. By this time everyone must surely have eyes to see and ears to hear the truth about Jesus and the inauguration of God's reign. The summaries with which the section concludes indicate that the this is *not* the case.

8:10-30. Conclusion of the Galilean ministry. The ministry of Jesus in Galilee and in gentile territory closes with three scenes that summarize the major themes of 1:14–8:9: words and deeds, controversy and opposition, blindness and deafness, scarcity and bread. The failure to hear, see, and understand that the audience has come to expect from the "outsiders" who oppose Jesus has by this time clearly become a problem for the "insiders" as well.

The last Galilean encounter with opponents (vv. 10-13) is bracketed by trips across the sea. In v. 10 Jesus and his disciples leave gentile territory and cross over to Dalmanutha. The place is unknown, but the encounter with Pharisees suggests a Jewish setting. Besides, the concluding boat trip, which begins in v. 13, is a crossing *to the other side* and the boat lands at Bethsaida on the eastern (gentile) side of the sea. Thus the setting of 8:11-12 is a Jewish one.

There are few surprises here. The audience already knows that the Pharisees and the Herodians are plotting to kill Jesus (3:6). The Pharisees are often associated with the scribes (7:1) who have been Jesus' opponents from the beginning (2:6, 16, 24).

The Pharisees' request for a sign is not equivalent to the requests for healing and exorcism that have been made to Jesus so far in the narrative. The evangelist makes this clear in two ways.

(1) They ask for a *sign* (v. 11), rather than making a specific request for a specific need. Mark's word for miracles that are portrayed in a positive light is δύναμις, "powerful act" (6:2, 5, 14; 9:39); σημεῖα, "signs," on the other hand, are understood negatively as acts done to establish one's identity or status (13:22). That is what the Pharisees request here: a sign *from heaven* as proof that Jesus is someone they should take seriously.

(2) Their motive is revealed to the audience by the omniscient narrator who knows everyone's motives in the story: they ask in order to put Jesus to the test (v. 11). Since the activity of "testing" Jesus has already been identified as the program of Satan (1:13), it is clear that the Pharisees remain opposed to Jesus' mission.

Jesus' refusal to give a sign makes two points that are theologically important to the evangelist:

(1) The miracles in the Gospel are not to be understood as "signs." They prove nothing about Jesus' identity or status. This will become even more clear

when the audience learns that *false* messiahs perform signs in order to prove who they are (13:22).

(2) The opponents' request for a sign from heaven shows that they have not understood that every aspect of Jesus' life is "from heaven." They do not recognize that God is the ground and source of Jesus' ministry (cf. 3:20-35; 6:1-6).

The last of the three boat scenes in the Gospel (vv. 14-21) brings to a climax the disciples' incomprehension. In 4:35-41 they had asked, *Who then is this?* and Jesus had asked, *Have you still no faith?* In 6:45-52 the disciples had failed to recognize Jesus and he had answered their previous question with the divine self-definition, "I am." The narrator had remarked that *they did not understand about the loaves, but their hearts were hardened* (6:52).

In this final scene it becomes clear that the disciples still do not understand about the loaves. Even after two miraculous feedings they are worried about their scarcity of bread. This is more than the Markan Jesus can tolerate, and he fires questions at them faster than they can answer: *Why are you talking about having no bread? Do you still not perceive or understand? Are your hearts hardened? Do you have eyes, and fail to see? Do you have ears, and fail to hear? And do you not remember?* (vv. 17-18). Even his review quiz on the number of baskets of leftovers after each feeding leaves them baffled.

The audience comes to the chilling realization that indeed the disciples are deaf and blind, indeed their hearts are hardened. Worse yet, these are the characteristics of *those outside* (4:10-12; Isa 6:9-10). If the disciples are to be counted among the outsiders, who is left on the inside? And how can one be sure of remaining inside, when the boundaries seem so fluid?

Finally in v. 22 Jesus and the disciples arrive in gentile Bethsaida, their destination ever since 6:45. There, Jesus heals a man of a particularly stubborn case of blindness. The story is narrated in such a way as to provide a parallel to 7:31-37 (the healing of a deaf man): Jesus arrives (7:31; 8:22a); people bring to him an afflicted person and beg Jesus to touch him (7:32; 8:22b); Jesus takes the person aside and performs some healing action (7:33; 8:23); the healing is confirmed (7:35; 8:25b); and Jesus attempts to conceal the healing from public notice (7:36; 8:26). After the devastation of vv. 14-21 these two stories hold out hope that Jesus may yet be able to heal the disciples' spiritual blindness and deafness as well.

The issue of Jesus' identity closes the large section 6:14–8:30. Is Jesus John the baptizer come back to life? Is he Elijah? Is he some other prophet? Just when it appears that the disciples have found the right answer (*You are the Messiah, v. 29*), the audience learns that there is more to messiahship than anyone bargained for. With that unsettling revelation, the evangelist begins the third major section of the Gospel.

On the Way, 8:22–10:52

The healing of the blind man at Bethsaida (8:22-26) and the story of Peter's confession at Caesarea Philippi (8:27-30) both have dual functions in the structural plan of the Gospel. Their functions in the narrative of the Galilean ministry have already been discussed, and we now turn to a study of the third major section of the Gospel in which the Markan Jesus teaches his disciples about the community implied by God's reign and about the role of suffering in Jesus' life and in the lives of his followers. Of course, the teachings of Jesus in this section have become the vehicle by which the evangelist teaches *his* audience on these topics.

We have already seen how Mark takes over Isaiah's imagery of sight and hearing, blindness and deafness. The material in 8:27–10:45 is framed by two stories about the healing of blindness—the only two such stories in this Gospel. Within this frame there is a narrative introduction (8:27-30) that sets the stage for the section. The subsequent material is arranged in three units of similar structure but differing length: 8:31–9:29; 9:30–10:31; and 10:32-45.

Each of these units begins with a prediction of Jesus' suffering and death (PASSION prediction). The prediction is followed by a response by disciples indicating that they do not understand the significance of what Jesus is telling them. This provides the Markan Jesus with an opportunity to engage in further teaching about the nature of discipleship.

The author of Mark has already indicated that although the disciples have eyes, they cannot see (8:18). Even though they have been given the secret of the reign of God, they have not perceived or understood it because their hearts are hardened (4:11; 6:52; 8:17). The teaching on the way to Jerusalem is Jesus' attempt to penetrate their blindness with the light of understanding. To indicate that purpose the evangelist begins the teaching section with the story of the healing of a blind man.

This is the only healing story in any Gospel that suggests difficulty or partiality in achieving the result.

Jesus puts saliva on the man's eyes and lays his hands on him, then checks to see how the healing is going: *Can you see anything?* (v. 23). The man reports partial sight (8:24). Jesus lays his hands on his eyes again and this time the man *looked intently and his sight was restored, and he saw everything clearly* (v. 25). This two-stage healing prepares for the encounter with the disciples that follows it.

That encounter takes place *on the way* to the villages of Caesarea Philippi. Of the sixteen references to "the way" (ὁδῷ) in Mark, half are concentrated between 8:27 and 11:8. In this section "the way" is the way to the cross, which becomes clear for the first time in the passion predictions. It is also *the way of the Lord* about which Isaiah wrote in the citation that began the Gospel (1:2-3). This way out of bondage into freedom, this second Exodus is a way the disciples are going to find especially distasteful. But then Isaiah also wrote, "My plans are not like your plans nor are your ways like my ways (ὁδοί, LXX), says the Lord."

Introductory Narrative, 8:27-30

This is the moment the audience of Mark has been waiting for. In 4:41 the disciples had asked, *Who then is this, that even the wind and the sea obey him?* In 6:50 Jesus had answered their question: *I am* (cf. Exod 3:14; Isa 43:10, 25; 45:18; 51:12). But their concern over bread in the last boat scene (8:14-21) showed that they were still blind to what they had seen.

Now the Markan Jesus asks them directly about his identity, beginning with what others are saying (v. 27). The speculations are those heard in Herod's court back in 6:13-15. Then comes the question that has challenged would-be disciples in the centuries since Mark first wrote it: *But who do you say that I am?* (v. 29).

Peter, speaking for the other disciples as he so often does in Mark, replies, *You are the Messiah* (v. 29; "Christ" is the Greek word for the messianic role or office). The audience breathes a sigh of relief. At last the disciples have seen the light. But Jesus interrupts the applause with a command to silence: *He sternly ordered them not to tell anyone about him* (v. 30). The audience knows that Peter is right (1:1), but apparently there is more to learn about who Jesus is before the news can be spread.

First Passion Prediction Unit, 8:31–9:29

The evangelist places the first passion prediction immediately after Peter's confession and Jesus' command to silence in order to show that before Jesus can be proclaimed as the Messiah, the component of suffering must be integrated into the messianic role.

Jesus' suffering is interpreted as a necessary part of the coming of God's eschatological reign by the use of the word translated *must* (δεῖ) in the NRSV (v. 31). The inbreak of God's reign can be seen in Jesus' miracles and exorcisms, but before its final consummation Jesus will have to be killed and to rise from death. By contrast with his usual mode of speech *in parables*, the passion prediction is crystal clear (v. 32).

Peter, as the representative of all the disciples, rejects the necessity of the passion. Jesus' retort means that to reject the necessity of suffering is to identify with Satan, Jesus' cosmic opponent (1:13; 3:22-27). The critique of Jesus' opponents in 7:6-13 here becomes the critique of the disciples: they are substituting human values and attitudes for the values and attitudes characteristic of God. From God's point of view there is no contradiction in a suffering healer, a victimized rescuer, a dying life-bringer. That the disciples see a contradiction indicates that they are looking with human half-sight. Like the blind man at Bethsaida, they need a second touch before they can see clearly.

Having added the component of suffering to the definition of messiahship, the Markan Jesus proceeds to add it to the definition of discipleship in 8:34–9:1. To follow behind the miracle worker is not enough; followers will deny themselves and accept the instruments of their own execution. Real life is found in losing one's life for the sake of Jesus and his good news. The desire for self-protection is the surest way to lose everything.

The concept of self-denial here must be interpreted in the context of the Gospel of Mark. It does not mean giving up certain pleasures or desires. It does not mean adopting the posture of a doormat by abandoning all sense of self. It means, rather, abandoning all claims to self-definition and accepting God's program for and God's claim upon one's life.

This is what the Markan Jesus does in 14:36. He has a will of his own, but he chooses God's will instead. In 14:62 Jesus denies himself publicly by the paradoxical act of boldly *claiming* his God-given identity and role. As a result, he takes up his cross and saves his life by losing it. Peter, by contrast, becomes the example of one who tries to save his life by denying *his* God-given identity and role as a follower of Jesus. For a Christian to deny herself, then, is to have the courage to be who she truly is. A Christian who tries to protect himself from persecution as a follower

of Jesus denies Jesus and loses the ground and center of his life.

Denying Jesus, or *being ashamed* of him and his teaching, has serious consequences. Of such a person Jesus will *be ashamed* when he comes as eschatological judge (8:38), and that judgment will be very soon (8:39). It is clear that the evangelist finds it necessary to issue a strong warning about the consequences of apostasy during persecution.

The next scene in this unit is the transfiguration. Exodus symbolism is again prominent: Moses, a high mountain, a cloud, the shining appearance of God's messenger, the building of tabernacles (9:5, NRSV *dwellings*). Along with Moses the lawgiver appears the prophet Elijah, with whom the evangelist has linked John the baptizer (1:2-8; 6:17-29).

John (Elijah) was present at Jesus' baptism, the first time the voice from heaven spoke (1:9-11). On that occasion Jesus received the Holy Spirit's presence and power for his ministry of teaching, healing and exorcism. Now the voice from heaven speaks again in the presence of Elijah and Moses to confirm the necessity of Jesus' humiliation and suffering just announced in 8:31. The *beloved son* will die (cf. Gen 22:2). At the baptism the voice was addressed only to Jesus; now the voice addresses the disciples: *Listen to him!* But this is not a message they are able to hear.

On the way down the mountain Jesus again enjoins silence *until after the Son of Man had risen from the dead* (9:9). The disciples raise the question about Elijah's coming as the forerunner (Mal 4:5). Indeed he has come, says Jesus, and you see what happened to him! (6:17-29).

The final story in the first passion prediction unit is the healing of the demon-possessed boy (9:14-29). Here the author of Mark has two points to make: (1) God's miraculous power and human confidence in that power are inextricably linked, and (2) God's power is not an impersonal force to be manipulated, but a gift to be prayed for. In order to make these two points, the evangelist uses this story of a botched exorcism to criticize the father and the crowd for their lack of faith and to criticize the disciples for their prayerlessness.

Having been disappointed once, the father is understandably skeptical and desperate: *If you are able to do anything, have pity on us and help us* (9:22). But in Mark, Jesus' *ability* to help is never at issue; the leper was right when he said, *If you choose, you can . . .* (1:40). So Jesus answers, *If you are able!—All things can be done for the one who believes* (9:23). Still desperate and still honest, the father cries out, *I believe; help my unbelief* [by healing my son]! (9:24). To this request Jesus immediately responds.

Faith is needed for miracles in Mark, but sometimes miracles are needed to awaken faith in Jesus' power (Dowd 1988, 107-14).

But the father's lack of faith is not the whole story. When the disciples get Jesus alone *in the house*, where all private teaching takes place, they ask the reason for their failure (9:28). Jesus' answer is that *this kind* of demon comes out only for those who cultivate the habit of prayer (as Jesus himself does 1:35; 6:46). Disciples do not give orders to God as magicians in the ancient world were known to do; rather, they make requests out of the quality of their relationship with God.

Second Passion Prediction Unit, 9:30–10:31

This unit is carefully organized, with a number of overlapping structures. After the passion prediction and the disciples' failure to understand (9:30-32), the teaching material that follows is held together by an inclusio: *Whoever wants to be first must be last* (9:35) and *Many who are first will be last, and the last will be first* (10:31).

Within this frame, two major subjects are dealt with. First the Markan Jesus holds out hope for the powerless in 9:33–10:16. This material has its own frame: receive children (9:33-37) and receive God's reign as a child (10:13-16). The second topic is hope for the powerful (10:17-27); their salvation is impossible for humans but possible for God (10:27).

The last item in the unit is a conversation between Jesus and his disciples on the rewards awaiting those who give up everything to follow Jesus (10:28-31). This conversation concludes with the saying on last/first that closes the frame on the entire unit.

The material in 9:30-50 is set in Galilee. The movement from the mountain of transfiguration south toward Jerusalem has begun. The second passion prediction introduces for the first time in the disciples' hearing the notion that Jesus will be betrayed. The audience, of course, has known of the betrayal and the identity of the betrayer since 3:19. The disciples do not understand and are afraid to ask questions (9:32).

All the teaching in chap. 9 takes place *in the house* in Capernaum. It begins with Jesus' awareness of an argument among the disciples (9:33) and ends with his admonition that they have peace among themselves (9:50). According to the narrator, the argument was about who was the greatest; this gives the Markan

Jesus the opportunity to emphasize that the values of God's reign are the reverse of those of this age. The one who serves everyone else is the greatest.

Jesus follows up by identifying with one of the "last" of society—a child. To welcome a powerless child is to welcome Jesus himself. The high infant mortality rate in antiquity contributed to the marginalization of children. Perhaps fewer than half lived to their fifth year (Wiedemann 1989, 16). They had only recently come from the divine realm and were likely to leave this life at any time; thus, they were not fully human beings.

On the other hand, this marginal status conferred on children a certain mystery. They were thought to be closer to the gods than adults and sometimes even their casual utterances were regarded as omens. (The best-known instance of this belief occurs in Augustine's account of his conversion, *Conf.* 8.12.) This context enables the evangelist to portray Jesus as designating children as the bearers of his presence when they are welcomed in his name.

The phrase "in your/my name" links this story with the one that follows. Although the disciples want to limit exorcism in Jesus' name to their own group, the Markan Jesus insists that all who minister wholeness in his name are to be recognized as *for us* (v. 40). The use of *the name* makes it clear that the issue here is not the ultimate status of non-Christians who do good works; rather, the issue is openness toward the ministry of Christian groups other than one's own. But anyone (even a non-Christian) who shows mercy toward the Christian community will be rewarded (9:41; cf. Matt 25:31-46).

Calling attention back to the child in his arms, the Markan Jesus pronounces an ominous warning against influencing a believing child (or any new Christian?) to commit apostasy (v. 42). On the topic of apostasy in general, the sayings in vv. 43-48 make it clear that "it is better to enter life having renounced certain cherished acts than to go into hell having done it all without restraint" (Via 1985, 18). Self-fulfillment is not to be equated with "entering into life," and self-indulgence may lead to self-destruction.

In 10:1 the scene shifts even further south. The mention of Judea anticipates the setting of chaps. 11–16. At this point the Pharisees reenter the picture and raise the question about divorce. The Markan Jesus explains that the Mosaic permission of divorce was not an expression of God's intent, but reflected the situation of fallenness and human *hardness of heart*.

The appeal to creation serves Mark's eschatology; God's reign, which is breaking through in Jesus' ministry, restores the possibility of relationships as they were intended in the beginning. The conversation with the disciples (vv. 10-12) changes the status of women from victims to responsible moral agents. No longer merely passive in marriage and divorce, they too must take responsibility for their decisions and actions. It should be noted that the evangelist believes divorce and adultery can be forgiven. The only unpardonable sin is blasphemy against the Holy Spirit (3:29).

The second reference to children portrays the disciples as still unable to get the point. Just as in the second feeding story, they have learned nothing from their previous experience. Despite 9:37 they try to prevent children from having access to Jesus (Tannehill 1977, 401). Jesus now says that the childlike are the primary citizens of God's realm (v. 14) and that everyone who enters God's realm must enter *as a little child* (v. 15).

This is "not an invitation to childlike innocence and naivete but a challenge to relinquish all claims of power and domination over others" (Fiorenza 1983, 148). God's reign cannot be achieved or earned; it must be received in the way that children in antiquity received what they needed for life. According to the Markan Jesus, people enter the reign of God, not in a proud triumphal procession, but in complete vulnerability, with no claim to any rights or status. It was not what the disciples had in mind.

Their amazement that it is humanly impossible for a rich person to enter God's reign (v. 26) reflects the relationship between wealth and religion in which prosperity was regarded as a blessing from God and therefore a sign of righteousness (Deut 28:1-14; Prov 13:25; 15:6; 37:25-26). In the world of Greco-Roman polytheism, wealth made it possible to persuade the gods with fine sacrifices and to be initiated into a variety of mystery religions (Apuleius, *The Golden Ass*).

The fact that Jesus expects a rich and religious person to renounce all the possessions and righteousness that he has acquired (v. 21) shocks the rich man and the disciples. They want to know who *can* be saved, if not this one. Jesus' answer is consistent with his earlier sayings about the advantage of the powerless. Humans cannot achieve salvation; God gives it away for free. Those who are accustomed to living on handouts will find it easier to enter God's reign than those who are accustomed to paying their own way. But God can do anything—even save a rich person (v. 27).

Peter misses the point about having no claim and attempts to convert his abandonment of possessions into an asset (v. 28). This gives the Markan Jesus an opportunity to recapitulate the theme of 3:31-35. The family that has been lost as a result of Christian conversion is replaced by the Christian community in the present and eternal life in the future (vv. 29-30).

This new family is radically different from the old, however, because it includes no fathers. In antiquity, the father had almost absolute control over the other members of the family. Control from above by a person who has power over others is repudiated by the vision of Christian community articulated by the Markan Jesus. God is the only father (8:38; 14:36; 11:25). The fatherhood of God in the context of Markan theology has the same function as the kingship of God: it guarantees a church made up of equals. God rules precisely in order to make sure that no one else does.

The evangelist cannot resist one wry addition to the list of blessings Christians receive *in this age*. Along with the new family, houses, and fields come persecutions (v. 30). Besides, *many who are first will be last, and the last first* (v. 31). For Peter, the disciple who was called first, this could be construed as a warning.

Third Passion Prediction Unit, 10:32-52

Much shorter than the previous two units, this one nevertheless begins with the longest and most detailed of the three passion predictions; it is virtually an outline for Mark 14:43–16:8. "The way" has taken Jesus and his disciples almost to Jerusalem and all of the instruction Jesus has given his followers so far has not made a dent in their amazement and fear (v. 32).

The placement of vv. 35-40 immediately after the passion prediction results in dramatic irony. The story about the request of James and John is narrated in such a way that the audience sees them stepping up briskly, as though they had been waiting impatiently for Jesus to stop talking. Their request is a boorish *non sequitur* after Jesus' solemn recitation of the tortures about to be inflicted on him.

In the first passion prediction unit the Markan Jesus had spoken about his coming in glory as eschatological deliverer (8:31, 38; 9:12). Peter's acclamation of him as the Messiah (8:29) was qualified, but not rejected, and the heavenly voice at the transfiguration alluded to one of the royal psalms (9:7; Ps 2:7). The narrative suggests that although James and John had no understanding about the passion (9:32) or the resurrection

(9:10), they had understood the part about glory and royalty and were determined to participate in it. They ask to be seated next to Jesus *in your glory* (v. 37).

Jesus begins his response with a warning: *You do not know what you are asking* (v. 38). Indeed they do not, for the positions they request on Jesus' right and left will be the positions of two crucified criminals (15:27). Taking up their vision of royalty, Jesus then reminds them that those closest to the king have to drink from his cup; if the wine is poisoned, they share the death intended for the ruler (v. 38; cf. Gen 40:1-13; 41:9-13; Neh 1:11b-2:1; Xenophon, *Cyropaedia* 1.3.9, Suetonius, *Claudius* 44.2).

There may be a pun on the word "baptize" in v. 38, since one of the meanings of the verb was "to destroy (e.g., a person by drowning, or a ship by sinking)" (Beasley-Murray 1990, 85). James and John apparently understand the question in the sense of ritual washing and answer brashly, *We are able* (v. 39). The gospel song based on their reply perpetuates their naivete.

As it turns out, their quest is frustrated. Jesus can guarantee martyrdom for James and John, but not glory (v. 40). The prediction of their martyrdoms here suggests that their blindness and self-seeking will finally be replaced by faithfulness.

The anger of the other disciples upon learning that the two brothers were seeking special privileges gives the Markan Jesus an opportunity to teach about the up-side-down values of Christian leadership (vv. 41-45). The community is not to be modeled on secular Roman ("gentile") structures. The teachings of 9:35 and 10:31 are recapitulated for emphasis: The one who wants to be great must be a servant; the one who wants to be first must be the slave of all.

In v. 45 the evangelist provides the christological rationale for this role reversal. Christian leaders must be servants because *the Son of Man came not to be served but to serve, and to give his life a ransom for many*. The first half of this saying interprets the ministry of Jesus up to this point as "service." All of his miracles and exorcisms, his teaching with authority, his winning arguments with the religious leaders, were done not to call attention to his status or power, but to serve. This is the point most often missed by interpretations of Mark that attempt to set miracle working and service in opposition to each other. They are synonyms, not opposites.

The second half of the saying points forward to the passion narrative. The word usually translated "ransom" here has the general meaning of a price paid for the release of a slave or prisoner of war. It is one of at least three understandings of the efficacy of Jesus' death that the author of Mark has incorporated into his Gospel. As we will see, the PASSION NARRATIVE is based primarily on the theme of the suffering righteous man, derived from the thought of ancient Israel and developed in the Hellenistic Jewish wisdom literature. To this general picture the author of Mark adds the metaphors of (1) covenant sacrifice (14:24) and (2) liberation from bondage (10:45).

The related verb, meaning "redeem," "ransom," or "set free," is important in the theology of Deutero-Isaiah, although the noun used in Mark 10:45 appears only once (45:13). Isaiah connects the concept of ransom/redemption/liberation with the interpretation of the return from exile as a second Exodus (41:14; 43:1, 14; 44:22-24; 51:11; 52:3; 62:12; 63:4, 9). Since this Isaian theme is central to Mark's theology, it is possible that the evangelist intends the saying to be understood as a metaphor for the freedom from bondage that will be effected by Jesus' death. This would be an understanding of the cross that would correspond with the freedom experienced by the human beneficiaries of Jesus' ministry of exorcism. The powerful one who has served by healing the broken bodies and psyches of humanity will also effect their ultimate freedom by giving his life.

The "way" section of Mark ends with the story of Bartimaeus, which closes the frame on the entire section, but is also linked explicitly with the previous request of James and John. Like the brothers, Bartimaeus brings a request. Jesus asks him exactly the same question he asked James and John: *What do you want me to do for you?* (10:36, 51). The repetition signals the audience that the misguided ambition expressed in the previous story is about to be corrected. Bartimaeus asks for the one thing that all the characters in Mark need most—sight. Jesus heals him with a word; the contrast with the two-stage healing of the blind man at Bethsaida is dramatic.

Bartimaeus's response to his healing is the response Jesus has been calling for throughout this section of the Gospel. As soon as he can see, he begins to follow Jesus *on the way* to Jerusalem, the place of crucifixion. To see aright is to walk the way of the cross unflinchingly. This vision and faithful response however, is not a human achievement. It is a divine miracle.

Ministry and Passion in Jerusalem, 11:1–16:8

The healing of Bartimaeus on the way out of Jericho marks the end of the "way" section. The rest of the narrative is set in Jerusalem and its environs. This final division of the Gospel falls into two parts. The passion and resurrection narrative (14:1–16:8) is preceded by a literary unit focused on Jesus' actions and sayings in and about the Temple (11:1–13:37).

Jesus and the Temple, 11:1–13:37

This unit of deeds and words is bracketed by references to the Mount of Olives. In 11:1-11 Jesus leaves the Mount of Olives and enters Jerusalem and the Temple; in 13:1-37 Jesus leaves the Temple, predicting its destruction, and goes to the Mount of Olives, where he delivers an apocalyptic discourse on the coming of the Son of Man.

The material between Jesus' entry into and exit from the Temple begins with two stories about Jesus' actions (the fig tree incident and the expulsion of the merchants and moneychangers, 11:12-25). This is followed by a series of teachings and controversies (11:27–12:44).

11:1-25. Deeds. This section is marked by a continual shift in location between Bethany and the Jerusalem Temple, whereas the setting for all the controversy and teaching material in 11:27–12:44 is the Temple itself. Of course, even this action material is not devoid of teaching, as the Markan Jesus interprets his actions to his opponents and to his disciples.

Jesus' power and authority are the primary emphases of the narrative of his initial actions in Jerusalem. The finding of the colt for the ride into Jerusalem (vv. 1-6) and the similar story of the finding of the room for the final meal (14:12-16) demonstrate Jesus' powers of prediction and his authority to requisition what he needs. Now that he has three times redefined his messiahship by combining access to divine power with vulnerability to rejection and death, the Markan Jesus has no need to conceal his identity as the one who inaugurates the reign of God.

The acclamation of the disciples in chiastic form (vv. 9b-10: hosanna, blessed, blessed, hosanna) is based partly on Ps 118:26. This psalm portrays a procession of thanksgiving to the Temple and emphasizes national sovereignty and defeat of Israel's enemies. Here translated into an apocalyptic mode, the psalm fragment is incorporated into a shout of welcome for the eschatological savior promised by Isaiah (33:22). Both Jewish and gentile members of Mark's audience would have recognized this as a procession to celebrate a victory, but unlike the group of disciples pictured in the narrative, the audience would have appreciated the irony of the scene. Whereas Roman triumphal processions ended with the execution of the prisoners of war, this one will end with the execution of the victor.

Only in Mark is Jesus' provocative action in the Temple sandwiched between the beginning and the end of the strange story of the withered fig tree. Unlike his modern interpreters, the author of Mark was completely unconcerned about the propriety of Jesus' destroying a helpless tree. The evangelist is interested in the way in which the destruction of the fruitless tree foreshadows the destruction of the Jerusalem Temple which, in his view, had also failed to bear the expected fruit.

Although Isaiah had written that the Temple was to be "a house of prayer for all the gentile nations" (56:7, author trans.), the Temple hierarchy had made it into a "robbers' hideout" (v. 17, author trans.) where they huddled together, claiming the protection of the holy place. This had been Jeremiah's complaint in his famous Temple sermon (7:11), from which the Markan Jesus quotes. The objection is not that dishonest merchants are cheating the public. The word ληστῶν means not cheats, but muggers or pirates, who use their "hideouts" not for robbing people but for evading detection and punishment.

The author of Mark interprets Jesus' actions not as a cleansing or reform of the Temple, but as a cancellation of Temple worship altogether. The Markan Jesus makes it impossible, not only for proper sacrificial animals to be procured and money changed for the Temple taxes, but also for the priests to carry through the Temple the vessels necessary to perform the rituals. Because the gentiles had been excluded from prayer in God's house, God's authoritative representative signals the end of all prayer in the Temple.

This, however, requires a reinterpretation of the conditions for effective prayer. Like all ancient religions, JUDAISM had a tradition of understanding the temple of the deity as the place where petitions were sure to be granted (1 Sam 1:1-29; 2 Kgs 19:14-37; 2 Macc 3:24-40). If the Temple, the holy place where God is especially present, is rejected, how can the followers of Jesus expect their prayers to be effective?

The answer comes with the reassurances about prayer in vv. 22-25. There are two conditions for effective prayer: faith (vv. 22-24) and forgiveness (v. 25). To *have faith* means to maintain the confidence that God is able to do what is otherwise impossible (9:23; 10:29). This faith is not "saving faith" but certainty about a worldview that early Christians shared with Hellenistic Jews and adherents of Neopythagorean philosophy. By contrast, the Platonists held that some things were impossible for the gods and the Epicureans argued that the gods did not intervene to perform miracles in response to human prayer.

But confidence in God's power must be combined with the clean slate provided only by God's forgiving disciples' sins. The catch is that in order to be forgiven, they will have to forgive each other (v. 25).

The evangelist replaces the holy place with the holy people who forgive and are forgiven and who stubbornly maintain their Christian worldview in the face of the philosophical alternatives. This is the ideal. But the Markan Jesus has already shown that God reserves the option of providing miraculous assistance to those who have inadequate faith (4:40; 8:4; 9:24). In Mark, the power of God overcomes even human unbelief.

11:27–12:44. Words in the Temple. In this teaching section, set in the Temple, the evangelist places a three-part discussion of theology and ethics between two three-part discussions which focus on christology (A—11:27-33; 12:1-9, 10-12; B—12:13-17, 18-27, 28-34, A'—12:35-37, 38-40, 41-44). The section begins with Jesus walking around in the Temple like a peripatetic philosopher (11:27) and ends with Jesus sitting to teach his disciples like a Jewish rabbi (12:41). These two postures correspond to the types of argumentation used throughout the section. Thoroughly Jewish modes of scriptural exegesis are combined with thoroughly Hellenistic rhetorical ploys, and all are set into an apocalyptic frame of reference.

The first christological subsection (11:27–12:12) makes the point that like the Davidic king who celebrates victory over his enemies (Ps 118), Jesus will be vindicated by God. His rejection and death are not the last word. The stone the builders rejected has become the cornerstone of the new temple, replacing the fruitless Jerusalem Temple. This new temple, the Christian community, is the house of prayer for all the gentiles that the previous Temple had failed to become. Thus, Isaiah's apocalyptic vision of the inclusion of the gentiles in the people of God is fulfilled in the Christian community (Isa 2:2-3; 56:6-7; Marcus 1992, 111-29).

Subsection A begins with a conversation with Jesus' opponents that links the teaching section with the series of actions that preceded it. The religious leaders confront Jesus over the issue of his authority to suspend the Temple cult. The audience, of course, knows the right answer to the leaders' question and Jesus' counterquestion: both John's and Jesus' authority came not from human beings, but from God (1:11; 9:7). Jesus' opponents are caught in the trap of their own cowardice, but their answer, *We do not know* (11:33), is ironically true. Indeed, their ignorance and blindness mark them as *those outside* (4:10-12).

The confrontation with the opponents continues as Jesus takes the initiative in the parable of the vineyard (12:1-9). Developing the imagery of Isa 5:2, the Markan Jesus takes an accusation that Isaiah directed against the whole people of Israel and focuses it specifically on the religious leaders. As interpreted by the Psalm quotation in 12:10-12, the parable becomes another prediction of Jesus' rejection, death, and vindication.

Subsection B consists of three encounters arranged in a chiastic structure with a central focus on the reality of the resurrection (Donahue 1982). This issue is dealt with in the conversation with the Sadducees (12:18-27). The form of Jesus' response is the rhetorical device known as an enthymeme (a syllogism in which one of the members is implied rather than stated):

Major premise (implied): God speaks accurately
   in scripture.
Minor premise: In scripture God speaks
   of the dead in the present tense (Exod 3:6).
Conclusion: The dead live in the presence of God.
   Resurrection is true.

The centrality of the resurrection is bracketed by conversations dealing with the ethical implications of theological claims. In 12:13-17 the Markan Jesus uses another enthymeme to escape a rhetorical trap designed to get him in trouble either with the people, who disliked paying Roman taxes, or with the Romans who demanded the payment. The implied major premise is: Ownership is established by the seal imprinted on something. Since the denarius bears Caesar's image, it is to be given to Caesar. What then is to be given to God? Obviously, that which bears God's image, that is, human beings (Gen 1:26-28). They are preeminently the "things of God," which must be surrendered completely to God. It is this self-giving to

God that characterizes the Markan Jesus, as 14:32-42 will make strikingly clear.

The question about the great commandment (12:28-34) completes the theological discussion. The stress is on monotheism and its implications. God was contrasted with Caesar in 12:13-17; here the obligation to love God with the entire self is combined with the obligation to love one's neighbor as oneself. The scribe who recognizes that Jesus' emphasis accords with the theology of Deutero-Isaiah (45:21, "There is no other god besides me") is not far from the eschatological reign of God foreseen by the prophet and inaugurated in Jesus' ministry.

By having the scribe cite the prophetic critique of sacrifice without obedience (1 Sam 15:22; Hos 6:6; Mic 6:6-8) the evangelist delivers a final blow to the Temple system. Its fruitlessness is conceded by one of its own scholarly elite. After this coup, no one puts any more questions to the Markan Jesus (12:34b).

In subsection A', the initiative shifts. Now it is Jesus' turn to ask the questions. He turns the conversation back to christology by making the point that the expectation of a royal Davidic messiah is inadequate. Although the evangelist clearly makes Davidic claims for Jesus with his use of Pss 2, 118, and 110, Jesus' messiahship is both more and less than the title *Son of David* suggests. Whereas the Davidic messiah was merely a human ruler who would defeat human enemies, Jesus is the divine warrior who defeats the demonic powers and ushers in God's reign. Unlike the expected Davidic messiah Jesus' victory is won by losing—by humiliation and death (Marcus 1992, 130-50).

The theme of judgment on the religious leaders is sounded again in 12:38-40. The scribes who *devour* widows' houses (Isa 1:17, 23; 10:2; Ezek 22:25) clearly do not live by the standard advocated by one of their own number in 12:32-33 (Beavis 1989, 102). By contrast, the widow in 12:40-44 performs the exemplary action. Like Jesus, she gives God everything she has, even "her whole life" (12:44, author trans; cf. 12:17, 30). This giving of one's life recalls 10:45. The widow gives all she has to live on; Jesus will give his life to set God's people free.

13:1-2. Transition. Having been in the Temple since 11:27, the Markan Jesus now leaves the Temple and predicts its destruction: *Not one stone will be left here upon another.* What was implicit in 11:15-17 here becomes explicit. This closes the section of teaching in the Temple and prepares for the following teaching *opposite the temple* (13:3).

13:3-37. Words opposite the Temple (the apocalyptic discourse). This second long speech by the Markan Jesus has a number of common features with the parable discourse in chap. 4. Both assume the cosmic conflict myth so fundamental to apocalyptic thought. Both contain repeated admonitions to pay attention (4:3, 9, 23, 24; 13:5, 9, 23, 33, 35, 37). Both use parables from nature (4:3-9, 26-32; 13:28-29), and both contain allegorical applications of parabolic material to discipleship (4:13-20; 13:34-37, Donahue 1988, 61).

It is characteristic of both speeches that an extended discourse punctuated by second-person-plural imperatives tends to blur the distinction between the addressees at the story level and the audience of the Gospel as a whole. The "you" of the teaching material reaches out to include the listeners in any subsequent time (Tannehill 1980, 141).

The scene in chap. 13 is the Mount of Olives. The cast of characters is exactly the same as that of the first scene of the Galilean ministry (11:16-20): Jesus, Peter, James, John, and Andrew. The only function of the disciples in this scene is to ask two questions. They are not mentioned again.

The disciples' questions are: (1) When will these things happen? and (2) What will be the sign? They are portrayed as regarding the destruction of the Temple, which Jesus has just predicted, as a catastrophic event that would surely be preceded by a significant omen. They understand themselves as insiders who are entitled to be let in on the secret (cf. 4:11).

Jesus, however, has more important information to impart. He never mentions the Temple again; rather, he begins to talk about false and true signs of the eschatological consummation of God's reign. Although he is answering a question the disciples have not asked, he takes up the two issues they have raised in reverse order, beginning with how to recognize the sign of the end (vv. 5-27) and moving to the issue of the time of the end (vv. 28-37).

The Markan Jesus first explains that no historical event can be read as a sign of the eschaton (vv. 5-23). This material is arranged chiastically:

A Danger of deception, 5-6
   B Prediction of future events, 7-8
      C Persecution and mission, 9-13
   B' Appropriate response to future events, 14-20
A' Danger of deception, 21-23

The section begins and ends with warnings that there will be deceivers who will make messianic claims for themselves and others and perform miracles in order to lead Christians astray (vv. 5-6, 21-23). Their apocalyptic interpretations of events are to be ignored (vv. 21, 23).

B and B' describe historical and natural events that might be misinterpreted as signs of the end (vv. 7-8) and prescribe the proper way to respond to such difficult times (vv. 14-20). Christians must always be ready to move quickly in times of crisis. Attachment to possessions will have to be put aside and even the most natural relationships will pose a problem (vv. 15-17). But although the suffering will be terrible, God is in control and will provide for God's chosen people. The right response is prayer and trust (vv. 18-20).

The center of the chiasm focuses on the persecution of the church (vv. 9-13). Like Jesus, Christians will be handed over, betrayed, brought to trial, and put to death. They are not to be afraid, because the Holy Spirit will enable them to bear witness. In the midst of their persecutions, they must continue to preach the gospel to the gentiles, because this is part of the divinely ordained prelude to the end (v. 10). *The one who endures to the end will be saved* (v. 13).

Scholars usually assume that the events described in vv. 5-23 were already taking place at the time of the writing of the Gospel. Jesus is portrayed as speaking in the past about events in the future, which is the evangelist's present. It is likely that the audience of the Gospel is facing some of the things described in this section. Some may already be in the past. But there is no way of knowing that all the events in this description are past or present. The evangelist may anticipate that some of these difficulties lie ahead for the church and may wish to prepare them to respond appropriately.

After an extensive discussion of events that are *not* signs of the end, the Markan Jesus turns to the real sign of the end: the coming of the Son of Man on the clouds, amid cosmic upheaval, to gather the elect from all over the earth (vv. 24-27). When they see Jesus coming for them again, they will know that the end is about to take place; no natural or political disasters that take place before that are to distract them from their mission.

As for the question of "When?" the Markan Jesus takes care of that in short order. This brief section (vv. 28-37) begins and ends with a parable. The parable of the fig tree makes the point that when the disciples see "these things" (i.e., the coming of the Son of Man, vv. 24-27), they will know that he is *at the very gates* (v.

29). In other words, when you see it happening, you will know that it is happening, and not before!

This is reinforced by repeated reminders that *you do not know when* (vv. 33, 35). In fact, no one knows except the Father. The futility of calculation based on "signs of the times" could not be more dramatically portrayed. But if "biblical prophecy" workshops are not appropriate, neither is complacency. The parable of the returning landlord (vv. 34-36) emphasizes the suddenness of the arrival of the eschaton. Since you do not know, be ready and alert at all times. The final exhortation is addressed explicitly to the audience: *What I say to you I say to all: Keep awake* (v. 37).

Passion and Resurrection Narratives, 14:1–16:8

Jesus' death in Mark. In their struggle to interpret the humiliation and crucifixion of Jesus, early Christians made use of a variety of biblical and cultural resources. Ancient people, both Jews and pagans, knew that life was often unfair. The individual psalms of lament preserved the complaints of the righteous person who suffered unjustly at the hands of enemies. In Plato's *Republic* (361e-362a), Socrates is challenged by dialogue partners who suggest that the truly righteous person will "hold his course unchangeable, even unto death," having "to endure the lash, the rack, chains," and "finally, after every extremity of suffering, he will be crucified." That the execution of just persons was not merely a theoretical possibility is made clear by the interpretations of Socrates' own death at the hands of the state (Plato, *Apology*, *Phaedo*; Xenophon, *Memorabilia*).

But human beings recoil from the notion that the death of the upright is meaningless. The psalmist cries out for vindication. The Isaian Servant Songs interpret the death of the servant as vicarious suffering for the sins of others. The author of the Wisdom of Solomon transforms the victims into the judges of their persecutors (4:16–5:2). The Greeks made heroes of kings and soldiers who died to save the lives of others. The Maccabean martyrs are portrayed as giving their lives to atone for the sins of their compatriots (2 Macc 7:38; 4 Macc 6:28-29).

The Gospel of Mark draws upon a number of these biblical and extrabiblical patterns to interpret the death of Jesus as a necessary part of God's eschatological victory over all that enslaves and distorts human life. Although blameless, Jesus is unjustly condemned and crucified. His death redeems enslaved humanity (10:45) and seals a covenant (14:25) that brings even gentiles into the people of God. Vindicated in the resurrection, he leaves the tomb empty as he leads his followers on the way of mission and martyrdom.

The overall organization of the Markan passion narrative is controlled by chronology; within that framework the individual episodes are carefully crafted for rhetorical and theological effect. The sense of speed and energy so characteristic of the Galilean ministry is replaced by a series of solemn notices of the passing of time (14:1, 12, 17; 15:1, 26, 33, 34, 42) as the evangelist tolls the agonizing final hours of Jesus' life.

The story of the anointing woman (14:3-9) has two literary functions in the outline of the Gospel. With the story of the widow's offering (12:41-44), it forms a frame (INCLUSIO) around the apocalyptic discourse in chap. 13. In both cases, women are praised for their actions, which point forward to Jesus' giving of his life and to his burial. The women are contrasted with the religious leaders, who exploit them (12:40) and oppose Jesus (14:1-2).

With the story of the three women who go in search of Jesus' corpse to anoint it for burial (16:1-8), the story of the anointing woman in 14:3-9 forms a frame around the passion narrative. Her act makes theirs unnecessary. Jesus has already left the tomb and is on the way to Galilee.

14:1-11. Plot and anointing. The story of the anointing woman is sandwiched into the narrative about the plot to kill Jesus (vv. 1-2, 10-11; cf. Ps 10:7-8; Wis 2:12). Judas provides the missing link that will enable the religious leaders to "arrest Jesus by stealth" away from the crowds.

Having redefined the concepts of clean and unclean verbally in 7:1-23, Jesus now acts on that redefinition by having dinner in the house of an "unclean" leper. In an act reminiscent of the OT prophets, a woman comes in and anoints Jesus' head, signifying his royal authority (2 Kgs 19:1-3; 1 Sam 10:1; 1 Kgs 1:38-49; Ps 133:2). Like many of Jesus' own words and actions, the woman's deed is misunderstood by those present; they criticize her extravagance.

But Jesus defends the woman and reinterprets her action as an anointing for burial. Just as Peter's confession of Jesus as the Messiah had to be reinterpreted in terms of the passion, so the woman prophet's confession of Jesus as the Messiah by her action requires reinterpretation. The royal anointing becomes a burial rite. It is the only anointing that the Markan Jesus will receive, since by the time his women disciples arrive at the tomb with their spices, Jesus will be gone.

14:12-31. The Last Supper. The preparation for the Passover meal again confirms Jesus' foreknowledge of events (cf. 11:1-6). The two sent ahead to prepare are joined in v. 17 by Jesus and THE TWELVE, suggesting that the evangelist wanted to make clear that attendance at this important meal was not limited to the group named in chap. 3.

Jesus predicts his betrayal by one of those at table with him (Ps 41:9). The disciples are portrayed as claiming innocence in the form of a question that implies a negative answer: Surely, not I? (v. 19). Jesus' response reflects the apocalyptic viewpoint that all is happening in accordance with God's plan (v. 21a) and human beings are nevertheless culpable for their opposition to God's elect (v. 21b).

Ignoring the symbolic actions usually associated with Passover meals, the narrator introduces new symbols. The broken bread is Jesus' body; the cup of wine is his blood. The reference to covenant sacrifice (v. 24; cf. Exod 24:8; Zech 9:11) points backward to God's faithfulness in the past. The reference to the messianic banquet in "the reign of God" (v. 25, author trans.) points forward to eschatological vindication and celebration in communion with God (Isa 25:6).

On the way to the Mount of Olives, Jesus predicts the apostasy of all his disciples and their reunion with him in Galilee (vv. 27-28; cf. Zech 13:7-9; 14:4). Their tentative Surely, not I? of moments before now becomes a bold assertion of loyalty even to the point of death (v. 31b). But by this time the audience is more inclined to believe Jesus. If he says that the disciples will flee and Peter will deny him three times, that is what the audience expects.

14:32-42. Gethsemane. This scene is carefully constructed. The prayer of Jesus is at the center. Leading up to the prayer, three verbs of motion (vv. 32a, 33, 35a) are followed by three requests by the Markan Jesus: to the larger group of disciples (v. 32b), to Peter, James, and John (v. 34), and finally to God (v. 35b).

The prayer itself expresses confidence in God's power (for you all things are possible) and makes a direct request (remove this cup from me). Thus the evangelist shows that Jesus follows his own instructions; he has faith and he asks for a miracle every bit as stupendous as tossing a mountain into the sea (11:22-24). He asks to be spared the cross, after having repeatedly acknowledged its necessity in the preceding narrative. But now in his practice of prayer the Markan Jesus adds something that was not in his earlier teaching about prayer: submission to the will of God. This is what distinguishes the Markan Jesus from the numerous other miracle workers and magicians of antiquity; he does God's will, not his own.

After the prayer, Jesus returns to find his disciples sleeping. They have fallen into the trap about which he warned them in the parable of the absent landlord (13:34-36). Again, as at the transfiguration, they do not know how to respond (v. 40; cf. 9:6).

It is important to notice that the Markan theology of prayer does not *substitute* submission to God's will for petitionary prayer. The two are combined as the Markan Jesus wrestles with God three times *saying the same words* (v. 39). Finally he wakes the sleeping disciples in time to confront Judas and his lynch mob.

14:43-52. Arrest. With the arrival of the arresting party, Jesus' predictions begin to be fulfilled in rapid-fire succession. He is betrayed by Judas (cf. 14:18) into the hands of the religious leaders (cf. 10:33). Despite their boasting of a few hours before (14:27), all his disciples desert Jesus to save themselves (8:34-38). Mark emphasizes the complete abandonment of Jesus by repeating the *all* of 14:31b in v. 50. The story of the terrified youth who flees naked has two functions: it reminds the audience that the group that attended the supper and followed Jesus to Gethsemane was larger than "the twelve" and it makes a graphic comment on the cowardice and shame of the flight of the disciples. Nowhere in Mark is there any suggestion that the young man is to be identified with the author of the Gospel.

14:53-72. Sanhedrin trial/denial of Peter. The evangelist weaves together the story of the Sanhedrin TRIAL OF JESUS, which takes place inside the residence of the high priest, and the story of Peter's denial, which is set outside in the courtyard. He narrates the introduction to the trial scene (15:53), then the introduction to the denial (15:54), proceeds with the trial narrative (15:55-65), and then completes the denial story (15:66-72). This emphasizes the point that these events are to be understood as occurring simultaneously, even though they must be narrated sequentially.

From this point forward the passion narrative is riddled with dramatic irony. Jesus' enemies bungle their plot against him because their false witnesses (Pss 27:12; 35:11) cannot get their stories straight. Ironically, though, their *false* testimony is true; although the Markan Jesus has not said that he will destroy the Temple and replace it with one *not made with hands* (v. 58), that is in fact exactly what will happen. The

Christian community will replace the Temple as the *house of prayer for all the nations* (11:17).

Since the opponents fail in their attempt to condemn him, Jesus has to condemn himself. In order for his commission from God to be fulfilled, Jesus has to give true testimony about himself, which the Sanhedrin then misinterprets as blasphemy. Here the evangelist brings together all the aspects of Jesus' identity. In response to the high priest's question, *Are you the Messiah, the Son of the Blessed One?* (v. 61, a reverent Jewish circumlocution for "God"), Jesus answers with the divine self-designation, *I am* (v. 62; cf. Isa 43:10, 45; 43:25; 45:18; 51:12; cf. Wis 2:13-20a), and adds the Danielic image used already in 8:38–9:1 and 13:26—the Son of Man coming on the clouds (Dan 7:13-14). All this identifies the one who will shortly die the most shameful possible death in the company of criminals.

By thus identifying himself correctly, Jesus "denies himself," doing God's will rather than his own. As a result, he will take up his cross, saving his life by losing it. Meanwhile, out in the courtyard, Peter is denying Jesus, forfeiting everything by attempting to save his own life. And the evangelist arranges for Peter to fulfill Jesus' prophecy of his denial in excruciating detail at the exact moment that Jesus is being mocked by the Sanhedrin as a false prophet (14:65; cf. Isa 50:6).

But in his denial, Peter ironically tells the truth. The fact is that he does not really *know this man* (v. 71). He never has. He breaks down in tears. Having "been ashamed" of Jesus, he has put himself into the category of those of whom the eschatological judge will ultimately *be ashamed* (8:38). Peter "the Rock" is rocky soil indeed (4:16-17).

15:1-15. Trial before Pilate. This section of the passion narrative begins with Jesus' being "handed over" to Pilate (15:1) and ends with his being "handed over" by Pilate to the crucifixion squad (15:15). The unit is held together by the vocabulary of "binding" (15:1, 7) and "releasing" (15:6, 9, 11, 15; Robbins 1992, 1165-67). The title "King of the Jews" is heard first on the lips of Pilate (15:2, 9, 12) then in the taunts of the soldiers (15:18), and finally on the lips of the religious leaders (15:32). Although the evangelist has spoken of God's kingship, and implied Jesus' kingship by the titles "Messiah" (one who is anointed) and "Son of God," he does not allow Jesus to be called "king" openly except by his enemies. They do not know how right they are because they cannot imagine a king who reigns from a gallows and triumphs by dying in public disgrace.

Jesus, the one who calls God "Abba" (father, 14:36) has been falsely arrested as though he were a rebel bandit (14:48). The crowd chooses death for the one who restored life to others, while a genuine rebel bandit who has committed murder (15:7) goes free. "Barabbas," ironically, means "son" (*bar*, cf. Bartimaeus, 10:46) of the "father" (*abba*, cf. 14:36).

15:16-20a. Mocking. This short unit highlights the humiliation of Jesus and the irony of the kingship motif. It is arranged chiastically:

A Jesus is led into the courtyard, 16
  B Jesus is clothed and crowned as a king, 17
    C The soldiers mock Jesus in speech:
      "Hail, King of the Jews!" 18
    C' The soldiers mock Jesus in actions:
      knelt down in homage, 19
  B' Jesus is stripped and clothed
    in his own clothes, 20a
A' Jesus is led out of the courtyard, 20b

15:20b-25. Crucifixion. The repetition of the verb "to crucify" marks the beginning and end of this unit (vv. 20b, 24, 25). Simon, an African from Cyrene with a Jewish name (probably to be understood as having come to Jerusalem for Passover), is conscripted to carry Jesus' cross. He thus becomes the first of those who pick up the cross and follow Jesus (cf. 8:34). His sons Alexander and Rufus (typical gentile names) must have been well known to the original audience of Mark, since Simon is identified for the audience by association with his sons' names.

The soldiers' offer of myrrhed wine is further mockery; this drink was a delicacy (Pliny, *NatHist* 14.15.92-93). It would have served as a numbing agent as well, which is why the Markan Jesus refuses it; he follows his own advice to stay alert (13:37; Gundry 1993, 944, 956). Jesus is then crucified naked while the soldiers gamble for his clothing, the mere touching of which had once conferred healing (5:27-29; 6:56; cf. Ps 22:18).

15:26-32. Ridicule of Jesus on the cross. This section is tied together by repetition. The mocking inscription on the cross, *"The King of the Jews"* (v. 26), is picked up by the religious leaders when they ridicule Jesus as *Messiah, King of Israel* (v. 32a). Those crucified with Jesus are mentioned in v. 27 and v. 32b (cf. Isa 53:12). Jesus is *blasphemed* (NRSV mg.) by passersby, "mocked" by the religious leaders, and *taunted* by the revolutionaries on his regal right hand and left

hand (cf. 10:37; Ps 22:7-8; Wis 2:17-20). Twice he is invited to save himself (v. 29, 30).

Again Jesus' enemies say more than they know. They articulate the paradox of the passion with the words, *He saved others; he cannot save himself* (v. 31). Only by not saving himself can Jesus save the *many* for whom his life is given as ransom (10:45) and with whom God initiates a covenant in his blood (14:24). If anyone is ever to see and believe it is essential that Jesus *not* come down from the cross now (v. 32a).

15:33-39. Death of Jesus. The darkness recalls Isa 13:9-10; 50:3. Jesus' first loud cry (and the only word from the cross in Mark) is the beginning of Ps 22. Having begun his references to this psalm in 15:22 with Ps 22:18 and moved backward to Ps 22:6-7 in 15:29-30, the narrator ends at the beginning of the psalm with a cry of desolation rather than with the victorious note on which the psalm ends (Robbins 1992, 1175-80).

These last words of Jesus are a prayer, but they contrast sharply with his prayer of submission in 14:36. The evangelist apparently believes that there is no contradiction between commitment to doing the will of God and the anger and abandonment one feels when God's will leads to unbearable suffering and Godforsakenness. The Markan Jesus models the expression of honest anger in the prayers of the faithful.

But like everything else that he has said, these words of the Markan Jesus meet with misunderstanding. Bystanders think that he is calling on Elijah rather than on God (v. 35). Not only that, but Elijah's role is interpreted in terms of his miracle-working power, whereas the Gospel of Mark understands Elijah/John the baptizer as Jesus' predecessor in rejection and suffering (6:14-29; 9:11-13).

The offer of sour wine recalls Ps 69:21: "for my thirst they gave me vinegar to drink." The irony of the misunderstanding is heightened for those members of the audience who would have been familiar with the next verses of Ps 69: "Let their eyes be darkened so that they cannot see" (23a). The three hours of darkness mirror the spiritual blindness of those who see Jesus without understanding and cannot comprehend his words, his actions, or the significance of his passion (Marcus 1992, 183-84).

Jesus' death is portrayed in such a way as to recall the moment of his baptism. The spirit that went into Jesus then (1:10, τὸ πνεῦμα . . . εἰς αὐτόν) now bursts forth from the dying Jesus (15:37, 39, ἐξέπνευσεν) with a loud cry. At the same time, a portent occurs at the Temple inside the city walls. There was an ornate tapestry hanging in front of the outer doors of the Temple, on which, according to JOSEPHUS, "was portrayed a panorama of the heavens" (*BJ* 5.5.4.212-14). This tapestry is ripped apart (ἐσχίσθη) from above by unseen hands (15:38), just as the heavens had been ripped apart (σχιζομένους) at the baptism (1:10) prior to the descent of the Spirit into Jesus (Ulansey 1991).

The tearing of the Temple tapestry has two functions in Mark: (1) it portends the destruction of the Temple that had been prophetically enacted by the Markan Jesus in 11:15-16 and explicitly predicted by him in 13:2; (2) it minimizes the significance of that destruction by interpreting the death of Jesus as the release of the divine Spirit into the world. No longer is the presence of God to be found in a special way in the Temple; instead, the apocalyptic inbreaking of God's reign, inaugurated by Jesus' victory over the demons, is now marked by the pouring out of that same eschatological Spirit into the world as it struggles to give birth to the new creation. Before his own martyrdom, John had prophesied that Jesus would "baptize in the Holy Spirit." The Markan crucifixion account shows that the baptism in the Holy Spirit that empowers the church for ministry and bold witness (13:11) is made possible by the death of Jesus.

The response of the centurion to Jesus' death is a "confession" only in the ears of Mark's audience. On the level of the story it is a sarcastic comment on the lips of a jaded professional executioner who has just watched one more peasant revolutionary die calling on his God: "Oh sure—*that's* a son of Zeus all right!" (v. 39; Fowler 1991, 205–208). His attitude is the same as that of the others at the foot of the cross: if Jesus had really been anybody special, he would have been translated to heaven before dying such a shameful death (Origen, *CCel* 2.68).

Ironically, however, the centurion represents all the gentiles who will hear the gospel and make a sincere confession as a result of Jesus' death (13:10; cf. Isa 52:15; 2:1-4; 56:6-8). Their inclusion has already been prefigured in the proclamation of the gentile man whom Jesus freed from demonic oppression (5:20) and in the insistence of the gentile woman that Jesus is the "Lord" at whose table even the *dogs* will be satisfied (7:24-30).

15:40-47. Burial. This unit is framed by the description of Jesus' female disciples who watch (from a safe distance) as he is crucified and buried (v. 40, 47). These women are followers of Jesus and participants

in the servanthood that he has described as the essence of his mission (v. 41; cf. 1:31; 10:45). They do not come forward to bury him, however.

John's disciples had taken his decapitated corpse and laid it in a tomb (6:29) but there is no one to perform this service for Jesus except one of the enemies who condemned him. Joseph is portrayed as a pious but misguided member of the Sanhedrin (v. 43; not a secret disciple as in Matthew and John) who buries Jesus out of adherence to the requirements of Torah. Deuteronomy 21:22-23 specifies that a criminal who has been impaled must be buried before sundown, lest the land be defiled (Brown 1988, 236). The fact that Joseph is still *waiting expectantly* (v. 43) for God's reign shows that he has missed the whole point; God's reign began to burst into existence before his very eyes, but he condemned the messenger (not dissenting from the verdict as in Luke). Now he tosses Jesus' body into a nearby tomb (not his own tomb or a new tomb as in Matthew, Luke, and John) without even washing it, let alone anointing it for burial.

16:1-8. Empty tomb. After his burial, the Markan Jesus is neither seen nor heard again, although his message is conveyed to the women by the young man at the empty tomb. Mark is the only canonical Gospel that narrates no appearances of the risen Jesus. The spurious later additions to the Gospel show how unsatisfactory this decision was to subsequent readers of the text. Later editors would add stories of appearances, creating the long ending of Mark that continues to puzzle devotional and scholarly readers alike.

It would be a mistake, however, to conclude that since the resurrection is not narrated the evangelist wished to emphasize the absence of Jesus between the resurrection and the eschaton. The Markan miracle stories provide abundant evidence that the author of Mark wanted to encourage beleagured Christians to have confidence in the presence and power of the risen Lord in the midst of their difficulties (e.g., 4:35-41). The abrupt ending is deliberate, but it puts the emphasis on mission rather than on the absence of Jesus.

At the beginning of chap. 16 the women followers of Jesus are seen belatedly making their way to the tomb to anoint Jesus' body. They are not expecting a resurrection, despite Jesus' repeated predictions, but at least they are still on the scene, unlike the men, whose absence is highlighted by the women's conversation about who is going to do the heavy work of rolling away the "very large" stone from the entrance to the tomb (vv. 3-4).

After this conversation, the rest of the narrative is framed by the women's entering the tomb in v. 5 and exiting the tomb in v. 8. In the tomb they encounter a young man in white, whose numinous quality is established by his resemblance to the transfigured Jesus (9:3). The response of these three disciples, like that of the three disciples at the transfiguration, is fear (16:5; cf. 9:6), but the messenger begins with the greeting, "Fear not!" (v. 6, author trans.).

Stating the obvious, he continues: "You are looking for Jesus of Nazareth, the crucified one. He has been raised (cf. Isa 52:13). He is not *here*" (v. 6, author trans.). Seeking for Jesus is never the right response in Mark (cf. 1:37); following Jesus is. So the messenger now shifts into the imperative mood: "Go tell his disciples (even Peter!) that he is leading you into Galilee; *there* you will see him, just as he told you" (v. 7, author trans.).

Several things are significant about this message. First, the message is delivered in indirect discourse and uses the second person plural. This makes it clear that the women are among those who are to go to Galilee; the messenger does not say, "Tell his disciples that he is leading them into Galilee; there they will see him just as he told them."

Second, the encounter with Jesus that is promised in the message is an example of unmerited grace based solely on the earlier promise of Jesus (*just as he told you*, v. 7). Nothing accounts for the inclusion of the apostate disciples in the community of the resurrection except for Jesus' promise to them in 14:28. Persistently blind, deaf, and hard of heart, they proved themselves "ashamed of Jesus" when the chips were down and by every criterion operative in the narrative so far they should be counted among the outsiders who have no part in God's reign. Even Peter is included, his denial forgiven.

The amazing grace according to Mark is that even those who fail all the tests articulated by the Markan Jesus may yet hear the reconciling call of the Risen Lord and be given another opportunity to follow him on his way. And this good news is "just as it is written in the prophet Isaiah," (cf. Mark 1:2), where the author of Mark had read

> Fear not, for I have ransomed you; I have called you by name; you are mine. . . . I will say, "Lead my sons from far away and my daughters from the end of the earth—everyone who is called by my name. For I created [them] for my glory and I formed them and made them. I led out the people

who are blind, yet have eyes, who are deaf, yet have ears . . . I, I am the Lord and besides me there is no savior" (Isa 43:1-11, LXX).

The message is given to the women disciples who flee in fear and silence. That, of course, made no difference, since everyone knew that if the women had told about the resurrection, they would not have been believed (Luke 24:10-11). But somebody must have met Jesus on the way of ministry and martyrdom because the story has just been told again. The abrupt ending of the Gospel of Mark leaves no one else to bear witness to the Risen but unseen Lord except the audience of the story's most recent telling. And that is as it should be.

Works Cited

Anderson, Janice Capel. 1992. "Feminist Criticism: The Dancing Daughter," *Mark and Method*, ed. J. C. Anderson and S. D. Moore, 103–34.

Beasley-Murray, G. R. 1990. "Baptism," MDB.

Beavis, Mary Ann. 1989. *Mark's Audience*.

Boring, M. Eugene. 1987. "The Kingdom of God in Mark," *The Kingdom of God in Twentieth-Century Interpretation*, ed. W. Willis.

Brown, Raymond E. 1988. "The Burial of Jesus (Mark 15:42-47)," *CBQ* 50:233–45.

Dewey, Joanna. 1980. *Markan Public Debate*. SBLDS 48.

Donahue, John R. 1982. "A Neglected Factor in the Theology of Mark," *JBL* 101:563–94. 1988. *The Gospel in Parable*.

Dowd, Sharyn. 1988. *Prayer, Power, and the Problem of Suffering*. SBLDS 105.

Dufton, Francis. 1989. "The Syrophoenician Woman and Her Dogs," *ExpTim* 100:417.

Fiorenza, Elisabeth Schüssler. 1983. *In Memory of Her*.

Fowler, Robert M. 1991. *Let the Reader Understand*.

Grimes, Betty J. 1991. "The Syrophoenician Woman," M.Div. paper, Lexington Theological Seminary.

Gundry, Robert H. 1993. *Mark*.

Marcus, Joel. 1986. *The Mystery of the Kingdom of God*. SBLDS 90. 1992. *The Way of the Lord*.

Montgomery, Helen Barrett. 1924. *The New Testament in Modern English*.

Robbins, Vernon K. 1989. "Rhetorical Composition and the Beelzebul Controversy," *Patterns of Persuasion in the Gospels*, by B. L. Mack and V. K. Robbins, 161–93. 1992. "Psalm 22 in the Markan

Crucifixion," *The Four Gospels 1992*. Festschrift Frans Neirynck. BETL 100.

Schüssler-Fiorenza, Elisabeth. *See* Fiorenza, Elisabeth.

Tannehill, Robert C. 1977. "The Disciples in Mark: The Function of a Narrative Role," *JR* 57:386–405. 1980. "Tension in Synoptic Sayings and Stories," *Int* 34:138–59.

Ulansey, David. 1991. "The Heavenly Veil Torn: Mark's Cosmic *Inclusio*," *JBL* 110:123–35.

Via, Dan O, Jr. 1985. *The Ethics of Mark's Gospel*.

Waetjen, Herman C. 1989. *A Reordering of Power*.

Wahlberg, Rachel Conrad. 1975. *Jesus according to a Woman*.

Wiedemann, Thomas. 1989. *Adults and Children in the Roman Empire*.

Luke

J. Bradley Chance

Introduction

Luke is the third Gospel in the NT. Like the other Gospels it describes the life and teachings of Jesus of Nazareth. Unlike the other Gospels it has a sequel attached to it, the Acts of the Apostles. That both Luke and Acts, commonly referred to simply as Luke-Acts, were written by the same person can be seen by comparing the prologues of each work. The employment of geography to structure the story depicts God's universal offering of salvation. The centrality of JERUSALEM in the narratives serves to remind the reader of God's promises to Israel. The movement of the story in Acts "to the ends of the earth" (Acts 1:8) gives expression to God's salvific concern for everyone, everywhere.

Luke and the Other Gospels

Luke shares much in common with the other two synoptic Gospels, Mark and Matthew, leading interpreters to conclude that some type of direct literary relationship exists between them. Since the nineteenth century, biblical scholars have generally agreed that the Gospel of Mark was employed as a source both by the authors of Luke and Matthew. In addition, interpreters argue that both Luke and Matthew employed a source called Q which consisted primarily of sayings of Jesus. A significant minority of biblical scholars rejects this "two-document hypothesis," arguing that Luke's primary source was the Gospel of Matthew. Luke also shares certain affinities with the Fourth Gospel, such as the somewhat similar story found in Luke 5:4-9 and John 21:5-11 about a miraculous catch of fish. Few scholars have concluded, however, that there existed a direct literary relationship between these two gospels.

Authorship

IRENAEUS (ca. 180 C.E.) expresses the common view of the church fathers concerning the authorship of Luke-Acts: "Luke, too, the companion of Paul, set forth in a book the Gospel as preached by him" (*Adv-Haer* 3.1, 1). Colossians 4:14 and Phlm 24 do refer to a certain Luke, implying that he was an occasional associate of PAUL. Irenaeus also viewed the so-called "we sections" of Acts (cf. Acts 16:10) as the author's indication of his close relationship with Paul (*AdvHaer* 3.14, 1). Modern interpreters note that neither the Gospel nor Acts offers any explicit word concerning the author's identity. Furthermore, the author of Luke-Acts seems to offer a very different portrait of Paul than that offered by Paul himself in his letters. In fact, the author of Acts shows no awareness that Paul was even a prolific letter writer. This evidence leads many scholars to reject the conclusion that the author of Acts was a companion of Paul, much less the specific person named Luke. Some current interpreters have reasonably defended the traditional identification of Luke as the author of Luke-Acts (e.g., Fitzmyer 1981, 35-51). The issue cannot be resolved, so it is best not to base one's interpretation of the narrative on any particular hypothesis concerning the actual identity of the real author. "Luke" is a name used primarily for convenience.

Date and Place of Composition

Luke's description of the fall of Jerusalem (19:43-44; 21:20; cf. the much more general reference in Mark 13:14), leads most interpreters to conclude that Luke was composed after the fall of Jerusalem (70 C.E.). The fact that Luke shows no knowledge of Paul's letter writing activity suggests a date of composition 100 C.E., before the approximate time when Paul's letters began to circulate as a collection. Any author as informed as Luke claims to be (Luke 1:1-4) would surely have known of such a collection. Hence, one may suggest a date of composition between 70 and 100 C.E. No one knows the place of composition, although many suggestions have been offered, both by ancient and modern readers of Luke-Acts.

Genre

Knowing the genre of an ancient text can guide the modern reader in reading the text as an ancient might have. Regrettably, modern scholars can reach no consensus concerning the genre of Luke and Acts. Do they represent separate genres, with the Gospel showing affinities with ancient biography (Burridge 1992) and Acts looking something like an ancient historical novel (Pervo 1989)? Does Luke-Acts represent a type of ancient history (Aune 1987)? Ancient biography (Talbert 1988)? Clearly, the subject of the Gospel is Jesus, allowing the conclusion that readers are reading an ancient biography. But Jesus is a character within a larger story describing God's dealings with Israel and the rest of the world; hence, readers should not hesitate to look for a bigger story within this story about Jesus.

For Further Study

In the *Mercer Dictionary of the Bible*: APOSTLE/APOSTLE-SHIP; APOSTLES, ACTS OF THE; DISCIPLE/DISCIPLESHIP; ESCHATOLOGY IN THE NT; GOSPELS, CRITICAL STUDY OF; HOLY SPIRIT; KINGDOM OF GOD; LORD'S SUPPER; LUKE; LUKE, GOSPEL OF; PASSOVER; Q; REDACTION; SON OF GOD; SON OF MAN; SOURCE CRITICISM; SYNOPTIC PROBLEM; TRAVEL NARRATIVE; TWELVE, THE; WOMEN IN THE NT; WORSHIP IN THE NT.

In other sources: D. E. Aune, *The N.T. in Its Literary Environment*; R. A. Burridge, *What Are the Gospels? A Comparison with Graeco-Roman Biography*; J. A. Fitzmyer, *The Gospel according to Luke I-IX*, AncB; R. Pervo, "Must Luke and Acts Belong to the Same Genre?" *SBLSP* (1989): 309-16; C. H. Talbert, "Once Again: Gospel Genre," *Semeia* 43 (1988): 53-73.

Commentary

An Outline

I. Prologue, 1:1-4
II. Preparing the Way, 1:5–4:13
   A. Preparation through Announcement, 1:5-56
   B. Preparation through Wondrous Births
      and Childhoods, 1:57–2:52
   C. Preparation through John's Preaching, 3:1-20
   D. Preparation through Jesus' Baptism
      and Temptation, 3:21–4:13
III. The Galilean Ministry
     of the Spirit-Anointed Prophet, 4:14–9:50
   A. Release to the Captives, 4:14–6:16
   B. Proclaiming the Favorable Year
      of the Lord, 6:17-49
   C. Release to the Oppressed, 7:1–9:50
IV. The Anointed Prophet's Journey
     to Jerusalem, 9:51–19:44
   A. Beginning the Journey, 9:51–10:42
   B. Understanding the Present Time, 11:1–13:35
   C. The Leaven of the Pharisees, 14:1–16:31
   D. Persistence for the Journey to Come, 17:1–18:30
   E. Approaching Jerusalem, 18:31–19:44
V. Exodus from Jerusalem, 19:45–24:53
   A. The Temple Ministry, 19:45–21:38
   B. The Hour of Darkness, 22:1–23:56
   C. Entering into Glory, 24:1-53

Prologue, 1:1-4

Luke is the only one of the four Gospels to begin with a formal, literary prologue. This prologue has a number of characteristics found in the formal prologues of other ancient biographies, historical narratives, and even fictional works. First, one finds a statement concerning the author's awareness of earlier, similar works ("many have undertaken to compile a narrative," 1:1 RSV). This may be a reference to Mark and Q, assuming the two-document hypothesis. Luke may have known of other narratives. Second, a statement of the contents of the work (*events that have been fulfilled among us*, v. 1) and a plan of presentation (*to write an orderly account for you*, v. 3). Third, a statement rehearsing the author's qualifications (vv. 2-3). Such statements were often rhetorical attempts to gain the reader's confidence rather than literal records of the author's research techniques. Fourth, a statement of purpose (v. 4). Fifth, identification of the addressee (*Theophilus*, v. 3). Finally, a very good literary style, which is discernable even in most English translations. Regrettably, the prologue offers no help in identifying specifically the author of the narrative, since it lacks what was a common feature of prologues: the author's name.

Although readers learn nothing of the author's identity, the text does imply some things about the author. First, he uses a masculine participle in the word translated as *investigating* (v. 3) to describe himself. Second, he makes no claims to having been an eyewitness, but rather describes himself as the recipient of tradition which goes back to *eyewitnesses and servants* (v. 2). Third, the author presents himself as informed and educated. Such an impression is made not only by what he says about how carefully he has investigated everything, but the very style of the prologue itself. It is clear that the author is calling the reader to take the forthcoming narrative seriously.

The prologue also implies certain things about the reader, whom the author identifies as *Theophilus*. If this were an actual person, his identity is unknown. Luke may be addressing the gospel to any "lover of God," which is what the name literally means. Regardless, the text assumes a reader who has had some previous instruction in the Christian tradition. The text also assumes an inquisitive reader who wishes to be better informed and who desires to *know the truth* (v. 4) about these matters. The very use of a formal prologue, inviting readers to compare this narrative to other works of history and biography, implies readers who would appreciate a narrative about Jesus and his followers written from a cultured, even cosmopolitan perspective.

In short, any reader, ancient or modern, who assumes the role of the reader implied by the text will approach the narrative as an informed, inquisitive, and cosmopolitan reader sympathetic with the Christian tradition. That is the perspective that shall be employed in the following commentary.

Preparing the Way, 1:5–4:13

In this first section of the narrative Luke will provide a context in which readers can understand the public ministry of Jesus. Hence, the "way" is not only being prepared for Jesus, but for the reader. This narrative of preparation indicates that Jesus' story finds its roots in the story of the OT, the story of Israel and Israel's God. Jesus' story is the realization of the hopes of Israel and the promises made by God to Israel's ancestors, Abraham, Isaac, and Jacob. Further, this coming salvation will be not only for Israel's glory but will offer revelation to the gentiles also.

John's public preaching announces that the time of the Lord's coming is at hand, placing the people of Israel and the reader at the edge of the time of the ac-

tual realization of the promises and hopes. Jesus' BAPTISM and testing by the devil offer some real insight into the profound significance of the work he is about to accomplish.

Preparation through Announcement, 1:5-56

Like the Gospel of Matthew, Luke begins his "narrative concerning the things which have been fulfilled among us" (author trans.) with an account of the birth of Jesus. Each of them likely constructed their infancy narratives on the basis of limited yet common traditions for the purpose of conveying to their readers something of the purpose and significance of Jesus' life—a common function of ancient biographical birth accounts. (See Fitzmyer 1981, 305-309.)

Readers of Luke's birth narrative should note in Gabriel's announcements to ZECHARIAH and MARY similarities with birth announcements of OT worthies (such as ABRAHAM), including the presence of an ANGEL, a message about the child, and sometimes even human questioning (cf. Gen 16:7-13; 17:1-22; Judg 13:3-20). These OT allusions, combined with a literary style reminiscent of the LXX, the Bible of Luke's readers, and the primary setting of Jerusalem and the Temple, places Luke's story and, hence, his readers into the world of the OT.

1:5-25. Announcement to Zechariah. Zechariah and ELIZABETH are introduced as stock, pious characters out of the OT, being described as righteous, blameless, and of priestly descent. Even their childless state puts them in company with OT heroes like Abraham and SARAH. During his priestly service Zechariah receives the vision of Gabriel concerning John's birth. Like heroes who have preceded them, Zechariah and Elizabeth will have a child late in life. This child will also resemble OT heroes, especially Elijah (1:16-17). Comparison with ELIJAH raises a note of expectation: the Lord is coming! Israel must be prepared! (cf. Mal 4:5-6).

Zechariah is struck dumb as an immediate and concrete sign to address his skepticism. It also renders Zechariah unable to offer the priestly blessing to the people waiting outside, perhaps implying that the old way of receiving the blessing of God is about to pass away. The story ends with a clear word that the announcement has come true—Elizabeth has experienced the favor of God.

1:26-38. Announcement to Mary. This angelic announcement also refers to a wondrous birth—but it is even more wondrous than that of John. Mary's child will be conceived by the power of the HOLY SPIRIT.

While John was compared to the great prophet Elijah, Jesus is called *the Son of the Most High* and will sit on the throne of DAVID and *reign over the house of Jacob forever* (vv. 32-33). Long awaited hopes for the messianic king are finally going to be realized. Gabriel's talk of the Holy Spirit, denoting the dynamic presence of God, Elizabeth's conception, and his concluding words, *nothing will be impossible with God* (vv. 35-37), serve to indicate the direct intervention of God into the story of the people of Israel. Mary's obedient response (v. 38) offers a model for all who experience God's favor (v. 28) to emulate.

1:39-56. Announcement of the mothers. When the two relatives meet, Elizabeth, being filled with the Holy Spirit, offers Mary a blessing. Mary is blessed because she is an instrument of God, bearing the Lord as *the fruit of [her] womb* (v. 42), and because she has responded to God by believing (having faith in) the word spoken to her (v. 45). The stirring of John in Elizabeth's womb and her filling with the Spirit confirm once again the power and immediate presence of God.

Mary offers up a hymn of praise (the MAGNIFICAT, vv. 46b-55), making explicit what has been intimated in the narrative: God is accomplishing great things. Specific blessings are coming Israel's way in fulfillment of God's promises to Israel's ancestors. Among these blessings is a great reversal of stations (vv. 51-53) commonly associated with the messianic age.

Preparation through Wondrous Births and Childhoods, 1:57–2:52

1:57-66 The circumcision and naming of John. The angelic announcement now finds fulfillment. John's circumcision continues the theme of Jewish piety (v. 59). In obedience to the vision (v. 13), Zechariah confirms Elizabeth's statement that the child shall be named "John" (vv. 60-63). His tongue is then loosed, evoking praise from him and fear from the neighbors and relatives (v. 65). Exciting expectations are raised among the people as they ask *what then will this child become?* (v. 66).

1:67-80. The Benedictus. Zechariah, filled with the Spirit, answers their question through *prophecy* in vv. 68-79. Zechariah repeats an important theme of Mary's Magnificat: God is fulfilling promises made of old to Israel's prophets (v. 70) and ancestors (vv. 72-73). Themes of deliverance abound: *redeemed, mighty savior for us, saved from our enemies, rescued from the hands of our enemies.* John, as *prophet of the Most High*, shall prepare the Lord's ways offering *knowledge of salvation, the forgiveness of their sins* (v. 77), leading to *the dawn from on high* to break in and offer *light to those . . . in darkness*, and *the way of peace* (vv. 78-79). But Israel, and the reader, must wait until the day when John appears *publicly to Israel* (v. 80).

2:1-20. The birth of Jesus. Luke is aware of the tradition that Bethlehem was the place of Jesus' birth. He uses a vague reminiscence of a census around the time of Jesus' birth as a means of explaining how Joseph and Mary came to be in Bethlehem. What confuses interpreters is the fact that the *registration . . . taken while Quirinius was governor of Syria* (v. 2) occurred in 6 C.E., long after "the days of King Herod" (1:5, d. 4 B.C.E.). Luke notes that Joseph, Mary's fiancee, was a descendant of David and Bethlehem was *the city of David* (v. 3) to emphasize the point that Jesus is to be the one to inherit *the throne of his ancestor David* (1:32).

The announcement to and visitation of the shepherds (vv. 8-20) allows for a number of important themes to be reiterated or introduced. The angelic announcement, which includes a *sign* (v. 12), indicates the activity of God. Shepherds as the recipients of this *good news of great joy* denote the lowly whom God is lifting up (1:52). Jesus is specifically identified as *a Savior* and *the Messiah* (v. 11). Just as expectations were raised among the people regarding John, all who hear the shepherds' report are *amazed* (v. 18). The shepherds' *glorifying and praising God* (v. 20) represents appropriate response to the great thing God is accomplishing.

2:21-40. The presentation of Jesus. The piety of Jesus' parents is made evident as they circumcise Jesus, name him in obedience to the angelic vision (v. 21), and do all that is necessary *according to the law of Moses* (v. 22). The favored status of the lowly, the poor, and humble (cf. 1:51-53) is reinforced by notification that Jesus' parents offer the sacrifice of those who are poor (v. 24. cf. Lev 12:8).

SIMEON too embodies pious characteristics, being guided by the Spirit, *righteous and devout, looking forward to the consolation of Israel* (v. 25). His hope is fulfilled as he is permitted to see Jesus. His words of praise introduce a new element into this story: this salvation is for "all of the peoples"—glory for Israel, *revelation to the Gentiles* (v. 32). Even Mary and Joseph *were amazed at what was being said about him* (v. 33), inviting readers to pause and reflect on what was so amazing about what Simeon has just said: even the gentiles will benefit from this savior! But then Simeon offers a final, ominous word: *the falling and rising of many in Israel* is coming. Jesus will be *a sign that will be opposed.* Even Mary will not be spared this dividing sword (v. 35). ANNA, a PROPHET, further shows how the truly pious of Israel recognize the significance of Jesus and what he has to offer those *looking for the redemption of Jerusalem* (v. 38).

2:41-52. Jesus at the Temple. This final story serves to foreshadow Jesus' ultimate obedience to God (v. 49), even over family (cf. Mary's experiencing the sword of division, v. 35), and his authority as an interpreter of God's law. The latter is evidenced by the astonishment of *teachers . . . at his understanding and his answers.* A final note (v. 52) confirms the favored status of Jesus.

Preparation through John's Preaching, 3:1-20

3:1-6. Historical introduction. The historical details offered by Luke serve to root the story of Jesus in world history. *The fifteenth year of the reign of Emperor Tiberius* is most likely 28/29 C.E. Pontius PILATE, who governed Judea 26–36 C.E., will play a role in Jesus' trial (chap. 23), as will HEROD (*ruler of Galilee* 4 B.C.E.–39 C.E.). Philip, Herod's brother, and Lysanias play no role in the story. Verse 2 leaves the impression that Annas and CAIAPHAS jointly held the office of high priest. Annas, the father-in-law of Caiaphas, actually held the office from 6–15 C.E. Caiaphas was the actual ruling high priest during Jesus' ministry (18–36 C.E.). Neither Annas nor Caiaphas appears by name anywhere else in Luke's story, but Luke must have one of these in mind when he refers to Jesus' hearing at the *high priest's house* (Luke 22:54).

This detailed introduction also provides for John the kind of historical introduction that is found in OT prophetic books (cf. Isa 1:1; Jer 1:1-3). This is a most fitting introduction since John has already been referred to as *prophet of the Most High* (1:76). John prepares the way by *proclaiming a baptism of repentance for the forgiveness of sins* (v. 3). Luke does not interpret the connection between baptism, repentance, and forgiveness. Perhaps he understood John's baptism as a kind of foreshadowing of (preparation for) Christian baptism (cf., e.g., Acts 19:1-7). John had already been introduced as one whose work would involve repentance, or turning (1:16-17), and forgiveness of sins (1:77). Now he is carrying out that role. The quotation from Isa 40:3-5 (vv. 4-6) is longer than that offered in

either Matthew or Mark and emphasizes the cosmic and universal significance (*all flesh shall see the salvation of God*; cf. 2:32) of what is about to happen.

3:7-17. The preaching of John. John's preaching focuses on three issues. Verses 7-9 make clear the necessity of repentance in the face of the eschatological wrath that is coming. Talk of wrath might seem surprising, but both Mary (1:51-53) and Zechariah (1:71-73) have already spoken of reversals that are necessary to set the world right. Despite such declarations as 1:55 and 1:73, John makes clear that repentance is needed even from the children of Abraham.

Verses 10-14 offer specific examples of repentance—a radical change of priorities, values, and ethical behavior. The fact that even *tax collectors* and *soldiers* are depicted among *the crowds that came out to be baptized by him* indicates that all are afforded the opportunity to prepare themselves for the coming of the Lord.

Verses 15-18 begin with people wondering whether this one *might be the Messiah.* The crowds clearly recognize the eschatological implications of John's message. Their inquiry leads John to point their attention to another: *one who is more powerful than* he is coming. Readers know that this is Jesus. John proclaims that this mighty one will carry out the baptism of salvation (*Holy Spirit*) or damnation (*fire*), dividing humanity into wheat and chaff. Recall Simeon's prophecy concerning the *falling and rising of many in Israel* (2:34).

3:18-20. The imprisonment of John. Neither Matthew (4:12; cf. 14:3-4) nor Mark (1:14a; cf. 6:17-18) informs the reader of John's arrest until after Jesus had been baptized. In Luke, however, John exits the stage prior to Jesus' baptism when Herod throws John in prison because he openly preached against Herod's marriage to his brother's wife. (JOSEPHUS confirms this fact, although he states that Herod feared the political implications of John's preaching [*Ant* 18.5.2].) The way has now been prepared for the Lord.

Preparation through Jesus' Baptism and Temptation, 3:21–4:13

Although the way has been prepared for Jesus through the proclamation of repentance and forgiveness, Jesus must be prepared through divine commissioning and a period of testing.

3:21-22. The baptism of Jesus. Unlike Matthew (3:13-17) and Mark (1:9-11), Luke does not state that

John baptized Jesus; in fact, he leaves exactly the opposite impression. Rather, Luke speaks of Jesus' baptism in an almost parenthetical statement associating Jesus' baptism with that of *all the people*. Luke offers no clues that Jesus was in need of repentance and forgiveness. But such identification prepares for the special ministry of Jesus to outcasts and sinners of Israel.

Luke notes that the Spirit descends upon Jesus while he is praying. The eschatological mission that is about to commence requires prayer and the enabling of the Spirit. No hint is given that any other than Jesus heard the voice confirming the identity of Jesus as God's *Son, the Beloved* with whom God is *well pleased* (contra? Matt 3:17). Informed readers would catch the allusion to Ps 2:7, a psalm of enthronement in which the LORD declares "you are my son," and recall the promise made to Mary (1:32). They would also note the allusion to Isa 42:1, an oracle concerning God's servant who receives God's spirit "to bring forth justice to the nations" (ἔθνη), and recall Simeon's prophecy that Jesus would be *a light for revelation to the Gentiles* (ἔθνη, 2:32).

3:23-38. The genealogy of Jesus. Matthew also offers a genealogy of Jesus (Matt 1:2-16), although it is not the same genealogy. The genealogies of Matthew and Luke, like other ancient genealogies, served to make a statement about the identity of Jesus. From Luke's genealogy one learns that through Joseph, Jesus' legal father (*the son [as was thought] of Joseph*, [v. 23]), Jesus is indeed of the line of David, although, interestingly, not of the royal line (cf. v. 32; Jesus is descended from David's son Nathan, not Solomon). Perhaps Luke was aware of specific prophecies such as those found in Jer 22:24-30; 36:30-31, stating that the Davidic dynasty would end with JEHOIACHIN (Coniah in Jer 22:24), son of JEHOIAKIM (cf. esp. Jer 22:30). Further by tracing Jesus' genealogy back to ADAM and God (v. 38) the genealogy also "serves to explain in still another way the relation of Jesus . . . to God and to the human beings he has come to serve" (Fitzmyer 1981, 498). The genealogy reinforces the impression made by the baptism story: that Jesus identifies with "all the people" and is God's son.

4:1-13. The temptation of Jesus. Luke's narration of the temptation, or testing, of Jesus is most similar to the account found in Matt 4:1-11 (cf. Mark 1:12-13), although the order of temptations is not the same. Luke introduces the temptation narrative by twice noting Jesus' close association with the *Holy Spirit* (v. 1), stating that Jesus was *full of the Holy Spirit*, and that he *was led by the Spirit in the wilderness*. Recall that Luke has closely juxtaposed the descent of the Spirit and the affirmation of Jesus' sonship in 3:22 and has just concluded the genealogy of Jesus with the phrase *son of God* (3:38). This allows the conclusion that it is Jesus, in his role as Son of God, who is being led by the Spirit into the wilderness. Twice Jesus' adversary begins his challenges to Jesus by saying *if you are the Son of God* (vv. 3, 9), confirming that, indeed, this narrative is primarily about Jesus and his work as God's Son.

The reason for Jesus' pilgrimage to the wilderness is clearly stated: Jesus *for forty days . . . was tempted by the devil* (v. 2). By portraying the time of testing as extending throughout the time of the forty days (contra Matt 4:1-3), Luke portrays a most intense and significant struggle.

The reference to *forty days* might be nothing more than a way of indicating an extended duration of time. One would not be reading too much into the text to find some sort of symbolic significance. For example, Moses and Elijah, two great figures of the OT whose names will often appear in Luke's narrative (and they will even appear as characters in the action! [cf. 9:28-36]), also experienced a period of forty days of solitude from other people at significant periods in their lives (cf. Exod 24:18; 1 Kgs 19:8). Perhaps Luke wishes the reader to compare the work of Jesus to the important influence of these great men of old.

The number *forty* might also allude to the forty years of testing in the wilderness experienced by Israel during the exodus. In all three temptations, Jesus' retorts to the devil consist of quotations from Deuteronomy. In the first (v. 4) Jesus quotes Deut 8:3. In Deut 8:2, Moses refers explicitly to Israel's testing for "forty years in the wilderness" and Israel's experiencing hunger and being fed with manna "in order to make you understand that one does not live by bread alone." Jesus' second retort to the devil (v. 8) quotes Deut 6:13, found in a context referring to Israel's impending possession of the land. It is emphasized that God gave Israel the land and Israel should, therefore, serve only God (cf. Deut 6:10-15). Notably, Jesus rebuffs the devil's offer to give him *all the kingdoms of the world* if Jesus will only worship him (vv. 5-7) with a quotation from the OT found in a context emphasizing that it is *God* who gives the land. It is also relevant that Ps 106, which rehearses the rebellious story of Israel in the face of God's mercy, notes that one of Israel's iniquitous acts "in the wilderness" was the false worship offered to the calf (Ps 106:14, 19-20). Jesus, unlike Israel, does not succumb to the temptation of false worship. In the final retort, v. 12, Jesus quotes Deut 6:16. Moses specifically commanded Israel, "Do not put the LORD your God to the test, as you tested him at Massah." Psalm 106:14b also states that Israel "put God to the test in the desert." Collectively, these rejections of the devil's tests show that Jesus accomplished in the wilderness what Israel could not. Such an impression cannot help but leave the reader sensing that indeed good times may be ahead for Israel. Where Israel had failed in the past, Jesus, the one who brings God's salvation prepared *for glory to [God's] people Israel* (2:32), succeeds. And yet, such reminders of Israel's failings might leave the reader feeling ambiguous. If Israel failed before, might failure come again?

Although informed readers can easily detect a comparison between Jesus and Israel, they cannot overlook the fact that this narrative is about a direct conflict between Jesus, the Spirit-anointed Son of God, and the devil. Luke does not need to introduce the devil; informed readers know who he is. He is Satan (cf., e.g., 10:18; 11:18; 13:16), Beelzebul, the ruler of demons (11:15), and even the ruler of *all the kingdoms of the world* (v. 5).

This, the last story told before Jesus begins his public ministry, makes clear that the way that has been prepared is a way that involves conflict of the most serious proportions. Jesus' nemesis will be Satan himself. To be sure, Jesus wins this round: *when the devil had finished every test, he departed from him* (v. 13). Luke has made clear to the reader that the Spirit-anointed Son of God is more powerful than Satan. But this battle is not over, for the devil *departed [only] . . . until an opportune time.* As subsequent stories will make clear, Satan, this ruler of demons, has allies everywhere.

The Galilean Ministry of the Spirit-Anointed Prophet, 4:14–9:50

This second section of Luke's narrative hurls Jesus into action and into confrontation with the allies of Satan. The first pericope sets the tone of the entire section and for Jesus' ministry: it will be a ministry of liberation, or release. In parts one (4:14–6:16) and three (7:1–9:50) of this section, Jesus' ministry of liberation comes primarily through his and his followers' actions. In part two (6:17-49) he offers his liberating word in the sermon on the plain.

Release to the Captives, 4:14–6:16

4:14-30. The rejection at Nazareth. Luke prefaces the story of the Nazareth incident with a summary statement (vv. 14-15) of Jesus' public ministry, leaving the impression Jesus has been at work for some time. This summary of Jesus' activities differs from that of Matt 4:13-17 and Mark 1:14b-15, both of which make explicit reference to Jesus' proclamation of the "kingdom of God." This has led some to believe that Luke does not wish to emphasize the eschatological significance of Jesus' work. The remainder of chap. 4 challenges this conclusion.

Luke's story of Jesus' Nazareth rejection is longer than the accounts found in Matt 13:54-58 and Mark 6:1-6a. The length of the story and Luke's use of this story to inaugurate Jesus' public ministry indicate its significance. The text from which Jesus reads (Isa 61:1-2a; 58:6) refers to familiar issues, especially *the Spirit of the Lord*, and *anointed* (having same Gk. root as the word "Christ"). Since readers already know Jesus to be the "anointed one" (2:11) and "full of the Spirit" (4:1), they will associate this text with Jesus and the work he is going to perform.

Captives and *oppressed* (v. 18) describe similar types of people. The words translated *release* and *go free* represent the same word in Greek (ἄφεσις). Reference is being made to the "setting free," the liberation, of oppressed persons. Such liberation is juxtaposed with references to bringing *good news to the poor, recovery of sight to the blind*, and proclaiming *the year of the Lord's favor* (vv. 18-19). Thus, several important issues pertaining the upcoming ministry of Jesus, particularly preaching and healing, are set in an overall context of liberation.

The eyes of all . . . were fixed on him (v. 20). Something significant is happening. Jesus declares that *today this scripture has been fulfilled in your hearing.* Thus, it is not surprising that *all spoke well of him and were amazed at the gracious words* (v. 22). Of course, readers know that Jesus is not merely *Joseph's son* (v. 22). Still readers share with the audience the expectation that liberation is coming, and wonder just what kind of liberation. Just who are the oppressed and the captives?

Jesus does not warmly receive the reaction of his hometown audience. He predicts that his people will quote Jesus the proverb, *Doctor, cure yourself* (v. 23), which he then interprets and applies specifically: *Do here also in your hometown the things we have heard* you did at Capernaum (v. 23). Despite an initially positive response, relations will cool. Such cooling has to do with Jesus' hometown citizens wanting to make sure that no other town receives anything that they do not. There are evidenced here hints of possessiveness and even jealousy.

Jesus' next words offer further interpretation, applying to himself the title prophet and stating that he will not be accepted by his own. Rejection, however, does not stop the prophet from doing his work. Elijah had certainly experienced rejection from his own, being the object of AHAB's and JEZEBEL's wrath requiring that he flee for his life (1 Kgs 19). Yet his prophetic work continued even in the midst of such struggle as indicated by his being sent to a non-Israelite widow (1 Kgs 17). ELISHA, upon whom the spirit of Elijah had come to rest (2 Kgs 2:15), further demonstrated that God's blessings were not reserved for Israel in that he healed the Syrian Namaan (2 Kgs 5).

The application to Jesus' own situation is clear: he will experience rejection from his own—but that will not stop him from performing the liberating work to which God has called him. He will move on from NAZARETH. In the larger setting of Luke-Acts readers may also sense something of an ominous foreshadowing: will Jesus ultimately be rejected by Israel just as he has predicted that he will be rejected by his hometown? If so, readers are assured that such rejection will not stop the liberating work of God. Elijah and Elisha went to the others—so can Jesus.

The reaction of Jesus' hometown is violent beyond reason. The very hint that God's blessings will not be halted by the rejection of his messenger drives the people to fury. Their violent protest against the prophecy that they will reject Jesus leads them to do precisely what Jesus predicted: they drove him out of town and tried to hurl him off the cliff (v. 29). Already the "rising and falling of many in Israel" has begun. Jesus' first public word to Israel has shown him to be the sign that will be opposed (2:34).

4:31-44. The liberating work of God's reign. Luke offers four pericopes that quickly demonstrate precisely the kind of liberation Jesus was talking about in Nazareth.

The first is 4:31-37. Jesus' word in 4:23 has prepared readers for something significant to happen in Capernaum. This pericope fulfills the expectation. The significant thing that happens is Jesus' confrontation with an unclean demon (v. 33), clearly an ally of the devil. The demon, speaking for himself and his band

of fellow hosts of Satan, sums up the essence of the conflict: Have you come to destroy us? (v. 34) Jesus' answer is clear as he rebuked him and thereby demonstrated his authority and power to command the unclean spirits, and out they come! (v. 36) Jesus' liberating ministry has begun.

Jesus' liberating work continues as he assaults not only demons but disease (vv. 38-39). The clause, he rebuked the fever (v. 39), recalls how he had earlier rebuked the demon (v. 35). The connection with Jesus' announced ministry of "release" (4:18) is found in the statement that the fever left her, which literally is translated "it released her." The service Peter's liberated mother-in-law renders to them demonstrates that she is indeed well. A deeper meaning is suggested in that the word used for service (διακονέω) is often used of "Christian service" (e.g., Luke 22:24-27). Those liberated by Jesus are liberated for service to him and others.

The third pericope (4:40-41) again juxtaposes Jesus' healings and exorcisms. Readers are told that Jesus rebuked the demons, not permitting them to reveal his identity as the Messiah and Son of God. No specific clue is given as to why Jesus will not permit such revelations. Perhaps Jesus wishes to define these titles on his own terms.

In the final pericope (4:42-44) of this section, Luke uses a phrase he has not yet used: the kingdom of God. Finally, readers know what all this is about. The proclaiming of good news to the poor and release to the captives (4:18), the rebuking of demons and disease, even the head-to-head encounter with the devil in the wilderness—all of these come under the straightforward clause: to proclaim to good news of the kingdom of God (v. 43). The reign of God himself is coming—and with it comes liberation from that which has oppressed and held captive God's people. CAPERNAUM has enjoyed these blessings. Capernaum must learn what Nazareth failed to learn: these blessings are not only for them. Jesus must proclaim this good news in other cities also.

5:1-11. Calling disciples. Luke introduces the story by referring to the pressing crowd, a mass-character already introduced (cf. 4:42). This is one of the many references portraying the masses as responding favorably to Jesus (cf. 5:15; 6:17; 7:11, et al.).

The story indicates the work of Jesus will involve the help of others, of whom Simon and James and John, sons of Zebedee, are the first chosen. Luke introduced Simon rather abruptly in 4:38. It is clear that he has seen the many mighty works of Jesus, works that point to Jesus' authority and power (cf. 4:36). The miraculous catch of fish offers one more demonstration of Jesus' power, a power to which Simon responds in amazement (v. 9). *He fell down at Jesus' knees, saying, "Go away from me, Lord, for I am a sinful man"* (v. 8). The call of Jesus transcends the sinful human condition. In spite of Peter's condition as a sinner Jesus calls him to *be catching people* (v. 10), a peculiar phrase literally rendered "catching alive." Surely, the implication is that Simon will be catching people alive for the kingdom of God (4:43). Simon and his companions respond with total allegiance: *they left everything and followed him* (v. 11).

5:12-16. Healing of a leper. Luke offers another example of the liberating power of Jesus. Here Jesus heals a man inflicted with a disease that ostracized him from the community of the people, due to uncleanness (Lev 13:45-46). The leper, therefore, desires to be made clean (5:12). Jesus' concern to restore the leper to community is shown in his command that the leper go immediately to the priest to *make an offering for your cleansing*, an offering that resulted in restoration to the community (cf. Lev 14:2-9). The liberating power of Jesus has genuine communal and sociological concern.

Luke now offers a series of controversy stories, extending from 5:17 through 6:11. In these stories, Jesus will continue to manifest his power and authority through the miracles by which he confronts oppressive disease. Jesus will also demonstrate his authority through confrontation with a new set of characters, the religious authorities. These people offer a different, yet no less real, kind of oppression of human beings: scrupulous religion.

5:17-26. The forgiveness of sins. Luke sets the stage for the next story by introducing the *Pharisees and teachers of the law* (v. 17). Readers would associate them with religious authorities, an association reinforced by reference to their being *from Jerusalem*. Notification of the presence of the crowd (v. 19), whom Luke has already shown to be positively disposed to the work of Jesus, raises a question as to whether the religious leaders will also respond positively to Jesus' work.

Luke sets readers up for another healing miracle, stating that *the power of the Lord was with him to heal* (v. 17). The story then takes a strange turn. When the paralytic is presented to Jesus, he declares, *"Your sins are forgiven"* (v. 18). Two things become clear. One,

the religious leaders react negatively to Jesus' word of forgiveness. Readers know the power of the Lord to be with Jesus (cf. 5:17; 3:21-22; 4:1); the leaders obviously do not. Their reaction is quite the opposite of the crowd who *glorified God* (v. 26). The division of Israel has begun! Ironically, in their skepticism the leaders ask what is a crucially important question: "Who is this man . . . ?" (author trans.) Two, readers are invited to consider that the power of Jesus to liberate from demons and disease can also liberate people from sin. The word used for "forgiveness" shares the same Gk. root as the word for "release" found in 4:18. "Release from sins" is part of a much larger ministry of liberation—the liberation from the oppressive grip of the devil from which the kingdom of God has come to release humanity. Jesus associates this dimension of the liberation with the title *Son of Man*, thereby answering his opponents' question.

5:27-6:11. Controversy with the religious leaders. Luke now offers a number of dramatic controversies. Jesus' word of forgiveness in the preceding pericope sets the stage for this story of calling a notorious sinner (a tax collector) to follow Jesus (5:27-32). The *Pharisees and their scribes* (5:30) are both equally scandalized by this act of Jesus. Jesus employs another physician proverb (cf. 4:23) to make clear that the invitation of sinners to repentance is why he has come, implying that the liberation from sin that Jesus offers requires a genuine change of heart and mind in the life of the sinner.

The following PARABLES offered by Jesus (5:33-39) make clear that this way of offering God's liberating power is something radically new. Jesus has not come to confirm the old ways of piety and religion, such as fasting, but to bring a joyful new way of life that calls for celebration. The seemingly innocuous metaphors about cloth and patches, wine and wineskins, illustrate a most ominous principle: the new and the old won't mix—indeed they cannot mix.

The incident of plucking grain on the SABBATH (6:1-5) demonstrates the *Pharisees'* brand of religiosity. Jesus appeals to the story of David (1 Sam 21:1-7) to declare that human need takes precedence over legal scruples. Speaking again of the *Son of Man* he declares himself (implicitly) to be lord even of the Sabbath. Luke seems to be presenting Jesus as the one whose authority alone as the lord of the Sabbath allows for this radically new understanding of Sabbath law, rooted in Jesus' unique and authoritative interpretation of scripture.

Luke concludes this section with one final Sabbath controversy (6:6-11). The intensity of the conflict between Jesus and the religious leaders may have led readers to wonder just how far these leaders might go to stop Jesus. Verse 11 invites readers to assume the worst. Could it be that even these religious leaders, like demons and disease, are on the side the devil? Luke leaves readers wondering.

6:12-16. Naming of the apostles. Luke concludes this section by completing the circle of those whom he is calling to "catch people." That this is to be the mission of the *apostles* (v. 13), these men whom Jesus will "send out," is suggested by the fact that Simon, whom Jesus specifically called to "catch people" (5:10) heads the list. The number twelve is reminiscent of the twelve tribes of Israel, suggesting that Jesus' liberating work does indeed involve a renewal and possibly redefinition of Israel. The statement that JUDAS *became a traitor* is particularly ominous in light 6:11. Will the leaders and Judas form some alliance?

Proclaiming the Favorable Year of the Lord, 6:17-49

In the preceding section, Jesus has demonstrated the liberating power of God through miracle and confrontation. In this section, the sermon on the plain, Jesus offers the liberating word.

6:17-19. Introduction. Here Luke introduces two important details: notification of the audience and a reminder of the eschatological context. The audience consists of the apostles (*them*), *a great crowd of his disciples* v. 17; (Jesus' followers are not limited to the circle of the apostles), and *a great multitude of people. People* is almost a technical term denoting "the people of Israel." It is often synonymous with the "crowd(s)" (cf. 5:19). Conspicuous by their absence is the Jewish leadership. The eschatological context is noted with reference to healing and exorcisms. This word of Jesus is to be heard within the context of his ministry of liberation.

6:20-26. The beatitudes and woes. Beatitudes are words of blessing that announce the happy condition of someone. They are not exhortations. The first beatitude, for example, does not say, "Be poor and God will give you the kingdom." Rather, the poor, the hungry, the sorrowful, and the despised and excluded are pronounced as blessed now because of what God will offer in the future: the kingdom, satisfaction, joy, and reward in heaven (cf. 1:52b, 53a). Present blessing on the basis of God's future action is no numbing

opiate for the masses. Recall the demonstrations of Jesus' power already manifested. God's reign is already breaking in to set right a corrupt world whose *kingdoms, authority,* and *glory* now lay in the hand of the devil (cf. 4:5-6). For those who have no claim or stake in the kingdom of this age, the liberation of God's kingdom comes.

For those who have staked their claim in the *kingdoms of the world* (cf. 4:5)—the rich, the satiated, the happy-go-lucky, and the respected (cf. 1:51b, 52a, 53b)—God's action brings *woe.* The demonic grip on the world is already being loosened—the sandy and shifting foundation of that world is being washed away (cf. 6:49). Indeed, *woe to you* who have staked your lives on this!

6:27-42. Response to God's initiative. God's action now, serving as a foretaste of his action to come, requires response. At the heart of that response is the command, *Be merciful, just as your Father is merciful* (v. 36). The one who benefits from God's merciful reclamation of his world and its inhabitants from the grip of evil must extend that mercy to others.

Such mercy manifests itself primarily in two ways. First, one is to love radically, even one's enemies (vv. 27-31), and without the expectation of reciprocity (vv. 32-35a). The word of Jesus offers concrete (although not casuistic or exhaustive) illustrations of such radical love. It involves the love of enemies (might this be how, in God's reign, enemies are conquered? [cf. 1:71, 74]), prayer for the abusive, turning the other cheek, giving both to the one who would beg and the one who would take, and even loving the one who has no intention of returning such love. The shock of Jesus' examples is no doubt intentional, leading the reader to "feel" just how radical the expectations of God's mercy really are. Such expectations, however, are grounded in the fact that God *is kind to the ungrateful and the wicked* (v. 35b). Readers cannot help but ask whether God's mercy to them has been as radical as loving those who despise, abuse, and take advantage of them.

The second concrete way that one exhibits the mercy received is to refuse to judge and condemn, and to extend forgiveness and generosity (vv. 37-38). Being merciful as God is merciful does not justify being the judge as God is the judge. Such refusal to judge does not mean refusal to acknowledge and address the corrupting evil of the present age. To conclude this is to forget the eschatological context of the sermon (cf. 6:17-19). It does require, however, that one's concern with sin and corruption begin with the logs that obscure one's own vision, not the specks that one is so sure pervert the vision of one's neighbor.

6:43-49. Concluding parables. The first concluding parable (vv. 43-45) teaches that the kind of good *fruit* required of those called to be *children of the Most High* (v. 35) can only come from good trees. Verse 45 interprets the metaphor, indicating that Jesus is talking about *the good person [who] out of the good treasure of the heart produces good*. Transformed persons and hearts are the prerequisites to the response demanded of the kingdom. The whole of this Gospel clearly implies that such transformation is possible only in light of the merciful liberation Jesus has come to offer. In short, God is the source of this "goodness" (cf. 18:19). Nonetheless, as the second concluding parable (vv. 46-49) indicates, a life built on the solid foundation which can survive the onslaught of God's discerning judgment, is the life of one who *hears my words, and acts on them*. Obedience, not just good intentions (what many call a "good heart") is demanded.

Release to the Oppressed, 7:1–9:50

This section provides further illustration of Jesus' ministry of liberation. In this section Jesus will encounter and conquer demons, disease, and even death. As these encounters progress, characters in the story will address the central question: Who is Jesus?

7:1-10. The centurion's slave. Jesus returns to Capernaum having finished offering his words of liberation to the *people*. He hears of a *centurion*, a gentile. Simeon's words about Jesus being *a light for revelation to the Gentiles* (2:32) come to mind. Unlike Matthew's version, Jesus does not deal with the gentile directly, but through intermediaries, Jewish leaders and the gentile's friends. Perhaps Luke views this as representative of the indirect way gentiles of his time encounter Jesus. The Jewish elders appeal to Jesus on the basis of the centurion's merits saying, *"He is worthy of having you do this for him"* (v. 4). However, when the centurion speaks for himself, through friends he sent to Jesus, he says, *"I am not worthy to have you come under my roof"* (v. 6). The centurion bases his request entirely on his simple faith that the *word* of Jesus carries with it *authority*. The centurion shows by this simple statement that he recognizes what Jesus has been demonstrating since the initiation of his ministry: he is the one with the authority to vanquish the corrupting powers within the world (cf. 4:36; 5:17, 24; 6:19). Jesus' statement indicates that such recognition

is exactly the appropriate response to Jesus. *Not even in Israel have I found such faith* (v. 9). Faith in the absolute power and authority of Jesus over evil is what renders such power effective (cf. 5:20).

7:11-17. Jesus confronts death. While this story offers Jesus' greatest challenge yet, Luke makes clear that compassion for the plight of a widow, now without a son, is what moves Jesus to act. This woman could now look forward only to an anxious existence in a world where orphans and widows served as proverbial models of the oppressed (cf. Jas 1:27). The story reminds readers that behind the awesome power that vanquishes evil is the love of God. Through his characters, Luke comments on the larger implications of the event. The people recognize that *a great prophet has risen among us* (cf. Jesus' own words [4:18-24]). Further, the crowd recognizes that *God has visited his people* (RSV cf. 1:78; "the dawn from on high has visited us" [author trans.]). The conquering of death shows clearly that the oppressive forces of evil and corruption are being conquered.

7:18-23. The Baptist's question. John is in prison (3:19-20), so he asks his question to Jesus through his *disciples*. The question, *Are you the one who is to come?*, is reminiscent of John's declaration of 3:16: *one who is more powerful than I is coming*. John predicted that this powerful one would separate the wheat from the chaff (3:17). John's question now can only imply that he does not recognize that Jesus is accomplishing the mission of this "powerful one" of 3:17. Jesus' response is a summary of his healing activity (v. 22; cf. Isa 35:5,6; 61:1; Luke 4:18). This summary, combined with Jesus' blessing of those who do not take offense at him, certainly communicates a positive response to John. Readers know these activities of Jesus to be demonstrations of his authority over evil. Readers also should recognize that the division Jesus is creating in Israel, manifested to this point primarily by the different responses to him by the masses and the leaders, is the realization of John's prediction that Jesus would separate the wheat from the chaff.

7:24-30. Jesus' view of John. Jesus invites his audience to consider the role of John. He is a prophet, but more than a prophet. Jesus reviews the role of John already spoken of by Luke. He is the *messenger* sent *to prepare your way before you* (cf. 1:17, 76: 3:4). John is more than a prophet, for he is a prophet whose role was itself a fulfillment of prophecy (cf. Mal 4:5). Yet John, as great as he is, pales in significance when compared to that for which his primary role was to prepare the people: the reign of God. The least of those who share in the reign of God are greater than the best of those who prepared the way for it. So much greater is the time of fulfillment than the time of promise. Verses 29-30 note the division created by John's preaching, a division between the masses and the leaders continued by Jesus. "The people . . . justified God" (RSV); the leaders "rejected the purpose of God" (RSV).

7:31-35. This generation. Luke introduces a new term to denote those opposed to Jesus and his work: *this generation*. In this pericope *this generation* denotes those who are like spoiled children who reject both the strict asceticism of John and the openness of Jesus. In this context, *this generation* denotes *the Pharisees and the lawyers* (v. 30). To be contrasted with *this generation* are the *children of wisdom*. These "children" by whom "wisdom is justified" (RSV) clearly denote the "the people" who "justified God" (7:29). *This generation* is clearly a group to which one does not wish to belong.

7:36-50. The sinner and Simon. The sinner woman and Simon the Pharisee offer concrete illustrations of the two types of people spoken of in the previous episode. No duplicity is hinted at in Simon's invitation to Jesus. Still, in the end, Simon refuses to acknowledge that Jesus is a prophet (v. 39), for Jesus allowed the sinner to touch him. By this lack of acknowledgment Simon showed himself to be one of "this generation" who rejected Jesus because he showed himself to be *a friend of tax collectors and sinners* (7:34). On the other hand, the sinner woman's act of heartfelt affection showed her to be one who "justified God," that is, "to acknowledge the rightness of [God's] call in John and Jesus and to repent and be forgiven" (Talbert 1986, 85).

Jesus' parable about the two debtors indicates that the operative principle in this story is that great forgiveness renders great love. In short, the woman is not forgiven because she treats Jesus lavishly. She treats Jesus lavishly because she has experienced the "release from sins" (v. 48). She has been a recipient of the ministry of liberation, which serves as the hallmark of Jesus' work in Luke (Luke 4:18-19). *Her sins, which were many, have been forgiven, hence she has shown great love*. The following statement, *But the one to whom little is forgiven, loves little*, can only be directed at Simon who has demonstrated "little love" for Jesus. The question of Simon's guests, *Who is this who even forgives sins?* echoes the question of other

Pharisees in 5:21. The woman who has experienced "release," salvation, and *peace* shows by her *faith* in Jesus that she knows the answer to the detractors' question.

8:1-21. The word of the kingdom. Luke sets the stage by reiterating and expanding upon some themes already introduced, reminding readers that Jesus is preaching the *kingdom of God* and is accompanied by *the twelve*. Yet he also has other followers, *some women who had been cured of evil spirits and infirmities* (vv. 1-2). Talk of Jesus' healing reminds readers of the nature of Jesus' kingdom work: liberation from the corrupting powers of evil. Inclusion of women among his followers offers an expanded definition of Jesus' followers. He has come to liberate all persons and to call all persons to follow him.

The parable of the sower and its interpretation (vv. 4-15) serves to explain how the preaching of the kingdom of God brings division among the people. Verses 9-10 offer a partial explanation. As offensive as it may appear to modern readers, these verses declare that the will of God stands behind this division. To the disciples *it has been given to know the secrets of the kingdom of God*. Such "giving" can only come from God. The others are described as *looking* although *they may not perceive* and *listening* although *they may not understand* (v. 10). Jesus is offering a loose quotation of Isa 6:9. This prophet, to whom Jesus has already compared himself (4:18-19), was called to preach to a people whom God knew would not heed his word. Jesus too has been called to preach to a people, not all of whom will perceive or understand, for Jesus has been *destined for the falling and the rising of many of Israel* (2:34).

Verses 11-15 provide further explanation as to why many reject the *seed* that is *the word of God*. Satan and his hosts hinder the planting, nurturing, and growth of the seed. For some, *the devil comes and takes away the word from their hearts*. For others faith lasts only until *a time of testing comes* and they *fall away*. Luke 4:2 and 13 imply the devil to be the source of such *testing*. Other people *are choked by the cares and riches and pleasures of life*. One who suspects the devil to be behind such life-killing concerns is correct (cf. Acts 5:1-3). The seed of the word proves fruitful only in those who *hold it fast in an honest and good heart*. Jesus here is speaking of the same kind of person about whom he spoke in 6:45.

Verses 16-18 exhort those who possess the *secrets of the kingdom of God* (8:10) to share the light of revelation that has been offered them. The world must continue to hear that God's victorious reign is breaking in. This is how one must *listen* to the word preached. A good example of the kind of persons about whom Jesus is talking are his *mother and his brothers* (v. 19), for such *are those who hear the word of God and do it* (v. 21). Readers are invited to recall how Mary responded obediently to the Lord, *according to [his] word* (1:38) and proclaimed openly his mighty works of salvation (1:46-55).

8:22-25. Rebuking the forces of chaos. This is the first of four miracles that make up a unit prior to the pericope of the sending forth of the twelve (9:1-6). Together they offer powerful testimony to the authority and power of Jesus over the forces of evil—a power and authority he will soon share with his followers.

This appears initially to be a story about Jesus' power over nature. Luke may wish the reader to discern a deeper meaning. The *windstorm [that] swept down on the lake* placed Jesus' disciples in *danger*, leading them to believe that they were *perishing*. In response Jesus *rebuked the wind and raging waves*. *Rebuked* is the same word used in 4:35, 39 where Jesus "rebuked" a demon and a fever. Luke might be intimating that even "forces of nature," which modern persons interpret in the context of the naturalistic laws of nature, can also be used by the "forces of evil" to harm people.

Jesus' question to his disciples, *Where is your faith?*, implies that if they truly trusted Jesus as the one who could "release" people from the threatening grip of evil, they would have realized that even the demonically manipulated forces of nature could be subdued by their *master*. Their concluding question, *Who then is this?*, shows that even those to whom *the secrets* have been given (8:10) can manifest a lack of perception like those of *this generation* (cf. 7:31, 49).

8:26-39. The Gerasene demoniac. Jesus has entered gentile territory, as evidenced by the presence of a *herd of swine* (v. 32). Jesus' first miracle in Jewish territory was an exorcism (4:31-37). So it is in gentile territory. This case of demon-possession seems particularly acute (cf. vv. 27, 29), suggesting that Satan's grip on the non-Jewish world was even tighter than his grip on Jesus' homeland.

The demons fear being sent *back into the abyss* (v. 31), which would spell the end of their earthly dominion. Jesus tricks them by granting their request to be sent into the swine. However, the swine *rushed . . . into the lake and drowned* (v. 33). The drowning of the demon-possessed swine in the lake results in the return of the demons to the abyss, for large bodies of water, such as lakes, were considered the entrance into the abyss (cf. vv. 22-25).

Again, Jesus offers release from the oppressive forces of the devil; as in Jewish territory, his work creates division. The *people of the surrounding country . . . asked Jesus to leave them* (v. 37). The one who had been *healed* (v. 36; lit. "saved"; cf. 7:50) wished to remain with Jesus. Jesus, however, commands that he return to his home and *declare how much God has done for you* (cf. 8:16). Luke states that he *proclaimed . . . how much Jesus had done for him*. Although anachronistic trinitarian thinking is not to be assumed, Luke clearly invites the reader to acknowledge that Jesus' work is actually God's work.

8:40-56. Jairus's daughter and the hemorrhaging woman. These two intertwined miracle stories conclude this section. Jesus has returned to Jewish territory, as evidenced by the presence of *Jairus, a leader of the synagogue*. Verse 42 indicates that the *crowds*, who have tended to respond positively to Jesus, are back on the scene as well.

On the way to Jairus' house, *a woman who had been suffering from hemorrhages for twelve years* and who had been unable to find help from doctors approached Jesus from behind *and touched the fringe of his clothes* (v. 43-44). This woman would have been considered as living in a perpetual state of uncleanness (cf. 4:12-16; Lev 15:25-27) and not welcome in the community. When touched, Jesus discerns *that power had gone out from* him (v. 46) and demands to know who touched him. In fear, the woman confesses what she had done. Jesus' statement is, in the Gk. text, exactly the same as that offered to the sinner woman who dared to approach him: "Your faith has saved you. Go in peace" (v. 48, author trans.; cf. 7:50). The trust that brings salvation manifested in "release from sins" also brings salvation manifested in being released from uncleanness. The ministry of liberation continues.

Upon arriving at the ruler's house, it is announced that Jairus' daughter is dead. Jesus can liberate from this evil as well: "Only believe and she shall be saved" (v. 50, author trans.). Again, "faith" and "salvation" are explicitly juxtaposed. The cynical skepticism of the crowd, offering notice to readers that the crowds do not fully trust in Jesus as one might hope, does not dissuade him. Taking his closest disciples and the girl's parents, he enters the house and raises her from the dead. His command to silence (v. 56) indicates that this mighty deed was in response to faith, not to convince the skeptics.

Four miracle stories have spoken clearly of "faith" (8:25, 48, 50) and "salvation" (8:36, 48, 50). The kind of salvation Jesus has come to offer is becoming increasingly clear: liberation from *all* forms of evil demonic oppression. The power that unleashes Jesus' liberating power is faith. THE TWELVE who have been with Jesus for the events of this entire chapter (cf. 8:1) are now ready to share in the work of Jesus.

9:1-6. The sending out of the twelve. *The twelve* have been with Jesus since 6:12-16. They have witnessed the mighty deeds of liberation. Now they share in that mission as Jesus gives them *power and authority over all demons and to cure diseases* (v. 1). The work that they do, like that of Jesus, is *to proclaim the kingdom of God* (v. 2). Jesus will not do his work alone. They travel without provision showing that those who accomplish the work of Jesus accomplish it by faith.

9:7-9. Herod's question. This brief notice serves three functions. One, it informs readers of the Baptist's fate—he is dead. Two, it raises the question of the precise identity of Jesus, an issue readers have seen before (cf. 5:21; 7:49; 8:25). Three, it raises an ominous note in that the one who had killed the Baptist now wants to see Jesus.

9:10-17. Feeding of the five thousand. *The apostles* have returned and *told Jesus all they had done. The crowds* are also back on the scene (v. 11). Readers are offered still another reminder of what the mission of Jesus is all about: he *spoke to them about the kingdom of God, and healed those who needed to be cured.*

Having established the audience and the eschatological setting and context, Luke narrates the miraculous feeding. One should not hunt only for symbolic meaning, as though the actual feeding of people in need of literal food is not at all the issue. Still, it seems that *the crowds* who have *followed him* (v. 11) are hungry for more than just bread—after all, one does not live by bread alone (4:4). One cannot ignore the language of the last supper (cf. vv. 16; 22:19) or the Lukan interest in the "breaking of bread" as an expression both of Christian fellowship (Acts 2:42, 46; 20:7) and recognition of fellowship with the risen Lord (24:30-31, 35). The fact that the apostles assist with the distribution of the food conjures up post-Easter images of Christian community as well. In short, a Christian reader (cf. 1:4) would recognize in this incident a foreshadowing of the spiritual nourishment that was to come in the context of the "breaking of bread." It is this spiritual hunger that the Messiah has come to fill (v. 17; 6:22). This too is a very real part of the liberating reign of God.

9:18-36. Recognizing Jesus. If in Luke's narrative world recognition of the risen Lord comes in the context of the *breaking of bread* (cf. 24:35), it is no surprise that after Jesus first breaks bread in the narrative (9:16), his disciples explicitly come to recognize who Jesus is. Readers too will learn some new things.

First, Peter confesses Jesus to be *the Messiah of God* (v. 20), something readers have known for some time. Second, Jesus, in defining his role as Messiah, talks in terms of his death and resurrection as the *Son of Man* (v. 22). Jesus' language is quite strong: *The Son of Man must undergo.* . . . The Greek word for *must* (δεῖ) is almost a Lukan code word to denote "divine necessity." The "Son of Man" has functioned in other capacities to this point (5:24; 6:5; 7:34). The implication is that this death and resurrection will play a decisive role in the work of liberation. Third, *the Son of Man* is spoken of by Jesus as the glorious judge of the end time. Fourth, after Jesus, Peter, James, and John ascend to the mount of transfiguration, the glory of Jesus is revealed even now to these men (v. 32). Luke may wish to emphasize that the glorious Son of Man to come is *this* Jesus whom the disciples are now following. Fifth, Moses and Elijah appear with Jesus and speak of his departure, which he was about to accomplish (lit. fulfill) at Jerusalem (v. 31). The OT, which these two so thoroughly embody, finds its realization in Jesus and in some significant event he is to fulfill in Jerusalem. Finally, God himself speaks to the disciples to identify Jesus: *This is my Son.* This provides the warrant for the concluding exhortation: *Listen to him* (v. 35). Readers will later learn from Acts 3:22-23 that this Jesus is the "prophet like Moses" to whom one must listen or "be utterly rooted out of the people."

The disciples also learn about following Jesus. Just as they have been called and sent out to share in his work of liberation (cf. esp. 9:1-6), so too they are called to share in his life of self-denial (vv. 23-24).

Luke has portrayed Jesus as the minister of the liberating power of the reign of God. Readers might expect that this climactic section offering the strongest testimony thus far concerning the identity (MESSIAH, SON OF MAN, SON OF GOD) and work (death and resurrection, exodus at Jerusalem) of Jesus might very well have some connection with this mission of God's liberating kingdom. Such a connection seems warranted, even if not fully explained, given the specific declaration of Jesus in the middle of this section: *some standing here . . . will not taste death before they see the kingdom of God* (v. 27).

This tantalizing declaration is followed by the experience of Peter, James, and John on the mountain where they not only behold Moses and Elijah, but experience the direct and immediate presence of God. This raises expectations that the disciples have come to the highest and best possible moment in their relationship with Jesus. Such expectations are shattered in the very next scenes.

9:37-50. Failing disciples. The conclusion to this section (4:14–9:50) ends on a low note. This disappointing conclusion is made even more noticeable by the "high notes" resonating from the preceding scenes.

The first scene, vv. 37-43, depicts the followers of Jesus as unable to use the power they had only recently been given (cf. 9:1) to heal the demoniac child. Jesus' response, *you faithless and perverse generation,* which has the disciples in view, is particularly strong for two reasons. One, *this generation* is a term already used by Jesus to denote those who *rejected God's purposes* (cf. 7:30-31). Two, the miracle stories that have preceded chap. 9 have emphasized the importance of faith in the actualization of Jesus' liberating power (cf. 8:48, 50). The disciples lack this faith and hence are unable to accomplish the ministry assigned to them.

Jesus reiterates his upcoming rejection (9:43b-45). Jesus' introduction, "*Let these words sink into your ears*" (v. 44; cf.8:18), highlights the significance of his words. *But they did not understand this saying; its meaning was concealed from them* v. 45). Not only do the disciples fail in doing what Jesus has given them authority to do, they have not at all grasped what lies at the heart of his mission of liberation. Luke does not say who or what concealed the meaning from them, but in light of the parable about the devil and his means of robbing people from the fruition of the planted word (8:12-14), one may suspect demonic foul play.

The disciples do not understand the role of self-denial to which Jesus had earlier called them (vv. 46-48; cf. 9:23-25), for on the heels of Jesus' speaking of his own rejection, they argue *as to which one of them was the greatest* (v. 46). Jesus must repeat his exhortation to self-denial, using a child as an illustration.

Finally, the disciples do not recognize that the work of Jesus is about the conquering of evil, not merely being associated with the inner circle which *follow[s] with us* (v. 49). The fact that the unknown exorcist was doing what the disciples themselves could not do (cf. 9:37-43a) and thereby accomplishing the work of the Spirit-anointed Son of God, is not within the purview of the disciples' perception.

The Anointed Prophet's Journey to Jerusalem, 9:51–19:44

The transfiguration scene of 9:28-36 sets the stage for this upcoming journey. There Moses and Elijah spoke of Jesus' "exodus which he was about to fulfill in Jerusalem" (9:31; author trans.). This section narrates the journey to that city. Later the voice of God spoke to the disciples of Jesus declaring, "*This is my Son . . . listen to him!*" (9:35; cf. Acts 3:22-23). The low notes on which Luke ended the previous section indicate that they have much listening to do. Hence, this journey section is rich with sayings material that the Son offers to his disciples, as well as the crowds and even his adversaries. On this journey, "Israel" will have opportunity to listen to God's Son, the Spirit-anointed prophet like Moses.

Beginning the Journey, 9:51–10:42

9:51-56. Rejection of the Samaritans. This pericope twice states that Jesus' *face was set toward Jerusalem,* the goal of Jesus' journey. For the prophet to "set his face against" something implies judgment (cf. Ezek. 21:2). On the surface, the Samaritans' rejection of Jesus is explained by the long-standing antipathy between Jews and Samaritans (cf. Neh 4:2-9; John 4:9). In the context of the story, Jesus' rejection by the Samaritans places the whole journey to Jerusalem under the ominous cloud of rejection. Jesus' refusal *to command fire to come down from heaven* (vv. 54-55) to destroy the Samaritans for their rejection, however, makes clear that rejection of Jesus is not unforgivable or irreversible. The fact that Jesus *rebuked* (cf. 4:35, 39; 8:24) his disciples for suggesting such irreversible judgment implies the ungodly, even demonic, character of such a sentiment.

9:57-62. Following Jesus. "Following" and its demands are the themes of this pericope (vv. 57, 59, 61). One is called to *follow the Son of Man,* whose mission is defined by rejection (v. II 58; cf. 9:22, 44). One is called to a thorough-going commitment to the *kingdom of God,* even at the expense of essential family duty or loyalty, such as burying one's father or bidding *fare-well* to one's family. Since following Jesus involves a decision to enter into the fray against the devil himself who will stop at nothing to hinder fruitful discipleship (8:11-14), commitment must be unequivocal.

10:1-16. Mission of the seventy. As the previous pericope implied, Jesus is willing to gather new disciples as he journeys to Jerusalem (9:57), and to specify the demands of such discipleship as well. Jesus has now gathered *seventy others* as followers and is sending them out on a mission similar to that of the twelve (cf. 9:1-6).

Only Luke has a mission of the seventy (some ancient mss. read "seventy-two"). The instructions to the seventy echo the instructions Jesus gives to the twelve in Matt 9:37-38; 10:7-16. The seventy might symbolize the traditional seventy nations (cf. Gen 10), foreshadowing the mission to the nations. They may be similar to the seventy elders whom Moses appointed (cf. Num 11:16-25), comparing Jesus to Moses (cf. Acts 3:22-23). The focus of their mission is to be the same as that of Jesus and the twelve: *cure the sick* and proclaim that *the kingdom of God has come near* (vv. 9-11). The authority of the seventy is emphasized as Jesus declares that *whoever listens to you listens to me* and, ultimately, whoever *rejects you rejects me and . . . the one who sent me.*

Such an authoritative message demands response. Thus Jesus lays forth the consequences of rejecting the messengers and their message in a series of woes (v. 13) and explicit threats of judgment (vv. 14-15). The particularly harsh words directed at CAPERNAUM (v. 15) where Jesus has spent so much time (cf. 4:31-42; 7:1-10) convey that repentance is required especially of those blessed with witnessing Jesus' ministry (cf. 13:26-27).

10:17-24. Return of the seventy. Having returned, the seventy joyfully report what readers already knew: the work of healing and proclamation subjected *even the demons.* Jesus reports a vision that interprets what the subjection of the demons means: the fall of Satan from heaven (cf. Rev 12:7-9). Such a fall is not the final defeat of Satan. In fact, such a *fall from heaven* can portend intensified struggle here on earth (cf. Rev 12:10-17). In this struggle Jesus' followers have been given *authority to tread on snakes and scorpions; and over all the power of the enemy* (vv. 19-20). More importantly, Jesus' followers should rejoice in the assurance of their final salvation, their names having been *written in heaven* (v. 20; cf. Rev 3:5).

In vv. 21-22 *these things* refer to this demise of Satan. Jesus' prayer states that the impending fall of Satan is not apparent to all. Failure of the *wise and intelligent* to recognize the significance of the present time serves only to show that they are not among the *infants* (cf. 7:35) to whom God, in his *gracious will,* has chosen to *reveal* these things. The affirmation of v. 22, reminiscent of the language of John's Gospel, indicates that recognizing the meaning of *these things* is dependent on revelation from *the Son.* Apart from following Jesus in the work of the kingdom (cf. 9:57-62), *these things* shall remain *hidden.*

Verses 23-24 show *the disciples* to be among those privileged to *see* and *hear* what the worthies of old only hoped for. One, however, must "perceive" as well as *see,* and "understand" as well as *hear* (cf. 8:10).

10:25-37. The lawyer's challenge. Luke introduces this scholar of the Jewish law negatively, explicitly stating that he wished *to test* Jesus, an activity attributed to the devil (cf. 4:2, 13). Like the devil who tested Jesus, the lawyer knows his scripture. He can answer rightly what one must *do to inherit eternal life*: love God wholly and one's neighbor. The lawyer, however, wishes to limit his definition of *neighbor* (v. 29). Luke's statement that he wished *to justify himself* echoes 7:29-30, where Jesus contrasted the crowds who "justified God" with the "Pharisees and lawyers" who "rejected the plan of God."

The parable of the good Samaritan is Jesus' response to the lawyer. Two points are clear. One, Jesus substitutes the broadest possible definition of neighbor for the lawyer's attempt to offer a restrictive definition. One is to be neighbor to any who must be shown *compassion* (v. 33, RSV) and *mercy* (v. 37). Two, by making a non-Jew the hero of the parable, over even the Jewish priest and Levite, Jesus suggests that doing what the law requires to inherit eternal life is not the exclusive privilege of the Jews (cf. 3:7-8). God's offering of eternal life is for all (cf. 2:31-32; 3:6) and attempts to limit God's saving grace to one's own group will be rebuffed by Jesus (cf. 4:24-30; 5:30-32).

10:38-42. Mary and Martha. The universalistic concern of Luke extends to women (cf. 8:1-3). This story continues that theme while offering commentary on the notion of "service" (RSV; NRSV reads *tasks,* v. 40). Given the choice between "serving" and sitting at the feet of *the Lord* and "hearing his word" (lit. trans.), Mary has chosen the latter. Jesus explicitly states that she *has chosen the better part.* Women too can hear the word. Martha is described as *distracted by many things.* These many distracting things are described earlier as "much serving" (v. 40; RSV). The word used for service is used elsewhere by Luke to denote Christian ministry (cf. 22:26; Acts 1:17, 25; 6:1-4). Luke does not wish to belittle such "service" (cf. the good Samaritan), but this story reveals that *there is need of only one thing*: "hearing the word." Service not rooted in such hearing becomes busy work. Yet, one who truly "hears" will serve (cf. 6:47; 8:21).

Understanding the Present Time, 11:1–13:35

As the Spirit-anointed prophet like Moses makes his way toward Jerusalem offering the word to which Israel should listen, he will devote a major portion of his teaching to the issue of the eschatological significance of his work and response to that work.

11:1-13. Teaching on prayer. Prayer has empowered Jesus during his ministry of eschatological liberation (cf. 4:21; 5:16; 9:18; et al.). *His disciples* need to pray as well.

The Lord's prayer. Disciples are charged to approach God even as Jesus does, as *Father* (cf. 2:49; 10:21-22), implying a direct and intimate approach to God. The prayer presents five petitions.

The first, "let your name be made holy" (author trans.), requests that God act so as to establish before all his sovereignty and holiness. An ancient Jewish prayer captures the sense: "Exalted and hallowed be his great name in the world which he created according to his will" (Marshall 1978, 457).

Two, *your kingdom come* (v. 2). This petition is no empty plea, for even now Jesus and his disciples are proclaiming and demonstrating that the "kingdom of God is drawing near" (cf. 10:9).

Petition three requests the provision of daily sustenance. Luke 9:3-5 and 10:8 inform readers that such sustenance comes from the hands of God's people. Luke 4:4 and 9:12-17 offer reminders that essential sustenance is not confined to literal "bread alone."

The fourth petition, *forgive us our sins*, (v. 4) asks God to make effective for his disciples the "releasing" benefits (cf. 4:18; 5:17-26) of God's salvation (cf. 7:48-50). Disciples must remember that God releases "because we ourselves release everyone owing us" (author trans.), for disciples must be merciful just as their *Father is merciful* (cf. 6:36).

The final petition acknowledges the reality of *trial* (v. 4; lit. "testing," cf. 4:2, 13; 8:13; 10:25) that will come the way of the disciple. "The kingdom of God is caught up in a struggle of powers. . . . This is not a struggle for humans to enter armed only with their 'free will'" (Tiede 1988, 214).

Verses 5-13 exhort persistence in prayer. The parable about the friend (vv. 5-8) is not saying that God responds only to nagging. This is an argument "from the lesser to the greater." If a friend, merely wanting to be left alone, will respond to one's request, surely God will respond to the requests of those who call him "Father." A similar message is conveyed by vv. 11-13.

The concluding statement that *the heavenly Father [will] give the Holy Spirit to those who ask him* (v. 13) is most appropriate in the Lukan context. Prayer focuses on the KINGDOM OF GOD and what is needed from God to engage in the struggle of the kingdom (cf. vv. 2-4). The greatest power for this struggle is that of the Spirit, which empowers Jesus himself.

11:14-36. Controversy over Jesus' power. Reference to the HOLY SPIRIT in the preceding verse sets the stage for this conflict over the source of Jesus' power in exorcising demons. Jesus' antagonists charge that he is in league with Beelzebul. These antagonists are *some of . . . the crowds* (vv. 14-15), which is not a good sign, since to this point the crowds have generally responded well to Jesus. *Others*, presumably from *the crowds* as well, wish *to test* Jesus by *demanding* a *sign from heaven* (cf. 4:9-12). Testing is the work of the devil (cf. 11:4) and that too does not bid well for the crowds.

Jesus rebukes their charge (vv. 17-23) and their demand for a sign (vv. 29-36). He rebukes the charge, first, by pointing out its obvious absurdity. Satan would not be casting out his own demons (vv. 17-18). Second, Jesus declares that his exorcisms demonstrate that *the kingdom of God has come to you*. Further, such works demonstrate that Satan, the *strong man, fully armed*, is being *attacked, overpowered*, and *plundered* (vv. 21-22). Jesus concludes his defense with an emphatic demand for total allegiance in this eschatological struggle: *whoever is not with me is against me* (v. 23).

Before responding to the sign-seekers Jesus offers a warning. Verses 24-25 assume that exorcised demons can return and make matters worse. "It is not sufficient to cast out demons if there is no acceptance of the kingdom whose presence is attested by the expulsion of demons" (Marshall 1978, 479). Hearing and obeying the word of God is the only sure cure, which, if applicable even to Jesus' mother, is surely applicable to everyone else (vv. 27-28). Such hearing and obeying of God's word is linked with hearing and obeying Jesus and his message of the kingdom (cf. 6:46-49; 9:26-27).

Jesus addresses *the crowds* demanding a sign in harsh terms (vv. 29-32). He identifies them with *this generation*, the term used by Luke to denote those who reject God' purpose (cf. 7:30). Non-Israelites, like the *queen of the South* who listened *to the wisdom of Solomon* and the *people of Nineveh [who] repented at the proclamation of Jonah*, know how to respond to God. The Jewish crowds are now confronted with something much greater than either of these OT figures or events: *the kingdom of God has come to you!* (v. 20). In the face of this, *this generation* (cf. above commentary on 7:31-35) is headed for judgment and condemnation.

Jesus concludes with a collection of sayings having to do with light, a general metaphor for that which pertains to God (vv. 33-36). He exhorts the crowds to have a healthy eye, which denotes one who "focuses his or her eye on God alone" (Garrett 1991, 99). Most especially the crowds are exhorted to *consider whether the light in you is not darkness* (v. 35), that is, whether they have a vision of life which is so perverse (such as imagining that "Satan is divided against himself" [v. 18]) that, in fact, *your body is full of darkness* (v. 34). At this juncture, the crowds stand in peril of eschatological judgment.

11:37-54. Controversy with Pharisees and lawyers. Luke has just identified the crowds with *this generation*, the generation epitomized by the PHARISEES and lawyers (cf. 7:30-31; 11:50-51 [Moessner 1989, 92-114]). Jesus has exhorted the crowds not to live in utter darkness. Now Luke uses Pharisees and lawyers to illustrate a kind of "light" that is, in fact, "darkness" (cf. 11:35).

The Pharisees (vv. 37-44) demonstrate "darkened light" in their meticulous concern for external piety, such as cleaning *the outside of the cup and of the dish* (v. 39) and tithing *mint and rue and herbs* (v. 42) at the expense of *those things that are within* (v. 41) and more important matters such as *justice and the love of God* (v. 42). Thus, *inside you are full of greed and wickedness* (v. 39), i.e., their bodies are *full of darkness* (v. 34).

The lawyers (vv. 45-48), the scholars of the Law and Prophets, show their concern for the law through their interpretations and teachings. In fact, they *only load people with burdens hard to bear* (v. 46). They claim to honor the prophets because they have built tombs for them, a boast Jesus turns on them: *you . . . approve the deeds of your ancestors* by building these tombs (vv. 47-48).

The judgment pronounced on *this generation* (vv. 50-51) is unequivocal. It will *be charged with the blood of all the prophets shed since the foundation of the world*. From the first murder recorded in Hebrew scriptures (Abel, Gen 4:8), to the last (Zechariah, 2 Chr 24:20-22), *it will be charged against this generation*. When one considers that *all*, not only Jewish leaders, but the "crowds" (cf. 11:29-32) and even the disciples (cf. 9:37-43) have been linked with *this generation*, things are looking quite gloomy indeed. In the face of this gloom, Luke's closing comment, that *the scribes . . . and Pharisees* now *began to be very hostile toward* Jesus (v. 53; cf. 6:11), borders on wry understatement.

12:1-12. Warnings to the disciples. Jesus has just offered a harsh judgment against *this generation*, epitomized by the Pharisees. Jesus has also identified both the crowds and the disciples with *this generation*. It is fitting, therefore, that as *the crowds gathered by the thousands* Jesus would tell *his disciples* to *"beware of the yeast of the Pharisees, that is, their hypocrisy"* (v. 1; see Moessner, 1990).

Verses 2-3 state that there will eventually come total disclosure of one's cover-ups, secrets, and whispers. Judgment *is* coming. Do not be associated with *this generation*, for its inner *greed and wickedness* (11:39) will be exposed. This exhortation anticipates the clear call of Peter to the masses of Jerusalem in Acts 2:40: "Save yourselves from *this* corrupt *generation*" (emphasis added).

Verses 4-7. The eschatological fray into which Jesus' followers are called to enter can bring death. Jesus calls upon his *friends* in the struggle to remember to whom ultimate allegiance, even *fear*, belongs. *Fear of him who . . . has authority to cast into hell* exhorts the disciple to stand firm before *those who kill the body*. The realization that one's total allegiance belongs to the one who does not even forget the sparrow or who has *counted* the *hairs of your head* can bring a deeper comfort which warrants the exhortation, *do not be afraid*.

Verses 8-12. The one who calls the disciples *my friends* (v. 4) is also the one who will come as the eschatological judge, *the Son of Man*. As the SON OF MAN, Jesus will judge according to whether one has *acknowledged* or *denied* him *before others*, presumably *the synagogues, the rulers, and the authorities*. Denial of Jesus, speaking *against the Son of Man, will be forgiven* (cf. 22:31-34, 61-62). Blasphemy *against the Holy Spirit*, however, *will not be*. Clearly, Luke has a post-Easter understanding of the Spirit in view here, given the statement *the Holy Spirit will teach you [the disciples] at that very hour what you ought to say*. The disciples do not receive the Spirit until after Easter (cf. Acts 2:1-4). In this context, to blaspheme against the Spirit is to persist in rejecting and opposing the gospel message spoken by God's Spirit-inspired people. "As long as that obstinate mindset perdures, God's forgiveness cannot be accorded . . . " (Fitzmyer 1985, 964).

12:13-34. Concern over possessions. The word of Jesus offered in 8:14 has already warned that an improper view of riches can choke the word. Here he offers a more detailed word about possessions.

Verses 13-21. *Someone in the crowd* misunderstands the nature of Jesus' authority, thinking that Jesus is concerned to offer judgment over matters of the *family inheritance*. Rather, Jesus warns the crowd to be on guard against greed that can distort one's perception of what life truly consists. The parable of the rich fool illustrates the folly of those who think life *consists in the abundance of possessions* and the storing *up of treasures for themselves but are not rich toward God* (v. 21). In the end, he has absolutely nothing.

Verses 22-31. Using arguments from the lesser (*ravens, lilies*) to the greater (people), Jesus offers assurance that God does care about the basic needs of life. Still, Jesus requires acceptance of the principle that *life is more than food, and the body more than clothing* (v. 23). Most importantly, one is to *strive for [God's] kingdom*. The promise that *these things will be given to you as well* must be heard rightly (*pay attention to how you listen!* [cf.8:18]). This is no carte blanche. To strive for the kingdom involves following the rejected Son of Man (9:58) into the fray of battle that can lead even to death (12:4). Only when heard in such a context is this promise heard rightly.

Verses 32-34. What is involved in being *rich toward God* (v. 21) and striving *for his kingdom* (v. 31) is a radical detachment from one's possessions. Possessions only bind one to an age that is passing (cf. 1 Cor 7:31). Detachment allows one to receive "the kingdom from your Father and to make for yourselves treasure in heaven" (author trans.). What one treasures reveals what type of *heart* one has (cf. 6:45; 8:15).

12:35-59. Eschatology: future and present. This subsection offers three parables (vv. 35-48) dealing with the future and three clusters of sayings, including one parable, dealing with the significance of the present time (vv. 49-59).

The three parables dealing with the future all involve the theme of readiness. One must be ready for the future coming of the *master* (vv. 36, 43), that is, *Son of Man* (v. 40), for when he comes he will bring judgment. Luke's readers know this master/Son of Man to be Jesus and the subject to be the PAROUSIA.

Verses 41-48 show that these warnings of readiness are not just *for us [but] for everyone*. All disciples, not just the inner circle of Jesus' time, need to hear these exhortations to readiness. This last parable not only speaks of readiness, but helps to define it. Readiness consists of the disciples being faithfully *at work* when the master arrives. The *manager* or *slave*, who represents the disciple, *who knew what his master wanted, but did not prepare himself or do what was wanted, will receive a severe beating (v. 47)*. In the parable itself, doing *what was wanted* is described as giving the other slaves *their allowance of food at the proper time*. This is a metaphorical reference to responsible discipleship that is defined for readers by the teachings of Jesus in this entire journey section. The parable concludes with an explicit warning to *everyone to whom much has been given*: *much will be required* (v. 48). With the privileged call of discipleship comes responsibility.

Verses 49-59 focus on the eschatological significance of the present time. The present time is not significant just because the master or Son of Man is coming at some point in the future. The present is significant because the reign of God is breaking in even now.

Verses 49-53 offer a word on the intensity and importance of Jesus' present mission: it brings the *fire* of judgment *to the earth*. It is a mission—a *baptism*—which consumes him completely: *what stress I am under until it is completed!* (v. 50). The judgment Jesus brings involves *division* (cf. 2:34-35 [the *falling and rising of many in Israel*]; 3:16-17 [the separation of the wheat and the chaff]; 7:29-35 [the *children of wisdom* vs. those who *reject the plan of God*]). Such division reaches into the intimacy of the *household*. In the present time one must decide to gather with Jesus or to scatter, to be for Jesus or against him (cf. 11:23).

Verses 54-59. This chapter began with a warning to Jesus' disciples in the presence of the crowds to beware of the *yeast of the Pharisees* (12:1). These verses continue Jesus' warning to *the crowds*. He calls them *hypocrites*—which is the very *yeast of the Pharisees* (12:1). Apparently the crowds are being overcome by the pervasive influence of *this generation* (cf.7:31-35). They must come to see the present time as a time for radical decision. They can *interpret the appearance of the earth and sky,* but they cannot see *the present time* as a time for decision that carries eternal significance. It is the time prophets and kings had longed to see (10:24). It is the time of Satan's demise (10:18). *The kingdom of God has come to you!* (11:20).

This generation is on its way to court (vv. 57-59). One must come to terms with one's *accuser* before one gets to the judgment bench. In short, one must come to terms with Jesus now. It will be too late once one is *dragged before the judge.*

13:1-9. The need to repent. The preceding talk of judgment and decision leads to the issue of repentance. In vv. 1-5 the essential message is that all need to repent. Persons cannot take comfort in the fact that life is going relatively well for them, that they have escaped the sword of Pilate or the catastrophe of falling buildings. Jesus indicates here that such fortune or lack of misfortune does not denote one's innocence before God: *No, I tell you; but unless you repent, you will all perish just as they did.*

The theme of repentance is continued with the parable of the fruitless fig tree (vv. 6-9). Trees that do not bear fruit are cut down. Readers recall echoes of John's preaching about *bearing fruits worthy of repentance* and trees not bearing good fruit being *cut down and thrown into the fire* (3:8-9). In this parable the fruitless tree is given a brief reprieve—it is given one more year to bear fruit. The implication is that the time is short.

13:10-17. Healing on the sabbath. Two important themes are reiterated. One, Luke offers a clear reminder of what is so significant about this present time: it is time when those bound by Satan are set free from his bondage (cf. 4:1-44). Two, the story reiterates the theme of division. The *leader of the synagogue,* whom Jesus identifies with the *hypocrites,* the Pharisees and *this generation* (cf. 11:50–12:1), is trying to persuade *the crowd* to his point of view. He is spreading the "yeast" of "hypocrisy" (cf. 12:1). His view is that strict, external sabbath observance takes precedence over human need. This is the kind of religiosity Jesus has condemned in 11:37-44. In this story, *the entire crowd* sides with Jesus. Is the crowd heeding Jesus' warning and call to repentance (13:5)?

13:18-21. Parables of the kingdom. Talk of the release from the bonds of Satan leads logically *(he said therefore)* to talk of the kingdom of God. Both parables are contrast parables—the point of the parable is found in contrasting the beginning with the end result.

Jesus' healings and even resuscitations, impressive as they are, hardly justify the claim that God reigns totally and Satan is now completely bound. True. What one sees now is but the beginning, the *mustard seed* which will *become a tree;* the little bit of *yeast* that will leaven the whole *three measures of flour.* The comparison of the kingdom with *yeast* invites contrast between the leaven of the kingdom and that of the Pharisees (cf. 12:1). The parable affirms that, in the end, the leaven of the kingdom will prevail.

13:22-30. Further warnings. After offering a reminder of the "journey theme" and what is so central to this journey *(Jesus* was *teaching as he made his way to Jerusalem* [v. 22]), Luke presents Jesus giving more warnings to his listeners. Verses 24-27 prevent one from being too optimistic about the ultimate response of the crowd to Jesus (contra 13:17). The door leading to salvation is *narrow* and although *many . . . will try to enter,* they *will not be able.* Reflection upon the "demands of discipleship" makes clear why (cf. 9:57-62). When judgment day comes, having been in the presence of Jesus (as are the crowds, Jewish leaders, and even disciples as he journeys to Jerusalem) will not be sufficient. When the festive banquet of the kingdom begins (vv. 28-30) *you* will be *thrown out,* while *people* from all over the world *will eat in the kingdom of God.* Jesus could hardly offer a more dire warning to his audience: some of these who have been *the first* to hear this word of the kingdom *will be last* when judgment comes.

13:31-35. The Pharisees warn Jesus. The way that Pharisees have been presented to this point (cf. esp. 11:37-44; 12:1) hardly allows readers to view their motives as above suspicion. They bear bad news. HEROD, who killed John (8:9), now wishes to kill Jesus. Jesus' work of liberation (exorcisms and cures) will not be deterred, for his mission is driven by divine necessity. (The *must* of v. 33 translates the Gk. δεῖ [see comment on 9:18-36]). The reference to *today, tomorrow, and . . . the third day/next day* should not be taken literally—that Jesus' work will be completed within the next seventy-two hours. Such wording points to the deliberateness of God's plan.

Jesus' work of liberation culminates in JERUSALEM, where the prophets are destined to die (vv. 33b-34). Jesus' "exodus" (9:31) and being "taken up" (9:51) will occur in the city which *kills the prophets and . . . those who are sent to it* (cf. Jer 26:20-23). Jesus falls short of explicitly predicting his death there, but readers will get the point. Sadly, Jesus wishes *to gather your children together* but *you are not willing.* Consequently, "your house is abandoned" (author trans.). "House" may refer either to the city, the temple, or the leadership—the meaning is still the same. The irony is that the word translated "abandoned" is the same Gk. word translated as "release" or "forgiveness" in many significant texts (4:18; 5:20; 7:48; 11:4). Jesus came to offer "release"; Jerusalem's response ensures "abandonment." Jesus concludes with a curious prophecy about what must happen before Jerusalem will *see* him. Is Jesus talking about literal sight, or more in-depth sight (cf. 8:10; 19:38)?

The Leaven of the Pharisees, 14:1–16:31

Jesus has warned his audience of disciples and crowds to beware of the Pharisees' leaven (12:1), the quintessential example of *this generation* (cf.7:31-35). This section is devoted primarily to an exposure of that corrupting yeast and some of the consequences of yielding to it.

14:1-24. Dining with the Pharisees and lawyers. Luke wastes no time in continuing his indictment of these Pharisees and their allies, the lawyers. Jesus is on his way to eat with them, but their invitation should not fool readers. They want to *watch him closely.* Such watching is motivated by sinister intentions: *to catch him in something that he might say* (see 11:54). On the way, Jesus performs a sabbath healing which again exposes the contrast between Jesus' and the Pharisees' notion of what is *lawful.* The Pharisees are not persuaded by Jesus' rhetorical question. They have learned only that they cannot successfully challenge him. Jesus' question of v. 5, reminiscent of 13:15-16, reminds readers that this healing is ultimately about liberation of people from the bonds of evil.

Verses 7-14. Noting how the Pharisees jockey for *the places of honor* (vindicating Jesus' charge of 11:43), Jesus offers a parable that puts their lack of humility into the proper perspective. On the level of social decorum, the jockeying of the Pharisees was most inappropriate (cf. Prov 25:6-7). Verse 11 gives this parable about the public humiliation of the arrogant a more general application. Yet talk of the proud being humbled and the humble being exalted gives the whole scene an eschatological application (cf. 1:51-53; 6:20-26; 13:29-30). These Pharisees show themselves to belong to the proud and mighty whom God's judgment will bring down.

Jesus presses his point further, still using the meal setting as context for his teaching. He encourages *the*

one *who had invited him* (a Pharisee, 14:1), to invite to his *banquet* those who cannot reciprocate (*the poor, crippled, lame, and blind*). This is consistent with what Jesus taught earlier in 6:30, 34. Why should one do such a thing? Because *you will be repaid at the resurrection of the righteous.* Nothing in the story indicates that Jesus' host would consider inviting such people, implying that he does not show concern for those whom Jesus, God's Spirit-anointed prophet, shows concern. Such lack of concern further implies that the Pharisee does not belong to "the righteous" destined for resurrection.

Verses 15-24. A guest catches the eschatological allusions of Jesus and pronounces a blessing on those *who will eat bread in the kingdom of God.* Jesus' parable about *someone [who] gave a great dinner* offers a rather direct message: only those who respond positively to the invitation to the banquet of the kingdom will participate in that banquet. Jesus and his followers have thus far in Luke's Gospel made reference to the reign of God some twenty times, as early as 4:43 and recently as 13:29. Yet the Pharisees and their kind (*this generation*) have yet to say yes to the invitation. Who is saying "yes"? The kind one would not think of inviting to a banquet in the first place: *the poor, crippled, blind, and lame* (v. 21; cf. 14:13) and those who reside in the *roads and lanes* (v. 22). These social outcasts represent not only literally those whom Jesus is inviting to share in the kingdom's blessing (cf. 7:22), but the spiritual outcasts as well—the tax collectors and sinners—whom Jesus also invites (cf. 5:27-32). The concluding line of the story serves as Jesus' closing line to his Pharisaic hosts: *none of those who were invited will taste my dinner* (v. 24). Why? The parable gives the answer: they chose not to come.

14:25-35. Counting the costs. The audience changes from Pharisees to *large crowds . . . traveling with him.* The crowds' being with Jesus offers another hopeful sign that they will heed Jesus' warning concerning the Pharisees' leaven (12:1). Jesus refuses to soften his message, however: the door into salvation is narrow (13:24) and he does the crowds no favors not to spell out clearly the demands if they are to continue to travel with him.

Jesus demands loyalty beyond family and even self (vv. 26-27). Literal hatred of anyone is not consistent with the message of Luke's Jesus (cf. 6:27; 10:27-28). The strong language confronts the crowds (and the reader) with how thorough and radical the demand of Jesus is. Are the crowds willing to risk what Jesus ldemands? Just as one does not begin to *build a tower* unless one is sure that he can finish the project; just as a king does not go to war unless he is sure that he can successfully oppose the approaching army, one should not pick up the cross (v. 27) unless one is ready to follow through with total commitment—and that includes that one *give up all [one's] possessions.* Would-be disciples who turn back after putting their hands to the plow (cf. 9:62) are worth less than worthless salt that one would not even throw on the dung-heap (vv. 34-35). Although Luke's Jesus would want to take the masses "under his wing" as he would even Jerusalem (cf. 13:34), he will pull no punches with them to persuade them to follow.

15:1-32. Pharisees and scribes oppose the mercy of God. The Pharisees and scribes show their contempt for Jesus' association with the spiritual equivalent of those types whom they would *not* invite to *their* banquets (cf. 14:13). While the *tax collectors and sinners* wish *to hear* Jesus, the Pharisees and scribes *were grumbling and saying* that Jesus *welcomes sinners and eats with them.* They have raised this objection before and Jesus has before responded to their objection (5:29-32). Now Jesus offers three parables that not only address why he associates with such types but that challenge their attitudes as well.

The parables of the lost sheep (vv. 3-7) and the lost coin (vv. 8-9) carry the same message. Both the shepherd and the woman value highly what is lost. Such extraordinary concern is indicated by shepherd's willingness to *leave the ninety-nine in the wilderness and go after the one that is lost* and the care he shows the sheep, laying *it on his shoulders.* Concern is shown in the way the woman searches for the lost coin (lighting the lamp and sweeping the house). To be sure, the parables end with a word about repentance—but repentance is preceded by persistent searching on the part of characters who represent God. Why would God take the initiative to look for sinners in the way depicted by these parabolic characters and react with such joy over their repentance? The reader must supply the only possible answer. God is merciful (cf. 6:36).

The parable of the prodigal son (vv. 11-32) offers insight into three different characters, each easily representing characters in Luke's story. The father, so anxious and willing to forgive the erring son, provides a glimpse of the mercy and love of God. Clearly the father was mistreated by his younger son who literally could not wait until he was dead to inherit his *share of the property* (v. 12). In receiving back his son with

joyous celebration—the best robe, rings, sandals, and veal (v. 22-23)—he portrays the God who *is kind to the ungrateful and the wicked* (see 6:35).

The younger son illustrates well that as much as God may take the merciful initiative (as demonstrated by the first two parables), sinners are not really passive sheep or inanimate coins. The younger son *came to himself* (v. 17) and resolved to confess his sin before his father (v. 18). The parable expresses no interest in the motives of the son. One can argue that he was seeking his own best interest—being a slave is better than eating pig slop. The father, however, is not interested in pure motives. He is interested in receiving the lost. That too is merciful.

The elder son illustrates the *grumbling* Pharisees and scribes (v. 2). He begrudges the father's forgiveness of the younger brother (whom the elder brother can only bring himself to call *this son of yours,* v. 30). What is further exposed in his conversation with his father is how baseless the elder brother's fear and jealousy is. The father loves the obedient son no less simply because he also loves the son who was lost: *Son, you are always with me, and all that is mine is yours* (v. 31). Thus his son simply has no good reason not to *rejoice* because *this brother of yours was dead and has come to life.* Likewise, the Pharisees and scribes who are opposed to God's sharing of his love with those who need his forgiveness have no good reason either.

16:1-15. The dishonest manager and wealth. The primary audience of this section is *the disciples,* although *the Pharisees* (v. 14) are also present. The portion of the story has three sections. Verses 1-8a present the parable of the dishonest manager. Verses 8b-13 offer general application of the meaning of the parable. Verses 14-15 offer specific application to and judgment of the Pharisees.

The parable of the dishonest manager is confusing to many because *the master commended the dishonest manager because he had acted shrewdly* (v. 8). What impresses the master, despite the fact that he will still have to fire the manager, is that the manager, when faced with the prospect of being turned out into the streets either to *dig* ditches or *to beg,* devised a plan to protect himself. He took a course of action to ensure that *people may welcome [him] into their homes* once he was dismissed. What the manager did, of course, was to reduce the amount due from his master's debtors. Whether the manager was stealing one last time from his master by fixing the books or merely writing off his own healthy commission is not clear nor that significant. The point is that he used money to lay a foundation for the future.

In vv. 8b-15 Jesus invites the disciples to use wealth as a means of laying a foundation for the future—the ultimate future. Surely if *the children of this age* can do this, *the children of light* can. Just as the dishonest manager used wealth that people might welcome him into their homes (v. 4), Jesus exhorts the disciples to use *dishonest wealth* (lit. "unrighteous mammon," used here to denote "money") *that they* [probably a circumlocution for God] *may welcome you into the eternal homes.*

Jesus continues his application in vv. 10-13. Verse 10 makes clear that the issue here is *faithful* use of that to which one has been entrusted. On this earth, God entrusted his children to deal with money (*dishonest wealth*). If they cannot deal responsibly with that, *who will entrust you with true riches?*, which probably denotes spiritual wealth. If disciples cannot be *faithful with what belongs to another*, an allusion to money that is "on trust from God" (Marshall 1978, 623), *who will give you what is your own?*, an allusion most likely to *treasure in heaven* (see 12:33). Verse 13 indicates that what is at stake in the way one uses money is the issue of whether one is truly devoted to God or something else. Unfaithful use of wealth, of which the upcoming parable offers an excellent illustration, renders one a *slave* to *wealth* and a despiser of God.

The Pharisees, described as *lovers of wealth*, ridicule such a notion. By their own response they show where their loyalties lie. They are people more concerned to *justify* themselves (cf. 10:29) than God (cf. 7:29-30). Thus, what they value *is an abomination in the sight of God* (v. 15). No wonder theirs is a leaven which must be utterly avoided!

16:16-18. The law and the prophets. Hans Conzelmann (1982, 157-69) argued that v. 16 served as the key to Luke's view of history: phase one was the period of the *law and the prophets*, which *were in effect until [and including the time when] John came. Since then*, phase two, the proclamation *of the kingdom of God* by Jesus, is in effect. Phase three, the era of the church, will begin with the outpouring the Spirit. Conzelmann drew the lines too sharply between the old and the new. As Jesus himself says in the very next verse *the law* is still very much in force; in fact *it is easier for heaven and earth to pass away* than for even one *stroke . . . in the letter to be dropped.*

Verse 18 illustrates just how much in force it is! In fact, the demand of the law, interpreted in the context of the kingdom of God, is intensified. *Adultery* is no longer confined to "sleeping with another person's spouse." It includes even the perverse legal niceties people use to justify breaking a marriage covenant.

With respect to the *kingdom of God*, Jesus says that *everyone tries to enter it by force*. Perhaps a better translation is the NRSV marginal note: *everyone is strongly urged to enter it.* This kingdom is something to which one *must* respond. The consequences for not entering the kingdom are disastrous, as the next parable clearly shows.

16:19-31. The rich man and Lazarus. This is a fitting parable to conclude this section aimed at the Pharisees' corrupting brand of religion. The audience is still the disciples (16:1), to whom the parable offers warning, and the Pharisees to whom the parable offers judgment as lovers of money (16:14).

The rich man, traditionally known as Dives (Latin for "rich man"), clearly does not use his wealth in such a way so as to be "welcomed in eternal homes" (16:9). After reading this parable, no one is left wondering just what Jesus meant by not being "faithful with dishonest wealth" (16:11). Ignoring the plight of the poor and oppressed, whom Jesus and the kingdom have come to liberate, is to oppose the liberating work of the kingdom and to be against Jesus (11:23).

The words of ABRAHAM in vv. 29 and 31 allude back to Jesus' comments concerning the law and the prophets in 16:16-17. The implication is that one who truly "hears" (*listen*, NRSV) *Moses and the prophets* will know that such contemptuous use of wealth is eternally damnable. The message of the kingdom is not adding anything new to the Law and the Prophets, nor is it diminishing this aspect of the Law's and the Prophets' demand for justice. Dives, as an example of one who embodies the Pharisees' love of money, offers clear reason to the disciples and readers why the leaven of the Pharisees must be utterly avoided.

Verse 31 offers an ironic allusion to the resurrection of Jesus. People who cannot "hear" the message of the Law and the Prophets will not be convinced even by one rising from the dead (cf. Acts 13:26-41). This concluding word offers a harbinger of the ultimate reaction of the Jewish leadership to the message of the kingdom—and an ominous warning as to what side of the eternal *chasm* they and people like them will end up on.

Persistence for the Journey to Come, 17:1–18:30

The disciples are not the exclusive focus of this section, but they are certainly the primary focus. Furthermore, many of Jesus' words concern issues that would be facing the church of Luke's time—the time of the church's journey.

17:1-10. Demands and duty. Verses 1-4 offer two difficult demands for life among disciples. Verses 1-2 acknowledge that *occasions for stumbling* will come. Jesus requires that disciples not be the ones to *cause one of these little ones* (other followers) *to stumble*. The second demand, vv. 3-4, requires disciples to forgive—offer "release" to (cf. 4:18)—those who sin against them and *turn back* (meaning "repent"). Disciples share in the liberating work of the kingdom is by the offering of forgiveness to others.

Such demands require faith (vv. 5-6), even for *apostles*. The Greek construction of Jesus' answer *does* assume such faith—little as it may be (contrary to NRSV). Only a little faith is needed to accomplish great things, such as watching out for and forgiving others.

Verses 7-10 offer a parable making clear that when disciples *have done all that [they] were ordered to do* it is not cause for self-adulation, for they *have done only what [they] ought to have done.*

17:11-19. The ten lepers. Luke offers another story of healing, the meaning of which readers are now accustomed to hearing: faith in Jesus brings salvation (v. 19, lit., "your faith has saved you"). It is important that such words are pronounced on a *Samaritan foreigner.*

First, v. 11 refers to Jesus being *on the way to Jerusalem* and *going through the region between Samaria and Galilee*, which recalls 9:51 where Jesus, on his way to Jerusalem, was rejected by the Samaritans. Here Jesus pronounces the same word of salvation upon a Samaritan that he has pronounced on Jews earlier (cf. 7:50; 8:48). The fact that this Samaritan *turned back* (v. 15, same Gk. word found in 17:4), allows Jesus to illustrate how *he* responds to those who "turn back": he offers salvation. Second, this Samaritan's *praising God* serves to foreshadow the response that Samaria would give to the gospel later in Acts (Acts 8:5-25).

17:20-37. The kingdom of God and seeing the Son of Man. The question of *the Pharisees* (vv. 20-21) concerning *when the kingdom of God was coming* lets Luke reiterate that the power of God's reign is already active in the world *among you* (v. 21). ("Within you"

[NIV, NRSV mg.] assumes an inner-spiritualistic view of God's reign that does not do justice to the kind of reign Luke's Jesus proclaims.) The Pharisees' inability to see the kingdom reveals their blindness (cf. esp. 11:14-36).

Attention is turned again to the disciples and *the days of the Son of Man* (v. 22; cf. vv. 24, 26). The subject here is the PAROUSIA. The coming of the Son of Man, like the reign of God, is not something that one can localize *there* or *here*. Unlike the reign of God, whose presence in the world can be missed, the coming of the Son of Man cannot be missed, for it is like the *lightening* flash which *lights up the sky from one side to the other*. Thus disciples need not be distracted by over-zealous cries that the Son of Man is already *there* or *here* (cf. 2 Thes 2:1-2). To silence any speculation that Jesus' current ministry represents the *days of the Son of Man*, Jesus reminds the disciples that he must first *be rejected by this generation*. Such words remind readers of the severe judgment Jesus has already pronounced on this *generation* (cf. 11:49-52).

Verses 26-37 envisages the judgment on the generation that rejects the Son of Man. The judgment will fall with complete surprise as *in the days of Noah* and *the days of Lot*. Verses 31-32 offer images of persons facing catastrophe. There is no time to gather one's possessions! No time to look back! One must escape to safety! These vivid illustrations show that in the *days of the Son of Man* (v.22) there will be no escape: *one will be taken and the other left*. Only those who were willing to *lose their life* for the sake of Christ (cf. 14:26-27) and the kingdom of God (cf. 18:29) *will keep* their lives. Where will those be who are left? *Where . . . the vultures will gather*—as food for the birds (v. 37).

18:1-14. Persistent and genuine prayer. The stark images of judgment make Jesus' following comments on prayer most appropriate. Jesus' question of 18:8, *When the Son of Man comes, will he find faith on earth?*, indicates that these words on prayer should be heard in the context of the preceding words on the *days of the Son of Man* (17:22). The Greek construction implies that the question is asked in an anxious frame of mind, betraying the seriousness of the question. Only each disciple, and each reader, can answer the question for him or herself. Hard times are coming. Will the disciple endure? Only by prayer.

The parable and application of the widow (vv.1-8) offers another example of Jesus arguing from the lesser to the greater (cf. 11:5-8). If an *unjust judge . . .*

will grant her justice simply not to be bothered, surely God *will . . . grant justice to his chosen ones who cry to him day and night.* Indeed, he will do it *quickly*.

The parable of the Pharisee and tax collector (vv. 9-14) is directed at persons *who trusted in themselves that they were righteous and regarded others with contempt*. Fittingly, Jesus uses a Pharisee as the example of that kind of person. Yet the words are not addressed only to Pharisees. Disciples in the journey to come need to beware of such a disposition. Jesus has come to invite sinners and the many types of social outcasts to repent and share in the reign of God (5:32; 14:21). In his mercy God is anxious to receive such persons (cf. chap. 15). The one who recognizes this, such as the tax collector of this parable, is the one who will go *down to his home justified*.

18:15-17. Jesus and the children. This story illustrates that *disciples* were not (or are not) immune from holding others in contempt, as they *sternly ordered* people not to bring their *infants* to Jesus. Jesus does not call upon *the little children* to repent or to become disciples, but he does command that people *let* (lit. "release"!) *the little children come to him . . . for it is to such as these that the kingdom of God belongs*. While the story does affirm God's love of *even infants*, it is also about the spirit with which one must receive the kingdom—*as a little child*: complete trust in the care and mercy of God—like the tax collector of the preceding parable.

18:18-30. A final word on wealth. Wealth is an important issue to Luke (cf. e.g., 6:30, 34; 8:3, 14; 12:13-34; 14:33; 16:1-14, 19-31). It is fitting, therefore, that this section, which offers teachings for the journey to come conclude with a word on the topic. This final word offers three sub-sections: the story of the rich ruler (vv. 18-23), Jesus' interpretation (vv. 24-26), and Jesus' final word to Peter (vv. 28-30).

Jesus' response to the appellation *Good Teacher* (v.18) should be viewed neither as a denial that he is good nor as a coy way of identifying himself with God. His response reminds the ruler and readers that all that is genuinely good, including *eternal life*, is found in *God alone*. The ruler wants to know what he must *do to inherit eternal life*. Jesus has heard the question before (10:25). Here, as there, Jesus looks to the law. The ruler insists that he has *kept all these [commandments] since [his] youth*. Jesus insists that *there is still one thing lacking*. This ruler is bound by his possessions. Hence, Jesus requires of him what he said in 12:33 that he requires of all disciples: *sell your*

possessions, and give alms. Make . . . for yourselves . . . an unfailing treasure in heaven. The ruler counts the costs and realizes that the price of eternal life is too high.

Jesus' interpretation assumes what he has tried to make clear throughout the Gospel. *Total* surrender to him is necessary: family, life, and possessions (14:26-33). The sad fact is that the rich are too blessed for their own good. They have so much to surrender. Thus, it is *hard . . . for those who have wealth to enter the kingdom of God!* (v.24). It is *hard* for everyone. Family, life, and even meager possessions are humanly impossible to abandon. *What is impossible for mortals is possible for God* (v.26). This echoes what the angel said to Mary (1:37). God does not force his possibilities on people. One must respond to what he makes possible even as Mary did: *let it be with me according to your word* (1:38).

Peter reminds Jesus that he and the disciples *have left [their] homes and followed* Jesus (cf. 5:11). The word translated *homes* is literally "our own things" and is used in Acts to denote friends (4:23; 24:23), financial resources (4:32; 28:30), and homes (21:6). The disciples are not perfect, but they have left it all behind to follow Jesus. He promises them *much more in this age* ("perhaps a reference to the new family in the church" [Talbert 1986, 173]) and *in the age to come eternal life*. A most fitting promise to end a section offering guidance to disciples for the "journey to come."

Approaching Jerusalem, 18:31–19:44

This last portion of the "journey to Jerusalem" begins with a final prediction of the passion of Jesus in Jerusalem (18:31-34) and ends with Jesus approaching and weeping over the city (19:41). In between, some important events and words performed and spoken in Jericho are narrated (18:35-19:28).

18:31-34. The passion foretold. This is the fourth PASSION prediction in Luke (cf. 9:22, 44-45; 17:25). It is by far the most detailed and specific: Jesus will die in Jerusalem in order to accomplish *everything that is written about the Son of Man by the prophets*. As horrifying as the Jerusalem events will be, they are according to the plan of God. The disciples do not understand (cf. 9:45), and Luke seems purposefully mysterious as to the cause. More important than who or what has *hidden . . . what he said . . . from them* is whether they will ever come to see.

18:35-43. The first Jericho story: healing a blind man. It is not accidental that word of the disciples' lack of understanding sets the stage for a story about a blind man. In this story readers encounter one who can see who Jesus is and what he is all about. The blind man hails Jesus as *Son of David*, a designation of Jesus as the Messiah (cf. 1:32, 69). He also knows the mission of this *Son of David*: to show *mercy* (cf. chap. 15). He approaches Jesus with the kind of *faith* that others have demonstrated before and Jesus pronounces a word with which readers have become familiar: literally, *your faith has saved you* (v. 42; cf. 7:50; 8:48, cf. v. 50; 17:19). The blind man has come truly "to see" as evidenced by his reaction: he *followed him, glorifying God*. Perhaps *the people* as well are seeing more clearly, for *all the people, when they saw it, praised God.*

19:1-10. The second Jericho story: Zacchaeus. This too involves a man who wanted *to see who Jesus was*. Unlike the blind man, Zacchaeus is restricted by more than his physical limitations—his profession as a *chief tax collector* who *was rich* makes him an example of the rich whom it is virtually impossible to save (cf. 18:23-26). Zacchaeus, this *Son of Abraham*, however, is willing to let go of that which binds him to this age. Like the daughter of Abraham whom Jesus released from the bondage of Satan (cf. 13:16), Jesus releases Zacchaeus. Unlike the rich ruler who was *sad* (cf. 18:23), Zacchaeus bears *fruits worthy of repentance* which characterize the true *children of Abraham* (cf. 3:8). For Zacchaeus declares, *Half of my possessions . . . I will give to the poor; and if I have defrauded anyone of anything, I will pay back four times as much* (v. 8; cf. 3:12-13).

The reaction of *all who saw it*, presumably the same people who just moments ago were praising God (cf. 18:43), is identical to the reaction of the Pharisees and scribes when they saw Jesus associating with tax collectors and sinners (cf. 15:1-2). In both instances there was grumbling (v. 7; cf. 15:2). Jesus' mission as the *Son of Man* is *to seek out and save the lost*. Will the masses ever come to see this?

19:11-28. The third Jericho story: the parable of the pounds. Luke indicates that the parable is prompted by the fact that *he was near Jerusalem, and because they supposed that the kingdom of God was to appear immediately* (v. 11). The parable as a whole informs readers that the kingdom of God did not appear with Jesus' arrival in Jerusalem. Talbert is perhaps correct that "in Luke's church . . . some disciples were regarding events in Jerusalem (Jesus' resurrection and ascen-

sion) as the PAROUSIA. In response the evangelist is saying 'not yet'" (Talbert 1986, 178).

There are three main characters, *a nobleman, slaves,* and *citizens of his country*, all of which are open to allegorical interpretation, representing, respectively, Jesus, his disciples, and the Jews who reject him. The parable directs attention away from the false notion that the *kingdom of God* appeared with Jesus' arrival in Jerusalem and redirects attention to the future.

The *nobleman* is going away for a while *to get royal power for himself and then return* (v. 12). In the meantime his *slaves* are given equal amounts of responsibility, represented by the *ten pounds* given to *ten of his slaves*, presumably one to each. They are to *do business with these until I come back. . . . When he returned, having received royal power* (vv. 14-15), he summoned the slaves to see what they had done with the pounds for which they had been given responsibility. The overall message is clear: those who used fruitfully what the nobleman had given them are rewarded; those who did not will not be rewarded. In fact, even what they have will be taken away. The message is harsh, but it is quite consistent with the message heard throughout the Gospel: following Jesus requires total commitment and dedication.

The citizens reject *the nobleman* because they *do not want this man to rule over* them. Their punishment was most harsh *when he returned*. He calls these citizens *these enemies of mine who did not want me to be king over them* and orders that they be slaughtered in his presence (v. 27).

Luke concludes bluntly: *After he had said this, he went on ahead, going up to Jerusalem* (v. 28). This journey section is about to come to a close. Israel, consisting of disciples, crowds, and the Jewish leadership have had opportunity to hear the word of God's Son (cf. 9:35). This concluding parable makes clear the consequences of not hearing.

19:29-40. Descending the Mount of Olives. Jesus' preparation to enter the city of Jerusalem is introduced by the story of the disciples' securing a colt for him. The impression left is that some sort of supernatural prescience on Jesus' part is involved. This impression reinforces the notion that what lies ahead in Jerusalem is according to some larger plan. As Jesus descends down the Mount of Olives he is greeted by the cry of *the whole multitude of the disciples*. Their cry, *Blessed is the king who comes in the name of the Lord* (v. 38), is a clear echo of 13:35 where Jesus said that Jerusalem would not see him until it offered a similar cry.

Two things stand out. One, it is not Jerusalem that makes this cry. Only the disciples do. Jerusalem has not offered the cry Jesus says it must if it is truly to "see" him. In fact, *the Pharisees*, the closest representatives to "Jerusalem" in this story, want Jesus to rebuke his disciples into silence. Jerusalem, it seems, does not "see" who Jesus really is. Will it ever? Two, the disciples hail Jesus as *the king*. This harks back to 19:27. These disciples are not like the citizens of that parable who did not want the nobleman to be their king. Like the blind man of Jericho (18:35-43), the disciples have come to see who Jesus is. No one else seems to. This does not bid well for the citizens of Jerusalem, but it does seem that at least a portion of Israel, the disciples, has listened to the SON OF GOD during the journey to the city (cf. 9:35).

19:41-44. Jesus weeps over Jerusalem. Jesus has still not reached Jerusalem, but as he approached it *he wept over it*. Jerusalem, unlike the disciples who cried *Peace in heaven!* (19:38), does not "see" *the things that make for peace;* in fact, *these things are hidden from [its] eyes* (v. 42). The consequences are devastating: Jerusalem and its inhabitants will be destroyed. "God has visited his people" (author trans. of 7:16b) in Jesus, but Jerusalem, the city of God's people, *did not recognize the time of [its] visitation* (v. 44).

The fate of Jerusalem and its people now seems a foregone conclusion. Jesus had earlier said that *this generation* would be charged with the blood of the prophets (cf. 11:49-50), including, it seems, the blood of the prophet Jesus (cf. 13:33-35a). Luke 17:25-37 envisaged the judgment to come to *this generation* that rejects the Son of Man.

Apparently, part of the punishment of *this generation* will include judgment against Jerusalem and its inhabitants as *they will crush you [Jerusalem] to the ground, you and your children within you* (v. 44). There seems only one means of escape: to separate oneself from *this generation* and accept Jesus as king. That will not save Jerusalem, but at least one might save oneself. Upon entering Jerusalem Jesus will present the word one more time to all the people of Israel. How will they respond?

Exodus from Jerusalem, 19:45–24:53

With the arrival of Jesus at the Temple (19:45), Jesus arrives in Jerusalem. He can now fulfill the exodus from this city about which MOSES and ELIJAH

had spoken (9:31). There are three steps to fulfill this exodus: one, Jesus' teaching of *all the people* of Israel in the Temple (19:45-21:38); two, Jesus' passion, the *hour of darkness* (cf. 22:53; 23:44); three, Jesus' *entrance into glory* (24:26).

The Temple Ministry, 19:45–21:38

19:45-46. The cleansing of the Temple. Before Jesus can teach from the Temple, he must possess it. He must transform this place, intended as a *house of prayer* (Isa. 56:7) but *made* into a *den of robbers* (Jer 7:11), that it might be worthy the king's (19:38) presence.

19:47-48. The opening notice of Jesus' teaching. Luke 19:47-48 and 21:37-38 mark the beginning and ending of this section. Both passages state that every day *he was teaching in the temple* and that his audience was "all the people." Luke consistently uses "people" to denote "Israel" (cf. 1:68) and, thus, in a sense Jesus, the Messiah, is teaching "Israel" in its holy Temple, calling it to a decision.

Here Luke presents a division between *all the people* and *the chief priests, scribes, and the leaders of the people*. The Pharisees have disappeared. It is clear that their role is now assumed by these representatives of Jerusalem leadership—the officers of the SANHEDRIN, or ruling assembly (cf. 22:66), who are *looking for a way to kill him. The people* of Jerusalem failed to welcome Jesus as the king. Now, if they will only remain on the side of Jesus and opposed to their leaders, perhaps they can escape the fate of Jerusalem (19:41-44) and *this generation* (11:49-52; 17:25-37).

20:1-8. Jesus' authority. The Jerusalem leadership begins its attack on Jesus by questioning the source of his *authority* to do *these things*, referring to seizing the Temple and teaching the people from it. This is a legitimate question for the religious leadership to ask, assuming they are sincere in their question. Jesus asks them to decide the source of John's authority—and, implicitly, his own. Was it human or divine? They deliberate, not because they are really interested in the issue itself (although as the leaders of Israel they certainly should be!), but only for jaded, political reasons. Is there any way to win this bout with Jesus? They decide they cannot win and retreat, exposing their insincere motives in asking the question. Having exposed their motives, Jesus is under no obligation to answer their question.

20:9-19. Parable of the tenants. Jesus goes on the offensive against his opponents (v. 19), offering a parable and interpretation. The parable, vv. 9-16, is open to allegorical interpretation, with the *vineyard* representing Israel (cf. Isa 5:1-7), *the owner* representing God, *the tenants* representing the Jewish leadership, and *the son* representing Jesus. The meaning is clear: the Jewish leadership rejects all of God's messengers, including even his son, whom they kill. As a consequence, God will *destroy those tenants [the leaders] and give the vineyard [Israel] to others* (v. 16). Israel is *not* destroyed—only its leaders! Who are the others? (cf. 22:28-30).

The people, to whom Jesus is telling the parable, react in horror (*Heaven forbid!*, v. 16), recognizing the ominous tone of his message. Jesus drives his message home, quoting from Ps 118:22 and Isa 8:14-15. He is the *stone* the *builders* (the leaders) will reject. He will be vindicated; he will *become the cornerstone*. In addition, he will become a stone that will trip up and crush those who opposed him. The option of the people seems clear: do not side with *the builders*!

20:20-26. Taxes to Caesar. The *spies*, sent from the leadership, possess the pseudo-righteousness of the Pharisees (NRSV *honest*; lit. "righteous"; cf. 18:9). They flatter Jesus (v. 21) with words they do not mean, but with words which are, nonetheless, absolutely true. Their goal is to place Jesus in the untenable position of either loosing credibility *in the presence of the people* by advocating payment of taxes, or placing himself in legal jeopardy with the *authority of the governor* by advocating refusal to pay taxes.

Jesus' answer (v. 25) does not speak of divided loyalties, but of legitimate obligations. Jesus does not deny the legitimacy of giving the Roman emperor back his due of his own money, money that, ironically, not Jesus but only his opponents carry in their pockets. One must give to God what is God's due. Readers should recall 10:27-28. God's due is total love and devotion. Such total devotion does require that when obligations to human beings conflict with loyalty to God, one must "obey God rather than any human authority" (as Peter proclaims in Acts 5:29).

20:27-40. The question of the resurrection. *Some Sadducees* now try to challenge Jesus. The *chief priests* and perhaps even some of *the elders* of 20:1 would have been aligned with this aristocratic, conservative party of Jewish society. Apparently they want to force Jesus either into rejecting the idea of resurrection, an idea to which the Sadducees did not adhere, or into advocating marital infidelities in the afterlife. Either way, he will loose credibility with the people.

They appeal to the Jewish law of Levirate marriage, wherein a widow married the brother of her dead husband (Deut 25:5-6). The Sadducees set up a comical situation, seeming to require Jesus to approve either of bigamy *in the resurrection*, with the woman now having seven husbands for eternity, or of multiple divorces, a practice Jesus has already forbidden (16:18).

Jesus responds, first, by rejecting the assumptions of the Sadducees who wrongly believe that life in *that age* is a continuation of life in *this age* (vv. 35-36). *Marriage* is a divinely sanctioned rite of *this age* to perpetuate the human race (cf. Gen 1:28). It is not necessary for the *children of the resurrection* for *they cannot die anymore*. Second (vv. 37-38), Jesus affirms the idea of resurrection by appealing to the Torah (Exod 3:6), the portion of scripture which the Sadducees recognized as authoritative. He asserts that God would not refer to himself as the God of Moses' ancestors if they were dead at the time God spoke to Moses, for God *is not God of the dead, but of the living*. Hence, the three ancestors must have been *living*. Thus, *the dead are raised*.

Even *some of scribes* had to acknowledge that Jesus was right (v. 39). Verse 40 indicates that attempts to *question* Jesus are finished. Will the leadership give up or resort to other means to kill Jesus?

20:41-47. Jesus' conclusion. In vv. 41-44, Jesus addresses the question of authority raised in 20:2. Jesus acts on the authority of *the king* (19:38) and the Messiah (2:11; 9:20), the son of David (1:32, 69; 18:35-43). How is Jesus this son of David? Ps 110:1 provides the answer. Jesus is rightly understood as the Messiah and son of David when he is understood as the one who is also David's Lord, who sits at the *right hand* of God until his *enemies* are subdued. By this kingly authority Jesus does *these things* (cf. 20:2).

Earlier Jesus warned the disciples in the presence of the crowd to *beware of the yeast of the Pharisees* (12:1). In vv. 45-47, Jesus, *in the hearing of all the people*, offers a word of warning *to the disciples* to *beware of the scribes*. His description of the scribes is similar to what he said about the Pharisees (cf. 11:43; 14:7). The people and the disciples must beware of all elements of the Jewish religious leadership: the Pharisees, the scribes, and the chief priests and elders. It is they who evict *widows* while they *say long prayers*, and who are destined for *the greater condemnation*.

21:1-4. The widow's offering. Having just spoken of widows, Luke now tells a story about a widow's offering. While the rich contribute to the Temple *out of their abundance, the poor widow* contributes *out of her poverty.* While Jesus may admire her devotion, readers might well wonder how this woman who *has put in all she had to live on* will now live at all. One way that the Temple has become a *den of robbers* (19:46) is by taking the last of the poor's pennies, knowing that they will soon be evicted.

21:5-38. The destruction of Jerusalem and the end of the world. This speech must be read carefully, for it is presented to two audiences *in the story* and an audience *outside the story.* The audience outside the story is Luke's readers. For them, the destruction of the Temple is a past event (70 C.E.) and they would read from that perspective. One audience in the story is Jesus' disciples (20:45). The other audience in the story is the people who call Jesus *teacher* (v. 7). In Luke's Gospel, "only non-disciples refer to Jesus by the title 'teacher'" (Chance 1988, 135–36). Hence, readers of Jesus' words cannot ignore that Jesus is speaking not only to disciples outside and inside the story, but to non-disciples, the people of Jerusalem, inside the story as well. Careful reading is required to maintain a proper focus.

21:5-7. The destruction foretold. The *some* who are with Jesus who speak *about the temple,* includes both the disciples (20:45) and *some* of *all the people* whom Luke describes as *spellbound by what they heard* (19:48). Mention of the Temple prompts Jesus to predict its destruction and to address the question *when will this be?*

21:8-19. Coming catastrophes and persecution. In the story, Jesus is presenting to his audience predictions of what will come prior to destruction of the Temple: the rise of false messiahs, predictions that the *time is near,* political, economic, and even natural upheavals as well as *dreadful portents and signs from heaven.* Luke's readers know these to be past events. The Jewish historian JOSEPHUS wrote of such things occurring before the destruction of Jerusalem (*Ant* 18.4.1; 20.5.1; 20.8.6; *BJ* 6.5.3-4).

Verses 12-19 are directed to the disciples in Jesus' story audience, for they speak of persecutions to come to Jesus' followers *before* the destruction of the Temple and the events of vv. 8-11 (cf. v. 12a). Luke will write of these persecutions in Acts.

21:20-24. The destruction of Jerusalem. These words are addressed to both of Jesus' story audiences, the disciples and the people. After the events of vv. 8-19 *you [will] see Jerusalem surrounded by armies.*

Jesus then begins to talk in the third person about those who will actually experience the destruction of Jerusalem. This allows Jesus' words to apply to any who might live in Jerusalem and its environs when Jerusalem's *desolation has come near,* not just the story audiences. Jesus' words make clear that the destruction of Jerusalem exhibits the *days of vengeance* and speaks *wrath against this people.* Both elements of Jesus' audience must know that the destruction of Jerusalem is God's emphatic word of judgment against *this people.* The gentiles will trample God's holy city, but only *until the times of the Gentiles are fulfilled* (cf. Dan 8:1-14). Both elements of Jesus' audience hear that Jerusalem's trampling is of limited duration. What will happen to Jerusalem, and more importantly its people, after this?

21:25-28. The Son of Man and your redemption. From v. 25 through the remainder of Jesus' speech, Luke's readers and Jesus' story audience are on equal footing, for they are both hearing Jesus speak of things yet-to-come. Great cosmic and natural upheavals will create *distress among the nations* and *foreboding.* Then *they will see "the Son of Man coming." They* probably denotes everybody, the *people* of v. 26 (lit. "humans" [ἄνθρωποι]).

With the coming of the Son of Man comes the end (17:22-37). With the coming of this end comes *your redemption.* Hence, when *these things* [the events of vv. 25-26] *begin to take place* "you" can know that *your redemption is drawing near.* What is the antecedent of "your"? Jesus' story audience consists of both disciples and the people of Jerusalem. Is Jesus promising the people of Jerusalem, as well as the disciples, that when *the times of the Gentiles are fulfilled* (v. 24) they will experience redemption? Might this be the time when Jerusalem will declare, *Blessed is the one who comes in the name of the Lord?* (13:35b)?

21:29-33. Concluding predictions. Jesus offers *them a parable.* "Them" denotes immediately his two story audiences and implies his reading audience. In this parable the same message of v. 28 is reiterated: *the kingdom of God is near* when *you see these things taking place.* Verse 33 offers an emphatic affirmation of the sure authority of Jesus' words. Verse 32 is saying more than all these things will happen before Jesus' contemporaries die. *This generation* denotes those who reject the Son of Man (cf. 17:25) who will experience severe judgment (cf. 11:49-51). *This generation* will not escape the *days of vengeance* (21:22) or the *great distress* and *wrath* (21:23). It shall by no means disappear from the stage until all these things have come upon it.

21:34-38. A final warning. Jesus concludes with a word to his audiences to stay on the alert so that *that day* (the "day of the Son of Man," cf. 17:24; 21:27) will not be one's undoing. Prayer will not allow one to avoid the hard times that are coming, but will allow one *to escape* the judgment that will fall upon *the whole earth* and *to stand before the Son of Man*. Jesus' disciples (both inside and outside the story) must continue in their faithfulness to obey his exhortation. The thus-far uncommitted people must decide whose side they are on.

The comments on 19:47-48 also apply to 21:37-38. What opened in chap. 19 comes to a close in chap. 21.

The Hour of Darkness, 22:1–23:56

This section tells of Jesus' PASSION. The other Gospels tell broadly the same story, with the other two synoptics being most similar to Luke (cf. Matt 26:1–27:66; Mark 14:1–15:47; John 13:1–19:42). John's is much longer in part because of the great attention given to Jesus' discourses (cf. esp. chaps. 14-17). Many interpreters believe a PASSION NARRATIVE to have been one of the earliest connected narratives to be composed by Jesus' early followers. Some argue that Luke had access to two passion narratives: Mark's and an independent narrative (see Fitzmyer 1985, 1359-68).

Luke began the story of Jesus' ministry by telling of direct confrontation between Jesus and the devil (4:1-13), described as a period of "testing." Now Satan reemerges as a direct player in the action (22:3), marshaling his allies of darkness (22:53) in this final time of "testing" (22:46). During this passion story, the three sets of characters with whom Jesus has been dealing in the preceding narrative, disciples, crowds (people), and the Jewish leadership, will have to make firm choices whether they are for or against Jesus (cf. 11:23).

22:1-6. The plot to kill Jesus. *The chief priests and scribes* still seek to kill Jesus (cf. 19:47). There is no question whose side they are on in this struggle. *The people* are not on their side in this plot (cf. 19:48), for an *opportunity* must be found for the leadership to catch Jesus *when no crowd was present*. Sadly, *Judas, one of the twelve*, will provide this *opportunity*. Will all the disciples side with evil? Judas' plot offers a warning that any can be corrupted by the leaven of the Pharisees (cf. 12:1) and join forces with *this genera-*

tion (cf. 17:25). *Satan* is directly involved in creating the *opportunity* to betray Jesus—the *opportune time* he has been waiting for since 4:13. The conflict of the two kingdoms (cf. 11:18-20) is about to reach a critical moment.

22:7-13. Preparing the Passover. The time for the sacrifice and preparation of *the Passover lamb* was the afternoon of 14 Nisan (March/April). The story displays Jesus' prescience (cf. 19:29-34), implying that things are unfolding according to plan.

22:14-23. The last supper. There are some significant textual critical issues in this passage (see NRSV mg.). The commentary below follows the NRSV text.

The Passover meal was eaten the evening after preparation. The Jewish day goes from sundown to sundown, hence, sundown brought the 15th of Nisan. Verses 15-16 imply that Jesus did not share the meal with his disciples, but only led in their eating of it. He declares that he *will not eat it until it is fulfilled in the kingdom of God*. He makes a similar statement about drinking with the disciples (v. 18). Jesus has given notice that the reign of God is already here (cf. 11:20; 17:21). He recently spoke of the reign that is to come (21:31) with the coming of the Son of Man (21:27). It is this reign to which Jesus primarily refers. Jesus promises his disciples that they will eat and drink together at the kingdom's table (cf. 13:28-29).

In vv. 19b-20 Jesus offers an interpretation of the *bread* and *cup* that need not await fulfillment in the kingdom of God to be meaningful. He speaks of the giving of his body and pouring out of his blood *for you* and *the new covenant*. Jesus' mission to inaugurate the reign of God, manifested in the offering of liberation ("release/forgiveness" [cf. 4:18; 5:20] and "salvation" [cf. 7:50]), will include his dying. Jesus' many predictions of his death have implied that. Jesus' relating of his death to *the new covenant* strongly implies that this death is most significant in the accomplishment of his ministry of liberation.

In vv. 21-23 Luke conveys that the tragic plot of Jesus' enemies will succeed. But Jesus' words also make clear *the Son of Man is going as it has been determined*, assuring readers that God is in control of the action.

22:24-34. The flawed, yet faithful, disciples. Readers have read the many attempts on the part of Jesus to lead his disciples into a mature following. The betrayal by Judas (cf. vv. 21-22) reminds readers that even one of the twelve can fall away. The dispute that arises concerning who *was to be regarded as the greatest* shows that even the balance of the disciples have much to learn. Having just spoken of his own death, Jesus calls upon the disciples not to pattern themselves after gentile lords. Rather they are to take their cues from Jesus who is among them *as one who serves*.

The disciples must learn the proper way to lead, for Jesus is conferring upon them *a kingdom*. This promise assures the disciples and the readers that despite their failings the disciples will share rule with Jesus in his kingdom *judging the twelve tribes of Israel*. Why? It is because they are *those who have stood by [Jesus] in [his] trials* (lit. "testing" cf. 4:13). Jesus does not expect perfection. He does demand faithfulness in standing with him in the trials that come in the struggle with evil.

Despite their failures, the disciples have, to this point, stuck with Jesus. Following his resurrection, Jesus will ascend to his throne and begin his reign as Messiah (cf. Acts 2:34-36). It is in this context that the apostles *will sit on thrones* (v. 30) and lead Israel—at least that portion of Israel which comes to recognize Jesus as Messiah and saves itself from "this corrupt generation" (cf. Acts 2:40).

The sad dialogue with Peter (vv. 31-34) communicates that Satan will harass the apostles. Their hitherto "standing" with Jesus will begin to unravel. Even those who want to be faithful will fail. Jesus' prayer will prevent the total failure of faith. When Peter has *turned back* (cf. 17:3-4) he will *strengthen [his] brothers*. Readers will discover in Acts just how effective a leader Peter becomes.

22:35-38. Two swords. Jesus' question of v. 35 refers back to 10:4. *But now*, points to a change of circumstances. The disciples, as they "stand by" Jesus (22:28), are about to enter into the thickest flack in the fray against evil. They must take full provisions, including a *sword*. This makes clear how intense the struggle is to become. The reference to the *sword* is metaphorical, although the disciples take Jesus literally. *It is enough* is Jesus' rebuke of their philistine interpretation. Verse 37 appeals to Isa 53:12 and prepares readers for 23:32.

22:39-46. Prayer in the time of trial. Jesus and the disciples are about to enter *the time of trial* (lit. "testing"). Will the disciples stand with Jesus during the upcoming testing as they have to this point (cf. 22:28)? Testing is not something anyone should want to endure. Thus Jesus exhorts his disciples to pray that they might *not come into* such a *time* (cf. 11:4). Prayer

is the best "provision" (cf. 22:36) one has for the struggle to come. Jesus himself prays a prayer of deliverance (v. 42). Verse 43 is textually questionable (see NRSV mg.), but offers a valid interpretation of why one must pray: it offers *strength*. Prayer for deliverance must include the willingness to do God's will, not one's own (v. 42). The disciples, *sleeping because of grief*, do not rise to the occasion. Satan's sifting (cf. 22:31) has begun. They may not continue to stand with Jesus. Readers recall hopefully the promise Jesus made in 22:32.

22:47-53. The arrest of Jesus. *Judas*, who has chosen to side with evil in the struggle against evil, leads *a crowd* to arrest Jesus. Verse 52 defines the *crowd*: *chief priests . . . the temple police, and the elders*. The disciples *strike with the sword* indicating that they do not grasp that prayer is how they are to engage the enemy in this present time of testing.

The Jewish leaders come to arrest Jesus *as a bandit*. Yet it is they, not Jesus, who have made the Temple a *den of robbers* (19:46, same Gk. word). Such blatant hypocrisy is to be expected, for they have assumed the role of the hypocritical Pharisees (cf. 12:1). More importantly, the Jewish leadership, being led by Judas, whom Satan is leading (22:3), are now explicitly in league with Satan, *the power of darkness* (cf. Acts 26:18). The arrest and subsequent execution of the Son of God is evil's finest *hour*. It will also be evil's undoing.

22:54-65. Peter's denial. Satan's sifting (22:21) continues. As Jesus was led to *the high priest's house* (cf. 3:2 for possible identity), *Peter was following*, but only *at a distance*. Peter's threefold denial shows that he completely fails as a thoroughly loyal disciple willing to give his life for Jesus (cf. 22:33).

Readers should recall that Jesus has promised a kingdom to his disciples because they have "stood with him" (22:28-29). They should also recall the many radical demands that Jesus laid upon those who wished to follow him (cf. esp. 9:23-26, 57-62; 12:49-53; 14:25-35). Throughout this passion narrative, one can hardly be impressed by how the disciples have "stood" or how faithfully they have devoted their lives to Jesus. If, indeed, Jesus does follow through on his promise to give the disciples a kingdom, it will be through no merit of their own. At this point readers may recall Jesus' word that he has prayed for Peter that his faith will not fail utterly. He demands repentance, to be sure (cf. *once you have turned back* [22:32]), but it is Jesus' action on behalf of his disciples that will restore and sustain them. The message of radical mercy rings through. Perhaps Peter realized this as *he wept bitterly.*

The abuse of Jesus (vv. 63-65) shows the utter contempt of Jesus' opponents as they mockingly encourage Jesus to *prophesy!* Readers catch the irony in that they have just witnessed a prophecy of Jesus come to realization as *the cock crowed.*

22:66-71. Hearing before the assembly. *The assembly* is the SANHEDRIN, the Jewish high court. This assembly as depicted in Luke has little interest in justice. In 20:20 the leadership schemed to secure politically incriminating testimony from Jesus. Getting Jesus to acknowledge his messianic status is similarly motivated. He refuses to cooperate.

Verse 68 alludes to 20:1-8, a narrative exposing the duplicity of the Jewish leadership which explains why they *would not believe* even if Jesus did answer their inquiry. He does affirm, however, that the Son of Man will assume royal power (*the right hand of God*). Readers know Jesus is talking about himself. Jesus' questioners suspect so, given the follow-up question of v. 70. Jesus' implicit affirmation gives them grounds to pursue legal action, although as the subsequent narrative will show they will have to offer a most twisted interpretation of Jesus' admission if they hope to get the governor to pass sentence.

23:1-5. The first hearing before Pilate. The charge concerning *taxes* is simply false (cf. 20:20-26). The charge of claiming to be the *Messiah* is a half-truth at best. Jesus has made no explicit claim, and certainly he has not portrayed himself as the kind of *king of the Jews* that PILATE would be interested in executing. Pilate quickly dismisses the charges before *the chief priests and the crowds.* The latter have perhaps arrived expecting to hear Jesus' teaching (cf. 21:38). The *they* of v. 5 who respond to Pilate are likely the chief priests who insist that Jesus *stirs up the people.* This charge gives Pilate further reason to execute their enemy Jesus.

23:6-12. Hearing before Herod. Readers recall that HEROD, having killed JOHN THE BAPTIST, had been wanting to see Jesus (9:9) and was seeking to kill him (13:31). Even corrupt Herod, after *he questioned him at some length* and heard *the chief priests and the scribes . . . vehemently accusing him* found nothing worthy of execution and *sent him back to Pilate* (vv. 9-11). On *that same day* they became *friends.* It is a perverted friendship, rooted in their willingness to appease the Jewish leadership. Although Herod did not recommend

execution, he is held fully accountable for his complicity in Jesus' death in Acts 4:25-28.

23:13-25. The second hearing before Pilate. Again, the leadership and the people are present. Pilate, however, seems more interested in addressing his comments to the leadership, reminding them of the charges they had made against Jesus earlier in the day: *this man . . . was perverting the people.* Since Pilate cannot find *this man guilty of any of your charges against him* he will flog Jesus *and release him* (vv.14-17).

Then they all shouted out together, "Away with this fellow!" Who are *they*? The leadership and the people, or the leadership who had been making the charges against Jesus? Luke is not clear. Whether *the people* at this juncture join the leaders of *this generation* (cf. 7:31-35) in demanding Jesus' crucifixion or simply acquiesce out of fear, the consequences are the same, as subsequent pronouncements by Jesus (23:27-31) and his followers (Acts 3:14-15) make clear: they are guilty. The implications of 11:23 become clear: *Whoever is not with me is against me.* The people have shown themselves not to be "with Jesus." Their failure, like that of the disciples, cannot be excused—it can only be forgiven. The early chapters of Acts will tell of the apostles preaching to the people offering them the opportunity to repent and be forgiven (Acts 2:38) and to separate themselves from "this corrupt generation" (Acts 2:40).

23:26-31. The walk to crucifixion. Luke again is unclear concerning the identity of the *they* who *led him away.* Romans? Jewish leaders? Jewish people? Luke distinguishes *a great number of the people* from those taking Jesus away to crucify him. Yet even those bemoaning Jesus' fate will not escape the punishment to befall *the daughters of Jerusalem* and their *children.* Terrible days are coming when even death would be better than life—clearly a reference to Jerusalem's destruction (cf. 19:43-44; 21:6, 20-24). The enigmatic saying of v. 31 means "If this kind of violent thing can happen to an innocent man (the *green wood*), imagine what will happen to a guilty city and its people (*dry wood*)."

23:32-56. The crucifixion of Jesus. This scene has three sections: the mocking of Jesus by the Jewish leaders and the soldiers (vv. 32-38); the two criminals (vv. 39-43); the death and burial of Jesus (vv. 44-56).

Verses 32-38. The scoffing and mocking of Jesus by *the leaders* (Jewish) and *the soldiers* (gentiles; cf. 18:32) centers around the spectacle of a supposed *Messiah* and *King of the Jews* not being able to *save* himself. The Jews and the gentiles share in the ridicule of the Lord's anointed (Acts 4:25-28). *The people stood by, watching*, not sharing in the ridicule of Jesus. The later sermons of Acts will condemn them, nonetheless (Acts 3:12-15).

Readers know Jesus to be the savior (1:69; 2:11) and Messiah (2:11; 9:20) and have seen him demonstrate his saving power over sin (7:48-40), disease (8:43-48), even death (8:49-50). Jesus accomplishes his saving mission through his self-giving. Luke may offer no explicit doctrine of the atonement, but the emphasis Jesus himself places upon his rejection and death as the divinely necessitated culmination of his earthly work as the Son of Man and prophet (see comments on 9:18-36; 13:33-34) allows readers to know that this death does play a role in his work of liberation and salvation. To mock him is to show that one simply does not understand "the plan of God" (cf. 7:30).

The first sentence of v. 34 may not be original (see NRSV mg.). But it is fitting here. Jesus offers ("release/liberation"; cf. 4:18)—saving others even as they mock him for saving others while he cannot save himself. It also prepares for Acts 3:17.

Verses 39-43. One *criminal* joins the scoffers. The other criminal implies his recognition of Jesus as the Messiah as he requests that Jesus remember him *when [he] comes into [his] kingdom*. Jesus' promise assures him of salvation, and even sooner than the criminal expected: *today*. *Paradise* was a common term to denote heaven and its blessings (2 Cor 12:4; Rev 2:7). The Messiah demonstrates his saving power as he dies, even as the scoffers scoff.

Verses 44-56. Reference to the failing of *the sun's light* recalls Jesus' word concerning *the power of darkness* (22:53). Jerusalem will pay a heavy price for aligning itself with darkness. The tearing of *the curtain of the temple* (v. 45) serves as an omen that the Temple will be destroyed, adding weight to what Jesus had predicted (19:43-44; 21:6). Jesus' last words show his trust in the *Father*, Jesus' favorite designation for God in the Gospel, even from childhood (cf. 2:49).

Luke narrates a number of reactions. The CENTURION, representing the mocking soldiers of 23:36, recognizes Jesus as *innocent* (Gk.: righteous). Jesus' opponents had thought they were "righteous" (18:9; 20:20 [NRSV "honest"]), but their brand of righteousness killed the one who truly was righteous. Does the centurion's response hold out hope for the gentiles?

The people react in gestures of mourning, *beating their breasts* (v. 48). The time for *weeping for them-*

selves and their children has begun (cf. 23:27-30). The phrase translated *returned home* is literally "turned back," sharing the same Greek root as a word Jesus has related to repentance (cf. 17:3-4), yet the verb does not actually mean "repentance." Their reaction is ambiguous. Is there hope for them?

THE TWELVE (eleven?), if present at all, are buried away in the anonymity of Jesus' *acquaintances* (v. 49). Theirs and the women's response to the scene (watching from a distance) is really no less ambiguous than that of the people. The report of the women's going to prepare spices is touching, but it also makes clear that they did not grasp Jesus' own predictions of his resurrection. Is there hope for Jesus' followers?

Joseph of Arimathea, *a member of the council*, is described most positively as *good and righteous*. His action is also the most courageous, having gone *to Pilate* to ask for *the body of Jesus*. It is made clear that he did not consent to the *plan and action* of the *council* (vv. 50-56). Readers might find some comfort in knowing that not all the Jewish leadership is utterly corrupt. Is there hope even for them?

Representatives from all groups involved in the execution of Jesus, Jewish and gentile, are present. Yet it is curious how Luke has presented them: the apostles are anonymous at best; the representative from the Jewish leadership—Joseph—is *good and righteous*. These last scenes of Jesus' passion are unsettling enough to dissuade readers from thinking that what happens in the story of Jesus is predictable. Glimmers of hope are offered for all the representative characters, especially when one remembers the prayers of Jesus on behalf of the "sifted" followers (22:31-32) and those who mocked and watched (23:34-46).

Entering into Glory, 24:1-53

For background discussion of the resurrection narratives and the resurrection of Jesus, see Fitzmyer 1985, 1533-43.

As readers reach the end of a story they look for resolution of issues raised in what has preceded (Parsons 1986, 201-204). Having arrived at the end of the story, Luke will now need to bring some closure to his story. Review of previous sections of the narrative recalls the issues of the story in need of resolution.

First, Jesus has come to offer redemption to Israel in fulfillment of scriptural promises, with clear hints of inclusion of the gentiles into God's salvation. There will be division among the people (1:5–4:13).

Second, Jesus has come to offer liberation ("release") to the captives and the oppressed. This section makes clear that Satan, later called *the power of darkness* (22:53), is behind this oppression. Jesus' shorthand expression for this liberation from Satan's power is *the reign of God* (4:16–9:50).

Third, Jesus is the PROPHET, indeed the Son of God, to whom Israel must listen (9:35). As he journeys to JERUSALEM, ISRAEL, consisting of disciples, the people, and the leadership, the last represented primarily by the Pharisees, are given ample opportunity to hear him. The leadership is hostile. The people vacillate. The disciples stay with Jesus, but they lack understanding. Despite these evidences of division among Israel, to all have been applied the negative appellation *this generation* (9:51–19:44).

Fourth, in Jerusalem Jesus called Israel to decision. No reader can be impressed by the response of any element of Israel in the passion narrative. With the death of Jesus, one must ask, will there be redemption in fulfillment of scriptural promises, liberation from the power of darkness, and a positive hearing of the word of Jesus by Israel? Readers, anticipating the resurrection, know that if resolution is to come it must come from the resurrected one.

24:1-12. The empty tomb. The women, later identified in v. 10, come to the tomb on Sunday (*the first day of the week*) morning. They have come for the wrong reason, to anoint a dead man, but *they did not find the body*. The description of *the two men in dazzling clothes* implies angelic beings (cf. 24:23). They announce the resurrection and recall the prediction that Jesus himself had made (v. 6; cf. 9:22). With Jesus alive expectations of resolution are raised. The women *told all this to the eleven* but they thought it *an idle tale*. PETER does go to inspect the tomb, however (v. 12, although this text is disputed [see NRSV mg.]). He is amazed, but does not see Jesus. So far, no resolution of any issues.

24:13-35. The road to Emmaus. It is still Sunday (v. 13). Hopes for resolution are raised as *Jesus himself* proceeds to walk with two persons journeying to EMMAUS. *But their eyes were kept from recognizing him* (v.16); a phrase hauntingly reminiscent of what Jesus had said of Jerusalem (19:42). Hopes for resolution are quickly taken away.

The conversation of CLEOPAS and his companion reminds readers of issues in need of resolution: Will there be redemption for Israel in fulfillment of scriptural promises? They certainly do not think so (cf. v.

21). The unrecognized Jesus is emphatic that the suffering of the Messiah is part of the fulfillment of the scriptural promises, although the two do not see it and the reader is even left clueless as to exactly how. Still, it is clear that the resurrected Jesus affirms the fulfillment of scripture. This hope is not to be abandoned.

What of the work of liberation and the reign of God? The fact of Jesus' resurrection, which by the end of the story, even the characters come to recognize, affirms the effectiveness of the liberating power of God. Jesus' act of taking, blessing, breaking, and giving bread is reminiscent of 22:19. In that context Jesus had said he would *not eat . . . until it is fulfilled in the kingdom of God*. What readers are witnessing is hardly the fulfillment of the kingdom of God; Luke 21:25-33 has made clear that such will accompany the coming of the Son of Man *in a cloud with power and great glory*. Still the picture of the resurrected Jesus breaking bread with his followers instills confidence that bread will be broken again when it is fulfilled in the kingdom of God. Here one may not find the realization of the reign of God, but one does find justification to hope for such realization.

What of the response of Israel? The disciples respond affirmatively; once *their eyes were opened* (v. 31), Jesus *appeared* to them (v. 34), and *had been made known* (v. 35) to them. Response, even after being "sifted by Satan" (22:31), is possible, but it can come only at the initiation of the resurrected Lord. Will the rest of Israel have opportunity to respond to this resurrected one? Comments concerning the leadership are thoroughly negative, leaving little hope (v. 20). What of the people? They are not explicitly indicted in v. 20, but neither is any explicit word offered to indicate that they will respond to the word of Jesus. The final phrase, stating that Jesus *had been made known to them in the breaking of the bread* (v. 35), might offer a clue that recognition of Jesus apart from life in the community of faith is not possible, for in Acts "breaking bread" serves to denote Christian fellowship at the table of the Lord (cf. 22:30; Acts 2:42, 46; 20:7, 11).

24:36-53. Appearance and exodus. It is now Sunday evening (cf. vv. 29, 33, 36). Jesus' appearance to the group (vv. 36-42) affirms for them and the readers the reality of his resurrection. Jesus invites them to *touch* him and to see his *flesh and bones*. He even eats *in their presence* (v. 43) to confirm the reality of his resurrection.

Jesus' pronouncement of *peace be with you* (v. 36) recalls the disciples acclamation of peace when Jesus approached Jerusalem (19:38) and especially the angelic announcement of 2:14. There the angels promised peace due to the birth of the Messiah. In this scene, Jesus fulfills this hope. He had wanted to offer such peace to Jerusalem, but it could not see it (19:42). This appearance reinforces resolution of the issue concerning the response of the disciples to Jesus. At least this part of Israel sees who this Jesus is.

In vv. 44-49, numerous issues are offered resolution, although new expectations are also raised. Jesus affirms again that, indeed, *everything written about [him] in the law of Moses, the prophets, and the psalms must be fulfilled.* Jesus affirms that the story of his passion itself was *written* in the scriptures. This story readers have just read is the realization, or at least an integral part of the realization, of the fulfillment of Israel's scriptures.

Still readers are not told exactly what scriptures are fulfilled. But Jesus *opened their minds to understand the scriptures.* This assures readers that the resurrected Lord can lead believers to see to exactly how the "Jesus story" fulfills "scripture's story." In Acts, readers will have several opportunities to hear the scriptures interpreted and to see how exactly Jesus fulfills the scriptures.

The ministry of liberation, or "release," is addressed explicitly in the charge Jesus makes to his followers. This work of liberation, which included in Jesus' ministry the offering of *forgiveness* (or "release") *of sins* is to continue (v. 47). In fact, this very continuation of the ministry of liberation is itself said to be part of the fulfillment of what *is written* (v. 46). What is more, this proclamation of *repentance and forgiveness of sins* will begin *from Jerusalem.* Jerusalem and its people (even its leaders?) will hear the message of repentance and be offered the opportunity to experience the liberation they rejected just a few days before. The proclamation will not stop in Jerusalem. It shall be offered to *all the nations* (same Gk. word as "gentiles").

Will redemption come to Israel as she once again is given opportunity to hear the message? Jesus' predictions about the destruction of Jerusalem create tension. Is there a way that redemption, liberation, and forgiveness can still come to Israel if, indeed, Jerusalem must fall? Will the nations (gentiles) respond positively? These questions are not answered. But Luke approaches the conclusion with hopeful expectations.

Finally in this section, Luke raises the expectation that the mission in which he is calling his disciples to engage will be assisted by something promised by the *Father* himself that Jesus will send: *power from on high.* Attentive readers will recall such texts as 3:16; 11:13; 12:12. Less attentive readers will have to wait until Acts to find out what Jesus is talking about.

In vv. 50-53, Jesus' exodus (departure [cf. 9:31]) and "taking up" (9:51) are to be realized. The journey of Jesus is coming to an end. Before he leaves he offers his followers a priestly blessing, *lifting up his hands.* The Temple may be destined to fall someday (and from the perspective of Luke's readers it has fallen), but the blessing of God's anointed will not be impeded by the lack of a Temple and priesthood, just as the existence of a Temple and priesthood cannot insure blessing (cf. 1:22).

The brief description of Jesus' ascension *up into heaven* allows readers to experience and witness the realization of Jesus' bold claim before his oppressors in 22:69: *the Son of Man will be seated at the right hand of . . . God.* Jesus has been vindicated.

The disciples return *to Jerusalem* whence the continuing mission of liberation will commence, *continually in the temple blessing God.* Jerusalem and the Temple will fall one day. But for now, the Temple has been cleansed by the Messiah (19:45-46) and is a most fitting place for his people to congregate.

Luke ends the story where he began it: in the holy city and sanctuary of Israel, the people of God. As readers prepare to turn the page to begin Luke's second book—the Book of Acts—this closing scene calls them back to the opening scenes and to hopes raised by such characters as Mary, the mother of Jesus, and Zechariah, the father of the Baptist, but perhaps expressed best by Simeon, the righteous man longing for the consolation of Israel. *My eyes have seen your salvation . . . a light for revelation to the Gentiles and for glory to your people Israel* (2:30-32).

Works Cited

Aune, David E. 1987. *The New Testament in Its Literary Environment.*

Burridge, Richard A. 1992. *What Are the Gospels? A Comparison with Graeco-Roman Biography.* SNTSMS 70.

Chance, J. Bradley. 1988. *Jerusalem, the Temple, and the New Age in Luke–Acts.*

Conzelmann, Hans. 1982 [1960]. *The Theology of St. Luke.*

Fitzmyer, Joseph A., S.J. 1981, 1985. *The Gospel according to Luke.* 2 vols. (pages numbered consecutively). AncB.

Garrett, Susan R. "'Lest the Light in You Be Darkness': Luke 11:33-36 and the Question of Commitment," *JBL* 110/1 (1991): 93-105.

Marshall, I. Howard. 1978. *Commentary on Luke,* NIGTC.

Moesnner, David P. 1989. *Lord of the Banquet: The Literary and Theological Significance of the Lukan Travel Narrative*; 1990. "The 'Leaven of the Pharisees' and 'This Generation': Israel's Rejection of Jesus according to Luke," *Reimaging the Death of Jesus,* ed. Dennis D. Sylva, 79–107.

Pervo, Richard I. 1989. "Must Luke and Acts Belong to the Same Genre?" SBLASP, 309-16.

Parsons, Mikeal C. 1986. "Narrative Closure and Openness in the Plot of the Third Gospel: The Sense of Ending in Luke 24:50-53," SBLASP.

Talbert, Charles H. 1986. *Reading Luke: A Literary and Theological Commentary on the Third Gospel.* 1988. "Once Again: Gospel Genre," *Semeia* 43:53-73.

Tiede, David L. 1988. *Luke.* AugCNT.

John

Gerald L. Borchert

Introduction

The fourth Gospel is one of the most fascinating books in the Bible. Its poetic-like stories have engulfed many, and a number of its verses are among the most familiar in scripture. Although its vocabulary is simple and verges on being redundant, the Gospel is one of the most complex compositions in the Bible in terms of the interweaving of theological themes. It is like a complex symphony that periodically repeats earlier themes with refreshing variations so that the reader is caught in the awe-inspiring work of a masterfully sophisticated artist.

John and the Synoptics

When one reads John after reading one of the Synoptics (Matthew, Mark, or Luke), one has the feeling of being in familiar territory. Yet, in spite of the similarities, it is strangely different. JESUS certainly performs miracles (in John called "signs"), but, except for the multiplication of bread and the walking on the water in chap. 6, the sign stories are all different. There is a great catch of fish in chap. 21 that reminds the reader of Luke 5, but it takes place after the resurrection in John so that scholars have a field day trying to work out the relationship between the two stories.

In terms of organization the Synoptics have Jesus moving from GALILEE to JUDEA to die, whereas John moves Jesus at will between the two regions. It is likely this Gospel's movement of Jesus is more reflective of what actually happened, but we are not quite sure. The question of the cleansing of the Temple points to the problem. Because the story appears in John near the beginning of the Gospel (chap. 2) and in the Synoptics in the final stages of Jesus' life, many readers automatically begin to think there are two cleansings of the Temple. But there is only one in any one Gospel. This fact raises the important question of organization in John.

Organization of the Gospel

When many readers are asked "How long did Jesus live?" the normal reply is thirty-three years. The reason is that they take the thirty years of preparation from Luke 3:23 and then go to John and count the number of Passovers recorded there. But to count Passovers in this manner is to misunderstand this Gospel (Borchert 1993).

The Gospel of John is organized according to cycles, and PASSOVER is a key to understanding John's cycle-thinking. The Gospel begins with a prologue (1:1-18, probably written after the Gospel was finished as an introduction to the Gospel) that relates Jesus to God and to the very beginning of time. Then there is a series of short stories (1:19-52) that introduces Jesus in terms of a variety of titles including MESSIAH, SON OF GOD, and King of Israel, with the focal designation being *the Lamb of God who takes away the sin of the world!* (1:29, 36). That lamb is meant to be understood as the world's Passover Lamb.

This introductory chapter is followed by a series of three cycles in which Passover plays a significant role. The Cana cycle (chaps. 2–4) has at its heart the Passover and the cleansing of the Temple (2:13-25). The Festival cycle (chaps. 5–11) after an introduction to feast thinking (chap. 5) moves from Passover (6:4) to Passover (11:55). Chapter 12 serves as a saddle text between the public ministry of Jesus and his private ministry to his disciples. The setting is just before the Passover (12:1). The farewell cycle (chaps. 13–17) begins with an announcement of Passover (13:1), and these chapters seek to prepare the disciples for Passover and the coming of a new era.

The Passover sequence is drawn to a conclusion in the death story (chaps. 18–19) with the dying of the perfect Passover lamb on the specific day of Preparation when the Passover lambs were killed (19:14, 31).

The resurrection stories (chaps. 20–21) then move the reader beyond Passover to the new era of the spirit-led community (20:22) of Jesus Christ (Borchert, *John*).

The Context of the Gospel

Behind this Gospel lies a community of faith that tradition situates in EPHESUS. Its history cannot be fully detailed but its BELOVED DISCIPLE (13:23; 19:26; 20:2; 21:20) may have been the unnamed disciple of JOHN THE BAPTIST (1:35-40).

Some time during its formative period, as J. Louis Martyn (1979, 37–62) has forcefully argued, members of the community undoubtedly encountered hostility from the SYNAGOGUE. Whether they moved from Israel first to Antioch or immediately to Ephesus is not certain. Neither is it clear whether their numbers included SAMARITANS, as might be argued from John 4:39-42.

The hostility with the synagogue seems clearly behind the story of the blind man (9:22, 34, 40) as well as the entire argument of Jesus in 8:31-59 and the warning in 16:2-4. Whether the *Birkath ha-Minim* (the curse of the heretics that was inserted into the Jewish benedictions) is directly related to this community, it is clear that the context of hostility is very similar. In this context, the reader cannot help but be reminded of the Christian evaluation of the Jews as the "synagogue of Satan" in the Apocalypse (Rev 2:9; 3:9).

The entire Gospel seems to be written from the perspective of the way Jesus filled the expectations of the OT. He is viewed, for example, as the new Temple (2:19-21), the successor to the hope of the lifted-up serpent (3:14), the interpreter of SABBATH (5:9-18), the true bread from heaven (6:48-51), the living water of Tabernacles (7:37-38), and the true shepherd king expected in Ezek 34 and Jer 23 (John 10:1-30). Such views undoubtedly raised the ire of many Jews.

Authorship

The traditional view has been that John the son of Zebedee was the author of this Gospel. Such a view was enunciated by Irenaeus in the second century C.E. (*AdvHaer* 3.1.1) and maintained until the late eighteenth and early nineteenth centuries. The theology then was challenged by some as being later dualistic and Platonic thinking (e.g., D. F. Strauss). Some began to point to the probability that the Gospel was written by a second-century disciple of the apostle (19:35; 21:25; e.g., H. Paulus). The next stage in thinking was that a school or community was responsible for the

Gospel (e.g., J. B. Lightfoot) and this theory received an expanded treatment recently by Culpepper (1975).

Clearly the epilogue is suggestive in terms of authorship because three parties are there identified. The first is the disciple or witness (21:24), the second is the church or community that authenticates the work (e.g., *we*, 21:24), and the third party is the *I* (21:25) who appears to be the writer of at least the last two verses and probably more. The text itself, therefore, indicates a multiplicity of persons involved in the writing and transmission of this Gospel. The Beloved Disciple, however, is clearly viewed as the source of the tradition or basis for the message. In this commentary the designations evangelist and John are used interchangeably, recognizing the complex nature of the issue.

Date

The traditional date for the writing of the Gospel has been the decade of 90–100 C.E. This date had been called into question by some who supposed the theology was second-century. The discovery of a fragment of the Gospel in Egypt (containing 18:31-33, 37-38, and housed in the Rylands Library in Manchester), which probably dates from the early second century, has resulted in the earlier date being resubstantiated.

Theology

This Gospel was early regarded as a very special work. Clement of Alexandria designated it as the "spiritual gospel." That name has adhered to it throughout the centuries. Even before Clement, however, Gnostic mythologizers and spiritualizers found it to be a powerful vehicle for their distorted message (see Borchert 1981, 249). Indeed works like the Gospel of Truth (*Evangelium Veritatis*) found at NAG HAMMADI and reputed to have been written by Valentinus made use of the Gospel of John. Moreover, Gnostic spiritualizers like Heracleon were the first commentators on the Gospel.

Such facts have led some to suspect the Gospel to be marginally heretical. Its theology is certainly lofty and its CHRISTOLOGY is among the most elevated in the NT. The Gospel does not begin with the birth of Jesus but with the LOGOS/WORD at the beginning of time. But while the christology is elevated, it is important to see that on the basis of the purpose of John the Jesus of this Gospel cannot be an adoptionistic, nonsuffering, alien messenger from without. The Jesus of this Gospel is very real, very human but also God-directed and divinely empowered. He is truly a God-man.

His concern is for his suffering community and for leading people from one stage of believing to the next. In John, Jesus is the divine-human rescuer of faithless, doubting people. He, the creator of the world (1:3), has come to his own people and place and has been rejected (1:9-11) but he continues to build a community from those who will believe (1:12), the purpose for which John wrote his Gospel (20:30-31).

In reaching this purpose the evangelist has interwoven many great themes. Those themes include seeing, believing, knowing, light, darkness, life, death, truth, hour, signs, judgment, love, "I am," freedom, bread, water, and a host of others. Each theme can make for interesting research studies and each can be developed as windows into the nature of the Gospel.

The careful reader will also discover that this Gospel can be studied on various levels so that its wells of insight seldom run dry. It is a work that is loved by many new Christians although they may not understand what it means to *eat the flesh of the Son of Man* (6:53). It will challenge the minds and hearts of the most mature believer. It is indeed a book that is used by the Spirit of God to touch the world.

For Further Study

In the *Mercer Dictionary of the Bible*: BELOVED DISCIPLE, THE; CHRISTOLOGY; FEASTS AND FESTIVALS; GNOSTICISM; GOSPELS, CRITICAL STUDY OF; INCARNATION; JESUS; JOHN THE APOSTLE; JOHN THE BAPTIST; JOHN, GOSPEL AND LETTERS OF; LAMB OF GOD; LAZARUS; LOGOS/WORD; MESSIAH/CHRIST; MIRACLE STORY; PHARISEES; RESURRECTION IN THE NT; SIGNS AND WONDERS; WOMEN IN THE NT; WORSHIP IN THE NT. In other sources: G. R. Beasley-Murray, *John*, WBC; G. L. Borchert, *John*, NAC; R. E. Brown, *The Gospel according to John*, AncB; D. A. Carson, *The Gospel according to John*; J. Charlesworth, ed., *John and the Dead Sea Scrolls*; E. Haenchen, *John*; R. Schnackenburg, *The Gospel according to St. John*.

Commentary

An Outline

Introduction, 1:1-51

The Gospel of John is one of the most fascinating documents in the NT. While it may appear to be simple in vocabulary and style, it is one of the most highly organized and sophisticated works in the Bible (Borchert 1981, 249). Although scholars suggest some variations in detail concerning organization, most agree in the primary divisions of the book, with a major-segment break at either chap. 12 or 13. My particular contribution (Borchert 1987, 86-152; and Borchert, *John*) is the view that the Gospel was written in cycles (the Cana cycle, chaps. 2-4; the Festival cycle, chaps. 5-11; the farewell cycle, chaps. 13-17) framed by other sections that provide special developmental emphases (the prologue, 1:1-18; stories of witness, 1:19-51; transition to death, chap. 12; the death story, chaps. 18–19; the resurrection stories, chap. 20; and the postscript, chap. 21). Moreover, the book hangs together as a magnificent testimony to Jesus, *the Lamb of God who takes away the sin of the world* (1:29), and provides a model of authentic life for the community of believers.

The Purpose, 20:30-31

To understand the thought and goal of John, one would do well to begin with the first ending of the book—its purpose statement. This purpose statement is formulated to provide readers with a window into what has been written. There it is said that

> Many other signs, indeed, Jesus did before his disciples that are not recorded in this book, but these are recorded that you might believe that Jesus is the Christ, the Son of God, and that in [the genuine act of] believing you might have life by [or in the power of] his name (author trans.).

From this statement it is evident that the evangelist expects a response from the reader. Clearly nothing less than active believing in Jesus which issues in a new way of living is adequate to encompass what this Gospel intends for its readership (Borchert 1987, 91). True life is the goal, authentic believing is the means, and relationship to Jesus (the SON OF GOD) is the basis. Furthermore, this purpose statement also indicates some of the most important themes that permeate the Gospel such as the understanding of signs, the importance of believing and life, the nature of Jesus, the importance of names and confession, and the significance of discipleship. In addition, readers of this Gospel should be alert to repetitive themes, words, phrases, and questions that arise in the Gospel. Attending to them should bring a new vitality to the study of this magnificent book. But all study should be related to the evangelist's purpose for the book and should result in a personal response involving one's own life. Only in such a context will the purpose be realized.

The Prologue, 1:1-18

The Gospel begins with one of the most profound statements concerning Jesus in the NT. The lofty CHRISTOLOGY is scarcely approximated elsewhere except perhaps in Heb 1:1-13 or Col 1:15-20. Moreover, its poetic-like style has led scholars to speculate on whether it was originally a poem or a hymn (e.g., J. Sanders 1971, 20–24; R. Brown 1966, 3–4). Some have sought to find a core document in Aramaic (Burney 1922, 40) while others like Bultmann have thought they found its roots in a gnostic logos hymn (1971, 23–28). Käsemann has countered that it was probably an early Christian hymn that was incorporated into the Gospel (1969, 138–67). Whatever may have been its roots, as it stands it has been thoroughly Johanninized in the editing process.

1:1-5. The eternal Word. In contrast to the synoptic Gospels, the evangelist begins at *the beginning* and builds upon the first and sixth orders of the creation account in Gen 1. He does not repeat those earlier presuppositions but identifies the *Word* (λόγος) with the very beginning and with God's divine selfhood, not in terms of subjugation of the *Word* but in a pattern of mutual interaction (Newman and Nida 1980, 8). The *Word* here is to be understood as a persona of God, not "a god" of subordination as argued by the Jehovah's Witnesses (see Metzger 1953).

In the prologue the contrast between the Greek verbs for "being" (ἦν) and "becoming" (ἐγένετο) is very crucial. The verb for "being" is used in vv. 1, 2, 4, 8, 9, 10, and 15 and refers to an existence without precondition, whereas the second word is used in vv. 3, 6, 10, 14, and 17, and implies moments within history. The *Word* in v. 1, however, is not a mere philosophical term to be identified simply with divine rationality as in Philonic speculation or Jewish Wisdom literature (cf. Dodd 1958, 274–75). Instead, it is to be understood as an early stage in the Trinitarian formulation concerning the various *personas* of God.

Not only is the preexistence of the *Word* here clearly implied, but it is also asserted that the *Word* has been active in the entire process of creation (v. 3). Indeed, the *Word* is here identified with the age-old quest of human beings for the essence of life (v. 4) and this pre-life-existing one is designated as the light-giver whose light is unquenchable (v. 5).

Many scholars today reject the translation of *overcome* (κατέλαβεν) in v. 5, arguing that the idea here could hardly be related to the ancient struggle between light and darkness—viewed as a conflict picture, symbolic of the warfare between good and evil (Beasley-Murray 1987, 32; Brown 1966, 8; Schnackenburg 1987, 1:245–49). My suggestion (*John*) is that there is a conflict to be understood here related to the rejection or nonreception (παρέλαβον) of the *Word* (cf. v. 11). For John the coming of Jesus divides persons and realities, and the underlying postresurrection perspective in the entire Gospel means that evil and rejection will not triumph (Borchert, *John*, and 1988, 502).

1:6-8. John the witness. The next three verses are prose and focus attention on *John* (the baptizer or *witness*). They function like a window from the lofty, poetic stance of the hymn on the *Word* down to the human context of witness, which is the first subject of concern following the lofty prologue. As such these verses provide a clear contrast: namely, John the witness is not to be considered in the same category or on the same level as the *Word* (cf. also 1:15), a view some of John's disciples apparently could not accept (John 3:25-30; see Borchert, *John*). Yet the designation of John as a witness is not to be considered a minor matter because witness, as J. Boice (1970, 31–38) argued, is a major theme in the Gospel. John the witness, like many persons in the Gospel, is more than an ancient person. He is an exemplar or representative.

1:9-13. Receiving the light. The *Word* is next identified as authentic light and linked to the idea of "the coming one," a designation derived from OT texts such as Zech 9:9 and used to identify the coming of the Messiah (cf. 4:25). According to the evangelist, however, although the *true light* entered the world in the midst of those who should have been expecting him, the tragic reality was that the *Word* encountered rejection rather than reception. This theme of rejection is often repeated in the Johannine stories of Jesus. But the evangelist is quick to assert that, despite rejection by many, those who believed are named the children of God not because of human lineage, desire, or power but because they have received the active *Word* of God.

1:14-18. The Incarnation and its implications. The second appearance of λόγος (*Word*) in the prologue signals the changed state of the *Word*'s work. In the first stage the emphasis was upon creation. The second stage, the work of the coming one, is redemption. In the language of the TENT OF MEETING in the EXODUS story, the evangelist describes the "enfleshment" of the *Word* in "tent" (σκηνόω) terminology. The *Word* is said to have actually "presenced" itself among humans. The idea of tent here implies no mere gnostic appearance theology. Instead, the meaning is that the *Word* actually entered the historical context and *became* (ἐγένετο) *flesh* or truly human. INCARNATION theology is one of the basic theses of historic Christianity.

As Israel experienced the glory of God at the wilderness tent (Exod 40:34), so both John (*we*, v. 14) and the early witnesses experienced divine glory in the enfleshed *Word* (Borchert, *John*). This sense of divine presence and glory was given to the world in God's

"only" (μονογενής, see Moody 1953, 213–19) son. In him was vested divine "fullness" (πλήρωμα), a term later used by the Gnostics to describe their godhead. But here the fullness of the *Word* is said to be the source for the Christian experience of abundant *grace* (v. 16). Such grace (a term used only in the prologue of John) is contrasted directly with the divine gift of law that came through Moses (remember: law is also gift).

Then in v. 17 the *Word* is finally named: *Jesus Christ*, the divine-human agent of grace and truth. Truth or authenticity is one of the major themes in John and is a mark of both Jesus and his genuine followers. Clearly no one has ever seen the full semblance of God. But Jesus—the only SON OF GOD, whose intimacy with God the Father is described by the term "bosom" (v. 18; *heart* NRSV)—has portrayed, detailed, or narrated (ἐξηγήσατο) the nature of God for the world. With this idea of portrayal, the evangelist concludes the prologue of his Gospel (see Borchert, John) and sets the stage for the introduction of Jesus by John, the witness.

The Baptizer's Witness, 1:19-28

Each of the canonical Gospels focuses on John the Baptizer prior to introducing the ministry of Jesus. This means that for the early Christians the work of the Baptizer was seen as a strategic signal for the beginning of the Gospel (cf. Mark 1:1). In this Gospel the Baptizer almost appears to be an intruder into the prologue. Yet for the evangelist the Baptizer is no intruder. Everything in this Gospel treats the Baptizer as an ideal model of witness. There is no suggestion here of doubt concerning Jesus by the Baptizer (as in Matt 11:3). His disciples may have doubts (3:26), but not John.

1:19-23. Questioning of John. Without further introduction, John is set in a defense posture by the investigating committee of Jews (the term *Jews* in this Gospel is applied primarily to adversaries; see Freeman 1991). In successive questions he is asked whether he is MESSIAH (cf. 1QS 9.1), ELIJAH (cf. Mal 4:5), or the *prophet* (cf. Deut 18:15). When these questions fail to elicit the anticipated response, the next question posed is a demand for self-definition. As a former lawyer, I usually ponder both such questions and their answers. Many scholars have noted that these questions reflect the confusing nature of the messianic expectations of the time. But it is also important to draw attention to the fact that the first two of John's answers are similar to Peter's first two answers in his denial, namely, *I am not* (οὐκ εἰμί, v. 21). As such these answers are a direct contrast to the constant affirmation in this Gospel of Jesus as "I am" (ἐγώ εἰμι, see Borchert, *John*). The clarity of the final "no" gives rise to John's self-definition as a non-self-centered "voice" of witness. Using Isaiah's reference to the unevenness of Israel's natural geography, the Baptizer calls his hearers to prepare a new highway of reformation.

1:24-28. Criticism and John's response. Undeterred by the Baptizer's call for preparing a new way, the PHARISEES questioned his right to testify. To set this story in the context of the time of writing it is important to remember that the Pharisees were major opponents of Christian witnesses. Other parties such as the SADDUCEES are not mentioned because they had vanished with the destruction of Jerusalem. The Baptizer's response then can be viewed from two perspectives: the time of Jesus and the time of the early Christians. Moreover, the Baptizer's words are a proclamation of the presence of true authority in their midst and an assertion of his own personal unworthiness even to be a slave (one who touches feet) of this worthy one.

Three Cameos of Witness, 1:29-51

The next three witness stories form a unit that emphasizes seeing and finding the Messiah who is identified by a series of names such as the LAMB OF GOD, SON OF GOD, teacher or RABBI, CHRIST, King of Israel, and SON OF MAN. Each segment begins with the notation *the next day* indicating the interrelationship of these three pericopes.

1:29-34. Witness to the Lamb. The Passover in John is not merely a time designation. It is a theological organizing principle for the Gospel (see Borchert 1993) and it is introduced by the Baptizer/Witness when he identifies Jesus as *the Lamb of God who takes away the sin of the world* (v. 29). To his earlier statements of self-humiliation or unworthiness the Baptizer here added his admitted lack of full understanding by his confession that he did not know the Lamb until he gained insight through the descent of the Spirit upon Jesus.

Some scholars take pains to seek a harmonization with Luke's infancy accounts of the relationship between the mothers of Jesus and the Baptizer by suggesting that the latter's solitary life may explain the text (see e.g., Brown 1966, 65). But "knowing" in John is not mere acquaintance. Recognizing Jesus for who he is takes spiritual insight (Borchert, *John*). When spiritual insight comes then there follows both the ability to distinguish between mortal and spiritual realities (baptism with water vs. the Holy Spirit) and the willingness to confess that Jesus is the *Son of God* (v. 34; a better translation than "elect of God" as in some texts).

Readers of John should not interpret the descent of the Spirit upon Jesus as an adoptionistic view whereby Jesus becomes Son of God, but as a divine witness to the Baptizer concerning the existing divine nature of Jesus. Readers should also note that the confirming voice from heaven at the baptism in the Synoptics (e.g., Mark 1:11 and par.) is reserved in John for the personal confirmation of Jesus' Passover death (John 12:28-30). They should likewise note that nowhere in John is the Baptizer said to baptize Jesus. Such a reference would have run counter to the evangelist's goal of arguing against the views of the remaining disciples of the Baptizer who had not understood the Baptizer's mission of witnessing to Jesus (see John 3:25-30).

1:35-42. Witness to the first disciples. The next stage of witness involved the turning over of the Baptizer's disciples to Jesus by the announcement to them that Jesus was God's Lamb. ANDREW and an unnamed disciple (some suggest Philip) responded and followed this Lamb. Bultmann reminds us that upon seeing them, Jesus began his transforming invitation with a simple question: "What do you want?" (Bultmann 1971, 99–100). This dialogue, I would argue, is crucial because "Where are you remaining [abiding]?" (v. 33, author trans.) initiates one of the great themes of discipleship in John and the response *come and see* (v. 39) identifies another of those themes (Cullmann 1953).

What this Gospel teaches us concerning the making of disciples is that witness and invitation are far more important than argument and apologetics. That is the pattern with Andrew who found PETER. It was the same with PHILIP who found Nathaniel in the next pericope. The theme of finding is important in these two pericopes because the witnesses not only find the prospects but also say they have found the expected one. The irony in the stories is that while disciples may say they find Jesus, it is not Jesus who is lost or unknowing.

Readers will also note in this pericope several interpretive statements: Rabbi means teacher, Messiah means Christ, and Cephas means Peter (today, we would probably say "Rocky"). These and other notations in the Gospel indicate that the intended readers were probably unfamiliar with Jewish or Hebrew/Aramaic terminology and needed guidance from an interpreter.

1:43-51. Witness to Nathaniel. The theme of finding again forms the background of this story. But here Nathaniel is introduced with a protest or argument: *Can anything good come out of Nazareth?* The response of Philip is not argument but witness: *Come and see* (v. 46).

Jesus recognized in Nathaniel (v. 47) as he did in Simon (v. 42) that which was authentic, and he named him an Israelite without guile (a contrast to the pre-Jabbok Jacob, Gen 32:27-28). In answer to Nathaniel's puzzlement—*Where did you get to know me?* (v. 48)—Jesus identified him as a serious student seeking God's way (for studying under a FIG TREE, cf. Str-B 2:371).

When Nathaniel responded to Jesus with some exalted titles of messianic expectation (*Son of God* and *King of Israel* v. 40), Jesus virtually said that you are just at the beginning of understanding who I am. Instead of prediction, however, Jesus pointed back to the strategic dream of JACOB (Gen 28:10-17) and identified himself both as a new BETHEL ("house of God") and as *Son of Man* (a favorite self-designation of Jesus which involves a number of theological possibilities from the embodiment of humanity to an apocalyptic figure). With this self-witness of Jesus these cameos both reach their conclusion and provide an introduction to the actions of Jesus in the Cana cycle.

The Cana Cycle, 2:1–4:54

The five stories that form this cycle move the reader's mind from Galilee and Cana to Jerusalem, then with ever widening ripples of the darkness of the Judean context to the acceptance of Jesus by the rejects of SAMARIA, and then back to the more open setting of GALILEE (4:47, 54). The cycle also moves from the first (beginning) sign to the second sign, both of which take place in Cana and are the only signs in the Gospel designated by numerical order.

The First Cana Sign: Water to Wine, 2:1-12

The attentive reader should learn quickly that this wonderful little wedding story which is cited in some wedding services is fraught with a number of interpretive pitfalls that can easily distract from the main points of the pericope. Briefly reviewing some of these

traps, the reader should note that *the third day* (v. 1) is not a sequential time designation following the three "next days" of chap. 1. Moreover, Jesus did not mistreat his mother when he called her *Woman* and added "What is it between me and you?" (v. 4, author trans.). And for those troubled by Jesus turning water into wine (οἶνος), it is a non sequitur to argue that such wine has no alcoholic content. It is also illegitimate to use this text as an authorization by Jesus for or against drinking alcohol today or as an authorization for or against a certain kind of wedding pattern.

2:1-4. A troubled wedding ceremony. In this story the mother of Jesus apparently had an important relationship with those in charge of the wedding party in which embarrassment was on the horizon either because of something such as inadequate planning or lack of funds to cover the long celebration (perhaps a week or longer, cf. Tob 8:19; 11:18). Typical of any Jewish mother in such a tense situation, the mother of Jesus began to use her parental relationship to solve the crisis of another relationship. It was at this initial stage that Jesus reminded her that he was not to be some magical solution or amulet to prevent disaster from striking, nor was she the one who directed his life. He was directed by a divine purpose or *hour* (v. 4, a theme of John).

2:5-10. Water to wine. His mother (she is not called Mary in this Gospel) quickly caught his meaning and redirected her attention from Jesus to the servants with the words *Do whatever he tells you* (v. 5). The message is clear: humans, including his mother, cannot use Jesus (or God) for their purposes. Instead, God uses persons to bring about the divine purpose.

The six large *stone water jars* used for purification in this story probably contained nine gallons each (Newman and Nida 1980, 59). A great deal of water! When the changed water was carried to the banquet master (who was responsible for keeping the guests happy), he was confused by the quality of the wine at this late point in the festivities. He *knew* nothing of the involvement of Jesus and could only judge that something strange had occurred.

2:11-12. The sign. While the banquet master viewed the results as strange, the evangelist reflected that the incident served as a *sign* (not "miracle" as in KJV) to the disciples. Indeed it was the beginning (or a key) to signs because in it Jesus *revealed his glory* (v. 11 a Johannine theme) and the disciples believed. In this strange act, the disciples saw something more than water and wine, and it led to commitment.

The pericope ends with a brief pause in the action as Jesus spends a few days with his family (mother and brothers—not cousins) and friends before the storm of the next pericope.

The Temple Cleansing, 2:13-25

Many persons with mindsets focused on chronology become sidetracked with comparisons here between John and the Synoptics and argue either for the priority of the Synoptics or of John, minimizing the theological concerns of both (cf. Brown 1966, 117–19). The alternative is to argue for two cleansings of the Temple, but such an approach is a construct of the interpreter, and no Gospel has two such cleansings. The problem is a presupposition that insists on turning the Gospels into pedantic prose/chronological reports and fails to allow a great literary figure like the Johannine evangelist to write the way he wishes. Instead, this story seems to serve the evangelist in a way similar to the literary or dramatic vehicle called *in medius res* ("in the thing's middle") where decisive moments are transported to the beginning of a story to involve readers immediately in the trauma of the story (see Borchert, *John*). Such does not minimize history and chronology but allows both to serve the purpose of theology and witness.

2:13-17. Jesus' confrontation in the Temple. The story opens with the strategic notation that it was PASSOVER time (see Borchert, *John*) *and Jesus went up to Jerusalem* (always "up" in the minds of the Jews). The time was the significant celebration of God's deliverance or salvation. Rather than being focused on God and worship, however, the Temple here is pictured as a combination of a noisy bank or exchange ("tables," the Greek term for banking) and a farmer's market. This misuse of God's house irritated Jesus, and he reacted with zeal by forcefully stopping all business transactions (not a "namby-pamby" Jesus).

2:18-22. The meaning of the act. The attack on the Temple business brought a demand from the Jews for an explanation or *sign* (a Johannine theme). Jesus' response was a three-day prediction concerning his death and resurrection. The Jewish reaction of forty-six years in building the Temple is significant because this story would then be dated at ca. 27 C.E., since the Temple rebuilding began ca. 20–19 B.C.E. (Josephus, *Ant* 15.11.1).

The entire conversation is important because it is packaged in a play on words for Temple. In vv. 14

and 15 ἱερόν means the "Temple complex" with its courts, whereas ναός (vv. 19, 20, 21) means "sanctuary" and is here used not of a building but of Jesus' body. This text also supplies an important post-resurrection perspective for this Gospel (v. 22), a fact that should be remembered by all readers of John (see Borchert 1988, 502–503).

2:23-25. The nature of believing. The evangelist adds a crucial postscript to this Temple confrontation by referring again to Passover and by reminding readers that Jesus does not accept everyone's believing because he knows human nature. The distinction about true and authentic believing is not a linguistic nicety of Greek, as some have suggested, but a matter of commitment to Jesus (cf. Carson 1981, 249–50n.37).

This postscript or summary statement is, like the entire Gospel, written from a holistic or post-resurrection view of the work of Jesus. The responses to him are reckoned from such a perspective. Thus, when one encounters the plural word *signs* (v. 23; cf. 3:2) before the *second sign* at 4:54 and when one meets a variety of believing responses so early in the Gospel, one should be alerted to the necessity of reading this Gospel from a holistic or post-resurrection point of view.

Nicodemus and Teaching on Salvation, 3:1-21

The pericope involving Nicodemus contains some of the best-known verses in the Bible. It is also the first of John's longer units that combine to form superb teaching vehicles.

3:1-4. The opening exchange. In the introduction Nicodemus is described as a significant Jewish Pharisee who was recognized as a ruler (ἄρχων) or member of the Jewish high council (SANHEDRIN), composed of the high priest and his seventy advisers (cf. 7:44-52). He came to Jesus by night (not merely a time notation in John but also a reflection of a spiritual state).

His polite assessment, based upon his supposed knowledge of Jesus' role with God, received a startling response. He was told in no uncertain terms that he needed to be born ἄνωθεν ("again" or "from above") or he would not experience the KINGDOM OF GOD. His initial knowledge vanished with his question: how could he as an adult re-enter the tiny womb of his mother? It was illogical.

3:5-10. Clarification and confusion. Jesus' response to Nicodemus' question of logic was to present two levels of discourse based on the word ἄνωθεν. Nicodemus understood the term to signify *again* (implying an earthly context), while Jesus meant that the new-ness or birth was *from above* (a spiritual context; cf. 3:31). *Spirit* and *flesh* are thus regarded as different realms.

Spiritual (new) birth here is identified with the combination symbol of water and the spirit. *Spirit* should not be capitalized in v. 5 as in NRSV because it usually results in the "and" being treated disjunctively (cf. Harris 1971, 3:1178, and Carson 1991, 191–96). This combination reflects the interconnection between the water of cleansing and newness of heart or new spirit in the OT (e.g., Ezek 36:24-27). Some scholars would argue that this verse reflects a baptismal concern and I have so argued, but the major focus of the text is not on an event or a sacrament/ordinance but upon spiritual life. Bultmann dismisses the baptismal question completely by attributing the words "water and" to a later ecclesiastical redactor (1971, 139). But such is unnecessary, if one understands the OT roots.

Flesh (σάρξ) in John refers to the realm of humanity with all its weakness and mortality. The word here is not per se antagonistic to God as is the expression "according to the flesh" in Paul, which implies that a person has made this existence the center of life (cf. Rom 8:4-8). Here the spirit (πνεῦμα) is used to designate the empowerment of weak humanity by the Spirit of God (v. 6).

The expression "spiritual birth" thus should not lead the believer to puzzlement (v. 7) because an enlightened person should perceive the two levels of discourse, illustrated here by the fact that spirit and wind are the same word (πνεῦμα). Yet a teacher like Nicodemus, if he could not perceive the two levels, would remain confused (vv. 9-10).

3:11-13. The witness of the Son of Man. Clarification of human confusion concerning divine realities is possible only through the in-breaking of Jesus as the divine witness who descended to earth from the heavenly realm. No one else than the SON OF MAN, according to John, has been able personally to bring such a firsthand account of heaven to the realm of earth. This Son of Man figure, however, is *not* to be identified as a nonhuman, nonsuffering gnostic alien messenger from outside our realm but as the divine one who truly became human and suffered the passover death for the world.

3:14-15. Jesus and the Mosaic serpent. The work of this Son of Man is thus identified as a healing agent, like the bronze serpent that Moses had fashioned and set on a pole in the wilderness epic of the poisonous snakes (Num 21:4-9). When the bronze snake was raised and the people looked upon it, healing came to the stricken. So believing in the *lifted up* Jesus (cf. also John 8:28 and 12:32, a symbol primarily of his death but not unrelated to his resurrection/exaltation) provides the agency for healing or salvation, here called eternal life.

The expression *eternal life* (ζωὴ αἰώνιος) is a particularly important Johannine theme that is used only once in the LXX (Dan 12:2) to render the rare OT idea of "life to the end of the age" or possibly "life of eternity." In John the qualitative nature of such life is stressed, although the long duration of such life is not to be dismissed.

3:16-18. Eternal life and judgment. These three verses contain one of the best known theological summations concerning salvation in the Bible. While many have memorized 3:16, however, I have consistently insisted that the three verses belong together in providing a proper theological balance (e.g., Borchert 1987, 104–105). The middle verse (17) states God's intention or purpose in sending his only son: not for destruction but for salvation. In v. 16 both the encompassing, self-giving love of God for the world is asserted and the necessary human response of believing is defined. Then in v. 18 the harsh reality of the situation is acknowledged: namely, believing provides the rescue whereas failure to believe means condemnation—not merely in the future but already in the present. This dark side of the gospel is an *integral part* of the message of salvation.

In sending his "one and only Son" (3:16; cf. Moody 1953), however, God made clear that his intention was not destruction. The God of the entire Bible is a loving and caring God whose concern is acceptance and salvation (v. 17). But there is pathos in the divine sacrifice that was illustrated beautifully on the human level in Abraham's near sacrifice of his "only" son Isaac (Gen 22:1-14). Yet the cost of human salvation was far more significant because the price was the life of God's only Son.

3:19-21. Actions, the measure of life. Love and hate, like believing and unbelieving, are action words in John. They define the nature of a person's life like the motifs of obedience and disobedience. Accordingly, as in the Book of James, this Gospel is concerned about the evidence of Christian life (v. 21). The one who acts authentically is associated with light, but the one who does evil hates light because it reveals the dark side of one's life.

The Baptizer and Salvation, 3:22-36

The Baptizer, as witness, here takes center stage for a final time. Scholars often debated the sequence of events in this Gospel, particularly since in the Synoptics the Baptizer was imprisoned before the Galilean ministry began and Jesus had in the Gospel of John performed a sign in Cana at 2:1-11. Unlike the Synoptics, however, Jesus in John moves with regularity between south and north, leading some like Bultmann to posit displacements in segments of the Gospel. Schnackenburg (1987, 1:380–96) places 3:31-36 before 3:13 to combine the salvation discussions, but I find most displacement theories including this one unconvincing because of the failure to recognize the evangelist's totalistic perspective of time.

3:22-24. Jesus and John's baptizing. The notations at v. 22 and 4:1-2 are the only places in the Gospels where Jesus and his disciples are said to be associated with baptism prior to the resurrection. Many questions therefore arise as a result of these statements, including the question of the significance of such baptism at this stage and its relation to the baptism of John.

The assertion that John had not yet been imprisoned in v. 24 indicates that the evangelist is clearly aware of chronological issues and is making a point. Perhaps the reference to the two baptisms of Jesus and John is here made in the context of John's forthcoming imprisonment because some of his disciples (vv. 25-30) had not understood the differences in the two baptisms indicated in 1:33. In any case, Jesus is said to have been baptizing in the territory of Judea and John is identified with Aenon meaning "a place of springs" near a town called Salim meaning "a place of peace." The identification of these places is not certain, although some possibilities include a northeast DEAD SEA site and a place near SHECHEM.

3:25-30. Concerns of the Baptizer's disciples. A dispute over water purification arose between the disciples of the Baptizer and a Jew (Loisy 1921, 71, speculated that the original may have been "and of Jesus"). The reason was consternation over the popularity of Jesus. Seeking consolation, John's disciples confronted their teacher with his diminishing status. True to his earlier stance, however, John reminded them of his former witness (cf. 1:19-28) and asserted that Jesus' calling was given from heaven (a typical Jewish circumlocution for God). Then he confirmed his witness by identifying Jesus symbolically with a bridegroom and his own role as the friend of the bridegroom, whose task was to listen for the bridegroom's expression of joy in the marriage (for marriage customs see Str-B 1:45–46 and 500–502).

Acts 19:1-5 (cf. 11:16) provides evidence that the Baptizer's disciples apparently were still active at a later time. It is doubtful, however, as some have suggested that a direct connection can be made between the Baptizer and the later Mandeans (cf. Borchert, John).

3:31-36. Summation concerning the Son. The evangelist then unites the stories of Nicodemus and of the Baptizer in a reaffirmation of two levels of discourse. Only the one from above can provide authentic witness concerning divine reality. The tragedy is the general lack of acceptance (no one, a literary hyperbole) of this witness from above (v. 32). But fortunately some do accept (cf. 1:11-12) and by their acceptance here have confirmed, sealed, or certified the authenticity of this divine witness.

While God has sent many on missions (including the Baptizer), the Son is God's model for mission (having the Spirit without limitation v. 34). Into his hand the Father "has given" (a timeless perfect) all things (v. 35). Such an assertion does not mean that the Father has abandoned the world but that in the love of God there is epitomized the unity of purpose between Son and Father. Accordingly, believing (πιστεύων εἰς) the Son provides the assurance of life eternal, whereas disobeying (ἀπειθῶν) the Son guarantees the horrifying reality of God's abiding (μένει) wrath (v. 36). There is thus no room for sitting on the fence concerning Jesus because of the present reality of judgment (cf. also 3:18).

The Samaritan Woman: An Unlikely Witness, 4:1-42

This pericope is one of the most fascinating in the Gospel. It not only challenges certain set prejudices of some religious people but it offers insights for ministry such as evangelism (Borchert 1976, 62).

4:1-6. Transition and introduction. This section may provide some rationale for the departure of Jesus to GALILEE via SAMARIA, namely: Pharisaic suspicion because of his popularity (4:1-3, cf. 4:44). But the use of ἔδει ("It was necessary" [author trans.], 4:4) in John may suggest once again that Jesus was moving according to the divine plan (cf. the use of hour in 2:4). This section certainly serves to correct any possible misconception that Jesus was a baptizer (only his disciples did so). In addition, it supplies a general description of the setting for the encounter. The meeting place was at the ancient town well near *Sychar* (a site not identified but probably on the slope of Mt. Ebal across from Mt. Gerizim) and near land owned by Jacob and Joseph (Gen 48:22). Sources of water were often places of meeting (cf. Gen 24:10-15; 29:1-12). The time was *about noon* (v. 6).

4:7-9. The meeting and the first exchange. The unusual circumstances are quickly defined: a Samaritan woman seeking to draw water during the heat of the day and a tired Jewish man asking her for a drink. It was the kind of setting that would cause heads to turn.

In fact, the encounter was unusual for the woman. Jesus did not fit the pattern and she sought an explanation to his request for a drink. SAMARITANS were rejected by Jews as half-breeds, a people with mixed origins (cf. Ezra 9–10), resulting from the settlement patterns of the Assyrians after the fall of SAMARIA in 722 B.C.E. (2 Kgs 17:6, 24). Their temple was later ruthlessly destroyed by the Jewish Hasmonean king John Hyrcanus (128 B.C.E.) and relations with the Jews continued to deteriorate until a major engagement in 52 C.E. (cf. Josephus, *Ant* 20.118–136). Although the temple was not rebuilt, Samaritans have continued even today to hold their Passover celebrations on that site.

While Jesus was resting, the disciples were engaged in a shopping tour. The quest was for food, acceptable food in Samaria. They probably settled on some bread and fruit (allowable items) after their search.

4:10-15. The second exchange: on water. Picking up the water themes from previous chapters that focused on baptism and water into wine, water now becomes the subject of the two levels of discourse. The woman was concerned with water and Jesus offered her *living water* (v. 10). Her mind, however, remained fixed on the earthly plane but her question in v. 12 (*Are you greater than our ancestor Jacob?*), although anticipating a negative response, provided Jesus the necessary opening to move the conversation back to the eternal realm.

The point is that water here temporarily quenches thirst, but the water of Jesus results in *eternal life* (v. 14). Yet the woman was stuck in the concerns of worldly tasks and asked for help to ease her burden (v. 15). She was in for a surprise.

4:16-19. The third exchange: the woman's life. The response of Jesus was to address her life and relationships. Although she tried to bypass the issue, Jesus spelled out her story in greater detail. The only way to avoid the issue was to change the subject to Jesus and focus on his perceived wisdom (*a prophet*), then ask him some questions. It was a sure way to discussion.

4:20-26. The fourth and fifth exchanges: ecclesiastical and theological issues. What better way is there to create religious tension than to ask which is the best place to worship, especially since the Jews had destroyed the Samaritan temple? Carson, however, apparently thinks such an explanation is too psychological (1991, 221–22). But I think there is more to the story than Carson sees because Jesus did not fall into the trap of a changed subject. Instead, he once again turned the discussion from the level of earthly institutionalism (v. 21) to the realm of the divine goal (*hour*) for worship and to God who is the subject of such worship (v. 23-24). Moreover, he reminded the woman that proper worship, like salvation, is a matter of divine revelation (*from the Jews*) and not a human construct concerning a God who is unknown (v. 22). It was a stinging rebuttal of Samaritan worship.

The woman's next response (v. 25) is intriguing because she has been moved in her concern to speak of the future era. Yet it is not entirely clear if she is using messianic talk to counter the rebuttal of Jesus by reminding him of a higher source for information (i.e., the Messiah) since she had already politely acknowledged him as *a prophet*. Or is this statement her honest anticipation? One thing seems clear: she had not yet connected Jesus with the Messiah or the coming of the messianic age.

That connection Jesus quickly made is an important self-identification. English readers of most translations may not recognize that the Greek at v. 26 is ἐγώ εἰμί (*I am*), the primary thematic self-designation of Jesus for his role as God's anointed one (Messiah) in this Gospel.

4:27-30. The disciples' interruption and the woman's witness. The return of the disciples signals the end to this part of the story. Their surprise which is indicated by their confused thinking (v. 27) only confirms the unusual nature of Jesus' conversation with the woman. Jewish men seldom talked to women in public. Yet here he was speaking with a Samaritan woman, and one not having the best reputation.

But the evangelist wanted readers to understand that the woman's concern had shifted from the mundane realm of the water pot (she left it) to the realm of messianic visitation. The Greek text says she sought out the "men" of the town and informed them she had met a man *who told me everything I have ever done* (v. 29). I wonder if *people* (v. 28) in the RSV and NRSV is the best translation? It seems that some of the implications for the initial interest which the men had in Jesus may be lost in these versions. But her question—*He cannot be the Messiah, can he?*—certainly had its desired effect because they left the city to meet Jesus (vv. 29-30).

While Craddock (1982, 36–37) makes a point that her believing was hardly ideal, I would insist that her story must be seen in the context of how John organized the Cana cycle through increasing stages of more adequate patterns of believing. Here she carries her understanding of Jesus to the point of telling others what she is thinking.

4:31-38. The disciples miss the point. While the woman had moved from the mundane level in her thinking to that of messianic expectation, the disciples were stuck in the physical realm of food (vv. 31, 33). So Jesus tried to raise the level of their thinking from the mere search for food to the quest for nourishment that comes by fulfilling their calling of doing the will of God. He modeled for them the concern that satisfied his hunger (v. 34) and he challenged them to accept their role of harvesting *fruit for eternal life* (v. 36).

The *four months* mentioned in the proverbial statement of v. 35 is generally regarded as the shortest time between the last of the seeding season and the start of harvest. Jesus was thus calling for his disciples to recognize that the messianic era of reaping had dawned. The evangelist, as Morris argues (1986, 150–51), undoubtedly considered this message also to be an urgent call for the church to evangelization, especially since he included the notation for the disciples that reaping is a crucial task even when the reaper had not been the sower (v. 38). Yet both sower and reaper can rejoice together at the harvest (v. 36) because the division of labor here does not exclude the sower from the returns of harvest as many ancient proverbs might suggest (cf. Beasley-Murray 1987, 64 and Brown 1966, 182–83), but both laborers are seen as partners with God in this important work of ingathering.

4:39-42. The Samaritans' belief and confession. The conclusion to this magnificent story indicates both the openness of Jesus to the rejects of the world (he stayed with them for *two days*, dispensing with proprietary living patterns of status and purity) and the fact that such rejects could make the most important confession in the Cana cycle. The Samaritan rejects came to discover Jesus through the witness of a rejected woman and then to confess him as *the Savior of the world* through direct encounter (v. 42). The motif of Savior in the OT is used of God (e.g., Isa 12:2 and 43:3, cf. Luke 1:47) and not elsewhere in the Gospels of the preresurrected Jesus, except in the prediction of the angel (Luke 2:12). It is a familiar Christian confession following the resurrection (e.g., Acts 5:31; Phil 3:20; 2 Pet 1:11). Since the designation was used by Jews of God and by others of Hellenistic deities and even the Roman emperor, the Christians' use of the term for Jesus was probably one of their identifying marks.

This confession signals for readers of the Gospel the great scope (i.e. *the world*) of the mission of Jesus and agrees with the intention of God in blessing Abraham (Gen 12:3). While Jesus told the Samaritan woman that *salvation is from the Jews* (v. 22, the historical womb of God's blessing), this village of rejects discovered that God really loves *the world* (3:16) and *all who receive* Jesus can become children of God (1:12).

4:43-45. Transition to Galilee. These verses serve as one of the typical "saddle" or "shoulder" texts between pericopes in a similar way that "saddles" unite mountain peaks in a mountain chain. The evangelist uses this saddle to move attention from Samaria to Galilee and to remind readers that Galileans are not unaware of what had been taking place in Jerusalem at the Passover.

The Second Cana Sign:
Healing the Official's Son, 4:46-54

By focusing on Cana in Galilee for the second sign (only two are numbered by John) the first and second signs serve as an INCLUSIO (contrary to Beasley-Murray) whereby the stories in chaps. 2 to 4 form a unit. The first story identifies the role of signs in believing (2:11) and the second argues for a new level of believing that questions the very need for signs (4:48).

The second sign is in the form of a healing story with a twist. A person (a boy) is seriously ill and a request is made for healing (in this case by the father). Jesus then responds and the person is made well. But unlike the healing of the centurion's servant in the Synoptics (Matt 8:5-13; Luke 7:1-10), the royal official here (probably an administrator or soldier in the service of the Herodian dynasty or the Roman Caesar) begs for Jesus to come to his home. In the synoptic story the centurion begs for healing but he tells Jesus it is not necessary to come to his home. There Jesus greatly commends such gentile faith (e.g., Luke 7:9).

Here, however, Jesus must tell the father to go because his son is living (v. 50). This word of Jesus then engenders believing in the father, even though he is unable to see the reality of the healing. But when the father confirms the healing, he again and for the first time his house are said to believe (v. 53).

This pericope thus is important because it may suggest a Johannine view of stages in believing. Certainly when people in John believe, they are usually called to the next stage of believing (Brown and Carson think they can distinguish such levels by variants in the Greek form of "believe," but such linguistic distinctions should not be pushed in John). This story also seems to foreshadow the kind of believing without seeing to which Thomas is called at the end of the book (20:29).

The Festival Cycle, 5:1–11:57

Many patterns of organization have been suggested for chaps. 4–12 of this Gospel. Bultmann has chaps. 7–10 as a unit; Brown has chaps. 5–10; Carson has two segments involving chaps. 5 to 7 and 8 to 10; and Sloyan has chaps. 5 to 7 and 8 to 12. Beasley-Murray, Morris, and Schnackenburg eschew finding a unit principle and settle for much smaller sections from chaps. 4 to 12. Bultmann and Schnackenburg are impressed by some topical and geographical variations in the stories and advocate theories of displacement to settle their uneasiness with these chapters.

Aileen Guilding proposed a theory that the Gospel had been organized as a festival lectionary (1960). While her overall theory found little acceptance, her focus on the Jewish festivals sparked renewed attention by some commentators on the festival context of several chapters. Brown in particular highlights the festivals in chaps. 5 to 10. I suggest (Borchert 1993) that chaps. 5–11 are a festival cycle with an introduction involving the overarching Jewish festival of Sabbath (chap. 5) and a cycle running from Passover (chap. 6) to Passover (chap. 11). The focus of this cycle is on the growing hostility that led inevitably to the Passover death of Jesus.

In this section the Jews are frequently mentioned. It is important for the reader to realize that the context in which this Gospel was written was one of persecution of Christians by the Jews, similar to that suggested by Rev 2:9 and 3:9. But such historical realities must not be made the basis for hatred of any group today.

The Sabbath and the Healing at Bethesda, 5:1-47

The festival cycle opens with a notation concerning a feast of the Jews (v. 1) but it remains undesignated except that it soon becomes evident that the issue focuses not on that unnamed feast per se, but on a SABBATH conflict. This conflict quickly touches many other underlying concerns like Jesus' authority, identity, and relationship to the Father as well as themes such as hour, judgment, life, and witness. As Sabbath became for the Jews a pervasive, haunting factor in their lives (witnessed by its importance in the Mishnah), so the Sabbath controversy was important for the evangelist. Yet it is used only in the festival cycle and serves the evangelist as one of the factors leading to the inevitable death of Jesus.

Some scholars are not satisfied here to discuss Sabbath alone and seek to posit possibilities for this feast such as PENTECOST, TABERNACLES, etc. I think the focus here falls on Sabbath, but it is intriguing to note that the evangelist speaks of "the great day of the Sabbath" (19:31, author trans.) in connection with Passover. The problem for most commentators is that they are concerned with filling in the chronology of John and fail to realize the cyclical pattern of John that focuses on Passover.

5:1-9a. The healing of the paralytic. When Jesus went up to Jerusalem he visited the pool area below the Temple where the helpless dregs of society existed in a pathetic state. While most people avoided the area, Jesus went out of his way to visit the place and found a paralytic who had experienced the wilderness of abandonment for thirty-eight years (equal to the time of Israel's wilderness experience from Kadesh to the brook Zared, cf. Deut 2:14).

The man's response to Jesus' question concerning healing revealed his hopelessness. His only expectation was a trust in a myth concerning angelic visitations to the pool (vv. 3b-4 are later additions to the text). His hopelessness was highlighted by the fact that he thought God was not interested in the most helpless. Jesus did not argue with his erroneous presupposition or his theological perspectives about receiving healing. Instead, Jesus merely told him to get up, pick up his bed roll, and be on his way. Healing was the immediate result. •

5:9b-16. Sabbath controversy. The next statement that this day was the Sabbath strikes the reader with the force of a bomb. The opponents pounce on the helpless man who has just experienced the unbeliev-able joy of entering the promised land of a new exis-tence. They focus not on his healing but on his break-ing of their carefully articulated Sabbath rules, formu-lated to support the TORAH principle in Exod 31:12-14. The bewildered man can only defend himself by quot-ing his healer's words, even though he did not know who he was (vv. 12-13). The evangelist, however, re-minds us that Jesus did not simply leave victims to the wolves but *found* them (v. 14, cf. 9:35; cf. also the theme at 1:41ff.).

The warning of Jesus not to *sin any more* is not to be understood here as a reference to a direct cause and effect relationship between sin and illness. That issue is treated at 9:2ff. Here Jesus is alluding to sin and judgment, which are treated in the next section (5:24). While Jesus had evidenced a self-giving-healing spirit, the healed paralytic (in contrast to the healed blind man of chap. 9) may have displayed a spirit of self-preservation in reporting to the Jews. In any case, the result was that Jewish sabbatarians turned their hostili-ty on Jesus.

5:17-18. Jesus' first response: Sabbath. The re-sponse of Jesus confronted these sabbatarians and led to a new charge. Carson (1991, 247–48) notes that the rabbis would basically agree with Jesus that provi-dence demands that God should continue to work on the Sabbath. The issue for the rabbis is that humans are not God. That, of course, is the question. So, if God continues to work positively on the Sabbath and Jesus' works are the works of God, then why are his works not legitimate? The battle was joined when Jesus called God his Father. The Jews recognized the equation immediately. Now the charge was not merely Sabbath breaking but also blasphemy.

5:19-24. Jesus' second response: relationship to the Father. The double ἀμήν (*truly*) signals again that two crucial statements are being made in this section. While the Jews have focused on equality, Jesus had highlighted his dependency on the Father. That depen-dency would be the means by which humans would come to understand the Son's role in the giving of life and the rendering of judgment. In that context there would come a recognition of the relationship between Father and Son. Moreover, obedience is not defined by Jesus in relation to rules such as observation of the Sabbath, but in terms of dynamic life patterns involv-ing honoring the Son (v. 23) and believing (v. 24). Such obedient response is the basis for gaining the assurance of eternal life and avoiding judgment.

5:25-29. Jesus' third response: the two resurrec-tions. In these responses the questioners have almost faded into the background as the evangelist's interest is directed only to the words of Jesus. The double ἀμήν once again announces a significant statement. The previous response identified a division between life and judgment. In this response the announcement is sounded concerning the coming of the decisive hour and the future eschatological separation between life and judgment represented in the idea of two resurrec-tions.

Bultmann (1971, 258–61), who is committed to a perspective of realized eschatology, finds such futuris-tic suggestions to be "dangerous" editorial additions to the early message. But the perspective of the text is that both present and future are genuine realities. Yet these realities are intertwined because present hearing (obedience) leads to the resurrection of life. Moreover, the idea of resurrection from the evangelist's under-standing was hardly a mere spiritual experience. For Jews the resurrection meant dealing with dead bodies and that is the reason why John has no hesitation in including a reference to persons emerging from tombs (v. 28). The point of the discussion is that Jesus' oppo-nents and the evangelist's hearers are being clearly warned that relationship to Jesus has immense eschato-logical consequences.

5:30-47. Jesus' fourth response: witnesses to his authority. The statements in vv. 30 and 31 seem to presuppose challenges both to Jesus' authority in judg-ment and the validity of his God-directed claims. The responses on the part of Jesus are a forthright denial of his self-seeking and the articulation of a four-fold testi-mony supporting his claims.

The first witness he called was John the Baptizer. He chose John not because he wished to rely on hu-man testimony but because such a testimony might help lead humans to salvation (v. 34). The second testimony is rated by Jesus at a higher level than the first, namely, his works. These works he was doing in accordance with the Father's will and the Jews could hardly deny their existence (v. 36).

The third witness he called was the Father. What does the evangelist mean by such a statement? It was a type of shorthand. Was it some voice from heaven (e.g., 12:28) or a sense of divine presence (e.g., 11:41-42)? Greater clarity would help. But the difficulty of using the Father as a witness for them was immediate-ly apparent to Jesus and he highlighted it. They could not accept such a witness because, unlike the prophets, they had not heard God speak. Moreover, unlike Isaiah (Isa 6:1) or Jacob at Jabbok (Gen 32:30), they had no vision of him or sense of his form. But perhaps most devastating of all was that they who claimed to uphold the Torah did not have God's *word* inwardly resident in them (vv. 37-38).

The mention of God's word provides the fourth and final witness: *the scriptures*, to which they by profession had committed themselves (v. 39). Here Jesus forthrightly condemns them because of their refusal to accept him (v. 40) and recognize the testimony of the texts they supposedly defended. Human religious confirmation of his role, however, was not required by Jesus (v. 41) because humans are confused in their offering of praise (vv. 43-44). So Jesus asserted that the religious leaders should clearly realize that he did not need to play the roles of both accuser and judge concerning them. Their accuser would be none other than Moses on whom they said they relied but failed in fact to believe (vv. 45-46).

Passover and the Exodus Motif, 6:1-71

The crossing of the sea (v. 1) and the coming of people out to a lonely mountainside (v. 3) formed a picture-perfect setting for reflecting about Jesus and the EXODUS. Accordingly, it should be no surprise that in this chapter the linkage of a miraculous feeding and a control of the sea is compared to the experience of MOSES in the wilderness.

It should also be no surprise that in such a context the evangelist announces it was PASSOVER time (v. 4). Even within the Passover Haggada today, in the introduction before the pronouncing of the "three words" and the "Halelya," two of the great "benefits" that are rehearsed are the control of the sea and the feeding of manna (see e.g., Fisch 1965). Likewise, when detailing God's great mercies both the Psalmist (Ps 78:13-30) and Paul (1 Cor 10:1-4) link these two events of water control and food supply as crucial for remembrance.

It is most likely, therefore, that as the early Christians told the stories of their Lord, bread and water miracles from his earthly life were also recited. Thus, when Mark first set the gospel in written form, it was quite natural that these two events would be narrated in a related context (Mark 6:30-52). Another highly significant event for Mark was the decisive point of discipleship in which Mark includes a confession by Peter (Mark 8:27-30). John brings all of these elements together in his development of this strategic Passover chapter and hints at the fact that the death of Jesus (flesh and blood) will be a key to eternal life (v. 54).

6:1-13. The distribution of food. In the unfolding of the text, following the crossing of the Sea of Tiberias (the Roman designation usually called Galilee, but also Gennesaret in Luke 5:1 [from the Heb. *kinnereth*], because it had the outline of a lyre), Jesus is pictured as sitting on a mountain side (v. 3), reminiscent of an ancient dispenser of divine wisdom. The linkage with the Mosaic experience at SINAI may be in mind (cf. Matt 5:1).

The feeding is introduced by Jesus questioning PHILIP (the company logician) concerning resources. Philip's answer was that the crowd was so large (5,000) that even 200 days' pay would have been insufficient to feed them. ANDREW (the company helper) found a small amount of food among the crowd (five barley loaves and two dried fish), but for Jesus it was sufficient (total, seven; cf. also the seven loaves and a "few" fish in feeding 4,000 of Mark 8:6-7). Thus, when Jesus acted, everyone had enough (v. 11).

Indeed, there was so much remaining that the disciples (Brown 1966, 233, wonders whether they are synonymous with the Twelve) collected twelve baskets of bread. The number twelve is symbolic for the people of God. This story was of such significance to early Christians that it is the only miracle per se reported in all four Gospels. The sea miracles vary, but their impact is the same. For John the bread miracle served as an important sign and became the basis for the following discourse.

6:14-15. The people's messianic expectations. In the minds of the Jews awaiting the MESSIAH, this act of feeding spurred the people's messianic hopes. Their immediate reaction was that this Jesus had to be the long expected *prophet* like Moses (Deut 18:15; cf. John 1:21). The additional reference to the one *who is to come* (v. 15) was, as Mowinckle has argued, also viewed as a messianic designation (1954, 213–41, 295–321, 385–93).

The expectations of the people were ignited to such an extent that they were ready to give Jesus the throne of DAVID and force the realization of their hopes (v. 15; cf. Jer 23:5; Ezek 34:23). But Jesus instead took to the mountains again because their understanding and timing were both skewed.

6:16-21. Walking on water. This pericope begins with a note that night and darkness fell. Such designations in John are usually theologically instructive (cf. 3:2 and 13:30), especially here since a storm arose and the disciples were caught in the middle of the sea (which was between five and seven mi. wide; cf. Josephus, *BJ* 3.10.7; 506). Despite the conditions, Jesus calmly walked on the sea. The Exodus symbolism is hard to miss.

No doubt the evangelist regarded this appearance as a Christophany (like the appearances of God in the OT) for here are present both the familiar sense of fear and the calming words, *Do not be afraid* (v. 20). While the expression "I am" (ἐγώ εἰμι) may be interpreted as a simple self-identification (*It is I,* as in many translations), the reader familiar with John cannot help but connect these words with God's revelation to Moses (Exod 3:14).

The joy of the disciples then replaced their fear as Jesus entered the boat. Moreover, their goal of reaching a safe harbor was immediately realized. Jesus thus is like the God of the OT who brings his people from a stormy sea to a safe haven (Ps 107:23-32).

6:22-25. The people sought Jesus. While the geography is a little vague, these stories suggest that the feeding may have taken place on the east side of the sea where there are hills (less likely is the traditional northeast side). The boats came from the west side (TIBERIAS) and the people took their boats from *near* the feeding place and found Jesus on the northwest side (CAPERNAUM). The people's query of Jesus concerning his coming to that place set the stage for a discourse on the sign of bread.

6:26-34. The sign of bread. The familiar Johannine double ἀμήν (*truly*) formula once again introduces a key perspective. The people were following because of the physical food, not because they recognized the *signs* (v. 26). The KJV incorrectly reads "miracles" here. The nature of the sign is to point beyond miracle to the one who nourishes to eternal life. When one understands such a sign, one should perceive the relationship of the acts of the *Son of Man* (Jesus' self-definition, cf. 1:51) to the works of the Father.

The response of unperceiving Jews, however, was tragic. Their request for a sign that would lead them to believe thus inspired yet another double-level Johannine insight framed, as Borgen (1965) has argued, like a midrashic interpretation of Exod 16:15, etc. They missed the point because their desire was for a return to a physical preservation model like that of manna in the wilderness (v. 31). But the bread was not merely a gift from a deliverer like MOSES; it had been given by God. The real gift of God's bread was not physical; it was life *come down from heaven* (v. 33). The misun-

derstanding inherent in their subsequent request for continual supplying of such bread (6:34) introduces an "I am" discourse.

6:35-40. Jesus' proclamation: the bread of life. The self-identification of Jesus as *I am the bread of life* (v. 35) is made here, but the motif of eating is expanded to include drinking (important for the next section). This affirmation merges into a discussion of separation and preservation. The opponents of Jesus are judged as unbelieving. But those whom the Father gives to Jesus will not be castaways (vv. 37, 39). Instead, they will have eternal life and experience resurrection in *the last day* (vv. 39-40). This concept of the resurrection on the last day is defuturized in Bultmann (1971, 233) but would have been perfectly understandable to a futuristically oriented Jewish Christian audience of the first century.

6:41-48. Reaction and defense. The reaction of the Jews is by John defined in Exodus terminology: "murmured" (NRSV, *complained*). The text implies they understood that he was claiming divine descent and mission. As a result they launched into a discussion of his family tree, which they said they knew (v. 42). The irony is obvious. Jesus responded in terms of his relationship to the Father and the eschatological hope of those drawn to him by God (v. 44). His response was based on the proclamation of the prophets that in the messianic era God's people would be instructed by God (cf. Isa 54:13; Jer 31:33-34).

Employing another double ἀμήν saying, he then identified their concern for physical bread and their earthly messianic hope with the hopeless state of those who perished in the wilderness even though they ate physical MANNA. But those who are nourished by *the living bread*, Jesus said, would have eternal life (v. 51). The problem for them was that such bread was his *flesh*.

6:52-59. Identification of flesh and blood. This identification of bread and flesh was too much for the Jews to swallow. The response of Jesus was another double ἀμήν saying that linked the inward acceptance (eating) of his sacrificial death (flesh and blood) to the reception of eternal life and resurrection on the last day (v. 54). The Jews, however, were stuck in the physical realm of reality with their fathers who ate manna and died (v. 58).

This section has been the focus of much theological discussion concerning the relationship to the LORD'S SUPPER. Brown (1966, 287–93), for example, sees it as the Johannine "institution," whereas Carson (1991,

295) thinks that the use of "flesh" rather than "body" argues against such a primary eucharistic sense. It is impossible in this space to detail the arguments on this matter but our attention should be kept on the major focus of the passage: namely, the familiar Johannine theme of receiving Jesus (cf. 1:12). That the evangelist probably saw in the supper a symbolic representation of the reception of Jesus is quite likely. But it is a question of what gives birth to what in John. This Gospel is certainly very symbolic. The issue is: Is sacrament a primary focus here?

6:60-71. Reaction of the disciples. The reader of John may be confused here by the designation *disciples* in this passage because disciples are said here to be troubled by Jesus' saying and, like the wilderness people, they murmured (v. 60). Indeed, Jesus said, they did not believe (v. 64) and in fact they departed and no longer walked with him (v. 66).

The insertion of the distinction between flesh and spirit in this context (v.63) is a reminder that the evangelist frequently employs words with two levels of meaning as he did when he used the term *believe* at 2:23-24. The confession of Peter and the mention of Judas is here a clear indication of this double level in discipleship.

The mention of Jesus choosing Judas Iscariot (vv. 70-71) must not be made the basis for a theology of reprobation (election or determinism to destruction). The text does not say that Jesus determined Judas to be a devil-man. The designation Iscariot is not totally clear. He may have been a man (*ish*; or the son of a man) from Kerioth or one of the "sicarii" (revolutionary knife men). But John will not let the reader forget the dark side of this disciple in contrast to the self-sacrifice of Jesus.

Tabernacles and the Motif of Deliverance, 7:1–9:41

This section of the Festival cycle involves the popular (Josephus *Ant* 8.100) post-harvest Feast of Booths or Tabernacles. If the Messiah were to come, it would be expected that he would put in an appearance in the month of Tishri, the most celebrated month of the Jewish year. The month started with the joyous celebration of the New Year on the first and second. It was followed on the tenth by the most sacred day of *Yom Kippur* (Day of Atonement) and it was climaxed with the joyous celebration of Tabernacles on the fifteenth to the twenty-second when the faithful devo-

tees left their houses and dwelt in booths as a reminder of God's preservation and deliverance.

This section, which highlights controversy, begins with the issue of timing concerning the adoption of Jesus' messianic role (7:1-13) and the reaction he engenders (7:14-36). The focus then moves to Jesus as water (7:37-39) and returns to the question of Jesus' messiahship (7:40-52). It moves next to Jesus as light (8:12) and returns again to his messiahship in terms of the question of his origin and purpose (8:13-29). Then it moves to the question of freedom (8:31-32) and leads to an outright confrontation on lineage and bondage (8:33-59). The evangelist then illustrates the importance of both light and deliverance in the story of the blind man (9:1-34) and concludes with Jesus' verdict about the parties in the dispute (9:35-41).

The pericope of the adulterous woman (7:53–8:11) is a fascinating story that wound up as a somewhat disconnected segment in the framework of the message of Tabernacles, and will be treated in an appendix at the end of the commentary. This style of treatment is no reflection on the worthiness of the story or its legitimacy to be regarded as a canonical pericope.

7:1-13. The brothers' question of messiahship at Tabernacles. The mood of this section is set by the opening notation of hostility. The issue is focused by the demand of the brothers (Mary's other children, not cousins) that Jesus adopt their time frame for his messianic revelation at Tabernacles (v. 3). The dialogue that follows is somewhat reminiscent of Jesus' rejection of his mother's timing (2:4).

Many readers become confused by the fact that Jesus said he was not going up to the feast (v. 8) when he did so almost immediately (v. 10). Like many other issues in John, the reader needs to recognize the two levels of discourse that are taking place. Jesus' timing is PASSOVER not TABERNACLES, and his role is not that of conquering hero but of dying Messiah. It was not Jesus' time for public show (v. 4) but for personal ministry (vv. 4, 10). Expectation concerning Jesus was obviously very high at this feast (vv. 11-12) although fear muted some open expression of it (v. 13). That Jesus could not help but engender public reaction (v. 26), however, does not change the fact that for John the actual public work of Jesus is his hour of glorification (12:31-32; 17:1).

7:14-36. Reactions to Jesus' messiahship. The appearance of Jesus in a teaching mode raised a question immediately. The *am ha'erez* (the "people of the land," who worked with their hands like carpenters and fishermen) were not trained in the technicalities of religious dialogue. Their insecurity in religious discussion would be obvious. Yet to the surprise of his hearers, Jesus (who was one of them) assumed the authority to teach (v. 15). Indeed, he claimed divine authority (v. 16) and criticized his opponents (the Jewish leadership) for not obeying Moses.

Their intention was to kill him (v. 19) because he healed on the Sabbath (v. 23; cf. 5:18). Of course, the argument could have turned on the rabbinic interpretations of the priority of Sabbath laws (Exod 31:12-17) over murder laws (Exod 20:13) but here they denied any intention to kill him. Indeed, they categorized him as a misguided, demon-possessed lunatic (v. 20). But Jesus did not accept their designation and attacked their motives and their Sabbath law logic by reference to circumcision (v. 22). The point was to critique their lack of tenderness for hurting people (vv. 23-24).

This open confrontation on religious logic with the religious elite raised for the people the issue of his role and their theories of an unknown origin for the Messiah. The questions of *where?* (origin, v. 27) and *where?* (goal, v. 35) are an undercurrent in this Gospel and once again John employs an ironic double-level meaning for the word *know* (v. 27) to focus attention on who Jesus is.

The leadership's answer to this threat was an attempt to silence this religious interloper by dispatching their guard to seize him (7:32).

7:37-39. Jesus and the water ritual. When the Jewish people moved in large numbers from the rural areas to the cities, the festive experiences of harvest were not as significant. But following long dry summers, cisterns were usually depleted and urbanites prayed for the coming of rain. The PHARISEES (mostly urbanites) promoted the addition of rain prayers in the celebration of Tabernacles (cf. Zech 14:16-19; *m. Sukk.* 5:1). The SADDUCEES generally had resisted this insertion as revisionist and conflict over this matter came to a head in the time of the Sadducean high priest and king, Alexander Janaeus, who poured the water offering at his feet. A rapprochement with the Pharisees was gained by his successors and the water ritual was retained. While the festival was eight days in length (including a Sabbath climax) the water ritual was conducted for seven days. On the seventh day the priests brought water seven times from the pool of Siloam. It may be that the evangelist means this seventh day by his designation *the last day* (v. 37) or perhaps he means the solemn Sabbath that followed.

The evangelist here draws together several themes in reflecting on Jesus at this event. Water in the OT is linked with the people's expectation of salvation (Isa 12:3; 55:1). Also, as life-sustaining water flowed from the rock (Exod 17:6), so life-giving water comes from Jesus (v. 38; cf. the visions of the future in Ezek 47:9-12 and Rev 22:1-2). Moreover, the evangelist notes that such a life-enhancing experience is to be connected with the coming of the Spirit following the glorification of Jesus (v. 39).

There is a minor textual variation in vv. 37 and 38. The NRSV, which links believing and drinking and forms a parallelism, is to be preferred over the earlier RSV rendering.

7:40-52. Evaluations of Jesus' messiahship. Division of opinions followed. Some affirmed him and answered positively the questions directed at John the Baptist (cf. 1:20-21). Some were frustrated by their theories concerning his origin. Others wanted to be rid of him. The guard returned empty-handed, stunned by the power of his words (v. 46). But the authorities and Pharisees remained undeterred. Their arrogant question (Had any of them believed? v. 48) was for the evangelist a double-edged irony when compared to their opinion of the stupid *crowd* (v. 49). Even the logic of fairness proposed by *Nicodemus* (v. 50-51) was rebuffed by their intolerance and name-calling. The issue for them was closed.

8:12. The light. The joyousness of the ritual of lights, which was accompanied by singing and dancing and which permeated the seven festival days of Tabernacles, was a reminder of God's leading of the people by fire in the darkness of the wilderness (Exod 13:21). Here the *I am* saying affirms the role of Jesus in lighting the darkness for his followers.

8:13-29. Return to the conflict: A legal argument. The rejection of Jesus' messiahship is again raised by a Pharisaic charge of bearing witness to himself, a charge Jesus preemptively argued in 5:30-47. In this passage, however, the issue of "whence" and "whither" (origin and goal; v. 14) are brought to center stage in the context of truth or authenticity.

The scene here is reminiscent of a legal argument. The opponents have rendered their verdict by rejecting Jesus (v. 15). His rebuttal was that he was not yet at the judgment stage (cf. v. 26), but if he were to render a verdict, it would be true because of his divine connection (v. 16). Instead, he was at the witness stage and while he provided the required two witnesses (cf. Deut 19:15) their problem was that they did not know the Father who functioned as his confirming witness. Moreover, their failure to regard him made it impossible for them to know the Father (v. 19). This testimony is certainly a tight one, but it is not necessarily convincing to the unconvinced.

On the other hand, the opponents were unable to carry out the sentence attached to their verdict because of a fundamental Johannine thesis: the *hour had not yet come* (v. 20). So the conflict continued.

There is no question, however, that Jesus understood that the opponents' desire for his death would be fulfilled. But it was not to be interpreted as their victory. Rather it was a divinely directed departure (v. 21) or "lifting up" (v. 28) that would bring a verdict on them: namely, they would die in their sin (v. 21). Yet Jesus did supply a verdict. They would not be able to join him in his realm above (vv. 22-23) because the basis for entrance to that realm was believing that he was the *I am* (v. 24; cf. Exod 3:14).

The dialogue that follows confirms the fact that Jesus and the Jews were operating on different wave lengths (v. 27). While the text of v. 25b is not entirely clear, the remaining verses indicate that recognition and condemnation would follow upon his death.

8:30-59. The conflict continues: truth and freedom. The notation in the midst of the conflict that many believed (v. 30) is followed by a statement that to those who believed Jesus issued his famous logion concerning truth and freedom (v. 32). The result was an immediate defensive response on the part of those addressed, involving both an assertion of kinship with father Abraham and a denial of any bondage experience (v. 33). These verses thus provide an illustration or commentary on 2:23-25 and the fallacy of much human believing.

Because the logion in v. 32 is frequently removed from its context and used as a justification for academic education, it is well to remember that knowing truth here is not related to academic information. The point is knowing Jesus. Moreover, freedom is not mere liberty; it is freedom in Christ and freedom from sin (vv. 34-36).

These "believers" are thus not to be categorized as legitimate disciples because their reliance for acceptance was built upon human descent patterns (father Abraham, vv. 37, 39) and their style of life was linked to those who would kill Jesus (vv. 37, 40). True believing in Jesus and true children of God would reflect the attitude of loving Jesus (v. 42). Instead, Jesus judged them harshly as *liars* and as children of the devil (v. 44). Accordingly, Jesus asked them to respond to two underlying questions: (1) Who can bring a verdict of sin upon Jesus? and (2) Why did they not in fact believe (v. 46)?

Their reaction was predictable. Like the priests and Pharisees who dismissed Nicodemus with a name (cf. 7:52), these "believers" categorized Jesus as a despised Samaritan (cf. 4:9) and as one possessed of a demon (v. 48). This interaction between Jesus and the so-called "believers" raised the issue of honor and shame (v. 49) in that society (for discussion, see e.g. Malina 1981, 25–50), a reality that runs extremely deep, particularly in many non-Western cultures.

The response of Jesus was another double ἀμήν (*truly*) saying, this one concerning obedience and death (v. 51). The promise of no death was for his opponents the proof of his authenticity. Even Abraham died. Who did he think he was? *Greater than . . . Abraham* (v. 53)? This question, like the woman's concerning Jacob (4:12), was seen by the evangelist to provide the coup de grace for his argument. Abraham acknowledged the priority of Jesus and not the reverse (vv. 56-58). The second double ἀμήν saying here (v. 58) is fascinating because it explodes our natural reasoning concerning time and reminds the reader that Jesus is the *I am*.

Such a response was too much for his opponents and although they would have stoned him, he departed and left them with their frustrations (v. 59).

9:1-12. Healing a blind man. The Tabernacles motif is brought to a climax with the story of the blind man. The connection with Tabernacles and chap. 8 is assured by the repetition of the *I am* saying concerning the light of the world (v. 5; cf. 8:12). The story is thus to be regarded as an illustrative outworking of earlier issues.

The question of theodicy (God's goodness and power in the face of evil) serves as the starting point of the story. It was raised by the disciples who sought a simplistic rationale to the problem OF BLINDNESS (v. 2). They were not unlike the pessimistic friends of JOB and they certainly had hardly digested the message of Ezek 18:20 concerning blame and the role of parents. But here was a man born blind. Who was to blame for this tragedy? Rather than agreeing to their easy solutions of blame, Jesus shifted the discussion to the grace of God in the face of human need (v. 3) and called attention to the shortness of his mission by reference to the theme of light and darkness (vv. 4-5).

Then he put mud cakes on the man's eyes and sent him to wash at Siloam ("sent," vv. 6-7). Following his healing the neighbors were filled with questions (vv. 8-9) and he was called upon to answer their queries concerning this strange happening (vv. 10-12).

9:13-34. A predetermined controversy. Verses 13 and 14 serve as early warning signals in the story that trouble was on the horizon. Bringing the man to the Pharisees had all the earmarks of a kangaroo court and the notation that it was Sabbath is like a prediction of doom (cf. 5:9b).

The interrogation began with a simple question about what happened (v. 15). It quickly led to a division of opinion concerning the relative weights to be attached to Sabbath and healing in the evaluation process (v. 16). So the man was asked for his judgment about the healer. His response that the healer was a *prophet* would seem on the surface to be a minimally safe assessment (v. 17). But for judges who have predetermined the case and who are unimpressed by a caring, merciful spirit, such logic carries little or no casuistic force in an argument.

Instead, the interrogation sought for a reason to debunk the impressive miracle. First, they questioned the authenticity of the man's former blindness. So they called for a confirmation from his parents about his blindness and for an explanation of his transformed state (vv. 18-19). The parents were of little help in the debunking process. Moreover, in seeking to avoid excommunication from the synagogue the parents refused to become involved and referred the interrogators back to their son as fully capable of answering for himself (vv. 20-21).

Next the interrogators tried to set the parameters for the man's answers so they could accept his present state and reject the healer (v. 24). But the man refused their theological gymnastics by reminding them of the legitimacy of the miracle (v. 25). So they began their questioning again. The exasperated man then questioned both their motives (v. 27) and their evaluation (vv. 30-32) concerning the healer. His logic proved impeccable because healing and a good God belong to the same side of reality and are not opposites as the interrogators were trying to make him believe.

These teachers (who relied on Moses and did not know who sent this healer) refused to accept correct teaching, called the man a name (sinner), dismissed his testimony, and excommunicated him (v. 34). The relationship of this story to the early Christians who were designated heretics (*minim*) and excluded from the synagogue would hardly be missed by the early readers.

9:35-41. The verdict of Jesus. The verdict of the interrogators and their dismissal, however, was followed by the searching Jesus who *found* (v. 35, cf. 1:43 and the ironic uses in 1:41, 45) the abandoned man and began a brief, alternative interrogation geared to his acceptance.

The man's witness to the Pharisees had been firm although he had not seen his healer. Now he had the chance to behold the *Son of Man* and confirm his belief (vv. 35-37). Forged in the context of deliverance and defense and faced with his God-sent healer, his confession became a firm *I believe* and his worship of Jesus (v. 38) has stood as unique in this Gospel's pre-resurrection stories of Jesus. He is a model of faith and commitment to the fulfillment of the messianic hope (cf. 4:23-26).

Accordingly, Jesus as judge judged the parties. In his coming as light to the world the blind were enabled to see and those who thought they saw became blind (vv. 39-41). The verdict was clear.

Dedication and the Motif of the Shepherd, 10:1-42

The Gospel is filled with many symbolic ideas, ironic statements, and double-level presentations. But in this long symbolic or parabolic chapter the evangelist for the first time identifies his treatment as figurative (παροιμία; cf. 16:25, 29). This mashal or extended parable provides several insightful portrayals of who Jesus is and his relationship to his followers. Moreover, he is symbolically contrasted with his opponents and the pseudoservants of God.

The chapter begins with a portrayal of Jesus as shepherd (vv. 1-6) which merges into a more involved picture of him as both door or gate and shepherd (vv. 7-18) which then leads to a familiar theme of division (vv. 19-21). In the heart of the discussion the note is sounded that it was the feast of Dedication at the Temple (vv. 22-23) that celebrated the cleansing of the defamed altar and Temple in the time of Judas Maccabeus, who himself became a messianic symbol. The discussion, accordingly, moves to the messianic role of Jesus as shepherd and his relationships with both believers and unbelievers as well as with the Father (vv. 24-30). It concludes with the attempt to stone Jesus which results in his departure across the Jordan (vv. 31-42).

10:1-6. Jesus the shepherd. The double ἀμήν introduces a new section and a new series of *I am* sayings focusing on the role of Jesus as the Messiah (cf.

10:24). The first picture is of Jesus as a shepherd leader, who fits the prophetic picture of the coming messianic shepherd-king like DAVID (Jer 23:5-6; Ezek 34:23-24). To watch shepherds leading (cf. vv. 3-4) sheep in Israel today with a song or tune even in urban areas points to the intimacy of relationship between shepherd and sheep that is often missed in the hard driving patterns of much contemporary life. Thieves and strangers cannot participate in such a close relationship and the evangelist points his judgmental finger at the opponents of Jesus with the words *they did not understand what he was saying to them* (v. 6).

10:7-18. Jesus as door and shepherd. The second double ἀμήν saying adjusts the focus slightly to describe Jesus as *the gate* or door of the sheepfold (v. 7). Many sheepfolds were built of rock walls but without gates. So once the sheep were safely inside, the shepherd took his position at the entrance serving as the guard.

The shepherd who is thus symbolized as the means of safety and security for the sheep is contrasted to thieves (v. 10) and wolves (v. 12) who plunder, devour, and devastate the flock. The implication would have been very clear in that day because the prophets likened the leaders of God's people to such destructive portraits (cf. Jer 23:12; Ezek 34:3-5).

The shepherd is likewise contrasted to the hired servant (v. 12) who received pay for work but was hardly invested in the sheep. Thus, when danger threatened, the paid worker was more concerned with payment and self-survival than with the security of the sheep (v. 13; cf. Ezek 34:8b-10).

The good shepherd, however, was invested so much in the sheep that he was ready to die for the sheep (vv. 11, 17). The picture of the dying shepherd is clearly to be associated in John with the dying *Lamb of God that takes away the sin of the world* (1:29), an image that coordinates with the fact that the goal of the death and resurrection for Jesus reaches beyond the Jews to the whole world (v. 16). The death and resurrection are here clearly implied (vv. 17-18) and the death is to be understood as Jesus' authoritative self-sacrifice and certainly not in terms of the power of world authorities over Jesus. The meaning is one of divine control and timing even in death.

10:19-21. Division. By now the reader is familiar with the theme that Jesus caused division (cf. 1:11-12). His words brought hostile reactions so that he was identified by many as demon possessed (v. 20; cf. 7:20; 8:48; etc.). Yet his works often caused others to evaluate him differently (10:21, 32-33; cf. 2:23; 4:48; 7:31; 9:32-33; etc.).

10:22-30. Dedication and the messianic question. On the twenty-fifth of Kislev 164 B.C.E., a new festival of Hanukkah (Dedication) was inaugurated into the Jewish year that celebrated the rededication of the Temple after the Syrians of Antiochus IV (Epiphanes) desecrated the Temple by slaughtering a pig on the altar and by setting up a statue of Zeus in the Temple. The defeat of the Syrians, the liberation of Jerusalem, and the cleansing of the Temple under the Maccabees electrified Jewish messianic dreams. These dreams of a messianic state bubbled into sporadic uprisings until they were crushed by the Roman destruction of Jerusalem in 70 C.E. and finally put to rest by the defeat of Bar-Kochba (135 C.E.).

These dreams were undoubtedly behind the question of the Jews concerning the possibility of Jesus being the *Messiah* (Christ, v. 24). But a shroud may be cast over the question by the fact that John announced it was Dedication and *it was winter* (v. 23). Obviously, Dedication came in winter time, but time designations in John often have theological import. Could it be that John was again thinking on two levels? In any case, their request that he should speak *plainly* (v. 24) is set in contrast to the "figurative" nature (10:6) of most of this chapter.

The response of Jesus to their request has the earmarks of frustration with their unwillingness to accept his words and to recognize the divine origin of his works (v. 25). The issue was not one of having information concerning Jesus but of being his sheep and believing the reality to which his words and works witnessed (vv. 26-27).

The reintroduction of the shepherd motif serves an important function in this argument. After operating on the thesis that his sheep knew him and heeded his voice (cf. 10:3-4, 14), Jesus moved their thinking from the level of safety in the sheepfold to safety and security in terms of eternal life of the believer and security from the powers of destruction (v. 28). This verse has often been used as a proof text in discussions of the security of the believer and sometimes linked with theories of predestination (here *given me* v. 29) to advocate concepts like "eternal security." It is important to recognize both that the term "eternal security" is a multi-meaning construct that does not appear in the Bible, and that any theory of security must take seriously the warnings of God and the idea of "following" the shepherd (v. 27—see Borchert 1987).

For the believer, life and security are gifts of God which are vested in the unified leading of the shepherd and the Father (vv. 27-30).

10:31-42. The hostile reaction. The identification of Jesus with the Father (10:30) once again raised the ire of the Jews (v. 31; cf. 5:18). Stoning for them was the answer (cf. 8:59). The Romans were in charge of capital punishment cases, but mob violence was frequent in the uneasy context of Judea. The charge here of blasphemy (v. 33; using God's holy name) was not technically satisfied (*m. Sanh.* 7:5) but mobs are hardly concerned with technicalities.

Jesus' defense (v. 34) was to cite a passage from Ps 82:6 where others are called gods (the meaning of that text is not clear but it may refer to sons of God at Sinai, corrupt judges who act like gods, or angelic beings). The purpose of the citation was to challenge their judgment patterns by reference to their indisputable source of argument, *the scripture* (v. 35). The reference to *law* here (v. 34) is obviously not to be understood technically as the written five books of Moses but as a general reference to scripture.

Jesus' concern was to help them understand his role in the overall work of God. So in the context of Dedication he referred to himself as *the Father's* consecrated (or *sanctified*) one, *sent* on mission by the Father (v. 36; cf. 17:17-19). He then turned to remind them that he was not blaspheming as the Son of God. He called them to think about his works as a basis for understanding his words of identification with the Father (vv. 37-38).

His defense, however, failed to convince them because they could not accept the premise of the relationship of Jesus and the Father (v. 38). Instead, they once again attempted to arrest him, but they were unsuccessful (v. 39). Accordingly, he left Judea and crossed the Jordan. He stayed in the area where John the Baptizer began his witness. People there, in contrast to Judea, *believed in him* (vv. 40-42).

A Climactic Sign and the Passover Plot, 11:1-57

In this strategic chapter the Festival cycle has come full circle. Beginning with a SABBATH introduction (chap. 5) the evangelist leads the reader from PASSOVER (6:4) to Passover (11:55) and from a desire to kill Jesus (5:18) to the decisive death plot (11:47-53). As the earlier Cana cycle began (2:11) and ended (4:54) with miraculous signs, so this cycle that has five signs begins (5:8) and ends (11:43) with miraculous events.

Unlike the portraits of Jesus in the Synoptics where the cleansing of the Temple is viewed as the last straw for the Jewish opposition, the event in John that welded the opposition into its climactic verdict (v. 50) is the raising of LAZARUS. The story of Lazarus (vv. 1-44) and the Passover plot (vv. 45-57) are thus intimately bound together in a stirring conclusion to the Festival cycle.

11:1-16. The setting: The death of Lazarus and reactions of the disciples. The story begins with the introduction of a sick man, Lazarus, and his two sisters from BETHANY (probably a town on the eastern ridge of the Mount of Olives, a short distance from Jerusalem). Mary is further identified, prior to the event, as *the one who anointed* Jesus (v. 2; cf. 12:3). This note provides perspective later when the reader learns that the anointing was for his burial (12:7).

The message the sisters sent to Jesus, *he whom you love is ill* (v. 3), has led Filson (1963, 22–25) to speculate that the BELOVED DISCIPLE and thus the author of this Gospel was Lazarus. While this argument is intriguing, it has been accepted by very few scholars. However, it does point out that speculation is always with us.

The reaction of Jesus that the sickness is *not to* (πρός) *death* but *for God's glory* (v. 4) may seem to the reader to conflict with the statement that *Lazarus is dead* (v. 14). But the author, who is in control of the story, employs the earlier statement as a window into the development of the story so that the reader will realize that Jesus is in control of the situation and that the events of the story will lead to the glorification of the *Son of God* (v. 4).

This window can be helpful in understanding both the actions of Jesus and the reactions of his followers. It may seem from a modern perspective that Jesus' love for Lazarus and his sisters (v. 5) cannot be coordinated with his delay of *two days* in coming to them (v. 6). Indeed, later Martha and Mary seem to express such a feeling (11:21, 32).

The disciples on the other hand were relieved to be outside of Judea and had no desire to return. So when Jesus announced to them an intention to return (v. 7), resistance seized their minds and they reminded him of the Judean threat of stoning (v. 8). The sermonette of Jesus about walking in the daylight hardly calmed their troubled hearts (vv. 9-10). When, therefore, Jesus told them he was going to awaken the sleeping Lazarus, they pled that he would not do anything rash because sick and sleeping people recover and wake up (v. 12).

His announcement that Lazarus was dead stunned them and they failed to hear his words that the situation would ultimately support their believing (v. 15). THOMAS, the model of earthly realism, voiced their hopelessness in the decision. But it was hardly the perspective of a coward. It was the voice of resignation in the face of a perceived reality, the acceptance of hopelessness for what it seemed to be. It was a willingness to die (v. 16). History has generally treated Thomas superficially. But the foundations for the major confession in this Gospel (20:28) can already be seen in the realism of the man popularly called "doubter."

11:17-44. The dialogues with the grieving and the work of Jesus. This scene opens with Lazarus already *in the tomb four days* (v. 17). Hope even for any word from the deceased was thus totally gone because, in popular thinking, the spirit no longer hovered around the tomb but departed for SHEOL (the place of the dead) on the third day.

As Jesus made his way towards his friends, a grieving Martha met him with the emotion-filled words *if you had been here . . . but even now . . .* (vv. 21-22). Those words indicate her strong belief in the power of Jesus but also reflect her sense of hopeless resignation. The words of Jesus, *Your brother will rise again,* were met with a strong affirmation of her trust in Jewish resurrection theology (vv. 23-24). The rejoinder of Jesus that he is the resurrection and the agent against death was met by Martha with an affirmation of belief in his messiahship and his descent from God.

The last statement represents the third time within a few verses that the title SON OF GOD is used (10:36; 11:4, 27) and indicates a definite movement in the Johannine message that earlier employed SON OF MAN as Jesus' self-designation (cf. 9:35). The linkage was of course already suggested in the Nathaniel pericope (1:49, 51).

Because the confession of Martha is such a strong theological statement, preachers using this chapter may tend to conclude their sermons with the high note of 11:27. But that is not the end of the story. Indeed, when one adds Martha's reaction at the tomb "Lord . . . he stinks" (NRSV, *there is a stench,* v. 39), it becomes quite clear that Jesus and Martha have been talking on two different levels of reality. Confession and belief do not always match.

Sandwiched between the two segments of the Martha story is a pericope about the hopeless state of Mary and the mourners. In spite of Martha's theological assertions nothing had changed. Indeed, Mary re-

peated the first hopeless statement of Martha *if you had been here* (v. 32; cf. 11:21). The text says that when Jesus saw her and the mourners weeping and beheld the situation at the tomb of Lazarus, "Jesus wept" (RSV, cf. NRSV, *Jesus began to weep,* v. 35).

Many interpreters accept the mourner's view of the weeping Jesus (vv. 36-37), but I am not so sure that an interpretation of mere "love" for Lazarus is fully sufficient to explain the weeping of Jesus. The mourners thought that all was lost (*kept this man from dying,* v. 37) but Jesus was hardly a helpless mourner. It is, therefore, not unlikely that their lack of comprehension (failing to understand the power that could open blind eyes could also touch a dead man) greatly contributed to the emotion of Jesus. Indeed, the next event begins to confront their puny presuppositions.

The events that followed are a study in contrast. Jesus' command to remove the stone (it is not clear here whether the tomb stone was a slab or a roller) brought forth Martha's protest against the stench. But Jesus was undeterred. In fact he gently censured her for her lack of believing in his role of bringing the glory of God (v. 40). The prayer of Jesus here begins with the typical Johannine address, *Father,* and moves to Jesus' concern for his mission (vv. 41-42; cf. 12:27-28 and esp. comments at chap. 17). But his prayer is not for his benefit (10:42). The cry of Jesus to the dead man and the command to release the resuscitated Lazarus was a stunning example of the power of Jesus to deal with human presupposition and doubt and at the same time to give incredible meaning to the theological formulations of Martha.

The story is a masterpiece of narrative writing. It is a reminder that theological answers can be very shallow in life application. It is, moreover, a story that moves the reader to the conclusion of the Festival cycle and towards the end of the public ministry of Jesus. Unlike the other stories in the cycle, however, most of the theological dialogue here precedes the act of Jesus.

But it must be added that not all the dialogue precedes because the Festival cycle has a major focus on conflict and up to this point the story has involved only the friends of Jesus. The foes of Jesus and the conflict dialogue are introduced next as the raising of Lazarus is seen as the climactic event that stirred the Passover plot (v. 53).

While many believed, some reported the event to the Pharisees (v. 45). The council members (SANHEDRIN) were frustrated by the implications of Jesus and they sought to avoid the possibility of confrontation with the Romans and the loss of their power and devastation of the nation (vv. 47-48). This section of the story is filled with irony (cf. Duke 1985, 86–89), especially when the reader remembers that the Gospel was written after the fall of Jerusalem (70 C.E.). The protective efforts of the Jews, from the Johannine perspective, proved to be futile.

Indeed, the argument of the high priest (which for the evangelist was the equivalent of an *ex cathedra* statement, v. 51) was also laced with irony. The high priest declared that saving the people would take the death of one man (10:50). It was a typical argument of the end justifying the means but for the evangelist it was an insight into the gospel of salvation. Moreover, the words of Jesus were not limited to the nation but were for all of God's scattered children (v. 52).

This section like several others in John may raise for readers questions of historicity: e.g., how did the author know the mind of the high priest? Such a question has been answered both skeptically and positively. Some posit a witness such as Nicodemus reporting the incident. In general, however, such discussions are attempts to use silence and are best recognized as speculation.

The Passover, the time of cleansing, was on the horizon (v. 55). The orders for the arrest of Jesus had been issued (v. 57). Jerusalem was in a state of upheaval and excitement (v. 56), but Jesus had departed from there and stayed with his disciples on the edge of the desert (v. 54). It is not entirely clear where this town of *Ephraim* was located. It may have been in the hill country between Jerusalem and the Jordan River but in spite of speculation, no archaeological confirmation has yet been made.

The Festival cycle is thus concluded. The remainder of the Gospel involves the outworking of Passover in the death and resurrection of Jesus.

The Anointing and Entry into Jerusalem, 12:1-50

Positioned between the Festival cycle and the Farewell cycle is the strategic chapter which announces the forthcoming death of Jesus. For mountain climbers it functions like a saddle that unites peaks of mountains and provides the opportunity to move from one place to another. In that sense this chapter contains elements of both what has been said and what is yet to be said. It is one reason why scholars have sometimes wrestled with the relationship of chaps. 11–13.

Most scholars begin a new section with chap. 13 because of the summary type section at 12:44-50, but chap. 12 should not be totally divorced from chap. 13 any more than it should be completely segmented from chap. 11. Chapter 12 is a literary conjunction and should be treated as such. But it is more than a conjunction between chaps. 11 and 13; it also is a preparation for chap. 18 and the death story.

This chapter is the work of a literary genius because of the multiplicity of cords that are being struck. In this chapter is the familiar story of the entry into Jerusalem and the several reactions that are raised by it (vv. 12-22). But the entry story is sandwiched between the anointing scene (vv. 1-11) and the Johannine Gethsemane-like scene (vv. 23-36a), both of which give the entry scene the ominous sense of a dirge. The chapter then concludes with two summations, one on believing (vv. 36b-43) and another on judgment (vv. 44-50).

12:1-11. The anointing for death. The opening announcement that it was six days before Passover sets the stage for the interpretation of this chapter as a window into the death of Jesus. Verses 1 and 10, which refer to Lazarus, underline the fact that the raising of Lazarus was viewed by the evangelist as a crucial event in the coming death of the Passover lamb.

The mention here of Martha and Mary together with brief references concerning their activities (vv. 2-3) is intriguing because the Johannine statements are quite consistent with the picture presented in Luke 10:38-42, the only other pericope in the NT where the sisters are mentioned together. In the Lukan context Martha is busy in the serving role and Mary is at Jesus' feet listening to his teaching. Here Martha is serving a meal and Mary is at the Lord's feet anointing him. In both stories Mary is commended for her activity (v. 7; cf. Luke 10:42).

It is also intriguing that the name Lazarus appears elsewhere in the NT only in the Lukan pericope with the rich man (Luke 16:19-31), although in Luke he was not a dead man but a helpless beggar who was full of sores. Dual texts like these involving the sisters and Lazarus make scholars ask questions concerning possible links between Johannine and Lukan traditions, at least at the oral or pre-canonical stage of the texts.

The anointing material has been variously translated into English as an "ointment" (KJV, RSV) or perhaps better a *perfume* (NRSV, TEV) since the emphasis seems to fall on its smell (v. 3c). The vial of *nard* or "spikenard" (KJV) used here was probably a plant oil extracted from the root (and "spike") of the Indian nard plant. The point here is its expensiveness (v. 3a) since the vial was valued by Judas as the equivalent of a year's wages (v. 5: *three hundred denarii* is of course one denarius per day for about six working days per week for a year, less the festival days).

The contrast here is between the self-giving Mary and Judas Iscariot (see comment at 6:70-71), whom John designates as the thieving treasurer of the band. While it could be argued with Judas that the anointing was a waste of resources that could have been used on the poor (v. 6), in censuring Judas Jesus was not rejecting the needs of the poor (v. 8). Instead, Jesus regarded the breaking of the fragrant vial as a symbol of his forthcoming burial (v. 7; cf. the commendation at Mark 14:8-9). It was an anointing fit for a king (cf. the elaborate burial spicing of the body at 19:39-41).

The scene closes with an expanded death plot that includes Lazarus (v. 10) because of the dead man's living testimony. The reference to departing and believing (v. 11) may have been viewed by the evangelist as a foretaste of the conflict which the early Christians would have with the synagogue and the subsequent departure of believers from their Jewish cradle.

12:12-22. The entry to Jerusalem and the reactions. While many Christians refer to the Palm Sunday event as a "triumphal entry," the designation scarcely does justice to the Johannine perspective. There is no question that the crowd was excited. The people shouted *Hosanna!* (v. 13), which is either an exclamation of salvation or an emotional petition for salvation (cf. Ps 118:25). The attached blessing makes it clear that the people were ready to install Jesus as *King of Israel* (v. 13; cf. Nathaniel's similar messianic exclamation 1:49). *The one who comes* (v. 13) from Ps 118:26 was viewed as a messianic designation and the early Christians regarded the entrance on a donkey to be a fulfillment of Zech 9:9. It was for the crowd the hoped-for beginning of the messianic age and the Lazarus event seemed to confirm their hope (vv. 17-18).

The disciples are pictured as being in the event but as those who were trying to piece together the strange puzzle of Jesus. Their problem was that they did not yet have the key of his death and resurrection (his glorification) so it did not yet make sense (v. 16).

The Pharisees were exasperated. The world seemed to be changing around them and they could not integrate Jesus into their socio-theological structures. The events were passing them by and they did not like it (v. 19).

The Greeks (Ἕλληνες, not merely Greek-speaking Jews) are next introduced (v. 20). The obvious implication is that the gentiles are interested in meeting ("seeing") Jesus. Andrew, the helper, and Philip, the programmer (cf. 14:8), are called upon to deal with this new situation (vv. 21-22; cf. 6:5-9). The mission of Jesus was expanding and they needed his direction (v. 22). The request of the Greeks, however, was not in fact answered in this story. Instead, it is as though the coming of the Greeks is merged into the Gethsemane-like experience recorded in the Synoptics (cf. Matt 26:36-39 and par.). Did the evangelist view it as the signal for the next stage of the story and part of the overall purpose of the gospel? It certainly seems so because Jesus declared in John 12:23 that his hour had come.

12:23-36a. The agony of Jesus and his purpose. The evangelist drew together the anointing and entry scenes into an integrated focus with the announcement that the hour had arrived for the glorification of the *Son of Man* (v. 23). Moreover, he provided another double ἀμήν *truly*) saying involving the dying of a grain of wheat to make it absolutely clear that the glorification of Jesus had to involve his death (v. 24).

But the metaphor of the seed contains an important Johannine statement of reversal. The dying of seed brings multiplication of life (v. 24). In the same manner losing or gaining eternal life actually is rooted in a reversal (v. 25) and following Jesus is indelibly linked to being a servant (v. 26).

Nevertheless, such reversal is often costly for it can be an agonizing experience, one that involved pain for Jesus. Avoidance of pain is a human desire and even Jesus wrestled with such avoidance (v. 27, *save me from this hour*). Yet, recognizing God's hand in pain was the method and model of Jesus. His prayer of yielding to the will of the Father and accepting his divinely given purpose in life (see also Borchert, "Prayer") was answered by an assuring voice from heaven.

Because the Synoptic scenes of the BAPTISM of Jesus (cf. Mark 1:9-11, and par.) and the TRANSFIGURATION (Mark 9:2-8 and par.) have been eliminated in John, the evangelist employed the confirming voice from heaven as an assurance that Jesus' acceptance of his death was affirmed in heaven (v. 28). The statement that the voice was not for his sake (v. 30), however, is somewhat confusing in the light of the fact the crowd thought it thundered (v. 29). It is a little speculative to argue that the evangelist was here making a distinction between the crowd and the disciples who heard. But it seems clear that he is once again clarifying for the reader that Jesus was not in danger of choosing the wrong way.

With this decisive moment concluded, Jesus declared that judgment-time had arrived together with the defeat (driving out) of the world ruler (v. 31), the deeper mystery about which C. S. Lewis wrote in his tale of Aslan (1950). The lifting up of Jesus (his death) was the hope of life for all (vv. 32-33; cf. 3:14-15). But the death of the Messiah did not fit the crowd's messianic expectations (v. 34) because they did not understand the deeper mystery of victory beyond death. Light was now with them for a short while. Their task was to believe the light so that they might become the children of light (vv. 35-36a).

12:36b-50. Summations: believing and judgment. The seven signs of the two cycles have been concluded and the final sign (the death and resurrection of Jesus) has been unequivocally introduced. But the reality was that the people would not believe (v. 37) and so the evangelist brings his story of Jesus' public ministry to a close with Jesus hiding himself from the people (v. 36b; cf. 8:59).

This rejection must have been hard for John to accept but he provided a rationale for such a rejection by including a composite text from sections of Isaiah (vv. 38-40; cf., e.g., Paul's use of such a florilegium in Rom 3:10-18).

The rationale here began with the haunting questions of who and why earlier addressed in Isa 53:1, a text frequently used by early Christians (cf. Rom 10:16). The answer, as Isaiah reflected in his call (6:6-9), was understood and determined by God alone. While Isaiah referred to both hearing and seeing problems of the people, the focus here is on seeing (v. 40), undoubtedly because of the Johannine emphasis on signs (v. 37).

The concept of God's hardening in this proof text (v. 40), as Beasley-Murray (1987, 216) has well observed, should not be made a basis for a view of reprobation (see notes at 6:70-71 and 10:27-28). The OT can speak at the same time of God hardening Pharaoh's heart (e.g., Exod 7:13) and of Pharaoh hardening his own heart (Exod 8:15, etc.). The tension between God's work and human reaction is never fully resolved in the Bible and must remain a mystery. Here John says *they did not believe* (v. 37) and at the same time *many, even of the authorities, believed* (v. 42). The broad sweep of Johannine categorizations may

disturb some Western readers but the point is that the tension must always be understood in John.

But the evangelist added that believing by itself is not adequate because some believed yet failed to confess openly their loyalties to Jesus because they yielded to human pressures and affirmations rather than seeking divine acceptance (vv. 42-43; cf. 2:23-25). Such a situation brought forth a concluding analysis from Jesus: believing in him is the equivalent of believing in the one who sent him (v. 44) and such believing is enlightening in a dark world (vv. 45-46). Failure to hear and keep (obey) his word will result in judgment (v. 48), although that was certainly not the purpose of Jesus' coming (v. 47; cf. 3:17). Both the Father and Jesus have been of one purpose, namely the provision of eternal life (vv. 49-50).

The Farewell Cycle, 13:1–17:26

Scholars have long recognized that in chaps. 13–17 Jesus was preparing his disciples for his departure. Moreover, Leon Morris (1971, 610) and other writers have designated these chapters as the "Farewell Discourses," but these chapters are clearly more than discourses.

The cycle begins with the reminder that it was almost time for the PASSOVER and that Jesus' hour of destiny had come. This cycle is therefore epitomized in an act that has become the model of the self-giving love of Jesus for his disciples (chap. 13). The cycle ends with a prayer that epitomizes both Jesus' self-giving love for his disciples who must live and witness in a hostile world and the assuring expectation that his followers would be with him (chap. 17). Between these two "book-end" segments the evangelist placed some very tender discussions concerning the disciples' perceived sense of abandonment (chap. 14) but also Jesus' promise of the supportive Paraclete (chaps. 14–16). These three middle chapters then frame a central magnificent mashal or parable concerning the vine and the branches (15:1-11) and a crucial reminder of the importance of the love command (15:12-17) introduced earlier (13:34-35). This central segment thus forcefully illustrates the relationship between Jesus and his followers.

The Footwashing and Authentic Discipleship, 13:1-38

This chapter is regarded by many as a model of Christian discipleship. It is also a strategic introduction to the farewell cycle.

13:1-11. Jesus, the footwashing, and Judas. The story opens with the notation again that it was almost Passover. The dull ring of those words is joined by the reminder that the hour of darkness had arrived. Judas, the devil's agent, was about to act (vv. 1-2). The evangelist makes sure that the reader knows that the events were not unexpected for Jesus.

In the midst of this fateful time one would expect a dirge, yet a melody of "love" is sharply sounded (v. 1). Love is a theme used in chaps. 13–21 four times more frequently than in chaps. 1–12. Here love is portrayed by Jesus in the moving scene of laying aside his clothes and taking up the slave's towel. He assumed the demeaning role of washing the disciples' feet (a role usually reserved for the lowest gentile slaves, women, and people of little status; cf. Str-B 1:121).

This act was undoubtedly repulsive to the disciples. Peter voiced the common shock in his halting words (v. 6) "Lord, *you* are washing my feet?" (author trans.) Peter's response to such an idea was equivalent to "Stop!"

The reply of Jesus was virtually: "No washing of your feet, then no part in me!" That answer sent another shock wave through Peter. He did not know the meaning. Understanding would come later because the act was a symbolic prediction (v. 7).

Peter immediately changed his tune from refusal to a request for a bath or a shower (vv. 8-9). It is a humorous note of good intention that misses the point. A bath was not the issue (v. 10). Bath terminology is here symbolic of the OT concern for CLEAN/UNCLEAN (purity). In many OT contexts uncleanness is linked to sinfulness (cf. Lev 16:16-30; Ps 51:2; Isa 1:16, 64:6; Zech 13:1).

It was not, therefore, the amount of water nor the number of body parts being washed that counted with Jesus. He was concerned with the nature of a person. Moreover, the issue is probably not even BAPTISM as some have thought, although it may be a related idea. The cleansing of Christ is the issue.

The disciples were cleansible, but one of them was not (v. 11). The evangelist never whitewashes Judas. He was the devil's agent, and the verdict was firm (vv. 2-18, 26-27). For John, Judas was bad news because as a friend he *lifted his heel against* Jesus (v. 18; cf. Ps 41:9). He was certainly numbered among the *chosen* (v. 18; cf. 6:70), but he was, nonetheless, a traitor.

13:12-20. The meaning of the event. The actions of Judas like the denials of Peter (cf. 13:38), however, did not take Jesus by surprise. For John all these events are within Jesus' messianic mission. They are viewed as fulfilling scripture and said to have contributed to believing that Jesus was indeed the *I am* (v. 19; cf. Exod 3:14).

The disciples' designations of Jesus as *Teacher* and *Lord* (v. 13) were fundamentally correct but incomplete. Jesus was their master and instructor, but they also needed to understand that self-giving humility was a mark of Jesus. Indeed, it was also to be a mark of his followers (vv. 14-15).

Accordingly, two double ἀμήν (*truly*) sayings were added to remind readers of the need to accept this servant role (vv. 16-17) and to receive both Jesus and anyone sent by him (v. 20). In these sayings the evangelist has again developed a dual level of discourse. Here one can sense John has in mind both the settings in the life of Jesus and that of the readers of this Gospel. Receiving a sent one is clearly an illusion to the post-resurrection work of Jesus' followers.

13:21-30. The painful tragedy and Judas. This section opens with the pain of Jesus (v. 21; cf. 12:27) and with a double ἀμήν saying concerning betrayal (v. 21). The announcement created confusion among the disciples, and Peter sought clarification (vv. 22, 24).

The evangelist uses the event to introduce one of his famous contrasts between PETER and the BELOVED DISCIPLE. Here the Beloved Disciple reclines next to Jesus at an oriental style meal (vv. 23-24; cf. 20:4; 21:7, 20-22). As in other cases Peter seems to emerge "second best," perhaps reflective of some struggle between the early Johannine community and others. But these statements in John are not a denigration of Peter as much as a positioning of him.

The identification by the dipped morsel (probably bread or perhaps some Passover herbs, v. 26) was also the effective signal for Judas to accept his role as the instrument of the devil (v. 27). The restraining power of God was removed from him and Satan took over. Therefore, there was no necessity for further delaying his tragic work (v. 27). The meaning of the signal, however, was not yet clear to the other disciples who assumed he was engaged in some economic enterprise (v. 29). But the evangelist understood that this event was decisive. Judas' departure finally brought the tragedy of "night" (v. 30; cf. 12:35-36).

13:31-35. The new command. Segovia (1991, 59) and others think the first unit of the discourses begins at this point. Perhaps, but this section also serves as a summation of the introduction to the farewell cycle and as a window into the discourses.

The coming of the hour (v. 1) had brought the imminent glorification of the SON OF MAN (v. 31). The departure of Judas signaled the coming "departure" of Jesus (v. 33). In this context Jesus enunciated for his disciples (*little children*, v. 33; cf. 1 John 2:1) one of his most famous statements: the new commandment of love. Love was to epitomize his followers and was to be the means by which everyone would recognize them as disciples of Jesus (vv. 34-35).

This command is one of the core statements of Christianity because the mark of discipleship was not formulated in terms of a statement of faith but in terms of a way of living. In the history of the church the last day of Jesus with his disciples is remembered in the celebration of MAUNDY THURSDAY (a name derived from a defective form of the Latin *mando*, "I command," in honor of this crucial saying of Jesus). The mandate of discipleship applies more than once a year.

13:36-38. Peter's denial foretold. The announcement of Jesus' departure (13:33) drew from Peter the question: *Where are you going?* (v. 36). This question formed the foundation for Peter's strong assertion of faithfulness and Jesus' prediction of Peter's threefold denial (vv. 37-38). It also served the evangelist as the introduction to the next chapter with Thomas's question and Jesus' discussion of going away (14:1-11, 18). Moreover, it undoubtedly influenced the second-century C.E. story of the return of Peter to face death in Rome when according to one tradition Jesus appeared as Peter was fleeing and asked, *Quo vadis?* ("Where are you going?"; see *ActsPet* 35; cf. Brown 1970, 607–608).

The Question of Anxiety and Loneliness, 14:1-31

Chapter 14 is the first of the three central discourse chapters of the farewell cycle. The focus in these chapters is on the disciples' relationship to God and to others. In this chapter the evangelist seeks to confront the disciples' fear and anxiety from loneliness. Also woven into the discussions here are the first two of five Paraclete sayings.

This chapter breaks naturally into four sections involving the departure of Jesus (vv. 1-3, previously introduced in 13:33 and 36), questions of Thomas and Philip concerning the way to the glorified Jesus and the Father (vv. 5-11), the relationship of believing, working, and asking through Jesus (vv. 12-14), and the promise of the Paraclete's presence in loneliness and frustration (vv. 15-31).

14:1-3. Departure and preparation for the future. The chapter begins with two crucial commands: one negative—"Don't let your troubled hearts (wills) control you"—and one positive—"Commit yourselves to (believe in) God and me" (author trans., v. 1). The reason given for heeding these exhortations is that in God there is security. God's home has many secure dwelling places, and the role of Jesus was to prepare for our future (vv. 2-3).

14:4-11. Questions of our destiny. Jesus' comment that the disciples now know their destiny with him (v. 4) brought utter confusion among them. Thomas, like Nicodemus, had difficulty in thinking about the realm of God (v. 5; cf. 3:12). He wanted a road map to his destiny. The *I am* saying of Jesus concerning *way*, *truth*, and *life* (v. 6) failed to clarify the situation because the disciples really did not understand the relationship of Jesus to the Father. Philip's practical request for a genuine vision of the Father (v. 8) revealed that the key to their understanding was still missing. Later Thomas would know the key (20:28), but not before the resurrection.

Seeing Jesus did not yet mean for them having a vision of God (vv. 9-10). So Jesus once again reminded them of his works (v. 11).

14:12-14. Elements of discipleship. Having mentioned his works, Jesus turned the conversation to discipleship. Believing was basic to accepting the disciples' work on behalf of Jesus. Indeed, they would expand his ministry (*do greater works*; v. 12) after his departure if they were properly attuned to him (*ask in my name*; v. 14). Such asking was not merely repeating Jesus' name in prayer, but asking according to his nature. God would thus be glorified in their working for Jesus (v. 13).

14:15-31. The coming of the Paraclete. While talk of Jesus' departure left them feeling empty and lonely, Jesus was not abandoning them (v. 18). He had been their companion; now they would have *another Advocate* (v. 16; one who would stand alongside of them). This term *Advocate* (or Paraclete) includes various meanings such as support, counsel, comfort, and exhortation. The disciples would not be orphaned because the authentic Spirit (of Truth) would be an internal resource for them (v. 17).

The distinction between *with* and *in* (v. 17) must not be made the basis of two levels of Christian life, as argued in some charismatic discussions concerning the Spirit. Rather, it is to be related to John's historical view of the coming of the Spirit and John's understanding of transformation (e.g., the nature of external and internal knowing and believing God). *On that day* (v. 20) they would understand (*know*) internally the relationship between Jesus and the Father and the true meaning of obedience (keeping Jesus' commands) which is rooted in love (vv. 20-21; cf. the love command in 13:34).

Living in the love of God and obediently loving others (cf. the two great commands of Mark 12:28-31 and par.) is the basis for sensing the divine presence in one's life. Such presence dispels loneliness (vv. 18, 21-24). The purpose of the first ADVOCATE/PARACLETE saying is thus to clarify the nature of God's presence in the disciples' life.

The second Advocate/Paraclete saying is built upon the first. In theophanies (appearances of God), angelophanies, and christophanies of the Bible, the presence of God usually brings a sense of fear and the need for a calming word of assurance (cf., e.g., Judg 6:22-24; Matt 14:26-27; see Thornton and Borchert, 1989).

The word of assurance normally is "Don't be afraid," or "Peace/Shalom." Here Jesus offers his shalom—a peace unlike that which the world can offer. It is a message not to be afraid or troubled by this new sense of presence and the departure of Jesus (vv. 27-28).

The role of the Advocate/Paraclete in the lives of Jesus' followers would be that of instructor to help them live in a hostile world (vv. 26, 30). The idea of instruction is deeply rooted in the OT faith. The Torah or Law was the center of instruction (Deut 6:4-9). Paul then argued that the Law's instructional value was to lead to Christ (Gal 3:24). Here the Spirit's, i.e., the Advocate/Paraclete, instructional role is to remind the disciple of Jesus (v. 26).

The pain of Jesus' departure was not to be magnified. Instead, the disciples were to rejoice at this new stage in God's unfolding work and in the fact that God's enemy (*the ruler of this world*) is not ultimately in control (vv. 28-30). Indeed the departure would turn out to be a witness to the world (v. 31).

The chapter ends with a note *Rise, let us be on our way* (v. 31). Some scholars have suggested that this note indicates that chaps. 15–17 are an insert. Others would argue that 15–17 take place in the garden (18:1) or somewhere between the site of the last supper and the garden. Perhaps the easiest answer is that it was a note retained from an earlier stage in the editing process and is one of the few literary seams in the Gospel (cf. Brown 1970, 656–57).

The Vine and the Branches, 15:1-17

In the midst of the painful discussion of farewell involving the disciples' fears and Jesus' promises of the Paraclete, the evangelist has inserted the captivating *mashal* or allegory of the vine and the branches together with the powerful reminder of the love command, both of which focus on the intimate relationship between Jesus and his followers.

This beautiful poetic passage contains the second *mashal* of John. The other in chap. 10 also focuses on Jesus' relationship to his disciples and pictures Jesus as the good shepherd. The opponents of Jesus are there likened to thieves, wolves and hired servants. Here are portrayed various aspects of authentic (true) and inauthentic discipleship in vineyard terminology.

Scholars hold varying opinions on the relationship of this section of the Gospel to the Lord's Supper or Eucharist. Its placement within the farewell cycle certainly is related to the death (glorification) of Jesus. The linkage of the love command here (v. 12) with the command in the footwashing scene (13:34) is hard to miss. But it is probably safe to conclude that the *mashal* per se was probably not eucharistic in orientation and should only be seen secondarily as such (for the contrary see: Beasley-Murray 1987, 269 and Brown 1970, 672–74).

15:1-11. Discipleship and the allegory of the vine. The vineyard had long been a symbol of Israel, God's people (cf. for example Isa 3:14; 5:1-7; Ps 80:8-18). Here the vineyard keeper is pictured as God the Father. Jesus is the authentic vine and his followers are branches (vv. 1-2). Genuine disciples know they are utterly dependent on Jesus and his word for cleansing (v. 3), fruitfulness (vv. 4, 8), and a proper understanding of their identity (v. 5). Failure to live in the vine is devastating in its implications (v. 6) but abiding in the vine is the key to prayer (v. 7, cf. 14:13), the glorification of God, and authentic discipleship (v. 8).

Such abiding is defined in terms of love (v. 9) and obedience (v. 10). Both are modeled on the relationship between Jesus and the Father. Indeed, such abiding should lead to the joy of the Lord becoming evident in the life of the disciple (v. 11).

15:12-17. Love and chosen disciples. The command to *love one another* announced at 13:34 is forcefully repeated here and identified with a call for the sacrificial death of the disciples (vv. 12-13). The strong summons undoubtedly reflects not only the circumstances in the farewell of Jesus but also the evangelist's context of a persecuted community. To love one another is the glue that enables the Christian community to stand together in times of suffering.

But this love is more than comradeship. It is rooted in the identification of the disciple with Jesus. Therefore, the evangelist includes the reminder that dying disciples are not merely obedient slaves but are participating friends in the mission of Jesus (vv. 14-15). Moreover, they are not self-directed actors but chosen and appointed agents of Jesus. Their mission is to bear fruit that lasts (v. 16).

Two important principles emerge in this central section of the cycle. First, divine chosenness or election in the Bible is not to privilege but to mission. God chooses not for the person's own benefit but to serve God's desire to bless the world (cf. Abraham's call in Gen 12:1-3). To reject the mission is tantamount to rejecting the call.

Second, the theme of "abiding," "remaining," or "lasting" is foundational in the Bible for inheritance or salvation texts. Accordingly, all assurance texts have a stated or implied warning or condition attached to them (cf. John 15:4, 6; 3:18). Thus, the promises made to successive patriarchs or kings are renegotiated between God and each generation. Moreover, each warning text has a stated or implied promise or assurance attached to it because God's intention is not the destruction of the world but the hope of salvation for all humanity (cf. 15:7, 10-11; 3:17).

It is in this context of the tension between assurance and warning that texts concerning asking God (or prayer) must be understood (15:7, 16; 14:14). God is not an unthinking Santa Claus-like figure supplying endless human desires or prayers. If such were the case, he certainly would have supplied the request of Jesus to avoid "the cup" of death (cf. Mark 14:36). God loves us and desires to commune with us but to pray in the name of Jesus is to accept the Lord's nature in our lives when we pray (cf. Borchert 1970).

The Question of Anxiety and Persecution, 15:18–16:33

This second major section dealing with the anxiety of the disciples is like a reversal or mirror image of chap. 14, except that the focus shifts from loneliness to world hatred. The earlier section ended with an announcement of the world ruler's limited power (14:30) and this section begins with world hatred and persecution (15:18-25). The earlier section began with Jesus confronting the anxiety of the disciples' loneliness

over his departure (14:1-11) and this section ends with Jesus confronting their anxiety over his departure, the forthcoming persecution, and their superficial understanding of the implications of what was to happen (16:16-33).

Embedded in both sections is a reminder that they are to pray or to ask for divine help concerning their situations (14:13; 16:23-24). Both sections also contain Paraclete sayings: two in the first part (14:16-17; 14:26-27) and three in this second part (15:26; 16:7-11; 16:12-15). These three chapters thus form an INCLUSIO framed around the central *mashal* and love command (15:1-17).

15:18-25. World hatred and persecution. The world in this farewell section is viewed from a negative, anti-Jesus perspective (cf. 3:16 where the world was viewed as the place of mission). Because the disciples have become identified with Jesus' select group, they stand over against this orientation of the world and thus receive the same hatred that was directed at Jesus (vv. 18-19).

The dual setting of the Gospel is once again in mind—for example, the life of Jesus and the early church. The maxim concerning *master* and *servant* is again used to recall the pattern. Not only were the disciples to be like their teacher in their life of service (13:13-16; cf. Luke 6:40), but here it is clear that the disciples would also not be able to avoid the hostility directed at their Lord (v. 20; cf. Matt 10:24). Persecution of the disciples and the church was therefore inevitable because the enemies would not accept (*do not know*) Jesus (v. 21).

Moreover, the hatred of Jesus meant the enemies also despised and did not know God the Father (vv. 21, 23). But they would not be excused for their sinful actions because their rejection of Jesus and his works preempted any defense on their part (vv. 22, 24; cf. the testimony section in 5:30-47). The unjustified nature of their hatred is supported here by a quotation from Ps 69, which early Christians viewed as messianic (v. 25 and Ps 69:4; cf. Ps 35:19. Note also the use of Ps 69:9 in John 2:17). *Law* (Torah) is the general use of the term for the OT. The enemies in mind here are Jewish persecutors but the early Christians would have expanded this negative orientation of world to include other persecutors as well (see Brown, 1979).

15:26–16:15. Three more Paraclete sayings. To face the world's hostility Christians are again reminded of their resource: the Paraclete or Spirit (cf. 14:15-31). The disciples' task was/is that of witness in the midst of hostility, but their witness was not self-induced or self-motivated. They had been with Jesus from the start of his ministry and were to bear witness to him (v. 27). In this third Paraclete saying Jesus indicated that their support for witness would be the Paraclete or Spirit of truth that was to be sent by Jesus and to come from the Father.

During the centuries when Christians were formulating the early creeds a dispute arose between the Eastern and Western churches about whether the Spirit proceeds from the Father "and the Son" (Lat. *filioque*). While much ink has been spilled over this Trinitarian formulation, it is best not to view the statement in v. 27 as involving a concern for relations within the Godhead per se. As Schnackenburg (1987, 3:118-19) has argued, it is a mission statement of the Spirit that in parallel form involves both Jesus and the Father. The point is that the Paraclete is intimately involved in the witness of Christians.

The concern of the evangelist was that Christians who were faced with persecution, death, and exclusion from the synagogues would be tempted to "abandon," "stumble," "fall away," "become scandalized" ($\sigma\kappa\alpha\nu\delta\alpha\lambda\iota\zeta\omega$) by the persecution (16:1-2). Such persecution was in the time of the evangelist not merely a vague threat; it was a reality. In the Apocalypse of John one can sense the scope of that threat because there the synagogue is called "a synagogue of Satan" (Rev 2:9 and 3:9; cf. the *birkath ha-minim* or so-called Jewish curse of the Nazarenes and heretics in the twelfth benediction [see Martyn 1979]). The Christian community was under attack and the evangelist wanted to remind the members (16:4) that Jesus understood their plight and that, like their Lord, Christians also would have their hour. But in that hour of danger they had a God-given resource to prevent their capitulation.

The fourth Paraclete saying is introduced by another statement concerning Jesus' departure, the disciples' accompanying sorrow (16:5-6; cf. 14:1-11), and the promise of consolation (16:7; cf. 14:18). Here the coming of the Paraclete is said to be an advantage. Certainly the statement does not suggest superiority of the Spirit to Jesus but the meaning probably implies that the extent of the personal ministry of Paraclete in the world is to expand the implications of the coming of Jesus.

In this fourth saying the threefold role of the Spirit in the world is outlined. The governing term ($\dot{\epsilon}\lambda\dot{\epsilon}\gamma\chi\omega$) that introduces *sin and righteousness and judgment* is multidimensional (16:8). Its meanings include "ex-

pose," "convict," demonstrate," "correct," and "convince." Obviously in using such a word with these three roles, the evangelist implies that the Paraclete is prepared to use Christians in confronting all orientation to evil in the world. In so doing the Paraclete will expose the world's sinfulness, identify the standards of righteousness in Jesus, and judge all sin as connected with Satan, the prince of evil (16:9-11). The role is a powerful one.

The fifth and final Spirit statement (Paraclete is not used here but follows by implication) involves future counsel or direction for the disciples. Recognizing that it was impossible to spell out everything, the function of the Spirit in relation to the disciples themselves was to be that of guide (16:13). But the guide would not operate independently of the revelation in Jesus. Indeed, in all communication the Spirit would glorify Jesus and in so doing affirm the unity between Jesus and the Father (16:13-15).

16:16-33. Confronting the implications of Jesus' departure. Following upon the sorrow of the disciples (16:6) and the last two Spirit sayings, Jesus' mention of *a little while* in reference to both not seeing him and seeing him, especially in the context of going to the Father, left the disciples confused (vv. 16-18). In response Jesus replied with the first of two double $\dot{\alpha}\mu\dot{\eta}\nu$ (*truly*) sayings. Sorrow would come to them, but it would be followed by joy (v. 20).

The combination of pain followed by joy is like the delivery process for a woman concluding in the birth of a child (v. 21). The mention of birth pangs immediately brings to mind the idea of the birth pangs of the Messiah. Israel developed a sense of hope and an expectation of deliverance in the midst of their experiences under foreign rulers. Grist for the idea was supplied by important texts such as Isa 66:5-14 and Mic 4:9-10; 5:2-3. In v. 22 the event does not signify joy at the birth of the Messiah but joy at the resurrection of Jesus and his ascent to the Father (cf. v. 17) following the painful experience of the crucifixion.

In the light of such an anticipated victory the second double $\dot{\alpha}\mu\dot{\eta}\nu$ saying is employed to remind the disciples that the Father takes seriously the prayers of Jesus' followers (v. 23). God's desire is to respond to Christians so that they will be filled with joy (v. 24; but for further perspective on asking in the name of Jesus see the discussions at 15:16 and at 14:14 and 15:7).

The pattern of Jesus in his ministry was to describe his life and work in word-pictures. With the coming of the hour, however, the disciples would have the key to understanding Jesus' mission and such figurative patterns would be unnecessary (v. 25). They would understand prayer and the relationship between Jesus and the Father at that point (vv. 26-28).

But the disciples jumped to the conclusion that they had the key before the crucial events (v. 29). Clearly they perceived that Jesus was God-sent (v. 30). Yet they still did not have the kind of perception that Jesus was seeking. Accordingly, Jesus announced that they would abandon him (vv. 31-32). While Jesus would not abandon them (cf. 14:18), their perception did not result in commitment. Yet Jesus did not give up on them. He reminded the disciples that he (*in me*) was the source of authentic *shalom* (*peace*; v. 33). The world was not the basis for peace. It provided the opposite, namely persecution or trouble. But the disciple should not despair because the disciples' Lord has *conquered the world* (v. 33).

The Great Prayer, John 17:1-26

In recent years many scholars have commented on this great prayer (see Borchert, "Prayer"). Some (such as Schnackenburg, Malatesta, and Black) have emphasized structural analysis based on theological or linguistic studies and many have focused on the theme of unity. Some have divided the text into three parts following Westcott, and others have opted for a four-part division.

In an earlier study on prayer, I showed that chap. 17 breaks naturally into seven petitions all except one of which follow the Johannine formula of invoking the *Father* (πάτερ). This formula is also present in other prayers in the Gospel (cf. 11:41; 12:27, 28). Also similar is that each of the petitions, no matter what the context, deals with some aspect of Jesus' mission. Although the invocation *Father* is used only six times (vv. 1, 5, 11, 21, 24, and 25), there are actually seven petitions because of the interconnection of the prayers. Taken as a whole the chapter is a magnificent summary not only of the farewell cycle but of the entire Gospel.

17:1-3. The first petition. The lifting up of Jesus' eyes and the announcement that the hour had come following the first *Father* signals the conclusion to the farewell cycle. The emphasis in vv. 2 and 3 is really a restatement of the mission of Jesus and the purpose statement for the Gospel in 20:30-31.

17:4-8. The second petition. The emphasis on *finishing the work* and "the glory before the world be-

gan" (author trans.) is a clear reminiscence of the "Word" who was "at the beginning" intimately related to God (1:1) and was the "only" Son who came to make God known (1:14, 18). The petition in 17:5 for the restoration of glory (cf. 1:14) is striking. Also striking is the fact that 17:7-8 concerning the disciples' receiving, knowing, and believing Jesus and his words echoes the key verses of the prologue (1:10-12) as well as the major emphasis of the Cana cycle—seen in the disciples at Cana (2:11), the crucial perspective on believing after the Temple incident (2:23-25), Nicodemus (3:12), the Samaritans (4:42), and the official (4:48-49).

17:9-19. The third and fourth petitions. *I am asking* or "I pray" (v. 9) begins a new emphasis on the situation of the disciples in a hostile world. The strong invocation *Holy Father* (v. 11) together with the repeated request for protection (vv. 11-15) in the *name* of God appears to be an allusion to the OT idea of power in the name of God and to the idea that God's name must never be spoken irreverently (e.g., Exod 20:7). The perceived hostility in these verses echoes the repeated hostility to Jesus in the festival cycle with the paralytic (5:18), the bread of life (6:41 and 70), the statement on truth (8:41-48), the blind man (9:24), the good shepherd (10:31-33), and Lazarus (11:45-50). Evil or *the evil one* is real (v. 15) and the disciples need the protection of God to survive.

The fourth petition, which does not include the invocation "Father," is a prayer for holiness or sanctification (v. 17) that picks up the holiness idea in the earlier invocation (v. 11). The use of *holiness* terminology is exceedingly rare in this Gospel and the only other use is in the good shepherd *mashal* (10:36; it is also used in 1 John 2:20 in a conflict situation). The purpose of the disciples on mission here (v. 18) is similar to that at 10:36.

17:20-26. The fifth, sixth, and seventh petitions. Again the words *I ask* signal a shift of emphasis (v. 20). These last three petitions are related to the farewell cycle but in fact go beyond them.

The prayer for oneness (v. 21) immediately reminds one of the central *mashal* of the vine and the mission of fruit bearing (15:5), which is mirrored in the purpose of the world believing in the one who was sent (vv. 21, 23). Moreover, the *through their word* reminds one of the post-Thomas expectation concerning those who will have to rely for believing on testimony (v. 20; cf. 20:29). The theme of love is also very significant here (v. 23) and reminds one of the command to love (13:34; 15:12) and the questions to Peter (21:15-17; cf. Peter's earlier scene in 13:37-38).

The sixth petition is the wish for the disciples to share in the glory of Jesus. The words *where I am* (v. 24) are exactly the same words as in 14:3, which emphasize the future the disciples can expect.

The final petition begins with the invocation *Righteous Father* and forcefully distinguishes the world from Jesus and his followers (vv. 25-26). The petition is intriguing because it remains unexpressed, but the interpretation seems clear. The only two places in the entire Gospel where the righteousness motif is used are here and at 16:10 of the farewell cycle where the role of the Paraclete is again introduced because Jesus is going *to the Father* (13:1; 14:6, 12, 28; 16:10, 17, 28; 20:17).

The task of the Paraclete there (16:8-10) was to define for the sinful world the nature of righteousness in and through the followers of Jesus. It is significant, therefore, that the nature of the community that should provide the standard for the world's judgment is here (v. 26) defined not in theological formulas but in terms of the love of the community.

Thus in bringing the farewell cycle to a close the evangelist ends where he began in chap. 13 with the model of Jesus' love lived out in the lives of his followers.

The Death Story, 18:1–19:42

The death story of John is one of the most fascinating pieces of NT literature. Throughout the story Jesus is portrayed as serenely in control of everything from the betrayal and arrest (18:1-11) to the mock trial before Annas (18:12-14, 19-24), the denials of Peter (18:15-18, 25-27), the skillfully crafted seven scenes before Pilate that move in and out of the praetorium (18:28–19:16), the crucifixion and death scenes (19:17-37), and finally the burial (19:38-42).

All the actors in the story pale in comparison to the king of Israel (Jesus). He is in charge of his own death and everyone connected with it. The skill of the evangelist is evident throughout the story; irony is a great tool that makes the portrait of Jesus stand out in bold relief when compared to the hollow characters who think they are in charge of his death.

In this story there is no kiss of Judas (cf. Mark 14:45), no washing of the hands of Pilate (cf. Matt 27:24), no carrying of the cross by Simon of Cyrene (cf. Mark 15:21), no identification of the two who were crucified with him (contrast Mark 15:27 and Matt 27:38 with Luke 23:32, 39-43), no acknowledgement of sin by Judas and report of his death (contrast Matt 27:3-10 with Acts 1:16-20), no cry of forsakenness or tearing of the Temple veil (cf. Mark 15:33-38, etc.), and no centurion's confession of the Son of God (cf. Mark 15:39). It is not that these events did not happen, but that for John the focus is upon Jesus' control of his death and the guilt of all the world before the enthroned king on the cross. Jesus as king is the central figure in this story and everything points towards his yielding of his spirit in death as the sacrificial LAMB OF GOD.

18:1-11. The garden scene. Separating the Mount of Olives and the Temple Mount runs the Kidron Valley. At the base of the Mount of Olives still today lies a garden that tradition marks as the place of the arrest of Jesus. But in John the scene is pictured in a unique manner.

The soldiers are there with Judas. Indeed, the *detachment* is designated by John (vv. 3, 12) in Greek as a σπεῖρα, normally used to refer to a battalion or cohort of at least 600. The leader is called a χιλιάρχος, a rank just under that of a general in the Roman army (v. 12). The picture is clearly intended to be one of imperial force coming out against Jesus, and to this political force was added the power of the religious establishment (v. 3). But the irony is that with all their human weaponry this great force needed lanterns and torches to find their way (v. 3), a reminder that night had come (13:30) and they did not know where they were going (cf. 12:35; 11:9-10).

The story is ironic in another way because it was Jesus who asked them: "Whom do you seek? (v. 4, author trans.)" The powerful ones were on a search-and-seize mission but it was Jesus who identified himself. And the identification words of Jesus echo the identification of God to Moses (Exod 3:14): "I am." The devil-man, Judas, is merely mentioned (vv. 2, 5) and then melts into the background. He does not identify Jesus in John. The evangelist wanted the reader to realize that Jesus was in control, even of his arrest. When therefore the religious leaders and powerful soldiers heard the self-identification of Jesus, they were rendered absolutely helpless in his presence (v. 6). Worldly power met supreme power, and human power faded.

It was Jesus who then gave the human pawns permission to arrest him but not before he cared for his disciples (vv. 8-9). Yet brash Peter had to act for the disciples. Impressed with these events, Peter determined he would try to rescue Jesus (only in John do we learn that the disciple is Peter, v. 10). The puny sword of Peter could damage a human ear but it could not deter a divine mission. The cup of death was the will of God. Inconsistent Peter was in the way of the divine mission and Jesus censured him. But Peter would still have his chance to prove his commitment.

18:12-27. The mock priestly trials and Peter's denials. For John the verdict had already been delivered by CAIAPHAS, the reigning high priest. The verdict was death, a sacrificial death (vv. 13-14; cf. 11:49-52). The trial therefore was a sham.

It was conducted by *Annas . . . the father-in-law of Caiaphas* (v. 13) whom John also designates as *the high priest* (v. 19). While Annas was no longer technically the high priest because he had been deposed in 15 C.E. by the Roman general Valerius, he continued to be the power broker of the high priestly family, acting through his sons, son-in-law, and grandson. The power-hungry corruption of the high priesthood was well known at this time and Ananais, the high priest at the time of Paul (cf. Acts 23:2), was so despised that the Jews themselves assassinated him before the fall of Jerusalem.

The arguments before Annas in John are little more than a late-night interrogation and are a contrast to the openness of Jesus' teaching in the synagogues and Temple (v. 20). The blow to Jesus by the high priest's servant could be explained as a defense of God's prince (Exod 22:28). But such a defense was firmly challenged by Jesus' own question concerning unjust punishment and false witnesses (v. 23). The interrogation became a standoff between justice and injustice so Jesus was shuttled to Caiaphas, the high priest (v. 24).

Alternating with these interrogation scenes, the evangelist inserts Peter's denial scenes. Both scene-patterns take place at night—the interrogations are inside while the denials are outside. The denial scenes take place in the context of *a charcoal fire* (ἀνθρακία, a term used only here at v. 18 and at 21:9). The threefold denial of Peter will later be paralleled in chap. 21 by a threefold question of love and service.

The responses of Peter in these denial scenes are striking when contrasted with the response of Jesus in the garden. Jesus had responded *I am* (ἐγώ εἰμι, vv. 5-6), but Peter responded to his question of commitment and identity with *I am not* (οὐκ εἰμί, vv. 17, 25). The implications are enormous. The disciple was ready to fight but would not accept the way of Jesus. But in his third response even his willingness to fight is shown

to be a mere shadow, for Peter, when confronted with his own slashing of the servant in the garden, denied even that involvement. The denial was thus complete and the cock immediately crowed (v. 27), fulfilling Jesus' prediction indicating that Peter's commitment was a matter of hollow words (13:36-38).

18:28–19:16. The mock trial before Pilate. The setting was the praetorium or Roman judgment hall, and the scenes once again alternate between inside and outside. The Jewish leaders, who had already determined Jesus' guilt even before the trial (v. 31; cf. 11:50), desired to maintain their ritual purity by remaining outside the gentile court at PASSOVER time (v. 28). The irony for John is clear because the lamb was being readied for Passover and the leaders were responsible for the fact that he was delivered (παραδίδωμι, v. 30; the same word frequently used of Judas, the betrayer) to be killed (v. 32).

The next scene shifts as PILATE, the procurator or prefect, entered the praetorium to question Jesus. Judea was a subdivision of the imperial province of Syria and unlike the senatorial provinces imperial provinces were viewed as hostile to Rome. The question of treason and rebellion was always a concern in such provinces.

From Pilate's viewpoint the question *Are you the King of the Jews?* (v. 33) was directed at determining the possibility of such a treasonable situation. The dialogue that ensued over Jesus' kingship left Pilate asking *What is truth?* (v. 38) and Jesus affirming his kingship but redefining the nature of such kingship (v. 37).

The third scene moves outside again and reveals a frustrated Pilate who found that Jesus was hardly a political rebel as Pilate had been led to believe. Accordingly, he sought to release Jesus because in his judgment Jesus was innocent. Realizing the determination of the Jews to condemn Jesus, however, Pilate tried the gimmick of a tradition or custom established for the Jews at Passover in releasing a confirmed criminal (v. 39). He gave them what seemed an easy choice—a hardened criminal BARABBAS, a thief who had no doubt robbed some of them, or the seemingly facile preacher Jesus. His strategy failed, and they chose Barabbas.

The fourth scene reveals Pilate's next strategy. Inside the fortress his troops whipped Jesus and played their mocking kingly game with him. Then in the fifth scene Pilate brought Jesus out to the hostile crowd, hoping that the sight of the beaten Jesus ("Behold the man," 19:5 KJV) might engender sympathy. But the crowd had tasted blood and wanted more. *Crucify him,* they shouted, to which Pilate finally responded, *Take him.* Yet he added his evaluation of innocence (v. 6; cf. 18:38; 19:4). Political expediency was carrying the day.

But the Jews countered Pilate's declaration of innocence with their own judgment that he was guilty of blasphemy because he declared himself to be the *Son of God* (v. 7). That announcement stunned Pilate who wanted a "time-out." Yet as Garland (1988, 491) and others have indicated, the Jews' reliance on the law to condemn Jesus set the stage for their own condemnation. They broke the law in their unjust pursuit of Jesus' death and ultimately in their affirmation of Caesar as their only king (v. 15).

Pilate's time-out forms the sixth scene. At this point his fear at the breach of the Roman peace by a mob uprising was countered by his fear of the unknown, and he reentered the praetorium to requestion Jesus (v. 8). His question, couched in the Johannine theme of origin, brought nothing but silence from Jesus. Pilate retorted by reminding Jesus of his power to condemn and to free, but Jesus finally broke the uneasy silence with a reminder that Pilate was not the source of power. Dispensing power was in the hands of God but guilt was the result of human action. So the theme of the deliverer is once again brought to focus and it serves as a forewarning to Pilate (v. 11).

The seventh and final scene took place before the Jews. It began with Pilate's renewed attempt to release Jesus but it was countered by the Jewish threat to identify Pilate as a foe of Caesar and a supporter of treason (v. 12). The threat proved effective and brought Pilate to the judgment seat to render the verdict.

Scholars today debate whether the *Pavement* (*lithostratus*, v. 13) was at the Herodian Palace on the west side of Jerusalem near the Jaffa Gate or at the Tower of Antonio to the north of the Temple (see Mackowski 1980, 91–111). While a few translations suggest that Pilate sat Jesus on the judgment seat in a defiant act, most translations correctly have Pilate seated to begin the final phase. To think that a Roman puppet would turn over his seat to a Jewish peasant seems highly unlikely.

The time of this event is duly noted by the evangelist, namely, *the day of Preparation . . . about noon.* The time is significant for John and it is repeated (19:14, 31) because the *day of Preparation* was the day for killing the Passover lambs. In the Synoptics the day of crucifixion is merely related to Passover, but theologically for John the death of Jesus has to be related specifically to the slaying of the lambs. Because of the apparent differences in such time statements, scholars have sought to reconcile John and the Synoptics by a number of arguments, including an argument based on the differences in the calendar of official Judaism and the calendar of the ESSENES. Such attempts usually prove to be fruitless. What is clear in John is the theological nature of the time designations.

In the final trial scene Pilate made one last attempt to free Jesus, but he was rebuffed by the ultimate Jewish hypocrisy: *We have no king but the emperor* (i.e., Caesar, v. 15). Throughout Israel's history it was God that was to be their king (cf. 1 Sam 8:7). So finally Pilate also joined the deliverers and handed Jesus over to be crucified (v. 16). Judas, the Jews, and Pilate are all guilty.

19:17-27. The crucifixion of the king. John simply notes that Jesus bore his own cross to the place of the skull and was crucified between two others. While Luke mentions Simon of Cyrene and the death confession of one of the criminals (Luke 23:26, 40-42), John's focus is on Jesus and the cross itself. Charges of condemned victims were nailed to their crosses. The charge against Jesus was treason because he was *the King of the Jews* (v. 19).

For John two facts were important. The charge was written in three languages: Hebrew, the language of the chosen people; Latin, the language of Roman authority and government; and Greek, the language of international commerce (v. 20). So the evangelist regards the charge as in fact a confession to the whole world concerning the kingship of Jesus. Moreover, while the Jews sought to modify the charge/confession to that of a pretender, John sees the weakling Pilate as finally having a backbone (vv. 21-22).

The conclusion is obvious: Pilate is not in control of this death. He has indeed finally received strength to stand against the Jews so that the integrity of the death scene is maintained. Jesus was indeed *the King of the Jews.*

The evangelist highlights two groups around the cross for attention. The soldiers in disposing of the clothing of Jesus are seen as fulfilling scripture (cf. Ps 22:18).

The women are briefly mentioned as a means to introduce Jesus' mother and *the disciple whom [Jesus] loved.* Traditionally that disciple was regarded as John.

The thesis of Filson (1963, 22) that the disciple was Lazarus has little support. As the eldest son, Jesus cared for his mother and in this text Jesus made his choice (vv. 26-27). The implications were significant. The Johannine community was special and Jesus cared for his own.

19:28-37. The death of the lamb. Two more statements from the cross bring to a conclusion the death of the lamb. The *I am thirsty* (v. 28) reminds the reader that the death scene was real and the *It is finished* (v. 30) accentuates the fact that the death was part of God's intention to bring Jesus to this hour. With this last statement Jesus *gave up his Spirit*. The point is clear: people were not ultimately in charge of the death of the lamb.

With the ending of *the day of Preparation* (and the killing of the Passover lambs), the Jews sought to ready the land ritually for SABBATH by having the crucified ones quickly dispatched. But surprisingly, the soldiers found the Passover lamb was already dead and there was no need to break Jesus' legs. John sees that fact to be very significant because the lamb died without blemish (Exod 12:46; Num 9:12). Yet he was appropriately stabbed, a fact that must have reminded the evangelist of some allusions to a pierced Messiah (cf. Zech 12:10).

But when he was pierced there came out *blood and water* (v. 34). Some writers and preachers who are opposed to ideas of Johannine symbolism have often been tempted to interpret blood and water as mere signs of death. But to a symbolic writer like John *blood and water* carry multifaceted meanings related to salvation, including but not limited to the ordinances or sacraments of the church.

The fact that the evangelist makes a special note to the effect that these symbols or signs are testimonies and are important for believing (v. 35) immediately reminds the careful reader of the purpose statement of the Gospel (20:30-31).

19:38-42. The burial of the king. The picture presented in this burial is that of a king. He was buried in *a new tomb* (v. 41) with the appropriate bindings and a hundred (Roman) pounds of spices (seventy-five by modern measure), sufficient to bury a king. The attendants, Joseph and Nicodemus, were undoubtedly among the PHARISEES who believed in the resurrection but who were still somewhat fearful of the Jewish leadership. With the burial of the king, the story seemed to be finished. But everyone was in for a big surprise.

The Resurrection Stories, 20:1-29; 21:1-23

The great PASSOVER had taken place; the lamb was slain; the king had died. No more would the theme of Passover be mentioned in this Gospel. A new day was ready to dawn. The night was ready to pass away. The stories of the resurrection in John are thus the stories of the transition into the new era.

In the Synoptics the appearance stories are set either in Galilee (in Matthew, except 28:9-10, and apparently in Mark) or in the Jerusalem area (in Luke). In John the main appearances occur in Jerusalem (chap. 20) but in the postscript the context is Galilee (chap. 21). The stories in John are unique although they are not different in kind from those in the Synoptics.

Chapter 20 contains three stories: the story of Mary Magdalene (20:1-2, 11-18), the episode of the two disciples visiting the tomb (20:2-10), and the appearances to the disciples and Thomas (20:19-29). Chapter 21 is a threefold story of the miraculous catch of fish, the breakfast, and the restoration of Peter (21:1-23).

20:2-10. The visit of the two disciples to the tomb. Although the resurrection stories begin with the note that Mary is the first one to the tomb, the story quickly shifts to the two disciples: Peter and the disciple whom Jesus loved (v. 2). The comparison between the two disciples that began at 13:23-24 is peculiar to John.

After being informed by Mary that the tomb was open, the BELOVED DISCIPLE outran Peter and first saw the tomb with the empty grave wrappings (vv. 4-5). Why he did not enter has been variously interpreted by commentators from a sense of reverence to waiting for Peter. Ecclesiologies often determine perspectives. But in spite of the order of entrance the text indicates that other disciple *saw and believed* (v. 8). This text is the only statement in the canonical Gospels where it is said that the empty tomb was a sufficient basis for belief. In all other cases the basis was the appearance of Jesus. What stage of believing was implied here is not quite clear because the evangelist seems anxious to move the people in the narratives from one level of belief to the next. Clearly he suggests that they did not yet fully understand the scriptural warrant for Jesus' resurrection (v. 9).

20:1-2, 11-18. Mary Magdalene. After her initial visit to the tomb and the notification to the disciples that the tomb was empty (vv. 1-2), Mary returned to the tomb weeping (v. 11). Then after the appearance of angels in the tomb she conversed with someone (who seemed to be a gardener, v. 15) about her sorrow and the missing body. But all the pain vanished with one word: *Mary!* He spoke her name and everything was changed (v. 16).

She grabbed at him and uttered the intensive word *Rabbouni!* But Jesus stopped her with the words, *Do not hold on to me* (v. 17). The reason given by the risen Lord is that he had not yet ascended. This statement has led a few commentators and preachers to pose an ascent and then a descent so that Jesus could be later touched. Such thinking is a complete misunderstanding of the text. Assurance of Christ's presence and support does not come via his physical presence (see Borchert 1987, 142). Mary wanted to hold on to him but such was not possible. Instead she had to leave him and carry her testimony to others (v. 18).

20:19-29. The disciples and Thomas. It was again *evening* and fear still plagued the disciples as they gathered on the *first day of the week* (v. 19). But they were in for a shock. Locked doors like a shut tomb did not deter the risen Jesus. He entered their room and like the theophanies or angelophanies of the OT the appearance of Jesus was accompanied by his word of *Peace* (vv. 19, 21) and followed by a commission to carry the message of forgiveness to others (v. 23).

Interpreters of this text must not concentrate on the "retaining" aspect here any more than they should concentrate on the "binding" aspect of the Matthean statement at Caesarea Philippi (Matt 16:19; 18:18). The role of the authentic rabbi (and believer) was to bring persons into a proper relationship with God.

The breathing on the disciples and the command to receive the Holy Spirit is the Johannine summation of the pentecostal promise (v. 22; cf. Luke 24:49, 51; Acts 1:8, etc.). Interpreters of these stories should avoid detailed, Tatian-like (as found in the DIATESSARON), Western attempts to fit these stories into neat packages. The testimonies are authentic messages concerning God's Son and our faith. They stand as faithful statements of the evangelists. For this reason Tatian was never accepted as a substitute for the Gospels.

While the disciples who were gathered on the first day of the week received a blessing, Thomas missed the first church service. When he heard the report, he stoutly refused to accept the word of testimony from others without the authentication of the nail holes and the stab wound (v. 25).

But the next Lord's Day, that is, *the first day of the week* (v. 19), he was at the service. Eight days later is one week later according to our system of reckoning where the first day is not counted (v. 26). Again Jesus entered and gave his "peace" or "shalom to those gathered. The ecclesiastical implications are obvious. The church meets each Lord's Day to receive the peace of the risen Lord.

Thomas had challenged the other's testimonies. At this gathering his failure to believe was challenged by Jesus' offer to touch his wounds. The experience was more than convincing for Thomas, and he uttered what has come to be Christianity's premier confession of faith: *My Lord and my God!* (v. 28). But the doubter turned confessor was nonetheless reminded that the church that would thereafter be built upon testimony would not have the same opportunity for verification. Thus a blessing was issued by the risen Lord to those who would believe "without seeing" (v. 29).

21:1-23. The epilogue, a triple story. The first segment of this story once again begins at night but this time it is in Galilee. The disciples decided to return to fishing and as in Luke 5:1-11 they toiled all night without success. At daybreak Jesus appeared on the shore and suggested to these seasoned fishermen that they try the other side of the boat (v. 6). The result was a large catch of fish. The BELOVED DISCIPLE first recognized the Lord and informed Peter (v. 7). Once again the comparison is made. And once again Peter, the second best, impetuously dashed off to see Jesus.

This story has been the subject of considerable form analysis and comparison with the Lukan story. These two texts are the only two places where a miraculous catch is recorded. Some argue that it is the same story with Luke being a transposed resurrection narrative. But some also suggest that part of the story is not unlike Peter walking on the water in Matt 14:28-33. Such suggestions have led to speculation that the entire story may be a construction from segments of other stories.

Others have asked about the significance of the number of fish. Some have suggested that maybe the author thought there were 153 varieties of fish in the sea or 153 language patterns at the time of the evangelist's writing, both of which might be the symbol of the worldwide scope of the Christian mission. Clearly this text is the subject of a great deal of speculation and analysis. While the story can stand on its own, further reflection may be helpful (see Brown 1970; Bultmann 1963; Schnackenburg 1987, v. 3).

The second part of the story takes place on land. The *charcoal fire* (v. 9) is a reminder of the one burning when Peter denied Jesus three times (cf. 18:1-8). In this story the risen Lord had prepared a meal of fish and bread (clearly reminiscent of the feeding of the five thousand at Passover time in the pre-resurrection era; cf. 6:1-14). The statement that Jesus *took the bread and gave it to them* as well as *the fish* (v. 13) is related to the words of the church's supper. The point is that in this event the disciples recognized that it was *the Lord* (v. 12), a theme related to the breaking of bread in the Lukan EMMAUS story (Luke 24:30).

The third part of the story involves the threefold question to Peter in his restoration. That threefold question of the Lord involved Peter's love. Would his relationship to others get in the way of his love for Jesus? It had done so on the horrible night of his betrayal. It was therefore review time. When Peter answered three times that his love for Jesus was primary, Jesus gave him a commission to feed the flock (vv. 15, 16, 17), a commission that Peter faithfully passed on to subsequent church leaders (cf. 1 Pet 5:2).

In preaching on this text some ministers become enamored with linguistic discussions about *love*. But the point of Peter's grief is not primarily a linguistic nicety. The text indicates that Peter was grieved because Jesus asked *the third time, "Do you love me?"* (v. 17). The third time was a haunting reminder that Jesus was right and he was wrong in his boast of commitment to Jesus (cf. John 13:37-38).

But when Peter's restoration was completed, the story was not ended because his boast of dying for Jesus (13:37) was accepted by the Lord. He would indeed die for Jesus, the stretched out death of crucifixion (v. 18).

Yet like all of us Peter was still Peter. If he were to die, what about the BELOVED DISCIPLE (vv. 20-21)? That question, Jesus told Peter, was totally irrelevant to him. His task was to follow Jesus (v. 22).

But that question was relevant for the Johannine community because some thought that Jesus said the Beloved Disciple would not die (v. 23). Obviously that disciple was either dead by the time the Gospel was being circulated or very near death. So the correction of false theories needed to be made.

Conclusions, 20:30-31 and 21:24-25

This Gospel contains two conclusions, the first at the end of chap. 20, which originally was intended to serve as the conclusion to the book, and the second at the end of chap. 21, which concludes the epilogue and expands the force of the earlier conclusion.

20:30-31. The first ending. As indicated earlier, these verses in fact contain a summary purpose statement for the entire book and tie together a number of the major themes of the Gospel. So complete did Loisy consider the work to be at the end of chap. 20 that he wrote: "The book is complete, quite complete" (1921, 514). The first twenty chapters—despite the displacement theories of Bultmann, the organizational weavings of MacGregor and Morton, and the structural arguments of Fortna—appear to be a continuous theological argument of the evangelist. This conclusion is therefore a masterfully tied knot that encircles these twenty chapters.

21:24-25. The second ending. While the epilogue should definitely be viewed as an afterthought or a postscript, it is important to recognize with Westcott (1889, 359) that there is no textual support for thinking that the other twenty chapters ever circulated without this epilogue. It was from the earliest times an attachment to the text. In theology and style the epilogue is truly Johannine.

In form this ending has two parts: an authentication and a conclusion. The authentication is a community-written testimony (*we know*, v. 24) that this Gospel represents the genuine witness of the disciple who stands behind the written text. The conclusion is an affirmation of the selective nature of materials included in the Gospel and the hyperbolic statement reflects the writer's (*I*, v. 25) grand opinion that the selection is drawn from a vast resource of material concerning Jesus.

The *I* of v. 25 may imply that the writer is a recorder who differs from the witness of v. 24. But this final verse stands as a striking invitation to discover the magnificent testimony of John that is drawn from an immense storehouse of information concerning Jesus, the word of God come in human flesh (1:14).

Appendix.
The Woman Taken in Adultery,
7:53–8:11

This pericope has been regarded by most textual analysts as an insertion into the Johannine Gospel. In style, form, and content it was hardly written by the author of the other parts of the Gospel. But that does not mean it should not be considered canonical. Early Christians were convinced that it was a reflection of an authentic Jesus tradition.

The major question seemed to be where it should be placed. Some manuscripts contain it here in the context of Johannine conflict stories but other manuscripts have it after Luke 21:38 and before the plot to kill Jesus. While it is more like the Lukan stories that emphasize the care of the Lord for the unfortunate, the setting at the end of Luke 21 is also a misfit. The best solution is to regard the pericope as an independent story going back to Jesus.

Adultery was regarded as a violation of the will of God in accordance with the seventh statement of the TEN COMMANDMENTS (Exod 20:14). But a double standard had emerged that held women more liable than men. This story reflects that same double standard because the woman's partner was not brought forward by the condemning men.

Jesus recognized the double standard and the Pharisees' attempt to entrap him in his care for the helpless (v. 6). His response therefore was aimed at the self-righteousness of the accusers (v. 7). When he disposed of those self-righteous ones and was alone with the woman, he addressed her in a forgiving spirit without dismissing the reality of her sin (v. 11).

The pericope is thus an excellent example of Jesus' firm confrontation of hypocritical self-righteousness and caring salvation of sinners who need to find transformation.

Works Cited

Beasley-Murray, G. R. 1987. *John.* WBC.

Black, D. 1988. "On the Style and Significance of John 17," *CTR* 3:141–59.

Boice, J. M. 1970. *Witness and Revelation in the Gospel of John.*

Borchert, G. L. 1981. "The Fourth Gospel and Its Theological Impact," *RE* 78:249–58. 1987. *Assurance and Warning.* 1988. "The Resurrection Perspective in John," *RE* 85:501–13. 1993. "Passover and the Narrative Cycles in John," *Perspectives in John,* ed. M. Parsons and R. Sloan, 303–16. Forthcoming. *John.* NAC. Forthcoming. "Prayer in John 17," in *Prayer in Biblical Research.*

Borgen, P. 1965. "Bread from Heaven," NovTsup.

Brown, R. E. 1966, 1970. *The Gospel according to John.* AncB. 1979. *The Community of the Beloved Disciple.*

Bultmann, R. 1963. *The History of the Synoptic Tradition.* 1971. *The Gospel of John.*

Burney, C. F. 1922. *The Aramaic Origin of the Fourth Gospel.*

Carson, D. A. 1991. *The Gospel According to John.*

Craddock, F. 1982. *John.* Knox Preaching Guides.

Culmann, O. 1953. *Early Christian Worship.*

Culpepper, R. A. 1975. *The Johannine School.* SBLDS 26. 1983. *Anatomy of the Fourth Gospel.*

Dodd, C. H. 1958. *The Interpretation of the Fourth Gospel.*

Duke, P. 1985. *Irony in the Fourth Gospel.*

Filson, F. 1963. *John.* LBC.

Fisch, H., ed. 1965. *Haggada.*

Fortna, R. 1988. *The Fourth Gospel and Its Predecessor.*

Freeman, C. H. 1991. "The Function of Polemic in John 7 and 8," Ph.D. diss., The Southern Baptist Theological Seminary.

Garland, D. E. 1988. "John 18–19: Life through Jesus' Death," *RE* 85:485-99.

Guilding, A. 1960. *The Fourth Gospel and Jewish Worship.*

Harris, M. 1971. "Prepositions and Theology in the Greek NT," *NIDNTT,* 1171–1215.

Haenchen, E. 1984. *John.* Herm.

Käsemann, E. 1969. "The Structure and Purpose of the Prologue to John's Gospel," *NT Questions of Today,* 138–67.

Lewis, C. S. 1950. *The Lion, the Witch and the Wardrobe.*

Loisy, A. 1921. *Le Quatrieme Evangile.*

MacGregor, G., and A. Morton. 1961. *The Structure of the Fourth Gospel.*

Mackowski, R. M. 1980. *Jerusalem, City of Jesus: An Exploration of the Traditions, Writings, and Remains of the Holy City from the Time of Christ.*

Malatesta, E. 1971. "The Literary Structure of John 17," *Bib* 52:190–214.

Malina, Bruce. 1981. *The NT World: Insights from Cultural Anthropology.*

Martyn, J. L. 1979. *History and Theology in the Fourth Gospel.*

Metzger, Bruce M. 1953. "The Jehovah's Witnesses and Jesus Christ: A Biblical and Theological Appraisal," *TT* 10:65–85.

Moody, D. 1953. " 'God's Only Son': John 3:16 in the RSV," *JBL* 72:213–19.

Morris, L. 1971. *The Gospel according to John.* NIGNT. 1986–1990. *Reflections on the Gospel of John.* 4 vols.

Mowinckle, Sigmund. 1956. *He That Cometh.*

Newman, B., and E. Nida. 1980. *A Translator's Handbook on the Gospel of John.*

Sanders, J. T. 1971. *The NT Christological Hymns.* SNTSMS 15.

Schnackenburg, R. 1987. *The Gospel according to John*.

Segovia, F. 1991. *The Farewell of the Word*.

Sloyan, G. 1988. *John*. Interp.

Thornton, Edward E., and Gerald Borchert. 1988. *The Crisis of Fear*.

Westcott, B. F. 1887 [1954]. *The Gospel according to St. John*.

Acts of the Apostles

Mikeal C. Parsons

Introduction

The Acts of the Apostles is the only book that presents the story of the early church in the apostolic age. As such it is a foundational document for understanding the life and work of the earliest Christian communities much as the four Gospels are the foundational documents for understanding the life and work of JESUS of Nazareth. The placement of Acts in the NT CANON between the fourfold gospel and the collection of Pauline epistles is reflective of its function in the canon: Acts is a bridge between the time of the founder of the community and the time of his first followers.

Authorship

Early Christian tradition argues that Luke the physician, the traveling companion of PAUL (see Col 4:14; 2 Tim 4:11; Phlm 24), was the author of Acts (see Irenaeus, *AdvHaer* 3.14). Although this traditional view still has its ardent supporters (see Fitzmyer 1981, 35–51), many scholars today are skeptical about identifying the author of Acts with any certainty. Since Cadbury, appeals to the "medical language" of Acts to support the traditional view of Lukan authorship is neither fashionable nor persuasive. Even the view that Luke and Acts were written by a gentile author has met strong resistance by those who view the conflict in Acts as an inter-Jewish problem. The identity of the author will probably remain a point of contention, but accepting an anonymous author in no way detracts from the message of the book. The name "Luke" is used throughout this commentary as a matter of convenience to refer to the implied author of Acts without any assumptions about the identity of the real author.

Relationship between Luke and Acts

Acts is the sequel to the Gospel of Luke. As such, one document is best read in light of the other, much like the fourth Gospel is best understood in the light of the Johannine Epis tles. That Luke and Acts were written by the same person seems indisputable; to argue that these two writings comprise a single, continuous narrative (represented by the hyphenated title "Luke-Acts"), however, is to make too much of the evidence. There is no manuscript evidence that these two writings ever existed as one document in a "precanonical" form. In fact, the longer Western text of Acts supports the notion that the writings enjoyed basically independent reception in the early church and were probably composed as discrete, although interrelated, narratives. In other words, the separation of Luke from Acts in the NT canon is not simply the result of a "botched" job by the "canonical" editors, but rather an accurate reflection of the independent character of each writing. Maintaining the individual character of each Lukan writing allows the reader to see both the similarities and the differences between the Gospel of Luke and the Acts of the Apostles.

Date and Place

Most scholars assume Acts was written after the third Gospel and near the end of the first century C.E., although the date assigned ranges from as early as pre-70 C.E. to as late as 150 C.E. The concerns reflected in Acts are similar to those of the Pastoral Epistles and tend to support a late first-century date. ACHAIA, CAESAREA, ANTIOCH, and more recently EPHESUS have been suggested as the locale of the Lukan community. Still others argue there was no one "Lukan community" but that Luke was addressing Christians in various locales. As with authorship, however, the questions of date and place remain unsettled; furthermore, a detailed understanding of those issues is essentially irrelevant for purposes of interpretation.

Genre and Literary Forms

The form of a writing helps interpret its content. Unfortunately, the genre of Acts is a much disputed issue. The book contains features often found in ancient biography, history, and novel, and scholars variously assign Acts to one of those forms. Although the overall genre of Acts is difficult to establish, understanding the constituent literary forms may be helpful in the reading process. The speeches, travel narrative (including the WE-SECTIONS), miracle stories (including "punitive" miracles), stories of edification, and summary statements all share literary conventions typical of other ancient literature, al though Luke has given his material a distinctive Christian "spin." Whatever sources were at Luke's disposal, the Book of Acts reflects an author in control of his materials. Above all, Acts is a story and employs literary conventions typical of ancient narrative.

For Further Study

In the *Mercer Dictionary of the Bible*: APOSTLE/APOSTLE-SHIP; APOSTLES, ACTS OF THE; BARNABAS; CHRISTOLOGY; FELLOWSHIP; HOLY SPIRIT; JAMES; JERUSALEM COUNCIL; LUKE; LUKE, GOSPEL OF; MIRACLE STORY; PAUL; PETER; PHILIP; RESURRECTION IN THE NT; ROMAN EMPIRE; SEVEN, THE; STEPHEN; TWELVE, THE; WE-SECTIONS; WOMEN IN THE NT. In other sources: J. Chance, "Luke," *MCB*; J. Fitzmyer, *The Gospel according to Luke I–IX*, AncB; R. Funk, *The Poetics of Biblical Narrative*; S. Garrett, *The Demise of the Devil: Magic and the Demonic in Luke's Writings*; D. Gill, "The Structure of Acts 9," *Bib* 55:546–48; E. Haenchen, *The Acts of the Apostles*; G. Krodel, *Acts*, AugCNT; J. Polhill, *Acts*, NAC.

Commentary

An Outline

I. The Sense of a Beginning, 1:1–5:42
  A. The Beginning of the Church, 1:1-26
  B. Pentecost, 2:1-47
  C. The Healing of a Lame Man, 3:1–4:31
  D. Tensions Within and Without, 4:32–5:42
II. Problems and Personalities, 6:1–12:25
  A. Stephen: His Witness and Death, 6:1–8:3
  B. Philip: A Man on Mission, 8:4-40
  C. Paul: His Conversion and Call, 9:1-31
  D. Peter: His Words and Deeds, 9:32–11:18
  E. Barnabas, Peter, and Herod:
    Contrasting Examples, 11:19–12:25
III. Paul's Mission to the Gentile World, 13:1–19:41
  A. Paul's Initial Missionary Campaign, 13:1–14:28
  B. The Conference in Jerusalem, 15:1-35
  C. Paul in Macedonia, 15:36–17:15
  D. Paul in Achaia, 17:16–18:17
  E. Paul in Ephesus, 18:18–19:41
IV. Paul's Farewell Journey, 20:1–28:31
  A. Paul's Last Journey to Jerusalem, 20:1–21:16
  B. Paul in Jerusalem, Acts 21:17–23:35
  C. Paul before Felix, Festus,
    and Agrippa, 24:1–26:32
  D. The Sea Voyage to Rome, 27:1–28:31

The Sense of a Beginning, 1:1–5:42

The Beginning of the Church, 1:1-26

The opening chapter of Acts refers to the previous story of the founder of the earliest Christian communi-

ty, Jesus of Nazareth, and sets the stage for the emergence and spread of that community. Acts 1:1-14 orients the reader to the story, and the remainder of chap. 1 (vv. 15-26) tells of the defection of Judas and the selection of his successor.

1:1-14. Introduction. Acts contains a brief, retrospective summary that describes the contents of the third Gospel (vv. 1-2). A prospective outline of the contents of Acts is given in v. 8 (this pattern is one of several used in narrative writings in antiquity: see, e.g., Polybius, *Hist* 2.1.4-8; 3.1.5–3.3.3; Philo, *Life of Moses* 2). Significantly, the outline is given by Jesus and is couched in the narrative as a promise.

The ascension account in Acts (vv. 6-11) follows the form of Greco-Roman assumption stories, while its terminology is heavily dependent on the assumption story of ELIJAH (2 Kgs 2:1-12). Just as ancient assumption stories accentuate the elevated status of their subjects, the ascension of Jesus underlines his exaltation. It is the fitting conclusion to the ministry of Jesus (so Luke 24:50-53); and here, it makes the life of the church both possible and intelligible. The ending of the story of Jesus then serves as the appropriate beginning of the story of the church.

Although after chap. 1 Jesus is absent as a character from the narrative of Acts (but see Acts 7:56), his influence throughout the rest of the narrative is profound. The name of Jesus occurs no less than sixty-nine times in Acts. He is at the center of the church's controversy with the Jews. He guides the church in its missionary efforts; he empowers the disciples to perform miracles. The ascended and exalted Christ, although absent as a character, is present throughout the narrative.

The ascension is significant for Luke's story and theology, but these opening verses actually focus on the response of the disciples to Jesus. This second section (vv. 6-11) contains two parts, and each one concludes with a reproof of the disciples (vv. 7, 11a) followed by a promise to them (vv. 8a, 11b; see Talbert 1984, 6–7). Despite the reproaches, the fact that both dialogues end with promises to the disciples invites a favorable judgment of the disciples by the audience.

In the summary of vv. 12-14, Luke lists the disciples who have gathered together in the *room upstairs*. The names of the disciples in Acts 1 are the same as those in Luke 6:13-16, although the order is slightly different. The list of followers is extended in Acts to include women and the family of Jesus. To mention women in ancient genealogies is unusual. Mary, the mother of Jesus, stands as a bridge figure between the women who followed Jesus (see Luke 8:2; 23:49, 55; 24:10) and the family of Jesus, who, except for James, receive no further mention in the text. The omission of Judas's name from the list, of course, prepares the reader for the report of his death and the choice of his replacement.

1:15-26. The death of Judas and the election of Matthias. Before Luke narrates the fulfillment at Pentecost of Jesus' promise that the disciples will be empowered by the Holy Spirit, Luke addresses what was for him a problem of the first magnitude. The circle of THE TWELVE has been broken and must be restored.

Peter stands in the midst of the believers to address this problem (v. 15). The situational irony of this first apostolic speech in the post-Easter community should not be lost. The irony is created by the similarities in the pre-Easter actions of JUDAS and PETER. Judas betrayed Jesus (Luke 22:47), thus fulfilling Jesus' prophecy (Luke 22:21-22). Peter denied knowing Jesus three times (Luke 22:54-62), thus fulfilling Jesus' prophecy (Luke 22:34). The actions of both Judas and Peter were associated with the work of Satan (Luke 22:3; 22:31). And so in Acts v. 15, we have the ironical predicament of the one who denied Jesus standing up to retell the story of the one who had betrayed him.

Before leaving v. 15, we should note the narrator's use of a narrative aside to address the reader directly about the size of the assembly gathered with Peter: *together the crowd numbered about one hundred twenty*

persons. The number is significant since 120 is not only a multiple of the Twelve but also because 120 males were required to constitute a local Jewish SANHEDRIN or council (Sanh 1.6). Luke may be arguing that the early church is also a "properly constituted" community according to Pharisaic standards. Regardless, it is clear that in this newly formed community, women also count (see v. 14; also Luke 8:1-3; 23:49).

Peter's speech (vv. 16-22) turns upon the OT quotation cited in v. 20. The first half of the quotation taken from Ps 69:26 deals with the demise of Judas; the second half, a citation of Ps 109:8, addresses the election of Judas's successor. The double use of the verb for divine necessity ($\delta\epsilon\hat{\iota}$) in vv. 16 and 21 is the narrative clue for dividing the speech into these two parts.

Peter depicts the defection of Judas and his subsequent judgment in the language of economics (Johnson 1977, 179–81). Judas does not repent and return the betrayal money (contra Matt 27:3-5), but rather purchases a farm (v. 18). This purchase not only stands in contrast to the believers who sold their farms and laid the proceeds at the apostles' feet (see 4:32-35); it also is juxtaposed to Peter who, along with James and John, "left everything" to follow Jesus (see Luke 5:11). Judas's purchase of property is a symbol of his apostasy from the circle of the Twelve.

Ironically, Judas dies on this same property. There is no hint of suicide here (as in Matt 27). The death is apparently the result of divine judgment, and the field is called the *Hakeldama, that is, Field of Blood* (v. 19). And just as the purchasing of a field symbolized Judas's defection, so also the fact that his property is doomed to perpetual desertion (v. 20) is a sign of his judgment.

Joseph and Matthias are put forward as apostolic candidates, and the assembly prays for divine guidance in the selection process. Matthias is chosen as the replacement. Note the play on words throughout this scene: Judas has forfeited his "share" ($\kappa\lambda\hat{\eta}\rho\sigma\varsigma$) in the apostolic ministry and gone to his own "place" ($\tau\acute{o}\pi\sigma\varsigma$). In contrast, the "lot" ($\kappa\lambda\hat{\eta}\rho\sigma\varsigma$) now falls to Matthias, and he takes his "place" ($\tau\acute{o}\pi\sigma\varsigma$) alongside the eleven in the apostolic ministry. The scriptures are fulfilled, the circle of Twelve is reconstituted, and the stage is set for Pentecost.

Pentecost, 2:1-47

The Holy Spirit descended on Jesus at the outset of his public ministry (Luke 3:22; 4:1; 4:14). Now the Holy Spirit comes upon the disciples at the inauguration of their public ministry. The disciples are worthy successors of Jesus.

2:1-13. The miracle of Pentecost. All narratives have gaps in the telling of a story, and what a narrator decides *not* to say is sometimes as important as what is said. The story of Pentecost is such a story. The story itself fills a gap created when Jesus instructs the disciples to stay in the city for an indeterminate length of time until they *receive power when the Holy Spirit has come upon* them (1:8). In v. 1 the length of time is fifty days. That time has not been idle time for the disciples: they spend forty days being instructed by the risen Lord about the kingdom of God (1:3) and an unspecified time electing Judas's replacement.

But gaps still remain within the story itself. In this Pentecost narrative, the reader encounters rather large lacunae over the nature of the miracle of glossolalia and the overall background against which the passage should be read. How one chooses to fill those gaps will determine in large measure the interpretation assigned to this particular passage.

What is the nature of the miracle recorded in Acts 2? The coming of the Spirit is joined by two manifestations: a loud noise and *tongues, as of fire.* But the function of these audial and visual signs in this narrative is unclear. When the apostles speak "in other tongues" (v. 4 RSV; NRSV *languages*) are they speaking in ecstatic, unintelligible speech (see 1 Cor 12–14), or are they speaking in the languages of the many foreign peoples gathered together there? There is evidence for both interpretations. Those gathered there heard in their own languages (vv. 6-7); but others mistook the disciples as drunk (v. 13), suggesting that, at least for some, the apostles' speech was unintelligible. The weight of the evidence seems to favor a miracle of hearing, but the "correct" interpretation is perhaps finally undecidable. Such rich ambiguity may underscore the multilayered understanding that Luke himself had of this event.

In the Pentecost narrative, the reader, standing at a crossroads, is faced with choosing among these various options. The road signs are few, and the exegetical path one chooses will determine the direction of interpretation when one encounters the next crossroad. Reading the passage against these various backgrounds at times sheds new light; at other times, such choices perpetuate certain misreadings.

Whichever of these paths the interpreter chooses to follow, one often-neglected emphasis of this passage remains constant. Alongside the theme of the Holy

Spirit empowering the disciples (Acts 1:4) is the countertheme that Pentecost also hints at the benefits of waiting, of being patient (Luke 24:52; Acts 1:8, 12; 2:1). So Pentecost celebrates both an empowered church as well as a patient God who endures the church's abuse of that power. Filling the interpretive gap left by the Pentecost narrative with an emphasis on the patience of waiting disciples and a faithful God also picks up on a major point of the text from Joel, which serves as the basis for Peter's sermon.

2:14-40. Peter's Pentecostal sermon. Peter's interpretation of the Pentecost experience is almost three times longer than the narrative detailing the event itself. The speech divides into two main parts (vv. 17-21; 22-36), with an introduction (vv. 14-16) and conclusion (vv. 37-40).

Peter stands again (see 1:15-22) to strengthen the brothers and sisters (vv. 14-15). The narrator's introduction (v. 14a) anchors the speech firmly within the narrative framework of 2:1-13. The linguistic connections are strong. Peter raises his *voice* (φωνή, v. 14) in harmony with the *sound* (φωνή, v. 6) that had drawn the multitudes to the company of believers in the first place. Furthermore, the word Luke uses to describe the address of Peter to the crowd is the same word used to describe the inspired speech the Spirit gave to the believers who were speaking in "other tongues" (see 2:4). Not only are the "tongues" at Pentecost divinely inspired, but Peter's interpretation of that event is likewise authoritatively inspired.

The introduction to the speech itself is a response to the exasperated question some of them were posing to one another, *What does this mean?* (v. 12). If Peter rejects the mockery of some that the believers are drunk (v. 15; see v. 13), he also affirms the understanding of others that the believers are rehearsing the *God's deeds of power* (v. 11). This citation of Joel 2:28-32 (LXX 3:1-5) functions as the bridge both to what precedes and follows it.

Note first the inclusive nature of this citation. This community Joel speaks about and that Peter says is realized in the earliest Christian community is remarkably inclusive. It is gender inclusive: *your sons and your daughters* (v. 17); *my slaves, both men and women* (v. 18). It is age inclusive: *your young men* and *your old men* (v. 17). And if we are to take seriously the opening of this citation (*all flesh,* v. 17), then this community is also destined to be ethnically inclusive.

The Joel citation has been modified by the addition of several significant terms and phrases. That this new community itself is an eschatological sign is underscored by the change from "after these days" in the LXX text of Joel (cf. Joel 2:29) to *in the last days* found here in Acts. That this sermon is inspired speech is further underscored by the addition in v. 17 of *God declares*. Peter had assumed the role of the narrator in this speech, but quickly yields the floor to Joel who in turn defers to God. The effect of these narrative layers—Luke said that Peter said that Joel said that God said—is to reinforce the utterly reliable and authoritative character of the speech here. This point is made again by the next Lukan addition to the quotation at the end of v. 18: *and they shall prophesy.* This promise is fulfilled not only in the Pentecost event; Peter is fulfilling it himself in this very speech.

The last element added to the Joel citations, *signs* (v. 19), is perhaps the most significant addition. The phrase "wonders and signs" or SIGNS AND WONDERS becomes something of a refrain throughout the first half of Acts. It first recurs in the context of this very speech when Peter refers three verses later to *Jesus of Nazareth, a man attested to you by God with deeds of power, wonders, and signs . . .* (v. 22). Jesus is the primary referent to the prophecy that God would work wonders and signs as eschatological portents of the coming Day of the Lord.

But Jesus is not the only referent. Later in this chapter we find wonders and signs being done through the apostles (cf. 4:30; 5:12). Stephen, one of THE SEVEN Hellenists selected to assist the Twelve (see 6:1-6), is himself described as one who *did great wonders and signs among the people* (6:8). Stephen next describes Moses as *having performed wonders and signs in Egypt, at the Red Sea, and in the wilderness for forty years* (7:36). Philip also works *signs* (8:6—note the absence of "wonders"). Finally, the Lord grants *signs and wonders to be done* by the hands of Paul and Barnabas (14:3; see 15:12).

Signs and wonders, then, accompany the ministries of the leaders of God's community in unbroken succession, from Moses to Jesus, to the Twelve, to Stephen and Philip the Hellenists, and to Paul and Barnabas, the leaders of the gentile mission. Luke demonstrates that the early church has been more faithful to the tradition of Moses than other groups making the same claims. Membership in this radically inclusive community is restricted in only one way: *Then everyone who calls on the name of the Lord shall be saved* (v. 21). The identity of this "Lord" is explored in the second part of this sermon (vv. 22-36), and the call to

"be saved" is the focus of the invitation at the end (vv. 37-41).

Acts 2:22-36 is marked with several appeals for attention that serve as indicators of rhetorical shifts. This part of the speech forms the following chiastic structure (Krodel 1986, 83):

A the kerygma, 22-24
  B proof from scripture, 25-28
    C interpretation of scripture, 34a
      D exaltation of Jesus and the
          mediation of the Holy Spirit, 32-33
    C' interpretation of scripture, 29-31
  B' proof from scripture, 34b-35
A' the kerygma, 36

The heart of the Pentecost sermon is to be found in vv. 32-33. Peter identifies the unnamed Christ as Jesus (v. 32), which distinguishes early Christian messianic exegesis from that of Jewish contemporaries. The identification is further strengthened by the use of resurrection language. David foresaw and spoke of the *resurrection of the Messiah* (v. 31) who is *this Jesus God raised up* (v. 32a).

These verses also serve to link the speech with the Pentecost narrative and its interpretive framework provided by the Joel citation. The reference to the *promise* Jesus *received from the Father* (v. 33) recalls the Pentecost event; v. 33 identifies that promise as the *Holy Spirit*. That Jesus *poured out this that you both see and hear* (v. 33) echoes the Joel prophecy ("I will pour out my Spirit," Joel 2:28) and explicitly interprets Pentecost as a miracle of both sight and sound.

The conclusion of Peter's sermon (vv. 37-39) is interrupted by the audience who are cut to the heart and ask Peter and the rest of the apostles, *Brothers, what should we do?* (cf. Luke 3:10). Peter then offers a soteriological conclusion to his sermon: *Repent, and be baptized every one of you in the name of Jesus Christ so that your sins may be forgiven* (v. 38a). He also promises that they too will receive the "gift which is the Holy Spirit" (v. 38b, author trans.). This promise (see v. 33) is not only for Peter's audience, but for their children and *for all who are far away* (v. 39). The final phrase of Peter's speech, *everyone whom the Lord our God calls to him*, takes the last phrase of the Joel citation (v. 21=Joel 2:32) and turns it on its head. The invitation to salvation is reciprocal: "Everyone who calls on the name of Lord" will be those "whom the Lord our God calls to him."

2:41-47. Narrative summary. Luke concludes this section with the first of a series of long summary statements. Some summaries, such as Acts 1:12-14, are brief (see 6:7; 8:14; 9:31-32; 11:19-20); others, such as vv. 41-47, are longer and more detailed (cf. 4:32-35; 5:12-16). These summaries are quite common in the early chapters of Acts and serve a double purpose. They divide the narrative into segments but serve also as connective tissue or "narrative glue," shaping the episodes into a continuous account.

The summary begins and ends with reference to the numerical growth of the community (vv. 41b, 47b). In between, the narrator depicts the shared life of the community, which for Luke is the life of the Spirit. The believers who accepted the word and were baptized, now devote themselves to the teaching of the apostles, to the shared life, to the breaking of bread, and to prayer. These four elements characterize the life of the Spirit and are illustrated by the examples given in vv. 43-47.

The Healing of a Lame Man, 3:1–4:31

This section is clearly set off from the rest of Acts by narrative summaries on either side (2:41-47; 4:32-35). The passage itself displays a certain internal coherence and is divided into four segments or scenes that are marked by shifts in space, time, and/or participants (Funk 1988, 83). While these changes in time, setting, and characters provide clear rhetorical markers for dividing the text into four scenes, these segments are also united by several thematic links. The theme of healing is found in every scene, either with specific reference to the lame man at the Beautiful Gate (3:7, 16; 4:9-10, 22) or to healing in general (4:30). Likewise, references to "the name of Jesus" are found throughout this stretch of narrative on the lips of Peter (3:6, 16; 4:10, 12), the religious leaders (4:7, 17, 18), and the community of believers (4:30).

3:1-10. Scene 1. At the Beautiful Gate. The opening verses (vv. 1-2) particularize the general description of the community of believers found in the preceding narrative summary. Two of these apostles, PETER and JOHN, are going to worship in the Temple on a specific day at a specific time, three o'clock in the afternoon, the hour of prayer. With the setting, time, and characters in place, the stage is set for a specific *sign* of healing (2:43; see 4:22).

This beggar sits at the Beautiful Gate of the Temple doing the only thing he knows to do: he begs for alms. But to his surprise, he receives the mercies of God. *I have no silver or gold*, Peter responds, *but what I have I give to you; in the name of Jesus Christ of Nazareth, stand up and walk* (v. 6). The name of Jesus Christ is introduced into this story for the first time and will remain the focus of attention throughout this stretch of narrative. The lame man's feet and ankles are made strong, and Peter and John, like Jesus before them (Luke 5:17-26) and Paul after them (Acts 14:8-18), command the lame to walk, confirming and extending the programmatic ministry of Jesus (Luke 7:22).

The once-lame man leaps and praises God (echoing Isa 35:6; see also Luke 7:22). A third group of participants now enter the scene, *all the people*, who recognize the man as the one who sat for alms (vv. 9-10). For the second time, the Beautiful Gate of the Temple is mentioned. With this second reference to the gate, one wonders if the narrator may be less interested in its specific locale and more interested in working a wordplay between the repetition of *hour* (ὥρα, *hour of prayer*, v. 1) and the Beautiful (ὡραία) Gate. Within the semantic domain of this word is the meaning "opportune moment" or "timely" (see Rom 10:15 quoting Isa 52:7). Could the narrator be hinting that this ninth hour (three o'clock in the afternoon), the hour of prayer, is the "timely" moment of opportunity for this lame man who sits begging, ironically, at the Gate of Opportunity?

3:11–4:4. Scene 2. In Solomon's Portico. The change in locale from the Beautiful Gate to Solomon's Portico indicates a scene change (v. 11). The pattern of Pentecost is repeated here: a miraculous event (vv. 1-10; cf. 2:1-4) draws a crowd (v. 11; cf. 2:5-12) and Peter delivers a speech (vv. 12-26; cf. 2:14-40).

The outer frame of the first half of Peter's speech (vv. 12-16) deals with the healing of the lame man (vv. 12, 16) which is interpreted by the inner frame, a traditional christological kerygma (vv. 13-15). This kerygmatic statement is arranged in a chiastic pattern:

A *The God of Abraham, the God of Isaac,*
   and the God of Jacob . . .
      has glorified his servant Jesus, 13a
  B *whom you handed over and rejected*
     in the presence of Pilate, 13b
  B' *But you rejected the Holy and Righteous One*
     . . . and you killed the Author of life, 14-15a
A' *whom God raised from the dead,* 15b

The loaded christological titles, *servant, Holy and Righteous One*, and *Author of life*, along with this traditional kerygma, provide the foundation for the correct interpretation of the healing of the lame man. Some observers of this sign might conclude that Peter and John through their *own power or piety . . . made him walk* (v. 12), but Peter denies this interpretation and argues rather that "the faith that is through Jesus has given him this perfect health in the presence of all of you" (v. 16).

And now, friends is the rhetorical clue that marks the beginning of the second half of Peter's sermon (vv. 17-26). Here Peter extends an invitation to repentance undergirded by various citations of and allusions to scripture. He begins by acknowledging that his audience, although culpable for the death of Jesus, *acted in ignorance, as did also your rulers* (v. 17). Still, this ignorance produces a guilt that stands in need of repentance (v. 19).

The call to *repent, therefore* is accompanied by the promise of a number of benefits (vv. 19-22). These benefits carry with them the responsibility to listen to the prophet like Moses (v. 22). The addition in v. 22 of the words *tells you* in this quotation from Deut 18:15-20, is a rhetorical device the Lukan Peter employs to sharpen the challenge to his audience. The speech ends on a salvation-historical note: God, having raised up his servant (see v. 12), *sent him first to you* (v. 26), hinting at least at the gentile mission that will soon follow in Acts led by Peter himself (see Acts 10).

In the concluding verses to this scene (4:1-4), new participants are introduced—priests and the captain of the Temple and the SADDUCEES—who take Peter and John into custody for "teaching the people and proclaiming that in Jesus there is the resurrection of the dead" (v. 2). It is late, so their interrogation will have to wait until tomorrow. The major temporal break between the first two scenes and the last two does not occur, however, before the narrator reports in a brief aside that *many of those who heard the word believed; and they numbered about five thousand* (v. 4). Even in the face of danger, the community of believers continues to add to its numbers.

4:5-22. Scene 3. Before the Sanhedrin. The next two scenes take place on the following day, and a formidable group of religious leaders gather for the interrogation of Peter and John (v. 6). The apostles are set in their midst, and the inquiry by the leaders links with Peter's previous speech: *By what power* (see 3:12) *or by what name* (see 3:16) *did you do this?* (v. 7). Before recording Peter's response, the narrator reports that Peter was *filled with the Holy Spirit* (v. 8), thus fulfilling Jesus' words of encouragement that

when his followers are oppressed "the Holy Spirit will teach you at that very hour what you ought to say" (Luke 12:12). Peter, then, recapitulates his previous speech, echoing the traditional christological kerygma: the one "whom you crucified, whom God raised from the dead" (v. 10; see 3:13, 15); reiterating the rejection of Jesus by his audience: *This Jesus is the stone that was rejected by you, the builders* (v. 11; see 3:13-14); and underscoring the fact that the healing was through *the name of Jesus Christ of Nazareth* (v. 10; see 3:16).

Peter introduces a new element into his summary; he identifies the healing as a *good deed*, or "benefaction" (v. 9). Later in Acts, Peter will characterize the healing ministry of the earthly Jesus with the same word (10:38). This is the technical word associated with the benefac tor/client system so prominent in the social structures of the ancient Greco-Roman world. Benefactors gave support, financial and otherwise, to individuals, groups, and sometimes whole cities. In return the recipients of such benefaction pledged and gave their loyalty to these benefactors (Danker 1982). The disciples here have taken over the role of benefactor, and, like Jesus, that which they have to give— wholeness of life—is far more precious than the typical benefits of *silver and gold*.

Unable to rebuke Peter and John because the lame man stood beside the apostles as empirical proof of the truth of Peter's words, the religious leaders order them out of the council (SANHEDRIN) and discussed what they should do. This scene heightens in tension when the council reaches the conclusion to issue a restraining order to the apostles (v. 17).

The apostles are called back in and warned *not to speak or teach at all in the name of Jesus* (v. 18). They respond with the boldness the SANHEDRIN has already observed: *we cannot keep from speaking about what we have seen and heard* (v. 20). The narrator depicts Peter and John speaking these words in unison (v. 19), highlighting the unity of the apostolic witness. The Sanhedrin further threatens them and then releases them, unable to follow through on their threats because of the people (v. 21).

This scene ends with a reference to the healing event of 3:1-10 (v. 22). The reader learns that the lame man was more than forty years old, although the narrator does not disclose the significance of that reference. Is he old enough to be a reliable witness to the event? Does his age underscore the miraculous nature of the healing of this one who had been *lame from birth* (3:2)? The reader must fill this gap.

More significant, perhaps, is the reference to this event as a *sign of healing* (v. 22) linking this miracle closely to the *wonders and signs* done through the apostles (2:43). The Sanhedrin had just acknowledged that this healing was *a notable sign* (v. 16). Earlier Peter had made the connection between this man who had been *healed* (σώζω, v. 9) *by the name of Jesus Christ* and his soteriological conclusion that *there is no other name under heaven given among mortals by which we must be saved* ("saved" = σωθῆναι, v. 12). The use of this word, which bears the double meaning of "heal" and "save," suggests that this healing story is more permeated with soteriological content.

The healed lame man has become the paradigm of salvation through Jesus' name in Acts. Just as the blind man who regains his sight in John 9 is a model disciple in the fourth Gospel where believing is symbolized as a kind of seeing, so the lame man who walks in Acts 3 is the symbol of salvation in a story where journey narratives occupy much narrative space, and where the Christian movement is referred to simply as "the Way" (see 9:2; 19:9, 23; 22:4; 24:14, 22).

4:23-31. Scene 4. Reunited with friends. The finale to this episode is set in some unnamed place in Jerusalem where the apostles return to *their friends* (Gk. "their own") and recount to them what the reader already knows about the threats of the chief priests and elders. This recapitulation prompts the community to pray with one voice to God in a show of solidarity with their beleaguered colleagues.

The prayer (vv. 24b-30) begins with an invocation of the Sovereign Creator. Psalm 2 is then interpreted in light of the passion of Jesus. The kings (HEROD and Pontius PILATE) and rulers (by inference the Sanhedrin, see 4:5) gathered with the gentiles and the peoples of Israel against the Lord and his Anointed. Of course, even these acts are according to God's hand and plan that God *predestined to take place* (v. 28; see 2:23).

But this psalm is also interpreted in light of the present circumstances of the believers. The believers pray that the Lord will *look at their threats* and grant to his servants *to speak your word with all boldness* (v. 29). The final verse of the prayer is a precis of many of the issues already addressed in this episode: *While you stretch out your hand to heal, and signs and wonders are performed through the name of your holy servant Jesus* (v. 30), with emphasis placed on the role of Jesus as the power source for the wonder-performing servant.

The entire episode is brought to a close in v. 31. The place in which they were gathered was shaken, and they were filled with the Holy Spirit (recalling Pentecost, 2:1-4). The first part of their petition, to speak *the word of God with boldness*, is fulfilled. In fact, this theme of speaking the word of God with "boldness" or "openness" (παρρασίας) is another dominant theme not only in this episode (see vv. 13, 29, and here in v. 31), but throughout the Book of Acts (see 2:29; 9:28; 13:46; 14:3; 18:26; 26:26; 28:31). Such boldness will surely be needed, as in the next episode the believers face conflict both within and without the community.

Tensions Within and Without, 4:32–5:42

Attention is turned again by way of a narrative summary (4:32-35) to the shape of this company of believers. Two case studies follow, providing positive and negative examples of how believers dealt with their possessions and commitments within the community. The final episode, 5:12-42, depicts the life of the community from an outsider's perspective. Here many of the themes found in 3:1–4:31 are repeated: the apostles are found healing the sick (5:12-16; cf. 3:1-10), which prompts the religious authorities to arrest them again and to bring them before the Sanhedrin for their second interrogation (5:17-42; cf. 3:11–4:22, see Tannehill 1990, 59–79). As the community is marked by unity and tension within, so it is characterized by similar challenges from without.

4:32–5:11. Tensions within. In 4:32-35, Luke reiterates the point of emphasis of the summary in 2:41-47. But this summary also provides an interesting variation to the themes found in chap. 2. Now, the believers took the proceeds from their sales and *laid it at the apostles' feet* (v. 35). To assume the posture of being at another's feet is a gesture of submission in the OT (Josh 10:24; 1 Sam 25:24, 41; 2 Sam 22:39; Pss 8:7; 110:1). Luke also employs this language of being at another's feet as a symbol of submission (Luke 7:38, 44, 45, 46; 8:35, 41; 10:39; 17:16; 20:43; Acts 2:35; 10:35; 22:3). So here in v. 35, laying the proceeds at the apostles' feet is more than just a way of taking care of an administrative detail. As Luke Johnson has noted: "When the believers lay their possessions at the Apostles' feet, therefore, they were symbolically laying themselves there, in a gesture of submission to the authority of the Twelve" (Johnson 1977, 202). In just such an act of submission, Barnabas lay his gift at the apostles' feet (vv. 36-37—see further comment on Barnabas at 11:19-30; 12:25).

Not everyone submitted themselves to the authority of the apostles, as the story of ANANIAS and Sapphira indicates (5:1-11). This story is linked linguistically to the previous two scenes by the words *at the apostles' feet* (v. 2) and depicts a negative example of community life. Ananias and Sapphira sell a piece of property, but they mock the community's Spirit of unity, and they usurp the authority of the apostles when they lay only a part of the proceeds at their feet.

Peter assumes the role of prophet when he confronts Ananias with the conspiracy (v. 3). Like Judas, Ananias has fallen prey to Satan (v. 3; cf. Luke 22:3), and like Judas, Ananias will not live to enjoy the material gains of his deceit (v. 5; see 1:17-18). Although Ananias has not lied verbally, the act of conspiracy itself was a *lie to the Holy Spirit* (v. 3).

Peter's remaining questions suggest that Ananias and Sapphira were not required to dispose of their property in this way, but could have retained authority over it (v. 4). But by taking this duplicitous action, they usurped the authority of the apostles. The offense was not simply against the community, Peter argues; it was against God. The problem was not simply a human one; it had serious spiritual dimensions, and as Ananias soon found out, serious repercussions. Upon hearing Peter's words, *he fell down and died* (v. 5).

After the disposal of Ananias and an interval—the narrator tells us—of *about three hours* (v. 7), Peter confronts Sapphira in what resembles a legal trial. The story drips rich with irony because the reader has knowledge Sapphira does not possess: the conspiracy is broken. Unknowingly Sapphira compounds the conspiracy with a verbal lie. Yes, she tells Peter, they sold the land *for such and such a price* (v. 8).

Peter's role as prophet becomes even more active when he predicts that this one who with her husband conspired against the community and God would now suffer the same fate as he (v. 8). And the final note of irony: Sapphira falls dead at Peter's feet. She who had feigned to lay her possessions at the apostles' feet now literally does fall at Peter's feet. The submission to apostolic authority she failed to give in life, she now gives permanently in death.

This grizzly story fulfills the threat of Peter's earlier sermon: *everyone who does not listen to that prophet will be utterly rooted out of the people* (3:23). No wonder that a *great fear seized the whole church and all who heard of these things* (v. 11).

5:12-42. Tensions without. This third and final summary (vv. 12-16), which describes the Jerusalem church, in several ways recalls a previous episode (3:1–4:31). First, there is the setting of Solomon's Portico that was the site of Peter's speech and the apostles' arrest (3:11–4:4). Second, the other half of the believers' prayer that *signs and wonders* be performed (4:30) is now fulfilled when the narrator reports: *Now many signs and wonders were done among the people through the apostles* (v. 12). Finally, the healing of one man in chap. 3 has now been generalized so that people carried their sick into the streets (vv. 14-15) where the apostles continue their benefaction (see 4:9), and *they were all cured* (v. 16). And, of course, the narrator does not miss an opportunity to record that *more than ever believers were added to the Lord, great numbers of both men and women* (v. 14). This summary is, however, distinct from the previous two in at least one important way. In contrast to the previous summaries (2:41-47; 4:32-35), "which looked inward at the internal life of the community, Luke's new summary looks outward at the public effect of the apostles on the Jewish people" (Krodel 1986, 124).

The public character of this summary scene is presumed in the closing episode of the chapter, vv. 17-42. The reader now learns of another response to the apostles than that of the people who *held them in high esteem* (v. 13). The high priest and the party of the Sadducees were *filled with jealousy* (v. 17). This response also explains further the timidity of the people who dared not join the believers (v. 13).

There is also remarkable redundancy between vv. 17-42 and Acts 4:1-22 (Tannehill 1990, 59–79). Both include the arrest of the apostles, their appearance before the Sanhedrin, short speeches that highlight the apostolic witness to Jesus and their commitment to obey God rather than the Sanhedrin, deliberation by the Sanhedrin out of the presence of the apostles, and the decision to release the apostles with the warning not to preach in Jesus' name. But variations in detail between these two accounts serve to heighten the tension of the narrative between the believers and the religious establishment. How will the church respond to these challenges from without?

In this closing episode, the conflict broadens: all of the apostles are placed in prison, not just Peter and John (cf. 4:3). This scene also adds the new dimension of divine intervention with an ironic twist. The narrator winks at the reader when he reports that the apostles are released from prison by an "angel," whose very existence the Sadducees deny (see 23:8). On the next morning, the officers find the prison guards standing watch over an empty cell (v. 23). The liberated apostles are found teaching in the Temple as they were instructed to do (v. 20), and they are quietly returned to the Sanhedrin (vv. 25-26).

The stage is set for the second interrogation (vv. 27-32). The old charge of teaching *in this name* (v. 27; cf. 4:7) is coupled with a new reaction by the Sadducees to the accusation that the apostles' teaching is intended to *bring this man's blood on us* (v. 28). The stakes have been raised considerably since the last confrontation. Peter responds with a confession similar to the one he made at the first interrogation (see 4:19): *We must obey God rather than any human authority* (v. 29). What had been a conditional sentence becomes a divine imperative, and the duet of Peter and John now becomes an apostolic chorus led by Peter.

They then employ the christological kerygma typical of the previous speeches (2:23-24, 36; 3:13-15; 4:10): *The God of our ancestors raised up Jesus, whom you had killed by hanging him on a tree* (v. 30). But rather than calling down this man's blood upon the Sadducees as the high priest had feared, the apostles argue that the exalted Jesus is the Leader and Savior who gives repentance and forgiveness of sins (v. 31). The speech concludes with the apostles reaffirming in unison their role as witnesses along with *the Holy Spirit whom God has given to those who obey him* (v. 32).

The apostles' insistence on the culpability of the religious leaders in Jesus' death, the need for Israel's repentance, and the reference to the gift of the *Spirit* (in which the Sadducees also did not believe—see 23:8) now not only annoys the Sadducees (see 4:2), but enrages them to the point of contemplating murder (v. 33). GAMALIEL, a PHARISEE member of the Council who was *respected by all the people*, swiftly stands and orders the apostles taken outside. In this tense moment, he offers a brief speech marked by restraint and caution. Citing the historical examples of Theudas and Judas the Galilean who were leaders of revolutionary movements that *came to nothing*, Gamaliel advises the council that *if this plan or this undertaking is of human origin, it will fail; but if it is of God, you will not be able to overthrow them* (vv. 38-39).

Of course, Luke's reader already knows from the divine intervention, the miraculous healings, and other signs and wonders, that *this plan* and *this deed* are, indeed, *of God*. The only conclusion to be drawn from the narrator's point of view is that the Sanhedrin has already been found opposing God (v. 39). An angel had intervened earlier on behalf of the apostles in freeing them from prison; now the agent of intervention is a human one, a Pharisee, who compels by the wisdom of his argument.

So the Sanhedrin took Gamaliel's advice and released the apostles (v. 40). Again, the religious leaders charge them not to speak in the name of Jesus (see 4:18), but the conflict is heightened as the threats turn into beatings. Once again, the apostles boldly defy the Sanhedrin's instructions, and every day in their expressions of corporate worship, publicly in the Temple and privately at home (see 2:46), the apostles *did not cease to teach and proclaim Jesus as the Messiah* (v. 42). This plan and this deed must surely be of God.

Problems and Personalities, 6:1–12:25

The first five chapters of Acts focus on the action in and around Jerusalem, and the second half of Acts (chaps. 13–28) narrates the spread of the gospel by focusing on the places where the apostle Paul and his companions travel. These middle chapters, however, explore personalities more than places. The adventures of STEPHEN, PHILIP, PAUL, PETER, and BARNABAS fill these pages. Of course, the success of the gospel in overcoming problems in the community is still the underlying theme that holds these stories together (see the INCLUSIO formed by the references to the spreading of the word of God in 6:7 and 12:24), but this middle division provides perhaps the best justification for the title assigned to this work in the second century, the "Acts of the Apostles."

Stephen: His Witness and Death, 6:1–8:3

6:1-7. Structures and the spirit. This first scene serves two purposes: to provide another example of how conflict in the early Christian community is resolved (and schism thus avoided) and to introduce Stephen and Philip into the narrative.

To fulfill the first purpose, Luke employs a narrative pattern remarkably similar to the OT form for choosing auxiliary leadership (Exod 18 and Num 27): (1) statement of the problem—a grumbling among the Hellenists that Greek-speaking Jewish-Christian widows were being excluded from table fellowship (vv. 1-2; cf. Exod 18:14-18; Num 27:12-14); (2) the proposed solution—the apostles thus propose that they continue to devote themselves to *serving the word* (v. 4b) and that the newly appointed auxiliary leadership be responsible to *wait on tables* (vv. 2c-3; cf. Exod 18:19-23; Num 27:15-17); (3) requisite qualifications for new leadership—they are to be *of good standing, full of the Spirit and of wisdom* (v. 3), and, judging from their Greek names, they came from the part of the church that had complained about mistreatment of some of its constituency (v. 3b; cf. Exod 18:21; Num 27:18-21); (4) *setting apart the new leader ship*—the Seven are set apart by prayer and the laying on of hands (vv. 5-6; cf. Exod 18:25; Num 27:22-23; on this pattern, see Talbert 1984, 29).

This unit ends with a second reference to the way *the number of the disciples increased greatly in Jerusalem* (v. 7; cf. v. 1). The point is further emphasized by the notice that "the word of God grew" (author trans.: on this phrase, see the comments below, at 12:24). The narrator goes on to add that *a great many of the priests became obedient to the faith* (v. 7). The upshot for Luke, of course, is that despite the conflicts that threaten the unity of the fledgling community, the church is able to solve its problems and continues to grow.

6:8–7:1. The controversy. The tensions between the followers of Jesus and the leaders of the Jewish community, recounted in Acts 4 and 5, now continue with the story of Stephen, one of THE SEVEN. Stephen, whom the narrator again reminds the reader is *full of grace and power* (v. 8) and *wisdom and the Spirit* (v. 10) performs signs and wonders like the apostles before him (4:30). Stephen is soon engaged in a dispute by some diaspora Jews (originally from various places, but probably belonging now to one synagogue; cf. v. 9) who stir up the people and bring him before the Council (v. 12).

The scene before the Sanhedrin parallels (and intensifies) the encounters of the apostles with the Council with one significant variation. In the previous conflict scenes, the "people" sided with the apostles (cf. 4:21, 5:26; see Tannehill, 84); here the people are stirred up against Stephen, thus removing the buffer that had previously protected the apostles. Instead, the scene now more closely parallels the arrest and trial scene of Jesus. Like Jesus, Stephen is led into the Sanhedrin (v. 12; Luke 22:66); and the people are stirred first against Jesus, now against Stephen (see Luke 23:13-25).

The tension has escalated here in Acts to unprecedented proportions. Only during the ministry of Jesus had such tensions been previously experienced, a fact that only intensifies the suspense for the readers.

The charge of blasphemy against Stephen (see Luke 5:21) is specified by false witnesses: Stephen had proclaimed that Jesus would destroy the Temple and change the customs of Moses. Stephen will ultimately address both these charges (see comments on the speech below). The charges do not die with Stephen; they will resurface later against Paul (21:28). In response to the high priest's question regarding the validity of the charges, Stephen speaks.

7:2-53. The speech. The speech of Stephen is the longest in Acts and is very important for understanding the nature of the conflict in the Jewish community about the role and purposes of Jesus. The speech is not a comprehensive retelling of Jewish history; in fact, it is very selective. Nor is the story a dispassionate, neutral account; it is revisionist history from a Christian perspective. As is the case in so many discourses, both oral and written, the purpose of Stephen's recounting Israel's history comes into focus only at its conclusion. At the end of the speech, Stephen accuses his listeners of *opposing the Holy Spirit, just as your ancestors used to do* (v. 51). Specifically, just as the ancestors had persecuted the prophets, so now their descendants had betrayed and murdered the Righteous One whose coming the prophets had foretold (v. 52). Both ancestors and contemporaries had rejected the law they had received. In short, Stephen argues that the death of Jesus fit into the overall pattern of rejection that was characteristic of Israel's history. All that goes before this part of the speech leads, in one way or another, to this climax.

The speech itself is organized into five parts: (a) the story of Abraham, vv. 2-8; (b) the story of Joseph and the patriarchs, vv. 9-16; (c) the story of Moses in three parts of forty years each, vv. 17-29, 30-34, 35-43; (d) the story of the tent and the Temple, vv. 44-50; and finally (e) the invective against Stephen's listeners, vv. 51-53. In the speech, Stephen at times will quote the LXX, summarize its content, or at least in one significant instance, expand the story with more explicit details. All of the parts fit together to make up Stephen's Christian interpretation of Jewish history.

MOSES receives more attention in the speech than any other OT character. His life is divided into three periods of forty years each (see above). Although Jesus is not explicitly mentioned until v. 52 (and even there not by name), the retelling of Moses' story has striking similarities to the story of Jesus. These parallels are most clearly seen in the first and last units (vv. 17-29 and 35-43). In Stephen's reconstruction, the infancy and childhood of Moses is parallel with that of Jesus. Moses was beautiful before God (v. 20; cf. Exod 2:2); Jesus was in favor with God (Luke 2:52). Moses was instructed in wisdom (v. 22) as was Jesus (Luke 2:52). As an adult Moses, like Jesus, was "powerful in words and deeds" (v. 22; cf. Luke 24:19; Acts 2:22).

In the last unit (vv. 35-43), the parallels continue. Both Jesus and Moses (and Stephen—see v. 8) performed signs and wonders (v. 36; see 2:22). Both Moses and Jesus are prophets. The typology is made explicit in Moses' words to the Israelites, *God will raise up a prophet for you from your own people as he raised me up* (v. 37).

This theme of Jesus as the *prophet like [Moses]* (see 3:22) is the most important parallel and lies at the heart of the Stephen speech. The ignorance of the people regarding Moses' call (v. 25) and their subsequent rejection of him (v. 35) foreshadow the rejection of Jesus by the people (v. 52).

The rejection of God's representatives is no less than a rejection of God himself. That is the point made at the end of the episode about Moses. Not knowing what had happened to Moses (v. 40), the people turn to idolatry, making a calf and sacrificing to it (v. 41). God then turns away from them and gives them up to their idolatry (vv. 42-43). The people have not only rejected Moses; they have rejected God.

The Moses' episode also contains Stephen's first response to his accusers that Stephen had claimed that Jesus would change the *customs that Moses handed on to us* (6:14). The rhetoric of Stephen's argument indicates that the Jewish leadership, not the followers of Jesus, are responsible for abandoning Moses and the law (v. 39; cf. v. 53). From Stephen's (i.e., Luke's) perspective, the Christian community is the "true Israel," i.e., the group within Judaism that is authentically preserving the customs of Moses as they reflect the purpose and destiny of what it means to be the people of God.

The second charge against Stephen, that he claimed that Jesus would destroy *this place* (6:14, i.e., the Temple), is addressed in the next unit (vv. 44-50). Here Stephen's complaint is not against the existence of the Temple per se, but rather against the view that God's presence is limited to a particular place. To worship God in "this place" was not to be understood as limiting God's self-disclosure to the Temple. Although Stephen does not make explicit the consequences for violating the purposes of the Temple as he

did the claim that God would judge the people's misunderstanding of Moses and his *customs* (6:14; cf. vv. 42-43), Luke's readers no doubt understood this invective against the background of the destruction of the Temple. Luke, then, in Stephen's speech, is not only drawing on the content of OT history, he is employing the familiar pattern of the Deuteronomistic history of disobedience, punishment, call to repentance, and restoration to make sense of the Temple's destruction. The people had defied the purpose of Temple worship and suffered then the destruction of that institution.

The climax of the speech, as we noted above, occurs here at the end. Both ancestors and contemporaries were guilty of *forever opposing the Holy Spirit* (v. 51). They had rejected the prophets from Moses to Jesus, they had an inadequate understanding of where and how they were to worship, and they had rejected the laws and customs of Moses. They had not kept the things that had been *ordained by angels* (v. 53), and now they were about to reject the one whose *face was like the face of an angel* (6:15).

7:54–8:3. The martyrdom. The speech results in the stoning of Stephen (reminiscent of the stoning of NABOTH in 1 Kgs 21:8-13). Earlier in the Pentecost sermon, Peter had leveled similar accusations against his listeners that *cut to the heart* (2:37) and led to their repentance. Here those whose hearts and ears are *uncircumcised* (7:51) harden their hearts and cover *their ears* (v. 57) and drag Stephen out of the city to stone him, with one Saul aiding and abetting them.

Actually this violent action only occurs after Stephen has recounted his vision of *the Son of Man standing at the right hand of God!* (v. 56). The term SON OF MAN, occurs only here outside the Gospels, and the curious detail that the Son of Man is standing rather than sitting (see Luke 22:69) may be taken in a juridical sense where Jesus stands as in advocacy for Stephen before God.

The last words of Stephen continue the parallels with Jesus begun in 6:8-15: *Lord Jesus, receive my spirit*, spoken by Stephen in 7:59 is reminiscent of Jesus' word from the cross: "Father, into your hands I commend my spirit" (Luke 23:46); and Stephen's final words, *Lord, do not hold this sin against them* (v. 60), echo Jesus' prayer: "Father, forgive them, for they do not know what they are doing" (Luke 23:43). Stephen, like Jesus in the third Gospel, dies the death of an innocent martyr and thus takes his place as yet another example of a prophet who, because he spoke of *the coming of the Righteous One* (7:52), is the victim of *stiff-necked people* who continue to persecute the representatives of God (7:51).

Luke concludes this section (8:1-3) with the notice that this persecution was not limited to Stephen, but was against the whole Jerusalem church (v. 1). Chief among those persecuting the church is one Saul who by dragging the believers to prison (v. 3; cf. Luke 21:12) is inadvertently contributing to the growth of the Word, as the next unit indicates.

Philip: A Man on Mission, 8:4-40

Philip is the other member of the Seven who, with Stephen, plays a major role in the story. With Philip's ministry, the gospel enters the area of the Samaritans. In chap. 8, he is the focus of two very important episodes and is in dialogue with two of the most interesting characters in Acts: SIMON MAGUS and the ETHIOPIAN EUNUCH.

8:4-25. Philip and Simon: miracles vs. magic. From the second century, Simon has been characterized as the first Gnostic and archrival to Christianity (Justin, *Apol* 1.26.1-3; 1.56.2; *Trypho* 120; Irenaeus, *AdvHaer*, 1.23). The text of Acts, however, is silent on the final destiny of Simon, and unfortunately these later reflections have preoccupied most interpreters of Acts 8. Comments here will be limited to what can be gleaned from the narrative of Acts itself (see Garrett 1989, 61–78, for a detailed exposition).

One of Luke's purposes in recording Philip's encounter with Simon was to respond to charges that the signs and wonders performed by early Christian missionaries were indistinguishable from the magical practices of antiquity. Luke concedes (contra later apologists) that outwardly there are similarities between Christian miracle workers and magicians, but then argues that the similarities are only superficial: at a deeper level there are profound differences between "Christian miracles" and "pagan magic." Luke makes this point forcefully in the Simon Magus episode.

On first reading there are striking parallels between the acts of Philip and Simon. Only closer reading of the text demonstrates the fundamental difference between the two: Simon's deeds point to himself in an act of self-aggrandizement; Philip's signs point to the kingdom of God and corroborate his proclamation of the Christian gospel. In fact, the opening passage about Philip ties his words and deeds very closely together: *The crowds with one accord listened eagerly to what was said by Philip, hearing and seeing the signs that*

he did (v. 6). What was the content of this message? Luke fills it out later in the narrative claiming that Philip *was proclaiming the good news about the kingdom of God and the name of Jesus Christ* (v. 12).

So to preach the gospel for Philip was to proclaim (1) that Jesus was the "Christ," the one God had anointed for *doing good and healing all who were oppressed by the devil* (as Peter would put it in 10:38); (2) that the KINGDOM OF GOD, inaugurated in the ministry of Jesus, would be completed when all of Christ's enemies—surely including Satan himself—had been brought into submission at Christ's feet (cf. 2:34); and (3) that this proclamation "in the name of Jesus" would issue forth in the forgiveness or liberation from sin and Satan's authority to the power of God. In other words, "Philip's message about the Christ, the Kingdom of God, and the name of Jesus was implied also to be a message about release from Satan's authority" (Garrett 1989, 65). Hence, Philip's signs and wonders—the healings and exorcisms—were outward signs reinforcing his message: Satan is being overcome, and the kingdom of God is being established.

In contrast to Philip, the deeds of Simon Magus were performed only to bring glory to himself. In a flashback (v. 9), the readers learn that Simon had been amazing the Samaritans with his magic and that they have designated him as the *power of God* (vv. 9-11). This claim stands in direct contrast to Luke's depiction of Jesus. From Luke's perspective, *the power of God* (v. 10) was in Jesus, or upon Jesus, or with Jesus, but the power of God was always distinct *from* Jesus. That Simon does not reject this title (as Paul and Barnabas do in Acts 14:11-15) but rather encourages it through his magic, places him in the tradition of the "false prophets" who throughout Jewish history, and now in Christian history, reject the way of God (now most clearly revealed in the ministry of Jesus and his followers) in favor of idolatry (cf. Luke 6:22-23; Acts 7:51-52). As such, Simon is depicted as an agent of Satan who is an opponent to God and the "true prophets" of Christianity. Nonetheless, this section ends with Simon believing, being baptized, and being constantly amazed (cf. v. 11) at *the signs and great miracles* of Philip (v. 13).

The sincerity of Simon's conversion has long been questioned because of this closing climactic scene. The opening notice (vv. 14-17) that the Jerusalem apostles prayed for the new believers and that they received the HOLY SPIRIT *after* their BAPTISM stands in contrast with the sequence in Acts 2:38 and argues against basing any *rigid* doctrine of the relationship between baptism and the gift of the Spirit on Acts.

More important, however, is Luke's report that Simon tried to buy the Holy Spirit from the apostles (v. 18). This detail confirms the earlier impression that Simon is portrayed as a false prophet, an agent of Satan. Magicians practiced their art for money, and as Hermas noted, the false prophet "accepts rewards for his prophecy, and if he does not receive them he does not prophesy" (*Man* 11:12). Although it is true that here Simon is offering money and not receiving it, clearly if he is willing to pay money for the use of the Spirit, he will later accept payment when he employs its power. In contrast, Peter makes it clear that the apostles would never take money for what they do (see 3:6). "Thereby Luke demonstrates that the Christians do not share one of the most widely recognized traits of practitioners of magic" (Garrett 1989, 70).

The fate of Simon is ambiguous. The language of Peter's curse is reminiscent of OT curses of idolatry (see esp. Deut 29:17-19). Either Simon is to repent of his wickedness, i.e., his idolatry, or he (and his money!) is to be condemned to eternal destruction at the judgment (vv. 20-22). Although he has supposedly entered the Christian community, Simon is still in *the chains of wickedness* (v. 23), i.e., still under the authority of Satan, and has not fully experienced Philip's message of liberation from sin. Simon beseeches Peter and John to pray for him that he might be spared this judgment. Luke perhaps does not know the fate of Simon and thus leaves the conclusion uncertain. More important to Luke is the fact that in this encounter Satan and his agent have been overcome, and the path is cleared for the preaching of the gospel in Samaria. So Peter and John (one of the two who had earlier offered to call fire down to consume the Samaritans! Luke 9:54) do indeed proclaim *the good news to many villages of the Samaritans* (v. 25).

8:26-40. Philip and the Ethiopian eunuch: What hinders me? The next pericope involving Philip is foundational to Luke's theology and certainly is the most exotic in its details. Philip is characterized as a prophet and preacher, and his entrance and exit in the story is reminiscent of ELIJAH and EZEKIEL (1 Kgs 18:12; 2 Kgs 2:16; Ezek 11:24). The story also echoes another foundational story in Luke and Acts: the two on the road to EMMAUS (see also the parallels with Luke 4:16-30 and Acts 13:13-43). Just as Jesus opens the scriptures to CLEOPAS and his companion, so Philip explains Isa 53:7-8 to the eunuch. Both Jesus and Philip make

quick exits from the story (Luke 24:31; Acts 8:39). Finally the two stories relate to the two ordinances of the church—the Emmaus story to the LORD'S SUPPER and the Ethiopian eunuch episode to Baptism. Also noteworthy are the parallels between this episode and the other three conversion stories recorded in this immediate context: the conversion of the Samaritans (8:4-13), the conversion of Paul (9:1-31), and the conversion of CORNELIUS (Acts 10:1–11:18). Most striking is the way Luke intensifies the element of divine intervention and providence in the last three episodes as the Spirit directs Philip, Paul (and Ananias), and Peter (and Cornelius; for other parallels with the Cornelius episode, see Tannehill 1990, 110–11).

Another way of understanding the meaning of the passage is by probing its form. Most scholars agree that a chiastic structure shapes the unit, although they disagree about its details. At the heart of any structure, however, lies the citation from the OT and the eunuch's questions. The quotation of Isa 53:7-8 is the only time in Luke or Acts when the narrator quotes the OT directly, apart from the lips of an individual character. Philip uses this OT text to tell *the good news about Jesus* (v. 35).

This kind of messianic exegesis was not as unusual as is sometimes thought. In first-century Judaism, interpreters were using a method of messianic exegesis to interpret the Hebrew scriptures, often providing messianic interpretations of scriptures that originally were not messianic prophecies. The messianic exegesis of Christians was not unique because they saw the Messiah foretold in the scriptures (their Jewish contemporaries saw that as well); the uniqueness lay in the fact that they believed this Messiah had already come in the person of Jesus Christ. Convinced of the truth of Philip's message, the eunuch lets forth with the refrain of an unhindered gospel that runs throughout Acts: *Look, here is water! What is to prevent me from being baptized?* (v. 36; cf. 10:47; 28:31). How is it, though, that the story of the Ethiopian eunuch bears witness to this "unhindered" gospel?

The answer may be found in the very description of this new convert: the Ethiopian eunuch. Implicit in each of those words are two very important characteristics. First, he is an Ethiopian, which informs the readers of the geographic and ethnographic significance of this conversion. Ethiopia was viewed by people of antiquity as lying at the southernmost end or limit of the earth (see e.g., Homer, *Iliad* 23.205–97; Herodotus, *Hist* 3.114–15; Strabo, *Geog* 1.2.27–28;

2.2.2). Thus the conversion of an Ethiopian represents "the symbolic (and partial) fulfillment of Acts 1:8c of mission to 'the end of the earth' " (Martin 1989, 120). Second, it is also well documented in ancient literature that skin color was an Ethiopian's most distinctive feature. Homer (*Odyssey* 19.244-48), Herodotus (*Hist* 2.29-32; 3.17-24; 4.183, 197), and Seneca (*Naturales Questiones* IV A. 218), among others, all refer to the dark skin of the Ethiopians. What is the ethnographic significance of the Ethiopian's conversion? Clarice Martin (1989, 114) argues that "the story of a black African . . . from what would be perceived as a distant nation to the south of the empire is consistent with the Lukan emphasis on 'universalism,' a recurrent motif in both Luke and Acts, and one that is well known."

The Ethiopian is also a eunuch, from which the readers infer two additional items. He is, first of all, an outsider, since Deut 23:2 forbids a castrated person from entrance into the assembly of the Lord and probably precluded even proselyte status. In the Acts passage, he has just returned from Jerusalem where he had gone to worship and was, no doubt, relegated to the outermost chambers of the Temple. For Luke, then, the Ethiopian eunuch is a God-fearing gentile and, as such, is the first gentile convert to Christianity. Commentators who resist this conclusion normally do so to preserve Cornelius as the first gentile convert and Peter as the founder of the gentile mission. The significance of Cornelius notwithstanding, the conversion of the Ethiopian eunuch is Luke's report of how, through Philip, the gospel reached the "end of the earth" and the gentile mission was initiated. Again, the reader is put in the superior position of knowing more about the story of the early church's progress than any of its characters.

Philip in these two stories is depicted as a man on mission. He is pressing the boundaries, with the apostles scrambling to keep up. He preaches the gospel, and Samaritans and a representative from the "ends of the earth" are converted. Evidently, it will take the Jerusalem church some time before it comes to the same position and then only through the insistence of the apostle to the gentiles, Paul. Later, Paul finds Philip in Caesarea (21:8) where the narrator left him. But now Philip is not alone; he has four unmarried daughters *who had the gift of prophecy* (21:9), and no doubt Philip's encouragement to exercise it. Not only is Philip's adventuresome spirit reaffirmed for the reader, but his openness to the fresh winds of God's Spirit has been passed on to another generation.

Paul: His Conversion and Call, 9:1-31

It would be difficult to overestimate the significance of the conversion of Paul for the narrative of Acts or, indeed, the course of early Christian history. Acts 9 is the first of three accounts in Acts of Paul's conversion (see chaps. 22 and 26). The accounts are slightly different in detail and tone (see the comments on chap. 22 for a discussion of the variations), but the repetition of the event indicates its importance for Luke. The passage in Acts 9 is not only about the conversion of Paul; it is also the narration of his call and commission to become the "apostle to the gentiles." As such, it shares similar formal features with other commissioning stories, both within Luke and Acts (e.g., Luke 1:5-25, 26-38; 2:8-20; 24:36-53; Acts 5:17-21; 10:1-8, 9-23; 16:9-10; 18:9-11; etc.) and throughout the biblical narratives (see e.g., Gen 17:1-4; Exod 3:1–4:16; Judg 6:11-24; 1 Kgs 19:1-19a; Matt 28:1-8; Mark 16:1-8; John 20:19-23; see Hubbard for other references and a list of the formal features associated with the commissioning story). Acts 9 then is about the conversion of Paul from a persecutor of Christ to one persecuted for Christ and Paul's call to be apostle to the gentiles.

9:1-25. Paul in Damascus. The unit is organized into two parts. The first part describes the events in and around DAMASCUS; the second details Paul's preaching ministry in JERUSALEM. The following chiastic arrangement for this first unit has been suggested (see Talbert 1984, 40):

A Paul plots against the Christians in Damascus, 1-2
  B Paul sees the vision, is blinded, and fasts, 3-9
    C Ananias sees a vision,
      is commissioned to go to Paul, 10-14
      D Paul's mission is foretold by Christ, 15-16
    C' Ananias goes to Paul, reports his vision, 17
  B' Paul's sight is restored,
    he is baptized and eats, 18-19a
A' Paul preaches Christ in Damascus,
  the Jews plot to kill him, 19b-25

Paul reappears in the opening verses of chap. 9. He was last mentioned in 8:3 where he was *ravaging the church*. Here in chap. 9 he is still *breathing threats and murder against the disciples of the Lord* (v. 1) and seeks permission to extend his persecution beyond Jerusalem to Damascus. The description of Paul here recalls Stephen's invective against those who *are forever opposing the Holy Spirit* (7:51-52).

Paul is not the only character to receive a vision in this episode; the Lord also visits Ananias, a disciple in Damascus (vv. 10-14). This "double vision" provides for Paul a (reluctant) deliverer from his blindness. Ananias's vision also supplies the content of Paul's call (vv. 15-16). In the CHIASM above, these verses lie at the heart of the passage and should be taken as its primary focus. Two points are made: (1) Paul is to be an *instrument whom I* [Christ] *have chosen to bring my name before Gentiles and kings and before the people of Israel* (v. 15) and (2) that Paul *must suffer for the sake of my name* (v. 16). Paul's call to the gentile mission cannot be separated from his call to suffer. His entire ministry throughout Acts is characterized by a mission in which he experiences rejection and persecution (cf. 13:46-47; 20:19-21; 22:15-18). As such, he stands in the long line of persecuted prophets that extend from Moses to Jesus and more recently to Stephen. But Paul does not have to wait until his "first" missionary journey to experience this suffering. His first preaching tour in Damascus ends with a narrow escape from his persecutors in a basket.

9:26-31. Paul in Jerusalem. This emphasis on the suffering character of Paul's ministry continues in this next episode of Paul in Jerusalem. The events in Damascus and Jerusalem are almost exact parallels (Gill 1974, 547-48).

Damascus	Jerusalem
Ananias hesitates to believe that Paul has been converted, 13-14.	The disciples fear Paul, "not believing that he is a disciple," 26.
The Lord reassures him, 15-16.	Barnabas reassures them, 27.
Ananias goes to Paul, cures, and baptizes him, 17-192.	
Paul is *with* the disciples in Damascus, 19b.	"Paul was *with* them going in and out at Jerusalem," 28a.
Paul preaches immediately in the synagogues, 20-22.	Paul speaks freely in the name of the Lord, 28b-29a.
The Jews plot to kill Paul, 23-24.	The Hellenists try to kill him, 29b.
Paul escapes, 25.	Paul escapes, 30.

Gill has commented on the significance of this parallelism: "The Jerusalem episode acts out for a second time the theme of preaching and persecution which Luke has placed as a heading over the whole chapter" (Gill 1974, 548). The zealous persecutor of Christ and his church has become the zealous missionary persecuted in Christ's name and for his church.

Peter: His Words and Deeds, 9:32–11:18

The next three scenes, the healing of AENEAS, the raising of Tabitha, and the conversion of Cornelius, may all be grouped under the larger heading "the acts of Peter." Theologically, all three stories serve to underscore the inclusive nature of the gospel, as well as to reveal further the complex character of PETER. Pairing stories of men and women is typical of Luke. Further, to join two shorter stories with a longer third one to make basically the same point is not uncommon to Luke. In fact, these stories are similar to Luke 15 where we have the two briefer stories of the lost sheep and the lost coin standing alongside the much longer story of the lost sons—with all three describing the joy in the kingdom when that which was lost is found. As with these three parables, readers can also detect the movement in these three stories in Acts to open the gospel to all persons.

9:32-43. Peter's raising of Aeneas and Tabitha. While evidently on a preaching tour, Peter encounters a paralyzed *saint* in Lydda who had been bedridden. Now for the second time (see Acts 3:1-10), Peter heals a lame man. The story is bare and unadorned with details; the narrator gets right to the point. Peter informs Aeneas that "Jesus Christ heals you; get up and make your bed!"

The reader is led to empathize more deeply with Tabitha and her mourners in the next scene. Tabitha (which the narrator tells us means DORCAS or "Gazelle") is described as one who is *devoted to good works and acts of charity* (v. 36—cf. the description later of Cornelius in 10:1 of the next episode). The products of her benevolence are made explicit when the widows who are mourning her death show to Peter *the tunics and other clothing Dorcas had made while she was with them* (v. 39). Quite possibly, they are wearing the garments (the verb is in the middle voice); for the widows to lose Dorcas was to lose their benefactor.

Once again, the problem of helpless Greek-speaking Jewish-Christian widows resurfaces in the narrative (cf. 6:1). Peter orders everyone outside (like Jesus, see Luke 8:51) and commands, *Tabitha, get up* (again reminiscent of Jesus' words in Mark 5:41). She, too, is raised, and he presents her alive to the saints and widows (v. 41).

These two stories share much in common: they echo the ELIJAH-ELISHA cycles of 1–2 Kings, as well as events in the career of Jesus (Acts 9:32-35 = Luke 5:18-26; Acts 9:36-43 = Luke 8:40-56). Further, unlike most healing stories in Luke and Acts, the healed persons here are named (contra Luke 5:17-26; 11:14-23; 18:35-43; Acts 3:1-10; 14:8-18). Both Aeneas and Tabitha are healed through divine power (vv. 34, 40). In their respective locales, both healings result in many conversions to the faith (vv. 35 and 42).

Finally, the raising of a lame man and the resuscitation of a dead woman are more similar than might appear at first glance. In the ancient Mediterranean world, the body was divided into three symbolic zones: (1) the heart-eyes, which is the zone of emotions and thoughts; (2) the mouth-ears, which is the zone of self-expressive speech; and (3) the hands-feet, which is the zone of purposeful action (Pilch 1991, 204). Aeneas's healing obviously falls into the zone of purposeful action. But resuscitations are also related to this zone; the dead can perform no purposeful act (Pilch 1991, 205). Thus, both healings share in the same symbolic zone; Aeneas and Tabitha are healed so they can resume their places as contributing members of the Christian community and walk in *the Way* (9:2).

10:1–11:18. The conversion of Cornelius and Peter. Many scholars focus in this story on the significance of the conversion of CORNELIUS and his household for the spread of the gospel to the gentiles in Acts. This episode does represent a critical turning point in the narrative of Acts. Equally as important, though, is the conversion of Peter to a new point of view, namely, that salvation knows no human boundaries and that *God shows no partiality* (v. 34). The chapter divisions here (as in many other places in scripture) are misleading. The episode actually divides into seven scenes (see Haenchen 1971, 357–59), interrelated by much repetition (the vision of Cornelius is reported four times; Peter's vision is twice related; and all of chap. 11 is basically a summary of chap. 10).

Scene 1. 10:1-8. Cornelius's vision in Caesarea. Cornelius, a centurion (see Luke 7:1-10), is favorably described by Luke as a *devout* man who practiced traditional Jewish piety in almsgiving and prayer, although he was himself a gentile "God-fearer." In this opening scene, Cornelius has a vision in which he is told his prayers and alms have been heard and accepted (v. 4) and that he should send to Joppa for a certain Simon Peter. Without further question, Cornelius complies by dispatching two personal servants and a soldier to

fetch Peter. Throughout the narrative the activities are directed from above (cf. chap. 9), but that does not mean there is no human response to this divine activity. Rather, the pattern here is that the divine revelations or epiphanies of both Cornelius and Peter are incomplete (Tannehill 1990, 129) and are only understood after further reflection and interaction with other human characters. Revelation here is depicted in contextual and interrelational terms, which means that both Cornelius and Peter have to move with the light they have before they can receive further illumination.

Scene 2. 10:9-16. Peter's vision in Joppa. Peter, like Cornelius, experiences a vision while at prayer (v. 10). This vision, too, is incomplete. Three times Peter is shown a sheet with all kinds of animals on it and is commanded to eat. Three times he refuses, claiming, *By no means, Lord, for I have never eaten anything that is profane or unclean* (v. 14). Is he thrice resisting temptation (cf. Luke 3) or thrice denying his Lord (cf. Luke 23)? The final response of the heavenly voice makes Peter's resistance clear: *What God has made clean, you must not call profane* (v. 15). What remains unclear is the subject of this vision. Is Peter to disregard Jewish dietary laws or is something else at stake?

Scene 3. 10:17-23a. Cornelius's men in Joppa. While Peter is wondering about the vision, Cornelius's emissaries arrive in JOPPA. The puzzled Peter is still obedient enough to respond to the Spirit's call to go with these men *without hesitation* (v. 20) or "without discrimination" (author trans.). Peter takes the first step in understanding his vision by extending hospitality to these gentile visitors and giving them a night's lodging.

Scene 4. 10:23b-33. Peter in Caesarea. The vision comes more into focus with Peter's visit to CAESAREA. After correcting Cornelius's mistaken assumption that Peter is a god (vv. 25-26), Peter takes the next step in correctly interpreting his vision when he sees the crowd of gentiles gathered in Cornelius's house and says, *You yourselves know that it is unlawful for a Jew to associate with or to visit a gentile* [Peter now has done both], *but God has shown me that I should not call anyone profane or unclean* (v. 28; cf. the restrictions of *Jub* 22:16; *JosAsen* 7:1).

Sociologists use the term "map" to designate "the concrete and systematic patterns of organizing, locating, and classifying persons, places, times, actions, etc. according to some abstract notion of 'purity' or order" (Neyrey 1991, 278). Peter understands that the vision of the sheet is not just about what can or cannot be eaten, that is, a cultural "map of the body"; but more importantly it addresses the question of who is and is not clean, i.e., the question of a radically new cultural "map of persons." Just as Stephen proposed a new map of holy places (which did not limit "holy space" to the Temple), so Peter is being directed to draw a new cultural map of people which was radically inclusive and gave gentiles a place on the map. The issue of the vision is not whether gentiles can be included in salvation: Peter has heard Jesus say as much (Luke 24:47) and has himself preached it (Acts 2:39; 3:25-26). The obstacle for the Jewish Christian to launch the gentile mission is gentile uncleanness that obstructs Jewish-gentile social relationships. The vision of the sheet now removes that obstacle.

Scene 5. 10:34-43. Peter's speech. After Cornelius recounts his vision (vv. 30-33, now for the third time), Peter responds to Cornelius's invitation to address the assembly. His speech falls into three parts: the introduction (vv. 34-36), the kerygma (vv. 37-41), and the conclusion (vv. 42-43). Peter's conversion to this new perspective of gentile cleanness is completed in the opening line of this speech: *I truly understand that God shows no partiality* (v. 34).

The next two verses are grammatically troublesome, and their meaning is obscured by both RSV and NRSV. Perhaps the best way to understand these verses is reflected in the following translation:

> Truly I perceive that God shows no partiality, but in every nation anyone who fears him and practices righteousness is acceptable to him. This [namely, the statement just made] is the word which he sent to the children of Israel, preaching good news of peace through Jesus Christ—He is Lord of all (vv. 34b-36, cited by Krodel 1986, 196).

This translation makes "He is Lord of all" the centerpiece of the thought unit rather than a disruptive or intrusive phrase (in parentheses in RSV). Both God (who "shows no partiality") and Jesus (who is "Lord of all") support Peter's perspective on the radically inclusive nature of the Gospel. The kerygma that follows (vv. 37-41) characterizes Jesus' ministry as one of benefaction, a particularly appropriate image for a gentile audience familiar with patronage and especially the audience in Cornelius's house who no doubt had personally enjoyed the benefits of Cornelius's benefaction.

Peter ends his speech (vv. 43-44) by returning to the theme of universality: *everyone who believes in him receives forgiveness of sins through his name.*

Scene 6. 10:44-48. The gentile Pentecost. Before Peter could finish speaking (v. 44), a second Pentecost occurs: the Holy Spirit falls on these gentiles. As in the first Pentecost, the gift of the Spirit is con firmed for the "circumcised believers" when *they heard them* [the gentiles] *speaking in tongues and extolling God* (v. 46). Peter strikes a major theme of Acts again when he asks, "Is anyone able to hinder the water for baptizing these who have received the Holy Spirit just like us?" (author trans.). The answer for Luke is, of course not. Just as earlier nothing could hinder the Ethiopian eunuch from being baptized (8:36) and later not even prison could hinder Paul from preaching the gospel (28:31), so now the barrier of gentile uncleanness could no longer hinder the inclusion of gentiles into the kingdom although it would indeed be the subject of one more debate (see chap. 15).

Scene 7. 11:1-18. Reporting to the Jerusalem church. The conversion of Cornelius and his household, as noted earlier, is important not because Cornelius is the first gentile converted in Acts (that honor belongs to the Ethiopian eunuch), but because his is the first gentile conversion publicly acknowledged by the Jerusalem church. Most of chap. 11 is a recapitulation (with some interesting variations) of the events reported in chap. 10. Most important are the opening verses that set the context: Peter is asked to defend his actions, not of ordering these gentiles to be baptized, but of eating with the "uncircumcised," i.e., of rewriting the "cultural map" of persons (see above). After recounting the incident (again the repetition points out the significance of this event for Luke), Peter asks, *Who was I that I could hinder God?* (v. 17; on "hinder" see the comments on scene 6 above). The question is not intended to be rhetorical, and the silence is finally broken when these Jewish Christians from Jerusalem praise God saying, *Then God has given even to the Gentiles the repentance that leads to life* (v. 18).

The issue of gentile inclusion in the church is by no means resolved, as Acts 15 demonstrates, but at least Peter's conversion is as complete as that of Cornelius and his household. For Peter, at least, as far as Jews and gentiles were concerned, God *has made no distinction between them and us* (15:9).

Barnabas, Peter, and Herod: Contrasting Examples, 11:19–12:25

In Luke's version of the last supper, a dispute arose among the disciples as to who was to be regarded as the greatest. In Luke 22:25-26, Jesus says, "The kings of the Gentiles lord it over them; and those in authority over them are called benefactors. But not so with you; rather the greatest among you must become like the youngest, and the leader like one who serves." In a sense, this episode (Acts 11:19–12:25) provides an exegesis by example of the saying in Luke 22. The contrasts between displays of divine and earthly power are striking.

11:19-30; 12:25. Barnabas and the church at Antioch. Luke presents the fledgling church at ANTIOCH as a case study of the mission of the early church. The church at Antioch receives considerable attention from Luke. It is established just after the conversion of Cornelius. Antioch was primarily a "Hellenistic city" (although there was a significant Jewish population of between 25,000 and 50,000). Antioch's population of 500,000 to 800,000 ranked it third largest in the Roman Empire (Polhill 1992, 268–69). The church was founded by Hellenists who *were scattered because of the persecution that took place over Stephen* (v. 19). Although some Hellenists spoke only to Jews, Christians from Cyprus and Cyrene evangelized the gentiles in Antioch. These Hellenistic Jewish-Christians who themselves had grown up in the gentile environment of the dispersion were sensitive to the cultural back ground of the Antiochenes and spoke not of Jesus as the Jewish Messiah, but rather proclaimed *the Lord Jesus* (v. 20), a title more familiar to those gentiles.

After the church was established and then encouraged and confirmed by BARNABAS and PAUL (vv. 22-26), the church at Antioch had the opportunity to minister to the believers in the church at Jerusalem, a clear sign that those first missionaries encouraged mission not only *to* but *with* the Antiochenes.

The Antiochenes' sensitivity to the plight of Judea is remarkable for several reasons. First, the famine was not confined to Judea, but rather evidently Antioch itself was gripped by famine during this time (ca. 46–47 C.E.). Second, the city of Antioch had experienced numerous disasters itself over the past one hundred years that must have left their mark on the collective memory of the inhabitants. In the midst of their own suffering, the Antiochene Christians reached out to those in need, not out of plenty but out of want.

Barnabas embodies this spirit of generosity so characteristic of the Antiochene Christians. When the disciples decide to send relief *to the believers living in Judea,* they send it by the hands of Barnabas and Saul (vv. 29-30). Like Saul (Acts 7:58), Barnabas makes a cameo appearance before assuming the center stage of the gentile mission (4:36-37; see Acts 11, 15). He provides a concrete example of those believers who demonstrated their commitment to the apostles' authority by laying the proceeds from the sale of his property at the apostles' feet (4:35).

The narrator supplies several interesting details about Barnabas; he is a LEVITE (who in the OT had no portion in the land!—see Deut 12:12; 14:29) and a native of Cyprus. But the most important detail is that the apostles have given him a surname, Barnabas. That the apostles have given this name is another indication that Barnabas has submitted himself to the authority of the apostles.

By having one of the two great leaders of the gentile mission express submission to the Twelve by receiving from them a new name and laying his goods at their feet, Luke is subtly but effectively creating an image in the reader's mind: the image of the Gentile mission under the authority of the Twelve (Johnson 1977, 202).

Also noteworthy is the translation the narrator provides for Barnabas's name, *Son of encouragement* (4:36). The significance lies less in the etymology of the Aramaic than it does in the role Barnabas will play later in this story. Barnabas is a sign both of submission to the apostles and of encouragement to fellow believers. While the Jews plot to kill Saul and the believers are afraid of him and doubt that he is a disciple (9:23-27), Barnabas takes the risk of befriending Saul, bringing him before the apostles, and confirming Saul's Damascus-road experience before them (9:27). When the church in Jerusalem hears about Greeks who had *turned to the Lord* in Antioch (vv. 19-21), they send Barnabas to Antioch, and he "encouraged [see 4:36] them all to remain faithful to the Lord with steadfast purpose" (v. 23, author trans.).

But Barnabas's submission to apostolic authority is not blind loyalty. When he turns his attention to the gentile mission, he is sent out, not by the apostles, but by the Holy Spirit (13:4; see also 13:43, 46, 50). The active role of Barnabas in the Apostolic Conference (chap. 15) is direct testimony to the way in which he (and Paul) held respect for the apostles' authority in tension with submission to the guidance of the Holy Spirit. This Barnabas who is (not blindly) loyal to the apostles and a continuing source of encouragement to the community (see also 15:36-40) stands in sharp contrast not only to the story of Ananias and Sapphira, but to the following story about Herod.

12:1-24. Herod: unmasking the powers. With the note of true Christian benefaction ringing in their ears, the readers are introduced to the manufactured benefaction of a tyrant, HEROD. In between is sandwiched the story of Peter's deliverance from prison. This chapter is one of the most delightful in Acts, but it is not only entertaining; it is also profitable, for it demonstrates Luke's understanding of the nature and locale of true power.

In the opening scene (vv. 1-5), Herod (whom the first- and twentieth-century reader might mistakenly identify as the wicked king of the Gospels) had JAMES, John's brother, *killed with the sword* (v. 2). Seeing this curried the favor of the Jews, Herod determines to serve them Peter as well. Perhaps aware of Peter's reputation as an escape artist (see 5:19-26), he places Peter under close watch around the clock (v. 4).

In an aside, the narrator notes that the arrest of Peter occurred during the PASSOVER (v. 3). This detail is important for several reasons. First, it accounts for the reason Peter did not immediately suffer the same fate as John; Herod wished to avoid a tumult of the people (see v. 4). This setting also parallels this deliverance scene with the passion of Jesus, which also occurred during the festival of Unleavened Bread (Luke 22:1, 7). (By now, the reader has noted the frequency with which the experience of the church parallels the experiences of Jesus.) Finally, the setting creates the biting irony of Peter in chains during the very festival that celebrated the deliverance of Israel from bondage in Egypt (see Pervo 1990, 41). This should not be surprising to the readers since Luke in his first volume had already described the passion of Jesus as an "exodus" (Luke 9:31).

The Passover setting, then, is very important in understanding the next scene, the deliverance of Peter from prison (vv. 6-11). The Exodus imagery continues, particularly in Luke's choice of language: *the night before* (v. 6; Exod 12:12); *Get up quickly* (v. 7; Exod 12:11); *put on your . . . sandals* (v. 8, Exod 12:11); *the Lord has rescued* (v. 11; Exod 18:4, 8-10). As in the Cornelius episode, everything is directed "from above" by an angel of the Lord who gives specific instructions to Peter even on how to dress himself. Peter's passivity is emphasized by the fact that he thought what was happening was another vision (cf. chap. 10), not realizing the reality of the situation. He does at least respond again to the call, *Follow me* (v. 8). Clearly, this is the story of Peter's divine deliverance from bondage (like the Israelites), not his escape.

Realizing finally the reality of his deliverance, Peter goes to the house of Mary, mother of John Mark, where the believers have gathered to pray (v. 12). This scene is filled with drama, punctuated with irony and comic relief. Peter encounters a second gate, only this time it does not open miraculously (cf. v. 10). Vulnerable to anyone who might see him, Peter knocks and a maidservant named *Rhoda* or "Rose" comes to answer. In Luke and Acts, this is Peter's second encounter with a maidservant (cf. Luke 22:56-57), neither of which is very successful. Rhoda is so overjoyed at recognizing Peter's voice that she runs inside to tell the others, leaving Peter standing at the gate (v. 14). The believers who presumably had gathered to pray for Peter (see vv. 5, 12) refuse to believe that their prayers have been answered. Rather, they inform Rhoda that she is out of her mind and suggest that what she has seen is not Peter but his ghost. This is evidently another sign that they did not trust that God would deliver Peter since, in popular Jewish tradition, it was believed that a person's "guardian angel" often appeared immediately following the person's death. As Polhill remarked, "They found it easier to believe that Peter had died and gone to heaven than that their prayers had been answered" (1992, 282). Like the two on the road to Emmaus, these believers refused to believe female testimony (cf. Luke 24:22-23).

But Peter continues to knock, and finally they open the gate and find him there, much to their amazement (v. 16). After recounting his rescue, Peter asks them to tell these things to James (presumably the brother of Jesus) and the believers. This is the key verse in this scene since it marks the beginning of the changing of the guard in the Jerusalem church from Peter to James, a transition that will be completed in chap. 15. Peter then departs, and Herod's frustrated search for Peter ends in the death of the guards from whom he escaped (vv. 18-19). With this note, attention turns again to Herod.

Already Herod has killed the other James, imprisoned Peter with the intentions of putting him to death, and executed the four squads of guards (a total of sixteen men) who had watched over him. Now he cuts off food supplies from the people of Tyre and Sidon (in Phoenicia) because he is angry with them for some unspecified reason (v. 20). After negotiations between the king and the Phoenician citizens brokered by the king's personal servant Blastus result in reconciliation, a celebration is held for the king to receive the people's praise for his benefaction (which, of course, is only necessary because of Herod's own vindictiveness). His speech garners the people's favor, and he is hailed as a god (v. 22). When Herod accepts this praise without protest and without giving "glory to God," he receives his own tap from an angel (v. 23; see v. 7) and meets the fate he intended for Peter. Like other tyrants (according to Josephus, *Ant* 19.343-52), Herod dies a grisly, worm-infested death.

The story of Peter is the second of three rescues from prison, and the demise of Herod is the third punitive miracle where the opponent of God is struck down (see JUDAS and ANANIAS and SAPPHIRA). These stories "unfold in inverse symmetry" (Pervo 1990, 43). The result is that the earthly powers, here represented by Herod, are unmasked for the impostors they are, and the power of God is demonstrated through the Antioch church, Barnabas, and Peter. Like the seed sown on good earth (see Luke 8:4-15), the *word of God* (meant here by Luke as figurative language to refer to the church) *grew* in the face of opposition and continued to produce a remarkable yield, just as it did at the beginning of this section (v. 24; see 6:7).

Paul's Mission to the Gentile World, 13:1–19:41

This next major division of Acts narrows its vision from the activities of the Twelve and the Seven to focus on the gentile mission of PAUL and his apostolic company. To speak of these chapters as Paul's "three missionary journeys" is inaccurate since Luke himself never refers to Paul's campaigns in such fashion. In fact, only Paul's first "foray" into the gentile world (13:1–14:28) has the character of an intentional journey, in this case a round trip beginning in and returning to Antioch. The second section revolves around the controversy surrounding Paul's missionary efforts and its resolution (15:1-35). The next three sections focus on Paul in MACEDONIA (15:36–17:15), the Achaian cities of ATHENS and CORINTH (17:16–18:17), and EPHESUS (18:18–19:41). The shift then is from persons (chaps. 5–12) to places (chaps. 13–19), but the spread of the gospel remains the central theme.

Paul's Initial Missionary Campaign, 13:1–14:28

13:1-12. Commissioned and tested. This scene begins with the commissioning of Paul and Barnabas by the church at Syrian Antioch (vv. 1-3). Two things are noteworthy about this opening. First is the diversity of the Antiochene church evidenced by this short list: SIMEON or Niger, a black person, perhaps from North

Africa; Lucius, who is originally from CYRENE and perhaps among those broad-minded enough to evangelize among the gentiles (see 11:20); and Manaen, who is of aristocratic Jewish stock, having been brought up in the court of Herod Antipas (see Luke 3:1; Acts 4:27). Barnabas and Saul are also counted as prophets in this list. The second important feature is the role of Holy Spirit in the commissioning. Luke wants it clear that just as the Holy Spirit was involved in the beginning of Jesus' public ministry, the Antiochene church sets Saul and Barnabas apart only under the direction of the Holy Spirit (v. 3).

The parallel between Paul and Jesus continues in the next scene (vv. 4-12). Saul and Barnabas are sent out by the Holy Spirit (v. 4) after their commissioning, as was Jesus (see Luke 4:1). For the second time in Acts, a Christian missionary confronts a magician (see Acts 8). Here the opponent is Bar-Jesus, known also as ELYMAS, a *Jewish false prophet* (v. 6). Elymas, who is in the service of a leading Roman official—Sergius Paulus—fears that Sergius might be persuaded to turn to the Christian faith by Paul and Barnabas so he opposes them (vv. 7-9). Elymas is closely related to Satan in Paul's curse where he is called *a son of the devil* and an *enemy of all righteousness*. He is also described as being *full of all deceit and villainy* (v. 10).

The confrontation here is between Paul, a true prophet full of the Holy Spirit, and Bar-Jesus, who seeks to make *crooked the straight paths of the Lord* (v. 10)—thus undoing the work of another true prophet, JOHN THE BAPTIST. It is nothing less than a confrontation between the Holy Spirit and the devil and echoes the conflict between Jesus and Satan at the beginning of Jesus' public ministry (Luke 4). Paul's curse of blindness on Elymas is especially fitting: as an idolater who serves as an agent of Satan, Elymas is cursed to the darkness from which he has come (see Deut 28:28-29; 1 QS 2:11-19).

Note also the irony here: Paul, who has himself just made the transition from darkness to light (see chap. 9), now pronounces a curse of "mist and darkness" that causes Elymas to search for *someone to lead him by the hand* (v. 11). The point of this scene for the ministry of Paul is crucial: Like Jesus, Paul has demonstrated his authority over the forces of Satan and thus has proven himself worthy of the mission set before him. The conversion and commission of Paul that began in chap. 9 is now complete, and perhaps this explains why from this point on, Saul is consistently referred to as Paul (see v. 9). With the fulfillment of his change in status from one who opposed.God to one who now serves him comes a change in name (see Garrett 1989, 85). That the church also gains a prominent convert in Sergius Paulus is a nice by-product of this encounter, but by no means the central focus.

13:13-52. Paul's speech at Pisidian Antioch. This next scene has three parts: (1) the setting (vv. 13-16), (2) the speech (vv. 17-41), and (3) the aftermath (vv. 42-52). After a whistle stop in Perga, Paul and his company come to Antioch of Pisidia. As would prove to be his pattern in Acts, Paul enters the synagogue on the Sabbath (v. 14). After the reading of scripture (see Luke 4), Paul is given the opportunity to speak and delivers the first of the major addresses in Acts (cf. Acts 17:22-31; 20:18-35).

Paul's inaugural speech (vv. 17-41) is remarkably similar to Jesus' inaugural address in Luke 4 and Peter's first major speech recorded in Acts 2 (see Tannehill 1990, 160). All three speeches use scripture to interpret the mission (Luke 4:18-19; Acts 2:17-21; 13:47) and include gentiles in God's salvation (Luke 4:25-28; Acts 2:39; 13:45-48). The speech itself narrates God's promises to Israel (vv. 16b-25), the fulfillment of those promises in Christ (vv. 26-37), and an invitation and warning (vv. 38-41). Each of these units is introduced with a form of direct address (*You Israelites* . . . [v. 16b]; *my brothers* . . . [v. 26]; *my brothers* [v. 38]). These direct addresses make it clear that Paul is addressing Jews (*you Israelites*) and those who are deeply interested in Judaism (*others who fear God*).

The first part of the speech (vv. 16b-25) is similar to Stephen's speech in that it recounts Israel's history; its focus however differs by concentrating not on Israel's rebelliousness, but rather on God's faithfulness. After this brief summary of Israel's history from the ancestors to David, the central claim of the section is made in v. 23: *Of this man's* [David's] *posterity God has brought to Israel a Savior, Jesus, as he promised.* Paul then cites the words of John the Baptist as corroborating evidence to support his claim that God's faithfulness has climaxed in Jesus.

That Jesus is the fulfillment of God's promises to Israel is worked out in more detail in the second part of Paul's speech (vv. 26-37). Having appealed to the content of Jewish history (vv. 17-22) and the witness of John the Baptist, Paul now employs two favorite scriptures (Pss 2, 16) and the rules of Jewish messianic interpretation (see comments on Acts 8). But Christian messianic exegesis once again takes a startling turn (see 3:20); this Messiah, whom God promised and to

whom the scriptures point, has already come in the person of Jesus (vv. 32-33).

The conclusion of the sermon is twofold. First, Paul extends an invitation for the hearers to receive the forgiveness of sins that can come only through Jesus, not through the Law of Moses (vv. 38-39). He also issues a prophetic warning (quoting Hab 1:5, cf. 1QpHab 2:1-10) that to reject Paul's message is to reject God's salvation and to be condemned to play the part of *scoffers* whose fate it is to *perish* (v. 41).

Immediately following the sermon, the people urge Paul and Barnabas to return the next Sabbath, and in the meantime the people follow these Christian missionaries who continue to exhort them (vv. 42-43). The rest of this unit falls into two parallel scenes (vv. 44-48; 49-52) summarizing Paul's ministry in Antioch (see Talbert 1984, 59; Krodel 1986, 246–47).

A The gathering of the whole city
    to hear the word of the Lord, 44
  B The rejection of unbelieving Jews, 45
    C Response of Paul and Barnabas:
        turning to the Gentiles, 46-47
      D The Gentiles rejoice, 48
A' The word of the Lord
    spread throughout the region, 49
  B' Unbelieving Jews stir up persecution
    against Paul and Barnabas, 50
    C' Response of Paul and Barnabas:
        shaking off the dust from their feet, 51
      D' The Disciples are filled with joy, 52

This pattern of (1) the proclamation of the gospel that leads to (2) division among those listening, (3) rejection by the unbelievers, (4) withdrawal by the Christian missionaries, and, finally, (5) Luke's report of the progress despite the opposition continues to the end of Acts. It will be repeated in the very next scene of Paul and Barnabas in Iconium.

14:1-28. Paul in Iconium, Lystra, and elsewhere. The description of the scene in ICONIUM (vv. 1-7) prevents the readers from reducing Paul's ministry to the simple formula of rejection by the Jews and success among the gentiles (Tannehill 1990, 176). Rather, Luke reports that a *great number of both Jews and Greeks became believers* (v. 1). Likewise, both Jews and gentiles persecute the apostles (v. 5) who withdraw to the surrounding country and continue to preach the good news (vv. 6-7). Paul's words in 13:46-47 are not to be understood in any rigid sense; division is not always along ethnic lines, certainly not in Iconium. The division is not between Jews and gentiles, but between those who hear the word and accept and those who reject the message and persecute the messengers.

In LYSTRA, Paul heals a man lame from birth (vv. 8-10; cf. Acts 3:1-10). As a result, the crowds cried out that *the gods have come down to us in human form* (v. 11), specifically Zeus (Barnabas) and Hermes (Paul). This story echoes an ancient legend no doubt familiar to the ancient reader that Zeus and Hermes had once visited the region of Phrygia and Lycaonia but had not been recognized nor warmly received until they came upon an elderly couple Baucis and Philemon (see Ovid, *Metamorph.* 8.626). Perhaps the hasty conclusion reached here by the Lycaonians was an attempt to avoid making the same mistake twice.

In sharp contrast to Simon Magus (Acts 8) and Herod (Acts 12), Paul and Barnabas are quick to deny their newly acquired divinity. In a quickly composed speech that anticipates the AREOPAGUS address (Acts 17), Paul is still barely able to restrain the people from honoring them with sacrifice. This turmoil gives way quickly to more serious trouble when Jews from Antioch and Iconium who have been pursuing Paul and Barnabas persuade this fickle crowd to join them in stoning Paul, dragging him outside the city, and leaving him for dead (v. 19). Suffering for Christ's name, foretold to Ananias in an epiphany (9:16), now becomes a painful reality. Surrounded by the support of other disciples, Paul gets up and continues his ministry in DERBE. This symbolic death and resurrection bear witness again to the "unhindered" nature of the gospel.

Luke quickly narrates the story of how Paul and Barnabas retrace their steps, and this episode ends in Syrian Antioch where it began, forming a literary inclusio (vv. 21-28). On this first missionary endeavor, Paul had fulfilled his calling first revealed to Ananias that Paul would *bring* [Jesus'] *name before Gentiles and kings and before the people of Israel* and that *he must suffer for the sake of* [Jesus'] *name* (9:15-16). So in Antioch, they reported to the church how God *had opened a door of faith for the Gentiles* (v. 27). Very shortly, however, some in the church would seek to close that door or at least severely limit its access.

The Conference in Jerusalem, 15:1-35

Acts 15 stands at the center of the Book of Acts both literarily and theologically. Finally the issue of gentile inclusion into the family of God is addressed and resolved. The episode is structured in four scenes: a description of the nature of the conflict (1-5); the debate in Jerusalem focusing on the three speeches by Peter, Paul, and Barnabas, and James (6-21); the solution (22-29); and the report to Antioch (30-35).

15:1-5. The conflict. The success of Paul and Barnabas reported in Acts 13 and 14 prompts some unnamed individuals to come down from Judea to Antioch to assert the official position of the Jerusalem church: *Unless you are circumcised according to the custom of Moses, you cannot be saved* (v. 1). *No small dissension and debate* (v. 2) between them and Paul and Barnabas resulted, and delegates were sent to Jerusalem to resolve the matter.

Verse 2 introduces the major players: the circumcision party (whom Luke refers to as *believers who belonged to the sect of the Pharisees* [v. 5]) which has no individual spokesperson but rather speaks as a group; the apostles, represented by Peter; and the elders, represented by James. The only group missing are the Hellenists, and Luke may intend for the reader to understand that Paul and Barnabas have been appointed by the Antioch church to represent their concerns (v. 2; cf. 13:1). The issue is stated sharply by the sect of the PHARISEES: GENTILES cannot become Christians without first becoming JEWS, that is, they must be circumcised and observe the Law of Moses.

15:6-21. The debate. The other representatives are then allowed to present their position. Peter speaks first. By recounting briefly the Cornelius story (without mentioning his name), Peter appeals to his own experience to justify including without restrictions the gentiles within the family of God. Two points are of special interest in Peter's speech. First, Peter's argument is not a mere autobiographical argument from personal experience; it is a theological argument (Tannehill 1990, 184). The speech throughout de scribes what God was doing in those events. God is the subject of most of the verbs and participles in this speech: God made a choice; God knows the human heart; God testified to them (gentiles); God gave them the Holy Spirit; God cleansed their hearts; God has made no distinction between them and us (vv. 7-9). The upshot is that God, not Peter (or Paul), is responsible for the inclusion of the gentiles. In light of this appeal to divine mandate, Peter's question, *Why are you putting God to the test by placing on the neck of the disciples a yoke that neither our ancestors nor we have been able to bear?* (v. 10), reduces the assembly from *much debate* (v. 7) to *silence* (v. 12).

The other point of emphasis in Peter's speech is on justification by grace through faith. The speech ends with these words: *we believe that we will be saved through the grace of the Lord Jesus, just as they will* (v. 11; cf. v. 9). The emphasis is, of course, a very common theme in Paul's letters (cf. e.g., Gal 3:15), but it is also found in the message of the Lukan Paul. At the end of his synagogue speech in Antioch, Paul asserts "everyone who believes is justified" (13:38-39, author trans.). Peter then represents the most liberal position on this issue: gentiles need only to believe in order to be saved. Salvation is an act of God's grace, not the result of human effort.

After Paul and Barnabas support Peter by relating the *signs and wonders that God had done through them among the Gentiles* (v. 12), James, representative of the Jerusalem elders, addresses the assembly. As Peter had offered a theological argument for gentile inclusion on the basis of his personal experience, James offers a theological argument based on another source of authority—scripture. James begins his speech with a reference to Peter's speech: *Simeon has related how God first looked favorably on the Gentiles to take from among them a people for his name* (v. 14). The Greek word for "people" is used in Luke almost exclusively for the Jews, but here it unmistakably identifies believing gentiles with God's chosen "people."

James argues further that the inclusion of gentiles into the people of God was foretold by the prophet Amos. James's interpretation of Amos 9:11-12 rests on the LXX version of that passage, which claims that the house of David will be restored *so that all other peoples may seek the Lord—even all the Gentiles over whom my name has been called* (v. 17; cf. Amos 9:12 where the sense is very different). Since no mention is made in Amos of the gentiles being circumcised or obeying the Mosaic law, James concludes that scripture confirms Peter's experience that the gentiles should not have to become Jews in order to become Christians: *we should not trouble those Gentiles who are turning to God* (v. 19).

James does, however, go one step further toward compromise with the sect of the Pharisees by suggesting that the council write to the gentiles, instructing them to observe certain dietary laws (v. 20). The council is persuaded by James's words and decides to communicate its decision to the gentile believers in Antioch, Cilicia, and Syria (15:23). But what exactly have they decided? Is this last addition by James a soteriological requirement or social compromise? In other words, has James removed circumcision only to substitute dietary laws as a requirement for gentile sal-

vation, or is he addressing a social problem of how gentiles and Jews are to live together peaceably in the church? A closer examination of the decree itself and the context of Acts in general may help resolve this question.

15:22-29. The solution. The four requirements demanding abstention from food offered to idols, from sexual immorality, from meat of strangled animals, and from blood (possibly based on Lev 17:8–18:18) are repeated in the letter composed for gentile consumption. The immediate context of the letter suggests these requirements should not be viewed as necessary for salvation, since the letter has been sent to correct those *certain persons who have gone out from us, though with no instructions from us,* and who *have said things to disturb you and have unsettled your minds* (v. 24). Further, these four requirements are "all basically ritual requirements aimed at making fellowship possible between Jewish and Gentile Christians" (Polhill 1992, 331). This view is supported by other clues in the text. In 16:1-3, Timothy (whose mother is Jewish and father Greek) is circumcised by Paul, not to insure his salvation, but to remove any obstacle that would hinder fellowship with the Jews with whom he came into contact. These regulations are recalled again in 21:21, where Paul is accused of leading Jews living among gentiles to *forsake Moses.* The situation has changed: "The problem is no longer the demands being made on Gentiles to become Jews but the pressure being felt by Jews to conform to a Gentile way of life" (Tannehill 1990, 191). The problem is still basically a social one of fellowship between Jewish and gentile Christians.

15:30-35. The report distributed. The appointed delegation—Paul, Barnabas, Judas BARSABBAS, and SILAS—depart, and the letter is delivered to the church at Antioch. It achieves the desired results: the congregation read it and *they rejoiced at the exhortation* (v. 31). The gentile mission has won a significant dispute; and, equally important for Luke, the church has resolved another major dispute in an orderly and peaceable fashion. Once again, church unity has been restored, and Paul and Barnabas can return to the task of teaching and proclaiming the word of the Lord (v. 35).

Paul in Macedonia, 15:36–17:15

15:36–16:10. Paul and the Apostolic company. Following the conference, Paul proposes to Barnabas that they retrace the steps of their first missionary campaign to see how the fledgling churches are faring (v. 36). This plan does not materialize because of a dispute about whether John Mark should accompany them. Again the conflict produces a positive result. The division actually leads to a multiplication of missionary efforts: Barnabas and Mark sail to Cyprus; and Paul and Silas travel through Syria and Cilicia, *strengthening the churches* (v. 41).

Paul's choice of traveling companions, Silas (15:40) and Timothy (16:1-3), deserves further comment. Timothy's mother was a Jewish Christian (on his circumcision, see comments on 15:22-29 above), and he himself *was well spoken of by the believers in Lystra and Iconium* (16:2). As a companion of Paul, he insured that the concerns and interests of these newly founded churches would be well represented. Silas, along with Judas, was one of the *leaders* of the Jerusalem church (15:22) who had been chosen to bear the apostolic decree to the gentile churches. In Antioch, Silas had shown his mettle by saying much *to encourage and strengthen the believers* (15:32). In fact, Luke identifies him as a *prophet*. Rather than exclude the Jerusalem church from further participation in the mission because they were on the losing side of the debate, Paul chooses to include Silas in his apostolic company. Silas, therefore, embodies the Jerusalem church's commitment to support the Jewish-gentile mission of Paul (see Tannehill 1990, 196).

So when Luke reports that *they went from town to town,* delivering the accord reached by apostles and elders in Jerusalem (16:4), it is significant that the *they* includes both a member of one of these diaspora churches and a member of the Jerusalem congregation. As a result of such strategy the churches grew daily both qualitatively (*in the faith*) and quantitatively (*in numbers* [16:5]).

Despite these positive references, Luke does not avoid reporting the limitations and failures of Paul's mission. With Paul and his company traveling as it were by trial and error, Luke twice reports that Paul was forbidden by the Spirit, first from speaking the word in Asia (16:6) and next from entering into Bithynia. The floundering mission is finally given focus in Troas when Paul experiences a vision (cf. chap. 10) in which a Macedonian man pleads with Paul to travel to Macedonia to *help us* (16:9). Guided now by the conviction that the campaign had divine endorsement, Paul sets sail for Macedonia (16:10).

Actually, the text says *we immediately tried to cross over to Macedonia* (16:10). Here Luke introduces the first of several so-called WE-SECTIONS, where the narrator seems to become a participant in the story.

The use of first-person narration is important because: "Geographically, it is prominent in the Aegean coastal region, but not limited thereto. Thematically, it emphasizes major moments and events. Literarily, the 'we' brings readers into the story. Its intimacy makes this story *our* story" (Pervo 1990, 56). The use of the first person, then, signals that important events are about to follow.

16:11-40. Conversions and imprisonments. The reader is certainly not disappointed, for what follows is another household conversion story (vv. 11-15; cf. Acts 10–11), an exorcism (vv. 16-24), and the third rescue from prison (vv. 25-40). Paul and his companions pass quickly through Samothrace and Neapolis to Philippi, *a leading city of the district of Macedonia and a Roman colony* (vv. 11-12), where they encounter some women at prayer, the most notable of whom is LYDIA (vv. 13-14). The story of Lydia actually frames this unit (vv. 13-15, 40).

The reader learns several things about Lydia: she is a *worshiper of God* (like Cornelius, a devout gentile who had not yet fully converted to Judaism [cf. 10:2]) and a dealer in purple cloth from Thyatira, which indicates that she is a rich businesswoman (v. 14). After she and her household are converted, she adopts the role of a gracious Christian hostess and patroness (see Rom 12:13; Heb 13:2; 3 John 5-8) in opening her home to and sharing her possessions with Paul and his company.

During their time with Lydia, Paul and his companions encounter a slave girl with *a spirit of divination* whose fortune-telling was very lucrative for her owners (v. 16). She rightly identifies the missionaries as *slaves of the Most High God, who proclaim to you a way of salvation* (v. 17). After *many days* of this, Paul commanded the spirit to leave the girl, reminiscent of Jesus's exorcisms (v. 18; cf. Luke 4:34; 8:28).

With the departure of the spirit went also the fortune of the slave-girl's owners. Once again, the material effect of the missionaries efforts leads to adverse results. The owners drag Paul and Silas into the marketplace before the authorities and hide their rage at economic loss behind political charges that will stick: *These men are disturbing our city; they are Jews and are advocating customs that are not lawful for us as Romans to adopt or observe* (vv. 20-21). The crowds join in, and the local authorities acquiesce. Stripped and flogged, Paul and Silas are thrown into prison where they are put in the innermost cell, what we would call the dungeon (vv. 22-24).

The next scene resembles a rescue-from-prison scene, but there is a significant difference. Prayers, hymn singing, and an earthquake lead not to the rescue of Paul and Silas from prison, but rather the deliverance of the Philippian jailer and his household to salvation. When the jailer awakens to discover the prison doors opened, he draws his sword to take his own life before the local authorities can (cf. 11:18-19). But Paul interrupts; the earthquake had opened the prison doors and unfastened the prisoners' fetters, but Paul and Silas were still there (vv. 27-29). Trembling, the jailer asks, *Sirs, what must I do to be saved?* (v. 30). Paul and Silas respond with the kerygma in a nutshell, *Believe on the Lord Jesus, and you will be saved, you and your household* (v. 31). In the middle of the night these words come true. Both parties receive cleansing waters—one for wounds, the other for baptism—and a symbolic Lord's Supper follows as the jailer sets food before them (vv. 32-34). Like Lydia, the jailer demonstrates the authenticity of his faith by acting as the proper host.

The scene has come to a proper denouement with the conversion of the jailer, but Luke has one more important detail to report. Only now in the story does the reader learn that Paul and Silas have been illegally beaten and imprisoned—they are Roman citizens (v. 37). This disclosure of citizenship comes too late in the story to offer protection, but it does set the stage for later encounters with political authorities when Paul's Roman citizenship becomes important again (22:25). This scene ends where it began, in Lydia's house (v. 15) with Paul and Silas strengthening the brothers and sisters there.

17:1-15. Conflict in Thessalonica. Paul and Silas's journeys next take them to THESSALONICA where there is a Jewish synagogue (v. 1). Luke reminds us that it was Paul's custom to speak in the synagogue; he has not yet abandoned the Jewish mission. His message is strikingly similar to the message of the risen Christ in Luke 24 (Tannehill 1990, 206): Paul "opens" the scriptures (*explaining and proving*, v. 3a; see Luke 24:32); he speaks of the necessity of the Messiah's suffering (v. 3b; Luke 24:26, 46). The result is that a few of the Jews were converted as well as *a great many of the devout Greeks and not a few of the leading women* (v. 4).

The notice given to these women converts is interesting. Although Luke has consistently given attention to the role of women in the Christian community (e.g., 1:14; 5:14; 8:12), they receive even greater attention in chaps. 16–18 (see 16:13-14, 16; 17:4, 12, 34; 18:2, 18, 26). The notice of leading women in the Macedonian churches is "very much in keeping with inscriptional evidence that in Macedonia women had considerable social and civic influence" (Polhill, 361). Even more important for the role of women in these churches, no doubt, was the gospel of freedom and radical inclusion that Paul preached.

A familiar pattern emerges in Acts 17:5-8. The Jews become jealous and join with some *ruffians* to form a lynch mob against Paul and Silas. When their searching fails to turn up Paul, they settle for Jason and some other believers instead (v. 6). Knowing that religious differences will matter little to the city authorities, they hurl political charges again (see 16:21), claiming the Christians *have been turning the world upside down* and that they *are all acting contrary to the decrees of the emperor saying that there is another king named Jesus* (vv. 6-7; see 1 Thes 1:1-20; 5:3). The officials are disturbed, but choose only to fine Jason and the others before releasing them (v. 8).

Meanwhile, Paul and Silas are carried off to Beroea where they repeat the pattern of going to the synagogue (v. 10). Luke reports that these Beroean *Jews were more receptive than those in Thessalonica* (v. 11). Whereas in Thessalonica only *some* Jews believed, Luke reports that in Beroea *many of them believed,* along with *not a few Greek women and men of high standing* (v. 12). Although the Beroean Jews are receptive, the Thessalonian Jews are equally persistent; they come to Beroea and again stir up the crowds (v. 14; cf. 14:19-20). And again, believers intervene, accompanying Paul ultimately all the way to Athens (v. 15). These believers receive instructions from Paul that Silas and TIMOTHY (who had been left behind, v. 14) are to join him as soon as possible, and they depart (v. 15).

Paul in Achaia, 17:16–18:17

This next episode takes place in the region of ACHAIA. In Athens, Paul gives his only missionary speech addressed to a gentile audience. As such it stands as a model for preaching to the gentiles. Paul next spends an extended period of time in Corinth. Both of these cities were well known in the ancient world. ATHENS, although it had faded from its period of prominence (4th–5th century B.C.E.), was still highly regarded as the cultural and intellectual center of the ROMAN EMPIRE, and CORINTH had emerged as the largest, most cosmopolitan city in Greece. Thus, in Achaia

Paul continues his pattern of evangelizing in significant urban centers.

17:16-34. Paul in Athens. The scene in Athens is divided into three parts: the setting leading up to the sermon is described in some detail (vv. 16-21); the sermon itself is the centerpiece of the episode in Athens (vv. 22-31); and the scene ends with a report of the responses to Paul's message (vv. 32-34).

While waiting for Silas and Timothy to join him, Paul has the opportunity to see Athens. Rather than being impressed by its magnificent art and architecture, Luke reports that Paul was "infuriated" (author trans.) to see the city full of idols (v. 16), a point Paul will address in his sermon. Again Paul follows the normal pattern of arguing with the Jews in the synagogue, but Luke goes on to say that he also engages in debate with people, especially Epicurean and Stoic philosophers, in the marketplace or agora (v. 17).

The EPICUREANS and STOICS represented two of the leading philosophical schools of the day. The Epicureans were committed to an ethical system that tolerated the existence of gods, but gave them no vital role. The Stoics were pantheists who held a more dynamic view of the gods, believing that the divine "spark" was present in all of creation. Paul will allude several times in his speech to certain views of these philosophers.

Evidently, Paul had not been terribly successful in communicating his views, for his audience assumed that he, too, was a pantheist presenting his view about Jesus (which in Greek is grammatically masculine) and his consort "Anastasia" ("Resurrection," which in Greek is grammatically feminine). Before he was through, however, Paul would dispel any notions that he was a polytheistic thinker.

Enamored with intellectual fads (see Demosthenes, *Oration* 4:10), the Athenians took Paul to the AREOPAGUS to present his new ideas (vv. 19-21). There is some debate whether Luke means that Paul was taken to a hill located beneath the acropolis and above the agora called the Areopagus (see, e.g., the KJV "Mars Hill") or whether he had in mind the court known by that name (an analogy is "Wall Street," which may refer either to the place or the stock exchange named after the street).

Internal evidence, such as the conversion of Dionysus, a member of the court of Areopagus (v. 34), suggests that Paul addressed the court of the Areopagus (which by this time was probably meeting in the *Stoa Basileios* or Royal Portico) in the northwest corner of the agora (Polhill 1992, 368). This view is further sup-

ported by the possible parallel that the ancient reader might have drawn between Paul's experience and the trial of Socrates. The accusation that Socrates had "introduced" other new gods (Plato, *Apologia* 24B) may be echoed in the description of Paul "introducing" a *new teaching* (v. 19) that had earlier been identified as *foreign divinities* (v. 18). Paul, of course, escapes here the fate of Socrates, and one does not have to posit a formal trial before the Areopagus to acknowledge the parallels with Socrates' trial.

The Areopagus sermon is the fullest and most dramatic speech of Paul's missionary career (vv. 22-31). Anticipated by the shorter address in Lystra (14:15-17) and consistent with the kerygma Paul presents to the gentiles in his letters (cf. Rom 1; 1 Thes 1), this address provides a window into how Paul dealt with the gentiles in other places. The speech itself is composed of five couplets following a chiastic pattern (see Polhill 1992, 37).

A Introduction: evidence of the ignorance
　　of pagan worship, 23-24
　　B The object of true worship
　　　　is the one Creator God, 25-26
　　　　C Proper relationship between humanity
　　　　　　and God, 26-27
　　B' The objects of false worship are the idols
　　　　of gold, silver, or stone, 28-29
A' Conclusion: the time of ignorance
　　is now over, 30-31

The sermon begins with a typical convention of ancient rhetoric, the *captatio benevolentia*, in which the speaker attempts to curry the favor of his audience with a compliment. Here Paul says, *Athenians, I see how extremely religious you are in every way* (v. 22). His evidence is taken from his tour of the city, during which he has seen an altar with the inscription *"To an unknown god"* (see Pausanias 1.1.4; Philostratus, *Life of Apollonius of Tyana* 6.3.5). But within the compliment is an implicit criticism, *What . . . you worship as unknown* [or perhaps in ignorance], *this I proclaim to you* (v. 23). The Athenians had been worshiping an object not a personal God, a "what" not a "whom."

Paul then claims that this unknown God is none other than the Creator God (vv. 25-26). There is no other god worthy of worship; indeed, Paul would argue, there is no other God. Although Paul does not quote scripture, his monotheism is biblically grounded (e.g., Paul's description that God *does not live in shrines made by human hands* (v. 24)—cf. 1 Kgs 8:27;

also Acts 7:48-50), as is his language used to speak of God creating all nations *from one ancestor* (presumably Adam) as well as the human response to search for God (vv. 26-27).

What Paul does quote, however, is not the OT, but rather the Stoic philosopher Aratus: *For "in him we live and move and have our being"; as even some of your own poets have said, "For we too are his off-spring"* (v. 28). Here then is the basis for Paul's attack on idolatry that follows: since humans are God's off-spring and in the true image of God, then no image *formed by the art and imagination of mortals* could possibly be anything other than a distortion of the image of the one, true God (v. 29).

Paul concludes his sermon by announcing that the time of ignorance is over. God will no longer *overlook* this ignorance (cf. 14:16; Rom 3:25); now is the time for repentance (v. 30). Just as God had made all the nations *to inhabit the whole earth* from *one ancestor* (v. 26), so God will judge the world through *a man* whom God appointed (cf. Rom 5). That this man is Jesus is confirmed when Paul says that God raised him from the dead (v. 31).

The sermon gets mixed reviews (vv. 32-34). The resurrection is viewed as "folly" by some of the Greeks in Paul's audience (v. 32; cf. 1 Cor 1:23), but to view the Areopagus speech as a failure would be a mistake. Some pledge to hear Paul speak again (v. 32); others, Dionysius and Damarius among them, became believers. Neither Paul nor the gospel failed in Athens; only those who heard the good news and did not respond in faith have failed.

18:1-17. Paul in Corinth. In the opening section (vv. 1-4), Paul leaves Athens and travels to Corinth. There he meets PRISCILLA AND AQUILA who had recently come to Corinth from Italy where they and other Jews had been expelled by the emperor Claudius (cf. Suetonius, *Life of Claudius* 25.4). Like Paul, they were tentmakers (v. 3). Paul stayed and worked with them (see Acts 20:34; cf. 1 Cor 4:12; 1 Thes 2; 2 Cor 11:7), while continuing to follow his customary pattern of trying to persuade Jews and gentiles that Jesus was Messiah (v. 4).

The rest of this passage preserves three "type scenes," defined as "when a basic situation, with similar characters and plot elements, recurs several times in a given literature" (Tannehill 1990, 202, 221–29). The first type scene is a kind of "synagogue rejection" that occurs three times in Acts and in which Paul turns to the gentiles in the face of Jewish rejection. The first

such scene takes place in Pisidian Antioch (13:44-47); the third occurs in Paul's speech to the Jews in Rome (28:23-28; cf. also 19:8-9; 22:17-21). In each instance, Paul makes a speech in which he announces that from that point on he is turning to the gentiles (13:46; 19:6; 28:28). Why does Paul continue to preach to the Jews in the face of such resistance? His prophetic act of shaking the dust off his feet (cf. 13:51; Luke 9:5) combines with his prophetic words *Your blood be on your own heads* (v. 6; cf. Ezek 33:4) and his symbolic shift from the synagogue to the house of a believer, Titius Justus, to demonstrate that Paul is fulfilling his responsibility as witness to the Jews. The Jews are responsible for their reaction. In fact, individual Jews continue to convert (witness Crispus the synagogue ruler and his household in this very scene, v. 8). Paul is obligated only to present the gospel; he cannot coerce converts.

The second type scene is that of a "divine commissioning" (see Tannehill 1990, 223). This scene was familiar to the readers from their reading of the OT (Exod 3:2-12; Josh 1:1-9; Jer 1:5-10; Isa 41:10-14) and Acts (5:17-21; 9:10-18; 16:6-10; 27:23-24). The scene consists of a confrontation (v. 9a, *The Lord said to Paul in a vision*), the commission to undertake a task (v. 9b, *speak and do not be silent*), reassurance (esp. prominent here in vv. 9-10, *Do not be afraid . . . for I am with you, and no one will lay a hand on you to harm you*), and a conclusion where the commissionee usually fulfills the assigned task (v. 11, *He* [Paul] *stayed there a year and six months, teaching the word of God among them*). Paul can continue his mission in the confidence that the Lord is present with him. The reality of this presence is felt in the next scene.

The third type scene has been identified as a scene of public accusation before an official, here Gallio (vv. 12-17). Twice already the reader has encountered this pattern (16:19-24; 17:5-7; cf. also 18:23-41) that has three elements (Tannehill 1990, 202): (1) Christians are compelled to appear before an official person or body (v. 12); (2) they are accused of wrongdoing, political or religious (v. 13); (3) the outcome is reported (vv. 14-17). This scene differs from the others in the outcome because, rather than being beaten and imprisoned (16:19-24) or fined (17:5-7), Paul is acquitted and SOSTHENES, the official of the synagogue, is beaten instead. Perhaps the difference in outcome is due to the fact that in the first two "public accusation" scenes, the charges are political; here they are religious—*This man is persuading people to worship God in ways that are contrary to the law* (v. 13)—giving Gallio an excuse to pay *no attention to any of these things* (v. 17). In any case, this scene proves the truthfulness of the previous unit: at least in Corinth no one will lay a hand on Paul.

Paul in Ephesus, 18:18–19:41

The final episode (18:18–19:41) of this division (chaps. 13–19) focuses on the city of Ephesus. The unit is organized into the following scenes: (1) Paul visits EPHESUS, JERUSALEM, and ANTIOCH (18:18-23); (2) the baptism of John (18:24–19:7); (3) Paul and the sons of Sceva (19:8-20); (4) Paul's resolve (19:21-22); and (5) the riot in Ephesus (19:23-41).

18:18-23. Paul visits Ephesus, Jerusalem, and Antioch. The first scene is transitional and could as easily be included at the end of the preceding section. Paul returns to Antioch where he began these missionary endeavors (15:35-41), but he also makes a quick stop in Ephesus where he leaves Priscilla and Aquila and enters into a quick debate with the Jews in the synagogue there (v. 19). Along the way, Paul shaves his hair to fulfill a vow (a Nazirite vow?—see Num 6:1-21), signifying that he continues to be a practicing Jew despite charges otherwise (see Acts 21:21). Paul also stops in Jerusalem to greet the church (v. 22); the tie between the gentile mission and the Jerusalem church remains unbroken. This passage then looks back to Antioch where Paul began his missionary career and forward to Ephesus where he will spend his last three years as a free man.

18:24–19:7. The baptism of John. The connection between the next two scenes, 18:24-28 and 19:1-7, may not be immediately obvious. In the first, Luke does a rare thing by shifting the spotlight away from Paul to APOLLOS. Apollos is described in glowing terms. He is *an eloquent man, well-versed in the scriptures. . . . instructed in the Way of the Lord* (vv. 24-25). He "spoke being fervent in the Spirit" (author trans.), and *taught accurately the things concerning Jesus* (v. 25). The only thing lacking is that Apollos *knew only the baptism of John* (v. 25).

Here then is the point of contact with the next unit (19:1-7) where Paul encounters some disciples in Ephesus who likewise have only experienced the baptism of John (v. 3). In both cases, "those knowing or having experienced John's baptism have their knowledge (18:26) or experience (19:4-6) completed by the associates of Paul (18:26) or by Paul himself (19:6)" (Talbert 1984, 81).

Nonetheless, there are significant differences in these two stories. Apollos is depicted much more favorably than the "disciples" encountered by Paul. The disciples were not only limited to the baptism of John; they had not heard that there was a Holy Spirit! (19:2). Apollos, on the other hand, spoke, "being fervent in the Spirit" (18:25). Further, these Ephesian disciples had to be instructed about the meaning of John's baptism for the coming of Jesus, while Apollos, limited as he was to John's baptism, is still able to teach *accurately the things concerning Jesus* (18:25). Further, with a little fine-tuning instruction from Priscilla and Aquila (note a woman instructing an evangelist here in a post-Pauline document, cf. 1 Tim 2:12), Apollos is able to secure a letter of recommendation from the Ephesians to continue his ministry in Corinth (18:27-28; 19:1).

These contrasts explain why the Ephesian disciples needed to receive baptism in the name of Jesus and the gift of the Holy Spirit (confirmed again by glossolalia, cf. 2:21-24; 10:44-48) while Apollos did not, even though both knew only the baptism of John.

19:8-20. Paul and the sons of Sceva. In this scene, the pattern of synagogue rejection continues. After three months, Paul's sermons in the Ephesian synagogue are met with such resistance by the Jews that he leaves and takes up residence elsewhere, in this case, the lecture hall of Tyrannus, where he preaches both to Jews and Greeks (18:8-10). As in the portrayal of Philip, Paul's healing ministry (vv. 11-12; cf. 8:6-7; also 5:15) confirms his message. By healing illnesses and casting out unclean spirits, Paul confirms the Christian kerygma that the authority of Satan has been overturned (on this passage, see Garrett 1989, 89–99).

Now for the third time (see Acts 8, 13), a Christian missionary confronts a practitioner of magic. In Ephesus, *some itinerant Jewish exorcists tried to use the name of the Lord Jesus over those who had evil spirits* (v. 13). The language used to describe the activities of these *seven sons of a Jewish high priest named Sceva* (v. 14) echoes magical practices of antiquity, especially "exorcist" and "adjure." That these exorcists are using the formula *the Jesus whom Paul preaches* probably implies that they, like Simon Magus, have mistaken Christian miracles for feats of magic. Thus they try to use Jesus' name in a way typical of magical technique, but Luke makes it clear that Jesus' name is not some magical name vulnerable to manipulation. Rather there is a close tie between Jesus' authority and the authority of the one calling upon his name. In Acts

16:16-17, e.g., the spirit in the slave girl recognizes Paul and his companions as *slaves of the Most High God*. But here the evil spirit replies to the sons of Sceva, *Jesus I know, and Paul I know; but who are you?* (v. 15). The demon does not know them, i.e., does not acknowledge their authority, and therefore refuses to obey them. Instead, the demon becomes master over them, sending them out of the house *naked and wounded* (v. 16). "The seven sons failed to mobilize Jesus' power because they lacked the authority to invoke his holy name, and so the demon remains in control" (Garrett 1989, 94).

The defeat of the sons of Sceva makes the accomplishments of Paul's exorcisms even more impressive, a fact not lost on the Ephesians (vv. 17-19). This incident demonstrates that the name of Jesus cannot be manipulated and therefore is worthy of praise (v. 17). Further, these Jews and Greeks had already heard the word of the Lord (v. 10) and seen the defeat of Satan confirmed in the healing ministry of Paul (vv. 11-12); now they reckon with the fact that magic itself is obsolete. "The magic books are useless now—emblems of a defeated regime—and so must be burned" (Garrett 1989, 95). The value of the books burned (*fifty thousand silver coins*) has been reckoned as having a current market value of about $1 billion.

The burning of the magical books is not to be viewed as an act of believers who had secretly practiced magic until now, but rather as part of the act of repentance on the part of those who, as a result of this incident, forsake their belief in and practice of magic and become believers. Thus, Luke uses language—"extol" and "awestruck"—that is intimately associated with conversion (cf. 9:31; 10:46). Furthermore, as noted earlier (see on 12:24), the phrase that concludes this section, *the word of the Lord grew mightily,* is one way Luke refers to the addition of believers to the church (see also 6:7, 12:24). Ironically, the victory of the demon over Sceva's sons is actually a defeat for the devil, because both sides serve Satan. Satan's kingdom is divided and thus doomed (Luke 11:18), and the Word of the Lord continues to grow.

19:21-22. Paul's resolve. In the next unit composed of only two verses (vv. 21-22), Luke anticipates the rest of Paul's ministry as it is recorded in Acts. Paul resolves in the Spirit (v. 21) to go through Macedonia and Achaia (see 20:1-12), to visit Jerusalem once again (see 21:15-38), and finally to go to Rome (see 28:14-16). The language is quite strong; Paul says that he *must* see Rome, a word characteristically used in

Acts to describe divine purpose. As such it is reminiscent of Jesus' resolve to go to Jerusalem (Luke 9:51). Although suffering is not mentioned explicitly, there is good reason to see here that the parallels between Jesus' journey to Jerusalem and Paul's journey to Rome include the dimension of suffering. For Paul, this insight becomes clearer the farther he journeys (20:22-24), but here we have the first step taken by Paul in understanding his divine destiny to travel to Rome.

19:23-41. The riot in Ephesus. Although Paul is largely absent from this scene, he remains at the center of controversy. The unit opens with one DEMETRIUS, a silversmith who made shrines of ARTEMIS, the Asian mother goddess of nature, addressing his fellow artisans. Demetrius has accurately perceived that Paul's invectives against idols would be bad for business (v. 26). To this economic argument, Demetrius adds a religious one: *the temple of the great goddess Artemis will be scorned, and she will be deprived of her majesty that brought all Asia and the world to worship her* (v. 27).

Even here, economics is not far beneath the surface; the temple of Artemis was a central pillar in the financial structures of Asia (Dio Chrysostom, *Oration* 31.54) as well as one of the seven wonders of the world bound to beef up the tourist industry in Ephesus.

Demetrius is successful in stirring up the crowd who drag GAIUS and Aristarchus, two of Paul's companions, into the theater. In the midst of mass confusion and shouts of *Great is Artemis of the Ephesians!* Paul is urged by some officials of Asia, who were friendly to him, to stay clear of the theater (v. 31). Finally, Alexander, a Jew, stepped forward to *make a defense before the people* (v. 33). Did Alexander intend to disassociate the Jews from the Christians or to defend Jewish rejection of idols? We will never know, but the crowd at least identifies this Jew with the Christian rejection of idols and drown him out in a verbal filibuster, resuming their chant: *Great is Artemis of the Ephesians!* (v. 34).

A speech by Demetrius began the riot; finally a speech by the town clerk ends it (Tannehill 1990, 243). With appropriate rhetorical flourish (cf. Acts 17:23), the town clerk begins by identifying with the point of view of the crowds, speaking of the *great Artemis* whose statue *fell from heaven* and whose temple is entrusted to the keeping of the city of the Ephesians (v. 35). In Gamaliel-like fashion, he points out the innocence of Gaius and Aristarchus and that the danger to the Ephesians was not Paul, but rather *the danger of being charged with rioting* (v. 40).

This scene shares similarities with previous public accusations (in chaps. 16, 17, and 18). Here, as in the first scene in Philippi, the accusers are gentiles (Jews are accusers in Thessalonica and Corinth, see Tannehill 1990, 202–203), making it a mistake to view opposition to the Christian movement as only and characteristically Jewish. The scene also bears remarkable similarity to the riot in the Jerusalem Temple (21:27-36). Especially similar is the reason for the riot in both instances: "Members of an established religion are protesting the effect that Paul's mission is having on their religion and its temple" (Tannehill 1990, 242). The riot subsides, order is restored, and Paul is prepared to make his final journey to Jerusalem and Rome (Acts 20–28).

Paul's Farewell Journey, 20:1–28:31

This last division of Acts (20–28) narrates Paul's farewell journey. For much of this part of the story Paul is under arrest, and the narrative is punctuated with Paul's defense speeches.

Paul's Last Journey to Jerusalem, 20:1–21:16

This first section describes the beginning of Paul's journey to Jerusalem (20:1-16), recounts his farewell address to the Ephesians (20:17-38), and records the resolve of Paul to continue to Jerusalem despite several warnings otherwise. Throughout the section, Paul exchanges good-byes with those whom he thinks he will never see again.

20:1-16. The beginning of the farewell journey. After the riot in Ephesus has been quieted, Paul gathers the disciples, encourages and bids them good-bye, and heads for Macedonia (vv. 1-6). Paul is accompanied by seven named companions who represent various areas of the gentile mission. Perhaps the number "seven" not only indicates a certain completion or fullness of the apostolic company, but represents the gentile mission itself (cf. the "seven" appointed to represent the concerns of the "Hellenists" in Acts 6). Yet another of Paul's companions reappears here when the narrator employs the first-person narration, the second such "we-passage" in Acts (cf. 16:17). This farewell ministry is characterized by the continued opposition of the Jews to Paul's witness (v. 3) and Paul *had given the believers much encouragement* (v. 2).

This encouragement is given further detail in the next scene (vv. 7-12). Paul's companions, separated at Philippi, are reunited in Troas, where they stay for a week (v. 6). Paul meets with the believers there on Sunday to share in the Lord's Supper, to *break bread* as Luke preferred to call it (v. 7; see Acts 2:42, 46). Since this was his last message to these believers, Paul continues to preach until midnight (v. 7). A young man named EUTYCHUS ("Lucky") has the misfortune of falling asleep and then falling out of a window of the upstairs room where they had met (v. 9). Pronounced dead by the time Paul gets to him, Paul takes the boy in his arms (cf. 2 Kgs 4:34) and announces that *his life is in him* (v. 10). Like Jesus (Luke 7:11-17) and Peter (Acts 9:36-42) before him, Paul now restores to life one who was presumably dead.

This story has a symbolic dimension: in the context of Paul's passion Luke places a story that foreshadows the resurrection power of the gospel to overcome death. Along these lines, the seemingly irrelevant detail about the *many lamps* in the meeting place (v. 8) may be read both literally, as an explanation of why, in the face of heat and lack of oxygen, Eutychus went to the window, and symbolically, as a contrast between the meeting room where the Word of God was proclaimed and the Lord's Supper as a place of light (13:47; 26:18, 23) and the place of death and darkness where Eutychus falls when he falls asleep. Eutychus's story is an exegesis by example of Paul's later admonition to the Ephesians to "stay awake" (author trans.) in his absence (v. 31). They may not be so fortunate as Eutychus ("Lucky"), who had Paul to reverse the misfortunes of his lack of moral diligence.

The story ends with Luke's report that the Troas believers were "not a little encouraged" (v. 12, author trans.), picking up on the word used to describe Paul's ministry throughout Macedonia and Greece (v. 2). The encouragement here derives from the integrity between Paul's *word* through preaching and sacrament (v. 11) and his *deed* in raising Eutychus.

The episode ends with a brief summary of Paul's travels from TROAS to MILETUS (vv. 13-15). The readers learn that a temporal goal has been added to Paul's spatial goal: he hopes to be in Jerusalem by the day of Pentecost (v. 16). He also chooses not to stop in Ephesus (because he dreaded the grief of leaving that Christian community again?) but rather sends for the leaders of the community to join him in Miletus (v. 16).

20:17-38. Paul's farewell address to the Ephesians. Sandwiched between the report of the arrival (v. 17) and departure (20:26-38) of the Ephesian elders is the speech given by Paul to them (vv. 18-35). Before examining the structure and content of the speech itself, it may help the reader to place the speech in several contexts. First in the context of Acts, this speech is the third by the Lukan Paul. The first in Antioch of Pisidia (Acts 13:16-41) is addressed to Jews; the second is the Areopagus speech delivered to the Greeks in Athens (17:22-31). The audience partly determines the shape and content of those first two speeches, and this is no less true for this last speech addressed to the Christian leaders from Ephesus who had gathered in Miletus to hear Paul. This speech serves as a window on the problems not only associated with the Ephesian church during Paul's day, but also with the problems faced by Luke's community in a post-Pauline time period. Luke's story about the time of Paul now gives way to Paul's story about Luke's time. As such, this speech has much in common with the Pastoral Epistles (1, 2 Timothy; Titus) that, like Acts, evidently address ecclesiastical problems in a post-Pauline situation. These problems will be given more attention in the exploration of the speech itself.

In form, the speech shares many similarities with the ancient genre of the farewell address. Farewell speeches were common in late Judaism (Gen 49; Josh 23–24; 1 Sam 12; Tob 14; *AsMos*; *T.12 Patr.*) and early Christianity (Mark 13; John 13–17; Luke 22:14-38; 2 Tim 3:1–4:8; 2 Pet) and shared certain constituent elements: (1) the assembling of the speaker's family and/or friends; (2) notice that the speaker is about to leave or die; and (3) a speech that exhorts the listener to emulate desired behavior and predicts events that will follow the speaker's departure/death (Polhill 1992, 423). The Miletus address reflects all these features.

The speech itself defies neat organization, although Talbert (1984, 85) has offered the following helpful proposal (here slightly modified). The speech divides into three parts (18b-27; 28-31a, 31b-35), each with its own chiastic or concentric structure:

1. Defense and Prediction, 18b-27
   A Paul's review and defense of his past ministry
       with the Ephesians, 18b-21
   B Paul's prediction of his future suffering—
       marked by "and now," 22-24
   B' Paul's prediction of his death—
       marked by "and now," 25
   A' Paul's defense of his past ministry, 26-27
2. Exhortations and a Prediction, 28-31a
   A Exhortation to elders to watch
       over the church, 28

   B Prediction that heresies will arise, 29-30
   A' Exhortation to elders to "stay awake," 31a
3. Exhortation and a Blessing, 31b-35
   A Paul's past exhortation, 31b
   B Paul's present blessing, 32
   A' Paul's past example, 33-35

At the heart of this speech lie the predictions that heresies will arise (vv. 29-30). These predictions function at two levels; a narrative level in which the predictions are fulfilled within the course of Acts, and a historical level in which these predictions have already come to pass in Luke's community. Thus, within the narrative itself there is good reason to view those external opponents (*savage wolves will come in among you*, v. 29) as Jews, such as the ones who in the very next episode (21:27-28) are found in opposition to the church (note that in 21:27 these Jews are identified as being from Asia, strengthening this argument), and the internal opponents as Jewish Christians or gentiles influenced by Judaism (21:20-21). There is also ample historical evidence for heresy in Ephesus at the end of the first century (see Eusebius, *EccHist* 3.32.7-8). The crisis faced here is how, in the face of internal and external pressures, to insure that the Christian traditions are preserved in the passing from one generation to the next.

21:1-16. Warnings to avoid Jerusalem. With tears and farewells, Paul and his company set sail again. After passing through Cos, Rhodes, and Patara, they land at Tyre to unload the ship's cargo (vv. 1-3) and stay there seven days. *Through the Spirit* the believers at Tyre gave Paul his first warning *not to go on to Jerusalem* (v. 4), probably because they, like Paul, knew that suffering and persecution were awaiting him there (cf. 20:23). Still, in spite of this weighty testimony to the contrary, Paul persists in continuing his journey to Jerusalem (vv. 5-6).

After a brief stop in Ptolemais, Paul and his company arrive in Caesarea and encounter several characters already familiar to the readers. They stay in the home of Philip the evangelist (see Acts 8) who has *four unmarried daughters who had the gift of prophecy* (v. 9). While it is unclear whether Paul will make it to Jerusalem by Pentecost, it is clear that already in Caesarea he is seeing evidence of the fulfillment of Pentecost prophecies, in this case, that both *sons and . . . daughters shall prophesy* (Acts 2:17).

Paul also meets with the prophet AGABUS who had prophesied a famine in Judea (11:27-30). Through

Agabus, the Holy Spirit again describes the persecution awaiting Paul in Jerusalem (cf. 20:23). Like an OT prophet, Agabus combines a prophetic sign, binding his own hands and feet with Paul's belt, with a prophetic warning: *This is the way the Jews in Jerusalem will bind the man who owns this belt and will hand him over to the Gentiles* (v. 11). This time, the believers, not the Holy Spirit, interpret this sign as a warning to Paul not to continue the journey to Jerusalem.

In the face of this third prediction of his passion (20:23; 21:4, 11), Paul remains resolute: *I am ready not only to be bound but even to die in Jerusalem for the name of the Lord Jesus* (v. 13). Unlike Peter who made a similar promise (Luke 22:33) but failed to fulfill it (at least in the narrative of Luke), Paul remains true to his oath. Seeing they could not persuade him otherwise, the believers pray that *the Lord's will be done* (v. 14). In language that echoes Luke 22:42, Paul is depicted here as facing his own Gethsemane, where he, like Jesus, finally prays, "Lord not my will, but yours be done."

This scene ends with some of the disciples from Caesarea escorting Paul and his company to the house of Mnason of Cyprus with whom they lodged in Jerusalem (v. 16).

Paul in Jerusalem, 21:17–23:35

21:17-40. Paul's arrival and arrest in Jerusalem. Paul and his companions are warmly received by the Jerusalem believers (v. 17), and on the next day, Paul meets with James and the Jerusalem elders (v. 18). In a scene reminiscent of the Jerusalem conference (Acts 15), Paul recounts what *God had done among the Gentiles through his ministry* (v. 19). The Jerusalem elders, in turn, invite Paul to see *how many thousands of believers there are among the Jews* (v. 20). But herein lies the problem: the Jewish believers have been told that Paul was teaching Jews living among gentiles to forsake Moses and abandon Jewish customs (v. 21).

This is the third church conflict involving Jewish-gentile relations (see Tannehill 1990, 268). First the question of baptizing gentiles was resolved in Acts 11. Then the controversy over requiring gentiles to be circumcised was addressed in Acts 15. The problem before the church now has to do with pressure, real or perceived, on Jewish Christians to forsake their Jewish customs, values, and practices. Paul is at the center of this problem because as leader of the gentile mission, he is creating a social situation that is not particularly supportive of Jewish Christians who wish also to honor their Jewish heritage. As the gentile mission continues to be successful and the Jewish population in the church becomes more and more of a minority, this problem intensifies.

The solution proposed by James and the elders is for Paul to demonstrate tangibly his support for Jewish Christians to live as Jews (v. 23). Paul is to join four Jewish believers who are under a vow in going through a seven-day rite of purification in the Temple (vv. 23-24). This will provide the evidence needed to dispel the rumors about Paul. Further, they argue, this solution in no way compromises the agreement reached at the Jerusalem conference regarding the gentiles (v. 25). Paul, despite all the Spirit's previous warnings of persecution and suffering, agrees and engages in the very public act of Temple purification (v. 26).

While Luke reports nothing of the response by Jewish believers to Paul's acts, he has much to say about the reaction of the Jewish community. Jews from Asia, who had seen Paul in the Temple and had also previously seen the gentile TROPHIMUS from Ephesus with Paul, jump to the conclusion that Paul has defiled the Temple by taking Trophimus into it (vv. 27, 29). Thus they stir up the crowd milling around the Temple charging that Paul is *the man who is teaching everyone everywhere against our people, our law, and this place* (v. 28)—charges similar to the ones leveled against Stephen (cf. 7:13). These Asian Jews incite a riot that would rival the one Paul had just endured in Ephesus. Paul was dragged from the Temple, and the Temple doors ominously were shut, never to be open to Paul again (v. 30).

Only the intervention of a Roman tribune prevents Paul from meeting his death (vv. 31-32). Paul is arrested and bound (cf. Agabus's prophecy in v. 11), and efforts by the tribune to learn Paul's identity are thwarted by the uproar of the crowd (v. 34). Instead, the pursuing mob becomes so violent that Paul has to be carried away by Roman soldiers in the midst of shouts of *Away with him!* (v. 36), the very cry of the crowds who called for Jesus' death (Luke 23:18).

While Jesus went to his death with no defense speech, Paul requests to address the crowd (vv. 37, 39). The tribune is surprised to learn that Paul speaks Greek, for he had mistakenly supposed that Paul was an Egyptian insurrectionist (v. 38). Paul identifies himself to the Roman tribune as a Jew from a leading city and then stands to clarify his identity to the Jewish mob (v. 40).

22:1-29. Paul addresses the crowd and the Roman tribune. Paul gestures for the crowd to be silent, but when they hear him speaking in their own language they become even more quiet (v. 2). Paul's speech addresses three issues: his Jewish piety and former life (vv. 1-5), his conversion (vv. 6-12), and his divine commission to go to the gentiles (13-21).

In the first unit (vv. 1-5), Paul again follows the conventions of ancient rhetoric and tries to identify with his audience: he is a pious Jew. He makes this point by (1) speaking in Hebrew (probably here meaning Aramaic), (2) addressing the audience as *brothers and fathers* (v. 1), (3) claiming immediately to be a Jew (v. 3), (4) recounting his impeccable Pharisaic education at the feet of Gamaliel (v. 3; cf. 5:34-38), (5) claiming to share a zeal for God with his audience (v. 3), and (6) appealing to the high priest and the whole council of elders as witnesses to his persecution of the church (vv. 4-5).

This affinity with his audience continues as Paul recounts his conversion experience in the form of a commissioning story, a form familiar to an audience steeped in the similar stories found in scripture (vv. 6-11). This is the second time Paul's conversion is narrated in Acts (see Acts 9:1-18), and there are both significant similarities and differences between the two accounts (and the third to be related later in chap. 26). Many of the differences may be explained by the fact that the audience with whom Paul is trying to relate to is Jewish (see Polhill 1992, 459–61 for a discussion of other differences). The dialogue between Paul and Jesus in the two accounts is nearly verbatim (compare vv. 7-8 with 9:4-5). The addition of *of Nazareth* to Jesus' name (v. 8) is appropriate for such a Jewish audience. Likewise, the description of Ananias as a pious Jew (v. 12) rather than a devout Christian (as in 9:10) again helps Paul establish his Jewishness with this Temple mob.

Also important in explaining the differences is the fact that Paul, not an omniscient narrator (as in chap. 9), is recounting the story, and thus Paul relates events as they unfolded to him. Hence the commission to go to the gentiles comes to Paul (vv. 17-21) and not to Ananias (9:15-16).

Again, Paul, like a good Jew, is praying in the Temple when Jesus commands him, *Go, for I will send you far away to the Gentiles* (v. 21). The brief mention of Stephen's stoning (where Paul was present, giving his approval, v. 20) prepares the readers for the response of the crowd.

Once Paul mentions the gentile mission, the mob is stirred against him again, throwing off their garments, tossing dust in the air, and shouting, *Away with such a fellow from the earth! For he should not be allowed to live* (vv. 22-23). In that sense, Paul's *defense* (as he calls it in v. 1) is a failure; his efforts to prove his "Jewishness" to the crowd finally give way to his conviction that he is called to be apostle to the gentiles.

Once again the tribune intervenes and decides to get to the bottom of this conflict by literally beating the answers out of Paul (v. 24). But just before he is to receive lashes, Paul reveals to the centurion what the reader already knows (see 16:37), namely, that Paul is a Roman citizen (v. 25), and flogging a Roman citizen was simply not an acceptable practice (see, e.g., Cicero, *Verrine Orations* 2.5.66). Paul has not purchased his Roman citizenship as did the tribune (who probably mentions the fact out of suspicion that Paul is lying); even better, he is a citizen by birth. Realizing he has bound and nearly flogged a Roman citizen, the tribune looks for an alternative plan for finding out the nature of the differences between Paul and the Jews.

22:30–23:11. Paul before the Sanhedrin. The tribune convenes a meeting of the SANHEDRIN and places Paul before them to speak (22:30). Paul begins with the assertion, *Brothers, up to this day I have lived my life with a clear conscience before God* (23:1). He is saying, in effect, that he has been obedient to his calling to the gentile mission (cf. 26:19). The high priest simply cannot accept that Paul's mission is indicative of his obedience to God and so orders Paul struck on the mouth (v. 2). Paul immediately responds with a sharp retort, *God will strike you, you white-washed wall! Are you sitting there to judge me according to the law, and yet in violation of the law you order me to be struck?* (v. 3). When observers point out to Paul that he has insulted the high priest (v. 4), Paul's tone changes rapidly, *I did not realize, brothers, that he was high priest; for it is written, "You shall not speak evil of a leader of your people"* (v. 5). The reader who notes a little irony here is probably not mistaken: Paul did not recognize the high priest (for whose organization he previously worked) because he was not acting like one might expect the leader of the people to act.

Paul then notices that both Sadducees and Pharisees are present on the council, and he attempts to redirect the focus of the debate from whether or not Paul is an observant Jew to a weighty theological issue, the question of the resurrection of the dead. Paul is really attempting to do more, however, than simply start a controversy among members of the Sanhedrin. Rather, his concern about *hope and resurrection* raised here continues to be an important theme throughout the defense even when it no longer creates controversy (see 24:15, 21; 28:20; see Tannehill 1990, 286–87). Nonetheless, Paul's words about resurrection here do spark a debate between the Sadducees who deny the doctrine of resurrection (as well as the existence of angels and spirits) and the Pharisees who affirm it. Note that Paul is speaking about a final eschatological resurrection of the dead (plural), not specifically of the resurrection of Christ. The Lukan Paul is seeking to emphasize the similarities between Christianity and segments of Judaism and thus lay the groundwork for more explicit claims later about the resurrection of Jesus (26:23). The Pharisees proclaim Paul's innocence (v. 9), much as Pilate, Herod, the penitent thief, and the centurion pronounced Jesus innocent (cf. Luke 23).

Once again, the tribune, fearing for Paul's safety, has him delivered back to the barracks. This scene ends with Paul as the recipient of yet another nocturnal christophany: *That night the Lord stood near him and said, "Keep up your courage! For just as you have testified for me in Jerusalem, so you must bear witness also in Rome"* (v. 11). The reason for the divine necessity for Paul to go to Rome is made clear: he is to *bear witness* there as he has in Jerusalem.

23:12-35. An ambush avoided. The resolve of the Jerusalem Jews against Paul is demonstrated by the next scene in which forty Jews take a solemn oath neither to eat nor drink until they had killed Paul (v. 12). They approached the Temple establishment (Sadducean chief priests and elders) with a plan to take Paul by ambush (the absence of the more sympathetic Pharisees from this conspiracy is noteworthy).

The plan is thwarted by Paul's nephew, his sister's son. The young man reports the conspiracy first to Paul and then to the tribune with detailed accuracy (vv. 16-21). The tribune again acts decisively in Paul's behalf. After ordering Paul's nephew to tell no one of their conversation, the tribune orders an impressive guard (200 soldiers, seventy horsemen, and 200 spearmen) to transport Paul to Caesarea where the procurator FELIX resides (vv. 23-24). In addition, the tribune drafts a letter to be delivered to Felix.

This letter is interesting for both its form and content. In form, the letter follows the threefold salutation typical of ancient letter writing: the sender, the recipient, and the word of greeting. For the first time, the

readers learn the tribune's name, CLAUDIUS LYSIAS (v. 26). Lysias is a complex character. He has acted decisively in Paul's behalf, thrice intervening in life-threatening situations (21:31-36; 23:10; 23:23-25). He has also been persistent in his investigations to learn the facts about Paul, and he has been willing to accept new information about Paul (to believe that he was an Egyptian insurrectionist, to accept that he was a Roman citizen, and now to believe the reports of Jewish conspiracy to kill Paul). But his letter reveals that Lysias also is willing to rearrange and suppress the facts to put himself in a better light. In the letter to Felix, Lysias suggests that he intervened in Paul's behalf after learning that he was a Roman citizen (v. 27). If this account were true, Paul presumably would not have been bound. But the reader knows that Lysias had at first thought Paul was a revolutionary and learned of Paul's citizenship only *after* he had placed him in chains and nearly had him flogged. Lysias's self-assurance in decision making is marred with interests of self-protection. Other political figures encountered later will demonstrate a similar complexity in character.

Both Paul and the letter are safely delivered to Felix (vv. 31-33). After learning that Paul is from Cilicia and within his jurisdiction, Felix promises to give Paul a hearing when his accusers arrive. Meanwhile Paul is kept under house arrest in Herod's headquarters (v. 35).

Paul before Felix, Festus, and Agrippa, 24:1–26:32

This section is filled with legal scenes and defense speeches. Here Paul confronts the political establishment—the Roman officials Felix and FESTUS and the Jewish king AGRIPPA. But a close reading of these passages reveals that Paul is not the only one "on trial": he is joined by the Christian gospel. Paul not only defends himself; he bears witness to the Christian faith whether before the Jews, the Roman PROCURATOR, or even Caesar himself.

The political establishment presents a less than consistent picture. On the one hand, the Romans protect Paul and testify to his innocence. On the other, they are willing to distort the facts in order to portray themselves in the most favorable light—this is true of Lysias, Felix, and Festus. Both Felix and Festus withhold justice from Paul, despite his innocence, in their desire to "do a favor for the Jews" (see 24:27). Each episode is examined in more detail below.

24:1-27. Paul before Felix. When Ananias and some of the elders arrive in Caesarea some five days after Paul, they bring with them their own attorney, TERTULLUS, who uses his persuasive skills in oration to present the case against Paul to Felix (v. 1). There are several interesting points about Tertullus's speech. The *captatio benevolentia*, in which Felix is praised, is nearly as long as the formal complaint lodged against Paul (vv. 2-4). Further, this section of praise is excessive. Tertullus uses all the right phrases to curry Felix's favor. Felix has brought much *peace* to the Jews (v. 2). He has enacted reforms that grew out of his *foresight* or "providence" (v. 2). And, Tertullus continues, all Jews everywhere and in every way are grateful to Felix for his benevolence (v. 3). The reader who knows the facts of Felix's reign, flawed as it was with countless rebellions by disgruntled Jews, however, will see through this poorly veiled attempt to influence Felix through flattery (see Tacitus, *Ann* 12:54; Josephus, *Ant* 20.181-182).

When Tertullus finally gets to the charges against Paul, the reader notes that the accusation has taken a decidedly political direction from the complaints lodged earlier in 21:21. Here Tertullus combines the charge that Paul is profaning the Temple (v. 6) with the more serious charge, from Felix's point of view, that Paul is a *pestilent fellow* who is *an agitator among all the Jews throughout all the world, and a ringleader of the sect of the Nazarenes* (v. 5). This charge of sedition would not be taken lightly by Felix, in light of the previous Jewish riots in Felix's territory of Judea (see Josephus, *BJ* 6.124-28). Tertullus concludes his speech by inviting Felix to examine Paul for himself, but Tertullus does not supply any supporting evidence or witnesses for his accusations (a point Paul will capitalize on in his rebuttal). The best Tertullus can do is produce other Jews who simply maintain the truth of his charges (v. 9).

Rather than conduct his own investigation at this point, Felix nods to Paul (v. 10) to present his defense, which he does (v. 10-21). Like Tertullus, Paul begins with a *captatio benevolentiae*, but Paul limits his "praise" to the simple acknowledgement that Felix's experience as *judge over this nation* ought to qualify him to judge the veracity of the charges brought against Paul (v. 10). Paul counters Tertullus's sweeping and ambiguous charges with a detailed narration of the events of twelve days ago. Paul had no past history of inciting people to riot (v. 12); Paul had come to Jerusalem to worship, not stir up a rebellion (v. 11).

His accusers have no way of making their case stand up under scrutiny (v. 13).

After this string of denials, Paul is willing to make a confession: he is a member of *the Way,* what the Jews call a *sect,* and as such, Paul confesses, he worships *the God of our ancestors, believing everything laid down according to the law or written in the prophets* (v. 14). Such a confession could hardly be found objectionable to Paul's opponents.

Paul then goes on to point out that he shares a hope in the resurrection of the dead with his accusers (Sadducees notwithstanding). Then in vv. 17-19, he responds to Tertullus's charge that he had tried to desecrate the Temple (v. 6). To the contrary, Paul was conducting himself as a pious Jew, bringing alms, making sacrifice, and completing the rite of purification—all without any disturbance (v. 18). The uproar, Paul claims, was caused by Jews from Asia who are not even at the trial to bring their charges firsthand (v. 19).

Paul concludes his speech by making explicit the true nature of the charge against him. His crime, he says, *was this one sentence that I called out while standing before them, "It is about the resurrection of the dead that I am on trial before you today"* (v. 21). Paul is not guilty of political sedition or even violation of Jewish law. What is at stake here is the *resurrection of the dead*—the "fundamental issue that unites Pharisaic Judaism with Christianity and divides non-Christian Judaism" (Krodel 1986, 441).

Felix's decision to postpone judgment until Lysias arrives appears at first reading to be a cautious and reasonable choice by a competent judge: he is, after all, *rather well informed about the Way* (v. 22). Felix even gives Paul some freedom under a loosely designed house arrest and arranges to hear him again (v. 23). But this initial favorable impression of Felix changes quickly.

Felix and his Jewish wife Drusilla (on the infelicities of this marriage, see Josephus, *Ant* 20.139-44) hear Paul *speak concerning faith in Jesus Christ* (v. 24). However offensive such talk may have been to the Jewess Drusilla is left to the imagination of the reader. What does disturb Felix is Paul's discussion of *justice, self-control, and the coming judgment* (v. 25). Felix's own inadequacy in the area of self-control is revealed in his hope to receive bribe money from Paul, a desire that motivates frequent conversations between Felix and Paul. His lack of justice is demonstrated when he leaves Paul in prison for two years in order *to grant the Jews a favor* (v. 27). "Thus Roman justice is undermined by an unjust administrator" (Tannehill 1990, 302).

25:1-12. Paul before Festus. The change in administration from Felix to Festus raises new hope that justice may be done for Paul. This hope is sustained when Festus refuses to grant a favor to the Jews against Paul, a favor they no doubt had come to expect from the Roman procurator through their dealings with Felix. Underlying the request to transfer Paul to Jerusalem was the old plot to ambush him along the way (v. 3). Festus replies that Paul would stay in Caesarea and if they had any accusations against Paul, those with authority should travel there along with Festus and present them personally before him (vv. 5-6).

In little more than a week, both Festus and the Jews have arrived to hear Paul (v. 6). Unsubstantiated charges are once again hurled against Paul (v. 7). And within these eight or ten days, Festus has evidently learned the political necessity of doing favors for the Jews (v. 9; see Tannehill 1990, 306-307) and asks Paul if he wishes to go to Jerusalem for trial. Paul's response is no little shock: rather than a simple yes or no, Paul once again maintains his innocence and appeals to Caesar for his trial (v. 11). That Paul is aware that he can receive no fair trial at the hands of Festus is hinted at in his words, "No one can *grant* me as *a favor* to them [the Jews]," echoing the narrator's statement that Festus wished "to grant the Jews a favor" (author trans.).

Historically, Paul's appeal to the emperor, the *provocatio*, is shrouded in mystery. Whether Paul thought he could have a fairer hearing before the emperor (then Nero) than before Festus is probably less important than his desire to fulfill his destiny to bear witness to the gospel before the emperor in Rome (19:21; 23:11; 27:24). Festus and his council, sensing an opportunity to rid themselves of a difficult case, formally ratify Paul's request with the terse judgment, *You have appealed to the emperor; to the emperor you will go* (v. 12).

25:13–26:32. Paul before Agrippa. After a few days, King Agrippa and his sister, Bernice, arrive to greet the newly appointed Festus (v. 13). Festus uses this opportunity to involve Agrippa in the proceedings against Paul, and more importantly, to offer a public defense of his own actions. In these two speeches by Festus (25:14-22 and 24-27), Luke subtly discloses Festus's hypocrisy without explicitly labeling it as such (see Tannehill 1990, 310–15). Like Lysias and Felix before him, Festus tries to put his public image

in the best light possible. His concern for justice that permeates his speech is notably absent from the narrator's account (25:1-12). His summary of the events surrounding Paul are decidedly biased toward his own self-interests. Festus correctly reports that he refused to turn Paul over to the Jews without a proper trial (25:16), but he glosses over his real purpose in proposing a Jerusalem trial for Paul (to gain the favor of the Jews, 25:9) by claiming that he *was at a loss how to investigate these questions* (25:20). Agrippa responds by requesting an audience with Paul, which Festus promptly arranges (25:22).

In his second address, however, Festus continues his distortion. First he exaggerates the pressure he is under from the Jews. He claims that the *whole Jewish community . . . both in Jerusalem and here* [Caesarea], petitioned him (25:24), while the narrator indicates only *the high priests and the leaders of the Jews* brought charges against Paul (25:2). Despite this (albeit exaggerated) pressure, Festus claims that Paul *had done nothing deserving death* (25:25). But when Paul had appealed to Caesar, there was nothing Festus could do but grant the request. If one takes Festus's remarks at face value, then Paul's request is incomprehensible. If, however, his speeches are understood as a cover-up, then Paul's appeal to Caesar to escape the incompetence if not corruption of this judge is even more understandable.

The decision to send Paul to Rome relieves one problem but creates another. Festus is no longer responsible for rendering a judgment in Paul's case, but he must specify the charges against Paul in a letter to the emperor. Perhaps his motivation to include Agrippa in the process is grounded in the desire to have someone to share the responsibility should the emperor determine the charges against Paul are of no substance, but rather are due to the incompetence of the local administration. Whatever the reason, Paul's address before Agrippa is "his most important speech before his most distinguished audience. The King Agrippa scene is as close as we shall get to seeing a speech before the king at Rome" (Pervo 1990, 87).

Indeed, Paul's speech in this scene allows him to fulfill the words of Jesus directed at his followers: "You will be brought before kings and governors for my name's sake" (Luke 21:13). The speech falls into five parts: (1) the *captatio benevolentiae* in which Paul (again following convention) curries the favor of Agrippa (26:2-3), (2) a summary of his Jewish background and credentials (26:4-8), (3) his work as persecutor of Christians (26:9-11), (4) a recounting of his conversion that here has more of the character of a prophetic call or commissioning (26:12-18), and (5) a brief summary of his missionary activity (26:19-23). The speech climaxes with Paul's assertion that the *Messiah must suffer* and be *the first to rise from the dead* (26:23). Paul's defense speech has a thorough christological grounding.

Festus interrupts Paul's speech at this point and accuses him of being *out of your mind* (26:24). For the first time in this scene, Paul addresses Festus, but only to make the point that Agrippa is fully aware of the things about which Paul speaks. None of the things associated with the Christian community has been *done in a corner* (26:26); rather Paul has made his case publicly in the marketplace and in the synagogues.

Agrippa replies to Paul's question about whether he believes the prophets with a sharp retort: *Are you so quickly persuading me to become a Christian?* (26:28). Paul concludes his defense with an object lesson: *Whether quickly or not, I pray to God that not only you but all who are listening to me today might become such as I am* [i.e., a follower of Jesus]—*except for these chains* (26:29).

But Agrippa has heard enough and rises to leave with Festus and Bernice. He does not depart without making this observation, *This man is doing nothing to deserve death or imprisonment* (26:31), and for the fifth time Paul's innocence is declared (see 23:9, 29; 25:18-19, 25). By now, the response that Paul could have been set free if he had not appealed to the emperor (26:32) sounds more than a little lame. The readers have no reason to think that Festus and Agrippa would have released Paul, regardless of his innocence or his appeal. The voyage to Rome begins.

The Sea Voyage to Rome, 27:1–28:31

In the last unit of Acts, the long-awaited journey to Rome is narrated. Luke returns to his use of first-person narration in these chapters, and much of the material shares common features with other sea voyage stories: shipwreck, narrow escapes, suspense, conflict, and high drama. This unit falls into two parallel panels, with the first and last being the most detailed.

A Paul journeys to Malta, 27:1-44
   B Paul in Malta, 28:1-10
A' Paul journeys to Rome, 28:11-16
   B' Paul in Rome, 28:17-31

Of course, Paul's voyage to Malta is determined by where he and his companions are washed ashore while his voyage to Rome has been an intentional destination for much of the second half of Acts. These units are examined in more detail below.

27:1-44. To Malta. The journey begins in Caesarea when Paul is entrusted to the custodial care of a centurion named Julius, who shows kindness to Paul (vv. 1-3). Verses 1-12 are both a prologue and a summary: in eight verses Luke describes Paul and the others on board setting sail for Italy and stopping at four different ports along the way, culminating with Paul's warning not to continue past *Fair Havens*. The storm (vv. 13-38) and shipwreck (vv. 39-44) are narrated in detailed and technical nautical language.

In a way typical of sea-voyage stories, Luke describes a variety of settings through which Paul and his fellow prisoners, the sailors, and Julius and his fellow soldiers pass: Sidon, Myra (in Lycia), Cnidus (or nearby), Fair Havens (on Crete), and Malta. In the process, they pass near several other cities, regions, or islands: Cilicia and Pamphylia, Lasea, Phoenix, Cauda, and Syrtis. But the one setting that remains constant throughout this voyage is the sea (both the Mediterranean and the Adriatic), and this setting is the most important for understanding the significance of this passage.

In both ancient Jewish and Greek literature, the sea was viewed sometimes as an evil or hostile place of chaos and confusion, sometimes as a vehicle through which divine forces punish wickedness. Homer tells how Odysseus's crew was killed in a shipwreck as punishment for destroying Helios's cattle (*Odyssey* 12.127-41, 259-446). In Chariton's *Chaereas and Callirhoe*, evil persons are drowned at sea and the just are spared (3.3.10, 18, 3.4.9-10; cited by Talbert 1984, 101). In the OT, God uses the sea to reverse creation and judge evil humanity (Gen 6–8); God uses a sea to destroy the Egyptians and rescue the Israelites (Exod 14); God employs a storm to persuade a recalcitrant prophet to speak (Jonah 1). The same view is held in postbiblical Judaism. In the Babylonian Talmud (*B.Mes.*, 58b-59), Rabbi Gamaliel is spared from the raging sea only after declaring his innocence before God (see Talbert 1984, 102).

Thus, both Greek and Jewish readers would understand the potential disasters involved here. If Paul perishes at sea, he is no doubt guilty of the charges leveled against him; if he is spared, then he is honored with divine vindication. The closing note to this section, where Paul and his traveling entourage are brought safely to land, reveals God's evaluation of Paul and his mission (v. 44).

Luke also uses this sea voyage with all its colorful details and rich imagery to depict the symbolic death and resurrection of Paul, much as he narrates the imprisonment and release of Peter in Acts 12. Both prison and shipwreck are common metaphors for death in antiquity. Night, the disappearance of heavenly luminaries (v. 20; cf. Luke 23:44-45), and the loss of hope (v. 20; cf. Luke 24:21) all echo the passion of Jesus and allude to Paul's symbolic death. On the other hand, references to daylight, the third day (21:19), a shared meal (vv. 33-35; cf. Luke 24:30-31), and Paul's deliverance from the tomb of the sea (v. 44) all point to a kind of symbolic resurrection.

Luke also deepens the characterization of Paul as a Christian benefactor through a description of his words and deeds. Two are especially noteworthy. After taking harbor in *Fair Havens* (v. 8), Paul predicts the dangers that lie before him and his fellow travelers: *Sirs, I can see that the voyage will be with danger and much heavy loss, not only of the cargo and the ship, but also of our lives* (v. 10). Like a prophet of old, Paul's words are ignored by his audience (vv. 11-12), and finally under divine direction he modifies his original prophecy to assure his companions that *God has granted safety to all those who are sailing with you* (v. 24). Still, Paul's heroic role as leader and visionary is strengthened by these words of prophetic insight, not to mention that Paul alone is granted direct discourse throughout this passage.

Equally important is the scene described in vv. 33-35 where Paul urges his companions to take food. The eucharistic symbolism of this passage is quite apparent: *After he had said this, he took bread; and giving thanks to God in the presence of all, he broke it and began to eat* (v. 35; cf. Luke 22:19). While perhaps not strictly bespeaking an observance of the Lord's Supper since most of the company are not believers, this meal anticipates deliverance in some sense similar to the promise of deliverance present in the Lord's Supper. This position is supported by the repeated references to "salvation" or "deliverance" throughout this section (vv. 20, 31, 34, 43, 44; 28:1, 4), no doubt "a reminder to a Christian reader that the same God who delivered the storm-tossed voyagers from physical harm is the God who in Christ brings ultimate salvation and true eternal life" (Polhill 1992, 527).

28:1-10. In Malta. Paul and all his companions are delivered safely from the shipwreck and find themselves on the island of Malta. Here the theme of Paul's vindication continues. Just as nature was understood to be a vehicle of divine vindication or retribution, so also was the animal kingdom (see *t.Sanh.* 8:3; *y.Ber.* 5:1; cited by Talbert 1984, 102). Paul survived the shipwreck, but will he survive the bite of the viper who fastened itself to Paul's hand while he gathers firewood (vv. 2-4)? The natives think not, assuming the snakebite is punishment for some heinous crime such as murder and that Paul is being punished by the Greek goddess of "Justice" (v. 5). But once gain, Paul is vindicated by God, and, unharmed, he shakes the serpent into the fire. By now there is no need to correct for the reader the native's misperception that Paul is a god (v. 6; cf. 10:25-26; 14:11-15).

The final act of Paul on Malta also confirms his role as a righteous representative of a beneficent God. When the leading man of the island, Publius, falls ill, Paul cures him *by praying and putting his hands on him* (v. 8). In return, Paul the Christian benefactor is the recipient of great honor and provisions at the hands of the Maltese. Christians, Luke seems to say, have no corner on hospitality and benefaction.

28:11-16. To Rome. After three months of winter, Paul and company set sail again. Three days in Syracuse, one day at Rhegium, and they join a community of believers in Puteoli where they lodge for a week. Paul next travels to Rome and takes the decisive step in fulfilling the earlier theophanic prophecy (*Do not be afraid, Paul; you must stand before the emperor*, 27:24). Having literally survived hell and high water (symbolized by the Satanic serpent and the storm at sea), Paul and crew finally come to Rome (see Pervo 1990, 92). The scene ends with a reminder that Paul, despite his immediate past heroism, is still a prisoner: *When we came into Rome, Paul was allowed to live by himself, with the soldier who was guarding him* (v. 16).

28:17-31. In Rome. The end of a book is no less important than its beginning. Luke chooses to end this narrative neither with a confrontation between Paul and the emperor, nor with a narration of Paul's martyrdom, but rather by focusing on Paul's dialogue with the Roman Jews. The closing scene is organized into three parts: Paul's first (vv. 17-22) and second (vv. 23-28) encounters with the Jews, and the final summary statement about Paul's ministry in Rome (vv. 30-31).

In the first encounter with the Roman Jews, Paul recounts the events of Acts 22–26. In so doing, Luke preserves what is most important for his readers to retain from that long stretch of narrative and speeches. Most important is Paul's claim that he *had done nothing against our people or the customs of our ancestors* (v. 17). Further, his appeal to Caesar did not mean that Paul intended to bring a charge against the Jewish nation (v. 19). To the contrary, Paul insists that *it is for the sake of the hope of Israel that I am bound with this chain* (v. 20). Throughout this speech, Paul maintains that he has remained a loyal Jew and that his mission to the gentiles is not based on an anti-Jewish foundation. The Jews respond by saying that they would like to hear more of Paul's thinking, especially regarding the Christian *sect* that is spoken against everywhere (v. 22).

In the second encounter with the Roman Jews, a familiar pattern emerges: Paul is first heard favorably by the Jews, is then resisted, and finally turns to the gentiles (see 13:42-48; 18:5-7; 19:8-10). Once again, his proclamation of Jesus divides his audience: *Some were convinced by what he had said, while others refused to believe* (v. 24). In his parting statement to them Paul quotes Isa 6:9-10, a harsh indictment of the dullness of ears, eyes, and heart of the Jewish people. Individual Jews may continue to believe, but Israel as a nation, at least at the time of Luke's writing, has rejected the new thing God has done in and through Christ Jesus. Now for the third and final time, Paul turns to the gentiles and thus opens up the *salvation of God* to all who would come (v. 28; cf. 13:46; 18:6).

The Book of Acts ends with the notice that Paul spent the next two years living under house arrest at his own expense (v. 30). Mention of *two years* in Acts often refers to periods of special blessing (see 18:11; 19:10; see Talbert 1984, 104; although cf. 24:27). The last claim of the book is that Paul preached the kingdom of God (cf. 1:6) *without hindrance* (v. 31), or "unhindered." The focus subtly shifts from Paul the messenger to the message he is proclaiming, the Christian gospel.

Frank Stagg has persuasively demonstrated that this final word—unhindered—sums up the message of Acts: the Gospel has overcome all human-made prejudice and every geographical, social, ethnic, gender, and theological barrier (Stagg 1955). In this regard, Pervo's words are apropos: "Luke's own last word is a perfect summary of his writings, a one-word closure, i.e., at the same time, an opening, a bright and invigorating

bid to the future, an assurance that 'the ends of the earth' is not the arrival at a boundary, but realization of the limitless promises of the dominion of God" (Pervo 1990, 96).

The gospel is unhindered because of the sovereignty of God who ultimately insures its triumph in the face of adversity. But from Luke's perspective, this "unhindered" gospel remains an "unfinished" gospel. The gospel is unfinished because of the grace of God who ultimately insures that its completion can occur when all have had the opportunity to hear about the "kingdom of God" and the "Lord Jesus Christ." Unfettered yet unfinished, the gospel can only be completed when the readers finally take up the challenge to fulfill the prophecy uttered at the beginning of the first of Luke's two volumes proclaimed by John the Baptist (who also quotes the words of the prophet Isaiah): "all flesh shall see the salvation of God" (Luke 3:6).

Works Cited

Danker, Frederick. 1982. *Benefactor: Epigraphic Study of a Graeco-Roman and N.T. Semantic Field.*

Fitzmyer, Joseph A. 1981. *The Gospel according to Luke I–IX.* AncB.

Funk, Robert. 1988. *The Poetics of Biblical Narrative.*

Garrett, Susan R. 1989. *The Demise of the Devil: Magic and the Demonic in Luke's Writings.*

Gill, David. 1974. "The Structure of Acts 9," *Bib* 55:546–48.

Haenchen, Ernst. 1971. *The Acts of the Apostles.*

Krodel, Gerhard. 1986. *Acts.* AugCNT.

Johnson, Luke T. 1977. *The Literary Function of Possessions in Luke-Acts.* SBLDS 39.

Martin, Clarice J. 1989. "A Chamberlain's Journey and the Challenge of Interpretation for Liberation," *Semeia* 47: 105–35.

Neyrey, Jerome H. 1991. "The Symbolic Universe of Luke-Acts: 'They Turned the World Upside Down'," in *The Social World of Luke-Acts: Models for Interpretation,* ed. Neyrey, 271–304.

Pervo, Richard I. 1990. *Luke's Story of Paul.*

Pilch, John J. 1991. "Sickness and Healing in Luke-Acts," in *The Social World of Luke-Acts,* 181-209.

Polhill, John B. 1992. *Acts.* NAC.

Stagg, Frank. 1955. *The Book of Acts.* 1990. "Apostles, Acts of the," MDB.

Talbert, Charles H. 1984. *Acts.* Knox Preaching Guides. 1990. "Luke, Gospel of," MDB.

Tannehill, Robert C. 1990. *The Narrative Unity of Luke-Acts.* Vol. 2. *The Acts of the Apostles.*

Romans

Dan O. Via

Introduction

Across the centuries the Christian church has found Paul's letter to the Romans to be one of its richest theological resources.

Genuineness, Unity, and Place in the Canon

Genuineness and unity. Scholars have generally concluded that PAUL was in fact the author of the whole original letter as established on the basis of the best manuscripts. Although the argument is inevitably somewhat circular, Romans is held to be in broad agreement with the other letters considered to be genuine writings of Paul in style, vocabulary, and thought. We shall see below that in light of the textual (i.e., manuscript) evidence there has been debate about whether the original letter was composed of chaps. 1–14, 1–15, or 1–16.

One should note that there have been some exceptions to the general consensus that Paul is the author of the whole original letter and that the letter is a coherent unity. Three examples will be mentioned. Rudolf Bultmann argued that Romans contains several later glosses (2:1; 2:16; 6:17b; 7:25b; 8:1; 10:17; 13:5) (Bultmann 1967). Walter Schmithals maintained that our Romans is composed of two earlier letters of Paul plus some fragments. According to Schmithals, letter A contained Rom 1:1–4:25; 5:12–11:36; 15:8-13, and letter B consisted of 12:1-21; 13:8-10; 14:1–15:4a, 7, 5-6; 15:14-32; 16:21-23; 15:33 (Schmithals 1975, 180, 189). Gloss and partition theories are not supported by ms. evidence.

Perhaps the most radical challenge to the genuineness and unity of Romans came from J. C. O'Neill, who argued that not only had short marginal comments of others been taken into the text but also editors had supplemented the text with substantial interpolations. Among the extensive sections that O'Neill denied to Paul are 1:18-32; 2:1-16; 2:17-29; 5:12-21; 7:14-25;

9:1-29; 10:16–11:36; 12:1–15:13 (O'Neill 1975, 14, 41–42, 49, 53, 96, 131–32, 155, 177, 192). O'Neill strained hard to explain why the manuscript evidence does not support his position (O'Neill 1975, 14–15) and generally based his argument on three questionable presuppositions: (1) that Paul always argued in a single-mindedly logical line and that, therefore, any inconsistencies have to be attributed to someone else; (2) that an author (Paul) is more likely to be consistent than a commentator; and (3) that Paul always used terms in the same sense.

Canonical Location. The individual title "To the Romans" suggests that Paul's letters became widely known as parts of a collection with a comprehensive title something like "The Letters of Paul." The most plausible explanation for this collection is that Paul's associates began a continuing "Pauline school" that sought to preserve and extend his influence. The first clear evidence for the existence of the Pauline collection, however, is provided by the second-century semignostic MARCION, whose arrangement places Romans after Galatians and 1 and 2 Corinthians (Knox 1982, 356–57; Gamble 1985, 41).

While Marcion gives us the first definite evidence, it seems probable that the collection originated earlier, in the late first or early second century. Had Marcion's collection been the first one, there would likely have been "orthodox" suspicion of Paul. But there is no indication of second-century hostility to Paul except from heterodox Jewish Christianity. Moreover, the reference of IGNATIUS (early second century) to "Paul in every letter" suggests that he knew a Pauline collection. The order of letters in this early collection was based on the length of the letters, but there seem to have been two editions of the collection based on the fact that length was assessed in different ways. In both cases the order ran from longest to shortest. The first approach regarded all letters to a given community as one unit and produced the order 1–2 Corinthians, Romans, Ephesians, 1–2 Thessalonians, Galatians, Philippians, Colossians (Philemon?). The second approach considered each individual letter as a separate unit and produced the order Romans, 1 Corinthians, 2 Corinthians, Ephesians, Galatians, Philippians, Colossians, 1 Thessalonians, 2 Thessalonians, (Philemon?) (Gamble 1985, 40–45; Knox 1982, 356–57).

Place of Writing and Date

Place. As Paul draws to the conclusion of the letter, he tells his readers that he has evangelized the Mediterranean world from JERUSALEM to ILLYRICUM (roughly the former modern Yugoslavia and Albania) and therefore has no more place to work in the East (15:19, 23). He hopes to extend the preaching of the gospel to Spain and to visit Rome on his way there (15:23-24, 28), but first he must go to Jerusalem to carry the money that he has collected in MACEDONIA and ACHAIA for the poor among the Jerusalem Christians (15:25-26).

Where is he as he writes? CORINTH is the most likely place. In the CORINTHIAN CORRESPONDENCE Paul is also concerned about the offering to be sent from the gentile churches of Achaia and GALATIA to Jerusalem, and he contemplates that he may make the trip to Jerusalem himself (1 Cor 16:1-4; 2 Cor 8:1-14; 9:1-5). In addition, PHOEBE, whom he recommends and who may be the bearer of the letter, is a deacon in the church of CENCHREAE, the port of Corinth (16:1-2). Beyond that GAIUS, his host (16:23), may well be the Gaius of 1 Cor 1:14, one of Paul's Corinthian converts. And ERASTUS (16:23) also could be loosely associated with Corinth (Acts 19:21-22; 2 Tim 4:20).

Date. Paul was apparently in Corinth three times, and Romans would have been written during the third of these sojourns. That means the writing occurred late in his life. The three-missionary-journey scheme in Acts would call for dating the letter late in the third journey (Acts 20:1-3). While the Acts format may contain individual items that are historically accurate, the scheme as a whole, and especially its stress on Paul's dependence on Jerusalem, is historically suspect. Nevertheless, Paul's letters confirm that he was a travelling missionary and suggest that he wrote Romans late in his career.

The one certainly datable event during Paul's missionary activities is the proconsulship of the Roman GALLIO in Corinth, whose tenure in office lasted from the spring of 51 to the spring of 52. During his first stay in Corinth Paul was haled before Gallio, according to Acts 18:12-17, by hostile Jews. It is plausible to suppose that the third visit to Corinth, the occasion for writing Romans, was sometime around 55 or 56.

Manuscript Evidence and Destination

Paul did not found the church in Rome and had not visited it prior to the writing of the letter. Why did he write this letter to Rome? Did he in fact write it *to* Rome? It seems altogether probable that the original letter was addressed by Paul directly to the Roman church, but that contention has not gone unchallenged.

One reason for challenging an original Roman destination is that the words "in Rome" are omitted in 1:7, 15 in a few manuscripts of a Western textual type. If this omission were the original reading, then it might be argued that Paul wrote the letter as a circular one, not intended for any one particular church. But the evidence is strongly in favor of including "in Rome" in the text. The great preponderance of manuscript evidence supports it. Romans 1:13 shows that the letter is written to a particular church that he has wanted to visit but has thus far been prevented from visiting. It can also be demonstrated that Romans as a whole can be rather specifically connected with a particular situation in the church at Rome.

The major textual problem in Romans is that the final doxology (16:25-27) appears in several different places in the manuscript tradition. The doxology itself is probably post-Pauline (see commentary), but it must have been composed quite early, and its placement bears on the question of the various versions of Romans that circulated in the early church. The complex manuscript tradition supports the following six configurations:

(1) 1:1–16:23 + doxology
(2) 1:1–14:23 + doxology + 15:1–16:23 + doxology
(3) 1:1–14:23 + doxology + 15:1–16:24
(4) 1:1–16:24
(5) 1:1–15:33 + doxology + 16:1-23
(6) 1:1–14:23 + 16:24 + doxology

(Metzger 1975, 534)

The evidence suggests that at an early date three versions of Romans were in circulation: Rom 1–14, Rom 1–15, and Rom 1–16. Each will be briefly assessed.

Romans 1–14 is probably not the original. The manuscript evidence is weaker than it is for the other alternatives, and the thought of 15:1-13 shows no break with that of chap. 14. A tradition going back to

ORIGEN says that Marcion cut off chaps. 15–16, and we can understand why he might have. He would have wanted to remove the personal material in 15:14-33 and chap. 16. And his antipathy for the OT would have prompted him to excise 15:1-13 as he did chaps. 4 and 9–11 (Manson 1991, 9–11).

A somewhat stronger case can be made for Rom 1–15 as the original. Only one manuscript supports it (the PAPYRUS P[46] which shows the concluding doxology after 15:33), but it is the oldest Greek manuscript of Paul (ca. 200) and represents the early Alexandrian text, generally considered the best. Moreover, Rom 16 with its many greetings to named individuals and its biting criticism of false teachings in 16:17-20a seems very different in content from chap. 15. The preceding factors have generated some arguments that Rom 16 was a separate letter of Paul and that it was sent to EPHESUS, not Rome. (1) Paul knows more people than he would have known in Rome, but he would have had many friends in Ephesus where he had a long ministry. (2) Some of the people greeted in Rom 16 are explicitly connected with ASIA, the province surrounding Ephesus: Prisca and Aquila (Acts 18:24-26; Rom 16:3), Epaenetus (Rom 16:5). (3) Paul knows some of these people too well for them to belong to a church he has never visited. For example, he knows who have house churches meeting in their homes (16:5, 15) and knows the identity of household groups (16:10, 11). (4) Rom 16:17-20 is inappropriately sharp for the Roman situation but could have been directed to a church like Ephesus where Paul had long worked. (5) Rom 15:33 has the solemn tone of a conclusion (Kümmel 1965, 222–26; Knox 1982, 364–68; Manson 1991, 12–13).

Similar arguments can be used to support the view that Paul wrote all of Rom 1–16 to Ephesus and 1–15 to Rome (Manson 1991, 11–13).

On the other side arguments have been brought forward against a connection between Rom 16 (or 1–16) and Ephesus and against the independence of chap. 16. (1) While there are other examples of letters composed primarily of greetings, there seems to be no other case in the Pauline corpus of combining letters to more than one church. (2) Inscriptions support the currency of the names Urbanus, Phlegon, Persis, and Asyncritus in Rome in the first century but not in Ephesus. (3) Paul seems not to have singled out individuals for greetings in churches that he did found. (4) Rom 15:33 is not a characteristic Pauline conclusion. Typically the peace wish (Rom 15:33) preceded (Gal 6:16; 1 Thes 5:23)

the concluding benediction, which always makes reference to grace, an element lacking in Rom 15:33 (Lampe 1991, 216–17; Gamble 1977, 53–54, 84, 90; Ziesler 1989, 21). It should be pointed out, however, that this is not a strong argument because it could be held that an original fifteen-chapter version of Romans contained a grace benediction following 15:33.

John Knox maintained that the arguments for Ephesus and Rome cancelled each other out and that neither should be regarded as the destination of Rom 16. Rather that chapter was written after Paul's time by someone in the Roman church in order to claim Paul's authority in the fight against false teaching (Knox 1954, 364–68). Knox's position has a good bit to commend it. However, the strongest manuscript evidence places the final doxology at the end of chap. 16. Moreover, in recent years additional arguments have been articulated in favor of connecting Rom 16 with the situation of the Roman church and of regarding that chapter as an integral part of Paul's original letter to the Romans. That is now the consensus position (Donfried 1991a, lxx).

These arguments in support of it may here be considered: (1) Paul might well have known many people in the Roman church because Jewish Christians expelled from Rome by the edict of CLAUDIUS (see next section), whom Paul met in Ephesus (and elsewhere), could have returned to Rome after Claudius' death. (2) Movement was easy in the ROMAN EMPIRE. (3) Paul need not actually have known all whom he greeted. (4) Rom 16:1-2 does resemble a letter of recommendation, but there are other examples of notes of recommendation within the conclusions of longer letters. (5) Other letters of Paul display the same concluding structure: (a) travel plans (1 Cor 16:5-9; Rom 15:22-29); (b) recommendation of a third party (1 Cor 16:10-11, 15-18; Rom 16:1-2); (c) final greeting (1 Cor 16:19-21; Rom 16:3-16) (Gamble 1977, 47–51, 85, 87, 89; Donfried 1991b, 48–49). (6) As for 16:17-20 the sterner tone may suggest that Paul realizes there are other issues in Rome than the ones he had addressed or he may have outside infiltrators in mind. Changes of tone within Paul's letters are not unusual (1 Cor 16:22; Phil 3:2, 18-19; 1 Thes 2:15-16), and in any case his addressing the readers here as "brothers" shows that his posture is not strongly polemical (Ziesler 1989, 23; Lampe 1991, 219; Wedderburn 1991, 15; Gamble 1977, 52).

Paul's purpose for the multiple greetings is to support the individuals who are named but even more to undergird his own credibility by associating himself with these people whom the Roman church knows and trusts. This would be important to do in a church that he did not establish (Lampe 1991, 219; Gamble 1977, 48, 92).

We have seen that it is quite plausible to suppose that Paul knew a number of people in the Roman church and that he knew at least some of them well and was in close touch with them. That would be because mobility was high in the Roman Empire and mail communication was quick and easy—seven or eight days between Corinth and Rome. Paul then could have had a good deal of specific knowledge about the situation of the church at Rome.

Occasion and Purpose

A good case then can be made for connecting Romans closely to a specific situation in the Roman church. But Paul's own situation and the one that he addresses in Rome both have many aspects, and the purposes that motivate his writing of the letter are more than one.

In assessing the occasion and purpose we have to take account not only of the situation in Rome but also of Paul's own situation and experiences. How do his successes, hardships, and conflicts in Galatia, Corinth, Ephesus, and elsewhere and his sense of having completed the evangelization of the East affect his posture? What impact do his intentions to visit not just Rome but also Jerusalem and Spain have on the content of the letter? And we must consider the character of the letter itself. While it is not at all a full, constructive statement of Paul's theology, it is relatively systematic and tightly argued. Whether or not it was Paul's intention to write such a letter, that nevertheless defines its nature. And while a convincing case can be made that the letter addresses a particular situation in Rome, it is by no means immediately obvious in what precise ways that situation is reflected in the letter.

Sometimes those who argue for a close relationship to a precise historical setting speak as if the only two alternatives are that the letter either is totally conditioned historically or is a timeless theological compendium unrelated to a specific setting. But that is not an adequate grasp of our interpretive task. The letter *is* historically conditioned. Thus the two real alternatives become is its meaning exhausted by its historical connectedness or does the meaning both reflect and transcend the setting? The more probable alternative is that the historical situation affects the meaning but does not account for everything in it.

Because the historical and theological context is complicated and the precise relationship of the letter to the Roman situation is not obvious, many have found the governing key to the meaning and purpose of Romans in some other factor: (1) it is a general theological treatise; (2) it reflects *Paul's* situation; (3) it has the imminent trip to Jerusalem primarily in view; (4) it is controlled by the hope of a mission to Spain. No one of these alone is an adequate explanation for the letter, but each must be considered for what it contributes to our understanding of it.

(1) According to Anders Nygren, Paul in Romans is dealing with a great theological issue on which hangs human life itself. It would be a misunderstanding of Romans and a constriction of its meaning to try to interpret it in the light of the accidental circumstances of the Roman setting, of which Paul had very little knowledge anyway (Nygren 1949, 4–8). Günther Bornkamm in a famous article held that while Paul had only a general knowledge of the Roman church, the letter grew out of the specifics of *Paul's* situation and is not a timeless theological treatise. However, Bornkamm ended up asserting that Romans lifts Paul's theology above the moment of definite situations and conflicts and into the sphere of the eternally and universally valid (Bornkamm 1991, 20, 21, 28). This unexpected turn in Bornkamm's argument shows how hard it is to confine the meaning of Romans within any specific historical situation.

(2) That Romans is to be explained not in light of the Roman situation but in light of Paul's own was also argued by T. W. Manson. Paul sums up the position that he had reached as a result of his controversies in Galatia and Corinth over the relationship of law to gospel (Manson 1991, 14–15). Robert Karris sees Romans as dealing with theological and ethical issues in the light of solutions to problems Paul had reached in his earlier missionary work, and Karris questions why we should assume that all of Paul's letters must have been addressed to specific church situations (Karris 1991a, 82–123; 1991b, 127).

(3) Peter Lampe maintained that the purpose of the whole letter was to gain the confidence of the Romans so that they would support Paul's mission to Spain (Lampe 1991, 218). Paul does want their support (15:24, 28)—spiritual, material, or both. This reference, however, is too brief and casual and Paul's concern to clarify his understanding of the gospel for its own sake is too strong for the Spanish mission to be a major part of Paul's purpose (Klein 1991, 33).

(4) The collection that he was about to carry to Jerusalem was important to Paul because it grew out of his agreement with the Jerusalem leaders (Gal 2:10) and symbolized the oneness of Jewish and gentile believers. Jacob Jervell argues that the prominence of Jewish issues in Romans—the status of the law (7:7), whether Israel has an advantage (3:1), the ultimate fate of Israel (11:1, 11-12) and others—shows that the content of Rom 1:18–11:36 is the defense Paul expects to make in *Jerusalem*. He presents it to the Romans because he wants them on his side when he goes to Jerusalem (Jervell 1991, 56, 62–64).

It is certainly the case that Paul wants the Roman church to pray for his Jerusalem mission, to pray that the unbelieving Jews will not harm him and that Jewish Christians in Jerusalem will be willing to accept his offering (15:30-31). Paul is intently looking over his shoulder at Jerusalem as he writes to Rome, and that undoubtedly affects the content of the letter, but the prominence of Jewish issues is also explained by his own origin in Judaism and by the gentile-Jewish conflict in the Roman church. And that brings us to Rome.

The intended visit. Although Paul's past longing to visit Rome has been thwarted (in chap. 1 he does not say why), he now intends to come for the purpose of exercising his apostleship by preaching the gospel and gaining a harvest of obedient faith (1:5-7, 13, 15). The Romans fall within his obligation to preach to all categories of people (1:13-15). He modestly—or prudently—suggests also that he expects to receive a spiritual blessing from them (1:11-12).

How does this eagerness to preach in Rome square with Paul's statement in 15:20 that it has been his intention to preach where Christ has not already been named? This principle of action he now offers as the explanation for why he has not been able to come to Rome (15:22). He was preaching where the gospel had not been heard. But since Christ has been named in Rome and the church has been established independently of Paul, how can he now come to preach in Rome since he does not want to build on another's foundation (15:20)?

Most scholars have taken his statement in 15:20 to be a fixed policy. And if that is the case, there seems to be a conflict between that policy and his present hope to preach in Rome. Can the conflict be resolved?

According to Günter Klein, Paul's non-interference policy does not renounce all missionary activity in already Christianized areas. He will not build on another's foundation, but if there is a church that in Paul's view lacks an apostolic foundation, he is free to preach there. What is at stake is whether the church in Rome has actually been founded on Christ (see 1 Cor 3:10-11). Paul will preach in Rome because the Roman church lacks the fundamental kerygma (proclamation) and grounding in Christ (Klein 1991, 38–43).

This is an attractive theory that could explain much in Romans. But if Paul's posture in principle were that he could preach wherever a church was not founded on the apostolic preaching of Christ, and if Rome were such a church, he could have gone to Rome at any time. He need not have waited until he had evangelized the East (15:19-22).

Peter Stuhlmacher deals with the issue by connecting Paul's eagerness to preach in Rome (1:15) with his *past* desire in 1:13: he *had* intended to come and preach, but having been prevented, that is no longer his hope, and he will be satisfied with the mutual sharing of faith described in 1:11-12. That is not in conflict with the noninterference policy (Stuhlmacher 1991, 236–37).

But Paul's concrete elaboration of his strong sense of obligation to preach to all and the use of the present tense in 1:14 make it difficult to relegate his eagerness to preach in Rome in 1:15 to the past.

Karl Donfried has suggested the most convincing approach (Donfried 1991c, 45). Paul is not stating an unexceptional policy in 15:20 but simply explaining why he has not been able to come to Rome. It has been his first responsibility to preach to those who have not heard the gospel. But now that he has completely evangelized the East—according to his understanding of his calling—and has no further place to work there, he is free to come to Rome where the gospel has already been heard. The purpose of Paul's visit will be to preach in Rome.

The visit and the letter. For the Hellenistic world generally and for Paul in particular a letter is understood as a substitute or surrogate for the presence of the sender and also the recipient. Paul states at one point that what he says by letter when absent, he does when present (2 Cor 10:11). In a somewhat formal and indirect way a letter represents what happens in face-to-face human meetings: greeting-dialogue-farewell (Funk 1967; Petersen 1985, 53–55). The purpose of the letter then is the same as the purpose of the visit: to preach the gospel—in light of the Roman situation, his own situation, the intended missions to Jerusalem and Spain, and in light of the capacity of the gospel to generate a certain logic or structure of thought irrespective of a particular situation.

The specific setting in the Roman church. This now needs further attention. The following scenario has been gaining increasing acceptance as the situation in the Roman church that Paul was addressing.

The Roman writer Suetonius (ca. 75–160) reports that the emperor CLAUDIUS expelled the Jews from Rome (in 49) because of rioting instigated by Chrestus. Chrestus is probably a corruption of Christus, and Suetonius may have thought that Christ was there in Rome at the time. These disturbances in the Jewish community probably refer to the conflict between law-abiding Jews and Jews who had come to believe in Jesus as the Messiah and had freed themselves from the Law of Moses. Among the Jews forced to leave the city would have been a number of Jewish Christians. There is no evidence that Claudius's edict of expulsion was ever rescinded, but it was probably allowed to lapse after his death in 54, and that would have made it possible for Jews who had left Rome to return. We can imagine that many Jewish Christians availed themselves of the opportunity. Jewish Christians were then returning to a Christian community that had for several years been entirely—or almost so—in the hands of gentile Christians. Differences would have been present, and tensions would have developed. Paul's purpose is to interpret the gospel so as to present the theological basis upon which these groups with different experiences and theological positions can live with mutual acceptance and love as one body in Christ (12:3-8; 14:1; 15:7-10). How are the gentile majority and Jewish minority to relate to each other (e.g., Donfried 1991c, 48–49; Wiefel 1991, 92–96; Ziesler 1989, 11–12; Dunn 1988, xlviii–xlix, liii; Wedderburn 1991, 55–56)?

The composition of the Roman Christian community needs to be further examined. The Jewish quarrels that Claudius addressed show that Christianity was in Rome by the 40s. We do not know who the first missionaries were, but the fourth-century writer "Ambrosiaster" suggests that they were Jewish Christians faithful to the Law of Moses, and that may well be correct. It could be that the absence of a central governing council for Roman Jews made it easier than it might have been for Christian missionaries to win converts from individual synagogues (Wiefel 1991, 108). By the time of Paul's letter, we may suppose that there were at least five groups in the Roman Christian community, representing at least three different theological positions: (1) Jewish Christians who were faithful to the Law of Moses; (2) Jewish Christians who were law-free; (3) gentile Christians who were law-abiding because of deep attachment to the synagogue prior to their conversion to Christianity; (4) gentile Christians who were law-free; (5) gentile Christians who stretched Paul's belief that salvation is by grace and not by works of the law to mean that the Christian stands under no moral obligation. Paul appears to assume that the Roman church was composed primarily of gentiles (1:5-6, 13-15; 9:3-4; 10:1-3; 11:13, 17-18, 24, 28, 30-31; 15:15-16, 18). But that it also contained Jewish members is seen in 15:7-12; 16:3, 7, 11. It would seem probable that the various house churches were marked and divided by these differing theological and ethnic characteristics.

We may also observe other social differences. Chapter 16 suggests that women had important places of leadership. If the Roman Christian community reflected the general population, it would have contained about two-thirds slaves and freedpersons and one-third free. Probably a majority of the members would have been from the lower socio-economic strata and a small minority from the upper classes (Lampe 1991, 222–30).

The letter is pervaded by Paul's concern about Jewish-gentile relationships (1:16; 2:12-16, 25-29; 8:33; 9:1–11:32; 15:8-12). His defense of the law and affirmation of God's faithfulness to Israel (3:1-8; 3:31; 7:7a, 10a, 12, 14a, 16; 11:1-2, 11, 23, 28-29) bespeak his own conviction about the continuity of the Christian community with Israel (4:11-12; 11:17-18). And he hereby supports the commitments of law-abiding Jewish Christians and gentile Christians who had firm attachments to JUDAISM as well as opposes the antinomian position (that faith has no moral requirements) of some. At the same time his proclamation of the gospel and his critique of the law (3:19-30; 4:1-5; 6:14; 7:1-6, 7b-9; 9:30–10:4) expound his own conviction about salvation by GRACE, not works of the LAW, and support the position of law-free gentile and Jewish Christians as well as confront his law-affirming Jewish Christian opponents.

The discussion up to this point may be summarized in the following way. Paul purposes to offer the Romans a universally valid gospel that is the power of God for the salvation of all humankind and in fact of the whole cosmos. This gospel, which has been worked out through his own experiences, is addressed to Rome for the sake of the gospel's own truth and for the well-being of the Romans. That is, Paul hopes to win converts to the Christian faith (1:5-6, 14-15) and to strengthen the faith of believers (15:14-15). And because of the all-encompassing capacity of the gospel, it can be the key for resolving the gentile-Jewish tension in the Roman church. At the same time Paul also wants to win the Romans' assent to his understanding of the gospel in the interest of gaining their support for his trip to Jerusalem and his Spanish mission.

Three additional topics that bear on the question of the letter's relationship to its historical situation call for brief discussion.

Historical setting and theological structure. Neither all of the elements in Romans nor the way they are related or structured can be accounted for—at least not exhaustively—by the historical situation. For example, it cannot be demonstrated, as is sometimes suggested (Campbell 1991, 252–53, 258–60), that the purpose of the gospel is the transformation of Jewish-gentile relationships.

It is clear from the syntactical indications of purpose in 3:25-26 that the *purpose* of the gospel is the demonstration of God's righteousness and the justification of believers. The new equality of Jews and gentiles (3:28-30) is the result of carrying out this purpose. It will also be argued in the commentary that justification and faith (3:21–4:25) have a structural relationship to life and freedom (5:1–8:36) that grows out of the inner logic of Paul's gospel and not out of the Roman situation.

Historical setting and letter type. The evidence of a certain sub-type of the letter genre in the first century augments the probability that Romans does both respond to a specific historical situation and also transcend that situation. A letter belonging to the subgenre known as the letter-essay is addressed to a real situation and has the framework of a regular letter (greeting and closing), but what is framed inside is more nearly a treatise than a personal message. This type of letter has an instructional purpose that reaches beyond the immediate addressees (Stirewalt 1991, 147–48; Donfried 1991d, 121–25; Dunn, lix).

Paul apparently felt free to mix genres, and evidence of this is seen in the fact that what is framed inside the greeting and closing of Romans displays certain characteristics of the *logos protreptikos* or "speech of exhortation." This type had the purpose of winning the hearers to a particular way of life or thought and had the following parts: (1) a critique of other ways of life or thought (Rom 1:18–3:20); (2) a positive presentation of the true way (Rom 3:21–15:13); (3) a personal appeal (15:14-33) (Aune 1991, 278–82, 295–96).

Historical setting and diatribe style. Karl Donfried has acknowledged that the claim that Romans was addressed to a specific situation would be undermined if it could be shown that the diatribe exercised a pervasive influence on the letter. However, Donfried has argued that the diatribe was not a definite genre but rather a series of rhetorical devices, that it did not seriously influence Romans, and that it does not in fact bring into question the historical specificity of the letter to the Romans (Donfried 1991d, 112–19; 1991b, lxx). We need to consider Stanley Stowers's work on the relationship of Romans to the diatribe.

The most distinctive feature of the diatribe is its dialogical nature. If the objections of the one who questions the speaker/writer in the dialogue grow out of a misunderstanding of the *subject matter*, then these objections do not need to be explained by the *situation* of the letter. The objector is a literary, not a historical, figure (Stowers 1981, 2). Is that the case for Romans?

With regard to the social setting an older scholarship held that the diatribe was a type of popular moral or philosophical propaganda directed to the masses by wandering preachers with the intention of converting the former. Stowers' own view is that the setting from which the diatribe emerged is the philosophical school (Stowers 1981, 18, 35, 44–48, 75–76).

The diatribe was not a fixed form or technical genre but was a distinct style though subject to variation. It was first of all the record of a school lecture or discussion and not a literary tractate (Stowers 1981, 29, 44, 47–48, 75).

The dialogue proceeded by address from the teacher, objections from the students, and response to the objections. When there were no real questions or objections, the teacher manufactured them. The mode of discussion was not polemical, for the teacher was not trying to damage the student/opponent or his credibility. He did want, however, to expose and indict his error and lead him to truth. The goal was not simply to impart knowledge but to transform the student. The concern of Paul's questioning objections throughout Romans is what is to become of the law if JUSTIFICATION is by faith and not works (Stowers 1981, 20, 40, 56, 76–77, 105–106, 117, 166).

What gives the diatribe its rhetorical effect is the interplay between two audiences: the real one and the one that provides the fictitious objectors (Stowers 1981, 106, 140). We might imagine that the real audience identifies sympathetically with the indictment of the fictitious one because it thinks it is not being indicted. Then when it discovers that it is, there is no escape.

In summary fashion we may note that the following diatribal features appear in Romans: (1) address to the imaginary questioner or interlocutor as distinguished from the real addressees (2:1-5, 17-24; 9:19-21; 11:17-24; 14:4, 10); (2) objections to or false conclusions drawn from the writer's position (3:1-9; 7:7, 13-14); (3) dialogical exchange between writer and questioner (3:27–4:2) (Stowers 1981, 79, 119, 128–29, 134, 155, 164).

In Stowers's view, these similarities show that Paul was dependent on the diatribe in Romans though he adaptively made it his own. The diatribe element in Romans is not an accident, not Paul's preaching style unconsciously coming through, but is rather central to his message and his self-presentation as a *teacher* (Stowers 1981, 176–79).

Stowers concludes that the objections and false conclusions that Paul cites in Romans do not reflect specific positions of the addressees of the letter. The dialogical interaction grows out of Paul's theological argument and represents what is typical for Paul. But the typical is addressed to a specific historical situation of whose pedagogical needs Paul has some knowledge (Stowers 1981, 180).

The issue of rhetoric having now been introduced, a somewhat more comprehensive look at the relationship of Romans to Greco-Roman rhetoric is in order.

Romans and Rhetoric

The term "rhetoric" refers both to the use of and critical reflection about persuasive language. It has been strongly recognized in recent years that rhetoric as spoken or written discourse is a matter of argumentation and persuasion and not of stylistic ornamentation. Style, of course, is a part of rhetoric, but for the best speakers and critics style should serve argument and not be gratuitous ornamentation. The speaker/writer hopes to modify a situation of exigence or urgency by using discourse to change human attitudes or action (Mack 1990, 14–15; Kennedy 1984, 25, 34–35; Wuellner 1991, 128; 1987, 449). When "rhetoric" is used to refer to reflection about discourse, it deals with the rules that a society agrees are acceptable for debate and argumentation (Mack 1990, 16, 19).

Rhetoric emerged in the Greek city-states during the sixth and fifth centuries B.C.E. By the first century B.C.E., it pervaded the Greco-Roman world, permeating both the system of education and public discourse (Mack 1990, 25, 28). Rhetoric would have been a part of the cultural air breathed by Paul and the Evangelists (Kennedy 1984, 9–10).

While Donfried considers the indispensability of rhetorical criticism on Romans an open question (Donfried 1991b, lxxi), Wuellner clearly believes it is the necessary wave of the future. Studies of the literary form of the letter can illuminate the letter frame but not the structure and nature of the body. Rhetorical criticism will allow us to grasp the structure of the argument found in the letter body as addressed to a particular situation. Rhetorical criticism will enable us also to comprehend the letter as a social act inseparable from other social relationships as well as to appreciate the role of rhetoric in appealing to our emotions and imaginations and not just to our rationality (Wuellner 1991, 129–32; 1987, 453, 461; Jewett 1991, 266).

Ancient rhetoricians identified three species, genres, or types of rhetoric on the basis of the kind of judgment the speaker is seeking. Each may take a positive or negative form. (1) In forensic or judicial rhetoric the speaker is trying to persuade the audience to make a judgment about past events. It may take the form of prosecution or defense. (2) In deliberative rhetoric the attempt is to move the audience to take some action in the future. It may take the form of exhortation or dissuasion. (3) In epideictic or demonstrative rhetoric the writer wants the audience to accept or reaffirm some value or point of view in the present. It may take the form of praise (encomium) or blame (invective) (Kennedy 1984, 19–20). This present-time perspective is a frequent but not necessary characteristic of epideictic (Beale 1978, 223).

It seems reasonably obvious that Romans belongs primarily to the epideictic genre. Paul wants to persuade the Romans to accept and/or reaffirm his understanding of the gospel and salvation right now in the present. Some would say that Romans is thoroughly epideictic (Wuellner 1987, 460) on the ground that the moral teaching in Romans (12:1–15:13) has to do with belief and attitude and not with action (Kennedy 1984, 154). It is true that Paul praises such attitudes or dispositions as humility (12:3), love (12:9), and self-consistency (14:5, 22-23). But his exhortations about paying taxes (13:1-7) and eating and drinking (14:15, 20-21) pertain to specific actions and refer to possible future behavior and so take certain parts of the letter over into the sphere of deliberative rhetoric.

It has recently been argued that the main defining feature of epideictic rhetoric is "rhetorical performative." Epideictic participates in or performs the action to which it refers, and brings the audience to participate in the community act that is the speech (Beale 1978, 225–26, 236). This accords well with Paul's claim in Romans that the gospel which he presents in the letter is the power of God.

For Further Study

In the *Mercer Dictionary of the Bible*: GRACE; JUSTIFICATION; PAUL; RIGHTEOUSNESS IN THE NT; ROMAN EMPIRE; ROMANS, LETTER TO THE; ROME; SALVATION IN THE NT; SIN.

In other sources: C. K. Barrett, *A Commentary on the Epistle to the Romans*; C. E. B. Cranfield, *A Critical and Exegetical Commentary on the Epistle to the Romans*, ICC; K. P. Donfried, ed., *The Romans Debate*; J. D. G. Dunn, *Romans 1–8* and *Romans 9–16*; H. Y. Gamble, *The Textual History of the Letter to the Romans*; E. Käsemann, *Commentary on Romans*; S. K. Stowers, *The Diatribe and Paul's Letter to the Romans*; A. J. M. Wedderburn, *The Reasons for Romans*.

Commentary

An Outline

I. Letter Opening, 1:1-15
  A. Paul's Greetings to the Saints in Rome, 1:1-7
  B. Paul's Thanksgiving
    for the Roman Community, 1:8-15
II. Theme: The Gospel of Righteousness
    as Power, 1:16-17
III. The Revelation of God's Righteousness, 1:18–4:25
  A. Righteousness as Wrath, 1:18–3:20
  B. Righteousness as Justification by Faith, 3:21–4:25
IV. Life as Liberation from Victimizing Powers, 5:1–8:39
  A. Transition from Justification
    to Peace and Life, 5:1-11
  B. Freedom from Adam, 5:12-21
  C. Freedom from Sin, 6:1-23
  D. Freedom from the Law, 7:1-25
  E. Freedom from Death and Flesh, 8:1-39
V. God's Word and the Destiny of Israel, 9:1–11:36
  A. God's Rejection of Israel, 9:1-29
  B. Israel's Rejection of Righteousness
    through Faith, 9:30–10:21
  C. The Final Salvation of all Israel, 11:1-36
VI. God's Mercy (Righteousness)
    and the Behavior of Believers, 12:1–15:13
  A. Ethical Renewal as the Appropriation
    of Mercy, 12:1-2
  B. Love in One Body in Christ, 12:3-21
  C. The State and Taxes, 13:1-7
  D. Love as the Fulfillment of the Law, 13:8-10
  E. The Pressure of the Imminent End, 13:11-14
  F. Eating and Drinking among the Weak
    and the Strong, 14:1–15:13
VII. Concluding Personal Statement, 15:14-32
  A. Paul's Feelings about the Roman Church
    and his Self-evaluation, 15:14-21
  B. Travel Plans, 15:22-29
  C. Emotional Appeal for Their Prayers, 15:30-32

VIII. Closing, 15:33–16:27
  A. Peace Wish, 15:33
  B. Commendation of Phoebe, 16:1-2
  C. Greetings, 16:3-23
    (Interrupted by Exhortation, 16:17-20a)
  D. Grace Benediction, 16:20b or 16:24 or both
  E. Doxology, 16:25-27

In the Greco-Roman period there was no sharp distinction between a private, personal letter and a public, literary one (epistle). The most ordinary personal letters were shaped by stylized letter-writing conventions. Paul's letters were personal in that they were written to real household churches, but they were meant to be read publicly in the whole assembly and perhaps circulated in other cities (Stowers 1989, 18–19).

The structure and content of Romans conforms broadly to the shape of the Greco-Roman letter form: greeting, prayer or thanksgiving, body, and closing. The outline above includes both greeting and thanksgiving in the opening. Items II–VII form a connected argument and should all be regarded as parts of the body. Especially should the ethical part not be excluded from the body since it has both a logical and syntactical ("therefore") relationship to the preceding theological parts—which themselves contain ethical implications. The personal statements in 15:14-32 close the body of the letter while 15:33–16:27 is the closing for the letter as a whole.

For the conventional term "greetings" (*chairein*) in the Greco-Roman letter Paul has substituted his theological term "grace" (*charis*, 1:7). Paul also preserves a characteristic of the semitic letter when he adds a peace wish to the greeting: grace to you and peace (1:7). Instead of the conventional "farewell" at the end Paul uses a benediction such as *The grace of our Lord Jesus Christ be with you* (16:20b) (Stowers 1989, 21–22).

The Greco-Roman letter genre was constituted by adding an initial greeting and final closing, as a frame, to the form of a proper speech as defined by the rhetoricians (Kennedy 1984, 141). The structured argument of Romans, then, can be illuminated by displaying its relationship to the speech form. This form had the following parts although speeches would not necessarily have all the parts.

(1) The *proem* or *exordium* (introduction) seeks to obtain the attention and good will of the audience.

(2) The *narration* provides the facts or background information.

(3) The *proposition* or *thesis* states the major contention to be proved and is followed immediately by a justifying reason. The thesis is the transition from exordium and/or narration to the proof.

(4) The *proof* or *confirmation* contains the arguments to support the thesis. Arguments could be creatively invented or could be "non-technical" proofs drawn from the traditional stock of laws, contracts, scripture, witnesses, and the like. The distinction between invented and non-technical proofs seems not to have been a firm one. The kinds of material available were classified as historical examples, analogies, and fables.

(5) The *refutation* neutralizes opposing views.

(6) The *epilogue* or *peroration* summarizes the argument and seeks to arouse the emotions of the audience to take action or make a commitment (Kennedy 1984, 23–24; Jewett 1991, 272–74; Mack 1990, 32–40; Wuellner 1991, 133–46).

Because the theological argument of Romans is complex and because the letter's theological intention is the chief item of debate within contemporary Romans scholarship (Donfried 1991a, lxxii), it seems well to begin the commentary proper by presenting a tentative "rhetorical-theological" overview of the letter as a whole.

The greeting (1:1-7) has already taken on a rhetorical function since it contains brief narration about both Paul himself and the SON OF GOD who is the content of the gospel. The rhetorical exordium corresponds to the letter thanksgiving in which Paul seeks the good will of the Romans by thanking God for their faith which

is proclaimed worldwide and by expressing his strong desire to see them. This also continues the narration about Paul.

Paul's thesis (1:16-17), which is the letter theme, is that the gospel is the power of God unto salvation for all who believe. This claim is grounded on the justifying reason that in the gospel the righteousness of God is revealed. The commentary will show that the thesis truly is a transition closely connected syntactically to both exordium-narration and proof.

The rhetorical proof (1:18–15:13) corresponds to the letter body except for the body's concluding personal statement (15:14-32). Several fundamental proofs are offered for the power of God's righteousness.

(1) It is demonstrated in God's wrath that delivers rebellious human beings to the ruinous consequences of their own actions (1:18–3:20).

(2) It is seen in God's providing justification equally for Jews and gentiles (3:21–4:25). This section displays Paul's use of Abraham as a historical example.

(3) God's power is manifested in God's liberating deliverance from the victimizing power of Adam (5:12-21), sin (6:1-23), the law (7:1-25), and flesh and death (8:1-39). Justification opens up freedom as a new quality of life, a relationship to be examined in the commentary.

(4) God's righteousness will finally be able to save all Israel despite the rebellion of the latter (9:1–11:36). In this section we find Paul using analogies with the potter and his clay (9:19-24) and with the olive tree (11:17-24) in order to clarify the human situation (Jewett 1991, 272–74).

(5) The ethical section is also a proof because it is God's power that enables ethical renewal (12:1–15:13).

Paul has taken the refutation of opposing views up into his proof by his employment of the diatribe style. At certain points he mentions objections to or false conclusions drawn from his positions and then refutes these mistakes (3:1-9; 3:31; 4:1-2a; 6:1-3, 15-16; 7:7, 13-14; 9:14-15, 19-20; 11:1-3, 11; 11:19-20) (Stowers 1981, 119–22).

The rhetorical peroration corresponds to the personal conclusion of the letter body (15:14-32). Here Paul compliments the Romans for their spiritual achievements yet affirms his right to instruct them. This moves into a favorable evaluation of his own ministry, which in turn melds into a brief narration (recall the exordium) of the scope of his past mission. Then he "narrates" the future as his hope to visit the Romans on his way to Spain and his present need to go to

Jerusalem first. Finally he makes an emotional appeal for their prayers.

The letter closing (15:33–16:27) continues the rhetorical function of the peroration—to cement personal connections.

Letter Opening, 1:1-15

Paul's Greetings to the Saints in Rome, 1:1-7

Paul's greeting expands the simplest conventional greeting form (Theon to Tyrannus, greetings): *Paul to God's beloved in Rome, grace and peace from God our Father and the Lord Jesus Christ.* The Romans are designated as saints, set apart for God.

Paul introduces two expansions into the greeting. (1) He identifies himself as set apart for the GOSPEL, as the OT prophets had been set apart or elected to preach (Isa 49:1; Jer 1:5), and identifies himself as an apostle. A NT apostle is one sent with an authoritative commission to represent the sender. For Paul the commission is from the risen Lord to preach to the gentiles (1:5; Gal 1:15-16). According to Acts 1:21-22 to be an APOSTLE one must have been a follower of the earthly Jesus and a witness to his RESURRECTION. Paul did not meet the first of these criteria, but he was fully convinced that his having seen the risen Lord and having been commissioned by him was quite enough to make him an apostle equal in authority to the others (Rom 1:1, 5; 1 Cor 9:1; 15:8-11; Gal 1:15-16).

(2) In addition Paul defines the gospel in terms of a Christological confession that he probably received from the tradition existing before or alongside him. This confession portrays Jesus' mission as moving in two stages (not two natures): (a) according to the flesh—in his historical phase—he was the descendant of David; (b) then he was appointed or installed (*not* declared to be who he already was) SON OF GOD in power in the spiritual realm by the resurrection of the dead. Notice it is not by *his* resurrection from the dead but because he anticipates the future general resurrection of the dead. The CHRISTOLOGY of this early confession is broadly adoptionistic. Jesus was not eternally Son of God but became Son at a certain point. However, there is no assertive denial of his pre-existence.

Paul provides a frame for this confession. He introduces it as a confession about the Son, thereby anticipating its second part, and he concludes by naming the Son, Jesus Christ our Lord, the one to whom the believer owes total obedience. For Paul the term Son of God connotes Jesus' close bond with God and his role

as redeemer, but it is probable that no Pauline passage clearly connects pre-existence with the title Son. In Rom 1:3, 9 the content of the gospel is the Son while in 1:16-17, it is the righteousness of God. This shows that for Paul the inner meaning of christology is the standing of human beings before God.

Paul's Thanksgiving for the Roman Community, 1:8-15

Paul first of all thanks God for the faith of the Roman Christians and assures them of his prayerful concern for them. Apparently in his enthusiasm he forgets to follow up "first" with a "second." (On Paul's desire to visit Rome see Introduction: Occasion and Purpose, The Intended Visit.)

Paul wants to preach in Rome because his obligation to preach is unlimited. He must preach to those who have been cultivated by the use of the GREEK LANGUAGE and those who are barbarian. He is a debtor to both wise and foolish. Hence he is eager to proclaim the gospel in Rome. In the thematic statement that follows—his thesis—he begins to explain further the reason why.

Theme: The Gospel of Righteousness as Power, 1:16-17

Paul wants to preach in Rome because he is not ashamed of the gospel. "I am not ashamed" might have a psychological tone. He is not tempted to think he will be shamed for having trusted something unreliable. Or the term might be confessional and be roughly equivalent to "I confess" or "I acknowledge" (see Mark 8:38). Paul is not ashamed of the gospel because it is the power of God for salvation. The gospel proclaimed is not words *about* God's power but *is* God's power in action (see 1 Cor 1:18, 21, 24). Salvation—ultimate well-being—is characteristically future for Paul (5:9-10) but can also be past (8:24) and present (1 Cor 1:18; 2 Cor 2:15).

The righteousness of God means God's action in being faithful to God's COVENANT intention, and faith is the human appropriative response to this. Righteous or righteousness when attributed to human beings refers to being in a right relationship. But see the commentary on 3:21-31 for a fuller discussion of these important terms. Paul finds the essence of the gospel to have been expressed in Hab 2:4—the one righteous by faith shall live. Paul is able to do this by changing the meaning of the prophetic passage. The Greek text of the Habakkuk passage should probably be translated "the one righteous by my (God's) faithfulness shall live." And the Hebrew text of the prophet should probably be translated "the righteous one shall live by his (own) faithfulness." But for Paul the meaning is that the one righteous by faith (in Paul's sense of faith) shall live.

The strong interconnections linking the end of the thanksgiving, the thesis as transition, and the beginning of the letter body are noteworthy. Verses 16-18 are closely tied to v. 15 by a fourfold use of the word *for* (i.e., "because"; vv. 16a, [16b], 17a, 18a), and this formation overarches the formal distinctions involved. Verse 15 belongs to the thanksgiving, vv. 6-17, to the theme or thesis, and v. 18, to the beginning of the body. The causal sequence binds these three together.

Verse 16a states why Paul is eager to preach in Rome (v. 15): because he is not ashamed of the gospel. Verse 16b states why he is not ashamed of the gospel: because it is the power of God. *Gospel* has to be understood as the subject of *is* in v. 16b. Verse 17a explains why the gospel is the power of God: because the righteousness of God is revealed in it. Verse 17a is dependent on v. 16b because the *it* of v. 17a has to have *gospel* as its antecedent. The gender agreement of *it* is with *gospel*, not with *salvation* or *power*.

In the light of both terminology and concept, v. 18a would seem to be parallel to v. 17a: wrath is conceptually related to righteousness (both refer to God's actions), and righteousness in v. 17a and wrath in v. 18a both have the same predicate: *for . . . the righteousness of God is revealed* is parallel to *for the wrath of God is revealed*. Therefore both would be dependent on v. 16b and would thus express causes for the gospel's being the power of God: because righteousness is revealed in it and because wrath is revealed.

Although the terminology and parallelism seem to support that conclusion, some of the conceptual content points in another direction. Righteousness and wrath have a different *temporal* qualification here. The righteousness of God has been manifested in the *present* eschatological moment—now (3:21). But 1:18-32 shows that the wrath of God has been happening *since creation* (1:20). Therefore, although it goes against the parallel structure (meanings and interpretations are rarely, if ever, certain), 1:18 is best referred back to v. 15 as another cause for Paul's wanting to come to Rome: because the WRATH OF GOD is being revealed. He hopes that his coming with the gospel—God's power—will save some from that wrath. Thus Paul has both positively and negatively stated

reasons for coming—to bring the gospel and to save from wrath. And since the letter is a substitute for his presence, these are also his reasons for writing.

The Revelation of God's Righteousness, 1:18–4:25

Righteousness as Wrath, 1:18–3:20

1:18-32. Against the gentiles or all humankind. The wrath of God is being revealed against the ungodliness and wickedness of *all* human beings. This is not unjust of God. All are without excuse (v. 20) regardless of their religion or culture because God has made God's eternal power and deity known and perceptible in the created order since the beginning. But human beings in the interest of having finite gods (idols) that they can manipulate (vv. 23, 25) have refused to thank and honor God and have suppressed the truth of God which they have (vv. 18, 21, 25). The result is that the senseless human mind has become darkened and futile (vv. 21b, 22b). Thus, the human situation is that universal knowledge of God is a possibility only in principle—a possibility "before the fall" so to speak and still a latent possibility. The actual situation in historical existence is that people do not have knowledge of God (vv. 21b, 22b; 1 Cor 2:10-14). But the possibility in principle is enough to hold people responsible (v. 20), for the lack of knowledge results from their *choice* not to have it.

The wrath of God here is God's reaction to humankind's rejection of the truth and knowledge that God has plainly revealed in creation. It is not just a cosmic principle of retribution working automatically in the moral universe (Dodd 1954, 21–24) but God's personal action, God's giving people up (vv. 24, 26, 28) to the consequences of their rebellion.

This giving up has three manifestations.

1. God gave them up to the dishonoring of their bodies in homosexual relationships (2:24-27). HOMOSEXUALITY then is not in Paul's view so much SIN itself as a consequence of sin, and yet it is evil for Paul in that it is destructive of the human self.

Present knowledge makes it difficult to agree with Paul that sinful rebellion is the sole or even a primary cause of homosexuality. But Paul's apparent underlying principle may be right. Rebellious rejection of God deforms the inner depth of human life where the roots of all sexuality lie.

Some Greek moralists defended pederasty (sexual relations between adult men and young boys) as superior to heterosexuality. Among the arguments were: (1) it contributes to the wisdom of youth; (2) it is more masculine; and (3) it is more "according to nature" (Scroggs 1983, 44–49). Other moralists condemned pederasty with such arguments as: (1) it is effeminate; (2) it lacks mutuality and permanence; (3) it is exploitative; (4) it is the expression of insatiable lust; (5) it is contrary to nature (Scroggs 1983, 49–65; Furnish 1979, 62–66).

Paul essentially agreed with the opponents of pederasty. He held homosexuality to be generated by insatiable lust—consumed with passion (v. 27). And he believed that it was chosen—they exchanged (v. 26). And perhaps most emphatically he held it to be contrary to nature, against God's created intention as an order immanent in the world and humankind (Cranfield 1980, 125–26; Käsemann 1980, 48).

People will debate whether homosexuals are more lustful than heterosexuals. That homosexuality is simply chosen and not biologically or socially determined is too facile an assumption. What about "contrary to nature"?

For Paul and the ancient world generally there is no such thing as a homosexual nature or orientation. There is one nature—what we would call a heterosexual one. Thus what Paul is condemning as unnatural is homosexual acts by people whom he takes to have a heterosexual nature. His underlying principle, then, is that people when they act sexually should do so in accordance with their nature. If Paul then could be confronted with the reality of a homosexual nature, he would not be consistent with himself if he claimed that homosexual acts by people with a homosexual nature are contrary to nature.

2. God gave them up to a base mind—a mind that cannot tolerate crisis and that collapses under testing (v. 28). The wrath of God is that God ratifies the darkened thinking that people visit on themselves (vv. 21b, 22b) and turns it into a destiny that they cannot escape on their own.

3. God gave them up to improper conduct (v. 28). The vices that Paul then lists as illustrative of this conduct are behaviors that destroy the coherence of the social order and turn it into a tissue of conflict and reciprocal hostility (vv. 29–32).

2:1-16. Against the Jews—or all humankind. In v. 1 Paul addresses every person who judges another, and he tells such a person that he or she is without excuse because in judging another, one condemns oneself. This is because the judge is guilty of the same offens-

es. Who is the "man" whom Paul addresses here in the second person as the guilty judge?

In v. 1 Paul has shifted from the third person description of 1:18-32 to second person address—you, O man, the judge. The *you* is not the real letter audience—usually designated as "brother/brothers" (cf. 1:13; 16:17) by Paul—but the imaginary questioner of the diatribe. Such a shift of addressee along with a strong indictment, as here, is typical of the diatribe style. Paul indicts the false conclusion that some are in a position to judge others. This address to "you" personalizes and concretizes the "them" of 1:18-32. Yet despite the slight distance created by the insertion of the imaginary questioner the real audience is still in view (Stowers 1981, 81–86, 91, 96, 106, 110–12). Who is it?

The initial *therefore* in v. 1 suggests a close relationship between 1:18-32 and vv. 1-16. In the former he is describing primarily the situation of the gentiles, but the allusion to *Israelite* IDOLATRY in 1:25 (see Ps 106:20; Jer 2:11) shows that he has Jews also in mind. Thus the *you* in v. 1 includes everybody.

However, as the gentile is primarily in view in 1:18-32, the Jew is primarily in view in vv. 1-11, and for these reasons: (1) He is explicitly referring to the Jew in 2:17-29, and 2:1-11 is similar to 2:17-29 in that both criticize inconsistent behavior. (2) The standard of judgment in 2:1-16 is Jewish in nature—works or deeds in obedience to the law (vv. 6, 12-13). (See Pss 18:20-24; 62:12; Prov 24:12; Job 4:9-10; Sir 16:12-14.) (3) Rom 2:4 seems to criticize the Jewish attitude described in Wis 3:9-10; 4:15; 11:9-10, 23; 12:8-11, 19-22; 15:1-6; 16:9-10. These passages suggest that Israel will be judged but with mercy, and Israel will accept the opportunity to repent. The gentiles, on the other hand, are judged without mercy and do not accept the opportunity to repent. Paul's position is that Israel has not repented but is as guilty as the gentiles.

While the wrath of God that Paul describes in 1:18-32 is the historical anticipation of the final judgment, vv. 5-10 speak about that future day of wrath and retribution itself. God will repay people according to their works (*erga*). Those who do good will receive ETERNAL LIFE, but those who do evil will get anguish and fury. This is the situation for both Jew and Greek (vv. 9-11).

The term "works" (v. 6, author trans.) has a very specific meaning for Paul and can hardly be thought to mean something like acts of *faith* or looking beyond human achievement (Barrett 1957, 45–48). Works of the law are human achievements, and here Paul seems to allow that some will be justified by doing the law (v. 13). This appears to contradict his statements elsewhere that no one can be justified by works of the law (3:20, 28; 4:2-5; 9:30–10:3).

On the other hand, here in vv. 6-13, Paul may be speaking hypothetically, speaking from the Jewish point of view for the sake of argument. If the law is the medium of the divine-human relationship, as Judaism says, then only obedient works count for salvation. Since the Jews have not been obedient, they are out on their own terms. But Paul's own real position is that the law is not and cannot be the medium of the divine-human relationship (3:21). For Paul it is in fact possible to be perfectly obedient to the law (Phil 3:6), but fallen human beings will turn that righteousness of the law into a claim of self-salvation rather than accepting righteousness as a gift from God (Phil 3:4b, 6, 9; Rom 9:30–10:3). The righteousness of the law is not the righteousness of God.

To underline the equality of Jew and gentile Paul states that while the gentile does not have the law as the Jew does, gentiles—or some gentiles— nevertheless do by nature what the law requires and thus show that the work of the law is written on their hearts (vv. 14-15). No one, regardless of religion or culture, is without moral sensibility.

Paul is not necessarily expressing the Greek belief that the reason of every person is stamped by the divine cosmic reason. He may rather be stating that the transcendent will of God encounters gentile as well as Jew in concrete situations (Käsemann 1980, 63–64) and is affirmed from within.

Whether the gentile is obedient to this inner law is judged by CONSCIENCE. For Paul and the ancient popular philosophy from which he learned the concept of conscience, the latter is the self in its *judging* mode. Conscience does not *determine* what is right or wrong but is the self judging itself on the basis of a standard of right that is independent of conscience. Here the standard is the law written on the heart, and it is distinct from conscience, whose judging function is expressed in the conflicting thoughts which accuse or excuse.

The statement about the law on the heart in vv. 14-15 should probably be taken as a parenthesis. If it is, then v. 16 flows from v. 13 in a smooth and natural way. The doers of the law will be justified (v. 13) on the day when God carries out the judgment (v. 16). The operation of conscience then (vv. 14-15) is something that goes on in history prior to the judgment day

and perhaps anticipates it. But if 2:14-15 is not taken as a parenthesis, it interrupts the flow and makes the operation of conscience coincident with and a kind of ratification of God's final judgment. That is probably not what Paul wanted to say. For Paul conscience has a relative authority and should be heeded (1 Cor 8:7-12). But it is not infallible and is subject to correction by God's judgment (1 Cor 4:4-5).

2:17-29. Religion, obedience, and circumcision. Here Paul explicitly addresses the Jew: the Jew who has persuaded himself that because he knows the law he has a secure relationship with God on which he can depend and a right to instruct others about how to live in the light. But this Jew who knows the law and the will of God and preaches against theft and adultery does the very things he condemns. Paul indicts this discrepancy between religious claims and moral performance. Again only obedience counts if the Jew is faithful to his own position.

It occurs to Paul that some Jew will say: we have circumcision that counts for us with God. Paul rejoins that circumcision is a benefit only if you obey the law, but disobedience renders it void. You have been disobedient, so circumcision is of no value. Moreover, real circumcision is a matter of the heart. The uncircumcised person who keeps the law is better than the circumcised person who breaks it. True Judaism is an inward and spiritual matter.

3:1-8. Then has the Jew any advantage? We more-or-less expect Paul to say "no." He has argued that the Jew—despite knowing God and the law, despite being mercifully given the opportunity to repent, despite offering moral instruction to others and having the gift of circumcision—is as disobedient and as subject to wrath as the gentile. So what advantage has the Jew? Paul surprises us with "much in every way." The Jews were entrusted with the oracles of God. Paul does not say that the law (*nomos*) is an advantage but that the oracles (*logia*) are. The Jewish scripture is more than law. The Jews know from scripture that if some of them were unfaithful God is still faithful. Paul uses three terms in this context to express the reliability of God—faithfulness (*pistis*, v. 3), righteousness (*dikaiosynē*, v. 5) and truth (*alētheia*, v. 7). This knowledge is the Jews' advantage.

All of this seems to mean that our unrighteousness brings out the righteousness of God. That will prompt some diatribal objector to ask then whether God is not unjust to condemn us. Paul replies "absolutely not" (v. 6, author trans.), for how could God judge the world if he were unjust. Paul's answer could mean that since God is surely judge of the world, he must be just. Or it might mean that God could not be a just judge if he did not take into account the intention of people—to do evil—and not just the result—the confirmation of God's righteousness.

The fact that human unrighteousness leads to the faithfulness of God might also prompt some people to the closely related assertion—which Paul says some people slanderously attribute to him—let us do evil in order that the good might come. Paul does not really deal with this problem here; he dismisses it contemptuously. But he raises the issue again in 6:1 and then gives a substantive theological-ethical response.

3:9-20. Are we Jews then any better off? The meaning of the verb translated "are we better off?" is very problematical, and only the briefest account of the possibilities can be given (see the longer commentaries). The verb could have three possible meanings: (1) Are we making a defense? (2) Are we excelled, at a disadvantage? (3) Are we better off, at an advantage? The first two possibilities seem ruled out by what precedes. The third makes most sense in context even though the middle voice of the verb with this sense is not attested elsewhere. But there are cases of other verbs in the middle voice with an active sense.

Paul's answer to the question is also ambiguous. It could mean either "not absolutely" or "absolutely not." The latter seems more probable in context. Thus question and answer should read: Are we Jews any better off? Absolutely not!

Romans 3:1 and 3:9 then stand in a paradoxical relationship to each other. The Jews have an advantage but are no better off. Their knowledge of God's faithfulness from scripture does not mean that they are any less sinful than the gentiles. The Jews are no better off because all people, Jews and gentiles, are equally under the power of sin. When Paul uses "sin" in the singular, as here, it means, not an act, but a power that controls human beings, especially since he speaks of people as being *under* it. And yet Paul can also speak of sins in the plural to mean acts (4:7; 7:5; 11:27). Sin as power produces sin/sins as dispositions and acts.

Not even one person is righteous. Paul quotes scripture to illustrate and confirm this universal sinfulness. The sin/sins that he details embrace both dispositions and actions. They are both religious and moral. Humankind is without understanding (v. 11). Religiously speaking people do not fear or seek God (vv. 11, 18). Morally speaking they show no kindness but rather

deceive, curse, poison, and shed the blood of their neighbors (vv. 12-15).

Interestingly, none of these OT passages comes from the books of the law. They are primarily from Psalms but also from Ecclesiastes and Isaiah, and yet Paul comprehensively includes them under the category of law (v. 19). The accusations against all Jews and Greeks in vv. 10-18 are the accusations of the law (v. 19), for the purpose of the law is precisely accusation—to stop every mouth (undermine every self-defense) and hold the whole world accountable to God. Proper works of the law are implicitly defined as fear of God and concern for the neighbor—the opposite of the offenses here condemned. But none can be justified by such works because the law's purpose is to hold people guilty, knowingly guilty. The law brings knowledge of sin (v. 20); it does not bring obedience.

But the law can make people aware of their sin only because they have in fact sinned, violated the law, and the law also has a role in the latter connection. The knowledge of sin that the law gives is the knowledge that comes from *doing* it. That is, the claim that the law gives knowledge of sin for Paul means that the law makes people sin (Rom 7:5, 7-8; see commentary on Rom 7).

Since the theme of the works of the law has been introduced by Paul and since Paul's interpretation of Israel's law is one of the most hotly contested issues in Romans scholarship (Donfried 1991a, lxii, lxxi), it seems well to look at the debate at this point.

Excursus: The Law in Paul

In recent years, certain claims have been made that minimize Paul's differences with his ancestral religion and his critique of the law and thus challenge the so-called "Lutheran" interpretation of Paul. Some of these arguments for the "non-Lutheran" Paul will be presented here.

1. Palestinian Judaism in Paul's time had no legalistic merit doctrine of salvation. Election into the covenant people—getting in—and ultimately salvation are by God's grace. E. P. Sanders states that obedience is *either* a response to electing grace *or* a meritorious means of salvation. The correct interpretation of the Jewish sources is that obedience to the law is a response to grace and a means of staying in the covenant, not a way of earning salvation. Thus Paul is not attacking the righteousness of the law on the grounds that it leads to self-righteousness and pride (Sanders

1977, 81–83, 420, 422, 426; Dunn 1988, lxv; Ziesler 1989, 42–43).

2. The works of the law that Paul does oppose are not meritorious acts that earn salvation but such sociological boundary markers as circumcision, sabbath observance, and food laws that mark Israel off from other peoples and give her a sense of privilege or special status. Such an attitude fails to see that what God demands is the obedience of the heart (Dunn 1988, lxv–lxxi, 124, 137, 191–92, 382, 627).

3. Paul did not reject the law as the way to salvation because of any inherent flaw in the law itself, but because of two other factors that grow out of Paul's Christian theological standpoint. (a) Salvation is for all and therefore cannot be by the law because only the Jews have the law. Salvation by the law would exclude the gentiles. (b) Salvation cannot be by the law because dogmatically, as a matter of definition, it comes through Christ, through faith in Christ (Sanders 1977, 489–90, 496–97; 1983, 20, 27, 31–35, 47, 155).

The following counterarguments can be made.

1. Let it be gladly affirmed that grace is an important theme in first-century JUDAISM. That, however, does not mean that Judaism was not legalistic. The two modes of obedience—obedience as response to grace and obedience as a meritorious condition for salvation—are by no means an "either/or" but rather a highly ambiguous "both/and." It is not possible to separate the two experientially, and theo-*logically* grace as enabling power and salvation by works—theological legalism—go hand in glove. By theological legalism is meant the religious belief that human behavior, obedience, performance of God's requirements, counts with God as a condition for salvation.

In Leviticus Israel's salvation depends on the grace of atonement provided by God (17:11). On the other hand, Israel must maintain herself in life in the land by obedience to the law (18:5; 20:22; 23:11; 26:3-39). Similarly in Deuteronomy God chooses Israel out of God's love and not because of Israel's merit, and God graciously intervenes in history on Israel's behalf (1:30-32; 7:7-8; 8:17; 9:4; 10:15). Israel's OBEDIENCE then is the appropriate response to GRACE (5:6-21; 6:20-25; 7:6; 8:4; 14:1-2; 26:5-11; 27:9-10). On the other hand, Israel maintains herself in the land and purges her guilt by right actions (4:1, 5; 6:18; 7:12; 8:1; 11:26-28; 16:20; 21:9). This legalistic strand can be seen in many places (Job 34:11; Pss 18:20-24; 62:12; Prov 24:12; Jer 17:10; Hos 12:2; Tob 4:9-10; Sir 16:12-14): performance issues in salvation.

Stating this point is not a chauvinistic effort to make Christianity look better than Judaism. The NT also has its legalistic strand. For example, despite Paul's strong polemic against JUSTIFICATION by works, his appeal to judgment on the basis of deeds (Rom 14:11; 2 Cor 5:10) is legalistic. Even more strongly in Matthew, while grace is a reality (13:16, 17, 20, 23, 37-38) that enables the response (7:16-20; 12:33-37; 13:23), human beings must achieve salvation by their own efforts (5:20; 6:14-15; 7:24-25; 16:27; 18:35). Given the legalistic strand in the daughter religion (Christianity) it would be strange indeed if it were not in the parent (Judaism). The paradoxical theo-logic running through all this material is that God's grace as forgiveness and power enables people to do what *they* must do to be saved.

2. Returning to Paul, acts performed to express Jewish separateness, like circumcision, cannot be neatly distinguished from meritorious acts to gain salvation since God could be expected to approve such boundary markers. Moreover, Paul does not say that people seek the righteousness of the law—perform works of the law—in order to mark themselves off as distinct but in order to have something of their own to trust (Rom 9:30–10:3; Phil 3:4, 9): a righteousness of their own based on the law. This boasting or trust in self (3:27) is not before other people but before God (10:2). And while works of the law include cultic boundary markers (Gal 2:11-16), they also include strictly religious attitudes and moral acts as the commentary on 3:19-20 showed. Works of the law for Paul are cultic, religious, and moral acts performed in order to gain a standing with God based on one's own achievements.

3. Paul did not reject the law as the way to salvation *because* salvation by law would have excluded the gentiles. It would not have excluded them, because all are under the law already. There is an obvious sense in which the Jews have the Law of Moses, and the gentiles do not. But there is a running subtext in Paul that reveals that in the actual struggles of existence the gentiles are as much under the law in principle as the Jews. For example, what the law requires is written on the hearts of gentiles (2:14-15). It is the purpose of the law to hold everyone accountable, all the world; therefore all are under the law (3:19-20). The "all" of 3:19-20 are the same as the "all" of 3:9: Jew and gentile. Since the whole church—Jew and gentile—is said to have died to the law (7:4), all must have been under the law. In 5:12-14 the command to Adam is equiva-

lent to law, and ADAM symbolizes the whole human race.

4. Nor did Paul reject the law as the means of salvation because by definition salvation is through faith in Christ. He rather rejected it because there is a substantive opposition between the righteousness of the law and the righteousness of faith. The righteousness of faith is not relatively better but is a qualitatively different antithesis. The righteousness of faith is willing to receive from God while the righteousness of the law asserts itself against God and is an instance of living according to the flesh (see commentary on 9:30–10:3).

5. The pursuit of salvation or justification by works of the law is not just a failure to see that God requires the obedience of the heart but is a deformation of the heart, a rupture of the wholeness of the self, in which three different levels of self-awareness are both in conflict with each other and out of touch with each other. These levels are: (1) I am righteous and wise (Rom 3:27-28; 1 Cor 1:29; 3:18-21). (2) Why then do I compulsively pursue righteousness and wisdom (Rom 10:2-3; 1 Cor 1:20-22; Gal 1:13-14; Phil 3:4-6, 8-9)? (3) My righteousness and wisdom are really foolishness and wickedness—trash (Rom 3:10, 20, 23; Phil 3:6, 8-9; 1 Cor 3:19) (see Via 1990, 29–33).

6. Paul makes positive statements about the law: it is connected with faith (9:30-32) and promises and promotes life (7:10, 14a, 16b, 22-23). But he also makes negative statements: the law causes sin (7:5, 7-10). This is only an apparent contradiction because Paul is not stating opposing things about the law under the same category but is distinguishing yet relating two different categories—intention and result. Paul's basically consistent position, which accounts for most of his statements on the law, is that the law intends faith and life, but human beings as flesh try to use the law to save themselves with the result that they subvert the law's original intention and produce sin. Romans 5:13-14 and 5:20 are in conflict with the generally consistent position (see commentary).

7. God's original intention for the law is subverted not only because human beings as flesh try to make themselves secure through a righteousness of their own (Rom 8:3, 7; Phil 3:4, 9-10) but also because the law as a personified power deceives people (Rom 7:10-11). Paul associates the law with sin and death (1 Cor 15:56) and death with the demonic cosmic powers (1 Cor 15:24-26; Rom 8:38). Thus by implication the law is a demonic power that seduces people into the false belief that it is the source of salvation (7:10; 9:30–10:3) (Via 1990, 38–44, and commentary on 8:31-39).

Righteousness as Justification by Faith, 3:21–4:25

3:21-26. Righteousness, faith, and grace. But *now*—now when the *future*, final, eschatological revelation has become a *present* reality—God has manifested his righteousness apart from the law. Righteousness, faith, and grace will be distinguished for analysis, but for Paul they are inseparable parts of the divine-human transaction. Although manifested apart from the law, Paul shows (for example, in 1:17; 4:1-25; 10:5-13) how this righteousness is continuous with the law and prophets that bear witness to it. Righteousness must come apart from the law since the law has left all people sinful without distinction. Sin as falling short of the glory of God may refer to humankind's loss of the image of God (1 Cor 11:7). (On sin, see commentary on 1:18-32; 5:12-21; 7:1-25.)

Paul's understanding of righteousness is derived from OT and Jewish usage. In the OT we may discern three senses: (1) God's righteousness is God's character or nature—readiness to be faithful to the covenant relationship. (2) God actively manifests this character by intervention in human affairs to establish life. This manifestation of righteousness is salvation (Isa 46:12-13; 51:5-6; 61:11; 62:1-2; Ps 98:2-3). (3) Since God's righteousness or salvation can be received by people, it is also referred to as *theirs* (Isa 62:1-2; 54:17).

Paul essentially repeats these three usages. (1) Righteous is something God is (Rom 3:26)—God's character. (2) This character is revealed in action: God's righteousness is manifested (1:17; 3:21). (3) People who receive God's righteousness exist in the righteousness of faith—the state of human beings who have a right relationship with God (Rom 4:3, 5; 9:30). The righteousness of the law is the attempt of human beings to establish a relationship with God based on their own works (Rom 10:3; Phil 3:9; Williams 1980, 259–65; Wedderburn 1991, 116–23).

God's manifestation of his covenant righteousness occurs as the justification of the believer (3:22, 24, 26). In Greek the righteousness family of words and the justification family have the same root (*dikai-*). Justification is God's establishment of the new right relationship. It is not making the sinner *ethically* righteous in either action or intention. Nor is it treating the sinner *as if* he or she were ethically righteous—a legal fiction. Justification is rather a *relational* term, and its social setting is the law court. To justify is to acquit. Paul's usage begins in the law court but surpasses that frame of reference, for the OT forbids that a guilty person be acquitted (Isa 5:22-23; Prov 17:15) and asserts that God will not acquit the wicked (Exod 23:7). But that is exactly what Paul says God has now done: God justifies, acquits, pronounces not guilty the one who is sinful, ungodly, guilty (vv. 23-24; 4:5). This is not a legal fiction but a relationship that is real. The guilty person has with the judge the relationship of a not guilty person that cannot be broken (8:33-36). The unacceptable one is accepted.

Faith is the human acceptance or reception of God's justifying action (vv. 22-25). It is the opposite of works: that is, it is receiving from God rather than depending on one's own righteousness (9:30-32). Faith involves two closely connected moves: (1) It is willingness to believe that the proclaimed death and resurrection of the Son of God constitute God's saving action. (2) It is a surrender to this divine action and a reversal of self-understanding based on it, a renunciation of boasting or self-trust. The two acts of faith merge into one because Paul came to know Jesus as Lord and Son of God in coming to understand himself as having nothing on which to depend for salvation (Phil 3:6-11; Gal 2:19-20) (Bultmann 1951, 300–301).

Faith as response to God's justifying act is a *human* decision. It is acceptance of the preached word *as* word of God (1 Thes 2:13); therefore faith involves a committed interpretation of the human word that is the vehicle of God's righteous action. That faith is a human decision for which people are responsible is seen in the fact that Paul puts his readers under the *imperative* to have and live by faith (1 Cor 7:29-31; 2 Cor 5:20; Rom 11:20-22). Yet faith is not a posture human beings produce in themselves but one that God generates in them through the power of the preached word (Rom 1:16; 10:8, 17). Faith is given—"graced" (Phil 1:29). Both sides are seen in Phil 2:12-13: *you* work out your *own* salvation *because God* is working in you.

Faith in Jesus (Christ) (vv. 22, 26) is more literally translated "faith of Jesus Christ," and it has been argued that it means the "faithfulness of Jesus Christ" that is the medium of the divine activity rather than the faith of the believer in the divine activity (Hays 1981, 168, 196; Williams 1980, 271–76; Cousar 1990, 39). Actually the expression and its contexts (see also Gal 2:16) are ambiguous and it could mean one as

well as the other, or both. It is not possible to determine that one of these meanings is the only right one.

Grace for Paul is both God's act in which God gives faith as response to the saving event and the act that is the saving event itself. These are two sides of the same event. Grace underlines the *gift*—undeserved—character of the event. Grace as event and gift extends what Paul has expressed in his understanding of the righteousness of God as the justification—acquittal—of the sinner: justification by grace. The eventful gift is the redemption accomplished in the sacrificial death of Christ Jesus.

The term "redemption" (*apolytrōsis*) was used for the liberation of slaves or prisoners of war and could be an allusion to the deliverance of Israel from Egyptian slavery. Therefore, it images Jesus' death as a liberation from sin.

The background of "sacrifice of atonement" by his blood has several facets. The term "sacrifice of atonement" (*hilastērion*) is generally used in the LXX (and in Heb 9:5) to refer to the mercy seat, which was the cover of the ark of the covenant in the holy of holies in the Temple (Exod 25:21). This is where God's presence is manifested (Exod 25:22; Lev 16:2) and where the blood of the sin offering is sprinkled to atone for sin (Lev 16:11-16). Closely associated with the sin offering is the ritual in which the scapegoat bears away Israel's sins into the wilderness (Lev 16:20-22). Romans 3:25 probably makes some reference to this material although "mercy seat" is too restricted a meaning, especially since *hilastērion* could mean "expiation" more broadly (4 Macc 17:22).

In Isa 53:6, 10, 12 the death of God's servant is a sin offering and a bearing of Israel's sins. It is difficult to believe that the NT text makes no allusion to this, even though Jewish sources did not interpret the Isaiah text as teaching expiatory vicarious suffering (Williams 1975, 111, 120).

In 4 Macc 17:22 (see also 1:11; 6:28-29) the deaths of the Jewish martyrs are interpreted as a *hilastērion* that preserves and purifies Israel. This Hellenistic-Jewish text was probably influenced by the classical Greek notion of a hero or heroine dying for the city, fatherland, family, or piety. Either directly or through such a Jewish source as 4 Maccabees this idea reached early Christianity (Williams 1975, 111, 120, 145–63, 230, 233). It should be pointed out that Rom 3:25-26a or 3:24-26 is probably a pre-Pauline confession.

The term *hilastērion* can mean either *propitiation* (a human act to appease or placate God—primarily in nonbiblical sources) or *expiation* (a divine act to deal with sin—primarily in the LXX). In Paul there is a hint of the idea of propitiation. The death of Jesus does after all avert the wrath of God (Rom 5:8-9). But the overall context in Paul shows that expiation is much the stronger sense: it is what God does to cover and forgive human sin. This interpretation is supported by several points.

(1) In speaking of Christ's death for human beings Paul does not say that it was *in place of* us (*anti*) (to appease God's wrath) but rather *for our sakes* or *in behalf of* us (*hyper*) (to affect us: Rom 5:8; 1 Cor 15:3; 2 Cor 5:14; Gal 3:13).

(2) Christ does not die in our place. Rather *our* old self also must die, and Christ's death is for us in that it draws us into itself and enables us to die to the old person we were (Rom 6:4-6; 7:4, 6; 2 Cor 5:14-15).

(3) It is humankind that needs to be reconciled, not God. We are the enemy, not God (Rom 5:10; 2 Cor 5:18-19).

(4) The cross confronts us as word (1 Cor 1:18) and as sacrament (Rom 6:4-6; 1 Cor 10:16; 11:26). The cross as word becomes effective by creating faith in us (Rom 10:8-9, 17). The cross as word, then, is toward us and affects us. It is not directed toward God.

In vv. 25b-26 the purpose of God's expiating act is to demonstrate God's own righteousness. God needs to make this active move because in the past God has passed over (not forgiven) former sins in God's restraint or inactivity (see Isa 63:15; 64:10-12). That is, God has not dealt with the sinful situation of the past (Williams 1975, 21–34). Perhaps the main reason for seeing the past as negative or neutral (unforgiven) is that it is contrasted with the present which is positive: righteousness is *now* demonstrated. The manifested righteousness has a dually stated purpose: in order for God (1) to be righteous, and (2) to justify the one who has faith in Christ (or the one redeemed by Christ's faithfulness). Since the latter purpose is positive, the fact that the former is mentioned at all probably (or possibly) means that it is a negative contrast. That is, the demonstration of God's righteousness entails judgment or justice as well as acquittal. This judgment is not in addition to justification by grace but is included within it. When one accepts the *undeserved* gift of a new standing with God, no longer under condemnation (8:33-34), then one must acknowledge—judge—oneself as *undeserving*.

In recent years René Girard has developed a complex theory to explain the origin and structure of both

societies and religions. In his view societies project their internal, reciprocal violence and hostilities onto a sacrificial victim or scapegoat in order to remove from the society the violence that would otherwise destroy it. By deciding unanimously to kill the scapegoat, the society's violence and the guilt for it are transferred to the sacrificial victim. Thus social conflicts are eliminated or curtailed and the community can exist in accord. The victim is regarded as both guilty and sacred. The community conceals from itself the fact that it is really the violent and guilty party. The great difference that the biblical tradition inserts into this picture is that guilt is shifted away from the victim and back onto society where it belongs (Girard 1986, 27, 38, 101–103, 109–10, 117; 1989, 3–4, 7–8, 53, 94–96, 104).

Whatever one may think of the generalizability of Girard's theory, the structure of Romans, with its own modifications and transformations, reflects Girard's depiction of the development of religion and society. In the letter the whole human community is portrayed as totally divided (1:18-32) and involved in ruinous, reciprocal violence (3:10-18). In this situation God acted redemptively through the sacrificial death of Christ (vv. 21-26). Paul understands the social violence as sin (3:9), and the way to freedom from the violence of sin is to die sacramentally with the sacrificial victim (6:4-6). This communal participation in baptism creates a unified community—one body in Christ (12:5). But the redemption, both individual and communal, is never complete; and the individual is exhorted to keep redemption in process by the continual appropriation of the death to sin (6:11-12); and the church is exhorted to continue cementing communal bonds (12:3, 6, 9).

3:27–4:2. Boasting, faith, and the validity of the law. This section is a diatribal exchange in which Paul deals with the impact of justification by grace on the continuing validity of the law (Stowers 1981, 164–65). The dialogue is generated by the interlocutor's question about what has happened to boasting if justification is through faith.

To boast is to put one's confidence in or to affirm one's confidence in. It is virtually synonymous with to trust in (*peithō*) (Phil 3:3). The object of this confidence can be God (Jer 9:24) or Christ (1 Cor 1:31; 2 Cor 10:17; Gal 6:14; Phil 3:3), on the one hand, or one's own achievements—wisdom, power, righteousness (Jer 9:23; 1 Cor 1:29; Phil 3:3, 9), on the other hand (Bultmann 1951, 242–43; Käsemann 1980, 69–70). Paul's questioner wants to know what has become of our basis for having confidence in our own righteousness based on the law. What becomes of boasting?

Paul answers that it has been excluded on the law or principle of faith. The word translated "law" here is Paul's normal word for law (*nomos*). But it could mean principle, norm, or order. On the other hand, Paul could be understood as saying *law* of faith. That is, boasting is excluded on the basis of the Law of Moses understood, not as demanding works, but as intending faith (see commentary on 9:31-32). There is *one* God, of Jew and gentile; therefore, there is *one* condition for justification, for both Jew and gentile. It is faith.

Paul's questioner then asks: do we overthrow the law, since justification by faith rules out works performed in obedience to the law as a way to justification. Paul answers: absolutely not, we rather establish the law.

The interlocutor then wonders how justification by *faith* can uphold the law since ABRAHAM belongs to the law but was justified by *works* and thus has something of his own to boast about. JUDAISM understood Abraham as the prime example of the devout Jew who was received as righteous because of his faithful obedience to the law (Jub 23:10; 1 Macc 2:52; Kidd 4:14) (Dunn 1988, 196). Paul replies that whatever boastful claims Abraham might have been able to make, they would have no standing with God.

In the remainder of chap. 4 Paul proceeds to develop the point that justification does not overthrow the law because justification by faith is already in the law in the case of Abraham. Clearly Paul understands the law as including much more than demands, and he is going to interpret Abraham very differently than his fellow Jews did.

It is true that Paul affirms the continuity between Israel and Christianity in Rom 4 (Dunn 1988, 197). Paul does this, however, by Christianizing Abraham. He does not say: proper Christian faith is like the faith of Abraham, the father of Israel. He rather says: Abraham, the father of Israel, already had Christian faith. That is, Paul finally defines Abraham's faith as *resurrection* faith. Since Paul's strategy is to use Abraham to prove that the Christian gospel of justification by faith does not overthrow but rather establishes the law, he logically has to argue that Abraham already had the faith of justification by faith.

4:3-15. Abraham's faith is reckoned as righteousness. For Paul it was not Abraham's works but his *believing* God that was reckoned to him as righteousness. Paul interprets the faith and righteousness attributed to Abraham in Gen 15:6 as being qualitatively the same as the righteousness of faith that Christians have.

In vv. 4-5 Paul makes a clear distinction between the self-understanding that accompanies works and the one that accompanies faith. The person who does works for salvation regards these works as meritorious; that is, the reward from God is a debt or obligation (*opheilēma*) which God owes to the worker. But the one who simply accepts in faith the new relationship that God establishes, knows herself or himself as *ungodly*, not deserving.

Verses 7-8 connects the *reckoning* of righteousness with not *reckoning* sin in Ps 32:1-2 (Ps 31 in LXX). Thereby Paul identifies justification with the forgiveness celebrated in the Psalm. But this LXX quotation is the only place where Paul uses this common verb for "forgive" (*aphiēmi*).

Paul goes on to underscore the non-meritorious quality of Abraham's righteousness by pointing out that his faith was reckoned as righteousness *before* he was circumcised. Then he was circumcised as a seal of the righteousness. Therefore, Abraham can be the father of the gentiles, who have faith but are not circumcised, and of the Jews, who are circumcised but also follow the example of Abraham's pre-circumcision faith.

4:16-25. Abraham's faith as faith in the resurrection. The specific promise of God that Abraham believed and as a result had his faith reckoned as righteousness was the promise that he would have many heirs. The promise was given at a time when he was old and Sarah was barren and they had no legitimate heir.

The fact that Paul describes the God in whom Abraham believed as the one who gives life to the dead and calls into existence the things that do not exist shows that Paul is interpreting Abraham's experience of God in the light of the Christian experience of the God who raised Jesus from the dead (v. 24). The Abraham story may also have contributed to his understanding of Jesus' death and resurrection. The dialectical interaction between the two is seen in the fact that the discussion of Abraham moves immediately into the kerygmatic (preaching) statement about Jesus' death and resurrection for our justification.

Paul's appropriation of the Abraham story is a clear case of his Christian understanding governing his reinterpretation of the pre-Christian past.

We could say that Paul posits a "resurrection situation" in Abraham's history and a corresponding faith arising from it. The resurrection situation is what the Christians' and Abraham's situations have in common—the promise of life in the midst of death.

The broader import of Rom 4 is that for Paul the death-resurrection-faith situation is a possibility—in principle and in actuality—at any point along the line of the history of God's saving acts. Not only Abraham but also other Israelites had the kind of faith Abraham had (4:11-12). Yet Paul can speak of the time before Christ as the time before faith came (Gal 3:23-25). These two points of view can be reconciled by pointing out, with Käsemann, that salvation history is not uninterrupted but contains discontinuities (Käsemann 1971, 88). The "before faith came" does not mean there had been no instances of Christian faith before Christ but that these instances had come intermittently, separated by gaps. There were times of faith before Christ but also times before faith came.

Romans 4 constitutes a certain modification—or deconstruction—of Paul's customary position. Generally faith in Christ (Rom 3:22; Gal 2:16) or in his death and resurrection (Rom 10:9; Gal 2:20; 3:1-2, Phil 3:9) is the condition for salvation. Being in a right relationship with God comes through faith in Christ (Rom 10:10). Faith in Christ is *in itself* the way to, or the consequence of (Phil 1:29), salvation. But in Rom 4, faith in Christ is not itself the way to justification. Rather faith in Christ has become a paradigm or model for other analogous situations that are not specifically faith in Christ but are qualitatively similar to it. If that were not Paul's real point, he would not be able to show that the faith of justification was present in Abraham and thus does not overthrow the law.

The medium for this shift in Paul's position is the hermeneutical move of interpreting X *as* Y; that is, interpreting Abraham's faith in God's promise (X) *as* the Christian's faith in the death and resurrection of Jesus (Y). The substance of the shift is that faith in Christ has ceased to be the focus and has been replaced in the center by the category of having righteousness reckoned to one. This is what happened for both Abraham and the Christian believers—the reckoning of righteousness. What the two have in common is that faith is reckoned as righteousness (vv. 22-24a).

The focus or fundamental category is having faith reckoned as righteousness, and the faith in which righteousness—a right relationship with God—becomes a reality has a certain character. Having this faith is the content of salvation, and this content is what Paul wants to define here. But the faith in which righteousness becomes a reality does not have to be faith in Christ. It has to be *like* faith in Christ. It has to be holding in hope to God's promise of life in the face of the impossible. Faith in Christ is the paradigm for faith as righteousness but not the only actual access to the right relationship.

Life as Liberation
from Victimizing Powers, 5:1–8:39

Romans 5:1 is an important transitional verse. *Since we are justified* sums up 3:21–4:25, and *peace* encompasses the new *life* of *freedom* that 5:1–8:39 will unfold. Paul makes the discussion in Rom 5–8 engage issues connected with the Jewish-gentile conflict in the Roman church—for example, the ethical dimension of the gospel (6:1-4, 12-13; 8:13) and the role of the law (chap. 7). That historical connection, however, is not the generating source of Rom 5–8, for both the juxtaposition of 5–8 to 1:18–4:25 and the content of 5–8 flow theo-*logically* from the content of 1:18–4:25. For Paul the new relationship with God—JUSTIFICATION—issues in a new quality of life—FREEDOM; and yet that freedom is experienced ambiguously. Therefore, it is necessary to explicate the powers that assail the life of freedom: ADAM, SIN, the LAW, flesh, and death. But Paul's real interest is in affirming deliverance from the destructive powers. In his paradoxical and dialectical way Paul both declares that the liberation has occurred (6:6-8; 7:6; 8:1-2) and expresses the hope that it will occur (5:5; 8:20-25). In the ending of each of the major sub-divisions of this section he affirms that life has come to believers in and through Christ (5:21; 6:23; 7:25a; 8:39).

Justification and liberation are not identical with each other, but they do merge into each other in the process of SALVATION. Justification gives the sinner the new *relationship* of a sinless person, no longer under condemnation. The new relationship confers upon the believer's life a new center—Christ (2 Cor 5:15)—rather than oneself. Thus the believer no longer lives toward achieving his or her salvation through good works. Since it was this misguided effort that brought one under the power of sin and the law (7:13-25), the justification that provides the new relationship is also a deliverance into a new kind of life. Proceeding from the other direction, it is the liberation from the power of sin and death—the overwhelming ruinous drive to manipulate all reality—that makes it possible to accept the new relationship. Faith is a gift.

Justification and liberation are immanent in each other, but they are not identical. By analogy the relationship of justification is the shape of the new life, and freedom from the powers is the content that is shaped. Moreover, justification sees the guilty sinner as freely and responsibly rejecting God and pronounces him *not guilty*. The *justified* sinner is still *sinner*. Deliverance sees the sinner as the victim of superhuman powers and frees her from these powers. The liberated sinner has a new character, is on the way toward not being sinner. Justification and liberation continue to interact with each other in salvation understood as an ongoing process (2 Cor 3:18; 4:16).

Transition from Justification to Peace and Life, 5:1-11

Romans 1:18–4:25 is unified on the basis of its depiction of the negative (wrath) and positive (justification) sides of God's righteousness. Romans 5:12–8:39 coheres on the basis of its portrayal of the interconnected destructive powers—Adam, sin, law, FLESH, DEATH—and the proclamation of God's liberation from these through Jesus Christ. Romans 5:1-11 points transitionally in both directions.

Our transitional passage looks backward to justification and grace (vv. 1-2, 9), Jesus' death for sinners (vv. 6-9), salvation (vv. 9-10), and wrath (v. 9). It points forward to the hope of sharing eschatological glory (v. 2; 8:18, 21), suffering (v. 3; 8:18), ethical concerns (v. 4; 8:4-5, 13-15), and the death of Christ (vv. 6-9; 6:3; 7:4, 25a; 8:3).

According to some manuscripts Paul says "since we are justified by faith, therefore *we have* (indicative mood) peace." According to other manuscripts (slightly better) he says "since we are justified by faith, therefore *let us have* (subjunctive mood) peace." In terms of the larger context of Rom 5–8, either is compatible with Paul's thought. He can refer to God's salvation in human beings as an accomplished reality (6:3-4) or he can put believers under the imperative to make it a reality (6:11-13). Justification and peace are related as cause and effect—justification, therefore PEACE. They are not identical.

Peace does not mean the subjectivity of peace of mind. Its background is the Hebraic concept of *shalōm*—total well-being. Within the context of Romans, it refers to the reconstitution of the deformed self (1:21-23, 24-28; 3:23) and the restructuring of a soci-

ety torn by reciprocal hostility and violence (1:29-32; 3:10-18).

Having strongly criticized boasting (trusting) in our own works, Paul proposes boasting in the hope of sharing God's glory as the fitting Christian posture. More than that, believers boast in their afflictions. Suffering is not a contradiction to standing in grace but the condition in which grace is effective (Dunn 1988, 264). We boast in our suffering because suffering leads through endurance and character—the quality of being proved by testing—to HOPE. And hope does not disappoint us because—it would seem—of our strength of character. But Paul surprises us. Hope does not disappoint us because the LOVE of God has been poured in our hearts by the Holy Spirit. It is God's love for us, not our love for God, which the HOLY SPIRIT has established in our hearts, the inner core of our being.

The Spirit for Paul is the power of God that makes God's reality and action present in human experience. In this context the action of God that the Spirit makes present is the love God demonstrated by sending God's Son to die for humankind. Our radical undeservingness of this love Paul underscores by means of a vivid contrast. While a person will hardly die for another who is righteousness (correct according to law or moral principle), a person perhaps would dare to die for someone who is good (more than correct). But Christ died for us ungodly sinners who are neither righteous nor good.

As in 3:24-25, the consequence of Jesus' saving death is expressed as justification (v. 9)—a new relationship. This is paralleled in v. 10 by defining the new situation as RECONCILIATION. This category takes its meaning from the reality of personal, group, and national hostilities, and it draws out the significance of peace with God in v. 1. In reconciliation hostility is overcome, and here it is human beings, not God, who are the enemy that needs to be reconciled. Justification and reconciliation overlap in meaning. Reconciliation is neither identical with nor the consequence of justification. Each describes the new situation that results from Christ's death, with reconciliation underlining the personal element in the relationship between God the judge and the justified sinner (Cranfield 1980, 265–67; Dunn 1988, 259).

Now that justification and reconciliation are a present reality through the love of God, total salvation in the future is assured. Paul typically, but not always, uses the term salvation for the future completion of redemption.

Freedom from Adam, 5:12-21

With this section the theme of sin takes on a new intensity and a somewhat different focus. Prior to this, sin is seen as universal but primarily as a matter of individual responsibility. Now with the role of Adam the supra-individual cause of sin comes clearly into the picture. Romans 6:1-23 then treats sin as a concrete everyday problem and struggle in the life of the believer. Chapter 7 deals with the relationship of sin to the law and chap. 8, with its connections to flesh and death. Yet throughout the discussion all these destructive powers are interconnected.

Adam is not the originating *source* of sin, but he is the agent through which sin as a demonic personalized power entered the world and infected all humankind and brought death in its wake. And yet death spread to *all* because *all sinned*. Paul maintains the paradox that sin and death are both freely chosen and fated, but the fated side is emphasized in vv. 12-21.

Structurally v. 12 is the first member of a comparison between ADAM and Christ, the second member of which occurs only at v. 18b: *as* through the one man Adam sin came (v. 12), *so* through the other one's act of righteousness justification came (v. 18b). Verses 13-17 is a parenthesis clarifying the difference between Adam and Christ, and v. 18a essentially repeats v. 12 as a preparation for the second member in v. 18b (Cranfield 1980, 272–73).

For Paul the presence of the law makes sin a transgression, makes it guilt-laden, causes it to count or incur wrath (vv. 13-14; 4:15). Adam's sin was such a guilty transgression because God's command to him not to eat from the tree (Gen 2:16-17) was the functional equivalent of law. But Paul holds here that between Adam and Moses' giving of the law, since there was no law, although people sinned and died, this sin was different from Adam's and was not counted. That declaration contradicts Paul's more general position in two ways. (1) There are many indications in Paul elsewhere that the whole human race has always been under the law in principle (see excursus on the law in the commentary on 3:9-20). Thus there could be no time when sin was not counted. (2) For Paul death is the wages or *result* of *sin* (Rom 6:23; 8:5-6); therefore, since Paul grants that death did in fact rule from Adam to Moses (when there was allegedly no law) and holds in 6:23 that death is the wages of sin, he cannot say consistently in v. 13 that sin is not counted. The reality of death shows that sin did count.

If Adam was not the originating *source* of sin, he is nevertheless the *cause* of the plight of all other human beings. His sin causes the sin (v. 19), death (vv. 15, 17), and condemnation (vv. 16, 18) of all others.

Adam and Christ are alike in that in each case what the one does affects the many—all others—and each of them represents the whole (or potentially the whole) of humankind. On the other hand, while Adam began a history, the history of sin, Christ reversed that history. Thus Adam represents humankind as sinful and Christ, humankind as righteous. And the righteousness of Christ does not just balance the sin of Adam and its consequences. It much more overbalances them, producing justification and life (vv. 15b, 16b, 17b, 18b, 19b).

In v. 16b the word signifying the opposite of condemnation should be translated justification, as it is. But in Greek it is not Paul's usual word for justification (*dikaiōsis*) but rather the cognate term *dikaiōma*, which ordinarily means requirement or righteous deed. *Dikaiōma* has a more normal meaning in v. 18 where it is used of Christ's righteous deed as a synonym for his obedience (v. 19).

Paul probably believed Adam to have been the first historical man, a difficult belief in the modern world. Nevertheless, Adam is also profoundly employed by Paul as a symbol for what the human situation always is in historical existence. In Rom 7 Paul can use the Adam story to express his own implication in sin and also to say what is true typically for other individuals. At the same time Adam symbolizes the whole of humankind, the structural human situation, the totality that overwhelms the individual. As Paul Ricoeur puts it, Adam is the always already there of evil in every situation into which the individual enters (Ricoeur 1969, 241, 243, 251, 257–58).

It has been held that Paul bases the participation of all humans in Adam on the physical-psychic solidarity of the human race and that he thinks of the participation of all in Christ in an analogous way. There is only the slightest hint of the role of faith. All share in Christ's work as a matter of the unity of the race (Best 1955, 35–37).

But Paul does *not* treat the effects of Adam's and Christ's actions in an analogous way. When he speaks of our involvement with Adam, he uses the past (aorist) tense and indicative mood—signs of factuality (vv. 15a, 17a, 19a, 21a). But when he speaks of the effect of Christ's obedient righteousness, although he once states that grace has already abounded (v. 15b), he characteristically here speaks of our involvement in Christ by using the future tense or subjunctive mood (vv. 17b, 19b, 21b)—signs of possibility. And he implies that this possibility—not a natural fact—will become a reality when it is *received* by faith (v. 17b).

Paul concludes the Adam section by stating that the law slipped or stole in *in order that* (probably a purpose rather than a result clause) the trespass might increase or become greater. This contradicts Paul's more typical position that sin is the *result rather than* the *purpose* of the law (see excursus on the law in commentary on 3:9-20). But the good news is that when sin increased, grace super-abounded; and the purpose of this grace is that it might reign through righteousness to produce eternal life. Grace, righteousness and eternal life are compactly distinguished and related. Grace (the gift and act of God) establishes righteousness (a right relationship with God) that issues in eternal life.

Freedom from Sin, 6:1-23

In Rom 6:1 Paul has his diatribal questioner draw a false conclusion, phrased as a question: What then shall we say? If grace superabounds where sin increases, should we not remain in sin in order that grace might abound? Paul answers "absolutely not" (author trans.). He then spends this chapter giving his reasons why the believer should not continue in sin. Thus he takes up in a substantive way the question that he summarily dismissed in 3:8. Sin in Rom 6 is both a personalized power (vv. 6-7, 12, 16, 20) and deeds of rebellion (vv. 12, 19, 21).

What are the reasons for not remaining in sin? It has been argued that since Paul rejects the law as a standard for performing good works that merit salvation and since he does not appeal to the inherent authority of the law, he has no logical basis for claiming that the believer must not continue in sin (Knox 1954, 471). Paul, however, does have powerful arguments of a different kind to justify his contention that the believer should live an ethical life. It is not Paul's position that the believer in consequence of his or her renewal will necessarily live an ethical life but rather that the morally responsible life is now a possibility that ought to be enacted—and for good reasons.

6:1-14. Sin and baptism. Paul tells the Romans that Christians should not sin because in BAPTISM they have shared in Jesus' death and potentially in his resurrection. Jesus' death was a victory over sin (v. 10); therefore, our baptismal participation in his death frees us

from sin (vv. 6-7). We should enact in our daily ethical lives what we have become in baptism—freed from sin. The believer should not continue in sin because to do so shatters wholeness or integrity, ruptures the correspondence between what we are in baptism and what we are in our daily lives. Sin violates the newness (v. 4) and life (v. 13) that have been created in us in consequence of the death of our old self (v. 6).

Baptism has a real effect. It is not just a pointer to a faith experience that happens independently of baptism. It is a symbol in which the meaning or effect is actualized in and through the symbol. Since in baptism we are united with Christ's death (v. 5), the benefits of that death are extended to us, and we are freed from sin (v. 7). Baptism does something.

This freedom from sin, however, is not a fixed, inalienable condition or possession. It is a reality but a reality that is a possibility that must be appropriated by the believer. You must become what you are. The believer is placed under the imperative to understand herself as dead to sin and alive to God (v. 11) and to yield her members to God and not to sin (v. 13).

The movement of this section is from indicative affirmations about the reality of freedom from sin (vv. 1-10) through imperative calls to appropriate this reality-possibility (vv. 11-13) and back to the affirmation in v. 14 that sin will not lord it over you because you are not under law but under grace. Since the law is the power of sin (1 Cor 15:56), if it is done away with (v. 14b), sin is reduced in power (v. 14a).

It is important that for Paul while the believer has already shared in Christ's *death* through baptism (vv. 4a, 5a, 6a, 7) sharing Christ's *resurrection* is "reserved" (Käsemann 1980, 166–67) for the future (v. 5b). Through sharing Christ's death a new quality of life is possible in this life (vv. 4, 6), but we are not yet raised with Christ (Phil 3:10). This means that salvation is never possessed but is a continuing process in which grace and faith interact (2 Cor 3:18; 4:16).

It has often been held that the MYSTERY RELIGIONS of the ancient world (the worship of Attis, Osiris, Dionysus, etc.) focused on a dying-rising deity with whom the worshiper could attain unity and deification through ritual acts. By means of the cultic celebration the worshiper passed from death to life with the deity. This influenced Paul's view of baptism.

It has been questioned, on the other hand, whether any sources truly substantiate the idea that the mysteries were in existence in Paul's time, and real differences have been pointed out between Paul's understanding of baptism and the mystery rites.

For example, the mystery rites were believed to be effective in themselves, automatically, while for Paul baptism is effective only when appropriated by faith. Or in the mysteries the worshiper is absorbed into the deity while in Paul the believer retains his or her identity but has a new relationship with God (Best 1955, 47–48; Wagner 1967, 117–18, 195, 198, 202, 212, 217).

Whatever the chronological relationship between Paul and the mysteries and however many very real differences there were between them, they had one important thing in common. Redemptive power extends from the deity to the worshipers by means of symbolic acts. This is also true in Judaism where, for example, the liberating power of the EXODUS is re-experienced through the celebration of PASSOVER.

6:15-23. Sin and death. Paul begins his discussion of the second reason for not remaining in sin by repeating the initial words from 6:1: *What then?* Should we sin because we are not under the law but under grace? And again: "Absolutely not." The central point is that one should not sin because sin produces death.

Paul interweaves four kinds of material in this section: theological reflection, indicative affirmations about their being set free from sin, the imperative to be righteous, and observations about the Romans' past way of life.

Paul's theological reflections deal with the paradoxical interaction of freedom and slavery. A person is the slave of whatever lord or power he or she obeys. But the choice to acknowledge and obey *no* lord is not a human possibility. As finite creatures human beings must obey some higher power. The only choice is whether one will obey sin or obey God (or righteousness) (vv. 16, 18, 22). To be free from sin is to be the slave of God or righteousness. But to be free from sin is at the same time to be free for God and obedience, which one was not when one was a slave of sin (v. 20). Real freedom for Paul is slavery to the power that can give life (v. 22). Romans 6 emphasizes that freedom from sin is *slavery to God* which is *freedom for God* and obedience. But 1 Cor 3:21-23 adds that one who belongs to Christ and God is grounded in a reality beyond the world. On the basis of this ground the believer is also free *for the world*, free to engage in the totality of the world's reality without being enslaved by it.

Paul declares to the Romans that they have in fact been liberated from sin (vv. 18, 22). But as is typical of him, he also places them under the imperative to make that freedom/slavery—which is both a reality and a possibility—into an actuality. Present your bodily members as slaves to righteousness which leads to sanctification (v. 19c).

Käsemann has argued that for Paul the righteousness that God establishes in believers includes obedi-ence. The ethical imperative does not stand alongside the indicative statements about the reality of justification or righteousness but coincides with them or is integrated into them (Käsemann 1980, 174–75). SANCTIFICATION is the believer's being for God in his or her everyday existence in the secular world (183), and for Käsemann justification includes sanctification; they coincide (174, 183). Or he can say that gift (justification) and task (sanctification) coincide (175). Obedience must verify the gift (174). Christ is no longer the Lord of the one who does not obediently serve him (175). If one fails at the task, he or she loses the gift.

Käsemann's interpretation ignores the fact that for Paul it is the *ungodly* or *sinful* person who is justified (3:23-24; 4:5). The person who is justified is still sinful. The justified believer who performs acts deserving of condemnation is still justified by God and is still the object of the crucified and risen Christ's intercession (8:33-34). Nothing can separate us from the love of Christ (8:35-39).

At the same time it is certainly the case with Paul that the proper and intended result of justification is sanctification. Righteousness is toward or into sanctification (v. 19; but also, see commentary on 14:10-12).

The one who is justified by grace without regard to his or her religious or moral achievements is nevertheless not to continue in sin because to do so: (1) causes the self to be divided against itself and (2) produces death. The juxtaposition of these two reasons implies that one dimension of death is self-division. The other—and more fundamental—dimension of death is that it is hostility to and estrangement from God (8:6-8). To go on in sin is to be both against God (vv. 16, 18, 22; 8:7) and against oneself (6:2, 4, 6; 7:5, 9; 8:10). The fundamental sinful reality is being against God (1:21a, 23, 25), and being against oneself is its consequence (1:21b, 24b, 27). Death is the slave wages paid by sin when one serves sin.

The free gift of God is life—a new relationship of reconciliation with God, the reconstitution of a shattered society and the reuniting of the divided self.

Freedom from the Law, 7:1-25

7:1-6. A death frees from the law. Paul introduces this topic by stating a broad principle (v. 1) which he illustrates (vv. 2-3) and then extends into its theological application (vv. 4-6). The connections of the parts are far from obvious or smooth, but the whole thing may hold together better than it appears to. And the main point is clear: the believer has been freed from the law.

The principle taken literally is a truism. A person is freed from obligation to the law by his or her own death. In the illustration a wife is freed from the legal requirement to be faithful to her husband by her husband's death. Thus one person is freed from the law by the death of another (vv. 2-3).

The theological application (7:4-6) makes metaphorical use of both preceding motifs, one's own death and the death of another. Under the conditions of fallen existence—the flesh—sinful passions aroused by the law worked in our members to produce death. But believers have been discharged from the law by dying to it. They are dead as far as the law's enticement to earn salvation by works is concerned. The old self has died through the body of Christ—probably a reference to Christ's death. The believer participates in the redemptive effects of Christ's death by dying with him (6:4; 2 Cor 5:14-15).

7:7-25. The law, sin, and internal conflict. First Corinthians 15:56 states concisely that the law is the power of sin, and Rom 7 probes that relationship in an elaborate way. Both sin and the law are personified by Paul as cosmic powers, suprahuman persons. Sin has dominion, reigns, enslaves (Rom 6:6-7, 12-14, 16, 20). It lies dead, revives, deceives, and kills (vv. 8-9, 11). Similarly, the law comes in (5:20; 7:9), arouses sin (vv. 5, 7), takes us captive (v. 6), and promises life but deceives by serving up death (v. 10).

Sin uses the law (vv. 8, 13). But the law as the instrument of sin is so closely tied to sin as a power, sin as the initiator of sinning, that the law itself can appear as the initiator. Sin employs the law, but the law is the power (7:5; 1 Cor 15:56) that brings latent sin to active life (v. 9). Therefore, the law itself can be spoken of as the provoker that causes sin (v. 7) and that, installed in the flesh, works against God's redemptive intention (vv. 22-23).

The law provokes or arouses sin (vv. 7-14), and existence under the law is rent by internal conflict (vv. 15-25). Paul makes use of the Adam myth to interpret his own experience as typical of humankind. There are three questions (which interpenetrate each other) to be pursued in interpreting this passage.

1. What phase of Paul's life is he talking about when he speaks of himself as engaged in all kinds of covetousness and torn asunder by conflict between intention and result?

He can hardly be referring to his Jewish life because as a Jew he saw himself as blameless regarding the righteousness of the law (Phil 3:6). It can also be argued that his description ill fits his Christian life. While there are other places where he attributes conflict to the Christian life (8:10), in such places the redemptive forces are victorious (8:11, 16). But in Rom 7 the law and sin seem to have the upper hand. Moreover, the structure of Romans suggests that he is not talking about Christian experience in this chapter. Just as 1:18–3:20 provides a negative foil for 3:21–5:11, and 5:12-21 provides a negative foil for 6:1-23, and 9:1–10:21 does for chap. 11, so 7:1-25 provides a negative foil for 8:1-39 (Käsemann 1980, 205, 210).

The most likely possibility is that since Paul as a Jew felt blameless (Phil 3:6), Rom 7:7-25 is describing his past Jewish life from the standpoint of his Christian faith. Looking back on his pre-Christian past he sees that he was in fact sinful and self-divided, but prior to his conversion he was unconscious of his true condition. Here he is describing the human situation as fallen—fleshly—and under the power of sin (v. 14), a part of cosmic fallenness (1:18–3:20; 8:22-23) (Bultmann 1951, 246-49; Käsemann 1980, 192, 199).

The chief problem with the immediately preceding interpretation is that the past tenses with which Paul has been describing his experience in vv. 7-13 are replaced by the present tense when he begins to speak about his inner conflict (vv. 14-24). Must we not then say that the present tense verbs present his pre-Christian and unconscious self-dividedness as if it were present and conscious. Does not the present tense in fact extend the inner conflict into the present of Paul and his Christian readers? Believers are only in the process of being renewed (2 Cor 3:18; 4:16). As long as they bear the image of the old Adam (1 Cor 15:39) and do not have Christ fully formed in them (Gal 4:19), which means as long as time lasts (Phil 3:10-11), they struggle with sin and self-division.

2. What exactly is the nature of the sinful covetousness or desire that Paul describes or in exactly what sense does the law provoke sin?

The most obvious answer is that the law provokes acts of covetousness. That wrong acts are in view is supported by the fact that the passions of sin aroused by the law are plural (7:5). Also the reference to members of the body and fruit for death (7:5) alludes to the similar language in 6:19, 21 where sin is rebellion upon rebellion.

The law is not sin, yet Paul would not have sinned but for the law. The very prohibition against coveting generated every coveting in him (vv. 7-8). The dynamic is that the law as a demand for obedience is a reminder of human limitations and thereby provokes in people a will not to submit (8:7).

At the same time vv. 9-10 seems to be a transition to sin in a different sense incited by the law (Theissen 1987, 209–10). Sin (v. 9) is closely related to the fact that the law promises life but causes death (v. 10). The law promises life, and under the conditions of fallen existence (in the flesh) people assume that life is attained by doing the law (10:5). They attempt a righteousness of the law that is a righteousness of their own (10:3; Phil 3:9), a human righteousness that puts God in their *debt* (Rom 4:4). This also is a refusal to submit to God (10:3). The law incites sin in the sense of offering a means to establish one's own righteousness, which is a rejection of God's righteousness.

Perhaps the connecting link between these two dimensions of sin is the function that Paul assigns to the law in 3:19—to shatter every self-defense and hold people accountable. The law provokes sin in the sense of overt acts of disobedience. Then people, knowing from the law that they are accountable and without a word to say, attempt to establish their own righteousness by obedience to the law and to put God in their debt.

3. What is the nature of the inner conflict Paul describes in vv. 15-24? Its nature is governed by the two dimensions of sin that Paul has brought to light. It is not an either/or but a both/and.

Paul in anguish declares that he does not do what he intends but rather does what he hates. He can will the good, but he cannot do it (vv. 15, 18-19). He rather does evil.

This self-division is in some part moral. The law was for Paul as a Jew, and still is in some sense, an ethical standard (13:8-10; 1 Cor 7:19). Paul wills to do the moral good that the law requires but finds that he lacks the resources and does the opposite.

With this sense of failure—at some level of consciousness—he then tries to use the law to establish

righteousness and life for himself. Here the conflict is existential. He agrees that the law is good and spiritual (vv. 14, 16). He appropriates its promise to give life (v. 10a) but discovers that it gives death instead (v. 10b). The good he wills is life—salvation—but the evil he achieves is death, because he pursues his own righteousness rather than accepting God's.

We have seen that broadly speaking Paul evaluates the intention of the law positively but sees its results in the context of fallen human existence as negative. This paradoxical view of the law is seen in Rom 7. The law is not sin but is holy, just, good, spiritual, and promises life (vv. 7, 10, 12, 14, 16). Yet the law is the cause of sin (vv. 8-9) and deception and finally issues in death (v. 10). This ambiguity is seen compactly in vv. 22-23. He delights in the law in his inner person or mind—the law in its redemptive intention. But at war with this law there is another law, the law of sin in his members, the law misunderstood as demanding works. This law takes him captive.

Paul calls out in his wretchedness—the wretchedness of his pre-Christian but also Christian existence—and asks who will deliver him from this body of death, the death of self-division. And now in his explicit Christian voice he offers his thanks to God through Jesus Christ for deliverance (v. 25a). But in the last sentence of this discussion he returns with great realism to the self-dividedness that even existence in faith never escapes during this historical life: I serve in my mind the law of God, but in the flesh—the condition of fallenness—I serve the law of sin (v. 25b).

Freedom from Death and Flesh, 8:1-39

8:1-11. Law, flesh, death, Christ, and Spirit. The affirmation that there is therefore now no condemnation for those in Christ is based on the rescue from the law accomplished by Christ (7:25a) despite the continuing struggle of the life of faith (7:25b). The ground of this absence of condemnation is further specified as our liberation from the law of sin and death by the law of the Spirit. The law of the Spirit and the law of sin and death could mean two principles of reality or two ways of understanding the Law of Moses—in terms of its intention (to give life and the Spirit) and in terms of its result (to cause death).

The law is a *power* that overpowers human beings and entices them against their wills into sin. But the ambiguity of the law expresses itself in yet another way. The law is also *weak*. Its weakness is its inability to do what God intended it to do—give life and faith. This weakness was caused by the flesh—human being in its fallenness—which is also a power. But God has done what the law could not do by sending his own Son.

The sending is probably not thought of as a sending from a preexistent heavenly state. There is no reference to a preexistent mode of being or activity, as in Phil 2:6; Col 1:15, 17; 1 Cor 8:6; Heb 1:2. The sending is more like an earthly appointment, as in the commissioning of the prophets (Isa 49:1, 5-6; Jer 1:5, 7) or the sending of the son to the vineyard in the parable of The Wicked Tenants (Mark 12:6; Fuller 1978, 41-44). That Jesus was sent in the *likeness of sinful flesh* does not mean that Paul questions Jesus' real humanity. Jesus was a man of flesh (1:3) and suffered the human condition under the power of wrath or curse (Gal 3:13) and the law (Gal 4:4). But Paul's insertion of the word *likeness* suggests that in the case of Christ the sin that is endemic to the flesh was overcome (2 Cor 5:21).

The purpose of sending the Son is that the law's requirement (*dikaiōma*) might be fulfilled in us who walk according to the Spirit. This requirement is probably the faith that the law intends. But the reference to walking also includes the ethical life that both the law and faith have in view.

For Paul flesh is not a *part* of human being but the *whole* self from a certain point of view. Paul has deepened and developed the OT notion of flesh as weakness (Ps 56:41; Isa 31:3; Davies 1948, 18-20) and given it a range of meanings. The flesh is the visible or physical (1 Cor 15:39; 2 Cor 12:7) and as such is weak and perishable in comparison with God (Gal 4:13; 1 Cor 15:50; 2 Cor 4:11). Yet it is the sphere of human existence created by God in which believers and all others live, and it is not judged to be evil (Gal 2:20; Phil 1:24). But the concept takes on a darker connotation when it is denied that believers still live in the flesh (Rom 7:5; 8:9). Then flesh becomes fully evil, virtually identical with sin. The mind of the flesh is hostile to God, refuses to submit, and those in the flesh cannot please God (vv. 6-8). The mind of the flesh prefers its own righteousness to God's (10:1-3). Observe that when the flesh is physical it is not evil, and when it is identical with sin it is not physical. The flesh as evil is a stance of the whole self. It is the self as trusting in itself or in some other aspect of finite reality. Paul's term for mind here (*phronēma*) does not just mean thought but the orientation or direction of one's whole existence (Käsemann 1980, 219).

This direction of one's existence *is* death. Death is not a punishment added to this hostility to God, but death is already present in it.

The power that liberates from flesh and death Paul refers to interchangeably as the Spirit, Spirit of God, Spirit of Christ, and Christ in you (vv. 9-10). The tension and ambiguity of existence in faith are still in view: although *your* body is dead because of sin, the Spirit of *God* is life because of the new relationship that is righteousness. Clearly here the Spirit of the one raising Jesus from the dead is the power of God operative in human existence to give life to dying bodies.

The body for Paul, like flesh, is not a *part* of a human being but is the *whole* self or person from a certain point of view. The body is the person in his or her physicality as a part of the material world (1 Cor 12:12-26; 13:3; 2 Cor 10:10; Gal 6:17). This shades off, however, into the body as the whole person, something one *is*, not something one has (Rom 6:12; 12:1). More specifically the body is the self in its *relatedness* in principle to other dimensions of reality (Bultmann 1951, 192-96, 201-203; Käsemann 1969, 135; 1971, 17-23).

In the relationship of self to self the body is perhaps most characteristically the self as the object of the self's will (Rom 6:12-14; 12:1; 1 Cor 9:27; 13:3; Phil 1:20). But the body as having deeds of its own is also subject (Rom 8:13). In fact the parallelism between body and spirit in 1 Cor 6:15, 17 shows that the body has a spiritual dimension. It is the place where death and resurrection with Christ is both understood and actualized (2 Cor 4:7-12).

A part of the meaning of body is its identity with flesh (1 Cor 6:16; 2 Cor 4:10-11). As such it is the self as the object of the world's physical violence (Gal 6:17; 2 Cor 11:23-29) and the self as sexually related (1 Cor 6:16). But the body is also the self as intended for the Lord (1 Cor 6:13, 15). The body can be given over to the power of death (Rom 7:24; 8:10-11), but the body is also the vehicle of eternal life (1 Cor 15:44), the spiritual body, the self fully assimilated to the realm of the Spirit. Here its fleshly physicality is explicitly denied (1 Cor 15:44-50). The *identity* of the self in relation to God and self is maintained in the resurrection, but *not* its *physicality* (Via 1990, 68-70).

8:12-17. Life in the Spirit as an obligation or task. In the previous section the Spirit's overcoming of the believer's death and self-division is spoken of as an assured reality. But in this passage the transformation of death into life is a task and obligation of the believer. It is in some way not certain that the believer will carry out this task.

Paul says: *If you live according to the flesh*—and you *will* (a condition determined as true)—*you will die*. But immediately thereafter he also states: *If by* (or in) *the Spirit you put to death the deeds of the body*—and you *will* (again a condition determined as true)—*you will live*. Each of these conditions is stated as equally possible. Paul perhaps leans toward the latter since he moves on to affirmative statements about the leading and witness of the Spirit. Body here is the equivalent of flesh in its evil sense (see Gal 5:16-17, 19).

Thematically for Paul (eternal) life is the gift of GRACE (Rom 1:16-17; 5:21; 6:23), but in 8:13 life is conditioned on the believer's putting an end to sinful acts. The believer must do what God has done in him or her.

The role of the Spirit here is to make being a child of God a *present* reality. The Spirit bears witness to our spirit that we are in fact God's children. The human spirit here is not a fragment or apportionment of the divine Spirit, but the strictly human spirit. The Spirit in bearing witness with our spirit is not talking to itself; rather, divine and human spirits are distinguished.

The human spirit is not a *part* of the self but the *whole* self from a particular standpoint. The spirit is the self as knowing subject. As spirit the self knows itself (1 Cor 2:11) and knows the public world and other people (1 Cor 16:18; 2 Cor 2:13; 7:13). Perhaps most importantly, as Rom 8:16 shows, the human spirit is the self in its openness to the testimony of God's Spirit (Via 1990, 70–73).

If we are children of God, we are fellow heirs with Christ, provided we suffer with him in order that we might be glorified with him. This note of suffering becomes the theme of the next section.

8:18-27. Suffering the wait for redemption. Present suffering cannot be compared to the overcompensating GLORY to be revealed—glory being Paul's term for the full manifestation of eschatological redemption. Glory is the substance of resurrection existence that believers will finally share with Christ (8:17; 2 Cor 3:18; 4:17; Phil 3:20-21).

Just as human beings struggle and groan against the power of sin, law, flesh, and death, so the nonhuman creation waits and longs for release from the decay and futility that God has allowed the cosmic powers to impose on the world. The human and non-human

creation form a solidarity—they struggle and groan together—so that neither will be fully redeemed apart from the other (cf. Gen 3:17-19; 4 Ezra 7:11-14). In 8:14-16 being a child of God is a *present* reality. But in vv. 22-23 while the Spirit gives a *foretaste* of this reality, full adoption as a child of God is identified with the resurrection of the body and is projected into a future for which we wait. Yet we wait with the hope in which salvation resides. Although we do not yet see our full redemption, hope is confident about the future which is in God's hands.

8:28-30. God's predetermining purpose. According to some manuscripts (reliable and diversified) Paul states that *all things* work toward the good—a happy outcome—for those who love God. According to other manuscripts (reliable but less numerous and less diversified) he says that *God* works with all things toward the good for those who love God. Whichever reading one takes, Paul has God's sovereign intention in view. Things do not work on their own. The *all things* probably refers especially to the suffering struggle in which believers are engaged.

The good is worked for those *who are called according to [God's] purpose*. These people God foreknew and predestined. God's redemptive intention is always there ahead of us. The eternal purpose of God becomes concrete historical reality in calling and justification, which have already happened. But here Paul goes further and also affirms our glorification—our final resurrection existence—as a part of the salvation that has already happened. This is in tension with his general tendency to reserve glorification for the future.

8:31-39. The certain security of the believer. What then shall we say? What is the outcome of our being already glorified (8:30)—despite being not yet glorified (8:17; Phil 3:21)? The outcome is that nothing can undo our redemption. Even if we do something deserving of condemnation, God's giving his Son for us guarantees our justification against which no charge can stand. Christ who died and was raised is interceding for us at God's right hand. This mythological image gives concrete expression to the never ending validity of Christ's death for us. Nothing can separate us from the love of Christ (v. 35) or, interchangeably, from the love of God in Christ (v. 39).

Our own deeds that are worthy of condemnation cannot separate us (vv. 31-37). Neither can the afflictions and reversals of the historical process separate us (v. 35). Nor can anything that life or death, present or future, might hand out separate us (v. 38). Not even cosmic fate can pull us away from the love of God. That is what Paul means by the principalities and powers (vv. 38-39). Paul presupposed the worldview of his time, which held that there are personal, hostile, supernatural powers that victimize and control human beings. Christ has overcome them (Via 1990, 40–44).

God's Word and the Destiny of Israel, 9:1–11:36

This section is not a parenthesis or excursus in which Paul merely indulges his Jewish patriotism by claiming for Israel a permanent place in the purpose of God. Paul rather addresses here an issue that grows essentially out of the preceding discussion. Can the word of God be trusted? For Paul the gospel of the righteousness of God as justification by faith is the fulfillment of God's promise to save Israel (Rom 4:13, 16, 20). *Israel* is the people of the COVENANT, the LAW, the sonship, the promises (9:4-5). But when the promises were fulfilled in the manifestation of God's justifying RIGHTEOUSNESS the result has been that most Jews are not justified believers while most believers are gentiles. Is justification by faith apart from the law then a nullification of God's promise to save Israel? Is God's promise unreliable? Has the word of God failed (9:6)?

Paul develops a three-fold argument to show that the word of God has *not* failed. This demonstration is of great theological importance to Paul, for if God's promising word to Israel is not reliable, then God's word is not reliable for anyone.

God's Rejection of Israel, 9:1-29

9:1-5. Paul's deep sorrow about his people. Paul is in anguish because most of his kinspeople according to the flesh—the Israelites—stand outside the realm of salvation. He would give up his own salvation for them if that were possible. It is ironical that Israel is mostly lost, for these are the very people who have had the tokens of salvation—sonship, the covenants, the law, the patriarchs, the promises. And from Israel the Christ is physically descended. To the word "Christ" (NRSV *Messiah*) Paul adds *who is over all, God blessed forever. Amen.*

How God is related to Christ here is a difficult interpretive problem (for various possible readings see Cranfield 1981, 464–70; Metzger 1975, 520–23) because the lack of punctuation in the original manuscripts leaves the relationship ambiguous. The two main alternatives are as follows: (1) Understand God as in apposition to Christ and read "Christ, who is God

over all." (2) Put a period rather than a comma after Christ thus separating God from Christ in an independent doxology and read " . . . Christ. God who is over all be blessed." Probably syntax and Pauline style favor the first. But the Pauline theological pattern seems to favor the second. Nowhere else does Paul directly identify Christ with God, and in 1 Cor 15:24, 27 he clearly subordinates the Son to God the Father.

9:6-29. The sovereign electing will of God. God's word promised salvation to Israel (Rom 4:16-18) (see commentary on Rom 11 for Paul's ambiguity regarding the constitution of the saved Israel). But most of Israel is not saved. Does that mean that God's word has failed? *No.* Here Paul gives his first argument to support the reliability of God's promise. It has never been the case that all of Abraham's descendants are saved. God's dealings with Israel have been consistent, for God has always distinguished among the descendants of ABRAHAM between the physical descendants and the children of the promise who alone are the children of God. Everything depends on God's electing will; nothing depends on human position or performance. Paul makes much use of the OT throughout this section.

For example, when twin sons were born to the patriarch ISAAC and his wife REBECCA, before they were born or had done anything good or bad, God chose JACOB and rejected ESAU. Only God's decisive action counts, not human works. This action of God can be spoken of as his promise (vv. 6-8), his calling (vv. 11-12), or his purpose of ELECTION (v. 11). All of these are expressions of his will (v. 18). God's will prompts God to show MERCY toward some (vv. 15-16) and to harden the hearts of others (vv. 17-18).

If then everything comes from God in deciding salvation or rejection and nothing from human beings—Paul's diatribal questioner will ask—how can God find fault since no one can resist his will (v. 19)? Paul's answer is that people have no more right to question God than the clay has to question the potter who molds it. But Paul does go on to say that in all of this God's purpose has been to create vessels of mercy destined for glory from among both gentiles and Jews.

The salvation of the gentiles Paul grounds on the promise in Hos 1:10; 2:1, 23 that God will make his people from those who are *not* his people. Paul, however, has changed the meaning of the OT text, for in HOSEA, the "not my people" refers to unfaithful, sinful Israel and not to the gentiles. Paul grounds the salvation of the relatively few believing Jews on the prediction that he attributes to Isaiah (but which actually amalgamates Isa 10:22-23 and Hos 1:10) that only a REMNANT of the huge number of Israelites will be saved.

God's word has not failed because from the beginning (with Abraham) until now the identity of Israel does not depend on birth (not all of Abraham's descendants are children of God) nor on performance of works, but solely on who God says it is by the exercise of his sovereign electing will. The failure of most of Israel to be saved is determined by God's doing, and God has been consistent.

Israel's Rejection
of Righteousness through Faith, 9:30–10:21

It is then highly paradoxical when Paul states as his second argument against the failure of God's word that Israel has missed out on salvation because *Israel* has rejected God's way of dealing with humankind. Everything depends on God; everything depends on Israel.

9:30–10:4. Israel's pursuit of righteousness by works. Paul notes an irony. The gentiles, who did not pursue righteousness, attained righteousness by faith. Israel, on the other hand, did pursue the law that affords righteousness. This pursuit of the law was not a mistake in itself, for the law can lead to righteousness.

The law as limit (Rom 7:7) and as accuser (3:19) makes people aware of their finitude and guilt and thus should point them in faith to God as the source of salvation. But under the conditions of fallen existence the law enticed Israel to attempt her own salvation. That is, Israel wrongly thought that the law called for works rather than faith. Thus Israel failed to attain the *law*. This shows that the real intention of the law was faith.

Paul acknowledges Israel's zeal for God but denies that her zeal is enlightened. In ignorance of the righteousness that comes from God Israel sought to establish her own righteousness by means of the law. What is wrong with the righteousness of the law for Paul is that it asserts itself to establish a right relationship with God rather than receiving the relationship from God. It does not submit (*hypotassō* in the passive) *to God's righteousness* (10:3). This is parallel to Paul's statement in 8:7-8 that *the mind that is set on the flesh is hostile to God [and] does not submit* (*hypotassō* in the passive) *to God's law*, that is, to the intention of the law to evoke faith. The parallelism between the two passages shows that pursuing the righteousness of

the law is an expression of the mind of the flesh in its hostility to God.

Paul then says "for Christ is the end (*telos*) of the law, leading to righteousness for every believer" (author trans.). The *for* (*gar*) does not express the reason for what Paul has just said. That is, Christ's being the end of the law is not the reason for Israel's not submitting. Rather it is the reason for something that Paul implies but does not state: Israel *should have* submitted to God's righteousness, *for* Christ is the end of the law (Williams 1980, 283–84).

Christ is the end of the law (10:4) in two senses, corresponding to Paul's dialectical—yes and no—understanding of the law. Christ is the *fulfillment* of the law's intention—to evoke faith and give life. But Christ is the *termination* of the law from the standpoint of its result—its being understood as a demand for works that produces death.

There is a difference between the attitude that Paul criticizes here—trusting in one's *obedient* works of the law as able to establish one's own righteousness with God—and the attitude he criticizes in 2:17-24—trusting that one is secure with God because one knows God's will in the law and approves what is excellent while at the same time *disobeying* the law. It should be remembered that Paul regards *all* people as under the law in principle; therefore, these sinful postures toward the law are not peculiarly Jewish but rather characteristically human.

10:5-13. Word, faith, and resurrection. Here Paul draws a line through the OT distinguishing between what is invalid and valid in the Jewish scriptures. To MOSES in Lev 18:5 he attributes the view that the righteousness of the law promises life to those who live by achieving obedience (v. 5; see Käsemann 1980, 285). *But* (adversative *de* indicating a contrast, v. 6) the righteousness of faith—replacing Moses as the speaker in Deut 30:11-14—calls, not for the achievement of obedience, but for believing and confessing the word. Paul interprets this word in Deuteronomy as the saving proclamation of Jesus' lordship and resurrection.

The very surprising thing about Paul's interpretation of Deut 30:11-14 is that the "word" in the Deuteronomy passage means the "law" (30:11, 14)—just as Leviticus speaks about the law—and not the righteousness of faith. Paul has read a fully Christian understanding of word back into the Deuteronomy passage, but his interpretation is not wholly arbitrary. "Word" in Deuteronomy does mean "law," but it also means the effective preaching about the God of Israel who gives life by bringing people through death (Deut 32:1-3, 6-13, 19-35, 36-43; esp. 32:39). This theme would have had a close affinity with Paul's preaching of the death and resurrection of Jesus. Thus while Paul clearly over-Christianized Deut 30:11-14, we can understand why he saw a connection between his preaching and the message of Deuteronomy. As in Rom 4 so also here he finds moments of the gospel in the OT.

Judaism prior to and in Paul's time used Deut 30:11-14 to speak about the inaccessibility of WISDOM. Wisdom is accessible only to God, but God has brought her near in the law (Bar 3:29–4:1). Paul may have Baruch as well as Deuteronomy in mind. In Rom vv. 6-8 Paul uses spatial imagery—up, down, near—of both the resurrected Christ and the preached word. Thus Christ and the word are in effect made identical. The word of the righteousness of faith says: Do not seek the risen Christ in a cosmically distant place but seek him in the near word which enters your heart and brings you to faith.

Paul personifies the righteousness of faith and has it speak of the nearness of the resurrected Christ in vv. 6-9. Righteousness first speaks of the nearness of Christ in negative terms (not far) and then in positive terms. But the fact that the category of nearness holds together the negative and positive ways of speaking suggests that they both have the same subject. Speaking negatively righteousness says: Do *not* seek the risen Christ up there in heaven to bring him down or down there in the abyss among the dead to bring him up (vv. 6-7). Then when righteousness speaks of the nearness of Christ positively or directly, it replaces the risen Christ with the preached word (v. 8). Righteousness does not say that Christ is near but that the word is near, on your lips and in your heart.

It is evident from the negative expression of Paul's theme (Christ is not far) that his point is the nearness of *Christ*. Therefore, it makes no sense to speak of the nearness of the *word* if the word does not represent Christ. Thus when Paul replaces Christ with the word, puts the word in Christ's place, he is interpreting the risen Christ *as* the power of the proclaimed word about Christ to bring people to faith (vv. 8, 17). Faith calls upon the Lord who is present in the heart by means of the word. Everyone who calls upon this Lord will be saved.

10:14-21. Preaching, faith, and understanding. Paul unfolds a series of stages that are necessary to lead to salvation: the sending of preachers, preaching, hearing,

believing, and calling upon. Paul then affirms, by appealing to the predictions of scripture rather than to historical evidence, that preachers have been sent, have preached, and have been heard. But not all of Israel has obeyed or believed what was heard (v. 16). Paul then at v. 19 introduces a new category into his series—understanding. Did Israel not understand? He answers the question by again appealing to the OT. The gentiles who were not seeking God have found God. Evidently Paul means to say that the gentiles at least have understood. But Israel has been disobedient and contrary.

Paul's point is less than clear, and his answer to the question whether Israel understood and his view about how understanding is related to believing (faith) can be interpreted in two ways.

(1) Paul distinguishes faith from understanding and means to say that since the gentiles understood the gospel surely Israel understood it although they did not (all) believe it.

(2) For Paul faith and understanding overlap extensively. Understanding is the intellectual element of faith itself and like faith shapes human existence (Rom 12:1-2; 2 Cor 3:12-18). Thus Israel no more understood than she believed, and that is made all the more ironical by the fact that the gentiles did understand and believe. This seems to be the more probable interpretation.

Paul has argued that only a few Jews are believers: (1) because God alone has decreed who among the descendants of Abraham shall be the spiritual Israel and (2) because Israel in the interest of self-assertion has neither believed nor understood. The relationship between these two opposing explanations can be understood in at least two ways.

1. The relationship is radically paradoxical. From one side God's act of will determines everything, and from the other side it is totally a human decision. If this is not seen as a hopeless contradiction, both sides are taken as necessary to account for the mystery of human destiny while acknowledging that there is no way to explain how they meet and interact.

2. There is finally an insoluble paradox, but to some extent the divine and the human can be seen as fusing and their point of contact, as definable. This presupposes that the divine and human are to some degree commensurate and comparable.

In 1 Cor 1:18 and 2 Cor 2:14-16 the divine, initiating activity occurs in the preaching of the gospel and thereby creates a situation in which a decision is inescapable for those who hear. Some respond with a "yes" and gain life while others respond with a "no" and inherit death. These are human decisions. The opposite destinies of the gentiles and Israel depend on how *they* decide (vv. 19-21; cf. 9:30-32). Yet the divine action in preaching made the decisions inescapable and necessary, determined that the decisions would in fact be made. Therefore, the yes leading to life and the no leading to death are at the same time in some sense divine actions or divine determinations.

The Final Salvation
of All Israel, 11:1-36

Paul's third argument in favor of the reliability of God's promise to Israel is that in the end God will save all Israel.

11:1-6. The present salvation of a remnant. Paul himself—a saved Israelite—is proof that God has not abandoned God's historical people. Beyond that there is now, as in the past (Elijah's time), a REMNANT chosen by grace, not rewarded for works.

11:7-10. Election and hardening. Israel (as a whole) did not attain the right relationship with God (9:31-32) that it sought, but the elect attained it. The rest were hardened. Note that Israel contains both the elect and the hardened. Paul reiterates the point made in 9:14-18 that both the election of the saved and the hardening of the lost are God's doing. Using scripture Paul underlines the assertion that the failure of the hardened to see and to understand God's intention was visited upon them by God. The wrong choice establishes an inescapable destiny.

11:11-16. The stumbling of Israel and the salvation of the gentiles. Israel has stumbled but not so as to fall, that is, not so as to be finally lost. Israel's stumbling, her temporary rejection of and by God, has provided the opportunity for the salvation of the gentiles. The purpose of the gentiles' salvation is to make Israel jealous, and that will lead to the salvation of *some* Jews by means of Paul's apostolic ministry. Evidently Paul's point is that Israel's seeing the gentiles' attaining the salvation promised to Israel will make her want to claim her own lost heritage. If Israel's rejection has had beneficial results for the gentiles and the world, how much more consequential will be her inclusion. It will bring about—or be brought about by—the resurrection from the dead.

In v. 16 Paul states a principle that will turn out to have far-reaching implications (see commentary on 11:25-32). In the OT (Num 15:17-21; Lev 23:14) a holy offering to God from the first fruits released the rest of the harvest for general or *non-holy* uses. Paul reversed this and stated that the holiness of the first fruits makes the whole *holy*. But the principle is the same in both cases, and it is reiterated with the root and branches image. What is true for the part is also true for the whole to which the part belongs. What is actual in the part—first fruits and root—is latent or potential in the whole—the full lump or harvest and the branches. The part represented by the first fruits and root is probably Abraham and/or the believing Israelite remnant through the centuries. The whole imaged in the full harvest and the branches is all Israel. Before drawing out the implications of this (in 11:25-32) Paul continues—in 11:17-24—his specific address to the gentile Christians in Rome, which he began at v. 13.

11:17-24. The relationship of saved gentiles to the historical Israel. Here Paul takes the root and branches image of 11:16 and develops it into an allegory of the history of salvation in which the people of God throughout history are portrayed as a cultivated olive tree (vv. 17, 24) or its root (v. 18), unbelieving Israelites are represented as branches cut off from this tree, and believing gentiles are imaged as *a wild olive shoot* grafted into the tree.

Several indications of diatribe style are seen here. (1) The gentile Christians are identified with the personified *wild olive shoot*. (2) This olive shoot is the diatribal interlocutor who raises an objection (v. 19). (3) Paul issues admonitions and warnings (Stowers 1981, 99–100).

Olive cultivation of the time included both grafting wild shoots into cultivated trees and cultivated shoots into wild trees (Cranfield 1981, 565–66; Dunn 1988, 661). Paul's meaning depends less on particular agricultural practices than on his metaphorical use of them. He does seem to want to suggest that there is something unnatural—unexpected—about finding gentiles among the Israelite people of God (v. 24).

In this passage the believing community, which extends from Abraham down into the church of Paul's time, does not exist because individual believers decide to get together and form it. Rather the historical community is always there prior to the individual, and individuals are saved by being placed in the community by God. The root (the historical believing community) supports the grafted in shoots, not vice versa.

The gentile Christians are not to think themselves superior to the Jews (branches) who have been cut off. The latter were cut off because of their unbelief, and the gentile Christians are in only because of their faith. They are dependent on both the prior existence of the tree and God's gift of faith. But *they* have a responsibility to continue in faith. If they let thinking highly of themselves replace awe and faith, God will cut them off also.

However strongly Paul affirmed in 8:31-39 that nothing can separate believers from the love of God, here he allows that believers may in fact renounce faith and be cut off. From the standpoint of God's intention salvation is certain. From the standpoint of possible human lack of resolution, salvation is not so certain. And yet since faith is *God's* work in believers as well as the latter's own decision, can faith finally be renounced?

Paul makes a transition to the next section by reminding the gentile Christians that if they have been unnaturally grafted into the saved community, how much more will God graft the cut off natural branches (Jews) back into the tree.

11:25-32. The mystery of Israel's final salvation. Having pronounced severe judgment on the Jews (chap. 2) and declared that most of them now stand outside of salvation (9:30–10:3; 10:18-21; 11:7-10), Paul here affirms that once the hardening of Israel allows the full number of gentiles to come in, then all Israel will be saved. By *the full number of the Gentiles* he probably means all the elect among the gentiles or gentiles as a whole. By *all Israel* Paul probably means Israel as a whole but not necessarily every single Jew. That would be consonant with the contemporary Jewish understanding of "all Israel" (Mishnah, *Sanh* 10). Paul anticipated this development in 4:16 where he says that grace is to avail for *all* the seed of Abraham— those who belong to the law and those who share the faith of Abraham.

Evidently Paul believes that the salvation of Israel will be accomplished by the eschatological return of Christ (vv. 26-27), whose preaching will bring Israel to faith. Faith is the only way that either gentiles (1:16-17; 3:21-26; 9:30-31) or Jews (1:16-17; 3:19-20; 4:12; 10:6-10, 13; 11:5-6) have ever come to salvation. So will it be at the end.

It is not possible that all Israel would not be finally saved because in choosing the patriarchs God has irrevocably called all Israel. The call, the covenant, the promises (9:4-5) cannot be nullified (vv. 28-29).

Paul concludes his argument and his vision of the future with the affirmation that God has consigned all to disobedience in order that he might have mercy on all. Mercy can be fully appropriated only when sin has been fully experienced and acknowledged (3:19-20; 7:7, 13, 15, 24-25). This belongs to the purpose of God. When Paul reaches this stage of his argument, it is no longer just that all Israel will be saved. It is now that *all human beings* will finally be the recipients of God's mercy (v. 32).

This vision of the future moves Paul to praise God for God's riches, wisdom, and inscrutable ways whose depths are unknowable to humankind and to give God glory.

In the course of Rom 9–11 Paul's thought about ELECTION undergoes a decided change. He moves *from* a quantitative division of human beings in which some are chosen and others are rejected (9:6-18) *to* a qualitative division in which rejection (disobedience) and election (mercy) are two stages through which *all* pass (v. 32). It is impossible to say how conscious Paul might have been of the shift.

This change is mediated by the principle articulated in 11:16 that what is actual in the part is latent in the whole. Some Jews and some gentiles have actual faith; therefore, all Jews and all gentiles have latent faith and ultimately will have actual faith (v. 32). Romans 11:16 in the context of Paul's thought leads by an inevitable logic to v. 32—the salvation of all human beings as the recipients of God's mercy.

The change in point of view leaves some tensions in Paul's theological argument. In 2:4, 17-18, 22-24 he criticizes Jews who presume upon the kindness of God and assume that their relationship with God is secure whether or not they are obedient. He implicitly condemns the assumption that being a member of the covenant people (9:4-5) places one among the elect (11:5-7). And yet he himself takes the position that belonging to the covenant people constitutes an irrevocable call (11:28-29) to salvation.

The affirmation of the salvation of all stands in tension with Paul's frequently expressed clear belief that God will execute a final judgment that will leave some outside of God's kingdom in final death (6:23; 14:10-12; 1 Cor 6:9-10; 2 Cor 5:10; Gal 5:19-21; 6:7; Phil 3:18-19; 1 Thes 5:3).

Perhaps both sides of these tensions are necessary to disclose the mystery of human destiny as Paul sought to grapple with it and to express the uncertain certainty of existence in faith. Paul's logic leads to the affirmation of universalism, the salvation of all people. But it would be presumption and an offense against God's sovereignty to tell God that God *will* save all human beings individually. The final judgment motif protects against that presumption. Yet the sweep of Paul's argument makes it impossible to assert that any particular individual will not be saved. One is assured of the final salvation of all (11:32) but must not assume one's own security (2:4, 17-18, 22-24). One is assured of the final victory of God's intention to save all (11:32) and redeem the cosmos (8:18-25), but in the course of the historical process one is not sure whether one belongs to the true believing remnant (11:5-7). The believer hopes (8:24-25; Phil 3:10-14)—with confidence (Rom 5:3-5).

God's Mercy (Righteousness) and the Behavior of Believers, 12:1–15:13

The *therefore* of 12:1 demonstrates a close relationship between Paul's theological interpretation of salvation in chaps. 1–11 and the ethical exhortation which he is going to give in 12:1–15:13—salvation, and for that reason, moral action.

Ethical Renewal as the Appropriation of Mercy, 12:1-2

Paul uses the expression *the mercies of God* (v. 1) to summarize the meaning of the gospel as he has developed it in Rom 1–11. The word for *mercy* here (*oiktirmos*) is different from the root for mercy which he used prominently in chaps. 9–11 (*eleeō* and *eleos*), but the two are synonymous (9:15).

Mercy represents the event of grace which changes human existence and *enables* the ethical posture which is called for. This *enablement* generates and implicitly contains a *motive* or justifying reason for the action or disposition required. The motive is wholeness or integrity: to be and act in accord with the new self or life which one has become through the mercies of God.

The required ethical stance is a *result of* the new life and is not identical with the latter (1 Cor 5:7; Gal 5:25), but it is the expected and appropriate result. The relationship of new life to ethical behavior is paradoxical. The new life given through God's mercy in justification and liberation is a reality and not just a possibility. Yet the very existence of the imperative—*become what you are* by presenting your bodies as living sacrifices—shows that the new life is not quite real but is a possibility to be realized in the process of moral action (Via 1990, 50–51).

Body for Paul means the *whole self* in its *relatedness* to the multiple dimensions of reality. By use of the cultic terms *sacrifice* and *service* (*latreia*) Paul extends worship to include the behavior of the body-self in all of its life relationships in a way pleasing to God.

The ethical imperative is extended in the call to *not be conformed to this world but [to] be transformed by the renewing* of the mind. One's whole existence is changed by the reshaping of the mind. This entails a move from the old age of sin and law to the new eschatological time. Mind here means the power of critical judgment, the ability to test and differentiate (Käsemann 1980, 330), and also suggests moral perceptiveness (Cranfield 1981, 609).

The transformation of the self by the renewal of the mind is something that the believer is to do. It is his or her own responsibility: transform yourself. This possibility, however, has been enabled by God's enacted mercy.

The renewal of the mind reverses the situation of a person in sin and under the wrath of God as portrayed in 1:18-32. Paul's use of cognate terms makes this clear. Humankind tested reality and chose (*dokimazō*) not to have God in its knowledge (1:28a). In consequence God gave it up to a mind that cannot cope with the tests of reality (an *adokimos* mind) (1:28b). But now in the eschatological time of salvation the realizable purpose of the mind's renewal is that it might discover or discern (*dokimazō* again) the will of God. For Paul the ethical norm is the will of God. That will, however, has not been exhaustively given in ethical rules but must be newly discovered in the changing situations of life.

Love in One Body in Christ, 12:3-21

The quality of *sober judgment*, which is to characterize the believer, Paul borrows from the Greek philosophical tradition where it connotes moderation, restraint, or a sense of proportion. For Paul, however, the content of this moderation will be drawn from the renewal of the mind through the gospel and the believer's sense of his or her place in the Christian community, imaged in this passage as one body in Christ.

The application of moderation that Paul makes here is the avoidance of excessive self-estimation. The key to this is the unity and diversity of the community. The church is *one* entity, not because of good feelings the members have for each other, but because they are all grounded together in a single reality that transcends them all—the crucified-risen Christ in his self-identification with his people. Common participation in Christ enables risky involvement with one another.

But as in the human body, so in the one body in Christ the members have different functions. Each member has a gift (*charisma*) given by grace, and each gift includes a role or calling and a function: a servant serves, a teacher teaches, et cetera. That these gifts are *different* from each other is a consequence of *God's grace*. Therefore, no one gift in its difference can be regarded as more or less important than another.

An additional check on over self-estimation is the suggestion that God has given each person a measure of faith that accords with that person's capacities. One's self-evaluation is to be in line with the measure of faith one has been given (v. 3b). The gift of grace then that comes with faith confers both a calling and a limit (Käsemann 1980, 334). Each gift is to be exercised by carrying out the function that is proper to it, and one should not attempt more functions than one has been given. The teacher, for example, exercises his or her calling by teaching and should not think of himself or herself too highly by claiming the functions of other callings.

That love should *be genuine* takes on here (v. 9) a thematic significance. Heretofore in Romans Paul has used the term *agapē* of God's love (5:5, 8; 8:39) in its surprising concern for the radically underserving. Now Paul uses *agapē* for the love that believers should extend both to fellow members of the body (vv. 9-10) and to enemies on the outside (vv. 14, 20). The love that believers have received they are to share.

For Paul love as an ethical disposition and mode of action means to seek the good or advantage of the other person rather than one's own. Paul expresses this in a number of places and with different vocabulary (15:1-2; 1 Cor 10:24, 33-34; 13:5; Phil 2:4; 1 Thes 5:15). This central ethical norm is an open or formal one. What constitutes the good of the other is left undefined and is to be determined in differing social contexts (Via 1990, 60–63). In this particular passage seeking the advantage of the other takes such expressions as showing honor (v. 10), meeting physical needs (v. 13), emotional identification (v. 15), living in harmony (v. 16), and renouncing vengeance (vv. 19-20). Love does not passively accept evil but overcomes it (v. 21).

The State and Taxes, 13:1-7

Paul calls on every person [to] *be subject to the governing authorities*. Paul's terms (*exousia*—13:1; *archōn*—13:3) are subject to varying interpretations. Some think that he has in mind primarily or exclusive-ly human officials (Cranfield 1981, 656–59) while others hold that the terms refer both to the civil rulers and the cosmic or angelic powers that act through them (esp. Cullmann 1957, 63, 66, 98). Probably both dimensions are in view with the emphasis being on the human.

The political rulers have authority at all because it has been delegated to them by God, the ultimate source of authority, for the purpose of preventing wrongdoing and promoting the common good (vv. 1b, 4). Since God has appointed the rulers, to resist them is to resist God.

A part of the believer's responsibility is to pay taxes, both direct (taxes—*phoros*) and indirect (revenue—*telos*). The admonition to pay taxes and to show respect and honor to all to whom they are due may mean that Paul is addressing an actual situation in the Rome of the fifties—unrest about the collection of indirect taxes (Wedderburn 1991, 62).

Paul offers here—explicitly or implicitly—four reasons for being subject to the authorities. (1) It should be done out of respect for the authority of God (vv. 1-2). (2) One should obey in order to escape punishment from the rulers, which is also an instrument of the wrath of God (vv. 2b-5). (3) One should obey for the sake of conscience. This assumes that those addressed know that they have an obligation to obey and would have a painful conscience if they did not (v. 5b). (4) Paul implies that one obeys and pays taxes in order to promote the good of the socio-political order (v. 4).

Paul affirms that God's governance of the world requires the political order in *principle*, but since he can also be critical of *particular* government officials in *particular* circumstances (1 Cor 2:8; 6:4), he is not saying that the believer is obligated to support any and every particular political system.

Since Paul's admonition to obey *the governing authorities* and pay taxes (vv. 1-7) is surrounded (12:9; 13:8-10) and framed by his affirmation of the love principle, these two motifs interpret each other. Paying taxes is seen as an expression of love—the seeking the advantage of the other that flows from receiving the undeserved love of God. And in the exhortation to pay taxes love is seen to have expressions that are public, political, and unsentimental.

Love as the Fulfillment of the Law, 13:8-10

If the believer pays all of his or her debts—respect, honor, taxes—the only remaining—and continuing—obligation is the obligation *to love one another*. That obligation can never be exhausted. Love to the neighbor is the fulfillment and summing up of all the individual commandments in the law. This probably does not mean that all the commandments of the law are still to be obeyed as such but now with a loving attitude. It rather means that love to the neighbor has superseded the many individual commands of the law because it actualizes what the law has always intended—not to do any harm to the neighbor. And yet the OT commandments of God retain a certain relative validity for Paul (7:7-12; 1 Cor 7:19; 7:7-12) in that they suggest how love can be made concrete. The individual laws are traces of God's will (Via 1990, 63–65). And Paul uses an OT command—"love your neighbor as yourself" (Lev 19:18)—to disclose the full intention of the whole law.

The Pressure of the Imminent End, 13:11-14

Paul reminds his readers to wake up because salvation is nearer than when we first believed. Salvation here means the return of Christ, the final judgment, and the eschatological completion of redemption, the resurrection of the body. Having moved from dealing with a specific ethical issue (political involvement) and a broad ethical norm (love for the neighbor) Paul now interprets the situation of believers in the temporal process both theologically and ethically by using the imagery of *night* and *day*. The night is far advanced and day has drawn near. Believers live in this in-between time that is no longer darkest night but is not yet quite day. Yet the day—the last day—is near enough to put pressure on the believer to live as if it were day. Cast off the works of darkness—drunkenness, debauchery, quarreling—and walk (live) as in the day. The principle is that the believer is to live in a way that is appropriate to his or her situation in the temporal process of salvation. The problem is that while the present situation of salvation is ambiguously neither night nor day, the moral demand is to live unambiguously as in the day.

That the believer is not yet fully in the day is underscored by the imperative to *put on . . . Christ* (v. 14). If one is told to put on Christ, then one has not yet put him on. But Paul can also tell baptized believers that they have already put on Christ (Gal 3:27) and are already "children of the day" (1 Thes 5:5). Living in the day and putting on Christ as the power of new life is both an actualized reality (1 Thes 5:4-5; Gal 3:27) and an unactualized reality (Rom 13:11-14)—the possibility of actualization through moral living.

Eating and Drinking among the Weak and the Strong, 14:1–15:13

This passage seeks to promote mutual acceptance (14:3-4, 13; 15:7), peace and harmony (14:19; 15:5), and mutual upbuilding (14:19) between two groups in the church at Rome that hold different opinions and apparently live in some tension with each other.

Paul designates them as the *weak in faith* (14:1) and the *strong* (15:1) and includes himself among the strong (15:1). The weak are vegetarians (14:2) who observe certain holy days (14:5) and apparently reject the drinking of wine (14:21). The strong eat anything (14:2, 21), consider all days alike (14:5), and drink wine (14:21). The meat avoidance seems not to be a matter of rejecting meat from animals sacrificed to idols, as at Corinth (1 Cor 8:1, 4, 7, 10), but rather to be a vegetarian rejection of all meat.

Regarding the history-of-religious sources of these differences the strong would be Christians of either gentile or Jewish background who had accepted a law-free position similar to Paul's that permitted their behavior on these issues. The weak are more difficult to categorize. Jews observed holy days, the SABBATH and other festival times, but Jews did not characteristically reject wine drinking. And while certain animals were forbidden as food (Lev 11), and Judaism permitted animals had to be slaughtered in the proper cultic manner (Lev 17:14; Deut 12:16, 23), Judaism did not reject the eating of meat in principle (Lev 11:1-3; Deut 12:15). On the other hand, some gentile religions did teach vegetarianism (e.g., Orphics and Pythagoreans).

Yet there is some evidence (Dan 1:12, 16; *Testament of Isaac* 4:5, 6, 41) that certain Jewish groups living under the pressure of a gentile environment did adopt vegetarianism and teetotalism (Wedderburn 1991, 33–34). Moreover, since 15:7-13 makes the point that the purpose of Christ's mission was to save both Jews and gentiles, it seems probable that the two groups designated as the weak and the strong were primarily, though not exclusively, respectively Jewish Christians and gentile Christians. Paul offers three perspectives for their living together in peace.

14:1-12. The theological perspective. That the weak person is weak specifically *in faith* suggests that he or she feels that faith alone is not sufficient for salvation but must be supplemented by the behaviors at issue here (Dunn 1988, 798). Interestingly Paul does not go on to condemn this position though he distinguishes himself from it (15:1—*we . . . are strong*).

The strong are not to treat the weak with contempt; the weak are not to condemn the strong. The important thing is that each should be convinced in his or her *own* mind that he or she is doing the right thing (v. 5).

The basis for this mutual acceptance is that both groups do what they do to honor the Lord. Moreover, all persons must finally *stand before the judgment seat of God* and give an account of themselves to God (vv. 10-12). Being accountable to the judgment of God lifts one above the position of being judged by a fellow human being. It is a Pauline paradox that God confronts us as both gracious redeemer (3:21–4:25) and demanding judge (1 Cor 6:9-11; 2 Cor 5:10; Gal 5:16-24).

14:13-23. The ethical perspective. Paul clearly believes that certain *ethical* acts and dispositions are inherently wrong (1:28-32; 1 Cor 6:9-10; Gal 5:19-21). But he rejects the Jewish distinction between cultic cleanness and uncleanness that rests on the belief that certain *physical* objects (like foods, Lev 11) or processes (like menstruation, Lev 15:19; marital sex, Lev 15:18; or childbearing, Lev 12:1-5) are inherently unclean (Via 1985, 88–96). Thus when he that *nothing is unclean in itself* (v. 14, emphasis added) Paul means nothing like food or drink. But such things are unclean to those who think they are unclean (v. 14b).

Paul is concerned that the strong should not cause harm to the weak who think that meat and wine should be avoided. Since meat and wine are not unclean in themselves (vv. 14, 20), he will not deal with the issue in terms of such unexceptionable rules as: do not eat meat, do not drink wine, observe the sabbath.

Paul rather applies the love principle (v. 15)—seek the good of the other—to this situation. It *is* wrong to eat meat or drink wine *if* it causes the ruin of a brother or sister for whom Christ died. It is all right to eat or drink if your faith's self-understanding allows it (vv. 22-23). But the person of weak faith believes it is wrong. If by your example you entice your weak brother or sister to eat meat or drink wine, you cause his ruin, cause her to fall or stumble (vv. 15, 20, 21). That is, you cause the weak one the inner pain of doubt and self-judgment because he or she will be going against what his or her own faith permits (vv. 22-23). The weak sin if they eat meat, not because it is wrong in itself, but because it violates what their faith allows; it violates the unity of their being. The strong do wrong if they cause this to happen to the weak.

Paul calls for mutual acceptance, but he really asks more of the strong than of the weak because they are capable of more. The strong have the freedom to eat

meat and drink wine or not without suffering internal disruption. The weak do not have that much freedom. If they want to avoid inner conflict, they are free only not to eat or drink. So the strong are called on to give up their freedom to eat or drink in those situations where it causes harm to the neighbor.

15:1-13. The christological perspective. Here the strong are specifically asked to bear the weaknesses of those who are not strong and not to please themselves. This appeal is based on the model of Christ who *did not please himself.*

The weak and strong are admonished to accept each other as Christ accepted both of them. Christ became a servant in order to confirm God's faithfulness to his promises to Israel's forefathers and to bring the gentiles to glorify God.

Concluding Personal Statement, 15:14-32

Paul's Feelings about the Roman Church and His Self-Evaluation, 15:14-21

Paul is satisfied with the spiritual stature of the church at Rome but also claims justification for having written to them boldly on the ground that God's grace has made him *a minister . . . to the Gentiles* (v. 16). Paul describes his preaching of the gospel as priestly activity, and the offering he makes to God through the gospel is the gentiles. The term he uses of himself as *a minister* (v. 16, Gk. *leitourgos*) means priest in Neh 10:39; Isa 61:6; Sir 7:30; Heb 8:2. The verb *hierougeō* (serve as a priest) underscores this.

Paul believes that his work for God is something to boast about (v. 17). The word he uses for boasting (*kauchēsis*) is the same word that he uses for the boasting that is excluded by justification by grace in 3:27. But here in v. 17 he is proud, not of his attainments, but of what Christ has achieved through him.

For further discussion of this section see Introduction: Occasion and Purpose, The Intended Visit.

Travel Plans, 15:22-29

On this passage see the discussion of Paul's plans to visit Jerusalem and Spain in Introduction: Occasion and Purpose.

Emotional Appeal for Their Prayers, 15:30-32

This last part of the concluding personal statement (body closing) fulfills the rhetorical function of making an emotional appeal to the Roman church for their prayerful concern about Paul.

Closing, 15:33–16:27

For the issues raised by chap. 16, see above, Introduction: Manuscript Evidence and Destination. And for the structure of the Closing, refer to the outline at the beginning of the commentary. Only a few brief comments will be made here.

It could be that Paul intended to end the letter with the grace benediction in 16:20b and that Paul's scribe *Tertius* (16:22), added the greetings from Paul's associates, requiring a repetition of the grace benediction in 16:24. Manuscripts differ on the placement of this benediction (Gamble 1977, 91–94).

Among those for whom Paul requests greetings are *Andronicus and Junia*(s) (16:7) whom Paul designates as fellow Jews and as persons who are well known among the apostles. The Greek name Iounian, as far as spelling is concerned, could be the accusative case of the male name Iounias (Junias) or the accusative of the common Roman female name Junia. But apart from this verse there is no evidence for a male name Junias (Cranfield 1981, 788). The name should be read as the female Junia, and it should be recognized that there were women apostles.

The final doxology (16:25-27) is probably a post-Pauline addition. Such terminology as *the eternal God* (*tou aiōniou theou*), *the only wise God* (*monō sophō theō*), and *the mystery . . . made known* (*mystēriou . . . gnōristhentos*) is not characteristic of Paul. Especially strange is the idea of the gospel as a mystery kept secret through the ages but now made known through the prophetic writings (Kümmel 1965, 223). Paul's own position in Romans is that the righteousness of faith, recently made manifest through the redemption in Christ Jesus (3:21-26), was already proclaimed in the law (10:6-8), and actualized by Abraham (4:3-8).

Works Cited

Aune, David E. 1991. "Romans as a *Logos* Protreptikos," in Donfried 1991a.

Barrett, C. K. 1957. *A Commentary on the Epistle to the Romans*, BNTC.

Beale, Walter H. 1978. "Rhetorical Performative: A New Theory of Epideictic," *Philosophy and Rhetoric* 11/4 (Fall 1978): 221–46.

Best, Ernest. 1955. *One Body in Christ*.

Bornkamm, Günther. 1991. "The Letter to the Romans as Paul's Last Will and Testament," in Donfried 1991a.

Bultmann, Rudolf. 1951. *Theology of the N.T.*, vol. 1. 1967. "Glossen im Römerbrief," *Exegetica*.

Campbell, William S. 1991. "Romans III as a Key to the Structure and Thought of Romans," in Donfried 1991a.

Cousar, Charles B. 1990. *A Theology of the Cross, Overtures to Biblical Theology*.

Cranfield, C. E. B. 1980. *A Critical and Exegetical Commentary on the Epistle to the Romans*, 2 vols., ICC.

Cullmann, Oscar. 1957. *The State in the N.T.*

Davies, W. D. 1948. *Paul and Rabbinic Judaism*.

Dodd, C. H. 1954. *The Epistle of Paul to the Romans*.

Donfried, Karl P. 1991a. *The Romans Debate*, rev. ed. 1991b. "Introduction 1991: The Romans Debate since 1977," in Donfried 1991a. 1991c. "A Short Note on Romans 16," in Donfried 1991a. 1991d. "False Presuppositions in the Study of Romans," in Donfried 1991a.

Dunn, James D. G. 1988. *Romans 1–8*. 1988. *Romans 9–16*.

Fuller, Reginald H. 1978. "The Conception/Birth of Jesus as a Christological Moment," *JSNT* 1 (1978): 37–52.

Funk, Robert W. 1967. "The Apostolic Parousia: Form and Significance," *Christian History and Interpretation*.

Furnish, Victor Paul. 1979. *The Moral Teaching of Paul*.

Gamble, Harry. 1977. *The Textual History of the Letter to the Romans*. 1985. *The N.T. Canon*, GBS/NT.

Girard, René. 1986. *The Scapegoat*. 1989. *Violence and the Sacred*.

Hays, Richard B. 1981. *The Faith of Jesus Christ*, SBLDS 56.

Jervell, Jacob. 1991. "The Letter to Jerusalem," in Donfried 1991a.

Jewett, Robert. 1991. "Following the Argument of Romans," in Donfried 1991a.

Karris, Robert J. 1991a. "Romans 14:1–15:13 and the Occasion of Romans," in Donfried 1991a. 1991b. "The Occasion of Romans: A Response to Professor Donfried," in Donfried 1991a.

Käsemann, Ernst. 1969. *New Testament Questions of Today*. 1971. *Perspectives on Paul*. 1980. *Commentary on Romans*.

Kennedy, George A. 1984. *N.T. Interpretation through Rhetorical Criticism*.

Klein, Günter. 1991. "Paul's Purpose in Writing the Epistle to the Romans," in Donfried 1991a.

Knox, John. 1954. "The Epistle to the Romans," *IB*.

Kümmel, Werner Georg et al. 1965. *Introduction to the N.T.*, 14th rev. ed.

Lampe, Peter. 1991. "The Roman Christians of Romans 16," in Donfried 1991a.

Mack, Burton L. 1990. *Rhetoric and the N.T.* GBS/NT.

Manson, T. W. 1991. "St. Paul's Letter to the Romans—and Others," in Donfried 1991a.

Metzger, Bruce E. 1975. *A Textual Commentary on the Greek N.T.*

Nygren, Anders. 1949. *Commentary on Romans.*

O'Neill, J. C. 1975. *Paul's Letters to the Romans.*

Petersen, Norman R. 1985. *Rediscovering Paul.*

Ricoeur, Paul. 1969. *The Symbolism of Evil.*

Sanders, E. P. 1977. *Paul and Palestinian Judaism.* 1983. *Paul, the Law, and the Jewish People.*

Schmithals, Walter. 1975. *Der Römerbrief als historisches Problem.*

Scroggs, Robin. 1983. *The N.T. and Homosexuality.*

Stirewalt, Martin Luther, Jr. 1991. "The Form and Function of the Greek Letter-Essay," in Donfried 1991a.

Stowers, Stanley Kent. 1981. *The Diatribe and Paul's Letter to the Romans.* 1989. *Letter Writing in Greco-Roman Antiquity.*

Stuhlmacher, Peter. 1991. "The Purpose of Romans," in Donfried 1991a.

Theissen, Gerd. 1987. *Psychological Aspects of Pauline Theology.*

Via, Dan O. 1985. *The Ethics of Mark's Gospel.* 1990. *Self-Deception and Wholeness in Paul and Matthew.*

Wagner, Günther. 1967. *Pauline Baptism and Pagan Mysteries.*

Wedderburn, A. J. M. 1991. *The Reasons for Romans.*

Wiefel, Wolfgang. 1991. "The Jewish Community in Ancient Rome and the Origins of Roman Christianity," in Donfried 1991a.

Williams, Sam K. 1975. *Jesus' Death as Saving Event*, HDR 2. 1980. "The Righteousness of God in Romans," *JBL* 99/2 (June 1980): 241–90.

Wuellner, Wilhelm. 1987. "Where Is Rhetorical Criticism Taking Us?" *CBQ* 49/3 (July 1987): 448–63. 1991. "Paul's Rhetoric of Argumentation in Romans," in Donfried 1991a.

Ziesler, John. 1989. *Paul's Letters to the Romans.*

First Corinthians

Marion L. Soards

Introduction

First Corinthians is considered one of Paul's four *great* letters (along with Romans, 2 Corinthians, and Galatians) in part because of the actual length of this letter in comparison to the other writings attributed to Paul in the NT; but even more, 1 Corinthians is regarded as a great epistle because of the range of the topics and the depth of the reflections that it contains. The "great letters" are regarded by all students of Paul's writings as the central documents for the interpretation of the apostle's theology, and 1 Corinthians is particularly significant for its treatment of important aspects of basic Christian faith and practice.

Authorship

Since the writing of *1 Clement* in the late first century the letter we refer to today as 1 Corinthians has been attributed to the apostle Paul (see *1 Clem* 47.1-7). No one has ever seriously questioned whether Paul wrote this letter. Even the most radical critics, F. C. Baur and his so-called Tübingen School, accepted 1 Corinthians as authentic. From time to time isolated scholars have raised questions about the unity of the letter, sometimes suggesting either that the epistle as we know it was composed from parts of several letters by Paul that were assembled by a later editor or that it contains a significant number of major and minor glosses that were written into the letter by later scribes. Such broad theories have not attracted a following, though scholars regularly question the authenticity of a few verses of the letter. (We shall consider these verses as we work through the sections of the letter in the commentary that follows.)

Paul and the Corinthians

First-century CORINTH existed because the city had been reconstructed by order of Julius Caesar in 44 B.C.E., long after the Romans destroyed old Corinth in 146 B.C.E. In antiquity Corinth lay in a particularly cru-cial location on the isthmus that connected the mainland of Greece with the Peloponnesian peninsula that separated the Corinthian Gulf of the Adriatic Sea on the west from the Saronic Gulf of the Aegean Sea on the east. The new city was reestablished as a strategic military and economic outpost for Rome. The population of new Corinth was originally composed of Italian freedmen, given their freedom as a reward for military service. Other merchants and traders looking for new and rich opportunities joined the former soldiers, so that the new city had a complex, cosmopolitan population despite an initially shallow culture. The goods of the East and the West moved through Corinth's harbors and across the short roadways connecting them. The city was an exciting place—genuinely pluralistic with a penchant for SYNCRETISM; fortunes and fame were made and lost in Corinth.

From PAUL's letters to Corinth and from a judicious reading of Acts, especially Acts 18, we can reconstruct a portrait of Paul's experiences in Corinth and of his dealings with the members of the Corinthian church. Apparently, shortly after Paul arrived in Corinth he sought out the Jewish quarter of the city where he met Prisca and Aquila (see PRISCILLA AND AQUILA), a Jewish couple recently arrived in Corinth as part of the emperor Claudius's expulsion of certain Jews from Rome. Historians conclude that Prisca and Aquila were Jewish Christians, indeed that the Jews expelled from Rome were the Christian Jews who created a disturbance in the capital of the ROMAN EMPIRE by preaching the gospel of Christ among the Jews. This couple shared both their faith and their trade of tentmaking with Paul, and we learn as no surprise that Paul lived and worked with this couple in Corinth.

In the time that followed, Paul, Prisca, Aquila, TIMOTHY, SILAS, and perhaps others who remain unnamed, preached to Jews in the SYNAGOGUE that Jesus was the Christ. The success of this mission is clear from the memory that Crispus, the leader of the synagogue, and his household became Christians. Severe opposition arose, however, so that the mission moved out of the synagogue into the house next door that belonged to a God-fearer named Titius Justus (Acts 18:7). According to Acts many Jews and God-fearers came to believe through the preaching of Paul and his colleagues. This work in Corinth lasted for eighteen months before the unbelieving Jews launched a united attack against Paul and his colleagues. They brought him before the Roman tribunal of the proconsul Lucius Junius Annaeus GALLIO, whose term of office extended either from 1 May 51 to 1 May 52 or 1 May 52 to 1 May 53 C.E. Gallio refused to hear the case, which produced a sharp outcry and demonstration by Paul's Jewish adversaries.

According to Acts, Paul stayed in Corinth "many days longer" (18:18 RSV), although eventually he departed from Corinth with Prisca and Aquila. After a time of travels, Paul and his companions settled in EPHESUS for over two years. From Ephesus Paul wrote a series of letters to the Corinthians, and he even had conversations with representatives of the Corinthian congregation who visited him in Ephesus. From 1 Cor 5:9 we see clearly that prior to the writing of 1 Corinthians Paul had already written at least one other letter to the Corinthians. Scholars debate whether that earlier letter is completely lost or whether it may, in part, be preserved in 2 Corinthians. Whatever the case, we should understand that our canonical work, 1 Corinthians, is at least the "second" letter to the Corinthians. At the time that Paul wrote our 1 Corinthians, he had been in Ephesus for an extended period, for he mentions his plans to leave Ephesus in 1 Cor 16:5-9.

The Situation and the Problems

As Paul lived and worked in Ephesus, he learned of the situation in Corinth both from visitors and from a letter that the members of the Corinthian congregation sent to him. First, near the beginning of the letter, in 1:11, the apostle mentions *Chloe's people* with whom he has been in conversation. This designation indicates members of the household of Chloe and could be a reference to family members, slaves, or both. Later, near the end of the letter, in 16:17, Paul names *Stephanus and Fortunas and Achaicus* who had visited him, and so, made up for the absence of the other members of the congregation. We cannot determine whether the early reference to *Chloe's people* are to be identified with the three men (apparently the letter delegation)

named toward the end of the letter, but we do see that Paul had firsthand observations concerning the circumstances in Corinth. In the course of the letter Paul refers explicitly to matters of which he learned from his visitors—see 5:1-2 (and perhaps the material in 5:3-6:20). Second, at 7:1 Paul refers directly to the letter with the phrase *Now concerning the matters about which you wrote*. Subsequently he uses the phrase *now concerning*, still apparently referring to the letter from the Corinthians, in 7:25, 8:1, 12:1, and 16:1. The items considered in relation to the letter from Corinth include sex and marriage, food offered to pagan idols prior to being sold in the market for consumption, the GIFTS OF THE SPIRIT, and the method for the collection that Paul was assembling for the poor in Jerusalem.

Behind all the issues Paul addresses in 1 Corinthians lies a preoccupation of the Corinthians with wisdom. The wisdom with which they were concerned was not mature or reasonable judgment, but special information that gave those "in the know" special status in relation to others who did not share those data. The Corinthians wanted involvement with supposedly deeper meanings and lofty unseen things. Some of them apparently thought of their life in Christ as if it were participation in MYSTERY RELIGIONS. Paul pejoratively calls such wisdom "human wisdom" (1:20; NRSV *wisdom of the world*), and he contrasts it with God's powerful wisdom, shown in the cross of Christ, in order to castigate the Corinthians for their inappropriate attitudes and behaviors.

Paul's remarks reveal that he understands the preoccupation with wisdom to result from the basic will of the Corinthians to boast. By claiming to have wisdom the Corinthians elevate themselves above others who do not share their information. Indeed, the will to boast of one's status through possession of wisdom was so great one group of Corinthians even compared their wisdom over against another's, to establish their spiritual superiority (or the other's inferiority). Throughout this letter Paul criticizes the particular actions of the Corinthians, but above all he denounces the will to boast. The will to be superior and to brag about it was the fundamental problem that generated the other symptomatic problems in Corinth.

Date

Since we know from the mention of Gallio in Acts 18 that Paul was active in Corinth sometime between 1 May 51 and 1 May 53 C.E., by taking 1 May 52 as a starting point and by tracing Paul's travels up to the time he arrived in Ephesus (Acts 18–19), we can safely understand that Paul arrived in Ephesus in late 52. He labored in Ephesus until the spring of 55. Moreover, from 1 Cor 16:5-9 we learn that Paul wrote 1 Corinthians toward the end of his Ephesian sojourn, so that this letter was most likely written early in 55 (or, less likely, very late in 54).

Primary Themes

First Corinthians presents a kaleidoscope of themes, touching on various aspects of basic Christian faith and practice. Among the prominent topics treated are the forming of factions in the church, the value of human wisdom versus divine wisdom or power, the nature of spirituality, blatant forms of misconduct, sex and marriage, social status, the eschatological character of Christian existence, food offered to pagan gods prior to sale in the marketplace, the nature of Christian freedom, orderly worship, the gifts of the Spirit, the church as the BODY OF CHRIST, the superior way of love, TONGUES and PROPHECY, resurrection, the collection for the SAINTS in Jerusalem, and Paul's future plans. In the course of reflecting on these topics, Paul comments on a number of items of concern for people

today—to name but a few: the essence of the GOSPEL, the shape and substance of Christian ministry, Christian involvement in lawsuits, appropriate and inappropriate sexual relations, DIVORCE, SLAVERY, the role of women in the life of the church, charismatic practices, the reality of Jesus' resurrection, and Christian giving.

For Further Study

In the *Mercer Dictionary of the Bible*: CORINTH; CORINTHIAN CORRESPONDENCE; EPISTLE/LETTER; ESCHATOLOGY IN THE NT; GIFTS OF THE SPIRIT; LOVE IN THE NT; MEAT SACRIFICED TO IDOLS; PAUL; RESURRECTION IN THE NT; SUFFERING IN THE NT; WISDOM IN THE NT.

In other sources: C. K. Barrett, *The First Epistle to the Corinthians*, HNTC; J. M. Bassler, "1 Corinthians," *WmBC*; R. B. Brown, "1 Corinthians," BBC; H. Conzelmann, *1 Corinthians*, Herm; G. D. Fee, *The First Epistle to the Corinthians*, NICNT; R. A. Harrisville, *1 Corinthians*, AugCNT; E. Fiorenza, "1 Corinthians," *HBC*; J. Murphy-O'Connor, "First Letter to the Corinthians," NJBC, *1 Corinthians*, and *St. Paul's Corinth*; W. F. Orr and J. A. Walther, *1 Corinthians*, AncB; C. H. Talbert, *Reading Corinthians*; M. E. Thrall, *First and Second Letters of Paul to the Corinthians*.

Commentary

An Outline

> I. Salutation, 1:1-3
>   A. Senders, 1:1
>   B. Recipients, 1:2
>   C. Greetings, 1:3
> II. Thanksgiving, 1:4-9
>   A. The Corinthians' Endowments, 1:4-7a
>   B. The Lord's Faithfulness, 1:7b-9
> III. Body of the Letter, 1:10–15:58
>   A. The Gospel and Wisdom, 1:10–4:21
>   B. Specific Problems and Questions, 5:1–11:1
>   C. Orderly Worship and Spiritual Gifts, 11:2–14:40
>   D. The Truth of the Resurrection, 15:1-58
> IV. Parenesis, 16:1-18
>   A. Future Plans, 16:1-12
>   B. Principles for Life, 16:13-14
>   C. Saluting Special Persons, 16:15-18
> V. Closing, 16:19-24

Salutation, 1:1-3

The letter opens with a fairly standard greeting, presenting the normal three elements an ancient reader would have expected at the beginning of a letter:

sender(s), recipients, and a greeting. Although standard, these verses are pregnant with theological significance through Paul's adaptation or modification of the basic letter form.

Senders, 1:1

In naming the senders, Paul refers to himself as *an apostle*. For modern readers this word has become a technical title, so that we miss Paul's point that he is a "sent one," which is the literal sense of the word "apostle" (ἀπόστολος) in Greek. Not only is Paul one who is sent, he was sent in behalf of Christ Jesus. Moreover, his being sent came about through God's will, not by Paul's own choice. Thus, Paul says he was *called*, meaning that God intervened in his life and established the priority of God's own will. Furthermore, Paul does not write alone, for he works in conjunction with others whom God also directs into action. Here, Paul names *Sosthenes* as his coauthor. Remarkably, Sosthenes is the name of the leader of the Jews who brought charges against Paul before Gallio in Corinth (Acts 18:17). If the Sosthenes named here is the same person about whom we read in Acts, he surely experienced a radical change of heart and a reorientation of his life.

Recipients, 1:2

Paul refers to the Corinthians in a nuanced fashion. They are a *church* (ἐκκλησία). The Greek word can mean "church," or "congregation," or "assembly." In Greco-Roman literature it indicated a political assembly, but as Paul would have known the word from its use in the Greek translation of the Hebrew Bible, ἐκκλησία was used for the Hebrew word קהל that named the children of Israel both in their EXODUS wanderings and in their worshipful assemblies at the Temple. Paul says the church is *the church of God*—that is, God has priority in the formation of the congregation, so that only secondarily does the apostle refer to the geographical location of the church *in Corinth*. Moreover, he declares the Corinthians are *sanctified in Christ Jesus*, indicating that the Corinthians were made holy by Christ—not by their own efforts. The Corinthians are (literally) "called saints," as Paul was (literally) "called apostle." Paul and the Corinthians share the experience of God's calling them and actually naming the purpose of their lives. Furthermore, Paul refers to the Corinthians as being saints *together with all those who in every place call on the name of our Lord Jesus Christ, both their Lord and ours*. With these phrases Paul recognizes the common bond of the Corinthians with all other Christians. They are not an isolated holy group simply set apart from the world; rather, the Corinthians (and Paul and Sosthenes) live in a dependent relationship to Christ that establishes a mutuality that transcends the normal boundaries of human relations.

Greetings, 1:3

The greeting pronounces *grace* and *peace* upon the Corinthians *from God our Father and the Lord Jesus Christ*. Thus, we see the true source of GRACE and PEACE. Grace is a divine gift that produces the divine result of peace in the lives of those who experience it.

Thanksgiving, 1:4-9

Scholars have long recognized that as a formal element of Paul's letters the thanksgiving (or, thanksgiving-prayer) serves several purposes. First, the thanksgiving terminates the opening portion of the letter. Second, it signals the basic theme or themes of the letter that will follow. Third, the thanksgiving can some-

times even outline the major topics to be treated in the epistle. Here, for example, Paul acknowledges God's grace as active among the Corinthians to the end that they are *in every way . . . enriched in* [Christ Jesus], *in speech and knowledge of every kind*. Among the Corinthians the real gifts of "speech" and "knowledge" are at the heart of their problematic thoughts and actions. At once Paul names the genuine strengths and weaknesses of the Corinthian church. The members experience the endowments of grace, but, as the remainder of the letter reveals, their concern with and use of these gifts is completely out of hand.

The Corinthians' Endowments, 1:4-7a

Paul acknowledges and qualifies the spiritual gifts with which the Corinthians have been blessed. The goal of God's gifts of speech and knowledge relates to the testimony about Christ that comes to confirmation among the Corinthians. As God endows the Corinthians with spiritual gifts, God demonstrates the reality of God's gracious work in Christ. The Corinthians experience grace unto the glory of Christ, not for their own aggrandizement. God's authority is recognized in the words *the grace of God . . . has been given you*; God gave grace, the Corinthians merely (though really) received it.

The Lord's Faithfulness, 1:7b-9

The true status of the Corinthians becomes clear in these verses; they are *waiting* for the revelation of the Lord Jesus Christ. *Already* they experience grace, but *not yet* is the Lord fully present. The Corinthians live in relation to a promise. The full experience of God's grace lies beyond the present in the future, and the sole basis of hope in that future is that *God is faithful*. The grace that the Corinthians experience in the present is not the guarantee of their hope for the future; rather, God who grants grace now is himself the hope of the future. Grace is no guarantee; it is a sign of God's goodness, a manifestation of God's faithfulness, which itself underwrites the future. God called the Corinthians into communion with Jesus Christ and, in turn, with one another. The fellowship they experience is not of their own doing; it is God's work. The church is not theirs; it is God's—by will and by work. The Corinthians are called into the community of faith created by God's grace at work in the Lord Jesus Christ. Seeing this much should inform the Corinthians who they are as a church; and so, they should see how they are to live.

Body of the Letter, 1:10–15:58

The Gospel and Wisdom, 1:10–4:21

This first major portion of the body of the letter is a coherent reflection treating basic matters of Christian belief and the particular situation in Corinth. Paul argues against an understanding of the gospel as a kind of esoteric or mysterious wisdom teaching, especially a teaching that would elevate those who have the information above the masses to whom the teaching would not be available.

1:10-17. Factions in the congregation. At the outset Paul takes up the issue of factions (*divisions*, v. 10; *quarrels*, v. 11) in the Corinthian church. He expresses his astonishment at the situation and implies his disapproval of the matter, but he does not yet offer a full resolution to the problem. Paul's choice of vocabulary (*appeal*, v. 10) indicates his earnestness in admonishing the Corinthians, and his reference to *the name of our Lord Jesus Christ* expresses the means and authority of his appeal. Paul's goal for the Corinthians is that they will be united in thought and disposition.

As Paul talks about the factions in Corinth, he identifies the groups in relation to prominent persons: PAUL, APOLLOS, Cephas (PETER), and CHRIST. It is not clear whether he means to name three or four groups, for it is not certain whether there is a "Christ party" or whether Paul means that all, regardless of their relationship with Paul, Apollos, or Cephas, are related to Christ. At root the problem is that the Corinthians have turned relationships into status-giving identities or positions. Paul works to inform the Corinthians that they have direction in life, they do not merely have positions to defend or declare. The three rhetorical questions in v. 13 are answered "yes," "no," and "no." The first question about the division of the church names the problem, and the following two questions make it clear that the situation is absurd.

At first reading, the statements in vv. 14-16 seem to display a shockingly cavalier regard for BAPTISM. There is certainly sarcasm in the remarks as Paul attempts to jolt the Corinthians out of their boastful comparisons concerning their status in the church. Yet, as one sees by continuing to read Paul's words in v. 17, he is able to relativize the importance of baptism (which the Corinthians value as giving them special identities and status) because he understands his call as a call to preach. Baptism is a part of the larger picture of Christian faith and practice, but for Paul proclama-

tion of the gospel is the cutting edge. Given the particular problem in Corinth with its baptismal parties and boasting, Paul is genuinely thankful that baptism per se was not his primary ministry. Further clarification comes in his words contrasting "wisdom" and the CROSS. The good news of God's saving work in the cross of Christ is not a slick message that is sold through elegant packaging. Sheer manipulative eloquence is not a medium that can bear the weight of the message of the cross. Above all, the shocking claim that God saves humanity in the cross of Jesus Christ demonstrates that God works in defiance of this world's norms.

1:18-25. God's peculiar, powerful way. God works in a most peculiar way—not only in defiance of the standards of this world, but also in such a powerful way that it incapacitates, reverses, even turns upside down the values (objectively established) of this world. Paul declares this way of God's working as a fact. In v. 18 Paul sets up a rhetorical contrast scheme that drives home the heart of the gospel as he understands it. In relation to the theme of "the word of the cross," that is, the proclamation of the saving death of Jesus Christ, Paul refers to humanity in two groups. On the one hand, there are those who regard the word of the cross as *foolishness*; Paul says they are perishing. On the other hand, there are those who are *being saved*. The passive voice of the verb indicates that God is doing the saving here. Moreover, in the scheme of this contrast with *perishing* versus *being saved*, one finds *foolishness* contrasted with *the power of God*. The natural opposite of *foolishness* in this context would be *wisdom*. Remarkably Paul says that it is what God does, not what humans know, that saves. God acted in the cross of Christ and it produces a division among humanity that itself implies God's power.

To make this argument Paul quotes Isa 29:14, although he changes the verb in the quotation from "conceal" to *thwart* (v. 19). With this slight alteration Paul makes the citation fit more exactly the context to which he writes. As the apostle offers a scriptural precedent for the way God works through the cross of Christ, he does more than prooftext his point. His use of scripture shows that he understands scripture to be absolutely authoritative, absolutely essential for comprehending God's ways, but of an ultimately penultimate significance. God's work in Christ directs the use of the Bible; the Bible does not control God.

The argument here locates where the wisdom of the merely human wise one, scribe, and debater originate—in *this age*. God's "age," however, exposes the shallowness and inaccuracy of merely human wisdom. Even the loftiest theology that is disengaged from the primary revelation of God in Jesus Christ is *foolishness*. Humans do not reason their way to God; God saves humanity (and the world!) by the cross of Christ, which is, by this world's standards, *foolishness*. Christ preached as crucified brings a crisis of separation. Denial of the saving significance of the cross reveals that one is in bondage to "this world," whereas "those who believe" are shown to be called by God, to be grasped by the power of God—a demonstration that Christ is God's "wisdom." Verse 25 summarizes the whole section saying that God's wisdom or power expressed in the cross of Christ renders worldly wisdom into foolishness as a demonstration of the reality of the power of God.

1:26-31. Before and after God's call. In these theologically loaded verses, Paul calls the Corinthians to consider themselves both *before* (or, at) the time of their call and *after* (or, in) their calling. Before their calling Paul suggests that in a variety of ways the Corinthians were for the most part nobodies; after being called by God, however, the Corinthians are instruments of God's power with Christ Jesus as the source of their lives. To make this argument Paul engages in a careful, deliberate play on the LXX version of Jer 9:22-24. The reference to scripture is clear in v. 31, but already in vv. 28-29 the language echoes Jeremiah, especially in the reference to "the wise" and "wisdom" and to "the powerful" and "the strong." Paul's contrast scheme is designed to humble the Corinthians in order to heighten their appreciation for the saving work of God in Jesus Christ. Paul tells the Corinthians that in light of what God has done in Jesus Christ the only legitimate boasting that Christians do is about what God has done—not about what humans know, do, are, or achieve.

2:1-5. Paul's apostolic ministry and message. This section is an exposition of Paul's *apostolic* message and ministry. It comes in two moves: First, vv. 1-2 demonstrate the continuity between the form and content or the style and substance of the apostle's proclamation. Second, vv. 3-5 demonstrate the continuity of the message and the demeanor of the preacher or messenger. Paul's language is intensely personal. The statements make clear that his approach and practice of ministry were deliberate. The statements are, nevertheless, ambiguous. Paul is not saying, "I preached only the cross instead of the cross plus something

more." Rather, he insists that he laid aside all other devices for persuasion and proclaimed the cross without frills.

Paul's portrait of himself refers to *weakness* and explains this idea by using the traditional Jewish image of *fear and trembling*—a reference to the reverent recognition of the reality of God! Paul says that his message was such that his speech allowed the Spirit and God's power to show themselves as they worked through his message. The Corinthians came to believe, not by showy human effort, but by the very working of God's power. Although humans are God's agents, God alone is the one who saves humanity.

2:6-16. Meditation on the operation of revelation. These verses are an excursus on the wisdom of God and the spiritual discernment of Christians, or a meditation on the operation of REVELATION. Interpreters ask whether Paul contradicts himself here. Does he have a two-leveled message with one word for some and a "deeper" teaching for others? No. One should recall that Paul designated his message "the word of the cross" (1:18 RSV). Clearly he interprets the saving significance of the cross throughout his letters by regularly applying the meaning of the cross to the lives of his readers. The cross is not only something that happened to Jesus. Paul declares that by the mysterious grace of God the cross affects, or effects (!), the lives of Christians. Paul does not have a special teaching for some. He can, however, explicate more to some than to others because of the differing degrees of their own spiritual maturation. This situation seems to be the basis for Paul's distinction between the "mature" and the "spiritual" on the one hand and the "unspiritual" or "natural" on the other.

Paul declares that God's wisdom is not available simply to inquiring minds. Paul refers to the scriptural precedent for this teaching, although it is impossible to identify precisely the passage he cites. His "quotation" in v. 9 seems to be a pastiche from perhaps Ps 3:20; Isa 52:15; 64:3-4; 65:16-17; Jer 3:16; Sir 1:10; and *AscIsa* 11.34. The depths of God's will and work come to humanity only as God chooses to reveal them through the Spirit. Paul explains the necessity of divine revelation through an argument on the principle of "like by like"—saying that a person is the only one who knows the inner secrets of himself or herself. It is likewise with God. Paul states that an unspiritual human is unable to receive the things of the Spirit of God because these things are only discernible by the Spirit. Moreover, in vv. 12 and 16 Paul boldly declares that Christians have the *Spirit that is from God* and *the mind of Christ*, so that they have God's wisdom imparted to them through the Spirit.

3:1-17. Working toward unity and edification. Paul ties together what he has said to this point in vv. 1-4 in order to show why he did not impart God's wisdom to the Corinthians. The chief implication of his remarks is that the Corinthians are immature, as is seen in their factionalization. Notice, however, that Paul at least regards the Corinthians as *infants* (v. 1) so that he does not completely deny they are persons of faith. Paul's words would prove insulting, nevertheless, for he repeatedly says the Corinthians are *of the flesh*. Although the Corinthians value wisdom and declare their status as mature believers or "spiritual ones," Paul refutes their claims.

Then, Paul takes up a series of metaphors in order to instruct the Corinthians. The entire set of remarks is aimed at correcting the Corinthians' misunderstandings and at directing them toward unity and mutual edification. In vv. 5-9 Paul offers a lesson by taking himself and APOLLOS as examples. Paul and Apollos are cast as field servants who serve the higher authority of their Lord. Their assignments are different, though they are both merely functionaries. The reality of divine farming is that God does the growing while the field hands simply execute God's will. As servants Paul and Apollos are equal and they get paid according to their labor. The NRSV provides a helpful translation of v. 9. Other translations may read "we are God's fellow workers" (RSV), an idea that makes little sense in the context of the previous lines; but the NRSV more accurately renders the ambiguous Greek as *we are God's servants, working together*. God's servants labor together; they do not form competitive groups, for they are united in their efforts under the sole authority of God. Paul recognizes God's authority over the apostles and over the church in Corinth, which he calls *God's field*.

At the end of v. 9 Paul shifts metaphors. Not only are the Corinthians *God's field*, they are also *God's building*. With that image established, Paul assumes the point of view of a sophisticated master builder and tells of the foundation he laid, the foundation of Jesus Christ. That foundation cannot be changed, although now others may erect an edifice on the foundation. Yet, Paul declares that even in the activity of building on the foundation of Jesus Christ, not all buildings are equal. Verse 12 catalogues a variety of building materials. Then, the following discussion promises a testing

of the materials, an eschatological testing in the future, promised *Day* (of the Lord). Those who built on the foundation of Jesus Christ may anticipate reward or loss in accordance with the quality and durability of the material they used. Paul means to admonish the Corinthians to a careful selection of materials, that is, to a way of life as a church that is fitting for the foundation of Jesus Christ. Christian works may not bring salvation—God accomplished that in the cross of Christ—but what Christians do with their lives makes a difference in God's eyes. As Paul applies the metaphor of *God's building* to the Corinthian situation, he informs them of their identity as God's Temple as they experience the indwelling of the Holy Spirit among them. Finally, Paul plainly warns that a just reward will be given to any who *destroy* God's Temple. Behavior that destroys the church will ultimately be destroyed by God.

3:18-23. Evaluating by God's standards. In these verses Paul returns to the original issues he identified and began to discuss at 1:18-25, namely, the contrast between God's mysterious saving activity in the cross of Christ and the elitist attitude of the Corinthians that resulted from their preoccupation with "wisdom." Paul identifies the behavior of the Corinthians for what he perceives it to be, sheer self-deception. By focusing on their own knowledge as a key to their spiritual standing, they have shunned the amazing power of God. Paul calls for the Corinthians to take a proper attitude toward wisdom: in comparison with the saving power of God it is of little value. In order to establish his point Paul cites Job 5:13 and Ps 94:11 (93:11 LXX). Here Paul is essentially underscoring his argument with prooftexts. The citation from JOB is very loosely related to the original text; literally the LXX refers to God as "the one who takes the wise ones in [their] prudence," whereas Paul names God as "the one who catches the wise ones in their craftiness" (v. 19b NASV). Paul comes closer to the psalm text in v. 20, simply altering the word "humans" in the psalm to read *wise*.

Having scored his basic point and documented it from the LXX Paul continues by informing the Corinthians that they do not claim enough. By dividing themselves into cliques or factions they fail to embrace the larger reality that God has called into being through the saving and unifying cross of Christ. The Corinthians belong to Christ, and because Christ belongs to God all that belongs to God belongs to Christ; so that all this is available to the Corinthians as they are faithful followers of Christ. In and through Christ God unifies a redeemed creation, and the Corinthians are called to a new life in that grand unity.

4:1-5. God as the only real judge. Nothing about Christian life leads to boasting. Paul illustrates why. He also identifies Christ as the only real or true judge. The lines begin by informing the Corinthians how they are to regard Paul, Apollos, Cephas, and all other early Christian workers. They are merely *servants* and *stewards*, called to serve Christ as agents of the proclamation of the mysteries of God's GRACE. Only one key quality must characterize stewards, trustworthiness or, more literally, faithfulness. God requires that Paul and the others be faithful executors of the charge with which they have been entrusted. What the Corinthians think of God's stewards is actually of little or no importance. In fact, Paul says the opinions God's stewards have of themselves is irrelevant. Why? Because of one simple fact: The Lord is the one who does the judging. In a sense Paul is freed by the Lord's being his sole judge, for he needs neither to worry about what others think nor even to be obsessed with evaluating his own performance. Paul is free to strive to be faithful, not worrying about his success, for in the end Christ will judge him (and all others) and then God will mete out whatever praise is appropriate.

The promise of judgment comes in striking eschatological form. The language is that of apocalyptic eschatology. Paul expects the coming of Christ in the end. That coming will create a separation of "light" and "darkness," apocalyptic language for good and evil. Christ's final judgment will be universal, disclosing and exposing all things, even *the purposes of the heart*. Then, in the end the focus turns to God who enacts the results of the judgment that Christ effected.

4:6-13. Exposing inappropriate boasting. Paul has illustrated matters with reference to himself and Apollos, but what he has said was intended to apply to the Corinthians, as is clear from v. 6. This verse, while stating that Paul wanted the Corinthians to draw a lesson from his discussion of himself and Apollos, is difficult to comprehend precisely. The grammar seems to suggest that Paul wants the Corinthians to learn for two purposes: (1) so that they will understand and apply the saying, *"Nothing beyond what is written"* (v. 6); and (2) so that they will not form factions because of arrogant prejudices. While these purposes are plain, exactly what lesson Paul would have the Corinthians gain from his metaphors about farming and building is not immediately apparent; and the meaning of the quoted saying itself is not clear. By *what is written*

Paul most likely is referring to the scripture he quoted in the sections prior to the metaphorical arguments in 4:1-5. If that is the case, we can return to Paul's basic point in 3:18-23, namely, by forming factions the Corinthians defy the unity that God in Christ is creating and to which the Corinthians themselves are called.

Paul's argument in the ensuing verses comes in two strokes. Verse 7 lays the basis for an attack on the Corinthians' practice of judging, comparing, and boasting. Verses 8-13 form the attack. At the outset in v. 8 Paul is quite sarcastic, mocking the Corinthians for their pride, or false pride as Paul would see it. In the face of Corinthian arrogance Paul counters with the example of the apostles themselves. Paul insists that God uses the real oppression of the apostles to a positive end. He then contrasts the state of the apostles with the claimed status of the Corinthians to show that something is wrong in their lives. His rhetoric is patterned: we . . . you; we . . . you; you . . . we. Paul's wording draws the attention of the Corinthians away from themselves and creates focused emphasis on the sufferings of the apostles. Thus, he lays out the nature of a genuine apostolic style of ministry characterized by "weakness."

This line of argument raises a question: What is the purpose of the suffering that the apostles endure? The last two clauses of v. 13 speak to this question, but they are notoriously difficult. The NRSV translates the verse, *We have become like the rubbish of the world, the dregs of all things, to this very day*. Thus, the translators take Paul's statement to indicate that the apostles have become "rubbish" and "dregs" in their sufferings, that is, Paul offers two negative descriptions in apposition. Orr and Walther (1976), however, suggests translating v. 13, in part, "until now the dirt scoured from the world, that which cleanses all"; so that Paul's phrases are read as a negative image that is superseded by a contrasting positive one. Remarkably, the Greek word (περικαθάρμα) translated as "rubbish" or "dirt scoured" occurs in Prov 21:18 (LXX) and means "expiation" or "ransom," and the Greek word (περίψημα) translated as "dregs" or "that which cleanses" occurs in Tob 5:19 and means "ransom" or "scapegoat." Rather than ending with two negative images in apposition ("rubbish," "dregs") or in a negative image that is superseded by a contrasting positive one ("dirt scoured," "that which cleanses"), Paul may ultimately define the positive meaning of the genuine suffering he and the others apostles endure. Thus, perhaps one should translate v. 13: "Being slandered, we call out, having become like an expiation for the world, a ransom for all until now." If this reading is correct, then, Paul is not saying that Christian suffering is a bad fate that can be endured; rather, Christian suffering plays a vital role in reconciliation.

4:14-21. A paternal appeal and threat. Paul's tone changes as he explains his motives for writing and issues an appeal to the Corinthians. The apostle employs the image of a "father" in relation to the congregation. Paul cites the special relationship he has with the Corinthians, and he recognizes this intimate association to be the natural result of his having founded the church through the preaching of the gospel of Jesus Christ. Paul works with the image of a father in terms the Corinthians would easily comprehend. As the father of the Corinthian church Paul is an example whom the Corinthians are to imitate. They are urged to take on Paul's *ways in Christ Jesus*. In order to direct the Corinthians Paul sends his "beloved and faithful child" Timothy, who in the pattern of relations named here would be a sibling to the Corinthians. Paul's call to imitation may seem egotistical, but we see later in 11:1 that Paul is urging the Corinthians to Christlike living (*Be imitators of me, as I am of Christ* [11:1]). The call here is an appeal for the Corinthians to take up or return to the standards of life that informed all of the congregations Paul founded.

Again, the Corinthians are called away from idiosyncratic, arrogant behavior as Paul reminds them they are part of the larger church that God in Christ is calling into being. Then, with the directions given, Paul continues in vv. 18-21 to write as a father to rowdy children as he issues a clear, pointed parental threat.

Specific Problems and Questions, 5:1–11:1

This lengthy and important part of the letter takes up a remarkable complex of materials that may be viewed as three major clusters of material: First, 5:1–6:20 treats a set of concrete misunderstandings. Paul has taught and written the Corinthians, but they have not accurately interpreted his remarks. Second, 7:1-40 deals with the topics of marriage, divorce, and social status. Again, the behavior of the Corinthians indicates that they have not taken the teachings of Paul to heart for the living of everyday life. Third, in an extended and spiraling segment of this section of the letter, 8:1–11:1, Paul discusses Christian rights and responsibilities in order to correct and direct the activities of the Corinthians.

5:1-13. Shocking sexual immorality. Verses 1-5 identify an incident of sexual immorality in the Corinthian congregation, wherein literally "someone has his father's wife." Paul declares his shock and announces that he has already passed judgment; he instructs the church about what to do and tells them why.

The problem is unclear in many ways. The situation is most likely that a man is living with his former stepmother. From Paul's discussion the man's father is quite likely dead. In turn, the language related to Paul's judgment, his instructions to the Corinthians, and his explanation are difficult and produce a number of challenges for interpretation.

First, Paul's directions concerning the action the Corinthians are to take are worded ambiguously. Yet, since Paul wrote to the "holy ones in Christ Jesus" (author trans.) at 1:2 and since he believes in the presence and the active power of the Risen Lord, one should probably take 5:4-5 to read, "When you are assembled in the name of the Lord, and I am with you in spirit along with the power of our Lord Jesus, give this one to Satan . . . " (author trans.).

Second, what is Paul's purpose in telling the Corinthians, literally, "Give this one to Satan unto destruction of the flesh, in order that the spirit may be saved in the day of the Lord?" What does "unto destruction of the flesh" mean? Whose "spirit" is it that "may be saved"? There are no easy solutions, but one should avoid interpretations that attribute to Paul ideas such as that Christians receive an indelible character in BAPTISM or that salvation comes by death.

In vv. 6-8 Paul turns on the community and their problem of boasting. The arrogance mentioned in v. 2 is a theme. Here Paul criticizes the Corinthians' boasting by using the image of leaven in relation to his directions for expulsion of the flagrantly immoral member. Paul's point is that a little undesirable boasting goes a long way. He advances his argument by employing the Jewish ritual of PASSOVER housecleaning to insure the full removal of all "leaven," that is, immorality and boasting.

Paul continues by declaring the motivation for Christian purity and discipline, namely, Christ, the paschal lamb. This traditional image registers the reality of the saving significance of Jesus' death and reminds the Corinthians that what God has done in Christ calls forth an altered manner of living for those who hear and believe the message of Christ.

A new, related line of thought comes in vv. 9-13. Paul refers to a former letter he says the Corinthians badly misunderstood. Paul means for the Corinthians to dissociate themselves from immoral persons in the church, not from those outside. Paul says that God attends to those outside the church. The directions not to eat with the immoral probably assume the context of the LORD'S SUPPER, which will occupy Paul in detail in chap. 11. Here, v. 13 is crucial. This verse is a quotation of Deut 17:7, although Paul uses the second person plural form of "drive out" rather than the second singular of the LXX. Thus, Paul tailors the biblical word to the Corinthians' situation, so that v. 13 helps one to comprehend Paul's difficult directions in 5:4-5. By expelling the immoral member from the church, the Corinthians assure that he comes under God's judgment. His condition is not, therefore, hopeless, but hopeful. The church, as those called by God in Christ, cannot tolerate such immorality; but if the church does allow such behavior, the sinner has no cause for change and no hope of reconciliation to God. God, on the other hand, can judge and call the sinner to the righteousness of faith.

6:1-11. Going to judgment before non-Christians. Having raised the issue of the relations of Christians both to other Christians and to those outside the church, Paul's mind seems to move to the matter of how Christians relate to one another outside the life of the church. Paul's discussion focuses on the issue of Christians suing each other in pagan courts of law. One cannot determine how Paul knows about this problem, nevertheless, he discusses the matter in some detail. Interpreters regularly refer to these verses as an excursus, although the discussion is not simply a digression from the main lines of thought.

Paul views Christians taking one another into pagan courts over lawsuits as an example of the degree of the Corinthians' lack of understanding, or better, lack of love, as will become clear later in the letter (chap. 13). The image of the "saints" judging the world adapts a motif of Jewish apocalyptic eschatology found in DANIEL, ENOCH, and the WISDOM OF SOLOMON. Does this statement contradict what was said about the church's capacity to judge in 5:9-13? No, for the judgment in view here is an anticipation of future judgment. Paul's argument is from greater to lesser, from future to present. If Christians will judge the world in a great apocalyptic future judgment, then, Paul argues, they should certainly be capable of exercising judgment over their own affairs here and now. Paul admonishes the Corinthians to take the full extent of life in Christ's community seriously.

In vv. 7-8 Paul advances his argument by declaring bluntly that the will to assert one's own rights at the expense of others—and at the expense of the general image of the community—is defeat. Verses 9-11 offer a catalogue listing in an illustrative, not exhaustive, manner certain characteristics and conditions that will not gain entry into the kingdom of God. The section becomes a brief meditation on "unrighteousness" (ἄδικος). The NRSV translation of *wrongdoers* (for ἄδικοι) rightly catches Paul's focus on actions, but this accurate translation runs the danger of minimizing Paul's point throughout this discussion that improper behavior results from a faulty theological attitude. Verse 11 is the most important statement in the section. From a frank recognition of the character of "some" of the Corinthians before their conversion, Paul elaborates why they now are—and, in turn, ought to be—different. They are *washed*, *sanctified*, and *justified* (v. 11); that is, Paul locates the Corinthians theologically, identifies them in relation to Christ, and recognizes the priority of God in their salvation and, now, in the conduct of their lives. In hearing this line, the Corinthians would likely think of their baptism, the gift of the Holy Spirit, and their new, right relationship with God. All of this transformation that the Corinthians have experienced comes, as the passive verbs show, through the work of God in Christ.

6:12-20. The character of Christian freedom. These nine verses form a complex segment of the letter. One finds here quotations from the Corinthians and a citation of the LXX. The verses are largely cast in the diatribe style of popular Hellenistic philosophy. One also encounters traditional elements of early Christian "doctrine." All of this material is woven together in service to Paul's deliberate line of argumentation.

Paul builds and argues a case in vv. 12-17 in response to the thinking and declarations of the Corinthians. As the NRSV and other translations recognize by placing the statement *All things are lawful for me* in quotations, Paul employs a pattern of rhetoric wherein he quotes the position of those with whom he is in imaginary dialogue in order to respond to their thinking. The conversation goes back and forth:

[Corinthians] *"All things are lawful for me,"*
[Paul] *but not all things are beneficial.*
[Corinthians] *"All things are lawful for me,"*
[Paul] *but I will not be dominated by anything.*
[Corinthians] *"Food is meant for the stomach and the stomach for food,"*
[Paul] *and God will destroy both one and the other.*

The Corinthians' slogan literally says, "All things [are] to me permissible." They may have learned this statement from Paul himself, for he never denies its validity; rather, he qualifies the idea with his argument. For the Corinthians, what they know or think they know has given them an abstract principle that can and has produced less than desirable results. Paul concretizes this idea. Freedom, according to Paul, is characterized by pursuing what it best; freedom does not lead to a new form of slavery. The Corinthians mistakenly claim an inner freedom that places them above the mundane realities of the world, and they are eager to demonstrate their liberation.

If Paul's remarks about the Corinthians' attitude toward food and sexual activity is accurate, the will to display freedom had gotten completely out of hand (although one should not forget that Paul creates deliberate distortions in his arguments in order to score his points). The Corinthians seem to assume that freedom means they are at liberty to gratify their every appetite. Paul expresses mild shock that from the notion that all foods are fit for consumption by those who are aware of their freedom, some in Corinth engage in casual sex with prostitutes in celebration of their freedom.

Paul's critique calls the Corinthians into a responsible relationship to "the Lord." Freedom, Paul tells the Corinthians, is "for the Lord," not merely for personal pleasure. To make his point with all possible force, Paul alludes to Gen 2:24 in v. 16b. On the one hand, he uses scripture to denounce involvement with prostitutes; on the other hand, the citation sets up a crucial statement of the nature of the spiritual union of Christians with the Lord.

In vv. 18-20 Paul's rhetoric takes the form of a clear frontal attack. He directs the Corinthians to *Shun fornication!* Then, he informs the Corinthians that their *body* is *a temple of the Holy Spirit within [them]*. Paul bluntly tells the Corinthians, *You are not your own.* Why? Because they *were bought with a price.* The language is a metaphorical reference to redemption as "ransom," and it alludes in an undeveloped way to the death of Jesus.

That the Corinthians belong to God is the ultimate qualification of their freedom. One should see that throughout this section Paul jabs his readers with the rhetorical refrain, *Do you not know . . . ?* The implication is that the Corinthians do not know what they ought to know. Paul writes to factor into the Corinthians' thinking new information that should correct their ignorance.

7:1-7. General remarks on marriage. Paul's statements in these verses are more often misunderstood than grasped and appreciated for what they say. At the outset, one should recognize that in v. 1 Paul is taking up the letter sent to him from Corinth with its variety of inquiries. Paul refers to the letter and, then, as the quotation marks in the NRSV around the words *"It is well for a man not to touch a woman"* recognize, he quotes a line from the letter. It is the position of some of the Corinthians that "It is well for a man not to touch a woman." Obviously the point was debated, for now the Corinthians have written to get Paul's own thinking on this point. Paul's position comes in v. 2. In Greek Paul uses an imperative in this statement, so that literally he declares, "Because of instances of sexual immorality, let each man have his own wife and let each woman have her own husband" (author trans.). This position is often called a concession, but the imperative force of the declaration calls that description into question.

From this opening exchange with the Corinthians Paul continues in v. 3 working with the assumption that people are already married. If so, then Paul instructs the husbands to give the wives their due and, likewise, the wives to give their husbands their due. At issue are so-called conjugal rights, which Paul assumes do exist. Verse 4 offers the social or anthropological assumptions behind Paul's directions. Remarkably, at this point Paul assumes a genuine mutuality in marital relations. The *authority* over each spouse's body is attributed to the other marital partner. There is little to no historical or cultural precedent for what Paul says here.

In v. 5 Paul initially encourages sexual union in the context of marriage, but he does allow for abstinence for special times of devotion *to prayer*. Some of the Corinthians seem to assume that ascetic restraint is a clear indication of spirituality, but Paul does not follow their line. Refraining from sexual union in a marriage is not the path of spirituality, although Paul allows for limited abstinence in special circumstances. When in the following verse Paul says, *This I say by way of concession, not of command*, he is merely qualifying his previous statement in v. 5 that allowed for sexual continence for prayer. In other words, Paul himself does not think that married persons need necessarily to refrain from sexual activity *by agreement for a set time* in order to devote themselves to prayer.

The heart of Paul's thinking about marriage and sex in marriage comes through in v. 7. Chastity, the capacity not to marry, freedom from a desire for sex in the context of a marriage, is a spiritual gift from God. For Paul, not marrying is preferable only if the capacity to remain single is given by God, but the gift of chastity is not universal and it is not necessary. Paul's own prejudices come out clearly in his remarks here, for he understands the gift of remaining unmarried to be an opportunity for freedom from marital responsibilities. Paul develops this dimension of this thinking later in 7:32-35.

7:8-9. Directions to the unmarried. Having discussed marriage, the advisability of sexual union in marriage, and the spiritual gift of remaining single, Paul turns directly to the unmarried members of the Corinthian congregation. He declares that he himself considers it better to remain unmarried than to marry, and his manner of expression shows that Paul is offering his own thinking on this subject. Later in this chapter he explains that he is of this opinion because of the eschatological character of the time in which he believes he and the Corinthians live. Nevertheless, Paul informs the unmarried members of the church that they should marry in certain circumstances. Paul reasons here from the assumption that the capacity to remain unmarried is a spiritual gift. The translation of this line in the NRSV and other translations, *But if they are not practicing self-control, they should marry*, is easily misunderstood. Paul is not saying, "If you cannot control yourself, get married." In Paul's well-known list of the fruit of the Spirit at Gal 5:23 one finds the noun "self-control" (ἐγκράτεια), so that although Paul uses the verbal form of "self-control" here (ἐγκρατεύεσθαι meaning "to practice self-control"), he is referring to a Spirit-empowered directing of one's self. If an unmarried person in Corinth does not have the Spirit-given ability to be chaste, then Paul says that person should marry.

7:10-11. Directions to the married. In turn, Paul writes again to the married. As he begins his remarks, Paul makes plain that he is not simply giving his own opinion; instead, he is delivering a word from the Lord to the Corinthians. The tradition to which Paul refers may lie behind the materials in passages such as Mark 10:2-9 and Luke 16:18 or Matt 5:32. This dominical word is a firm denial of the validity of DIVORCE. The NRSV correctly places v. 11 in parentheses. The statement is not an exception clause, however; rather, it provides directions in the event that persons practice divorce despite the word from the Lord. Remarkably Paul does not turn the Lord's word into a new law.

Moreover, facing the possibility of a divorce that is obviously contrary to the advice from the Lord, Paul does not denounce the divorced person. He has other advice. Paul's comments at this juncture once more assume that in marriage both wives and husbands have responsibilities and can take initiatives.

7:12-16. Regarding "mixed" marriages. Having directed remarks to unmarried Christians and to Christians married to each other, Paul writes *to the rest*, that is, to those Christians who are married to *unbelieving* partners. Paul works from the assumption that divorce is contrary to the teaching of the Lord (7:10-11); yet, he recognizes that the involvement of an *unbelieving partner* in a marriage creates a different set of circumstances. Paul's advice to the Christian partners is that they remain in their marriages if their non-Christian spouses agree. Paul's reasoning supports or maintains Christian freedom, although the ideas of reconciliation and peace are the foundations of his thought. Peace, not the conflict of a divorce, is the characteristic of Christian life.

Verse 14 is enigmatic. Paul probably assumes that non-Christian spouses are involved in pagan religions and makes these statements to recognize that no pagan deity plays a part in the Christians' dealings with pagan spouses. Thus, his reference to the children of "mixed" marriages aims at illustrating the ultimate power of the Lord. Christians are not defiled by pagan spouses, rather the Christian's presence in the family and the Spirit's presence in the life of the believer actually sanctifies the relationship. In turn, v. 16 summarizes the reason Paul advises Christians to remain married to pagans. Critical editions of the Greek text suggest the two sentences are questions, not assertions as the NRSV translates. The basic sense of the sentences is clear whether the words are taken to declare or to inquire, and what Paul says may seem peculiar at a glance. One sees clearly from Paul's total writings that he does not think humans ever save themselves or one another, God does the saving through Christ; so these lines are best understood to say that God may work through a Christian spouse to save an unbelieving partner.

7:17-24. God's gifts and the Corinthians' calling. The reference *to the rest* in v. 12 probably indicates that having addressed the question of how men and women are to relate in terms of sex, Paul thinks he is done with that topic. Nevertheless, he sums up the matter and elaborates a bit in this next segment of the letter. Paul tells the Corinthians they are to live according to the gift the Lord gave them in the state in which they were called. Paul applies this idea to CIRCUMCISION and to SLAVERY. The concluding lines of this section reiterate the basic idea that the Corinthians are to remain before God in the state in which God called them. How is a modern reader to take this notion? Some observations may aid comprehension. One should notice that Paul offers an off-balance contrast in v. 22:

    (A) a Christian slave is the Lord's free person
       in the Lord;
    (B) a free person is the Lord's slave.

The idea of being *in the Lord* transcends simple social conventions. Moreover, Paul's thought here is completely relativized in relation to his thoroughgoing apocalyptic eschatology as is clear from 7:31b, *For the present form of this world is passing away*. For Paul, God saves regardless of worldly social status, and remaining in the social state in which one was called demonstrates that it is not something that humans do that effects salvation; indeed, worldly social change is not equivalent to salvation.

Finally, the calling of Christians by God creates real freedom. All who are called are freed, in spite of social circumstances, to obey God (v. 19). The saving work of God actually eliminates the boundaries of sacred and profane, for God's saving work knows no confines.

7:25-40. Issues and eschatology. These verses are a contorted series of statements about "virginity," the eschatological nature of the time, and the death of a spouse. An amazing variety of issues are treated in rapid succession. Verses 25-28 are difficult, in part, because of the uncertain (for us) identity of the VIR-GINS. Verse 25 clearly states that Paul is offering his opinion, not a word from the Lord, but he suggests his opinion is informed and valuable. Paul's thinking is determined by his eschatological conviction that the worldly future is to be but a brief span of time. Therefore, Paul advises the virgins to stay as they are, as everyone else should; but Paul says if the virgins marry they do not sin.

Paul's eschatology becomes more explicit in vv. 29-31. All of human existence is relativized in light of the conviction that God's work is bringing this world to its end. The passage should be taken in relation to Paul's earlier teaching about freedom and the aim of Christian life to glorify God. Paul's point: The time left is short, so live it fully for God. In turn, vv. 32-35 are well intended (v. 35) but odd advice. Paul's atti-

tude is decidedly ascetic. There are certainly other possibilities that simply do not occur to Paul. The apostle seems capable of understanding marriage only as a responsibility that will create anxiety. Paul writes out of his own Spirit-endowed gift of singleness with little understanding of the broad range of possible relationships in marriage. The idea that the love and mutual support of a marriage might actually foster more effective Christian living does not appear to cross Paul's eschatologically riveted thinking.

The enigma of the virgins comes around again in vv. 36-38, although the NRSV resolves the matter (rightly) by rendering the Greek *fiancée* rather than "virgin." The language of these lines reflects the male-dominant character of the first-century culture in which Paul wrote. Although the focus and the language are somewhat different from the earlier discussion in 7:8-9 and 7:25, Paul's thinking is consistent: if passions are strong, then marry; whoever marries does well, but whoever is able to remain single does better.

8:1-13. Eating meat sacrificed to idols. Paul takes up a theme here that, despite the seeming lack of coherence, continues through 11:1: Christian rights and responsibilities, especially regarding "knowledge" and "freedom" in relation to idol sacrifices. As the opening words show, Paul is again responding to an issue brought to his attention by the Corinthians. He probably quotes the Corinthians' own position as the NRSV recognizes with the quotation marks around *"all of us possess knowledge."* Paul's critique of this declaration follows as he contrasts "knowledge" and "love." Paul remarks that knowledge is of no value in itself. The appropriate criterion is not knowledge but love for God. To focus on knowledge demonstrates an inadequate understanding. What really matters is to be known by God; and the evidence of God's knowing a believer is the believer's love for God. God's will and work must be the first priority of a believer, not a self-inflated estimation of the value of what one knows.

In v. 6 Paul offers a confessional statement that seems creedal in character. This "creed" assumes a Christian perspective and focuses on creation, call, Christ, and redemption. From the discussion one sees that the Corinthians had turned the confession into a speculative thesis that led to an artificially sophisticated lifestyle that easily denied the reality of *idols*. Paul, by contrast, takes pagan gods and lords more seriously than do the Corinthians. Later, at 10:20, Paul relates such gods and lords to demons, so that he considers them to be dangerous entities.

Verse 7 explicitly refutes the Corinthians' claim concerning knowledge. Every believer does not share the conviction that idols are not real. Paul's concern is to correct the arrogant behavior of those denying idols toward "weak" believers who assume the idols are real. Those who deny the idols insist their knowledge frees them to eat meat that had been previously sacrificed to idols (as most meat for sale had been), despite the objections of other believers who believed in idols and were scandalized by the eating of idol meat. Paul teaches that freedom is not abstract, but concrete. Real freedom is being freed from the necessity to assert only, or primarily, one's own rights. Knowledge alone is dangerous. What ultimately matters is that believers will the well-being of others rather than simply insist on their own rights and privileges.

9:1-27. Illustrative observations on the "rights" of an apostle. This chapter may appear to be an intrusion into the discussion of idols and eating idol meat, but Paul simply takes himself and the matter of his rights as an apostle as an illustration of a proper demeanor for Christians. Paul declares his freedom in a rhetorical question. Then, he explains the real meaning of freedom in his own life. Paul reminds the Corinthians that he could make claims as others do (vv. 4-5) or as soldiers, planters, and shepherds (v. 7). Moreover, he recognizes that God ordained that the apostles be able to derive their living from the work they do as ministers. To underscore this point Paul offers a midrashic exposition on Deut 25:4 in vv. 9-11. Yet, he continues by stating that he does not use the right of support by the churches, lest his taking pay for his ministry be misunderstood as bilking the congregation (v. 12). Paul elaborates the matter of his right to support by referring to the practice of supplying the needs of those in Temple service from the proceeds given to the Temple. Then, in v. 14 he cites a word from the Lord (cf. Luke 10:7) to the effect that *those who proclaim the gospel should get their living by the gospel.* Yet, Paul explains that he does not take his rightful support. Amazingly, Paul's reward is that he takes no reward! Paul preaches because he was commissioned to do so, but by not taking his due he gives up his own rights as an offering to God.

In vv. 19-23 Paul describes the style of his ministry and its motivations. He reiterates his freedom and declares that while he is free from all, nevertheless, he enslaves himself to all. Paul reports that he varies his personal behavior depending upon his audience. In relation to Jews who are *under the law* (v. 20) Paul

takes on their patterns of living, although he himself is not under the law. In relation to those *outside the law* (v. 21) he lives as they do, but he is not free from God's law because he lives under "Christ's law." Paul says he varies his behavior in order to "win" both Jews and those outside the law. Paul strives to become all things to all people in all ways so that he may serve as God's agent in saving "some." Paul's remarks in v. 23 show that the power of the gospel presides over Paul; it is the senior partner in a partnership. Thus, the gospel is not relativized to worldly social conditions that are no more than contemporary social structures and sensibilities; rather, the apostle himself becomes relativized in order to preserve the integrity of the gospel.

Paul brings his discussion of apostolic rights to a conclusion in vv. 24-27. He takes up a set of athletic images as metaphors, explaining and advocating discipline. Paul's metaphors are inexact and should not be allegorized. First, Paul writes of *runners*. Basically he seeks to admonish the Corinthians to an active and disciplined life. Appropriate Christian living takes definite direction. With that point in mind Paul shifts to the image of boxing. He says he does not "fan the air" in the style of an untrained fighter; he works like an expert pugilist whose punches count because they hit their mark. Paul is focused through discipline.

Paul's final comments on boxing are almost shocking. He reveals that his opponent is himself. Surely this is a lesson for the Corinthians whose attitude leads to the kind of easy, self-indulgent living that merely presumes upon God's grace and does not relate in obedience to God's saving acts. Paul explains that he "blackens the eye of [his] body" (v. 27, author trans.) lest he be disqualified himself—a strong word of warning to the readers.

10:1-13. Relating the Exodus experience to Christian life. Having raised the frightening, serious matter of disqualification, Paul moves immediately to deliver a midrash on the EXODUS that is laced with scriptural allusions. Paul applies the Exodus story to the Corinthian situation as a further word of warning. Then, he specifies the heart of his concern by again taking up the matter of eating meat that had been offered to idols. Paul returns to the Corinthians' slogan about freedom and offers further rebuttal, clarification, and directions.

Verses 1-5 form the midrash. One finds here allusions to the book of Exodus, selected Psalms, the Wisdom of Solomon, and Numbers. Paul's style of biblical interpretation may strike modern readers as strange, but this manner of interpreting the biblical materials is neither unique nor was it unusual in Paul's day. Indeed, both PHILO and the RABBIs developed the idea of a peripatetic or divine rock. Paul may simply be "christianizing" a standard theme of Jewish wisdom teaching, or he may appropriate images and ideas from developed wisdom traditions in his own creative reflection. The idea of Christ's preexistence is inherent in Paul's comments, although preexistence per se is not the focus of the discussion.

The application of the Exodus imagery is made through typological analogy (see τυπικῶς in v. 11). The typological analysis and application lay the foundation for the stark warning that comes in v. 5, where *nevertheless* says a great deal. Indeed, in spite of the ancestors having been *baptized into Moses* (v. 2) and having participated in an archetypal LORD'S SUPPER, God was not pleased with most of them and they were overthrown in the wilderness. Thus, according to Paul, baptism and participation in the Lord's Supper are not unequivocal assurances against negative divine judgment. The sacraments are not magical charms that guarantee an absolute claim on salvation.

Verses 6-13 make further application of the midrash by adding and applying other Exodus materials to the exhortation. Primarily the story is brought to bear on the Corinthians in relation to the issue of idolatry, especially in relation to the theme of idol-meat. Verse 6 introduces the application in a general manner. Verse 7 applies the scriptural lesson directly to the issue of idolatry and in doing so quotes a portion of Exod 32:6 verbatim. Finally, vv. 8-10 form a trilogy of negative directions against immorality, testing the Lord, and grumbling. These verses also report the terrible results of such wrongful behavior—the death of *twenty-three thousand . . . in a . . . day* (v. 8, although in Num 25:9 one reads that "twenty-four thousand" died). Verse 11 explains the application, and one should notice two items. First, Paul's exegesis clearly reveals that he understands the scriptures to be typological as a result of the Christ-event. Second, Paul locates himself and the Corinthians at the juncture of the ages, as the NRSV recognizes with the correct translation, *they were written down to instruct us, on whom the ends of the ages have come.* This line is generally mistranslated and misunderstood as a reference to either a general summary of all previous times or epochs (*ends of the ages* [v. 11]) or a general summary of all previous nonepochal time ("end of the age"). But, these under-standings fail to take seriously Paul's apocalyptic eschatological temporal dualism. From this perspective Paul understands that he and the Corinthians live at the point where "the present evil age" (Gal 1:4) and the "new creation" (2 Cor 5:17) are both *already* and *not yet* present. They live between the cross and the coming of Christ at a time when the ages are mingled. In this interim the old is already dying and the new is already being born, though the old has not yet passed away and the new has not yet fully arrived.

Verse 12 issues a sobering warning, probably because of Paul's convictions about the danger of the volatile times, that recognizes the continuing threat of opposition to God. More directly, v. 13 declares that the real crisis (temptation) besetting the community is indeed manageable and conquerable. Paul proclaims the theological basis of such management: God is faithful. God provides the antidote to the temptation. While there is no avoidance of the problem, mixed with the problem in this mingling of times is God's saving provision. Paul's confidence is in God's sustaining grace. Although one can imagine different ways in which Paul would name this divine provision—the Spirit, Christ, the power of God—the apostle does not name God's grace; rather, he declares God's faithfulness. Above all, Paul establishes here the necessity of the relationship of the Corinthians to God who saves.

10:14-22. Directions against idolatry. Paul elaborates and makes even more direct application of his warning to the Corinthians. He understands himself to be building on his preceding remarks and inferring conclusions in relation to them as is evident in his first word in this section, *Therefore*—or better, "On account of" (Διόπερ). Paul tells the Corinthians to *flee from the worship of idols*. Then, he states in eucharistic metaphors the unified nature of Christian life (vv. 15-16). By analogy to Israel Paul identifies the demonic forces associated with pagan religion and, in turn, with sacrificial food (vv. 17-20). One should note that Paul's reference is to the food, not to the act of eating. Then, Paul doubly reiterates the exclusive nature of Christian life in terms of the elements of the Lord's Supper, mentioning the cup before the bread. Finally, he instructs the Corinthians through two rhetorical questions. Paul informs them that their *eating*, an insistent practice of personal freedom, may and does provoke God. Thus, the apostle contrasts human and divine strength in such a way that he issues an indirect threat.

10:23–11:1. Further clarification of the nature of Christian freedom. Verses 23-24 repeat the Corinthians' slogan from 6:12, but this time there is no *for me* with the words *All things are lawful*. As in chap. 6 Paul states and qualifies this slogan twice. First, he repeats and qualifies exactly as in 6:12, *but not all things are beneficial*. Then, he repeats the slogan and qualifies it in relation to edification or "building up." This reasoning recalls 3:10-15, so one sees that, above all, Paul desires the unity of the church. Paul builds on these qualified statements by declaring a maxim, *Do not seek your own advantage, but that of the other*. In other words, he teaches them to live so that each may say, "Not my good but your good be done."

Verses 25-30 make practical application of this principle. In fact, one sees Paul pluck a principle out of the thin air of abstraction and put it down with the power of particularity in the actual affairs of the Corinthians. In so doing, the principle of Christian freedom is maintained; but, the matter of one's conscience is not raised as governing one's actions! Rather, the conscience of others is brought in relation with one's freedom so that freedom is interpreted as an established opportunity for putting others before one's self.

In 10:31–11:1 Paul sums up and concludes by again declaring the goal of Christian life to be the *glory of God* in all that believers do. Paul continues to make matters concrete by reference to his own attitude, aim, and style of ministry. He calls for the Corinthians to imitate him as he imitates Christ. Thus, he issues a call to Christlikeness.

Orderly Worship and Spiritual Gifts, 11:2–14:40

This third major section of the body of the letter contains reflections on a variety of topics that are particularly interesting for contemporary Christian practices. Here, Paul discusses the role of women in worship, the celebration of the Lord's Supper, charismatic gifts and practices, and the essential traits of Christian life and relationships.

11:2-16. Keeping church customs. The section opens with a commendation that may or may not be in response to a claim the Corinthians have made about their own preservation of tradition as Paul delivered it. Verse 3, however, follows by taking exception to a practice Paul views as outside the boundaries of normal church *custom* (cf. v. 16). Paul begins his argument by articulating a scheme of priority of authority. There are three distinct and related statements, but the scale here is not a simple stepladder or hierarchy:

Christ	>	the head	>	of every man
the husband	>	the head	>	of his wife
God	>	the head	>	of Christ

One should notice, above all, that the scheme begins with the authority of Christ and ends with the authority of God. While the notion of the husband having authority over his wife offends progressive sensibilities, Paul's point here is to recognize the authority of Christ over humanity and the ultimate authority of God. The scheme is a Stoic-like system of "natural order" that values order over chaos. Verses 4-6 unpack one line of argumentation concerning this scale in relation to the worship activities of praying or prophesying, specifically focusing on the practice of women wearing head coverings.

There are immediate problems for interpretation: Which instances of *head* are literal and which are metaphorical? Are all uses of *head* literal, all metaphorical, or is there some mix? Clearly the first occurrence of *head* in both v. 4 and v. 5 are literal because of the issue of covering and not covering. But, what of the second use of *head* in each verse? Are they metaphors for Christ and husband respectively, or are they literal? (The third mention of *head* in v. 5 in the NRSV is a supplying of the word by the translators. In Greek the perfect passive participle ἐξυρημένη "having been shaved" is simply preceded by the definite article τῇ, probably meaning "the woman," not "her head"; so that the line reads "it is one and the same thing as her having been shaved.") From what follows in v. 7, the explication of a man's not covering his head in terms of his existing as the image and the glory of God and the woman' covering her head in terms of her being the glory of man, one sees that the dishonored "heads" of vv. 4-5 are metaphorical.

The strange sense of the argument begins to make sense when one sees that Paul understands *nature* (v. 14) to *give indication* of the God-ordained pattern of life. Nevertheless, there are several problems raised by these verses that are not easily resolved: (1) How can a woman, veiled or otherwise, pray or prophesy if she is to be silent in the church as 14:33-35 indicates? (2) Has not Paul confused nature and humanly determined fashion? Are male and female hairstyles given by nature or set in style? (3) How is one to understand the amount of energy Paul invests in this section, vv. 2-16? Does the show of creative effort indicate the severity of the problem? Or, is Paul simply biased? (4) What kind of attitude do these lines reflect—Greek, Jewish, or Christian? It is easier to raise difficult questions than to find gratifying answers. One needs to follow the remaining course of the argument.

Verses 7-12 continue the argument from the perspective of a set of biblical texts. Verse 7 restates the idea with which Paul is working, bringing in the language of Gen 1:26-27; yet, the idea clearly controls the exegesis. Then, vv. 8-9 extend the argument by taking recourse to the creation story of Gen 2:18-22.

Verse 10 is an enigma. The opening words, *For this reason*, can relate either to previous or to ensuing comments. The words probably refer to what went *before* (vv. 8-9 or vv. 2-9), since still another *because of* ends the line. Thus, because of the relationship of men and women, women ought to have *a symbol of authority* on their heads, and this wearing of a symbol is related to *the angels*.

What does Paul mean by *because of the angels*? The statement is obscure. Perhaps he is thinking of the fallen angels of Genesis 6 who took human women for wives; or, perhaps he means the angels who were thought to be protectors of the order of creation and who are present, according to early Christian thought, in the assembly of Christians at worship.

Verses 11-12 form a statement in peculiar juxtaposition to what Paul has said to this point. One should note the all-important phrase *in the Lord*. This location allows the balanced statement in v. 12 to be made. Paul understands the situation concerning men and women as he did the issues of circumcision and slavery in chap. 7. *In the Lord* one recognizes the eschatological abrogation of sexual distinctions, but as Christians await the Day of the Lord they are not to act as if the Day has already come. One remains in the state in which one was called as the only valid demonstration of freedom.

Verses 13-16 put the issue before the Corinthians for a last time and from another angle. Paul calls for the Corinthians to judge the matter of a woman's being unveiled at prayer. The basis of the evaluation is the teaching of nature; Paul understands that nature indicates God's will and how one is to style one's self as a copy of nature. Paul surely did not reflect on this weak example or argument, for what he attributes to nature is merely human fashion, reflecting culture, not necessarily God—unless Paul thinks somehow that culture derives from nature and, in turn, that fashion ultimately goes back to God. Strikingly, in denouncing his opposition Paul cannot cite revelation or the Lord; rather, he is reduced to custom for his standards and authorization. The issues here may elude resolution,

although one should not fail to see that v. 16 recognizes the potential denial of Paul's argument.

In sum, at its root the alteration of custom often (although not always) stems from individualism, that is, the claiming of personal rights in the name of the Lord—a problem already identified by Paul. Christians, Paul tells the Corinthians, are "not to confuse a direct desecularization that is carried on by ourselves with the eschatological desecularization brought about by Christ, but to maintain the imperceptibility of this unworldliness—by dint of Christians wearing their hair normally and clothing themselves in normal ways" (Conzelmann 1975, 191).

11:17-22. Problems in the assembly. Paul identifies and criticizes a problem or problems arising when the Corinthians *come together*. Paul says their gathering is not for the better but for the worse. The results of the congregational assembly are negative. Paul recognizes divisions among the members of the church. Oddly, he rationalizes this problem by explaining that factions are necessary in order that those who are approved may be recognized. It is debatable whether he is being sarcastic or whether he discerns God creating confusion in Corinth.

Verse 20 broaches the matter of the LORD'S SUPPER, declaring that at their assemblies the Corinthians do not eat a meal that can be so named. Then, vv. 21-22 identify individualistic self-gratification—in the extreme—as the social reality that Paul opposes. But, he puts a theological twist on his denunciation by showing that self-interest undermines community. Thoughtlessness toward others causes humiliation and, as becomes clear in what follows, is antithetical to love. From Paul's rhetorical questions in v. 22 one must ask whether the Corinthians are interpreting divisiveness as a pluralism that deserves praise. If so, Paul's remarks indicate that unity is essential and without it diversity is meaningless.

11:23-26. Recalling the origins of the Lord's Supper. These four verses recapitulate the early Christian tradition concerning the institution of the Lord's Supper. Paul reiterates this tradition as the foundation of his ensuing teaching in vv. 27-34. In light of the Corinthian situation he explicates matters related to the tradition but does not explain or theologize the tradition directly.

These verses are enormously important for the church in belief and practice, and must be studied along with parallels in Mark 14:22-24, Matt 26:26-28, and Luke 22:17, 19-20 for full appreciation of the tradition. A full-scale comparative analysis is not attempted here.

Verse 23 claims the Lord as the ultimate source of this tradition since the words go back to the Lord whom Paul understands to be raised and who is alive in the Spirit. Paul's language concerning *receiving* and *handing on* is technical vocabulary in both Greek schools and Jewish synagogue thought. This manner of speaking establishes both the authority and reliability of the teaching. Remarkably, nothing in the tradition necessitates the PASSOVER setting found in the Gospels, but mention of the betrayal shows the fixed nature of this tradition and points to its association with the larger PASSION NARRATIVE.

Verse 24 narrates the first act. Thanksgiving and breaking of bread are Jewish table customs that were performed by the head of a household or a host. The words *this is my body* refers to the bread alone. Brokenness is not in view here. The emphasis is on the phrase *that is for you*, words that recognize the vicarious nature of Jesus' death. Some interpreters contend this clause is inherently sacrificial in focus, but that is not necessary. The words translated *do this in remembrance of me* are ambiguous in Greek, though they clearly interpret the ritual. In Greek the phrase literally says "do this unto my memory." Does this mean (1) that as Christians do and remember what Jesus said that they perceive the power and presence of Christ, or (2) that as Christians do these things, God's memory of Christ or Christ's own memory of his disciples is jogged toward realization of the parousia. Both interpretations are suggested by scholars, although the first option finds the most support.

Verse 25 narrates the second similar act. The focus is the cup, not its contents. This observation helps one see that the interpretation attaches to the administration of the Supper, not the elements themselves. Moreover, the acts stand separately as well as together as sacramental communications. One should notice that the COVENANT is related to the cup. The blood defines or establishes this covenant. The type of covenant is not determined by the statements, though the relationship of the covenant to blood recalls, in the context of 1 Corinthians (see 5:7), the motif of the paschal lamb. The motive of remembrance anticipates repetition of the acts.

Verse 26 extends the repetition theme and brings together the bread and cup in the declaration, *you proclaim the Lord's death until he comes*. These words hold open God's future in relation to the Lord's death

as they refer to the Lord's coming. This note places the whole observation of the Lord's Supper in the larger conceptual framework of apocalyptic eschatology and takes the Supper as prescribed foundational behavior for life between the cross and the coming.

11:27-34. Proper and improper attitudes at the Supper. These verses are concerned with one's attitude toward the Supper. They give advice for eliminating an improper disposition at the celebration. The final lines, vv. 33-34, are practical and elucidate the more abstract materials in vv. 27-32.

Verses 33-34 begin *So then*, and aim at correction or circumvention of the previously named problem(s). Note the advice:

(1) *When you come together to eat, wait for one another*—from 11:21 one knows that the Corinthians individually or in small groups are going ahead with their meals.

(2) Parenthetically, Paul separates satiation of hunger from the community meal or celebration—cf. 11:22.

(3) Paul's advice aims at preventing condemnation ensuing from the inappropriate gathering in which the Corinthians are already engaging—cf. 11:17-19.

Thus, 11:33-34 and 11:17-22 form a bracket or INCLUSIO around Paul's reflections and directions on the Lord's Supper in the material between 11:23-32. This fact grants a perspective from which to view vv. 27-32. First, a pair of negative observations: (1) Paul is not directly or indirectly concerned with the nature of the sacramental elements; (2) the matter at hand is not one's personal piety or lack thereof. A second, positive observation is that Paul's concern is for an appropriate attitude that fosters appropriate behavior.

Verses 27-32 take up the issue of appropriate attitudes and behavior. Eating and drinking in an unworthy way is eating and drinking with an attitude of self-centeredness, individualism, or arrogance. Even hyperpious individualism would fall under the rubric *unworthy*. Unworthy participation—coming to the Supper without regard for the result of Christ's reconciling work that draws the Christian community into a new selfless relatedness—makes one *answerable for the body and the blood of the Lord*. To deny the reconciling, unifying effects of Christ's death casts one into the role of those who crucified Jesus. Thus, one must examine one's self to insure the appropriate Christ-like attitude and, then, in a spirit of self-giving and interrelatedness one eats and drinks. Otherwise, Paul says, one participates in the Supper unto judgment, that is, one casts one's self outside the pale of redemptive reconciliation into the context of God's eschatological wrath.

Verse 29 mentions *discerning* the body. This statement should not be reduced to an abstract level. Rather, to discern the body (notice the absence of blood) means to comprehend and appropriate into one's own life the transforming significance of Christ himself. *Body* metaphorically identifies the Christ-event with its power to transform lives and create the new Christian community of reconciliation. Furthermore, v. 30 is Paul's explanation of illness and death in the Corinthian community. He speaks from the perspective of his belief in Christ's real presence in the *remembrance* of the Supper. Surely his explanation is descriptive and dramatic, not a declaration. Finally, v. 31 mentions judgment—not eschatological, but present judgment in this world as in v. 30. This explains the importance of the Corinthians' heeding Paul' directions.

12:1-3. The nature of Christian enthusiasm. This section addresses a new topic, namely, *spiritual gifts* or the gifts of the "spiritual ones." The language at the outset of the discussion is ambiguous in Greek, but the basic sense of Paul's remarks comes through however one decides to translate the Greek word πνευματικοί—translated *spiritual gifts* in the NRSV. A note in the NRSV indicates the possible translation "spiritual persons." One should notice that throughout the remainder of the section Paul continues the discussion by referring to spiritual gifts (χαρίσματα, an unambiguous designation); so the initial reference (to πνευματικοί) is most likely to "spiritual persons."

Verse 1 shows that the Corinthians brought this topic to Paul's attention. Paul's stated wish may imply that the Corinthians do lack adequate information. Then, vv. 2-3 identify the problem as the practice of ecstasy. Ecstasy may be contrasted with enthusiasm to explicate Paul's point here. Ecstasy is the effort to "stand outside" oneself, to grasp or be grasp by a vital power that provides one with an extraordinary experience. Enthusiasm is the result of one's being indwelt by the power of God, so that one's quality of experience is transformed. At a glance it is hard or impossible to distinguish the frenzy of ecstasy from the empowering of enthusiasm, but according to Paul genuine enthusiasm affirms the lordship of Jesus whereas the practice of ecstasy generates behavior contrary or hostile to the affirmation of Jesus' lordship. The recognition of the lordship of Jesus is the criterion that forms the parameters of legitimate enthusiasm.

One should notice that Paul assumes the reality of extraordinary spiritual experiences. He battles a particular theological explanation given to the experiences, not the experiences per se. The situation seems to be that the Corinthians are taking spiritual gifts as the grounds for comparison that leads to ranking of gifts and boasting. The more flamboyant gifts according to the Corinthians, are to be cherished and more highly esteemed. Some people apparently become so elevated in their spirituality that they have no use for, indeed they even express disdain for, the all-too-human Jesus who suffered the disgrace of dying on the cross. Paul will have none of this kind of spiritual expression.

12:4-11. Unity and diversity of gifts. This section argues concerning the spiritual gifts that there is a unified purpose in a variety of expressions because of the common divine origin of one's gift. The gifts Paul discusses here are not natural, birthright propensities.

In vv. 4-6 there are three parallel statements based on an underlying triad of Spirit/Lord/God. In relation to each of these three "persons" Paul recognizes variety. There are varieties of gifts of grace and there is one Spirit; there are varieties of services and there is one Lord; there are varieties of activities and there is one God. Diversity in the human sphere exists, relates to, and is unified by unity in the sphere of the divine. By drawing these phrases together Paul creates the theological matrix for valid interpretation of the phenomenon of *spiritual gifts*. Ultimately all gifts extend from God and are given for the good of the church. These gifts are not rendered according to the disposition of those who receive them. They are given and established under the Lordship of Jesus the Lord.

Verses 8-10 catalogue gifts without offering an exhaustive inventory. The list seems, in light of the rest of the letter, particularly relevant to the situation in Corinth. In this list, *discernment of spirits*, that is, the capacity to judge rightly for which Paul calls throughout the letter, is itself recognized to be a charismatic reality (v. 10).

12:12-31a. The body of Christ. In three striking movements these verses introduce (vv. 12-13), develop (vv. 14-26), and apply (vv. 27-31) Paul's best-known ecclesiastical metaphor: *body of Christ*. Scholars debate the exact background from which Paul may have drawn inspiration for developing this memorable image for the church. His contemporaries, certain Stoic philosophers, spoke of the cosmos in its unity as a body, and Jewish wisdom thinking often reflected upon the idea of corporate personality among a whole people. While Paul's image is not unique, his thinking does not exactly match any background, and his use of the image of "body" is extraordinary. One should notice that this metaphor applies both to the local church and to the church universal (see Romans 12). Furthermore, philosophically, being a "body" is the very basis of human relation; and, in context, as Paul speaks of "body" he refers to the absolute antithesis of that over which the Corinthian pneumatics were in orbit, namely, "spirit."

The metaphor BODY OF CHRIST serves to explicate a powerful thesis, *So it is with Christ*! Christ means variety but essential unity. From the outset of this discussion it is clear that this metaphor is possible because of the unifying work of the Spirit. The emphasis on unity cuts sharply across all social boundaries. Then, as Paul develops the metaphor, he ponders the significance of "body" from alternating points of view. First, vv. 14-19 approaches the metaphor from the perspective of *differentiation* of body members. Paul elaborates this perspective and articulates the necessity of differences. He states that such differences are by divine design and volition and, then, concludes by summarizing the necessity of differences. Second, vv. 20-26 return to the perspective of *unity*. Again, Paul elaborates his thought and declares that unity reflects divine design. Paul declares that unity is necessary, relating his thought to the motif of mutual care in the church. Paul concludes this phase of the meditation by summarizing the value of relatedness in the church.

Verses 27-31a apply and explain the metaphor in specific relation to the Corinthians' situation. Paul delineates the godly order of spiritual gifts, probably placing speaking in TONGUES last in order to devaluate the desirability of this flamboyant gift. Paul pursues the theme of the necessity of differentiation or variety of gifts in rhetorical questions (vv. 29-30). Then, in v. 31a he states his desire for the Corinthians. Even though the gifts are granted by God, Paul advises, the Corinthians to aspire toward the "greater" gifts!

12:31b–14:1a. The superlative way of love. These verses are often referred to as an excursus on love, and there are good reasons for this description. From Paul's admonition to aspire for the greater gifts—literally, he says, "Earnestly seek the higher gifts of grace" (v. 31a)—Paul declares that he shows the Corinthians *a still more excellent way* (v. 31b). The transition from v. 31a to 31b is awkward, and the material that follows in 13:1–14:1a is remarkable. First, it intrudes. 1 Cor 12:31a flows well into 14:1b; and the theme of

love in chap. 13 relates only indirectly to the particular situation being addressed to this point in the epistle. Second, the material on love seems to be a self-contained, quite polished unit. Third, there are comparable Greek and Hellenistic-Jewish parallels to this meditation on love found in such diverse materials as Tyrtaeus, Plato, Maximus of Tyre, and especially 3 Ezra 4:34-40. Fourth, the chapter seems unconcerned with Christ. This array of observations produces a variety of suggestions; but, in any case the material seems to be an originally independent piece (or, originally independent pieces) of developed tradition that Paul inserted into this context and applied to the Corinthian situation. Paul is likely to have worked minor adaptations on this material in order to fit it into this letter, and it is not impossible that the piece, although originally independent, was composed by Paul himself.

Verses 1-3 establish the necessity of love, for love alone confers worth to all other spiritual gifts. The mention of *tongues* has immediate relevance to the Corinthian situation, and the *gong* and *cymbal* are naturally associated with pagan religious ecstasy; so that Paul's words form a poetic critique of the Corinthians' behavior as one knows it from the previous chapters. Yet, in the next lines *prophetic powers* names a gift highly regarded by Paul. Thus, even manifesting a gift Paul values is useless without love, so one sees here no simple condemnation of those who have values different from the apostle and his cohorts. In turn, the reference to FAITH in v. 2 seems odd. In this line *faith* seems to be something akin to "miraculous power," a traditional definition, rather than Paul's own understanding of faith as "fruit of the Spirit" (Gal 5:22; 1 Cor 12:9).

A minor textual problem makes it uncertain whether Paul says that without love it is no gain to hand over one's body "in order to boast" (13:3) or "in order to be burned" (see NRSV mg.). Whichever reading is original, the sense of Paul's statement is that either the pride or the selflessness of sacrifice is worthless without the authenticating motivation of love. Paul's twin verdicts here are that without love *I am nothing* and *I gain nothing*. Whatever characterizes human lives and whatever achievements humans attain are ultimately judged by the presence or absence of love.

A change of style occurs in vv. 4-7. The content and style are those of Jewish parenesis, and the form is didactic (instruction) not hymnic (praise). The phrase "Love *is*" supplies the verb in English which is absent in Greek, but the translation accurately captures the descriptive intention of the lines. In brief, vv. 4-6 create a listing that is epitomized in v. 7. Love is presented as the essential Christian characteristic: Love is selflessness and is not self-centeredness. Love is patient and kind. It is not jealous, boastful, arrogant, rude, irritable, and resentful. The lines critique the Corinthian situation elegantly but abstractly. Then, with a shift from the nature of love to the activities of love, one finds that love does not insist on its own way or rejoice at wrong; rather, love rejoices in the right, bears all things, believes all things, hopes all things, and endures all things. In short, love defines and directs Christian life.

Once again the style shifts in 13:8–14:1a. Now instead of pithy wisdom sayings one encounters elaborated arguments. The preceding verses of this meditation on love took the position that charismatic gifts are worthless without love, but now love and the charismatic gifts are set over against each other with the end of establishing the enduring, eternal, eschatological nature of love. Verse 8 opens with a contrast between love and prophecy, tongues, and knowledge—declaring the enduring quality of love and indicating that prophecy, tongues, and knowledge will come to an end or will cease. One recalls 1 Cor 7:31 where Paul said *the present form of this world is passing away*; so that one infers that prophecy, tongues, and knowledge belong to this world, not to God's new creation. Thus, v. 9 can identify the basis for the cessation of knowledge and prophecy—they are imperfect.

Verse 10 declares the eschatological end of imperfection and promises survival of that which is perfect, so that one recalls 1 Cor 3:10-15. This point is dramatized through the metaphor of putting away childish things. Immaturity gives way to maturity. Moreover, the ensuing metaphor of seeing in a mirror *dimly* articulates a contrast between current existence and the promised eschatological vision of seeing *face to face*. In these metaphors Paul states the idea of knowledge seen in earlier chapters. Current knowledge is labeled *partial*, whereas eschatological knowledge is promised to be *full*. Here, Paul writes that all full eschatological knowledge, as well as current partial knowledge, is based on our being fully known by God, so that one learns again of God's genuine priority in salvation. As stated in chap. 1, what matters is not what humans comprehend but what God has done and will do.

Finally, 13:13–14:1a heightens and concludes the previous lines of thought. There is a slight contrast between these statements and what went before, for now

one hears of the three highest gifts—faith, hope, and love. Faith was mentioned in 13:2, but it is not clear that the same sense of "faith" is intended here. Nevertheless, faith becomes the foundation for Christian life. In turn, hope emanates from faith (13:7); but as the lines continue one sees that the point here is to establish the superiority of love, as stated in 12:31b. Interpreters debate whether 13:13 means that (1) faith, hope, and love are and remain valid eternally or (2) faith, hope, and love are now valid, but only love will endure eternally. In either case, one should see the superior and eternal character of love. The supreme characteristic and motivation—now and forever—for Christian life is nothing other than love.

14:1b-40. Practicing the gifts and maintaining orderly worship. This chapter returns to the direct consideration of spiritual gifts that was left off after 12:31a. Paul's general concern is with orderly worship, but there are bends and turns to the argumentation that are hard to follow and highly debated.

At the outset (vv. 1b-5) Paul compares and contrasts only two of the gifts, *tongues* and *prophecy*. His discussion makes clear that so-called TONGUES are unintelligible assertions (glossolalia), not foreign languages. He declares his own strong preference for PROPHECY over tongues. In his consideration of these two gifts Paul informs the readers that those who speak in tongues do not address people but God, and no human understands them because they utter the mysteries of the Spirit; whereas those who prophesy speak to humans for the edification, encouragement, and consolation of their hearers. Paul tells the Corinthians that tongues edify the one speaking and prophecy edifies the whole church. Paul states that he wants all to speak in tongues, but even more he desires that all prophesy. Paul's concern is not so much with the content of tongue-speech and prophecy as with the mode and orientation of these utterances. Paul declares the superior merit of an utterance that is oriented away from one's self to speech, even spiritual speech, that merely serves one's self.

In vv. 6-12 Paul shifts into a diatribe style of disputation, issuing a series of rhetorical questions in various forms that are followed by illustrative analogies and a concluding exhortation. Verse 6 begins with a false first person statement, declaring an irreality to make the point that giving one's self to the practice of glossolalia necessarily precludes one from engaging in sensible, understandable communication. Paul refers to the flute, harp, and trumpet and the muted playing of such instruments to illustrate the unintelligibility and inferiority of speaking in tongues (vv. 7-8). Tongues are no more useful than indistinct music, for one is as good as *speaking into the air* (v. 9).

Paul continues to illustrate his point with a similar analogy indicating the pointlessness of speaking in a foreign language to those who do not understand the language (vv. 10-11). Finally, v. 12 redirects the energies of the Corinthians. Paul calls for them to excel in edification as genuine manifestation of the Spirit. He reiterates his earlier point (see 12:31a) that the Corinthians are to seek the preeminent gifts, not merely the flashy ones. While the point is clear, Paul's phraseology is not, for his sentence could mean either "Seek spiritual gifts that edify the church in order to excel" or "Seek to excel in the spiritual gifts that edify the church." Given the thrust of the general argument against self-directed spiritual practices, the second option is preferable over the first.

Paul continues (vv. 13-19) by explaining his position. He offers an argument against a sheer enthusiasm that would be indistinguishable from ecstasy. In genuine enthusiasm one's mind stays engaged. A Christian caught up in the Spirit does not unplug the mind and feel a lot. Rather, the concern for others, both Christians and non-Christians—named here as "outsiders," or more literally, "the uninitiated"—orients the enthusiast and grounds enthusiasm in sensible reality. Paul reports his own practice of tongues and his clear preference for prophecy. He speaks in tongues and is thankful to God for it, but in church he prefers that which makes clear sense to others. One suspects that Paul must, therefore, have practiced glossolalia privately, though he does not impose such a restriction on the Corinthians' speaking in tongues. Nevertheless, the degree of Paul's preference of prophecy over tongues is clear from the numbers he articulates: five words with the mind are better than ten thousand words in a tongue—odds of two thousand to one. The reason for this preference is that in church prophecy benefits others whereas tongues edify only the self.

A further section of the reflection follows in vv. 20-25 with language and concerns reminiscent of 2:6 and 3:1. Paul calls the Corinthians away from childishness—perhaps meaning a fascination with things that dazzle—to maturity. He literally calls for them to "become perfect" or "complete ones," and in an aside he expresses his desire that they be naive in terms of evil. In v. 21 the apostle cites Isa 28:11-12 as a text on the topic of tongues. The citation is a very loose paraphrase that alters vocabulary, word order, subjects, and verbs alike, as is necessary since the original passage in Isaiah referred to foreign languages, not to glossolalia. Nevertheless, Paul finds in Isaiah a scriptural precedent for his position, and the citation leads into his next statements.

Verses 22-25 are striking. The individual sentences are clear, but the sequence of thought is nevertheless hard to follow. Verse 22 states a principle, claiming to do exegesis of the cited biblical passage ("then" or "thus"; Gk. = ὥστε). From the citation Paul concludes that tongues are a *sign* to unbelievers, not to believers; yet, prophecy speaks to believers, not to unbelievers. The way forward in this application should be clear, but it is not. From this lead, given that the whole church assembles and all speak in tongues and the uninitiated or unbelievers enter, one would expect that the uninitiated would be struck by the *sign* (and moved to believe?); but, instead Paul says that the uninitiated will say that the tongue-speaking believers are raving mad. Furthermore, given that all believers prophesy and the uninitiated enter, one expects that the uninitiated would not perceive; but, instead Paul says the uninitiated will be convicted by all, held accountable by all, and they will worship God and say that God is truly among the believers. Some sense for this strange sequence of statements comes clear if, for Paul, *sign* in v. 22a means "that which is obscure," not that which indicates something. Yet, v. 22b remains cryptic. In any case, Paul is marshaling still another argument for the preferance of prophecy to tongues.

In vv. 26-33a Paul delineates regulations for orderly assembly and worship. He names certain elements of worship: HYMNs, lessons, revelations, tongues, and interpretations. All of these must produce edification. Thus, Paul restricts the practice of tongues to two or three tongue-speakers per assembly. Moreover, he allows tongues only if someone is present who can interpret the tongues, for otherwise glossolalia is unintelligible, useless, and so, not permissible. Similarly, two or three prophets may speak in a single assembly, and curiously some prophecy is recognized to be more urgent than other prophecy. Here, v. 32 is difficult. Paul means either "each prophet controls the spiritual gift he or she possesses" or "one who prophesies is subject to evaluation by other prophets who are present." Given (a) that 12:10 recognizes *discerning the spirits* as an identifiable gift of the Spirit and (b) the emphasis on mind and Spirit in 14:13-19 and (c) the expectation that tongue-speakers can limit their expression to instances when interpreters are present, the first option seems most likely. Most importantly, however, Paul articulates the central theological position that underlies what he has said and will say, namely, *for God is a God not of disorder but of peace.*

No verses cause more difficulty in the late twentieth century than vv. 33b-36. The problems are complex for exegetical and sociological reasons. Thus, some preliminary observations are in order.

First, the phrase *the churches of the saints* in v. 33b is peculiar, for in the context of the undisputed Pauline letters there is no such designation. Rather, churches are referred to as the church(es) of God or Christ and as the church(es) of a region or city. Thus, divine proprietorship and geographical setting are the normal ways of identifying Pauline congregations.

Second, the command to silence in vv. 34-35 seems to contradict the expectation in chap. 11 of women praying and prophesying, albeit they should be veiled.

Third, the verb *to speak* in vv. 34-35 is *not*, as some commentators suggest, equivalent with "to chatter" as an activity distinct from other sensible speech or prayer or prophecy. Through the rest of chap. 14 *to speak* refers to inspired speech (cf. vv. 2, 3, 4, 5, 6, 9, 11, 13, 18, 19, 21, 23, 27, 28, 29, 39).

Fourth, the issue in chap. 11 is somewhat different in focus. There the focus was on "men and women," but here, as v. 35 makes clear, the issue concerns "husbands and wives."

Fifth, at 11:6 one finds that it is "shameful" (αἰσχρόν; NRSV *disgraceful*) for a woman to be shorn, whereas in 14:35 it is *shameful* (αἰσχρόν) for a wife to speak in church.

Sixth, some few and inferior manuscripts transpose vv. 34-35 to a position after 14:40. While the manuscript evidence is not strong, it shows both (a) scribal grappling with the illogical intrusion of these verses in the discussion of worship from the perspective of tongues and prophecy (two specific forms of verbal expression) and (b) the scribal recognition of a naturally smoother transition from 14:33a to 14:36.

Seventh, a very similar position is articulated in 1 Tim 2:11-12.

What can be made of the evidence? Because of the unusual character of the language and the textual problems associated with these verses, a strong case can be mounted that this section of the letter is an interpolation, perhaps of an early scribe's marginal gloss. Or, the shift of focus from men and women to husbands and wives may provide a key, indicating that

Paul is advocating the preservation of traditional Jewish patterns of family relations. This understanding is problematic since Paul is writing to Corinth, which is not a Semitic social context. Or, the speaking of the wives to which these verses refer may be simply a specific instance of enthusiasm that amounts to no more than the importing of pagan ecstasy into the context of Christian worship, so that Paul's advice applies only to a single situation and is not meant to be followed elsewhere. Still other solutions, none entirely gratifying, are offered by various interpreters. The lack of specific information about the situation(s) Paul faced in Corinth may make it impossible for later readers of the letter to understand these lines—even if they do come from Paul. Of late, however, the increasing tendency among both conservative and radical scholars is to regard the verses as an interpolation into Paul's original text.

In any case, the fact that the argument in v. 33b and v. 36 is based purely on custom, not on revelation or a word of the Lord, gives the statements a restricted force. Moreover, it is astounding that these verses (coupled with 1 Timothy 2) became the church's norm when one finds in 11:11-12, Gal 3:28, and in the frequent mention of prominent Christian women ministers in Paul's letters both declarations and assumptions about women taking active roles of leadership in the life of the church.

Finally, in vv. 37-40 Paul boldly confronts the Corinthians. He states a criterion that puts the burden of proof on anyone wishing to disagree. Agreement, by contrast, would verify one as a prophet or a spiritual one. It is not clear how Paul relates his teaching to a *command of the Lord*, although the point of discussion is concerned with the issue of prophecy, not with the immediately preceding matter of wives speaking in church (see v. 39). The passive form *is not to be recognized* in v. 38 suggests God's involvement in the life of the church. Ultimately tongues are permissible but prophecy is preferable and all is to be decent and orderly. Such are God's ways, and such is God's will.

The Truth of the Resurrection, 15:1-58

The letter moves toward its conclusion with the long, crucial discussion of the resurrection in chap. 15. In general this section is a long defense of the truth of the resurrection and its intrinsic importance for all of Christian belief and life.

15:1-11. Back to the basics. Paul takes the Corinthians back to the basics, to the very foundation of their faith. In vv. 1-2 he identifies what follows in vv. 3-11 as *the good news that I proclaimed to you*, and he qualifies this gospel with the phrases *which you in turn received*, *in which also you stand*/have stood, and *through which also you are being saved*. Then, he recognizes the troubling possibility that the Corinthians may have believed *in vain*. It is a moot point whether Paul refers to a reality or an irreality when he says the Corinthians may have believed *in vain*.

Verses 3-8 communicate the foundational content of the teaching of Paul in Corinth. Interpreters generally recognize that in these verses there are one or two early Christian confessional formulae to which Paul adds his own commentary. When the apostle says he delivered this tradition to the Corinthians *as of first importance* (ἐν πρώτοις), he may mean either that he delivered this teaching logically "above all" or temporally "in the first instance." The lines, in either case, state Paul's starting point.

Paul recalls the substance of his primary teaching in a complex that finds its structure in a series of "that" (ὅτι) clauses: *that Christ died . . . that he was buried . . . that he was raised . . . that he appeared*. These phrases form the backbone of the confessional material in vv. 3-5, and there is additional information both embedded in this basic framework and attached to it in vv. 6-8. Thus, some interpreters suggest perhaps two "competitive" confessions are amalgamated and adapted—although no polemical note occurs in the lines and the phrase *that he appeared* is merely extended through the ensuing series of *he appeared . . . then he appeared* statements in vv. 6-8.

Of interest and importance is the material that is embedded in vv. 3-5. First, in v. 3 one learns of Christ's vicarious, sacrificial, atoning death (*for our sins*) that occurred as part of God's will and work (*in accordance with the scriptures*). In v. 4 one learns of the timing of Jesus' resurrection (*on the third day*), which also occurred as part of God's will and work (*in accordance with the scriptures*); and in v. 5 one learns of the initial appearance to *Cephas*, a partial explanation of the prominence of PETER in the life of the early church. One also learns of the subsequent appearance to *the twelve*, an odd note since for a time after the demise of Judas Iscariot there were only eleven disciples in the inner group. Nevertheless, one sees the early presence and importance of *the twelve*. Thus, one finds here evidence of the early interpretation of Jesus' death and resurrection and an indication of the early church's recognition of authorizing appearances that ac-

tually identified and formed the structures of the church.

The additional information in vv. 6-8 reports the appearance to *five hundred [believers] at one time* and declares that most of them were *still alive* at the time Paul wrote. These lines both document the reality of the appearances by taking them out of the realm of private hallucination and register the point that even those who saw the risen Lord die. Moreover, the mention of JAMES (the brother of the Lord) recognizes and perhaps explains his prominence in the early church; indeed, the remark may explain his being a believer since he was not a disciple of Jesus. Commentators remark, "James' new status as a believer offers an indirect proof that there was nothing he could remember from his acquaintance with Jesus in the family that would make such belief impossible" (Orr and Walther 1976, 322). But, the facts of James' coming to leadership in the early church cut two ways: That *James* did not believe before and without this appearance is a direct proof that there was nothing he knew from the family or from his acquaintance with Jesus that compelled him to believe in Jesus!

The mention in v. 7 of the appearance to *all the apostles* seems to name a central criterion, perhaps *the* criterion, for apostleship from Paul's perspective. Then, v. 8 tells of the final appearance of the risen Lord, this one to Paul. This appearance occurred after the appearances to the others, but at the time of Paul's writing to Corinth, this last appearance had taken place about twenty years earlier. Paul's language is that of violent metaphor. He literally says he was born as of an abortion. Thus, he aims at communicating the abnormal manner in which he became an apostle.

In turn, vv. 9-11 explicate Paul's point so that there is no need to speculate about the sense of his metaphorical language. Paul tells of his behavior that should have disqualified him as an apostle. Then, he grounds the reality of his calling in the reality of God's transforming grace. The degree of the power of God's grace is clear in that Paul was not merely redirected, so that his own zeal took new directions; rather, God's grace grasped his life and made it into something new and different. Throughout this section, Christ's death, burial, resurrection, and appearances are taken in their full soteriological force; they are not reported as isolated propositions.

15:12-19. Controversy in Corinth. These verses move from the foundational issues to a controversy in the Corinthian church, and the verses declare in a tough-minded logic the invalidity of the Corinthians' position. The problem is that some of the Corinthians said *there is no resurrection of the dead*. Perhaps they meant (1) there is no resurrection at all, or (2) they advocated "immortality" rather than "resurrection," or (3) they denied a future resurrection and claimed a fully realized this-worldly resurrection (as in 2 Thess 2:1-2 and 2 Tim 2:17-18). Option two is not likely given the full discussion by Paul. Option one makes the plainest sense of the words; but given the Corinthians' penchant for enthusiasm, sacramentalism, and the futuristic christocentric argument that follows in this chapter, option three may be preferable.

This whole section resists viewing Christ's resurrection in isolation as a mythic theme or as an eternal timeless truth. Paul's argument exposes the errors of the Corinthians' denial of a future resurrection of the dead. Paul argues a tight logical loop: *Christ is raised* > the gospel is preached > the Corinthians have faith > the dead in Christ are raised > *Christ is raised*. To falsify one element of this loop is to invalidate the whole, and to invalidate the loop exposes the testimony of the apostles as false testimony about God. If, moreover, the testimony about God's gracious saving work is false, then, the dead are lost and Christians have no hope, but are to be pitied as deluded.

15:20-28. Christ, the resurrection, and the end. These verses form a remarkably rich section of Paul's reflections and teachings about resurrection (see RESURRECTION IN THE NT). One encounters quotations of and allusions to several passages from the LXX, and Paul employs other traditional materials in formulating his argument. Despite the seemingly straightforward nature of the lines, they are subtle. In vv. 20-22 Christ is presented as the one through whom there is a resurrection of the dead, but one should notice that *all* will *be made alive in Christ* (emphasis added). Resurrection is reality in Christ, but the resurrection of others—dead or living—is cast as a future phenomenon. Moreover, commentators debate who the *all* of v. 22 are—the "all" who die in Adam certainly refers to all humanity; but does *all* [who] *will be made alive in Christ* indicate all humans or merely all believers? The matter cannot be settled simply from the words in these verses or even from examining these lines in the context of the entirety of 1 Corinthians. Paul's remarks in 1 Thess 4:13-18, 5:1-11, Phil 2:5-11, and Rom 9–11 are critical parallels for interpretation.

Verses 23-28 delineate the events of the end, though Paul is probably not concerned here with a strict chronological ordering. Rather, all Paul's teaching follows from Christ's having been raised by God. In rapid succession these lines tell of the PAROUSIA (Christ's so-called second coming), the destruction of the forces set in opposition to Christ, Christ's delivery of the kingdom to God, Christ's reign that is now underway, and death as the last enemy of Christ. The implication of Paul's scenario is that Christians necessarily face death as an inevitable foe until Christ's achieves the end. Though Christ reigns and defeats his foes, including death, one should not miss the thoroughly theological cast of Paul's teaching. As v. 27 makes clear, God and God's power are active in Christ's accomplishing that good of which Paul tells and even predicts. Finally, v. 28 clarifies the ultimate purposes of God's power at work in Christ: *so that God may be all in all!*

15:29-34. Arguments against misunderstanding. Paul offers another set of arguments against the Corinthians' denial of resurrection. He makes statements and asks questions in a loose sequence, with all that he says aimed to refute and reverse the Corinthians' position. In form and thrust the argument is similar to vv. 12-19.

Through rhetorical questions Paul attempts to bring the thinking of the Corinthians into proper line. First, in v. 29 he uses two questions about a practice of the Corinthians to expose the inconsistency between their activities and the denial of the resurrection. Exactly what Paul means by referring to people *who receive baptism on behalf of the dead* is not clear. Dozens of theories have been proposed, and none is fully satisfactory. Whatever Paul means we should (1) note that he does not criticize or deny the practice but uses it to score his point: The dead will rise; and (2) resist any interpretation that bases its understanding on either the idea of necrobaptism or a doctrine of baptismal regeneration, for elsewhere Paul demonstrates no such thinking (compare 1 Cor 1 and Rom 6).

Verses 30-31 pose another question: Why would Paul jeopardize himself for a hopeless lie? He would not, but he does risk his very life for the sake of calling the Corinthians and others to believe the gospel truth of Jesus Christ's death and resurrection. Thus, the resurrection is no lie. In turn, v. 32 uses another question to illustrate the serious degree of Paul's perils in ministry. One cannot know whether Paul's reference to fighting with beasts is literally true or hyperbolically metaphorical, although the difficult phrase *with merely human hopes* (κατὰ ἄνθρωπον) may signal the metaphorical nature of the remark. Nevertheless, even if he speaks in picture language Paul means to identify the seriousness of the threat he faced. Paul cites Isa 22:1-3b to establish the necessity of the truth that the dead are raised. The apostle's remarks have been labeled "opportunistic," but when read in their specific context the statements are in no way unscrupulous.

Paul quotes a well-known Greek proverb from the poet Menander in v. 33 to make the point that association with those in Corinth who deny the resurrection presents a danger to those forming such affiliations. This proverb leads into a blunt upbraiding in v. 34. The call to sobriety is plain enough, and such language was standard rhetoric for urgent eschatological exhortations in early Christianity; literally Paul says, "Sober up righteously and by all means don't sin!" He avers that some have an active lack of knowledge about God (ἀγνωσία, usually translated "no knowledge"). There is a difference between ignorance that actively disregards the truth and naivete that is simply as yet uninformed.

15:35-49. Pondering the reality of resurrection. Paul offers another complicated segment of his argument that quotes the LXX; alludes to stories from Genesis; and develops analogies related to seed, fleshes, body and glory, and Adam. The lines open in the style of a diatribe with a dialogical argument. Verse 35 states the question from Paul's supposed opponent, and v. 36 issues the first, scoffing reply that leads into an analogy on seed. Paul's point becomes clear in v. 38: God is sovereign and supreme in relation to all creation.

This argument in v. 38b sets up the analogies following in vv. 39-41, which themselves lead to the summary application of all the analogies in vv. 42-44. Paul's point is that the resurrection or "spiritual" body is a kind of its own, unique as are other bodies; but the spiritual body is like all other bodies in that it is given by God (v. 38a).

The series of arguments concludes with a discussion using Adam typology (vv. 45-49). Paul uses this new style of reasoning and this fresh illustration to underscore three items: (1) The spiritual body will be distinctive; (2) God gives the spiritual body; and (3) the resurrected *will* have/be/get this body in the future as they are transformed by God from being like Adam to being like the risen Christ.

15:50-58. Concluding comments. Verse 50 introduces a new idea or line into the reflection. Naturally, from Paul's statement that *flesh and blood cannot inherit the kingdom of God*, one would ask, "Then

how?" Paul assumes that unstated question and uses the following lines to answer the query.

The anticipated transformation of *flesh and blood* into the God-given spiritual body is *a mystery*. This mystery is not known by reason but, if at all, by God's revelation of this truth. Thus, Paul scores the point that the transformation of earthly existence into spiritual reality is purely God's work. Paul writes in traditional terms and language of divine transformation, using mysterious images designed to inspire awe and confidence. He continues by extending his reasoning in a didactic fashion. Verse 53 gives a prophecy that *will* be fulfilled. Paul offers a prooftext for his point from Isa 25:8, and to amplify his position Paul adds the words *in victory* to Isaiah's *death has been swallowed up*. The victory is God's, through Christ, and this divine victory has implications for Christian hope and life (v. 54). Paul continues in v. 55 with a quotation from Hos 13:14, and again he adapts it to suit the context. Both quotations from the LXX relate to the statement made earlier in 15:26.

Verse 56 is Paul's own exegesis of the quotations from the prophets, as is clear from the mention of "law" at the end of the line. Paul continues with a doxological declaration of the meaning of all that he has written (v. 57). Then, v. 58 builds a final admonition (*Therefore*) on the tradition. This statement is not a mere work ethic, but an assurance of the Lord's preserving of vital Christian efforts (cf. 3:10-15). Thus, Paul argues for the reality of resurrection, basing his argument on God's work in Christ and calling for the Corinthians to embrace his teaching as the basis for their future hope and current living.

Parenesis, 16:1-18

Chapter 16 concludes the letter, offering a parting report about the apostle's personal appointment book and expressing his ultimate regard for the church in Corinth.

Future plans, 16:1-12

16:1-4. The collection. Paul may or may not be responding to an inquiry at this point, but the words *Now concerning* identify a topic that was likely brought to Paul's attention by the letter or the delegates from Corinth. Paul moves to discuss the collection he was assembling for the poor saints in Jerusalem. One sees that giving in the church had not yet been systematized. There was no standard timetable and there was no formula for how much one should give. Tithing apparently was not yet an idea in the church. Paul does, however, say that he did not wish to do fund-raising when he arrived in Corinth. Moreover, he wanted the giving to be done naturally and willingly, so that generosity was more charismatic than duty-bound. Similarly, Paul's plans for delivering the collection were open to development or to the guidance of the Spirit.

16:5-9. Paul's travel plans. Paul's travel plans seem cryptic to twentieth-century readers, but they are related to the seasonal conditions of travel in the first-century Mediterranean world. Paul intended to spend the winter, the season when travel was impossible, in Corinth; then, when spring came and travel was possible he could go either East or West as the Spirit directed. Paul refers to his stay in Ephesus, indicating success and opposition; yet, he sees that the end of that stay is at hand. In speaking of his work in Ephesus, Paul says, *a wide door for effective work has opened to me*. The form of the statement shows that Paul understood both opportunities and successes in ministry to be the results of God's own involvement in his life and work.

16:10-12. Mentioning fellow workers. Paul refers to Timothy and Apollos as he moves toward the end of his letter. Timothy was apparently working on or was about to work on some commission, probably from Paul, and apparently the Corinthians requested Apollos to come to them. But, Paul says this development (literally) "was not the will." Whose will, Apollos's or God's? The sentence is ambiguous. In any case, Paul and Apollos could and did discuss the matter, plainly disagreed with each other, but continued to relate without friction.

Principles for Life, 16:13-14

These two verses are a bit of stock parenesis. The tone is traditional and eschatological. The Corinthians are admonished to *watch*. They are told to stand courageously "in their faith"—the foundation of their existence—and they are to do everything *in love*—the chief criterion for all Christian living (see chap. 13).

Saluting Special Persons, 16:15-18

Paul passes out praise for the prominent Christian workers in Corinth. The *household of Stephanas* (see STEPHANAS) especially shows spiritual gifts and should be rightfully acknowledged, not because of status, but because of the presence and the power of the Lord at work in their lives. Moreover, the Corinthians who visited Paul in Ephesus (*Stephanas and Fortunatus and Achaicus*) are praised for representing the Corinthians and bringing Paul encouragement on the mission field. Paul declares that these persons who have served faithfully are worthy of recognition.

Closing, 16:19-24

Paul passes greetings in vv. 19-24. He mentions *the churches of Asia*, conceiving the distinct assemblies in a region (see ASIA) as a network of congregations. *Aquila and Prisca* (see PRISCILLA AND AQUILA) send greetings through Paul to the Corinthians. Paul offers a generally greeting, and, then, he mentions an enigmatic form of greeting, the *holy kiss*. Though many have guessed what this *holy kiss* was, no one really knows.

The last lines are Paul's autograph. A scribe had written for Paul to this point, but now Paul takes pen in hand and gives the letter a truly personal touch. As he writes he couples a curse (ἀνάθεμα) on those who oppose the Lord with an eschatological cry for the Lord to come (μαράνα θά), a cry that shows the proper attitude toward the Lord. Although the anathema is in good Greek and the eschatological call is Aramaic transliterated into Greek, the words form a sound pair that contrast spiritual discord and spiritual concord. The last line of the letter is remarkable, for Paul ends with an unusual passing of his love to all the Corinthians in Christ Jesus.

Works Cited

Conzelmann, Hans. 1975. *1 Corinthians*. Herm.
Orr, William F., and James Arthur Walther. 1976. *1 Corinthians*. AncB.

Second Corinthians

W. Hulitt Gloer

Introduction

While no Pauline Letter demands more from its readers, none rewards its readers more fully than 2 Corinthians. Forged in the crucible of controversy, it has been called the "paradise and the despair of the commentator" (Martin 1986, x). Writing with an unmistakable intensity and urgency, Paul sets before his readers an unusually vivid picture of himself in this most personal of all his letters. At the same time he sets before us a most powerful portrayal of the nature of the gospel and the lifestyle of all who would be its ministers. In 2 Corinthians we discover the essence of what Paul understood the gospel and the nature of ministry to be.

First-Century Corinth

First-century CORINTH was a teeming urban center of relatively recent vintage. Once the chief city of the Achaian League, it had been destroyed by the Romans in 146 B.C.E. Recognizing its strategic military and commercial significance, Julius Caesar refounded the city in 44 B.C.E. and populated it with Roman freedmen. Beginning in 27 B.C.E. it functioned as the capital of the Roman province of ACHAIA. Archeological and literary evidence suggests that the city grew rapidly during the first century and was home to tens of thousands by the time of Paul's arrival.

Located on a narrow isthmus connecting the Peloponnesus with the mainland of Greece and separating the Gulf of Corinth and the Saronic Gulf, Corinth was situated at the crossroads of trade and travel. It controlled all trade and travel between the Peloponnesus and the mainland, and with its two harbors, one leading to Asia (Cenchreae) and one leading to Italy (Lechaeum), it controlled the safest and most direct trade route between Italy and ASIA.

As a result of its location, the city played host to tradespeople from all over the world and grew rich from taxes levied on the movement of goods it supervised and controlled. Its coffers were further lined as a result of banking, the production of bronze, an active terra-cotta industry, and the production of pigments, lamps, and small bone implements. In addition to all this, every two years Corinth played host to the Isthmian games, which brought to it people from all over the Mediterranean world.

Corinth was a microcosm of first-century religious life. Pagan cults of every stripe were represented: Apollo, Athena, Poseidon, Hera, Heracles, Jupiter Capitolinus, Asklepius, Isis, and Serapis. The city was especially well known as a center for the worship of Aphrodite whose temple stood high above the city atop the Acrocorinth, and throughout the Roman world the mention of Corinth elicited images of sexual license and excess. Philosophers of all persuasions plied its streets, and the presence of a Jewish colony is well attested. Paul's proclamation of the gospel added yet another ingredient to this diverse religious mix.

The Corinthian Church

PAUL founded the Corinthian church during his initial eighteen-month visit to the city during his second missionary journey (Acts 18:1-18). The fact that this visit coincides in part with the term of the Roman governor GALLIO (who ruled July 51–June 52 C.E.) suggests that Paul probably first arrived in Corinth early in 50 C.E.. During his stay he preached Christ crucified (1 Cor 2:1-2), and his preaching was accompanied by "a demonstration of the Spirit and of power" (1 Cor 2:4; cf. 2 Cor 12:12). While he began his ministry in the SYNAGOGUE, opposition from the Jews eventually compelled Paul to move next door to the home of Titius Justus. An effort on the part of the Jews to bring charges against Paul for preaching an unlawful religion was rejected by Gallio, after which Paul stayed in Corinth for "many days" continuing his ministry.

While the church was born as a result of Paul's preaching in the local synagogue, it is likely that its membership was made up of both Jews and gentiles (1 Cor 1:22-24). Sociologically the membership seems to have been reflective of a cross section of the urban society from which it was drawn. Some of its members represent positions of high social standing: Crispus (Acts 18:8; 1 Cor 1:14) was a synagogue ruler who had a house; SOSTHENES (Acts 18:17; 1 Cor 1:1) was a synagogue ruler; Erastus (Rom 16:23) was the city treasurer; GAIUS (Rom 16:23; 1 Cor 1:14) had a house large enough to accommodate the whole church. Many, perhaps most of its members, however, did not enjoy such a position in their society and seem to have been drawn from the lower classes (1 Cor 1:26-29).

Paul's Continuing Ministry to the Corinthians

While the NT contains two Corinthian letters, a careful reading of the CORINTHIAN CORRESPONDENCE suggests that Paul may have written as many as five letters to the church in Corinth. The following scenario, based on the Corinthian correspondence and the Acts narrative, details Paul's continuing ministry to the church after his initial visit and the place of the letters in that ministry.

Leaving Corinth after the founding of the church and an eighteen-month ministry there, Paul returned to JERUSALEM by way of EPHESUS and then proceeded to ANTIOCH. After a brief stay in Antioch he returned to Ephesus for an extended ministry of two and one-half years from autumn of 52 to spring of 55 (Acts 18:18ff.). While in Ephesus he wrote his first letter to the Corinthians urging them not to associate with Christians who were immoral, greedy, idolaters, slanderers, drunkards, or swindlers. This letter, which we will call *Corinthians A*, is the "previous" letter mentioned in 1 Cor 5:9.

Subsequently, Paul learned from visitors from Corinth of factiousness in the church (1 Cor 1:11), and received a letter from the Corinthians asking for advice and counsel regarding a number of issues (1 Cor 7:1ff.). He responded to the oral report and the letter by writing *Corinthians B* (our 1 Corinthians, 54 C.E.). Paul sent TIMOTHY on a special mission to Corinth (1 Cor 4:17; 16:10), and Timothy returned with news of a crisis fomented by a ringleader who had launched a personal attack on Paul (2 Cor 2:5-11; 7:8-13). Paul made a *painful visit* to Corinth to deal with the crisis (2 Cor 2:1). He was humiliated and returned to Ephesus (spring 55) where he wrote a "tearful" or "severe" letter (*Corinthians C*) calling on the Corinthians to

take action against the one who had offended him thereby demonstrating their influence in the matter and their affection for him (2 Cor 2:3-4; 7:8, 12). He sent this letter (which is either lost or partially preserved in 2 Cor 10–13) with TITUS (summer 55).

Anxious to learn of the Corinthian's response to his "severe letter," Paul left Ephesus hoping to meet the returning Titus in Troas. Though he found an "open door" for ministry there, when Titus did not appear, anxiety prompted Paul to leave for MACEDONIA in hopes of intercepting Titus there (2 Cor 2:12-13).

Upon meeting Titus in Macedonia and learning that the crisis was over and the rebellion quelled (2 Cor 7:6-16), Paul wrote *Corinthians D* (our 2 Corinthians) either in part (chaps. 1–9) or, less likely, in its entirety (in which case chaps. 10–13 are aimed at clearing up any remaining pockets of resistance) and sent it from Macedonia with Titus and two other brothers (2 Cor 8:16–9:5; fall 55).

Sometime later Paul learned of a renewed crisis in Corinth prompted by the arrival of "false apostles" who challenged his authority and introduced a rival teaching (2 Cor 10:10; 11:27; 12:6-7). He then wrote *Corinthians E* (2 Cor 10–13) to answer the accusations of the *false apostles* (2 Cor 11:13), dispel suspicions, and warn the Corinthians of a planned third visit when he would demonstrate his authority in no uncertain terms (2 Cor 12:14; 13:1-4, 10; 56 C.E.). This third visit is probably reflected in Acts 20:2-3.

Paul's Opponents in 2 Corinthians

Paul's polemic in 2 Corinthians is directed at a group he refers to as *super-apostles* (11:5; 12:11), *false apostles, deceitful workers* (11:13), ministers of Satan in disguise (11:14-15), *fools* (11:19), and *peddlers* of the word (2:17) who preach a *different gospel* about *another Jesus* that results in a *different spirit* (11:4). While he gives no systematic description of their teaching and practice, careful reading suggests they are outsiders (11:4) who have invaded Paul's mission field attempting to take credit for what he has done (10:13-18). Arriving with *letters of recommendation* (3:1), they claim to have a special relationship with Christ (10:7), a superior apostolate (11:5; 12:11), superior knowledge (11:6), and superior rhetorical abilities (11:6; 10:10). Flaunting their Hebrew pedigree (11:22), they refer to themselves as *ministers of righteousness* (11:15) and *of Christ* (11:23) who carry out their mission on the same basis as Paul (11:12). They place great significance in *visions and revelations*

(12:1), and emphasize the importance of *signs and wonders* as the true signs of apostleship (12:11-13; 5:12).

These *super-apostles* criticize Paul, charging that he acts in a "worldly manner" (10:2), that Christ does not speak through him (12:3, 19), that he does not perform the SIGNS AND WONDERS that are the true signs of an apostle (12:12), that he lacks a commanding presence (10:9-10), is unimpressive as a speaker (10:10; 11:6), and has an inferior knowledge (11:6). Furthermore, they suggest that Paul is bold when absent but that this boldness disappears when they are face to face (10:1), that his unwillingness to receive support from the Corinthians indicates a lack of love for them (11:7-11), and that he has been duplicitous with regard to his travel plans (1:17ff.) and the Jerusalem collection (12:14-18).

Efforts to identify these opponents have focused in three basic directions. While some have identified them as Judaizers, the absence of the kind of polemic found in Galatians makes such an identification questionable. Others have identified them as Gnostics and while they exhibit some traits characteristic of later GNOSTICISM, these traits are also common to Hellenistic thought in general, including Hellenistic JUDAISM. It is probably best to see them as Jewish-Christian propagandists who have been influenced by the HELLENISTIC WORLD and have incorporated into their own understanding of apostleship certain Hellenistic ideas such as a stress on rhetorical skills and a fascination with signs and wonders, visions and revelations.

In essence, there are two fundamental differences between Paul and his opponents in Corinth. The first relates to the nature of the GOSPEL itself. From Paul's perspective, his opponents preach *a different gospel* presenting a different Jesus by which *a different spirit* is received (11:4). Thus, the very nature of the gospel is at stake in the controversy reflected here.

The second difference relates to the nature of apostleship and the criteria by which it is evaluated. Paul's opponents present a triumphalist perspective in which the apostle is authenticated by his or her impressive bearing, commanding presence, eloquent speech, the performance of signs and wonders, the reception of visions and revelations, and displays of apostolic power. In such a view there is no place for weakness and suffering.

Paul, on the other hand, presents a perspective in which it is precisely in our weakness and suffering that the power of God is made manifest for all to see, in which the true apostolic ministry is recognized by its fruits (3:2-3), and in which one shares in Christ's sufferings (4:8-12; 11:23-28). Those who preach the gospel of Christ crucified as Lord will exemplify in their ministry both the weakness in which Christ was crucified and the power exercised by Christ as risen Lord (4:7-12; 12:9-10; 13:3-4).

Thus, while in no way denying the importance of power and authority, Paul understands that these do not inhere in the apostle. They depend wholly on the activity of God who chooses to allow his power to rest upon the servant in his/her weakness and thereby to manifest that power (12:9-10). Such a perspective set Paul in direct opposition to the cultural conventions of his day, conventions that undergirded his opponents' view and must have made that view seem reasonable and very attractive to the Corinthians.

Authenticity and Integrity

The authenticity of 2 Corinthians has never been seriously questioned. The internal evidence supporting Pauline authorship is so strong that it is accepted without debate. The writer claims to be Paul and the letter is unmistakably Pauline in vocabulary, style, tone, and character.

The integrity of 2 Corinthians, however, has been the subject of much debate especially with regard to the relationship between chaps. 1–9 and 10–13. Because of the marked difference in tone that characterizes these two sections, there is widespread consensus that these two sections of our canonical 2 Corinthians represent two separate letters. Chapters 1–9 are confident, conciliatory, and full of praise for the Corinthians. They appear to be a response to a crisis resolved, a crisis precipitated by the actions of an individual. Chapters 10–13, on the other hand, are characterized by anxious pleading, defensiveness, and sharp attacks on rival apostles who are undermining Paul's ministry in Corinth. In short, chaps. 10–13 reflect a crisis brought about by a group of intruders referred to as *false apostles* that is far from being resolved, and the scathing rhetoric of these chapter is quite unexpected after the tactful, carefully reasoned remarks of chaps. 1–9.

Proponents of the unity of the letter (see, e.g., Hughes) point to the fact that there is no manuscript evidence that any part of our canonical 2 Corinthians ever circulated independently or as a part of another letter. They argue that the supposed differences between chaps. 1–9 and chaps. 10–13 are overdrawn and can be explained without resorting to a partition theory. After writing chaps. 1–9 Paul received distressing news of a deteriorating situation in Corinth and then penned chaps. 10–13 before sending chaps. 1–9, or chaps. 10–13 are addressed to a recalcitrant minority in Corinth, or the dramatic difference in tone can be attributed to the ups and downs of the apostles' mercurial temperament.

Proponents of a two-letter theory fall into two camps. On the one hand there are those who argue that chaps. 10–13 are to be identified with the "tearful" or severe letter mentioned in 2 Cor 2:3-4, 9, and 7:8, 12 which was written before chaps. 1–9 (see, e.g., Talbert). Those who hold this view suggest that certain things in chaps. 10–13 seem to precede chaps. 1–9: 12:11 precedes 3:1 and 5:12; 13:2 precedes 1:23; 13:10 precedes 2:3, 4, 9; 10:6 precedes 2:9 and 7:15. Furthermore, in 3:1 and 5:12 Paul speaks of commending himself *again* suggesting that he is thinking of his boasting in chaps. 10–13, and his announcement in 10:16 that he is looking forward to preaching *in lands beyond you* makes more sense if he is writing from Ephesus than from Macedonia from which he writes chaps. 1–9.

Others argue that the identification of chaps. 10–13 with the "tearful" or severe letter is too problematic. First, chaps. 10–13 make no reference to the one thing that we are certain must have been in the "tearful" letter, namely, the demand that a certain offender be punished (2:5-6; 7:12). Second, chaps. 10–13 promise an imminent visit and are written so as to make the impending visit more productive (10:2; 12:14; 13:1-2), but the "tearful" letter was sent so that Paul would not have to make a painful personal visit (1:23; 2:1). Third, when Paul describes what the "tearful" letter has achieved (7:5-12) there is no mention of the subject that dominates chaps. 10–13, the threat to the Corinthians' faith and to Paul's apostleship posed by the false apostles. Fourth, 12:18 assumes that Titus has made at least one visit to Corinth to assist in the collection, thus presupposing 8:6a or 8:16-19. Fifth, Paul is aware in chaps. 10–13 of suspicions that he is collecting money for the Jerusalem church under false pretenses (12:14-18) and that there are rumors of deceit and fraud (14:16-17), yet there is no suggestion of such suspicions in chaps. 8 and 9, but rather a confidence that the process he is engaged in will prevent any such suspicions from arising (8:20).

Factors such as these have led to an emerging consensus among recent commentators that chaps.

10–13 represent a separate letter written sometime after chaps. 1–9 when Paul had received news of another crisis in Corinth (Barrett, Bruce, Danker, Furnish, Kruse, Martin). The two letters probably became joined early in the manuscript tradition by an editor who removed the closing of one and the opening of the other in a kind of redactional activity employed by editors of other ancient letters. This is the view adopted in this commentary.

Noting a certain redundancy in Paul's discussion of the collection in chaps. 8 and 9, Paul's use of Greek particles in 9:1 (*peri men gar* similar to the *peri de* used to introduce new topics in 1 Corinthians), the fact that 9:2 is addressed to *Achaia* rather than Corinth, and the different reasons given for the sending of *the brothers* in 8:20 and 9:3-5, some have argued that these two chapters do not belong together and that chap. 9 represents a separate letter. However, given that Paul is not above redundancy, that there is no evidence that *peri men gar* would be recognized as a formal introduction, that 1:1 indicates the letter is also addressed to the churches of Achaia, and that the two reasons given for the sending of *the brothers* are not incompatible, it seems best to see chaps. 8 and 9 as a single, integrated treatment of the collection. Furthermore, when Paul mentions *the brothers* in 9:3, 5 he assumes his readers know about whom he speaks, yet they are only identified in 8:6, 16ff.

Noting a somewhat abrupt transition and a seeming lack of thematic continuity between chap. 7 and Paul's introduction of the collection in chap. 8, and pointing out that while in chap. 7 Titus has just returned from Corinth and in chap. 8 he is preparing to leave for Corinth, some have argued that chap. 8 does not go with chap. 7. Careful reading of the text, however, reveals that the two chapters are linked by the repetition of key terms (earnestness/zeal [*spoudē*], 8:7, 11 and 7:11, and boasting [*kauchēseōs*], 8:24 and 7:14), and an emphasis on Paul's love for the Corinthians and his request for their affection in return (6:11-13; 7:2; 8:7-8). The allusions to Titus are understandable if chaps. 1–9 were written after Titus's return from Corinth with good news and in preparation for his upcoming trip to Corinth in connection with the collection. This commentary assumes that chaps. 8 and 9 stand together with chaps. 1–7.

Some have argued that 2:14–7:4 constitutes an interpolation because the lengthy defense of Paul's apostleship that is contained in these verses seems to interrupt the flow of thought between 2:13 and 7:5.

While in 2:12-13 Paul is discussing his travel plans with regard to Corinth, in 2:14 he launches into a lengthy discourse concerning apostleship that continues until 7:4. In 7:5 he returns to the subject of his travel plans. However, Paul's references to *Macedonia* in 2:13 and 7:5 would be unduly repetitive if they stood side by side. Furthermore, there is a strong verbal linkage between 7:4 and 7:5-7 as three of the words employed in 7:4 are repeated in some form in 7:5-7 (*paraklēsis, chara/charēnai, thlipsis/thlibomenoi*). There is thematic continuity as well as the idea of comfort in affliction found in both 1:1–2:13, and 7:5-16 runs like a thread through 2:14–7:4. We shall assume, therefore, that chaps. 1–7 are a unity consisting of an apology (2:14–7:4) framed by two sections of itinerary (1:18–2:13 and 7:5-16).

Finally, much attention has also been focused on 6:14–7:1. It has been argued that Paul's admonition against being mismated with immoral and idolatrous pagans can be seen as a self-contained unit that interrupts the flow of thought of the surrounding context. Furthermore, when these verses are removed, 6:13 joins easily with 7:2. Thus, these verses have been seen as an interpolation. Some have held that these verses represent a fragment of the lost letter to the Corinthians mentioned in 1 Cor 5:9 in which Paul had charged them not to associate with Christians who were living an immoral lifestyle.

Noting the presence of eight key words not found elsewhere in the NT and the presence of certain elements that resemble the language and thought of Qumran (the dualistic antitheses, the reference to Beliar, the idea of community as a temple, the conflation of OT citations, and the general emphasis on separation), others have argued that the passage is a non-Pauline fragment that has been incorporated into the text by a later editor.

While these verses contain features characteristic of Qumran, these features were not peculiar to Qumran. Furthermore, Paul is perfectly capable of digressing and these verses may represent an intentional digression (known in classical rhetoric as an apostrophe). In this case while pleading for a mutual openheartedness

Paul reflects that the reason for the lack of openheartedness among the Corinthians lies in their unwillingness to break with idolatrous associations as he had charged them to do in 1 Cor 10:14ff. ("Therefore, my beloved, flee from idolatry . . . ").

Literary Form

Our canonical 2 Corinthians falls naturally into four sections after the pattern of a typical first-century letter. A *salutation* in which Paul includes a brief self-description (1:1-2) is followed by a *thanksgiving* that functions to introduce the main theme(s) and express Paul's perspective on the theme while inviting the readers to share in that perspective (1:3-11). The *body* of the letter follows and falls into three main sections. In 1:12–7:16 Paul defines the nature of his ministry. In 8:1–9:15 he challenges the Corinthians to complete their participation in the collection for the saints in Jerusalem. In 10:1–13:10 Paul defends his ministry in response to the criticisms of *super-apostles* who are seeking to undermine his authority. Finally, the *closing* of the letter consists of final exhortations and greetings followed by a benediction (13:11-13).

For Further Study

In the *Mercer Dictionary of the Bible*: ACHAIA; APOSTLE/APOSTLESHIP; CORINTH; CORINTHIAN CORRESPONDENCE; EPISTLE/LETTER; GNOSTICISM; HELLENISTIC WORLD; MACEDONIA; OPPONENTS OF PAUL; ROMAN EMPIRE; SATAN IN THE NT; SUFFERING IN THE NT.

In other sources: W. Baird, *1 Corinthians/2 Corinthians*; C. K. Barrett, *A Commentary on the Second Epistle to the Corinthians*; G. R. Beasley-Murray, "2 Corinthians," *BBC*; E. Best, *Second Corinthians*, Interp; H. D. Betz, *2 Corinthians 8 and 9*; F. F. Bruce, *I and II Corinthians*, NCB; F. Danker, *II Corinthians*; V. Furnish, *II Corinthians*, AncB; P. E. Hughes, *Paul's Second Epistle to the Corinthians*, NICNT; C. Kruse, *2 Corinthians*; R. Martin, *2 Corinthians*, WBC; J. Murphy-O'Conner, "The Theology of the Second Letter to the Corinthians," *RE* 86/3 (1989); C. H. Talbert, *Reading Corinthians*; F. Young and D. Ford, *Meaning and Truth in 2 Corinthians*.

Commentary

An Outline

Salutation, 1:1-2

As a typical first-century Greek letter, 2 Corinthians begins with the identification of the author and the recipient(s) followed by a short greeting. Writing to a congregation where his apostleship was being challenged, PAUL includes a brief self-description that functions as a clear statement of his apostolic authority. He is *an apostle of Jesus Christ*, that is, Christ's commissioned representative, not by human appointment but by *the will of God*. With these words Paul sets the stage for the defense of his apostleship that will occupy much of what follows. At issue in Corinth is the nature of authentic apostleship, and it is to address this issue that Paul writes. The mention of TIMOTHY indicates that Timothy endorses what is written.

The letter is addressed to the Corinthian church and *all the saints throughout Achaia*, the Roman province of which Corinth was the capital including, for example, the Christians at Cenchreae (cf. Rom 16:1). As *saints* ("holy ones") they are set apart for obedience to the will of God, and if Paul is an apostle by the will of God this means allegiance to him and the gospel he proclaimed to them. Therefore, what is at stake in Corinth is not so much the apostleship of Paul but the genuineness of the faith of the Corinthians.

In 1:2 Paul combines the conventional Greek greeting (*grace*) with the traditional Hebrew greeting (*peace*) and indicates that these gifts come from God through Jesus Christ.

Thanksgiving, 1:3-11

In these verses, which take the form of a typical Jewish benediction ("Blessed be . . . "), Paul introduces the central theme of the letter: *the consolation of God in the midst of affliction and suffering*. He gives thanks to God for the fact that both he and the Corinthians have experienced God's consolation in the midst of affliction. This God is the *father of mercies* (i.e., the most merciful Father, one whose outstanding characteristic is mercy; cf. Ps 86:5, 15; Mic 7:18) and *God of all consolation* (i.e., encouragement and cheer), a description of God that goes back to the OT (Ps 103:13, 17; Isa 51:12; 66:13). Paul has experienced the reality of God's consolation in the midst of affliction so that he will be able to console others in their affliction with the same consolation with which he has been consoled, that is, the consolation of God (v. 4). In short, Paul's ability to console others is a direct result of God's prior work in his life. Furthermore, God's consolation for us in our affliction is sufficient, that is, abundant, even as Christ's sufferings for us are sufficient, indeed abundant. Thus, we can count on God's consolation to be abundant even as we have counted on Christ's sufferings to be abundant (v. 5).

In vv. 6 and 7 Paul writes that his afflictions and consolations would doubly benefit the Corinthians. First, whether he is afflicted or consoled, the result is the same: their comfort. Second, the Corinthians can also experience this consolation if they *patiently endure* the kinds of afflictions Paul is experiencing. This "endurance" is not Stoic resignation nor the power of positive thinking. It is the obedient faith of those who trust in God's power to sustain and deliver his people in affliction. Paul knows that those who share in his experience of suffering will also share in his consolation precisely because where God is at work there is consolation in the midst of affliction.

In vv. 8-11 Paul explains why he is so sure about the reality of God's consolation by recalling for his readers a recent example of his affliction. The occasion and nature of this affliction in Asia is unknown (some have identified it with the experience mentioned in 1 Cor 15:32). Whatever it was, his suffering was so severe that he saw no way out but death; and, helpless in the face of this *deadly . . . peril*, Paul was forced to trust no longer in himself but in God who raises the dead.

Paul sees his deliverance from this death as a type of the resurrection. Just as Christ was called in his death to trust in God who raises the dead, so Paul was called in the face of death to trust this God whose deliverance of Paul became a demonstration of his power. In short, it is Paul's suffering that becomes the revelatory vehicle by which the power of God is made known so that it is precisely in his suffering that the legitimacy of his apostleship is demonstrated. In his affliction and consolation he becomes an embodiment of that truth first seen in Christ's death and resurrection, that God's power is made known and perfected in our weakness (cf. 12:9).

Paul concludes his thanksgiving by calling for the continuing prayers of the Corinthians so that many will join in thanking God for his suffering and deliverance, for it is precisely in this that the power of God is made known. To all who would deny his apostleship on the basis of his suffering, Paul announces that it is in his suffering that his apostleship is authenticated.

Defining the Nature of His Ministry, 1:12–7:16

Responding to Charges, 1:12-14

Paul moves to respond to charges of vacillation in his relationship with the Corinthians because he has postponed a promised visit. His CONSCIENCE is clear because his actions have been motivated by *the grace of God* and not by *earthly wisdom* (lit. "the wisdom of the flesh"). He has acted with *frankness* and *godly sincerity* and is not hesitant to write openly about his recent change of plans in the hope that the Corinthians will hear him out and understand him fully.

Reaffirming His Credibility, 1:15-22

The charge of vacillation (v. 17) stems from a change in Paul's travel plans. While he had originally planned to visit Corinth after passing through MACEDONIA (1 Cor 16:5), he later indicated that he would visit Corinth both before and after passing through Macedonia (vv. 15-16). But after the first of these projected visits he decided not to make *another painful visit* (2:1) and sent a stinging letter instead (2:3-4). Thus, the charge of vacillation, of making *plans according to ordinary human standards* (v. 17, lit. "according to the flesh"), of being ready to say "yes, yes" and "no, no" at the same time.

Paul's questions in v. 17 are constructed in Greek so as to require "no" for an answer. He responds by saying that just as God is faithful to his people, so he has been faithful to the Corinthians (v. 18). He is concerned, however, lest questions about his credibility lead to questions about the credibility of the gospel. He insists there is no equivocation in this gospel (v. 19). Indeed, all the promises of God find their *yes* in Jesus (v. 20) and it is through him that we are able to say *amen* to the glory of God. It is this God who has established Paul, his colleagues, and the Corinthians in Christ, anointing them with his Spirit which functions as both God's seal (the mark of his ownership) and *a first installment* guaranteeing their full participation in the blessings of the age to come (vv. 21-22).

Explaining His Actions, 1:23–2:4

Having argued that his change of plans was a result of his faithfulness to God and to the Corinthians, Paul explains that his change of plans was to spare the Corinthians *another painful visit* (1:23; 2:1). Instead, he wrote them *out of much distress and anguish of heart and with many tears* to let them know of his abundant love for them (2:4).

Restoring the Offender, 2:5-11

The circumstances surrounding Paul's painful visit to Corinth and prompting the severe letter are implied in vv. 5-11. During his *painful* visit to Corinth a member of the Corinthian church had acted in some way so as to injure Paul and, by derivation, the whole congregation (v. 5), and the congregation had neither supported Paul nor reprimanded the offender. Rather than make a return visit Paul had written the severe letter *to test* the obedience of the whole congregation (v. 9). This letter had prompted the majority to take sufficient disciplinary action against the offender (v. 6), and Paul, whose concern is reconciliation rather than retaliation, calls for forgiveness (v. 7) and love (v. 8) to be extended to the repentant offender lest their disciplinary action fail to be redemptive. Failure to respond in this way would be to fall prey to Satan's designs of destroying the love and forgiveness that are to characterize God's people as the sign of God's redemptive work (v. 11).

Going to Macedonia, 2:12-13

Anxious for news of the Corinthian's response to his severe letter (2:3-4), Paul left EPHESUS and went north to Troas, the embarkation point for Macedonia, hoping to intercept the returning Titus there. Though a *door was opened* for him as he preached the gospel there, his anxiety was so great that he left Troas and crossed the Aegean Sea hoping to find Titus in Macedonia.

Being Led in Triumph, 2:14-17

Interrupting the account of his movements, Paul launches the most detailed defense of his apostleship to be found in any of his letters, a defense that runs through 7:4. In v. 14 he employs a striking image of apostolic service that sets the tone for all that follows. In the Greek term *thriambeuein* (translated *leads us in triumphal procession*) Paul's readers would recognize an allusion to the Roman "triumph" in which a victorious general would parade through the streets of Rome leading a long procession of captives whose afflictions and sufferings became a demonstration of the power and glory of the conqueror.

While it is possible Paul sees himself as a partner with Christ in his triumph, it seems more likely that in this context Paul sees himself as a captive of Christ whose ministry, beset by afflictions and sufferings as it is, becomes a demonstration of Christ's power and glory. This image becomes a graphic expression of the significant role suffering plays in apostolic ministry, a significance rejected by Paul's critics in Corinth. Yet it is precisely through Paul's ministry of suffering that God *spreads in every place the fragrance that comes from knowing him* (v. 14), that is, through Paul's ministry the knowledge of God is spread abroad and the suffering apostle becomes *the aroma of Christ* (v. 15).

Paul knows that not all will respond positively to this understanding of the nature of ministry even as all do not respond positively to the word of the cross. In fact, Paul describes the reaction to this understanding

of ministry in terms of the same twofold response described for the word of the cross in 1 Cor 1:18-25. For those who acknowledge that God reveals himself in Paul's suffering, this aroma is the fragrance of life. For those who reject it, the fragrance is the smell of death. To those being saved, suffering is an appropriate expression of apostleship. To those who are perishing, it is foolishness (vv. 15-16).

This reflection on the nature of apostolic ministry prompts Paul to ask, *Who is sufficient for these things?* (v. 16). Who, that is, is adequate for such a ministry? While his answer does not come until 3:5-6, in 2:17 he makes it clear that the "sufficient one" is not a *peddler of the word*, that is, someone who preaches and teaches for his or her own gain, even adulterating the message to make it more marketable. Those who are "sufficient" speak in Christ as persons of sincerity, as persons who speak for God (saying what God wants said), and as persons who speak as if standing in the presence of God (i.e., with God as judge, cf. 5:10).

Acknowledging His Commendation and Competence, 3:1-6

Paul raises two questions in v. 1 that are intended to distinguish him from those who have come to Corinth bearing letters of recommendation. The implied answer to both is "no." He need not commend himself and does not need letters of recommendation because the Corinthians themselves are his letter of recommendation, authored by Christ, *written . . . with the Spirit of the living God . . . on tablets of human hearts* (vv. 2-3; for the background of this image see Jer 31:33; cf. Ezek 11:19-20; 36:26-27). This letter is *to be known and read by all.*

In short, the Corinthians owe their very lives as Christians to the ministry of Paul and to deny his apostleship would be tantamount to denying their conversion. Their experience legitimates Paul's apostleship. Indeed, there is no better evidence of the validity of Paul's ministry than the existence of the Corinthian church.

The Corinthian church is itself the basis for Paul's confidence (v. 4), but he is quick to point out that his competence for this ministry is not in himself but from God *who has made us competent to be ministers of a new covenant*, a covenant not of letter but of spirit *for the letter kills, but the Spirit gives life* (v. 6). Thus, Paul sets up a contrast between the old covenant and the new, and implies that his ministry is an essential part of the dawning of the new age promised in Jer

31:33 and Ezek 11 and 36. This new spiritual covenant served by his ministry is the subject of 3:7-18.

Ministering under the New Covenant, 3:7–4:6

In a *midrash* on Exod 34:29-35 Paul develops further the contrast introduced in 3:6. In 3:7-11 he employs the rabbinic principle of arguing from the lesser to the greater (*qal wa-homer*) to demonstrate the surpassing glory of this new COVENANT and the ministry that accompanies it. While the old covenant is *chiseled in letters on stone tablets* (cf. 3:3 and Exod 31:18), the new is written *on tablets of human hearts* (3:3). While the old covenant results in *condemnation*, the new results in *justification* (3:9). While the ministry that accompanies the old covenant is *the ministry of death* (3:7), the ministry of the new covenant is *the ministry of the Spirit* (3:8) that *gives life* (3:6). While the old covenant has been *set aside* (3:11), the new covenant is *permanent* (3:11). While the old covenant came with *glory* (3:7, 9, 10, 11), the new covenant has come with *greater glory* (3:8, 9, 10, 11) so that *what once had glory has lost its glory* in the light of the new that has come.

As a minister of this new covenant, Paul acts *with great boldness* (3:12), unlike Moses who put *a veil* over his face to conceal the temporary character of the glory of the old covenant (3:13). In 3:14 and 15 this *veil* becomes a metaphor for the spiritual blindness that lies over the hardened minds of those who continue to live under the old covenant. When they turn to the Lord, however, this veil is removed and they are able to see *the glory of the Lord* as it is revealed in Jesus, and beholding him to be *transformed into the same image from one degree of glory to another* (3:18).

Paul reaffirms the fact that he is engaged in this ministry of the new covenant as a result of *God's mercy* (4:1; cf. 3:5). Therefore, he does not *lose heart* despite the suffering he may experience. The nature of this ministry is then described both negatively and positively. Those engaged in this ministry do not resort to methods that bring shame when exposed. They do not engage in deceptive methods for their own advantage and they do not adulterate the message to make it more palatable. Rather they commend themselves to the conscience of everyone in the sight of God by *the open statement of the truth* (4:1-2).

If Paul's message is veiled, it is veiled only to unbelievers who lack the enlightenment of the Spirit and have been blinded by *the god of this world*. In this blindness they see only Paul's suffering and are blind to the power of his message (4:3-4).

Paul's message does not center on himself. He preaches nothing but *Jesus Christ as Lord* and unlike those who would exploit the congregation, he postures himself as their "slave" (4:5). The basis for both his message and the manner of his ministry is to be found in his own experience of discovering *the light of the knowledge of the glory of God* [i.e., all that God is and wills] *in the face of Jesus Christ* (4:6).

Recognizing Treasure in Clay Jars, 4:7-15

In v. 7 Paul employs another powerful image for the apostolic ministry. *We have this treasure in clay jars.* In the ancient world treasure was often buried in clay jars. The jar was fragile and expendable and often had to be broken so that the treasure inside could be revealed. So the treasure of apostleship is carried within the life of a fragile human being *so that it may be made clear that this extraordinary power belongs to God and does not come from us* (v. 7). In the weakness and the brokenness of the vessel the power of God is made manifest, and, therefore, weakness and suffering are integral to authentic apostolic ministry.

In support of this view Paul presents a list of the tribulations accompanying his ministry in vv. 8-10. He is *afflicted, perplexed, persecuted,* and *struck down,* and in these sufferings he is carrying in his own body the death (lit. "dying") of Jesus. But he is *not crushed, driven to despair, forsaken,* or *destroyed* because the power of God sustains him, and, therefore, the life of Jesus is *made visible in [his] mortal flesh.* In short, Paul's apostolic sufferings are a manifestation of Jesus' death and resurrection, and his suffering to bring the gospel to the Corinthians assures them of life in Christ (vv. 11-12).

So Paul does not *lose heart* even though his ministry is beset by suffering. He has the same spirit of faith as the Psalmist who wrote, *"I believed, and so I spoke."* The quotation is taken from Ps 116, a hymn of thanksgiving for deliverance from death. What Paul believes that enables him to speak is the gospel that *the one who raised the Lord Jesus will raise us also with him, and will bring us with you into his presence* (v. 14).

Living in the Light of the Future, 4:16–5:10

In v. 16 Paul picks up on the theme of future glory as a reason that he does not *lose heart* amidst the suffering of his apostolic ministry. The contrast between present, momentary affliction, and future, eternal glory is a reason for apostolic confidence. While the *outer nature* (i.e., mortal existence) is passing away, the *inner nature* (i.e., identity as children of God) is being renewed day by day (4:16), and the affliction we encounter serves to prepare us for *an eternal weight of glory beyond all measure* (4:17). Thus, we are able to look beyond present, temporary, and seen affliction to the future, eternal, not-yet-seen glory that lies ahead (4:18).

In 5:1-5 Paul employs a series of metaphors to describe the resurrection life. In 5:1 he contrasts the transience of our *earthly tent* (a common idiom for life in the body) with the permanence of our *building from God*, a *heavenly dwelling* which is *eternal, not made with hands*. In 5:2-3 he employs the image of putting on a garment over a garment already being worn. Similarly in 5:4 he pictures the putting up of another tent around one already inhabited. In both cases, Paul's desire is to receive the new garment or tent without having to give up the old one so as not to be *naked* (5:3) or *unclothed* (5:4), that is, to avoid the threat of nonbeing (death).

So in this life we groan, longing for the mortal to be swallowed up by life, knowing that the Spirit of God that we have already received is the guarantee of the reality of this resurrection life (5:5).

In 5:6-8 Paul introduces yet another metaphor, that of being *at home* and *away from home*. To be *at home in the body* (i.e., mortal existence) is to be *away from the Lord*. It is to walk *by faith* and not *by sight*. While he prefers to be *away from the body and at home with the Lord*, his eschatological hope is the foundation of his confidence (5:6, 8). This eschatological hope is more than just a source of confidence. It is also a challenge to right living. Since we all must appear before the *judgment seat of Christ*, our aim, whatever our state, must ever be to please him (5:9-10).

Being Ministers of Reconciliation, 5:11–6:10

In 5:11-15 Paul discusses the motivation for his ministry. He carries out his apostolic ministry *knowing the fear of the Lord*, knowing, that is, that he will give an account for his service *before the judgment seat of Christ* (5:10). His motives and actions lie open before God and the Corinthians, who he hopes will listen to their consciences rather than to his critics (5:11). Paul's intention in writing is not self-commendation. His aim is to provide the Corinthians a basis for re-

sponding to his critics who boast in external appearances rather than the things of the heart (5:12).

In 5:13a Paul responds to charges that he is either mad (in which case he responds that his behavior is determined by his faithfulness to God) or that his ministry is not truly apostolic because it does not give sufficient evidence of ecstatic experiences (in which case he responds that such experiences are between him and God, and are not to be worn on one's sleeve as evidence of one's apostleship). Whatever his behavior, whether he is *beside* himself, or in his *right mind*, it is for God and his glory, and for the benefit of the Corinthians. Paul's primary motivation is *the love of Christ* (Christ's love for him), a love demonstrated in the fact that *one has died for all; therefore all have died*, died, that is, to a sinful, self-centered existence so that they might live a Christ-centered life (5:14-15).

The new life in Christ is characterized by two things. First, there is a new way of knowing (5:16) in which we no longer evaluate either Christ or others *from a human point of view* (lit. "according to the flesh," i.e., knowledge without reference to God and God's purposes). Second, there is a new way of being, *a new creation* (5:17). The old self-centered humanity *has passed away*; the new Christ-centered humanity has come (cf. Paul's treatment of the two humanities in Rom 5:12ff.). *All this is from God who reconciled us to himself through Jesus Christ* (5:18).

Reconciliation, a major soteriological motif in Paul (cf. Rom 5:10; Col 1:21ff.; Eph 2:11-22), is summarized in 5:18-21.

First, it is initiated and accomplished by God (5:18, 19).

Second, it is accomplished *through* (5:18), *in Christ* (5:19) who was made *to be sin* (5:21). While this phrase has been interpreted to mean (a) that God caused him to assume our sinful nature or (b) that God allowed him to be condemned as a sinner, it is probably best to understand it to mean that (c) God made him a sin offering. In any case, God has so acted that *in him* [Christ] *we might become the righteousness of God*, that is, sinners are given a righteous status before God through the righteous one who absorbed their sin and its judgment in himself.

Third, all who are reconciled become ministers of *reconciliation* (5:18), charged with announcing the *message of reconciliation* (5:19) as *ambassadors for Christ* (5:20).

This message contains the plea to *be reconciled to God*, a plea addressed in this case to the Corinthians whose alienation from Paul has become a denial of the reality of the gospel of reconciliation in their lives. This reconciliation is a relationship with God and others that must be continually reaffirmed and realized. Thus, quoting Isa 49:8, Paul exhorts the Corinthians not to accept the reconciling grace of God in vain by acting in a way that is contrary to their experience of God's grace for every day is the *today* of salvation.

Paul has attempted to live and minister so as not to hinder the message he proclaims. In 6:4b-5 he presents a catalog of afflictions that he has borne with *great endurance* (cf. 11:23-33 for a second and more detailed listing). In 6:6-7 he lists moral and spiritual characteristics necessary to conduct his ministry. These are the *weapons of righteousness for the right hand and for the left*. In 6:8-10 he gives seven pairs of antithetical ways of viewing his ministry that contrast the visible appearance and essential reality of that ministry. Those who evaluate on the basis of human standards will have one perception of Paul's ministry. Those who judge according to the standards of the new creation will have quite another perception.

Appealing to the Corinthians, 6:11-13

In all his dealings with the Corinthians Paul has spoken frankly with a heart wide open to them. If there is any lack of openness between Paul and the Corinthians, the fault lies with them (vv. 11-12). So as a father speaking to his children (cf. 1 Cor 4:14-15), Paul appeals to them to open wide their hearts to him (5:13).

Calling for a Holy Life, 6:14–7:1

These verses (seen by many as an interpolation: see "Integrity," above) are a digression suggesting that one reason for the Corinthians' alienation from Paul is that they are still accommodating too much to the pagan environment in which they live (a problem amply attested in 1 Corinthians). The passage begins with an exhortation not to be *mismatched with unbelievers*. The term *mismatched* means "unequally" or "unnaturally" yoked, such as harnessing an ox and an ass together (a practice prohibited in Deut 22:10). This is followed by five rhetorical questions presupposing a negative answer illustrating the incongruity of a believer being yoked to an unbeliever. Righteousness, light, Christ, believers, and God's temple have nothing in common with lawlessness, darkness, Beliar (an evil spirit in intertestamental literature, under, or identified with, Satan), unbelievers, and idols (6:14b-16a).

Verses 16b-18 characterize the church as God's *temple* and depict the nature of that community with a series of OT quotations (Lev 26:12; Isa 52:11; a combination of Ezek 20:34, Isa 43:6, and 2 Sam 7:14). The section closes with an exhortation in 7:1 to be a holy people in reverent fear of their God (cf. 5:10).

Continuing the Appeal, 7:2-4

In v. 2 Paul repeats his plea of 6:13. The basis for that appeal is found in vv. 2b-3. He has been totally honest in all of his dealings with the Corinthians, and his purpose for writing is not condemnation but an expression of his life-and-death commitment to them. Verse 4 is an expression of his confidence in the Corinthians.

Rejoicing in Reconciliation, 7:5-16

In v. 5 Paul resumes the account of his movements begun in 2:12-13. The affliction he had experienced in Troas (2:13) continued in Macedonia as he awaited Titus's return from Corinth with a report of their reception of his severe letter (2:3-4). On receiving Titus's report his regrets about sending the letter vanished (v. 8) and he was *overjoyed* (v. 4) because it had led the Corinthians to a *godly grief* that led them to repentance and salvation rather than a *worldly grief* which leads only to death.

As a result of his letter the Corinthians had (1) rallied to Paul's side and reaffirmed their solidarity with him (vv. 5-6); (2) acted to discipline the offender, realizing that the offender's actions not only injured Paul but ultimately the whole congregation (2:5-7; 7:11-12); and (3) lived up to Titus's expectations of them based on Paul's boasting about them as Titus witnessed their obedience to Paul's apostolic leadership (vv. 13-15).

Paul concludes this section with another affirmation of his *complete confidence* in the Corinthians (v. 16; cf. v. 4) that serves to set the stage for the request he is about to make in chaps. 8 and 9. Such expressions of confidence typically functioned to undergird the subsequent request by creating a sense of obligation through praise.

Challenging the Corinthians to Complete the Collection, 8:1–9:15

Chapters 8 and 9 focus on Paul's collection for the saints in Jerusalem (see 1 Cor 16:1-4 and Rom 15:25-27). Having expressed his *complete confidence* in the

Corinthians (7:16), Paul calls upon them to fulfill their obligation to this collection.

Excel in Giving, 8:1-8

Paul challenges the Corinthians to follow the example of the Macedonian churches. Using the ancient rhetorical technique of comparison to evoke competition between two individuals or groups, Paul seeks to motivate the Corinthians by alluding to the generosity of the Macedonians. Though experiencing *a severe ordeal of affliction* and *poverty*, they have voluntarily given generously, even *beyond their means*, out of the overflow of their gift of themselves to the Lord and to Paul (vv. 1-5). So Paul encourages the Corinthians to demonstrate their commitment to the Lord and to him as he sends Titus to complete their gift to the collection (v. 6). Playing on their pride, he calls upon them to excel in this *generous undertaking* as they excel in everything else (v. 7). Here is an opportunity for them to demonstrate the *genuineness* of their love as the Macedonians have done (v. 8).

Follow Christ's Example, 8:9-15

In these verses Paul challenges the Corinthians to fulfill their obligation on the basis of the example of Christ who *though he was rich, yet for your sakes he became poor, so that by his poverty you might become rich* (v. 9) Paul advises them to match the eagerness they had previously shown with the necessary action to complete their gift (vv. 10-12). They are encouraged to give (1) according to their means and (2) in keeping with the principle of equality (vv. 13-15) whereby those who have share out of their abundance with those who have not so that there is a *fair balance*. Citing Exod 16:18 Paul finds scriptural support for this practice in the story of the gathering of the manna in the wilderness (v. 15).

Receive the Representatives, 8:16–9:5

Paul is sending a delegation to receive the contribution of the Corinthians. The delegation includes Titus (8:16-17), the brother *who is famous among all the churches for his proclaiming the good news* and who has been appointed by the churches to travel with them perhaps as a kind of independent auditor (8:18-19), and *our brother whom we have often tested and found eager in many matters* (8:22). These arrangements have been made so there can be no charges of deceit leveled against Paul or this project. The purpose for the delegation is clearly stated in 8:20-21:

We intend that no one should blame us about this generous gift that we are administering, for we intend to do what is right not only in the Lord's sight but also in the sight of others.

Titus comes as Paul's representative, while the other two come as representatives of the churches (8:23). Paul encourages the Corinthians to show them proof of their love and the reason for Paul's boasting about them. In other words, complete the collection (8:24).

9:1-5 extend and support the commendations in 8:16-24 (for the view that chap. 9 represents a separate letter, see "Integrity," above), and together with 9:6-15 provide the conclusion for Paul's treatment of the collection in 8:1–9:15. The subject of Paul's *boasting* about the Corinthians is given in 9:1-2. He has boasted to the Macedonians about the eagerness of the Corinthians to participate in the *ministry to the saints*. They have been ready to participate *since last year*. This boasting has *stirred up most* of the Macedonians, and Paul hopes that his boasting about the Macedonians in 8:1-5 will stir up the Corinthians.

In 9:3-5 Paul gives a second reason for sending *the brothers* (Titus and the two unnamed brothers of 8:16-24; the first reason was given in 8:20-21). They will *arrange in advance* for the *bountiful* gift the Corinthians have promised so that neither the Corinthians nor Paul will be humiliated when he arrives with representatives of the Macedonian churches because the Corinthians, about whom Paul has been boasting, are not prepared with their gift.

Give Bountifully and Cheerfully, 9:6-15

Paul concludes his appeal on behalf of the collection by challenging the Corinthians to "sow bountifully" so that they may *reap bountifully* (v. 6; cf. Gal 6:7-8). To "sow bountifully" is to give *not reluctantly or under compulsion* but "cheerfully" (v. 7; cf. 9:5 and LXX of Prov 22:8a). To *reap bountifully* is to be *enriched in every way* (v. 11) by the God who is able *to provide you with every blessing in abundance*, not to be self-sufficient, but so that *having enough of everything, you may share abundantly in every good work* (v. 8).

In v. 9 Paul quotes from the description of the man who fears the Lord in Ps 112:9, whose *righteousness* [i.e., acts of piety, esp. almsgiving] *endures forever*.

The generosity of the Corinthians in sharing in the collection will supply the needs of the saints (v. 12) and will be a sign of their obedience to the gospel that will bring glory to God (v. 13). It will result in thanksgiving to God (v. 11b); in fact, it will overflow *with many thanksgivings to God* (v. 12b) because God is the ultimate source of both the spirit of generosity and the abundance from which the Corinthians are able to give.

All of our giving is done in light of and in response to God's *indescribable gift* (v. 15) for which Paul gives thanks as he closes this discussion. Romans 15:25-27 (probably written from Corinth after 2 Corinthians), suggests that the Corinthians heeded Paul's appeal with regard to the collection.

Defending His Ministry, 10:1–13:10

Because of the abrupt change of tone, there is a widespread consensus among NT scholars that chaps. 10–13 represent a separate letter. While some identify it as the "tearful" or "severe" letter referred to in 2:3-9 and 7:8-12 that was written before chaps. 1–9, a growing number of commentators—including the present one—argue that it was written some time after chaps. 1–9 in response to a fresh outbreak of trouble in Corinth precipitated by the arrival of *false apostles* (11:13) who were attempting to undermine Paul's ministry there (on the relationship between chaps. 1–9 and chaps. 10–13, see "Integrity," above). In any case, these chapters contain a passionate and vigorous defense of Paul's apostolic ministry.

Responding to Criticism, 10:1-11

Paul appeals to the Corinthians on the basis of *the meekness and gentleness of Christ* and in light of a series of criticisms leveled at him by his unnamed opponents in Corinth.

The first criticism, as reflected in vv. 1 and 10, is that while Paul is bold from a distance, he is weak and unimpressive in person. The charge probably reflects on his oratorical skills (cf. 1 Cor 2:3-4; 2 Cor 11:6), his physical appearance, and his behavior on the painful visit when in the face of opposition he left Corinth and, rather than returning in person, fired off the severe letter. Paul responds with the veiled threat in vv. 2 and 11, that he is prepared to back up his strong words with action if necessary when he arrives in Corinth.

The second charge is that he acts *according to human standards* (v. 2, lit. "according to the flesh"). This may mean either that he acts according to egocentric, worldly motives or that he acts without spiritu-

al power. Paul responds that while he lives as a human being, he wields weapons with *divine power* (vv. 3-4a). Employing military images, he describes these weapons as capable of destroying *strongholds* (i.e., *arguments and every proud obstacle raised up against the knowledge of God*), taking captives (i.e., *every thought captive to obey Christ*) and punishing *every disobedience* (vv. 4b-6). While he wields these weapons in *the meekness and gentleness of Christ* (v. 1), this must never be confused with weakness. He will wield them in Corinth if necessary but hopes that the Corinthians will not force a showdown.

In response to the claims of his opponents, Paul reminds the Corinthians that he too belongs to Christ (v. 7) and that the Lord has given him the apostolic authority (v. 8) for the purpose of building up rather than tearing down.

Seeking the Lord's Commendation, 10:12-18

In v. 12 Paul focuses specifically on his opponents, ironically stating that he does not "dare" to compare himself with those who nonsensically measure themselves by one another and make themselves the measure of genuine apostleship. In reality no comparison is possible, for Paul sees them as *false apostles* who serve Satan rather than Christ (11:13-15). Unlike Paul, his opponents *boast beyond limits*, demonstrating the kind of excessive self-praise characteristic of the sham philosopher (v. 13). Furthermore, they boast *in the labors of others* (v. 15) and take credit for *work already done in someone else's sphere of action* (v. 16).

The clear implication is that Paul's opponents have invaded the sphere of action assigned to Paul and are seeking to take it over for themselves. In so doing they are not building up but destroying the Corinthian congregation (v. 8; 13:10). Paul, on the other hand, keeps within the field assigned to him (v. 13) preaching the gospel in places where it was not already known (cf. Rom 15:20-21). It was in keeping with that charge that Paul had come to Corinth as the first to preach the gospel there (v. 14). Corinth was, therefore, in his jurisdiction, and he now hoped to proclaim the good news in the lands beyond Corinth without boasting of work already done (v. 16).

Citing Jer 9:24 (LXX), Paul asserts that if any boasting is to be done it is to be boasting in the Lord, *For it is not those who commend themselves* [as do his opponents] *that are approved, but those whom the Lord commends* (v. 18). Once again Paul needs no letter of recommendation, for the very existence of the

Corinthian church is evidence of the Lord's commendation, the only commendation that matters.

Playing the Fool for Love: the Fool's Speech, 11:1–12:13

This passage has been called Paul's "fool's speech" on the basis of Paul's introduction of it as *a little foolishness* (11:1) and his comment at the end, *I have been a fool* (12:11). The necessity of defending his apostolic status in the face of the boasting of his opponents forces Paul to engage in the kind of self-commendation he has just repudiated in 10:12-18. That such boasting is foolishness is clear; that it is necessary at this point is also clear, lest he lose the Corinthian congregation to even greater fools.

Careful reading of this "fool's speech" reveals that it is a devastating attack on Paul's boastful opponents. His emphasis throughout on the foolishness of such boasting (11:1, 17, 21; 12:1, 11) becomes an indictment of his opponents who practice such boasting. Furthermore, by boasting of humiliating experiences rather than of glorious accomplishments, he reveals the great gulf that separates his understanding of apostleship from theirs.

Having invited his readers to bear with him in *a little foolishness* (11:1), Paul explains that it is motivated by his concern for the Corinthians. Comparing himself to the father of a bride who has been betrothed, he sees his role as that of guarding his daughter's virginity between the time of the betrothal and the consummation of the marriage (11:2). He fears that the Corinthians are in danger of being led astray from *a sincere and pure devotion to Christ* by *super-apostles* who have come to Corinth preaching *another Jesus*, a *different Spirit* and a *different gospel* (11:3-5).

Paul emphasizes that he is in no way inferior to these *super-apostles*—an ironic designation of his opponents that makes light of their pretentious claims. Apparently Paul was being unfavorably compared with them on several accounts.

First, his style as a public speaker had been criticized because it lacked the rhetorical sophistication displayed by his opponents (11:6). This may also lead to the suggestion that he lacked the knowledge that according to his opponents an apostle should have. While not disputing his critics' evaluation of his eloquence, Paul will not allow their evaluation of his knowledge, a knowledge that has been made evident to the Corinthians in every way. In short, he is *not in the least inferior* to the *super-apostles*.

Second, in a culture where many considered it degrading for a philosopher to work, Paul's insistence on supporting himself while in Corinth with his refusal to accept support from the Corinthians had been seen as an indication of an inferior status and even as a lack of love for the Corinthians. Paul responds that his behavior was certainly not an indication of a lack of love; rather he has acted so as not to burden them (11:7-11). Finally, Paul will have nothing of his opponents' claim to an equal status with him (11:12). Disguising themselves as apostles of Christ, they are in reality *deceitful workers, false apostles, ministers* of Satan (11:13-15).

In 11:16 Paul repeats his plea of 11:1 asking indulgence for his foolish boasting. Nevertheless he will engage in the foolishness of boasting according to human standards as his opponents do (11:16-18). With powerful sarcasm he indicates that this is possible because in their "wisdom" the Corinthians *put up with fools* who would exploit them (11:19-20), something that he was *too weak* to do (11:21).

Paul begins his boasting by establishing that while his ethnic and religious credentials are no less Jewish than his opponents (11:22), his credentials as a minister of Christ are superior (11:23a). Ironically, the evidence he brings to support his claim is not a list of glorious triumphs but of the trials and hardships he has suffered as an apostle (11:23b-33). While some have understood this litany as an attempt at one-upmanship (the opponents bragged about what they had suffered for Christ, so Paul recounts what his service to Christ had cost him), the irony that pervades the context suggests that it is better seen as a kind of parody of the opponents' exalted claims. While they boast of things that demonstrate their strength, Paul boasts of things that show his weakness (11:29a-30) for in his weakness the transcendent power of God is made known (4:7-15; 12:9).

The incident at DAMASCUS (11:32-33) illustrates *danger in the city* (11:26). It stands as an example of Paul's weakness especially when viewed against the backdrop of the Roman *corona muralis* (wall crown) that was presented for valor to the first soldier to ascend the wall of an enemy city. The marked contrast between such a courageous ascent and Paul's inglorious descent of the city wall would not be missed by the Corinthians and could only have been seen as another evidence of his weakness and humiliation.

In response to the claims of his opponents, Paul finds it necessary to boast about *visions and revela-*

tions (12:1). Using the third person (a reflection of his reticence about boasting of his own experiences), Paul tells of being *caught up to the third heaven* (considered in some Jewish cosmologies to be the highest heaven), which is here synonymous with Paradise. He says nothing of what he saw, and what he heard he cannot repeat because it was either inexpressible or impermissible to repeat (12:2-4).

While such experiences have a personal benefit for the one who experiences them, they have no real benefit for others. Therefore, Paul chooses to boast of his *weaknesses* (12:5-7) because he had learned that it is in weakness that God's power is made manifest. Paul had learned this from his experience of the *thorn . . . in the flesh* that had been given him to keep him from *being too elated*.

While the *thorn* has been the subject of much speculation, it is probably best understood as a physical illness or infirmity that left Paul open to public ridicule (cf. Gal 4:13-14). Paul's persistent plea for its removal was greeted by the promise of God's sufficient grace and the knowledge that God's *power is made perfect in weakness* (12:8). If this is the case, then it is not in our strength but in our weakness that God's power is revealed, and, therefore, it is in our weakness that we should boast (12:9). It is as we suffer *weaknesses, insults, hardships, persecutions, and calamities* that we become the showplace of God's power (12:10).

Thus, while Paul's vision had provided nothing that could be uttered for the benefit of others, the thorn in the flesh communicated the grace and power of God each day. In his weakness, therefore, Paul embodied the folly of the cross that reveals the power of God (1 Cor 1:18-31; 2 Cor 4:7-12).

Paul concludes his "fool's speech" by reasserting that he is in no way inferior to the *super-apostles* (12:11). He has performed the signs of a *true apostle* (12:12). His ministry was of both word and deed and had included *signs and wonders and mighty works* (cf. Rom 15:18-19). He has held back nothing from the Corinthians except that he has not asked them for support, and ironically he asks to be forgiven for not exploiting them as his opponents have (12:13).

Anticipating His Third Visit, 12:14-21

As Paul anticipates his third visit to Corinth, he makes it clear that he will continue his practice of not burdening the Corinthians. As a genuine apostle, he does not want what the Corinthians have but the Corinthians themselves. He cares for them as a parent for a child (v. 14) knowing that apostolic authenticity is demonstrated when one is willing *to spend and be spent* for the Corinthians (v. 15).

Verses 16-18 suggest that Paul has been charged with defrauding the Corinthians with regard to the collection for the saints in Jerusalem. Perhaps his critics were saying that while Paul asked for no money for himself, he was actually using the collection to line his own pockets. He responds by pointing to the exemplary behavior of his representatives (*Titus* and *the brother*). Just as they had not taken advantage of the Corinthians, neither had he.

Paul's concern is not for his own reputation but for the building up of the Corinthians (v. 19). As he approaches his third visit, he fears (1) that he may not find the Corinthians to be as he wished and that they might not so find him; (2) that there will be quarreling, jealousy, anger, selfishness, slander, gossip, conceit, and disorder; and (3) that the congregation will still be plagued by impurity, sexual immorality, and licentiousness (vv. 20-21).

Warning the Corinthians, 13:1-4

Citing Deut 19:15 Paul views his upcoming third visit as a third witness against his opponents and their followers. He had previously warned them on his second visit and then by means of the severe letter. When he arrives he will not be lenient but will vigorously assert his apostolic authority. He will give compelling evidence that Christ speaks through him in powerful action with regard to the unrepentant. Such powerful action is modeled after the pattern of Christ who was *crucified in weakness, but lives by the power of God* (v. 4).

This does not mean that the crucifixion represents weakness and the resurrection power; the cross is the supreme expression of God's power (1 Cor 1:24) and the resurrection shows that what appears to be weakness (the crucifixion) is in truth the power of God (see Rom 1:4). Similarly the apparent weakness of Paul—his unimposing presence (10:10) and his suffering service (6:4-10; 11:25-29)—is in fact the sign that God's power is at work in his ministry (12:10). Since Paul shares the suffering of Christ (Phil 3:10; Gal 2:10), he is "weak in him" (v. 4); since he shares the power of Christ's resurrection (Phil 3:10), he will exercise the power of Christ when dealing with the Corinthians (Baird 1988, 108).

Challenging the Corinthians, 13:5-10

Paul challenges the Corinthians who question whether Christ speaks through him to examine whether Christ lives in them (v. 5). While Paul hopes that they will recognize the authenticity of his apostleship and thus his authority (v. 6), his overarching concern is that the Corinthians will do what is right, regardless (v. 7). He is happy to appear weak so long as the Corinthians are strong (v. :8) and prays that they will *become perfect* (v. 9; lit. "upright again").

In v. 10 Paul states the purpose for his writing. He has written so that when he comes he might not have to be severe in using the apostolic authority that had been given to him for the building up of the church.

Closing 13:11-13

Closing Exhortations and Greeting, 13:11-12

These verses contain the briefest of paraeneses (cf. Rom 12:9-13; 1 Cor 16:13-15; 1 Thes 5:12-22). Attention to Paul's fourfold admonition will allow the Corinthian church to become what God intends and will assure the Corinthians of God's presence.

Benediction, 13:13

This is the fullest Pauline benediction to be found in any letter. It is distinguished from others by its clearly trinitarian form. The grace of the *Lord Jesus Christ* expresses and leads us to know the love of *God* whose *Spirit* produces communion with God and with one another.

Works Cited

Baird, William. 1988. *1 Corinthians/2 Corinthians*.
Ralph P. Martin. 1986. *2 Corinthians*. WBC.

Galatians

Charles H. Cosgrove

Introduction

Galatians is addressed to a group of gentile-Christian congregations founded by PAUL and located in central Asia Minor (modern Turkey). The date and place of composition are uncertain. Paul's so-called third missionary journey (ca. 52–56) is a possibility, in which case he may have composed the letter in EPHESUS, CORINTH, or in some part of MACEDONIA.

The Occasion of the Letter

Since Paul's founding visit, the Galatians have been influenced by certain persons who Paul claims are *confusing* them and wanting *to pervert* the gospel (1:7; cf. 5:10, 12). These persons may be Jewish-Christian teachers from JERUSALEM who disagree with Paul about the nature of the GOSPEL for the gentiles. They insist above all on CIRCUMCISION (5:2-6; 6:12-13), and will be referred to here as "the Circumcisers."

To judge from Paul's argument, the Circumcisers have urged the Galatians to accept the Law as a way of promoting the power and wondrous works of the Spirit (3:5). Paul's letter is an effort to refute this teaching and persuade the Galatians to return to the way of life in Christ that Paul first taught them.

Paul's Argument

Paul makes his appeal in three stages. The first stage is an "apostolic autobiography" (1:11–2:21) in which Paul claims that his apostolic authority and his gospel preaching come directly from God, the implication being that the Galatians had better listen to him. At the same time Paul depicts himself as the only apostle who has consistently defended the gentile cause in the gospel. The Galatians can trust him. Thus the primary aim of the apostolic autobiography is to encourage the Galatians to trust Paul, so they will accept his interpretation and logic in the central argumentation of the letter.

The second phase of Paul's appeal (3:1–4:31, with a certain anticipation in 2:15-21) consists largely of theological argument from scripture and Christian tradition. Paul argues that the Galatians enjoy eschatological life (manifest in the wondrous power of the Spirit, 3:5) solely because they believed Paul's gospel and not because of any relationship they may now have with the Law of Moses. In fact, if they practice works of the Law, they will put themselves under a curse and forfeit the blessing they now experience in Christ.

The third phase of Paul's appeal is an apostolic exhortation (5:1–6:10). Paul defines the relationship between the Law and FREEDOM in the Spirit. He admonishes the Galatians in a way that suggests their ethical life has been deteriorating—as if their adoption of the Law might itself be the cause of an increase among them of *works of the flesh*. In this way the exhortation functions as an implicit argument against Law-keeping.

Galatians and Anti-Judaism

In our time all Christian commentary proceeds in the shadow of the Holocaust, hence a word is in order about the impression Galatians gives today of sanctioning "anti-Judaism." For Paul, as for most Jews in his day, JUDAISM was defined by the Law, but in Galatians Paul says that all those "in the Law" are in slavery. That amounts to a harsh attack on Judaism, even if Paul was in some sense seeking to redefine Judaism on the basis of his conviction that the Messiah had come with a new revelation about the Law.

As part of the Christian Bible, Galatians has an anti-Jewish ring that is amplified by the political power of Christianity in the world. But when Paul wrote Galatians, the letter represented a critique that barely tinkled within the world of ancient Judaism; it certainly did not pose any social or political threat to Jews. As an ancient Jewish scholar Paul had every right to reinterpret Judaism by his own lights, and

Jews and Christians of all ages have every right to quarrel with him about that reinterpretation. They also have an opportunity to learn from him.

For Further Study

In the *Mercer Dictionary of the Bible*: CIRCUMCISION; FREEDOM; GALATIA; GALATIANS, LETTER TO THE; JERUSALEM COUNCIL; LAW IN THE NT; NT USE OF THE OT; OPPONENTS OF PAUL; PAUL.

In other sources: H. D. Betz, *Galatians: A Commentary on Paul's Letter to the Churches of Galatia*, Herm; F. F. Bruce, *The Epistle to the Galatians: A Commentary on the Greek Text*, NIGTC; C. H. Cosgrove, *The Cross and the Spirit: A Study in the Argument and Theology of Galatians*; R. B. Hays, *The Faith of Jesus Christ: An Investigation of the Narrative Substructure of Galatians 3:1–4:11*, SBLDS; D. Lührmann, *Galatians: A Continental Commentary*; F. J. Matera, *Galatians*, SP; R. C. Tannehill, *Dying and Rising with Christ*, BZNW.

Commentary

An Outline

> I. The Opening, 1:1-5
> II. A Thanksgiving Parody, 1:6-10
> III. The Letter Body, 1:11–6:10
>   A. Apostolic Autobiography, 1:11–2:21
>   B. Central Apostolic Argument, 3:1–4:31
>   C. Apostolic Exhortation, 5:1–6:10
> IV. A Personal Postscript, 6:11-18

The Opening, 1:1-5

Instead of simply stating his name as "sender," Paul opens the letter by elaborating on his apostleship, declaring that he became *an apostle* directly through *Jesus Christ and God the Father*. What Paul means is that God has given him a direct commission to preach the gospel to the gentiles (1:16; cf. Rom 1:1-6, 13-14; 15:15-18), and in that commission God has also revealed the gospel to him (1:11-12). Being an apostle and knowing the gospel go together in Paul's self-understanding because he attributes both to the same source and revelatory moment.

The point of stating and defining his apostleship in the letter opening is to establish (probably by way of reminder) two things. First, the Galatians must heed what Paul says because he is God's messenger to them, the unspoken insinuation being that the Circumcisers have not gotten their message from God. Second, and by obvious implication, Paul's teaching is true because he got it straight from God.

Paul encapsulates that teaching in several brief expressions. He identifies God as *the Father, who raised* [Jesus] *from the dead* (v. 1), and he calls Jesus *the Lord*, who *gave himself for our sins to set us free from the present evil age*. The idea that the gospel means liberation from an EVIL cosmic condition (in which human beings are trapped) recurs elsewhere in the letter. That liberation, in Paul's understanding, comes to pass through Jesus' death, about which he will have more to say in 2:15-21, 3:10-14, and 6:14-15.

A Thanksgiving Parody, 1:6-10

In Paul's other letters rather elaborate "thanksgiving statements" follow his epistolary openings. But not in Galatians. Instead of celebrating their increasing growth and steadfastness in the gospel, Paul berates the Galatians for abandoning the gospel and turning to *another gospel*. He even goes so far as to pronounce a "curse" on anyone who might preach a gospel other than the one that he himself first taught the Galatians.

In the ancient Mediterranean world, it was widely assumed that the utterance of a curse, especially by a person who enjoyed special connections with the divine world (as Paul claims he does), could bring harm (including the possibility of death) to its object. Thus Paul is not simply expressing his own depth of concern; he is implementing his apostolic power (cf. 1 Cor 5:3-5) in a spiritual attack on his opponents (whom he later suggests—3:1—have themselves practiced witchcraft on the Galatians).

The Letter Body, 1:11–6:10

Apostolic Autobiography, 1:11–2:21

1:11-24. Paul's call and commission. In vv. 11-12 Paul claims that he did not receive his gospel *from* any human beings; it came directly *through a revelation of Jesus Christ*. This probably means a REVELATION by God of the risen Jesus. In 1 Cor 15:8 Paul reports that the resurrected Christ appeared to him, and in v. 16 he says that God "revealed his Son *in* me." We don't know exactly how Paul experienced this revelation (which may also be what he has in mind in 2 Cor 12:1-4), but clearly he understood it as a miraculous event in which God commissioned him to preach the gospel of Christ to gentiles without the requirement that they receive CIRCUMCISION and practice the Law of Moses. Admittedly, Paul does not say anything about the Law in vv. 11-24, but his insistence that he has always preached the same gospel (see esp. the stories that follow in 2:1-21) indicates that by *the gospel* he always means a gospel that does not require Law-keeping from gentiles.

According to some interpreters, the Circumcisers claimed that Paul received his apostolic commission from the Jerusalem apostles. In that case (so the argument goes) he would be obliged to conform his preaching to the Jerusalem version of the gospel, which the Circumcisers purport to represent. This conjecture seems very likely, considering the oath Paul takes in v. 20. But even if the Circumcisers did not claim that Paul stood under the authority of Jerusalem, Paul might well have made the argument he develops in the narrative of vv. 13-24. For that narrative backs up his claims to apostolic authority (vv. 1, 11-12) on the basis of which he instructs the Galatians about the gospel and the law, interprets scripture, and tells them how to live their lives in Christ.

Paul begins by describing his *earlier life in Judaism*, which provides a contrast to his life after receiving his call from God. It also implies that he knows more about the Law than the Circumcisers themselves do (see v. 14). Next Paul explains that after receiving his apostolic commission from God he had no contact with any of the apostles in Jerusalem. Instead he went directly to *Arabia* and then *returned to Damascus* (v. 17), which indicates that his call-revelation occurred in DAMASCUS. The point of vv. 13-17 is to refute any actual or potential claim that he received his knowledge of the gospel or any kind of commission from the Jerusalem church.

But three years later, Paul says, he did go up to JERUSALEM, evidently for the first time after receiving his call. His purpose was "to *see* Cephas" (v. 18, author trans.), Cephas probably being PETER. Paul uses a word in v. 18 (*historēsai*) that typically means to "inquire" or to "see someone about something." This shows that Paul is no longer at this point arguing that he didn't learn anything from any of the other apostles. When he says that he went up "to *see* Cephas" and that he didn't see any of the other apostles except JAMES (v. 19), he is making it clear that he had no meetings with the Jerusalem apostles that might be construed as occasion for any apostolic commissioning. Perhaps Paul finds it important to stress the unofficial nature of his meetings with Cephas and James because he has not yet arrived at the point in his life story where he began his apostolic ministry. His first mention of "preaching the gospel" appears only after the story of his first visit to Jerusalem, which was followed by trips to *Syria and Cilicia* (v. 21). Anyone who had been told (evidently correctly) that Paul began his apostolic ministry only after his first visit to the Jerusalem church might have inferred that the Jerusalem apostles commissioned him for this work. Paul makes it clear that he was party to no official meetings of the Jerusalem apostles, and he certifies this with an oath (v. 20).

2:1-10. God leads the Jerusalem apostles to confirm Paul's gospel. In vv. 1-11 Paul describes his first official meeting with the Jerusalem apostles. Whatever the Galatians may have been told about this meeting, Paul maintains that by the end of it, thanks to his own witness (v. 2), the chief Jerusalem apostles had come to full agreement with him about the nature of his apostleship and about the gospel for the gentiles (vv. 7-9).

Cephas, James, and JOHN may have invited him or even "summoned" him to Jerusalem. But Paul says that he went up in obedience *to a revelation* (v. 2), as if to ward off any impression that he was following directives from Jerusalem. At Jerusalem he presented his gospel, apparently in both public gatherings of the church and in private conferences with church leaders (v. 2). He did so, he says, in order to make sure that he had not been laboring for nothing (v. 2). But, as it turned out, *even Titus, who was with me, was not compelled to be circumcised, though he was a Greek* (v. 3). Verses 1-3 suggest that if the Jerusalem leaders had rejected Paul's understanding of the gospel for the gentiles and had insisted that TITUS be circumcised, then Paul would have accepted this as God's will. That seems surprising in the light of how Paul has argued thus far and how he continues to underscore his independence from Jerusalem in what follows. But it is nonetheless the impression Paul leaves, perhaps as if to say, "There came a time when God (to whom I am alone obedient) told me to go to Jerusalem and submit my gospel to the test of the Jerusalem authorities, and the result was, in God's providence, that the Jerusalem apostles approved my gospel." Nevertheless, the Jerusalem apostles were really only "seeing" and "recognizing" the activity of the divine "grace" already at work in Paul apart from any agency or authorization on their part (vv. 7-9).

But there were some *false believers* (v. 4) who *slipped in to spy on the freedom we have in Christ Jesus*. This FREEDOM must be the practice of living "free" from obedience to the Law. One guesses that the "false" believers saw Paul and BARNABAS breaking the Law (perhaps in their dietary practice) or discovered that Titus was not circumcised, and then denounced Paul and his party before the Jerusalem apostles (in order to *enslave us*, Paul says). But, as v. 5 describes it, Paul and his company stood heroically steadfast "in order that the truth of the gospel might be preserved for you" (RSV)—"you" being the Galatians, whom he has not yet even met! The rhetorical point of v. 5 is to imply that even before the Galatians became Christians, Paul was on their side. From first to last he remains the hero of the gentile cause.

By contrast the pillar apostles couldn't have been more affirming of Paul. Not, Paul says, that he cared anything about their status. He, like God, doesn't pay attention to such things (v. 6). But, we might add, Paul is in fact only too pleased to point out that the pillars affirmed his gospel. So he trades on their prestige at the same time that he denies owing them any obedience or special regard.

The pillars recognized that the same God who entrusted Cephas with the *gospel for the circumcised* (v. 7, meaning a gospel for the Jews) also entrusted Paul with the *gospel for the uncircumcised* (v. 7, meaning a gospel for the gentiles). The *gospel for the uncircumcised* is a Law-free gospel, and Paul probably assumed that since there is only "one" gospel, Jewish Christians are also not *required* by the gospel to keep the Law. The pillars at Jerusalem may have understood the agreement about the gospel (vv. 6-10) to mean that Jewish Christians must keep the Law while gentile Christians are not obliged to do so. That would explain how the controversy at ANTIOCH (2:11-21) could have arisen after the agreement made in Jerusalem. The understanding achieved at Jerusalem involved a fundamental misunderstanding between the two parties.

2:11-21. Paul champions the gentile cause at Antioch. In a story about the church at Antioch Paul again portrays himself as the hero who defends the gentile cause in the gospel. As he recounts it, Jewish and gentile Christians were accustomed to eating together in the Antioch church, evidently without observing any of the Jewish dietary laws. But when a certain group *from James* came, all the Jewish Christians (except for

Paul but including Cephas, and even Barnabas) abandoned table fellowship with the gentiles. Paul accuses these Jewish Christians of *hypocrisy* (v. 13), meaning they acted in a way inconsistent with what they knew and affirmed to be the *truth of the gospel* (v. 14).

We should not assume that the party *from James* carried the same message to Antioch that the Circumcisers later brought to Galatia, except in the general sense that both groups promoted the Law and linked it positively with life in Christ. The Galatians were in a position to discern points of correspondence between the Antioch incident and their own situation. We can only guess about these similarities.

Paul accuses Cephas of "compelling" (v. 14) the gentiles to *live like Jews* (i.e., by practicing the Law). Cephas, Paul says, knows better than to pressure the gentiles into Law-keeping, for he himself lives *like a Gentile and not like a Jew*. And this way of living—which Cephas's present behavior so glaringly contradicts—is in accord with the truth of the gospel. That means that in Paul's understanding neither Jewish nor gentile Christians are obliged to keep the Law. Considered in the context of the Antioch incident, it also means that when Jewish and gentile believers are together, Jewish Christians ought to live as gentiles.

The theological rationale for Jewish-Christian freedom from the Law is found in a dense and obscure argument presented, ostensibly, as the speech Paul made at Antioch. Since it was a customary practice of the time to compose speeches in the course of a historical narrative, we need not assume that Paul reproduces in vv. 14b-21 exactly what he said at Antioch. That helps explain why it is difficult to see the immediate relevance for the Antioch controversy of everything he says in these verses.

According to Paul, Jewish Christians "know" that they owe their righteousness before God to the "faith of Jesus Christ" (v. 16; NRSV mg.). Paul does not say how they know this. The Galatians are to take his word for it, Paul himself being a Jewish Christian. The phrase, "the faith of Jesus Christ," is the most natural way to translate the Greek expression found here, which may refer to Christ's own faith or, more likely, to "Christian faith" as an eschatological way of salvation. The traditional translation, *faith in Christ* forces the Greek and should be avoided unless there is no other coherent way to interpret the phrase. In 1:23 Paul says that he preaches *the faith*. In 3:23, 25 he speaks of faith as a transcendent reality that comes into the world, like Christ himself. And in 3:22 he speaks of "what was promised from the faith of Jesus Christ" (author trans.). These texts suggest that "the faith" and "the faith of Jesus Christ" are names Paul uses for the way and means of salvation that God has brought in Christ.

In v. 20 Paul speaks of "the faith of the Son of God" (NRSV mg.), meaning the faith Jesus himself exercised, which may also be the sense of "the faith of Jesus Christ" in v. 16. In either case—whether the expression means Jesus' own faithfulness or stands in a larger sense for the way of salvation in Christ—the faith of Jesus Christ, according to Paul, effects what the works of the Law could not: it alone makes Jewish Christians righteous before God.

In his discussion of salvation, Paul uses a verb (*dikaioun*) that is used in the SEPTUAGINT in the passive voice to render Hebrew expressions that mean "be righteous" or "become righteous." It makes sense to follow this usage in translating the passive form of the verb (*dikaiousthai*) in Paul. Thus, we may render v. 16, "we know that a person does not become righteous by works of the Law but by the faith of Jesus Christ." The passive form occurs three times in v. 16. It is also found at v. 17, 3:11, 3:24, and 5:4.

Does righteousness (or JUSTIFICATION) by this faith imply that Jewish Christians are not obligated to keep the Law? In v. 17 Paul links seeking to be righteous in Christ with a way of living that leaves Christians open to the charge that they are sinners—sinners because they do not keep the Law. Presumably the party from James leveled this charge at the Jewish Christians at Antioch. Paul's answer to this charge is that if seeking to be righteous in Christ makes Jewish Christians sinners, then Christ himself is an agent of sin. That is, the rhetorical question in v. 17 is a *reductio ad absurdum*. As an argument it has force only if one already accepts Paul's premise that seeking to be righteous in Christ rules out seeking to be righteous by the Law. The party from James no doubt sees righteousness in Christ and righteousness in the Law as compatible. Paul doesn't. He "knows" that God commissioned him, a Jew, to evangelize and live among gentiles, without imposing the Law on them. This probably explains why he is so certain about the distinction between the righteousness provided in Christ—which both Jews and gentiles have—and the righteousness of the Law (which, according to Phil 3:6, he once had). According to v. 18, Paul would make himself a sinner before God only if he were to reinstate the requirements of the Law (*the very things that I once tore down*). The same

holds for the Jewish Christians at Antioch, who have in fact reinstated those requirements, thus making themselves sinners before God by abandoning the righteousness they have in Christ—a righteousness constituted in part by their table fellowship with gentile Christians.

Verses 19-20 take another approach. In Christ, believers "die" to the Law, just as they die *with Christ* to the present world order (6:14; cf. Rom 7:4-6). They die *through the law* (v. 19) because Christ's death took place through the Law, namely, through the *curse of the law* (3:13). Thus, to be a Christian is to be *crucified with Christ*, which transfers one to the sphere of being in Christ. Only by dying with Christ does one come to experience eschatological life, signified in v. 19 by the Hellenistic Jewish expression *live to God* (cf. 4 Macc 7:19; 16:25). It follows from this interpretation of Christ's death that Christians are righteous because Christ lives through them and that they owe no obedience to the Law because they have died to it.

Paul closes off this argument with another *reductio ad absurdum*. If righteousness before God could be achieved through the Law, *then Christ died for nothing* (v. 21). Paul's point is that since Christ obviously did not die for nothing, righteousness must not be "from the Law." But this argument does not refute the view that righteousness before God depends on both the Law (as norm) and Christ (as source of atonement and moral power in the Spirit), which may be the theological opinion of the party from James (and the Circumcisers at Galatia).

Central Apostolic Argument, 3:1–4:31

3:1-5. Faith mediates the Spirit. With this paragraph Paul addresses the Galatians directly, suggests they have been *bewitched*, and gives some important clues about what he understands the "other gospel" (1:7) in Galatians to be. The passage moves from a question about the past to an inference about the present. The Galatians know that they received *the Spirit* (when Paul first preached to them) because they heard and believed, not because they began practicing the Law (v. 2). *Therefore*—the Greek text of v. 5 contains the illative particle *oun*—they should draw the same conclusion about the basis of their present experience of the Spirit: "Does the one who supplies you with the Spirit and works miracles among you do so because of the works of the Law or because you heard and believed [the gospel]?" (author trans.). The implied answer is that God's present provision of the Spirit and its mighty works has nothing to do with whether or not the Galatians keep the Law. Or, as vv. 3-4 suggest, if the Galatians continue on their present course with the Law they will end up with the flesh and, presumably, lose the Spirit (see FLESH AND SPIRIT).

This is the first argument aimed directly at the Galatians in their own situation, and it suggests that the Circumcisers told the Galatians that doing the Law mediates the power of the Spirit.

3:6-14. Faith brings the Spirit as the blessing of Abraham. In vv. 6-14 Paul develops a somewhat intricate argument to show that the blessing of the Spirit comes through the death of Christ alone, apart from the Law. First, he cites a scripture text that makes "faith" a basis for "righteousness" (Gen 15:6 quoted in v. 6) and concludes from this that *those who believe* (lit. "those from faith") are Abraham's children (v. 7). He then uses this bit of exegesis to interpret another, more famous, scriptural promise about all the gentiles (or "nations") being blessed through Abraham (Gen 12:3; cf. 18:18). By associating Gen 15:6 and Gen 12:3, Paul is able to draw the conclusion he needs to make his point: the blessing of Abraham on the gentiles belongs to those who share Abraham's faith, that is, to gentiles like the Galatians (v. 9).

But what is the blessing of Abraham? Since Paul seems to interpret this blessing in an all-encompassing sense in Rom 4:13 (as "inheriting the world"), we should perhaps not limit it in any way here. But the explicit content that Paul identifies as the substance of the promise to Abraham is *the Spirit* (v. 14). And we should note here the following implication of this identification: The blessing of Abraham is fulfilled among the Galatians in their present experience, namely, in God's ongoing gift of the Spirit to them, which includes *miracles* (v. 5).

Verses 10-14 develop the argument from Abraham in a way that relates that blessing to two of the letter's central themes: the Law and the cross of Christ. While it was a well-established Jewish tradition, based in the Bible, that faithfulness to the Law brings God's blessing, Paul radically disjoins the two. Those who *rely on* the Law fall *under a curse*, the Law's own curse upon the unrighteous (v. 10). This happens because "in the Law (i.e., in the sphere of the Law) no one is righteous before God" (v. 11a, author trans.; on the translation "no one is righteous," see the comments on 2:16). Paul does not attempt to prove this by arguing that no one can keep the Law perfectly. Instead he quotes the words of Hab 2:4 as proof that no one in

the Law is righteous before God. *"The one who is righteous will live by faith,"* Paul declares (v. 11b), citing a version of Hab 2:4 that does not contain the possessive pronoun "his" (as the Hebrew scriptures do) or "my" (as the LXX does) before the word "faith." Nor does Paul mark it as a quotation from scripture by introducing it with a phrase such as "as it is written." He apparently expects the Galatians to recognize the words, probably because he himself made this text central to his foundation teaching (cf. Rom 1:17).

Scripture prophesies that the righteous person will *live by faith* (v. 11b). The Law, by contrast, *does not rest on faith* (v. 12a). As proof Paul now cites another scripture text, again without identifying it as such: "The one who does them [the works of the Law] will live by them" (v. 12b; author trans.). This is a paraphrase of Lev 18:5, a passage sometimes echoed in Jewish formulations of the Law's promise of life (cf. Neh 9:29; Ezek 20:13; Luke 10:28; CD 3:16; PssSol 14:3). The Circumcisers might have quoted this text to the Galatians as proof that doing the Law mediates eschatological life (the ongoing power of the Spirit). By contrasting Hab 2:4 and Lev 18:5, Paul demands that the Galatians choose between *faith* (meaning "Christian faith") and *works of the Law*, which comprise two ways of relating to God. The Circumcisers no doubt integrated these two ways by combining faith with works of the law. If so, Paul sharply distinguishes what they join. Nevertheless, nothing in the contrast itself, but only the preceding argumentation (in vv. 1-5 and vv. 6-9) and the weight of Paul's apostolic authority, are likely to persuade the Galatians to treat Hab 2:4 (and not Lev 18:5) as the definitive biblical word for the new age.

In v. 13 Paul declares that Christ *redeemed us from the curse of the law by becoming a curse for us*. According to the Law-text cited here (Deut 21:23), victims of crucifixion are an abomination (or "curse") in God's sight. Paul equates this curse with the curse of the Law already mentioned in v. 10. The death of Christ lifts this curse *for us*, a phrase that refers to those under the Law's curse and therefore may refer strictly to Jews.

With the transference of the curse to Christ the blessing of Abraham in Christ can flow to the gentiles (v. 14a) so that *we might receive the promise of the Spirit through faith* (v. 14b). Paul doesn't explain how the lifting of the curse from the unrighteous in the Law lets the blessing flow to the gentiles, with the reciprocal effect that "we" (which must mean we Jews who believe in Christ) receive the promise of the Spirit by faith. The Galatians are to take Paul's authoritative word for it. But they may also find his interpretation appealing, since it implies that Jewish Christians (such as the Circumcisers) enjoy the life of the Spirit solely by faith and only because God has first given this blessing to gentiles (such as the Galatians)!

3:15-18. Christ the sole heir of Abraham. Paul supplements his argument about how the blessing of Abraham (the Spirit) comes by comparing the Abrahamic covenant to a will. Even in human affairs it is illegal to add a codicil to a covenant (or a "will") once it has been ratified. God ratified the covenant with Abraham, in which God promised the inheritance to Abraham's offspring, long before God gave the Law. Therefore God could not, with justice, add the Law as a kind of later codicil, thus making the inheritance conditional upon keeping the Law. Since the very idea that God might attempt such an unfair thing is blasphemous, Paul qualifies his argument from the outset by explaining that he is going to speak "like a (mere) human being" (which is what v. 15 literally says).

The aim of vv. 15-18 is to reinforce Paul's contention that the Law has no say about the promise God made to Abraham, which Paul has already indicated is the *promise of the Spirit* (v. 14). God's promise to Abraham concerned an inheritance for a single *offspring* (v. 16), Paul says, quoting God's promissory words, *"And to your offspring,"* in Gen 13:15 (cf. Gen 12:7). In fact, the word *offspring* can be used in both the collective and the singular sense. In Gen 13:15 it is used as a collective (meaning "descendants"), but Paul interprets it as singular and takes it as referring to Christ. This exegetical move makes Christ the sole heir of the promise, thus excluding all those "in the Law" along with everyone else in the world! In 3:22-29 Paul explains how others come to be included with Christ as heirs of the promise.

3:19-22. The purpose of the Law. After disconnecting the Law from the promise and attributing to the Law the power only to curse and not to bless, Paul must explain why God gave the Law in the first place. He offers a brief and rather obscure answer to this question in vv. 19b-20. The Law was given "for transgressions" (v. 19b, author's trans.), which may mean to inhibit them. But, in view of Rom 5:20, it might mean "to create them" by making sin legally punishable as transgression. The remainder of vv. 19-20 poses an exegetical conundrum that continues to vex interpreters. Paul is perhaps arguing that the Law came

only indirectly from God and therefore enjoys a lower status than the covenant with Abraham (which God made directly with Abraham).

In vv. 21-22 Paul seeks to dispel any impression that he views the Law as an opponent of the promise. The opponent is sin, which dominates all things (v. 22). The Law was never endowed with any power to *make alive*, hence it is not able to produce righteousness in a sin-enslaved world (cf. 1:4, *the present evil age*).

3:23-29. Becoming heirs with Christ. Having offered a brief defense of the Law in order to defend his own interpretation of its place in history, Paul now takes up an unfinished line of argument begun in 3:15-18. How can anyone become an heir of the promise to Abraham if Christ himself is the sole heir (3:15; cf. 3:19)?

Those under the Law are enslaved to sin. During this enslavement the Law serves as a kind of "guardian" (*paidagōgos*) until the arrival of Christian faith (3:23-25). In the Greco-Roman world the *paidagōgos* had charge of a boy during his minority, that is, until the boy came into his inheritance (see the comments on 4:1-11). Thus, being under the Law's guardianship, Paul says, coincides with the time of *waiting* for the inheritance. But now that *faith* has arrived (v. 25), this time of waiting under the guardianship of the Law is over.

The arrival of *faith* with Jesus Christ has transformed the Galatians into God's children (lit., "sons of God"). Through baptism they have "put on Christ" (RSV) and become "one" in Christ (vv. 27-28). That makes them part of the "one offspring" of Abraham, and in this process of unification with Christ they become heirs of the promise given to Christ alone (v.29).

4:1-11. The limited time of the Law. In 4:1-11 Paul explains what he meant by saying (in 3:23-25) that being under the Law is like being under a guardian. To be an heir during one's minority (childhood) is to be in a position no better than a slave, without access to the goods of one's inheritance. During this time the heir (typically a male) is under various overseers until a time set by his father. In the same way, Paul says, Jews and gentiles alike lived in a period of minority until the time of fulfillment set by God. But now that the *fullness of time* [has] *come* (v. 4), those redeemed by God through divine *adoption* receive the goods of the *inheritance*, namely, the Spirit itself (vv. 6-7).

In vv. 8-11 Paul equates serving the Law with bondage to the *elemental spirits* of the world. Many

Jews in Paul's day attributed cosmic wisdom to the Law. Perhaps the Circumcisers taught the Galatians that by observing the Jewish calendar, informed by the Law's cosmic wisdom, Christians may live safely and prosperously in the present age (see v. 10). Paul calls this a path to cosmic bondage. Accepting the Law only brings the Galatians right back to the situation of futility in which Paul found them, when they were *enslaved to beings that by nature are not gods* (v. 8).

4:12-20. A "pathos" appeal. In 4:12-20 Paul makes an emotional appeal, what ancient rhetoricians called an argument from "pathos." He reminds the Galatians of the kindness and honor they bestowed upon him during his first visit (vv. 13-16), and wonders whether his letter, with its blunt truthfulness, will make him their enemy (v. 16). He attributes ulterior motives to the Circumcisers (v. 17) and describes himself, by contrast, as a mother who is perplexed by the fact that she is in labor pangs all over again with the same child (vv. 19-20)!

4:21-31. The law bears children for slavery. Before issuing apostolic exhortation to the community, Paul presents an allegorical interpretation of the story of Abraham's two wives and two sons. Paul identifies the slave wife HAGAR with the covenant of the Law from Mount SINAI. The Law, as a slavewoman, bears children for slavery. These enslaved children comprise the present Jerusalem, which stands for the Jewish people as a whole. The freewoman SARAH (who represents God's covenant with Abraham) stands, allegorically, for the heavenly Jerusalem, where the free children of the Spirit are born. This Jerusalem is *our mother* (v. 26), Paul says, including himself and the Galatians (v. 28) among her children.

The Mosaic covenant and the Abrahamic covenant are not only distinct, their children are at odds with each other: *But just as at that time the child who was born according to the flesh persecuted the child who was born according to the Spirit, so it is now also* (v. 29, quoting Gen 21:9), a citation that the Galatians are likely to construe as a call to expel the Circumcisers from their midst.

Apostolic Exhortation, 5:1–6:10

5:1-12. Stand fast in freedom. The logically inseparable themes of SLAVERY and FREEDOM have been running through the letter since the beginning (see 1:4; 2:4-5; 3:13, 22-25; 4:1-11, 21-31). According to Paul, Christ's death liberates people from slavery to sin. It redeems those under the Law from the Law's curse on

the unrighteous. At the same time it also establishes freedom from the Law as a way of righteousness, an idea first broached in chap. 2 (2:4-5; 2:15-21). In v. 1 Paul calls the Galatians to stand fast in this (threefold) freedom to which Christ has set them free. He follows up this basic exhortation with a series of warnings (vv. 2-6). Accepting circumcision removes one from the sphere of Christ's blessing (v. 2). It also obligates a person to keep the entire Law (v. 3), which the Galatians may not realize if the Circumcisers have so far insisted only on circumcision and the Jewish calendar (cf. 4:10 and 6:12-13). In v. 4 Paul reiterates the point of v. 2, telling the Galatians that by becoming "righteous in the Law" (author trans.; on this translation, see the comments on 2:16) they lose Christ and fall from grace.

Next Paul describes his own view of Christian existence in ways that prepare for the ethical exhortation to follow. *For through the Spirit, by faith, we eagerly wait for the hope of righteousness* (v. 5). The words *hope of righteousness* probably mean the hope of salvation that belongs to righteousness and not the hope of becoming righteous. Thus far Paul has described the ethics of this righteousness only once. In 2:17 the expression *our effort to be justified in Christ* describes the way of life that Paul has adopted by giving up the practice of the Law in order to be in communion with gentile Christians. In v. 6 he defines the ethics of this righteousness as *faith working through love*. Paul would probably call the originally integrated community life at Antioch (2:12a) an expression of this love-working faith. In 5:13–6:10 he elaborates on his view that "love" is the basic form and guiding principle of righteousness in Christ.

Verses 7-12 resemble the "pathos appeal" of 4:12-20 in emotional tone and strategy. Paul celebrates the Galatians' beginnings in Christ, expresses confidence about their future, and blames the Circumcisers for the Galatians' defection from *the truth*. It may be that one of the Circumcisers is *confusing* the Galatians by telling them that in other churches Paul himself preaches circumcision (vv. 10-11).

5:13-26. Love as the way of freedom in the Spirit. Verses 13-26 show how the theme of *love* is related to basic themes of the earlier argumentation, namely, *freedom*, *the Law*, *the cross*, and *the Spirit*. Believers have died in Christ to the Law as a way of righteousness (2:17-20). The resultant freedom in Christ is to take ethical form as serving one another in love (v. 13). This is what it means to "walk by the Spirit" (v.

16 RSV; cf. v. 25). Opposed to this way of living is what Paul terms *the flesh* and its desires (v. 17), which he personifies as a kind of independent power. The passions of the flesh produce the *works of the flesh* described in vv. 19-21. These passions are in opposition to the Spirit, which produces the *fruit* described in vv. 22-23. The opposition of the flesh and the Spirit hinders Christians from doing what they *want* (v. 17). That means that the choice created for them by their freedom is to follow one of these two powers (cf. v. 13). If they *live by the Spirit* (i.e., yield to its desires, following the principle of love), they will not satisfy the passions of the flesh (v. 16).

Walking by the Spirit in love fulfills a basic intent of the Law (v. 14). In saying this Paul cites Lev 19:18, *You shall love your neighbor as yourself.* Early Christians identified Lev 19:18 as a summary of the Law, having learned to do so from Judaism (and especially from Jesus' own prophetic Jewish teaching). Paul is not saying that Christians must show love because the Law tells them to, but that the love commanded by the Spirit is in continuity with a basic interest of the Law itself. Dying with Christ (see the comments on 2:19-20) crucifies the flesh with its passions and cravings (v. 24). This enables believers to fulfill this way of love, which is embodied in the *fruit of the Spirit* (vv. 22-23). And, with a touch of wry humor, Paul comments that *there is no law* against such things as *love, joy, peace, patience, kindness,* and so forth.

6:1-10. Concluding exhortations. The ethical exhortation in vv. 1-10 presents additional and more specific admonitions. The community is to treat those who sin with gentleness and humility, renouncing spiritual rivalry (vv. 1-5). By bearing one another's burdens they will *fulfill the law of Christ* (v. 2). Paul does not define this law. Perhaps he expects the Galatians to recognize it as something he taught them about during his first visit. The law of Christ is probably the way of Christ exemplified in Christ's self-giving love (the way of Christ *who . . . gave himself for me*, 2:20; who "did not please himself," Rom 15:3; and who "became poor" for the sake of others, 2 Cor 8:9).

In vv. 7-10 Paul takes up the themes of the flesh and the Spirit once more (cf. 5:13-26), encouraging the Galatians to *sow to the Spirit* in order to inherit *eternal life* (cf. 5:21). Paul defines *sowing to the Spirit* in ethical terms as *doing what is right* (v. 9), which

means *work for the good of all, and especially for those of the family of faith* (v. 10). The Greek expression behind *work for the good* is typically used in Hellenistic Jewish Greek to designate assistance to the poor, and this nuance (which echoes 2:10) should be heard in v. 10 as well.

A Personal Postscript, 6:11-18

The concluding postscript indicates that Paul followed the custom of having a trained writer (an *amanuensis*) take down the letter. But now at the end, as was also common, Paul inscribes something in his own (evidently clumsy) hand (v. 11). In this last word to the Galatians, Paul claims that the Circumcisers themselves don't even keep the Law (v. 13). Perhaps the Circumcisers think that only certain requirements of the Law (above all regarding CIRCUMCISION but apparently also the Jewish calendar; see 4:10) are obligatory for gentile Christians. In that case, Paul may be alleging, the Circumcisers prove themselves unfaithful to the very Law they are promoting. For circumcision (as Paul says in 5:3) obligates one to keep the entire Law, not just certain parts of it.

Paul also accuses the Circumcisers of seeking to avoid suffering for the cross (v. 12) and being interested only in their own glory ("boasting" in the Galatians' circumcised flesh, v. 13). He contrasts himself with them by declaring that he boasts only in *the cross of . . . Christ* (v. 14). The cross, Paul says, means death to the world (v. 14) and establishes a *new creation* in which *neither circumcision nor uncircumcision* counts for anything (v. 15; cf. 5:6). In Christ's death the present world itself also dies, at least as far as those in Christ are concerned. This implies that the community of those in Christ is the locus of the new creation.

Righteousness in this new creation constitutes itself in the erasure of distinctions between Jew and Gentile, male and female, slave and free (6:15; 3:28). These distinctions represent hierarchies by which the present age is ordered. But they come to an end in the death of the present world through Christ's crucifixion. Thus Paul closes his letter on a revolutionary note, declaring that the new social order, which embodies the apocalyptic hope of new creation, has already dawned in Christ. And the church is to be the place in the world where this new social order is sown.

Ephesians

Frank Stagg

Introduction

Ephesians is the most comprehensive writing in the NT on the church, both goal and instrument in God's *eternal purpose* to create in Christ Jesus *one new humanity*. It was *through the cross* that God broke down *the dividing wall* between Jew and gentile, replacing *hostility* with *peace*.

Opening with a doxology praising God for carrying through his redemptive purpose which antedates *the foundation of the world* and prayer for the illumination and empowering of the readers, the letter continues with an exposition of the origin, nature, and mission of the CHURCH, with a call to unity, freedom from old vices, and practice of virtues proper to God's people.

Authorship and Destination

PAUL as author is explicit in the first word of the text, supported by autobiographical references to bonds, afflictions, and *chains* (3:1, 13; 4:1; 6:20). Matters of style, word usage, and theology leave scholars divided as to whether authentically from Paul, a pseudonym, or an insoluble problem (see Tolbert 1990 and Kümmel 1975, 357-63). It does follow that the letter is from Paul or from some cogent, unknown writer with amazing insight into Paul's mind and experience.

No theory of destination is compelling. The superscription "To the Ephesians" was probably added when letters of Paul were first collected and published as a corpus. MARCION (ca. 140) listed this letter as "To the Laodiceans," probably influenced by Col 4:16. The words *in Ephesus* (1:1) are absent from the earliest known manuscripts (including ₱46, Vaticanus, and Sinaiticus) and were unknown to Tertullian and Origen, in which no place name appears. Nothing in the letter implies Ephesus. TYCHICUS, bearer of the letter (6:21), may have been authorized to insert a place name if the letter was to be read in various churches, but this is speculation.

Date

If not from Paul, there are no criteria for dating the letter. If from Paul, either his Caesarean or Roman imprisonment is likely. If, as held here, Ephesians is Paul's response to his eviction from the Temple and arrest in JERUSALEM, the likely date is around 60 C.E.

Relationship with Colossians

About one-third of Colossians appears also in Ephesians. Verbal parallels are found throughout the letter with the exception of 2:6-9, 4:5-13, and 5:29-33. Whether by common authorship or not, it is generally recognized that Ephesians is dependent upon Colossians and not vice versa. Both letters feature Christ and the church, differing in focus. In Colossians, Christ is the head of the church; in Ephesians, the church is the body of Christ. These two foci are not mutually exclusive or improbable for the same author, different situations calling for different emphases.

Occasion and Purpose

The theme that dominates Ephesians, God's purpose to reconcile Jews and gentiles to himself and to one another, in Christ Jesus and through the cross, also runs through Paul's undisputed writings, and it is emphatic in Romans and Acts. A flood of light falls upon Romans and Ephesians as well as Acts if it is perceived that Romans was written on the eve of Paul's visit to Jerusalem (cf. 15:25) and Ephesians after his eviction from the Temple and arrest leading to years of imprisonment in CAESAREA and ROME.

The *dividing wall* seen as *broken down* (2:14) seems to echo Paul's eviction from the Temple when charged that he has "actually brought Greeks into the temple and has defiled this holy place" (Acts 21:28). A wall separated the Court of the gentiles from that of the Jews, with plaques warning that anyone of another nation caught beyond that wall would be responsible for his death which would follow. That wall stood materially until the destruction of the Temple by Roman armies in 70 C.E.; but to Ephesians, that wall was in effect already broken down in that what it represented was rejected.

Before reading Ephesians, it is illuminating to read in Acts 20–28 Paul's last-recorded visit to Jerusalem and also Paul's own compulsion to make that visit as anticipated in 1 Cor 16:1-4, 2 Cor 8-9, and Rom 15:22-33 (see Stagg 1990, 259—78).

Wanting to go to Spain by way of Rome, Paul felt compelled to go first to Jerusalem with an offering called a *koinōnia* from MACEDONIA and ACHAIA for the poor among the *saints* in Jerusalem (Rom 15:26). Paul's strategy was to get gentile churches to give not only money but themselves to the Jews (2 Cor 8–9) and to get the Jewish saints in Jerusalem to accept not only the money but the gentile Christians who gave it (Rom 15:31). Thus, Paul's mission to Jerusalem intended both to provide relief for the poor and to unite Jew and gentile in Christ. Instead, the mission led to his eviction from the Temple and the closing of Tem-

ple doors not only to gentiles but also to a Jew such as Paul (Acts 21:30).

Paul was held prisoner for two years in Caesarea and under house arrest in Rome for at least two years (Acts 28:30). It is plausible that sometime during those years he looked back upon that traumatic experience in Jerusalem and wrote his classic on the Church. At the heart of Ephesians is the vision of "the broken wall" (Barth 1959). Along with the sign of the veil in the Temple "torn in two, from top to bottom" (Matt 27:51) stands that in Ephesians of "the broken wall." Much of the gospel is dramatized in these two signs.

For Further Study

In the *Mercer Dictionary of the Bible*: BAPTISM; CHURCH; COLOSSIANS, LETTER TO THE; EPHESIANS, LETTER TO THE; EPHESUS; MARCION; PAUL; RECONCILIATION; ROMAN EMPIRE; SLAVERY IN THE NT; SATAN IN THE NT. In other sources: M. Barth, *The Broken Wall*; *Ephesians*; W. G. Kümmel, *Introduction to the N.T.*; N. H. Keathley, ed., *With Steadfast Purpose*; J. A. Robinson, *St. Paul's Epistle to the Ephesians*; A. Van Roon, *The Authenticity of Ephesians*.

Commentary

An Outline

I. Salutation, 1:1-2
II. Doxology and Prayer, 1:3-23
III. The Unity of All Humankind in Christ, 2:1–3:21
IV. Practical Exhortations, 4:1–6:20
V. Personal Words and Benediction, 6:21-24

Salutation, 1:1-2

The greeting is similar to that in Colossians, the most striking difference being the absence of a place name, except in later manuscripts. There is no compelling explanation for this absence. Origen took the phrase *tois ousin* ("those being") in an ontological sense, that is, "the saints who truly are!" The NRSV mg. reading is possible, "saints who are also faithful."

Doxology and Prayer, 1:3-23

1:3-14. Doxology. These twelve verses consist of one sentence in the Greek text. They fall into three strophes, each ending with *to the praise of his glory* (vv. 6, 12, 14). A trinitarian motif may be implied, for the first strophe praises *the God and Father of our*

Lord Jesus Christ, the second praises *Christ*, and the third praises the *Holy Spirit*. This could argue for a post-Pauline development, but it is anticipated in 2 Cor 13:13. No formal doctrine of trinity appears, for the letter begins and closes with *God our (the) Father and the Lord Jesus Christ*, with no reference to the Holy Spirit.

The first strophe (vv. 3-6) traces our calling to a holy and blameless life and destiny as God's children to God's having elected us *before the foundation of the world*. ELECTION and destiny do not imply unilateral determination; they simply mean that God calls us before we are able to answer.

The second strophe (vv. 7-12) is laden with heavy theological terms about God's accomplishments *in Christ. Redemption* is liberation from the bondage of sin. This liberation is effected through Christ's *blood*, his life given for us. *Forgiveness* is not indulgence; it is not only acceptance of the sinner but overcoming of *trespasses*, all traceable to God's *grace*. In Christ is seen God's *plan for the fullness of time*, that is, *to gather up all things in him*.

The third strophe (vv. 13-14) praises the *Holy Spirit*, the present possession of whom gives us the *pledge* (*arrabōn* = a down payment making a transaction binding) of our full redemption as God's people.

1:15-23. Prayer. This is one long sentence in Greek. It is a prayer that the readers be illuminated so as to know *the hope* implied in God's call, *the riches* of the *inheritance* God has offered, and the *power* which is inherently God's and which expresses itself in overcoming all resistance. It is the prayer that the readers experience within themselves the very power that *raised [Jesus] from the dead.*

The Unity of All Humankind in Christ, 2:1–3:21

Chapters 2–3 form the theological base for the CHURCH as the new humanity composed of Jew and gentile, God's new creation in Christ. With this is Paul's understanding of his own ministry to the gentiles and his prayer for his readers.

2:1-10. From death to life. Two foci appear: *You were dead. . . . But God . . . made us alive together with Christ* (vv. 1, 4-5). The emphasis is upon God's act of GRACE in giving new life to gentiles; but the *You* (v. 1) is expanded to *All of us* (v. 3), Jew and gentile alike, dead in sin until brought to life by God's grace.

In fact, several contrasts appear in this passage: Jew and gentile once dead, now made alive; Jew and gentile once divided, now together; not our work, but God's work; not by good works but for good works.

Trespasses (*paraptomasin*) refer to willful acts of disobedience. *Sins* (*hamartiais*) may refer to failure or "missing the mark," but even this term implies guilt. Sin is not only an act of disobedience, it results in spiritual death (Rom 6:23).

Paul shared the widely held view that powerful, evil spirits under an evil ruler (SATAN) are behind human sin, but this does not imply that we are mere victims and not *disobedient* sinners. He also saw that Jews as well as gentiles followed *the desires of flesh and senses*; but again, they were not merely victims. *Flesh* stands for disposition and life apart from God, with no special reference to the literal flesh (cf. Gal 5:19-21 for "the works of the flesh" as nonsensual as well as sensual). Also, Jews as well as gentiles are seen as *by nature children of wrath* (v. 3). This does not imply that they were mere victims of Adam's sin or of God's anger. "Wrath" to Paul was not God's anger so much as God's letting us follow our own choices even if they lead to our self-destruction (cf. Rom 1:18-32). Sinners "by nature" means that Jew and gentile alike are sinners in their natural state.

But God introduces the positive side of "from death to life." Salvation for gentile and Jew is new life and new life together, grounded in God's rich *mercy*, out of his *great love*, and by his *grace*. Sin and death are the works of Jew and gentile. Life, including life together with God and with one another, is God's act out of his love, mercy, and grace.

Verse 5 may intend that God makes each Jew and gentile alive *with Christ*. Probably it intends that "in the Christ" (so in p^{46}, Vaticanus, et al.), God makes Jew and gentile alive with one another. This parallels the picture in v. 6 (obscured in NRSV): "both raised together and seated together in the heavenlies in Christ Jesus" (author's trans.). This is the major theme of Ephesians. Overcoming hostility between Jew and gentile will *show the immeasurable riches of his grace in kindness toward us in Christ Jesus* (v. 7).

Salvation is *by grace* through the *faith* that is trust; and though not of our own doing, it is *for good works*. Jew and gentile as a new creation is in eternal design and achievement God's *poiema, what he has made us!*

2:11-22. One fresh humanity in Christ. Continuing his "before and after" theme, Paul contrasts the gentile status before Christ and now. They once were called *"the uncircumcision"* by those called *"the circumcision"* (v. 11). Paul himself had once built his faith and practice upon such an arbitrary and superficial distinction. He now exposes it in three Greek words: "in flesh, handmade." It is "in flesh," thus superficial; it is "handmade," thus artificial—a little skin removed with a knife.

The gentile's real privation was not genetic or cultic; it was the alienation from God and thus alienation from the people of God. The privation was not "uncircumcision" or being born gentile; it was being *without Christ*. It was in being *in the world* (a world like this) *without God*. Paul's word is *atheoi*, literally "atheists." Gentiles were not atheists in a philosophical sense; they were strangers to the true God, thus *strangers to the covenants of promise, having no hope*. They had their gods and their hopes; but they did not have "the hope of glory" (Col 1:27).

Verse 13 introduces the mighty newness *in Christ Jesus*. Those once *far off have now been brought near by the blood of Christ*. Again, the union of Jew and gentile in Christ is the overriding theme of Ephesians.

Verses 14-22 comprise the heart of Ephesians. This paragraph seems to look back on Paul's trauma of eviction from the Temple in Jerusalem, charged with having taken uncircumcised gentiles beyond the dividing wall separating the Court of the gentiles from that of the Jews (Acts 21:27-30). Although the wall stood materially until destroyed by Roman soldiers in 70 C.E., Paul saw that Christ Jesus had already in effect broken it down, rejecting the principles upon which it had been built.

Christ himself (*autos*) *is our peace*! This means peace with God, but the emphasis is upon peace between Jew and gentile, for *in his flesh he has made both groups into one.* Jesus not only rejected in words the holiness code that superficially ruled some "clean" and others "unclean" (cf. Mark 7:23); he rejected that code in his actions, touching a leper (Mark 1:41) and eating with "tax gatherers and sinners" (Luke 15:1-2). He defined his true family in terms not of flesh but of obedience to the will of God (Mark 3:35).

Christ broke down the separating wall when he *abolished the law with its commandments and ordinances* (v. 15). He not only rejected such ordinances as kosher foods and purification rites but also the holiness code that rested upon externals (e.g., Lev 15:19-20; 21:18-24; Deut 23:1-6). He followed the tradition already found in such scriptures as Ps 24:3-6 and Mic 6:8. His holiness code had to do with moral and ethical principles and the attitudes and dispositions behind such principles and actions. When one holiness code replaced another, the dividing wall was broken down. (see HOLY SPIRIT).

Peace was made when Christ created in himself *one new humanity in place of the two* (v. 15). "Fresh" is a better rendering of *kainon* than "new." The church, the body of Christ, is not simply novel; it is a fresh kind of humanity where worldly criteria that separate are replaced by principles that unite. The old humanity was bent on excluding; the new humanity seeks to include.

The *one body* in which Jew and gentile are reconciled (v. 16) is the CHURCH. This is achieved *through the cross*, where the principle of self-serving is overcome by that of self-giving. The Jew-gentile hostility, like every hostility, was based on the self-serving principle. The CROSS is the ultimate in the self-denial which is salvation (Mark 8:34-35; John 12:24-26). The "enmity" (KJV; NRSV *hostility*) that is slain at the cross is life centered upon itself, the sin behind all sins.

The *peace* proclaimed to those *far off* and those *near* is peace between gentile and Jew; but it is first of all peace with God and peace with and within themselves (v. 17). This peace occurs when the love that serves and includes replaces the selfishness that exploits and excludes.

Jews and gentiles now have the same *access* to the Father, through Christ and *in one Spirit* (v. 18). Gone are the old courts, walls, barriers, and doors segregating Jews from gentiles, men from women, and priests from laypersons, as was built into the architecture of the Temple and imposed upon people. The "broken wall" and the "rent veil" mean now that all in Christ and by faith may enter the "Holy of Holies" into the very presence of *the Father*.

Using a political model, gentiles *are no longer strangers and aliens*, foreigners merely tolerated in another's land. They are *citizens with the saints and also members of the household of God* (v. 19). In Christ, Jews and gentiles alike are at home in God's house, unlike Temple discrimination.

The model having the church built upon *the foundation of the apostles and prophets* (v. 20) is seen by some as impossible to Paul, for whom the only possible foundation is Jesus Christ (1 Cor 3:11). The point is weighty and, to many, decisive against Pauline authorship of Ephesians. On the other hand, models are flexible; and different models are not necessarily competing. Ephesians holds to the centrality of Christ, whatever is intended here. *The foundation of the apostles and prophets* is ambiguous. This may intend either the apostles and prophets themselves as the foundation, or the foundation upon which they built. Christ is the unrivaled creator and lord of the church, the model here being *cornerstone*, not a mere ornamental stone but a keystone holding walls together.

Unlike the old Temple with dividing walls and veil, Jews and gentiles in Christ now form a new *holy temple*, built together into *a dwelling place for God* (vv. 21-22). God dwells in the fellowship of His people.

3:1-13. Paul's ministry to the gentiles. In 3:1 Paul began to pray, and then he paused to describe his role in ministry to the gentiles before resuming his prayer in 3:14 (each unit introduced with *Toutou charin*, "because of this"). In effect, vv. 2-13 form a digression, although highly relevant and instructive.

Identifying himself as *prisoner for Christ Jesus for the sake of you Gentiles*, Paul breaks off to give the background against which his prayer is best understood. NRSV obscures by seeing "this cause" (KJV; NRSV *reason*) as explaining Paul's imprisonment rather than why he presumes to pray for the gentiles.

To understand why Paul thus prays for the gentiles requires that they understand his special commission as minister to the gentiles. The explanation revolves around *the mystery* given him *by revelation* and his commission to proclaim the good news of God's eternal purpose to unite Jews and gentiles in Christ.

The commission given Paul translates *oikonomian*, a term for stewardship or management of a house. "Dispensation" (KJV) is misleading when confused with modern dispensational ideas. Paul simply means that the REVELATION given him carries with it a stewardship obligation to proclaim it (see 3:9). *Diakonos* (servant or minister) carries the same idea in v. 7. By the grace of God, Paul has received this revelation and the commission to proclaim it.

Paul calls this revelation a *mystery*, about which he has written briefly (v. 3), presumably in the early part of this letter (see also Col 1:26-27). This mystery is now an open secret, known first to God alone, and then revealed to his servant who is to proclaim it to Jews and gentiles. It is not apparent who were the *holy apostles and prophets* to whom this mystery was revealed. This understanding was offered the Twelve, but for the most part they resisted it (cf. Mark 9:38-41; Acts 1:6; 10:1-11:3; Gal 2:11-14). STEPHEN, PHILIP, and unnamed men from CYPRUS and CYRENE anticipated Paul in this VISION (Acts 6:8-8:1; 8:4-40; 11:20).

Verse 6 states the basic provision of the *mystery*, the union of Jew and gentile in Christ. NRSV interprets, but obscures some powerful wordplay: *gentiles have become fellow heirs, members of the same body, and sharers in the promise* (v. 6). The Greek text has it "heirs with and bodied with and partakers with." The second of these terms is possibly a new coinage, *syssōma* (synsomatic). These three terms strain to stress the oneness of Jew and gentile in Christ.

Verses 7-9 stress the marvel of Paul's part in showing forth the mystery. Of this mystery he became a *servant* (*diakonos*), and this by the *gift of God's grace* given him by the "energizing of his power" (author trans.). Seeing himself as *the very least of all the saints*, he marvels at the grace given him "to proclaim to the gentiles the untraceable (*anexichniaston*) wealth of Christ" (author trans.). He might strike its trail but could not trace it out, so vast it was.

In bringing to light this mystery, hidden in God for ages, *the wisdom of God in its rich variety* now could be made known to *the rulers and authorities in the heavenly places* (v. 10). This "multicolored (*polypoikilos*) wisdom of God" is seen at last *through the church*! Even the heavenly creatures do not understand God's wisdom until the emergence of the church, God's new creation out of hitherto hostile Jews and gentiles.

This great achievement was "according to the purpose of the ages" (NRSV *the eternal purpose*). God has had one plan through the ages, in Christ Jesus thus to unify Jew and gentile in giving them *access to God in boldness and confidence through faith* (vv. 11-12). Now that his readers see that Paul sees his mission to the Jews as God's gracious gift to him, they have no reason to *lose heart* over his sufferings.

3:14-19. Paul's prayer resumed. After several digressions in which Paul describes the mystery he is commissioned to proclaim, with its special relation to gentiles, Paul resumes the prayer begun in 3:1, repeating "For this cause" (*Toutou charin*).

A play on the words *Father* (*patera*) and *family* (*patria*) serves further to stress the theme of oneness. The intention may be "every fatherhood" rather than *family*, God seen as the archetype of all fatherhood. Either way, all peoples are seen as deriving from the same divine fatherhood, thus all "families" are united under "the Father of our Lord Jesus Christ." Although this sexually exclusive language is problematic today, the concern of Ephesians was elsewhere, to overcome ethnic bias.

The prayer is that they be strengthened in their *inner being* as Christ dwells within them. Salvation does not come as an abstraction; it comes only as Christ becomes a transforming presence within the inner self.

Paul next prays that not only may they be *rooted and grounded in love* (v. 17) but that they may be empowered *to comprehend, with all the saints* (v. 18) the love of Christ in its full magnitude: breadth, length, height, and depth. *The love of Christ* may be intended objectively, love *for* Christ, or subjectively, the love Christ has *for us*, presumably the latter. Such understanding is not for "loners," but for those who learn *with all the saints*.

To know the love of Christ is to know *that which surpasses knowledge* (v. 19). Again, here is a play on words, knowing which surpasses knowledge! To "know" the love of Christ is experiential knowledge, and it surpasses cognitive knowledge.

A reply to gnostic claims may appear in v. 19. Christ's love surpasses *knowledge* (*gnosis*) from which gnostics took their name and of which they were so proud. Again, in Christ gentiles and Jews *may be filled with all the fullness* (*plērōma*) *of God*. In Col 1:19, "all the fullness of God" was pleased to dwell in Christ, not in a gnostic hierarchy of eons or emanations. Also, where one is "in Christ" and Christ dwells in that one, that one is *filled with all the fullness of God* (v. 19; cf. Col 2:10).

3:20-21. Doxology. Paul could not talk about God's grace and his marvelous "plan of the ages" without breaking into prayer and praise. He praises God for his power working within us, achieving *far more than all we can ask or imagine!*

Practical Exhortations, 4:1–6:20

Although theology continues, this section is primarily practical, with attention to the individual life, the life and work of the church, and guiding principles for the extended family: wives/husbands, children/parents, slaves/masters.

4:1-6. Basis for unity. In his capacity as *the prisoner in the Lord*, Paul calls for life worthy of *the calling* by which the readers were *called*. Salvation in Christ is our *calling* (*klesis*) or vocation. Initiative always is with God: creation, revelation, redemption. Calling and ELECTION refer to the same thing, divine initiative. God's calling opens the option, it does not dictate the response.

Those in Christ ought to be characterized by *humility and gentleness, with patience*. Humility was despised in the Greek world, proper to slaves alone. In the NT, servanthood and humility are seen as virtues, exemplified in Jesus and proper to his followers (John 13:4-5; Phil 2:3ff.).

Bearing with one another in love, is best rendered "holding back" or "forbearing," recognizing the fact that we tend to antagonize one another and strike back. It is *love* that gives us the disposition and strength to hold back.

Love demands more than simply holding back; it requires that we make every effort "to guard" (*terein*) *the unity of the Spirit in the bond of peace* (v. 3). Though unity is the divine provision, it is not unilaterally bestowed. It belongs to Christian vocation. *Peace* like *shalom* is well-being under the sovereignty of God.

Seven (the number for perfection) unities are named, in three groups: *one body, one Spirit, one hope; one Lord, one faith, one baptism; one God and Father of all* (vv. 4-6). The *one body* is the church, the body of Christ. Only context is clue to whether Spirit or the human spirit is intended. The *one hope* is "Christ in you" (Col 1:27). The one Lord is Christ. *One faith* is not one creed but one trust or faith commitment. *One baptism* is not only the one initiation rite but the commitment it signifies. *One God* is not only

affirmation of the MONOTHEISM basic to OT and NT, but also the ultimate ground for the unifying of humanity.

4:7-16. Diversity in unity. The ascended Christ as prime minister of the church gives gifts of grace, varying with the individual, designed to equip all the saints for ministry. The receiving church is to be the serving church, both means and goal in the purpose of God.

The quotation, apparently from Ps 68:18, is freely adapted. The psalm celebrates the triumph of "the God of Sinai" as he came into "the holy place" and "ascended the high mount," that is, "the sanctuary," the "temple at Jerusalem." He did so "leading captives" and "receiving gifts," changed here to *gave gifts*. In Ephesians, Christ both *ascended* and *descended*, the order unclear. The descent may be the incarnate experience leading to his death, the ascent being the resurrection and ascension. What is clear is that the descending and ascending one is the same. Christ is not dead but alive; not absent but present; not ghostly but embodied; not passive but active in the life and ministry of the church, his body.

Verses 11-16 form a classic statement as to the ministry of the church. Christ is *the Minister*. He gives to the church its various ministries, *some . . . apostles, some prophets, some evangelists, some pastors and teachers*. This catalogue is illustrative rather than complete, as comparison with other catalogues shows (Rom 12:6ff.; 1 Cor 12:28). There is no mention of bishops, presbyters, or deacons! These, too, although unmentioned here, belong to the equipping ministers of the Church. They are servants, not rulers.

The function of equipping ministers is *to equip the saints for the work of ministry* (v. 12). All in Christ are *saints*, ones set apart in Christ (with no implication of special sanctity). All are called to ministry. The whole Church is in intention the ministering body of Christ. Ministries vary with the gifts present in the members of the Body. The total ministry includes Christ, the equipping ministers, and all the saints.

The Church is intended to be both servant and minister and the goal of all ministry, itself "a perfect man, unto the measure of the stature of the fullness of Christ" (v. 13, author trans.). Unity and maturity are marks proper to the body of Christ, with each member functioning in terms of its role, and all members blended into one growing body. The saints are not to remain *children*, vulnerable to deceit; but they are to reach maturity and unity in variety. *Speaking the truth in love* could be rendered "holding the truth in love" or "being true in love."

4:17-24. Former vices to shun. Those *in the Lord* are no longer to live like *gentiles*, seen here as pagan (the readers were ethnically gentiles). The gentile plight was living *in the futility of their minds*. Alienated from God, their minds were not only uninformed but *darkened*, incapacitated and immoral. Those in Christ are called to a new quality of life, new and constantly *renewed*, a new creation in *the likeness of God in true righteousness and holiness*.

4:25–5:2. Sins of the spirit that destroy unity. A catalogue of wrong feelings, attitudes, and dispositions is matched in each case with positives. *Falsehood* is to be replaced with *the truth*. Since we are *members of one another*, in being true or false to others, we are that to ourselves. *Be angry but do not sin?* How? Anger is recognized as a reality; it is what we do with it that matters. To *let the sun go down on your anger* is to *make room for the devil*. It is to let anger eat away at us, even while we sleep. Stealing is to be replaced with honest work, providing not only for ourselves but *to have something to share with the needy*.

Evil talk is any talk that is like inedible fruit (*sapros*; cf. Matt 12:33, where "bad fruit" is not rotten but the wrong kind). In its place is to be talk *useful for building up* and for *giving grace*. There is no place for bitterness, wrath, anger, wrangling, slander, and malice. Instead, we should be kind, tenderhearted, and forgiving. All this follows, if as imitators of God, we *live in love, as Christ loved us*. This is the fragrant *sacrifice* to be offered to God.

5:3-20. Sins of sensuality that corrupt and degrade. Gross acts of sensuality like *fornication, impurity*, and *greed*, seen as pagan, are to be so far removed that they are not even mentioned among the *saints*. Even *obscene, silly, and vulgar talk*, making light of sensuality, is *out of place*.

The warning in v. 5 is severe (cf. 1 Cor 6:9-10). The Greek text may be imperative, "This know ye, knowing" or indicative, "This ye know, knowing." The warning that *no fornicator or impure person, or one who is greedy* (worship of things seen as a form of idolatry) will inherit the kingdom of Christ is not softened. This is impossible to assimilate into the soteriology that equates salvation with what is perceived as confessional orthodoxy. For the most part, it is ignored as are such warnings as attributed to Jesus (cf. Matt 7:15-27; 25:31-46). Verse 5 is weighted on the side of orthopraxy rather than orthodoxy.

Light and *darkness* are the themes through vv. 6-14. The gentile readers were once *darkness*, but now they are *light* and *the children of light* (v. 8; cf. Matt 5:14-16). As in biblical usage generally, light and darkness are moral and ethical terms, not cognitive. A benighted person is evil, not necessarily ignorant; and an enlightened person is good, not simply informed. To walk in darkness is to live in evil. To walk in light is to live in goodness.

Light and darkness are disclosed by their *fruit*. The fruit of light includes what is *good and right and true* (cf. Gal 5:22). Darkness, in fact, is *unfruitful* in that it bears no edible fruit.

It is the function of light to give light, exposing darkness and turning darkness into light (vv. 13-14). The darkness to be exposed are the *shameful* acts of darkness. The children of light are to be in action what they are in nature. The DEAD SEA SCROLLS belonged to a priestly group who saw themselves as "the sons of light," but they were hiding their light in their withdrawal at QUMRAN. Jesus countered as he addressed an ordinary group, saying: "You are the light of the world . . . let your light shine before others" (Matt 5:14-16).

Although light and darkness are moral and ethical terms, they are not indifferent to wisdom or foolishness. The children of light are to be *wise* and not *foolish* (vv. 15-17). For example, getting drunk with wine is not simply evil; it is foolish. Getting *filled with the Spirit* and "singing songs to God in praise and thanksgiving" (cf. Col 3:16) is both good and wise.

5:21–6:9. The extended family. This passage is a domestic code for the extended family: wife-husband, child-parent, slave-master. Parallels with commonalities and differences are found in Col 3:18–4:1; 1 Pet 2:13–3:7; Titus 2:1-10; and 1 Tim 2:1ff., 2:8ff.; 3:1ff., 3:8ff.; 5:17ff.; 6:1-2. The code in Ephesians seems to be built upon that in Colossians.

The extended family in the Greco-Roman world gave rise to codes designed to regulate relationships within domestic and civil structures of society, traceable in Aristotle (*Politics* 1.3) and Philo (*Hypothetica* 7.14). No direct dependence upon such codes is traceable here, but some influence is probable. The NT codes offer moral and ethical principles that should humanize and Christianize these relationships (Stagg and Stagg 1978, chap. 8).

Ephesians 5:21 is linked grammatically to what precedes, but in intention it governs what follows: *Be subject to one another out of reverence for Christ*. This applies to all who are in Christ; it is egalitarian; and it follows Jesus' basic law that, contrary to the pagan disposition to rule, his followers are to find their greatness in servanthood (Mark 9:33-37; 10:35-45). All codes must be subordinated to this principle.

All codes are historically conditioned, as here. Jewish and Roman law decreed that the husband was head of the family; and both laws gave slave owners legal authority over slaves. These were legal realities, whatever their injustices. The early church had no worldly power sufficient then to change such structures and laws. It did have the disposition to bring them under the claims of Christ.

Codes at best intend to articulate and apply values and principles in a given historical situation. They are never one and the same as such principles, and they are not failsafe. For example, kindness is a principle, universally and eternally valid. How kindness is expressed can never be defined in any code. Because all codes are historically conditioned and by nature not one and the same as that which they seek to apply, they are not to be uprooted from one situation and imposed upon another. Codes, like wineskins (Mark 2:22), are to be replaced as necessary if the "wine" of principle or value is to be preserved.

5:22-33. Wives-husbands. *Wives, be subject to your husbands* (NRSV) is a questionable translation, for there is no verb in the Greek text of v. 22. *Be subject* translates a participle in v. 21, and this carries over to v. 22, with imperative force. In form it is middle voice and probably middle in force, "subject yourselves" instead of passive, "be subject." If middle voice, at least wives are recognized as responsible and competent to shape their side of the marital relationship, not subordinates to be commanded. If applied, v. 21 would call upon the husband to do likewise, with mutual choice of voluntary submission, each to the other.

In affirming husband as *head of the wife*, the code follows the legal structures then obtaining, not the ideal cited by Jesus from Gen 2:24: " 'For this reason a man shall leave his father and mother and be joined to his wife, and the two shall become one flesh.' So they are no longer two, but one flesh" (Mark 10:7-8). Significantly, the code itself gives way to the principle of Jesus in v. 31!

Christ as *head* and *Savior* of the church is the model here for wives as subject to their husbands. *In everything* heightens the demand over that in Col 3:18. Husbands normally were providers and protectors of the family, but surely a husband is not "savior" of his wife in the sense that Christ is Savior of the church. Many husbands are not themselves "saved," much less saving. The code is best understood within its own limits as historically conditioned. To absolutize the code as binding on wives today is to open the door to any abuse of which fallible husbands are capable and often disposed.

The appeal to "love" as the controlling principle in the husband's relationship with his wife follows what Jesus verified as "the first" commandment of all (Mark 12:29). A husband is to love his wife *as Christ loved the church and gave himself up for her*. Should a wife love a husband any less?

At this point, the focus turns to the church itself. What is intended by *cleansing her with the washing of water by the word* is difficult. Taken literally, this serves as a text for baptismal regeneration, as problematic as the contention that circumcision was a means to salvation, rejected outright in 2:11ff. *By the word* (NRSV) translates *en remati*, literally "in a word." This may imply a baptismal confession of the name of Christ (cf. 1 Cor 6:11), but this is speculation.

That a husband should love his wife "as his own body" may be understood two ways. He may love her the way he loves himself, or in loving her he does love himself, since the two have become one flesh.

Verse 31 recaptures the mutual and egalitarian ideal of v. 21. All are to be *subject to one another out of reverence for Christ*, and husband and wife are to become *one flesh*. It follows that husband should *love his wife* and wife should *respect her husband* (v. 33), but surely a wife should love her husband and a husband should respect his wife.

6:1-4. Children-parents. The code here differs somewhat from that in Colossians. In both letters, both parents are to be obeyed by their children; but "in everything" drops out in Ephesians! Instead, many manuscripts have *in the Lord*; but this phrase is absent in some strong Greek and Latin manuscripts and several early church fathers. Thus Ephesians does not impose obedience unconditionally, a significant factor today when many children are abused by their fathers and/or mothers.

Ideally, obedience to parents is *right*, for parental responsibility requires corresponding authority. Authority is forfeited when abused.

The text here builds upon the fifth commandment (Exod 20:12; Deut 5:16), *the first commandment with a promise*. Significantly, the egalitarian principle is in force here, for mothers and fathers are to be obeyed alike in the Decalogue and in Ephesians.

What precisely is intended by the promise *live long on the earth* is unclear. If individual longevity is the promise, it is unclear why many obedient children die young and many disobedient ones live long. In the Decalogue the promise may be long life "in the land" for a nation obedient to parents, not individuals.

Verse 4 goes beyond Colossians in adding a positive to the negative in discipline. Fathers are not only to refrain from provoking their children to anger, but also to *bring them up in the discipline and instruction of the Lord.*

Not including mothers here is in keeping with the distrust of mothers in much of the ancient world, deeming them unfit to teach even their own children. Such distrust of women does not accord with the manner of Jesus. Neither does it agree with the recognition that Timothy's "sincere faith" was in his maternal heritage, a faith that lived first in his maternal heritage, "a faith that lived first in your grandmother Lois and your mother Eunice" (2 Tim 1:5), not from his Greek father (Acts 16:1). Of course, there is no evidence today that mothers are less competent than fathers in teaching or parenting.

6:5-9. Slaves-masters. This part of the code parallels that in Colossians, with no significant variations. Slavery as such is not challenged, for whatever reason. What does concern the code is the quality service given by the slave, service which is a credit to a follower of Christ. As *slaves of Christ* they are to render service in deed and in spirit worthy of a servant of Christ. Ultimate reward is from the true Master, under whom the distinction between *slaves* and *free* persons is transcended (v. 8; cf. Gal 3:28).

Without condoning slavery, *masters* are warned that they are answerable to the ultimate "Master" for how they relate to those whom they hold as slaves.

6:10-20. The whole armor of God. This section sees the Christian as embattled, threatened by *cosmic powers* seen as *spiritual forces of evil in the heavenly places* (vv. 10-17), and also by human forces to whom the gospel is to be preached with boldness (vv. 18-20).

The present world retains the language about demonic forces, and there is yet sincere belief in the reality of such threats; but nothing today compares with fear in the ancient world of such powers believed to inhabit the stars, mountains, trees, and human beings. The word "disaster" preserves the belief that human sufferings are traceable to some star god. Modern space travel and even mining of mountains would be problematic to the ancient world, for fear of disturbing cosmic powers.

The *whole armor of God* implies nothing of worldly militarism. All the armor is defensive except the *shoes* that *will make you ready to proclaim the gospel of peace* (v. 15) and *the sword of the Spirit, which is the word of God* (v. 17; cf. Rev 1:16).

Defensive armor includes *the belt of truth.* The injunction anticipates our "fasten your seatbelts!" In a world like this, the Christian pilgrimage can be a rough ride. "Truth" is our defense, and it requires no defense. *The breastplate of righteousness* is a reminder that although we are not saved by our goodness, righteousness belongs properly to followers of Jesus. *Faith* is more than a shield, but it is that. *Salvation* is more than security, but it is that too.

Prayer rightly includes self, but there is a special duty to pray *for all the saints.* Paul includes himself in his prayer requests, but it is not a self-serving request. Imprisoned for preaching a gospel inclusive of Jew and gentile, he prays that he have the "boldness" to speak *the mystery of the gospel,* the very gospel for which he is *an ambassador in chains.* No threat is to silence him or cause him to modify his proclamation of "the mystery of the gospel" (cf. 3:1-6).

Personal Words and Benediction, 6:21-24

Tychicus is apparently the bearer of the letter (no postal system then for civilians). His further mission is to inform the readers more fully as to Paul's situation. This is for their encouragement in difficult times.

Peace, love, faith, and *grace* are primary in the benediction, as a reminder of what is received from *God the Father and the Lord Jesus Christ* and also of that by which *the whole community* is to be characterized. The final appeal is for *an undying love for our Lord Jesus Christ.*

Works Cited

Barth, Marcus. 1959. *The Broken Wall.* 1974. *Ephesians.* AncB.

Kümmel, W. G. 1975. *Introduction to the N.T.*

Robinson, J. A. 1904. *St. Paul's Epistle to the Ephesians.*

Roon, A. Van. 1974. *The Authenticity of Ephesians.*

Stagg, Frank. 1990. "Paul's Final Mission to Jerusalem," in *With Steadfast Purpose,* ed. N. Keathley.

Stagg, Evelyn, and Frank Stagg. 1978. *Woman in the World of Jesus.*

Tolbert, Malcolm O. 1990. "Ephesians, Letter to the," MDB.

Philippians

Charles H. Talbert

Introduction

Philippians is one of thirteen letters attributed to PAUL in the NT. It belongs to the group of nine Pauline letters addressed to seven churches that is arranged in order of descending length. It is to devotional literature what Romans is to doctrinal and 1 Corinthians to ethical writing. The Marcionite prologue to Paul's letters (late second century) gives perhaps the oldest Christian view of the letter.

> The Philippians are Macedonians. They persevered in faith after [they] had accepted the word of truth and they did not receive false apostles. The Apostle praises them, writing to them from Rome from the prison, by Epaphroditus.

Genre

Philippians is both like and unlike ancient non-Christian letters (Soards 1990, 660). Like them, it begins with a salutation (A to B, greeting) followed by a prayer form (thanksgiving and petition), moves to a body, and ends with a conventional closing (e.g., greetings). Unlike them, its components are Christianized, for example, Salutation—*Grace and peace from God our Father and the Lord Jesus Christ* (1:2); Closing— *The grace of the Lord Jesus Christ be with your spirit* (4:23).

Author and Recipients

The letter's claim to be by Paul is universally accepted today. It is addressed to Christian converts in the Macedonian city of PHILIPPI. That church, founded during Paul's second missionary journey (Acts 16:9-40), stayed in close contact with the apostle (2 Cor 11:8-9; Phil 4:15-16; Acts 20:1-2, 3-6). It was basically gentile Christian in composition.

Integrity

There is diversity of opinion about whether or not Philippians is a unity. Some take 3:1b–4:3 as a fragment of a second letter. Others regard 4:10-20 as one note; 1:1–3:1 + 4:4-7 as another; and 3:2–4:3 + 4:8-9 as a third. If so, then these different letters were collected, edited, and published as one when the Pauline letter collection was made near 100 C.E. Still others believe that Philippians can best be explained as one letter. One's position on the matter of integrity affects one's decisions about other issues.

Date, Locale, and Occasion

If Philippians is not a unity, then its different components may come from different locales at different times and have different purposes. (1) If three independent letters are assumed, then 4:10-20 may be the earliest, written from an alleged imprisonment in EPHESUS, on the third journey, to thank the Philippians for their gift; 1:1–3:1 + 4:4-7 (perhaps 4:21-23) may be next, also from an Ephesian imprisonment, calling for unity and joy; while 3:2–4:3 + 4:8-9 may be the latest, written shortly after leaving Ephesus, perhaps from CORINTH, warning about false teachers (Koester 1976, 665–66). (2) If there were two original letters, then 1:1–3:1a + 4:4-23 may have been written from prison in Rome (Acts 28), Ephesus (an alleged imprisonment on the third journey), or CAESAREA (Acts 23:23–26:32) to thank the church for its gift and to exhort them to Christian unity; 3:1b–4:3 may have come from a time when Paul was not in prison, close to that of Galatians and warning about similar problems with false teaching (Michael 1928). (3) If the letter is a unity, it was written from prison in Rome, Ephesus, Caesarea, or elsewhere (2 Cor 11:23—Paul was imprisoned a number of times before the Caesarean imprisonment of Acts 23; *1 Clem* 5:5—Paul was imprisoned seven times) to serve multiple functions: giving thanks for a gift, encouragement to unity, warning about heresy, information about travel plans (Hawthorne 1983, xxix–xlviii).

Although no consensus exists, this commentary assumes the unity of Philippians, for which a good case has been made by Garland 1985, Kurz 1985, and Watson 1988. Again, although consensus does not exist and certainty is impossible, this reading of Philippians assumes a Roman origin, near the beginning of Paul's imprisonment there. The only serious obstacle against this ancient view, the great distance between Rome and Philippi that allegedly renders the travel undertaken and proposed difficult, is removed by the comment of Philostratus (*Life of Apollonius* 7.10), that the distance from Puteoli (near Rome) to Corinth (fairly close to Philippi) was crossed in five days. The similarities with Romans and Galatians are then explained by locating Philippians early in Paul's imprisonment in Rome. (For an outline of Paul's life and the place of his letters in it, see Soards 1990, 660.)

For Further Study

In the *Mercer Dictionary of the Bible*: PAUL; PHILIPPI; PHILIPPIANS, LETTER TO THE; PRISON EPISTLES.

F. W. Beare, *A Commentary on the Epistle to the Philippians*, HNTC; W. G. Doty, *Letters in Primitive Christianity*; D. Garland, "The Composition and Literary Unity of Philippians: Some Neglected Factors," *NovT* 27 (1985): 141–73; G. F. Hawthorne, *Philippians*, WBC; H. Koester, "Philippians, Letter to the," *IDBSupp* 665–66; W. S. Kurz, "Kenotic Imitation of Paul and of Christ in Philippians," in *Discipleship in the New Testament*, ed. F. Segovia, 103–26; R. P. Martin, *Carmen Christi: Philippians 2:5-11 in Recent Interpretation*; J. H. Michael, *The Epistle of Paul to the Philippians*, MNTC; S. K. Stowers, *Letter Writing in Greco-Roman Antiquity*; C. H. Talbert, "The Problem of Preexistence in Philippians 2:6-11," *JBL* 86 (1967): 141–53; D. Watson, "A Rhetorical Analysis of Philippians and Its Implications for the Unity Question," *NovT* 30 (1988): 57–88.

Commentary

An Outline

Introduction, 1:1-11

Salutation, 1:1-2

The letter's beginning adopts and adapts the customary form of ancient letters: A to B, greeting. PAUL is the author but TIMOTHY (Acts 16:1-3; 19:22) is included to lay the foundation for his future visit (2:19-23) and to demonstrate Paul's humility (2:3-4; 3:17). The letter is sent *to all the saints in Christ Jesus* in Philippi; we would say to all the Christians there. *With the bishops and deacons* might better be translated "overseers and helpers" to convey the idea that they

are not officials in the second-century sense but administrative functionaries manifesting the gifts of service (Rom 12:7—ministry [διακονία]; 1 Cor 12—helpers) and oversight (Rom 12:8—the leader; 1 Cor 12:28—administrators). These functionaries would be addressed because, in part, Philippians is a response to a gift sent to the prisoner Paul by the church and doubtless supervised by these overseers and helpers. The greeting of v. 2 invokes *God our Father* (Matt 6:9; Luke 11:2; Rom 8:15; Gal 4:6; 2 John 3) and the *Lord Jesus Christ* (Rom 15:6; 2 Cor 1:3; 11:31; Col 1:3), making it distinctively Christian.

Prayer, 1:3-11

Ancient letters often used a prayer form after the salutation. A THANKSGIVING (vv. 3-6) and a petition (vv. 9-11) are joined by an expression of personal affection (vv. 7-8). Thanksgiving and petition are organized in similar ways: reference to prayer followed by its two objects, ending with an eschatological note, the *day of Jesus Christ*. In this section one hears themes that will recur throughout the letter: Paul's joy, the Philippians' gift, the completion of salvation at the last day, Paul's imprisonment, and Christian growth.

1:3-6. Thanksgiving. Paul gives thanks for two things: (1) either for his every remembrance of them or for their every remembrance of him (the Greek allows either; so does the context), which is always in every prayer, for all of them, with joy (vv. 3-4); and (2) for their sharing in the gospel, that is, their gift to him in prison (v. 5; 4:10). The thanksgiving ends with a reference to their eschatological hope, the day of Christ, when God's saving activity in them, begun in the past, will find its completion (v. 6).

1:7-8. Expression of personal affection. Paul's hope for the Philippians verbalized in v. 6 is grounded both in their sharing in God's grace (v. 7, here, ministry as in 1 Cor 3:10; Gal 2:9) and in Paul's deep affection for them (v. 8).

1:9-11. Petition. Paul asks for two things for the Philippians: (1) that their love *may overflow* with knowledge and full insight (1 Cor 12:8, 10) so that they may *determine what is best* (vv. 9-10a), and (2) that, at the day of Christ, they *may be pure and blameless, having produced the harvest of righteousness.* The petition, like the thanksgiving, ends on the note of eschatological hope, the day of Christ.

Body of the Letter, 1:12–4:20

The body of Philippians unfolds in a concentric pattern: A (1:12-26), B (1:27–2:16), C (2:17–3:1a), B' (3:1b–4:9), A' (4:10-20).

Paul's Rejoicing, 1:12-26

This section, A in the pattern, is held together by an INCLUSIO: *spread/progress* (προκοπήν) in v. 12 and v. 25. It consists of two units, vv. 12-18 and vv. 19-26, the first focused on Paul's rejoicing in the present, the second on his rejoicing in the future.

1:12-18. Paul's rejoicing in his present status. Being a prisoner and having heard that some preach out of bad motives does not keep Paul from rejoicing for two reasons: (1) because his imprisonment, rather than hurting the Christian cause, has advanced it among pagans (vv. 12-13; the *imperial guard* could refer to soldiers, members of the court, or officials of a government house, none of which were restricted to Rome) and Christians (v. 14); and (2) because even those seeking to afflict Paul advance the Christian cause (vv. 15-18; these opponents, whose message is acceptable but whose motives are questionable, are not those of 3:2-19, whose message is erroneous).

1:19-26. Paul's rejoicing in the future. Whether he dies as a martyr or is released from prison will not keep Paul from rejoicing for two reasons: (1) because if he dies as a martyr, Christ will be honored and he will be with Christ (vv. 19-23; cf. 2 Cor 5:8); and (2) because if he is released, it will mean *fruitful labor* for him and glory for Christ (vv. 22-26; cf. 2 Cor 5:9).

Paul's Exhortations, 1:27–2:16

This section, B in the pattern, consists of three paragraphs, 1:27-30, 2:1-13, and 2:14-16. The focus of the first is on the church's relation to the world while that of the second is on the community's inner life. The third offers general exhortations to round off the two prior paragraphs.

1:17-30. The church's relation to the world. Verse 27a is best translated: "Live, as citizens of heaven, worthily of the gospel of Christ." Just as the Philippians strove to live as citizens of Rome, worthily of their privilege in a Macedonian context, so the Philippian Christians, as citizens of heaven (3:20), are to live in line with their citizenship in this present evil age. Verses 27b-30 give two specific examples of what this means.

1:27b. Christian unity. To live in line with their heavenly citizenship in relation to the world means maintaining Christian unity. Military (*standing firm*) and athletic (*striving side by side*) metaphors describe the desired unity on behalf of *the faith of the gospel*. Paul calls for a new Macedonian phalanx and a new Olympic team of athletes to be formed, composed of Philippian Christians who manifest the same unity as successful military units and athletic teams do.

1:28a-30. Christian fearlessness. Living worthily of their heavenly citizenship means also fearlessness in the face of pagan hostility (v. 28a). Two bases for such fearlessness follow: (1) it is a sign to pagans of the ultimate outcome of history (v. 28b); and (2) not only faith in Christ but also suffering for Christ is a gift from God, as Paul's example shows (vv. 29-30; 1 Thes 2:2).

2:1-13. The community's inner life. This section is held together by an inclusio: the theme of vv. 1-2 echoed in v. 13. The section focuses on the inner life of the community. It is composed of three subsections, vv. 1-2, vv. 3-11, and vv. 12-13, each consisting of injunctions and their bases. All call for Christian unity.

2:1-2. Relate to one another as you are related to by God. Verse 1 offers four bases: "Since there is [1] *encouragement in Christ*, [2] *consolation from* God's *love*, [3] *sharing in the Spirit*, and [4] *compassion and sympathy* shown by God to us." The "if" clauses should be translated "if (and there is)" or "since." Verse 2 follows with four injunctions: (1) *be of the same mind*, (2) have *the same love*, (3) be *in full accord*, and (4) be *of one mind*. Relate to one another in a way that is consonant with the way God relates to you.

2:3-11. Relate to one another as Christ related to God. Verses 3-4 offer two injunctions: (1) *Do nothing from selfish ambition or conceit, but in humility regard others as better than yourselves*; and (2) *Let each of you look not to your own interests, but to the interests of others*. The problems Paul addresses were recognized by the philosopher Epictetus to be indigenous to the human condition. He said: "It is a general rule—be not deceived—that every living thing is to nothing so devoted as to its own interest" (*Discourse* 2.22.15).

The basis for these injunctions is in vv. 5-11. Verse 5 is missing a verb in the second half of the sentence. Translated literally, it reads: "Think this among yourselves, which also _____ in Christ Jesus." Different verbs may be supplied—either "was" or "think." This explains the difference in modern translations. If "think" is supplied, then the result is: "Let your bearing towards one another arise out of your life in Christ Jesus" (NEB). If "was" is supplied, then one finds: "The attitude you should have is the one that Christ Jesus had" (TEV). The RSV second edition reflects the former; the RSV third edition employs the latter. In terms of meaning, the former would mean, "Relate to one another as you relate to Christ" (i.e., with humility and submission); the latter, "Relate to one another as Christ related to God" (i.e., with humility). The former is an appeal to experience, the latter an appeal to tradition. The latter seems to fit the context better.

Verses 6-11 are almost universally regarded as an early Christian HYMN taken up and employed by Paul as the basis for his call to humility. The hymn divides into two parts, vv. 6-8 where Jesus is the subject of the action, and vv. 9-11 where God is the subject. In the first part, Jesus *humbles* himself, even to the point of death. In the second part, God exalts Jesus, giving him the name and position of Lord. Modern interpreters of the hymn disagree over whether vv. 6-8 refer to preexistence (v. 6), INCARNATION (v. 7), and death on the cross (v. 8), or only to Jesus' human existence as an antitype of Adam's experience in Gen 1–3: being in God's image (v. 6a; Gen 1:27); not trying to be like God (v. 6b; Gen 3:5); being obedient to God (vv. 7-8; Gen 2:16-17; 3:11). Either way, it is Jesus' humility that serves as the basis for the injunctions in vv. 3-4. Relate to one another as Jesus related to God, with humility.

2:12-13. Relate to one another, in obedience to Paul, as the God who indwells you enables you. In vv. 12-13 the two bases are split, v. 12a being the first, v. 13 the second. The injunction comes in v. 12b. It reads: *Work out your* [plural] *own salvation with fear and trembling*. This is not a call to personal salvation by works (Eph 2:8-9); the Philippians' salvation is assumed. Nor is it a call for individuals to grow spiritually (as in 3:12-15); it speaks rather about corporate wholeness. In Pauline thought, salvation involves not only individuals but also human community (Eph 4:1-16). Since groups as well as individuals sin, groups as well as individuals need to be delivered from sin. Moreover, groups as well as individuals need to grow spiritually. Here the community that has experienced God's saving power is asked to work out that initial deliverance from sin in all of the community's life. With a sense of seriousness, work out the implications of your corporate salvation in the many relationships of the community's life. The bases are two: (1) *For it is God who is at work in you* [plural], *enabling you* [plural] *both to will and to work for his good pleasure* (v. 13); and (2) *just as you have always obeyed me, not only in my presence, but much more now in my absence* (v. 12a).

2:14-16. General exhortations. Having exhorted the Philippians to right relations with the world (1:27-30) and proper relations within the community (2:1-13), Paul ends this section with the general exhortation *Do all things without murmuring and arguing*, that is, with cheerful obedience (v. 14; cf. 1 Cor 10:1-12; Exod 14:12; Num 16:41, 49). Two reasons for such behavior follow: (1) it benefits the world (vv. 15b; cf. Matt 5:14-16), and (2) it will benefit the Philippians (vv. 15a, 16a) and Paul (v. 16b).

Paul's Plans: Travelogue, 2:17–3:1a

Just as in 1 Cor 4:17-19 and 2 Cor 8:16-19, information about the travel plans of Paul and his coworkers appears in the middle rather than at the end of the letter (Rom 15:14-29). This paragraph functions as C, the centerpoint, in the concentric pattern of the letter's body. It consists of three parts: (1) about TIMOTHY (vv. 19-23), (2) about PAUL (v. 24), and (3) about EPAPHRODITUS (vv. 25-30). It is held together by an inclusio: "rejoicing" in 2:17-18, echoed in 3:1a.

2:19-23. Hope plus commendation. Paul hopes to send Timothy to see the Philippians soon to gather news about them. He will send Timothy because there is no one like him *who will be genuinely concerned* for their welfare. Others *are seeking their own interests* (2:4). Paul will send his best.

2:24. Paul's hopes for himself. In 1:24-25 Paul concluded that, since his remaining in the flesh was better for the Philippians, he expected to live and be released from prison. Here, in v. 24, he voices his *trust in the Lord that I will also come soon.* If he is to be released, it will be not because he wishes it but because God enables it.

2:25-30. Decision plus commendation. When the Philippians sent their latest gift to Paul (4:10), they not only sent it by Epaphroditus, but sent Epaphroditus himself to stay with Paul and assist him in his ministry while the apostle was in prison (vv. 25, 30). Epaphroditus became ill and nearly died (vv. 27, 30). Even though he survived, he became emotionally distraught, longing for home (v. 26). Paul, therefore, determined to send him back to Philippi. Lest the Philippians be unhappy with him on his return for not finishing his mission, Paul commends him for his labors and asks that he be welcomed and honored (v. 29).

Paul's Exhortations, 3:1b–4:9

This section is B' in the letter body's pattern, corresponding to Paul's exhortations in 1:27–2:16. The section begins with an introduction, 3:1b, and ends with a conclusion, 4:9. In between are two panels, each with three parts. Panel One appeals to apostolic example against error and consists of 3:2-11, 3:12-15, and 3:16–4:1. Panel Two utilizes apostolic teaching for the church's benefit and consists of 4:2-3, 4:4-7, and 4:8.

3:2–4:1. Panel one: apostolic example. In this segment of text Paul uses his own example to argue against three distortions of religious existence: legalism (vv. 2-11), perfectionism (vv. 12-15), and libertine behavior (3:16–4:1). Debate rages about whether these three issues reflect one, two, or three groups of opponents. Issues one and two could be explained by opponents who were either Jews or Jewish Christians. Issue three, if representative of the same group as one and two, requires a legalistic, perfectionistic, libertine opposition, perhaps Jewish-Christian GNOSTICISM. Unanimity reigns only on the conclusion that the opponents of chap. 3 are not the same as those of 1:15-18. In 1:15-18 Paul expressed reservations about his opponents' motives, not their message. In chap. 3 Paul defends against a wrong message.

3:2-11. Against legalism. A warning is issued, using terms of disparagement for the opponents: *dogs* (Rev 22:15; Matt 15:21-28), *evil workers* (Rom 2:17-

24), *those who mutilate the flesh* (Rom 2:25-29). Christians are the true *circumcision* (Col 2:11). Paul then uses his own situation as a paradigm. He has every reason for confidence in the flesh—to trust human achievement to gain God's approval. A list of seven Jewish virtues is given (vv. 5-6), beginning with *circumcised on the eighth day* (Lev 12:3) and ending with *as to righteousness under the law, blameless.* Yet he regarded (perfect tense) them all as loss because of Christ (v. 7) and regards (present tense) everything as loss *because of the surpassing value of knowing Christ Jesus my Lord* (v. 8).

Paul's motivation for considering all things as rubbish is threefold : (1) *in order that I may gain Christ* (v. 8c; cf. Matt 13:44-45); (2) *in order that I may . . . be found in him* (Gal 3:27; Eph 4:24) with a righteousness not from law but from either the faith of Christ or faith in Christ (v. 9; Rom 3:21-22; 10:1-13; Gal 2:15-16); and (3) *I want to know Christ and the power of his resurrection and the sharing of his suffering by becoming like him in his death* (2:8; cf. Rom 6:5, 10), *if somehow I may attain the resurrection from the dead* (vv. 10-11; cf. Rom 6:8; 8:17). These three reasons are different aspects of the same reality—trusting Christ for one's relation with God instead of reliance on one's own achievements. Legalism, reliance on one's own productivity and achievements to gain a relation to God, is ruled out of order for the Philippians by Paul's example.

3:12-15. Against perfectionism. *Not that I have already obtained this or have already reached the goal* (v. 12). Paul claims to have experienced neither complete victory over sin nor the resurrection from the dead, as some perfectionists in the early church did (sinlessness—1 John 1:8; resurrection—2 Tim 2:18). Rather, like a long-distance runner, he presses on towards the goal (v. 14; cf. Eph 4:12-13; Heb 12:1-2). In Pauline thought, SALVATION involves three tenses: past ("We were saved"—Rom 8:24); present ("We are being saved"—1 Cor 15:2); and future ("We shall be saved"—Rom 5:9). It is inappropriate, then, to claim in the present what only belongs to the future. The paragraph concludes with the exhortation: *Let those of us then who are mature be of the same mind* (v. 15). Paul's example is again appealed to, this time against perfectionism.

3:16–4:1. Against libertine behavior. This unit is held together by an inclusio: 3:16, *Only let us hold fast to what we have attained,* and 4:1, *Stand firm in the Lord in this way.* Verse 17 begins with an explicit appeal to the Pauline example. *Brothers and sisters, join in imitating me, and observe those who live according to the example you have in us* (1 Cor 4:16; 11:1; 1 Thes 1:6; 2 Thes 3:7, 9). On the mission field, new converts need an embodied gospel. The apostle offers them himself and those who follow his example. Unlike those who make their belly their god (cf. Rom 16:18), with their minds set on earthly things (v. 19; 1 Cor 6:12-20), Christians are citizens of heaven whose bodies will be transformed at the PAROUSIA to be like their Savior's glorious body (3:20-21; 1 Cor 6:14). This eschatological hope is the basis for Christians' standing firm in the Lord (4:1). Paul's point here is captured by the early Christian author of the *Epistle to Diognetus*:

> For the distinction between Christians and other men is neither in country nor language nor customs. For they do not dwell in cities in some place of their own, nor do they use any strange variety of dialect, nor practice an extraordinary kind of life. . . . Yet while living in Greek and barbarian cities . . . following the local customs . . . they show forth the wonderful and confessedly strange character of the constitution of their own citizenship. They dwell in their own fatherlands, but as if sojourners in them; they share all things as citizens, and suffer all things as strangers. Every foreign land is their fatherland, and every fatherland is a foreign country. . . . They pass their time upon the earth, but they have their citizenship in heaven (5:1-2, 4-5, 9; Lake 1970, 2:358–61).

Throughout the section, 3:2–4:1, Paul's example has been held up as a norm for the readers. "Keep your eye on the goal if you can see it. If not, keep your eye on one who knows the way to the goal and who is going there" (Robertson 1917, 118).

4:2-9. Panel two: apostolic instruction. In this segment of text Paul deals with three topics: (1) a specific need for Christian unity in the Philippian church (vv. 2-3); (2) the call for perpetual joy (vv. 4-7); and (3) an appeal to meditation on what is noblest and best (v. 8).

4:2-3. Christian unity. Two women in the Philippian church, Euodia and Syntyche, are urged to be of the same mind (1:27; 2:2; 3:15). An unnamed loyal companion, an individual, or perhaps the church as a whole, is urged to help the women agree (v. 3). They are worth the effort because they have *struggled beside me in the work of the gospel, together with Clement*

and the rest of my coworkers (v. 3). Paul here makes no gender distinctions in ministry (cf. Rom 16:1-2, 7), just as he makes none in church membership (Gal 3:27-28).

4:4-7. Perpetual joy. The apostle asks for perpetual joy: *go on rejoicing in the Lord always* (v. 4). What follows are two injunctions and two promises.
Injunction: *Let your gentleness be known to everyone* (4:5a)
Promise: *The Lord is near* (4:5b).
Injunction: *Do not worry about anything, but in everything by prayer and supplication with thanksgiving let your requests be made known to God* (4:6).
Promise: *And the peace of God . . . will guard your hearts and your minds in Christ Jesus* (4:7).
"If anything is big enough to worry about, it is not too small to pray about" (Baille 1962, 47). Neither the hostility of others nor adverse circumstances need interrupt Christians' joy because of the resources provided by God: his nearness (either spatially, Ps 34:18, or temporally, 1 Thes 4:17; 1 Cor 15:52), his answers to prayer (cf. Ps 84:11; Jas 4:2; Matt 7:7), and his peace (cf. John 14:27).

4:8-9. Meditation on what is noblest and best. Just as the ancient Jew meditated on God, his acts and his precepts (Josh 1:8; Ps 1:2; 63:6; 77:12; 119:23, 48, 78, 97, 99, 148; 143:5), so the Christians are to think about things that are uplifting and ennobling. *Whatever is true, whatever is honorable, whatever is just, whatever is pure, whatever is pleasing, whatever is commendable, if there is any excellence* [and there is], *and if there is anything worthy of praise* [and there is], *think about these things*. The entire section of exhortations, 3:1b–4:9, ends with a generalizing command and a promise:
Command: *Keep on doing the things that you have learned and received and heard and seen in me* (4:9a; cf. 3:17)
Promise: *and the God of peace will be with you* (4:9b). The apostle's concern is that his converts live according to what he taught and modelled. In this respect Paul mirrored the views of the philosophical schools of his time. The philosopher's word alone, unaccompanied by the act, was regarded as invalid and untrustworthy (Chrysostom, *Discourse* 70.6). Being a disciple meant imitating a teacher's acts and words so as to become like him (*Discourse* 55.4-5). "Plato, Aristotle, and the whole company of sages . . . derived more benefit from the character than from the words of Socrates" (Seneca, *Epistle* 6:5-6). Paul's appeal both

to his words and to his deeds would have been what the Philippians expected from their apostle.

Paul's Rejoicing, 4:10-20

This section is A' in the body's pattern, corresponding to 1:12-26. It falls into two parallel panels (vv. 10-14 and 15-18) in which a rejoicing Paul (v. 10) thanks the Philippians for their gifts to meet his need, past (vv. 15-18) and present (vv. 10-14). The section concludes with a promise (v. 19) and a doxology (v. 20).

4:10-14. Panel one: present generosity. This panel is organized in terms of basically the same three components that will be found in panel two: (1) thank you, (2) but, (3) nevertheless.

4:10. Statement of the Philippians' act of generosity in the present. Now that an opportunity has presented itself for the Philippian church to give Paul material assistance again, they have done so. Paul rejoices in their concern for him.

4:11-13. Not that (oủx ὅτι) Paul speaks out of great want. He has learned *to be content* (αὐτάρκης) *with whatever I have* (v. 11). He knows how to deal both with plenty and with deprivation (v. 12). The Greek term translated *content* was widely used in Stoic circles to refer to a state of being independent of external circumstances. Epictetus, for example, praised Agrippinus, a distinguished Roman Stoic of the mid-first century C.E. because: "His character was such . . . that when any hardship befell him he would compose a eulogy upon it; on fever, if he had a fever; on disrepute, if he suffered from disrepute; on exile, if he went into exile" (*Fragment* 21). The Stoic discovered within himself the resources to allow contentment no matter what situation might arise. For Paul the resources came from his relation to Christ. Verse 13 might better be translated: "I have the strength for everything (poverty or plenty) in union with the one who infuses me with power" (cf. 2 Cor 12:9-10; Col 1:29). Paul's independence of circumstances came through his dependence on the Lord (cf. Heb 13:5-6).

4:14. Nevertheless the Philippians did well in sharing in Paul's distress. Even though he could have done without their gift, yet Paul affirms their care and concern shown for him by their contribution.

4:15-18. Panel two: past generosity. Three similar components to those in vv. 10-14 make up the second panel, vv. 15-18.

4:15-16. Statement of the Philippians' acts of generosity on two or more occasions in the past. Although Paul refused to allow the Corinthian church

to give him money in order to avoid any charges of self-interest on his part (1 Cor 9:3-18; 2 Cor 12:13), he accepted aid from the Philippian church more than once prior to the present gift.

4:17. Not that (oủx ὅτι) Paul seeks the gift in and for itself. Paul does not want his acknowledgment of the Philippians' past generosity to be interpreted as his desire for more from them. It is what they gain by it that he seeks (cf. 2 Cor 8:1-5).

4:18. A pleasing sacrifice.. Commercial language used in v. 18a indicates that this part of the letter is Paul's receipt for the Philippians' gift (*paid in full*). Sacrificial language in v. 18b points to their gifts as their participation in the Christian liturgy of life (2:17; Rom 12:1-2).

4:19-20. A promise and a doxology. The conclusion to the two panels, 4:10-14 and 15-18, comes in the form of a promise and a doxology.

4:19. A promise. Verse 19 is a promise or a petition depending upon which textual variant is chosen for the main verb: *my God will fully satisfy every need* (future tense) or "may my God fully satisfy your every need" (aorist optative). The NRSV reflects the better textual alternative. Paul speaks as a prophetic figure, certain that God will act in a certain way because of who he is. *My God will fully satisfy every need of yours.* What follows is better rendered: "in a glorious manner in Christ Jesus." (Hawthorne 1983, 208). As in 2 Cor 9:6-11, Paul believes God gives prosperity to his children to enable their generosity.

4:20: A doxology. *To our God and Father be glory forever and ever. Amen.* For similar doxologies to end a letter, compare Rom 16:25-27; 2 Pet 3:18b; Jude 24–25. The letter ends (v. 20) as it began (1:2) with a reference to God the Father.

Conclusion, 4:21-23

The conclusion to a Pauline letter often contained one or more of the following: a peace wish, greetings, reference to the holy kiss, a grace or benediction. Two of these components are found here: greetings (vv. 21-22) and a grace (v. 23). *Caesar's household* refers to that body of officials and servants involved in imperial administration. They would be found in most of the great cities of the empire, for example, Rome and Ephesus. That the saints of Caesar's household greet you (v. 22) indicates how far the gospel had penetrated Roman society. Without Paul's imprisonment (1:12-13), would this have happened?

Works Cited

Baille, John. 1962. *Christian Devotion.*

Garland, D. 1985. "The Composition and Literary Unity of Philippians: some Neglected Factors," *NovT.*

Hawthorne, G. F. 1983. *Philippians.* WBC 43.

Koester, Helmut. 1962. "Philippians, Letter to the." IDBsup.

Kurz, W. S. 1985. "Imitation of Paul and of Christ in Philippians," in *Discipleship in the New Testament.*

Lake, Kirsopp. 1970. *The Apostolic Fathers.*

Michael, J. H. 1928. *The Epistle of Paul to the Philippians.* MNTC.

Robertson, A. T. 1917. *Paul's Joy in Christ: Studies in Philippians.*

Soards, M. 1990. "Paul." MDB.

Watson, D. 1988. "A Rhetorical Analysis of Philippians and Its Implications for the Unity Question," *NovT.*

Colossians

Frank Stagg

Introduction

Colossians is a creative response to heresy. Instead of merely condemning it, PAUL exposed its fallacies and countered with a fresh statement of the Christian calling. Paul clarified his own theology and the moral and ethical practice it implied as he met what apparently was a strange new syncretism of pagan, Jewish, and Christian thought and practice.

Authorship

Whether Colossians is from Paul or his followers is debated. Arguments relate to style, word usage, and theology as compared with the undisputed letters of Paul. Variances are real, but theories accounting for them are not compelling. Extensive use of traditional materials (hymnic, paraenetic, domestic codes) plus Paul's dependence upon scribal help (cf. Rom 16:22) may account for the variants (Cannon 1983, chaps. 2–4). Seeming linkage with Philemon (probably the letter out of LAODICEA, 4:16) argues for Paul as author.

Time and Place

Paul's many imprisonments (2 Cor 11:23), leave uncertain the place from which he wrote Colossians. Options generally considered are ROME, CAESAREA, and EPHESUS. Evidence is not compelling for any one of these. Fortunately, this does not vitally affect interpretation. Date is tied to place; mid-fifties to early sixties, if written from Caesarea or Rome.

Occasion and Purpose

The threat at COLOSSAE was for Paul a *philosophy and empty deceit* (2:8), falsifying the nature of Christ, human nature, and the world, with dire implications for faith, worship, and practice. It subordinated Christ to a hierarchy of spiritual beings, teaching the worship of angels, ascetic disciplines, and bondage to a religious calendar. Paul contended for the all-sufficiency of Christ, the fullness of God embodied, creator, redeemer, and sustainer.

The heresy behind Colossians can be identified only as reflected in the letter. It had strong affinities with what appeared later as GNOSTICISM, with a mixture of pagan, Jewish, and Christian elements. It assumed a DUALISM of spirit and matter, the former good and the latter worthless or evil. This low view of matter could lead to rigid ASCETICISM or permissiveness. Such dualism posed the problem of how an evil creation could come from the goodness of spirit. The gap was bridged by a theory of a series of aeons or emanations called the pleroma or "fullness," issuing from God and ending with a demiurge (worker) as agent in creation.

The church in Colossae seemingly was founded out of a pagan past (1:21, 27; 2:13) by EPAPHRAS (1:7f.; 4:12f.), as yet not visited by Paul (1:4, 7-9; 2:1). Paul's appeal is that they continue in the tradition already received, that represented by the Christian hymn quoted in 1:15-20.

For Further Study

In the *Mercer Dictionary of the Bible*: CHRISTOLOGY; COLOSSAE; COLOSSIANS, LETTER TO THE; DUALISM; EPISTLE/LETTER; GNOSTICISM; PAUL; PRISON EPISTLES; SALVATION IN THE NT; WOMEN IN THE NT.

In other sources: G. E. Cannon, *The Use of Traditional Materials in Colossians*; E. Lohse, *Colossians and Philemon*, Herm; R. P. Martin, *Colossians: The Church's Lord and the Christian's Liberty*; R. McL. Wilson, *Gnosis and the New Testament*.

Commentary

An Outline

Salutation, 1:1-2

Paul alone in Colossians appears as an *apostle*. It was under this authority that Paul warned his readers against new traditions that threatened the authentic faith of the church, which had been proclaimed by Paul's *beloved fellow servant* Epaphras (v. 7).

TIMOTHY alone is associated with Paul in the salutation, though eight others are named later. Possibly Timothy served as scribe, even sharing in the composition, Paul taking the pen only at 4:18.

Grace . . . and peace was a familiar Christian greeting, modeled on current usage but changing the Greek "greeting" (*charein*) to grace (*charis*). *Peace*, like the Hebrew *shalom*, is well-being under the rule of God.

Thanksgiving and Prayer, 1:3-14

1:3-8. Faith, love, hope. This triad, in this order, appears in 1 Thes 1:3 and 5:8, possibly Paul's first letter. To Paul faith was primarily trust. Love (*agape*) is a disposition to relate to others for their good, whatever the cost to self, with no self-serving motive (1 Cor 13:5). *Hope* is eschatological, *laid up for you in heaven* (v. 5; see also 1:27). It sustains and gives meaning to life, overcoming the futility of fate in angel worship.

From Epaphras they had received *the word of the truth, the gospel* (v. 5) and had *truly comprehended the grace of God* (v. 6). The *truth* they received should not be lost to some new tradition presented as *philosophy* (2:8). The gospel derives from *the grace of God*, excluding the need for alleged merits like ascetic practice, angel worship, or worldly regulations (2:6-23).

Paul sees the gospel validated through its worldwide acceptance (not provincial) and its fruitbearing (v. 6; see Gal 5:22-23). It yields a new quality of life (see Matt 7:16-20).

1:9-14. Wisdom and fruitful lives. Along with Paul's confidence in the Colossians is concern that they be *filled with the knowledge* (*epignosin*) *of God's will in all spiritual wisdom and understanding* (v. 9). Paul's *epignosis* (thorough knowledge) may be his answer to the *gnosis* (knowledge) sought by the Gnostics, their claim to a higher revealed knowledge of their origin and destiny. Paul stands in the Hebrew tradition of *knowledge* as acquaintance with God (v. 10). Such saving knowledge includes a knowledge of God's will, validated by obedience and fruit, the resulting quality of life. This is not human achievement but the working of God's *glorious power* (v. 11).

The community of the DEAD SEA SCROLLS saw themselves as "the sons of light," as did the later Gnostics; but Paul sees all God's people as children of light. Like a new Exodus, God has *rescued us from the power of darkness and transferred us into the kingdom of his beloved Son* (v. 13). *Redemption* is not paying off God. It is God's act of liberation (*apolytrosis*) by *the forgiveness of sins* (v. 14).

Preeminence of Christ, 1:15-23

1:15-17. Creator of the universe. An early Christian hymn may be preserved in vv. 15-20, even though there is no agreement as to its extent or structure, whether in two strophes or more. Christ is seen as creator of all that is (vv. 15-17), head of the church (vv. 18-20), and redeemer and sustainer of his people (vv. 21-23).

Christ is *the image* [*eikon*] *of the invisible God* (v. 15). When we see him, we see "the Father" (John 14:9). "Jesus" means "YHWH Savior," and as "Emmanuel" he is "God with us" (Matt 1:21, 23). New Testament writers would never have said that Jesus is "the second person of the trinity," for this says too little and implies division in deity.

That Christ is *the firstborn of all creation* must be harmonized with the claim that he is *before all things* (v. 17). *Firstborn* (*prototokos*) indicates not time but primogeniture, the rights of the firstborn.

That *in him all things in heaven and on earth were created* (v. 16) counters the claim that created matter is worthless or evil. It reflects the idea that people are ruled by a hierarchy of spiritual beings, called *thrones or dominions or rulers or powers* (v. 16). Ancient people thought the stars were inhabited by angels or demons and that these determined human fate ("disaster" implies that a star is against us). Christ is creator, but he is not created. He is *before all things* and the power holding together all things (v. 17).

1:18-20. Head of the church. Paul made much of the CHURCH as the body of Christ (1 Cor 12:12-30; Rom 12:1-8; Eph 1:22-23). Against the threat at Colossae, he changed the focus to Christ as the head of this body. He is *the beginning* (*archē*), understood absolutely as in John 1:1 or as the originator of the church. He also is *the firstborn* [*prototokos*] *from the dead*. As in v. 15, *prototokos* means primogeniture, rights over creation (v. 18).

That all the *fullness* (*pleroma*) *of God* dwells in Christ (v. 19) strikes at the heart of the Colossian heresy. *Pleroma* was a term for all the spiritual beings (æons or emanations) supposedly between God and the universe, bridging the gap between spirit and matter. For Paul there is no gap, for in Christ is the fullness of deity, and he is the creator (cf. 2:9).

The "fullness of deity" was pleased not only to dwell in Christ but also *to reconcile to himself all things* (v. 20). Creator and redeemer are the same, and redemption includes all creation (cf. Rom 8:19-23). Rejected is the gnostic idea that spirit and matter are by nature antithetical. Estrangement is moral, and Christ brings about reconciliation by moral means, *making peace through the blood of his cross*. Language here is to be taken seriously, not literally. The cross as timber has no blood, but RECONCILIATION comes through the self-giving of Christ, ultimately in giving his life on the cross. Christ's death becomes effective in our salvation not as an external transaction but only as we are crucified with him (cf. Gal 2:19-21; Rom 6:5-11).

1:21-23. Redeemer and Preserver. The Colossians probably were gentiles (1:27), alienated from God and with a mind-set hostile to God, reflected in their evil works. That was "once," but "now" they have been reconciled to God. God in Christ is the agent in reconciliation, not the problem. Reconciliation has to do with relationship, but salvation in its fuller dimensions intends a new quality of life, holy and blameless and irreproachable. Salvation is not God's unilateral action: it requires the faith that endures (v. 23).

Paul's Apostolic Ministry, 1:24–2:7

1:24-25. The sufferings of Christ. It is a bold claim, yet Paul declared that in his ministry he completed things lacking in the sufferings of Christ. He did so as a part of Christ's *body, that is, the church*. The human

body was a primary model for the church to Paul (see 1 Cor 12:12-26; Rom 12:5), one body comprised of many members. Not only does Christ suffer for the church, but it suffers for him. What is done to the church is done to Christ (see Matt 25:40, 45; Acts 9:4). Paul's sufferings included "chains" and more (4:18; 2 Cor 11:23-29).

1:26-29. God's open secret. The *mystery* long hidden but now revealed is summed up as *Christ in you*. As apostle to the gentiles, Paul gave himself to both Jews and gentiles, all alike in sin and called to a new relationship and quality of life in Christ. "You" is plural in v. 27, *Christ in you* all! This eternal purpose of God, overcoming the estrangement between Jews and gentiles as well as that between Jew and gentile and himself, is the revealed *mystery* (Eph 3:9) as well as *the hope of glory*. Life together in Christ is a glorious hope and the only hope offered us by the God of glory.

2:1-7. Faithfulness to heritage. The concern of this unit is that those at Colossae and Laodicea hold fast to the *treasures of wisdom and knowledge* which already they have in Christ, not letting anyone *deceive* them with *plausible arguments*, that is, the art of persuasion. The heresy threatening them made bold claims to something superior, but it was in fact inferior, false, and empty. Although Paul warns his readers of this subtle threat, he affirms them for their *morale and . . . firmness* and encourages them to remain true to their heritage of faith. Here and throughout Colossians, the basic theme is the all-sufficiency of Christ. They need only to hold to and cultivate what already they have been taught.

Warnings against Entrapments, 2:8-23

This unit is the heart of Colossians, exposing the nature of the threatening heresy and pointing to Christ as the *fullness of deity* (v. 9) and as providing for our *fullness in him* (v. 10).

2:8. Captured by human traditions. Paul uses a rare word (*sulagogein*) for capturing and taking booty. This implies the self-serving motive of those who seek to entrap others as well as the fraud suffered by the victims of *human tradition* posing as *philosophy* but in fact only *empty deceit*. Paul's term for this fallacy is *the elemental spirits of the universe*. "Elements" (*stoicheia*) was a term used variously, including what were thought to be the elements of the cosmos (earth, fire, water, air) and the stars thought to be composed of these elements. The stars were thought to be inhabited by angels who controlled the universe and the fates (dis-aster) of humans.

2:9-10. The fullness of deity. Paul takes the gnostic *pleroma (fullness)* and applies it to Christ. In him *the whole fullness of deity dwells bodily.* The KJV "Godhead" intended what we mean by "godhood" (NRSV *deity*), but it mistakenly came to stand for "persons of the godhead." The NT knows only one God, and the fullness of deity came bodily into the world in Christ (John 1:1, 14).

Fullness also is offered us in Christ. Salvation is seen as becoming fully human: nothing more, nothing less, and nothing other. Christ, who is above *every ruler and authority,* is our sufficiency for our own fulfillment as human beings.

2:11-15. The old and the new. "A circumcision made without hands" (RSV) is the inward "circumcision" of the heart (Rom 2:29). Just as in literal CIRCUMCISION some flesh is removed, so there is *the circumcision of Christ* (i.e., made by Christ) that removes *the body of the flesh* (i.e., sinful nature). Literal circumcision serves here as a paradigm for the cleansing that comes under the lordship of Christ.

Literal BAPTISM also serves as a paradigm for what could be called "a baptism not made with hands." Literal baptism is no more saving than literal circumcision, but each dramatizes something that is saving. "Fullness of life" comes not by religious rites but by the very power that raised Christ from the dead.

New life comes when God forgives us all our trespasses. We are freed from all legalism, whether the cultic laws of Judaism or regulations imposed by *rulers and authorities.* Christ has set aside the record against us with its *legal demands . . . nailing it to the cross* (v. 14). In Christ we are free from the tyranny of rules and from "rulers and authorities" themselves.

2:16-19. Food laws and calendars. God alone is our ultimate judge (1 Cor 4:1-5), and we are judged by his requirements, not those of other people. The Colossians are not to let Gnostics or others judge them by food laws or religious calendars (v. 16). Jesus freed us from calendars (Mark 2:27-28) and kosher laws (Mark 7:15, 19). Such arbitrary rules are but a *shadow.* Christ is the *substance.*

The imperative in v. 18, *Do not let anyone disqualify you,* could be rendered, "do not let anyone award you a prize unjustly." Paul's opponents offer the prize for those who qualify by *self-abasement and worship of angels* instead of *holding fast to the head,* that is, Christ. Such is an empty prize. The true prize is

growth that is from God, attained only as the body of Christ holds fast to the head.

Dwelling on visions translates difficult syntax. This may be a quotation from the mystery religions, including the Greek *embateuon* ("setting foot upon"; NRSV *dwelling on*), a term used for entering a sanctuary in initiation rites where *visions* were sought (Lohse 1971, 118–20). Paul warns against such *visions* as displacing what God has done in Christ.

2:20-23. Impotence of rules. Since *the elemental spirits of the universe* are but human creations, why be subservient to their rules? We belong not to *the world* but to Christ.

Rules like *Do not handle, Do not taste, Do not touch* relate only to such things as perishable food, not to lasting significance. They are merely human rules. They may have the appearance of wisdom as they impose devotion, self-abasement, and ascetic practice, but they are powerless to check *self-indulgence.*

Moral and Ethical Admonitions, 3:1–4:1

3:1-4. Heavenly vs. earthly claims. That Christians *have been raised with Christ* means that they are under the claim of heaven, the world *above, where Christ is, seated at the right hand of God,* the place of honor and power. Although they have *died* and *been raised,* Christians yet live *on earth,* caught between two claims, those from above taking precedence.

We are to live now a life suited to heaven, not to get there but because already we belong there in Christ. The life above is assured by Christ's present enthronement and by his promised return in glory. Life on earth for those in Christ may have the appearance of dishonor and defeat (e.g., Paul's *chains* [4:18]), but its true honor will be revealed eschatologically when Christ is revealed in his glory.

3:5-11. What to put off. Five *earthly* sins are listed, four as sexual abuses: *fornication, impurity, passion, evil desire.* The fifth is more deadly: *greed (which is idolatry).* The material as such is not evil; it is God's creation. It is materialism that is evil. When it owns us, it becomes a god and we idolaters. The *wrath of God* (v. 6) coming upon this is the outworking of God's moral law (Rom 1:18-32). It is reaping what we sow (Gal 6:7-8).

A second list of five *earthly* things are antisocial vices: *anger, wrath, malice, slander, and abusive language.* Anger in itself is not the problem; it is what we do with it or let it do with us. *Wrath* here is anger become chronic. Malice, slander, and abusive language intend harm to others. In the new life, worldly distinctions are transcended, for in Christ *there is no longer Greek and Jew, circumcised and uncircumcised, barbarian, Scythian, slave and free. Greek* stands for gentile. *Scythian* was a term for that ethnic group as more savage than *barbarian*, a questionable stereotype. This enlarges upon Gal 3:28 but significantly drops "no longer male and female" (see 3:18-19).

3:12-17. What to put on. Five virtues to put on displace the evils to put off. These have to do with conduct serving others, unlike the self-serving vices. Forbearance (RSV) or bearing with one another (NRSV) is holding back from one another when tempted to retaliate. Unlike indulgence, forgiveness is creative. It seeks to free from sin as well as restore relationships.

The main adornment for *God's chosen ones* (God chooses us first) is *love*. This fruit of the Spirit (Gal 5:22), abiding and greatest gift of Cod's grace (1 Cor 13), *binds everything together in perfect harmony*.

The peace of Christ is not the world's "peace" (John 14:27). Augustus Caesar boasted of *Pax Romana*, but the peace of Rome was imposed by military might. *Pax Christi* is inner peace, attained by the cross, not by the sword.

The *word of Christ* is to dwell in each Christian, and all are to *teach and admonish one another in all wisdom*. Nothing here excludes women or laypersons from teaching or admonishing. *Psalms, hymns, and spiritual songs* imply the full range of songs to God, not precise distinctions.

3:18–4:1. Domestic relationships. This is the first appearance in the NT of an early domestic code (also in Eph 5:22–6:9; 1 Tim 2:8-15; 6:1-2; Titus:1-10; 1 Pet 2:13–3:7; see Stagg and Stagg 1978, 187–204).

Wives, be subject to your husbands mistranslates the middle imperative *hypotassesthe*. The text reads, "Wives, subject yourselves." This at least recognizes the right of a wife to order her own life *as is fitting in the Lord*. From the NT as a whole, more is to be said. Codes are historically conditioned, never final or complete. Husbands are to love their wives and not mistreat them; but silence here does not imply that wives are not to love their husbands or may mistreat them.

The code for children and parents rightly implies that parental responsibility requires the child's obedience; but when the code is absolutized, problems arise. The code here does not cover the problems of child abuse, a modern scandal.

Slaves are to give a quality of service that is a credit to them and to Christ, not for self-serving purposes or because the master deserves it. Masters themselves are reminded that they must answer to the master in heaven (see PHILEMON, LETTER TO for another approach to slavery).

Closing Appeals and Greetings, 4:2-18

4:2-4. Prayer. Paul's prayer request was not that the doors of his prison be opened for his release but that *a door for the word* be opened, that he might *declare the mystery of Christ*, the very gospel for which he was in prison. Paul was not imprisoned for preaching Jesus as the Christ, for others did that without arrest. It was because he preached that "in Christ" there was no Jew and Greek that he was evicted from synagogues and Temple and imprisoned. If given an open door, he would preach *clearly* the very gospel for which he suffered chains.

4:5-6. Outsiders. The Colossians are urged to conduct themselves wisely toward outsiders and to make their speech gracious, *seasoned with salt*, appealing as well as informed and honest.

4:7-17. Colleagues. *Tychicus* seemingly was the bearer of the letter, commissioned to add his report to the letter. *Onesimus* is doubtless the runaway slave of Philemon. Once estranged from *Mark* (Acts 15:37-40), Paul now warmly commends him. *Aristarchus, Mark,* and *Jesus Justus* are the only Jews now with Paul, a price paid for his gospel of no distinction between Jew and gentile in Christ. This letter and one *from Laodicea* (probably Philemon) are to be exchanged, with *Archippus* charged to "fulfil the ministry" (RSV) already given him, possibly the release of Onesimus (Knox 1959, chap. 3).

4:18. Paul's autograph. Paul now takes the pen for his autograph. Remembering his *chains*, they should also remember the *mystery of Christ* (4:3) for which he was in chains.

Works Cited

Cannon, George E. 1983. *The Use of Traditional Materials in Colossians.*

Knox, John. 1959. *Philemon among the Letters of Paul.*

Lohse, Eduard. 1971. *Colossians and Philemon.*

Stagg, Evelyn, and Frank Stagg. 1978. *Woman in the World of Jesus.*

Wilson, R. McL. 1968. *Gnosis and the New Testament.*

First Thessalonians

Linda McKinnish Bridges

Introduction

First Thessalonians deserves careful reading. Dwarfed by the giant literary shadows of Romans, Galatians, and the Corinthian letters, 1 Thessalonians has often been overlooked by Pauline scholars. Yet, this small but significant letter offers the reader an opportunity to explore an early sample of Christian literature (certainly the earliest in our CANON), to hear the burning theological and ethical issues of a young, inexperienced Christian community in THESSALONICA, and to see the passion and tender care given to them by their extraordinary leader, the apostle PAUL.

The Writer

That Paul wrote 1 Thessalonians is not contested. The literary style, vocabulary usage, and parallels in Acts point to Paul as the author. *When* he wrote the letter, however, is much more difficult to establish.

Some scholars date the letter around 40 C.E. (Luedemann 1984; Donfried 1985; Richard 1990; Jewett 1986), while others situate the writing around 50 C.E. (Koester 1982; Malherbe 1983, 1987). The reason for lack of consensus is that a detailed itinerary of Paul's missionary activity is impossible to reconstruct from either Luke's story of Paul in MACEDONIA (Acts 17–18) or Paul's own letter to the church in Thessalonica. Neither writer wrote for the sole purpose of relating travel itineraries; therefore, exact dates are conjectures, at best.

Just as the exact date of the writing is difficult to determine, so is the precise setting and surrounding circumstances. Not only are Luke's and Paul's accounts sketchy, sometimes they do not agree. The reader, therefore, must be familiar with both accounts in order to establish background information for the Thessalonian letter.

The Acts Account. How did Paul arrive in Thessalonica? According to the Acts account, Paul was imprisoned in PHILIPPI at the beginning of the mission to Europe (Acts 16:19-24). Paul, along with SILAS and TIMOTHY, then left Philippi, traveled through AMPHIPOLIS and Appolonia and then arrived in Thessalonica. When they arrived, Paul went into the synagogue, as was his custom, and proclaimed Jesus as Messiah (17:3).

How long did Paul stay? Paul stayed in Thessalonica for three Sabbaths (three weeks). As a result, some Jews, a number of gentiles, and many women were converted. Their success angered the Jews, however, and a hostile crowd attacked the home of a new convert, Jason. Jason and other believers were dragged to the city magistrate. Paul, although not present, was charged with treason (17:7). Paul and his colleagues secretly left Thessalonica by night. They traveled to Beroea, where the Thessalonican Jews continued to agitate the crowds. Silas and Timothy remained in Beroea, and Paul went on to ATHENS alone.

When did Paul write the letter? Acts does not give us information about any of Paul's letters. From the Acts account, however, we surmise that Paul wrote a letter after visiting the community of believers in Thessalonica.

The Account from 1 Thessalonians. How did Paul arrive in Thessalonica? Paul does not give details of his initial arrival in Thessalonica. We must learn that information from Acts 17.

How long did Paul stay? In the Acts account, we read that Paul stayed in Thessalonica for three weeks. In Paul's letter, however, the visit appears longer. Again, the details are sketchy. We do know that Paul was in the city long enough to establish his trade of tentmaking and to provide a model of behavior for the Christians (2:9-10). We also know that on several occasions Paul received gifts sent from Philippi by a traveling courier (Phil 4:15). Philippi was about 100 miles distant. The time spent in travel would have taken longer than three weeks (4:15).

When did Paul write the letter? First Thessalonians does not give a date. The letter was written after Timothy reported his visit to Paul. No other churches are mentioned in the letter. We can surmise that Paul wrote 1 Thessalonians shortly after leaving the city of Thessalonica, perhaps in CORINTH in 50 C.E., in the company of Timothy and Silas.

The Letter

Traditionally scholars have viewed 1 Thessalonians according to its thematic structure. The letter has been divided into the categories of thanksgiving, personal remarks, and ethical and doctrinal teaching. Recently, scholars have proposed new readings of 1 Thessalonians, using the exegetical methods of structuralism (Malbon 1983), feminist reading (Gaventa 1990), and Graeco-Roman rhetorical conventions (Wanamaker 1990).

Although various methods are used to outline and interpret the epistle, 1 Thessalonians, nonetheless, remains a letter. This epistle is an authentic piece of correspondence between two parties, Paul and the church at Thessalonica. Unfortunately we only have clear access to one part of the conversation—Paul's. To hear the voice of the other party, the novice Christians in the church at Thessalonica, we must listen carefully.

The Community

Paul's letter was not intended to be a systematic theological treatise. Paul wrote to a community, composed predominantly of gentile believers who were struggling with their new faith (see the description by Blevins 1990, 909, of the setting of the community). Paul does not present dogmatic rules for life; nor does he prescribe a quick fix for their theological anxiety. Rather, in this letter Paul shares himself and pastoral words of comfort with "the beloved ones" in Thessalonica (2:8).

The occasion for the letter comes from the community. Timothy returns to Paul from Thessalonica with a good report and with a list of questions from the community. These questions, either in written or oral form, articulate the basic concerns of the community. The questions also reveal a troubled congregation. Paul writes to comfort them.

As we read Paul addressing the concerns of the Thessalonian church in this intimate letter, we can also hear the anxious voices from the church. The community is experiencing persecution (1 Thes 1:6; 2:14-16). They are concerned about the recent death of church members (4:13-18). They remain confused about the meaning of an incalculable PAROUSIA (5:1). The community in Thessalonica also question Paul's style of leadership (2:1-12). Sexual ethics are also a major concern (4:1-8).

For Further Study

In the *Mercer Dictionary of the Bible*: APOSTLE/APOSTLESHIP; EPISTLE/LETTER; ESCHATOLOGY IN THE NT; PAROUSIA; PAUL; THESSALONIANS, LETTERS TO THE; THESSALONICA.

In other sources: E. Best, *The First and Second Epistles to the Thessalonians*; L. McK. Bridges, "Paul as a Nursing Mother," *Lectionary Homiletics* (Nov 1993); R. Collins, *The Thessalonian Correspondence*; Beverly Gaventa, "The Maternity of Paul," in *The Conversation Continues*, ed. R. Fortna and B. Gaventa; R. Jewett, *The Thessalonian Correspondence: Pauline Rhetoric and Millenarian Piety*; H. Koester, "I Thessalonians—Experiment in Christian Writing," in *Continuity and Discontinuity*, ed. F. Church; A. J. Malherbe, *Paul and the Thessalonians: The Philosophic Tradition of Pastoral Care*; E. S. Malbon, "'No Need to Have Any One Write?' A Structural Exegesis of 1 Thessalonians," *Semeia* 26 (1983): 57–83; I. H. Marshall. *1 and 2 Thessalonians*; L. Morris, *The First and Second Epistles to the Thessalonians*; J. M. Reese, *1 and 2 Thessalonians*; C. Wanamaker, *The Epistles to the Thessalonians: A Commentary on the Greek Text*.

Commentary

Greeting the Church, 1:1

Paul begins the letter with the familiar, traditional epistolary greeting (cf. Rom 1:1-7; 1 Cor 1:1-3; 2 Cor 1:1-2; Gal 1:1-4). *Silvanus*, the SILAS of Acts 15:22, and *Timothy*, Paul's missionary colleague, were probably the couriers of the Thessalonian letter. They transported the letter from CORINTH to THESSALONICA.

Paul does not identify himself as servant as he does in the greeting of Romans, or as an apostle as seen in 1 and 2 Corinthians and Galatians. Perhaps Paul's position as leader is not as unstable in the Thessalonican church as it would later become in the other churches. The liturgical prayer, a traditional Pauline greeting, offers *grace . . . and peace* to the church.

Encouraging the Church, 1:2-10

Central to the skill of a good communicator is the ability to make contact with the audience. Paul, an excellent communicator, gains the attention of the listeners by talking directly to them. He praises them and their accomplishments. In this tribute, the themes of the entire epistle are also introduced.

1:2-4. Praise. Paul offers thanks for the believers. The tone of praise is repeated in 2:13-14, 2:20, 3:6-10, and 4:1. A familiar triad—faith, love, and hope—describe the people (1 Thes 5:8; Rom 5:1-5; 1 Cor 13:12-13). The church at Thessalonica is noted for their work that comes from their faith, their labor that proceeds from their love, and their steadfastness that follows their hope (v. 3). Paul also gives thanks because he knows that his friends, "the beloved ones,"

have been called by God (v. 4). Paul continues to offer tribute for the "beloved ones" throughout the epistle (see 2:19-20; 3:6-10).

The language used in these verses instills community and intimacy. The presence of the second personal pronouns, the use of familial term, "brothers" (ἀδελφοί), translated inclusively as *friends* (NRSV), and the use of the word calling or ELECTION (ἐκλογήν) in v. 4 are used to create intimacy between the speaker and the audience.

1:5-7. Paul's ministry of imitation. Paul encourages the readers to imitate him. At first glance, the injunction sounds self-serving. Paul, however, was not establishing his life as the authoritarian model for morality for the community. Rather, Paul is saying, "imitate me as I imitate Christ." See the further development of the idea of imitation in 1 Thes 2:13-16 and 2 Thes 3:6-9.

Verses 6b-8 clarify the metaphor of imitation. To imitate Paul means to be willing to experience the joy of the Spirit even in times of distress (v. 6b). The persecution may have been emotional or physical suffering, or both. To break from the past, either from the Jewish tradition or gentile cultic worship, required emotional anguish for the neophyte Christians. Persecution may have also been more visible, like political oppression or economic hardship.

Paul's understanding of imitation suggests that believers are to become an example to others as he had been an example to them. As Paul had been instrumental in bringing the Thessalonians to faith, so should the community of faith, in turn, be responsible for spreading the gospel (vv. 7-8).

1:9. Ethics. The community received Paul and his gospel. That reception was manifested in clear and visible ways. The believers left their former way of life; they turned from idols to embrace a new life-style with Christ. Paul clarifies this new ethical behavior in 4:12.

To leave a cultic life-style and embrace the strict, ethical admonitions of Paul was no easy task for the novice, Thessalonian Christian. Religious cults were popular in the city of Thessalonica. Archaeological evidence points to the presence of the cults of Serapis, Dionysus, Cabirus, and Samothrace in Thessalonica. Sexual symbols, mystical rites, and frenzied, orgiastic worship characterized the cults.

1:10. Eschatology. The theme of eschatology is briefly introduced here, foreshadowing further development in 4:13. The community of believers have not only left their former life-styles, they are waiting patiently for the return of Christ.

Notice the didactic use of the relative clauses. The community "waits for God's son *who* is from heaven, *who* was raised from the dead, and *who* is Jesus, our deliverer" (author trans.). With characteristic literary flair, Paul packs a thought unit, using every opportunity to teach the gospel, even through a preponderance of relative clauses.

Serving the Church, 2:1–3:10

Soon after Paul's arrival in Thessalonica he incurred much agony (ἀγῶνι) in opposition (see Acts 17:1-9). Paul had also endured much agony in his previous missionary stop in PHILLIPI (Phil 1:30). Paul ministered in the face of considerable obstacles. His motives for ministry were pure, and the opposition unwarranted.

As a Nursing Mother, 2:1-9

Paul, who is perhaps being maligned by opponents in the church, uses literary energy to explain his innocence. Paul's ministry is not to please people, as he has perhaps been accused. Paul did not minister to the Thessalonians with words of flattery, nor with the motive of greed. Nor did Paul come looking for glory from them or others.

How did Paul come to the people? Although he could have come as a heavy, apostolic tyrant or dictator, "throwing his weight around" in the congregation, he chose to come gently, as a nursing mother, ὡς ἐὰν τροφὸς θάλπῃ τὰ ἑαυτῆς τέκνα (vv. 6-7). This striking contrast of images provides a vivid picture of Paul's relationship with the people. As a mother would nurse her child, giving of her life, sharing her time, being accessible, providing life-sustaining nourishment whenever needed, so does Paul care for the people of Thessalonica. The maternity of Paul challenges the contemporary abuses of pastoral leadership.

As an Encouraging Father, 2:10-16

A second familial metaphor describes how Paul serves the church. Paul responded to them as father, πατὴρ (vv. 10-11). Paul's images of pastoral leadership do not come from Roman military structure or the ancient business world, but from the arena of the household. Verse 12, which continues the thought of vv. 10-11, describes the role of the father: to exhort or teach, to encourage or cheer, to witness or affirm. The father in the first-century home was the primary parent responsible for moral guidance. Paul's maternal and paternal images form a unified image that challenges contemporary views of pastoral leadership and power in the church.

Some scholars view vv. 13-16 as an interpolation, added later and not written by Paul. Most argue for the interpolation view because of the anti-semitic tone of the passage. Others argue that although it was written by Paul, vv. 13-16 provide a digression, or interruption of his train of thought.

I suggest, however, that the unit vv. 13-16 is not an interpolation. Rather, these verses are used by Paul to support and expand the familial metaphor given in vv. 10-12. Verses 10-13 illustrate the role of the fatherly pastor. Just as the role of the first-century father was to encourage the children, so Paul encourages the people (v. 13). Paul likewise takes on the role of teacher as he reminds the Thessalonians to imitate him (v. 14). Finally, Paul affirms the congregation by reminding them of his own personal suffering. Paul is fulfilling the role of the traditional Jewish father who brings the memory of past experiences as lesson to be learned for the present (v. 16).

As an Orphan, 2:17–3:10

Paul loves the people of Thessalonica, and he is not ashamed to show his emotion for them. In their absence, he feels like an orphan (ἀπορφανισθέντες), like a child without parents. Again, this potent image reinforces Paul's style of leadership. Paul has not only given these people the gospel, he has given them *himself* (2:8). They have become family to him. The community of believers becomes his *crown of boasting* (2:19-20).

Paul sent Timothy back to the Thessalonians as Paul's official courier (3:2). Paul received a glowing report. Paul is encouraged (3:6).

Praying for the Church, 3:11-13

We already know that Paul prays for this church as seen in 1:2. Verses 11-13 give us some of the content of those prayers.

The verses are linked by verbs found in the optative mood, a grammatical expression for prayer: *may . . . direct* (v. 11), *may . . . make you increase and . . . abound in love* (v. 12). Paul prays so that the church might be blameless and holy (v. 13).

Teaching the Church, 4:1–5:22

Commonly called the paranesis, which means teaching or exhortation, this section deals with ethical behavior in the community. Paul's concern for the ethics of the congregation has already been foreshadowed in 1:9 and reinforced in Paul's prayer in 3:12-13.

Theology and Praxis, 4:1-2

Paul understands that loving God, a horizontal relationship, also means loving the community, a vertical relationship. A sense of urgency is heard in Paul's voice as he begs (ἐρωτῶμεν) the members of the church to have their walk with others parallel their talk about Christ (v. 1). Ethics, for Paul, is not a philosophical abstraction. Rather, Paul summarizes Christian behavior by giving practical guidelines for holy living.

Sexual Ethics, 4:3-8

Paul does not mince words when he says: *Abstain from fornication* (v. 3). In v. 4, Paul exhorts the believer to control one's own "vessel" (σκεῦος). Some English translations, however, render this Greek word as *wife*. For example, the RSV translates v. 4a as, "each one of you know how to take a wife for him." This biased translation limits the exhortation to married men and misses the force of the paragraph. To control one's own sexual urges is the point of this verse. The reason for sexual discipline relates to issues of justice for the entire community, not only within marriage (v. 6). To exploit another person sexually damages both individuals and the life of the community suffers. Paul acknowledges that to live a life with sexual limits is not easy. This is God's way, however, and the HOLY SPIRIT has been given for assistance (vv. 7-8).

Relationships, 4:9-12

Paul begins a new thought unit with the words, *Now concerning*. The new topic continues to highlight the horizontal mandate of the gospel—*love one another* (v. 9). Four verbal infinitives provide the grammatical structure for this section: to love more, to be quiet, to mind your own affairs, and to work with your own hands. Some of Paul's converts may have been refusing to earn their own keep. Some of the church members may have also stopped working thinking that

Jesus would return soon. Paul urges them to wait quietly, while working and relating to people.

Return of Christ, 4:13–5:11

A new topic begins in v. 13. Paul addresses directly the questions given to Timothy by the congregation. Their dilemma is this: The church members have had relatives to die since Paul's last visit. They understood that Paul taught the imminent return of Christ, the PAROUSIA. Then their relatives began to die, and the parousia had not yet happened. They are confused. They are also grieving. They grieve over the loss of their loved ones. They also grieve because their teacher is not present with them in their time of mourning.

In response, Paul makes two important points. One, Paul says that those who have died will not be disadvantaged at the parousia (4:13-18). God will take care of them. Reunion with them and union with Christ will occur in the end. Two, the exact time of Jesus' return cannot be determined in advance (5:1-11). Therefore, the Thessalonians should relax and be comforted.

Paul's initial reaction is to comfort his grieving friends (5:11). To do so he recalls a word from the Lord (4:15). He uses powerful, visual images—"the archangel's voice," "a trumpet," "the clouds"—to describe the majestic event that is to come. The most comforting point is found in the tiny Greek word σύν (together with) in v. 17. Paul wants the community to know that we will be all *together with* the Lord (v. 17).

This epistle draws the confused, grieving believers in Thessalonica closer *together with* Paul, their teacher and friend. Paul promises that the return of Christ will bring a grand reunion, where loved ones will be brought *together with* one another (2:17–3:10).

Final Instructions, 5:12-22

Last-minute imperatives of ethical behavior are given in the closing of 1 Thessalonians. Paul earnestly begs that the believers recognize and respect their leaders (vv. 12-13). Paul encourages the community to consider those who are idlers (ἀτάκτους), fainthearted, and weak with generous and forgiving grace (v. 14). Do not return evil for evil (v. 15).

The imperatives also guide the liturgical life of the congregation. *Rejoice* (v. 16). *Pray* (vv. 17-18). Do not restrain the Holy Spirit (v. 19). Do not despise prophecy (v. 20). *Test everything* (v. 21). Keep away from evil (v. 22).

Blessing the Church, 5:23-28

Using the grammar of prayer, the optative mood, Paul offers a concluding prayer for the Thessalonians. The ethical behavior of the Thessalonians remains a primary focus (see the prayer in 3:11-13). Energy for the task, however, comes not from the believer but from God.

Paul's understanding of apostolic authority surfaces in the conclusion (see 2:1–3:10). Paul not only offers prayers for the people, but he is also eager to receive them (v. 25) The *holy kiss* (φιλήματι ἁγίῳ) became a liturgical gesture in the second or third centuries (v. 26). The letter is to be read aloud in the meetings of the church (v. 27). The ending of the letter echoes the beginning with the word *grace* (χάρις, 1:2 and 5:28).

Works Cited

Blevins, James L. 1990. "Thessalonians, Letters to the," in *MDB.*

Donfried, K. P. 1985. "The Cults of Thessalonica and the Thessalonian Correspondence," *NTS* 31:336–56.

Gaventa, Beverly, 1990. "The Maternity of Paul: An Exegetical Study of Galatians 4:19," in *The Conversation Continues: Studies in Paul and John in Honor of J. Louis Martyn*, ed. Robert Fortna and B. Gaventa.

Jewett, R. 1986. *The Thessalonian Correspondence: Pauline Rhetoric and Millenarian Piety.*

Koester, H. 1982. *Introduction to the New Testament.* 2: *History and Literature of Early Christianity.*

Luedemann, G. 1984. *Paul, Apostle to the Gentiles: Studies in Chronology.*

Manson, T. W. 1953. "St. Paul in Greece: The Letters to the Thessalonians," *BJRL* 35:428–47.

Malbon, E. 1983. "'No Need to Have Any One Write?' A Structural Exegesis of 1 Thessalonians," *Semeia* 26:57–83.

Malherbe, A. J. 1983. "Exhortation in First Thessalonians," *NovT* 25:238–56. 1987. *Paul and the Thessalonians: The Philosophic Tradition of Pastoral Care.*

Richard, E. 1990. "Contemporary Research on (1 & 2) Thessalonians," *BTB* 20:107–15.

Wanamaker, C. 1990. *The Epistles to the Thessalonians: A Commentary on the Greek Text.*

Second Thessalonians

Linda McKinnish Bridges

Introduction

Although 2 Thessalonians continues the conversation with the church in THESSALONICA, this epistle must be read separately. It is not simply the second half of 1 Thessalonians. Let 2 Thessalonians be 2 Thessalonians!

To note the dissimilarities between the two letters helps to separate the readings. Second Thessalonians does not contain the personal warmth and affective language as seen in 1 Thessalonians. Absent in 2 Thessalonians is the frequent use of first- and second-person pronouns. Although a basic epistolary structure remains the same, the syntax and style is more complex in 2 Thessalonians, using more relatival clauses and dependent phrases. Furthermore, while 1 Thessalonians addresses many concerns of the community, 2 Thessalonians focuses on one issue, namely, how to be faithful in persecution.

The Writer

Did PAUL write 2 Thessalonians? Although scholars generally conclude that Paul wrote 1 Thessalonians, consensus has not yet been reached regarding the authorship of 2 Thessalonians. The authorship question, first raised at the turn of the century, still lingers.

Wolfgang Trilling (1981) and others, for example, oppose Pauline authorship on the basis of a study of vocabulary and style. On the other hand, Robert Jewett (1986) and others, argue for Pauline authorship on the basis of vocabulary and style. Both arguments are compelling. Although Pauline authorship was not questioned in the first few centuries of the church, recent linguistic analyses show significant variation in Greek syntax between the two letters. Paul either wrote in a totally new style when he composed the second letter, or another person used Paul's apostolic authority to gain a hearing for 2 Thessalonians.

Questions regarding the author, however, do not diminish the powerful voice of the letter, either for first-century or twentieth-century readers. The writer, whether Paul or another, writes a real letter to real people with real problems. We listen in on the conversation.

The Letter

Traditional, first-century, epistolary conventions are seen in 2 Thessalonians. This carefully constructed letter includes a greeting, body, and closing. Particular attention is given to chap. 2, the central chapter. This crucial section introduces the primary focus of the letter—the community's response to the PAROUSIA of Christ.

Which letter was written first? The question is valid, for canonical sequence has more to do with length of the letters than with chronological concerns. Some scholars, H. Grotius 1679, J. Weiss 1937, T. W. Manson 1953, and others, posit that 2 Thessalonians was actually written first. They assume Paul wrote 2 Thessalonians while in ATHENS. TIMOTHY delivered the letter to the church, as Paul later records in the second letter (1 Thes 3:1-6). First Thessalonians, Paul's second letter, was written from CORINTH and composed after Timothy returned from his previous visit.

Contemporary scholarship remains divided on the issue of the sequence of 1 and 2 Thessalonians. Robert Jewett (1986) presents a cogent argument for canonical sequencing. By contrast, Charles Wanamaker (1990) offers a detailed argument for the reversal.

The question of sequence is valid; the answers, however, remain questionable. For our purposes here, we follow the traditional sequencing and assume that 2 Thessalonians was written after 1 Thessalonians. The second letter continues the conversation with the community. The style of conversation, however, is strikingly dissimilar.

The Community

At least three problems concern this community of believers. One, they are theologically confused (2 Thes 2:2). They think *that the day of the Lord* has already come. Paul describes what will take place before Christ comes to assure them that the parousia, or coming of Christ, has not happened yet.

Two, some members of the community have become social problems and economic burdens for the church. These people, believing that Christ had already come, have become lazy (3:6). They are not working. They depend on others for their economic support.

The third problem, related to the first two, has to do with false teachers in the church. OPPONENTS OF PAUL and his teachings have infiltrated the life of the community (1:4-12). They have introduced faulty theologies and weak ethics. They have also brought suffering and persecution to the members of the community who do not heed their teachings.

Who are these false teachers? We know more about what they said than where they came from. Various options regarding the identity of the opponents have been given, such as gnostic infiltrators, millenarian radicals, or enthusiastic revivalists. We, however, can only guess at their identity and place of origin.

Could it be that these opponents were members from the church in JERUSALEM? The chasm between Paul's ministry and the intended ministry goals of the Jerusalem church was great. The Jerusalem church often sent missionaries to check on Paul's work (Acts 15:22f.; Gal 2:4-10). It is not unlikely that a group of anti-Paul, energetic, Judaizers from Jerusalem also entered Thessalonica causing disruption and distressing the Thessalonican Christians. They contradict Paul's teachings, assuring the neophyte Christians that the *day of the Lord* has already come (2:2).

Furthermore, these opponents oppose Paul's ethical teachings by encouraging the Thessalonican community to relax, not bother with working (3:12). The opponents demand conformity, and the community labors under great pressure and persecution (1:4-12). To this community of new believers in Thessalonica, who have been influenced by these infiltrators, Paul says, "Be faithful, don't give up, hang in there."

For Further Study

In the *Mercer Dictionary of the Bible*: ESCHATOLOGY IN THE NEW TESTAMENT; MAN OF LAWLESSNESS; PAUL; THESSALONIANS, LETTERS TO THE; THESSALONICA.

In other sources: *See also* "1 Thessalonians," above; J. Bailey, "Who Wrote II Thessalonians?" *NTS* 25 (1978–1979): 131–45; E. Krentz, "Traditions Held Fast: Theology and Fidelity in 2 Thessalonians," in *The Thessalonian Correspondence*, ed. R. Collins; M. J. J. Menken, "The Structure of 2 Thessalonians," in *The Thessalonian Correspondence*, ed. R. Collins; R. Russell, "The Idle in 2 Thess. 3:6-12: An Eschatological or a Social Problem," *NTS* 14 (1988): 105–19; D. Schmidt, "The Authenticity of 2 Thessalonians: Linguistic Arguments," *SBLSP* 1983.

Commentary

An Outline

I. Greeting the Church, 1:1-2
II. Thanking the Church, 1:3-12
III. Warning the Church, 2:1-17
    A. The Coming of Christ
       and the Person of Lawlessness, 2:1-12
    B. The Gathering of Christians, 2:13-17
IV. Teaching the Church, 3:1-15
    A. The Prayer for Discipline, 3:1-5
    B. The Discipline in the Community, 3:6-15
V. Blessing the Church, 3:16-18

Greeting the Church, 1:1-2

Note the similarities between the epistolary greeting in 1 and 2 Thessalonians. Three major characters are introduced—PAUL, SILVANUS, and TIMOTHY. Traditionally we focus on the missionary activities of Paul, often to the exclusion of Paul's colleagues. It is important to note, however, that the missionary activity of the early church was not accomplished through the efforts of one, but of many. Paul worked with BARNABAS, JOHN MARK, LYDIA, Phoebe, and a host of others, some of whom are not even mentioned in the letters. Together, they planted churches and nurtured young congregations in the faith.

Thanking the Church, 1:3-12

Paul's letters exhibit liturgical qualities. The depth of emotion is best revealed in the Greek syntax. This section, although containing ten verses in English, is constructed from only two Greek sentences, vv. 3-10 and 11-12. The Greek embedded clauses and phrases give power and personal drama to the moment of thanksgiving.

The thanksgiving section, while liturgical in tone, also has a rhetorical function. The use of second-person pronouns and words of praise urges people to stop and listen to the important points of the presentation. Likewise, the first-century reader hears Paul's affective language and is compelled to listen. While listening to Paul's praise (vv. 3-4), they are also introduced to the main themes of the letter (vv. 5-11).

Two themes are introduced in this section and then further clarified in the body of the letter. First, the theme of *the day of the Lord* is introduced in vv. 5-10 and then discussed in greater detail in 2:1-12. Likewise, the theme of the community is introduced here and is given fuller treatment in the paranetic section of 2:13–3:15.

1:3-4. Praise and prayer. The church is congratulated on their faithful persistence in spite of local opposition. In a spirit of prayer, Paul praises the congregation for their faith in God and love for one another. The Thessalonican church has become a model of faith for other churches (v. 4).

1:5-10. Reversal of fortunes. The *day of the Lord* will bring both reward and punishment. This theology of suffering includes rewards for those who have been faithful and affliction for those who have caused the persecution. This reversal of fortunes, repaying those who caused affliction with affliction, belongs to God's righteous judgment (vv. 5-7). Those who have been faithful, even in persecution, will be able to relax when Jesus returns. To be able to relax at *the day of the Lord* stands in sharp contrast to those who, not knowing God and not obeying the gospel of Christ, will be given punishment. The punishment will be total separation from the face of the Lord and from the glory of his strength (vv. 7-9).

1:11-12. Praise and prayer. The section closes with a prayer (vv. 11-12) just as it began with a spirit of prayer (1:3-4). Attention shifts, however, within the INCLUSIO from the explanation of *the day of the Lord* to the response of the community to Christ's coming. With an understanding of *the day of the Lord*, expressed with apocalyptic images and predicted reversal of fortunes, the community is still faced with the question, "How are we supposed to live in the meantime?" It is this question that lingers in the minds of the young believers. Living in the meantime requires intercessory prayer by Paul and ethical behavior by the Thessalonian Christians (v. 12).

Warning the Church, 2:1-17

The predominant theme of 2 Thessalonians, subtly introduced in the thanksgiving section of chap. 1, is given full treatment in chap. 2. The parousia (παρουσίας), the coming of the Lord, and our coming together with him (ἐπισυναγωγῆς) are crucial concerns of the community.

Perhaps the young Christians have been asking particular questions concerning the manifestation of Christ, when and how it might occur. Paul responds by describing not only the details of Christ's coming but also our "assembling" with him.

The Coming of Christ and the Person of Lawlessness, 2:1-12

The believers at Thessalonica were confused, literally "shaken in their mind and continually disturbed" (v. 2, author trans.). Someone, somewhere told the congregation that the parousia had already occurred. It is not clear how they received this information, perhaps by a supposedly spirit-inspired utterance, an oral report, or maybe a letter purported to be written by Paul. By whatever means, the young Christians have been deceived.

The purpose of this section is to prove that *the day of the Lord* positively could not have already arrived. Verses 3-7 detail the events that must precede the Lord's coming, and vv. 8-12 point to the events that have not yet happened.

Paul warns that the day of the Lord will not come unless the APOSTASY comes first and the person of lawlessness, the son of destruction, is revealed. Who is this person of lawlessness? This person represents for both the first and twentieth-century reader the epitome of EVIL. The person of lawlessness opposes God, proclaiming to be God.

By wrapping the abstract concept of evil into human form, the readers can visualize its reality and menace. Many comparable historical figures, like Antiochus Epiphanes, Pompey, Gaius Caesar, probably entered the mind of the first-century reader. The first-century reader, most likely, expected a future historical figure to appear whose power could only be restrained by the preaching of the gospel. Full victory over such a person, which also signals victory over pervasive evil, is only possible in the parousia (v. 8).

What about the people? The person of lawlessness deceives the people. Those who have been deceived, therefore, receive not the love of truth and ultimately perish (vv. 10-11). This rather harsh language describes why some people have chosen to reject the gospel. Perhaps Paul is describing the opponents, those people who saw the radical freedom of Christians as a direct threat to their own religious traditions.

Obviously, *the day of the Lord* has not yet come, Paul asserts. In other words, it is going to become much worse before it becomes better.

The Gathering of Christians, 2:13-17

In tones of worship and praise, Paul gives thanks for God's initiative in calling the young Christians into salvation. The appropriate response to the glory of God in Christ is clear to the young Christians in Thessalonica: *Stand firm and hold fast to the traditions that you were taught by us* (v. 15). Capsuled in elegant, apocalyptic descriptions, complemented by beautiful, liturgical phrases, and supplemented by deep, theological insights stands the core of Paul's thought—ethical behavior. It makes a difference how you live. Talk about the end of time does not make much sense unless one also talks about what the parousia means for the gathered people of God in the present. Paul introduces the concept here of the community's response to the coming of Christ and then gives greater detail in the final chapter.

Teaching the Church, 3:1-15

A small word of transition, *finally* (λοιπόν), marks this new section. This word is used often to signal a change of thought and to mark the beginning of the ethical or paranetic portion of the letter (cf. 1 Thes 4:1; 2 Cor 13:11; Phil 4:2). The chapter begins with praise and prayer and concludes with specific instructions for ethical behavior.

The Prayer for Discipline, 3:1-5

Prayer is crucial for Paul. Prayer is also reciprocal between leader and people. Just as the Thessalonians need prayer, so does Paul. The ultimate goal of righteous living for Paul is not for self-glory. Rather, one is to live righteously so that the gospel of Christ, the word of the Lord, might run on ahead and triumph (v. 1). The progress of the gospel can be encouraged by one's life. Not all people, however, will contribute to the progress. Some are not responsive to the word of God (v. 2).

Paul refers to those people who oppose the progress of the Christian mission as the "out-of-place ones" (ἀτόπων). These opponents are consistent dialogue partners throughout this letter, as well as 1 Thessalonians (see 1 Thes 2:13-16). Paul speaks to them and against them as he communicates to the entire church.

The opponents are also a convenient literary foil to show the young believers how not to act. Paul condemns the behavior of the opponents while at the same time he exhorts the others to obedience.

The Discipline in the Community, 3:6-15

Unlike the paranetic section in 1 Thessalonians that contains many instructions (see 1 Thes 4–5), 2 Thessalonians is concerned with only one issue. Its solitary position makes the single exhortation clear and dramatic: Keep away from every friend who is living in *idleness* (ἀτάκτως) (v. 6).

The word *idleness* (see also 1 Thes 5:14 and 2 Thes 3:6, 7) can denote either undisciplined or disorderly actions or persons, or idle or lazy individuals. In the Thessalonian correspondence, the word seems to denote idle behavior that leads to disorderly lives.

Members of the congregation have not been working. They are living in irresponsible idleness. By depending on the wealthier members of the congregation to provide their economic sustenance, they are creating havoc in the community.

Paul reminds them that he and the ethical tradition that he taught does not advocate laziness (v. 8). His own life is an example. Paul did his missionary work without payment (see 1 Thes 2:9; 1 Cor 9:1-18; 2 Cor 11:7). According to the law of Moses and to traditional religious practices, he could, however, have demanded a salary.

A maxim summarizes Paul's position in v. 10: "If you don't work; you don't eat." The instruction given by Paul is plain and simple. The believer is to work, eat one's own bread, and not meddle in the affairs of others. The church is to take special notice of those who cannot obey this instruction. The church is instructed to isolate the person until the behavior is modified. Ostracizing deviant persons becomes necessary for the preservation of the larger community. Notice, however, that the idle person who is undergoing rehabilitation is still to be considered as friend, not enemy.

Blessing the Church, 3:16-18

Second Thessalonians concludes with a prayer of blessing. Paul notes that he is writing this letter with his *own hand* (v. 17). For some scholars, this is a critical clue that this letter may not have been written by

Paul, but rather by someone who needed Paul's authority to gain a hearing in the church. Another position is to see v. 17 as Paul's own personal, written signature to a letter actually written by an AMANUENSIS, or secretary. Paul, or his authority, is an important component of the conversation to the Thessalonians.

As the letter began, so it ends. *Grace* (χάρις), the beginning and ending of the life of an individual believer and the community of faith, also becomes the beginning and ending of a letter written by a faithful follower of the gospel, Paul, to a group of young believers in Thessalonica.

Works Cited

Grotius, H. 1679. *Operum Theologicorum.*

Jewett, R. 1986. *The Thessalonian Correspondence: Pauline Rhetoric and Millenarian Piety.*

Manson, T. W. 1953. "St. Paul in Greece: The Letters to the Thessalonians," *BJRL* 35:428-47.

Trilling, W. 1972. *Untersuchungen zum zweiten Thessalonicherbrief.*

Wanamaker, Charles. 1990. *The Epistles to the Thessalonians: A Commentary on the Greek Text.*

Weiss, J. 1959. *Earliest Christianity: A History of the Period A.D. 30–150.* Vol. 1. Trans. F. C. Grant.

First and Second Timothy and Titus

E. Glenn Hinson

Introduction

First and Second Timothy and Titus, referred to since 1703 as the PASTORAL EPISTLES, pose one of the intriguing dilemmas of NT scholarship. Claiming both strong internal and external support as the work of the PAUL, they display enough peculiarities by comparison with other letters bearing his name that many question whether Paul could have written them.

The Problem of Authorship

Five issues have been raised regarding Paul's authorship: (1) Vocabulary, grammar, and style differ from those found in Paul's other letters, especially Romans, 1 and 2 Corinthians, and Galatians. (2) The doctrine of the Pastorals differs from Paul's in some ways. (3) The ecclesiastical organization depicted in them is unlike that existing in Paul's lifetime. (4) The heresy attacked is late. (5) The historical data presented in the letters do not square with the framework of Paul's life sketched in Acts.

Theories about Authorship

Scholars have offered a number of theories about authorship. (1) Some scholars attribute the letters to an admirer of Paul responding to a different set of problems and circumstances, dating them variously as early as 90 to 100 C.E. and as late as 140 to 150 C.E. (against MARCION). (2) Others have developed a "fragments hypothesis." A pious follower of Paul had fragments of letters by Paul which he incorporated into these letters, mostly into 2 Timothy. (3) Still others have argued for the genuineness of 2 Timothy and disputed that of 1 Timothy and Titus.

Paul as Author

Those who sustain Paul's authorship of the Pastoral Epistles make the following responses to the arguments against it: (1) Variations in vocabulary, grammar, and style can be explained by (a) the use of a secretary to whom considerable freedom was given, (b) Paul's aging, (c) natural variations in the vocabulary and style of any writer in different contexts writing to different addressees (individuals in this case), and (d) incorporation of formal elements such as hymns, catalogues of virtues and vices, codes for Christian conduct, and confessions of faith. (2) The doctrine agrees with that of Paul's other letters for the most part. Where it varies, it is not post- but *pre*-Pauline, found in hymns or confessions cited in the letters. (3) The ecclesiastical organization of the Pastorals is that of the twofold office of presbyter-bishops and deacons, as in Philippians, and not the threefold office of IGNATIUS (d. 110–117). The roles of Timothy and TITUS, moreover, do not fit the model of bishops in the second century. (4) The heresy attacked in the Pastorals was not second-century GNOSTICISM or Marcionism but some sort of Judaistic, possibly Essene, aberration. Even if it had a gnostic cast, this does not require a post-Pauline date, for the date of Gnosticism has been moved back to Paul's day. (5) Although the historical setting does not fit the scheme of Acts, Luke did not tell the complete story of Paul's life. There is strong early Christian tradition favoring Paul's release after trial, travels, and reimprisonment. In addition, (6) some have questioned whether early Christians accepted the custom of writing under an assumed name as readily as sometimes assumed by scholars who consider the Pastorals pseudonymous.

Purpose

Those who question whether Paul wrote the Pastorals usually envision them as anti-gnostic or anti-Marcionite. The author used basically the same approach Ignatius, Bishop of Antioch, did in the early second century, that is, strengthening ecclesiastical organization. The names of Paul and his disciples, Timothy and Titus, gave an authoritative ring to the proposal. If there were genuine "fragments" which could be incorporated into the letters, they would add further certification. If the pious forger made up personal reminiscences, he did so deliberately to enhance the Pauline nuances.

Those who interpret the Pastorals as Paul's own must try to interpret them as they project themselves. First Timothy presents itself as the instructions of an old soldier to his young aide-de-camp about mission work—public worship, ministry, behavior in the church, and so on. Second Timothy is much more personal, Paul's last will and testament during his second imprisonment and plea for Timothy to join him. Titus contains directions for a seasoned missionary about his work on the island of Crete. Opponents do not figure very prominently in the letters, but they may have been Judaizers with some gnostic tendencies as in Paul's other writings.

Date

If by Paul, the Pastorals would have to have been written during a period after his release from prison in Rome about 62 C.E. If by some later author, they should not be dated later than the last decade of the first century.

For Further Study

In the *Mercer Dictionary of the Bible*: PASTORAL EPISTLES; CHURCH; PAUL; TIMOTHY; TITUS.

In other sources: W. Barclay, *The Letters to Timothy, Titus, and Philemon*; C. K. Barrett, *The Pastoral Epistles in the New English Bible*; E. G. Hinson, "1–2 Timothy and Titus," *BBC* 11; J. N. D. Kelly, *A Commentary on the Pastoral Epistles*.

Commentary

An Outline

First Timothy
I. Greeting and Affirmation of Apostolate, 1:1-2
II. General Orders to Timothy, 1:3-20
III. Orders Concerning the Churches, 2:1–6:2a
A. Public Worship, 2:1-15
B. The Ministry, 3:1-16
C. Behavior in the Church, 4:1–6:2a
IV. Final Orders to Timothy, 6:2b-19
V. Closing Charge and Salutation, 6:20-21

Greeting and Affirmation of Apostolate, 1:1-2

The letter opens with a strong assertion of apostleship as in Romans and Galatians. Paul addresses Timothy in an intimate way as his legitimate child in faith.

General Orders to Timothy, 1:3-20

A military motif prevails throughout this letter. As a commander to his aide, Paul orders TIMOTHY to stay at his post in EPHESUS and to put a stop to teaching other than Paul did and to wrangling about the Law. The goal is agape-love that comes from a pure heart, good CONSCIENCE, and authentic faith. Some have gone astray by ignoring these and plunging into meaningless speculation, wanting to be teachers of the Law but not understanding what they were doing.

Paul agrees with the Judaizers, or Jewish Gnostics, that the Law is good if properly applied. Its proper use is to show what is wrong, as a catalogue of vices based on the TEN COMMANDMENTS confirms, and not what is right. We learn what is right from the gospel with which Paul was entrusted. The gospel is what reveals God as God truly is.

Frequently a target of attacks from Judaizers, the old apostle cannot help lapsing into a defense (vv. 12-17). Paul is "exhibit A" of the grace of God to which the gospel bears witness. What else could Paul do but give thanks to Christ for appointing him as apostle despite what he had once been—a blasphemer, persecutor, and bad-mouther. He was no better than a pagan. Yet the grace of God overflowed with the faithfulness and love that are in Christ. Yes, Paul has to agree with the saying, *Christ Jesus came into the world to save sinners* (v. 15; cf. Luke 19:10), for he was the prime example. Why? So that Christ might display his incredible patience as an example for future believers.

In typical Pauline fashion these thoughts touch off a doxology (v. 17). Praise of God as the only God may be the apostle's way of negating the emperor cult that burgeoned under Nero.

Paul reinforces his general orders with an appeal to their close ties as father and son in faith (vv. 18-20). Yet the command is clear. Timothy, selected by prophets for the job (cf. Acts 13:1-3), must wage a good battle in Ephesus. He has the qualities Paul wants for the whole community, faith and a good conscience. At least *Hymenaeus and Alexander* have suffered shipwreck in the faith and Paul has *turned them over to Satan*. This phrase probably referred to a formula used in cutting them off from the community (cf. 1 Cor 5:5) with physical illness as a possible consequence.

Orders Concerning the Churches, 2:1–6:2a

Paul next issues more specific orders about the church in Ephesus. He addresses the three major areas of concern for young churches—public worship, the ministry, and behavior of their members.

Public Worship, 2:1-15

Appropriately his directions concerning public worship begin with insistence on prayer for all persons and not just for believers (vv. 1-7). The main point is the universality of the prayer. By contrast with some sects in JUDAISM such as the ESSENES, Christians should entreat God on behalf of the emperor and all persons in authority so that they may live peacefully in their own religious commitment.

Paul predicates this appeal on MONOTHEISM. The one and only God wants all persons to be saved and converted to the truth of Christianity. A snippet from an early Christian hymn or confession of faith buttresses the point. Not only is there one God but also one mediator between God and humankind, the man Christ Jesus, who gave himself as *a ransom* not just for the few but *for all*. The gospel cannot be narrowed to an elect. It is for everyone.

Predictably, mention of the universal gospel touches Paul's defense mechanism. It is to this that God appointed him as preacher and apostle and teacher of the gentiles.

To counter the debates that fractured the assembly, Paul appealed for tranquillity in the conduct of worship (vv. 8-15). *Men should pray* with pure lives and *without anger* or disputes. Early Christians, like both Jews and Gentiles, prayed standing, with eyes open

and hands lifted toward heaven. Paul was underscoring character and conduct. They should lift up *holy hands* and leave tempers and taunts behind. We relate to God better with peaceful expressions.

Women, likewise, should do things that would promote harmony in the worship services. One dimension would be to dress modestly. Early Christian women tried to set themselves apart from their contemporaries by simplicity of habit—shunning costly clothing, jewelry, elaborate hair styles (cf. 1 Pet 3:1-6). Instead of majoring in dress, they majored in good deeds.

Another dimension for promotion of harmony would be humility in conduct. Although in the church Paul wanted equality (Gal 3:28), practical realities forced women to accept subordinate roles in public worship (cf. 1 Cor 15:34-35). Context may well have dictated concessions at EPHESUS for the sake of preserving peace.

Paul argues like a RABBI in support of the subordinate role for women. (1) God created man before woman (v. 13; cf. Gen 2:22). (2) The serpent deceived Eve and not Adam (v. 15; cf. Gen 3:1-6). The statement that "woman will be saved through bearing children" (RSV) is difficult, maybe impossible, to interpret. A simple interpretation is probably best, that the gift of women through bearing children offsets her failure if she has other Christian qualities—faith, love, purity, and modesty.

The Ministry, 3:1-16

Paul speaks first about the office of presbyter or bishop. The office (Gk. *episkopos*) may have derived from the "superintendent" (*mebaqqer*) of the ESSENES. The term was used interchangeably with the word presbyter (Titus 3:5-7). From this brief instruction one can surmise that presbyter-BISHOP superintended the churches (v. 5), taught, watched over the charities, and led in public worship. The chief concern in this passage, however, was character and not duties.

The phrase "husband of one wife" (RSV) has been interpreted in several ways: (1) faithful to one wife, (2) monogamous, (3) never remarried even after death of a spouse, (4) never divorced, and (5) necessarily married. The first two are the more likely, although in the NRSV, *married only once*, favors the first, second, and third options.

Paul envisioned the church as an extended family and the presbyter-bishop as the head of it. The bishop needed, therefore, the qualities of a good father. How he presided over his own family would give a good clue to his ability to lead this larger family. In a mission situation such as Timothy served in Ephesus, moreover, the bishop should not be a newly baptized Christian and should have a good reputation with outsiders. These early communities became victims of Christian failing and the attacks of adversaries in times of persecution. *Devil* here probably means "Satan," however, rather than human adversary.

The office of DEACON (vv. 8-13), unlike that of bishop, probably did not have a direct antecedent in JUDAISM except in the servant model of JESUS. The qualifications listed would indicate that deacons shared leadership in worship, visited the sick and imprisoned, played a leading role in the LORD'S SUPPER or Agape meals, handled money for the poor, and taught. They needed careful scrutiny regarding their ministry. Like bishops, they needed to demonstrate in their families the character and gifts of leaders.

There is much debate concerning the reference to women in v. 11. Does it mean women deacons, wives of deacons, or women in general? The last two interpretations have had few advocates. In favor of women deacons are: (1) the reference to Phoebe as a deacon in Rom 16:1; (2) the absence of "their" which one would expect if Paul meant wives; (3) the nature of the virtues listed; and (4) the use of *likewise* to break the train of thought. In favor of wives of deacons are: (1) the brevity of the statement; (2) the way it is sandwiched between statements about male deacons; (3) the discussion of ministry of women in connection with *widows* in 5:3-16; and (4) the likelihood that a more definite term than *women* would have been used if women deacons were meant. The weight of argument slightly favors women deacons. The qualifications suggest a role similar to that of deacons. Women deacons in the late second century assisted in the baptism of women, visited the sick, discharged a ministry of prayer, and did other diaconal tasks.

Paul interjects another personal note explaining why he was writing (vv. 14-16). If Paul is delayed, Timothy should go right ahead with his task, for he knows very well what to do in the CHURCH.

Mention of the church brings to Paul's mind a hymn about Christ as *the mystery of our religion* (v. 16). The hymn emphasizes the universality of God's saving plan to which the church bears witness.

Behavior in the Church, 4:1–6:2a

At this point Paul turns to a series of miscellaneous orders concerning behavior in the church at Ephesus.

He refutes the false ASCETICISM of the Judaizers regarding prohibition of marriage and abstinence from certain foods. He instructs Timothy to avoid debating and instead to focus on his own personal piety, remembering especially the spiritual gift he has received for ministry. He follows this with directives about the proper behavior of groups within the Christian family—older and younger persons, widows, presbyters, slaves, and masters.

Casting his refutation (4:1-5) in the form of a prophecy, Paul cites some specific errors, all of which sound like the kind of teachings which would have originated with the ESSENES. They either spent a lot of time talking about demons or evil spirits or, alternatively, teaching things inspired by them. Having bad consciences as a result, they prohibited marriage and observed certain food laws. Paul rebuts these two practices by citing the OT concept of creation and the Christian concept of thanksgiving. Everything God created is good. Giving thanks further validates it for believers.

By contrast with the false ascetics, Timothy should be a good MINISTER of Christ (4:6-10). For this Paul prescribes three ingredients. First, he should nourish himself on the sound teaching that he received under Paul's tutoring and avoid the speculative interpretations of scriptures the ascetics propounded. In Titus 1:14 Paul called these "Jewish myths" and human concoctions.

Second, Timothy should train himself spiritually. Using an athletic metaphor (cf. 1 Cor 9:24-27; Phil 3:12), the apostle underscores how important this is for a minister. If physical exercise is of great benefit, how much greater must be spiritual exercise, for it bears not merely on the present life but also on the life to come. The promise of ETERNAL LIFE is what Christians strive to attain because they have placed their hope in the living God, the Savior of all persons, as believers amply attest. The main accent falls once again on the universality of God's saving work.

Third, combining command and personal plea, Paul directs Timothy's attention to his spiritual gift as the ground on which he can do what ministry requires (4:11-16). Timothy, now in his thirties, should stop hiding behind the excuse, "I'm too young." He should be an example of believers in all dimensions of Christian life—speech, conduct, love, faith or faithfulness, and sexual purity. A weighty expectation! Until Paul could get there, he should continue with the key duties—reading OT scriptures, preaching, and teaching new converts. The wherewithal for all of this would come from his charisma.

How Timothy received this "spiritual gift" is somewhat unclear. Obviously God gave it, but was Paul (as in 2 Tim 1:6) or the "presbytery" the means? As in 1:18, prophets discerned Timothy's spiritual gifts. It would be unlikely, therefore, that Paul or the presbyters would be required to convey the Spirit he already possessed. Laying on of hands accompanied and confirmed what prophetic utterance indicated, that is, Timothy's God-given capacity for ministry. This aspect Timothy must not forget. The gift of God would assure his progress.

Paul sums up his urgent charge. Timothy must pay heed both to himself and to what he teaches, for the stakes are high. He has responsibility both for his own spiritual welfare and for that of the people who listen to him.

This comment opens the way for a transition to the four groups within the household of faith for whom Timothy is responsible: young and old, widows, presbyters, and slaves. Concerning the first group (5:1-2), the apostle emphasizes the familial approach. Timothy should treat older men and women like fathers and mothers, younger men and women like brothers and sisters. Obviously with the latter he had to be circumspect about sex.

Widows (5:3-16) must have constituted a considerable segment of the Ephesian community and their numbers posed a problem. The main objective of this directive was to enroll on the church's charitable list only those whose needs and manner of life established them as genuinely bereft. Paul lists two basic requirements: (1) need and (2) record of Christian service *before* being widowed.

Regarding need, Timothy should see first whether personal family members, children or grandchildren, could care for the widows, thus relieving the overburdened extended family. An allusion to the fifth commandment undergirds the point. A Christian who does not watch out for members of his or her own family is worse than an unbeliever, for Christian faith makes it a principle (v. 8).

Paul's "real widow" would be truly dependent on God, praying night and day. The early churches, of course, knew some not like that, the kind who abandoned themselves to pleasure and comfort, perhaps even prostitution.

As a safeguard against such self-indulgence, Paul established three practical tests: (1) age over *sixty*,

(2) *married only once*, and (3) having good reputation for charitable works. "Wife of one husband" (RSV) probably means a single marriage, but the same possibilities exist here as for presbyters and deacons (3:2, 12; Titus 1:6).

Emphasis on reputation for charity suggests that some widows functioned as deacons. Paul lists four specific items that perhaps hint at duties of women deacons. They reared children, practiced HOSPITALITY, washed the feet of the saints, and relieved the sick. As a catchall, Paul adds, widows should have devoted themselves to every sort of good deed.

In vv. 11-15 Paul explains why younger women should not be enrolled as widows, indicating three sets of problems: (1) sexual passion, (2) idleness, and (3) gossiping. He uses very strong language. Their strong sex drive may cause them to violate their pledge to Christ as their bridegroom, made either when baptized or when enrolled as widows. Moreover, they may become troublemakers within the Christian community. Consequently Paul urges in no uncertain terms the remarriage of young widows. Confronted here with a specific problem, he proposes marriage, child-bearing, and care of a home as the way to safeguard the church's reputation. Paul knew that the mission could not afford scandal.

Once again returning to the problem of overtaxed social aid, Paul urges any faithful woman to take needy widows into her household. Some early manuscripts read "believing man," but wealthy women often headed households (e.g., LYDIA in Acts 16:14, 40).

Elders (5:17-25) should be understood in the nontechnical sense of "older men" here to avoid dividing them into two classes. Most leaders, if not all, came from this group. *Honor* would have a dual meaning, both respect and pay, as quotations from the OT would imply. At this early stage pay consisted of gifts of food and necessities rather than MONEY. The older leaders would receive twice the allotment for widows and others on the charitable roll.

Where leaders required discipline, Paul had two bits of advice: (1) Do not accept an accusation against a presbyter unless two or more witnesses confirm it. (2) Reprove the offender publicly, either before the elders or the CONGREGATION. Here Timothy must not let personal bias intrude, a point underlined with an oath.

The best DISCIPLINE is, of course, preventive. Thus Paul counsels Timothy not to baptize or ordain anyone hastily. Laying on of hands accompanied both BAPTISM and ordination. Since Timothy played a key role in choosing people, he must take care lest he be implicated in their offenses. The goodness and wickedness of people are sometimes evident, sometimes not.

Thrown in (v. 23) is a little aside about Timothy's personal health. The ancients ascribed medicinal value to wine.

Slaves (6:1-2a) also constituted an important element of the Christian community. Here Paul distinguished the motives of slaves under pagan and under Christian masters. Slaves should treat pagan masters respectfully to avoid bringing reproach on the name of God and Christian teaching. They should show still greater respect for Christian masters because they are *believers and beloved.* Many slaves must have chafed more under Christian than under pagan owners!

Final Orders to Timothy, 6:2b-19

The apostle shifts from orders concerning behavior in the church to warn about the profit motive in religion (vv. 2b-10), deliver a personal charge to Timothy, and give a special word to the wealthy.

Early Christianity attracted some, like SIMON MAGUS (Acts 8:18-24), who tried to turn it into a profit-making enterprise. Paul suspected that the wranglers at Ephesus were inspired by such motives. They could not square these with the teachings of Jesus. Religion, Paul had to admit, is immensely profitable, but not in the way these people pursued it. Rather, Christians must seek contentment with food and clothing, the necessities. People who crave wealth are headed for destruction, for obsession with money is the root of all evils. That is what has caused many to end up in heartache already.

Timothy (vv. 11-16) should shun this and aim at genuine virtue. In what has the ring of a baptismal or ordination charge Paul challenges his favorite son in faith to keep the pledge he made at baptism, a solemn commitment before God and Jesus Christ. Like a good soldier, Timothy must fight valiantly and discharge the orders given him until Christ returns.

Allusion to the appearance of Christ again touches off a doxology, this time mixing Jewish and Greek elements, probably from an early Christian HYMN. The words throw out a stout challenge to the emperor cult. Christ alone rules, possesses immortality, dwells in unapproachable light, and is thus due honor and dominion.

'As for the rich (vv. 17-19), who would have been in a minority in early Christian communities, Timothy must charge them not to trust in their wealth but only in God and to be generous. Paul wants them to consider their wealth a stewardship that would give them a solid foundation in eternity. The Christian's goal is not wealth but "real life."

Closing Charge and Salutation, 6:20-21

Paul ends as he began. Almost plaintively, he commands his sometimes vacillating aide to keep the orders given, that is, the true Christian faith. In sum, avoid silly speculation, so-called knowledge, which has led others astray.

An Outline

Second Timothy
I. Greeting and Affirmation of Apostolate, 1:1-2
II. Recollections and Personal Encouragement, 1:3–2:13
III. Counsels for Timothy, 2:14–4:8
IV. Farewell and Concluding Benedictions, 4:9-22

Written after Paul's reimprisonment in ROME, 2 Timothy is his last will and testament (cf. 4:6-8). It sounds two notes: (1) how much PAUL expects of Timothy and (2) what he hopes Timothy will do as his successor in mission.

Greeting and Affirmation of Apostolate, 1:1-2

This greeting differs only slightly from that in 1 Timothy. As one might expect of someone anticipating his death, Paul throws in a hopeful note. He is *an apostle* through God's will according to *the promise of life* attested in Christ's resurrection.

Recollections and Personal Encouragement, 1:3–2:13

Paul initiates his last will and testament with some remembrances that would offer encouragement to his successor (1:3-5). As in other letters, he begins with a prayer of THANKSGIVING to God, whom he served with the same clarity of purpose as his Jewish forbears did. He prayed night and day for his son in the faith. Remembrance of Timothy's tears at their parting aroused a longing to see him. Paul recalled the sincere faith that both Timothy's Jewish grandmother LOIS and his Christian mother EUNICE had exhibited. So Paul was confident he would find the same in Timothy.

His imprisonment notwithstanding, Paul directed Timothy to have confidence in God (1:6-14). Timothy should *rekindle the gift* God had given as indicated by Paul's *laying on of . . . hands* (cf. 1 Tim 4:14). God did not equip him with a spirit of timidity but of power, love, and self-control. He, therefore, should not hesitate to offer his witness to Christ or to defend Paul. As Christ and Paul had suffered, so too should Timothy suffer for the gospel in the power of God.

Mention of God's power stirs up in Paul's mind a HYMN or confession of faith (1:9-10). The first stanza praises God for God's saving work in Christ, calling humankind on the basis of MERCY rather than merit. The second stanza praises Jesus Christ as the one through whom God carried out the eternal plan. The third stanza declares what Christ did—abolished death and brought life and immortality through the gospel.

The word *gospel* triggers an instinctive apology on the part of the aged apostle (1:11-14). It is to this that God appointed Paul as preacher, apostle, and teacher (cf. 1 Tim 1:11) and it explains his suffering. Yet he has no regrets. He has complete confidence in God, that God will see to it that he keeps his pledge.

Paul appeals to Timothy to look to him as an example of reliable teaching he had heard from him that is grounded in faith and love in Christ. Timothy must guard the truth of the gospel committed to him. Although some have detected in the reference to a deposit a succession theory like that of *1 Clem* 42:2-4; 44:2, the statement here does not have to do with succession of bishops. It is about preservation of truth. The ultimate guardian is the HOLY SPIRIT indwelling us.

Paul recounts briefly his own sad plight (1:15-18). All the Christians from the province of ASIA living in Rome had deserted him, notably *Phygelus and Hermogenes.* Well, there was an exception, *Onesiphorus,* an Ephesian who had sought Paul out and done everything he could to aid him. The prayer for his household would seem to indicate that he may have given his life to help Paul.

Having built a foundation for faithfulness from the example of Timothy's family and himself, Paul comes to the main point. His dear child in faith must be strong and endure suffering (2:1-7). What he had heard from Paul, he must hand on to other faithful persons who will have the ability to teach others. Here again is an embryonic form of succession but of doctrine and not of office.

Paul invokes three images of perseverance: the soldier, the athlete, and the farmer. The soldier models stalwart endurance of hardships, non-entanglement, and desire to please. The athlete image emphasizes the need for *discipline.* The farmer image underlines the importance of hard work. Paul underscores his point with a sort of "Are you listening?"

Ultimately the apostle directs Timothy to the example of Christ (2:8-13). The gospel itself, briefly summarized (cf. Rom 1:3-4), is the reason for faithfulness. It is for the sake of the gospel that Paul suffers imprisonment. Though he is fettered, the word of God is not. The apostle has endured what he has for the sake of those God has chosen to take part in the eternal purpose. Their eternal glory, the antithesis of suffering, is the object of God's plan.

Reflections on God's assurances brings another hymn or confession of faith to mind (2:11-13). The first stanza has an exact parallel in Rom 6:8, suggesting a baptismal context. BAPTISM entails dying and rising with Christ. The second stanza echoes Jesus' words about endurance (Matt 10:22; 24:13; Mark 13:13) and promises participation in Christ's messianic kingdom. The third stanza warns against denial (cf. Matt 10:33). However shaky our faith, God is always faithful.

Counsels for Timothy, 2:14–4:8

Having laid his foundation, Paul turns to more specific directions about the Ephesian problem. His main counsel is to avoid getting entangled in meaningless debates and to discipline those who need it with humility and gentleness. Timothy has to set the example.

By way of contrast with the wranglers Timothy should avoid destructive debating and be a constructive workman (2:14-26). Constant disputation only upsets hearers. Timothy should model constructiveness, steering clear of harmful chatter that spreads through the body like cancer. Prime examples of the type Timothy should shun are *Hymenaeus* (2:17; cf. 1 Tim 1:20) and *Philetus,* who taught that the *resurrection has already taken place.* Some early gnostic groups taught that the resurrection took place in baptism, possibly on the basis of Paul's own teaching (cf. Rom 6:4).

Paul uses two metaphors to draw the line between himself and the wranglers: (1) the solid *foundation* of a strong building (2:19) and (2) the varied utensils in a household (2:20-21). God has established the foundation and inscribed it. God knows his own in an intimate way, and everyone claiming the Lord's name should avoid wrong. Why would any other type be in the church? Because it is a mixed body, like a large household. The key issue is not type of utensil or vessel, but the purity of each.

The apostle once again places the weight of responsibility on Timothy's shoulders (2:22-26). He should flee uncontrolled impulses and aim at the Christian virtues especially suitable in these circumstances, thus putting himself in the company of authentic believers. In handling the disputants he should do two things: (1) stay out of arguments; and (2) treat them with patience and kindliness. The accent falls on gentleness in handling opponents. The aim is to rescue the offenders from the Devil's snare and bring them back to the authentic Christian message.

Paul interjects a kind of apocalyptic warning (3:1-9). Jewish apocalypticists expected dire happenings in the *last days*. To describe these, Paul lists a catalogue of vices similar to the one used in Rom 1:29-31 but not dependent on it. The first two vices—*lovers of [self]* and *lovers of money*—epitomize the whole list. They are arrogant persons who act insensitively toward other persons and toward God. Timothy must shun them.

Paul describes a subtle method of operation. They preyed especially on women burdened by an extreme sense of guilt, always seeking a solution to problems but never able to arrive at the truth. Such charlatans, however, Paul assures Timothy, will not succeed. They will fail like the Egyptian magicians, JANNES AND JAMBRES, who tried their occult powers against MOSES. Everybody will be able to see their counterfeit faith, as they saw the Egyptian magicians' (Exod 8:16-19).

Operating on the assumption that he would have to maximize his plea, Paul invokes again his personal example and Timothy's training (3:10-17). Timothy had shared Paul's missionary labors and knew the price he had paid. He should not be surprised, for the faithful always suffer while the evil imposters get worse and worse. This called for steadfastness. Bedrock for Timothy would be confidence he could place in persons he learned from (his grandmother and mother) and in scriptures.

Scriptures, learned from infancy, furnished the ultimate ASSURANCE. Verse 16 could be translated either "Every scripture is inspired and profitable" or "Every inspired scripture is also profitable" with the latter more likely (ERV, NEB, et al.). The doctrine of inspiration allows room for human agency, but it emphasizes scriptures as the one fully reliable means of REVELATION. They serve, therefore, as the basis of Christian teaching, reproof of SIN, correction, and constructive educa-

tion in Christian life. Religious leaders like Timothy can count on them.

The apostle buttresses his appeal to example with a solemn exhortation to preach the gospel (4:1-8). With a solemn OATH, he pleads with his sometimes timid colleague to stand fast and do his duty with patience and care. This is urgent because an apocalyptic situation seems at hand when novelty will have more followers than the truth at the time when Paul senses that the end is near. His life about to be poured out on the altar, Paul counts on Timothy.

In this poignant passage the apostle had to reassure himself as much as Timothy. He had *fought the good fight, finished* the race, and *kept the faith* (4:7). Now he could look forward to receiving his eternal reward given to all who have loved Christ's coming.

Farewell and Concluding Benedictions, 4:9-22

The remainder of 2 Timothy consists of personal notices and instructions (vv. 9-18), greetings (vv. 19-21), and a benediction. Scholars who hold the "fragments hypothesis" ascribe all or most of this passage to Paul.

At this point Paul needed Timothy desperately. Demas, his fellow worker during his first imprisonment (Col 4:14; Phlm 24), had deserted him. Crescens and TITUS had taken mission assignments in GALATIA and Dalmatia. LUKE was now the only one with him. Paul, therefore, needed as much help as possible, even John Mark, with whom he must have become reconciled after their rupture (Acts 15:38). MARK would replace TYCHICUS, whom Paul sent to Ephesus with the letter.

Winter approaching (v. 21), Paul wanted Timothy to bring warmer clothing, the heavy blanket-like cloak he had left in Troas with Carpus. He also needed the books, especially the parchments, containing important writings—perhaps parts of the OT, collections of testimonies, and other documents.

Paul could not help inserting a warning about *Alexander the coppersmith*, perhaps the person "turned over to Satan" (1 Tim 1:20) but the name was a common one. Paul was confident God would pay him back, but he knew the danger Alexander posed to Timothy.

After this brief digression the apostle recounts his own sad circumstances. During his first defense, meaning either his first trial or a preliminary hearing in Rome, all deserted him. Yet he would not hold that against them and prayed they not be held accountable in the Judgment. The Lord, God or Christ, stood by him and rescued him from extreme danger. The very thought evokes from Paul a confession of faith and doxology.

The concluding paragraph adds a greeting to longtime missionary associates *Prisca and Aquila* (Acts 18:2, 18; 1 Cor 16:19; Rom 16:3f.) and to Onesiphorus's *household*, a note suggesting Onesiphorus was dead. Paul throws in a couple of other tidbits about mutual acquaintances and passes on some greetings from others. The fact that he mentions them need not be seen as a conflict with the fact that all deserted him in his first defense (v. 16). These persons did not qualify for a formal defense.

An Outline

Titus
I. Greetings and Affirmation of Apostolate, 1:1-4
II. Instructions for the Community, 1:5–2:15
III. Instructions Regarding the World, 3:1-11
IV. Some Final Instructions, 3:12-14
V. Concluding Salutation and Benediction, 3:15

PAUL did not have as intimate personal ties with TITUS as with TIMOTHY, but he counted heavily on him for effective mission work. Titus had handled the Corinthian problem more effectively than Timothy (2 Cor 8:6; 12:18). At Paul's request (3:12) Titus evidently joined him in ROME. Before writing 2 Timothy Paul sent him to Dalmatia (2 Tim 4:10). From there he went to CRETE.

The letter to Titus has essentially the same objectives as 1 Timothy: to instruct an associate about the ordering of church life and about defense of the mission against agitators. It is both personal and official, intended to be read publicly.

Greetings and Affirmation of Apostolate, 1:1-4

OPPONENTS OF PAUL's mission turned up wherever Paul and his associates worked. Consequently the apostle had constantly to assert his commission. His commission had three aims: to enhance the faith of the elect, to bring them to godly knowledge of the truth, and to share the hope of ETERNAL LIFE. This hope never disappoints because God never lies and has revealed it at the right time through preaching. It is this that God entrusted to Paul.

The greeting to Titus is a bit stiffer than those to Timothy. Titus is an authentic child in a common faith, rather than "beloved" (2 Tim 1:2).

Instructions for the Community, 1:5–2:15

The bulk of the letter gives instructions about the ordering of church life with some warnings about disturbers thrown in. Predictably the qualifications of presbyter-bishops gets attention first (1:5-9). The APOSTLE had left Titus in Crete to set up proper organization and to appoint qualified persons to continue the mission. As in other areas, Paul specified an urban pattern.

Qualifications for presbyter-bishops (NRSV *elders*) correspond closely with that for bishops and deacons in 1 Tim 3. Here too Paul envisioned the church as a family. Success in heading his own household would provide a good clue to management of an extended family. The BISHOP is God's steward. He should be mature, unselfish, and other-directed, able to preach healthy doctrine and refute those who oppose it.

Worthy leadership will be essential in order to counter those who stand opposed to what Paul has taught. Judaistic leanings of the troublemakers are quite clear. Some belonged to the "circumcision party" (cf. Gal 2:12; Col 4:11) and taught Jewish myths. Evidently they also adhered to Jewish dietary laws. They may also have engaged in some kind of magical rites.

Paul had no patience for them because they upset whole families for base motives. The Cretan poet Epimenides characterized them correctly (1:12). Titus must silence them, reprove them sharply, act forcefully to put a stop to them.

Here the apostle offers an antidote to the Cretan troublemakers, exemplary behavior within the Christian community (2:1-10). For this Titus himself offered the key. He had to teach healthy doctrine. Paul directs Titus's attention to four groups—older men, older and younger women, younger men, slaves.

For *older men* (2:1-2) Paul lists essentially the same qualities as he demands of presbyter-bishops and deacons. Christianity does not have two standards of behavior.

For *older women* (2:3-5) he lists qualities similar to those he gives for women deacons or wives of deacons in 1 Tim 3:11. In Crete they would have a special responsibility for the Christian education of younger women, for whom Paul's main concern was strong and stable families. Love of women for husbands and children is the key to the family. As in social codes in other letters of Paul (Col 3:18; Eph 5:22), Paul enjoins wives voluntarily to accept the authority of their husbands lest Christianity's reputation suffer harm in societies that were not yet ready for equality of male and female (Gal 5:28).

For *younger men* (2:6-8) the apostle uses more decisive directions. Titus should set the example of gentlemanly behavior Paul expected. How these individuals behaved would silence the kind of criticism that arose so easily from pagan lips or from the troublemakers in Crete.

For *slaves* (2:9-10) Paul prescribes acceptance of their status and exemplary service. Christians should not act like typical slaves, talking back and stealing. Rather, they should model reliability so as to make the message of the Savior God noble and attractive to all.

The allusion to God as Savior causes Paul to lapse into a HYMN or confession of faith on God's saving grace as the basis for Christian behavior (2:11-14). GRACE was manifested at a definite moment in history, in the birth of JESUS of Nazareth. It instructs us to lay aside irreligious and worldly behavior, to live godly lives, and to await the consummation of the Christian hope. The signal for the latter will be the return of Christ. Christ came to do two things: liberate us from sin and prepare us to be God's own people. Christ's death furnished the ransom price needed to free us from evil, and it laid a foundation for the church.

At this point (2:15) Paul interjects a general charge to Titus. He must not act indecisively but with full authority, that is, Paul's.

Instructions Regarding the World, 3:1-11

Whereas in chap. 2 Paul gave directions on behavior within the Christian community, in chap. 3 he widens them to the larger world in which Christians live. He wants the Christians of Crete to be model citizens—obedient to their rulers (cf. Rom 13:1-7), honest, and courteous to all (vv. 1-2). They were not always like that (v. 3), but God pulled off a mighty work of recycling.

In support of this plea the apostle cites an early Christian baptismal hymn on regeneration and renewal. Whatever the human situation prior to the Christian era, God decisively changed it in the coming of Christ. Out of goodness and generosity God saved us in one decisive intervention in human history. God acted out of MERCY and not on the basis of our righteousness. We, however, appropriated this mercy through BAPTISM and the gift of the Spirit, which God poured out upon us generously through Jesus Christ. The purpose of the whole divine act is that we may become heirs of eternal life after God has rightwised us. The formula *The saying is sure* (v. 8) looks backward rather than forward.

Concluding the main body of the letter (vv. 8b-11), Paul takes one last shot at the troublemakers. Titus must be insistent on what Paul has said so that believers may apply themselves to good deeds beneficial to humankind. Contrariwise, he must avoid divisive debates deadly for Christian witness. He should shun the factious person after one or two warnings (cf. Matt 18:15-17). If such a person refused to relent, he or she would be self-condemned.

Some Final Instructions, 3:12-14

Paul intersperses in his conclusion some personal notes with his final instructions. When he dispatched *Zenas . . . and Apollos* with the letter, he had evidently not yet decided whether to send *Artemas* and *Tychicus*. He intended to do so soon, however, and to meet Titus in *Nicopolis* where they would *spend the winter*. Zenas and Artemas are not mentioned elsewhere in the NT. Thinking of the needs of these missionary travelers, Paul throws in a final comment about the need for consistent charity, the distinguishing mark of early Christians.

Concluding Salutation and Benediction, 3:15

Paul closes this letter as he did those to Timothy with concluding greetings and a benediction. Probably written earlier, this greeting is more optimistic than 2 Tim 4:9-22.

Philemon

Charles H. Cosgrove

Introduction

Paul writes to PHILEMON on behalf of Philemon's slave ONESIMUS, who has become a convert through Paul's own witness. By comparing the names in Philemon with those in Col 4:7-17, we may conclude that Philemon is a member of a house church at COLOSSAE. While PAUL addresses almost every sentence directly to Philemon, as if the letter were for him alone, he also identifies the church as recipient (along with APPHIA and ARCHIPPUS).

Date and Place of Writing

Although Paul does not state his location at the time of writing, except to indicate that he is in prison (v. 10), he probably writes from EPHESUS around 52–54 C.E. (see Harrison 1950).

The Occasion of the Letter

We know from v. 16 that Onesimus is Philemon's slave. Paul writes in order to persuade Philemon to act graciously toward Onesimus in the wake of some alleged (and unnamed) misdeed by the slave (see v. 18).

Since Paul addresses the letter not only to *Philemon* but *to the church*, he probably intends for it to be read aloud in the assembly. The CONGREGATION is supposed to "overhear" Paul's words to Philemon, which makes the slave-owner accountable not only to Paul but to them as well.

Traditionally it has been assumed that Onesimus is a fugitive slave, and interpreters have reconstructed his story more or less as follows. Once there was a slave named Onesimus who ran away from his master Philemon, and (somehow or other) came in contact with Paul, founder of the CHURCH to which Philemon belongs. Under Paul's influence Onesimus came to faith in the God of Jesus Christ and decided to do the right thing by returning to his master.

The difficulty with this reconstruction is that it fails to provide a plausible explanation of how the runaway slave happens to wind up in Paul's company. It strains credulity to think this is sheer coincidence.

Some have therefore suggested that the fugitive Onesimus grew remorseful and deliberately sought out his master's friend, Paul, in the hopes that Paul might be willing to smooth things over with Philemon. Paul nowhere indicates that Onesimus has had a change of heart about running away.

The suggestion that Onesimus intentionally went to Paul for help is, nevertheless, a step toward a better reconstruction. We should abandon the assumption, nowhere confirmed by the letter itself, that Onesimus is a fugitive slave. It happens that in Roman case law, which was widely respected even outside of ROME, there are precedents establishing the propriety of a slave seeking out a third party, usually an esteemed "friend of the master" (*amicus domini*), in order to resolve a difficulty with a master. If a slave left the household in order to speak with this third party (who may have been in another city), the slave was not considered a runaway.

It is probable that Onesimus, fearing reprisal from his master for some alleged misdeed, sought out Paul as an *amicus domini* who might mediate between him and Philemon. In that case, Paul's letter and his upcoming visit (v. 22) are actions of mediation on behalf of Onesimus.

For Further Study

In the *Mercer Dictionary of the Bible*: ONESIMUS; PAUL; PHILEMON, LETTER TO; PRISON EPISTLES; SLAVERY IN THE NT.

In other sources: J. M. G. Barclay, "Paul, Philemon, and the Dilemma of Christian Slave-Ownership," *NTS* 37 (1991): 161–86; P. N. Harrison, "Onesimus and Philemon," *ATR* 32 (1950): 268–94; John Knox, *Philemon among the Letters of Paul*; L. A. Lewis, "An African-American Appraisal of the Philemon-Paul-

Onesimus Triangle," in *Stoney the Road We Trod: African-American Biblical Interpretation*, ed. Cain Hope Felder; J. B. Lightfoot, *St. Paul's Epistles to the Colossians and to Philemon*; E. Lohse, *A Commentary* on the Epistles to the Colossians and to Philemon; N. R. Petersen, *Rediscovering Paul*; B. M. Rapske, "The Prisoner Paul in the Eyes of Onesimus," *NTS* 37 (1991): 187–203.

Commentary

An Outline

> I. Opening, 1-3
> II. Thanksgiving, 4-7
> III. Letter Body: Appeals for Onesimus, 8-22
>   A. First Appeal: "For Love's Sake," 8-10
>   B. Second Appeal: For Usefulness' Sake, 11-14
>   C. Third Appeal: The Rights
>   of Apostolic Paternity, 15-16
>   D. The Fourth Appeal: "Receive Him as Me," 17-20
>   E. A Statement of Confidence
>   and Final Instructions, 21-22
> IV. Closing, 23-25

Opening, 1-3

Paul, writing from PRISON (cf. vv. 9-10, 13) and naming *Timothy* as coauthor, identifies himself as a *prisoner* (δέσμιος) *of Jesus Christ*. Later in the letter he will voice his wish that Onesimus continue to serve him in the "bonds" (δεσμοῖς) of the gospel (vv. 10-13). The literal chains of Paul symbolize the metaphorical chains that bind Paul as Christ's *prisoner*. Onesimus is also in chains, namely, the metaphorical chains of (literal) slavery to Philemon—and may be clapped into literal chains upon his return. If he has been serving with Paul in the chains of the gospel, he is also, like Paul, Christ's prisoner. Thus at the very beginning of the letter Paul hints that Onesimus shares Paul's status. This hint prepares for v. 17, where Paul says, "Receive him as . . . me" (RSV).

Paul describes Philemon as "our beloved coworker." He next names *Apphia our sister*, and after her *Archippus*, "our comrade in arms." We know practically nothing about these three persons, although ARCHIPPUS appears in Col 4:17. APPHIA might be the wife of Philemon or of Archippus, if she is married to either of them. *Your house* (v. 2), in which the CHURCH meets, may be the house of Philemon or Archippus. The singular *your* would most naturally be taken with the last person named (Archippus), but it could also refer to Philemon as the one most directly addressed throughout the letter.

After naming the recipients Paul gives one of his customary liturgical greetings (v. 3).

Thanksgiving, 4-7

Paul constructs an elaborate epistolary THANKSGIVING in vv. 4-8. In the presence of those gathered to hear the reading of the letter, Paul thanks God for Philemon's many virtues. This is an example of what the Latins called a *captatio benevelentiae*. We might say that Paul "butters up" Philemon before bringing up the matter of Onesimus.

As Petersen (1985, 72) points out, the rhetorical function of the thanksgiving is to inaugurate the basic strategy of persuasion that governs the letter as a whole. Paul's *I hear* therefore *I . . . appeal* (vv. 5, 9) means "you have refreshed the hearts of the saints with your faith and love, now refresh my heart also" (author trans.; cf. vv. 7 and 20). Philemon is about to learn how he can continue to be his virtuous self and refresh Paul's heart.

Letter Body: Appeals for Onesimus, 8-22

For analysis we can divide the body of the letter into five parts: an opening expression of apostolic authority and general introductory appeal (vv. 8-10), followed by three additional appeals (vv. 11-14, 15-16, and 17-20), a closing statement of confidence (v. 21), and an announcement of an impending visit (v. 22).

First Appeal: For Love's Sake, 8-10

"For love's sake," Paul says, he is appealing rather than commanding, but the command is rhetorically present nonetheless in two ways. First, by calling the content of his appeal "what is necessary," Paul rules out the possibility that Philemon can act honorably without doing what Paul requests. Second, as Petersen (1985, 65) rightly notes, Paul's appeals are a convention used by persons in authority (esp. royalty) to express commands. The language of request functions as a command when the one who requests has the authority to command. Paul includes a reminder of his authority in v. 8 ("Although I have the boldness in Christ to command you," author trans.) and again in v. 9, where he refers to himself by means of a term πρεσβύτης, which carries the general meaning of *old man* and the specialized technical meaning of "ambassador," which best seems to fit here. In 2 Cor 5:20 (cf. Eph 6:20) Paul uses a cognate verbal form to depict himself as God's ambassador. There, too, he describes his ambassadorial mode of discourse as *appeal*.

In v. 10 Paul discloses the purpose of his letter as an appeal for Onesimus. It becomes clear in what follows that Onesimus, whether justly or unjustly by Greco-Roman convention and law, is in trouble with Philemon. Paul does not need to point this out, nor does he anywhere in the letter dispute any complaint that Philemon may have against Onesimus. He tacitly presumes Philemon's interpretation of what has happened, and so his appeal "for my child, whom I have fathered in my chains" (author trans.) sounds initially like an appeal for mercy. The expression "for love's sake" (author trans.) in v. 9 has already prepared Philemon to hear the appeal in this way. Nevertheless, in what follows Paul progressively displaces his argument from love with arguments from usefulness and paternal apostolic rights.

There is, in fact, already a hint of these subsequent arguments when Paul says in v. 10 that he "fathered" Onesimus. This metaphor means that Paul, as apostle, converted Onesimus and now enjoys fatherly apostolic rights over him (cf. 1 Cor 4:14-15; 2 Cor 6:13; 12:14-15). Hence, in calling Onesimus his "child" Paul implicitly lays claim to Onesimus and, in effect, disputes Philemon's prior claims on Onesimus.

Second Appeal: For Usefulness' Sake, 11-14

Having hinted at his rights to Onesimus, Paul goes on in vv. 11-14 to suggest that he might retain the "use" of Onesimus. "Onesimus," a common slave name, means "useful," and it is a synonym of that word (εὔχρηστος) used in v. 11. Onesimus, Paul says, was once *useless* (ἄχρηστον) but now he is *useful* (εὔχρηστον), both to Philemon and to Paul. This is how one talked about slaves in the Greco-Roman world: as property valued for their instrumentality. Since Onesimus suggests servile identity, we should bring this out in English by calling him Useful.

Although Paul calls Useful his child, his argument from usefulness in these verses treats Useful as chattel. Even though Paul has already spoken of himself as a *prisoner*, this does not put him on the same level with Onesimus. Paul's bondage to Christ gives him considerable authority, whereas Useful's status as a slave makes him powerless.

Paul's evaluation of Useful as formerly *useless* probably expresses what he takes to be Philemon's

own opinion. We don't know how or for exactly what reasons Philemon may have regarded Useful as a worthless slave. In any case, Paul adopts the perspective of the slave owner. The only question is whether the property called Useful will revert to Philemon or be retained by Paul. The decision is to be made in the interests of usefulness, not those of Useful himself.

Nevertheless, Useful is not merely property to Paul. Paul calls him *my own heart* (lit. "inward parts," the locus of deepest affection). Paul had wished to hold on to his beloved child, so that Useful might "serve" him "in the bonds of the gospel" (v. 13, author trans.). But, he says, "I didn't want to do anything without your opinion" (author trans.). The word "opinion" can mean *consent*. It is not, however, an unambiguous term for consent. By choosing this word rather than, say, "assent" or "agreement," Paul manages to be courteously deferent to Philemon without giving away the right to hold on to Useful. As he goes on to say, the reason he is sending Useful back to Philemon (along with the letter) is so that Philemon can do the right thing ("what is good") voluntarily and not by compulsion. All of this suggests that if Paul did not send Useful back, Philemon would have no choice but to accept the loss of Useful. As it now stands, he can make Paul a gift of Useful.

Third Appeal:
The Rights of Apostolic Paternity, 15-16

Paul suggests that divine PROVIDENCE has separated Useful from Philemon for a time. He states the aim of this providence in terms of Philemon's and not Useful's interest. The separation is, "perhaps," so that Philemon *might have him [Useful] back forever, no longer as a slave but more than a slave, a beloved brother . . . both in the flesh and in the Lord*. As a follower of Christ, Onesimus *is* a brother, whether Philemon receives him as such or not. Do Paul's appeals oblige Philemon to give Onesimus his freedom? Paul's suggestion in vv. 15-16 clearly implies this, for brotherhood may exist in the Lord between master and slave, as Paul's letters otherwise suggest, but brotherhood cannot exist in the flesh between master and slave. To put it differently, if Paul had meant to restrict brotherhood to a "purely spiritual" plane, leaving social relations undisturbed, he should have written simply *in the Lord* and not added *in the flesh* as well. So there is scarcely any room to doubt that Paul is appealing for Useful's freedom.

Verse 16 seems therefore to undermine the argument that Paul has been building since v. 10. That argument, at least in part, treated Useful as property and focussed delicately on the question of whose property Useful really is. Verse 16 declares Useful *no longer a slave but . . . a brother*, thus effectively undercutting either Paul's or Philemon's "ownership" of Useful. Useful is no longer to be slave to Paul or Philemon. He is now *brother* to Philemon and, we can add, recalling v. 10, *child* to Paul.

The effect of Paul's rhetoric, however, is in fact to undercut all of Philemon's authority over Useful while maintaining Paul's apostolic fatherly authority over the former slave. Thus Paul comes out ahead, and Useful comes under a new patriarchal authority. Although Philemon gets his property *back forever,* his property is no longer property and he really ought to send Onesimus back to Paul.

Verses 15-16 displace the argument begun in v. 10, which treated Useful as disputed property, with an argument that treats him as a person. This implicit recognition of him as a person scarcely acknowledges that Useful has any rights in Christ. While naming Useful's new status in Christ, Paul does not make it the basis of his mandate that Philemon free Useful. In v. 16 he does not say, for example, that Philemon should receive Useful as a brother *in the Lord* and therefore also *in the flesh.* He leaves it to his hearers to construe the relationship between *in the Lord* and *in the flesh.* Later Christian readers must do the same. We must also confront the fact that in Philemon the mandate for Useful's freedom rests on Paul's authority and not on any stated principle of the gospel. It is the apostle-patriarch Paul who decides Useful's fate, and Philemon is expected to obey not because the gospel requires him to accept Useful as *a beloved brother . . . in the flesh* but because Paul does. Thus Paul acts as a kindly monarch, God's own vice-regent, and Useful is entirely dependent on Paul's paternalistic favor.

By basing Useful's fate on his own decision as father and not directly on the gospel, Paul avoids the general question of Christian slave-ownership. If that question posed a dilemma for Paul, he never treats it as such in this letter.

Fourth Appeal: "Receive Him as Me," 17-20

The fourth appeal contains the first formal imperative in the letter. Referring to the fact that he is Philemon's partner, Paul tells Philemon to receive Useful as if he were Paul himself. Now, in effect, Useful becomes Paul's ambassador and is therefore elevated above Philemon. At the same time all Useful's debts

are canceled by Paul's promise (witnessed by an autograph, v. 19) to settle accounts with Philemon. Since Philemon owes Paul his own self, a fact that Paul mentions by saying he's not going to mention it, this settling of accounts really takes place in the letter itself. Paul is calling in part of the debt Philemon owes him, a debt that can, of course, never be fully paid since Philemon owes Paul everything—just as Useful now does. Thus, before any detailed calculation of Useful's debts is made, Useful is in the clear with Philemon, and Philemon and Useful are *both* hopelessly in debt to Paul.

In v. 20 Paul says that he wants to "profit in the Lord" from Philemon, a statement that recalls his "suggestion" that Philemon might grant him the "use" of Useful (vv. 11-14). Then, echoing the language of his opening thanksgiving, Paul urges Philemon to "refresh" his "heart" (again, the word is "inward parts") in Christ.

A Statement of Confidence and Final Instructions, 21-22

If there was ever any doubt that Paul's suggestions through appeal were commands requiring OBEDIENCE, v. 21 dispels it. Paul says that he is confident of Philemon's *obedience* and knows that Philemon will *do even more* than what Paul has requested.

Paul closes the body of the letter with a request that the church *prepare a guest room* for him, informing them that he intends to pay them a visit. He asks for their prayers to help make this possible. An unspoken purpose of these requests is no doubt to back up the letter with a promise of his personal apostolic presence.

Closing, 23-25

Paul concludes the letter with greetings from EPAPHRAS, MARK, Aristarchus, Demas, and LUKE. We may assume that these persons are esteemed by Philemon (and the Colossian church) and that Paul mentions them as further witnesses to Philemon's handling of the case of Useful (vv. 23-24). A liturgical blessing brings the letter to a close (v. 25).

Works Cited

Harrison, P. N. 1950. "Onesimus and Philemon," *ATR* 32:268–94.

Petersen, Norman R. 1985. *Rediscovering Paul: Philemon and the Sociology of Paul's Narrative World.*

Hebrews

Marie E. Isaacs

Introduction

The King James Version confidently designates this work as "The Epistle of Paul to the Hebrews." Modern scholarship, however, has shown this to be improbable on all counts. It is more a sermon than a letter, almost certainly not by the apostle Paul, and written to a Christian congregation rather than to the Jewish nation. About little else can we be certain, however. We know virtually nothing about the circumstances that led to Hebrews's composition, original destination, date, or authorship. What evidence we have is largely to be inferred from Hebrews itself—and that is far from unambiguous.

A Sermon

Only in its final greetings (13:22-25) does Hebrews resemble a first-century letter. Otherwise, from its opening prologue (1:1-4) to its closing warnings (12:29), it exhibits all the features of an expository sermon. (Some scholars think the sermon extends as far as 13:21.) Thus the work is highly rhetorical throughout, especially in those passages where the preacher interrupts his theological exposition and addresses the audience directly (see 2:1-4; 3:7-4:13; 5:11-6:20; 10:19-39; 12:1-29).

Although Ps 110 seems to be the homily's main text, it is by no means its only one. Thus the author of Hebrews uses a number of OT passages (mostly drawn from the Pentateuch and the Psalms) in his attempt to draw out the implications of Christ's death and ascension for the particular situation of the group to whom he is writing. Like all Christian preaching, Hebrews tries to grapple with contemporary experience on the one hand, and inherited religious tradition on the other, in order to make sense of them both.

The Situation Addressed

From the work itself we can infer a number of things about the congregation. It was a group whose knowledge of the Christian message had not come firsthand from the earthly JESUS but via the preaching and teaching of the earliest disciples (2:1-3). Although the preacher accuses them of spiritual immaturity (5:12-14), they were not recent converts. In fact theirs was an admirable record of fidelity even in the face of persecution and suffering, which they had encountered in the past (10:32-34; cf. 12:4). Now, however, that enthusiasm was on the wane.

Exactly what has caused this crisis of confidence we cannot say. Various suggestions have been made: the delayed PAROUSIA, the outbreak of the Jewish war against Rome in 66 C.E., the Neronian persecution in 64 C.E., the fall of the Jerusalem Temple in 70 C.E., and so forth. What is clear is that they were a congregation in danger of drifting (2:2; 3:12; 4:11), tempted to go backward rather than forward. Many commentators have interpreted this to mean that they were tempted to revert to their original ancestral faith, JUDAISM. There is nothing in Hebrews that would suggest that the preacher is inveighing against Judaism, however. Rather, he finds examples of both fidelity (11:1-40) and infidelity (3:7-19) among the people of God in the past, and uses these by way of warning and encouragement to God's people in the present.

It is impossible to be sure as to the location of this particular group. JERUSALEM, ALEXANDRIA, CORINTH, SYRIA, and Asia Minor have all had their proponents. The current favorite is ROME, although this suggestion too is not without its difficulties. Both religiously and culturally its members seem to be Christian converts from the Greek-speaking Judaism of the dispersion. That of itself does not tell us where they were currently located, however.

As to Hebrews's date, it could have been written any time between the 60s and the 80s C.E.. It is first attested by Clement of Rome at the end of the first century. He cites parts of it, but not by name or title.

Central Theme

The main aim of this sermon is clearly pastoral. The author calls it *a word of exhortation* (13:22). The fundamental message to the group addressed could be summed up as:

Don't give up! See in Jesus, seated at the right hand of God in heaven, the assurance that God's sovereignty will ultimately reign on earth. In the meantime, understand that the Christian's pilgrimage to final salvation inevitably involves suffering, just as surely as Jesus' own route to God was via the cross.

In conveying this message Hebrews expounds biblical texts that enable the author to interpret salvation as the process whereby access to God is achieved. To this end he focuses upon divinely appointed places of rendezvous between God and the people. In Jewish tradition these were, par excellence, the promised LAND of CANAAN (cf. 3:1–4:13; 11:1–12:3), and the cult place, where God was approached via sacrifice (cf. 4:14–10:8). In neither territory, Hebrews argues, has but a partial encounter with God occurred, since the barrier of sin, which hindered true access to God, remained. Hence, the only one who truly entered into the presence of God, that is, heaven, was Jesus. He was the *pioneer* who entered into the promised land (2:10; 12:2), the Melchizedekian high priest who has entered the superior Holy of Holies (8:1–10:18), namely, heaven itself. And that by virtue of his death, which, by analogy, was the expiatory sacrifice that enabled the HIGH PRIEST to gain access to God. Other NT authors describe the work of Christ in sacrificial terms. Hebrews, however, is unique in comparing it to the sin offering of the Day of Atonement. Moreover, nowhere else in the NT do we find Jesus' death and entry into heaven depicted in priestly terms.

Author

From the second century, Christian tradition attributed Hebrews to Paul. Not until the fourth century was the Western church convinced, however. Even in the East there were those who were aware that there were problems, on stylistic grounds alone, of ascribing it to the APOSTLE. Hence, Clement of Alexandria suggested that Hebrews was originally written by Paul in Aramaic and then translated into Greek by Luke. Most NT characters have been suggested as the author of Hebrews, including BARNABAS, APOLLOS, and even a wom-

an—Priscilla. Perhaps we should leave the last word on the identity of the author of Hebrews to Origen. "As to who actually wrote the epistle God alone knows the truth of the matter" (Eusebius, *EccHist* 6.12-14).

Nonetheless, from Hebrews itself we can deduce quite a lot about its author. There is nothing to suggest that the work was originally written in Aramaic or Hebrew. Its author (as well as presumably his audience) was, therefore Greek rather than semitic-speaking. Hence he uses the LXX version(s) of the OT. Indeed, in places (eg. 1:6,7) his argument would have made no sense had he been using the Hebrew of the MT. He also seems to be at home not only with the scriptures themselves, but also with accepted Jewish exegetical methods and traditions current in the first century.

Scholars are divided as to how far Hebrews has been influenced by current Hellenistic philosophy. Most agree that at the very least he draws upon the same wealth of literary vocabulary, and moved in the same circles of educated thought, as diaspora Jews such as PHILO of Alexandria, and the authors of the *Wisdom of Solomon* and the *Epistle of Aristeas*. Undoubtedly, he was trained in the rhetorical skills that loomed so large in the higher education of the Greco-Roman world of his day.

Equally evident is that the author stood firmly within first-century Christian tradition. Thus his homily—for all its unique features—is built upon two major tenets of Christian faith, which he assumes that his readers share: (1) that Jesus is now exalted in heaven; and (2) that his death was the means whereby that exaltation was achieved. He not only reaffirms these beliefs; he reinterprets and extends them to meet the needs of the situation of his audience. In so doing he has created a new and powerful theology of access to God, which has spoken to generations ever since.

For Further Study

In the *Mercer Dictionary of the Bible*: ATONEMENT, DAY OF; EPISTLE/LETTER; EXPIATION IN THE NT; HEBREWS, LETTER TO THE; HELLENISTIC WORLD; HIGH PRIEST; JUDAISM; MELCHIZEDEK; RESURRECTION IN THE NT.

In other sources: H. W. Attridge, *The Epistle to the Hebrews*, Herm; F. F. Bruce, *The Epistle to the Hebrews*, NICNT; J. Héring, *The Epistle to the Hebrews*; F. L. Horton, *The Melchizedek Tradition: A Critical Examination of the Sources to the Fifth Century AD and the Epistle to the Hebrews*; G. Hughes, *Hebrews* and Hermeneutics: The Epistle to the Hebrews as an Example of Biblical Interpretation; P. E. Hughes, A Commentary on the Epistle to the Hebrews; M. E. Isaacs, Sacred Space: An Approach to the Theology of the Epistle to the Hebrews; W. G. Johnsson, "The Pilgrimage Motif in the Book of Hebrews," JBL 97 (1971): 239-51; E. Käsemann, The Wandering People of God; H. Koester, "'Outside the Camp': Hebrews 13.9-14," HTR 33 (1962): 299-315; W. L. Lane, Hebrews, WBC; B. Lindars, The Theology of the Letter to the Hebrews; H. Montefiore, The Epistle to the Hebrews, BNTC; D. Peterson, Hebrews and Perfection: An Examination of the Concept of Perfection in the Epistle to the Hebrews; R. Williamson, "The Eucharist and the Epistle to the Hebrews," NTS 21 (1975): 300-12; R. McL. Wilson, Hebrews, NCC.

Commentary

An Outline

Prologue: The Exaltation of Jesus, the Son of God, 1:1-4

Hebrews opens with a prologue that extols the Son as God's supreme agent of REVELATION, creation, and salvation. These claims are put forward as commonly accepted Christian tradition. The tone, therefore, is confessional rather than argumentative.

1:1-2b. The Son, as God's definitive spokesman, supersedes all his predecessors. The genuine inspiration of the OT and its prophetic voice is not in dispute. Reference to the plurality and diversity of revelation in the past (in many and various ways), therefore, should not be understood pejoratively (contra NEB in fragmentary and piecemeal fashion). Nonetheless, it gives way to the single, definitive word articulated in Jesus.

Son is the name he has inherited (unlike Phil 2:11 where it is "Lord"). It signals his superior status to prophets (v. 1) and angels (v. 4) alike. This theme is developed in 1:5–2:18 concerning angels, and in 3:1-6 it is taken up with regard to MOSES (counted among Israel's prophets in Jewish tradition).

1:2c-3b. The Son as agent in creation. Here terms and functions, previously ascribed in Judaism to divine wisdom (Job 28:23-28; Prov 8; Sir 24:3-24; Wis 7:1–8:1), are applied to the Son. Thus he is God's agent in bringing the worlds (lit. "the ages") into being, and in the ongoing work of sustaining the universe. We find the selfsame functions ascribed by PHILO (the Alexandrian Jewish rabbi and older contemporary of the apostle Paul) to God's word (λόγος). In most respects Philo's logos is but wisdom (σοφία) in another guise.

Like wisdom in Jewish writings (cf. Wis 7:25f.), so the Son in Hebrews is described as God's reflection. Like the word in Philo (cf. On Planting 18) he is the exact imprint. The language of the divine wisdom/word is applied to the Son somewhat obliquely, however. Thus, unlike Paul in 1 Cor 1:24, 30, Hebrews does not directly describe Jesus as God's wisdom. Nor, unlike the prologue of John's Gospel, is he identified with the preexistent logos who became flesh.

The closest parallel in the NT to these verses is Col 1:15-20. It is possible that both Colossians and Hebrews are drawing upon an early Christian HYMN or confession. If so, Hebrews does not use it to stress the Son's preexistence so much as to assert his preeminence. Above all, the prologue is concerned to affirm the sovereignty of Christ in his postexistence.

1:3c-4. The Son as agent of salvation. Unique to Hebrews is the analogy that it draws between the death and ascension of Jesus and the actions of the Levitical high priest on the Day of Atonement (see Lev 16 and ATONEMENT, DAY OF). Thus the CROSS is likened to the sacrificial offering that was the essential prerequisite for entry into the shrine's inner sanctum, and heaven becomes that inner sanctum, the Holy of Holies in which Jesus is now situated.

This theme, developed at length in 4:14–10:18, is announced at the very outset: *When he had made purification for sins, he sat down at the right hand of the Majesty on high* (v. 3). The motif of session (sitting at the right hand of God) alludes to Ps 110:1, one of the most widely cited texts in the NT. It is used throughout this homily (1:13; 8:1; 10:12-13; 12:2) to affirm that Jesus is now in heaven, seated at God's right hand. A psalm that originally celebrated the enthronement of a Davidic king as God's son and viceroy is seen to find its fulfilment in the exalted Christ.

He Excels the Very Angels, 1:5–2:18

A discussion of Jesus' status vis-à-vis the angels arises out of the session theme of the prologue. From his heavenly location should not be inferred that Jesus is one of the angels, however. As Son he has a different status from the other occupants of heaven.

Scriptural Proof of the Son's Incomparable Status, 1:5-14

Seven OT texts are cited as confirmation. They are used to advance a carefully constructed argument:

1:5. Jesus is not an angel. He is Davidic Messiah, SON OF GOD. Ps 2:7 and 2 Sam 7:17 (texts that addressed the Davidic king as Son of God) are cited as twin testimonies to this.

1:6. Jesus receives homage. Jesus is the one who receives rather than pays homage, since he is God's *firstborn* (a term used of the Davidic king in LXX Ps 88 (MT 89):17).This is confirmed by Deut 32:43 (to be found only in the LXX).

1:7. Angels are changeable. Using the LXX Ps 103:4, Hebrews can claim that scripture shows that angels are so unstable that God can reduce them to the elemental forces of wind and fire, if he so chooses. (The MT Ps

104:4 says something quite different, i.e., that God can use winds and flames as his messengers.)

1:8-12. The Son, on the other hand, exercises eternal sovereignty. Ps 45:6-7 (LXX Ps 44:6-7), originally addressed as an encomium to the Davidic king, is here applied to Jesus. In both its Hebrew and Greek versions there are ambiguities in this psalm. Hence v. 6 (=Heb 1:8) can either be translated as, "Thy throne O God is forever," or "God is your throne forever," or "Your throne is a throne of God forever." Whether or not the original psalmist addressed Israel's king as "God" (cf. Exod 7:1; Ps 82:6), or Hebrews so designates Jesus, is far from certain. What is clear is that the emphasis here is upon the eternal sovereignty exercised by the Lord's anointed on God's behalf (1:9; cf. Isa 61:1). With the citation (vv. 10-12) of Ps 101:26-28 (MT 102:25-27), the permanence and stability of this rule is contrasted with the impermanence and instability of the created order.

1:13-14. Jesus is now enthroned in heaven. The section concludes with the text first cited in the prologue, Ps 110:1. Christ's heavenly session demonstrates his sovereignty over all things, angels included.

A Warning Aside:
Heed the Christian Message, 2:1-4

This is the first of a number of instances where the author interrupts his exposition to address his audience directly. Here it is to issue a warning against the dangers of drifting away from the Christian faith.

The rhetorical question in v. 3 introduces an *a fortiori* argument. If the revelation mediated by angels is to be heeded, *how much more* so should the message of salvation, which was originally proclaimed by the Lord and validated by his original disciples? *The message declared through angels* (v. 2) probably reflects the tradition that had grown up in Judaism that angels were present when Moses was given the Law on Mount Sinai (cf. also Acts 7:28, 35; Gal 3:19). *Signs, wonders and various miracles,* together with the gifts of the *Holy Spirit,* act as corroborative testimony. Here the empowering work of the Spirit is to the fore (cf. also 6:4; 10:29). Elsewhere (3:7; 9:8; 10:15) the emphasis is on the HOLY SPIRIT as the source of scripture's inspiration.

The Sovereignty and Solidarity of the Son of Man, 2:5-18

2:5-9. The sovereignty of the son of man. Psalm 8:4-6 (MT vv. 5-7) is cited to show that God originally entrusted the exercise of sovereignty over the created order, not to angels, but to Man (=Adam; cf. Gen 1:26-30). The NRSV *human beings, mortals* (together with the plural verbs and pronouns) brings out well the corporate emphasis. This translation, however, obscures the singular *Man, Son of Man* of the original text. Whereas the psalmist was indeed using this language in a corporate rather than a titular sense, it was precisely the singular of the original that enabled Hebrews to see in the exaltation of one man, Jesus, the fulfilment of God's purposes for all humanity.

The MT of the psalm marvels that we should be made "a little lower than God" (*Elohim*). Following the LXX, however, Hebrews has *for a little while lower than the angels. Little while* is given a dual interpretation: (1) Applied to the earthly Jesus it refers to the interlude between his death and his heavenly exaltation. (2) Applied to the present it refers to the equally brief interlude between Jesus' heavenly enthronement and his exercise of sovereignty on earth. As yet the latter awaits its fulfilment until his return (see 9:28). In the meantime Jesus is the pioneer; the Son who leads *many sons* (NRSV *many children*) to their destiny of sovereignty (v. 1).

2:10-18. Jesus' solidarity with his followers. Three additional OT texts are used (vv. 12-13) to confirm this. As fellow members of the assembly (ἐκκλησία) of God he addresses them as his siblings (Ps 22:22), united with him in their praise of and trust in God (Isa 8:17), and counted as his (God's) children (Isa 8:18).

The chapter concludes with a statement of the genuine humanity of Christ. Unlike angels, he was subject to human limitations—including temptation (*testing*), suffering, and death. Therefore his help is directed, not towards angels in whose heavenly domain he now resides, but to human beings whose frailty he shared throughout the span of his earthly life. It is precisely Jesus' common humanity that qualifies him to act as *a merciful and faithful high priest* on our behalf.

Fidelity and Infidelity, 3:1–4:14

Picking up the word *faithful* from 2:17, the homily now moves to the topic of fidelity and infidelity. This section is predominantly an exhortation to remain steadfast and not to lose hope.

Jesus the Faithful Son Contrasted with Moses the Faithful Servant, 3:1-6

Both envoys (cf. v. 1, *apostle*) of God are comparable in their fidelity. Both were "faithful in my (i.e.,

God's) house." This is an allusion to Num 12:7 (LXX). Unlike the MT of this verse ("He is entrusted with all my house"), which points up Moses' status as Israel's supreme leader, the LXX stresses his constancy. He alone of all the wilderness generation continued to have faith in God's purposes for his people (=his *house*, household). On the other hand, Moses' status is lower than that of Jesus, and may be likened to that of a servant rather than the son of the house.

A Warning Example: The Faithlessness of the Wilderness Generation, 3:7-19

3:7-11. Israel's loss of faith in the past. In contrast to Moses' fidelity is the loss of faith on the part of those he sought to lead. Verses 7-11 cites Ps 94 (MT 95):7-11, which recalls Israel's resolve, in the face of the hardships of the wilderness, to turn her back on the promise of a homeland, and to return to a life of bondage in Egypt (cf. Num 14:1-35). The psalm also contains an allusion to an incident (Exod 17:1-7; Num 20:2-13) in which the people's complaint at their lack of water gave rise to the place names *Meribah* (=strife or contention) and *Massah* (=proof or test). The LXX translates rather than transliterates these Hebrew names. Hence they become: *as in the rebellion*, and: *as on the day of testing* (v. 8). The psalmist saw Israel's demand for water as putting God to the test—itself a demonstration of her loss of faith. By altering the punctuation and adding *therefore* (v. 10) Hebrews makes *forty years* refer, not to the duration of God's anger, but to the length of time Israel had been privileged to experience God's works (v. 17 reverts to the more usual reading). The effect of this is to heighten the enormity of the people's ingratitude.

3:12-4:11. A commentary on Psalm 95. Here the preacher applies the psalm to the present situation of his Christian audience. He draws an analogy between the experience of the wilderness generation and that of the group he is now addressing. Like their predecessors, they too are living through testing times. Unlike them, however, they should stand firm and not lose hope in the promises of God's future. They should take warning from the fate that befell the faithless of the past, whose punishment was that they were forbidden to enter the promised land of Canaan.

Like the psalmist, the author of Hebrews confines himself at this point to the threat of disinheritance. *They will not enter into my rest.* He does not mention that, in the case of CALEB, JOSHUA, and those Israelites under twenty years of age, God relented, in response to Moses' pleading (see Num 14:29ff.). To have done so would have detracted from the main purpose of this particular sermon. The preacher wants to use the words of the psalm as an exemplary warning to his own generation of the dangerous consequences of abandoning their faith.

Beware Lest You Fail to Enter God's Promised Rest, 4:1-11

By *enter* and *rest* Hebrews is not simply referring to Israel's possession of the land of CANAAN. He is well aware that that was achieved under Joshua (cf. 4:8). In Jewish tradition however, the land had come to represent more than a place of rest from Israel's wanderings (cf. Deut 3:20; Josh 1:3), or from the assaults of her enemies (cf. Deut 25:19; Josh 11:23). The land, more specifically Jerusalem (cf. Ps 132:14) and its Temple (cf. Deut 12:18), came to be thought of as God's abode or resting place. Thus *rest*, understood as the presence of God (cf. Exod 3:14; LXX Deut 33:14), could be a metaphor for salvation. Clearly that is how it is understood by the author of Hebrews.

Linking the psalm's noun *rest* with the verb "to rest" found in (LXX) Gen 2:2 enables Hebrews to move from the idea of salvation as the possession of the LAND to its depiction as the attainment of heaven itself. Salvation is thus to be in the presence of God in heaven, there to share that "rest" that he himself enjoyed on the seventh day, having created the universe. *Sabbath rest* (σαββατισμός) is the word coined by Hebrews (4:9) to characterize salvation as heavenly rather than earthly in its locus. Understood thus, the promised "rest" was not obtained when JOSHUA (v. 8) entered Canaan. (Chapter 11 reverts to this theme. The land sought in faith by Israel's patriarchs was not the earthly Canaan but a heavenly inheritance.)

What is more, neither the promise nor threat of this particular word of God was intended for the wilderness generation alone. Hence the psalmist (assumed by Hebrews to be DAVID) could and did address both to the *today* of his own time. Had the promise been fulfilled in Joshua's day there would have been no need for the psalmist of a later generation to have repeated it. For Hebrews this demonstrates that the promise is still outstanding (vv. 7-10). Thus he uses the psalm to challenge his contemporary audience to seize the *today* of God's word, lest they fail to become heirs of salvation. Like the wilderness generation, they stand on the brink of entry. They are *in the process of entering* God's rest. The NRSV *enter* (v. 3) obscures the

continuous force of the Greek at this point. The recurrent warnings in this section (3:12-14; 4:1,11) remind the readers that, even for them, salvation *remains* (3:9) to be attained in the future.

A Coda: The Penetrative Power of God's Word, 4:12-13.

The homiletic exposition of Ps 95 concludes with a coda in praise of the word (λόγος) of God. Clearly this is not a reference to Jesus, but to God, speaking through the scriptures that have just been cited. The Bible is seen as no dead letter of the past, but *living and active*; of continuing and contemporary relevance.

The image of divine judgment as a sword is a traditional one (cf. Isa 34:5-6). Wis 18:14-16 depicts the word as a warrior, wielding the divine sword of judgment against Israel's enemies at the EXODUS (cf. Eph 6:17; Rev 1:16; 2:12; 19:15). *Spirit* and *soul*, *joints* and *marrow*, and *thought* and *intentions* are used as three pairs of synonyms to emphasize the penetrative power of God's word and its ability to bring judgment even to the seemingly impenetrable.

Jesus the High Priest, 4:14–10:18

In this central section the principal soteriological model employed is that of the high priest, and the role he played in the Day of Atonement ceremonies. In this analogy, the death and ascension of Jesus represent both the offering and the offerer, the expiatory sacrifice that was the essential prerequisite for entry into the Holy of Holies and the high priest who was thus enabled to enter into the presence of God on the people's behalf.

Not only are comparisons made but contrasts are also drawn. Thus Jesus is superior both to the Day of Atonement's sacrificial victim, and its high priest. Furthermore, the cult place that Christ has entered far excels even the Holy of Holies, since it is nothing less than heaven itself. When in 8:7-13 and 9:15-22 Hebrews moves from the image of Jesus as expiatory sacrifice to one whereby he is seen as a COVENANT offering, we find a similar stress on his supremacy over what has gone before. His was a superior sacrifice that inaugurated a new and better covenant.

Merciful and Compassionate, 4:14–5:10

Hebrews 4:14-16 acts as a transition from the theme of access to God in terms of entry into the promised land (3:1–4:13), to its depiction in terms of the Jewish cult that dominates 4:14–10:18. Christ's priesthood, hinted at 1:3 and first stated at 2:17, *a merciful and faithful high priest*, is now pursued.

By way of encouragement to hold fast to their faith, the readers are once more reminded that Jesus is now in the presence of God in heaven. Earlier images of heaven as a royal court where Christ is enthroned now give way to its depiction as the inner sanctum of Israel's cult place. Thus it contains a *throne of grace* (4:16), i.e., the *mercy seat* located in the tabernacle's Holy of Holies (cf. 9:5). This is a reference to the lid or covering of the ark, upon which the victim's blood was sprinkled by the high priest on the Day of Atonement. Since the effect of this action was expiatory, the ARK could be spoken of as the place where mercy was dispensed. In the light of Jesus' expiatory work, Christians should be confident (NRSV *approach . . . with boldness*; cf. 3:6; 10:19) that they may approach God.

The source of Jesus' compassion as HIGH PRIEST lies in his genuine humanity—*one who in every respect has been tested as we are* (4:15). This picks up the theme of testing from 3:8 where it referred to the wilderness generation's desire to put God to the test. Thereby their own faith was tested and found wanting. By contrast, Jesus' response to testing was quite different. He was *without sin*.

Excursus: Priesthood in Postexilic Israel.

With the demise of the Davidic monarchy in postexilic Judaism, it was the institution of priesthood that came to the fore. Hence the covenant made by God with LEVI came to be seen as analogous to the one he made with Moses (cf. Jer 33:14-26—a passage regarded by many scholars as a postexilic interpolation). Like the Davidic covenant (2 Sam 7:12-16), the Levitical one was portrayed as permanent (Num 25:11-13; Sir 45:6-21)—*forever*.

The dominance of the priestly model of leadership in the postexilic period is evident from the second century B.C.E., with the installation of the Hasmonean high priesthood. In 140 BCE, Simon Maccabeus claimed the dual role of high priest and ethnarch both for himself and in perpetuity for his heirs (cf. 1 Mac 14:41). JOSEPHUS tells us (*Ant* 13.301) that by the time of John Hyrcanus (130–104 B.C.E.) the Hasmoneans had adopted the title "king" as well as high priest.

The QUMRAN community seems to have come into being originally as a protest, not against Hasmonean claims to (non-Davidic) kingship, but to their right to the high priesthood. According to the Covenanters,

although of the tribe of Levi, they were not descended from the Zadokite line (cf. *1QpHab* 12:7-8; 10:10; *CD* 12:2). They therefore regarded Hasmonean incumbency of the office to be invalid. The restoration of the true Zadokite line became part of their eschatological vision of the cult in the future. Thus, unlike Hebrews, the Qumran Covenanters looked forward to the purification of Judaism's Levitical high priesthood, rather than to its replacement by something wholly other—a Melchizidekian order.

5:1-4. The Aaronic priesthood. The major qualifications for the Aaronic priesthood are: (1) Common humanity. The priest must be part of what he represents. Hence he is *chosen from among mortals* (v. 1). (2) He should display a tolerant understanding towards those who err (v. 2), since he himself has human weaknesses (cf. 4:15) that require that he offer sacrifice, not only for the people, but for himself (v. 3). Here Hebrews has in mind the Day of Atonement ritual, where the two separate offerings were clearly distinguished (cf. Lev 9:7; 16:6-17). Later (7:27; 9:7) he is to assert the superiority of Christ's priesthood over that of the Levitical order, not least in his sinlessness (cf. 4:15), which precluded the need for two sacrifices and two entries into the Holy of Holies. (3) Priesthood requires a call and appointment that has God rather than oneself as its instigator (v. 4). "Appointed" (RSV) is preferable (as in 7:28 and 8:3) to the NRSV *put in charge of* (v. 1). 5:5-10 applies these qualifications to Jesus in inverse order:

5:5-6,10. His is a divine appointment. He has not only been called by God as his Son (Ps 2:7; cf. Heb 1:5); he has also been designated *a priest forever according to the order of Melchizedek* (Ps 110:4). In their original setting both Pss 2 and 110 were addressed to a Davidic king. Although Israel's preexilic kings could and did exercise what were later to become the exclusive functions of the priesthood (cf. 2 Sam 6:13-18; 24:17; 1 Kgs 3:15), since they were of the tribe of JUDAH rather than Levi, they were not priests. Hence the Psalmist addressed the Davidic king as of *the order of Melchizedek*, rather than Levi. Hebrews can therefore appropriately designate Jesus, the Davidic Messiah, as priest. In what sense he is *after the order of Melchizedek* will be developed in chap. 7.

Although Ps 110:1 is widely used in the NT, it is striking that Hebrews is the only Christian writer before JUSTIN MARTYR in the second century to use verse 4. Even those Qumran writings that feature MELCHIZEDEK (*11QMelch*; *1QapGen*) make no use of it.

5:7-10. Jesus shares human weakness. He is thus part of the humanity he represents. Unlike the Levitical high priest, however, in the case of Jesus it is not sin that is the common bond between representative and people; it is suffering and mortality (cf. 2:14-15). *Having been made perfect* (v. 9) is not a reference to moral perfectibility, and should not be understood as parallel with, *He learned obedience through what he suffered* (v. 8). That would be to suggest that Jesus' death was designed to correct his prior disobedience, whereas Hebrews stands firmly within the tradition that regarded him as sinless (cf. 2 Cor 5:21; 1 Pet 2:22; 1 John 3:5). His suffering is certainly portrayed as educative—but not in a punitive sense. Rather, it developed (cf. Luke 2:52) and expressed his filial obedience to God.

The language of *perfection* (τελείωσις) and its cognates (τελείουν and τελειωτής) in Hebrews, whether applied to Jesus or his followers, never loses the sense of achieving an end or goal (τέλος). In terms of the Jewish cult that end was access to God, symbolized by the entry of the high priest into the Holy of Holies. *Perfection* (cf. 7:11) for the Christian author of Hebrews is the attainment of that goal in terms of entry into heaven. It is, moreover, a process (*being made perfect*) that includes not only the end, but the means to that end. In the case of Jesus, his passion was the path to his perfecting (cf. 2:10; 5:9; 7:28). His disciples also, if they follow Jesus the *perfecter* (12:2), may achieve access to the presence of God, that is, heaven (cf. 10:4; 12:23), although, unlike Christ, for them that lies in the future.

Verse 7 is unlikely to refer to Jesus' prayer in Gethsemane (cf. Matt 26:36-46 ‖ Mark 14:32-42 ‖ Luke 22:40-46), since there his petition, "Remove this cup from me," was not granted. Here, however, *his prayer was heard*. Far from being a fearful entreaty, this prayer exudes the confidence that is the hallmark of the truly *reverent*. It displays that frank expression of emotion (*loud cries and tears*) that, according to Jewish tradition, characterized the prayer of the righteous. Thus Philo can say of Moses' prayer: "But the man of worth has such courage of speech that he is bold not only to speak and cry aloud, but actually to make an outcry of reproach, wrung from him by real conviction, and expressing true emotion" (*Who Is the Heir of Divine Things* 19). As vv. 6 and 10 make clear, this is the confidant prayer of Jesus, the Melchizedekian high priest, which accompanied the offering of the sacrifice of his own life.

An Exhortatory Aside: Grow Up! There Can Be No Going Back, 5:11-6:20.

Before further developing the theme of Jesus' Melchizedekian high priesthood, Hebrews urges his readers to become more mature (v. 1 *maturity* is preferable to NRSV *perfection*).

5:11-6:3. In spiritual matters they are mere babes. They have yet to progress beyond the ABCs of the faith. These are listed in vv. 1-2. *Repentance from dead work*s = behavior that will ensue in spiritual death. There is nothing here to suggest the contrast that we find in Paul between faith and works. *Contra* NRSV, *instruction on baptisms* (6:2) is unlikely to refer to Christian baptism since: (1) The NT word for baptism is neuter, whereas here it is masculine, and (2) it is in the plural. If it were baptism we would expect the singular. It is better understood, therefore, as referring to purificatory rites of ablution in general.

Similarly, we should not confine *laying on of hands* to any one specific Christian rite of initiation. In biblical tradition it occurs in a whole variety of different contexts as the mode whereby power was transferred and blessings bestowed (Lohse 1974). *Resurrection of the dead* refers to the general resurrection that lies in the future (see 11:19) rather than to the resurrection of Christ that has already taken place. Only once in Hebrews (13:10) do we find a reference to Jesus' resurrection.

All these beliefs and practices can be found in JUDAISM. Nonetheless, for the author of Hebrews, convinced as he was that Judaism's scriptures are *about Christ* (6:1), they may be described also as Christian *basic teaching*. This is therefore no call to reject the inspiration of the past in order to embrace Christianity, but a call to see in Jesus the true fulfilment of God's previous revelation.

6:4-12. Hope versus despair. Here the hopelessness that comes from giving up one's Christian discipleship is contrasted with the hope that is held out to those who remain steadfast. It is impossible for renegades to be readmitted to the community of faith once they have left (6:4-6; cf. 10:26-31), not because they have committed postbaptismal sin. Nor because there is a special category of "mortal" sins for which there can be no forgiveness. Like Num 15:30-31, Hebrews believes that there can be no expiatory sacrifice for one who *acts high-handedly*, that is, for one who refuses to accept the very jurisdiction of God. To *fall away* in this context means to deliberately place oneself outside the new covenant community. To abandon Christian discipleship is to ally oneself with that very rejection that originally brought about Christ's crucifixion. As the rest of this homily goes on to assert, that sacrifice was unique and cannot be repeated.

All this is merely by way of warning. So far the recipients have remained loyal (v. 9). So they are not only warned; they are encouraged (vv. 10-12) to look forward in hope rather than go back via a path that can only lead to a dead end.

6:13-20. God has confirmed his promise by an oath. Christian hope is grounded in the twofold character of God's word: (1) the *promise* that is the believer's inheritance, and (2) the *oath* that guarantees the promise (v. 17). Hebrews cites the example of ABRAHAM. God's promise that he would father a great nation (Gen 12:1-4) was emphatically renewed (by God swearing an oath) after the patriarch had demonstrated his willingness to sacrifice his son (Gen 22:16-18). Both promise and oath are to be trusted (v. 18, *two unchangeable things*), but the word accompanied by the oath is the superior, definitive, last word of God.

This argument paves the way for chap. 7. It enables the author to claim that Melchizedekian high priesthood is superior to the Aaronic order since it was confirmed by an oath. Although v. 16 acknowledges the problem, unlike some Jewish authors (cf. Philo, *Allegorical Commentaries* 3.207), Hebrews does not discuss how it is possible for God to swear by himself.

According to the Order of Melchizedek, 7:1-28

In order to pursue the analogy of Christ's death and ascension in priestly terms, it is essential for the author to establish the non-Levitical order of his priesthood. Jesus could not at one and the same time be Davidic Messiah of the tribe of Judah (vv. 13-15) and Aaronic high priest of the tribe of Levi.

7:1-3. The order of Melchizedek. In the two references to MELCHIZEDEK in the OT (Gen 14:17-20; Ps 110:4) Hebrews finds a type of priesthood that is non-Levitical. In vv. 1-2 he focuses on two things mentioned in Gen 14: (1) Melchizedek's blessing of Abraham, and (2) his receiving tithes from the patriarch. In these actions is to be found evidence of Melchizedek's superiority (vv. 4-8).

Melchizedek was probably originally a Canaanite priest-king. Little more can be said of this figure from the mists of Israel's prehistory. Perhaps precisely because of this he came to exercise the creative imagination of both Jewish and Christian writers.

Verse 2 reflects first-century Jewish exegetical belief that the *zedek* of the priest-king's name was derived from the Hebrew *sedeq* (righteous-ness) and therefore meant *king of righteousness*. In fact it may have had its origins in Zedek, the name of a Canaanite deity, and meant "Zedek's king." By the time of Hebrews, Melchizedek had become associated in Jewish thought with the city of *Salem* (=Jerusalem), whose name was supposedly derived from the Hebrew *shalom, peace*.

The Qumran Covenanters were also interested in Melchizedek (cf. *1QapGen* 14; *11QMelch*). Their interest in him was not as a priestly figure but as a heavenly being, whom they thought would come in the final jubilee year to exercise judgment on God's behalf.

From scripture's silence as to Melchizedek's origins and final destiny v. 3 infers that he was *without father, without mother, without genealogy, having neither beginning of days nor end of life*. He therefore typifies a kind of priesthood that is neither inherited nor bequeathed. Jesus' resurrection, *the power of an indestructible life* (v. 16), demonstrates that he *remains a priest forever* (v. 3 = Ps 110:4), and therefore has no successor (cf. 7:24). From this the reader might be led to think that Melchizedek was the model for Christ. Yet, as v. 3 shows, for Hebrews it is Melchizedek who resembles the SON OF GOD rather than *vice versa*.

7:4-10. Melchizedek is superior to both Abraham and Levi. Abraham acknowledged this in receiving his blessing and giving him tithes. And Levi, although as yet unborn, did likewise, since he may be regarded as seminally present (= *in the loins of*) in his great grandfather.

7:11-19. Failure of Levitical order. The Levitical order failed to effect access to God, which was its whole purpose. Therefore it has been superseded by a new priesthood. Hebrews (vv. 12, 18) is aware that to abrogate the Aaronic office is effectively to overthrow the Mosaic Law that legislated for its provision. Apart from a brief mention at 10:1, however, the issue of the Law is not pursued further. The discussion is confined to priesthood.

7:20-28. The superiority of Jesus' high priesthood. Psalm 110:4, initially introduced at v. 17 to stress the eternity (*forever*) of Christ's priestly order, is now used to assert that Melchizedekian priesthood is God's final word—*The Lord has sworn and will not change his mind*. Just as 6:13-20 argued that in the case of Abraham God's promise was even better when con-

confirmed by an oath, so here the asseveration that prefaced the address to a Davidic king in Ps 110 is seen to confirm that it is Melchizedekian rather than Levitical priesthood that is God's definitive word. This priesthood is *the guarantee of a better covenant* (cf. 8:7-13; 9:15-27).

7:23-25. Christ's priestly ministry is singular and permanent. It is therefore better than that of AARON, since it requires no line of succession (cf. 7:3). The ministry of the ascended Christ is that of *intercession* (cf. Rom 8:34) rather than sacrifice. The latter was but the means whereby Jesus entered heaven.

7:26-28. He was a high priest who was sinless. Unlike the Aaronic high priest, who needed to offer two sacrifices and therefore make two entries into the Holy of Holies on the Day of Atonement, Jesus had no need of personal expiation. He entered the presence of God but once. He *has been made perfect* (v. 28) does not imply his own need of moral perfectibility. Rather, the language of "perfection" in Hebrews refers to the process whereby he achieved the goal of entry into heaven (see note on 5:9).

The Sacrificial Work of Christ, 8:1–10:18

At this point the cultic imagery is expanded to make way, not only for Christ as priest, but Christ as sacrificial victim, whose death was the essential prerequisite for his access to God. This is worked out in terms of Jesus as (1) the new covenant sacrifice (8:7-13; 9:15-22), and (2) the superior Day of Atonement offering.

The whole purpose of expiatory sacrifices in the Jewish cultic system was to remove the barrier of sin which separated the profane from the holy. They were the divinely appointed means whereby the worshiper could approach God. Above all this was exemplified in the Day of Atonement ceremonies. Using this model, Hebrews compares the death of Christ to that offering, and his ascension to heaven with the entry of the high priest into the Holy of Holies. Thus the goal of all sacrifice has been achieved, making the cult itself redundant.

8:1-6. Jesus is now in the presence of God. With yet another allusion to Ps 110:1, *seated at the right hand*, the preacher brings us back once more to this *the main point* (v. 1) of his sermon. He cites (v. 5) Exod 25:40 (LXX), *"See that you make everything according to the pattern that was shown you on the mountain,"* to claim that the plans of the tabernacle shown to Moses by God were but a shadowy copy (NRSV, v. 5, *a sketch and shadow*) rather than the real thing. That superior reality, which now replaces the earthly shrine, is heaven itself—*the sanctuary and the true tent* which Christ has entered.

Hebrews 8:6 at once concludes this section on Jesus as *minister* in the superior shrine, and introduces the new theme of him as *the mediator of a better covenant.*

8:7-13. The promise of a new covenant. Here the Mosaic covenant on Mount Sinai (see Exod 19) is contrasted with that promised by JEREMIAH (31:31-34). COVENANT, especially as developed in Deuteronomistic circles in the years leading up to the EXILE, became the term that encapsulated Israel's faith that she had been chosen as God's people. The bond between God and Israel was not thought of as a contract between two equal partners. Nonetheless, it was bilateral in nature. God's commitment to his people carried with it a solemn obligation to serve him alone and to be obedient to his commandments. It was because of Israel's lamentable failure to fulfil her side of the obligation that Jeremiah looked forward to a new covenant.

8:8-12. The prophecy of Jeremiah. This is cited from the LXX (=Jer 38:31-34). Hebrews goes further than Jeremiah, however. He suggests that failure to keep the covenant was not merely weakness on the people's part; it was inherent in the Mosaic covenant itself, as the very mention of *a second* one demonstrates. *For if the first had been faultless, there would have been no need to look for a second one* (v. 7).

What lies at the heart of Jeremiah's promise of a new covenant is the same notion of adoption that lay behind the Mosaic covenant. To this, however, the prophet has added some striking new features: (1) *I will put my laws in their minds and write them on their hearts* (v. 10). It is this interiorization of the will of God that leads to radical obedience. (2) With the universal knowledge of the Law's demands will come the redundancy of its teachers and interpreters. *For they shall all know me from the least of them to the greatest* (v. 11).

8:13. The new covenant. This new covenant has been inaugurated by the death of Christ. It heralds a new order (a theme that runs throughout 7:1–10:18) that makes what went before *obsolete, growing old* and *soon to disappear*. For Hebrews, the new covenant is thus part of the new age that, like the promised land, has yet to be attained. It is the promise held out to the believer of God's future, to be experienced in the present as hope.

9:1-10. The inadequacy of the earthly cult. The author returns to the theme that dominates this central section—the Day of Atonement.

9:1-5. The layout and contents of the shrine. Clearly, the simple twofold division of the wilderness TABERNACLE (Exod 25-26) rather than the more complex structure of the Jerusalem Temple (see TEMPLE/TEMPLES) is in mind. In the former was an outer tent (*the first one*), *the Holy Place* (v. 2), beyond which was an inner sanctum, *the Holy of Holies* (v. 3).

In the accounts in Exodus (25:1–31:11; 36:2–39:43; 40:1-15; 40:16-38) the only furnishing in the Holy of Holies was the ARK. The final fate of the ark remains unknown. It was probably removed and/or destroyed by the Babylonians when they sacked the Temple (cf. Jer 3:14-17). JOSEPHUS (*BJ* 5.219) tells us that in the Temple of his day the inner sanctum was completely empty. In Hebrews's account the ark is made to contain within it certain sacred objects: the *tablets of the covenant* (cf. Deut 10:2; 1 Kgs 8:9; 2 Chr 5:10); the urn containing the *manna* (cf. Exod 16:33-34); and *Aaron's rod* (cf. Num 17:16-24). Furthermore, unlike Exod 30:1-10; 38:25-28, Hebrews (v. 4) locates the *altar of incense* inside rather than outside the Holy of Holies.

9:6-10.The regulations for worship on the Day of Atonement. These are briefly alluded to. Two points are emphasized: (1) The Holy of Holies was the exclusive domain of the high priest, who was permitted to enter on but one day of the year. (2) Expiatory sacrifice was the *sine qua non* without which even he was not permitted access. He in fact made two sacrifices and two entries into the inner sanctum. First he offered a bull to expiate for the sins of himself and his household (cf. Lev 16:6,11). Then he sacrificed a goat to purify both the people and the cult place (cf. Lev 16:16). *Sins committed unintentionally* (v. 7), reminds us that Israel's sacrificial system (including its "sin" and "guilt" offerings) was largely intended to expiate unwitting rather than "high-handed" sins (see Num 15:30-31).

The sins of the people were laid upon the head of a second goat (the "scapegoat") by the high priest. Since nothing that is sinful can be offered to God, this animal was not sacrificed, but driven out live into the wilderness (cf. Lev 16:20-22). Nowhere in the NT is Jesus depicted as the scapegoat. The emphasis rather (v. 14) is upon Jesus as the spotless victim.

The Mosaic ritual itself (= *the first tent*, v. 8) was a parable in action (= *symbol*, v. 9) of the fact that it provided no definitive, lasting access to God. Even during the period of its dispensation (=*standing*, v. 8), it could only deal with external rather than internal purification. It could not cleanse the *conscience* (v. 9). That had to await the sacrifice of Christ (= *the time . . . to set things right*, v. 10).

9:11-14. The superiority of Christ as priest and victim. This lies in the fact that Jesus has entered the presence of God, not through the sacrifice of an animal, but through the superior offering of himself. Verse 13 alludes to another of Israel's expiatory rites—the ceremony of the red heifer (Num 19:2-20) in which the animal was burned with cedar wood, along with hyssop and scarlet "stuff" (cf. Heb 9:19). The resultant ashes were then mixed with water and sprinkled upon the people (see HEIFER, RED).

It is the contrast between the exterior and the interior that is drawn at this point in the homily. Judaism's expiatory rites could only cleanse what is outside (= the *flesh*, v. 13), whereas Jesus' sacrifice dealt with the interior sense of guilt (= *conscience*), that inner accuser that condemns a way of life that leads to death. (*Dead works*, v. 14, should not be understood in the Pauline sense of "works of the law" over against faith.)

By capitalizing *Spirit* the NRSV gives a trinitarian interpretation to v. 14. It is better understood, however, as a reference to Jesus' own spirit or person, which is *eternal* by virtue of his resurrection (cf. 7:16).

9:15-22. The new covenant and its sacrifice. This resumes the theme of 8:7-13. Now the death of Christ is likened, not to the Day of Atonement offering, but to the sacrifice that accompanied the ratification of the Mosaic covenant (Exod 24:1-8). Apart from Luke 20:20 and 1 Cor 11:25, Hebrews is the only NT work to depict Jesus as the *new* covenant victim. (Mark 14:24 || Matt 26:28 mentions covenant but not new covenant.) Unlike them, however, Hebrews does not place this within the context of the last supper. In fact, Hebrews displays no interest in the Eucharist whatsoever.

9:15. The death of Jesus ratifies a new covenant. *Redeems* (cf. 9:12) conjures up a picture of God's manumission of his people from slavery in Egypt. The bondage envisaged here, however, is that of sin.

9:16-17. A testator must first die before a will can take effect. This argument depends upon the double meaning of διαθήκη, the LXX's translation of the Hebrew word for *covenant (berith)*. In secular Greek it means "will" (cf. Gal 3:15-17).

9:18-22. A death was also necessary to ratify the Mosaic covenant. Whereas in Exodus the covenant offering was concerned with consecration, here it is interpreted as expiatory. This is probably because the Day of Atonement, rather than the inauguration of the covenant, dominates Hebrews's thinking. The one becomes interpreted in terms of the other. Thus, unlike the biblical account, not only the people, but the book (v. 19) together with the contents of the tabernacle (v. 21) are sprinkled with the blood of the covenant victim. Hebrews 9:19 also contains elements drawn, not from the covenant, but from the ceremony of the red heifer (see note on 9:13).

9:23-28. Christ's death as the means whereby he entered heaven. Once more we are back with the dominant motif of the Day of Atonement. Hebrews 9:23-24 is another *a fortiori* argument. If the contents of the material shrine needed cleansing, *how much more* the *heavenly things themselves.* The latter is probably a metaphor for that which is interior, namely, the CONSCIENCE. Thus this section looks back to 9:11-14 and forward to 10:1-10, which focus upon the internal as opposed to the external.

9:25-28. Levitical sacrifices and the death of Christ. The repetitive character of Levitical sacrifices is contrasted with the *once for all* (vv. 26, 27, 28) of the death of Christ. A *reductio ad absurdum* argument is employed to show that if this were not the case Jesus would have had to die repeatedly. As we all know, however, humans die but once! Jesus' return will not be to atone for sin, but to bring final salvation. Throughout Hebrews salvation is held out as a future hope—not a present possession.

10:1-18. The sacrifice to end all sacrifices. This passage functions as both a recapitulation of the argument of 8:1–10:18 and as its climax. Thus it reiterates:

(1) 10:1-3. Christ's sacrifice needs no annual renewal. Sacrifices of the cult, on the other hand, had to be repeated. This proves that they, together with the Mosaic Law that legislated for them, were not God's final revelation (*true form*) but only a precursor (*shadow*). Far from absolving guilt (*consciousness of sin;* cf. 9:14), they merely acted as its constant reminder.

(2) 10:4-10. Unlike animal sacrifice, that of Jesus was a voluntary self-offering. Ps 40:6-8 is cited (vv. 5-7) in its LXX form (=Ps 39:7-9). *A body you have prepared for me* (v. 5) is the LXX translation of the obscure Hebrew phrase, "Ears you have dug for me," which the NRSV of Ps 40 freely renders, "You have given me an open ear." This is used to echo the Psalmist's insistence upon the supremacy of obedience over sacrificial offerings *per se* (v. 9). Above all, Jesus' death is seen as superior to that of animals, since they had no option. Putting the psalm on the lips of Jesus (v. 5; cf. 2:12-13) is not to claim his preexistence, but to identify his death with the superior self-offering spoken of by the psalm.

(3) 10:11-18. Since it was effective, it does away with all further need of sacrifice. Having offered the definitive sacrifice, Jesus is now enthroned in heaven (Ps 110:1). His enemies have as yet to be subjugated on earth (cf. 2:8; 9:28). Nonetheless, he has gained access to God (= *perfected*) not only for himself but ultimately for his followers (= the *sanctified*). His death has thus fulfilled the two promises that lay at the heart of Jeremiah's new covenant: (a) a genuine change in humanity that affects the interior and not simply the exterior; and (b) the removal of sin. With this achieved, there is no further need of a sacrificial system at all.

An Exhortation to Persevere in the Faith, 10:19–12:29

The sermon proper is concluded by a series of encouragements and warnings aimed at a readership who may be tempted to abandon their discipleship in the face of present hardships. Once more the theme of pilgrimage (cf. 3:1–4:14) is taken up.

Perseverance: Some Encouragements and Warnings, 10:19-39

10:19-25. Trust in the faithfulness of God. An appeal to the fidelity of the Christian is grounded in a belief in the fidelity of God: *He who has promised is faithful* (v. 23). Heb 10:19-20 is best understood as an allegorization of the *curtain* that divided the Holy of Holies from the rest of the shrine. It now represents the death (= *flesh*) through which Jesus passed in order to gain access to God.

10:26-31. Go forward rather than back. The warning of 6:4-6 is renewed. *Anyone who has violated the law of Moses dies without mercy* (v. 28) alludes to Deut 17:8. Here what is condemned is not every breach of the Law, but idolatrous APOSTASY. What makes that unforgivable is that it constitutes a refusal to accept God's jurisdiction. That is as true of the new covenant as it was of the old. To go back on Christian discipleship is to spurn the Son of God, to treat the cross as if it were merely a profane death, rather than a sacred sacrifice that inaugurated a new covenant, and thus to outrage the spirit of God that mediated that grace (v. 29).

10:32-39. Be encouraged by your own past good record. *Enlightened* (v. 32) became a metaphor for BAPTISM from the second century onwards. Here, however, it is used as an image of spiritual conversion in general. The references to public ridicule (= *exposed to abuse*), *persecution,* and the *plundering of . . . possessions* (vv. 32-34) are too vague and general to enable us to pinpoint either the date or destination of this epistle. Habakkuk 2:3-4 (LXX) is cited (vv. 37-38) to affirm, by way of encouragement: (1) that Jesus will shortly return (*in a very little while*); and (2) that his readers will not be among those who renege on their commitment.

The Faithful of the Past, 11:1-40

The theme of faith is now picked up from the Habakkuk quotation cited at the end of chap. 10. *By faith* is the repetitive refrain by which a list of various heroes and martyrs of Israel's past are introduced as exemplars of faith. Nowhere in the biblical accounts themselves are their exploits attributed to faith.

Such listings of the achievements of people and events of the past in order to bolster up the resolve of the faithful of the present seem to have been traditional. Thus Wis 10 appeals (although not by name) to ADAM, ABEL, NOAH, JACOB, JOSEPH, MOSES, and the EXODUS generation as examples of those who triumphed over adversity with the aid of God's wisdom. An even closer formal parallel is PHILO (*On Rewards and Punishments* 11-14), in his definition and exposition of hope. He, however, confines himself to types in general of those who have exemplified hope. Hebrews, on the other hand, cites particular individuals and events that have demonstrated faith, i.e., a belief and trust in God's as-yet-unseen future, which was to find its fulfilment in Jesus.

11:1-3. What is faith? Commentators disagree as to the meaning of two crucial words in v. 1. The NRSV choice of *assurance* for ὑπόστασις and *conviction* for ἔλεγχος find no parallel in first-century Greek usage. It is therefore preferable to translate v. 1: "Now faith is the *title deed* of things hoped for, *the evidence* of things not seen."

Faith is not purely subjective. It is trust in the reality of God's consummation of his purposes in the future. Our ancestors "received confirmation" (v. 2, lit. "testimony," *contra* NRSV, *approval*) of God's promises. In their case, that final salvation was as invisible as

was the material, visible world, before God brought it into existence through his divine command (v. 3).

11:4-7. Abel, Enoch, and Noah. Genesis 4:3-10 does not explain how or why Abel's was the superior sacrifice. Here (v. 4) it is ascribed to his faith. Hebrews 11:5 follows the LXX of Gen 5:21-24 and understands the enigmatic, "and he was not because God took him" of the MT, as implying that Enoch was translated to heaven (cf. *1 Enoch* 12.3; 15.1; *2 Enoch* 27.8; 71.14; *Jub* 4.23; Philo, *On the Changing of Names* 38; Josephus, *Ant* 1.2.4). Noah (cf. Gen 6:13-22) believed in God's warning of the impending flood (v. 7, *events as yet unseen*).

11:8-12. Abraham and Sarah. The story of Abraham's migration in response to God's call (Gen 12:1-8) enables Hebrews to link faith with obedience (v. 8). Like that of his successors ISAAC and JACOB, Abraham's sojourn in Canaan was but temporary (v. 9; cf. Gen 17:8; 23:4), since God's promise was not of an earthly but of a heavenly reality (v. 10). (The theme of the heavenly city will be resumed at 12:12.) Unlike those traditions that looked forward to the descent of the heavenly Jerusalem to earth (e.g., *4 Ezra* 13:36; Rev 21:2, 10), for Hebrews the land/city that is the true destination of pilgrimage is wholly transcendent.

11:13-16. The goal of faith. The true goal of faith is a heavenly rather than an earthly homeland. This recapitulates the main point of the chapter. None of these heroes of the past lived to see God's promises fulfilled. They lived in the faith that a *better country, a heavenly one* was to be theirs in the future.

11:17-22. Isaac, Jacob, and Joseph. Abraham was willing to offer his *only son* Isaac since he had faith in God's power to raise the dead (v. 19). A belief in a future resurrection of the dead was widespread in the first century. It is not, however, attributed to Abraham in the biblical account.

The NRSV translation *figuratively speaking* (v. 19) is to be rejected. Rather, as in 9:9, it means a *symbol* of future salvation: "Isaac's rescue from virtual death on the sacrificial pyre is symbolic of the deliverance that all the faithful can expect" (Attridge 1989, 336). Isaac's blessing of his sons (Gen 27:27-29, 39-40) is also seen to have a future reference (v. 20).

By adopting the LXX of Gen 47:31, "bowing in worship over the top of his staff" (v. 21), Jacob's blessing of his sons (Gen 48:8-22) is seen as an act of homage to God. (The MT, "Israel bowed himself on the end of his bed," means rather that he was prostrated by old age.)

11:23-27. Moses. Even Judaism's supreme agent of revelation (cf. Exod.33:11; Num 12:1-8) was motivated by a vision of the future. It was this, rather than fear (v. 27), that led him to leave Egypt. (His murder of an Egyptian overseer [Exod 12:11-12] is not mentioned.)

Abuse suffered for the Christ (v. 26) could either have Jesus the Messiah, or Moses the Lord's *anointed* (cf. LXX Ps 88:51-52 [MT 89:50-51]) as its referent. Probably both are intended. Thus, Moses, in obedience to and solidarity with the reproach that will be endured by the future Christ, accepted his fate as an exile. This glimpse of the future motivated his endurance.

11:28-31. The Passover, the Exodus, the fall of Jericho, and Rahab. These (cf. Exod 12:21-30; 14:21-31; Josh 6:12-21; 2:1-21; 6:22-5) all similarly reflect a faith in the future.

11:32-8. Other heroes and martyrs. Beginning with various military and political leaders of the postsettlement period (vv. 32-34), the list now includes not simply the victors, but the persecuted, many of whom lost their lives (vv. 35-38). *Women received their dead by resurrection* (v. 35), probably refers to the miracles performed by ELIJAH (1 Kgs 17:17-24) and ELISHA (2 Kgs 4:18-37). The picture of torture and death in vv. 36-38 has probably been colored by the stories of the Maccabean martyrs (see 2 Macc 6:18-31; 7; 4 Macc 6–12).

11:29-40. A summary. Their faith was to find its fulfillment in Christ. They awaited a *better* resurrection. This was what inspired them to endure—even in adversity.

The Faithful Endurance Required Now, 12:1-29

12:1-3. Look to the example of Jesus, the pioneer and perfecter of faith. The array of *witnesses* paraded in chap. 11 find their climax in Jesus. He has not only blazed the trail (= *pioneer*); he has reached its goal (= *perfecter*)—heaven. In their preparation for and participation in the contest (cf. *race*) of faith, Christians should take courage from his example.

12:4-13. View suffering as God's fatherly discipline. The readers, unlike Jesus, have not yet had to face a martyr's death. Their present *trials* (v. 7) should be seen as a sign of their true membership of the household of God. Far from being evidence of God's displeasure, they are signs of his fatherly care (cf. Wis 11:9-10). The educative value of suffering (cf. Prov 13:24; 22:15; Wis 3:3-5; Rom 5:3-4; 1 Cor 11:32) is

confirmed by way of a citation (vv. 5-6) from Prov 3:11-12 (LXX). Painful though their present plight might be (v. 11; cf. the athletic imagery of vv. 1-2), its aim is educative rather than punitive.

12:14-17. Take warning from the example of Esau. Hebrews 12:14-15 appeals for harmony (= *peace*) within the Christian community. *See . . . that no root of bitterness springs up and causes trouble* (v. 16) alludes to Deut 29:17 (LXX)—a passage which, in its original context, warned against APOSTASY from the covenant community. Similarly, the author of Hebrews is concerned that his readers should not abandon their Christian commitment. Otherwise they could become like Esau (cf. Gen 25:27-34; 27:30-40), who sold his birthright cheap. The biblical account has no reference to Esau's belated and futile repentance. In introducing it (v. 17), Hebrews echoes the previous warning (6:4-6; 10:26-31) that repentance for the apostate is impossible.

12:18-24. The heavenly Zion contrasted with Mount Sinai. Although not explicitly named, vv. 18-21 clearly alludes both to the site (Mt. Sinai) and the events that surrounded the ratification of the Mosaic covenant and the giving of the Law. In his summary the author of Hebrews combines features drawn from Exod 19:12-19; 20:18-21 with those of Deut 4:11-12; 5:23-27 in order to stress the distance imposed upon the people by the very awesomeness of that theophanic revelation. Mount Sinai's site was so sacred that not so much as an animal was permitted to set foot upon it. Unlike the Exodus account, Hebrews will not even exempt Moses from the taboo. He, too, was terrified.

Verses 22-24 contrasts this with Mount Zion. This is not to be identified with the Jebusite stronghold captured by David (cf. 2 Sam 5:6-9), which became the capital city, Jerusalem. For Hebrews, heaven, not earth, is God's abode. This *heavenly Jerusalem*, unlike Mount Zion, may be *touched* (cf. v. 18).

Even so, that salvation has yet to be achieved by the believer. As yet only Christ has attained it. "You have approached" is a better translation than the NRSV *you have come* (v. 22). Meanwhile, the author has a proleptic vision (v. 23) of that future heavenly Jerusalem, peopled by the faithful of all ages, who, having been perfected through the work of Christ, will finally make up the completed assembly of the people of God. Chief among their number is Jesus. The blood of his new covenant sacrifice speaks of forgiveness and reconciliation, unlike that of Abel (cf. Gen 4:10-11) which cried out for vengeance.

12:25-29. A final solemn warning. The awesome responsibility of having access to God is to be taken seriously. The theme of the infidelity of the wilderness generation (cf. 3:7–4:13) is once more touched upon (v. 25). Part of an oracle, originally a promise to the postexilic remnant of the restoration of the Jerusalem Temple, is cited: *"Yet once more I will shake not only the earth but also the heaven"* (v. 26 = Hag 2:6). Here it is used, however, as an assurance of the replacement of all that is earthly and transient (= *what is shaken*, v. 27) by the heavenly and permanent (i.e., what *cannot be shaken*, vv. 27, 28). Verses 28-29 conclude with a call to worship. The offering now acceptable to God is that of gratitude and reverence on the part of the worshiper.

Epistolary Exhortation and Conclusion, 13:1-25

An abrupt change in tone and style signals the beginning of the author's epistolary conclusion. Here he appends a number of injunctions concerning the implications of his sermon for Christian living.

Christian Holiness and Its Obligations, 13:1-6

The ethical hallmarks that should characterize the new covenant community are briefly listed: (1) *Mutual love* between its members. (2) Hospitality. Probably this refers also to fellow Christians; visitors, who are *strangers* to the particular community. Heb 13:2 alludes to Abraham and Sarah's unrecognised guests (Gen 18:2-15). (3) Empathy towards those who have been imprisoned or otherwise maltreated (NRSV *tortured* is too specific) for their faith. (4) Marital fidelity and sexual chastity. (5) An absence of material greed. This is reinforced in v. 5 by the citation of a combination of Deut 31:6,8 and Josh 31:8, and in v. 6 by LXX Ps 117 (MT 118):6. These texts exhort reliance upon God.

The Implications of Jesus' Sacrifice, 13:7-19

Between an injunction to remember leaders—past (v. 7) and present (vv. 17-19)—is now placed a parenthetical summary of the epistle's main argument. Its condensed style makes this passage initially difficult to follow. Once "unpacked", however, it becomes clear. What is being said is: (1) The gracious act of God (= *grace*) in the death and exaltation of Jesus is superior to the Mosaic cult (=*regulations about food*, v. 9). (2) Christians have an expiatory sacrifice (= *an altar*)

which, like those offered on the Day of Atonement, was not eaten (v. 10). Just as the carcases of these animals were *burned outside the camp* (v. 10; cf. Lev 16:27), so Jesus was disposed of *outside the city gate* (v. 12; cf. Mark 15:20 = Matt 27:31). (3) Therefore, look beyond the fate of Jerusalem and its sanctuary, which is but transitory. Follow instead the way of Jesus. *Abuse* (cf. 11:26) will be the necessary lot of those who journey with him to the heavenly city (vv. 13-14). (4) Now, the only sacrifice required of the Christian is the praise of God in worship and the performance of good works in life (vv. 15-16).

A Closing Benediction, 13:20-21

This takes the form of a prayer for the recipients, and a doxology in praise of Christ.

13:20. Led up from the dead. "Led up from the dead" is a better translation than the NRSV *brought back*: Hebrews presents Christ's victory over death as exaltation rather than resurrection. In keeping with Jewish traditions of the Messiah as the shepherd of God's flock (cf. *PsSol* 17:40), Jesus is the *great shepherd of the sheep* (cf. John 10:11,14; 1 Pet 2:25; 5:4).

A Farewell Note, 13:22-25

Here more practical matters are dealt with. The author describes what he has written as a *word of exhortation* (v. 22)—the usual designation of a sermon (cf. Acts 13:15). The mention of *Timothy* (v. 23) led later interpreters to link Hebrews with PAUL (cf., e.g., Rom 16:21; 2 Cor 1:1; 1 Thes 1:1), and to conclude that the apostle was its author. It is unclear whether Timothy *has been set free* (v. 23) means from prison, or from some task that has, until recently, detained him. Equally ambiguous is *those from Italy* (v. 24). This could mean that Italy was the place from which Hebrews was written. It could, however, designate Italians who were sending their greetings home, in which case Italy would be its destination. Given these ambiguities (and that some scholars do not attribute vv. 21-25 to the original author), it is impossible to determine from these verses either the epistle's origin or destination.

Works Cited

Attridge, H. W. 1989. *The Epistle to the Hebrews*, Herm.

Lohse, Eduard. 1974. "The Laying on of Hands." TDNT 9:431-34.

James

R. Alan Culpepper

Introduction

James is an eminently practical letter, manifesting a passionate concern for the role of faith in the concrete circumstances of life. Rather than deal with SANCTIFICATION, James challenges believers to control their tongues. Rather than debate the meaning of JUSTIFICATION, James calls on Christians to treat the POOR and the rich with equal respect. James, therefore, shuns abstract arguments and pointedly calls for PURITY and faithfulness in all areas of life.

Literary Character

Although James begins with an epistolary greeting, it lacks other characteristics of the letter form. Instead, one finds a series of exhortations with affinities to Jewish wisdom materials and Greco-Roman philosophical, ethical instruction: lack of topical continuity, eclecticism, repetition of motifs, and admonitions that do not apply to a single audience or situation.

Some fifty to sixty imperatives have been counted in James's 108 verses. Lists of traditional virtues and vices are featured (3:16-17). Occasionally, various maxims are gathered around one topic, as in Jas 5:13-18, where prayer is discussed from several perspectives. In Jas 2 one finds the only sustained argument in the letter, on the dangers of partiality and the relationship between FAITH and works. More often, however, the reader of James finds a series of different maxims or exhortations, often organized by a mnemonic device called *catchword linkage*. Sayings are strung together in such a way that a significant term in one saying also appears in the following saying. For example, note the succession of linking terms in Jas 1:2-6: *trials* (v. 2)–*testing* (v. 3); *endurance* (v. 3)–*endurance* (v. 4); *lacking* (v. 4)–*lacking* (v. 5); *ask* (v. 5)–*ask* (v. 6). The exhortations in James are carefully selected; it is not just a random collection of sayings. At the same time, the paraenetic character and catch-word linkage employed in James make it difficult to reduce the letter to an orderly topical outline.

Social Setting

James is concerned about oppression of the poor by the rich and reciprocal hostility from the poor. The Christians meet in assemblies (2:2) led by *elders* (5:14), and one might be expected to aspire to the role of teacher (3:1). Some justify their lack of faithfulness by boasting Pauline slogans (2:14-26), and echoes of words of JESUS recur frequently. Envy and malicious talk are constant threats to the fabric of community life (4:2, 11). Laborers work for unfair wages (5:4). Life itself poses trials for the believers, who are encouraged to endure hardship patiently, anoint the sick with oil, and replace oaths with prayer.

James 1:1 contains the address and greeting: *To the twelve tribes in the Dispersion: Greetings*. Three interpretations of this address have been advanced: (1) all Jews living outside of Palestine; (2) Christendom conceived as the fulfillment of Israel; and (3) Jewish Christians living outside of Palestine who still looked to Jerusalem for leadership. The first has largely been abandoned because the epistle is clearly from a Christian leader to other Christians. The figurative interpretation is held in one form or another by all who claim that the epistle is pseudonymous and hold to a late date. The third position is compatible with the view that the epistle derives directly or indirectly from James, the brother of Jesus and leader of the Jerusalem church.

Authorship and Date

Among the factors that must be accounted for are the following: JAMES does not claim to be an APOSTLE, only *a servant of God and of the Lord Jesus Christ* (1:1). There is no claim to a familial relationship with Jesus. In fact, there are only two references to Jesus in the entire letter (1:1; 2:1). Although James seems to know both the tradition of the sayings of Jesus and some of the tenets of Paulinism, it does not quote any other NT book and is not quoted elsewhere in the NT. At most, one may argue that Jude 1 echoes Jas 1:1. James is also written in excellent Greek and reflects both Hellenistic and Jewish Christian features.

The traditional view is that James was written by James the Just, the brother of Jesus, prior to his death in 62 C.E. Alternatively, some scholars maintain that James is a pseudonymous work, written in the name of James late in the first century. It has also been suggested that the letter was originally a Jewish document that was subsequently reworked by a Christian, but this position has failed to gather much support.

A mediating position seems to be gaining favor. It holds that James contains material from the teachings of James in Jerusalem that was later compiled or edited by someone else. It was then sent to Jewish Christians who had been dispersed from Jerusalem during the turbulent events of the 50s and 60s. On this reading, James gives us a glimpse of the early Palestinian church just before it was dispersed by the war of 66–74 C.E. (see Davids 1982).

For nearly two centuries the early church was remarkably silent about James. The first clear reference to the letter appears in Origen (third cent.), who referred to it as scripture and attributed it to James the Just. In his "Preface to the New Testament" in 1552, Luther concluded, "Therefore St. James' epistle is really an epistle of straw, compared to these others, for it has nothing of the nature of the gospel about it." His reasons for discrediting James were that it opposed Paul in "ascribing justification to works" (*Luther's Works*, 35:396) and because of its apparent lack of organization.

Nevertheless, evidence for the origin of the material in James in the early days of the church (before the composition of the Gospels or the collection of Paul's letters) seems strong. The absence of anything peculiar to James the Just is also significant. The epistle preserves the traditional, ethical concerns of early Jewish Christianity, but drops its emphasis on the Law, circumcision, and dietary restrictions. At the same time, it embraces and endorses the authority of James and combats a misinterpretation of Paul. The letter, therefore, appears to be the work of one who gathered up the teachings of the early church in Jerusalem, attached the name of the late head of the church (since it contained his teachings), and sent it to Jewish Christians who had been dispersed as a result of the anarchy in Judea in the 60s.

For Further Study

In the *Mercer Dictionary of the Bible*: FAITH AND FAITHLESSNESS; JAMES, LETTER OF; GENERAL LETTERS; JAMES. In other sources: P. H. Davids, *The Epistle of James: A Commentary on the Greek Text*, NIGTC; M. Dibelius, *James*, Herm; D. E. Hiebert, *The Epistle of James: Tests of a Living Faith*; S. Laws, *A Commentary on the Epistle of James*, HNTC; R. P. Martin, *James*, WBC; D. P. Scaer, *James, the Apostle of Faith: A Primary Christological Epistle for the Persecuted Church*; H. S. Songer, "James," BBC.

Commentary

An Outline

I. Introductory Address and Greeting, 1:1
II. The Obedience of Faith, 1:2-27
    A. Testing Produces Joy, 1:2-4
    B. Prayer Produces Wisdom, 1:5-8
    C. Wealth Is Transient, 1:9-11
    D. Sin Results in Death, 1:12-16
    E. God Gives Perfect Gifts, 1:17-21
    F. The Obedient Persevere, 1:22-25
    G. The Obedient Care for the Oppressed, 1:26-27
III. The Obedience of Faith in Worship
    and Works, 2:1-26
    A. The Heresy of Partiality, 2:1-13
    B. The Relationship of Faith and Works, 2:14-26

IV. The Obedience of Faith in Words
    and Wisdom, 3:1-18
    A. The Power of Words, 3:1-12
    B. The Wisdom from Above, 3:13-18
V. The Obedience of Faith in Community, 4:1–5:6
    A. Faith as a Response to Dissension, 4:1-12
    B. Faith as a Response to Presumption, 4:13-17
    C. A Warning to the Rich, 5:1-6
VI. The Obedience of Faith
    in Patience, Oaths, and Prayer, 5:7-18
    A. A Call for Patience, 5:7-11
    B. Rejection of Oaths, 5:12
    C. The Power of Prayer, 5:13-18
VII. Concluding Exhortation:
    Restoring the Wayward, 5:19-20

Introductory Address and Greeting, 1:1

James, the brother of Jesus and leader of the early church, greets the Jewish Christians dispersed from Jerusalem.

The Obedience of Faith, 1:2-27

The first chapter is composed of a series of ethical instructions. A definition of pure religion concludes the chapter.

Testing Produces Joy, 1:2-4

Appropriately, the first word is one of encouragement for those who face trials. The term *trials (peirasmos)* can mean either (1) temptation to do evil, or (2) trial or stress. Here it means the latter. The main thrust of these verses is that trials are an opportunity for joy and growth. Stubbornly refusing to give in to anxiety, despair, or grief is both the test and the testimony of authentic faith. These verses echo the saying of Jesus in Matt 5:11-12 (= Luke 6:22-23) and call not just for brave endurance but for joy in the midst of trial.

Prayer Produces Wisdom, 1:5-8

Two new concepts are introduced in these sayings: WISDOM (cf. 3:13-18) and double-mindedness (4:8). Wisdom is the ability to transcend our circumstances and see life from God's perspective.

Care must be taken to let James be James. Do not read James's words with Paul's meanings. By *faith* James does not mean a saving belief but loyalty and commitment under trial, faithful living. By *wisdom* James means God's gift of discernment and empowerment, something akin to Paul's understanding of the role of the Spirit, or being "in Christ." Unlike the rabbis, James does not depend on the study of TORAH for wisdom but on prayer. If wisdom is a gift from God, it is natural to insist that the Christian ask for it (Luke 11:13 = Matt 7:7-8). By *double-mindedness* James does not mean doubt but divided loyalty or conflict of interest.

Verses 7 and 8 have been handled variously by the translators: as distinct but related statements (KJV), as subject and predicate (RSV), or as appositional (NEB, JB, NIV, GNB, NRSV).

The doubter is a "two-souled person" who is unwilling to trust God completely, contrary to the SHEMA that calls for the faithful to love God with all their heart, soul, and might (Deut 6:4-5). The double-mind-

ed vacillate; they are uncommitted, refuse to take sides, and do one thing wishing they were doing another. When James encourages us to ask without doubting, he is not talking about drumming up a particular kind of feeling when we pray but about living out a steadfast trust in God.

Wealth Is Transient, 1:9-11.

These verses introduce James's concern for poverty and WEALTH. This theme too is deeply rooted in the teachings of Jesus, especially in Luke. The humble person is a Christian, but does James think of the rich person as a Christian or not? In contrast to the NEB, JB, and GNB, it is doubtful that James considered the rich man to be a brother also.

James contrasts the humble, lowly person with the arrogant, godless person. *Rich* and *poor* are not exclusively economic terms but carry contrasting connotations of pious humility and wicked arrogance. Here the social location of James's readers must be kept in mind.

Boasting usually carries a negative connotation in the NT, but it can also mean rejoicing and glorifying God. The reversal of fortunes is a common biblical theme (e.g., Luke 12:13-21; 16:19-31). The humble should rejoice because God has chosen them and will exalt them. Both the present grace of God and its future fulfillment call for exultation. James challenges us to see life from the vantage point of the fulfillment of God's redemptive work.

The lowly will be exalted and the wealth of the rich will pass away. The only thing that is worthy of our glory and praise is the completion of God's work. Wealth is meaningless in the face of death (Isa 40:6-7; Ps 103:15). James returns to the dangers of wealth in 2:5-7, 4:13-16, and 5:1-6.

Sin Results in Death, 1:12-16

This unit deals with both trials and temptations. Verse 12 returns to the theme of enduring trials (cf. 1:2-4). It offers two good reasons for enduring trials: (1) one who endures is blessed, and (2) that one will receive *the crown of life*, eternal life. The term for standing the test is one that was also used in connection with the testing of coins to determine whether they were genuine. The goal for the Christian is keep faith genuine in the midst of life's tests. The reward is salvation.

Verse 13 is the first instance of diatribe style: entering dialogue with an imaginary opponent. Does

God test persons of faith or tempt us to sin? Commentators are divided on the issue of whether the term *peirasmos* has the same meaning in v. 13 as it has had previously (i.e., "trial") or whether it now means "temptation." If the meaning is temptation, then v. 13 is the beginning of a new section that is joined to v. 12 by catchword linkage. Trials are to be endured, but temptations are to be resisted. Still, the two cannot be completely separated; some temptations may call for endurance also.

James warns us that we cannot blame our sin on God. God is not tempted, and God tempts no one. Neither does James introduce the notion of the demonic here (cf. 3:15; 4:7). Instead, he requires us to face our own culpability. James emphasizes the human side of sin. Whatever the origin of the temptation, we are the ones who choose to sin.

The EVIL we do begins with the desire we enjoy. The imagery is drawn from hunting and fishing. The fish is lured, and the prey is enticed to a trap (2 Pet 2:14, 18). The image is also used of the harlot enticing to FORNICATION. Hiebert (1979, 105) comments: "Temptation has its source not in the outer lure but in the inner lust."

Evil is seldom born full-grown. James therefore unveils the process of its growth. Sin always has the insidious power to grow into something we never intended. At its birth SIN is hardly recognizable, but when it has grown up it is death. Many people would like to sin and then be done with it; but sin, once born, always grows up. The problem with sin, therefore, is not that we may get caught but that sin itself kills.

God Gives Perfect Gifts, 1:17-21

These verses speak of God's good gifts and our need to receive them with gladness. Verse 17 sets forth the principle of God's goodness and changelessness. If God is good and cannot change, then God cannot entice people to evil. There is no variation in God's goodness either. It does not wax or wane. As the creator of the stars, God is the "father of lights." The technical terms in v. 17b, which have been translated variously, can all refer to astronomical phenomena. God neither changes nor is changed.

Verse 18 supplies an illustration of God's goodness. The issue is whether it refers to God's giving life in creation or in redemption. The reference to our being *a kind of first fruits of his creatures* tilts the matter in favor of God's activity in redemption. God's work, therefore, stands in opposition to sin. Sin brings

death; God brings forth new life. The new life begins in God's resolute will. The instrument of regeneration is the gospel message, but Christians are responsible for demonstrating the reality of the new life by the way they live. Our changeless, steadfast, creative God gives only good gifts, the chief of which is salvation; but this is just the beginning of God's work.

The cluster of three related, short sayings on receiving the word (vv. 19-21) is typical of Jewish wisdom (e.g., Prov 13:3; 15:1; 29:20; Eccl 7:9; Sir 5:11; 6:33). The reference to being *quick to listen* indicates a ready, responsive attitude. It is probably tied to hearing the preached word. *Slow to speak* counsels against hasty, ill-considered reactions. *Slow to anger* guards against a flash of temper, but it does not mean that anger has no place in Christian life.

Verse 21 begins with the common image of taking off clothes, which was often used to speak of repentance and BAPTISM (Rom 13:12; Eph 4:22; Col 3:8; 1 Pet 2:1). The word *all* reminds us that God is never satisfied with partial purity. Then, receive God's word with meekness—which means not weakness but humility. *The implanted word* is not inborn or "engrafted" (KJV). It is the seed planted in us through the word of God or the preaching of the gospel (compare Jesus' seed PARABLES). Salvation is still future, but *the implanted word* has the power to bring it about. Like sin, the word grows in a dynamic process. Rather than death, however, it results in salvation.

The Obedient Persevere, 1:22-25

These sayings continue James's refrain that the only faith that makes any difference is the faith that is obedient to God's direction. In the previous section he said that we should be quick to receive the word. Now he tells us what he means by that: be quick not only to listen but to obey. Hearing and doing was a common theme both in Jewish wisdom and in the teachings of Jesus (Deut 6:4-5; Matt 7:24-27; Rom 2:13). Having stated the principle in v. 22, James illustrates the point in vv. 23-24, and then draws a positive conclusion (v. 25). The illustration of the mirror was common in ancient ethical teachings (cf. 1 Cor 13:12). Mirrors were made of polished copper or bronze and were neither common nor very clear. The person who hears the word and does not seize the opportunity to respond with obedience is like the person who gets a chance to see what he or she looks like and then forgets.

By *the perfect law, the law of liberty* (v. 25), James probably means the higher standard of righteousness in the teachings of Jesus. Literally, James enjoins the reader to be not a "forgetful hearer but a workful doer." The beatitude then pronounces blessing on the doer *in their doing*.

The Obedient Care for the Oppressed, 1:26-27

These verses aptly sum up most of the message of the letter. The Christian is instructed to control the tongue, care for others, and resist temptation. Here is the positive side of hearing the word.

James echoes the prophets' critique of religion that is vain and futile. Some persons may do all the right, religious things, but if they *do not bridle their tongues,* their religion is futile. These persons are not hypocrites who pretend in order to deceive others; they themselves are deceived. They think they are religious but show no inner character that is consistent with the religion they profess.

Verse 27 offers a penetrating definition of pure religion that stands in contrast to the vain religion James has just described. The language is drawn from the practice of ritual cleanness. *Pure and undefiled* here means that which is free from moral pollution and corruption in the presence of God—the Father of those who are hurt by an abusive tongue, the Father of the widows and orphans also. *Orphans and widows* were traditional examples of the powerless and neglected (Isa 1:10-17; Deut 14:29; 24:17-22; Jer 5:28).

James spotlights both the personal and the social elements of true piety in v. 27: care for the helpless and moral purity, or as one commentator put it, "charity" and "chastity."

The Obedience of Faith in Worship and Works, 2:1-26

Chapter 2 offers the most sustained argument in the letter. Essentially it has two parts, one dealing with showing partiality and one demanding works of faithfulness.

The Heresy of Partiality, 2:1-13

Most commentators treat v. 1 as a prohibition, but it may also be an opening question (NRSV). The author gives an illustration of partiality in the context of a meeting of the church either for worship or to hear a legal case. The term for partiality or favoritism literally means "face receiving."

Two men enter the assembly. We are not told whether they are Christians or visitors. The rich person is distinguished by his rings and fine clothing. By contrast the POOR person (a *ptōchos*—one almost has to spit to say the word!) has dirty or shabby clothes and no rings. Both enter. How does the church respond? They do not see the persons. Instead, they take note of the clothing. The man in fine clothing is shown to a prominent seat. The poor man is told to stand out of the way or sit at someone's feet.

Verse 4 issues the first of the condemnations by means of a question that expects an affirmative answer. Yes, they have made judges of themselves, and they have *become judges with evil thoughts* (cf. Lev 19:15; Luke 18:6). Distinguishing between persons robs Christian community of its distinctive character.

Verses 5-7 expose the awful consequences of such partiality. God has chosen *the poor of the world* (cf. Deut 4:37; 7:7; 14:2; 1 Cor 1:26). God has refused to favor the wealth of the rich and has thereby nullified social distinctions. The role reversal is dramatic. In God's eyes it is not a person's *face* but one's *faith* that matters. The oppressed are favored and exalted. They will be *rich in faith*, heirs of the inheritance coveted by others. Verse 5 contains the only reference to the *kingdom* in James; it is promised to those who love God (1:12).

Two penetrating questions follow. James charges that the church shows favor to the rich, but it is the rich who oppress them. The next charge is the most devastating: the rich also blaspheme the excellent name that was invoked over you—which is probably an allusion to the name of Christ invoked in the context of BAPTISM. By siding with the rich, the church has taken the side of oppressors and blasphemers. Care must be taken today, of course, to distinguish the first-century connotations of rich and poor. These verses should not be treated as a general condemnation of wealth or as a blessing of poverty. The issue here is partiality, not possessions.

The argument of vv. 8-13 is that the law commands love of neighbor. Therefore, anyone who shows partiality has violated the law, and anyone who has violated any part of the law has violated the whole law. Love of neighbor (Lev 19:18) was viewed as the essence of the law. *Royal law* (v. 8) may mean the supreme law, God's law, or the OT law as interpreted by Jesus. Partiality, therefore, is a serious offense, not something to be tolerated or excused. Love, on the other hand, is partial to the needy and the neglected.

One cannot despise or dishonor another person by showing partiality and still please God. The principle of the unity of the law was taught by the rabbis. Since every commandment expresses the lawgiver's will, the violation of any commandment is an offense against the lawgiver. To drive home the point, James appeals to two central laws of the Decalogue, ADULTERY (IN THE OT) and MURDER. One who violates any commandment is a transgressor of the whole law.

Verse 12 draws the practical conclusion: speak and act as persons who are about to be judged by the law of FREEDOM (cf. 1:25). As elsewhere in James, an eschatological urgency is brought to bear on the ethical dimensions of life. The closing verse of this section reflects the paradox of judgment under the gospel. No MERCY will be shown to one who shows no mercy (Matt 5:7; Luke 16:19-31). Mercy does not triumph at the expense of JUSTICE, but the cross is the greatest testimony to the triumph of mercy.

The Relationship of Faith and Works, 2:14-26

James is apparently confronting a situation in which people in the church were professing faith in Christ but felt no need for moral purity or ethical living. Faith alone was regarded as essential, while works were unnecessary. James is not addressing the question of how one "gets saved." He is concerned about Christians who have grown complacent about living faithfully.

The argument takes the form of a question: *What good is it . . . if you say you have faith but do not have works?* (v. 14). In this hypothetical instance the person's faith is confirmed only by the claims he or she makes for it. This kind of argument by constructing an imaginary dialogue was characteristic of a diatribe between CYNICS and STOICS, but may have been common in synagogue sermons as well. The second question, *Can faith save you?* (v. 14) expects a negative answer. The question is deliberately provocative. One hardly wants to admit that a person of faith will not be saved. The implications are disturbing. The question, therefore, forces reflection on the nature of faith. Underlying James's attack may be his concern over misinterpretation of Paul's insistence that we are saved by faith alone.

Verses 15-16 give an illustration, and v. 17 draws the obvious conclusion. The illustration has parallels with Matt 25:35-45 and 1 John 3:17. A Christian meets a brother or sister who is in need of food and clothing, but all the Christian does is extend sympathy and best wishes. But prayer and sympathy are of little value when one refuses to share the basic necessities of life with those in need. The question, "What good

is it?" echoes v. 14. The obvious conclusion is that faith without works is dead. James is not arguing for the superiority of works over faith but for the inseparability of faith and works. An authentic faith will make a difference in how a person lives.

Verse 18 is difficult, and no solution to its difficulties is entirely satisfactory. An imaginary speaker interjects a comment, but is the speaker James's ally or his opponent, and how far does the comment extend? Is the comment only *"You have faith and I have works,"* or does it extend through v. 19? The problem is that the comment seems to express James's point, not that of an opponent. Although no satisfactory solution is evident, the gist of the objection is that faith and works may be separated, and it is this separation that James disallows. Works demonstrate the existence of a vibrant faith.

Even orthodox belief is no substitute for a living faith. Verse 19 seems to be part of James's response to the interlocutor, pointing to the intellectual content of faith: *you believe that.* The affirmation that *God is one* was the central affirmation of Jewish worship (Deut 6:4). Knowledge, even confession, without commitment is of no value. *Even the demons believe!*

The rhetorical question in v. 20 sets up an appeal to biblical characters: ABRAHAM and RAHAB. The question plays on the contrast between *works* (*ergōn*) and *barren* (*argē*). Abraham demonstrated faith by offering ISAAC. Verse 23 cites Gen 15:6, just as Paul does in Rom 4:3. The next statement, *You see that a person is justified by works and not by faith alone* (v. 24), seems to be a rebuttal to Rom 3:28: "For we hold that a person is justified by faith apart from works prescribed by the law." The difficulty is largely resolved when one pays close attention to the different problems JAMES and PAUL were addressing, and the difference in the meaning of the terms in each context. Paul was arguing that one is justified by reliance on God's grace rather than by works of the law. James was addressing complacent Christians, arguing that intellectual belief in God is of no value unless it gives rise to deeds that demonstrate one's faith.

Even recognizing these differences, it still appears that James is responding to Christians who are misinterpreting Paul and quoting Pauline slogans. James uses language that echoes Paul's teaching (the formula, *by faith alone* (v. 24), occurs elsewhere only in Paul's letters); appeals to Abraham as Paul does in Rom 4; quotes Gen 15:6 as Paul does in Rom 4:3; and his affirmation reverses the points of Paul's affirmation in

Rom 3:28. James was probably not responding directly to Paul, however, but to distortions of his teachings.

Rahab was a popular heroine in contemporary literature (Matt 1:5; Heb 11:31). She was considered to be a model of the ideal proselyte. Verse 26 concludes the chapter with an analogy: *faith without works* is as dead as a *body without . . . spirit* (cf. v. 17).

The Obedience of Faith in Words and Wisdom, 3:1-18

James 3 treats two subjects of vital importance to Christian living: controlling the tongue (vv. 1-12) and recognizing true wisdom (vv. 13-18).

The Power of Words, 3:1-12

The tongue can easily serve as a barometer of character and spiritual maturity (Matt 12:34-37), so control of one's speech is not optional for Christians. The chapter begins with a specific warning that *not many . . . should become teachers*. The reason given is that teachers will be judged more strictly than others.

As sensitive as James is to the many subtle forms of sin that can insinuate themselves into the life of a Christian, it still holds out the ideal of perfection. By steadfastness "you may be perfect" (1:4, NRSV *mature*), and faith is perfected by works (2:22). An echo can again be found in the sermon on the mount: "You, therefore, must be perfect, as your heavenly Father is perfect" (Matt 5:48). James does not require perfection but uses it to underscore the difficulty of complete mastery over one's speech.

Two metaphors drive home the point that a small member can control the whole body: *bridle* and *rudder*. Although the metaphors lend themselves to the positive sense that one small member could actually harness and control the whole body, James emphasizes the difficulty of harnessing the tongue rather than its power to subdue a wild or undisciplined body. The paragraph reaches a pointed conclusion in v. 5a. The tongue's influence does not correspond to its size. James paints graphic, disturbing pictures of the tongue's potential for perversity and leaves it up to each individual to decide what to do about the problem of unrestrained speech.

The third metaphor introduces the tongue's potential for destruction: a spark can destroy a whole forest. Verse 6 is so difficult to translate that commentators have often suggested the text is corrupt. The NRSV, however, renders it intelligible by simply reversing the sequence of the second and third clauses and translating the verb as passive (*is placed*). The tongue can stain, defile, or render a person unclean before God.

The phrase *the cycle of nature* is peculiar. It reflects the view that life is an eternal, cyclical procession. The phrase had entered into common usage, however, and James uses it without adopting the philosophy it once conveyed. The tongue not only exposes the whole realm of evil within us; like a spark it sets on fire the whole arena of human life. Consequently, the tongue can ignite far greater EVIL than we may ever intend. The source of the tongue's iniquity is finally revealed: hell itself.

The progressive growth of evil can be charted through this tangled verse. GEHENNA, place of torment and home of demons, the inexhaustible source of iniquity, lights the fiery tongue. The tongue introduces the whole world of evil into our bodies and puts to flame the whole order of life. Paul would have introduced a list of vices; James paints a graphic picture of the most destructive fire imaginable.

Verses 7 and 8 advance James's series of hyperboles on the evils of the tongue by comparing its untamed and poisonous nature to that of wild beasts. The second point of comparison follows quickly: the tongue is *full of deadly poison*. Few things evoke fear more quickly than the sight of a scorpion or a poisonous snake. The hissing tongue is full poison (Ps 140:3; Rom 3:13). Who can still claim, "but words will never hurt me"?

Having condemned the wild, poisonous nature of the tongue, James finally gives specific examples. The tongue is fickle. James did not know the idiom "forked tongue," but it expresses the tongue's inconsistency. The tongue is used both to curse and to bless, and that *ought not to be so*. This admonition may refer to casual cursing, but James may be referring to the church's worship, and specifically to preachers who both praise God and invoke curses on others in God's name. One cannot bless God and curse those made in his image. Such speech is evidence of the double-mindedness James condemns (1:8; 4:8).

Two further metaphors follow, illustrating the incompatibility of blessing and cursing. Springs were vital to life in Palestine. Yet, in the same area one found both fresh and bitter water—but never from the same opening. Each spring was known for the water it produced. Similarly, a fig tree cannot produce olives, nor can a grapevine produce figs (cf. Matt 7:16). Verse 12 ends abruptly. The shorter text reads: *No more can salt water yield fresh.* The longer text draws the statement in line with the previous metaphors: "Thus no spring can yield both salt water and fresh water." The longer text, however, says no more than v. 11, while the shorter text maintains that one product cannot become another.

The Wisdom from Above, 3:13-18

Verses 13-17 form a unit that contrasts the evidences of wisdom from above with earthly wisdom. Verse 18 provides a transition to the sayings on conflict that follow in 4:1-12.

The unit begins with a question that invites self-examination. An imperative follows. If one has both wisdom and discernment, then let that person demonstrate spiritual maturity not in devastating arguments but in the good works that come from *gentleness born of wisdom* (v. 13). If faith results in works (2:14-26), so too true wisdom is manifested in one's conduct and manner of life. True wisdom produces humility not arrogance.

Verse 14 conveys the implication that the church is plagued by bitter jealousy and ambition. These may be especially evident in its teachers and would-be leaders. James echoes words of Jesus again at this point: these sins come from the heart (cf. Matt 15:19). The admonitions that follow may stand in coordinate relationship to one another ("do not boast about it or deny the truth," NIV) or causal relationship ("do not be arrogant and so lie against the truth," NASB).

Verse 15 explains why boasting is excluded. Ambition and arrogance are the fruit of a kind of wisdom, but not the true wisdom that comes down *from above*. True wisdom is one of God's good and perfect gifts (1:17). Nevertheless, the wisdom of the arrogant and ambitious who create dissension in the church is indeed inspired: it is inspired by the devil. The three adjectives form a crescendo of sinful alienation from God. Such wisdom is *earthly, unspiritual, and devilish* (v. 15).

Verse 16 pushes the argument one step further: if counterfeit wisdom is exposed by jealousy and selfish ambition, these in turn give rise to disorder and every kind of evil. True wisdom bears seven identifying marks (v. 17):

1. *Pure*. Like the works of God, the life of his people should be morally perfect and undefiled.

2. Ready for peace (*peaceable*). The wisdom from above is therefore diametrically opposed to the divisiveness of the earthly, sensual, and demonic inspiration of the arrogant and ambitious.

3. *Gentle* or "considerate" (NEB, NIV). In a position of strength, the wise person is considerate of those who might otherwise be dominated or manipulated.

4. Compliant (*willing to yield*). In a position of weakness, the wise one is reasonable, yielding, and obedient.

5. *Full of mercy and good fruit*. True wisdom results in the true religion (acts of mercy, 1:27) and true faith (acts of charity, 2:15-17).

6. *Without a trace of partiality* or "unwavering" (NASB). The sense is either that true wisdom does not "make a distinction" or that it is not fickle and inconsistent—like the tongue that both blesses and curses (vv. 9-12).

7. Sincere. Having nothing to hide, wisdom is *without . . . hypocrisy*, genuine. It can be taken at face value.

The aphorism in v. 18 closes this section on the contrasting effects of the two wisdoms. Its interpretation hinges on two issues: (1) is *the harvest of righteousness* (a) an appositional genitive (in which case the fruit is righteousness) or (b) a subjective genitive (in which case righteousness produces its own fruit); and (2) is the fruit *sown in peace* (a) by or (b) *for* those who make peace? The similarity to the blessing of the peacemakers (Matt 5:9) is unmistakable. Peace and righteousness are mutually dependent; each requires the other. The mark of true wisdom is, therefore, its capacity to produce peace and righteousness. Peacemaking and jealousy are antithetical; one creates unity, the other division.

The Obedience of Faith in Community, 4:1–5:6

As with most of James, the section that follows is composed of loosely related instructions for ethical living. Various divisions of the chapters have been proposed. Here Jas 4:1–5:6 is viewed as a series of exhortations on living faithfully in community. Three of the chief dangers to the communities of faith are dissension (4:1-12), presumption (5:1-6), and inappropriate use of wealth (5:1-6).

Faith as a Response to Dissension, 4:1-12

This section is an extension of the previous one in that it exposes the consequences of earthly wisdom: the quarrels that destroy (vv. 1-3), the world that corrupts (vv. 4-6), the humility that restores (vv. 7-10), and the judgment on those who judge (vv. 11-12).

The first verse raises two questions. The first diagnoses the situation; the second challenges the readers to accept James's diagnosis of the cause of quarreling and infighting. The wars and fightings are generally understood as metaphorical references to quarrels and factions within the community. The second question suggests that the quarrels are caused by "pleasures" that war in your members. The thought that our pleasures are the cause of fighting among members of the Christian community places pride, ambition, and vanity in their true context.

The charge *you . . . murder* seems so harsh as a charge concerning the church that Erasmus (1519 ed. of Greek NT) proposed that the text was corrupt and that "you envy" (*phthoneite*) should be read instead of "you murder" (*phoneuete*). This conjecture was accepted by Calvin and the KJV, but is now generally rejected. There is no manuscript support for the conjecture. On the other hand, murder is often connected metaphorically with sins of the tongue.

The tragedy is that by fighting we do not obtain what we desire. On the other hand, we have only to ask God for what we need. God is the giver of every good and perfect gift (1:17). Again, we ask but we do not receive because we do not ask rightly. James does not say that we are asking for sinful things, but we are asking sinfully. We are not praying for forgiveness or righteousness, but to further our own interests. We may ask for good things for the wrong reasons. This does not mean, of course, that all unanswered prayer is due to praying wrongly.

Using a term that evokes echoes of Hosea's condemnation of Israel, James charges that such Christians are adulterers and adulteresses (v. 4). *World* is used here in the hostile sense found in the Johannine literature (1 John 2:15-17). God and the world are set in opposition to one another, so that friendship with one means hostility toward the other (Matt 6:24; Luke 16:13). The desire for pleasure divides and distorts our entire existence. This forced choice means that neutrality toward God is impossible.

Verse 5 announces a quotation from scripture, but the remainder of v. 5 cannot be found anywhere in the OT. Psalms 41:2 and 83:3 come as close as any reference, but James may paraphrase material such as Gen 6:3 or Exod 20:5. The first part of v. 6 promises that God does not readily give us up. Instead, he gives more grace. God helps wavering Christians!

There are ten imperatives in vv. 7-10. Together they provide an expanded definition of repentance.

1. *Submit . . . to God.* The imperatives that follow explain this first, basic demand. It is a military term meaning to put oneself under the command of a superior.

2. *Resist the devil.* The second command is the counterpart to the first. The first requires the second. Again, James uses a military metaphor: to stand against.

3. *Draw near to God.* This is a cultic term for worshiping God.

4. *Cleanse your hands.* This is the language of ceremonial cleansing (Exod 30:19-21; 2 Cor 7:1).

5. *Purify your hearts.* Again, ceremonial language. To cleanse one's heart means to cleanse one's entire inner being (cf. Ps 24:4).

6. *Lament* (lit. "be wretched"). True repentance is accompanied by remorse.

7. *Mourn.*

8. *Weep* (Luke 6:25; Mark 14:72).

9. *Let your laughter be turned to mourning and your joy to dejection.*

10. *Humble yourselves.* Any other road to exaltation is the result of sinfulness.

True repentance, however, does not lack for results. Three promises follow the ten imperatives: (1) the devil *will flee from you*; (2) *God will draw near to you*; and (3) God *will exalt you.*

Verses 11-12 form a conclusion to Jas 3:1–4:12 in that they return to the sins of speech and dissension within the community. Verse 11 begins with the only imperative in these two verses. The command is not to disparage or belittle one another. The present tense implies that such disparagement is currently taking place. The issue is not whether what is being said is true or not. James leaves no room for those who would justify their damaging words by saying, "Well, I am just telling the truth." The rest of vv. 11-12 gives a theological justification for this command: (1) The one who disparages or judges a brother disparages or judges the law: "inasmuch as ye have done it unto the least of these my brethren ye have done it unto God's law" (cf. Matt 25:40).

The command not to slander appears both in the OT (Lev 19:16) and in the NT (Rom 1:30; 2 Cor 12:20). (2) Breaking the law highhandedly implies that we are not bound by the law. (3) If we place ourselves above the law, as judges, we have usurped God's prerogative. We have taken God's place as the lawgiver. Are we able to give a better law or a more righteous judgment? God is the only one who is able to save and to destroy. Breaking the law by disparaging others is therefore a disparagement of God. It is blasphemy. The conclusion of v. 12 puts us in our place again: *So who, then, are you to judge your neighbor?*

Faith as a Response to Presumption, 4:13-17

This section turns again to the rich and the results of love of the world. James has in mind here the merchants in particular, the small businessmen who worked ambitiously and industriously, traveling to whatever place held the prospect of profit. James does not condemn their business dealings as dishonest. What he condemns is the presumptuous disregard of God's sovereignty as they make their plans. The businessmen are merely an illustration of the attitude that ignores God in our daily affairs. Their plans assume that they are in full control of their lives. First, they do not know the future. Second, their lives are mortal and transitory. James is not saying that it is wrong to make plans, only that we ought to live our lives under God's sovereignty.

The saying "If the Lord wills" (RSV) is common in hellenistic writings. It may express either genuine or superficial piety. James, therefore, may intend a bit of irony. If the pagans at least say, "If God wills," then should not Christians recognize their finiteness and place the planning of their lives under God's sovereignty? By placing our lives under God's will we also have a sure defense against dread, despair, and fear of the future. In contrast, those who worship God on Sunday and live in complete disregard of God's sovereignty the rest of the week show an attitude of sinful arrogance.

Verse 17 is a maxim or proverb, such as James quotes in 2:13 or 3:18. If we know what is good and do not do it, we sin. The word order emphasizes that such compromise is nothing less than sin. Sin is not related just to certain absolutes, therefore, but also to the level of our spiritual maturity and discernment.

A Warning to the Rich, 5:1-6

With this paragraph James shifts both his target and his tone. He offers a sharp, prophetic warning to the rich landowners who oppress the poor. These are apparently not members of the community because he never calls them brothers (as in 5:7-11). He does not call them to repent; he laments the judgment on them. His primary concern, however, is to dissuade Christians from falling into envy towards the power and privilege of the wealthy.

The call to weep and howl (RSV) depicts a scene of utter despair and misery. The present participle vividly describes the scene as already occurring. In vv. 2-3 James describes the effects of the judgment upon the wealth of the rich. Perfect tense verbs are used, as though the judgment had already been accomplished.

1. Their wealth is ruined, decayed, *rotted.* We may have a list of three types of wealth: foodstuffs, garments, and metals.

2. Their garments are *moth-eaten.*

3. Their *gold and silver have rusted.* These metals, of course, cannot rust. So James is either thinking of the coins of the time that had so much alloy that they did rust, or else he is describing the corruption of riches by a power greater than rust.

Moreover, the rich will be condemned by their wealth. The rust will bear witness against them that they did not use their wealth responsibly. The rust that eats at the metals in an awful turn of events will eat at their flesh. The final irony of this verse is that they have been storing up treasure *in the last days.* While they should have been preparing for the Lord's coming by righteous living, they have hoarded their goods and oppressed the poor. The goods they hoarded now condemn them (Matt 6:19-21; Luke 12:15-21; 16:19-31).

Verse 4 describes the charges against landowners. The charges, though, are brought by the wages they have wrongfully held back from those who labored in their fields. Jewish law required that laborers be paid at the end of each day, since some depended on the day's wage for food. The harvest, of course, was a time of great income for the landowner, but he defrauds the poor who work his fields. These cries rise to the Lord, the Lord of Hosts! (cf. Isa. 5:7-9). The wealth of the rich has been gained at the expense of the poor.

The rich have lived a life of ease and pleasure, supported by the suffering and oppression of others. They have fattened their hearts (cholesterol!) like fatted calves that continue eating even on the day of their slaughter. Now the day of the Lord has come, and they themselves are the fatted calves. Yet they live in complete disregard for the imminence of the Judgment.

Verse 6 states the third and most serious offense. These landowners have condemned and killed the righteous. They have killed the righteous sufferer, perhaps by means of judicial proceedings. Some see it as an allusion to the crucifixion of Jesus or the martyrdom of James the Just. Neither is really called for, however. "The righteous" is probably a collective term (NIV).

The Obedience of Faith
in Patience, Oaths, and Prayer, 5:7-18

The remaining verses of the letter can be divided into four sections: a call for patience (vv. 7-11), rejection of profanity (v. 12), the power of prayer (vv. 13-18), and restoring the wayward (5:19-20). The main themes of the letter are found in this closing section: rich—poor, the need to control speech, concern for harmony within the community, and the need for endurance.

A Call for Patience, 5:7-11

The word for patience means literally to have a long temper, or we might say "a long fuse." James turns from condemnation of the rich in 5:1-6 to concern for the community. Although the poor may be abused by the rich, James calls on Christians to be patient. Some have understood *the coming of the Lord* as a reference to God's coming in judgment, as in the OT prophets, but most interpreters are convinced it is a reference to the PAROUSIA of the risen Lord.

James draws an illustration from the life of the small farmer. The farmer awaits the "precious fruit from the earth" (RSV). His livelihood depends on the harvest. He plants his carefully saved seed, hopes, waits, and stretches his resources and rations—everything depends on the harvest. *The early and late rains* are characteristic of the climate of the east end of the Mediterranean. The early rains came in October and November, the late rains in April and May. Without the early rains the crops would not survive; without the late rains the harvest would be small.

Verse 8 draws the conclusion: "So you be patient also." The best response to impatience is new resolve. The basis for such resolve is offered by the promise that the coming of the Lord is "at hand" (RSV).

Discouragement and impatience can easily lead to grumbling, and grumbling to disunity. James therefore warns the Christians not to "moan" about one another. Even if some complaining about the rich might be tolerated (vv. 1-6), the Christians should not turn their impatience against one another. Both hope and judgment are expressed by the rest of v. 9. Don't complain about one another lest you be judged also. The judge is standing at the doors even now (Mark 13:29; Rev 3:20). He is coming to judge both the rich and the poor. Wait on his judgment and do not incur condemnation at the last minute by sowing dissension within the community of believers.

Christians are not in a unique situation just because they have suffered. The prophets suffered too. The Christians will do well to take the prophets as an example of suffering and patience. They too spoke in the name of the Lord. Verse 11 turns to a specific example of patience: Job. Actually JOB does not seem all that patient in the OT book, so James may be referring to contemporary tradition regarding Job. This is the only reference to Job in the NT, and James speaks of Job's endurance or steadfastness rather than his patience. The main point is that Job remained faithful in spite of his suffering. The issue is whether we will endure and not lose faith.

The Lord is full of compassion and mercies. The one who is patient and endures trial faithfully will see the good that the Lord is doing.

Rejection of Oaths, 5:12

This verse appears with little context. It may be that James has in mind again the dangers of the tongue and the ways it disrupts community. Harold Songer (1972, 136) finds the sequence of admonitions meaningful: "Suffering Christians (vv. 7-11) must guard their speech and not grumble (v. 9) or swear (v. 12) . . . but pray (vv. 13-18) and confess their sins (v. 16)."

This verse is closely paralleled by Matt 5:33-37 (cf. Matt 23:16-22). James's concern is not oaths sworn in court but the practice of using oaths in everyday discourse. This practice had developed to the point that some oaths were binding, while other, similar formulas were not. One could give the appearance of swearing a sacred oath, therefore, but actually use a defective form with no intention of being bound by it. Jesus and James both condemn such hypocrisy. If this is the central concern, then James is saying that Christians should always speak in such a way that no one would ever doubt our word. Oaths would then no longer be needed.

The Power of Prayer, 5:13-18

Following the warning against swearing in the previous verse, James turns to the positive admonition to be diligent in prayer. The section opens with three questions: Is anyone *among you suffering*? Is *any cheerful*? Is *any among you sick*? The answers give his response: Let him *pray*. Let him *sing praise*. Let him call for the *elders of the church*. Prayer is not just an aid in time of distress; it is the appropriate response to every circumstance in life.

The first question seems not to have illness in view but rather distress, misfortune, or calamity. In the NT the term for singing is used of singing praises to God in public worship (1 Cor 14:15; Eph 5:19). Don't forget God in the good times.

Is any sick? The term can denote any illness or weakness, here apparently a serious illness. *The elders of the church* were probably the senior, respected men of the community. Prayer is primary. The anointing with OIL is mentioned in a participle. There is no instruction to consecrate the oil. It is the common term for olive oil, which was at times used medicinally (Mark 6:13; Luke 10:34). Here it is an external sign of the inward power of prayer. James is apparently describing a common practice of the church rather than prescribing a new procedure. James does not prescribe this procedure for every illness, nor does he assure that we will always be cured or spared from death. Obviously that is not the case. Instead, James is describing a procedure by which one in need is upheld by the church and God's mercy and healing power is invoked.

The last part of v. 15 forms a transition to James's closing emphasis—rooting sin out of our lives. Sin and sickness were closely connected in popular thought. James does not contend that sickness is always the result of sin, but he allows that it may be. Prayer can deal with both sickness and sin. In times of need we are to pray for God's care and deliverance.

James exhorts Christians to confess their sins to one another. He does not say the sick person is to confess his or her sins to the elders. He seems to have in mind open, public confessions of specific sins in the context of worship and prayer for one another. Apart from confession we cannot experience forgiveness. Excesses are to be avoided, of course. In some instances specific, public confession would not lead to restoration or harmony.

The latter part of v. 16 states the theme of the whole section. The entreaty or petition *of the righteous [person] is powerful and effective.* The prayer of ordinary persons has great power when God makes it effective. James is not just talking about the prayer of saints. He illustrates the power of prayer by appealing to the example of ELIJAH. The period of three and a half years is based on a rabbinic estimate of the time of the drought based on 1 Kgs 18:1. Elijah is the fourth OT character James has used, following Abraham (2:21-24); Rahab (2:25); Job (5:11). James takes pains to say that Elijah was human and subject to the same suffering the rest of us endure. Legend emphasized the effectiveness of Elijah's prayer. James argued that it wasn't Elijah; it was the power of prayer at work.

Concluding Exhortation: Restoring the Wayward, 5:19-20

A Christian's responsibility for sinners does not stop with prayer. James closes the letter by calling on us to take responsibility for erring Christians. To wander *from the truth* means to turn aside from God's will and live in moral corruption. James is not talking about converting an unbeliever but restoring an erring brother or sister. He does not specify how this restoration takes place. Death is the final result of sin. If we minimize the gravity of the erring one's position, we also minimize the significance of restoration.

One who restores another also covers a multitude of sins. The term to *cover* comes from the OT and means to secure their forgiveness (Ps 32:1; 85:2). Some commentators take this to mean that the agent of restoration has secured forgiveness for his or her own sins, but the idea that meritorious works bring forgiveness cuts against the NT emphasis that sin is forgiven by grace.

This last admonition, to be active in turning others from sin, captures the purpose of the letter. So, with no closing greetings, it ends abruptly, leaving us to consider its claim upon our lives.

Works Cited

Davids, P. H. 1982. *The Epistle of James: A Commentary on the Greek Text.* NIGTC.

Hiebert, D. Edmond. 1979. *The Epistle of James: Tests of a Living Faith.*

Luther's Works. Ed. Theodore G. Tapert. 1955–1958.

Songer, Harold S. 1972. "James." *BBC.*

First Peter

J. Ramsey Michaels

Introduction

First Peter is one of two NT letters bearing the name of the apostle PETER. Nothing in the letter itself identifies it explicitly as the "first" of the two. In the NT it is given the title "First Peter" or "the First Epistle of Peter" because of 2 Pet 3:1, where that work refers to itself as "this second letter," and perhaps also because in "Second Peter" the apostle is represented as expecting his own death very soon (2 Pet 1:14). First Peter presents itself not as the beginning of an ongoing correspondence, but as a once-for-all directive from the apostle to a large number of Christian congregations spread over five Roman provinces of Asia Minor (1:1).

Authorship and Genre

The authorship of 1 Peter is disputed because its elegant Greek style is believed to be inconsistent with the tradition that Simon Peter was an uneducated Galilean (Acts 4:13). Defenders of Petrine authorship, such as E. G. Selwyn and Peter Davids, have resorted to the theory that Peter's coworker *Silvanus* (5:12) was responsible for putting some of Peter's ideas into good Greek style. This in effect makes Silvanus the real author of the letter. More likely, Silvanus (or Silas) was simply the messenger who delivered the letter to its Asian destination, just as he helped deliver the decree of the JERUSALEM COUNCIL to ANTIOCH according to Acts 15:22-32.

A better theory is that 1 Peter was a semiofficial communication from the church at ROME. Like *1 Clement* at the end of the first century C.E., 1 Peter claims to be written from a congregation in *Babylon* (5:13), which by the latter half of the century had become a designation for the city of Rome (cf. Rev 17:4-5, 18). If Peter was the Roman congregation's resident apostle at the time, it is not surprising that a circular letter from Rome to Christians scattered throughout the Asian provinces might have been written under his supervision and authority. If so, the letter's style can be attributed to an anonymous learned scribe without resorting to theories about Silvanus.

The appropriateness of a circular letter from *Babylon* (5:13) to the Diaspora, or *Dispersion* (1:1) is unmistakable, for Babylon was the city that had first scattered the Jews from their homeland in 587/6 B.C.E. Peter is drawing an analogy between the Jewish community scattered throughout the world and the world-wide Christian community of his day (5:9). The church at Rome is telling its sister churches in the provinces that they all share a common lot as *aliens and exiles* in the ROMAN EMPIRE (1:1; 2:11), and that they must know how to respond to slander, hostile questioning, and even persecution, whether from the populace or the imperial authorities.

Another major objection to the traditional view that Peter wrote 1 Peter is the assumption, itself based on tradition, that the apostle Peter died in the persecution under Nero in 64 C.E., a decade before Jews and Christians began referring to Rome as "Babylon." The traditions about Peter's death are relatively late, and the later they are the more detailed and specific they become (as, e.g., in *ActPet* 30-41). John 21:18-19 may or may not suggest that Peter was martyred, but in any case gives no information as to when or under what circumstances. The same is true of the reference to his death in 2 Pet 1:14. What is usually considered the earliest explicit reference to Peter's martyrdom merely states that Peter "suffered not one or two, but many trials, and having thus given testimony went to the glorious place which was his due" (*1 Clem* 5.4).

Although there is no consensus on the authorship of 1 Peter, the letter is well known and well attested in the ancient church (POLYCARP, PAPIAS, IRENAEUS, Tertullian, Clement, and Origen; see Michaels 1988, xxxi–xxxiv). The burden of proof still rests with those who want to assign it to someone other than Peter.

Integrity

Many questions have been raised in the past about the integrity of 1 Peter. The apparent sharp break between 4:11 and 4:12 has suggested to some that a letter consisting of 1:1–4:11 dealt with persecution as a rather remote possibility, and that 4:12–5:11 was added as a postscript when the persecution suddenly broke out. Alternatively, some have argued that 1:3–4:11 was not a letter at all but a baptismal sermon, or even a baptismal liturgy, later framed into a letter by the addition of 1:1-2 and 4:12–5:14.

In keeping with more recent literary approaches to the NT, the tendency in the past two or three decades has been rather to interpret 1 Peter as a literary unit, and in most instances as an actual letter. Although there has been continued recognition of rhetorical forms in 1 Peter such as "household duty codes" (2:18– 3:7), and even of possible hymnic or creedal fragments (e.g., 1:18-21; 2:21-25; 3:18-22), these are now generally discussed under the heading of Peter's "sources" (along with the OT and the sayings of Jesus), not as generic features which somehow call into question the work's integrity or its identity as a real letter.

For Further Study

In the *Mercer Dictionary of the Bible*: ESCHATOLOGY IN THE NT; ETHICS IN THE NEW TESTAMENT; GENERAL LETTERS; PERSECUTION IN THE NT; PETER; PETER, LETTERS OF; ROME; SUFFERING IN THE NT.

In other sources: W. J. Dalton, *Christ's Proclamation to the Spirits: A Study of 1 Pet 3:18–4:6*; P. H. Davids, *The First Epistle of Peter*, NICNT; J. N. D. Kelly, *A Commentary on the Epistles of Peter and of Jude*, HNTC; J. R. Michaels, *1 Peter*, WBC, and *Word Biblical Themes: 1 Peter*; E. G. Selwyn, *The First Epistle of St. Peter*; C. H. Talbert, ed., *Perspectives on First Peter*, NABPR/SSS 9.

Commentary

An Outline

I. Greetings, 1:1-2
II. The Identity of the People of God, 1:3–2:10
   A. The Great Salvation, 1:3-12
   B. The New Way of Life, 1:13-25
   C. The Chosen Community, 2:1-10
III. The Responsibilities of the People of God, 2:11–4:11
   A. Respect for Everyone, 2:11-17
   B. Slaves and Masters, 2:18-25
   C. Wives and Husbands, 3:1-7
   D. Seeking Peace, 3:8-12
   E. The Hope of Vindication, 3:13–4:6
   F. Christian Community, 4:7-11
IV. The Responsibilities of Elders, 4:12–5:11
   A. The Fiery Ordeal, 4:12-19
   B. Elders and Their Congregations, 5:1-11
V. Conclusion, 5:12-14

Greetings, 1:1-2

Peter, like PAUL, identifies himself as *apostle of Jesus Christ*, but writes to a far larger audience than Paul. While Paul wrote only to individual congregations, or (in one instance) "the churches of Galatia" (Gal 1:2), Peter's audience encompasses five Roman provinces roughly equivalent to present-day Turkey. He addresses his readers as Christian believers chosen by the God of Israel and thereby alienated from the religion and culture of the ROMAN EMPIRE. Like the Jews, they are a Diaspora (cf. Jas 1:1), a chosen people scattered throughout the empire. Peter attributes their conversion to God's foreknowledge and the purifying work of the HOLY SPIRIT. Like the Jews in Moses' time who promised to obey God as the blood of sacrificial animals was sprinkled over them (Exod 24:3-8), these Christians have obediently accepted the blood of Jesus Christ poured out for them. Peter wishes them abundant *grace and peace*.

The Identity of the People of God, 1:3–2:10

The Great Salvation, 1:3-12

A long introductory "blessing" embraces the present experience and future hope of Christians, setting both against the background of biblical (and extrabiblical) prophecies out of the Jewish past. The whole section is loosely held together by relative pronouns (e.g., vv. 6, 8, 10, 12), as Peter moves back and forth between praise of God and the instruction of his readers.

1:3-9. Salvation as revelation and joy. Peter praises God for the power evident in raising Jesus Christ from the dead, and for the mercy evident in giving Christians (himself included) a new birth as children of God with a sure promise of eternal salvation (v. 3). Shifting from *us* to *you*, he assures his readers that God will keep them safe through whatever persecutions they may now be facing (vv. 5-6). His knowledge of their actual circumstances in the Roman provinces seems general and rather limited, yet he is confident that whatever is happening to them now is God's way of testing their faithfulness, as gold is tested and purified *by fire* (v. 7; cf. Ps 66:10 and Wis 3:5-6). He is confident that their faith will turn out stronger than ever, bringing them *praise and glory and honor* at the time "when Jesus Christ appears" (v. 7b).

Peter's mention of the "appearing," or "revealing," of Jesus in v. 7b reinforces and personalizes his reference to *salvation ready to be revealed in the last time* (v. 5b; cf. 1:13; 4:13; 5:4). "Salvation" *is* JESUS, now invisible, but soon to become visible in power and splendor. To be saved is to see him when he appears, and know the joy of his presence (vv. 6, 8). Until then, one must love him and trust in him sight unseen (v. 8). *Indescribable and glorious joy* (v. 8; cf. 4:13b) is still future, reserved in HEAVEN for all who love Jesus even though he is now hidden from human view (cf. 1 Cor 2:9; 2 Tim 4:8).

1:10-12. Salvation's witnesses. Salvation to Peter is the "end," or goal, of Christian faith (v. 9), not its beginning, but he reminds his readers that this future salvation and the sufferings that made it possible were prophesied long ago (v. 10). By mentioning both *prophets* (v. 10) and *angels* (v. 12b), Peter places his audience at the end of time, and at the center of the universe. The ancient Jewish prophets were already Christians in that the *spirit of Christ* (v. 11) was speaking through them about the *sufferings* intended for Christ (i.e., his death on the cross), and the "glorious events" to follow: his resurrection from the dead, his journey to heaven (cf. 3:19, 22), and his final "appearing" again on earth. Not even the prophets understood when or how this would all take place. They tried to find out, but God told them it was not for them or for their time. Instead, Peter claims, it is for our benefit today (cf. Matt 13:17 = Luke 10:24). The Holy Spirit sent from heaven has made the good news known through missionaries in Asia Minor, and even God's angels long to look down from heaven on the wonders of human salvation (v. 12b).

The New Way of Life, 1:13-25

1:13-21. Hope and holiness. *Therefore* in v. 13 introduces a call to action on the basis of the salvation just described. Yet Peter cannot stop celebrating the salvation itself. The section begins, like the preceding one, with *hope* (v. 13; cf. 1:3), and ends on the same note (v. 21). Peter keeps weaving into his call to

action reminders of what God has done and will do for Christian believers (compare such phrases as *the grace that Jesus Christ will bring you when he is revealed*, v. 13; the holy one *who called you*, v. 15; and all of vv. 18-21). Consequently, the call to action is general, not specific. The imperatives of hope (v. 13) and godly fear (v. 17) have more to do with attitudes of mind than with behavior, and are directed not toward other people but toward God. Only the command to *be holy* (vv. 15-16) focuses on day-by-day Christian living. To be holy as God is holy (cf. Lev 19:2, which Peter cites) was traditionally understood as a religious or cultic goal, but Peter identifies holiness here as something expressed in *conduct* (v. 15). "Holy conduct" for Peter is something that runs counter to the values of Roman society (i.e., *the futile ways inherited from your ancestors* [v. 18]), but only in later sections of his letter (e.g., in 2:11–3:12), will he define it more concretely.

In vv. 18-21 Peter resumes his celebration of God's saving work through Jesus Christ. He describes Christian salvation here as "redemption" (*ransom*) or release from slavery by the payment of a price. The price is not *silver or gold* (cf. Isa 52:3), but something far more precious—the blood of Christ understood as a ransom (cf. Mark 10:45; Titus 2:14). Drawing on the Exodus story (e.g., Exod 12:1-7), Peter compares the blood of Christ to *that of a lamb without defect or blemish* (v. 19; cf. Exod 12:5), and places Christ's death in the context of God's eternal plan, from *before the foundation of the world* to *the end of the ages* (v. 20). By the shedding of Christ's blood (cf. v. 2) and his *resurrection . . . from the dead* (cf. v. 3), the readers of this letter have become for the first time "believers in God" (v. 21)—the God of Israel—and sharers in Israel's redemption. The implication is clear that these Christian readers are gentiles by birth and not Jews.

1:22-25. Undying love. Peter now brings his argument to a focus in a single ethical command: *love one another deeply from the heart* (v. 22b). The love command proper is framed by references to purification through OBEDIENCE (v. 22a; cf. vv. 2, 18-19), and spiritual rebirth (v. 23; cf. v. 3). The key word is *deeply* or "constantly" (cf. 4:8). Love among Christians should be as strong and as lasting as their faith *tested in the fire* (cf. v. 7). Theirs is an undying love because they have been reborn by the planting of *imperishable seed*—that is, by the preaching of the Christian gospel understood as *the living and enduring word of God*

(vv. 23-25). Peter drives home his point with a citation of Isa 40:6b, 8: all humanity fades away like the grass and the flowers, but *the word of the Lord endures forever*. To Peter the word of the eternal God, the message spoken by Jesus the Lord (cf. Mark 13:31), and the good news about Jesus announced by his followers (cf. v. 12) all amount to the same thing—an eternal Word summoning those who hear it to eternal and genuine love for each other.

The Chosen Community, 2:1-10

2:1-3. Growing toward salvation. For the time being, Peter continues on the theme of hearing the word of God, without exploring further the love command. With the image of rebirth still in mind, he compares his readers to *newborn infants* (v. 2), urging them to do what comes naturally to babies—that is, to long for the *pure, spiritual milk* consisting of *the Lord* (v. 3) and the Lord's message. This means rejecting all other spiritual food as impure: all the *malice* and *guile*, all the *insincerity, envy, and all slander* evident to Peter in Roman society (v. 1). *Milk* here is not elementary Christian instruction intended to give way later to "solid food" (as, e.g., in 1 Cor 3:2, and Heb 5:12-13). It is not teaching or instruction at all, but the very life of God given in *mercy* (1:3; 2:10b) to those who are reborn, in the same way a mother nourishes her children. "Milk from the breasts of the Lord" later became a striking metaphor in the collection of early Christian hymns known as the *Odes of Solomon* (see, e.g., *Odes* 4.10; 8.14; 14.2-3; 19.2; 35.5; 40.1, in *OTP* 2:725–71). Like babies, Christians need this *pure, spiritual milk* in order to grow. The end of the growth process is *salvation* (v. 2b)—the salvation Peter had said is now *ready to be revealed* in Christ (cf. 1:5). Here as in chap. 1, salvation is the assured and appropriate outcome of a faithful life.

2:4-10. Becoming the people of God. In vv. 4-10, Peter's metaphor shifts from that of growth to that of building under construction (cf. Eph 2:21; 4:12, 16). At the same time his attention shifts from Christians as individuals to their corporate identity as a people. As more and more of them come to Christ in the course of the Christian mission (v. 4)—by "tasting" Christ's mercy (2:3)—they are being built into a kind of temple (*a spiritual house, to be a holy priesthood*, v. 5).

From Isa 28:16, a text Peter assumes is referring to Christ as *a stone, a cornerstone chosen and precious* (v. 6), he draws the implication that Christians too are *living stones* (v. 5) out of which God is building this

new "temple." He plays on a contrast almost universal in his time between honor and shame. His text from Isaiah concludes that those who trust in the great cornerstone *will not be put to shame* (v. 6b), and Peter applies this to Christians because they have believed in Jesus (v. 7a). Theirs is the "honor," while "shame" is reserved for those who reject Jesus (vv. 4, 7b; cf. Ps 118:32). God's CORNERSTONE becomes for them *a stone that makes them stumble, and a rock that makes them fall* (cf. Isa 8:14). To this fate, Peter says, God has appointed them (v. 8b), just as surely as God has "appointed" Jesus Christ the cornerstone of faith.

Christian believers, on the other hand, are *God's people*, and the recipients of God's MERCY (v. 10). Although they are gentiles, whatever was true of the Jewish people is now true of them. They are *a chosen race, a royal priesthood, a holy nation*, and *God's own people* destined for vindication (v. 9a; cf. Exod 19:6; Isa 43:20-21). The last of these phrases refers not to the present but to the future, like Peter's references to future salvation in 1:5, 9, and 2:2. Although God has called these gentile Christians "out of darkness" (cf. 1:14, 18) to *marvelous light* (v. 9b), the *marvelous light* of salvation has not quite dawned (cf. *1 Clem* 36.2). They must still undergo suffering for a while longer (cf. 1:6-7). Living as they do between the darkness of their gentile past and the light of God's future, these Christians have the responsibility of praising the God of Israel both with their words and their lives. Like Israel itself (cf. Hos 1:6-9), they were once *not a people* and once *had not received mercy*. Now they are *God's people*, now they have *received mercy* (v. 10; cf. 1:3), and they await their inheritance.

The Responsibilities of the People of God, 2:11–4:11

The expression *Beloved, I urge you* introduces a new section in which Peter will enlarge on his readers' responsibilities to the society in which they live. This section extends all the way to 4:11 (note the repetition of *Beloved* in 4:12 and *I exhort* [lit. "I urge"] in 5:1).

Respect for Everyone, 2:11-17

Building on the designation *exiles* back in 1:1, Peter now focuses on the potential hostility between Christians and a culture where they are *aliens and exiles*. Their struggle is both inward and outward. It is first a struggle between the *soul* of Christian believers (i.e., their new life destined for salvation) and certain *desires of the flesh* within them carried over from their pagan past (v. 11), but it finds outward expression in social conflicts and tensions between Christians and their unbelieving neighbors in the Roman Empire (v. 12). Peter's main concern is with this social dimension of his readers' life in Christ. The conflict in which they find themselves is to be won not by aggressive behavior in society, but by "conducting themselves honorably" among those who ridicule or mistreat them (v. 12; cf. 2:15, 20; 3:6, 11, 17).

Peter writes in the spirit of Paul, who had urged Christians in Rome not to "be overcome by EVIL, but overcome evil with good" (Rom 12:21). He also echoes Jesus in the SERMON ON THE MOUNT: "Let your light shine before others, so that they may see your good works and give glory to your Father who is in heaven" (Matt 5:16). Peter has adapted the saying—or one like it—to the social situation of Christians in the empire. Their task in such circumstances is to live in such a way that those who denounce or accuse them will come to appreciate, even worship, the God of Israel. Peter's advice is much like that of the Jewish (or Jewish-Christian) TNaph 8.4: "If you work that which is good, my children . . . God shall be glorified among the Gentiles through you, and the devil shall flee from you." The main difference is that Peter's vision—here as elsewhere—is focused on the coming day *when Jesus Christ is revealed* (cf. 1:7, 13), here understood as a day of judgment or reckoning (v. 12). His hope is that opponents of the Christian movement will see the error of their ways and turn to God, so that on that day they will "give glory to God" and share in the honor in store for those who believe (cf. 1:7, 2:7a). Yet he knows that a different outcome is also possible—not honor but shame (cf. 2:7b)—and he will look more closely at such a scenario later in his argument (cf. 3:16; 4:17-18).

"Good conduct among the gentiles" is defined in vv. 13-17 in relation to Roman imperial authority, and in vv. 18-25 and 3:1-7 in relation to the family or household. For this reason, 2:18–3:7 is commonly viewed as a "household duty code" comparable to other such codes in contemporary Greek and Roman literature (cf. Col 3:18–4:1; Eph 5:21–6:9). Peter does not distinguish sharply between responsibility to the state and responsibility within the family. Both involve a command to defer to the authority of others (vv. 13, 18; 3:1, 5). By giving this command its widest possible application in v. 13 (lit. "every human creature"), Peter makes it clear that he is not urging some kind of abstract subjection to institutional authority (as in the

NRSV, *every human institution*), but voluntary deference or respect to individuals simply because God created them. It is in this context that he commands respect for the emperor and the local magistrates who represent him (compare the similar transition in 1 Tim 2:1-2 from "all people" to "kings and all who are in authority").

Unlike Paul in Rom 13, Peter makes no claim that God put the emperor in power or that imperial authority is God's authority. The emperor should be respected *for the Lord's sake*, not because he is divine but because he is human (cf. v. 17, *Honor everyone. . . . Honor the emperor*). His job is to maintain order in society by punishing wrongdoers and rewarding those who do good (v. 14). Peter is confident that the emperor will honor those who honor him, and that if Christians in the provinces "do right," they will silence even their most vocal critics (v. 15). At the same time he insists that they must have their priorities straight. He reminds them that they are "free" in Jesus Christ—not free of all obligation to the empire, but certainly free of its values (i.e., *the futile ways inherited from your ancestors*, 1:18). Because God has set them free, they are at the same time God's *servants* (v. 16). Their reverence for God and their love for each other (cf. 1:22) take precedence even over the respect they owe the emperor and *everyone* (v. 17).

Slaves and Masters, 2:18-25

Peter now shifts attention from all Christians as "servants of God" to those who were actual slaves in Roman households (οἰκέται, lit., "household servants," v. 18), but within a few verses he shifts back again to all the readers of his letter. The household serves as an appropriate context in which to introduce the sobering thought that all Christians may soon have to suffer for their faith in Roman society. Unlike Paul (Col 4:1; Eph 6:9), Peter addresses only slaves, not slaveowners, because he wants to make a point about suffering, and slaves are the ones who suffer. What counts with God is not suffering as such, or even the patient endurance of suffering, but *suffering unjustly* (v. 19) or "doing right and suffering for it" (v. 20). Endurance of suffering is a virtue only when suffering is undeserved, like the suffering of JESUS (vv. 21-23). This is the case when slaveowners are harsh or cruel (v. 18).

It is difficult to specify a point at which Peter widens the application of his words from household servants in particular to Christian believers in general.

He allows the former to be stand-ins for the latter because he does not want to temper the optimism about the empire expressed in vv. 13-17. But his readers could hardly miss the point. What could happen to Christian slaves at the hands of a cruel master could happen to any Christian if the mood of the populace took an ugly turn. Christ died for all believers, not just slaves (v. 24). All of them, not just slaves, are called to follow in his footsteps (v. 21). All were *going astray like sheep*, and all have *returned to the shepherd and guardian of your souls* (v. 25).

Because he has all believers in view, Peter puts his emphasis as much on verbal as on physical abuse. Actual physical suffering was not yet widespread among Christians, but they knew what it was to be denounced, ridiculed, and accused of crimes against the social order (cf. 2:12, 15). Peter wants to make sure they do not retaliate in kind. In language drawn from Isa 53, he describes Christ's behavior at his arrest and trial, accenting the fact that "no deceit was found in his mouth" (v. 22; cf. Isa 53:9b). "Deceit" to Peter is not deception, but malice or ill will of any sort (cf. 2:1). He elaborates Isaiah's words with the observation that Christ never denounced his accusers, and never threatened them with divine vengeance, as martyrs were said to have done in the time of the MACCABEES (cf. 2 Macc 7; 4 Macc 9–10). He simply left them to God, and to the prospect of God's righteous judgment (v. 23; cf. 1:17; 4:5).

Still drawing on Isa 53, Peter takes the opportunity to insist that Christ's suffering was more than an example. Adopting the confessional "we" and "our" from Isa 53, he includes himself with his readers (for the first time since 1:3) as sharers in a common salvation. Christ on the cross took "our" sins away (cf. Isa 53:4, 12b). He did not merely atone for sins or secure forgiveness; he actually carried the sins in his body to the cross and left them there (v. 24). With "our" sins gone, "we" are free to live for what is right, even in the face of hostility and slander. Peter quickly shifts back to his customary "you" as he reflects on his gentile readers' "healing" or conversion from paganism (vv. 24b-25; cf. Isa 53:5b-6). Without mentioning Christ's resurrection explicitly, he describes the Christ of the cross as now alive from the dead, carrying out the role of SHEPHERD over his flock (for the risen Christ as shepherd, cf. Mark 14:27-28; John 10:15-17; Heb 13:20-21). Later he will explain how Christ functions as shepherd over his congregations through the ministry of elders (5:2-4).

Wives and Husbands, 3:1-7

3:1-6. Advice to wives. Just as Peter, in addressing slaves, gave special attention to those who served cruel or hostile masters (2:18), so in addressing wives he focuses on those who are married to unbelieving husbands (v. 1). His goal is that husbands might be *won over* not with words but by reverent and pure conduct (v. 2; cf. 2:12). Taking over certain stereotyped denunciations (by Jewish, Greek, and Roman teachers alike) of some women's flamboyant tastes, he adapts them to this purpose. What counts as lavish *adornment* in God's sight is not hairdo or jewelry or clothes (extravagant or otherwise), but rather *the inner self with the lasting beauty of a gentle and quiet spirit* (v. 4). Peter associates flamboyant dress with flamboyant behavior and domestic rebellion, and modest dress with modest behavior and domestic peace. He knows nothing of the Christian "Total Woman" of the 1970s, for whom big hair and excessive makeup became the badge of wifely submission!

Peter does command wives to defer to their husbands' authority, and he does so even when the husband does not *obey the word* (i.e., not a Christian believer, v. 1). But a woman does not carry out this command by denying or concealing who she really is. Her obligation to defer to an unbelieving husband does not extend to adopting his religion—as Roman society expected—for the *conduct* to which she is called includes reverent fear toward her God (v. 2). Her role models are the *holy women* of Israel's past (probably SARAH, REBEKAH, RACHEL, and LEAH) who *hoped in God* (v. 5), and in particular Sarah, who once called Abraham *lord* (v. 6)—even though she laughed when she said it (Gen 18:12)!

Peter is probably aware not only of the irony of Sarah's laughter, but of the deeper irony of using Sarah and the *holy women* as examples in the first place. The women he is addressing here are not married to godly patriarchs like ABRAHAM, ISAAC, and JACOB, or anyone like them. They would have found it truly laughable to call their unbelieving husbands "lord" as they called Jesus "Lord," or "obey" them as they "obeyed" God (cf. the accent on "obedience" in 1:2, 14, 22). Yet by faith they are "Sarah's children." Peter's argument is from the greater to the lesser: if Sarah called Abraham "lord" (even in her laughter), Sarah's children should at least show deference and respect to their less than ideal marriage partners. The real social setting in which these wives lived emerges in Peter's final words of advice: *do what is good, and never let fears alarm you.* The appropriate submission of a wife to her husband is defined by "doing good" (i.e., doing the will of God, cf. 2:15), not the other way around. This means there is always a possibility that the unbelieving husband might not be *won over* by the *purity and reverence* of her life, or even be willing to tolerate her alien religion—hence the comforting but ominous last command to the wives, *never let fears alarm you* (v. 6b; cf. Prov 3:25).

3:7. Advice to husbands. Peter has a few words for husbands as well. If a wife must accept her husband's authority, the husband has a corresponding obligation to *show consideration* and *honor* to his wife—first, because she is physically *weaker* than he, and second, because a Christian husband and wife are together *heirs of the gracious gift of life.* Because society's expectation was that a wife would adopt her husband's religion, the likelihood was that the wife of a Christian husband had become a Christian too. If so, husband and wife are partners in faith and prayer—a kind of church in miniature. If not, the Christian husband must understand and honor his wife simply as God's creature (cf. 2:13, 17a), and as someone weaker than he, knowing that God values weakness above strength (cf. 5:5-6; 1 Cor 1:26-29; 12:22-24).

Seeking Peace, 3:8-12

Peter now generalizes from the advice just given about specific relationships in 2:18–3:7. He urges his readers to show kindness in all their dealings with each other (v. 8), and to seek peace even toward those who do not share their faith, but who ridicule and insult them (v. 9). In particular, he urges them not to trade insults with their oppressors, but always to speak words of kindness and blessing (vv. 9-10; cf. the appeal to Christ's example in 2:22-23). Drawing on words from Ps 34:12-16, Peter concludes that God will reward such an attitude on the part of his people and punish those who oppress them (vv. 10-12). Like the married couples in the preceding paragraph, they will find that God answers their prayers (v. 12).

The Hope of Vindication, 3:13–4:6

3:13-17. Encouragement "just in case." On the basis of the psalm just quoted, Peter urges his readers to maintain integrity before Christ their Lord in situations where they might have to face opposition and hostile questioning, whether from fellow citizens or the ruling authorities (vv. 14b-15). His confidence in such cases is that those who denounce them will be *put to shame* (v. 16), probably on the day of reckoning (cf. 2:12) when God comes to judge the world (cf. 3:12). Like those "persecuted for righteousness' sake" in the SERMON ON THE MOUNT (cf. Matt 5:10), faithful Christians are *blessed* (v. 14a), for their lot will be infinitely *better* on the day of judgment than that of their oppressors (v. 17).

3:18-22. The victory Christ won. Peter again introduces Jesus Christ as his example, picking up where 2:21-25 left off. There he had spoken of Christ's behavior in his PASSION (2:23), of his actual death (2:24), and (implicitly) of his resurrection (2:25). Now, illustrating the notion of suffering for "doing good" (3:17), Peter refers to Christ's death, RESURRECTION (vv. 18b, 21b), and journey to heaven (vv. 19, 22)—all the "glorious events" the prophets had only partially understood (cf. 1:11). Possibly he and his readers were familiar with a three-part confession of faith about Jesus Christ *put to death in the flesh / made alive in the Spirit / gone into heaven*—a symmetrical expression consisting of three participles in Greek, each with the same ending (θείς).

The third of these participles (πορευθείς, *gone* in the phrase, *gone into heaven,* in v. 22) is anticipated already in v. 19 with the claim that Jesus *went* (πορευθείς) *and made a proclamation to the spirits . . . who in former times did not obey, when God waited patiently in the days of Noah* (vv. 19-20a). This suggests that throughout vv. 19-22 Peter is elaborating the third element in the three-part confession—Christ's journey to heaven. Building on Jesus' analogy between *the days of Noah* and the present (Matt 24:37 = Luke 17:26), Peter links the evil or unclean spirits Jesus faced in his ministry of exorcism with the state of the world just before the flood. He focuses especially on the illicit union described in Gen 6:1-4 between "sons of God" (usually understood as evil angels) and women on earth. According to some Jewish traditions, this union produced "giants" who would "be called evil spirits upon the earth" (*1 Enoch* 15.8). Peter's point is that the victory over demons which began in Jesus' earthly ministry was completed after his resurrection, in the course of his journey to heaven. This victory established Jesus' lordship over all *angels, authorities, and powers* (v. 22)—even those that are hostile—and so reinforces Peter's assurances to his readers (vv. 13-17) that they have nothing to fear from those who question or denounce their Christian way of life.

One difficulty with the passage is the apparent statement that the disobedient spirits were *in prison* (Gk. ἐν φυλακῇ, v. 19b). If they were in prison, what did Christ announce to them? Their release? This would not have been good news! Their salvation? Nothing here or in any other NT text suggests that evil spirits will be saved. Their subjection to him? If they are already in prison, what would further subjection mean? For these reasons, it is possible that ἐν φυλακῇ should be understood as "in refuge" or "in hiding," rather than *in prison*. According to *1 Enoch* evil angels are said to be chained or imprisoned (cf. also 2 Pet 2:4; Jude 6), but not evil spirits, and the word φυλακή is not used. In Revelation, the only other NT use of φυλακή in connection with evil spirits, Babylon is doomed to be "a haunt of every foul spirit" (Rev 18:2). Such a translation suggests that Peter viewed the "disobedient spirits" as free and very active in the world until Jesus tamed them by his resurrection (vv. 18b, 21b) and journey to heaven (vv. 19, 22). At that point their safe havens (whether on earth, under the earth, or in the air) were no longer safe from his universal lordship, and in the course of his journey he invaded their haunts and announced their subjection.

Within his reflection on Christ's journey, Peter extends the analogy between Noah's day and his own by comparing the waters of the flood to Christian BAPTISM (vv. 20-21). Like NOAH and *a few* others then, Christians are *saved through water* now, not in the sense of being washed clean from their sins, but because they have already been purified through Christ's death and resurrection (cf. 1:2, 22; see also Josephus's explanation of John's baptism, *Ant* 18.117).

4:1-6. Sharing in victory over sin and death. The triumphant tone of 3:22 is at once muted by a reminder that no one can share in Christ's resurrection and victorious journey without first preparing for the same kind of suffering he experienced (cf. 2:21-25). Christ is the one who *has finished with sin* (v. 1b) in that he did away with it *once for all* (3:18a) by his death on the cross (cf. 2:24). Now he has nothing more to do with sin (cf. Heb 4:15; 7:26; 9:28), and the same must be true of his followers (vv. 2-3). They must make an absolutely clean break with the immoral culture out of which they came (cf. 2:1, 11). If they do, they can expect to be ridiculed and slandered (lit., "blasphemed"), just as Christ was before he suffered (v. 4; cf. 2:23a). But like Christ, they too can expect vindication from God, *who stands ready to judge the living and the dead* (v. 5; cf. *the one who judges justly*, 2:23b).

As a postscript to the paragraph, the set phrase *the living and the dead* reminds Peter that God's vindication of the righteous did not begin with Jesus, but embraces many who died long before his coming (cf. Heb 11). They too heard God's *gospel* (cf. Heb 4:2, 6), accepted it, were condemned for it, but have the sure hope of resurrection from the dead. Peter echoes here the thought that "the souls of the righteous are in the hands of God and no torment will ever touch them. In the eyes of the foolish they seemed to have died . . . but they are at peace. For though in the sight of men they were punished, their hope is full of immortality" (Wis 3:1-4, RSV).

Christian Community, 4:7-11

A series of short generalized commands (vv. 7-11a) leading up to a doxology (v. 11b) gives the impression that Peter is now bringing his letter to an end (cf. Paul in 1 Thes 5:12-24). His reminder that *the end of all things is near* (v. 7) follows appropriately the reference to God as *him who stands ready to judge the living and the dead* (4:5). The prospect, however remote, of official persecution requires unity and cohesion among Christian believers, and Peter sees the source of this unity in worshipping and ministering congregations. In contrast to 2:18– 3:7, his focus is on congregations rather than households, and mutuality is at the heart of all his commands: mutual love (v. 8), mutual HOSPITALITY (v. 9), and mutual ministry (vv. 10-11). There are no fixed roles here comparable to slaves and masters or wives and husbands. There are no offices, no clergy-laity distinctions, no leaders or followers. All believers have a responsibility to love, show hospitality, and MINISTER to each other. Precisely who ministers to whom is determined not by status or seniority, but solely by *the manifold grace of God* (v. 10). By repeating the word *God* three times in v. 11a, Peter drives home the point that all ministries are from God, and therefore accountable to *him who stands ready to judge the living and the dead* (4:5).

The Responsibilities of Elders, 4:12–5:11

The address *Beloved* in 4:12, as in 2:11, introduces a new section of the letter. The accompanying appeal, however, does not follow immediately as it does in 2:11, but is deferred until 5:1, where it turns out to be directed to *elders* in particular. The whole section from 4:12 through 5:11 has much the same function as 4:7-11—to build congregational unity in the face of impending trouble—but it does so at greater length, and with a more specific audience in view. Having spoken generally to all the congregations reading his letter, Peter now turns his attention more specifically to those ruled (like his own congregation in Rome) by elders on the basis of seniority. This means that 4:12-19 is something of a digression, laying a basis for the appeal to elders in 5:1-11 by reiterating and reinforcing the themes of 2:11–4:6.

The Fiery Ordeal, 4:12-19

4:12-16. True suffering and true joy. The reiteration carries a new note of urgency, echoing the concern early in the letter about *various trials* testing believers as fire tests gold (cf. 1:6-9). Peter now urges joy in suffering, not because suffering is a good thing in itself or a reason for joy, but because those who suffer for Christ are sharing in Christ's own experience. Consequently, when Christ's glory is revealed, they will rejoice all the more (v. 13; cf. 1:6, 8). Those who are ridiculed for his sake are *blessed* (v. 14a; cf. 3:14), not because they are suffering but because they are suffering for the right reasons (cf. Matt 5:11). At such times the Spirit of God (and the coming glory) rests on them just as Jesus said it would (cf. Luke 12:11-12). Many manuscripts add that if the Spirit is blasphemed (cf. Luke 12:10), the guilt of blasphemy rests not on those who are ridiculed, but on their oppressors (v. 14b KJV).

Such promises do not apply to those who suffer for the wrong reason. Christians who are accused of crimes against Roman society, or even of antisocial behavior that is not explicitly criminal (e.g., as "busybodies" [KJV], or self-appointed guardians of public morality), must make sure that such charges are untrue (v. 15). Only when they have no reason to be ashamed of their actual conduct are Christians free to *glorify God* in the face of hostile questions (cf. 2:12, 15, 19-20; 3:15-16). This, to Peter, is what it means to suffer *as a Christian*.

4:17-19. Judgment at the house of God. Peter's imagery for divine judgment centers on the Christian community as the "house," or temple, of God (cf. 2:5). His point of departure is Ezek 9:6 (LXX), where God orders the judgment on Jerusalem to begin "from my sanctuary" and "from the men who are elders, who are inside the household." Peter refers to the house or sanctuary here and to the "elders" in 5:1-5. To him the judgment of God (cf. 1:17; 2:23; 4:5) is one universal judgment, and is now under way. If a *fiery ordeal* is breaking out even among God's people, how much worse is the fate in store for the "disobedient" (vv. 17-

18; cf. 2:8)? This could have led to a kind of vengeful joy in the punishment of the wicked, but it does not. Instead, Peter reminds his readers of the common humanity they share even with their oppressors (cf. 2:13). The judge to whom believer and unbeliever alike are accountable is also the creator who made them all. Peter urges continued trust in that *faithful Creator*, and a renewed commitment *to do good* in the face of unjust suffering (v. 19; again cf. 2:12, 14-15, 20; 3:6, 11-12, 13, 17).

Elders and Their Congregations, 5:1-11

5:1-4. Elders. Peter now resumes the appeal begun in 4:12. For the benefit of congregations ruled by elders, and in keeping with the notion that judgment begins from the elders in "the house of God" (Ezek 9:6), he reminds elders of their responsibilities (vv. 1-4). This he does as an *elder* himself (v. 1), whether as a leader in his own congregation at Rome, or as one of the Twelve chosen by Jesus (cf. 1:1) and therefore an *elder* to all Christians everywhere (cf. v. 9b, *your brothers and sisters in all the world*). He shares with the elders to whom he writes a special responsibility to testify to Christ's sufferings—which he has done repeatedly in this letter (cf. 1:11; 2:21-25; 3:18; 4:1, 13)—and a special hope of reward when Christ's glory is revealed (v. 1b; cf. v. 4). Peter urges elders to be good shepherds over *the flock of God* (v. 2; cf. Acts 20:28), not for financial gain or even "their own satisfaction on the job, but as glad volunteers in God's service" (Kelly, 201). They must lead by example instead of lording it over their respective congregations (lit. "lots" or "assigned portions"), so that *the chief shepherd*, Jesus Christ (cf. 2:25), will reward them when he appears in glory (v. 4).

5:5-11. Their congregations. Peter turns his attention briefly to the *younger* (v. 5a), adapting to his purpose a formalized code of behavior similar to the household codes of 2:18–3:7 (cf. Titus 2:1-6; *1 Clem* 1.3). His actual interest is not in those who are young in age, nor in some subordinate order of ministry, but simply in all who are not elders. He quickly moves from the elder/younger distinction to a strong emphasis on mutuality reminiscent of 4:7-11: *And all of you must clothe yourselves in humility in your dealings with one another* (v. 5b). Such words, like those of 4:7-11, are relevant to all congregations whether ruled by elders or not.

The theme of humility before God continues in the next few verses, as Peter reflects on Prov 3:34 LXX:

God opposes the proud, but gives grace to the humble (v. 5c; cf. Jas 4:6). The call to humility, with its promise of exaltation or vindication (vv. 6-7, 10-11; cf. Matt 23:12; Luke 14:11; 18:14), frames a related call to resist the devil (vv. 8-9; cf. Jas 4:7-10). Despite Christ's victory over the evil spirits (3:18-22), the devil remains on the loose *like a roaring lion* (v. 8), ready to *devour* those who are unprepared (cf. *JosAsen* 12.9). To Peter, being "devoured" by the devil does not mean persecution as such, or even martyrdom, but APOSTASY or loss of faith. Resisting the devil and trusting God are not two commands but one (cf. Jas 4:7). He reminds his readers that the conflict they face is worldwide (v. 9), and that God's *eternal glory* is their destiny (v. 10; cf. *his marvelous light* in 2:9). Their sufferings are indeed few and brief (v. 10; cf. 1:6) when weighed against that glory to come (cf. Paul in Rom 8:18 and 2 Cor 4:17).

Conclusion, 5:12-14

Peter ends with a word acknowledging *Silvanus*, probably not as scribe or coauthor, but as the bearer of the letter to the Asian provinces (v. 12a). The expression *through Silvanus* is echoed in Ignatius's letters, where the proposition "through" consistently has this meaning (e.g., *Phld* 11.2, *Smyrn* 12.1, Rom 10.1). Playing down the letter's scope (*this short letter*, cf. Heb 13:22), Peter nevertheless claims that it is *true grace of God*, for which those who read it must "stand" (v. 12b). With greetings from a sister congregation *in Babylon* where he resides (probably Rome), and from Mark (cf. Col 4:10, Phlm 24), his associate whom he calls his *son* (v. 13), Peter urges that his greeting (*Peace to all of you*) be passed along through the Asian congregations as through a family, *with a kiss of love* (v. 14; cf. 1:22; 2:17; and 4:8).

Works Cited

Kelly, J. N. D. 1969. *A Commentary on the Epistles of Peter and Jude.*

Michaels, J. Ramsey. 1988. *1 Peter.* WBC.

Second Peter

Edwin K. Broadhead

Introduction

Second Peter was accepted into the NT CANON as one of the GENERAL LETTERS—apostolic letters addressed to the CHURCH as a whole. Nonetheless, 2 Peter has proven elusive and problematic. The enigmatic nature of this text was recognized early within church history, and numerous questions remain unanswered. These problems will be identified and addressed by giving attention to the role of 2 Peter in canonical perspective, in historical perspective, and in contemporary perspective.

Second Peter in Canonical Perspective

Origen (ca. 185–254 C.E.) provides the first written acknowledgement of the existence of 2 Peter (in Eusebius, *EccHist* 6.25.8, 11), yet he also expresses doubts about its authenticity. EUSEBIUS (ca. 260–339 C.E.) himself was hesitant to accept the letter. Jerome (ca. 346–420 C.E.) wholly endorsed the letter and assigned it to apostolic authorship. He supposed the difference in style between 1 and 2 Peter could be explained by Peter's use of two different scribes. Probably based on Jerome's endorsement, 2 Peter gained wide acceptance within the Latin and Greek churches. When the canon of the NT was fixed in the fourth-century church, the place of 2 Peter was established.

Second Peter presents itself as an epistle with an apostolic foundation and a postapostolic focus. While other general letters tend to limit apostolic attestation to the opening and closing lines, 2 Peter insists throughout upon its apostolic foundation. In addition to the apostolic address (1:1) the letter recalls the presentation of the apostolic preaching (1:12) and makes plans for its preservation (1:13-15). Peter's role as an eyewitness and his experience of the TRANSFIGURATION are recalled (1:16-18). The continuity and vitality of interpretation are confirmed (1:19). A prior letter is recalled (3:1), and the christological foundation is confirmed on the witness of the apostles (3:2). The witness of PAUL is recalled (3:15-16), and the testimony of scripture is evoked (3:16).

The primary concern of this letter is for the time after the death of the apostles. The departure of the earliest leaders will bring a time of crisis (3:4). This period will be marked by eschatological doubt (3:3-13) and moral failure (2:2, 9-22). The destruction of the world and its judgment lie close at hand (3:5-13). The letter warns against these troubles (2:1; 3:3) and seeks to prepare the reader to face this forthcoming crisis (1:12-15; 3:17-18).

This trauma involves the activity of false teachers from within the Christian tradition (2:1-3, 15; 3:16). They will take advantage of the newly converted and the unstable (2:14, 18-22). The letter prepares its readers for this postapostolic trauma through warning about the future (2:1; 3:3) and remembrance of the past (1:12-15; 3:1-2).

Several issues shape this apostolic challenge. The apostolic faith is foundational. This faith is based upon knowledge of Jesus Christ as Lord and Savior (1:1, 14, 16; 2:1, 20; 3:2, 18). The apostle is an eyewitness to the work of Jesus (1:16-18) and continues to receive REVELATION from Christ (2:14). This apostolic faith is based on the prophetic tradition (1:19-21; 2:3; 3:2, 13). The readers of the letter share in this faith (1:1-2, 12; 3:1-2, 17-18).

The scriptures provide a sure witness and warning for the recipients of the letter. The scriptures are understood as a body of literature which believers hold in common. Among the writings considered as scripture are the prophetic warnings (1:19-21; 2:3; 3:2, 13), the stories and sayings of the OT (2:4-9, 15-16, 22a; 3:5-6, 8), the writings of Paul (3:15-16), and other writings (3:16).

Attention is given as well to the formulation of the faith. The reader is warned against clever myths (1:16) and esoteric interpretation of prophecy (1:21). More importantly, the letter seeks to restore ethical stability (1:3-11; 3:11, 14, 17-18) in the face of moral failure (2:9-22). At the heart of the letter lies a warning against eschatological delusion: the promised judgment and renewal of the earth will not fail (3:4-13).

Second Peter thus presents a strategic approach to the problems at hand. The warning against false teachers is framed as a final letter of challenge from one of the last of the apostles. With prophetic foresight, the apostle warns the readers of the trauma that will engulf believers in the postapostolic age. False teachers practicing corrupt ethics and preaching a failed eschatology are countered by the sure foundation of the apostolic faith, the words of scripture, the consistent righteousness, and the sure hope of the believer.

Within this canonical perspective 2 Peter presents itself as a general epistle based on a final apostolic testimony. From this standpoint, the letter is seemingly addressed to a specific group of Christians by Peter near the time of his death (in ROME ca. 64–65 C.E.).

Second Peter in Historical Perspective

Second Peter presents a quite different image in historical perspective. Current knowledge about language, theological development, and church history raise serious questions about the relationship of 2 Peter to the apostolic era and to the other writings of the NT.

Second Peter is only formally related to 1 Peter. The greeting (1:1), the blessing (1:2), and the benediction (3:18) are on the same model as those of 1 Peter. Beyond this, 2 Peter is framed as the second letter from the apostle (3:1). This formal framework does not bear up in the substance of the letter. Differences in language and style were noticed as early as Jerome (*Ep* 120.11), and modern statistical analysis confirms this. The style of 2 Peter tends to be more formal and grandiose than 1 Peter. The two letters share few themes or concerns in common.

In reality, the epistle closest to 2 Peter is JUDE. Indeed, large parts of Jude are found in 2 Peter:

2 Pet 1:2	=	Jude 2
2 Pet 1:12	=	Jude 5a
2 Pet 2:1-3	=	Jude 4
2 Pet 2:6	=	Jude 7
2 Pet 2:10b-15	=	Jude 8–12a
2 Pet 2:17	=	Jude 12b–13
2 Pet 2:18	=	Jude 16
2 Pet 3:2-3	=	Jude 17
2 Pet 3:14	=	Jude 24
2 Pet 3:18b	=	Jude 25

Beyond this, various elements of organization and numerous themes are shared in common between Jude and 2 Peter.

This common ground has been explained through three theories: (1) Jude is a reduction of 2 Peter; (2) Second Peter is an expansion of Jude; (3) Jude and 2 Peter are two different applications of one traditional work. The third opinion is the most likely. The relatively low level of precise verbal agreement in the common material speaks against direct dependence of one letter upon the other. Both works may be based on an apostolic testimony that circulated in a variety of forms. The letter of Jude, employing a midrashic approach with various allusions to the OT and to apocryphal writings, represents a more Jewish form of the tradition. Second Peter shows less interest in the Jewish traditions and structures and represents a more Hellenized form of the apostolic testimony.

Of primary concern for most interpreters is the relationship of 2 Peter to the apostolic era and to Peter. The language and conceptualization of the letter seem far removed from the world of a Galilean fisherman. The desire to escape the corruption of the world and participate in the divine nature (1:4) is more akin to Hellenistic thought than to the Palestinian world of Peter. Common authorship of 1 and 2 Peter is unlikely. Various images in the letter point to a postapostolic period. While the crisis is foreseen as a future event (2:1; 3:3), it is addressed as a present reality (2:10; 3:4, 16). The death of the earliest leaders is seemingly acknowledged (3:4). The apostolic experience of faith is now expressed in more fixed and formulaic terms (1:1; 3:2). The tension between Paul and Peter is absent (3:15). A fixed body of scripture is assumed, and includes Paul's writings (3:16). The proper interpretation of scripture has become an issue (1:20-21). The remembrance of JESUS has been framed primarily as *power* and *majesty*, and it has been focused in one event—the Transfiguration (1:16-18). Second Peter is almost unknown in the first and second century, and its apostolic origin is questioned from the beginning. The letter first emerges in the manuscripts from Egypt, and it is accepted last among the Syrian church.

Second Peter also stands at a distance from the major lines of NT thought. The experience of faith has been formulated as apostolic commands (3:2). The CHRISTOLOGY posed here tends to focus on formal titles (1:11; 2:20; 3:18), to be docetic in outlook (1:1, 3), and to emphasize power and glory (1:3, 16-17). FAITH is framed as revelation (1:14) and recognition (1:3, 8,

12; 2:20; 3:18). Missing are the teachings of Jesus, the cross and the resurrection, and the experience of GRACE and RECONCILIATION. The outlook is closer to Hellenism than to Palestinian Judaism. The moral demands likely reflect the virtues of Hellenistic Judaism. The expected collapse of the universe is similar to Stoic thought. The heresy addressed sounds similar to the developing gnostic tendencies of the late first and early second centuries. This outlook is also evident in the language of 2 Peter. There are fifty-seven words in 2 Peter not found elsewhere in the NT; thirty-two of these are not found in the Greek OT (i.e., LXX) either. Fifteen of these thirty-two words are found in other Jewish Hellenistic writings. Three words in 2 Peter have no parallel in Greek literature. Thus, the historical perspective makes doubtful the identity of 2 Peter as an epistle from the apostolic age.

A more likely framework for 2 Peter is the literary form known as the "Testament" (see TESTAMENTS, APOC-RYPHAL). In this literature a heroic figure gives words of instruction and warning before departing. Without exception, these texts are composed after the death of the hero to recall and preserve the impact of the leader. Often these texts are used to address particular problems faced by a later generation. The pattern for Peter's Testament may be drawn from the story of MOSES in Deuteronomy. Told that his death is imminent, Moses ascends the mountain to see what lies ahead (Deut 3:23ff.). Moses' mountaintop experience with God is remembered (Deut 4:9-14). The earlier COMMANDMENTS are recalled (Deut 4:13). Warnings to OBEDIENCE are issued, and the people are instructed in how they should face the trials of the future without their leader. This Mosaic model is taken up in the writings of Josephus (*Ant* 4.8.2) and in the *Testament of Moses*. Examples of the Testament form may be found in the OT, in Jewish literature, and in the NT.

Seen from a historical perspective, 2 Peter belongs to the postapostolic stage of church history in which the teaching and authority of the apostles was brought to bear against contemporary controversies. From this historical perspective, 2 Peter is a Testament framed in the form of a letter. It seeks to draw upon the apostolic era to address a postapostolic situation, likely between 90 and 110 C.E. Likely addressed to a general audience, the author and place of composition are unknown.

Second Peter in Contemporary Perspective

Second Peter continues to hold value in a contemporary perspective. Second Peter provides key historical insights into the postapostolic age and the development of the institutionalized church. Seen in terms of its own context and purposes, this letter provides crucial information about the controversies which underlie the formation of the CHURCH.

Beyond this, 2 Peter offers a theological contribution. This epistle provides a primary example of how the Christian church handled the literature and the traditions which it inherited. The traditions of the OT, of Judaism, and of apostolic Christianity converge within this text. Of key interest is the manner in which the early church appropriated these traditions for its own age and task. Beyond this, the interaction of the church with the world is modeled. The ongoing dialogue of Judaism and Christianity with the Hellenistic environment echoes through this epistle. Second Peter also demonstrates the in-house arguments that form the matrix of early church history. The definition of scripture, the naming of heresy, and the fixing of church patterns are all underway in this letter.

Thus, 2 Peter provides information on how early Christianity handled its heritage, articulated its identity, and found its way in the world. The church, which lives yet between the age of the apostles and the day of judgment, has much to learn from this work.

For Further Study

In the *Mercer Dictionary of the Bible*: EPISTLE/LETTER; ESCHATOLOGY IN THE NT; GNOSTICISM; JUDE, LETTER OF; LORD IN THE NT; PAROUSIA/SECOND COMING; PETER; PETER, LETTERS OF; SAVIOR IN THE NT; TESTAMENTS, APOCRYPHAL. In other sources: R. Bauckmam, *Jude, 2 Peter*, WBC; C. Bigg, *A Critical and Exegetical Commentary on the Epistles of St. Peter and St. Jude*, ICC; J. Calvin, "2 Peter," *Calvin's Commentaries*; L. Johnson, *The Writings of the New Testament*, 442–52; E. Käsemann, "An Apologia for Primitive Christian Eschatology," in *Essays on New Testament Themes*, 169–95; K. Schelkle, *Die Petrusbrief, der Judasbrief*, HTKNT 13/2; W. Schrage and H. Balz, *Die katholischen Briefe: Die Briefe des Jakobus, Petrus, Johannes, und Judas*, NTD; R. Summers, "2 Peter," BBC.

Commentary

Salutation, 1:1-2

Typical of ancient letters, 2 Peter opens with mention of the sender and the receiver and with a word of greeting. The apostolic nature of the letter is established from the beginning in the titles associated with the author: *servant and apostle of Jesus Christ*. The author names himself as *Simeon Peter*. Simeon represents an unusual spelling based on the Hebrew form and is found elsewhere in the NT only in Acts 15:14. Many interpreters see here an attempt to convince the reader of the ancient and apostolic nature of the letter.

The recipients of the letter are specified only as fellow believers. Later they are identified as the recipients of a prior letter (3:1). The word of greeting is framed upon 1 Pet 1:2b, and it enhances the apostolic appearance of the letter. Three elements within the salutation, however, point to a postapostolic period: faith is understood more as a possession than an experience (v. 1); Jesus is seemingly addressed as *God* (v. 1); and the title of *Savior* is applied to Jesus. While these elements have parallels within the NT, they typify the later, more marginal stages of NT thought.

The reference to the believer's *knowledge* (ἐπί-γνωσις) *of God and of Jesus* may be a subtle rebuke of the false teachers. They are, perhaps, among those who claim a special knowledge (γνῶσις) of the divine, later known as Gnostics. If so, the greeting already sets the true knowledge of believers over against that of false teachers (see KNOWLEDGE IN THE NT).

Theological Exposition, 1:3-11

The Gift, 1:3-4

The body of the letter opens with a brief theological exposition that sets the background for the apostolic challenge. The reader is first reminded of all that has been given to believers. The knowledge and the promises of Christ provide life and deliverance. The gift is understood primarily in terms of knowledge. While the basis of this message is primitive Christianity, the language and concepts are those of Hellenism.

The Demand, 1:5-7

Demand is built upon gift. The believer is to support the gift of faith with a life of virtue. This list combines normative biblical values (*faith, mutual affection, love*) with ethical categories common to popular Greek philosophy (*knowledge, goodness, self-control, endurance*). Again, a basic NT pattern is expressed in the concepts of Hellenism.

The Result, 1:8-11

The result is focused, both in its positive and its negative aspects. At the center of this discussion echoes the theme of knowledge. Depending on how one practices morality, the *knowledge of . . . Jesus Christ* may be cultivated or lost. The discussion alternates between gift and demand. BAPTISM, calling, and ELECTION form the basis of the Christian life; these may be lost through moral neglect. Entrance into the kingdom is a gift; it may be forfeited. The reduction of the kingdom of God wholly to the kingdom of Christ is further evidence of a later stage of Christian thought.

The Author's Situation and Purpose, 1:12-15

The situation of the author clarifies the purpose of the letter. The apostle has received revelation of his imminent death (v. 14). While the apostle remains, his purpose is twofold: to remind the readers of the apostolic faith (v. 13) and to prepare them for the postapostolic period (v. 15). These two goals shape the remainder of the letter.

The Apostolic Foundation, 1:16-21

The Certainty of the Witness, 1:16-18

The author assures the readers of the validity of the tradition they have received. Not *cleverly devised myths*, but the apostolic message provides the foundation of their faith. Perhaps the author seeks to counter the timeless mythical structures of Hellenistic thought with a salvation-history focus on God's activity. Here the authority of the entire apostolate is confirmed through the use of the plural (*we* is used twice in v. 16; in v. 18; and in v. 19). This authority is based on eyewitness experience, and the TRANSFIGURATION of Jesus is recalled as an example. Those who preach the future coming of Christ are qualified to do so by their experience of his past revelation in honor and glory. The faith of the postapostolic church is founded on its sure witness to God's saving activity within history.

The Certainty of the Message, 1:19-21

Further confirmation is provided by the certainty of the message. Behind the prophetic and apostolic word stands the activity of the HOLY SPIRIT. As God spoke on the mount of Transfiguration, so God speaks through the prophecy that the church possesses. This tradition is confirmed over against all alternatives as the message for the church.

The Coming Crisis: Ethics, 2:1-22

The apostolic heritage is now applied to the postapostolic situation. Apostolic instruction is set against false teachers in two specific areas: ethics and eschatology.

The Appearance of False Teachers, 2:1-3

Emphasizing the continuity between OT and apostolic tradition, the *false prophets* of the OT reemerge within the postapostolic church. Their leadership is set against that of apostolic tradition—*the way of truth* (v. 2). Their teaching will be marked by subtlety, destructiveness, immorality, heresy, and deceptive words. Both their appearance and their judgment have been prophesied.

Old Testament Lessons, 2:4-10a

The continuity of OT and apostolic traditions is filled out through three examples: the fallen angels (drawn from apocryphal sources such as *EthEnoch* 20:2; *SibOr* 4:185); Noah's generation (Gen 6:6-8; 8:18); *Sodom and Gomorrah* and *Lot* (Gen 19:16, 24,

29). The point of these examples becomes clear in 2:9-10a: God is able to preserve the godly and to judge the unrighteous. Second Peter applies this truth directly to the situation of the postapostolic church.

The Character of the False Teachers, 2:10b-22

A full range of vocabulary and imagery describes the opponents' moral failure. Evocative similes are employed: irrational animals, cursed children, waterless springs, storm-driven mists, and slaves of corruption. Numerous descriptions clarify their immorality: bold, willful, slanderous, revelers, blots, blemishes, adulterous, insatiable, greedy, cursed, bombastic, and licentious. The OT story of BALAAM (vv. 15-16) and two graphic proverbs describe those who follow their path (v. 22).

The Coming Crisis: Eschatology, 3:1-13

The second heresy addressed by the letter is the failed eschatology of the false teachers. A similar pattern of argument is followed.

The Appearance of Scoffers, 3:1-4

The warnings of 2 Peter are grounded upon four foundations: the word of *the holy prophets*, the commandments of Jesus, the teaching of the apostles, and a previous letter. The specific threat addressed in the remainder of this epistle is the loss of faith in the return of the Lord. In this threat both ethical and eschatological failure are combined (v. 3). The death of the fathers (v. 3) points to the end of the apostolic era. Historically, this transition meant that expectation of the return of Christ faded into the distance and with it the threat of imminent judgment. The author of 2 Peter fights against this tendency.

The Apostolic Answer, 3:5-13

The early church sought in various ways to deal with the delayed PAROUSIA of Christ. A unique approach to this problem is given in 2 Pet 3:5-13. Four arguments are given against those who have abandoned the apostolic tradition of the imminent parousia. First, the word of God does not fail. Upon the dynamic of God's word the ancient world was both founded and judged by water. Upon the same divine word, the present world will undergo a judgment of fire. A second answer, based on Ps 90:4, argues that God's time is relative. A third response sees purpose behind the delay: God has allowed time for REPENTANCE and salvation. The fourth reply focuses the unexpected nature of the judgment; the lack of present signs is no indication of its failure or its lack of intensity. The apostolic reply concludes with an appeal that again unites ethics and eschatology: the certainty of judgment should produce lives of holiness and godliness. As with the OT models, both destruction and renewal are envisioned. Here the renewal extends beyond the interests of the individual or even of the church to include the entire creation.

The Challenge to Endure, 3:14-18a

In view of the coming trauma, believers are challenged to wait with upright behavior. The delay is to be seen as a particular moment of grace within God's salvation history. The reader is warned that attempts to twist the apostolic message are not new: Paul's letters and other scripture suffer the same abuse. In light of the ethical and eschatological crisis, the believer has received an apostolic warning. Rather than fall away or turn back, the believer is to *grow in the grace and knowledge of . . . [the] Savior Jesus Christ.*

Final Benediction, 3:18b

Even the final words of the apostolic message recall its focus. Over against the unstable ways of the false teachers, believers are to give glory to Jesus Christ, both in their present living and until the day of judgment.

First, Second, and Third John

John B. Polhill

Introduction

The three Johannine Epistles can be classified in two ways. Along with the Petrine Epistles, James, and Jude, they belong to the category of "general" or "catholic" epistles. They have also traditionally been grouped with the Gospel of John and Revelation in the "Johannine corpus." Their affinity with the fourth Gospel is unmistakable. The relationship to Revelation is more remote.

Literary Form

In form, all three have traditionally been denoted epistles. This is most accurate for the latter two. Second John follows the standard conventions of first-century epistles and is addressed to a Christian congregation. Third John is a private epistle from a church leader to an individual. The writer of both identifies himself as *the elder* (2 John 1; 3 John 1).

First John is anonymous. It does not have the usual form of an epistle: no address, no conclusion, none of the conventions of a Greek letter. It is still probably best described as general epistle—a written communication, probably to a group of churches by a church leader concerning matters of mutual concern. The language and thought are so close to that of the other two that it was probably also written by "the elder."

Authorship and Date

Who was this *elder*? Tradition identifies him with the apostle JOHN, who is said to have lived to a ripe old age, ministering in Ephesus. This view identifies John with the BELOVED DISCIPLE and sees him as author of the Gospel and Epistles of John. A second view builds upon a tradition from POLYCARP that there were two Johns in Ephesus, the apostle and a disciple of the apostle known as the Elder John (EUSEBIUS, *EccHist* 3.39.4-6). Many would see this "elder John" as "the elder" of the three epistles. A third view emphasizes the communal aspect in the Johannine Epistles and sees the entire Johannine corpus as coming from a "Johannine School" of thought. The traditions in which this community grounded itself are taken back ultimately to the beloved disciple of the fourth Gospel.

Although some argue otherwise, the majority of scholars place the epistles in a Johannine milieu according to one of these three views. They are usually placed in Asia Minor around the last decade of the first century. Throughout this commentary, the writer will be designated as John or the elder with no distinction implied between the two.

Life Setting

All three epistles depict a CHURCH in conflict. False teachers have separated from the church. The elder accuses them of three errors. First, they have an inadequate view of the INCARNATION, failing to give full due to the humanity of Jesus (1 John 2:22; 2 John 7). Second, they have a deficient view of SIN, failing to keep God's commandments while at the same time claiming to be above sin (1 John 1:8, 10; 2:4). Finally, they have a failure in FELLOWSHIP, not loving their Christian brothers and sisters (1 John 2:9; 4:20).

These separatists have often been identified with GNOSTICISM, and more specifically with Cerinthus, a Gnostic precursor whom IRENAEUS depicts as an opponent of John in Ephesus. There are problems with this identification, however, since Cerinthus does not seem to have held all the views applied to the false teaching in 1 John, nor are all Cerinthus's main views attacked in the epistles. That the elder was fighting some sort of incipient Gnosticism seems likely. Later Gnostics often maintained a spiritual perfectionism that saw itself as above sin. They were elitist and tended to disdain others (lack of love), and they held a docetic CHRISTOLOGY, denying the humanity of Jesus.

For Further Study

In other sources: R. E. Brown, *The Epistles of John*, AncB; R. A. Culpepper, *1 John, 2 John, 3 John*, Knox Preaching Guides; I. H. Marshall, *The Epistles of John*, NICNT; S. S. Smalley, *1, 2, 3 John*, WBC.

Commentary

An Outline

Prologue, 1:1-4

With its reference to *what was from the beginning* and *the word of life*, the prologue to 1 John is reminiscent of the fourth Gospel's prologue (John 1:1-18). There are differences, however. In 1 John *the beginning* probably refers to the tradition of the Christian witness to Christ rather than to the preexistence of the Word. There is also a stronger emphasis on the eyewitness TESTIMONY to the real humanity of Christ: *what we have seen with our eyes, what we have looked at and touched with our hands* (v. 1). Already John focuses on the false teachers. In response to the innovations of the false teachers, John calls his readers back to their roots—to the original apostolic testimony to Christ, to the word of the gospel they first heard. He especially concentrates on the false teachers' inadequate CHRISTOLOGY, as he expands on the "word made flesh" of the fourth Gospel's prologue (John 1:14).

Of particular concern to John is the unity of his community. It is a triangular fellowship—among Christians with both *the Father* and *Son* (v. 3). This emphasis persists throughout 1 John, particularly in the motif of "abiding." John expresses his personal purpose for writing in verse 4—*that our joy may be complete*. John is concerned with restoring the joy of the

fellowship, which has been threatened by the withdrawal of the false teachers from the community.

Part One: God Is Light, 1:5–3:10

First John is difficult to outline, because its themes are constantly repeated. The division followed here is based on the recurrence of the phrase *this is the message* in 1:5 and 3:11. In 1:5 the message is defined in terms of light, in 3:11 in terms of love.

The Johannine Epistles are marked by dualistic language. There is either darkness or light, no in-between. One belongs either to the realm of light or to that of darkness. Darkness is marked by sin, falsehood, hate, and death. Life is characterized by righteousness, TRUTH, love, and life. The first main division contrasts these two realms. The contrast is explicit in the first two subdivisions: those who walk in light are cleansed from sin (1:5–2:2); they keep the commandments (2:3-11). The light and darkness imagery is not explicit in the following sections but is implicit in the dualistic contrasts. The world is to be shunned as the world of darkness (2:12-17). The true confession in the Son is contrasted with the lie of the false teachers (2:18-27). Finally, *the children of God*, children of light, are contrasted with the children *of the devil* (2:28–3:10).

Dealing with Sin, 1:5–2:2

John's first subject is the place of sin in the believer's life. His basic premise is that God is wholly light (v. 5). Since sin is darkness, there is no room for sin in the lives of those who have FELLOWSHIP with God. Yet, sin is a reality even for believers, and God has provided means for dealing with it.

This section is constructed in a series of six antitheses, expressed in conditional sentences ("if anyone should . . . "). There are three negative statements describing those who walk in the darkness of sin (1:6, 8, 10). Alternating with these are three positive statements, treating the believer's relationship to sin (1:7, 9; 2:1-2).

The negative statements are best seen as describing the false teachers. They are not walking in the light but continue to sin (v. 6). This is so because they claim to have no sin, and this is sheer self-delusion (v. 8). They even claim to have never sinned (v. 10), and this makes God a liar, who throughout scripture asserts the sinfulness of all humanity (cf. Prov 20:9; Ps 14:2-3). Much like later Gnostics, John's opponents seem to have claimed a spiritual perfection in which they either viewed themselves as above sin or considered moral behavior a matter of indifference. John did not agree with this spirit/flesh DUALISM, but rather saw one's behavior in the flesh as indicative of one's spiritual state.

In three positive antitheses, John presents his readers with a realistic program for dealing with sin. His conviction is that sin has no place for those who walk in the light. The atoning blood of Christ has cleansed them of sin (1:7). If they do sin, however, they should confess it, and God will forgive and cleanse them (1:9). In such a case, the believer has an ADVOCATE to intercede with the Father (2:1). (Note the term "paraclete" applied to Jesus in his intercessory role. In the Gospel of John, the term is used of the Spirit.) The word "just" refers to the righteousness of Christ which qualifies him as intercessor for our unrighteousness. Christ is further described as the atonement (*hilasmos*) for our sins, a term with sacrificial overtones (cf. *blood* in 1:7). John is a realist. The goal of every Christian is to have fellowship with God, to walk in his light, to be free of sin (2:1). But we still live in an imperfect world where temptation is a reality. When we do sin, we have forgiveness through Christ.

Keeping His Commandments, 2:3-11

This section can be divided into two subsections. The first (vv. 3-6) is closely related to the previous treatment of sin, as it deals with keeping the commandments. The second (vv. 7-11) moves the thought forward to the supreme command to love. In both sections the argument is built around a recurring participial construction ("the one who says, loves . . . ").

Verse 3 begins with the theme of "being known" by God. This is an experiential knowledge, closely related to the theme of "abiding" that permeates this section: the truth is *in* a person (v. 4); we are *in him* (v. 5); one claims to *abide in him* (v. 6). For John, salvation is a relationship—to be personally known by God; to live in him and in the Son; to live in a community of love with fellow Christians. In this section John depicts the keeping of the commandments as a mark of this relationship to the Father. Probably he has in mind the whole moral tradition of the Johannine

community. Verse 6 focuses on the specific example of Christ. In contrast to the false teachers, who seem to have put little stock in Christ's human life, John presents it as a model for Christian living.

Verse 7 moves to a particular COMMANDMENT—that of love. It is both old and new. It is old because the Christians have heard it from the beginning of their Christian life (v. 7). It is also the *new commandment* that Christ gave (John 13:34; 15:12). Verses 8-11 reflect the close relationship of light and love. Because God is both light and love, to walk in his light is also to walk in his love. John again looks to the false teachers. They are likely the ones who *hate* (v. 11). Johannine dualism allows no in-betweens: To fail in love is to hate. Throughout the epistle love applies to love between Christian brothers and sisters. John is concerned with the conflict in his own community and does not address the Christian's relationship to outsiders—except, that is, the false teachers. Once they belonged to John's community; now they have left (2:19). They have no love for their former sisters and brothers in Christ.

Shunning Worldliness, 2:12-17

With vv. 12-14 one comes upon the address that was lacking at the epistle's beginning. The section raises many questions. Who are the *little children*, *fathers*, and *young people*? Elsewhere in 1 John *little children* addresses the whole community, and indeed the things said about the little children (forgiveness of sin, knowledge of the Father) apply to every Christian, but who are the fathers and young people? Do these terms designate age, or office, or stages in Christian maturity? Why does v. 14 virtually repeat vv. 12-13? For emphasis? The main function of the section seems clear. These are words of assurance to the Johannine Christians that they need not shrink from the disdain of those who have left nor doubt their own status with God. Their roots are firm: their sins are forgiven, they know the Father and the Son, and they have conquered the devil (*evil one*).

Verses 15-17 link up with the reference to conquering the devil in v. 14. In Johannine thought the devil holds sway over the world (John 12:31; 16:11). To *love the world* is to place oneself under his dominance. John does not depict the world as EVIL in itself; on the contrary, Christ died for the world, God sent his Son to save it (1 John 2:2; John 3:16). In the Johannine dualism, however, one cannot live within the world's sphere of POWER and God's at the same time. Verse 16 aptly summarizes the world's enticements—physical appetites, things which please the eye, boasting in self-achievement. To center oneself on these rather than on God is to invest in the transient.

Making the True Confession, 2:18-27

The reference to the world's *passing away* in 2:17 serves as a transition to the announcement that it is the *last hour* in v. 18. The term *antichrist* seems to have originated in Johannine circles, but the idea of false prophets and messiahs coming in the last days before Christ's return was well established in early Christianity (cf. Mark 13:22; 2 Thes 2:8). Usually ANTICHRIST is depicted as a single figure, but John speaks of many of them because he identifies antichrist with those who separated from his community (v. 19). For John the separation proves they never really belonged in the first place. They are guilty of the cardinal lie, denying that JESUS is the Christ (v. 22). This is the primary doctrinal error of the separatists. They held an inadequate view of the INCARNATION, emphasizing Christ's divinity and neglecting his humanity. The example of his life (2:6), his mediatorial role (2:1f.), and his atoning death (5:6) held no importance for them. Because they did not have the Son, neither did they have the Father nor the *eternal life* which is in him. It is not so for John's *little children*. They have the anointing of the Spirit (v. 20). They make the true confession and have both Son and Father (v. 23). Theirs is the life eternal (v. 24). John was concerned lest the separated group lead his community astray (v. 26). He thus assures them they need no experience in the Spirit that they had not already received, no teaching other than what they had been given from the beginning (v. 27).

Living as Children of God, 2:28–3:10

John returns to the theme of the last days, continuing his note of assurance in v. 28. His *little children* will have boldness to appear before the Lord at his return because they abide in him. The mark of their abiding is their righteous living. Since God is righteous, their righteousness is a sign that they have been begotten by God and are his true children (v. 29). The style of this section is again antithetical, constructed with the phrase "everyone who. . . ." It is interrupted in 3:1-2 by an encomium on being a child of God. Because God has begotten us in his love, we are now his children (3:1). Our final state does not yet appear, but John assures us we will be like Christ, *for we will see him as he is* (3:2).

Returning to the "everyone who . . . " style, 3:3 urges that those who share this hope of glory maintain their conformity to Christ even now by sharing in his purity. This links with the reference to doing righteousness in 2:29 and contrasts with the reference to *commits sin* in 3:4. Those who live in sin and iniquity will not share in Christ's coming. Christ came to take away sin (cf. John 1:29). Sin finds no place in him, and the sinner has neither seen nor known him (3:6). In fact, those who sin are the children of sin's originator, the devil (3:8, 10). Here again John's dualistic treatment of sin appears. The one abiding in Christ does not sin (3:6). The one begotten of God *cannot sin* (3:9). One must bear in mind John's treatment of sin in the life of the believer (2:1-2). He was well aware of that reality and faulted those who claimed to be sinless (1:8, 10). Many have noted that John used the present tense throughout this section, indicating a continual state of sinning: the one who abides in Christ does not "live in" sin. One must be careful not to water down John's point. Christ and sin are incompatible. The one who abides in Christ must seek to perfect that relationship by conquering sin.

Part Two: God Is Love, 3:11–5:12

The same themes recur in 1 John 3:11–5:12 that are found in 1:5–3:10—right living, the right confession of Christ, love. The balance differs. Whereas God's righteousness dominates the first part, God's love commands the last half of the epistle. The word used for love throughout 1 John is *agape*, a rather bland word in secular Greek, which often meant little more than "like, prefer." The NT writers seized the word and filled it with new meaning in the light of God's gift of love in Christ. No one does this more profoundly than John.

Loving in Deed and Truth, 3:11-24

Using his normal antithetical style, in vv. 11-18 John contrasts love and hate. CAIN's murder of ABEL is held up as the archetype of all hatred. Cain's disposition is traced to the devil, and his motivation is linked to his jealousy over his brother's righteous deeds (v. 12). Thus, in dualistic fashion, John makes of a single piece hatred, unrighteousness, murder, and the devil. Ultimately, death is added to the fabric. To hate is to murder, and no murderer has a share in eternal life (v. 15). This is the way of the unrighteous world which, like Cain, abhors the righteous. Christians should thus not be surprised when they encounter the world's hatred (v. 13; cf. John 7:7; 15:18, 19).

If the way of hatred is death, the way of love is life, life in God's own Son who laid down his life for us. This is how we *know* what love is (v. 16). How we *demonstrate* that love abides in us is in concrete deeds of charity to needy brothers and sisters (v. 17). Love is not a feeling or a profession for John. It is active, expressed in concrete deeds (v. 18; cf. Jas 1:22). Perhaps such lack of concern for the needy was the clearest evidence of the lovelessness of those who had separated from John's community.

Verse 19 introduces the theme of confidence before God's judgment. It is closely connected to v. 18, because it is this active, charitable love that gives such confidence. John assures his readers that even should they experience qualms of GUILT at their own imperfection in love and righteousness, God knows the hearts of those who truly abide in his love (v. 20). Indeed, because we abide in him, God hears our prayers and grants our requests (v. 22). Verses 22b-23 summarize the three main traits of the one who abides in God, the three which run like a thread throughout the epistle: keeping God's commandments, loving one another, and believing in the Son. There is also a witness that God abides in his children—the HOLY SPIRIT (v. 24). The mention of the Spirit serves as a transition to the next section.

Testing the Spirits, 4:1-6

The early CHURCH was alive with spiritual experience, but it soon became apparent that not all such experience came from God. It became necessary to *test the spirits* (v. 1). Much like PAUL (1 Cor 12:3), John laid down the basic confession of Jesus Christ as the main test (v. 2). But John adds a qualifying clause: they must confess Jesus Christ as having *come in the flesh*. He has the Christology of the separatists in mind, their failure to acknowledge the significance of Jesus' humanity. Theirs is not God's Spirit, but the spirit which opposes God, that *of the antichrist* (v. 3; cf. 2:18, 22).

Verses 4-6 contrast *the Spirit of God* and *the spirit of the antichrist* (vv. 2-3). John's *little children* may take assurance that the victory is theirs, because God's Spirit is more powerful (v. 4; cf. 2:14). One certain contrast is that *the world* listens to the message of false spirits; it does not heed God's Spirit (vv. 5-6a). This is perhaps indicative that the separatists who had *gone out* into the world (2:19) were having more

success in spreading their message than John. It certainly reflects John's conviction that *the world* is under the sway of the evil one and naturally heeds the spirit of deceit rather than *the spirit of truth* (v. 6).

Being Perfected in God's Love, 4:7-21

First John 4:7-21 is the most profound treatment of God's love in the NT. Verses 7-11 depict the priority of God's love. Verse 12 is transitional, introducing the main themes of the following verses: abiding in God's love (13-16), and being perfected in God's love (17-21).

True love, perfect love, begins with God (v. 7-11). The main thrust of this section is that John's readers should *love one another*. This exhortation begins and ends the treatment (vv. 7, 11). In between John establishes the basis of all love—God's love. It is significant that throughout this section John addresses his readers not as *little children* but as *beloved* (3:21; 4:1, 7, 11); that is, as those who have received God's love. Within the Christian community all love begins with God. *God is love* (v. 8). The evidence of God's love is his sending his Son into the world to die as a sacrificial atonement (*hilasmos*; cf. 2:2) for our sins so that we might have life (vv. 9-10; cf. John 3:16). Through acceptance of God's sacrificial love in Christ, the believer is begotten of God and comes truly to know him (v. 7). It is not a matter of the believer's striving after God and finding him but of God reaching down in love; he loved us first (v. 10; cf. v. 19). There is thus a triangle of love which begins with God's love, is manifested in the love of Christ, and comes to life in the believer who accepts God's sacrifice of love in Christ. But this love is not genuine until it becomes a quadrangle, reaching out to others (vv. 7, 11).

The theme of abiding in God (vv. 13-16) is closely related to that of being "begotten" by (*born of*) God and "knowing" him in v. 7. "Abiding" is a favorite Johannine term. It describes the intimate, mystical relationship between Father, Son, Spirit, and believer. The evidence of this relationship is the presence of the Spirit in the believer's life (v. 13; cf. 3:24). The basis of the relationship for the believer is confessing that Jesus is the Son of God sent to save the world (vv. 14-15; cf. vv. 9-10). The stuff of the relationship is love—God's active love in the believer's life. God is love; abiding in love and abiding in God are one and the same (v. 16).

Verses 17-20 treat the "perfection" or "completion" of God's love in the believer. The very concept of perfection points to the relational character of love. It grows in proportion to the depth of one's abiding in God. It models itself after the example of Christ's sacrificial love (v. 17). As it deepens, fear is dispelled, for there is *no fear* in a genuine relationship of love (v. 18). Abiding in God's love, the believer has no room for fear, only for confidence on the day of judgment (v. 17). This confidence is only justified when love is perfect, and love is perfect only when it reaches out to others. Just as God loved us first and reached out to us, so must his love in us reach out to others (v. 19). Love is tangible (cf. 3:17-18). To claim love for an invisible God, a love that cannot be visibly demonstrated, is a sham. The arena for showing one's love for God is the visible world of the brother or sister in need (v. 20). As John has said before, none of this is new (2:7-8). It is *the commandment* of the Lord (v. 21; cf. John 13:34, 15:12).

Finding Life in the Son, 5:1-12

The concluding section of the body of 1 John is a final word of ASSURANCE to John's readers that they have obtained life in the Son (v. 12). Three characteristics in them demonstrate this (vv. 1-5), and three witnesses confirm it (vv. 6-12).

Verses 1-5 are a final summary of the three traits that mark one as begotten of God. First, they *love God*, and because they love the Father they love his children as well (v. 1). Second, they keep God's *commandments*, and this is not burdensome because God gives them the power to conquer the world (vv. 3-4; cf. Matt 11:30). Finally, they have the right faith, believing and confessing Jesus as the Christ, *the Son of God* (vv. 1, 5).

Verses 6-12 point to the witnesses that confirm that there is life in the Son. Verse 6 is a crux of interpretation: the proper confession of Jesus affirms that he came through *the water and the blood*. Do these refer to the INCARNATION, the water and blood of childbirth? Do they refer to his atoning death, the water and blood that flowed from his side at the CRUCIFIXION (John 19:34)? Or does the water refer to his BAPTISM and the blood to his atoning death? The last seems the more likely. The separatists from the community may have held a view much like that of Cerinthus, who maintained that the divine Spirit descended on the man Jesus at his baptism and departed before the crucifixion. It was the coming of the Spirit that counts, not the life of the man nor his death. No, replies John. He came by water and by blood, by his divine Spirit and by the outpouring of his human blood in his atoning death. The Spirit associated with his baptism and the blood of his crucifixion are thus two witnesses to who Christ is. The inner testimony of the Spirit is a third (v. 8). Finally, there is a fourth witness, *the testimony of God* (vv. 9-12). What is this witness of God? Is it his giving of his Son, as v. 11 seems to indicate? Or, is it his raising him from the dead and thus assuring the life that is in the Son?

Epilogue, 5:13-21

In vv. 13-21 John brings together themes which have run throughout the epistle. Verses 13-15 are words of assurance. Verse 13 gives John's main purpose in writing—that his readers might fully know that they *have* ETERNAL LIFE through their faith in the Son (cf. John 20:31). The false teachers may have raised doubts for some. John assures they need not fear for their salvation—they already have life in Christ. (Note the Johannine "realized eschatology.") Verses 14-15 give the further assurance that God answers their prayers. There is a qualification: the petitions must be *according to his will* (3:22 should also be read with this qualifier).

Verses 16-17 treat intercessory prayer of one Christian for another. John's readers are assured that God hears and grants such requests. But there is a sin for which John does not recommend intercession—the sin "unto death" (*mortal sin*). It is not altogether clear what he had in mind. Perhaps it was the sin of those who had left the community and rejected the significance of Christ's atoning death.

In vv. 18-19 John returns a final time to the subject of sin in the Christian. The one *born of God* does not live in the realm of sin, the world dominated by the evil one. Instead, children of God belong to God and Christ (the most likely referent for *gennetheis* in v. 18) keeps them from the devil's clutches.

The false teachers may have claimed special knowledge. John assures his readers that the SON OF GOD has come and given them insight into the truth (v. 20). He is himself the truth (John 14:6) and the only way to knowledge of the one true God (cf. John 1:18, 17:3).

Why John concludes with an abrupt command to shun idols is anybody's guess. The warning may be quite literal. The Greek world, and Ephesus in particular, was filled with idols. The reference may be figurative, as it often is in the NT. The error of the separatists with their proud claims to sinless perfection was itself a form of self-idolatry.

An Outline

Salutation, 1-3

Second John follows closely the customary Greek letter form. The sender is *the elder*. The recipient is *the elect lady,* which most likely refers to a sister CHURCH. The church is one within the Johannine community, as the elder's implicit authority and the customary Johannine language would indicate (e.g., *all who know the truth . . . that abides in us*). In place of the usual Greek word of salutation, *chairein,* the NT writers characteristically substitute *grace* (*charis*) and add the Hebrew greeting *peace.* John adds a third greeting *mercy* (cf. 1 Tim 1:2; 2 Tim 1:2). At the end he tacks on two more distinctly Johannine blessings—*truth and love.*

Body of the Letter, 4-11

Reminder of Love Commandment, 4-6

The main body of 2 John is divisible into three parts: vv. 4-6, 7-9, and 10-11. In the first part (vv. 4-6) John reminds the sister church of the Lord's *new* commandment of love. John's main concern in the letter is to warn the congregation of the false teachers, and as is clear from 1 John, one of their primary faults was their lack of love. Another was their moral deficiency; so John reminds the congregation that genuine love

for God is demonstrated by living according to the *commandments* (v. 6).

False Teachers Described, 7-9

In vv. 7-9 John focuses on the false teachers more directly. Once a part of the community, they have now *gone out* into the world (cf. 1 John 2:19). They belong to the deceiver, *the antichrist* (cf. 1 John 2:18, 26). They do not confess that Jesus Christ has come in the flesh; that is, they have a deficient view of his humanity (cf. 1 John 2:22f.; 4:2f.). John describes them as "progressives." They have gone out into the world and "gone ahead" in their theology, departing from the true teaching of Christ (v. 9). Johannine theology could itself be described as "progressive" in the sense of "advanced." The trouble with the separatists was in having gone too far in their accommodation to the world.

Warning Not to Receive False Teachers, 10-11

The false teachers do not yet seem to have reached the *elect lady,* and in vv. 10-11 John advises the congregation to shun them altogether should they arrive. They are not to accept them in their homes, not even to greet them. This should be understood in light of early Christian HOSPITALITY. Itinerant missionaries depended on local Christians to provide their basic needs as they traveled. In the case of false teachers, to show them the customary hospitality would only further their cause.

Conclusion, 12-13

As with the salutation, the conclusion to 2 John closely follows conventional letter form with its exchange of greetings. Even in the note that he had more to write but hopes to share it in person, the elder is following literary convention.

Like 2 John, 3 John is quite brief, the length of a single PAPYRUS page. It too follows customary epistolary form. Unlike 2 John, it is written to an individual. It makes no mention of false teachers, but it does have an ironical relationship to 2 John. The refusal of hospitality *the elder* recommended to the "elect lady" (2 John 1) is now experienced by the elder himself.

An Outline

Salutation, 1-2

The writer again identifies himself as *the elder* and addresses *Gaius*. We know nothing else of GAIUS. He may have been a member of Diotrephes' church (v. 9) or, as is more likely, one nearby. The prayer that all be well and the recipient *in good health* (v. 2) is a standard feature of private letters in John's day.

Body of the Letter, 3-12

The body of the letter falls into 3 parts: Gaius's hospitality (vv. 3-8), Diotrephes' opposition (vv. 9-11), and a commendation of *Demetrius* (vv. 11-12).

Gaius's Hospitality, 3-8

Verses 3-4 commend Gaius for the good report "the brothers" have given him, that he is walking in the truth. Most likely, this refers to his giving hospitality to "the brothers" (vv. 5-8). These were probably co-workers of John, itinerant missionaries who had been provided for by Gaius while they were working in his region. On returning to John's church, they had reported Gaius's generosity to the congregation. The passage reflects the early Christian practice of providing for traveling missionary workers. They were given food and lodging and on their departure enough provision to take them to their next stopping place. They refused help from non-Christians, depending wholly on the Christian community. Verse 8 states a basic principle of Christian missions—those who give support to missionaries participate in the ministry.

Diotrephes' Opposition, 9-11

Verses 9-11 reflect a breakdown in this arrangement. John had written a letter to *the church*, presumably regarding the provision of hospitality for his co-workers, but an individual in the congregation named *Diotrephes* had opposed him. Diotrephes' opposition was expressed in four ways: he spoke idle, gossipy words against John; he refused hospitality to the traveling Christian workers; he forbade others to give them

hospitality; he expelled any member who did offer them support. We know nothing else of Diotrephes. John does not accuse him of any doctrinal or moral failure; so he doesn't seem associated with the separatists. We don't know from what he derived his POWER over the CHURCH, whether from office or personal prestige. John accuses him of liking *to put himself first* (v. 9).

The whole situation betrays a power struggle. Diotrephes may have been exerting the autonomy of his congregation against the authority of the elder John. The situation may reflect a transition stage in church organization. The old order of centralized apostolic authority was dying out. Whatever the situation, the irony is that Diotrephes was following the elder's own advice (cf. 2 John 10). The elder's emissaries were certainly not false teachers, but Diotrephes may have turned John's prohibition of supporting false teachers into a blanket principle covering all itinerant workers. Verse 11 is best understood in this connection. For John there is no greater work than loving one's fellow Christian. Refusing hospitality was an unloving, evil work, and evil workers have *not seen* God. Here John comes close to linking Diotrephes with the separatists.

Commendation of Demetrius, 11-12

The commendation of *Demetrius* (v. 12) is probably linked to the problem with Diotrephes. DEMETRIUS may have been the bearer of 3 John, and Gaius's accepting him and furnishing hospitality the whole purpose for John's writing.

Conclusion, 13-15

Third John's conclusion follows conventional epistolary form. The claim to have more to write and the desire to talk face-to-face are literary conventions (cf. 2 John 12). In this instance, however, John's desire for a visit may have been substantive. The problem with Diotrephes may have urged the elder to come *soon* (v. 14) and deal with the matter personally (cf. v. 10).

Jude

Watson E. Mills

Introduction

Jude ranks, along with 2 and 3 John, among the most neglected and least well known of the twenty-seven books of the NT. The neglect of Jude is especially deplorable since Jude is a crucial document from a period of Christian history when rigid lines were being drawn between orthodoxy and heresy. In the strongest terms, the book of Jude posits a definite relationship between belief and practice.

Jude is included in a division of the NT CANON known variously as the GENERAL LETTERS or sometimes the "apostolic epistles" (James, 1, 2 Peter, 1, 2, 3 John, and Jude). These letters are said to be "catholic" (or universal) in their appeal since the letter opening does not name a single, specific recipient as do most of Paul's letters. The universal letters rather are addressed to all Christians everywhere (cf. 1 Pet 1:1). Yet despite this tradition, it would appear that the words of warning in Jude are directed to a very specific, though unnamed, community of Christians. In fact, the author appears to know the specific situation so well, that he is even aware of the movements of the "opponents" (see below, Opponents).

Authorship

The JUDE referred to in v. 1 is almost certainly JUDAS, the brother of Jesus, whose brother JAMES is James "the Just," a leader of the Jerusalem church. Both names were common in the early Christian community. For instance, the two disciples Judas Iscariot and Judas son of James; Judas Barsabbas (Acts 15:22-33); and, in the Maccabean era, Judas Maccabeus.

Jude is the short form for Judas (and is used only here in the NT for Ἰούδας, otherwise translated Judas) and James is the English form for Jacob. In the NT there are several men by each name. There is only one combination of brothers by those names, however—the James and Jude who are listed as two of the four brothers of Jesus (Matt 13:55; Mark 6:3). While most modern commentators agree on the referents, they disagree as to whether the author was the Jude referred to, or someone who used his name. The hypothesis that the author used the name of Jude has prevailed in many recent commentaries (Barnett, Grundmann, Reicke, Schelkle, Sidebottom), if only because arguments for a date too late for Jude's lifetime are held by the commentators.

We know little about Jude the brother of Jesus. He was one of four brothers of Jesus (with James, Joseph, and Simon), probably younger than James (Matt 13:55; Mark 6:3). Apparently, like Jesus' other brothers, Jude did not become a follower of Jesus during Jesus' earthly ministry (John 7:5) but only after the resurrection (Acts 1:14). According to 1 Cor 9:5, the brothers of the Lord became traveling missionaries, and, presumably, Jude is included in that reference. His missionary work was probably among the Jews, but not necessarily limited to PALESTINE. Julius Africanus (Eusebius, *EccHist* 1.7.14) says that the relatives of Jesus spread the gospel throughout Palestine, starting from Nazareth and Cochaba (in TRANSJORDAN). According to the *Acts of Paul* (*NTApoc* 2:388), Judas, the Lord's brother, befriended Paul in DAMASCUS—a tradition based only on identifying the Judas of Acts 9:11 with the brother of the Lord.

The fact that the writer refers to himself as Jude the *brother of James* (v. 1) and not the brother of Jesus could be a telling argument against the hypothesis of pseudonymity. Such a description is much more easily explicable on the hypothesis of authenticity. The humility that prompted this description must in itself be regarded as a mark of genuineness, matched by his more eminent brother's similar behavior (Jas 1:1).

Date, Relationship to 1 Peter, Recipients

Many of the scholars who doubt the traditional authorship do so on the grounds that the content of the letter suggests it is of a late composition. Bo Reicke (1964), for example, settled on a date of 90 C.E. Verse 3 supposes that the faith is already becoming a systematic body of doctrine, and vv. 17, 18 speak as if the generation of the apostles has died out. If Jude was indeed the younger brother of Jesus then is it not impossible that he was alive well into the latter part of the first century. J. A. T. Robinson argues that if *James* (v. 1) had already died, the author would have given some epithet such as "blessed" or "good" or "just" in referring to him. In the absence of any such reference Robinson holds that Jude must be dated before James's death in 62 C.E.

The date of the writing is inevitably related to the question of the relationship between Jude and 2 Peter. Except for a few opening and closing words, virtually all of Jude is included in 2 Peter:

Jude		2 Peter
2	=	1:2
3	=	1:5
5a	=	1:12
5b-19	=	2:1-3:3
24	=	3:14

Not only is the material common to the two letters, but each reflects a similar organizational approach. Both letters (1) warn against false teachers; (2) use three illustrations of God's judgment, two of which are identical (*angels* and *Sodom and Gomorrah*; (3) use BALAAM as an example of false teachers; (4) characterize the false teachers as those who are defiant toward divine authority; (5) use materials from apocryphal writings; and (6) use the same strong metaphors to characterize the false teachers (i.e., irrational animals, doomed to eternal darkness; spots and blemishes; arrogant boasters, etc.).

These literary similarities may be explained in one of three ways: (1) Second Peter borrowed heavily from Jude; (2) Jude borrowed heavily from 2 Peter; (3) both 2 Peter and Jude used a common source either oral or more probably written, but in either case no longer extant.

Since the early nineteenth century, a majority of scholarly opinion has favored the priority of Jude (option 1 above). Essentially the evidence is that (1) it is far more likely that the writer of 2 Peter would incorporate Jude into 2 Peter than that Jude would have lifted one chapter out of 2 Peter and presented it as a separate epistle; (2) the unknown writer of 2 Peter made use of the epistle from Jude, the brother of James and Jesus, to lend authority to his letter; (3) the

writer of 2 Peter removed from Jude the explicit references to apocryphal books (*1 Enoch* in Jude 6, 14, and 2 Peter 2:4) and the identifiable materials of apocryphal books (the *Assumption of Moses* in Jude 9 and 2 Peter 2:11) to make his letter more acceptable to Christian readers.

There is nothing to indicate to whom the letter was written, or where the writer was situated, except that the author is addressing Christian people (v. 1) who are apparently beset by the same kind of problems that have plagued the recipients of 2 Peter. This reality may well suggest an identity of the two groups, but in no way proves it.

Opponents

The most universally held opinion is that these false teachers were Gnostics. Indeed, GNOSTICISM was a very widespread threat to the mainstream of Christian thought by the late first and early second centuries. By that time it was firmly entrenched in the Mediterranean world—Palestine, ASIA, Africa, and ROME. Some scholars, however, contend that this letter comes too early for it to contain specific refutations of a fullblown Gnosticism such as that found in the second century. Moreover, if it were a refutation of Gnosticism, it is surprisingly timid in its denunciation. Bauckham (1983) suggests the opponents were itinerant charismatics who have caused trouble for the Christian community elsewhere (Matt 7:15; 2 Cor 10-11; 1 John 4:1). Whoever they were, the "opponents" were not just casual passersby, but rather active members of the Christian community who were involved directly in its various functions, and thus had a fertile ground and opportunity to promulgate their heretical teachings.

Purpose and Structure

The purpose of the letter is to demonstrate how these false teachers pose a threat to the Christian community and how the readers must carry on the fight for the faith.

The statement of the theme (vv. 3-4) contains two parts: (1) an appeal to Jude's readers to carry on the fight *for the faith* and (2) the background to this appeal, that is, specific references to the false teachers, their character and their judgment. Similarly the body of the letter contains two parts that correspond to this division: (1) the background (vv. 5-19) establishes that these false teachers are condemned and that their judgment has been prophesied in the Hebrew Bible since the days of Enoch. Thus these false teachers constitute a genuine and serious threat to the churches. Thereby the way is prepared for the second, and central, part the of body of the letter; (2) the appeal (vv. 21-23) calls on his readers to fight for the faith.

Jude cites a series of four "texts" although they are not actual quotations so much as textual allusions. The arrangement is such that each text is followed by an interpretative section:

Text	Interp.	Location	Drawn from
one		vv. 5-7	three types from
	one	vv. 8-10	the Hebrew Bible
two		v. 11	three types from
	two	vv. 12-13	the Hebrew Bible
three		vv. 14-15	the Book of Enoch
	three	v. 16	
four		vv. 17-18	the Apostles
	four	v. 19	

The first two "texts" are summary references to two sets of three OT types (vv. 5-7, 11). It is evident from the way he quotes the material in two of these instances (Prov 25:14 and Isa 57:20) that here Jude is depending upon the text of the Hebrew Bible and not that of the LXX as has been often supposed. The writer then quotes a prophecy of *Enoch* (vv. 14-15) and a prophecy *of the apostles* (vv. 17-18). Each is followed by a passage of interpretation (vv. 8-10, 12-13, 16, 19) which, by pointing to the character and behavior of the false teachers, identifies them as those to whom this type of prophecy applies. In text one, a secondary text (v. 9) is introduced in the course of the passage of interpretation.

Ellis (1978) has demonstrated that vv. 5-19 are actually cast in the form of a midrash. The term "midrash" is used in this instance to describe Jude's exegesis of the scriptures and other ancient materials and his application of these results to a specific historical situation. The term does *not* imply that Jude's midrash bears any close resemblance to the highly developed and stylized forms of later rabbinic midrashim.

The function of this section is to provide the background for the ultimate purpose of the letter: the appeal for its readers to *contend for the faith* (v. 3).

The midrash demonstrates the clear danger that these false teachers bring to the church, and prepares the way for the clarification and expansion of the purpose of the letter (vv. 20-23) already hinted at in v. 3.

In vv. 20-23 the author brings his readers to a dramatic conclusion, the urgency and relevancy of which has been heightened. Jude issues the call for his readers to fight to keep the faith.

For Further Study

In the *Mercer Dictionary of the Bible*: ENOCH, FIRST; ENOCH, SECOND; GENERAL LETTERS; GNOSTICISM; JAMES; JUDE, LETTER OF; PETER, LETTERS OF.

In other sources: R. J. Bauckham, *Jude, 2 Peter*; J. D. Charles, "Jude's Use of Pseudepigraphical Source-Material as Part of a Literary Strategy," *NTS* 37 (1991): 130–45; J. N. D. Kelly, *A Commentary on the Epistles of Peter and Jude*; B. Reicke, *The Epistles of James, Peter, and Jude*; E. M. Sidebottom, *James, Jude, and 2 Peter*.

Commentary

An Outline

> I. Greeting, 1-2
> II. Purpose, 3-4
>   A. Appeal, 3
>   B. Background, 4
> III. Development of the Background, 5-19
>   A. Description of the False Teachers as Sinners, 5-10
>   B. Description of How These False Teachers
>   Are Leading Others into Sin, 11-13
>   C. A Prophecy Adapted from Enoch, 14-16
>   D. A Prophecy Adapted from the Apostles, 17-19
> IV. The Appeal, 20-23
> V. Closing Doxology, 24-25

Greeting, 1-2

This section follows the form of the Jewish letter with the parties formula (from sender "X" to recipient "Y") and salutation or greeting. The authority rests upon the term "servant" (δοῦλος) not upon identification of the writer with Jesus' blood line. *Those who are called* reflects the fact that "the called" (κλητοῖς) has become a technical term within the Christian community, indicating those who have responded to the gospel. The tripartite formula *called, beloved,* and *kept* could possibly reflect an understanding of the servant songs of Isaiah (41:9; 42:1; 42:6). Jude omits "grace" (χάρις) in the salutation. The *mercy, peace, and love* offered here is also found in 1 and 2 Timothy.

Purpose, 3-4

The present less-finished treatise has been substituted for the one planned because of the danger of the present situation, that is, there are those present who refuse to follow the teachings of the faith and are ready to lead others in this heretical vein. The writer is thinking not so much of any creed or dogma, but rather an erroneous and unacceptable mode of conduct. There is a contemptuous ring in the phrase *certain intruders* who *have stolen* their way into the community. This threat is real; the author calls his readership to their responsibility to face up to this threat.

Development of the Background, 5-19

Description of the False Teachers as Sinners, 5-10

Next, the author describes the certainty of the judgment upon any who fail to live out the faith. Examples from the Hebrew Bible make it abundantly clear that status alone is no guarantee of a saving relationship with God. These false teachers, and any who follow them, are sinners and must face the consequences of their actions.

Description of How These False Teachers Are Leading Others into Sin, 11-13

Here the author points out, rather graphically, how as in the cases of CAIN, BALAAM, and KORAH, these false teachers are trying to lead others into immorality and away from their calling. These false teachers are motivated by jealousy and pride—a pride so great that it cannot tolerate any knowledge or power greater than its own.

A Prophecy Adapted from Enoch, 14-16

Jude quotes Enoch's prophecy as dramatic evidence of the impending punishment upon the false teachers. Apparently the Book of Enoch was well known in the first century, and Enoch himself was remembered as one "who walked with God" (Gen 5:22, 24). Here the Lord has come to bring judgment upon the ungodly, their character, their behavior. *Grumblers* (see Exod 16:2, 9) calls to mind the experience of the Israelites as they wandered aimlessly in the wilderness. These false teachers are chronic faultfinders, who, while incessantly complaining about others, follow their own lustful desires without regard for others.

A Prophecy Adapted from the Apostles, 17-19

Taken from the words spoken earlier by the apostles (though the specific tradition quoted remains unknown), this apostolic prophecy is expressed as a warning. That such persons as these would appear among the faithful is itself a sign that the "end times" are near. These false teachers cause serious divisions within the community by setting themselves up as superior to ordinary Christians. Jude maintains it is *these ungodly people* who are *devoid of the Spirit*.

The Appeal, 20-23

All that has come before has pointed the reader to this final appeal. Here Jude offers an exhortation to the faithful, a kind of "Christian antidote" to countermand the work of the false teachers. This appeal to action begins *But you, beloved* to heighten the contrast between the faithful and the false teachers. The contrast is further sharpened when he adds praying *in the Holy Spirit* as a quantifier for the faithful. This theme calls to mind a similar note found in the writings of Paul (Rom 8:26; 1 Cor 12:3; Gal 4:6; Eph 6:18). The referent here is in no way equivocal since the false teachers are without the Spirit. Jude offers these specific ingredients for his "antidote": (1) *build yourselves up on [the] most holy faith*; (2) *pray in the Holy Spirit*; (3) *keep yourselves in the love of God*; (4) *look forward to the mercy of our Lord Jesus Christ*.

Verses 22-23 abruptly shifts the focus to the way in which in the readers should respond toward those have been taken in, to greater and lesser degrees, by the false teachers. The text here is uncertain and it is not immediately clear whether Jude refers to two or three groups of individuals. The NRSV follows ℵ and A (three groups) while the NEB follows B and Clement of Alexandria. If we are to understand three groups, Jude's advice becomes progressively more drastic: (1) those who have not made up their minds—they must be convinced by argument; (2) those who are already involved with the false teachers—spare no effort in trying to rescue these (*save others by snatching them out of the fire*, v. 23); (3) those who have strayed so far they are only to be pitied—these must be feared by the faithful so as to avoid contamination.

Closing Doxology, 24-25

Beyond the responsibilities of the recipients is the sure presence of God's support and protection that in effect guarantees that their efforts to avoid spiritual heresy will not be in vain. These closing words call to mind an eschatological celebration of worship. The believers celebrate the final consequence of God's purposes, that is, they are found to be a suitable sacrifice before God.

Works Cited

Barnett, A. E. 1962. "The Epistle of Jude. Introduction," *IB*.

Bauckham, Richard J. 1983. *Jude, 2 Peter*. WBC.

Ellis, E. Earle. 1978. *Prophecy and Hermeneutic in Early Christianity*.

Grundmann, W. 1974. *Der Brief des Judas und der zweite Brief des Petrus*. THKNT.

Robinson, J. A. T. 1976. *Redating the New Testament*.

Reicke, Bo. 1964. *The Epistles of James, Peter, and Jude*. AncB.

Schelkle, K. H. 1980. *Die Petrusbriefe, der Judasbrief*. HTKNT.

Sidebottom, E. M. 1967. *James, Jude, and 2 Peter*. NCB.

Revelation

Mitchell G. Reddish

Introduction

Few writings have captured the imagination of as many people as has the book of Revelation. Artists, musicians, and writers have been intrigued by its rich imagery and symbolism and have mined its treasures as inspiration for their own works. Examples include Olivier Messiaen's musical composition *Quartet for the End of Time* and Handel's *Messiah*; Dürer's woodcuts and Michelangelo's *Last Judgment* in the Sistine Chapel; William Blake's *America, a Prophecy*; and Ernesto Cardenal's *Apocalypse*. People in despair and in crisis situations have turned to Revelation for comfort and hope, finding assurance in the book's confident assertion that God is in control of the universe and that good will ultimately triumph over EVIL. Its hymns, prayers, and words of praise have greatly enriched the church's liturgy.

In spite of its tremendous influence, Revelation remains for many readers a mysterious, enigmatic, even frightening work. The bizarre symbolism and repetitive structure of the book have caused many readers to abandon hope of making sense of John's message. On the other hand, some people claim to possess the key to unlocking the mysteries of this work, viewing it as a book of predictions of soon-coming world events. Armed with fanciful interpretations often more bizarre than the images of the book itself, these individuals transform John's writing into a propaganda sheet for their own futuristic views. Both reactions to the book—bewilderment and sensationalism—need to be avoided. Properly understood, Revelation contains a message of hope and comfort, as well as a call to faithfulness, that is still as valid to the CHURCH of today as it was to the church of the first century.

Literary Form

The Book of Revelation exhibits characteristics of several literary types. The work contains the major elements of ancient letters: greeting (1:4-5a), blessing or thanksgiving (1:5b-6), body (1:7–22:20), and closing (22:21). Embedded within the work are also seven messages to local churches, each cast in a form similar to a letter. Some scholars have argued that Revelation should be understood as prophetic literature. Indeed the author calls his writing a *prophecy* (1:3; 22:7, 10, 18, 19) and refers to the prophets as his brothers (22:9, NRSV *comrades*). Other scholars have viewed Revelation as modeled after the form of ancient Greek drama.

As valid as these insights may be, most scholars agree that Revelation is best understood as belonging to the literary form of an apocalypse, a type of writing popular in certain Jewish and Christian circles. The name of the genre is derived from the opening words of Revelation in which the author calls the contents of his work an *apocalypsis* (revelation). Ancient apocalypses were writings that purported to contain revelations of cosmic secrets, mediated to human recipients by supernatural beings either directly or in visions or dreams. The contents of the revelations usually consisted of both eschatological and otherworldly information. Although the social setting for many of the ancient Jewish and Christian apocalypses is unclear, apocalypses seem to have been produced in response to some sort of crisis situation (political, military, social, theological), either real or imagined. APOCALYPTIC LITERATURE was written to offer its readers a message of hope and comfort by providing an alternative view of reality from that dominant in the current sociohistorical setting. Apocalyptic writings assured their readers that, in spite of how the situation appeared, God was in control of history and the universe. Eventually God would triumph, rewarding the faithful and destroying evil.

Several literary and theological characteristics, while not definitive of the genre, are commonly found in apocalypses. Among the literary characteristics are pseudonymous authorship, historical reviews in the form of *ex eventu* prophecy ("prophecy" after the event has happened), mythological and symbolic language, visionary and auditory revelations, and rapture experiences. Theological characteristics include a dualistic theology (God versus the powers of evil), a dualistic view of history (two ages: the present, evil age and the glorious age to come), expectation of the imminent end of this age, and a deterministic understanding of world events.

Provenance and Social Setting

Evidence from Revelation indicates that the author and his audience were residents of Asia Minor, located in present day Turkey. The author states that he received the revelation contained in the Apocalypse while he was on the island of PATMOS, located off the coast of Asia Minor in the Aegean Sea. In addition, churches in seven cities of Asia Minor are recipients of special messages in Revelation.

John states he is on Patmos *because of the word of God and the testimony of Jesus* (1:9). Whereas this could mean John went to the island to share the Christian faith with the people there, the usual understanding is that John was banished by the Roman authorities to Patmos for being a Christian. Some islands in this area were used by the Romans as penal colonies, although there is no evidence that Patmos was ever so used. Similar phrasing elsewhere in the book supports the understanding that John's presence on Patmos was due to persecution (cf. 6:9; 12:11; 20:4).

The social and political setting reflected in Revelation is one of persecution and even martyrdom. Not only has John been banished because of his faith, but he also knows of other Christians who have been killed, even singling one out by name, *Antipas* (2:13; see also 2:9-10; 6:9-11; 16:6; 17:6; 18:24; 19:2; 20:4). Martyrdom is a major interpretive key for Revelation, with martyrs receiving special praise and reward. Calls to faithfulness and endurance resound throughout the book. Whereas some persecution seems to be based on Jewish hostilities (2:9-10), the majority derives from the Roman government. Enforcement of emperor worship and punishment of those who refuse is a major cause of the persecution (chap. 13).

This sociopolitical setting of suffering and persecution has been questioned by scholars who correctly point out that evidence for such persecution is meager or even nonexistent. No empire-wide persecution against Christians occurred in the first century. Furthermore, the portrayal of the emperor Domitian as a cruel despot by Roman and early Christian writers is likely due more to bias and imagination than to historical fact. Yet even if this is true, the author of Revelation was aware of some cases of persecution and martyrdom, no matter how limited in scope or duration. From his vantage point as a recipient of such persecution, the situation did indeed seem perilous. Reality is a matter of perspective, and from the perspective of John and his audience persecution was a present experience and a future threat. Although all Christians in Asia Minor might not have viewed the social and historical situation as life-threatening, John certainly did. Thus the setting for Revelation can be correctly labeled a persecution setting, even if that persecution was not widespread.

Date and Authorship

The writing of Revelation is commonly placed during the time of Domitian, emperor of Rome 81–96 C.E. The statement of IRENAEUS (ca. 140–ca. 202 C.E.) that the VISION of the Revelation was seen at the end of the reign of Domitian is the earliest external evidence attesting the date of Revelation (*AdvHaer* 5.30.3). Several writers in the following centuries also support a Domitianic dating for the book. Other early writers mention the reigns of Claudius, Nero, and Trajan as the setting for Revelation. Internal evidence lends additional support to the claim of Irenaeus. In Revelation *Babylon* (14:8; 16:19; 17:5; 18:2, 10, 21) is used as a symbolic name for ROME, a practice that would be appropriate only after 70 C.E. As Babylon had destroyed Jerusalem in the sixth century B.C.E. and had persecuted the people of God, Rome had also destroyed Jerusalem (70 C.E.) and was now persecuting God's people. A further indication of dating appears in the use of the Nero *redivivus* myth in chaps. 13 and 17. This belief in the return of Nero was popular during the last half of the first century, following the death of Nero in 66 C.E. Since the internal evidence coheres with Irenaeus's dating of the book during the time of Domitian, most scholars place its composition around 95 C.E.

The author of Revelation identifies himself as *John* (1:9). Christian writers as early as the second century identified this John as the disciple of Jesus. This identification is almost certainly ruled out, however, by the way in which the author refers to *the twelve apostles* as the *foundations* of the new Jerusalem (21:14). The writer is looking back on a venerated group of heroes of the faith. Furthermore, the author never claims apostolic authority for his writing. He describes himself simply as *your brother who share with you in Jesus the persecution and the kingdom and the patient endurance*" (1:9). Whereas the majority of Jewish and Christian apocalypses were written pseudonymously, such does not seem to be true of Revelation. The writer of the Apocalypse apparently does not claim to be anyone other than who he is: John, a Christian leader who has received a revelation from God while on the island of Patmos. John was obviously well known to the Christians in Asia Minor and knew the churches and their backgrounds intimately (2:1–3:22). Since he referred to his message as a *prophecy* (1:3), he viewed himself as a Christian prophet and had possibly functioned in this role among the Christians in Asia Minor. His extensive use of the Hebrew Bible and the many semitisms in his Greek suggest that he was a Jewish Christian, likely originally from Palestine.

Literary Structure

The literary structure of Revelation has been the focus of much debate among interpreters. All commentators recognize the importance of the number seven as a structuring device in the book—seven messages, seven seals, seven trumpets, seven bowls. How are these series of sevens related? The seven messages in 2:1–3:22 have sometimes been viewed as disconnected to the remainder of the work. A close examination, however, reveals otherwise. The clearest example of such connections occurs in the introductions to each of the seven messages, which borrow phrases from the description of the exalted Christ in chap. 1. Furthermore, the themes of persecution, faithfulness, endurance, rewards for the righteous, and the new Jerusalem, which are prominent in the seven messages, are also the major themes in the remainder of the book.

Some interpreters see the four series of sevens as consecutive series; that is, John presents in chronological order his vision of coming events. A progression is certainly intended in the events described, as evidenced by the opening of the seventh seal that introduces the seven trumpets. Yet the progression is not strictly linear. Rather, later events sometimes recapitulate earlier events. For example, the plagues and calamities of the seven trumpets describe in a new way the punishments and judgments of the end times depicted by the seven seals. Instead of a straight linear progression, the structure of Revelation presents a movement that is spiral. Earlier events are presented in different forms and use different images. As in certain musical pieces, a theme is played, then variations of that theme occur, each variation moving the piece forward. In Revelation, the movement of the work is from John's historical situation to the arrival of the new Jerusalem, the fulfillment of God's ultimate plan for creation. Within that overall forward movement, however, are numerous instances of overlapping and parallel scenes.

Interpreting Revelation

Fascinated and intrigued by the often bizarre imagery in Revelation, interpreters throughout the centuries have attempted in various ways to understand this writing. One of the more popular approaches today understands the book as a catalogue of unfulfilled prophecies of the final days of history. Proponents of this view believe that they are now living in the last days and that informed readers can see predictions in Revelation being fulfilled in current world events. Wars, natural disasters, societal ills, and economic catastrophes are all interpreted as signs of the end times. The beasts and other symbols of evil are identified as actual persons and institutions now in existence or soon to appear. According to this view, John was not addressing the concerns of his own time and situation, but was speaking about the events unfolding today. One of the major problems with this method of interpreting Revelation is that it divorces the work from its first-century historical context. The message of Revelation would have been virtually incomprehensible and meaningless to the Christians of Asia Minor to whom it was addressed. Another problem with this approach is that it fails to take seriously the apocalyptic genre of Revelation with its extensive use of ancient myths and symbols.

A proper interpretation of the Apocalypse must take account of the sociohistorical context and the literary genre of the work. In addition, the function of the language of Revelation needs to be understood. The language of the book is primarily pictorial and symbolic. It is not propositional language. The message of Revelation cannot be condensed into neat, concise theological statements. The language of Revelation is evocative, powerful, emotive language, more akin to poetry than to prose. The Book of Revelation should overwhelm the reader (or hearer) with visual and auditory symbols. Revelation needs to arouse the imagination. It must be experienced, not deciphered. A skilled exegete can explain the origin of many of John's symbols and images by pointing to the Hebrew

Bible, Jewish APOCALYPTIC LITERATURE, and ancient myths as the sources for much of the writing. A scholar can also help us understand how John's original readers may have understood the book's message in their sociohistorical context. As helpful and necessary as these insights are, however, they do not exhaust the meaning of the Apocalypse. The symbols in the book are multivalent and open-ended. They continue to speak to new generations of perceptive readers who realize that the monstrous evils of pride, idolatry, abuse of power, and dehumanization represented by the beasts of Revelation continue to appear in ever new forms, manifesting themselves in individuals and institutions. Likewise, the images of hope and assurance that empowered and comforted John's first-century audience still function in that manner for modern readers.

For Further Study

In the *Mercer Dictionary of the Bible*: APOCALYPTIC LITERATURE; CHURCHES OF REVELATION; LAMB OF GOD; MYTH; NT USE OF OT; REVELATION, BOOK OF; PERSECUTION IN THE NT; SYMBOL; VISION.

In other sources: G. R. Beasley-Murray, *The Book of Revelation*, NCB; I. T. Beckwith, *The Apocalypse of John*; J. L. Blevins, *Revelation as Drama*; M. E. Boring, *Revelation*, Interp; G. B. Caird, *The Revelation of St. John*, HNTC; A. Y. Collins, *The Apocalypse, N.T. Message, Crisis and Catharsis: The Power of the Apocalypse*, and "Revelation, Book of," *AncBD* 5:694-708; E. Schüssler Fiorenza, *The Book of Revelation*, and "Revelation: Vision of a Just World," *ProcI*; C. J. Hemer, *Letters to the Seven Churches*; R. L. Jeske, *Revelation for Today*; J. P. M. Sweet, *Revelation*, WPelC; L. L. Thompson, *The Book of Revelation*.

Commentary

An Outline

Prologue, 1:1-8

The first two verses serve as a title to the work and describe it as a revelation (Gk. *apocalypsis*) from God mediated to John by a heavenly messenger, dealing with soon-occurring events. This description contains many of the elements of the literary genre of an apocalypse as defined by scholars. Indeed, the genre derives its name from the opening word of v. 1 in the Greek text. Although God is the ultimate source of the revelation, it comes to John from Jesus through an ANGEL. John is described as one *who testified to the word of God and to the testimony of Jesus Christ* (v. 2). Testifying, or bearing witness (*martyreō*), is an important theme in Revelation (cf. 1:5, 9; 2:13; 3:14; 6:9; 11:3; 12:11, 17; 17:6; 20:4). One of the purposes of the writing was to call all Christians to be faithful witnesses. The benediction in v. 3 (the first of seven benedictions in the work) indicates that John intended his work to be read aloud to the Christians in Asia Minor as they gathered for worship. Like other apocalyptic writers, John saw himself as living in the final days of history.

These verses comprise an epistolary introduction, describing both the sender and the recipients of the message. *The seven churches* (v. 4) refer to the churches in the Roman province of Asia mentioned in 1:11 and 2:1–3:22. Although addressed to these seven churches specifically, the work is intended for all Christians because the number seven often symbolized completeness or totality. The description of God as the one *who is and who was and who is to come* (vv. 4, 8), an adaptation of Exod 3:14, affirms the continuing presence of God in the lives of believers. Note the change in structure at the end of this trilogy. John does not describe God as the one "who will be" but uses a more dynamic phrase, the one *who is to come*. God is active, not static. *The seven spirits* before God's throne symbolize the power and presence of God active throughout the world (cf. 5:6; Zech 4:1-14), later expressed in Christian theology by the doctrine of the HOLY SPIRIT. The titles attributed to Christ—*the faithful witness, the firstborn of the dead, and the ruler of the kings of the earth*—would have been especially appropriate to John's first-century readers who were faced with persecution and martyrdom. If they too are faithful witnesses, refusing to concede to the divine claims of earthly rulers, they will share in Christ's resurrection.

After the doxology to Christ in vv. 5b-6, John, in language borrowed from Dan 7:13 and Zech 12:10, delivers a prophetic pronouncement of the coming of Christ. The coming, or PAROUSIA, of Jesus Christ, which symbolizes the fulfillment of God's goal for the universe, is portrayed in the subsequent visions (19:11-21), is divinely promised (22:7, 12, 20), and is the final plea of the book (22:17, 20). The prologue closes with a threefold declaration from God, giving divine assurance of the authenticity of John's revelation. This is one of only two places in the book where God speaks directly (cf. 21:5). The ascription *the Alpha and the Omega*, the first and last letters of the Greek alphabet, identify God as the beginning and the end of all history. God is the creator and the consummator of the universe.

The Commissioning of John, 1:9-20

Like many of the Hebrew prophets, particularly ISAIAH and EZEKIEL, John relates a dramatic experience of being commissioned as a PROPHET. *In the spirit* means overcome by the Spirit of God, perhaps in a trance. This phrase identifies John's experience as a visionary experience. *On the Lord's day* probably refers to Sunday, the day of Christ's resurrection. The selection of these particular seven churches to be recipients of the revelation to John is not clear. Perhaps they were the churches with which John was most familiar.

John's vision of the SON OF MAN combines features from the "Ancient One" in Dan 7:9 and the mighty figure of Dan 10 (cf. also Ezekiel's vision of God in 1:26-28). The phrase *one like the Son of Man* (v. 12, lit. "one like a son of man," i.e., one in human form) is also drawn from Daniel (7:13). The exalted Christ stands among the churches, a symbol of power, majesty, and judgment.

Overwhelmed by the spectacle, John falls to his feet (cf. Dan 10:8-9). Both the description of the Son of Man and his first words to John (*I am the first and the last*) indicate his unity with God. He is the resurrected Christ who has conquered death and the place of the dead (*Hades*). For John's readers faced with the possibility of death, that claim would indeed be comforting. The imagery of *the seven stars* in Christ's right hand is perhaps drawn from contemporary depictions of the emperors holding the seven planets or stars in their hands, symbolizing their power over the world. For John, Christ and not the emperor is sovereign. Christ identifies the stars as *the angels of the seven churches*. These angels are the guardian angels of the churches, but even more, they are the heavenly counterparts of the churches. (Cf. the assertion in Dan 10 that nations have such heavenly guardians/counterparts.) When the angels receive the message, the churches do also. The imagery of *the seven lampstands* is derived from Zech 4 where a seven-branched lampstand represents the presence of God (cf. Exod 25:31-40). For John *the seven lampstands are the seven churches* (v. 20), in the midst of whom Christ stands to strengthen and uphold them.

The Messages to the Seven Churches, 2:1–3:22

Often called letters, these messages are cast more in the form of court decrees or proclamations. With slight variations, the messages follow a typical pattern: address to the angel of the church, description of Christ (in terms borrowed from the attributes of the Son of Man in chap. 1), words of praise and/or admonition and condemnation, exhortation, a call to hear, and a promise to the ones who conquer. The information stated or implied about each of the churches bespeaks John's deep familiarity with each of the cities (see Hemer 1986; see also CHURCHES OF REVELATION).

2:1-7. Ephesus. EPHESUS, a seaport and major trading center, was the most important city in Asia Minor. The city was renowned for its temple to the goddess ARTEMIS (cf. Acts 19:21-41), and was also one of the centers of the imperial cult in Asia Minor. Christianity had been established early in Ephesus and had prospered (cf. Acts 18:24–19:41). Christ praises the church at Ephesus on two accounts: its patience and endurance, apparently in the face of some sort of persecution, and its faithfulness in discerning good from evil, truth from falsehood. The latter commendation includes the church's wisdom in rejecting the works of the NICOLAITANS, a group mentioned more fully in the letter to the church at Pergamum. The Ephesian church, apparently in its zeal to preserve the integrity of its faith and root out evil, has become overzealous and forgotten that love is the first responsibility of Christians. The church is admonished to repent of this error or Christ will come in judgment on the church. To *remove your lampstand from its place* means that the people will no longer be a part of the body of Christ. As in all the letters, a closing promise is given to those who conquer, that is, the faithful believers. The promises in all the letters are variations of the same theme—the faithful are assured of participation in the kingdom of God. The *paradise* imagery in v. 7 is found in many apocalyptic writings. The world to come will be a restored and transformed Garden of Eden where the faithful will enjoy a blessed existence.

2:8-11. Smyrna. Like Ephesus, SMYRNA was an important seaport, located approximately thirty-five miles north of Ephesus. It was a city loyal to Rome. In 195 B.C.E. the city erected a temple to the goddess Roma and in 26 C.E. was given the right to build a temple in honor of the emperor TIBERIUS. Nothing is known of the beginnings of Christianity in Smyrna. During the reign of Trajan (98–117 C.E.), IGNATIUS, bishop of ANTIOCH, was martyred. On his way to Rome to be executed, Ignatius stayed in Smyrna, and later on the journey wrote a letter back to the church there and one to Polycarp, bishop of Smyrna. Around 156 C.E. Polycarp himself suffered the fate of martyrdom (see POLYCARP, MARTYRDOM OF). Christ issues no criticisms of the church at Smyrna, only encouraging and extolling the Christians there. Although outwardly poor and afflicted, they are rich in faith and in spirit. The church is suffering persecution from Jews in Smyrna, who because of their attacks on God's people no longer deserve to be called Jews but *a synagogue of Satan*. This statement should not be generalized to mean that John condemns all Jewish people. His harsh words here are aimed only at those who were persecuting the church. John warns the church at Smyrna that more persecution is to be expected. They are to remain faithful, however, even if martyrdom is required. The faithful will receive eternal life, symbolized by the *crown of life*. In Greek athletic contests, the victors were awarded a crown or wreath. To be exempted from *the second death* is another metaphor for ETERNAL LIFE (cf. 20:6, 14).

2:12-17. Pergamum. The capital of the Roman province of Asia, PERGAMUM was home to numerous temples, among them the spectacular temple to ZEUS and the famous ASCLEPION, devoted to Asclepius, the god of healing. Pergamum was an important center for the imperial cult also, having been the first city in the province of Asia to erect a temple to the deified Augustus. The references to *Satan's throne* and *where Satan lives* (v. 13) likely refer to the imperial cult, although some commentators see them as references to the temples of Zeus or Asclepius. The Christians in Pergamum are commended for their faithfulness even in the face of martyrdom. Strong in resisting this external threat, they have been weak in resisting internal threats to their faith. Some in their group have accepted the false teaching of BALAAM, a Mesopotamian diviner who was blamed for leading the Israelites into idolatry and sexual immorality (see Num 22–25, 31). The Nicolaitans at Pergamum are accused of a similar heresy. They eat food sacrificed to idols and practice FORNICATION. They were likely libertine Christians, similar to those in CORINTH (1 Cor 8–10), who believed it was acceptable to eat meat that had been ritually slaughtered and offered to pagan gods or even to the emperor. Whether fornication here is to be understood literally as sexual immorality or figuratively for participation in pagan cults (as often in the Hebrew Bible) is unclear. The faithful will receive MANNA and a white stone. In some Jewish traditions the miracle of the manna in the wilderness (Exod 16:13-36) was expected to be repeated in the messianic age. White stones were used to indicate acquittal in a jury trial and also served as admission tickets to certain events. Either meaning could apply here.

2:18-29. Thyatira. THYATIRA was the least important of the seven cities whose churches are sent messages in Revelation. LYDIA, the dealer of purple cloth whom PAUL met in PHILIPPI (Acts 16:11-15), was originally from Thyatira. The city was home to a large number of trade and craft guilds, organizations that served both social and religious functions. The church at Thyatira is praised highly for its works and for its increasing faithfulness. Like the church at Pergamum, the Thyatirans have not been diligent enough, however, in resisting false teachings and practices. A woman referred to as *Jezebel* (cf. the stories of JEZEBEL in 1–2 Kings) was serving as a prophet and teacher in the church. Her practices were similar to those of the Nicolaitans at Pergamum. Perhaps she was claiming that Christians could participate in the religious rituals and practices of the trade guilds without compromising their faith. Having been warned previously, perhaps by John, she has persisted in her practices. Now she and her followers will be punished by God. The *bed* upon which the woman is to be thrown (v. 22) is likely a sickbed. *Adultery* here is almost certainly figurative. The woman and her followers may have claimed to be so "spiritual" and so in touch with the supernatural world that they could fathom even *'the deep things of Satan'* (v. 24). On the other hand, this phrase may be John's sarcastic parody of their claim to be in touch with the deep mysteries of God. In language borrowed from Ps 2, the faithful are promised that they will triumph over evil and rule with Christ, *the morning star* (v. 28; cf. 22:16).

3:1-6. Sardis. The city of SARDIS had once been the capital of the ancient kingdom of Lydia and a wealthy city. Under Roman rule it was still a prosperous commercial center but did not match its former glory. Sardis was located on an almost impregnable acropolis. On two occasions in its history, however, the city had been conquered due to the lack of diligence on the part of its defenders. John may be alluding to these events in the city's past when he tells the church that it must *wake up* (vv. 2-3) and be diligent in its work. The church in Sardis receives only mild praise (v. 4). The majority of the message to the church is an admonition to wake up and be more alive. The church suffers from lethargy and apathy. Outwardly it appears vital, but its inward condition is critical. The church is on the point of death. If the church does not change, then Christ will come in judgment on them. Their lack of watchfulness will prove disastrous, for Christ *will come like a thief* (cf. Matt 24:42-44; 1 Thes 5:2). The faithful at Sardis will be clothed in white garments, a symbol of purity, and their names will not be removed from *the book of life*. Ancient cities kept registries of their citizens. The book of life is the list of heavenly citizens (cf. Exod 32:32; Dan 12:1). The promise of Christ to confess the name of the faithful before God echoes a similar saying in the Gospels (cf. Matt 10:32; Luke 12:8).

3:7-13. Philadelphia. Founded in the second century B.C.E. by either Attalus II Philadelphus or his older

brother Eumenes II (who succeeded one another as kings of Pergamum), the city of PHILADELPHIA and the surrounding area were subject to frequent earthquakes. In 17 C.E. Philadelphia (as well as Sardis) suffered major destruction from an earthquake. Philadelphia, like Smyrna, was visited by Ignatius on his way to martyrdom and the church there received a letter from Ignatius. The *key of David* imagery is borrowed from Isa 22:22. Here, Christ, as the holder of the key, grants or withholds entrance into the KINGDOM OF GOD. The church at Philadelphia receives no condemnation, only commendation, exhortation, and promise. The *open door* (v. 8) provided by Christ leads to God. Access to God is at the heart of the struggle for this church. The local Jews were perhaps denying the validity of the Christians' approach to God and excluding them from the synagogues (v. 9). The words of Christ offer them assurance that they do indeed have access to God, an access that cannot be denied. Even their Jewish opponents will eventually have to admit that the Christians are indeed beloved by God. The faithful will be preserved from the *hour of trial that is coming*, a reference to the eschatological woes that will come in judgment upon the earth. These cataclysmic events are described in detail in the remainder of the book. The conqueror will become *a pillar*, that is, will have a secure place in the presence of God.

3:14-22. Laodicea. Located in the Lycus River valley, the city of LAODICEA was founded by Antiochus II around the middle of the third century B.C.E. and named after his wife Laodice. Because of its location at an important crossroads, Laodicea became a major commercial center. The church at Laodicea is mentioned in Col 4:13-16. Nothing worthy of praise is found among the Laodicean Christians. They receive only criticism from Christ, who condemns them for being ineffective, describing them as neither cold nor hot. This imagery was likely suggested by the beneficial hot springs at nearby Hierapolis and the pure, cold water at COLOSSAE. Laodicea, on the other hand, was plagued with a bad water supply that was both lukewarm and foul. The emetic quality of the water at Laodicea provides the background for the description of Christ who is nauseated by the Laodiceans and spits (or vomits) them from his mouth (v. 16). Although the Laodiceans think they are successful and self-sufficient, they are in reality *wretched, pitiable, poor, blind, and naked* (v.17). To correct their bankrupt spiritual condition, the Laodiceans must turn to Christ. The offer of white robes, symbols of PURITY, is particularly appropriate at Laodicea for the city was famous for its clothing industry, and particularly for its black wool. The salve for their eyes likewise draws upon local information. Laodicea was famous for an eye salve manufactured there. The memorable image of Christ knocking at the door and inviting those inside to eat with him is a promise of Christ's presence, both now and particularly at the messianic BANQUET in the coming age. Those who conquer are promised a share in Christ's reign in the coming kingdom (cf. 22:5).

The Heavenly Throne Room, 4:1–5:14

Chapter 4 begins a new section in the Apocalypse. Whereas chaps. 2 and 3 dealt primarily with the immediate concerns of John's readers, the remainder of the book, while still addressing the first-century situation, is more eschatological in orientation. A characteristic of many apocalypses is the otherworldly journey in which the author claims to have been taken away to another domain (heaven, the underworld, the extremes of the earth) and shown the secrets of those places. Chapter 4 begins in that fashion, but the motif of a journey is not carried through. John's "visit" to the heavenly regions is a visionary experience and not a physical journey.

4:1-11. The throne of God. The open door (cf. 3:8) leads to God's dwelling place. God and his throne are described in images drawn from Ezekiel's vision of the throne-chariot of God (Ezek 1–2; cf. Dan 7 and Enoch's vision of God's throne room in 1 Enoch 14:8-24). The vision is intended to overwhelm and awe the reader with a sense of the majesty and mysteriousness of God. The scene serves as a forceful reminder that God, and not the Roman emperor or any other power, is sovereign over the universe. God, and God alone, is worthy of worship. The *twenty-four elders* seated on thrones constitute the heavenly council. Who they represent is not clear. The most popular suggestion is that they represent the twelve patriarchs of Israel and the twelve disciples of Jesus. The *sea of glass, like crystal* (v. 6) likely draws from the mythological imagery of the sea as representative of chaos, the untamed part of creation, threatening to overcome the created order. Here the sea is still a potential threat, but it has been subdued (the sea is smooth like crystal, instead of turbulent). In the *new heaven* of chap. 21, the sea no longer exists. The *four living creatures* (John has creatively transformed Ezekiel's imagery) lead the heavenly entourage in continual worship of God. Liturgical elements are prevalent in Revelation.

5:1-14. The lamb and the scroll. John then sees *a scroll* in the hand of God. The SCROLL is sealed to guarantee its authenticity and to keep secret its contents. The scroll contains the destiny of the world, the purposes and plans of God for all creation (cf. Ezek 2:9-10; Dan 10:21). As in many apocalyptic writings, in Revelation the course of history is already determined. The heavenly council is at an impasse because no one in the universe has been found who is able to break the seven seals and open the scroll. The dramatic tension of the scene is heightened by the reaction of John, who begins to weep because no one is *worthy to open the scroll*. Then one of the elders informs him that indeed there is one who can open the scroll—the Messiah, described as the Lion of the tribe of JUDAH (Gen 49:9) and the Root of David (Isa 11:1, 10).

Christ stands among the elders as a slain *Lamb*. Whether the specific referent for this metaphor is the sacrificial lamb of the Jewish cultus, the PASSOVER lamb, or the imagery of Isa 53, sacrifice is certainly a part of the message of this slaughtered Lamb figure. But there is a deeper meaning in the imagery. The slain Lamb is the crucified Christ, that is, the martyred Christ. This Lamb is more than victim, however. He is also a powerful, conquering Lamb, similar to the great horned sheep in *1 Enoch* 90:9-42. In fact, as the book of Revelation emphasizes, martyrdom is the means of conquering for both Christ and his followers. The *seven horns and seven eyes* on the Lamb emphasize his strength and wisdom—all-powerful and all-knowing. When the Lamb takes the scroll, the twenty-four elders and the four living creatures fall down in worship before him and once more break forth in song, praising the Lamb for the redemption he has effected for those *from every tribe and language and people and nation* (v. 9). Like the Israelites in Exod 19:6, the redeemed community is to be *a kingdom and priests serving our God* (v. 10). Soon the twenty-four elders and four living creatures are joined by a countless multitude of angels singing in full voice a resounding chorus of praise to the Lamb. Next the whole universe joins in the doxology of adoration and praise, not just for the Lamb but for *the one seated on the throne* as well. Christ is not just the agent of God, but is one with God. For that reason the worship and honor that are due God are appropriate for the Lamb as well.

The Seven Seals, 6:1–8:5

The Lamb proceeds to open the seals on the scroll one by one, unleashing a series of destructive events on the earth. Series of cataclysms such as these are a stock element of many apocalyptic writings (cf. 2 Esdr 4:51–5:13; 6:11-28; 8:63–9:13; 2 Bar 27:1-15; *TMos* 10:4-6; Mark 13:3-27 par.). Often called the eschatological woes, these events are presented as signs of the end times and serve as a part of God's punishment of the earth. As mentioned earlier, the events associated with the seven seals, as well as the other calamities in the book, should not be taken literally, nor assumed to be presented in chronological order. The destructive punishments unleashed by the seven trumpets and seven bowls are different representations of the same eschatological occurrences.

The First Six Seals, 6:1-17

6:1-8. The first four seals. The opening of the first four seals lets loose on the earth the four horsemen of death and destruction, one of the most memorable of the images in the entire Apocalypse. The symbolism of the riders on four different colored horses (*white, red, black,* and *pale green*) is adapted from Zech 1:8-11 (four horsemen are sent out by God to patrol the earth) and Zech 6:1-8 (chariots with four different colored horses are sent out over the earth). The first four seals are opened with a dramatic flourish—the seal is opened and one of the four living creatures cries, *"Come!"* The first rider, on *a white horse,* symbolizes warfare and conquering. White is an appropriate color, since victorious military commanders often rode a white horse in a triumphant procession. "Wars and rumors of wars" (Mark 13:7) are often associated with the end times. When the second seal is opened, a rider on *a red horse,* symbolizing violence and bloodshed, marches across the stage of history, leaving in its path disorder, violent death, and the absence of peace. The opening of the third seal brings forth the rider on *a black horse,* representing famine. The prices for the wheat and the barley are so exorbitant that the average person could not afford to buy food. Luxury items, olive oil and wine, would not be affected however. While the poor starve, the wealthy can continue their indulgent, selfish lifestyle. The fourth rider appears on *a pale green horse.* He is identified as *Death* (the Gk. word can also mean "pestilence") and is accompanied by *Hades,* the place of the dead. Together they wreak destruction upon the earth in a variety of forms (cf. Ezek 5:15-17; 14:21). Their destruction is not complete, however, for they kill only a fourth of the inhabitants of the earth.

6:9-17. The fifth and sixth seals. The opening of the fifth seal reveals to John the souls of the martyrs under the heavenly altar. Their location under the altar derives from their lives having been poured out as a sacrifice. The cry of the martyrs (*How long?*) is a cry for justice, for divine vindication. The cry is both one of personal vengeance and a cry for God to avenge the cause of justice and righteousness. How long will the forces of evil continue to dominate? How long will God allow the people of God to suffer? In outward appearances, the death of the martyrs seemed in vain. Their God was powerless to save them. The forces of evil had conquered. The prayer of the martyrs is that God will reverse the judgment of the world so that the purpose of their dying, as well as the sovereignty of God, might be revealed. The martyrs are each given *a white robe,* symbols of purification and victory, and told to wait until the number of martyrs would be complete. This idea of a predetermined number of righteous who must die before the end arrives is found in other apocalyptic writings (cf. *1 Enoch* 47:3-4; 2 Esdr 4:33-37). The deaths of the martyrs are not meaningless. Their deaths help fulfill the predetermined number and thus hasten the coming of the end when God's justice will be established.

A series of new cataclysms breaks forth when the sixth seal is opened. Described in traditional apocalyptic language, the cosmic disturbances and catastrophes bring judgment upon all the earth, particularly upon the rich and the powerful (v. 15). The punishment is so severe that the people cry out for mercy, asking who is able to withstand such judgment.

Interlude, 7:1-17

Before the seventh seal is opened, the action pauses. In the midst of all the punishment and judgment, John stops to give a word of assurance to God's people. The two visions that comprise this interlude reassure the faithful that they will be saved from the punishments that will affect the earth.

7:1-8. The sealing of the 144,00. vision John sees four angels hold back the winds that are set to unleash destruction on the earth. Another angel commands them to delay their punishment until God's servants have been given a mark on their foreheads for protection. Ezekiel 9:3-4 is the source for this imagery of a mark on the forehead for protection (cf. also the mark on the doorposts that saved the people of God from the plague of the death angel in Exod 12:21-32). Those who are thus protected comprise a throng of 144,000, with 12,000 taken from each of the twelve tribes of Israel. The number 144,000 should be understood figuratively. As a multiple of 12 and 10, both of which often symbolized completeness, 144,000 also represented completeness. But who comprises this complete group? Although some interpreters have argued that the 144,000 are Jews or Jewish Christians, in Revelation neither of these groups receives preferential treatment. Just as the numerical size of the group should not be understood literally, neither should the description of the group as being drawn from the twelve tribes. Instead the imagery depicts the church as the new people of God, the new Israel (cf. Jas 1:1). Although it is possible that the groups in the two visions both symbolize the complete number of God's people, the 144,000 more likely represent a complete subgroup—the martyrs (see the further descriptions of this group in 14:1-5). John gives special attention to them because they must bear the ultimate witness to their faith.

7:9-17. The great multitude. In contrast to the 144,000 in the first vision, the people who comprise the group in the second vision are too numerous for anyone to count. Whereas the first group was solely martyrs, the second group includes all the people of God, *from every nation, from all tribes and peoples and languages* (v. 9). They have *come out of the great ordeal* (v. 14), that is, the persecution that precedes the end. In a paradoxical metaphor, John says that they have washed their robes *in the blood of the Lamb* and made them white. Christ's sacrificial death has purified the people and rendered them righteous. This innumerable crowd of the faithful is in heaven, where they wave palm branches, symbols of joy and celebration, and sing a song of praise to God. Once more the heavenly chorus composed of the angels, the twenty-four elders, and the four living creatures join in with their doxology to God. The interlude ends with a comforting description of the existence awaiting the faithful. Neither hunger, nor thirst, nor scorching heat will afflict them for the Lamb will care for them. The Lamb, paradoxically, will be their shepherd who provides for their needs. Suffering and pain will be absent, for *God will wipe away every tear from their eyes* (cf. 21:3-4).

The Seventh Seal, 8:1-5

A climactic moment has been reached. The seventh seal is opened. One expects a final vision of what is to come. Instead, a short period of silence follows the opening of the last seal. The silence is not only for dramatic effect, but also indicates reverence, awe, and anticipation. The opening of the seventh seal does not yield the expected end but inaugurates a new series of woes, the seven trumpets. Before the trumpet series begins, another angel appears. Standing before the heavenly altar, the angel mixes incense with the prayers of the people and offers them on the altar. Although not restricted to them, the prayers of the martyrs under the altar in 6:9-11 would certainly be included in this offering. The prayers of the people are prayers for justice and the coming of the kingdom of God. *The smoke of the incense, with the prayers of the saints, rose before God* (v. 4), indicating that God hears the people's prayers. The angel takes fire from the altar and casts it down upon the earth, resulting in thunder, lightning, and an earthquake. The prayers of the people have been effective. The judgment on the earth has begun, as the blowing of the seven trumpets will make clear.

The Seven Trumpets, 8:6–11:19

The blowing of *the seven trumpets* sets forth a new series of eschatological woes on the earth. What was begun with the opening of the seven seals is portrayed here in a different set of images. The two series overlap rather than succeed one another. There is a progression from the seals to the trumpets, however. Whereas the destruction wrought by the opening of the seals was basically limited to humanity, the destruction from the trumpet blasts affects the entire universe: the earth (8:7), the oceans (8:8-9), fresh water (8:10-11), the heavenly bodies (8:12), and persons (9:1-20). A further advance is noted in the extent of the destruction of human lives. When the fourth seal is opened, Death and Hades kill one-fourth of the population. In contrast, the trumpet punishments affect one-third of the world. Again, one must remember that this is poetic, not mathematical, language. The numerical statements convey that the destruction is not yet complete. The trumpet judgments are dependent on the Egyptian PLAGUES in Exod 7–10. Plagues of hail and fire (8:7), water turning to blood (8:9), darkness (8:12), and locusts (9:1-11) match the Egyptian plagues.

The First Six Trumpets, 8:6–9:21

8:6-11. The first three trumpets. The first trumpet blast sends fire that scorches the earth, affecting a third of the plant life. The second trumpet causes *something like a great mountain* (8:8) to fall into the sea, turning the water to blood. Not only are the fish in the sea killed but ships are also destroyed. The plague from the third trumpet blast is an extension of the second one. Whereas the second trumpet blast affected only the salt water, the third affects fresh water, turning them poisonous. *Wormwood,* the name of the star that poisons the water, is a popular name for any of several related plants. The wormwood mentioned several places in the Bible is probably a small shrub with hairy, gray leaves that was known for its extremely bitter taste. This latter characteristic explains why in the Bible "wormwood" is used figuratively for bitterness and sorrow. The plant is not actually poisonous, but John intensifies its effect.

8:12-13. The fourth trumpet. The results from the blowing of the fourth trumpet provide a good example of why the imagery in Revelation cannot be taken at face value. If a third of the sun and moon were darkened, then the length of a day and a night would not correspondingly be shortened by one third. John's imagery is not limited by reality or scientific accuracy, however. Between the sounding of the fourth and fifth trumpets, an announcement is made by an eagle flying through the sky. The announcement serves as a preview of what is to come and as a warning to the inhabitants of the earth. The first three trumpets have unleashed their punishments, but even more terrifying are the calamities yet to come. This announcement is a dramatic technique that heightens the suspense of John's vision.

9:1-11. The fifth trumpet. After the eagle warning, the fifth angel blows his trumpet and a fallen star takes a key and opens the bottomless pit. The star is an angel, as is often the case in APOCALYPTIC LITERATURE (cf. *1 Enoch* 86, 88). *The bottomless pit,* or abyss, is the place where demons or fallen angels were imprisoned. (Cf. *1 Enoch* 1–36, known as the "Book of the Watchers." This work, elaborating on the tradition in Gen 6:1-4, describes the rebellion against God of a group of angels. As punishment they are consigned to the abyss, described as a desert place and a place of burning fire.) The pit is the reservoir of EVIL. When the shaft to the pit is opened, smoke billows out and blocks the sun. Out of the smoke comes a swarm of locusts who look *like horses equipped for battle* (v. 7). The imagery of destructive horse-like locusts is drawn from Joel 1:1–2:11. The plague of locusts in Joel is also accompanied by darkness throughout the land. Locusts were (and still are) a devastating terror in the Near East. Swarms of locusts can destroy an entire

region due to their numbers and their voracious appetite. John is even more creative than Joel in his description of the locusts. Not only do they have the appearance of horses, they wear

> *what looked like crowns of gold; their faces were like human faces, their hair like women's hair, and their teeth like lions' teeth; they had scales like iron breastplates, and the noise of their wings was like the noise of many chariots with horses rushing into battle.* (vv. 7-9)

The surreal locusts of John's vision are told not to harm the vegetation. Instead their task is to torture the wicked of the earth, those *who do not have the seal of God on their foreheads* (v. 4). They do not kill, but only inflict agonizing torture with their scorpion tails for five months, a limited amount of time. These demonic locust figures are grotesque and frightening representations of evil. They symbolize war, destruction, and chaos, but on a much grander scale than anything seen before. These evil forces, released in the last days, serve God's purposes by inflicting pain and punishment on the wicked. Evil itself, however, after this final resurgence will eventually be defeated by God. The idea of the last assault of evil is given in a different form in 19:11–20:15. The name of the leader of the locust monsters is given in Hebrew (*Abaddon*) and in Greek (*Apollyon*). The word *Abaddon* means "destruction" and is used figuratively in the Hebrew Bible for death or the place of the dead (see Job 26:6; 28:22). *Apollyon* is from a Greek word meaning "to destroy." (Some scholars have seen here a reference also to Apollo, whose symbol was a locust and of whom Domitian claimed to be an incarnation. See Beasley-Murray 1974, 162–63.)

9:12-21. The sixth trumpet. The sixth trumpet, which is the second woe foretold by the eagle, brings forth another invading army, cavalry from the *river Euphrates.* This woe is set in motion by the command of a voice from the heavenly altar, the place where the prayers of the people have been poured out (8:3-5) and from underneath which the cries of the martyrs have been heard (6:9-11). The sixth trumpet, then, is in part a response to the prayers of God's people. It is part of God's punishment of the wicked and the vindication of the righteous. As with the earlier punishments, this one is limited. Only a third of humankind is killed. The EUPHRATES River was the eastern boundary of the ROMAN EMPIRE. On the other side were the Parthians, the dreaded enemy of the Romans. The Parthian cavalry may have provided the rudimentary image for John, but John's army is no earthly force. Like the locust plague of the fifth trumpet, the cavalry is a grotesque, supernatural force that will wreak destruction. Their appearance is frightening; their effect is devastating. John envisions God using these demonic agents to carry out God's will. The angels who lead the destruction are *bound* (v. 14), that is, they are part of the fallen angels who were bound and thrown into the pit according to apocalyptic writings (see comment on 9:1).

The EXODUS motif that is so prevalent in Revelation explains the statement that, even after these plagues, the remainder of the people do not repent. The people of the world will follow in the footsteps of the PHARAOH. They will continue their idolatrous and rebellious ways.

Interlude, 10:1–11:13

As was the case between the sixth and seventh seals, so between the sixth and seventh trumpet blasts John inserts an interlude to provide reassurance to the faithful that they will not be harmed by the eschatological woes. This interlude, like the earlier one, contains two visions.

10:1-11. The mighty angel with the little scroll. John sees a mighty angel coming down and standing with one foot *on the sea* and one *on the land*. The physical description of the angel owes much to the description in Dan 10 of a similar heavenly being and the description of God in Ezek 1:26-28. This scene draws also upon the vision in Dan 12 in which two angels appear to Daniel, "one standing on this bank of the stream and one on the other" (12:5). The angel speaks like a roaring lion, causing the seven thunders to break forth. The seven thunders deliver a message that John is able to understand and that he is about to write down when he is told to seal up the message, that is, keep it secret. The reader is left puzzled and curious about the contents of the message from the seven thunders. The secrecy motif heightens the drama, but it plays a more important role. The refusal to reveal the message of the seven thunders is a way of saying that even such revelatory visions as John experienced and wrote down for his readers are incomplete. God's purposes and plans are not all revealed, because God is beyond full comprehension by mortals. The ineffable MYSTERY of God remains intact.

The angel *raised his right hand to heaven and swore by him who lives forever and ever* (vv. 5-6; cf. Dan 12:7) that there would be no more delay. The

time for the fulfillment of God's purposes is near. John believed that he and the church of his time were living in the last days. The final onslaught of evil was breaking forth upon the world. Soon God would act decisively and would triumph over the evil forces. This word would have been a message of great comfort to John's readers who were facing persecution and perhaps martyrdom. The cry "How long?" has been answered: "No more delay!"

The voice from heaven speaks once more to John, commanding him to take the open scroll from the angel's hand and *eat it*. A similar episode is reported by Ezekiel as part of his experience of being called to be a prophet (2:8–3:3). For John, eating the scroll is a reinforcement of his commissioning to the role of the prophet. The scroll is *sweet as honey*, but makes his *stomach . . . bitter* (v. 10). This scroll, like the scroll in chaps. 4–5, contains God's plan for all creation, the message John is to make known as a prophet of God. Eating the scroll is symbolic of taking in the message, of "consuming" God's word, so that God's message is now John's message. The scroll is both bitter and sweet, because both judgment and mercy, punishment and blessing, are a part of the divine plan. A close parallel with the scroll is found in Dan 12. There Daniel is told to keep the book sealed "until the time of the end" (12:4). Now, however, the book is unsealed because *there will be no more delay* (v. 6). The long-awaited time of God's vindication has arrived.

11:1-13. The measuring of the Temple and the two witnesses. The second vision of the interlude begins with John being given a measuring rod and told to go and measure the Temple. Only the inner courts are to be measured. The measuring is a sign of protection. Whereas the inner court is preserved, the outer court will be trampled by the nations. Many scholars have postulated that this was an earlier prophecy that was put forth by ZEALOT defenders of Jerusalem prior to its destruction by the Romans in 70 C.E. After the outer part of the Temple was captured by the Romans, the defenders barricaded themselves in the inner courts. If the suggestion by some interpreters is correct, this prophecy would have been a prediction by the Zealot defenders that even though the Romans might trample the outer courts, God would not allow the inner sanctuary to fall to them. Sadly, they were in error. John has perhaps taken this earlier prophecy and adapted it for his purposes. The Temple has already been destroyed by the time John writes, so his concern is not with the actual Temple in Jerusalem. Rather, for John the people of God are now the Temple. The church is what is marked for protection. This vision then serves as a word of encouragement and assurance to the faithful. The unrighteous will be "trampled" (v. 2) during the time of the eschatological woes, but God's people will not be harmed. The period of the trampling will be forty-two months, three and one-half years. In Daniel three and a half years (or "times") is the predicted length of time before the end arrives (7:25; 12:7). The figure should not be pressed. As half of seven, a number for completeness or totality, three and one half represents incompleteness, a short period of time.

The introduction of the *two witnesses* (v. 3) seems disconnected to the vision of the Temple. The abruptness of their appearance supports the contention that the measuring of the Temple is an earlier tradition that John has reworked. The two witnesses are given authority to prophesy for 1260 days (three and one half years), the same amount of time mentioned in v. 2. To prophesy is to proclaim God's message to the world, to be faithful witnesses of God and Christ. The content of their message is likely indicated by their garb, *sackcloth*. Since sackcloth was worn as a sign of penitence, the prophecy of the two witnesses is a call to repentance. The two witnesses are further described as *the two olive trees and the two lampstands that stand before the Lord* (v. 4). In Zech 4 the image of two olive trees is used for ZERUBBABEL the governor and JOSHUA the high priest, both of whom are viewed as messianic figures. The two olive trees provide oil for the lampstand. John applies both images, the olive trees and the lampstands, to the two witnesses. For John, however, the two witnesses are not messianic figures. They are further described in terms reminiscent of ELIJAH and MOSES (11:6; cf. 1 Kgs 17:1; Exod 7:8–11:10).

The two witnesses must give the ultimate testimony—their lives—when they are attacked and killed by the beast *from the bottomless pit*. This beast John will describe more fully in the coming chapters. The place where they are killed is *prophetically called Sodom and Egypt, where also their Lord was crucified* (v. 8). Jerusalem, like Sodom and Egypt, has become for John a symbol of rebellion against God. Jerusalem is representative of the entire world that rejects God and the prophets of God. John's portrayal of Jerusalem as the place where the prophets are killed is not an anti-Jewish statement. In the Hebrew Bible, Jerusalem is often condemned for its disobedience to God and its rejection of God's spokespersons. John is simply

adapting that tradition here. Of course, for him that condemnation of Jerusalem is even more pointed because Jerusalem was the place of Jesus' martyrdom. Even after death, the two witnesses are treated shamefully, their bodies allowed to lie on the streets to be the subject of taunts and ridicule.

God will not allow his prophets to die in vain, however. After a short span of time (*three and a half days*), they are resurrected and ascend into heaven in the sight of their enemies. Following their ascension, a great earthquake strikes the city, killing seven thousand people. Those who are left *were terrified and gave glory to the God of heaven* (v. 13). The witness of the two martyrs produces results. Their testimony in word and in blood leads to repentance by the people.

The Seventh Trumpet, 11:14-19

Verse 14 serves as a reminder of the action of the work prior to the interlude. The lengthy interlude had interrupted the three woes that were announced by the eagle (8:13). Verse 14 ties the earlier section with what is to follow. The third woe, though announced, is not described. It is hinted at in the first part of v. 18 (*the nations raged, but your wrath has come*). The seventh trumpet blast brings the action to an end. God's purposes have been fulfilled. The heavenly voices declare the completion of God's plan when they announce, *The kingdom of the world has become the kingdom of our Lord and of his Messiah* (v. 15). God's reign no longer lies in the future, but is a present reality. In a way, the seventh trumpet blast is anticlimactic. After all the destruction and punishment leading up to the last days, John provides no description of God's new order. It is completed. Instead of a picture of the kingdom of God, John lets his readers hear the celebration that takes place over God's victory. The twenty-four elders sing a song of triumph, saying, *We give you thanks, Lord God Almighty, who are and who were, for you have taken your great power and begun to reign* (v. 17). God is no longer described as the one who is and who was and who is to come. The last element is no longer needed. God has already come; the future has become the present. John could have ended his message here. The consummation of the kingdom has been achieved. John has more to reveal, however. He will present new images of punishment and salvation, eschatological woes and eternal reward.

Chapter 11 ends with a brief glimpse into the heavenly Temple in which the ark of the covenant is seen. The ARK had sat in the Holy of Holies in Solomon's

Temple, a visual reminder of the presence of God in the midst of the people. The ark of the covenant was probably carried away or destroyed when the Babylonians captured Jerusalem in the sixth century B.C.E. When God's kingdom has arrived in its fullness, John sees the ark in the heavenly Temple, a symbol of God's presence with the people.

The Great Conflict, 12:1–14:20

Chapters 12–14 portray the life-and-death struggle of the church with the evil forces aligned against it. For John and his readers, evil is incarnated primarily in the Roman emperor and his claims to divinity. This confrontation with the imperial cult is the major focus of this section. But John realizes that the conflict he and other Christians are facing is larger than what it appears. John sees this struggle in the context of the great cosmic conflict between the forces of good and evil. The evil powers have always rebelled against the sovereignty of God and attempted to thwart God's purposes. The suffering of the Christians of John's day was not isolated or insignificant. John paints their trials on a cosmic canvas, one that stretches back in history to primeval times. The struggles in which the church is engaged is simply another chapter in the ancient story of chaos versus order, obedience versus disobedience, rebellion versus loyalty. By giving his readers a new perspective on their ordeal John gave meaning to their suffering. Their persecution and martyrdom were not in vain. By their patient endurance and faithful witness, they were contributing to the overthrow and defeat of the powers of evil. John also offers assurance to his readers by revealing to them the ultimate outcome of this cosmic conflict of which they are a part.

The Vision of the Great Dragon, 12:1-18

Chapter 12 draws heavily upon ancient mythology for its images, adapting a popular cosmic combat MYTH found in many cultures of the ancient world. The closest parallel to the story told by John is the Greek version of the myth which tells of the birth of Apollo, son of Zeus and Leto. Python, the great dragon, pursues the pregnant goddess Leto, seeking to kill the unborn Apollo and his mother. Leto is carried away to safety to an island where Poseidon, god of the sea, hides her by sinking the island under the sea. When Python's search is unsuccessful, he finally gives up and goes away. The island is raised and Leto gives birth to Apollo, who goes and kills Python. John

adapts this universal myth to convey the story of the defeat of the forces of evil by Jesus. John's use of this myth may have been particularly significant for his readers who were confronted with the claims of the imperial cult. Several of the Roman emperors used this myth for their own propaganda purposes, presenting themselves in the role of Apollo, the destroyer of evil. John and his readers know otherwise, however. Christ, not the emperor, is the real victor over the malevolent forces of chaos, darkness, and wickedness. As such, Christ and not the emperor is the one worthy of obedience and worship.

12:1-6. The woman, the dragon, and the child. The woman is presented as the cosmic queen, *clothed with the sun, . . . the moon under her feet, and . . . [wearing] a crown of twelve stars* (the zodiac). The *great red dragon* has *seven heads and ten horns, and seven diadems on his heads* (v. 3). In the Babylonian story of creation TIAMAT, the monster of the deep, also has seven heads. LEVIATHAN, the serpent-like monster of chaos in Hebrew folk-lore, also had many heads (cf. Ps 74:14). The *ten horns* (cf. Dan 7:7) symbolize the monster's power, the crowns his dominion. He is a powerful figure, as evidenced by his knocking a third of the stars out of the heavens (a traditional motif in many of the ancient myths). The application of Ps 2:9 to the child—he *is to rule all the nations with a rod of iron* (v. 5)—identifies him as the Messiah. The dragon fails in his attempt to kill the child, who is snatched away and taken to God. In John's story the birth and ascension of Christ are compressed into a single event. The woman escapes to the wilderness and is protected there by God for 1,260 days, the same three-and-a-half-year period John has mentioned before (see 11:2-3).

12:7-12. Michael and the dragon. Verses 7-12 appear to be an insertion into the cosmic combat myth. In reality they contain simply another version of the same struggle. That John is adapting a Jewish story here is evidenced by the role played by MICHAEL. He is the hero of the story, the one who defeats the dragon and his angels. The story of the ouster from heaven of rebellious angels is found in several Jewish sources (cf. *1 Enoch* 6–16) and has been popularized in John Milton's *Paradise Lost*. The great dragon is identified as *that ancient serpent, who is called the Devil and Satan, the deceiver of the whole world* (v. 9). In the Hebrew Bible Satan (literally the "accuser" or "adversary") is not the leader of the forces of evil who are arrayed against God. Rather Satan is the accuser of the righteous, the "prosecuting attorney" who brings charges against God's people. In later nonbiblical Jewish writings, likely due to the influence of the Zoroastrian religion of Persia, Satan (or Belial, or Beliar, or Azazel, or Semyaza) begins to be seen as the leader of the demonic forces of evil. Satan is portrayed as the archenemy of God. That understanding of the role of Satan was taken over by NT writers and is evident in Revelation also (see SATAN IN THE NT).

The ancient Jewish myth that John is using would have portrayed Michael as the one who defeats Satan and casts him out of heaven. John alters that story. Satan has been overthrown *by the blood of the Lamb and by the word of their testimony* (v. 11), that is, the testimony of the martyrs. For John the defeat of Satan is not a primeval event, but one that occurs in the death and exaltation of Christ and continues in the faithful witness of the martyrs who give their lives for the sake of God. John is saying to the persecuted church that their deaths have meaning. The faithful are contributing to the overthrow of the forces of evil. Their deaths may look like defeat, but John gives them a new vision in which death is victory.

12:13-18. The pursuit of the woman. Thrown out of heaven, Satan turns his attack upon the woman on earth. The woman, however, is given divine protection. She is *given the two wings of the great eagle* and carried off to the wilderness where she is protected during the coming period of trouble (cf. Exod 19:4, "I bore you on eagles' wings and brought you to myself"). Unable to defeat the woman, the dragon then goes off to make war on her children, the faithful witnesses (v. 17). The woman is a multivalent image. She is at the same time Mary (mother of Jesus), Israel (from whom the Messiah comes), the church, and the people of God of all ages, whose "children" are still being persecuted. John is adapting a universal myth here for his Christian message. Exact correspondence between the characters in the myth and the Christian story is not possible. One should not press for consistency in the role of the woman in the story.

The Two Beasts, 13:1-18

Whereas chap. 12 depicted the heavenly battle with Satan, chap. 13 reveals the earthly counterpart of that struggle. Thrown down to earth, the dragon stands poised to unleash his fury against God's faithful.

13:1-10. The beast from the sea. The first beast arises from the sea, the primordial realm of chaos and rebellion. The description of the beast is dependent on the four beasts from the sea in Dan 7, whose characteristics are merged into this one beast. John makes clear the source of this beast's power: *the dragon gave it his power and his throne and great authority* (v. 2). In awe and fear of this great beast, the people follow after the beast and worship him. Who is this beast? Even though the term is not used in Revelation, he is the ANTICHRIST, the eschatological opponent of Christ and his followers (see Reddish 1990, 34.) The Antichrist has taken on a particular identity for John. As the clues John gives elsewhere make clear, the beast is the ROMAN EMPIRE, and particularly the emperors themselves (see chap. 17). The many heads symbolize the various emperors who have ruled over the empire. The statement that one of the heads of the beast *seemed to have received a death-blow, but its mortal wound had been healed* (v. 3) is a reference to the Nero *redivivus* myth. Nero occupied a special place in the minds of the Christians, for Nero had instigated the first persecution against Christians when he blamed the fire in Rome on them in 64 C.E. Later, Nero committed suicide by stabbing himself in the throat. The rumor soon spread, however, that Nero was not really dead or that he would come back to life and rule over the people again. By saying that this mortal wound had been healed, John is warning the church that Nero's persecution has returned in the present emperor, Domitian.

For forty-two months (three and a half years) the beast wages war against God's people. Without attributing evil to God, John states that the beast *was allowed to make war on the saints* (v. 7). Satan and his cohorts may have the upper hand at the moment, but ultimately God will assert control and the beast will be allowed to persecute the saints no longer. Those who succumb to the lures of the beast and worship it are the ones whose names are not written in *the book of life*, the register of the citizens of heaven (cf. 3:5). The last part of v. 10 is a refrain that sounds throughout the Apocalypse: *Here is a call for the endurance and faith of the saints*.

13:11-18. The beast from the earth. The second beast, also called *the false prophet* (19:20), is a beast from the land who deceives the people and enforces worship of the first beast. He performs SIGNS AND WONDERS like prophets of God, but he is a *false* prophet. Those who refuse to worship the first beast are killed. Those who comply, who pay homage to the first beast, receive a mark on their right hands or on their foreheads. This "mark of the beast," a parody of the sealing of the 144,000 in chap. 7, allows them to buy and sell in the marketplace. The mark of the beast requires wisdom, John says, for the number of the beast is the number of a person. That number is 666. The ancient practice of *gematria*, the assigning of numerical values to words, is at work here. In the ancient world, letters were used for numbers. (In our alphabet, A=1, B=2, C=3, etc.) One could easily convert a person's name into a number. Since the numerical value of several names could equal 666, the identification of the person John had in mind is not certain. The most likely referent for John's 666 number code, however, is Caesar Nero, whose name in Hebrew equals 666. The beast is not Nero, for he is dead. But Domitian, the current emperor, is a reincarnation of Nero. (Some commentators have argued for the symbolic meaning of 666. Since six is one less than seven, the perfect number, then 666 represents triple imperfection or evil.)

The background for this chapter is obviously emperor worship. The first beast who is worshiped represents the Roman emperor. Who, then, is the second beast? He represents everyone who encourages and supports emperor worship (local magistrates, imperial priests, provincial councils). By depicting the emperor and the promoters of the imperial cult as beasts who operate under the authority of the great dragon, John pulls back the curtain and reveals to his readers the true identity of those who are persecuting them. The imperial cult is an instrument of Satan, for it usurps the worship that belongs only to God.

Interlude, 14:1-20

Once more John pauses in the midst of scenes of suffering to offer words of encouragement and assurance. Twice already John has reassured his readers that the faithful will receive divine protection during the coming trials. This protection is protection from the effects of God's punishment, not protection from persecution and death. John is fearful that many of his Christian comrades may have to bear witness through death. Even if that happens, however, they can be assured that God will not abandon them. They will still share in God's new kingdom. That is the assurance that the marks of protection convey.

14:1-5. The Lamb and the redeemed. These verses reveal the ultimate destiny of the faithful. Chapter 13 portrayed the apparent defeat of God's people who died a martyr's death. The opening section of chap. 14 reverses that judgment, depicting the faithful not as defeated but as triumphant. John sees Christ (the Lamb) standing on Mt. Zion, the center of the messianic kingdom. With him are the 144,000 that were introduced in chap. 7. Like the heavenly chorus in 5:8-10, the 144,000 sing a new song of praise to God, a song that no one else could learn. While it is tempting to interpret the 144,000 as symbolic of all the redeemed of humanity, a closer reading of the description of them suggests that they are specifically the martyrs, the ones who have been the victims of the beasts in chap. 13. These with the Lamb *have not defiled themselves with women, for they are virgins* (v. 4). This description is figurative, not literal. One of the regulations for HOLY WAR required sexual abstinence before battle (cf. 1 Sam 21:4-5). John uses this requirement for ceremonial purity to symbolize moral and religious purity. The 144,000 have not been defiled by idolatry or by the enticements of the great whore of Babylon (chap. 17). They *follow the Lamb wherever he goes*, even unto death. They are described as *first fruits*. This is sacrificial language, appropriate for those who have sacrificed their lives for God. Finally, *in their mouth no lie was found*. The martyrs maintained their witness even under persecution, refusing to proclaim Caesar as lord.

14:6-13. The message of three angels. The central section of this chapter presents three angels who move across the stage, each proclaiming the coming judgment of God. The message of the first angel is a call to repentance and a warning of the impending judgment. The second angel issues a proleptic announcement of the fall of Babylon (Rome). The third angel pronounces judgment upon those who have succumbed to the power of the beast and its cult. Once more a call for the endurance of the saints is sounded (v. 12). The second beatitude of Revelation pronounces blessings upon those *who from now on die in the Lord* (v. 13). Those who are called to die as martyrs can face their ordeal with the knowledge of the glorious rest that awaits them. After death, they will no longer have to endure trials and persecutions.

14:14-20. The final judgment of God. This section depicts the final judgment of God in imagery that is borrowed from Joel 3:13. The first scene shows the harvesting of the earth, like wheat that is cut with a sickle (cf. Matt 13:24-30). John does not make clear whether this harvesting is a complete gathering of all people, the wicked for punishment and the righteous for rewards, or whether, like the second scene, this one portrays only the judgment of the unrighteous. Either of these options is preferable to the attempt by some commentators to argue that the first scene depicts only the ingathering of the faithful, whereas the second scene (vintage), portrays the punishment of the wicked. In Joel both images are used to show God's judgment against the wicked. In both scenes in chap. 14 an angel from the presence of God (*the temple . . . the altar*) gives the comand for the divine judgment to begin. The imagery of blood flowing *as high as a horse's bridle, for a distance of about two hundred miles* (v. 20) conveys the magnitude and severity of God's punishment on the wicked.

The Seven Bowl Plagues, 15:1–16:21

The seven seals and the seven trumpets have already disclosed the eschatological woes that are to strike the earth. John now introduces a different series, this one composed of seven bowls, that will present a different perspective on these calamities. Like the seven trumpet plagues, the bowl plagues are modeled after the PLAGUES on Egypt in the book of Exodus.

The Martyrs on the Heavenly Shore, 15:1-4

Verse 1 gives a brief announcement of the new series of seven plagues that are soon to break forth. These will be the last plagues, *for with them the wrath of God is ended* (v. 1). Before beginning the bowl plagues, John presents another vision of the faithful whom he sees standing beside *a sea of glass mixed with fire* (v. 2). This is the sea that stands before the throne of God (4:6). Here the sea also connotes the RED SEA of the Exodus tradition. As the Israelites traveled safely through the Red Sea and arrived in the Promised Land, so the faithful in John's vision have passed through their Red Sea (persecution and martyrdom) and now stand on heaven's shore. Moses and the Israelites sang a song of THANKSGIVING and praise after reaching the distant shore (Exod 15:1-18.) Likewise the victorious martyrs now sing *the song of Moses . . . and the song of the Lamb* (v. 3).

The Seven Angels with Bowls, 15:5-8

John sees seven angels who are to inflict the seven plagues come out of the heavenly Temple. Each is given a bowl containing the wrath of God that is to be poured out on the earth. The imagery of the bowls is likely a composite of two ideas from the Hebrew Bible. Bronze basins or bowls were used by the priests to carry away the ashes from the altar after sacrifices were offered (Exod 27:3). In John's vision the angels

who are given the bowls have just exited the Temple where the heavenly altar is located (cf. the angel with the censer at the altar in 8:3-5). The bowls are *full of the wrath of God* (v. 7). Several passages in the Hebrew Bible speak of the cup of God's wrath (Isa 51:17; Ps 75:8; Jer 25:15-29; 49:12) that God's enemies drink, symbolizing God's punishments on them.

The Pouring of the Seven Bowls, 16:1-21

16:1-7. The first three bowls. In response to a command by a voice from the Temple, the seven angels pour out their bowls of judgment on the earth. The bowl plagues are very similar to the trumpet plagues, both of which draw upon the plagues inflicted on Egypt. The pouring out of the first bowl results in painful sores on *those who had the mark of the beast and who worshiped its image* (v. 2). This plague is similar to the sixth Egyptian plague (Exod 9:8-12). The second and third bowl plagues, like the second and third trumpet plagues, affect first the sea and then the fresh water. Here both are turned to blood, which is seen as fitting because the wicked had *shed the blood of saints and prophets* and now they must drink blood (v. 6). John proclaims that God is a God of justice. The people deserve the punishment they receive. The altar (the angel attending the altar, or the souls of the martyrs under the altar?) agrees in the assessment that God's judgments are true and just. The result of the second bowl plague is more severe than the result of the second trumpet plague. With the latter, only one-third of the earth is affected. With the former, *every living thing in the sea died* (v. 3).

16:8-11. The fourth and fifth bowls. The pouring of the fourth bowl on the sun brings about a scorching heat on the earth. Like the Egyptian PHARAOH, the people are obstinate in their rebellion against God and refuse to repent. The first four plagues have already affected all parts of the cosmos (land, waters, sea, and the sun). The focus of the fifth plague is narrower than that of the previous four plagues. The fifth bowl is poured *on the throne of the beast*. The ROMAN EMPIRE receives special punishment because it is responsible for leading many people into idolatry. Reminiscent of the ninth plague on Egypt (Exod 10:21-29), the fifth bowl plague produces an agonizing darkness over the whole land. Once more John states that the people do not repent of their evil ways. Some people are so hardened against God that nothing is able to bring them to repentance.

16:12-16. The sixth bowl. The sixth bowl plague has many similarities with the sixth trumpet plague in 9:13-19. Both describe invading armies from across the Euphrates who invade the west. In both scenes John is making use of the Roman fear of a Parthian invasion. John sees *three foul spirits like frogs* (v. 13) coming out of the mouths of the dragon, the beast, and *the false prophet* (that is, the second beast). The imagery of the frogs comes from the second Egyptian plague (Exod 7:25–8:15) in which the land is overrun by an abundance of frogs. John has greatly modified the imagery, however. These are no ordinary frogs. They are demonic spirits who gather together the kings of the earth for the great eschatological battle. The place where they are assembled *is called Harmagedon* (v. 16, or, ARMAGEDDON). The name Harmagedon is likely derived from Hebrew words meaning "mountain of Megiddo." Megiddo was an important city guarding the pass through the JEZREEL Valley in Israel. Several important battles had been fought at Megiddo throughout Israel's history. Thus the name Megiddo would have connoted a battlefield for people familiar with Israel's past. John is not predicting a literal battle that is to take place at Megiddo. *Harmagedon* is figurative language. It symbolizes the final attempt by the forces of evil to defeat God. John does not give any description here of the confrontation. He will do that in a later chapter (19:11-21). Instead, he gives an admonition from Christ: *"See, I am coming like a thief! Blessed is the one who stays awake and is clothed, not going about naked and exposed to shame"* (v. 15). This call to watchfulness is a warning about being unprepared for the coming of Christ which will occur unexpectedly. The wise person will live in anticipation and preparedness.

16:17-21. The seventh bowl. The emptying of the seventh bowl into the air brings down the curtain on the eschatological drama. A loud voice from the Temple announces, *"It is done!"* (v. 17). A cataclysmic earthquake, accompanied by lightning and thunder, rips through the earth, destroying *the great city . . . and the cities of the nations* (v. 19). The great city is called *Babylon,* but in reality is Rome. It is singled out for special mention because of its role in the persecution of God's servants and its idolatrous and blasphemous claims. The following chapters will present a fuller description of the downfall of Rome. The plague of hail that also occurs when the seventh angel pours his bowl is a part of the Exodus motif that is so strong in this section of the Apocalypse.

The Fall of Babylon, 17:1–19:10

For John, Rome represented the ultimate rebellion against God. The divine claims of the emperor, the imperial cult, and the persecution of God's people were all components of Rome's sinfulness and resistance to God. John goes to great lengths in this section to expose the true character and identity of this "great city" and to show reactions both on earth and in heaven to the city's demise.

The Great Whore, 17:1-18

Invited by an angel to see the judgment that befalls the great city, John is carried away *in the spirit* (in a vision) into a wilderness. John introduces a new imagery for Rome. The city is portrayed as a *great whore* who rides on a scarlet beast *full of blasphemous names* who has *seven heads and ten horns.* The beast is the same as the one John described in 13:1-10 and represents the Roman Empire. The blasphemous names refer to the divine claims made for the emperors. The woman riding on the beast is dressed in luxurious clothes and adorned with expensive gold and jewels. In her hand she holds a golden cup full of filth, representing her idolatry and wickedness. To the world, Rome appeared to be a dazzling, enticing city. John unmasks the true identity of the city. It is a repulsive, drunken prostitute. Like prostitutes in ancient Rome who wore their name on a headband, the woman bears her name stamped on her forehead. The use of sexual imagery for IDOLATRY is prominent in biblical traditions (cf. Rev 2:20-22). The most damning indictment of the city is the statement that the woman is *drunk with the blood of the saints and the blood of the witnesses to Jesus* (v. 6).

The angel describes the beast as the one who *was, and is not, and is about to ascend from the bottomless pit and go to destruction* (v. 8). This description is a parody of God, *who is and who was and who is to come.* In addition, the description is a reference to Nero who lived, then died, and was expected to return to lay claim to the throne once more (see 13:3). Through the voice of the angel, John tells his readers that the vision of the woman and the beast has more than a surface meaning for those who are wise enough to understand. As the woman represents Rome, the beast upon which she rides symbolizes the Roman Empire. The seven heads of the beast have a dual meaning. They represent seven mountains (Rome was known as the city of seven hills) and seven kings (the emperors). John's explanation of the beast has intrigued commentators for centuries. Who are the specific emperors John has in mind when he says that *five have fallen, one is living, and the other has not yet come; and when he comes, he must remain only a little while* (v. 10)? What about the beast who *is an eighth but it belongs to the seven* (v. 11)?

Scholars have given various answers to these questions. The problem is that by the time of John there had been more than seven emperors. Where does John start? Whom does he omit? Rather than attempt to decipher the listing of emperors, one should interpret the number seven as symbolic. The number seven is derived from the ancient myth of a seven-headed monster. That myth, not the actual number of emperors, controls John's imagery. The seven-headed beast symbolizes all the emperors up to and including Domitian. *Five have fallen*, meaning that Rome has already seen the majority of its rulers; *one is living* (Domitian); and the seventh will last only a short time (because the end is near). The claim that the beast is the eighth, but also part of the seven, is another reference to the Nero myth. Domitian (one of the seven) is, figuratively, the reincarnation of Nero.

The ten horns represent the rulers of other nations who are cohorts of the beast. They will join forces in the war against the Lamb. Their power is limited (*for one hour*), however. They will meet their defeat at the hands of Christ and his faithful followers (cf. 19:11-21). Verses 15-18 present a surprising development. The beast and the ten kings turn on the great whore and destroy her. They unwittingly become agents of God in inflicting punishment on Rome for its arrogance, idolatry, persecution, and greed.

Laments on Earth, 18:1-24

Chapter 18 is similar in form to a funeral dirge. It is composed of several laments over the fall of Babylon (Rome). Examples of these abound in the writings of the prophets in the Hebrew Bible, from which John has freely borrowed in constructing the present songs of doom (cf. Isa 13; 23–24; 34; Jer 50–51; Ezek 26–27). An angel first announces the fall of the city, an event John narrated earlier in 17:15-18. The destruction of the city will be complete. It will become a place haunted by demons and foul animals. Not only has Rome committed evil itself, but it has lead astray other nations, kings, and merchants who have drunk her wine and committed fornication with her.

In this chapter, the chronological perspective shifts. In vv. 2-3, Babylon has fallen. In vv. 4-8, the fall has not yet occurred and the people of God are given advance warning to leave the doomed city before its destruction occurs. Even though for John the destruction is future, he is so certain of God's ultimate triumph that he can speak of it as an accomplished fact. A similar chronological shift occurs several times in the following verses. The command to come out of the doomed city, modeled after Jeremiah's words in Jer 51:45, has a figurative meaning as well as perhaps a literal one. The people are to come out, or separate themselves, from the idolatry and wickedness of the city. God's people are called to reject the values and lifestyle of Rome and its followers. Rome's arrogance and pride are aptly stated in v. 7, *"In her heart she says, 'I rule as a queen; I am no widow, and I will never see grief'."*

Verses 9-20 report the laments of three groups of people who witness the fall of the great city (cf. Ezek 26–28). Each of these groups (kings, merchants, and mariners) has profited from its association with Rome. They weep and mourn because the fall of Rome means economic and political ruin for them. The wealth and extravagance of Rome is indicated by the vast amount of goods sold by the merchants. The last item in the list of v. 13 is rather jarring and indicates the depth of Rome's depravity: *cattle and sheep, horses and chariots, slaves—and human lives.*

After the laments are finished, an angel takes up a huge millstone and throws it into the sea, stating that such will be the fate of Babylon. This imagery of destruction is adapted from Jer 51:63-64 where the prophet is told to take the scroll on which his oracle against Babylon is written, tie a stone to it, and throw it into the Euphrates River, saying, "Thus shall Babylon sink, to rise no more." The totality of Rome's destruction is expressed in vv. 21-23. No music will be heard, no artisans will be found, no sounds of millstones or bridal parties will be heard, and no light will shine any longer. The city will be desolate. Rome has deserved this punishment, for in the city *was found the blood of prophets and of saints, and of all who have been slaughtered on earth* (v. 24). The destruction of the city is divine retribution for the suffering and persecution that Rome had inflicted on God's people.

Celebration in Heaven, 19:1-10

Strictly speaking, this section is an audition, rather than a vision. Each part of this section describes what

John has heard. The fall of Rome brings about a reaction of celebration in heaven. The heavenly multitude sings praises to God because God has exacted judgment on Rome. Their song is a song of victory. The cry of the martyrs (6:10) has been answered and God has avenged *the blood of his servants* (v. 2). The songs of the heavenly chorus are not primarily songs of gloating, but celebrations of justice and vindication. The *twenty-four elders and the four living creatures* join in the worship and praise of God. Then a heavenly voice invites all God's people to join in the celebration. Heaven and earth are united in glorious peals of praise to God as Hallelujahs! reverberate throughout all creation. (This chapter is the only place in the NT where the word HALLELUJAH occurs.)

The final hallelujah song in this section offers praise not for the destruction of Rome but for *the marriage of the Lamb* (v. 7). The bride of the Lamb is the church. In the Hebrew Bible the metaphor of Israel as the bride of God is found often (see esp. Hos 1–3). Since Christians saw themselves as the new Israel, the application of the bride imagery to the church was a natural one. In the NT the author of Ephesians gives an extended application of this metaphor (Eph 5:23-32; cf. 2 Cor 11:2). The bride is dressed in *fine linen, bright and pure*, which is interpreted as the righteous deeds of the saints. The contrast between the church and Rome is unmistakable. Rome is the great prostitute, drinking from a cup of abominations and impurities. The church, on the other hand, is the pure bride of Christ, adorned in fine, bright linen.

The fourth beatitude of Revelation (v. 9) declares: *Blessed are those who are invited to the marriage banquet of the Lamb.* Who are the guests? They too are the church. One cannot press John's imagery for consistency. John's language is poetic, imaginative language, not analytical or scientific language. In John's creative presentation, the church can be both the bride and the wedding guests. The imagery of a wedding and a wedding feast convey the mood of the kingdom of God. God's kingdom is filled with joy and celebration, happiness and intimacy.

In response to all that he has heard, John falls down in worship before his angel guide. The reaction of the angel is quick and decisive: *"You must not do that! I am a fellow servant with you and your comrades who hold the testimony of Jesus. Worship God!"* (v. 10). The words of the angel were apt words for John's readers as well. Tempted to compromise their faith and participate in emperor worship, they should hear these words as a warning. No one, not even the angels and certainly not the beastly emperor, is worthy of worship. Worship belongs to God alone.

The Final Victory, 19:11–20:15

Several times John has either intimated or directly stated that the decisive victory over evil has been accomplished. In this section he gives the final and most complete portrayal of the defeat of all the forces aligned against God. Like all of the Apocalypse, the scenes here are not literal predictions of coming events, arranged in chronological order. Instead, John presents the reader with powerful images of judgment, punishment, and the righteousness of God.

19:11-16. The triumphant Christ. This passage portrays the coming of Christ as judge and warrior. Heaven opens and John sees a rider on *a white horse.* (This horse and rider should not be confused with the one that appeared at the opening of the first seal in 6:1-2.) The rider is Christ, *called Faithful and True* (cf. 3:14, *the faithful and true witness*). His eyes are *like a flame of fire* (cf. 1:14; 2:18). His many diadems are evidence of his royal position. His name *that no one knows but himself* (v. 12) signifies the mystery of Christ who surpasses all human understanding. His robe is dipped in blood, like that of God the Divine Warrior in Isaiah 63 whose robe is stained with the blood of his enemies. *His name is called The Word of God* (cf. John 1:1, 14; and esp. Wis 18:14-16). The sword from his mouth, his ruling with a rod of iron, and his treading the wine press (v. 15) are all images of judgment upon the earth. In case any doubt exists concerning the identity of this splendid figure, emblazoned on his robe and on his thigh are the words *King of kings and Lord of lords.* Christ is accompanied by the armies of heaven, also riding white horses. Although some commentators understand the heavenly armies to be composed of angels, the forces here are probably identical with the *called and chosen and faithful* of 17:14, the martyrs. They do not engage in actual combat (notice they wear festal garb, not battle vestments), but they accompany Christ to share in his victory. They are witnesses of their own vindication.

19:17-21. The final battle. An angel calls to the birds and invites them to *the great supper of God* to eat the bodies of God's enemies who will be killed (cf. Ezek 39:17-20). This is a grotesque counterpart to 19:9. Like the redeemed who are invited to the marriage supper of the Lamb, the wicked of the earth will also participate in a great feast. The difference is that they will be the main course! In the final battle the beast and false prophet are captured and thrown into *the lake of fire that burns with sulfur* (v. 20). The lake of fire is GEHENNA, the place of torment for the wicked. The remainder of the forces arrayed against Christ are killed *by the sword that came from his mouth* (v. 21). The identification of Christ's weapon as the sword of his mouth (i.e., the word of God) should be a caution to anyone who is tempted to interpret the battle imagery of Revelation literally.

20:1-6. The millennial reign. As a result of the battle, Satan is bound by an angel and thrown into *the bottomless pit* (see 9:1; cf. Isa 24:21-22). There he is to remain for a thousand years. The imprisonment of Satan is certain, for he has been bound with a chain, locked in the pit, and a seal placed over the door. All the evil forces have now been removed from the earth.

The millennial reign of Christ and his followers now begins. The concept of an interim earthly rule prior to the consummation of the KINGDOM OF GOD in heaven is found in several apocalyptic writings. The idea apparently developed from the attempt to combine the older prophetic idea of a this-worldly kingdom of God centered in Israel that would occur in the last days with the apocalyptic notion of a new heaven and new earth as the locale for God's kingdom. The interim reign of the messiah, followed by the otherworldly kingdom of God, preserves both concepts. The length of this interim reign varies in different traditions. John pictures it lasting for *a thousand years*; in 2 Esdr 7:28 the messianic reign lasts 400 years. Among the many other limits set for this reign are 4,000 years, 600 years, 60 years, 365 years, or even 365,000 years.

According to v. 4 the millennial reign is not for all believers, but only for the martyrs. This interim period is a special reward for those who have given their lives for the sake of God's kingdom. The rest of the dead (righteous and unrighteous) will not be raised until the end of the millennium. The first resurrection is only for those who have paid the ultimate price for their witness. They are the *firstfruits* (14:4) of the harvest. The remainder of the faithful will be united with them after the second resurrection. The millennium should not be taken literally. Instead it should be seen as powerful imagery offering reassurance that God knows and values the tremendous sacrifices that some believers are called upon to make for the sake of God's kingdom.

20:7-10. The final conflict. Satan is loosed from his imprisonment after the millennium is ended and mounts one last assault on the people of God. Why, in John's scheme, Satan must be released after he has been bound is not clear. Perhaps it is John's way of emphasizing the formidable power of evil. Even when it appears that evil has been contained and is no longer a threat, it has the capacity to rebound and wreak havoc in one's life. A more mundane reason for having Satan released is so John could introduce one more image in his apocalyptic drama, the figures of *Gog and Magog*. Satan is joined by Gog and Magog, representing *the nations at the four corners of the earth* (v. 8). The symbolism of Gog and Magog is taken from Ezek 38–39 where Gog, the leader of the land of Magog, leads a group of nations in an attack on Jerusalem. John adapts that tradition, making Gog as well as Magog the names of nations. Satan and his army attack the people of God, described as *the camp of the saints and the beloved city* (v. 9). God intervenes, however, destroying the rebellious forces of Satan. Satan is thrown into the lake of fire, there to be *tormented day and night forever and ever* (v. 10), along with his cohorts, the beast and the false prophet. Finally, and definitively, Satan is defeated.

20:11-15. The last judgment. The final judgment takes place in front of the *great white throne* of God. The earth and heaven flee from God's presence because as part of the old, rebellious order no place exists for them anymore. A new heaven and new earth will be needed. All people stand before the throne, while two types of books are brought and examined. In one book, *the book of life* (cf. 3:5; 13:8; 17:8), are recorded the names of all the people of God. It is the heavenly register of the redeemed. In the other books are recorded all the deeds of humanity. The imagery here appears in conflict. If one's name is in *the book of life*, how can one also be judged by works? If one's name is not in the book of life, can one be saved by works? The resolution of this tension lies in the creative juxtaposition of these two images. John is reminding his readers that salvation is a matter of God's grace, not their achievement (the book of life). On the other hand, one's actions do matter. They are an indication of the seriousness of one's commitment to God. Grace and works are held together in this scene in creative tension. No one escapes God's judgment. Even Death, the last enemy and the destroyer of life, is not exempt. *Death and Hades* (the place of the dead), along with *anyone whose name was not found written in the book of life*, are cast into the lake of fire, the second death.

The New Jerusalem, 21:1–22:5

All of John's visions have been leading up to this final section. The eschatological woes, the punishments, the words of assurance, the last judgment, all are left in the shadows of this final spectacular scene of God's glorious kingdom. As has been the case throughout the Apocalypse, John draws heavily upon motifs and images from the Hebrew Bible and apocalyptic traditions. The reader must keep in mind that John's language is imaginative and symbolic. A literal reading of the text produces a distorted understanding of John's message. The imagery of *the new Jerusalem* and *the new heaven and the new earth* are symbols of life lived in intimate communion with God.

New Heaven and New Earth, 21:1-8

Not only do earth and heaven give way for a new heaven and new earth (cf. Isa 65:17; 66:22), but the sea no longer exists in John's vision of the new world. The sea is a symbol of chaos, rebellion, and evil. John sees the new Jerusalem coming down out of heaven. This is no human construct. Its origin is from God. The city is *prepared as a bride adorned for her husband* (v. 2). John has earlier painted a graphic picture of another city, "the great city," Rome. The new Jerusalem is in direct contrast to that city. Rome was portrayed as a prostitute; the new city is like a bride. The hallmark of this new city is that God dwells here with God's people. Nothing separates the people from their God, not physical distance, not emotional nor physical pain.

God speaks directly in vv. 5-8, declaring that the re-creation of all things is completed. The end has arrived through the actions of the one who is Alpha and Omega, beginning and end. The faithful (the conquerors) are assured that they will inherit the blessings of God and will be God's children. The wicked, however, are excluded from God's kingdom. The list of those who will be cast into the lake of fire is probably traditional, but some of its elements would have had special significance for John's situation. The cowardly and the faithless are those who did not resist the beast of Rome; the liars are those who confessed the emperor as lord (cf. 14:5).

The Holy City, 21:9-27

An angel comes and takes John up to a high mountain from which he can view the new Jerusalem. The city has *twelve gates* named for the *twelve tribes of Israel* and *twelve foundations* named for the *twelve apostles*. This symbolizes the city as the total people of God. The measurement of the city reveals that it is a cube, symbolizing the perfection of the city. In the Greek text the measurements are multiples of twelve (twelve thousand stadia), symbolizing the enormity and completeness of the city. The city is built of precious metals and jewels (cf. Isa 54:11-12). Much of this description is borrowed from other traditions, including the listing of the precious stones on the breastplate of the high priest (cf. Exod 28:17-20). The presence of these stones support the claims made earlier that the people of God are a priestly people. The gates of the city are made of pearls and the streets are made of gold. The total effect of the description is to overwhelm the reader with the magnificence and glory of this dwelling place for God's people.

No need exists in the city for a temple, symbolic of the presence of God, because in the new Jerusalem God and the Lamb dwell with the people. Likewise no sun or moon are needed because the glory of God and Christ shine throughout the city. The glory of the city is such that it will draw nations and kings into it. It is a place of safety where the gates of the city need never be shut (v. 25). It is also a place of purity and righteousness into which everyone and everything that is unclean are forbidden to enter.

The River of Life, 22:1-5

John's description of the new Jerusalem is heavily dependent on Ezekiel's vision of the restored Jerusalem (chap. 47). In Ezekiel, as well as in other writings (particularly in APOCALYPTIC LITERATURE), future hope is expressed in terms of a restored Garden of Eden. That imagery is prevalent in these verses in the tree of life and in the river that flows through the city. John borrows from Ezekiel the idea that the leaves of the tree will be for healing. The most revealing characteristic of life in the new Jerusalem is that God's servants *will see his face* (v. 4), a feat not possible before (cf. 1 Cor 13:12; Matt 5:8). This act expresses intimacy, fellowship, and complete knowledge. Life in God's new kingdom is eternal, for *they will reign forever and ever* (v. 5).

Epilogue, 22:6-21

The book concludes with a series of warnings, exhortations, and assurances. The identity of the speaker is not clear in all cases. Verses 7, 12, 16, and 20 come from Christ. Verses 6 and 10 may be from Christ or an angel. In v. 6 the speaker declares the message of John to be authentic because its ultimate source is God. Verse 7 presents a blessing for those who hold fast to the message John has revealed in this writing.

Once again (cf. 19:10) John falls down to worship his angelic guide and is strongly rebuked (vv. 8-10). Worship should be directed to God alone. Apocalyptic writings often claim to have been written by venerable figures of the distant past, but their message has only recently come to light. To explain why the works, if ancient, had not been known earlier, a command to secrecy is often included. The works have been sealed up until the last days, which are the present time (cf. Dan 8:26; 12:4, 9). John does not use an ancient pseudonym. He writes in his own name for his own time. There is no need to seal up his message, *for the time is near* (v. 10). In fact the end is so near that little time is left for people to change their ways (v. 11).

Christ declares that he is coming soon to bring punishment and reward (v. 12). He applies to himself the same titles that have been used in the book for God (cf. 1:8; 21:6). The final blessing of the book is pronounced upon *those who wash their robes*, that is, those who have been redeemed by Christ's death (cf. 7:14). While the redeemed may enter the new Jerusalem, the wicked (*dogs* was a derogatory term often applied to the godless) must remain outside. Once more the authenticity of the message is declared

(v. 16). In v. 17 the Spirit and the bride (the church) respond to the promise that Christ is coming by issuing their own invitation, *"Come."* (In the Gk. text, *come* is singular, indicating that the invitation is addressed to Christ and not to people in general.) Everyone is urged to join in extending the invitation, and finally the invitation is opened to all who want the water of life to come (cf. John 7:37-38).

Verses 18-19 contain a curse formula to safeguard the accuracy and authenticity of the work. Formulas of this nature, found in many ancient writings, were an attempt to prevent copyists from altering the text. John believes that his message is a true word from God and wants to preserve its integrity. For the third time in this section, Jesus exclaims, *"I am coming soon"* (v. 20). This time John answers in words that are both a shout of jubilation and a prayer for fulfillment: *Amen. Come, Lord Jesus!*

The book ends with an epistolary conclusion similar to those in Paul's letters.

Works Cited

Beasley-Murray, George R. 1974. *The Book of Revelation*, NCB.

Hemer, Colin J. 1986. *The Letters to the Seven Churches of Asia in Their Local Setting.*

Reddish, Mitchell G. 1990. "Antichrist," MDB.